Jon Courson's
APPLICATION COMMENTARY

Jon Courson's APPLICATION COMMENTARY

OLD TESTAMENT

VOLUME 1: Genesis—Job

Foreword by

CHUCK SMITH

THOMAS NELSON
Since 1798

NASHVILLE DALLAS MEXICO CITY RIO DE JANEIRO

Published in Nashville, Tennessee, by Thomas Nelson. Thomas Nelson is a trademark of Thomas Nelson, Inc.

Thomas Nelson, Inc. titles may be purchased in bulk for educational, business, fund-raising, or sales promotional use. For information, please email SpecialMarkets@ThomasNelson.com.

Scripture quotations, unless otherwise indicated, are from the King James Version of the Bible.

Cover Illustration: "The Disciple" by Lyle Trimmer © 1992. Used by permission.

ISBN 10: 1-4185-0146-8
ISBN 13: 978-1-4185-0146-4

Printed in United States of America
25 26 27 28 /TRM/ 19 18 17 16

FOREWORD

Many commentaries on the Bible are available today. Most are expositional or exegetical; and they often seek to be so exacting with respect to the letter of the law, or the possible meaning of a particular word, that they lack life and inspiration. It is hard to find a good devotional commentary on the Bible—one that brings both understanding and life to the passage, so that you are inspired to worship the Lord as you gain new insights into the truth of His love and grace toward us.

This commentary is one that does just that.

In Nehemiah, chapter eight, we are told that "the people gathered themselves together" and "they read in the book in the law of God distinctly, and gave the sense, and caused them to understand the reading." I find this to perfectly describe what Jon Courson has done in his commentaries. Giving understanding and meaning to the Word is one of the greatest needs in the church today. In Nehemiah's time, this method of commentary brought great conviction upon the people, and a genuine turning to God. The ultimate result was that the people went their way rejoicing, "because they had understood the words that were declared unto them."

I am convinced that you also will go your way rejoicing after reading the insights that the Holy Spirit has given to Jon on the Scriptures.

Pastor Chuck Smith
Senior Pastor, Calvary Chapel
Costa Mesa, California

TABLE OF CONTENTS

TOPICAL TABLE OF CONTENTS

Faith

Family

Grace

Guidance

Holy Spirit

Jesus Christ

Ministry

Prayer

Salvation

Sin

Spiritual Growth

Spiritual Warfare

Trials & Suffering

The Word

Jon Courson's APPLICATION COMMENTARY

GENESIS

Background to Genesis

The word *genesis* means "beginning." Therefore, Genesis is a fitting title for the book before us, for its pages record the beginning of everything—the beginning of creation, man, sin, family, culture, and industry. It deals with the beginning of everything one could possibly imagine—except it does not deal with the beginning of God.

Why?

First, because God has no beginning.

Secondly, the Bible being, in a sense, the autobiography of God, He needs no introduction. Think about it. If you were to write your life story, you would not spend chapters trying to prove that you exist because the very fact that you were writing the book would be verification of your being.

The more I study the Bible, the more I realize it was composed supernaturally. Comprised of sixty-six different books written by forty different authors over a span of 1,600 years in three different languages, there isn't one contradiction. Instead, there is a unified theme that begins here in Genesis, the Book of Beginning, and extends through the Book of Revelation. That theme is the story of God's gracious, glorious work of redemption.

GENESIS

1

Genesis 1:1
In the beginning God created the heaven and the earth.

Lots of people get hung up on verse 1 of chapter 1. And this presents a problem, for if one doesn't agree with the opening statement of the first sentence, it will be difficult for him to accept what follows.

"You don't *really* believe that God created heaven and earth in six days, do you?" scoffs the cynic. "That might be a nice legend, even a practical parable—but you can't really take this seriously. It's just not scientific!"

Gang, the book in your hand doesn't claim to be a book of science. Yet whenever it touches on issues of science, it is absolutely infallible. There is no proven scientific fact that contradicts a single statement written in the pages of this book.

> Have ye not known? have ye not heard? hath it not been told you from the beginning? have ye not understood from the foundations of the earth? It is he that sitteth upon the circle of the earth . . . Isaiah 40:21, 22

Every culture, every nation, every people throughout world history believed the earth to be flat as a pancake—until Christopher Columbus proved the validity of Isaiah's words.

> He stretcheth out the north over the empty place, and hangeth the earth upon nothing.
> Job 26:7

God hangs the earth on *nothing?*

Learned scholars in India would have said, "We all know the world is held up on the backs of giant elephants." The Greeks maintained that the earth was held in place by the bulging biceps and massive shoulders of Atlas. South Sea islanders believed the earth was supported on the backs of giant tortoises.

Sure enough, the more we learn, the more we find the Bible is right all along. I like that!

"Wait a minute," some say. "Genesis 1:1 may address spirituality and theology, but it can't be taken literally—not in this day, when the theory of evolution has been accepted so completely."

Keep in mind that evolution at best is a theory—and a bankrupt one at that. Many men of science who are neither believers in Jesus Christ nor students of the Bible have turned away from the evolutionary hypothesis because it violates the most foundational, fundamental principles and laws of known science. For example, one of the most important laws of science is the Second Law of Thermodynamics. It's not a theory, not a hypothesis, but a basic principle which says everything goes from order to disorder.

If I create the outline of a horse by arranging marbles on a sheet of plywood, place my finished work in the backseat of my VW, drive around town for half an hour, when I stop the car, will the horse be more intricate? Will the horse become even finer in detail, more elaborate artistically? Or will there be a bunch of marbles on the floor?

One of the principles upon which science is predicated is the fact that everything goes from order to disorder. The theory of evolution completely violates this understanding, maintaining as it does, that things go from disorder to greater order, from simplicity to complexity.

"But the great minds embrace the theory of evolution," some insist. Do they?

> *The man* Discover Magazine *rated as the greatest scientific thinker in history is Sir Isaac Newton. Newton was mocked because his contemporaries couldn't understand why he believed there really was a God who created the world in six days. One day, Sir Isaac made an elaborate model of the solar system, which took up the entire front room of his house. Impressed by its details, his colleagues asked him where he got the model.*
>
> *"I didn't get it," Newton said.*
>
> *"Oh. You made it?"*
>
> *"No, I didn't buy it. I didn't make it. No one put it here. It just appeared."*
>
> *And suddenly they got his point.*

> The heavens declare the glory of God; and the firmament sheweth his handywork. Day unto day uttereth speech, and night unto night sheweth knowledge. There is no speech nor language, where their voice is not heard.
> Psalm 19:1–3

The grandeur of the universe undeniably points to the existence of a Creator. But men suppress this truth, not wanting to be accountable to this Creator (Romans 1). That is why you can defend the Genesis account on the basis of science until you're blue in the face—and still fail to convince the skeptic.

You can engage people intellectually, banter with people philosophically, appeal to people rationally only to have them oppose you adamantly. The bottom line isn't biology or philosophy, academics or genetics, Darwin or doctrine. The bottom line is the same as it is for every controversy or concern, debate or dilemma.

The bottom line is Jesus.

"I and My Father are one," He said. And the people listening to Him that day clearly understood the implication. So incensed were they by His claim to deity that they picked up rocks to stone Him on the spot (John 10:30, 31).

> *"Show us a sign," they said, "to verify You are who You claim to be."*
>
> *"One sign only will I give you," He said. "Destroy this body and in three days, I will rise again" (John 2:18–21).*

Thus, the entire burden of proof for Jesus' claim to deity lies in His empty tomb. And the door of faith to believe everything He ever said swings on the hinge of the Resurrection. His Resurrection, documented by over five-hundred eyewitnesses proves Jesus is God.

As God, Jesus speaks with absolute authority. As God, Jesus fashioned the Garden of Eden creatively (John 1:3). As God, Jesus referred to Adam and Eve specifically (Mark 10:6). Therefore, when talking to a skeptic, take the argument away from all of the scientific debate, and back to the single issue that matters: Who is Jesus Christ? That's the key.

Genesis 1:2 (a)
And the earth was without form, and void . . .

The Hebrew phrase here is *tohuw va bohuw.* Suddenly, the earth was 'tohuw va bohuw.' We see this phrase again in Isaiah 45:18, where we read that God created the heaven and earth *not* in vain—*not* "tohuw va bohuw."

Now, if Isaiah says God did not create the earth without form and void, but Genesis 1 says the earth was without form and void, what's going on?

Along with many Bible scholars, I believe an event took place between Genesis 1:1 and 1:2 described in Isaiah 14 and Ezekiel 28, wherein an archangel named Lucifer launched a rebellion against God and was kicked out of heaven. Along with one-third of the angels who followed him in his rebellion, he came to earth, where he would become "the god of this world" (2 Corinthians 4:4). So great was the impact when, in a sense, hell hit earth, that our planet suddenly became "without form and void."

Genesis 1:2 (b)
. . . and darkness was upon the face of the deep. And the Spirit of God moved . . .

God is always coming in on something which has been messed up by the enemy. Here, the world is a mess, without form and void, wiped-out, wasted. And God begins to move.

Genesis 1:2 (c)
. . . upon the face of the waters.

Throughout Scripture, water is a symbol of the Word.

> Now ye are clean through the word which I have spoken unto you. John 15:3

> Husbands, love your wives, even as Christ also loved the church, and gave himself for it; That he might sanctify and cleanse it with the washing of water by the word. Ephesians 5:25, 26

How does the Spirit of God move?

Upon the face of the water—upon the Word.

Suddenly you hear a Bible study, listen to a radio program, watch a crusade on TV, or talk to a buddy and as the water of the Word is shared, the Spirit of God moves.

Genesis 1:3
And God said, Let there be light: and there was light.

The Hebrew literally reads: "Light be! And light was." Here we see the recreation of planet earth.

Genesis 1:4
And God saw the light, that it was good: and God divided the light from the darkness.

In the beginning, God created the heaven and the earth; the earth became wiped out; the Spirit moved on the face of the water; and God said "Let there be light."

That's *your* story. You were created in God's image, but sin wiped you out. The Spirit of God moved in through the Word. You saw the light—and you were born again. Then God separated the darkness from the light, and good things began to happen—not only in creation physically, but in your life personally because of God's sovereign grace and mercy.

Genesis 1:5
And God called the light Day, and the darkness he called Night. And the evening and the morning were the first day.

Notice the phraseology. "The evening and the morning were the first day." That's still the way the Jewish people reckon their days. They begin in the evening and end in the morning. They go from darkness to light. I like that!

Genesis 1:6–8
And God said, Let there be a firmament in the midst of the waters, and let it divide the waters from the waters. And God made the firmament, and divided the waters which were under the firmament from the waters which were above the firmament: and it was so. And God called the firmament Heaven. And the evening and the morning were the second day.

Scripturally, "heaven" refers not only to the stars above us, and the destiny awaiting us, but to the atmosphere around us. This passage makes it clear that when God recreated earth, there was water above the firmament, or atmosphere—which means that, with a water canopy surrounding its atmosphere, earth would have been a great big greenhouse. It means nothing would get wiped out by ultraviolet rays. It means the whole planet would have shared the same climate. It explains why fossils of tropical vegetation are found in the Arctic Circle. It explains why man could live nine hundred years.

To cause the Flood in Noah's day, God collapsed the protective canopy, which deluged the earth with water. And as a result, cataclysmic changes took place. The climate was altered radically. And man had to wear SPF40 sunscreen just to live to seventy.

Genesis 1:9–13
And God said, Let the waters under the heaven be gathered together unto one place, and let the dry land appear: and it was so. And God called the dry land Earth; and the gathering together of the waters called he Seas: and God saw that it was good. And God said, Let the earth bring forth grass, the herb yielding seed, and the fruit tree yielding fruit after his kind, whose seed is in itself, upon the earth: and it was so. And the earth brought forth grass, and herb yielding seed after his kind, and the tree yielding fruit, whose seed was in itself, after his kind: and God saw that it was good. And the evening and the morning were the third day.

On the first day, light was created. On the second day, the atmosphere was created. On the third day, life is created. Why does life appear on the third day? Because Jesus—the Way, the Truth, *the Life*—rose on the third day.

Genesis 1:14–19
And God said, Let there be lights in the firmament of the heaven to divide the day from the night; and let them be for signs, and for seasons, and for days, and years: And let them be for lights in the firmament of the heaven to give light upon the earth: and it was so. And God made two great lights; the greater light to rule the day, and the lesser light to rule the night: he made the stars also. And God set them in the firmament of the heaven to give light upon the earth, And to rule over the day and over the night, and to divide the light from the darkness: and God saw that it was good. And the evening and the morning were the fourth day.

On the fourth day, God made the sun and the moon.

Jesus is the Light of the world (John 8:12). He said we are also to be lights (Matthew 5:14). He is the greater light—the sun. We are the lesser light—the moon—reflecting His light to our dark world.

I recently watched the moon appear smaller and smaller in an eclipse, and was reminded that to whatever extent the world gets between the sun and the moon is the extent to which the light of the sun upon the moon is diminished. The same thing is true with me and you. Jesus is the sun; we're the moon; and to whatever degree we allow the world to come between us, His light in our lives will fade proportionately. If you were to chart your own life tonight, would you be a full moon, a three-quarter moon, half moon, quarter moon, or eclipsed moon? It all depends on how much of the world you allow to creep in between you and the Son.

Genesis 1:20–25
And God said, Let the waters bring forth abundantly the moving creature that hath life, and fowl that may fly above the earth in the open firmament of heaven. And God created great whales, and every living creature that moveth, which the waters brought forth abundantly, after their kind, and every winged fowl after his kind: and God saw that it was good. And God blessed them, saying, Be fruitful, and multiply, and fill the waters in the seas, and let fowl multiply in the earth. And the evening and the morning were the fifth day. And God said, Let the earth bring forth the living creature after his kind, cattle, and creeping thing, and beast of the earth after his kind: and it was so. And God made the beast of the earth after his kind, and cattle after their kind, and every thing that creepeth upon the earth after his kind: and God saw that it was good.

This passage deals a deathblow to theistic evolution—the idea that God started the process and then let the species evolve one into another. The language in the Hebrew is emphatic: "after their kind," "after his kind," "after its kind." In other words, there could be changes within a species but not changes from one species to another. Scientists have been able to breed fruitflies into millions of generations. And guess what. They're still fruitflies. Not one has become a honeybee.

Genesis 1:26 (a)
And God said, Let us make man in our image, after our likeness . . .

The Hebrew word translated "God" is *Elohim. El* is the singular form. "Elohim" refers to three or more. Thus, the very word "God" in Hebrew speaks of the Trinity.

We, too, are triune beings. We are body, soul, and spirit. The body refers to our physical being. The soul refers to our mind and our emotions, and relates to people. The spirit refers to our eternal being, and relates to God. Animals have bodies and souls. But they do not have spirits because they're not made in God's image. Only man is a spiritual being.

Genesis 1:26 (b)–28 (a)
. . . and let them have dominion over the fish of the sea, and over the fowl of the air, and over the cattle, and over all the earth, and over every creeping thing that creepeth upon the earth. So God created man in his own image, in the image of God created he him; male and female created he them. And God blessed them, and God said unto them, Be fruitful, and multiply, and replenish the earth, and subdue it . . .

Before things go haywire due to the Fall, God gives an assignment to man: Subdue the earth.

Subdue it from what?

From Satan.

From the very beginning, God said, "This little rock called earth is the place where there is to be a cosmic showdown between Me and Satan. So I'm going to use you, mankind, to partner with Me as part of the process to drive out the enemy."

How?

By being fruitful and multiplying.

How are you to subdue your earth, your world, your family which seems to be in the grasp and grip of the enemy?

By being fruitful.

Because the fruit of the Spirit is love (Galatians 5:22), and because love covers a multitude of sins (1 Peter 4:8), you'll be fruitful if you don't criticize, gossip, or find fault with things, people, or situations. You'll be fruitful if you speak words of love and peace, patience and gentleness, for such is the fruit of the Spirit.

James talks about the tongue being an instrument of fire (James 3:6). If you find fault with your neighbor, your job, your school, your church, your family—you will hand your world over to the hellish flames of the enemy. But if you speak words of affirmation and encouragement, of faith and joy—you will replace the fires of hell with the fruit of heaven.

I talked to a mom and dad who had opinions about the church and the country, the politicians and the government. All their kids ever heard was Mom and Dad putting something down. And now Mom and Dad can't figure out why their kids don't want to go to church.

"Could it be that you've poisoned your own well?" I asked.

"But we only complained to our own family," they said.

Ah, but their own family was the very world in which they were to be fruitful, in which they were to multiply.

How do we multiply?

Acts 6 tells us the Word of God increased, and the number of disciples multiplied when the Word was shared.

If you talk to your kids, your classmates, your coworkers about the Word, you will see multiplication of life and love. And suddenly the world in which you live will be subdued, won back from the enemy.

We now know that every solid object retains the imprint of a sound wave. The very principle which allows a CD to be pressed or a tape to be made affects this chair, this microphone, my tennis shoe. Jesus could have been hinting at this when He said, "If I tell My disciples to be quiet, the rocks would cry out" (see Luke 19:40). Thus, I challenge you to live tomorrow as though everything you say to your husband or wife, family or friends is being recorded to be replayed to the whole church. Such is the way to live, for every word you say produces life or death, fruit or fire. Kids who grow up hearing Mom and Dad talk about the Word and how good God is, how much they appreciate fellowship and prayer and praise, plug in and worship God, and walk with Him all of their days.

Subdue your world, gang, by speaking love and by sharing the Word—by being fruitful and multiplying.

Genesis 1:28 (b)–31
. . . and have dominion over the fish of the sea, and over the fowl of the air, and over every living thing that moveth upon the earth. And God said, Behold, I have given you every herb bearing seed, which is upon the face of all the earth, and every tree, in the which is the fruit of a tree yielding seed; to you it shall be for meat. And to every beast of the earth, and to every fowl of the air, and to every thing that creepeth upon the earth, wherein there is life, I have given every green herb for meat: and it was so. And God saw every thing that he had made, and, behold, it was very good. And the evening and the morning were the sixth day.

Our God is awesome. He could have said, "For nourishment, take a pill." Instead He said, "For food, here's a thrill—the colors and textures and tastes of bananas and mangoes and guavas and avocadoes and tomatoes and celery are all yours to enjoy."

- "He satisfies our mouth with good things," David declares (Psalm 103:5).
- "Every good and perfect gift comes from above," James echoes (1:17).
- "He has given us richly all things to enjoy," Paul affirms (1 Timothy 6:17).

- "If you being evil know how to give good gifts to your kids, how much more will the Heavenly Father give good things to them that ask Him?" Jesus says (see Matthew 7:11).
- "Then why haven't I received what I've been asking for?" you wonder.

The answer is, "Because it's not a good gift." If it was good, God would give it to you, for He withholds no good thing from them that walk uprightly (Psalm 84:11).

2 **Genesis 2:1–3**
Thus the heavens and the earth were finished, and all the host of them. And on the seventh day God ended his work which he had made; and he rested on the seventh day from all his work which he had made. And God blessed the seventh day, and sanctified it: because that in it he had rested from all his work which God created and made.

At the time the Law was given, no culture had ever taken a day off of work. In agrarian societies, this would have been unthinkable. But here in the very beginning of time, we see the institution of the Sabbath.

"But I don't need a Sabbath because I'm not tired," you might be thinking.

Gang, God wasn't saying, "Whew, am I beat! This creating stuff is really draining." No, He was saying to you and me, "I'm your Father, and here's a key to navigate life successfully: Shut it down one day in seven."

"But I can get ahead if I just do a little bit of work on the seventh day."

As an observer, as a Bible teacher, as a pastor, I tell you with surety that if you don't take a Sabbath day, it will catch up with you either mentally, emotionally, physically, or spiritually. Ever wonder how Samson could sleep through the looming of his hair? He was exhausted! I am convinced that many people—men in particular—find themselves sleeping on the lap of Delilah because they haven't kept the Sabbath. I'm convinced many people have physical problems they wouldn't have if they took one day in seven and said, "I'm going to rest and relax, be refreshed and renewed." I'm convinced many people are seeing psychiatrists and taking pills because, failing to take a Sabbath, they're just mentally fried. I'm convinced many people have collapsed spiritually because the weekend finds them revving up their ski boats rather than finding renewal and refreshment in the Lord.

Be renewed, gang. I'm not saying what you should or shouldn't do on the Sabbath day because that's where the Pharisees erred. Instead, I would just remind you that because God rested on the seventh day, we get to as well.

The principle He modeled on the seventh day of creation continues to be a healthy one for us.

Genesis 2:4
These are the generations of the heavens and of the earth when they were created, in the day that the LORD God made the earth and the heavens,

Notice the word "heavens" is plural. Some people say this contradicts Genesis 1:1, which declares "In the beginning God created the *heaven* and the earth." But they fail to understand that Scripture speaks of the heavens in three dimensions . . .

- The first heaven is where the birds fly (Daniel 4).
- The second heaven is where the stars are (Psalm 19).
- The third heaven is the place Paul went when he beheld things too wonderful to articulate (2 Corinthians 12:2)—the place all believers will ultimately be.

These are three dimensions of heaven—and God created all three.

Genesis 2:5, 6
And every plant of the field before it was in the earth, and every herb of the field before it grew: for the LORD God had not caused it to rain upon the earth, and there was not a man to till the ground. But there went up a mist from the earth, and watered the whole face of the ground.

The Lord evidently had a built-in sprinkler system on automatic timer which kept everything watered, for before the days of Noah, there was no rain on the earth, which explains why the sight of him building an ark would have seemed laughable to his contemporaries.

Genesis 2:7 (a)
And the LORD God formed man . . .

Genesis 1 and 2 both deal with the creation story. Chapter 1 uses a wide-angle lens to give us the big picture. Chapter 2 uses a zoom lens to deal specifically with the creation of man.

Genesis 2:7 (b)
. . . of the dust of the ground . . .

Adam's name literally means "man." But the root of his name comes from that from which he was fashioned: dust.

Genesis 2:7 (c)
. . . and breathed into his nostrils the breath of life; and man became a living soul.

The words "breath," "wind," and "spirit" are all the same word in Hebrew, the language of the Old Testament: *ruach.* The same is true in Greek, the language of the New Testament, where the words translated "breath," "wind," and "spirit" are all *pneuma.* Formed of dust, man does not become a living soul until God breathes into him.

Genesis 2:8–14
And the LORD God planted a garden eastward in Eden; and there he put the man whom he had formed. And out of the ground made the LORD God to grow every tree that is pleasant to the sight, and good for food; the tree of life also in the midst of the garden, and the tree of knowledge of good and evil. And a river went out of Eden to water the garden; and from thence it was parted, and became into four heads. The name of the first is Pison: that is it which compasseth the whole land of Havilah, where there is gold; And the gold of that land is good: there is bdellium and the onyx stone. And the name of the second river is Gihon: the same is it that compasseth the whole land of Ethiopia. And the name of the third river is Hiddekel [Tigris]: that is it which goeth toward the east of Assyria. And the fourth river is Euphrates.

We know where the Tigris and Euphrates Rivers are. But we don't know the location of the other two. Of this much, however, we are certain: "Eden" means "delight." This garden in which the Lord placed man was a delightful place indeed.

Genesis 2:15
And the LORD God took the man, and put him into the garden of Eden to dress it and to keep it.

Before the Fall, before the advent of thorns and thistles, before the collapse of the water canopy that kept the earth perfectly temperate, gardening was not hard work. Thus, Adam was a gardener not only by vocation, but also for recreation.

Genesis 2:16, 17 (a)
And the LORD God commanded the man, saying, Of every tree of the garden thou mayest freely eat: But of the tree of the knowledge of good and evil, thou shalt not eat of it . . .

Why would God place in the Garden a tree from which Adam and Eve were not to eat? Because God desires a loving relationship with man. And true love is built on choice. Therefore, in placing the Tree of Knowledge of Good and Evil in the Garden, God said to mankind, "If you want to kill our relationship, if you want to turn your back on Me, I must provide this opportunity. All you have to do, Adam, to end our relationship is to eat from that tree."

Genesis 2:17 (b)
. . . for in the day that thou eatest thereof thou shalt surely die.

The Lord is so good because He made it as scary as possible. He said, "If you eat from that tree, it's going to kill you." What else could the Father have done to provide a choice, but also to say, "Don't do that."?

Notice God does not say, "If you eat of that tree, I'm going to kill you." He says, "If you eat of the tree, *it* will kill you." For many years, I thought that if I did something wrong, God would track me down. No, the Bible says, "Be sure your sin will find you out" (Numbers 32:23). It is *sin* that tracks us down, our *sin* that wipes us out. In the fruit of the Tree of the Knowledge of Good and Evil, perhaps there was something carcinogenic, something that would cause men to begin to die.

Genesis 2:18 (a)
And the LORD God said, It is not good that the man should be alone . . .

Adam's single state was the only thing God created that He declared not good.

Genesis 2:18 (b)–20
. . . I will make him an help meet for him. And out of the ground the LORD God formed every beast of the field, and every fowl of the air; and brought them unto Adam to see what he would call them: and whatsoever Adam called every living creature, that was the name thereof. And Adam gave names to all cattle, and to the fowl of the air, and to

every beast of the field; but for Adam there was not found an help meet for him.

"Mr. and Mrs. Giraffe, Mr. and Mrs. Rhinoceros, Mr. and Mrs. Orangutan, Mr. and Mrs. Hippopotamus"—Adam called out their names as the animals paraded before him. And as he did, there must have come a point when he came to the realization that everyone but him had a counterpart.

"I gotta make something happen," Adam could have said, climbing trees and beating bushes to find a mate. He could have searched the world to find his counterpart—but the closest he would have come would have been an orangutan or a chimpanzee. And that's what happens to a lot of people today. Aware of their single state, they say, "I gotta find somebody." So off they go to Rockin' Rodeo and they come back with an orangutan. "So she's a little hairy? So he's kind of big and overbearing, this is as close as I can get to a perfect match," they say. That is no more God's plan for us than it was for Adam.

Genesis 2:21, 22
And the LORD God caused a deep sleep to fall upon Adam and he slept: and he took one of his ribs, and closed up the flesh instead thereof; And the rib, which the LORD God had taken from man, made he a woman, and brought her unto the man.

When Adam was in a deep, death-like sleep, from out of his side came a bride. Down the tunnel of time, another Bride would come forth from the side of another Adam, the last Adam, Jesus Christ. When a Roman soldier stuck a spear in His side and the birthing fluids of blood and water poured forth, a Bride was born: the church—you and me.

"Husbands, love your wives as Christ loved the church and gave himself for it," Paul instructed the Ephesians (Ephesians 5:25). Husband, you are to love your wife like Christ loved the church. In other words, you're to die—to your needs, your desires, your dreams because that's what Christ did for us.

"Father, if it be possible, let this cup of death pass from Me," He prayed. "Nevertheless not my will, but Thy will, be done" (Luke 22:42).

Wife, you came from the side of man, and you will find fulfillment at the side of your man—neither leading him nor lagging behind him, but standing by him, standing with him, submitting to him. But know this, wives: Your husband will never be all you want or need him to be. A rib was taken from Adam and men have been missing something ever since. There is only One who has it all together. He's not called the Second Adam, which means there might be a third one. He is called the Last Adam because there is no other. And He's not missing a thing. Why? Because He wasn't born the way every man since the first Adam is born. And *He* will be the One who will listen to you by the hour and walk with you in the garden in the cool of the day. *He* will be the One who will hear not only the words of your lips, but also the cry of your heart. *He* will be the One who will truly understand you.

Thus, when we start seeking what we crave from the Last Adam, from Jesus Christ, we take pressure off our husband or wife and are then able to enjoy them without expecting something from them that they cannot give us.

Genesis 2:23 (a)
And Adam said, This is now bone of my bones, and flesh of my flesh . . .

"Bone of my bone, flesh of my flesh" is a Hebrew idiom meaning, "exact counterpart." God is a triune Being: Father, Son, and Spirit. And because He made us in His image, man is triune as well.

Our body is the physical part of us that relates to the material world around us. Our soul speaks of our mind and emotions and relates to the people around us. Our spirit is the part of us that relates to God and will live forever.

I believe it was a matching of body, soul, and spirit that caused Adam to realize Eve was truly bone of his bone, flesh of his flesh. And I believe the same can be true for us.

With regard to the body, there must be a physical attraction between you and the one you marry. Secondly, with regard to the soul, one must be able to communicate on the same wavelength with the one he or she marries. Thirdly, with regard to the spirit, one's love for the Lord, commitment to the Lord, involvement with the Lord must equal that of the one he or she marries.

Body, soul, spirit—when those three are mirrored in another, it is a match made in heaven.

The problem is, we usually settle for two out of three.

"I feel a spark for her romantically," he says. "And she has that same feeling for me. Spiritually, we both love the Lord, go to Bible study, and pray together. But the soul? She likes malls and I like backpacking. She likes to talk and I don't. But we can make this work." Yes, they can make it work. But it will take a lot of work to make it work.

"With regard to the soul, we're best friends," she says. "We talk by the hour and love just

hanging out with each other. And spiritually, we both love the Lord and are committed to the kingdom. But physically? I can't explain it, but he doesn't do much for me." This relationship can work—but, again, it will take a lot of work to make it work because someday, someone will come along who will spark that physical connection, and then there will be problems.

"We've got the romance thing wired," he says. "We're also buddies and best friends. But spiritually? I want to be a missionary, and she's content going to church only on Christmas and Easter." This relationship is destined for hardship because, due to different commitment levels spiritually, each will view life through a different lens.

Body, soul, and spirit. It's amazing to me how many couples connect only in two out of three, or even one out of three. When people settle for one out of three, their marriage almost inevitably ends in divorce. When couples settle for two out of three, they can make it work, but it takes a lot of work. It is those who connect on all three levels who, like Adam, are able to say, "Bone of my bone, flesh of my flesh. Wow!"

"Marriage and misery go hand in hand," wails the world. Not God. He says, "I want marriage to be a taste of heaven for you. If you'll go My way it can be just that."

"It's a little late for me to hear this," you might be thinking. "I am one of those who settled for only one match out of three and married the wrong person."

That's what Jacob could have said . . .

After seven years of working and waiting, he woke up to find he had wed Leah instead of Rachel—the older sister instead of the girl of his dreams. But at the end of his life, when deciding near whom he would be buried, Jacob again had to choose between the two women. And this time with eyes wide open, he chose Leah. Why? Because Leah produced a son whose name was Judah, from whom would come Yeshua, Messiah, Jesus.

So, too, as I look over this congregation, I see people who have difficult marriages, but who have developed out of necessity a deep walk with the Lord which never would have been developed if they'd had an easier, simpler marriage. I see people who have hung in there and could now say, "If I could do it all over again, I would choose my husband or wife again because our marriage has brought me to a richness with Jesus I never would have known had our marriage been easier."

If you have gone through a divorce, if you dropped the ball, if you missed the mark, know this: We all have. Every one of us has totally blown it (Romans 3:23). But the good news is that the work of the Cross completely takes care of my failure, my shortcoming, my sin. And it takes care of yours as well. All we have to do is say, "Lord, I've failed. I determine by Your grace and with Your help to walk rightly to the greatest possible degree. And if my hurts or mistakes can help others, use my wounds." If we confess our sin rather than cover it up, excuse it, or justify it, our points of failure can be our point of greatest ministry.

Genesis 2:23 (b)
. . . she shall be called Woman, because she was taken out of Man.

The Hebrew word for man is *Ish;* the word for woman is *Isha.* In other words, in this first marriage, Eve was given Adam's name.

Genesis 2:24, 25
Therefore shall a man leave his father and his mother, and shall cleave unto his wife: and they shall be one flesh. And they were both naked, the man and his wife, and were not ashamed.

True one-ness, true unity is based on two requirements:

Leaving. Leaving Mom and Dad is not a problem for most of us. The problem lies in leaving the relationship at work, in leaving the man or woman at the office to whom you pour out your heart, with whom you share your dreams.

"But it's nothing sensual whatsoever," you protest.

Really? Jesus said no man can serve two masters, for he will eventually begin to hate one of them. Therefore, if you hold on to any outside relationship, almost imperceptibly at first, your husband or wife will slowly begin to bug you. "I wish she would cut her hair," or "I wish he wasn't such a slob," you'll find yourself thinking. So she cuts her hair and he cleans himself up—but then you'll wish her hair was long or that he wasn't so concerned about his appearance—because no matter what he or she does, it won't be quite right.

It's all too easy to invest time and energy into relationships outside of marriage—and that will be hugely problematic in every instance because Jesus says wherever a man's treasure is, there will his heart be also (Luke 12:34).

That's why Paul says, "If any woman has a question, let her ask her husband" (1 Corinthians 14:35).

Therefore, whenever a wife says, "But my husband doesn't know anything about spiritual matters. Pastor, you're so wonderful. Could I please talk to you?" it is the wise pastor who says, "If he doesn't know the answer, he'll ask me and I'll have the privilege of sharing with him, after which he'll come home and share with you."

I say this tonight because in the past few weeks alone, I've seen five or six good brothers and sisters hit the skids due to this very issue. They did not leave every other. And you can say, "Well, I don't know if I buy this," and you can continue to joke with the woman or laugh with the man at the office—but in so doing, they'll become your treasure and later your heart will be sure to follow. There are no exceptions.

Cleaving. Although the world doesn't understand this, the Bible tells us that physical intimacy is more than simply two bodies coming together. It's two souls being made one (see Proverbs 6:32). That's why we are not to defraud our partner (see 1 Corinthians 7:5).

> *"Well, I would cleave to him if I felt more love for him," or, "I would cleave to her if I had feelings for her," some say.*
>
> *But that's backwards. As in every other area of spiritual life, the Lord says, "Step out and I'll part the water."*
>
> *"Part the water and I'll step out," we say.*
>
> *"That's not the way it works," the Lord says, "because that's not faith."*

Begin to give yourself to your spouse, and the feelings will come because by making him or her your treasure, your heart will follow. In the very first marriage seminar ever given, held in the Garden of Eden, God told Adam and Eve to leave and cleave. The degree to which we do this is the degree to which we'll experience unity and joy in our marriages.

3 **Genesis 3:1**
Now the serpent was more subtil than any beast of the field which the LORD God had made. And he said unto the woman, Yea, hath God said, Ye shall not eat of every tree of the garden?

"Are you sure you heard God right?" Satan asked Eve. The Fall of mankind began with a question. The same is still true. Even in Christian circles, Satan's strategy is to get believers to doubt their ability to understand the Word. Don't fall prey to his tactics, gang. The Word of God is incredibly profound. But it is also amazingly simple.

Genesis 3:2 (a)
And the woman said unto the serpent . . .

Eve begins to dialogue with the devil—always a dangerous thing to do.

Genesis 3:2 (b), 3
. . . We may eat of the fruit of the trees of the garden: But of the fruit of the tree which is in the midst of the garden, God hath said, Ye shall not eat of it, neither shall ye touch it, lest ye die.

God didn't tell Adam and Eve they were not to touch the forbidden fruit, but Eve added an extra rule, a protective parameter to make sure she didn't violate what God had said. And that is the beginning of legalism.

Adding to the Word always leads to bondage, bitterness, and backsliding. Our intent might be to try and prevent ourselves or others from getting too close to forbidden fruit, but in reality, our rules and barriers only burden people and ultimately cause them to forget the whole thing and walk away from God.

***For topical study of Genesis 3:3 entitled "He Didn't Say That!" turn to page* 14.**

Genesis 3:4, 5
And the serpent said unto the woman, Ye shall not surely die: For God doth know that in the day ye eat thereof, then your eyes shall be opened, and ye shall be as gods, knowing good and evil.

After questioning the *Word* of God, Satan questions the *way* of God as he intimated to Eve that God was holding something back from her that would be good for her. Again, this is the same strategy he uses today. Satan slithers up to our friends, our children, our neighbors, and hisses in their ears saying, "You know why you're not ssssupposed to do that? Because it's really fun. And God doesn't want that for you. He wants you to be ressstricted and missserable."

Not true. As I tell my kids, "If you think sin is fun, if you want to eat from the tree of forbidden fruit, look first at another tree—the tree of Calvary—and you'll see what sin will ultimately do. It will crucify you. And if you think God is holding something back from you, or doesn't want the best for you, look at that tree again, and you'll see Him with outstretched arms, nails piercing His palms, proving to you unequivocally that He loves you passionately."

Satan's three-pronged old lie is now part of the

New Age: "You're not going to die. Your eyes will be opened. You'll be a god."

What's the New Age philosophy? "You don't die; you just reincarnate. By embracing everything, you receive illumination. When you are enlightened, you become a god." Here in the Garden of Eden, at the very outset of time, Satan lays out a strategy he will maintain throughout human history.

Genesis 3:6 (a)
And when the woman saw that the tree was good for food, and that it was pleasant to the eyes, and a tree to be desired to make one wise, she took of the fruit thereof, and did eat, and gave also unto her husband with her . . .

John tells us all sin falls into one of these three categories: the lust of the flesh—it tastes good; the lust of the eyes—it's nice to look at; the pride of life—it'll make you wise (1 John 2:16). Eve bought and bit into Satan's lie, and invited Adam to do the same.

Genesis 3:6 (b)
. . . and he did eat.

Timothy tells us Eve was deceived (1 Timothy 2:14). Not so with Adam. By eating of the forbidden fruit, he said in essence, "I want to be with Eve more than I want to obey God. I would rather be doomed with the woman than trust God to resolve the situation." If Adam had turned to God, I am convinced God would have somehow reconciled Eve's fallen state. But rather than turn to God, Adam chose to join Eve.

Genesis 3:7 (a)
And the eyes of them both were opened . . .

"In the day ye eat thereof, then your eyes shall be opened," Satan had said to Eve, "and ye shall know good and evil." Unfortunately, Satan was right. You see, before man ate of the Tree of the Knowledge of Good and Evil, he had to ask the Father about every matter, about every situation in order to discern good from evil. God and Adam walked together in the cool of the day in constant communion because Adam had to depend solely upon God for his knowledge. After the Fall, Adam grew independent from God—and knowledge without God is always deadly.

The Tree of the Knowledge of Good and Evil is as deadly for us as it was for Adam. It can squeeze the life out of our relationship with the Lord if we're not oh, so careful. Even Bible knowledge can be deadly to anyone who says, "I've been to Bible school; I've been to seminary; I've been reading the Word for years. I know good from evil."

"Aren't we supposed to know the Bible?" you ask.

Yes. But as we study the Word we are to fellowship with the Lord intimately, talk to Him personally, worship, praise, commune, and listen to Him constantly. You see, as parents our job is to get our kids to become independent. When they take their first steps, we say, "Way to go!" When they learn to tie their shoes, ride a bike, drive a car, move out, we say, "Hooray!" But our Heavenly Father wants just the opposite for you and me. He wants us to be totally dependent upon Him. He wants us to be constantly talking to Him just as Adam used to do before he ate of the forbidden fruit.

Genesis 3:7 (b)
. . . and they knew that they were naked . . .

Before their Fall, it would seem as though Adam and Eve were, like God, clothed with a garment of light (Psalm 104:2). After the Fall, their garments of light were replaced with darkness, and the beauty of their sexuality became an embarrassment, a perversion, a problem.

Genesis 3:7 (c)
. . . and they sewed fig leaves together, and made themselves aprons.

The only identifiable tree in the Garden of Eden is this one—the fig tree. The national symbol of Israel, the fig tree speaks of man's attempt to cover the nakedness of his sin with his own effort.

Genesis 3:8
And they heard the voice of the LORD God walking in the garden in the cool of the day: and Adam and his wife hid themselves from the presence of the LORD God amongst the trees of the garden.

Attired in their scratchy, itchy fig leaves, Adam and Eve hear the voice of the Lord and they hide. That's what sin always does. It causes us to hide from the Lord. Like Adam and Eve, if there's rebellion in my life, I'll run from the voice of the Lord—I'll lose my appetite for Scripture.

Genesis 3:9
And the LORD God called unto Adam, and said unto him, Where art thou?

Because none seeks God (Romans 3:11), it had to be God who sought Adam. And His question is not, "Why did you?" or, "How could you?" but simply, "Where *are* you?"

Genesis 3:10, 11
And he said, I heard thy voice in the garden, and I was afraid, because I was naked; and I hid myself. And he said, Who told thee that thou wast naked? Hast thou eaten of the tree, whereof I commanded thee that thou shouldest not eat?

Because God knew precisely what Adam had done, He's not after information from Adam, but confession from him. So, too, God wants to get me to a place where I confess to Him—not because He wants to embarrass me or needs information about my sin, but because when I confess sin, it loses its grip on me. That's why confession is so important. Confession doesn't bring forgiveness because forgiveness was already granted to us at the Cross. Confession doesn't forgive us—it simply frees us from the grip of sin on our lives.

Genesis 3:12
And the man said, The woman whom thou gavest to be with me, she gave me of the tree, and I did eat.

Rather than confessing his sin, Adam blames the woman for his sin, and, indirectly, God Himself for giving the woman to him. The same is still true. Anytime I blame someone else—be it a spouse, a parent, a boss, an employee, a neighbor—I am ultimately blaming the One who put that person in my life.

Genesis 3:13, 14 (a)
And the LORD God said unto the woman, What is this that thou hast done? And the woman said, The serpent beguiled me, and I did eat. And the LORD God said unto the serpent . . .

You gotta love the Father here. He's not heavy-handed with Adam and Eve. Rather, He just lets them play out their blame game.

Genesis 3:14 (b)
. . . Because thou hast done this, thou art cursed above all cattle, and above every beast of the field; upon thy belly shalt thou go, and dust shalt thou eat all the days of thy life:

The lustrous serpent becomes the lowly snake. Interestingly, according to Isaiah 65:25, even in the Millennium, when earth is restored back to her Eden-like condition, everything will return to its pre-Fall state—except the snake. The snake will remain in its cursed condition, crawling on its belly.

Genesis 3:15 (a)
And I will put enmity between thee and the woman . . .

One of the practical outcomes of the Fall was that women and snakes would become enemies. So, too, when people base their relationship on sin, they inevitably become enemies. How many times have we seen people who want nothing to do with each other and won't even acknowledge each other because their relationship was built on sin?

Genesis 3:15 (b)
. . . and between thy seed and her seed; it shall bruise thy head, and thou shalt bruise his heel.

Not only is there the practical outcome of enmity, but there is a prophetic message as well because within this verse lies the Proto Evangelicum—the first mention of the Gospel. The term "her seed" is an apparent impossibility unless One would come from the woman in a way that would be supernatural. And who would that One be? Of course, it's Jesus—the Promised Seed of Galatians 4:4. Christ would come and we are told here that He would bruise, or literally crush the head of the serpent. But the serpent would bruise the heel of the Promised Seed. And therein we see a picture of the Cross, where Christ was bruised for our iniquities (Isaiah 53), and where He cleansed our sin with His own blood, thereby crushing the head of Satan's authority in our lives.

Genesis 3:16 (a)
Unto the woman he said, I will greatly multiply thy sorrow and thy conception; in sorrow thou shalt bring forth children . . .

"You'll have children, Eve, but it won't be like it was supposed to be—painless, glorious, and easy. It will be difficult."

Genesis 3:16 (b)–19
. . . and thy desire shall be to thy husband, and he shall rule over thee. And unto Adam he said, Because thou hast hearkened unto the voice of thy wife, and hast eaten of the tree, of which I commanded thee, saying, Thou shalt not eat of it: cursed is the ground for thy sake; in sorrow shalt thou eat of it all the days of thy life; Thorns also and thistles shall it bring forth to thee; and thou shalt eat the herb of the field; In the sweat of thy face shalt thou eat bread, till thou return unto the ground; for out of it wast

thou taken: for dust thou art, and unto dust shalt thou return.

The desire of the woman would be for her husband. The man, on the other hand, would work by the sweat of his brow. And therein lies a foundational dilemma in marriage to this day.

"Why won't my husband slow down? I want him to take a walk with me, talk to me, listen to me," she cries.

"I show my love most clearly by providing for my family," answers the weary husband. "That's why I work three jobs."

She wants to talk. He needs to work. She wants to enjoy. He can't wait to get going. It's all part of the curse. When husbands and wives realize what the curse has done and how it works, no longer will they try to change each other. Lowered expectations will replace futile ideas of transformation. Don't raise the bar for your marriage. Lower it. And as you lower your expectations on earth, raise your sights toward heaven.

This is what Paul meant when he said, "Let those who are married be as though they're not" (1 Corinthians 7:29). In other words, "Life is short. Keep your focus on the kingdom, your eyes on eternity." Set your sights on the Lord and what will that do? It will make you a better husband or a better wife because as His love flows from you, your times with your husband or wife will be sweet and rich.

It's amazing what happens when we do what the Lord tells us to do. When we seek first the kingdom, everything else will be added to us (Matthew 6:33). When a woman and man both deeply love Jesus Christ, they each find their ultimate satisfaction in their walk with Him. The pressure is removed. The bickering stops. They are a joy to be around.

Tammy can only enjoy me if she keeps her expectations real low. If she reads too many books and attends too many seminars, her expectations will increase, disappointment will set in, and frustration will follow. God is so incredibly practical. "Life is short," He says. "There's coming a time when you'll be free, when all will be right, so seek first the kingdom."

Genesis 3:20
And Adam called his wife's name Eve; because she was the mother of all living.

In chapter 2, Adam called Eve *Isha* which means "from the man." Here, he changes her name to "Eve" which means "the giver of life." The implication is astounding. No longer does Adam say, "Woman, you're from me. You're mine. Listen to me," for now he realizes that from her will come his Savior. So, too, husband, there will be a transformation in the mind of any man who understands that in his wife dwells his Lord.

Genesis 3:21
Unto Adam also and to his wife did the LORD God make coats of skins, and clothed them.

To replace Adam and Eve's itchy fig leaves, a sacrifice was made—illustrative of the fact that mankind's sin and nakedness would never be covered by his own efforts, but by the sacrifice of an innocent One, the Lamb of God, Jesus Christ.

Will we see Adam in heaven? I believe so. Verse 20 indicates Adam understood that from Eve would come a Savior. Verse 21 says he received the substitutionary death of another to cover his nakedness. And I believe both of these indicate faith at work.

***For topical study of Genesis 3:21 entitled "Go Fig-ure," turn to page* 16.**

Genesis 3:22, 23
And the LORD God said, Behold, the man is become as one of us, to know good and evil: and now, lest he put forth his hand, and take also of the tree of life, and eat, and live for ever: Therefore the LORD God sent him forth from the garden of Eden, to till the ground from whence he was taken.

Adam and Eve could no longer stay in the garden lest they ate of the Tree of Life and lived forever in their fallen condition. Can you imagine what you would look like at 30,000 years of age at your present rate of decay? It would be sad. So God in His mercy ruled out that possibility.

Genesis 3:24
So he drove out the man; and he placed at the east of the garden of Eden Cherubims, and a flaming sword which turned every way, to keep the way of the tree of life.

A sacrifice had been made to cover Adam and Eve's nakedness. Cherubim and a flame followed. This same picture will be painted again in the tabernacle, for over the mercy seat, sprinkled with sacrificial blood, were cherubim and the bright Shekinah glory of God.

But the place we see this picture painted most powerfully is not in the Garden, nor in the tabernacle, but in an empty tomb where two angels clothed in light sat at either end of a slab stained with the sacrificial blood of the Lamb of God.

Genesis 3 keeps man away from the Tree of Life; but Jesus Christ invites mankind to eat of the Bread of Life (John 6:57). And as we do, we begin to experience power over the curse as well as a sneak preview of coming attractions when the curse will be obliterated in heaven. Oh, glorious day!

HE DIDN'T SAY THAT!

A Topical Study of GENESIS 3:3

Several years ago, a medical mystery baffled the physicians at Palnomie Hospital in Free State, South Africa, when, for ten consecutive weeks, whichever patient was in Bed #4 of the Intensive Care Unit would be dead on Friday morning. After double checking medical procedures, air-conditioning vents, and room structure surrounding Bed #4, it was discovered that at 3 A.M. every Friday morning, the cleaning lady would unknowingly pull the plug of the life support system of Bed #4 so that she could plug her floor polisher in to the vacant socket.

People look around our world and see disaster, disease, and death. They see problems, pollution, and pain. They scratch their heads and say, "How did the world get this way? Why are there earthquakes and volcanoes and hurricanes and tornadoes? Why are there wars? Why can't people get along with each other? Why is there cancer?"

The answer is that someone pulled the plug of our planet's life support system.

When Adam chose to rebel against God, the whole world was plunged into sin. Nature was impacted. Earth's ecology changed radically. Disease and death entered in, and from that point on, man would be born with the nature of depravity.

Why should we pay the price for Adam's failure?

Because if it was you or I in the Garden, we would have done worse.

If I said, "I will pay you one million dollars to come up here right now and go ten rounds with Mike Tyson. If you survive ten rounds in a small ring with an angry, bitter Tyson, then one million is yours. Or, if you would rather, you can have someone represent you. You can have Evander Holyfield stand in for you"—every one of you with any sense would say, "I'll go with Evander."

Adam was Evander. Hot off the press, freshly made by God, he was a champion. Thus, because even Adam bombed out, we can be assured that if you or I were in the Garden, we would have surely blown it a whole lot sooner.

With eyes wide open, Adam chose to join Eve in eating of the forbidden fruit; and in so doing, chose creation over Creator. It's a tragedy repeated to this day with the same inevitable results.

Whenever a man or woman says, "I don't care what the cost might be, I know this is wrong, but I'm going to have her anyway; I'm going to be with him no matter what"—

a decision is made which will ultimately bring about prolonged, permanent pain. Those who choose creation over Creator say, "Oh, I know there will be repercussions. I know there will be a price to pay, but I'll suck it up and take it because I love him or I've just got to have her. I know it'll be tough for a while, but our love can endure. My baby and I will sail through the seas of adversity together to a port of tranquility and tropical beauty." They have it all figured out. But the price they expect to pay is not what it will cost. That's the trick. That's the catch. And that's the truth.

Inevitably, invariably, eventually, their cry will be, "I didn't know *this* would be the result of my sin. God have mercy. I'm a fool."

When Adam chose to join Eve in eating of the Tree of the Knowledge of Good and Evil, the fruit of his choice would bring bloodshed, perversion, destruction, sorrow, death, and disease into his family. It would change the earth's topography. And it would plunge all of mankind into depravity. Although he didn't understand the consequences, Adam's choice was a matter of out and out rebellion. Eve, on the other hand, was deceived into making her choice (1 Timothy 2:14).

When did this deception begin?

Some would say it began the moment Eve started dialoguing with the serpent, always a dangerous thing to do.

Others would say, "No, it began when Eve started hanging around the forbidden tree. If she hadn't been there, she wouldn't have entered into conversation with the deceiver."

Others would say, "No, it began when she left Adam's side. The man and woman were to be traveling together, fulfilling each other, and yet here we see the woman alone."

But I suggest the deception began when legalism began . . .

> *But of the tree of the knowledge of good and evil, thou shalt not eat of it: for in the day that thou eatest thereof thou shalt surely die.* Genesis 2:17

> *And the woman said unto the serpent, We may eat of the fruit of the trees of the garden: But of the fruit of the tree which is in the midst of the garden, God hath said, Ye shall not eat of it, neither shall ye touch it, lest ye die.* Genesis 3:2, 3

A phrase was added to complicate the beautiful simplicity God gave to Adam and Eve in the Garden of Eden. I understand Eve's rationale, don't you? After all, if they weren't to eat of the tree, why should they touch it? That seems like a wise rule.

The only problem is, God didn't tell them not to touch it. Eve could have made that choice for herself, and that would have been fine. But when she ascribed that rule to God, legalism was born. The conception of deception begins with legalism—adding rules, conditions, regulations. Mankind says what we need are some parameters to protect us from sin. It's always been this way.

"Israel, I want you to have what no other nation in the history of humanity has ever had," said God. "I want you to do what no other civilization has ever done. I want you to set aside one day in seven for rest, refreshment, renewal. Take a day off. Enjoy!"

So what did God's people do? They did what we do. They said, "We better add some rules and regulations to make sure we keep this vacation . . ."

Anyone who had a wooden leg had to unscrew it on the Sabbath lest he be guilty of carrying a burden.

Anyone who spat on the ground was in violation of the Sabbath because he would be making clay, which could be used for construction.

Books were written, libraries filled with rules for keeping the Sabbath. But what happened?

All but the Pharisees eventually said, "We can't keep these rules," and they drifted away from their desire to know, love, and walk with God.

The same can still be true. So much of what we see in churches today is nothing more than man saying things God never said . . .

> Why do we dress nicely to come to church?
> "Because God is there."
> And He's not in our homes? He's not with us in our backyards?
> "It just shows respect."
> Says who?

God never said, "When you seek Me show Me respect by dressing nicely." Others may say that. But not God.

Mom and Dad, we must tell our kids what God said—nothing more, nothing less, nothing else—for, like the Jews, our kids will turn away from a vibrant walk with God, and like Eve, they'll fall prey to deception whenever barriers are erected which come between them and God. If your kids are reeling under the weight of rules and regulations, if they're feeling condemned and confused, don't blame God. He came to share truth. He came to set them free (John 8:32).

Keep it simple, gang. Stay away from the deception that begins with the conception of legalism. Simply do what God tells you to do and you'll do well.

GO FIG-URE

A Topical Study of GENESIS 3:21

1962: It was the best of times; it was the worst of times. It was the year my beloved San Francisco Giants made it to the World Series. And it was the year our school adopted SMSG—Student Mathematic Study Group—into its curriculum. SMSG was the dreaded "new math" in which algebraic theory replaced long division, multiplication tables, and fractions. By the time the program was dumped four years later, we had the theories down, but we couldn't multiply or divide. As a result, math has never been my strongest suit. But even if math came easy to me, sometimes God's math doesn't seem to add up . . .

An owner of a vineyard headed to the marketplace at sunrise to hire harvesters. "I'll pay you a denarius," he told them, which was the day's wage of a top-ranking Roman soldier. A few hours later, in need of more workers, he returned to the town square and hired additional help. He did the same thing at noontime, and again at 3:00 in the afternoon. Finally, at 5:00—an hour before quitting time—the vineyard owner hired his last crew.

At the end of the day, the owner of the vineyard paid the men he'd hired at 5:00 a full day's wage. "This is great!" said those who had been hired at 6:00 in the morning. "If the guys who only worked an hour got a full day's wage, we're going to walk away loaded!" But such was not the case, for the owner of the vineyard gave the guys hired at 3:00 a denarius, the guys hired at noon a denarius, the guys hired at 9:00 a denarius, and the guys hired at 6:00 a denarius (Matthew 20).

One hour's work equals a full day's work? Go figure!

Observing a widow place two mites—less than one penny—in the offering, Jesus told His disciples that she had given more than all those who were contributing much larger sums of money to the temple treasury (Mark 12).

Less than a penny was worth more than hundreds of dollars? Go figure!

When the shepherd discovered one of his flock was missing, he left ninety-nine of his sheep to search for the one that was missing. (Luke 15). Wait a minute. If he leaves ninety-nine sheep unattended, by the time he returns, twenty-five of them could be picked off. Besides, there's no guarantee he'd even find the missing sheep.

Leaving ninety-nine in the hand for one in the bush? Go figure!

As He sat in the home of Simon the Pharisee, Jesus allowed His head to be anointed with perfume which cost the equivalent of a year's salary. No wonder the accountant took offense. Why waste so much money when there were so many poor to feed? (John 12).

Yet Jesus rebuked the practical treasurer and commended the extravagant worshiper. Go figure!

A man had two sons, one of whom wasted his entire inheritance on loose living. The older son made no demands of his father, and remained by his side, working the family farm. When the younger son's inheritance was completely gone, he returned home. Now, if I were telling this story, I would have said, "The father rewarded the faithful older son, while the younger son was happy simply to be offered a position as a hired hand." But that isn't the way Jesus told the story. In His version, who got the ring of authority, a robe, new shoes? The younger son (Luke 15).

What? The son who stayed got a warning, and the son who left got a party? Go figure!

I know these stories well, and so do you. But if we were hearing them for the first time, we would agree that they don't add up. It should have been the older brother who got the party, the big donor who got the attention, the ninety-nine sheep who got the care, and the hard worker who got the pay.

Because that's not the way it worked out, it becomes clear that God's math is entirely different than mine. That is the only way I can explain the text before us, where instead of leaving Adam and Eve to suffer in their scratchy fig leaves, God covers them with fur; where instead of dressing them down for turning their back on Him, He dresses them up. Go figure!

God's computations are based on an entirely different system than ours.

Ours are based on logic, practicality, hard work. His are based solely on grace.

The world says, "There's no free lunch. Work hard. Make it happen." But not God.

He says, "My ways are not your ways. My ways are based upon unmerited, undeserved, unearned favor."

There is nothing you can do to make God love you more. Nothing. There's nothing I can do to make God love me one ounce more than He loves me right now. If I pray all day today; if I fast for a week or a month; if I worship constantly, He will not love me any more than He loves me right now. Likewise, there is not one thing you could do to make Him love you less.

This amazes me because, like you, I am under the impression that I have to do something to earn God's favor.

"No," says God. "Your efforts will be like fig leaves. They will be scratchy. They will crumble. They won't work. Let Me give you that which you could never provide for yourself: Matchless grace and infinite mercy which will cover you completely and eternally."

God's ways are not our ways. Therefore, His math is not ours. His grace and mercy, His goodness and blessings lavished upon sinful people like me just don't add up.

And I'm so glad.

---

4 **Genesis 4:1**
And Adam knew Eve his wife; and she conceived, and bare Cain, and said, I have gotten a man from the LORD.

"I have gotten a man from the Lord," said Eve, or literally, "I have gotten a man, even the Lord." In naming her firstborn son, Cain, or "acquired," it is clear Eve believed he was the Seed promised to her in Genesis 3:15, the Promised One, the Messiah.

Genesis 4:2 (a)
And she again bare his brother Abel . . .

It wasn't very long before Eve discovered what every one of us who has kids knows to be true: Kids are born with a sin nature. Therefore, since Cain wasn't who she hoped he'd be, Eve knew her second son wouldn't be either—and named him Abel, which means "vanity" or "empty." The problem with Cain and Abel is that they were born of the seed of man. The promise of Genesis

3:15 would not be fulfilled until One was born of the seed of woman. And that One is Jesus Christ.

Genesis 4:2 (b)–4 (a)
. . . And Abel was a keeper of sheep, but Cain was a tiller of the ground. And in process of time it came to pass, that Cain brought of the fruit of the ground an offering unto the LORD. And Abel, he also brought of the firstlings of his flock and of the fat thereof . . .

According to Hebrews 11:4, what Abel did, he did by faith. The fact that faith comes by hearing, and hearing by the Word of God (Romans 10:17), means God had spoken to Cain and Abel concerning what an acceptable sacrifice would be. Abel chose to do what the Lord told him to do. Cain, on the other hand, evidently said, "I don't like the idea of bloodshed. It's dreadful."

But that was precisely the point. Sin *is* dreadful. Sin causes death. Sin brings sorrow. God did not institute the sacrificial system because He's gory. He instituted it to pointedly communicate the fact that sin causes blood to be shed, lives to be lost.

"I have a better, neater, cleaner idea," said Cain. "I'll sacrifice fruits and vegetables—the fruit of my own labor."

Genesis 4:4 (b), 5 (a)
. . . And the LORD had respect unto Abel and to his offering: But unto Cain and to his offering he had not respect . . .

Abel's offering was accepted because it was made by faith, according to God's Word. Cain's was rejected because it was based on his own ideas and efforts.

Genesis 4:5 (b)
. . . And Cain was very wroth, and his countenance fell.

His offering rejected, Cain became angry and bitter. The phrase, "his countenance fell," constitutes the first mention of depression in the Bible. Thus, according to the Principle of First Mention which holds that the first place a subject appears in Scripture contains foundational principles regarding said subject—Cain's depression holds truths for us . . .

Genesis 4:6, 7 (a)
And the LORD said unto Cain, Why art thou wroth? and why is thy countenance fallen? If thou doest well, shalt thou not be accepted?

In other words, "If you choose to do well, your countenance will be lifted up as it was previously."

Genesis 4:7 (b)
. . . and if thou doest not well, sin lieth at the door. And unto thee shall be his desire, and thou shalt rule over him.

"If you choose not to do well, Cain, sin lies at the door like a lion ready to attack. You will either be lifted up, or you will be attacked. It's your choice."

Although I feel like a prophet crying in the wilderness as I go against the flow of what our culture says about depression, I remain biblically persuaded that many people today are seeking medical help for depression when in reality it is often a spiritual issue. Interestingly, even the research done by the pharmaceutical companies who manufacture antidepressants corroborate this, for their studies indicate that, due to the reduction of serotonin—a chemical in the brain which governs emotional stability, it is impossible for those who are clinically depressed to simply will themselves out of depression. I believe this is what Scripture has indicated all along, for bitterness and anger, sin and resentment affect the chemistry of one's brain. Thus, the pharmacist and the pastor differ not in the diagnosis of depression, but in the cure. The pharmacist says, "Take a pill."

The pastor says, "Make a choice."

Gang, we can choose to put on the garment of praise for the spirit of heaviness (Isaiah 61:3). We can choose to rejoice in the Lord (1 Thessalonians 5:16). We can choose to pray without ceasing (1 Thessalonians 5:17). We can choose to give thanks in everything (1 Thessalonians 5:18). We can choose to think on whatever is pure and lovely and praiseworthy (Philippians 4:8).

"If you choose right," God said to Cain, "you'll be lifted up. But if you don't, the lion of depression will eat you for lunch."

I am not suggesting that we should never use medication. But as a pastor, I am concerned and saddened by how many Christians in our country are popping pills.

"Why art thou cast down, O my soul?" David asked when he faced depression like ours. What was his prescription? "Hope thou in God" (Psalm 42:11).

"My bones ache. My eyes weep. I feel as though there's gravel in my teeth," cried Jeremiah in his own deep, dark depression. His cure? "I will lift up my heart with my hands unto the heavens" (Lamentations 3:41).

Although I am increasingly convinced that

there are people who, because of difficulties in life, can benefit from wise and prudent medical help in this arena, such is not the norm because as you read the Bible from cover to cover, it becomes clear that the issue regarding depression is primarily an issue of choice.

God didn't say, "I know you're sad, Cain. Here, drink this; swallow that; and you'll be better in the morning." No, He said, "Your bitterness is causing your countenance to fall. If you choose to do well—to obey My Word—you'll be lifted up. If you don't choose well, you'll be eaten up."

Genesis 4:8, 9
And Cain talked with Abel his brother: and it came to pass, when they were in the field, that Cain rose up against Abel his brother, and slew him. And the LORD said unto Cain, Where is Abel thy brother? And he said, I know not: Am I my brother's keeper?

Sin says, "I don't care about him. He hurt me. I don't care about her. She offended me. I don't care about them. They wronged me." That explains how, after killing Abel, Cain could say, "I don't care about him. I'm not his keeper." If there is someone in your life whom you would just as soon disappear, be careful because you're walking in the way of Cain (Jude 11). Your hostility and bitterness towards him or her will alter the course of your life as surely as Cain's did his.

Genesis 4:10 (a)
And he said, What hast thou done? the voice of thy brother's blood . . .

If in the margin of your Bible the word "blood" is translated "bloods," it is due to the fact that the Jewish people believe that he who kills one person also kills that person's potential children, grandchildren, great-grandchildren and so on. Conversely, he who saves one person saves generations, which is why trees are planted at the Holocaust Museum in Israel in honor of Gentiles who harbored Jews during World War II.

So in this I am reminded that unforgiveness and hate and bitterness have repercussions far bigger than I might think. That is why in the Book of Jude, God specifically says to watch out for the way of Cain, which is bitterness, unforgiveness, hatred. Make sure there's no one you're mad at, upset with, or angry about because it only takes one to affect many. Ask Cain.

Genesis 4:10 (b)
. . . crieth unto me from the ground.

"The blood of your brother cries out to Me." The writer of Hebrews picks up this metaphor when he declares, "Jesus' blood speaks better things than the blood of Abel" (12:24). What does Abel's blood cry? It's a message of condemnation, judgment, accusation. What does Jesus' blood cry? It cries, "Forgiven."

If there is an old boyfriend, ex-spouse, parent, or boss you're mad at, whose name still comes up when you talk to people, God would say, "My Son was slaughtered on the Cross for the very sin that person committed against you. Let it go. Give it up. Put it under the blood that speaks better things. Lay it at the Cross."

Genesis 4:11–13
And now art thou cursed from the earth, which hath opened her mouth to receive thy brother's blood from thy hand; When thou tillest the ground, it shall not henceforth yield unto thee her strength; a fugitive and a vagabond shalt thou be in the earth. And Cain said unto the LORD, My punishment is greater than I can bear.

Cain didn't say, "Father forgive me." He said, "My punishment is not fair." Cain remained in his cursed condition because he chose to be mad rather than to ask for mercy.

Genesis 4:14
Behold, thou hast driven me out this day from the face of the earth; and from thy face shall I be hid; and I shall be a fugitive and a vagabond in the earth; and it shall come to pass, that every one that findeth me shall slay me.

The language here is most interesting, for notice that Cain doesn't say, "You're going to hide from me," but rather, "I'm going to hide from You." In other words, Cain declares, "Even though everyone will be out to get me, I'm not going to be looking to You anymore," as he shakes his fist at God.

Genesis 4:15
And the LORD said unto him, Therefore whosoever slayeth Cain, vengeance shall be taken on him sevenfold. And the LORD set a mark upon Cain, lest any finding him should kill him.

God looks at this man who continues to be oh, so wrong, and says, "Don't anyone bother him." The grace and mercy of our Father amazes me.

Genesis 4:16
And Cain went out from the presence of the LORD, and dwelt in the land of Nod, on the east of Eden.

Cain could have pressed in *to* the presence of the Lord. Instead he went out *from* the presence of the Lord—to Nod, or literally, "Wandering."

Genesis 4:17 (a)
And Cain knew his wife . . .

Where did Cain get his wife? This is one of the questions that has been asked of me more than any other single question. The answer? Because Adam lived to be 930 years old, he and Eve had many, many children. Therefore, Cain married one of his own relatives because mankind had not yet gone down the road of depravity long enough chronologically to cause the kinds of problems now present in intermarriage. What I wish people would ask is not where did Cain get his wife, but what the Philippian jailor asked when he said, "What must I do to be saved?" (Acts 16).

Genesis 4:17 (b)
. . . and she conceived, and bare Enoch: and he builded a city, and called the name of the city, after the name of his son, Enoch.

Cain wanders away from the Lord, and builds a city which he dedicates not to God, but to his son. He's desiring, determining, attempting to build his own empire. But watch what happens to his family . . .

Genesis 4:18 (a)
And unto Enoch was born Irad . . .

The name *Irad* literally means "Fugitive" or "Wild Ass."

Genesis 4:18 (b)
. . . and Irad begat Mehujael . . .

Mehujael literally means "blot out that Yah is El." In other words, "wipe out the name of God."

Genesis 4:18 (c)
. . . and Mehujael begat Methusael . . .

Methusael literally means "They are dead who are of God."

In other words, "Those who believe in God are dead." It's a skeptical, scornful kind of name.

Genesis 4:18 (d)
. . . and Methusael begat Lamech.

Lamech literally means, "Poor and lowly."

Genesis 4:19 (a)
And Lamech took unto him two wives . . .

Here, in the degenerate line of Cain, we see the first mention of polygamy.

Genesis 4:19 (b)
. . . the name of the one was Adah, and the name of the other Zillah.

Adah means "ornament." *Zillah* can either mean "seductress" or "shabbiness." Because nothing in the Bible is coincidental, I find this account interesting. You see, it could be that Zillah seduced Lamech. Or, more possibly, it could be that after Lamech took two wives, one became beautiful, the other shabby in his sight.

If you're toying with an affair, an infatuation, a fantasy, a pictorial excursion on the Internet, understand this: the degree to which anyone else becomes attractive to you is the degree to which your spouse will become increasingly unattractive. No man can serve two masters. That's just the way the human soul is made.

Genesis 4:20
And Adah bare Jabal: he was the father of such as dwell in tents, and of such as have cattle.

The word "cattle" is literally "possession," or "production." Before this, people lived in community. From the line of Cain, however, independence is born, as Jabal became the father of the nomad.

Genesis 4:21
And his brother's name was Jubal: he was the father of all such as handle the harp and organ.

From whence comes the entrepreneurial spirit? From whence comes those who developed music? From the line of Cain. In other words, no longer were the harp and organ solely employed in worship around the throne of God as an act of worship and adoration. They now become a means of livelihood.

Genesis 4:22
And Zillah, she also bare Tubal-cain, an instructer of every artificer in brass and iron: and the sister of Tubal-cain was Naamah.

Tubalcain was an instructor, or, literally, a "whetter" or developer of cutting instruments—that is, weapons.

Genesis 4:23
And Lamech said unto his wives, Adah and Zillah, Hear my voice; ye wives of Lamech, hearken unto my speech: for I have slain a

man to my wounding, and a young man to my hurt.

Like his forefather, Lamech kills a man. This is called the Song of the Sword, as Lamech says arrogantly, "I killed a man who was hassling me."

Genesis 4:24
If Cain shall be avenged sevenfold, truly Lamech seventy and sevenfold.

The literal rendering of "seventy and sevenfold" is "seventy times seven." Does that ring a bell? Jesus applied the same mathematics to the subject not of vengeance but of forgiveness (Matthew 18:22).

It's sad to realize that arms, music, and an independent, entrepreneurial spirit—these things which our culture esteems highly—have their roots in Cain.

Ah, but there's a ray of sun breaking through . . .

Genesis 4:25, 26
And Adam knew his wife again; and she bare a son, and called his name Seth: For God, said she, hath appointed me another seed instead of Abel, whom Cain slew. And to Seth, to him also there was born a son; and he called his name Enos: then began men to call upon the name of the LORD.

From Seth came those who called upon the name of the Lord, or literally those who were called *by* the name of the Lord. In today's terminology, they would be called "Christians." That's us. We're not Jubalites or Jabalites. We're not musicians or entrepreneurs or military men. We're believers. That's our identity. Oh, we might raise cattle or play a harp. But that's not who we are. We find our sole identity not in the line of Cain, but in the line of Seth—as believers in the One who loves us.

5

Genesis 5:1, 2 (a)
This is the book of the generations of Adam. In the day that God created man, in the likeness of God made he him; Male and female created he them . . .

Before tracing Adam's family tree through the godly line of Seth here in verses 1 and 2, chapter 5 pauses to look back to the day God created Adam and Eve . . .

Genesis 5:2 (b)
. . . and blessed them, and called their name Adam, in the day when they were created.

God Himself presided over the first wedding ceremony. God Himself was the One who, in calling Adam and Eve "Adam," called them one.

"Is it lawful for a man to put away his wife for every cause?" the Pharisees asked Jesus, seeking to entrap Him in the raging controversy of the day (Matthew 19:3). Would He side with the school of Shammai, a conservative rabbi who maintained there was virtually no reason for divorce? Or would He side with Hillel, a rabbi who interpreted the Law of Moses so liberally that even a wife who over-salted her husband's eggs, causing him to lose his temper, could be considered "unclean" and therefore a candidate for divorce?

In answering, Jesus referred neither to Shammai nor Hillel, nor even to Moses. Jesus took the issue of divorce all the way back to the verse before us when He simply said, "Moses because of the hardness of your hearts suffered you to put away your wives: but from the beginning it was not so" (Matthew 19:8).

"*Their* name is Adam," God declared. They are one. There is only one reason for divorce: fornication, or adultery (Matthew 19:9).

"I'm so sorry," she cried. "I shouldn't have jeopardized my marriage. I shouldn't have allowed myself to become vulnerable to that situation. But God forgives me. So why can't my husband?"

"Yes," I told her. "God does indeed forgive you. Instantly, totally, completely. When Jesus hung on the Cross, He took the very sin of your adultery and died for it. And His blood washes it away so completely that it doesn't even enter the mind of the Father. But—the problem is that the same physical union which was powerful enough to bind you and your husband into one flesh initially is also powerful enough to tear you asunder tragically."

You see, gang, this is what our culture doesn't understand; this is where so many miss the boat and end up crashing on the rocks of heartache and despair. Adultery kills. It deals a deathblow to marriage. Contrary to what our culture espouses, the idea of "safe sex" outside of marriage is an absolute lie. When two become one intimately, it is not simply their bodies or emotions which are linked together. It is their very souls (Proverbs 6:32). Thus, Jesus cites fornication or adultery as the only force strong enough to render a marriage irreparable.

"But I thought that if we confess, the blood of Christ cleanses us from all sin—from the sin of gossip as well as from the sin of pride; from the sin of anger as well as from the sin of adultery," you might be thinking.

It does (1 John 1:9). All sin is equivalent to God.

All sin is equally hideous in the sight of our Father. But not all sins carry the same repercussions. "Don't be deceived," Paul declared. "God is not mocked. Whatever a man sows, that shall he reap" (Galatians 6:7).

If a man puts a gun to his wife's head and pulls the trigger, he can cry with remorse, saying, "Oh, I'm so sorry. I had a hard day today. I lost my stability. I didn't mean to do that." But none of his remorse will alter the results of his firing a single bullet into her head. As amazing as it sounds, if he confessed even that sin, God would forgive him. But his marriage would nonetheless be over.

Such is the power of adultery. "Well, then, I'll get divorced and move on," you might be thinking.

Yes, you'll move on. But you'll take with you the very problems that caused adultery in the first place. Gang, no one will make you happier than your present spouse. Why? Because even if you married your husband or wife without seeking God's guidance, will, or direction; even if there are 4,999 people who would have been more suited to you, in God's economy, the moment you said "I do" to that person, #5,000 instantly became #1.

You see, knowing our propensity to think the grass is always greener on the other side of the fence, knowing our tendency to want to trade this year's car for next year's model, God made it real simple for us. He ordained marriage for life. And those who understand this find glorious peace and freedom when they look at their spouse because they know there's no one down the line or around the corner who will give them a greater thrill; that there's not another person on earth who will make them happier, more content, or more fulfilled. Such is the amazing mystery of matrimony.

There are couples in our church who weren't perfectly matched body, soul, and spirit—but they stayed together because they understood the way of the Lord. And as I've watched them over the years, as I've seen their hair turn gray and their back bow a bit; as I've seen them blessed with children and grandchildren, I've heard them say, "Wow. It's worth it to go God's way."

There is no greater joy than watching your kids grow and walk in the way of the Lord. But all that is thrown away by the one who says, "If I have an affair, I'll be forgiven." There is nothing, there is no one, worth losing your family. God talks more about the sin of adultery than about any other single sin because adultery uniquely brings long-term, irreversible repercussions.

If you have been one of the fortunate few who have experienced a miraculous resurrection of your marriage following the deathblow of adultery, rejoice. You have been graced. Go your way and sin no more.

Dear people, determine that no matter what you've been through, no matter where you've been, you will do whatever it takes to guard the sanctity of your family.

Genesis 5:3 (a)
And Adam lived an hundred and thirty years . . .

Adam literally means "man."

Genesis 5:3 (b)
. . . and begat a son in his own likeness, after his image; and called his name Seth:

Seth literally means "appointed."

Genesis 5:4, 5
And the days of Adam after he had begotten Seth were eight hundred years: and he begat sons and daughters: And all the days that Adam lived were nine hundred and thirty years: and he died.

Concerning the Tree of the Knowledge of Good and Evil, God said, "In the day that ye eat thereof ye shall surely die" (Genesis 2:17). Adam did indeed eat of the Tree of the Knowledge of Good and Evil—and yet he obviously didn't die the day he ate of it. He lived 930 years. Wait a minute. What does God say concerning how He reckons time? With Him, a day is as a thousand years, and a thousand years is as a day (2 Peter 3:8). Therefore, because even Methuselah died thirty-one years short of 1,000—in God's economy, man did indeed die the "day" he ate of the forbidden tree.

Genesis 5:6–8
And Seth lived an hundred and five years, and begat Enos: And Seth lived after he begat Enos eight hundred and seven years, and begat sons and daughters: And all the days of Seth were nine hundred and twelve years: and he died.

Enos literally means "subject to death."

Genesis 5:9–11
And Enos lived ninety years, and begat Cainan: And Enos lived after he begat Cainan eight hundred and fifteen years, and begat sons and daughters: And all the days of Enos were nine hundred and five years: and he died.

Cainan literally means "sorrowful."

Genesis 5:12–14
And Cainan lived seventy years, and begat Mahalaleel: And Cainan lived after he begat Mahalaleel eight hundred and forty years, and begat sons and daughters: And all the days of Cainan were nine hundred and ten years: and he died.

Mahalaleel literally means "from the presence of God."

Genesis 5:15–17
And Mahalaleel lived sixty and five years, and begat Jared: And Mahalaleel lived after he begat Jared eight hundred and thirty years, and begat sons and daughters: And all the days of Mahalaleel were eight hundred ninety and five years: and he died.

Jared literally means "one comes down."

Genesis 5:18–20
And Jared lived an hundred sixty and two years, and he begat Enoch: And Jared lived after he begat Enoch eight hundred years, and begat sons and daughters: And all the days of Jared were nine hundred sixty and two years: and he died.

Enoch literally means "dedicated."

Genesis 5:21
And Enoch lived sixty and five years, and begat Methuselah:

Methuselah literally means "dying He shall send." Why? The year Methuselah died, what did God send? The Flood.

Genesis 5:22, 23
And Enoch walked with God after he begat Methuselah three hundred years, and begat sons and daughters: And all the days of Enoch were three hundred sixty and five years:

After his first son was born, Enoch began to walk with God. Having kids will do that to you! Raising kids brings a unique awareness of one's need for the Lord.

Genesis 5:24 (a)
And Enoch walked with God: and he was not . . .

"Who shall I say sent me?" asked Moses of God.

"Say I AM that I AM hath sent you" (Exodus 3:14).

And with this, Moses must have come to the realization that if God is I AM, like Enoch, he was "not."

John the Baptist came to the same conclusion when, asked if he was the Messiah, he emphatically declared, "I am not" (John 1:20). Oh, how we as a culture, as a body, as individuals need to grasp what Enoch, Moses, and John the Baptist understood so clearly: that God is, and we are not. You see, I believe the problem for most of us is that we are constantly trying to figure out who we are, what we should do, how we should minister, where we should go. Yet the more we think about how we're doing, where we're going, what we're thinking; the more we talk about ourselves, make reference to ourselves, draw attention to ourselves—the more misery we heap upon ourselves.

Do you ever get tired of hearing your own voice, of dealing with your own stuff, of taking your own pulse? I do. That's because we were created not for self-indulgence or self-introspection, but solely to give pleasure to God (Revelation 4:11). It is only logical, then, to join Enoch, Moses, and John the Baptist in decreasing so that He might increase, in losing our lives in the wonder of His glory.

Genesis 5:24 (b)
. . . for God took him.

Because Adam sinned, and because the wages of sin is death—everyone in Adam's family tree ends up the same way: they die. There is, however, one exception. There is one guy who never dies. After walking with Him three hundred years, one day the Lord simply snatches, grabs, raptures Enoch.

The wages of sin is still death. But, like Enoch, there will be people who will not die. Paul put it this way: Then we which are alive and remain shall be caught up together with them in the clouds, to meet the Lord in the air: and so shall we ever be with the Lord (1 Thessalonians 4:17). I believe we are the generation who will see the Rapture of the church. But even before that glorious day, you and I can experience rapture in our hearts presently. You see, the Latin word, *raptus*, speaks of the physical event that will take place when Jesus comes to call His church home. But it also speaks of an emotional event that can take place right now.

"I was enraptured by that music," we say. Or, "The poem she sent me enraptured me." Is your heart enraptured? Maybe you've walked with the Lord for ten years; maybe you've been a believer for twenty years; but maybe you haven't found the Lord to be all that enthralling lately. Instead, maybe you're discouraged, defeated, depressed. Maybe you read that happy is the people whose God is the Lord (Psalm 144:15), and the joy of the

Lord is my strength (Nehemiah 8:10), but you're feeling anything *but* happy and joyful.

Why is this?

It is because you're not doing what Enoch did. Look at our text: Enoch pleased God. That is, as he walked *with* God, Enoch brought pleasure *to* God. The closer you walk to God today, the more you'll be enraptured, taken, caught up with Him. The godliest people I know don't talk about themselves. The happiest people I know are not focused on themselves. The folks I truly admire are not those who live to please themselves. The people who are most godly and happy, the people who are just such a joy to be around are those who live for one reason: to simply walk with and please God. May we be such people.

Genesis 5:25–27
And Methuselah lived an hundred eighty and seven years, and begat Lamech: And Methuselah lived after he begat Lamech seven hundred eighty and two years, and begat sons and daughters: And all the days of Methuselah were nine hundred sixty and nine years: and he died.

Lamech literally means "to the poor and lowly."

Genesis 5:28–31
And Lamech lived an hundred eighty and two years, and begat a son: And he called his name Noah, saying, This same shall comfort us concerning our work and toil of our hands, because of the ground which the LORD hath cursed. And Lamech lived after he begat Noah five hundred ninety and five years, and begat sons and daughters: And all the days of Lamech were seven hundred seventy and seven years: and he died.

Noah literally means "rest" or "comfort."

Perhaps you wonder if it was really necessary to devote an entire chapter of the Word to a list of men who begat and died. But look at the names again: The Man appointed to death, sorrowful. From the presence of God, One comes down, dedicated. Dying, He shall send to the poor and lowly, rest and comfort.

I must have read Genesis 5 a hundred times before I realized that the entire gospel message is embedded in what seems to be a boring genealogy. Such is the wonder of the Word . . .

Genesis 5:32
And Noah was five hundred years old: and Noah begat Shem, Ham, and Japheth.

We now come to the end of the first section of the Book of Genesis—which deals with creation—and to the beginning of the next section which will deal with the destruction of all that was created—save for one human family and a boatload of fortunate animals.

HOW TO READ YOUR BIBLE

A Topical Study of GENESIS 5

This book of the law shall not depart out of thy mouth; but thou shalt meditate therein day and night, that thou mayest observe to do according to all that is written therein: for then thou shalt make thy way prosperous, and then thou shalt have good success.
Joshua 1:8

Perhaps no one epitomized "good success" more than Job. He, who was the most prosperous and successful man on the face of the earth in his day said this: "I have esteemed the words of His mouth more than my necessary food" (Job 23:12). In other words, if Job had our Bible, he would have said, "If it's a choice of breakfast or the Bible, I choose the Bible. If it's lunch or Luke, I'll take Luke. If it's dinner, or Daniel, I'll go with Daniel. Nothing will have priority for me over the reading of the Scriptures—not even eating."

Job lived out what Joshua promised. That is, he had genuine prosperity and great success. "Yeah, but that's only part of the story," you might be thinking. "He had a lot of troubles, too."

Yes, he did. But when everything fell apart in a single day—his family destroyed, his health demolished, his material blessings decimated—what did Job say? He said, "The Lord gives and the Lord takes away. Blessed be the name of the Lord" (Job 1:21). Job went through his trial—and came out on the other side twice as blessed (Job 42:12).

So it is that I suggest to you today that if you want prosperity and good success, the best piece of advice you can follow is to be one who, like Job, is committed to reading, studying, meditating upon the Word.

"But I've tried reading through the Bible," you might be thinking, "and I just never seem to get it."

Let me give you four simple yet very significant keys which I believe will help you in your study of God's Word . . .

Read Consistently

The first key is to read the Bible with consistency. From cover to cover, chapter by chapter, verse by verse, read the Bible consistently. Don't worry about those things you don't understand. If you're reading through the Bible, you will come across some things which will confuse you initially—but there will also be a bunch of things that will jump out at you—important things for you to do, essential things for you to know.

Why does the Lord make the Scriptures so difficult in so many ways? Why didn't He simply write a section on marriage, a section on finances, a section on parenting? Why all the stories and rules and ordinances and parables and pictures and types and illustrations? Solomon, another prosperous man shed light on this question when he wrote, "It is the glory of God to conceal a thing: but the honour of kings is to search out a matter" (Proverbs 25:2). God purposely conceals some things because even though initially a certain story, passage, or section of Scripture might not make sense to you, as you meditate on it, pray about it, and wrestle with it—a week, or a month, or a year later when a light goes on and you finally understand it, you'll never forget it.

I have often found that the passages with which I wrestle the longest are the passages I learn the deepest. How many wonderful truths I would have missed had I not read the Word consistently—even when I didn't necessarily understand it. Jesus promised the Holy Spirit will "bring all things to your remembrance, whatsoever I have said unto you" (John 14:26). In other words, the Holy Spirit will bring to our minds and make application of that which the Lord has said to us in His Word. He cannot, however, bring to mind that which we haven't read.

The first time I went skiing, I was a junior in high school. My buddy, Bruce, and I went with a couple of girls who were accomplished skiers to Donner Pass in the Sierras. After purchasing our lift tickets, we trekked to the "bunny slope" where the girls promised they'd teach us to ski. Unfortunately, Bruce and I did not learn as quickly as they had hoped. So, after a miserable morning, we told the girls to take the higher lifts and leave us on the bunny slope to practice what they had shown us.

As the 4:00 closing time drew near, still having made no headway, Bruce and I were near the top of the bunny slope when, suddenly, a previous wrestling injury caused Bruce's knee to pop to the side of his leg. "My knee, my knee," he cried, as he tumbled into a snowdrift.

"I'll get help," I said, and, without thinking, I skied all the way down to the bottom of the hill—without falling. So amazed was I by this, that I immediately forgot all about Bruce until my third run down the hill. Thankfully, help had already arrived by the time I remembered him.

When you learn to ski, you find yourself saying, "I don't get this. This is miserable. I'm wet. I'm cold. Why even bother?"—when suddenly it all comes together and you find yourself sailing down the bunny slope. And that's the way it is in reading the Word. "I don't get this," we say. "What does this mean? What's it about?" But then, if you just keep doing it, it begins to click. The pieces begin to fit. The applications are made. The tie-ins are there. That's why it is an honor and a joy to search out what God has concealed.

The armies of Israel and Judah, arrayed in the desert of Edom for battle against the armies of Moab, were desperately in need of water. "Thus saith the Lord," declared the prophet Elisha. "Make this valley full of ditches" (2 Kings 3:16). So ditches were dug and the next morning the ditches were filled with water.

If you want to be full of the water of the Word, you just keep digging—even in the dry times, even in the desert hour. You just say, "I'm going to keep reading. I'm going to keep studying because I know that as I dig ditches consistently, they will be filled with the water of the Word eventually."

Read Expectantly

Wondering why God was doing certain things and why He wasn't doing other things, Habakkuk said, "I will go up into a high tower and I will wait and see what the Lord will say unto me" (Habakkuk 2:1).

The Lord did indeed speak to Habakkuk, saying, "Write the vision" (Habakkuk 2:2)—and Habakkuk didn't have to borrow a pencil.

What does it mean to read with expectancy? I believe it means you come to your devotions, to Bible studies, to church with pencil and paper in hand, ready to take note of that which the Lord would speak to you.

I wonder if, in our morning devotions and study times, we're not speaking volumes through our casual, lethargic approach. "Ho hum, Lord," our actions say, "I don't expect You to say anything to me today. You never do. So let's see, where should I read today . . ." No wonder the Lord doesn't speak to us. No wonder the Word isn't real to us.

I want you to do well, gang. And that comes by approaching the Word with anticipation and expectation, for he that comes to God must believe He is a rewarder of those who diligently seek Him (Hebrews 11:6).

Read Conversationally

As Daniel read the writings of Jeremiah, he realized the time for Israel's release from Babylon was drawing near. So what did Daniel do? He asked the Lord what his people should do in light of Jeremiah's prophecy (Daniel 9:2, 3). I have found this to be such a key for me. As I read the Word, I pray. I read a sentence or two, and I stop and talk it over with the Lord.

True communication requires two-way conversation. If I said to Tammy, "Listen very carefully. I'm going to talk to you for fifteen minutes. Talk, talk, talk, talk, talk. Now it's your turn." And she talk, talk, talk, talk, talked to me—our conversation would not be very natural or intimate. If, on the other hand, I said a sentence or two, and she said a sentence or two and we responded to each other conversationally, true communication would take place.

I am convinced that's the way it's supposed to be in spiritual life. I used to think it was, "Okay, Lord, You talk to me through the Scriptures." Read, read, read, read, read. "Now I'll talk to You through prayer." Pray, pray, pray, pray, pray. And although we can communicate that way, it's very stilted, and not very intimate. That is why I suggest you read a verse or two or three, and talk to the Lord about what you read. If you do, you will find yourself truly communicating with, and hearing from the Lord.

The same holds true even in a corporate setting, for if you pray as the Word is taught, you will find yourself engaged and growing rather than bored and drifting. If you hear something that convicts you in a sermon or a study, say, "Oh, Father, I hear You on that. Forgive me for the way I treated him today," right where you're sitting. If you hear something comforting say, "Thank You for that promise, Lord."

If you learn to pray as you're studying corporately, if you learn to pray while you're reading the Scriptures personally, the Word will come to life for you in ways that will warm your heart and blow your mind.

Read Obediently

Simply put, our Lord is so awesomely kind that He's not about to load us down with a whole bunch of stuff which causes our spiritual desks to stack up with papers. He won't allow my spiritual "in-box" to fill up to the point where it's overflowing and overwhelming and depressing. Instead, He graciously gives me only one thing to do at a time.

To those who say, "I just don't get anything out of Bible study or morning devotions," my question is: Have you done the last thing God told you to do? After all, why should God give us more information and more instruction and more input if we have not been obedient to what He's already brought to our attention?

In the midst of a huge revival, God told Philip to go to the desert. Philip obeyed, and was able to share the Word with a man who, in turn, so impacted Ethiopia and Africa with the gospel that the effects are still seen today (Acts 8).

God doesn't give me fifteen things to do. He simply gives me one thing to do at a time. And I have found that as I do the one thing the Lord asks of me, He proceeds to tell me the next step. That is why we are to be doers of the Word, not hearers only (James 1:22), for it is when we say, "Lord, You are God, and with Your grace and by Your strength, I desire and determine to do whatever You say," that He will open doors before you and give direction to you.

Read with consistency. Read with expectancy. Don't approach the Word halfheartedly, lethargically, apathetically, or lazily. Read conversationally. Pray while you read; read while you pray. And read obediently. When God speaks to your heart, do what He tells you to do and more revelation will follow.

In the course of my forty-year pilgrimage with the Lord, I have found these elements to be essential to my love for, understanding of, and delight in the Word.

6

But as the days of Noe were, so shall also the coming of the Son of man be. For as in the days that were before the flood they were eating and drinking, marrying and giving in marriage, until the day that Noe entered into the ark, And knew not until the flood came, and took them all away; so shall also the coming of the Son of man be. Matthew 24:37–39

Knowing this first, that there shall come in the last days scoffers, walking after their own lusts, And saying, Where is the promise of his coming? for since the fathers fell asleep, all things continue as they were from the beginning of the creation. For this they willingly are ignorant of, that by the word of God the heavens were of old, and the earth standing out of the water and in the water: Whereby the world that then was, being overflowed with water, perished: 2 Peter 3:3–6

The last days before Jesus' return will be similar to the days before the Flood. Surely the day of His return is near, for in the text before us, we see striking parallels between Noah's day and ours . . .

Genesis 6:1, 2

And it came to pass, when men began to multiply on the face of the earth, and daughters were born unto them, That the sons of God saw the daughters of men that they were fair; and they took them wives of all which they chose.

When you read the genealogy of chapter 5, you realize, among other things, that people lived a long time—nine hundred years and more. Now, think with me. If a man has four kids and lives to see his kids have kids, in five generations his family will number ninety-six. In ten generations, the population will jump to 3,070. In twenty generations, the population soars to 3,120,000. And in thirty generations, it skyrockets to 3,220,000,000. If a generation is forty years, with at least forty generations listed in Genesis 5, the population on earth in Noah's day would have conservatively been billions and billions of people. In other words, Noah lived in a world more densely populated than ours is presently.

We're experiencing a similar population growth in our own last days. You see, from the time Noah got off the ark, it took until 1867 for the world to reach the one billion mark. But it only took from 1867 to 1935—less than one hundred years—for the population to reach two billion. And from 1935, it only took until 1965 to reach over six billion. Due to the 250,000 people added to our planet every twenty-four hours, the earth's population will now double every fifteen years.

Genesis 6:3
And the LORD said, My spirit shall not always strive with man, for that he also is flesh: yet his days shall be an hundred and twenty years.

Sociologists have studied the effects of the exponential population growth we are experiencing by placing a group of rats in the same proportional density as New York City. Two things took place: The crowded conditions caused the maternal instinct to be suppressed to the point that mother rats no longer cared for their young; and, secondly, the rats started eating each other even though there was adequate food supplied for them.

Population growth carries with it definite sociological implications. Those who study such things say this explains why inner city life is the way it is today. This makes sense to me because we're sinners. We're a bunch of rats. Pack us close together and you have a whole bunch of sin condensed in one spot. That's why God graciously gave man one hundred-twenty years to turn to Him. Longer than that, he surely would have destroyed himself.

Genesis 6:4
There were giants in the earth in those days; and also after that, when the sons of God came in unto the daughters of men, and they bare children to them, the same became mighty men which were of old, men of renown.

The Hebrew word translated "giants" is *nephalim,* which literally means "fallen ones." These "fallen ones" are the legendary figures spoken of in many cultures—the giants. Where did these giants come from? There are two schools of thought. Some suggest that the term, "daughters of men," refers to the descendants of Cain. But because a union of the ungodly daughters of Cain and the godly sons of Seth would not inherently produce giants, others—myself included—believe their origin is due to something else.

The phrase "sons of God" is *benai elohim.* Every time "benai elohim" appears in the Old Testament, it is in reference to angels. Angels are divided into two groups: the exalted angels around the throne of God who do the work of the Lord, and fallen angels, or demons. Lucifer was an exalted angel who led a rebellion against the Lord in heaven. When he fell and became the devil, Revelation tells us one-third of the angelic host joined his rebellion and became demons. I believe it is to these demons that Genesis 6:4 refers. Some of these demons, evidently, had sexual relations with human women, resulting in *nephalim*—giants, legendary men, men of renown. That is why every culture contains stories of giants similar to those found in Greek mythology and Roman folklore.

The best explanation for these nephalim, however, isn't found in mythology or folklore, but in the Word. We know that certain demons are held in prison (1 Peter 3:19) because their deeds were so diabolically dark. I believe the demons who "left their own habitation" (Jude 6), are the "benai elohim" through whom Satan futilely attempted to pollute the seed of woman to such a degree that the promise of Genesis 3:15 would be thwarted.

I suggest to you we also live in a day of similar aberrant sexual behavior. We can say, "We're okay. Our culture's doing fine. Our economy's doing well." But underneath the surface, the perversion in our society is unbelievable. The largest industry in America today is not airplanes or automobiles, not even agricultural production. The largest industry in America today is entertainment. And the fastest-growing segment of the entertainment industry is hard-core pornography. We no longer even question things that once would have shocked and scandalized us. As in Noah's day, our society insists everything is fine, when underneath the surface lurks a strong current of horrific sexual behavior that will eventually sink us.

Genesis 6:5–7
And GOD saw that the wickedness of man was great in the earth, and that every imagination of the thoughts of his heart was only evil continually. And it repented the LORD that he had made man on the earth, and it grieved him at his heart. And the LORD said, I will destroy man whom I have created from the face of the earth; both man, and beast, and the creeping thing, and the fowls of the air; for it repenteth me that I have made them.

What are evil imaginations? Break the word down, and you get to the essence of it: images. Throughout the Old Testament, idols were worshiped in groves of trees which were planted to cover up the "shady" activities that took place therein (Judges 3:7). I cannot help but think how this applies to our day, as the images on our television screens are continually evil.

Genesis 6:8–10
But Noah found grace in the eyes of the LORD. These are the generations of Noah:

Noah was a just man and perfect in his generations, and Noah walked with God. And Noah begat three sons, Shem, Ham, and Japheth.

That Noah found grace in the eyes of the Lord does not mean that God showed grace to Noah exclusively. Yes, a flood wiped everyone else out eventually, but not before God gave them one hundred years to repent of their wickedness and receive salvation. Yes, the planet was deluged, but every man had opportunity to hear His message as they observed Noah building the huge barge. But the world refused to grab hold of the good news of salvation, and they drowned in their sin. It wasn't that God looked at Noah with grace and everyone else with condemnation. God looked at *everyone* with eyes of grace and mercy. It's just that Noah *found* the grace.

The question I want to ask you today is this: What have *you* found in the eyes of the Lord?

A London traffic jam prevented C. S. Lewis from arriving at a certain religious symposium on time. The panel, comprised of the world's most highly esteemed religious thinkers, began without him, their first question being: What is unique about Christianity? Although the Buddhist, Muslim, Jew, and Taoist discussed the question they could arrive at no conclusive answer. In the midst of their debate, C. S. Lewis burst into the room.

"Dr. Lewis," said the moderator, "tell us what is unique to Christianity."

"That's easy," Lewis replied. "It's grace."

C. S. Lewis was right. No other religion or philosophy provides unmerited, undeserved, unearned favor. Every other religion, every other philosophy says there are things we must do—devotional exercises, good deeds, or righteous acts—to earn blessings from Allah or to gain favor from Buddha. Only biblical Christianity says, "It's all grace, nothing more, nothing less, nothing else."

Noah found grace in the eyes of the Lord. Peter was another who, like Noah, looked in the eyes of the Lord. And what he saw therein caused him to weep. What did Peter see in the Lord's eyes? I believe your answer is a good indication of where you are in your relationship with God. You see, Peter fell asleep when he should have prayed; denied the Lord when questioned by a young maid; and forsook the Lord because he was afraid. Thus, it would be natural to think that it was the look of disappointment in the eyes of the Lord that caused Peter to weep. But such was not the case, for Jesus had already told Peter that Satan sought to sift him like wheat, but that he would eventually make it through regardless of his failure on the way (Luke 22:31, 32). No, Peter didn't find disappointment or discouragement in the Lord's eyes. He found the same thing Noah found. He found grace.

The writer to the Hebrews says, "Let us therefore come boldly to the throne of grace that we shall obtain mercy and find grace to help in time of need" (Hebrews 4:16). If you want to experience the blessings of God in a world that's falling apart, if you want to experience the blessings of God no matter your situation, you have the privilege of gazing constantly in the eyes of the Lord. You have an invitation to find grace.

Genesis 6:11–13

The earth also was corrupt before God, and the earth was filled with violence. And God looked upon the earth, and, behold, it was corrupt; for all flesh had corrupted his way upon the earth. And God said unto Noah, The end of all flesh is come before me; for the earth is filled with violence through them; and, behold, I will destroy them with the earth.

The fourth sign of a culture about to be judged is violence. Violence was celebrated, exalted, and practiced in Noah's day, just as it is in our own. "It used to be when I started my job, the crime on the streets of Brooklyn would follow this pattern: Your money or your life," said William Flack, Brooklyn's District Attorney. "But that's no longer true. Now it's your money *and* your life." It's what he calls "joy killing"—killing for the sake of killing. By the time they graduate from junior high, young people in our country have seen an average of more than 35,000 murders on TV. Add to that the 1.2 million couples who use guns, knives, or other lethal weapons on each other, and it is evident that the home has become a battleground in much of our society.

Wise is the woman, wise the man who has the understanding and discernment to see a world of exploding population, sexual perversion, evil imagination, and rampant violence—and is able to draw the parallel with Noah's day. Wise are all who, knowing the Lord's coming is at hand, say to everyone they can, "Come on board the Good Ship Salvation because we're sailing to heaven."

Genesis 6:14 (a)

Make thee an ark of gopher wood . . .

Not coincidentally, I believe, due to its density and strength, gopher wood was the wood used to make coffins. "If any man come after Me, let him deny himself and take up his cross," Jesus declared (Matthew 16:24).

Salvation begins with death. It begins when we say, "I'm dying to self. I no longer demand my own way, but rather give myself completely to You."

Genesis 6:14 (b)
. . . rooms shalt thou make in the ark . . .

The Hebrew word translated "rooms" is literally "nests." On the Good Ship Salvation, there is an abundance of rooms, where Episcopalians and Presbyterians, Baptists and Lutherans, Catholics and Applegaters alike can nest. How careful we must be to allow room, to give our fellow brothers and sisters in Christ space to "work out their own salvation" (Philippians 2:12). Each of us thinks we see perfectly clearly. But Paul reminds us that this side of eternity, each of us only sees "through a glass darkly" (1 Corinthians 13:12). Therefore, we need each other. The ark had plenty of room. So does the kingdom.

Genesis 6:14 (c)
. . . and shalt pitch it within and without with pitch.

This is the only time in the Old Testament where the Hebrew word *kapher* is translated "pitch." In the seventy other passages this word is used, it is translated "atonement"—a wonderful word that essentially means "at-one-ment." Just as the salvation God provided Noah was surrounded by the pitch of atonement, so God provided us "at-one-ment" with Him by sending His Son to die for our sin.

Genesis 6:15
And this is the fashion which thou shalt make it of: The length of the ark shall be three hundred cubits, the breadth of it fifty cubits, and the height of it thirty cubits.

Constructed to float atop the water rather than to navigate through it, the ark Noah built looked more like a covered barge than a boat. If a cubit is eighteen inches, as most people believe, the ark was four hundred and fifty feet long, seventy-five feet wide, and forty-five feet high.

Genesis 6:16 (a)
A window shalt thou make to the ark, and in a cubit shalt thou finish it above . . .

As we will see, Noah had no control over the door of the ark. But he did have control over the window. I control how much illumination and understanding I have in life by how much I allow the Word of God to be in my thinking (Psalm 119:105). I can either remain in the dark, or I can gain light and insight by opening up the window of the Word—just like we're doing right now. Sure, sometimes it would be easier to just watch Jeopardy. Sometimes it would be easier to sleep in and skip morning devotions. Sometimes it would be easier not to take the time to study Scripture—but I will walk in light only to the extent that I choose to open the window and allow the light of the Word to flood my soul and renew my thoughts.

Genesis 6:16 (b)
. . . and the door of the ark shalt thou set in the side thereof . . .

There was only one door in the ark. There was no back door, no emergency exit. "Why can't you just be broad-minded? Why can't you just say there are many ways to enter into a relationship with God?" people ask us. The reason is because Jesus said, "No man comes to the Father but by Me" (John 14:6). And I'm real glad about that. You see, if God had five ways to enter in to salvation, five ways to be able to make it to heaven, five ways to cultivate a relationship with Him, Satan would come back with twenty-five counterfeit ways. If God had ten ways, Satan would come back with 10,000. God says, "I don't want anyone to choose the wrong door. I'm going to keep it real simple. There's only one."

Genesis 6:16 (c)
. . . with lower, second, and third stories shalt thou make it.

Just as there were three levels on the ark, the apostle John makes it clear that there are three segments of the Christian family (1 John 2:13, 14). There are "little children" who know the Father. There are "young men" who have overcome the Wicked One and in whom the Word of God abides. And there are "fathers" who, because they have "known Him from the beginning," have an intimate, deep relationship with God. There are three different levels of maturity on the Good Ship Salvation, but *all* aboard are sailing toward heaven.

Genesis 6:17, 18
And, behold, I, even I, do bring a flood of waters upon the earth, to destroy all flesh, wherein is the breath of life, from under heaven; and every thing that is in the earth shall die. But with thee will I establish my covenant; and thou shalt come into the ark, thou, and thy sons, and thy wife, and thy sons' wives with thee.

Eight souls were to enter into the ark. Yes, there would be some bobbing up and down, some noise and confusion, some questions and concerns—but guess what. They would be headed to a fresh start, a new beginning, a new world. And that's what's happening with you and me. The reason we're here tonight, the reason we have morning devotions, the reason we keep plugging away is because we're saved. And when all is said and done, that's all that matters. Let's never lose sight of that. Let's never get so caught up in the esoteric understanding of Scripture that we miss the underlying base of all things—that God so loved the world that He gave His only begotten Son, that whosoever believes in Him should not perish but have everlasting life (John 3:16).

Genesis 6:19–21
And of every living thing of all flesh, two of every sort shalt thou bring into the ark, to keep them alive with thee; they shall be male and female. Of fowls after their kind, and of cattle after their kind, of every creeping thing of the earth after his kind, two of every sort shall come unto thee, to keep them alive. And take thou unto thee of all food that is eaten, and thou shalt gather it to thee; and it shall be for food for thee, and for them.

Three-storied, the ark contained 97,000 square feet of space. How big is that? It's equivalent to five hundred and twenty boxcars. Would this be enough space to hold all of the animals? Taxonomists tell us that on the earth today there are 3,500 species of mammals, 8,600 species of birds, 5,500 reptiles and amphibians. (Fish, obviously weren't on the ark; and the 25,500 species of worms could fit in the cracks). Added together, there were 17,600 species of animals. Double that to include male and female, and the figure becomes 35,200. The average size of the 17,600 species of animals on the ark is equivalent to a full-grown sheep. 35,200 sheep would easily fit in only one hundred and twenty boxcars. Even doubling the number to include species which may have become extinct since Noah's day would only require two hundred and forty boxcars—leaving two hundred and eighty boxcars worth of space for Noah's family and food.

"But what about dinosaurs?" you ask. Due to the biblical account in Job 40 and 41, as well as the discovery of fossilized footprints of dinosaurs adjacent to footprints of men, I believe dinosaurs and men lived simultaneously. If that be so, dinosaurs would have to have been on the ark.

Wouldn't they take up the whole ark?

Not if they were babies.

Genesis 6:22
Thus did Noah; according to all that God commanded him, so did he.

What if Noah didn't do all that God commanded him to do? What if he completed the sides of the ark, but didn't put the roof on? If Noah gave it a pretty good shot, but then said, "Oh, well, close enough,"—we wouldn't be here. Noah did *all* that God commanded him. He finished the ark. As great an accomplishment as Noah's was, however, it speaks of a far greater accomplishment by another carpenter—the Carpenter from Galilee, Jesus Christ . . .

- Noah held a hammer in his hand.
- Jesus absorbed the blows of a hammer *upon* His hand.
- Noah built with wood.
- Jesus was pinned to wood.
- Noah constructed a door.
- Jesus said, "I am the Door."
- Noah covered the ark with pitch.
- Jesus covers us with His blood.

May God give us the ability to understand and remember that we are of all people most blessed. No matter what's happening in our lives tonight, we're most blessed because we're saved.

7

Genesis 7:1 (a)
And the LORD said unto Noah, Come . . .

"Come." This is the first time this word is spoken in the Bible. But it is not the last, for from cover to cover the Lord says . . .

> *Come* now, let us reason together, though your sins be as scarlet, they shall be white as snow.
> Isaiah 1:18

> *Come* unto Me, all ye that are weary and heavy laden, and I will give you rest. Matthew 11:28

> Whosoever is thirsty, let him *come* and drink of the water of life freely. Revelation 22:17

Genesis 7:1 (b)
. . . thou and all thy house into the ark; for thee have I seen righteous before me in this generation.

What a fabulous thing it is to realize that our Lord is interested in saving not only individuals, but entire families.

Genesis 7:2–6
Of every clean beast thou shalt take to thee by sevens, the male and his female: and of beasts that are not clean by two, the male

and his female. Of fowls also of the air by sevens, the male and the female; to keep seed alive upon the face of all the earth. For yet seven days, and I will cause it to rain upon the earth forty days and forty nights; and every living substance that I have made will I destroy from off the face of the earth. And Noah did according unto all that the LORD commanded him. And Noah was six hundred years old when the flood of waters was upon the earth.

Noah was told to take the animals two by two unless they were clean animals. Of the clean animals, he was told to take seven. Why? Clean beasts would be sacrificed to the Lord. Therefore, if there were only two and one was killed, that specie would become extinct.

Genesis 7:7–9
And Noah went in, and his sons, and his wife, and his sons' wives with him, into the ark, because of the waters of the flood. Of clean beasts, and of beasts that are not clean, and of fowls, and of every thing that creepeth upon the earth, There went in two and two unto Noah into the ark, the male and the female, as God had commanded Noah.

"There went in two and two unto Noah." In other words, Noah didn't have to round up the animals. As He did in the Garden of Eden when He brought the animals to be named by Adam (Genesis 2:19), God brought the animals to Noah. How could the wolf and the pig, the fox and the rabbit come together into the ark? Second Corinthians 5 declares that if any man be in Christ, he is a new creature. So somehow in preparation for the new creation which would take place after the Flood, the Lord caused the animals to enter the ark by twos and sevens without antagonizing each other. This shouldn't be that hard to understand, however, since similar miracles occur daily in the animal world . . .

Sitting on ice floes, dressed in identical tuxedoes, millions of Emperor penguins are mirror images of each other. And yet, after she lays her egg and dives into the Arctic waters for a three-month eating binge while the father incubates the egg, Mama Penguin is able to pick her husband out of the look-alike crowd upon her return.

From the North Pole, terns fly to Hawaii for the winter. But they leave their young behind because the young aren't ready to fly. Several months later, having gained enough strength to make the journey, the young terns fly in formation on their own—without a single travel agent or map—straight to their parents in Hawaii.

I can't explain terns or penguins but I do know this: God can do whatever He chooses to do with the animal kingdom, just as He can do whatever He chooses to do with you and me in changing our beastly behavior.

Genesis 7:10 (a)
And it came to pass after seven days . . .

Evidently it took the animals seven days to make their way into the ark. When they got on board, wouldn't they start fighting? Wouldn't the cats start chasing the mice and the dogs start barking at the cats? God did something when He brought all these different kinds of animals on to the Good Ship Salvation—just like what He does with us. People who normally would be biting and barking and devouring each other begin to realize they have a commonality in Christ and something wonderful happens.

Genesis 7:10 (b)–12
. . . that the waters of the flood were upon the earth. In the six hundredth year of Noah's life, in the second month, the seventeenth day of the month, the same day were all the fountains of the great deep broken up, and the windows of heaven were opened. And the rain was upon the earth forty days and forty nights.

Throughout Scripture, the number forty appears again and again with relation to judgment, trials, difficulty. The rain fell forty days. The Israelites wandered forty years. Jesus was tempted forty days.

Genesis 7:13
In the selfsame day entered Noah, and Shem, and Ham, and Japheth, the sons of Noah, and Noah's wife, and the three wives of his sons with them, into the ark;

Noah and his family boarded the ark. But notice: Noah went first.

For topical study of Genesis 7:13 entitled "Get On Board . . . Your Family Will Follow," turn to page 36.

Genesis 7:14–16
They, and every beast after his kind, and all the cattle after their kind, and every creeping thing that creepeth upon the earth after his kind, and every fowl after his kind, every bird of every sort. And they went in unto Noah into the ark, two and two of all flesh,

wherein is the breath of life. And they that went in, went in male and female of all flesh, as God had commanded him: and the LORD shut him in.

Now the door is shut, and Noah and his family are sealed in the ark. There's no way for them to open the door and escape or change their minds. This speaks to me because the One who said, "I am the Door," lets us know we are likewise secure in our salvation. "You are in My hand," Jesus declares, "and no man can pluck you out" (see John 10:28).

Do I believe in eternal security? Yes, I do. I am absolutely secure, because the Lord has "shut me in." You see, it wasn't Noah who shut the door of the ark, hoping he latched it right and that it would stay shut. *God* shut the door of the ark, just as He seals our salvation on our journey to heaven.

"Wait a minute," you say. "I thought there will be some who won't make it into heaven even though they once made a profession of faith."

That's also true. And I believe the story that most clearly explains this dichotomy deals with a ship—like the ark, and a storm—like the Flood . . .

On a ship bound for Rome, Paul advised the captain to winter in port, due to bad weather. Ignoring Paul's advice, they sailed on—right into a storm which grew so fierce that the sailors feared for their lives. "Be of good cheer," Paul said. "There stood by me this night an angel of God whose I am, whom I serve, saying, Fear not Paul, thou must be brought before Caesar. And lo, God hath given thee all them that sail with thee" (Acts 27:22–24).

When the storm continued, some of the sailors decided to bail out. But just as they were about to leave, Paul said, "Except these abide in the ship, you cannot be saved." In other words, "If you choose to go overboard, you'll be wiped out. You are secure, safe, sealed only as long as you stay on board."

Gang, no one can pluck us out of God's hand, but that doesn't mean we can't leave on our own. I'm shut in the Good Ship Salvation because I have no intention of going overboard, of sailing off in another direction. Yes, I sin. But I am determined and decided that I will love the Lord all the days of my life. I pray you are, too.

Genesis 7:17, 18
And the flood was forty days upon the earth; and the waters increased, and bare up the ark, and it was lift up above the earth. And the waters prevailed, and were increased greatly upon the earth; and the ark went upon the face of the waters.

The waters continued to rise even after the rain stopped because the source of the flood was not only from the skies above, but also from the fountains of the deep, from below the surface of the earth (Genesis 7:11).

Genesis 7:19–23
And the waters prevailed exceedingly upon the earth; and all the high hills, that were under the whole heaven, were covered. Fifteen cubits upward did the waters prevail; and the mountains were covered. And all flesh died that moved upon the earth, both of fowl, and of cattle, and of beast, and of every creeping thing that creepeth upon the earth, and every man: All in whose nostrils was the breath of life, of all that was in the dry land, died. And every living substance was destroyed which was upon the face of the ground, both man, and cattle, and the creeping things, and the fowl of the heaven; and they were destroyed from the earth: and Noah only remained alive, and they that were with him in the ark.

The waters rose fifteen cubits—approximately twenty-four feet—above the highest mountain peaks. Some have suggested that this was not a worldwide flood, but rather a local flood in one section of the world. The problem with this viewpoint is that if it was merely a local flood, why didn't God simply tell Noah to leave the area? The waters were above the mountains—which speaks of a *global* flood. That is why virtually every culture on the face of the earth has stories about a flood, and why fossils of sea life have been found underneath ice packs in the Himalayas.

The idea of a local flood doesn't make sense logically, culturally, paleontologically, and certainly not Scripturally. Peter wrote that, just as the world was wiped out by water in Noah's day, it will be destroyed by fire in the last day (2 Peter 3:7). Thus, if the Flood was local, the end-time fire will be local as well. And that's just not so.

Genesis 7:24
And the waters prevailed upon the earth an hundred and fifty days.

Although Noah had heard the voice of the Lord telling him to go into the ark, there is no record of God speaking to Noah while he was on the ark. In fact, he would not hear the voice of God again for a total of three hundred and seventy-seven days.

Maybe that's your situation presently. Maybe three hundred and seventy-seven days ago, the Lord made Himself known to you through a very real revelation of some sort and you said, "Okay, Lord. This is awesome!" And you did what you knew you should do. But now, as you are cooped up and bouncing around on rough seas, you wonder why God isn't speaking.

Folks, all of us wish God would speak more frequently than He does. But unlike some people, God isn't a chatterbox. Why doesn't He speak with greater regularity dealing with specific issues? It is not because He is callous. It's not because He doesn't care. It's because there's a bigger issue at stake . . .

> But we glory in tribulations also: knowing that tribulation worketh patience; And patience, experience; and experience, hope: And hope maketh not ashamed . . . Romans 5:3–5

Bobbing around on the ark, sometimes there's nothing to do but learn patience. Then, when I finally settle down, when I finally quit squawking, God says, "Good. Now you're getting it." And it is then I begin to gain some experience . . .

There we were at the county hearings, requesting approval for a new sanctuary from a planning commission which was not very open to our plan. Ahead of us on the agenda, were the Buddhists, who were requesting approval for a twelve-bed retreat center in Ashland. When their request was denied, their lawyer immediately said, "Well, what about Applegate Christian Fellowship? They have a one hundred and twenty-bed retreat center."

"They have what?" said the surprised commissioners.

And as the story unfolded, it came to light that when three separate meetings were called to give us clearance for the retreat center, the commissioners failed to attend. So the decision was left to a single county officer—who approved it!

I was reminded once again that the Lord came through back then in ways I see only now. Tribulation does indeed work patience, and when I finally calm down, I begin to log some experiences. I begin to see how God works. Experience, then, brings hope—the absolute expectation of coming good. And hope "maketh not ashamed." Looking back over the years, I have discovered that the things I've done, the words I've said, the attitudes I've held of which I'm ashamed are all directly linked to a loss of hope.

I suggest the same is true for you. What you are ashamed of today are the times you thought, "What's the use? Why even bother? Why try so hard to follow the Lord?" That's precisely why hard times—times we feel like we're shut up in an ark with no word from God—are vital to our development. They make us patient, which gives us experience, which leads to hope.

GET ON BOARD . . . YOUR FAMILY WILL FOLLOW

A Topical Study of GENESIS 7:13

How important is it to read the fine print? Ask Richard Lusk. A Florida newspaper recently carried his story . . .

The large print on the Sweepstakes mailing screamed, "Richard Lusk has won it all and will definitely receive 12 million dollars!" So Mr. Lusk, age 88, traveled 6,000 miles to insure his winning ticket didn't get lost. The trip was in vain. The fine print told the story. The lead-in to the won-it-all pitch on the American Family Publishers entry said in small print *if you have and return the top winning entry.*

"The thing to do was get the ticket back to them and that's what I was trying to do," Lusk said Friday from his home near Victorville—a desert town east of Los Angeles. After all, he said he received six such announcements and returned all of them, but he still wasn't a millionaire. So he assumed that the tickets were getting lost in the mail. This time he decided to fly across country and deal with it personally. For several years, Lusk had been entering sweepstakes, thinking he had to order magazines with the entry. His family estimates he spent $100,000 on magazine subscriptions. One-quarter of his house is filled with periodicals.

Upon his arrival, Richard Lusk found out about the small print. He returned home and yet mailed in his most recent ticket for the next drawing sometime in November. He still hopes to win the twelve million. "But this is the end of it," he said emphatically. "I've got more magazines than I know what to do with."

Sometimes it's the small print that causes big headaches and heartbreaks. But such is not the case with Scripture, for even the small print carries big blessings—as is true of the text before us. There's something in the small print of our story, which perhaps you've never seen before, and which I believe will warm your heart.

Expectation in Faith

And Noah was five hundred years old: and Noah begat Shem, Ham, and Japheth. Genesis 5:32

And the L*ORD said, My spirit shall not always strive with man, for that he also is flesh: yet his days shall be an hundred and twenty years.* Genesis 6:3

And Noah was six hundred years old when the flood of waters was upon the earth. Genesis 7:6

Putting together the "fine print" of Genesis 5:32, Genesis 6:3, and Genesis 7:6, we know that Noah was four hundred and eighty years old when he began building the ark, five hundred years old when his first son was born, and six hundred years old when the Flood began. This means that when God instructed Noah to make a place for his sons in the ark, He did so twenty years before Noah's first son was even born!

Twenty years before his sons were born, God said to Noah, "You, as the leader of the family, you as the patriarch of the clan, you as the father, Noah, are to expect your sons and their wives to be in the ark—the place of salvation—with you and your wife."

- Could this be why blood on the doorposts during Passover spared not only the one who applied it but the entire house? (Exodus 12:13)

- Could this be why the Holy Spirit fell on Cornelius *and his house?* (Acts 10)
- Could this be what Paul meant when he said to the Philippian jailer, "Believe in the Lord Jesus Christ and thou shalt be saved *and thy house*"? (Acts 16:31)
- Could this be what the writer of Hebrews referred to when he wrote: By faith, Noah, being warned of God of things not seen as yet, moved with fear, prepared an ark to the *saving of his house?* (Hebrews 11:7)

I believe so. Am I suggesting a new doctrine? Dad, get saved and everyone else is included? No, I'm not talking about a doctrine, but about a dynamic. By faith, Noah prepared a place for his family on the ark even before his kids were conceived. So you open your heart, Dad, to the Lord Jesus Christ, and by faith say, "I am believing my sons and daughters and their spouses and our grandchildren will be on board the Good Ship Salvation."

Certainly, each man, woman, and child must make his own decision regarding salvation, but they can do so, seeing the reality of faith lived out before them, just as Noah's family observed him pounding away on the ark day after day.

Exemplification of Faith

When it was time for Noah and his family to enter into the ark, Noah went first. He didn't say, "There's the ark, kids. Go ahead. I'll catch up." No, Noah led the way. He was an example—and that's the key. Mom and Dad, what you are personally will be communicated to your kids individually and it will impact them very powerfully.

Think with me. When David was a young man, he killed a giant. The list of David's "mighty men" in 2 Samuel 23 includes those who also killed giants.

This means that even though most of David's men didn't see him kill Goliath, they became giant-killers simply because of their linkage to David.

Contrast this with Saul. Saul was intimidated by Goliath. In Saul's catalogue of mighty men, not one is a giant-killer because Saul wasn't.

Dad, you be a prayer warrior and watch how your kids will be prayer warriors, too. You witness at work, and watch your kids follow your example at school.

Who we are very definitely affects what our kids become. Therefore, if I am a man who loves the Word, is devoted to prayer, is committed to the kingdom, my kids will be impacted very deeply. Your kids will either be spiritual wimps who get wiped out and are intimidated by the enemy, or they will be giant-killers who overcome and are successful in the things of God.

Mom and Dad, lead the way in the things of God—and your family will follow.

8 Genesis 8:1 (a)
And God remembered Noah, and every living thing, and all the cattle that was with him in the ark . . .

The idea here is not that God momentarily forgot about Noah, but rather that even though Noah was in the dark, bouncing around in the ark, God remembered him constantly. This is the key that will help you and me in times when we're bobbing around in a barge on the verge of despair. God remembered Noah, and God remembers us.

I remember God remembers me when I do what Jesus asked of me when He said, "Do this in remembrance of Me" (Luke 22:19). As I kneel at the Table, as I hold the broken body and shed blood of Jesus, I remember what He did for me. Although, like Noah, I might not understand His silence at any given time, I am reminded at the Table that even if I never hear from Him again, He spoke loudly and clearly for all eternity when He laid down His life for me.

Genesis 8:1 (b)
. . . and God made a wind to pass over the earth, and the waters asswaged.

The Hebrew word translated "wind" is *ruach* which is also translated "spirit." In other words, the world was covered with water and the Spirit moved across the water just as He did at creation (Genesis 1:2), and land became visible. Water being a picture, or type of the Word, it is always when the Spirit moves across the pages of Scripture that my world becomes clear again.

Genesis 8:2–4
The fountains also of the deep and the windows of heaven were stopped, and the rain from heaven was restrained; And the waters returned from off the earth continually: and after the end of the hundred and fifty days the waters were abated. And the ark rested in the seventh month, on the seventeenth day of the month, upon the mountains of Ararat.

What took place on the seventeenth day of the seventh month?

The Resurrection of Jesus Christ.

***For topical study of Genesis 8:4 entitled "Resting on the Resurrection," turn to page* 41.**

Genesis 8:5, 6 (a)
And the waters decreased continually until the tenth month: in the tenth month, on the first day of the month, were the tops of the mountains seen. And it came to pass . . .

"It came to pass." Don't you love that phrase? I do—because, like Noah, I have found that the storm, the water, the waves *always* pass.

Genesis 8:6 (b)–9 (a)
. . . at the end of forty days, that Noah opened the window of the ark which he had made: And he sent forth a raven, which went forth to and fro, until the waters were dried up from off the earth. Also he sent forth a dove from him, to see if the waters were abated from off the face of the ground; But the dove found no rest for the sole of her foot, and she returned unto him into the ark, for the waters were on the face of the whole earth . . .

The dove, a picture of the Holy Spirit, found no place to land. So today, the Holy Spirit is looking for people like you and me to land upon, to empower. Is there room in our lives for Him? Second Chronicles 16:9 tells us the eyes of the Lord go throughout the earth, looking for a person in whom He might show Himself strong. Is there a place in this congregation corporately and in our hearts individually wherein that might happen?

Genesis 8:9 (b)
. . . then he put forth his hand, and took her, and pulled her in unto him into the ark.

A raven and a dove were released from the ark. Noah reached out for the dove.

***For topical study of Genesis 8:9 entitled "Reach Out and Touch the One," turn to page* 45.**

Genesis 8:10–12
And he stayed yet other seven days; and again he sent forth the dove out of the ark; And the dove came in to him in the evening; and, lo, in her mouth was an olive leaf pluckt off: so Noah knew that the waters were abated from off the earth. And he stayed yet other seven days; and sent forth the dove; which returned not again unto him any more.

The third time the dove was released, it stayed away, signaling to Noah the dawn of a new beginning. In this, I see a powerful prophetic portrait . . .

Due to the fact that in God's economy, one day is as 1,000 years, and 1,000 years is as a day

(2 Peter 3:8), Jesus rose again from the dead 2,000 years—or "two days"—ago. In Hosea 6, the nation of Israel cries out collectively, "We've been smitten and torn because we've rejected the Lord. But after two days He will revive us." After being smitten for 2,000 years, the Jews are back in their homeland and they're about to be revived spiritually, for in the third Millennium after Christ's death—or the "third day" of God's calendar—a new beginning will dawn—when the repercussions of sin will be reversed, when the lion will lie down by the lamb, when men will study war no more, when Jesus Christ will rule and reign in Jerusalem.

Genesis 8:13
And it came to pass in the six hundredth and first year, in the first month, the first day of the month, the waters were dried up from off the earth: and Noah removed the covering of the ark, and looked, and, behold, the face of the ground was dry.

Noah saw the new world, the rejuvenated earth, in the first year, in the first month, on the first day of the seventh century of his life. The number seven is significant in Scripture, for it speaks of completion, as portrayed, for example, by the Sabbath rest and by the freeing of slaves every seventh year (Exodus 21:2).

According to the biblical account, Adam was on the scene around the year 4000 B.C., which means there have been 6,000 years of human history, or, in God's economy, "six days" (2 Peter 3:8). This means in the year 2,000, we enter into the 7,000th year, or "seventh day" of human history—the day of rest, the day of freedom from the slavery of sin and depravity, the day of the completion of human history.

Genesis 8:14, 15 (a)
And in the second month, on the seven and twentieth day of the month, was the earth dried. And God spake unto Noah . . .

According to the previous verse, Noah knew the ground was dry when the dove did not return. Why did Noah remain in the ark? After all, he had been cooped up for 377 days with a boatload of seasick animals. Why didn't he climb out the window the first chance he got? I believe it was because Noah experienced the same thing you have experienced when you've been in troubled waters. Noah sensed the unmistakable presence of God; and He wasn't about to leave it until God told him to do so.

Genesis 8:15 (b), 16 (a)
. . . saying, Go . . .

In chapter 7, God had said, "Come." Here in chapter 8, He says, "Go." That's always the way it is. God calls us to come unto Him, (Matthew 11:28). And then He says, "Now that you've been filled, now that you've taken in, there's work for you to do. Go into all the world" (see Matthew 28:19).

Genesis 8:16 (b)–19
. . . forth of the ark, thou, and thy wife, and thy sons, and thy sons' wives with thee. Bring forth with thee every living thing that is with thee, of all flesh, both of fowl, and of cattle, and of every creeping thing that creepeth upon the earth; that they may breed abundantly in the earth, and be fruitful, and multiply upon the earth. And Noah went forth, and his sons, and his wife, and his sons' wives with him: Every beast, every creeping thing, and every fowl, and whatsoever creepeth upon the earth, after their kinds, went forth out of the ark.

At this point, if I were Noah, I would have thought, "Get the Frisbee, grab the picnic baskets. This is great!" But even though God didn't tell him what to do, that's not what Noah did . . .

Genesis 8:20 (a)
And Noah builded an altar unto the LORD . . .

The first thing Noah did was build an altar. I know Noah had enjoyed the presence of God in the ark because he emerged from the ark an "altared" man.

Genesis 8:20 (b)
. . . and took of every clean beast, and of every clean fowl, and offered burnt offerings on the altar.

"Noah, what are you doing?" the world would say. "There's a whole planet to repopulate, and you're burning up limited, valuable resources. It's a waste, Noah. Be practical."

Whenever I find myself thinking this, I realize I'm in very, very bad company . . .

A woman poured an alabaster box full of perfume upon Jesus. "Wait a minute," said Judas. "That's a waste of resources. The poor could be helped with that money."

"What she has done, she has done unto Me," said Jesus (Matthew 26:12).

And in this I begin to understand that God values worship more than work.

"Thou shalt worship the Lord thy God, and Him only shalt thou serve," declared Jesus (Matthew 4:10). Did you notice the order? Worship comes first, service second. You might not be able to be a missionary in Africa, an evangelist in a big stadium, or a singer on the radio—but every single person can do that which most blesses God, for the highest priority of ministry is not work, but worship.

Some of us will go home tonight and worship God. We'll wake in the morning and worship the Lord. It's the highest, most precious ministry you will ever perform. Worship will bless you the most, and honor God in the greatest way. Worship will "altar" your life—it will change who you are.

Genesis 8:21, 22
And the LORD smelled a sweet savour; and the LORD said in his heart, I will not again curse the ground any more for man's sake; for the imagination of man's heart is evil from his youth; neither will I again smite any more every thing living, as I have done. While the earth remaineth, seedtime and harvest, and cold and heat, and summer and winter, and day and night shall not cease.

And GOD saw that the wickedness of man was great in the earth, and that every imagination of the thoughts of his heart was only evil continually. And it repented the LORD that he had made man on the earth, and it grieved him at his heart. And the LORD said, I will destroy man whom I have created from the face of the earth; both man, and beast, and the creeping thing, and the fowls of the air; for it repenteth me that I have made them. Genesis 6:5–7

And the LORD smelled a sweet savour; and the LORD said in his heart, I will not again curse the ground any more for man's sake; for the imagination of man's heart is evil from his youth . . . Genesis 8:21

There seems to be a contradiction here. Is God being fickle?

No. You see, even though the external flood couldn't deal with the internal depravity of man, the fragrance of Noah's sacrifice—a sweet-smelling savor unto the Lord—overpowered the stench of sin. A burnt offering was made, and that made all the difference.

Every Old Testament sacrifice points to and speaks of Jesus Christ—the ultimate sacrifice, the Lamb of God slaughtered on the Cross for the sin of the world. It's the fragrance of the work of Christ that overrides the stench of my depravity. The Flood didn't clean up culture. The Flood didn't solve the problem. No, it was the sacrifice that caused God to say, "Neither will I again smite every living thing."

You might feel terrible tonight. You might feel like you've blown it badly. But even on your drive home you can worship God and He will smell a sweet savor. He knows our imaginations are evil continually, yet He still finds sacrifice sweet. God doesn't command you to worship Him tonight, but some of you will. He won't command you to worship Him tomorrow, but some of you will. And in so doing, you'll bless Him.

RESTING ON THE RESURRECTION

A Topical Study of GENESIS 8:4

In the seventh month, on the seventeenth day of the month, on a mountain named Ararat, the ark came to rest. The seventh month would become the first month in the Hebrew religious calendar when the Jews were delivered from their Egyptian bondage (Exodus 12:1–5). And it was on the fourteenth day of the first month—Passover—when Jesus Christ, the Lamb of God was nailed to a cross.

Maybe now you're beginning to see the significance of the text before us. But wait. The ark rested on the seventeenth day—that's three days *after* Passover. What took place three days after Jesus was crucified? He rose again. Therefore, the ark rested on the mountain the very day Christ would rise from the dead.

The Fact of the Resurrection

Just as the ark rested on Resurrection Day, so too, our faith rests on the fact of the Resurrection. Perhaps you find yourself feeling confused when people come your way, saying, "We love the teachings of Jesus. But you must understand that there are some good people in the Mormon church down the road. And there are some wonderful people in Ashland who follow Tao. You can't just wipe them out and say they're going to burn in hell. And what about Islam? The very word means Submission. Or the Buddhist who is committed to breaking free of his selfish desires? You can't just write them all off."

"Hmm," we say. "These *are* good people," as we begin to bob up and down on the sea of confusion. Our ark comes to rest, however, when we remember one thing: Jesus said, "I am the Way, the Truth, and the Life. No man comes to the Father but by Me" (John 14:6).

"We don't believe You," countered the Pharisees. "Show us a sign."

"One sign I will give to you," Jesus said. "Even as Jonah was in the belly of the whale three days, so shall the Son of man be in the center of the earth," speaking of His burial and resurrection (Matthew 12:40).

Our faith rests on the fact of the Resurrection. If Christ has not risen, then we are, as Paul said, most miserable (1 Corinthians 15:19). We don't know what to say to the Taoist, to the Mormon, to the Buddhist. If Christ did not rise from the dead, we do not know if we're headed in the right direction. But if, on the other hand, He did rise from the dead, He did something no one else in history has ever done. The Resurrection is conclusive proof that we are on the right track. Our ship of faith rests on the mountain of the Resurrection.

I am in Israel almost every year. Every time I go, I check the tomb. And guess what. It's empty.

"That *sounds* good," says the scoffer, "but maybe it's the wrong tomb."

Believe me, when word started spreading that Christ had risen, the enemies of Jesus would have searched frantically to make sure that the empty tomb was not a case of mistaken identity. You see, the leaders of Judaism desperately desired to see Christianity wiped out. All they would have had to do would be to say to the Christians, "Here's the body of this One who claimed to be the exclusive Way to heaven. Here's proof He couldn't validate His claim." But they didn't.

"Well, maybe the disciples stole His body to perpetuate the myth of a resurrected Jesus," claims the cynic.

Peter was crucified upside down. Thomas was speared in the back. James was sawn in half. Matthew's brains were beaten out with a club. With the exception of John—who was banished to the isle of Patmos after an unsuccessful attempt to boil him in oil—each of the disciples died a tortuous death. To believe that eleven men would have allowed their wives and children to be martyred, and their own bodies slaughtered to propagate what they knew to be a lie requires an incredible leap of faith.

"It was the Romans who took the body," declares the doubter.

Christianity was such a threat to the Roman Empire that they launched ten waves of persecution in which sixty million Christians were killed. Indeed, Christianity would eventually cause the Empire to split in two—east and west—and ultimately fall. Certainly the Romans didn't have the body, for producing it would have saved their Empire.

"No one stole the body because Jesus didn't really die," muses the mocker. "One of the disciples put some drugs in the vinegar that was lifted up to Jesus as He hung on the Cross, which caused Him to go into a coma. After the cool air of the tomb revived Him, He appeared as though He had resurrected."

The scourging Jesus suffered before His Crucifixion was in itself enough to kill a man. Jesus went on, however, to endure spikes through His hands and feet and a spear thrust in His side. Then He was put in a tomb for three days without food, water, or medical attention. To suggest He then stood up, single-handedly rolled away a two-ton stone, and took on the one hundred Roman soldiers guarding His tomb requires infinitely more faith than I could possible muster.

He who studies the Resurrection honestly and intellectually must rest finally on the mountain of evidence that says, "He is risen."

The Act of the Resurrection

The act of the Resurrection impacts my entire understanding of spirituality and Christianity. Paul put it this way:

> *I am crucified with Christ: nevertheless I live; yet not I, but Christ liveth in me: and the life which I now live in the flesh I live by the faith of the Son of God, who loved me, and gave himself for me.* Galatians 2:20

The Resurrection means that Christ lives *in* you. It's not imitation—trying to be a "good little Christian boy or girl." It's impartation . . .

A film loop I watched constantly as a high-school discus-thrower was the world-record throw of four-time Olympian Al Oerter. Over and over, I'd watch him drive his hip, thrust his shoulder, cock his arm, steady his grip, and make the toss. Then I'd go out to the rink and I'd try to do it all just like Al. But although I knew exactly what to do, did I ever do it like he did? I didn't even come close.

And that's the problem with religion and philosophy. They tell you what to do—but fail to give you the power to do it. Not so with Christianity. If Al Oerter could have squeezed into my body and thrown the discus through me, I could have set world records just like he did. Because Jesus is risen, His Spirit lives *in* me. It's not a matter of me trying to figure out what to do, reading certain books, going to certain seminars, listening to certain tapes. It's a matter of Him living in me, giving me the power to do what the Word tells me to do.

The Pact of the Resurrection

"Because I live, you shall live also," declared Jesus. "It's a pact I'm making with you." If Christ did not rise, we would have no hope of eternal life ourselves. But because He lives, we shall as well.

Jesus is risen, and He is returning. And while that gives me great peace, it also stirs me. You see, Peter tells us that when the Chief Shepherd shall appear, we will receive a crown of glory (1 Peter 5:4). The events in the Middle East indicate to me that Jesus' coming is very near. And even if it's not as soon as I think it's going to be, life goes by oh, so rapidly. Very soon I'm going to face Jesus personally. I will stand before the Chief Shepherd and give an account for what I did with all that He gave me so graciously. So will you.

God has given you money, talents, time, ability, freedom, health, opportunity, calling. He's given you vision, direction, instruction. And, because He lives within you, He's given you power. One day, you will give an account of what you did with the graces and gifts He gave you.

"I hear what you're saying," you might be thinking. "But I'm still young. As soon as I get married, I'll serve Jesus."

So you get married, and then not too much later, you hear yourself saying, "We're really serious about serving Jesus. But right now, we've got a home to build and diapers to change. When our kids are in elementary school, then we'll get busy and serve the Lord."

But with elementary school comes Cub Scouts, piano lessons, and Little League. And church gets shoved down further because, after all, who's going to cheer junior on if you're not there? So he misses Sunday school—he's learning to hit a curve ball!

Then you say, "As soon as our kids are out of the house, we're going to get real serious about serving God."

But then a funny thing happens. I have discovered that right about the time the kids leave is the time people start to remodel their houses.

Gang, there will never be a day easier than this one for you to say, "I will seek first the kingdom."

- May the fact of the Resurrection strengthen your faith.
- May the act of the Resurrection empower your life.
- May the pact of the Resurrection stir your heart.

In Jesus' name.

REACH OUT AND TOUCH THE ONE

A Topical Study of GENESIS 8:9

Most of us need pictures and stories to understand theology. I know I do. The text before us provides just such a picture, for it pointedly and powerfully portrays what it means to be empowered by the Spirit . . .

The first animal to leave the ark was a raven—a black bird that goes "to and fro" eating the carcasses of dead animals.

When Satan came before the Lord one day in heaven, the Lord said, "Where have you been?"

"I've been going to and fro," said Satan—cruising around just like the raven (Job 1:6, 7).

Peter tells us Satan is always on the lookout for those whom he may devour (1 Peter 5:8). But the good news is that as the raven circled, Noah released a dove—which, throughout Scripture, speaks of the Holy Spirit.

Why?

The dove is the purest of all birds, for not only is it white in color—but it secretes more dirt-repelling oil on its feathers than any other flying bird. The dove is also sensitive because it is one of few animals who mates for life. The dove is also a symbol of peace because, unlike vultures or buzzards, doves vacate places where there is frenzy or fighting.

As Noah saw the dove circling overhead, he could have said, "If the dove wants to land on me, he can. I'm open." But that's not what he did. Noah extended his hand, grabbed the dove, and brought it in.

So often, with regard to the power and presence of the Spirit, people say, "If the Holy Spirit wants to bless me and empower me, I'm open." But that kind of passivity will never bring the potency of the Spirit in its greatest possible degree. If you want to be empowered by the Spirit, you cannot be passive about the work of the Spirit any more than you were passive about the work of salvation.

This is where so many people err. You see, God is looking for those who will partner with Him rather than merely being passive about Him. Noah didn't simply fold his arms and watch. He stretched forth his hand and reached.

"Wait a minute," you might be saying. "I'm born again, therefore I already have the Spirit" (Romans 8:9).

That's true. The moment you were born again; the Spirit came in you. You've got the Spirit. The question is: Does the Spirit have you? Jesus taught us there are three different relationships a person can have with the Holy Spirit . . .

The Spirit *with* You

Even the Spirit of truth; whom the world cannot receive, because it seeth him not, neither knoweth him: but ye know him; for he dwelleth with you . . .

John 14:17 (a)

The first relationship a person has with the Spirit is "with" you. The Greek word translated "with" is *para*, which means "alongside of." You wouldn't be here today, you would never have opened your heart to Jesus had not the Holy Spirit come alongside you and whispered in your heart, "You need to become a Christian. You need to open your heart to Jesus." Every person has the Spirit *with* them at some point in their life.

The Spirit *in* You

. . . and shall be in you. John 14:17 (b)

Once you become a believer, the Holy Spirit comes *in* you. When did this happen to the disciples? After Jesus had risen from the dead, He breathed on His disciples and said, "Receive ye the Holy Spirit" (John 20:22). At that point, they were born again, and the Spirit came *in* them.

The Spirit *upon* You

But ye shall receive power, after that the Holy Spirit is come upon you . . .

Acts 1:8 (a)

People refer to the baptism in the Spirit, the fullness of the Spirit, or the empowering of the Spirit. The Bible calls this the "coming upon" of the Spirit. Whenever the Spirit of God came upon a man in both the Old and New Testaments, it was always to empower him for service, to dynamically impact him for ministry.

How does this happen?

By reaching out, just as Noah did . . .

Reach Out in Faith

Blessed are they which do hunger and thirst after righteousness: for they shall be filled. Matthew 5:6

Have you hungered and thirsted for righteousness? Have you hungered and thirsted for the "coming upon" of the Spirit? Jesus said if we being evil know how to give good gifts to our children, how much more will the Heavenly Father give the Holy Ghost to them that ask (Matthew 7:11). If you want to be filled with the Spirit, reach out with a faith that's based upon God's promises.

Reach Out with Hope

Looking for that blessed hope, and the glorious appearing of the great God and our Saviour Jesus Christ . . . Titus 2:13 (a)

The biblical definition of hope is "the absolute expectation of coming good." What does this mean practically? It means I reach out in faith, with hope, *expecting* the Lord will answer. It might take some time. After all, the disciples sought the Lord for ten days before the mighty rushing wind of the Spirit filled their upper room (Acts 2:2).

Am I saying we have to wait for ten days? No. We no longer have to wait *for* the Spirit, because the Spirit was given on the Day of Pentecost. But we do wait *on* the Spirit. Isaiah said those who wait on the Lord shall renew their strength (Isaiah 40:31). Why would He have us wait on Him? I suggest one reason is that although many of us want to be filled, the real issue is that we first must be emptied—of sin.

You see, if the Lord filled me with His Spirit in my sinful condition, it would be detrimental because it would justify my carnality. Consequently, the Lord often says, "I want you to wait on Me and allow Me to search your heart, to show you that which needs to be adjusted. It might take ten days, ten weeks, or ten months. Wait on Me."

People wait for days to get tickets to a Rolling Stones concert, but when it comes to the empowering of the Holy Ghost, we say, "Okay, Lord, I'm going to ask You for it. You've got fifteen seconds, and if it doesn't happen, then I guess it's not for me." How little we know of waiting on the Lord.

Reach Out for Love

Though I speak with the tongues of men and of angels, and have not charity, I am become as sounding brass, or a tinkling cymbal. 1 Corinthians 13:1

First Corinthians 12 and 14 deal with the gifts and workings of the Holy Spirit. First Corinthians 13—the definition of love—appears right in the middle of Paul's discussion of the Spirit because love is the center of it all. Love is the key. That's what Jesus meant when He said, "The Spirit is in you. Now go to Jerusalem and wait for the Spirit to come upon you," (see Acts 1:4).

Jerusalem? The collective cry of Jerusalem had been, "Away with Him. Let His blood be upon our heads. Crucify Him." For Jesus to pour out His Spirit at Jerusalem doesn't make sense. For Him to pour out His wrath at Jerusalem—that makes sense. For Him to pour out His judgment at Jerusalem—that's understandable. But to pour out His Spirit in the place that wanted nothing to do with Him, that turned its back on Him, that killed Him? I would have thought the Lord would blast Jerusalem. Instead He blessed Jerusalem.

If you want to be filled with the Holy Ghost, reach out in faith, with hope, for love. Love the person who really messed up, who let you down, who fired you unfairly. Who is your Jerusalem? Who has wronged you, hurt you, offended you? Do good to him, bless her, love them. And as you do, you'll find that the Spirit of God will begin to flow through you. You'll be filled and anointed and empowered whenever you choose to love your Jerusalem. When you choose to love the wife who left you, the child who rejected you, the boss who hurt you, you will be empowered with the Spirit of God. I guarantee it. It all starts in Jerusalem.

9

Genesis 9:1 (a)
And God blessed Noah . . .

God blessed Noah; for, in building an altar, Noah had blessed God. So, if you choose to bless the Lord by sacrificing to Him, like Noah, you will be blessed, for God will be a debtor to no man. You will always get back more than you give.

Genesis 9:1 (b), 2
. . . and his sons, and said unto them, Be fruitful, and multiply, and replenish the earth. And the fear of you and the dread of you shall be upon every beast of the earth, and upon every fowl of the air, upon all that moveth upon the earth, and upon all the fishes of the sea; into your hand are they delivered.

Noah, here, is essentially told to start over. Even as God had initially told Adam and Eve to be fruitful and multiply, Noah and his sons and their wives are hearing the same command. This time, however, earth is not paradise, but neither is it perdition. Due to man's perpetual propensity to sin, our planet is not what it was in Adam's day—but neither is it as bad as it could have been.

I say this to remind you that, although you may not think your life is going great, it's going a whole lot better than you deserve. We deserve to be frying in hell. God is so *good* to us. Anything we have, everything we enjoy is due to His mercy and kindness. We're headed for heaven, where all things are right and perfect. Yet even in the meantime, we have so much today for which to be thankful.

The text before us is known as the Noahic covenant. A covenant is a sovereign proclamation from the lips of God that puts Him into a relationship of responsibility with a man, a family, or a nation. Such proclamations are usually—but not always—unconditional. That is, they're God saying, "This is what I'm going to do, regardless of what you do." In one notable exception, the covenant is conditional. A conditional covenant is God saying, "I'm going to do this if you do your part, too."

There are essentially eight covenants in Scripture—each of which further unfolds the drama of the redemption of humanity . . .

- The Edenic Covenant (Genesis 2).
  This is when God sovereignly said to Adam, "The Garden of Eden is for you to enjoy. Except for the Tree of the Knowledge of Good and Evil, eat freely and enjoy completely."
- The Adamic Covenant (Genesis 3).
  This is the covenant made to Adam after he had fallen into sin. In it, God declares man would work by the sweat of his brow, and woman would give birth in pain. But it also contains great hope in that it promises a Savior.
- The Noahic Covenant (Genesis 9).
- The Abrahamic Covenant (Genesis 12).
  This is the covenant wherein God declares that all nations would be blessed through Abraham and his seed—that Seed, of course, being Jesus.
- Mosaic Covenant (Exodus 20)
  Also known as the Law, the Mosaic covenant is the one covenant that is conditional. Over and over, God says, "You'll be blessed if you do these things, cursed if you don't."
- Palestinian Covenant (Deuteronomy 30)
  In the Palestinian covenant, God declares that, though they would be driven out of their land, God would re-gather His people and restore to them perpetual ownership of the land of Israel.
- Davidic Covenant (2 Samuel 7)
  This is the covenant wherein God promised that from David would come a Ruler who would reign forever and ever—again, pointing to the Son of David, Jesus Christ.
- The New Covenant (Hebrews 8)
  In the new covenant, God declares, "No longer will My will be external, written on

stone—but internal, written in hearts." This is why when He broke bread with His disciples right before His death, Jesus said, "This is the blood of the new covenant. My Spirit shall reside in you, give direction to you, and provide power for you to be the kind of people I want you to be."

The Noahic covenant, as seen in the text before us, is comprised of three basic components: Diet, Discipline, and Declaration . . .

Genesis 9:3, 4
Every moving thing that liveth shall be meat for you; even as the green herb have I given you all things. But flesh with the life thereof, which is the blood thereof, shall ye not eat.

Following the Flood, man would no longer be a vegetarian. Why? It wasn't that God said, "You guys have gone without meat long enough." No, there are those who believe that history indicates and Scripture hints that meat was necessary not only for flavor, but to repel the demonic entities and spirits which had interacted with women previously (Genesis 6:2). I'm not saying if you're a vegetarian, you'll be inflicted by demons. I am suggesting, however, that meat has a way of repelling those forces. Presently, cultures that are heavily influenced by demonic religious thought, such as the Hindus in India, embrace vegetarianism. Prophetically, in the last days, there shall be those who fall away from the faith, who fall prey to "seducing spirits" that forbid them from eating meat (1 Timothy 4:1–3).

Scripture does not prioritize nor point to a vegetarian diet as being more spiritual, deeper, better. In fact, after Jesus died for our sins, rose again, and had a glorified body, He appears to the disciples, saying, "Have you any meat?" (Luke 24:41). Don't let anyone tell you that to be a vegetarian is to be more spiritual, for, if anything, Scripture points in the opposite direction.

Genesis 9:5–7
And surely your blood of your lives will I require; at the hand of every beast will I require it, and at the hand of man; at the hand of every man's brother will I require the life of man. Whoso sheddeth man's blood, by man shall his blood be shed: for in the image of God made he man. And you, be ye fruitful, and multiply; bring forth abundantly in the earth, and multiply therein.

The second element of the Noahic covenant is Discipline. God declares that if a man kills another, humanity is required to deal with it with great severity because, man being made in God's image, the murder of a man is ultimately a strike at God Himself. Thus, the foundation of human government was laid.

There are three institutions God establishes: the family, the church, and government. And the basis of human government is capital punishment—no small controversy in our culture today. Scholars debate it. Philosophers argue it. Politicians waffle back and forth on it. But the average person intuitively, innately understands that in a world where man's imagination is evil continually, capital punishment does indeed deter chaos. That is why presently the fastest growing religion in Western culture is Islam—with mosques outnumbering churches in the city of London.

Moving away from capital punishment as our country has done has a domino effect on our entire culture. It used to be that if a man committed first-degree murder, he was sent to his eternal destiny. That meant the rapist served fifteen to twenty years in prison, the shoplifter ten years. But now with the first-degree murderer serving fifteen years in prison, the rapist serves five and the shoplifter six months. As the punishment for crime is diminished, society begins to discover that crime *does* pay—and things begin to go terribly awry.

Following the Flood, at the outset of recreated history, God gave man the obligation and responsibility of governing himself, predicated upon the foundational understanding that he who commits murder must himself be put to death.

"But that's an Old Testament principle," you protest.

Turn to the New Testament.

> For rulers are not a terror to good works, but to the evil. Wilt thou then not be afraid of the power? do that which is good, and thou shalt have praise of the same: For he is the minister of God to thee for good. But if thou do that which is evil, be afraid; for he beareth not the sword in vain: for he is the minister of God, a revenger to execute wrath upon him that doeth evil. Romans 13:3, 4

The phrase, "execute wrath," is understood by Greek scholars and Bible teachers to mean that the law enforcement system is in place to execute capital punishment upon those who deserve it. Thus, capital punishment is a New Testament concept as well as an Old Testament precept.

"Well, Jesus didn't believe in capital punishment," you argue. "After all, He put a stop to those who were trying to stone the woman taken in adultery in John 8."

Wait a minute. The Law of Moses declared that

if a person was caught in adultery, both the man and the woman were to be stoned. So Jesus said that day, "Go ahead. But let he who is without sin cast the first stone." Jesus knew these men weren't interested in justice because had they been seeking justice, they would have brought the woman's partner as well as the woman. Nevertheless, even though He knew the mob wasn't interested in justice, Jesus didn't dismiss capital punishment as seen in the Law.

Genesis 9:8–17
And God spake unto Noah, and to his sons with him, saying, And I, behold, I establish my covenant with you, and with your seed after you; And with every living creature that is with you, of the fowl, of the cattle, and of every beast of the earth with you; from all that go out of the ark, to every beast of the earth. And I will establish my covenant with you; neither shall all flesh be cut off any more by the waters of a flood; neither shall there any more be a flood to destroy the earth. And God said, This is the token of the covenant which I make between me and you and every living creature that is with you, for perpetual generations: I do set my bow in the cloud, and it shall be for a token of a covenant between me and the earth. And it shall come to pass, when I bring a cloud over the earth, that the bow shall be seen in the cloud: And I will remember my covenant, which is between me and you and every living creature of all flesh; and the waters shall no more become a flood to destroy all flesh. And the bow shall be in the cloud; and I will look upon it, that I may remember the everlasting covenant between God and every living creature of all flesh that is upon the earth. And God said unto Noah, This is the token of the covenant, which I have established between me and all flesh that is upon the earth.

The third and final element of the Noahic covenant is Declaration. God declared that He would never again destroy the earth with a flood, and that He would underscore His commitment with a rainbow. So if you see the rainbow, the covenant still applies.

What is a rainbow? It's a mixture of storm and sunshine. So often you see a rainbow—the emblem of God's grace and glory throughout Scripture—when you're coming out of a storm. The Son breaks through and there's a beauty, a reminder of God's presence even in the remnants of the storm.

The bow is emblematic of the bow used by an archer, without an arrow. The rabbis say the reason the bow is empty is because the arrow has already been shot, never again to be pointed in the direction of humanity. No matter what scientists say about global warming or rising oceans, a flood will not destroy the world because that particular arrow has already been shot.

Genesis 9:18–21
And the sons of Noah, that went forth of the ark, were Shem, and Ham, and Japheth: and Ham is the father of Canaan. These are the three sons of Noah: and of them was the whole earth overspread. And Noah began to be an husbandman, and he planted a vineyard: And he drank of the wine, and was drunken; and he was uncovered within his tent.

It's when things are going well that we must be especially careful. When the storms are brewing, when trials are coming, we have a tendency to pray and seek the Lord. But when things are on "automatic pilot" we, like Noah, often fall into trouble.

Genesis 9:22, 23
And Ham, the father of Canaan, saw the nakedness of his father, and told his two brethren without. And Shem and Japheth took a garment, and laid it upon both their shoulders, and went backward, and covered the nakedness of their father; and their faces were backward, and they saw not their father's nakedness.

Ham exposed his father's nakedness. Shem and Japheth, however, chose a much better way.

***For topical study of Genesis 9:23 entitled "A Loving Covering," turn to page* 51.**

Genesis 9:24, 25
And Noah awoke from his wine, and knew what his younger son had done unto him. And he said, Cursed be Canaan; a servant of servants shall he be unto his brethren.

Ham was the one who exposed his dad's sin. Yet it would be his son, Canaan, who would experience the repercussions. We see the same thing today when the son of an alcoholic grows up to be an alcoholic himself, when the son of a child abuser grows up to, himself, abuse children. This is one of the great tragedies of sin. Toss a pebble into a pond, and the circles will grow ever wider. The same is true of sin. The consequences and ramifications grow to include many more people than we ever guess.

Genesis 9:26 (a)
And he said, Blessed be the LORD God of Shem . . .

Shem's name means "Glory." Shem is the father of the Semitic people—the Jews and Arabs. They settled primarily in the Middle East. Blessed be the Lord God of Shem, indeed, for the God of Shem is the True and Living God.

Genesis 9:26 (b)
. . . and Canaan shall be his servant.

Depending on the lexicon used, Ham's name means either "black" or "hot." The Hamitic people settled in Africa. You may have heard sermons to the effect that the reason the people of Africa have been enslaved is due to Ham's sin and subsequent curse. No. Ham was not cursed. It was his son, Canaan, who was cursed. Canaan was the father of the Canaanites, a people so perverted and polluted that God ordered their annihilation in order to put them out of their misery.

Genesis 9:27–29
God shall enlarge Japheth, and he shall dwell in the tents of Shem; and Canaan shall be his servant. And Noah lived after the flood three hundred and fifty years. And all the days of Noah were nine hundred and fifty years: and he died.

The family of Japheth, whose name means "Ruler," settled in Europe. For centuries, the European people were considered uncouth and primitive. But as history unfolded, the sons of Japheth would ultimately become the geo-political rulers of the world. Yet Japheth would nonetheless dwell in the tents of Shem. That is, his covering would come not from his own pagan deities which the Europeans worshiped for centuries—but from the True and Living God of Shem.

A LOVING COVERING

A Topical Study of GENESIS 9:23

The storm had passed. After being a carpenter for one hundred years, pounding away on the ark; after being a preacher, warning the people of judgment; after being a sailor for 377 days, sailing atop the Flood—Noah changes occupations. He becomes a farmer, a "husbandman" or, literally, "a man of the earth." And in so doing, he will indeed become quite earthy . . .

The Reality of Noah's Sins

Evidently, after sampling some of the fruit of his vines, Noah was drunk and lay uncovered in his tent. The original language makes it clear that his nakedness was related to immorality of some sort.

How could this be? After all, Noah was the one who preached for one hundred years to the whole world. Noah was the one who built the ark, and who didn't complain when he was sealed for 377 days within a floating zoo. Noah was the one who built an altar, who blessed God, who found grace in the eyes of the Lord.

When he was going through challenging times, difficult days, thundering storms, Noah walked with God. But when things became normal, he became vulnerable. And the same is true with us. It's when everything is going well, when our vines are growing, when our job is going fine, when life is on automatic pilot, that we are in danger. No longer are we on guard, no longer are we dependent upon the Lord or desperately crying out to Him. Such is what happened to Noah. He got drunk and sinned greatly.

Regardless of your stand on social drinking, this is without controversy for anyone who claims to be a believer: From Genesis through Revelation, drunkenness is absolutely forbidden. "Getting high" or "getting a buzz" is absolutely forbidden. Why? Is it because God is mean? No. It's because when a person gets drunk, like Noah, he is exposed. You see, exposure can happen in all sorts of ways. Drunk people say things they wish they wouldn't have said; they get involved in discussions which never should have started; they do things they wish they never had done. Drunkenness leads to exposure in one way or another.

In the course of twenty years in ministry, I've talked with people whose hearts were broken because they were involved in immoral behavior brought on by drinking. When people drink, their thinking becomes fuzzy and there will be a vulnerability to get involved in stuff they wouldn't have otherwise. Such was the reality of Noah's sin.

The Reaction of Noah's Sons

Ham saw his father's nakedness. That's always the way it is, for whether it's regarding our birth family or our church family, those closest to us are those who will see our weaknesses. Why Ham talked about his father's nakedness, I do not know—just as I don't know why we are so eager to talk about one another's weaknesses. But this I do know: Shem and Japheth wouldn't look at their father's nakedness themselves. Why did they stretch a garment between them? Because they didn't want anyone outside the tent to look in and see their dad's nakedness. They didn't want those outside of the tent to be distracted by their father's condition.

Folks, people are looking for reasons not to believe our message of hope and salvation. And hearing us talk about each other's weaknesses gives them reason not to come in and join us.

But not only did Shem and Japheth keep others from viewing their father's nakedness—they did not look upon it themselves.

Why?

Because even though I know someone may be forgiven, even though I know sin is common to everyone, looking at someone's sin, listening to reports of someone's iniquity taints the way I view him in the future. You see, if you come home from work upset with your boss and you start complaining and exposing his mistakes and weakness to your wife, although you end up feeling much better, your wife stores that information away. And the next time she sees your boss, there are daggers in her eyes, and you wonder why she no longer wants to go to the company picnic. If I listen to reports of the sin or iniquity of another, it will taint the way I view that person. Exposure is damaging, destructive, and divisive.

Shouldn't we talk about problems? If it's *your* problem, yes. But if it's someone else's problem, someone else's sin, someone else's weakness, nakedness, or vulnerability, follow Shem and Japheth's example: Walk in backwards and conceal it from others. Not only will this protect the one who sins, but it will protect you as well, for the person who talks to you about someone else will invariably also talk to someone else about you.

How do I know this?

Because Paul warns, "Take heed that you do not bite and devour one another because you will be consumed one of another. On the other hand," Paul continues, "the entire law is fulfilled in the one word: love" (Galatians 5:14, 15).

The Reason for Noah's Sayings

When Noah awoke from his drunken state, he knew what Ham had done and cursed Ham's son. No doubt Ham thought, "I've got big shoulders. I can handle the repercussions of my sin." Unbeknownst to him, however, was the fact that the repercussions didn't fall on him. They fell upon his son. How bad were the repercussions? The Canaanites were the worst culture in the history of the world. Totally immoral and completely perverted, they were eventually absolutely annihilated.

Dad and Mom, if we sin we must not think we alone will pay the price. Sin doesn't work that way. The consequences will often come in ways that will break your heart as they relate to your family. The children of parents who expose the weaknesses of bosses and neighbors, sisters and brothers; of parents who are dour and sour and critical, grow up not wanting to go to church, bitter about the things of God, and uninterested in the Bible.

So what are we to do?

We are to say, "I've been forgiven of so much that I will not talk about the weakness of my boss, my neighbor, my pastor, the person sitting next to me, my friends, or my enemies. I will not speak or listen to negativity." Every one of us will fail at some point or another. But if you choose today to be like Shem and Japheth—to cover the nakedness of others—you will be likewise covered when you fail.

> *Be ye therefore merciful, as your Father also is merciful. Judge not, and ye shall not be judged: condemn not, and ye shall not be condemned: forgive, and ye shall be forgiven: Give, and it shall be given unto you; good measure, pressed down, and shaken together, and running over, shall men give into your bosom. For with the same measure that ye mete withal it shall be measured to you again.*
>
> Luke 6:36–38

Maybe you've heard this passage quoted by a preacher, saying, "Support my ministry financially, and watch and see how goodness will be heaped upon you in return." However, this verse has nothing to do with giving money, and everything to do with showing mercy. Jesus says we will be recipients of mercy, forgiveness, and compassion to the degree we forgive others. Therefore, may we be like Shem and Japheth. May we cover rather than expose the nakedness of others, for love covers a multitude of sins.

10 The Flood is over. Earth is being repopulated. And in chapter 10, we come to what is known as the Table of Nations—the beginning point of an understanding of world history and anthropology . . .

Genesis 10:1
Now these are the generations of the sons of Noah, Shem, Ham, and Japheth: and unto them were sons born after the flood.

From the following sixty descendants of the three sons of Noah will come all of the world's races and language groups.

Genesis 10:2 (a)
The sons of Japheth; Gomer . . .

Gomer is present-day Germany.

Genesis 10:2 (b)
. . . and Magog . . .

Magog is present-day Russia. According to famed historian, Herodotus, ancient peoples universally recognized Russia as Magog. Even the Great Wall of China, erected to keep out the Russians, is called the Wall of Magog by the Chinese people. Magog will come into play in a key prophetic event—the invasion from the North into Israel (Ezekiel 38, 39).

Genesis 10:2 (c)
. . . and Madai . . .

Madai refers to the Medes and the Persians—present-day Iran. The reason Iraq and Iran are always at odds historically is because Iraq is peopled by Arabs—descendants of Shem, while Iran is peopled by Persians—descendants of Japheth.

Genesis 10:2 (d)
. . . and Javan . . .

Javan is present-day Greece.

Genesis 10:2 (e)
. . . and Tubal, and Meshech, and Tiras.

Meshech is the ancient name for Moscow.

Genesis 10:3 (a)
And the sons of Gomer; Ashkenaz . . .

Ashkenaz is in the area of present-day Eastern Germany and Eastern Europe. The Jewish people are divided into two groups: the Ashkenazi Jews and the Sephardic Jews. In A.D. 70, when the Romans crushed the nation of Israel, a great number of the Jewish people settled in Germany and Eastern Europe. These are the Ashkenazi Jews. The Sephardic Jews settled in the Mediterranean region. The Ashkenazi Jew has traditionally been the power broker, resulting in ethnic tension between the two groups.

Genesis 10:3 (b)
. . . and Riphath, and Togarmah.

The descendants of Togarmah settle in Turkey and are the descendants of Japheth, which, again, explains the political tension between Turkey and Israel.

Genesis 10:4, 5
And the sons of Javan; Elishah, and Tarshish, Kittim, and Dodanim. By these were the isles of the Gentiles divided in their lands; every one after his tongue, after their families, in their nations.

Tarshish is the area of either Spain or England. Although there is debate, most scholars believe it refers to present-day Spain. You might recall Tarshish as the intended destination of a certain Hebrew prophet who had a whale of a time getting there.

Genesis 10:6
And the sons of Ham; Cush, and Mizraim, and Phut, and Canaan.

The Hamitic people settled primarily in the region of Africa, with some in the Middle East. Cush settled in the area of the Nile, present-day Ethiopia. Those who descend from Cush in the Bible are talked about as those who have very distinctive skin (Jeremiah 3:23), and being very tall (Isaiah 45:14). Mizraim is the area of Egypt. Phut is present-day Libya. Canaan is present-day Israel. Some of the descendants of Ham, the Canaanites, would settle in that region and would ultimately have to be exterminated because of their perpetual pollution and perversion—but not before God gave them four centuries to repent.

Genesis 10:7
And the sons of Cush; Seba, and Havilah, and Sabtah, and Raamah, and Sabtecha: and the sons of Raamah; Sheba, and Dedan.

Sheba and Dedan is present-day Saudi Arabia. Sheba and Dedan will pop up in Scripture again and again, especially in relation to Ezekiel 38, 39.

Genesis 10:8 (a)
And Cush begat Nimrod . . .

The name, *Nimrod,* literally means "rebel." The quintessential rebel, Nimrod was a prototype of the ultimate rebel—antichrist. Based out of the revived Roman Empire—or the European Union—antichrist will head a one-world government and seek to establish a one-world religion. He will be powerful, charismatic, and amazingly persuasive.

Genesis 10:8 (b)
. . . he began to be a mighty one in the earth.

Like the rebel of whom he is a prototype, the language here indicates that Nimrod did things that amazed and confounded people.

Genesis 10:9
He was a mighty hunter before the LORD: wherefore it is said, Even as Nimrod the mighty hunter before the LORD.

Newer versions properly render this verse, "He was a mighty hunter *against* the Lord." Nimrod was a mighty, powerful rebel who hunted souls and ripped people off.

Genesis 10:10
And the beginning of his kingdom was Babel, and Erech, and Accad, and Calneh, in the land of Shinar.

Originally Babel was *Bab-El,* which means "Gateway to God." As the story unfolds, however, Babel will come to mean "confusion."

Genesis 10:11
Out of that land went forth Asshur, and builded Nineveh, and the city Rehoboth, and Calah.

This verse literally begins, "*He* went out . . ." Who went out? Nimrod.

Nimrod not only founded Babylon, but he also is the founding father of the Assyrian Empire, whose capital was Nineveh. It was the Assyrians who carried away the ten northern tribes of Israel into captivity in 722 B.C. And it was the Babylonians who destroyed Jerusalem one hundred and thirty-six years later in 586. Babylon and Assyria both figure greatly in Bible history—and both were founded by a rebel named Nimrod.

Genesis 10:12–14
And Resen between Nineveh and Calah: the same is a great city. And Mizraim begat Ludim, and Anamim, and Lehabim, and Naphtuhim, And Pathrusim, and Casluhim, (out of whom came Philistim,) and Caphtorim.

"Philistim" brings to mind a certain Philistine named Goliath.

Genesis 10:15–17
And Canaan begat Sidon his firstborn, and Heth, And the Jebusite, and the Amorite, and the Girgasite, And the Hivite, and the Arkite, and the Sinite,

Sino refers to China. The Chinese, Japanese, and Asian people are descendants of Ham.

Genesis 10:18–21
And the Arvadite, and the Zemarite, and the Hamathite: and afterward were the families of the Canaanites spread abroad. And the border of the Canaanites was from Sidon, as thou comest to Gerar, unto Gaza; as thou goest, unto Sodom, and Gomorrah, and Admah, and Zeboim, even unto Lasha. These are the sons of Ham, after their families, after their tongues, in their countries, and in their nations. Unto Shem also, the father of all the children of Eber, the brother of Japheth the elder, even to him were children born.

This is the first mention of the children of Eber, or the Hebrews. *Eber* simply means "crossing over"—a fitting name for a people who, in Abraham would leave Ur and under the leadership of Moses would cross over into the land which God had promised them.

Genesis 10:22–32
The children of Shem; Elam, and Asshur, and Arphaxad, and Lud, and Aram. And the children of Aram; Uz, and Hul, and Gether, and Mash. And Arphaxad begat Salah; and Salah begat Eber. And unto Eber were born two sons: the name of one was Peleg; for in his days was the earth divided; and his brother's name was Joktan. And Joktan begat Almodad, and Sheleph, and Hazarmaveth, and Jerah, And Hadoram, and Uzal,

and Diklah, And Obal, and Abimael, and Sheba, And Ophir, and Havilah, and Jobab: all these were the sons of Joktan. And their dwelling was from Mesha, as thou goest unto Sephar a mount of the east. These are the sons of Shem, after their families, after their tongues, in their lands, after their nations. These are the families of the sons of Noah, after their generations, in their nations: and by these were the nations divided in the earth after the flood.

The Hebrew word translated "earth" in verse 25 is *erets,* which always refers to the geological, physical earth rather than to the people on the earth. The fact that the earth was divided explains how the animals were able to spread from Mount Ararat into all corners of the world.

According to Dr. Dolph Hooker's book, *The Astounding Ice Ages,* the Ice Ages, triggered when the water canopy collapsed at the time of the Flood, did not happen gradually but were cataclysmic moments in time, which explains why fossils of woolly mammoths have been found with fresh vegetation in their mouths. Dr. Hooker goes on to say that the immediate coming of an Ice Age would cause a recession of the oceans due to the fourteen million cubic miles of water needed to form the glaciers in the North and South Poles. This, in turn, would create land bridges which would connect every continent to another at some point, making the journey from Ararat to Australia possible for the kangaroo.

Thus, the cynic who scoffs at the truth of the account of the Flood and of Noah's ark on the grounds that it doesn't explain how animals ended up all over the world—is silenced again.

11

Genesis 11:1, 2 (a)
And the whole earth was of one language, and of one speech. And it came to pass, as they journeyed from the east, that they found a plain in the land of Shinar . . .

The plain of Shinar is located in present-day Iraq.

Genesis 11:2 (b), 3 (a)
. . . and they dwelt there. And they said one to another, Go to, let us make brick, and burn them thoroughly. And they had brick for stone . . .

Man builds with brick. Because brick is manmade, it cracks and chips easily. That's why God uses stone.

The massive stones used for the temple were cut to size in a rock quarry a mile away from the temple site so that when the stones arrived at the building site, the Bible says the sound of neither hammer nor chisel was heard (1 Kings 6:7). How close did the stones fit? So close that not even a knife could fit between them. There was no need for cement or mortar, for the stones fit perfectly.

And God still uses stones to build His temple. We are living stones being fit together for a spiritual house (1 Peter 2:5). This means the world is the rock quarry wherein the chipping is taking place so that when we get to the true temple in heaven, there will not be the sound of a hammer or chisel heard.

Therefore, we should not be surprised when the living stone we're sitting next to or married to rubs us the wrong way. It's all part of God's plan to knock off our rough edges so that when we get to heaven, we'll fit together perfectly.

Genesis 11:3 (b)
. . . and slime had they for morter.

Man's efforts are always held together with slime.

Genesis 11:4 (a)
And they said, Go to, let us build us a city and a tower, whose top may reach unto heaven; and let us make us a name . . .

The tower was actually a ziggurat, used for the pagan practice of astrological observation. Ancient tradition tells us ziggurats were also communication towers by which people were able to communicate with each other through the use of crystals. How this worked we do not know—which is not surprising since when you look at structures like Stonehenge and the pyramids, we realize ancient civilizations were doing things we still do not know how to do today.

Genesis 11:4 (b)
. . . lest we be scattered abroad upon the face of the whole earth.

"Be fruitful, multiply, and replenish the earth," God said to Noah (Genesis 9:1).

"Let's not spread throughout the earth," countered Nimrod. "Let's all stay here together."

Genesis 11:5, 6
And the LORD came down to see the city and the tower, which the children of men builded. And the LORD said, Behold, the people is one, and they have all one language; and this they begin to do: and now nothing

will be restrained from them, which they have imagined to do.

Our generation is the first generation since the tower of Babel where man is speaking one language. What language is that? The language of mathematics. Thanks to the mathematical marvel of the computer, a person can type English in America and it will appear as Japanese in Japan. And as it did in Nimrod's day, the universal language of our day is growing increasingly evil because man's imagination remains "evil continually."

Genesis 11:7
Go to, let us go down, and there confound their language, that they may not understand one another's speech.

Father to Son to Spirit says, "We're going to go down and undo this one-world technology, one-world government, one-world religion led by Nimrod"—just as Jesus Christ will come down and undo antiChrist's evil domain.

Is this mean? No, it's merciful. Whether you're talking about brick and slime or microchips and Microsoft, here's the reality: God says, "Now that man is unified, there is nothing to stop him from what he's imagining to do. Unified technology will lead to devastation, destruction, and eternal damnation."

"Without Me, ye can do nothing," Jesus said (John 15:5).

But humanity answers, "Yes we can. We can build whatever we want to with our super computers and brilliant technology. We are the world."

Genesis 11:8
So the Lord scattered them abroad from thence upon the face of all the earth: and they left off to build the city.

No matter how hard they try, no matter how sincere their attempts might be, people can no longer communicate. So they separate into language groups and begin to form their own cultures. The good news, however, is that the necessary curse of Genesis 11 was reversed in Acts 2 when one hundred and twenty believers in the Upper Room began to praise God in languages they had never learned, causing the people from Mesopotamia, Cappadocia, Egypt, Arabia, Galatia, and from all parts of the world on the streets below to hear the gospel in their own language.

And now I begin to understand that the only way for people to truly communicate cross-culturally is to be focused on the Cross of Christ and to be empowered by His Spirit, for apart from Christ, all of our efforts at unity are nothing more than slime and chipped brick. Without Christ, we can try to build a foundation of unity; we can have all kinds of rallies and seminars and marches—but there will be no unity apart from the power and Person of the Holy Spirit coming upon us. It is only in Christ that there is neither male nor female, bond nor free, Jew nor Gentile (Galatians 3:28). It is only in Jesus that division is obliterated.

Genesis 11:9
Therefore is the name of it called Bab-El; because the Lord did there confound the language of all the earth: and from thence did the Lord scatter them abroad upon the face of all the earth.

Bab-El, or "Gateway to God" became "Confusion" when Nimrod's technology led only to chaos. Does the story end here? No. God now shifts the storyline to focus on a single family—the family of Abraham—through whom He will bring the solution for man's sin . . .

Genesis 11:10–26
These are the generations of Shem: Shem was an hundred years old, and begat Arphaxad two years after the flood: And Shem lived after he begat Arphaxad five hundred years, and begat sons and daughters. And Arphaxad lived five and thirty years, and begat Salah: And Arphaxad lived after he begat Salah four hundred and three years, and begat sons and daughters. And Salah lived thirty years, and begat Eber: And Salah lived after he begat Eber four hundred and three years, and begat sons and daughters. And Eber lived four and thirty years, and begat Peleg: And Eber lived after he begat Peleg four hundred and thirty years, and begat sons and daughters. And Peleg lived thirty years, and begat Reu: And Peleg lived after he begat Reu two hundred and nine years, and begat sons and daughters. And Reu lived two and thirty years, and begat Serug: And Reu lived after he begat Serug two hundred and seven years, and begat sons and daughters. And Serug lived thirty years, and begat Nahor: And Serug lived after he begat Nahor two hundred years, and begat sons and daughters. And Nahor lived nine and twenty years, and begat Terah: And Nahor lived after he begat Terah an hundred and nineteen years, and begat sons and daughters. And Terah lived seventy years, and begat Abram, Nahor, and Haran.

Here we see Abraham's family tree.

Genesis 11:27–30
Now these are the generations of Terah: Terah begat Abram, Nahor, and Haran; and Haran begat Lot. And Haran died before his father Terah in the land of his nativity, in Ur of the Chaldees. And Abram and Nahor took them wives: the name of Abram's wife was Sarai; and the name of Nahor's wife, Milcah, the daughter of Haran, the father of Milcah, and the father of Iscah. But Sarai was barren; she had no child.

Whereas in verses 10–26, we see Abraham's family tree, in verses 27–32, we see his family ties—ties that will be germane to the story that unfolds.

Genesis 11:31 (a)
And Terah took Abram his son, and Lot the son of Haran his son's son, and Sarai his daughter in law, his son Abram's wife; and they went forth with them from Ur of the Chaldees, to go into the land of Canaan;

As we will see in chapter 12, Abram was supposed to leave his family in Ur and go to a land God would show him. Here, however, we see his father, Terah, leading the way.

Genesis 11:31 (b), 32
. . . and they came unto Haran, and dwelt there. And the days of Terah were two hundred and five years: and Terah died in Haran.

Located halfway between Ur and Canaan, Haran was the border town of the Babylonian region. The modern-day equivalent of this event would be God saying to us, "I want you to leave Oregon and meet Me in Mexico City," and us stopping in San Diego.

Abram, Sarai, Lot, and Terah traveled to Haran—adjacent to, but not inside the Promised Land—and stayed there until Terah died, which was a minimum of fifteen years later. No wonder *Terah's* name means "Delay."

"Follow Me," Jesus said.

"Let me first go and bury my dad," answered the young man. This didn't mean his dad was awaiting burial. It meant after his dad died, he'd be free to follow Jesus.

"Let the dead bury the dead," Jesus replied. In other words, "I understand family obligations. But obeying Me has even a higher priority" (Matthew 8:18–22).

When Terah dies, Abram gets going again—and we'll follow his story in chapter 12.

12

Genesis 12:1 (a)
Now the LORD had said unto Abram . . .

"The Lord *had* said unto Abram . . ." When had the Lord said this? Twenty-five years previously, when Abram was approximately fifty years old. By virtue of the fact that he lived in the city of Ur—the "hot spot" of the day where bathtubs were first invented—Abram had done pretty well for himself. In addition to riches, Abram had respect, for he was a leader, with a stunningly beautiful wife. Also, Abram was religious. Joshua tells us he worshiped the moon god. Yet although he was rich, respected, and religious, Abram was also lost. He was headed for hell, until the Lord sovereignly in His mercy and grace reached down to Hot Tub City and made Himself known to Abram.

Genesis 12:1 (b)
. . . Get thee out of thy country, and from thy kindred, and from thy father's house, unto a land that I will shew thee.

When God said, "Leave your country, leave your family, and follow Me," Abram had a choice. He could either cling to his riches, religiosity, and respectability—or he could respond. Abram chose the latter, and in so doing, became the father of faith.

Genesis 12:2, 3
And I will make of thee a great nation, and I will bless thee, and make thy name great; and thou shalt be a blessing: And I will bless them that bless thee, and curse him that curseth thee: and in thee shall all families of the earth be blessed.

Not only did God extend salvation to Abram personally, but He would make of Abram a new nation miraculously. Following are three reasons why . . .

To Be a Witness of God's Ways

> And he said, It is a light thing that thou shouldest be my servant to raise up the tribes of Jacob, and to restore the preserved of Israel: I will also give thee for a light to the Gentiles, that thou mayest be my salvation unto the end of the earth. Isaiah 49:6

The Jews were to be a light for the Gentiles. "This one nation will be a light for all other people to see practically what it means to believe in Me and walk with Me," God declared.

To Be a Keeper of God's Word

> What advantage then hath the Jew? or what profit is there of circumcision? Much every way: chiefly, because that unto them were committed the oracles of God. Romans 3:1, 2

To their credit, and to our benefit, the Jews were fierce protectors of the Scriptures.

To Be a Channel for God's Wonder

> For unto us a child is born, unto us a son is given: and the government shall be upon his shoulder: and his name shall be called Wonderful, Counsellor, The mighty God, The everlasting Father, The Prince of Peace. Isaiah 9:6

Messiah would come through the Jewish people. That is why through the Jewish people all people would be blessed.

God said to Abram, "I'm going to give you a name, make you a nation, and protect you. Those who bless you will be blessed; those who curse you will be cursed. In other words, you're going to have primacy, identity, and security."

I find this intriguing because those were the three things man had wanted so desperately at Babel. "Let us build a tower," said man, "whose top may reach unto heaven (primacy); and let us make us a name (identity), lest we be scattered abroad upon the face of the whole earth" (security).

The same is still true. We want something meaningful to do in life—primacy. Or we want to discover who we are—identity. Or we need security relationally or financially. Jesus said, "If you seek first the kingdom, all these other things will be added to you" (see Matthew 6:33).

Every one of us is either walking in chapter 11, the Babel mentality—or in chapter 12, simply obeying and seeking first the kingdom.

Genesis 12:4
So Abram departed, as the LORD had spoken unto him; and Lot went with him: and Abram was seventy and five years old when he departed out of Haran.

Abram was fifty years old when he initially heard God's call. But he didn't leave Haran until he was seventy-five. Obviously, Abram faltered in his obedience. But guess what. God doesn't give up *on* Abram. Rather He waits *for* Abram.

> And therefore will the LORD wait, that he may be gracious unto you . . . Isaiah 30:18 (a)

"Lord, why aren't You directing me?" we cry.

"I already did," He answers. "Twenty-five years ago, I told you what to do. And I won't give you more to do until you do what I've already told you."

Many people are confused about God's will because, like Abram, they've delayed doing what He has already asked of them. It might concern intercessory prayer, witnessing, Bible study. I encourage people to keep journals—to write down things God lays upon their hearts because so often we ask, "What's going on?" when, if we just looked back at what God told us previously, we could see what the problem is.

God wasn't mad at Abram—and He's not mad at you. When your kids take their first steps, you don't yell at them when they fall down. You celebrate their steps rather than berate their stumbling. God's the same way. He knows this is how we learn to walk by faith. Take hope, stumbling saint, Abram was in a twenty-five-year slump, and God didn't give up on him. God gives us a second chance and a third and a ninety-ninth. His mercy is new every morning. His grace is limitless.

Genesis 12:5–7 (a)
And Abram took Sarai his wife, and Lot his brother's son, and all their substance that they had gathered, and the souls that they had gotten in Haran; and they went forth to go into the land of Canaan; and into the land of Canaan they came. And Abram passed through the land unto the place of Sichem, unto the plain of Moreh. And the Canaanite was then in the land. And the LORD appeared unto Abram, and said, Unto thy seed will I give this land . . .

Concerning possession of the West Bank, Gaza strip, and Golan Heights, God says, "They are Mine to give to Abraham, Isaac, and Jacob (Exodus 32:13). I am giving the entire land to the Jews."

Genesis 12:7 (b), 8 (a)
. . . and there builded he an altar unto the LORD, who appeared unto him. And he removed from thence unto a mountain on the east of Bethel, and pitched his tent . . .

When the astronauts went to the moon, they planted a flag. So, upon entering the Promised Land, Abram leaves a mark. As we will see, wherever Abram goes he builds an altar—which shows he's a worshiper; and he pitches a tent—which shows he's a pilgrim. Abram never builds a house. Why? Because he looked for a city with foundations, whose builder and maker is God

(Hebrews 11:10). For fifty years he did the big house, hot tub, and Lexus thing in Ur. But he realized that what he really craved was heaven.

Abram, the father of faith, the friend of God, shows us the real way to live. Wherever you go, build the altar of worship. It will altar who you are, how you feel, the way you think. And wherever you go, go with a "tent" mentality. We may think we're looking for a house in the country or a house on the lake, a ski boat or a ski cabin, a dream car, or a dream date. But what we're really craving is heaven. No other city has foundations. Everything else is shaky and wobbly.

Genesis 12:8 (b), 9
. . . having Bethel on the west, and Hai on the east: and there he builded an altar unto the LORD, and called upon the name of the LORD. And Abram journeyed, going on still toward the south.

Abram pitched his tent with Bethel on the west and Hai on the east. *Bethel* meaning "House of God," and *Hai,* meaning "heap" or "dump," Abram had the House of God ahead of him, and a dump on the other side of him. That's basically where you and I live. With heaven before us, and the world behind us, we're camped out in the middle, waiting for the culmination.

Genesis 12:10
And there was a famine in the land: and Abram went down into Egypt to sojourn there; for the famine was grievous in the land.

Throughout Scripture, whenever people go to Egypt, they always go "*down* to Egypt" because Egypt is a type, or symbol of the world. Abram was doing well, but now he falls again because he didn't remain in the land God showed him. A famine made him think he had to take matters into his own hands—always a dangerous place to be.

Genesis 12:11, 12
And it came to pass, when he was come near to enter into Egypt, that he said unto Sarai his wife, Behold now, I know that thou art a fair woman to look upon: Therefore it shall come to pass, when the Egyptians shall see thee, that they shall say, This is his wife: and they will kill me, but they will save thee alive.

Here's the father of faith faltering in the arena of faith because man always struggles and stumbles in his area of strength . . .

- Righteous Noah fell when he got drunk in his tent.
- Moses, the meekest man on the face of the earth, struck his rod against a rock and said, "You rebels, must we fetch water for you?"
- Unsheathing his sword, Peter was ready to take on a whole army in order to defend Jesus in Gethsemane. Yet, only hours later, he faltered when a little girl asked him, "Aren't you one of His?"

The area in which you're strongest is the area you'll be most vulnerable because you'll depend on your own strength. At the point you say, "That's not a problem for me; I'll never fall there"—watch out because that's the very area where you'll experience difficulty. Where you know you're weak, you rely on God.

Genesis 12:13
Say, I pray thee, thou art my sister: that it may be well with me for thy sake; and my soul shall live because of thee.

Sarai and Abram were actually half-brother and sister, but a half-truth is a total lie. "Thou shalt not bear false witness," declared God on Mount Sinai. What is false witness? We see false witnesses in those who testified against Jesus. "This fellow said, I am able to destroy the temple of God, and to build it in three days," they said concerning Him (Matthew 26:61). While Jesus did indeed say that, their witness was false because they were giving the right information with the wrong implication. Jesus was talking about the temple of His body.

Thus, as defined in the Bible, bearing false witness is not just lying. It's giving the right information, but with the wrong implication. Sarai was Abram's sister. But she was really his wife.

Genesis 12:14–16
And it came to pass, that, when Abram was come into Egypt, the Egyptians beheld the woman that she was very fair. The princes also of Pharaoh saw her, and commended her before Pharaoh: and the woman was taken into Pharaoh's house. And he entreated Abram well for her sake: and he had sheep, and oxen, and he asses, and menservants, and maidservants, and she asses, and camels.

Sheep, oxen, camels, and servants were the Rolexes, Infinitis, and fancy stuff of the day. "Take the goods," Pharaoh said to Abram, "and I'll take your sister."

Genesis 12:17
And the LORD plagued Pharaoh and his house with great plagues because of Sarai Abram's wife.

Pharaoh was taken ill, as was his whole house, and somehow, he understood why . . .

> And Pharaoh called Abram, and said, What is this that thou hast done unto me? why didst thou not tell me that she was thy wife? Why saidst thou, She is my sister? so I might have taken her to me to wife: now therefore behold thy wife, take her, and go thy way. And Pharaoh commanded his men concerning him: and they sent him away, and his wife, and all that he had.

Sarai, the wife of Abram, is the one woman whom the Bible holds up as a picture of what a Christian wife should be.

> But let it be the hidden man of the heart, in that which is not corruptible, even the ornament of a meek and quiet spirit, which is in the sight of God of great price. For after this manner in the old time the holy women also, who trusted in God, adorned themselves, being in subjection unto their own husbands: Even as Sara obeyed Abraham, calling him lord: whose daughters ye are, as long as ye do well, and are not afraid with any amazement. 1 Peter 3:4–6

Abram was making a big mistake here. He was leading his wife in a way that was not the best—down into Egypt. And then he chickened out and left her in a vulnerable spot, where she was taken into Pharaoh's harem. Nonetheless, Sarai called him lord. She reverenced him. She honored her husband even when he was not walking in wisdom. And God protected her. Wife, submit to your husband even if he's walking in a less than perfect way, and God will protect you just as He protected Sarai.

Not only did God protect Sarai, but He prospered the family. With the flocks and herds and servants they were given, Abram and Sarai were again wealthy. Do you want to enrich your family, wife? Submit to your husband, and God will bless your family.

"That sounds awfully chauvinistic," you say. "After putting his wife in danger to save his own skin, Abram walks away smelling like a rose."

Not quite. Abram doesn't get off scot-free, for one of the maidservants given to Sarai was named Hagar, who will break Abram's heart as well as his family. Be not deceived, gang, God is not mocked. Whatever a man sows, that shall *he* also reap (Galatians 6:7). If I blow it in my role as leader, there will not only be heartbreaks in my family, but in my life personally.

13

Alexander Whyte was right on when he said, "The Christian life is basically a series of new beginnings." How true that is. We stumble and fall, but the Lord's grace is sufficient, His mercy matchless. He reaches down to you and me and puts us on our feet again, just as He did to Abram . . .

Genesis 13:1 (a)
And Abram went up out of Egypt . . .

Abram went down to Egypt as a saved man, but he comes up from Egypt a spiritual man. When you fall, be like Abram: Pick something up. Learn from the experience.

Genesis 13:1 (b)–4
. . . he, and his wife, and all that he had, and Lot with him, into the south. And Abram was very rich in cattle, in silver, and in gold. And he went on his journeys from the south even to Bethel, unto the place where his tent had been at the beginning, between Bethel and Hai; Unto the place of the altar, which he had made there at the first: and there Abram called on the name of the LORD.

There is no record of Abram pitching a tent or building an altar in Egypt. Here, however, we see him return to the place where he had pitched his tent; we see him going to the altar once more.

When you find yourself in Egypt, when you know things aren't the way they're supposed to be, what do you do? "Remember therefore from whence thou art fallen, and repent, and do the first works . . ." Jesus told the Church of Ephesus—a group of believers who had strayed from their passion for Him (Revelation 2:5). Maybe your relationship with the Lord was great five years ago. Maybe things were really happening spiritually four months ago. Jesus' word to you is the same as it was to the Church of Ephesus. Remember, repent, and repeat: Go back and do what you used to do. Perhaps you were enjoying a season of morning devotions. Maybe you were coming out to worship on Friday nights. Maybe you were memorizing Scripture, or aggressively sharing your faith. What were you doing when you were on fire, when things were really cooking? Do it again.

Abram went back to where it all began—where he had pitched his tent previously, where he had built an altar initially.

Genesis 13:5, 6
And Lot also, which went with Abram, had flocks, and herds, and tents. And the land was not able to bear them, that they might dwell together: for their substance was great, so that they could not dwell together.

Abram and Lot had such large flocks and herds that the land couldn't hold them both.

Genesis 13:7, 8 (a)
And there was a strife between the herdmen of Abram's cattle and the herdmen of Lot's cattle: and the Canaanite and the Perizzite dwelled then in the land. And Abram said unto Lot . . .

Notice how Abram emerged from Egypt a wiser man, for here he shows *directness.* That is, he goes to Lot and deals with the issue directly. "There's strife between our herdsmen," he says, "and the heathen are watching us fighting. It ought not be." Such is often the case today. Christians fight and bicker while the world watches and wonders. It ought not be.

Genesis 13:8 (b)
. . . Let there be no strife, I pray thee, between me and thee, and between my herdmen and thy herdmen . . .

Notice also Abram's *deference*. He doesn't place blame on Lot. He says, "Let there be no strife between *me* and thee, between *my* herdmen and thy herdmen." While he will assume the secondary position when it comes to choosing the land, Abram assumes the primary position when it comes to shouldering responsibility.

Genesis 13:8 (c)
. . . for we be brethren.

Notice Abram's *discernment* when he says, "We be brethren." In other words, "There is more that unites us than divides us. Sure, there are some complications with the cattle, some hassles with the herdmen—but we're brothers."

How we need to realize the truth of this within the Christian community in our country and around the world. Because we all embrace the Person and Work of our Lord Jesus, there is more that unites us than could possibly divide us.

Genesis 13:9
Is not the whole land before thee? separate thyself, I pray thee, from me: if thou wilt take the left hand, then I will go to the right; or if thou depart to the right hand, then I will go to the left.

Notice the *dignity* of Abram. Not only does Abram put himself in the equation of the problem, but he says to his younger nephew, "Take your pick. If you go to the right, I'll go to the left. If you want the left, I'll take the right."

George Washington said, "When there is an elder man and a younger man in the same room, the elder man should never mention it, but the younger man should never forget it." I like that! Abram doesn't mention the fact that he is the elder, the leader, but Lot chooses to forget it. Abram nonetheless demonstrates hugeness of heart and dignity of character.

Genesis 13:10 (a)
And Lot . . .

Contrast the wisdom of Abram with the worldliness of Lot. Lot was *weak in devotion,* for we never read of him building an altar. Like Lot, you may possess a "tent mentality" knowing you're headed for heaven; and you may even have a ministry, with herds to take care of—but if you're not an altar-builder, you'll be weak in devotion which will lead to real problems.

Genesis 13:10 (b)
. . . lifted up his eyes, and beheld all the plain of Jordan, that it was well watered every where, before the LORD destroyed Sodom and Gomorrah, even as the garden of the LORD, like the land of Egypt, as thou comest unto Zoar.

Lot was *worldly in desires.* He lifted up his eyes, but not high enough. He didn't lift his eyes to heaven and say, "Lord, show me the best place for me and my family." Instead, he lifted up his eyes only high enough to check out the financial possibilities and the greenest pastures. Lot saw a good place to raise cattle, but failed to see that it would be a lousy place to raise kids because he fixed his gaze short of heaven.

Genesis 13:11–13
Then Lot chose him all the plain of Jordan; and Lot journeyed east: and they separated themselves the one from the other. Abram dwelled in the land of Canaan, and Lot dwelled in the cities of the plain, and pitched his tent toward Sodom. But the men of Sodom were wicked and sinners before the LORD exceedingly.

Thirdly, Lot was *wrong in decision.* Lot made a series of wrong decisions based on his own reasoning . . .

- In verse 10, he looked toward Sodom.
- In verse 12, he pitched his tent toward Sodom.
- In chapter 19, we'll see him became a leader in Sodom.

Lot left Ur, but he became entrenched in Sodom. A lot of people are like that. They say yes to heaven, but they never say no to the world. And, like Lot, they end up in a terrible predicament.

Genesis 13:14–17
And the LORD said unto Abram, after that Lot was separated from him, Lift up now thine eyes, and look from the place where thou art northward, and southward, and eastward, and westward: For all the land which thou seest, to thee will I give it, and to thy seed for ever. And I will make thy seed as the dust of the earth: so that if a man can number the dust of the earth, then shall thy seed also be numbered. Arise, walk through the land in the length of it and in the breadth of it; for I will give it unto thee.

Abram didn't demand his own way, and what happened? God promised him the entire land—including Lot's portion.

> Then Peter began to say unto him, Lo, we have left all, and have followed thee. And Jesus answered and said, Verily I say unto you, There is no man that hath left house, or brethren, or sisters, or father, or mother, or wife, or children, or lands, for my sake, and the gospel's, But he shall receive an hundredfold now in this time, houses, and brethren, and sisters, and mothers, and children, and lands, with persecutions; and in the world to come eternal life.
> Mark 10:28–30

If my house burned down tonight, I know there are one hundred people or more in this Fellowship who would say, "Stay with us." So, I can travel anywhere in the world and find Christians who would say, "Come on in." The same is true for you. We have brothers and sisters a hundredfold, parents a hundredfold, houses a hundredfold. Even this side of heaven, you just can't outgive God. And Abram finds this out.

Genesis 13:18
Then Abram removed his tent, and came and dwelt in the plain of Mamre, which is in Hebron, and built there an altar unto the LORD.

Mamre meaning "Fatness," and *Hebron* meaning "Communion," Abram is saying, in type, "I'm not interested in the people, pleasures, prosperity, politics, or perversity of Sodom. Instead, I'm going to enjoy the fatness, the richness, the satisfaction which comes from Communion."

14

Genesis 14:1 (a)
And it came to pass in the days of Amraphel king of Shinar . . .

Amraphel is Hammurabi, author of the ethics system known as the Code of Hammurabi.

Genesis 14:1 (b), 2
. . . Arioch king of Ellasar, Chedorlaomer king of Elam, and Tidal king of nations; That these made war with Bera king of Sodom, and with Birsha king of Gomorrah, Shinab king of Admah, and Shemeber king of Zeboiim, and the king of Bela, which is Zoar.

Four kings took on five kings in battle and were victorious.

Genesis 14:3
All these were joined together in the vale of Siddim, which is the salt sea.

The salt sea is the Dead Sea in Southern Israel.

Genesis 14:4 (a)
Twelve years they served Chedorlaomer . . .

Scripturally, twelve is the number of government.

Genesis 14:4 (b)
. . . and in the thirteenth year they rebelled.

Scripturally, thirteen is the number of rebellion.

Genesis 14:5–7
And in the fourteenth year came Chedorlaomer, and the kings that were with him, and smote the Rephaims in Ashteroth Karnaim, and the Zuzims in Ham, and the Emims in Shaveh Kiriathaim, And the Horites in their mount Seir, unto El-paran, which is by the wilderness. And they returned, and came to En-mishpat, which is Kadesh, and smote all the country of the Amalekites, and also the Amorites that dwelt in Hazezon-tamar.

Chedorlaomer and the other three kings wipe out a bunch of smaller nations and then engage in battle against the five kings of verse 2 who are rebelling after twelve years of servitude.

Genesis 14:8–10
And there went out the king of Sodom, and the king of Gomorrah, and the king of Admah, and the king of Zeboiim, and the king of Bela (the same is Zoar;) and they joined battle with them in the vale of Siddim; With Chedorlaomer the king of Elam, and with Tidal king of nations, and Amraphel king of Shinar, and Arioch king of Ellasar; four kings with five. And the vale of Siddim was full of slimepits; and the kings of Sodom and Gomorrah fled, and fell there; and they that remained fled to the mountain.

I find it appropriate that the kings of Sodom and Gomorrah fell into the slime pit.

Genesis 14:11, 12
And they took all the goods of Sodom and Gomorrah, and all their victuals, and went their way. And they took Lot, Abram's brother's son, who dwelt in Sodom, and his goods, and departed.

The four kings put down the insurrection and carried goods and hostages—of which Lot was one—back to their home countries.

Genesis 14:13–16
And there came one that had escaped, and told Abram the Hebrew; for he dwelt in the plain of Mamre the Amorite, brother of Eshcol, and brother of Aner: and these were confederate with Abram. And when Abram heard that his brother was taken captive, he armed his trained servants, born in his own house, three hundred and eighteen, and pursued them unto Dan. And he divided himself against them, he and his servants, by night, and smote them, and pursued them unto Hobah, which is on the left hand of Damascus. And he brought back all the goods, and also brought again his brother Lot, and his goods, and the women also, and the people.

Abram does something amazing. He arms and trains three hundred and eighteen of his servants, and launches a guerilla war against the four victorious kings. Because God was with him, Abram and his company overcame tremendous odds and were victorious. This is important for a number of reasons—but the one I want to consider is this: This is the first mention of war in the Bible.

Is war moral? Is war just? James says the reason there are so many wars in the world today is because of lust: one country wants another country's resources. But there is also a justifiable war, and that is what we see here. The war Abram launches is not about territory, possessions, politics, ideology, economy, or free enterprise. It's about family. Thus, I believe warfare is justified for the reason of liberating family. When people are being carried away, when family is held in captivity, I believe war is justifiable and necessary.

Genesis 14:17
And the king of Sodom went out to meet him after his return from the slaughter of Chedorlaomer, and of the kings that were with him, at the valley of Shaveh, which is the king's dale.

Returning from his victorious military raid, Abram is met by the king of Sodom—the prince of perversity—a picture of Satan himself.

Genesis 14:18 (a)
And Melchizedek king of Salem . . .

Abram is also met by a mysterious, marvelous monarch named Melchizedek, King of Salem. *Melchizedek* meaning "King of Righteousness," and *Salem* meaning "Peace," this is most likely a Christophany—an Old Testament appearance of Christ.

Genesis 14:18 (b)
. . . brought forth bread and wine . . .

Two thousand years before Christ came to die for our sin, Melchizedek brings a symbol of His death—bread and wine, the elements of Communion. Just as we are saved by looking *back* to Christ's death on the Cross, Old Testament saints were saved by looking *ahead* to Christ's death on the Cross—of which their sacrifices were a picture. When we partake of Communion it is in *remembrance* of Jesus. Abram partook of Melchizedek's bread and wine in *anticipation* of Jesus.

Genesis 14:18 (c)–20 (a)
. . . and he was the priest of the most high God. And he blessed him, and said, Blessed be Abram of the most high God, possessor of heaven and earth: And blessed be the most high God, which hath delivered thine enemies into thy hand . . .

The author of the Book of Hebrews gives further illumination as to Melchizedek's identity when he describes Him as being

Without father, without mother, without descent, having neither beginning of days, nor end of life; but made like unto the Son of God; abideth a priest continually. Hebrews 7:3

As Melchizedek's name means Righteousness, Jesus is our Righteousness (1 Corinthians 1:30). As Salem means Peace, Jesus is the Prince of Peace (Isaiah 9:6). As Melchizedek had no beginning and no end, Jesus is Alpha and Omega (Revelation 22:12, 13). As Melchizedek was a priest, Jesus is our Great High Priest (Hebrews 7:25, 26).

Genesis 14:20 (b)
. . . And he gave him tithes of all.

It is fitting that in Genesis, the Book of Beginnings, we find the beginning of the tithe—and the beginning of a glorious way of living . . .

For topical study of Genesis 14:20, see "Blest Be the Tithe that Unbinds" below.

Genesis 14:21
And the king of Sodom said unto Abram, Give me the persons, and take the goods to thyself.

The Hebrew word translated "persons" is literally "souls." As he still does today, the king of Sodom—a picture of Satan—says, "Help yourself to the toys and trinkets. I want the souls."

Genesis 14:22–24
And Abram said to the king of Sodom, I have lift up mine hand unto the LORD, the most high God, the possessor of heaven and earth, That I will not take from a thread even to a shoelatchet, and that I will not take any thing that is thine, lest thou shouldest say, I have made Abram rich: Save only that which the young men have eaten, and the portion of the men which went with me, Aner, Eshcol, and Mamre; let them take their portion.

From whence comes the ability to say *No* to the temptation of Sodom, the seduction of Satan? By saying *Yes* to the King of Salem, the Lord Jesus.

How do you say *Yes* to Him? Through Communion with Him and tithes to Him—for as you come to His Table and remember all He gave *for* you, it will only be natural to give what He asks *of* you.

BLEST BE THE TITHE THAT UNBINDS

A Topical Study of GENESIS 14:20

"If you don't support this ministry, we're going to go off the air," threatens the radio evangelist. "If you don't support this work, we can't go on," cries the televangelist. "You have an obligation to supply the needs of this ministry. If you don't, we're going to sink," says the traveling evangelist. And so it is that I understand why people dread teachings on tithing. After all, the principle has been misused and abused by so many for so long.

"I have never seen the righteous begging for bread," David declared (Psalm 37:25). Truly, if there is righteousness in a ministry or in a person individually, such a one will never need to beg for bread, for when God guides, God provides. Impassioned fund-raisers to the contrary, God is not broke, gang, for Haggai reminds us that all silver and gold are His (2:8). God doesn't need our money. Therefore, tithing is not His way of raising cash, but His way of raising kids. Tithing is not God's way of getting money, but His way of developing maturity—as we will see in the text before us. Consider with me four reasons why the tithe was instituted here in Genesis, the Book of Beginnings—and why it continues throughout the entire Scripture . . .

Liberation

Tithing is the way to liberation. Our tendency is to be greedy and grabby. And Satan, king of Sodom, knows this. That's why he comes our way day after day, saying, "You deserve that trinket. You've earned that bauble. Keep the goods." But God knows greediness leads only to unhappiness . . .

> A billionaire himself, Andrew Carnegie said this: "I have seldom seen millionaires laugh."
>
> "I am not a happy man," said Donald Trump. "Frankly, my best friends are buildings."

God, on the other hand, says, "I'm totally content. I have infinite peace, and endless joy. I lack nothing. And I want you to be like Me."

God is a Giver—seen most obviously in His giving of His only Son. He wants us to be givers as well, because every time we give to Him, we give away a part of our greediness. Thus, tithing is the way to liberation.

Destination

From cover to cover, the Bible calls us to set our hearts on things above and not on things of this world (Colossians 3:2). Jesus put it this way: "Seek first the kingdom of God and His righteousness, and all these other things will be added to you" (Matthew 6:33).

How do we practically seek first the kingdom and set our hearts on heaven? Jesus told us how when He said, "Where your treasure is, there will your heart be also" (Matthew 6:21). If your treasure is on earth, that's where your heart will be. So God in His wisdom, kindness, and love for you and me says, "Lay up your treasure in heaven where neither moth nor rust destroys, where thieves don't break in and steal. Put your treasure in heaven because, in so doing, your heart will follow."

> I entered the business world for the first time as a freshman in high school when I bought one share of American Motors stock for twelve dollars. And what happened after that amazed me. You see, normally every morning I would grab the *San Jose Mercury News* and immediately open to the Sports Page to find out, depending on the season, how the Giants, Warriors, or 49'ers were doing. But after investing my treasure in the stock market, I found myself turning first to the Business Section to find out how American Motors was doing.
>
> Then, in my sophomore year, our church youth group planned a big banquet at a fancy restaurant in San Francisco. Wanting to take part, but short of

cash, I sold my stock—for eight dollars. The next morning, something interesting happened. I skipped the Business Page altogether, for once my treasure was no longer in American Motors, neither was my heart.

If your treasure is in your house or your IRA or your Mercedes, that's where your heart will be. Knowing this, the Lord demands that the first tenth of whatever we make on any given day, in any given week be given to Him in order that our hearts will be set on our heavenly destination.

Jesus talked more about money than He did about heaven. He talked more about money than He did about hell. In fact, He talked more about money than He did about heaven and hell combined. Why? Because He knows it's a huge issue for you and me—and that it speaks of larger principles. One of the things Jesus said about money was this:

And I say unto you, Make to yourselves friends of the mammon [*money*] *of unrighteousness; that, when ye fail, they may receive you into everlasting habitations.* Luke 16:9

In other words, the money you have made friends of—or that you have used rightly—will greet you when you die. Now, the old adage is true: You can't take it with you. But you *can* send it ahead. And what you send ahead—through the tithe that God demands, and through the offering which He deserves—will meet you there.

"But I don't make much money, so there won't be much to greet me," you say. Consider this: When Jesus saw a widow giving two mites—less than a penny—He told His disciples that she had given more than they who, out of their abundance, had given much because she gave all that she had (Mark 12:41–44). Jesus acknowledged even two mites—and that woman will receive a mite-y big welcome in heaven!

Evaluation

How we deal with money determines how we'll do in ministry . . .

If therefore ye have not been faithful in the unrighteous mammon, who will commit to your trust the true riches? Luke 16:11

If you want to be used by the Lord, you must understand that according to Luke 16, the foundational question is: How do you deal with money? Jesus said, "If you can't be entrusted with money, how can you be entrusted with the true riches of the kingdom?"

"I can tell more about the spirituality of a man by looking at his checkbook than I can by looking at his prayerbook," said D.L. Moody.

It's true. We can sing, "I love You Lord, and I lift my voice . . ." and, "I have decided to follow Jesus . . ." but if we don't put our money where our mouth is, it's all meaningless words and cheap talk.

Liberation, destination, evaluation—they're all wrapped up in the principle of tithing.

"Wait a minute," you say. "Tithing is part of the Law. And aren't we free from the Law?"

Yes, because of the Finished Work of the Cross, we are no longer under the Law—but as seen in the text before us, tithing predates the Law by five hundred years. Not only that, Jesus said tithing should not be left "undone" (Matthew 23:23). In addition, tithing is seen in the early church (1 Corinthians 16:1, 2). Thus, seen before, during, and after the Law, the tithe is timeless.

And so passionate is God about this issue that He says something He never says again in any other place . . .

> *Will a man rob God? Yet ye have robbed me. But ye say, Wherein have we robbed thee? In tithes and offerings.* Malachi 3:8

"In not giving Me the tithe, you have robbed Me," God declares. The tithe is God's. It's not an option. The first ten percent is the Lord's. Scripture, I believe, is crystal clear on this issue.

"What if I don't tithe?" you ask.

Malachi goes on . . .

> *Ye are cursed with a curse: for ye have robbed me, even this whole nation.* Malachi 3:9

If you don't tithe, you're cursed. Oh, it's not God Who curses you. Rather, you curse yourself. How? Haggai explains . . .

> *Now therefore thus saith the* LORD *of hosts; Consider your ways. Ye have sown much, and bring in little; ye eat, but ye have not enough; ye drink, but ye are not filled with drink; ye clothe you, but there is none warm; and he that earneth wages earneth wages to put it into a bag with holes.* Haggai 1:5, 6

By not tithing, we curse ourselves because the money we save disappears through the holes in our pockets, and the money we spend doesn't bring satisfaction.

> *Bring ye all the tithes into the storehouse, that there may be meat in mine house . . .* Malachi 3:10 (a)

God wants us to bring tithes to His storehouse—to the place where the Word is taught and praise ascends—even though we won't get a plaque for it, be applauded because of it, or have a say in where it goes.

And then God says something He says nowhere else in all of Scripture . . .

> *. . . and prove me now herewith, saith the* L*ORD of hosts . . .* Malachi 3:10 (b)

The only time God says, "Test Me" is with regard to tithing.

Notice three promises God makes to those who take up His challenge . . .

> *. . . if I will not open you the windows of heaven, and pour you out a blessing, that there shall not be room enough to receive it.* Malachi 3:10 (c)

"I will reward your faith."

> Immediately after lending Jesus his fishing boat for use as a floating podium to teach the multitude on the shore, Peter caught so many fish his net broke (Luke 5:2–7).
>
> The little boy who gave his lunch to Jesus was himself "glutted" along with the rest of the 5,000 (John 6:9–12).

If you've ever given anything to God, you know from experience that it's impossible to out give Him.

> *And I will rebuke the devourer for your sakes, and he shall not destroy the fruits of your ground; neither shall your vine cast her fruit before the time in the field, saith the* L*ORD of hosts.* Malachi 3:11

"I will rebuke your foe." Some people are perpetually plagued with problems. The money they make goes through their pockets; the labor of their hands never comes to fruition. To them, God says, "If you tithe, I will rebuke the world's hold on you which devours your happiness and eats away at your possessions."

> *And all nations shall call you blessed: for ye shall be a delightsome land, saith the* L*ORD of hosts.* Malachi 3:12

"I will renew your fruit."

"Put your trust in Me, and I will make you a fruitful land," declares the Lord, for he who tithes will experience renewal and revival.

There is not a subject I would less rather teach than this one. But the Bible has much to say about tithing because it represents where a person's heart is. Therefore, I would be shirking my responsibility to declare to you "all the counsel of God" (Acts 20:27), were I to ignore it. The tithe is the Lord's. It's not yours. Whether it's ten cents or ten thousand dollars, the first tenth is the Lord's—to be brought into the storehouse, the place where the Word is proclaimed and worship ascends.

Heaven is right around the bend, gang. And we will soon regret all the stuff we've accumulated with God's tithe, all the ways we've indulged ourselves with His offerings.

Maybe you have been robbing God. Maybe you have been wasting your time and treasure and talents. The good news is: It's not too late! Today you can say, "As I race towards heaven, I understand the wisdom of God's way, the rightness of His Word. Therefore, I am going to give Him the tithe. And I am going to see, even as He asked me, what He will do in blessing, in rebuking, and in renewing."

Precious people, you'll be blessed all of your days if you go God's way.

Start today.

Then watch and see what God will do.

15

Genesis 15:1 (a)
After these things . . .

After what things? Chapter 14 gives the account of the daring military raid Abram made to rescue his nephew Lot; the subsequent appearance to him of two kings—the king of Sodom and Melchizedek, king of Salem; Abram's worship of Melchizedek; and his refusal to take even a shoelace from the king of Sodom.

Genesis 15:1 (b)
. . . the word of the LORD came unto Abram in a vision, saying, Fear not, Abram . . .

That God said, "Fear not," to Abram indicates Abram was fearful. This is not surprising. After all, in the wake of his spiritual victory in resisting the material temptation of the riches offered him by the king of Sodom, as well as his military victory in rescuing Lot, Abram hit an emotional slump. This happens. Challenge often follows victory. Think of Jesus. When He was baptized in the Jordan, He heard a voice from heaven, saying, "This is My beloved Son in Whom I am well pleased." Then, the Holy Spirit came upon Him and empowered Him for ministry. (Matthew 3:16, 17). It was a great day. But immediately following this, He was driven into the wilderness to be tempted of Satan, to wrestle against the enemy for forty days (Matthew 4). Therefore, don't be surprised, if, after you experience victory spiritually, like Abram you face a time of discouragement emotionally.

"Fear not." This is the first time this glorious command appears in Scripture. But it is certainly not the last . . .

- "Fear not," the angel said to a flock of frightened shepherds (Luke 2:10).
- "Fear not," Jesus said to a crew of seasick disciples (Mark 4:40).
- "Fear not," the angel said to a disheartened Paul (Acts 27:24).

Genesis 15:1 (c)
. . . I am thy shield, and thy exceeding great reward.

Perhaps it suddenly hit Abram that he and his rag-tag army of servants had made enemies of four powerful kings with four huge armies. "*I* am your shield," God told him. "Yes, you came home empty-handed materially, but *I* am your reward."

In this, I am reminded that what every person ultimately desires is not something *from* the Lord, but simply more *of* the Lord.

- "I'm not going to show you the way," Jesus declared, "I *am* the Way" (John 14:6).
- "I'm not going to give you bread; I *am* the Bread" (John 6:35).
- "I'm not going to share with you truth; I *am* the truth" (John 14:6).

Those who come to the Lord not looking for something *from* Him, but simply to cling *to* Him find all kinds of blessing in all sorts of areas they never expected. Are you disappointed with God because you asked Him for something you have yet to receive? Maybe it's because you're looking for some thing. God loves you too much to toss a boxed little package your way. The issue is bigger; and He wants you to discover today that *He* will satisfy your need; that *He* will be your reward.

Genesis 15:2 (a)
And Abram said, Lord God, what wilt thou give me . . .

"Fear not; I am your reward," the Lord had declared. Yet, like us, Abram responded by saying, "But what wilt Thou give me?"

Genesis 15:2 (b), 3
. . . seeing I go childless, and the steward of my house is this Eliezer of Damascus? And Abram said, Behold, to me thou hast given no seed: and, lo, one born in my house is mine heir.

Like me, Abram doesn't get what the Lord is saying. He goes on babbling—just like I do. The custom of the day was such that if a man had no son, his highest-ranking servant would inherit his wealth. And this prospect was bothering Abram.

Genesis 15:4
And, behold, the word of the Lord came unto him, saying, This shall not be thine heir; but he that shall come forth out of thine own bowels shall be thine heir.

"I am your reward," said God.
"But what will you give me?" asked Abram.
"I'll give you a son," said God.

The bigness of our Father's heart absolutely staggers me. He's so patient with Abram, so patient with you, so patient with me.

Genesis 15:5
And he brought him forth abroad, and said, Look now toward heaven, and tell the stars, if thou be able to number them: and he said unto him, So shall thy seed be.

With his naked eye, Abram would have been able to see at most 1,200 stars. "I'm going to have a family of *1,200?!*" Abram must have thought. But wait. God is able to do exceeding abundantly above all that we can ask or think (Ephesians 3:20). Abram could see approximately 1,200 stars. But how many stars are there? Far beyond anything Abram could even begin to ask for or imagine in his wildest dreams.

How many stars are there? Scientists tell us that there are as many stars in the sky as there are grains of sand on the seashore of all the beaches in the world. This should not surprise the student of Scripture, for God made the same correlation when He told Abram not only would his family number as the stars, but as the sand (Genesis 22:17).

According to the Psalmist, the only other thing as innumerable as the grains of sand are the thoughts of God towards us (Psalm 139:17, 18). This fascinates me because the Pentium computer chips made of silicon, of sand, perform one trillion calculations per second. Clear back in antiquity, God measured His thoughts with the substance that would come to epitomize our own computer age.

Genesis 15:6
And he believed in the Lord; and he counted it to him for righteousness.

So important is this verse that Paul anchors his definition of salvation upon it (Romans 4; Galatians 5). "I'm going to bless you," God said to Abram.

And simply because he believed God would do what He promised, God looked at Abram as being righteous.

The Hebrew word translated "righteous" is literally "rightly clothed." When Adam and Eve sinned, they realized they were naked—and man has been naked ever since. But just as God sacrificed an animal to clothe Adam and Eve, He sacrificed His Son to clothe us.

> I will greatly rejoice in the Lord, my soul shall be joyful in my God; for he hath clothed me with the garments of salvation, he hath covered me with the robe of righteousness, as a bridegroom decketh himself with ornaments, and as a bride adorneth herself with her jewels.
>
> Isaiah 61:10

To be righteous means to be rightly clothed. That is what we are when, like Abram, we simply take God at His Word.

- Righteousness:
  God thought it.
  Jesus bought it.
  The Spirit taught it.
  Satan fought it.
  But, gang, we got it!

We're robed in *His* righteousness.

Genesis 15:7, 8
And he said unto him, I am the Lord that brought thee out of Ur of the Chaldees, to

give thee this land to inherit it. And he said, Lord God, whereby shall I know that I shall inherit it?

Like the one who said, "Lord, I believe. Help my unbelief" (Mark 9:24), Abram says, "I believe, but how will I know the land is mine?"

I would think that at this point, the Lord would tire of Abram. I mean, God told him He would be his reward only to have Abram ask what He would give him. The Lord promised Abram a grand family and a glorious land only to have Abram ask for proof.

If I were God, I'd say, "So long, Abram." But that's not what our Father does, and I'm oh, so glad because even when giants of the faith like Abram have their struggles and doubts—God continues to walk with them and work through them.

Genesis 15:9, 10
And he said unto him, Take me an heifer of three years old, and a she goat of three years old, and a ram of three years old, and a turtledove, and a young pigeon. And he took unto him all these, and divided them in the midst, and laid each piece one against another: but the birds divided he not.

In answer to Abram's request for proof that God would give him an inheritance, God instructs Abram to draw up the equivalent of a modern-day contract. You see, in Abram's day, when two people entered in to a legal agreement, they did so by splitting an animal in two, standing in the midst of the carcass, and clasping each other's wrist to show that they were deadly serious about keeping up their end of the bargain.

Genesis 15:11
And when the fowls came down upon the carcases, Abram drove them away.

Throughout Scripture, birds almost always symbolize evil. The picture here is that while Abram waited for God to meet him, he did his best to keep evil at bay, shooing away the birds of doubt and unbelief.

Genesis 15:12
And when the sun was going down, a deep sleep fell upon Abram; and, lo, an horror of great darkness fell upon him.

Exhausted by his own efforts, Abram fell asleep.

Genesis 15:13, 14
And he said unto Abram, Know of a surety that thy seed shall be a stranger in a land that is not theirs, and shall serve them; and they shall afflict them four hundred years; And also that nation, whom they shall serve, will I judge: and afterward shall they come out with great substance.

As he slept, God told Abram that although He would indeed give Abram's descendants a grand and glorious land, they would first spend four hundred years as slaves in a foreign land—which, of course, was Egypt.

Genesis 15:15, 16
And thou shalt go to thy fathers in peace; thou shalt be buried in a good old age. But in the fourth generation they shall come hither again: for the iniquity of the Amorites is not yet full.

"The Amorites"—a generic term for all of the people living in the land of Canaan—refers to a culture so diseased, defiled, and depraved that it was doomed. Nonetheless, God gave them four hundred years—the period in which the Jews were held captive in Egypt—to repent.

While it may be popular to construct the false image of an angry Old Testament God who needed Jesus to come and calm Him down, nothing could be further from the truth. God waited *four hundred* years for the Amorites to turn to Him. It would take four *centuries* before their iniquity demanded that He order their extermination at the hand of Joshua.

Genesis 15:17
And it came to pass, that, when the sun went down, and it was dark, behold a smoking furnace, and a burning lamp that passed between those pieces.

When Abram awoke, he saw that the meat on either side of him was barbequed. God had been there—not meeting Abram halfway as was the custom—but walking the entire length alone.

This is still the way of God. Oh, we try and chase away the birds of evil which threaten our families and our country. We hold rallies and sign pledges; we make vows and make promises. But, because "in our flesh dwells no good thing" (Romans 7:18), like Abram, we eventually become exhausted in trying.

Although numbering over one million in attendance, the recent Promise Keepers rally in Washington, DC was not the biggest Promise Keepers convention in history, for one three times as big took place when three million people heard the voice of God, and witnessed a Divine pyrotechnic display at the foot of Mt. Sinai which so impressed them that they said, "All the words which the Lord hath said, we will do" (Exodus 24:3).

Those in attendance at that first Promise Keepers convention weren't playing a game. They were sincere. They truly meant to keep the Ten Commandments. After all, they had heard God speak and had seen a mountain quake. But Moses came down the mountain forty days later to find them worshiping a golden calf.

Times don't change. People with sincere hearts say, "We will keep our promises." The problem with signing contracts, making vows, keeping promises is that they fail to factor in to the equation a huge component: the flesh.

> For that which I do I allow not: for what I would, that do I not; but what I hate, that do I. If then I do that which I would not, I consent unto the law that it is good. Now then it is no more I that do it, but sin that dwelleth in me. For I know that in me (that is, in my flesh,) dwelleth no good thing: for to will is present with me; but how to perform that which is good I find not. For the good that I would I do not: but the evil which I would not, that I do. O wretched man that I am! who shall deliver me from the body of this death?
>
> Romans 7:15–19, 24

God's aware of this, gang. That's why He says, "I will wait until you're as tired as Abram was. Then I'll come through on My own. I don't want you to sign a contract or make a promise. I know what you're made of. I know your frailty. So I'm not going to meet you halfway. I'm going to do the whole thing."

> For all the promises of God in him are yea, and in him Amen, unto the glory of God by us.
>
> 2 Corinthians 1:20

There is only one Promise Keeper, only One in Whom all the promises are yea and amen. Jesus came on the scene and did what we were unable to do. He kept the covenant, the promises, the commandments. All of the promises of God are *in* Him and kept *by* Him. They're fulfilled *through* Him and point *to* Him. What, then, is our part? Our part is not to stand in the midst of an animal cut in two—but to kneel at a Table, to hold in our hands a Body that for us was cut in two, and to remember *Him* (Luke 22:19).

Genesis 15:18–21

In the same day the LORD made a covenant with Abram, saying, Unto thy seed have I given this land, from the river of Egypt unto the great river, the river Euphrates: The Kenites, and the Kenizzites, and the Kadmonites, And the Hittites, and the Perizzites, and the Rephaims, And the Amorites, and the Canaanites, and the Girgashites, and the Jebusites.

God promised Abram the land from the Nile to the Euphrates—300,000 square miles. The most Israel has ever possessed of this land was 30,000 square miles under Solomon's reign.

16

Genesis 16:1 (a)

Now Sarai Abram's wife bare him no children . . .

The promise had been given. God said to Abram, "You're going to have a family as numerous as the stars in the heavens." But time passes, and guess what. Abram starts wondering. Abram is now eighty-six, Sarai seventy-six, and they think, "This is not working."

Always remember this, folks: When God gives a promise, there is often a gap of time between the giving of the promise and the fulfillment of the promise. In Abram's case, there will be a thirteen-year gap.

Is God's delay due to procrastination on His part? No. Is it due to preoccupation—is He just too busy? No. God's delay is due to *preparation,* for He is preparing us in the arena of faith. You see, the gaps between God's promise and the fulfillment of His promise provide opportunities for the muscle of faith to be exercised—for, like a butterfly emerging from a cocoon, if there is no struggle, faith never soars.

Genesis 16:1 (b)–3

. . . and she had an handmaid, an Egyptian, whose name was Hagar. And Sarai said unto Abram, Behold now, the LORD hath restrained me from bearing: I pray thee, go in unto my maid; it may be that I may obtain children by her. And Abram hearkened to the voice of Sarai. And Sarai Abram's wife took Hagar her maid the Egyptian, after Abram had dwelt ten years in the land of Canaan, and gave her to her husband Abram to be his wife.

This was not a strange practice, but common in the cultures of Ur and Babylon. Women unable to bear children offered their handmaidens to their husbands, and the child produced was considered the child of the husband and wife.

Genesis 16:4, 5
And he went in unto Hagar, and she conceived: and when she saw that she had conceived, her mistress was despised in her eyes. And Sarai said unto Abram, My wrong be upon thee: I have given my maid into thy bosom; and when she saw that she had conceived, I was despised in her eyes: the LORD judge between me and thee.

Even though it was her idea to follow the cultural norm, Sarai, whose name means "Contentious" was angry with Abram for impregnating Hagar.

Genesis 16:6
But Abram said unto Sarai, Behold, thy maid is in thy hand; do to her as it pleaseth thee. And when Sarai dealt hardly with her, she fled from her face.

In trying to give God a hand, in trying to help Him out, Abram and Sarai unwittingly gave birth to the Middle East tension that exists to this day.

Genesis 16:7
And the angel of the LORD found her by a fountain of water in the wilderness, by the fountain in the way to Shur.

This is the first time the phrase, "the angel of the Lord," appears in Scripture. The word translated "angel" means "messenger." Throughout Scripture, angels adamantly refuse to be worshiped. Thus, because the angel of the Lord receives worship, we know He is no ordinary angel. The angel of the Lord refers to the Second Person of the Trinity—Jesus Christ.

How like Jesus to appear not to a man, but to a woman; not to one who sought faith, but to one who was running from the family of faith. After all, Jesus is the Good Shepherd who left the ninety-nine to find the single sheep who had gone astray.

So, the person in here who is in the greatest need, who feels as though he's blown it the worst is the person whom the Lord is most interested in this evening. It would seem more logical to stay with the ninety-nine. But that's not the heart of our Shepherd. He goes after the one. He goes after Hagar. He goes after you.

Genesis 16:8–12
And he said, Hagar, Sarai's maid, whence camest thou? and whither wilt thou go? And she said, I flee from the face of my mistress Sarai. And the angel of the LORD said unto her, Return to thy mistress, and submit thyself under her hands. And the angel of the LORD said unto her, I will multiply thy seed exceedingly, that it shall not be numbered for multitude. And the angel of the LORD said unto her, Behold, thou art with child, and shalt bear a son, and shalt call his name Ishmael; because the LORD hath heard thy affliction. And he will be a wild man; his hand will be against every man, and every man's hand against him; and he shall dwell in the presence of all his brethren.

Although Sarai's proposal was expedient, it was not obedient. Although it was accepted culturally, and had merit logically, it was wrong spiritually, for Abram and Sarai failed to seek the Lord about it. As a result, to this day, world leaders try to figure out what to do concerning the tension, hatred, animosity, and bloodshed stemming from this singular event.

Genesis 16:13, 14
And she called the name of the LORD that spake unto her, Thou God seest me: for she said, Have I also here looked after him that seeth me? Wherefore the well was called Beer-lahai-roi; behold, it is between Kadesh and Bered.

Hagar called the name of the Lord "The God who Sees." Hagar hadn't been looking for God, hadn't seen God, hadn't found God. It was God who saw Hagar.

Genesis 16:15, 16
And Hagar bare Abram a son: and Abram called his son's name, which Hagar bare, Ishmael. And Abram was fourscore and six years old, when Hagar bare Ishmael to Abram.

When the angel of the Lord told Hagar to return to Sarai, she could have said, "No way." Instead, she said, "Okay." Hagar not only made a confession of faith by acknowledging God as Lord, but she was obedient to the Lord in returning to Sarai. Therefore, I firmly expect to see Hagar in heaven. Sarah will be there, too. But gone will be the animosity between them.

17

Genesis 17:1 (a)
And when Abram was ninety years old and nine, the LORD appeared to Abram . . .

Keep in mind there are great gaps and spans of time between these appearances of the Lord to Abram. This intrigues me. Abraham is called the friend of God (James 2:23). Why, then, would God wait fifteen years between conversations? Perhaps you're wondering the same thing with regard to your own situation: "Why don't I hear more frequently from the Lord? Why do I go through weeks or months or years when I don't seem to hear direct words from Him in my spiritual ears?" Keep in mind that Abraham was not only called the friend of God, but he is also called the father of faith. Consequently, God is making a man of faith out of Abram, and he's making a man or woman of faith out of you. Faith means we walk not by what we see physically, by what we hear audibly or by what we know intellectually. Faith means we hang on to what God said previously. We just hang on.

Think back for a moment to a time in the not too distant past when you thought, "This will never work. Everything's going wrong. I'll never make it." Yet here you are today. Why did God allow those things to happen in that way? To teach you to be a man or woman of faith, to teach you to quietly and confidently believe that God is on the throne, that He is in control, that all things work together for good.

Genesis 17:1 (b)
. . . and said unto him, I am the Almighty God . . .

"I am El Shaddai, the Almighty God." Here is the first mention of this name that appears over and over throughout Scripture. *El* signifies the right arm, and speaks of strength. *Shaddai* speaks of a woman's breast, and speaks of nourishment. Thus, God is the mighty One who sees us through with the right hand of His strength as He nurtures us as tenderly as a mother does her newborn baby.

Genesis 17:1 (c)
. . . walk before me, and be thou perfect.

To a ninety-nine-year-old Abram, God doesn't say, "It's time to retire." He says, "I want you to go higher. I want you to be perfect." How is Abram to do this? By walking in the strength and drawing upon the nourishment of El Shaddai.

Genesis 17:2
And I will make my covenant between me and thee, and will multiply thee exceedingly.

Please note four elements in the following summation of the Abrahamic covenant presented in chapters 12—15 . . .

Genesis 17:3–6
And Abram fell on his face: and God talked with him, saying, As for me, behold, my covenant is with thee, and thou shalt be a father of many nations. Neither shall thy name any more be called Abram, but thy name shall be Abraham; for a father of many nations have I made thee. And I will make thee exceeding fruitful, and I will make nations of thee, and kings shall come out of thee.

Notice the *principle* of the covenant. The principle is grace. Twenty-four times in the Abrahamic covenant, God says, "I will." In other words, it's all by His grace. To underscore this, the fifth letter of the Hebrew alphabet is added to Abram's name, changing it from Abram to Abraham because biblically, five is the number of grace—of unmerited, undeserved, unearned favor.

Genesis 17:7 (a)
And I will establish my covenant between me and thee and thy seed after thee in their generations . . .

Secondly, notice the *people* of the covenant. The covenant is not only between God and Abraham, but also between God and the Jewish people as a whole.

Genesis 17:7 (b), 8 (a)
. . . for an everlasting covenant, to be a God unto thee, and to thy seed after thee. And I will give unto thee, and to thy seed after thee . . .

Thirdly, notice the *period* of the covenant. Contrary to what the Palestinians maintain, the Abrahamic covenant did not become null and void in A.D. 70 when the Jews were scattered. No, it is an *everlasting* covenant, as reiterated in Ezekiel 11:17.

Genesis 17:8 (b)
. . . the land wherein thou art a stranger, all the land of Canaan, for an everlasting possession; and I will be their God.

Fourthly, notice the *place* of the covenant. God promised the Jews 300,000 square miles. Although at most, they only possessed ten percent under Solomon's reign, a day is coming when they will inherit all of the land God promised them.

Genesis 17:9–14
And God said unto Abraham, Thou shalt keep my covenant therefore, thou, and thy seed after thee in their generations. This is my covenant, which ye shall keep, between me and you and thy seed after thee; Every man child among you shall be circumcised. And ye shall circumcise the flesh of your foreskin; and it shall be a token of the covenant betwixt me and you. And he that is eight days old shall be circumcised among you, every man child in your generations, he that is born in the house, or bought with money of any stranger, which is not of thy seed. He that is born in thy house, and he that is bought with thy money, must needs be circumcised: and my covenant shall be in your flesh for an everlasting covenant. And the uncircumcised man child whose flesh of his foreskin is not circumcised, that soul shall be cut off from his people; he hath broken my covenant.

The sign of God's covenant with His people would manifest itself in the flesh. That is, there was to be a sensitivity and purity in them that they hadn't known previously. Circumcision was an outward sign, but it would speak of an inward reality, the same way the ordinances of Baptism and Communion do presently.

Genesis 17:15
And God said unto Abraham, As for Sarai thy wife, thou shalt not call her name Sarai, but Sarah shall her name be.

By adding grace, signified by the fifth letter of the Hebrew alphabet to her name, Sarai became Sarah; "Contentious" became "Princess."

Genesis 17:16, 17
And I will bless her, and give thee a son also of her: yea, I will bless her, and she shall be a mother of nations; kings of people shall be of her. Then Abraham fell upon his face, and laughed, and said in his heart, Shall a child be born unto him that is an hundred years old? and shall Sarah, that is ninety years old, bear?

Abraham's is not the laugh of mockery or unbelief, but of ecstasy and elation. Abraham's hilarity turns to heaviness, however, his delight to anguish, when he remembers he already has a son . . .

Genesis 17:18
And Abraham said unto God, O that Ishmael might live before thee!

The Hebrew text makes it clear that this is the passionate cry of a father who says, "I already have a son who I love deeply. Let *him* be the one through whom the covenant and blessings come." In other words, Abraham is saying, "I know I got ahead of You when Ishmael was conceived. I know that was not Your plan. I know I made a mess, but, Lord, bless my mess."

Have you ever done that? Maybe your motives were sincere, your intensions were right. But you didn't wait on God or talk things over with Him. Instead, you just plunged into that relationship, that job opportunity, that ministry. And when it turned out to be a mess, you asked God to bless it anyway.

I used to think prayer was giving God orders: "Bless this, bless that, bless the other," I'd pray, as if I could ring a bell through prayer (the more faith I had, the louder it would ring), and God would grant me my wishes as if He were a genie. I used to think I knew what God should do. Now I know I don't have a clue. I have found that God gives His best to those who leave the choice with Him. Thus, prayer is not giving God orders. Prayer is simply reporting for duty. Prayer is not "Bless my mess." It's, "Lord, have *Your* way."

Genesis 17:19 (a)
And God said, Sarah thy wife shall bear thee a son indeed . . .

Ishmael was not the child of God's promise, therefore he could not be the channel of God's blessing.

Genesis 17:19 (b)
. . . and thou shalt call his name Isaac: and I will establish my covenant with him for an everlasting covenant, and with his seed after him.

Only *Isaac*, or "Laughter," could be the one through whom the covenant would be established, for only Isaac was the product of God's miraculous grace.

Genesis 17:20–22
And as for Ishmael, I have heard thee: Behold, I have blessed him, and will make him fruitful, and will multiply him exceedingly; twelve princes shall he beget, and I will make him a great nation. But my covenant will I establish with Isaac, which Sarah shall bear unto thee at this set time in the

next year. And he left off talking with him, and God went up from Abraham.

"Although the covenant will not be established through Ishmael, I have heard your prayer, Abraham, and he will become a great people," said God. And Ishmael, father of the Arab nation, did just that.

I can't help but wonder what would have happened if instead of saying, "Bless Ishmael," our dear brother Abraham had said, "Lord, I've messed up. What do *You* want to do now?"

Genesis 17:23
And Abraham took Ishmael his son, and all that were born in his house, and all that were bought with his money, every male among the men of Abraham's house; and circumcised the flesh of their foreskin in the selfsame day, as God had said unto him.

Notice Abraham's *parental obedience.* Although Ishmael at this point was thirteen years old, Abraham didn't tell him to get circumcised—he circumcised Ishmael himself. I have noticed that it makes all the difference in the world when instead of telling their kids to pray, a mom or dad prays *with* them; that instead of telling them to go to Bible study, a mom or dad goes *with* them. Here, our brother Abraham leads the way.

Genesis 17:24–26
And Abraham was ninety years old and nine, when he was circumcised in the flesh of his foreskin. And Ishmael his son was thirteen years old, when he was circumcised in the flesh of his foreskin. In the selfsame day was Abraham circumcised, and Ishmael his son.

Notice Abraham's *personal obedience.* It would have been tempting for Abraham to say, "It's important that these young guys deal with the flesh. But, Lord, I'm ninety-nine. Certainly You don't expect me to deal with the flesh in this way." But that's not what Abraham said. The very day he heard the word, he submitted to it. I like that!

As one advances in age, there can be a tendency to say, "I'm glad the young people are going to Bible study; I'm glad the next generation is sharing their faith. But I'm old. Don't expect me to be stretched or to enter in to a new experience spiritually." Not so with Abraham. Even though he's ninety-nine, he says, "Okay, let's do it."

How I want to be that kind of man. How I want you to be that kind of person. How I want us to be that kind of Fellowship—where we don't say, "Those were great days back in 1982," but rather, "What do You have for us *now,* Lord?"

Genesis 17:27
And all the men of his house, born in the house, and bought with money of the stranger, were circumcised with him.

Notice Abraham's *professional obedience.* Abraham said, "Look boys, if you're working for me, this is the way it's going to be. . . ." I like that! Due to the fear of repercussions legally, or being misunderstood in the business community, Christian employers are reticent to make a stand for God professionally. If you have someone working for you, I encourage you to be like Abraham and say, "This company is run on the principles of God's Word. I know I can't change your heart—but I can set the standard"—and watch God bless you.

18

Genesis 18:1
And the LORD appeared unto him in the plains of Mamre: and he sat in the tent door in the heat of the day.

The heat of the day in Scripture is often a picture of the hard times that come our way. So often in my walk, I've seen the Lord in a fresh way in the heat of the day, in fiery trials. You have, too. This is not surprising. After all, it was when Shadrach, Meshach, and Abed-Nego were cast into a fiery furnace that they saw the Lord (Daniel 3:25). Consequently, when I hear of people in the body who are going through fiery trials and hot times, on one hand my heart goes out to them, but on the other hand, in a sense, I'm envious of them because I know the Lord will make Himself known to them in a special way in the heat of the day.

Genesis 18:2 (a)
And he lift up his eyes and looked, and, lo, three men stood by him . . .

As we shall see, the three men are the Lord and two angels.

Genesis 18:2 (b)
. . . and when he saw them, he ran to meet them from the tent door, and bowed himself toward the ground,

I like this! Here's a ninety-nine-year-old man who *runs* to meet the Lord. How do you and I greet the Lord when the alarm clock goes off for devotions and prayer, for meditation and worship?

Genesis 18:3–5
And said, My Lord, if now I have found favour in thy sight, pass not away, I pray thee, from thy servant: Let a little water, I pray you, be fetched, and wash your feet, and rest yourselves under the tree: And I will fetch a morsel of bread, and comfort ye your hearts; after that ye shall pass on: for therefore are ye come to your servant. And they said, So do, as thou hast said.

Abraham realized these were no ordinary visitors.

Genesis 18:6–8 (a)
And Abraham hastened into the tent unto Sarah, and said, Make ready quickly three measures of fine meal, knead it, and make cakes upon the hearth. And Abraham ran unto the herd, and fetcht a calf tender and good, and gave it unto a young man; and he hasted to dress it. And he took butter, and milk, and the calf which he had dressed, and set it before them . . .

Prodigal meaning "extremely generous, or lavish," here we see a prodigal Abraham running to meet his Lord and serving Him a tender calf—a parallel to another prodigal whose father would run to greet him and welcome him with a fatted calf (Luke 15).

Genesis 18:8 (b)
. . . and he stood by them under the tree, and they did eat.

Fellowship took place under the tree. Such is always the case, for it is only through Christ's death on the tree of Calvary that we have fellowship with Him.

Genesis 18:9–12
And they said unto him, Where is Sarah thy wife? And he said, Behold, in the tent. And he said, I will certainly return unto thee according to the time of life; and, lo, Sarah thy wife shall have a son. And Sarah heard it in the tent door, which was behind him. Now Abraham and Sarah were old and well stricken in age; and it ceased to be with Sarah after the manner of women. Therefore Sarah laughed within herself, saying, after I am waxed old shall I have pleasure, my lord being old also?

In chapter 17, Abraham had laughed at this prospect with ecstasy. Here, his wife laughs incredulously.

Genesis 18:13, 14 (a)
And the LORD said unto Abraham, Wherefore did Sarah laugh, saying, Shall I of a surety bear a child, which am old? Is any thing too hard for the LORD?

Is anything too hard for the Lord? We have a tendency to think of God's ability in relation to degrees of difficulty . . .

If someone comes to me and says, "I'm struggling with a headache. Would you pray for me?" I say, "Sure. Bless Bob, Lord. Take away the tension and allow him to experience a healing touch from Your hand."

But if someone comes to me saying, "I just came back from the doctor's office and he told me I have a malignant tumor. Would you pray for me?"—I act as if it's a whole different deal! "Pastors, brothers, gather round," I say. And I fervently plead with the Lord as though cancer is harder for Him to heal than a headache.

Oh, there's nothing wrong with praying passionately, but not because there are degrees of difficulty or because we need to get God's attention emotionally. The prophets of Baal slashed their bodies and cried loudly to get his attention, all to no avail. Elijah, on the other hand, simply prayed two sentences, and thereby moved the hand of God (1 Kings 18).

Genesis 18:14 (b), 15
. . . At the time appointed I will return unto thee, according to the time of life, and Sarah shall have a son. Then Sarah denied, saying, I laughed not; for she was afraid. And he said, Nay; but thou didst laugh.

The Lord doesn't condemn Sarah for laughing; but simply reminds her that He knows exactly what's going on in her heart and what she's doing behind closed tent flaps.

Genesis 18:16–19
And the men rose up from thence, and looked toward Sodom: and Abraham went with them to bring them on the way. And the LORD said, Shall I hide from Abraham that thing which I do; Seeing that Abraham shall surely become a great and mighty nation, and all the nations of the earth shall be blessed in him? For I know him, that he will command his children and his household after him, and they shall keep the way of the LORD, to do justice and judgment;

that the LORD may bring upon Abraham that which he hath spoken of him.

The Lord would give Abraham information and revelation based not upon the accumulation of his knowledge, but upon the communication to his family. "I will give Abraham understanding of what I'm about to do," said the Lord, "because I know he is a man who will teach his children."

The same is true today. The revelation God wants to give us concerning what He's doing, how He's moving, where He's going is based not upon our journal entries or our Bible Study notes. It's based upon whether or not we will share what He tells us with our children.

People often say to me, "If I could go back and do it all over again, I would not go into the profession I'm in presently. I would go into the ministry." And I understand that, for I have found the ministry to be absolutely delightful. It's a fabulous calling. But here's the fact: If you have children or grandchildren, you *are* in the ministry. No clerical collar or pulpit compares to gathering your family around you, giving a simple Bible lesson, singing songs, sharing with each other, and praying together. *That* is the ministry. And anyone who takes seriously this call will, like Abraham, receive fresh revelation. I know this to be so, for the most wonderful insights and sweetest revelations of God to my heart have not come as I have prepared sermons, but as I have simply shared in worship with my family.

Genesis 18:20, 21 (a)
And the LORD said, Because the cry of Sodom and Gomorrah is great, and because their sin is very grievous; I will go down now . . .

It was the cry of Sodom and Gomorrah that caused the Lord to "go down." And in the last days, it will be the cry of man's Sodom-like culture (Luke 17:30) that will cause the Lord to come down again—this time to rapture His church (1 Thessalonians 4:17).

Genesis 18:21 (b), 22
. . . and see whether they have done altogether according to the cry of it, which is come unto me; and if not, I will know. And the men turned their faces from thence, and went toward Sodom: but Abraham stood yet before the LORD.

God knows everything. Why, then would He have to come down and see what's going on? God says, "I will come down and see firsthand so that you will know that My judgment will not be uninformed or capricious."

Genesis 18:23
And Abraham drew near, and said, Wilt thou also destroy the righteous with the wicked?

Knowing his nephew Lot's family lived in Sodom, Abraham enters into a dialogue with God on their behalf . . .

Genesis 18:24, 25
Peradventure there be fifty righteous within the city: wilt thou also destroy and not spare the place for the fifty righteous that are therein? That be far from thee to do after this manner, to slay the righteous with the wicked: and that the righteous should be as the wicked, that be far from thee: Shall not the Judge of all the earth do right?

"No man comes to the Father but by Me," Jesus declared (John 14:6).

"There is none other name under heaven given among men, whereby we must be saved," Peter preached (Acts 4:12).

If there is no way to heaven other than through Jesus, how shall the Judge of all the earth rightly judge the person in Africa who has never had an opportunity to hear the gospel? In the first two chapters of his epistle to the Romans, Paul maintains that creation round about and conscience deep within all of humanity testifies to the reality of a Creator. Therefore, people will be judged according to the light they had—which is why in Revelation 19:2, we see all of heaven saying, "True and righteous are Your judgments, O Lord. You judged *perfectly*."

The Judge of all the earth shall do right. He will not, cannot, does not wink at sin. So He left the throne of heaven to come down and pay the price for any who will accept His free gift of salvation.

Genesis 18:26–33
And the LORD said, If I find in Sodom fifty righteous within the city, then I will spare all the place for their sakes. And Abraham answered and said, Behold now, I have taken upon me to speak unto the Lord, which am but dust and ashes: Peradventure there shall lack five of the fifty righteous: wilt thou destroy all the city for lack of five? And he said, If I find there forty and five, I will not destroy it. And he spake unto him yet again, and said, Peradventure there shall be forty found there. And he said, I will not do it for forty's sake. And he said unto him, Oh let not the Lord be angry, and I will speak: Per-

adventure there shall thirty be found there. And he said, I will not do it, if I find thirty there. And he said, Behold now, I have taken upon me to speak unto the Lord: Peradventure there shall be twenty found there. And he said, I will not destroy it for twenty's sake. And he said, Oh let not the Lord be angry, and I will speak yet but this once: Peradventure ten shall be found there. And he said, I will not destroy it for ten's sake. And the LORD went his way, as soon as he had left communing with Abraham: and Abraham returned unto his place.

As we will see in chapter 19, Lot had two daughters living in his house (19:8). He also had at least two married daughters (19:14). This means Lot's family, including his sons-in-law, numbered eight at the very least. Perhaps Abraham stopped negotiating with the Lord at ten because he thought there was bound to be two other righteous people in the entire cities of Sodom and Gomorrah.

But God didn't stop at ten, for, as we will see, when He saved Lot and his household from destruction, He stooped all the way down to four.

19

Genesis 19:1 (a)
And there came two angels to Sodom at even . . .

Although three men had appeared to Abraham in chapter 18, only two go to Sodom because the Lord Himself does not enter into the city. Why? Psalm 66 tells me that if I regard iniquity in my heart the Lord will not hear me. That is, if I am purposely, rebelliously, intentionally, arrogantly holding on to sin, when I pray, the Lord won't hear my prayer; He'll not come into my city; He'll not enter in to my situation.

You see, even though the sin to which I so stubbornly cling was paid for completely on the Cross of Calvary, the Lord loves me so much He says, "I love you too much to let you go on your merry way day after day as though there's nothing wrong because if I did that, you would continue in that sin, and that sin would destroy you. Consequently, you won't feel My hand. You won't sense My presence—not because I'm not there, for I will never leave you, nor forsake you—but because your spirit senses something is not quite right."

When I feel as though my prayers bounce off the ceiling, it's not because the Lord is angry *with* me or mad *at* me, disappointed *in* me or turning away *from* me. Rather, it's an indication He's lovingly giving *to* me that something's not right.

The angels went into Sodom—but not the Lord.

Genesis 19:1 (b)
. . . and Lot sat in the gate of Sodom . . .

Like every other city gate in biblical times, the gate in which Lot sat was a large area at the entrance of the city wherein the city leaders would give advice and render civic decisions. The fact that Lot sat in Sodom's gate indicates he had become a leader of Sodom.

How had Lot arrived at this point?

- In Genesis 13:10, he had looked *at* Sodom.
- Two verses later, he pitched his tent *toward* Sodom.
- In chapter 14, he moved *into* Sodom.

In other words, he arrived there one step at a time.

Genesis 19:1 (c), 2
. . . and Lot seeing them rose up to meet them; and he bowed himself with his face toward the ground; And he said, Behold now, my lords, turn in, I pray you, into your servant's house, and tarry all night, and wash your feet, and ye shall rise up early, and go on your ways. And they said, Nay; but we will abide in the street all night.

The angels initially turned down Lot's hospitality in order to check out the situation in the streets of Sodom.

Genesis 19:3
And he pressed upon them greatly; and they turned in unto him, and entered into his house; and he made them a feast, and did bake unleavened bread, and they did eat.

Knowing what would befall these visitors in the streets of his city, Lot finally persuaded them to stay with him.

Genesis 19:4, 5
But before they lay down, the men of the city, even the men of Sodom, compassed the house round, both old and young, all the people from every quarter: And they called unto Lot, and said unto him, Where are the men which came in to thee this night? bring them out unto us, that we may know them.

In this case, to "know" means to have homosexual relations.

Genesis 19:6, 7
And Lot went out at the door unto them, and shut the door after him, And said, I pray you, brethren, do not so wickedly.

A man who began on a spiritual pilgrimage years previously now calls a mob of crazed homosexuals brothers. How low can Lot go? He's about to go lower still . . .

Genesis 19:8
Behold now, I have two daughters which have not known man; let me, I pray you, bring them out unto you, and do ye to them as is good in your eyes: only unto these men do nothing; for therefore came they under the shadow of my roof.

This story is so unbelievably sordid and shocking that I've researched it thoroughly and carefully in order to find a cultural or historical explanation for a dad who would offer his daughters in this way. But there is none to be found—other than the fact that Lot was completely desensitized to what was happening. He had been in Sodom so long that he had become accustomed to perversion—just as we have. Things that once shocked and scandalized our community are now totally acceptable, for, like Lot, we as a nation have been so seduced that we have lost our moral compass.

Genesis 19:9 (a)
And they said, Stand back. And they said again, This one fellow came in to sojourn, and he will needs be a judge: now will we deal worse with thee, than with them . . .

"Who are you to judge us?" said the men of Sodom to Lot. "You hang out with us; you've become like us; how do you think you can be a judge over us?"

Genesis 19:9 (b)–11
. . . And they pressed sore upon the man, even Lot, and came near to break the door. But the men put forth their hand, and pulled Lot into the house to them, and shut to the door. And they smote the men that were at the door of the house with blindness, both small and great: so that they wearied themselves to find the door.

What a story. The angels reach out, pull Lot in, and smite the men outside with blindness. Yet even in their blindness, the men of Sodom still try to break into Lot's house in order to fulfill their sexual desires.

Genesis 19:12–14
And the men said unto Lot, Hast thou here any besides? son in law, and thy sons, and thy daughters, and whatsoever thou hast in the city, bring them out of this place: For we will destroy this place, because the cry of them is waxen great before the face of the LORD; and the LORD hath sent us to destroy it. And Lot went out, and spake unto his sons in law, which married his daughters, and said, Up, get you out of this place; for the LORD will destroy this city. But he seemed as one that mocked unto his sons in law.

Why didn't Lot's sons-in-law listen to him? Because when he moved his family to Sodom and became a leader of the community, Lot lost his credibility. And the same is still true. A dad loses credibility whenever his kids see glaring inconsistencies between his words and his walk. Poor Lot. His peers told him to "stand back." His family simply scoffed.

Genesis 19:15, 16 (a)
And when the morning arose, then the angels hastened Lot, saying, Arise, take thy wife, and thy two daughters, which are here; lest thou be consumed in the iniquity of the city. And while he lingered . . .

If some angels came to you and said, "Get out of here as fast as you can," what would you do? The only reason I can think of for Lot's lingering is that he was hoping against hope that his daughters and sons-in-law would show up.

Genesis 19:16 (b)
. . . the men laid hold upon his hand, and upon the hand of his wife, and upon the hand of his two daughters; the LORD being merciful unto him: and they brought him forth, and set him without the city.

"Wilt Thou destroy the righteous with the wicked?" Abraham had asked the Lord (18:23). The answer, as illustrated here, is "No"—for before judgment could be poured out upon Sodom, before fire and brimstone would come down to destroy Gomorrah, God rescued Lot and those of his house; He rescued the righteous.

Lot righteous? A guy who calls perverted people his brothers? A guy who offers his daughters to a homosexual mob? A guy who lingers when angels tell him to leave? Lot *righteous?*

Yes, for that is what Peter calls him (2 Peter 2:7). How can Lot possibly be considered righteous? Because righteousness is imputed solely on the basis of simple faith. I am righteous and so are you if you have confessed with your mouth that Jesus is who He claimed to be, and believed in your heart that God raised Him from the dead (Romans 10:9, 10).

I love this chapter because there are a lot of people I care about deeply who, like Lot, made a profession of faith but ended up in Sodom, not living the way they know they should. If you're worried about a friend or a family member, take hope. While we don't want anyone to follow Lot's example because sin brings all kinds of pain and problems presently as well as empty-handedness eternally, know this: If that son of yours confesses with his mouth that Jesus is who He claimed to be, and believes in his heart that God raised Him from the dead, he will go up in the Rapture—of which this account is an illustration.

I don't know how the Lord could have painted any more powerful a picture than this to say, "I'm going to rescue people you may have thought were hopelessly lost."

Genesis 19:17 (a)
And it came to pass, when they had brought them forth abroad, that he said, Escape for thy life . . .

"Escape for thy life," the Lord said to Lot. Of the Tribulation, Jesus said, "Pray that ye may be accounted worthy to escape all these things" (Luke 21:36).

"The reason you guys at Applegate always talk about the Rapture happening before the Tribulation is because you just want to escape the Tribulation," say our critics. And they're exactly right!

Genesis 19:17 (b)
. . . look not behind thee, neither stay thou in all the plain; escape to the mountain, lest thou be consumed.

In telling Lot to escape to the mountain, the Lord wanted to turn a city-boy into a mountain man. Throughout Scripture, the Lord continually calls His people to the mountains . . .

- With Abraham, who was ready to sacrifice his son in obedience to the Lord's command, He calls us to Mt. Moriah, the Mount of Devotion.
- With the Israelites, who gathered to receive His commandments, the Lord calls us to Mt. Sinai, the Mount of Instruction.
- With Moses, who viewed the Promised Land, He calls us to Mt. Pisgah, the Mount of Vision.
- With Elijah, whose prayer brought down fire from heaven, He calls us to Mt. Carmel, the Mount of Passion.
- With Peter, James, and John, who beheld the glory of the Lord, He calls us to Mt. Hermon, the Mount of Transfiguration.

Genesis 19:18, 19
And Lot said unto them, Oh, not so, my Lord: Behold now, thy servant hath found grace in thy sight, and thou hast magnified thy mercy, which thou hast shewed unto me in saving my life; and I cannot escape to the mountain, lest some evil take me, and I die:

The most important mountain to which God calls us is to Mt. Calvary, the Mount of Crucifixion, of death to self. As is our tendency, Lot was fearful to make such a journey.

Genesis 19:20
Behold now, this city is near to flee unto, and it is a little one: Oh, let me escape thither, (is it not a little one?) and my soul shall live.

"I know you're calling me to the mountain, Lord," said Lot, "but let me go to this little city. Things can go wrong on the mountain."

Genesis 19:21, 22
And he said unto him, See, I have accepted thee concerning this thing also, that I will not overthrow this city, for the which thou hast spoken. Haste thee, escape thither; for I cannot do any thing till thou be come thither. Therefore the name of the city was called Zoar.

Zoar means "little one." This is just like us. "To the mountain!" says the Lord—"to the mount of passion, instruction, vision, crucifixion."

"No thanks, Lord," we say. "I know You're calling me to a new elevation and a greater revelation, but, Lord, I've got clients to meet, a quiche in the oven, a dripping faucet to fix. Going to the mountain just doesn't fit in my schedule right now."

"The winter has passed; the rain is gone; the flowers appear on the earth. Come away, my beloved," said the bridegroom to His bride.

"You go ahead," answers the bride, "I'm going to snooze" (see Song of Solomon 2).

That's what the bride said. That's what Lot said. That's all too often what we say.

Genesis 19:23–25
The sun was risen upon the earth when Lot entered into Zoar. Then the LORD rained upon Sodom and upon Gomorrah brimstone and fire from the LORD out of heaven; And he overthrew those cities, and all the plain,

and all the inhabitants of the cities, and that which grew upon the ground.

Located near what the people who have lived in the region for centuries call the Sea of Lot—what we know as the Dead Sea—the site where Sodom and Gomorrah once stood looks like the aftermath of an atomic bomb. This area which was once so green that Lot chose it above any other region, is now totally, completely, awesomely arid.

Genesis 19:26
But his wife looked back from behind him, and she became a pillar of salt.

"Remember Lot's wife," Jesus said in a powerful exhortation only three words long (Luke 17:32). Could it be that Lot's wife was thinking of family and friends she had left in Sodom? Whatever the reason, Lot's wife looked back, and became a pillar of salt in the process. What happens to the person who has been saved, but looks back longingly at the life from which he or she was rescued? His or her walk doesn't progress. Like Lot's wife, he or she is paralyzed.

Genesis 19:27–30 (a)
And Abraham gat up early in the morning to the place where he stood before the LORD: And he looked toward Sodom and Gomorrah, and toward all the land of the plain, and beheld, and, lo, the smoke of the country went up as the smoke of a furnace. And it came to pass, when God destroyed the cities of the plain, that God remembered Abraham, and sent Lot out of the midst of the overthrow, when he overthrew the cities in the which Lot dwelt. And Lot went up out of Zoar, and dwelt in the mountain, and his two daughters with him; for he feared to dwell in Zoar . . .

After seeing judgment in the form of fire and brimstone poured out on Sodom and Gomorrah, Lot decides maybe the mountain wasn't such a bad idea after all.

Genesis 19:30 (b)
. . . and he dwelt in a cave, he and his two daughters.

At last Lot is on the mountain—but he's in a cave—and now things are really going to cave in on top of him.

He had called down fire from heaven; he had seen a powerful victory. But now he's on a mountain in a cave of depression.

"What are you doing here?" the Lord asked Elijah.

"I'm the only one who hasn't bowed his knee to Baal," came Elijah's voice from the darkness.

"No you're not," said God. "There are seven thousand more. Get busy. Get going. There's a king to anoint. There's work to do" (see 1 Kings 19).

Like Elijah, following an incredible display of God's power, Lot found himself in the cave of depression.

Genesis 19:31
And the firstborn said unto the younger, Our father is old, and there is not a man in the earth to come in unto us after the manner of all the earth:

Among other things, the problem with the cave of depression is that it distorts reality. Just as Elijah thought he was the only believer left on earth, Lot's daughters thought their father was the only man left on earth.

Genesis 19:32 (a)
Come, let us make our father drink wine . . .

The time when things are caving in around you is usually the time a voice will whisper in your ear, "Why don't you have a glass of wine to soothe your nerves? Have a beer. Relax!"

Genesis 19:32 (b)–36
. . . and we will lie with him, that we may preserve seed of our father. And they made their father drink wine that night: and the firstborn went in, and lay with her father; and he perceived not when she lay down, nor when she arose. And it came to pass on the morrow, that the firstborn said unto the younger, Behold, I lay yesternight with my father: let us make him drink wine this night also; and go thou in, and lie with him, that we may preserve seed of our Father. And they made their father drink wine that night also: and the younger arose, and lay with him; and he perceived not when she lay down, nor when she arose. Thus were both the daughters of Lot with child by their father.

Lot's daughters didn't look to God to solve their problem. They simply came to their own immoral, irrational decisions. But whose fault was that? Certainly Lot must lay the blame squarely upon his own shoulders, for he led his daughters into Sodom, and had educated them in the ways of Sodom.

Genesis 19:37, 38
And the firstborn bare a son, and called his name Moab: the same is the father of the Moabites unto this day. And the younger, she also bare a son, and called his name Benammi: the same is the father of the children of Ammon unto this day.

As you read through the Old Testament, you see the Moabites and the Ammonites hassling God's people continually. It all started with a believer drinking wine in the cave of depression because he didn't leave the city when he should have.

May God give us wisdom.

20

Genesis 20:1
And Abraham journeyed from thence toward the south country, and dwelled between Kadesh and Shur, and sojourned in Gerar.

On the move once again, Abraham heads south to Gerar, a Philistine city twelve miles south of the Gaza Strip on the West coast of Israel.

Genesis 20:2
And Abraham said of Sarah his wife, She is my sister: and Abimelech king of Gerar sent, and took Sarah.

In this story, we see Abraham falling into the same sin with which he had become entangled twenty-five years earlier.

Genesis 20:3
But God came to Abimelech in a dream by night, and said to him, Behold, thou art but a dead man, for the woman which thou hast taken; for she is a man's wife.

Finding himself inexplicably exhausted, Philistine King Abimelech, was not interested in meeting the new addition to his harem. Thus, it was in a dream that God told him the truth about Sarah.

Genesis 20:4–6
But Abimelech had not come near her: and he said, Lord, wilt thou slay also a righteous nation? Said he not unto me, She is my sister? and she, even she herself said, He is my brother: in the integrity of my heart and innocency of my hands have I done this. And God said unto him in a dream, Yea, I know that thou didst this in the integrity of thy heart; for I also withheld thee from sinning against me: therefore suffered I thee not to touch her.

As was the case with Abimelech, the man, woman, or nation who chooses to live in integrity will be kept from further sins which would wipe them out personally or nationally. The first time the word "integrity" is seen in the Bible is in this story with regard to Abimelech. God help America that once again we would see the importance and value of integrity.

***For topical study of Genesis 20:6 entitled "A Matter of Integrity," turn to page* 86.**

Genesis 20:7 (a)
Now therefore restore the man his wife; for he is a prophet, and he shall pray for thee, and thou shalt live . . .

Herein is the first time in the Bible where the word "prophet" appears. Now, if there was ever a time God wouldn't want to introduce Abraham as a prophet, I would think it would be right here. I would think God would be embarrassed by, upset with, and ashamed of Abraham. But such is not the case, for God says to Abimelech, "That man who told a lie, who misled you, who jeopardized his wife and your nation—he's My man; he's My spokesman; he's My prophet."

Romans 11:29 tells us that "the gifts and calling of God are without repentance." This means when God gives a spiritual gift, a calling, a ministry to a man, woman, or church, He doesn't change His mind. He doesn't take it back. If God has given you a gift, be it ministry, music, prophecy, teaching, or evangelism—if He's given you a skill, be it carpentry, mechanic ability, athletic ability, it's yours to keep.

Perhaps you've seen people stumble, fall, drop the ball, and you wonder how God could still use him, her, or them. The answer is that the gifts and calling of God are without repentance. Sin will always bring about its own sadness, depression, defeat, and despair, for the way of the transgressor is hard (Proverbs 13:15). The fact remains, however, that because the gifts and callings of God are without repentance, God will still use sinners.

I say this because I have found that the thing which hobbles so many people in their service for the Lord is thinking, "God can't use me. God wouldn't use me. God won't use me because I've failed so miserably; I've botched it so badly." That's the voice of the enemy, for the voice of the Lord says, "Because you didn't earn the gifts I gave you or the calling I sovereignly placed upon you, there's no way you can lose them either."

If you've been on the sidelines because you

think you've messed up once too often, remember this story and the mercy of our Master, the grace of our God, the kindness of our King. Truly, there's no one like Him.

Genesis 20:7 (b)–11 (a)
. . . and if thou restore her not, know thou that thou shalt surely die, thou, and all that are thine. Therefore Abimelech rose early in the morning, and called all his servants, and told all these things in their ears: and the men were sore afraid. Then Abimelech called Abraham, and said unto him, What hast thou done unto us? and what have I offended thee, that thou hast brought on me and on my kingdom a great sin? thou hast done deeds unto me that ought not to be done. And Abimelech said unto Abraham, What sawest thou, that thou hast done this thing? And Abraham said, Because I thought . . .

There's the problem. Doesn't that pretty much sum up everything in your situation and mine when we do things that we ought not to do? Abraham didn't say, "I did what I did because I prayed and the Lord led me to lie to you." No, Abraham did what he did because he *thought.*

Genesis 20:11 (b), 12
. . . Surely the fear of God is not in this place; and they will slay me for my wife's sake. And yet indeed she is my sister; she is the daughter of my father, but not the daughter of my mother; and she became my wife.

Because Sarah was Abraham's half-sister, Abraham had told a half-truth. But a half-truth is a complete lie. "Thou shalt not bear false witness," thundered God from Mt. Sinai (Exodus 20). What is a false witness? A false witness is the right information with the wrong implication. In other words, it's saying the right thing, but using it in the wrong way. Abraham gave the right information for, technically, Sarah was his half-sister, but he gave it with the wrong implication, because he failed to tell Abimelech that she was also his wife.

Genesis 20:13
And it came to pass, when God caused me to wander from my father's house, that I said unto her, This is thy kindness which thou shalt shew unto me; at every place whither we shall come, say of me, He is my brother.

Abraham wasn't caught off guard by Pharaoh and Abimelech wanting to add Sarah to their harems. No, the verse before us makes it clear that Abraham's lie was part of a predetermined strategy. And in this I am reminded once again that a person doesn't fall into sin, but rather walks into sin one step at a time. If Abraham hatched this plan way back in Ur, we can only wonder how many other kings besides Pharaoh and Abimelech he fooled. It was a pattern that had been going on for years because in this situation, rather than pray, Abraham thought.

Genesis 20:14, 15
And Abimelech took sheep, and oxen, and menservants, and womenservants, and gave them unto Abraham, and restored him Sarah his wife. And Abimelech said, Behold, my land is before thee: dwell where it pleaseth thee.

Why does Abimelech give Abraham gifts and tell him to live wherever he wants? It isn't because he was impressed with Abraham, but because he was impressed with Abraham's God.

Genesis 20:16 (a)
And unto Sarah he said, Behold, I have given thy brother a thousand pieces of silver . . .

Abimelech refers to Abraham the same way Abraham had initially referred to himself—as Sarah's brother.

Genesis 20:16 (b)
. . . behold, he is to thee a covering of the eyes, unto all that are with thee . . .

The implication is that Abraham shouldn't have exposed his wife to danger in the way he had. Rather than hiding behind her, he should have been a covering for her.

Genesis 20:16 (c)
. . . and with all other: thus she was reproved.

The meaning of the word translated "reproved" is actually "vindicated." In other words, Abimelech didn't blame Sarah for what had happened.

Genesis 20:17, 18
So Abraham prayed unto God: and God healed Abimelech, and his wife, and his maidservants; and they bare children. For the LORD had fast closed up all the wombs of the house of Abimelech, because of Sarah Abraham's wife.

Although Abraham would be used in other arenas and would go on to live a life of blessing before Abimelech, at this point, Abraham couldn't preach to Abimelech because he was a liar and a coward in his eyes. Yet even though Abraham couldn't preach to, or share with Abimelech, he could still pray for him.

Because you have fallen short in their eyes or hurt them badly, there are people to whom you may not be able to preach or with whom you may not be able to share. But this story tells me that although I may not be able to preach to them or share with them, I get to effectively bless them through prayer.

When I pray for my enemies, not only does it release blessing upon them, but it keeps me from getting involved in a cycle of bitterness which will only destroy me. You cannot pray blessing on a person and stay angry with him. It's impossible. That's why Jesus said, "Pray for your enemies" (Matthew 5:44).

I challenge you to pray for the people toward whom you feel bitterness or hostility; for the people you just don't like. Pray that they'll be healed, that they'll prosper, that they'll do well. God will answer your prayer, and you'll be blessed in the process.

A MATTER OF INTEGRITY

A Topical Study of GENESIS 20:6

America has at last "come of age." We have shaken off our Puritanical frontier past, for we have joined Europe in thinking that it doesn't matter what our leaders do in private as long as they are effective in their elected positions. At the state funeral of France's President François Mitterand, his wife stood on one side of his casket, his mistress on the other side—a scene completely acceptable to the French populous. What does it really matter, the Europeans ask, if a person has certain personal inconsistencies as long as he can function effectively in his position governmentally?

It *does* matter. Read your history books . . .

> Joseph Stalin turned a backwater, third-world Russia into a force of great strength militarily and rising power economically. He made Russia a great nation. He got the economy rolling, the military growing—but at what cost? Twenty million Russians were sent to gulags or shot in the back.
>
> Or how about the most efficient leader in European history—Adolf Hitler. "He may hate Jews, and he may have all kinds of quirks, but as long as he can build a Third Reich, he's our man," Germany declared.

Even if you don't believe the Bible, study what's happened in Europe over the last century, and ask if morals matter, if character counts, if integrity is an issue. The dictionary defines integrity as "an unimpaired condition or soundness; an adherence to a code of moral values; the quality or state of being complete or undivided, integrated." What is integrity? It's solidness, soundness, firmness.

Why should we care about integrity?

The Bible gives four reasons . . .

Integrity Protects Us from Sin

And God said unto him in a dream, Yea, I know that thou didst this in the integrity of thy heart; for I also withheld thee from sinning against me . . .

Genesis 20:6 (a)

If we choose to walk in integrity, to value honesty, God will protect us from sins which otherwise would have victory over us.

"What's the big deal about sin?" you might be saying. "I can cover my tracks. I can deal with the repercussions."

"Be sure your sin will find you out," the Word declares (Numbers 32:23). Sin will bring you humiliation, consternation, and real depression. No one gets away with sin.

"But I thought Jesus died for our sin," you say. "I thought our sin was washed away from the Father's memory because of what Christ did on the Cross."

That's absolutely true. "Your sin and iniquity will I remember no more," God declares (Hebrews 10:17). Every confessed sin you've ever done, are doing, or will do is forgiven and forgotten by God. You're forgiven—but your sin itself will track you down, humiliate, and hurt you (Numbers 32:23). That is why integrity is so vital. It protects us from the destructiveness of sin.

Integrity Profits Our Children

The just man walketh in his integrity: his children are blessed after him.

Proverbs 20:7

If you choose integrity, your children will be blessed. That is, they will be prosperous and happy. I know this to be true. My dad was not a powerful, flamboyant person, but he was one of the greatest men I have ever known. And the thing that characterized my dad was this word integrity . . .

> For a season, our family car was a VW beetle. Our family of six traveling in our VW beetle—sometimes accompanied by our German Shepherd named Sam—was a sight to see. Then one day, my bank president dad came home with a brand new company car. I was so excited about the prospect of family trips in that 1966 blue Ford Fairlane—until I heard my dad say, "This car is meant to be used only to go to the bank."
>
> "Let's take the Fairlane out for a spin," I'd say.
>
> "So, you want to go to the bank?" he'd reply.

You see, my dad was a man of real integrity, a man of his word. And his children have been abundantly blessed by his legacy.

Integrity Promotes Stability

A double minded man is unstable in all his ways. James 1:8

A man who lives in integrity is single-minded. His yea is yea, his nay, nay (Matthew 5:37). He is one who is emotionally solid. As a pastor, I'm convinced that many people are emotionally unstable and depressed because they're double-minded. They're like waves being tossed to and fro in the sea.

People who don't have integrity are emotionally distraught, vulnerable to depression, and unstable internally because they don't exactly know what story they told whom. He who lacks integrity forgets what truth is. His story shifts, and pretty soon, all he can say is, "No comment; talk to my lawyer."

Integrity Provides Guidance and Direction

The integrity of the upright shall guide them: but the perverseness of transgressors shall destroy them. Proverbs 11:3

The best guidance system you'll ever have is integrity. The Hebrew word translated "integrity" is *tummah,* from which comes the word "thummim." In Old Testament days, when a person had a question—should he go there, attack them, do this—he would go to the High Priest who would consult the Urim and the Thummim. *Urim* means "lights." *Thummim* means "perfection" or "direction." The Urim and Thummim was part of the High Priest's breastplate. It would seem to refer to the twelve gems on his breastplate—one for each tribe—which would light up in such a way as to spell an answer, each stone representing the first letter of its tribe.

The difference between the Old Testament believer who sought direction from the High Priest and the New Testament believer who seeks direction from a pastor or counselor is a big one, however, for the Old Testament believer had to follow the counsel of the High Priest, or die.

We live in a culture where there's endless counseling and running to this guy and that meeting, trying to find what we want to hear. Integrity, on the other hand, says, "I'm coming to You, Lord. No games, no agenda. Whatever You say, I'll do."

"*That's* integrity," God says. "And I will definitely guide you."

Integrity protects from sin, profits one's children, promotes stability, and provides guidance. How can we incorporate integrity into our own lives? I believe the answer can be seen in the life of Job . . .

"Do you still retain your integrity?" asked his wife. "Curse God, and die" (Job 2:9).

Although his children, possessions, and health had all been decimated, Job answered, "I will not cave in on the issue of integrity."

His friends came to him, saying, you must be doing *something* wrong, Job.

"Even though you want me to confess to this stuff, even though that might sound humble and seem spiritual, it lacks integrity because what you are saying I have done is just not true. It might sound noble and humble and spiritual—but I must not compromise honesty and integrity," declared Job.

What made Job this way? What made Job a man about whom God would say to Satan, "Here's a man who will hold fast his integrity no matter what you do, no matter what happens"?

"I made a covenant with mine eyes; why then should I think upon a maid?" Job declared (Job 31:1). "I made a decision about my life that I would not look at a woman lustfully. I drew a line in the sand, and made my stand." Such was Job's mentality. He wasn't making a deal with his Lord. He was making a decision about his life.

If someone offered me a bunch of heroin, I would have lots of options: I could call the cops, witness to him, or tell him to beat it. But partaking of his heroin would not be an option because somewhere along the way in my life I decided heroin is non-negotiable. When I finally, seriously decide that lying is not an option, that twisting the truth is non-negotiable—I will no longer be tempted to lie; I will walk in integrity. Whenever we make such a decision, God makes the provision which enables us to carry it out. That's what Job had done.

"But he lost everything," you say.

Not true. At the end of the story, Job had twice as much as he had originally.

When you make a decision to start living in integrity and honesty, God will bless you just as He blessed Job, just like He blessed Abimelech. Our culture is so confused on this issue. Let us go out and be salt and light. Let us choose to be people of integrity that we might see blessings in our lives personally, in our families, and in our country.

21

Genesis 21:1, 2

And the LORD visited Sarah as he had said, and the LORD did unto Sarah as he had spoken. For Sarah conceived, and bare Abraham a son in his old age, at the set time of which God had spoken to him.

And so at last we see the promise that was given to Abraham twenty-five years previously coming to pass. As we have noted, more often than not, there is a time gap between the promise and performance of God—a period which is invariably longer than we thought it would be, or than we think it should be. Because our implicit trust in the Lord will be a key ingredient in allowing us to function in the coming kingdom, it is essential that we be people of faith. So Abraham, the father of faith, was himself put into a place where his faith was stretched.

Genesis 21:3–7

And Abraham called the name of his son that was born unto him, whom Sarah bare to him, Isaac. And Abraham circumcised his son Isaac being eight days old, as God had commanded him. And Abraham was an hundred years old, when his son Isaac was born unto him. And Sarah said, God hath made me to laugh, so that all that hear will laugh with me. And she said, Who would have said unto Abraham, that Sarah should have given children suck? for I have born him a son in his old age.

Abraham named the child exactly what God said he should be named: Isaac, or Laughter—signifying the amazing miracle of his birth to a ninety-year-old mom and a hundred-year-old dad.

Genesis 21:8
And the child grew, and was weaned: and Abraham made a great feast the same day that Isaac was weaned.

Abraham celebrated when Isaac was no longer dependent upon his mother's milk, but was able to take in meat. So, too, there's great joy not only in the heart of the heavenly Father, but in an earthly parent when we see our kids move from milk to meat—when they can sink their teeth into the Scriptures and extract truth, when they no longer need to be fed by their dad or mom from a spiritual bottle, when they begin to see things in the Word that apply to them personally.

I had such a reason to rejoice a few weeks before my daughter, Jessie, went to heaven. We were on the Mountaintop, where I was teaching through the Book of Revelation one weekend. I came to a certain point where I sent the "retreatants" away to contemplate certain sections. During the sharing time which followed, Jessie raised her hand and said, "Dad I don't know if you've ever seen this before, but in my assigned section concerning the seven bowl judgments, it struck me that the seven bowls match up chronologically with the seven last sayings of Christ on the Cross." She made the correlation between God pouring out His wrath and Christ absorbing the wrath that should have been ours. And I was "bowled" over.

As I rushed out the door last night, Christy said, "Stop, Dad. Could I lay hands on you and pray blessing for you?" Oh, my. Watching your kids grab spiritual principles causes celebration.

How do you become a deeper person in the Word? The writer of Hebrews tells us that strong meat belongs to those who by reason of use have exercised their sense to discern good and evil (Hebrews 5:14). In other words, strong meat is given to those who use what they already have been given. As you put into practice the milk, pabulum, or strained vegetables before you, strong meat will be added to you.

Genesis 21:9
And Sarah saw the son of Hagar the Egyptian, which she had born unto Abraham, mocking.

At this point, Isaac is approximately three years old, Ishmael approximately seventeen. If you wonder how a seventeen-year-old could tease a three-year-old, you haven't had kids yet!

Genesis 21:10, 11
Wherefore she said unto Abraham, Cast out this bondwoman and her son: for the son of this bondwoman shall not be heir with my son, even with Isaac. And the thing was very grievous in Abraham's sight because of his son.

"Ishmael and his mother have got to go!" Sarah said. The thought was grievous to Abraham because, as any father would, he deeply loved his son.

Genesis 21:12
And God said unto Abraham, Let it not be grievous in thy sight because of the lad, and because of thy bondwoman; in all that Sarah hath said unto thee, hearken unto her voice; for in Isaac shall thy seed be called.

It's amazing how often we as husbands quote Ephesians 5:22: Wives, submit to your husbands. We know that verse well! But, dear brothers, understand that Ephesians 5:22 follows Ephesians 5:21: Submit yourselves one to another in the fear of God. The correct picture is husbands submitting to wives, wives submitting to husbands, listening to each other, receiving from each other. So it is that God says, "Abraham, listen to your wife."

Genesis 21:13
And also of the son of the bondwoman will I make a nation, because he is thy seed.

"Ishmael is important to you," God said to Abraham. "And because he is your child, I'm going to make a great nation of him." Ishmael did indeed become a great nation—the Arab people of today. But although Ishmael was made a great nation eventually, this was not the plan of God initially.

I think of D. L. Moody—a powerful evangelist, a wonderful man of God, the Billy Graham of the 1800's. Through him, not only were hundreds of thousands of people converted, but the Moody Memorial Church in Chicago—which is to this day a powerhouse of preaching and a lighthouse of the gospel—and Moody Bible Institute—which has trained tens of thousands of Christian workers very effectively—came to being under his direction.

Yet there's something else D. L. Moody began, about which at the end of his life he said, "God has blessed this, but it is the blessing of Ishmael." His intention was very sincere. His motives were right.

He truly wanted to begin a ministry that would help young men develop their bodies physically, as well as their souls spiritually. But in putting this into play, he was talked into certain compromises—namely that this particular ministry would be overseen by prominent members of the community. Thus, the YMCA was born—blessed to a certain extent, but far from what it could have been.

Ishmael is also blessed, but he will prove to be a perpetual problem to the people of Israel, the descendants of Isaac.

Genesis 21:14 (a)
And Abraham rose up early in the morning, and took bread, and a bottle of water, and gave it unto Hagar, putting it on her shoulder, and the child, and sent her away . . .

At first this story troubled me greatly. At this point, Abraham was a very wealthy man. In addition to the herds too numerous to share land with Lot's, Abraham had been given riches from both Pharaoh and Abimelech. Why, then, wouldn't he have sent Hagar and Ishmael away with a huge caravan of supplies?

But upon further study, his actions make perfect sense for a man of faith.

Genesis 21:14 (b)
. . . and she departed, and wandered in the wilderness of Beer-sheba.

The biblical use of the word "wilderness" refers to the desert, a dry, barren region—whereas the biblical use of the word "desert" refers to a wilderness, a refreshing, wooded area. This is why Jesus was tempted in the wilderness, yet retreated with His disciples to the desert (Mark 6:31).

For topical study of Genesis 21:14 entitled "Make No Provision for the Flesh," turn to page 93.

Genesis 21:15
And the water was spent in the bottle, and she cast the child under one of the shrubs.

No doubt Ishmael was beginning to experience dehydration, so Hagar put him under a shrub in an effort to shade him from the sun.

Genesis 21:16, 17 (a)
And she went, and sat her down over against him a good way off, as it were a bowshot: for she said, Let me not see the death of the child. And she sat over against him, and lift up her voice, and wept. And God heard the voice of the lad; and the angel of God . . .

Who is the angel of God, or the angel of the Lord? It's Jesus.

Genesis 21:17 (b)
. . . called to Hagar out of heaven, and said unto her, What aileth thee, Hagar? fear not; for God hath heard the voice of the lad where he is.

"What's wrong, Hagar?" asked Jesus—just as centuries later He would say to His disciples, "Why are ye fearful, O ye of little faith?" (Matthew 8:26). Referring to the Sea of Galilee, "Let us go over to the other side," He had said (Matthew 8:18). He hadn't said, "Let us go under out in the middle," or, "Let us go down in an attempt." No, Jesus had given the Word to His disciples that day that they would indeed make it to the other side. Jesus had already told Hagar Ishmael would be blessed (Genesis 16). Thus, the Lord here is lovingly rebuking Hagar. "Didn't I give you My Word, Hagar? Have you already forgotten?"

What Word has God given us? He's told us all things work together for good (Romans 8:28), that He will never leave us nor forsake us (Matthew 28:20), that He will give us the desires of our heart (Psalm 37:4). He's told us that our sins are forgiven (1 John 1:9), that His love for us is everlasting (Jeremiah 31:3), that we are more than conquerors (Romans 8:37). What aileth *us?*

Genesis 21:18–21
Arise, lift up the lad, and hold him in thine hand; for I will make him a great nation. And God opened her eyes, and she saw a well of water; and she went, and filled the bottle with water, and gave the lad drink. And God was with the lad; and he grew, and dwelt in the wilderness, and became an archer. And he dwelt in the wilderness of Paran: and his mother took him a wife out of the land of Egypt.

I find it more than coincidental that in the story of Ishmael, we see the entire plan of God for Israel . . .

For topical study of Genesis 21:14–21 entitled "God's Faithfulness to the Jew . . . And to You," turn to page 96.

Genesis 21:22, 23
And it came to pass at that time, that Abimelech and Phichol the chief captain of his host spake unto Abraham, saying, God is with thee in all that thou doest: Now therefore swear unto me here by God that thou wilt not deal falsely with me, nor with my son, nor with my son's son: but according to the kindness that I have done unto thee, thou shalt do unto me, and to the land wherein thou hast sojourned.

This is a very ordinary event—a contractual dispute in the everyday life of this giant of the faith. No wonder Abimelech asked Abraham not to deal falsely with him. This is the same Abimelech who, years previously having been told Sarah was Abraham's sister, took her into his harem until God spoke to him of her true identity.

Genesis 21:24
And Abraham said, I will swear.

Abraham shows a tremendous amount of humility in that he never defends himself. In this regard, I am reminded of a journal entry I made recently during an Alaskan cruise on which I was speaking . . .

So many blessings, so many thoughts cruising the waters of the inland passage of Alaska and seeing the mountains tower above us, the stars shining over us, the unseen but teeming life beneath us, I am deeply impacted. Not only by His majesty, or creativity, or power and glory but especially and surprisingly by His humility, for this majestic, creative-beyond-genius Being tells us that He stretches the heavens out like a curtain, He sits upon the circle of the earth (Isaiah), He measures the heavens with the span of His hand (Isaiah)—yet He did not give us the take-your-breath-away data, facts and figures of the size of other stars, the range of our galaxy, the puniness of our planet in comparison to the billions and trillions of other objects. He simply allows the vastness of space, the mysteries beneath the sea, the power of the atom that He holds together (Colossians) to slowly be discovered. As man's technology and ability increases, he only discovers more wonder. And I wonder at His humility. I would have laid it all out, let it be known what I have done, how great I am with facts and figures and data. But God allowed Himself to be discovered, uncovered, in due season. And that season will fill all eternity. Real power, true genius, creative ingenuity, spiritual authority if indeed real, can wait, indeed should wait to be discovered slowly, quietly. For only what is real can dare to wait. And only what is humble will ultimately be exalted.

God is the Epitome of humility. Only true greatness can be humble. And that's what Abraham is showing us as well. He doesn't try to prove he's a great guy. He just goes about his work, and, after years of observation, Abimelech says, "I can see that God is with you."

Genesis 21:25
And Abraham reproved Abimelech because of a well of water, which Abimelech's servants had violently taken away.

If someone said to me, "I can see you're blessed," I would be quiet about any dispute we may have. Not Abraham. He showed humility, but he also showed honesty.

Genesis 21:26
And Abimelech said, I wot not who hath done this thing: neither didst thou tell me, neither yet heard I of it, but to day.

Thirdly, Abraham shows charity in taking what Abimelech said at face value.

Genesis 21:27
And Abraham took sheep and oxen, and gave them unto Abimelech; and both of them made a covenant.

Fourthly, Abraham shows wisdom in that he makes a covenant with Abimelech to ensure they don't have this problem in the future.

Genesis 21:28–32
And Abraham set seven ewe lambs of the flock by themselves. And Abimelech said unto Abraham, What mean these seven ewe lambs which thou hast set by themselves? And he said, For these seven ewe lambs shalt thou take of my hand, that they may be a witness unto me, that I have digged this well. Wherefore he called that place Beer-sheba; because there they sware both of them. Thus they made a covenant at Beer-sheba: then Abimelech rose up, and Phichol the chief captain of his host, and they returned into the land of the Philistines.

Finally, Abraham shows generosity in giving Abimelech seven lambs, which would be a living reminder of the agreement they made.

Humility, honesty, charity, wisdom, and generosity—Abraham provides a wonderful model of maturity.

Genesis 21:33, 34
And Abraham planted a grove in Beer-sheba, and called there on the name of the LORD, the

everlasting God. And Abraham sojourned in the Philistines' land many days.

As your margin notes may indicate, Abraham planted a tamarisk tree, and in so doing, he finds a creative, spontaneous, innovative way of worshiping.

Three-year-old Benny came out of his room holding a picture attached to a helium balloon.

"What's that, Benny?" I asked.

"It's a picture of me and Jesus," he said, as he went in the backyard and watched as the balloon soared heavenward.

Such is innovative, creative worship from the heart of one who loves God.

When you love God, it's not enough just to sing the same songs as everyone else. It's not enough to go through the motions during worship sessions.

- A lover of God finds a way to plant a tree and say, "Lord, this is for You."
- A lover of God finds a way to break the alabaster box and say, "This is my dowry, and I'm giving it to You," (see Mark 14).
- A lover of God finds a way to dance in his undergarments before the Lord (2 Samuel 6:14).

A lover of God finds ways of fresh, personal, intimate expressions others may never see. As a result, Abraham discovered the "everlasting God"—a new aspect of God's nature—for fresh revelation only follows true worship.

MAKE NO PROVISION FOR THE FLESH

A Topical Study of GENESIS 21:14

I'm in Abraham's sandals—wealthy like he is—and I must send my son to the desert. What do I do? I call for the mules and donkeys and load them down with water bottles, McDonald's milkshakes, and Gatorade. I call for the camels and load them with tents and umbrellas and ice chests. I do whatever I can to ensure my son's safety. But that's not what Abraham did. All he gave his son was a single water bottle, a bit of bread and a "See ya later."

This initially seemed so odd to me. Why would a dad who had lots of money send his son away into a deathly region with just a little bit of bread and water?

I suggest three reasons . . .

An Indication of His Faith

God made a promise to Abraham and reiterated it several times that Ishmael would become a mighty nation. And here, evidently because he believed God would do what He promised, Abraham wisely decided not to give God a hand in fulfilling what He had promised. After all, that's how Ishmael was conceived in the first place.

Consequently, Abraham shows incredible peace. He gives Ishmael and Hagar a bit of water, a bit of bread, so saying, "I trust the Lord is going to do what He said—not because of my provision, but because of His promise."

Mom and Dad, let this be a comfort to you today. The promises of God toward my children are the same as toward yours: Train up a child in the way he should go and when he is old he will not depart from it (Proverbs 22:6). No matter what desert your child is in, no matter in what dry region he finds himself, even when he is old he won't depart from the way he's been trained.

"For I know whom I have believed," said Paul, "and am persuaded that He is able to keep that which I've committed unto Him" (2 Timothy 1:12). Have you committed your kids to the Lord? God is able to keep them. This doesn't mean He's merely capable. It means He's *committed* to keeping that which has been entrusted to Him.

Mom, you may be heartbroken. Dad, you may be discouraged. It may seem your kids aren't going the right way. But God isn't through with them, for He who has begun a good work in them will be faithful to complete it (Philippians 1:6).

I hate it when I panic. I get worried. I get uptight. And I run around like a chicken with my head cut off, trying to make something happen. Faith is the opposite of panic. I love it when I'm not panicking, when I'm walking in faith. When I walk in faith, I'm not irritated, anxious, or upset. There's a peace deep within me, and a serenity that overflows from me. I like it when I walk in faith like Abraham.

Abraham said, "I've heard Your voice, Father. Ishmael, Hagar, here's some water and some bread. God be with you." He is maturing, this mighty man of God. He is growing, this giant of faith. He'll miss Ishmael—but he trusts God completely, knowing God will do exactly what He said He would.

An Illustration of Our Flesh

Secondly, looking at this account from an entirely different angle, the story before us is not only an indication of Abraham's faith, but also an illustration of our flesh.

How do I know this?

Paul calls the story of Ishmael and Hagar an allegory (Galatians 4:22–29) in which Ishmael is a type of the flesh, and Isaac a type of the Spirit. You see, the mockery that took place in this story from Ishmael towards Isaac happens in each of our hearts constantly.

> *For the flesh lusteth against the Spirit, and the Spirit against the flesh: and these are contrary the one to the other: so that ye cannot do the things that ye would.* Galatians 5:17

There's a constant battle going on, and here's the question: Who are we going to allow to win? The Bible says the solution is to cast out Ishmael, the flesh.

> *For to be carnally minded is death; but to be spiritually minded is life and peace.* Romans 8:6

If I choose to be carnally minded and allow the stuff of the flesh to have dominion over me, it will lead to death, depression, discouragement, despair, and defeat. If, on the other hand, I say, "Ishmael, you're out of here," and choose to walk in the Spirit, I will have life and peace.

How do we cast Ishmael out?

By doing what Abraham did: by giving him no provision.

Abraham didn't give Ishmael a Visa card and a Ford Explorer. He gave him nothing more than prisoner's rations—a little bread and water. That is why Paul emphatically tells us to "make no provision for the flesh" (Romans 13:14).

I don't care if everyone else is going to the dance. If you know flesh is there, you stay away. I don't care if everyone else is going to see the show. If you know flesh is on the screen, you make no provision.

> *Be not deceived; God is not mocked: for whatsoever a man soweth, that shall he also reap. For he that soweth to his flesh shall of the flesh reap corruption; but he that soweth to the Spirit shall of the Spirit reap life everlasting.*
>
> Galatians 6:7, 8

Every fleshly thing I see or hear is a seed planted in the soil of my soul, and will come up eventually. Likewise, every Godly thing I take in will also come to fruition. Perhaps the best illustration of this is one I shared recently with a group of junior-highers . . .

> It's as if there are two dogs inside of you: one black, one white. The white dog is life, the black dog, death. And at any given point, you're feeding one of the dogs through the type of people with whom you associate, through what you choose to listen to, watch, and take in. If you feed the black dog, he gets bigger and stronger. He bares his fangs and starts ripping on the white dog, as the white dog gets smaller and smaller. Once the black dog decimates the white dog, he turns on you and begins to sink his jaws into your innermost being—leaving you wondering why you're so down, defeated, depressed, and discontent. On the other hand, if you feed the white dog—the Spirit—by doing what's right in God's sight, the white dog grows bigger and stronger, as the black dog grows punier and weaker until he's no bigger than a Chihuahua. At any given moment, you'll feed one of the two dogs. Which will it be?

"Who is that?" Samuel asked.

"That's Agag, king of the Amalekites," Saul answered.

"God told you to destroy every Amalekite," said Samuel.

"Yeah, but I'm keeping him as a trophy," Saul said. "He's no problem. I've got him in chains" (see 1 Samuel 15).

Twenty three years pass. Saul is doing battle with the Philistines on Mt. Gilboa. He takes a shot, falls to the ground, and when he comes to, he's looking into the face of a young man with sword in hand.

"Who are you?" Saul asks.

"I am an Amalekite," answered the young man before killing Saul (2 Samuel 1).

Thus Saul was done in by what he himself was supposed to kill.

So, if you say, "I know God told me to deal with this thing I've got tucked away in the garage or locked in the cabinet, but it's not that big a deal; I've got it under control"—watch out. It's Agag—and it will eventually get you. If you provide for your flesh, your flesh will rise up and give you great pain and difficulty. But if you finally come to the place where you say, "Ishmael's got to go *today*," God will give you the energy, the will, the power, the strength to send him on his way.

Illumination about My Failure

The story of Hagar provides illumination about my failure, for in the Galatians 4 passage, Paul says not only is Ishmael a type of the flesh and Isaac a type of the Spirit, but Hagar is a type of the Law and Sarah a type of the new covenant. Hagar represents Mt. Sinai, where the Law was given. Sarah represents the heavenly Mt. Zion, from whence grace flows.

My natural tendency is to say, "The best way to deal with the flesh is to lay down the law. I'm going to set up rules and regulations to keep my flesh in check." But whenever I do, I am bound to fail badly because, although the rules and regulations might be wonderful, I cannot keep them. Oh, for a while I might be able to, during which time I'll say, "What's wrong with you? Why is your Ishmael running about wildly? Why can't you deal with the flesh like I have?"

But eventually I will fall under the weight of my own rules, and I will fail miserably. Then I'll say, "I was doing so well for three days, or three months, or three years—but then I blew it. So why even go to Bible study, why even pray? I'm a failure. The Lord will never use me."

This is why the law doesn't work. It makes you either a self-righteous prude or a self-condemned dude. It causes us to say either, "What's wrong with you?" or, "What's wrong with me?"

So what's the answer? Do what Abraham did. Send Hagar away, and embrace Sarah. Don't put yourself or others under regulations or rules. Rather hold fast to the new covenant, and walk in grace.

GOD'S FAITHFULNESS TO THE JEW . . . AND TO YOU

A Topical Study of GENESIS 21:14–21

Although Ishmael is the father of the Arab genetically, he could be considered a type of Israel spiritually, for it is Israel who is under the Law, of which Hagar is a picture (Galatians 4:25). In this light, look with me at the vignette before us, and see how it encapsulates the historic and prophetic plan of God for His people, Israel.

Sent Away Wandering

> *And Abraham rose up early in the morning, and took bread, and a bottle of water, and gave it unto Hagar, putting it on her shoulder, and the child, and sent her away: and she departed, and wandered in the wilderness of Beer-sheba.*
>
> Genesis 21:14

Because Ishmael mocked Isaac, he was sent away. This is precisely what happened to Israel. In A.D. 32, in accordance with Zechariah's prophecy (9:9), Jesus presented Himself to the people of Israel when He rode into Jerusalem on the back of a donkey. But they mocked Him when they shook their collective fist at Him, saying, "Away with Him. Crucify Him."

Aware of what the consequence of this would be, Jesus cried, "O, Jerusalem, Jerusalem. I would gather you under My wings as a mother hen gathers her chicks, but you would not, therefore your house shall be left unto desolation. Your nation will be destroyed" (see Matthew 23:37, 38).

Indeed, approximately thirty-eight years after Israel declared, "We will not have this Man rule over us," Roman General Titus destroyed the city of Jerusalem and burned the temple, causing the Jewish people to flee for their lives. Those who stayed tried to launch a revolt against the Roman authorities which so incensed Emperor Hadrian that he ordered them either to be exterminated in the land of Israel or dispersed throughout the world. So it was that the Jews were sent into every continent of the world save Antarctica.

> *If thou wilt not observe to do all the words of this law that are written in this book, that thou mayest fear this glorious and fearful name, THE LORD THY GOD; And the LORD shall scatter thee among all people, from the one end of the earth even unto the other; and there thou shalt serve other gods, which neither thou nor thy fathers have known, even wood and stone. And among these nations shalt thou find no ease, neither shall the sole of thy foot have rest: but the LORD shall give thee there a trembling heart, and failing of eyes, and sorrow of mind: And thy life shall hang in doubt before thee; and thou shalt fear day and night, and shalt have none assurance of thy life:*
>
> Deuteronomy 28:58, 64–66

"If you reject Me," the Lord told His people, "you'll be scattered into every nation, but you'll find no comfort. You'll be hunted and persecuted everywhere you go." And as one studies history, one sees that is exactly what happened—for every culture the Jews entered attempted to annihilate them. But here's the irony: They were also blessed incredibly. Intellectually, academically, financially, wherever the Jews went, they left their mark. Though they were persecuted, yet they prospered.

One rabbi said it best when, on the eve of the Spanish Inquisition, he stood before King Ferdinand and declared, "You cannot curse us because we are blessed; and you cannot bless us because we are cursed."

Miraculously, the Jews kept their identity—an occurrence unique to the Jewish nation, as no other people in history has ever been robbed of their homeland and survived longer than two generations. The Jews are a people who have been scattered yet preserved, cursed yet blessed, blessed yet cursed. Why? Because God said, "When you reject Me, this will happen." We see Ishmael sent away and wandering. Such is the story of the Jews.

Water Spent

> *And the water was spent in the bottle, and she cast the child under one of the shrubs.*
> Genesis 21:15

After Hagar was sent away, the water she was given dried up very quickly. Scripturally, water is a type of two things: the Spirit (John 7:37), and the Word (John 4). When the Jews rejected Jesus, they became spiritually dry. As a whole, the Jewish people are fascinated by, and committed to the Old Testament. Rabbis today have lots of questions and wonderful interaction, but no conclusions and no answers. An ex-rabbi named Paul who was converted from Judaism to Jesus explained it this way . . .

> *But their minds were blinded: for until this day remaineth the same vail untaken away in the reading of the old testament; which vail is done away in Christ.*
> 2 Corinthians 3:14

Without Christ, the eyes of the Jew are blinded because the Spirit has departed, leaving the Scriptures dry.

Weeping

> . . . *And she sat over against him, and lift up her voice, and wept.*
> Genesis 21:16 (b)

In the minor key foundational to the music of the Jew, one can hear the weeping of Hagar to this day. Although the temple was filled with the sounds of trumpets and cymbals, lyres, horns, and harps, in Jewish Orthodox services today you will hear a cantor, but no musical instruments because when the temple was destroyed in A.D. 70, Orthodox Jews said, "We must never play instruments again until we have a temple."

The only part of Solomon's temple that remains today is actually a retaining wall known as the Wailing Wall. Over what do the Jews wail? The loss of their temple, for they know that without the shedding of blood there is no forgiveness of sin (Hebrews 9:22). According to the Law, the only place acceptable for sacrificial atonement being the temple, the Jews cannot be ceremonially forgiven. Thus, like Hagar, the weeping of the Jew continues.

Rise

Arise, lift up the lad . . . Genesis 21:18 (a)

Responding to her cry, God told Hagar to arise. There is coming a day when God will say to the Jew, "Rise up." When will this be? "Come and let us return unto the Lord," writes Hosea, "for he hath torn, and he will heal us; he hath smitten, and he will bind us up. After two days will he revive us: in the third day he will raise us up, and we shall live in his sight" (6:1, 2).

According to 2 Peter 3:8, in God's economy, a day is as a thousand years, a thousand years as a day. In accordance with Hosea's prophecy, for 2,000 years, the Jewish people had indeed been torn. Now they're home again in Israel. In the third day, they'll see the light and be revived. When will this happen? It's been "two days" thus far—2,000 years. We come to the "third day" at the turn of the century in the year 2000. Am I saying the Rapture should have happened in 2000? No. No one knows the day or the hour. But this we do know: We are in the "third day." The Lord's coming is near.

Opened Eyes

And God opened her eyes, and she saw a well of water . . . Genesis 21:19 (a)

Hagar didn't see the water that was right before her until God opened her eyes. The same is true of Israel . . .

For I would not, brethren, that ye should be ignorant of this mystery, lest ye should be wise in your own conceits; that blindness in part is happened to Israel, until the fulness of the Gentiles be come in. Romans 11:25

A day is coming indeed when Israel's eyes shall be opened—when she, like Hagar will see the well that was before her all along . . .

In that day there shall be a fountain opened to the house of David and to the inhabitants of Jerusalem for sin and for uncleanness. Zechariah 13:1

Became an Archer

And God was with the lad; and he grew, and dwelt in the wilderness, and became an archer. Genesis 21:20

In biblical times, leaders were archers (1 Samuel 20). When the Lord comes to rule and reign in His millennial kingdom, He will do so from the city of Jerusalem. The Jews will be His archers—His leaders. As the church, we will rule and reign with Christ. We're spiritual Israel. But physical Israel will provide His base of operations humanly speaking.

Wilderness of Paran

And he dwelt in the wilderness of Paran . . . Genesis 21:21 (a)

The word "wilderness" means "desert." *Paran* means either "beauty" or "glory." Ishmael dwelt in the desert of beauty or glory. We see this happening today, for, as Isaiah prophesied, the Jews have made a desert "blossom like a rose" (35:1)—so much so that Israel has become the number one exporter of flowers and the third largest exporter of fresh fruits in the world today. But this is only a sneak preview of coming attractions, for in the millennial kingdom, Israel will be as glorious as the Garden of Eden (Ezekiel 36).

Wife of Egypt

. . . and his mother took him a wife out of the land of Egypt.
Genesis 21:21 (b)

Just as Ishmael married an Egyptian woman, so Israel will be joined with Egypt. "How can this be?" you ask. "The Jews and the Egyptians are perpetual enemies." Truly, there has been no people more difficult for Israel throughout history than the Egyptians—except for the people of Assyria: present day Iraq, Iran, and Syria.

In that day shall there be a highway out of Egypt to Assyria, and the Assyrian shall come into Egypt, and the Egyptian into Assyria, and the Egyptians shall serve with the Assyrians. In that day shall Israel be the third with Egypt and with Assyria, even a blessing in the midst of the land: Whom the LORD of hosts shall bless, saying, Blessed be Egypt my people, and Assyria the work of my hands, and Israel mine inheritance. Isaiah 19:23–25

All we may see is Saddam Hussein shouting, "Death to the great white Satan" and hanging our leaders in effigy. God, however, views the situation entirely differently, for He looks down the tunnel of time and sees the Egyptian and the Assyrian (the Syrian, Iraqi, and Iranian) walking hand in hand to Israel—not for warfare, but for worship. What a day it will be when centuries of enmity will be replaced with unity.

So it is that through Ishmael we see the plan of God for Israel. And in God's plan for Israel redemptively, we glimpse His heart for us personally . . .

Who shall separate us from the love of Christ? shall tribulation, or distress, or persecution, or famine, or nakedness, or peril, or sword? As it is written, For thy sake we are killed all the day long; we are accounted as sheep for the slaughter. Nay, in all these things we are more than conquerors through him that loved us. For I am persuaded, that neither death, nor life, nor angels, nor principalities, nor powers, nor things present, nor things to come, Nor height, nor depth, nor any other creature, shall be able to separate us from the love of God, which is in Christ Jesus our Lord. Romans 8:35–39

After stating that nothing can separate us from God's love, Paul launches in to Romans 9—11, three chapters which deal with God's faithfulness to the Jewish people.

Thus, Paul's point is clear: We know that nothing shall separate us from God's love for us because we see nothing separated the Jews from His love for them. Even if you've been wandering, stumbling staggering; even if you've been faithless, God is faithful still (2 Timothy 2:13). That's the message of Ishmael's story.

I've walked with the Lord for over forty years, and I tell you, God is faithful. No matter what you go through, God is faithful even when we are faithless. But don't take my word for it. Look at Israel. See both in her history and in her future, God's amazing grace and faithfulness. God's not through with Israel, gang—neither is He through with you.

22

On my desk sits a picture of Tammy taken in Israel at the Garden of Gethsemane. In it, she is sitting on a wall, lifting her hands to the Lord, with her eyes closed in worship. Beside her is an open Bible, and around her neck is her ever-present camera. I like this picture because, to me, it captures the essence of my wife. And because I love her, even though I see this picture every time I'm at my desk, I never tire of it.

I find the same to be true of the chapter before us, for it is a picture of Jesus Christ. And Jesus is One I never grow weary of looking at or looking on. As you will see, the picture in our text is actually a Polaroid—one that develops and becomes more clearly focused as we go along . . .

Genesis 22:1, 2 (a)
And it came to pass after these things, that God did tempt Abraham, and said unto him, Abraham: and he said, Behold, here I am. And he said, Take now thy son, thine only son Isaac . . .

Because God does not remember our sin (Hebrews 10:17), He doesn't even acknowledge Ishmael—the fruit of Abraham's impatience.

Genesis 22:2 (b)
. . . whom thou lovest . . .

Isaac is a picture, a type of Christ . . .

- Conceived miraculously when a heretofore-barren Sarah was ninety years old, Isaac was a miracle baby.
- Born of a virgin, Jesus was a miracle Baby.
- Isaac's birth was promised long before he showed up—twenty years before he was born.
- Jesus' birth was promised clear back in Genesis 3:15—approximately 4,000 years before His birth in Bethlehem.
- Abraham and Sarah were told what to name their son.
- Mary and Joseph were told what to name their Son.
- To his father, Isaac was obedient to the point of death.
- To His Father, Jesus was obedient to death.

The parallels are many. Isaac and Jesus are linked together. Isaac is the type; Jesus the fulfillment.

Genesis 22:2 (c)
. . . and get thee into the land of Moriah . . .

Moriah literally means "Foreseen of Jehovah." Therefore, it is as if God is saying, "Take your son, your only son, where you will provide a sneak preview of coming attractions." You see, God would sacrifice His only Son on the same spot to which He called Abraham.

Genesis 22:2 (d)
. . . and offer him there for a burnt offering upon one of the mountains which I will tell thee of.

The Hebrew word translated "offer" is *alaw,* which means "to lift up." Thus, God tells Abraham to lift Isaac up upon Mt. Moriah. "If I be lifted up, I will draw all men to Myself," declared Jesus. "And this spake He signifying His death" (John 12:32, 33), as He was lifted up on Calvary's Cross.

Genesis 22:3 (a)
And Abraham rose up early in the morning . . .

This is incredible to me. Here Abraham is told to offer his son as a sacrifice to the Lord—and rather than hesitate, he rises early to obey.

Genesis 22:3 (b)
. . . and saddled his ass, and took two of his young men with him, and Isaac his son . . .

Jesus Christ, the fulfillment of this picture, would also travel to the same mountain with two men. Our Lord would be crucified between two thieves—which I find poetically correct, for in my opinion, He is the greatest thief in human history, stealing our hearts through His death on our behalf.

Genesis 22:3 (c)
. . . and clave the wood for the burnt offering, and rose up, and went unto the place of which God had told him.

Abraham and Isaac leave for Mt. Moriah, the place foreseen of the Lord. Mt. Moriah is a ridge that runs from north to south through the city of Jerusalem, peaking right outside of the north wall of the city at a place called Calvary.

***For topical study of Genesis 22:3 entitled "The Moriah Moment," turn to page* 104.**

Genesis 22:4
Then on the third day Abraham lifted up his eyes, and saw the place afar off.

Isaac and Abraham walked side by side for three days on their way to Moriah—just as Jesus and the Father walked together for three years during Jesus' public ministry that would climax at His death on Calvary.

Genesis 22:5 (a)
And Abraham said unto his young men, Abide ye here with the ass; and I and the lad will go yonder and worship . . .

The Hebrew word translated "lad" could speak of a man in his thirties—the age Jesus was when He climbed Mt. Calvary.

Genesis 22:5 (b)
. . . and come again to you.

"This is as far as you can go," said Abraham to the young men accompanying him. "But we will come back to you." In other words, Abraham knew Isaac would return with him.

> By faith Abraham, when he was tried, offered up Isaac: and he that had received the promises offered up his only begotten son, Of whom it was said, That in Isaac shall thy seed be called: Accounting that God was able to raise him up, even from the dead; from whence also he received him in a figure. Hebrews 11:17–19

Even though it had never happened before, Abraham believed God would resurrect Isaac.

Genesis 22:6 (a)
And Abraham took the wood of the burnt offering, and laid it upon Isaac his son . . .

Isaac carried the wood upon which he would be laid, just as Jesus carried the wooden cross upon which He would be nailed.

> For unto us a child is born, unto us a son is given: and the government shall be upon his shoulder: and his name shall be called Wonderful, Counseller, The mighty God, The everlasting Father, The Prince of Peace. Isaiah 9:6

What was on the shoulder of the Wonderful Counselor, the Mighty God, the Everlasting Father, the Prince of Peace? The Cross. That's why He has the right to rule over me. That's why He has the right to reign over you. He alone died in our place.

Genesis 22:6 (b)
. . . and he took the fire in his hand . . .

Isaac carried the wood, but Abraham carried the fire. Why? The fire speaks of the holy, righteous indignation that the Father would hurl on His Son as He who knew no sin became sin on our behalf (2 Corinthians 5:21).

As a result, God—who is too pure to look on sin—would turn His back upon His Son. This is what terrified Jesus, for He knew that for the first time in all eternity, He and His Father would be out of fellowship, signified by the darkness that blanketed the earth for three hours the day Jesus died.

We can be terrified by a lot of things—cancer, bankruptcy, broken relationships, death. But those things didn't terrify our Lord. The one and only thing that terrified Him was being out of touch with His Father. Oh, that this may be my heart as well.

Genesis 22:6 (c)
. . . and a knife . . .

The knife Abraham carried speaks of the spear that would pierce Jesus' side as He hung on the Cross in our place.

Genesis 22:6 (d)
. . . and they went both of them together.

Abraham and Isaac traveled together. So, too, the Father and Son travel together. Contrary to what many imagine, it wasn't as though Jesus loved us and died for us in order to appease His angry Father. No, salvation was the Father's heart and plan from before the foundation of the world (Ephesians 1:3, 4).

Genesis 22:7, 8 (a)
And Isaac spake unto Abraham his father, and said, My father: and he said, Here am I, my son. And he said, Behold the fire and the wood: but where is the lamb for a burnt offering? And Abraham said, My son, God will provide himself a lamb for a burnt offering . . .

"God will provide himself a lamb," Abraham told Isaac—not, "God will provide *for* Himself a lamb"—but, "God will provide *Himself* a lamb. He will *be* the Lamb."

Genesis 22:8 (b), 9
. . . so they went both of them together. And they came to the place which God had told him of; and Abraham built an altar there, and laid the wood in order, and bound Isaac his son, and laid him on the altar upon the wood.

As He prayed in the Garden the night before He was to be crucified, two hundred Roman soldiers led by Judas Iscariot, came to arrest Jesus.

"Whom seek ye?" He asked.

"Jesus of Nazareth," they answered.

"I AM," Jesus declared, and—boom—the entire regiment fell down backwards (John 18:6).

After regaining their balance, the soldiers bound Jesus with ropes and led Him away. But it certainly wasn't ropes which bound this One who flattened the Roman army with the simplest of statements. It was submission to His Father and love for His brethren that bound Him.

Genesis 22:10, 11 (a)
And Abraham stretched forth his hand, and took the knife to slay his son. And the angel of the Lord . . .

Who is the angel of the Lord? It's Jesus Himself. This means Jesus was in heaven watching this drama unfold, knowing it depicted what He would go through centuries later.

Genesis 22:11 (b), 12
. . . called unto him out of heaven, and said, Abraham, Abraham: and he said, Here am I. And he said, Lay not thine hand upon the lad, neither do thou any thing unto him: for now I know that thou fearest God, seeing thou hast not withheld thy son, thine only son from me.

"Stop, Abraham," God said. "You've clearly demonstrated to yourself and to all who will read your story that you love Me."

Genesis 22:13
And Abraham lifted up his eyes, and looked, and behold behind him a ram caught in a thicket by his horns: and Abraham went and took the ram, and offered him up for a burnt offering in the stead of his son.

That Abraham saw a ram instead of a lamb caught in the thicket speaks of the fact that this was not the fulfillment of God's promise to provide Himself a lamb (v. 7), for that promise would not be fulfilled until Jesus came as the Lamb of God to take away the sin of the world (John 1:29).

Genesis 22:14
And Abraham called the name of that place Jehovah-jireh: as it is said to this day, In the mount of the Lord it shall be seen.

As your margin might indicate, *Jehovah-jireh* means "The Lord will provide" or "The Lord will see." Both are true. God provided a ram in place of Isaac. Whatever you want to see about God's provision for you will always be seen on Mt. Moriah. When you doubt God's love for you, provision for you, care for you—go to Mt. Moriah, to Calvary, and lift up your eyes. You will be reminded that God indeed saw your need—and provided perfectly.

Genesis 22:15–18
And the angel of the LORD called unto Abraham out of heaven the second time, And said, By myself have I sworn, saith the LORD, for because thou hast done this thing, and hast not withheld thy son, thine only son: That in blessing I will bless thee, and in multiplying I will multiply thy seed as the stars of the heaven, and as the sand which is upon the sea shore; and thy seed shall possess the gate of his enemies; And in thy seed shall all the nations of the earth be blessed; because thou hast obeyed my voice.

Because Abraham obeyed, the Lord would make of him a great nation. And because Jesus was obedient to death, He became the first of many who would follow (1 Corinthians 15:20–23). In other words, we have been blessed because He obeyed.

Genesis 22:19
So Abraham returned unto his young men, and they rose up and went together to Beer-sheba; and Abraham dwelt at Beer-sheba.

The two men and Abraham travel back to Beersheba together without Isaac. It must be this way, for it was on the third day that Isaac was set free—just as on the third day after He died, Jesus rose again.

Genesis 22:20–24
And it came to pass after these things, that it was told Abraham, saying, Behold, Milcah, she hath also born children unto thy brother Nahor; Huz his firstborn, and Buz his brother, and Kemuel the father of Aram, And Chesed, and Hazo, and Pildash, and Jidlaph, and Bethuel. And Bethuel begat Rebekah: these eight Milcah did bear to Nahor, Abraham's brother. And his concubine, whose name was Reumah, she bare also Tebah, and Gaham, and Thahash, and Maachah.

At first reading, I thought this genealogy to be a somewhat odd ending to the glorious story of crucifixion and resurrection. But upon further consideration, this ending makes perfect sense, for in this passage, we are introduced to Rebekah, the bride of Isaac. After a spear was thrust into the side of our Greater than Isaac as He hung on the Cross, blood and water—the fluids of birthing—gushed forth.

What was birthed from His side?

Look again at the first Adam, and you'll see that from his side was taken a rib, from his side came Eve, from his side came a bride. Likewise, from the side of the Last Adam, Jesus Christ, came a Bride—the church, you and me.

And the story continues . . .

THE MORIAH MOMENT

A Topical Study of GENESIS 22:3

It was at 11:30 A.M., May 29th, 1953 that the BBC declared, "No man has, or ever will, climbed higher," as Sir Edmund Hillary's successful ascent of Mt. Everest was announced to the world. While the BBC's statement that May morning was true geographically, I suggest the ascent of the mountain in the passage before us was an infinitely higher climb.

Sitting only a couple hundred feet above the city of Jerusalem, Mt. Moriah is technically only a ridge. But when the Lord said to Abraham, "I want you to take your son, your only son to Mt. Moriah," father and son set off on the greatest mountain-climbing expedition in world history—second only to the one another Father and Son would later make to the very same destination centuries later.

Put yourself in Abraham's sandals and you will see this is an incredible journey, for God had asked him to sacrifice his son—his only son, the promised son, the one of whom he was so proud, the one in whom he saw such potential. How could Abraham have had such a heart to obey such a command? I couldn't have done it. But Abraham did.

How?

The reason Abraham could climb Mt. Moriah is the same reason Sir Edmund Hillary could climb Everest. You see, prior to Hillary's ascent up Mt. Everest, he spent five years acclimating his body to the altitude, five years allowing his lungs to expand to deal with the lack of oxygen he would encounter at that height, five years to get in shape, five years to make preparations and gather gear.

So, too, Abraham would climb his infinitely higher mountain because, like Hillary's team, there had been great preparation.

"It came to pass after these things God did tempt, or test, Abraham" (22:1) After what things? Fifty-seven years of things.

- Leaving his home in Ur for a land God would show him was Step #1 in training for the Moriah moment.
- Saying goodbye to his nephew as Lot headed for Sodom was Step #2.
- Refusing the spoils of battle offered him by the king of Sodom was Step #3.
- Obeying God's command to send his son Ishmael into the desert was Step #4.

Nothing in Scripture is accidental, nor incidental. Thus, when we read, "It came to pass after these things that God did tempt Abraham," it means that the testing didn't take place until *after these things*—each of which prepared Abraham for this moment.

God will never, ever give you a test He has not thoroughly and painstakingly prepared you to navigate successfully. Never.

We look at Abraham's Moriah moment and think, *"I couldn't do that."* And we're right. We couldn't, because God hasn't prepared us for that—yet.

> *There hath no temptation taken you but such as is common to man: but God is faithful, who will not suffer you to be tempted above that ye are able; but will with the temptation also make a way to escape, that ye may be able to bear it.*
> 1 Corinthians 10:13

"Wait a minute," you say. "This deals with temptation—but Abraham wasn't being tempted. He was being tested."

The original language does not differentiate between a temptation and a test.

Therefore, when it says God did tempt Abraham, it means God did test Abraham. In reality, there is no difference between a temptation and a test, for in any situation that comes our way, Satan means it for a temptation to pull us down—but God intends it as a test to pull us through. Satan means to destroy us, to shake us up. God uses the same event to edify us and show us off.

> Upon its completion, Chrysler gives a new Jeep Grand Cherokee to *Car And Driver. Car And Driver,* in turn, takes the jeep out on the track and through its paces to shake it down, to see if it's going to rattle and fall apart.
>
> "We're not worried about it," Chrysler says. "We've already taken it through tests, and this one is not going to shake it apart. It's going to show it off."

Satan says, "Aha! I'm going to shake you up. I'm going to wipe you out."

But God says, "I'm allowing this because I want to show My strength through you and show you what I can do."

People say to me, "I don't know if I could deal with some of the things you've dealt with. If I lost a spouse or a child, I'm not sure I could pass such a test."

And to them I say, "I have had blessing in my life. I've walked with the Lord for over forty years—and all along the way He has always been faithful to prepare me for every test He's given me. Always."

"Even if God is faithful to prepare us through a series of events, each perhaps more difficult than the one before, what kind of life is that?" you may wonder. "Why would a person choose to walk such a path?"

Following are three reasons . . .

Completion

Paul tells us there are three great virtues: faith, hope, and love (1 Corinthians 13:13). Abraham's faith was developed first when God called him out of Ur . . .

> *By faith Abraham, when he was called to go out into a place which he should after receive for an inheritance, obeyed; and he went out, not knowing whither he went.*
>
> Hebrews 11:8

But God didn't stop there, for He proceeded to build hope into Abraham, as Abraham waited for his promised son . . .

> *Who against hope believed in hope, that he might become the father of many nations; according to that which was spoken, So shall thy seed be.*
>
> Romans 4:18

Nor did God stop there, for the greatest of these is love. Our text contains the first use of the word "love" in Scripture. It's as if God is saying, "Let the one you love go in your greater love for Me. Love is a chance for you take a quantum leap in growth."

If you say, "I don't want faith or hope or love. I want to be frazzled and afraid and frustrated"—don't go down the path that leads to Moriah, the path that leads you on a journey of trials and testing. But if you want to be entire and complete, lacking nothing, there's only one way . . .

> *My brethren, count it all joy when ye fall into divers temptations; Knowing this, that the trying of your faith worketh patience. But let patience have her perfect work, that ye may be perfect and entire, wanting nothing.*
>
> James 1:2–4

There's no other way to be complete than to say "Okay" to tests, temptations, and trials.

Contemplation

"I've prepared you, Abraham," God says, "to do something seemingly unbelievably difficult because I want to show people a picture of My Son. Even though it will be difficult for you, Abraham, your trial will touch multiplied millions of people throughout history."

Gang, your Christian life will change radically when it finally sinks in that God does not exist for you. Most believers go through a chunk of time believing God does indeed exist for them. "Bless my marriage. Bless my house. Bless my job. Give me abundant life. Give me joyful days," we pray—as if God exists for our pleasure.

> With mountains on either side of them, their backs to the Red Sea, and Pharaoh's army barreling down on them, Moses cried to the Lord.
>
> "Know this, Moses," He answered, "I will get Me honor upon Pharaoh and upon all his hosts. And the Egyptians shall know that I am the Lord." In other words, "Moses, this isn't about you or even the people with you. I've got work to do. I want to show the Egyptians who I am. To do that, I'm putting you in a tight spot, a tough place. But word will get back to the Egyptians that there is no God like the God of Israel" (Exodus 14:17, 18).

So, God says to us,

"I've got a big job to do—to let people around you know who I am. That means the doctor may say, "It's cancer." That means the business may go under. That means the relationship may not work out so people can see in your pain, in your difficulty, in your dilemma how I come through not to solve your problem, but to be with you in your problem. I will show Myself in the way that can most effectively reach the people I want to reach through and around your life. That may mean you go through real problems physically, or that things don't work out in the way you thought they would in your family. It may even mean death. But it's not about you. I love you deeply, but there's a bigger thing happening than simply your comfort."

Because we exist for God, gang—not the other way around—our part is to say, "However He wants to direct His drama on the stage of my life, be it a comedy or a tragedy, so be it."

Communion

Abraham was the friend of God (James 2:23). Why, then, would God ask Abraham to sacrifice his son? Friends don't let friends have Moriah moments—or do they?

Paul put it this way:

> *That I may know him, and the power of his resurrection, and the fellowship of his sufferings, being made conformable unto his death . . .* Philippians 3:10

Most of us attain to the power of Jesus' Resurrection, but know little about the fellowship of His sufferings. Yet the power of His Resurrection doesn't come without the fellowship of His sufferings.

I love to laugh with people. But the people I'm closest to are not the ones I've laughed with. They are the ones with whom I've shed tears. The same is true with you, for there's a closeness that occurs when people navigate deep waters together.

Thus, God the Father says to Abraham, "I want you to experience something of what I will do because when you do, you and I will be bonded together uniquely."

> There they were—walking around in the fiery furnace.
>
> "How many men did we throw in?" asked Nebuchadnezzar.
>
> "Three," said one of his aides.
>
> "Then how is it that I see four, and the fourth is like the Son of God?" asked Nebuchadnezzar.
>
> Shadrach, Meshach, and Abed-Nego could have walked out of that oven anytime they wanted and no one would have put them back in. I mean, if you are strolling around in a fire so hot it killed the guys who threw you in, and you decide to leave—no one would say, "Get back in there."
>
> Shadrach, Meshach, and Abed-Nego could have come out anytime they wanted. But they didn't come out until Nebuchadnezzar commanded them to because it was in the fire that they had fellowship with the Lord, a vision of the Lord, a closeness to the Lord they had never before known (Daniel 3).

You have found this to be true as well. It's when you're in the fire of affliction and adversity that you have real communion.

Don't fear, flock. Don't shy away from the Moriahs that loom over you. God will train you. And when you're there, He'll see you through. You'll come out saying, "I would have it no other way—entire and complete in communion so sweet."

It came to pass *after these things* that God did test Abraham. And Abraham rose up early in the morning because God had fully and faithfully prepared him.

23 In chapter 22, Abraham had been asked to offer his son. Here in chapter 23, I believe he faces an even harder test as he is asked to give up his wife. As the chapter before us unfolds, we see Abraham's grief in verses 1–6, Sarah's grave in verses 7–9 and Ephron's gift in verses 10–20.

Genesis 23:1
And Sarah was an hundred and seven and twenty years old: these were the years of the life of Sarah.

I find it interesting that, whereas over and over throughout Scripture, men's ages are given, Sarah is the only woman in the entire Bible whose age is revealed. Why is Sarah's age recorded? It's not to embarrass her or to expose her—but to exalt her, for Sarah was truly an incredible lady. After all, so beautiful was she that even in her eighties, Abimelech, king of Gerar, wanted her for his harem.

Genesis 23:2 (a)
And Sarah died in Kirjath-arba; the same is Hebron in the land of Canaan . . .

Sarah died in Hebron. This is neither accidental nor coincidental, for *Hebron* means "fellowship." Sarah was in fellowship with her husband. She and Abraham traveled together. Yes, they had some challenges, but they stayed by each other's side, and found themselves in fellowship the day Sarah died. Sarah was also in fellowship with her Lord—a godly woman of whom Peter says, "That's the kind of woman a Christian wife should be" (1 Peter 3:5, 6).

It's wonderful when a person moves into eternity being in fellowship . . .

The Sunday night before the Monday morning that my first wife, Terry, was taken to heaven, she was on stage leading worship. We stayed up late that night, talking about the blessings we were enjoying in the Fellowship and of what God was doing at that time. The next morning, on our way to a day of skiing at Mt. Bachelor, our car hit ice and the Lord took Terry home.

I think of my daughter, Jessie, who, immediately before she was taken to heaven, was here in the Sanctuary having Communion, offering prayer. She walked out the door, and a few minutes later she was in heaven.

I cannot tell you how thrilled I am to know that those who were linked to me intimately died in Hebron, died in fellowship.

Genesis 23:2 (b)
. . . and Abraham came to mourn for Sarah, and to weep for her.

Even though he was a giant of a man, the friend of God, the father of faith, we see Abraham was also a man who mourned and wept. This being the first mention of weeping or tears in the Bible, God waits until chapter 23 to introduce this concept. It's curious to me that there is no record of tears at the Fall of man, or when the Flood came, or when the people were scattered at Babel. The Holy Spirit purposefully waits to record weeping until the time a giant of a spiritual man was separated from a godly woman.

"Put thou my tears into thy bottle," David wrote. "Are they not in thy book?" (Psalm 56:8). Evidently, God keeps scrapbooks in heaven. Malachi 3 tells us every time one of His children talks to another person about Him, God hearkens to it and writes it in a book. And here, we see Him keeping another book—a book of our tears.

Concerning hard times, God doesn't say, "Deal with it." He says, "I understand what you're going through. It's precious to Me."

In Jesus' day, women wore tear bottles—little vials which fit against their cheek and caught their tears. A very precious possession, a woman would give this bottle of tears to the one she loved most. It could be this practice to which the account of the woman washing Jesus' feet with her tears refers (Luke 7:38).

Tears are unique. Under a microscope, you'll see the saline crystals in a tear are shaped in the form of a cross. It's as though the Lord would say, "I understand. I know. I wept, too" (John 11:35).

Genesis 23:3, 4 (a)
And Abraham stood up from before his dead, and spake unto the sons of Heth, saying, I am a stranger and a sojourner with you . . .

"I am a stranger and a sojourner." It is after he sees Sarah move on into eternity that Abraham looks at those around him and says, "This world is not my home." When someone dear to you departs, life becomes a whole lot clearer, for what previously may have been theoretical or theological becomes very real and powerful. That is, it becomes very evident that you are only a pilgrim here.

"Wherever your treasure is, there will your heart be also," Jesus declared (Matthew 6:21). And when you begin to see your treasure—family and loved ones—deposited in heaven, your heart follows. That's why the departure of loved ones is an important process in spiritual development. It's a way in which you suddenly wake up and say, "My heart is in heaven. Worldly things don't last." You find yourself truly free when someone close to you moves on into eternity.

Genesis 23:4 (b)
. . . give me a possession of a buryingplace with you . . .

Although he's standing right in the middle of his own property, it doesn't mean a thing to Abraham because he's a pilgrim to such a degree that when his life ends, the only thing he will own is Sarah's grave.

Genesis 23:4 (c)
. . . that I may bury my dead out of my sight.

Abraham didn't want to make a monument to Sarah. He wanted to bury her out of his sight and continue on in the pilgrimage God had ordained for him. This doesn't mean he would forget about her. It means he realized that what would make Sarah most happy would not be his mourning perpetually, but his moving on to the finish line victoriously.

Concerning those who have gone on before us, Hebrews 12 says we are surrounded by a great cloud of witnesses, saying, "Go for the finish line! Go for the gold. It's real!" Therefore, I honestly believe I do a disservice to those who have gone on ahead of me if I have not, like Abraham, made a decision to sprint to the finish line.

Genesis 23:5, 6
And the children of Heth answered Abraham, saying unto him, Hear us, my lord: thou art a mighty prince among us: in the choice of our sepulchres bury thy dead; none of us shall withhold from thee his sepulchre, but that thou mayest bury thy dead.

"You're a mighty prince," said the children of Heth to Abraham. This intrigues me because, although Abraham lived very simply in a tent, he had a huge impact on the heathen. Abraham's nephew, Lot, on the other hand, wanted to be involved in the cultural climate of Sodom. Yet when he tried to correct them, the men of Sodom said, "Who are you?" (Genesis 19:9).

You will hear, "You're so heavenly minded, you're no earthly good." Abraham proves just the opposite—that you're no earthly good until you're heavenly minded. If you want to make a difference on earth, your focal point, priority, and passion in whatever you do should be as one who lives for eternity.

"Master, should we pay taxes to Caesar?" they asked Jesus, seeking to lure Him into the hot political debate of the day.

"Let Me see a coin," Jesus said. "Whose image is this?"

"Caesar's," they answered.

"Then give it to Caesar. But give God that which is His," Jesus responded (Matthew 22)—the implication being that man is made in God's image and therefore should live for Him.

Genesis 23:7–9
And Abraham stood up, and bowed himself to the people of the land, even to the children of Heth. And he communed with them, saying, If it be your mind that I should bury my dead out of my sight; hear me, and intreat for me to Ephron the son of Zohar, That he may give me the cave of Machpelah, which he hath, which is in the end of his field; for as much money as it is worth he shall give it me for a possession of a buryingplace amongst you.

"I don't want any of your carved tombs or sepulchres," said Abraham. "I'm interested in the cave owned by Ephron because it's at Machpelah." *Machpelah* means "double doors." In other words, there's a way in and there's a way out.

"Yea," said the psalmist, "though I walk *through* the valley of the shadow of death, I will fear no evil" (Psalm 23:4, italics added). There is a door in and a door out because when we die, our last breath on earth becomes our first breath in heaven. We're just passing through.

Genesis 23:10, 11
And Ephron dwelt among the children of Heth: and Ephron the Hittite answered

Abraham in the audience of the children of Heth, even of all that went in at the gate of his city, saying, Nay, my lord, hear me: the field give I thee, and the cave that is therein, I give it thee; in the presence of the sons of my people give I it thee: bury thy dead.

Three times in one sentence, Ephron says, "I'm giving this to you"—which was simply the beginning of the Middle Eastern bargaining process.

Genesis 23:12–15
And Abraham bowed down himself before the people of the land. And he spake unto Ephron in the audience of the people of the land, saying, But if thou wilt give it, I pray thee, hear me: I will give thee money for the field; take it of me, and I will bury my dead there. And Ephron answered Abraham, saying unto him, My lord, hearken unto me: the land is worth four hundred shekels of silver; what is that betwixt me and thee? bury therefore thy dead.

Was the true price of the land four hundred shekels? Historians say no. Four hundred shekels was meant to be the starting figure. Perhaps Ephron was hoping for one hundred shekels out of the deal.

Genesis 23:16
And Abraham hearkened unto Ephron; and Abraham weighed to Ephron the silver, which he had named in the audience of the sons of Heth, four hundred shekels of silver, current money with the merchant.

Abraham pays the full price because regardless of what Ephron said, this man who had refused even a shoelace from the king of Sodom realizes nothing in the world is free.

Running from the Lord, Jonah goes to the dock where there just happens to be a ship ready to take him away. Scripture says Jonah went down to the boat and paid the fare (Jonah 1:3). And as the story unfolds, we see Jonah paying in more ways than one.

Don't take Ephron's gift, gang. You will experience a peace that passes understanding if you don't take what the world is trying to sell you. Jesus is the Prince of Peace, and His is a peace completely unlike that which the world can only promise.

Genesis 23:17–20
And the field of Ephron, which was in Machpelah, which was before Mamre, the field, and the cave which was therein, and all the trees that were in the field, that were in all the borders round about, were made sure Unto Abraham for a possession in the presence of the children of Heth, before all that went in at the gate of his city. And after this, Abraham buried Sarah his wife in the cave of the field of Machpelah before Mamre: the same is Hebron in the land of Canaan. And the field, and the cave that is therein, were made sure unto Abraham for a possession of a buryingplace by the sons of Heth.

As Abraham buried his wife at Machpelah, he did so knowing she had simply passed through one door and out the other into eternity.

I am so glad we're saved. We're sojourners and strangers, yet we have a peace in the meantime that passes understanding as we head for heaven. Life only makes sense in the framework of eternity. If there's no other reason to get saved, surely that is reason enough.

24 It has been said that a picture is worth a thousand words. I have found this to be true. So have you. Every parent knows how important it is to read to his children, and how much more involved they are if there's a picture on the page. We're children, gang. And our Father knows that, as kids, we need pictures—pictures that allow us to understand the principles of the Scriptures.

Pictures not only help one understand the subject—they often reveal the nature of the artist . . .

Legend has it that in painting the Last Supper, Leonardo Da Vinci used a younger version of his own face as a model for the face of Christ—and the face of his worst enemy as a model for the face of Judas Iscariot. Upon completion, Da Vinci was dismayed with the result. The lighting was wrong. The colors weren't what they were supposed to be. Nothing was right. So he painted over the canvas and began again. This time, however, he painted his enemy's face in the place of Christ, and his own face in the place of Judas Iscariot. The result is the masterpiece we know today.

A painting often reveals the passion and priority of the artist. Such is the nature of the passage before us . . .

Genesis 24:1 (a)
And Abraham was old, and well stricken in age . . .

Abraham was probably one hundred and forty years old at this time.

Genesis 24:1 (b)
. . . and the LORD had blessed Abraham in all things.

"Seek first the kingdom of God," Jesus said, "and all these things shall be added unto you" (Matthew 6:33). Abraham did just that. He left everything he had to follow the leading of the Lord. And here we read he was blessed in all things.

Genesis 24:2 (a)
And Abraham said unto his eldest servant of his house, that ruled over all that he had . . .

In this particular portrait, Abraham represents the Father; Isaac represents the Son; and the servant—who is not named—represents the Holy Spirit. Why is the servant not named? Because the Holy Spirit does not speak of Himself. Rather, the ministry of the Holy Spirit is to draw attention to Jesus Christ.

In Paul's epistles, you will read, "Greetings in the name of the Father," or "Blessings upon you in the name of the Father and His Son." But you will never read, "Blessings upon you in the name of the Father and His Son and the Holy Ghost" because the Spirit—He Who inspired Paul to write these salutations and blessings—does not speak of Himself.

Genesis 24:2 (b), 3 (a)
. . . Put, I pray thee, thy hand under my thigh: And I will make thee swear by the LORD, the God of heaven, and the God of the earth . . .

Putting one's hand under another's thigh sounds strange to us—but in Abraham's day, when a man gave an order to an employee or servant, this was a way of saying, "I want you to give me your full attention. Therefore I am sitting on your hand so you can't scoot away."

Genesis 24:3 (b), 4
. . . that thou shalt not take a wife unto my son of the daughters of the Canaanites, among whom I dwell: But thou shalt go unto my country, and to my kindred, and take a wife unto my son Isaac.

Abraham sent his servant to find a bride for Isaac, just as it is the Holy Spirit who tugs on our hearts and draws us to Christ as His bride.

Genesis 24:5, 6
And the servant said unto him, Peradventure the woman will not be willing to follow me unto this land: must I needs bring thy son again unto the land from whence thou camest? And Abraham said unto him, Beware thou that thou bring not my son thither again.

Fulfilling the type most wonderfully, just as Abraham's servant was to bring the bride to Isaac rather than bringing Isaac to the bride, we will one day join our Greater than Isaac, our Bridegroom, Jesus Christ in *His* kingdom—in heaven.

Genesis 24:7–9
The LORD God of heaven, which took me from my father's house, and from the land of my kindred, and which spake unto me, and that sware unto me, saying, Unto thy seed will I give this land; he shall send his angel before thee, and thou shalt take a wife unto my son from thence. And if the woman will not be willing to follow thee, then thou shalt be clear from this my oath: only bring not my son thither again. And the servant put his hand under the thigh of Abraham his master, and sware to him concerning that matter.

"If the woman won't follow you, you'll be free from this responsibility," said Abraham to his servant. As symbolized by the servant, the Holy Spirit will never force anyone to come to Christ, for He is a perfect Gentleman.

Concerning the manifestations of the Spirit, Paul said, "Know this: The spirit of the prophet is subject to that prophet" (1 Corinthians 14:32). In other words, contrary to what many propound, the Holy Spirit is not some bizarre force that overpowers people, making them do things they wouldn't have done otherwise.

"You are to give an invitation to her," said Abraham, "but not force your will upon her."

Genesis 24:10 (a)
And the servant took ten camels of the camels of his master, and departed . . .

These ten camels are subtle yet significant players in the unfolding drama, as they illustrate how a person is brought from a far-off land into the embrace of the Bridegroom, into the embrace of grace.

For topical study of Genesis 24:10 entitled "Being Brought to Christ," turn to page 116.

Genesis 24:10 (b)–14
. . . for all the goods of his master were in his hand: and he arose, and went to Mesopotamia, unto the city of Nahor. And he made his camels to kneel down without the city by a well of water at the time of the evening, even the time that women go out to draw water. And he said, O LORD God of my master Abraham, I pray thee, send me good speed this day, and shew kindness unto my master Abraham. Behold, I stand here by the well of water; and the daughters of the men of the city come out to draw water: And let it come to pass, that the damsel to whom I shall say, Let down thy pitcher, I pray thee, that I may drink; and she shall say, Drink, and I will give thy camels drink also: let the same be she that thou hast appointed for thy servant Isaac; and thereby shall I know that thou hast shewed kindness unto my master.

The task the servant suggested was hardly an easy one. It would take hours for a woman to lower her pitcher into the well enough times to quench the thirst of ten dry camels.

Genesis 24:15, 16
And it came to pass, before he had done speaking, that, behold, Rebekah came out, who was born to Bethuel, son of Milcah, the wife of Nahor, Abraham's brother, with her pitcher upon her shoulder. And the damsel was very fair to look upon, a virgin, neither had any man known her: and she went down to the well, and filled her pitcher, and came up.

It is interesting but not surprising to me how many men in the Scriptures find their brides by a well, for Isaiah 12:3 speaks of the well of salvation as a place of refreshment. If you want to find someone who's very fair, go to the well. Go to morning worship. Go to the place offering refreshment in the Lord.

Genesis 24:17–20
And the servant ran to meet her, and said, Let me, I pray thee, drink a little water of thy pitcher. And she said, Drink, my lord: and she hasted, and let down her pitcher upon her hand, and gave him drink. And when she had done giving him drink, she said, I will draw water for thy camels also, until they have done drinking. And she hasted, and emptied her pitcher into the trough, and ran again unto the well to draw water, and drew for all his camels.

When you see a man or woman going out of his or her way to minister, you have found someone very special.

Genesis 24:21
And the man wondering at her held his peace, to wit whether the LORD had made his journey prosperous or not.

Rebekah not only watered the camels, but she was also "a virgin fair to look upon."

"Wait a minute," you say. "If Abraham is a picture of God the Father, Isaac a picture of Jesus, the servant a picture of the Spirit, and Rebekah a picture of the Bride of Christ—this is where it breaks down, for, unlike Rebekah, I am not fair to look upon. I drop the ball continually and fail miserably."

So do I. But in the perspective of the Artist of this portrait, we *are* very fair to look upon because, having been cleansed by the blood of the Cross, we are the very righteousness of God (2 Corinthians 5).

Genesis 24:22–25
And it came to pass, as the camels had done drinking, that the man took a golden earring of half a shekel weight, and two bracelets for her hands of ten shekels weight of gold; And said, Whose daughter art thou? tell me, I pray thee: is there room in thy father's house for us to lodge in? And she said unto him, I am the daughter of Bethuel the son of Milcah, which she bare unto Nahor. She said moreover unto him, We have both straw and provender enough, and room to lodge in.

The servant—a type of the Spirit—gave Rebekah—a type of the church—beautiful gifts. This is still the way of the Spirit. We see His gifts in 1 Corinthians 12 and 14, Romans 12, and Ephesians 4, given to beautify His bride.

Genesis 24:26–28
And the man bowed down his head, and worshipped the LORD. And he said, Blessed be the LORD God of my master Abraham, who hath not left destitute my master of his mercy and his truth: I being in the way, the LORD led me to the house of my master's brethren. And the damsel ran, and told them of her mother's house these things.

Many times, people wonder how God will lead them. "How will I know whether to take that job, get involved in this relationship, or take on a new ministry?" they ask.

The servant says, "Being in the way, the Lord led me." I find his phraseology interesting, for centuries later, Jesus would declare, "I am the Way" (John 14:6); and the early church itself was called "the Way" (Acts 19:23).

If you are walking in the Way, gang, if you're obeying Jesus, you will end up at the right spot. You don't have to waste your time struggling and striving to find God's will. Simply walk day by day in the Way, and, as He did Abraham's servant, the Lord will lead you.

Genesis 24:29–31
And Rebekah had a brother, and his name was Laban: and Laban ran out unto the man, unto the well. And it came to pass, when he saw the earring and bracelets upon his sister's hands, and when he heard the words of Rebekah his sister, saying, Thus spake the man unto me; that he came unto the man; and, behold, he stood by the camels at the well. And he said, Come in, thou blessed of the LORD; wherefore standest thou without? for I have prepared the house, and room for the camels.

As we will see, Laban is a very worldly man—yet he welcomed the servant because of the gifts he saw on his sister. We must never diminish or quench the work of the Spirit because the world—the Labans out there—are watching to see the reality of the living Lord through His people as evidenced by the manifestations of His gifts within the church.

Genesis 24:32–36
And the man came into the house: and he ungirded his camels, and gave straw and provender for the camels, and water to wash his feet, and the men's feet that were with him. And there was set meat before him to eat: but he said, I will not eat, until I have told mine errand. And he said, Speak on. And he said, I am Abraham's servant. And the LORD hath blessed my master greatly; and he is become great: and he hath given him flocks, and herds, and silver, and gold, and menservants, and maidservants, and camels, and asses. And Sarah my master's wife bare a son to my master when she was old: and unto him hath he given all that he hath.

Just as Abraham had given all things to his son, so God the Father gave all He had to His Son (John 3:35).

Genesis 24:37–49
And my master made me swear, saying, Thou shalt not take a wife to my son of the daughters of the Canaanites, in whose land I dwell: But thou shalt go unto my father's house, and to my kindred, and take a wife unto my son. And I said unto my master, Peradventure the woman will not follow me. And he said unto me, The LORD, before whom I walk, will send his angel with thee, and prosper thy way; and thou shalt take a wife for my son of my kindred, and of my father's house: Then shalt thou be clear from this my oath, when thou comest to my kindred; and if they give not thee one, thou shalt be clear from my oath. And I came this day unto the well, and said, O LORD God of my master Abraham, if now thou do prosper my way which I go; Behold, I stand by the well of water; and it shall come to pass, that when the virgin cometh forth to draw water, and I say to her, Give me, I pray thee, a little water of thy pitcher to drink; And she say to me, Both drink thou, and I will also draw for thy camels: let the same be the woman whom the LORD hath appointed out for my master's son. And before I had done speaking in mine heart, behold, Rebekah came forth with her pitcher on her shoulder; and she went down unto the well, and drew water: and I said unto her, Let me drink, I pray thee. And she made haste, and let down her pitcher from her shoulder, and said, Drink, and I will give thy camels drink also: so I drank, and she made the camels drink also. And I asked her, and said, Whose daughter art thou? And she said, The daughter of Bethuel, Nahor's son, whom Milcah bare unto him: and I put the earring upon her face, and the bracelets upon her hands. And I bowed down my head, and worshipped the LORD, and blessed the LORD God of my master Abraham, which had led me in the right way to take my master's brother's daughter unto his son. And now if ye will deal kindly and truly with my master, tell me: and if not, tell me; that I may turn to the right hand, or to the left.

"You've heard my story. You've seen the miraculous way in which God has led me. It's obvious something special has taken place. Are you willing to let your daughter go?" asked the servant.

Genesis 24:50–53
Then Laban and Bethuel answered and said, The thing proceedeth from the LORD: we cannot speak unto thee bad or good. Behold, Rebekah is before thee, take her, and go, and let her be thy master's son's wife, as the LORD hath spoken. And it came to pass, that, when Abraham's servant heard their words, he worshipped the LORD, bowing himself to the earth. And the servant brought forth jewels of silver, and jewels of gold, and raiment, and gave them to Rebekah: he gave also to her brother and to her mother precious things.

Not only did Rebekah receive gifts, but Rebekah's family did as well. Paul says if two people are married and one becomes a Christian while the other remains a pagan, the unbeliever will be blessed simply by being married to a believer (1 Corinthians 7:14). That is what was happening here. Because gifts were heaped upon the bride, some overflowed to her family.

Genesis 24:54, 55
And they did eat and drink, he and the men that were with him, and tarried all night; and they rose up in the morning, and he said, Send me away unto my master. And her brother and her mother said, Let the damsel abide with us a few days, at the least ten; after that she shall go.

If you have a reference Bible you will see the phrase "at least ten" translated "at least ten months." In other words, Rebekah's family is now saying, "Let's not be fanatic. Let Rebekah stay here for a year—or at least ten months."

This is always what the world says. "Don't get so radical," they insist. "You don't need to go to church on Wednesdays. Sunday is enough. Or better yet—Christmas and Easter, that's all you need. Don't go overboard. Relax. Stay with us."

Genesis 24:56–58
And he said unto them, Hinder me not, seeing the LORD hath prospered my way; send me away that I may go to my master. And they said, We will call the damsel, and inquire at her mouth. And they called Rebekah, and said unto her, Wilt thou go with this man? And she said, I will go.

I love this! Rebekah said, "I will go." Where? To a man she has never met. To a place she has never seen. Why? Because although she had never seen Isaac, she liked what she had heard about him and what she had seen of him in the gifts.

We have not yet seen our Bridegroom. But we like what we have caught glimpses of, and what we have heard of Him. There is coming a day when we will see Him with our eyes, but, as Peter declared, even though we haven't yet seen Him, we love Him (1 Peter 1:8).

Genesis 24:59, 60
And they sent away Rebekah their sister, and her nurse, and Abraham's servant, and his men. And they blessed Rebekah, and said unto her, Thou art our sister, be thou the mother of thousands of millions, and let thy seed possess the gate of those which hate them.

At last bidding farewell to Rebekah, her family blessed her saying, "May no one have power over you. May you have victory."

Genesis 24:61, 62
And Rebekah arose, and her damsels, and they rode upon the camels, and followed the man: and the servant took Rebekah, and went his way. And Isaac came from the way of the well Lahai-roi; for he dwelt in the south country.

Knowing his father had sent the servant to find a bride for him, Isaac doesn't go and look for her himself. In Jewish tradition, the father would arrange the marriage for his son. Upon agreement of both fathers, the bride and groom-to-be would then be betrothed at a simple ceremony in which cups of wine were exchanged and a dowry given. Then the son would return to his father's house to build a dwelling place for his bride either close to or adjoining the house of his father. When the father deemed all had been properly prepared, he would send his son out to call for his bride—and she would run out to join him.

"In My Father's house are many dwelling places," Jesus, our Bridegroom, said. "I go to prepare a place for you. And if I go and prepare a place for you, I will come again, and receive you unto myself; that where I am, there ye may be also" (John 14:2, 3).

When will this day be? "No man knows the day or the hour—not even Me," Jesus answered (Mark 13:32).

But this much is sure: Like the brides of old, when our Bridegroom calls for us, we will run to meet Him—not, however, in the streets—but in the air (1 Thessalonians 4).

Most of us are watching for the Lord. But there is something more important than that. That is, the Lord—as seen in the person of Isaac, being at the well of *Lahairoi*, or "The Lord sees"—is watching for us. The Lord longs for us more than we long for Him. Why? Because while we can only speculate concerning the wonderful things God has prepared for those who love Him (1 Corinthians 2:9), He knows all about them and is eager to share them with us.

Genesis 24:63 (a)
And Isaac went out to meditate in the field at the eventide . . .

As it might say in your margin, Isaac literally went out to pray. What's Jesus doing right now for you and me? While He's preparing a place for us to dwell with Him eternally, He's praying for us constantly (Hebrews 7:25).

Genesis 24:63 (b)–67
. . . and he lifted up his eyes, and saw, and, behold, the camels were coming. And Rebekah lifted up her eyes, and when she saw Isaac, she lighted off the camel. For she had said unto the servant, What man is this that walketh in the field to meet us? And the servant had said, It is my master: therefore she took a vail, and covered herself. And the servant told Isaac all things that he had done. And Isaac brought her into his mother Sarah's tent, and took Rebekah, and she became his wife; and he loved her: and Isaac was comforted after his mother's death.

This last verse speaks volumes. Notice Isaac brought Rebekah into his mother Sarah's tent. Sarah represents Israel. Rebekah represents the Bride of Christ. Rebekah is not Sarah. But Rebekah is brought into the place that Sarah occupied previously. The Bride of Christ moves into that place where Israel once was. When Israel turned her back on the Lord and wouldn't submit to the rule of the Lord, Israel was put away and the church moved into the tent where Sarah once was. The church is not Israel anymore than Rebekah was Sarah, but we move into the place that Israel once enjoyed because Israel is now temporarily put away.

However, before you think this means God is through with the Jews, you must read on to see it's not the end of the story for Israel, not by a long shot . . .

BEING BROUGHT TO CHRIST

A Topical Study of GENESIS 24:10

We all know people to whom we're related, with whom we work, about whom we care, who just don't seem to get it. That is, we've shared with them what we've found in Christ and the blessings of being a believer only to have them look at us with glazed eyes and say, "I'm glad you found something that works for you. But please don't bother me." Over and over again, we have encountered people who seem completely immune to the gospel. It might be a son or daughter, a parent or spouse, a sister, brother, friend, or schoolmate. If someone you personally care about is not saved—this is just the story for you . . .

Setting out to find a bride for his master's son, Abraham's servant loaded ten camels to accompany him on the journey. Biblically, the number ten points to, alludes to, reminds us of the Ten Commandments. In our text, we see the Ten Commandments, the ten camels kneeling at the well. Seeing the thirsty camels, a young woman named Rebekah offered to draw water for them. When does salvation come to the person with the glazed look on his face, the blank look in his eye? It is when he is aware of the ten camels, the Ten Commandments, the Law.

"The Law of the Lord is perfect," the psalmist declared, "converting the soul" (Psalm 19:7). Paul would say the same thing when he wrote:

> *Now we know that what things soever the law saith, it saith to them who are under the law: that every mouth may be stopped, and all the world may become guilty before God. Therefore by the deeds of the law there shall no flesh be justified in his sight: for by the law is the knowledge of sin. Wherefore the law was our schoolmaster to bring us unto Christ, that we might be justified by faith.* Romans 3:19, 20; Galatians 3:24

"Get saved and you can be happy like me," we say to our friends, our kids, or our parents who don't know the Lord.

"I'm already happy," they say.

"But you can have abundant life," we say.

"I'm fine the way I am," they answer.

People need to understand they are in big trouble. They don't think they are. They basically think they're pretty good because they compare themselves with their friends and neighbors.

> A sheep on a green pasture looks pretty white. But when the snow falls, the same sheep against pure white snow looks pretty dusty. Did his wool change? No. The background did.

The Law provides the only true background, for only the Law shows us God's standard of perfection.

> Once a cruise ship pulls away from its berth, an alarm sounds, calling passengers to a designated spot in order to receive instructions concerning lifejackets and exit procedures in case of an emergency. Research indicates that until recently, forty-two percent of the passengers didn't show up for these meetings. Now, however, virtually every passenger responds to the alarm. Why? A movie called *Titanic* came out that made people aware of potential disaster.

The Law of the Lord shows people one thing: Not that they need abundant life or a peaceful life or a loving life. It shows them they are headed for disaster, that they are headed for hell because James says he who breaks one part of the law breaks the entire law (James 2:10).

Why?

Think of it this way . . .

> You're in a helicopter, and you accidentally fall out the door. On your way down, the pilot quickly throws you a chain made of ten links. "Don't worry," he yells.

"This chain is pretty good. Nine of the ten links are strong. Ninety percent isn't bad, is it?"

What does the Law say?

Thou shalt have no other gods before Me. If you have any god before God—that is, if any hobby, relationship, person, or possession occupies your thoughts or energies to a greater degree than does God, you have broken Commandment #1—and the soul that sins shall surely die (Ezekiel 18:20).

Thou shalt not make unto thee any graven image. What is an image? It comes from the imagination. "I can't believe a loving God would send anyone to hell—so my god won't," people say.

God says, "You are not to remake My image to fit your personality. I AM who I AM (Exodus 3:14). I am holy. I am love. I am pure. I am just. I am compassionate. I am a consuming fire." And he who says otherwise has broken Law #2.

Thou shalt not take the name of the Lord thy God in vain. Have you ever taken the Lord's name in vain? Have you ever cheapened or degraded it in any way? If so, you're guilty.

Remember the Sabbath day to keep it holy. Do you reserve one day to slow everything down and worship God? If you don't, you've broken the law.

Thou shalt honor thy father and thy mother. If you have ever been disrespectful either in thought or deed to your parents, you are guilty of breaking the Law of God.

Thou shalt not kill. "At least I don't break this one," you say, breathing a sigh of relief. Really? Jesus said if you're even angry with another, you are guilty of the equivalent of murder (Matthew 5:22).

Thou shalt not commit adultery. "I know I haven't broken this one," you insist. But Jesus said if you even look at someone else with desire adultery has already taken place in your heart (Matthew 5:28).

Thou shalt not steal. Have you ever failed to tithe or to give God that which is His? God calls this stealing (Malachi 3:8).

Thou shalt not bear false witness. Giving the right information with the wrong implication, making a correct statement but in the wrong spirit, "spinning" the truth are all instances of what is known as bearing false witness and will damn a person.

Thou shalt not covet. What is coveting? Simply wanting more of what you already have enough of. If you have ever wanted more, join me in being guilty of the sin of covetousness.

"What shall I do to inherit eternal life?" asked the rich young ruler.

"Keep the Commandments," Jesus said.

"I have kept them from my youth," answered the young man.

"What about coveting?" asked Jesus. "Go sell your stuff" (see Matthew 19).

How was the rich young ruler made aware of his covetousness? Jesus didn't talk to him about abundant life or love or peace. He said, "Look at the Law."

When people see they've broken ten out of the Ten Commandments, they realize the price paid on their behalf is immense. That is how the Law of the Lord,—the ten camels—converts the soul.

When Rebekah saw Isaac, she stepped down from her camel. Once we come to Christ, the camels have done their job, for just as Isaac and Rebekah were made one, when a man or woman opens their heart to Christ, oneness and intimacy transpires which allows Him to rule in them and live through them.

The law is the divinely-designed artillery to tear down the strongholds, to break down the walls of our imagination (2 Corinthians 10:5). "The weapons of our warfare are not carnal," Paul declares (2 Corinthians 10:4).

What does "carnal" mean?

It refers to anything I do which is powered by my flesh.

"I thought it was the *goodness* of God which leads men to repentance," you say. It is (Romans 2:4). But we'll never know how good God is until we see how bad we are. We'll never understand God's goodness until we see our sinfulness.

Grace is for the humble. The Law is for the proud. The humble person will welcome grace because he knows he's a sinner. The proud man, on the other hand, thinks he's OK. To the humble person, you share grace. With the proud person, you share the Law.

> "Master, what must I do to inherit eternal life?" asked the lawyer.
>
> "How readest thou the Law?" Jesus answered, knowing the heart of the lawyer (Luke 10:25, 26).

Jesus loved people enough to say, "The issue is the Law. If you have violated any of the Ten Commandments, you're a sinner. You're in trouble. You need forgiveness. You need redemption. You need Me."

Dear parent, brother, sister, child, friend, neighbor—if you really love those with whom you're linked, you'll care more about seeing them saved than about what they think of you. Therefore, you must be totally honest with them and say, "You have broken every Law in the Book. You are headed for disaster. But God wants to save you. He's provided a Lifeboat for you in the Person of Jesus Christ. If you take His hand, you'll be saved. If not, you'll be damned and doomed forever."

Those are strong words for a strong reality. Gang, if we care about one neighbor, friend, or loved one, the time has come to realize that the Law of the Lord is perfect, converting the soul. The Law is the schoolmaster that will drive them to the warm embrace of grace.

25

Genesis 25:1
Then again Abraham took a wife, and her name was Keturah.

After twenty years of being single following the death of Sarah, Abraham marries *Keturah* whose name means "Incense"—perhaps signifying the sweet fragrance she added to Abraham's life.

Genesis 25:2–4
And she bare him Zimran, and Jokshan, and Medan, and Midian, and Ishbak, and Shuah. And Jokshan begat Sheba, and Dedan. And the sons of Dedan were Asshurim, and Letushim, and Leummim. And the sons of Midian; Ephah, and Epher, and Hanoch, and Abida, and Eldaah. All these were the children of Keturah.

I believe the names of the sons born to Abraham and Keturah parallel the prophetic picture of the people of Israel. You see, when the church is taken up in the Rapture, the veil will be lifted from the eyes of the Jewish people, and all of Israel will be saved at the end of the Tribulation. Then, she will play a primary role as God rules and reigns from Jerusalem in the millennial kingdom (Revelation 20). What a glorious time that will be! Nature will be restored to what it was originally meant to be: the mountains shall sing; the trees of the field shall clap their hands; the lion will lie down with the lamb. Not only will nature react, but, also, a complete disarmament by all nations and people will result in swords being turned into plowshares and spears into pruninghooks (Isaiah 2).

But wait. There's a dark side—as seen in the sons of Keturah. *Zimram* means "Song." *Jokshan* means "Snare." *Medan* means "Strife." *Midian* means "Man will leave." *Shuah* means "From the pit." What begins with a song ends in the pit.

You see, Scripture tells us man will live to be 1,000 years old in the millennial kingdom. Consequently, the world's population will mushroom to the point that at the end of the millennial kingdom, there will be multiplied generations that, because they have never known anything else, become bored with peace, love, and prosperity. Thus, perfection will be a *Snare* to them. *Strife* and *Contention* will follow. Although many of them will want to do their own thing and *Leave* the way of the Lord, they'll not be able to because righteousness will be enforced in the millennial kingdom. But, because God will not force His will on anyone, He will allow Satan to be released *from the pit* for a short season at the end of the Millennium. Satan will lead a rebellion, before he is cast permanently into the lake of fire along with those who, bored with perfection, choose to follow him.

Although the names of Abraham and Keturah's sons paint a prophetic portrait, they also point to a very practical principle. That is, we too live in the age of the kingdom of God—not where the lion is lying down with the lamb externally—but internally where righteousness, peace and joy in the Holy Ghost abound (Romans 14:17). This being the case, like those living in the millennial kingdom, we are at risk of taking the righteousness, peace, and joy of the present kingdom for granted. Dear brother, precious sister, may we never be those who take lightly the work God has done in our hearts, for if we stop singing the sweet song of salvation, we will become ensnared in strife and contention, lured away from the rule of our King by lies from the pit.

Genesis 25:5
And Abraham gave all that he had unto Isaac.

Here we see Abraham disposing of his wealth to his son, Isaac, even as the Father in heaven gave all things to His Son (John 17).

Because all things will find their ultimate destination in Christ, anything I do which isn't for Him results in hopelessness, while everything I do for and in Jesus positions me in the center of God's will.

How does this work practically?

Suppose you are a UPS driver. God's will for you is that you be a UPS driver for His glory. As you pull up to every stop, pray that God will gift those inside. And suddenly, your job will not be a matter of how many deliveries you can make in a day, but of how many people God can bless through you in a day. To the extent that you do this in any given day is the extent to which you will experience purpose and contentment.

Genesis 25:6
But unto the sons of the concubines, which Abraham had, Abraham gave gifts, and sent them away from Isaac his son, while he yet lived, eastward, unto the east country.

As a type of the heavenly Father, Abraham sent his other sons away because there's coming a day when every knee shall bow and every tongue shall confess that Jesus is Lord singularly (Philippians 2:10, 11).

Genesis 25:7
And these are the days of the years of Abraham's life which he lived, an hundred threescore and fifteen years.

"The days of the years" is a Hebrew phrase which speaks of quality of life because life is made up of days—individual, specific days. In his 64,000 days, Abraham, the friend of God, walked with God. The Christian life is not called the Christian leap, the Christian jump, or the Christian bounce. It's called the Christian walk because it takes place one step, one day at a time.

What am I going to do tomorrow? Will I choose to walk with God—or do I expect somehow to bounce, leap, skip, or hop and end up a spiritual man at age fifty? What I do today will affect how I arrive at the end of my life. One of the greatest misconceptions in spiritual life is that when we're old, we'll automatically be spiritual. I need to know God's Word *today*. I need to know God's ways *today*. If I don't, the end of my life will find me nothing more than an old fool.

Genesis 25:8 (a)
Then Abraham gave up the ghost, and died in a good old age, an old man, and full of years . . .

Abraham was full of years. The words "of years" being in italics, this phrase was added later. Thus, the original text reads Abraham "died full." I want to die full—full of the joy and love of the Lord—don't you?

Genesis 25:8 (b)
. . . and was gathered to his people.

Abraham was gathered to his people. Who are *your* people? Does the church say, "You're one of us"? Do those who populate heaven say, "We know you"? Or do you feel more at home in the world?

Genesis 25:9, 10
And his sons Isaac and Ishmael buried him in the cave of Machpelah, in the field of Ephron the son of Zohar the Hittite, which is before Mamre; The field which Abraham purchased of the sons of Heth: there was Abraham buried, and Sarah his wife.

We see Ishmael and Isaac brought together at the death of their father, Abraham, because true reconciliation can only happen through death.

For topical study of Genesis 25:9 entitled "Someone's Gotta Die," turn to page 123.

Genesis 25:11
And it came to pass after the death of Abraham, that God blessed his son Isaac; and Isaac dwelt by the well Lahai-roi.

We come now to Isaac's story. But before we do, we must round out the story of Ishmael . . .

Genesis 25:12–17
Now these are the generations of Ishmael, Abraham's son, whom Hagar the Egyptian, Sarah's handmaid, bare unto Abraham: And these are the names of the sons of Ishmael, by their names, according to their generations: the firstborn of Ishmael, Nebajoth; and Kedar, and Adbeel, and Mibsam, And Mishma, and Dumah, and Massa, Hadar, and Tema, Jetur, Naphish, and Kedemah: These are the sons of Ishmael, and these are their names, by their towns, and by their castles; twelve princes according to their nations. And these are the years of the life of Ishmael, an hundred and thirty and seven years: and he gave up the ghost and died; and was gathered unto his people.

The names of Ishmael's twelve sons portray the history of Islam—the base of which is idolatry and paganism. In Mecca, the most holy site of Islam, stands a silver holder containing a black stone which fell from the sky long before Mohammed was even born. In his desire to unify the region's numerous nomadic tribes, Mohammed designated Allah as the single god over the three-hundred-plus existing deities. Allah is a moon god, a pagan entity, linked to the black meteorite worshiped at Mecca. Thus, to think Islam is one of the great monotheistic religions is unsophisticated intellectually and inaccurate historically. Islam is pagan worship of a moon god.

Genesis 25:18
And they dwelt from Havilah unto Shur, that is before Egypt, as thou goest toward Assyria: and he died in the presence of all his brethren.

If you have a reference Bible, you see the word "died" is "fell." It's a different word for death than Abraham's death. Abraham died full. Ishmael simply fell.

Genesis 25:19–21 (a)
And these are the generations of Isaac, Abraham's son: Abraham begat Isaac: And Isaac was forty years old when he took Rebekah to wife, the daughter of Bethuel the Syrian of Padan-aram, the sister to Laban the Syrian. And Isaac intreated the LORD for his wife, because she was barren . . .

The daughter of a Syrian, when Rebekah married Isaac she became one of God's chosen. We who once walked in darkness can be linked to our Greater than Isaac—and yet, like Rebekah, remain barren.

Genesis 25:21 (b)
. . . and the LORD was intreated of him, and Rebekah his wife conceived.

Isaac does for his bride what our Bridegroom does for us. He doesn't pout. He doesn't pity himself. He prays (Hebrews 7:25). The best thing a person can do if he's aware of his own or another's spiritual barrenness is to pray.

Genesis 25:22
And the children struggled together within her; and she said, If it be so, why am I thus? And she went to inquire of the LORD.

Rebekah was saved; she was no longer barren. But now there was something troubling within her. So she booked a counseling appointment with the wonderful Counselor (Isaiah 9:6)—the only One who could identify the source of her struggle.

Genesis 25:23
And the LORD said unto her, Two nations are in thy womb, and two manner of people shall be separated from thy bowels; and the one people shall be stronger than the other people; and the elder shall serve the younger.

Like Rebekah, we're no longer barren because we've been prayed for. Why, then, is there a rumbling, an unsettledness inside us? It is because our flesh and spirit wage war within us. What can we do about this? The answer is very simple: We must decide which one we want to be stronger. If we choose to feed our flesh, our flesh will get bigger and stronger, and our spirit will become the runt of the litter. If, on the other hand, we choose to feed our spirit, our spirit will grow stronger and our flesh will grow weaker and weaker.

I recommend the latter, for to be fleshly minded is death, but to be spiritually minded is life and peace (Romans 8:6).

Genesis 25:24, 25
And when her days to be delivered were fulfilled, behold, there were twins in her womb. And the first came out red, all over like an hairy garment; and they called his name Esau.

Esau, whose name means "hairy," is the quintessential outdoorsman.

Genesis 25:26
And after that came his brother out, and his hand took hold on Esau's heel; and his name was called Jacob: and Isaac was threescore years old when she bare them.

Jacob, whose name means "heel snatcher" is an indoor kind of guy with a propensity to want to be first in everything—as evidenced by his wanting to be firstborn.

Genesis 25:27
And the boys grew: and Esau was a cunning hunter, a man of the field; and Jacob was a plain man, dwelling in tents.

Jacob and Esau represent the two natures warring within us: Jacob represents the spirit. Esau, the older twin brother, represents the flesh. He's the older brother because each of us walked in the flesh before we were born again and touched by the Spirit.

Genesis 25:28
And Isaac loved Esau, because he did eat of his venison: but Rebekah loved Jacob.

While Isaac loved Esau because he enjoyed Esau's venison, Rebekah loved Jacob—period. In this, I understand that the flesh tries to give reasons for being loved. But Jacob, a picture of the Spirit, reminds me that God does not love me because I'm lovable or lovely. He loves me because He is love. Period.

Genesis 25:29, 30
And Jacob sod pottage: and Esau came from the field, and he was faint: And Esau said to Jacob, Feed me, I pray thee, with that same red pottage; for I am faint: therefore was his name called Edom.

Not only does *Edom,* or "red," reflect the color of the bean stew Jacob cooked, but it also calls to mind the color of the dust from which Adam's name was derived. Descendants of Esau, the Edomites will cause perpetual problems for the people of Israel.

Genesis 25:31–34
And Jacob said, Sell me this day thy birthright. And Esau said, Behold, I am at the point to die: and what profit shall this birthright do to me? And Jacob said, Swear to me this day; and he sware unto him: and he sold his birthright unto Jacob. Then Jacob gave Esau bread and pottage of lentiles; and he did eat and drink, and rose up, and went his way: thus Esau despised his birthright.

According to Old Testament law, as owner of the birthright, the oldest son would receive a double inheritance (Deuteronomy 21:17). Secondly, he would assume the spiritual leadership of the family—making sure the family was taken care of financially and that they walked with God spiritually. In other words, as priest of the home, he would have a significant role to play in ministry.

A type of the flesh, Esau couldn't care less about ministry. He simply wanted to satisfy the appetites of his flesh. In Hebrews, he's called a "profane man," "profane" meaning "outside of the temple" (Hebrews 12:16).

Jacob, on the other hand, for all of the faults we shall see he has, had this going for him: he hungered and thirsted after the things of the kingdom. He placed a great importance on the birthright from the very beginning. So he traded Esau a bowl of beans for it. And both his and Esau's lives took a different course as a result of a ten-second exchange . . .

SOMEONE'S GOTTA DIE

A Topical Study of GENESIS 25:9

Genesis is a foundational book, for in it lies every foundational principle of spiritual life. The text before us is no exception, for embedded in it we find the foundation, the basis, the bottom line of reconciliation. From the day Ishmael and his mother were sent away, he and his half-brother, Isaac, would remain estranged from each other—to be reconciled only at the grave of their father.

While it's sad that it took the death of their father to bring them together, I'm glad it took that, for in their story we see that if there is ever to be reconciliation between you and the son or daughter who is estranged from you, between you and the mother or father who doesn't understand you, between you and the friend who betrayed you, between you and the spouse who hurt you—someone has got to die. There is no other way.

We see this principle most powerfully in our relationship with our Father. Because of sin, we were estranged from Him.

> *And all things are of God, who hath reconciled us to himself by Jesus Christ, and hath given to us the ministry of reconciliation; To wit, that God was in Christ, reconciling the world unto himself, not imputing their trespasses unto them; and hath committed unto us the word of reconciliation.*
>
> 2 Corinthians 5:18, 19

God reconciled us to Himself through His own death. Then, once we were reconciled, He gave us the ministry of reconciliation—to reconcile people to God as we share with them the Good News of the gospel—and also to reconcile people to each other.

So big is Jesus on reconciliation that He said something quite shocking when He said, "If, while you are at the altar worshiping the Lord, you become aware that something is not quite right with someone you know or once knew, leave the altar and reconcile yourself to the one who is offended" (see Matthew 5:24).

The Greek word translated "reconcile" is *diallasso*—a word used by tailors and garment-makers with regard to alteration. Thus, Jesus was saying, "If, at the altar, you realize a relationship doesn't fit right, get it altered." In other words, the ill-fitting garment is not to be discarded, taken to Goodwill, or stuffed in the back of the closet and forgotten. "If a relationship isn't right," Jesus declared, "I want you to deal with that matter before you continue in worship."

How will reconciliation happen practically? There's only one way: Someone has got to die. If there's to be reconciliation with your wife, your husband, your daughter-in-law, your boss, your coach, your neighbor—you have to die.

"I don't want to die," we protest. "How come *she* can't die? It's *his* turn to die. I'm sick and tired of dying. Why does it have to be *me?*"

For several hours last night, Tammy and I talked with two people we think the world of. He's been a pastor for years; she's a godly woman with a passion for Jesus. But they're on their way to divorce. And it's a tragedy. There's no real issue—just irritations that have grown over the years. Both argued their points, yet as the hours passed, all we could say is, "One of you has got to die, or there will be no reconciliation."

Their answer? "Why me? It's his turn. It's her turn."

Many couples drove out to church this morning in virtually the same situation. As the husband sat behind the wheel, his words were few, but his thoughts many. "Why is she so cold?" he wondered. "Why doesn't she see my needs? I've been good to her. I've been faithful. I've provided for her. I've tried to be helpful. But months and years have passed, and I've had enough."

Meanwhile, as she sat on her side of the car, hugging the door handle, she thought, "Why is he so demanding? Why doesn't he understand I'm not a thing to be used. Why can't he see me and love me the way the Bible says he ought to?"

And the silence is deafening—broken only by the sounds of construction on the wall between them which grows higher and higher every day. And they come out to church and lift their hands and worship—when the Lord would say, "If you're bringing your gift to the altar and you remember that he or she has something against you, don't even continue worshiping until you alter the hurtful situation."

Why should you be the one to die?

Three reasons . . .

Reconciliation Delights our Father

Every parent knows the delight of reconciliation. When I hear one of my kids say to another, "It's *your* turn. *You* go first," all I can say is, "Glory hallelujah! The age of miracles is not over! These kids are working it out. They're dying to self. They're letting the other have his way!"

If you are fortunate enough to have a child who goes out of his way to be a peacemaker, you know the place he has in your heart. Any one of us who says, "I'm going to die so that there can be reconciliation" brings a great deal of joy to the heart of the Father.

Reconciliation Defeats our Foe

Satan has one tactic he's used from the very beginning: division. As the worship leader of the angelic chorus, Lucifer persuaded one-third of the angels to see things his way. They joined his rebellion, and are now demons, destined for eternal damnation. Because Satan's strategy remains the same, he who says, "I will die before I allow separation between me and another" deals a death blow to Satan.

The person who binds Satan is not the one who loudly declares, "I bind you, Satan." The person who binds Satan is the one who dies to self and reconciles with another person. The binding of Satan comes about not through a statement we make verbally—but through a choice we make actively.

Reconciliation Destroys our Flesh

The reason we're depressed, the reason for the gnawing ache within us is found in one word: flesh. We think if we could indulge or pamper our flesh, we'd be happier. The opposite, however, is true. Jesus taught that the one who loses His life will find it (Matthew 10:39); that the one who follows Him must deny himself and take up his cross (Matthew 16:24).

The cross you are to bear is not getting the flu or losing your job. It's not even divorce or death in your family—as tragic as those events are. The cross is not something that comes uninvited. Rather, it's something we choose to do which causes pain and agony to our flesh. The cross is what Jesus endured when He prayed, "Not My will, but Thine be done."

"I'm tired of being married to her," or "I'm tired of my dad treating me this way," or "I'm tired of my in-laws. Nevertheless, Lord, not my will but Thine be done. And Your will is that there be reconciliation, which means I must die"—*that's* the cross.

The Roman soldier knew Jesus had died when he stuck a spear in His side and there was no reaction, other than the blood and water that flowed forth. So, when that person with whom you've had a hard time pokes you yet again and you don't respond, you don't react, you don't retaliate—you'll know you've died to your flesh.

Designed to be the most tortuous death possible, crucified victims often hung on a cross for two or three days before they died. Jesus hung on the cross for six hours. He was in a hurry because He knew the sooner He died and completed the Work of redemption, the sooner Easter Sunday would come. What if He had decided to struggle hour after hour, day after day? Easter couldn't happen until He died. That's why He said, "If you deny yourself, you'll have life. But if you seek to hang on to your life, you'll only prolong your misery."

Precious people, it's not that we *have* to die. It's that we *get* to. Will you be the one today who loves God so much that you will delight Him by dying to your rights, your way, your self?

If so, reconciliation is sure to follow as you race towards resurrection day.

---

26 Genesis 26:1
And there was a famine in the land, beside the first famine that was in the days of Abraham. And Isaac went unto Abimelech king of the Philistines unto Gerar.

Abimelech being a family name, this is the son of the king who had an encounter with Abraham regarding Sarah in chapter 20.

Genesis 26:2–5
And the Lord appeared unto him, and said, Go not down into Egypt; dwell in the land which I shall tell thee of: Sojourn in this land, and I will be with thee, and will bless thee; for unto thee, and unto thy seed, I will give all these countries, and I will perform the oath which I sware unto Abraham thy father; And I will make thy seed to multiply as the stars of heaven, and will give unto thy seed all these countries; and in thy seed shall all the nations of the earth be blessed; Because that Abraham obeyed my voice, and kept my charge, my commandments, my statutes, and my laws.

"Don't go to Egypt," God says to Isaac. "I'll bless you if you remain in the land to which I have called you." Egypt being a type of the world, God says the same thing to us. I know you experience dry times. I do too. I know there can be a famine in your soul. It happens to me as well. But resist the temptation to wander into Egypt in those times because if you do, you'll get burned and miss God's blessing.

Genesis 26:6
And Isaac dwelt in Gerar:

A border town, Gerar is the closest one can get to Egypt without crossing the line. God tells Isaac to stay in the Land, and what does Isaac do? He dwells right on the edge. Do you know anyone who might do this from time to time? How about you? How about me? We see how far we can go, how close we can get to the education, ethics, or entertainment of Egypt and still remain in the Promised Land to which we are called.

Genesis 26:7
And the men of the place asked him of his wife; and he said, She is my sister: for he feared to say, She is my wife; lest, said he, the men of the place should kill me for Rebekah; because she was fair to look upon.

Does any of this ring a bell? Abraham said the same thing at the same exact spot concerning his own wife (Genesis 20:2). Let every father be convicted and challenged. You see, the problem with going to the border is this: Your son will follow you. Camp out in Gerar, and that's where your son will most likely choose to dwell. Walk righteously, on the other hand, and your son will most likely follow in your footsteps to the Land of blessing.

Genesis 26:8, 9
And it came to pass, when he had been there a long time, that Abimelech king of the Philistines looked out at a window, and saw, and, behold, Isaac was sporting with Rebekah his wife. And Abimelech called Isaac, and said, Behold, of a surety she is thy wife: and how saidst thou, She is my sister? And Isaac said unto him, Because I said, Lest I die for her.

On one hand, Isaac is to be corrected for his cowardice. "I lied about my wife because I didn't want to die for her," he said. Yet the biblical command is the exact opposite: "Husbands love your wives even as Christ loved the church, and gave Himself for it" (Ephesians 5:25). In other words, husbands, just as Christ died on the Cross for His Bride, we are to die to our own desires, our own dreams, our own intentions, our own pleasures. On the other hand, Isaac is to be commended for his candor. He didn't try to rationalize, justify, or put a positive spin on his lie. He simply said, "I lied because I was afraid."

Genesis 26:10, 11
And Abimelech said, What is this thou hast done unto us? one of the people might lightly have lien with thy wife, and thou shouldest have brought guiltiness upon us. And Abimelech charged all his people, saying, He that toucheth this man or his wife shall surely be put to death.

Why would Abimelech say this? Just as Isaac followed in Abraham's footsteps, Abimelech had no doubt heard his dad's account of what had happened regarding Sarah—and warned his people accordingly (Genesis 20:6, 7).

Genesis 26:12 (a)
Then Isaac sowed in that land . . .

Humbled at "Border Town," Isaac returns to the Promised Land, where he belongs.

Genesis 26:12 (b)
. . . and received in the same year an hundredfold: and the Lord blessed him.

When did Isaac receive a hundredfold? After he said, "I made a mistake, Abimelech. I told you Rebekah was my sister because I'm a chicken. I didn't want to die." That's all confession is, gang—simply admitting the real deal. Isaac's sin was exposed; confession was made; and now he can go on.

Genesis 26:13 (a)
And the man waxed great, and went forward . . .

Yes, Isaac stumbled. Yes, he fell a bit. But he got up and went forward.

Genesis 26:13 (b)
. . . and grew . . .

Isn't this what you would like to be said about you? You might have stumbled, we all have fallen—but you waxed great by God's grace, you went forward, and you *grew.* That's what I desire my story to be.

Genesis 26:13 (c), 14
. . . until he became very great: For he had possession of flocks, and possessions of herds, and great store of servants: and the Philistines envied him.

So blessed was Isaac that even the mighty Philistines took notice.

Genesis 26:15
For all the wells which his father's servants had digged in the days of Abraham his father, the Philistines had stopped them, and filled them with earth.

As did the Philistines to Isaac, those who don't understand the grace of God will look at you and say, "It's not fair that you're blessed. I know you fell. I knew you back then. I heard about what you did," as they dig up dirt in a futile effort to plug the flow of God's forgiveness.

Genesis 26:16–18
And Abimelech said unto Isaac, Go from us; for thou art much mightier than we. And Isaac departed thence, and pitched his tent in the valley of Gerar, and dwelt there. And Isaac digged again the wells of water, which they had digged in the days of Abraham his father; for the philistines had stopped them after the death of Abraham: and he called their names after the names by which his father had called them.

On the move, restoring wells his father had dug, Isaac strikes water again.

Genesis 26:19
And Isaac's servants digged in the valley, and found there a well of springing water.

The term, "springing water," is correctly rendered "living water" in some translations. "If any man thirst," Jesus said, "let him come unto Me and drink, and out of his innermost being shall gush forth torrents of living water. This spake He of the Holy Ghost" (John 7:38). When did Isaac find living water? When he was in the valley. That's often the way it is. At least it was for me . . .

As a twenty-year-old teaching the Book of Jonah at a junior-high retreat, it hit me in the middle of my teaching that I didn't care at all about the kids sitting before me. It was as if the Lord held up a mirror and I saw the ugliness of my soul. I saw that I wanted to teach—but that I didn't care about those I was teach-

ing. I realized, much to my dismay, that they were just a means for me to do what I wanted to do. Here I was, studying for the ministry, involved in teaching and serving—and yet I knew my heart was calloused and hard. At the end of the weekend, in deep despair, I hopped in my van and drove for a couple of days. I finally pulled in to the parking lot of the church I was attending—Calvary Chapel in Costa Mesa. As I did, I saw a pastor I recognized from the Saturday night concerts I had attended there. His name was Tom Stipe.

"I know you're a pastor here," I said to him. "I'm just really sad."

"Oh?" he said. "What's up?"

I told him what was going on.

"That's easy," he said. "You need the Holy Spirit." He laid hands on me and prayed for me—and something happened to me. I felt a warm sensation in my inner being, and I began to worship the Lord in a way I had never done before.

That was a huge watershed for me, for I understood that, although previously I had the Holy Spirit inside of me, I lacked the overflow of the Spirit through me. And so I say to you, if you are in a valley spiritually—you're in the perfect place to find the living water because you realize your own inadequacy. Jesus said, "Blessed are those who hunger and thirst after righteousness—those who realize their need—for they shall be filled," (Matthew 5:6).

When, like Isaac, you say, "I want to be used to water the flock around me"—be it your family, your friends, your neighbors, a Sunday school class—the Lord will truly empower you in a fresh and dynamic way (Acts 1:8).

Genesis 26:20

And the herdmen of Gerar did strive with Isaac's herdmen, saying, The water is ours: and he called the name of the well Esek; because they strove with him.

Now that Isaac had found living water in the valley, was everything smooth sailing for him from that point on? No, for *esek* means "contention." It was immediately after Jesus' baptism in the Jordan River—where He was filled with the power and presence of the Holy Spirit—that He was led to the desert to be tempted and challenged by Satan. When we are filled with the living water of the Spirit, we must understand that challenges are sure to follow.

Genesis 26:21

And they digged another well, and strove for that also: and he called the name of it Sitnah.

Again, Isaac found water, and, again was challenged—thus the name, *Sitnah*, or "Hated."

With the exception of Moses, there is not a man in the Old Testament meeker than Isaac. After all, when Ishmael taunted and teased him, did Isaac fight back? No. When his dad laid him on the altar to sacrifice him, did thirty-year-old Isaac try to escape? No. When his father's servant selected a bride for him, did Isaac question his choice? No. When Abimelech rebuked him, did he rationalize his cowardice? No. When his water rights were challenged, did he stand his ground? No.

"Blessed are the meek," Jesus said, "for they shall inherit the earth" (Matthew 5:5). And here we see that happening. Isaac is a man of remarkable meekness. And he will indeed inherit earthly blessings.

Genesis 26:22

And he removed from thence, and digged another well; and for that they strove not: and he called the name of it Rehoboth; and he said, For now the LORD hath made room for us, and we shall be fruitful in the land.

When I was sixteen years old, a man in our church offered me a summer job washing windows for five dollars an hour—big money in that day. My first assignment was a ten-story building, using a dilapidated scaffolding system that had to be hand-cranked one side at a time. The already terrible situation was made worse by the fact that I hate heights. So there I was—cranking myself up floor after floor, leaning over and washing these windows day after day, coming home sick every night. After about four days of this, a dear brother called me and said, "Is there any way you would consider changing jobs and working at camp for us this summer?"

"You bet!" I said. By God's grace and providence I was delivered!

So I went to work in the Santa Cruz Mountains where I got to work with kids, teach the Word, and play games. I returned summer after summer, eventually working my way up to camp speaker and director.

After I was filled with the Spirit when I was twenty, the brother who had hired me initially called me into his office and said, "There's a rumor going around that you're attending a church that believes in the gifts of the Spirit." So I told him my story. "That's not our denominational position," he said. "I want you to stay here as long as you wish—just don't talk about the baptism of the Spirit." Loving my work there, I agreed.

But not long after this, I was approached by three counselors who said, "We have a problem. We were up late last night talking, and we realized we just don't have compassion for these kids. We prayed about it and felt like we should come to you and ask what we should do."

Oh, no! I thought. *I love working here, yet my boss told me not to talk about the baptism of the Spirit. But here these counselors are feeling as dry as I did when I was in my own spiritual valley previously.*

Finally, I said, "Here's the deal . . ." and went on to share with them my own experience.

They listened eagerly. I laid hands on them, prayed for them, and they were filled with the Spirit that evening in a remarkable way. As a result, I realized the doors were closing for me at camp. I also realized the doors were closing for the denomination I had planned to work with after graduation. "What should I do?" I wondered. "I guess I'd better let my pastor know."

Having attended Calvary Chapel for over three years, but having never personally met Pastor Chuck Smith, I wrote him a long letter about my situation, including a resume and a big color picture of myself. The following Sunday night found me sitting in the third row, listening to Chuck teaching through Psalms. When he came to Psalm 75:6, where the psalmist declares, "Promotion does not come from the north or the south, the east nor the west; it is the Lord who raises up one and sets down another," Chuck paused and said, "You know, people send me resumes and lists of their accomplishments and rewards. Don't do that. That's the way of the flesh. It's the Lord who will raise up one, who will set down another. You don't need to advertise yourself." And I wanted to melt through the crack in the pew and disappear.

I walked along the beach that evening for a long time thinking, *Lord, I am so dumb.* Ever feel that way? The next day I got a call from Chuck Smith's secretary saying, "Pastor Chuck wants to see you."

Oh, no! I thought, *A personal rebuke! I'm so far out of line he has to call me into his office and deal with me personally.* The problem was, the appointment was for seven weeks later. So for seven weeks, I lived in terror and repented constantly, wondering what I was going to do after graduation.

When my appointment finally arrived, I was so nervous that I just started talking—apologizing for my stupidity, asking forgiveness for my arrogance, explaining my predicament, rationalizing my behavior. All the while, Chuck just looked at me. Finally, when I came up for air, he said, "As a matter of fact, I called you because we're starting a Bible college in the mountains, and I want to hire you as one of our professors." I couldn't believe it! So off I went to Twin Peaks to teach Bible college—staying up late every night in order to get the next day's lesson ready just to keep ahead of my students.

The following year, my brother Dave came to see me and said, "Let's go back to San Jose and start a church." San Jose being our hometown, I was excited about the prospect. Dave, a great guy who I respect immensely and who has since gone on to impact many countries as an effective missionary, was a suit and tie man, while I was a Levis and sandals kind of guy. Thus, we thought Dave would relate to the IBM group, I'd relate to the hippies, and together we'd relate to everyone. Although we thought we'd have this great coming together, in reality, when I taught, one group would come out; and when Dave taught, an entirely different group attended. Neither group understood each other—and, as was the case with Jacob's wells, strife and contention were the result.

In the meantime, a few couples heard my tapes from San Jose and asked if I could meet with them for a weekend at a place called Applegate. Terry and I met together with about twenty people, and had a glorious time. They asked us back, and we eventually felt the Lord would have us move here. That was twenty years ago.

As I look back, I see my life as a series of digging wells and moving on—until finally I found my Rehoboth, for *rehoboth* means "room." Over the years, I've watched lots of gifted and talented men and women who had anointing, calling, and gifting miss great opportunities because they dug a well and there was strife; and they dug a second one, and there was contention; and instead of digging a third well, they gave up, thinking, *What's the use? I won't be used. Why go on?* God's plan is that we keep digging, keep digging, keep digging until we find our Rehoboth—where there's room.

Every one of you without exception has a Rehoboth awaiting you. But the enemy will try to discourage you through contention and strife. Why does God allow this to happen? Because He has a two-fold task: Not only to prepare a place for you, but to prepare you for the place. That means you'll go through some trying times, some stretching points, some questions—but you must not throw in the towel and give up. You keep digging, move down the road, dig again, move down the road, dig again—and eventually you'll find your Rehoboth. I promise.

Genesis 26:23–33
And he went up from thence to Beer-sheba. And the LORD appeared unto him the same night, and said, I am the God of Abraham thy father: fear not, for I am with thee, and will bless thee, and multiply thy seed for my servant Abraham's sake. And he builded an altar there, and called upon the name of the LORD, and pitched his tent there: and there Isaac's servants digged a well. Then Abimelech went to him from Gerar, and Ahuzzath one of his friends, and Phichol the chief captain of his army. And Isaac said unto them, Wherefore come ye to me, seeing ye hate me, and have sent me away from you? And they said, We saw certainly that the LORD was with thee: and we said, Let there be now an oath betwixt us, even betwixt us and thee, and let us make a covenant with thee; That thou wilt do us no hurt, as we have not touched thee, and as we have done unto thee nothing but good, and have sent thee away in peace: thou art now the blessed of the LORD. And he made them a feast, and they did eat and drink. And they rose up betimes in the morning, and sware one to another: and Isaac sent them away, and they departed from him in peace. And it came to pass the same day, that Isaac's servants came, and told him concerning the well which they had digged, and said unto him, We have found water. And he called it Shebah: therefore the name of the city is Beer-sheba unto this day.

Here, Isaac's one-time enemies seek him out to make a covenant with him. If you keep on digging, your life will impact the people around you. Oh, Satan will use them to bring strife and contention into your life initially because he doesn't want you to expand the borders of the kingdom. But if you resist him, he will flee from you ultimately (James 4:7), and even the Philistines will be drawn to you eventually.

Genesis 26:34, 35
And Esau was forty years old when he took to wife Judith the daughter of Beeri the Hittite, and Bashemath the daughter of Elon the Hittite: Which were a grief of mind unto Isaac and to Rebekah.

While Jacob was digging wells, Esau was taking wives. Unfortunately, because the women he chose were pagans, in so doing he broke the hearts of his parents—she who had followed Abraham's servant to a new life (Genesis 24:58), and he who had prayed in the field, waiting for God's best (Genesis 24:63).

27

Genesis 27:1
And it came to pass, that when Isaac was old, and his eyes were dim, so that he could not see, he called Esau his eldest son, and said unto him, My son: and he said unto him, Behold, here am I.

Perhaps because his half-brother Ishmael died at the age of one hundred and thirty-seven, Isaac now being one hundred and thirty-seven years old himself, is keenly aware of his mortality and that his body is beginning to fail him.

Genesis 27:2
And he said, Behold now, I am old, I know not the day of my death:

Although at one hundred and thirty-seven years of age, Isaac was indeed an old man, he was correct in realizing he didn't know the day of his death—for he would live an additional forty-three years.

Genesis 27:3, 4
Now therefore take, I pray thee, thy weapons, thy quiver and thy bow, and go out to the field, and take me some venison; And make me savoury meat, such as I love, and bring it to me, that I may eat; that my soul may bless thee before I die.

In your Sunday school mind's eye, you probably see Esau as being fifteen, eighteen, or twenty-one years old. Esau is, in fact, seventy-seven years old at this point—which makes the story all the more incredible to me.

Genesis 27:5–10
And Rebekah heard when Isaac spake to Esau his son. And Esau went to the field to hunt for venison, and to bring it. And Rebekah spake unto Jacob her son, saying, Behold, I heard thy father speak unto Esau thy brother, saying, Bring me venison, and make me savoury meat, that I may eat, and bless thee before the LORD before my death. Now therefore, my son, obey my voice according to that which I command thee. Go now to the flock, and fetch me from thence two good kids of the goats; and I will make them savoury meat for thy father, such as he loveth: And thou shalt bring it to thy father, that he may eat, and that he may bless thee before his death.

As we saw earlier, it was clear Jacob was to be the blessed one (Genesis 25:23). Because Rebekah knew this, when she heard Isaac was about to bless Esau, we see her doing what you and I can fall into oh, so subtly: knowing God's Word and doing God's work—but not in God's way. You might have a sincere heart and pure motives in wanting to see God's work done in the ministry or in your family. But God's work must be done God's way. Ask Moses . . .

Wanting to see his Israelite brothers set free from the tyranny of the Egyptians, one day when Moses saw an Egyptian beating one of the Hebrew children, he rescued his Hebrew brother, and killed the Egyptian, thinking he would be a hero in the eyes of the Hebrew people. But because God didn't direct Moses to do this, the end result was rejection by the very people he was trying to help.

God's work must be done God's way. Ask David . . .

He knew the people would be blessed, the glory of God would be experienced if the ark of the covenant was brought into the capital city of Jerusalem. To transport the ark from where it was, six miles outside of Jerusalem, David built a cart and stationed a man named Uzzah, *or "Strong," upon it. In front of the ark, leading the way was a man named* Ahio, *or "Friendly." Talk about a great set-up—Mr. Strong controlling the cart, Mr. Friendly leading the way. It seemed like such a wonderful way to bring in the glory of God. But you know the story: On the way, the cart hit a rut in the road, and the ark began to wobble. Thinking he had better give God a hand, Uzzah reached out to stabilize the ark. But when his hand touched it, God killed him (2 Samuel 6:7).*

Completely disheartened, David pouted for several months. But when he got back in the Word again, he discovered that the ark of the covenant was to be carried on the shoulders of priests rather than on a cart. Why? Because carts are nothing more than boards and big wheels, whereas priests are people who praise and pray. All too often, people call board meetings and bring in big wheels to make God's work happen. But such is Philistine mentality. God's way is to work through people who praise and pray.

As the priests carried the ark, they stopped every six steps, built an altar and sacrificed a bull to the Lord. The world would say, "It's not efficient to stop every six steps on a six-mile journey—especially in this age of technology." However, what God is concerned about in spiritual life is not efficiency, but effectiveness. Efficiency is doing things right. Effectiveness is doing the right thing. Why did David stop every six steps? Because six is the number of man and the flesh. It's a reminder that the Mr. Strong and Mr. Friendly mentality won't make it spiritually.

Only by stopping every six steps to sacrifice did the ark make it to Jerusalem. Only by waiting on, walking with, and looking to God will His presence be evident in our lives.

Genesis 27:11, 12 (a)

And Jacob said to Rebekah his mother, Behold, Esau my brother is a hairy man, and I am a smooth man: My father peradventure will feel me, and I shall seem to him as a deceiver . . .

Jacob doesn't say, "If I do this, I'll *be* a deceiver." He says, "If I do this, I'll *seem like* a deceiver." Isn't this where our culture finds itself? Reputation is what people think I am. Character is what I know I am. And most people today, like Jacob, are concerned about reputation over character. How do you know what your character really is? You'll know by what you do when no one is around.

Genesis 27:12 (b)–15

. . . and I shall bring a curse upon me, and not a blessing. And his mother said unto him, Upon me be thy curse, my son: only obey my voice, and go fetch me them. And he went, and fetched, and brought them to his mother: and his mother made savoury meat, such as his father loved. And Rebekah took goodly raiment of her eldest son Esau, which were with her in the house, and put them upon Jacob her younger son:

An outdoorsman, Esau had a distinct aroma about him. Realizing this, Rebekah put some of Esau's garments on Jacob.

Genesis 27:16, 17

And she put the skins of the kids of the goats upon his hands, and upon the smooth of his neck: And she gave the savoury meat and the bread, which she had prepared, into the hand of her son Jacob.

Rebekah is sharp. She takes the skins of the goats and straps them around the arms and neck of her son, Jacob, so that if Isaac feels his skin, he'll feel like Esau.

Genesis 27:18–23

And he came unto his father, and said, My father: and he said, Here am I; who art thou, my son? And Jacob said unto his father, I am Esau thy firstborn; I have done according as

thou badest me: arise, I pray thee, sit and eat of my venison, that thy soul may bless me. And Isaac said unto his son, How is it that thou hast found it so quickly, my son? And he said, Because the LORD thy God brought it to me. And Isaac said unto Jacob, Come near, I pray thee, that I may feel thee, my son, whether thou be my very son Esau or not. And Jacob went near unto Isaac his father; and he felt him, and said, The voice is Jacob's voice, but the hands are the hands of Esau. And he discerned him not, because his hands were hairy, as his brother Esau's hands: so he blessed him.

Although Jacob didn't sound like Esau, he smelled like Esau and felt like Esau. Therefore he must be Esau, thought Isaac, trusting his senses rather than the word that he heard.

Whenever we make decisions based upon what we feel or what we smell or what we see rather than upon what we hear in the Word, we will be deceived. If an experience, trend, or phenomena isn't seen throughout the New Testament record of the life of Christ and of His church—be it barking, laughing, or falling down—it's Jacob parading as Esau, and we will be as deceived as Isaac was if we choose to follow our senses rather than the Word.

Genesis 27:24, 25 (a)
And he said, Art thou my very son Esau? And he said, I am. And he said, Bring it near to me, and I will eat of my son's venison, that my soul may bless thee . . .

A key component of Hebrew life, the blessing was pronounced by the patriarch primarily upon the oldest son. A declaration of who one is and a revelation of where one is headed, Orthodox Jewish fathers understand the significance of the blessing and bestow it upon their children to this day. Following, we see the four elements that compromise this blessing . . .

Genesis 27:25 (b), 26
. . . And he brought it near to him, and he did eat: and he brought him wine, and he drank. And his father Isaac said unto him, Come near now, and kiss me, my son.

First, the blessing involves *a tender, meaningful touch.* In a study of girls who had numerous unwanted pregnancies, a common denominator was found: they all had fathers who did not show them affection. Consequently, they sought this missing ingredient in the arms of strangers.

A pure and tender touch upon our kids is so important. That's why Jesus didn't call out a blanket blessing upon the children who were brought to Him. He tenderly and lovingly *touched* them (Mark 10:13).

Genesis 27:27
And he came near, and kissed him: and he smelled the smell of his raiment, and blessed him, and said, See, the smell of my son is as the smell of a field which the LORD hath blessed:

Secondly, the blessing includes *a spoken message of valued, valuable evaluation.* "You have the fragrance of the field. You are an outdoorsman. This is what I see in you," said Isaac, as he affirmed Esau's strengths through the spoken blessing.

Many kids never hear their parents' perception of them. Many parents never say, "This is what I see in you. This is how I see God made you. This is what is great about you." Speak a word of valuable evaluation today, Dad, for not hearing from you at all hurts far more than hearing a word of correction from you.

Genesis 27:28, 29
Therefore God give thee of the dew of heaven, and the fatness of the earth, and plenty of corn and wine: Let people serve thee, and nations bow down to thee: be lord over thy brethren, and let thy mother's sons bow down to thee: cursed be every one that curseth thee, and blessed be he that blesseth thee.

Thirdly, the blessing gives *a word of destination.* Our kids and grandchildren need to hear not only what we see in them presently, but what we see ahead for them eventually. Here again, the Orthodox Jewish families understand this concept so well. When you go into an Orthodox home, the parents will say, "Here is Joey the doctor, and Benny the lawyer"—even though Joey and Benny are only four and five years old. In so doing, they are giving their kids a special future. And they do indeed grow up becoming doctors and lawyers, scientists and rabbis because that is what is pronounced on them.

What do you see your son or daughter becoming, Dad?

Let them know!

Genesis 27:30–33
And it came to pass, as soon as Isaac had made an end of blessing Jacob, and Jacob was yet scarce gone out from the presence of Isaac his father, that Esau his brother came in from his hunting. And he also had made savoury meat, and brought it unto his

father, and said unto his father, Let my father arise, and eat of his son's venison, that thy soul may bless me. And Isaac his father said unto him, Who art thou? And he said, I am thy son, thy firstborn Esau. And Isaac trembled very exceedingly, and said, Who? where is he that hath taken venison, and brought it me, and I have eaten of all before thou camest, and have blessed him? yea, and he shall be blessed.

Realizing that God will ultimately have His way, Isaac conceded that Jacob would indeed be blessed.

Genesis 27:34 (a)
And when Esau heard the words of his father, he cried with a great and exceeding bitter cry . . .

In the Hebrew language, this is an emphatic expression describing a painful, plaintive wail. Here Esau, this man's man, sobs bitterly.

Genesis 27:34 (b)–37
. . . and said unto his father, Bless me, even me also, O my father. And he said, Thy brother came with subtilty, and hath taken away thy blessing. And he said, Is not he rightly named Jacob? for he hath supplanted me these two times: he took away my birthright; and, behold, now he hath taken away my blessing. And he said, Hast thou not reserved a blessing for me? And Isaac answered and said unto Esau, Behold, I have made him thy lord, and all his brethren have I given to him for servants; and with corn and wine have I sustained him: and what shall I do now unto thee, my son?

Finally, the blessing contained *a promise of continued commitment.* Because it was nonnegotiable, the blessing says, "Not only do I see this *in* you, but I am committed to see it through *for* you, and am determined to stand *with* you regardless of reversals, setbacks, or disappointments."

Job, the most righteous man on the face of the earth, rose early every morning and offered a sacrifice for each one of his sons and daughters—a lot of hard, bloody, dirty work. And I can do that as a dad for my kids through intercessory prayer, through doing whatever I can to see God's power upon them and His work flowing through them.

Genesis 27:38
And Esau said unto his father, Hast thou but one blessing, my father? bless me, even me also, O my father. And Esau lifted up his voice, and wept.

Even though the birthright included a double inheritance, Esau regarded it so lightly that he traded it for a bowl of beans. But so desperately did Esau desire the blessing, that even at seventy-seven years of age, he wept passionately over its loss.

Maybe you're saying, "I never had a father or grandfather pronounce a blessing on my life." You can. Your heavenly Father is just waiting to bless you. He will pronounce blessing upon your life, give direction for your life, and place His hand tenderly upon you anytime you choose to come into His presence. Each of us has a Father who's always there, who is as close to us as a simple prayer. May God give us wisdom to bless our own kids as we declare to them who they are and reveal to them what they can be. And may He give us the desire to continually seek His blessing upon our own lives.

Genesis 27:39, 40 (a)
And Isaac his father answered and said unto him, Behold, thy dwelling shall be the fatness of the earth, and of the dew of heaven from above; And by thy sword shalt thou live, and shalt serve thy brother . . .

Isaac says to Esau, "You're not going to be in a place of permanence, but rather you are going to live off the land and by the sword, serving your brother." And then he inserts an interesting clause . . .

Genesis 27:40 (b)
. . . and it shall come to pass when thou shalt have the dominion, that thou shalt break his yoke from off thy neck.

In other words, "You'll be under your brother's authority, Esau, fighting for your very life. But there will come a season when you will break loose from the yoke of his dominion over you."

I believe what is spoken here has huge prophetic implication. You see, God's anger at the Edomites, the descendants of Esau, appears throughout the Old Testament—seen nowhere more clearly than in the Book of Obadiah, the only book in the Old Testament devoted to an indictment against a single group of people.

Why does God wage war against the Edomites? An Edomite named Haman sheds light on the reason, for in the Book of Esther, we read of his plan to annihilate the Jews.

Then, around the year 300 B.C., a group called the Nabateans took control of the area where the Edomites lived southeast of Israel. Driven out of their homeland, the Edomites settled around Hebron—part of the West Bank today—and became known as Idumeans. Years later, when the Macabbeans rose up and overthrew the Syrians who had taken control of Jerusalem, the Macabbeans said to the people living in Idumea, "We'll let you stay here only if you convert to Judaism." So the Idumeans became Jews religiously, although they remained Edomites ethnically.

Around the year 47 B.C., Julius Caesar appointed Antipater—an Idumean—as governor of the region. Antipater was the father of Herod, and Herod being a family name, all of the Herods who followed were Idumean, including the Herod who ordered the death of every male child under two years of age in an attempt to kill the Babe of Bethlehem. From generation to generation, God declares, "I wage war against the descendants of Esau" (Ezekiel 25:14) because from the very beginning there's a spirit at work. It's the spirit to destroy the Jewish nation and prevent Messiah from surviving. It's the spirit of antichrist.

In the year A.D. 70, the Romans, led by General Titus, were positioned to destroy the city of Jerusalem. Josephus tells us 20,000 Idumeans were let in the city gates by the Jews because they promised to help fight the Romans. But once inside, the Idumeans turned against the Jews and slaughtered them. The surviving Jews scattered; the Idumeans migrated to Italy, settling around the city of Rome, where their descendants are to this day. Why Rome? Because through Herod, there was a linkage to the Romans.

According to Daniel 9, antichrist shall be of the people who destroyed the city of Jerusalem. Who destroyed Jerusalem? The Romans. Thus, the nationality of antichrist will most likely be Roman, but his ethnic background will be Idumean because prophecies throughout the Old Testament indicate that he will be linked ethnically to Esau. God is not capricious or unfair when He says, "I hate Esau" (Romans 9:13) because there's a spirit which travels through Esau's descendants directly to antichrist.

When is the day Esau will beat the yoke of Jacob from off his neck? I suggest it is the day antichrist rises to power and sets up his image in the temple in Jerusalem (Matthew 24:15).

Genesis 27:41–45
And Esau hated Jacob because of the blessing wherewith his father blessed him: and Esau said in his heart, The days of mourning for my father are at hand; then will I slay my brother Jacob. And these words of Esau her elder son were told to Rebekah: and she sent and called Jacob her younger son, and said unto him, Behold, thy brother Esau, as touching thee, doth comfort himself, purposing to kill thee. Now therefore, my son, obey my voice; and arise, flee thou to Laban my brother to Haran; And tarry with him a few days, until thy brother's fury turn away; Until thy brother's anger turn away from thee, and he forget that which thou hast done to him: then I will send, and fetch thee from thence: why should I be deprived also of you both in one day?

"Go to Uncle Laban's house and stay there for a few days until Esau simmers down," Rebekah said to Jacob. But guess what. Those few days would turn into twenty-plus years, and Rebekah would never see her son, Jacob again. Trying to manipulate, trying to pull the strings, trying to make it happen in her own energy, Rebekah will lose her son. Trying to help God out would prove to be a heartbreaking disaster for this mother who loved her son deeply.

Moms, be careful that you don't try to protect or direct your kids in your own energy because, like Rebekah, you will end up making a mess that will ultimately break your heart. Don't pry. Pray. Fight the right battle, for the Word says we wrestle not against flesh and blood, but against principalities and powers (Ephesians 6:12).

Genesis 27:46
And Rebekah said to Isaac, I am weary of my life because of the daughters of Heth: if Jacob take a wife of the daughters of Heth, such as these which are of the daughters of the land, what good shall my life do me?

"If Jacob marries a girl like the girls Esau chose—a girl who doesn't love God—I would just want to die," said Rebekah. That's why she was determined that Jacob, her pride and joy, would not be sucked in to the ways of the world as was his twin brother.

---

28 The next eight chapters of the Book of Genesis all focus on God's work in and on Jacob. We see the saving of Jacob here in chapter 28, the subduing of Jacob in chapters 29—32, the separating of Jacob in chapters 33—34, and the sanctifying of Jacob in chapter 35.

Genesis 28:1, 2
And Isaac called Jacob, and blessed him, and charged him, and said unto him, Thou shalt not take a wife of the daughters of Canaan. Arise, go to Padan-aram, to the house of Bethuel thy mother's father; and take thee a wife from thence of the daughters of Laban thy mother's brother.

Abraham sent a servant to find a bride for his son, Isaac. Isaac, however, sent his son, Jacob, to find his own bride. Paul would write, "work out your *own* salvation with fear and trembling, for it is God who is at work within you both to will and to do of His good pleasure" (Philippians 2:12, italics added).

Your salvation is going to be worked out, exercised, a little bit differently than the salvation of the person sitting next to you or that of the generation that went before you. Oh, we're all saved by grace through faith in Jesus Christ. But it's all going to work out a little bit differently in each of us.

This allows me to give freedom to people whose salvation is being worked out a little differently than mine might be. We can give each other lots of space because, within the parameters of grace and faith, God deals with each of us uniquely.

Genesis 28:3–9
And God Almighty bless thee, and make thee fruitful, and multiply thee, that thou mayest be a multitude of people; And give thee the blessing of Abraham, to thee, and to thy seed with thee; that thou mayest inherit the land wherein thou art a stranger, which God gave to Abraham. And Isaac sent away Jacob: and he went to Padan-aram unto Laban, son of Bethuel the Syrian, the brother of Rebekah, Jacob's and Esau's mother. When Esau saw that Isaac had blessed Jacob, and sent him away to Padan-aram, to take him a wife from thence; and that as he blessed him he gave him a charge, saying, Thou shalt not take a wife of the daughters of Canaan; And that Jacob obeyed his father and his mother, and was gone to Padan-aram; And Esau seeing that the daughters of Canaan pleased not Isaac his father; Then went Esau unto Ishmael, and took unto the wives which he had Mahalath the daughter of Ishmael Abraham's son, the sister of Nebajoth, to be his wife.

Realizing his choice of Canaanite wives had upset his father, Esau takes an Ishmaelite wife hoping to rectify the situation. Poor Esau. All he can do at this point is think carnally as he wades deeper into the murky waters of polygamy. It is not only Esau who will get mired in the perils of polygamy, but his brother, Jacob will as well.

The Bible is, in a sense, like a newspaper. It reports the facts—but certainly doesn't condone all of them. The fact that the *San Francisco Chronicle* reports a shooting in Arkansas doesn't mean the *Chronicle* approves of the shooting.

Where there's polygamy or immorality, the Bible will tell it like it is, but that doesn't mean God approves of it. The Law would later put some very real parameters around this issue of polygamy, as it would with divorce. But due to the heartaches and heartbreaks they both cause, neither are God's will.

Genesis 28:10
And Jacob went out from Beer-sheba, and went toward Haran.

Knowing Esau is planning to kill him, Jacob runs for his life.

Genesis 28:11
And he lighted upon a certain place, and tarried there all night, because the sun was set; and he took of the stones of that place, and put them for his pillows, and lay down in that place to sleep.

If it is true that a clear conscience makes a soft pillow, it is appropriate that Jacob slept on a pillow of rocks, for, after cheating Esau out of his birthright and blessing, Jacob's conscience was anything but clear.

Genesis 28:12 (a)
And he dreamed . . .

God is about to appear to Jacob in a most remarkable manner—not when Jacob was trying to be a good guy, but when he was running away. That's because everything God does is solely, completely, and totally by grace.

Genesis 28:12 (b)
. . . and behold a ladder set up on the earth, and the top of it reached to heaven: and behold the angels of God ascending and descending on it.

Notice the order: In both this account and the comments Jesus will make in John 1 which refer to this story, the order is that the angels ascend to heaven and come back down—which means that angels hang out here. We tend to think of angels as being only in heaven. But angels hang out on earth as ministering spirits (Hebrews 1:14).

So commonplace was the angelic presence in the early church that when Rhoda told a group of believers that Peter had been released from prison in answer to their prayers and was standing at the door, they thought it was simply his angel and didn't even bother to break up their prayer meeting to check it out (Acts 12).

Later on, Paul would say, "When spiritual gifts are being exercised and prophecy is being spoken keep in mind, women, that the angels are present, so make sure you don't present yourself in a way that is out of order" (see 1 Corinthians 11:10).

The angels are extremely sensitive about people being out of order, about people not living in submission. Why? Because one-third of their company was kicked out of heaven when they moved out from under the authority of God and linked themselves to Lucifer. The angels are also extremely concerned about the issue of submission because they saw what happened in the Garden of Eden when Eve was left uncovered by her husband and thus in a position of vulnerability.

I truly believe there are angels in this room tonight because Peter said, "When you talk about the things of salvation, the angels are diligent to look into those things" (1 Peter 1:12). We are a living laboratory, gang, to help the angels understand the grace, goodness, and lovingkindness of God. You see, angels experience firsthand the holiness of God, the omnipotence of God, the omniscience of God—but the idea of God loving failures and sinners like us is a constant source of amazement to them.

Genesis 28:13 (a)
And, behold, the LORD stood above it, and said, I am the LORD God of Abraham thy father, and the God of Isaac . . .

Alluding to this story, Jesus told Nathanael he would see angels ascending and descending upon the Son of God. In other words, "The ladder spanning the gap between earth and heaven is Me. The Ladder bridging the gap between man and God is Me" (see John 1:51).

Genesis 28:13 (b)–15 (a)
. . . the land whereon thou liest, to thee will I give it, and to thy seed; And thy seed shall be as the dust of the earth, and thou shalt spread abroad to the west, and to the east, and to the north, and to the south: and in thee and in thy seed shall all the families of the earth be blessed. And, behold, I am with thee . . .

The first thing God promised Jacob was His presence.

Genesis 28:15 (b)
. . . and will keep thee in all places whither thou goest . . .

Secondly, God promised Jacob His protection.

Genesis 28:15 (c)
. . . and will bring thee again into this land . . .

Thirdly, God promised Jacob preservation—that he would return to the Promised Land.

Genesis 28:15 (d)
. . . for I will not leave thee, until I have done that which I have spoken to thee of.

Finally, God reiterated to Jacob His promise—that He would complete the work which He had begun.

Genesis 28:16
And Jacob awaked out of his sleep, and he said, Surely the LORD is in this place; and I knew it not.

"God is here, and I didn't know it." Why wouldn't Jacob know this? Because of his circumstances. He knew he was nothing but a conniver, hiding out in a seemingly God-forsaken, rocky region.

That may be your story today. You may feel like you're stuck in a rocky situation, a rocky marriage, rocky finances, or on a rocky road. But God would say to you tonight, "I'm with you in this place—even though you may not know it."

What can separate us from the love of God? Neither death, nor life, nor angels, nor principalities, nor powers, nor things present, nor things to come, nor height, nor depth, nor any other creature (Romans 8:38, 39).

Why? Because there is no condemnation to them who are in Christ Jesus (Romans 8:1). There is no separation because there is no condemnation. Why is there no condemnation? Because Jesus Christ, our Hero, our Lord took all of the stuff that would separate us from the Father—the stuff we did last year, the stuff we're doing today, the stuff we'll do tomorrow—and paid for it *all*.

If you find yourself in a rocky situation, you have a choice: You can either say, "God is nowhere"—or, like Jacob, you can look at your surroundings with new eyes and say, "God is now here." On what basis? On the basis of grace.

Genesis 28:17, 18
And he was afraid, and said, How dreadful is this place! this is none other but the house of God, and this is the gate of heaven. And Jacob rose up early in the morning, and took the stone that he had put for his pillows, and set it up for a pillar, and poured oil upon the top of it.

In Jacob, we see three characteristics of the person who truly encounters God . . .

First, *true conversion is seen in his worship.* You'll know when a person is converted because he'll want to worship God. Whether it be singing, lifting hands, or building a monument like Jacob did—the heart of a true believer will look for a way to express love and thanksgiving to his Lord.

Genesis 28:19
And he called the name of that place Bethel: but the name of that city was called Luz at the first.

Bethel means "house of God." *Luz* means "separation." *I was separated from God,* thought Jacob, *but now I realize I'm right in the house of God.* The same is true of you. There are people who, if they caught wind that you're at a Bible study, would be shocked. They knew you ten years ago, or two weeks ago. But since then, you've moved from Luz to Bethel. And everything is changed.

Genesis 28:20, 21
And Jacob vowed a vow, saying, If God will be with me, and will keep me in this way that I go, and will give me bread to eat, and raiment to put on, So that I come again to my father's house in peace; then shall the LORD be my God:

Jacob isn't saying, "Okay, God, if You do this, then You'll be my God." No, the idea here is, "If You'll have me, God—far out!"

Genesis 28:22
And this stone, which I have set for a pillar, shall be God's house: and of all that thou shalt give me I will surely give the tenth unto thee.

Secondly, *true conversion is seen in one's work.* Faith without works is dead, and one of the most practical ways a person shows he has faith that works is when he gives the tithe, which is God's. Every Christian should understand that the first tenth of whatever comes his way is God's. If I keep the tenth, I'm robbing God (Malachi 3:8). But if I let it go, God says, "I will open the windows of heaven and bless you" (Malachi 3:10). You see, God has a job to do: to make us less selfish. So He requires the first tenth, knowing that every time we put our tithe in the basket, along with it goes a bit more of our selfishness.

True conversion manifests itself in one's worship and one's work. We'll see a third manifestation in chapter 29 . . .

29

Genesis 29:1
Then Jacob went on his journey, and came into the land of the people of the east.

If your Bible has margin notes, perhaps you see the phrase "went on his journey" rendered "lifted up his feet." In Hebrew, the literal idea is that of "happy feet." As we saw in chapter 28, Jacob's conversion was seen in his witness and his work. Here we see *true conversion in Jacob's walk.* As he heads to Padanaram, he does so with "happy feet." He does so with enthusiasm.

Enthusiasm, or *en theos,* simply means "full of God." An encounter with God—the Giver of joy, the Source of all true happiness—manifests itself in a changed walk. And such was Jacob's case. But even though Jacob is saved, he's not yet subdued. So in the chapter before us, as well as the three following, we'll see God dealing with Jacob as He moves Jacob along on his spiritual journey.

Genesis 29:2–4
And he looked, and behold a well in the field, and, lo, there were three flocks of sheep lying by it; for out of that well they watered the flocks: and a great stone was upon the well's mouth. And thither were all the flocks gathered: and they rolled the stone from the well's mouth, and watered the sheep, and put the stone again upon the well's mouth in his place. And Jacob said unto them, My brethren, whence be ye? And they said, Of Haran are we.

The words, "of Haran are we" must have been music to Jacob's ears, for, after traveling over four hundred miles through rough, rocky regions, he had finally reached his destination.

Genesis 29:5
And he said unto them, Know ye Laban the son of Nahor? And they said, We know him.

A real character, Laban will prove to be the perfect match for Jacob.

Genesis 29:6, 7
And he said unto them, Is he well? And they said, He is well: and, behold, Rachel his daughter cometh with the sheep. And he said, Lo, it is yet high day, neither is it time that the cattle should be gathered together: water ye the sheep, and go and feed them.

Spotting Rachel in the distance, Jacob said to the men gathered around the well, "Hey, guys, this is the time of day for you to water these sheep and take them to pasture." Could it be that Jacob was trying to clear the field in order to spend some time with Rachel?

Genesis 29:8
And they said, We cannot, until all the flocks be gathered together, and till they roll

the stone from the well's mouth; then we water the sheep.

Could it be that the men gathered around the well were waiting for the shepherdess who was "beautiful and well favored" (29:17)?

Genesis 29:9, 10 (a)
And while he yet spake with them, Rachel came with her father's sheep: for she kept them. And it came to pass, when Jacob saw Rachel the daughter of Laban his mother's brother, and the sheep of Laban his mother's brother, that Jacob went near, and rolled the stone from the well's mouth . . .

Rachel shows up and suddenly, with Herculean strength, Jacob single-handedly rolls the stone from the well—no doubt hoping to impress her.

Genesis 29:10 (b), 11
. . . and watered the flock of Laban his mother's brother. And Jacob kissed Rachel, and lifted up his voice, and wept.

Rebekah had watered the camels of her future husband (Genesis 24:20). Here, her son waters the flock of his future wife.

Genesis 29:12, 13
And Jacob told Rachel that he was her father's brother, and that he was Rebekah's son: and she ran and told her father. And it came to pass, when Laban heard the tidings of Jacob his sister's son, that he ran to meet him, and embraced him, and kissed him, and brought him to his house. And he told Laban all these things.

Laban didn't know Jacob, but he did know that Jacob came from a wealthy family, as evidenced by the gifts he had received from them prior to his sister Rebekah's marriage to Isaac (Genesis 24:53).

Genesis 29:14 (a)
And Laban said to him, Surely thou art my bone and my flesh . . .

As we will see, Jacob and Laban are two birds of a feather, for they are both quintessential con men.

Genesis 29:14 (b), 15
. . . And he abode with him the space of a month. And Laban said unto Jacob, Because thou art my brother, shouldest thou therefore serve me for nought? tell me, what shall thy wages be?

"You've been here for a month," Laban said to Jacob. "I see that you have some real talent. I want you to work for me. What's your price?"

Genesis 29:16, 17
And Laban had two daughters: the name of the elder was Leah, and the name of the younger was Rachel. Leah was tender eyed; but Rachel was beautiful and well favoured.

Some commentators say "tender eyed" means Leah couldn't see well. Others say it means she had blue eyes as opposed to the more acceptable brown eyes of that culture. Others say her loving eyes were her best feature. But contrasted with the fact that Rachel was beautiful of face and well-favoured in form, this much is sure: Rachel was the more physically desirable of the two.

Genesis 29:18
And Jacob loved Rachel; and said, I will serve thee seven years for Rachel thy younger daughter.

"I will work for you for seven years for Rachel's hand," Jacob said to Laban.

Genesis 29:19, 20
And Laban said, It is better that I give her to thee, than that I should give her to another man: abide with me. And Jacob served seven years for Rachel; and they seemed unto him but a few days, for the love he had to her.

Jacob worked seven years and they seemed but a few days because love is patient (1 Corinthians 13).

- Love gives.
- Lust takes.
- Love waits.
- Lust won't.
- Love is patient.
- Lust is pressure.
- Lust says Now.
- Love says No.

There's a world of difference between love and lust.

Genesis 29:21
And Jacob said unto Laban, Give me my wife, for my days are fulfilled, that I may go in unto her.

"My seven years are complete," Jacob said to Laban. "Now it's time for you to come through with your end of the bargain."

Genesis 29:22–25
And Laban gathered together all the men of the place, and made a feast. And it came to pass in the evening, that he took Leah his daughter, and brought her to him; and he went in unto her. And Laban gave unto his daughter Leah, Zilpah his maid for an handmaid. And it came to pass, that in the morning, behold, it was Leah: and he said to Laban, What is this thou hast done unto me? did not I serve with thee for Rachel? wherefore then hast thou beguiled me?

Dressed in traditional wedding attire, Leah was veiled from head to toe. Thus, it wasn't until the next day that Jacob realized he had been tricked.

Genesis 29:26
And Laban said, It must not be so done in our country, to give the younger before the firstborn.

"In our country, we have rules," said Laban. "And the rules dictate we take care of the firstborn." Firstborn? That would strike a chord in the heart of Jacob, for he knew what he had done to Esau—the firstborn in his own family—had come right back on him. "Whatever a man sows, that shall he also reap" (Galatians 6:7)—and Jacob discovered this to be true.

Genesis 29:27
Fulfil her week, and we will give thee this also for the service which thou shalt serve with me yet seven other years.

"Fulfill her *week*. . . . Thou shalt serve *seven years.*" Here it is clear that a biblical "week" can refer to seven years—an especially important understanding with regard to the prophecy concerning the seventy weeks of Daniel (Daniel 9).

Genesis 29:28–30
And Jacob did so, and fulfilled her week: and he gave him Rachel his daughter to wife also. And Laban gave to Rachel his daughter Bilhah his handmaid to be her maid. And he went in also unto Rachel, and he loved also Rachel more than Leah, and served with him yet seven other years.

Jacob loved Rachel more than Leah. But watch what happens in the space of just one verse . . .

Genesis 29:31
And when the LORD saw that Leah was hated, he opened her womb: but Rachel was barren.

At first the text indicates that Jacob loved Rachel more than he loved Leah. But here we read that he hated Leah. This is the problem with polygamy. Completely contrary to the recent reports that affairs can be healthy for a marriage, the Bible says man cannot serve two masters, for he'll love one and hate the other (Matthew 6:24).

You see, the heart is constructed in such a way that we cannot be in love with two people simultaneously. We might think we can. The world might say we can. But the Bible says it can't be done. We can't serve two masters. And this is the problem with polygamy, or with any relationship with the opposite sex outside of marriage.

If a man is having even an occupational or ministerial relationship with any woman other than his wife, he's headed for trouble because Jesus taught that where a man's treasure is—his thoughts and dreams—there will his heart be also (Matthew 6:21). An innocent relationship with a member of the opposite sex other than your spouse is a subtle, sad, serious situation because as you begin to share even innocently with each other, your heart follows.

That's why when a couple comes in for marital counseling, the first thing I ask is if there's someone else they're involved with, talking to at work, or sharing with in a Bible study.

When Jesus chose His disciples, He didn't choose six men and six women. He chose twelve men. Otherwise, there were sure to be problems among His disciples. Men are to work with men, talk to men, disciple men. Women are to work with women, disciple women, talk to women. This isn't legalism, gang. It's wisdom.

Genesis 29:32
And Leah conceived, and bare a son, and she called his name Reuben: for she said, Surely the LORD hath looked upon my affliction; now therefore my husband will love me.

Leah made the mistake of thinking a baby would bring her and Jacob together.

Genesis 29:33
And she conceived again, and bare a son; and said, Because the LORD hath heard that I was hated, he hath therefore given me this son also: and she called his name Simeon.

The phrase, "the Lord hath heard that I was hated" is more properly rendered, "the Lord has heard that I *am* hated." *Reuben,* whose name means "see a son" didn't bring Jacob and Leah together in the way Leah hoped. So when the Lord gave her *Simeon,* whose name means "the

Lord has heard," Leah thought he would be the answer to her prayer.

Genesis 29:34
And she conceived again, and bare a son; and said, Now this time will my husband be joined unto me, because I have born him three sons: therefore was his name called Levi.

Levi means "join." "This will do it," Leah thought. "Surely after giving him three sons, Jacob's heart will be joined to mine." But it wasn't.

Genesis 29:35
And she conceived again, and bare a son: and she said, Now will I praise the LORD: therefore she called his name Judah; and left bearing.

This time, there's no mention of her husband. By son number four, Leah realized that no matter how many kids she gave Jacob, he still wouldn't feel toward her the way she wished he would. *Judah* means "praise"—an appropriate name if Leah had indeed drawn closer to the Lord as a result of her failed bid for Jacob's devotion.

30 Genesis 30:1 (a)
And when Rachel saw that she bare Jacob no children, Rachel envied her sister . . .

Probably for the first time in her life, Rachel envied her older sister because Leah had four sons, while Rachel was barren—a curse in that culture.

Genesis 30:1 (b), 2
. . . and said unto Jacob, Give me children, or else I die. And Jacob's anger was kindled against Rachel: and he said, Am I in God's stead, who hath withheld from thee the fruit of the womb?

Rachel thought she'd die if she didn't have children. Ironically, it will be childbirth itself that will kill her.

***For topical study of Genesis 30:1 entitled "Give Me Children or I Die," turn to page* 143.**

Genesis 30:3
And she said, Behold my maid Bilhah, go in unto her; and she shall bear upon my knees that I may also have children by her.

As was the custom of the day, the child conceived by Jacob and Rachel's handmaid would be considered Jacob and Rachel's.

Genesis 30:4–6
And she gave him Bilhah her handmaid to wife: and Jacob went in unto her. And Bilhah conceived, and bare Jacob a son. And Rachel said, God hath judged me, and hath also heard my voice, and hath given me a son: therefore called she his name Dan.

In naming the baby *Dan,* or "Judge," it was as if Rachel said, "God has seen my situation and has ruled in my favor."

Genesis 30:7, 8
And Bilhah Rachel's maid conceived again, and bare Jacob a second son. And Rachel said, With great wrestlings have I wrestled with my sister, and I have prevailed: and she called his name Naphtali.

In naming her second son *Naphtali,* or "My Wrestling," it was as if Rachel said, "I'm catching up with my sister in the child-bearing contest."

Genesis 30:9–11
When Leah saw that she had left bearing, she took Zilpah her maid, and gave her Jacob to wife. And Zilpah Leah's maid bare Jacob a son. And Leah said, A troop cometh: and she called his name Gad.

In naming the son conceived by her handmaid, *Gad,* or "Troop," it was as if Leah said, "Reinforcements are here!"

Genesis 30:12, 13
And Zilpah Leah's maid bare Jacob a second son. And Leah said, Happy am I, for the daughters will call me blessed: and she called his name Asher.

In naming Zilpah's second son *Asher,* or "Happy," Leah expressed her joy in having so many children—a cultural sign of sure blessing.

Genesis 30:14, 15 (a)
And Reuben went in the days of wheat harvest, and found mandrakes in the field, and brought them unto his mother Leah. Then Rachel said to Leah, Give me, I pray thee, of thy son's mandrakes. And she said unto her, Is it a small matter that thou hast taken my husband? and wouldest thou take away my son's mandrakes also?

The *mandrake,* or "love apple," was a rare, small plant of Middle Eastern origin that grew close to the ground much like a strawberry vine. From its white blossoms would come round, red fruit which looked like small apples, believed to be aphrodisiacs. In addition, because eating the carrot-like root was believed to enhance a woman's fertility, mandrakes were highly valued.

Genesis 30:15 (b)
. . . And Rachel said, Therefore he shall lie with thee to night for thy son's mandrakes.

"If you give me the mandrakes your son found," said Rachel to Leah, "I'll let Jacob lie with you tonight."

Genesis 30:16, 17
And Jacob came out of the field in the evening, and Leah went out to meet him, and said, Thou must come in unto me; for surely I have hired thee with my son's mandrakes. And he lay with her that night. And God hearkened unto Leah, and she conceived, and bare Jacob the fifth son.

Rachel manipulates to get the mandrakes—and Leah gets pregnant. Isn't that the way it often is? We scheme and plan and connive—only to see the opposite of what we intended.

Genesis 30:18
And Leah said, God hath given me my hire, because I have given my maiden to my husband: and she called his name Issachar.

Perhaps Leah named her newest son *Issachar,* or "Hire" because she saw him as payback, or reward, for her having given her handmaid to her husband.

Genesis 30:19, 20
And Leah conceived again, and bare Jacob the sixth son. And Leah said, God hath endued me with a good dowry; now will my husband dwell with me, because I have born him six sons: and she called his name Zebulun.

Zebulun means "Habitation"—perhaps reflecting Leah's desire to experience security in Jacob's elusive love for her.

Genesis 30:21–24
And afterwards she bare a daughter, and called her name Dinah. And God remembered Rachel, and God hearkened to her, and opened her womb. And she conceived, and bare a son; and said, God hath taken away my reproach: And she called his name Joseph; and said, The LORD shall add to me another son.

At long last Rachel has a baby—and what does she say? In naming him *Joseph,* or "May God Add," she was saying, "I want more."

How reflective of human nature. "I want this job. I want that car. I want that home. I want that position," we say. And when we get them, like Rachel, we find we only want more.

Genesis 30:25–27
And it came to pass, when Rachel had born Joseph, that Jacob said unto Laban, Send me away, that I may go unto mine own place, and to my country. Give me my wives and my children, for whom I have served thee, and let me go: for thou knowest my service which I have done thee. And Laban said unto him, I pray thee, if I have found favour in thine eyes, tarry: for I have learned by experience that the LORD hath blessed me for thy sake.

As we'll see in the next chapter, Laban isn't even a believer, yet even he recognizes he has been blessed by God because of Jacob. The number of his herds, flocks, and grandsons had multiplied radically. Everything was going well for Laban. And in a rare moment of honesty, he says to Jacob, "You have brought the Lord's blessing to my household."

No wonder Laban wanted Jacob to stay. In addition to being supernaturally blessed, Jacob was industrious—which isn't surprising since, throughout Scripture, God often called men who were already hard at work . . .

- Moses was watching his father-in-law's sheep (Exodus 3:1).
- Elisha was plowing behind the oxen (1 Kings 19:19).
- Peter was casting his net into the sea (Matthew 4:18).
- Matthew was collecting taxes (Matthew 9:9).

"Whatever you do in word or deed, do all in the name of the Lord Jesus" (Colossians 3:17). "You have not chosen Me, but I have chosen you," Jesus said, "and *ordained you*" (John 15:16, italics added). We're *all* in the ministry, gang. When I stand in the amphitheatre and see sixty, seventy, eighty people come forward to receive Christ and to be baptized Sunday after Sunday, I'm looking at the fruit of all you ministers who pound nails, teach classes, bus tables, and repair pipes all to the glory of God. Christians must be, can be, get to be the very best worker in the company, for then even the Labans will be drawn to the One we serve.

Genesis 30:28
And he said, Appoint me thy wages, and I will give it.

"Tell me what you need in order to stick around," said Laban to Jacob.

Genesis 30:29, 30
And he said unto him, Thou knowest how I have served thee, and how thy cattle was with me. For it was little which thou hadst before I came, and it is now increased unto a multitude; and the LORD hath blessed thee since my coming: and now when shall I provide for mine own house also?

"I've served your needs for fourteen years," Jacob answered. "You've become a wealthy man. But now I, too, have a family I must provide for."

Genesis 30:31
And he said, What shall I give thee? And Jacob said, Thou shalt not give me any thing: if thou wilt do this thing for me, I will again feed and keep thy flock:

And thus a contest between two con men is set up . . .

Genesis 30:32
I will pass through all thy flock to day, removing from thence all the speckled and spotted cattle, and all the brown cattle among the sheep, and the spotted and speckled among the goats: and of such shall be my hire.

To this day in the Middle East, sheep are primarily white, goats predominantly brown or black. There's an occasional spotted or multicolored sheep or goat—but the solid color gene being dominant, solid-colored sheep and goats are the ones most highly valued. "I will go throughout your flock and pick out the few which aren't solid-colored," said Jacob. "They will be my pay."

Genesis 30:33
So shall my righteousness answer for me in time to come, when it shall come for my hire before thy face: every one that is not speckled and spotted among the goats, and brown among the sheep, that shall be counted stolen with me.

In other words, Jacob said, "I will take care of the flocks here. Then, when it's time for me to leave, I'll take the spotted ones."

Genesis 30:34
And Laban said, Behold, I would it might be according to thy word.

Thus, the two con men struck a deal.

Genesis 30:35, 36 (a)
And he removed that day the he goats that were ringstraked and spotted, and all the she goats that were speckled and spotted, and every one that had some white in it, and all the brown among the sheep, and gave them into the hand of his sons. And he set three days' journey betwixt himself and Jacob . . .

True to his nature, Laban removed all the spotted and speckled goats and sheep—and sent them three days away with his other sons.

Genesis 30:36 (b)
. . . and Jacob fed the rest of Laban's flocks.

The next day, Jacob goes out to find no speckled or spotted livestock whatsoever. Laban had tricked him again. But Jacob had only just begun to fight . . .

Genesis 30:37, 38
And Jacob took him rods of green poplar, and of the hazel and chesnut tree; and pilled white strakes in them, and made the white appear which was in the rods. And he set the rods which he had pilled before the flocks in the gutters in the watering troughs when the flocks came to drink, that they should conceive when they came to drink.

Jacob strips the bark off poplar, hazel, and chestnut branches in such a way that they appeared striped. Then he placed them in the watering troughs of Laban's flocks.

Genesis 30:39–43
And the flocks conceived before the rods, and brought forth cattle ringstraked, speckled, and spotted. And Jacob did separate the lambs, and set the faces of the flocks toward the ringstraked, and all the brown in the flock of Laban; and he put his own flocks by themselves, and put them not unto Laban's cattle. And it came to pass, whensoever the stronger cattle did conceive, that Jacob laid the rods before the eyes of the cattle in the gutters, that they might conceive among the rods. But when the cattle were feeble, he put them not in: so the feebler were Laban's, and the stronger Jacob's. And the man in-

creased exceedingly, and had much cattle, and maidservants, and menservants, and camels, and asses.

Not only did the striped branches cause the herds and flocks to come into heat, but the offspring produced were speckled and spotted. Does this mean the Bible gives validity to the idea of prenatal suggestion? No. As we will see in chapter 31, God spoke to Jacob in a dream, saying, "Ask for the spotted and speckled livestock." Did the striped branches cause the livestock to bear spotted and speckled offspring? I don't think so. Rather, I think God simply put His stamp of approval on a man who showed some initiative and industry.

"Daddy, can I help you wash the windows?" asked not-yet-three-year-old Christy.

"Sure!" I said.

So she toddled into the kitchen and began washing the windows with what she thought was window cleaner, but which was actually furniture polish. What a mess! But you know what? I was so blessed! Christy was doing something from her heart—and it truly touched mine.

When we get to heaven, we're going to be surprised by the things we thought were helping God, but were, in fact, equivalent to using furniture polish on glass. Nonetheless, just as He did in the life of Jacob, God will bless even our simplest efforts for His glory.

GIVE ME CHILDREN OR I DIE

A Topical Study of GENESIS 30:1

All her life, she had been the pretty one—the one who was invited to all the parties, the one who received all the attention. But now it was her older sister who seemed to be blessed, for it was her older sister who was bearing children. In her spirit of envy, Rachel said, "I want kids. There's nothing to live for if I don't have kids. Without kids, I just can't go on. Give me children, Jacob, or else I die."

And at last anger was ignited in the heart of her husband who loved her so deeply that the seven years he had to work to secure her as his bride seemed but a few days. "*I'm* not the problem," he said. "I have four kids with Leah. Therefore don't look to me for the solution."

Please note two important points that relate to any of us who find ourselves desperately seeking a solution to our barren condition . . .

Looking to the Wrong Person

Maybe you have been looking to your husband, wife, friend, or pastor to meet the barrenness, emptiness, lack of productivity in your life. "Meet this need," you cry, "or I'll die." But the reality is, they can't.

When asked who he was, John the Baptist identified himself by who he was *not.* "I am not the Christ," he said. "I'm not the answer. I'm not the Savior. I'm not the solution. My whole role is to point to the One who *is* the Christ" (John 1:20).

> *For the creature was made subject to vanity, not willingly, but by reason of him who hath subjected the same in hope.* Romans 8:20

- *For the creature—*
  You and me
- *Was made subject to vanity—*
  Or emptiness
- *Not willingly—*
  We don't want to feel empty.
- *But by reason of Him—*
  By God's divine design
- *Who hath subjected the same in hope—*
  In order that we would look to Him.

God says, "I'm going to create in the soul of every man and woman a hole which cannot be satisfied by anything but Me because otherwise they'll look to her, to him, to it, to that—and they will be disillusioned. They will fall into deep despondency and dark depression. On the other hand, if they look to Me to fill the hole in their soul, they'll discover I'll never let them down."

God made you to be totally dependent upon Him. Therefore, the person who finally gives up looking to the wrong person and looks to God exclusively, like Leah, will be set free and end up praising the Lord (Genesis 29:35).

The only way you'll be truly satisfied is to be extremely close *to* God, totally dependent *on* God, and passionately in love *with* God.

Sunday morning Christianity will never fill the hole in your soul. The hunger in your heart can only be filled through intimacy, dependency, and an ever-deepening relationship with the One who created you for His own pleasure (Revelation 4:11).

Asking in the Wrong Fashion

"Give me children, or else I die. I demand that You give me kids." Such are the prayers of those in the so-called "Faith Movement," the "Name It and Claim It" gang who say, "We need to speak the word and demand from God that we don't want to be barren, that we want to be rich and healthy and successful."

Wait a minute. When Rachel finally had a son, she named him Joseph. Why? Because *Joseph* means, "May God Add." In other words, Joseph wasn't enough. Rachel wanted more.

That's always the way it is. When you're looking to something or someone to meet the need of your soul, it's never enough. And here's the real irony: As a result of having another son, Rachel did, in fact, die.

As she was dying in childbirth, what did she say? Not, "Oh, praise God, another son;" not, "Oh, Lord, You're awesome to give this barren woman two children." No, as she was dying in childbirth, Rachel named her son *Benoni*, or "Son of my Sorrow." The last word on beautiful Rachel's lips was "sorrow" (Genesis 35:18).

Rachel demanded her way and it killed her.

Why did Rachel's life end this way? Because she looked to the wrong person and asked in the wrong fashion. A husband, wife, friend, pastor, or parent cannot fill the hole in your soul because you were created for a deep yet humble relationship with God.

A broken Rachel named her son *Benoni*, "Son of my Sorrow." But a wiser Jacob renamed him *Benjamin*, "Son of my right hand." As the Son of Man, Jesus was called the "Man of sorrows" (Isaiah 53:3), but as the Son of God, He sits at the Father's right hand (Colossians 3:1). And as He does, He prays for us.

Rachel said, "Give me children, or I die."

The Father says, "For My children, I will die."

God says, "I am so in love with you, I'm not demanding something *from* you, but I'm dying *for* you. I love you to death. And the sins and mistakes you've made so foolishly, I will wash away completely in order that you can live with Me eternally."

Trust in the LORD with all thine heart; and lean not unto thine own understanding. In all thy ways acknowledge him, and he shall direct thy paths.

Proverbs 3:5, 6

- *Trust in the Lord with all thine heart;*
  Don't look to anyone else to fill the hole in your soul.
- *And lean not unto thine own understanding.*
  Don't demand God to do things your way.
- *In all thy ways acknowledge Him,*
  Realize God alone is your Satisfaction, your Reason for living.
- *And He shall direct thy paths.*
  He will fill every need.

Precious people, don't trust in your own demands or desires, your own plans or perspective. If you do, you'll die with the word "sorrow" on your lips. Instead, trust in the Lord with all your heart, and He will direct you not to the place of Rachel's sorrow—but to the place Leah found her ultimate satisfaction: He will direct your paths to Himself.

31 Although Jacob was saved in chapter 28, he was not yet subdued. He's converted, but he still has a carnal nature within him that seems to have control of him.

Like Jacob, our flesh can still be in control even though we are born-again believers. It doesn't need to be this way, for we can be, as Paul would go on to say, spiritual men (1 Corinthians 3:1). That is, we can let the Holy Spirit guide us and lead us. And that's where real joy, purpose, and peace are found, as Jacob will begin to discover . . .

Genesis 31:1
And he heard the words of Laban's sons, saying, Jacob hath taken away all that was our father's; and of that which was our father's hath he gotten all this glory.

Laban, Jacob's uncle/father-in-law, was a real match for Jacob. In chapter 30, these two con men had set up a con-test to see which of them would end up with the greater number of sheep, goats, and cattle. Here in chapter 31, as Jacob's herds increase, Laban's sons are angry, realizing that Jacob's success would eventually cut into their own inheritance.

Genesis 31:2
And Jacob beheld the countenance of Laban, and, behold, it was not toward him as before.

Many times, we're in a place where we wonder if God is trying to get us to make a move—geographically, professionally, or in ministry? I believe Jacob's story provides key clues to this question.

First, notice that *the situation around Jacob soured.* Jacob could see in his father-in-law's face that Laban was no longer looking kindly upon him.

Genesis 31:3
And the LORD said unto Jacob, Return unto the land of thy fathers, and to thy kindred; and I will be with thee.

Secondly, *the Word of the Lord within Jacob sweetened.* As Jacob's situation soured, the Word within him stirred. The same thing happens today. When the Lord wants to move us, the Scriptures we read day after day all seem to point in that direction.

Genesis 31:4
And Jacob sent and called Rachel and Leah to the field unto his flock,

Jacob would now have to convince his wives to make the journey with him hundreds of miles across a rough desert area to a land they had never seen.

Genesis 31:5–7
And said unto them, I see your father's countenance, that it is not toward me as before; but the God of my father hath been with me. And ye know that with all my power I have served your father. And your father hath deceived me, and changed my wages ten times; but God suffered him not to hurt me.

While Jacob was right in his assessment of Laban's deceitful ways, he failed to see the most obvious truth about Laban: That is, Laban was in actuality a full-length mirror, a life-size reflection of Jacob's own flawed character.

I have discovered that the flaws and faults I see most clearly in others are my own. The more flawed a person is, the more he will see other's flaws. Jacob will point out over and over that Laban is a deceiver, because it was Jacob's own tendency to be a deceiver, a conniver, a cheater. My prayer is that, before I die, God will deliver me from a Jacob mentality and will work in me the agape love that doesn't even notice when others do it wrong (1 Corinthians 13:5).

Genesis 31:8–12
If he said thus, The speckled shall be thy wages; then all the cattle bare speckled: and if he said thus, The ringstraked shall be thy hire; then bare all the cattle ringstraked. Thus God hath taken away the cattle of your father, and given them to me. And it came to pass at the time that the cattle conceived, that I lifted up mine eyes, and saw in a dream, and, behold, the rams which leaped upon the cattle were ringstraked, speckled, and grisled. And the angel of God spake unto me in a dream, saying, Jacob: And I said, Here am I. And he said, Lift up now thine eyes, and see, all the rams which leap upon the cattle are ringstraked, speckled, and grisled: for I have seen all that Laban doeth unto thee.

And now we understand where Jacob got the idea for his seemingly outlandish plan seen in chapter 30. The business plan that proved to be hugely successful came to him in a dream.

But notice gang, when Jacob's name was called, he answered, "Here I am." If you want the dream God has placed on your heart, the dream God has put in your mind to come true—the only way it will happen is if you, like Jacob, get out of bed and let the Lord do His work through you as you partner with Him. Why doesn't God just do it Himself? Because this life is to prepare us for one thing: Heaven. Thus, God wants us to exercise faith and to get involved in the process because such will be key ingredients in the ages to come.

Genesis 31:13–16
I am the God of Bethel, where thou anointedst the pillar, and where thou vowedst a vow unto me: now arise, get thee out from this land, and return unto the land of thy kindred. And Rachel and Leah answered and said, Is there yet any portion of inheritance for us in our father's house? Are we not counted of him strangers? for he hath sold us, and hath quite devoured also our money. For all the riches which God hath taken from our father, that is ours, and our children's: now then, whatsoever God hath said unto thee, do.

Thirdly, *the plan proposed by Jacob was seconded.* Not only can we find confirmation from our own family as did Jacob, but within the family of God lies great wisdom, for in the multitude of counselors there is safety (Proverbs 11:14).

Genesis 31:17, 18
Then Jacob rose up, and set his sons and his wives upon camels; And he carried away all his cattle, and all his goods which he had gotten, the cattle of his getting, which he had gotten in Padan-aram, for to go to Isaac his father in the land of Canaan.

Jacob, his two wives, eleven sons, one daughter, and his livestock are all ready to embark on their journey.

Genesis 31:19
And Laban went to shear his sheep: and Rachel had stolen the images that were her father's.

Although Laban acknowledged the God of Jacob, he was in reality a worshiper of the idols Rachel stole. "How primitive!" we are prone to say of idol worship. But what about our own culture? We may not have the multi-breasted goddess Ashteroth—but we have the Playboy bunny. We don't have the stocky little god Mammon—but we have square little Visa cards. These people weren't any more primitive or backward than our own culture is today.

Genesis 31:20–24
And Jacob stole away unawares to Laban the Syrian, in that he told him not that he fled. So he fled with all that he had; and he rose up, and passed over the river, and set his face toward the mount Gilead. And it was told Laban on the third day that Jacob was fled. And he took his brethren with him, and pursued after him seven days' journey; and they overtook him in the mount Gilead. And God came to Laban the Syrian in a dream by night, and said unto him, Take heed that thou speak not to Jacob either good or bad.

As perhaps your margin indicates, a more correct rendering of this last phrase would be "speak not to Jacob from good to bad." In other words, God said to Laban, "Don't greet Jacob warmly only to later turn on him as is your usual custom."

Genesis 31:25–27
Then Laban overtook Jacob. Now Jacob had pitched his tent in the mount: and Laban with his brethren pitched in the mount of Gilead. And Laban said to Jacob, What hast thou done, that thou hast stolen away unawares to me, and carried away my daughters, as captives taken with the sword? Wherefore didst thou flee away secretly, and steal away from me; and didst not tell me, that I might have sent thee away with mirth, and with songs, with tabret, and with harp?

"If you told me you were planning to leave, I would have sent you off with a big party."

Sure you would, Laban.

Genesis 31:28, 29
And hast not suffered me to kiss my sons and my daughters? thou hast now done foolishly in so doing. It is in the power of my hand to do you hurt: but the God of your father spake unto me yesternight, saying, Take thou heed that thou speak not to Jacob either good or bad.

"The only thing keeping me from doing you bodily harm is the warning I received from your God," Laban said to Jacob.

Genesis 31:30–32
And now, though thou wouldest needs be gone, because thou sore longedst after thy father's house, yet wherefore hast thou stolen my gods? And Jacob answered and said to Laban, Because I was afraid: for I said, Peradventure thou wouldest take by force thy daughters from me. With whomsoever thou findest thy gods, let him not live: before our brethren discern thou what is thine with me, and take it to thee. For Jacob knew not that Rachel had stolen them.

Completely unaware of Rachel's doing, Jacob said, "If someone in my camp has taken your gods, let him die."

Genesis 31:33, 34
And Laban went into Jacob's tent, and into Leah's tent, and into the two maidservants' tents; but he found them not. Then went he out of Leah's tent, and entered into Rachel's tent. Now Rachel had taken the images, and put them in the camel's furniture, and sat upon them. And Laban searched all the tent, but found them not.

Rachel hid the idols in her camel's saddle, and then sat upon it.

Genesis 31:35, 36 (a)
And she said to her father, Let it not displease my lord that I cannot rise up before

thee; for the custom of women is upon me. And he searched, but found not the images. And Jacob was wroth, and chode with Laban . . .

The word translated *wroth* literally means "to burn to the place of igniting." The word translated *chode* means "to tear into." Consequently, here we see Jacob burning up and lashing out at Laban over the fact that he had been furiously chased, falsely charged, and financially cheated.

Jacob had reason to be ticked off, but not as much as he thought. For while Laban had indeed cheated him on numerous occasions, this time Laban's cry of "Stop! Thief!" was actually warranted, as, unbeknownst to Jacob, the missing idols were in the possession of his own wife.

When, like Jacob, I find myself lashing out, "How could he do that?" or, "How could she say that?" or, "How could they think that?"—I must remember this story. None of us knows as much as we think we do about any given situation, because, at best, we see through a glass darkly (1 Corinthians 13:12). There is only One who sees perfectly, and that's our Lord because all things are naked and open before Him (Hebrews 4:13).

Jacob thought his anger was completely justified. The fact is, he was unaware of a key component in the equation.

Genesis 31:36 (b), 37
. . . and Jacob answered and said to Laban, What is my trespass? what is my sin, that thou hast so hotly pursued after me? Whereas thou hast searched all my stuff, what hast thou found of all thy household stuff? set it here before my brethren and thy brethren, that they may judge betwixt us both.

"If you've found something I shouldn't have taken, bring it here and let the people around us decide who's right or wrong in this matter," Jacob said.

Genesis 31:38–40
This twenty years have I been with thee; thy ewes and thy she goats have not cast their young, and the rams of thy flock have I not eaten. That which was torn of beasts I brought not unto thee; I bare the loss of it; of my hand didst thou require it, whether stolen by day, or stolen by night. Thus I was; in the day the drought consumed me, and the frost by night; and my sleep departed from mine eyes.

Continuing with his defense, Jacob said to Laban, "I have served you faithfully for twenty years—even to the point where if one of your livestock was eaten by wild beasts, I paid for it out of my own pocket. If one was stolen, you held me responsible, and I paid for it. Day and night I protected your investment."

Genesis 31:41, 42
Thus have I been twenty years in thy house; I served thee fourteen years for thy two daughters, and six years for thy cattle: and thou hast changed my wages ten times. Except the God of my father, the God of Abraham, and the fear of Isaac, had been with me, surely thou hadst sent me away now empty. God hath seen mine affliction and the labour of my hands, and rebuked thee yesternight.

"Even though I have been faithful to you," Jacob continued Laban, "if God hadn't spoken to you, you'd be ripping me off even now."

Genesis 31:43
And Laban answered and said unto Jacob, These daughters are my daughters, and these children are my children, and these cattle are my cattle, and all that thou seest is mine: and what can I do this day unto these my daughters, or unto their children which they have born?

"Those are *my* daughters, *my* grandchildren, and *my* livestock," Laban insisted.

Genesis 31:44–47
Now therefore come thou, let us make a covenant, I and thou; and let it be for a witness between me and thee. And Jacob took a stone, and set it up for a pillar. And Jacob said unto his brethren, Gather stones; and they took stones, and made an heap: and they did eat there upon the heap. And Laban called it Jegar-sahadutha: but Jacob called it Galeed.

Jegar-sahadutha and *Galeed* simply mean "the heap of witness." Unable to locate his missing idols, a reluctant Laban drops his accusations against his son-in-law.

Genesis 31:48, 49
And Laban said, This heap is a witness between me and thee this day. Therefore was the name of it called Galeed; And Mizpah; for he said, The LORD watch between me and thee, when we are absent one from another.

"The Lord watch between me and thee when we are absent one from another." Sometimes you'll see this inscribed on a necklace in a romantic context. While that's a sweet sentiment, the fact of the matter is that what's being said here is, "You scoundrel. I don't trust you as far as I can spit. But even though I can't keep my eye on you, God will be watching you."

Genesis 31:50–53
If thou shalt afflict my daughters, or if thou shalt take other wives beside my daughters, no man is with us; see, God is witness betwixt me and thee. And Laban said to Jacob, Behold this heap, and behold this pillar, which I have cast betwixt me and thee; This heap be witness, and this pillar be witness, that I will not pass over this heap to thee, and that thou shalt not pass over this heap and this pillar unto me, for harm. The God of Abraham, and the God of Nahor, the God of their father, judge betwixt us. And Jacob sware by the fear of his father Isaac.

"This heap is a line in the sand," declared Jacob and Laban in effect. "You stay on your side. I'll stay on mine."

Genesis 31:54, 55
Then Jacob offered sacrifice upon the mount, and called his brethren to eat bread: and they did eat bread, and tarried all night in the mount. And early in the morning Laban rose up, and kissed his sons and his daughters, and blessed them: and Laban departed, and returned unto his place.

Laban kisses his daughters and grandchildren, but does he kiss Jacob? No. He wants nothing to do with Jacob. He doesn't even tell him goodbye as he passes out of Jacob's life and out of the Scriptural account on his way back to Padanaram.

32

After twenty years as an exile, Jacob is on his way home—knowing his brother Esau may very well still feel anger and hostility towards him . . .

Genesis 32:1, 2
And Jacob went on his way, and the angels of God met him. And when Jacob saw them, he said, This is God's host: and he called the name of that place Mahanaim.

As he's on his way with his cattle, his servants, his kids, his wives, Jacob looks around and sees a band of angels traveling with him. Amazed, he names the area *Mahanaim* or "Two Hosts"—for he saw the reality of the heavenly escort which would escort him and his family.

Genesis 32:3–5
And Jacob sent messengers before him to Esau his brother unto the land of Seir, the country of Edom. And he commanded them, saying, Thus shall ye speak unto my lord Esau; Thy servant Jacob saith thus, I have sojourned with Laban, and stayed there until now: And I have oxen, and asses, flocks, and menservants, and womenservants: and I have sent to tell my lord, that I may find grace in thy sight.

Initially, we see Jacob *requesting peace.* He sends his servants ahead, saying, "Go find Esau and tell him I'm coming back home. Tell him I'm a rich man, and that I want nothing from him. Tell him there's no more competition, and ask him if I could have his permission to travel through his territory to make my way home."

Genesis 32:6–8
And the messengers returned to Jacob, saying, We came to thy brother Esau, and also he cometh to meet thee, and four hundred men with him. Then Jacob was greatly afraid and distressed: and he divided the people that was with him, and the flocks, and herds, and the camels, into two bands; And said, If Esau come to the one company, and smite it, then the other company which is left shall escape.

After requesting peace, Jacob *reacts in panic.* Upon hearing that Esau and four hundred of his men were coming to meet him, Jacob divided his company in two so that half could escape in the event of an attack.

Genesis 32:9, 10 (a)
And Jacob said, O God of my father Abraham, and God of my father Isaac, the Lord which saidst unto me, Return unto thy country, and to thy kindred, and I will deal well with thee: I am not worthy of the least of all the mercies, and of all the truth, which thou hast shewed unto thy servant . . .

After requesting peace and reacting in panic, Jacob *resorts to prayer* . . .

Genesis 32:10 (b)
. . . for with my staff I passed over this Jordan; and now I am become two bands.

When Jacob crossed the Jordan initially, he held only a staff in his hand. Here, as he again crosses the Jordan, he acknowledges that, due to the grace and goodness of God, he does so a rich man.

Genesis 32:11, 12

Deliver me, I pray thee, from the hand of my brother, from the hand of Esau: for I fear him, lest he will come and smite me, and the mother with the children. And thou saidst, I will surely do thee good, and make thy seed as the sand of the sea, which cannot be numbered for multitude.

Here, Jacob is doing something oh, so right: He's praying with insistence. He's taking the promise that God gave him and saying, "Father, You promised . . ." I have found that when I pray the promises of God, my faith begins to soar. And that's when things begin to happen, for "he that comes to God must believe that He is, and that He is a rewarder of those who diligently seek Him" (Hebrews 11:6).

Genesis 32:13–20

And he lodged there that same night; and took of that which came to his hand a present for Esau his brother; Two hundred she goats, and twenty he goats, two hundred ewes, and twenty rams, Thirty milch camels with their colts, forty kine, and ten bulls, twenty she asses, and ten foals. And he delivered them into the hand of his servants, every drove by themselves; and said unto his servants, Pass over before me, and put a space betwixt drove and drove. And he commanded the foremost, saying, When Esau my brother meeteth thee, and asketh thee, saying, Whose art thou? and whither goest thou? and whose are these before thee? Then thou shalt say, They be thy servant Jacob's; it is a present sent unto my lord Esau: and, behold, also he is behind us. And so commanded he the second, and the third, and all that followed the droves, saying, On this manner shall ye speak unto Esau, when ye find him. And say ye moreover, Behold, thy servant Jacob is behind us. For he said, I will appease him with the present that goeth before me, and afterward I will see his face; peradventure he will accept of me.

After requesting peace, reacting in panic, and resorting to prayer, Jacob *resumes his plotting,* as he sends wave after wave of gifts ahead of him, hoping to appease Esau.

Genesis 32:21, 22

So went the present over before him: and himself lodged that night in the company. And he rose up that night, and took his two wives, and his two womenservants, and his eleven sons, and passed over the ford Jabbok . . .

Knowing he'd face Esau the next day, Jacob couldn't sleep. Yes, he prayed. And it was a good prayer. But, as you and I so often do, he took the burden back again.

Genesis 32:23

And he took them, and sent them over the brook, and sent over that he had.

A second huge event in Jacob's life is about to take place. The first had transpired twenty years earlier at Bethel. Running away from Esau, Jacob found himself in the middle of nowhere at a place called Luz, where God appeared to him in a dream. Realizing God was indeed with him, Jacob changed the name of Luz to Bethel, from "Separation" to "House of God," and became a believer at that point (Genesis 28).

At Bethel, Jacob was saved. But here at Peniel, on the other side of the brook Jabbok, he will be sanctified, for a deep work is about to take place in his heart.

Genesis 32:24

And Jacob was left alone; and there wrestled a man with him until the breaking of the day.

This man was the God-Man, Jesus Christ.

Genesis 32:25 (a)

And when he saw that he prevailed not against him . . .

In Jacob, the Lord found one who put up a good fight, one who didn't give up.

Genesis 32:25 (b)

. . . he touched the hollow of his thigh; and the hollow of Jacob's thigh was out of joint, as he wrestled with him.

Jacob's hip is dislocated—which means he will no longer be able to do something he's relied on for years: He'll no longer be able to run.

Genesis 32:26

And he said, Let me go, for the day breaketh. And he said, I will not let thee go, except thou bless me.

Even though he was pinned to the ground in pain, Jacob innately, intuitively understood he deeply, desperately needed to be blessed.

***For topical study of Genesis 32:26 entitled "Prevailing in Prayer," turn to page* 152.**

Genesis 32:27 (a)
And he said unto him, What is thy name? . . .

Does this mean the Lord didn't know who He was wrestling? No. The Lord knew Jacob's name, and now He's giving Jacob an opportunity to be reminded of it as well. You see, years earlier, his dad had asked him, "Who are you?"

"I am Esau," Jacob had answered (Genesis 27:19).

It's as if here, the Lord is saying, "Let's try it again, Jacob. What is your name?"

Perhaps the great majority of people wish they were someone else. Jacob certainly did. "I want to be firstborn. I want the blessing. I want to be Esau," he said. So, too, you can go through life trying to be someone you're not. You can copy the way she dresses, or the way he talks, but it will lead to nothing but frustration until you come to the moment when in total honesty you say, "I've tried to be this guy, tried to do that thing, but now I admit who I am. I'm Jacob."

Genesis 32:27 (b)
. . . And he said, Jacob.

"Jacob. Heel Snatcher. One who trips people up, one who is a conniver, a con man, a scoundrel—that's who I am."

Genesis 32:28 (a)
. . . And he said, Thy name shall be called no more Jacob, but Israel . . .

No sooner does Jacob confess and come clean regarding his true identity than the Lord changes his name entirely—from Jacob to Israel, from "Heel Snatcher" to "Governed By God."

Genesis 32:28 (b)
. . . for as a prince hast thou power with God and with men, and hast prevailed.

"When did I prevail?" Jacob must have wondered.

And God would answer, "It was when you were broken, when you were pinned by Me, when you were weeping, but wouldn't let go of Me, when you said, 'I can't go through another day without You'—*that's* when you prevailed."

Genesis 32:29
And Jacob asked him, and said, Tell me, I pray thee, thy name. And he said, Wherefore is it that thou dost ask after my name? And he blessed him there.

"You know who I AM, Jacob. Unlike you, My name doesn't change—for I am the same yesterday, today, and forever" (Hebrews 13:8).

Genesis 32:30, 31
And Jacob called the name of the place Peniel: for I have seen God face to face, and my life is preserved. And as he passed over Penuel the sun rose upon him, and he halted upon his thigh.

Twenty years earlier at Bethel, Jacob left with "happy feet." Here at Peniel, he'll leave not with a spring in his step, but with a limp for the rest of his life.

Genesis 32:32
Therefore the children of Israel eat not of the sinew which shrank, which is upon the hollow of the thigh, unto this day: because he touched the hollow of Jacob's thigh in the sinew that shrank.

To this day, the Orthodox Jews don't eat the thigh meat of an animal in honor of their great-great-great-great-great-great-great grandfather Jacob. Thus, down the tunnel of time, Jacob's descendants commemorate not his cleverness, intelligence, or charisma. They commemorate his pain.

A can-do kind of guy, Jacob was clever, charming, skilled, intelligent—a man any smart CEO would want to hire. God, on the other hand, said, "I have big plans for you, Jacob. You are going to have a huge impact on the history of the world—for from you will come an entire nation. And from that nation will come Messiah. I have big plans for you—but you're too smart, too self-confident, too clever. Therefore I'm going to break you."

Dear sister and brother, you must understand that no matter how charming or intelligent or clever you are, or how good you may be in any given area, your skill is puny, your intelligence is nothing, your strength is scrawny in comparison to God's. So God says, "I'm going to allow this pain in your life because then, and only then, will you lean on Me every step of the way, knowing that if you don't, you'll fall flat on your face. And as you lean *on* Me, you'll draw strength *from* Me and you'll be governed *by* Me instead of trying to make things happen in your own energy."

"Okay, Lord," we say. "I understand I have to be broken that I might learn to lean on You. But once I'm broken, can't You heal me? Once I've wrestled with You about a certain issue, can't You make me like new again?"

I am reminded of the story of another man who was lame . . .

He had laid on the deck of a pool in Jerusalem day after day for thirty-eight years, hoping against hope that somehow when, according to tradition, an angel stirred the waters, he would be the first one in the pool and would be healed. Then, one day a young Rabbi came his way and asked him, "Wilt thou be made whole?"

"I can't," he answered, "because I don't have anyone to help me into the water."

And then something amazing happened—for when the Rabbi told him to take up his bed and walk, the once-lame man was able to do just that.

"Whee!" he said. "I can walk! I can run! I can leap!"

"Hold on," said some Pharisees who had observed the scene. "It's the Sabbath Day. You're not supposed to carry your bed on the Sabbath Day. Who told you to do this? Who is this One who healed you?"

"Hmm," said the newly-healed man. "I don't know. I'm just so happy to be walking. I don't know who it was" (John 5:13).

That's the issue, gang. We all would like to be healed, to have the pain go away, to have the hurt be gone. But the fact is, if that were to happen, like the lame man, we would say, "Whee!" And we wouldn't know who healed us. Therefore, the pain stays; the limp continues day after day, year after year that we might lean on Him, talk to Him, and draw strength and insight from Him which we would never have received if we were just saying, "Whee!"

That's why Jacob's descendants would say, "To this day, we honor the fact that our dad was a broken man. He limped through life. He leaned on God. He wasn't Mr. Whee! But there was a richness and a depth of character that we will honor for all our generations throughout our nation's history."

Mom and Dad, Grandma and Grandpa, the degree to which your kids and grandchildren see you limp through life, leaning on God and drawing from Him strength and character and depth is the degree to which they will value your legacy. They won't remember how successful you were in climbing the corporate ladder, how big your bank account was, how skilled you were mechanically, or how gifted you were musically. What they will remember is what they learned as they watched you limp.

"I know I have to lean on Him," you might be saying. "But sometimes I lose my way. Sometimes I forget. What do I do then?"

"Do this in remembrance of Me," Jesus would say to you. "It wasn't just My hip that was dislocated. My entire body was broken for you."

Thus, it is at the Cross that I am reminded that in light of what Jesus did for me, the pain He's allowing in my life is because He wants the very best for me. Communion is essential because we can get mixed up; we can get confused by pain and sadness and sorrow. But when we come to the Lord's Table and are reminded once again of His inexpressible love for us, we gladly exchange the leap of the lame man for the limp of Jacob because it is in limping that we remain close to Him all the days of our life.

PREVAILING IN PRAYER

A Topical Study of GENESIS 32:26

Many things could be said about Jacob—some good, some bad. But one thing *must* be said about him, and that is this: Jacob was a man who was able to prevail in prayer. Of that there can be no question.

Like you, I want to see my prayer life develop and deepen. I want to see my prayers be more effective and more impacting. I want to be a man of prayer. To that end, I join with the disciples who came to our Master, saying, "Lord, teach us to pray." They didn't say, "Lord teach us to preach." They didn't say, "Lord, teach us to heal the sick." They didn't say, "Lord, teach us to cast out demons." They said, "Lord, teach us to pray"—because they rightly understood that the key to His ministry, indeed the key to His entire life was His communion with His Father. That's why they said, "Lord, teach *us* to pray" (Luke 11:1).

I'm glad the Lord doesn't simply give us theories about prayer or theological treatises on prayer, but that He gives us stories which depict prayer, for I can understand stories much more easily than I can theory or theology. And here in our text is just such a story—one I have found exceedingly helpful to see what it means to prevail in prayer.

Here's the situation: After being gone for twenty years, Jacob is headed back home. With two wives, eleven sons, one daughter, numerous servants, and abundant cattle in tow, his should have been a triumphant return. But there was a difficulty ahead, for Jacob's brother, Esau—the one he had cheated, the one who had vowed to kill him—was on his way to meet Jacob, accompanied by four hundred men.

Once again, fearing for his life, Jacob does a wise thing: He prays. Notice two qualities that are essential for anyone who wants to prevail in prayer . . .

Jacob Was Insistent in Prayer

> *And Jacob said, O God of my father Abraham, and God of my father Isaac, the* LORD *which saidst unto me, Return unto thy country, and to thy kindred, and I will deal well with thee:* Genesis 32:9

> *And thou saidst, I will surely do thee good, and make thy seed as the sand of the sea, which cannot be numbered for multitude.* Genesis 32:12

Both at the beginning and at the conclusion of his prayer, Jacob is insistent in that he says, "Lord, You are the One who told me to go back home. You are the One who promised You would save my life." In so doing, Jacob takes the promises given to him and lifts them back to the Lord in prayer.

This is a great, great key to praying effectively. "Concerning the work of my hands, command ye me," the Lord declares (Isaiah 45:11).

"Command Him?" you say. "That sounds an awful lot like the 'Name It and Claim It' mentality."

No, for contextually you will see God is talking about the promises and prophecies He had already made to the people. Listen to what Jesus would say along the same line: "If ye abide in me, and my words abide in you, ye shall ask what ye will, and it shall be done unto you" (John 15:7). In other words, "If you're abiding in Me, hanging around Me, clinging to Me, you can ask anything of Me because within you will be My Word."

What word?

"Exceeding great and precious promises!" (2 Peter 1:4).

It has been said that there are between three and five *thousand* promises given to us in the Word. Therefore, it is as if God says, "I want you to take these exceedingly great and precious promises—and I want you to command Me."

George Mueller, the great prayer warrior of the last century, who founded scores of orphanages and funded them solely through prayer said this: "I take the promises of the Word and I argue with the Lord—not in order to convince God, but to convince myself." You see, as we repeat the promises God has so graciously given to us regarding provision, health, peace, salvation, understanding, guidance, direction, we are reminded of them ourselves. That's why we come to Bible study. That's why we take in the Scriptures. The Word is our bank account—and we're far, far richer than we think.

Too often, we live like spiritual paupers. We don't see blessings in our family, for our friends, or throughout our country. Why? We have not because we ask not (James 4:2). Why don't we ask? I'm convinced it's because we don't know what's in the Word. We have time to study the *Wall Street Journal* to figure out how we should invest; we have time to study *Good Housekeeping* to learn how to create a warm home; we have time to study *Parents Magazine* to enhance our parenting skills—but we fail to study the one book that contains promises concerning *all* of these areas. It is only as we pray the promises of God that we are able to withdraw from the inexhaustible resources the Lord has provided. Jacob understood this. That is why he was insistent in prayer.

Jacob Was Persistent in Prayer

> *And Jacob was left alone; and there wrestled a man with him until the breaking of the day. And when he saw that he prevailed not against him, he touched the hollow of his thigh; and the hollow of Jacob's thigh was out of joint, as he wrestled with him. And he said, Let me go, for the day breaketh. And he said, I will not let thee go, except thou bless me.* Genesis 32:24–26

From Hosea's commentary on this wrestling match, we gain further insight . . .

> *He took his brother by the heel in the womb, and by his strength he had power with God: Yea, he had power over the angel, and prevailed: he wept, and made supplication unto him: he found him in Bethel, and there he spake with us . . .*
> Hosea 12:3, 4

When did Jacob have power and prevail?

When he "wept and made supplication." In other words, although Jacob was the one who said, "I will not let thee go except thou bless me," Jacob was the one who was weeping; Jacob was the one who was pinned. Even though he was weeping, even though he was "losing" the match, even though he was pinned to the ground in pain, nonetheless Jacob didn't give up. He prayed with persistence.

In Prayer Jacob Found Intimacy

Why did God wrestle Jacob?

Why does He want to wrestle with you and me?

For the same reason I like to wrestle with Benny. It's something called intimacy. God likes to wrestle things through with me and you because He enjoys us. It's as if He says to us, "Let's wrestle this thing through hour after hour, day after day, even month after month because not only will you find that I'll come through eventually—but in the process, we will develop a wonderful intimacy."

That's why the original Greek text makes it clear that we are to "*keep* asking, *keep* seeking, *keep* knocking" (Matthew 7:7), for that is how intimacy is developed; that is how prayer is answered.

Through Prayer Jacob Made Discovery

Wrestling provides unique opportunities for discovery. As you measure your strength against that of your opponent, as you assume various positions and are held in numerous holds, you discover things about yourself and your opponent you couldn't have known otherwise.

God also invites us to wrestle with Him in order that we might discover things about Him and ourselves we could learn in no other way. As you wrestle in prayer, you might find that what God gives to you and does for you is entirely different than what you expected. Jacob asked to be blessed, instead he was broken—but the answer was better, because our Father knows best.

This classic prayer was found in the breast pocket of a Civil War soldier shot at Gettysburg:

I asked for strength that I might achieve.
He made me weak that I might obey.

I asked for health that I might do great things.
He gave me grace that I might do better things.

I asked for riches that I might be happy.
He gave me poverty that I might be wise.

I asked for power that I might have the praise of men.
He gave me weakness that I might feel a need for God.

I asked for all things that I might enjoy life.
He gave me life that I might enjoy all things.

I received nothing I asked for.
He gave me everything I hoped for.

Keep on wrestling, gang. You'll have intimacy *with* the Lord. You'll make discoveries *about* the Lord. And you'll be changed radically *by* the Lord in the very process of praying.

33 In wrestling with the angel Jacob had been blessed—but he had also been broken. So it is now, limping on his cane, that Jacob continues on his way back home . . .

Genesis 33:1, 2
And Jacob lifted up his eyes, and looked, and, behold, Esau came, and with him four hundred men. And he divided the children unto Leah, and unto Rachel, and unto the two handmaids. And he put the handmaids and their children foremost, and Leah and her children after, and Rachel and Joseph hindermost.

Jacob positioned the handmaidens and their children in the front of the procession, with Leah and her children following them. He positioned Rachel and Joseph at the back, the safest place, because his heart was with Rachel.

Genesis 33:3, 4
And he passed over before them, and bowed himself to the ground seven times, until he came near to his brother. And Esau ran to meet him, and embraced him, and fell on his neck, and kissed him: and they wept.

Jacob bows to the ground, afraid to look at Esau's face. But Esau rushes towards him and smothers him in a warm embrace.

Genesis 33:5 (a)
And he lifted up his eyes, and saw the women and the children; and said, Who are those with thee?

"Who are all these kids and women?" Esau asked.

Genesis 33:5 (b)
. . . And he said, The children which God hath graciously given thy servant.

"This is the family God has graciously given me," said Jacob.

Genesis 33:6–8 (a)
Then the handmaidens came near, they and their children, and they bowed themselves. And Leah also with her children came near, and bowed themselves: and after came Joseph near and Rachel, and they bowed themselves. And he said, What meanest thou by all this drove which I met?

Esau asked the meaning of the waves of camels and goats and sheep Jacob had sent ahead to try and appease him.

Genesis 33:8 (b)
. . . And he said, These are to find grace in the sight of my lord.

"I sent them to you in order that I might find grace in your sight," Jacob answered.

And in Jacob we see an illustration of our tendency to think we have to give something to the Lord in order to receive grace from the Lord. Why is it so difficult for us to receive grace graciously? It's because we've been so convinced that "there's no free lunch." But guess what. There *is* a free lunch—and breakfast and dinner, too! "Come and dine," says the Lord. "Ho every one that thirsteth, come ye to the waters. He that hath no money, come ye buy and eat" (Isaiah 55:1).

Genesis 33:9
And Esau said, I have enough, my brother; keep that thou hast unto thyself.

Now if Esau, who is a type of the flesh, says, "That's not the way it works,"—how much more our Lord, who is the epitome of grace and goodness, would say, "You don't have to do this, do that, or give up the other before you come into My presence." Therefore, let us come *boldly* unto the throne of grace that we may receive mercy and find grace to help in time of need (Hebrews 4:16).

If you're in need today, know this: There's nothing keeping you from going boldly to the throne and saying, "Father, I'm stuck," or, "Father, I don't understand," or, "Father, I need help."

This is the genius of true spirituality, the uniqueness of biblical Christianity. Every other philosophy and religion is based upon responsibility—the responsibility of its adherents to fast, to chant, to give, to work. Christianity isn't based on responsibility. It's based on response—the response to unconditional love, unrestrained mercy, undeserved grace.

For many years, I thought my salvation was based on my responsibility to pray, my responsibility to tithe, my responsibility to be at church. But then I began to understand that God blesses, God gives, God avails Himself not on the basis of what I do or don't do—but on the basis of what *He* did in sending His Son to die on the Cross in order to pay the price for my sin. And when that pressure was taken off me, I *wanted* to study the Word. I *wanted* to be in church. I *wanted* to pray—not to earn blessing, but because I had *already* been so blessed.

Genesis 33:10
And Jacob said, Nay, I pray thee, if now I have found grace in thy sight, then receive my present at my hand: for therefore I have seen thy face, as though I had seen the face of God, and thou wast pleased with me.

At first, Jacob said, "I gave you gifts in order to find grace." Now he gets it right, for he says, "I'm giving you gifts in response to the grace you've *already* shown me."

Genesis 33:11
Take, I pray thee, my blessing that is brought to thee; because God hath dealt graciously with me, and because I have enough. And he urged him, and he took it.

Here, Esau is being gracious. He doesn't need Jacob's gifts.

Genesis 33:12
And he said, Let us take our journey, and let us go, and I will go before thee.

"Let's travel together," Esau said.

Genesis 33:13
And he said unto him, My lord knoweth that the children are tender, and the flocks and herds with young are with me: and if men should overdrive them one day, all the flock will die.

"With all these young ones, I won't be able to keep up with you," said Jacob.

Genesis 33:14
Let my lord, I pray thee, pass over before his servant: and I will lead on softly, according as the cattle that goeth before me and the children be able to endure, until I come unto my lord unto Seir.

Seir was Edom, Esau's home, so Jacob says, "You go ahead, and I'll meet you at your place." Does Jacob in fact go to Seir? Evidently not. Even though Jacob is once again less than forthright, perhaps, remembering his relationship with Laban, he knew he shouldn't go to Seir because of the inevitable heartache and heartbreak which come when a believer is yoked with an unbeliever (2 Corinthians 6:14).

Genesis 33:15 (a)
And Esau said, Let me now leave with thee some of the folk that are with me . . .

"I'll leave some of my men to help you on your journey," Esau said.

Genesis 33:15 (b)
. . . And he said, What needeth it? let me find grace in the sight of my lord.

"That's not necessary," Jacob answered.

Genesis 33:16
So Esau returned that day on his way unto Seir.

Even though he had reason to be angry, Esau does not hold a grudge against Jacob. Furthermore, he only accepted Jacob's gift when pressed. Finally, he offered to accompany Jacob on his way as a means of protection for Jacob and his family. Thus, Esau would be considered refined and polished in our society. Yet the Bible says he is an uncouth man spiritually.

> Lest there be any fornicator, or profane person, as Esau, who for one morsel of meat sold his birthright. For ye know how that afterward, when he would have inherited the blessing, he was rejected: for he found no place of repentance, though he sought it carefully with tears. Hebrews 12:16, 17

Esau is a picture of the flesh—a doomed and damned man for whom there was found no place to repent.

"But my unsaved neighbor, or coworker, or uncle is so nice, so generous, so kind, so giving" we say. They may be. They may be gems, real diamonds. In comparison, the Christian you're sitting next to may be a cabbage. But there's a big difference. A diamond is brilliant, polished, and highly esteemed—but dead. A cabbage is common, lowly, and ugly—but alive.

People get real mixed up about this. They say, "I see Christians and they're rude and mean." The real issue, however, is this: We may be cabbage heads, but we're alive.

But God, who is rich in mercy, for his great love wherewith he loved us, Even when we were dead in sins, hath quickened us together with Christ, (by grace ye are saved;) And hath raised us up together, and made us sit together in heavenly places in Christ Jesus. Ephesians 2:4–6

Diamond-like as we may have been, we were nonetheless dead—but God made us alive. And now, cabbage-like as we may be, we're growing . . . We're not what we should be, but we're not what we used to be, and we're not what we're going to be, for when we see Him, we shall be like Him (1 John 3:2). Oh, glorious day!

Is Esau polished? Yes. Kind? Yes. But there is a basic flaw in Esau that will send him to hell: He doesn't have a heart for God, and therefore has no need of grace. A self-made man, he says, "I have enough" (v. 9).

Jacob, on the other hand, has lots of problems, but beneath them all, he has a heart for God and, therefore embraces grace. A believer, he says, "God hath dealt graciously with me" (v. 11). God is looking for men and women who truly, deeply know they don't deserve His goodness. The reason Jacob goes down in spiritual history as a giant is because he understands grace.

Genesis 33:17 (a)
And Jacob journeyed to Succoth . . .

Situated on the other side of the Jordan River, *Succoth* means "Tent Town."

Genesis 33:17 (b)
. . . and built him an house . . .

Jacob is the first patriarch to build a house. He's backsliding. He was supposed to live in a tent in the Promised Land. Instead, he builds a house on the wrong side of the river.

Genesis 33:17 (c)
. . . and made booths for his cattle: therefore the name of the place is called Succoth.

Jacob builds a house and booths for his cattle. In other words, he becomes a farmer.

Genesis 33:18 (a)
And Jacob came to Shalem, a city of Shechem, which is in the land of Canaan . . .

Perhaps realizing his dream house wasn't what he thought it would be, Jacob crosses over the Jordan River and goes to Shechem. Located on the right side of the Jordan River, Shechem was technically in the Promised Land, but, as we shall see, it was a carnal, evil place.

Genesis 33:18 (b)
. . . when he came from Padan-aram; and pitched his tent before the city.

Reminiscent of Lot, Jacob didn't go into the city, but pitched his tent toward the city.

Genesis 33:19, 20
And he bought a parcel of a field, where he had spread his tent, at the hand of the children of Hamor, Shechem's father, for an hundred pieces of money. And he erected there an altar, and called it El-elohe-Israel.

El-elohe-Israel literally means, "The God, the God of Israel." Jacob says the right thing—but with his tent facing Carnal City, he's saying it from the wrong place.

34

Genesis 34:1
And Dinah the daughter of Leah, which she bare unto Jacob, went out to see the daughters of the land.

Surrounded by twelve brothers, it's understandable why Dinah would want to see her girlfriends!

Genesis 34:2, 3
And when Shechem the son of Hamor the Hivite, prince of the country, saw her, he took her, and lay with her, and defiled her. And his soul clave unto Dinah the daughter of Jacob, and he loved the damsel, and spake kindly unto the damsel.

This is a mystery to me. After Shechem raped Dinah, he spoke kindly to her. Evidently, in his lustful passion, he developed feelings for her.

Genesis 34:4–7
And Shechem spake unto his father Hamor, saying, Get me this damsel to wife. And Jacob heard that he had defiled Dinah his daughter: now his sons were with his cattle in the field: and Jacob held his peace until they were come. And Hamor the father of Shechem went out unto Jacob to commune with him. And the sons of Jacob came out of the field when they heard it: and the men were grieved, and they were very wroth, because he had wrought folly in Israel in lying with Jacob's daughter; which thing ought not to be done.

Dinah's brothers were understandably angry. "What's going on here?" they demanded. "Our sister Dinah has been defiled."

Genesis 34:8, 9
And Hamor communed with them, saying, The soul of my son Shechem longeth for your daughter: I pray you give her him to wife. And make ye marriages with us, and give your daughters unto us, and take our daughters unto you.

"Let's merge our families together," Shechem's father suggested.

Genesis 34:10
And ye shall dwell with us: and the land shall be before you; dwell and trade ye therein, and get you possessions therein.

"It'll be good for business," said Shechem.

Genesis 34:11, 12
And Shechem said unto her father and unto her brethren, Let me find grace in your eyes, and what ye shall say unto me I will give. Ask me never so much dowry and gift, and I will give according as ye shall say unto me: but give me the damsel to wife.

"Name your price," Shechem said, hoping to close the deal.

Genesis 34:13–17
And the sons of Jacob answered Shechem and Hamor his father deceitfully, and said, because he had defiled Dinah their sister: And they said unto them, We cannot do this thing, to give our sister to one that is uncircumcised; for that were a reproach unto us: But in this will we consent unto you: If ye will be as we be, that every male of you be circumcised; Then will we give our daughters unto you, and we will take your daughters to us, and we will dwell with you, and we will become one people. But if ye will not hearken unto us, to be circumcised; then will we take our daughter, and we will be gone.

"We cannot do as you suggest," said the sons of Jacob to the father of Shechem, "because you are not circumcised. However, if your men become circumcised, then we can join our families together."

Genesis 34:18, 19 (a)
And their words pleased Hamor, and Shechem Hamor's son. And the young man deferred not to do the thing, because he had delight in Jacob's daughter:

Hamor and Shechem agreed to the demand of Jacob's sons.

Genesis 34:19 (b)
. . . and he was more honourable than all the house of his father.

In other words, Shechem was making a deal he meant to keep.

Genesis 34:20
And Hamor and Shechem his son came unto the gate of their city, and communed with the men of their city, saying,

Hamor and Shechem now have a big job ahead of them: They have to sell this idea to the men of their city.

Genesis 34:21–23
These men are peaceable with us; therefore let them dwell in the land, and trade therein; for the land, behold, it is large enough for them; let us take their daughters to us for wives, and let us give them our daughters. Only herein will the men consent unto us for to dwell with us, to be one people, if every male among us be circumcised, as they are circumcised. Shall not their cattle and their substance and every beast of theirs be ours? only let us consent unto them, and they will dwell with us.

"We know this will be a little painful," Hamor and Shechem admitted, "but here's the deal: Eventually, we'll take these people over. And all of their stuff will ultimately be ours. We'll have it made."

Genesis 34:24
And unto Hamor and unto Shechem his son hearkened all that went out of the gate of his city; and every male was circumcised, all that went out of the gate of his city.

The men of Shechem bought into Hamor's and Shechem's plan.

Genesis 34:25–29
And it came to pass on the third day, when they were sore, that two of the sons of Jacob, Simeon and Levi, Dinah's brethren, took each man his sword, and came upon the city boldly, and slew all the males. And they slew Hamor and Shechem his son with the edge of the sword, and took Dinah out of Shechem's house, and went out. The sons of Jacob came upon the slain, and spoiled the city, because they had defiled their sister. They took their sheep, and their oxen, and their asses, and that which was in the city, and that which was in the field, And all their wealth, and all their little ones, and their

wives took they captive, and spoiled even all that was in the house.

Completely incapacitated, the men of Shechem were unable to defend themselves when Simeon and Levi showed up and began chopping away.

Genesis 34:30, 31
And Jacob said to Simeon and Levi, Ye have troubled me to make me to stink among the inhabitants of the land, among the Canaanites and the Perizzites: and I being few in number, they shall gather themselves together against me, and slay me; and I shall be destroyed, I and my house. And they said, Should he deal with our sister as with an harlot?

"When word gets out to the other cities in the area concerning what you've done, we, too, will be annihilated," said a distraught Jacob to his sons.

Why would God take a whole chapter to tell such a sad, sordid story? It is a wise man and a wise woman who says, "Lord, if you're telling us this, we better listen." You see, every time I have failed, every time I have erred, every time I have missed the mark, dropped the ball, stumbled about—God was faithful to warn me ahead of time. The problem was, I didn't listen.

The story we have just read serves as just such a warning to every mom and dad wise enough to understand that he who pitches his tent toward the world must not be surprised when his kids act like the world. The parent who says to his children, "The way you're behaving, the way you're dressing, the way you're living is causing me to stink," is almost invariably the one who has allowed his kids to go places and do things he knew in his heart weren't right—for if we allow our Dinahs and Daniels to interact with the heathen, confusion in our kids and problems in our homes are sure to follow. Heed the warning so clearly given here, dear dad and precious mom. It's not legalism. It's plain old wisdom.

35 His daughter raped, his sons mass murderers, Jacob's family is falling apart. The whole place stinks in his estimation. Things look real grim. And the story continues . . .

Genesis 35:1 (a)
And God said unto Jacob, Arise, go up . . .

In light of his situation, what God says to Jacob amazes me. He doesn't say, "Sit down. You're benched," or, "Back off. You're done," or, "That's it. You're through." He says, "Arise. Go up"—because our God is a God of unbelievable grace.

Genesis 35:1 (b)
. . . to Bethel, and dwell there . . .

Bethel—previously called Luz until the night Jacob had an encounter with God—was the place where Jacob was saved. Now the Lord says, "Go back to the place you met Me." How I appreciate our Lord—because that's what He says to you and me. We tend to think God is mad *at* us, is angry *with* us, has had enough *of* us. But our brother Paul would come on the scene and say, "Where sin abounds, grace abounds *more*" (Romans 5:20, italics added). Jacob and his clan are neck-deep in sin. And yet God says, "Rise up. Let's get going again."

Genesis 35:1 (c)
. . . and make there an altar unto God, that appeared unto thee when thou fleddest from the face of Esau thy brother.

"I want to 'altar' you once more," God said to Jacob.

Genesis 35:2–4 (a)
Then Jacob said unto his household, and to all that were with him, Put away the strange gods that are among you, and be clean, and change your garments: And let us arise, and go up to Bethel; and I will make there an altar unto God, who answered me in the day of my distress, and was with me in the way which I went. And they gave unto Jacob all the strange gods which were in their hand, and all their earrings which were in their ears . . .

Evidently, Jacob's family had added pagan gods and trinkets to the idols Rachel had stolen from her father. Here, Jacob says, "We're going to Bethel. We're going to the house of God. So give me all of those earrings and bracelets and stuff you picked up from the heathens."

Notice God didn't say to Jacob, "If you deal with the pagan gods in your family, then I might give you a second chance." No, God said, "Rise and let us go to Bethel."

Perhaps it was because Jacob was so amazed by this that he said, "It's time to clean up—not *so* God will call us, but because He *has* called us."

That's what grace does. When I realize how kind and good and benevolent and merciful God is to me day after day after day, it causes me to want to put away my trinkets and toys that are not of Him. Too often, we think, *I've got to get my life cleaned up and maybe then I can hear God's voice; maybe then He'll lead me again.* No. God is ready to lead us today right where we are—and because of that we say, "Lord, You're so good. I don't want the things of the world any more."

Genesis 35:4 (b)
. . . and Jacob hid them under the oak which was by Shechem.

The tree in Scripture, of course, speaks of the Cross. In other words, the picture is that Jacob left his sin at Calvary. When Jesus died on the Cross, not only was the penalty of sin paid for completely, but power over sin was provided fully. This is an amazing and potent truth. You can leave here tonight and say, "Lord, truly You are good in allowing me to go to Bethel once more. I'm tired of my sin, and I want to make my way free and unencumbered of the junk which entangles me."

But, practically, how does this happen? You reckon the old man dead. You say, "Lord, on the basis of Your Word, I no longer have to do that, go there, be involved with the other—not because of positive thinking, but because of what You did on Calvary's tree." Just as by faith you receive forgiveness, so too by faith you gain victory.

Thus, I can truly say to that Double Quarter Pounder with cheese, "I no longer have to submit to the demand you are placing on me. I reckon the old man dead to that sin." And I truly, honestly, absolutely, unequivocally can turn away from that Quarter Pounder and walk free—if I choose to! If you haven't spent time in Romans 6 lately, I encourage you to marvel at it and say, "Thank You, Lord, that because on the Cross You not only removed the penalty of sin, but broke the power of sin, I don't have to give in. I can walk away a free man." Gang, I am simple-minded enough to believe this applies to a heroin addict, to a gossiper, to a person who's hooked on pornography, to a person with a negative attitude. *Whatever* the sin might be, its power was shattered on the Cross.

"Give me that stuff," Jacob said to his family.

"No, it's too strong. No, it can't be done. No, it's too important," they could have said. Instead, they responded to the command given them by Jacob, just as you can respond to the Word given you by the Lord.

Genesis 35:5
And they journeyed: and the terror of God was upon the cities that were round about them, and they did not pursue after the sons of Jacob.

With the old gods and the old stuff buried at the base of the tree, as Jacob's family makes their way to Bethel, the fear of God keeps the people round about from attacking.

Genesis 35:6, 7
So Jacob came to Luz, which is in the land of Canaan, that is, Bethel, he and all the people that were with him. And he built there an altar, and called the place El-beth-el: because there God appeared unto him, when he fled from the face of his brother.

Jacob has his problems indeed. Jacob has all kinds of baggage without question. But through it all, he's growing because when he comes to Bethel the second time, he no longer calls it *Bethel*, "the house of God," but *El-Bethel* or, "The God of the House of God." This shows monumental maturity, for Jacob understands that it's not the house of God that is important, but the God who dwells therein. So, too, it's not worship that's important, but the God whom we worship. It's not the Bible that's important, but the God of the Bible. You see, the Word is not an end in itself. The goal of Bible study is not to try and gain more intellectual or theological understanding. It's much more than that. The Word of God is simply a door I go through many times a day to meet the God of the Word.

"That's obvious," you say.

Not really. A lot of people initially delight in church or Bible study or worship. But eventually they lose interest in church and Bible study and worship because those things are not God.

Genesis 35:8
But Deborah Rebekah's nurse died, and she was buried beneath Bethel under an oak: and the name of it was called Allon-bachuth.

Allon-bachuth means "the oak of weeping." As Jacob enters the Promised Land, he re-connects with Deborah, the woman who raised him, his nanny. Rid of his idols, Jacob is back at Bethel with a deeper understanding. But when Deborah dies, he weeps.

Genesis 35:9, 10
And God appeared unto Jacob again, when he came out of Padan-aram, and blessed him. And God said unto him, Thy name is Jacob: thy name shall not be called any more Jacob, but Israel shall be thy name: and he called his name Israel.

God speaks to Jacob again, assuring him the promise He had given him was still in place. Changed from "Heel-Snatcher" to "Governed by God," from "Con Man" to "Israel," Jacob was reminded that God had given him a *personal name*.

Genesis 35:11
And God said unto him, I am God Almighty: be fruitful and multiply; a nation and a company of nations shall be of thee, and kings shall come out of thy loins;

After a personal name comes *promised fame*, as God promised Jacob he would be fruitful and powerful.

Genesis 35:12, 13
And the land which I gave Abraham and Isaac, to thee I will give it, and to thy seed after thee will I give the land. And God went up from him in the place where he talked with him.

Finally, the Land being God's to give, He gives it to Israel as a *perpetual claim*.

Genesis 35:14 (a)
And Jacob set up a pillar in the place where he talked with him, even a pillar of stone . . .

Stone in Scripture speaks of the Rock of Ages, the Chief Cornerstone, Jesus Christ.

Genesis 35:14 (b)
. . . and he poured a drink offering thereon . . .

The wine of the drink offering speaks of the work of the Cross, when Jesus' blood was poured out for us.

Genesis 35:14 (c)
. . . and he poured oil thereon.

The oil speaks of the work of the Holy Spirit. What did the Good Samaritan pour into the wounds of the man who was beaten up? Wine and oil (Luke 10:34). The oil being provision for success, and the blood payment for failure, the Lord says, "The way to be successful is not by might, not by power, but by My Spirit (Zechariah 4:6). But if you fall, My blood will cleanse you." What a wonderful combination!

Genesis 35:15, 16 (a)
And Jacob called the name of the place where God spake with him, Bethel. And they journeyed from Bethel . . .

To this man who experienced devastation in his family, God said, "Go to Bethel and dwell there. Go to Bethel and stay put." Jacob went there, found refuge and renewal, revival and refreshment—and then he left! *Why?* Why do people leave Bethel? Why do people leave the House of God? Let me give you the only answer we see in the text: After talking about Jacob's revival in Bethel in verse 7, verse 8 says, "But Rebekah's nurse died." In other words, although he had met God, heard the promises of God, and fellowshipped with God at Bethel, Jacob evidently couldn't deal with the fact that his nanny was no longer there.

Both Abraham and Jacob would leave the House of God because of changes. Abraham left Bethel because of famine. His grandson leaves Bethel because of family. Abraham left because things were changing financially. Jacob leaves because he can't handle it emotionally.

"Why isn't our church small like it used to be?" people ask. "Why are there different people leading worship? Why isn't my nanny here anymore?"

The answer is singular: Because things change. Why do things change? Because God is not static. Spiritual life will always be in motion. Therefore, it is the unwise man, the foolish woman who says, "If nanny's not here anymore, I'm not coming either." Precious fellow pilgrim, on our spiritual journey, we must build our altar, offer our praise, receive instruction and *remain* in Bethel.

Genesis 35:16 (b)–18 (a)
. . . and there was but a little way to come to Ephrath: and Rachel travailed, and she had hard labour. And it came to pass, when she was in hard labour, that the midwife said unto her, Fear not; thou shalt have this son also. And it came to pass, as her soul was in departing, (for she died) . . .

"Give me children or else I'll die," Rachel had demanded (Genesis 30:1). But it was in bearing a child that she did, in fact, die.

Genesis 35:18 (b)
. . . that she called his name Ben-oni: but his father called him Benjamin.

A picture of our Lord Jesus Christ in this story, Benjamin brought sorrow to his mother. A sword would pierce Mary's heart when she saw her Son on the Cross (Luke 2:35). But to Jacob, Benjamin was the "son of my right hand"—just as to the Father, Jesus would bring great delight (Matthew 3:17).

Genesis 35:19
And Rachel died, and was buried in the way to Ephrath, which is Bethlehem.

Rachel died in labor—perhaps unnecessarily as a result of the journey from Bethel.

Genesis 35:20, 21
And Jacob set a pillar upon her grave: that is the pillar of Rachel's grave unto this day. And Israel journeyed, and spread his tent beyond the tower of Edar.

Notice that Jacob buried Rachel—but Israel journeyed on. Jacob was exceedingly sorrowful, but he will eventually soar higher.

Genesis 35:22 (a)
And it came to pass, when Israel dwelt in that land, that Reuben went and lay with Bilhah his father's concubine: and Israel heard it . . .

If Jacob had heard what Reuben had done, he would have reacted. But Israel heard it. Broken, limping, governed by God, Israel does not react immediately.

Genesis 35:22 (b)–29 (a)
. . . Now the sons of Jacob were twelve: The sons of Leah; Reuben, Jacob's firstborn, and Simeon, and Levi, and Judah, and Issachar, and Zebulun: The sons of Rachel; Joseph, and Benjamin: And the sons of Bilhah, Rachel's handmaid; Dan, and Naphtali: And the sons of Zilpah, Leah's handmaid; Gad, and Asher: these are the sons of Jacob, which were born to him in Padan-aram. And Jacob came unto Isaac his father unto Mamre, unto the city of Arbah, which is Hebron, where Abraham and Isaac sojourned. And the days of Isaac were an hundred and fourscore years. And Isaac gave up the ghost, and died, and was gathered unto his people, being old and full of days . . .

Once again, sadness enters Jacob's heart, as his father dies.

Genesis 35:29 (b)
. . . and his sons Esau and Jacob buried him.

As Ishmael and Isaac had done before them, now Jacob and Esau meet at the grave of their father.

36

All scripture is given by inspiration of God, and is profitable for doctrine, for reproof, for correction, for instruction in righteousness . . . 2 Timothy 3:16 (a)

The word "inspired" literally means "God-breathed." *All* Scripture is given by inspiration. That means God breathed life into each word He spoke. We live in a time when people are saying, "Oh, yes, the Bible is inspired." But they're using the word "inspired" the same way they say Shakespeare was inspired—and that's not what Paul was saying to Timothy. According to Paul, God personally breathed life into and uttered each word specifically. Therefore, the modern theologian who says the Bible contains the Word of God is in grave and, I believe, damnable error. The Bible does not contain the Word of God, gang. The Bible *is* the Word of God.

Am I splitting hairs? No. The implication of those who say the Bible contains the Word of God is that the Bible also contains the words of men. The problem with that is, even if I say most of the Bible is the Word of God, as I decide which part is inspired and which isn't, I become the judge of the Bible rather than allowing the Bible to judge me. And guess how I'll judge it. Concerning the things I agree with, I'll say, "That's God speaking." Concerning the things that convict me, however, I'll say, "That's man speaking."

Every book in the Bible, every chapter of every book, every verse of every chapter, every word of every verse, every letter of every word is inspired. It's *all* God-breathed. It's *all* important. Even the passage before us . . .

Genesis 36:1 (a)
Now these are the generations of Esau . . .

Chapter 36 is a genealogy of the family of Esau. Esau is the epitome of the flesh, the old nature, the part of you and me that wants its own way, that demands to be satisfied. Whether it concerns an easily identifiable sin, or a much more subtle desire, the flesh is always contrary to the spirit.

Genesis 36:1 (b)
. . . who is Edom.

Esau is also called Edom because he settled across the Jordan River in the southern area directly east of the Promised Land known as Edom. The flesh also lives outside the Promised Land, removed from the blessings and promises of God.

Genesis 36:2 (a)
Esau took his wives of the daughters of Canaan . . .

In Deuteronomy 7:3, God would say, "Do not take Canaanite women to be your wives." Paul would say, "Don't be unequally yoked with unbelievers" (2 Corinthians 6:14). Determined to have his way, however, Esau went to the pagan communities and married Canaanite women.

Genesis 36:2 (b)
. . . Adah the daughter of Elon the Hittite, and Aholibamah the daughter of Anah the daughter of Zibeon the Hivite;

When Esau took his wife Adah back home to meet Isaac and Rebekah, there must have been immediate tension, for Adah was the name of the woman married to Lamech in the days preceding the Flood (Genesis 4:19). Lamech being one who rebelled against the Lord, what does Esau do? We know from other genealogies (Genesis 26:34), that Esau changes her name to the name of one of his cousins: *Bashemath,* or "Spice."

Esau changed her name. So, too, the flesh has a tendency to change the name of sin into something more palatable, which makes it easier to swallow. That is why committing adultery is now called "having an affair;" why fornication is now a "fling;" why a Sodomite is now "gay."

The problem is, every time Esau says the name of his wife, he's reminded of his cousin—to such a degree that he ends up marrying her as well.

Genesis 36:3
And Bashemath, Ishmael's daughter, sister of Nebajoth.

Now Esau has two Bashemaths. So we see him change the original Bashemath's name in 28:9 to Mahalath. *Mahalath* literally means "sickness." Why would Esau name her this? Because he's getting ready to take a third wife. The flesh still does the same thing today, evidenced whenever someone says, "I'm going to brand my spouse as one who makes me sick, who is incompatible, who is emotionally abusive, so I can move on to someone else."

Genesis 36:4, 5 (a)
And Adah bare to Esau Eliphaz; and Bashemath bare Reuel; And Aholibamah bare Jeush, and Jaalam, and Korah . . .

Aholibamah, or literally, "Tent of the High Place" was a temple prostitute. At the high places, where pagan gods were worshiped and pagan idols served, there would be a tent close by called "the tent of the high place." The "priestesses" within were nothing more than prostitutes and, like Aholibamah, were known as residents of the tent of the high place.

Realizing his marriage to a temple prostitute would not set very well with his parents, in 26:34, we see Esau change Aholibamah's name to Judith.

As a temple prostitute, Aholibamah would have been very beautiful. But she was also quite powerful, for in verse 41, we see she was actually a duke, or a *sheikh*—as rare for a woman in that day as it is in ours.

In Esau's genealogy, we see many characteristics of the flesh, the first being that the flesh is *pious,* as it changes names to make sin sound acceptable—even at times religious. Gossip can parade as a prayer request and judgment can masquerade as a concern in an effort to make the "Aholibamahs" in our own lives appear righteous.

Genesis 36:5 (b)
. . . these are the sons of Esau, which were born unto him in the land of Canaan.

Secondly, the flesh is *prolific.* As you read this genealogy, you see numerous groups of people whose line goes back to Esau because the flesh is prolific. Yes, when we sin, when we give in to our flesh, our sin past, present, and future is forgiven because Christ paid for it so completely that God says, "Your sin and iniquity will I remember no more" (Hebrews 10:17). However, Paul says, "Be not deceived. If a man sows to the flesh, then of the flesh he shall reap corruption" (Galatians 6:8). If I plant seeds of the flesh, although I'm forgiven, the crop will still come up. There's no way around this. That is why the chapter before us contains such a long list of people who are descendants of Esau.

Genesis 36:6–8
And Esau took his wives, and his sons, and his daughters, and all the persons of his house, and his cattle, and all his beasts, and all his substance, which he had got in the land of Canaan; and went into the country from the face of his brother Jacob. For their riches were more than that they might dwell together; and the land wherein they were strangers could not bear them because of their cattle. Thus dwelt Esau in mount Seir: Esau is Edom.

The flesh is *prosperous.* Esau was prosperous. And herein lies a problem. "How come the fleshly guy at work gets the promotion?" we ask. "Why does the guy who cheats on his taxes get the new ski boat? Why does the girl who cheats on her exam get an A?" These questions are what caused the psalmist to cry, "My feet slipped when I saw the prosperity of the wicked" (Psalm 73).

If you cheat, you'll get ahead, but only for a season. You might make an A when you should have received a C; you might get money because you beat the system—but it will haunt you. It'll bite you. It'll catch up with you every single time without exception.

Genesis 36:9–13
And these are the generations of Esau the father of the Edomites in mount Seir: These are the names of Esau's sons; Eliphaz the son of Adah the wife of Esau, Reuel the son of Bashemath the wife of Esau. And the sons of Eliphaz were Teman, Omar, Zepho, and Gatam, and Kenaz. And Timna was concubine to Eliphaz Esau's son; and she bare to Eliphaz Amalek: these were the sons of Adah Esau's wife. And these are the sons of Reuel; Nahath, and Zerah, Shammah, and Mizzah: these were the sons of Bashemath Esau's wife.

The flesh is *persuasive.* It was Eliphaz the Temanite who came to Job, saying, "Look at the jam you're in. Life is not happening the way it's supposed to. It must be that God is mad at you."

The flesh will say to you, "So you've been going to church, walking with God, reading the Bible—where is it getting you? You've got more problems, more trials, more difficulties than ever."

Genesis 36:14–16
And these were the sons of Aholibamah, the daughter of Anah the daughter of Zibeon, Esau's wife: and she bare to Esau Jeush, and Jaalam, and Korah. These were dukes of the sons of Esau: the sons of Eliphaz the firstborn son of Esau; duke Teman, duke Omar, duke Zepho, duke Kenaz, Duke Korah, duke Gatam, and duke Amalek: these are the dukes that came of Eliphaz in the land of Edom; these were the sons of Adah.

The flesh is *pernicious.* The Amalekites picked on the folks in the back as Moses led the people to the Promised Land (Deuteronomy 25).

The most dangerous place to be in spiritual life is in the back of the pack, for it is there that we get picked off by the flesh. Go for the kingdom with all your might. Stay as close to the things of God as you possibly can. Otherwise, you're an easy target for Amalek.

Genesis 36:17–23
And these are the sons of Reuel Esau's son; duke Nahath, duke Zerah, duke Shammah, duke Mizzah: these are the dukes that came of Reuel in the land of Edom; these are the sons of Bashemath Esau's wife. And these are the sons of Aholibamah Esau's wife; duke Jeush, duke Jaalam, duke Korah: these were the dukes that came of Aholibamah the daughter of Anah, Esau's wife. These are the sons of Esau, who is Edom, and these are their dukes. These are the sons of Seir the Horite, who inhabited the land; Lotan, and Shobal, and Zibeon, and Anah, And Dishon, and Ezer, and Dishan: these are the dukes of the Horites, the children of Seir in the land of Edom. And the children of Lotan were Hori and Hemam; and Lotan's sister was Timna. And the children of Shobal were these; Alvan, and Manahath, and Ebal, Shepho, and Onam.

The flesh is *powerful.* We know from the Book of Deuteronomy that the Horites were powerful men related to the Anakim, the giants. The descendants of Esau were able to wipe out even the mighty Horites because the flesh is powerful. "I kicked that habit. I dealt with that addiction. I beat that problem," some say as they glory in their flesh, for the flesh can overcome giants.

The problem is, the flesh can also *become* a giant, for when you feed the flesh, it doesn't become calmer, it grows stronger. "I'll just satisfy this fleshly tendency a little bit," we say. But each time we give in, the flesh grows stronger.

Genesis 36:24–31
And these are the children of Zibeon; both Ajah, and Anah: this was that Anah that found the mules in the wilderness, as he fed the asses of Zibeon his father. And the children of Anah were these; Dishon, and Aholibamah the daughter of Anah. And these are the children of Dishon; Hemdan, and Eshban, and Ithran, and Cheran. The children of Ezer are these; Bilhan, and Zaavan, and Akan. The children of Dishan are these: Uz, and Aran. These are the dukes that came of the Horites; duke Lotan, duke Shobal, duke Zibeon, duke Anah, Duke Dishon, duke Ezer, duke Dishan: these are the dukes that came of Hori, among their dukes in the land of Seir. And these are the kings that reigned in the land of Edom, before there reigned any king over the children of Israel.

The flesh is *proud.* "We, the descendants of Esau, had kings before the children of Israel had a king. We're way ahead of the game. We're on the cutting edge. We know where it's at." The flesh is proud, boasting of what it accomplishes, of what it has achieved, of what it has brought about in its own power.

Genesis 36:32–39
And Bela the son of Beor reigned in Edom: and the name of his city was Dinhabah. And Bela died, and Jobab the son of Zerah of Bozrah reigned in his stead. And Jobab died, and Husham of the land of Temani reigned in his stead. And Husham died, and Hadad the son of Bedad, who smote Midian in the field of Moab, reigned in his stead: and the name of his city was Avith. And Hadad died, and Samlah of Masrekah reigned in his stead. And Samlah died, and Saul of Rehoboth by the river reigned in his stead. And Saul died, and Baal-hanan the son of Achbor reigned in his stead. And Baal-hanan the son of Achbor died, and Hadar reigned in his stead: and the name of his city was Pau; and his wife's name was Mehetabel, the daughter of Matred, the daughter of Mezahab.

The flesh is *persistent.* Concerning the succession of kings, we read "in his stead," "in his stead," "in his stead." So, too, even though one aspect of the flesh may die, there's always another to take its place.

Genesis 36:40–43
And these are the names of the dukes that came of Esau, according to their families, after their places, by their names; duke Timnah, duke Alvah, duke Jetheth, Duke Aholibamah, duke Elah, duke Pinon, Duke Kenaz, duke Teman, duke Mibzar, Duke Magdiel, duke Iram: these be the dukes of Edom, according to their habitations in the land of their possession: he is Esau the father of the Edomites.

The flesh is pious, prolific, prosperous, persuasive, pernicious, powerful, and proud. But it's something else, as well: It's *pitiful.*

Go to Edom today, and you'll see there's absolutely nothing there. The once-impregnable city of Petra, of which the Edomites were so proud is nothing but a ghost town. Whatever is done through the flesh will ultimately be as empty as Edom. What, then, are we to do? If you don't want to end up a great big zero, turn to the Book of Romans.

> For to be carnally minded is death; but to be spiritually minded is life and peace. Because the carnal mind is enmity against God: for it is not subject to the law of God, neither indeed can be. So then they that are in the flesh cannot please God. But ye are not in the flesh, but in the Spirit, if so be that the Spirit of God dwell in you. Now if any man have not the Spirit of Christ, he is none of his. And if Christ be in you, the body is dead because of sin; but the Spirit is life because of righteousness. But if the Spirit of him that raised up Jesus from the dead dwell in you, he that raised up Christ from the dead shall also quicken your mortal bodies by his Spirit that dwelleth in you.
>
> Romans 8:6–11

The same Spirit that raised Jesus from the dead dwells in you—not only to raise you up eternally, but to raise you up presently, away from the flesh which so easily ensnares and seduces and snags us. So what are we to do? We say, "No more flesh"—and the Spirit takes it from there, telling us moment by moment what to do. This doesn't mean there won't be obstacles, but the Spirit of God is more powerful than any obstacle if we choose to obey, for to be carnally minded is death, but to be spiritually minded is life and peace. May God help us make the choice moment by moment to draw from *His* strength to see us through.

37

We come to the account of Joseph—one of the greatest men in the Bible, and along with Daniel, one of only two major characters in the Old Testament of whom there is no mention of sin.

A full one-quarter of the Book of Genesis is devoted to Joseph's story. In Genesis 1:16, God devotes a mere five words to His creation of the universe, while in Genesis 37—50, He spends twelve chapters on a single individual. I would have thought it would be the other way around because stars, space, that which is beyond our world, and how it came to be are what interest us. But those things are not God's priority. He spends His time talking about Joseph—for Joseph is a wonderful picture of Jesus. And Jesus is a subject that interests God greatly.

As we will see, in the story of Joseph, we find insights *about* Jesus, prophecies that point *to* Jesus, and understandings concerning the nature *of* Jesus. In fact, wherever you touch Joseph, you'll find Jesus . . .

Genesis 37:1, 2
And Jacob dwelt in the land wherein his father was a stranger, in the land of Canaan. These are the generations of Jacob. Joseph, being seventeen years old, was feeding the flock with his brethren; and the lad was with the sons of Bilhah, and with the sons of Zilpah, his father's wives: and Joseph brought unto his father their evil report.

Joseph was not being a tattletale. Rather, because he was in harmony with his father and cared about his father, he was accountable to his father. Jesus is in the same category. "I always do the things that please My Father," He said (John 8:29). "Don't you know I have to be about My Father's business?" He asked (Luke 2:49). "The Son does nothing of Himself, but what He sees and hears of the Father, that will He do," He declared (John 5:19).

At any given moment, in any given situation, the Bible tells me I will either seek to please God or seek to please man (Galatians 1:10). I'm either going to be concerned about what the Father thinks of the way I'm talking, the things I'm doing, the plans I'm making—or I'll be concerned about the opinion of those around me regarding those things.

The Bible says the fear of the Lord is the beginning of wisdom (Proverbs 9:10), but the fear of man is a snare (Proverbs 29:25). There is no middle ground. We're either living in the fear of the Lord or in the fear of man.

Joseph realized his brothers wouldn't be happy when he told his father about them, but he cared more about his father than he did about his brothers. It's a beautiful illustration not of a tattletale, but of one living life in harmony with his father.

Genesis 37:3
Now Israel loved Joseph more than all his children, because he was the son of his old age: and he made him a coat of many colours.

This is a coat of many pieces, actually a coat of big sleeves.

Genesis 37:4
And when his brethren saw that their father loved him more than all his brethren, they hated him, and could not speak peaceably unto him.

Who else was hated by His brothers because He was in harmony with the Father? Jesus. Of Jesus, John says, He came unto His own, but His own received Him not (John 1:11).

***For topical study of Genesis 37:3, 4 entitled "Big Sleeves . . . Big Problems," turn to page* 170.**

Genesis 37:5–7
And Joseph dreamed a dream, and he told it his brethren: and they hated him yet the more. And he said unto them, Hear, I pray you, this dream which I have dreamed: For, behold, we were binding sheaves in the field, and, lo, my sheaf arose, and also stood upright; and, behold, your sheaves stood round about, and made obeisance to my sheaf.

"I had a dream last night that all of your sheaves bowed down to mine" is a gutsy statement for seventeen-year-old Joseph to make to ten grown men.

Genesis 37:8 (a)
And his brethren said to him, Shalt thou indeed reign over us? or shalt thou indeed have dominion over us?

Listen closely to Joseph's brothers, and you're sure to hear the nation of Israel say, "We will not have this man rule over us" (John 19:15).

Genesis 37:8 (b)–11
. . . And they hated him yet the more for his dreams, and for his words. And he dreamed yet another dream, and told it his brethren, and said, Behold, I have dreamed a dream more; and, behold, the sun and the moon and the eleven stars made obeisance to me. And he told it to his father, and to his brethren: and his father rebuked him, and said unto him, What is this dream that thou hast dreamed? Shall I and thy mother and thy brethren indeed come to bow down ourselves to thee to the earth? And his brethren envied him; but his father observed the saying.

The sheaves speak of the world's resources. The stars speak of the world's rulers. In other words, both the world's resources and rulers will bow down to the Greater than Joseph, Jesus Christ (Colossians 1:16–18).

Knowing that his first dream made his brothers hate him, why would Joseph share Dream number two with them? It would have been very easy for Joseph to say, "I already have the big sleeves. Why should I complicate matters with these dreams about sheaves and stars?" But, like Jesus, Joseph knew that truth had to be shared, let the chips fall where they may.

Genesis 37:12
And his brethren went to feed their father's flock in Shechem.

The site their sister was raped, the place where Levi and Simeon had become mass murderers, Shechem was a worldly place.

Genesis 37:13
And Israel said unto Joseph, Do not thy brethren feed the flock in Shechem? come,

and I will send thee unto them. And he said to him, Here am I.

"Your brothers are in Shechem—a place of wickedness and depravity," said Jacob to his son. "Will you go help them?"

And Joseph said, "Here am I."

This scene is an insight into the interaction between the Father and the Son. "For God so loved the world that He gave His only begotten Son" (John 3:16). God the Father sent His Son to this Shechem. No wonder Jesus would hear the Father's voice thunder from heaven, "This is My beloved Son in whom I am well pleased" (Matthew 3:17)—signifying that He knew He was to die; that He was willing to go all the way not only to Shechem, but to Calvary.

Genesis 37:14
And he said to him, Go, I pray thee, see whether it be well with thy brethren, and well with the flocks; and bring me word again. So he sent him out of the vale of Hebron, and he came to Shechem.

Jacob sent Joseph as a messenger. Jesus told the story of the vineyard owner who went on a journey and sent some messengers to pick up the rent from the vineyard—only to have the vineyard workers beat up messenger after messenger. Finally, the owner said, "They're not respecting my servants. Therefore, I'll send my son. Him they will receive." But what did they do with the son? They killed him (Matthew 21).

Genesis 37:15, 16 (a)
And a certain man found him, and, behold, he was wandering in the field: and the man asked him, saying, What seekest thou? And he said, I seek my brethren:

Jesus would then say, "The Son of man came to seek and save those who are lost" (Luke 19:10).

Genesis 37:16 (b)–18
. . . tell me, I pray thee, where they feed their flocks. And the man said, They are departed hence; for I heard them say, Let us go to Dothan. And Joseph went after his brethren, and found them in Dothan. And when they saw him afar off, even before he came near unto them, they conspired against him to slay him.

Even while he was afar off, Joseph's brothers plotted and planned to kill him. In the same way, before they even knew Him, the Jewish leaders had launched their damnable plot to destroy Jesus (John 5:18).

Genesis 37:19–21
And they said one to another, Behold, this dreamer cometh. Come now therefore, and let us slay him, and cast him into some pit, and we will say, Some evil beast hath devoured him: and we shall see what will become of his dreams. And Reuben heard it, and he delivered him out of their hands; and said, Let us not kill him.

A man who wavers back and forth, oldest brother Reuben doesn't exactly know how to handle this situation. In this, he's a lot like Pontius Pilate (Matthew 27:24).

Genesis 37:22
And Reuben said unto them, Shed no blood, but cast him into this pit that is in the wilderness, and lay no hand upon him; that he might rid him out of their hands, to deliver him to his father again.

"Maybe putting Joseph in a pit will satisfy my brothers," Reuben hoped. So, too, hoping to satisfy the cry of the Jew, the brothers of Jesus, Pilate ordered Him scourged (John 19:1).

Genesis 37:23
And it came to pass, when Joseph was come unto his brethren, that they stript Joseph out of his coat, his coat of many colours that was on him;

Who else had a coat—a seamless robe—stripped from Him?

Jesus.

Genesis 37:24 (a)
And they took him, and cast him into a pit: and the pit was empty . . .

The empty pit is a picture of the tomb in which Jesus would be buried, for the tomb had never held a body before (Luke 23:53).

Genesis 37:24 (b)–27
. . . there was no water in it. And they sat down to eat bread: and they lifted up their eyes and looked, and, behold, a company of Ishmeelites came from Gilead with their camels bearing spicery and balm and myrrh, going to carry it down to Egypt. And Judah said unto his brethren, What profit is it if we slay our brother, and conceal his blood? Come, and let us sell him to the Ishmeelites, and let not our hand be upon him; for he is our brother and our flesh. And his brethren were content.

"Let's sell Joseph to these Gentiles," said Judah. "Then we won't be responsible for his blood."

In the same way, the Jews handed Jesus over to a Gentile Pilate because they said it was against Roman law for them to execute Him themselves. Interestingly, however, they were more than ready to execute the woman taken in adultery (John 8)—and even had been ready to push Jesus over a cliff (Luke 4:29). Why, then, did they bow to Roman law here? To unknowingly fulfill prophecy. You see, crucifixion was a Gentile form of execution, and prophecy was clear that the manner in which Messiah would die was definitely crucifixion.

Genesis 37:28 (a)
Then there passed by Midianites merchantmen; and they drew and lifted up Joseph out of the pit, and sold Joseph to the Ishmeelites for twenty pieces of silver . . .

Who else was sold for silver?
Jesus.

Genesis 37:28 (b), 29 (a)
. . . and they brought Joseph into Egypt. And Reuben returned unto the pit; and, behold, Joseph was not in the pit . . .

Absent when the sale of Joseph had taken place, Reuben returns to find the empty pit which had previously held his brother—just as Pilate would receive word that the tomb which held Jesus was now empty.

Genesis 37:29 (b)
. . . and he rent his clothes.

There are two strong traditions about Pontius Pilate. The Coptic Church in Egypt holds that years after the Resurrection, Pilate became a born-again believer. Other historical traditions indicate he went insane. Either way, like Reuben, Pilate was deeply impacted.

Genesis 37:30, 31
And he returned unto his brethren, and said, The child is not; and I, whither shall I go? And they took Joseph's coat, and killed a kid of the goats, and dipped the coat in the blood;

Here we see Jacob deceived by the blood of a kid, just as he had deceived his own father with the skin of a kid (Genesis 27:16). "Be not deceived," Paul said, "whatever a man sows, that will he also reap" (Galatians 6:7).

Genesis 37:32
And they sent the coat of many colours, and they brought it to their father; and said, This have we found: know now whether it be thy son's coat or no.

Joseph's brothers lied about the disappearance of their brother whom they knew to be alive.

What did the religious leaders of Israel do when they heard the truth about the empty tomb? They paid the Roman soldiers to lie. Had not the religious leaders joined forces with Rome in an attempt to cover up the Resurrection, these Roman soldiers who claimed to have fallen asleep during their watch would have been executed, guarding, as they were, something with the seal of the Emperor upon it. Instead of being executed, however, they were rewarded—which should have been highly suspicious.

Genesis 37:33
And he knew it, and said, It is my son's coat; an evil beast hath devoured him; Joseph is without doubt rent in pieces.

"An evil beast has devoured him," cried Jacob. Jesus also was devoured by the evil beast of my own sin. But, like Joseph, Jesus would eventually emerge the victor.

Genesis 37:34, 35
And Jacob rent his clothes, and put sackcloth upon his loins, and mourned for his son many days. And all his sons and all his daughters rose up to comfort him; but he refused to be comforted; and he said, For I will go down into the grave unto my son mourning. Thus his father wept for him.

We're going to see how wrong Jacob was here. Later on, thinking he lost Benjamin, Jacob will cry out in despair, "Everything is against me." He lacked the faith to see that everything was, in fact, working out beautifully. That is why it is Jacob—not Israel—who rent his clothes.

Genesis 37:36
And the Midianites sold him into Egypt unto Potiphar, an officer of Pharaoh's, and captain of the guard.

Following a break in chapter 38, Joseph's story will continue as his life goes on to illustrate the life of Jesus.

The Father says to us, "You exist to cause people to appreciate My Son, to focus on My Son, to give pleasure to My Son. Therefore, I want you to know Him and to make Him known." As living epistles (2 Corinthians 3:2), may our lives be Joseph-like; may they be pictures of Christ.

BIG SLEEVES . . . BIG PROBLEMS

A Topical Study of GENESIS 37:3, 4

The legend is told of a godly man who lived in a cave in order to give himself to prayer, worship, and contemplation. Wanting to lure him away from his life of piety, Satan sent some demons to tempt him through lust, selfishness, and greed. But demon after demon reported back to Satan, saying, "The man doesn't budge. He doesn't waver. He doesn't give in."

Finally, Satan said, "Let me show you how it's done." He made his way to the hermit's cave, perched on his shoulder, and whispered, "Your brother has just been made Bishop."

And as the spiritual man's expression turned from serenity to a scowl, the demons could see that Satan had succeeded where they had failed, as the hermit's heart filled with envy.

Many times, we are not as vulnerable to the things of earthly materialism or fleshly temptation as we are to spiritual honor or recognition. Satan knows this. That is why envy is one of his favorite tools. In the Book of Acts, Stephen refers to the text before us, saying that Joseph's brothers were moved with envy against him (Acts 7:9). Of what were they envious? Joseph's coat. Although your King James Bible describes this coat as being "of many colors," a better rendering is that it was a coat of "many pieces" or, literally, a coat of "big sleeves."

You see, in Joseph's day, most coats were actually vests because most men were workingmen and sleeves would only hinder their movement. However, those who held the position of boss or foreman would be given garments with sleeves. A coat with sleeves was not only a symbol of authority—but it was also a matter of practicality, for—in those days before briefcases and hand-held computers—documents, writing instruments, and supplies would be kept in the sleeves secured by drawstrings at the wrists. Consequently, a man on the job site with sleeves was equivalent to a man carrying a briefcase, talking on a cell phone, wearing Oakley sunglasses. In other words, the man with sleeves was clearly the boss.

And that's the issue in the story before us. Joseph's ten older brothers said, "Hey, what's the big idea? Why did Dad give the coat with big sleeves to little Joey? Why should *he* be the boss, the big cheese, the big shot? It's not right. It's not fair. It's not acceptable!" And so envious were they that they threw Joseph in a pit and sold him as a slave.

The story continues. Joseph ended up down in Egypt, purchased by a man named Potiphar. Realizing Joseph had a lot on the ball, Potiphar made him his right-hand man. And, as number two man in the Egyptian conglomerate known as Potiphar Inc.,

Joseph was given another coat with big sleeves. Shortly thereafter, however, Joseph found himself the object of desire when his boss's wife looked at him lustfully. Being a man of integrity, and refusing to succumb to her ways, Joseph wiggled out of his coat and ran for his life. Using his coat as phony evidence of Joseph's advances toward her, however, Mrs. Potiphar managed to get Joseph thrown into prison.

In this, I see something most interesting . . .

> "Why can't I be the manager at McDonald's?" we say. "Why do I have to work the drive-thru year after year?"
>
> "Why can't I be the boss at the company? I've been there longer than he has."
>
> "How come I didn't get the contract? My bid was lower; my work is better. I don't understand."

In other words, we are prone to say, "*I* should have the big sleeves."

Whether it's on the job, at school, or in church—there will always be opportunity for you and me to say, "How come I'm not noticed or acknowledged, elevated or rewarded?" Yet I believe the real question is: Are you sure you want to be?

> The story is told of a tear traveling down a river, who, seeing another tear, called out, "Who are you?"
>
> "I am the tear that rolled down the face of a fair young maiden whose man left her for another young maiden. And who are you?"
>
> "I am the tear of the young maiden who ended up with the man."

We think we know what we want. But the fact is, the coat of big sleeves caused Joseph big headaches. Therefore, it is the wise person who says, "Lord, I think I want that. I think I deserve that. I think I should be that. But, Lord, I understand that inherent in that position there may be headaches, problems, and pressures of which I am completely unaware."

> There was a man who was known throughout the land—and now throughout history—as a man who was exceedingly godly. Although he worked faithfully in a monastery, he never climbed the ladder to a position of prominence, but remained a dishwasher. Day after day, month after month, Lawrence washed pots and pans in the kitchen of the monastery—and as he did, he talked to the Lord. So intense was his fellowship in that place of simple service that word got out into the community, "There's a revival going on at the monastery."
>
> "Where? In the chapel?"
>
> "No, in the kitchen."
>
> "Which abbot is leading it?"
>
> "There's no abbot—just a dishwasher."
>
> Brother Lawrence eventually wrote a little book about his experience called *Practicing The Presence of God,* which went on to become one of the best-sellers of all time. He was a lowly dishwasher, but while the other monks

were busy with administration and sermon preparation, Brother Lawrence was able to simply enjoy God.

Sometimes we complain that we don't have this, lack that, are unacknowledged here, or aren't noticed there. But getting what we think we want, reaching the position we think we deserve, having the recognition we think we're worthy of often turns out to be a distraction and a burden. "The Lord will withhold no good thing from those who fear Him," declares the psalmist (Psalm 84).

Therefore, if I don't get the promotion, the notice, the relationship—I must remember it's because it wouldn't be good for me. "Oh, Lord," I may argue, "it would be great to have those big sleeves. I could use them for ministry."

But the Lord answers, "You would regret them. Otherwise, I wouldn't withhold them from you."

And if I question this, I have only to look at another robe—a robe without seams (John 19:23) . . .

It was the only possession of One who was born in a borrowed manger, preached from a borrowed boat, rode a borrowed donkey, ate in a borrowed room, and was buried in a borrowed grave.

There was something about this One who, while others were trying to climb the ladder materially or religiously, was so free that people flocked around Him, listened to Him, and hung on His every word—until He was stripped of His robe to hang on the Cross and die for their sin.

Because Jesus was disrobed for me, if the robe I have my eye on doesn't come my way, it's because He who loved me enough to give His very life for me knows it wouldn't be best for me.

Thus, it is the wise man or woman who says, "Lord, if You don't give me prestige or honor at work or in ministry, that's okay because You see what I can't. Therefore I will learn to be content because You proved Your love for me at Calvary."

38

Jewelers wisely display diamonds against black velvet, knowing the dark background highlights the beauty of the gems. Such is the case of the chapter before us, for sandwiched between chapter 37—which shows us Joseph's piety at home—and chapter 39—which shows us his position abroad—the sad, sordid story of Judah serves as the dark background which highlights the luster of Joseph's life . . .

Genesis 38:1
And it came to pass at that time, that Judah went down from his brethren, and turned in to a certain Adullamite, whose name was Hirah.

Judah began to associate with a man outside the family of faith—a man named Hirah.

Genesis 38:2, 3
And Judah saw there a daughter of a certain Canaanite, whose name was Shuah; and he took her, and went in unto her. And she conceived, and bare a son; and he called his name Er.

Continuing his linkage to those outside of the believing community, Judah married a Canaanite woman.

Genesis 38:4–6
And she conceived again, and bare a son; and she called his name Onan. And she yet

again conceived, and bare a son; and called his name Shelah: and he was at Chezib, when she bare him. And Judah took a wife for Er his firstborn, whose name was Tamar.

Arranged marriages being the custom of the day, Judah chooses a wife for his oldest son.

Genesis 38:7
And Er, Judah's firstborn, was wicked in the sight of the LORD; and the LORD slew him.

"And the Lord slew him." Oftentimes, when people read a phrase like this, they say, "How brutal of God to slay a man for being wicked." But they fail to realize that a man can become so wicked it is actually an act of mercy for the Lord to put him out of his misery. When the Bible talks about the sin unto death (Romans 6:16), it is not referring to a single sin, but rather to a life of sin. There comes a time when the Lord will put such a person out of his or her misery, and in so doing, protect others. You see, the problem with wickedness is that it's contagious. Wicked people draw other people into their depravity. So, the Lord in His wisdom and mercy, deals with the problem decisively.

Genesis 38:8
And Judah said unto Onan, Go in unto thy brother's wife, and marry her, and raise up seed to thy brother.

This practice of marrying a widow to her brother-in-law is one of thirty-four Old Testament laws which have their beginning in the Book of Genesis (Deuteronomy 25:5–10). Accordingly, if the older brother had not yet had children, it would be up to the next oldest brother to marry the woman and produce children—the first of whom would be considered his dead brother's son, in order to continue the family name.

Genesis 38:9, 10
And Onan knew that the seed should not be his; and it came to pass, when he went in unto his brother's wife, that he spilled it on the ground, lest that he should give seed to his brother. And the thing which he did displeased the LORD: wherefore he slew him also.

This verse is often misused as a statement against birth control. The issue here, however, isn't about family planning. It's about family plotting—for in his actions, Onan is saying, "I'm going to despise the directive of my father and trample on the casket of my brother." Thus, this scenario has nothing to do with God's opinion about family planning—and everything to do with a man determined to manipulate the situation.

Genesis 38:11 (a)
Then said Judah to Tamar his daughter in law, Remain a widow at thy father's house, till Shelah my son be grown: for he said, Lest peradventure he die also, as his brethren did . . .

Fearing for his third son's life, Judah says, "Listen, Tamar, you married my first son. He's dead. You married my second son. He's dead. Why don't you go home to your parents, and I'll let you know when Shelah is ready to marry you." Judah is afraid. He's beginning to suspect that Tamar isn't good for the family.

Genesis 38:11 (b)
. . . And Tamar went and dwelt in her father's house.

Tamar obediently did what Judah suggested.

Genesis 38:12 (a)
And in process of time the daughter of Shuah Judah's wife died; and Judah was comforted . . .

Literally, Judah was desiring to be comforted.

Genesis 38:12 (b)
. . . and went up unto his sheepshearers to Timnath . . .

Who else went to Timnath?
Samson.

Genesis 38:12 (c)
. . . he and his friend Hirah the Adullamite.

"I need to recover from my grief," Judah said, "so I'm going to go hang out at Timnath with my pagan pal, Hirah."

Genesis 38:13
And it was told Tamar, saying, Behold thy father in law goeth up to Timnath to shear his sheep.

At some point, it dawned on Tamar that Judah had no intention of giving her his third son in marriage. So she decided to take action herself . . .

Genesis 38:14, 15
And she put her widow's garments off from her, and covered her with a vail, and wrapped herself, and sat in an open place, which is by the way to Timnath; for she saw that Shelah was grown, and she was not given unto him to wife. When Judah saw her, he thought her to be an harlot; because she had covered her face.

The Hebrew word translated "harlot" implies Tamar was dressed up like a temple prostitute—a woman employed by the pagan temple system.

Genesis 38:16
And he turned unto her by the way, and said, Go to, I pray thee, let me come in unto thee; (for he knew not that she was his daughter in law.) And she said, What wilt thou give me, that thou mayest come in unto me? And he said, I will send thee a kid from the flock.

"I don't have any money on me right now," said Judah. "I'll pay you later."

Genesis 38:17
And she said, Wilt thou give me a pledge, till thou send it?

"How will I know that you're going to come through?" asked Tamar.

Genesis 38:18
And he said, What pledge shall I give thee? And she said, Thy signet, and thy bracelets, and thy staff that is in thine hand. And he gave it her, and came in unto her, and she conceived by him.

Notice what Tamar asked for. Used as a seal on business transactions or correspondence, the signet spoke of the person, of identity. The bracelets spoke of possession of wealth. The staff spoke of position—even as it does to this day.

Thus, Tamar, playing the role of a prostitute, is saying, "I want your person, your possessions, your position." And that's exactly what happens to anyone who gives himself or herself to immorality. Person, possessions, position are all lost. "What do I want?" asked Tamar. "I want it all."

Genesis 38:19, 20
And she arose, and went away, and laid by her vail from her, and put on the garments of her widowhood. And Judah sent the kid by the hand of his friend the Adullamite, to receive his pledge from the woman's hand: but he found her not.

So I messed up. So I cashed out. I can get it back. That's what Judah had initially thought.

Genesis 38:21–23
Then he asked the men of that place, saying, Where is the harlot, that was openly by the way side? And they said, There was no harlot in this place. And he returned to Judah, and said, I cannot find her; and also the men of the place said, that there was no harlot in this place. And Judah said, Let her take it to her, lest we be shamed: behold, I sent this kid, and thou hast not found her.

"We've got to get this payment to her," Judah fretted, "or else I'll be accused of not keeping my end of the bargain." Wasn't that what he was already guilty of concerning giving his son to Tamar?

Genesis 38:24 (a)
And it came to pass about three months after, that it was told Judah, saying, Tamar thy daughter in law hath played the harlot; and also, behold, she is with child by whoredom . . .

"*My* daughter-in-law would be involved in immorality? I can't believe it!" thundered Judah. It's amazing how bad my sin looks on someone else. We are often most angry at, upset with, scandalized by the very sins in others we struggle with ourselves.

Genesis 38:24 (b)
. . . And Judah said, Bring her forth, and let her be burnt.

Leviticus 21:9 will later say that if a woman who is the daughter of a priest is a whore, she is to be burnt in the fire. Consequently, in ordering Tamar to be burned, Judah evidently saw himself as a priest. The priestly line, however, would not come through Judah, but through Levi. Such is often the case. When a person says, "Burn them!" it can be because he thinks of himself more highly than he ought to think.

If anyone is burnt in this story, it's Judah . . .

> Can a man take fire in his bosom, and his clothes not be burned? Can one go upon hot coals, and his feet not be burned? So he that goeth in to his neighbour's wife; whosoever toucheth her shall not be innocent. Men do not despise a thief, if he steal to satisfy his soul when he is hungry; But if he be found, he shall restore sevenfold; he shall give all the substance of his house. But whoso committeth adultery with a woman lacketh understanding: he that doeth it destroyeth his own soul.
> Proverbs 6:27–32

The Father devoted an entire chapter in the middle of Joseph's story as if to say, "You can either be Joseph or Judah. You can be a person of purity—which leads to success, or you can be a person of immorality—which leads to burn-out."

Genesis 38:25
When she was brought forth, she sent to her father in law, saying, By the man, whose these are, am I with child: and she said, Discern, I pray thee, whose are these, the signet, and bracelets, and staff.

"Dad," said Tamar to Judah, "do you know who this ring with the great big J on it belongs to?"

Genesis 38:26
And Judah acknowledged them, and said, She hath been more righteous than I; because that I gave her not to Shelah my son. And he knew her again no more.

"She is more righteous than I." What a grand statement. Too bad it had to be made in these circumstances, for even though Judah was forced to admit his sin, at this point he virtually disappears from the Scriptural account.

Genesis 38:27–30
And it came to pass in the time of her travail, that, behold, twins were in her womb. And it came to pass, when she travailed, that the one put out his hand: and the midwife took and bound upon his hand a scarlet thread, saying, This came out first. And it came to pass, as he drew back his hand, that, behold, his brother came out: and she said, How hast thou broken forth? this breach be upon thee: therefore his name was called Pharez. And afterward came out his brother, that had the scarlet thread upon his hand: and his name was called Zarah.

Zarah provides a picture of the death and Resurrection of our Lord . . .

- The scarlet thread on the wrist of Zarah pictures the blood-stained wrist of Jesus Christ.
- Zarah appeared first, just as Jesus is the Firstfruit of the brethren (1 Corinthians 15:20–23).
- Zarah remained in the womb, just as Jesus would be placed in a tomb.
- At last Zarah was seen in totality, just as the resurrected Jesus was seen in His Deity.

Tamar and her two sons are seen again, in the genealogy of Jesus Christ. It's as if the Lord says, "This woman did things that were very questionable and deceptive, and yet she will be connected to My Son."

That's *grace!* We may blow it big-time, gang, but the Lord has a way of saying, "If you look to Me and live for Me, I'll turn even your mistakes around and link you to My Son."

And although the person of Judah is no longer important in Scripture, Jesus chooses to identify Himself as the Lion of the Tribe of Judah. Including Tamar in His genealogy is grace. But identifying with Judah is *amazing* grace!

39

Genesis 39:1 (a)
And Joseph was brought down to Egypt . . .

Joseph went to Egypt a seventeen-year-old in chains of iron. He'll return a one hundred and ten-year-old in chains of gold.

Genesis 39:1 (b)
. . . and Potiphar, an officer of Pharaoh, captain of the guard, an Egyptian, bought him of the hands of the Ishmeelites, which had brought him down thither.

A man of power and prestige in Pharaoh's court, Potiphar saw something useful in Joseph and purchased him.

Genesis 39:2
And the LORD was with Joseph, and he was a prosperous man; and he was in the house of his master the Egyptian.

Why is Joseph referred to as a "prosperous man" even though he is a slave? I suggest it is because, like Paul, he inherently understood that it is not great gain that brings contentment, but rather contentment that brings great gain (1 Timothy 6:6). Joseph was prosperous because he was *content.*

Genesis 39:3, 4
And his master saw that the LORD was with him, and that the LORD made all that he did to prosper in his hand. And Joseph found grace in his sight, and he served him: and he made him overseer over his house, and all that he had he put into his hand.

Joseph became Potiphar's right-hand man.

Genesis 39:5 (a)
And it came to pass from the time that he had made him overseer in his house, and over all that he had, that the LORD blessed the Egyptian's house for Joseph's sake . . .

"Whatever you do in word or deed, do all to the glory of God," said Paul (Colossians 3:17). If you, like Joseph, bring the Lord into the situation, your workplace will be blessed simply because you're there.

Genesis 39:5 (b), 6 (a)
. . . and the blessing of the LORD was upon all that he had in the house, and in the field. And he left all that he had in Joseph's hand; and he knew not ought he had, save the bread which he did eat . . .

Such trust did Potiphar have in Joseph that he didn't even know the state of his own finances.

Genesis 39:6 (b)
. . . And Joseph was a goodly person, and well favoured.

If I were in Joseph's sandals, would I give myself wholeheartedly, enthusiastically, energetically to serving an Egyptian taskmaster—or would I say, "Lord, You've given me dreams and talents and abilities. But they're all being wasted because I'm just a slave"? One of the many things that impress me about Joseph is that he didn't focus on what he lacked, but instead threw himself into the task at hand.

One Arizona dad, watching the tears on the faces of the boys who were too slow, too small, and too clumsy to make it on to the roster of one of the five North Phoenix Little League teams asked if he could form a sixth team from the kids who were cut.

"Sure," said the officials, "if you'll coach them and pay for their uniforms."

So the dad did, naming his team the Phoenix Diamondbacks.

Last Friday, the Phoenix Diamondbacks won their last game by a score of 19–0.

It was the League Championship game.

Some say, "I could have really been used if I had made the team," or, "I'll really be used as soon as my situation changes." Others, however, join Joseph in saying, "So what if I'm a slave? It's a great opportunity to work hard for the glory of God and see what He'll do."

Genesis 39:7
And it came to pass after these things, that his master's wife cast her eyes upon Joseph; and she said, Lie with me.

As a young man totally cut off from his family, how easy it would have been for Joseph to justify accepting Mrs. Potiphar's invitation.

Genesis 39:8, 9
But he refused, and said unto his master's wife, Behold, my master wotteth not what is with me in the house, and he hath committed all that he hath to my hand; There is none greater in this house than I; neither hath he kept back any thing from me but thee, because thou art his wife: how then can I do this great wickedness, and sin against God?

Notice Joseph doesn't say to Potiphar's wife, "In light of what he's given me, how can I sin against your husband?" Nor does he say, "How can I sin against you?" He says, "How can I sin against *God?*"

This is what is known throughout Scripture as "the fear of the Lord." Joseph was in constant awareness of the "there-ness" of God—an awareness equally convicting and comforting. Yes, he was severed from his family and his country, but Joseph knew he was never alone.

Genesis 39:10
And it came to pass, as she spake to Joseph day by day, that he hearkened not unto her, to lie by her, or to be with her.

Joseph didn't say to Potiphar's wife, "Let's share a cup of coffee and I'll show you why you shouldn't be so seductive," or, "I can see you have an unhappy marriage. Let's just talk things over." No, Joseph avoided her from that point on. Thus, he goes down as a huge hero for all eternity and his family will be blessed to a great degree because of his bedrock integrity.

Genesis 39:11, 12
And it came to pass about this time, that Joseph went into the house to do his business; and there was none of the men of the house there within. And she caught him by his garment, saying, Lie with me: and he left his garment in her hand, and fled, and got him out.

"Flee youthful lusts," said a wise Paul to a young Timothy (2 Timothy 2:22)—and that's exactly what Joseph is doing. He doesn't minister to Mrs. Potiphar. He doesn't witness to her. He runs for his life.

Genesis 39:13–19
And it came to pass, when she saw that he had left his garment in her hand, and was fled forth, That she called unto the men of her house, and spake unto them, saying, See, he hath brought in an Hebrew unto us to mock us; he came in unto me to lie with me,

and I cried with a loud voice: And it came to pass, when he heard that I lifted up my voice and cried, that he left his garment with me, and fled, and got him out. And she laid up his garment by her, until his lord came home. And she spake unto him according to these words, saying, The Hebrew servant, which thou hast brought unto us, came in unto me to mock me: And it came to pass, as I lifted up my voice and cried, that he left his garment with me, and fled out. And it came to pass, when his master heard the words of his wife, which she spake unto him, saying, After this manner did thy servant to me; that his wrath was kindled.

Scripture says Potiphar's wrath was kindled, but it doesn't say against whom. In Egypt, attempted rape was a capital offense—so much the more if the crime was committed by a slave against the wife of a government official. So here's the question: If Potiphar's wrath was kindled against Joseph, why didn't he demand immediate execution? I suggest it's because, knowing his wife's history and personality, Potiphar's wrath was kindled not against Joseph but against his wife for concocting a story that forced his hand to send the man who had so blessed his house to prison.

Genesis 39:20
And Joseph's master took him, and put him into the prison, a place where the king's prisoners were bound: and he was there in the prison.

Just as Joseph went to prison, so, too, did Jesus. In Ephesians 4 and 1 Peter 3, we read that before He ascended to heaven, Jesus first descended into the lower parts of the earth and led "captivity captive"—or set the captives free.

You see, according to Jude 6, the very worst of the demons—those who many commentators believe are the demons referred to in Genesis 6:2—are not free to roam about, but are chained. To these hellions, Jesus preached, letting them know that their darkest, most dastardly and demonic power over people had been broken because His blood was potent enough to cleanse even the most depraved sin of mankind.

Genesis 39:21
But the LORD was with Joseph, and shewed him mercy, and gave him favour in the sight of the keeper of the prison.

Joseph will go from pit to Potiphar's house to prison to palace. But everywhere he goes, he knows the Lord is with him.

Genesis 39:22
And the keeper of the prison committed to Joseph's hand all the prisoners that were in the prison; and whatsoever they did there, he was the doer of it.

Because of his boundless industry and bedrock integrity, Joseph was blessed immeasurably—even in prison.

Genesis 39:23
The keeper of the prison looked not to any thing that was under his hand; because the LORD was with him, and that which he did, the LORD made it to prosper.

The keeper of the prison turned the whole operation over to Joseph. Why? Because it was obvious the Lord was with him.

40

Genesis 40:1 (a)
And it came to pass after these things . . .

"Lie with me," Potiphar's wife had repeatedly said to Joseph. Unjustly accused of succumbing to her demand, Joseph was thrown into prison. And we see how his story continues to depict Jesus, for even as Joseph faced this very real temptation, Jesus was driven into the wilderness and tested by Satan for forty days. Like Joseph, Jesus passed His test victoriously, beating back Satan decisively (Matthew 4).

Genesis 40:1 (b)–4
. . . that the butler of the king of Egypt and his baker had offended their lord the king of Egypt. And Pharaoh was wroth against two of his officers, against the chief of the butlers, and against the chief of the bakers. And he put them in ward in the house of the captain of the guard, into the prison, the place where Joseph was bound. And the captain of the guard charged Joseph with them, and he served them: and they continued a season in ward.

Of Jesus, Isaiah says, "And he was numbered with the transgressors and made intercession of them" (Isaiah 53:12)—which speaks ultimately of the two thieves between whom Jesus hung on the Cross.

Likewise, here, we see two criminals with Joseph—one who will hear words of salvation, the other, words of damnation . . .

Genesis 40:5–13
And they dreamed a dream both of them, each man his dream in one night, each man according to the interpretation of his dream,

the butler and the baker of the king of Egypt, which were bound in the prison. And Joseph came in unto them in the morning, and looked upon them, and, behold, they were sad. And he asked Pharaoh's officers that were with him in the ward of his lord's house, saying, Wherefore look ye so sadly to day? And they said unto him, We have dreamed a dream, and there is no interpreter of it. And Joseph said unto them, Do not interpretations belong to God? tell me them, I pray you. And the chief butler told his dream to Joseph, and said to him, In my dream, behold, a vine was before me; And in the vine were three branches: and it was as though it budded, and her blossoms shot forth, and the clusters thereof brought forth ripe grapes: And Pharaoh's cup was in my hand: and I took the grapes, and pressed them into Pharaoh's cup, and I gave the cup into Pharaoh's hand. And Joseph said unto him, This is the interpretation of it: The three branches are three days: Yet within three days shall Pharaoh lift up thine head, and restore thee unto thy place: and thou shalt deliver Pharaoh's cup into his hand, after the former manner when thou wast his butler.

The position of butler, or cupbearer, was a very important office in any administration in Pharaoh's day because, with constant access to the king, cupbearers were often a king's closest advisor.

"If it be possible, let this cup pass from Me," Jesus prayed. What cup? The cup of suffering. But because Jesus drank the cup of suffering, we can drink freely of the cup of salvation and thereby gain access to and fellowship with the King of kings.

Genesis 40:14
But think on me when it shall be well with thee, and shew kindness, I pray thee, unto me, and make mention of me unto Pharaoh, and bring me out of this house:

"Think on me, make mention of me when it shall be well with thee," said Joseph.

"Remember me when You come into Your kingdom," said the thief on the cross (Luke 23:42).

"This do in remembrance of Me," said Jesus (Luke 22:19).

True fellowship is based on *remembrance*.

How do we remember Him?

Through Communion. Communion is the way we most clearly remember what Jesus did when He freed us from the prison of our sin.

Genesis 40:15
For indeed I was stolen away out of the land of the Hebrews: and here also have I done nothing that they should put me into the dungeon.

"I have done nothing that they should put me in the dungeon," said Joseph.

"I find no fault in this man," said Pilate of Jesus (Luke 23:4).

Genesis 40:16, 17 (a)
When the chief baker saw that the interpretation was good, he said unto Joseph, I also was in my dream, and, behold, I had three white baskets on my head: And in the uppermost basket there was of all manner of bakemeats [breads] . . .

The butler dreamed of a cup. The baker dreamed of bread. What are the two elements of Communion? Bread and wine.

Genesis 40:17 (b)–19
. . . for Pharaoh; and the birds did eat them out of the basket upon my head. And Joseph answered and said, This is the interpretation thereof: The three baskets are three days: Yet within three days shall Pharaoh lift up thy head from off thee, and shall hang thee on a tree; and the birds shall eat thy flesh from off thee.

If the cup and the bread both speak of Communion, why does the butler's dream end in salvation, while the baker's end in damnation? Because he who understands and accepts what Christ did on the Cross, as signified by the bread and wine of Communion, will be set free. But he who goes to the Lord's Table haphazardly and doesn't embrace what Jesus did on his behalf will remain in the grip of sin.

Genesis 40:20
And it came to pass the third day, which was Pharaoh's birthday, that he made a feast unto all his servants: and he lifted up the head of the chief butler and of the chief baker among his servants.

What does the third day speak of? The Resurrection. Those who believe and receive shall be lifted up, and those who don't will miss out.

Genesis 40:21
And he restored the chief butler unto his butlership again; and he gave the cup into Pharaoh's hand: But he hanged the chief baker: as Joseph had interpreted to them. Yet did not the chief butler remember Joseph, but forgat him.

"Remember me," Joseph said. And the butler forgot him for approximately ten years.

"Remember Me," Jesus says. Yet there are

people who haven't had Communion in ten years because they can't expend the energy, can't find the time to do the one thing the Lord asks them to do. It's amazing how we can become so callused, so unappreciative, so forgetful.

41

Genesis 41:1 (a)
And it came to pass . . .

Joseph has been in prison for ten years for a crime he didn't commit. You might be in a place where you feel completely forgotten and in the dark—but, as it will for Joseph—your situation could change radically even in the next hour. Be patient, fellow pilgrim. Look to the One who is the epitome of patience; look to the Greater than Joseph, who, although He could have risen immediately to power and prominence, said instead, "My hour is not yet come" (John 2:4).

Genesis 41:1 (b)–8
. . . at the end of two full years, that Pharaoh dreamed: and, behold, he stood by the river. And, behold, there came up out of the river seven well favoured kine and fatfleshed; and they fed in a meadow. And, behold, seven other kine came up after them out of the river, ill favoured and leanfleshed; and stood by the other kine upon the brink of the river. And the ill favoured and leanfleshed kine did eat up the seven well favoured and fat kine. So Pharaoh awoke. And he slept and dreamed the second time: and, behold, seven ears of corn came up upon one stalk, rank and good. And, behold, seven thin ears and blasted with the east wind sprung up after them. And the seven thin ears devoured the seven rank and full ears. And Pharaoh awoke, and, behold, it was a dream. And it came to pass in the morning that his spirit was troubled; and he sent and called for all the magicians of Egypt, and all the wise men thereof: and Pharaoh told them his dream; but there was none that could interpret them unto Pharaoh.

In Pharaoh's day, Thot was the god called upon to give interpretation. But Thot had nothing to say.

Genesis 41:9–16
Then spake the chief butler unto Pharaoh, saying, I do remember my faults this day: Pharaoh was wroth with his servants, and put me in ward in the captain of the guard's house, both me and the chief baker: And we dreamed a dream in one night, I and he; we dreamed each man according to the interpretation of his dream. And there was there with us a young man, an Hebrew, servant to the captain of the guard; and we told him, and he interpreted to us our dreams; to each man according to his dream he did interpret. And it came to pass, as he interpreted to us, so it was; me he restored unto mine office, and him he hanged. Then Pharaoh sent and called Joseph, and they brought him hastily out of the dungeon: and he shaved himself, and changed his raiment, and came in unto Pharaoh. And Pharaoh said unto Joseph, I have dreamed a dream, and there is none that can interpret it: and I have heard say of thee, that thou canst understand a dream to interpret it. And Joseph answered Pharaoh, saying, It is not in me: God shall give Pharaoh an answer of peace.

"Only God can give you an interpretation for your situation," said Joseph.

Like Joseph, Jesus continually drew attention to His Father. "Let your light so shine before men that they will glorify your Father," He said (Matthew 5:16). That is why you'll never read about people glorifying Jesus. You see, Jesus was able to minister in such a way that people would see the light, but glorify the Father.

Those who are successfully used by the Lord are those who cause people to say, "God is good," without taking any credit themselves.

Genesis 41:17–25
And Pharaoh said unto Joseph, In my dream, behold, I stood upon the bank of the river: And, behold, there came up out of the river seven kine, fatfleshed and well favoured; and they fed in a meadow: And, behold, seven other kine came up after them, poor and very ill favoured and leanfleshed, such as I never saw in all the land of Egypt for badness: And the lean and the ill favoured kine did eat up the first seven fat kine: And when they had eaten them up, it could not be known that they had eaten them; but they were still ill favoured, as at the beginning. So I awoke. And I saw in my dream, and, behold, seven ears came up in one stalk, full and good: And, behold, seven ears, withered, thin, and blasted with the east wind, sprung up after them: And the thin ears devoured the seven good ears: and I told this unto the magicians; but there was none that could declare it to me. And Joseph said unto Pharaoh, The dream of Pharaoh is one: God hath shewed Pharaoh what he is about to do.

The dreams of the cattle and corn contain a single message . . .

Genesis 41:26–31 (a)
The seven good kine are seven years; and the seven good ears are seven years: the dream is one. And the seven thin and ill favoured kine that came up after them are seven years; and the seven empty ears blasted with the east wind shall be seven years of famine. This is the thing which I have spoken unto Pharaoh: What God is about to do he sheweth unto Pharaoh. Behold, there come seven years of great plenty throughout all the land of Egypt: And there shall arise after them seven years of famine; and all the plenty shall be forgotten in the land of Egypt; and the famine shall consume the land; And the plenty shall not be known in the land by reason of that famine following . . .

The plenty of the first seven years will be eaten up by the seven years of famine to follow.

Genesis 41:31 (b)
. . . for it shall be very grievous.

The Hebrew word translated "grievous" literally means "heavy." Seven years of unparalleled prosperity would be followed by seven years of unparalleled problems and heaviness—which speak of the Tribulation. Described in Revelation 6—19, the Tribulation is referred to as "Jacob's Trouble." Just as Jacob and his sons will be so troubled by famine that they will be forced to go to Joseph for grain, one of the purposes of the Tribulation is to force Israel to turn to Jesus.

Never in the history of humanity has the world been as prosperous as it is presently. Are these the years of prosperity preceding the Tribulation?

Perhaps.

Genesis 41:32
And for that the dream was doubled unto Pharaoh twice; it is because the thing is established by God, and God will shortly bring it to pass.

In other words, "This is a done deal, and it is about to happen shortly."

Genesis 41:33–36
Now therefore let Pharaoh look out a man discreet and wise, and set him over the land of Egypt. Let Pharaoh do this, and let him appoint officers over the land, and take up the fifth part of the land of Egypt in the seven plenteous years. And let them gather all the food of those good years that come, and lay up corn under the hand of Pharaoh, and let them keep food in the cities. And that food shall be for store to the land against the seven years of famine, which shall be in the land of Egypt; that the land perish not through the famine.

"You dreamed a dream," Joseph said to Pharaoh, "but a nightmare is about to unfold. Reserve twenty percent of the output in the upcoming seven prosperous years in order to be prepared for the upcoming years of difficulty."

Genesis 41:37, 38
And the thing was good in the eyes of Pharaoh, and in the eyes of all his servants. And Pharaoh said unto his servants, Can we find such a one as this is, a man in whom the Spirit of God is?

"No one has the spirit of God like Joseph does," said Pharaoh. Oh, but One would come after Joseph in whom dwelled the Spirit fully, for Scripture records that Jesus was given the Spirit without limitation (John 3:34).

Genesis 41:39, 40
And Pharaoh said unto Joseph, Forasmuch as God hath shewed thee all this, there is none so discreet and wise as thou art: Thou shalt be over my house, and according unto thy word shall all my people be ruled: only in the throne will I be greater than thou.

He who had been in the dungeon only an hour earlier is now elevated to the position of Prime Minister.

Genesis 41:41–43 (a)
And Pharaoh said unto Joseph, See, I have set thee over all the land of Egypt. And Pharaoh took off his ring from his hand, and put it upon Joseph's hand, and arrayed him in vestures of fine linen, and put a gold chain about his neck; And he made him to ride in the second chariot which he had; and they cried before him, Bow the knee . . .

"Bow the knee." rang out the command concerning Joseph. In the same way, when Jesus comes, every knee shall bow (Philippians 2:10)—but a command won't be necessary.

Genesis 41:43 (b), 44
. . . and he made him ruler over all the land of Egypt. And Pharaoh said unto Joseph, I am Pharaoh, and without thee shall no man lift up his hand or foot in all the land of Egypt.

No one could do anything without Joseph's permission.

"Without Me, ye can do nothing," said Jesus, the Greater than Joseph (John 15:5).

Genesis 41:45 (a)
And Pharaoh called Joseph's name Zaphnath-paaneah . . .

It has been suggested that *Zaphnath-paaneah* means "Revealer of Secrets." If so, it would be a fitting name for this one who is a picture, a preview of Jesus—for many mysteries are revealed in Him (Romans 11:25). But there is no consensus regarding the meaning of the name, which is also fitting—for Revelation 19 says that written on Jesus is a name no man knows. In other words, we'll never fully discover the richness of Christ Jesus. We'll be intrigued by Him, fascinated with Him, and explore His nature for eternity—yet never come to the point where we say, "I've got Him all figured out."

If you've been married for a long time, you probably know exactly what your wife will say or your husband will do at any given time. But you'll never be able to say that about Jesus, and you'll never become bored exploring His glory.

Genesis 41:45 (b)
. . . and he gave him to wife Asenath the daughter of Poti-pherah priest of On . . .

Joseph, a picture of Jesus, is given a Gentile bride whose name means "She who is of Nath." Who was Nath? The Egyptian goddess of provision and protection, known in the Greek culture as Helena, and in the Roman culture as Minerva. Interestingly, this goddess finds her way into our country, for it is her likeness that sits atop the United States Capitol Building.

Not only does Joseph make this Gentile woman his bride, but she also becomes spiritual Israel in a very real way, for she will give birth to Manasseh and Ephraim, two of the tribes of Israel.

The Gentile Bride—the church—has been swept up into the Greater than Joseph's embrace and has been made spiritual Israel. While there is a physical, literal Israel that plays very definitely into God's economy, we, the church, are spiritual Israel.

Genesis 41:45 (c), 46 (a)
. . . And Joseph went out over all the land of Egypt. And Joseph was thirty years old when he stood before Pharaoh king of Egypt . . .

How old was Jesus when He began His public ministry?

Thirty.

Genesis 41:46 (b)–49
. . . And Joseph went out from the presence of Pharaoh, and went throughout all the land of Egypt. And in the seven plenteous years the earth brought forth by handfuls. And he gathered up all the food of the seven years, which were in the land of Egypt, and laid up the food in the cities: the food of the field, which was round about every city, laid he up in the same. And Joseph gathered corn as the sand of the sea, very much, until he left numbering; for it was without number.

So prosperous was the land that the provision was too great to number.

Genesis 41:50, 51
And unto Joseph were born two sons before the years of famine came, which Asenath the daughter of Poti-pherah priest of On bare unto him. And Joseph called the name of the firstborn Manasseh: For God, said he, hath made me forget all my toil, and all my father's house.

Sold into slavery by his own brothers, lied about by his boss's wife, thrown into prison and forgotten—if anyone had a reason to be dysfunctional, it was Joseph. Yet *Manasseh* meaning "Forget," Joseph is saying, "God made me forget the brothers who picked on me unfairly, the pit I was thrown into cruelly, the dungeon I suffered in unjustly."

"This one thing I do," Paul said, "forgetting that which lies behind, I press on toward the high calling" (Philippians 3:13, 14). Those who can't forget about their past walk through life crippled. On the other hand, there is no stopping those who, like Joseph and Paul, forget about that which they can't do anything about.

Genesis 41:52
And the name of the second called he Ephraim: For God hath caused me to be fruitful in the land of my affliction.

Ephraim means "Fruitful." I find the order of Joseph's sons intriguing, for we'll never be fruitful until we quit living in the past.

Genesis 41:53, 54 (a)
And the seven years of plenteousness, that was in the land of Egypt, were ended. And the seven years of dearth began to come, according as Joseph had said: and the dearth was in all lands . . .

Just as the dearth was in all lands, so the seven-year Tribulation will affect the entire planet.

Genesis 41:54 (b)
. . . but in all the land of Egypt there was bread.

Egypt weathered the difficult days because, under Joseph's direction, she had brought grain to the storehouse. In this, I am reminded of another storehouse . . .

> Bring ye all the tithes into the storehouse, that there may be meat in mine house, and prove me now herewith, saith the LORD of hosts, if I will not open you the windows of heaven, and pour you out a blessing, that there shall not be room enough to receive it. Malachi 3:10

Just as the Egyptians were to bring of their plenty to the granary in order that they would later be fed physically, we are to bring our tithe to the place wherein we are fed spiritually.

"Wait a minute," some protest. "We're no longer under the Law. And tithing is the Law."

Not true. Tithing precedes the Law, for we see Abraham give tithes to Melchizedek—or Christ—before the Law was even given (Genesis 14). Not only does tithing precede the Law, but it postdates the Law as well, for Jesus said the tithe was not to be left undone (Luke 11:42). Later, Paul goes on to tell the Church at Corinth to bring to the storehouse of that which the Lord had blessed them (1 Corinthians 16).

It is because the tithe is God's, that he who doesn't give the first ten percent of whatever he makes robs God (Malachi 3:9). But he who tithes will be rewarded to such a degree that there won't be room to contain it. According to a recent study, not only would every church, ministry, and charitable work be free of debt, but every hungry person in the world would be fed—if for two years, Christians would simply not rob God of the tithe.

> And I will rebuke the devourer for your sakes . . . Malachi 3:11 (a)

Not only does God reward the one who brings Him the tithe, but He rebukes the forces which seek to devour him. When I have ignored this principle and disobeyed the command to tithe, I have experienced exactly what Haggai said would happen when he wrote, "Ye have sown much, and bring in little; ye eat, but ye have not enough; ye drink, but ye are not filled with drink; ye clothe you, but there is none warm; and he that earneth wages earneth wages to put it into a bag with holes" (Haggai 1:6). Finances get devoured—eaten up needlessly when I fail to tithe.

> And all nations shall call you blessed: for ye shall be a delightsome land, saith the LORD of hosts. Malachi 3:12

Not only does tithing bring *reward* to us and a *rebuke* to the devourer—it also ushers in *revival* to those around us as they see firsthand the blessings and goodness of God in our lives.

Tithing is not God's way to raise money, gang. It's His way to raise kids. You see, every time the offering basket passes by, it is an opportunity for me to let go of a portion of my earthiness, of my greediness, of my selfishness. Jesus said wherever our treasure is, there will our heart be (Matthew 6:21). God doesn't need our money, but He desires our heart. Therefore, when we seek first the kingdom, and invest our treasure therein, our heart follows.

Genesis 41:55 (a)
And when all the land of Egypt was famished, the people cried to Pharaoh for bread . . .

To whom will people cry during the Tribulation? Initially they'll cry to antichrist.

Genesis 41:55 (b)
. . . and Pharaoh said unto all the Egyptians, Go unto Joseph . . .

Unlike Pharaoh, antichrist will not direct people to the Greater than Joseph. Nonetheless, he will know in his soul that Jesus is their only hope.

Genesis 41:55 (c)
. . . what he saith to you, do.

Concerning a lack of bread, Pharaoh said of Joseph, "What he saith to you, do."

Concerning a lack of wine, Mary said of her Son, "Whatsoever He saith unto thee, do" (John 2:5).

Genesis 41:56, 57
And the famine was over all the face of the earth: and Joseph opened all the storehouses, and sold unto the Egyptians; and the famine waxed sore in the land of Egypt. And all countries came into Egypt to Joseph for to buy corn; because that the famine was so sore in all lands.

"And all countries came . . . to Joseph." This is a key component in understanding what the Tribulation is all about. Without question, the greatest revival in history will take place in the seven-year Tribulation period. And even though you won't be here at that time, your witness to those around you—the books you gave them, the tapes you left them, the words you shared with them—will flood their hearts and minds. And in the famished condition of their soul, they'll begin to realize that the key is not to cry to Pharaoh, but to run to Jesus.

42

Genesis 42:1
Now when Jacob saw that there was corn in Egypt, Jacob said unto his sons, Why do ye look one upon another?

As the famine continued, word reached Jacob that there was grain in Egypt.

Genesis 42:2
And he said, Behold, I have heard that there is corn in Egypt: get you down thither, and buy for us from thence; that we may live, and not die.

Although Jacob's sons will try to buy bread from Joseph, they will be unable to because Joseph is a type of Christ—whose provision of salvation cannot be bought (Isaiah 55:1).

Genesis 42:3
And Joseph's ten brethren went down to buy corn in Egypt.

The ten brothers speak of the law. The law always wants to purchase salvation through the expenditure of its own energy. That is why people have a propensity to think they can earn God's favor, to want to work for God's blessing, to try to purchase salvation.

Genesis 42:4
But Benjamin, Joseph's brother, Jacob sent not with his brethren; for he said, Lest peradventure mischief befall him.

Benjamin was the full brother of Joseph. Jacob's refusal to send him with his ten half-brothers indicates that perhaps Jacob had strong suspicions concerning what had happened to Joseph years earlier.

Genesis 42:5, 6 (a)
And the sons of Israel came to buy corn among those that came: for the famine was in the land of Canaan. And Joseph was the governor over the land, and he it was that sold to all the people of the land . . .

Because Joseph had unlimited resources, there was food available for all who came to him. Because His mercy and grace are inexhaustible, Jesus is unlimited in His resources to bless you and me. He will supply all our needs according to His riches (Philippians 4:19)—and His riches are without limitation.

Genesis 42:6 (b)
. . . and Joseph's brethren came, and bowed down themselves before him with their faces to the earth.

At the end of the Tribulation period, when the nation of Israel realizes that Jesus is Messiah, she will bow to Him—even as Joseph's brothers are bowing down before him.

Genesis 42:7 (a)
And Joseph saw his brethren, and he knew them, but made himself strange unto them . . .

Joseph knew and felt great love for his brothers, but he didn't make himself known to them. For 2,000 years, Jesus has looked on the nation of Israel with compassion. Yet because blindness has come upon Israel (Romans 11:25), she does not see Jesus. That is why you can open up the Scriptures to the Jews and show them how the prophecies have all been fulfilled in Him, yet, for the most part, a veil will remain over their eyes.

"We don't want You to rule over us, to have any part of us," the Jews said concerning Jesus. And so Jesus has withdrawn from them—just as He withdraws from anyone who says, "I don't want You in my life; I don't want You as my Lord."

Does God still love Israel? Of course. Does He have a plan for Israel? Absolutely. For when her eyes are finally opened, and she asks Him, "Where did You get these wounds?" He won't say, "I got them from a bunch of strangers." He'll say, "I got them in the house of My *friends*" (Zechariah 13:6).

Genesis 42:7 (b)
. . . and spake roughly unto them . . .

In other words, Joseph spoke a different language to them. He spoke the language of the Egyptians. The Jewish people say the New Testament was written in a language they don't understand. Oh, they understand Greek intellectually—but they don't accept it theologically.

Why would Joseph speak a language his brothers didn't understand? For the same reason the Lord does. It's called conviction. You see, a person needs to realize he's a sinner because no one is saved *by* the Lord until he realizes his need *for* the Lord. To that end, the law was given as a "rough" schoolmaster—rapping people on the knuckles, showing them they're sinners, making it clear to them that they don't measure up (Galatians 3:24). "I read the Bible," people say, "and I don't like it because it makes me feel bad." Good! That's the whole point, for in seeing your sin, you will see your need for a Savior.

"The one who is forgiven much loves much" (Luke 7:47). Therefore, I will not love the Lord much until I realize how badly I've blown it and how much I've been forgiven. Those who don't have a passion for the Lord are those who don't realize what sinners they are. But when they understand the price paid for them on the Cross, the work Jesus did on their behalf, the mercy and grace lavished upon them—their love for Him grows.

Genesis 42:7 (c)–9
. . . and he said unto them, Whence come ye? And they said, From the land of Canaan to buy food. And Joseph knew his brethren, but they knew not him. And Joseph remembered the dreams which he dreamed of them, and said unto them, Ye are spies; to see the nakedness of the land ye are come.

"You're spies come to check out how weakened we may be in order to plan your military strategy," said Joseph to his brothers.

Genesis 42:10, 11 (a)
And they said unto him, Nay, my lord, but to buy food are thy servants come. We are all one man's sons; we are true men . . .

"We are true men," said the brothers. Tilt. What had they done to Joseph?

Are they honest? Are they righteous? Are they true men?

In our fleshly condition, in our fallen state, we say, "We're pretty good, we're true." And that is the reason for the ordeal that follows. Joseph must show his brothers that they're *not* true men.

Genesis 42:11 (b)–13
. . . thy servants are no spies. And he said unto them, Nay, but to see the nakedness of the land ye are come. And they said, Thy servants are twelve brethren, the sons of one man in the land of Canaan; and, behold, the youngest is this day with our father, and one is not.

"We're not spies," say the brothers to Joseph. "We simply came for food."

Genesis 42:14, 15
And Joseph said unto them, That is it that I spake unto you, saying, Ye are spies: Hereby ye shall be proved: By the life of Pharaoh ye shall not go forth hence, except your youngest brother come hither.

"If you're really telling the truth, have your youngest brother come here," answered Joseph.

Genesis 42:16
Send one of you, and let him fetch your brother, and ye shall be kept in prison, that your words may be proved, whether there be any truth in you: or else by the life of Pharaoh surely ye are spies.

Why does Joseph want to see Benjamin? I suggest it's because he wants to know if his brothers had done to Benjamin what they had done to him.

I find it interesting that Benjamin was the only one of Joseph's brothers who had no part in selling him into slavery, for from what tribe was the apostle Paul? From the tribe of Benjamin. You see, even though the nation of Israel has, by and large, rejected Him, there is always a remnant, always a Benjamin, always those who do understand and embrace Jesus.

Genesis 42:17
And he put them all together into ward three days.

For three days, Joseph's brothers were held in captivity. So, too, because in God's economy one day is as a thousand years, and a thousand years as one day (2 Peter 3:8), the Jewish people are entering their "third day" in "captivity," beginning with the time they were driven from their homeland in 1026 B.C.

Genesis 42:18 (a)
And Joseph said unto them the third day . . .

Jesus died 2,000 years—"two days"—ago. And I believe at the breaking of the "third day"—the third Millennium, He will come again and establish His kingdom on earth.

Genesis 42:18 (b)
. . . This do, and live; for I fear God:

"I fear Elohim," said Joseph—which should have startled his brothers, *Elohim* being a Hebrew rather than an Egyptian God. They should have thought, *There's something about the man standing before us we don't understand.* But they couldn't get past the fact that he was a Gentile.

The same way the Jewish people can't figure

us out. "You claim to know our God," they say, "but where are your kosher foods and prayer shawls?"

Genesis 42:19–21
If ye be true men, let one of your brethren be bound in the house of your prison: go ye, carry corn for the famine of your houses: But bring your youngest brother unto me; so shall your words be verified, and ye shall not die. And they did so. And they said one to another, We are verily guilty concerning our brother, in that we saw the anguish of his soul, when he besought us, and we would not hear; therefore is this distress come upon us.

"We're guilty," Joseph's brothers said amongst themselves, not realizing Joseph could understand what they said. "Our brother cried out and we didn't respond. Our brother was in anguish and we didn't care. We are not true men, and now we're paying the price."

Genesis 42:22
And Reuben answered them, saying, Spake I not unto you, saying, Do not sin against the child; and ye would not hear? therefore, behold, also his blood is required.

"His blood is now upon us," said Reuben of Joseph.

"Let His blood be upon us," said Israel of Jesus (Matthew 27).

Genesis 42:23
And they knew not that Joseph understood them; for he spake unto them by an interpreter.

They didn't know Joseph was taking in this whole conversation—just as Jewish people today don't realize Jesus is listening to their conversation.

Genesis 42:24 (a)
And he turned himself about from them, and wept . . .

Following their final rejection of Him, Jesus looked over the city of Jerusalem and wept (Luke 19:41). Here, Joseph does the same thing.

Genesis 42:24 (b)
. . . and returned to them again, and communed with them, and took from them Simeon, and bound him before their eyes.

Simeon means "Hearing." Nine brothers will return to the Promised Land—but they'll go without hearing. Concerning Jesus, Isaiah said of the Jews, "In hearing you shall hear, but not understand; in seeing you shall not perceive," (Isaiah 6:9, 10).

The same remains true today, for, in May, 1948, the Jews returned to Israel—but they returned without Simeon because they still can't hear Jesus.

Genesis 42:25
Then Joseph commanded to fill their sacks with corn, and to restore every man's money into his sack, and to give them provision for the way: and thus did he unto them.

Joseph didn't accept his brother's money. Neither will Jesus accept our efforts to purchase either our own salvation or His continued favor. Grace isn't the starting point of our salvation, gang. It's the *only* point.

Genesis 42:26–28
And they laded their asses with the corn, and departed thence. And as one of them opened his sack to give his ass provender in the inn, he espied his money; for, behold, it was in his sack's mouth. And he said unto his brethren, My money is restored; and, lo, it is even in my sack: and their heart failed them, and they were afraid, saying one to another, What is this that God hath done unto us?

As did Joseph to his brothers, even though they have been scattered, God has faithfully provided silver for His people—to such a degree that one of the reasons the Third Reich rose to power was in reaction to the prosperity of the Jews in Europe.

Genesis 42:29–35
And they came unto Jacob their father unto the land of Canaan, and told him all that befell unto them; saying, The man, who is the lord of the land, spake roughly to us, and took us for spies of the country. And we said unto him, We are true men; we are no spies: We be twelve brethren, sons of our father; one is not, and the youngest is this day with our father in the land of Canaan. And the man, the lord of the country, said unto us, Hereby shall I know that ye are true men; leave one of your brethren here with me, and take food for the famine of your households, and be gone: And bring your youngest brother unto me: then shall I know that ye are no spies, but that ye are true men:

so will I deliver you your brother, and ye shall traffick in the land. And it came to pass as they emptied their sacks, that, behold, every man's bundle of money was in his sack: and when both they and their father saw the bundles of money, they were afraid.

The hearts of Jacob and his sons must have stopped when they discovered not one piece of incriminating evidence—but *ten*.

Genesis 42:36
And Jacob their father said unto them, Me have ye bereaved of my children: Joseph is not, and Simeon is not, and ye will take Benjamin away: all these things are against me.

Notice it's not *Israel*—"Governed By God"—who declares, "All these things are against me." It's Jacob. "Everything is against me," he cries. Not true, Jacob. Hang in there for another chapter, and you'll see that all these things are working out gloriously.

For topical study of Genesis 42:36, see "It's All for Good" below.

Genesis 42:37, 38
And Reuben spake unto his father, saying, Slay my two sons, if I bring him not to thee: deliver him into my hand, and I will bring him to thee again. And he said, My son shall not go down with you; for his brother is dead, and he is left alone: if mischief befall him by the way in the which ye go, then shall ye bring down my gray hairs with sorrow to the grave.

The plot thickens, and the picture becomes more vivid in color and texture in chapter 43 . . .

IT'S ALL FOR GOOD

A Topical Study of GENESIS 42:36

Certain things we *don't* know—like how honeybees fly when, theoretically, their wings are too short and too light to support them when carrying pollen.

Some things we *can't* know—like the day or hour of the Rapture (Matthew 25:13), or who will be in heaven (Matthew 13:24–30).

Several things we *should* know—like the fact that Jesus is coming again (1 Thessalonians 4:13), and the manifestation of spiritual gifts (1 Corinthians 12).

But there is one thing we *do* know . . .

The Promise Given *to* Us

"And we know that all things work together for good to them that love God, to them who are called according to his purpose," wrote Paul (Romans 8:28).

How do we know this?

Because it's in the Bible.

Alright. But what about the guys in Rome to whom Paul was writing? They had never heard of Romans 8:28. How, then, could Paul assume they knew its truth?

The Price Paid *for* Us

A few verses down, in Romans 8:32, Paul writes, "God spared not His own Son, but delivered Him up for you and me." If He loved you enough to send His Son to be slaughtered in your stead, don't you know God will do what's good for you continually? When I begin to doubt the love of God, or wonder if things are really working out for good, all I need to do is look to Calvary and see Jesus dying for me.

The Peace *within* Us

God's goodness was known and understood by Old Testament saints long before the Cross of Calvary because deep within their hearts, in the midst of tragedy, in the face of difficulty, all those who love God know that all things are truly working together for good—even though at first they question God's goodness.

Jacob was such a man. In the passage before us, we see how he initially deceived himself by thinking God was not working everything together for good in his own life.

Here's the situation; Jacob had twelve sons. Although he loved them all, Joseph was his favorite. Jealous of his standing with his father, Joseph's brothers threw him into a pit, where they were going to leave him to die until one of them suggested they could make some money if they sold him as a slave. So sell him they did, after which they smeared blood all over his coat, and took it to Jacob, saying, "Bad news, Dad. Joseph was eaten by wild animals."

Meanwhile, through an incredible series of events, Joseph became Prime Minister of Egypt—Number Two to Pharaoh himself. When famine hit Israel, Jacob called his sons together, and said, "I've heard there's a man in Egypt who has food. Go ask him if we can buy some grain."

So his sons, ten in number, appeared before the Prime Minister, whom they didn't recognize as their brother.

"Why are you here?" asked Joseph.

"We're here to buy grain, your Highness," they answered.

"I think you're lying," said Joseph. "I think you've come to spy out the land."

"No," insisted his brothers. "We're brothers. In fact, there were twelve of us originally, but one is dead, and the youngest is at home."

"If that's true," countered Joseph, "go bring your youngest brother to me. That will validate your story. Meanwhile, the oldest of you will stay in prison as security until the youngest one is brought back."

Upon his sons' return, what was Jacob's answer to this demand? "Joseph is not, and Simeon is not, and ye will take Benjamin away: all these things are against me" (Genesis 42:36).

What does Romans 8 say? "All things work for good."

But what does Jacob declare? "Everything is working against me. Simeon is a hostage. Joseph is dead. And my son Benjamin is soon to disappear." Jacob was completely wrong: Simeon would be released; Joseph was in perfect health; Benjamin would return.

Yet even though Jacob said, "Everything is against me," I suggest that deep down inside, he didn't believe it. Why? Because in the next chapter we read that the brothers did indeed return to Egypt—with Benjamin in tow. Knowing Jacob, if he *really* believed Benjamin would die in Egypt, he would not have allowed Benjamin to go. Clever, cunning Jacob would have figured out another way. But his sending Benjamin proves he didn't *truly* believe everything was working against him.

Joseph identified himself to his brothers, and as they fell at his feet, he said, "Don't fear. Although you meant evil against me, God meant it for good" (Genesis 50:20).

Here's the question: How will I react to difficulty? Will I be like Jacob and say, "All things are working against me"—even though I know in my heart such is not the case? Or will I be like Joseph and say, "Man may have meant this for evil, but God meant it for good"?

Unfortunately, all too often, I choose the sniveling of Jacob over the security of Joseph. Why? To elicit sympathy. What is it about our flesh that wants people to think we have it tough? What is in us that wants people to think we have it hard? While this may seem an insignificant quirk, in reality, it borders on blasphemy because, in getting you to feel sorry for me, I get you to question God's goodness, provision, and protection in my life. Thus, your pity for me is at God's expense.

Who will I be? I can be self-indulgent and allow God to be cast in a bad light even though I know in my heart the promise given to me, the price paid for me, the peace available within me. I can deny all of this and say, "I want you to feel sorry for me. Listen to my tragedy."

Or, I can say, "I will not dishonor this good, gracious, loving God, who has been so kind to me, so good for me. He's my Creator and my Father. Therefore, I will not bring shame to His name in seeking sympathy from anyone." That is called the fear of the Lord. It's saying, "Father, I care more about Your reputation than I do about getting sympathy from the congregation. I don't want them to think questioningly, negatively, or blasphemously of You."

Where are the men and women who say, "We fear God. We will not snivel. God is good and we know deep within our hearts that He is working all things together for good"?

Here's the question: In the name of compassion, are you one who constantly weeps with others? Perhaps what we need in the Christian community during this time of self-centered Christianity are men and women who say, "I fear God. So, dear brother, precious sister, even if you don't understand—even if you think this is cold-hearted or lacking compassion—you *know* that this difficulty or tragedy will work for good. Stand on that knowledge. Cling to it. I will weep for you if you don't get it. But I'm not going to weep with you as you question God. He's too good for that."

May God give us wisdom.
May God give us peace.
May God give us understanding.

All things work together for good to them that love God, to them called according to His purpose. I *know* it.

And so do you.

43 Genesis 43:1–6

And the famine was sore in the land. And it came to pass, when they had eaten up the corn which they had brought out of Egypt, their father said unto them, Go again, buy us a little food. And Judah spake unto him, saying, The man did solemnly protest unto us, saying, Ye shall not see my face, except your brother be with you. If thou wilt send our brother with us, we will go down and buy thee food: But if thou wilt not send him, we will not go down: for the man said unto us, Ye shall not see my face, except your brother be with you. And Israel said, Wherefore dealt ye so ill with me, as to tell the man whether ye had yet a brother?

Out of food again—yet realizing his sons couldn't return to Egypt for replenishment without taking Benjamin with them, Jacob said, "Why did you open your big mouths, boys? Why did you even bring up the fact that you had another brother?"

Genesis 43:7–9

And they said, The man asked us straitly of our state, and of our kindred, saying, Is your father yet alive? have ye another brother? and we told him according to the tenor of these words: could we certainly know that he would say, Bring your brother down? And Judah said unto Israel his father, Send the lad with me, and we will arise and go; that we may live, and not die, both we, and thou, and also our little ones. I will be surety for him; of my hand shalt thou require him: if I bring him not unto thee, and set him before thee, then let me bear the blame for ever:

"I will guarantee with my own life that Benjamin will be brought back safely," Judah promised his father.

Genesis 43:10

For except we had lingered, surely now we had returned this second time.

"We can't delay any longer; we're wasting time; the life of our whole family is in jeopardy," Judah continued.

Genesis 43:11–14

And their father Israel said unto them, If it must be so now, do this; take of the best fruits in the land in your vessels, and carry down the man a present, a little balm, and a little honey, spices, and myrrh, nuts, and almonds: And take double money in your hand; and the money that was brought again in the mouth of your sacks, carry it again in your hand; peradventure it was an oversight: Take also your brother, and arise, go again unto the man: And God Almighty give you mercy before the man, that he may send away your other brother, and Benjamin. If I be bereaved of my children, I am bereaved.

Finally, Jacob gave permission for Benjamin to accompany his brothers to Egypt, nonetheless insisting that if he lost Benjamin, he would live out his life in continual grief.

Genesis 43:15, 16

And the men took that present, and they took double money in their hand, and Benjamin; and rose up, and went down to Egypt, and stood before Joseph. And when Joseph saw Benjamin with them, he said to the ruler of his house, Bring these men home, and slay, and make ready; for these men shall dine with me at noon.

In the midst of famine and tribulation, Joseph—a picture of Jesus—made provision for his brothers even though they didn't know who he was. So, too, when Israel as a nation goes through the Tribulation of Revelation 6—19, God will protect them, provide for them, work through them, and work on them, even before they recognize Him.

Genesis 43:17, 18

And the man did as Joseph bade; and the man brought the men into Joseph's house. And the men were afraid, because they were brought into Joseph's house; and they said, Because of the money that was returned in our sacks at the first time are we brought in; that he may seek occasion against us, and fall upon us, and take us for bondmen, and our asses.

"Oh, no!" said Joseph's brothers. "He's calling us to his table because he wants to send us away as prisoners—and take our donkeys, too."

People still have this view of the Greater than Joseph, Jesus Christ. People still say, "I've blown it so badly; I've erred so greatly; I know the Lord will yell at me, put chains around me, and take my donkey from me if I come to His house."

Not true! Even though these guys had sinned greatly, they will discover incredible grace and unbelievable mercy because Joseph is a picture of Jesus, and where sin abounds His grace abounds more (Romans 5:20). When you are aware of your failings, your weakness, your inconsistencies, your stubbornness, rebellion, and sin, there's a tendency to say, "I can't go to church because I know Jesus is mad at me. If I go, I'll be bound with rules and regulations; I'll be sent away to the prison of condemnation; and on top of all that, I'll lose my donkey."

> For my thoughts are not your thoughts, neither are your ways my ways, saith the LORD. For as the heavens are higher than the earth, so are my ways higher than your ways, and my thoughts than your thoughts.
>
> Isaiah 55:8, 9

Through Isaiah, God says, "When someone offends you, is mean or nasty to you, I know that your ways and your thoughts center on one thing: Revenge. But I don't think like you do. Therefore, I don't work like you do," declares God.

We need to realize how much different the Lord is than we are in our fallen condition, in our depraved nature. God is good, declares the psalmist (Psalm 73:1). He's just flat out, plain old *good*—looking for ways not to blast, but to bless.

Some people are afraid to go to the Lord's Table. On the basis of 1 Corinthians 11:29, they've been wrongly taught that if there's sin in their life and they partake of the elements of Communion, they will do so to their own damnation. But that's like saying to someone who's sick, "Before you go to the doctor, get well. Before you go into the hospital, make sure there are no germs within you." No, we go to the doctor *because* we're sick. We go to the hospital *because* we have a problem. So, too, we go to the Lord's Table *because* we realize we're sinners—for it is at the Lord's Table that we are reminded of the work Jesus did on our behalf when He shed His blood to cleanse us from our sin.

Paul's admonition to the Corinthians regarding Communion speaks volumes about how the early church viewed the Lord's Table. They didn't view it with the somber, heavy, fearful, introspective mentality that has crept into Protestant theology. They viewed it as a celebration to such a degree that Paul had to caution against drunkenness (1 Corinthians 11:21).

Even though his brothers had blown it incredibly, Joseph says, "Get the meat ready! It's time to feast with my family!"

Genesis 43:19–23

And they came near to the steward of Joseph's house, and they communed with him at the door of the house, And said, O sir, we came indeed down at the first time to buy food: And it came to pass, when we came to the inn, that we opened our sacks, and, behold, every man's money was in the mouth of his sack, our money in full weight: and we have brought it again in our hand. And other money have we brought down in our hands to buy food: we cannot tell who put our money in our sacks. And he said, Peace be to you, fear not: your God, and the God of your father, hath given you treasure in your sacks: I had your money. And he brought Simeon out unto them.

"I had your money." This is a great picture of the way of our Lord as it relates to money. You see, we give the Lord our tithe—which is already His. And what does He do? He puts it back into our sack. Whatever you give to the Lord will come back in a way that will blow your mind—mysteriously, timely, wonderfully; spiritually, financially, relationally. Whatever the combination, the fact remains: You cannot out give God. Never forget that.

Genesis 43:24, 25

And the man brought the men into Joseph's house, and gave them water, and they washed their feet; and he gave their asses provender. And they made ready the present against Joseph came at noon: for they heard that they should eat bread there.

Rather than finding rebuke in Joseph's house as they had feared, the brothers found refreshment. And rather than losing their donkeys, their donkeys were fed.

Genesis 43:26

And when Joseph came home, they brought him the present which was in their hand into the house, and bowed themselves to him to the earth.

In all, we will see Joseph's brothers bow to him on five separate occasions in fulfillment of the dreams which they had so vehemently denied.

Genesis 43:27–30 (a)
And he asked them of their welfare, and said, Is your father well, the old man of whom ye spake? Is he yet alive? And they answered, Thy servant our father is in good health, he is yet alive. And they bowed down their heads, and made obeisance. And he lifted up his eyes, and saw his brother Benjamin, his mother's son, and said, Is this your younger brother, of whom ye spake unto me? And he said, God be gracious unto thee, my son. And Joseph made haste; for his bowels did yearn upon his brother . . .

In other words, there were butterflies in Joseph's stomach upon at last seeing his full brother, Benjamin.

Genesis 43:30 (b)
. . . and he sought where to weep . . .

This is the first of two times Joseph will weep concerning his brothers.

Jesus also wept on two occasions: once in a cemetery at the tomb of His friend Lazarus (John 11:35), and the other over His people in the city of Jerusalem (Luke 19:41).

Genesis 43:30 (c)
. . . and he entered into his chamber, and wept there.

Joseph's heart was pounding, his stomach churning, his eyes were weeping, yet he didn't reveal himself to his brothers. Why? Because there was still work to do. There was still testing to take place.

Just the same way Jesus passionately wants to be with you and me, His Bride. But He hasn't yet come for us because there's still work to do in us. It is true that Jesus is in heaven preparing a place for us (John 14:2). But He's also preparing us for the place. And when we're ready, He'll take us home—either through the Rapture or through death. When the time is right, when the work He wants to do has come to completion, He'll take us home one way or the other. Therefore, if we're still here, it means there's still work to do—not just *through* us, but *in* us.

Genesis 43:31, 32
And he washed his face, and went out, and refrained himself, and said, Set on bread. And they set on for him by himself, and for them by themselves, and for the Egyptians, which did eat with him, by themselves: because the Egyptians might not eat bread with the Hebrews; for that is an abomination unto the Egyptians.

In order to maintain his disguise, Joseph would have to sit with the Egyptians rather than with his brothers.

Genesis 43:33
And they sat before him, the firstborn according to his birthright, and the youngest according to his youth: and the men marvelled one at another.

Beginning with Reuben, Joseph seated his brothers in their birth order.

Genesis 43:34 (a)
And he took and sent messes unto them from before him: but Benjamin's mess was five times so much as any of theirs . . .

Benjamin was given five times as much food as the others. Why did Joseph do this? I suggest it was in order to observe the reaction of his brothers. When Joseph was given the coat with the big sleeves, what was their response? Envy, jealousy, hostility, anger. Therefore, Joseph wanted to see if his brothers would deal with Benjamin the same way they had dealt with him years earlier.

The Lord also measures the changes that have taken place in my life by how I react to my brothers not just when they're hurting, but when they, like Benjamin, succeed. It's easy to weep with those who weep. It's harder to rejoice with those who rejoice. If someone undergoes a tragedy, a catastrophe, a problem, most of us feel a certain amount of sympathy rather easily. But it's a little tougher for us to rejoice with the one who has everything go his way.

You'll know a deep work has taken place in your life when you not only weep with those who weep, but rejoice with those who rejoice, without being jealous or envious, hostile or cynical.

"All men will know you are My disciples," said Jesus, "by your love one for another" (John 13:35). And "one another" includes the happy as well as the hurting.

Genesis 43:34 (b)
. . . And they drank, and were merry with him.

Prior to the time Joseph will reveal himself to his brothers, he communes with them. Prior to the time when the Jews at last recognize Jesus as Messiah, He will commune with them from afar as He walks them through the Tribulation.

People tend to think that until the Jewish people understand who He is, the Lord will have nothing to do with them. But this story proves otherwise. Because Jesus cares passionately about His people, He is blessing and enjoying them even before they know exactly who He is. Even though they don't yet sit at the same table, there is interaction nonetheless.

That is why in talking to the Jewish people, you can't help but sense a real interaction with God even though they do not yet know what they will know in the time of the Tribulation—that Jesus is their Redeemer, their Savior, their Messiah.

44

Genesis 44:1, 2 (a)
And he commanded the steward of his house, saying, Fill the men's sacks with food, as much as they can carry, and put every man's money in his sack's mouth. And put my cup, the silver cup . . .

Egyptian rulers had silver divining cups which spoke not only of their authority, but were used to determine the will of their gods.

Jesus also had a "divining cup" through which he determined God's will—the cup of suffering of which He prayed, "Father, if it be possible, let this cup pass from Me; nevertheless not My will but Thine be done" (Luke 22:42).

Genesis 44:2 (b)–5
. . . in the sack's mouth of the youngest, and his corn money. And he did according to the word that Joseph had spoken. As soon as the morning was light, the men were sent away, they and their asses. And when they were gone out of the city, and not yet far off, Joseph said unto his steward, Up, follow after the men; and when thou dost overtake them, say unto them, Wherefore have ye rewarded evil for good? Is not this it in which my lord drinketh, and whereby indeed he divineth? ye have done evil in so doing.

Putting the cup in Benjamin's sack and then asking why he had taken it was all part of Joseph's plan.

Genesis 44:6–8
And he overtook them, and he spake unto them these same words. And they said unto him, Wherefore saith my lord these words? God forbid that thy servants should do according to this thing: Behold, the money, which we found in our sacks' mouths, we brought again unto thee out of the land of Canaan: how then should we steal out of thy lord's house silver or gold?

"Why would we take your master's cup?" the brothers asked Joseph's steward. "We're not thieves."

Genesis 44:9, 10
With whomsoever of thy servants it be found, both let him die, and we also will be my lord's bondmen. And he said, Now also let it be according unto your words: he with whom it is found shall be my servant; and ye shall be blameless.

"So sure are we of our innocence that you can kill whoever of us has the cup, and the rest of us will be your slaves," insisted the brothers.

"No," said Joseph's steward, "whoever has the cup will be a slave. The rest of you can go free."

Genesis 44:11, 12
Then they speedily took down every man his sack to the ground, and opened every man his sack. And he searched, and began at the eldest, and left at the youngest: and the cup was found in Benjamin's sack.

Like his older brother, Benjamin is also a picture of Jesus. The silver cup was in his sack because it would be Jesus who would hold the cup of redemption, of which silver is a picture.

Genesis 44:13
Then they rent their clothes, and laded every man his ass, and returned to the city.

At Joseph's table, the brothers had been tested for envy. Here, they're tested for loyalty. What will they do now? All they have to do is leave Benjamin, and they can go home free men. Will they let him be taken into slavery? Or will they jeopardize their own freedom and stand with him?

Genesis 44:14, 15
And Judah and his brethren came to Joseph's house; for he was yet there: and they fell before him on the ground. And Joseph said unto them, What deed is this that ye have done? wot ye not that such a man as I can certainly divine?

"I knew what you were up to in stealing my silver cup," Joseph said to his brothers.

Genesis 44:16 (a)
And Judah said, What shall we say unto my lord? what shall we speak? or how shall we clear ourselves? God hath found out the iniquity of thy servants: behold, we are my lord's servants . . .

Judah didn't say, "Sorry, Benny, you're now a slave." He said, "We're to blame," and continues in marvelous confession . . .

Genesis 44:16 (b)–23
. . . both we, and he also with whom the cup is found. And he said, God forbid that I should do so: but the man in whose hand the cup is found, he shall be my servant; and as for you, get you up in peace unto your father. Then Judah came near unto him, and said, Oh my lord, let thy servant, I pray thee, speak a word in my lord's ears, and let not thine anger burn against thy servant: for thou art even as Pharaoh. My lord asked his servants, saying, Have ye a father, or a brother? And we said unto my lord, We have a father, an old man, and a child of his old age, a little one; and his brother is dead, and he alone is left of his mother, and his father loveth him. And thou saidst unto thy servants, Bring him down unto me, that I may set mine eyes upon him. And we said unto my lord, The lad cannot leave his father: for if he should leave his father, his father would die. And thou saidst unto thy servants, Except your youngest brother come down with you, ye shall see my face no more.

"You won't see my face unless Benjamin comes with you," Joseph had said to his brothers. In the same fashion, unless Jesus had died for our sins, we could not see the face of the King of all creation.

Genesis 44:24–31
And it came to pass when we came up unto thy servant my father, we told him the words of my lord. And our father said, Go again, and buy us a little food. And we said, We cannot go down: if our youngest brother be with us, then will we go down: for we may not see the man's face, except our youngest brother be with us. And thy servant my father said unto us, Ye know that my wife bare me two sons: And the one went out from me, and I said, Surely he is torn in pieces; and I saw him not since: And if ye take this also from me, and mischief befall him, ye shall bring down my gray hairs with sorrow to the grave. Now therefore when I come to thy servant my father, and the lad be not with us; seeing that his life is bound up in the lad's life; It shall come to pass, when he seeth that the lad is not with us, that he will die: and thy servants shall bring down the gray hairs of thy servant our father with sorrow to the grave.

"If you don't let Benjamin go, our father will die from sorrow," said Judah.

Genesis 44:32, 33
For thy servant became surety for the lad unto my father, saying, If I bring him not unto thee, then I shall bear the blame to my father for ever. Now therefore, I pray thee, let thy servant abide instead of the lad a bondman to my lord; and let the lad go up with his brethren.

"I'll be your slave, but let Benjamin go," pleaded Judah.

Genesis 44:34
For how shall I go up to my father, and the lad be not with me? lest peradventure I see the evil that shall come on my father.

The two underlying themes of Judah's powerful, effectual intercessory "prayer" to Joseph are: "I can't let Dad go through this," and, "I won't let Benjamin remain here in slavery."

And it is to this intercession by Judah on behalf of Jacob and Benjamin that Joseph will respond . . .

45

Genesis 45:1 (a)
Then Joseph could not refrain himself before all them that stood by him; and he cried, Cause every man to go out from me . . .

Upon hearing Judah's confession, Joseph dismissed all of his aides.

Genesis 45:1 (b)
. . . And there stood no man with him, while Joseph made himself known unto his brethren.

It was Judah's confession combined with intercession that caused Joseph's heart to be moved with compassion and resulted in revelation.

Genesis 45:2
And he wept aloud: and the Egyptians and the house of Pharaoh heard.

If you want to move the heart of your Lord, pray. Confess your sin. Acknowledge your love for the Father. And be loyal to your brothers.

Genesis 45:3
And Joseph said unto his brethren, I am Joseph; doth my father yet live? And his brethren could not answer him; for they were troubled at his presence.

What must Joseph's brothers have thought? Terror must have filled their hearts. Confusion must have flooded their minds. Yet following the revelation of his person in verses 1–3, Joseph will go on to reveal his purpose in verses 4–16.

When will Jesus reveal who He is?

> I will go and return to my place, till they acknowledge their offence, and seek my face: in their affliction they will seek me early.
>
> Hosea 5:15

Through Hosea, Jesus said prophetically, "I will return to My place until My people acknowledge their offense." What offense? Their rejection of Him. In their affliction, they will seek Him early. What affliction? The Tribulation, the time of Jacob's trouble, the seven-year period described in Revelation 6—19 in which the world undergoes judgment and the horrific outpouring of God's wrath on a Christ-rejecting world. In their affliction, the nation Israel will seek the Lord. They'll acknowledge their offense. They'll realize Jesus is Messiah. And then He will make Himself known to them.

Genesis 45:4, 5

And Joseph said unto his brethren, Come near to me, I pray you. And they came near. And he said, I am Joseph your brother, whom ye sold into Egypt. Now therefore be not grieved, nor angry with yourselves, that ye sold me hither: for God did send me before you to preserve life.

After revealing his person, Joseph reveals his purpose. The first purpose for Joseph's position was *pardon.* "Don't be upset with yourselves," he said to his brothers. "Your selling me into this foreign land as a slave was all part of God's plan."

I love these words of Joseph because they express the heart of Jesus. "Father, forgive them," He prayed from the Cross, "for they don't know what they're doing" (Luke 23:34). Those who crucified Jesus were indeed forgiven. The price was paid. And Peter would go on to declare that it was all part of a Divine design, a grand plan—that Jesus would die for the sins of every man (Acts 2:22–24). "I know you are aware of your flaws and failings," Jesus would say to us, "but don't be grieved. I've forgiven you."

> *"I can't believe I did what I did. I can't believe I blew it so badly," someone said to me recently.*
>
> *And I had to say to him, "Your being down on yourself simply proves you didn't believe what God said about you in the first place—that in your flesh dwells no good thing" (Romans 7:18).*

Whenever we say, "How could I have done that?" we show how little we understand the need for Calvary because God clearly tells us that He had to send His Son to die for us because there is *no* good in us.

"Don't be angry with yourself," He would say to you and me tonight. "Accept the fact that you're a sinner. Remember you are but dust" (Psalm 103).

Christianity is unique because it is not a matter of us cleaning ourselves up and getting our act together. It is a matter of constantly rejoicing in the fact that the blood of Jesus cleanses us continually, that our sin is washed away constantly by what He did for us on the Cross sacrificially. Thus, Christianity is celebration of what He's done, not condemnation for what we have or haven't done.

"Don't be angry with yourselves," Joseph said to his brothers. "God had a plan in all of this."

And God has a plan in all of the stuff *you're* involved in: to make you appreciate what He's done for you—not to boast in your own righteousness, your own purity, your own holiness—but to say, "Lord, Your forgiveness and kindness and goodness and mercy are awesome."

Genesis 45:6–11

For these two years hath the famine been in the land: and yet there are five years, in the which there shall neither be earing nor harvest. And God sent me before you to preserve you a posterity in the earth, and to save your lives by a great deliverance. So now it was not you that sent me hither, but God: and he hath made me a father to Pharaoh, and lord of all his house, and a ruler throughout all the land of Egypt. Haste ye, and go up to my father, and say unto him, Thus saith thy son Joseph, God hath made me lord of all Egypt: come down unto me, tarry not: And thou shalt dwell in the land of Goshen, and thou shalt be near unto me, thou, and thy children, and thy children's children, and thy flocks, and thy herds, and all that thou hast: And there will I nourish thee; for yet there are five years of famine; lest thou, and thy household, and all that thou hast, come to poverty.

The second purpose for Joseph's position was *provision.* I don't think there's anything more powerful than a person who goes through hard times yet keeps his faith in the Lord intact. That's what Joseph was doing, as he said to his brothers, "It's okay that you sold me into slavery because it was all part of God's plan to keep you guys alive."

Genesis 45:12, 13
And, behold, your eyes see, and the eyes of my brother Benjamin, that it is my mouth that speaketh unto you. And ye shall tell my father of all my glory in Egypt, and of all that ye have seen; and ye shall haste and bring down my father hither.

The third purpose for Joseph's position was *praise.* "Tell Dad what you see in me," he said. Any of you who are fathers know there's nothing more delightful than hearing someone tell you what you already know: that your kids are great. The Father already knows all about His Son, and yet here's what we can do to delight His heart: We can talk to Him about His Son. When I take time to talk to the Father about the blessings of His Son—my Savior, Jesus Christ—it blesses His heart immensely. That is why Joseph says, "Go tell Dad everything you've seen."

Genesis 45:14, 15 (a)
And he fell upon his brother Benjamin's neck, and wept; and Benjamin wept upon his neck. Moreover he kissed all his brethren, and wept upon them . . .

The fourth purpose of Joseph's position is *proximity.* As Joseph and his brothers weep together and hug each other, intimacy grows. This is what the Lord wants with you, and what He desires of me.

Genesis 45:15 (b)
. . . and after that his brethren talked with him.

"Get out of here, dreamer," his brothers had said to Joseph when he first came to them with visions of what God had shown him (Genesis 37:8). But the second time he appears to them here in our story, they receive, submit to, and have a great appreciation for Joseph. As Stephen pointed out (Acts 7), this has been the tendency of Israel throughout her history . . .

When Moses attempted to rescue a man being beat up by an Egyptian taskmaster, did the Jews welcome him? No. But when he came to them forty years later as their deliverer, they embraced him.

When Joshua first came on the scene and, along with Caleb, gave a good report concerning the Promised Land, the Jews refused to believe his report. Forty years later, however, it was Joshua who they followed into the Promised Land.

When David first came to his brothers as they quivered before Goliath, they said, "Go back home, runt"—only to later crown him king.

The first time Jesus came and dwelt among His people, they said, "We will not have this Man rule over us." But the second time He comes, every knee will bow to Him (Romans 14:11).

Genesis 45:16–20
And the fame thereof was heard in Pharaoh's house, saying, Joseph's brethren are come: and it pleased Pharaoh well, and his servants. And Pharaoh said unto Joseph, Say unto thy brethren, This do ye; lade your beasts, and go, get you unto the land of Canaan; And take your father and your households, and come unto me: and I will give you the good of the land of Egypt, and ye shall eat the fat of the land. Now thou art commanded, this do ye; take you wagons out of the land of Egypt for your little ones, and for your wives, and bring your father, and come. Also regard not your stuff; for the good of all the land of Egypt is yours.

Pharaoh told Joseph to say to his brothers, "Take these U-hauls back to Canaan; get your families and possessions; and come live in my land—the best part of the land of Egypt."

Genesis 45:21, 22
And the children of Israel did so: and Joseph gave them wagons, according to the commandment of Pharaoh, and gave them provision for the way. To all of them he gave each man changes of raiment; but to Benjamin he gave three hundred pieces of silver, and five changes of raiment.

The brothers didn't seem to notice that Benjamin had three hundred more pieces of silver and four more suits than they did. So blown away were they by Joseph's forgiveness that there was no room for envy or jealousy. I am so looking forward to that time when our Greater than Joseph is revealed, when we are living with Jesus, when there is no more competition. What a great day it will be when we don't notice if someone has five times more or three hundred pieces more, for one of the heavenly things about heaven is that everyone will be 1,000% thrilled for everyone else. Our competition-based society places a high premium on getting ahead. But this is not the way of the kingdom . . .

When the water stirred, the first one in to the pool of Siloam would be the one who would be healed. So what did Jesus do? He didn't go to the ones close to the pool. He went to the guy in the back, the one who had been there for thirty-eight years, and said, "Let's split this competitive scene" (see John 5:8).

When you're caught up in the "Joseph moment," everything else fades. The brothers didn't even notice that Benjamin was three hundred pieces of silver richer and four suits ahead of them because those things no longer mattered.

Genesis 45:23, 24
And to his father he sent after this manner; ten asses laden with the good things of Egypt, and ten she asses laden with corn and bread and meat for his father by the way. So he sent his brethren away, and they departed: and he said unto them, See that ye fall not out by the way.

Because Jesus identified Himself as the Way, early Christians were known as those who walked in the Way. Here, Joseph says, "I'm giving you everything you need to make the journey from where you are to where I am. Just see to it that you don't fall out by the way."

It's easy to fall out of the Way. It's easy to say, "My body is hurting. My stocks are dropping. My head is spinning. And it's time to kick back a bit." But our Greater than Joseph would say to us, "Don't do it. Don't fall back. Don't give up." In this regard, it's sobering to realize that Jesus told us only one-fourth of the seeds scattered would go on to bear significant fruit . . .

In some people, the seed of the Word falls in soil and springs up quickly. But then comes the heat—the tragedies, setbacks, and difficulties—that cause it to shrivel. In others, the cares of this world, the lust for riches, and the desire for other things are like weeds that choke out the Word. In others, the Word doesn't take root at all. But some falls on soil where its roots grow deep and where it goes on to bring forth much fruit (Matthew 13).

Over the years, I've known those whose roots have gone deep in the soil of the Word, whose lives have borne much fruit, who, despite setbacks and shortcomings, have not fallen out of the Way.

Genesis 45:25–28
And they went up out of Egypt, and came into the land of Canaan unto Jacob their father, And told him, saying, Joseph is yet alive, and he is governor over all the land of Egypt. And Jacob's heart fainted, for he believed them not. And they told him all the words of Joseph, which he had said unto them: and when he saw the wagons which Joseph had sent to carry him, the spirit of Jacob their father revived: And Israel said, It is enough; Joseph my son is yet alive: I will go and see him before I die.

Jacob didn't believe the word he heard, but that didn't stop the wagons from coming in his direction. Even though our faith might falter from time to time, the wagons are on their way to carry us home.

THE WAGONS ARE COMING

A Topical Study of GENESIS 45:27

"Smile first thing in the morning," joked W. C. Fields, "and get it over with."

"If you find anything to laugh about," echoed Groucho Marx, "it's only because you're not paying attention."

People often have reasons why they're so cynical . . .

In the midst of their phone conversation, a lady said to her friend, "Did you wake up grouchy?"

"No," said her friend, "I let him sleep."

Indeed, there can be reasons why people are grouchy or even why they sting people with cynicism . . .

> Bees fly 100,000 miles from flower to flower in order to gather enough nectar for just one pound of honey—only to have someone steal it from them. No wonder they sting us!

Perhaps, humanly speaking, Jacob had reason to be pessimistic. When his sons came to him, saying, "Dad, Joseph has been killed," he believed their untrue report. But when the same sons came to him, saying, "Dad, Joseph is alive, and he's governor of Egypt," he couldn't believe their true report. He believed what wasn't true because it was bad; and he didn't believe what was true because it seemed too good.

That's pessimism—the tendency to dismiss the light and embrace the dark.

"I would have fainted had I not believed to see the goodness of the Lord in the land of the living," declared the psalmist (Psalm 27:13). Jacob is indeed fainting because of his failure to believe God's goodness. Yet even though he didn't believe his son's words, he couldn't deny the wagons Joseph had sent to carry him and his possessions to the land of Goshen—the best part of Egypt. And Scripture says, when he saw the wagons his soul revived.

Notice it was the heart of Jacob which fainted (v. 26), but it was the mouth of Israel—the one "Governed by God," that said, "Joseph is alive" (v. 28).

This passage hit me in a way that delighted my heart, for, you see, even though pessimistic Jacob was ready to believe the bad lie, and unwilling to believe the good truth—he was convinced when he saw the wagons. This reminds me of Thomas . . .

> "I won't believe the report you guys are sharing about Jesus being risen from the dead," he said to the other disciples, "unless I can touch the holes in His hands and put my finger in His side." But when Thomas came face to face with Jesus, he became a believer (see John 20:28).

So, Jacob said, "I'm not going to believe the word"—but when he saw the wagons outside, his spirit revived.

Like Jacob, many times we don't believe the Word we heard. But the good news is that Jacob's disbelief did not derail the wagon train Joseph had sent his way to pick him up and bring him to Goshen. You might be going through dry times right now in which you're famished spiritually. But I have good news for you: The wagon has been sent your way.

What wagon?

The Lunch Wagon

> *Ho, every one that thirsteth, come ye to the waters, and he that hath no money; come ye, buy, and eat; yea, come, buy wine and milk, without money and without a price. Wherefore do ye spend money for that which is not bread? and your labour for that which satisfieth not? hearken diligently unto me, and eat ye that which is good, and let your soul delight itself in fatness.* Isaiah 55:1, 2

You might feel like things aren't going your way today, but that doesn't derail the lunch wagon God has sent in your direction. Society says, "There's no free lunch." Scripture, however, says, "Yes there is." You can come and buy and eat even if you don't have any money. The invitation is given you to freely delight your soul in fatness. The lunch wagon is headed in our direction, gang. And the Marriage Feast of the Lamb is right around the bend!

The Station Wagon

Train up a child in the way he should go: and when he is old, he will not depart from it. Proverbs 22:6

Not only is the lunch wagon coming—but the station wagon is headed your way as well. Your kids might have wandered away, but even if you're pessimistic or full of doubt about them God promised that He will keep that which is committed to Him (2 Timothy 1:12), and will finish the work He began (Philippians 1:6).

"Believe on the Lord Jesus Christ and not only you, but your family will eventually be saved as well," declared Paul (see Acts 11:14). The promises of God are intact, gang. And even if you don't believe it, the station wagon is headed in your direction to scoop up you and your family.

The Welcome Wagon

But as it is written, Eye hath not seen, nor ear heard, neither have entered into the heart of man, the things which God hath prepared for them that love him. 1 Corinthians 2:9

Even if you doubt it, the fact is, if you're a believer, you're on board and you're going to heaven. And when you get there, you're going to see the ultimate Welcome Wagon as you take in all that Jesus has prepared for you during the past 2,000 years.

"I go to prepare a place for you," He said (John 14:2).

And when I see it, I'll say, "Perfect, Lord! This is amazing! It's beyond anything I ever imagined. How did you know this is *exactly* what would make me happy?" He will welcome me into my new home. And He will do the same for you.

The Bandwagon

Praise ye the LORD. Sing unto the LORD a new song, and his praise in the congregation of saints. Psalm 149:1

"Can I be in the band? Please let me be in the band. C'mon guys, I wanna be in the band." It's going to happen! The bandwagon is coming—and I'm going to be there—singing in heavenly harmony right along with the best of them!

The Covered Wagon

For sin shall not have dominion over you: for ye are not under the law, but under grace. Romans 6:14

The wagon coming our way is a covered wagon. Our inadequacy, stupidity, and sin are all covered by the blood of the Lamb. And even if you don't believe the word you've heard, the fact remains that God has everything covered because of the finished work of the Cross.

It has been rightly said that "none lives so pleasantly as he who lives optimistically." How much easier it is to live pleasantly, to live optimistically, when we know for certain that the wagons are coming.

"A little bit of faith will get your soul to heaven, but a lot of faith will bring heaven to your soul," C. H. Spurgeon astutely said. And how right he was! The wagons are on their way. And heaven is just around the bend.

46 Joseph has revealed himself to his brothers, and has invited them—along with Jacob—to live with him in Egypt. And the story continues . . .

Genesis 46:1
And Israel took his journey with all that he had, and came to Beer-sheba, and offered sacrifices unto the God of his father Isaac.

I admire Jacob here because, although accepting this invitation to live among royalty and to be with his son, Joseph, again seems like the right thing to do, he stops and offers sacrifice to God to ensure that what he is doing is truly acceptable in the Lord's sight.

Appearances can be deceiving. I'm learning that, aren't you? Jacob stops and says, "I want to make sure I'm going to Egypt with God's blessing." Why would he be so reticent? Perhaps it was because his grandfather had also gone down to Egypt in a time of famine, returned with a servant girl named Hagar, and set in motion a series of events for which the Middle East is paying the price to this day.

Genesis 46:2–4
And God spake unto Israel in the visions of the night, and said, Jacob, Jacob. And he said, Here am I. And he said, I am God, the God of thy father: fear not to go down into Egypt; for I will there make of thee a great nation: I will go down with thee into Egypt; and I will also surely bring thee up again: and Joseph shall put his hand upon thine eyes.

God says, "Jacob, I do want you to go to Egypt. I'm not going to hold something from you that would be good for you. Your son will touch your eyes—you'll be in fellowship with him once again."

Romans 12 says this about God's will: It's good and acceptable and perfect. So often we think, "I hate the heat and can't stand snakes. Therefore, I know God will send me as a missionary to Africa." But that's not the way the Father works! His will for you is good, acceptable, and *perfect*. Understand this, precious people: Whatever God tells you to do will be good—*really good* for you.

In a recent newspaper article, I read the following . . .

Attending religious services lowers blood pressure more than tuning into religious TV or radio, a new study says. People who attend a religious service once a week and prayed or studied the Bible once a day are forty percent less likely to have high blood pressure than those who don't go to church every week or pray and study the Bible less than once a day. Says David B. Larson, head of the National Institute for Health Care Research, "If they relied on TV or radio for their religious service, it wasn't as beneficial. It shows that church attendance is better for your health than even watching religious TV." The link between religious activity and blood pressure was surprisingly strong. Previous studies showed other health benefits from prayer. A 1988 study found that patients who were prayed for needed fewer antibiotics and had fewer complications in surgery. Last year, re-

searchers found monthly church visits improved the mental health of the elderly. And researchers found earlier this year that adults who attend church once a week were more likely to have high levels of an immune system protein associated with age-related diseases. The new findings, part of a National Institute of Health initiative, came from a study of 2,391 people. They say more research is needed to understand these links, but going to church is healthy.

I like that! The will of the Father is perfect—and Jacob is about to find this out . . .

Genesis 46:5–7
And Jacob rose up from Beer-sheba: and the sons of Israel carried Jacob their father, and their little ones, and their wives, in the wagons which Pharaoh had sent to carry him. And they took their cattle, and their goods, which they had gotten in the land of Canaan, and came into Egypt, Jacob, and all his seed with him: His sons, and his sons' sons with him, his daughters, and his sons' daughters, and all his seed brought he with him into Egypt.

The whole family is saved from the famished condition of where they were previously and called to live with Joseph in a land of luxury. I personally believe the Lord wants to save entire families. "Believe in the Lord Jesus Christ," Paul said to the Philippian jailor, "and you will be saved—and your house" (Acts 16:31). This doesn't mean the whole family is automatically saved if the parent is a believer. But it does mean that a believing father or mother can expect the Lord to work in the rest of the family as he or she is obedient to the Word.

I'm simple enough to expect that my kids and grandchildren, should the Lord tarry, will travel with me, to be with the Greater than Joseph—Jesus Christ—in the land He is preparing for us.

This note was left on my windshield yesterday . . .

I was so glad to see your car here, Brother Jon. I have the opportunity to share with you some wonderful news. While visiting my mother a few months ago, I accidentally left a set of tapes at her house. The tapes were of services I had missed from our current Genesis study. Now my mother thought I had left them there with hopes of converting her. But it truly was a mistake. I had really wanted to listen to them myself. But God is so faithful. For whatever reason, Mom started listening to the tapes, and she accepted Jesus as her Savior and is going to be baptized this Sunday in a church in Kennewick, Washington. My mother is saved. She's saved, she's saved! God used this chain of events just for her, and I couldn't be happier.

That's not coincidence. That's providence! Grandpa, believe it. Mom, don't doubt it. Parents, lay hold of it. Believe. Believe that the Lord will work in your family.

Genesis 46:8–13
And these are the names of the children of Israel, which came into Egypt, Jacob and his sons: Reuben, Jacob's firstborn. And the sons of Reuben; Hanoch, and Phallu, and Hezron, and Carmi. And the sons of Simeon; Jemuel, and Jamin, and Ohad, and Jachin, and Zohar, and Shaul the son of a Canaanitish woman. And the sons of Levi; Gershon, Kohath, and Merari. And the sons of Judah; Er, and Onan, and Shelah, and Pharez, and Zerah: but Er and Onan died in the land of Canaan. And the sons of Pharez were Hezron and Hamul. And the sons of Issachar; Tola, and Phuvah, and Job, and Shimron.

Issachar had a son named Job. Many Bible commentators—with whom I'm inclined to agree—believe this is the Job of the Book of Job. If you chart the chronology, you find that Moses—who most scholars believe to be the author of the Book of Job—would have been fifty-five years old at the time when this particular Job was on the scene, making him the right age to have penned the book that uniquely chronicles the patience and power of faith under fire.

Genesis 46:14–20
And the sons of Zebulun; Sered, and Elon, and Jahleel. These be the sons of Leah, which she bare unto Jacob in Padan-aram, with his daughter Dinah: all the souls of his sons and his daughters were thirty and three. And the sons of Gad; Ziphion, and Haggi, Shuni, and Ezbon, Eri, and Arodi, and Areli. And the sons of Asher; Jimnah, and Ishuah, and Isui, and Beriah, and Serah their sister: and the sons of Beriah; Heber, and Malchiel. These are the sons of Zilpah, whom Laban gave to Leah his daughter, and these she bare unto Jacob, even sixteen souls. The sons of Rachel Jacob's wife; Joseph, and Benjamin. And unto Joseph in the land of Egypt were born Manasseh and Ephraim, which Asenath the daughter of Poti-pherah priest of On bare unto him.

As we noted previously, Joseph's Gentile wife speaks of us, the church, the Bride of Christ,

while the nation Israel is the wife of Jehovah (see Hosea 12:12).

Genesis 46:21–26
And the sons of Benjamin were Belah, and Becher, and Ashbel, Gera, and Naaman, Ehi, and Rosh, Muppim, and Huppim, and Ard. These are the sons of Rachel, which were born to Jacob: all the souls were fourteen. And the sons of Dan; Hushim. And the sons of Naphtali; Jahzeel, and Guni, and Jezer, and Shillem. These are the sons of Bilhah, which Laban gave unto Rachel his daughter, and she bare these unto Jacob: all the souls were seven. All the souls that came with Jacob into Egypt, which came out of his loins, besides Jacob's sons' wives, all the souls were threescore and six;

Sixty-six come out of Canaan. Six is the number of man.

Genesis 46:27
And the sons of Joseph, which were born him in Egypt, were two souls: all the souls of the house of Jacob, which came into Egypt, were threescore and ten.

Jacob, Joseph's two sons, and Joseph bring the number to seventy. Seven is the number of perfection. This is not surprising, for whenever Jesus—of whom Joseph is a picture—is added to the equation, He makes it perfect.

Genesis 46:28
And he sent Judah before him unto Joseph, to direct his face unto Goshen; and they came into the land of Goshen.

Goshen means "To Draw Near." *Judah* means "Praise." Therefore, it is not coincidental that Judah led the way to Goshen, for, as the psalmist declared, we enter the gates of our heavenly Father with thanksgiving, and into His courts with praise (Psalm 100).

Praise is the soil that allows the fruit of joy to thrive. Praise draws us in and causes us to be cognizant of the Lord's presence. Thus, it was additionally fitting for Judah to lead the way to Goshen, for from Judah would come Jesus, the Praiseworthy One (see Revelation 5:5).

Genesis 46:29, 30
And Joseph made ready his chariot, and went up to meet Israel his father, to Goshen, and presented himself unto him; and he fell on his neck, and wept on his neck a good while. And Israel said unto Joseph, Now let me die, since I have seen thy face, because thou art yet alive.

The father who was certain his son was dead now encounters him face to face and says, "Let me die. This is great! My life is complete!" What a reunion! What a picture of the reunion which must have taken place when the heavenly Father and Son met together after Jesus, our Greater than Joseph, had died for our sins, risen from the dead, and returned to heaven.

Genesis 46:31, 32
And Joseph said unto his brethren, and unto his father's house, I will go up, and shew Pharaoh, and say unto him, My brethren, and my father's house, which were in the land of Canaan, are come unto me; And the men are shepherds, for their trade hath been to feed cattle; and they have brought their flocks, and their herds, and all that they have.

Following the reunion with his father, Joseph becomes a mediator for his family as he goes before Pharaoh on their behalf. After He died for our sins and ascended to heaven, Jesus sat at the right hand of the Father, where He continues to intercede for us (Hebrews 7:25).

Genesis 46:33, 34
And it shall come to pass, when Pharaoh shall call you, and shall say, What is your occupation? That ye shall say, Thy servants' trade hath been about cattle from our youth even until now, both we, and also our fathers: that ye may dwell in the land of Goshen; for every shepherd is an abomination unto the Egyptians.

Joseph not only intercedes for his brothers, but he also instructs them, saying, "When you go before Pharaoh, and he asks your occupation, tell him you're shepherds." Why did Joseph instruct his brothers to answer this way? Because Egyptian society at that time was based on a caste system. And guess who was at the bottom of the heap, the lowest rung on the social ladder. Shepherds. Shepherds were untouchable. People didn't interact with them. They weren't allowed in the temples of Egyptian deities. Thus, as shepherds, Joseph's brothers would be marked men—completely separated from the worldly Egyptian system. Joseph knew that were his brothers not marked, they would be assimilated into Egyptian culture.

I have discovered that a Bible in my hand, a bumper sticker on my car, or a Christian logo on my shirt makes me a marked man. Secret, closet

Christians get in all kinds of trouble and are susceptible to walk into temptation needlessly. Identify yourself at every opportunity, gang—even if it makes you look like a "shepherd" in the eyes of society. Don't say, "I'm going to a meeting." Say, "I'm going to Bible study. Why don't you come with me?"

Joseph—a picture of Jesus—said, "I want you to be marked in this land in order that you might keep your purity and identity intact." Wise is the one who follows his instruction.

47

Genesis 47:1, 2
Then Joseph came and told Pharaoh, and said, My father and my brethren, and their flocks, and their herds, and all that they have, are come out of the land of Canaan; and, behold, they are in the land of Goshen. And he took some of his brethren, even five men, and presented them unto Pharaoh.

Joseph takes five of his brothers and presents them to Pharaoh. Five in Scripture being the number of grace, the picture is perfect. You see, like Joseph's brothers, we've been fickle in our faith. We've said things we shouldn't have said and done things we shouldn't have done. And yet, like Joseph, Jesus will present us faultless before God with exceeding joy (see Jude 24).

Joseph doesn't bring up his brothers' failures, foibles, and flaws. No, he brings them to Pharaoh and says, "This is my *family.*" And that's what the Lord will do with us.

Genesis 47:3–6
And Pharaoh said unto his brethren, What is your occupation? And they said unto Pharaoh, Thy servants are shepherds, both we, and also our fathers. They said moreover unto Pharaoh, For to sojourn in the land are we come; for thy servants have no pasture for their flocks; for the famine is sore in the land of Canaan: now therefore, we pray thee, let thy servants dwell in the land of Goshen. And Pharaoh spake unto Joseph, saying, Thy father and thy brethren are come unto thee: The land of Egypt is before thee; in the best of the land make thy father and brethren to dwell; in the land of Goshen let them dwell: and if thou knowest any men of activity among them, then make them rulers over my cattle.

When asked their occupation, Joseph's brothers said they were shepherds—just as Joseph had instructed them. And Pharaoh said if any of them were so inclined, they could care for his cattle as well.

Genesis 47:7
And Joseph brought in Jacob his father, and set him before Pharaoh: and Jacob blessed Pharaoh.

Jacob blesses Pharaoh because, according to tradition, the greater always blesses the lesser (Hebrews 7)—and, despite the fact that he's an old man from a poverty-stricken land, in God's economy Jacob was the greater indeed.

Genesis 47:8, 9
And Pharaoh said unto Jacob, How old art thou? And Jacob said unto Pharaoh, The days of the years of my pilgrimage are an hundred and thirty years: few and evil have the days of the years of my life been, and have not attained unto the days of the years of the life of my fathers in the days of their pilgrimage.

"Life has been kind of tough," Jacob said, "but it's not over yet because my dad and grandfather lived longer than this."

Genesis 47:10
And Jacob blessed Pharaoh, and went out from before Pharaoh.

The next section of our text pictures the Millennium—when Jesus will rule and reign on earth.

- In verses 11 and 12, we see Joseph's grace to Israel.
- In verses 13–22, we see Joseph's government over Egypt.
- In verses 23–26, we see Joseph's goodness for all.

***For topical study of Genesis 47:10 entitled "Being and Bestowing a Blessing," turn to page* 205.**

Genesis 47:11 (a)
And Joseph placed his father and his brethren . . .

After Joseph revealed his identity to his brothers and presented them before Pharaoh, he placed them in the land. Once Jesus comes back and Israel at last understands His true identity, a one-thousand-year period of unparalleled peace and prosperity will follow.

Genesis 47:11 (b)
. . . and gave them a possession in the land of Egypt, in the best of the land, in the land of Rameses, as Pharaoh had commanded.

First, we see Joseph showing grace to Israel in their position. He placed them in the best part of the land of Egypt. Just as Egypt is a type of the world, the Millennium takes place on planet earth. And just as Jacob and his sons were placed in the best part, Israel will have the best of the land. Israel will be the head and not the tail (Deuteronomy 28:13). Right now, Israel gets kicked around. A pariah in the international community, she's constantly voted against in the United Nations and put down by virtually every nation. But in the Millennium, that will all change. Israel will have preeminence and predominance as God fulfills the promises made to her throughout Scripture.

Genesis 47:12
And Joseph nourished his father, and his brethren, and all his father's household, with bread, according to their families.

According to Ezekiel 48, in the millennial kingdom, there will be portions of land given each of the Twelve Tribes.

Genesis 47:13, 14
And there was no bread in all the land; for the famine was very sore, so that the land of Egypt and all the land of Canaan fainted by reason of the famine. And Joseph gathered up all the money that was found in the land of Egypt, and in the land of Canaan, for the corn which they bought: and Joseph brought the money into Pharaoh's house.

As Prime Minister of a people devastated by famine, Joseph pulls everything to the throne—beginning with their purses. Money is a problem. Those who have it are worried about keeping it; those who don't are concerned about getting it. That's why Joseph does something Jesus will do as well: He brings all of the money to the throne.

Genesis 47:15–17
And when money failed in the land of Egypt, and in the land of Canaan, all the Egyptians came unto Joseph, and said, Give us bread: for why should we die in thy presence? for the money faileth. And Joseph said, Give your cattle; and I will give you for your cattle, if money fail. And they brought their cattle unto Joseph: and Joseph gave them bread in exchange for horses, and for the flocks, and for the cattle of the herds, and for the asses: and he fed them with bread for all their cattle for that year.

Not only did the Egyptians bring Joseph their purses, but they also brought him their possessions. "Bring everything to the throne," Joseph said, "and I'll take care of you."

So, too, in the millennial kingdom, there will be no need for the possessions that so easily possess us because our Greater than Joseph, Jesus Christ, will fully provide for us.

Genesis 47:18–20
When that year was ended, they came unto him the second year, and said unto him, We will not hide it from my lord, how that our money is spent; my lord also hath our herds of cattle; there is not ought left in the sight of my lord, but our bodies, and our lands: Wherefore shall we die before thine eyes, both we and our land? buy us and our land for bread, and we and our land will be servants unto Pharaoh: and give us seed, that we may live, and not die, that the land be not desolate. And Joseph bought all the land of Egypt for Pharaoh; for the Egyptians sold every man his field, because the famine prevailed over them: so the land became Pharaoh's.

After bringing their purses and possessions to Joseph, the Egyptians give him their property. Why does Joseph want property? Because he doesn't want the divided loyalties or human rivalries property so often brings.

Genesis 47:21
And as for the people, he removed them to cities from one end of the borders of Egypt even to the other end thereof.

After calling purses, possessions, and property under his control, Joseph took charge of the people themselves—relocating them throughout the land of Egypt.

"Let's stick together and build a tower which will reach to the heavens," said the inhabitants of Babel.

The Lord, however, scattered them throughout the earth (Genesis 11:9).

It's always been God's intention to have people spread out. That's why Christians were told to fan out throughout the world and preach the gospel (Acts 1:8).

Genesis 47:22
Only the land of the priests bought he not; for the priests had a portion assigned them of Pharaoh, and did eat their portion which Pharaoh gave them: wherefore they sold not their lands.

The pagan priests were allowed to remain where they were. So, in the coming millennial kingdom, there will be people who will do their own thing. Oh, they'll be living under an enforced righteousness, but they will do so with rebellion in their hearts. The Lord will invite all people to celebrate the Feast of Tabernacles. Those who come will be blessed, but those who don't will experience drought (Zechariah 14).

This is a key to understanding what life is about. Paul says God has made known to us the mystery of what life is really about. It's all about Jesus. Everything in heaven and on earth is being gathered together in Him and for Him. As seen in the life of Joseph, the degree to which your purse, possessions, property, and person are brought to the Throne will be the degree to which you are in the flow of history and destiny, for everything will one day be brought together under the authority and for the pleasure of Jesus (Revelation 4:11).

Everything you are, think about, and do is to be under the authority of Jesus Christ, our Greater than Joseph. In our text, those who did so were blessed, while others were starving, struggling, and dying. Yes, it meant they had to give up purse, possessions, property, and person, but once they did, they could relax and rest. In the same way, we'll choose to either go against God's flow—or we'll say, "I surrender *all*."

Genesis 47:23, 24
Then Joseph said unto the people, Behold, I have bought you this day and your land for Pharaoh: lo, here is seed for you, and ye shall sow the land. And it shall come to pass in the increase, that ye shall give the fifth part unto Pharaoh, and four parts shall be your own, for seed of the field, and for your food, and for them of your households, and for food for your little ones.

Joseph had taken care of them through treacherous times and now says, "Here's seed for you. You keep eighty percent and twenty percent goes to the king."

Genesis 47:25, 26
And they said, Thou hast saved our lives: let us find grace in the sight of my lord, and we will be Pharaoh's servants. And Joseph made it a law over the land of Egypt unto this day, that Pharaoh should have the fifth part; except the land of the priests only, which became not Pharaoh's.

The Egyptians gladly gave twenty percent to the king. Zacchaeus gladly gave fifty percent to the Lord (Luke 19:8). The widow with two mites gave one hundred percent to the temple (Mark 12:42–44). And we complain about giving ten percent?

Genesis 47:27
And Israel dwelt in the land of Egypt, in the country of Goshen; and they had possessions therein, and grew, and multiplied exceedingly.

Jacob and his sons thrived in Goshen. So, too, in the millennial kingdom, Israel will prosper and grow.

Genesis 47:28
And Jacob lived in the land of Egypt seventeen years: so the whole age of Jacob was an hundred forty and seven years.

Joseph was seventeen years old when he was sold into slavery. Jacob was able to live near him for seventeen years in the land of Goshen. Therefore, I believe the picture is that I will enjoy heaven to the same degree that I have invested time with the Lord on earth. You who have walked with the Lord, invested in your knowledge of the Lord, been close to the Lord for seventeen years will, I believe, have a capacity seventeen times greater to enjoy heaven than will the believer who made only a meager investment into the things of eternity and who followed God at a distance.

Genesis 47:29 (a)
And the time drew nigh that Israel must die: and he called his son Joseph, and said unto him, If now I have found grace in thy sight, put, I pray thee, thy hand under my thigh, and deal kindly and truly with me . . .

As seen when Abraham sent his servant to find a bride for Isaac in Genesis 24, the practice of putting one's hand under another's thigh said, "I want your undivided attention. Don't pull away. This is of utmost importance."

Genesis 47:29 (b)–31
. . . bury me not, I pray thee, in Egypt: But I will lie with my fathers, and thou shalt carry me out of Egypt, and bury me in their buryingplace. And he said, I will do as thou hast said. And he said, Swear unto me. And he sware unto him. And Israel bowed himself upon the bed's head.

"Even though I've been here in Egypt, my heart is in Canaan," said Jacob. "Yes, I've had it easy here, Joseph. And it's been glorious. But my heart is in another land."

Even though we'll be here on earth in the millennial kingdom, our hearts will be drawn to the new heaven and the new earth—the true land of Canaan (Revelation 21:1).

BEING AND BESTOWING A BLESSING

A Topical Study of GENESIS 47:10

The scene would have been unusual, illogical, surreal. Here was Pharaoh at his prime—powerful potentate of Egypt; here was Pharaoh in all of his splendor; here was Pharaoh, ruler of the known world's mightiest empire; here was Pharaoh—being blessed by a travel-weary exile from an impoverished land.

And without all contradiction the less is blessed of the better. Hebrews 7:7

The greater blesses the lesser. Jacob blessed Pharaoh because, although Jacob couldn't hold a candle to Pharaoh politically, financially, or militarily—he was unequivocally the greater spiritually because he was linked to the God of the Universe.

The privilege of bestowing blessing—of proclaiming prosperity, happiness, and success—was reserved for patriarchs. Thus, Jacob was perfectly justified in pronouncing blessing, for he was a patriarch.

But guess what. It is equally proper for us to pronounce blessing, for, it was also a privilege for priests and kings—and, according to 1 Peter 2:9, we are a chosen generation, a royal priesthood.

What, then, are we to do?

Instructing the priests, the Lord said,

Speak unto Aaron and unto his sons, saying, On this wise ye shall bless the children of Israel, saying unto them, The LORD bless thee, and keep thee: The LORD make his face shine upon thee, and be gracious unto thee: The LORD lift up his countenance upon thee, and give thee peace. And they shall put my name upon the children of Israel; and I will bless them. Numbers 6:23–27

In other words, God said, "Priests, this is what you're to do: You're to fan out among the people and place My name upon them. You're to speak blessing to them. You're to pronounce this benediction upon them. And I will work accordingly."

Whether a person is a friend or a Pharaoh, whether he is a brother or a boss—we get to be the ones to bless him.

How?

Two ways . . .

The Words We Say

Wherever we go, we hear people mock God, dishonor God, trivialize God. But you and I get to be those who say, "The Lord *bless* you." We get to be those who speak the Lord's name upon someone's life, into someone's day.

When you go to work on Monday, you have the opportunity to walk into your Pharaoh's office and say, "The Lord bless you. May His grace be upon your life. May He cause His face to shine upon your day."

It's radical! And it's doable. Every one of us has the opportunity to cause blessing to be bestowed upon someone.

"But I'm old," you say.

So was Jacob.

"But I'm poor," you say.

So was he.

"But I'm nothing," you say.

In the eyes of men, neither was Jacob.

"But I'm not godly," you say.

Neither was Jacob.

Yet he walked into the palace of Pharaoh and blessed him. And that's what you can do. It just takes a moment or two, but in the words you say you can bless people by speaking God's name in their ear, by adding God's presence to their day.

The Way We Pray

Not only can you speak words *of* blessing, but you can also pray *for* blessing . . .

Two nights ago, I had an opportunity to go for a walk through my neighborhood and as I did so, it was a fabulous time to go down the street and pronounce blessing upon each house, to say, "Lord, may Your Spirit be moving in that house this evening. Those people probably don't know You, but You know them, and I pray Your blessing upon them."

Maybe you're wondering why you would want to say to your in-laws,

"May the Lord fill your house with His peace,"

why you would go to your boss and say,

"May the Lord bless your day,"

or why you would walk up to kids on the street and say,

"May the Lord smile upon you."

The reason is because not only will pronouncing blessing change the lives of others, but it will radically change yours as well. You see, I've learned that if I'm mad at people, if I can't believe they did that, if I can't believe they said the other, if I curse people in my heart—my own life will be cursed.

But if I bless people, my own life is blessed. That's why Jesus said, "When you are put down or bugged or unfairly treated, you will be blessed if you bless" (see Matthew 5:10, 11).

In other words, what flows *through* me sticks *to* me. If I murmur and complain, grumble and snivel, I will be a small, bitter person. But if I speak blessing and beauty, peace and prosperity, I will become expansive and delightful.

I challenge you to be like Jacob. No matter what Pharaoh you may face, no matter where you go—pronounce blessing; offer prayer. In so doing, you will open the door for God to work in the lives of those around you.

And in yours as well!

48

Genesis 48:1, 2
And it came to pass after these things, that one told Joseph, Behold, thy father is sick: and he took with him his two sons, Manasseh and Ephraim. And one told Jacob, and said, Behold, thy son Joseph cometh unto thee: and Israel strengthened himself, and sat upon the bed.

While it was Jacob who was sick, it was Israel who strengthened himself when he heard his son was coming. We might not be able to do a lot of things, but every one of us can visit someone who's hurting, sick, or in need. Joseph did, and his father felt a surge of strength as a result.

Genesis 48:3–5 (a)
And Jacob said unto Joseph, God Almighty appeared unto me at Luz in the land of Canaan, and blessed me, And said unto me, Behold, I will make thee fruitful, and multiply thee, and I will make of thee a multitude of people; and will give this land to thy seed after thee for an everlasting possession. And now . . .

As Joseph enters with his sons Ephraim and Manasseh in tow, they who had blessed Jacob in coming are about to be blessed themselves.

Haven't you discovered that when you go to share with someone in need, you might set out, saying, "I don't know if I'll be able to help, say the right thing, or do enough"—only to find that when you get there, *you* are the one who is blessed?

Jesus wants us to minister to each other because He taught that whatever measure a man gives out, it will be given back to Him (see Matthew 7:2). It's in giving that we get. It's in praying for the sick that we become healthier. It's in cheering the discouraged that our own emotions begin to soar. It's in explaining truth to others that we begin to see things more clearly.

Whenever you give, you get back—and Joseph models this.

Genesis 48:5 (b), 6
. . . thy two sons, Ephraim and Manasseh, which were born unto thee in the land of Egypt before I came unto thee into Egypt, are mine; as Reuben and Simeon, they shall be mine. And thy issue, which thou begettest after them, shall be thine, and shall be called after the name of their brethren in their inheritance.

At this point, Jacob does something amazing: He claims Joseph's sons as his own—elevating Ephraim and Manasseh to the status of patriarchs. "Wow," Joseph would have thought. "What a blessing. You take my two boys who were born in Egypt and are dressed like Egyptians—and you're bringing them into your family, where they will have a legacy, where their names will be recorded for all eternity, where they will be key players in God's economy. Wow!"

The addition of Ephraim and Manasseh brought the total number of tribes to fourteen. But Ephraim and Manasseh usually take the place of two other tribes in the accounting, one of which is the tribe of Joseph. Although the tribe of

Joseph appears in the Book of Revelation, throughout the Bible his two sons usually assume his place. The other tribe taken out of the numeration is the tribe of Levi because, as priests, the Levites would have a high and holy calling, but not a piece of property.

Genesis 48:7, 8
And as for me, when I came from Padan, Rachel died by me in the land of Canaan in the way, when yet there was but a little way to come unto Ephrath: and I buried her there in the way of Ephrath; the same is Bethlehem. And Israel beheld Joseph's sons, and said, Who are these?

His eyesight failing, as Ephraim and Manasseh come closer, Jacob says, "Which is which? Who's who?"

Genesis 48:9–11
And Joseph said unto his father, They are my sons, whom God hath given me in this place. And he said, Bring them, I pray thee, unto me, and I will bless them. Now the eyes of Israel were dim for age, so that he could not see. And he brought them near unto him; and he kissed them, and embraced them. And Israel said unto Joseph, I had not thought to see thy face: and, lo, God hath shewed me also thy seed.

"I didn't think I would ever see you again, Joseph. I thought you were dead. But now we're living together as a family—and I get to see your children, too!" Jacob is blown away, exceedingly blessed.

Genesis 48:12 (a)
And Joseph brought them out from between his knees . . .

The little guys were clinging to Dad's legs.

Genesis 48:12 (b), 13
. . . and he bowed himself with his face to the earth. And Joseph took them both, Ephraim in his right hand toward Israel's left hand, and Manasseh in his left hand toward Israel's right hand, and brought them near unto him.

Joseph positioned Manasseh so that Jacob could put his right hand on him, for as the older son, Manasseh would receive the blessing of the firstborn.

Genesis 48:14
And Israel stretched out his right hand, and laid it upon Ephraim's head, who was the younger, and his left hand upon Manasseh's head, guiding his hands wittingly; for Manasseh was the firstborn.

Jacob intentionally crosses his arms.

Genesis 48:15, 16 (a)
And he blessed Joseph, and said, God, before whom my fathers Abraham and Isaac did walk, the God which fed me all my life long unto this day, The Angel which redeemed me from all evil . . .

"Angel" is capitalized because it refers to Jesus Christ.

Genesis 48:16 (b), 17
. . . bless the lads; and let my name be named on them, and the name of my fathers Abraham and Isaac; and let them grow into a multitude in the midst of the earth. And when Joseph saw that his father laid his right hand upon the head of Ephraim, it displeased him: and he held up his father's hand, to remove it from Ephraim's head unto Manasseh's head.

"Wait a minute, Dad. You're a bit mixed up here," Joseph said as he tried to put Jacob's right hand back on Manasseh's head.

Genesis 48:18, 19
And Joseph said unto his father, Not so, my father: for this is the firstborn; put thy right hand upon his head. And his father refused, and said, I know it, my son, I know it: he also shall become a people, and he also shall be great: but truly his younger brother shall be greater than he, and his seed shall become a multitude of nations.

"The Spirit of God has revealed to me that the younger son will be the greater," insisted Jacob. "Manasseh will be blessed, too—but there's a greater plan for Ephraim."

And that's exactly what happened. Ephraim became the greater tribe by far. The ten northern tribes of Israel are called Israel—but they're also referred to as Ephraim because Ephraim was the predominant of the ten northern tribes.

Culturally and traditionally, the elder son, the firstborn was to receive all of the benefits and assume the greater position. But the Lord seems to tweak that a lot . . .

- Cain was the firstborn, but Abel was blessed.
- Ishmael was the firstborn, but it was Isaac who was blessed.
- Esau was the firstborn, but it was Jacob who was blessed.

- Reuben was the firstborn, but it was Joseph who was blessed.
- Aaron was the firstborn, but it was Moses who was blessed.

Throughout the Word, the Lord often makes the lesser the greater, and uses the younger to rule the older. Why? I think the basic message is simply this: What is coming is always better than what has been. We tend to wax eloquent about the good old days. The Lord, however, says, "The best is yet to come. I'm going to take you from glory to *greater* glory" (see 2 Corinthians 3:18).

This gives me real hope, because I truly believe for our churches, for our families, for us personally the best is yet to come. It just seems to be the way of the Lord if we choose to believe on Him and walk with Him.

Genesis 48:20
And he blessed them that day, saying, In thee shall Israel bless, saying, God make thee as Ephraim and as Manasseh: and he set Ephraim before Manasseh.

"May God bless you like He's blessed Ephraim" would become a saying throughout the land.

Genesis 48:21, 22
And Israel said unto Joseph, Behold, I die: but God shall be with you, and bring you again unto the land of your fathers. Moreover I have given to thee one portion above thy brethren, which I took out of the hand of the Amorite with my sword and with my bow.

If you want to see how God can work in your family and through your children, read on . . .

BEHOLD I DIE, BUT . . .

A Topical Study of GENESIS 48:21, 22

There comes a moment in the life of every man when he becomes keenly aware, acutely aware of his mortality. In the text before us, Jacob is at just such a point. In light of this, please notice with me four elements in his words to his son, Joseph . . .

A Sobering Realization

And Israel said unto Joseph, Behold, I die . . . Genesis 48:21 (a)

At one hundred forty-seven years of age, it was Jacob's body that no doubt let him know the end of his life was near.

> When I was younger, I could eat as much as I wanted. It was wonderful! In college, just about every single night after track practice, we'd all go to Love's Charcoal Broiler and order hot fudge sundaes—not just ordinary ones, but the specialty of the house: Fifteen-gallon sundaes. And they didn't affect me at all. But then something happened when I hit middle age. No longer could I eat like that without consequences. I can't explain it—but you can certainly observe it!

Young people don't understand this, but at some point in every man's life, he realizes his days are numbered. And such was the case for Jacob.

Confident Expectation

. . . but God shall be with you . . . Genesis 48:21 (b)

"Behold I die," said Jacob, "but God shall be with you."

What a fantastic thing it is for us to be able to say to our children, "Behold, I die, but God will see you through. I guarantee it because He has seen me through."

Because Jacob was one who had lots of failings, tons of shortcomings, all sorts of problems, he was one who knew that God's faithfulness was not dependent upon his own deservedness. Jacob was a man who knew even when he was failing and faltering, that God would be faithful, that God would come through. And he passed that assurance on to his son.

Due to the aging of the baby boomer generation, you may have noticed there seems to be a flood of life insurance advertisements lately. Let me tell you, as important as it might be to have life insurance, it's infinitely more important to have life *assurance*, to be able to say to your son, your daughter, your grandchildren, "You *will* make it through, because even as God has been faithful to me, He will be faithful to you."

Don't settle for a piece of the rock from Prudential, gang. Seek the *peace* of the Rock of Ages. Being in good hands with Allstate doesn't compare to being in the Good Hands of the Almighty. Dad, listen; Grandpa, take heed: Nothing is more important for your family than your confident expectation that the same God who walks with you every step of the way will do the same for them.

Personal Application

. . . and bring you again unto the land of your fathers. Genesis 48:21 (c)

Jacob had problems just like we do. Jacob had troubles and inconsistencies just like ours. Nonetheless, he was able to say, "Joseph, God's going to bring you to the land of your fathers."

Dad, Grandpa—where's your land? Because that's where your kids and grandchildren will land when you're gone. If your land is the kingdom, if you have a love for the Lord, if you're a student of the Word, if you pray and seek first the kingdom day after day—that's where your kids and grandchildren will land. Conversely, chances are, statistics prove, and experience has shown that if your land is Blockbuster Video, Rockin' Rodeo, or HBO—those are the places your kids will end up.

Ultimately, the land of the fathers is the land of the Father. "In my Father's house are many mansions," Jesus said, "If it were not so, I would have told you. I go to prepare a place for you" (John 14:2). *That's* where I desperately desire my kids land. Therefore, I can no longer goof around. The stakes are too high—not just for me, but for my kids and future grandchildren. Oh, I'm Jacob. I still have struggles and failures and problems. But I'm also Israel—Governed by God because I've committed my heart and life to Him. And that is my desire, and prayer for those who follow me.

Glorious Continuation

Moreover I have given to thee one portion above thy brethren, which I took out of the hand of the Amorite with my sword and with my bow. Genesis 48:22

"I'm giving you an extra portion," Jacob says, "a parcel of property I took with my bow and sword from the Amorite." Here's the problem, Bible students: There's no record of Jacob ever doing this. Not only is there no mention in Scripture that Jacob ever took territory of an Amorite, but doing so was not even in his nature. Esau was the hunter, the warrior. But Jacob was a man who dwelt in tents and cooked. So what did Jacob mean when he said he took territory with his bow and sword?

The language indicates this speaks of an event that would take place in the future, an event so certain to happen that Jacob speaks of it as though it had already taken place.

Romans 8 tells us we are glorified. Have we actually, physically been glorified? No. But it's going to happen with such certainty that the Bible speaks as though it has already taken place. Jacob is saying, "The portion of land I took with my bow and sword is yours. The foundation has been laid, and what you do will be a continuation of who I am."

Last Sunday when I was taken violently ill after first service, I called my son, Peter-John, and said, "PJ, you're on." Listening to him on the radio, I was so blessed. And then Sunday night, so many, many young people opened their hearts to Jesus and were baptized by Peter-John, only twenty-two years old.

God is raising up a generation that will take more territory, see further, do better, claim a bigger portion as they stand on our shoulders and go on to greater victory.

That's why I'm so glad I'm a believer. I know those who come after me will do better than I have done. They'll take territory I was unable to claim. They'll do things I could never do.

Our kids, precious people, will do better than us because God takes His people from glory to *greater* glory. That's His promise. That's His way.

And I can't wait.

49

Genesis 49:1
And Jacob called unto his sons, and said, Gather yourselves together, that I may tell you that which shall befall you in the last days.

The phrase, "in the last days" is used fourteen times in the Old Testament—each time dealing with prophecy. Thus, Genesis 49 is one of those incredibly rich passages that deals with future events.

Genesis 49:2
Gather yourselves together, and hear, ye sons of Jacob; and hearken unto Israel your father.

On his deathbed, Jacob gathers his twelve sons around him and speaks to them concerning what lies ahead for them. Although he will begin with Reuben, Jacob won't address his sons in their birth order, as would have been customary in such a blessing. Instead, we will see Jacob address his sons in a way that will portray the history and future of the nation of Israel.

Genesis 49:3, 4
Reuben, thou art my firstborn, my might, and the beginning of my strength, the excellency of dignity, and the excellency of power: Unstable as water, thou shalt not excel; because thou wentest up to thy father's bed; then defiledst thou it: he went up to my couch.

This is in reference to what Reuben had done forty years previously, when, following Rachel's death, he had relations with her handmaid, Bilhah—through whom Jacob had fathered Dan and Naphtali. Perhaps Reuben thought he had gotten away with this, but here—forty years later—it comes back to bite him. "You're my firstborn," Jacob said to Reuben. "You had every opportunity, but you're unstable as water. And what you did forty years ago has caused you to be less than what you would have been had you not partaken in that sin."

Reuben speaks of the earliest days of Israel's history, where we see *a disappointing people,* as they committed spiritual fornication while Moses was on the mountain getting the Word of the Lord for them. So disappointed was Moses that he threw down the tablets when he realized that, just like Reuben, Israel was unstable as water.

Genesis 49:5–7
Simeon and Levi are brethren; instruments of cruelty are in their habitations. O my soul, come not thou into their secret; unto their assembly, mine honour, be not thou united: for in their anger they slew a man, and in their selfwill they digged down a wall. Cursed be their anger, for it was fierce; and their wrath, for it was cruel: I will divide them in Jacob, and scatter them in Israel.

When Dinah, their sister, was raped by Shechem, it was Simeon and Levi who hatched the plan that would result in the destruction of the people of Shechem.

Simeon and Levi speak of the next phase of Israel's history, wherein we see *a dispersed people*—for just as Simeon and Levi depended on their own plan to retaliate against Shechem, the nation of Israel began to depend upon her own ingenuity and alliances with other nations. The result? The Assyrians in 722 B.C., and the Babylonians in 586 would carry the people of Israel into captivity, thereby dispersing them throughout the globe.

Genesis 49:8
Judah, thou art he whom thy brethren shall praise: thy hand shall be in the neck of thine enemies; thy father's children shall bow down before thee.

After becoming a disappointing people and a dispersed people, there is good news for Israel as they become *a delivered people* as seen in Judah—for from the tribe of Judah, their Deliverer, their Messiah would come. Here, with His enemies at His mercy, the Deliverer is seen as an invincible Leader.

Genesis 49:9
Judah is a lion's whelp: from the prey, my son, thou art gone up: he stooped down, he couched as a lion, and as an old lion; who shall rouse him up?

Here, the Deliverer is seen as an unstoppable lion.

Genesis 49:10
The sceptre shall not depart from Judah, nor a lawgiver from between his feet, until Shiloh come; and unto him shall the gathering of the people be.

Here, the Deliverer is seen as an unvanquished Lord.

According to historian Josephus, "The scepter shall not depart from Judah until Shiloh come" was the phrase that caused the rabbis to run through the streets of Jerusalem screaming in anguish in the year A.D. 12.

You see, it was in that year that the Romans—who were occupying the land of Israel—withdrew the ability of the Sanhedrin to mete out capital punishment. Having taught that the mark of a nation's sovereignty resided in its ability to execute capital punishment, when this power was taken from them, the Jews thought the scepter had indeed departed from Judah—that God had broken His promise to them. After all, Shiloh, Messiah, had not yet come.

Oh, but He had. For right in their midst sat Shiloh, Messiah, Jesus as a twelve-year-old boy, astounding the teachers and rabbis with His wisdom (Luke 2:46).

Genesis 49:11, 12
Binding his foal unto the vine, and his ass's colt unto the choice vine; he washed his garments in wine, and his clothes in the blood of grapes: His eyes shall be red with wine, and his teeth white with milk.

Finally, the Deliverer is seen as an uncontested landowner, as He purchases property with His own blood.

Genesis 49:13
Zebulun shall dwell at the haven of the sea; and he shall be for an haven of ships; and his border shall be unto Zidon.

In Zebulun we see *an exiled people.* Forty years after Israel rejected Jesus, saying, "We will not have this man rule over us," the Romans destroyed Jerusalem, and burned the temple. The Jewish people were dispersed and scattered once again, and the name "Israel" was replaced by the name of her enemies: "Philistine"—or, "Palestine."

Genesis 49:14, 15
Issachar is a strong ass couching down between two burdens: And he saw that rest was good, and the land that it was pleasant; and bowed his shoulder to bear, and became a servant unto tribute.

Issachar speaks of *an exploited people,* for although the Jews were exiled, they remained as stubborn and strong as a donkey. Although they were scattered into virtually every corner of the world, the Jews prospered to such a degree that they were persecuted, blamed, and exploited as seen in the pogroms of Russia and the concentration camps of Nazi Germany.

Genesis 49:16, 17
Dan shall judge his people, as one of the tribes of Israel. Dan shall be a serpent by the way, an adder in the path, that biteth the horse heels, so that his rider shall fall backward.

Dan speaks of *a poisoned people.* After they are exiled, a snake will come on the scene that will poison Israel. This is why to this day the rabbis believe a false Messiah will appear who will come from the tribe of Dan. As Christians, we call this snake the antichrist.

Genesis 49:18
I have waited for thy salvation, O LORD.

This heart-cry of Jacob speaks of the fact that, although ultimately antichrist will seek to destroy Israel, initially she will trust him and pin her hopes to him.

Genesis 49:19
Gad, a troop shall overcome him: but he shall overcome at the last.

In Gad, we see *a persecuted people.* Because his hatred for Israel will be venomous, antichrist will lead a worldwide persecution against the Jews. Antichrist and the forces of Satan will mobilize the world in the Valley of Megiddo in order to destroy Jerusalem. But in the end, they shall be overcome themselves.

Genesis 49:20
Out of Asher his bread shall be fat, and he shall yield royal dainties.

Asher speaks of the fact that even though the Jews will be a poisoned people and a persecuted people, they will also be *a protected people* as they at last recognize their Redeemer, and God tucks them away in a place He has prepared for them in the wilderness—most likely the rock city of Petra—where they will be cared for royally.

Genesis 49:21
Naphtali is a hind let loose: he giveth goodly words.

Naphtali speaks of *a preaching people.* After antichrist appears, 144,000 evangelists—12,000 from each of the twelve tribes—will go throughout the world preaching the "goodly word" of the gospel. The greatest revival in all of history will take place during the Tribulation because it is the destiny of the Jewish people to be a preaching people.

Genesis 49:22
Joseph is a fruitful bough, even a fruitful bough by a well; whose branches run over the wall:

Joseph, of course, speaks of Jesus.

***For topical study of Genesis 49:22 entitled "The Secret of a Satisfied Life," turn to page* 215.**

Genesis 49:23–26
The archers have sorely grieved him, and shot at him, and hated him: But his bow abode in strength, and the arms of his hands were made strong by the hands of the mighty God of Jacob; (from thence is the shepherd, the stone of Israel:) Even by the God of thy father, who shall help thee; and by the Almighty, who shall bless thee with blessings of heaven above, blessings of the deep that lieth under, blessings of the breasts, and of the womb: The blessings of thy father have prevailed above the bless-

ings of my progenitors unto the utmost bound of the everlasting hills: they shall be on the head of Joseph, and on the crown of the head of him that was separate from his brethren.

Joseph speaks of the One who was rejected, separated from His brethren, the *Virtuous Ruler*— Jesus Christ.

***For topical study of Genesis 49:24 entitled "Don't Shoot Back," turn to page* 218.**

Genesis 49:27
Benjamin shall ravin as a wolf: in the morning he shall devour the prey, and at night he shall divide the spoil.

Benjamin speaks of a *victorious remnant.* Throughout history, others have castigated and almost annihilated the Jews. But the story is not over yet, for Benjamin will ultimately be as strong as a ravenous wolf.

God is not through with the Jews, gang—not by a long shot. In Romans 8:38, 39, Paul, a Benjamite himself, says we know nothing will separate us from the love of God, and uses the Jewish people as proof, for even when they are fickle, God will continue to prove Himself faithful to them.

Genesis 49:28 (a)
All these are the twelve tribes of Israel:

Interestingly, this is the first time the phrase "the twelve tribes of Israel" is seen in the Bible.

Genesis 49:28 (b)–32
. . . and this is it that their father spake unto them, and blessed them; every one according to his blessing he blessed them. And he charged them, and said unto them, I am to be gathered unto my people: bury me with my fathers in the cave that is in the field of Ephron the Hittite, In the cave that is in the field of Machpelah, which is before Mamre, in the land of Canaan, which Abraham bought with the field of Ephron the Hittite for a possession of a buryingplace. There they buried Abraham and Sarah his wife; there they buried Isaac and Rebekah his wife; and there I buried Leah. The purchase of the field and of the cave that is therein was from the children of Heth.

After giving a blessing to his sons, Jacob now gives an admonition to them as he says, "Make sure you bury me at Machpelah, where Abraham and Sarah are buried, where Isaac and Rebekah are buried, and where I buried Leah." This is interesting because for seventeen years, Jacob had been living in the splendor of Egypt. Father of the Prime Minister of the land, had he so desired, he could have ordered a huge monument to be built in his honor—a grand tomb in which he could have been placed like other nobles in Egypt. But that's not what he says. He says he wants to go back to Hebron, back to Machpelah, back to Leah.

***For topical study of Genesis 49:31 entitled "Don't Jump Ship!" turn to page* 222.**

Genesis 49:33
And when Jacob had made an end of commanding his sons, he gathered up his feet into the bed, and yielded up the ghost, and was gathered unto his people.

Jacob let go of his spirit, and was gathered unto his people. We will all be gathered unto our people. The only question is: Who are your people? Who are the people with whom you're most comfortable? They're the ones with whom you'll spend eternity.

Sometimes people say, "Hell won't be so bad. At least all my friends will be there." But nothing could be further from the truth. No one will be playing poker with his buddies and listening to country music in hell. No, hell is completely dark and totally hot. In hell, everyone is isolated.

Why would a loving God send anyone to a place like that?

He doesn't.

God being Light, he who doesn't want God in his life gets darkness. God being Love, he who doesn't want God in his life gets hate. God being a Father, he who doesn't want God in his life will be an orphan—alone for all eternity. God being the Wellspring of joy and Source of happiness, he who doesn't want God in his life will experience nothing but drought and depression. The person in hell isn't there because God wants to torture him. He's there because he doesn't want God in his life.

"Please reconsider," God says. "If you choose to kick Me, step on Me, and turn your back on Me, I will give you that option. But the only way I'll let you go is over My dead body. You'll have to walk over the body of My Son."

THE SECRET OF A SATISFIED LIFE

A Topical Study of GENESIS 49:22

What is the secret of a satisfied, successful life? Rabbis and ministers, gurus and philosophers throughout history have attempted to answer this question. The Bible, however, gives us the answer very succinctly, for in Revelation 4:11, we read this:

> *Thou art worthy, O Lord, to receive glory and honour and power: for thou hast created all things, and for thy pleasure they are and were created.*
>
> Revelation 4:11

That's the key. All things were created to please God—including you and me. That is why the first component of the Westminster Catechism states that the chief end of man is to glorify God and to enjoy Him forever.

If we exist to bring pleasure to God, the question then becomes, "How?"

"Herein is My Father glorified:" Jesus said directly, "That you bear much fruit" (John 15:8). Thus, when you bear fruit, you glorify the Father. And when you glorify the Father, you fulfill the very reason for your existence.

And that brings us to our text. At the end of his life, Jacob draws his attention—and ours—to his son, Joseph . . .

The Reality of His Fruitfulness

Joseph is a fruitful bough . . . Genesis 49:22 (a)

The Bible defines fruit in five specific areas . . .

In Romans 1:13, Paul tells us that the winning of souls is fruit unto God. Did Joseph win souls? Indeed! He saved his whole family from famine and drought. So, when you share with your family, neighbors, or friends the Good News of the gospel, saving them from the drought in their own souls and from the fires of hell, you bear fruit that pleases God.

Romans 6:22 identifies holiness as fruit. Perhaps best epitomized by his flight from the advances of Potiphar's wife, Joseph lived a holy life. In fact, he is one of only two major Old Testament characters of whom there is no recorded sin.

Philippians 4:17 identifies tithes and offerings as fruit. Joseph gave more than money in Egypt. He gave his life.

Colossians 1:10 says good works are a fruit unto God. Did Joseph do good works? Yes. He saved an entire nation from starvation by storing up goods to distribute when there was need.

Hebrews 13:15 names praise as fruit. When Joseph came to Pharaoh with the interpretation of Pharaoh's dream, he directed all praise to God (Genesis 41:16).

These five areas, so evident in Joseph's life, are summed up in a sixth New Testament reference to fruit:

But the fruit of the Spirit is love, joy, peace, longsuffering, gentleness, goodness, faith, meekness, temperance: against such there is no law. Galatians 5:22, 23

The fruit of the Spirit is love as defined by joy, peace, longsuffering, gentleness, goodness, faith, meekness, and self-control. The fruit of the Spirit is love. That's why we give of our money. That's why we lift our hands in praise. That's why we share with others.

With all of these qualities flowing through his life, no wonder Jacob said to Joseph, "You are a fruitful bough."

"Good for Joseph," you might be saying. "But why should I be fruitful?"

Turn to Mark 11 . . .

And on the morrow, when they were come from Bethany, he was hungry: And seeing a fig tree afar off having leaves, he came, if haply he might find any thing thereon: and when he came to it, he found nothing but leaves; for the time of figs was not yet. And Jesus answered and said unto it, No man eat fruit of thee hereafter for ever. And his disciples heard it. And in the morning, as they passed by, they saw the fig tree dried up from the roots.

Mark 11:12–14, 20

Why should we be fruitful? Because if we don't satisfy Jesus, not only will we not satisfy anyone else, but we won't satisfy even ourselves. Jesus went out of His way to teach a powerful lesson in cursing the fig tree, saying, "Whatever doesn't satisfy Me will satisfy no one."

Listen, gang, if you are not living to please God, then your life will dry up from the roots, from below the surface, from deep within—and you will experience emptiness, frustration, depression, and a lack of satisfaction.

The Reason for His Fruitfulness

Joseph is a fruitful bough, even a fruitful bough by a well . . . Genesis 49:22 (a)

Blessed is the man that walketh not in the counsel of the ungodly, nor standeth in the way of sinners, nor sitteth in the seat of the scornful. But his delight is in the law of the Lord*; and in his law doth he meditate day and night. And*

> *he shall be like a tree planted by the rivers of water, that bringeth forth his fruit in his season; his leaf also shall not wither; and whatsoever he doeth shall prosper.* Psalm 1:1–3

> *I am the true vine, and my Father is the husbandman. Every branch in me that beareth not fruit he taketh away . . .* John 15:1, 2 (a)

The Greek word translated "taketh away" is *airo*— the same word John uses when he says "Jesus *lifted up* His eyes at the tomb of Lazarus" (John 11:41). *Airo* is always used in Scripture to mean "lift up." Therefore, in Jesus' analogy, the husbandman would *lift up* the branch which didn't bear fruit because the branches on the grape vine would sometimes grow heavy, fall to the ground, and get stuck in the mud. And that's just what Jesus does with us. When we're in the mud, He lifts us up.

> *. . . and every branch that beareth fruit, he purgeth it, that it may bring forth more fruit. Now ye are clean through the word which I have spoken unto you.* John 15:2 (b), 3

The Greek word translated "purge" is *kathairo,* from which we get our word "catharsis." *Kathairo* means "to wash, to clean." Again, in the analogy, the vinedresser would come by and wash the mud off the branch that had fallen to the ground. To amplify this, Jesus says, "You are lifted up, washed off by the water of the Word." The key is the Word.

> *If ye abide in me, and my words abide in you, ye shall ask what ye will, and it shall be done unto you. Herein is my Father glorified, that ye bear much fruit; so shall ye be my disciples.* John 15:7, 8

Like Joseph, whose roots went into the well, if the Word abides in you, you'll bring forth much fruit.

> If I went out to my backyard, cut off a limb from the apple tree and said, "Great news, kids: You no longer need to go outside to pick apples. Here's a branch we're going to keep right in the kitchen"—they would wonder about me!
>
> "You can't cut off a branch and have it bear fruit," they'd say. "It has to be connected to the tree."

It's as if Jesus says, "The sap of the Scriptures must flow from Me to you in order for there to be fruit in your life."

As I observe the apple tree bring forth apples, never once have I seen the branches connected to the trunk struggling to bear fruit. Not once. The branches just hang there. They abide, and the fruit is produced naturally. You might decide to be loving, to do good works or to praise the Lord in your own energy. And you might be able to fake it for an hour or two, for a day or three—but ultimately you'll come up empty. The only way to produce genuine fruit morning by morning and day by day is to hang in there, abide in Christ, and allow the Spirit to flow to you and through you. Fruit cannot be faked for very long. You've got to have the Word in your life.

The Results of His Fruitfulness

> *Joseph is a fruitful bough, even a fruitful bough by a well; whose branches run over the wall . . .* Genesis 49:22 (a)

So fruitful was Joseph that even the next-door neighbors—all of Egypt—were able to glean from his life. When we are fruitful, not only are we fulfilled, but our fruit extends over our own boundaries and spills over to our neighbors, coworkers, friends, and family.

The key to satisfaction is so simple: Be a fruit-bearer. In so doing, your life will be prosperous without question. Let the Word abide in you. Have devotions every morning. Read the Word every evening. Get involved in Bible studies. Let the Word of God fill you up. Plant yourself by the well of the water of the Word.

God will be glorified.
Others will be edified.
And you will be satisfied.

DON'T SHOOT BACK

A Topical Study of GENESIS 49:24

Someone recently handed me this list entitled, "A Few Thoughts to Ponder. . . ."

- Do vegetarians eat animal crackers?
- Why isn't phonetic spelled the way it sounds?
- On a flight from Portland to Chicago, why are there flotation devices under the seats instead of parachutes?
- Why are cigarettes sold at gas stations when smoking is prohibited there?
- How does the guy who drives the snowplow get to work?
- If nothing sticks to Teflon, how does Teflon stick to the pan?
- If you are driving at the speed of light and turn on your headlights, what happens?
- Why are Braille dots on the keypad of the drive-up ATM?

- Why don't sheep shrink in the rain?
- What does Geronimo scream when he jumps out of a plane?
- If con is the opposite of pro, is congress the opposite of progress?
- Why are there interstate highways in Hawaii?

I have one more thought to add to the list . . .

How does one measure the strength of a man?

I'm convinced the strength of a man can be measured by what he doesn't do with the power he possesses. In our text, we see this principle clearly portrayed.

Joseph was a successful man, a strong man, a spiritual man. He was, really, a super man. A man of whom there is no recorded sin, Joseph was one who walked closely to the Lord, and had total confidence in the Lord. But in our text, we also note that being one with a big calling and a big future made Joseph a big target—for the archers were out to get him.

To me, archery is a coward's way of attacking a person. Archers hide behind a bush and wait. Then, when their victim is a few hundred feet away, they fire from a safe distance. Throughout his life, there was no shortage of such archers who took potshots at Joseph . . .

- He was shot at by his brothers because they were envious.
- He was shot at by Potiphar's wife because he was righteous.
- He was shot at by the butler who was thankless.

Joseph's brothers fired the arrow of envy; Potiphar's wife, the arrow of fury, and the butler, the arrow of apathy. Wherever Joseph went, there would be those who would view him as a target and let their arrows fly.

But what did Joseph do when he was shot at?

When he came into power, he could have nailed them all. He could have pinned his brothers to the wall, put Mrs. Potiphar in her place, and done in the butler. He had the power, the opportunity, the legal right. But he didn't fire back. He didn't defend himself. His bow abode in strength. His bow remained silent.

Why didn't Joseph fire back?

According to our text, Joseph's God kept him from grabbing his bow and letting the arrows fly. Joseph's God kept Joseph's hand in His.

It was 1968, the "Summer of Love," and our family, along with the Jones family, decided to check out the scene at Haight Ashbury. While there, we discovered that San Francisco wasn't all flowers and peace. There was also lots of violence and danger, long since forgotten these days. As we walked down the street, one of the hippies looked at Anita Jones and made a lewd remark to her. Her brother, my buddy Bill—who was eighteen years old and a tackle on his high school football team—hearing the remark to his sister, immediately clenched his fist and was ready to let it fly right in the guy's face. At that moment, my dad grabbed Bill's fist mid-air and stopped it instantly. The big tackle was stopped mid-punch by a banker. I saw Bill a few months ago—and to this day, he says, "Your dad was one strong guy!"

So it was with God the Father who prevented Joseph from letting his arrows fly. And that's the key. You see, I can't control the tendency to want to defend myself, to retaliate, to get revenge. When I hear or see things I feel are unfair or untrue, everything within me says, "Fire back. Clear the record. Straighten it out."

Thus, the only way to refrain from this tendency is to say, "Father, I want to stand up for my reputation, my right, my point of view. Restrain me, Lord."

Why shouldn't you clear the air and fire back for what you think is right?

Because those who find fault with you, those who come against you, those who shoot at you from a distance are ultimately instruments of God for your growth and for your good. You see, it was his brothers, Potiphar's wife, and the butler who were used by the Lord to create in Joseph character, strength, and a depth he would not have had if he hadn't been shot at, or if he had fired back.

I'm reminded of another man who was shot at unfairly. His name was David . . .

> Jealous of him, Saul grabbed a javelin and threw it at David while David played his harp. David ducked, and the spear lodged in the wall. Young, strong, and athletic, David could have easily grabbed the spear and thrown it right back at Saul. And the people of Israel most likely would have applauded him. But he didn't. Instead, David simply returned the next day and played for Saul once again.
>
> A second time, anger boiling within Saul caused him to throw the spear. David ducked again, and didn't fire back. After this happened a third time, David got the point and left. Later, accompanied by 3,000 soldiers, Saul chased him all the way to the caves of En Gedi.
>
> When David happened upon Saul asleep in one of the caves, his men said, "This is your chance, David! God has delivered Saul into your hand. Chop off his head!" And David did indeed unsheath his sword—but only to cut off a small piece of Saul's robe.
>
> When Saul later awoke, David waved the piece of material, and called to him, saying, "Although I had the chance to lop off your head, I didn't."
>
> But Scripture records that David's heart "smote him." "I shouldn't have done even that," he said. "I shouldn't have touched the Lord's anointed" (1 Samuel 24:5, 10).

David knew something—namely that Saul was the anointed instrument in God's hand to make him into the man God wanted him to be. No wonder David went on to greatness. No wonder David became the sweet psalmist of Israel. No wonder he was a man after God's own heart.

Years later, after his son launched an insurrection against him, we see David again running for his life. As he does, a little pipsqueak of a man throws stones at him, calling him a bloody man because of what David had done to Uriah the Hittite.

"Why should this dead dog curse you?" asked David's general. "Let me chop off his head."

"Leave him alone," David said. "God has allowed him to say these things to do a work in me. Let it be" (2 Samuel 16).

If, like David, you go to work on Monday and when you're put down, misunderstood, or wrongly accused, you say, "God has allowed this to make me humble before Him and totally dependent upon Him,"—like David, you will grow immensely in your understanding of Him.

Unfortunately, there's no way to be humble without being humiliated. I wish there was. I wish I could go to a humble seminar, or take a humble pill. But humility and humiliation go hand in hand. David knew this, and that's why "his bow abode in strength." Don't fire back, gang. Don't defend yourself, for once you do, that's all you'll ever do. Straightening the record, ironing out the falsehoods will become your full-time job.

"Stand still," said the prophet, "and see the salvation of the Lord . . ."

> The Amonites and Moabites were attacking the people of Judah.
>
> "You're surrounded by your enemies," God said. "Here's what you're to do: Don't send the soldiers; don't send the chariots; don't send your defenders into battle. Send the choir."
>
> Jehoshaphat did just that. And so confused were his enemies by seeing a choir instead of an army and hearing praise to the Lord instead of a battle cry that they unsheathed their swords and attacked each other—leaving nothing more for Jehoshaphat and his boys to do but pick up the spoils (2 Chronicles 20).

The secret of strength is to refrain from using the power you have, to keep from trying to outmaneuver your enemy intellectually or retaliating physically, to let the Lord fight for you and do a work within you.

Will you be a more satisfied person if you don't fire back?

Yep.

Will God stand up for you if you don't become your own defense attorney?

Yep.

Will you see good things happen in your character if you let the Shimeis in your life throw stones?

Yep.

How, then, do we do this?

By doing what Jesus did. They shot at Him not just with an ordinary bow, but with a Cross-bow. Jesus was able to go to the Cross and absorb the arrows shot in His direction because the night before He had prayed, "Father, not My will, but

Thine be done." And because Jesus had talked to the Father, He was able to say of His enemies, "Father, forgive them for they know not what they do."

If I want to be like Joseph, like David, like Jesus, I first must talk to the Father and surrender to Him my tendency to want to fire back at those who fire at me. After I talk to the Father, I then need to pray for my enemy. If I talk to my Father, and pray for my persecutor, then, like Jesus, like David, like Joseph, I, too, will be "made strong by the hands of the mighty God of Jacob."

DON'T JUMP SHIP!

A Topical Study of GENESIS 49:31

He was young, single, footloose—and looking for a wife. Arriving in Padanaram, he found a group of shepherds milling around a well. Industrious by nature, Jacob couldn't understand this—until he saw a beautiful shepherdess approaching, bringing her flock with her. Immediately, Jacob flexed his muscles, single-handedly removed the stone that covered the well, and gallantly said, "Come and water your flock." She did; he kissed her; and then he cried aloud, for she had smitten his heart.

When Jacob discovered this beautiful maiden was the daughter of his uncle, he went to her father and said, "I want to marry your daughter."

"Okay," said Laban. "Work for me for seven years, and I'll give her to you."

Jacob agreed, and the Bible says it seemed to him but a few days because of the great love he had for her.

The big night finally came. Jacob took his beloved bride—veiled from head to toe according to Jewish tradition—to his tent where they consummated the marriage. The next morning, when Jacob opened his eyes, he couldn't believe what he saw. It wasn't Rachel he had married—it was her older sister, Leah. Jacob stormed out of the tent, found Laban and said, "You tricked me!"

"I'm sorry, Jacob," his uncle said, "but we have a custom that the older daughter must marry before the younger daughter. But I'll tell you what I'll do. Work seven more years, and you can marry Rachel."

Now, if anyone ever had a right to say, "I got tricked—I want out," it was Jacob. "Listen, Leah," he could have said, "I realize we went through the ceremony, but I didn't know who you were. I'm in love with Rachel. So I'm out of here."

But that's not what Jacob did. He agreed to Laban's proposal, and thus ended up with both Leah and Rachel as his wives.

Time passed. Between Leah, Rachel, and their handmaidens, Jacob fathered twelve sons, who became, of course, the Twelve Tribes of Israel. Giving birth to the youngest, Rachel died, and Jacob buried this one about whom he was so passionate in Canaan. Years later, Leah died, and Jacob buried her in the Promised Land, in a place called Machpelah.

In our text, Jacob gathers his twelve sons around him, and, after blessing each one, he says, "I am going the way of my fathers. When I die, bury me in—" Now, I would have thought he would have said, "Canaan. Bury me by the love of my life. Bury me by Rachel."

But that's not what he said.

He said, "Bury me at Machpelah—by Leah."

Why did he say that? I suggest it was because, at the end of his life, Jacob realized that what he thought was a trick, a gyp, unfair, was in reality the biggest blessing in his life because from Leah—not Rachel—came Judah. And from Judah came the Messiah, Jesus Christ.

Wife, you might look at the man next to you and say, "I was tricked. He's not the man I thought he would be." Husband, you might look at the woman you married, and say, "She's not the passion of my life. I didn't know she would turn out this way." But if you jump ship, know this—if you bail out, understand this: You will miss the blessing of the birthing of Jesus in a supernatural, incredible, wonderful way because there are no tricks in the life of a child of God.

Employee, you might look at your boss and say, "When I signed that contract, I didn't know he would be such a jerk. I don't care what I signed. I'm going to find a legal loophole. I'm jumping ship." But when you initially put pen to paper and signed your name, your Father was there. And to the child of God, there are no tricks.

Teenager, you might look at your parents and say, "I was tricked. I must have been switched at birth. God couldn't have chosen *these* people to raise me." But know this: You are not only their child—you are a child of the King. He, in wisdom, handpicked them for you, and God makes no mistakes.

I think of our brother Paul . . .

After jumping through legal hoops in Caesarea, he was finally sailing towards Rome to plead his case before Caesar. En route, a storm arose which threatened the lives of the two hundred and seventy-five soldiers, sailors, and fellow-prisoners on board with him. After the crew readied a lifeboat in order that they alone might escape the inevitable crashing of the ship against the rocks, Paul, the little rabbi who was a tentmaker by trade and a prisoner by decree, said, "Except ye abide in the ship, ye cannot be saved" (Acts 27:31).

"If you jump ship, you'll lose your life," Paul said. And the centurion on board—knowing how tempting it would be for the sailors to bail out, to jump ship, to give up—ordered the soldiers to cut the lines so there would be no possibility of escape.

There are times—maybe you're in one right now—when the wind howls, the waves rise, and you find yourself thinking,

> "I can't take this marriage one more day."
> "I can't take this job one more hour."
> "I can't take my parents one more minute."

Or maybe you're saying, "haven't jumped ship yet. I've only lowered a lifeboat over the side. I'll give it three more weeks, or two more months, or one more year."

The problem with that is, if you keep an escape option open in your mind, I guarantee you will end up using it. Think about divorce, and you'll jump ship. Think about changing jobs, and you'll bail out. Think about leaving home, and you'll never see His reality.

Get rid of the lifeboats.

Cut the lines.

"It's easy for you to pontificate," you say. "But you don't know the storm I'm in. You don't know how vehemently the wind is blowing, how violently the waves are pounding. You just don't understand."

You're right. I don't.

But there is One who does . . .

> In 1902, a fire broke out which flared up rapidly in the home of an elderly woman. Asleep in the upstairs bedroom was her grandson, who she tried to rescue before she died in the process. Someone outside heard the screams of the five-year-old boy, however, and found a way to climb hand-over-hand up a drainpipe until he made it to the roof, broke through a window, and pulled the boy to safety.
>
> This story, which appeared in the *St. Louis Globe Herald*, generated quite a bit of interest in the orphaned boy. During the hearings that followed, a schoolteacher came forward and gave reasons why he felt he should be appointed the boy's guardian. So did a wealthy businessman, a minister, and several other upstanding people of the community. The boy, however, looked down and never raised his eyes—until a man came through the back door of the courtroom, walked up to him, and opened his hands. With one look at the badly blistered hands of the stranger, the boy jumped into his arms, saying, "This will be my dad."

I'm asking you to look at the hands of the One who loves you so much that He absorbed the heat of hell to pull you out of eternal destruction. I'm asking you to listen to this One who says, "Trust Me. Don't jump ship, or all will be lost."

Precious people, Jesus will come in a way that will blow your mind if you don't jump ship. Ignore what the sailors of society are saying about breaking commitments, bailing out, giving up. Cut the ropes. Let the lifeboats crash in the sea below.

Stay on board, and, like Jacob, you'll look back and see that the blessing was in Leah all along.

50

Genesis 50:1–3
And Joseph fell upon his father's face, and wept upon him, and kissed him. And Joseph commanded his servants the physicians to embalm his father: and the physicians embalmed Israel. And forty days were fulfilled for him; for so are fulfilled the days of those which are embalmed: and the Egyptians mourned for him threescore and ten days.

As Prime Minister of Egypt, Joseph orders the Egyptian physicians to embalm his father—a very sophisticated process that took forty days, and which to this day we don't fully understand.

Genesis 50:4–6
And when the days of his mourning were past, Joseph spake unto the house of Pharaoh, saying, If now I have found grace in your eyes, speak, I pray you, in the ears of Pharaoh, saying, My father made me swear, saying, Lo, I die: in my grave which I have digged for me in the land of Canaan, there shalt thou bury me. Now therefore let me go up, I pray thee, and bury my father, and I will come again. And Pharaoh said, Go up, and bury thy father, according as he made thee swear.

Joseph expresses his desire to fulfill the request of his father to be buried in Hebron—a request Pharaoh grants.

Genesis 50:7–9
And Joseph went up to bury his father: and with him went up all the servants of Pharaoh, the elders of his house, and all the elders of the land of Egypt, And all the house of Joseph, and his brethren, and his father's house: only their little ones, and their flocks, and their herds, they left in the land of Goshen. And there went up with him both chariots and horsemen: and it was a very great company.

Consisting of Egyptian dignitaries, chariots, horsemen, and soldiers, along with Jacob's family members, it was a great host which made its way to Canaan.

Genesis 50:10, 11
And they came to the threshingfloor of Atad, which is beyond Jordan, and there they mourned with a great and very sore lamentation: and he made a mourning for his father seven days. And when the inhabitants of the land, the Canaanites, saw the mourning in the floor of Atad, they said, This is a grievous mourning to the Egyptians: wherefore the name of it was called Abel-mizraim, which is beyond Jordan.

Observing the week-long funeral given to Jacob, the Canaanites must have thought an important official was being buried in their midst. And in the eyes of the world, Jacob was indeed an important figure. But his importance in their eyes was all predicated upon his relationship to his son, Joseph.

Because Joseph is a picture of Jesus, the same is true of you and me. We are defined solely by our relationship with Him. Thus, whatever happens in our lives presently, and at the end of our lives ultimately will be based not on what we have or haven't done—but on our linkage to God's Son.

Genesis 50:12–15
And his sons did unto him according as he commanded them: For his sons carried him into the land of Canaan, and buried him in the cave of the field of Machpelah, which Abraham bought with the field for a possession of a buryingplace of Ephron the Hittite, before Mamre. And Joseph returned into Egypt, he, and his brethren, and all that went up with him to bury his father, after he had buried his father. And when Joseph's brethren saw that their father was dead, they said, Joseph will peradventure hate us, and will certainly requite us all the evil which we did unto him.

Oh, no! thought Joseph's brothers. *Now that Dad's dead, Joseph will get back at us for throwing him in the pit, for selling him into slavery.*

Genesis 50:16, 17 (a)
And they sent a messenger unto Joseph, saying, Thy father did command before he died, saying, So shall ye say unto Joseph, Forgive, I pray thee now, the trespass of thy brethren, and their sin; for they did unto thee evil: and now, we pray thee, forgive the trespass of the servants of the God of thy father . . .

"Before he died, Dad said you'd forgive us if we asked you to," Joseph's brothers said hopefully.

Genesis 50:17 (b)
And Joseph wept when they spake unto him.

Joseph cries. The word translated "wept" isn't the word for sobbing. It's the word for quiet weeping. Tears just rolled down his cheeks. His brothers didn't get it. They thought he was holding a grudge against them. They thought he was simply waiting for the right time to pounce on them. They thought he was angry with them, bitter towards them.

The same way, we often think of our Lord Jesus as keeping a record of our previous failures; that He must be getting tired of us, exhausted by us. But we are told that, like Joseph, Jesus wept . . .

"If you had only been here, our brother would not have died," cried Martha and Mary. "We told You he was sick. We sent You word—but You didn't come. And now he's dead." And Jesus wept. He knew what He would do. He knew He would bring Lazarus back to life. So it wasn't for Lazarus He wept. It was for the unbelief of Martha and Mary (John 11).

Jesus wept a second time when He said, "O Jerusalem, Jerusalem, I would gather you under My wing and nestle You close to My heart, but you wouldn't let Me" (Matthew 23:37).

If you're thinking, *I've botched it so many times that the Lord must be just about ready to throw in the towel with me*—you don't understand the heart of our Lord. It was for the man most in need, upon the man who couldn't handle things all that well, towards the man with the paralyzed hand that Jesus had compassion (Mark 3). So, if you are struggling tonight, barely able to hold things together—you are the very one for whom Jesus has the most compassion. The person who's not reaching out, not doing well, unable to handle life is the one for whom Jesus has special affection and on whom He has a laser-like focus.

Each of us has come limping into this place in one way or another. Each of us is struggling with something or another. Thus, Jesus would say to all of us, "No matter how withered it might be, stretch out your hand. Grab hold of Me. Receive from Me that which I long to give you."

No matter what pit you've dug, or what brother you've sold, our Greater than Joseph has washed away your sin with His own blood. Therefore, there is now no condemnation to you who are in Christ Jesus (Romans 8:1).

What can separate you from God's love?

Absolutely nothing (Romans 8:35–39).

Genesis 50:18, 19
And his brethren also went and fell down before his face; and they said, Behold, we be thy servants. And Joseph said unto them, Fear not: for am I in the place of God?

"I am not God," Joseph declared. What a wonderful day it is when we realize we don't have to judge people because we're not God.

What a great day it was for me when the Lord spoke to me early in my ministry, saying, "Jon, you love them and let Me judge them"—for prior to that time, I had it reversed!

At best, we only see through a glass darkly. That's why our judgments are so often wrong . . .

With spit running down his beard and his nails clawing the gates of a Philistine city, I would have written him off.

"What are you doing, David?" I would have said. "You killed Goliath, and now you're hanging out in his city? You're crazy!" (1 Samuel 21:13)

But when we read the rest of the story, we realize that, although everyone else would have written him off, at that very time, David was composing some of the most potent psalms ever penned.

Man looks on the outward appearance. Only God sees the heart. And Joseph knew this.

Genesis 50:20
But as for you, ye thought evil against me; but God meant it unto good, to bring to pass, as it is this day, to save much people alive.

"I know you meant evil when you threw me in the pit and sold me into slavery," Joseph said, "but it was all part of God's plan to get me to Egypt to save your lives."

Don't you love Joseph? Don't you desire a heart like his that says, "Whatever happens today, God is at work"?

Our Greater than Joseph would say, "Father, forgive them. They don't know what they're doing" (Luke 23:34).

Joseph says, "You meant it for evil, but God had a plan."

Genesis 50:21–23
Now therefore fear ye not: I will nourish you, and your little ones. And he comforted them, and spake kindly unto them. And Joseph dwelt in Egypt, he, and his father's house: and Joseph lived an hundred and ten years. And Joseph saw Ephraim's children of the third generation: the children also of

Machir the son of Manasseh were brought up upon Joseph's knees.

No longer Prime Minister, Joseph brought up his grandchildren on his knees in two ways: He bounced them on his knees, telling them stories of God's work. And he prayed for them on his knees that they would follow God all of their days.

If you are a grandparent, you have an opportunity for ministry like at no other time in your life. Be like Joseph. Scoop up your grandchildren physically and talk to them about God while bouncing them on your knee. And scoop them up spiritually as you pray for them continually.

Genesis 50:24, 25
And Joseph said unto his brethren, I die: and God will surely visit you, and bring you out of this land unto the land which he sware to Abraham, to Isaac, and to Jacob. And Joseph took an oath of the children of Israel, saying, God will surely visit you, and ye shall carry up my bones from hence.

All other Egyptian leaders built monuments and pyramids. Joseph had none of that. His one request was that his bones be carried back to the Promised Land. Hundreds of years passed, but finally the day came when Moses lead the Israelites out of Egypt. And as he did, he took the bones of Joseph with him (Exodus 13). The Egyptians must have wondered why. But Moses and the children of Israel knew they were a reminder of the promise that they would indeed return to the land which the Lord "sware to Abraham, Isaac, and Jacob," that the Lord would indeed bring them home.

Genesis 50:26
So Joseph died, being an hundred and ten years old: and they embalmed him, and he was put in a coffin in Egypt.

Thus ends Genesis. The book that began with creation ends with a coffin. The book that began in glory, ends in a grave. The book that began with the living God, ends with a dead man. The book that began with the brightness of heaven, ends with bones in Egypt.

Why?

It's the Holy Spirit's commentary on
the condition of man,
the repercussions of sin,
the need for a Savior.

Joseph is the most Christ-like man in the Bible, and yet we see him in a coffin. Although Satan said otherwise, God had said, "In the day you eat of the forbidden fruit, thou shalt surely die" (Genesis 2:17). Joseph was a very good man, but the fact is that *all* have sinned and come short of the glory of God, and that the wages of sin is death (Romans 3:23, 6:23).

Is there any way out? Is there any hope? Is there any plan?

Yes! We'll see God's redemptive plan unfold in Exodus. We'll not stay in a coffin in Egypt indefinitely, gang. We're going to heaven. We're on our way Home!

EXODUS

Background to Exodus

The theme of Genesis, the Book of Beginnings, is Creation. But because the apex of God's creation—man—sinned, and although it begins on a high note wherein we read of God declaring everything He created to be good (1:31), the last verse of Genesis ends on a low and tragic note. The book that begins with creation, ends with a coffin (50:26).

But that's not the end of the story, for in the book before us, God sees the condition of man and begins to work in a way that is heart-warming and mind-blowing. The Book of Exodus is the Book of Redemption, wherein we see God's heart is for us and that He has a plan to set us free. Exodus is a picture book of God's redemptive character, of His desire to set at liberty those who were enslaved by sin and stuck in a coffin in Egypt.

Between Genesis 50 and Exodus 1 is a time gap of approximately four hundred years—a time gap during which something quite amazing happens . . .

EXODUS

1 **Exodus 1:1–7**
Now these are the names of the children of Israel, which came into Egypt; every man and his household came with Jacob. Reuben, Simeon, Levi, and Judah, Issachar, Zebulun, and Benjamin, Dan, and Naphtali, Gad, and Asher. And all the souls that came out of the loins of Jacob were seventy souls: for Joseph was in Egypt already. And Joseph died, and all his brethren, and all that generation. And the children of Israel were fruitful, and increased abundantly, and multiplied, and waxed exceeding mighty; and the land was filled with them.

How fruitful were the children of Israel? The seventy souls who originally entered the land of Egypt in Genesis 50 numbered approximately three million in Exodus 1, four hundred years later.

Why were the children of Israel in Egypt?

Two reasons . . .

First, God planted His people in Egypt in order to prepare them for the Land of Promise. Safe and warm, Egypt was an "incubator" for Jacob's growing family.

Secondly, and equally important, God planted His people in Egypt to prepare the Promised Land for them. In Genesis 15, God told Abraham that, although his offspring would eventually number as many as the stars in the sky or the grains of sand on the seashore, they would also spend four generations—or four hundred years—in Egypt until the iniquity of the Amorites was full, until the sin of the Canaanites had risen to the place where He had no other option but to judge them. The sins of the Canaanites were horrific. They were a people who sacrificed their children and tortured each other. Yet in His incredible kindness and mercy, God gave them four hundred years to repent and turn from their sin. But they wouldn't. So, like a rabid dog, they had to be exterminated not only in order that others wouldn't be infected by their debauchery, but also that they might be put out of their own misery.

I camp on this point because the tendency for people who don't know this is to think God is cruel when they read His commands in the Book of Joshua to wipe out the Canaanites. Nothing, however, could be further from the truth. God is exceedingly kind, unspeakably patient. For four hundred years, He waited for the Canaanites to turn from their sin, to turn to Him. And now He's ready to see His people take over their land.

Exodus 1:8–11
Now there arose up a new king over Egypt, which knew not Joseph. And he said unto his people, Behold, the people of the children of Israel are more and mightier than we: Come on, let us deal wisely with them; lest they multiply, and it come to pass, that, when there falleth out any war, they join also unto our enemies, and fight against us, and so get them up out of the land. Therefore they did set over them taskmasters to afflict them with their burdens. And they built for Pharaoh treasure cities, Pithom and Raamses.

Seti I, the new king who arose up over Egypt, knew he had a problem: The Hittites to the north threatened his empire. Although in and of themselves they may not have posed a serious threat, Seti understood that were the Israelites living in his land to join forces with them, he would have a huge problem militarily. His solution was to enslave the Israelites, hoping that their enslavement would reduce their population.

Exodus 1:12 (a)
But the more they afflicted them, the more they multiplied and grew . . .

The historical reason for this affliction was the possibility of a Hittite invasion. But the spiritual reason behind it is the same reason Haman sought to destroy the Jews in the Book of Esther, why Herod sought to destroy them at the time of Jesus' birth, and why Hitler sought to do so in recent history. That is, Satan has always sought to destroy the Jews.

Why?

Because knowing that Messiah would come from the nation of Israel, Satan mistakenly believed that if he could destroy the Jews, he could thwart God's plan of redemption. Even after failing to prevent Jesus' First Coming, Satan continues to try to prevent Him from coming a second time to rule and reign from Jerusalem. Satan hates the Jewish people. There is no other explanation for history's continuing undercurrent of anti-Semitism.

In addition to a historical and spiritual reason for the affliction of God's people, there's also a practical reason. And it is for this reason that I have this verse underlined in my Bible. God allows His people to be afflicted because He knows the same thing Coach Dominguez knew. Coach Dominguez told us guards and tackles and centers on the Del Mar High School football team that the only way to increase our strength was to break down our muscles. And he was right. The foundational premise of weight training is that hard exercise allows a muscle to break down, eventually repairing itself stronger than it was before.

The same thing holds true spiritually. Because faith is a muscle that needs to be worked, if I am to grow in depth, in strength, in maturity, there's no other way than to go through testing, trial, and affliction. Therefore, when I feel like I'm breaking down, falling apart, caving in, if I listen, I'll hear the voice of the Ultimate Coach, Jesus, saying, "Trust Me. I know what I'm doing. These hard times are necessary to build your strength, to give you victory."

Exodus 1:12 (b)–14
. . . And they were grieved because of the children of Israel. And the Egyptians made the children of Israel to serve with rigour: And they made their lives bitter with hard bondage, in morter, and in brick, and in all manner of service in the field: all their service, wherein they made them serve, was with rigour.

In other words, the Egyptians cracked the whip on the Israelites.

Exodus 1:15, 16
And the king of Egypt spake to the Hebrew midwives, of which the name of the one was Shiphrah, and the name of the other Puah: And he said, When ye do the office of a midwife to the Hebrew women, and see them upon the stools; if it be a son, then ye shall kill him: but if it be a daughter, then she shall live.

Any male babies were to be executed immediately.

Exodus 1:17
But the midwives feared God, and did not as the king of Egypt commanded them, but saved the men children alive.

Because those in positions of authority are placed there by God, we are told to obey them (Romans 13:1–5). Shiphrah and Puah, however, refused to obey the command of the king because they feared God. Their example tells me that I'm to obey those in authority over me governmentally, spiritually, in my family—unless I'm told to violate what God has decreed I should do.

After beating Peter and John, the temple soldiers prohibited them from speaking in the name of Jesus. But because Jesus had told them to go into the world and preach the gospel, they said they were to obey God rather than man (Acts 5:29).

The injunction for us is clear. Yes, we are to submit to those in authority over us, realizing it is God who placed them in their position. But when their commands clearly violate the Word of God, like Peter and John, we are to obey God rather than man.

Exodus 1:18, 19
And the king of Egypt called for the midwives, and said unto them, Why have ye done this thing, and have saved the men children alive? And the midwives said unto Pharaoh, because the Hebrew women are not as the Egyptian women; for they are lively, and are delivered ere the midwives come in unto them.

"By the time we show up, the babies are already born," said Puah and Shiphrah.

Exodus 1:20, 21
Therefore God dealt well with the midwives: and the people multiplied, and waxed very mighty. And it came to pass, because the midwives feared God, that he made them houses.

Midwives were midwives because they were barren. But God blessed these midwives and gave them children of their own.

"Wait a minute," you protest. "Hadn't these women lied?"

Yes, but God blessed them anyway. It isn't that God approves of lying. Rather than focusing on the fault of these women, however, He sees that they feared Him, that they disobeyed Pharaoh and risked their own lives to do what was right in His sight.

God the Father has a way—not only with Shiphrah and Puah, but with you and me—of finding what is good, and celebrating that. Aren't you glad that God doesn't focus on our failings and shortcomings, but rather has a way of looking at us and approving the things which are excellent—just as Paul tells us we all should do (Philippians 1:10)? This doesn't mean God doesn't convict us of sin and call us to repent and change direction. But it does mean that our God is exceedingly kind. We might judge these women for lying. God, however, declares, "They did something good in My sight and I'm going to honor them."

Exodus 1:22
And Pharaoh charged all his people, saying, Every son that is born ye shall cast into the river, and every daughter ye shall save alive.

While we do not know the number of people who obeyed Pharaoh's command, in chapter 2, we'll see one woman who didn't.

2

Exodus 2:1–3
And there went a man of the house of Levi, and took to wife a daughter of Levi. And the woman conceived, and bare a son: and when she saw him that he was a goodly child, she hid him three months. And when she could not longer hide him, she took for him an ark of bulrushes, and daubed it with slime and with pitch, and put the child therein; and she laid it in the flags by the river's brink.

Jochabed, Moses' mother, was a woman of vision, for she saw that her son was "a goodly child." Not only was she a woman of vision, but she was a woman of the Word—for what else would explain her decision to place her son in the very river in which all other male babies his age were being drowned? My tendency would be to stay as far from the river as possible. But not Jochabed. Why? I suggest it was because she knew the story of another "goodly" man who was saved in a time of destruction and judgment. I suggest it was because she knew the story of Noah. You see, the Hebrew word translated "ark" in verse 3 is used only one other place in all of Scripture: in reference to Noah. Thus, I believe it was not mere coincidence that prodded Jochabed to fashion an ark and to line it with pitch, just as Noah had done (Genesis 6:14).

How I encourage you who are parents to follow the pattern of Jochabed. Ask God to give you a vision for your child. Even if others think he is ordinary or not all that special, in God's sight that child of yours has a wonderful, huge, important, unique calling. Ask God to show a portion of it to you. Secondly, immerse yourself in the Word. Believe in it, act on it in faith, and don't be surprised if, in so doing, like Jochabed, you raise a hero of the faith.

Exodus 2:4, 5 (a)
And his sister stood afar off, to wit what would be done to him. And the daughter of Pharaoh came down to wash herself at the river . . .

Josephus tells us Pharaoh's daughter, Thermutus, was his only child.

Exodus 2:5 (b), 6
. . . and her maidens walked along by the river's side; and when she saw the ark among the flags, she sent her maid to fetch it. And when she had opened it, she saw the child: and, behold, the babe wept. And she had compassion on him, and said, This is one of the Hebrews' children.

As Thermutus sees the baby crying, her heart goes out in compassion towards him.

Exodus 2:7–9
Then said his sister to Pharaoh's daughter, Shall I go and call to thee a nurse of the Hebrew women, that she may nurse the child for thee? And Pharaoh's daughter said to her, Go. And the maid went and called the child's mother. And Pharaoh's daughter said unto her, Take this child away, and nurse it for me, and I will give thee thy wages. And the woman took the child, and nursed it.

Isn't this a great story? I mean, here Jochabed is, nursing her own baby, and getting paid to do it. Not a bad deal! Does it pay to believe the Bible? Does it pay to have vision? Ask Jochabed!

Exodus 2:10
And the child grew, and she brought him unto Pharaoh's daughter, and he became her son. And she called his name Moses: and she said, Because I drew him out of the water.

Moses means "drawn out" or "drew."

Exodus 2:11 (a)
And it came to pass in those days, when Moses was grown, that he went out unto his brethren, and looked on their burdens . . .

Approximately forty years of age at this point, and most likely next in line to assume the throne of Egypt, Moses looked out on the burdens of his brethren, the Jewish people.

Exodus 2:11 (b)–14
. . . and he spied an Egyptian smiting an Hebrew, one of his brethren. he looked this way and that way, and when he saw that there was no man, he slew the Egyptian, and hid him in the sand. And when he went out the second day, behold, two men of the Hebrews strove together: and he said to him that did the wrong, Wherefore smitest thou thy fellow? And he said, Who made thee a prince and a judge over us? intendest thou to kill me, as thou killedst the Egyptian? And Moses feared, and said, Surely this thing is known.

At the prime of his life, Moses wanted to do something to help God. So, seeing an Egyptian beating one of his Hebrew brothers, he killed the Egyptian. But it backfired. Why? Because, although Moses wanted to be involved in service, and although he "looked this way and that way," he didn't look up to hear what God had to say.

Moses made a mistake I often make. That is, he ministered according to need rather than according to obedience. What's the Lord telling you to do? It's not a matter of looking this way and that way. It's a matter of looking up. On any given day, in any given situation, it's a matter of saying, "Lord what would *You* have me do?"

Exodus 2:15
Now when Pharaoh heard this thing, he sought to slay Moses. But Moses fled from the face of Pharaoh, and dwelt in the land of Midian: and he sat down by a well.

Because it was a capital offense for an Egyptian to kill another Egyptian, Pharaoh knew his empire would expect him to deal decisively with Moses' offense. Knowing this as well, Moses fled.

Exodus 2:16–20
Now the priest of Midian had seven daughters: and they came and drew water, and filled the troughs to water their father's flock. And the shepherds came and drove them away: but Moses stood up and helped them, and watered their flock. And when they came to Reuel their father, he said, How is it that ye are come so soon to day? And they said, An Egyptian delivered us out of the hand of the shepherds, and also drew water enough for us, and watered the flock. And he said unto his daughters, And where is he? why is it that ye have left the man? call him, that he may eat bread.

Perhaps it was as a somewhat weary father that Reuel, (later called Jethro), said, "Ladies, this is your golden opportunity! I've had you seven girls for years—and now a man shows up? Grab him!"

Exodus 2:21 (a)
And Moses was content to dwell with the man . . .

In Acts we read that not only was Moses "mighty in works"—which means he was a military hero—but that he was "full of the wisdom of Egypt." In other words, he was schooled in philosophy and astronomy, in science and history, in language and botany. And yet here he is in a desert with one man and his seven daughters. From Genesis 46:34, we know that in the eyes of the Egyptian, shepherds were an abomination. Therefore, the man who had been most respected was now utterly rejected.

And yet he was content.

According to Paul, contentment is precisely what you and I are to study (Philippians 4:11). "Learn to be content," he tells us, understanding that if we're not content where we are today, we'll not be content wherever we plan on going tomorrow.

If asked whether we're content right here, right now, most of us would answer, "Not yet—but I'm going to be tomorrow, next month, real soon, around the corner, coming up. Any day now, things will be perfect." Moses, however, wouldn't have answered this way, for he had learned the hugely important lesson of contentment.

Exodus 2:21 (b), 22
. . . and he gave Moses Zipporah his daughter. And she bare him a son, and he called his name Gershom: for he said, I have been a stranger in a strange land.

"I know I'm supposed to learn to be content," people say. "But how?"

I believe verse 21 tells us how: Be a Gershom. You see, *Gershom* means "stranger." Therefore, in naming his son Gershom, Moses, in essence, said, "I'm just passing through. This world is not my home."

Contentment is not hard to learn if you realize what you really long for is heaven. Once I understand that I'm just a stranger here, that I won't ever fit in, that I'm just passing through, I enjoy life because I'm not expecting the job, the car, the house, the relationship, or the bank account to do what those things can never do. If I am truly Gershom, I'll take a whole lot more things a whole lot less seriously, and, as a result, my life will be characterized by relaxation and joy.

Exodus 2:23–25
And it came to pass in process of time, that the king of Egypt died: and the children of Israel sighed by reason of the bondage, and they cried, and their cry came up unto God by reason of the bondage. And God heard their groaning, and God remembered his covenant with Abraham, with Isaac, and with Jacob. And God looked upon the children of Israel, and God had respect unto them.

When the children of Israel finally reached the point of crying to the Lord, as we'll see in chapter 3, things started happening; things started cooking; things started igniting—literally!

3

Exodus 3:1 (a)
Now Moses kept the flock of Jethro his father in law, the priest of Midian: and he led the flock to the backside of the desert . . .

It seems God often plants His people in the desert before He uses them . . .

Elijah was a man of the desert.

John the Baptist grew up in the desert regions of the Dead Sea in southern Israel.

Paul spent three years following his conversion in the deserts of Arabia.

John the Revelator was banished to the desert isle of Patmos.

Like you, I have gone through desert times, dry seasons when I have wondered, "Lord, where's Your presence and where's Your power?" But, as the years have gone by, I have come to understand that those desert times are imperative if I am to be one who is not dependant upon my feelings or my emotions. Desert seasons are essential for me to come to a place where I can say, "Lord, You promised You would be with me. You promised You would never leave me no matter how dry the times might be or how solitary the setting might seem. The fact of the matter is, Your Word has been given and You're teaching me to stand upon it rather than sinking in my own emotions."

Over the years, I have seen lots of talented people in all sorts of ministries fall away because their emotions, rather than the Word, dictated their walk. Emotions go up and down. Emotions are fickle. Emotions are affected by how our job is going, how our family is doing, how much pizza we had the previous evening. But because God wants us to be stable and solid, to walk by faith and not by feelings, He will put us into a desert place where we, like Moses, must learn to be content and say, "Lord, You've given me the promise of Your Word. And that is all I need."

Exodus 3:1 (b)
. . . and came to the mountain of God, even to Horeb.

Once a most respected man, now a most rejected man, Moses had logged time in the desert. And the work has taken root. Now God is about to move and make Himself known to him in a most amazing way . . .

Exodus 3:2 (a)
And the angel of the LORD appeared unto him in a flame of fire out of the midst of a bush . . .

I love the fact that when the Lord wanted to speak to Moses, He didn't use a strong oak tree, a stately pine tree, or a fragrant cedar tree—but a garden variety bush, just like me . . .

***For topical study of Exodus 3:2 entitled "Burning Bushes," turn to page* 235.**

Exodus 3:2 (b), 3
. . . and he looked, and, behold, the bush burned with fire, and the bush was not consumed. And Moses said, I will now turn aside, and see this great sight, why the bush is not burnt.

Would Moses have turned aside to study this situation—this interesting phenomenon of a bush burning but not being consumed—if he was in the city, if he was engaged in lots of activity, if he was in the palace of Pharaoh as he was forty years previously? I don't think so.

And now I see that the Lord places me in desert regions because it's only then that I have eyes to see and ears to hear that which He desires to tell me. When things are humming, active, and hectic, I believe I miss many of the key indicators God sends my way. So if you're in a desert place, a desert job, a desert marriage—rejoice, for it will give you opportunity to see the Lord in ways, to sense the Lord in ways that, if you were more active, more engaged, even more fulfilled you would miss.

Exodus 3:4
And when the LORD saw that he turned aside to see, God called unto him out of the midst of the bush, and said, Moses, Moses. And he said, Here am I.

"Why don't I hear from the Lord more?" we wonder. It could be because we're buzzing around with too much activity. It could be because things are going too smoothly. It could be that the Lord wants us to log in some desert times quite regularly—times when things seem lonely and dry. It was only when Moses turned to see the burning bush that God called his name. So, there's a bush burning in your desert, dear saint. And when the Lord sees that you're not on automatic pilot, that you're not running here, there, and everywhere, but that you've quieted yourself and you're in a place where you're curious about what He might say to you, He'll call your name as well.

Exodus 3:5
And he said, Draw not nigh hither: put off thy shoes from off thy feet, for the place whereon thou standest is holy ground.

"You are in a special spot, Moses," God said. "You're in My presence."

Exodus 3:6 (a)
Moreover he said, I am the God of thy father, the God of Abraham, the God of Isaac, and the God of Jacob . . .

Even in identifying Himself as the God of Abraham, the God of Isaac, and the God of Jacob, the trinity is seen.

Exodus 3:6 (b)
. . . And Moses hid his face; for he was afraid to look upon God.

In God's presence, Moses is acutely aware of his inadequacies, his fleshly tendencies, his unworthiness. Centuries later, Isaiah (Isaiah 6:5), and Peter (Luke 5:8) would be two others who would come to the same conclusion.

Exodus 3:7–10
And the LORD said, I have surely seen the affliction of my people which are in Egypt, and have heard their cry by reason of their taskmasters; for I know their sorrows; and I am come down to deliver them out of the hand of the Egyptians, and to bring them up out of that land unto a good land and a large, unto a land flowing with milk and honey; unto the place of the Canaanites, and the Hittites, and the Amorites, and the Perizzites, and the Hivites, and the Jebusites. Now therefore, behold, the cry of the children of Israel is come unto me: and I have

also seen the oppression wherewith the Egyptians oppress them. Come now therefore, and I will send thee unto Pharaoh, that thou mayest bring forth my people the children of Israel out of Egypt.

So eager was Moses to be used forty years earlier that he went out in his own strength and killed an Egyptian taskmaster who was beating one of his Jewish brothers. Now, however, as he has matured and grown in the desert region, in the days of dryness and boredom, humility has replaced impetuosity in the life of Moses.

Exodus 3:11
And Moses said unto God, Who am I, that I should go unto Pharaoh, and that I should bring forth the children of Israel out of Egypt?

"Who am I?" asked Moses. Forty years earlier, he would have said, "Here am I," or, "I'm your guy." But no longer. The self-confidence is gone. And in its place is a brokenness, a depth, a richness. Interesting. The most qualified men and women are often those who are the most reluctant to take the challenge, to respond to the call because they're aware of their own unworthiness and frailty.

Exodus 3:12
And he said, Certainly I will be with thee; and this shall be a token unto thee, that I have sent thee: When thou hast brought forth the people out of Egypt, ye shall serve God upon this mountain.

"You're going to see, Moses, that I certainly am with you," said God, "for the time will come when you and the entire congregation will worship Me at this very site." And indeed they would, for Mt. Horeb is also known as Mt. Sinai.

Exodus 3:13, 14
And Moses said unto God, Behold, when I come unto the children of Israel, and shall say unto them, The God of your fathers hath sent me unto you; and they shall say to me, What is his name? what shall I say unto them? And God said unto Moses, I AM THAT I AM: and he said, Thus shalt thou say unto the children of Israel, I AM hath sent me unto you.

Like "Mr. President" or "Your Highness," "God" is a title. Moses, here, is asking for more then God's title. He's asking for His Name, His Nature. Interestingly, the children of Israel never asked Moses what God's name was. God knew they wouldn't. And yet, honoring Moses' desire to know Him more intimately, He answered his request . . .

For topical study of Exodus 3:13 entitled "I AM . . . Whatever You Need," turn to page 238.

Exodus 3:15, 16
And God said moreover unto Moses, Thus shalt thou say unto the children of Israel, The LORD God of your fathers, the God of Abraham, the God of Isaac, and the God of Jacob, hath sent me unto you: this is my name for ever, and this is my memorial unto all generations. Go, and gather the elders of Israel together, and say unto them, the LORD God of your fathers, the God of Abraham, of Isaac, and of Jacob, appeared unto me, saying, I have surely visited you, and seen that which is done to you in Egypt:

"Surely I have visited you," God says. "I'm aware of what you're going through," He declares. "I know the cracking of the whips on your back, the unreasonable demands placed upon your shoulders. I have surely visited you."

God visited us in the Person of Jesus Christ. He continues to visit us—to chat with us, to comfort us, to cheer us, to give direction to us. There is no need for us to feel uncared for, untended, disenfranchised, forgotten, for God is the great Visitor.

Exodus 3:17, 18 (a)
And I have said, I will bring you up out of the affliction of Egypt unto the land of the Canaanites, and the Hittites, and the Amorites, and the Perizzites, and the Hivites, and the Jebusites, unto a land flowing with milk and honey. And they shall hearken to thy voice . . .

"When you communicate to My people that I have visited them, that I know their situation and have come to set them free, they'll listen to your voice," God promised Moses.

Exodus 3:18 (b)
. . . and thou shalt come, thou and the elders of Israel, unto the king of Egypt, and ye shall say unto him, The LORD God of the Hebrews hath met with us: and now let us go, we beseech thee, three days' journey into the wilderness, that we may sacrifice to the LORD our God.

Was it really God's intent to set His people free for only three days? No. But by denying even three days off—a reasonable vacation for people who had been performing slave labor for forty years—Pharaoh's obstinance and hard-heartedness would come to light.

Exodus 3:19–22
And I am sure that the king of Egypt will not let you go, no, not by a mighty hand. And I will stretch out my hand, and smite Egypt with all my wonders which I will do in the midst thereof: and after that he will let you go. And I will give this people favour in the sight of the Egyptians: and it shall come to pass, that, when ye go, ye shall not go empty: But every woman shall borrow of her neighbour, and of her that sojourneth in her house, jewels of silver, and jewels of gold, and raiment: and ye shall put them upon your sons, and upon your daughters; and ye shall spoil the Egyptians.

"At first, Pharaoh will say No. But when you finally leave, you'll leave enriched," God promised.

I can't help but think of Another who would not only set captives free, but would give gifts freely (Ephesians 4:8). Our Greater than Moses, Jesus Christ, did just that when He delivered us from Satan's dominion and gifted us through His Holy Spirit.

BURNING BUSHES

A Topical Study of EXODUS 3:2

Apart from Jesus, without a doubt, the greatest leader in world history would have to be the man who led a congregation of three million people for forty years across the desert from Egypt to the borders of the Promised Land. Moses had a task and he did it successfully. He did it remarkably. And when he died at the age of one hundred and twenty, Scripture tells us his sight wasn't dimmed; his strength wasn't diminished (Deuteronomy 34:7).

The life of this remarkable man can be divided into three forty-year segments. In his first forty years, Moses became somebody. Adopted by Rameses II, he was educated by the best scholars of Egypt, was a military hero, and was in line to become the next Pharaoh of the Egyptian empire.

The next forty years, however, Moses was a nobody—for at the age of forty, after killing an Egyptian taskmaster, he fled for his life to the desert.

In the text before us, we see God reaching out to Moses, causing his final forty years to be spent as a model for everybody.

I love the fact that when He wanted to bring Moses to the place of service and ministry, the Lord used a bush just like me . . .

The Lord Can Use Me

To speak to Moses, I would have thought the Lord would use a mighty oak tree strong and sturdy, or a majestic pine tree tall and stately, or a fragrant cedar smelling sweetly. But the Lord didn't use any of those. He used a bush. The Hebrew word translated "bush" is *cenah,* and literally refers to a thorny bush. According to botanists, thorns are basically aborted branches. That is, they should have been branches, but just didn't get that far. So here's this bush. It's common; it's prickly; and even its attempts at growing branches were too weak to amount to anything. In other words, it's just like me.

The Lord loves to use bushes like you and me . . .

> *For ye see your calling, brethren, how that not many wise men after the flesh, not many mighty, not many noble, are called: but God hath chosen the foolish things of the world to confound the wise; and God hath chosen the weak things of the world to confound the things which are mighty; and base things of the world, and things which are despised, hath God chosen, yea, and things which are not, to bring to nought things that are: that no flesh should glory in his presence.* 1 Corinthians 1:26–29

God chooses those who are bushes, those who are bush-league, those who feel bushed because when He uses a bush, all of the glory goes to Him.

> Paganini, the great violinist of a generation ago, did something amazing when, in a Viennese concert hall one evening, he walked on to the stage, violin in hand, and broke a string. He followed this by breaking a second string, then a third. With only one string remaining, Paganini nestled the violin under his chin and, for the next eighteen minutes, played magnificently. As the crowd rose to its feet in ovation, Paganini said, "One string and Paganini." And, realizing they had heard a true master, the crowd erupted in applause.

I might feel like I only have one string. I might feel strung-out, strung-along, or third-string. But the reality is, the Lord loves to use that which is weak, unimportant, unimpressive because then He, the Master Musician, gets the ovation, the glory, the adoration.

Why does God reserve all glory for Himself? Because He knows that if He shares His glory with you—if people look up to you, lean on me, become impressed with us, every one of us will ultimately disappoint them. Therefore, He says, "I alone will receive glory because I alone will never disappoint anyone who looks to Me, who trusts in Me, who leans on Me." Only God is solid and stable enough to see us through day after year after decade on through eternity. So He uses bushes, one-stringed violins, common people like you and me in order that He alone receives praise.

The Lord Is with Me

Here's Moses on the backside of the desert day after week after month after year. Decades go by. And then something happens. Among the many bushes in the wilderness, one burns brightly without being consumed, causing Moses to eventually realize that the Lord was with him.

Where is God tonight? He's in the bush sitting next to you.

"That prickly person?" you ask.

Yes. God is here in the person sitting next to you, in the person you're married to, in the person you work with.

"Wait a minute," you protest. "The Lord certainly can't speak through my husband, my parents, my boss. They're not on fire."

Oh, but there's what you need to see: the bush was not on fire. The fire was in the bush. You might think people around you aren't on fire. That may be true. But if they're believers, the fire is in them . . .

> Although Jesus did mighty works in Capernaum, there were those who scoffed and said, "We know him. He's the son of the carpenter. Aren't his brothers and sisters among us?" (Matthew 13). They thought He was the son of a carpenter, failing to realize He was the Son of the Creator.
>
> In Mark 6, the disciples are toiling; the waves are mounting; the wind is howling. And in the middle of the night, they see Someone walking towards them. A legend of the day said that right before fishermen drowned, they saw a spirit coming towards them. No wonder their fear was rising. "It's a ghost!" the disciples cried—until Jesus said, "Be of good cheer. It is I."
>
> As two disciples walked towards Emmaus, they were joined by One who asked them why they were so sad. "Are you a stranger here?" they asked incredulously, not recognizing it was Jesus Himself who walked beside them (Luke 24).
>
> Finding the tomb empty that Easter morning, Mary Magdalene wept. Seeing a Man she supposed to be the gardener, she said, "Sir, if you have moved the body, tell me where you have taken Him." But when the "gardener" answered and spoke her name, she recognized Him for who He was (John 20).

Jesus dwells with us in the carpenter's son—in those we think we know. He speaks to us through people that may frighten us as they dare to rattle the bars of our beliefs. He reaches out to us through strangers walking alongside us. He speaks to us through gardeners, through plumbers, through those who work beside and for us. Oh, they might not be on fire. But the fire is in them, and the Lord can use them as easily, as powerfully, as surprisingly as He can use a common, everyday bush like you.

Bushes burning in the desert are common. Lightning bolts strike them and they ignite. Nomads burn them to keep warm at night. Therefore, assuming lightning had struck the bush, or that it was simply the remnant of a campfire, Moses could have easily walked right by. But he didn't. He stopped long enough to notice this bush was different, that it was not being consumed.

The problem with too many of us too much of the time is that we don't stop long enough to ponder the bushes around us. We're usually in such a hurry that we don't take the time to say, "Maybe my dad has the Word of the Lord for me today. Maybe this stranger in my life is being used to speak to me in some way. Maybe my son has a word from the Lord for me this morning. I'd better investigate." I'm convinced we miss many things the Lord would say, many directions He would give, many blessings He would bestow because we hurriedly walk right by.

The Lord wants to guide, direct, and bless if we'll simply take the time to stop and check out the bush sitting right beside us. May we be those who have eyes that see, ears that hear, and feet that stop in order that we might receive illumination and warmth from the bushes surrounding us.

I AM . . . WHATEVER YOU NEED

A Topical Study of EXODUS 3:13

At the ripe old age of eighty, Moses was given a massive, monumental task to do. He was called by God to lead the children of Israel out of bondage and into Egypt to the Land of Promise. For the previous forty years, he had been on the backside of the desert, seemingly forsaken and forgotten. No wonder he said, "Lord, who am I? I'm eighty years old. I've been out of the loop for forty years. I've been out here in the desert for four decades. Lord, who am I?"

"Certainly I will be with thee," God answered. In other words, "The question isn't who are you, but Who's with you. And the answer is I AM."

Like Moses, we might say, "Who are we?"

And, as He said to Moses, the Lord would say to us, "The issue isn't who are you, but Who's with you."

Fifteen hundred years later, Jesus said to His disciples, "Go into the world and preach the gospel. Make disciples and baptize them in the name of the Father, Son, and Holy Spirit." Jesus commissioned His disciples to see people set free.

"Who are we to do this massive, monumental task?" they must have wondered.

But Jesus went on to say, "And lo, I am with you even to the end of the world" (Matthew 28:20). "It's not who are you, but Who's with you. *That's* the key."

After hearing the Lord is with him, Moses asks, "What shall I say Your name is?" Moses asks this question not for the sake of identification. He already knows Who this God is talking to him. God had already identified Himself in verse 6. So it wasn't a matter of identification. Nor was it a matter of conversation. Moses wasn't simply trying to make small talk—not with the lives of three million at stake.

Moses' question was neither for identification nor idle conversation. It was for the purpose of communication . . .

Communication

"I know You are the God of Abraham, Isaac, and Jacob. I know You are the Supreme Entity. Those are Your titles. But what's your *Name?*" Moses asked God.

When you know someone's name, you can communicate with him very effectively. For example, if you're in the parking lot of Wal-Mart and someone calls your name, your ears perk up in a way they never do when you hear, "Hey, bro," or "Hey dude."

I love it when I'm walking through town and someone calls out, "Pastor Jon!" If we both have time, rich fellowship is sure to take place right there. If, however, I'm walking through Jacksonville, and hear, "Jonny!"—it's even better, for I know it is a family member or long-time friend calling me.

So, too, Moses is asking God's name in order that he can communicate with Him more deeply, more intimately. It's as if he's saying, "Lord, if I'm going to lead three million people across the wilderness, I need to be able to reach You."

Revelation

Secondly, the name deals not only with communication, but, more importantly, with revelation. In Bible days, a person's name was an indication of his nature. That's why we're told to pray in Jesus' name. "If you ask anything in My name," He said, "I will do it" (John 14:14).

"In Jesus' name," is not merely a phrase to tack on to the end of your prayers, like "over and out." No, praying in Jesus' name means praying according to His nature, praying in harmony with His heart, praying as He would pray if He were in our situation. So in asking God's name, Moses in essence is saying, "What's Your nature?" And God, for the first time, here in Exodus 3, identifies His name as literally, I AM THAT I AM.

The *tetragrammaton*—the pronunciation of which we don't know to this day. You see, because the Jewish people felt God's name to be so holy that it should only be spoken by the high priest once each year, they abbreviated in their scrolls to YHWH. Whenever you read the word LORD in the Old Testament, it's the tetragrammaton, YHWH. What is the pronunciation of YHWH? Although the high priest knew, it was eventually lost. For years, people pronounced it Jehovah. In the last few decades, it's been pronounced Yahweh. But no one knows for sure because the vowels were left out. Moses, however, knew. Moses knew God's name. Why? The answer is simple: He asked.

"I AM . . . what?" Moses may have wondered.

"I AM whatever you have need of," God must have intimated. "Moses you're on a journey. The task before you is huge and you want to know who I am. I AM whatever you need. Not I USED TO BE, not I'M GONNA BE, but I AM presently. Immutable. Unchangeable. The same yesterday, today, and forever. Rock-solid. I AM. That's My name I AM whatever you need."

Fifteen hundred years later, Jesus would shed further light on God's name by declaring,

I AM the Bread.
I AM the Way.
I AM the Truth.
I AM the Life.
I AM the Light of the world.
I AM the Good Shepherd.
I AM the Door.
I AM the Vine.

Jesus took the name of God and filled in the blank.

"Show us the Father," said Philip.

"He that has seen Me has seen the Father," Jesus answered (John 14:9). No wonder two hundred armed soldiers seeking to arrest Jesus fell down backwards upon hearing His irrefutable declaration of Deity, upon hearing Him say, "I am He," or, literally, "I AM."

For many years, I didn't fully understand this and thought Jesus was not I AM but I GIVE, as in "I give bread, deliverance, strength, healing." Now I understand that He's infinitely more than that. We think we need bread, healing, deliverance, companionship. In actuality, however, we're craving Jesus. It's not something He gives us, but who He will be for us step by step, day by day.

If you face a monumental task—raising your son, being the wife you're supposed to be, shining for the Lord in a dark jobsite, just physically or financially making it through the week ahead—understand that Jesus is your I AM, that He is the Bread which satisfies and strengthens you, the Shepherd who laid down His life for you. He wants to whisper His name in your ear, to write His nature on your heart in a way that others may not understand or even be able to pronounce. But it will be as personal and powerful to you as it was to Moses.

The issue tonight isn't loneliness or cancer, finances or relationships. The issue is a revelation of the nature and presence of God the Father. He will be all you need and He'll make Himself known to you personally.

All you have to do is ask.

4

Exodus 4:1
And Moses answered and said, But, behold, they will not believe me, nor hearken unto my voice: for they will say, the LORD hath not appeared unto thee.

In verse 13 of chapter 3, God had told Moses the people would listen to him. Here, Moses tells God the people won't listen to him. It's one thing to be humble. But here Moses crosses the line. And in the upcoming chapters we'll see him argue with God seven times, saying, "This can't be. It's not going to happen. You got the wrong guy."

Exodus 4:2
And the LORD said unto him, What is that in thine hand? And he said, a rod.

To those who say, "I can't be used. If I try to serve in some way, the people won't respond; if I try to be used at work or in Sunday school, in my neighborhood or in my family, no one will listen; if I try to pray with my wife, she won't receive from me; that's for other guys not me," God gives the same three tools He gave to Moses . . .

The first is *ability.*

"What's in your hand?" God asked Moses.
"A shepherd's rod," Moses answered.
"That's what I'll use," said God.

"What's in your hand, Paul?"
"A pen. I'm a scholar."
"I'll use that," said God. "You will write a great portion of My Word."

"What's in your hand, Peter?"
"A net. I'm a fisherman."
"I'll use that," said God. "You will be a fisher of men and haul people into the kingdom."

If you wonder how you can serve God, how you can be used by Him, take a look at what's in your hand. God gave you gifts when you were born simply waiting to be activated when you were born again. You're already doing that which He will energize and empower for ministry. What's in your hand? A computer? A hammer? A basketball? That's what He will use for His glory.

Exodus 4:3
And he said, Cast it on the ground. And he cast it on the ground, and it became a serpent; and Moses fled from before it.

You may be an accountant, a carpenter, or a surgeon. God says, "Throw down your occupation, your profession and see what it is in and of itself: It's a snake. If you're living for it, if you're all caught up in it, if you're depending on it, you will be bitten by it." The same holds true—maybe *especially* true—with regard to ministry. Moses had been a faithful shepherd for forty years. Here, God makes it clear that nothing could compare to an empty hand lifted and open to Him. It's as if, at the outset of the monumental ministry to which He was calling Moses, God said, "*I* must be your passion—not service for Me, not your talents or abilities, not your spiritual gifts. Nothing must take the place of an open hand, an open heart to embrace Me personally."

Maybe you've been forced to throw down some skill, some calling, some position you were good at, gifted for. Don't despise this, for now you can say, "Lord, now that I don't have that in my hand anymore, I'm rediscovering it's not doing something for You that I crave, but simply You. I'm not looking for an opportunity to exercise my gift or to be used in ministry. I'm just looking for more intimacy with You. No wonder it had to be pried out of my hand. I get it. It's a snake." And once you understand this, you're in a position to pick it up once again . . .

Exodus 4:4, 5
And the LORD said unto Moses, Put forth thine hand, and take it by the tail. And he put forth his hand, and caught it, and it became a rod in his hand: That they may believe that the LORD God of their fathers, the God of Abraham, the God of Isaac, and the God of Jacob, hath appeared unto thee.

To avoid getting bitten, the wisest thing to do is to grab a snake by the back of the head. God, however, tells Moses to grab it by the tail as if to say, "Now that you see that ministry is not the priority, pick it up again, only this time by the tail. It's not going to have priority in your life. It's not going to be the thing that drives you. No longer will it be the head. It will be the tail."

Exodus 4:6–8
And the LORD said furthermore unto him, Put now thine hand into thy bosom. And he put his hand into his bosom: and when he took it out, behold, his hand was leprous as snow. And he said, Put thine hand into thy bosom again. And he put his hand into his bosom again; and plucked it out of his bosom, and, behold, it was turned again as his other flesh. And it shall come to pass, if they will not believe thee, neither hearken to the voice of the first sign, that they will believe the voice of the latter sign.

The second tool God gave Moses was *a testimony.* Leprosy is a picture of sin in Scripture. Therefore, the illustration of a leprous hand made whole is one of being born again. What God has done in each of our lives is a powerful tool in ministry. Share your story. Share your testimony. It's powerful and cannot be denied.

Exodus 4:9
And it shall come to pass, if they will not believe also these two signs, neither hearken unto thy voice, that thou shalt take of the water of the river, and pour it upon the dry land: and the water which thou takest out of the river shall become blood upon the dry land.

The third tool God gave Moses was *authority.* He was to pour water from the Nile River—the river that sustained the entire Egyptian Empire—on the ground, where it would become blood. And in so doing, the people would see that no matter how "cool" they might seem, no matter how refreshing their surroundings might be, apart from God, even their best efforts at life were doomed to die.

With regard to ministry, never underestimate the power of telling the truth directly, of saying, "The path you're on will lead to death. But here's what God has done: He died on the Cross that you might live. The water you're drinking will lead to death. But if you drink of Jesus, the Water of Life, you will never thirst again."

Regarding ministry, a lot of people have gifts, callings, and good intentions. But they never get to the root issue. They never directly address a family member, neighbor, relative, or friend with the message of, "That which you're drinking will kill you. You need to be born again." When is the last time you truly shared the message of the Cross with a non-believer? As good as simply being nice to people, helping them out, making them feel loved, welcomed, or affirmed might be, they can't hold a candle to the power of the Cross. There is nothing as powerful as a clear, simple presentation of the Cross. God told Moses that if the people didn't believe his ability, that if they doubted his testimony, when he showed them the blood, they would understand that what they were drinking was death.

Exodus 4:10
And Moses said unto the LORD, O my Lord, I am not eloquent, neither heretofore, nor since thou hast spoken unto thy servant: but I am slow of speech, and of a slow tongue.

A "slow tongue" implies Moses may have had some type of speech impediment.

Exodus 4:11, 12
And the LORD said unto him, Who hath made man's mouth? or who maketh the dumb, or deaf, or the seeing, or the blind? have not I the LORD? Now therefore go, and I will be with thy mouth, and teach thee what thou shalt say.

One of the great evangelists of all time and founder of the YMCA, D. L. Moody was very impacting but not very polished. A woman came to him after one service and said, "Mr. Moody, I noticed in your message that you made eighteen grammatical mistakes."

"Ma'am," Moody replied, "I'm using all the grammar I got for the Lord. What are you doing with yours?"

God loves to use the foolish things of the world to confound the wise. He loves to use those who stutter spiritually, who don't have perhaps the greatest skills or the most talent because that way, He gets the glory (1 Corinthians 2:1).

Exodus 4:13
And he said, O my Lord, send, I pray thee, by the hand of him whom thou wilt send.

Forty years earlier, Moses was an eager beaver. But now he's in a whole different place, saying, "I'm not your man. I'm not the guy who can do the job. Send someone more qualified than I am, someone more capable than I am, someone worthier than I am."

Exodus 4:14 (a)
And the anger of the LORD was kindled against Moses . . .

One of the very few times in Scripture we see God's anger kindled, it was toward Moses, a man who doubted His call. Sometimes people say, "I just feel burnt out. Church has become a drag. I don't have a desire to pray. Spiritual things seem to have gone up in smoke. Why?" It's very likely that, in a sense, the anger of the Lord is kindled against you because, like Moses, you have doubted what He has called you to do.

Exodus 4:14 (b)–16
. . . and he said, Is not Aaron the Levite thy brother? I know that he can speak well. And also, behold, he cometh forth to meet thee: and when he seeth thee, he will be glad in his heart. And thou shalt speak unto him, and put words in his mouth: and I will be with thy mouth, and with his mouth, and will teach you what ye shall do. And he shall be thy spokesman unto the people: and he shall be, even he shall be to thee instead of a mouth, and thou shalt be to him instead of God.

The Lord is angry with Moses, but He doesn't give up on Moses. He simply expands His call to include Aaron as Moses' mouthpiece. I'm so thankful that the gifts and calling of God are without repentance (Romans 11:29). Perhaps you're like me. Perhaps you've waffled and wavered a time or two. Maybe you've been intimidated by the task you know you ought to do, the opportunity placed before you, the people who live beside you. But the Lord didn't give up on Moses. And He won't give up on you.

Exodus 4:17, 18
And thou shalt take this rod in thine hand, wherewith thou shalt do signs. And Moses went and returned to Jethro his father in law, and said unto him, Let me go, I pray thee, and return unto my brethren which are in Egypt, and see whether they be yet alive. And Jethro said to Moses, Go in peace.

Here we see an eighty-year-old Moses asking his father-in-law's permission to move. I like that, for it speaks of a humble heart and a submitted life. Here was this man who at one time was the Number Two power in all of Egypt. Here was the one who had it all together. Here was one who was called by God to lead a mighty move. And yet he still shows incredible humility and submission even at the age of eighty. I admire that tremendously.

Exodus 4:19
And the LORD said unto Moses in Midian, Go, return into Egypt: for all the men are dead which sought thy life.

Moses outlived the men who were out to get him. There will be people who are out to get you, some one or some group who doesn't like you, some who might want to destroy you. Here is what to do: Outlive them. "Oh, no," I used to worry, "this person thinks that," or, "the other guy is saying this." But over the years, I've learned that if I just keep doing what God has called me to do, I "outlive" them because they move on.

"By their fruit ye shall know them," Jesus said (Matthew 7:20). The fruit of the Spirit produced in your life, the fruit borne in your ministry, in your family, in your walk personally is undeniable, irrefutable and will outlive any criticism unfairly hurled against you.

Exodus 4:20, 21
And Moses took his wife and his sons, and set them upon an ass, and he returned to the land of Egypt: and Moses took the rod of God in his hand. And the LORD said unto Moses, When thou goest to return into Egypt, see that thou do all those wonders before Pharaoh, which I have put in thine hand: but I will harden his heart, that he shall not let the people go.

Although the Lord is sending Moses to demand that Pharaoh let His people go, He makes it clear to Moses that He would harden Pharaoh's heart, knowing the confrontation would eventually prove to the entire Egyptian culture that He alone is the true and living God.

It's a dangerous thing to harden your heart against God because if you persist in that mentality, God will eventually agree with you. "All manner of sin but one is forgiven all men," Jesus said, referring to the blasphemy of the Holy Spirit—when a man hardens his heart against the work of the Spirit drawing him to God (Matthew 12:31). Because God's Spirit won't always strive with us (Genesis 6:3), if you keep saying, "I don't want Jesus in my heart; I won't believe He is who He claimed to be; I absolutely refuse to submit to Him," God will say, "Have your way. I'll no longer speak to you." And at that point a decision to be saved is impossible.

Exodus 4:22, 23
And thou shalt say unto Pharaoh, Thus saith the LORD, Israel is my son, even my firstborn: And I say unto thee, Let my son go, that he may serve me: and if thou refuse to let him go, behold, I will slay thy son, even thy firstborn.

God's message to Pharaoh carried the death penalty for disobedience because God is deadly serious about sin. Yet, although we see two sons spoken of in this scenario, there are actually three . . .

Exodus 4:24
And it came to pass by the way in the inn, that the LORD met him, and sought to kill him.

"Let My Son go," God said to Pharaoh, "or your son will die." Two sons are being talked about, but there are three sons in the story, for Moses had a son as well. And Moses couldn't pronounce judgment on Pharaoh's house while his own house was in error (1 Peter 4:17). You see, in Genesis 17:11, God instituted circumcision as an outward sign of an inward belief—its counterpart seen in the New Testament ordinance of baptism (Colossians 2:11, 12). Circumcision was given to the Jewish nation as a mark of differentiation between them and every other culture round about them. Yet Moses never circumcised his son. A descendant of Abraham, Moses certainly knew the significance of this act. Why, then, wouldn't he have circumcised Gershom?

It could be that he was preoccupied with his occupation. It could be that he was so into watching sheep that he forgot about the spiritual needs of his son. And before we wonder how watching sheep in the desert could be that consuming, we would do well to ask ourselves why we expend so much time and energy simply to make another sale, to get another client, to climb another step, to make another dollar? When we get to heaven, on the other side of eternity, we will surely say, "What was I thinking? Why did I take my career so seriously? Why wasn't I there for my son, helping him to grow in his walk with the Lord?"

Or perhaps the reason Moses didn't circumcise his son was a little more subtle. Perhaps it was because he was caught up in ministry. Listen carefully, Dad. There is no ministry in which you will ever be engaged that is more important, more fulfilling, more satisfying, gratifying, or thrilling than discipling your own children. God tapping you on the shoulder and saying three million people will listen to you would be incomparable to seeing your son or daughter discipled and trained. And lest you think your family isn't a big enough ministry for a man of your skills and abilities, consider this: Jesus, the perfect Man, the ultimate Minister, chose only twelve disciples into whom to pour His life. Therefore, one, two, or three kids are more than enough for even the best of us. Besides, by the time people come to me for counsel or help, they're already messed up. As a parent, however, you get your kids fresh from the oven, so to speak, as clean pieces of paper. And from day one you get to pray for them, love them, model God to them. It's an incredible opportunity.

Preoccupation with his occupation or a false understanding of ministry could have been factors in Moses' failure to circumcise his son. But I believe there is a third, more likely reason . . .

Exodus 4:25, 26
Then Zipporah took a sharp stone, and cut off the foreskin of her son, and cast it at his feet, and said, Surely a bloody husband art thou to me. So he let him go: then she said, A bloody husband thou art, because of the circumcision.

Moses' wife, *Zipporah,* whose name means "sparrow" was a Midianite. The language is clear she wasn't into the rite of circumcision. Therefore, I suggest Moses didn't circumcise his son because of pressure from his wife. And his capitulation nearly cost him his life.

"As for me and my house, we will serve the Lord," Joshua declared (Joshua 24:15). And he didn't ask Mrs. Joshua's permission. Because Moses failed to take a similar stand, in seeking to kill him, it's as if God is essentially saying, "Moses your life will be basically meaningless if you continue to neglect your primary ministry, your family."

Seeing the severity of the situation, Zipporah did something she wouldn't have had to do had Moses taken the leadership earlier. And his life was spared. But his wife walked away bitter.

The lesson for us? Hebrews 4:12 tells us the Word of God is quick and powerful and sharper than any two-edged sword. Therefore, it is the Word that deals with the flesh.

> And these words, which I command thee this day, shall be in thine heart: And thou shalt teach them diligently unto thy children, and shalt talk of them when thou sittest in thine house, and when thou walkest by the way, and when thou liest down, and when thou risest up.
>
> Deuteronomy 6:6, 7

Get the Word in your heart and share it with your children constantly. When you're driving together in the car, working together in the yard, playing together at the beach, you have opportunity to pour the Word into your children. It's the Word, the Word, the Word that cuts away the flesh. David put it this way: "How shall a young man cleanse his way? By taking heed to the Word" (Psalm 119:9).

Satan would whisper in your ears, "It's too late to tend to the flesh of your sons and daughters, your grandchildren, your family." No. It's never too late. Ask Zipporah, the one who saved the life of her husband. From this point on, take the sword of the Spirit—the Word of God —and apply it regularly, consistently in your family. Carve out time for family devotions, family prayer, and family discussion.

"But my kid's not into it," you say.

That's irrelevant. It's a matter of you saying, "We take time to eat together. We take time to vacation together. And we take time to honor the Lord together. I hope you're into it, but even if you're not, it's still going to happen because God said I am to teach my family constantly."

"But my teenage son is rebellious," you say.

Ah, but God searched throughout all eternity and said, "You're the one who can handle him."

No one who has kids, grandchildren, nephews, or nieces ever need long for a bigger ministry or more opportunity. If you never speak in tongues, do a miracle, or have a big evangelistic ministry, but if you have family devotions, this pastor will go to heaven a happy man because the action is with the church under your roof, the congregation God uniquely chose just for you.

Exodus 4:27–31
And the LORD said to Aaron, Go into the wilderness to meet Moses. And he went, and met him in the mount of God, and kissed him. And Moses told Aaron all the words of

the LORD who had sent him, and all the signs which he had commanded him. And Moses and Aaron went and gathered together all the elders of the children of Israel: And Aaron spake all the words which the LORD had spoken unto Moses, and did the signs in the sight of the people. And the people believed: and when they heard that the LORD had visited the children of Israel, and that he had looked upon their affliction, then they bowed their heads and worshipped.

The people heard how the Lord had visited them, that He knew and understood their affliction. We, too, have been visited by the Lord, for when the Word was made flesh and dwelt among us (John 1:14), God communicated everything He ever wanted to say to us perfectly in the Person of His Son (Hebrews 1:1, 2).

5

Exodus 5:1, 2(a)

And afterward Moses and Aaron went in, and told Pharaoh, Thus saith the Lord God of Israel, Let my people go, that they may hold a feast unto me in the wilderness. And Pharaoh said, Who is the Lord, that I should obey his voice to let Israel go?

Claiming to be a descendant of the sun, Pharaoh claimed Deity. As such, he refused to acknowledge a greater One than he lest he be required to submit to a greater authority.

> For the wrath of God is revealed from heaven against all ungodliness and unrighteousness of men, who hold the truth in unrighteousness;
>
> Romans 1:18

The Greek word translated "hold" in Romans 1:18 describes what sailors would do in purposefully sailing directly into the wind. That is, those who "hold the truth in unrighteousness" know the truth, but suppress it, determined not to go with the flow of what they know to be true. They feel the wind of the Spirit. They understand something of the truth. But they're determined to set their boat in the opposite direction and sail against what they know to be so. Such a man was Pharaoh.

Exodus 5:2 (b)

. . . I know not the LORD, neither will I let Israel go.

Revelation is directly linked to obedience. Pharaoh knew not the Lord solely because He had no intention of obeying Him.

Do you desire to be obedient to the Lord? If so, He will give revelation to you and will provide direction for you. But so good is our God that He will not give further revelation to us or further direction to us if we have not been obedient to that which He has already told us to do. Oftentimes, people say, "I just don't know what the Lord's plan or will for me is." And oftentimes, it's an issue of whether or not they've obeyed the last thing He told them to do.

The desk in my study is piled high with papers. My in-box is overflowing. The Lord is so good to us that He doesn't keep stacking up our spiritual in-boxes. He gives us one thing to do, one assignment, one memo, one piece of information, one directive. And then He waits until we do it before giving us another. "My burden is easy," He declared. "My load is light" (see Matthew 11:30). He gives us one thing to do. He doesn't overwhelm or overwork us.

Exodus 5:3

And they said, The God of the Hebrews hath met with us: let us go, we pray thee, three days' journey into the desert, and sacrifice unto the LORD our God; lest he fall upon us with pestilence, or with the sword.

Although it was God's intent to bring His people out of the land of Egypt and into the Land of Promise, they were first to offer sacrifice to Him. In denying even this simple request, however, the hardness of Pharaoh's heart would become clearly evident.

Exodus 5:4

And the king of Egypt said unto them, Wherefore do ye, Moses and Aaron, let the people from their works? get you unto your burdens.

"What are you doing, asking for three days off?" Pharaoh said, "Get back to work!"

Exodus 5:5–7

And Pharaoh said, Behold, the people of the land now are many, and ye make them rest from their burdens. And Pharaoh commanded the same day the taskmasters of the people, and their officers, saying, Ye shall no more give the people straw to make brick, as heretofore: let them go and gather straw for themselves.

Straw was an essential ingredient for making bricks. Nevertheless, Pharaoh decided that Moses' request for three days off was the last straw. Thus, the children of Israel would get no more.

Exodus 5:8
And the tale of the bricks, which they did make heretofore, ye shall lay upon them; ye shall not diminish ought thereof: for they be idle; therefore they cry, saying, Let us go and sacrifice to our God.

Although their straw was eliminated, the quota of bricks remained the same. Just how many bricks did the children of Israel make? Historical records indicate they made enough to build a wall ten feet high and five feet thick that would stretch from Seattle to New York City. That's a lot of bricks!

Exodus 5:9
Let there more work be laid upon the men, that they may labour therein; and let them not regard vain words.

Pharaoh referred to Moses' request to worship as "vain words," or a waste of time. And Pharaoh's mentality prevails to this day. "You don't have time for Communion. You don't have time for worship. You don't have time for devotions. There's work to do," our society barks.

Nowhere is this mindset seen more clearly than in Judas, the one who, observing Mary anoint Jesus with ointment which cost a year's salary, said, "That's a waste. That money could have been spent on the poor. That money could have been used to do some good work" (see John 12:4–6). Yet Jesus would later refer to Judas himself as "the son of perdition," or, literally, "the son of waste" because the biggest waste is that of wasting the opportunity to worship.

The moles in my backyard drive me crazy. To rid my yard of them, I've stuck a hose down their holes and flooded them for an hour at a time. I've tossed in little smoke bombs. I've stood vigilantly over their holes with shovel in hand—all to no avail. Then I read that in one night, a single mole will often dig 300 feet of tunnel. And, as my experience proves, the moles' efforts are not in vain—for even though they're digging under the surface where no one can see them—when the smoke bombs are thrown in or the water turned on, they can escape to their network of tunnels and bomb shelters.

That's exactly what the devotional life does for you and me. "What a waste of time staying up later or getting up earlier to study the Word. What a waste of time to go to church on a Thursday night," some might mutter. But that's because they fail to understand that those things are tunnels and bomb shelters that will protect you from the inevitable attacks of the enemy.

"Why couldn't we cast this demon out?" the disciples asked Jesus.

"This kind does not come out but by prayer and fasting," Jesus answered, (Matthew 17:21). In other words, we are to live a life of prayer and fasting, for if we wait to lay the spiritual groundwork until the challenge is before us, it will be too late. We won't be able to do what we could have done, to be who we might have been because there were no tunnels dug under the surface, in the dark, early in the morning and late at night.

Exodus 5:10–19
And the taskmasters of the people went out, and their officers, and they spake to the people, saying, Thus saith Pharaoh, I will not give you straw. Go ye, get you straw where ye can find it: yet not ought of your work shall be diminished. So the people were scattered. And the taskmasters hasted them, saying, Fulfil your works, your daily tasks, as when there was straw. And the officers of the children of Israel, which Pharaoh's taskmasters had set over them, were beaten, and demanded, Wherefore have ye not fulfilled your task in making brick both yesterday and to day, as heretofore? Then the officers of the children of Israel came and cried unto Pharaoh, saying, Wherefore dealest thou thus with thy servants? There is no straw given unto thy servants, and they say to us, Make brick: and, behold, thy servants are beaten; but the fault is in thine own people. But he said, Ye are idle, ye are idle: therefore ye say, Let us go and do sacrifice to the Lord. Go therefore now, and work; for there shall no straw be given you, yet shall ye deliver the tale of bricks. And the officers of the children of Israel did see that they were in evil case, after it was said, Ye shall not minish ought from your bricks of your daily task.

Although we sympathize with the children of Israel, we must make note of their mistake in crying to Pharaoh instead of calling out to God. Are you having a hard time at work? Is your boss cracking the whip? Is your supervisor loading you down? Are your coworkers demanding more of you than you think reasonable? Don't cry to your boss. Cry to the Lord first. Get direction from Him, for as the old hymn so rightly declares, "Oh, what peace we often forfeit, oh, what needless pain we bear, all because we do not carry everything to God in prayer."

This is so simple and we know it to be true. But I must be reminded of it over and over again. Maybe you do, too. It's so easy to cry to Pharaoh—to cry to a husband or wife, brother or sister, pastor or elder. It's easy to seek out people, when in reality, God would say, "Woe to the rebellious people who take counsel but not of Me" (Isaiah 30:1). Is the whip cracking? Is your back aching? Cry to the Lord.

Exodus 5:20, 21
And they met Moses and Aaron, who stood in the way, as they came forth from Pharaoh: And they said unto them, The LORD look upon you, and judge; because ye have made our savour to be abhorred in the eyes of Pharaoh, and in the eyes of his servants, to put a sword in their hand to slay us.

Because Pharaoh wouldn't help them, the children of Israel lashed out at Moses and Aaron.

Exodus 5:22, 23
And Moses returned unto the LORD, and said, Lord, wherefore hast thou so evil entreated this people? Why is it that thou hast sent me? For since I came to Pharaoh to speak in thy name, he hath done evil to this people; neither hast thou delivered thy people at all.

This is what made Moses great. We'll see him constantly falling on his face before the Lord. What a mighty man he was. And his secret was that, when people yelled at him, he didn't retaliate, but simply went before the Lord again and again.

6 **Exodus 6:1–5**
Then the LORD said unto Moses, Now shalt thou see what I will do to Pharaoh: for with a strong hand shall he let them go, and with a strong hand shall he drive them out of his land. And God spake unto Moses, and said unto him, I am the LORD: And I appeared unto Abraham, unto Isaac, and unto Jacob, by the name of God Almighty, but by my name JEHOVAH was I not known to them. And I have also established my covenant with them, to give them the land of Canaan, the land of their pilgrimage, wherein they were strangers. And I have also heard the groaning of the children of Israel, whom the Egyptians keep in bondage; and I have remembered my covenant.

This past week, I was reading an article describing a great revival which took place in Florida in the 1890s. As thousands of people were brought into the kingdom, reporters covering the story repeated an expression they heard the new believers use. They didn't say people were "born again." Nor did they say many people were saved. Nor did they say many people received Christ. Now, all of those things were true. People were indeed born again and were saved because they received Christ. But the phrase appearing most often in the written record was that people were "seized by a great affection." In other words, people were simply overwhelmed by the goodness and grace of God, swept up in His loving embrace. I like that!

In his epistle to the Romans, Paul tells us it is the *goodness* of God that leads men to repentance, which ushers people into the kingdom of God (2:4). After all, how could we not be "seized by a great affection" when we begin to understand what God has done for us? In the text before us, we'll see exactly what God does for His children not only historically, but presently . . .

Exodus 6:6 (a)
Wherefore say unto the children of Israel, I am the LORD, and I will bring you out from under the burdens of the Egyptians . . .

Salvation. Egypt is always an illustration of the world system, of the lost condition of man. "I will save you," God declares. "I will bring you out from there." And that's exactly what God did for you and me when He brought us out from under the burden of sin. Under the burning, blistering Egyptian sun, the children of Israel baked bricks that would be used to construct tombs for the Pharaohs. That was us as well—living meaningless lives, burdened by guilt, building our own tombs with our activities. But then God saved us. Great is the mystery, Paul would say, that God became a Man and dwelt among us in order that He might ultimately die for us (1 Timothy 3:16). Man's greatest need is forgiveness. God's greatest deed is salvation.

Exodus 6:6 (b)
. . . and I will rid you out of their bondage . . .

Liberation. God would not only remove His people from Egypt, but would rid them of their bondage. "The thing I have against you Christians is that you live such restricted lives," said a man to me at the YMCA.

"Not true," I said. "I drink as much as I want whenever I want. Not only that, I go to all the parties I want because the Bible says all things are lawful to me (1 Corinthians 6:12). So I get to do whatever I want."

It's true. I drink all I want to. And the amount I want to drink is none. While alcohol of any kind has always been as tempting to me as slug bait, even that which used to pull me no longer does because I'm absolutely free.

I've had many people tell me, "It's been two weeks, three months, or four years since I smoked. It's not that I made a pledge or a promise, but I've just been so into the Lord, so excited about walking with Him, that I forgot to light up." That's what God means when He says, "I will rid you out of their bondage."

Exodus 6:6 (c)
. . . and I will redeem you with a stretched out arm, and with great judgments:

Redemption. To the children of Israel, an outstretched arm referred to God's judgment against Pharaoh. To us, it refers to the outstretched arm of Jesus pinned to the Cross of Calvary, for that's what it would take to redeem us.

Exodus 6:7 (a)
And I will take you to me for a people, and I will be to you a God . . .

Adoption. "I will claim you as My family," God said to the children of Israel. Christ adoped us into His family, Paul tells us. And what a family it is. Oh, we're not perfect by any stretch. But we are being perfected. And as a result, we find in the family of God an agape love and a reality we find in no other place.

Exodus 6:7 (b)
. . . and ye shall know that I am the LORD your God, which bringeth you out from under the burdens of the Egyptians.

Revelation. "You will know Who I am. And you'll realize what I've done," God declares.

Exodus 6:8 (a)
And I will bring you in unto the land, concerning the which I did swear to give it to Abraham, to Isaac, and to Jacob . . .

Direction. "I will bring you into the land I told Abraham, Isaac, and Jacob about," God told His people—"the Promised Land, the place I prepared for you."

"I go to prepare a place for you," Jesus told us (John 14:2). If you're not a Christian, this world is the best it's ever going to be for you. But for those who know the Lord, this world is the worst it's ever going to be because it's only going to get better and better when we move into eternity.

Exodus 6:8 (b)
. . . and I will give it you for an heritage: I am the LORD.

Provision. "I will not only bring you into the Land of Promise," God declared, "but I will provide a heritage for your children." I have great news for you, Dad: God has a plan not only to direct you, but to direct your family—your children and grandchildren as well.

"Believe on the Lord Jesus Christ and thou shalt be saved and thy house," Paul told the Philippian jailer (Acts 16:31). In other words, "Your decision to believe will impact and affect your family."

In verses 4–8 we see seven "I wills," seven statements of promise made by God. The one thing we don't see is a single, "If you . . ." because such is the nature of the gospel. The gospel is the expression of God's furious love toward us. It's all about what He has done and nothing about what we must do. The gospel is nothing short of the best news the world has ever heard: Our sin is forgiven. The price is paid. The work is done.

About to be beheaded, when Paul wrote to his protegé Timothy, he didn't say, "Be strong in righteousness" or "Grow in your understanding of theology." No, as good as those things may be, Paul's final word to Timothy was, "Grow in *grace.*" The degree to which we understand that grace is not the beginning point but the only point, is the degree to which we'll find ourselves wanting to study, desiring to pray, eager to worship as grace does its work in our hearts day by day.

Exodus 6:9
And Moses spake so unto the children of Israel: but they hearkened not unto Moses for anguish of spirit, and for cruel bondage.

Even though they doubted because of their anguish of spirit, God still did what He said He would do for His people. Exactly as He said He would, He delivered them from Egypt and planted their descendants in the Land of Promise. You're going to get to heaven. You can either go celebrating or you can go doubting. I recommend being a Tigger instead of an Eeyore. Say, "Oh, Lord, thank You that You're going to bless me today, not because of what I do but because of Who You are and what You've done."

Exodus 6:10–13
And the LORD spake unto Moses, saying, Go in, speak unto Pharaoh king of Egypt, that he let the children of Israel go out of his land. And Moses spake before the LORD, say-

ing, Behold, the children of Israel have not hearkened unto me; how then shall Pharaoh hear me, who am of uncircumcised lips? And the Lord spake unto Moses and unto Aaron, and gave them a charge unto the children of Israel, and unto Pharaoh king of Egypt, to bring the children of Israel out of the land of Egypt.

Even though Moses is still saying, "Pharaoh's not going to listen to me. I'm not the right guy," God charges him again and says, "I've given you a job to do. You're to go to Pharaoh." And, as God's ambassadors, the genealogy of Moses and Aaron is presented as their credentials . . .

Exodus 6:14
These be the heads of their fathers' houses: The sons of Reuben the firstborn of Israel; Hanoch, and Pallu, Hezron, and Carmi: these be the families of Reuben.

Reuben was the firstborn son of Jacob. But he wasn't the one from whom Moses and Aaron came.

Exodus 6:15
And the sons of Simeon; Jemuel, and Jamin, and Ohad, and Jachin, and Zohar, and Shaul the son of a Canaanitish woman: these are the families of Simeon.

Simeon was Jacob's second son. But he wasn't the one who would bring forth Moses and Aaron.

Exodus 6:16–19
And these are the names of the sons of Levi according to their generations; Gershon, and Kohath, and Merari: and the years of the life of Levi were an hundred thirty and seven years. The sons of Gershon; Libni, and Shimi, according to their families. And the sons of Kohath; Amram, and Izhar, and Hebron, and Uzziel: and the years of the life of Kohath were an hundred thirty and three years. And the sons of Merari; Mahali and Mushi: these are the families of Levi according to their generations.

Levi, Jacob's third son, was the one whose lineage would bear Moses and Aaron.

Exodus 6:20
And Amram took him Jochebed his father's sister to wife; and she bare him Aaron and Moses: and the years of the life of Amram were an hundred and thirty and seven years.

Amram was the father, Jochebed the mother of Aaron and his younger brother, Moses.

Exodus 6:21–23
And the sons of Izhar; Korah, and Nepheg, and Zichri. And the sons of Uzziel; Mishael, and Elzaphan, and Zithri. And Aaron took him Elisheba, daughter of Amminadab, sister of Naashon, to wife; and she bare him Nadab, and Abihu, Eleazar, and Ithamar.

These four sons of Aaron will be germane to the story, as we shall see.

Exodus 6:24–27
And the sons of Korah; Assir, and Elkanah, and Abiasaph: these are the families of the Korhites. And Eleazar Aaron's son took him one of the daughters of Putiel to wife; and she bare him Phinehas: these are the heads of the fathers of the Levites according to their families. These are that Aaron and Moses, to whom the Lord said, Bring out the children of Israel from the land of Egypt according to their armies. These are they which spake to Pharaoh king of Egypt, to bring out the children of Israel from Egypt: these are that Moses and Aaron.

Just as Moses and Aaron were descendants of the third son of Jacob, the one sign the ultimate Ambassador, Jesus Christ, offered as His credential was that He would rise on the third day (John 2:19).

Exodus 6:28–30
And it came to pass on the day when the Lord spake unto Moses in the land of Egypt, That the Lord spake unto Moses, saying, I am the Lord: speak thou unto Pharaoh king of Egypt all that I say unto thee. And Moses said before the Lord, Behold, I am of uncircumcised lips, and how shall Pharaoh hearken unto me?

This is the seventh time Moses protests. Like Moses, we have a tendency to argue. But, again, God didn't give up on Moses. And He won't give up on you.

---

7 Ever have a day where everything seemed to unravel? Yesterday was like that for me. So when I walked in to my study to prepare for tonight, my mind was full of the disappointments and problems I had faced. But when I opened the Word to the passage before us, I realized my foolishness. Seeing the plagues that these people endured, I had no other choice but to bow my head and say, "Lord, forgive me. What a baby I've been."

Not only did the people in the Exodus account

face difficulties that dwarf my own, but the world is headed for an unspeakably trying time called the Tribulation. Described in Revelation 6 through 19, the Tribulation is the seven-year period when God will pour out His wrath upon the world that rejected His Son.

I tie the plagues of Exodus with the Tribulation of Revelation because there is a remarkable correlation between the two . . .

In both the Exodus and the Revelation accounts, the nation Israel is afflicted. In Exodus, they were oppressed by Pharaoh. In the Tribulation period, they will be oppressed by antichrist specifically and by the whole world generally.

In both cases, God's people cry out to God in desperation. And in both cases, God hears their cry (Exodus 2; Jeremiah 31:18–20).

In both accounts, God demands that the oppressor let His people go (Exodus 5; Isaiah 43). Interestingly, we're seeing this begin to happen even now. The population of the state of Israel is presently 5,987,000, which intrigues me because in the Holocaust of World War II—which created the climate for the nation to come into existence—six million Jews were killed. This present population of Israel is very close to six million, which speaks to me of what God declared when He said, "I will restore to you the years the locust has eaten" (Joel 2:25).

In the Exodus story, Pharaoh didn't want the Jews to go. So, in the Tribulation period, there will be this same tendency. But God will demand that His people be set free, and, again, we have a sneak preview of that happening right now. In the wake of the collapse of the Soviet Union, 66,000 Jews returned to the Promised Land. Of that number, 54,600, or 83% came from Russia, from the north. But because nearly 60% of those returning to Israel from Russia are physicians, college professors, academicians, musicians, and artists, there is presently a brain drain from Russia. That is why it is commonly believed that there will be a closing of the door in the north.

In the Exodus story, two witnesses—Moses and Aaron—are raised up to speak to Pharaoh. In Revelation 11, two witnesses—Moses and Elijah—give understanding on the streets of Jerusalem.

In the Exodus story, we see water turn to blood, boils on the people, frogs hopping throughout the land, darkness covering the nation, swarming flies, locusts, and hailstones causing great consternation. So, too, in the Tribulation, we see water turned to blood, locusts swarming, boils upon the people, frogs, and hailstones.

Pharaoh hardened his heart in the Exodus account. The people not killed by the plagues in the Tribulation will harden their hearts as well (Revelation 9:20, 21).

Yet in both cases, Israel is delivered. In Exodus, they eventually arrive in the Promised Land. Romans 11:25–26 tells us that, although Israel will go through the time of Jacob's trouble in the Tribulation, eventually all of Israel shall be saved. And if God keeps His promises to Israel, He will keep the promises He made to you and me as well.

Exodus 7:1–5

And the LORD said unto Moses, See, I have made thee a god to Pharaoh: and Aaron thy brother shall be thy prophet. Thou shalt speak all that I command thee: and Aaron thy brother shall speak unto Pharaoh, that he send the children of Israel out of his land. And I will harden Pharaoh's heart, and multiply my signs and my wonders in the land of Egypt. But Pharaoh shall not hearken unto you, that I may lay my hand upon Egypt, and bring forth mine armies, and my people the children of Israel, out of the land of Egypt by great judgments. And the Egyptians shall know that I am the LORD, when I stretch forth mine hand upon Egypt, and bring out the children of Israel from among them.

"Go speak to Pharaoh," God instructed Moses. "He won't listen to you, but that will give Me opportunity to stretch out My hand upon the land of Egypt. As a result, the entire nation will know that I am the Lord and that there is none like Me." Yes, there would be problems. Yes there would be tribulation. Yes, there would be difficulty—all of which would affect God's people as well. But it was all part of God's purpose and plan to not only provide liberation for His children, but to give revelation to the Egyptians.

"Lord, liberate me," we cry. "Set me free from the snap of the whips of the Egyptian oppressors. Set me free from the bondage of baking bricks under the desert sun."

"Gladly, for that's my intention," the Lord says. "But I am also doing something else simultaneously. You see, I want the Egyptians, the unsaved, the lost souls to see My power, to understand My reality. And for that to happen, there will be a series of problems which will affect you, too."

"I'm tired of my situation," we say. "My boss is mean. My trials are great. Why don't You set me free, Lord?"

"I will," He says, "in due season. Heaven's around the bend."

"But why do I have to endure this trial, Lord? Why can't You take this cancer away immediately? Don't You have that ability? Why can't You solve the problem today? Why can't You work now?"

And the Lord answers, "I've got two things I'm doing simultaneously. Yes, I'm bringing you into the Land of Promise. But at the same time, there are Egyptians watching carefully to see how you handle the same trials they face. I want them to see My power. I want them to see what I can do. I want to show them that I can see you through."

Seeing you win the Publisher's Clearinghouse Sweepstakes doesn't cause the Egyptian to scratch his head and say, "Wow." No, the Egyptian scratches his head when he sees you facing problems on the job, difficulties in the family, setbacks financially, difficulties physically—and yet walk through them victoriously. God never promised to protect us *from* problems. He promised to see us *through* them. And as He does, the neighbor, the coworker, brother, sister-in-law, or father say, "There's something about the way you navigate life that I can't do."

And then you can say, "It's the power and reality, the grace and goodness of God. And He's available to you, too."

It is such an obvious truth, but one so easily forgotten: God does not exist for me. It's a shock to remember and a hard thing for me to grasp, but God has a bigger plan than merely my comfort, a greater concern than simply my ease. "I'm taking you to the land of milk and honey," He tells us, "where every tear shall be wiped way, where every problem will be solved. But in the meantime, Egyptians need to see that I am the Lord. And that will happen when they see you make your way through deep waters because I am with you."

Exodus 7:6–12 (a)
And Moses and Aaron did as the LORD commanded them, so did they. And Moses was fourscore years old, and Aaron fourscore and three years old, when they spake unto Pharaoh. And the LORD spake unto Moses and unto Aaron, saying, When Pharaoh shall speak unto you, saying, Shew a miracle for you: then thou shalt say unto Aaron, Take thy rod, and cast it before Pharaoh, and it shall become a serpent. And Moses and Aaron went in unto Pharaoh, and they did so as the LORD had commanded: and Aaron cast down his rod before Pharaoh, and before his servants, and it became a serpent. Then Pharaoh also called the wise men and the sorcerers: now the magicians of Egypt, they also did in like manner with their enchantments. For they cast down every man his rod, and they became serpents . . .

Aaron cast down his rod and it became a snake. The magicians cast down their rods and they became snakes as well. Paul identifies these magicians as Jannes and Jambres, "men of corrupt minds, reprobate concerning the faith" (2 Timothy 3:8). How were they able to duplicate this miracle? By tapping into demonic, occultist power with which the Egyptian culture was very familiar.

Exodus 7:12 (b)
. . . but Aaron's rod swallowed up their rods.

I like that, don't you? Aaron's snake just got bigger and bigger as the magicians' snakes were scarfed up. "Go into all the world and preach the gospel," Jesus said, "and if you come across any serpents, they will not hurt you" (see Mark 16:18). As Paul put wood on a fire, when a snake in the sticks felt the heat, it fastened its fangs into his hand. Observing this, the natives decided Paul must be a murderer to deserve such a fate. But when they saw him shake the snake into the fire and feel no harm, they changed their minds about him and he was able to give a grand and powerful witness for Jesus Christ (Acts 28).

As believers, we are not free from attack, but we are immune from its effect. Snakes show up and they strike. But we can eat them up, shake them off, and not be beaten down. Even though the enemy was able to produce snakes, Aaron's rod ate them up.

Joshua and Caleb were among the group of twelve spies who spied out the Land of Promise. "The land is a glorious place," they said to the children of Israel upon their return.

"But there are giants there. And we're like grasshoppers in their sight," argued the other ten.

"No, God's with us and these guys will be bread for us. We can eat them up," countered Joshua and Caleb (Numbers 14:9).

But the people listened to the ten instead of the two and wandered for forty years.

After their entire generation died, Joshua and Caleb were at last allowed to enter the Land of Promise. When they arrived, a now eighty-five-year-old Caleb said, "Joshua, for my inheritance give me the land where the giants are."

Why would Caleb make such a request? Because he knew something about giants. He knew they were bread. And he was hungry. "Give me the challenges which challenge others," he said. "Give me the giants—and pass the butter."

Don't run away from challenges or obstacles, gang. Instead, say, "This is a chance for me, like Aaron's rod, to grow bigger and bigger. It's a way for me, like Caleb, to grow spiritually strong."

Exodus 7:13–21
And he hardened Pharaoh's heart, that he hearkened not unto them; as the LORD had said. And the LORD said unto Moses, Pharaoh's heart is hardened, he refuseth to let the people go. Get thee unto Pharaoh in the morning; lo, he goeth out unto the water; and thou shalt stand by the river's brink against he come; and the rod which was turned to a serpent shalt thou take in thine hand. And thou shalt say unto him, The LORD God of the Hebrews hath sent me unto thee, saying, Let my people go, that they may serve me in the wilderness: and, behold, hitherto thou wouldest not hear. Thus saith the LORD, In this thou shalt know that I am the LORD: behold, I will smite with the rod that is in mine hand upon the waters which are in the river, and they shall be turned to blood. And the fish that is in the river shall die, and the river shall stink; and the Egyptians shall lothe to drink of the water of the river. And the LORD spake unto Moses, Say unto Aaron, Take thy rod, and stretch out thine hand upon the waters of Egypt, upon their streams, upon their rivers, and upon their ponds, and upon all their pools of water, that they may become blood; and that there may be blood throughout all the land of Egypt, both in vessels of wood, and in vessels of stone. And Moses and Aaron did so, as the LORD commanded; and he lifted up the rod, and smote the waters that were in the river, in the sight of Pharaoh, and in the sight of his servants; and all the waters that were in the river were turned to blood. And the fish that was in the river died; and the river stank, and the Egyptians could not drink of the water of the river; and there was blood throughout all the land of Egypt.

In rivers and streams, ponds and puddles, in wooden buckets and stone jugs, blood was everywhere. Pop machines and water purifiers, swimming pools and garden hoses were all filled with blood. Pharaoh's magicians turned water into blood as well. But here's the question: Where did they get the water? The answer is, they had to dig for it. Real brilliant. The whole nation is dying of thirst and what do Pharaoh's magicians do? Turn the remaining water supply to blood. Satan, demons, and dark forces can, and do perform powerful feats. But in every case, their actions only make things worse. Satan never does anything, demons never do a single thing which make things better. They do not have that within them. Yes, they can make more snakes, more blood, more frogs—but all they do is multiply the difficulty.

People can truly tap into demonic power through psychic hotlines and astrology, ouija boards and tarot cards. But know this: they only make things worse. Demonic power never, ever under any circumstance, in any way proves to make things better. It only makes a bigger mess.

Exodus 7:22–25
And the magicians of Egypt did so with their enchantments: and Pharaoh's heart was hardened, neither did he hearken unto them; as the LORD had said. And Pharaoh turned and went into his house, neither did he set his heart to this also. And all the Egyptians digged round about the river for water to drink; for they could not drink of the water of the river. And seven days were fulfilled, after that the LORD had smitten the river.

For seven days, the land of Egypt was a bloody mess, just as for seven years, the Tribulation will produce a horrific, awful mess. Moses, the Lawgiver, turned water to blood. Jesus, the Lifegiver, turned water to wine. The Law was a schoolmaster to show us that we can't be religious, that even our best efforts at spirituality produce nothing more than death—death of peace, death of freedom, death of hope. But once we realize that, once we embrace Jesus as the One who pulls us out of the quicksand of sin and death, we are free to drink deeply of the wine of great, great joy.

8

Exodus 8:1–6
And the LORD spake unto Moses, Go unto Pharaoh, and say unto him, Thus saith the LORD, Let my people go, that they may serve me. And if thou refuse to let them go, behold, I will smite all thy borders with frogs: And the river shall bring forth frogs abundantly, which shall go up and come into thine house, and into thy bedchamber, and upon thy bed, and into the house of thy servants, and upon thy people, and into thine ovens, and into thy kneadingtroughs: And the frogs shall come up both on thee, and upon thy people, and upon all thy servants. And the LORD spake unto Moses, Say unto Aaron, Stretch forth thine hand with thy rod over the streams, over the rivers, and over the ponds, and cause frogs to come up

upon the land of Egypt. And Aaron stretched out his hand over the waters of Egypt; and the frogs came up, and covered the land of Egypt.

The Egyptians considered frogs to be sacred, as evidenced by the discovery of frog-shaped amulets in recent archeological digs in the Nile River region. One of their goddesses was Heqt, a fertility goddess whose face was frog-like. Not only did frogs speak of fertility to the Egyptians, but also of productivity, for it was frogs that kept the insect population from destroying the crops in the Nile River region. But that which was once a blessing to the Egyptians is about to become a burden. That which they once honored would become a horror. That which once pleased them is about to plague them.

And that's always the way it is with sin.

Exodus 8:7

And the magicians did so with their enchantments, and brought up frogs upon the land of Egypt.

As when they turned water to blood, Pharaoh's magicians were able to duplicate the miracle of the frogs, but were unable to eradicate the mess. All they did was make the situation worse.

Exodus 8:8, 9

Then Pharaoh called for Moses and Aaron, and said, Intreat the LORD, that he may take away the frogs from me, and from my people; and I will let the people go, that they may do sacrifice unto the LORD. And Moses said unto Pharaoh, Glory over me: when shall I intreat for thee, and for thy servants, and for thy people, to destroy the frogs from thee and thy houses, that they may remain in the river only?

"Ask your God to take the frogs away," Pharaoh begged Moses and Aaron.

"When do you want this to happen?" asked Moses.

Exodus 8:10 (a)

And he said, To morrow . . .

In what is arguably the most amazing answer ever given in all of Scripture, when Moses asked him when he wanted the frogs to go, Pharaoh didn't say "Immediately!" or, "Right away!" He said, "Tomorrow."

For topical study of Exodus 8:10 entitled "One More Night with the Frogs," turn to page 255.

Exodus 8:10 (b)–13

. . . And he said, Be it according to thy word: that thou mayest know that there is none like unto the LORD our God. And the frogs shall depart from thee, and from thy houses, and from thy servants, and from thy people; they shall remain in the river only. And Moses and Aaron went out from Pharaoh: and Moses cried unto the LORD because of the frogs which he had brought against Pharaoh. And the LORD did according to the word of Moses; and the frogs died out of the houses, out of the villages, and out of the fields.

Suddenly, in a moment of time, the Word was spoken and the frogs died immediately.

Exodus 8:14

And they gathered them together upon heaps: and the land stank.

Even though the frogs were dealt with by the word that was spoken, a stench remained. That's the problem with sin. It leaves a stench that lingers long after the sin has been dealt with. However, even the stench of a dead frog can serve a great purpose. When my kids see me make a mistake, when there's an undeniable smell of dead frog in the air, I challenge them to learn from my mistakes, to stand on my shoulders and do better when they assume positions of leadership in their families, and in their ministries.

Exodus 8:15

But when Pharaoh saw that there was respite, he hardened his heart, and hearkened not unto them; as the LORD had said.

Pharaoh was given a break. He was freed and released from the frogs. Yet did he glorify God and thank Him for His mercy? No. He hardened his heart.

A farmer was nailing shingles on the peak of his roof when he suddenly lost his footing. Sliding down the roof, headed for destruction, he said, "Lord, if You're there, save me and I'll give you my life." Just then, as he reached the edge of the roof and was about to plunge to his demise, his belt loop caught on a nail and halted his fall—at which point he looked up to heaven and said, "Never mind, Lord. The nail saved me."

Like the farmer, Pharaoh was blind to the goodness of God. On the other hand, seeing God's hand in everything, "coincidence" is not a word in the vocabulary of the believer.

Exodus 8:16–18 (a)
And the LORD said unto Moses, Say unto Aaron, Stretch out thy rod, and smite the dust of the land, that it may become lice throughout all the land of Egypt. And they did so; for Aaron stretched out his hand with his rod, and smote the dust of the earth, and it became lice in man, and in beast; all the dust of the land became lice throughout all the land of Egypt. And the magicians did so with their enchantments to bring forth lice, but they could not . . .

Due to their size and availability, producing lice would have been the easiest of all the plagues to duplicate. But Pharaoh's magicians couldn't. Always under the sovereign control of God, they had their day in the sun, but now they will disappear from the account.

Exodus 8:18 (b)
. . . so there were lice upon man, and upon beast.

So terrible a curse did the Egyptian nobles consider lice that they shaved their bodies every other day—which explains their Yul Brynner-like portrayal.

Exodus 8:19
Then the magicians said unto Pharaoh, This is the finger of God: and Pharaoh's heart was hardened, and he hearkened not unto them; as the LORD had said.

The last time we will see these magicians, they are saying, "This is the finger of God."

- It was the finger of God that wrote on the tablet of stone, "Thou shalt have no other gods before me" (Exodus 31:18).
- It was the finger of God that wrote on Belshazzar's wall, "You have been weighed in the balance and found wanting" (see Daniel 5:5).
- It was the finger of God that wrote in the dust, causing the accusers of the woman taken in adultery to drop the stones they would otherwise have hurled at her (John 8:6).

Thus, the finger of God either points at you in judgment or calls you to forgiveness and salvation. The choice is yours.

Exodus 8:20, 21
And the LORD said unto Moses, Rise up early in the morning, and stand before Pharaoh; lo, he cometh forth to the water; and say unto him, thus saith the LORD, Let my people go, that they may serve me. Else, if thou wilt not let my people go, behold, I will send swarms of flies upon thee, and upon thy servants, and upon thy people, and into thy houses: and the houses of the Egyptians shall be full of swarms of flies, and also the ground whereon they are.

Psalm 78:45 refers to these flies as those which tormented and destroyed the people.

Exodus 8:22
And I will sever in that day the land of Goshen, in which my people dwell, that no swarms of flies shall be there; to the end thou mayest know that I am the LORD in the midst of the earth.

The first "no-fly zone" was over the land of Goshen wherein dwelt the children of Israel.

Exodus 8:23, 24
And I will put a division between my people and thy people: to morrow shall this sign be. And the LORD did so; and there came a grievous swarm of flies into the house of Pharaoh, and into his servants' houses, and into all the land of Egypt: the land was corrupted by reason of the swarm of flies.

When the water turned to blood, when frogs and lice covered the land, Egyptian and Hebrew alike were affected. But when it came to flies, there was a division between Egyptian and Hebrew. In certain areas there remains a division between the believer and the unbeliever. I can tell you categorically tonight that I will never suffer from alcoholism because I don't drink alcohol and never will. Does this mean, however, that I can say I'll never have cancer, a bad back, or heart trouble? No. Certain curses are universal. Others we bring upon ourselves when we live like the world.

Exodus 8:25
And Pharaoh called for Moses and for Aaron, and said, Go ye, sacrifice to your God in the land.

Egypt being a picture of the world, Pharaoh was, in essence, saying, "Worship your God—but stay in the world."

Exodus 8:26, 27
And Moses said, It is not meet so to do; for we shall sacrifice the abomination of the Egyptians to the LORD our God: lo, shall we sacrifice the abomination of the Egyptians before their eyes, and will they not stone us? We will go three days' journey into the wilderness, and sacrifice to the LORD our God, as he shall command us.

Shepherds being an abomination to the Egyptians (Genesis 46:34), the sacrifice of lambs would have been so abhorrent to them that they would have stoned the children of Israel. The Egyptians' failure to understand the sacrifice of a lamb prefigured the world's inability to understand the sacrifice of the Lamb of God who had come to take away their sin.

Exodus 8:28
And Pharaoh said, I will let you go, that ye may sacrifice to the LORD your God in the wilderness; only ye shall not go very far away: intreat for me.

Although Pharaoh offered a compromise to Moses, Moses chose to singularly, wholeheartedly follow the Lord. And therein lies a key to success in the walk of faith, for the object is not to see how closely we can walk to the world and still call ourselves Christians, but to see how far we can distance ourselves from the world's mentality.

Exodus 8:29–32
And Moses said, Behold, I go out from thee, and I will intreat the LORD that the swarms of flies may depart from Pharaoh, from his servants, and from his people, to morrow: but let not Pharaoh deal deceitfully any more in not letting the people go to sacrifice to the LORD. And Moses went out from Pharaoh, and intreated the LORD. And the LORD did according to the word of Moses; and he removed the swarms of flies from Pharaoh, from his servants, and from his people; there remained not one. And Pharaoh hardened his heart at this time also, neither would he let the people go.

From this point on, the plagues will not affect the people of God. Therefore, take heart dear saint, for the effects of the curse which plague our planet will not torment us forever. We're on our way to the Promised Land, to the land flowing with milk and honey where every tear shall be wiped away for once, for all, forever.

ONE MORE NIGHT WITH THE FROGS

A Topical Study of EXODUS 8:10

"No problem," he told me. "So I smoke a little grass now and then? I've got tensions during the day, problems at home. And if I can just get away and smoke a bit, I can relax."

"We only drink socially," they say. "After all, we don't want to be left out of the office parties and civic functions our jobs require us to attend."

"I know he's not a Christian," she says. "But he's getting there. And I know if I keep dating him, one of these days, he'll come to church with me. Sure, he's a bit "froggy" right now. But soon, he'll turn into a prince. I just know he will."

Pharaoh, evidently, came to the same conclusion. The frogs covering his land were troublesome indeed, but nothing he couldn't live with for one more night.

There are twenty-five million alcoholics in America today. Yet I guarantee not one of them opened his first beer or poured her first glass of wine and said, "Today

I'm going to become one of the twenty-five million alcoholics." No, everyone said, "I've got it under control. No problem. It's not going to bother me." And we say the same thing concerning everything from a questionable relationship to a hot temper, from a propensity to lie to a curiosity about pornography—until suddenly we wake up one day and realize our houses, ovens, beds, and kneading troughs are filled with frogs; until suddenly we realize that what we once thought we had under control has hopped out of its riverbed and is, instead, controlling us.

Pharaoh came to the stark realization that the frogs which he once encouraged his people to worship, that the frogs he depended on to keep the insect population at bay, were out of control. "They've got to go, Moses," he insisted. Yet when Moses asked him when, he answered, "Tomorrow."

Amazing. I would have thought he would have said, "Get them out of here right now! Today! Immediately! Quickly! I can't stand them another minute." But that's not what Pharaoh said. He said, "Tomorrow." Why? He wanted one more night with the frogs. Oh, he knew they had to go—but not quite yet. Not right now.

There are activities, people, places in our lives about which the Lord says, "You thought you had that under control, all hemmed in. But now it's hopped its banks and is taking over."

And we say, "You're right, Lord. It is. What I'm doing with my computer is out of control. What I'm watching on TV is out of control. What I'm reading, where I'm going, the way I'm living is out of control." But when the Lord asks us when we want to be set free, all too often our answer is the same as Pharaoh's: "Tomorrow."

The problem is, by saying, "Tomorrow," Pharaoh's heart grew harder and harder still. You see, he could have gotten off relatively easy had he been serious and said, "I want the frogs to go now, right now. I'm repenting of what I've been doing. I'm changing my way of living. Moses, you and your people are free to go." And had he done so, Pharaoh would have spared himself, his family, and his country the unbelievable horror that awaited them.

The Bible says, "Today if you hear His voice, harden not your hearts" (Hebrews 4:7) "because, although there is pleasure in sin for a season, the end result is always destruction" (see Hebrews 11:25).

So what are we to do concerning the sin that controls and plagues us?

I suggest four things . . .

Remember

Remember that sin is not bad because it's forbidden, but that it's forbidden because it's bad. You see, God doesn't arbitrarily say, "This, this, this, and this are forbidden. Therefore they're sin." No, He says, "This, this, this, and this will hurt you, so I forbid them because I know they'll eventually destroy you."

Every sin I've ever committed, might commit, will commit, is paid for, washed away completely by Jesus' blood shed for me on Calvary. That's the gospel. But because whatever a man sows, that shall he also reap (Galatians 6:7), every sin I plant carries its own inevitable repercussions. Therefore, wise is the man who, understanding this principle, stays as far away from that which he knows will hurt not only himself, but the people around him.

Repent

To repent simply means to change directions. Where you once said, "This is OK," change your mind. Make a U-turn. Instead of justifying, rationalizing, excusing sin, call it what it is and agree with the Lord that it's gotta go. Right now.

Reckon

Perhaps the most potent passage of Scripture regarding sin, Romans 6 tells us that when Jesus died on the Cross, not only was the penalty of sin paid for, but the power of sin was broken.

"Oh, but you don't know how strong my addiction is," you say.

Perhaps. But I do know this: The Bible says the power of all sin was dealt a deathblow on the Cross. Therefore, all that remains is for me to reckon it to be true and to quit saying, "My situation is different. I'm too involved. I'm too addicted"—for such statements only diminish the reality and potency of what Jesus did on Calvary in order to set us completely, wholly, totally free.

As believers, we may choose to sin; we may decide to sin; but we never *have to* sin because the power of Christ resides in us. And He who told us to go our way and sin no more, to be holy for He is holy, also gives us the power to carry out His commands.

Refuse

Refuse to go where the frogs are croaking. You know exactly who the people and the places are that you need to avoid to stay free—regardless of whether they're the cool crowd or the hot place to be.

I find it amazing that Pharaoh would say, "Tomorrow"—until I analyze my own life and see the same tendency within me. I can hear a truth and say, "That's right. That's gotta go. That's gotta be corrected, adjusted, changed, repented of. And I'm going to get right on it . . . tomorrow." How I desire to be one who says, "*This* is the time—right here, right now."

You who have heard God's Word, you who have heard His heart, don't be like Pharaoh and wait for your own heart to harden. Instead, say, "I'm going to go Your way, Lord, not tomorrow, not Tuesday, but today."

9

Exodus 9:1–3
Then the LORD said unto Moses, Go in unto Pharaoh, and tell him, Thus saith the LORD God of the Hebrews, Let my people go, that they may serve me. For if thou refuse to let them go, and wilt hold them still, Behold, the hand of the LORD is upon thy cattle which is in the field, upon the horses, upon the asses, upon the camels, upon the oxen, and upon the sheep: there shall be a very grievous murrain [fever].

God told Moses to tell Pharaoh that his cattle, sheep, oxen, and donkeys would all come down with a deadly fever. This meant that the Egyptian economy would be affected adversely without livestock to perform the tasks necessary in an agrarian society.

Exodus 9:4–6
And the LORD shall sever between the cattle of Israel and the cattle of Egypt: and there shall nothing die of all that is the children's of Israel. And the LORD appointed a set time, saying, To morrow the LORD shall do this thing in the land. And the LORD did that thing on the morrow, and all the cattle of Egypt died: but of the cattle of the children of Israel died not one.

The division between the Egyptians and the children of Israel seen in Exodus 8:23 with regard to the plague of flies continues here in chapter 9 concerning the death of livestock.

Exodus 9:7
And Pharaoh sent, and, behold, there was not one of the cattle of the Israelites dead. And the heart of Pharaoh was hardened, and he did not let the people go.

Not only is Pharaoh being hit with plague after plague, but he realizes that the Israelites aren't. It's hard enough to go through difficulty, but doubly hard when it seems like others aren't. Yet even this realization was not enough to soften Pharaoh's heart.

Exodus 9:8–12
And the LORD said unto Moses and unto Aaron, Take to you handfuls of ashes of the furnace, and let Moses sprinkle it toward the heaven in the sight of Pharaoh. And it shall become small dust in all the land of Egypt, and shall be a boil breaking forth with blains upon man, and upon beast, throughout all the land of Egypt. And they took ashes of the furnace, and stood before Pharaoh; and Moses sprinkled it up toward heaven; and it became a boil breaking forth with blains upon man, and upon beast. And the magicians could not stand before Moses because of the boils; for the boil was upon the magicians, and upon all the Egyptians. And the LORD hardened the heart of Pharaoh, and he hearkened not unto them; as the LORD had spoken unto Moses.

The furnace referred to here is generally believed to be that of the god Typhoon wherein humans were sacrificed in order to stave off boils and sores for the remaining population. The Lord telling Moses to throw the ashes of Typhoon's furnace into the sky was as much a slap in the face of Typhoon as the abundance of frogs was to Heqt. "I require obedience, not sacrifice," declared the true and living God. "I don't want you to burn your people in the fire, Pharaoh. I want you to let My people go."

Exodus 9:13–16
And the LORD said unto Moses, Rise up early in the morning, and stand before Pharaoh, and say unto him, Thus saith the LORD God of the Hebrews, Let my people go, that they may serve me. For I will at this time send all my plagues upon thine heart, and upon thy servants, and upon thy people; that thou mayest know that there is none like me in all the earth. For now I will stretch out my hand, that I may smite thee and thy people with pestilence; and thou shalt be cut off from the earth. And in very deed for this cause have I raised thee up, for to shew in thee my power; and that my name may be declared throughout all the earth.

God raised up Pharaoh in order that all people throughout history could know that He is singular, that He is omnipotent, that He is sovereign. And to those who would protest that it was unfair for God to use Pharaoh in such a way, Paul would say, "Who are you to question God? Can the clay say to the potter, "Why did you make me thus?" The potter has the right to do whatever he chooses with the lump of clay. And God has the right to do whatever he wants with us" (see Romans 9:21).

How arrogantly foolish of us to think that we can figure God out. Truly our God is an awesome God. Yes, He's a loving Father, our Abba, our Papa. But He is also the One who, without any explanation, told His friend to sacrifice his son (Genesis 22:2); the One who struck a king who served him well with leprosy for offering a sacrifice in the temple (1 Chronicles 26:20). I can't read my Bible without realizing that my Father is loving and kind, compassionate and tender. But He is also awesome and huge, powerful and "other." Yes, we rejoice in our Father. Yes, we understand His nature as we look at Jesus. But along with that, we must also understand that it is the fear of the Lord that is beginning of wisdom (Proverbs 9:10). We think we have God all figured out. But one can't read the Scriptures without coming to the conclusion that He doesn't fit into any box very easily.

Stand in awe of God. Be amazed by His greatness, by His size, by His sovereignty. And then marvel that He's allowed us to be brought into His family, that He's made Himself known to us through Jesus personally, that He placed us at a time in history where the gospel message surrounds us constantly. Sometimes I lift my hands in love and adoration to the Lord. Other times, I fall on my face on my living room floor, speechless in His presence. He raised up Pharaoh simply to show His power. And He stooped to save us to do the same.

Exodus 9:17–21
As yet exaltest thou thyself against my people, that thou wilt not let them go? Behold, to morrow about this time I will cause it to rain a very grievous hail, such as hath not been in Egypt since the foundation thereof even until now. Send therefore now, and gather thy cattle, and all that thou hast in the field; for upon every man and beast which shall be found in the field, and shall not be brought home, the hail shall come down upon them, and they shall die. He that feared the word of the LORD among the servants of Pharaoh made his servants and his cattle flee into the houses: And he that regarded not the word of the LORD left his servants and his cattle in the field.

It was the responsibility of the masters to care for their servants, to protect them from the storm that would otherwise take their lives. "Come unto Me all ye who are weak and heavy laden and I will give you rest," declares our Master. "Take My yoke upon you and learn of Me, for I am meek and lowly of heart" (Matthew 11:29). It is only in coming unto Jesus that we are spared from the hailstorm that would otherwise destroy us.

"Why is this happening?" we cry. "Why are these things taking place in my life? Why are these things coming down?" Many times the reason is because we did not take heed to the warning and call of our Master. There are people who are needlessly getting beat up and bruised by storms because they fail to come inside the household of God.

"Do not forsake the assembling of yourselves together as is the manner of some," warned the writer of the letter to the Hebrews (10:25). We get needlessly pelted and pounded when we ignore the Lord's Table; when we go it alone rather than joining the company of believers for times of instruction and worship, praise and prayer; when we fail to seek shelter in Jesus.

Exodus 9:22, 23 (a)
And the LORD said unto Moses, Stretch forth thine hand toward heaven, that there may be hail in all the land of Egypt, upon man, and upon beast, and upon every herb of the field, throughout the land of Egypt. And Moses stretched forth his rod toward heaven: and the LORD sent thunder and hail, and the fire ran along upon the ground . . .

Evidently, lightning ignited the fields and fire broke out.

Exodus 9:23 (b)–27 (a)
. . . and the LORD rained hail upon the land of Egypt. So there was hail, and fire mingled with the hail, very grievous, such as there was none like it in all the land of Egypt since it became a nation. And the hail smote throughout all the land of Egypt all that was in the field, both man and beast; and the hail smote every herb of the field, and brake every tree of the field. Only in the land of Goshen, where the children of Israel were, was there no hail. And Pharaoh sent, and called for Moses and Aaron, and said unto them, I have sinned this time . . .

Here we see a pseudo-confession made by Pharaoh. The problem is, he acknowledges his sin only "this time," failing to confess the series of sins that had brought him to this point.

Exodus 9:27 (b)
. . . the LORD is righteous, and I and my people are wicked.

Secondly, even Pharaoh's weakest of confessions is diluted by his eagerness to falsely implicate his people in the decisions he alone had made.

Exodus 9:28
Intreat the LORD (for it is enough) that there be no more mighty thunderings and hail; and I will let you go, and ye shall stay no longer.

Thirdly, the result of true confession is not reprieve but repentance—not a desire to save face, but a decision to make an about face; not insulation from correction, but a determination to change direction.

Exodus 9:29–32
And Moses said unto him, As soon as I am gone out of the city, I will spread abroad my hands unto the LORD; and the thunder shall cease, neither shall there be any more hail; that thou mayest know how that the earth is the LORD's. But as for thee and thy servants, I know that ye will not yet fear the LORD God. And the flax and the barley was smitten: for the barley was in the ear, and the flax was bolled. But the wheat and the rie were not smitten: for they were not grown up.

The flax and the barley were destroyed, but the wheat and rye would grow. Even in God's judgment there is mercy.

Exodus 9:33–35
And Moses went out of the city from Pharaoh, and spread abroad his hands unto the LORD: and the thunders and hail ceased, and the rain was not poured upon the earth. And when Pharaoh saw that the rain and the hail and the thunders were ceased, he sinned yet more, and hardened his heart, he and his servants. And the heart of Pharaoh was hardened, neither would he let the children of Israel go; as the LORD had spoken by Moses.

The hail ceased; the lightning dissipated; the thunder stopped. Yet Pharaoh's heart remained hard.

10

Exodus 10:1, 2
And the LORD said unto Moses, Go in unto Pharaoh: for I have hardened his heart, and the heart of his servants, that I might shew these my signs before him: And that thou mayest tell in the ears of thy son, and of thy son's son, what things I have wrought in Egypt, and my signs which I have done among them; that ye may know how that I am the LORD.

God's intent in baring His arm and raining plagues upon Egypt was not only that the Egyptians would see His power and superiority, but that His own people would know that He was indeed who He claimed to be to such an extent that they could pass this knowledge on to their children and grandchildren. They could learn a portion of this lesson by observing God's dealing with the Egyptians through the hail that fell upon them and the flies which tormented them. But the other part of the lesson could only be learned firsthand as they themselves experienced the effects of water turned to blood, of frogs swarming their houses, and of lice covering their bodies.

There's no testimony without tests. A vibrant, passionate, and authentic walk with the Lord does not come from secondhand theology. It only comes through the things we experience personally.

Exodus 10:3–6
And Moses and Aaron came in unto Pharaoh, and said unto him, Thus saith the LORD God of the Hebrews, How long wilt thou refuse to humble thyself before me? let my people go, that they may serve me. Else, if thou refuse to let my people go, behold, to morrow will I bring the locusts into thy coast: And they shall cover the face of the earth, that one cannot be able to see the earth: and they shall eat the residue of that which is escaped, which remaineth unto you from the hail, and shall eat every tree which groweth for you out of the field: And they shall fill thy houses, and the houses of all thy servants, and the houses of all the Egyptians; which neither thy fathers, nor thy fathers' fathers have seen, since the day that they were upon the earth unto this day. And he turned himself, and went out from Pharaoh.

You are about to be bugged, Pharaoh. The locusts are going to swarm over the land in a way you have never seen in all of your nation's history. They're going to fill your houses, destroy your crops, devour your trees. If you don't let My people go, God declared to Pharaoh, your land will be destroyed.

Exodus 10:7
And Pharaoh's servants said unto him, How long shall this man be a snare unto us? let the men go, that they may serve the LORD their God: knowest thou not yet that Egypt is destroyed?

"Let the men go," said Pharaoh's advisers. "Our land is already destroyed because of them." I believe the operative word in their request was the word "go." But, as we will see in verse 9, the operative word for Pharaoh was "men." Different people can indeed hear the same thing different ways. For example, in the sentence, "A woman without her man is nothing," men hear, "A woman, without her man, is nothing," while women hear, "A woman, without her, man is nothing."

Pharaoh's advisers said, "Let the men *go.*" But Pharaoh heard, "Let the *men* go."

Exodus 10:8
And Moses and Aaron were brought again unto Pharaoh: and he said unto them, Go, serve the LORD your God: but who are they that shall go?

"I'll be the one who will decide who can go," Pharaoh said.

Exodus 10:9–11 (a)
And Moses said, We will go with our young and with our old, with our sons and with our daughters, with our flocks and with our herds will we go; for we must hold a feast unto the LORD. And he said unto them, Let the LORD be so with you, as I will let you go, and your little ones: look to it; for evil is before you. Not so: go now ye that are men, and serve the LORD; for that ye did desire . . .

No doubt knowing that by leaving their families in Egypt, the men would return quickly if indeed they went at all, Pharaoh offered to let the men go.

Exodus 10:11 (b)
. . . And they were driven out from Pharaoh's presence.

Moses would not compromise on this point, for it wasn't merely a matter of men serving the Lord but of entire families serving Him together.

Exodus 10:12–15
And the LORD said unto Moses, Stretch out thine hand over the land of Egypt for the locusts, that they may come up upon the land of Egypt, and eat every herb of the land, even all that the hail hath left. And Moses stretched forth his rod over the land of Egypt, and the LORD brought an east wind upon the land all that day, and all that night; and when it was morning, the east wind brought the locusts. And the locusts went up over all the land of Egypt, and rested in all the coasts of Egypt: very grievous were they; before them there were no such locusts as they, neither after them shall be such. For they covered the face of the whole earth, so that the land was darkened; and they did eat every herb of the land, and all the fruit of the trees which the hail had left: and there remained not any green thing in the trees, or in the herbs of the field, through all the land of Egypt.

We will see locusts again in Scripture—most notably in the Book of Joel, where God uses them in judgment against His own people—but also in the mouth of one who would prepare the way of the One who would preach not judgment but joy (see Matthew 3:3, 4).

Exodus 10:16, 17
Then Pharaoh called for Moses and Aaron in haste; and he said, I have sinned against the LORD your God, and against you. Now therefore forgive, I pray thee, my sin only this once, and intreat the LORD your God, that he may take away from me this death only.

Pharaoh's arrogance is amazing. Here, he has the audacity not only to think he's playing Moses like a well-tuned violin, but to suggest that, either he would ask Moses to go to God on his behalf only once more, or, more incredibly, that he had sinned only once.

Exodus 10:18
And he went out from Pharaoh, and intreated the LORD.

Because Pharaoh played games time after time with him, Moses would have been justified in answering Pharaoh's request with, "Forget it." Instead, in praying on Pharaoh's behalf, his actions answered "Yes." Moses was a man of incredible patience, of unbelievable humility. No wonder the Lord could use him.

Exodus 10:19–22
And the LORD turned a mighty strong west wind, which took away the locusts, and cast them into the Red sea; there remained not one locust in all the coasts of Egypt. But the LORD hardened Pharaoh's heart, so that he would not let the children of Israel go. And the LORD said unto Moses, Stretch out thine hand toward heaven, that there may be darkness over the land of Egypt, even darkness which may be felt. And Moses stretched forth his hand toward heaven; and there was a thick darkness in all the land of Egypt three days:

The land that had been darkened by locusts (10:15) was now made dark with a darkness so dense it could actually be felt.

Exodus 10:23 (a)
They saw not one another, neither rose any from his place for three days . . .

For three days there was total darkness, even as there would be three hours of darkness when

Jesus hung on the Cross. The disciples would go on to experience three days of inner darkness between Good Friday and Easter Sunday until they understood that hope was not lost, that death had been conquered, that the Light of the world had indeed risen from the dead.

Exodus 10:23 (b)
. . . but all the children of Israel had light in their dwellings.

The light flooding the homes of the children of Israel must have been that of the Shekinah, the chabod, the glory of God.

Is there light in your home? Is the presence of the Lord there? Are your kids being taught to walk in His ways? Is your home a place where you love each other and pray together, where things are right? Let us live in the light; let us walk in the light; let us be obedient to that which God has illuminated for you and me.

Exodus 10:24–26
And Pharaoh called unto Moses, and said, Go ye, serve the LORD; only let your flocks and your herds be stayed: let your little ones also go with you. And Moses said, Thou must give us also sacrifices and burnt offerings, that we may sacrifice unto the LORD our God. Our cattle also shall go with us; there shall not an hoof be left behind; for thereof must we take to serve the LORD our God; and we know not with what we must serve the LORD, until we come thither.

Moses and Pharaoh had been duking it out, mixing it up, and sparring round after round . . .

Round 1:

After being punched with the plagues of blood, frogs, lice and flies, Pharaoh said to Moses, "I'll let you and your people serve the Lord—but you must remain in Egypt" (see 8:25).

"We'll be stoned if we stay here," said Moses. And both returned to their corners.

Round 2:

"I'll let you leave the country—but don't go very far" (see 8:28).

"We must go where God directs," said Moses.

Round 3:

Having been struck with boils and hail, Pharaoh said, "You and your men can go as far as you want. But your women and children must stay here" (see 10:11).

"We're taking our families," Moses countered. And both returned to their corners.

Round 4:

Here in our text, following the double punch of locusts and darkness, Pharaoh said, "You and your families can go. But your livestock must stay."

"No," said Moses. We're going to take our families and flocks. We're going to take our kids and our cattle. We're going to take the whole kit and kaboodle."

Egypt being a picture of the world, Satan seeks to make the same compromises to people today . . .

"Stay in the world," he says. "Sure, you might have to bake a brick or two, but at least you're familiar with the system. Why take a risk on that which you can't see? Why leave the known for the unknown? Why set your sights on a kingdom which claims to be eternal, yet is presently invisible?"

And when we choose to listen to God instead of to him, Satan changes his tactic to, "Alright, go ahead and believe in Jesus. But don't go too far. Don't get too radical."

And when we ignore him again, Satan says, "Be radical in your faith if you want. But don't rope your kids into it. When they're older, let them make their own decision about whether or not to follow Jesus. Until then, leave them in Egypt where they can play soccer and take ballet lessons."

And when we decide, like Moses, that we will worship as families, Satan comes up with a final compromise: "Go ahead. Throw in your lot with God. You and your family can even be radical in your faith. But don't spend money on it. Don't tithe. Don't give God His due. Don't invest in eternity."

"Where your treasure is, there will your heart be also," Jesus said, (Matthew 6:21). Were Moses to leave the livelihood of his people in Egypt, their hearts would remain there. And to the degree that we sink ours into the soil of this world, ours remain here as well.

Exodus 10:27–29
But the LORD hardened Pharaoh's heart, and he would not let them go. And Pharaoh said unto him, Get thee from me, take heed to thyself, see my face no more; for in that day thou seest my face thou shalt die. And Moses said, Thou hast spoken well, I will see thy face again no more.

Pharaoh's death threats notwithstanding, Moses would go on to lead every one of God's people out of Egypt, while Pharaoh would find himself at the bottom of the Red Sea.

11 Exodus 11:1–3
And the LORD said unto Moses, Yet will I bring one plague more upon Pharaoh, and upon Egypt; afterwards he will let you go hence: when he shall let you go, he shall surely thrust you out hence altogether. Speak now in the ears of the people, and let every man borrow of his neighbour, and every woman of her neighbour, jewels of silver, and jewels of gold. And the LORD gave the people favour in the sight of the Egyptians. Moreover the man Moses was very great in the land of Egypt, in the sight of Pharaoh's servants, and in the sight of the people.

The Hebrew word translated "borrow" is *sha'al.* It appears 168 times in Scripture—all but six times meaning "request" or "demand." Lest we wonder what right the Israelites had to request gold and silver of the Egyptians, we must bear in mind that they had served the Egyptians for centuries without any compensation whatsoever. The Egyptians owed much to the children of Israel.

Although it doesn't realize this, the world owes much to the community of faith. The building of hospitals and orphanages, the elevation of women, the dismantling of slavery, the institution of public education all find their roots in the church. Imperfect as she may be, as flawed as she is, the church has had a huge influence on world history, for wherever the gospel has gone, great change has followed. And it is the church that is restraining the forces of evil presently. When the church is taken up in the Rapture, although the world will rejoice initially, it will be plunged into such immorality and problems that it will see the difference the church made all along.

Exodus 11:4, 5
And Moses said, Thus saith the LORD, About midnight will I go out into the midst of Egypt: And all the firstborn in the land of Egypt shall die, from the firstborn of Pharaoh that sitteth upon his throne, even unto the firstborn of the maidservant that is behind the mill; and all the firstborn of beasts.

"Israel is my firstborn," God had declared (Exodus 4:22). Therefore, because Pharaoh had enslaved and ordered the systematic annihilation of Israel, God's firstborn, He was justified in ordering the annihilation of Pharaoh's firstborn.

Exodus 11:6, 7
And there shall be a great cry throughout all the land of Egypt, such as there was none like it, nor shall be like it any more. But against any of the children of Israel shall not a dog move his tongue, against man or beast: that ye may know how that the LORD doth put a difference between the Egyptians and Israel.

Were the children of Israel to be spared the death of their firstborn because they were better than the Egyptians? Hardly, for listen to God's own description of His people . . .

> And say unto them, Thus saith the Lord GOD; In the day when I chose Israel, and lifted up mine hand unto the seed of the house of Jacob, and made myself known unto them in the land of Egypt, when I lifted up mine hand unto them, saying, I am the LORD your God; In the day that I lifted up mine hand unto them, to bring them forth of the land of Egypt into a land that I had espied for them, flowing with milk and honey, which is the glory of all lands: Then said I unto them, Cast ye away every man the abominations of his eyes, and defile not yourselves with the idols of Egypt: I am the LORD your God. But they rebelled against me, and would not hearken unto me: they did not every man cast away the abominations of their eyes, neither did they forsake the idols of Egypt: then I said, I will pour out my fury upon them to accomplish my anger against them in the midst of the land of Egypt. But I wrought for my name's sake, that it should not be polluted before the heathen, among whom they were, in whose sight I made myself known unto them, in bringing them forth out of the land of Egypt. Ezekiel 20:5–9

The Israelites weren't delivered from the hand of the Egyptians because of their faithfulness, because of their devotion, because of their integrity. They were spared solely because of God's sovereignty.

Why are we here tonight? Certainly not because we're pure and holy, but simply because, by His sovereign will, God chose you and me to be part of His family. He's chosen to call us by His name, to be an example of His grace and mercy. We are just as prone to sin as anyone else. But we, who, because we were dead in trespasses and sins were unable to do anything for ourselves, were rescued and redeemed. God is indeed all-wise. But it wasn't His wisdom that chose you and me. It was simply, purely, completely His grace and mercy.

Exodus 11:8–10
And all these thy servants shall come down unto me, and bow down themselves unto me,

saying, Get thee out, and all the people that follow thee: and after that I will go out. And he went out from Pharaoh in a great anger. And the LORD said unto Moses, Pharaoh shall not hearken unto you; that my wonders may be multiplied in the land of Egypt. And Moses and Aaron did all these wonders before Pharaoh: and the LORD hardened Pharaoh's heart, so that he would not let the children of Israel go out of his land.

Keep in mind that in chapter 4, God had warned Pharaoh point-blank, "If you don't let My firstborn, the nation Israel, to go free, then I will deal most harshly with your firstborn." Pharaoh had heard the word of the Lord. But neither hail nor locusts, flies nor lice, boils nor frogs would soften his heart. Therefore, God had no other recourse but to deliver the knock-out punch which would finally force Pharaoh to say, "Go."

12

Exodus 12:1, 2
And the LORD spake unto Moses and Aaron in the land of Egypt, saying, This month shall be unto you the beginning of months: it shall be the first month of the year to you.

Monumental as it was, the Passover would not be the only event which would turn the calendar on its head, for when the Incarnation divided the global calendar into B.C. and A.D.—Before Christ and The Year of our Lord—all of history was impacted. But there is a time yet to come when antichrist will seek to change the calendar again in order to eradicate the name of Jesus altogether (Daniel 7:25). We're seeing a hint of this even today as the terms C.E. or B.C.E.—Common Era and Before Common Era—are increasingly used in Europe as replacements for A.D. and B.C. Has your calendar been changed personally? If so, no doubt you look at your life Before Christ and see yourself as a Neanderthal without Him.

Exodus 12:3
Speak ye unto all the congregation of Israel, saying, In the tenth day of this month they shall take to them every man a lamb, according to the house of their fathers, a lamb for an house:

The net of salvation grows ever wider in Scripture. In Genesis 4, Abel offered a lamb for a man. Here in Exodus 12, the children of Israel were to offer a lamb for a family. In Exodus 29, the priests were to offer a lamb for a nation. And in John 1, we see a Lamb who came to be offered for the whole world.

Exodus 12:4, 5 (a)
And if the household be too little for the lamb, let him and his neighbour next unto his house take it according to the number of the souls; every man according to his eating shall make your count for the lamb. Your lamb . . .

In *a lamb* (v. 3), *the lamb* (v. 4), and *your lamb* (v. 4), we see progressive revelation. Yes, Jesus is a Lamb. But He's more than a Lamb. He's not just one of the Great Teachers, the Great Masters. No, He's *the* Lamb. Yet He's more than that, for to be your Savior, He must be *your* Lamb.

Exodus 12:5 (b)
. . . shall be without blemish . . .

"He's done nothing wrong," said the thief crucified next to Jesus (see Luke 23:41).

"Truly this must be the Son of God," said the Roman centurion (Matthew 27:54).

"I find no fault in Him," said Pontius Pilate as he washed his hands nervously (Luke 23:4).

"I've betrayed innocent blood," said Judas desperately (Matthew 27:4).

Jesus was indeed the Lamb without blemish.

Exodus 12:5 (c)
. . . a male of the first year . . .

"Of the first year" can also be translated "firstborn."

Exodus 12:5 (d), 6 (a)
. . . ye shall take it out from the sheep, or from the goats: And ye shall keep it up until the fourteenth day of the same month . . .

A lamb was to be selected on the tenth day and slaughtered on the fourteenth day. The four days between the two, serving as a period of inspection to ensure that the lamb was not blemished or diseased. It was on the tenth of the month of Nissan A.D. 32 that Jesus went into Jerusalem during His final week. For the following four days, the Pharisees, Sadducees, and His enemies would try to challenge Him theologically and attempt to trap Him ethically. But they were, to a man, unable to find any flaw in Him, for truly He is the spotless Lamb.

Exodus 12:6 (b)
. . . and the whole assembly of the congregation of Israel shall kill it in the evening.

One for each household, thousands of lambs would have been slaughtered, yet they are referred to as "it," as one because they point to the singular Lamb, Jesus, the Lamb of God.

Exodus 12:7
And they shall take of the blood, and strike it on the two side posts and on the upper door post of the houses, wherein they shall eat it.

In verse 22, we read that the blood was to be applied with hyssop, a plant that speaks of humility. A person doesn't get saved until he's humble before God, until he realizes he's a sinner.

Exodus 12:8 (a)
And they shall eat the flesh in that night . . .

Confused by His words, it was after Jesus said, "If you do not eat of My body, you have no life in you," that many followed Him no more (John 6:66). This side of the Resurrection, we understand that we have to absorb, to assimilate Jesus into our lives, to allow Him to rule and reign from within—a principle of which Passover then and Communion now are pictures.

Exodus 12:8 (b)
. . . roast with fire . . .

The lamb was roasted with fire as a picture of the fact that, as Jesus hung on the Cross, God hurled upon His Son the fire of His wrath that He should have hurled upon me.

Exodus 12:8 (c)
. . . and unleavened bread . . .

Not only is leaven a picture of the sin which was completely absent from our Lord—but the unleavened bread eaten at Passover to this day is poked and striped, just as the back of Jesus was striped by the flagellum (Isaiah 53:5) and His side pierced with a spear (John 19:34).

Exodus 12:8 (d), 9 (a)
. . . and with bitter herbs they shall eat it. Eat not of it raw, nor sodden at all with water . . .

Choosing to absorb the full blow of His Father's fury, Jesus refused the vinegar offered to Him as a painkiller on the Cross. Therefore, the bitter herbs of Passover were not to be watered down.

Exodus 12:9 (b)
. . . but roast with fire; his head with his legs, and with the purtenance thereof.

The "purtenance" speaking of the insides, we're to feed on Jesus' mind, walk, and heart. We're to know what He said, to see how He walked practically, to feel His heart. And, in turn, we're to love Him with all our heart, soul, mind and strength (Mark 12:30).

Exodus 12:10
And ye shall let nothing of it remain until the morning; and that which remaineth of it until the morning ye shall burn with fire.

The children of Israel were to eat the Passover lamb in one sitting. They weren't to save any for leftovers. So, when Jesus died on the Cross, He didn't say, "To be continued . . ." He said, "It is *finished*." There is nothing left to be accomplished. The work is *complete*.

Exodus 12:11
And thus shall ye eat it; with your loins girded, your shoes on your feet, and your staff in your hand; and ye shall eat it in haste: it is the LORD's passover.

Just as the children of Israel were to partake of the Passover in a posture of being ready to go, in I Corinthians 11, Paul says in observing Communion, we show the Lord's death *until He comes*. In other words, the Communion Table, like the Passover meal, is not to be simply about absorbing the Lamb and appropriating the blood—but to realize the time is at hand when He will come back, when we'll move on, when we'll at last partake of the marriage feast of the Lamb with Him in eternity.

Exodus 12:12
For I will pass through the land of Egypt this night, and will smite all the firstborn in the land of Egypt, both man and beast; and against all the gods of Egypt I will execute judgment: I am the LORD.

After declaring He would pass through the land and smite the firstborn of man and beast, God gives this reason: "I am the Lord." And that's all the reason He needs.

Exodus 12:13
And the blood shall be to you for a token upon the houses where ye are: and when I see the blood, I will pass over you, and the plague shall not be upon you to destroy you, when I smite the land of Egypt.

It wasn't the expense of the house nor the righteousness of the people within the house which mattered. The only issue was the blood applied *to* the house. The shed blood was not enough to save their families. The children of Israel had to *apply* the blood to the doorposts of their own homes.

"Behold, I stand at the door and knock," Jesus said. "If any man hear My voice and open the door, I will come in to him and sup with him and he with Me" (Revelation 3:20). As the blood needed to be applied to the doorposts individually, so each man must open the door to his own heart personally.

Exodus 12:14–17
And this day shall be unto you for a memorial; and ye shall keep it a feast to the LORD throughout your generations; ye shall keep it a feast by an ordinance for ever. Seven days shall ye eat unleavened bread; even the first day ye shall put away leaven out of your houses: for whosoever eateth leavened bread from the first day until the seventh day, that soul shall be cut off from Israel. And in the first day there shall be an holy convocation, and in the seventh day there shall be an holy convocation to you; no manner of work shall be done in them, save that which every man must eat, that only may be done of you. And ye shall observe the feast of unleavened bread; for in this selfsame day have I brought your armies out of the land of Egypt: therefore shall ye observe this day in your generations by an ordinance for ever.

Passover was celebrated on the fourteenth day of the month. The following day, a seven-day celebration began called the Feast of Unleavened Bread. In the middle of the Feast of Unleavened Bread, a third feast began, which was the Feast of Firstfruits (Leviticus 23). Together, these three feasts paint a perfect prophetic picture. Yes, Jesus died on Passover. But was He truly without blemish, without leaven, without sin? His Resurrection answers that question with a resounding, "Yes!" And not only that, but the fact that He rose on the Feast of Firstfruits means that He is only the first One to do so—that we will follow. Oh, happy day that will be!

Exodus 12:18–20
In the first month, on the fourteenth day of the month at even, ye shall eat unleavened bread, until the one and twentieth day of the month at even. Seven days shall there be no leaven found in your houses: for whosoever eateth that which is leavened, even that soul shall be cut off from the congregation of Israel, whether he be a stranger, or born in the land. Ye shall eat nothing leavened; in all your habitations shall ye eat unleavened bread.

Psalm 105:37 tells us that after they ate the Passover Meal, the entire nation was in perfect health. Second Chronicles 30:13–20 goes on to say that when the Passover was reinstated by Hezekiah, the Lord healed all the people. What did Paul say about our celebration of Passover—the Table of Communion? Because some don't give it worth, many are sick or weak, and the implication is that some even died unnecessarily (see 1 Corinthians 11:30).

Exodus 12:21, 22
Then Moses called for all the elders of Israel, and said unto them, Draw out and take you a lamb according to your families, and kill the passover. And ye shall take a bunch of hyssop, and dip it in the blood that is in the bason, and strike the lintel and the two side posts with the blood that is in the bason; and none of you shall go out at the door of his house until the morning.

The word translated "bason" is actually the Egyptian word *sap,* which speaks of the basin used for washing one's feet that was built into the threshold of the door. With the basin filled with blood on Passover, and the side and upper doorposts marked with blood, the picture of a Cross is unmistakable.

Exodus 12:23–28
For the LORD will pass through to smite the Egyptians; and when he seeth the blood upon the lintel, and on the two side posts, the LORD will pass over the door, and will not suffer the destroyer to come in unto your houses to smite you. And ye shall observe this thing for an ordinance to thee and to thy sons for ever. And it shall come to pass, when ye be come to the land which the LORD will give you, according as he hath promised, that ye shall keep this service. And it shall come to pass, when your children shall say unto you, What mean ye by this service? That ye shall say, It is the sacrifice of the LORD's passover, who passed over the houses of the children of Israel in Egypt, when he smote the Egyptians, and delivered our houses. And the people bowed the head and worshipped. And the children of Israel went away, and did as the LORD had commanded Moses and Aaron, so did they.

In the Jewish Passover meal to this day, there are four cups of blessing. Between the first and second cups, three matzos stacked on top of each other are removed from a linen pouch, and the one in the middle broken. Half of the broken matzo is then wrapped in a linen napkin and hidden for the children of the family to find. The one who finds it is given a special prize and celebration follows. Ask the Jewish rabbis or read Jewish literature to determine the meaning of this custom and, although you will find lots of theories, you will find no consensus—for, although the Jews can explain the Passover in terms of their history, they can't explain this particular ceremony, known as *afikomen*. *Afikomen* is the only word in the Passover celebration which is not Hebrew. Rather, it's a Greek word, meaning, "I came."

The body of Jesus, the middle One of the Trinity comprised of Father, Son, and Spirit, was broken, wrapped in linen, hidden away, and discovered amidst great celebration. Why is only half of the matzo broken in the Passover tradition? Because as God-Man, it was only Jesus' humanity that died. Thus, the *afikomen* of the Passover perfectly pictures the Lamb of God Who came to die for the sins of the world.

Interestingly, at the completion of their Passover, Moroccan Jews take a piece of the *afikomen* and carry it with them for the full year until the next Passover celebration because tradition has it that if a storm comes up when they are out at sea, all they need do is toss a piece of the *afikomen* into the water and the sea will be calm—a tradition which finds its roots in the One who came, the One who quieted storms, the One who said, "Peace, be still."

Exodus 12:29, 30
And it came to pass, that at midnight the LORD smote all the firstborn in the land of Egypt, from the firstborn of Pharoah that sat on his throne unto the firstborn of the captive that was in the dungeon; and all the firstborn of cattle. And Pharaoh rose up in the night, he, and all his servants, and all the Egyptians; and there was a great cry in Egypt; for there was not a house where there was not one dead.

Hearing the haunting cries of Egyptian parents who realized death had struck their homes, perhaps God's people were afraid. Perhaps they doubted. But guess what. It mattered not whether they were at peace or feeling anxious, whether they were rejoicing or worried greatly. All that mattered was that the blood was on the door. No matter what they felt emotionally, it was all about the blood singularly.

Exodus 12:31, 32
And he called for Moses and Aaron by night, and said, Rise up, and get you forth from among my people, both ye and the children of Israel; and go, serve the LORD, as ye have said. Also take your flocks and your herds, as ye have said, and be gone; and bless me also.

It must have been a broken and brokenhearted Pharaoh who finally admitted that the true and living God was superior to his gods.

Exodus 12:33–36 (a)
And the Egyptians were urgent upon the people, that they might send them out of the land in haste; for they said, We be all dead men. And the people took their dough before it was leavened, their kneadingtroughs being bound up in their clothes upon their shoulders. And the children of Israel did according to the word of Moses; and they borrowed of the Egyptians jewels of silver, and jewels of gold, and raiment: And the LORD gave the people favour in the sight of the Egyptians, so that they lent unto them such things as they required . . .

"You can have anything you want," the Egyptians must have said. "Just leave before we all die."

Exodus 12:36 (b), 37 (a)
. . . And they spoiled the Egyptians. And the children of Israel journeyed from Rameses to Succoth . . .

With loins girded—robes cinched around the waist to give mobility to the legs—and shoes on their feet, with walking sticks in hands and kneading troughs on their shoulders, the children of Israel resembled backpackers. And, appropriately, their first stop was Succoth, or "Tent Town."

Exodus 12:37 (b)
. . . about six hundred thousand on foot that were men, beside children.

Six hundred thousand men means approximately three million people, including women and children, set out from Egypt.

Exodus 12:38
And a mixed multitude went up also with them; and flocks, and herds, even very much cattle.

Although they weren't children of Israel, others wanted to be part of their company.

Exodus 12:39–44
And they baked unleavened cakes of the dough which they brought forth out of Egypt, for it was not leavened; because they were thrust out of Egypt, and could not

tarry, neither had they prepared for themselves any victual. Now the sojourning of the children of Israel, who dwelt in Egypt, was four hundred and thirty years. And it came to pass at the end of the four hundred and thirty years, even the selfsame day it came to pass, that all the hosts of the LORD went out from the land of Egypt. It is a night to be much observed unto the LORD for bringing them out from the land of Egypt: this is that night of the LORD to be observed of all the children of Israel in their generations. And the LORD said unto Moses and Aaron, This is the ordinance of the passover: There shall no stranger eat thereof: But every man's servant that is bought for money, when thou hast circumcised him, then shall he eat thereof.

No pagan could eat of the Passover. However, pagan slaves willing to be circumcised were free to partake.

Exodus 12:45, 46
A foreigner and an hired servant shall not eat thereof. In one house shall it be eaten; thou shalt not carry forth ought of the flesh abroad out of the house; neither shall ye break a bone thereof.

Why was no bone to be broken? I suggest three reasons . . .

Restoration. David—a man who was a shepherd by trade and a sheep by nature—speaks of restoration when he writes, "Make me to hear joy and gladness; that the bones which thou hast broken may rejoice" (Psalm 51:8). You see, in Bible days, if a lamb continually placed its life in jeopardy by wandering away, the shepherd would break its legs, set the bones, and carry it on his shoulders for the following six to eight weeks until the bones were healed. During that period, the lamb would develop such a deep affection for the shepherd, that when its legs were healed, it would remain by the shepherd's side all the days of its life. Jesus, being the sinless Lamb of God, however, had no need to be broken.

Redemption. "Where sin abounds, grace abounds more," Paul declares (Romans 5:20). What is the basis of grace? The blood of Calvary. Where is blood produced? In the bone. Therefore, in insisting that not a bone be broken, it's as though God is saying, "I don't want any suggestion that there is a limitation to the blood. I want people to understand that where sin abounds, grace always abounds *more.*"

Reconciliation. To hasten death, soldiers would break the legs of those being crucified. However, when they came to do this to Jesus, so surprised were they that He had died in only six hours, that they poked a spear in His side to make sure (John 19:34).

If you are estranged from or at odds with someone to whom you were once close, the only way there can be reconciliation is if someone dies. Jesus models that for you and me. He died to reconcile us to the Father—but He died quickly. It was not unusual for victims of crucifixion to prolong their lives eighteen hours or more as they hung on the cross. Not Jesus. The work of reconciliation complete, He released His spirit relatively quickly in order that He might race to Easter—to Resurrection day. That's the key: the sooner we die, the sooner we'll be at Easter Sunday. A lot of people remain at Good Friday, saying, "I'm not going to give up. I'm not going to die. I'm going to stand up for my rights," only to prolong the pain and separation. Jesus showed us the way when He died quickly.

How do you know if you're really dead? They poked Jesus in the side with a spear to find out if He was really dead—and the same will happen to you. If you're dead, you won't react when you get poked. You won't say, "Ouch! Cut that out!" You'll know you're dead if, when you are poked, all that comes out is the blood of forgiveness, the water of refreshment. And that's when there can be reconciliation and resurrection.

Exodus 12:47–51
All the congregation of Israel shall keep it. And when a stranger shall sojourn with thee, and will keep the passover to the LORD, let all his males be circumcised, and then let him come near and keep it; and he shall be as one that is born in the land: for no uncircumcised person shall eat thereof. One law shall be to him that is homeborn, and unto the stranger that sojourneth among you. Thus did all the children of Israel; as the LORD commanded Moses and Aaron, so did they. And it came to pass the selfsame day, that the LORD did bring the children of Israel out of the land of Egypt by their armies.

Outsiders who wanted to take part in the Passover feast could do so if they were circumcised, if they would deal with their flesh.

13 Although the trip from Egypt to the Promised Land would have been a ten-day journey as the crow flies, it was God's intent that His people spend a full year getting there, stopping at seven specific campsites, learning seven important lessons on the way. Why? Because it was one thing for God to get His people out of Egypt—and quite another to get Egypt out of His people.

Egypt being a picture of the world, when we were saved, the Lord took us out of the world—and now He's taking the world out of us. He is not only preparing a place for us in heaven, but also preparing us for the place. If we fail to understand this, life will be constantly confusing and depressing as we wonder, "What is this about?" "Why is that taking place?" "What on earth is going on?" I will find myself discouraged, disoriented, and defeated unless I understand life is meant to prepare me for Heaven.

After stopping at Succoth, or, "Tent Town"—a perfect picture that this world is not our home—the children of Israel were headed for Campsite number two. But before they packed up, God had something He wanted to tell them . . .

Exodus 13:1, 2
And the LORD spake unto Moses, saying, Sanctify unto me all the firstborn, whatsoever openeth the womb among the children of Israel, both of man and of beast: it is mine.

"Every firstborn is to be sanctified, consecrated, set apart for Me," God declared. Why? When the Israelites left Egypt, they left behind a nation in agony, mourning the deaths of their firstborn sons. Therefore, in commanding the Israelites to sanctify their firstborn, God was, in effect, saying, "To help you remember you are My firstborn, I am commanding that your firstborn be dedicated to Me."

God's intent was that the firstborn son in every family would be in the priesthood, involved in ministry. The problem was, however, that the people of Israel fell prey to idolatry to such a degree that, at the golden calf, only one tribe responded to the Lord's call to rectify the situation. Thus, the tribe of Levi would be the only men who would be allowed to minister as priests.

Exodus 13:3–10
And Moses said unto the people, Remember this day, in which ye came out from Egypt, out of the house of bondage; for by strength of hand the LORD brought you out from this place: there shall no leavened bread be eaten. This day came ye out in the month Abib. And it shall be when the LORD shall bring thee into the land of the Canaanites, and the Hittites, and the Amorites, and the Hivites, and the Jebusites, which he sware unto thy fathers to give thee, a land flowing with milk and honey, that thou shalt keep this service in this month. Seven days thou shalt eat unleavened bread, and in the seventh day shall be a feast to the LORD. Unleavened bread shall be eaten seven days; and there shall no leavened bread be seen with thee, neither shall there be leaven seen with thee in all thy quarters. And thou shalt shew thy son in that day, saying, This is done because of that which the LORD did unto me when I came forth out of Egypt. And it shall be for a sign unto thee upon thine hand, and for a memorial between thine eyes, that the LORD's law may be in thy mouth: for with a strong hand hath the LORD brought thee out of Egypt. Thou shalt therefore keep this ordinance in his season from year to year.

The Israelites were not only to remember that they were God's firstborn, but they were to remember the day He delivered them. They were to celebrate Passover annually in order that they would be able to provide a tangible way that their children could understand what God did for His people in bringing them out of Egypt.

Exodus 13:11–16
And it shall be when the LORD shall bring thee into the land of the Canaanites, as he sware unto thee and to thy fathers, and shall give it thee, that thou shalt set apart unto the LORD all that openeth the matrix, and every firstling that cometh of a beast which thou hast; the males shall be the LORD's. And every firstling of an ass thou shalt redeem with a lamb; and if thou wilt not redeem it, then thou shalt break his neck: and all the firstborn of man among thy children shalt thou redeem.

And it shall be when thy son asketh thee in time to come, saying, What is this? that thou shalt say unto him, by strength of hand the LORD brought us out from Egypt, from the house of bondage: And it came to pass, when Pharaoh would hardly let us go, that the LORD slew all the firstborn in the land of Egypt, both the firstborn of man, and the firstborn of beast: therefore I sacrifice to the LORD all that openeth the matrix, being males; but all the firstborn of my children I redeem. And it shall be for a token upon thine hand, and for frontlets between thine eyes: for by strength of hand the LORD brought us forth out of Egypt.

The only way a donkey could live was if a lamb was slain for it. I like this analogy. Because we know the lamb speaks of Jesus, it's not too difficult to figure out who the donkey represents . . .

The donkey is mentioned twenty-five times in the Old Testament, among which are the following . . .

In Genesis 22, when Abraham took Isaac up to Mt. Moriah, a donkey was saddled for them, which speaks of a loss of liberty.

Later in the same chapter, the donkey was to be tied up while Abraham and Isaac ascended the mountain, which speaks of an inability to worship.

As Jacob pronounces blessing on his sons in Genesis 49, he likens Issachar to a donkey that is heavily laden.

In Deuteronomy 22, we read that the ox and donkey were not to plow together, the implication being that the donkey would only slow the ox down.

In 1 Samuel 9, we see Saul trying to locate his father's donkeys that had wandered away.

Jeremiah 22 speaks of a donkey left for dead and tossed outside the city gates.

Taken together, these references speak of you and me—laden down, tied up, lacking an ability to serve or worship the Lord, lost, left for dead, tossed out—not a very flattering picture. But the final mention of a donkey in the Old Testament is a glorious one indeed . . .

> Rejoice greatly, O daughter of Zion; shout, O daughter of Jerusalem: behold, thy King cometh unto thee: he is just, and having salvation; lowly, and riding upon an ass, and upon a colt the foal of an ass. Zechariah 9:9

A week before He would go to Calvary, Jesus said to His disciples, "Go into the village and you'll see a donkey. Untie it and bring it to Me. And if anyone asks why you are untying it, tell him the Lord has need of it" (see Matthew 21:3).

"I choose a donkey," Jesus said. "Let Alexander the Great ride on the back of his mighty black stallion. Let the Romans ride their dazzling white horses. I'll use a donkey."

Jesus wants to enter your city, your workplace, your family. And He chooses to use you as a means of getting there.

"How can He use me?" you ask. "I'm nothing but a donkey."

That's right. And He loves using donkeys—the foolish things of the world to confound the wise (1 Corinthians 1:27). But before He can use you, you first must be untied, released because you can't be used if you're bound up with guilt and sin and worry. So He sends disciples to untie you—maybe in a Bible study, maybe over the radio, with a word from the Lord just for you. Before the donkey was ridden, he was released. But before he was released, he had to be redeemed. The donkey would die unless a lamb died in his place. And that's exactly what the Lamb of God did when He died for us.

> When fishes flew and forests walked and figs grew upon thorn
> When some moment the moon was blood, then surely I was born
> With monstrous head and sickening cry and ears like errant wings
> The devil's walking parody on all four-footed things
> The tattered outlaw of the earth, of ancient, crooked will
> Scourge me, starve me, deride me. I am dumb. But I keep my secret still
> For I, too, had my hour, one far, fierce hour and sweet
> When there were shouts of Hosanna about my ears and palm branches about my feet.
> G. K. Chesterton

The donkey had his day. So can we. That's *amazing* grace.

Exodus 13:17
And it came to pass, when Pharaoh had let the people go, that God led them not through the way of the land of the Philistines, although that was near; for God said, Lest peradventure the people repent when they see war, and they return to Egypt:

"It seems like I'm on a merry-go-round, Lord," we cry. "It seems like I'm on a circuitous route. Why don't You take me straight to the Promised Land?"

"Because I see things you don't, know things you can't," the Lord answers. "If I took you in the way you think you should go, it would be disastrous for you. Trust Me. I'm preparing you for the land as well as preparing the land for you."

Exodus 13:18, 19
But God led the people about, through the way of the wilderness of the Red sea: and the children of Israel went up harnessed out of the land of Egypt. And Moses took the bones of Joseph with him: for he had straitly sworn the children of Israel, saying, God will surely visit you; and ye shall carry up my bones away hence with you.

Approximately 360 years earlier, Joseph had said, "I know I'm dying. I also know, as God's people, you will make it to the Promised Land. Therefore, don't leave me here in Egypt. Although I live here, worked here, and will die here, I'm not of Egypt. So take me to the Promised Land."

Our bones will be taken out of this Egypt as well. Even if you die tonight, your bones will not be left here, for the Lord Himself shall descend and the dead in Christ shall rise first—bones and all (1 Thessalonians 4:16).

Exodus 13:20
And they took their journey from Succoth, and encamped in Etham, in the edge of the wilderness.

When the Israelites left Succoth, they didn't go to the Land of Promise. They went to Etham—a town on the brink of disaster, a town on the edge of the wilderness. In the Bible, the word "wilderness" does not refer to a land of pine trees, mountain streams, rainbow trout, and wildflowers—but to the bleak, brutal, blistering desert.

"You brought us to the desert, Lord? With nothing but nothing before us?" the Israelites must have cried.

Oh, but the place is called *Etham* or literally, "With them."

"I'm with you," the Lord declares. "I know it looks like you're on the brink of disaster, like there's nothing good ahead. But I'm with you to see you through."

How can the Lord teach us He is truly with us except to take us to the desert? When everything is fine, we go on our merry way as if His presence in our life is optional. It's only when we're on the brink of disaster that we realize how much we need Him.

Exodus 13:21 (a)
And the LORD went before them by day in a pillar of a cloud, to lead them the way . . .

How did God lead His people? In the heat of the desert, He led them with a cool, comforting cloud.

For topical study of Exodus 13:20–22, see "The Leading of the Lord" below.

Exodus 13:21 (b), 22
. . . and by night in a pillar of fire, to give them light; to go by day and night: He took not away the pillar of the cloud by day, nor the pillar of fire by night, from before the people.

Biblically, fire is a symbol of trials. "Don't think it strange," Peter writes, "concerning the fiery trials that come your way" (1 Peter 4:12). How does God guide you? Not only with a cool, comfortable cloud—but sometimes through the fire of difficulty. Yet, as Shadrach, Meshach, and Abed-Nego learned, the hotter the trial, the greater the liberty. When the three Hebrews were thrown into Belshazzar's fiery furnace, their skin didn't burn; their hair wasn't singed; their clothes didn't even smell like smoke. The only physical effect of the fire was that the ropes which had once bound them were burned away.

"She dumped me? He fired me? This is terrible!" we cry.

Wait. Hold on. Hang in there. You'll look back and see that, in reality, you were actually set free.

And then, like the children of Israel, you'll be able to go on to Stop Number Three, where it gets even worse—and even more wonderful . . .

THE LEADING OF THE LORD

A Topical Study of EXODUS 13:20–22

Now what? Having been released from their slavery in Egypt, they knew there was a great destiny awaiting them: a land flowing with milk and honey, the Promised Land. The only question was, how would they know the way? How would God guide them day by day? And that is the question people still ask. "I know I've been freed from Egypt—they say, from the slavery of the sins to which I was once bound—and headed for a great destiny, that I'm going to heaven ultimately, but what do I do in the meantime? How will the Lord lead me practically, daily?"

Many people are in a fog about the way the Lord leads. But I believe the passage before us clears things up wonderfully as it replaces the fog around us with a cloud over us. In light of this, I submit three questions for your consideration, three questions to help you determine which way the Lord is leading in any given situation . . .

Is It Cool?

When I read this story in Sunday school, saw it on the flannel graph board, or watched it in the movies, it seems to me that the cloud was always in front of the congregation. That is, the Israelites would see the cloud off in the distance and simply follow wherever it lead. But I don't think this was what was really taking place, for in Psalm 105:39, we read that the cloud wasn't ahead of the congregation, but was above the congregation, a covering of the congregation.

This means that when God wanted His people to move, He got them to move in a very simple, practical way. With daytime temperatures reaching one hundred and twenty-five degrees in the desert, God put a cloud over the entire congregation to shade them. And when He wanted them to move, He would simply move the cloud, knowing His people would move as well, simply to stay in the shade.

And that's the way the Lord still directs us. "My burden is easy, My load light," Jesus declared (see Matthew 11:30)—a New Testament principle pictured in the Old Testament priesthood . . .

> *And it shall come to pass, that when they enter in at the gates of the inner court, they shall be clothed with linen garments; and no wool shall come upon them, whiles they minister in the gates of the inner court, and within. They shall have linen bonnets upon their heads, and shall have linen breeches upon their loins; they shall not gird themselves with any thing that causeth sweat.*
>
> Ezekiel 44:17, 18

When you want to know what God's will for you is, the first thing you should do is ask, Is it cool—or is it wool? Will it cause inspiration—or perspiration? "Delight yourself in the Lord," the psalmist declared, "and He will give you the desires of your heart" (Psalm 37:4). In other words, if you delight in, love, and enjoy the Lord, He will give you that which your heart desires. How can that be? Because He has already written His will on the table of your heart (Jeremiah 31:33), the desire of the heart in fellowship with Him is His desire.

Perhaps Augustine said it best when, asked how to determine God's will, he answered, "Love God—and do what you please."

> A few years ago, I talked to some missionaries in the mountainous area of Papua New Guinea where it rains forty-three days a year and where toads spit poison so potent it burns through clothing.
>
> "How can you do this?" I asked in amazement.
>
> "We love it," they answered. "Come and see our bug collections!"

> They love the bugs, the people, and even the weather because God fashioned them in such a way that they would fit in to His divine design for them to share His Word with the people of Papua New Guinea.

It has been rightly said that there are lots of cheap imitations of priceless masterpieces in the church today. "Look at him. Look at her. Look at them," we say. "I'm going to be just like him or her or them." But when we try to imitate or duplicate someone else's calling or ministry, the best we can be is only a cheap imitation. You are a masterpiece because the Master has pieced you together to do exactly what He intended you to do since before the world even began (Ephesians 1:4).

"You are His workmanship," Paul wrote to the Ephesians (2:10). *Poema,* the Greek word translated "workmanship," is the word from which we get our word "poem." You are God's poetry. He has created you specifically and uniquely to do that which He knows will satisfy you most completely. Therefore, when you get to heaven, the Lord is not going to say, "Why weren't you more like Moses? Why weren't you more like Abraham? Why weren't you more like Paul or Billy Graham?" No, He's going to say, "Why weren't you more like *you?* Why weren't you simply the person I made you to be—My Masterpiece, My poetry?"

Don't strive, dear saint. Don't sweat, fellow priest. Be who the Lord intended you to be—His unique Masterpiece, His inimitable poetry.

Will It Count?

> *And when he had spoken these things, while they beheld, he was taken up; and a cloud received him out of their sight.* Acts 1:9

> *Then we which are alive and remain shall be caught up together with them in the clouds, to meet the Lord in the air: and so shall we ever be with the Lord.* 1 Thessalonians 4:17

> *Behold, he cometh with clouds; and every eye shall see him, and they also which pierced him: and all kindreds of the earth shall wail because of him. Even so, Amen.* Revelation 1:7

Because Jesus is coming back in the clouds, the cloud causes us not only to consider what is cool, but what will count. You see, when we stand before Him, we'll give an account of what we did with our time, talents, and treasures. All that we did on earth will be tried by fire, and whatever remains will be our reward for eternity. And even if you don't think you're the type who cares about rewards, I promise you, you'll care then—for they will determine your capacity to enjoy eternity, your function in the kingdom.

"For the Lamb which is in the midst of the throne shall feed them, and shall lead them unto living fountains of waters: and God shall wipe away all tears from their eyes" (Revelation 7:17).

What could possibly be the reason for tears in heaven?

I believe there will be tears when we stand before the Lord and see the opportunities we lost, the time we wasted, the potential we took for granted. What we do now will affect who we are, how much we enjoy, the way we function forever. And there's no hint in Scripture that in heaven we can compensate for that which we didn't do on earth. So when I'm deciding whether to watch TV or worship the Lord, to focus my energy on my car or on the kingdom, to pursue pleasure or to love people, if I'm aware of the cloud which speaks of His coming, I'll choose correctly every time.

Does It Conform?

Seeing Jesus shine as He talked with Moses and Elijah on the Mount of Transfiguration, no wonder Peter exclaimed, "Lord, it's *good* for us to be here. Let's make three booths, three tents, three monuments—one for You, one for Moses, one for Elijah and camp out right here!"

It was at this point that a cloud appeared, with a voice thundering, "This is My beloved Son. Hear ye *Him*" (Matthew 17:5, italics added).

The cloud of the Transfiguration reminds me that, concerning any crossroad facing me, my decision must conform to the words and example Jesus gave me. The writer to Hebrews clarifies this even further when he says, "Wherefore, seeing we are compassed about with so great a cloud of witnesses, let us run the race set before us" (Hebrews 12:1). We're surrounded by a cloud of witnesses—heroes of the faith like Abraham, Moses, and David; Noah, Jacob, and Gideon.

If, when you were struggling with a decision, I asked if you'd be interested in a personal appointment with the apostle Paul, followed by a time of worship with David, and a Question and Answer session with Isaiah, you'd no doubt jump at the chance. But such a scenario is presently possible, for you hold in your hand the collective wisdom of the great cloud of witnesses. What an unspeakable privilege is ours to be counseled by forty different authors, each inspired by the Spirit of God. Oh, the wisdom, counsel, and direction I find when I read the Scriptures.

God's will is not hard to figure out. He leads us with a cloud. And when we follow, we have it made in the shade.

---

14 **Exodus 14:1, 2**

And the LORD spake unto Moses, saying, speak unto the children of Israel, that they turn and encamp before Pi-hahiroth, between Migdol and the sea, over against Baal-zephon: before it shall ye encamp by the sea.

Pi-hahiroth literally means "mouth of the gorges." *Migdol* means "tower." Therefore, it would seem that for Stop Number Three, God directed His people to camp between a cavernous mountain wherein enemy troops might be hidden and a military fortress of some sort, with their backs to the Red Sea.

"That's not strategically wise," Moses' advisors must have said. "If the Egyptians change their minds and pursue us, we would be sitting ducks." But the Lord would go on to explain His strategy to Moses . . .

Exodus 14:3, 4
For Pharaoh will say of the children of Israel, they are entangled in the land, the wilderness hath shut them in. And I will harden Pharaoh's heart, that he shall follow after them; and I will be honoured upon Pharaoh, and upon all his host; that the Egyptians may know that I am the LORD. And they did so.

Surely the Egyptians knew that the true and living God was Lord of all. If the frogs and flies hadn't convinced them of this, blood and boils, hail and lice, and the horror of the death of the firstborn would have done so. But they still had one ace up their sleeve—their awesome, legendary, invincible army. Thus, they needed to see God's preeminence over their military prowess.

Exodus 14:5, 6
And it was told the king of Egypt that the people fled: and the heart of Pharaoh and of his servants was turned against the people, and they said, why have we done this, that we have let Israel go from serving us? And he made ready his chariot, and took his people with him:

Realizing he had lost his work force, Pharaoh made ready to pursue the Israelites.

Exodus 14:7 (a)
And he took six hundred chosen chariots . . .

The Hebrew word translated "chosen" means "choice." In other words, these chariots were the most sophisticated weapons of the day. Inventors of the chariot, the Egyptian army seemed to have left its enemies in the dust technologically.

Exodus 14:7 (b), 8
. . . and all the chariots of Egypt, and captains over every one of them. And the LORD hardened the heart of Pharaoh king of Egypt, and he pursued after the children of Israel: and the children of Israel went out with an high hand.

That they "went out with a high hand" means the Israelites went out rejoicing, celebrating, giving each other "high fives," so to speak.

Exodus 14:9, 10 (a)
But the Egyptians pursued after them, all the horses and chariots of Pharaoh, and his horsemen, and his army, and overtook them encamping by the sea, beside Pi-hahiroth, before Baal-zephon. And when Pharaoh drew nigh, the children of Israel lifted up their eyes . . .

The children of Israel lifted their eyes only high enough to see the problem. They didn't lift their eyes high enough to see their Protector.

Exodus 14:10 (b), 11 (a)
. . . and, behold, the Egyptians marched after them; and they were sore afraid: and the children of Israel cried out unto the LORD. And they said unto Moses, because there were no graves in Egypt, hast thou taken us away to die in the wilderness?

Because Egyptian culture gave high priority to the afterlife—as evidenced by the pyramids and mummification—for the Israelites to insinuate there were no graves in Egypt was utter nonsense. I find it's amazing how easily I can get mixed up, how skewed my perspective becomes whenever I stray from the Word.

Exodus 14:11 (b)
. . . wherefore hast thou dealt thus with us, to carry us forth out of Egypt?

Why did the Lord lead His people out only to seemingly box them in? I suggest three reasons, the first being to show them His power.

"More love, more power, more of You in my life . . ." we sing.

"More love, more power, more of Me in your life?" the Lord says. "Okay. Here's Pi-hahiroth. There's Migdol. I'm going to plant you right between them with your backs to the Red Sea. I'm going to put you in a place that you can't strategize, rationalize, or compromise your way out of in order that I might show you My power to deliver you in ways you would never have imagined."

Exodus 14:12
Is not this the word that we did tell thee in Egypt, saying, let us alone, that we may serve the Egyptians? For it had been better for us to serve the Egyptians, than that we should die in the wilderness.

"Leave me alone," some people insist. "Leave me in Egypt. I'll just muddle through on my own because even though I've walked with the Lord and followed after Him, look where I am. My back is to the Red Sea; I'm between a mountain of caves and a fortified tower—and here comes Pharaoh's army bearing down on me."

Exodus 14:13
And Moses said unto the people, Fear ye not, stand still, and see the salvation of the LORD, which he will shew to you to day: for the Egyptians whom ye have seen to day, ye shall see them again no more for ever.

"Be strong and show thyself a man" a dying David said to his son, Solomon—or literally, "Play the part of a man" (1 Kings 2:2).

"Put on the whole armor of God," Paul tells us, "that ye may resist the devil . . . and having done all, to stand" (see Ephesians 6:11–13).

"Don't give in; don't fall down; don't go back; but stand," Moses said to the people—even as the Word would say to us today.

Exodus 14:14 (a)
The LORD shall fight for you . . .

I believe the second reason the Lord planted His people between Pi-hahiroth and Migdol was that they might experience His presence. Haven't you found that it's when you're between a rock and a hard place that you perceive the Lord's presence in your life most clearly?

Exodus 14:14 (b)
. . . and ye shall hold your peace.

In other words, Moses said to the people, "When you see the Lord fight for you, you'll regret your whining; you'll quiet down; you'll hold your peace."

Exodus 14:15
And the LORD said unto Moses, wherefore criest thou unto me? Speak unto the children of Israel, that they go forward:

There's a time to pray and a time to proceed; a time to stand and a time to move forward. Now was the time to move forward—and it was up to Moses to set the pace.

Exodus 14:16
But lift thou up thy rod, and stretch out thine hand over the sea, and divide it: and the children of Israel shall go on dry ground through the midst of the sea.

Water is emblematic of the Word. Therefore, Moses' dividing the sea is a picture of what you are to do, Dad, in dividing Scripture (2 Timothy 2:15). Hold out your rod of authority. Say to your son, "Follow me," as you set the pace and lead the way.

Exodus 14:17, 18
And I, behold, I will harden the hearts of the Egyptians, and they shall follow them: and I will get me honour upon Pharaoh, and upon all his host, upon his chariots, and upon his horsemen. And the Egyptians shall know that I am the LORD, when I have gotten me honour upon Pharaoh, upon his chariots, and upon his horsemen.

The third reason God boxed His people in between Pi-hahiroth and Migdol was as a demonstration of His Preeminence. Even more fundamental than our experiencing His power and His presence is the world's understanding of His sovereignty. "I'm going to put you in this horrible predicament, this tough spot, this brutal place," He says, "because I want to make Myself known to the Egyptians."

"I'm stuck in this marriage. I'm stuck with that parent. I'm stuck in a financial crunch," we cry—failing to understand that sometimes He can touch people who don't know Him by putting us in uncomfortable, difficult, heartbreaking, challenging situations. God doesn't exist for us. We exist for Him.

So scandalized was the church, that for decades she refused to acknowledge Copernicus' discovery. After all, how could the *sun* be the center of the planetary system? Surely the planets revolved around the earth, around man.

And it remains equally shocking today to discover that it is the Son rather than our own worlds, our own concerns, our own comfort at the center of God's creation. But it is not until we finally understand that we exist for God rather than He for us that the rotation of our worlds, our situations, and our lives makes sense. If the pain doesn't go away, if the business doesn't work out, if the marriage isn't great, God would say, "I love you. But it's not about you. I have a bigger plan. The Egyptians are watching, and when the people you work with see you continue to praise Me, when your neighbors see you worshiping Me, when your family sees you thanking Me, I will be glorified."

You can fight it until the day you die, or you can finally come to the place in your life where you say, "The Son is the center of everything. Come what may, the Son is the center of my universe."

And although life might not seem fair right now, it will eventually. The waters will part and you will be ushered into eternity where you will hear, "Well done, good and faithful servant. I had you boxed in. But you stood still. You didn't fall away. You didn't turn back. You didn't walk out. Enter in to the joy of the Lord" (Matthew 25:21).

Perhaps special teams football players have the best grasp of this idea. "Special teams" is suicide. Special teams charge down the field full steam ahead, throwing their bodies directly at men who are also running full steam ahead in their direction. They crack heads. They take hits. They endure pain. Why? So that the one carrying the ball can gain yards.

It's such a simple concept, but it sometimes takes decades to understand that we're not the sun, that we're not the ball carrier, but that we exist for the One who is. And the degree to which we allow Him to do what He wants to do through our lives is the degree to which we will be rewarded immensely, immeasurably, eternally.

Exodus 14:19 (a)
And the angel of God, which went before the camp of Israel, removed and went behind them . . .

The angel of the Lord is known as a "Christophany"—an appearance of Jesus in the Old Testament before He came as the Babe of Bethlehem. Jesus—He who previously went before them—now went behind them to be a rear guard, to cover their backs. I like that!

Exodus 14:19 (b), 20
. . . and the pillar of the cloud went from before their face, and stood behind them: And it came between the camp of the Egyptians and the camp of Israel; and it was a cloud and darkness to them, but it gave light by night to these: so that the one came not near the other all the night.

The cloud that was darkness to the Egyptians was light for God's children. The same is true of the Word. To those who choose to walk in darkness because they love darkness rather than light (John 3:19), the Bible is confusing. But to those who seek to walk in the light (1 John 1:7), it is a lamp unto their feet and a light unto their path (Psalm 119:105).

Exodus 14:21–25
And Moses stretched out his hand over the sea; and the LORD caused the sea to go back by a strong east wind all that night, and made the sea dry land, and the waters were divided. And the children of Israel went into the midst of the sea upon the dry ground: and the waters were a wall unto them on their right hand, and on their left. And the Egyptians pursued, and went in after them to the midst of the sea, even all Pharaoh's horses, his chariots, and his horsemen. And it came to pass, that in the morning watch the LORD looked unto the host of the Egyptians through the pillar of fire and of the cloud, and troubled the host of the Egyptians, and took off their chariot wheels, that they drave them heavily: so that the Egyptians said, Let us flee from the face of Israel; for the LORD fighteth for them against the Egyptians.

With their chariots bogged down in the middle of the Red Sea, the Egyptians knew they were in trouble. But it would prove to be too late.

Exodus 14:26–31
And the LORD said unto Moses, Stretch out thine hand over the sea, that the waters may come again upon the Egyptians, upon their chariots, and upon their horsemen. And Moses stretched forth his hand over the sea, and the sea returned to his strength when the morning appeared; and the Egyptians fled against it; and the LORD overthrew the Egyptians in the midst of the sea and the waters returned, and covered the chariots, and the horsemen, and all the host of Pharaoh that came into the sea after them; there remained not so much as one of them. But the children of Israel walked upon dry land in the midst of the sea; and the waters were a wall unto them on their right hand, and on their left. Thus the LORD saved Israel that day out of the hand of the Egyptians; and Israel saw the Egyptians dead upon the sea shore. And Israel saw that great work which the LORD did upon the Egyptians: and the people feared the LORD, and believed the LORD, and his servant Moses.

Finally, Pi-hahiroth and Migdol illustrate the plan of God prophetically. As seen in Psalm 65:7, Daniel 7:2, and Revelation 17:15, with regard to future events, the nations are often referred to as a sea. Here in the Exodus account, the sea—the nations—part in order that the Israelites can reach the Promised Land. From this we understand that any nation seeking to destroy Israel will ultimately see its plan parted in order that the people of Israel can go through on dry land to their destiny. And even as God is faithful to the Jews, He will be faithful to you and me, His family.

15

Exodus 15:1 (a)
Then sang Moses and the children of Israel . . .

The people who were once sighing (Exodus 2:23), are now singing. The first song recorded in

Scripture is sung by people who had been set free, redeemed miraculously.

Exodus 15:1 (b)
. . . this song . . .

This song is not only the first song recorded in Scripture, but also the last—for we see it repeated in Revelation 15, sung around the crystal sea by those who have been raptured. Between Exodus and Revelation, portions are also repeated in Psalm 118, when the people of God were set free from Babylonian captivity—and again in Isaiah 12 by those in the millennial kingdom.

Exodus 15:1 (c)
. . . unto the LORD . . .

Moses and the children of Israel weren't merely singing for the Lord or about the Lord. They sang *to* the Lord. And the Lord liked their song so much that He recorded it four times.

Exodus 15:1 (d), 2
. . . and spake, saying, I will sing unto the LORD, for he hath triumphed gloriously: the horse and his rider hath he thrown into the sea. The LORD is my strength and song, and he is become my salvation: he is my God, and I will prepare him an habitation; my father's God, and I will exalt him.

"I will prepare Him a habitation," says Moses. "The Lord inhabits"—or literally is enthroned upon—"the praises of His people," David declared (Psalm 22:3). When you sing from your heart to the Lord, you construct a habitation, a home, a throne from which He can rule over you. And because the Father seeks those who worship Him in spirit and in truth (John 4:23), when I feel distanced *from* the Lord, when I don't sense the presence *of* the Lord, when I lack intimacy *with* the Lord, the best thing for me to do is to sing *to* the Lord because then He seeks me. And it's a whole lot easier for Him to find me than it is for me to find Him.

Exodus 15:3–10
The LORD is a man of war: the LORD is his name. Pharaoh's chariots and his host hath he cast into the sea: his chosen captains also are drowned in the Red sea. The depths have covered them: they sank into the bottom as a stone. Thy right hand, O LORD, is become glorious in power: thy right hand, O LORD, hath dashed in pieces the enemy. And in the greatness of thine excellency thou hast overthrown them that rose up against thee: thou sentest forth thy wrath, which consumed them as stubble. And with the blast of thy nostrils the waters were gathered together, the floods stood upright as an heap, and the depths were congealed in the heart of the sea. The enemy said, I will pursue, I will overtake, I will divide the spoil; my lust shall be satisfied upon them; I will draw my sword, my hand shall destroy them. Thou didst blow with thy wind, the sea covered them: they sank as lead in the mighty waters.

"God is love," John tells us (1 John 4:8).

"The Lord is a man of war," Moses says.

Is this a contradiction?

No, because, although God is indeed love, there are forces all around us which are anything but lovely or lovable. And God wages war against these forces as surely as He waged war against Pharaoh. That is why, when you study the Old Testament, you'll see violence in virtually every book. And because the Old Testament is a picture book illustrating physically what we're to do spiritually, we're to be violent as well (Matthew 11:12).

How?

We're to do battle violently in prayer against the spiritual forces that seek to deceive, defile, and destroy those around us. Wife, did you do battle in prayer for your husband today? Did you pray passionately that the forces of the enemy would not gain a toehold in his life? Dad, did you do what Job did, who energetically sacrificed for each of his children before the break of day lest they sin against the Lord? (Job 1:5). Did you pray earnestly lest they fall prey to the enemy that seeks to derail and destroy them spiritually?

"The effectual *fervent* prayer of a righteous man avails much," James tells us (5:16). Praying, "Lord, help everyone to be nice," is neither effective nor fervent—and it doesn't make much of an impact. God is a Man of war, but He's a Gentleman nonetheless and, therefore, won't force His way into any situation but will wait for an invitation (Revelation 3:20). The question is, are we actively, fervently, passionately opening the door to Him and bidding Him to come in?

Exodus 15:11–14 (a)
Who is like unto thee, O LORD, among the gods? who is like thee, glorious in holiness, fearful in praises, doing wonders? Thou stretchedst out thy right hand, the earth swallowed them. Thou in thy mercy hast led forth the people which thou hast redeemed: thou hast guided them in thy strength unto thy holy habitation. The people shall hear, and be afraid . . .

"Other nations will tremble when they hear about what You do and how powerful You are," sang the children of Israel.

Exodus 15:14 (b)–17 (a)
. . . sorrow shall take hold on the inhabitants of Palestina. Then the dukes of Edom shall be amazed; the mighty men of Moab, trembling shall take hold upon them; all the inhabitants of Canaan shall melt away. Fear and dread shall fall upon them; by the greatness of thine arm they shall be as still as a stone; till thy people pass over, O LORD, till the people pass over, which thou hast purchased. Thou shalt bring them in . . .

God doesn't simply bring us *out* of Egypt, but He brings us *in* to the Land of Promise. He not only sets us free redemptively—as grand and glorious as that is—but He also brings us into a land flowing with milk and honey, the Spirit-filled life.

Exodus 15:17 (b)–19
. . . and plant them in the mountain of thine inheritance, in the place, O LORD, which thou hast made for thee to dwell in, in the Sanctuary, O Lord, which thy hands have established. The LORD shall reign for ever and ever. For the horse of Pharaoh went in with his chariots and with his horsemen into the sea, and the LORD brought again the waters of the sea upon them; but the children of Israel went on dry land in the midst of the sea.

This is quite a song. I'm anxious to hear it sung in heaven!

Exodus 15:20
And Miriam the prophetess, the sister of Aaron, took a timbrel in her hand; and all the women went out after her with timbrels and with dances.

After Moses finished his song, his older sister took up where he left off. Notice, however, that she led only women. "I don't allow women to teach," Paul would say, "because it was a woman who was deceived by Satan" (see 1 Timothy 2:12). This isn't chauvinism, but old-fashioned wisdom. Satan didn't tempt Eve by offering her a glass of wine or an R-rated movie. He tempted her by offering her a way to be more spiritual. A clever foe, Satan brought about the Fall of humanity through Eve's desire for spirituality. And to this day, a disproportionate number of cults have been founded by women desiring to be more godly.

Exodus 15:21
And Miriam answered them, sing ye to the LORD, for he hath triumphed gloriously; the horse and his rider hath he thrown into the sea.

As good as this song is, how much better it would have been had it been sung at Pi-hahiroth and Migdol, had it been sung *before* the Red Sea parted, had it been sung by the children of Israel *before* they were rescued.

To you who are boxed in between Pi-hahiroth and Migdol with your back to the Red Sea—*this* is your moment; *now* is your opportunity for greatness. You see, once the Red Sea parts—once the financial crisis is over, the relationship is restored, the disease is healed—you will no longer have before you the opportunity for greatness. Then you can be grateful—but only now you can be *great*.

When the hour was dark, when nothing was externally right, there in the middle of a black, bleak night, what did Paul and Silas do? They sang songs of praise. And so intriguing was this to their fellow-prisoners that when an earthquake caused the prison doors to open, they chose to stay in the dungeon with Paul and Silas rather than to flee, to remain imprisoned physically in order that their souls might be set free (Acts 16).

You who are in a dungeon financially, relationally, physiologically have a unique opportunity to show us greatness. And once this experience is over, you'll never have the same opportunity again.

"I want to be like David," we say. "I'd like to grab some stones and nail Goliath." You can. There's a huge giant before you—a giant headache, a giant heartache, a giant problem. Are you going to be like Saul and his men, murmuring and complaining, depressed and discouraged? Or are you going to praise the Lord in the face of the giant that seems to stomp up and down the valley of your life day after day? Ninety-nine percent of people will choose to be like Saul. This is your chance, however, to be a David.

The difficulties in the lives of any great man or woman in Scripture weren't pleasant, weren't easy. We know how their stories end—Joshua, Deborah and Gideon, Jeremiah, David and Paul—but when they were living out their stories, they were every bit as brutal as your situation. Yet they chose by God's grace to be great, to be heroic. And we are the richer for it.

When there's an ugly giant before you, or prison bars all around you, it's your chance to be great. Don't miss it—because although opportunities for greatness come to everyone, they usually only come once or twice in a lifetime. Will your story be one of mediocrity—or one of greatness? It all depends on what you do this side of the Red Sea.

Exodus 15:22
So Moses brought Israel from the Red sea, and they went out into the wilderness of Shur; and they went three days in the wilderness, and found no water.

It would have been nice to linger at the seashore, lounging on the beach, playing tambourines and singing songs of praise. But God says, "Yes, the Sea opened before you. But now we must continue on. There's more to learn." So He led them to the wilderness of Shur—and you can be "sure" He'll do the same with you.

Exodus 15:23
And when they came to Marah, they could not drink of the waters of Marah, for they were bitter: therefore the name of it was called Marah.

Feeling as though death was breathing down upon them, the Israelite's need for water was immediate and great when suddenly the report must have filtered through the congregation that water lay ahead. I can see in my mind's eye the people stampeding in the direction of the report, finding a pool, and diving in—only to come up sputtering and spitting out bitter water.

The same thing happens to us. We come to our own Marah—a situation, a relationship, an occupation, or even a ministry we think will be cool and refreshing—only to find it bitter, not what we thought it would be. Why did the Lord choose Marah as Stop Number Four for His people? I believe it was to teach them three lessons, the first being that life is a mixture of sweetness and bitterness—for were it only sweet, we would have no desire for heaven.

Exodus 15:24
And the people murmured against Moses, saying, what shall we drink?

I believe the second lesson God wanted to teach His people at Marah was that trials are the x-rays that allow us to see what's going on in our hearts. You see, although the children of Israel murmured against Moses, in reality, they were murmuring against God for bringing them to Marah in the first place. And the same is true of us. I will never know what's in my heart until I dive into a pool expectantly and find it isn't what I thought it would be. People do not make us bitter. Situations do not make us bitter. They simply show us what is already within us. I know this because, looking at Jesus, I see that, although He was spat upon, cursed at, and nailed to a cross, He said, "Father forgive them. They don't know what they're doing" (Luke 23:34). No bitterness came out of Him because there was no bitterness within Him.

Exodus 15:25 (a)
And he cried unto the LORD; and the LORD shewed him a tree, which when he had cast into the waters, the waters were made sweet . . .

Thirdly, notice that God didn't create this tree on the spot—but that it was there all along. The tree in Scripture being emblematic of the Cross (1 Peter 2:24; Galatians 3), it is the Cross of Calvary which still transforms bitter experiences, bitter people, bitter circumstances. How? By realizing that the wrongs done to us, the offenses against us, the disappointments registered by us have all been paid for, dealt with, washed clean by the blood of Calvary. In temple worship, every sin had to be named individually. On the Cross of Calvary, the Lamb of God paid for each sin specifically. Nowhere is this seen more clearly than in the little postcard of an epistle located near the end of the New Testament—the Book of Philemon.

A friend of Paul's, Philemon had a slave named Onesimus who evidently ripped him off and ran away. Ending up in prison as a cellmate of the apostle Paul, Onesimus had virtually no choice but to get saved—and when he was released, Paul sent him back to Philemon with a letter in hand which said, "If Onesimus has wronged you or owes you anything charge it to my account" (Philemon 18).

This is the heart of our Lord. "Whatever he, she, or they did to you," He says to us, "charge it to My account, for I died for it specifically."

How does this work out practically?

Read on . . .

Exodus 15:25 (b)
. . . there he made for them a statute and an ordinance, and there he proved them,

It is during the ordinance of Communion that we can say, "As I hold this cup, Lord, I realize that not only are my sins washed away, that I'm robed in Your righteousness, that You live within Me—but that the one who hurt me, who abandoned me, who disappointed me is forgiven as well by the same blood that cleanses me."

How long has it been since, at the Lord's Table,

you've embraced the grace that God shed not only on you, but on those who hurt you?

"But what she did to me was awful," you say. "What he said about me was unforgivable," you say. "How they hurt me was incomprehensible," you say.

Ah, but where sin abounds, grace abounds *more* (Romans 5:20). Come to the Lord's Table regularly—not just for yourself, but for the one who hurt you. Cast in the tree of the Cross of Calvary, and drink deeply of sweet water once again.

Exodus 15:26
And said, If thou wilt diligently hearken to the voice of the LORD thy God, and wilt do that which is right in his sight, and wilt give ear to his commandments, and keep all his statutes, I will put none of these diseases upon thee, which I have brought upon the Egyptians: for I am the LORD that healeth thee.

"I am *Jehovah-Rapha*"—the Lord who healeth thee. By linking this new revelation with what just took place at Marah, the implication is clear that if we want to be healthy, we are to be those who forgive. Certain types of heart diseases, cancers, and ulcers are medically linked to an unforgiving heart, to bitterness. Paul echoed this same idea when he told the Corinthians that many of them were unnecessarily sick or even dying because of their failure to give worth to the Lord's Table (1 Corinthians 11:30).

Exodus 15:27
And they came to Elim, where were twelve wells of water, and threescore and ten palm trees: and they encamped there by the waters.

Following their time at Marah, God led the children of Israel to Stop Number Five: *Elam,* or "Mighty ones." With twelve wells of water and seventy palm trees, God had led them to a wonderful oasis indeed. I'm so glad that the Lord not only takes us to the bitter water of Marah, but to the cool wells of Elam! The palm tree being the only tree in the world which bears more fruit as it gets older, and the numbers twelve and seventy reminding us of the twelve disciples and the seventy Jesus sent out in ministry, could it be that the Holy Spirit gives us this vignette to say that the place we'll find true refreshment is to be "mighty ones" in ministry?

"Whatever measure you give out will be the measure you'll get back," Jesus told us (see Luke 6:38). At Elam, there's no murmuring, nothing negative, nothing but refreshment in the place of service. Tomorrow, serve someone and bless someone, share your faith, intercede for someone—and be blessed and refreshed yourself in the process.

16

Exodus 16:1
And they took their journey from Elim, and all the congregation of the children of Israel came unto the wilderness of Sin, which is between Elim and Sinai, on the fifteenth day of the second month after their departing out of the land of Egypt.

Having left the oasis of Elim, the children of Israel find themselves in the wilderness once again—the perfect place for God to show them His power and provision yet once more . . .

Exodus 16:2, 3
And the whole congregation of the children of Israel murmured against Moses and Aaron in the wilderness: And the children of Israel said unto them, Would to God we had died by the hand of the LORD in the land of Egypt, when we sat by the flesh pots, and when we did eat bread to the full; for ye have brought us forth into this wilderness, to kill this whole assembly with hunger.

Flesh pots? Bread to the full? It's amazing how the mind plays tricks and how the enemy capitalizes on this. These ex-slaves replaced memories of baking bricks under the blistering Egyptian sun with fantasies of croissants and filet mignon. And such is our tendency as well whenever we think of the lives we lived before we left Egypt, the brutal days in bondage before we were rescued, redeemed, and saved.

Exodus 16:4 (a)
Then said the LORD unto Moses, Behold, I will rain bread from heaven for you . . .

To the murmurers and complainers did God say, "I'm going to rain fire and judgment upon you"? No, He said, "I'll rain bread upon you. I'll pour out blessing upon you." Such is the heart of our Father.

Exodus 16:4 (b)
. . . and the people shall go out and gather a certain rate every day, that I may prove them, whether they will walk in my law, or no.

What do you do with the bread God rains upon you—with the paycheck you get each week by

His grace? God has entrusted it to you and now, as He said to the children of Israel, He says to you, "Let's see what you're going to do with it."

Exodus 16:5
And it shall come to pass, that on the sixth day they shall prepare that which they bring in; and it shall be twice as much as they gather daily.

Providing twice as much as they would need on the sixth day in order that they could rest on the seventh day, here God reiterates what He Himself modeled at creation when He rested on the seventh day.

Exodus 16:6–8
And Moses and Aaron said unto all the children of Israel, At even, then ye shall know that the LORD hath brought you out from the land of Egypt: And in the morning, then ye shall see the glory of the LORD; for that he heareth your murmurings against the LORD: and what are we, that ye murmur against us? And Moses said, This shall be, when the LORD shall give you in the evening flesh to eat, and in the morning bread to the full; for that the LORD heareth your murmurings which ye murmur against him: and what are we? your murmurings are not against us, but against the LORD.

Verse 2 clearly states that it was against Moses and Aaron that the children of Israel murmured. Moses, however, correctly identifies their complaints as being against the Lord as well. And the same is true with us. Anytime we complain about our supervisors, parents, or circumstances, we are actually complaining against God for putting us in the situation in the first place.

Exodus 16:9–12 (a)
And Moses spake unto Aaron, Say unto all the congregation of the children of Israel, Come near before the LORD: for he hath heard your murmurings. And it came to pass, as Aaron spake unto the whole congregation of the children of Israel, that they looked toward the wilderness, and, behold, the glory of the LORD appeared in the cloud. And the LORD spake unto Moses, saying, I have heard the murmurings of the children of Israel: speak unto them, saying, At even ye shall eat flesh, and in the morning ye shall be filled with bread . . .

"I've heard your murmuring," God said. "Therefore, I'm going to send you meat tonight and bread tomorrow." Truly, our Father is *amazingly* merciful.

Exodus 16:12 (b)
. . . and ye shall know that I am the LORD your God.

The bread the Lord would send to the children of Israel provides a perfect picture of the bread He sends us in His Word and in His Son, the Word made flesh . . .

Exodus 16:13
And it came to pass, that at even the quails came up, and covered the camp: and in the morning the dew lay round about the host.

Numbers 11 tells us that the host, the bread, was covered by dew in order that it not be defiled by the ground. In addition to this practical reason, I believe it was so that we could see a wonderful illustration of both the written Word and the Word made flesh, Jesus Christ. You see, water in the Scriptures speaks of the work and Person of the Holy Spirit. No wonder, then, that the bread came in the dew, for it is only as the Spirit gives us understanding that we can read the written Word—and only by the Spirit that Jesus, the Word made flesh, was conceived (Matthew 1:20).

Exodus 16:14, 15 (a)
And when the dew that lay was gone up, behold, upon the face of the wilderness there lay a small round thing, as small as the hoar frost on the ground. And when the children of Israel saw it, they said one to another, It is manna: for they wist not what it was . . .

Manna being small and round speaks both of humility and eternity. The entire counsel of God—all we need to know to navigate life successfully—is contained in a book easily carried to Sunday school by kindergarteners. Yet so powerful is it that it will outlive our planet (Matthew 5:18). Jesus humbled Himself to come to us not only as a Baby, but as the servant of all (Mark 10:45), as One whose only autobiographical statement was that He was meek and lowly (Matthew 11:29). Yet, like the written Word, Jesus—the Word made flesh—is eternal, the great I AM (John 8:58).

Exodus 16:15 (b), 16
. . . And Moses said unto them, This is the bread which the LORD hath given you to eat. This is the thing which the LORD hath commanded, gather of it every man according to his eating, an omer for every man, according to the number of your persons; take ye every man for them which are in his tents.

Of the written Word, Jeremiah declared, "Thy words were found, and I ate them. And they were to me the joy and rejoicing of my heart" (15:16).

"Take, eat. This is My body, broken for you," Jesus declared (Matthew 26:26). Too many people analyze and theorize the Word without eating it, digesting it, allowing it to change their lives. And too many do the same concerning Jesus.

"Lord, Lord," they will call Him in the last day, only to hear Him say, "Depart from Me. I never knew you" (Matthew 7:22, 23) because they had no true intimacy or interaction with Him.

Exodus 16:17, 18
And the children of Israel did so, and gathered, some more, some less. And when they did mete it with an omer, he that gathered much had nothing over, and he that gathered little had no lack; they gathered every man according to his eating.

An omer was six pints. Therefore, if the children of Israel numbered even two million—a conservative estimate—God would have provided 4,500 tons of bread daily—or enough to fill ten trains with thirty boxcars each. Our God is a God of abundance. In the written Word He gives us *all* that pertains to life and godliness (2 Peter 1:3) and in His Son He gives us all that we need to live with Him forever (John 3:16).

Exodus 16:19, 20
And Moses said, Let no man leave of it till the morning. Notwithstanding they hearkened not unto Moses; but some of them left of it until the morning, and it bred worms, and stank: and Moses was wroth with them.

That which was gathered but not eaten began to stink. The same is true of the Word—for whenever we gather teaching or truth without applying it, whenever we take in without giving out, we'll begin to tire of it. When we are chewing on, digesting, and applying the Word, we will always be hungry for more. Therefore, when people say, "I'm not being spiritually fed," it's because they're simply taking in information without making application. When I'm not sharing with others that which I've learned, when I'm not incorporating into my life truth I've been given, I get critical. But when I'm sharing and incorporating, I'm always hungry for more. If Bible study "stinks," if your walk with Jesus seems stale, I encourage you to start serving once again. And not only will you find that your appetite returns, but you'll find yourself in Elim, the place of rest and refreshment.

Exodus 16:21
And they gathered it every morning, every man according to his eating: and when the sun waxed hot, it melted.

Once the sun arose, the day began, the manna disappeared—and I have found the same thing to be true still. Oh, I may have great intentions of personal Bible study in the afternoon or an evening time of devotion—but after walking with the Lord for over forty years, I am more convinced than ever that spending time in the Word, time in fellowship with Jesus in the morning hours is the key. This should come as no surprise, for Jesus Himself "rose a great while before morning" in order to spend time with His Father (Mark 1:35), in order to receive a word to speak to those who are weary (Isaiah 50:4).

Exodus 16:22–27
And it came to pass, that on the sixth day they gathered twice as much bread, two omers for one man: and all the rulers of the congregation came and told Moses. And he said unto them, This is that which the LORD hath said, To morrow is the rest of the holy sabbath unto the LORD: bake that which ye will bake to day, and seethe that ye will seethe; and that which remaineth over lay up for you to be kept until the morning. And they laid it up till the morning, as Moses bade: and it did not stink, neither was there any worm therein. And Moses said, Eat that to day; for to day is a sabbath unto the LORD: to day ye shall not find it in the field. Six days ye shall gather it; but on the seventh day, which is the sabbath, in it there shall be none. And it came to pass, that there went out some of the people on the seventh day for to gather, and they found none.

If we can gather this much in six days, thought some, *imagine how much we could get if we worked Sunday, too.* But they came back empty-handed because God's way is that His people take a day to rest and honor Him, a day to make Him our priority and to be renewed in our faith.

"Oh, but I work seven days a week," some might say, "and I don't come home empty-handed. My paycheck proves it."

To them, Haggai would say, "Watch and see what happens over the long haul—when you discover that regardless of all your labor, you are still empty" (see Haggai 1:9).

Exodus 16:28–31 (a)
And the LORD said unto Moses, How long refuse ye to keep my commandments and

my laws? See, for that the LORD hath given you the sabbath, therefore he giveth you on the sixth day the bread of two days; abide ye every man in his place, let no man go out of his place on the seventh day. So the people rested on the seventh day. And the house of Israel called the name thereof Manna: and it was like coriander seed, white . . .

The color white speaks of purity, of holiness. "How shall a young man cleanse his way?" the psalmist asked. "By taking heed thereto according to Thy Word," he answered (Psalm 119:9). In Jesus, the Word made flesh, we see nothing but purity. When we look at one another, we see flaws, gaps, and holes. When we look at Him, we see only holiness.

Exodus 16:31 (b)
. . . and the taste of it was like wafers made with honey.

The psalmist found the law to be sweeter than honey and the honeycomb (Psalm 19:10). And haven't we found Jesus to be just that? Jesus is never grumpy, never moody, never touchy. He never has a bad day. He's powerful, awesome, holy—and yet He's also sweeter than honey.

Exodus 16:32–34
And Moses said, This is the thing which the LORD commandeth, fill an omer of it to be kept for your generations; that they may see the bread wherewith I have fed you in the wilderness, when I brought you forth from the land of Egypt. And Moses said unto Aaron, Take a pot, and put an omer full of manna therein, and lay it up before the LORD, to be kept for your generations. As the LORD commanded Moses, so Aaron laid it up before the Testimony, to be kept.

This pot would be kept in the ark of the covenant along with Aaron's rod and the Ten Commandments (Hebrews 9:4)—as a reminder of God's provision, power, and plan for His people.

Exodus 16:35, 36
And the children of Israel did eat manna forty years, until they came to a land inhabited; they did eat manna, until they came unto the borders of the land of Canaan. Now an omer is the tenth part of an ephah.

It was in the wilderness that God gave manna to His people. And it is in our wilderness here on earth that He daily provides the Bread of His Word, the Bread of Himself. If I don't feast on the Scriptures daily, I become disillusioned, disoriented, confused. I get mixed up on the days I don't get away with the Lord in a quiet spot at a quiet time and enjoy the truths and promises of His Word. I think about fleshpots and the bread of Egypt; I become restless and troubled. But when I take in the Word, I find what Jeremiah said to be oh, so true. I find it to indeed be the very joy and rejoicing of my heart (Jeremiah 15:16).

Like manna, Jesus Christ, the Word made flesh, came to this wilderness—to murmurers, sinners, and complainers—and dwelt among us (John 1:14). God didn't wait for the children of Israel in the Promised Land. He joined them in the wilderness. And He does the same for us. You don't have to climb a mountain or clean up your act to find Him. You don't have to ascend into heaven or descend into the depths of hell and depression. He's already as close as the word in your mouth, as close as your confession (Romans 10:8–10).

It was hunger that inevitably drove the prodigal son home (Luke 15:17). And it is hunger—a hole in your heart, a longing in your soul—that will drive you home as well. All you must do is humble yourself, bow your knee, and stoop to pick up the manna of the Word, the manna of the Son, which God has provided so lavishly and lovingly, so freely and faithfully.

17

Exodus 17:1
And all the congregation of the children of Israel journeyed from the wilderness of Sin, after their journeys, according to the commandment of the LORD, and pitched in Rephidim: and there was no water for the people to drink.

Stop Number Seven was at *Rephidim*, or "Rest Stop." If you've ever pulled into a rest stop along the highway, feeling so thirsty you thought you'd die if you had to drive a mile more—only to find the drinking fountain out of order, you know how the children of Israel must have felt when they arrived at Rephidim.

Exodus 17:2–4
Wherefore the people did chide with Moses, and said, Give us water that we may drink. And Moses said unto them, Why chide ye with me? Wherefore do ye tempt the LORD? And the people thirsted there for water; and the people murmured against Moses, and said, Wherefore is this that thou hast brought us up out of Egypt, to kill us and our children and our cattle with thirst? And Moses cried unto the LORD, saying, What

shall I do unto this people? They be almost ready to stone me.

What a hard job it must have been for Moses to pastor this congregation. Every time there's a problem, they're ready to nail him.

Exodus 17:5–7
And the LORD said unto Moses, Go on before the people, and take with thee of the elders of Israel; and thy rod, wherewith thou smotest the river, take in thine hand, and go. Behold, I will stand before thee there upon the rock in Horeb; and thou shalt smite the rock, and there shall come water out of it, that the people may drink. And Moses did so in the sight of the elders of Israel. And he called the name of the place Massah, and Meribah, because of the chiding of the children of Israel, and because they tempted the LORD, saying, Is the LORD among us, or not?

Massah and *Meribah* mean "chiding" and "temptation." It was hot. The people were thirsty. And God said to Moses, "Here's what to do: Take the rod which had become a snake before Pharaoh, smite the rock, and out will come water." Paul gives the interpretation of this account in 1 Corinthians 10:4, where he tells us the Rock was Jesus Christ. This means that Jesus, the Rock of our salvation, was smitten by the "serpent" of Moses' rod—perfectly portraying the prophecy given in the Garden of Eden when God said to Satan, "You shall bruise His heel, but He will crush your head" (see Genesis 3:15). Was the heel of Jesus bruised? Yes. A spike was driven through it on the Cross of Calvary. But Satan was crushed—for the power he held over us was obliterated, washed away by the blood Jesus shed that day. What happened when Jesus was pierced with the spear? Blood and water flowed from His side (John 19:34). So, too, here at Rephidim, the Rock, smitten by the rod that was once a serpent pours forth water. The analogy is perfect. This passage points to Jesus.

Why would God lead His people from a place where they were being satisfied with manna to a rest stop where the drinking fountain was out of order? You might leave a Bible study or a retreat where you've been feasting on the manna of the Word only to find yourself in a place of dryness. "I don't understand," you say. "I was doing so well—but now there is a drought in my soul. Why am I so dry? Is there sin in my life?" Not necessarily. God led His people to Rephidim in order to do something very important. You see, after they ate of the manna, to make them aware of their need for a fresh drenching of water, God brought them to Rephidim to create in them a thirst for more of Him. Why would He do this? Because He knew what was about to happen . . .

Exodus 17:8 (a)
Then came Amalek . . .

Every time the Amalekites are mentioned in the Bible, they speak of the ongoing war we wage with our flesh. Here, it's as if God says, "I know you feasted on the bread. You've taken in the manna. But right around the bend, right up ahead, war is about to break out. And if you try and defeat Amalek in your own strength, you'll be trounced." Therefore, He took His people—as He does us—to a place where they were aware of their dryness in order that, after crying out to Him, they would be empowered afresh with the water of His Spirit.

If you are going through a desert season, God has led you there. For what purpose? To create within you a craving for more of Him. "Blessed are they who hunger and thirst for righteousness," Jesus said, "for they shall be filled" (Matthew 5:6). Who is filled? The one who hungers. The one who thirsts. The one who's at Rephidim, longing for water.

Exodus 17:8 (b)
. . . and fought with Israel in Rephidim.

Amalek was the descendant of Esau, Jacob's twin brother. Jacob was the one who, although he made mistakes as we all do, had a heart for God. Esau, on the other hand, was carnal, not interested in spiritual things, one who sold his birthright for a bowl of stew. Amalek, Esau's grandson, fathered a people who, like their forefather, Esau, were people epitomized by carnality. The Amalekites were a brutal people, intimidated by no one, who sought to wipe out the children of Israel as easily as they did other nations . . .

> Remember what Amalek did unto thee by the way, when ye were come forth out of Egypt; how he met thee by the way, and smote the hindmost of thee, even all that were feeble behind thee, when thou wast faint and weary; and he feared not God.
>
> Deuteronomy 25:17, 18

When the Israelites were set free from Egypt, headed for the Land of Promise, Amalek would ambush those in the back of the pack. And that's still the tactic of the flesh. That is, when a person is no longer front and center, no longer fully engaged like he once was, Amalek is sure to strike.

Whenever we say, "I've been on this journey a long time. I've gone to tons of Bible studies. I've been to countless prayer meetings. I've had my share of Communion"—that is when the flesh rises up, when the flesh takes control, when Amalek launches an ambush. Front and center, fully engaged is the best place, the safest place, the only place to be.

Exodus 17:9
And Moses said unto Joshua, Choose us out men, and go out, fight with Amalek: to morrow I will stand on the top of the hill with the rod of God in mine hand.

Moses told a young general named Joshua to engage in battle while he would take his position on the top of the hill, rod in hand.

Exodus 17:10, 11
So Joshua did as Moses had said to him, and fought with Amalek: and Moses, Aaron, and Hur went up to the top of the hill. And it came to pass, when Moses held up his hand, that Israel prevailed: and when he let down his hand, Amalek prevailed.

The lifting up of hands speaks of prayer (1 Timothy 2:8). As long as Moses reached out to the Lord on the mountain of intercession, there was victory below in the valley of interaction.

Exodus 17:12
But Moses' hands were heavy; and they took a stone, and put it under him, and he sat thereon; and Aaron and Hur stayed up his hands, the one on the one side, and the other on the other side; and his hands were steady until the going down of the sun.

"Men ought always to pray and not to faint," Jesus said (Luke 18:1). And as long as Moses was doing just that, there was victory. But once his hands got heavy—which can happen so easily—victory was in jeopardy. I have experienced this. You have, too. We know we should pray with passion. We know we should pray with greater fervency, greater frequency, greater intensity. But we get weary. The solution? Do what Moses did. Cultivate an Aaron and a Hur. Everyone needs a couple of people you can count on—that when your soul sags, when you know Amalek is on the attack, when you feel your flesh rising up within you, you can say, "Pray for me."

Exodus 17:13–16
And Joshua discomfited Amalek and his people with the edge of the sword. And the LORD said unto Moses, Write this for a memorial in a book, and rehearse it in the ears of Joshua: for I will utterly put out the remembrance of Amalek from under heaven. And Moses built an altar, and called the name of it Jehovah-nissi: For he said, Because the LORD hath sworn that the LORD will have war with Amalek from generation to generation.

When the battle was finally won, God instructed Moses to record what had transpired in a book—in order that future generations would know that the battle was won not with the sword in the valley of interaction, but through prayer on the mount of intercession.

Oftentimes, we think that if we were more skilled with the sword of Scripture, if we were better able to dialogue and counsel, if we could love more and do more, we'd see the salvation of our parents or grandchildren, our neighbors or friends. But this story tells us that is not where the battle is won. It's won through prayer.

Why is prayer so important? Because the old adage that prayer changes things is only partly true. I think it's more accurate to say, "Faith changes things. Prayer changes *me*."

Yes, God wanted the children of Israel to win the battle. But He also wanted to win the heart of Moses in a deeper way. And He wants to do the same with us. We may think that our situation needs to change. God, however, knows that even if it did, we'd still be unhappy, sleepwalking through life unless our hearts were changed. Therefore He says, "Because I want to fill your heart, enflame your soul, satisfy that ache within you which can be satisfied only by Me, you're going to have to come to Me time after time because when you do, you'll get to know Me in the process. And when you get to know Me, that is when, and only when you'll be content and fulfilled, blessed and happy." That's what prayer is about. It's not about seeing things change, but about seeing ourselves change; not about a change of circumstance, but about engagement of spirit and expansion of heart.

"Behold, I stand at the door and knock," Jesus says. "If any man hear My voice and open the door, I will come in to him and sup with him and he with Me." Addressed to the church, Revelation 3:20 tells us Jesus knocks at the door of the church, at the heart of believers. Therefore, when we pray, we are acting as doormen, opening the door and inviting Him in. He doesn't beat the door down. He doesn't bust His way in. He doesn't force His presence or force the issue. But whoever hears the knocking and is wise enough to open the door in prayer will enjoy His presence and company. Prayer opens the door.

By praying, I open the door. That doesn't mean Jesus is obligated to do what I ask or desire. That's up to Him. I have learned, however, that if He doesn't do what I suggest, He'll do something infinitely better. But if I don't open the door, if I don't pray, I'm left on my own with my kids, with my marriage, with my ministry—not a good place to be. "You have not because you ask not," James tells us (4:2). It's all about prayer.

Before leaving Rephidim, I draw your attention to one more consideration . . .

In the middle of the battle, were Joshua to look over his shoulder, he would have seen three men on a hill—the one in the middle holding a wooden rod. This makes us think of another Man on a hill, flanked by two others, arms outstretched, holding not a wooden rod, but pinned to a wooden beam. But His arms didn't sag; His soul didn't sag; His spirit didn't sag. No, Jesus our Savior hung in there for you and me. And the Man in the middle not only bled and died for me, but He rose again, where He lives to make intercession for me (Hebrews 7:25). Aaron might get busy sometimes. Hur might not always be available. But Jesus ever lives to make intercession for me. He lives to pray for me. Amazing.

"If that's the case," you say, "then why should we pray at all? Why not just let Him do the heavy lifting?" Because, although the victory is won, there are still mop-up operations going on. Do you want to be fruitful, successful, blessed in the daily skirmishes of life? Do you want to see your kids do well, the church blessed, the country changed? Jesus won the victory completely at Calvary. All the rest is mop-up stuff. And we have the privilege of taking part. "Seek Me," the Lord says. "Talk to Me. Call on Me with uplifted hands. And watch and see what I will do as you open the door for Me to work."

18

His was a high and holy calling indeed. He had been called into ministry—and what a ministry it was: to lead between two and three million people out of slavery into the land of their destiny. But on his way to do the bidding of the Lord, on his way to tell Pharaoh to let God's people go, Moses was pinned to the ground by the Lord Himself for his failure to minister to his own family, for his failure to circumcise his own son personally. Looking on the scene and understanding the severity of the situation, Moses' wife, Zipporah, circumcised their son immediately. As a result, Moses' life was spared and he would go on to incredible ministry. But, because his wife was forced to assume a role never intended to be hers, Moses' neglect cost him his family for a season when Zipporah took Gershom and left.

Months passed, and here at the outset of chapter 18, we pick up the story. Our God is the God of the second chance. And I'm so glad. I've dropped the ball, haven't you? I've messed up once or twice, maybe three times in my life—how about you? But look what happens. Moses' family is about to be reunited and restored . . .

Exodus 18:1, 2
When Jethro, the priest of Midian, Moses' father in law, heard of all that God had done for Moses, and for Israel his people, and that the LORD had brought Israel out of Egypt; then Jethro, Moses' father in law, took Zipporah, Moses' wife, after he had sent her back,

This story is not only one of the restoration of a family, but is rich as it relates to prophecy. You see, the manna of chapter 16 spoke of the Incarnation. Rephidim spoke of the Crucifixion. Moses' ministry on the mount of intercession during the battle with the Amalekites spoke of the Resurrection. And that brings us to this story that speaks of the next event on the prophetic timetable: Christ's return to establish His kingdom.

In this story, although Zipporah is a Gentile, she is a type of Israel. In Scriptures like Jeremiah 31:32 and Isaiah 54:6, Israel is called the wife of Jehovah. And Zipporah is a precursor to another who would represent Israel's relationship to God, a precursor to Gomer, the adulterous wife seen in the Book of Hosea. Calling Moses a "bloody husband," Zipporah fled from Moses because she was offended.

Paul would declare that Christ crucified was a stumbling block to the Jew (1 Corinthians 1:23). What offended the Jewish people? A bloody Messiah. After all, they were looking for Messiah to come with power and majesty—not some bloody Carpenter pinned to a Roman tree. And the idea of a meek and lowly, bloody and battered Messiah remains offensive to the Jewish people to this day.

Exodus 18:3 (a)
And her two sons . . .

Moses' two sons speak of the fact that Israel would be divided into two kingdoms.

Exodus 18:3 (b)
. . . of which the name of the one was Gershom; for he said, I have been an alien in a strange land:

Within forty years after the Jews rejected Jesus as Messiah, they became strangers in a strange land, scattered throughout every corner of the world. For 2,000 years they didn't have a home—yet they kept their identity. How? Read on . . .

Exodus 18:4
And the name of the other was Eliezer; for the God of my father, said he, was mine help, and delivered me from the sword of Pharaoh:

Even though the Jews were scattered, God would be their help. And just as *Eliezer*—whose name means God is my help—was not known until this section, so, too, the Jews will not know how much God has been their help until the time the kingdom is established. Presently they know they've been strangers in a strange land, but there is coming a day when they will see how God was with them.

Exodus 18:5 (a)
And Jethro, Moses' father in law, came with his sons and his wife unto Moses into the wilderness . . .

It was Jethro, the priest of Midian, the Gentile priest, who brought Zipporah back into unity with Moses. Paul declares that God will use the Gentiles, the church, us, to provoke His people to jealousy (Romans 11:11).

Exodus 18:5 (b)
. . . where he encamped at the mount of God:

Where will the reunion take place in which the wife of Jehovah, Israel, at last understands her history, her destiny? When Jesus Christ stands on the Mount of Olives and goes into the Holy City, Mount Zion, Jerusalem. Zechariah tells us that when the Jewish people see Jesus coming as their nation is about to be destroyed in the campaign of Armageddon, they'll ask Him where He got His wounds. "In the house of My friends," Jesus will answer (Zechariah 13:6). And they'll understand that it was by their own hand. Zechariah goes on to tell us that there will be a fountain that will be available to the Jewish people as a fountain of cleansing (Zechariah 13:1). And at that moment all Israel will be saved (Romans 11:26).

Exodus 18:6–12
And he said unto Moses, I thy father in law Jethro am come unto thee, and thy wife, and her two sons with her. And Moses went out to meet his father in law, and did obeisance, and kissed him; and they asked each other of their welfare; and they came into the tent. And Moses told his father in law all that the LORD had done unto Pharaoh and to the Egyptians for Israel's sake, and all the travail that had come upon them by the way, and how the LORD delivered them. And Jethro rejoiced for all the goodness which the LORD had done to Israel, whom he had delivered out of the hand of the Egyptians. And Jethro said, Blessed be the LORD, who hath delivered you out of the hand of the Egyptians, and out of the hand of Pharaoh, who hath delivered the people from under the hand of the Egyptians. Now I know that the LORD is greater than all gods: for in the thing wherein they dealt proudly he was above them. And Jethro, Moses' father in law, took a burnt offering and sacrifices for God: and Aaron came, and all the elders of Israel, to eat bread with Moses' father in law before God.

In the Millennium, a new temple will be built and sacrifices will be offered—not to atone for sin, for that work was finished completely on the Cross of Calvary, but to serve as visual aids in order to help the Tribulation saints understand the price Jesus paid as the sacrificial Lamb of God (Zechariah 14:16). It is only fitting, then, that here we would see sacrifice being made at the reunion of Moses' family.

Last night I took my dog, Sam, for a walk. It was one of those nights that was so clear it seemed as though I could see a zillion stars—one of which shot across the Milky Way in an almost magical display. Yet Sam missed the whole thing because he was sniffing the ground for traces of other dogs. Here was this grand and glorious scene—and he had his nose in the bushes. I'm convinced Sam misses ninety percent of what life is about because his understanding, his interests are oh, so small.

I'm convinced such is the case with a lot of us. We're sniffing around in small stuff, so caught up on the ground that we miss what's going on overhead. I become restricted, small-minded, and petty when I don't keep before me the big picture of eternity—of what God is up to, where we're going, what lies ahead. As I read my Bible, I understand that page after page is trying to get my nose out of the bushes and to look up and see the grand design of God's plan for eternity and how I fit in. When I was a younger believer, I wished there were books in the Bible devoted to practical stuff—how to have a better marriage, how to raise kids, how to handle money. But the older I get, the more I realize the practical stuff leads only to disappointment and legalism. I realize that Jesus was right when He said, "Seek first the kingdom and all these other things will take care of themselves" (Matthew 6:33). I realize His wisdom in saying "Look beyond. Understand My grand plan. Lift your eyes to the skies."

Exodus 18:13–18
And it came to pass on the morrow, that Moses sat to judge the people: and the people stood by Moses from the morning unto the evening. And when Moses' father in law saw all that he did to the people, he said, What is this thing that thou doest to the people? Why sittest thou thyself alone, and all the people stand by thee from morning unto even? And Moses said unto his father in law, Because the people come unto me to inquire of God: When they have a matter, they come unto me; and I judge between one and another, and I do make them know the statutes of God, and his laws. And Moses' father in law said unto him, The thing that thou doest is not good. Thou wilt surely wear away, both thou, and this people that is with thee: for this thing is too heavy for thee; thou art not able to perform it thyself alone.

Jethro told Moses that if he continued to try and tend to the needs of all of the people, he himself would burn out and the people would wear out trying to get the counsel they needed. And then he went on to offer a solution . . .

Exodus 18:19, 20
Hearken now unto my voice, I will give thee counsel, and God shall be with thee: be thou for the people to Godward, that thou mayest bring the causes unto God: And thou shalt teach them ordinances and laws, and shalt shew them the way wherein they must walk, and the work that they must do.

Moses was to continue to pray for and teach the people. But he was also to do something else . . .

Exodus 18:21–27
Moreover thou shalt provide out of all the people able men, such as fear God, men of truth, hating covetousness; and place such over them, to be rulers of thousands, and rulers of hundreds, rulers of fifties, and rulers of tens: and let them judge the people at all seasons: and it shall be, that every great matter they shall bring unto thee, but every small matter they shall judge: so shall it be easier for thyself, and they shall bear the burden with thee. If thou shalt do this thing, and God command thee so, then thou shalt be able to endure, and all this people shall also go to their place in peace. So Moses hearkened to the voice of his father in law, and did all that he had said. And Moses chose able men out of all Israel, and made them heads over the people, rulers of thousands, rulers of hundreds, rulers of fifties, and rulers of tens. And they judged the people at all seasons: the hard causes they brought unto Moses, but every small matter they judged themselves. And Moses let his father in law depart; and he went his way into his own land.

Here we see the establishing of eldership. Moses was to appoint a group of men with different responsibilities—some to oversee hundreds, some to oversee fifties, some to oversee tens—who would judge and counsel the people. Numbers 11:17 tells us that God would take the same spirit that was upon Moses and place it upon them. Thus, their leadership would be at one with his.

Jesus picks up this same model in appointing twelve to be with Him. In the Book of Acts, it is seen in the establishing of elders. Paul reiterates this principle in the epistles. And it crescendos and climaxes in the Book of Revelation, where we see twenty-four elders ministering in heaven, bowing before the throne, sitting quietly before the Lord, pointing to Jesus Christ, saying, "Righteous and true are Thy judgments, O Lord" (Revelation 19:9). God's plan from Exodus through Revelation is that of plurality and collegiality—to work through groups of men who stand together and care for His flock, brothers who fear God, who are committed to truth, who aren't in it for themselves. And mature is the church, wise is the believer who takes advantage of this wisdom.

19

In chapter 19, we arrive at the Israelite's final "campsite" on their pilgrimage from Egypt to the Promised Land. As with the previous six stops, this was a place God ordained them to be in order that He might prepare them for their land of destiny. But this stop would be different. The scene at Mt. Sinai is one of the most significant in the history of the world, for it was there that God spoke audibly.

Exodus 19:1
In the third month, when the children of Israel were gone forth out of the land of Egypt, the same day came they into the wilderness of Sinai.

Comparing this verse with Numbers 10:11, we see that the children of Israel would camp here for eleven months. Why so long? Because it was here that they would be given the entire Law of God and the instructions for the construction of the tabernacle.

Exodus 19:2
For they were departed from Rephidim, and were come to the desert of Sinai, and had pitched in the wilderness; and there Israel camped before the mount.

Here at Mt. Sinai, God will audibly speak to His people in a way unparalleled in human history. It seems only natural that God would choose Mt. Sinai to speak to this congregation of two to three million. After all, rectangular in shape, Mt. Sinai not only looks like a huge pulpit, but its name means "thorny"—an apt description of the Law God would give to Moses, a Law perfect and glorious but one which pricks mankind because of our inability to keep it.

Mt. Sinai is also called Mt. Horeb in Scripture. *Horeb* means "to kill or destroy." That's what the Law does—it destroys my concept of my own goodness and brings me to the realization that I'm a sinner in desperate need of a Savior.

Exodus 19:3, 4 (a)
And Moses went up unto God, and the LORD called unto him out of the mountain, saying, Thus shalt thou say to the house of Jacob, and tell the children of Israel; ye have seen what I did unto the Egyptians . . .

The first thing the children of Israel were to do in preparation to receive the Law was to remember—to remember how God had set them free from their bondage in Egypt. How important it is that I always remember what the Lord has done for me, how good He has been to me—for as I read the Word, I realize that what He asks of me is not because He's a mean ogre trying to make me miserable, but because He is a loving Father who truly wants the best for me. That's why Communion is so very important. Every time I come to the Lord's Table, I'm reminded again that He loves me to death.

Exodus 19:4 (b)
. . . and how I bare you on eagles' wings, and brought you unto myself.

With eagles soaring over their heads and eagles' nests perched on the ledges of the Sinai mountain range, this image would be very clear to the children of Israel.

> As an eagle stirreth up her nest, fluttereth over her young, spreadeth abroad her wings, taketh them, beareth them on her wings: so the LORD alone did lead him, and there was no strange god with him. Deuteronomy 32:11, 12

After selecting a site on a high precipice, the mother eagle builds her nest. And as her newly hatched eaglet grows, he's comfy and cozy—until one day the mother eagle overturns the nest and the young eagle is sent tumbling downward, squawking all the way. Just before he hits the rocks below, however, the mother eagle swoops down and rescues him, bearing him upon her wings. She returns him to the nest—only to overturn it a few days later and bear him on her wings yet again. This process is repeated six or seven times—until one time, the eaglet catches a thermal and starts flying. Higher and higher he goes, set free to experience life in an entirely different dimension with a higher perspective than he ever had previously.

Because faith cannot grow in comfort and security, we'll all be knocked out of our nests of cozy complacency from time to time. What do we do at such times? "They that wait upon the Lord shall renew their strength," Isaiah declares. "They shall mount up with wings as eagles" (40:31). To wait upon the Lord doesn't mean to passively wait, but to wait on Him like a skilled waiter would wait on the guest of honor. To wait upon the Lord means to lavish praise, to minister, to fellowship day by day, moment by moment. And those who do, mount up with wings as eagles.

God delivers His people on the wings of an eagle. Don't be a squawker. Say, "Okay, Lord. You're allowing this to happen in order to teach me to soar higher than I've ever flown before."

Exodus 19:5, 6
Now therefore, if ye will obey my voice indeed, and keep my covenant, then ye shall be a peculiar treasure unto me above all people: for all the earth is mine: and ye shall be unto me a kingdom of priests, and an holy nation. These are the words which thou shalt speak unto the children of Israel.

Peter picks up the same analogy when he calls us a royal priesthood (1 Peter 2:9). But the Jewish people made the same mistake that we so often make. That is, they turned inward to such a degree that if a Jewish person accidentally brushed against a Gentile, he would burn his clothes and ceremonially cleanse himself in order to rid himself of the pollution caused by the Gentile. We do virtually the same thing whenever we lose our passion for the lost, whenever we fail to share the gospel to a world so desperately in need.

Exodus 19:7, 8
And Moses came and called for the elders of the people, and laid before their faces all these words which the LORD commanded him. And all the people answered together, and said, All that the LORD hath spoken we will do. And Moses returned the words of the people unto the LORD.

A model of the priestly ministry, Moses told the people the words of the Lord and then told the Lord the words of the people.

Exodus 19:9
And the LORD said unto Moses, Lo, I come unto thee in a thick cloud, that the people may hear when I speak with thee, and believe thee for ever. And Moses told the words of the people unto the LORD.

To those of us who desire to hear the voice of the Lord more clearly, Moses would say we are to do the same three things the children of Israel were instructed to do . . .

Exodus 19:10, 11
And the LORD said unto Moses, Go unto the people, and sanctify them to day and to morrow, and let them wash their clothes, And be ready against the third day: for the third day the LORD will come down in the sight of all the people upon mount Sinai.

The people were to wash their clothes as an outward sign of inward expectancy. And to be those who truly and clearly hear the voice of God personally and powerfully, we must wash our clothes as well.

How?

- "How shall a young man cleanse his way?" David asked. "By taking heed according to the Word" (Psalm 119:9).
- "We are washed by the water of the Word" Paul said (Ephesians 5:26).
- "You are clean through the Word I have spoken" Jesus declared (John 15:3).

A much better way than rolling out of bed and dashing to church is to say, "Before I come to church this evening or this morning, Lord, I'm going to spend some time in Your Word that my mind might be purified, my heart sensitized; that I might be in a place to experience Your grace, a place to recognize Your voice."

Exodus 19:12, 13
And thou shalt set bounds unto the people round about, saying, Take heed to yourselves, that ye go not up into the mount, or touch the border of it: whosoever toucheth the mount shall be surely put to death: there shall not an hand touch it, but he shall surely be stoned, or shot through; whether it be beast or man, it shall not live: when the trumpet soundeth long, they shall come up to the mount.

Not only were the people to wash their clothes, but they were to watch their step. They were to stay away from the mountain, for, if they got too close to God's "pulpit," they would die.

"That doesn't sound very loving," you say.

Oh, but any dad who has wrestled with his two-year-old knows that it is.

Dad, when you wrestle with your toddler, you place restrictions upon yourself. You want the contact with your kids, but you place limits on yourself because otherwise they'd be wiped out. The same is true of God. His beauty, His glory, His splendor, majesty and holiness would be so powerful that were the children of Israel to get too close to Him, their hearts would simply stop beating in awe.

So often we trivialize God. Yes, through the Person of Jesus Christ, He is our Friend—but His grandeur and glory are undiminished nonetheless. Therefore, the fear of the Lord—the fear of doing anything that would grieve Him—should cause us to fall at His feet in speechless humility.

Exodus 19:14, 15
And Moses went down from the mount unto the people, and sanctified the people; and they washed their clothes. And he said unto the people, Be ready against the third day: come not at your wives.

Finally, in preparation to hear the voice of God, the children of Israel were to wake their soul. Paul would say just the opposite when he said, "Don't defraud your spouse unless there is mutual consent for the purpose of prayer and fasting" (see 1 Corinthians 7:5). Therefore, I believe God is declaring that for this particular moment, this prescribed day, He didn't want anything to distract His people or to lull them into a place of insensitivity towards Him.

There come times when a mature believer says, "I need to put away for a season any fleshly inclinations which normally preoccupy me in order that I might get a specific word from the Lord."

Exodus 19:16
And it came to pass on the third day in the morning, that there were thunders and lightnings, and a thick cloud upon the mount, and the voice of the trumpet exceeding loud; so that all the people that was in the camp trembled.

Does the sound of a trumpet ring a bell? Paul tells us that the Lord Himself shall descend from heaven with a shout and with the trumpet of God before we're raptured not to the top of Mt. Sinai, but to the top of the clouds where we'll meet Jesus in the air (1 Thessalonians 4:16).

Exodus 19:17
And Moses brought forth the people out of the camp to meet with God; and they stood at the nether part of the mount.

At the base of the rectangular Mt. Sinai is a vast plain whereupon there would have been room for the entire congregation.

Exodus 19:18
And mount Sinai was altogether on a smoke, because the LORD descended upon it in fire: and the smoke thereof ascended as the smoke of a furnace, and the whole mount quaked greatly.

Not only was this a monumental moment in Israel's history, but it was a picture of what would happen in Acts 2, when the events of Exodus 19 were fulfilled prophetically—when suddenly on the Day of Pentecost, God the Holy Spirit descended upon the disciples gathered together in the Upper Room and tongues of fire sat upon each of them (Acts 2:3).

Exodus 19:19
And when the voice of the trumpet sounded long, and waxed louder and louder, Moses spake, and God answered him by a voice.

On the Day of Pentecost, not only was fire seen, but God's voice was heard in the tongues that those on the street below the Upper Room heard, each in their own language (Acts 2:6).

Exodus 19:20–25
And the LORD came down upon mount Sinai, on the top of the mount: and the LORD called Moses up to the top of the mount; and Moses went up. And the LORD said unto Moses, Go down, charge the people, lest they break through unto the LORD to gaze, and many of them perish. And let the priests also, which come near to the LORD, sanctify themselves, lest the LORD break forth upon them. And Moses said unto the LORD, The people cannot come up to mount Sinai: for thou chargedst us, saying, Set bounds about the mount, and sanctify it. And the LORD said unto him, Away, get thee down, and thou shalt come up, thou, and Aaron with thee: but let not the priests and the people break through to come up unto the LORD, lest he break forth upon them. So Moses went down unto the people, and spake unto them.

Just as God came down and Moses went up, Jesus will come down and the church will go up to meet Him in the air (1 Thessalonians 4:17).

May we be those who see and embrace the three-fold illustration of Exodus 19: of God the Father coming down to give the Word, of God the Spirit coming down to empower His people, of God the Son coming down to take us Home.

---

20 As we come to the study of the Law, there can be a great deal of confusion, because throughout Paul's epistles, we are told that we are free from the Law because we live under grace. This confusion can be cleared up, however, by the understanding that there is a differentiation between the Law of God and the Law of Moses . . .

- The Law of God is given in Exodus 20.
- The Law of Moses is given in Exodus 21—23 and in the Book of Leviticus.
- The Law of God is referred to by Paul in Romans 7.
- The Law of Moses is referred to by Jesus in John 7.
- The Law of God was given to two to three million people audibly.
- The Law of Moses was given to Moses privately.
- The Law of God was written by God directly (Exodus 31:18).
- The Law of Moses was recorded by Moses.
- The Law of God was preserved in an ark.
- The Law of Moses was not.
- The Law of God is for all people at all times inclusively.
- The Law of Moses is for the Jews exclusively.

If, as Acts 15:5 tells us, we as believers are not under the Law of Moses, why study it at all? I suggest two reasons . . .

Why study the Law? Because in it we see interesting illustrations and awesome applications. When we read about the festivals and study the sacrifices, when we look at the regulations and ordinances, we gain great insight about Jesus, for they all point to, and picture, Him.

Secondly, we study the Law because it drives and directs us. Seeing our inability to keep its requirements, the Law drives us to our Savior (Galatians 3:24), and once there, it directs us in how we are to live (Matthew 5:17–19).

Exodus 20:1, 2 (a)
And God spake all these words, saying, I am the LORD thy God . . .

God doesn't say, "I am the Lord God." He says, "I am the Lord *thy* God"—as if to say, "I made you; I created you; I know what will make you happy." Thus, because of the incredible tenderness embedded in the little word "thy," the Ten Commandments could be called the "Ten-der" Commandments.

For this is the love of God, that we keep his commandments . . . 1 John 5:3 (a)

John doesn't say we'll *earn* God's love by keeping His commandments. No, he says keeping His commandments *is* the love of God.

"I'm not experiencing God's love," you say.

Are you keeping His commandments?

"I don't have to. I'm under grace."

Yes, you are. But you'll experience God's love when you keep His commandments because He alone knows how you are made, how you tick—and His commandments constitute His personal instruction book for you, straight from your Manufacturer.

. . . and his commandments are not grievous. 1 John 5:3 (b)

God's commandments are not grievous because rules provide liberty.

There is a rule I keep every single day. That is, in the morning—every morning—I brush my teeth. You might call this legalism. But I find it to be exceedingly refreshing. Not only that, it also releases me from philosophical questioning. I never once ask, "To brush, or not to brush? Do I have time? Is this the right day? Does brushing apply to me?" I could waste a great deal of energy debating and wondering if I should brush my teeth, but because brushing my teeth is a non-negotiable rule for me, I am released from all kinds of mental turmoil. And not only does brushing my teeth refresh and release me, but it relieves those around me. Thus, it's a win-win-win situation. The same is true of God's Law. It is the way I experience His love personally and express my love practically.

Exodus 20:2 (b)
. . . which have brought thee out of the land of Egypt, out of the house of bondage.

Commandments are vitally important for us not only because of who God is—our Creator—but because of where we were. Like the children of Israel, we grew up as slaves in Egypt, in bondage to sin. With whips cracking over us, orders shouted at us, burdens placed upon us, we didn't even know how to think. But our Creator, Redeemer, Liberator rescued us and brought us out of bondage—and teaches us to think rightly in order that we might live successfully in the Land of Promise.

Exodus 20:3
Thou shalt have no other gods before me.

In this simple phrase, we see a premise and a promise. The premise is that there are indeed other gods . . .

Baal was the god who supposedly hurled lightning down from heaven (1 Kings 18:24). Baal was the god of power. Munching on power bars, listening to power tapes, thinking they're powerful and in control, lots of people still unknowingly worship Baal today.

Ashteroth was the goddess of sensuality, of pleasure—a goddess worshiped extensively in our society by those with the "if it feels good, do it" mentality.

Mammon was the god of money, the god of prosperity. Because it is the love of money, rather than money itself, which is evil (1 Timothy 6:10), it is not only the wealthy who are prone to worship mammon. Anyone who places a priority on money, worries about money, strives for money is vulnerable.

Molloch was the god of practicality. To earn Molloch's blessing upon his new business, the Molloch worshiper would place his firstborn in an earthen jar and build the walls of his shop around it, believing that the baby entombed within the wall wasn't really dead, but would reappear in his next child. Many a parent does virtually the same thing today when, in the name of practicality, they ignore their children in the name of advancing their career, mistakenly thinking that once their business is successful, their place in the company secure, they can reconnect with their kids. The problem, however, is that kids grow up; time is lost; and opportunity dies on the altar of practicality.

In addition to the premise that there are indeed other gods, this first commandment carries a promise that other gods will not pull on God's people indefinitely.

Having captured the ark of the covenant, the gold-covered box which held the Ten Commandments—the Philistines placed it in the temple of their god, Dagon, a being which was half man and half fish. The next day, when the priests of Dagon went into the temple, they found Dagon knocked down before the ark. The priests returned Dagon to his original position—only to come in the following day to find him on the floor once again, his head and hands severed in the fall (1 Samuel 5).

The same thing happens today. "Let Me into the temple of your heart," God says, "and I'll knock Dagon down; I'll knock Baal out. I'll take care of Mammon. I'll deal with Ashteroth."

The Ten Commandments is the only law of antiquity that forbids the worship of other gods. All other codes and cultures allowed, even encouraged, the worship of other deities. Why? Because all other gods work as a team to bring hell into peoples' lives and to damn them eternally. There will be no other gods before the true and living God because those gods will not come through ultimately. In the last day, every knee shall bow, every tongue confess that Jesus alone is Lord (Philippians 2:10, 11). And what a day that will be.

Exodus 20:4
Thou shalt not make unto thee any graven image, or any likeness of any thing that is in heaven above, or that is in the earth beneath, or that is in the water under the earth:

To understand what God must look like, man has looked to nature for clues . . .

- Looking to the sky, the Native American saw the eagle soaring majestically overhead and decided God must be an eagle.
- Looking at the grassy plain, the Indian saw the powerful yet peaceful cow and decided God must be a cow.
- Looking down to the sea, the Pacific Islander saw the massive sea turtle with its impenetrable shell and decided God must be a sea turtle.

Although we know better than this, we as believers can fall prey to the same tendency. You see, there are those who say, "When I get to heaven, I'm going to sit on God's lap and feel His embrace." While I understand their sentiment, their image is faulty, for in the Book of Revelation, God is not described as having a long white beard, flowing hair, bulging biceps, and muscular calves, reaching out His finger to touch man as, Michelangelo portrayed Him in the Sistine Chapel. He's described primarily by color—the flame of His eyes; the red of His garment (Revelation 19). Jesus simply said, "God is Spirit" (John 4:24). Therefore, I don't believe we're going to see the Father as having arms, hands, and legs.

"But doesn't Scripture say He spans the universe with His hand?" you ask.

Yes, but it also says He covers us with His wings. Therefore, I believe it is as much a mistake to think that God the Father has two eyes, a nose, and ears as it is to think He has wings or feathers.

God cannot be contained by a body no matter how great. He's Spirit. He's everywhere. When we get to heaven, with our new bodies, we'll be able to bask in His glory—just as the high priest did in the Holy of Holies on the Day of Atonement. But I don't believe we will "sit on His lap," as we would with our earthly fathers. God is everywhere—all *around* us. The Holy Spirit dwells *within* us. Jesus relates *to* us.

> God, who at sundry times and in divers manners spake in time past unto the fathers by the prophets, hath in these last days spoken unto us by his Son, whom he hath appointed heir of all things, by whom also he made the worlds; who being the brightness of his glory, and the express image of his person, and upholding all things by the word of his power, when he had by himself purged our sins, sat down on the right hand of the Majesty on high;
>
> Hebrews 1:1–3

Christianity is not about making an image of God, no matter how noble or grand. It's about looking at Jesus, and allowing Him to conform us to His image.

Exodus 20:5 (a)
Thou shalt not bow down thyself to them, nor serve them: for I the LORD thy God am a jealous God . . .

God is not jealous *of* other gods. Rather, He's jealous *for* us. He wants the best for us. He wants us to be conformed to the image of His Son.

Exodus 20:5 (b)–6
. . . visiting the iniquity of the fathers upon the children unto the third and fourth generation of them that hate me; and shewing mercy unto thousands of them that love me, and keep my commandments.

Your lifestyle—the priorities you have, the philosophy you embrace—will impact your kids, your grandchildren, your great-grandchildren. If you live for Jesus, if you're a person of prayer, if you spend time in the Word and in fellowship, these qualities will be passed on to future generations.

Exodus 20:7
Thou shalt not take the name of the LORD thy God in vain; for the LORD will not hold him guiltless that taketh his name in vain.

Because virtually everyone would agree that societies and families work best when there is no murder, stealing, or lying, people have an easy time understanding the commandments that prohibit those activities. But in the minds of most people, the third commandment is a different story. After all, they reason, everyone takes the Lord's name in vain occasionally. God, however, does not agree. And to underscore this, although He prohibited stealing, coveting, killing, lying, committing adultery with a simple "Thou shalt not," He amplified the prohibition to take His name in vain as if to say "This is exceptionally serious."

Why?

I suggest three reasons . . .

First, when the Lord's name is used in vain, in a manner devoid of meaning, the result is desensitization. Satan is behind blasphemy and profanity because they trivialize both salvation and damnation. This commandment is not about God being offended, but about people being lost, desensitized to the reality of the name that will save them and the reality of where they will be if they don't receive Him.

In addition to desensitization, when the Lord's name is taken in vain, there are real ramifications. The man who accidentally hits his thumb while pounding a nail and says, "God damn it," is actually saying, "May this project be doomed to destruction." And because life and death are indeed in the power of the tongue (Proverbs 18:21), his words will, in one way or another, have a definite impact. The worst thing a person can do when he's frustrated is to take the Lord's name in vain, to use profanity—for in doing so, he only compounds the problem.

Mock Buddha and you'll hear from the ACLU. Make fun of an Indian religion and you'll be politically incorrect. But use the name of Jesus Christ in any manner whatsoever and no one will even raise an eyebrow. While we may not be able to keep this from happening outside of our homes, we can use it as an opportunity to talk about Jesus to the one who uses His name so freely, but does so blasphemously. And in sharing His reality, we can turn the situation around for His glory.

Dear brother, precious sister, child of God, do not take the name of the Lord in vain. Do not allow it to be profaned through your television, blasphemed through your radio. His name must be respected and protected because the stakes are too high to do anything less.

Exodus 20:8–11
Remember the sabbath day, to keep it holy. Six days shalt thou labour, and do all thy work: But the seventh day is the sabbath of the LORD thy God: in it thou shalt not do any work, thou, nor thy son, nor thy daughter, thy manservant, nor thy maidservant, nor thy cattle, nor thy stranger that is within thy gates: For in six days the LORD made heaven and earth, the sea, and all that in them is, and rested the seventh day: wherefore the LORD blessed the sabbath day, and hallowed it.

Having worked four hundred years as slaves in Egypt, the concept of a day off would have sounded radical indeed to the children of Israel. And not to them only, but to the surrounding civilizations as well, for no other society of antiquity entertained the idea of a day of sabbath, a day of rest.

With the Assyrians bearing down on them, the children of Israel set up an alliance with the Egyptians, failing to realize that it was only in God that their help would be found. Ever feel like financial, relational, physical problems are waging war against you? Ever feel like you can't get ahead or even catch up? Listen to what God says . . .

> For thus saith the Lord GOD, the Holy One of Israel; In returning and rest shall ye be saved; in quietness and in confidence shall be your strength: and ye would not. And thine ears shall hear a word behind thee, saying, This is the way, walk ye in it, when ye turn to the right hand, and when ye turn to the left.
>
> Isaiah 30:15, 21

The bills are mounting; the pressures are building; the Assyrians are coming. What am I to do? It's only in returning to God and resting in Him that I'll know. If I consistently take one day of every seven and say, "This is Yours, Lord," I am saying, "Lord, I acknowledge that what I have and enjoy is not because of my work ethic, my creativity, my business acumen, my energy. It's all from You. And I'm going to prove that to myself and to my family by stopping one day in seven. In so doing, I am acknowledging that You are the Giver of every good gift, the Provider of the bread I enjoy, that You are the One who truly holds my life together."

If I keep the Sabbath, I'll know which way to go as I hear a voice in my ear telling me how to walk. I'll experience a fullness in my heart, a richness in my soul. And so will you.

Spend time in worship. Take a break. Kick back. Chill out. Pray. Read. Talk. Enjoy. Fly a kite. Take a nap. Listen to your kids. When a day is set apart, conversations begin to flow; people begin to open up. But it takes a chunk of time—an entire day set aside. One day should be so free, so refreshing, so relaxing that dynamics take place that would not in any lesser amount of time. The Sabbath is a gift. Make it a time when your family, your health, your soul can be restored.

Exodus 20:12
Honour thy father and thy mother: that thy days may be long upon the land which the LORD thy God giveth thee.

The Fifth Commandment is unique indeed, for, as Paul reminds us, it is the only one with a promise attached to it (Ephesians 6:1–3). As evidenced by the fact that many saints die at a young age, while many sinners seem to live indefinitely, the long days promised to those who keep this commandment refer not necessarily to quantity but to quality—to a life full of rich and meaningful days. Living until the age of 930, the first Adam lived thirty times longer than the Last Adam, Jesus Christ, who died at the age of thirty-three. Yet no one would argue that the first Adam honored his heavenly Father thirty times more than did the Last Adam, for Jesus honored His Father perfectly. And the way He related to His heavenly Father provides a picture, a pattern, an example for how I am to relate to my earthly mother and father . . .

Jesus was a reflection of His Father (John 5:19). Because you are a reflection of your parents, if you're down on them, you'll be down on yourself. Therefore, the way to be well emotionally and relationally is to honor your father and mother.

Jesus was dependent on His Father (John 5:26), just as we are dependent upon our earthly parents. Given the fact that the chemical components that comprise our bodies are the same as those of a slug, we should be eternally grateful we were born as humans rather than slugs. Therefore, if there's no other reason to honor them, we should honor them because they gave us life, sustained our lives, and saved our lives probably many more times than we could even imagine.

Jesus was submitted to His Father (John 5:30). The two key qualities that will bring fulfillment and success to anyone's life are those of humility and submission. And those qualities are born only in the context of family. You see, if I don't like my job, I can quit; if I don't like my friends, I can avoid them; if I don't like my neighbors, I can move; if I don't like my school, I can drop out. But my relationship to my parents is the one relationship I can't change. And it is precisely when I don't agree with them or understand them that submission and humility are worked into my soul. At the peak of His maturity, Jesus said, "I am in submission to My Father." And so must I be.

Finally, Jesus was validated by His Father (John 5:37). Jesus said the only honor that matters is that which comes from the Father. The same is true with us. True validation comes when one's own parents or in-laws are able to say, "There's a great man."

"It was easy for Jesus to submit to His Father," some might say. "After all, His Father was God. My father, on the other hand, walked out on me or beat me, failed to provide for me or ignored me. How can I honor a man like that?"

In response, I would ask them to consider the following . . .

"My God, My God, why hast Thou forsaken Me?" Jesus cried from the Cross (Matthew 27:46). Jesus knows better than anyone what it is like to have a Parent turn His back.

Marred more than any other man, Jesus knows what it is like to be smitten by a Father (Isaiah 52, 53).

"If You're the Son of God, why are You hungry? Turn these stones to bread," Satan taunted—the implication being that Jesus' Father wasn't providing for Him (Matthew 4:3).

"If it be possible, let this cup pass from Me," Jesus prayed so intensely that He sweat blood (Luke 22:44). But the cup of suffering did not pass from Him—meaning that Jesus knows better than anyone what it's like for a Parent to seemingly ignore a request.

Jesus has experienced more of what has embittered you or angered me than we'll ever understand this side of eternity. And because this same Jesus who honored His Father and who knows what it's like to be beaten, forsaken, and ignored lives in you, trust Him to enable you to honor your father and mother—regardless of how difficult that may seem to be.

Exodus 20:13
Thou shalt not kill.

While working on a roof, two men stumbled and fell down the chimney. The first one down absorbed all the soot. When they got to the bottom, the first man down looked at his partner and assumed his own face was clean. The second man looked at his partner and assumed his own face was dirty. And both were wrong. Concerning the commandment before us, some who think they're clean may not be, while some who think they aren't may not be as dirty as they think.

I talked to a man who has recently become a believer. Years ago as a Marine in Vietnam, he killed a number of North Vietnamese soldiers. Now he wonders if he violated the command not to kill. In Matthew 19:18, we see that in commanding us not to kill, God is commanding us not to murder. The question, then, becomes, Is war murder? I believe the answer is *No* . . .

In the Old Testament, we see God ordering the destruction of the Canaanite culture after giving them four hundred years to repent from unspeakable evil (Acts 7:6).

Jesus Himself chose a man of war in Simon the zealot. Zealots were guerilla fighters who were trying to overthrow the Romans controlling Israel at that time. Far from castigating Simon for being a warrior, Jesus chose him to be one of His inner circle.

In Romans 13, Paul makes it clear that God raises up powers to bear the sword in order to keep evil in check.

Therefore, I believe Scripture clearly indicates that fighting in an army does not make one a murderer. Is capital punishment murder? Again, I believe the answer is *No.* Read Genesis 6 through 8 and see what happens when there is no capital punishment. And then you will understand God's mandate in Genesis 9 that those who murder must be put to death.

Who has the "dirty face"?

Not the soldier, not the executioner, but someone much closer to home . . .

> Ye have heard that it was said by them of old time, Thou shalt not kill; and whosoever shall kill shall be in danger of the judgment: but I say unto you, that whosoever is angry with his brother without a cause shall be in danger of the judgment: and whosoever shall say to his brother, Raca, shall be in danger of the council: but whosoever shall say, Thou fool, shall be in danger of hell fire. Matthew 5:21, 22

There are two Greek words translated "anger" in the New Testament. The first is *thumos,* and refers to the anger one feels that causes his veins to bulge and his face to get red. The word used here, however, is *orgizo*—a word that refers to the anger that smolders internally day after week after month after year. The person who harbors this kind of anger without a cause is the one with the black face, the one who is a murderer.

"Oh, but I have a cause. I have a reason to be angry," you say.

Do you?

In Matthew 18, we read the story of the master who forgave his slave's debt of ten million dollars only to discover that the slave threatened to kill a fellow slave over a debt of two thousand dollars. In telling this story, Jesus' point was that, as real as the $2,000 debt was, it was nothing in comparison to the debt of which he had been forgiven. In other words, if all of our mixed motives, evil intentions, and sinful imaginations were brought to light, we would see that we owe a debt far greater than any owed us, that we are worse than the worst offense committed against us.

> Therefore if thou bring thy gift to the altar, and there rememberest that thy brother hath ought against thee; leave there thy gift before the altar, and go thy way; first be reconciled to thy brother, and then come and offer thy gift. Agree with thine adversary quickly, whiles thou art in the way with him; lest at any time the adversary deliver thee to the judge, and the judge deliver thee to the officer, and thou be cast into prison. Verily I say unto thee, Thou shalt by no means come out thence, till thou hast paid the uttermost farthing.
> Matthew 5:23–26

The only way to keep from murdering others is to be reconciled. And the only way to be reconciled is to agree with your enemy. Even if his facts are wrong, you're a bigger sinner than he can even imagine. So you are to go to him and say, "I'm wrong. I'm sorry. Please forgive me." If you don't, you'll end up in court. What court? The court that exists in your mind. You practice law daily. You gather new witnesses and new evidence systematically. You build an airtight case, and every time court convenes, you win. The other guy never wins. Consequently, your relationships dwindle and your life grows smaller. Families divide. Hell breaks out. And although you may be technically, judicially, legally right, you're oh, so wrong when you fail to reconcile with your adversary.

I know this because Jesus absorbed the blame

for us totally. On the Cross, He absorbed the full punishment for our sin, paid the entire price for you and me. Even on the Cross, He said, "Father forgive them." And as a result, Jesus is free from the chains of death and the grave—just as you will be if you choose to absorb the blame wholly, completely, and unconditionally.

Exodus 20:14
Thou shalt not commit adultery.

Because the Seventh Commandment is the least understood, it is the most argued.

> But whoso committeth adultery with a woman lacketh understanding: he that doeth it destroyeth his own soul. Proverbs 6:32

The world thinks sex is about procreation and recreation, failing to understand that it's primarily about unification—about two souls being mystically and miraculously merged into one. The issue is not unwanted pregnancy, disease, AIDS. God says the issue of intimacy is the soul. That is why, after presiding over the first marriage ceremony, He looked at the couple and called their name Adam singularly (Genesis 5:2). Sex outside of marriage destroys one's soul irreparably, inevitably. Every time people are involved in sexual activity outside of marriage, there will be destruction as the soul is destroyed a piece, a layer, a step at a time. That is why Jesus was so emphatic when He dealt with the subject of adultery (Matthew 5:27–30). Knowing its danger, He told us to deal with it radically, brutally, severely—to do whatever it takes to keep it from our lives.

If there was a sign which read:

> Please proceed with great caution because behind these doors there are experiments taking place with chemical components which may be used one day to cause an explosive reaction at some future point.

I'd probably ignore it.

But if the sign said:

> Danger! Explosives!

I would stay away.

"Thou shalt not commit adultery." If you want to read the fine print, you can explore the Scriptures and find the reason why. But here, it is as if God is simply, clearly, undeniably saying, "Take My Word for it: Adultery is explosive. It is dangerous. It will destroy you."

Exodus 20:15
Thou shalt not steal.

Although the Eighth Commandment is straightforward and simple, it is even more so in Hebrew, where it reads simply, "Steal not." As a society, we know that stealing is wrong, so we teach our kids from the earliest age not to take what isn't theirs. And yet, according to the IRS, if no one cheated on his taxes, our national debt would be retired in one year. Perhaps the pervasiveness of stealing is seen even more clearly in the story of the New York City man who was able to get rid of his garbage every day during a two-week garbage strike by putting it in a wrapped package and leaving it on the front seat of his car every day while he was at work. But make no mistake—stealing is not limited to money or material goods. We can rob our employers through two-hour lunches or leaving early from work.

Following are four prescriptions for the epidemic of thievery that pervades our culture . . .

"Let him that stole steal no more: but rather let him labour, working with his hands the thing which is good . . ." (Ephesians 4:28). We are to work with our hands. When man fell in the Garden of Eden, God told Adam that he was to work by the sweat of his brow. This wasn't punishment but protection—for in his sinful state, man needed to work or else he would be vulnerable to stealing, taking shortcuts, cheating. One of the greatest ways to be free from thievery is to work hard. Why? If you're not working hard, you're a candidate for depression. You'll be down on yourself, disillusioned with yourself, sad about your situation. I believe depression can be linked to people who no longer work hard.

Jesus said if someone compels you to go a mile, go two (Matthew 5:41). Go twice as far, twice as hard as your boss expects. Satan will tell you that you deserve a break, but Jesus tells us to go twice as far because, His burden being easy, His load light, He knows it's for our benefit.

". . . that he may have to give to him that needeth" (Ephesians 4:28). We are to reach out our hands. If we're going the second mile, working harder than others, we'll inevitably experience a certain degree of success—not to accumulate more for ourselves, but to reach out our hands and give to others. In so doing, a dynamic takes place which leads to joy and liberty, happiness and freedom (Luke 19:8).

"Will a man rob God? Yet ye have robbed me. But ye say, Wherein have we robbed thee? In tithes and offerings" (Malachi 3:8). We are to open up our hands. God indicted His people of robbery when they failed to tithe. The whole earth is the Lord's (Psalm 24:1)—and we acknowledge that fact by tithing. He who robs God, also robs everyone around him in sneaky, subtle ways.

"He that spared not his own Son, but delivered him up for us all, how shall he not with him also freely give us all things?" (Romans 8:32). We are to look at His hands. The holes in Jesus' hands tell me that God loves me, that He cares about me, that He'll do what's best for me—which obliterates the need for thievery. I look at His hands, and in them I rest.

Exodus 20:16
Thou shalt not bear false witness against thy neighbour.

The biblical viewpoint of bearing false witness is not confined to the telling of bold-faced lies, but also includes being tricky with the truth. In the one account where the phrase "false witness" is used in Scripture, we see individuals falsely accusing Jesus of threatening to destroy the temple when, in fact, He was speaking of His own death (Matthew 26:59).

Because he is the father of lies, Satan is the ultimate false witness, accusing us day and night before God's throne as he points out our failings, our shortcomings, our sins (Revelation 12:10). Jesus, on the other hand, is the faithful and true Witness (Revelation 1:5, 3:14), our Advocate, our Defense Lawyer.

Are you a true witness or a false witness? If the person sitting next to you is a believer, he or she is righteously robed, heaven-bound, Spirit-filled, positionally pure. Speaking anything less of them is bearing false witness. Oh, you might give the right information—but in so doing do you convey the wrong implication? You might say lots of nice things about them, but do you add a "but . . . ," a "however . . . ," an "I don't know if I should share this, but . . ."? If so, you're a false witness because, although you might be telling the truth, you're not telling the whole truth. You're failing to factor in God's estimation of them.

If you're prone to bearing false witness, consider the following remedies . . .

Say less—for as Solomon so insightfully declared, "In the multitude of words there wanteth not sin: but he that refraineth his lips is wise" (Proverbs 10:19).

Pray more. "Remove from me the way of lying" David prayed (Psalm 119:29).

Think again. Before you say anything about anyone else, THINK:

T: Is what you are about to say the whole truth?
H: Is it helpful? Will people be edified?
I: Is it inspirational? Will God be praised as a result?
N: Is it necessary?
K: Is it kind?

The best way to keep from bearing false witness is to simply say less, pray more, and think again.

Exodus 20:17
Thou shalt not covet thy neighbour's house, thou shalt not covet thy neighbour's wife, nor his manservant, nor his maidservant, nor his ox, nor his ass, nor any thing that is thy neighbour's.

Of all the commandments, the last one is probably taken the least seriously. If a person breaks the Sixth Commandment, he might be executed. If he breaks the Eighth, he might end up in jail. If he breaks the Ninth, he might be sued. But if he breaks the Tenth Commandment, not only is he forgiven, but applauded—for coveting is a key component of our culture.

Essentially, to covet is simply to want more of that of which one already has enough. And our economy is based upon this. Society screams at us that the way to have real life is to have this car or that toy. But the Giver of life, the Author of life, the One who declared, "*I* am the Life," said, "That's not true. A man's life does not consist of the stuff he has materially." And to illustrate His point, He went on to give a parable of a man who had so many material goods that it was necessary for him to construct bigger barns to hold it all. Yet although the financial planners would consider him wise, although his culture might consider him blessed, God considered him a fool for failing to lay up treasure in the only place that matters: heaven (Luke 12:20).

If God blesses you materially—wonderful! God gives us richly all things to enjoy (1 Timothy 6:17). I find it interesting that in Jesus' parable, the rich man was planning to enjoy his wealth in the future (Luke 12:19). In other words, up to that point, he never truly enjoyed what he had. And such is all too often the case. The man living for things, wanting more things, focused on things will never, ever be satisfied, for he will always think he needs just a few more things to make him happy.

The solution? Not only are we to enjoy material blessings, but we are to employ them—not to make more money for ourselves, but to help others, to extend the gospel to others.

A wealthy man in Ur, Abraham left his comfortable life behind to seek a city whose Builder and Maker was God (Hebrews 11:10). He saw the big picture. He saw the kingdom. And so must we.

Jesus said it is the deceitfulness of riches that crowd out the Word in our lives (Matthew 13:22). No wonder, then, that God's last commandment,

His final audible word to His people was, "Don't covet."

Exodus 20:18, 19
And all the people saw the thunderings, and the lightnings, and the noise of the trumpet, and the mountain smoking: and when the people saw it, they removed, and stood afar off. And they said unto Moses, Speak thou with us, and we will hear: but let not God speak with us, lest we die.

So powerfully did God's power and potency, His glory and grandeur convict the people that they said, "You speak to us, Moses, because if God speaks to us, we'll die." And that's the way it's supposed to be.

The Word of God is powerful, sharper than any two-edged sword. It pierces. It divides. It kills our pride, our self-centeredness, our flesh (Hebrews 4:12). And because it does, the person who wants to pamper his flesh, the person caught up in sins of the flesh will often be one who doesn't want to hear from God anymore. If I choose to indulge my flesh day after day, week after week, I won't be at Bible study six months down the road.

If you're at a place where lately it's been hard to get into the Word, I have great news for you: God wants to do something special in you. Satan sees what God desires to do and is trying to keep you from that blessing. It's a big one, a great one. So pick up the Word; let God speak—and I guarantee you'll feel exhilarated in your spirit.

Exodus 20:20
And Moses said unto the people, Fear not: for God is come to prove you, and that his fear may be before your faces, that ye sin not.

Like the BMW engineer eager to take his car on a test drive to rev up the RPM's and fine tune it, God wants to "fine tune" us in order that we won't go careening off course.

Exodus 20:21–24
And the people stood afar off, and Moses drew near unto the thick darkness where God was. And the LORD said unto Moses, Thus thou shalt say unto the children of Israel, Ye have seen that I have talked with you from heaven. Ye shall not make with me gods of silver, neither shall ye make unto you gods of gold. An altar of earth thou shalt make unto me, and shalt sacrifice thereon thy burnt offerings, and thy peace offerings, thy sheep, and thine oxen: in all places where I record my name I will come unto thee, and I will bless thee.

After the Law is heeded, an altar is always needed. When we really hear the Law of God, we realize we're sinners in need of a sacrifice to take away our lawlessness, our iniquity, our failure, our sin.

Exodus 20:25
And if thou wilt make me an altar of stone, thou shalt not build it of hewn stone: for if thou lift up thy tool upon it, thou hast polluted it.

The altar was not to be ornate or artistic but rather very simple, made of dirt or uncarved stone. Why? So that the focus would be not on the altar but on the sacrifice. The sacrifice speaks of Jesus, the Lamb of God. Generally speaking, the farther a people stray away from a real relationship with God, the greater the tendency will be toward grandeur and glory in altar-building. When the Spirit of God is not moving, the artisans and architects try to figure out how to create a feeling to mask the lack. But the heart of the Father is that the focus always be on the Son.

Exodus 20:26
Neither shalt thou go up by steps unto mine altar, that thy nakedness be not discovered thereon.

Not only was there to be simplicity in worship, but there was to be humility as well. Clothed in robes, the higher the priests climbed, the more exposed they would be to the people below. To rectify this, the Lord ordered the priests to keep grounded.

"God be merciful to me a sinner," cried the publican, eyes downcast (Luke 18:13). The worship God honors is not a set of twelve steps whereby one climbs higher and higher. It is one step—the simple step to the Savior. Therefore, from the very beginning, as God gives the Law to His people, He says, "keep it simple. Focus on the sacrifice, not on the structure. And stay humble."

21 After seeing the Law of God presented in chapter 20, we come to the Law of Moses here in chapter 21. Although the Law of Moses is not directly applicable *to* us, it is definitely helpful *for* us because in studying the Law of Moses, we gain insight into the mind and heart of God, and into the Person and Nature of His Son—for the sacrifices, ordinances, and regulations which follow all ultimately point to Him.

Exodus 21:1–6 (a)
Now these are the judgments which thou shalt set before them. If thou buy an Hebrew servant, six years he shall serve: and in the seventh he shall go out free for nothing. If he came in by himself, he shall go out by himself: if he were married, then his wife shall go out with him. If his master have given him a wife, and she have born him sons or daughters; the wife and her children shall be her master's, and he shall go out by himself. And if the servant shall plainly say, I love my master, my wife, and my children; I will not go out free: then his master shall bring him unto the judges; he shall also bring him to the door, or unto the door post; and his master shall bore his ear through with an aul;

At various times in history, this passage has been a hotbed of controversy, for it deals with slavery. Is God instituting slavery? No. Slavery was already deeply embedded into the fabric of Hebrew culture. Therefore, God was not introducing or instituting slavery, but rather regulating it. The same principle is seen concerning divorce. In Matthew 19, Jesus makes it clear that divorce was not God's intent. But because of the hardness of men's hearts, God regulated it.

That said, the parameters God places on slavery are telling indeed. Male slaves were required to serve a maximum of six years. After that, if he wanted to remain in the service of his master, he would be taken to a doorpost, where his ear would be pierced, signifying that he was a slave by choice.

> Let this mind be in you, which was also in Christ Jesus: Who, being in the form of God, thought it not robbery to be equal with God: but made himself of no reputation, and took upon him the form of a servant, and was made in the likeness of men: Philippians 2:5–7

Jesus is the ultimate Servant, the perfect Servant . . .

Just as the six years the Old Testament slave was to serve speaks of the number of man, so Jesus left His throne in heaven to become a Man.

Just as the seventh year speaks of the number of completion, so Jesus completed the work He came to do to reconcile us to the Father (John 17:21).

Just as the Old Testament slave could choose to remain a slave for love of family and master, so Jesus chose to become a slave for the love of His Bride (Ephesians 5:25–27), His children (John 1:12), and His Father (John 8:29).

Just as the ear of the Old Testament slave would be pierced to show that he was a slave by choice, Jesus would be pierced—not through His ear, but through His hands and feet, His brow and side.

Why would the Old Testament piercing take place at a doorpost? Because it would bring to mind the posts which the children of Israel had recently marked at the top, bottom, and sides—in the shape of a cross—with the blood of the Passover Lamb. The picture is perfect. It all points to Jesus.

Exodus 21:6 (b)
. . . and he shall serve him for ever.

Although He finished the work, Jesus chose to be a servant forever. That is why He girded Himself with a towel and washed His disciples' feet (John 13). And that is why He will gird Himself again and serve all those who are watching for His coming (Luke 12:37). And as I accept this, I must then reflect it. What am I to be? A servant. Jesus sets the pace. Jesus shows the way. Ever wonder why you're not thanked, why you're not appreciated? It's a golden opportunity for you to see if you're a servant or not, if you're reflecting Jesus, if you're becoming more like Him.

Exodus 21:7
And if a man sell his daughter to be a maidservant, she shall not go out as the menservants do.

Although it initially seems unfair that male slaves could go free after six years, but female slaves couldn't, this was actually a blessing for the women. You see, when families were under extreme financial pressure, they would often sell their children into slavery. While a father might think his daughter could handle being a slave for six years, God says she would serve not for six years, but for life. Therefore, I believe this differentiation was God's intent that parents give serious and sober consideration to their actions concerning their daughters.

Exodus 21:8, 9
If she please not her master, who hath betrothed her to himself, then shall he let her be redeemed: to sell her unto a strange nation he shall have no power, seeing he hath dealt deceitfully with her. And if he have betrothed her unto his son, he shall deal with her after the manner of daughters.

If after making preparation to marry one of his slaves, a man changes his mind, he can't sell the woman he intended to marry to someone else but must return her to her family. And if a man buys a slave to be the bride of his son, he must treat her not as a slave, but as a daughter-in-law.

Exodus 21:10, 11
If he take him another wife; her food, her raiment, and her duty of marriage, shall he not diminish. And if he do not these three unto her, then shall she go out free without money.

Again, God is not endorsing polygamy, but regulating it. As you go through the Word and see God's unfolding revelation, there will be clarification on this matter. But at this point, the requirement to care for wives equitably and to treat slaves fairly would alone be a shock in the ears of the people. Other cultures knew nothing of this.

Exodus 21:12, 13
He that smiteth a man, so that he die, shall be surely put to death. And if a man lie not in wait, but God deliver him into his hand; then I will appoint thee a place whither he shall flee.

He who committed second-degree murder would not be held to the same standard as the one who committed first-degree, or premeditated, intentional murder.

Exodus 21:14
But if a man come presumptuously upon his neighbour, to slay him with guile; thou shalt take him from mine altar, that he may die.

If a man intentionally killed someone, he couldn't take refuge at the altar. Peter warned us that we are not to use our liberty for a "cloak of maliciousness" (1 Peter 2:16). Some people say, "I've come to the altar or to the Table of Communion, so now I can do whatever I want." But Peter says such a one doesn't understand that liberty and grace are not to be a cloak, a cover-up for sin.

Exodus 21:15
And he that smiteth his father, or his mother, shall be surely put to death.

There are no exceptions for this deadly serious sin.

Exodus 21:16
And he that stealeth a man, and selleth him, or if he be found in his hand, he shall surely be put to death.

Kidnapping merits death as well.

Exodus 21:17
And he that curseth his father, or his mother, shall surely be put to death.

Some of the most vicious murders are committed with the mouth. You might have lots of reasons to be angry or to feel bitter towards your parents, but when you speak against them, it is a capital offense in God's economy.

Exodus 21:18, 19
And if men strive together, and one smite another with a stone, or with his fist, and he die not, but keepeth his bed: If he rise again, and walk abroad upon his staff, then shall he that smote him be quit: only he shall pay for the loss of his time, and shall cause him to be thoroughly healed.

The man who strikes another must pay for the time lost and the expenses of the healing.

Exodus 21:20, 21
And if a man smite his servant, or his maid, with a rod, and he die under his hand; he shall be surely punished. Notwithstanding, if he continue a day or two, he shall not be punished: for he is his money.

God declares that if a servant is hurt permanently, there's a price to pay. But if the servant is only bruised, there is no price to pay—an interesting word indeed for our litigious society.

Exodus 21:22, 23
If men strive, and hurt a woman with child, so that her fruit depart from her, and yet no mischief follow: he shall be surely punished, according as the woman's husband will lay upon him; and he shall pay as the judges determine. And if any mischief follow, then thou shalt give life for life,

Imagine a barroom brawl in which one man hurls a chair at another. The intended target ducks, however, and a pregnant woman is hit. If she miscarries or gives birth prematurely, the perpetrator shall be punished. But if the woman dies, the perpetrator will be killed. Again, God is elevating the status of women, for, although her death was an accident, it was to be treated as first-degree murder.

Exodus 21:24, 25
Eye for eye, tooth for tooth, hand for hand, foot for foot, burning for burning, wound for wound, stripe for stripe.

This idea of life for life, eye for eye, tooth for tooth seems at first glance to be harsh—but in reality, it is an expression of God's mercy . . .

When Peter-John was in first grade, he came home from school one day with his shirt rumpled and tear stains on his cheek.

"What happened?" I asked.

"The biggest guy in my class beat me up," he answered.

The next morning, he came out of his room carrying his baseball bat. When I asked him why, he answered, "Today is show and tell."

But, having a pretty good idea to whom he was going to show his bat, I made him take a baseball card instead.

The tendency of people is to say, "If you push me down, I'm coming at you with my baseball bat. If you poke my eye, I'm going for both of yours. If you knock out one of my teeth, I'll give you a knuckle sandwich which will take out all of yours." Our flesh says, "Hit me once, I'll hit you twice."

The Lord, however, says, "No. It's *one* eye for an eye, *one* tooth for a tooth."

Later on, in Matthew 5, Jesus will say, "If someone smites your right cheek, offer him your left cheek as well" (see Matthew 5:39). Did God change His mind? No. As a Parent, He does the same thing we do when we have an entirely different set of standards for our eighteen-year-old than we do for our three-year-old. You see, here in Exodus, God's family was fresh from slavery in Egypt, surrounded by paganism. So that's where He begins with them. But as the centuries pass, His heart and His plan become increasingly clear to His people through progressive revelation—until His Final Word, His full heart was revealed in His Son (Hebrews 1:1, 2).

Exodus 21:26, 27

And if a man smite the eye of his servant, or the eye of his maid, that it perish; he shall let him go free for his eye's sake. And if he smite out his manservant's tooth, or his maidservant's tooth; he shall let him go free for his tooth's sake.

If a man struck his servant in such a way that a tooth or an eye was lost, the servant was to go free.

Exodus 21:28–30

If an ox gore a man or a woman, that they die: then the ox shall be surely stoned, and his flesh shall not be eaten; but the owner of the ox shall be quit. But if the ox were wont to push with his horn in time past, and it hath been testified to his owner, and he hath not kept him in, but that he hath killed a man or a woman; the ox shall be stoned, and his owner also shall be put to death. If there be laid on him a sum of money, then he shall give for the ransom of his life whatsoever is laid upon him.

The first time an ox gored someone, it would be considered an accident. But if the ox demonstrated a propensity towards this behavior and wasn't properly restricted, the ox must die and the owner must either die or settle monetarily. We live in a day of animal rights activism. God, however, makes it clear here that people are more important than animals.

Exodus 21:31, 32

Whether he have gored a son, or have gored a daughter, according to this judgment shall it be done unto him. If the ox shall push a manservant or a maidservant; he shall give unto their master thirty shekels of silver, and the ox shall be stoned.

If it was a servant who was gored, the owner of the ox was to pay thirty shekels of silver. And in this, a picture is being painted of One whose life, because He was a Servant, would be bought for a mere thirty pieces of silver (Matthew 26:15).

Exodus 21:33, 34

And if a man shall open a pit, or if a man shall dig a pit, and not cover it, and an ox or an ass fall therein; the owner of the pit shall make it good, and give money unto the owner of them; and the dead beast shall be his.

If an ox or ass fell into an open pit, the man who dug it and failed to cover it would be responsible to pay for the animal.

Exodus 21:35, 36

And if one man's ox hurt another's, that he die; then they shall sell the live ox, and divide the money of it; and the dead ox also they shall divide. Or if it be known that the ox hath used to push in time past, and his owner hath not kept him in; he shall surely pay ox for ox; and the dead shall be his own.

If an ox killed another ox, the owner of the dead ox would receive half the value of the live ox. But if the live ox was prone to aggressive behavior, the owner of the live ox would pay full price.

Commonplace and common sense as these laws may seem, in light of what other cultures were doing at this time, they were revolutionary.

And through them, the Jewish people understood that their God not only was exceedingly fair, but that He cared about every aspect of their lives.

22 Exodus 22:1
If a man shall steal an ox, or a sheep, and kill it, or sell it; he shall restore five oxen for an ox, and four sheep for a sheep.

If I steal your ox or lamb to either eat or sell, I am to restore the ox fivefold and the sheep fourfold. As God addresses such legal matters, He bases His justice on the very important principle of restitution. As a result, the Jewish people knew nothing of incarceration. Ours is the most jailed people in the world. With 1.8 million in prison, for every 1,000 people, sixty-six are incarcerated. But here in God's economy, justice was based not on incarceration, but on restitution.

Here, we see the penalty for stealing an ox was five oxen; the penalty for a sheep, four sheep. If a man was so poor he had to steal the ox or sheep in the first place, how was he to pay four or five times what he stole? The answer is that the whole family was responsible. Thus, there would be tremendous pressure within a family to obey the law because if one of their number failed to do so, the rest would pay.

Exodus 22:2, 3
If a thief be found breaking up, and be smitten that he die, there shall no blood be shed for him. If the sun be risen upon him, there shall be blood shed for him; for he should make full restitution; if he have nothing, then he shall be sold for his theft.

If a thief broke in at night and was killed in the process, the one who killed him was justified. But this was not the case if the crime occurred in broad daylight. It was not allowable to kill a thief if the crime occurred in the day. Why? Perhaps because in the dark, it would be confusing and hard to determine whether a man was out to kill or merely to steal. But in the daytime, there would be no confusion. In other words, with increased light comes increased responsibility. And in the broadest sense, he who has light must live up to it.

Exodus 22:4
If the theft be certainly found in his hand alive, whether it be ox, or ass, or sheep; he shall restore double.

If a thief was caught red-handed with whatever he had taken, he was to pay it back twofold. An exception found in Numbers 5:6, 7 says if a thief's conscience bothered him and he confessed without being apprehended, he was to pay back only twenty percent above that which he took.

Exodus 22:5
If a man shall cause a field or vineyard to be eaten, and shall put in his beast, and shall feed in another man's field; of the best of his own field, and of the best of his own vineyard, shall he make restitution.

If I allow my animal to graze in your field or your vineyard, I am to pay you back with the best of my field.

Exodus 22:6
If fire break out, and catch in thorns, so that the stacks of corn, or the standing corn, or the field, be consumed therewith; he that kindled the fire shall surely make restitution.

If I'm where I ought not be, I'm to pay for the damage done. The Book of James says the tongue is like a fire (James 3:6). Truly, a great deal of good fruit is burned by activities of the tongue. When we poke around in someone else's business and fire results, we have to make restitution. How? By replacing the fruit that was lost. How are we to do this? By saying to the people we talked to, "What I said was unfair and untrue and I was very wrong." We are to do whatever we can do to replace that which was lost due to the fire we set when we meddled in a field in which we ought not to have been.

Exodus 22:7, 8
If a man shall deliver unto his neighbour money or stuff to keep, and it be stolen out of the man's house; if the thief be found, let him pay double. If the thief be not found, then the master of the house shall be brought unto the judges, to see whether he have put his hand unto his neighbour's goods.

If you're watching your neighbor's goods while he's on vacation and they be stolen, the thief must pay double. But if no thief is found, it is up to the judges—the spiritual leaders of the community—to decide whether you actually were the thief.

Exodus 22:9
For all manner of trespass, whether it be for ox, for ass, for sheep, for raiment, or for any

manner of lost thing, which another challengeth to be his, the cause of both parties shall come before the judges; and whom the judges shall condemn, he shall pay double unto his neighbour.

Paul picks up this same principle in 1 Corinthians 6, when he says, "If something is wrong between you and a brother, you are to go to the church rather than to court because the world cares more about tricky legal maneuverings than it does about truth."

Exodus 22:10–13
If a man deliver unto his neighbour an ass, or an ox, or a sheep, or any beast, to keep; and it die, or be hurt, or driven away, no man seeing it: then shall an oath of the LORD be between them both, that he hath not put his hand unto his neighbour's goods; and the owner of it shall accept thereof, and he shall not make it good. And if it be stolen from him, he shall make restitution unto the owner thereof. If it be torn in pieces, then let him bring it for witness, and he shall not make good that which was torn.

God declares in this economy that a man's word was to be accepted at face value. "All things are naked and open before Him with whom we must deal" (Hebrews 4:13). Therefore, if a man gives his word, we're to accept it. If he's lying, God will deal with him.

Exodus 22:14, 15
And if a man borrow ought of his neighbour, and it be hurt, or die, the owner thereof being not with it, he shall surely make it good. But if the owner thereof be with it, he shall not make it good: if it be an hired thing, it came for his hire.

The one who borrowed something from his neighbor was responsible to maintain it. But if there was payment involved, if it was "rented," he would not be responsible to replace it.

Exodus 22:16, 17
And if a man entice a maid that is not betrothed, and lie with her, he shall surely endow her to be his wife. If her father utterly refuse to give her unto him, he shall pay money according to the dowry of virgins.

In God's economy, the point at which a man seduced a woman was the point at which he essentially said, "I do." Once there was sexual involvement, he was married. If, however, the woman's father didn't want the man in his family, he could refuse to give him her hand—yet the man would still be required to pay the dowry, which was a significant portion of one's income.

Exodus 22:18
Thou shalt not suffer a witch to live.

In the occult, in witchcraft there is a darkness that, because it dooms and damns, must be taken with deadly seriousness.

Exodus 22:19
Whosoever lieth with a beast shall surely be put to death.

This is an absolute command that bestiality is not to be countenanced.

Exodus 22:20, 21
He that sacrificeth unto any god, save unto the LORD only, he shall be utterly destroyed. Thou shalt neither vex a stranger, nor oppress him: for ye were strangers in the land of Egypt.

Although sacrifice to any strange god was punishable by death, merely being a stranger was not grounds for oppression.

Exodus 22:22–24
Ye shall not afflict any widow, or fatherless child. If thou afflict them in any wise, and they cry at all unto me, I will surely hear their cry; and my wrath shall wax hot, and I will kill you with the sword; and your wives shall be widows, and your children fatherless.

It seems as though our Father in heaven has a special place in His heart for fatherless children and for women who don't have a covering.

Exodus 22:25
If thou lend money to any of my people that is poor by thee, thou shalt not be to him as an usurer, neither shalt thou lay upon him usury.

God's people were not to charge one another interest.

Exodus 22:26, 27
If thou at all take thy neighbour's raiment to pledge, thou shalt deliver it unto him by that the sun goeth down: For that is his covering only, it is his raiment for his skin: wherein shall he sleep? And it shall come to pass, when he crieth unto me, that I will hear; for I am gracious.

If a man put down his coat as collateral on a loan, his coat was to be returned at the time he would have need of it. In this we see the graciousness of God—not only to us, but also to those who have to part with their coats to make ends meet, towards those who have made bad choices, towards those who we might deem lazy. Certainly, they have made errors. Certainly they have problems. But so have we all. And in this God says, "I'm gracious toward you. Be gracious toward others. If you can keep someone else warm, do so."

Exodus 22:28
Thou shalt not revile the gods, nor curse the ruler of thy people.

In newer translations, the word "gods" is correctly rendered "judges" or "leaders."

Exodus 22:29 (a)
Thou shalt not delay to offer the first of thy ripe fruits, and of thy liquors . . .

We are not to delay the tithe. "Concerning the collection for the saints . . . upon the first day of the week let every one of you lay by him in store," Paul declared (see 1 Corinthians 16:1, 2). It's not up to us when to give the tithe or to dictate how it will be used.

Exodus 22:29 (b)
. . . the firstborn of thy sons shalt thou give unto me.

At this time, the firstborn son in every family would be serving as priest, for initially, God desired that every family participate in this glorious calling (Exodus 13:2).

Exodus 22:30
Likewise shalt thou do with thine oxen, and with thy sheep: seven days it shall be with his dam; on the eighth day thou shalt give it me.

The tendency might be to extend the time a lamb or ox was to remain with its mother. Knowing this, God set a clear parameter at seven days.

Exodus 22:31
And ye shall be holy men unto me: neither shall ye eat any flesh that is torn of beasts in the field; ye shall cast it to the dogs.

A mark of one's holiness is his diet. In New Testament economy, this speaks of what we allow our minds to feed upon. All too often, we take in that which has been "torn," that which is violent. But because we're to be holy, we're not to partake of that which is either hurtful to us or to others—be it in the form of that which we read, which we watch, or which we talk about.

23

Ye have heard that it hath been said, an eye for an eye, and a tooth for a tooth: but I say unto you, that ye resist not evil: but whosoever shall smite thee on thy right cheek, turn to him the other also.

Matthew 5:38, 39

Many people are under the false impression that the God of the Old Testament is angry and uptight, while Jesus is kind and forgiving—that Jesus has to "calm God down" and remind Him that He loves us. Nothing, however, could be farther from the truth. The seeming disparity is because Jesus addresses the individual. God addresses the culture. For a culture to work, there must be boundaries and regulations. Without them, people would not survive. Thus, it is the love of God that declares the need for parameters.

Exodus 23:1
Thou shalt not raise a false report: put not thine hand with the wicked to be an unrighteous witness.

Our judicial system allows for the buying of "expert" witnesses—a practice prohibited in God's economy.

Exodus 23:2 (a)
Thou shalt not follow a multitude to do evil . . .

We must be those who tell the truth even if everyone else is moving in the opposite direction.

Exodus 23:2 (b)
. . . neither shalt thou speak in a cause to decline after many to wrest judgment:

Don't decline to testify—even if it seems unpopular.

Exodus 23:3
Neither shalt thou countenance a poor man in his cause.

In the judicial context of which God is speaking, poor people are not to be favored simply because of their poverty. Three verses later, God will say, "Don't rule against the poor simply because they're poor." Taken together, God is saying, "Treat people with integrity regardless of their social status." Our nation's understanding of blind justice is based upon this biblical precept.

Exodus 23:4
If thou meet thine enemy's ox or his ass going astray, thou shalt surely bring it back to him again.

Today's parallel would read, "If you see your enemy's car beginning to roll down a hill, give him a brake."

Exodus 23:5
If thou see the ass of him that hateth thee lying under his burden, and wouldest forbear to help him, thou shalt surely help with him.

I believe this speaks not only of the rescue of an animal, but of restoration between people. If you know your enemy is burdened or troubled by a marriage on the rocks or a business under stress, you can help them through prayer. I have found this to be exceedingly practical. Years ago, an older brother in the Lord taught me to see that the way to keep from having any bitterness in my heart was to pray for people with whom I might otherwise be upset or disappointed.

"Don't curse those who persecute you," Jesus would say. "Pray for them" (see Matthew 5:44). Lift the burden off your enemy through prayer and you'll be set free yourself of the burden of hostility or bitterness.

Exodus 23:6
Thou shalt not wrest the judgment of thy poor in his cause.

This is the counterpart to verse 3.

Exodus 23:7
Keep thee far from a false matter; and the innocent and righteous slay thou not: for I will not justify the wicked.

Speaking of society as a whole, God says He will not justify the wicked. But when it comes to individual sinners, Romans 4 tells us that God is the One who justifies the ungodly. What good news!

Exodus 23:8
And thou shalt take no gift: for the gift blindeth the wise, and perverteth the words of the righteous.

Those whose job it is to sort through judicial matters are not to take gifts in order that their judgment be not clouded.

Exodus 23:9
Also thou shalt not oppress a stranger: for ye know the heart of a stranger, seeing ye were strangers in the land of Egypt.

"Oppress not the stranger," God had said in the previous chapter (v. 21). And here, He repeats the injunction. When God repeats a matter, it's because He wants us to understand how important it is to Him. Prejudice can lurk in the farthest corners of a man's heart without him even being aware it's there. That is why we have to ask the Lord, as the psalmist did, to search our heart, to see if there be any wicked way in us (Psalm 139:23). Because we were all strangers and aliens, cut off from the blessings of God before He adopted us into His family, there is no room for oppression or prejudice in the heart of any believer (Ephesians 2:12).

Exodus 23:10–12
And six years thou shalt sow thy land, and shalt gather in the fruits thereof: But the seventh year thou shalt let it rest and lie still; that the poor of thy people may eat: and what they leave the beasts of the field shall eat. In like manner thou shalt deal with thy vineyard, and with thy oliveyard. Six days thou shalt do thy work, and on the seventh day thou shalt rest: that thine ox and thine ass may rest, and the son of thy handmaid, and the stranger, may be refreshed.

Those who think the Law is demanding have not read it, for passages such as this speak of God's tender heart toward us. God wants us to succeed, but not at the expense of our health or the well-being of others.

"Come unto Me," Jesus would say, "and I will give you rest. Yoke with Me. Take some time to be with Me. Learn of Me and you'll find rest in your soul" (see Matthew 11:29). In Exodus 20:10, God mandated one day off in seven so that one's sons and daughters could rest. Here, the circle is widened to include animals and servants.

Exodus 23:13
And in all things that I have said unto you be circumspect: and make no mention of the name of other gods, neither let it be heard out of thy mouth.

Paul said we should be ignorant concerning evil (Romans 16:19)—completely unfamiliar with the idols that dominate the heart of our culture.

Exodus 23:14–16
Three times thou shalt keep a feast unto me in the year. Thou shalt keep the feast of unleavened bread: (thou shalt eat unleavened bread seven days, as I commanded thee, in the time appointed of the month Abib; for in it thou camest out from Egypt: and none shall appear before me empty). And the feast of harvest, the firstfruits of thy labours, which thou hast sown in the field: and the feast of ingathering, which is in the end of the year, when thou hast gathered in thy labours out of the field.

The people of God were to gather three times a year: for the feast of Passover in the spring; for the Feast of Harvest, or Pentecost, fifty days after Passover; and for the Feast of Ingathering or Tabernacles in the fall. And when they gathered, none were to come empty-handed. Rather, they were to come ready to give. There are people today who come to the assembly not looking for something to get, but something to give. They come prayed up, prepared to worship, eager to tithe, ready to reach out to someone. And in so doing, they enrich the Fellowship greatly.

Exodus 23:17, 18
Three times in the year all thy males shall appear before the Lord God. Thou shalt not offer the blood of my sacrifice with leavened bread; neither shall the fat of my sacrifice remain until the morning.

Leaven being a type of sin, this is a reiteration of verses 8 and 10 of chapter 12.

Exodus 23:19 (a)
The first of the firstfruits of thy land thou shalt bring into the house of the LORD thy God . . .

The priority the Lord has in our lives is seen by what we do with the "firstfruits"—the first tenth of all He gives us.

Exodus 23:19 (b)
. . . Thou shalt not seethe a kid in his mother's milk.

Although observant Jews are very careful to never eat meat products with dairy products (e.g. no cheeseburgers), I don't believe such was the intent of this regulation. You see, this verse being connected with the topic of the Passover, I believe it refers to the fertility rites practiced by the heathen at the time of Passover, wherein they partook of the milk of a goat or cow along with the meat of a kid or calf in order that their gods might bless them with children. Writings dating from 1300 B.C. that record such practices have been recently discovered. Therefore, I believe God gives this regulation in order that His people stay completely clear of anything resembling pagan practices.

Exodus 23:20, 21
Behold, I send an Angel before thee, to keep thee in the way, and to bring thee into the place which I have prepared. Beware of him, and obey his voice, provoke him not; for he will not pardon your transgressions: for my name is in him.

The word "Angel" is capitalized because it unquestionably refers to Jesus—a Christophany, or an appearance of Jesus before He came to earth as the Babe of Bethlehem. This is the only explanation for why this Angel had the power to pardon sin.

Exodus 23:22, 23
But if thou shalt indeed obey his voice, and do all that I speak; then I will be an enemy unto thine enemies, and an adversary unto thine adversaries. For mine Angel shall go before thee, and bring thee in unto the Amorites, and the Hittites, and the Perizzites, and the Canaanites, and the Hivites, and the Jebusites: and I will cut them off.

The heart of God is that we obey the voice of His Angel in order that He might bless us, in order that we might have victory over those things that weigh us down, those things which hold us in bondage, those things which eat at our soul.

Exodus 23:24
Thou shalt not bow down to their gods, nor serve them, nor do after their works: but thou shalt utterly overthrow them, and quite break down their images.

The ultimate image in our day is the one beamed into our homes constantly on the screens of our televisions.

Exodus 23:25
And ye shall serve the LORD your God, and he shall bless thy bread, and thy water; and I will take sickness away from the midst of thee.

Aren't you tired of living in a sick society? God says, "If you obey what I say, if you break down those altars and do in these images, I'll heal your land."

Exodus 23:26, 27
There shall nothing cast their young, nor be barren, in thy land: the number of thy days I will fulfil. I will send my fear before thee, and will destroy all the people to whom thou shalt come, and I will make all thine enemies turn their backs unto thee.

I love this! Oh, may the enemies that wage war against our souls, the forces which seek to do us harm have no place in our lives. This is what I want for myself and my family, for the church and for our country. "Trust Me," says the Lord. "I will drive out your enemies—but I will do it in a way you would never have imagined. . . ."

Exodus 23:28
And I will send hornets before thee, which shall drive out the Hivite, the Canaanite, and the Hittite, from before thee.

God says, "I'm going to take care of all these problem people with hornets." *Hornets?* Some have suggested that the term "hornets" refers to the Assyrians. That may be, but I don't think so. I think the Lord is saying, "I have ways you can't comprehend to take care of the depression, the addiction, the sadness which plague you. My ways are not your ways. I'm going to send hornets."

Exodus 23:29, 30
I will not drive them out from before thee in one year; lest the land become desolate, and the beast of the field multiply against thee. By little and little I will drive them out from before thee, until thou be increased, and inherit the land.

"I've gone to Bible study for six weeks," some say, "and I'm still depressed, still defeated." Or, "I've been praying for three months and my situation still hasn't changed."

The Lord, however, says, "I'll not drive out your enemies as quickly as you might think because there's something else in play. If I drove them out in one year, the wild beasts would multiply. Therefore, until you're increased, until you're ready to occupy the land, I'm keeping them there in order to keep the fields tilled and the wild beasts at bay."

This is hard for me because patience is hard for me. I like things to happen immediately. But that's not the way God works. "Count it all joy," He says, "when you go through trials in order that patience might have her perfect work" (see James 1:2–4). I want to get ahead of God, but He says, "If the project was completed, if the answer was given on your schedule, you wouldn't be ready for it. My timing is perfect—any earlier and it would be disastrous. In the meantime, you'll be increased by talking the situation over with Me, by waiting on Me, by spending time with Me."

"I want this kind of ministry," we say, or, "that kind of girl to marry," or, "this type of family."

"Great!" the Lord says, "but I've got a lot of work to do to make you the kind of person who can handle that responsibility. It's not going to happen quickly. Little by little I'll drive out the obstacles. In the meantime, stay close to Me."

Exodus 23:31–33
And I will set thy bounds from the Red sea even unto the sea of the Philistines, and from the desert unto the river: for I will deliver the inhabitants of the land into your hand; and thou shalt drive them out before thee. Thou shalt make no covenant with them, nor with their gods. They shall not dwell in thy land, lest they make thee sin against me: for if thou serve their gods, it will surely be a snare unto thee.

"I'm going to do something big," the Lord says. "I'm going to bring you into a land that stretches from the Red Sea to the Mediterranean to the Euphrates. And when you get there, don't become involved with the gods you'll find, but keep your eyes on Me."

24

Exodus 24 is the Old Testament counterpart to the account of the Transfiguration in Matthew 17. In both we see a mountain. In both we see Moses. And in both we see Jesus . . .

Exodus 24:1 (a)
And he said unto Moses, Come up unto the Lord, thou, and Aaron, Nadab, and Abihu, and seventy of the elders of Israel . . .

Aaron was Moses' older brother, his spokesman. Nadab and Abihu were Aaron's sons. Along with his brother and nephews, Moses was to bring the seventy leaders he had appointed in response to his father-in-law's suggestion (18:13–27).

Exodus 24:1 (b)
. . . and worship ye afar off.

"Draw nigh to Me and I will draw nigh to you," God says to us (James 4:8). Yet to this group, God says, "Come and worship ye afar off." They were told to worship even though they were to worship from afar. Although I know that because of the work of Christ on the Cross, I can come boldly unto the throne of grace; I can draw nigh to God; I can call Him Abba, or Papa—the fact is, sometimes I don't feel that way emotionally. I feel like I'm worshiping Him from afar off. Ever feel that way? Take heart. I have learned that it's okay because God is worthy of worship whether I am emotionally engaged or not. Worship is not about how I feel. It's all about who God is. And He is worthy to receive glory and honor and power, for He has created all things and for His pleasure they are and were created—whether I feel this or not (Revelation 4).

Exodus 24:2, 3
And Moses alone shall come near the LORD: but they shall not come nigh; neither shall the people go up with him. And Moses came and told the people all the words of the LORD, and all the judgments: and all the people answered with one voice, and said, All the words which the LORD hath said will we do.

Although the people of Israel were determined to do right, the Word says there is none righteous, no not one (Romans 3:10). Therefore, it would have been better for them to say, "We want to do Your will, Lord. Now help us, for without You, we can do nothing."

Exodus 24:4 (a)
And Moses wrote all the words of the LORD, and rose up early in the morning . . .

I suggest Moses rose up early in the morning because, after hearing the claims of the people, yet knowing full well their frailty, he didn't sleep very well the night before.

Exodus 24:4 (b)–7
. . . and builded an altar under the hill, and twelve pillars, according to the twelve tribes of Israel. And he sent young men of the children of Israel, which offered burnt offerings, and sacrificed peace offerings of oxen unto the LORD. And Moses took half of the blood, and put it in basons; and half of the blood he sprinkled on the altar. And he took the book of the covenant, and read in the audience of the people: and they said, All that the LORD hath said will we do, and be obedient.

Knowing that without the shedding of blood there could be no remission of sin (Hebrews 9:22), Moses built an altar. The altar speaks of the Ultimate Altar—the place where our sins would be cleansed forever, the Cross of Calvary where the Lamb of God was slain for you and me.

Exodus 24:8
And Moses took the blood, and sprinkled it on the people, and said, Behold the blood of the covenant, which the LORD hath made with you concerning all these words.

While the sprinkling of the blood on the altar speaks of salvation, the sprinkling of the blood over the people speaks of sanctification—of being set apart. So, too, the blood was shed *for* us on the altar of Calvary. But it's sprinkled *on* us as we apply it presently. That is why Communion is oh, so important. We're saved, born again, heaven-bound—but how we need the blood sprinkled on us, to be sanctified, to be set apart, to be reminded that we can't get through a single day without the Lord living in us.

Exodus 24:9, 10 (a)
Then went up Moses, and Aaron, Nadab, and Abihu, and seventy of the elders of Israel: and they saw the God of Israel . . .

In talking about the grandeur of God, Paul writes, "No man can approach unto Him whom no man hath seen nor can see" (1 Timothy 6:16). John says the same thing when he writes, "No man hath seen God at any time" (John 1:18). It's not that man will be punished for seeing God, but rather, the sight of the glory and grandeur of the First Person of the Trinity would simply cause a man's heart to stop beating. Yet here we read that Moses, Aaron, Nadab, Abihu, and the seventy elders all saw God. To understand this seeming contradiction turn to the Book of Isaiah . . .

> In the year that king Uzziah died I saw also the Lord sitting upon a throne, high and lifted up, and his train filled the temple. Isaiah 6:1

Now turn to John's Gospel . . .

> Then Jesus said unto them, Yet a little while is the light with you. Walk while ye have the light, lest darkness come upon you: for he that walketh in darkness knoweth not whither he goeth. But though he had done so many miracles before them, yet they believed not on him: that the saying of Esaias the prophet might be fulfilled, which he spake, Lord, who hath believed our report? And to whom hath the arm of the Lord been revealed? These things said Esaias, when he saw his glory, and spake of him. John 12:35, 37, 38, 41

John identifies the Person Isaiah called the Lord as Jesus. Therefore, who did Moses and Aaron, Nadab, Abihu, and the seventy elders see? They saw Jesus.

Exodus 24:10 (b)
. . . and there was under his feet as it were a paved work of a sapphire stone, and as it were the body of heaven in his clearness.

Under Jesus' feet was transparent blue pavement. Ever feel like you're over your head? Whatever is over your head is under His feet. And it's beautiful. Peter experienced this. Looking around and seeing the waves over his head, he took his eyes off Jesus and sank. Like Peter, some people seem to always be in a state of panic because they take their eyes off Jesus, not understanding that the waves that were over Peter's head were under Jesus' feet as He walked upon them (Matthew 14:25).

Exodus 24:11
And upon the nobles of the children of Israel he laid not his hand: also they saw God, and did eat and drink.

The word "nobles" does not mean noble by birth, but literally "rooted ones." Who is noble in God's economy? Those who are rooted and grounded in Christ, rooted and grounded in their faith, rooted and grounded in love (Ephesians 3:17).

Exodus 24:12 (a)
And the LORD said unto Moses, Come up to me into the mount, and be there . . .

"Be there." Ever go to church or to a Bible study and you're not there? The Word is being taught, worship is being offered, and you're there—but you're not there. God says, "Come and be there"—not just physically, but wholly.

Exodus 24:12 (b)
. . . and I will give thee tables of stone, and a law, and commandments which I have written; that thou mayest teach them.

It was because God knew Abraham would "command his children and his household after him" in the way of the Lord that He told Abraham about the impending destruction of Sodom (Genesis 18:17–19). Who does God give His Word to? Those who He knows will teach or share with others.

Exodus 24:13
And Moses rose up, and his minister Joshua: and Moses went up into the mount of God.

The name "Joshua" being the Old Testament form of the name "Jesus," Moses took Jesus, if you would, with him. And it had to be this way, for without Joshua, Moses' ministry would be incomplete. You see, it was Joshua who would eventually lead the people into the Promised Land. Moses represents the Law. And although the Law can take us to the edge of the Promised Land as it shows us how things ought to be, we can't enter in to the Promises of God through the Law because we are unable to keep it.

"*I* am the Way," Jesus declared (John 14:6). The Law was given by Moses, but grace came by Jesus Christ (John 1:17). And it is only by grace that we are saved, that we enter the Promised Land.

Exodus 24:14
And he said unto the elders, Tarry ye here for us, until we come again unto you: and, behold, Aaron and Hur are with you: if any man have any matters to do, let him come unto them.

Although Aaron will fail miserably, Hur evidently didn't for he is not mentioned in the account of the golden calf debacle. God declares He will not tempt us above that which we are able, but will provide a way of escape (1 Corinthians 10:13). Hur evidently found the way of escape while Aaron chose not to.

Exodus 24:15, 16
And Moses went up into the mount, and a cloud covered the mount. And the glory of the LORD abode upon mount Sinai, and the cloud covered it six days: and the seventh day he called unto Moses out of the midst of the cloud.

Prophetically, the Lord Himself shall descend in the clouds and we'll hear His voice (1 Thessalonians 4:16). The picture portrayed here on Mt. Sinai is one seen throughout Scripture and one we'll see again.

Exodus 24:17, 18
And the sight of the glory of the LORD was like devouring fire on the top of the mount in the eyes of the children of Israel. And Moses went into the midst of the cloud, and gat him up into the mount: and Moses was in the mount forty days and forty nights.

Moses was in the mount forty days and forty nights, and in chapter 25, we'll see what God told him there . . .

25

The world is familiar with the pyramids of Egypt, the pagodas of Japan, and the cathedrals of Europe, but the greatest, most awesome place of worship ever constructed is largely unknown—that being the tabernacle, painstakingly and powerfully described in the chapter before us and the fifteen which follow . . .

Exodus 25:1, 2 (a)
And the LORD spake unto Moses, saying, Speak unto the children of Israel, that they bring me an offering . . .

Although the design of the tabernacle would be God's alone, He gave the people a definite part to play in the construction.

Exodus 25:2 (b)–7
. . . of every man that giveth it willingly with his heart ye shall take my offering. And this is the offering which ye shall take of them; gold, and silver, and brass, and blue, and purple, and scarlet, and fine linen, and goats' hair, and rams' skins dyed red, and badgers' skins, and shittim wood, oil for the light, spices for anointing oil, and for sweet incense, onyx stones, and stones to be set in the ephod, and in the breastplate.

In Exodus 36, we see that when this offering was actually collected, so generously did the people give that Moses had to say, "Enough! We have too much!" How often have you heard a preacher say that?! Keep in mind that, although the tabernacle would be outwardly simple, the interior would cost millions of dollars in today's standards—all provided by the hand of God's people.

In 2 Corinthians 9:7, Paul says we are not to give reluctantly or out of compulsion but according to that which is stirred in our hearts. We're to give cheerfully or, literally, hilariously. In other words, we're to be those who say, "Hooray! It's offering time. I've been looking forward to this all week!" If you give sparingly, you'll reap sparingly. If you give hilariously and generously, you'll get back with great blessing and liberality. It's an absolute principle of God (2 Corinthians 9:6, 7).

Exodus 25:8
And let them make me a sanctuary; that I may dwell among them.

The sanctuary the children of Israel were to construct was a tabernacle. Consider the following similarities between the tabernacle and the Word made flesh who dwelt, or literally *tabernacled* among us (John 1:14) . . .

The tabernacle was a temporary appointment. It served a specific purpose for a specific time until the temple was erected in Jerusalem, just as Jesus dwelt among us temporarily for thirty-three years until He ascended into heaven.

The tabernacle was erected in the wilderness. So, too, Jesus dwelt in the wilderness, for, although foxes have holes and the birds of the air have nests, the Son of Man had nowhere to lay His head (Matthew 8:20).

The tabernacle was humble in outward appearance. Covered with animal skins, it resembled the Bedouin tents of the day. So common was Jesus in appearance that Judas had to identify Him with a kiss (Matthew 26:48).

Although it was humble outwardly, the interior of the tabernacle was unbelievably beautiful—for not only was it filled with gold, silver, and fine tapestries—but, infinitely more importantly, it was filled with the Shekinah glory of God. Although Jesus resembled other men of His day in outward appearance, there was such a beauty within Him that people were drawn to Him like moths to a flame (Mark 12:37).

The tabernacle was not only God's dwelling place (verse 8), but His meeting place (verse 22). Just as Jesus not only dwells among us, but He is the only way we have oneness, fellowship communion with the Father (1 Timothy 2:5).

Exodus 25:9
According to all that I shew thee, after the pattern of the tabernacle, and the pattern of all the instruments thereof, even so shall ye make it.

"Make sure you build exactly according to the pattern," God said to Moses. Why? Because Hebrews 8:5 tells us that the tabernacle is a shadow or a picture of that which is in Heaven presently.

Exodus 25:10 (a)
And they shall make an ark . . .

After giving Moses the list of building materials, if I were God, at this point, I would have given him the blueprint, the plans for the tabernacle. Not until after the tabernacle itself was complete would I have moved on to give instruction for the furnishings within. But that's not what God does.

Directly following the list of building materials, He gives Moses the plans for the ark of the covenant—a box that was to be placed inside the Holy of Holies, inside the tabernacle. And in so doing, it's as if God is saying, "I know your tendency will be to think you have to work your way in to My presence. Therefore, I'm going to begin at that very point to show you there's nothing you can or must do to deserve a relationship with Me. It's all based on grace."

Exodus 25:10 (b)
. . . of shittim wood . . .

Shittim wood, or acacia wood, speaks of humanity. Acacia trees grow in desert regions, in dry ground, just as Isaiah declared that Jesus would be a "root out of dry ground" (Isaiah 53:2). Acacia wood has a unique property that Bedouins use to this day. That is, when pierced, it pours forth a gum resin that contains healing properties for cuts, sores, and abrasions. In the same way, Jesus was pierced with the flagellum, and by His stripes we are healed—spiritually, emotionally, physically.

Exodus 25:10 (c)
. . . two cubits and a half shall be the length thereof, and a cubit and a half the breadth thereof, and a cubit and a half the height thereof.

A cubit being the distance from one's fingertip to his elbow, the ark was to be a box four feet by two feet by two feet.

Exodus 25:11 (a)
And thou shalt overlay it with pure gold, within and without shalt thou overlay it . . .

Although Jesus became a Man, He was also God. Thus, to portray Jesus correctly, the acacia wood of humanity was covered with the gold of Deity.

Exodus 25:11 (b)
. . . and shalt make upon it a crown of gold round about.

Acacia wood is the only thorn-bearing tree which grows in the desert. Jesus would indeed be crowned with a crown of thorns—but He'll also be crowned with a crown of gold (Revelation 14:14).

Exodus 25:12–15
And thou shalt cast four rings of gold for it, and put them in the four corners thereof; and two rings shall be in the one side of it, and two rings in the other side of it. And thou shalt make staves of shittim wood, and overlay them with gold. And thou shalt put the staves into the rings by the sides of the ark, that the ark may be borne with them. The staves shall be in the rings of the ark: they shall not be taken from it.

The ark was to have a ring on each corner to hold the wooden poles by which the priests would carry it—for, like everything else in the tabernacle, the ark was to be portable, traveling with the people wherever they went.

Exodus 25:16
And thou shalt put into the ark the testimony which I shall give thee.

The testimony is the Ten Commandments, the two tables of stone written by the finger of God (Exodus 31:18).

"Come boldly before the throne of grace and find mercy and grace to help in time of need," God says to us (Hebrews 4:16).

"But I can't," we say. "I haven't prayed in days. I haven't been to church in weeks. I haven't witnessed in months. I haven't kept the commandments."

Where were the commandments kept?
In the ark.
Who kept the commandments?
Jesus. "I always do the things that please the Father," He said (John 8:29).

Jesus kept the commandments perfectly. And, as believers, we are in Him positionally (2 Corinthians 5:17). Therefore, the Father looks at us and doesn't see our sin. He looks at us and sees His Son (Romans 3:22).

Exodus 25:17–21 (a)
And thou shalt make a mercy seat of pure gold: two cubits and a half shall be the length thereof, and a cubit and a half the breadth thereof. And thou shalt make two cherubims of gold, of beaten work shalt thou make them, in the two ends of the mercy seat. And make one cherub on the one end, and the other cherub on the other end: even of the mercy seat shall ye make the cherubims on the two ends thereof. And the cherubims shall stretch forth their wings on high, covering the mercy seat with their wings, and their faces shall look one to another; toward the mercy seat shall the faces of the cherubims be. And thou shalt put the mercy seat above upon the ark . . .

Most Christians try to meet God at the ark by keeping the commandments, by going to this meeting, by doing those things, by not sinning, by living purely. God, however, says He'll meet us not at the ark, but at that which covers it—the mercy seat.

How do we walk with the Lord practically? Not by anything we do, how long our devotions are, how many chapters of the Bible we've read, how many prayers we offer—but simply and solely by the unmerited, undeserved, unearned favor of God. This is where so many people miss it. Although they know they're saved by grace, they think they're sanctified through works. Big mistake. True relationship with God is not about our witnessing, ministry or devotional life. It's all about what He did in and through Christ.

On that first Easter Sunday morning, had you looked into the empty tomb, you would have seen two angels sitting—one at the head, one at the foot of the blood-stained slab where the body of Jesus had lain (John 20:12). Leviticus 16:14 tells us that the mercy seat would be sprinkled with blood. Thus, the mercy seat paints a perfect picture of the only way we can have fellowship with God—that being through the finished work of the Son.

Exodus 25:21 (b), 22
. . . and in the ark thou shalt put the testimony that I shall give thee. And there I will meet with thee, and I will commune with thee from above the mercy seat, from between the two cherubims which are upon the ark of the testimony, of all things which I will give thee in commandment unto the children of Israel.

It was at the mercy seat that God would meet with man. And we err greatly whenever we forget this . . .

After capturing the ark, Philistines eventually put it in the temple of their god, Dagon—only to find Dagon face down before it the following day. Setting Dagon aright, they returned the next day to find him toppled over once again—this time with his head and hands severed (1 Samuel 5). While it would seem obvious that they needed a more powerful god to protect them, they instead decided to protect their god by sending the ark back to Israel. Seeing the ark on its way back to their border, the people of God were understandably excited. But their excitement soon turned to terror when God smote 50,070 of their number because they had looked inside the ark, perhaps for no other reason than to see if the commandments were still inside (1 Samuel 6).

"I will meet you at the mercy seat," God says. But sometimes we make a deadly mistake when we set aside mercy to get to the bottom of an issue, to lay down the law on someone. I have done this—and it always leads to death in relationships, in families, in friendships, in ministry.

"The letter of the law kills," Paul would write, "but the Spirit gives life" (2 Corinthians 3:6). Once we set aside mercy—even temporarily—to get to the bottom of an issue, to find out who's right and who's wrong, to get to the letter of the Law, the end result will always be death. Always. Friendships will die. Families will divide. Ministry will shut down. No good comes from removing the mercy seat. Be merciful. To whom? To the person you're angry with. Be gracious. To whom? To the person you feel has wronged you. *Blessed are the merciful, for they shall obtain mercy* (Matthew 5:7).

Whenever you feel far from God, a practical way you can be brought back into His presence is by building a mercy seat. That is, find people to whom you can show mercy. I have discovered over and over again in my own life that there are two uniquely practical ways I truly experience the presence of the Lord. The first is by praising Him, for Psalm 22 declares that He inhabits the praises of His people. The second is by showing mercy to people, for it was at the mercy seat that God chose to dwell.

Exodus 25:23 (a)
Thou shalt also make a table of shittim wood . . .

The only time the word "also" is seen in describing the tabernacle, its use here speaks of a connection with verse 22. Verse 22 speaking of the presence of God at the mercy seat, the implication is that we also experience the presence of God when we come to the table of showbread, described here. "Showbread" refers to the twelve loaves of bread—two rows of six each—which were set before the Lord each Sabbath (Leviticus 24:5–8). Showbread speaks of the Bread of Life, the Word made flesh, Jesus Christ.

Sometimes people come to me and say, "I don't feel God's presence."

And my question to them is always the same: "How long has it been since you've been to the Lord's Table?"

"Take, eat. This is My body given for you," Jesus said (Luke 22:19). Therefore, it always amazes me that people will wonder why they don't feel His presence, yet refuse to come to the place of His presence—the Table of Communion.

Exodus 25:23 (b)
. . . two cubits shall be the length thereof . . .

Why was the table of showbread to be two cubits long? Two is the number of union, communion, agreement (Amos 3:3). True communion with God takes place when we agree with Him and confess our sins. The Greek word translated "confession" is *homoligeo*, which means "to speak the same."

Thus, confession in the biblical sense is not a matter of promising not to sin again, but rather of simply agreeing with God and saying of any given sin, "This sin is depressing and defeating me, Lord. And it's detrimental to others."

Surely God knows our sins. Why, then, does He want us to confess them? Because every sin I specifically confess loses its grip on me to an ever greater degree. In addition, when I also confess that a specific sin is blotted out by the blood of Calvary, there is a dynamic which takes place in the Spirit that sets me free. Confession is not promising never to sin again, but simply to call it like it is. That's two cubits. That's union.

Exodus 25:23 (c)
. . . and a cubit the breadth thereof, and a cubit and a half the height thereof.

Whereas two is the number of union, one is the number of unity. Unity in the body of Christ does not usually come about through corporate Bible studies or times of worship because Christians don't always agree on the interpretation of any given passage or the style of any given type of music. But there is a place where people do agree—be they Episcopalian or Lutheran, Presbyterian, Catholic, or Baptist. At the Lord's Table, a unity takes place unlike during any other thing we do as Christians. The act of remembering the Lord through a piece of bread and the fruit of the vine has united believers of every culture, of every language for the past two thousand years.

Exodus 25:24, 25
And thou shalt overlay it with pure gold, and make thereto a crown of gold round about. And thou shalt make unto it a border of an hand breadth round about, and thou shalt make a golden crown to the border thereof round about.

There was to be a crown of molding around the outside edge of the table of showbread and a smaller crown inside. Why two crowns? Because Christ will be crowned twice: the first time He was crowned with a crown of thorns (Matthew 27:29). The second time it will be with a crown of glory and honor (Hebrews 2:9).

The smaller crown on the table of showbread was to keep the bread from falling off the table. The bread speaking of the body, no wonder this crown was measured by the hand breadth, for of His followers Jesus said, "I give them eternal life and no man shall pluck them out of My hand" (John 10:28). We think we're holding His hand, when, in reality, He's holding us. And in this we can rest. In this regard, I do not believe a person can lose his salvation. I do believe, however, if a person really wants to, he can leave it. But he's got to really want to jump off the table of showbread, over the crown of protection, past the boundary of God's love to finally fall to the ground.

Exodus 25:26–30
And thou shalt make for it four rings of gold, and put the rings in the four corners that are on the four feet thereof. Over against the border shall the rings be for places of the staves to bear the table. And thou shalt make the staves of shittim wood, and overlay them with gold, that the table may be borne with them. And thou shalt make the dishes thereof, and spoons thereof, and covers thereof, and bowls thereof, to cover withal: of pure gold shalt thou make them. And thou shalt set upon the table shewbread before me alway.

Just as the table of showbread was to be wherever the people were—to be carried, to be available—the Lord would say to us tonight, "I'm available. I'm the Bread of Life. Eat of Me."

Concerning Communion, in 1 Corinthians 11, Paul says, "Because you eat unworthily, you eat to your own damnation." This doesn't mean that if a person partakes of Communion with unconfessed sin in his life, he'll be damned. Rather, it means that he who doesn't assign a great worth to Communion, he who doesn't value it, he who ignores it, will be spiritually—and sometimes even physically—weak. The Table is portable. Take advantage of it. Be renewed and revived. Be healthy and strengthened as you remember God's mercy and His unspeakable love for you.

Exodus 25:31 (a)
And thou shalt make a candlestick . . .

The word translated "candlestick" is the Hebrew word *menorah*—which held oil lamps rather than wax candles.

Exodus 25:31 (b)
. . . of pure gold . . .

The lampstand was not made of wood covered with gold as was the ark and the table of showbread—but of pure gold.

Exodus 25:31 (c)
. . . of beaten work shall the candlestick be made: his shaft, and his branches, his bowls, his knops, and his flowers, shall be of the same.

A few chapters from now, we will see how Aaron made a golden calf from molten gold. Unlike that false god, this lampstand, which speaks of Jesus Christ, the Light of the world, was made of beaten gold. Many people say, "You Christians claim that Jesus is the single answer, the only Way, the one true Light. But how do you know what you're declaring is right?" The answer is that, like the gold of the candlestick, He was beaten—yet He rose again from the dead.

"What sign showest thou us?" the Jews asked Jesus.
"Destroy this temple and in three days I will raise it up," Jesus answered, speaking of the temple of His body (John 2:18–21).

Truly, the door of our faith swings on the hinge of the Resurrection.

Exodus 25:32
And six branches shall come out of the sides of it; three branches of the candlestick out of the one side, and three branches of the candlestick out of the other side:

There were to be seven lamps on the lampstand—a main stem and six branches. Six is the number of man; seven the number of completion or perfection. This brings to mind Jesus' words in John 15 when He said, "I am the Vine and you are the branches."

From Adam's side a rib was taken and fashioned into his bride (Genesis 2:21–25). Jesus is the Last Adam, and He, too, has a bride: the church. As He was pinned to the Cross, as He died for you and me, a soldier thrust a spear into His side, and out came blood and water, the fluids of birthing. From whence came we? Out of His side—for it was His death that gave birth to the church.

Exodus 25:33
Three bowls made like unto almonds, with a knop and a flower in one branch; and three bowls made like almonds in the other branch, with a knop and a flower: so in the six branches that come out of the candlestick.

Each of these six branches had three bowls, or flares, each of which contained a bud and a knop, or blossom, resembling those of an almond. An almond blossom is pure white and, even today, the almond tree is the first in Israel to blossom and the first to bear fruit. This speaks of the Resurrection of Jesus Christ, for He is the Firstfruit (1 Corinthians 15:20). That is, He is the first One risen from the dead.

Exodus 25:34, 35
And in the candlestick shall be four bowls made like unto almonds, with their knops and their flowers. And there shall be a knop under two branches of the same, and a knop under two branches of the same, and a knop under two branches of the same, according to the six branches that proceed out of the candlestick.

The side branches had three units consisting of a flare, a bud, and a flare. The middle shaft, however, was to have four such units. This meant it would be higher than the other six—just as Jesus Christ is preeminent. There is *none* like Him.

Exodus 25:36
Their knops and their branches shall be of the same: all it shall be one beaten work of pure gold.

The branches were to be of the same material as the main stem, the Vine. This means that, like Jesus, we shall be beaten. "I am the Light of the world," Jesus declared (John 8:12). But He also said we are the lights of the world (Matthew 5:14). When does the world see our light? When we are beaten. It's not when things are going well, when all is peaches and cream that the skeptic is converted. No, people are convinced of the reality of the Son when they see us beaten by problems, by hard times, by tragedy—and yet reflecting the light of the Son nonetheless.

Exodus 25:37
And thou shalt make the seven lamps thereof: and they shall light the lamps thereof, that they may give light over against it.

The Hebrew rendering of the last phrase is literally, "that they may light the face of it." In other words, although the lights on these branches were to illuminate the holy place, their primary purpose was to show the face of the main shaft. Truly, it's when you are beaten and yet continue to burn bright that the beauty, the reality of the Vine, Jesus, is seen. This means that the point at which you choose to embrace the difficulty that seems to beat upon you is the point where you will see Jesus in ways you've never seen Him before. It is when you're being beaten, when you're in the fiery trial that Jesus is clearer to you than you ever dreamed possible.

Ask Shadrach, Meshach, and Abed-Nego. As they were in the furnace, Who did they see? The Son of God in their midst. How real was He? So real they didn't want to leave the furnace (Daniel 3:25–26). A lot of people try to get out of the fire—when in reality, it is the fire itself which causes the Lord to be seen most clearly.

Exodus 25:38
And the tongs thereof, and the snuffdishes thereof, shall be of pure gold.

The instruments used to trim the wicks and snuff out the candles were to be pure gold. Just as there will be people in our lives who are there morning and evening, "snipping" and "snuffing." And, although my tendency is to belittle them, I am in error when I do because they provide golden opportunities for me to burn brighter.

Exodus 25:39
Of a talent of pure gold shall he make it, with all these vessels.

The only time the word "he" appears in conjunction with the making of an instrument for the tabernacle, the man spoken of is Bezaleel, as we will see in chapter 31—a picture or type of the Holy Spirit. I find it interesting that although the weight is given of the lampstand (132 lbs.), unlike the ark and the table of showbread, the dimensions aren't given. Could this be because there is no limit to how brightly we can shine, to how clearly we can reflect the Vine?

Exodus 25:40
And look that thou make them after their pattern, which was shewed thee in the mount.

Moses was to make everything according to the pattern given him on the mount. We, too, are to do everything according to the pattern given us on the mount—not Mt. Sinai, but Mt. Calvary, when, for the joy set before Him, Jesus endured the Cross, knowing that on the other side there would be a bud, a blossom, fruit—you (Hebrews 12:2).

26

Exodus 26:1 (a)
Moreover thou shalt make the tabernacle with ten curtains . . .

Ten is the number of human responsibility, as seen in the Ten Commandments and the ten plagues on Pharaoh's nation due to his failure to respond to God's command to let His people go.

Exodus 26:1 (b)
. . . of fine twined linen, and blue, and purple, and scarlet . . .

The curtains, which would serve as walls of the tabernacle, were to be made of four colors: white, blue, purple, and scarlet. The number four draws one's mind to the four Gospels which, not surprisingly, correspond perfectly to the four colors of the tabernacle. Luke speaks of the righteous humanity of Jesus, which would be typified by the fine white linen. John portrays Jesus as Deity, which would be typified by blue, the color of heaven. Matthew writes of Jesus as King of the Jews—as seen in purple, the color of royalty. Mark speaks of Jesus as the Suffering Servant—seen in the color scarlet . . .

The Hebrew word, *tola'ath*, can be translated either of two ways: "scarlet" or "worm." Why? Because in Old Testament times when people wanted to dye something scarlet, they would dip the material in ground-up worms and the material would take on a scarlet color.

"I am a worm and not a man," cried the psalmist, prophetically speaking of Jesus on the Cross (Psalm 22:6). And the word he used was *tola'ath*,— a most fitting word. You see, to reproduce, the *tola'ath* or worm, would fasten itself on the limb of a tree and die in the process of giving birth. As it died, it left a red spot that, according to the New International Bible Encyclopedia, turned white after three days and flaked off like snow. "Though your sins be as scarlet, they shall be as white as snow," Isaiah declares (1:18). The picture is perfect. Jesus fastened Himself to a tree that we might be born into His family. He sacrificed His life that we might live. Three days later, He rose again, and our sin that was scarlet was washed white as snow. Is it any wonder that scarlet was one of the colors in the tabernacle and in the vestures of the priest?

Exodus 26:1 (c)
. . . with cherubims of cunning work shalt thou make them.

When the priests went into the holy place, they would be aware that angels were in their midst.

The same is true of us, for Paul tells us that angels are in our company, learning about God's grace and mercy by observing how good He is to you and me (1 Corinthians 11:10). The tabernacle being a picture of Jesus, it is no wonder that angels would have been embroidered within its fabric, for angels were present at Jesus' birth (Luke 2), present during His life (Matthew 4), and present at the end of His life (Luke 22:43).

Exodus 26:2, 3
The length of one curtain shall be eight and twenty cubits, and the breadth of one curtain four cubits: and every one of the curtains shall have one measure. The five curtains shall be coupled together one to another; and other five curtains shall be coupled one to another.

The fabric of the ten curtains joined into two sections was beautiful, but it was still in two separate pieces—just as the Ten Commandments were written on two tablets of stone. There was still a gap between the curtains because, although the Law of the Lord is perfect, it is impossible to live up to, leaving an impassable gap for any who have tried.

Exodus 26:4–6
And thou shalt make loops of blue upon the edge of the one curtain from the selvedge in the coupling; and likewise shalt thou make in the uttermost edge of another curtain, in the coupling of the second. Fifty loops shalt thou make in the one curtain, and fifty loops shalt thou make in the edge of the curtain that is in the coupling of the second; that the loops may take hold one of another. And thou shalt make fifty taches of gold, and couple the curtains together with the taches: and it shall be one tabernacle.

Fifty is the number of salvation, as seen in the year of Jubilee which occurred every fifty years when all debts were cancelled (Leviticus 25:10), and in Noah's ark which was fifty cubits wide (Genesis 6:15). The curtains were brought together not with fasteners of wood covered with gold, but by pure gold—just as our lives come together and make sense not through a mixture of our efforts at keeping God's Law, but solely by His salvation, by His grace.

Exodus 26:7, 8
And thou shalt make curtains of goats' hair to be a covering upon the tabernacle: eleven curtains shalt thou make. The length of one curtain shall be thirty cubits, and the breadth of one curtain four cubits: and the eleven curtains shall be all of one measure.

There would be a total of four coverings over the tabernacle. This is the second—consisting of eleven curtains instead of ten, thirty cubits instead of twenty-eight. Middle Eastern goats being primarily black, this would be a black covering.

Exodus 26:9 (a)
And thou shalt couple five curtains by themselves . . .

Biblically, six is the number of man or the flesh; five the number of grace; eleven the number of disorder.

Exodus 26:9 (b), 10
. . . and six curtains by themselves, and shalt double the sixth curtain in the forefront of the tabernacle. And thou shalt make fifty loops on the edge of the one curtain that is outmost in the coupling, and fifty loops in the edge of the curtain which coupleth the second.

The eleventh curtain was to cover the opening of the tabernacle. Folded back, the only part of the curtain one would see upon entering the tabernacle would be the black curtain.

Exodus 26:11
And thou shalt make fifty taches of brass, and put the taches into the loops, and couple the tent together, that it may be one.

Brass is the metal of judgment . . .

It was when they looked at the brass snake upon a pole, signifying the judgment Christ would bear on the Cross as He was made sin for us that the children of Israel were saved from the deadly snakebites in the wilderness (Numbers 21). They were brass fetters which bound Samson after the Holy Spirit had departed from him (Judges 16:21). It was a brass helmet Goliath wore when David slew him (1 Samuel 17:5).

Seen in conjunction with the "disorder" of the eleventh curtain made of the blackness of the goats' skin, the brass tacks underscored the price Jesus would pay to become sin for us.

Exodus 26:12, 13
And the remnant that remaineth of the curtains of the tent, the half curtain that remaineth, shall hang over the backside of the tabernacle. And a cubit on the one side, and

a cubit on the other side of that which remaineth in the length of the curtains of the tent, it shall hang over the sides of the tabernacle on this side and on that side, to cover it.

On the inside of the tabernacle was beautiful, embroidered tapestry. Yet it was covered with the black curtain of goat's hair. This speaks of Jesus, who, although He was righteous and beautiful bore the black ugliness of our sin. I find it interesting that 1/11th of this second covering would be seen—the remainder covered by the third layer—because Jesus' public ministry was three years, or 1/11th of His life.

Exodus 26:14 (a)
And thou shalt make a covering for the tent of rams' skins dyed red . . .

Made of ram's skins, the third covering speaks of the Genesis 22 account where we read that, in obedience to God's command, Abraham took his son, Isaac, up Mt. Moriah—the very place Jesus would be crucified centuries later—to sacrifice him. Ready to plunge a knife into the chest of his son, Abraham was interrupted by God and told to sacrifice the ram caught in a nearby thicket instead. To this day, it is a ram's horn, or *shofar*, which is blown at the year of Jubilee because the ram's horn is a picture of grace.

Exodus 26:14 (b)
. . . and a covering above of badgers' skins.

In the Middle East, badger skins are considered even today to be common and ugly. Therefore, with a badger skin covering—atop the beautiful tapestry and goats' and rams' skin coverings—to the Moabites, Ammonites, and all the surrounding peoples, the tabernacle would appear ugly and common. It would be as if you had a wonderful house and you covered it with black trash bags. So, too, of Jesus, Isaiah said that there is no form or comeliness that when we see Him we should desire Him (53:2). And yet the beauty within Him broke through on the day He was on Mt. Hermon, when He was transfigured, when the glory of His Deity burst through His humanity.

Exodus 26:15
And thou shalt make boards for the tabernacle of shittim wood standing up.

Acacia wood grows in the desert, is gnarled, and speaks of us. "Know ye not that ye are the temple of God?" Paul would ask (1 Corinthians 3:16)—for gnarled and human as we are, the Spirit nonetheless dwells within us.

Exodus 26:16
Ten cubits shall be the length of a board, and a cubit and a half shall be the breadth of one board.

Just as the acacia wood had to be cut down and cut to size before it could be used, it is the humble man God uses (1 Peter 5:6).

Exodus 26:17, 18
Two tenons shall there be in one board, set in order one against another: thus shalt thou make for all the boards of the tabernacle. And thou shalt make the boards for the tabernacle, twenty boards on the south side southward.

Each board was to be one and one-half cubits. One and one-half being an unstable number, it would only be when two boards were linked together that they could stand, for three is the number of godliness, as seen in the Trinity. By ourselves, we'll be unbalanced. We must be linked to another brother or sister, for without accountability, we'll be unstable.

Exodus 26:19–21
And thou shalt make forty sockets of silver under the twenty boards; two sockets under one board for his two tenons, and two sockets under another board for his two tenons. And for the second side of the tabernacle on the north side there shall be twenty boards: And their forty sockets of silver; two sockets under one board, and two sockets under another board.

Each board was placed in silver sockets because silver is the metal of redemption. We who once had our roots in the dirt and dust of the world were chopped down—and now we stand because we've been redeemed. Held up by sockets of silver, we're still in the world—but not of the world (John 17:16–18). Why were there to be two sockets per board? Because we're redeemed both in this life and forever in Heaven.

Exodus 26:22–24
And for the sides of the tabernacle westward thou shalt make six boards. And two boards shalt thou make for the corners of the tabernacle in the two sides. And they shall be coupled together beneath, and they shall be coupled together above the head of it unto one ring: thus shall it be for them both; they shall be for the two corners.

There were to be twenty boards on the north, twenty boards on the south, six boards on the west, and two corner boards to tie the three walls together—leaving the east side open. When Christ comes, from what direction will He come? The east. Through which gate will He enter Jerusalem? The Eastern Gate. It all points to His coming.

Exodus 26:25–28
And they shall be eight boards, and their sockets of silver, sixteen sockets; two sockets under one board, and two sockets under another board. And thou shalt make bars of shittim wood; five for the boards of the one side of the tabernacle, and five bars for the boards of the other side of the tabernacle, and five bars for the boards of the side of the tabernacle, for the two sides westward. And the middle bar in the midst of the boards shall reach from end to end.

Because we are the righteousness of God in Christ Jesus (2 Corinthians 5:21), believers can have a tendency to think they don't need the church. "We'll just meet for coffee," two can say. "That will be our church." But those two can fall into error without even being aware of what's happening. Two boards are more stable than one—but what keeps the two boards from falling? The five bars God gave to the church to stabilize her: apostles, prophets, evangelists, pastors, and teachers (Ephesians 4). Each of these ministries is needed to keep the boards straight, to keep the church standing strong. Apostles govern the church. Prophets guide the church. Evangelists gather the lost. Pastors guard against wolves. Teachers ground believers in the Word.

Exodus 26:29
And thou shalt overlay the boards with gold, and make their rings of gold for places for the bars: and thou shalt overlay the bars with gold.

The bars were held in place by golden rings. Rings are emblems of love. If you have the tongue of men and angels but have not love, you're nothing. If you give your body to be burned, but have not love, your sacrifice is worthless. If you have faith to move mountains, but have not love, your faith is meaningless. First Corinthians 13 tells us that love is more important than having faith, being a prophet, doing miracles, speaking in tongues—more important than anything else in ministry, for love is what holds everything together. Do you love God? Do you love people? Love is the essence of true ministry.

Exodus 26:30
And thou shalt rear up the tabernacle according to the fashion thereof which was shewed thee in the mount.

And now, the tent was to be raised.

Exodus 26:31 (a)
And thou shalt make a vail of blue, and purple, and scarlet, and fine twined linen of cunning work . . .

Everything in the tabernacle points to Jesus—and we need not speculate on what the veil signifies because the author of the Book of Hebrews makes it clear . . .

> Having therefore, brethren, boldness to enter into the holiest by the blood of Jesus, by a new and living way, which he hath consecrated for us, through the veil, that is to say, his flesh . . .
> Hebrews 10:19, 20

The veil represented Jesus' flesh. Therefore, the colors are, again, fitting. Blue is the color of heaven. As a Man, Jesus was heavenly minded. Purple speaks of royalty. "My kingdom is not of this world," Jesus said in response to the crowd's clamor to make Him King (John 18:36). Blue and purple were linked together because Jesus never lost sight of the fact that His kingdom was a heavenly one.

Although we're concerned about our present comfort, our King is more concerned about our eternal state—who we'll be and how we'll function in the next billion years to come. Therefore, if things don't work out the way we think they should, the scarlet which speaks of sacrifice reminds us that the One who laid down His life for us will continue to do what's best for us. Finally, the white linen speaks of righteousness. Our flesh is depraved, infected by sin. Jesus, on the other hand, lived such a righteous life that Pilate could find no fault in Him (Luke 23:4), and even Judas had to admit, "I have betrayed innocent blood" (Matthew 27:4).

Exodus 26:31 (b)
. . . with cherubims shall it be made:

As with the curtains, cherubims, or angels, were to be embroidered into the veil, speaking of the angelic presence throughout Jesus' life.

Exodus 26:32, 33 (a)
And thou shalt hang it upon four pillars of shittim wood overlaid with gold: their hooks shall be of gold, upon the four sockets of silver. And thou shalt hang up the vail under

the taches, that thou mayest bring in thither within the vail the ark of the testimony . . .

The veil was hung on four pillars because there are four Gospels which portray the Word made flesh, which reveal to us who Jesus is. And just as the veil was to be hung on four wooden pillars, the One whose flesh it speaks of would be hung on a wooden Cross.

Exodus 26:33 (b)
. . . and the vail shall divide unto you between the holy place and the most holy.

Just as the beautiful veil which portrayed Jesus so perfectly separated the priests from the Holy of Holies wherein dwelt the Shekinah glory of God, it is the very loveliness and beauty of Jesus which keeps people from experiencing the glory of God because, compared to Him, even our most noble attempts at righteousness are as filthy rags (Isaiah 64:6).

Exodus 26:34, 35
And thou shalt put the mercy seat upon the ark of the testimony in the most holy place. And thou shalt set the table without the vail, and the candlestick over against the table on the side of the tabernacle toward the south: and thou shalt put the table on the north side.

The only way anyone but the high priest—and he only one day a year—could enter the Holy of Holies to fellowship with God at the mercy seat was if the veil was somehow opened to them. And that is precisely what happened. At the moment Jesus died on the Cross, the veil was ripped in two, God, in effect, saying, "Open House! Enter in! Come boldly to the throne of grace" (Hebrews 4:16). Thus, the perfection of Jesus' flesh that was previously a barrier to us became the bridge for us because it was ripped apart when He bore our sin.

Exodus 26:36
And thou shalt make an hanging for the door of the tent, of blue, and purple, and scarlet, and fine twined linen, wrought with needlework.

The tabernacle had only one door—for Jesus is the single Door (John 10:9), the only Way to the Father (Acts 4:12). If there were ten ways to heaven, Satan would counter with one hundred false ways and we would have to figure out which were true. So the Lord said, "I'm going to keep it real simple, real basic. There's only one Way to heaven. There's just one Door. It's My Son."

Exodus 26:37
And thou shalt make for the hanging five pillars of shittim wood, and overlay them with gold, and their hooks shall be of gold: and thou shalt cast five sockets of brass for them.

The door was to be held up by five pillars because five is the number of grace—and it is only by grace that we are saved (Ephesians 2:8). But notice that the five pillars were to be held with sockets of brass. Brass being the metal of judgment, the door would point to the fact that, although grace is free, it's not cheap. It cost Jesus everything. Jesus absorbed the judgment that should have been ours when He gave His life that we might live.

27

Exodus 27:1
And thou shalt make an altar of shittim wood, five cubits long, and five cubits broad; the altar shall be foursquare: and the height thereof shall be three cubits.

At seven and one-half by seven and one-half by four and one-half feet, this is not only the first object one would see when entering the tabernacle, but the largest. The place where sacrifices would be made, where blood would be shed, it speaks of the Cross.

Exodus 27:2
And thou shalt make the horns of it upon the four corners thereof: his horns shall be of the same: and thou shalt overlay it with brass.

The horns were used to tie the sacrifice to the altar. Jesus Christ was tied to the altar of the Cross—not by the spikes that pierced His hands and feet, but by the bands of His love for you and me. "He saved others, let Him save Himself," the crowd mocked (Mark 15:31)—failing to understand, unable to comprehend, blind to the fact that if He saved Himself, He couldn't save them.

Exodus 27:3–8
And thou shalt make his pans to receive his ashes, and his shovels, and his basons, and his fleshhooks, and his firepans: all the vessels thereof thou shalt make of brass. And thou shalt make for it a grate of network of brass; and upon the net shalt thou make four brasen rings in the four corners thereof. And thou shalt put it under the compass of the altar beneath, that the net may be even to the midst of the altar. And

thou shalt make staves for the altar, staves of shittim wood, and overlay them with brass. And the staves shall be put into the rings, and the staves shall be upon the two sides of the altar, to bear it. Hollow with boards shalt thou make it: as it was shewed thee in the mount, so shall they make it.

The altar would be carried by staves, or poles, slipped through the rings upon it. I like this because the Communion Table ought to be portable. That is, wherever we are, we are to remember and receive the work Christ did for us on the brass altar of Calvary.

The altar was the only piece of tabernacle furniture covered with purple (Numbers 4:13, 14). Purple is the color of royalty. Why is Jesus Christ our King? Not because of what He does for me, but because what He already did on the Cross. He's not our King so that we'll have a happy day or have our bills paid, so that we'll get a newer car or have better relationships. The purple cloth was over the brass altar exclusively because that is the basis of His kingly authority over our lives. He saved us from hell—and if He never answers another prayer or sends another blessing our way, that is reason enough to praise Him all the days of our lives.

Over the purple was a second covering—of badger skin. Royal purple and common badger skin covered the same altar because people look at the Cross in two different ways. One thief mocked and "badgered" Jesus; the other said, "Remember me when You come into Your kingdom" (Luke 23:42). Two thieves—equally needy, equal in proximity to Jesus. One saw the badger skin of His humanity and was lost, the other, the purple of His royalty and was saved.

Because Jesus paid the price for our sin, our lives have been permanently, eternally "altared." We're going to heaven because of the work He did on the brass altar of Calvary.

Exodus 27:9–15
And thou shalt make the court of the tabernacle: for the south side southward there shall be hangings for the court of fine twined linen of an hundred cubits long for one side: and the twenty pillars thereof and their twenty sockets shall be of brass; the hooks of the pillars and their fillets shall be of silver. And likewise for the north side in length there shall be hangings of an hundred cubits long, and his twenty pillars and their twenty sockets of brass; the hooks of the pillars and their fillets of silver. And for the breadth of the court on the west side shall be hangings of fifty cubits: their pillars ten, and their sockets ten. And the breadth of the court on the east side eastward shall be fifty cubits. The hangings of one side of the gate shall be fifteen cubits: their pillars three, and their sockets three. And on the other side shall be hangings fifteen cubits: their pillars three, and their sockets three.

We come to the description of the linen fence which formed the courtyard surrounding the tabernacle. At one hundred cubits long by fifty cubits wide, or one hundred and fifty feet by seventy-five feet, this area was not very big considering that it was for a congregation of possibly three million people. But perhaps in it the Lord was saying, "At a given time, I know not many people will seek Me."

Sixty pillars—twenty each on the north and south sides, ten on the east and west sides—kept the linen fence in place and kept out people who didn't belong inside, those who weren't part of the family. "Who says I can't go to heaven?" people say. "I'm a pretty good guy"—failing to understand that their righteousness is as filthy rags in comparison to the fine white linen of God's righteousness (Isaiah 64:6).

Exodus 27:16 (a)
And for the gate of the court shall be an hanging of twenty cubits, of blue, and purple, and scarlet, and fine twined linen, wrought with needlework . . .

The door into the outer courtyard was made of the same fabric as the veil and the door into the tabernacle itself because whether one is talking about the door into the courtyard—the place of salvation, the door into the holy place—the place of service, or the door into the Holy of Holies—the place of worship, it's all the same Door. It's all through Jesus.

You see, just as the tabernacle was comprised of three sections—the outer courtyard, the holy place, and the Holy of Holies—I believe there are three stages in our life in Christ . . .

There are those who are inside the courtyard. They're in Christ, part of the kingdom. They realize Jesus Christ, the Lamb of God was slain for their sins. They receive His salvation, they embrace His grace.

But there are others who say, "Because God has been so good to me, I want to serve Him." So they go into the holy place and serve the showbread, which speaks of the Word of God. They teach Sunday school, lead family devotions, share the Word with someone at work. They see the golden lampstand and desire to let their light shine through good works (Matthew 5:16)—

through helping in the nursery, through visiting shut-ins, through helping those in need. They smell the incense burning and are reminded that it speaks of intercession. So they pray consistently for the lost and for their brothers and sisters, for their families and the country.

But there are still others who, like the high priest himself, enter in to the Holy of Holies in order to simply spend time in the Lord's presence—to consider His character, ponder His nature, give Him praise, express their love, bring Him pleasure. All too often, we don't understand this. We think if we could lead worship, preach a sermon, or be a missionary, we'd be amazing. But those things don't hold a candle to the highest level—to coming in to the Presence of the Lord and worshiping Him intimately. And here's the irony: the highest form of ministry, the most satisfying aspect of ministry is available to every single person right now.

Jesus went to the home of His close friends in Bethany—the home of Mary, Martha, and Lazarus. Lazarus is not mentioned in the Luke 10 account. He was outside, in the outer courtyard, if you would. He was a friend of the Lord to be sure. But he was outside. Martha was in the kitchen, or the holy place, if you would—serving. She was baking bread, doing good works, and even praying, "Lord, tell my sister to get in here and help me!" Mary, however, was sitting at the feet of Jesus. She was in the Holy of Holies. And, of her, Jesus said, "Mary has chosen the better part" (Luke 10:42). Nothing compares to being in the Holy of Holies, to being in the Lord's presence. It's the highest calling, the most important aspect of ministry. And it's available to every one of us.

Salvation, service, and intimacy are all entered through the same door—through Jesus' finished work on the Cross. "God so loved the world that He gave His only begotten Son" (John 3:16). That's the door into the courtyard. "If any man come after Me, let him take up His cross and follow Me" (Mark 8:34). That's the door into the holy place, into service. "Take, eat. This is My body broken for you. Do this in remembrance of Me" (Luke 22:19). That's the door into the deepest place of ministry.

The longer we walk with the Lord, the deeper we go in the Lord, the more we return to the Cross—to that which first touched our hearts when we were born again. Paul put it this way: "It's the love of Christ that constrains me, motivates me to be a servant of His" (2 Corinthians 5:14). And, "Even as you received Christ Jesus, so walk ye in Him" (Colossians 2:6).

Exodus 27:16 (b)–20
. . . and their pillars shall be four, and their sockets four. All the pillars round about the court shall be filleted with silver; their hooks shall be of silver, and their sockets of brass. The length of the court shall be an hundred cubits, and the breadth fifty every where, and the height five cubits of fine twined linen, and their sockets of brass. All the vessels of the tabernacle in all the service thereof, and all the pins thereof, and all the pins of the court, shall be of brass. And thou shalt command the children of Israel, that they bring thee pure oil olive beaten for the light, to cause the lamp to burn always.

The people were not to come into the tabernacle empty-handed, but to bring the oil for the lamp—not just to be blessed, but to be a blessing. The priests were to make sure the lampstand was trimmed and in good order. But the people were to bring the oil—an unbeatable combination.

Exodus 27:21
In the tabernacle of the congregation without the vail, which is before the testimony, Aaron and his sons shall order it from evening to morning before the Lord: it shall be a statute for ever unto their generations on the behalf of the children of Israel.

Aaron and his sons were to keep the light burning bright from evening to morning. Since the beginning of time, the Lord has reckoned a day to be from evening to morning (Genesis 1:5). Our days begin bright and move towards night. In God's economy, things always go from dark to light. I like that!

28

"Wherefore, holy brethren, partakers of the heavenly calling, consider the Apostle and High Priest of our profession, Christ Jesus" (Hebrews 3:1). Here, we get to do just that—for, after considering the construction and configuration of the tabernacle, we now switch gears and focus our attention on the high priest, a picture of our Great High Priest, Jesus Christ . . .

Exodus 28:1 (a)
And take thou unto thee Aaron thy brother, and his sons with him, from among the children of Israel, that he may minister unto me in the priest's office, . . .

Here, we see the *priority of ministry.* The priority of ministry is not primarily to minister *for* the Lord, but to minister *to* the Lord. And that can be done in a back pew in morning worship. It can be done on a park bench with the Word open before you on your lunch hour. It can be done on your knees late at night as you lavish praise upon the Lord.

Exodus 28:1 (b)
. . . even Aaron, Nadab and Abihu, Eleazar and Ithamar, Aaron's sons.

Here, we see the *family in ministry*. Jesus is our Great High Priest and, because we are linked to Him by His grace, we are a royal priesthood (1 Peter 2:9). Therefore, each of us has a role to play in ministry.

Exodus 28:2–5
And thou shalt make holy garments for Aaron thy brother for glory and for beauty. And thou shalt speak unto all that are wise hearted, whom I have filled with the spirit of wisdom, that they may make Aaron's garments to consecrate him, that he may minister unto me in the priest's office. And these are the garments which they shall make; a breastplate, and an ephod, and a robe, and a broidered coat, a mitre, and a girdle: and they shall make holy garments for Aaron thy brother, and his sons, that he may minister unto me in the priest's office. And they shall take gold, and blue, and purple, and scarlet, and fine linen.

The high priest's garments were of the same materials as the tabernacle because there is a direct linkage between the high priest and the tabernacle, the place of worship. Sometimes people will say, "I love Jesus, but the church is so full of problems that I have no use for it."

In Hebrews, we see Jesus singing praises to His Father in the midst of His church. Yes, we're flawed. Yes, we have failed. But of us, Jesus says, "I'm in the midst of them; I'm not ashamed of them; I'm one with them. I'm proud of them" (Hebrews 2:11, 12). Therefore, never let the enemy whisper in your ear that you can separate Jesus, the Great High Priest from His church.

Exodus 28:6
And they shall make the ephod of gold, of blue, and of purple, of scarlet, and fine twined linen, with cunning work.

The *ephod* was an apron which extended to the knees—a most fitting garment for one involved in the work of preparing animals for sacrifice. The ephod speaks of Christ, the Authoritative One, because in Old Testament culture, the ephod spoke of authority. After Gideon led the people of Israel to victory over their enemies, the Midianites, the people asked him to be their king. Gideon refused, saying it was the Lord who would rule them. (Judges 8:23).

Not many people would turn down an opportunity for power or privilege or prestige. Gideon did. There are many wonderful lessons to be learned from the life of Gideon—and this is one of the great ones. He did not take advantage of an opportunity to put himself in a place of prominence. But then he made a critical mistake when he melted the golden earrings the men had collected as the spoils of war into a golden ephod. Evidently, he thought a golden ephod would help the people remember they were to get instruction and council from God through the high priest. But his plan backfired when the people began worshiping the ephod instead of worshiping God (Judges 8:27).

You and I have a Great High Priest who is the Authoritative One. Therefore, how careful we must be that we don't begin to say, "I've got some pretty good things to say, some very enlightening counsel to give, my own golden ephod to share with you."

"Woe to the rebellious people who take counsel but not of Me," the Lord declares. "In returning to Me and resting in Me you will be saved. And then you'll hear a voice in your ear, saying, 'This is the way, walk ye in it'" (Isaiah 30:1, 15, 21). Jesus alone wears the ephod. Jesus alone is the Anointed One.

Exodus 28:7, 8
It shall have the two shoulderpieces thereof joined at the two edges thereof; and so it shall be joined together. And the curious girdle of the ephod, which is upon it, shall be of the same, according to the work thereof; even of gold, of blue, and purple, and scarlet, and fine twined linen.

The "curious" or "embroidered" girdle was the sash worn around the waist. In John 13, Jesus in the Upper Room girded Himself with a towel in order that He could wash the disciples' feet. Thus, the girdle speaks of Christ, the Serving One. Just as the ephod and girdle were made of the same material, true authority is always linked to a servant mentality.

"Don't be like the Gentiles who seek to lord it over others," Jesus said. "If you want to be great in the kingdom, you must be the servant of all" (see Matthew 20:25, 26). Notice that Jesus didn't say, "If you want to be great, repent," but rather, "If you want to be great, here's how: Be the servant of all." Do you serve your wife, husband? Do you serve your kids—not spoiling them, but being sensitive to them, hearing their hearts, meeting their needs? Jesus shows us how this works. The Lord of all was the Servant to all; the Master of all was the Minister to all. I'm so glad we serve a Lord like that. Our Great High Priest, Jesus Christ, wears the ephod of authority. At His name, every knee shall bow and every tongue confess He's Lord (Philippians 2:10). But linked to the ephod He wears is a girdle—with which He girds Himself to wash the feet of sinners like you and me.

Exodus 28:9–11
And thou shalt take two onyx stones, and grave on them the names of the children of Israel: six of their names on one stone, and the other six names of the rest on the other stone, according to their birth. With the work of an engraver in stone, like the engravings of a signet, shalt thou engrave the two stones with the names of the children of Israel: thou shalt make them to be set in ouches [settings] of gold.

As we will see, each tribe will have its own gem, its own color, its own nature. Their names inscribed on these two onyx stones, however, speak not of their diversity but of their commonality. So, while we each have a unique flavor, we're all founded on the single Rock of Ages, Jesus Christ.

Exodus 28:12
And thou shalt put the two stones upon the shoulders of the ephod for stones of memorial unto the children of Israel: and Aaron shall bear their names before the LORD upon his two shoulders for a memorial.

As we will see, the twelve stones representing the Twelve Tribes were over the heart of the high priest. Here, however, we see their names on his shoulders, the place of burden-bearing. Are you willing to take some risks, to carry some weight? Will you lift others to the Lord as you intercede for them on your knees? Will you do some heavy lifting on behalf of others? Jesus did. He bore the heaviest thing in the world when He bore the weight of my sin.

Exodus 28:13–16
And thou shalt make ouches [settings] of gold; And two chains of pure gold at the ends; of wreathen work shalt thou make them, and fasten the wreathen chains to the ouches. And thou shalt make the breastplate of judgment with cunning work; after the work of the ephod thou shalt make it; of gold, of blue, and of purple, and of scarlet, and of fine twined linen, shalt thou make it. Foursquare it shall be being doubled; a span shall be the length thereof, and a span shall be the breadth thereof.

The breastplate was attached to the ephod with chains.

Exodus 28:17–20 (a)
And thou shalt set in it settings of stones, even four rows of stones: the first row shall be a sardius, a topaz, and a carbuncle: this shall be the first row. And the second row shall be an emerald, a sapphire, and a diamond. And the third row a ligure, an agate, and an amethyst. And the fourth row a beryl, and an onyx, and a jasper . . .

Each one of the twelve stones representing the Twelve Tribes was a different gem—each with its own distinct color. Wise, therefore, is the person who can learn to see everyone in the body as a gem of infinite worth. You will find a person in Scripture whom God honors and blesses and uses who is very similar to the people around you. Maybe you know someone who's always wrestling with issues. He's your Habakkuk. Maybe you know someone who is prone to tears. There's your Jeremiah. Each gem was distinctive and different, but all were valued, all beautiful. How I need to look at the whole family, the whole body, the whole kingdom and realize that each part of the body of Christ refracts the light uniquely, giving a different coloring, a distinct beauty—and all are gems to Him.

Exodus 28:20 (b), 21
. . . they shall be set in gold in their inclosings. And the stones shall be with the names of the children of Israel, twelve, according to their names, like the engravings of a signet; every one with his name shall they be according to the twelve tribes.

"Can a mother forget her nursing child?" God asks. "Neither will I forget you because you are engraved in the palms of My hands" (Isaiah 49:15, 16). Indeed, the nail that pierced my Savior's palms had my name on it, for it should have been mine. Our names are on the Lord's heart. They're not penciled in—they're indelibly, unalterably, permanently *engraved.*

Exodus 28:22–29
And thou shalt make upon the breastplate chains at the ends of wreathen work of pure gold. And thou shalt make upon the breastplate two rings of gold, and shalt put the two rings on the two ends of the breastplate. And thou shalt put the two wreathen chains

of gold in the two rings which are on the ends of the breastplate. And the other two ends of the two wreathen chains thou shalt fasten in the two ouches [settings], and put them on the shoulderpieces of the ephod before it. And thou shalt make two rings of gold, and thou shalt put them upon the two ends of the breastplate in the border thereof, which is in the side of the ephod inward. And two other rings of gold thou shalt make, and shalt put them on the two sides of the ephod underneath, toward the forepart thereof, over against the other coupling thereof, above the curious girdle of the ephod. And they shall bind the breastplate by the rings thereof unto the rings of the ephod with a lace of blue, that it may be above the curious girdle of the ephod, and that the breastplate be not loosed from the ephod. And Aaron shall bear the names of the children of Israel in the breastplate of judgment upon his heart, when he goeth in unto the holy place, for a memorial before the LORD continually.

Here we see Christ the Loving One. Where does He carry His people, His children? On His heart. He sees everyone as a priceless gem. And there is not one person that Jesus Christ loves on the face of the earth or in all of history more than He loves you.

Exodus 28:30
And thou shalt put in the breastplate of judgment the Urim and the Thummim; and they shall be upon Aaron's heart, when he goeth in before the LORD: and Aaron shall bear the judgment of the children of Israel upon his heart before the LORD continually.

Judgment refers to the decision-making process. The word *urim* means "light" or "lights." The word *thummim* means "perfection." The Greek translation of the Hebrew text renders them "truth" and "manifestation." Either way, the *urim* and the *thummim* speak of seeing true light in a perfect way.

***For topical study of Exodus 28:30 entitled "Divine Direction," turn to page* 328.**

Exodus 28:31, 32
And thou shalt make the robe of the ephod all of blue. And there shall be an hole in the top of it, in the midst thereof: it shall have a binding of woven work round about the hole of it, as it were the hole of an habergeon, that it be not rent.

Here we see Christ the heavenly One. John tells us it was because He knew from whence He came and where He was going that He washed His disciples' feet (John 13:3–5). Some people say, "You're so heavenly minded, you're no earthly good." Jesus, however, would show us we can be no earthly good *until* we're heavenly minded. Why? Because if I'm not heavenly minded, I'll get bogged down taking care of my toys, my trinkets, my trivial world. But as I choose to be heavenly minded, living for the big picture of eternity, I enjoy this life immensely because I don't take this life so seriously.

Exodus 28:33 (a)
And beneath upon the hem of it thou shalt make pomegranates of blue, and of purple, and of scarlet, round about the hem thereof . . .

Of all the fruits in the world, none has more seeds than the blood-red interior of a pomegranate. On the Cross, Jesus shed His blood in order that His Spirit might bear much fruit through seeds like you and me.

Exodus 28:33 (b)
. . . and bells of gold between them round about:

If pomegranates speak of the fruit of the Spirit, bells speak of the gifts of the Spirit.

Exodus 28:34
A golden bell and a pomegranate, a golden bell and a pomegranate, upon the hem of the robe round about.

The bells were made to have a beautiful sound in and of themselves. But if they hit each other, they would sound like nothing more than a "clanging gong or a crashing cymbal." But if they were separated by pomegranates, by the fruit of the Spirit, they would ring in harmony. That is why in 1 Corinthians 12, Paul talks about the gifts of the Spirit. In chapter 14, he talks about the gifts of the Spirit. But in between the two is a pomegranate, for in chapter 13, he talks about the fruit of the Spirit, which is love.

Exodus 28:35
And it shall be upon Aaron to minister: and his sound shall be heard when he goeth in unto the holy place before the LORD, and when he cometh out, that he die not.

Here, we see Christ the Living One. When the high priest went into the tabernacle to minister to the Lord, to trim the candles, to burn the incense, to take care of the showbread—and on the

Day of Atonement, to sprinkle blood on the mercy seat within the Holy of Holies—he would disappear from the sight of the people. But as long as they heard the beautiful sound of the bells on the hem of his robe, they would know he was ministering to the Lord on their behalf.

How do we know Jesus is living? We hear the bells, the sounding of the gifts of His Spirit. Ten days after He disappeared from sight and ascended into heaven, the sound of a mighty rushing wind and tongues of every language filled the Upper Room—and everyone knew Jesus was alive indeed, ministering on their behalf in the true tabernacle, the holiest of all, in heaven.

Exodus 28:36–38
And thou shalt make a plate of pure gold, and grave upon it, like the engravings of a signet, HOLINESS TO THE LORD. And thou shalt put it on a blue lace, that it may be upon the mitre; upon the forefront of the mitre it shall be. And it shall be upon Aaron's forehead, that Aaron may bear the iniquity of the holy things, which the children of Israel shall hallow in all their holy gifts; and it shall be always upon his forehead, that they may be accepted before the LORD.

Here, we see Christ the Holy One. Just as the words, "Holiness To The Lord" were on the mitre that covered the head of the high priest, Jesus our Great High Priest, has holiness on His mind. The word "holy" simply means to be whole. Sin robs. Sin erodes. Sin destroys. Holiness adds. Holiness completes. Holiness leads to happiness. Jesus lived life in such a way that fishermen would leave their nets, radical zealots their politics, tax collectors their money to follow Him. There was a quality, a vitality, a vibrancy about Him—all because He was holy. Holiness is not prudishness. Quite the opposite, because true holiness makes one's life whole, it is a quality which others find magnetic.

Exodus 28:39
And thou shalt embroider the coat of fine linen, and thou shalt make the mitre of fine linen, and thou shalt make the girdle of needlework.

Here, we see Christ the Perfect One. We know from the Talmud that the fine linen of this coat was woven with five hundred and forty threads per square inch. While linen speaks of righteousness, such fine linen speaks of perfection. And it had to be so, for Jesus, the spotless Lamb, the One in whom even Pilate could find no fault, is Perfection personified.

Exodus 28:40 (a)
And for Aaron's sons thou shalt make coats . . .

Just as we are a royal priesthood because we are linked to our Great High Priest, Jesus Christ, Aaron's sons were priests based on their linkage to Aaron. Made of linen, the coats they wore speak of salvation and righteousness (Psalm 132:9, 16). We are also robed in the righteousness of Christ (Isaiah 61:10). This means that when God looks at us, He doesn't see the stained Levis of our sin, but the fine linen of His Son.

Exodus 28:40 (b)
. . . and thou shalt make for them girdles . . .

In light of the fact that we're robed in the righteousness of God, we're to gird up our minds and bring into submission any stray thought which would exalt itself against Christ in order that nothing would trip us up, in order that we might minister effectively (2 Corinthians 10:5).

Exodus 28:40 (c), 41
. . . and bonnets shalt thou make for them, for glory and for beauty. And thou shalt put them upon Aaron thy brother, and his sons with him; and shalt anoint them, and consecrate them, and sanctify them, that they may minister unto me in the priest's office.

The third thing the sons of Aaron were to wear were bonnets, or turbans which symbolize submission. To this day, Jews wear yarmulkes as outward signs of submission to God's authority. We would do well to be mindful of the same. And one of the best places to cultivate this awareness is in prayer. Prayer is not giving orders, but reporting for duty. Prayer is saying, "Lord, I come before You to talk things over with You, but I know You see things I don't and know things I can't. Therefore, I submit to Your will."

Exodus 28:42
And thou shalt make them linen breeches to cover their nakedness; from the loins even unto the thighs they shall reach:

Even underneath the robe, out of the sight of people, there was to be righteousness. How important it is that we understand this. So often, we are concerned about our reputation. God isn't. He's concerned about our character. Reputation is what others think I am. Character is what I truly am. There are those who have a great reputation in the sight of others—but their character is sadly lacking. Conversely, there are those who may have been accused unjustly, but whose character is pure. Paul tells us Jesus made Himself of no reputation (Philippians 2:7). But never a man had more character.

Exodus 28:43
And they shall be upon Aaron, and upon his sons, when they come in unto the tabernacle of the congregation, or when they come near unto the altar to minister in the holy place; that they bear not iniquity, and die: it shall be a statute for ever unto him and his seed after him.

If the priests were not willing to wear the breeches or the turban, the girdle or the robe, they would die. They wouldn't survive the ministry. There are people now with great potential who end up on the sidelines because they fail to clothe themselves with the garments of righteousness and submission freely provided by the Father. Others, however, gird up their minds, concern themselves with their character rather than their reputation, and submit to the Father in all things. And they are those who continually move on to ever-widening spheres of authority, greater opportunity for ministry.

DIVINE DIRECTION

A Topical Study of EXODUS 28:30

Sometimes it seems to me that the children of Israel had it made in the shade because when they had questions or needed direction, they could go to the high priest who, after consulting the Urim and the Thummim, would give them the answer they sought. How did this work? Evidently, the Lord would make known the answer in some wonderful, miraculous, mysterious way through lights that would shine through the stones on the breastplate of the high priest. But, although this initially sounds like a perfect solution to our questions, there were two problems associated with this particular method of receiving direction. The first was proximity, the second priority.

The high priest would only be able to be in one place at any time. Therefore, if you were in Galilee, one hundred miles from the temple in Jerusalem, and had a question, you couldn't fax the high priest. You couldn't call him on your cell phone. You couldn't even get in a car and drive to Jerusalem. To get direction, it was necessary to leave family, livestock, and crops in order to make a long and difficult journey. But an even greater problem was priority, for the Urim and the Thummim could be consulted only concerning matters of grave consequence. Consequently, people would be very reluctant to bring their questions to the high priest.

Fifteen hundred years later, when Jesus came on the scene, it was a grand and glorious declaration He made when He said, "I am the Light of the world" (John 8:12). And "I am with you always, even to the end of the world" (Matthew 28:20).

And concerning the issue of priority, Peter doesn't say, "Don't bother God with the small stuff." No, he says, "Cast *all* your cares on Him for He cares for you" (1 Peter 5:7). Anytime, any place we need direction, all we have to do is ask.

How does this work out practically? I believe God directs us in three ways . . .

Impressions of the Heart

In the Old Testament, where were the stones that would give direction? Over the heart of the high priest. Now, however, the Lord gives direction not by a breastplate worn *over* the heart but by the branding He does *upon* our hearts.

> *But this shall be the covenant that I will make with the house of Israel; After those days, saith the LORD, I will put my law in their inward parts, and write it in their hearts; and will be their God, and they shall be my people.*
>
> Jeremiah 31:33

This is fantastic. Here, God declares we'll know what we ought to do not by some external stone but by impressions and desires within our hearts. That is why David could say, "Delight yourself in the Lord and He will give you the desires of your heart" (Psalm 37:4). What are we to do to find God's will? Augustine nailed it when he said, "Love God with all your heart and mind and soul and strength—and do whatever you want."

Why do I live in Oregon? Because I want to. Why do I teach the Bible? Because I enjoy it. You see, I am simple enough to believe God's promise that if I delight in Him, He will put desires in my heart which conform to His perfect plan for me. If you're not delighting in the Lord, don't follow the desires of your heart because they will lead you on a dangerous path. But if you say, "Although I know I have problems and flaws, but I do love the Lord and I want to delight in Him." He'll give you light and direction, the Urim and the Thummim in your heart.

Interaction with the Church

Because my heart can, at times, be a little hard and things can get a bit fuzzy, I need to understand that, just as God made His will known through the gems which represented the Twelve Tribes, He continues to make His will known through the living stones of His church (1 Peter 2:5). You may have an impression on your heart, a desire stirring within. That's great, for that's the way the Lord works in giving direction. Now get it confirmed through the gems, the living stones, the children of God's family.

It was as they were worshiping and praising the Lord that He said to the church in Antioch, "Separate Paul and Barnabas for the ministry" (Acts 13). Why would the Lord choose to work through the church? Because He's into this thing called family.

We have a tendency to think, *I don't need my sisters and brothers. I get irritated with them. I see all kinds of flaws in them. I'll just figure out my own life—just me and God.* But that's not the heart of the Father, for He said, "Whenever two or three meet together in My name, I will be in the midst of them" (Matthew 18:20). He wants His children to come together. Why? Any parent knows why. There's nothing more delightful than seeing the family discussing issues, working out problems, wrestling through dilemmas together. There's nothing better than seeing your kids talking and sharing, interacting and caring. It's as if our Father says, "You're going to be together for a billion years. Therefore, I want you to get to know each other and appreciate one another this side of eternity."

"Forsake not the assembling of yourselves together as is the manner of some," the author of the Book of Hebrews warns (Hebrews 10:25). Don't miss the opportunity to dialogue and to learn from your brothers and sisters in the Lord.

Instruction from the Word

People sometimes say to me, "I don't know what to do."

"What's the Lord been showing you in your Bible reading?" I ask.

"My what?"

"Your morning devotions."

"Ummmm. . . ."

The impressions of your heart might be fuzzy. Interaction with others may be flawed. But the Word of God is infallible and practical—the perfect lamp for our feet, the ideal light for our path (Psalm 119:105). We are so blessed to have this book in our hands, available night and day. More than any other way, this is how God speaks to me. Yes, He puts impressions and desires on my heart. Yes, He speaks through brothers and sisters in the family. But above all, He speaks through His Word.

When there is harmony between the impressions on my heart, interaction with the body, and instruction from the Word, I can be sure it is direction from the Lord as I cast all my cares and concerns upon Him. Are there any stipulations? Yes . . .

A Heart of Expectancy

"If any of you lack wisdom, let him ask of God Who gives to all men liberally," James writes. "But let him ask in faith, nothing wavering, for the man who doubts is like the waves of the sea and let not that man expect to receive anything" (James 1:5–7). Why does God want us to trust Him? Why is faith a prerequisite to answered prayer? Because faith is the language of eternity. Thus, this life is Language School—where we learn to speak the language we'll be speaking for the next billion years to come, where we learn to speak the language of faith.

A Spirit of Integrity

"The integrity of the upright shall guide them" (Proverbs 11:3). The Hebrew word translated "integrity" is *tummah,* which comes from the word *thummim.* Like its root word, *tummah,* or integrity, speaks of perfection, of an absence of double-mindedness. Many times, people say, "Lord, what's Your opinion on this? What would You see as being best for me?" But they want nothing more than to take

His direction into account when they make their own decision regarding whether they are to marry that girl, take this job, make that move. And theirs are the prayers God doesn't answer, for He doesn't direct people who aren't committed to obeying Him.

Why? Because He is a God of love. You see, God isn't saying, "If you don't come with integrity, I'm not talking." No, He's saying, "If you choose not to do what I tell you, the result will be disobedience. Therefore, I will remain lovingly silent, for you can't disobey what I don't tell you."

> *I beseech you therefore, brethren, by the mercies of God, that ye present your bodies a living sacrifice, holy, acceptable unto God, which is your reasonable service. And be not conformed to this world: but be ye transformed by the renewing of your mind, that ye may prove what is that good, and acceptable, and perfect, will of God.* Romans 12:1, 2

Because He's in love with us, God wants the best for us. Therefore, He says, "You'll know My good and acceptable and perfect will when you sacrifice your right to make your own decisions."

And when at last we come to the place where we say, "Lord, I'm tired of calling the shots. Please tell me what to do, for I intend to obey You fully, gladly, joyfully with integrity," He says "I'll be happy to."

29

Exodus 29:1 (a)
And this is the thing that thou shalt do unto them to hallow them, to minister unto me in the priest's office . . .

In 1 Timothy 1:12 , Paul says, "I thank Christ Jesus our Lord who hath enabled me in that he counteth me faithful putting me into the ministry." Like Paul, I am amazed at the goodness and grace of God that He would include me in this glorious privilege called ministry.

Ministry is a privilege because of the *present blessings.* "With what measure ye mete out, it shall be measured to you," Jesus said (Mark 4:24). That is, what we give out, we'll get back. And I have found that to be oh, so true. When I pray for others, *I* get blessed. When I share with others, *I* am confirmed in the truth of the Scriptures. When I witness to others, my *own* faith grows deeper, stronger, more powerful.

This should not be surprising. After all, Jesus promised we would receive power to become His witnesses (Acts 1:8). And the word He used for power was translated *dunamis,* from which we get our word "dynamite." This dynamic experience, this power is like an electrical charge. Therefore, like electricity, it will only enter that from which it can exit. The power, the electricity, the anointing of the Spirit is given to you that it might flow through you to others. The one who wants to be used by the Lord in the lives of others is the one who will experience the electric, dynamic power of the Spirit. That's why I love being in the ministry.

Secondly, I enjoy being in the ministry because of *future rewards.* What we do in ministry—even as simple as giving a cup of cold water in Jesus' name—will be rewarded by the Lord and will impact us eternally (Matthew 10). When we choose to do something no matter how simple in the name of the Lord, for His glory, in order that people will be drawn to Him, impressed with Him, refreshed by Him, we'll have rewards in heaven. You might think you don't care about rewards. But you will then. When we get to heaven and rewards are given, you'll say, "I wish I would have taken more seriously the admonitions to strive to run the race, to win the prize, to gain the crown" (Philippians 3:14).

Thirdly, I love the ministry because of *real needs.* People all around us are lost. Wandering around like sheep without a shepherd, they don't know what to do. They're depressed, discouraged, and, worst of all, without Jesus, they're headed for hell. They don't know that God sent His Son not to condemn them, but to save them, to die in place of them that they might be forgiven of their sins and might spend eternity in heaven (John 3:17). So I say, "Lord, thank You for allowing me to be in the ministry because I see people all around me who are confused and You've given such simple and significant answers for me to share with them."

And He's given the same opportunity to you—for, although you might earn a living as a schoolteacher, a carpenter, or an electrician, you are in the ministry every bit as much as I am. The division between the clergy and the laity is a man-made distinction completely without biblical basis, for Jesus said, "You have not chosen me, but I have chosen you, and ordained you, that ye should go and bring forth fruit, and that your fruit should remain . . ." (John 15:16).

"But I don't know if I'm properly prepared for ministry," you say.

Read on . . .

Exodus 29:1 (b)–4 (a)
. . . Take one young bullock, and two rams without blemish, and unleavened bread, and cakes unleavened tempered with oil, and wafers unleavened anointed with oil: of wheaten flour shalt thou make them. And thou shalt put them into one basket, and bring them in the basket, with the bullock and the two rams. And Aaron and his sons thou shalt bring unto the door of the tabernacle of the congregation . . .

Aaron and his sons were brought to the door. So were we. The Spirit of God directed someone to bring us to a church service, to witness to us, to talk to us and we were brought to the Door that leads to life eternal. We were brought to Jesus (John 10:7).

Exodus 29:4 (b)
. . . and shalt wash them with water.

Aaron and his sons didn't wash themselves. They were washed—which speaks of baptism.

Exodus 29:5, 6
And thou shalt take the garments, and put upon Aaron the coat, and the robe of the ephod, and the ephod, and the breastplate, and gird him with the curious girdle of the ephod: And thou shalt put the mitre upon his head, and put the holy crown upon the mitre.

After coming to the door of salvation and being plunged into the water of baptism, we see Aaron robed in garments he didn't make, buy, or even put on. He just stood there and the robes were put on him in this ordination ceremony.

Exodus 29:7
Then shalt thou take the anointing oil, and pour it upon his head, and anoint him.

Again, Aaron did not anoint himself. He simply stood still and the anointing oil was poured upon his head.

Exodus 29:8, 9
And thou shalt bring his sons, and put coats upon them. And thou shalt gird them with girdles, Aaron and his sons, and put the bonnets on them: and the priest's office shall be theirs for a perpetual statute: and thou shalt consecrate Aaron and his sons.

Just as Aaron was given priestly garments, so were his sons—through no effort of their own, but simply due to their linkage to Aaron, the high priest. Because we are a royal priesthood (1 Peter 2:9), we, too, are robed with the garments of salvation, the robes of righteousness (Psalm 132:9, 16). Our part is simply to receive the righteousness He wants to give to you and me as a free gift.

Exodus 29:10–14
And thou shalt cause a bullock to be brought before the tabernacle of the congregation: and Aaron and his sons shall put their hands upon the head of the bullock. And thou shalt kill the bullock before the LORD, by the door of the tabernacle of the congregation. And thou shalt take of the blood of the bullock, and put it upon the horns of the altar with thy finger, and pour all the blood beside the bottom of the altar. And thou shalt take all the fat that covereth the inwards, and the caul that is above the liver, and the two kidneys, and the fat that is upon them, and burn them upon the altar. But the flesh of the bullock, and his skin, and his dung, shalt thou burn with fire without the camp: it is a sin offering.

Here we see the first of three sacrifices as part of the ordination ceremony, for there can be no true ministry without sacrifice (Matthew 16:24). The sacrifice of the bullock was for a sin offering. The hands of Aaron and his sons placed upon the bullock signified that they acknowledged their sin and that they understood to deal with it required nothing less than shed blood.

Exodus 29:15–18
Thou shalt also take one ram; and Aaron and his sons shall put their hands upon the head of the ram. And thou shalt slay the ram, and thou shalt take his blood, and sprinkle it round about upon the altar. And thou shalt cut the ram in pieces, and wash the inwards of him, and his legs, and put them unto his pieces, and unto his head. And thou shalt burn the whole ram upon the altar: it is a burnt offering unto the LORD: it is a sweet savour, an offering made by fire unto the LORD.

Following the sin offering was the burnt offering—signifying entire devotion to God. The first offering dealt with sin; this one deals with service. The third offering, the peace offering, will deal with sanctification . . .

Exodus 29:19–21
And thou shalt take the other ram; and Aaron and his sons shall put their hands upon the head of the ram. Then shalt thou kill the ram, and take of his blood, and put it upon the tip of the right ear of Aaron, and upon the tip of the right ear of his sons, and upon the thumb of their right hand, and upon the great toe of their right foot, and sprinkle the blood upon the altar round about. And thou shalt take of the blood that is upon the altar, and of the anointing oil, and sprinkle it upon Aaron, and upon his garments, and upon his sons, and upon the garments of his sons with him: and he shall be hallowed, and his garments, and his sons, and his sons' garments with him.

As Aaron and his sons stood in this ordination ceremony, blood was put on their right ears, their right thumbs, their right big toes. Why? People often feel as though they've heard things they shouldn't have listened to, done things they shouldn't have been involved in, walked in places they ought not to have gone. Therefore, the blood was applied to the ear, to the thumb, to the toe to signify that our shortcomings in what we've heard, what we've done, where we've walked are all covered, cleansed, forgiven because of the blood.

Aaron and his sons were allowed to be in the ministry solely because they were a chosen family. Not one of the sons was left out. And the same is true of us—for we are in the family of the Great High Priest, Jesus Christ (John 1:12). Nothing was done *by* Aaron and his sons in this ordination ceremony. Rather, everything was done *for* them. They were amazingly passive. We tend to think, *I better do this,* or, *I must do that*—but this illustration shows us very clearly that it's not what we do that matters, but what Jesus has done *for* us.

Exodus 29:22–28
Also thou shalt take of the ram the fat and the rump, and the fat that covereth the inwards, and the caul above the liver, and the two kidneys, and the fat that is upon them, and the right shoulder; for it is a ram of consecration: And one loaf of bread, and one cake of oiled bread, and one wafer out of the basket of the unleavened bread that is before the LORD: And thou shalt put all in the hands of Aaron, and in the hands of his sons; and shalt wave them for a wave offering before the LORD. And thou shalt receive them of their hands, and burn them upon the altar for a burnt offering, for a sweet savour before the LORD: it is an offering made by fire unto the LORD. And thou shalt take the breast of the ram of Aaron's consecration, and wave it for a wave offering before the LORD: and it shall be thy part. And thou shalt sanctify the breast of the wave offering, and the shoulder of the heave offering, which is waved, and which is heaved up, of the ram of the consecration, even of that which is for Aaron, and of that which is for his sons: and it shall be Aaron's and his sons' by a statute for ever from the children of Israel: for it is an heave offering: and it shall be an heave offering from the children of Israel of the sacrifice of their peace offerings, even their heave offering unto the LORD.

The hands of Aaron and his sons—once empty enough to place on the head of the sin offering—are now filled.

On one mountain ridge stood the people of Israel. On the other were the Philistines. And in the valley between them, Goliath taunted the people of Israel day after day, challenging them to send someone to do battle with him. The Israelites were understandably terrified. After all, Goliath was at least 9′9″ and possibly as tall as 11′6″. So heavy was his spear that the tip alone weighed thirty pounds. To put that in perspective, shot-putters throw a ball weighing a "mere" sixteen pounds. The armor he wore to protect his chest was itself two hundred pounds. Goliath was indeed massive. When the young shepherd boy from Bethlehem arrived on the scene, hearing Goliath's jeers, he said, "Give me a chance. Let me take him on." You see, while everyone else thought Goliath was too big to hit, David thought he was too big to miss. Turning down the offer of armor too big for him, David went into the valley of Elah with the only thing he was accustomed to using: his sling. But it was empty until, there in the very valley in which he would do battle, he found five stones—one of which would slay Goliath (1 Samuel 17:40).

Just as it wasn't until David had already committed himself to the battle that he found the stones, just as it wasn't until Aaron and his sons were to make an offering to the Lord that they were given bread and meat, it won't be until you start sharing your faith and reaching out to people that you will be given exactly what you need for ministry (Matthew 10:19). Preparing to minister is not nearly as necessary as daring to minister—for it's when we are in the valley of confrontation that we'll look down and see five smooth stones waiting to be put to God's use.

Exodus 29:29, 30
And the holy garments of Aaron shall be his sons' after him, to be anointed therein, and to be consecrated in them. And that son that is priest in his stead shall put them on seven days, when he cometh into the tabernacle of the congregation to minister in the holy place.

Just as Aaron's garments would be passed on to his sons, your character, Dad, will be passed on to your children as well. If I want Peter-John to be a man of prayer, I must be a man who prays. If I want Benjamin to be a man who loves the Word, I must be one given to studying the Scriptures. If I want my kids to be honest, I must cultivate honesty and integrity because the garments I wear, for better or worse, will be passed on to my kids. Oh, our kids will make their own choices—but the most important thing we can do to help our kids choose to be godly is to cultivate our own private, personal walk with the Lord. Love God. Walk with Him and it will be passed on from generation to generation.

Not only is this a precept, but it's a promise—for when we see our One greater than Aaron, our Great High Priest, our Savior, we shall be like Him (1 John 3:2). "I cannot be satisfied until I awake in Thy likeness," David declared (Psalm 17:15). Oh, happy day that will be!

Exodus 29:31–37
And thou shalt take the ram of the consecration, and seethe his flesh in the holy place. And Aaron and his sons shall eat the flesh of the ram, and the bread that is in the basket, by the door of the tabernacle of the congregation. And they shall eat those things wherewith the atonement was made, to consecrate and to sanctify them: but a stranger shall not eat thereof, because they are holy. And if ought of the flesh of the consecrations, or of the bread, remain unto the morning, then thou shalt burn the remainder with fire: it shall not be eaten, because it is holy. And thus shalt thou do unto Aaron, and to his sons, according to all things which I have commanded thee: seven days shalt thou consecrate them. And thou shalt offer every day a bullock for a sin offering for atonement: and thou shalt cleanse the altar, when thou hast made an atonement for it, and thou shalt anoint it, to sanctify it. Seven days thou shalt make an atonement for the altar, and sanctify it; and it shall be an altar most holy: whatsoever toucheth the altar shall be holy.

For seven days, Aaron and his sons were to seek the Lord, offer sacrifices, consecrate, or dedicate the altar because it wasn't only the priest who needed to be consecrated, but the process; not only the minister, but the manner in which he was to serve. It is the wise person who prays, "Lord, I know I need to be consecrated. I need to be cleansed, anointed, empowered—and not me only, but also the things I do. May the process, the work, be "altared" by You, even as the altar was consecrated to You."

How does this happen?

Read on . . .

Exodus 29:38–43
Now this is that which thou shalt offer upon the altar; two lambs of the first year day by day continually. The one lamb thou shalt offer in the morning; and the other lamb thou shalt offer at even: and with the one lamb a tenth deal of flour mingled with the fourth part of an hin of beaten oil; and the fourth part of an hin of wine for a drink offering. And the other lamb thou shalt offer at even, and shalt do thereto according to the meat offering of the morning, and according to the drink offering thereof, for a sweet savour, an offering made by fire unto the LORD. This shall be a continual burnt offering throughout your generations at the door of the tabernacle of the congregation before the LORD: where I will meet you, to speak there unto thee. And there I will meet with the children of Israel, and the tabernacle shall be sanctified by my glory.

A lamb was to be sacrificed every morning and every evening. And there seems to be a wonderful principle for which the Lord is laying the groundwork here—that we are to start our day with the sacrifice of prayer and praise and end it in the same way. Prayer in the morning opens the door to blessing. Prayer at night locks it and makes us safe and secure. You see, the enemy doesn't snooze. Therefore, if you wake up feeling blue and wondering why, it could very well be that you've been a target of his. But you can shield yourself to a large degree from his attacks by turning off the TV and praying before you end your day.

I talk to the Lord all day long, you might be thinking. *Why do I need to have a specified time of prayer in the morning and evening?*

Think of it this way: If I came home from a week at camp and said, "Tammy, we don't need to sit down and talk. You can just follow me around and we'll talk on the go," what kind of relationship would we have? There needs to be a constant flow of conversation, true. But for a marriage to be strong, there must be not only a quantity of time, but quality of time—where both people are completely focused on each other.

And I suggest that same thing is true in our relationship with the Lord. While we are to indeed pray without ceasing all through the day, there also must be times where we say, "Lord, I'm here to talk to You, to hear from You, to offer You the sacrifice of thoughtful, articulate, emotional, intelligent praise. I'm here to press in to Your presence, to pour out my heart, to focus exclusively on You." It's not a "got to." It's a "get to."

Exodus 29:44–46
And I will sanctify the tabernacle of the congregation, and the altar: I will sanctify also both Aaron and his sons, to minister to me in the priest's office. And I will dwell among the children of Israel, and will be their God. And they shall know that I am the LORD their God, that brought them forth out of the land of Egypt, that I may dwell among them: I am the LORD their God.

While it was Moses who would consecrate Aaron and his sons, the garments and the altar—it was God alone who could sanctify them for His service. All that Moses could do was to portray through biblical typology that which only God could do in reality. And so it remains today, for the point at which communion or baptism, Bible study or worship become the end in themselves rather than pointing to Jesus is the point at which the Lord's presence will be tragically missing from our lives.

"And they shall know that I am the Lord their God," God declared.

"That I may know *Him,*" Paul prayed.

And may his prayer be ours.

30

Exodus 30:1, 2
And thou shalt make an altar to burn incense upon: of shittim wood shalt thou make it. A cubit shall be the length thereof, and a cubit the breadth thereof; foursquare shall it be: and two cubits shall be the height thereof: the horns thereof shall be of the same.

Every part of the tabernacle both pictures and points to Jesus Christ. And the altar of incense is no exception. The brass altar of chapter 27 portrays Jesus in His First Coming. The golden altar of incense speaks of His present work and His Second Coming. At one cubit by one cubit, or 18″x18″, the altar of incense is much smaller than the imposing brass altar of sacrifice because Jesus doesn't need to go to great lengths, wrestling and pleading with the Father through His intercessory prayer on our behalf. No, He's constantly, continually, consistently bringing us up before the Father in a comfortable confidence.

Sometimes our prayers don't get answered the way we hope because the Lord is answering previous prayers we forgot about. For example, we pray, "Lord, make me a godly man. Give me patience. Give me depth. Bring me into holiness."

"Okay," the Lord says. So a challenge comes our way, and what do we say?

"Get me out of here, Lord! Why am I in this predicament? What's going on? Have You forgotten about me? Don't You care?"

That's why we need an Intercessor, a High Priest who loves us, who sees the big picture, who knows what we asked for and what's coming down the road . . .

"Simon, Simon," Jesus said, "Satan desires to sift you like wheat, but I have prayed for you that your faith fail not. And when you are converted, when you get through this ordeal, strengthen the brethren" (Luke 22:32).

"But Peter's faith failed," you say.

No it didn't. His hope failed. "Hope maketh not ashamed" (Romans 5:5). That's why when Peter's hope failed, he was ashamed of his linkage to Jesus (John 18:17). Later on, after He rose again, Peter was unable to tell Jesus he loved Him because Peter knew Jesus' definition of love was by keeping His commandments (John 14:21). Peter's hope failed. Peter's love failed. But his faith never failed. He always believed.

Tonight Jesus says to us, "I know your Simon-like tendencies. I know you get shaken and that you are unstable. But I'm praying for you that your faith doesn't fail. I'm holding you up. So when you get through—and you *will* get through this—strengthen others."

Exodus 30:3 (a)
And thou shalt overlay it with pure gold, the top thereof, and the sides thereof round about, and the horns thereof; . . .

The altar of chapter 27—the altar in the courtyard of the tabernacle—was to be made of brass. Brass being the metal of judgment, Jesus was judged on the Cross when He bore our sins. The altar here in chapter 30, however, was not to be covered with brass, but with gold—the metal of Deity—because Jesus is now at the right hand of the Father, interceding for us. And when He comes back, He will come not as the Suffering Servant, but as King of kings and Lord of lords.

Exodus 30:3 (b)–5
. . . and thou shalt make unto it a crown of gold round about. And two golden rings shalt thou make to it under the crown of it, by the two corners thereof, upon the two sides of it shalt thou make it; and they shall be for places for the staves to bear it withal. And thou shalt make the staves of shittim wood, and overlay them with gold.

There was to be a crown, a molding of gold around the altar because when Jesus comes back, He'll not be wearing a crown of thorns but a crown of gold (Revelation 14:14). The crown, the molding around the altar of incense, served a practical purpose as well, in that it kept the incense from falling off.

Exodus 30:6
And thou shalt put it before the vail that is by the ark of the testimony, before the mercy seat that is over the testimony, where I will meet with thee.

Upon the golden altar of heaven seen in Revelation 8, the incense speaks not only of the prayers of the Savior on our behalf, but also of our intercessory ministry on behalf of others. Incense was burned on an altar because prayer requires sacrifice. There is nothing harder to do in spiritual life than pray. Why? I believe it's because Satan opposes it so vehemently. Why? He knows that's where the power is. Just as the altar of incense was the piece of furniture closest to the mercy seat, we are never closer to the Father than when we're in prayer.

"Son of David, have mercy on me," cried the Syro-Phoenician woman. Yet Luke tells us Jesus walked by as though He heard her not. "Son of David, have mercy," she cried again. But Jesus kept going. The phrase, "Son of David" was a Jewish term used by Jewish people to address the Jewish Messiah. This woman, however, was a Gentile. She had heard stories about what had taken place in Israel, about Jewish people who were blind or leprous crying out to the Son of David who healed them. So she used the formula. But it didn't apply to her. It was religion. It wasn't real. It wasn't until she said, "Lord help me," that Jesus stopped in His tracks and healed her daughter (Matthew 15:25).

Keep your prayer simple. Don't think you have to copy how someone else prays or the phrases someone else uses. The altar of incense was small. It's not the length of your prayers, but their strength, their sincerity that matters (Ecclesiastes 5:2).

Exodus 30:7 (a)
And Aaron shall burn thereon sweet incense every morning . . .

Just as the altar of incense was a sweet-smelling place, there is a sweetness about people who pray. "Pray for your enemies," Jesus said—the implication that we would pray for everyone because if we're praying for our enemies, it's assumed we'll pray for our friends and family. And, because it's impossible to be angry with those for whom one prays, a sweet-smelling fragrance will replace the stench of bitterness in our lives.

Exodus 30:7 (b), 8
. . . when he dresseth the lamps, he shall burn incense upon it. And when Aaron lighteth the lamps at even, he shall burn incense upon it, a perpetual incense before the LORD throughout your generations.

"Let my prayer be set forth before thee as incense; and the lifting up of my hands as the evening sacrifice," David prayed (Psalm 141:2). Incense in Scripture is always a picture of prayer. Jesus, our Faithful Friend and Great High Priest, is praying for us at this very moment (Hebrews 7:25). And not one of His prayers will "fall off." They are all heard—which is why He intercedes for us with exceeding joy (Jude 24).

Exodus 30:9
Ye shall offer no strange incense thereon, nor burnt sacrifice, nor meat offering; neither shall ye pour drink offering thereon.

Unlike the brass altar, blood was not to be shed on the altar of incense because it was by *one* offering that our salvation was secured (Hebrews 10:14). Jesus' offering on the Cross was *complete.*

Exodus 30:10
And Aaron shall make an atonement upon the horns of it once in a year with the blood of the sin offering of atonements: once in the year shall he make atonement upon it throughout your generations: it is most holy unto the LORD.

Horns in Scripture always speak of power. The horns on the four corners of the altar of incense remind us of the incredible power of prayer. More than anything else you do in spiritual life, Satan will try to keep you from praying.

Exodus 30:11–14
And the LORD spake unto Moses, saying, When thou takest the sum of the children of Israel after their number, then shall they give every man a ransom for his soul unto the LORD, when thou numberest them; that there be no plague among them, when thou numberest them. This they shall give, every one that passeth among them that are numbered, half a shekel after the shekel of the sanctuary: (a shekel is twenty gerahs) an half shekel shall be the offering of the LORD. Every one that passeth among them that are numbered, from twenty years old and above, shall give an offering unto the LORD.

Most of the offerings we have seen thus far and will see later on were to be voluntary offerings. The offering called "the ransom of souls," however, was mandatory—to be collected whenever a census was taken. In 1 Chronicles 21:1, we read that it was Satan who tempted David to number the people of Israel—something which God here forbids—in order to see how strong the nation was militarily. The result? Just as verse 12 warns of the plague that would be the result of numbering the people, 70,000 died of the plague that followed in 1 Chronicles.

Numbering the people was not to be done for reasons of pride, but for service and ministry. And the way this was to be done was by collecting half a shekel from every person twenty years of age and older. In this way, it was the money rather than the people that was counted.

Is it wrong for a church to number its members? It all depends on the reason for doing so. If it's done out of pride, it's wrong. If, on the other hand, it's done out of concern, it's necessary. After all, it was after counting his sheep that the shepherd realized one was missing and sent out to find it (Luke 15).

This offering came to be known as the temple tax in the New Testament, and was the one to which Jesus referred when He told Peter to "fish" their portion out of the sea (Matthew 17:27).

Exodus 30:15, 16
The rich shall not give more, and the poor shall not give less than half a shekel, when they give an offering unto the LORD, to make an atonement for your souls. And thou shalt take the atonement money of the children of Israel, and shalt appoint it for the service of the tabernacle of the congregation; that it may be a memorial unto the children of Israel before the LORD, to make an atonement for your souls.

There have been groups throughout history who, on the basis of this verse, have said atonement for souls can be made by paying money. Can atonement be purchased? Can man be "at one" with God for a price? No. The whole Bible argues against that. We can't purchase salvation. Yet salvation must indeed be purchased. And it was. Peter tells us we were redeemed not with corruptible things like silver and gold, but by the precious blood of the Lamb (1 Peter 1:18, 19).

Great is the day when we realize our lives are not our own, when we say, "If the Lord wants to take me through tragedy or difficulty, if He chooses to make me a pauper, send me to Africa, give me kids or give me none—I'm not my own. And because I've been bought with a price, I, who was once headed for hell, am destined for heaven."

"Why am I still single?"

You're not your own.

"Why am I stuck in this job?"

You were bought with a price.

"How come I'm going through this?"

God has your number and purchased you with something infinitely greater than silver when He bought you with the blood of His own Son.

Exodus 30:17, 18
And the LORD spake unto Moses, saying, Thou shalt also make a laver of brass, and his foot also of brass, to wash withal: and thou shalt put it between the tabernacle of the congregation and the altar, and thou shalt put water therein.

The first thing one would see upon entering the courtyard of the tabernacle was the brass altar. The second thing would be the brass laver, or basin, filled with water. The water was to provide restoration, refreshment, renewal, revival. The water was the Word (John 15:3; Ephesians 5:26).

Exodus 30:19–21
For Aaron and his sons shall wash their hands and their feet thereat: When they go into the tabernacle of the congregation, they shall wash with water, that they die not; or when they come near to the altar to minister, to burn offering made by fire unto the Lord: So they shall wash their hands and their feet, that they die not: and it shall be a statute for ever to them, even to him and to his seed throughout their generations.

Aaron and his sons were to wash their hands and feet *at,* rather than *in* the laver by drawing water from it in order that the water within would remain pure. Cultists have drawn all sorts of wrong conclusions from the Word—but they cannot spoil a drop of the truth within it. The water of the Word remains one hundred percent pure—the only agent pure enough to give us clear perspective, to cleanse our hands and feet, our work and walk.

***For topical study of Exodus 30:17–21 entitled "I'm the Leper," turn to page* 340.**

Exodus 30:22–25
Moreover the Lord spake unto Moses, saying, Take thou also unto thee principal spices, of pure myrrh five hundred shekels, and of sweet cinnamon half so much, even two hundred and fifty shekels, and of sweet calamus two hundred and fifty shekels, And of cassia five hundred shekels, after the shekel of the sanctuary, and of oil olive an hin: and thou shalt make it an oil of holy ointment, an ointment compound after the art of the apothecary: it shall be an holy anointing oil.

Here we see the "recipe" for the anointing oil which would be used throughout Israel's history to anoint three groups of people: prophets, priests, and kings. Oil in Scripture always being emblematic of the Spirit, the anointing of oil is a picture of the work of the Spirit. As the Prophet "like unto Me" of Deuteronomy 18:15, as our Great High Priest who ever lives to make intercession for us (Hebrews 7:25), as King of kings and Lord of lords at whose name every knee will one day bow (Romans 14:11), Jesus is the Anointed One. No wonder, then, that, comprised of the sweet-smelling spices of myrrh, cinnamon, and calamus, this oil was first of all sweet, for Jesus, the Anointed One is nothing but sweet. He is never grouchy, discouraged, or depressed. He never is out of sorts, under the weather, or in a bad mood. He is the sweetest Person you'll ever encounter day after day after day.

"Didn't He call the Pharisees blind guides, hypocrites, and white-washed sepulchres? That's not very sweet," you may say.

Actually, it was. Knowing it would take that kind of language to break through their thick skulls, hard hearts, and closed minds, Jesus used language intended to jar them into listening. And even though He called them white-washed tombs, hypocrites, and blind guides, some of their number sensed that He loved them—as seen in their desire to spend time with Him (Luke 11:37; John 3:1).

Exodus 30:26–30
And thou shalt anoint the tabernacle of the congregation therewith, and the ark of the testimony, and the table and all his vessels, and the candlestick and his vessels, and the altar of incense, and the altar of burnt offering with all his vessels, and the laver and his foot. And thou shalt sanctify them, that they may be most holy: whatsoever toucheth them shall be holy. And thou shalt anoint Aaron and his sons, and consecrate them, that they may minister unto me in the priest's office.

This anointing oil was not to be used sparingly, but was to be placed upon the tabernacle, all of the furniture, and the priests themselves. Because everything in the tabernacle was to picture Christ, everything in the tabernacle was to radiate His sweetness—just as we are to do (2 Corinthians 2:15; Ephesians 5:2).

Exodus 30:31, 32
And thou shalt speak unto the children of Israel, saying, This shall be an holy anointing oil unto me throughout your generations. Upon man's flesh shall it not be poured, neither shall ye make any other like it, after the composition of it: it is holy, and it shall be holy unto you.

In addition to being sweet, the anointing oil was not to be placed upon the flesh. The flesh being a picture of the sin nature, Jesus the Anointed One, never spent a moment living by the power or pull of sin. Therefore, the anointing oil was to have no contact with that which symbolizes sin.

Exodus 30:33
Whosoever compoundeth any like it, or whosoever putteth any of it upon a stranger, shall even be cut off from his people.

Thirdly, the anointing oil was inimitable. There was to be no imitation of it. Jesus, the Anointed One, our Savior, is one of a kind. There is no other like Him. All others are thieves and robbers indeed (John 10:1). Because Jesus was anointed with this oil of holiness—because He loved righteousness, because He hated sin—God anointed Him with the oil of gladness "above thy fellows," (Hebrews 1:9). If you have an image of Jesus like the icons in an old musty church where He looks mean, mystical, or upset, change your image—for Jesus was the "gladdest" Man who ever lived. No wonder He was always invited to parties (Matthew 11:19). Tax collectors and prostitutes, newlyweds and Pharisees understood He was the true Life of the party.

Exodus 30:34
And the LORD said unto Moses, Take unto thee sweet spices, stacte, and onycha, and galbanum; these sweet spices with pure frankincense: of each shall there be a like weight:

In addition to the holy anointing oil, Moses was to make perfume made of stacte, onycha, and galbanum. These three spices are all sweet-smelling—yet none were indigenous to Israel. They were all imported from a far away place. So, if there is to be any sweetness in you or me, it must be imported from a far country. We must allow the work of the Holy Spirit to be sent from heaven to indwell our lives. If you desire to be pleasing to the Father, you must realize it will not be by your own efforts.

In Leviticus 2:11, we read that sacrifices were not to be offered with honey, the sweetest substance known in antiquity. Why? Because honey loses its sweetness when it gets hot. And the same is true of us. We might think we're sweet—but when the temperature goes up, when the heat's turned on, when the trials come, suddenly we find our natural sweetness breaking down. Not so with the sweetness of the Spirit. It just becomes sweeter under pressure (James 1:2–4).

Exodus 30:35
And thou shalt make it a perfume, a confection after the art of the apothecary, tempered together, pure and holy:

Secondly, this perfume was to be salted. The Hebrew word translated "tempered" is actually "salted," as some Bibles correctly render it. We don't need to wonder what this means, for Colossians 4:6 says specifically, "Let your speech be always with grace, seasoned with salt that you may know how to answer every man." When we think of salty speech, we think of cursing or swearing. But salty speech in the biblical sense refers to speech that is gracious. Grace being unmerited, undeserved, unearned favor, our speech should always show unmerited, undeserved, unearned favor to whomever we talk to, for that is how we are to "answer every man." I don't know the answer to everyone's questions, but I know how the answer is to be given—it's to be given with grace.

Do you speak words of grace to those who raise questions, accusations, innuendoes? We must, for that is the only aroma that pleases our Father.

Exodus 30:36–38
And thou shalt beat some of it very small, and put of it before the testimony in the tabernacle of the congregation, where I will meet with thee: it shall be unto you most holy. And as for the perfume which thou shalt make, ye shall not make to yourselves according to the composition thereof: it shall be unto thee holy for the LORD. Whosoever shall make like unto that, to smell thereto, shall even be cut off from his people.

Thirdly, the perfume was to be sacred—for in addition to being gracious, we must remain holy. The winning combination is to be as gracious to other people as you possibly can be by importing the sweetness of the Spirit from heaven, and to seek to be pure and holy in your own life. All too often, we reverse this. We want others to be holy, but we want grace to be poured out upon us. Jesus, of course, is the perfect example of how grace and holiness are to function . . .

While in Samaria—a place Jews didn't usually visit—to whom does Jesus talk? In a day when rabbis didn't even speak to their own wives in public, Jesus talks to a woman. And when she told Him she didn't have a husband, rather than condemn her for her lie, He commends her for the part of her statement that was true (John 4:17). As a result, her heart was touched, and her city impacted (John 4:30). Although I would have thought Jesus would have addressed the issue of her living situation, that's not what Jesus did. Why? Divorced five times, the chances of this woman getting married again were nil. Therefore, leaving the man with whom she was living would have given her no other recourse than prostitution to support herself. Jesus knew this—and no doubt also knew that in due season she would grow in her understanding of who He was and what new life in Him would entail.

Do Samaritans and pagans love to be around you? They loved to be around Jesus. How we need to be like Him—in our own lives to be holy, to be pure, and in the lives of others to be sweet, to show grace, to share love.

I'M THE LEPER

A Topical Study of EXODUS 30:17–21

Some teachers say the brass laver in the courtyard of the tabernacle speaks of being born again, of regeneration. I do not believe that is what it depicts, however, for regeneration is pictured by the brass altar, the place of sacrifice. I believe the laver—where the priests were to wash their hands and feet—speaks not of regeneration but of reinvigoration, not of rebirth but of refreshment.

As Abraham sat in his tent, he saw three men in the distance. Somehow realizing that these men were unique—for indeed it was God Himself accompanied by two angels—he ran to meet them, saying, "Let a little water be fetched and wash your feet and rest yourselves under the tree, and I will fetch a morsel of bread and comfort your hearts" (Genesis 18:4, 5). The washing of feet, the sharing of bread, the image of a tree—it all speaks of what Jesus would do in the Upper Room the night before His Crucifixion (John 13).

Where are we to be refreshed in the priestly ministry to which we've been called? At the brass laver filled with water—at the place of renewal, restoration, and revival—in the pages of the Word.

Two elements appear to be missing in the description of the brass laver. The first is its dimensions. Concerning every other piece of furniture, every other aspect of the tabernacle, the dimensions are given. But of the brass laver, no dimensions are given. Why? I suggest the Lord is saying, "The refreshment and reinvigoration you'll receive from being in My Word is limitless, beyond measure, inexhaustible."

Secondly, there was no covering for the laver. Every other piece of furniture—the ark of the covenant, the golden candlestick, the table of showbread—were to have coverings made to protect them when they were moved. But for the brass laver there was no covering. I believe this is as if the Lord is saying that His Word is always available, never concealed, never closed off to you or me.

Psalm 119, the longest chapter in the Bible deals with one single issue: the benefits and blessings of being in the Word. Verse 1 of this Psalm declares that the person who obeys the Word will be blessed, or happy. Verse 7 tells us that the person who is in the Word will be a person who worships. Verse 9 says that the person who takes heed to the Word will be clean. Verse 24 tells us the Word is a delight; verse 50 that it is a comfort. Verse 72 declares the Word to be more precious than gold and silver; verse 99 that it brings understanding; verse 105 that it sheds light.

Most of us know these things. Most of us agree that when we study the Word countless blessings are ours. Here, then, is the mystery: If we know that being in the Word is a good place to be, why aren't we in the Word a whole lot more than we are? Why aren't we diving in the laver continually? I suggest it's because the laver is made of brass.

In the Bible, brass is the metal of judgment. Where did the children of Israel get the brass to make this laver? Exodus 38 tells the story. When construction of the tabernacle actually began, the women donated the brass looking glasses they had been given in Egypt. I find this more than coincidental because James likens the Word to a mirror (1:23–25). And therein lies the problem. You see, when we open the Word, we see our reflection—and it's not what it should be. We see our failures and flaws, our sins and shortcomings. And although we understand that the Word brings benefits to those who study it, sometimes we become exhausted by trying to live up to its standard.

The laver was made of brass. And it is the brass which judges us so decisively that, although we know what we see in the Word is true, right, good, and the way it ought to be—we don't know if we can take another sermon, another lesson, another study because we're so far from it.

But wait. The brass laver was filled with water. Without water, all one would see would be the reflection of his flaws and failures. But the addition of water made the laver refreshing, renewing, reinvigorating. "All you who thirst, come unto Me," Jesus said, "and out of your innermost being shall gush forth torrents of living water" (John 7:37, 38).

I was at a point some years ago where I was reading through the Gospels as I love to do. But I was weary. I came to the portion where Jesus touched a leper and the leper was cleansed. And I heard myself saying, "I need to be helping people physically just like Jesus did."

Then I turned the page and saw how Jesus touched the ears and tongue of a man unable to hear and speak. And I found myself thinking, *"I need to find some dumb guys and help them just like Jesus did."*

Then I turned the page and read how Jesus had compassion on the multitudes and fed five thousand hungry men. And I said, "That's the way it ought to be. I need to get involved in World Vision or Compassion International and help feed hungry people."

Then I saw Jesus blessing kids and thought, *"I need to work with kids."*

Then I saw how Jesus calmed the storm on the Sea of Galilee, and was reminded of those I knew whose marriages were on the rocks, whose lives were in turmoil, and decided I should do what I could to see those storms stilled.

Then I read how Jesus defended the woman caught in adultery, and felt that I should stand up for those who are socially or politically oppressed.

And at the end, I was exhausted. Finally, I said, "I just can't read another chapter. I can't do it. Jesus, I'm impressed with You. I see the rightness of what You do. But I can't do all the things You did."

And it was at that moment that the Lord whispered in my heart, "Exactly. You have yourself in the wrong position. *I'm* the One who touches the leper. *I'm* the One who blesses the children. *I'm* the One who feeds the hungry. *I'm* the One who makes the dumb to speak. *I'm* the One who stands up for the woman. *I'm* the One who calms the storms. It's not you. It's *Me*."

"I get it," I said. "You're the Christ. I'm not. That makes me the leper. I'm being eaten away every day by my sin and carnality. Yet every day You come my way and touch and restore my life. I'm the dumb guy. I say things I shouldn't say. I put my foot in my mouth. Yet You're there to forgive me and straighten me out. I'm the deaf man. But You never give up on me. You open my ears, you renew my thoughts. I'm the little child who needs a touch from You. I'm the hungry one and only You can meet the need within me. I'm the one caught in adultery and You're there to forgive me. I'm the one caught in the storm and You're the One who walks out to rescue me. I've been reading my Bible all wrong. No wonder I've been so weary, so reluctant to keep reading. I've placed myself in the wrong role. You're the Christ; I'm the leper. Thank You for Your mercy. Thank You for Your patience. Where would I be without You?"

And when the Lord adjusted my thinking, Scripture reading became a total joy once again.

Where did the water for the laver come from as the children of Israel wandered through the wilderness? It came from the Rock that traveled with them, the Rock that was smitten, the Rock 1 Corinthians 10:4 identifies as Jesus. What happened to Christ when He was smitten on the Cross with a spear? Out of His side flowed blood and water—redemption and refreshment.

If we dive into the laver of the Word without the water of the Spirit, the water of the Word made flesh, we'll crash into the brass of judgment. No wonder Jesus said, "Learn of Me and you will find rest in your soul" (Matthew 11:29).

Get back to the laver, gang, and dive in. Just make sure there's water there. Make sure it's filled with the water of the Spirit, the water of the Word, the water of the Rock of Ages.

---

31 **Exodus 31:1–5**

And the LORD spake unto Moses, saying, See, I have called by name Bezaleel the son of Uri, the son of Hur, of the tribe of Judah: and I have filled him with the spirit of God, in wisdom, and in understanding, and in knowledge, and in all manner of workmanship, to devise cunning works, to work in gold, and in silver, and in brass, and in cutting of stones, to set them, and in carving of timber, to work in all manner of workmanship.

In chapter 30, we saw the anointing oil for priestly ministry. Here, in chapter 31, we move from priestly ministry to practical ministry and, again, we see an anointing, a gifting of the Holy Spirit. Bezaleel was anointed, filled with the Spirit of God in order that he might accomplish practical work in the tabernacle. As "foreman" of the project, Bezaleel was to oversee the actual construction of the tabernacle and its furnishings, as well as the making of the garments the priests would wear.

I love this because the anointing for practical ministry is every bit as necessary as the anointing for priestly ministry. What gifts, ability has God given you? Ask God to anoint them, and He will use you just as surely as He used Bezaleel. Finding ministry is a lot easier than people think. It's whatever comes supernaturally natural to you. Bezaleel was, no doubt, already one who was skilled with his hands. But now he's empowered to do it for God's glory.

Exodus 31:6–11
And I, behold, I have given with him Aholiab, the son of Ahisamach, of the tribe of Dan: and in the hearts of all that are wise hearted I have put wisdom, that they may make all that I have commanded thee; the tabernacle of the congregation, and the ark of the testimony, and the mercy seat that is thereupon, and all the furniture of the tabernacle, and the table and his furniture, and the pure candlestick with all his furniture, and the altar of incense, and the altar of burnt offering with all his furniture, and the laver and his foot, and the cloths of service, and the holy garments for Aaron the priest, and the garments of his sons, to minister in the priest's office, and the anointing oil, and sweet incense for the holy place: according to all that I have commanded thee shall they do.

God empowered, energized, anointed carpenters, tailors, perfumers to do this work. Bezaleel was the foreman, but Aholiab was the assistant, along with others who served by his side.

When asked what was the hardest position in the orchestra to fill, a famous conductor said, "First chair, second violin. I can find all kinds of people who want to play first violin. But it's hard to find someone who wants to be excellent at second violin, who wants to play harmony."

Human tendency is to want to be mediocre at first violin rather than to excel at second. Not so with Aholiab. He was told he would be assistant to Bezaleel. And he was successful in that position. Thus, he is an example for all of history of the way God uniquely and powerfully uses "second fiddles" for His glory.

As chronicled in a 1970s bestseller entitled *The Peter Principle,* all too often the problem in corporate America is that people are promoted to the level of incompetence. That is, a man who does well in his position is promoted to the next level. After doing well there, he is moved to Level three. Succeeding there, he is moved to Level four. And he keeps being promoted until, towards the top, he's over his head. He was good going up the ladder, but he went one step too far. And when the corporation downsizes, guess who gets the ax. God doesn't want that for us. He wants us to fit into the place He's custom-designed for us. Am I saying we are not to take steps of faith? No, I'm saying that we must avoid the folly of taking one step too many. If God puts you in a number one spot, He will give you the grace and ability to handle it. But if you're in a number two position, rejoice and excel at that. Whether on the job or in ministry, if you're wanting to climb one more rung, be careful. If you're a Bezaleel, great. If you're an Aholiab, wonderful. Just be content and shine in the position the Lord places you.

Exodus 31:12–17
And the LORD spake unto Moses, saying, Speak thou also unto the children of Israel, saying, Verily my sabbaths ye shall keep: for it is a sign between me and you throughout your generations; that ye may know that I am the LORD that doth sanctify you. Ye shall keep the sabbath therefore; for it is holy unto you: every one that defileth it shall surely be put to death: for whosoever doeth any work therein, that soul shall be cut off from among his people. Six days may work be done; but in the seventh is the sabbath of rest, holy to the LORD: whosoever doeth any work in the sabbath day, he shall surely be put to death. Wherefore the children of Israel shall keep the sabbath, to observe the sabbath throughout their generations, for a perpetual covenant. It is a sign between me and the children of Israel for ever: for in six days the LORD made heaven and earth, and on the seventh day he rested, and was refreshed.

God here, after assigning the team that was to do the work in constructing the tabernacle and the furniture and the garments, now reiterates the Sabbath day command. This might seem out of place initially. But He did this because there is a tendency in our lives in times of construction, of building to say, "Okay, we've got the plan, the team, let's roll up our sleeves and let's get going."

"Wait a minute," the Lord says. "Let not the time of construction become a time of distraction—where you forget to rest in Me, worship Me, spend time with Me."

Exodus 31:18
And he gave unto Moses, when he had made an end of communing with him upon mount Sinai, two tables of testimony, tables of stone, written with the finger of God.

Here, Moses is given the Ten Commandments written with the finger of God's own hand. We see the fingers of God at work in creation—when He created the heavens (Psalm 8:3). We see the finger of God evident in condemnation—when even Pharaoh's magicians at last recognized the power of His judgment (Exodus 8:19). But nowhere do the fingers of God appear more wonderful than when we see them employed in compassion—when placed into the ears of a deaf man about to hear (Mark 7:33) and writing on the ground before a woman about to be set free (John 8:6).

32

Here in chapter 32, we will see Moses as a mediator. In chapter 33, we'll see him as an intercessor. In chapter 34, we'll see him as a worshiper. And I believe these qualities abounded in Moses because he was a man of the mountain, a man who spent time in the presence of God . . .

Exodus 32:1 (a)
And when the people saw that Moses delayed to come down out of the mount . . .

Moses stayed on Mt. Sinai for forty days and forty nights and didn't come down until he had the Word of the Lord. That's so unlike me. I'll be on the mountain in the presence of the Lord—but if I sense something going wrong down below, I'll scurry to the situation and try to solve the problem in my own energy. Moses didn't. He stayed on the mountain until the Lord "made an end of communing with him" (31:18), until he had the Word of the Lord in hand.

Exodus 32:1 (b)
. . . the people gathered themselves together unto Aaron, and said unto him, Up, make us gods, which shall go before us; for as for this Moses, the man that brought us up out of the land of Egypt, we wot not what is become of him.

"We wot not what is become of him," the people said of Moses—Moses, one of only a handful of men in Scripture referred to as a man of God; Moses, author of both the first and last hymn in the Bible (Exodus 15; Revelation 15), Moses, perhaps the greatest leader who ever walked the earth other than our Lord Jesus Christ.

"Where *is* he?" the people fret. "What are we paying him for, anyway? We don't know what's happened to him. So now, Aaron, you're our man."

Exodus 32:2–6
And Aaron said unto them, Break off the golden earrings, which are in the ears of your wives, of your sons, and of your daughters, and bring them unto me. And all the people brake off the golden earrings which were in their ears, and brought them unto Aaron. And he received them at their hand, and fashioned it with a graving tool, after he had made it a molten calf: and they said, These be thy gods, O Israel, which brought thee up out of the land of Egypt. And when Aaron saw it, he built an altar before it; and Aaron made proclamation, and said, To morrow is a feast to the LORD. And they rose up early on the morrow, and offered burnt offerings, and brought peace offerings; and the people sat down to eat and to drink, and rose up to play.

Moses' older brother, Aaron was a great man, too. But he was flawed particularly in that he was afraid of what people thought. The Bible says the fear of the Lord is the beginning of wisdom, while the fear of man is a snare (Proverbs 1:7; 29:25). At any given moment I will either be living in the fear of man—concerned about what people think, or living in the fear of God—concerned about what my Father thinks.

"We're going to offer burnt offerings and sacrifices to the Lord," said Aaron. "But if you want some help visualizing God, I'll make a golden calf like the ones they had in Egypt."

Exodus 32:7–10
And the LORD said unto Moses, Go, get thee down; for thy people, which thou broughtest out of the land of Egypt, have corrupted themselves: They have turned aside quickly out of the way which I commanded them: they have made them a molten calf, and have worshipped it, and have sacrificed thereunto, and said, These be thy gods, O Israel, which have brought thee up out of the land of Egypt. And the LORD said unto Moses, I have seen this people, and, behold, it is a stiffnecked people: Now therefore let me alone, that my wrath may wax hot against

them, and that I may consume them: and I will make of thee a great nation.

His anger against the people already kindled, God said, "I'm going to wipe them out and make of *you,* Moses, a brand new nation."

Exodus 32:11–13
And Moses besought the LORD his God, and said, LORD, why doth thy wrath wax hot against thy people, which thou hast brought forth out of the land of Egypt with great power, and with a mighty hand? Wherefore should the Egyptians speak, and say, For mischief did he bring them out, to slay them in the mountains, and to consume them from the face of the earth? Turn from thy fierce wrath, and repent of this evil against thy people. Remember Abraham, Isaac, and Israel, thy servants, to whom thou swarest by thine own self, and saidst unto them, I will multiply your seed as the stars of heaven, and all this land that I have spoken of will I give unto your seed, and they shall inherit it for ever.

The heart of Moses, this giant of a man, is revealed when he petitions God on the basis of His people in verse 11, His prestige in verse 12, and His promise in verse 13. "If You wipe out these people, what will the Egyptians think?" Moses said to God. "They will say You're unable to do what You promised, to finish what You began." His was honest prayer, selfless prayer, biblical prayer, prayer that would indeed move the hand of God . . .

Exodus 32:14
And the LORD repented of the evil which he thought to do unto his people.

The question becomes obvious. If God repented, does that mean He sinned when His anger waxed hot, when He planned on destroying the people? No, for who put the heart in Moses to stand up for the people, to plead on their behalf, to care so passionately about them? God Himself. Later, He will say, "I looked for a man to stand in the gap, but found none" (see Ezekiel 22:30). Here, however, in Moses, God found a man to be the recipient of a heart like His own.

Exodus 32:15–19
And Moses turned, and went down from the mount, and the two tables of the testimony were in his hand: the tables were written on both their sides; on the one side and on the other were they written. And the tables were the work of God, and the writing was the writing of God, graven upon the tables. And when Joshua heard the noise of the people as they shouted, he said unto Moses, There is a noise of war in the camp. And he said, It is not the voice of them that shout for mastery, neither is it the voice of them that cry for being overcome: but the noise of them that sing do I hear. And it came to pass, as soon as he came nigh unto the camp, that he saw the calf, and the dancing: and Moses' anger waxed hot, and he cast the tables out of his hands, and brake them beneath the mount.

The breaking of the tablets was a reflection of the true breaking of the Law that occurred with the fashioning of the golden calf.

Exodus 32:20
And he took the calf which they had made, and burnt it in the fire, and ground it to powder, and strawed it upon the water, and made the children of Israel drink of it.

In Moses, we see a leader who doesn't walk in the fear of man. His goal is not popularity but godliness.

Exodus 32:21–24
And Moses said unto Aaron, What did this people unto thee, that thou hast brought so great a sin upon them? And Aaron said, Let not the anger of my lord wax hot: thou knowest the people, that they are set on mischief. For they said unto me, Make us gods, which shall go before us: for as for this Moses, the man that brought us up out of the land of Egypt, we wot not what is become of him. And I said unto them, Whosoever hath any gold, let them break it off. So they gave it me: then I cast it into the fire, and there came out this calf.

Because verse 4 clearly says that Aaron fashioned the gold with a graving tool, he's lying when he says he cast the gold in the fire and out came a calf. This is not surprising, for if we live in the fear of man, there will always be the temptation to alter the truth.

Exodus 32:25, 26
And when Moses saw that the people were naked; (for Aaron had made them naked unto their shame among their enemies). Then Moses stood in the gate of the camp, and said, Who is on the LORD's side? Let him come unto me. And all the sons of Levi gathered themselves together unto him.

In Genesis 34, we read how Levi had become enmeshed in immorality, treachery, and butcherly activity. Perhaps having suffered the consequences, they were now ready to stand for integrity.

Exodus 32:27
And he said unto them, Thus saith the LORD God of Israel, Put every man his sword by his side, and go in and out from gate to gate throughout the camp, and slay every man his brother, and every man his companion, and every man his neighbour.

The Word of God is quick and powerful and sharper than any two-edged sword (Hebrews 4:12). Sometimes, like Levi, in obedience to the prompting of the Spirit, we must draw the sword of the Word when speaking to those we care about most. Even though it might cause pain initially, cleansing and healing will be the result eventually if we speak the truth in love (Ephesians 4:15).

Exodus 32:28
And the children of Levi did according to the word of Moses: and there fell of the people that day about three thousand men.

The day the Law came down in the hand of Moses, three thousand died. The day the Spirit came down in Acts 2, three thousand were saved. The Law brings death; the Spirit brings life (2 Corinthians 3:6).

Exodus 32:29
For Moses had said, Consecrate yourselves to day to the LORD, even every man upon his son, and upon his brother; that he may bestow upon you a blessing this day.

God's original intent was that the firstborn son in every family would serve in the priesthood. But because only the Levites were willing to stand strong and do what needed to be done, they now become the sole tribe involved in priestly ministry.

Exodus 32:30
And it came to pass on the morrow, that Moses said unto the people, Ye have sinned a great sin: and now I will go up unto the LORD; peradventure I shall make an atonement for your sin.

Our New Testament understanding of atonement is that of washing clean. But prior to the work of the Cross, the Old Testament meaning of atonement was not of washing away, but only of covering up.

Exodus 32:31
And Moses returned unto the LORD, and said, Oh, this people have sinned a great sin, and have made them gods of gold.

Notice the specific nature of Moses' confession. When we confess our sin, we need to identify the sin. We need to say, "Forgive me, Lord, I lied to him when I said this . . ." or, "I was wrong when I got angry with her about that. . . ." Be specific—and be equally specific in declaring that your sins are forgiven, cleansed, atoned by the blood of the Lamb.

Exodus 32:32
Yet now, if thou wilt forgive their sin—; and if not, blot me, I pray thee, out of thy book which thou hast written.

"If you don't forgive these people, Lord, blot my name out of Your book of life as well," Moses said.

Who gave Moses that kind of heart?

The same One who gave Paul a heart that said, "I would be accursed for the sake of my kinsmen according to the flesh. If they could be saved, I would go to hell" (see Romans 9:3). Who worked that in Paul? Who worked that in Moses? God. For God Himself so loves people that He gave His only Son (John 3:16). How I want that heart worked in me.

Exodus 32:33, 34 (a)
And the LORD said unto Moses, Whosoever hath sinned against me, him will I blot out of my book. Therefore now go, lead the people unto the place of which I have spoken unto thee . . .

God's directive to Moses to lead the people implies that Moses' request was granted, that the people would live, that they were forgiven.

Exodus 32:34 (b), 35
. . . behold, mine Angel shall go before thee: nevertheless in the day when I visit I will visit their sin upon them. And the LORD plagued the people, because they made the calf, which Aaron made.

Not only were the people forgiven, but God's Angel—His Son—would lead them. Nevertheless, there would still be repercussion for their sin. And that's the way it always is (Galatians 6:7).

33 After seeing Moses as a mediator in chapter 32, we'll see him as an intercessor here in chapter 33 . . .

Exodus 33:1–3
And the LORD said unto Moses, Depart, and go up hence, thou and the people which thou hast brought up out of the land of Egypt, unto the land which I sware unto Abraham, to Isaac, and to Jacob, saying, Unto thy seed will I give it: and I will send an angel before thee; and I will drive out the Canaanite, the Amorite, and the Hittite, and the Perizzite, the Hivite, and the Jebusite: unto a land flowing with milk and honey: for I will not go up in the midst of thee; for thou art a stiffnecked people: lest I consume thee in the way.

A Fire Department recently spent a great deal of money on fire helmets which included built-in microphones and other high-tech capabilities—only to discover to their dismay that the helmets melted in high heat. That's what God is saying here. It's not that He would kill the people for being in His presence—but that they would simply melt in the heat of His glory and grandeur.

Exodus 33:4–6
And when the people heard these evil tidings, they mourned: and no man did put on him his ornaments. For the LORD had said unto Moses, Say unto the children of Israel, Ye are a stiffnecked people: I will come up into the midst of thee in a moment, and consume thee: therefore now put off thy ornaments from thee, that I may know what to do unto thee. And the children of Israel stripped themselves of their ornaments by the mount Horeb.

If God told us He would send an angel to lead us into the Promised Land—into the fulfillment of prophecy and the actualization of promises, I think our tendency would be to say, "Terrific!"

But to the credit of the children of Israel, even though they were in a state of carnality, they mourned when they heard this. They didn't care about an angel. And they were no longer excited about the promise without God's presence. "This is terrible," they said. "We need God."

Exodus 33:7
And Moses took the tabernacle, and pitched it without the camp, afar off from the camp, and called it the tabernacle of the congregation. And it came to pass, that every one which sought the LORD went out unto the tabernacle of the congregation, which was without the camp.

The Hebrew word *ohel* translated "tabernacle" in this passage, the tabernacle spoken of here is not the tabernacle Moses had been given instruction to build, for that is defined by the Hebrew word, *mishken*. Rather, the tabernacle spoken of here is the meeting tent for the congregation. Moses packs up the meeting tent and repitches it outside the camp. Having heard the Lord declare that He would not be in the midst of the camp, it's as if Moses was saying, "If God's not there, I don't want to be there either."

You and I desperately need times of pitching our tent outside the camp of busyness in order that we might be made aware of God's presence once again. And sometimes this takes some effort . . .

A number of years ago, when my three kids were little, I took them camping at Indian Mary campground. As a single dad in those days, I was delighted that my college roommate, Rick, and his family joined us. But about five hours after we pitched our tents, a massive storm arose. Although we weathered it for a couple of days, staying in the tents and hanging out under whatever coverings we could find, finally it got so wet we packed up everything and all headed home. On my way back to Jacksonville, the kids and I stopped at McDonald's. And as they played on the playland equipment, the sun popped through. It was at that moment that I realized that, although we'd been camping for a couple of days, I missed my objective totally—which was to focus on my kids. We adults were playing games and enjoying fellowship, but I didn't accomplish what I had initially set out to do. So I loaded the kids back in the car, we went back to Indian Mary, re-pitched the tent, hung out all the wet stuff—and shared some of the best four days we ever spent together.

The same is true in your walk with the Lord. Sometimes you'll have devotions or Bible study—only to realize at the end that a storm blew through, that you were distracted by this, caught up in that, and lost focus. But if you don't give up, if you re-pitch your tent, if you change location and say, "Lord, I really need to be in Your presence"—just as we'll see Him do with Moses—God will meet you there.

Exodus 33:8–10
And it came to pass, when Moses went out unto the tabernacle, that all the people rose up, and stood every man at his tent door,

and looked after Moses, until he was gone into the tabernacle. And it came to pass, as Moses entered into the tabernacle, the cloudy pillar descended, and stood at the door of the tabernacle, and the LORD talked with Moses. And all the people saw the cloudy pillar stand at the tabernacle door: and all the people rose up and worshipped, every man in his tent door.

The people watched as Moses re-pitched the tent of meeting and as the cloudy pillar which symbolized God's presence descended upon the door. They watched the cloud. They were intrigued by the Presence of God. They bowed down. But they remained in their own tents. Just as people can be intrigued by spiritual life, read books about spiritual life, dialogue and write in their journals about spiritual life—they still do not budge from their own tents. Such were the children of Israel—all, that is, except one . . .

Exodus 33:11
And the LORD spake unto Moses face to face, as a man speaketh unto his friend. And he turned again into the camp: but his servant Joshua, the son of Nun, a young man, departed not out of the tabernacle.

Although anyone could have accompanied Moses to the tent of meeting pitched outside the camp, evidently only Joshua chose to go. And once he got there, he couldn't pull himself away. No wonder he would be the man God would use to bring His people into the Land of Promise.

Every one of us is as close to God as we want to be. God will gladly and readily take you and me as far as we want to go. But He won't take us one step further than we desire.

Exodus 33:12–14
And Moses said unto the LORD, See, thou sayest unto me, Bring up this people: and thou hast not let me know whom thou wilt send with me. Yet thou hast said, I know thee by name, and thou hast also found grace in my sight. Now therefore, I pray thee, if I have found grace in thy sight, shew me now thy way, that I may know thee, that I may find grace in thy sight: and consider that this nation is thy people. And he said, My presence shall go with thee, and I will give thee rest.

Was it because of the holiness, devotion, or piety of the people that God promised His Presence would go with them and give them rest? Obviously not, for just one chapter earlier, they were caught up in idolatry and immorality as they danced around the golden calf. No, God declared His presence would go with them and give rest to them not because they were worthy but because they had a mediator named Moses who stood between their sin and God's holiness. Sin requires judgment, but in Moses God found a way to bless His people rather than judge them.

> For there is one God, and one mediator between God and men, the man Christ Jesus; who gave himself a ransom for all, to be testified in due time. 1 Timothy 2:5, 6

Like the children of Israel, we drop the ball; we fall short; we mess up constantly. But, like them, we experience the presence of God because we, too, have a Mediator, a Greater than Moses—Jesus Christ.

As a result, like the children of Israel, we are given direction by a God who will go "in the way before you, to search you out a place to pitch your tents" (Deuteronomy 1:33).

As the people were preparing to enter the Promised Land, they were to follow the ark of the covenant—and yet there was to be 2,000 cubits—over half a mile—between them and the ark. In commanding this, it's as if God was saying, "Give Me space. I'm going ahead of you to prepare the place for you and to prepare you for the place to which I'm leading you" (Joshua 3:3, 4).

The Lord has promised direction for us. Our part is to give Him space to work.

Not only are we given direction, but, like the children of Israel, we are given protection by a God Who not only goes before us, but behind us . . .

> And the angel of God, which went before the camp of Israel, removed and went behind them; and the pillar of the cloud went from before their face, and stood behind them: and it came between the camp of the Egyptians and the camp of Israel; and it was a cloud and darkness to them, but it gave light by night to these: so that the one came not near the other all the night. Exodus 14:19, 20

There are times when I feel I made a bad decision, that I didn't hear God's voice clearly or discern His will properly. But even if that be so, our God not only goes before us, but places Himself between us and the enemies so eager to pursue us. He's got our backs covered. I like that!

Thirdly, in addition to receiving direction and protection, we are given satisfaction by God. We are told Moses fasted two, and perhaps three times for forty days on Mt. Sinai. I suggest it wasn't so much that he fasted in order to seek the Lord, as it was that, having already seen something of the Lord, Moses was so satisfied, so fulfilled, so satiated that he simply forgot to eat. Truly, when we're in the presence of the Lord, we find such satisfaction that we, too, begin to lose our appetite for the fleshly stuff which otherwise is attractive to us.

Direction, protection, satisfaction—all blessings of the Lord's presence.

Exodus 33:15
And he said unto him, If thy presence go not *with me,* carry us not up hence.

The words "with me" are in italics. Therefore, they are not present in the original text. Thus, Moses is saying, "Lord, it's not about Your presence being with me. It's about Your presence being with *us.*" The result of Moses spending time with the Lord on the mountain and in the tent of meeting outside the camp was that he not only had a passionate heart for God, but an incredible passion for God's people.

Exodus 33:16, 17
For wherein shall it be known here that I and thy people have found grace in thy sight? is it not in that thou goest with us? so shall we be separated, I and thy people, from all the people that are upon the face of the earth. And the LORD said unto Moses, I will do this thing also that thou hast spoken: for thou hast found grace in my sight, and I know thee by name.

I can see a smile on the face of God as He says, "Okay, Moses, I'll do what you ask. I'll not only go with you personally, but with the whole nation corporately." And if He responded to Moses' intercession on behalf of the children of Israel, how much more will He give ear to His Son's intercession on our behalf.

Exodus 33:18
And he said, I beseech thee, shew me thy glory.

The Hebrew word translated "glory" is *chabod,* which speaks of weight and substance. The chabod is what clothed Adam and Eve in the garden of Eden. But when they sinned, the chabod departed and they became aware of their emptiness. And man has been aware of the weightlessness, shallowness, nakedness in his soul ever since.

Exodus 33:19 (a)
And he said, I will make all my goodness pass before thee . . .

"Let me see Your glory," Moses said.

"I'll make My goodness pass before you," God answered. God's goodness and His glory are linked because the glory of God is good. It's just plain good.

Exodus 33:19 (b)
. . . and I will proclaim the name of the LORD before thee . . .

Keep in mind—the name of the Lord is always equivalent to His nature, His essence.

Exodus 33:19 (c), 20
. . . and will be gracious to whom I will be gracious, and will shew mercy on whom I will shew mercy. And he said, Thou canst not see my face: for there shall no man see me, and live.

"My goodness will pass before you and My name will be proclaimed to you," God declared. "But My face? No man can see Me and live."

> No man hath seen God at any time . . .
> John 1:18 (a)

Truly the greatness of God is overwhelming, overpowering—but, praise the Lord, John goes on . . .

> . . . the only begotten Son, which is in the bosom of the Father, he hath declared him.
> John 1:18 (b)

When people in Scripture had an encounter with God—as did Abraham in Genesis 18 and Isaiah in Isaiah 6—they were seeing Jesus. And truly no man can see Him and live, for every time we catch a glimpse of our Savior, something of our flesh dies.

Exodus 33:21–23
And the LORD said, Behold, there is a place by me, and thou shalt stand upon a rock: and it shall come to pass, while my glory passeth by, that I will put thee in a clift of the rock, and will cover thee with my hand while I pass by: and I will take away mine hand, and thou shalt see my back parts: but my face shall not be seen.

"Back parts" does not mean backside physically, but literally "afterglow." In other words, God says to Moses, "You can't see Me and live, but you can sense and experience My afterglow." The only way Moses could see God's afterglow was if he was in the cleft of the rock. Who is the Rock? Jesus. When was He cleft? On the Cross.

For ye are dead, and your life is hid with Christ in God. Colossians 3:3

The only way we'll ever see anything of God's glow or glory is to be hidden in Jesus.

34 **Exodus 34:1–3**
And the LORD said unto Moses, Hew thee two tables of stone like unto the first: and I will write upon these tables the words that were in the first tables, which thou brakest. And be ready in the morning, and come up in the morning unto mount Sinai, and present thyself there to me in the top of the mount. And no man shall come up with thee, neither let any man be seen throughout all the mount; neither let the flocks nor herds feed before that mount.

The first tablets had been broken because the Law had been broken (Exodus 32:19)—which isn't surprising since Paul said the reason the Law was given was to show that we couldn't keep it, that we're sinners in desperate need of a Savior (Galatians 3:24).

Exodus 34:4–6 (a)
And he hewed two tables of stone like unto the first; and Moses rose up early in the morning, and went up unto mount Sinai, as the LORD had commanded him, and took in his hand the two tables of stone. And the LORD descended in the cloud, and stood with him there, and proclaimed the name of the LORD. And the LORD passed by before him, and proclaimed, The LORD, The LORD God, . . .

Because God's name was to be spoken only one day each year by the high priest, His name was written without vowels in the Old Testament as YHWH. Some say this name was pronounced "Jehovah." Some say it was pronounced "Yahweh." Others have made other suggestions. While we can't be sure of the pronunciation of this holy name, we do know its meaning . . .

Exodus 34:6 (b)
. . . merciful and gracious , . . .

For their own safety, in verse 1, God told Moses to keep the people and even the livestock away from the mount where His power and presence would be. Therefore, in defining His name and nature, God could have said, "I'm powerful and holy, awesome and mighty." Instead, He said, "I'm gracious; I show mercy." Mercy is not getting what one deserves. Grace is getting what one doesn't deserve. We deserve torment, but because our God is merciful, we get blessing. We deserve hell, but because He is gracious, we're destined for heaven.

Exodus 34:6 (c)
. . . longsuffering . . .

Although I give the Lord plenty of reason to be exasperated with me, He doesn't get uptight. He doesn't drink coffee. He's not wired. He has no ax to grind. He's not wounded. He's not trying to prove His point. He's beyond patient. He's longsuffering.

Exodus 34:6 (d), 7 (a)
. . . and abundant in goodness and truth, Keeping mercy for thousands, forgiving iniquity and transgression and sin . . .

The picture in the Hebrew text is one of overflowing. Think of the broken automatic sprinkler in your front lawn. No matter what you do, it just keeps dispensing water. That's the way God is with goodness and truth, forgiveness and mercy.

Exodus 34:7 (b)
. . . and that will by no means clear *the guilty* . . .

The words "the guilty" are in italics. This means they were added by the translators. Thus, in the original text, God is saying He would not clear or erase that which He had spoken.

Exodus 34:7 (c)
. . . visiting the iniquity of the fathers upon the children, and upon the children's children, unto the third and to the fourth generation.

This verse seems to be jarringly out of place if taken to mean that if I sin it will affect my son, my grandson, my great-grandson and my great-great-grandson. However, linguistically, contextually, or theologically I do not believe that's what is being said. Ezekiel sheds further light on this . . .

What mean ye, that ye use this proverb concerning the land of Israel, saying, The fathers have eaten sour grapes, and the children's teeth are set on edge? As I live, saith the Lord GOD, ye shall not have occasion any more to use this proverb in Israel. Behold, all souls are mine; as the soul of the father, so also the soul of the son is mine: the soul that sinneth, it shall die. Ezekiel 18:2–4

"All souls are mine," God declares. "I make every person individually. And it is the soul that sins who will die." The question arises: If this passage doesn't mean God will punish future generations for the sins of the fathers, what does it mean? Taken in context, this passage speaks of God's grace and mercy. You see, if I sin, the Lord is going to visit me. He's going to deal with me, convict me, chasten me. If Peter-John sins, the Father will do the same with him. And if Peter-John's son sins, God will deal with him as well. In other words, God is saying, "I'm going to knock on the door of each generation; I'm going to deal with each person. I'm going to visit, correct and chasten—all for the purpose of restoration. I will not give up."

Exodus 34:8, 9 (a)
And Moses made haste, and bowed his head toward the earth, and worshipped. And he said, If now I have found grace in thy sight, O Lord, let my Lord, I pray thee, go among us; for it is a stiffnecked people . . .

A realization of the incredible grace and mercy causes Moses first to worship and then to intercede on behalf of a stiff-necked and hard-hearted people.

Exodus 34:9 (b)
. . . and pardon our iniquity and our sin, and take us for thine inheritance.

"Pardon *our* iniquity and *our* sin." Called to lead a rebellious people, Moses nonetheless identified with them. Is it any wonder God used him?

Exodus 34:10
And he said, Behold, I make a covenant: before all thy people I will do marvels, such as have not been done in all the earth, nor in any nation: and all the people among which thou art shall see the work of the LORD: for it is a terrible thing that I will do with thee.

"If you ask anything in My name, I will do it," Jesus said (John 14:14). For many years, I thought this meant I was to simply add the phrase "In Jesus' name" to the end of my prayers, sort of like "Over and out." But when I understood that praying in Jesus' name means to pray according to His nature, I found I couldn't pray a lot of prayers I had been praying—prayers like, "Lord deal with that guy who just cut me off on the highway," prayers like, "I want this to happen *now.*"

"Am I unmerciful, impatient, short-fused?" the Lord asked me. "Or am I longsuffering, merciful, slow to anger? I only work in ways that reflect who I am."

It was because Moses knew the name, the nature, the character of God that he was able to ask for His presence, His pardon, His eternal promise. Meditate on God's nature as seen in the Person of Jesus. Get a strong, firm grip on this, understand—and your prayers will become those God can answer.

Exodus 34:11 (a)
Observe thou that which I command thee this day . . .

After proclaiming His glory, His nature, God will reiterate certain aspects of the Law lest His goodness and grace not be experienced by the people.

Ninety-three million miles away, the sun is huge in size, awesome in power. And yet I can block it from my vision with only my thumb. I can let my flesh come between me and the sun and suddenly, I see it no longer. The sun doesn't leave—my flesh just gets in the way. So, too, the degree to which we allow our flesh to come between us and the Son is the degree to which we'll walk in darkness. And because God doesn't want this for His children, He reminds Moses to deal decisively with that which would cloud the people's perception of His nature.

"All things are lawful for me," Paul declared. As children of God, we are the freest people in the whole world, for who but the believer can say all things are lawful for him? Yet Paul went on to say that even though all things are lawful, not all things are expedient, profitable, wise (1 Corinthians 6:12). In this regard, the remainder of chapter 34 was given to Moses in order that the people would be wise, that they might experience all God wanted to do for them.

Exodus 34:11 (b)–16
. . . behold, I drive out before thee the Amorite, and the Canaanite, and the Hittite, and the Perizzite, and the Hivite, and the Jebusite. Take heed to thyself, lest thou make a covenant with the inhabitants of the land whither thou goest, lest it be for a snare in the midst of thee: But ye shall destroy their altars, break their images, and cut down their groves: For thou shalt worship no other god: for the LORD, whose name is Jealous, is a jealous God: Lest thou make a covenant with the inhabitants of the land, and they go a whoring after their gods, and do

sacrifice unto their gods, and one call thee, and thou eat of his sacrifice; And thou take of their daughters unto thy sons, and their daughters go a whoring after their gods, and make thy sons go a whoring after their gods.

"Be careful you don't get sucked in to the images of the world," God warns. God is jealous for us. He wants the very best for us. And He says images, altars, and worship in shady groves will destroy our lives by destroying our vision of Him.

Exodus 34:17
Thou shalt make thee no molten gods.

The ark of the covenant which represented the presence of the Lord was to be made of beaten gold whereas the gods of the Canaanites were made of molten gold. Molten gold is melted and poured into a mold—which is exactly what we see in the melt-down of spirituality where people mold God into what they think He should be in order to excuse their own sin. God chose to represent Himself through *beaten* gold. Why do I serve the True and Living God? Why am I committed to Jesus Christ? Because He was beaten for me and nailed to the Cross of Calvary.

Exodus 34:18
The feast of unleavened bread shalt thou keep. Seven days thou shalt eat unleavened bread, as I commanded thee, in the time of the month Abib: for in the month Abib thou camest out from Egypt.

"Remember and celebrate what I did for you when I delivered you from Egypt," God says. "This do in remembrance of Me," Jesus would echo, inviting us to the celebration of His Table (Luke 22:19).

Exodus 34:19
All that openeth the matrix is mine; and every firstling among thy cattle, whether ox or sheep, that is male.

The children of Israel being an agrarian people, cattle represented livelihood. The proof of one's dedication is seen in what he does with his livelihood. Yet giving to God materially is not only the proof *of* dedication, but the path *to* dedication. "Where your treasure is, there will your heart be also," Jesus said (Matthew 6:21). Therefore, giving God the first of our livelihood, of our cattle, "steers" our hearts toward heaven.

Exodus 34:20 (a)
But the firstling of an ass thou shalt redeem with a lamb: and if thou redeem him not, then shalt thou break his neck . . .

A donkey could be redeemed through the death of a lamb. If the Lamb speaks of Jesus Christ, the Lamb who was slain, guess what that makes us.

Exodus 34:20 (b)
. . . All the firstborn of thy sons thou shalt redeem. And none shall appear before me empty.

What a delight it is to see people come to church not empty-handed but looking for opportunities to give to the Lord and to encourage their brothers and sisters.

Exodus 34:21
Six days thou shalt work, but on the seventh day thou shalt rest: in earing time and in harvest thou shalt rest.

We'll experience the goodness of God to the degree that we take one day out of seven to put aside our normal activities in order to rest and refocus, in order to be revived, refreshed, and renewed in our vision of Him.

Exodus 34:22, 23
And thou shalt observe the feast of weeks, of the firstfruits of wheat harvest, and the feast of ingathering at the year's end. Thrice in the year shall all your men children appear before the Lord GOD, the God of Israel.

God called His people to come away three times each year for the Feast of Passover in the spring, the Feast of Pentecost fifty days later, and the Feast of Ingathering or Tabernacles in the fall.

Exodus 34:24
For I will cast out the nations before thee, and enlarge thy borders: neither shall any man desire thy land, when thou shalt go up to appear before the LORD thy God thrice in the year.

"I can't afford to get away," we say. "If I take time off, my competitors will eat me alive. My bank account will dwindle. Our family will suffer." That's what the children of Israel could have said as well, knowing that traveling to the feasts would leave their land vulnerable to the enemies surrounding them.

God, however, says, "If you obey Me, *I* will cast

out the nations; *I* will enlarge your borders; *I* will be your protection."

If you're trying to defend your family yourself, watch out. God may say, "If you want to do that, you're on your own. Good luck." I would much rather have the Lord take care of my family, wouldn't you?

Exodus 34:25
Thou shalt not offer the blood of my sacrifice with leaven; neither shall the sacrifice of the feast of the passover be left unto the morning.

Leaven being a picture of sin, it was not to be offered with the sacrifice.

Exodus 34:26 (a)
The first of the firstfruits of thy land thou shalt bring unto the house of the LORD thy God . . .

The firstfruits were not to be distributed by the children of Israel to whomever they deemed worthy or needy, but were to be brought to the house of the Lord. The same is true today. We are to bring the firstfruits, the tithe into the house of the Lord—into the place we're being spiritually fed—to be distributed as the Lord sees fit. That way, we have no control over it and receive no credit for it—which is as it should be (Matthew 6:3). If you want to give money to those people or ministries you deem needy or worthy, God bless you—but do so with your money, not God's, for the tithe belongs to *Him* (Malachi 3:8).

Exodus 34:26 (b)
. . . Thou shalt not seethe a kid in his mother's milk.

So careful are Orthodox Jews to keep the letter of this law that they have separate plates, utensils, cookware for meat and dairy products lest the two inadvertently come into contact with each other. But the children of Israel would have readily understood that the reference was to the Canaanite fertility practices of which they were to have no part.

Exodus 34:27, 28
And the LORD said unto Moses, Write thou these words: for after the tenor of these words I have made a covenant with thee and with Israel. And he was there with the LORD forty days and forty nights; he did neither eat bread, nor drink water. And he wrote upon the tables the words of the covenant, the ten commandments.

Because Moses had seen something of the glory of God, he was to remind the people that in order to keep an understanding of His glory fresh, they were to keep His commands—commandments that would define His nature, commandments which would point to and be fulfilled in His Son.

Exodus 34:29–35
And it came to pass, when Moses came down from mount Sinai with the two tables of testimony in Moses' hand, when he came down from the mount, that Moses wist not that the skin of his face shone while he talked with him. And when Aaron and all the children of Israel saw Moses, behold, the skin of his face shone; and they were afraid to come nigh him. And Moses called unto them; and Aaron and all the rulers of the congregation returned unto him: and Moses talked with them. And afterward all the children of Israel came nigh: and he gave them in commandment all that the LORD had spoken with him in mount Sinai. And till Moses had done speaking with them, he put a vail on his face. But when Moses went in before the LORD to speak with him, he took the vail off, until he came out. And he came out, and spake unto the children of Israel that which he was commanded. And the children of Israel saw the face of Moses, that the skin of Moses' face shone: and Moses put the vail upon his face again, until he went in to speak with him.

If we had only this account, we would think Moses covered his face in order that the people not be blown away with its brightness. But in 2 Corinthians, Paul gives us the real reason . . .

> Seeing then that we have such hope, we use great plainness of speech: and not as Moses, which put a vail over his face, that the children of Israel could not stedfastly look to the end of that which is abolished: 2 Corinthians 3:12, 13

Moses put a veil over his face because he didn't want the people to see that the glow was decreasing. And we do the same thing. As "mature" Christians, we don't want people to see that we're not shining as brightly as we once did or think we should. So we put a veil on ourselves. We learn the lingo; we learn how to appear pious; we learn to cover up. And we become exhausted as our lives become fake, phony, façades. But when we realize we don't have to pretend to be spiritual giants, prayer warriors, or heroes of faith—when we are free to be the dim bulbs we know we are, suddenly the burden lifts and our Christian experience becomes vibrant and alive once more as we simply reflect *His* light, *His* beauty, *His* grace and goodness and glory.

It's not about us and who we pretend to be, but about Jesus and His reality. Look at *Him*. Point others to *Him*. And you'll do well.

LET "GLOW" OF YOUR ISSUES

A Topical Study of EXODUS 34:29–35

Going without food for forty days does not usually help one's appearance—especially if one is eighty years old. But this was not true in the case before us, where, after spending forty days in the presence of the Lord on Mt. Sinai, Moses' face actually glowed.

Reflecting the glory he had experienced on the mountain, Moses didn't initially realize his face was glowing. That's always the way it is. When we spend time in the presence of the Lord—when we are at His feet, when we take time to pray, when we worship Him and spend time in the Word—our gloom is replaced by a glow.

"I don't feel like I glow," you say—but Moses didn't know he was glowing either.

When the Holy Spirit fell on the one hundred and twenty disciples in the Upper Room, a flame burned above each of their heads (Acts 2:3). This means that if you were one of the one hundred and twenty, you would look around and see one hundred and nineteen other people ignited, on fire, illuminated with the power of the Spirit. But you would not see the flame on top of your own head. And such is our tendency—to think everyone but us is aflame. Actually, it's the goodness and grace of God that doesn't allow us to see our own flame . . .

> "Come and see the zeal I have for the Lord," boasted Israel's King Jehu. In reality, however, Jehu was a hypocrite—as evidenced by his statement two verses later that "Ahab served Baal a little; but Jehu shall serve him much" (2 Kings 10:16, 18).

Unlike Jehu, Moses was a man of integrity, of humility. And it was a good thing there was a glow on his face, for he held the Law of the Lord in his hands. The children of Israel needed to hear the commands, the exhortations, the instructions of the Lord. But you know how kids are. They're not always receptive to commandments, instructions, or exhortations. We all tend to be rebellious by nature.

Yet when Moses came down from the mountain and talked to the children of Israel, what could they say? After all, his face was glowing.

Mom and Dad, if your kids aren't being very receptive to your instructions, it might be because there's a glare instead of a glow on your face. Moses glowed—and it made the Word he shared acceptable, the things he said palatable.

Why did Moses glow? Having been in the presence of the Lord, he was simply reflecting the glory inherent in the Lord. In other words, just by hanging out with the Lord, Moses' face glowed. Spending time in the presence of the Lord will impact you in a very real and special way even today. But here's the problem: Moses' glow began to diminish, decrease, decline. It wasn't until he spent time with the Lord that he began to glow once again.

And that's what needs to happen in our lives. We need to realize that we need to be renewed and recharged constantly. Oh, we can do well for a while, but then our glow turns to a glower or a glare. And we find ourselves dull. But when we return to the presence of the Lord, we get recharged, refueled constantly and consistently through prayer, through worship, through His Word.

Sometimes we forget this and instead of seeking renewal from the Lord, we seek it from other people. In this, I am reminded of an account in Luke's Gospel . . .

> *And a woman having an issue of blood twelve years, which had spent all her living upon physicians, neither could be healed of any, came behind him, and touched the border of his garment: and immediately her issue of blood stanched.* Luke 8:43, 44

She had been hemorrhaging for twelve years, going from clinic to clinic, spending everything she had to stop the blood from seeping from her body. According to the rabbis, her condition was the result of immorality. Consequently, she would be ostracized from her community, divorced from her husband, treated as a leper, unclean, a sinner. For twelve years, she had an issue bothering her greatly, hurting her deeply, draining her year after year.

How about you? Perhaps there's an issue with which you struggle, an issue causing pain deep within you, an issue constantly gnawing on you, nagging at you—a past hurt, a previous slight, a prior betrayal. You go to this person and that group trying to get help for the issue. But the more you try to get help, the more people pull away, feeling overwhelmed by your pain, your problem, your issue. Relationships are spent, friendships are spent, emotions are spent because of the ever-present issue that drains you.

Such was the case with the woman in Luke 8. Then her life changed. After twelve years of trying to get help from people, she finally heard about Someone who could deal with the issue of her situation. She heard about Jesus. And hearing that He was able to do what no other man ever could or would, she touched the border of His garment. And immediately, her issue was gone.

In Bible times, strings hanging from the hems of garments would be tied in certain knots that would identify lineage, family, vocation, heritage. That is why, in cutting the hem of Saul's robe in 1 Samuel 24, David was actually cutting off the symbol of his authority—an act of which David later repented.

Thus, in touching the hem of Jesus' garment, the woman in Luke 8 was actually submitting to His authority over her condition, her pain, her sadness, her issue. So, if you have an issue about the way you were brought up, about your ex-wife, former boss, or high school coach which causes your blood to boil, you can be set free right here, right now by simply touching the hem of Jesus' garment, by saying, "Lord, You are in authority and You are on the throne. You always have been and always will be. Therefore, nothing could have happened to me or come my way unless You allowed it. Therefore, I submit to your sovereignty. I'm not going to bleed on other people any longer. I won't camp on the issue of my lousy marriage, my deprived childhood, my financial setbacks another day. I'll submit it to You as I touch the hem of Your garment."

What garment? The garment for which the Roman soldiers rolled dice as Jesus hung on the Cross for me and for you (Matthew 27:35).

What will happen? Like Moses, you'll have a glow on your face and in your heart. You'll experience a newfound wholeness, healthiness, and beauty by spending time with Jesus. Don't bleed on others, gang. Instead, go to the One who shed His blood for you.

35

Exodus 35:1–3
And Moses gathered all the congregation of the children of Israel together, and said unto them, These are the words which the LORD hath commanded, that ye should do them. Six days shall work be done, but on the seventh day there shall be to you an holy day, a sabbath of rest to the LORD: whosoever doeth work therein shall be put to death. Ye shall kindle no fire throughout your habitations upon the sabbath day.

The penalty for violating the Sabbath command was death. And how true that is. Whenever I don't take advantage of the opportunity to be in the Lord's presence, to be refreshed and renewed, something within me dies.

Exodus 35:4–19
And Moses spake unto all the congregation of the children of Israel, saying, This is the thing which the LORD commanded, saying, Take ye from among you an offering unto the LORD: whosoever is of a willing heart, let him bring it, an offering of the LORD; gold, and silver, and brass, and blue, and purple, and scarlet, and fine linen, and goats' hair, and rams' skins dyed red, and badgers' skins, and shittim wood, and oil for the light, and spices for anointing oil, and for the sweet incense, and onyx stones, and stones to be set for the ephod, and for the breastplate. And every wise hearted among you shall come, and make all that the LORD hath commanded; the tabernacle, his tent, and his covering, his taches, and his boards, his bars, his pillars, and his sockets, the ark, and the staves thereof, with the mercy seat, and the vail of the covering, The table, and his staves, and all his vessels, and the shewbread, the candlestick also for the light, and his furniture, and his lamps, with the oil for the light, and the incense altar, and his staves, and the anointing oil, and the sweet incense, and the hanging for the door at the entering in of the tabernacle, the altar of burnt offering, with his brasen grate, his staves, and all his vessels, the laver and his foot, the hangings of the court, his pillars, and their sockets, and the hanging for the door of the court, the pins of the tabernacle, and the pins of the court, and their cords, the cloths of service, to do service in the holy place, the holy garments for Aaron the priest, and the garments of his sons, to minister in the priest's office.

"Whoever is of a willing heart, let him bring an offering to the Lord." I like that. I sometimes hear preachers say, "Give until it hurts"—but that's not the Lord. If it hurts to give, don't do it because Paul tells us the Lord loves a *cheerful*, or literally a *hilarious* giver (2 Corinthians 9:7).

As Jesus sat against the wall in the temple, we

are told He watched not what people gave, but *how* they gave (Mark 12:41). The Lord loves a cheerful giver because when I give cheerfully, I am freed from my fleshly, selfish, small tendencies and I become more like Him in the process. That is why Moses asked only for those with *willing* hearts to give.

How much would those with willing hearts give? By today's standards, approximately one billion dollars worth of gold and silver alone. That's a big offering!

Exodus 35:20
And all the congregation of the children of Israel departed from the presence of Moses.

I like this! They heard the invitation; they had a project before them; and they departed. In other words, Moses didn't pass the basket right then. He didn't pressure the people. He didn't try to manipulate the situation. He simply said, "Go home and think about this."

Exodus 35:21–26
And they came, every one whose heart stirred him up, and every one whom his spirit made willing, and they brought the LORD's offering to the work of the tabernacle of the congregation, and for all his service, and for the holy garments. And they came, both men and women, as many as were willing hearted, and brought bracelets, and earrings, and rings, and tablets, all jewels of gold: and every man that offered offered an offering of gold unto the LORD. And every man, with whom was found blue, and purple, and scarlet, and fine linen, and goats' hair, and red skins of rams, and badgers' skins, brought them. Every one that did offer an offering of silver and brass brought the LORD's offering: and every man, with whom was found shittim wood for any work of the service, brought it. And all the women that were wise hearted did spin with their hands, and brought that which they had spun, both of blue, and of purple, and of scarlet, and of fine linen. And all the women whose heart stirred them up in wisdom spun goats' hair.

Not only goods, but talents were offered to the Lord.

Exodus 35:27–29
And the rulers brought onyx stones, and stones to be set, for the ephod, and for the breastplate; and spice, and oil for the light, and for the anointing oil, and for the sweet incense. The children of Israel brought a willing offering unto the LORD, every man and woman, whose heart made them willing to bring for all manner of work, which the LORD had commanded to be made by the hand of Moses.

The leaders didn't merely say, "I'm glad the people are giving." No, the leaders gave the most. And that's the way it ought to be. Any elder, deacon, preacher, or pastor should be one who leads the way when it comes to giving.

Exodus 35:30–33
And Moses said unto the children of Israel, See, the LORD hath called by name Bezaleel the son of Uri, the son of Hur, of the tribe of Judah; and he hath filled him with the spirit of God, in wisdom, in understanding, and in knowledge, and in all manner of workmanship; and to devise curious works, to work in gold, and in silver, and in brass, and in the cutting of stones, to set them, and in carving of wood, to make any manner of cunning work.

Bezaleel was given wisdom, anointed, and gifted by the Holy Ghost to do practical construction. Maybe the Spirit has done the same in you. Because every good and perfect gift comes from above (James 1:17), if you can fix an engine or construct a building, yours is a good and perfect gift indeed.

Exodus 35:34, 35
And he hath put in his heart that he may teach, both he, and Aholiab, the son of Ahisamach, of the tribe of Dan. Them hath he filled with wisdom of heart, to work all manner of work, of the engraver, and of the cunning workman, and of the embroiderer, in blue, and in purple, in scarlet, and in fine linen, and of the weaver, even of them that do any work, and of those that devise cunning work.

Bezaleel and his coworker Aholiab were not only to do the work themselves, but to teach others as well. Paul was one who worked with his hands as a tentmaker, even as he taught others the Word (Acts 18:3). Sod, Bezaleel and Aholiab were able to work and to teach—an unbeatable combination.

36–40

Exodus 36:1
Then wrought Bezaleel and Aholiab, and every wise hearted man, in whom the LORD put wisdom and understanding to know how to work all manner of work for the service

of the sanctuary, according to all that the LORD had commanded.

Given both a calling and an anointing, Bezaleel and Aholiab put their hands to the plow and began working.

Exodus 36:2
And Moses called Bezaleel and Aholiab, and every wise hearted man, in whose heart the LORD had put wisdom, even every one whose heart stirred him up to come unto the work to do it:

Bezaleel and Aholiab were given ability to do the work that needed to be done practically. But we also read that they came. If you want your life to be impacting, the key is to have both ability and availability. There are people who have great abilities, but they're never available. When there is work to do, when opportunities open, when needs are presented, they're just not around. Bezaleel and Aholiab go down in history as models, their names recorded for eternity, as men who used the practical gifts God had given them for His glory. How we need men who will say, "I can't preach or sing, but I can fix an engine. I can't evangelize, but I can pour cement." We need you! Make yourself available—and your name will be added to the roster of Bezaleel and Aholiab.

Exodus 36:3–7
And they received of Moses all the offering, which the children of Israel had brought for the work of the service of the sanctuary, to make it withal. And they brought yet unto him free offerings every morning. And all the wise men, that wrought all the work of the sanctuary, came every man from his work which they made; and they spake unto Moses, saying, The people bring much more than enough for the service of the work, which the LORD commanded to make. And Moses gave commandment, and they caused it to be proclaimed throughout the camp, saying, Let neither man nor woman make any more work for the offering of the sanctuary. So the people were restrained from bringing. For the stuff they had was sufficient for all the work to make it, and too much.

So much did the people bring that Moses finally had to say, "We have too much!"

Amazing.

Exodus 36:8
And every wise hearted man among them that wrought the work of the tabernacle made ten curtains of fine twined linen, and blue, and purple, and scarlet: with cherubims of cunning work made he them.

And so began the construction of the tabernacle which would take approximately six months (40:2) as chronicled in the remaining four chapters.

In verses 33 and 34 of chapter 40, we read the following . . .

Exodus 40:33, 34
And he reared up the court round about the tabernacle and the altar, and set up the hanging of the court gate. So Moses finished the work. Then a cloud covered the tent of the congregation, and the glory of the LORD filled the tabernacle.

The pathways of Bible studies, conferences, and camps are strewn with the good intentions of people who began to do something but never finished. How I pray we would be those who say, "Lord, by Your grace, help me to finish what You've called and gifted me to do"—for it was only after Moses *finished* the work that the glory of the Lord filled the tabernacle.

FINISHING THE WORK

A Topical Study of EXODUS 40:33

The project was immense, but Moses finished the work. And because of this, the writer to the Book of Hebrews declares Moses was faithful in all his house (Hebrews 3:5). In other words, he was faithful in all that he did.

Even though it took him one hundred years, Noah was another one who finished the work—and I'm so glad he did, for if he hadn't we'd be all wet! Nehemiah was another Old Testament hero who was faithful to finish the task to which God had called him. Following the Babylonian captivity, Nehemiah was the man sent by God back to Jerusalem to rebuild the wall. But when he arrived, he found no shortage of opposition . . .

> "Even if you do finish the wall," mocked two men named Tobiah and Sanballat, "if a fox walks along the top of it, the whole thing will topple," (Nehemiah 4:3).
>
> In addition, Nehemiah's own helpers, the tribe of Judah, came to him and said, "This job is too difficult." But the Word says Nehemiah set his mind to the work and continued on (Nehemiah 4:6).
>
> Realizing the wall was indeed going up, Tobiah and Sanballat changed their tactic and sent messengers to Nehemiah, saying, "Meet us in the valley of the plain of Ono and let us talk together."
>
> "I'll not leave the task the Lord has called me to complete," answered Nehemiah (Nehemiah 6:3).
>
> A short time later, a man in the temple sent a message to Nehemiah, saying, "Come into the temple and let us seek God together."
>
> But perceiving something was wrong, Nehemiah said, "I'm not going to the temple even though it's seemingly spiritual because the Lord has set before me a task and I will not leave" (Nehemiah 6:11).

Within fifty-two days, the wall was completed because God honored Nehemiah's tenacity and anointed his perseverance.

Moses finished the work. Noah finished the work. Nehemiah finished the work. And in his last letter penned before his pending execution, the apostle Paul said, "I have fought the good fight. I have finished the course" (2 Timothy 4:7).

But no one had a greater task, no one a grander finish than the One who would say, "Father, I have glorified Thee and finished the Work Thou hast given Me to do" (John 17:4). Oh, there were still thousands who needed to be healed, thousands who needed to be taught, thousands who needed deliverance from demons. There was still much to be done. But Jesus always ministered according to the direction of His Father rather than according to the needs of those around Him.

That is why when His mother hinted that He should do something miraculous at the wedding in Cana, and when His brothers told Him He should go to the feast in Jerusalem, He was able to say, "Mine hour is not yet come," with confidence and serenity.

"Come quickly," said Mary and Martha. "The one whom Thou lovest is sick." Jesus didn't come immediately. Their brother died. And the Father worked a miracle when He resurrected Lazarus from the dead (John 11). Jesus always moved in obedience to the Father's directing. And thus, although there was much to be done in the eyes of men, He was able to say He had finished the work His Father had given Him to do.

How about you? Do you know the work God is calling you to do? If not, here are three principles for you to consider . . .

Receive Direction from God Daily

In the first chapter of Marks' Gospel, we see Jesus ministering all day long. He taught the Word, healed the sick, delivered the oppressed—so much so that the whole city came and gathered outside the door where He was preaching. Yet Mark records that the next morning, a great while before the sun rose, He went into a solitary place and prayed. If there was ever a time Jesus would have been justified in sleeping in, that would have been the day. But the One who was able to say, "I have finished the work Thou hast called Me to do," was One who received daily instruction from His Father.

This is such an important, foundational principle—for if we don't capture the day in the morning, we'll be held captive by the day as it unfolds. We'll find ourselves influenced by events, confused by opportunities, pressured by demands. Therefore, I believe the Lord would have us, morning by morning with pencil and paper in hand, say, "Father, what do *You* want me to do today?"

And His answer might be something as simple as, "Write a letter to your mother." Or the task might be something as complicated as purchasing a Greek Lexicon in preparation for further ministry. The Lord will lay on your heart specific things He wants you to accomplish. And at the end of the day, you will know if you finished the work. If this step is omitted, you'll wander and squander your years away, always under the deluded deception that next year you'll get it together, that next year your life will count, that next year you'll accomplish something of eternal value. But next year will never come.

Allow Reflection upon God Weekly

Our Maker and Master, Designer, and Creator said we should have a day of Sabbath, a day of reflection, a day of meditation. It doesn't matter which day it is, but, as His created beings, we need to follow His instructions.

"Man wasn't made for the Sabbath," Jesus said, "but the Sabbath for man" (Mark 2:27). The Sabbath is for man's benefit, for our well-being. If you set apart one day to concentrate on the things of God, to meditate on the Word of God, to reflect on where you've been that week and where you're going the next, you will find your other six days much more productive than if you sought to squeeze in some extra hours of work. The Sabbath provides perfect opportunity to slow down physically, to tune in spiritually, to be refreshed mentally.

Seek Specific Vision from God Periodically

Moses was able to finish the work of the tabernacle because he knew precisely how to build it. How did he know? As he spent forty days on Mt. Sinai in fasting and prayer, God laid out a perfect pattern for him to follow.

"I wish God would give me a blueprint," we say. "If He would give a plan to me, I would follow it." But do we take forty days to seek Him for it? How about four days—or even four hours? Paul spent three years in the deserts of Arabia getting the divine pattern for His life. Jesus spent thirty years tuned in to the Father before He ministered publicly for three years. So, too, we need times where we seek God fervently and expectantly.

For an example of how this happens, turn to the Book of Habakkuk . . .

Habakkuk's name means "Wrestler"—an appropriate name for this one who wrestled with why God wasn't doing more to combat the evil in the world around him. And in his life, we see three characteristics of those who seriously seek specific vision from God.

> *I will stand upon my watch, and set me upon the tower, and will watch to see what he will say unto me, and what I shall answer when I am reproved. And the* LORD *answered me, and said, Write the vision, and make it plain upon tables, that he may run that readeth it.* Habakkuk 2:1, 2

The first characteristic is *determination.* Habakkuk didn't say, "I should stand upon my watch," or, "I think I'll stand upon my watch," but, "I *will* stand upon my watch."

"You will find Me when you search for Me with all your heart," God declared (Jeremiah 29:13). As it did for Habakkuk, there must come a point in our lives when we are *determined* to seek the Lord if we truly expect to hear from Him.

Secondly, we see the *importance of isolation.* I have found that when I'm in desperate need of vision and direction, I must get away from the telephone, radio, television, away from the clamor and clutter of the world. Wherever your "high tower" might be, find a place where you won't be distracted by the needs that incessantly pull at you if you want to hear what it is God would have you do.

Finally, we see Habakkuk's *expectation.* He didn't say, "I'll watch to see *if* God will speak to me," but, "I'll watch to see what God *will* say to me."

"He that comes to God must believe that He is, and that He is a rewarder of them that diligently seek Him," declares the writer of the Book of Hebrews (11:6). James echoes this when he writes,

> *If any of you lack wisdom, let him ask of God, that giveth to all men liberally, and upbraideth not; and it shall be given him. But let him ask in faith, nothing wavering. For he that wavereth is like a wave of the sea driven with the wind*

> *and tossed. For let not that man think that he shall receive any thing of the Lord.*
> James 1:5–7

If I approach God but don't expect to receive from Him, I won't.

Determination, isolation, expectation—as these three components become part of my life, I'll find direction. And if I've dropped the ball, missed opportunities, failed miserably?

I simply go to the Cross, where the One who finished the Work died to cleanse me completely—and I begin again.

Oh, that we might be a people who find freedom in the Finished Work of the Cross, that we might finish the work God has called us to do, that we might hear Him say, "Well *done*, good and faithful servants."

In Jesus' name.

LEVITICUS

Background to Leviticus

If the Book of Genesis shows us depravity and condemnation, and the Book of Exodus illustrates redemption and salvation, then surely the book before us speaks of separation and consecration. *Leviticus* literally means "pertaining to the Levites." Therefore, the Book of Leviticus was a handbook for the tribe of Levi, those who were to serve the Lord in the tabernacle and later in the temple.

Because the people of God were to be holy, we'll see the word "holy" or "holiness" over eighty times in the Book of Leviticus. And because without blood, there can be no holiness, no remission of sin (Hebrews 9:22), we'll see the word "blood" over eighty-eight times. That is why this book is offensive to some. But it ought not be, for it speaks of the solution to the death of happiness, the death of joy, the death of a relationship with God sin brings to you and me. You see, not only does Leviticus speak of the severity of sin, but of the grace of God. That is why over and over again, we'll come across the phrase, "I will forgive your sin and iniquity." Forgiveness is a recurring theme in the Book of Leviticus. But it comes at a price.

Thirdly, and most importantly, in addition to the severity of sin and the grace of God, the Book of Leviticus portrays the sacrifice of Christ. Every offering and sacrifice give us understanding of the unspeakable price the Lamb of God paid that we might be forgiven, consecrated, separated.

The book before us instructs us concerning the sacrifices *to* the Lord and the festivals *of* the Lord. Through the sacrifices, we see the *way* to God; through the festivals we see our *walk* with God. And thus, it is a glorious book not only for the sons of Levi—but for each of us, the sons of God.

LEVITICUS

1 **Leviticus 1:1, 2**
And the LORD called unto Moses, and spake unto him out of the tabernacle of the congregation, saying, Speak unto the children of Israel, and say unto them, if any man of you bring an offering unto the LORD, ye shall bring your offering of the cattle, even of the herd, and of the flock.

Chapter 1 opens with the first of five offerings—in each of which we will see a purpose, procedure, picture, price, and point . . .

Leviticus 1:3
If his offering be a burnt sacrifice of the herd, let him offer a male without blemish: he shall offer it of his own voluntary will at the door of the tabernacle of the congregation before the LORD.

The purpose of the first offering—the burnt offering—was to consecrate or dedicate one's self. It was a voluntary offering, and had to be so, for true dedication can only be made from a heart filled with desire, true consecration comes not from responsibility, but from response.

Leviticus 1:4
And he shall put his hand upon the head of the burnt offering; and it shall be accepted for him to make atonement for him.

The procedure of the burnt offering was one of consecration through identification . . .

For topical study of Leviticus 1:1–4 entitled "A Hands-On Experience," turn to page 366.

Leviticus 1:5
And he shall kill the bullock before the LORD: and the priests, Aaron's sons, shall bring the blood, and sprinkle the blood round about upon the altar that is by the door of the tabernacle of the congregation.

The picture of Jesus as seen through the burnt offering is of tremendous significance. Just as the burnt offering was offered voluntarily, Jesus laid down His life willingly. When He prayed "If it be possible, let this cup pass from Me," He used a phrase translated into Greek as a first class conditional clause. This means it was indeed possible that He could bypass the cup of suffering and death. "*Nevertheless,*" He prayed, "not My will but Thine be done" (Luke 22:42). Had Jesus demanded to be released from suffering, He would not have had to go to Calvary—but we would be doomed and damned eternally.

Leviticus 1:6, 7
And he shall flay the burnt offering, and cut it into his pieces. And the sons of Aaron the priest shall put fire upon the altar, and lay the wood in order upon the fire:

Wood was laid on the fire of the altar in preparation for the sacrifice—just as a wooden cross was prepared for Jesus upon which He would absorb the fire of God's righteous wrath on our behalf.

Leviticus 1:8 (a)
And the priests, Aaron's sons, shall lay the parts, the head . . .

The head speaks of the mind. And Jesus' mind was perfect. "Should we pay taxes to Rome?" His enemies asked in a futile attempt to entangle Him in political controversy. A "yes" answer would incense the Jews who abhorred the Roman government. A "no" answer would provide the Romans grounds to arrest Him for anarchy.

"Whose image is on the coin?" Jesus asked in response. "Give to Caesar that which belongs to Caesar, and to God that which belongs to God." In other words, "The coin bears Caesar's image. Therefore, give the coin to Caesar. But man bears God's image. Therefore, give your life to God" (see Matthew 22:21).

Leviticus 1:8 (b)
. . . and the fat, in order upon the wood that is on the fire which is upon the altar:

Fat speaks of excess. Even the perjured testimony of hired witnesses could not blind Pilate to the fact that there was no excess, no fault in Jesus (Luke 23:4). And even the fire of ambition could not silence Judas' admission that he had indeed betrayed innocent, flawless blood (Matthew 27:3, 4).

Leviticus 1:9 (a)
But his inwards . . .

The "inwards" speak of inward purity. When were the inwards of Jesus revealed? When, on the Mount of Transfiguration, the pure brilliance of His glory shone through His outward humanity (Matthew 17:2).

Leviticus 1:9 (b)
. . . and his legs shall he wash in water . . .

The legs speak of one's walk, of one's lifestyle. No wonder, then, that it was as Jesus walked that John said, "Behold the Lamb of God who takes away the sin of the world" (John 1:29).

Leviticus 1:9 (c)
. . . and the priest shall burn all on the altar, to be a burnt sacrifice, an offering made by fire, of a sweet savour unto the LORD.

"What must I do to obtain eternal life?" the rich young ruler asked. If there are three qualities the world seeks, they are riches, youth, and power. This man had all three—but inwardly he knew he was lacking.

"Keep the commandments," Jesus answered.

"I have," he replied.

"This one thing you lack," Jesus said—which, in itself, is further proof of the young ruler's dedication, for if the Lord were speaking to me, He would surely say there are countless things I lack. "Go and sell your goods and come and follow Me."

Knowing he was dominated by money, Jesus put His finger on the rich young ruler's singular point of weakness. Hearing this, the young man walked away from Jesus, unwilling to consecrate his entire being (Matthew 19:22).

The burnt offering speaks of giving *all* that we are to the Lord—and he who does will never be disappointed because man simply cannot out give God.

Leviticus 1:10
And if his offering be of the flocks, namely, of the sheep, or of the goats, for a burnt sacrifice; he shall bring it a male without blemish.

The price of the offering differed according to one's possessions—yet their illustration was singular: The ox spoke of Jesus Christ the Strong One able to bear our burdens, *to pull us out* of sin. The lamb portrayed Jesus as the Perfect One who came *to take away* our sin. The goat represented Jesus as the Rejected One who, for us, *became* sin.

Leviticus 1:11–13
And he shall kill it on the side of the altar northward before the LORD: and the priests, Aaron's sons, shall sprinkle his blood round about upon the altar. And he shall cut it into his pieces, with his head and his fat: and the priest shall lay them in order on the wood that is on the fire which is upon the altar: But he shall wash the inwards and the legs with water: and the priest shall bring it all, and burn it upon the altar: it is a burnt sacrifice, an offering made by fire, of a sweet savour unto the LORD.

The lamb or goat was to be killed on the altar northward, which speaks of the ultimate altar—the Cross of Calvary—located north of the city of Jerusalem.

Leviticus 1:14
And if the burnt sacrifice for his offering to the LORD be of fowls, then he shall bring his offering of turtledoves, or of young pigeons.

In the ox, we see Jesus as the Burden-Bearer. In the lamb, we see Him as the One who takes away our sin. In the goat, we see Him rejected in our place. And in the birds, we see Him as One who left His home in heaven to lodge in a tree called Calvary in order that we might one day soar with Him in the heavenlies.

Leviticus 1:15
And the priest shall bring it unto the altar, and wring off his head, and burn it on the altar; and the blood thereof shall be wrung out at the side of the altar:

When the bird was brought to the altar, the priest was to wring off its head. Ringing Jesus' head was a crown of thorns piercing His skull. And as it did, I was on His mind. So were you.

Leviticus 1:16, 17 (a)
And he shall pluck away his crop with his feathers, and cast it beside the altar on the east part, by the place of the ashes: And he shall cleave it with the wings thereof, but shall not divide it asunder: and the priest shall burn it upon the altar, upon the wood that is upon the fire:

Jesus felt the pain and humiliation as His beard was plucked. And the arms outstretched on the Cross were the same wings under which He had longed to gather the entire city of Jerusalem (Matthew 23:37).

Leviticus 1:17 (b)
. . . it is a burnt sacrifice, an offering made by fire, of a sweet savour unto the LORD.

Jesus was completely consumed as He hung on the wood of the Cross, as He felt the fire of God's holy, righteous indignation. That is why when He was baptized at the age of thirty, the Father said, "This is My beloved Son in whom I am well pleased" (Matthew 3:17). Baptism being a picture of death, burial, and resurrection, Jesus knew what He was doing. He had come to die. As the prophet declared, He had set His face like flint towards Jerusalem on what would be a three-year journey to Calvary. And He did so voluntarily. Therefore, as I look at Jesus and see Him as the Ox, the Lamb, the Goat, the Dove who gave Himself willingly for me, I cannot help but join Paul in concluding that it is only reasonable that I present myself to Him (Romans 12:1, 2).

A HANDS-ON EXPERIENCE

A Topical Study of LEVITICUS 1:1–4

Composed of twenty muscles, fifteen tendons, and twenty-seven bones, the human hand is a most amazing instrument—at one moment able to precisely place a single thread through the eye of a needle, the next, able to form a fist to use as a powerful weapon. Yet the Word teaches that, in addition to its important role in our physical well-being, the hand is an instrument of spiritual importance . . .

Expression

In the first minute of the upcoming San Francisco/Miami game, without a doubt Forty-Niner Quarterback, Joe Montana will drop back seven yards into a perfectly formed pocket and fire an accurate strike to Dwight Clark for a huge gainer—the beginning of what will undoubtedly be a tremendous Forty-Niner victory over the Miami Dolphins. And when Joe completes that first pass, the fans will voice their expression of approval with hands raised in the air and thunderous applause.

If Joe Montana is worthy of applause, certainly our Lord Jesus is imminently more so. Therefore, Psalm 47 instructs all people to clap their hands. The clapping of hands in Scripture is more than a spiritual exercise we go through to get things warmed up. Rather, it is a way the Lord has chosen by which we can show appreciation for Him.

Yet not only is clapping a form of approval—it is also a form of warfare . . .

And the priest shall bring it unto the altar, and wring off his head, and burn it on the altar; and the blood thereof shall be wrung out at the side of the altar:

Leviticus 1:15

Here we see the enemies of the people of Jerusalem rebuking them by gnashing their teeth, by hissing, by clapping the hands. The clapping of hands in confrontation is also seen in Job 23, Ezekiel 25, and Nahum 3. I don't mean to be dogmatic, but during those times when it seems all the hordes of hell have gathered around me to hurl depression, discouragement, or temptation at me, I have found that as I use the name of Jesus Christ and rebuke them with the clapping of hands, something begins to happen miraculously. Years ago, the Lord gave me a practical illustration of why this might be so . . .

Christy, my three-year-old was in one of her giggly moods. Working on a school project at the kitchen table, Peter-John, my seven-year-old was in a sober mood. When Christy began to tickle him, he endured it for a while. But when she continued plaguing and oppressing him, I said, "Christy, leave Peter-John alone." But when she was unable to do so, I finally clapped my hands once and said, "Christy, stop." And she immediately returned to her side of the table.

If you're a parent, you know the power of the clap! And it seems as though spiritually, the same thing is true. When we're being plagued and harassed by the enemy, there's something that happens mystically and spiritually when we use the name of Jesus and clap. Try it and see if you don't experience freedom as you begin to use this form of confrontation.

In addition to using our hands to express appreciation and confrontation, we also use them to express affection. When we lift our hands to the Lord, we are, in a sense reaching out to His hand. That is why Jeremiah calls us to lift up our hearts with our hands unto the heavens (Lamentations 3). When your heart is defeated or discouraged, heavy or hardened, that is the very time you need to lift your hands in an act of worship, for in doing so you actually lift up your emotions, your spirit, and your heart with your hands into the heavens.

In lifting our hands, we also express surrender—surrendering all that we are to God for Him to use as He chooses.

Impartation

Throughout Scripture, we see examples of the blessing and power of God flowing through the hands of His people . . .

- In Exodus 17, it was when Moses lifted his hands that the army of Israel prevailed.
- In Leviticus 9, it was through Moses' lifted hands that God blessed the people.
- In Mark 16, Jesus said it was as hands were laid on the sick that they would recover.
- In Acts 6, it was when hands were laid upon the deacons that they were empowered for service.
- In Acts 8, it was as Peter and John laid hands on the Samaritan believers that they were filled with the Holy Spirit.

No wonder Paul said he would that men everywhere would lift up holy hands in prayer (1 Timothy 2:8)—for truly there is power imparted through the lifting up of hands.

Identification

In the text before us, we see a man coming to the courtyard of the tabernacle. He stands before the priest and next to him is his bull or lamb—an innocent, docile, harmless animal. The man would then lay his hand—the Hebrew language implies that he would press it—upon the animal's head. Then he would watch the priest slit the animal's throat, the animal slumping to the ground. If the man had any kind of compassion, he would be moved as he realized that, in a very real sense, he was transferring his sin to the animal, and that the animal was literally dying in his place.

> Short of men in his campaign through Europe, Napoleon began to draft heavily in France. However, when approached, one man answered, "I can't go. My father is very ill and my mother cannot manage the farm alone." So he was allowed to pay someone else to go in his place—a common practice of the time. The first day the substitute reported for duty, he was killed in battle and subsequently buried. A few months later, there was a knock on the door of the man who had hired the substitute. Once again, it was a recruiting officer who said, "Your number is up."
>
> "You can't take me," said the young man. "I'm already dead and buried."
>
> Baffled, the officer hauled him off to a military tribunal. The tribunal heard the case and sent it all the way to Napoleon himself, who, when he heard about the situation, agreed with the would-be soldier and said, "You're right. You're already dead. Go home."

The man was free because someone died in his place. I, too, I am free because the Lamb of God was butchered in my place. It is my sin He bore—the sin of being short with my kids today, the sin of being annoyed with the driver in front of me yesterday, the sin of saying things which shouldn't be said, the sin of thinking things that shouldn't be thought, the sin of doing things which shouldn't be done. My sin was transferred to Jesus—and He died in my place.

Suppose the man came with his bull to the tabernacle, but when the priest told him to put his hand upon the bull, the man said, "Let me teach you the significance of this particular sacrifice."

"I care not how knowledgeable you are theologically or how certain you are doctrinally," the priest would answer. "Put your hand on the bull and press in, for if you don't become involved, the sacrifice will be to no avail."

Many Christians have no shortage of understanding and theological insights about the substitutionary work of Jesus Christ. They have the teaching down, but there's no touching. That is why there will be those who say, "Lord, my theology is impeccable. I can explain to You the whole plan of salvation," only to hear Him say, "Depart from Me. I never knew you. Your teaching was correct, but your touching was nonexistent. You were not touching Me, nor were you touched by Me. Your heart was calloused and cold. Even when the gospel was preached, you slumbered. When the Cross was considered, your mind wandered. No longer were you touched by the sacrifice. No longer did you press in."

There are those who never weep, whose heart is never broken, whose sins are never confessed, who never press in and touch. "I don't delight in burnt offerings," the Lord says. "A broken and contrite spirit is what is acceptable to Me" (see Psalm 51:17).

David was an adulterer, a murderer, and a liar. But after spending one year refusing to acknowledge his sin, David fell down in humility and brokenness. David's was a heart of tenderness, a heart that laid its hand on the sacrifice. No wonder he could say, "Happy is the man whose transgression is forgiven, whose sin is covered. Happy is the man to whom the Lord does not impute iniquity" (Psalm 32).

Press in to the Sacrifice offered on your behalf, dear saint.

How?

The best place I know is at the Lord's Table. Confess your sins and transfer them to the Son, saying, "Father, I realize it was my sin that sent Jesus to the Cross."

Your hands can be used for any number of activities—but it is at the Lord's Table, as you use them to hold the broken body and the shed blood of the Lamb of God, that they reach their highest purpose.

---

2 The burnt offering of chapter 1 spoke of Christ's total dedication. The meal offering here in chapter 2 speaks of Christ's absolute perfection. The burnt offering was for the consecration of self. As we will see, the meal offering was for the consecration of service.

Leviticus 2:1 (a)
And when any will offer a meat offering unto the LORD, his offering shall be of fine flour . . .

In King James' day, meat referred to grain. Thus, this offering is actually a meal offering. Notice it was to be of fine, or sifted, flour—for after Jesus offered His life symbolically in the water of baptism, He was led to the wilderness, where He was tempted—sifted—for forty days, emerging as the perfect meal Offering.

Leviticus 2:1 (b)
. . . and he shall pour oil upon it . . .

Oil in Scripture is symbolic of the Holy Spirit. Any attempt I make to serve God in my own energy is doomed to fail. Therefore, everything I offer to God must be anointed with the oil of the Holy Ghost.

Leviticus 2:1 (c)
. . . and put frankincense thereon:

Incense speaks of prayer.

"Without Me," Jesus said, "you can do nothing" (John 15:5).

"You have not because you ask not," James tells us (4:2).

Oh, that we might be like Epaphras—one who "laboured fervently" in prayer (Colossians 4:12)—for prayer is an essential ingredient in an acceptable meal offering to the Lord.

Leviticus 2:2
And he shall bring it to Aaron's sons the priests: and he shall take thereout his handful of the flour thereof, and of the oil thereof, with all the frankincense thereof; and the priest shall burn the memorial of it upon the altar, to be an offering made by fire, of a sweet savour unto the LORD:

The meal offering was to be roasted with fire. So, if you want to be a servant of God, to be used by God, you can be sure you will go through fire. "Think it not strange," Peter warned, "concerning the fiery trials which beset you" (1 Peter 4:12). The Lord will take you through difficulty and trials because a man cannot relate to others until he has experienced the baptism of fire in his own life (2 Corinthians 1:4). Because the people who are most effective in ministering to us are those who have experienced the very trials we face, I believe God walks His most trusted servants through the fire of difficulty, the flames of tragedy.

Leviticus 2:3
And the remnant of the meat offering shall be Aaron's and his sons': it is a thing most

holy of the offerings of the LORD made by fire.

A handful of the meal offering was burnt upon the altar, the rest given to the priests. Yet even though the priests benefited directly, the sacrifice was nonetheless credited to the eternal account of the one who brought the offering, for it was indeed the Lord's. And the same is true of any offering we give today—for while the "priest and his sons" may be the visible beneficiaries, the Lord is the ultimate Receiver and will credit and bless accordingly.

Leviticus 2:4–6
And if thou bring an oblation of a meat offering baken in the oven, it shall be unleavened cakes of fine flour mingled with oil, or unleavened wafers anointed with oil. And if thy oblation be a meat offering baken in a pan, it shall be of fine flour unleavened, mingled with oil. Thou shalt part it in pieces, and pour oil thereon: it is a meat offering.

The cakes were to be mingled with oil, the wafers to be anointed with oil. Oil being a type of the Spirit, conceived by the Spirit, Jesus was "mingled with oil" at the moment of conception (Matthew 1:20). And He was anointed with oil when the Spirit came upon Him, empowering Him for service following His baptism (Matthew 3:16). We are mingled with oil when we are born again (John 14:17). We are anointed with oil when we come to the point where we say, "I want to be used by You, Lord" and the Spirit comes upon us, empowering us for service (Acts 1:5).

Leviticus 2:7–10
And if thy oblation be a meat offering baken in the fryingpan, it shall be made of fine flour with oil. And thou shalt bring the meat offering that is made of these things unto the LORD: and when it is presented unto the priest, he shall bring it unto the altar. And the priest shall take from the meat offering a memorial thereof, and shall burn it upon the altar: it is an offering made by fire, of a sweet savour unto the LORD. And that which is left of the meat offering shall be Aaron's and his sons': it is a thing most holy of the offerings of the LORD made by fire.

As was the case with the burnt offering, the price of the meal offering varied according to possession. If a person had an oven, his meal was to be baked. If he had a covered pan, it was to be baked in the pan. If all he had was a frying pan, it was to be fried. Again, this tells us we are accountable to God according to how He has blessed us. God will use whatever you have—be it an oven, a covered dish, or a simple frying pan. When Jesus taught the parable of the talents, the indictment was not given to the man with ten talents or even five—but with the man who buried his single talent (Matthew 25:28–30). If you only have one talent, if you possess nothing more than a frying pan, offer that one talent as a meal offering to God—and watch Him be glorified through it.

Leviticus 2:11 (a)
No meat offering, which ye shall bring unto the LORD, shall be made with leaven . . .

Leaven is a picture of sin. Meal offerings were not to contain leaven. So we must beware of using the ways of the world to expand the ministry to which we're called.

Leviticus 2:11 (b)
. . . for ye shall burn no leaven, nor any honey, in any offering of the LORD made by fire.

Because honey breaks down when the temperature rises, the Lord wanted nothing to do with that which would break down under pressure, which would lose its sweetness in the fire. Many people have learned how to be sweet—but the problem is, when the temperature goes up, they break down. Therefore, it's not about becoming sweeter people by our own will power. It's about the work of the Holy Spirit producing in us the sweet fruit of love—joy and peace, longsuffering and gentleness, faith, meekness, and self-control which will remain no matter how high the mercury rises.

Leviticus 2:12, 13
As for the oblation of the firstfruits, ye shall offer them unto the LORD: but they shall not be burnt on the altar for a sweet savour. And every oblation of thy meat offering shalt thou season with salt; neither shalt thou suffer the salt of the covenant of thy God to be lacking from thy meat offering: with all thine offerings thou shalt offer salt.

Why was salt to be offered with the meal offering? Because salt speaks of grace (Colossians 4:6). Thus, in this picture of Christ, the perfect One, it is only fitting that salt be incorporated, for there is none more gracious than Him (Luke 4:22).

Leviticus 2:14
And if thou offer a meat offering of thy firstfruits unto the LORD, thou shalt offer for the meat offering of thy firstfruits green ears of corn dried by the fire, even corn beaten out of full ears.

If you jump ahead 1,500 years, you will see Jesus, the perfect One of whom this meal offering speaks, allowing His disciples to partake of the corn in the field, even while He—the Corn which would be beaten for their sins and ours—was in their midst (Matthew 12:1).

Leviticus 2:15, 16
And thou shalt put oil upon it, and lay frankincense thereon: it is a meat offering. And the priest shall burn the memorial of it, part of the beaten corn thereof, and part of the oil thereof, with all the frankincense thereof: it is an offering made by fire unto the LORD.

Why did God choose burnt offerings and meal offerings to illustrate His Son? What would you have chosen? Sports? Technology? Anything we choose would not be understood by other cultures or by those living in other times in history. Like the tabernacle itself, every culture at any time in history can relate to barbequed beef and lamb, cakes and bread, roasted ears of corn. God chose to use things common not just to Americans in the twenty-first century, but to everyone around the globe throughout history. Such is the genius of our Father.

3 If the burnt offering spoke of Christ's total dedication and the meal offering of His absolute perfection, the peace offering before us speaks of Christ our Peace and Satisfaction . . .

Leviticus 3:1, 2
And if his oblation be a sacrifice of peace offering, if he offer it of the herd; whether it be a male or female, he shall offer it without blemish before the LORD. And he shall lay his hand upon the head of his offering, and kill it at the door of the tabernacle of the congregation: and Aaron's sons the priests shall sprinkle the blood upon the altar round about.

Just as the man bringing the burnt offering was to lay his hand upon the head of the animal as a sign of identification, so the one bringing an animal as a peace offering was to personally claim the peace and satisfaction only God can bring—ultimately fulfilled in Jesus, the One who would Himself be our peace (Ephesians 2:14).

Leviticus 3:3–15
And he shall offer of the sacrifice of the peace offering an offering made by fire unto the LORD; the fat that covereth the inwards, and all the fat that is upon the inwards, and the two kidneys, and the fat that is on them, which is by the flanks, and the caul above the liver, with the kidneys, it shall he take away. And Aaron's sons shall burn it on the altar upon the burnt sacrifice, which is upon the wood that is on the fire: it is an offering made by fire, of a sweet savour unto the LORD. And if his offering for a sacrifice of peace offering unto the LORD be of the flock; male or female, he shall offer it without blemish. If he offer a lamb for his offering, then shall he offer it before the LORD. And he shall lay his hand upon the head of his offering, and kill it before the tabernacle of the congregation: and Aaron's sons shall sprinkle the blood thereof round about upon the altar. And he shall offer of the sacrifice of the peace offering an offering made by fire unto the LORD; the fat thereof, and the whole rump, it shall he take off hard by the backbone; and the fat that covereth the inwards, and all the fat that is upon the inwards, and the two kidneys, and the fat that is upon them, which is by the flanks, and the caul above the liver, with the kidneys, it shall he take away. And the priest shall burn it upon the altar: it is the food of the offering made by fire unto the LORD. And if his offering be a goat, then he shall offer it before the LORD. And he shall lay his hand upon the head of it, and kill it before the tabernacle of the congregation: and the sons of Aaron shall sprinkle the blood thereof upon the altar round about. And he shall offer thereof his offering, even an offering made by fire unto the LORD; the fat that covereth the inwards, and all the fat that is upon the inwards, and the two kidneys, and the fat that is upon them, which is by the flanks, and the caul above the liver, with the kidneys, it shall he take away.

As we will see in chapter 7, the peace offering was the one offering in which three parties partook: the man who brought the offering, the priest, and the Lord Himself. Thus, the peace offering uniquely speaks of fellowship, and relationship.

Again, I believe this is highly emblematic of Communion, for at the Lord's Table, we experience a unique time of fellowship not only with the Lord, but with our "fellow priests" (1 Peter 2:9) as we eat of His body and drink of His blood. How I would encourage you to establish this practice in your life. You truly have peace with God through Jesus Christ (Romans 5:1). All that remains is for you to believe and receive it. The argument of the enemy will always be that God is upset with you, that you haven't been doing this or that, that you've missed the mark here or there. But it's all a lie. If you have received Jesus' gift of salvation, if you have embraced His finished work on the Cross on your behalf, you have peace with God tonight. The work is complete. Nothing more can be added to it. So celebrate what He's done.

Nothing smells better than a barbeque. As this peace offering was being prepared, surely the aroma would make everyone's mouth water. Spiritually, there is nothing more pleasant than the Lord's Table. And it makes my spiritual mouth water as I realize Jesus is my peace Offering.

Leviticus 3:16, 17

And the priest shall burn them upon the altar: it is the food of the offering made by fire for a sweet savour: all the fat is the LORD's. It shall be a perpetual statute for your generations throughout all your dwellings, that ye eat neither fat nor blood.

In ancient cultures, the fat was considered to be the best part of the animal. Therefore, think of all the people throughout the centuries who read this and thought that the Lord was taking the best part for Himself—when, in reality, He was keeping men from the one part of the animal that causes clogged arteries and heart attacks.

"Why must we have only one partner sexually?" we say.

"I'm saving you from heartbreak, disease, and misery," God answers.

"Why must I give the tithe to You?" we say.

"Because I'm protecting you from the disease of greediness," God answers.

"Why do You get the fat?" we ask.

"So you won't be," God says. "As time goes on—and ultimately when you get to heaven, you'll see everything I did was for your good."

Precious people, everything God does is based on love, for He is love itself. We might not understand this right now, but as time goes on, we'll see a reason for everything He did in our lives, the reason that He kept the fat for Himself.

4 While the burnt offering, the meal offering, and the peace offering were voluntary offerings, the sin offering here in chapter 4 and the trespass offering seen in chapter 5 were mandatory.

Leviticus 4:1–3

And the LORD spake unto Moses, saying, Speak unto the children of Israel, saying, If a soul shall sin through ignorance against any of the commandments of the LORD concerning things which ought not to be done, and shall do against any of them: If the priest that is anointed do sin according to the sin of the people; then let him bring for his sin, which he hath sinned, a young bullock without blemish unto the LORD for a sin offering.

"If we say that we have not sinned, we make God a liar," John declares (1 John 1:10). We may indeed sin through ignorance. But we cannot claim ignorance of the sin nature inherent within each of us,

Leviticus 4:4–11

And he shall bring the bullock unto the door of the tabernacle of the congregation before the LORD; and shall lay his hand upon the bullock's head, and kill the bullock before the LORD. And the priest that is anointed shall take of the bullock's blood, and bring it to the tabernacle of the congregation: And the priest shall dip his finger in the blood, and sprinkle of the blood seven times before the LORD, before the vail of the sanctuary. And the priest shall put some of the blood upon the horns of the altar of sweet incense before the LORD, which is in the tabernacle of the congregation: and shall pour all the blood of the bullock at the bottom of the altar of the burnt offering, which is at the door of the tabernacle of the congregation. And he shall take off from it all the fat of the bullock for the sin offering; the fat that covereth the inwards, and all the fat that is upon the inwards, and the two kidneys, and the fat that is upon them, which is by the flanks, and the caul above the liver, with the kidneys, it shall he take away, as it was taken off from the bullock of the sacrifice of peace offerings: and the priest shall burn them upon the altar of the burnt offering. And the skin of the bullock, and all his flesh, with his head, and with his legs, and his inwards, and his dung,

Again, as with the burnt offering and peace offering, we see the laying of a hand upon the sacrifice as a sign of identification with the deadly consequence of sin. Sin kills physically, mentally, morally, and spiritually. The stench of death surrounds everything sin touches. Thus, it was literally our sin placed upon the Lamb of God that killed Him.

Leviticus 4:12
Even the whole bullock shall he carry forth without the camp unto a clean place, where the ashes are poured out, and burn him on the wood with fire: where the ashes are poured out shall he be burnt.

The sin offering was to be taken out of the camp because when Christ, the One who knew no sin, was made sin for us, He was offered outside Jerusalem on the hill of Calvary.

Leviticus 4:13, 14
And if the whole congregation of Israel sin through ignorance, and the thing be hid from the eyes of the assembly, and they have done somewhat against any of the commandments of the LORD concerning things which should not be done, and are guilty; when the sin, which they have sinned against it, is known, then the congregation shall offer a young bullock for the sin, and bring him before the tabernacle of the congregation.

The price for the sin of a priest was the same as the price for an entire nation. And because we are a royal priesthood (1 Peter 2:9), if we drop the ball, if we fail in our calling, the whole nation is affected. We might bemoan the condition of our country, but the reality is, Jesus told us we are the salt of the earth. And if the salt loses its savor, there will not be the seasoning, the preservation, the healing there ought to be (Matthew 5:13).

Leviticus 4:15–21
And the elders of the congregation shall lay their hands upon the head of the head of the bullock before the LORD: and the bullock shall be killed before the LORD. And the priest that is anointed shall bring of the bullock's blood to the tabernacle of the congregation: And the priest shall dip his finger in some of the blood, and sprinkle it seven times before the LORD, even before the vail. And he shall put some of the blood upon the horns of the altar which is before the LORD, that is in the tabernacle of the congregation, and shall pour out all the blood at the bottom of the altar of the burnt offering, which is at the door of the tabernacle of the congregation. And he shall take all his fat from him, and burn it upon the altar. And he shall do with the bullock as he did with the bullock for a sin offering, so shall he do with this: and the priest shall make an atonement for them, and it shall be forgiven them. And he shall carry forth the bullock without the camp, and burn him as he burned the first bullock: it is a sin offering for the congregation.

When the congregation sinned, the elders were to lay hands on the sacrifice, thereby accepting responsibility for the sin of the entire congregation. No wonder James warns, "Let not many of you desire to be teachers, knowing you have the greater judgment" (3:1).

Leviticus 4:22–30
When a ruler hath sinned, and done somewhat through ignorance against any of the commandments of the LORD his God concerning things which should not be done, and is guilty; or if his sin, wherein he hath sinned, come to his knowledge; he shall bring his offering, a kid of the goats, a male without blemish: And he shall lay his hand upon the head of the goat, and kill it in the place where they kill the burnt offering before the LORD: it is a sin offering. And the priest shall take of the blood of the sin offering with his finger, and put it upon the horns of the altar of burnt offering, and shall pour out his blood at the bottom of the altar of burnt offering. And he shall burn all his fat upon the altar, as the fat of the sacrifice of peace offerings: and the priest shall make an atonement for him as concerning his sin, and it shall be forgiven him. And if any one of the common people sin through ignorance, while he doeth somewhat against any of the commandments of the LORD concerning things which ought not to be done, and be guilty; Or if his sin, which he hath sinned, come to his knowledge: then he shall bring his offering, a kid of the goats, a female without blemish, for his sin which he hath sinned. And he shall lay his hand upon the head of the sin offering, and slay the sin offering in the place of the burnt offering. And the priest shall take of the blood thereof with his finger, and put it upon the horns of the altar of burnt offering, and shall pour out all the blood thereof at the bottom of the altar.

Although a ruler was required to offer a male goat for his sin and a common person a female goat, the sacrifice of a priest was the same as the sacrifice of the entire nation. Such is the enormity of the responsibility for those in positions of leadership in God's economy.

Leviticus 4:31–35
And he shall take away all the fat thereof, as the fat is taken away from off the sacrifice of peace offerings; and the priest shall burn it upon the altar for a sweet savour unto the LORD; and the priest shall make an atonement for him, and it shall be forgiven him. And if he bring a lamb for a sin offering, he

shall bring it a female without blemish. And he shall lay his hand upon the head of the sin offering, and slay it for a sin offering in the place where they kill the burnt offering. And the priest shall take of the blood of the sin offering with his finger, and put it upon the horns of the altar of burnt offering, and shall pour out all the blood thereof at the bottom of the altar: And he shall take away all the fat thereof, as the fat of the lamb is taken away from the sacrifice of the peace offerings; and the priest shall burn them upon the altar, according to the offerings made by fire unto the LORD: and the priest shall make an atonement for his sin that he hath committed, and it shall be forgiven him.

The purpose of the sin offering was atonement. The word translated "atonement" here in Leviticus is the Hebrew word *kaphar,* whose root meaning is "to cover." We see the first use of this word in Genesis 6:14, where Noah was instructed to pitch—or cover—the ark within and without with pitch. The Greek word translated "atonement" in the New Testament, however, is *katallage,* which means not "to cover," but "to reconcile."

> For if, when we were enemies, we were reconciled to God by the death of his Son, much more, being reconciled, we shall be saved by his life. And not only so, but we also joy in God through our Lord Jesus Christ, by whom we have now received the atonement. Romans 5:10, 11

Oh, how great is our privilege as New Testament believers of having our sins not only covered, but *cleansed* by the blood of the Lamb (1 John 1:7).

5 The offering before us in chapter 5 is the trespass offering, different from the sin offering in that it deals with specific sins rather than the sin nature, with the acts of sin rather than the fact of sin. When Christ died, He died for the sin nature of mankind. But even as He hung on the Cross, He said, "Father forgive them," referring to the specific sin of those crucifying Him (Luke 23:34).

Leviticus 5:1
And if a soul sin, and hear the voice of swearing, and is a witness, whether he hath seen or known of it; if he do not utter it, then he shall bear his iniquity.

To "hear the voice of swearing" meaning to be under oath, the first sin on the list of trespasses is lying under oath, playing games with the truth.

Leviticus 5:2–4
Or if a soul touch any unclean thing, whether it be a carcase of an unclean beast, or a carcase of unclean cattle, or the carcase of unclean creeping things, and if it be hidden from him; he also shall be unclean, and guilty. Or if he touch the uncleanness of man, whatsoever uncleanness it be that a man shall be defiled withal, and it be hid from him; when he knoweth of it, then he shall be guilty. Or if a soul swear, pronouncing with his lips to do evil, or to do good, whatsoever it be that a man shall pronounce with an oath, and it be hid from him; when he knoweth of it, then he shall be guilty in one of these.

If I were God and were singling out trespasses, lying under oath or finding loopholes in contracts would not be at the top of my list. But because God sees differently than we do, it seems as though He is saying that compromise in our speech opens the door to a whole series of problems in our lives.

Leviticus 5:5
And it shall be, when he shall be guilty in one of these things, that he shall confess that he hath sinned in that thing:

Because God's demand for forgiveness was met fully and completely when Jesus died for our sins, confession is not for God's sake but for ours—that we might be free from the burden of guilt and condemnation which would otherwise plague us.

For topical study of Leviticus 5:1–5 entitled "True Confession," turn to page 375.

Leviticus 5:6–10
And he shall bring his trespass offering unto the LORD for his sin which he hath sinned, a female from the flock, a lamb or a kid of the goats, for a sin offering; and the priest shall make an atonement for him concerning his sin. And if he be not able to bring a lamb, then he shall bring for his trespass, which he hath committed, two turtledoves, or two young pigeons, unto the LORD; one for a sin offering, and the other for a burnt offering. And he shall bring them unto the priest, who shall offer that which is for the sin offering first, and wring off his head from his neck, but shall not divide it asunder: And he shall sprinkle of the blood of the sin offering upon the side of the altar; and the rest of the blood shall be wrung out at the bottom of the altar: it is a sin offering.

And he shall offer the second for a burnt offering, according to the manner: and the priest shall make an atonement for him for his sin which he hath sinned, and it shall be forgiven him.

"I'm poor," people say. "Poor me. I can't pay my bills. I can't afford a lamb." But God says no one gets off the hook, for if someone was too poor to bring a lamb or a goat, two pigeons would suffice.

Leviticus 5:11–13
But if he be not able to bring two turtledoves, or two young pigeons, then he that sinned shall bring for his offering the tenth part of an ephah of fine flour for a sin offering; he shall put no oil upon it, neither shall he put any frankincense thereon: for it is a sin offering. Then shall he bring it to the priest, and the priest shall take his handful of it, even a memorial thereof, and burn it on the altar, according to the offerings made by fire unto the LORD: it is a sin offering. And the priest shall make an atonement for him as touching his sin that he hath sinned in one of these, and it shall be forgiven him: and the remnant shall be the priest's, as a meat offering.

He who couldn't afford two pigeons was simply to bring some flour. God provided a way for even the poorest person to offer a trespass offering.

Leviticus 5:14–19
And the LORD spake unto Moses, saying, If a soul commit a trespass, and sin through ignorance, in the holy things of the LORD; then he shall bring for his trespass unto the LORD a ram without blemish out of the flocks, with thy estimation by shekels of silver, after the shekel of the sanctuary, for a trespass offering: And he shall make amends for the harm that he hath done in the holy thing, and shall add the fifth part thereto, and give it unto the priest: and the priest shall make an atonement for him with the ram of the trespass offering, and it shall be forgiven him. And if a soul sin, and commit any of these things which are forbidden to be done by the commandments of the LORD; though he wist it not, yet is he guilty, and shall bear his iniquity. And he shall bring a ram without blemish out of the flock, with thy estimation, for a trespass offering, unto the priest: and the priest shall make an atonement for him concerning his ignorance wherein he erred and wist it not, and it shall be forgiven him. It is a trespass offering: he hath certainly trespassed against the LORD.

Because man can never make restitution to God for his sin nature, no restitution was required with the sin offering. The trespass offering, however, offered for specific acts of sin, carried with it a penalty of twenty percent to be paid to the person wronged. This wasn't given to punish God's people, but to liberate them from the guilt we needlessly bear whenever we fail to deal openly and candidly with those we have wronged. That is why Jesus said if we even know our brother has something against us, we're to make it right before continuing in worship (Matthew 5:23, 24). It is a loving Father who tells us that restitution is required in order that relationship might be restored.

TRUE CONFESSION

A Topical Study of LEVITICUS 5:1–5

The Church of Jesus Christ is the only organization whose members describe themselves as wretches. And while some say we as Christians have an obsession with sin, in reality, we simply have a proper assessment of self. We realize that man is intrinsically, hopelessly, fundamentally selfish. But praise be to God, He has provided a solution for our sinfulness and selfishness in Jesus Christ—for as we see in the Book of Leviticus, He is the fulfillment of the sacrifices, His is the blood which not only covers our sin temporarily but cleanses it completely.

Yet, although I understand theologically that my sin is forgiven, sometimes I don't feel it personally. Realizing this would happen, the Father graciously provided a very practical tool to help alleviate the weight of guilt and condemnation we can sometimes feel. The name of this tool is confession.

Confession is an important element of forgiveness not because God needs us to confess, but because we need to confess. And nowhere do we see confession more powerfully, practically, or personally portrayed than in the life of the man after God's own heart, the sweet Psalmist of Israel, David.

In 2 Samuel chapters 11 and 12, we read that, after choosing to remain in Jerusalem rather than join his men in battle, after having an affair with another man's wife, after killing her husband to cover his tracks, David was finally brought to the point where he said, "I have sinned against the Lord." And in Psalm 51, as David pours his heart out to the Lord, we see what true confession really is . . .

A Right View of Sin

Have mercy upon me, O God, according to thy lovingkindness: according unto the multitude of thy tender mercies blot out my transgressions. Wash me thoroughly from mine iniquity, and cleanse me from my sin. For I acknowledge my transgressions: and my sin is ever before me. Against thee, thee only, have I sinned, and done this evil in thy sight: that thou mightest be justified when thou speakest, and be clear when thou judgest. Behold, I was shapen in iniquity; and in sin did my mother conceive me. Psalm 51:1–5

A right view of sin begins with the understanding that sin deserves judgment because sin always brings about heartache and hurt, death and destruction. David's sin began with a seemingly harmless peek at Bathsheba—but it ended in murder. God hates even so-called innocent, victimless sins because He knows where those sins will lead. And because He knows they will destroy us, He refuses to allow sin to go unchecked in the lives of His children.

Secondly, a right view of sin declares guilt. When we sin, there is a tendency to want to pass the proverbial buck. "The woman You gave me gave me of the tree," Adam said, blaming Eve and ultimately blaming God (Genesis 3:12). Adam's attitude has permeated every one of us. We all have a tendency to want to blame someone else—or, if need be, God—for our sin.

Thirdly, a right view of sin descends from Adam. The psychologist is wrong: babies are not born with a blank page that becomes polluted by his surroundings. The Word says we are born in sin. We're not sinners because we sin. We sin because we're sinners. And David understood this.

A Right View of God

Behold, thou desirest truth in the inward parts: and in the hidden part thou shalt make me to know wisdom. Purge me with hyssop, and I shall be clean: wash me, and I shall be whiter than snow. Make me to hear joy and gladness;

> *that the bones which thou hast broken may rejoice. Hide thy face from my sins, and blot out all mine iniquities. Create in me a clean heart, O God; and renew a right spirit within me. Cast me not away from thy presence; and take not thy holy spirit from me. Restore unto me the joy of thy salvation; and uphold me with thy free spirit.* Psalm 51:6–12

David had a right view of God's purity. God desires purity in the inward parts, not the outward actions. A person can have all sorts of outward purity while remaining inwardly defiled. Blessed are the pure *in heart* Jesus said, for they shall see God (Matthew 5:8). A right view of God begins with purity.

Secondly, David had a right view of God's power. God is so incredibly powerful that He not only says, "forgive you and cleanse you," but also, "I will remember your sins no more." He has chosen to remove my sin from His memory bank. No other being in this universe has the power to do this.

Thirdly, David had a right view of God's punishment. "Make me hear joy and gladness," he says, "that the bones You have broken may rejoice." The metaphor is one with which David, being a shepherd, was familiar. You see, if a lamb displayed a propensity to endanger himself by wandering away from the flock, the shepherd would break its legs, put splints upon them, and carry the lamb on his shoulders until the bones were healed. As a result, so closely would the lamb bond with the shepherd during the period of recovery that when its legs were healed, it remained close to the shepherd all the days of his life.

Sometimes our Good Shepherd will break us. "Ouch!" we say. "What are You doing?" But in our brokenness and pain, we find ourselves drawing closer to Jesus than we ever would have otherwise.

A Right View of Self

> *Then will I teach transgressors thy ways; and sinners shall be converted unto thee. Deliver me from bloodguiltiness, O God, thou God of my salvation: and my tongue shall sing aloud of thy righteousness. O Lord, open thou my lips; and my mouth shall shew forth thy praise. For thou desirest not sacrifice; else would I give it: thou delightest not in burnt offering. The sacrifices of God are a broken spirit: a broken and a contrite heart, O God, thou wilt not despise. Do good in thy good pleasure unto Zion: build thou the walls of Jerusalem. Then shalt thou be pleased with the sacrifices of righteousness, with burnt offering and whole burnt offering: then shall they offer bullocks upon thine altar.* Psalm 51:13–19

David understood he must confess his sin for sinner's sake—for it was only when his sin was confessed and his joy restored that he could teach transgressors God's ways, that sinners would be converted. If we harbor unconfessed sin, the result will undoubtedly be spiritual lockjaw. We won't witness; we won't share God's

Word with people; we won't be bold because to do so would be hypocritical. But when sin is confessed, joy overflows and we can't help but share the goodness of God with others.

David knew he must confess his sins for God's sake. "To what purpose is the multitude of your sacrifices unto me? saith the Lord: I am full of the burnt offerings of rams, and the fat of fed beasts; and I delight not in the blood of bullocks, or of lambs, or of he goats" (Isaiah 1:11). It's an abomination to the Lord for me to worship, praise, pray if there is unconfessed sin in my life.

Finally, David knew he must confess sin for the saints' sake. "Do good in thy good pleasure to Zion," he prayed. "Build thou the walls of Jerusalem." If I harbor unconfessed sin in my life, the walls will not be established, God's people will not be fortified, my prayers will not be answered.

In light of the necessity of confession, consider with me the following six ways we can make it practical . . .

Confess immediately. Don't wait until the end of the day, the end of the week, the end of the month. Not only will that keep you out of the flow of God's fullness, but you'll forget what it is you want to confess. Keep your accounts current. When you sin, confess immediately.

Confess specifically. Even as an individual's hand had to be placed upon the ram, so sin must be dealt with specifically.

Confess with sensitivity. I need to realize that it was *my* sin that brought about the death of the Lamb of God on Calvary. In this regard, Communion is essential because it keeps us sensitive.

Confess realistically. Concerning any specific sin, God never tells us to promise never to do it again. Because in us dwells no good thing (Romans 7:18), to promise not to commit a particular sin is unrealistic. The Greek word translated "confess" is *homologeo,* which simply means "to say the same." Thus, confession means that, rather than call lying "stretching the truth," we call it sin. It means rather than call gossiping "sharing a prayer request," we call it sin. It means rather than calling losing our temper "having a short fuse," we call it sin—just as God does.

Finally, sometimes confession needs to be made openly. James 5 says we are to confess our faults one to another. If you know you're forgiven, but can't get victory over a certain sin, share it with another believer—for not only will he be able to remind you that, on the basis of God's Word, your sin is forgiven, but as you become linked to him through honest accountability, you will be less likely to continue on in secret sins.

Confession is indeed good for the soul—a tremendous tool, a purifying power, a gracious gift from a loving Father.

6 Chapter 6 continues with the subject of the trespass offering . . .

Leviticus 6:1–7
And the LORD spake unto Moses, saying, If a soul sin, and commit a trespass against the LORD, and lie unto his neighbour in that which was delivered him to keep, or in fellowship, or in a thing taken away by violence, or hath deceived his neighbour; or have found that which was lost, and lieth concerning it, and sweareth falsely; in any of all these that a man doeth, sinning therein: Then it shall be, because he hath sinned, and is guilty, that he shall restore that which he took violently away, or the thing which he hath deceitfully gotten, or that which was delivered him to keep, or the lost thing which he found, Or all that about which he hath sworn falsely; he shall even restore it in the principal, and shall add the fifth part more thereto, and give it unto him to whom it appertaineth, in the day of his trespass offering. And he shall bring his trespass offering unto the LORD, a ram without blemish out of the flock, with thy estimation, for a trespass offering, unto the priest: And the priest shall make an atonement for him before the LORD: and it shall be forgiven him for any thing of all that he hath done in trespassing therein.

On the Cross, Jesus paid the price for the time we cheated on our income tax or short-changed a business partner. But because God chastens those He loves (Hebrews 12:6), He requires we pay an additional twenty percent to those we have wronged in order that we would learn not to do it again.

Leviticus 6:8–12 (a)
And the LORD spake unto Moses, saying, Command Aaron and his sons, saying, This is the law of the burnt offering: It is the burnt offering, because of the burning upon the altar all night unto the morning, and the fire of the altar shall be burning in it. And the priest shall put on his linen garment, and his linen breeches shall he put upon his flesh, and take up the ashes which the fire hath consumed with the burnt offering on the altar, and he shall put them beside the altar. And he shall put off his garments, and put on other garments, and carry forth the ashes without the camp unto a clean place. And the fire upon the altar shall be burning in it; it shall not be put out:

The fire on the altar was never to go out. Has the fire that once blazed in your heart and radiated from your life concerning the things of God been somewhat quenched? If so, go back to the Lord and offer Him your body as a burnt offering morning and evening. Dedicate yourself anew to Him and once again He will ignite your soul. Go for it in your witness, in your worship, in your work for Him. And light the darkness once again.

Leviticus 6:12 (b), 13
. . . and the priest shall burn wood on it every morning, and lay the burnt offering in order upon it; and he shall burn thereon the fat of the peace offerings. The fire shall ever be burning upon the altar; it shall never go out.

We will burn for the Lord through the burnt offering of sacrifice only to the degree that we share with Him the peace offering of fellowship. I can't help but wonder how many of the children of Israel took the Lord up on His invitation to celebrate and commune with Him over the peace offering. But then, I wonder how many of us accept His invitation to dine with Him at the Table of Communion . . .

Leviticus 6:14–23
And this is the law of the meat offering: the sons of Aaron shall offer it before the LORD, before the altar. And he shall take of it his handful, of the flour of the meat offering, and of the oil thereof, and all the frankincense which is upon the meat offering, and shall burn it upon the altar for a sweet savour, even the memorial of it, unto the LORD. And the remainder thereof shall Aaron and his sons eat: with unleavened bread shall it be eaten in the holy place; in the court of the tabernacle of the congregation they shall eat it. It shall not be baken with leaven. I have given it unto them for their portion of my offerings made by fire; it is most holy, as is the sin offering, and as the trespass offering. All the males among the children of Aaron shall eat of it. It shall be a statute for ever in your generations concerning the offerings of the LORD made by fire: every one that toucheth them shall be holy. And the LORD spake unto Moses, saying, This is the offering of Aaron and of his sons, which they shall offer unto the LORD in the day when he is anointed; the tenth part of an ephah of fine flour for a meat offering perpetual, half of it in the morning, and half thereof at night. In a pan it shall be made with oil; and when it is baken, thou shalt bring it in: and the baken pieces of the meat offering shalt thou offer for a sweet savour unto the LORD. And the priest of his sons that is anointed in his

stead shall offer it: it is a statute for ever unto the LORD, it shall be wholly burnt. For every meat offering for the priest shall be wholly burnt: it shall not be eaten.

As with the sin and trespass offerings, the meal offering, in addition to providing a sweet-smelling savor to God, would help support those in His service.

Leviticus 6:24–30
And the LORD spake unto Moses, saying, Speak unto Aaron and to his sons, saying, This is the law of the sin offering: In the place where the burnt offering is killed shall the sin offering be killed before the LORD: it is most holy. The priest that offereth it for sin shall eat it: in the holy place shall it be eaten, in the court of the tabernacle of the congregation. Whatsoever shall touch the flesh thereof shall be holy: and when there is sprinkled of the blood thereof upon any garment, thou shalt wash that whereon it was sprinkled in the holy place. But the earthen vessel wherein it is sodden shall be broken: and if it be sodden in a brasen pot, it shall be both scoured, and rinsed in water. All the males among the priests shall eat thereof: it is most holy. And no sin offering, whereof any of the blood is brought into the tabernacle of the congregation to reconcile withal in the holy place, shall be eaten: it shall be burnt in the fire.

Because we are earthen vessels (2 Corinthians 4:7), brokenness occurs when sin is dealt with. "Godly sorrow works repentance," Paul declares (2 Corinthians 7:10). Therefore, if there is not brokenness or repentance, the issue of sin hasn't really been dealt with. A lot of times, people are sad only because they get caught sinning. But to truly turn *away* from sin requires nothing less than brokenness.

7 Leviticus 7:1–10
Likewise this is the law of the trespass offering: it is most holy. In the place where they kill the burnt offering shall they kill the trespass offering: and the blood thereof shall he sprinkle round about upon the altar. And he shall offer of it all the fat thereof; the rump, and the fat that covereth the inwards, And the two kidneys, and the fat that is on them, which is by the flanks, and the caul that is above the liver, with the kidneys, it shall he take away: And the priest shall burn them upon the altar for an offering made by fire unto the LORD: it is a trespass offering. Every male among the priests shall eat thereof: it shall be eaten in the holy place: it is most holy. As the sin offering is, so is the trespass offering: there is one law for them: the priest that maketh atonement therewith shall have it. And the priest that offereth any man's burnt offering, even the priest shall have to himself the skin of the burnt offering which he hath offered. And all the meat offering that is baken in the oven, and all that is dressed in the fryingpan, and in the pan, shall be the priest's that offereth it. And every meat offering, mingled with oil, and dry, shall all the sons of Aaron have, one as much as another.

Here we see further instructions concerning the trespass, burnt, and meal offerings—particularly the portion of which was to be given to the priests.

Leviticus 7:11–12
And this is the law of the sacrifice of peace offerings, which he shall offer unto the LORD. If he offer it for a thanksgiving, then he shall offer with the sacrifice of thanksgiving unleavened cakes mingled with oil, and unleavened wafers anointed with oil, and cakes mingled with oil, of fine flour, fried.

The invitation is to come and express thanks to the Lord, to be unleavened—without sin, and to be mingled with oil—to come in the Spirit.

Leviticus 7:13
Besides the cakes, he shall offer for his offering leavened bread with the sacrifice of thanksgiving of his peace offerings.

Is the leavened bread seen here in verse 13 a contradiction of the unleavened bread spoken of in verse 12? No, leaven being a picture of sin, what's being said here is that, although we're not to justify our sin, neither are we to hold back because of it. In other words, we're not to say, "I can't offer the sacrifice of praise because I've been grouchy today," or, "I can't bring my tithe to the Lord because, as a cashier, I earned some of it by selling alcohol." No, bring your sacrifice anyway. We'll see a sacrifice which will consist of two loaves of leavened bread waved before the Lord (Leviticus 23:17) as a picture of Jews and Gentiles—sinful as each group was—being brought together into a new entity: the forgiven church.

Leviticus 7:14–18
And of it he shall offer one out of the whole oblation for an heave offering unto the LORD, and it shall be the priest's that sprinkleth the blood of the peace offerings. And the flesh of the sacrifice of his peace offerings for thanksgiving shall be eaten the same day that it is offered; he shall not leave any of it until the morning. But if the sacrifice of his offering be a vow, or a voluntary offering, it shall be eaten the same day that he offereth his sacrifice: and on the morrow also the remainder of it shall be eaten: But the remainder of the flesh of the sacrifice on the third day shall be burnt with fire. And if any of the flesh of the sacrifice of his peace offerings be eaten at all on the third day, it shall not be accepted, neither shall it be imputed unto him that offereth it: it shall be an abomination, and the soul that eateth of it shall bear his iniquity.

When the peace offering was brought before the Lord, it was to be eaten immediately. "Oh, taste and see that the Lord is good," the psalmist proclaimed (Psalm 34:8).

"Ho, everyone that thirsteth, come ye to the water. He that hath no money come buy and eat," the prophet declared (Isaiah 55:1).

"Come and dine," Jesus invited.

Leviticus 7:19–27
And the flesh that toucheth any unclean thing shall not be eaten; it shall be burnt with fire: and as for the flesh, all that be clean shall eat thereof. But the soul that eateth of the flesh of the sacrifice of peace offerings, that pertain unto the LORD, having his uncleanness upon him, even that soul shall be cut off from his people. Moreover the soul that shall touch any unclean thing, as the uncleanness of man, or any unclean beast, or any abominable unclean thing, and eat of the flesh of the sacrifice of peace offerings, which pertain unto the LORD, even that soul shall be cut off from his people. And the LORD spake unto Moses, saying, Speak unto the children of Israel, saying, Ye shall eat no manner of fat, of ox, or of sheep, or of goat. And the fat of the beast that dieth of itself, and the fat of that which is torn with beasts, may be used in any other use: but ye shall in no wise eat of it. For whosoever eateth the fat of the beast, of which men offer an offering made by fire unto the LORD, even the soul that eateth it shall be cut off from his people. Moreover ye shall eat no manner of blood, whether it be of fowl or of beast, in any of your dwellings. Whatsoever soul it be that eateth any manner of blood, even that soul shall be cut off from his people.

Aaron and his sons were to be given the shoulder and the breast of the peace offering because, as priests, they were to shoulder the burdens of, and have a heart for God's people.

Leviticus 7:28–38
And the LORD spake unto Moses, saying, Speak unto the children of Israel, saying, He that offereth the sacrifice of his peace offerings unto the LORD shall bring his oblation unto the LORD of the sacrifice of his peace offerings. His own hands shall bring the offerings of the LORD made by fire, the fat with the breast, it shall he bring, that the breast may be waved for a wave offering before the LORD. And the priest shall burn the fat upon the altar: but the breast shall be Aaron's and his sons.' And the right shoulder shall ye give unto the priest for an heave offering of the sacrifices of your peace offerings. He among the sons of Aaron, that offereth the blood of the peace offerings, and the fat, shall have the right shoulder for his part. For the wave breast and the heave shoulder have I taken of the children of Israel from off the sacrifices of their peace offerings, and have given them unto Aaron the priest and unto his sons by a statute for ever from among the children of Israel. This is the portion of the anointing of Aaron, and of the anointing of his sons, out of the offerings of the LORD made by fire, in the day when he presented them to minister unto the LORD in the priest's office; which the LORD commanded to be given them of the children of Israel, in the day that he anointed them, by a statute for ever throughout their generations. This is the law of the burnt offering, of the meat offering, and of the sin offering, and of the trespass offering, and of the consecrations, and of the sacrifice of the peace offerings; Which the LORD commanded Moses in mount Sinai, in the day that he commanded the children of Israel to offer their oblations unto the LORD, in the wilderness of Sinai.

At the end of this review of the five sacrifices, notice the portrayal of the life of Christ from His baptism to His Crucifixion . . .

In the burnt offering, we see Christ's baptism, for both speak of total dedication. In the meal offering, we see Jesus being tempted, for both show an absence of leaven, an absence of sin. In the peace offering, we see Jesus embarking on public ministry, for both proclaim speak of the good tidings of the gospel. At the Cross, we see the sin and trespass offerings, as Jesus died not only for our sin nature, but also for our specific acts of sin.

I find it interesting, however, that in the life of the believer, the sacrifices are illustrated in reverse order . . .

A person gets saved when he realizes he has trespassed. Then he discovers he sins because he's a sinner, because he has a sin nature. He confesses his sin, asks the Lord into His life, and communes with God through the peace offering—at the Lord's Table. Then he says, "Refine me, Lord. Take out the lumps and the leaven in my life." And finally, he says, "Don't only sift me, but consume me, Lord. I'm laying my life down as a burnt offering. I want to be consumed by You."

Where are you in this process? The further you choose to go, the happier you'll be. I can guarantee this because Jesus did when He told us it's when we lose our life that we truly find it (Matthew 10:39).

8 The first seven chapters of the Book of Leviticus deal with sacrifices. Chapter 8 deals with Aaron and his sons, the priests. As sinners, we need a Sacrifice; as believers, a High Priest. And we have both in Jesus, the Lamb of God and our great High Priest . . .

Leviticus 8:1–4
And the LORD spake unto Moses, saying, Take Aaron and his sons with him, and the garments, and the anointing oil, and a bullock for the sin offering, and two rams, and a basket of unleavened bread; and gather thou all the congregation together unto the door of the tabernacle of the congregation. And Moses did as the LORD commanded him; and the assembly was gathered together unto the door of the tabernacle of the congregation.

There is about to be a presentation of the priests. But before there can be presentation, there must first be preparation. That's always the way it is . . .

- God prepared Moses for eighty years—forty years as a prince in the courts of Pharaoh, forty years as a shepherd on the backside of the desert—before calling him to lead His people away from Pharaoh and to shepherd them across the wilderness.
- God prepared Paul for three years in the desert of Arabia before calling Him to take the gospel to the Gentiles.
- God prepared Jesus for thirty years through submission to His earthly parents. As a result, He grew in favor with both God and man (Luke 2:52).

To you, who, like me, want to be used by God, I would say as did Zechariah, "Don't despise the day of small things" (4:10). You may be on the backside of the desert, going through boring times or difficult situations, but know this: It's all part of God's preparation.

Leviticus 8:5, 6
And Moses said unto the congregation, This is the thing which the LORD commanded to be done. And Moses brought Aaron and his sons, and washed them with water.

How does the Lord prepare us for service? The first thing that happens is we must be washed with water. Ephesians 5 identifies water as the Word of God. "Now ye are clean through the Word which I have spoken unto you," Jesus declared (John 15:3). "Thy Word have I hid in my heart that I might not sin against Thee," David proclaimed (Psalm 119:11). The washing of the water of the Word cleanses our souls, purifies our spirits. That's why a person just can't get too much of Bible study. Even if you don't understand it all completely, even if you don't think it's making an impact, it is.

"When the Spirit comes, He shall bring to your remembrance all things I have spoken to you," Jesus promised (John 14:26). The work of the Holy Spirit is to remind us of the Word. He will not, however, be able to bring to our remembrance what we have not put in our memory. That's why we must read Leviticus, Ezekiel, and Haggai.

"But I don't get those books," you might protest. "They're boring."

Read them anyway because you're putting the Word in your soul, and in due season, at the right time, the Holy Spirit will put the pieces together in such a way that it will blow your mind.

Leviticus 8:7 (a)
And he put upon him the coat . . .

After being washed, Aaron was robed. According to Ezekiel (44:17, 18), God's servants were to wear linen rather than wool—garments which allowed them to be cool rather than those which caused them to sweat. That is why we don't see our great High Priest, Jesus Christ, panicked, frenzied, or crying in the streets (Isaiah 42:2).

There was a wonderful peace about Him because, although His ministry would cost Him His life, it was nonetheless linen to Him.

Leviticus 8:7 (b)
. . . and girded him with the girdle . . .

The girdle, or belt, speaks of service. Worn underneath the robe that was to follow, this girdle speaks of unseen service, of a heart simply willing to serve.

Leviticus 8:7 (c)
. . . and clothed him with the robe . . .

Along the hem of the robe of the high priest were alternating pomegranates and bells attached to a border of blue (Numbers 15:38). Blue speaks of heaven; the pomegranates of the fruit of the Spirit, the bells of the gifts of the Spirit. Our great High Priest is the Way to heaven, personifies the fruit of the Spirit, and ministers the gifts of the Spirit.

"The Spirit of the Lord God is upon me; because the Lord hath anointed me to preach good tidings unto the meek . . ." (Isaiah 61:1 (a)). This was the text of Jesus' first sermon. In the tenth verse of Isaiah 61, we read, "I will greatly rejoice in the Lord, my soul shall be joyful in my God; for he hath clothed me with the robe of righteousness." Surely, above all others, our great High Priest was clothed with the robe of righteousness—and yet He willingly laid aside this robe in exchange for the robe of scarlet placed upon Him by His enemies before they led Him to the Cross to die for my sin (Matthew 27:28).

Leviticus 8:7 (d)
. . . and put the ephod upon him . . .

The ephod speaks of authority. In Judges 8:24–27, we see a misuse of the ephod as it became a snare rather than a blessing to the people of Israel. Authority rightly used never draws people closer to a person or a program no matter how right or justified it might initially seem. Godly authority always draws people closer to God alone. That is why whenever Jesus ministered, the result was always singular: men glorified the Father (Luke 7:16).

Leviticus 8:7 (e)
. . . and he girded him with the curious girdle of the ephod, and bound it unto him therewith.

A "curious girdle" or belt, this time visible from the outside, held the ephod together because true authority always walks hand in hand with servanthood—seen nowhere more clearly than in the life of Jesus as He fed multitudes, touched lepers, washed feet.

Leviticus 8:8
And he put the breastplate upon him: also he put in the breastplate the Urim and the Thummim.

The breastplate contained the Urim and the Thummim which were used to determine the will of God. It also contained the gems that represented the Twelve Tribes of Israel. Not only does our great High Priest ever live to make intercession for us in order that we might know the way wherein we should walk, He also carries us as gems upon His heart

Leviticus 8:9
And he put the mitre upon his head; also upon the mitre, even upon his forefront, did he put the golden plate, the holy crown; as the LORD commanded Moses.

The golden plate and mitre speak of covering, of submission, of Jesus who was submitted completely to His Father (John 8:29).

Leviticus 8:10–12
And Moses took the anointing oil, and anointed the tabernacle and all that was therein, and sanctified them. And he sprinkled thereof upon the altar seven times, and anointed the altar and all his vessels, both the laver and his foot, to sanctify them. And he poured of the anointing oil upon Aaron's head, and anointed him, to sanctify him.

Not only was our great High Priest, Jesus Christ, anointed to preach good tidings unto the meek (Isaiah 61:1), But He was anointed with the oil of gladness above all His fellows (Hebrews 1:9). No wonder, then, that tax collectors and publicans loved to be with Him, that the common people heard Him gladly (Mark 12:37).

Leviticus 8:13 (a)
And Moses brought Aaron's sons . . .

As high priest, Aaron is a picture of our great High Priest, Jesus Christ. Aaron's sons, however, are a picture of you and me—a royal priesthood (1 Peter 2:9), and, by His grace, sons of God (John 1:12). While Aaron wore pomegranates and bells, gems and a gold plate, his sons were attired much more simply in only three items . . .

Leviticus 8:13 (b)
. . . and put coats upon them . . .

The coat, or linen garment, speaks of salvation. In Zechariah 3, we see a priest who stood before the Lord whose garments were filthy. "I will clothe them with change of raiment," the Lord declared.

- Which robe was placed on the prodigal upon his return?
  The best robe.
- Whose robe was the best?
  The father's.

When you accepted Jesus Christ, you were robed with the Father's best robe, for He robed you with His Son (Isaiah 61:10).

Leviticus 8:13 (c)
. . . and girded them with girdles . . .

The girdle, or belt, worn around the waist allowed the robes to be tucked in, freeing the legs for service.

Leviticus 8:13 (d)
. . . and put bonnets upon them; as the LORD commanded Moses.

Thirdly, we see the bonnets, or turbans, which speak of submission (1 Corinthians 11). In our priestly service, we're to be robed in Christ's righteousness. We're to be doing the work of service. And we're to be submitted to those who are over us. There is no room in the body of Christ for lone rangers or independent agents. There is to be linkage and submission, accountability and humility. You'll never be *in* authority unless you are *under* authority. And while it is easy to submit to those with whom I agree, it is when I submit to a decision with which I don't necessarily agree that a true spirit of submission and humility are worked within me.

Leviticus 8:14–24
And he brought the bullock for the sin offering: and Aaron and his sons laid their hands upon the head of the bullock for the sin offering. And he slew it; and Moses took the blood, and put it upon the horns of the altar round about with his finger, and purified the altar, and poured the blood at the bottom of the altar, and sanctified it, to make reconciliation upon it. And he took all the fat that was upon the inwards, and caul above the liver, and the two kidneys, and their fat, and Moses burned it upon the altar. But the bullock, and his hide, his flesh, and his dung, he burnt with fire without the camp; as the LORD commanded Moses. And he brought the ram for the burnt offering: and Aaron and his sons laid their hands upon the head of the ram. And he killed it; and Moses sprinkled the blood upon the altar round about. And he cut the ram into pieces; and Moses burnt the head, and the pieces, and the fat. And he washed the inwards and the legs in water; and Moses burnt the whole ram upon the altar: it was a burnt sacrifice for a sweet savour, and an offering made by fire unto the LORD; as the LORD commanded Moses. And he brought the other ram, the ram of consecration: and Aaron and his sons laid their hands upon the head of the ram. And he slew it; and Moses took of the blood of it, and put it upon the tip of Aaron's right ear, and upon the thumb of his right hand, and upon the great toe of his right foot. And he brought Aaron's sons, and Moses put of the blood upon the tip of their right ear, and upon the thumbs of their right hands, and upon the great toes of their right feet: and Moses sprinkled the blood upon the altar round about.

After being washed in water, robed in righteousness, anointed with oil, the fourth step of preparation for Aaron and his sons was to be symbolically covered with blood as blood was literally applied to the ear, the thumb, and the big toe. Because the things we hear, the things we do, the places we go can pollute us, we need the blood applied to us, the blood to cleanse us, the blood to protect us from future sin.

As time goes on, these priests would apply the blood not only when they entered the tabernacle, but when they exited as well—a principle I have found to be a real key in ministry. Before I teach or share, counsel or serve, I need to say, "Lord, I know I am a sinner. I know I am frail. I plead the blood to cleanse me in order that Your Spirit might flow through me." And when I finish teaching, sharing, counseling, or serving, I plead the blood as well because when I'm done ministering, one of two things invariably happens: either I am totally discouraged about how badly I did, or I'm proud of how well I did—and that's even more dangerous, for pride goes before destruction.

Pleading the blood takes care of both of these tendencies as I realize that, because I am a sinner through and through, it's only by God's grace that I am allowed to minister at all.

Leviticus 8:25–27 (a)
And he took the fat, and the rump, and all the fat that was upon the inwards, and the caul above the liver, and the two kidneys, and their fat, and the right shoulder: And

out of the basket of unleavened bread, that was before the LORD, he took one unleavened cake, and a cake of oiled bread, and one wafer, and put them on the fat, and upon the right shoulder: And he put all upon Aaron's hands, and upon his sons' hands . . .

In this offering of consecration, Aaron's and his son's hands were initially empty. The Hebrew word translated "consecration" means "to fill the hands." We usually think of consecration in terms of what we can bring to the Lord, what we can give Him, what we can do for Him—when in reality consecration means we come before the Lord with empty hands and let Him fill them as He chooses.

Leviticus 8:27 (b)–32
. . . and waved them for a wave offering before the LORD. And Moses took them from off their hands, and burnt them on the altar upon the burnt offering: they were consecrations for a sweet savour: it is an offering made by fire unto the LORD. And Moses took the breast, and waved it for a wave offering before the LORD: for of the ram of consecration it was Moses' part; as the LORD commanded Moses. And Moses took of the anointing oil, and of the blood which was upon the altar, and sprinkled it upon Aaron, and upon his garments, and upon his sons, and upon his sons' garments with him; and sanctified Aaron, and his garments, and his sons, and his sons' garments with him. And Moses said unto Aaron and to his sons, boil the flesh at the door of the tabernacle of the congregation: and there eat it with the bread that is in the basket of consecrations, as I commanded, saying, Aaron and his sons shall eat it. And that which remaineth of the flesh and of the bread shall ye burn with fire.

Aaron and his sons were to wave certain portions of the meat and bread before the Lord in an act of worship, presenting them to Him before placing them upon the altar.

Leviticus 8:33–36
And ye shall not go out of the door of the tabernacle of the congregation in seven days, until the days of your consecration be at an end: for seven days shall he consecrate you. As he hath done this day, so the LORD hath commanded to do, to make an atonement for you. Therefore shall ye abide at the door of the tabernacle of the congregation day and night seven days, and keep the charge of the LORD, that ye die not: for so I am commanded. So Aaron and his sons did all things which the LORD commanded by the hand of Moses.

The last step of preparation was one of isolation. Seven being the number of completion, Aaron and his sons were to remain in the tabernacle for seven days.

Ministry is like the measles. You can't give it unless you've got it. You can't give blessing unless you are blessed. And you won't be blessed until you're locked in, tucked away, set aside—for how long? Until God's preparatory work in you is complete.

Aaron and his sons were no doubt eager to begin, but they were to wait in order that they die not. Many ministries die because people don't know the meaning of a personal devotional life, of spending chunks of time locked away in the presence of God.

9

Leviticus 9:1
And it came to pass on the eighth day, that Moses called Aaron and his sons, and the elders of Israel;

The preparation complete, what day were the priests presented? The eighth day. Sabbath being the eighth day, the eighth day would have been the first day of the week, Sunday. The picture is perfect—for not only is eight the number of new beginnings, but Jesus, our great High Priest, rose on Sunday.

Leviticus 9:2–4
And he said unto Aaron, Take thee a young calf for a sin offering, and a ram for a burnt offering, without blemish, and offer them before the LORD. And unto the children of Israel thou shalt speak, saying, Take ye a kid of the goats for a sin offering; and a calf and a lamb, both of the first year, without blemish, for a burnt offering; also a bullock and a ram for peace offerings, to sacrifice before the LORD; and a meat offering mingled with oil: for to day the LORD will appear unto you.

As part of their presentation, Aaron and his sons were to bring three offerings to the Lord: a sin offering, a burnt offering, a meal offering. But notice which one was to be offered first. Before the burnt offering came the sin offering. This is a principle that applies to us as well. You see, before we can be used by the Lord in service, we must be right with the Lord in regard to sin, for the sins of God's people will hinder the flow of His power through them.

Leviticus 9:5–22
And they brought that which Moses commanded before the tabernacle of the congregation: and all the congregation drew near and stood before the LORD. And Moses said, This is the thing which the LORD commanded that ye should do: and the glory of the LORD shall appear unto you. And Moses said unto Aaron, Go unto the altar, and offer thy sin offering, and thy burnt offering, and make an atonement for thyself, and for the people: and offer the offering of the people, and make an atonement for them; as the LORD commanded. Aaron therefore went unto the altar, and slew the calf of the sin offering, which was for himself. And the sons of Aaron brought the blood unto him: and he dipped his finger in the blood, and put it upon the horns of the altar, and poured out the blood at the bottom of the altar: But the fat, and the kidneys, and the caul above the liver of the sin offering, he burnt upon the altar; as the LORD commanded Moses. And the flesh and the hide he burnt with fire without the camp. And he slew the burnt offering; and Aaron's sons presented unto him the blood, which he sprinkled round about upon the altar. And they presented the burnt offering unto him, with the pieces thereof, and the head: and he burnt them upon the altar. And he did wash the inwards and the legs, and burnt them upon the burnt offering on the altar. And he brought the people's offering, and took the goat, which was the sin offering for the people, and slew it, and offered it for sin, as the first. And he brought the burnt offering, and offered it according to the manner. And he brought the meat offering, and took an handful thereof, and burnt it upon the altar, beside the burnt sacrifice of the morning. He slew also the bullock and the ram for a sacrifice of peace offerings, which was for the people: and Aaron's sons presented unto him the blood, which he sprinkled upon the altar round about, and the fat of the bullock and of the ram, the rump, and that which covereth the inwards, and the kidneys, and the caul above the liver: and they put the fat upon the breasts, and he burnt the fat upon the altar: and the breasts and the right shoulder Aaron waved for a wave offering before the LORD; as Moses commanded. And Aaron lifted up his hand toward the people, and blessed them, and came down from offering of the sin offering, and the burnt offering, and peace offerings.

This description of the sacrifice is studied by Jewish scholars at great length because it's the only time the procedure of a sacrifice is seen. Why does the Lord go into such detail? Why does He take virtually an entire chapter to describe this procedure? Because He cares about the details of how He is to be worshiped just as He cares about the details of how we are to live. Our God is a God of incredible order. Not only does the Book of Leviticus attest to this, but His fingerprint can be seen on even the most minute aspect of nature, His concern over each sparrow His awareness of each hair (Matthew 10:29, 30).

A lady approached G. Campbell Morgan with a particular question.

"Why don't you ask the Lord about that?" he asked.

"Oh, it's too small a detail for the Lord," she replied.

"Tell me, madam," he countered, "what in your life is big to the Lord?"

G. Campbell Morgan was right. Because nothing is big to God, nothing is too small for Him.

Leviticus 9:23 (a)
And Moses and Aaron went into the tabernacle of the congregation, and came out, and blessed the people . . .

After going into the tabernacle, Moses and Aaron came out and blessed the people. That's what we're doing here tonight. We are coming into the tabernacle of the True and Living God in order to be refueled and refilled, in order that we might go out and be a blessing to others.

Leviticus 9:23 (b), 24 (a)
. . . and the glory of the LORD appeared unto all the people. And there came a fire out from before the LORD, and consumed upon the altar the burnt offering and the fat: which when all the people saw, they shouted . . .

After a time of consecration and presentation, after a time of going in before the Lord and coming out to bless the people, suddenly fire from heaven came down and consumed the offerings upon the altar. The glory of God was seen and people shouted—an understandable reaction for the Hebrew word for worship implies a shout of joy.

Leviticus 9:24 (b)
. . . and fell on their faces.

We see the highest joy in a shout and the deepest reverence in a falling on one's face. So awed and amazed were they by the presence of God, the people's first reaction was to shout, but it was followed by a very quiet reverence before the Lord. "The Lord is in His temple," Habakkuk declared. "Let all the earth keep silent" (Habakkuk 2:20). Sometimes the truest sign of an intense move of the Lord is not necessarily a shout, a clap, or even a word, but an awesome, quiet reverence.

10 Leviticus 10:1, 2
And Nadab and Abihu, the sons of Aaron, took either of them his censer, and put fire therein, and put incense thereon, and offered strange fire before the Lord, which he commanded them not. And there went out fire from the Lord, and devoured them, and they died before the Lord.

"For God so loved the world that He gave His Son" (John 3:16). In Old Testament times, to reveal to the world how much He cared for them and the way people were to walk with Him, God called a nation—the people of Israel—and separated them from other nations in order that He might bless them and that they, in turn, might be a witness, an example, a lighthouse to the dark, dying world around them. God raised up a priesthood, priests, who were to give instruction to His people, provide direction for them, and be an example to them. That is why, when Nadab and Abihu chose their own way instead of God's, He dealt directly and severely with them lest the people follow suit and the nation no longer be an example to the world.

***For topical study of Leviticus 10:1 entitled "Burnout!" turn to page* 388.**

Leviticus 10:3
Then Moses said unto Aaron, This is it that the Lord spake, saying, I will be sanctified in them that come nigh me, and before all the people I will be glorified. And Aaron held his peace.

Although the foundational sin of Nadab and Abihu was that of offering strange fire, evidently a second problem was that they were ministering in such a way as to draw attention to themselves, for it was in response to their sin that God said, "I alone will be glorified."

Is God saying He doesn't want any competition because He's insecure? No, it's because He knows if people depend on a person, a church, a ministry, they're sure to be disappointed ultimately. God is the only One without flaw. That's why He won't share His glory with any man or ministry.

Leviticus 10:4–7
And Moses called Mishael and Elzaphan, the sons of Uzziel the uncle of Aaron, and said unto them, Come near, carry your brethren from before the sanctuary out of the camp. So they went near, and carried them in their coats out of the camp; as Moses had said. And Moses said unto Aaron, and unto Eleazar and unto Ithamar, his sons, Uncover not your heads, neither rend your clothes; lest ye die, and lest wrath come upon all the people: but let your brethren, the whole house of Israel, bewail the burning which the Lord hath kindled. And ye shall not go out from the door of the tabernacle of the congregation, lest ye die: for the anointing oil of the Lord is upon you. And they did according to the word of Moses.

Neither father nor brother were to mourn the deaths of Nadab and Abihu because the implication would be that God was unfair.

Ezekiel was another who was told not to mourn when, as an illustration to the people, God took his wife (Ezekiel 24). "Righteous and true are thy judgments, O, Lord," say the multitudes in heaven (Revelation 19:2), seeing the full picture, understanding that God's ways are absolutely perfect without fail.

This side of eternity, our vision is so very limited. Yet even that which appears to be a tragedy to us is all part of a bigger plan. After all, do you think Ezekiel and his wife are in heaven right now feeling cheated that her life on earth was cut short—or do you think they're blown away by the goodness of God in allowing her to partake of the unspeakable splendor of heaven early? When you go through a hard time, a setback, a tragedy, it is oh, so easy to suck sympathy from people—but you always do so at the expense of God's reputation. This is why Aaron was not to mourn.

Leviticus 10:8, 9 (a)
And the Lord spake unto Aaron, saying, Do not drink wine nor strong drink, thou, nor thy sons with thee, when ye go into the tabernacle of the congregation, lest ye die . . .

Thirdly, from the text and context, it appears that Nadab and Abihu were drunk—which might partially explain the poor judgment which did indeed lead to their deaths.

Leviticus 10:9 (b)–11
. . . it shall be a statute for ever throughout your generations: And that ye may put difference between holy and unholy, and between unclean and clean; and that ye may teach the children of Israel all the statutes which the LORD hath spoken unto them by the hand of Moses.

The injunction against drinking wine is repeated in Ezekiel 44:21 and is explained in Proverbs 31:4, 5.

Leviticus 10:12–18
And Moses spake unto Aaron, and unto Eleazar and unto Ithamar, his sons that were left, Take the meat offering that remaineth of the offerings of the LORD made by fire, and eat it without leaven beside the altar: for it is most holy: and ye shall eat it in the holy place, because it is thy due, and thy sons' due, of the sacrifices of the LORD made by fire: for so I am commanded. And the wave breast and heave shoulder shall ye eat in a clean place; thou, and thy sons, and thy daughters with thee: for they be thy due, and thy sons' due, which are given out of the sacrifices of peace offerings of the children of Israel. The heave shoulder and the wave breast shall they bring with the offerings made by fire of the fat, to wave it for a wave offering before the LORD; and it shall be thine, and thy sons' with thee, by a statute for ever; as the LORD hath commanded. And Moses diligently sought the goat of the sin offering, and, behold, it was burnt: and he was angry with Eleazar and Ithamar, the sons of Aaron which were left alive, saying, Wherefore have ye not eaten the sin offering in the holy place, seeing it is most holy, and God hath given it you to bear the iniquity of the congregation, to make atonement for them before the LORD? Behold, the blood of it was not brought in within the holy place: ye should indeed have eaten it in the holy place, as I commanded.

Having just witnessed the deaths of Nadab and Abihu due to disobedience, Moses was angry with his remaining nephews for their disobedience in failing to eat the sin offering.

"If you do not eat of My body and drink of My blood, you have no part with Me," Jesus would declare (see John 6:53). Therefore, if the priests failed to eat the sin offering, the prophetic picture it was given to portray would not be realized.

Leviticus 10:19
And Aaron said unto Moses, Behold, this day have they offered their sin offering and their burnt offering before the LORD; and such things have befallen me: and if I had eaten the sin offering to day, should it have been accepted in the sight of the LORD?

"We did as much as we could," Aaron said. "but I can't eat. My two boys were just killed and we have no appetite."

Leviticus 10:20
And when Moses heard that, he was content.

Nadab and Abihu's sin was wickedness. They lit strange fire; they drew attention to themselves; their judgment was clouded with drink. Ithamar and Eleazar sinned as well, but theirs was a sin of weakness. God was severe with Nadab and Abihu's wickedness and iniquity. He was merciful with Ithamar and Eleazar's weakness and inability.

If you're committing the sin of Nadab and Abihu, the fear of our God as a consuming fire must come upon you. However, if yours is the sin of Ithamar and Eleazar, be free in the grace and forgiveness, the mercy and patience of our Father.

BURNOUT !

A Topical Study of LEVITICUS 10:1

"Come unto Me," Jesus said, "all ye who are heavy laden, and I will give you rest. Take My yoke upon you and learn of Me and you shall find rest in your souls" (Matthew 11:29). Why, then, are so many "mature" Christians burned out in their ministry to Him, their service for Him?

I believe Aaron's sons, Nadab and Abihu give us the answer. *Nadab* means "willing one." *Abihu* means "father of him"—perhaps in reference to his famous father, Moses' brother Aaron, the high priest of the nation of Israel.

Having been eyewitnesses to the glory of God filling the tabernacle, having seen the flames, having smelled the smoke of the fire from heaven mystically and miraculously igniting the sacrifice upon the altar, it is understandable why Nadab and Abihu would indeed be willing to join their famous father in ministry, to play a pivotal part in the "holy happening" unfolding before their eyes. After all, they had gone through the process of preparation—they had been washed, robed, anointed with both oil and blood—as well as that of isolation, having been shut up in the tabernacle for seven days. Surely now was the time to begin, their time to shine. So they lit their censers and set out to take part in the celebration.

The problem, however, was that Nadab and Abihu lit their censers with strange fire. Strange fire was fire that came from any source other than the altar which burned continually and which speaks of the place where the Lamb of God absorbed the fire of God's wrath that should have been poured out on you and me. The fire speaks of Calvary.

> *For the love of Christ constraineth us; because we thus judge, that if one died for all, then were all dead: and that he died for all, that they which live should not henceforth live unto themselves, but unto him which died for them, and rose again.*
> 2 Corinthians 5:14, 15

What Christ did on the altar of Calvary was that which motivated Paul day after day, year after year—for the love of Christ is a fire that never burns out.

Some people involve themselves in ministry simply because they want to be part of the action. But when the action shifts somewhere else, they shift along with it, leaving ministry behind. Others have a need to be used, so they serve the Lord to fulfill their own need. But when they're needed somewhere else, ministry takes a back seat. Still others serve the Lord out of concern for the lost. But when the lost don't respond as quickly as hoped, they eventually give up ministering altogether.

Ministry for ministry's sake, ministry for fulfillment's sake, ministry for others' sake is all strange fire which will eventually burn people out.

The only fire which will never burn one out or burn one up is the fire from the altar of Calvary. Those who, like Paul, are constrained, motivated, propelled by the love Christ demonstrated on Calvary will still be serving Him with passion, with effectiveness, with intensity until they draw their last breath their last breath this side of eternity.

How can one keep from the Nadab and Abihu mentality? The simplest way is to go to the altar over and over again, to go to the Lord's Table over and over again and remember what Christ Jesus did for us. When we bow our knee and commune with the Lord, when we handle His broken body and drink of His shed blood, all the dials are set back to zero as we remember the price He paid for us.

Jesus died for me so that I wouldn't have to go to hell. He died for me so I could go to heaven. He died for me so that my sins would be washed away. How can I *not* serve Him? True ministry has nothing to do with a need to be involved, a need to be fulfilled, or even a desire to help people. True ministry is all about what Christ did for us when He laid down His life for us at Calvary.

11 As seen in the sacrifices, chapters 1 through 10 dealt with worshiping the Lord. Here in chapter 11, and on through chapter 17, the subject matter is walking with the Lord.

Leviticus 11:1, 2
And the LORD spake unto Moses and to Aaron, saying unto them, Speak unto the children of Israel, saying, These are the beasts which ye shall eat among all the beasts that are on the earth.

The first topic God addresses in how He wanted His people to walk concerns dietary issues. And in so doing, He provided protection for the Israelites from the diseases that ravaged the cultures surrounding them.

When the Bubonic Plague killed one out of four Europeans, the Jewish community was remarkably immune. Because they followed the sanitary regulations of the Old Testament, not knowing the reason for them but simply being obedient to them, the Jews were protected to a remarkable degree.

Secondly, the dietary laws in this section would provide distinction or separation to God's people, setting them apart for His purposes.

Finally, in addition to providing protection and distinction to the Israelites, the dietary regulations of Leviticus 11—17 provide illustration to us as believers . . .

Leviticus 11:3
Whatsoever parteth the hoof, and is clovenfooted, and cheweth the cud, among the beasts, that shall ye eat.

The Jews were allowed to eat those animals that had a divided hoof and chewed its cud. In other words, cleanliness was determined by how an animal walked and how it ate.

The principle for us is obvious. Is there a "dividedness" in our walk? Are we separated from the world or do we walk like everyone around us? We are new creatures in Christ (2 Corinthians 5:17). Is there a difference in our walk? There needs to be.

Secondly, do we chew the spiritual "cud"? Just as a cow constantly chews and rechews its food, we are to be those who chew and rechew the Word, who think it through, pray it in, extract from it every nutrient to feed their inner man. No wonder the Hebrew word for chewing the cud is essentially the same word translated "meditation."

> This book of the law shall not depart out of thy mouth; but thou shalt meditate therein day and night, that thou mayest observe to do according to all that is written therein: for then thou shalt make thy way prosperous, and then thou shalt have good success. Joshua 1:8

We get to meditate on the Word. We get to look in the book. We get to think it through once more. And as we do, we'll have good success; we'll be healthy; we'll be clean.

Leviticus 11:4
Nevertheless these shall ye not eat of them that chew the cud, or of them that divide the hoof: as the camel, because he cheweth the cud, but divideth not the hoof; he is unclean unto you.

History makes note of the intestinal diseases that afflicted the ethnic groups which ate the meat of camels. Jesus would later indict the Pharisees for spiritually doing just that—for straining out gnats that would have done them no harm, yet swallowing camels that were forbidden, for analyzing minute details yet missing the big picture.

Leviticus 11:5, 6
And the coney, because he cheweth the cud, but divideth not the hoof; he is unclean unto you. And the hare, because he cheweth the

cud, but divideth not the hoof; he is unclean unto you.

A coney is like a rabbit without ears. He chews the cud, but his hoof is not divided. Before we point a finger at the Pharisees for swallowing camels, we need to consider whether we deceive ourselves by acting like coneys or hares. You see, Joshua was instructed to meditate on God's Word in order to *do* all that was commanded therein. The cud must be chewed and the hoof divided, for we are to both chew on the Word and walk in it.

Leviticus 11:7, 8
And the swine, though he divide the hoof, and be cloven-footed, yet he cheweth not the cud; he is unclean to you. Of their flesh shall ye not eat, and their carcass shall ye not touch; they are unclean to you.

The swine represents those who live moral lives, but who don't open the Word.

Leviticus 11:9–12
These shall ye eat of all that are in the waters: whatsoever hath fins and scales in the waters, in the seas, and in the rivers, them shall ye eat. And all that have not fins and scales in the seas, and in the rivers, of all that move in the waters, and of any living thing which is in the waters, they shall be an abomination unto you: They shall be even an abomination unto you; ye shall not eat of their flesh, but ye shall have their carcases in abomination. Whatsoever hath no fins nor scales in the waters, that shall be an abomination unto you.

Fins and scales being necessary for movement in the water, fish are determined to be clean or unclean based on how they move. In other words, the Jews were not to eat bottom feeders. So, too, water being emblematic of Scripture, we are clean or unclean based on how we move through the water of the Word. Do we seek to justify sin? Do we try to rationalize carnality? Is there a bottom feeding mentality? The scales speak of a sense of purity, the fins of the ability to navigate successfully. It's a wonderful analogy.

Leviticus 11:13–20
And these are they which ye shall have in abomination among the fowls; they shall not be eaten, they are an abomination: the eagle, and the ossifrage, and the ospray, And the vulture, and the kite after his kind; every raven after his kind; and the owl, and the night hawk, and the cuckow, and the hawk after his kind, And the little owl, and the cormorant, and the great owl, and the swan, and the pelican, and the gier eagle, and the stork, the heron after her kind, and the lapwing, and the bat. All fowls that creep, going upon all four, shall be an abomination unto you.

Ravens are an unclean bird and a symbol of evil in the Bible. Why, then, did God use them to miraculously deliver food to Elijah in the wilderness (1 Kings 17:6)? I suggest it was to show us that He can use anyone or anything to minister to us. Sometimes, we have a tendency to think we can't be instructed by him, or corrected by her because they're "unclean birds." In reality, however, we can learn from anyone God sends our way even if he or she might appear to be "unclean."

"I'm not going to listen to my parents because they're not as spiritual as I am," some might say. Big mistake. God can use all sorts of interesting creatures and situations to bring food to us, to minister to us, to admonish, nourish, and correct us.

Therefore, wise is the man who will say, "Lord give me eyes to see and ears to hear whatever You want to tell me, through whatever messenger You choose."

Leviticus 11:21–23
Yet these may ye eat of every flying creeping thing that goeth upon all four, which have legs above their feet, to leap withal upon the earth; even these of them ye may eat; the locust after his kind, and the bald locust after his kind, and the beetle after his kind, and the grasshopper after his kind. But all other flying creeping things, which have four feet, shall be an abomination unto you.

Certain kinds of beetles, locusts, and grasshoppers met the criterion for cleanness. And, no doubt, John the Baptist, for one, was glad they did (Matthew 3:4).

Leviticus 11:24–28
And for these ye shall be unclean: whosoever toucheth the carcase of them shall be unclean until the even. And whosoever beareth ought of the carcase of them shall wash his clothes, and be unclean until the even. The carcases of every beast which divideth the hoof, and is not clovenfooted, nor cheweth the cud, are unclean unto you: every one that toucheth them shall be unclean. And whatsoever goeth upon his paws, among all manner of beasts that go on all four, those are unclean unto you: whoso toucheth their carcase shall be unclean until the even. And

he that beareth the carcase of them shall wash his clothes, and be unclean until the even: they are unclean unto you.

The principle here is one the prophet Haggai will develop more fully (2:12). That is, while that which is clean cannot make holy that which is unholy, that which is unclean can make unholy that which is holy. Think of it this way: If I put a drop of clean water into a mud puddle, the drop of clean water becomes muddy. But if I put a drop of muddy water into a jar of clean water, the clean water is no longer clean. You might think you can enter an unclean situation and make it clean because you're holy—but more often than not, the situation will remain unclean and you'll be tainted in the process.

Leviticus 11:29 (a)
These also shall be unclean unto you among the creeping things that creep upon the earth; the weasel, and the mouse . . .

The carcass of a mouse is as unclean as the carcass of an elephant because neither part the hoof. This deals a death-blow to the concept of venial and mortal sin. This is no ranking of sin. Sin is sin, whether it be a mouse or an elephant. "It's just a white lie," we say, "a slight compromise," a "quirk." No, it's a mouse. It's sin.

Leviticus 11:29 (b)–33
. . . and the tortoise after his kind, And the ferret, and the chameleon, and the lizard, and the snail, and the mole. These are unclean to you among all that creep: whosoever doth touch them, when they be dead, shall be unclean until the even. And upon whatsoever any of them, when they are dead, doth fall, it shall be unclean; whether it be any vessel of wood, or raiment, or skin, or sack, whatsoever vessel it be, wherein any work is done, it must be put into water, and it shall be unclean until the even; so it shall be cleansed. And every earthen vessel, whereinto any of them falleth, whatsoever is in it shall be unclean; and ye shall break it.

Because we are earthen vessels (2 Corinthians 4:7), God in His love must break us when there is uncleanness found in us—not to punish us, for Christ bore all of our punishment on the Cross, but to purify us. Therefore, when I come into contact with uncleanness, I can expect breaking in my life.

Leviticus 11:34–36
Of all meat which may be eaten, that on which such water cometh shall be unclean: and all drink that may be drunk in every such vessel shall be unclean. And every thing whereupon any part of their carcase falleth shall be unclean; whether it be oven, or ranges for pots, they shall be broken down: for they are unclean, and shall be unclean unto you. Nevertheless a fountain or pit, wherein there is plenty of water, shall be clean: but that which toucheth their carcase shall be unclean.

If an unclean animal fell into an earthen vessel, the vessel had to be broken—but if an unclean animal fell into a fountain or pit that had an abundance of water, the water would not be affected. Jesus Christ is the Living Water (John 4; 7). You might feel like a mole, a chameleon, a lizard—but when you come to the fountain of Living Water, the Living Water can handle your uncleanness. That is why Jesus could call Judas "friend" even at the moment of betrayal (Matthew 26:50)—and why He is not ashamed to call unclean sinners like us brethren (Hebrews 2:11).

Leviticus 11:37–40
And if any part of their carcase fall upon any sowing seed which is to be sown, it shall be clean. But if any water be put upon the seed, and any part of their carcase fall thereon, it shall be unclean unto you. And if any beast, of which ye may eat, die; he that toucheth the carcase thereof shall be unclean until the even. And he that eateth of the carcase of it shall wash his clothes, and be unclean until the even: he also that beareth the carcase of it shall wash his clothes, and be unclean until the even.

If a bat or lizard falls in a bag of seed, if the seed is still in its shell, it's okay. But if the shell of the seed is no longer there because water has softened it, that seed is to be thrown out because the seed itself will have become polluted. The seed being a picture of the Word (1 Peter 1:23), if the seed is not encased by the armor of faith, rats of unbelief will gnaw at it, causing us to question if it truly is infallible, immutable, applicable. Can the Word become unclean? Yes—to people who no longer read it in faith, but find fault with it rather than allowing it to find and change the faults within them.

Leviticus 11:41–47
And every creeping thing that creepeth upon the earth shall be an abomination; it shall not be eaten. Whatsoever goeth upon the belly, and whatsoever goeth upon all four, or whatsoever hath more feet among all creeping things that creep upon the earth,

them ye shall not eat; for they are an abomination. Ye shall not make yourselves abominable with any creeping thing that creepeth, neither shall ye make yourselves unclean with them, that ye should be defiled thereby. For I am the LORD your God: ye shall therefore sanctify yourselves, and ye shall be holy; for I am holy: neither shall ye defile yourselves with any manner of creeping thing that creepeth upon the earth. For I am the LORD that bringeth you up out of the land of Egypt, to be your God: ye shall therefore be holy, for I am holy. This is the law of the beasts, and of the fowl, and of every living creature that moveth in the waters, and of every creature that creepeth upon the earth: to make a difference between the unclean and the clean, and between the beast that may be eaten and the beast that may not be eaten.

"Ye shall be holy, for I am holy." This is an exhortation—but it is also an expectation, as if God is saying, "If you choose to walk with Me and to walk in My ways, because I am holy, you will be holy, too."

12

It has been rightly said that the Bible is a book no man could write even if he would, and no man would write even if he could. You see, even if a man wanted to write the Bible, he would be unable to do so for this book was not authored by human ingenuity. It is unlike any other book in that it wasn't written by mortal men but by God, who inspired man specifically and exactingly concerning every word written. One example of the uniqueness of the book before you is that a full third of it deals with prophecy, with predicting events before they take place. Although no other religious writing dares to deal in the realm of prophecy, over three hundred prophecies were given concerning the coming of Christ in the Old Testament—each fulfilled to the letter.

> Produce your cause, saith the LORD; bring forth your strong reasons, saith the King of Jacob. Let them bring them forth, and shew us what shall happen: let them shew the former things, what they be, that we may consider them, and know the latter end of them; or declare us things for to come. Shew the things that are to come hereafter, that we may know that ye are gods: yea, do good, or do evil, that we may be dismayed, and behold it together.
> Isaiah 41:21–23

> Thus saith the LORD the King of Israel, and his redeemer the LORD of hosts; I am the first, and I am the last; and beside me there is no God. And who, as I, shall call, and shall declare it, and set it in order for me, since I appointed the ancient people? and the things that are coming, and shall come, let them shew unto them.
> Isaiah 44:6, 7

> Remember the former things of old: for I am God, and there is none else; I am God, and there is none like me, declaring the end from the beginning, and from ancient times the things that are not yet done, saying, My counsel shall stand, and I will do all my pleasure:
> Isaiah 46:9, 10

God challenges other gods to set things in order, to predict what is to be. Yet no other religion has dared accept the challenge lest their fraudulence come to light.

No man could write this book, even if he would. But also, no man would write this book even if he could. If someone were able to write a seemingly divinely inspired book in his own energy, he wouldn't write a book like this one. Why? Because of chapters like the one before us—a chapter that if I were writing the Bible, I wouldn't necessarily include . . .

Leviticus 12:1, 2
And the LORD spake unto Moses, saying, Speak unto the children of Israel, saying, If a woman have conceived seed, and born a man child: then she shall be unclean seven days; according to the days of the separation for her infirmity shall she be unclean.

After giving birth to a baby boy, a woman was considered ceremonially unclean, unable to take part in tabernacle worship for seven days.

Leviticus 12:3
And in the eighth day the flesh of his foreskin shall be circumcised.

The baby boy was to be circumcised on the eighth day because not only is eight the number of new beginnings, but, physiologically, the day when the blood coagulates. The rite of circumcision, a specific mark placed upon the Jewish male alone, spoke of dealing with the flesh. The fact that it was to take place as soon as it was physiologically possible speaks of the fact that sin is to be dealt with from the earliest of days.

Leviticus 12:4
And she shall then continue in the blood of her purifying three and thirty days; she shall touch no hallowed thing, nor come

into the sanctuary, until the days of her purifying be fulfilled.

Following the circumcision of her baby, the mother was considered to be ceremonially unclean for an additional thirty-three days.

Leviticus 12:5
But if she bear a maid child, then she shall be unclean two weeks, as in her separation: and she shall continue in the blood of her purifying threescore and six days.

If she gave birth to a boy, a mother was ceremonially unclean for a total of forty-one days. If she gave birth to a girl, she was ceremonially unclean for a total of eighty days. Why was she unclean twice as long if she gave birth to a girl? Because, through circumcision, the sin of the baby boy was addressed, but the sin of a baby girl could not be addressed in that way, leaving the mother alone to deal with the issue of sin.

Why would either mother or baby have to deal with sin? Why would the birth of either son or daughter be considered unclean? When we have babies, people send flowers, buy balloons, and celebrate. What, then, is the meaning of this chapter? Is the birth process something that is unclean? No, for it was God Himself who said, "Be fruitful and multiply" (Genesis 1:28).

In this passage, God is illustrating something that is difficult for people today to comprehend or embrace. He is declaring that when a baby is born—as glorious and wonderful an event as that is—it causes uncleanness because another sinner is added to the world.

In Psalm 51, under inspiration of the Spirit, David declares, "In sin did my mother conceive me" (51:5). At the moment of conception, there was sin—not in the act of procreation, but at the moment of conception a sin nature began. This is the doctrine of the depravity of man—politically incorrect, but true nonetheless. Contrary to current psychological thought, babies don't arrive with a "clean slate." Man is not a sinner because he sins. He sins because he is a sinner. And when I understand this, the implications and applications are profound.

First, an understanding of the depravity of man affects me parentally—how I view my kids and the way I raise my family. To understand that a baby comes into the world as a sinner and not an innocent little person who is bruised by culture or infected by civilization makes me realize that as great as he is and as much joy as she brings, they're sinners just like me.

> Foolishness is bound in the heart of a child; but the rod of correction shall drive it far from him. Proverbs 22:15

Foolishness, rebelliousness, and sin are built into the heart of a child. If you have kids, you know this to be so. Not one parent has ever had to teach his child how to have a temper tantrum when he didn't get his way. Not one had to teach his child how to lie, how to be sneaky, how to be deceptive. Not one says, "Today I'm going to teach my kids how to sin."

> He that spareth his rod hateth his son: but he that loveth him chasteneth him betimes. Proverbs 13:24

God knows exactly what He's doing when He says that the way to deal with the sin in our kids is to do so lovingly with the rod of correction. Tears flow, guilt is released, hugs follow. And they can go on free from the baggage of guilt and sin.

Secondly, an understanding of the depravity of man affects me politically. Communism made great strides as Karl Marx insisted there should be a comradeship, a brotherhood between all men because men are basically, intrinsically good. The Bible says men are basically, intrinsically bad. That is why Communism ultimately collapsed. Capitalism survived because it is actually based on the depravity of man—that man is greedy and will, therefore work to the degree that he is personally rewarded.

Thirdly, an understanding of the depravity of man affects how I see myself personally. In Romans 7, Paul declared, "In my flesh dwells no good thing." Therefore, I don't have to be shocked or down on myself when I am aware of sin within me. Instead, I can say, "Lord have mercy on me. Lord, take it from me. Lord, deal with me because I know the sin deep within me will destroy me and my family."

> But God commendeth his love toward us, in that, while we were yet sinners, Christ died for us. Romans 5:8

An understanding of my own depravity actually gives me a great deal of security because I realize who I am and the extent of God's love for me.

Finally, an understanding of the depravity of man affects me relationally. Because we're all sinners, I never need to be disappointed by someone else's sin. All we like sheep have gone astray (Isaiah 53:6). We have *all* rebelled against God. That is why Paul determined to know no man after the flesh (2 Corinthians 5:16). Paul didn't focus on the flesh. Instead, he chose to see people in the Spirit—to see what the Lord was doing in their lives.

Leviticus 12:6–8
And when the days of her purifying are fulfilled, for a son, or for a daughter, she shall bring a lamb of the first year for a burnt offering, and a young pigeon, or a turtledove, for a sin offering, unto the door of the tabernacle of the congregation, unto the priest: who shall offer it before the LORD, and make an atonement for her; and she shall be cleansed from the issue of her blood. This is the law for her that hath born a male or a female. And if she be not able to bring a lamb, then she shall bring two turtles, or two young pigeons; the one for the burnt offering, and the other for a sin offering: and the priest shall make an atonement for her, and she shall be clean.

Just as the woman would bring an offering, God says, "I have an Offering to cleanse you, to purify you, to wash away the sin you've done today, yesterday, or tomorrow." The lamb being the most costly offering required, it speaks of the Lamb of God, whose blood was shed that we might be a forgiven people. A lamb was brought by the woman who brought a sinner into the world—and a Lamb was brought by the Father who brought salvation to the world.

---

13 Chapters 13 and 14 both deal with the issue of leprosy, which, in the Word, is a picture of sin.

Like sin, leprosy began underneath the surface of the skin, out of sight initially, no big deal seemingly. But then it spread insidiously as it moved throughout the body, eventually causing the bones to soften and the fingernails to disappear, the teeth to recede into the gums and the nose to fall off.

Secondly, like sin, leprosy destroyed sensitivity. Most of the time, a person who contracted leprosy would not be aware anything was wrong until he spilled hot water on his hand or dropped something on his foot without feeling any pain. Concerning sin, Ephesians 4:17–19 says Gentiles walk in the vanity of their mind, being past feeling. Tragically, sin destroys sensitivity to the point that we are no longer bothered by that which at one time made us recoil.

Thirdly, like sin, leprosy was incurable. Although the Law contained regulations concerning the cleansing of leprosy, they were never utilized because, with the exception of Naaman, no one was ever cleansed. It wasn't until 1,500 years later, when an itinerant Rabbi from Nazareth appeared on the scene and told the lepers He healed to show themselves to the priests that the priests were able to put into practice the unused laws that had been on their books for centuries.

Fourthly, like sin, leprosy caused separation between people and their loved ones. When a person was infected with leprosy, he would be sent away from the community to live in isolation or at best in a leper colony. That's what sin does. It destroys relationships, splits families, breaks hearts.

Leviticus 13:1, 2 (a)
And the LORD spake unto Moses and Aaron, saying, When a man shall have in the skin of his flesh a rising . . .

What is sin? It is the flesh rising, the flesh demanding its own way. Lucifer launched a rebellion in heaven, was cast out, and became known as Satan all because of pride, all because he wanted his own way. Pride goes before destruction; a haughty spirit before a fall (Proverbs 16:18)—and Lucifer's fall was great indeed.

Leviticus 13:2 (b)
. . . a scab . . .

Like a scab, sin covers that which needs to be healed.

Leviticus 13:2 (c)
. . . or a bright spot, and it be in the skin of his flesh like the plague of leprosy; then he shall be brought unto Aaron the priest, or unto one of his sons the priests:

Like a bright spot on the skin, sin masquerades as a harmless "bright spot" in our day—be it from TV, books, music, or any other avenue of "innocent" pleasure.

Leviticus 13:3
And the priest shall look on the plague in the skin of the flesh: and when the hair in the plague is turned white, and the plague in sight be deeper than the skin of his flesh, it is a plague of leprosy: and the priest shall look on him, and pronounce him unclean.

Just as the priest would suspect leprosy if a blemish was deeper than the skin, the root problem of sin is deeper than the flesh. It's the heart. "The heart is desperately wicked," Jeremiah declares (17:9). The phrase "desperately wicked" in Hebrew means "gravely ill." Therefore, the flesh cannot be rehabilitated. Instead, the heart must be regenerated. We must be born again.

Leviticus 13:4–8
If the bright spot be white in the skin of his flesh, and in sight be not deeper than the skin, and the hair thereof be not turned white; then the priest shall shut up him that hath the plague seven days: and the priest shall look on him the seventh day: and, behold, if the plague in his sight be at a stay, and the plague spread not in the skin; then the priest shall shut him up seven days more: and the priest shall look on him again the seventh day: and, behold, if the plague be somewhat dark, and the plague spread not in the skin, the priest shall pronounce him clean: it is but a scab: and he shall wash his clothes, and be clean. But if the scab spread much abroad in the skin, after that he hath been seen of the priest for his cleansing, he shall be seen of the priest again: and if the priest see that, behold, the scab spreadeth in the skin, then the priest shall pronounce him unclean: it is a leprosy.

When a man was suspected of having contracted leprosy, he was put in isolation for two seven-day periods in order that the priest would have sufficient time to observe him and make a correct diagnosis. Mankind, too, has been under observation for six of seven "days" or dispensations as God has, throughout human history, given man opportunity to turn to Him: Innocence (Genesis 1:28), Conscience or Moral Responsibility (Genesis 3:7), Human Government (Genesis 8:5), Promise (Genesis 12:1), Law (Exodus 9:1), and the Church (Acts 2:1). And what, according to our great High Priest, is the diagnosis?

> There is none that understandeth, there is none that seeketh after God. They are all gone out of the way, they are together become unprofitable; there is none that doeth good, no, not one. Their throat is an open sepulchre; with their tongues they have used deceit; the poison of asps is under their lips: Whose mouth is full of cursing and bitterness: Their feet are swift to shed blood: destruction and misery are in their ways: and the way of peace have they not known: there is no fear of God before their eyes. Romans 3:11–18

The diagnosis is not good; the prognosis is death. But Romans goes on to tell of God's plan to cleanse us of our leprosy, to pay the price for our sin.

Leviticus 13:9–11
When the plague of leprosy is in a man, then he shall be brought unto the priest; And the priest shall see him: and, behold, if the rising be white in the skin, and it have turned the hair white, and there be quick raw flesh in the rising; it is an old leprosy in the skin of his flesh, and the priest shall pronounce him unclean, and shall not shut him up: for he is unclean.

When someone lovingly shows us that which needs changing in our lives, if we say, "Who are you to tell me what to do?," our response indicates a "quick raw rising" of our flesh.

Leviticus 13:12, 13
And if a leprosy break out abroad in the skin, and the leprosy cover all the skin of him that hath the plague from his head even to his foot, wheresoever the priest looketh; then the priest shall consider: and, behold, if the leprosy have covered all his flesh, he shall pronounce him clean that hath the plague: it is all turned white: he is clean.

Because leprosy that covered a person from head to foot was not active, such a one was pronounced clean. So it is, when I realize I am a sinner from head to toe, from top to bottom—that I can't cover my sin, defend myself, explain away my behavior, or justify my actions—that I am on my way to being pronounced clean.

After taking in a haul of fish so big it almost sank his boat, Peter realized Jesus was God. "Depart from me," he said in response, "for I am a sinful man" (Luke 5). And he was on his way to being converted.

Confession is a real key to salvation . . .

- "I was conceived in sin," David said (Psalm 51:5).
- "Woe is me," Isaiah cried, "for I am undone" (Isaiah 6:5).
- "I have sinned," the prodigal confessed (Luke 15:18).

Confession alone, however, does not guarantee salvation . . .

- "I have sinned against God," Pharaoh declared (Exodus 10:16).
- "I have sinned," Saul admitted (1 Samuel 15:24).
- "I have betrayed innocent blood," Judas confessed (Matthew 27:4).

Yet none of these confessions resulted in salvation. You see, while confession is indeed a key to salvation, the motive for confession is important as well. The second group of men were confessing because they knew they had been caught; the first group because godly sorrow had worked in them a true heart of repentance (2 Corinthians 7:10).

Leviticus 13:14–17
But when raw flesh appeareth in him, he shall be unclean. And the priest shall see the raw flesh, and pronounce him to be unclean: for the raw flesh is unclean: it is a leprosy. Or if the raw flesh turn again, and be changed unto white, he shall come unto the priest; and the priest shall see him: and, behold, if the plague be turned into white; then the priest shall pronounce him clean that hath the plague: he is clean.

The word "but" ties verse 14 to verse 13. Regarding the man covered from head to toe with leprosy, fresh eruptions were a problem because that would mean he wasn't clean after all. So, too, the person who is truly born again does not habitually, continually practice sin (1 John 3:6).

Peter writes about those who seemingly once followed the Lord, but are like pigs returning to the mud (2 Peter 2:22). There is a difference between a sheep and a pig. Both can fall in the mud—but while the pig loves it, the sheep hates it. We who are in God's flock can indeed end up in a mud puddle from time to time. But we don't feel comfortable there indefinitely.

The uncleanness here in verse 14 speaks not of the person who struggles with or, or even succumbs to sin, but of the person who practices sin as devotedly as a man practices his golf swing.

Leviticus 13:18–23
The flesh also, in which, even in the skin thereof, was a boil, and is healed, And in the place of the boil there be a white rising, or a bright spot, white, and somewhat reddish, and it be shewed to the priest; and if, when the priest seeth it, behold, it be in sight lower than the skin, and the hair thereof be turned white; the priest shall pronounce him unclean: it is a plague of leprosy broken out of the boil. But if the priest look on it, and, behold, there be no white hairs therein, and if it be not lower than the skin, but be somewhat dark; then the priest shall shut him up seven days: and if it spread much abroad in the skin, then the priest shall pronounce him unclean: it is a plague. But if the bright spot stay in his place, and spread not, it is a burning boil; and the priest shall pronounce him clean.

This passage speaks of boils or blemishes that had once appeared to be healed but that proved leprous in the end. Peter would allude to the same danger spiritually . . .

> For if after they have escaped the pollutions of the world through the knowledge of the Lord and Saviour Jesus Christ, they are again entangled therein, and overcome, the latter end is worse with them than the beginning. For it had been better for them not to have known the way of righteousness, than, after they have known it, to turn from the holy commandment delivered unto them.
>
> 2 Peter 2:20, 21

Leviticus 13:24–37
Or if there be any flesh, in the skin whereof there is a hot burning, and the quick flesh that burneth have a white bright spot, somewhat reddish, or white; then the priest shall look upon it: and, behold, if the hair in the bright spot be turned white, and it be in sight deeper than the skin; it is a leprosy broken out of the burning: wherefore the priest shall pronounce him unclean: it is the plague of leprosy. But if the priest look on it, and, behold, there be no white hair in the bright spot, and it be no lower than the other skin, but be somewhat dark; then the priest shall shut him up seven days: And the priest shall look upon him the seventh day: and if it be spread much abroad in the skin, then the priest shall pronounce him unclean: it is the plague of leprosy. And if the bright spot stay in his place, and spread not in the skin, but it be somewhat dark; it is a rising of the burning, and the priest shall pronounce him clean: for it is an inflammation of the burning. If a man or woman have a plague upon the head or the beard; then the priest shall see the plague: and, behold, if it be in sight deeper than the skin; and there be in it a yellow thin hair; then the priest shall pronounce him unclean: it is a dry scall, even a leprosy upon the head or beard. And if the priest look on the plague of the scall, and, behold, it be not in sight deeper than the skin, and that there is no black hair in it; then the priest shall shut up him that hath the plague of the scall seven days: and in the seventh day the priest shall look on the plague: and, behold, if the scall spread not, and there be in it no yellow hair, and the scall be not in sight deeper than the skin; he shall be shaven, but the scall shall he not shave; and the priest shall shut up him that hath the scall seven days more: and in the seventh day the priest shall look on the scall: and, behold, if the scall be

not spread in the skin, nor be in sight deeper than the skin; then the priest shall pronounce him clean: and he shall wash his clothes, and be clean. But if the scall spread much in the skin after his cleansing; then the priest shall look on him: and, behold, if the scall be spread in the skin, the priest shall not seek for yellow hair; he is unclean. But if the scall be in his sight at a stay, and that there is black hair grown up therein; the scall is healed, he is clean: and the priest shall pronounce him clean.

The physical burning spoken of in verses 24–28 puts one in mind of the burning of contention or strife which causes confusion in the body of Christ (James 3:14–16).

Leviticus 13:38–44
If a man also or a woman have in the skin of their flesh bright spots, even white bright spots; Then the priest shall look: and, behold, if the bright spots in the skin of their flesh be darkish white; it is a freckled spot that groweth in the skin; he is clean. And the man whose hair is fallen off his head, he is bald; yet is he clean. And he that hath his hair fallen off from the part of his head toward his face, he is forehead bald: yet is he clean. And if there be in the bald head, or bald forehead, a white reddish sore; it is a leprosy sprung up in his bald head, or his bald forehead. Then the priest shall look upon it: and, behold, if the rising of the sore be white reddish in his bald head, or in his bald forehead, as the leprosy appeareth in the skin of the flesh; he is a leprous man, he is unclean: the priest shall pronounce him utterly unclean; his plague is in his head.

Many people will not come to Christ due to the plague of pride in their head.

> But when he was strong, his heart was lifted up to his destruction: for he transgressed against the LORD his God, and went into the temple of the LORD to burn incense upon the altar of incense. And Azariah the priest went in after him, and with him fourscore priests of the LORD, that were valiant men: and they withstood Uzziah the king, and said unto him, it appertaineth not unto thee, Uzziah, to burn incense unto the LORD, but to the priests the sons of Aaron, that are consecrated to burn incense: go out of the sanctuary; for thou hast trespassed; neither shall it be for thine honour from the LORD God. Then Uzziah was wroth, and had a censer in his hand to burn incense: and while he was wroth with the priests, the leprosy even rose up in his forehead before the priests in the house of the LORD, from beside the incense altar. And Azariah the chief priest, and all the priests, looked upon him, and, behold, he was leprous in his forehead, and they thrust him out from thence; yea, himself hasted also to go out, because the LORD had smitten him. 2 Chronicles 26:16–20

Uzziah was a very good king—and yet it went to his head. He began to think, "Why is it just the priests who can burn incense? That doesn't make sense to me. My reasoning argues against the necessity of that kind of legalism. My mind tells me it would be alright if I also burn incense." So Uzziah did what he was not ordained to do, called to do, anointed to do—and as a result, he contracted leprosy. Such is the result of being ruled by one's intellect rather than according to what God proclaims in His Word.

Leviticus 13:45, 46
And the leper in whom the plague is, his clothes shall be rent, and his head bare, and he shall put a covering upon his upper lip, and shall cry, unclean, unclean. All the days wherein the plague shall be in him he shall be defiled; he is unclean: he shall dwell alone; without the camp shall his habitation be.

"He shall dwell alone." I was talking to an unbeliever today about hell. "I'm going to hell," he said, "because that's where all my buddies will be."

"You need to understand something," I said. "If the Bible is true, hell is not a place where you'll be playing poker with your buddies. It's outer darkness. You won't see one other soul. It's pitch black and yet the burning goes on for eternity."

Leviticus 13:47–49
The garment also that the plague of leprosy is in, whether it be a woollen garment, or a linen garment; whether it be in the warp, or woof; of linen, or of woollen; whether in a skin, or in any thing made of skin; and if the plague be greenish or reddish in the garment, or in the skin, either in the warp, or in the woof, or in any thing of skin; it is a plague of leprosy, and shall be shewed unto the priest:

In verses 47–59, we see a description of leprosy in the garments, a fungus which would evidently cause leprosy in the skin. While we don't have to battle this particular fungus today, wise is the mom or dad who does not allow leprosy or sin to enter their homes by way of questionable music, clothing, posters, or TV.

God takes a chunk of Scripture to instruct His people on the subject of purity and the dangers of seemingly small sin because the wages of sin is death. There will be a toll, a price paid for that to which we turn a blind eye. If you want to have kids who will warm your heart rather than break it, make sure they really have a grasp of the understanding that sin leads to sorrow, while holiness leads to happiness.

Leviticus 13:50–59
And the priest shall look upon the plague, and shut up it that hath the plague seven days: and he shall look on the plague on the seventh day: if the plague be spread in the garment, either in the warp, or in the woof, or in a skin, or in any work that is made of skin; the plague is a fretting leprosy; it is unclean. He shall therefore burn that garment, whether warp or woof, in woollen or in linen, or any thing of skin, wherein the plague is: for it is a fretting leprosy; it shall be burnt in the fire. And if the priest shall look, and, behold, the plague be not spread in the garment, either in the warp, or in the woof, or in any thing of skin; then the priest shall command that they wash the thing wherein the plague is, and he shall shut it up seven days more: and the priest shall look on the plague, after that it is washed: and, behold, if the plague have not changed his colour, and the plague be not spread; it is unclean; thou shalt burn it in the fire; it is fret inward, whether it be bare within or without. And if the priest look, and, behold, the plague be somewhat dark after the washing of it; then he shall rend it out of the garment, or out of the skin, or out of the warp, or out of the woof: and if it appear still in the garment, either in the warp, or in the woof, or in any thing of skin; it is a spreading plague: thou shalt burn that wherein the plague is with fire. And the garment, either warp, or woof, or whatsoever thing of skin it be, which thou shalt wash, if the plague be departed from them, then it shall be washed the second time, and shall be clean. This is the law of the plague of leprosy in a garment of woollen or linen, either in the warp, or woof, or any thing of skins, to pronounce it clean, or to pronounce it unclean.

"If You will, cleanse me," said the leper to Jesus.

And Jesus looked on him with compassion and said, "Of course I will. Be thou clean" (see Matthew 8:3).

Jesus wants to clean us, our houses, and our clothing. "Be thou clean," is His word to us, to our families, to our congregation.

14

Where chapter 13 dealt with the characteristics of leprosy, chapter 14 addresses the cleansing of leprosy . . .

Leviticus 14:1, 2 (a)
And the LORD spake unto Moses, saying, This shall be the law of the leper in the day of his cleansing:

Verses 1 through 7 paint a perfect picture of the death, Resurrection, and Ascension of Jesus Christ 1,500 years before the event took place . . .

Leviticus 14:2 (b), 3 (a)
. . . He shall be brought unto the priest: and the priest shall go forth out of the camp . . .

The leper was to be brought to the priest outside of the camp. So, too, when we were out of it—when we were in isolation, left for dead, when there was no hope—Jesus met us where we were, outside the camp.

Leviticus 14:3 (b), 4 (a)
. . . and the priest shall look, and, behold, if the plague of leprosy be healed in the leper; then shall the priest command to take for him that is to be cleansed two birds alive and clean . . .

There is no more insignificant a bird than a sparrow. Yet when even a sparrow falls to the ground, the Father takes notice (Matthew 10:29). In their insignificance, these sparrows speak of Jesus, who humbled Himself and assumed the frailty of humanity. Yet the Father's care and awareness of their every move speaks of the depth of His love for His only begotten Son.

Leviticus 14:4 (b)
. . . and cedar wood, and scarlet, and hyssop:

Wood in Scripture speaks of the wood of the Cross, and scarlet of blood. Hyssop was the little bush with which the Israelites applied blood on the doorposts of their homes during Passover. It was also the stalk to which a sponge was attached containing a drink refused by Jesus on the Cross (John 19:29). Thus, hyssop speaks of sacrifice.

Leviticus 14:5 (a)
And the priest shall command that one of the birds be killed in an earthen vessel . . .

Jesus would become an earthen vessel just like us (2 Corinthians 4:7). He would die an earthen vessel as well.

Leviticus 14:5 (b)
. . . over running water:

Scripturally, water speaks not only of the Word, but of the Spirit. Thus, the bird was to be killed in the earthen vessel over running water because Jesus would die according to the prophecies of the Scripture that were inspired by the Spirit. When the Sparrow of our salvation died, it was neither accident nor random tragedy. Rather, it was all part of prophecy, a preordained plan of God which the Spirit inspired the writers of Scripture to record over a century before it would take place.

Leviticus 14:6, 7
As for the living bird, he shall take it, and the cedar wood, and the scarlet, and the hyssop, and shall dip them and the living bird in the blood of the bird that was killed over the running water: and he shall sprinkle upon him that is to be cleansed from the leprosy seven times, and shall pronounce him clean, and shall let the living bird loose into the open field.

The remaining bird would be dipped in the blood, the first blood shed. Why? One bird would depict the death of our Savior, our Redeemer. But the story doesn't end there. He ascended to heaven. He rose again. So a second bird was needed to complete the illustration. After being dipped in the blood of the first bird, the second bird was allowed to fly away free. After Jesus died on the Cross, the Book of Hebrews tells us He took His blood into heaven and sprinkled it in the sanctuary of heaven (Hebrews 9). Thus, the analogy is perfect.

The Resurrection is the hinge on which the door of our faith swings for if there was no Resurrection, Paul was right: we are of all men most miserable (1 Corinthians 15:19).

The Resurrection is essential because it provides proof *to* us. "Show us a sign to validate Your claims," Jesus' contemporaries demanded.

"Destroy this body and in three days, I'll rise again," Jesus answered. And indeed that continues to be the sign that sets Him apart from all others.

Secondly, the Resurrection tells us He's present *with* us. On that first Easter Sunday, His followers weren't rejoicing in theological implications or dispensational ramifications but simply in the fact that their Friend—the One who had calmed the storm and fed them, the One who had healed and loved them—was with them once again. And the same is true for every believer. What storm is raging around you tonight? What leprosy is nibbling at you? What problem is pressing down heavily on your soul? You can cast all those cares upon Jesus, for He's with you even now.

Finally, the Resurrection reminds us that He's praying *for* us. Jesus ever lives to make intercession for us (Hebrews 7:25). Therefore, if any man sin, we have an Advocate with the Father (1 John 2:1). How does He win His case? Revelation 12:11 tells us the accuser of our souls is overcome by the blood. That's why, in our text, the leper was sprinkled seven times, for seven is the number of perfection, of completion.

The Sparrow of our salvation left His nest in heaven to lodge in a tree called Calvary, to die in place of you and me. But the story doesn't end there. Because He took His blood into heaven to cleanse each of us, we can come boldly before God no matter how inadequate, how unworthy, how leprous we feel (Hebrews 4:16).

Leviticus 14:8, 9
And he that is to be cleansed shall wash his clothes, and shave off all his hair, and wash himself in water, that he may be clean: and after that he shall come into the camp, and shall tarry abroad out of his tent seven days. But it shall be on the seventh day, that he shall shave all his hair off his head and his beard and his eyebrows, even all his hair he shall shave off: and he shall wash his clothes, also he shall wash his flesh in water, and he shall be clean.

After washing his clothes, shaving his hair, and waiting seven days, the leper was to repeat the process.

Just as the leper was to be washed and shaved twice, thereby taking on the appearance of a newborn babe, Peter says, "As newborn babes, desire the sincere milk of the Word" (1 Peter 2:2). He didn't say *if* you're a newborn babe, a new Christian, a new believer, but *as* newborn babes we should continually return to the place where our so-called maturity doesn't come into play, but where we are as eager and hungry to learn as when we were first born again. We all need to shave off our false sense of maturity and wisdom, our puffed-up estimation of our spirituality. The key is to come in humility, to say, "Lord, I need to hear these simple truths over and over again that I might continue to grow."

Leviticus 14:10
And on the eighth day he shall take two he lambs without blemish, and one ewe lamb of the first year without blemish, and three tenth deals of fine flour for a meat offering, mingled with oil, and one log of oil.

Eight is the number of new beginnings. A "log" is about three-fifths of a pint.

Leviticus 14:11
And the priest that maketh him clean shall present the man that is to be made clean, and those things, before the LORD, at the door of the tabernacle of the congregation:

Who is the Priest who makes us clean and presents us before the door of the heavenly tabernacle, the throne of God? Jesus. He can keep us from falling (Jude 24). But even when I do fail, even when I do fall, He can present me faultless before God because He has cleansed me with His blood.

Leviticus 14:12, 13
And the priest shall take one he lamb, and offer him for a trespass offering, and the log of oil, and wave them for a wave offering before the LORD: and he shall slay the lamb in the place where he shall kill the sin offering and the burnt offering, in the holy place: for as the sin offering is the priest's, so is the trespass offering: it is most holy:

The leper was to make a sin offering and a trespass offering to atone for both the sin nature inherent within him as is in every man, as well as for the specific acts of sin committed by him as are committed by every man.

Leviticus 14:14
And the priest shall take some of the blood of the trespass offering, and the priest shall put it upon the tip of the right ear of him that is to be cleansed, and upon the thumb of his right hand, and upon the great toe of his right foot:

What we've heard, what we've done, where we've been is all covered by the blood. It must be—for we've heard stuff we shouldn't have, done stuff and gone places we're ashamed of.

Leviticus 14:15–17
And the priest shall take some of the log of oil, and pour it into the palm of his own left hand: and the priest shall dip his right finger in the oil that is in his left hand, and shall sprinkle of the oil with his finger seven times before the LORD: and of the rest of the oil that is in his hand shall the priest put upon the tip of the right ear of him that is to be cleansed, and upon the thumb of his right hand, and upon the great toe of his right foot, upon the blood of the trespass offering:

The blood applied to the ear, thumb, and toe was followed by oil, the symbol of the Holy Spirit. The Holy Spirit can only be applied where the blood has been. Some people try to be filled with the Holy Spirit, failing to understand that the real issue is not to be filled with the Spirit as much as it is to be emptied of sin. Too often we seek the anointing of oil—the power and presence of the Spirit—when in reality, we first need to repent of sin.

Leviticus 14:18
And the remnant of the oil that is in the priest's hand he shall pour upon the head of him that is to be cleansed: and the priest shall make an atonement for him before the LORD.

Only four groups of people were anointed with oil upon the head: kings, prophets, priests—and lepers. Isn't that just like the Lord?

Every day, she made her way to the stream from which she would draw water enough to fill the two large pots she would carry half a mile back to the manor. One of the pots being cracked, by the time she arrived, only a pot and a half were full. After a few years, the cracked pot said, "I'm not worthy. I try to be. I want to be. I mean to be. But I never come through. I only make it half way. Why didn't you discard me long ago?"

"I want to show you something," the servant girl replied. And she took the pots on the walk again. "What do you see?"

"All kinds of flowers," the pot answered.

"That's right," the girl said. "They're there because every day, without you even knowing it, you watered the ground so they could grow."

I think we all feel like cracked pots. We want to do good, but it seems although we never do. But here's what we need to know: lepers were anointed to be the bouquet of grace. Lepers like us are producing something in which our Master delights. Sure, there's an anointing on the king and the prophet and the priest. But there's an anointing on the cleansed leper as well—if for no other reason than to be a trophy of God's grace.

Leviticus 14:19–21 (a)
And the priest shall offer the sin offering, and make an atonement for him that is to be cleansed from his uncleanness; and afterward he shall kill the burnt offering: and the priest shall offer the burnt offering and the meat offering upon the altar: and the priest shall make an atonement for him, and he shall be clean. And if he be poor, and cannot get so much; then he shall take one lamb for a trespass offering to be waved, to make an atonement for him . . .

If the leper was poor, one lamb would suffice. For us, one Lamb was indeed sufficient not only to take away our sin, but the sins of the whole word (John 1:29).

Leviticus 14:21 (b), 22 (a)
. . . and one tenth deal of fine flour mingled with oil for a meat offering, and a log of oil; and two turtledoves, or two young pigeons, such as he is able to get. . . .

Such as he is able to get. "I don't get a lot of this," you might be thinking. That's okay. All the Lord requires is that you apply what you are able to get.

Leviticus 14:22 (b)–31
. . . and the one shall be a sin offering, and the other a burnt offering. And he shall bring them on the eighth day for his cleansing unto the priest, unto the door of the tabernacle of the congregation, before the LORD. And the priest shall take the lamb of the trespass offering, and the log of oil, and the priest shall wave them for a wave offering before the LORD: and he shall kill the lamb of the trespass offering, and the priest shall take some of the blood of the trespass offering, and put it upon the tip of the right ear of him that is to be cleansed, and upon the thumb of his right hand, and upon the great toe of his right foot: and the priest shall pour of the oil into the palm of his own left hand: and the priest shall sprinkle with his right finger some of the oil that is in his left hand seven times before the LORD: and the priest shall put of the oil that is in his hand upon the tip of the right ear of him that is to be cleansed, and upon the thumb of his right hand, and upon the great toe of his right foot, upon the place of the blood of the trespass offering: and the rest of the oil that is in the priest's hand he shall put upon the head of him that is to be cleansed, to make an atonement for him before the LORD. And he shall offer the one of the turtledoves, or of the young pigeons, such as he can get; even such as he is able to get, the one for a sin offering, and the other for a burnt offering, with the meat offering: and the priest shall make an atonement for him that is to be cleansed before the LORD. This is the law of him in whom is the plague of leprosy, whose hand is not able to get that which pertaineth to his cleansing.

The requirement for those who couldn't afford a lamb was less fine flour and two birds, but the procedure was the same.

Leviticus 14:32–40
And the LORD spake unto Moses and unto Aaron, saying, When ye be come into the land of Canaan, which I give to you for a possession, and I put the plague of leprosy in a house of the land of your possession; and he that owneth the house shall come and tell the priest, saying, It seemeth to me there is as it were a plague in the house: then the priest shall command that they empty the house, before the priest go into it to see the plague, that all that is in the house be not made unclean: and afterward the priest shall go in to see the house: and he shall look on the plague, and, behold, if the plague be in the walls of the house with hollow strakes, greenish or reddish, which in sight are lower than the wall; then the priest shall go out of the house to the door of the house, and shut up the house seven days: and the priest shall come again the seventh day, and shall look: and, behold, if the plague be spread in the walls of the house; then the priest shall command that they take away the stones in which the plague is, and they shall cast them into an unclean place without the city:

Some translations render this plague as a stain, or mildew. How could leprosy exist in a house? Evidently, this was the manifestation of some kind of infectious disease—to be taken seriously and inspected carefully.

Leviticus 14:41–44
And he shall cause the house to be scraped within round about, and they shall pour out the dust that they scrape off without the city into an unclean place: and they shall take other stones, and put them in the place of those stones; and he shall take other morter, and shall plaister the house. And if the plague come again, and break out in the house, after that he hath taken away the stones, and after he hath scraped the house, and after it is plaistered; then the priest shall come and look, and, behold, if the

plague be spread in the house, it is a fretting leprosy in the house: it is unclean.

After replacing the plagued stones with new stones, if the plague reappeared, it was chronic and couldn't be dealt with simply by removing a few stones.

A house with leprosy speaks of the heart. In Ephesians 3, Paul prayed that Christ might dwell in our hearts, or literally be at home in our hearts. Is Christ at home in your heart—in every room of the home of your heart? Or are there closets and attics that are leprous? You can't simply lock the door or seal them off. No, the stones are to be ripped out and carried away. Otherwise, the leprosy will spread. We think if we've given the Lord five out of eight rooms, we're doing pretty well, when, in actuality, if there's even one room with leprosy, the entire house will ultimately be affected.

Secondly, leprosy in a house speaks of the family. As priest of the home, Dad, it is your responsibility not only to clean your homes continually, but to teach your kids what is clean and what is unclean. Some moms and dads take stuff off the wall, off the bookshelf, or out of the music collection, but the kids never understand why. If there's no other reason to immerse yourself in the Word, being able to show your kids or grandchildren what leprosy does, how it works, and what to do about it is reason enough.

Thirdly, leprosy in a house relates not only to our hearts or families, but also to the church. Because we are living stones, the household of God, we're connected (1 Peter 2:5). Therefore, if you see leprosy in another stone, it is your responsibility not to murmur or gossip, not to judge or complain, but to deal with it straightforwardly and biblically. In Matthew 18, Jesus declares that if there is a problem, an offense, a difficulty between you and a brother, you are to talk with him privately. If he won't listen, you're to take another brother to help explain the issue. And if he still won't listen, you are to go to the church leadership and the church will step in. Because we're one household, if we sweep any given problem under the rug, we'll find what they found in Joshua's day—that the whole country was defeated by the sin under Achan's rug (Joshua 7:21). Therefore, let's clean house, gang.

Leviticus 14:45–53
And he shall break down the house, the stones of it, and the timber thereof, and all the morter of the house; and he shall carry them forth out of the city into an unclean place. Moreover he that goeth into the house all the while that it is shut up shall be unclean until the even. And he that lieth in the house shall wash his clothes; and he that eateth in the house shall wash his clothes. And if the priest shall come in, and look upon it, and, behold, the plague hath not spread in the house, after the house was plaistered: then the priest shall pronounce the house clean, because the plague is healed. And he shall take to cleanse the house two birds, and cedar wood, and scarlet, and hyssop: and he shall kill the one of the birds in an earthen vessel over running water: and he shall take the cedar wood, and the hyssop, and the scarlet, and the living bird, and dip them in the blood of the slain bird, and in the running water, and sprinkle the house seven times: and he shall cleanse the house with the blood of the bird, and with the running water, and with the living bird, and with the cedar wood, and with the hyssop, and with the scarlet: but he shall let go the living bird out of the city into the open fields, and make an atonement for the house: and it shall be clean.

Here we see the same procedure as seen in verses 1 through 7. This time, however, it relates to the house.

Leviticus 14:54
This is the law for all manner of plague of leprosy, and scall,

As defined in 13:30 "scall" is a dry leprosy.

Leviticus 14:55–57
And for the leprosy of a garment, and of a house, and for a rising, and for a scab, and for a bright spot: to teach when it is unclean, and when it is clean: this is the law of leprosy.

This chapter ends with an admonition that God's people are to be able to determine themselves and to teach others what is clean and unclean as it relates to leprosy—whether it be on the flesh, in a garment, or within a house.

15

There are certain chapters in the Bible from which one would not necessarily choose to preach or teach. This is one of those. It deals with issues that are rather personal and can be a bit embarrassing, at least initially. But every part of God's Word has an amazing way of being applicable to our daily lives. So bear with me as we work through the text and discover applications I believe you will find to be helpful.

Chapters 13 and 14 deal with the law of the leper. Leprosy is an obvious uncleanness. The law presented in the chapter before us, however, addresses hidden uncleanness and speaks of the sins we are able to camouflage or hide from others but which are just as insidious and sometimes even more dangerous than those which are obvious.

David understood this. "Cleanse me from secret faults," and, "Thou desirest truth in the inward parts," he prayed (Psalm 19:12, 51:6). David understood that regardless of what people thought of him or how he presented himself outwardly, God desired truth integrity and rightness internally. And such is the matter before us . . .

Leviticus 15:1, 2
And the LORD spake unto Moses and to Aaron, saying, Speak unto the children of Israel, and say unto them, when any man hath a running issue out of his flesh, because of his issue he is unclean.

Although some commentators debate it, most believe the running issue spoken of here refers to a venereal disease. And before we condemn those who contract such an illness, let us remember Jesus' words in Matthew 5 when He said, "You have heard it said that you're not to commit adultery. But I say unto you, whoever looks at a woman with lust in his heart has already committed adultery," for suddenly none of us escape indictment.

"In me," Paul would declare, "dwells no good thing" (Romans 7:18). Even David, the man after God's own heart cried out, "Cleanse me and purge me" (see Psalm 51:7). No matter how spiritual we think we are, no matter how mature, we have all contracted uncleanness of one sort or another.

Leviticus 15:3–11
And this shall be his uncleanness in his issue: whether his flesh run with his issue, or his flesh be stopped from his issue, it is his uncleanness. Every bed, whereon he lieth that hath the issue, is unclean: and every thing, whereon he sitteth, shall be unclean. And whosoever toucheth his bed shall wash his clothes, and bathe himself in water, and be unclean until the even. And he that sitteth on any thing whereon he sat that hath the issue shall wash his clothes, and bathe himself in water, and be unclean until the even. And he that toucheth the flesh of him that hath the issue shall wash his clothes, and bathe himself in water, and be unclean until the even. And if he that hath the issue spit upon him that is clean; then he shall wash his clothes, and bathe himself in water, and be unclean until the even. And what saddle soever he rideth upon that hath the issue shall be unclean. And whosoever toucheth any thing that was under him shall be unclean until the even: and he that beareth any of those things shall wash his clothes, and bathe himself in water, and be unclean until the even. And whomsoever he toucheth that hath the issue, and hath not rinsed his hands in water, he shall wash his clothes, and bathe himself in water, and be unclean until the even.

In dealing with this chronic discharge of this disease, the key phrase is, there is to be a washing, a scrubbing, a cleansing with water. This predated medical knowledge by thousands of years, for it wasn't until the nineteenth century that doctors understood the importance of cleanliness. Prior to that time, a clean doctor was considered to be about as effective as a clean football player. They wore blood on their clothes and hands as a sign of success. But in the 1800s, one particular doctor made a correlation between the number of autopsies performed and the number of patients who, treated by the same doctors who performed the autopsies hours earlier, died from infectious disease. When he realized it was the doctors themselves who were spreading disease, he came to the revolutionary conclusion that doctors should wash after every operation.

"How shall a young man cleanse his way?" David asked. "By taking heed to the Word" (Psalm 119:9).

"We are washed by the water which is the Word" Paul said (Ephesians 5).

"Now ye are clean by the Word I have spoken unto you," Jesus declared (John 15:3).

There is indeed a washing, a cleansing from spiritual disease as we drink of the Scriptures. Like the doctors in the dark ages of medicine, we mistakenly think we don't have to wash ourselves spiritually all that often. But yet we wonder why we remain in an infected condition. God's way is that His Word would be the cleansing agent which would purify and protect us from the infection of lustful thoughts, bad attitudes, cynical spirits, and the host of other diseases which we think no one sees.

It's amazing how much better those who take time to be in the Word personally and fellowship with the Lord intimately do than those who think they don't need to wash. What we're doing here tonight is not just filling up an hour or two, but we're saying, "Lord, I'm trusting something is happening miraculously, supernaturally even now, that Your Word is doing a cleansing work in me."

Leviticus 15:12
And the vessel of earth, that he toucheth which hath the issue, shall be broken: and every vessel of wood shall be rinsed in water.

Throughout Scripture, the earthen vessel speaks of you and me (2 Corinthians 4:7). And this passage is no exception, for just as any ceramic plate or piece of pottery the diseased man touched was to be destroyed, so too, there is a price to pay for promiscuity—not the least of which is that everyone touched by such a one gets shattered and broken in the process.

Leviticus 15:13
And when he that hath an issue is cleansed of his issue; then he shall number to himself seven days for his cleansing, and wash his clothes, and bathe his flesh in running water, and shall be clean.

In John 13, Jesus said to Peter, "If I don't wash you, you can have no part with Me." In other words, "If you don't allow washing, there won't be intimacy between you and Me, fellowship the way there ought to be." That is why immersing ourselves in the water of the Word is absolutely essential and nonnegotiable.

Leviticus 15:14, 15
And on the eighth day he shall take to him two turtledoves, or two young pigeons, and come before the LORD unto the door of the tabernacle of the congregation, and give them unto the priest: and the priest shall offer them, the one for a sin offering, and the other for a burnt offering; and the priest shall make an atonement for him before the LORD for his issue.

When free of the infection, the man was to bring two sacrifices: the burnt offering that spoke of consecration, and the sin offering which spoke of confession. The fact that a sin offering was required is the reason this affliction, more than likely, was the result of this man's own sin.

Leviticus 15:16
And if any man's seed of copulation go out from him, then he shall wash all his flesh in water, and be unclean until the even.

Verses 16 through 19 deal not with the chronic discharge of venereal disease, but the sporadic discharge of a man's seed.

Leviticus 15:17, 18
And every garment, and every skin, whereon is the seed of copulation, shall be washed with water, and be unclean until the even. The woman also with whom man shall lie with seed of copulation, they shall both bathe themselves in water, and be unclean until the even.

Because sporadic discharge is natural and right in the context of marriage, there is no need for a sin offering. But even the most natural and beautiful things are unclean because everything is polluted and tainted by sin. That is why Romans 8 says all of nature groans, waiting for the day of redemption (8:22). All of nature is in a fallen condition. And as wonderful as it is to watch the sun set into the ocean, to be in the mountains on a beautiful winter day, or to experience the love of husband or wife, even the most beautiful aspects of nature are not what they once were. When Adam sinned, all of nature crashed. And what we see around us, as beautiful as it may be, is not what it was before the Fall and not what it will be when Christ comes back and restores the earth (Revelation 21:1).

Leviticus 15:19–24
And if a woman have an issue, and her issue in her flesh be blood, she shall be put apart seven days: and whosoever toucheth her shall be unclean until the even. And every thing that she lieth upon in her separation shall be unclean: every thing also that she sitteth upon shall be unclean. And whosoever toucheth her bed shall wash his clothes, and bathe himself in water, and be unclean until the even. And whosoever toucheth any thing that she sat upon shall wash his clothes, and bathe himself in water, and be unclean until the even. And if it be on her bed, or on any thing whereon she sitteth, when he toucheth it, he shall be unclean until the even. And if any man lie with her at all, and her flowers be upon him, he shall be unclean seven days; and all the bed whereon he lieth shall be unclean.

This speaks of the periodic uncleanness of a woman. And, again, because no sin is involved, the sacrifice of an animal is not required. What God declares here, reinforced in Leviticus 18:19 and 20:18, is that during this period of time, a man is to be careful with his wife, that he is to make allowances for her condition. If understood correctly, rather than having a restrictive effect on marriage, this can have a renewing effect, as is God's intent.

Leviticus 15:25
And if a woman have an issue of her blood many days out of the time of her separation, or if it run beyond the time of her separation; all the days of the issue of her uncleanness shall be as the days of her separation: she shall be unclean.

Verses 25 through 30 deal not with the monthy cycle of women, but with a chronic uncleanness which, due to the sin offering required in verse 30, appears to be linked to a sexually transmitted disease.

Leviticus 15:26–28
Every bed whereon she lieth all the days of her issue shall be unto her as the bed of her separation: and whatsoever she sitteth upon shall be unclean, as the uncleanness of her separation. And whosoever toucheth those things shall be unclean, and shall wash his clothes, and bathe himself in water, and be unclean until the even. But if she be cleansed of her issue, then she shall number to herself seven days, and after that she shall be clean.

While this disorder would have been uncomfortable for any woman, it would have been unbearable for a Jewish woman because as long as the problem persisted, she would be ceremonially unclean—unable to go into the tabernacle or temple, restricted in what she could do publicly and socially. Once seven days passed in which she had no issue, however, she would be declared clean.

Leviticus 15:29, 30
And on the eighth day she shall take unto her two turtles, or two young pigeons, and bring them unto the priest, to the door of the tabernacle of the congregation. And the priest shall offer the one for a sin offering, and the other for a burnt offering; and the priest shall make an atonement for her before the Lord for the issue of her uncleanness.

As concerning the man in verses 2 through 15, the burnt offering would speak of consecration—of rededication, renewal, recommitment—while the sin offering would speak of confession.

Leviticus 15:31
Thus shall ye separate the children of Israel from their uncleanness; that they die not in their uncleanness, when they defile my tabernacle that is among them.

Although physical hygiene is a primary factor in this discussion, it's not the only one, for God says that which comes form from a man or woman can cause a defiling in the tabernacle or in the congregation which can result in the death of fellowship, of unity, of victory . . .

Leviticus 15:32, 33
This is the law of him that hath an issue, and of him whose seed goeth from him, and is defiled therewith; and of her that is sick of her flowers, and of him that hath an issue, of the man, and of the woman, and of him that lieth with her that is unclean.

Some people come to a congregation, a community of believers with an ax to grind, a bone to pick, a fish to fry. While an occasional issue is understandable, the chronic issue is sin. And death is the result. Marriages die. Personalities shrivel. Congregations are sapped of their vitality, robbed of the joy that once was or the power that could have been.

What is the solution? It's found in Luke 8 . . .

"Someone touched Me," Jesus said—not brushed against Him, not bumped into Him, but really touched Him. And indeed someone had. A woman who had been unclean for twelve years had touched the border of His garment. Why? The border of the garment spoke of one's position. Therefore, in so doing, she was submitting to Jesus' authority.

Through prayer, we can do exactly as she did. We can say, "Lord, You have me married to this man or that woman. You have me working for that boss. You are in control. I'm touching the hem of Your garment and will submit to Your authority through them."

In addition to authority, the hem spoke of destiny, for in Numbers 15, God told the children of Israel to place upon it a ribbon of blue. Blue being the color of heaven, they would be reminded of their heavenly destiny with every step they took. "I go to prepare a place for you," Jesus told us (John 14:2). In the meantime, He's preparing us for the place through people around us who might rub us the wrong way in order to get us to be looking forward to heaven.

Finally, the garment spoke of intimacy, for just as Ruth, a pagan woman, said to Boaz, a godly man, "Put your garment over me," we can draw near to our Greater than Boaz, Jesus Christ, by placing ourselves under His authority and realizing He is our destiny.

16

We come to the section of Scripture that deals with the most holy day of the Jewish calendar—Yom Kippur, the Day of Atonement. *Kaphar*, the Hebrew word for "atonement," actually means "to cover." The Day of Atonement signified not a cleansing of sin, but a covering because sin could not be cleansed through the offering of a bull or a ram, a goat or a lamb. It could only be cleansed by the blood of a perfect Man. The Book of Hebrews argues that, because the Day of Atonement had to take place annually, it spoke of something better to come. And that was God's only Son.

Chapter 16 is divided into three sections. Verses 1 through 6 deal with the preparation of the priest, 7 through 19 with the preparation of the place, and 20 through 34 with the preparation of the people—all to be performed exactingly and painstakingly for they prefigured what Jesus would do as both our great High Priest and the Lamb of God.

Leviticus 16:1, 2
And the Lord spake unto Moses after the death of the two sons of Aaron, when they offered before the Lord, and died; and the Lord said unto Moses, speak unto Aaron thy brother, that he come not at all times into the holy place within the vail before the mercy seat, which is upon the ark; that he die not: for I will appear in the cloud upon the mercy seat.

Linked to chapter 10, these opening verses of chapter 16 hint that, in addition to burning strange fire, Nadab and Abihu violated God's Law by going in to the Holy of Holies.

Suppose you are an Amorite, Amonite, or a Jebusite watching the Israelites fervently engaged in pitching a huge tent. An Israelite happens across your path and you ask him what they're doing. "Erecting the tabernacle," he would answer, "the tent where God meets with His people."

"I want to go there and meet Him, too," you would say.

"Sorry, it's just for Israelites," he would answer.

"Then I wish I were an Israelite," you would say.

"It's not enough to simply be an Israelite," he would answer. "You have to be of the tribe of Levi. They're the only ones who get to put up the tabernacle."

"Then I wish I were a Levite," you would say.

"It's not that simple," he would say. "To go into the tabernacle, you must be a priest, which means you must be of the family of Aaron."

"Then I wish I were of the family of Aaron," you would say.

"It's not that simple," he would say. "Only the oldest member of the family can serve as the high priest. And only the high priest can actually meet with God."

"Then I wish I were the oldest member of the family of Aaron so I could meet with God whenever I wished," you would say.

"It's not that simple," he would say. "The high priest can only meet with God one day each year on Yom Kippur. And if he's not properly prepared, he'll die. See ya later."

We can have the tendency to read the Old Testament and think it would be wonderful to live in days when people saw firsthand the parting of the Red Sea, the drowning of Pharaoh's army, manna falling from heaven. Yet, in reality, we live in much better days because we experience every day that which only one of them could experience on only one day each year: the *chabod*, the glory of God. It's an unbelievable privilege God has given to you and me. Thus, these days are better indeed.

Leviticus 16:3
Thus shall Aaron come into the holy *place:* with a young bullock for a sin offering, and a ram for a burnt offering.

The word "place" is in italics. Therefore, the phrase should read, "Thus shall Aaron come into the Holy of Holies." The tabernacle was divided into two rooms. The first room was the holy place in which was the table of showbread, the altar of incense, and the golden candlestick. It was the room from into which the priests would go daily. But there was a second room—a smaller room, separated from the first room by a veil—called the Holy of Holies into which only the high priest could enter one day each year to experience the glory of God.

Leviticus 16:4
He shall put on the holy linen coat, and he shall have the linen breeches upon his flesh, and shall be girded with a linen girdle, and with the linen mitre shall he be attired: these are holy garments; therefore shall he wash his flesh in water, and so put them on.

Normally, the high priest would wear glorious garments—colorful robes bordered by pomegranates and bells, a jeweled breastplate, a golden plate across his forehead. But on Yom Kippur, he would lay aside his regal robes and wear only the simple linen garments worn by the priests. And that is what Jesus Christ, our great High Priest, did for us when He laid aside the attributes of His Divinity and clothed Himself with humanity in order to offer Himself a sacrifice for you and me.

***For topical study of Leviticus 16:4 entitled "Humility," turn to page* 410.**

Leviticus 16:5, 6
And he shall take of the congregation of the children of Israel two kids of the goats for a sin offering, and one ram for a burnt offering. And Aaron shall offer his bullock of the sin offering, which is for himself, and make an atonement for himself, and for his house.

The first offering was for the high priest himself because, unlike our great High Priest, Aaron was a sinner, and he had to deal with his own sin before he could deal with anyone else's.

Leviticus 16:7–10
And he shall take the two goats, and present them before the LORD at the door of the tabernacle of the congregation. And Aaron shall cast lots upon the two goats; one lot for the LORD, and the other lot for the scapegoat. And Aaron shall bring the goat upon which the LORD's lot fell, and offer him for a sin offering. But the goat, on which the lot fell to be the scapegoat, shall be presented alive before the LORD, to make an atonement with him, and to let him go for a scapegoat into the wilderness.

Because the wages of sin is death (Romans 6:23), one goat would be killed. But, because if we confess our sin, God is faithful and just to forgive us our sin (1 John 1:9), one goat would be spared.

Leviticus 16:11, 12
And Aaron shall bring the bullock of the sin offering, which is for himself, and shall make an atonement for himself, and for his house, and shall kill the bullock of the sin offering which is for himself: and he shall take a censer full of burning coals of fire from off the altar before the LORD, and his hands full of sweet incense beaten small, and bring it within the vail:

After offering a burnt offering for himself, Aaron was to take the coals from the altar of incense into the Holy of Holies.

Leviticus 16:13
And he shall put the incense upon the fire before the LORD, that the cloud of the incense may cover the mercy seat that is upon the testimony, that he die not:

Just as the Holy of Holies would be filled with the incense of prayer and intercession, the man or woman who experiences God's presence to the fullest degree is the man or woman who prays.

Leviticus 16:14
And he shall take of the blood of the bullock, and sprinkle it with his finger upon the mercy seat eastward; and before the mercy seat shall he sprinkle of the blood with his finger seven times.

Seven is not only the number of perfection, but when Jesus Christ, the Lamb of God, was sacrificed, He bled from seven points: There was a crown of thorns around His head. His back was whipped with the flagellum. His left and His right hands were pierced through with spikes driven into the wood of the Cross, as were His left and right feet. And finally, His side bled from the thrust of a spear. Thus, prophetically, the blood was to be sprinkled seven times prefiguring what Christ would do perfectly, completely.

Leviticus 16:15
Then shall he kill the goat of the sin offering, that is for the people, and bring his blood within the vail, and do with that blood as he did with the blood of the bullock, and sprinkle it upon the mercy seat, and before the mercy seat:

Easter Sunday was in reality a depiction, a fulfillment of Yom Kippur, for when the disciples looked in the empty tomb that morning, what would they have seen? A blood-splattered slab where the body of Christ had lain with an angel sitting on either end—a perfect picture of the mercy seat and the ark of the covenant.

Leviticus 16:16–19
And he shall make an atonement for the holy place, because of the uncleanness of the children of Israel, and because of their transgressions in all their sins: and so shall he do for the tabernacle of the congregation, that remaineth among them in the midst of their uncleanness. And there shall be no man in the tabernacle of the congregation when he goeth in to make an atonement in the holy place, until he come out, and have made an atonement for himself, and for his household, and for all the congregation of Israel. And he shall go out unto the altar that is before the LORD, and make an atonement for it; and shall take of the blood of the bullock, and of the blood of the goat, and put it upon the horns of the altar round about. And he shall sprinkle of the blood upon it with his finger seven times, and cleanse it, and hallow it from the uncleanness of the children of Israel.

As Aaron sprinkled the blood of the bull and goat to cleanse the Holy of Holies, he did so alone because Christ Jesus alone would do the work of atonement, of bringing us into oneness with the Father. That is why on the Cross of Calvary, He cried, "My God, My God, why hast thou forsaken Me?" (Matthew 27:46) He was utterly, completely, totally alone, for He alone could pay the price. No one else would, no one else could.

Leviticus 16:20–22
And when he hath made an end of reconciling the holy place, and the tabernacle of the congregation, and the altar, he shall bring the live goat: and Aaron shall lay both his hands upon the head of the live goat, and confess over him all the iniquities of the children of Israel, and all their transgressions in all their sins, putting them upon the head of the goat, and shall send him away by the hand of a fit man into the wilderness: and the goat shall bear upon him all their iniquities unto a land not inhabited: and he shall let go the goat in the wilderness.

One goat had been sacrificed because the wages of sin is death. But the other goat was brought before Aaron in order that he might lay his hands on its head and verbally, articulately, carefully confess the sins of the nation and, in a sense, transfer the sin to the goat. Symbolically bearing the sins of the whole nation, the goat was lead to the wilderness, where it symbolically carried the sins of the congregation out of sight.

The scapegoat is an illustration of God's declaration that He will remember our sins and iniquities no more (Jeremiah 31:34). When this understanding finally drops from one's head to his heart, it is so exhilarating, so liberating because most of us believe that God, like Santa Claus, is making a list and checking it twice, that God is keeping score. He's not. We remember each other's sin. But God has chosen to erase from His memory bank the sins we confess.

Most people know this doctrinally, but because they don't believe it in the deepest part of their soul, they believe God is disappointed in them because of what happened ten years ago or ten weeks ago or ten minutes ago. In Psalm 103, God says, "As far as the east is from the west, so I have put your iniquities from Me." In Isaiah 38:17, He says, "I have cast your sins behind My back." Isaiah 44:22 tells us He has blotted out our sins like a thick cloud; Job 14:17 that He puts our sins in a bag and sews it up; and Micah 7:19 that our sins are cast into the depth of the sea.

What the scapegoat pictured symbolically and temporarily, the Lamb of God achieved practically and eternally when He died on the Cross of Calvary for each and every sin of all of humanity.

Leviticus 16:23, 24
And Aaron shall come into the tabernacle of the congregation, and shall put off the linen garments, which he put on when he went into the holy place, and shall leave them there: and he shall wash his flesh with water in the holy place, and put on his garments, and come forth, and offer his burnt offering, and the burnt offering of the people, and make an atonement for himself, and for the people.

We who are involved in service plead the blood before we give a Bible study, witness to someone, lead in worship—but here is a key principle in ministry. It is not only when Aaron went into the Holy of Holies that he was to make a sacrifice and wash himself, but he did so again when his service therein was complete. So, when you're through singing your song or teaching a study, or witnessing to someone at work, you need to plead the blood again because you will be vulnerable to sin when you come out of ministry even more than you were going in because one of two things will happen. You will either feel inadequate and depressed, saying, "I forgot to share that," or, "I didn't hit those notes," or, "I am a miserable failure,"—or, if your witnessing is impacting, your music note-perfect, you'll be proud of your accomplishment. Either way, Satan has you right where he wants you. That is why when you're through ministering, you need to again plead the blood, to be cleansed and empowered once again.

Leviticus 16:25–34
And the fat of the sin offering shall he burn upon the altar. And he that let go the goat for the scapegoat shall wash his clothes, and bathe his flesh in water, and afterward come into the camp. And the bullock for the sin offering, and the goat for the sin offering, whose blood was brought in to make atonement in the holy place, shall one carry forth without the camp; and they shall burn in the fire their skins, and their flesh, and their dung. And he that burneth them shall wash his clothes, and bathe his flesh in water, and afterward he shall come into the camp. And this shall be a statute for ever unto you: that in the seventh month, on the tenth day of the month, ye shall afflict your souls, and do no work at all, whether it be one of your own country, or a stranger that sojourneth among you: for on that day shall the priest make an atonement for you, to cleanse you, that ye may be clean from all your sins before the LORD. It shall be a sabbath of rest

unto you, and ye shall afflict your souls, by a statute for ever. And the priest, whom he shall anoint, and whom he shall consecrate to minister in the priest's office in his father's stead, shall make the atonement, and shall put on the linen clothes, even the holy garments: and he shall make an atonement for the holy sanctuary, and he shall make an atonement for the tabernacle of the congregation, and for the altar, and he shall make an atonement for the priests, and for all the people of the congregation. And this shall be an everlasting statute unto you, to make an atonement for the children of Israel for all their sins once a year. And he did as the LORD commanded Moses.

The Day of Atonement took place in the seventh month, on the tenth day. Seven is the number of perfection, ten the number of the Law. Do we keep the law perfectly? No. And that is the reason for the Day of Atonement.

On the Day of Atonement, how would the children of Israel know if the offering was sufficient? They would know their sins were covered if the high priest emerged from the tabernacle—for if he was not properly prepared, if his offering was unacceptable, he would die in the Holy of Holies, in the presence of a Holy, Almighty God.

In the same way, I know with certainty that I am forgiven because our great High Priest, Jesus Christ, came out of the tomb. Therefore, the Book of Hebrews declares, "Let us come boldly unto the throne of grace that we might find grace and mercy to help in time of need" (4:16). Because the work of atonement has been accomplished completely and perfectly, God invites us specifically and personally to come in to the Holy of Holies, to come before His throne. The question is, Will we take advantage of the invitation?

The story is told of a telegraph company in the 1800s seeking to hire a telegraph operator. The salary offered being quite substantial, only the most qualified were encouraged to apply. On the day of the invitation, seven men showed up. As they sat outside the boss' office waiting for their interview, listening to the telegraph operators working in the background, suddenly, the last one to arrive stood up and went into the boss' office without being asked. The boss emerged a few minutes later and said, "Gentlemen, thank you for coming. But there will be no need for an interview. I've hired this man for the position."

"Wait a minute," one of the remaining six protested, "that's not fair. This man was the last to arrive. We should have had our chance to be interviewed for this position."

"You did," the boss said. "While you were sitting here, one of the operators was tapping out a message saying, 'If you receive this message, come into my office immediately. The job is yours.'"

All of the men were trained. All were qualified. All had knowledge of Morse Code—but only one of the seven was tuned in to the message being tapped out right then.

I can't help but wonder today if there is one in seven who has really heard the message being tapped out which says, "Come boldly to My throne. Talk with Me. Cast your care upon Me. Receive from Me help, strength, instruction."

Have you heard the message, Mom—the tap, tap, tap of the Morse Code of the Master saying, "Come and talk to Me about your son or daughter. This is the moment"?

Have you heard the message, husband? Do you hear the tapping of the Master, saying, "Come boldly to the throne of grace that you might find help for your marriage which is presently unraveling"?

If you're wondering if you should go to college, take the job, move away; if you're struggling with physical affliction or fighting depression, I wonder if there is one in seven who hears the Lord saying, "The stone is rolled away. The veil is rent. The way is open. Come on in!"

HUMILITY
A Topical Study of LEVITICUS 16:4

No wonder Yom Kippur held such significance for the people of God, for it was the day in which all unconfessed sins, all unknown sins, all unrecognized sins were covered.

As significant as Yom Kippur was for the nation, it was a day especially significant for the high priest, for it was the one day each year that he would enter the Holy of Holies and experience the physical, tangible glory of God. Thus, for the high priest especially, Yom Kippur was a glorious day of exaltation.

But before exaltation came humiliation. Before ministry came humility. You see, normally the high priest would be decked out in garments of glory—with a breastplate full of jewels, onyx stones on his shoulders, a golden mitre upon his head, robes of blue with pomegranates and bells circling the hem, a colorful belt around his waist. On Yom Kippur, however, he took off these garments of glory and exchanged them for the common linen garments worn by his brethren.

And in both his humiliation and exaltation, Aaron as high priest, paints a picture of our great High Priest, Jesus Christ.

Jesus will also have a day of exaltation . . .

> *Wherefore God also hath highly exalted him, and given him a name which is above every name: That at the name of Jesus every knee should bow, of things in heaven, and things in earth, and things under the earth; and that every tongue should confess that Jesus Christ is Lord, to the glory of God the Father.*
> Philippians 2:9–11

But before exaltation came humiliation . . .

> *Let this mind be in you, which was also in Christ Jesus: who, being in the form of God, thought it not robbery to be equal with God: but made himself of no reputation, and took upon him the form of a servant, and was made in the likeness of men: and being found in fashion as a man, he humbled himself, and became obedient unto death, even the death of the cross.* Philippians 2:5–8

Jesus stripped Himself of the royal robes of His divine attributes in exchange for the common linen robe of humanity.

Jesus was humbled at His birth when He, the Creator of the universe was born in a manger, surrounded by hay. He was humbled before His brethren when He girded Himself with a towel and washed their feet (John 13:4). He was humbled during His betrayal yet called His betrayer, "Friend" (Matthew 26:50). No wonder, then, that in the only autobiographical statement He ever made, He said, "I am meek and lowly of heart" (Matthew 11:29).

The mindset of Jesus Christ is to be ours as well. How does this happen? The text in Philippians offers important clues as to how humility can be woven into the very fabric of our personality . . .

> *Let nothing be done through strife or vainglory; but in lowliness of mind let each esteem other better than themselves.* Philippians 2:3

In his wonderful work on New Testament word studies, Dr. Kenneth Wuest points out that the idea of esteeming others better than oneself as seen in Philippians 2:3 does not necessarily mean looking at everyone as better than you, but rather looking on others as excelling themselves. Approving someone else is the very essence of humility.

Secondly, the truly humble person will look at himself honestly.

In 2 Samuel 16, we see David's son rebelling against him to the point where David and his men flee Jerusalem. Upon their departure, a man named Shimei called out to David, "You're a bloody man and you're getting what you deserve," while throwing rocks and dust in his direction.

"Let me lop off this guy's head," one of David's men said.

But David forbade it, saying, "He's right. I am a bloody man. The Lord is allowing this to happen."

Shimei would eventually lose his head as God dealt with him. But in the meantime, David accepted his words as being from the Lord. The Lord sometimes allows Shimeis to come into our lives to reveal to us our weaknesses that we might look at others compassionately and sympathetically rather than haughtily and hard-heartedly, that we might not be those who find fault or put down, but rather those who embrace and forgive.

"Woe unto the Edomites. Woe unto the Amonites. Woe unto the Moabites. Woe unto the Perizzites," Daniel declared in the first five chapters of his Book. But in chapter 6, he saw the Lord and cried, "Woe is *me*."

Why should we be humble? Because humility brings about unity. There will be unity in the body of Christ to the degree that there is humility. Secondly, humility brings about liberty. The humble person is the freest person of all because he is completely free from protecting his rights, promoting himself, or polishing his image.

- The world says, "Promote yourself."
  The Lord says, "Humble yourself."
- The world says, "Watch out for Number One."
  The Lord says, "Esteem others better than yourself."
- The world says, "Claw your way to the top."
  The Lord says, "The way up is down."

May God begin to work humility into our lives that we might be those who are like our linen-clad great High Priest, Jesus.

17

Leviticus 17:1–9

And the LORD spake unto Moses, saying, Speak unto Aaron, and unto his sons, and unto all the children of Israel, and say unto them; This is the thing which the LORD hath commanded, saying, What man soever there be of the house of Israel, that killeth an ox, or lamb, or goat, in the camp, or that killeth it out of the camp, And bringeth it not unto the door of the tabernacle of the congregation, to offer an offering unto the LORD before the tabernacle of the LORD; blood shall be imputed unto that man; he hath shed blood; and that man shall be cut off from among his people: to the end that the children of Israel may bring their sacrifices, which they offer in the open field, even that they may bring them unto the LORD, unto the door of the tabernacle of the congregation, unto the priest, and offer them for peace offerings unto the LORD. And the priest shall sprinkle the blood upon the altar of the LORD at the door of the tabernacle of the congregation, and burn the fat for a sweet savour unto the LORD. And they shall no more offer their sacrifices unto devils, after whom they have gone a whoring. This shall be a statute for ever unto them throughout their generations. And thou shalt say unto them, Whatsoever man there be of the house of Israel, or of the strangers which sojourn among you, that offereth a burnt offering or sacrifice, And bringeth it not unto the door of the tabernacle of the congregation, to offer it unto the LORD; even that man shall be cut off from among his people.

Ezekiel 20 tells us that when the Israelites were in Egypt for four hundred years, they were involved in idolatry. Therefore, because God the Father was very concerned about the tendency of His people to fall into heresy which would lead to idolatry, He said, "I want all sacrifices to be made at the tabernacle."

"We don't like the tabernacle. It's too confining," some might have protested. "Can't five of us just get together and sacrifice in the woods?"

"No," God said.

"Who needs priests?" others might have asked. "Aren't we all spiritual? Can't we all offer sacrifices?"

"No," God said.

There are those today who think they can worship God without going to church. "My church is on the golf course," they say. Or, "at the lake." Or, "on the beach" "Why go into a stuffy building?" they ask. "Isn't God the God of creation?"

This passage reveals God's heart concerning the way He wants to be worshiped—not because He is stuffy and contrary, but because He knows what will happen practically. You see, over the years, I have noticed that the people who choose to seek the Lord at their lake house rather than in the sanctuary with the congregation never do well over the long haul. There can be a tendency—especially for older Christians—to say, "Church was great for our first ten years, but now we just need some space on Sundays," failing to realize that it's when we're with our brothers and sisters—living stones being fit together for a holy habitation (1 Peter 2:5)—that sometimes we're rubbed the wrong way by necessity. That is, it is the interaction, the fellowship, the seeking God together that not only smoothes our rough edges, but also gives us stability.

Leviticus 17:10, 11

And whatsoever man there be of the house of Israel, or of the strangers that sojourn among you, that eateth any manner of blood; I will even set my face against that soul that eateth blood, and will cut him off from among his people. For the life of the flesh is in the blood: and I have given it to you upon the altar to make an atonement for your souls: for it is the blood that maketh an atonement for the soul.

When Peter Marshall, Chaplain of the United States Senate in the 1940s, first arrived in Washington DC to pastor the New York Avenue Presbyterian Church, an elderly lady greeted him, saying, "I do so hope you won't talk too much about the blood as our previous pastor did."

"I promise I won't talk too much about the blood," the young Scotsman assured her, "because it is impossible to talk too much about the blood."

Peter Marshall nailed it perfectly. It is impossible to talk too much about the blood of Jesus Christ. Why? Because this book is soaked in blood, saturated with blood. Ours is a bloody religion indeed. And there's a reason for that. The Book of Hebrews tells us that without the shedding of blood there can be no remission of sin (Hebrews 9:22). Therefore, man's greatest need being forgiveness, it only stands to reason that blood would be spoken of freely and consistently throughout the Word.

Why is blood the key to forgiveness? Because, as seen in our text, the life of the flesh is in the blood. That is why it was blood that cried out when the first murder was committed (Genesis 4:10). There is indeed a potency, a mystery, a power in blood for it is the essence of life. And in Leviticus, God uses these powerful properties of blood to not only show us the seriousness of our sin, but to point to the sacrifice of His Son.

Leviticus 17:12–14 (a)
Therefore I said unto the children of Israel, No soul of you shall eat blood, neither shall any stranger that sojourneth among you eat blood. And whatsoever man there be of the children of Israel, or of the strangers that sojourn among you, which hunteth and catcheth any beast or fowl that may be eaten; he shall even pour out the blood thereof, and cover it with dust. For it is the life of all flesh; the blood of it is for the life thereof . . .

Because the blood is sacred, orthodox Jews, as they do to this day, were exceedingly careful not to eat any meat not thoroughly drained of every drop of blood. And then an itinerant Rabbi from Galilee came along one day and had the audacity to proclaim, "Except you drink My blood, you have no life in you" (John 6:53). No wonder it was at that point that many walked away to follow Him no more (John 6:66).

I know what Jesus was saying. So do you. He wasn't talking about cannibalism, about drinking His blood literally in violation of Leviticus 17. He was talking about intimacy—how we are to devour the Word, how we are to open our hearts, how we are to embrace the Work He did when He shed His blood for our sin. Yet, when His followers turned away, Jesus didn't say, "Wait a minute. Let Me explain what I meant. It's not what you think." Why didn't He do that? Why didn't He clarify the issue? I believe it was for three basic reasons . . .

He knew what the Holy Spirit would do. That is, He knew that which He shared could only be made real when the Holy Spirit made it alive. And because it is the work of the Spirit to bring all things to remembrance (John 14:26), Jesus knew the Spirit would bring this occasion to their minds and make application in due season.

Secondly, Jesus knew what the Father alone could do. Only the Father can cause a person to come to Jesus (John 6:44). The Spirit gives revelation—but it is the Father who determines who will come to His Son.

Thirdly, Jesus knew what the true disciples should do. When asked if he was about to leave with the rest, Peter answered, "Where else would we go? You alone have the words of eternal life" (John 6:67, 68). Jesus didn't hurry to explain His words to those who left because He knew that they must learn to do what you and I must do—walk by faith. Why? Because only faith is strong enough to weather the storms ahead.

When we don't understand what's going on, when we're troubled by a teaching we've heard or a passage we've read, when we're going through a tragedy or a heartbreak, if we're not careful, we will be like those in John 6:66, failing to understand that the only way our faith becomes strong is when, like Peter, we believe in spite of that which we don't initially understand.

Jesus knew what the Holy Spirit would do. He knew what the Father alone could do. He knew what His true disciples should do. And knowing these things, Jesus ministered in a way that was wonderfully relaxed, incredibly peaceful.

Leviticus 17:14 (b)–16
. . . therefore I said unto the children of Israel, Ye shall eat the blood of no manner of flesh: for the life of all flesh is the blood thereof: whosoever eateth it shall be cut off. And every soul that eateth that which died of itself, or that which was torn with beasts, whether it be one of your own country, or a stranger, he shall both wash his clothes, and bathe himself in water, and be unclean until the even: then shall he be clean. But if he wash them not, nor bathe his flesh; then he shall bear his iniquity.

Here, verse 11 is repeated: The life of the flesh is in the blood. Physiologically, this understanding preceded medicine by thousands of years, for it wasn't until 1628 that an anatomist named Dr. Harvey identified the importance of the red fluid circulating within us. Spiritually, we know that just as our own blood keeps us alive temporarily, the shed blood of the Lamb of God gives us life eternally.

> Forasmuch as ye know that ye were not redeemed with corruptible things, as silver and gold, from your vain conversation received by tradition from your fathers; but with the precious blood of Christ, as of a lamb without blemish and without spot: Who verily was foreordained before the foundation of the world, but was manifest in these last times for you, who by him do believe in God, that raised him up from the dead, and gave him glory; that your faith and hope might be in God.
>
> 1 Peter 1:18–21

When Jesus died on the Cross, He paid for each one of our sins specifically. How could He have accomplished this in only six hours two thousand years ago on Calvary? Peter tells us He was slain before the foundation of the world. And John tells us that when we see Him, we'll see Him as a Lamb having just been slain (Revelation 5:6). Therefore, from the perspective of the time/

space continuum, the work of salvation was indeed complete in six hours on the Cross. But from the eternal perspective—where there is no future and no past (Ecclesiastes 3:15)—Jesus' suffering was infinitely greater than anything we can even begin to comprehend. This being the case, how can I lightly say, "It doesn't matter if I harbor an unforgiving spirit, have a lousy attitude, or engage in a questionable activity. It's all forgiven because of Calvary"?

The work of salvation is complete, finished, done. Yet as true as that is, it is also true that the price Jesus paid for each of our sins individually is unspeakably more than we can understand this side of eternity.

Because the life of the flesh is in the blood, Jesus gave His blood so that we could have life.

18 Chapter 18 deals with personal sanctity and moral propriety. It also paints a very humiliating picture of the depths of depravity of which man is capable. As we observe human nature and study the Scripture with regard to what God has to say concerning our fallen state, I am totally amazed that our Father could love us—a people who have wandered away from Him, taken advantage of Him, rebelled against Him. The Word paints a picture of the depravity of human nature, and yet, through it all, God says, "I love you anyway."

Leviticus 18:1–5
And the LORD spake unto Moses, saying, Speak unto the children of Israel, and say unto them, I am the LORD your God. After the doings of the land of Egypt, wherein ye dwelt, shall ye not do: and after the doings of the land of Canaan, whither I bring you, shall ye not do: neither shall ye walk in their ordinances. Ye shall do my judgments, and keep mine ordinances, to walk therein: I am the LORD your God. Ye shall therefore keep my statutes, and my judgments: which if a man do, he shall live in them: I am the LORD.

Here in chapter 18, God declares, "I am the Lord your God. You are to behave in a way unlike that which you saw in Egypt." During the four hundred-year period the children of Israel were in Egypt, the Egyptians were the most advanced culture in world history. Impressive in many ways, it was also an immoral culture. The Canaanites being even more immoral than the Egyptians, God said, "You are to be neither like those in the land from which you came nor like those in the land to which you're going. I am the Lord your God. I know how you were created. I know what will bring you lasting joy, true peace. If you do what I say, you'll experience the way life was meant to be."

Leviticus 18:6–20
None of you shall approach to any that is near of kin to him, to uncover their nakedness: I am the LORD. The nakedness of thy father, or the nakedness of thy mother, shalt thou not uncover: she is thy mother; thou shalt not uncover her nakedness. The nakedness of thy father's wife shalt thou not uncover: it is thy father's nakedness. The nakedness of thy sister, the daughter of thy father, or daughter of thy mother, whether she be born at home, or born abroad, even their nakedness thou shalt not uncover. The nakedness of thy son's daughter, or of thy daughter's daughter, even their nakedness thou shalt not uncover: for theirs is thine own nakedness. The nakedness of thy father's wife's daughter, begotten of thy father, she is thy sister, thou shalt not uncover her nakedness. Thou shalt not uncover the nakedness of thy father's sister: she is thy father's near kinswoman. Thou shalt not uncover the nakedness of thy mother's sister: for she is thy mother's near kinswoman. Thou shalt not uncover the nakedness of thy father's brother, thou shalt not approach to his wife: she is thine aunt. Thou shalt not uncover the nakedness of thy daughter in law: she is thy son's wife; thou shalt not uncover her nakedness. Thou shalt not uncover the nakedness of thy brother's wife: it is thy brother's nakedness.Thou shalt not uncover the nakedness of a woman and her daughter, neither shalt thou take her son's daughter, or her daughter's daughter, to uncover her nakedness; for they are her near kinswomen: it is wickedness. Neither shalt thou take a wife to her sister, to vex her, to uncover her nakedness, beside the other in her life time. Also thou shalt not approach unto a woman to uncover her nakedness, as long as she is put apart for her uncleanness. Moreover thou shalt not lie carnally with thy neighbour's wife, to defile thyself with her.

In the context of this passage, "to uncover the nakedness," "to take," "to approach," and "to lie with" are all phrases which speak of incest—forbidden in every form. Seen in verses 18 and 19, marrying sisters simultaneously was also forbidden, as was adultery.

God addresses issues that seem to be common sense because the Canaanite culture was caught up in these very practices. And so, I fear, will ours be. Should the Lord tarry, I believe we will be shocked by the widespread acceptance of once-taboo issues like incest and pedophilia within the next twenty years. Should the Lord tarry, they will be destined to join the rank of homosexuality—once abhorred, but now embraced.

God is not wasting His words here. As His people are poised to enter a new land, He warns them very straightforwardly of the pressures and temptations that will pull them into perversion. "I am the Lord your God," He says. "You're not to do these things. They are unacceptable, unallowable. If you do what I say, you'll live. If you compromise you'll die." God covers every possibility because He knows what people will do, where they will go if they allow themselves to set foot on the path to perversity.

Leviticus 18:21
And thou shalt not let any of thy seed pass through the fire to Molech, neither shalt thou profane the name of thy God: I am the LORD.

Molech was the god of prosperity. The Canaanites made idols of Molech—five feet high with a hollow stomach—out of cast iron. They built fires in the bellies of these idols, heated them to the point of incandescence, and placed their babies as sacrifices on their red-hot arms.

How could this happen? Because those involved in Molech worship thought the babies weren't real people. Sound familiar? Babies are burned in our culture not on the arms of Molech, but with a saline solution in the name of prosperity. "I can't afford a baby right now," we say. "I don't have the resources to raise this child. I'll be better off next time around." It's a lie as old as Molech.

Leviticus 18:22
Thou shalt not lie with mankind, as with womankind: it is abomination.

"We're not really sure how God feels about homosexuality," people say. Really? He calls it an abomination. How clear does He need to be?

Leviticus 18:23
Neither shalt thou lie with any beast to defile thyself therewith: neither shall any woman stand before a beast to lie down thereto: it is confusion.

"Confusion" speaks of insanity.

Leviticus 18:24, 25
Defile not ye yourselves in any of these things: for in all these the nations are defiled which I cast out before you: And the land is defiled: therefore I do visit the iniquity thereof upon it, and the land itself vomiteth out her inhabitants.

God declares the land itself will vomit out the cultures involved in homosexuality and incest, pedophilia and bestiality. And history has shown that cultures who have embraced these behaviors have collapsed.

Leviticus 18:26–30
Ye shall therefore keep my statutes and my judgments, and shall not commit any of these abominations; neither any of your own nation, nor any stranger that sojourneth among you: (For all these abominations have the men of the land done, which were before you, and the land is defiled). That the land spue not you out also, when ye defile it, as it spued out the nations that were before you. For whosoever shall commit any of these abominations, even the souls that commit them shall be cut off from among their people. Therefore shall ye keep mine ordinance, that ye commit not any one of these abominable customs, which were committed before you, and that ye defile not yourselves therein: I am the LORD your God.

Chapter 18 deals with physical purity—but I believe, as the family of God, we need to hear and heed what God would say to us on a spiritual level. That is, are we guilty of exposing the nakedness of a brother or sister in God's family?

In Genesis 9, Noah, a godly man, was exposed in a way that spoke of moral compromise. Ham told his brothers. But Shem and Japheth stretched a blanket between them, walked in backwards, and covered their father's nakedness. Realizing what had happened, Noah cursed Ham's son. Shem and Japheth, on the other hand, were blessed because love covers a multitude of sins (1 Peter 4:8).

When someone else stumbles, do you, like Ham, talk about it? Or, like Shem and Japheth, do you walk in backwards not wanting to look at the nakedness of those in your family?

As they entered the Promised Land, the children of Israel were told not to touch anything from the city of Jericho. But Achan saw a wedge of gold, a bar of silver, and a Babylonian garment he couldn't resist. No one will know, *he thought. So he took them and hid them under the floor of his tent. When the men of Israel went to their next battle in Ai, what should have been a walk in the park was a crushing defeat to God's people. When he asked God the reason, Joshua was told there was sin in the family. Thus, the congregation was defeated because a man and his family covered the problem.*

In Genesis 9, Shem and Japheth were blessed for covering Noah's sin. In Joshua 7, Achan's family was stoned for doing that very thing. The stories seem to be contradictory. Which are we to do? The solution, as always, is seen in Jesus . . .

There sat the disciples, arguing over who was the greatest. Not only did their pride fill the room, but so did the smell of their dirty feet. John 13 tells us that Jesus neither covered their sin nor exposed it, but dealt with it by washing their feet.

The Genesis and Joshua accounts come together in Jesus. So, I have no right to point out the dirt of any sister or brother unless I am willing to get on my knees and deal with it. When we're open and honest with people concerning our own flaws and failings, they can receive the work we see needs to be done in their lives. We must be careful not to uncover the nakedness of another. And yet we must realize the responsibility and privilege that is ours to deal with issues in order to see people do better. The only way I'll find a balance between the two is to be like Jesus, to cover and cleanse sin by uncovering myself on my knees.

19 I love the Law of God, for the Law of God reveals the love of God. God is a God of love. And He desires His people to live lives that reflect this attribute. He desires us to be a people who love each other. Consequently, when God established the nation of Israel, He laid down regulations for their society that would provide an atmosphere conducive to love. The first half of Leviticus 19 in particular deals with the regulations to establish a society that would move and grow in love . . .

Leviticus 19:1, 2
And the Lord spake unto Moses, saying, Speak unto all the congregation of the children of Israel, and say unto them, Ye shall be holy: for I the Lord your God am holy.

Chapter 19 is a continued call to holiness. Holiness is related to wholeness. And God wants us to be a whole people. When you understand this, the commands of God are no longer burdensome, but you'll find yourself wanting to embrace them, eager to learn them, ready to practice them. The Father wants us to be a blessed people—blessed in our families and our marriages, in our relationships and our occupations. He just wants us to be happy. Satan, the deceiver and liar, says holiness leads to strangeness. "You'll be miserable," he hisses. "You'll missss out on all the fun." Not so.

God doesn't look in the mirror and say, "I'm not really pleased with this aspect of Myself," or, "I wish I was a bit different in this area of My personality." No, because He is holy, God is totally, completely, absolutely happy with every part of His being. You see, in essence, the world "holy" simply means "whole." And because He's whole, because He lacks nothing, God is supremely happy with who He is. That's why He wants us to be happy, too.

Holiness leads to happiness. That's an absolute, nonnegotiable, irrefutable spiritual principle. God wants us to be holy for He is holy. He commands us to be holy, for He wants us to be happy.

Leviticus 19:3 (a)
Ye shall fear every man his mother, and his father . . .

Holiness begins at home. On Mt. Sinai, the children of Israel were commanded to honor their father and mother. Honor speaks of action. Here, they are commanded to fear—or revere—them. Reverence speaks of attitude. Notice there's no qualifier in either command. How we treat and feel about our parents has nothing to do with our perception of whether or not they were good parents. The fact is, none of us would be alive without our parents, so that in itself is reason enough to honor and revere them.

Leviticus 19:3 (b)
. . . and keep my sabbaths: I am the Lord your God.

To be whole people, we need to set aside one day in seven to rest our bodies, stretch our spirits, and consider spiritual things.

Leviticus 19:4
Turn ye not unto idols, nor make to yourselves molten gods: I am the Lord your God.

The problem with molten gods is that they can be molded according to whatever it is one wants them to be. People still do this today whenever they attempt to mold God into their image in order to justify their own behavior.

Leviticus 19:5–8
And if ye offer a sacrifice of peace offerings unto the LORD, ye shall offer it at your own will. It shall be eaten the same day ye offer it, and on the morrow: and if ought remain until the third day, it shall be burnt in the fire. And if it be eaten at all on the third day, it is abominable; it shall not be accepted. Therefore every one that eateth it shall bear his iniquity, because he hath profaned the hallowed thing of the LORD: and that soul shall be cut off from among his people.

Unlike the sin offering or the trespass offering, the burnt offering or the meal offering, the peace offering was unique in that it was offered simply to say, "Lord, I'm enjoying my relationship with You. You have forgiven me and been good to me. There's peace between You and me because of Your goodness and grace and mercy."

Also, unlike any other offering, the one offering it would eat of the meat of the peace offering. It was to be eaten on the day it was offered, or at the latest, leftovers could be eaten on the second day. In this, it's as if God is saying, "Don't nibble of My presence. Dive in! Eat until you're full, satiated, completely satisfied."

Leviticus 19:9, 10
And when ye reap the harvest of your land, thou shalt not wholly reap the corners of thy field, neither shalt thou gather the gleanings of thy harvest. And thou shalt not glean thy vineyard, neither shalt thou gather every grape of thy vineyard; thou shalt leave them for the poor and stranger: I am the LORD your God.

When they harvested their fields, the Israelites were to leave whatever was on the edges for those who were poor. Rabbinical scholars tell us that this would amount to approximately fifteen percent of one's crop. This was a wonderful welfare program because food was made available to anyone willing to roll up his sleeves and work for it. Cars and houses just keep getting bigger and bigger. But in time of prosperity, we are to make sure we care about those less fortunate than us. It's God's heart that we do so, an element of holiness, a part of the way we will become whole people.

Leviticus 19:11 (a)
Ye shall not steal . . .

While verses 9 and 10 would have spoken to the rich, verse 11, speaks to the poor.

Leviticus 19:11 (b), 12
. . . neither deal falsely, neither lie one to another. And ye shall not swear by my name falsely, neither shalt thou profane the name of thy God: I am the LORD.

We usually think of profaning the Lord's name in conjunction with using it as a curse word. But the word "profane" actually means "to make common." Therefore, in addition to those who use the Lord's name in cursing, believers can be guilty of profaning His name by speaking of it lightly, by saying, "The Lord told me . . ." or, "The Lord showed me . . ." so often that they actually make it seem common.

Leviticus 19:13
Thou shalt not defraud thy neighbour, neither rob him: the wages of him that is hired shall not abide with thee all night until the morning.

Do whatever it takes to pay whatever you owe. Don't say, "I'll pay you in the morning, when my financial situation looks brighter." No, God says, "Pay now." This is God's way—and it's one of the ways in which the rubber of holiness meets the road.

Leviticus 19:14
Thou shalt not curse the deaf, nor put a stumblingblock before the blind, but shalt fear thy God: I am the LORD.

In addition to the obvious injunction not to be hardened to those who are physically inflicted, blindness and deafness are pictures throughout Scripture of the spiritual insensitivity of a world that's lost.

Cursing the deaf is subtle. Do we have an attitude of cursing those who bother us, toward those who act worldly because their ears are closed to an awareness of God? How did Jesus deal with the deaf? Turn to the gospel of Mark . . .

> And they bring unto him one that was deaf, and had an impediment in his speech; and they beseech him to put his hand upon him. And he took him aside from the multitude, and put his fingers into his ears, and he spit, and touched his tongue; and looking up to heaven, he sighed, and saith unto him, Ephphatha, that is, Be opened. And straightway his ears were opened, and the string of his tongue was loosed, and he spake plain. Mark 7:32–35

Jesus not only took the deaf man aside from the crowd and gave him individual attention, but He put His fingers in the deaf man's ears and gave him an individual touch. Jesus didn't have to touch him. He could have spoken the word and that would have sufficed—but had He done so, the deaf man wouldn't have heard it. So He related to that man where he was. Then Jesus looked to heaven, showing the man from whence his healing would come. That's the pattern—touching people and relating to them where they're at concerning their knowledge and understanding. When Jesus spoke, the man's ears were opened. And it is as you and I speak the Word of God that spiritually deaf ears are opened as well.

Secondly, we're not to trip the blind. The concept of being a stumbling block is also seen in 1 Corinthians 8, where a controversy had arisen concerning meat that had been offered to idols before it was sold in discount markets. Looking for a good buy and knowing that idols were powerless to affect meat, some Christians would purchase the meat at discount prices. Others, however, said the meat was defiled and not to be eaten. Paul's answer was that while believers are the freest of men, we're not to use our freedom in a way that causes others to stumble. In any given situation, each of us will either be a stumbling block or a stepping stone. People will either be hindered in coming to Jesus or we'll be stepping stones on their path to Him.

Sometimes I feel we're the ones with blinded eyes, who don't see people properly; that we're the ones with deaf ears, unable to hear the cries of lost humanity. How can the Lord make us more like Himself? Turn again to Mark's Gospel . . .

> And he cometh to Bethsaida; and they bring a blind man unto him, and besought him to touch him. And he took the blind man by the hand, and led him out of the town; and when he had spit on his eyes, and put his hands upon him, he asked him if he saw ought. And he looked up, and said, I see men as trees, walking. After that he put his hands again upon his eyes, and made him look up: and he was restored, and saw every man clearly. Mark 8:22–25

Sometimes I think we who have been touched by the hand of Jesus Christ, we who have received divine enlightenment, still see men as trees, trees that are in our way, trees that are to be cut down and used for our own purposes. How did Jesus solve this problem? He touched the blind man a second time and made him look up. And then the man saw every man clearly.

You and I also need to look up, for when we fix our eyes on Jesus, we become like Him (1 John 3:2). When I don't look up to the Lord, I'll look down on men. I'll see them as trees. But when I focus on Jesus, I see people as He sees them.

Leviticus 19:15
Ye shall do no unrighteousness in judgment: thou shalt not respect the person of the poor, nor honour the person of the mighty: but in righteousness shalt thou judge thy neighbour.

We must be careful not to view poverty as a sign of spirituality or riches as a sign of carnality. God blessed Abraham to the point his wealth was incredible and blessed Solomon with unsurpassed wealth (1 Kings 3:13). And yet Amos was a poor farmer and Jesus had nowhere to even lay His head. Therefore, because wealth or the lack thereof is a matter of what God chooses to do in each individual life, rich and poor are to be treated as equals.

Leviticus 19:16
Thou shalt not go up and down as a talebearer among thy people: neither shalt thou stand against the blood of thy neighbour: I am the LORD.

A talebearer hurts three people: the person he talks about, the person he talks to, and himself.

In a very real sense, people are who we say they are—regardless of whether what we say is true. People will either be lifted up or put down in the estimation of others by what we say about them. Jesus draws a direct parallel between murder and the tongue because we have the power to kill another's reputation with our words (Matthew 5:21). Secondly, telling tales, or gossiping, hurts the person who listens because it affects the way he or she will view the person being talked about. Finally, gossip hurts the talebearer himself because every time we gossip, we become smaller and smaller. As has been wisely said, great minds talk about ideas or ideals; good minds about events; small minds about people. In which company are you?

Leviticus 19:17
Thou shalt not hate thy brother in thine heart: thou shalt in any wise rebuke thy neighbour, and not suffer sin upon him.

If you see a problem in the life of a sister or brother that needs to be addressed, don't gossip about it, but go directly to the one in error. Love him or her enough in the Lord to share your concern.

Leviticus 19:18
Thou shalt not avenge, nor bear any grudge against the children of thy people, but thou shalt love thy neighbour as thyself: I am the LORD.

"Thou shalt love thy neighbor as thyself," was identified as the second greatest commandment by the One who would live it out completely (Matthew 22:37–40).

Leviticus 19:19 (a)
Ye shall keep my statutes. Thou shalt not let thy cattle gender with a diverse kind:

In 2 Corinthians 6, Paul refers to this idea when he says, "Be not unequally yoked with an unbeliever." You might think you're an exception, but you are playing a risky game if you're entertaining the idea of marrying an unbeliever. For every marriage of a believer to an unbeliever that makes it, there are one hundred that end up in disaster.

Leviticus 19:19 (b)
. . . thou shalt not sow thy field with mingled seed . . .

As seen in Matthew 13, seed is a picture of the Word. There are those who say, "I appreciate this Bible study stuff, but I also want to explore other forms of theology which don't view the Bible as God's Word. I want to combine the best parts of all religions." God, however, forbids this.

Leviticus 19:19 (c)
. . . neither shall a garment mingled of linen and woollen come upon thee.

Linen breathes; wool causes sweat. That is why the priests were to wear linen rather than wool. So, we must be oh, so careful lest we say, "Grace is okay, but there needs to be some wool, some things we can do to earn God's favor, to merit His blessing." No. God's priests were to wear no wool, for grace isn't merely the starting point—it's the only point.

Leviticus 19:20–22
And whosoever lieth carnally with a woman, that is a bondmaid, betrothed to an husband, and not at all redeemed, nor freedom given her; she shall be scourged; they shall not be put to death, because she was not free. And he shall bring his trespass offering unto the LORD, unto the door of the tabernacle of the congregation, even a ram for a trespass offering. And the priest shall make an atonement for him with the ram of the trespass offering before the LORD for his sin which he hath done: and the sin which he hath done shall be forgiven him.

Although the man was to offer a trespass offering who had sexual relations with one of his servant girls, as seen in your margin, both he and the women were to be scourged. Why was the woman scourged? I believe that God is declaring that when men take advantage of women, the woman will pay a price even though she ought not to, for such is the tragic yet inevitable repercussion of sexual sin.

Leviticus 19:23–25
And when ye shall come into the land, and shall have planted all manner of trees for food, then ye shall count the fruit thereof as uncircumcised: three years shall it be as uncircumcised unto you: it shall not be eaten of. But in the fourth year all the fruit thereof shall be holy to praise the LORD withal. And in the fifth year shall ye eat of the fruit thereof, that it may yield unto you the increase thereof: I am the LORD your God.

Upon entering the Promised Land, for three years, the children of Israel were not to eat of the trees they planted. Horticulturists tell us that trees not allowed to bear fruit for their first three years are incredibly productive in the fourth year. Spiritually, I believe God is saying that when it comes to the bearing of spiritual fruit through ministry, before there is ordination there must be observation. Paul would put it this way: Be careful that you don't lay hands on any man too quickly (1 Timothy 5:22).

Leviticus 19:26
Ye shall not eat any thing with the blood: neither shall ye use enchantment, nor observe times.

Astrology and psychic matters are completely forbidden.

Leviticus 19:27, 28
Ye shall not round the corners of your heads, neither shalt thou mar the corners of thy beard. Ye shall not make any cuttings in your flesh for the dead, nor print any marks upon you: I am the LORD.

Tattooing and body piercing were commonly done for the dead in Egypt as part of their religion.

Leviticus 19:29
Do not prostitute thy daughter, to cause her to be a whore; lest the land fall to whoredom, and the land become full of wickedness.

While it would seem "Do not prostitute thy daughter" goes without saying, we need to be aware we don't allow our daughters' attire or appearance to cast them in a questionable light.

Leviticus 19:30–32
Ye shall keep my sabbaths, and reverence my sanctuary: I am the LORD. Regard not them that have familiar spirits, neither seek after wizards, to be defiled by them: I am the LORD your God. Thou shalt rise up before the hoary head, and honour the face of the old man, and fear thy God: I am the LORD.

Ours is a youth-obsessed culture. But God's heart, God's way, God's Word is to honor older people.

Leviticus 19:33, 34
And if a stranger sojourn with thee in your land, ye shall not vex him. But the stranger that dwelleth with you shall be unto you as one born among you, and thou shalt love him as thyself; for ye were strangers in the land of Egypt: I am the LORD your God.

"Be careful," God says to His people newly released from Egypt, "that when you're in the land, you don't treat the stranger differently than you treat each other for you know what it's like to be a stranger."

Leviticus 19:35, 36
Ye shall do no unrighteousness in judgment, in meteyard, in weight, or in measure. Just balances, just weights, a just ephah, and a just hin, shall ye have: I am the LORD your God, which brought you out of the land of Egypt.

God's people are to be those who deal justly.

Leviticus 19:37
Therefore shall ye observe all my statutes, and all my judgments, and do them: I am the LORD.

The chapter ends with, "I am the Lord," a statement repeated fifteen times in this chapter of only thirty-seven verses, a statement through which we are reminded that as Lord, God not only had the wisdom to establish laws He knew would lead to the happiness of holiness, but that He had the power to enforce them as well.

20

Leviticus 20:1–5
And the LORD spake unto Moses, saying, Again, thou shalt say to the children of Israel, Whosoever he be of the children of Israel, or of the strangers that sojourn in Israel, that giveth any of his seed unto Molech; he shall surely be put to death: the people of the land shall stone him with stones. And I will set my face against that man, and will cut him off from among his people; because he hath given of his seed unto Molech, to defile my sanctuary, and to profane my holy name. And if the people of the land do any ways hide their eyes from the man, when he giveth of his seed unto Molech, and kill him not: then I will set my face against that man, and against his family, and will cut him off, and all that go a whoring after him, to commit whoredom with Molech, from among their people.

Nothing was more abhorrent in the eyes of God than the worship of the Amonite deity, Molech. *Molech* means "king" because he was the main god in the Amonite pantheon of false gods. Molech promised pleasure and prosperity to those who placed their babies on the red-hot arms of the idols representing him. So abhorrent was Molech worship to God that not only were those directly involved to be stoned, but those who hid knowledge of them were to be cut off as well.

Stoning was God's prescribed form of execution and, because those who made the accusations were those who threw the stones, it would be a very sobering experience for the entire community. Not only would this cause people to be very careful about the testimony they gave, but, public as it was, it would be an unforgettable illustration of the horrendous price of sin.

Leviticus 20:6
And the soul that turneth after such as have familiar spirits, and after wizards, to go a whoring after them, I will even set my face against that soul, and will cut him off from among his people.

Those who became involved with psychic hotlines, tarot cards, fortune-telling, astrology were to be cut off from the believing community.

Leviticus 20:7
Sanctify yourselves therefore, and be ye holy: for I am the LORD your God.

"Sanctify," or *qadash* in Hebrew, means "to set apart"—set apart *to* God and set apart *from* sin. Can we really be set apart from sin? Can we truly be sanctified?

John Wesley and his brother, Charles, godly men both, believed that if people lived a disciplined life before God, they could achieve a state of sanctity in which they would never sin again. Determined to see this understanding come to fruition, they developed a method to do this—and the Methodist movement was born. On the other hand, John Calvin and others said it was impossible to be completely and totally sanctified in this life. And these two views remain in the church to this day.

When Jesus died on the Cross, He didn't say, "To be continued," or, "This will do for now." He said, "It is *finished*" (John 19:30). That is why Paul could address the Corinthian believers as those who have been sanctified (1 Corinthians 1:2). Practically, the Corinthian congregation was full of problems. So are we. But positionally, the Corinthians were sanctified. And so are we.

Leviticus 20:8
And ye shall keep my statutes, and do them: I am the LORD which sanctify you.

Verse 7 begins with "Sanctify yourselves." Verse 8 ends with, "I am the Lord which sanctify you." Is sanctification something we do, or is it something God does for us? It's both. God sanctifies us—yet He won't do it without our participation. We see this illustrated perfectly in 2 Kings 5.

Plagued by leprosy, a Syrian general named Naaman heard there was a prophet in Israel doing miracles. He traveled there and was told by Elisha to dip in the Jordan River 7 times.

Naaman was offended. "That dirty river? We have bigger, cleaner rivers in Syria," he protested.

But when his advisors said, "What do you have to lose?," he followed Elisha's instructions, and after his seventh dip, his leprosy was gone.

If we want to be free from the leprosy eating away at our marriages, our families, our joy, we have a part to play. Seven being the number of completion, and water being emblematic of the Word, we are to dip into the Word over and over and over again. And as we do, God meets us and we begin to see we are indeed sanctified. As we fellowship with Him, listen to Him, and obey Him, we experience the unmistakable sanctifying process. "Sanctify yourselves," God says, "and as you do, I will sanctify you." Without Him, we can't. Without us, He won't.

Leviticus 20:9
For every one that curseth his father or his mother shall be surely put to death: he hath cursed his father or his mother; his blood shall be upon him.

In the Fifth Commandment, God said, "Honor thy father and thy mother that thy days may be long upon the land" (Exodus 20:12). So important is this command in God's economy, that He strengthens it here by saying, "Honor your father and mother—lest you die."

Leviticus 20:10
And the man that committeth adultery with another man's wife, even he that committeth adultery with his neighbour's wife, the adulterer and the adulteress shall surely be put to death.

Adultery causes death. Families split apart. Hearts break. Tragedy follows.

Leviticus 20:11, 12
And the man that lieth with his father's wife hath uncovered his father's nakedness: both of them shall surely be put to death; their blood shall be upon them. And if a man lie with his daughter in law, both of them shall surely be put to death: they have wrought confusion; their blood shall be upon them.

Verses 10 through 21 deal with the issue of sexual purity—the same issues as seen in chapter 18 as God underscores the necessity for His people to walk in purity.

Leviticus 20:13
If a man also lie with mankind, as he lieth with a woman, both of them have committed an abomination: they shall surely be put to death; their blood shall be upon them.

God again declares homosexuality to be an abomination.

Leviticus 20:14–16
And if a man take a wife and her mother, it is wickedness: they shall be burnt with fire, both he and they; that there be no wickedness among you. And if a man lie with a beast, he shall surely be put to death: and ye shall slay the beast. And if a woman approach unto any beast, and lie down thereto, thou shalt kill the woman, and the beast: they shall surely be put to death; their blood shall be upon them.

That God goes into detail in this section concerning the sins already addressed in chapter 18 speaks of the prevalence of such sins in the surrounding nations as well as the tendency of the Israelites to follow culture—a warning no less necessary for us.

Leviticus 20:17–21
And if a man shall take his sister, his father's daughter, or his mother's daughter, and see her nakedness, and she see his nakedness; it is a wicked thing; and they shall be cut off in the sight of their people: he hath uncovered his sister's nakedness; he shall bear his iniquity. And if a man shall lie with a woman having her sickness, and shall uncover her nakedness; he hath discovered her fountain, and she hath uncovered the fountain of her blood: and both of them shall be cut off from among their people. And thou shalt not uncover the nakedness of thy mother's sister, nor of thy father's sister: for he uncovereth his near kin: they shall bear their iniquity. And if a man shall lie with his uncle's wife, he hath uncovered his uncle's nakedness: they shall bear their sin; they shall die childless. And if a man shall take his brother's wife, it is an unclean thing: he hath uncovered his brother's nakedness; they shall be childless.

The primarily application here is to incestuous matters. But the secondary issue, as addressed in the Talmud, is, an injunction against nakedness among family members—for such liberty leads to confusion. This matter is not one of prudishness, but of propriety.

Leviticus 20:22–27
Ye shall therefore keep all my statutes, and all my judgments, and do them: that the land, whither I bring you to dwell therein, spue you not out. And ye shall not walk in the manners of the nation, which I cast out before you: for they committed all these things, and therefore I abhorred them. But I have said unto you, Ye shall inherit their land, and I will give it unto you to possess it, a land that floweth with milk and honey: I am the LORD your God, which have separated you from other people. Ye shall therefore put difference between clean beasts and unclean, and between unclean fowls and clean: and ye shall not make your souls abominable by beast, or by fowl, or by any manner of living thing that creepeth on the ground, which I have separated from you as unclean. And ye shall be holy unto me: for I the LORD am holy, and have severed you from other people, that ye should be mine. A man also or woman that hath a familiar spirit, or that is a wizard, shall surely be put to death: they shall stone them with stones: their blood shall be upon them.

The children of Israel were to walk in the ways of the Lord lest the land "spew them out." In other words, built into creation are certain laws which, if violated, bring repercussions as inviolable as the law of gravity . . .

If I jumped off a ten-story building, saying, "I'm not sure the law of gravity still applies. Times have changed. It was okay in Newton's day, but we live in an enlightened age, in a day of greater understanding, education, tolerance, and freedom," I would end up splattered on the ground—not as a result of God punishing me, but simply as the result of thinking I could break the law of gravity.

So, any culture which chooses to walk deeper and deeper into perversion will experience natural, inevitable repercussions and will eventually collapse as God's laws of nature take effect and purge the land of their presence.

21

Because Jesus didn't rapture you when you asked Him into your heart, because we have been saved to serve, because we're to be priests standing before God on behalf of people and standing before people on behalf of God, the chapter before us, dealing with rules and regulations for priestly ministry, is applicable to each of us . . .

Leviticus 21:1–4
And the LORD said unto Moses, Speak unto the priests the sons of Aaron, and say unto them, There shall none be defiled for the dead among his people: but for his kin, that is near unto him, that is, for his mother, and for his father, and for his son, and for his daughter, and for his brother, And for his sister a virgin, that is nigh unto him, which hath had no husband; for her may he be defiled. But he shall not defile himself, being a chief man among his people, to profane himself.

The Old Testament paints material pictures of New Testament spiritual principles. And this passage is no exception. Barring their own families, Old Testament priests were to have no contact with dead people. As New Testament priests, we are to have no contact with those who are spiritually dead unless it is to bring them into the family of God. If you spend time with those who are spiritually dead solely because you enjoy their activities and like their company, you're compromising your calling as a priest. But if your purpose for hanging out with the spiritually dead is to share your faith with them, you're doing what our great High Priest did, who was the Friend of sinners because He had a desire to see them brought into the kingdom.

Leviticus 21:5
They shall not make baldness upon their head, neither shall they shave off the corner of their beard, nor make any cuttings in their flesh.

The shaving of the head, cutting of the beard, cutting of the flesh were all practices of the Egyptian death cult. Those who have been born again ought not bear the marks of death on their bodies or clothing.

Leviticus 21:6–8
They shall be holy unto their God, and not profane the name of their God: for the offerings of the LORD made by fire, and the bread of their God, they do offer: therefore they shall be holy. They shall not take a wife that is a whore, or profane; neither shall they take a woman put away from her husband: for he is holy unto his God. Thou shalt sanctify him therefore; for he offereth the bread of thy God: he shall be holy unto thee: for I the LORD, which sanctify you, am holy.

Marriage being foundational to ministry and providing credibility to ministry, the priests were to marry godly women.

Leviticus 21:9
And the daughter of any priest, if she profane herself by playing the whore, she profaneth her father: she shall be burnt with fire.

In this, it's as if God is saying, "I want this lesson burned into the fabric of your culture—that men, you're responsible to care for your daughters, to pray for them, to give training to them. And daughters, you're to realize that you will burn your parents and the ministry if you walk in compromise."

People read passages like this and say they are patently, grossly unfair and unkind—as if those of whom such passages speak are surely in hell. But such is not the case. For example, it could be that the most important ministry Achan and his family could ever do was to impress on people the importance of purity. Thus, even the punishment of death takes on a different perspective in light eternity.

Leviticus 21:10–12
And he that is the high priest among his brethren, upon whose head the anointing oil was poured, and that is consecrated to put on the garments, shall not uncover his head, nor rend his clothes; Neither shall he go in to any dead body, nor defile himself for his father, or for his mother; neither shall he go out of the sanctuary, nor profane the sanctuary of his God; for the crown of the anointing oil of his God is upon him: I am the LORD.

In times of difficulty and tragedy, we ought not to rend our clothes, but rather to keep on ministering and thereby experience the healing and help which come from serving others.

***For topical study of Leviticus 21:10–12 entitled "God's Solution to Sadness," turn to page* 426.**

Leviticus 21:13–15
And he shall take a wife in her virginity. A widow, or a divorced woman, or profane, or an harlot, these shall he not take: but he shall take a virgin of his own people to wife. Neither shall he profane his seed among his people: for I the LORD do sanctify him.

If the priests were to marry godly women (v. 7), how much more was the high priest to marry a godly woman. In ourselves, we are neither godly nor pure. Yet our great High Priest, Jesus Christ, has made us so in order that we might be His Bride.

Leviticus 21:16, 17
And the LORD spake unto Moses, saying, Speak unto Aaron, saying, Whosoever he be of thy seed in their generations that hath any blemish, let him not approach to offer the bread of his God.

He that had a blemish was not to serve in priestly ministry. In our day, these blemishes speak of spiritual principles, eternal truths, internal matters . . .

Leviticus 21:18 (a)
For whatsoever man he be that hath a blemish, he shall not approach: a blind man . . .

Blindness speaks of a lack of vision. The man or woman lacking vision won't be used in ministry successfully, for without vision, people perish (Proverbs 29:18).

Leviticus 21:18 (b)
. . . or a lame . . .

A priest must be able to walk—not leap in emotion, nor run in fervor, but simply walk in steadiness and consistency.

Leviticus 21:18 (c)
. . . or he that hath a flat nose . . .

Priests must have a good sense of smell in order to discern whether something is true or false, in order to sniff out and identify the strange winds of doctrine which can so easily cloud and confuse the church.

Leviticus 21:18 (d)
. . . or any thing superfluous,

Like six-legged frogs, some believers carry with them superfluous stuff—be it Far East philosophy or mystical spirituality. As priests, we are to keep ministry simple, focused on the Person of Jesus Christ.

Leviticus 21:19 (a)
Or a man that is brokenfooted . . .

Some people can't stand up. They keep getting blown away by emotions, knocked down by problems. Priests are to have the ability to stand firm no matter the obstacles or difficulties.

Leviticus 21:19 (b)
. . . or brokenhanded,

Unlike the priest of Luke 10, true priests must have the ability to reach out to those who are beaten and bruised.

Leviticus 21:20 (a)
Or crookbackt . . .

A priest must have backbone. I think of Pilate. He knew Jesus was innocent of the accusations levied against Him. He knew Jesus was not guilty of the crimes reported by those who lied about Him. But under political pressure, Pilate gave in.

Leviticus 21:20 (b)
. . . or a dwarf . . .

A person who isn't growing or expanding in his knowledge of the Word and of the Lord is not qualified for service because, like those to whom the Book of Hebrews was written, although they ought to be teachers, they still have need to be taught (Hebrews 5:12).

Leviticus 21:20 (c)
. . . or that hath a blemish in his eye . . .

This infection of the eye speaks of one unable to see clearly. Jesus spoke of such a one—a rich man who, because he didn't see things from an eternal perspective, was impoverished in the things of God (Luke 12:13–21).

Leviticus 21:20 (d)
. . . or be scurvy, or scabbed . . .

In ministry, a man cannot have thin skin because he who does is sure to become irritated and eventually give up.

Leviticus 21:20 (e)
. . . or hath his stones broken;

Priests must have the ability to reproduce. We must share our faith, for if we don't evangelize, we fossilize. It is no wonder that when one sinner comes to repentance, heaven rejoices (Luke 15:7, 10), for when we see sinners respond to the Lord, enthusiasm and joy are rekindled in our own hearts.

Leviticus 21:21–24
No man that hath a blemish of the seed of Aaron the priest shall come nigh to offer the offerings of the LORD made by fire: he hath a blemish; he shall not come nigh to offer the bread of his God. He shall eat the bread of his God, both of the most holy, and of the holy. Only he shall not go in unto the vail, nor come nigh unto the altar, because he hath a blemish; that he profane not my sanctuaries: for I the LORD do sanctify them. And Moses told it unto Aaron, and to his sons, and unto all the children of Israel.

Looking at this list, you might feel disqualified by a point or two or three or ten. The answer is, *Yes,* you are disqualified. That's why in Hebrews 3, we are told to consider, or literally focus on, the High Priest of our profession, Christ Jesus, for He is indeed the flawless One, the Perfect One . . .

Jesus had vision. "Master," they said to Him, "look at the magnificence of the temple," (Mark 13:1).

"I tell you the truth," He said in response, "not one of those stones will remain upon the other."

And a mere forty years later, in A.D. 70, the Roman Army burned the temple and toppled every stone into the Kidron Valley below. Jesus had vision concerning the big picture of what was to come.

Jesus wasn't lame. In John 1, we read that it was as Jesus walked that John the Baptist looked on Him and said, "Behold the Lamb of God which takes away the sin of the world." Watching Jesus walk, John could see that Jesus walked in righteousness.

Jesus had perfect discernment. "Master, what must I do to have eternal life?" asked the rich, young ruler.

"Sell your goods and follow Me," Jesus answered, putting His finger on the very thing which stood in the young man's way (see Luke 18:22).

Was there anything superfluous about Jesus? No, He simplified everything, reducing the entire law to two commands (hang).

Concerning surefootedness, no one stands stronger than Jesus. "Who seek ye?" He asked the Roman soldiers in the Garden of Gethsemane.

"Jesus of Nazareth," they answered.

"I AM," Jesus replied—and they fell backwards, leaving Him the only one still on His feet (John 18:6).

And whose hands reached out to others more than those of Jesus? Whether He was blessing little children or touching lepers, washing feet or touching the eyes of the blind, Jesus' hands were wonder-working hands indeed.

Did Jesus lack spine? No. He called the Pharisees whitewashed sepulchers full of dead men's bones—a heavy thing to say to the respected religious leaders of the day (Matthew 23:27).

As for His eyesight, Jesus not only appraised situations perfectly, but He looked on people compassionately (Matthew 9:36).

So far from being thin-skinned was Jesus that He not only called Judas "friend" even at the moment of his betrayal (Matthew 26:50), but He prayed forgiveness for the very soldiers who crucified Him, for the very crowd which mocked Him (Luke 23:34).

Concerning reproduction, shortly following His death, Jesus' followers would become those who filled Jerusalem with His doctrine (Acts 5:28) before going on to "turn the whole world upside down" (Acts 17:6)—all because they were indeed born again (John 3:3).

As a picture of what true ministry looks like, Jesus is flawless. And yet, as Isaiah tells us, He was marred—or blemished—more than any other man . . .

He was blinded when the temple guards put a blindfold on Him in the courtyard of Caiaphas. His nose would be flattened as they pummeled Him in the face. He was lame as He carried the Cross and fell to the ground. His hands and feet were broken when they were pierced through with spikes, His back made crooked when He was beat with the flagellum, His skin scarred and scabbed as a crown of thorns was mashed into His skull. He was dwarfed as the crowd taunted and belittled Him.

In other words, He who knew no sin became sin that we might be made the righteousness of God in Him (2 Corinthians 5:21).

GOD'S SOLUTION TO SADNESS

A Topical Study of LEVITICUS 21:10–12

And they took Joseph's coat, and killed a kid of the goats, and dipped the coat in the blood; And they sent the coat of many colours, and they brought it to their father; and said, This have we found: know now whether it be thy son's coat or no. And he knew it, and said, It is my son's coat; an evil beast hath devoured him; Joseph is without doubt rent in pieces. And Jacob rent his clothes, and put sackcloth upon his loins, and mourned for his son many days.

Genesis 37:31–34

Then David took hold on his clothes, and rent them; and likewise all the men that were with him: and they mourned, and wept, and fasted until even, for

Saul, and for Jonathan his son, and for the people of the L*ORD, and for the house of Israel; because they were fallen by the sword.* 2 Samuel 1:11, 12

Following the custom of the day, Jacob and David tore their garments in an expression of intense grief. In our text, however, we read that the high priest was not to rend his garments—even if it was his mother or father who died.

Is God being callous and cold, hard-hearted and harsh?

No.

You see, this passage gives priests an essential key about how they were to navigate tragedy and difficulty. And because we are all priests and because every single one of us will deal with heartbreak and sorrow, this word is essential for us as well.

When my first wife was taken to heaven, I was loved and cared for by a group of people who, wanting the best for me, said, "You need to get away, to be healed, to work through this emotionally." Theirs was a tender, caring suggestion—but as much as I appreciated their hearts of concern, I knew what they were telling me to do was exactly what I ought not to do, for God's Word to Aaron, even following the death of his own sons (Leviticus 10:6), was that he was not to rend his garments and not to leave the tabernacle or he, too, would die. He was to stay in the place of ministry, to remain in the place where he was serving others, where praise was ascending, where prayer was offered.

Knowing this principle, three days later I was back preaching—and it was the best thing for me. Thirteen years later, when my daughter, Jessie, was taken to heaven, well-meaning, good-hearted people again told me to take six months or a year off. And again, while I appreciated their intent, I knew that was precisely what I ought not do lest I die.

After parking his car, a man set out for a day-hike in the Sierra Nevada Mountains. Three miles into what was to be a relaxing afternoon outing, he noticed ominous storm clouds forming as the temperature dropped precipitously. Realizing a freak snowstorm was headed his way, the man began backtracking towards his car. He had a mile or so to go, when the storm became so intense that he couldn't see his hand in front of his face. Losing his way, he walked for two hours until he realized he was freezing. Feeling a deadly lethargy come over him, he knew if he sat down, he would never get up, so he fought it off for as long as he could. But finally, the desire to rest was just too overpowering, so he sat down at the base of a tree, the snow still falling intensely. As he sat down, he felt something next to him. Brushing away the snow, his suspicions were confirmed when he discovered the body of a man who had evidently stopped to rest only a few moments earlier. Finding a pulse, the young man stood to his feet and, with a burst of new-found energy, picked up the man who had almost frozen to death, put him on his shoulders, and began walking feverishly. After walking fifty hours or so, he bumped into the side of a cabin.

Feeling his way to the front, he banged on the door that was opened by a man who welcomed the pair inside to warm themselves by his roaring fire.

The application is obvious. In attempting to save someone else, the young man was himself saved. In caring for someone else, he himself was cared for. And that's what Jesus said would happen when He said, "The measure you give out will be measured back to you" (see Luke 6:38).

When tragedy strikes, when trials come, we'll either say, "This ought not to be. Poor me"—or we'll say, "This can be used for Your glory, so pour me, Lord. Pour me out to the people in need all around me."

What did our great High Priest do in His time of tragedy, in His time of pain? Even as He hung on the Cross in agony, He ministered to a man beside Him, to a woman below Him, to the crowd around Him . . .

> "This day you shall be with Me in paradise," He said to the needy thief beside Him (Luke 23:43).
>
> "Woman, behold your son," He said to his grieving mother standing at the foot of the Cross below Him (John 19:26).
>
> "Father, forgive them," He prayed concerning the jeering crowd surrounding Him (Luke 23:34).

No wonder Caiaphas rent his garments that day (Matthew 26:65)—for he was disqualified from priestly ministry at that moment, superceded by the great High Priest whose garment was not rent (John 19:24).

The garment of Caiaphas was torn. Not so the garment of Jesus—for Jesus will never lose control emotionally or grieve hysterically. Therefore, neither must we. I'm not talking about "keeping a stiff upper lip," having a "positive mental attitude" or a "Don't worry, be happy" mentality. I'm talking about the reality of our great High Priest living in you and me through both good days and bad.

Stay in the place of ministry, gang. Follow the example of Jesus. The best thing you can do when difficulties come your way is to go for it more than you ever have previously in giving out, in sharing with, in caring for those beside you and all around you.

---

22 Leviticus 22:1–3

And the LORD spake unto Moses, saying, Speak unto Aaron and to his sons, that they separate themselves from the holy things of the children of Israel, and that they profane not my holy name in those things which they hallow unto me: I am the LORD. Say unto them, Whosoever he be of all your seed among your generations, that goeth unto the holy things, which the children of Israel hallow unto the LORD, having his uncleanness upon him, that soul shall be cut off from my presence: I am the LORD.

Because he handles holy things, a defiled priest was to be discharged, put aside, let go, shown the door. As a royal priesthood, this applies directly to us as well, for we, too, handle holy things. We've been given the Word. We've been given the privilege of prayer. We've been linked to

God's children. We are a priestly company indeed.

Leviticus 22:4 (a)
What man soever of the seed of Aaron is a leper, or hath a running issue; he shall not eat of the holy things, until he be clean . . .

As we have seen, leprosy is a picture of sin. The tendency for us is to say, "Sin is not a big deal. Everyone bends the rules; everyone does that; everyone goes there." Passages like the one before us, however, say just the opposite. Sin brings about separation from service and ministry.

Knowing this, God goes on record saying, "No matter how seemingly insignificant, regardless of how society winks at it, sin is leprous. It will destroy you."

A priest's inability to eat of his prescribed portion of the sacrifices is equivalent to our inability to draw nourishment from the Word. The believer who compromises with sin will open the Bible only to find it as dry as a desert. Eventually, his appetite for it will disappear altogether. And spiritual weakness will be the result. There is no balance, strength, or stamina in the life of the one who doesn't eat of the holy things of the Word of God. Life can be exhausting if we don't eat. We *must* eat.

Leviticus 22:4 (b)–7
. . . And whoso toucheth any thing that is unclean by the dead, or a man whose seed goeth from him; or whosoever toucheth any creeping thing, whereby he may be made unclean, or a man of whom he may take uncleanness, whatsoever uncleanness he hath; the soul which hath touched any such shall be unclean until even, and shall not eat of the holy things, unless he wash his flesh with water. And when the sun is down, he shall be clean, and shall afterward eat of the holy things; because it is his food.

The remedy for uncleanness is first waiting then washing. The unclean person was to wait until evening time. Why evening? Because in Jewish economy, the setting of the sun signaled a new day . . .

It is of the LORD's mercies that we are not consumed, because his compassions fail not. They are new every morning: great is thy faithfulness. Lamentations 3:22, 23

Paul put it this way:

Brethren, I count not myself to have apprehended: but this one thing I do, forgetting those things which are behind, and reaching forth unto those things which are before, I press toward the mark for the prize of the high calling of God in Christ Jesus. Philippians 3:13, 14

The Lord ordered our lives in such a way that every day after about sixteen or eighteen hours, we go to bed and basically die. To me, His plan is ingenious because I find that after about sixteen hours of living, I've pretty much messed it up. I've dropped the ball once too often, fumbled one time too many. I need to die and start over in a fresh way. So I think it's wonderful that God lets us die every eighteen hours.

How I love the morning hours. Whether I spend them at church, in my prayer place at home, or walking the streets of town on a spring or summer morning, I love the morning when it's quiet, when I can receive a piping hot batch of mercy fresh from the oven of God's grace.

Secondly, the priest who was unclean—whether by his own flesh or through contact with the dead things of the world—was to wash. As New Testament priests, the washing refers to the water of the Word (John 15:3). Did you wash today in the water of the Word? We're bombarded every day by creeping things and dead carcasses, by that which would defile us and render us unable to serve or eat of that which would satisfy our soul. God would say, "The solution is simple, the remedy real: Wait on Me in this new day and wash in the water of My Word."

Leviticus 22:8
That which dieth of itself, or is torn with beasts, he shall not eat to defile himself therewith: I am the LORD.

Strict instruction was given to stay away from those animals that had died either as prey or by disease.

Leviticus 22:9–13
They shall therefore keep mine ordinance, lest they bear sin for it, and die therefore, if they profane it: I the LORD do sanctify them. There shall no stranger eat of the holy thing: a sojourner of the priest, or an hired servant, shall not eat of the holy thing. But if the priest buy any soul with his money, he shall eat of it, and he that is born in his house: they shall eat of his meat. If the priest's daughter also be married unto a stranger, she may not eat of an offering of the holy things. But if the priest's daughter be a widow, or divorced, and have no child, and is returned unto her father's house, as in her youth, she shall eat of her father's meat: but there shall no stranger eat thereof.

Not only does this speak of the familial relationship of slave to master, but of the fact that so separate, so sanctified was the sacrificial system to be, that only the priests and their families were to eat of the sacrificial meat.

Leviticus 22:14–16
And if a man eat of the holy thing unwittingly, then he shall put the fifth part thereof unto it, and shall give it unto the priest with the holy thing. And they shall not profane the holy things of the children of Israel, which they offer unto the LORD; Or suffer them to bear the iniquity of trespass, when they eat their holy things: for I the LORD do sanctify them.

If a priest found himself accidentally eating of the holy things when he was disqualified from doing so, he would have to pay back twenty percent above and beyond that which he took. In this, we see restitution that speaks of responsibility. One of the problems in society is that people sin without accepting responsibility or making restitution. To counteract this, the Lord wove into the fabric of the priesthood an understanding that even if a priest's sin was unknown to him at the time he partook of the offering, he was to acknowledge responsibility through the discipline of restitution.

Leviticus 22:17–25
And the LORD spake unto Moses, saying, Speak unto Aaron, and to his sons, and unto all the children of Israel, and say unto them, whatsoever he be of the house of Israel, or of the strangers in Israel, that will offer his oblation for all his vows, and for all his freewill offerings, which they will offer unto the LORD for a burnt offering; ye shall offer at your own will a male without blemish, of the beeves, of the sheep, or of the goats. But whatsoever hath a blemish, that shall ye not offer: for it shall not be acceptable for you. And whosoever offereth a sacrifice of peace offerings unto the LORD to accomplish his vow, or a freewill offering in beeves or sheep, it shall be perfect to be accepted; there shall be no blemish therein. Blind, or broken, or maimed, or having a wen, or scurvy, or scabbed, ye shall not offer these unto the LORD, nor make an offering by fire of them upon the altar unto the LORD. Either a bullock or a lamb that hath any thing superfluous or lacking in his parts, that mayest thou offer for a freewill offering; but for a vow it shall not be accepted. Ye shall not offer unto the LORD that which is bruised, or crushed, or broken, or cut; neither shall ye make any offering thereof in your land. Neither from a stranger's hand shall ye offer the bread of your God of any of these; because their corruption is in them, and blemishes be in them: they shall not be accepted for you.

We are not to give to the Lord blemished or blind or maimed sheep—leftover money, energy or time. The Lord deserves the best, the first, the finest of everything in our lives—not because He's a greedy God but because we're greedy people who, to be like Him, need to learn how to give.

Leviticus 22:26–33
And the LORD spake unto Moses, saying, When a bullock, or a sheep, or a goat, is brought forth, then it shall be seven days under the dam; and from the eighth day and thenceforth it shall be accepted for an offering made by fire unto the LORD. And whether it be cow or ewe, ye shall not kill it and her young both in one day. And when ye will offer a sacrifice of thanksgiving unto the LORD, offer it at your own will. On the same day it shall be eaten up; ye shall leave none of it until the morrow: I am the LORD. Therefore shall ye keep my commandments, and do them: I am the LORD. Neither shall ye profane my holy name; but I will be hallowed among the children of Israel: I am the LORD which hallow you, that brought you out of the land of Egypt, to be your God: I am the LORD.

When an Israelite willingly offered a sacrifice of thanksgiving, it was to be completely eaten on the same day it was offered. Why? Physically, it was to protect against pollution, against the food becoming spoiled for lack of refrigeration. Spiritually, I believe our thanksgiving can also become spoiled unless offered consistently. Over time, our minds have a way of explaining away God's miraculous hand in any given situation, of attributing His goodness in our lives to our own efforts, to luck, to coincidence. And thus, our thanksgiving becomes spoiled if not offered immediately, consistently, wholeheartedly.

Secondly, I believe this word was given to us to provide satiation. It is as if the Lord is saying, "When you bring Me the sacrifice of thanksgiving, I want you to leave with a full belly. I want you to be deeply satisfied, totally satiated, completely happy."

> By him therefore let us offer the sacrifice of praise to God continually, that is, the fruit of our lips giving thanks to his name. Hebrews 13:15

God wants us to offer the sacrifice of praise and thanksgiving not because He needs to be thanked but because we need to be thankful. Why? Thanksgiving is the antidote to depression, the remedy for a cynical spirit. Yes, there are very real battles facing each of us. We are not to pretend they don't exist. But neither are we to indulge in doubt and self-pity. Rather, we're to do what Jehoshaphat did . . .

With a confederation of Edomite, Ammonite, and Moabite troops arrayed against him, Jehoshaphat, king of Judah, called unto God for help. God responded through a prophet, saying, "Be not afraid nor dismayed by reason of this great multitude for the battle is not yours but God's. Ye shall not need to fight in this battle: set yourselves, stand ye still, and see the salvation of the Lord with you, O Judah and Jerusalem: fear not, nor be dismayed; tomorrow go out against them: for the Lord will be with you."

Jehoshaphat could have said, "What kind of battle plan is that?" Instead, he bowed his head and worshipped. Although all he had was a promise, the next morning, rather than sending his troops to battle, Jehoshaphat sent a choir to praise. And although this made no sense militarily, it disoriented the enemy to the point where they drew their swords in confusion and annihilated one another (2 Chronicles 20).

The same thing is true in the Spirit. We have an enemy that surrounds us constantly, an Adversary who wants to intimidate and depress us daily, whose goal is to rob us of the riches of our joy and peace. This enemy is beaten back, confused, overwhelmed through the power of praise and thanksgiving. Why? I believe it's because of who he once was. Before he rebelled against God, Satan was Lucifer, the worship leader of heaven. So when he hears praise, I believe it triggers something within him that reminds him of what he used to do, where he once was, how far he has fallen. Consequently, in his ears, the sound of praise is like the sound of a dentist's drill, or of fingernails on a chalkboard. He just wants to get as far away from it as possible.

Finally, I believe the thanksgiving offering was to be consumed the day it was offered in order to prevent procrastination. There can be a tendency for us to say, "Lord, I'm offering You this sacrifice of thanksgiving. But right now, there are demands on my time. My family's calling me. I've got to water my lawn. We'll finish this meal tomorrow. I'll put it in a Ziploc bag and we'll have leftovers."

But the Lord says, "No. I want you to take the time to consume as much as you can in this moment, at this time, right here, right now. Don't put it off, for there will never be an opportunity exactly like this one."

To protect against pollution, to provide satiation, to prevent procrastination—three reasons the Old Testament Jews were to consume the thanksgiving offering, and three reasons we as New Testament believers are to be ourselves consumed with thanksgiving.

23

The Pharisees also with the Sadducees came, and tempting desired him that he would shew them a sign from heaven. He answered and said unto them, When it is evening, ye say, It will be fair weather: for the sky is red. And in the morning, it will be foul weather to day: for the sky is red and lowering. O ye hypocrites, ye can discern the face of the sky; but can ye not discern the signs of the times? Matthew 16:1–3

The Pharisees and Sadducees should have known the times in which they lived were prophetically significant. Had they been students of Bible prophecy, they would have known the time Messiah was to come. But they didn't. And as a result, they missed the moment. My prayer is that, unlike the Pharisees and Sadducees, we will be those who understand the significance of the days in which we're living. Throughout Scripture, there are very clear indicators of God's plan for that which is to be. And the chapter before us is such a passage . . .

Leviticus 23:1, 2
And the LORD spake unto Moses, saying, Speak unto the children of Israel, and say unto them, Concerning the feasts of the LORD, which ye shall proclaim to be holy convocations, even these are my feasts.

In Leviticus 23, we see the seven major feasts the nation of Israel was to celebrate annually. These feasts had a two-fold purpose: commemoration and expectation. Like our Fourth of July celebrations, the feasts were to commemorate and celebrate what God had done for them as a nation historically. But they also served as prophetic illustrations in that they spoke of that which was to come.

Four of the feasts took place in the springtime and early summer. The remaining three took place in the fall. From our perspective, the events prophesied by the feasts which took place in the spring and summer have already taken place in the first coming of Christ. The events prophesied by the three feasts that took place in the fall have yet to take place, to be fulfilled when Jesus comes again.

Leviticus 23:3, 4
Six days shall work be done: but the seventh day is the sabbath of rest, an holy convocation; ye shall do no work therein: it is the sabbath of the LORD in all your dwellings. These are the feasts of the LORD, even holy convocations, which ye shall proclaim in their seasons.

After an initial reminder that the Sabbath day is to be honored on a weekly basis, the Lord begins His discourse on the feasts. Why are they called feasts? Because, with one exception, they were times of celebration and elation.

Leviticus 23:5
In the fourteenth day of the first month at even is the LORD's passover.

The Passover feast was to commemorate the freeing of the Israelites from their bondage in Egypt. After being enslaved for four hundred years, they cried out to the Lord and a deliverer was raised up. Moses went to Pharaoh and said, "Thus saith the Lord, Let My people go." But because Pharaoh refused, a series of plagues descended upon the Egyptians—the last of which was the death of the firstborn in any house not marked with the blood of a lamb on the doorposts (Exodus 12:29).

In looking ahead prophetically, however, Passover illustrated what Christ would do as the Lamb of God who would take away the sin of the world.

Leviticus 23:6–8
And on the fifteenth day of the same month is the Feast of Unleavened Bread unto the LORD: seven days ye must eat unleavened bread. In the first day ye shall have an holy convocation: ye shall do no servile work therein. But ye shall offer an offering made by fire unto the LORD seven days: in the seventh day is an holy convocation: ye shall do no servile work therein.

The day after Passover—on the fifteenth day of the first month of the religious year—there was to be the Feast of Unleavened Bread, commemorating the night the Israelites left Egypt with such haste that their bread didn't have time to rise.

Prophetically, the Feast of Unleavened Bread would speak to the Jews of the unleavened One, the sinless One, who would say, "Take, eat. This is My body, given for you" (Luke 22:19).

Leviticus 23:9–14
And the LORD spake unto Moses, saying, Speak unto the children of Israel, and say unto them, when ye be come into the land which I give unto you, and shall reap the harvest thereof, then ye shall bring a sheaf of the firstfruits of your harvest unto the priest: and he shall wave the sheaf before the LORD, to be accepted for you: on the morrow after the sabbath the priest shall wave it. And ye shall offer that day when ye wave the sheaf an he lamb without blemish of the first year for a burnt offering unto the LORD. And the meat offering thereof shall be two tenth deals of fine flour mingled with oil, an offering made by fire unto the LORD for a sweet savour: and the drink offering thereof shall be of wine, the fourth part of an hin. And ye shall eat neither bread, nor parched corn, nor green ears, until the selfsame day that ye have brought an offering unto your God: it shall be a statute for ever throughout your generations in all your dwellings.

The Feast of Firstfruits took place on the first day of the week following Passover and commemorated the fact that, having been released from Egypt, the children of Israel were headed to a Promised Land wherein there would be plentiful harvests in the land which "flowed with milk and honey."

Of what expectation did the Feast of Firstfruits speak? Christ was killed on Passover. On the Feast of Unleavened Bread, His body was put in the tomb. Yet on the very day of the Feast of Firstfruits, He rose from the dead—the Firstfruit of all who would follow Him (1 Corinthians 15:20). The Firstfruit, Jesus Christ, finished the work. And because He rose, we, too, shall rise.

Leviticus 23:15, 16
And ye shall count unto you from the morrow after the sabbath, from the day that ye brought the sheaf of the wave offering; seven sabbaths shall be complete: even unto the morrow after the seventh sabbath shall ye number fifty days; and ye shall offer a new meat offering unto the LORD.

Following the week in which the Feasts of Passover, Unleavened Bread, and Firstfruits were celebrated in Jerusalem, those in attendance returned to their homes. Fifty days later, they reconvened for the Feast of Weeks, or, as the New Testament calls it, the Feast of Pentecost.

Leviticus 23:17
Ye shall bring out of your habitations two wave loaves of two tenth deals: they shall be

of fine flour; they shall be baken with leaven; they are the firstfruits unto the LORD.

The firstfruits spoken of here were not those of the barley harvest, but of the wheat harvest. At Pentecost, two loaves made of wheat and leaven were to be waved before the Lord. What does this commemorate? According to the rabbis, the two loaves represent the two tablets of stone on which the Law was given when Israel became a nation.

Leaven, however, is a picture of sin. Therefore, the Law being perfect (Psalm 19:7), I believe the fullest explanation for the meaning of the two loaves lies not in what Pentecost commemorated, but what it anticipated, for it would be on the very Day of Pentecost that the church was born (Acts 2).

Prior to Acts 2, the world was divided into only two groups of people: Jews and Gentiles. But after the Spirit came down, after three thousand were born again in a single day, a third group came into being: the church, comprised of former Jews and former Gentiles. Thus, there was leaven in the bread—for, comprised of sinners, the church is far from sinless.

Leviticus 23:18–22
And ye shall offer with the bread seven lambs without blemish of the first year, and one young bullock, and two rams: they shall be for a burnt offering unto the LORD, with their meat offering, and their drink offerings, even an offering made by fire, of sweet savour unto the LORD. Then ye shall sacrifice one kid of the goats for a sin offering, and two lambs of the first year for a sacrifice of peace offerings. And the priest shall wave them with the bread of the firstfruits for a wave offering before the LORD, with the two lambs: they shall be holy to the LORD for the priest. And ye shall proclaim on the selfsame day, that it may be an holy convocation unto you: ye shall do no servile work therein: it shall be a statute for ever in all your dwellings throughout your generations. And when ye reap the harvest of your land, thou shalt not make clean riddance of the corners of thy field when thou reapest, neither shalt thou gather any gleaning of thy harvest: thou shalt leave them unto the poor, and to the stranger: I am the LORD your God.

The Book of Ruth, the story of a Jewish woman and her Gentile daughter-in-law, illustrates both the historical and prophetic application of the passage. You see, in this passage, God wisely and compassionately ordained that the edges and corners of any given field were not to be harvested, but were to be left for those who were poor. Ruth and Naomi being poor, Ruth gleaned in the field of a man named Boaz—a man she would eventually marry and by whom she would bear a son named Obed who, in turn, would become the father of Jesse. Jesse would become the father of David—who would ultimately be the father of the Son of David, Jesus Christ.

Thus, the Gentile, Ruth, learns about God from the Jew, Naomi. But Naomi does not receive the baby who would ultimately be the Babe of Bethlehem until Ruth conceived. And just as Ruth would eventually fade from the story, the church will leave the scene at the time of the Rapture. But in this, the Jewish nation will be awakened to the point that eventually those who remain will be saved (Romans 11) when they at last recognize Jesus as their Greater than Boaz, their longed-for Messiah.

Leviticus 23:23–25
And the LORD spake unto Moses, saying, Speak unto the children of Israel, saying, in the seventh month, in the first day of the month, shall ye have a sabbath, a memorial of blowing of trumpets, an holy convocation. Ye shall do no servile work therein: but ye shall offer an offering made by fire unto the LORD.

The Feast of Passover was immediately followed by the Feast of Unleavened Bread which was immediately followed by the Feast of Firstfruits. Fifty days later, people reconvened for the Feast of Pentecost—after which they returned home for approximately four months until the first day of the seventh month. Thus, the final three feasts—all of which took place in the fall—deal with the Second Coming of Christ, an event to which we are still looking forward.

Historically, the Feast of Trumpets commemorated the silver trumpets which were sounded for three reasons: to gather the people as they traveled through the wilderness on their way to the Land of Promise, to move to a new destination, and as a battle alarm.

Prophetically, the trumpets should "ring a bell" in the minds of students of prophecy, for in 1 Thessalonians 4:16, Paul writes that it is at the sound of the trumpet of God that the dead in Christ shall rise.

Why did God instruct Moses to make *two* trumpets (Numbers 10:2)? Because there are two times the trumpet of God is sounded: once when the Law was given (Exodus 19), and once when the Rapture takes place (1 Thessalonians 4:16).

Why did the Feast of Trumpets take place in

the seventh month? Because seven is the biblical number of completion, and it is not until the "fullness of the Gentiles" is come (Romans 11:25), not until the number of Gentiles to be saved is complete, that the Rapture will occur. So if you're not saved, do us all a favor and open up your heart to Jesus. Then we can all move out together to our heavenly Promised Land!

Leviticus 23:26–32
And the LORD spake unto Moses, saying, Also on the tenth day of this seventh month there shall be a day of atonement: it shall be an holy convocation unto you; and ye shall afflict your souls, and offer an offering made by fire unto the LORD. And ye shall do no work in that same day: for it is a day of atonement, to make an atonement for you before the LORD your God. For whatsoever soul it be that shall not be afflicted in that same day, he shall be cut off from among his people. And whatsoever soul it be that doeth any work in that same day, the same soul will I destroy from among his people. Ye shall do no manner of work: it shall be a statute for ever throughout your generations in all your dwellings. It shall be unto you a sabbath of rest, and ye shall afflict your souls: in the ninth day of the month at even, from even unto even, shall ye celebrate your sabbath.

Following the Feast of Trumpets, Yom Kippur, or the Day of Atonement, was unlike every other festival in that it was a time of somber reflection, the day the high priest would remove his priestly outer garments and sprinkle blood on the mercy seat to atone for the sins of the nation.

What does this speak of prophetically? Once the Rapture takes place, Israel will experience a time of soul-searching and affliction in the Tribulation, a time Jeremiah refers to as "Jacob's trouble," (30:7). During this time, in addition to the 144,000 Jewish evangelists who will be raised up to spread the gospel (Revelation 7), two witnesses—most likely Elijah and Moses—will come on the scene, preaching powerfully (Revelation 11). As a result, Zechariah tells us the remaining third of the nation of Israel will realize the wounds in the hands and feet of their Messiah were wounds they themselves inflicted when they said, "We will not have this Man rule over us" (Zechariah 13).

The understanding that God has not forsaken Israel is as important for the church to understand as it is for the Jews—for just as God is not through with the Jew, neither will He be through with us when we stumble and fall. The promises of Romans 1 through 8 are glorious—among them that we are justified by faith, that there is no condemnation to those who are in Christ Jesus, that all things work together for good for those who love God. And it is no coincidence that Romans 1 through 8 is followed by Romans 9 through 11—a passage which recounts God's faithfulness to the Jews—as verification that God's promises remain true, that He remains faithful even when we prove to be faithless (2 Timothy 2:13).

Leviticus 23:33–44
And the LORD spake unto Moses, saying, Speak unto the children of Israel, saying, The fifteenth day of this seventh month shall be the Feast of Tabernacles for seven days unto the LORD. On the first day shall be an holy convocation: ye shall do no servile work therein. Seven days ye shall offer an offering made by fire unto the LORD: on the eighth day shall be an holy convocation unto you; and ye shall offer an offering made by fire unto the LORD: it is a solemn assembly; and ye shall do no servile work therein. These are the feasts of the LORD, which ye shall proclaim to be holy convocations, to offer an offering made by fire unto the LORD, a burnt offering, and a meat offering, a sacrifice, and drink offerings, every thing upon his day: Beside the sabbaths of the LORD, and beside your gifts, and beside all your vows, and beside all your freewill offerings, which ye give unto the LORD. Also in the fifteenth day of the seventh month, when ye have gathered in the fruit of the land, ye shall keep a feast unto the LORD seven days: on the first day shall be a sabbath, and on the eighth day shall be a sabbath. And ye shall take you on the first day the boughs of goodly trees, branches of palm trees, and the boughs of thick trees, and willows of the brook; and ye shall rejoice before the LORD your God seven days. And ye shall keep it a feast unto the LORD seven days in the year. It shall be a statute for ever in your generations: ye shall celebrate it in the seventh month. Ye shall dwell in booths seven days; all that are Israelites born shall dwell in booths: That your generations may know that I made the children of Israel to dwell in booths, when I brought them out of the land of Egypt: I am the LORD your God. And Moses declared unto the children of Israel the feasts of the LORD.

The final festival, the one mentioned in Scripture more than any other, was the Feast of Tabernacles—a festival of joy and happiness. Historically, the Feast of Tabernacles commemorated God's provision for the nation of Israel when they dwelled in tabernacles, or tents, during their wilderness wanderings. To celebrate the Feast of Tabernacles, the Jews were to construct small booths, little lean-tos, within a Sabbath day's journey, or half a mile, from the temple. Consequently, if one was to travel to Jerusalem during the Feast of Tabernacles, he would see hundreds of thousands of these little booths, constructed in such a way that the families within would be shaded from the heat of the day, but able to look out and see the stars at night—a reminder of God's fulfillment of His promise to Abraham (Genesis 15:5)—of which they themselves were a part.

Prophetically, the Feast of Tabernacles speaks of Jesus' Second Coming—when it will be reinstated and celebrated throughout the Millennium.

Practically, the Feast of Tabernacles speaks to me of the connection between repentance and restoration. Taking place five days after the somber Day of Atonement, the Feast of Tabernacles speaks of the restoration of joy, which would be linked to a timely petition. You see, the fall months being the season of "early rains," if rain didn't fall, Israel's agrarian society would be in trouble. So at the Feast of Tabernacles, the Israelites came together not only to say, "Lord, You have been so good to us," but, "Lord, remember the season ahead. Pour out Your rain upon us."

Are you dry tonight? Is there a drought in your soul? It could be the result of unconfessed sin, of a neglect of a personal "day of atonement."

> Blessed is he whose transgression is forgiven, whose sin is covered. Blessed is the man unto whom the LORD imputeth not iniquity, and in whose spirit there is no guile. When I kept silence, my bones waxed old through my roaring all the day long. For day and night thy hand was heavy upon me: my moisture is turned into the drought of summer. Selah. I acknowledged my sin unto thee, and mine iniquity have I not hid. I said, I will confess my transgressions unto the LORD; and thou forgavest the iniquity of my sin. Selah. Psalm 32:1–5

On the Day of Atonement, the nation confessed their sin and afflicted their souls. The result? A party five days later at the Feast of Tabernacles, five being the number of grace. Every morning during the Feast of Tabernacles, the priests would divide into two processionals. One group would go directly to the east, the valley of Kidron, and gather willow, palm, myrtle, and citrus branches to pass out to the people and to lay in the courtyard of the temple where sacrifices were made. The second group of priests would go south to the pool of Siloam, carrying a golden pitcher, which they would dip into the water. Both companies of priests—those carrying the branches and those carrying the water—would meet at the temple, where the water was poured out from the pitcher before the altar as a reminder of God's provision of water for them during their wilderness wandering. On the eighth day, the great day of the feast, although the priests would go to the pool of Siloam, they would return with an empty pitcher, acknowledging the fact that, because they were now in the Promised Land, there was no longer need for supernatural provision of water. And as they did, the priest would say this prayer . . .

> Thus saith the LORD that made thee, and formed thee from the womb, which will help thee; Fear not, O Jacob, my servant; and thou, Jesurun, whom I have chosen. For I will pour water upon him that is thirsty, and floods upon the dry ground: I will pour my spirit upon thy seed, and my blessing upon thine offspring: and they shall spring up as among the grass, as willows by the water courses. Isaiah 44:2–4

Why would they read this passage?

Because they understand that Isaiah 44 was a prophecy of the pouring out of the Spirit that could transpire only when Messiah came to their land.

The year is approximately A.D. 32. On the great day of the feast, as everyone watched, as the processional returned from the pool of Siloam, poured out the empty pitcher and prayed for Messiah to come, a young thirty-three-year-old Rabbi from Galilee shouts out, "If any man thirst, let him come to Me and drink. And out of his innermost being shall gush forth torrents of living water" (John 7:37, 38), thereby presenting Himself as Messiah and offering the living water, the rain of the Holy Spirit.

But Jesus' declaration was not yet complete . . .

Every night during the Feast of Tabernacles the celebration of illumination took place wherein four huge menorahs on the temple mount, with wicks made of priest's robes which had been worn out, were lit—causing a light to shine so brightly it could be seen one hundred miles away. At the end of the feast, the menorahs would be extinguished, not to be relit until the following year. John tells us that it was on the day after the Feast of Tabernacles, the day after the menorahs were extinguished that Jesus declared, 'I am the light of the world,' (John 8:12)—the true Light which would never be extinguished.

What a perfect picture was painted at the Feast of Tabernacles.

Don't lose sight of the fact that the Lord's coming is near, gang. In the meantime, drink deeply of the water of His Spirit and illuminate your life not with a pillar of fire or a huge menorah which were used and then extinguished, but by the Presence and promises of the One who will never leave you or forsake you as you walk daily with Him.

24

Leviticus 23 deals with special days of rejoicing. Leviticus 25 deals with special years of refreshing. But between chapters 23 and 25 comes chapter 24, a chapter of responsibilities, wherein God assigns the responsibilities to His people of preparing holy oil, providing holy bread, and protecting His holy name . . .

Leviticus 24:1–4
And the LORD spake unto Moses, saying, Command the children of Israel, that they bring unto thee pure oil olive beaten for the light, to cause the lamps to burn continually. Without the vail of the testimony, in the tabernacle of the congregation, shall Aaron order it from the evening unto the morning before the LORD continually: it shall be a statute for ever in your generations. He shall order the lamps upon the pure candlestick before the LORD continually.

As high priest, it was Aaron's responsibility to keep the lamp burning brightly in the holy place of the tabernacle. But it was the peoples' responsibility to bring the oil. As pastor I have the opportunity in this congregation to make sure that the light of the Word is opened and allowed to shine brightly. But what I do is dependent to a very great degree upon you. Do you pray for the anointing of the Spirit that there might be illumination? C.H. Spurgeon was oh, so right when he said, "Great preachers do not make great congregations, but rather great congregations make great preachers." Truly, illumination is directly related to the faithfulness of the congregation.

Leviticus 24:5–9
And thou shalt take fine flour, and bake twelve cakes thereof: two tenth deals shall be in one cake. And thou shalt set them in two rows, six on a row, upon the pure table before the LORD. And thou shalt put pure frankincense upon each row, that it may be on the bread for a memorial, even an offering made by fire unto the LORD. Every sabbath he shall set it in order before the LORD continually, being taken from the children of Israel by an everlasting covenant. And it shall be Aaron's and his sons'; and they shall eat it in the holy place: for it is most holy unto him of the offerings of the LORD made by fire by a perpetual statute.

The people were to provide the holy bread in order that Aaron and his sons might be fed on the Sabbath day in the sanctuary. How thankful I am that people understand the importance of bringing the bread in order that there might be a feeding of the ministry, an expanding of the work here congregationally. If people didn't tithe, this ministry would not be fed in the way it is. God has blessed us because of your faithfulness in bringing the bread into the sanctuary.

Leviticus 24:10–12
And the son of an Israelitish woman, whose father was an Egyptian, went out among the children of Israel: and this son of the Israelitish woman and a man of Israel strove together in the camp; and the Israelitish woman's son blasphemed the name of the LORD, and cursed. And they brought him unto Moses: (and his mother's name was Shelomith, the daughter of Dibri, of the tribe of Dan). And they put him in ward, that the mind of the LORD might be shewed them.

Here we see the responsibility of the people to protect God's holy name. When, during a fight, the son of an Israelite woman and an Egyptian man blasphemed the name of the Lord, the people of God weren't sure whether he was to be held to the same standards as they were. So they put him in ward, in custody, and sought the mind of the Lord—always a wise thing to do.

Had Moses come to me asking what I thought he should do with a man who was half-Egyptian and half-Jew who blasphemed the Lord's name during a fight?" my tendency would have been to say, "Let's discuss this. He didn't have the background the rest of us have had. Here's a chance for us to be merciful, to show grace, to demonstrate to the Egyptian people how kind, bighearted, and loving we are. Let's not rush into this matter. Let's give him a warning, explain why we don't say those things around here, and let him go. After all, he's half-Egyptian."

But the following verse shows me just how far my thoughts are from God's, that I'm not nearly as wise as I think I am. Maybe you're like me. Maybe you think you know what's right and what's wise—but on the basis of this passage, I encourage you even as I remind myself, rather than making a decision based upon dialogue, discussion, and debate, to seek the Lord in prayer and see what *He* says concerning any given matter.

God speaks to those on their knees who seek Him sincerely, admitting they lack wisdom. God's will is not a mystery. The issue is, will we do what He tells us to do?

Leviticus 24:13, 14
And the LORD spake unto Moses, saying, Bring forth him that hath cursed without the camp; and let all that heard him lay their hands upon his head, and let all the congregation stone him.

In His answer, the Lord declares that, regardless of background or family history, genetics or individual tendencies, there was to be only one law for all of the people.

"But isn't stoning an extreme sentence for blasphemy?" we ask.

How do we know?

Maybe we'll see this man in heaven and hear him say, "My life was basically going nowhere, but God used me mightily to get people to think very seriously about the issue of blasphemy." It could very well be that it was His love and grace which caused God to take the lives of this man and others like Achan, seeing that, if left on earth, their lives would be meaningless. Of this much we can be sure: because God is good, loving, and just, all that He does will prove to be right when we finally get to heaven and see all parts of the equation.

Leviticus 24:15–18
And thou shalt speak unto the children of Israel, saying, Whosoever curseth his God shall bear his sin. And he that blasphemeth the name of the LORD, he shall surely be put to death, and all the congregation shall certainly stone him: as well the stranger, as he that is born in the land, when he blasphemeth the name of the LORD, shall be put to death. And he that killeth any man shall surely be put to death. And he that killeth a beast shall make it good; beast for beast.

The reason the discussion of murder comes on the heels of God's edict concerning blasphemy is because blasphemy is indeed a form of murder. You see, whenever the name of our God who is transcendent, holy, perfect, full of mercy, gracious, benevolent, kind, and good is profaned, blasphemed, trivialized, His reputation is slaughtered. And God takes issue with that, knowing that, because the people who listen to blasphemy day after day won't believe in Him or have an understanding of Him, they won't call out to Him in the time of their need, in the day of their difficulty. God cares about His name not because He's proud but because He wants people to understand who He is.

Leviticus 24:19–23
And if a man cause a blemish in his neighbour; as he hath done, so shall it be done to him; Breach for breach, eye for eye, tooth for tooth: as he hath caused a blemish in a man, so shall it be done to him again. And he that killeth a beast, he shall restore it: and he that killeth a man, he shall be put to death. Ye shall have one manner of law, as well for the stranger, as for one of your own country: for I am the LORD your God. And Moses spake to the children of Israel, that they should bring forth him that had cursed out of the camp, and stone him with stones. And the children of Israel did as the LORD commanded Moses.

Although people think this sounds like revenge, it's actually restraint. You see, if someone punches me in the eye, every part of me will be determined not to punch him in the eye, but to go for both of his eyes. If someone knocks out my tooth, I'll try to knock out his mouthful. Knowing this, God sets the price at only one eye for an eye, at only one tooth for a tooth.

Today's sociologist and psychologist would most likely say such things do not deter people from criminal behavior. God's Word, however, declares that equitable justice does in fact prove to be a deterrent to behavior that is the inevitable result of our depraved condition. Therefore, although we might not understand it initially, this passage pulsates with mercy.

25

Following a discussion on rejoicing in chapter 23 and responsibility in chapter 24 comes refreshment here in chapter 25 . . .

Leviticus 25:1–7
And the LORD spake unto Moses in mount Sinai, saying, Speak unto the children of Israel, and say unto them, When ye come into the land which I give you, then shall the land keep a sabbath unto the LORD. Six years thou shalt sow thy field, and six years thou shalt prune thy vineyard, and gather in the fruit thereof; but in the seventh year shall be a sabbath of rest unto the land, a sabbath for the LORD: thou shalt neither sow thy field, nor prune thy vineyard. That which groweth of its own accord of thy harvest thou shalt not reap, neither gather the grapes of thy vine undressed: for it is a year

of rest unto the land. And the sabbath of the land shall be meat for you; for thee, and for thy servant, and for thy maid, and for thy hired servant, and for thy stranger that sojourneth with thee, And for thy cattle, and for the beast that are in thy land, shall all the increase thereof be meat.

Every seventh year, the Israelites were to take a break. During this sabbath, or sabbatical year, the land wasn't worked and bills weren't paid (Deuteronomy 15). Agriculturally, we now know the wisdom of letting the land rest. And the same is true sociologically.

During this seventh year, the Book of Deuteronomy would be read (Deuteronomy 31:9–13) and people would be refreshed and renewed through the study of the Word. The people, however, deciding they needed to get ahead more than they needed to rest went four hundred and ninety years without observing a sabbath year. As a result, because they robbed God of seventy sabbaths, the children of Israel would spend seventy years held captive in Babylon (2 Chronicles 36:21).

Leviticus 25:8, 9
And thou shalt number seven sabbaths of years unto thee, seven times seven years; and the space of the seven sabbaths of years shall be unto thee forty and nine years. Then shalt thou cause the trumpet of the jubile to sound on the tenth day of the seventh month, in the day of atonement shall ye make the trumpet sound throughout all your land.

Every fiftieth year, the Year of Jubilee was to be observed—a year characterized by release, rest, and restoration . . .

Leviticus 25:10
And ye shall hallow the fiftieth year, and proclaim liberty throughout all the land unto all the inhabitants thereof: it shall be a jubile unto you; and ye shall return every man unto his possession, and ye shall return every man unto his family.

In the Year of Jubilee, there was to be a release of slaves and debt. That is, all slaves were to be set free and the slate of mortgages, car payments, and credit card debt was to be wiped clean.

Leviticus 25:11, 12
A jubile shall that fiftieth year be unto you: ye shall not sow, neither reap that which groweth of itself in it, nor gather the grapes in it of thy vine undressed. For it is the jubile; it shall be holy unto you: ye shall eat the increase thereof out of the field.

Secondly, during the Year of Jubilee—as in the sabbath year—there was to be rest for man as well as for the land.

Leviticus 25:13
In the year of this jubile ye shall return every man unto his possession.

Thirdly, in the Year of Jubilee, any land which had been sold was to be returned to its original owner. That is, if a piece of property was sold to cover a debt or to rescue a household financially, it would be restored to the family of the one who had sold it initially.

With release of debt, rest from labor, restoration of property, the Year of Jubilee seems like a golden opportunity. And yet neither the Bible nor extra-biblical writers give any indication it was ever observed.

Yet before we chide the Israelites for failing to take advantage of the glorious Year of Jubilee, we would do well to look in the mirror. If you want to experience jubilee in your own life presently, it begins with releasing people from the captivity in which you hold them because you think they let you down, disappointed, or hurt you. "For if ye forgive men their trespasses," Jesus said, "your heavenly Father will also forgive you: but if ye forgive not men their trespasses, neither will your Father forgive your trespasses" (Matthew 6:14, 15). It is the one who doesn't set the debtor free who remains bound in misery. Even though you don't feel it emotionally, you can decide today to do that which Israel never did: to cancel all debts and experience jubilee in your soul.

Secondly, I will experience jubilation only to the degree that I quit trying to earn blessings from God. When the trumpet was to have sounded signaling the beginning of the Year of Jubilee, it would have applied to everyone equally. Every person could have reaped the benefits of the blessings of Jubilee. All they had to do was receive it. So, too, because it is by grace that we're saved, the Year of Jubilee will dawn in your soul if you'll just relax and receive.

Thirdly, the Year of Jubilee was to be a year of restoring property. And therein most likely lies the reason as to why the Year of Jubilee was never celebrated. People didn't want to give back their land. However, had they done so, they would have received blessings far greater than anything they gave up.

Leviticus 25:14–17
And if thou sell ought unto thy neighbour, or buyest ought of thy neighbour's hand, ye shall not oppress one another: according to the number of years after the jubile thou shalt buy of thy neighbour, and according unto the number of years of the fruits he shall sell unto thee: according to the multitude of years thou shalt increase the price thereof, and according to the fewness of years thou shalt diminish the price of it: for according to the number of the years of the fruits doth he sell unto thee. Ye shall not therefore oppress one another; but thou shalt fear thy God: for I am the LORD your God.

If you were to buy a piece of property three months before the Year of Jubilee, knowing it would be restored to its owner in three months, you would pay only a fraction of its price. If the Year of Jubilee was three years away, you'd pay a little more. And if it was forty-nine years away, you'd pay full price.

In other words, the further away one was from the jubilee, the more valuable the property was. The same is true concerning the ultimate Jubilee that will take place in the kingdom, for the closer the kingdom seems to us, the less valuable our material possessions become to us. Conversely, my being caught up in my possessions, my hobbies, my agenda, is an indication that I'm not living for the kingdom the way I could be.

What are we to do? Let it all go. Jesus said, "Wherever your treasure is, there will your heart be also" (Matthew 6:21). The Lord wants to put His kingdom in your heart to a greater degree. May this be the day.

Leviticus 25:18–22
Wherefore ye shall do my statutes, and keep my judgments, and do them; and ye shall dwell in the land in safety. And the land shall yield her fruit, and ye shall eat your fill, and dwell therein in safety. And if ye shall say, What shall we eat the seventh year? Behold, we shall not sow, nor gather in our increase: then I will command my blessing upon you in the sixth year, and it shall bring forth fruit for three years. And ye shall sow the eighth year, and eat yet of old fruit until the ninth year; until her fruits come in ye shall eat of the old store.

"Wait a minute," people could have said. "If we're not to work on the seventh year and the next year is Jubilee,—with two years of no sowing or reaping—what will we eat?"

In response, God says, "In the sixth year, I'll give you enough for both the seventh year and the Jubilee year. I'll give you enough to see you through."

And He says the same thing to you and me when He says, "Bring the tithe into the storehouse. Trust Me and test Me to see if I don't provide for you" (Malachi 3:10).

Leviticus 25:23, 24
The land shall not be sold for ever: for the land is mine; for ye are strangers and sojourners with me. And in all the land of your possession ye shall grant a redemption for the land.

For forty-nine years men could buy and sell and build their own estates. The fiftieth year, the land was to be returned to its original owner. In other words, free enterprise for forty-nine years and compassion in the fiftieth year would have prevented monopolization and exploitation. It was a brilliant plan.

Leviticus 25:25
If thy brother be waxen poor, and hath sold away some of his possession, and if any of his kin come to redeem it, then shall he redeem that which his brother sold.

Here we are introduced to the concept of the kinsman redeemer, perfectly illustrated in the person of Boaz (Ruth 2—4), and perfectly fulfilled in the Person of Jesus Christ.

Leviticus 25:26–28
And if the man have none to redeem it, and himself be able to redeem it; then let him count the years of the sale thereof, and restore the overplus unto the man to whom he sold it; that he may return unto his possession. But if he be not able to restore it to him, then that which is sold shall remain in the hand of him that hath bought it until the year of jubile: and in the jubile it shall go out, and he shall return unto his possession.

If, after having sold his property, a man is later able to buy it back, he has the right to do so. Otherwise, he must wait until the Year of Jubilee for it to be returned to him.

Leviticus 25:29–31
And if a man sell a dwelling house in a walled city, then he may redeem it within a whole year after it is sold; within a full year may he redeem it. And if it be not redeemed within the space of a full year, then the house that is in the walled city shall be es-

tablished for ever to him that bought it throughout his generations: it shall not go out in the jubile. But the houses of the villages which have no wall round about them shall be counted as the fields of the country: they may be redeemed, and they shall go out in the jubile.

If I sell my house in a walled city but later decide I want it back, either I or a kinsman of mine can buy it back within a year. But if I don't buy it back within a year, the house is to become the buyer's forever. If my house was not in the city, however, I could buy it back at any point—or wait until the Year of Jubilee, at which time it would be returned to me. The rabbis teach that, in this, God is encouraging people not to live in cities. Whether or not such be the case, the fact remains that with a higher density of people comes greater opportunity to sin. A higher density of believers in any given area can result in a greater degree of lethargy. That is why, as salt and light, we are most effective when we are spread out.

Leviticus 25:32–34
Notwithstanding the cities of the Levites, and the houses of the cities of their possession, may the Levites redeem at any time. And if a man purchase of the Levites, then the house that was sold, and the city of his possession, shall go out in the year of jubile: for the houses of the cities of the Levites are their possession among the children of Israel. But the field of the suburbs of their cities may not be sold; for it is their perpetual possession.

Having been given no land of their own (Numbers 18:20), the tribe of Levi was given cities in which to live and a surrounding area as pasture land for their livestock. While a Levite could sell his house, which would be returned to him in the Year of Jubilee, he could not sell his land.

Leviticus 25:35–38
And if thy brother be waxen poor, and fallen in decay with thee; then thou shalt relieve him: yea, though he be a stranger, or a sojourner; that he may live with thee. Take thou no usury of him, or increase: but fear thy God; that thy brother may live with thee. Thou shalt not give him thy money upon usury, nor lend him thy victuals for increase. I am the LORD your God, which brought you forth out of the land of Egypt, to give you the land of Canaan, and to be your God.

Although Deuteronomy 23:20 allows for interest from a stranger having themselves been rescued by God when they were slaves in Egypt, the Israelites were to rescue their brothers from financial bondage with no-interest loans. In other words, they were not to take advantage of a brother in need.

Leviticus 25:39–46
And if thy brother that dwelleth by thee be waxen poor, and be sold unto thee; thou shalt not compel him to serve as a bondservant: but as an hired servant, and as a sojourner, he shall be with thee, and shall serve thee unto the year of jubile: and then shall he depart from thee, both he and his children with him, and shall return unto his own family, and unto the possession of his fathers shall he return. For they are my servants, which I brought forth out of the land of Egypt: they shall not be sold as bondmen. Thou shalt not rule over him with rigour; but shalt fear thy God. Both thy bondmen, and thy bondmaids, which thou shalt have, shall be of the heathen that are round about you; of them shall ye buy bondmen and bondmaids. Moreover of the children of the strangers that do sojourn among you, of them shall ye buy, and of their families that are with you, which they begat in your land: and they shall be your possession. And ye shall take them as an inheritance for your children after you, to inherit them for a possession; they shall be your bondmen for ever: but over your brethren the children of Israel, ye shall not rule one over another with rigour.

If an Israelite had to become a servant, his master was to treat him not as a slave, but as an employee until he was released in the Year of Jubilee. We were all slaves of sin, but because Jesus is our Jubilee, we have been set free.

Leviticus 25:47–55
And if a sojourner or stranger wax rich by thee, and thy brother that dwelleth by him wax poor, and sell himself unto the stranger or sojourner by thee, or to the stock of the stranger's family: after that he is sold he may be redeemed again; one of his brethren may redeem him: either his uncle, or his uncle's son, may redeem him, or any that is nigh of kin unto him of his family may redeem him; or if he be able, he may redeem himself. And he shall reckon with him that bought him from the year that he was sold to him unto the year of jubile: and the price of his sale shall be according unto the number of years, according to the time of an hired servant shall it be with him. If there be yet many years behind, according unto them he shall give again the price of his redemption out

of the money that he was bought for. And if there remain but few years unto the year of jubile, then he shall count with him, and according unto his years shall he give him again the price of his redemption. And as a yearly hired servant shall he be with him: and the other shall not rule with rigour over him in thy sight. And if he be not redeemed in these years, then he shall go out in the year of jubile, both he, and his children with him. For unto me the children of Israel are servants; they are my servants whom I brought forth out of the land of Egypt: I am the LORD your God.

Is God instituting slavery in these laws regarding the price of a slave's redemption prior to the Year of Jubilee? No, He's regulating what was already taking place. Why didn't God forbid slavery? Because God's way is to change people. Changed people, in turn—people like England's abolitionist William Wilberforce, an outspoken believer—will then change politics.

26 After carefully and thoroughly giving His Law to His people, here at the end of the Book of Leviticus, God will declare to them, "If you walk in My Law, you will be beautifully blessed. If you wander from My Law, you will be unbelievably burdened. The choice is yours."

We live in a universe regulated by physical laws. Therefore, if I start poking around in an electrical socket or jump off a ten-story building, I can't be shocked to find myself fried or to wake up broken and battered. The penalties for breaking the laws of electricity and gravity are consistent. There will always be a price to pay.

So, too, there are spiritual laws which are irrefutable, undeniable, absolute. And those who violate them suffer consequences as surely as if they violated physical laws. If they keep them, however, their lives will be illuminated as surely as is the one who obeys the law of electricity; their lives will be as grounded as those who choose to live by the law of gravity.

Leviticus 26:1
Ye shall make you no idols nor graven image, neither rear you up a standing image, neither shall ye set up any image of stone in your land, to bow down unto it: for I am the LORD your God.

The children of Israel were not to make standing images because, in reality, no image, no idol, no false god can ever stand.

***For topical study of Leviticus 26:1 entitled "Overcoming Idolatry," turn to page* 444.**

Leviticus 26:2
Ye shall keep my sabbaths, and reverence my sanctuary: I am the LORD.

The Israelites were to keep the holy day and come to the Holy Place.

Leviticus 26:3, 4
If ye walk in my statutes, and keep my commandments, and do them; then I will give you rain in due season, and the land shall yield her increase, and the trees of the field shall yield their fruit.

"If you do what I say, your land will be productive," the Lord promises.

Leviticus 26:5
And your threshing shall reach unto the vintage, and the vintage shall reach unto the sowing time: and ye shall eat your bread to the full, and dwell in your land safely.

"If you walk in My ways, you will experience prosperity," God declares.

Leviticus 26:6
And I will give peace in the land, and ye shall lie down, and none shall make you afraid: and I will rid evil beasts out of the land, neither shall the sword go through your land.

"Follow Me," God says, "and you will receive peace and protection."

Leviticus 26:7, 8
And ye shall chase your enemies, and they shall fall before you by the sword. And five of you shall chase an hundred, and an hundred of you shall put ten thousand to flight: and your enemies shall fall before you by the sword.

Power would be given to God's people if they kept His commands. Their enemies would be able to make no impact upon them.

Leviticus 26:9
For I will have respect unto you, and make you fruitful, and multiply you, and establish my covenant with you.

"My promises will be fulfilled in those who walk in My statutes," God declares.

Leviticus 26:10
And ye shall eat old store, and bring forth the old because of the new.

Provision will be made for those who walk God's way through an understanding of both the old and the new—in our case, the Old Testament truths and New Testament revelations.

Leviticus 26:11–13
And I will set my tabernacle among you: and my soul shall not abhor you. And I will walk among you, and will be your God, and ye shall be my people. I am the LORD your God, which brought you forth out of the land of Egypt, that ye should not be their bondmen; and I have broken the bands of your yoke, and made you go upright.

Productivity and prosperity, peace and protection, power, promise, and provision were topped off by the promise of God's presence to those who chose to obey Him. Jesus reiterated this same truth in the context of material blessings when He said, "Seek first the kingdom of God and all these things shall be added unto you" (Matthew 6:33).

"How can I walk in His ways if I can't remember what they are?" you ask.

Jesus reduced the entire Old Testament Law and prophets to two sentences when He said, "Thou shalt love the Lord thy God with all thy heart, soul, mind, and strength. And thou shalt love thy neighbor as thyself" (Mark 12:30, 31).

Leviticus 26:14 (a)
But . . .

Here is the three-letter pivotal word on which this chapter—if not the entire book—rests.

Leviticus 26:14 (b)–19
. . . if ye will not hearken unto me, and will not do all these commandments; And if ye shall despise my statutes, or if your soul abhor my judgments, so that ye will not do all my commandments, but that ye break my covenant: I also will do this unto you; I will even appoint over you terror, consumption, and the burning ague, that shall consume the eyes, and cause sorrow of heart: and ye shall sow your seed in vain, for your enemies shall eat it. And I will set my face against you, and ye shall be slain before your enemies: they that hate you shall reign over you; and ye shall flee when none pursueth you. And if ye will not yet for all this hearken unto me, then I will punish you seven times more for your sins. And I will break the pride of your power; and I will make your heaven as iron, and your earth as brass:

Do you ever feel like heaven is iron, like your prayers bounce off the ceiling? God says, "If you don't do what I tell you to do, heaven will be as iron, and earth as brass, the metal of judgment."

Leviticus 26:20–24
And your strength shall be spent in vain: for your land shall not yield her increase, neither shall the trees of the land yield their fruits. And if ye walk contrary unto me, and will not hearken unto me; I will bring seven times more plagues upon you according to your sins. I will also send wild beasts among you, which shall rob you of your children, and destroy your cattle, and make you few in number; and your highways shall be desolate. And if ye will not be reformed by me by these things, but will walk contrary unto me; then will I also walk contrary unto you, and will punish you yet seven times for your sins.

Disobedience to God affects one's health, one's family, one's livelihood. Why are *seven* plagues sent to those who choose to disobey God? Why *seven* punishments? Because God wants us to know we have two choices: a real good one and a real rotten one. It's not like choosing between the Toyota or the Nissan. It's, "Do you want prosperity, peace, and power—or do you want anger, curses and problems?"

"Do what I tell you and you'll be blessed," God says. "Don't, and you'll be distressed. It's just that simple."

Leviticus 26:25–31
And I will bring a sword upon you, that shall avenge the quarrel of my covenant: and when ye are gathered together within your cities, I will send the pestilence among you; and ye shall be delivered into the hand of the enemy. And when I have broken the staff of your bread, ten women shall bake your bread in one oven, and they shall deliver you your bread again by weight: and ye shall eat, and not be satisfied. And if ye will not for all this hearken unto me, but walk contrary unto me; then I will walk contrary unto you also in fury; and I, even I, will chastise you seven times for your sins. And ye shall eat the flesh of your sons, and the flesh of your daughters shall ye eat. And I will destroy your high places, and cut down your images, and cast your carcases upon the carcases of your idols, and my soul shall abhor you. And I will make your cities waste, and bring your sanctuaries unto desolation, and I will not smell the savour of your sweet odours.

The choice to walk contrary to God's ways would not only result in all of creation being at war with them through horrendous disease and famine, but, worse, because God would no longer "smell the savour of their sweet odours," their sacrifices would not be accepted.

Leviticus 26:32–35
And I will bring the land into desolation: and your enemies which dwell therein shall be astonished at it. And I will scatter you among the heathen, and will draw out a sword after you: and your land shall be desolate, and your cities waste. Then shall the land enjoy her sabbaths, as long as it lieth desolate, and ye be in your enemies' land; even then shall the land rest, and enjoy her sabbaths. As long as it lieth desolate it shall rest; because it did not rest in your sabbaths, when ye dwelt upon it.

Israel was given a command that would be an indicator of their obedience to God and their affection for God. The command concerned the sabbath year—the seventh year to be set aside during which there was to be no sowing of seed, no reaping of the harvest, no work done by man or beast. And when the people used the seventh year to work instead of to rest, God waited for them to repent. Because our Father is patient, slow to anger, full of mercy (Nehemiah 9:17), He waited year after year, for a change of heart. But after four hundred and ninety years passed, He said, "Enough." And His people were carried to captivity in Babylon for seventy sabbaths, or seventy years.

The laws of God are absolute. When violated, the consequences are inevitable. Thus, the captivity of His people was proof of the surety of God's Word. If I walk in it, I'm blessed. If I wander from it, I'm taken captive.

Leviticus 26:36–39
And upon them that are left alive of you I will send a faintness into their hearts in the lands of their enemies; and the sound of a shaken leaf shall chase them; and they shall flee, as fleeing from a sword; and they shall fall when none pursueth. And they shall fall one upon another, as it were before a sword, when none pursueth: and ye shall have no power to stand before your enemies. And ye shall perish among the heathen, and the land of your enemies shall eat you up. And they that are left of you shall pine away in their iniquity in your enemies' lands; and also in the iniquities of their fathers shall they pine away with them.

The prosperity and power, peace, protection, and provision of verses 3 through 10 would be replaced by the powerlessness, perishing, and pining of verses 36 through 39.

Leviticus 26:40–46
If they shall confess their iniquity, and the iniquity of their fathers, with their trespass which they trespassed against me, and that also they have walked contrary unto me; and that I also have walked contrary unto them, and have brought them into the land of their enemies; if then their uncircumcised hearts be humbled, and they then accept of the punishment of their iniquity: then will I remember my covenant with Jacob, and also my covenant with Isaac, and also my covenant with Abraham will I remember; and I will remember the land. The land also shall be left of them, and shall enjoy her sabbaths, while she lieth desolate without them: and they shall accept of the punishment of their iniquity: because, even because they despised my judgments, and because their soul abhorred my statutes. And yet for all that, when they be in the land of their enemies, I will not cast them away, neither will I abhor them, to destroy them utterly, and to break my covenant with them: for I am the LORD their God. But I will for their sakes remember the covenant of their ancestors, whom I brought forth out of the land of Egypt in the sight of the heathen, that I might be their God: I am the LORD. These are the statutes and judgments and laws, which the LORD made between him and the children of Israel in mount Sinai by the hand of Moses.

Even in the time of captivity, even in the place of bondage which was due to their own disobedience, of His people, God declares, "I won't forget them. I won't forsake them." And that is the Word of the Lord to you and me today. God is saying, "If you walk in My Law, you'll be blessed. If you wander from My Law, you'll be burned. But even if you're in captivity, know this: I have not forsaken you, for lo, I am with you always" (see Matthew 28:20).

Every broken commandment, every ignored precept can be forgiven because of what Jesus did for us on Calvary. Therefore, even if we're in the land of the enemy, God still cares about us. If we'll confess our sin to Him, if we'll call upon His name, He'll restore us once again. "If you wander from My ways, terror will come," God says. "If you walk in My ways, I'll bless you. It's your choice. The ball is in your court."

OVERCOMING IDOLATRY

A Topical Study of LEVITICUS 26:1

Throughout the Old Testament, the warning is sounded concerning the seduction of idolatry. Over and over again God's people are commanded to avoid idolatry and any type of imagery. Why? Is it because God is jealous of or threatened by idols? Is it because idols make Him feel insecure about who He is? Why does God over and over again warn against idolatry?

Turn to Psalm 115, where we see God's view of idols . . .

> *Their idols are silver and gold, the work of men's hands. They have mouths, but they speak not: eyes have they, but they see not: They have ears, but they hear not: noses have they, but they smell not: They have hands, but they handle not: feet have they, but they walk not: neither speak they through their throat.*
>
> Psalm 115:4–7

Throughout the Word, God's view of idolatry is always linked with stupidity and ignorance. And yet, although idols are powerless in the material realm, there is a reality behind them in the spiritual arena . . .

> *What say I then? That the idol is any thing, or that which is offered in sacrifice to idols is any thing? But I say, that the things which the Gentiles sacrifice, they sacrifice to devils, and not to God: and I would not that ye should have fellowship with devils.*
>
> 1 Corinthians 10:19, 20

The material idol in and of itself is nothing. It's simply a piece of wood or a carved stone. It has no life. It's blind, deaf, and dumb. However, there are spiritual powers, entities, personalities which flow through those idols. Although our tendency can be to think of the Canaanites and Old Testament Israelites as cavemen walking around worshiping idols because they were stupid, nothing could be further from the truth. In the fields of philosophy and science, medicine and architecture, ancient cultures were so advanced that to this day, we have no idea how they did some of the things they did. Likewise, their religion was highly developed—with parallels still seen today . . .

Mammon was the god of material prosperity. Although worship of mammon centered around an idol, no one believed the idol in and of itself possessed power. Rather, it merely represented a way to get to the idea of mammon, a way to reach material prosperity. We do the same thing today through financial seminars, publications, and investment clubs. Are these things wrong? Only if they become a higher priority than loving God or loving each other.

Baal was the god of the intellect. Those who wanted answers for natural phenomena worshiped Baal because Baal worship offered a rational explanation for everything from earthquakes and rain to lightning and famine. And because they had no God to answer to personally, they felt they had the freedom to plunge into moral laxity. The same holds true today. People are agnostics because they want to do their own thing. And if they don't have to give answer to a holy or just God, they can do whatever they want.

Molech and Ashteroth were the god and goddess of physical, sensual pleasure. Those who worshiped these gods were totally consumed with and motivated by the latest hedonistic thrill. Worshipers of Molech would place their children as sacrifices on the incandescent arms of his idol, believing they would thereby gain greater pleasure for themselves. "How cruel!," we say. And yet there isn't a day that goes by in our own culture when people don't sacrifice their children through adultery and immorality in pursuit of their own physical pleasure.

Fifty other gods are recorded in Scripture—each with a demonic entity behind it, each still present today. That's what Paul is driving at. There are the same spiritual entities, the same hordes of hell here today. And there are Christians who, perhaps unknowingly, bow the knee to mammon or Baal, submitting to those forces of evil that seek to destroy us and disrupt our walk with Jesus Christ.

> *For though we walk in the flesh, we do not war after the flesh: (For the weapons of our warfare are not carnal, but mighty through God to the pulling down of strong holds), casting down imaginations, and every high thing that exalteth itself against the knowledge of God, and bringing into captivity every thought to the obedience of Christ;* 2 Corinthians 10:3–5

We're in a war. And the war we're fighting deals with the idols of imagination—illustrated perhaps most vividly in the Book of Ezekiel . . .

> *And he brought me to the door of the court; and when I looked, behold a hole in the wall. Then said he unto me, Son of man, dig now in the wall: and when I had digged in the wall, behold a door. And he said unto me, Go in, and behold the wicked abominations that they do here. So I went in and saw; and behold every form of creeping things, and abominable beasts, and all the idols of the house of Israel, pourtrayed upon the wall round about. And there stood before them seventy men of the ancients of the house of Israel, and in the midst of them stood Jaazaniah the son of Shaphan, with every man his censer in his hand; and a thick cloud of incense went up. Then said he unto me, Son of man, hast thou seen what the ancients of the house of Israel do in the dark,*

every man in the chambers of his imagery? For they say, the L*ORD seeth us not; the* L*ORD hath forsaken the earth.* Ezekiel 8:7–12

A shocking vision was given to Ezekiel of the temple walls covered with abominable pictures. "This is what is happening in the chambers of imagery, in the imaginations of men of maturity." In the minds of these outwardly religious men who would never have an idol in their homes, Ashteroth and Baal have taken up residence.

We are involved in warfare, the warfare of the mind. I don't know which god is most effective in your life, which entity most pervasively preys on your chamber of imagery, but I do know Satan is sure to release his emissaries to launch an attack against you and me.

Why?

He attacks us first of all because of *perversion.* At the point Lucifer rebelled against God and fell from heaven, his wisdom became perversion. And one of his perverted desires is to destroy (John 10:10). That is why the ultimate manifestation of one given over to Satan is a suicidal tendency (Matthew 27:5).

A second reason Satan attacks is for *ransom.* It would seem as though Satan is going to use the host which he has caused to come into his kingdom of darkness as a bargaining chip against God in the last day.

Thirdly, Satan attacks God's people because he's desperate. When, standing near a swimming pool, I see the all-too-familiar sight of a group of guys headed my way, my reaction is always the same. I realize I'm going in—but my attitude is, if I'm going in, I'm taking as many of them with me as I can. So I grab arms, legs, and shirts of any within my reach. That's the way Satan is. He's seeking to pull as many as he can into the lake of fire with him.

If you're a believer in Jesus, Satan knows he's lost your soul. But he'll seek to neutralize and nullify your witness by attacking you, by sending out his demons to cause destruction and deception. What do we do with these images, these powers that plague and haunt us? Consider the following four suggestions . . .

In dealing with these entities, these spiritual realities which war against your soul, there must first of all be *realization.* We are at war. And because we're at war, there will be casualties. When a person sins, the reaction can be, "He has blown it. Shame on him." But we need to realize that he has been attacked and therefore look at him not as vicious but as a victim of the attack of the enemy.

Secondly, there must be *preparation.* When the disciples were unable to cast out a demon from a boy who was possessed, Jesus told them to do so required prayer and fasting (Matthew 17). Therefore, we must be prepared *before* the attack comes. How? Before running a marathon, runners stock up on carbohydrates. To prepare spiritually, we are to do just the opposite because something happens when we say "No" to our stomachs. Saying "No" to our appetites physically strengthens the inner man spiritually.

Thirdly, there must be *confrontation* against these entities. We can't run from them. We must move in authority, fervency, and intensity in dealing with them. And yet all too often when we sense a spiritual attack headed our way, we just give up and get depressed. It took a shout to bring down the walls of Jericho (Joshua 6:20). It took a spoken, authoritative command to cast out demons (Mark 5:8). Thus, if we are to wage war against the demonic entities that plague us we must confront them with authority—at times even vocally.

Finally, we move in *expectation*, for without faith it is impossible to please God (Hebrews 11:6). We can expect to be victorious knowing that our enemy and his hordes of hell are doomed to one day be thrown into the bottomless pit forever (Revelation 12).

The victory is ours, gang. All we have to do is take it and act upon it. May we be those who keep ourselves from idols as we recognize them, be prepared for them, and confront them in the name of Jesus.

27

Leviticus 27:1–8
And the LORD spake unto Moses, saying, Speak unto the children of Israel, and say unto them, when a man shall make a singular vow, the persons shall be for the LORD by thy estimation. And thy estimation shall be of the male from twenty years old even unto sixty years old, even thy estimation shall be fifty shekels of silver, after the shekel of the sanctuary. And if it be a female, then thy estimation shall be thirty shekels. And if it be from five years old even unto twenty years old, then thy estimation shall be of the male twenty shekels, and for the female ten shekels. And if it be from a month old even unto five years old, then thy estimation shall be of the male five shekels of silver, and for the female thy estimation shall be three shekels of silver. And if it be from sixty years old and above; if it be a male, then thy estimation shall be fifteen shekels, and for the female ten shekels. But if he be poorer than thy estimation, then he shall present himself before the priest, and the priest shall value him; according to his ability that vowed shall the priest value him.

Anyone who vowed to devote himself to service to the Lord, but was unable to keep his vow due to a change of heart, a physical disqualification, or because he was not needed, he was to pay a price of redemption based not upon the value he held in God's eyes, but upon how much work he was able to do.

Sometimes people say, "I really wanted to go to the mission field," or, "I really desired to be a youth pastor"—but if they prove to be unable, unwilling, or unneeded, they can still redeem the situation by supporting those who are called, those who are able and truly willing.

Leviticus 27:9, 10
And if it be a beast, whereof men bring an offering unto the LORD, all that any man giveth of such unto the LORD shall be holy. He shall not alter it, nor change it, a good for a bad, or a bad for a good: and if he shall at all change beast for beast, then it and the exchange thereof shall be holy.

If someone tried to trick God by switching an inferior animal with a spotless one to sacrifice, God was to get both animals—a reminder that playing games with God is always a lose/lose situation.

Leviticus 27:11–13
And if it be any unclean beast, of which they do not offer a sacrifice unto the LORD, then he shall present the beast before the priest: and the priest shall value it, whether it be good or bad: as thou valuest it, who art the priest, so shall it be. But if he will at all redeem it, then he shall add a fifth part thereof unto thy estimation.

If a worshiper changed his mind and wanted his sacrificial animal back, he was to buy it back at full price plus twenty percent.

Leviticus 27:14–25
And when a man shall sanctify his house to be holy unto the LORD, then the priest shall estimate it, whether it be good or bad: as the priest shall estimate it, so shall it stand. And if he that sanctified it will redeem his house, then he shall add the fifth part of the money of thy estimation unto it, and it shall be his. And if a man shall sanctify unto the LORD some part of a field of his possession, then thy estimation shall be according to the seed thereof: an homer of barley seed shall be valued at fifty shekels of silver. If he sanctify his field from the year of jubile, according to thy estimation it shall stand. But if he sanctify his field after the jubile, then the priest shall reckon unto him the money according to the years that remain, even unto the year of the jubile, and it shall be abated from thy estimation. And if he that sanctified the field will in any wise redeem it, then he shall add the fifth part of the money of thy estimation unto it, and it shall be assured to him. And if he will not redeem the field, or if he have sold the field to another man, it shall not be redeemed any more. But the field, when it goeth out in the jubile, shall be holy unto the LORD, as a field devoted; the possession thereof shall be the priest's. And if a man sanctify unto the LORD a field which he hath bought, which is not of the fields of his possession; then the priest shall reckon unto him the worth of thy estimation, even unto the year of the jubile: and he shall give thine estimation in that day, as a holy thing unto the LORD. In the year of the jubile the field shall return unto him of whom it was bought, even to him to whom the possession of the land did belong. And all thy estimations shall be according to the shekel of the sanctuary: twenty gerahs shall be the shekel.

"We need a 15,000 square foot house, Lord, because we're going to use it for ministry. We'll have people over constantly as well as hosting Bible studies consistently." But if this turns out to be a promise we're unwilling or unable to keep, we're to redeem the house—buy it back—at full price plus twenty percent. The same principle was to be followed with regard to property.

Leviticus 27:26
Only the firstling of the beasts, which should be the LORD's firstling, no man shall sanctify it; whether it be ox, or sheep: it is the LORD's.

A man could not dedicate to the Lord the first ox or the first sheep in his herd or flock because it was already God's. So, too, because the tithe is already the Lord's, why do we think we're doing something special when we give Him what is His already?

Leviticus 27:27
And if it be of an unclean beast, then he shall redeem it according to thine estimation, and shall add a fifth part of it thereto: or if it be not redeemed, then it shall be sold according to thy estimation.

Unclean animals were to be bought back for full price plus twenty percent.

Leviticus 27:28
Notwithstanding no devoted thing, that a man shall devote unto the LORD of all that he hath, both of man and beast, and of the field of his possession, shall be sold or redeemed: every devoted thing is most holy unto the LORD.

Jericho was an example of that which was to be devoted to the Lord. That is why the Israelites were forbidden to take anything from it, and why Achan was punished so severely for doing so (Joshua 7:25).

Leviticus 27:29
None devoted, which shall be devoted of men, shall be redeemed; but shall surely be put to death.

Under Old Testament Law, a person sentenced to die could not be redeemed, could not be "bought back." Praise be to God, however, because of the Cross of Calvary, we who were sentenced to death through the penalty of sin were indeed redeemed by the blood of the Lamb.

Leviticus 27:30, 31
And all the tithe of the land, whether of the seed of the land, or of the fruit of the tree, is the LORD's: it is holy unto the LORD. And if a man will at all redeem ought of his tithes, he shall add thereto the fifth part thereof.

If a man needed to withhold a portion of his tithe, he was to add twenty percent to it when he was able to offer it to the Lord.

Leviticus 27:32, 33
And concerning the tithe of the herd, or of the flock, even of whatsoever passeth under the rod, the tenth shall be holy unto the LORD.

He shall not search whether it be good or bad, neither shall he change it: and if he change it at all, then both it and the change thereof shall be holy; it shall not be redeemed.

"Passing under the rod" referred to the way a shepherd would hold forth his shepherd's rod in order to count his sheep as they passed under it. Thus, God was saying, "After you've counted it, tithe ten percent of your flock."

Leviticus 27:34
These are the commandments, which the LORD commanded Moses for the children of Israel in mount Sinai.

The Book of Leviticus ends with a teaching on tithing as if to say that holiness is proved by how one responds and reacts to that which costs him something. We can talk about holiness, sing songs about holiness, even pray about holiness—but holiness becomes real in our lives to the extent that we give the Lord His due, no matter the cost. And, as New Testament believers, His due is our all . . .

> I beseech you therefore, brethren, by the mercies of God, that ye present your bodies a living sacrifice, holy, acceptable unto God, which is your reasonable service. Romans 12:1

NUMBERS

Background to Numbers

The Book of Numbers gets its name from the numbering of the people—the first time seen in chapter 1, the second approximately thirty-nine years later in chapter 26. In the Hebrew Bible, the Torah, this book is titled "In The Wilderness" due to where it takes place. It is also known as "The Book of Murmurings" for reasons that will become clear as we read through it.

The five books penned by Moses—the five Books of the Pentateuch—of which Numbers is the fourth, chronicle the development of God's people . . .

- In Genesis, we see in the person of Abraham God's people waiting—waiting for the son promised to him, the first of a nation that was to number as the stars in the heavens, the sand on the seashore.
- In Exodus, we see God's people watching—as God raised up a deliverer named Moses and sent plagues upon the land of Egypt in order to set them free.
- In Leviticus, we see God's people worshiping—in response to what He had done for them so graciously.
- Here in Numbers, we see God's people warring—as they are organized in camps to do battle against the enemies they will encounter on their way towards the Promised Land.

The same sequence plays out in the life of the believer—for, after waiting for the Lord to work, after seeing what He does and worshiping in response, we are told to storm the gates of hell (Matthew 16:18), to roll up our sleeves, strap on our swords and take by force the territory promised to us—to be those who say, "God said all things work together for good, therefore I'm going to rejoice in the Lord always," to be those whose hearts are not troubled because we know Jesus is preparing a place for us.

You see, gang, although it's inevitable that we come to wilderness times in our walk, we don't need to live in the wilderness year after year, decade after decade.

It's not God's intention that we wander endlessly in the wilderness of depression and defeat, discouragement and despair. Such is the lesson of the Book of Numbers.

There will be a majority of teachers, speakers, and preachers who say such teaching is simplistic—that what we now know about the human psyche, about chemical reactions in the brain, about the pressures of culture render Scripture unrealistic. And we have a choice whether to believe the majority report that doesn't subscribe to the profound simplicity of the promises of God—or to believe God and determine we're not going to spend thirty-nine years, thirty-nine weeks or even thirty-nine days wandering in the wilderness of despair.

The book divides itself into three basic sections. Chapters 1 through 12 deal with the old generation—organized in chapters 1 through 4 and sanctified in chapters 5 through 12. In chapters 13 through 20, we see the failing of the old generation—their failure to believe, their murmuring, their disobedience. In chapters 21 through 36, a new generation is raised up that will take the Promised Land simply by taking God at His Word.

NUMBERS

1 **Numbers 1:1 (a)**
And the LORD spake unto Moses in the wilderness of Sinai . . .

It was in the wilderness that Moses heard the Word of the Lord. I point this out because sometimes when we go through a wilderness experience, although we try to extract things from the Word, although we spend time in prayer, we don't hear the voice of the Lord. All of us go through such times. But notice exactly where Moses was in the wilderness when the Lord spoke to him . . .

Numbers 1:1 (b)
. . . in the tabernacle of the congregation . . .

Moses was in the tabernacle of the congregation when he heard the voice of the Lord. And I believe the best place to hear the Lord speak is still the tabernacle of the congregation—in church. So many times in my walk when I have been dry, when I haven't heard the heart of the Lord, no sooner would I go into a church service and plop down on a back pew somewhere than I would begin to listen and wonder, *Who told this preacher what I'm going through?*, as he seemed to speak directly, specifically to my situation. I say this because sometimes we fail to remember when we talk about Bible study that the way to study the Bible most effectively is to consistently, faithfully come to church and travel through the Word with our brothers and sisters in the Lord.

Numbers 1:1 (c)
. . . on the first day of the second month, in the second year after they were come out of the land of Egypt . . .

After leaving Egypt, the children of Israel camped at the base of Mt. Sinai for one year during which time they received the Ten Commandments, the Law, and instruction concerning worship. Here in Numbers, the tabernacle has been constructed, the people have received instruction for worship, and they are beginning the second month of the second year of their journey through the wilderness.

Numbers 1:1 (d)–3
. . . saying, Take ye the sum of all the congregation of the children of Israel, after their families, by the house of their fathers, with the number of their names, every male by their polls; from twenty years old and upward, all that are able to go forth to war in Israel: thou and Aaron shall number them by their armies.

"Mobilize the congregation," the Lord commanded Moses. "Count the people and see who will be able to fight in Israel's army." Following are four possible reasons Moses was told to number the people . . .

Verification. God promised Abraham that he would one day be the father of a great nation (Genesis 12:2). This numbering would verify that God does what He promises. Even at this early point of their history, Israel was a big nation, an impressive group of people.

Identification. In referring to Himself as the Good Shepherd, Jesus said He calls His sheep by name (John 10:3). God cares about each and every individual. That is why He instructs Moses to number the people. Some people say, "I'm not into numbers with regard to church life." While I understand that we are not to be puffed up about numbers, I also know that we are to care about individuals, and sometimes that cannot happen without a numbering of the flock. After all, it was only after the Good Shepherd numbered the ninety-nine that He knew one was missing (Matthew 18:12). In the Book of Acts, we see that 3,000 were saved (Acts 2:41), which later grew to 5,000 (Acts 4:4). Admittedly, there can be a danger, a downside. David erred greatly when he numbered the people (2 Samuel 24:10). Is this a contradiction? No. David numbered the people not out of concern for them but in order to see how strong he had become. Numbering the people out of pride is wrong. But refusing to number them out of a reverse pride is also wrong, for it shows a lack of care.

Separation. There were those traveling with the Israelites who were not children of Israel. As we will see in verse 18, those not sure of their pedigree couldn't be used in the army. And the same thing is true for you and me. We must know our pedigree. We must know if we're part of the family. We must know whether or not we've been born again. If you're not sure of this, don't even think about going to war, about mobilizing for ministry. Romans 8:16 tells us that God's Spirit bears witness with our spirits that we are the sons of God. On this basis, I don't generally try to talk people into assurance of salvation. Instead, I'll say to them, "If you're not sure where you stand, wait on the Lord until you have the witness from His Spirit in your spirit that you are indeed His child."

Organization. We've been called to be soldiers in an army. We're involved in a war. Thus, there must be order. Anyone serious about serving God who is not part of any local church, who is not in submission to anyone, not linked with anyone, not accountable to anyone will sooner or later be a casualty. God is not into a lone ranger mentality.

Numbers 1:4
And with you there shall be a man of every tribe; every one head of the house of his fathers.

As seen in verses 5–15, each of the Twelve Tribes had a leader.

Numbers 1:16–18
These were the renowned of the congregation, princes of the tribes of their fathers, heads of thousands in Israel. And Moses and Aaron took these men which are expressed by their names: and they assembled all the congregation together on the first day of the second month, and they declared their pedigrees after their families, by the house of their fathers, according to the number of the names, from twenty years old and upward, by their polls.

As seen in verses 18 through 43, Reuben's tribe numbered 46,500. Simeon's 59,300. Gad 45,650. Judah 74,600. Issachar 54,400. Zebulun 57,400. Joseph was represented by his two sons, Ephraim and Manasseh who numbered 40,500 and 32,200 respectively. Benjamin numbered 35,400, Dan 62,700, Asher 41,500, and Naphtali 53,400.

Numbers 1:44–46
These are those that were numbered, which Moses and Aaron numbered, and the princes of Israel, being twelve men: each one was for the house of his fathers. So were all those that were numbered of the children of Israel, by the house of their fathers, from twenty years old and upward, all that were able to go forth to war in Israel; even all they that were numbered were six hundred thousand and three thousand and five hundred and fifty.

The census which will be taken of the new generation in chapter 26, will be amazingly close in number at 601,730.

Numbers 1:47–49
But the Levites after the tribe of their fathers were not numbered among them. For the LORD had spoken unto Moses, saying, Only thou shalt not number the tribe of Levi, neither take the sum of them among the children of Israel:

The above figures representing only the men of the congregation and excluding the tribe of Levi, the Israelites would have numbered between two and three million in totality.

Numbers 1:50–54
But thou shalt appoint the Levites over the tabernacle of testimony, and over all the vessels thereof, and over all things that belong to it: they shall bear the tabernacle, and all

the vessels thereof; and they shall minister unto it, and shall encamp round about the tabernacle. And when the tabernacle setteth forward, the Levites shall take it down: and when the tabernacle is to be pitched, the Levites shall set it up: and the stranger that cometh nigh shall be put to death. And the children of Israel shall pitch their tents, every man by his own camp, and every man by his own standard, throughout their hosts. But the Levites shall pitch round about the tabernacle of testimony, that there be no wrath upon the congregation of the children of Israel: and the Levites shall keep the charge of the tabernacle of testimony. And the children of Israel did according to all that the LORD commanded Moses, so did they.

The tabernacle was the place wherein dwelt the *chabod*, the glory of God—that which every person, whether he knows it or not, craves. You might think you're craving a bigger house, a faster car, a new boyfriend. But in reality, what you're truly craving is the *chabod*, the glory of God. And the degree to which you experience the glory of God is the degree to which you will be satisfied in this life presently. Otherwise, you'll fall into the trap of thinking, *I'm not content now, but I will be—as soon as I get the next promotion*—failing to understand that it is only the weight, the substance, the glory of God which will satisfy your soul.

Here we see that the Levites—those who served in the tabernacle—were those who had the privilege of camping closest to the place where the chabod resided. The same is true today. The way to experience the presence of God is to serve—be it teaching a Sunday school class, coaching a Little League team in a way that you are an example of what it means to be a lover of God, raising your kids in the ways of God, serving as a missionary, or being involved in intercessory prayer. Jesus said whatever measure we give out will be given back to us (Matthew 7:2). And I have found it to be oh, so true—that the key to be experiencing the glory of God is to be involved in service, for if we only take in, we become bloated and groggy, but if we share with others that which we're learning, that which we've been given, that which we've experienced, we will receive a continuous supply.

---

2 "If the Bible seems a bit dry, moisten it with sweat," someone once said. I like that because some passages, perhaps like the one before us, can seem a bit dry to us. And yet studying the entire Bible is a life-long project because even then, we'll only scratch the surface—even of passages like this one.

In our text, we see an entire chapter devoted to a repetition of the leaders and census of the tribes, along with the position in which they were to camp. I would think there should be chapter after chapter dealing with raising kids or marriage, and only a verse or two about this Numbers thing. And yet in His Word, God seems to reiterate certain principles, knowing that if the principles are properly understood, the practical stuff will take care of itself. We want the practical. God, however, places a great priority on principles. The practical—different trends—comes and goes, but principles are eternal. And the passage before us is no exception, for in it, God painstakingly paints a picture that, once seen, is extremely practical.

Numbers 2:1–9
And the LORD spake unto Moses and unto Aaron, saying, Every man of the children of Israel shall pitch by his own standard, with the ensign of their father's house: far off about the tabernacle of the congregation shall they pitch. And on the east side toward the rising of the sun shall they of the standard of the camp of Judah pitch throughout their armies: and Nahshon the son of Amminadab shall be captain of the children of Judah. And his host, and those that were numbered of them, were threescore and fourteen thousand and six hundred. And those that do pitch next unto him shall be the tribe of Issachar: and Nethaneel the son of Zuar shall be captain of the children of Issachar. And his host, and those that were numbered thereof, were fifty and four thousand and four hundred. Then the tribe of Zebulun: and Eliab the son of Helon shall be captain of the children of Zebulun. And his host, and those that were numbered thereof, were fifty and seven thousand and four hundred. All that were numbered in the camp of Judah were an hundred thousand and fourscore thousand and six thousand and four hundred, throughout their armies. These shall first set forth.

The tribes of Judah, Issachar, and Zebulun, numbering 186,400 in totality, were to camp to the east of the tabernacle.

Numbers 2:10–16
On the south side shall be the standard of the camp of Reuben according to their armies: and the captain of the children of Reuben shall be Elizur the son of Shedeur. And

his host, and those that were numbered thereof, were forty and six thousand and five hundred. And those which pitch by him shall be the tribe of Simeon: and the captain of the children of Simeon shall be Shelumiel the son of Zurishaddai. And his host, and those that were numbered of them, were fifty and nine thousand and three hundred. Then the tribe of Gad: and the captain of the sons of Gad shall be Eliasaph the son of Reuel. And his host, and those that were numbered of them, were forty and five thousand and six hundred and fifty. All that were numbered in the camp of Reuben were an hundred thousand and fifty and one thousand and four hundred and fifty, throughout their armies. And they shall set forth in the second rank.

The tribes of Reuben, Simeon, and Gad, numbering 151,450 in totality were to camp to the south of the tabernacle.

Numbers 2:17
Then the tabernacle of the congregation shall set forward with the camp of the Levites in the midst of the camp: as they encamp, so shall they set forward, every man in his place by their standards.

The Levites—those who served God—were those who camped closest to the tabernacle, closest to the ark of the covenant, closest to His Shekinah glory, closest to His presence. That's always the way it is. Those who serve God cannot help but experience His presence.

Numbers 2:18–24
On the west side shall be the standard of the camp of Ephraim according to their armies: and the captain of the sons of Ephraim shall be Elishama the son of Ammihud. And his host, and those that were numbered of them, were forty thousand and five hundred. And by him shall be the tribe of Manasseh: and the captain of the children of Manasseh shall be Gamaliel the son of Pedahzur. And his host, and those that were numbered of them, were thirty and two thousand and two hundred. Then the tribe of Benjamin: and the captain of the sons of Benjamin shall be Abidan the son of Gideoni. And his host, and those that were numbered of them, were thirty and five thousand and four hundred. All that were numbered of the camp of Ephraim were an hundred thousand and eight thousand and an hundred, throughout their armies. And they shall go forward in the third rank.

The tribes of Ephraim, Manasseh, and Benjamin, numbering 108,100 in totality were to camp to the west of the tabernacle.

Numbers 2:25–31
The standard of the camp of Dan shall be on the north side by their armies: and the captain of the children of Dan shall be Ahiezer the son of Ammishaddai. And his host, and those that were numbered of them, were threescore and two thousand and seven hundred. And those that encamp by him shall be the tribe of Asher: and the captain of the children of Asher shall be Pagiel the son of Ocran. And his host, and those that were numbered of them, were forty and one thousand and five hundred. Then the tribe of Naphtali: and the captain of the children of Naphtali shall be Ahira the son of Enan. And his host, and those that were numbered of them, were fifty and three thousand and four hundred. All they that were numbered in the camp of Dan were an hundred thousand and fifty and seven thousand and six hundred. They shall go hindmost with their standards.

The tribes of Dan, Asher, and Naphtali, numbering 157,600 in totality, were to camp to the north of the tabernacle.

Numbers 2:32–34
These are those which were numbered of the children of Israel by the house of their fathers: all those that were numbered of the camps throughout their hosts were six hundred thousand and three thousand and five hundred and fifty. But the Levites were not numbered among the children of Israel; as the LORD commanded Moses. And the children of Israel did according to all that the LORD commanded Moses: so they pitched by their standards, and so they set forward, every one after their families, according to the house of their fathers.

To understand the significance of the camping assignments of the twelve tribes, turn to Numbers 22.

On their way to the Promised Land, the children of Israel pitched their tents in the plain of Moab. This caused consternation in the heart of Balak, the king of Moab, for he had heard of the Israelite's victory over the Amonites. So, in addition to forming an alliance with the Midianites, Balak persuaded Balaam, a prophet of the Lord, to curse the Israelites.

Accompanied by Balak to the top of a mountain from which he could see the entire Israelite camp, Balaam looked down to see the tabernacle in the midst with a contingent of 108,100 to the west, 186,400 to the east, 157,600 to the north, and 151,450 to the south. In other words, he would have seen the configuration of a Cross. No wonder he was unable to curse the Israelites. You see, Balaam thought the Israelites were to be cursed because they were a bunch of complainers and idolaters. God, however, saw no iniquity in them because they were encamped in the Cross.

And the same is true for us. Because we're encamped in the Cross, because we're in Christ, we can go boldly before the throne of God today and receive that which we need (Hebrews 4:16). For whatever battle you're fighting or issue you're facing, the solution is found at the throne of grace simply because you're encamped in, cleansed by, forgiven through the Cross of Calvary.

3 Chapter 2 dealt with the position of the tribes. Chapter 3 deals with the organization of the Levites . . .

Numbers 3:1
These also are the generations of Aaron and Moses in the day that the LORD spake with Moses in mount Sinai.

A year after Moses received the Ten Commandments on Mt. Sinai, he climbs the mountain again to get God's mind, His heart, His plan. If your life feels disorganized or confused, don't look to a self-help book to solve it for you. The best thing we can do individually, as families or as a church is to go to the mountain. Although the temptation is to reverse the order, we need to agonize in prayer before we organize a plan. When you feel scattered or out of focus, when your family is frayed by all of its activities, follow the example of Moses. Find a place where you can hear from the Lord.

Numbers 3:2–10
And these are the names of the sons of Aaron; Nadab the firstborn, and Abihu, Eleazar, and Ithamar. These are the names of the sons of Aaron, the priests which were anointed, whom he consecrated to minister in the priest's office. And Nadab and Abihu died before the LORD, when they offered strange fire before the LORD, in the wilderness of Sinai, and they had no children: and Eleazar and Ithamar ministered in the priest's office in the sight of Aaron their father. And the LORD spake unto Moses, saying, Bring the tribe of Levi near, and present them before Aaron the priest, that they may minister unto him. And they shall keep his charge, and the charge of the whole congregation before the tabernacle of the congregation, to do the service of the tabernacle. And they shall keep all the instruments of the tabernacle of the congregation, and the charge of the children of Israel, to do the service of the tabernacle.And thou shalt give the Levites unto Aaron and to his sons: they are wholly given unto him out of the children of Israel. And thou shalt appoint Aaron and his sons, and they shall wait on their priest's office: and the stranger that cometh nigh shall be put to death.

In Leviticus 10, Nadab and Abihu were killed when, as a result of their disobedience, a fire came down from heaven and consumed them. Aaron and his remaining sons were to serve as priests. All of the priests throughout the history of the nation were to be descendants of Aaron. Aaron being a descendant of Levi, every priest was a Levite but not every Levite was a priest because only Aaron's family would serve in the priestly service. The other Levites would assist Aaron and his descendants.

I find it interesting that, although our culture is touchy about nepotism, Scripture indicates that it's good and right that families be involved together in service.

Numbers 3:11–13
And the LORD spake unto Moses, saying, And I, behold, I have taken the Levites from among the children of Israel instead of all the firstborn that openeth the matrix among the children of Israel: therefore the Levites shall be mine; Because all the firstborn are mine; for on the day that I smote all the firstborn in the land of Egypt I hallowed unto me all the firstborn in Israel, both man and beast: mine shall they be: I am the LORD.

Due to the fact that He not only created them but spared them at Passover, God owned the firstborn. In other words, they were His not only by creative right, but also by redemptive right. It was the Lord's original intent that the firstborn of every family of every tribe be priests. But when only the Levites came forward as those who were on the Lord's side, they became the exclusive tribe God chose to minister to Him. The men of Reuben, Gad, and Naphtali backed away, knowing they would have to deal with their friends and neighbors. The men of Judah, Benjamin, and Zebulun knew that they would have to inflict pain in order to save the nation. In the end, only one tribe was willing to say, "It's not a pleasant task, not an easy thing to do, but we're on the

Lord's side and this needs to be done. So we will do it." And, as a result, they were blessed (Exodus 32:29).

In this, I understand why oftentimes we are not used to the degree we would like to be or think we ought to be. Hebrews 4:12 tells us the Word of God is quick and powerful, sharper than any two-edged sword. Am I willing to unsheathe the sword of the Word and deal with situations which are detrimental, dangerous, or diseased in the lives of friends, neighbors, or family members? Or will I be like Simeon, Issachar, and Asher and shy away?

It's one thing to say, "I'll take the sword and deal with the Jebusites, the Philistines, the Canaanites." But will you deal with your own family, your own friends, your own coworkers? Proverbs 29:25 says the fear of man is a snare. It will trip me up. At any given moment, I am living in fear. So are you. The question is, who do I fear? I will either be walking in the fear of God—not wanting to disappoint Him or disobey Him—or I will be walking in the fear of man—concerned about what others think of me.

The fear of man says, "I care more about you liking me than I do about you doing well." The fear of God, on the other hand, says, "You might not like this, but I'm going to tell you the truth because I care more about you doing well than I do about you liking me."

Knowing the story of Levi, I would have thought it would be any tribe but his that would step up to the task. After all, it was Levi who, along with Simeon, decided to avenge the rape of their sister, Dinah, by unsheathing the sword and butchering all the men of Shechem (Genesis 34)—an offense of such magnitude that Simeon and Levi were cursed and denied an inheritance in the Promised Land (Genesis 49:5–7). Therefore, when Moses asked who would unsheathe the sword and mete out judgment upon Israel, I would have thought Levi would have said, "Not us. We've been down this road before. We're cursed to this day. Let Reuben do it." But that's not what happened—for even though they failed previously, Levi said, "We will do what's necessary." Amazing.

"How can I correct him?" we say. "I failed in the past the same way he's failing now." Or, "I have no right to confront her. I made the very same mistakes she's making." That's what Levi could have said. Instead, he did what Paul teaches us to do—he forgot that which was behind, pressed ahead, and did what had to be done (Philippians 3:13). And, as a result, although the curse remained, because the Levites chose to stand for the Lord, not only would they be used in ministry, but God Himself would be their inheritance ultimately (Joshua 13:33).

Does this mean we're to be those who unsheathe our swords and go sin-sniffing and fault-finding? No. It does mean, however, that we are to be those who love the Lord and love the family enough to say, "It's more important that you do well than that you like me."

There they were in the Garden, where Jesus had been praying. And now He and His disciples could hear the sound of soldiers approaching. After Judas' betrayal, as Jesus was being led away, Peter unsheathed his sword and severed the ear of a servant of the high priest. Thus, the last miracle Jesus did was to heal someone unnecessarily wounded by one of His disciples (Matthew 26).

Will we be like Peter, or will we be like Levi? Peter drew his sword out of frustration; Levi drew his for redemption. Whenever I feel the hair stand up on the back of my neck or my blood begin to boil, I must put away my sword. Otherwise, like Peter, I'll wound people unnecessarily for the wrath of man never works the righteousness of God (James 1:20). But there are other times when, like the Levites, the only way I can be involved in ministry is to be willing to unsheathe the sword, to speak the truth, to deal with the problems in the camp.

Numbers 3:14–20
And the LORD spake unto Moses in the wilderness of Sinai, saying, Number the children of Levi after the house of their fathers, by their families: every male from a month old and upward shalt thou number them. And Moses numbered them according to the word of the LORD, as he was commanded. And these were the sons of Levi by their names; Gershon, and Kohath, and Merari. And these are the names of the sons of Gershon by their families; Libni, and Shimei. And the sons of Kohath by their families; Amram, and Izehar, Hebron, and Uzziel. And the sons of Merari by their families; Mahli, and Mushi. These are the families of the Levites according to the house of their fathers.

The Levites were divided into three major family groups.

Numbers 3:21–26
Of Gershon was the family of the Libnites, and the family of the Shimites: these are the families of the Gershonites. Those that were numbered of them, according to the number

of all the males, from a month old and upward, even those that were numbered of them were seven thousand and five hundred. The families of the Gershonites shall pitch behind the tabernacle westward. And the chief of the house of the father of the Gershonites shall be Eliasaph the son of Lael. And the charge of the sons of Gershon in the tabernacle of the congregation shall be the tabernacle, and the tent, the covering thereof, and the hanging for the door of the tabernacle of the congregation, And the hangings of the court, and the curtain for the door of the court, which is by the tabernacle, and by the altar round about, and the cords of it for all the service thereof.

The Gershonites numbered 7,500 and were given the responsibility of caring for the woven material and animal skins which covered the tabernacle. The Gershonites weren't priests, but they fulfilled an important role nonetheless in that they provided the covering for worship.

Numbers 3:27–32
And of Kohath was the family of the Amramites, and the family of the Izeharites, and the family of the Hebronites, and the family of the Uzzielites: these are the families of the Kohathites. In the number of all the males, from a month old and upward, were eight thousand and six hundred, keeping the charge of the sanctuary. The families of the sons of Kohath shall pitch on the side of the tabernacle southward. And the chief of the house of the father of the families of the Kohathites shall be Elizaphan the son of Uzziel. And their charge shall be the ark, and the table, and the candlestick, and the altars, and the vessels of the sanctuary wherewith they minister, and the hanging, and all the service thereof. And Eleazar the son of Aaron the priest shall be chief over the chief of the Levites, and have the oversight of them that keep the charge of the sanctuary.

The Kohathites numbered 8,600 and were in charge of the furniture of the tabernacle—the altars, the table of showbread, the candlestick, the ark.

Numbers 3:33–37
Of Merari was the family of the Mahlites, and the family of the Mushites: these are the families of Merari. And those that were numbered of them, according to the number of all the males, from a month old and upward, were six thousand and two hundred. And the chief of the house of the father of the families of Merari was Zuriel the son of Abihail: these shall pitch on the side of the tabernacle northward. And under the custody and charge of the sons of Merari shall be the boards of the tabernacle, and the bars thereof, and the pillars thereof, and the sockets thereof, and all the vessels thereof, and all that serveth thereto, And the pillars of the court round about, and their sockets, and their pins, and their cords.

The family of Merari numbered 6,200 and was responsible for the framework of the tabernacle—its boards and bars, pillars and sockets.

Numbers 3:38
But those that encamp before the tabernacle toward the east, even before the tabernacle of the congregation eastward, shall be Moses, and Aaron and his sons, keeping the charge of the sanctuary for the charge of the children of Israel; and the stranger that cometh nigh shall be put to death.

The significance of the east is seen throughout Scripture. Jesus will come through the eastern gate into the city of Jerusalem (Ezekiel 43). Thus, the east speaks of the coming of the Lord.

Numbers 3:39–43
All that were numbered of the Levites, which Moses and Aaron numbered at the commandment of the LORD, throughout their families, all the males from a month old and upward, were twenty and two thousand. And the LORD said unto Moses, Number all the firstborn of the males of the children of Israel from a month old and upward, and take the number of their names. And thou shalt take the Levites for me (I am the LORD) instead of all the firstborn among the children of Israel; and the cattle of the Levites instead of all the firstlings among the cattle of the children of Israel. And Moses numbered, as the LORD commanded him, all the firstborn among the children of Israel. And all the firstborn males by the number of names, from a month old and upward, of those that were numbered of them, were twenty and two thousand two hundred and threescore and thirteen.

The total number of Levites was 22,000—a number remarkably close to the 22,273 firstborn males whose place they were to take.

Numbers 3:44–51
And the LORD spake unto Moses, saying, Take the Levites instead of all the firstborn

among the children of Israel, and the cattle of the Levites instead of their cattle; and the Levites shall be mine: I am the LORD. And for those that are to be redeemed of the two hundred and threescore and thirteen of the firstborn of the children of Israel, which are more than the Levites; thou shalt even take five shekels apiece by the poll, after the shekel of the sanctuary shalt thou take them: (the shekel is twenty gerahs), and thou shalt give the money, wherewith the odd number of them is to be redeemed, unto Aaron and to his sons. And Moses took the redemption money of them that were over and above them that were redeemed by the Levites: of the firstborn of the children of Israel took he the money; a thousand three hundred and threescore and five shekels, after the shekel of the sanctuary: and Moses gave the money of them that were redeemed unto Aaron and to his sons, according to the word of the LORD, as the LORD commanded Moses.

The principle of redemption was to be a life for a life. In place of a life, that which most closely touched a man's life was to be offered—namely, money. Because one's work is where one invests the bulk of his time and energy, that which reveals most about someone's priorities is the way he uses his money. Talk is cheap. The proof of the pudding is not in the song I sing, but what I do when the basket goes by.

Does this mean we can purchase our salvation? No. Our salvation was indeed purchased—not by our own efforts or money but by the blood of Christ on the Cross of Calvary. (1 Peter 1:3). Therefore, the way we spend money—as well as the way we spend our time, talents, and every other resource given to us—should reflect that which was so freely and sacrificially spent for us when our Lord gave His life to set us free.

4

Numbers 4:1–3 (a)
And the LORD spake unto Moses and unto Aaron, saying, Take the sum of the sons of Kohath from among the sons of Levi, after their families, by the house of their fathers, from thirty years old . . .

The Levites were to serve from the age of thirty. David was thirty when he became king of Israel. Jesus was thirty when He began His public ministry. Although we are often in a rush to jump into ministry, the Bible cautions against doing so (1 Timothy 5:22). Moses was in the wilderness forty years before God used him to deliver His people. And Paul spent years in the deserts of Arabia before being used in ministry.

Numbers 4:3 (b), 4
. . . and upward even until fifty years old, all that enter into the host, to do the work in the tabernacle of the congregation. This shall be the service of the sons of Kohath in the tabernacle of the congregation, about the most holy things:

Why were the priests to retire at the age of fifty? In chapter 8, we'll see that the Levites entered priestly service at twenty-five years of age. Therefore, from age twenty-five to thirty, the priests were to be trained. By whom? I suggest it was by those who had retired from priestly service at fifty. In other words, when a priest reached fifty years of age, he would step aside and pour his life and experiences into the next generation of priests. I think it's a wonderful model.

Numbers 4:5, 6 (a)
And when the camp setteth forward, Aaron shall come, and his sons, and they shall take down the covering vail, and cover the ark of testimony with it: and shall put thereon the covering of badgers' skins . . .

Although the badger skins covering the furnishings and ark were durable, they were ugly. Underneath the badger skins, however, were coverings of blue—the color of heaven. Therefore, although the Canaanites and others looking on would see the badger skin, they would miss altogether the blue underneath. And the same is true today. The world doesn't understand why we meet together, why we study the Word. They don't understand that we're learning about heaven.

Numbers 4:6 (b)–8 (a)
. . . and shall spread over it a cloth wholly of blue, and shall put in the staves thereof. And upon the table of shewbread they shall spread a cloth of blue, and put thereon the dishes, and the spoons, and the bowls, and covers to cover withal: and the continual bread shall be thereon: And they shall spread upon them a cloth of scarlet . . .

The table of showbread was the only item in the tabernacle covered by a scarlet cloth as well as a blue cloth. Why? Because it spoke of Communion.

Numbers 4:8 (b)–13
. . . and cover the same with a covering of badgers' skins, and shall put in the staves thereof. And they shall take a cloth of blue, and cover the candlestick of the light, and

his lamps, and his tongs, and his snuffdishes, and all the oil vessels thereof, wherewith they minister unto it: and they shall put it and all the vessels thereof within a covering of badgers' skins, and shall put it upon a bar. And upon the golden altar they shall spread a cloth of blue, and cover it with a covering of badgers' skins, and shall put to the staves thereof: and they shall take all the instruments of ministry, wherewith they minister in the sanctuary, and put them in a cloth of blue, and cover them with a covering of badgers' skins, and shall put them on a bar: and they shall take away the ashes from the altar, and spread a purple cloth thereon:

Why was purple to cover the altar where sacrifices were made, where blood was shed? Because the altar speaks of Jesus Christ. And what was placed on Jesus before He offered Himself as a sacrifice on the Cross of Calvary? A purple robe.

Numbers 4:14, 15 (a)
And they shall put upon it all the vessels thereof, wherewith they minister about it, even the censers, the fleshhooks, and the shovels, and the basons, all the vessels of the altar; and they shall spread upon it a covering of badgers' skins, and put to the staves of it. And when Aaron and his sons have made an end of covering the sanctuary, and all the vessels of the sanctuary, as the camp is to set forward; after that, the sons of Kohath shall come to bear it: but they shall not touch any holy thing, lest they die . . .

Aaron and his sons were to cover the instruments of sacrifice and worship before the Kohathites came to bear them.

Numbers 4:15 (b), 16
. . . These things are the burden of the sons of Kohath in the tabernacle of the congregation. And to the office of Eleazar the son of Aaron the priest pertaineth the oil for the light, and the sweet incense, and the daily meat offering, and the anointing oil, and the oversight of all the tabernacle, and of all that therein is, in the sanctuary, and in the vessels thereof.

Eleazar was to be the priest who would oversee the ministry of the Kohathites.

Numbers 4:17–20
And the LORD spake unto Moses and unto Aaron, saying, Cut ye not off the tribe of the families of the Kohathites from among the Levites: but thus do unto them, that they may live, and not die, when they approach unto the most holy things: Aaron and his sons shall go in, and appoint them every one to his service and to his burden: but they shall not go in to see when the holy things are covered, lest they die.

How could the Kohathites be cut off, how could they die? By looking at the holy things of the tabernacle. And in this lies a warning . . .

The Israelites were understandably elated to see the ark of the covenant returned to them after it had been captured by the Philistines. Wanting to make sure that the contents were still intact, they removed the mercy seat to look inside. But in so doing, 50,000 men died (1 Samuel 6).

So, whenever we remove mercy in the name of investigation, something in us dies. This doesn't mean we're not to have discernment and accountability. However, those who always think they have to get to the bottom of a matter, those who forsake mercy, become impotent spiritually and ineffective in ministry.

Numbers 4:21–28
And the LORD spake unto Moses, saying, Take also the sum of the sons of Gershon, throughout the houses of their fathers, by their families; from thirty years old and upward until fifty years old shalt thou number them; all that enter in to perform the service, to do the work in the tabernacle of the congregation. This is the service of the families of the Gershonites, to serve, and for burdens: and they shall bear the curtains of the tabernacle, and the tabernacle of the congregation, his covering, and the covering of the badgers' skins that is above upon it, and the hanging for the door of the tabernacle of the congregation, and the hangings of the court, and the hanging for the door of the gate of the court, which is by the tabernacle and by the altar round about, and their cords, and all the instruments of their service, and all that is made for them: so shall they serve. At the appointment of Aaron and his sons shall be all the service of the sons of the Gershonites, in all their burdens, and in all their service: and ye shall appoint unto them in charge all their burdens. This is the service of the families of the sons of Gershon in the tabernacle of the congregation: and their charge shall be under the hand of Ithamar the son of Aaron the priest.

Eleazar was to oversee the Kohathites, while the Gershonites were to be overseen by Ithamar, the brother of Eleazar.

Numbers 4:29–33
As for the sons of Merari, thou shalt number them after their families, by the house of their fathers; from thirty years old and upward even unto fifty years old shalt thou number them, every one that entereth into the service, to do the work of the tabernacle of the congregation. And this is the charge of their burden, according to all their service in the tabernacle of the congregation; the boards of the tabernacle, and the bars thereof, and the pillars thereof, and sockets thereof, And the pillars of the court round about, and their sockets, and their pins, and their cords, with all their instruments, and with all their service: and by name ye shall reckon the instruments of the charge of their burden. This is the service of the families of the sons of Merari, according to all their service, in the tabernacle of the congregation, under the hand of Ithamar the son of Aaron the priest.

In addition to overseeing the Gershonites, Ithamar was to oversee the family of Merari. In other words, Ithamar does double-duty. Why? Because how many sons did Aaron have initially? Four—one for each of these three families, with an extra in reserve. But when Nadab and Abihu lit strange fire (Leviticus 10:1), only two sons were left, leaving Ithamar with a double assignment.

When someone gets burned out on ministry—be it teaching Sunday school, giving financially, or covering the fellowship in prayer—and gives up or cuts back, others are left to fill in the gap, to do double and sometimes triple-duty in their absence.

Numbers 4:34–49
And Moses and Aaron and the chief of the congregation numbered the sons of the Kohathites after their families, and after the house of their fathers, from thirty years old and upward even unto fifty years old, every one that entereth into the service, for the work in the tabernacle of the congregation: and those that were numbered of them by their families were two thousand seven hundred and fifty. These were they that were numbered of the families of the Kohathites, all that might do service in the tabernacle of the congregation, which Moses and Aaron did number according to the commandment of the LORD by the hand of Moses. And those that were numbered of the sons of Gershon, throughout their families, and by the house of their fathers, from thirty years old and upward even unto fifty years old, every one that entereth into the service, for the work in the tabernacle of the congregation, Even those that were numbered of them, throughout their families, by the house of their fathers, were two thousand and six hundred and thirty. These are they that were numbered of the families of the sons of Gershon, of all that might do service in the tabernacle of the congregation, whom Moses and Aaron did number according to the commandment of the LORD. And those that were numbered of the families of the sons of Merari, throughout their families, by the house of their fathers, From thirty years old and upward even unto fifty years old, every one that entereth into the service, for the work in the tabernacle of the congregation, Even those that were numbered of them after their families, were three thousand and two hundred. These be those that were numbered of the families of the sons of Merari, whom Moses and Aaron numbered according to the word of the LORD by the hand of Moses. All those that were numbered of the Levites, whom Moses and Aaron and the chief of Israel numbered, after their families, and after the house of their fathers, From thirty years old and upward even unto fifty years old, every one that came to do the service of the ministry, and the service of the burden in the tabernacle of the congregation, Even those that were numbered of them, were eight thousand and five hundred and fourscore. According to the commandment of the LORD they were numbered by the hand of Moses, every one according to his service, and according to his burden: thus were they numbered of him, as the LORD commanded Moses.

The metal alone in the tabernacle weighed over ten tons. Therefore, God's wisdom is seen in placing the Merarites—the largest group—in charge of the transporting of the structure of the tabernacle. And yet, taken as a whole, the tribe of Levi numbered only one-fourth of the least of the other tribes, for those wholly devoted to the service of God are always few in number.

Oh, that we might number ourselves among them.

5 Having seen the people organized in chapters 3 and 4, we will see them purified here in chapter 5 . . .

Numbers 5:1–4
And the LORD spake unto Moses, saying, Command the children of Israel, that they put out of the camp every leper, and every one that hath an issue, and whosoever is defiled by the dead: both male and female shall ye put out, without the camp shall ye put them; that they defile not their camps, in the midst whereof I dwell. And the children of Israel did so, and put them out without the camp: as the LORD spake unto Moses, so did the children of Israel.

Those with leprosy, those with a running issue, those defiled by contact with the dead were to be removed from the camp. Why? Not because leprosy was contagious nor because running issues and dead bodies lead to all kinds of disease. The singular reason God gave for ridding the camp of this kind of impurity was because He dwelt therein.

The trend today in churches is that of being "seeker sensitive." To this end, we're not to sing too many songs, carry our Bibles, or talk about sin and repentance. I wholeheartedly disagree with this trend—for while we are indeed to be seeker-sensitive, it is not the sinner who is the seeker, but the Father who seeks those who will worship Him in spirit and in truth (John 4:23). "Behold, I stand at the door and knock," Jesus declares (Revelation 3:20). And here, God says, "Honor Me. Deal with the leprosy, the issues, the defilement not only because those things will destroy you, but more importantly because I'm in the camp."

Numbers 5:5–7
And the LORD spake unto Moses, saying, Speak unto the children of Israel, When a man or woman shall commit any sin that men commit, to do a trespass against the LORD, and that person be guilty; then they shall confess their sin which they have done: and he shall recompense his trespass with the principal thereof, and add unto it the fifth part thereof, and give it unto him against whom he hath trespassed.

If an Israelite hurt or cheated someone, he wasn't simply to say, "I'm sorry," but was to make up for that which he did—with an additional twenty percent. Such is God's heart. Why? Because restitution leads to restoration.

Numbers 5:8–10
But if the man have no kinsman to recompense the trespass unto, let the trespass be recompensed unto the LORD, even to the priest; beside the ram of the atonement, whereby an atonement shall be made for him. And every offering of all the holy things of the children of Israel, which they bring unto the priest, shall be his. And every man's hallowed things shall be his: whatsoever any man giveth the priest, it shall be his.

If the person sinned against moved or was otherwise unable to be located, the offender was to bring the restitution to the tabernacle. And the same is true today. You see, the Lord knows our tendency to weasel out of responsibility, to find a way to conveniently put off dealing with the restitution we know needs to be made. That's why He says, "It's never too late. Regardless of whether you know the location of the person you wronged, regardless of whether you know how to reach the company you cheated, you know the damage that was done, so pay what you owe plus twenty percent to Me." And in so doing, God teaches His people about growing up, about responsibility, about maturity.

Numbers 5:11–14
And the LORD spake unto Moses, saying, Speak unto the children of Israel, and say unto them, if any man's wife go aside, and commit a trespass against him, and a man lie with her carnally, and it be hid from the eyes of her husband, and be kept close, and she be defiled, and there be no witness against her, neither she be taken with the manner; and the spirit of jealousy come upon him, and he be jealous of his wife, and she be defiled: or if the spirit of jealousy come upon him, and he be jealous of his wife, and she be not defiled:

Whereas in Leviticus 13, we see God's instruction concerning the purification of leprosy, here we see His heart concerning the purification of immorality.

Numbers 5:15 (a)
Then shall the man bring his wife unto the priest . . .

If a husband suspected that his wife had been unfaithful to him, he was not to launch his own investigation. He was to bring her to the priest.

Numbers 5:15 (b)
. . . and he shall bring her offering for her, the tenth part of an ephah of barley meal; he shall pour no oil upon it, nor put frankincense thereon; for it is an offering of jealousy, an offering of memorial, bringing iniquity to remembrance.

The suspicious husband was also to bring a meal offering—devoid of the oil which speaks of the Spirit and of the sweet smell of frankincense.

Numbers 5:16–24
And the priest shall bring her near, and set her before the LORD: and the priest shall take holy water in an earthen vessel; and of the dust that is in the floor of the tabernacle the priest shall take, and put it into the water: And the priest shall set the woman before the LORD, and uncover the woman's head, and put the offering of memorial in her hands, which is the jealousy offering: and the priest shall have in his hand the bitter water that causeth the curse: and the priest shall charge her by an oath, and say unto the woman, if no man have lain with thee, and if thou hast not gone aside to uncleanness with another instead of thy husband, be thou free from this bitter water that causeth the curse: but if thou hast gone aside to another instead of thy husband, and if thou be defiled, and some man have lain with thee beside thine husband: then the priest shall charge the woman with an oath of cursing, and the priest shall say unto the woman, the LORD make thee a curse and an oath among thy people, when the LORD doth make thy thigh to rot, and thy belly to swell; and this water that causeth the curse shall go into thy bowels, to make thy belly to swell, and thy thigh to rot: and the woman shall say, amen, amen. And the priest shall write these curses in a book, and he shall blot them out with the bitter water: and he shall cause the woman to drink the bitter water that causeth the curse: and the water that causeth the curse shall enter into her, and become bitter.

Of what does this illustration speak? With regard to the woman, a swollen belly speaks of turmoil internally, a rotten thigh of an inability to walk spiritually. But in a larger sense, the illustration points to Jesus.

Jesus Christ came to earth as an earthen vessel when He became like you and me. He was filled with the water of the Word and absorbed the curse that should have been ours.

It was at the Feast of Tabernacles that they brought Jesus a woman caught in the act of adultery. When His teaching, His pouring forth of the water of the Word was interrupted, He stooped down and wrote in the dust on the floor of the temple compound, eventually freeing the woman to go and sin no more (John 8).

Thus, all the components of the purification of immorality come together in Jesus. Truly, Jesus came to free us from the curse that causes our walk to be rotten and our bellies bloated. We are the woman. But Jesus came to absorb our sin, to set us free—and I'm so glad.

Numbers 5:25–31
Then the priest shall take the jealousy offering out of the woman's hand, and shall wave the offering before the LORD, and offer it upon the altar: and the priest shall take an handful of the offering, even the memorial thereof, and burn it upon the altar, and afterward shall cause the woman to drink the water. And when he hath made her to drink the water, then it shall come to pass, that, if she be defiled, and have done trespass against her husband, that the water that causeth the curse shall enter into her, and become bitter, and her belly shall swell, and her thigh shall rot: and the woman shall be a curse among her people. And if the woman be not defiled, but be clean; then she shall be free, and shall conceive seed. This is the law of jealousies, when a wife goeth aside to another instead of her husband, and is defiled; or when the spirit of jealousy cometh upon him, and he be jealous over his wife, and shall set the woman before the LORD, and the priest shall execute upon her all this law. Then shall the man be guiltless from iniquity, and this woman shall bear her iniquity.

Why was the woman and not the man singled out as an illustration? Because the woman is a picture of you and me, for we're the ones who have been unfaithful, even though our Bridegroom, our Lord, our Savior remains faithful still (2 Timothy 2:13).

6

Whereas chapter 5 dealt with suspicion and conviction, chapter 6 deals with consecration and purification. And that's the way it always is, for there must be a dealing with the issue of moral purity before there can be the possibility of ministry.

Numbers 6:1, 2
And the LORD spake unto Moses, saying, Speak unto the children of Israel, and say unto them, when either man or woman shall separate themselves to vow a vow of a Nazarite, to separate themselves unto the LORD:

The Hebrew word, *zar*, means "to separate." Therefore, a Naz*ar*ite vow spoke of one who separated himself or herself for a period of time in order to totally focus on the Lord. According to rabbinical tradition, the length of a Nazarite vow was usually a month, but could last for a year, or even longer. Although priestly ministry was given to the Levites exclusively, through the Nazarite vow, every man and woman from every tribe was given opportunity to seek the Lord radically. But there were three demands God made of anyone choosing to do so . . .

Numbers 6:3, 4
He shall separate himself from wine and strong drink, and shall drink no vinegar of wine, or vinegar of strong drink, neither shall he drink any liquor of grapes, nor eat moist grapes, or dried. All the days of his separation shall he eat nothing that is made of the vine tree, from the kernels even to the husk.

Determination. In order that their minds remain clear, their vision unobstructed, Nazarites were to stay away from anything that would intoxicate them. Knowing our tendency to figure out a way to get intoxicated even on grapes or raisins, the Lord instructed the Nazarites to stay away from them as well.

> And I raised up of your sons for prophets, and of your young men for Nazarites. Is it not even thus, O ye children of Israel?, saith the Lord. But ye gave the Nazarites wine to drink; and commanded the prophets, saying, prophesy not. Behold, I am pressed under you, as a cart is pressed that is full of sheaves. Amos 2:11–13

> It is not for kings, O Lemuel, it is not for kings to drink wine; nor for princes strong drink: lest they drink, and forget the law, and pervert the judgment of any of the afflicted. Give strong drink unto him that is ready to perish, and wine unto those that be of heavy hearts.
> Proverbs 31:4–6

This is not legalism. Rather, God is declaring, "This doesn't apply to everyone. But if you want to be a leader in ministry, a leader in your family, if you want to be on the cutting edge of being used by Me, if you want to be a Nazarite, stay away from that which would cause you to forget the law and pervert judgment."

Numbers 6:5
All the days of the vow of his separation there shall no rasor come upon his head: until the days be fulfilled, in the which he separateth himself unto the LORD, he shall be holy, and shall let the locks of the hair of his head grow.

Identification. In Old Testament days, long hair on a man was such a rarity that his hair would make him readily identifiable. Today, being easily identified as a believer, letting everyone know you are a child of God, will keep you on course and out of trouble.

Numbers 6:6, 7
All the days that he separateth himself unto the LORD he shall come at no dead body. He shall not make himself unclean for his father, or for his mother, for his brother, or for his sister, when they die: because the consecration of his God is upon his head.

Separation. The Nazarite was to separate himself from death. You see, if I enjoy hanging around places where those who are spiritually dead congregate, I need to take a second look at my commitment to the One who came to give me life. Because our love for God should be so passionate and real that our love for any other person seems like hatred in comparison, Jesus said, "Unless you hate father, mother, sister, or brother, you can't follow Me" (Luke 14:26). Therefore, even if a family member wants you to join them in places which are spiritually dead, you're to honor the Lord rather than cater to your family. On the other hand, if, like Jesus, you frequent such places for the purpose of ministry, that's an entirely different story (Matthew 9:10–13).

Numbers 6:8
All the days of his separation he is holy unto the LORD.

Because the Nazarite vow speaks of a single-minded devotion, a single-hearted passion, it is a wonderful picture for single people. In 1 Corinthians 7, Paul says, "If you can handle it, there are advantages to being single because it allows you to focus solely on the Lord."

Numbers 6:9–12 (a)
And if any man die very suddenly by him, and he hath defiled the head of his consecration; then he shall shave his head in the day of his cleansing, on the seventh day shall he shave it. And on the eighth day he shall bring two turtles, or two young pigeons, to the priest, to the door of the tabernacle of the congregation: and the priest shall offer the one for a sin offering, and the other for a burnt offering, and make an atonement for him, for that he sinned by the dead, and shall hallow his head that same day. And he shall consecrate unto the LORD the days of his separation, and shall bring a lamb of the first year for a trespass offering . . .

If someone broke a Nazarite vow, he was to shave his head and bring two turtledoves or pigeons for a sin offering and burnt offering, as well as a lamb for a trespass offering. The lamb, of course, speaks of Jesus, who cleanses us from all broken vows, all failure.

Numbers 6:12 (b)
. . . but the days that were before shall be lost, because his separation was defiled.

If someone took a Nazarite vow for sixty days but on the fifty-ninth day came into contact with a dead body, he or she was to start all over again at Day One. While this may seem unfair initially, it actually speaks of the second chance, the new beginning God is willing to give us continually.

Numbers 6:13–21
And this is the law of the Nazarite, when the days of his separation are fulfilled: he shall be brought unto the door of the tabernacle of the congregation: and he shall offer his offering unto the LORD, one he lamb of the first year without blemish for a burnt offering, and one ewe lamb of the first year without blemish for a sin offering, and one ram without blemish for peace offerings, and a basket of unleavened bread, cakes of fine flour mingled with oil, and wafers of unleavened bread anointed with oil, and their meat offering, and their drink offerings. And the priest shall bring them before the LORD, and shall offer his sin offering, and his burnt offering: and he shall offer the ram for a sacrifice of peace offerings unto the LORD, with the basket of unleavened bread: the priest shall offer also his meat offering, and his drink offering. And the Nazarite shall shave the head of his separation at the door of the tabernacle of the congregation, and shall take the hair of the head of his separation, and put it in the fire which is under the sacrifice of the peace offerings. And the priest shall take the sodden shoulder of the ram, and one unleavened cake out of the basket, and one unleavened wafer, and shall put them upon the hands of the Nazarite, after the hair of his separation is shaven: and the priest shall wave them for a wave offering before the LORD: this is holy for the priest, with the wave breast and heave shoulder: and after that the Nazarite may drink wine. This is the law of the Nazarite who hath vowed, and of his offering unto the LORD for his separation, beside that that his hand shall get: according to the vow which he vowed, so he must do after the law of his separation.

After addressing the subject of contamination in verses 9–11, God addresses the subject of completion in verses 13–21. Except for rare instances, the Nazarite vow was only taken for a season. Therefore, if, as a single person, after a season of seeking the Lord with determination, dedication, and separation, He puts a desire in your heart to be married, understand that He will indeed fulfill that desire.

Before Adam even knew he had a need, God declared it was not good for man to dwell alone (Genesis 2:18). So He gave Adam the task of naming the animals (Genesis 2:19), and somewhere along the line, as he named Mr. and Mrs. Rhino, Mr. and Mrs. Giraffe, Mr. and Mrs. Hippo, it must have dawned on Adam that, although there was a male and female of every creature, there was no counterpart for him. "Go to sleep," God said to Adam. And it was when Adam was asleep, at rest, that God fashioned a woman for him so perfect for him that he declared her bone of his bone, flesh of his flesh (Genesis 2:23).

If you sense the single season is drawing to a close, I encourage you to follow Adam's example: Rest in the Lord and let Him provide the perfect counterpart for you.

Numbers 6:22, 23 (a)
And the LORD spake unto Moses, saying, Speak unto Aaron and unto his sons, saying, on this wise ye shall bless the children of Israel . . .

Most people today think God is angry with them. But, as seen here, it was never God's intention that His ministers blast people. God's intent was that His ministers *bless* people . . .

Numbers 6:23 (b), 24 (a)
. . . saying unto them, The LORD bless thee . . .

The Hebrew word translated "bless" here meant to transfer prosperity primarily in the realm of the financial, physical, and material. The heart of the Father is that you would be blessed physically, financially, and materially. Jesus put it this way:

> If ye then, being evil, know how to give good gifts unto your children, how much more shall your Father which is in heaven give good things to them that ask him? Matthew 7:11

Every parent or grandparent knows the joy, the thrill of blessing your kids or grandchildren with gifts. Jesus said, "You're evil and you love to do that. How much more, then, does your Father love to give good gifts to His children?" David declares in Psalm 84 that the Father will hold back no good thing from His children. James says every good gift you have—whether it's the house you live in, the car you drive, the health you enjoy, the clothes you wear—every single gift is from the Father (James 1:17).

Numbers 6:24 (c)
. . . and keep thee:

The priests were not only to say, "The Lord bless thee"—but, also, "the Lord *keep* thee." The Hebrew word translated "keep" means "guard." Why do we ask God first to bless us and then to keep, or guard us? Because if He does give us material blessings, we need to be protected from the evil prosperity may bring.

I like that. We all know people God has graciously and marvelously blessed—and yet sometimes those very blessings can become dangerous distractions to them. No longer are they studying the Word like they once did. No longer are they engaged in service like they once were. Therefore, it is the wise man who says, "May the Lord keep you lest you get distracted from that which is of eternal significance."

Numbers 6:25 (a)
The LORD make his face shine upon thee . . .

Even as the Father is the Giver, the Son is the Revealer. May you see His face. May you be enlightened in knowing who God is.

> For God, who commanded the light to shine out of darkness, hath shined in our hearts, to give the light of the knowledge of the glory of God in the face of Jesus Christ. 2 Corinthians 4:6

Anything you want to know about God, you'll discover, you'll be enlightened by looking at Jesus.

Numbers 6:25 (b)
. . . and be gracious unto thee:

As you look at Jesus, as you learn of Him and focus on Him, you'll discover what the crowds who gathered around Him discovered. You'll discover what the woman caught in adultery discovered. You'll discover what the tax collectors, prostitutes, and sinners discovered. You'll discover His tenderhearted, compassionate grace.

Numbers 6:26
The LORD lift up his countenance upon thee, and give thee peace.

To "lift up the countenance" simply means to smile. Here the priests were to say to the people, "May the Lord smile upon you and give you peace." In the blessing of verses 24–26, we see the name of the Lord repeated three times. In this, there is a suggestion of the Trinity—for in verse 24, the reference is to God the Father, in verse 25, to God the Son, and in verse 26, to God the Holy Spirit.

- In verse 24, we see God the Father as the Giver.
- In verse 25, we see God the Son as the Revealer.
- In verse 26, we see God the Holy Spirit as the Soother.

These three characteristics correspond to our needs. God is a Trinity and in a sense, made in His image, we are as well, for while God is Father, Son, and Holy Spirit, we are body, soul, and spirit. The body relates to the material—the realm wherein the Father blesses us physically. The soul is the mind and the emotions—that which we think and feel. Sometimes we get confused. Sometimes we have questions. Sometimes we're disturbed. That's where God the Son comes in. Any issue with which I'm wrestling, any struggle with which I'm dealing will ultimately find its answer in Jesus Christ. The spirit is the deepest part of my being, the part of me that will live forever. And because the spirit within me can lack peace, it's the Holy Spirit who inhabits my spirit, who indwells my spirit, who communes with me in the deepest part of my being and gives me peace.

Numbers 6:27
And they shall put my name upon the children of Israel, and I will bless them.

"The Lord bless thee and keep thee. The Lord make His face shine upon thee, and be gracious unto thee. The Lord lift up His countenance upon thee, and give thee peace." This was not a prayer, but a proclamation—upon every single person in the congregation. Because we who believe are also the children of Abraham (Galatians 3:29), this proclamation applies to us. And because we are a royal priesthood, we can offer it as a blessing to others.

7 Numbers 7 is the second longest chapter in the Bible. It seems to be rather redundant, causing the reader to wonder why so much space is devoted to this event. But, although it sounds like a broken record to us, it's a beautiful record to God of those who gave gifts to Him.

The longest chapter in the Bible is Psalm 119, a psalm in which virtually every verse deals with the same subject: God's Word. Over and over again in Psalm 119, we read about the benefits and blessings of being in the Word. So the longest chapter in the Bible deals with the Word. The second longest chapter deals with giving. Is this coincidental? I don't think so. James tells us we are to be doers of the Word and not hearers only (James 1:22). It's easy to be a hearer of the Word. But it's something else to be a doer. And one of the greatest indicators of whether I'm a doer of the word is what I do with money. It's easy for me to talk about spiritual life. But it's another matter when I need to put my money where my mouth is. Consequently, the chapter before us is a detailed account of what the leaders of Israel gave day by day over a twelve-day period.

If I want to be a leader in my family, in the Fellowship, or in the workplace, the proof of maturity is in giving.

> He that is faithful in that which is least is faithful also in much: and he that is unjust in the least is unjust also in much. Luke 16:10

Jesus said, "If you want to be entrusted with impact in ministry, prove yourself in that which is least—mammon." In other words, the one who is faithful in money matters will be the one entrusted with that which is truly important both now and eternally.

Not only is giving the proof *of* maturity, but it is also the pathway *to* maturity. Each time I give, I become a little more like my heavenly Father, for He is a Giver (1 Timothy 6:17). Conversely, when I hold back, when I don't give, I become more like the enemy, Satan, who is a thief and a robber (John 10:1).

Numbers 7 may be long to us, but to God it is of vital importance.

> For God is not unrighteous to forget your work and labour of love, which ye have shewed toward his name, in that ye have ministered to the saints, and do minister. Hebrews 6:10

Anything we give to the Lord, any act of ministry we do in the name of the Lord, any kindness we show on behalf of the Lord is noted by the Lord. Jesus said that even a cup of cold water being given in His name reaps a reward (Mark 9:41).

> Lay not up for yourselves treasures upon earth, where moth and rust doth corrupt, and where thieves break through and steal: but lay up for yourselves treasures in heaven, where neither moth nor rust doth corrupt, and where thieves do not break through nor steal: for where your treasure is, there will your heart be also. Matthew 6:19–21

If I'm putting my treasure in the things of eternity, my heart will be set on things above. That's why God wants us to be givers. And that is why Numbers 7 is here: to show us that God cares a great deal about everything we do for Him, every gift we bring to Him.

Numbers 7:1–9

And it came to pass on the day that Moses had fully set up the tabernacle, and had anointed it, and sanctified it, and all the instruments thereof, both the altar and all the vessels thereof, and had anointed them, and sanctified them; that the princes of Israel, heads of the house of their fathers, who were the princes of the tribes, and were over them that were numbered, offered: and they brought their offering before the LORD, six covered wagons, and twelve oxen; a wagon for two of the princes, and for each one an ox: and they brought them before the tabernacle. And the LORD spake unto Moses, saying, take it of them, that they may be to do the service of the tabernacle of the congregation; and thou shalt give them unto the Levites, to every man according to his service. And Moses took the wagons and the oxen, and gave them unto the Levites. Two wagons and four oxen he gave unto the sons of Gershon, according to their service: And four wagons and eight oxen he gave unto the sons of Merari, according unto their service, under the hand of Ithamar the son of Aaron the priest. But unto the sons of Kohath he gave none: because the service of the sanctuary belonging unto them was that they should bear upon their shoulders.

As seen in chapter 4, the tribe of Levi was divided into three groups: the Gershonites, Merarites, and Kohathites. Of the six covered wagons and twelve oxen brought as an offering, the Gershonites were given two wagons and four oxen. The Merarites were given four wagons and eight oxen. The Kohathites were given zero wagons and zero oxen.

"That's not fair!" we protest. But in reality it was . . .

***For topical study of Numbers 7:1–9 entitled "It's Not Fair . . . Or Is It?" turn to page* 467.**

Numbers 7:10–12

And the princes offered for dedicating of the altar in the day that it was anointed, even the princes offered their offering before the altar. And the LORD said unto Moses, they shall offer their offering, each prince on his

day, for the dedicating of the altar. And he that offered his offering the first day was Nahshon the son of Amminadab, of the tribe of Judah:

On the first day of this dedication of the altar at the tabernacle, Nahshon, representing the tribe of Judah made his offering.

Numbers 7:13–17
And his offering was one silver charger, the weight thereof was an hundred and thirty shekels, one silver bowl of seventy shekels, after the shekel of the sanctuary; both of them were full of fine flour mingled with oil for a meat offering: one spoon of ten shekels of gold, full of incense: one young bullock, one ram, one lamb of the first year, for a burnt offering: one kid of the goats for a sin offering: and for a sacrifice of peace offerings, two oxen, five rams, five he goats, five lambs of the first year: this was the offering of Nahshon the son of Amminadab.

On the day Nahshon made his offering, the Lord recorded every single item he gave.

The next day, Nethaneel of the tribe of Issachar gave exactly what Nahshon gave. On Day Three, Eliab from the tribe of Zebulun gave his offering and guess what. It was exactly the same as Nahshon's and Nethaneel's. The fourth day, Elizur of the tribe of Reuben gave nothing more, nothing less than that which the first three gave.

And on it goes to the twelfth day—each man giving exactly what the man before him gave.

Numbers 7:84–89
This was the dedication of the altar, in the day when it was anointed, by the princes of Israel: twelve chargers of silver, twelve silver bowls, twelve spoons of gold: each charger of silver weighing an hundred and thirty shekels, each bowl seventy: all the silver vessels weighed two thousand and four hundred shekels, after the shekel of the sanctuary: the golden spoons were twelve, full of incense, weighing ten shekels apiece, after the shekel of the sanctuary: all the gold of the spoons was an hundred and twenty shekels. All the oxen for the burnt offering were twelve bullocks, the rams twelve, the lambs of the first year twelve, with their meat offering: and the kids of the goats for sin offering twelve. And all the oxen for the sacrifice of the peace offerings were twenty and four bullocks, the rams sixty, the he goats sixty, the lambs of the first year sixty. This was the dedication of the altar, after that it was anointed. And when Moses was gone into the tabernacle of the congregation to speak with him, then he heard the voice of one speaking unto him from off the mercy seat that was upon the ark of testimony, from between the two cherubims: and he spake unto him.

This is the combination of all of their giving—twelve times what each gave individually. These leaders, princes, men that were used, men who had impact all gave the same. What does that say to us? If we are to be men and woman who are impacting, we all give exactly the same as it relates to the tithe. We all give ten percent.

"I don't like regulations like that," people say. "They're too legalistic, too restrictive, too confining." But in the twenty-three years I've been in ministry, I have yet to talk to one person who said, "Tithing is too regulated. I want to give forty percent," or, "I think tithing is restrictive because I want to give sixty percent." No, people argue against tithing not because they find it truly legalistic but because they simply don't want to do it.

On the other hand, those who tithe, discover that God's Word is true—that He opens the windows of heaven and blesses them both now and eternally (Malachi 3:10).

IT'S NOT FAIR . . . OR IS IT?

A Topical Study of NUMBERS 7:1–9

In our society, we place a high premium on fairness and equality. With that in mind, look at our text . . .

On the day the tabernacle was dedicated and anointed, the leaders of the tribes of Israel brought twelve oxen and six wagons as an offering to the Lord. The wagons and oxen were divided between the three groups of Levites. The first group, the Gershonites, were given two wagons and four oxen. So far so good. But when the next group, the sons of Merari, was given four wagons and eight oxen, the Gershonites must have said, "Wait a minute. This isn't fair. We only got four oxen and two wagons." But if the Gershonites didn't like this, imagine how the third group—the Kohathites felt when there was nothing left for them. "Unfair!" they must have cried. And we do the same.

"Wait a minute," we say. "We're all called to serve God, aren't we? Why, then, does he have four wagons and eight oxen and I have none? Look at the position he holds, the prosperity she enjoys, the prominence they have. Why don't I?" And then we fall into the subtle mindset that God is not truly fair, that He plays favorites. And we're not one of them.

Why were the wagons distributed the way they were? Does God indeed have favorites? The answer is found in a significant phrase in our text where it says the wagons were given according to their service. Earlier, we read that the sons of Gershon were in charge of the fabric and coverings of the tabernacle—to take them up and down and pack them along. But the Merarites had an even heavier load, for they were in charge of the boards, silver sockets, and bars which made up the walls of the tabernacle. In fact, those who study these things say the weight the sons of Merari carried would have been approximately twice as great as that which the sons of Gershon carried. Consequently, called to bear twice as great a burden, it makes sense the Merarites would have twice as many oxen and twice as many wagons.

Of those who appear to be more blessed than we are, we say, "Look at the wagons they have. Look at their oxen." Yes, they may have more oxen and more wagons. But they also have heavier burdens. They have obligations that you and I don't understand. God is fair. With those wagons come added responsibilities and burdens because to whom much is given, much is required (Luke 12:48).

The Kohathites were to carry the furniture of the tabernacle—including the ark of the covenant—upon their shoulders, which speaks of intimacy, of close proximity. And now I begin to understand. Maybe I don't have four wagons or eight oxen. Maybe I don't even have two wagons and four oxen. Maybe I'm on foot. But maybe that's because the Lord knows that not having the position or possessions others have will result in a deeper intimacy than if there were oxen and wagons rumbling around.

Jesus opted for this when He said, "Foxes have holes and the birds of the air have nests, but the Son of Man has nowhere to lay His head" (Matthew 8:20). The priests and Pharisees had an abundance of oxen and wagons. But Jesus chose a different direction. Yet He was so happy and so full of joy that even those with lots of oxen and wagons, so to speak, left everything to follow Him.

He was able to focus on that which mattered. And as a result, there was a sparkle in His eye, a smile on His face, and a winsome quality to His personality which caused multitudes—of which we are a part—to want to be around Him.

If God has given you four carts and eight oxen, rejoice. But be on guard lest these blessings distract you from walking with Jesus in simplicity. Carts and oxen aren't always as good as they look. Carts lose their wheels; oxen make messes; and life becomes complicated. Thus, it is the wise man who says, "Lord, *You* set the agenda. You give me what You know is best for me."

My tendency is to say, "I don't think things are fair. We're going to have a fund-raising campaign to raise money to buy carts for the Kohathites." But would that truly be best for the Kohathites?

To those with no wagons, no oxen, God says, "You have Me. And I'm all you need."

On a related note, sometimes I look at people and wonder how they bear the burden they carry, how God could allow certain events to happen in their lives. "I could never go through that trial, never carry that weight," I say. But then I realize it's because I haven't been given the necessary carts or oxen to do so, that if I were to go through that trial, my Father would give me the oxen and carts necessary to bear the burden.

We have a fantastic privilege, to say to people who are self-absorbed, self-focused, self-centered, "God has you in the place best for you. He's a fair Father who treats us all with passionate love, doing what's best for each of us. God is oh, so good. And He knows what's best."

---

8 **Numbers 8:1, 2**
And the LORD spake unto Moses, saying, Speak unto Aaron, and say unto him, when thou lightest the lamps, the seven lamps shall give light over against the candlestick.

This speaks of the lighting of the menorah—the lamp stand comprised of seven oil lamps.

Numbers 8:3, 4
And Aaron did so; he lighted the lamps thereof over against the candlestick, as the LORD commanded Moses. And this work of the candlestick was of beaten gold, unto the shaft thereof, unto the flowers thereof, was beaten work: according unto the pattern which the LORD had shewed Moses, so he made the candlestick.

Following this brief interlude about the candlestick being lit, we will spend the rest of chapter 8 in a discussion about the dedication of the Levites. Chapter 7 dealt with the presentation of gifts, chapter 8 with the dedication of Levites; chapter 7 with offering, chapter 8 with service. And I believe this insertion of the lamp stand between the presentation of gifts and the dedication of servants is as though the Lord is saying, "It all needs to be exposed to the light."

"When you give, do not sound the trumpet in order to be noticed by men," Jesus said. "When you give, don't let your right hand know what your left hand is doing. If you give in secret, your Father who sees will reward you openly" (Matthew 6). Do I give for tax purposes? Do I serve to be noticed of men? That's what the hypocrites did in Jesus' day. But Jesus sees not only what we do, but why we do what we do, not simply what we give, but *how* we give . . .

As He sat against the wall of the temple, He saw rich people giving with much fanfare. Then He saw a poor woman who gave less than a penny. And she was the one He commended because she gave in simplicity and sincerity (Mark 12:41–44).

That's why it's important for us to say, "Lord, search my heart."

Numbers 8:5–7 (a)
And the LORD spake unto Moses, saying, Take the Levites from among the children of Israel, and cleanse them. And thus shalt thou do unto them, to cleanse them: Sprinkle water of purifying upon them . . .

This passage speaks of positional truth. That is, according to the original Greek text of 1 John 1:7, the blood of Jesus Christ *continually* cleanses us from all sin. We can come boldly to our Father and fellowship with Him because we're constantly being cleansed.

Numbers 8:7 (b)
. . . and let them shave all their flesh, and let them wash their clothes, and so make themselves clean.

This passage speaks of practical truth. That is, although Moses sprinkled water on the priests, they were to shave themselves. The first part of their cleansing was passive, the second part required their participation. Although I am clean positionally, I must participate in my cleansing practically. "How shall a young man cleanse his ways?" David asked. "By taking heed to the Word (Psalm 119:9). Thy Word have I hid in my heart that I might not sin against thee" (Psalm 119:11).

Positionally, I'm being cleansed every day by the blood of Jesus Christ. But practically, there's a bunch of sin in my life and the only way it will be worked out is by the working in of the Word. I've got to wash myself in the water of the Word, take in the Scriptures, meditate on the Word, listen to the Word, learn the Word. That's why studying the Word together is so important.

Numbers 8:8–11
Then let them take a young bullock with his meat offering, even fine flour mingled with oil, and another young bullock shalt thou take for a sin offering. And thou shalt bring the Levites before the tabernacle of the congregation: and thou shalt gather the whole assembly of the children of Israel together: and thou shalt bring the Levites before the LORD: and the children of Israel shall put their hands upon the Levites: and Aaron shall offer the Levites before the LORD for an offering of the children of Israel, that they may execute the service of the LORD.

Hands were laid upon the Levites and they were presented to the Lord.

Numbers 8:12–18
And the Levites shall lay their hands upon the heads of the bullocks: and thou shalt offer the one for a sin offering, and the other for a burnt offering, unto the LORD, to make an atonement for the Levites. And thou shalt set the Levites before Aaron, and before his sons, and offer them for an offering unto the LORD. Thus shalt thou separate the Levites from among the children of Israel: and the Levites shall be mine. And after that shall the Levites go in to do the service of the tabernacle of the congregation: and thou shalt cleanse them, and offer them for an offering. For they are wholly given unto me from among the children of Israel; instead of such as open every womb, even instead of the firstborn of all the children of Israel, have I taken them unto me. For all the firstborn of the children of Israel are mine, both man and beast: on the day that I smote every firstborn in the land of Egypt I sanctified them for myself. And I have taken the Levites for all the firstborn of the children of Israel.

This passage describes how the Levites would take the place of the firstborn of every family for priestly service, such being God's original intent prior to the idolatry participated in by every tribe other than Levi (Exodus 34).

Numbers 8:19–22
And I have given the Levites as a gift to Aaron and to his sons from among the children of Israel, to do the service of the children of Israel in the tabernacle of the congregation, and to make an atonement for the children of Israel: that there be no plague among the children of Israel, when the children of Israel come nigh unto the sanctuary. And Moses, and Aaron, and all the congregation of the children of Israel, did to the Levites according unto all that the LORD commanded Moses concerning the Levites, so did the children of Israel unto them. And the Levites were purified, and they washed their clothes; and Aaron offered them as an offering before the LORD; and Aaron made an atonement for them to cleanse them. And after that went the Levites in to do their service in the tabernacle of the congregation before Aaron, and before his sons: as the LORD had commanded Moses concerning the Levites, so did they unto them.

In verse 11, we saw Aaron offering the Levites to God. In verse 19, we see God giving them back to Aaron. And that's always the way it is, for God is a debtor to no man. More is always given back to us than we could possibly ever give Him (Matthew 7:2).

Numbers 8:23–26
And the LORD spake unto Moses, saying, This is it that belongeth unto the Levites: from twenty and five years old and upward they shall go in to wait upon the service of the tabernacle of the congregation: and

from the age of fifty years they shall cease waiting upon the service thereof, and shall serve no more: but shall minister with their brethren in the tabernacle of the congregation, to keep the charge, and shall do no service. Thus shalt thou do unto the Levites touching their charge.

The original meaning of the phrase "wait upon the service" implied warfare. That's what ministry is. There's a war going on against principalities and powers and spiritual forces that want to defeat and distract, destroy and depress (Ephesians 6:12). But because greater is He that is in me is than he that is in the world, (1 John 4:4), we like the Levites, can do that which He requires of us.

9

Numbers 9:1–5
And the LORD spake unto Moses in the wilderness of Sinai, in the first month of the second year after they were come out of the land of Egypt, saying, Let the children of Israel also keep the passover at his appointed season. In the fourteenth day of this month, at even, ye shall keep it in his appointed season: according to all the rites of it, and according to all the ceremonies thereof, shall ye keep it. And Moses spake unto the children of Israel, that they should keep the passover. And they kept the passover on the fourteenth day of the first month at even in the wilderness of Sinai: according to all that the LORD commanded Moses, so did the children of Israel.

The Passover was to take place once each year to commemorate how the Lord delivered His people from Egypt. A year having passed, the children of Israel were to celebrate Passover.

Numbers 9:6, 7
And there were certain men, who were defiled by the dead body of a man, that they could not keep the passover on that day: and they came before Moses and before Aaron on that day: And those men said unto him, We are defiled by the dead body of a man: wherefore are we kept back, that we may not offer an offering of the LORD in his appointed season among the children of Israel?

After touching a dead body, a group of men asked Moses if they were still able to celebrate Passover.

For us, Passover is synonymous with Communion, for Jesus instituted Communion at the Passover meal He shared with His disciples (Luke 22:15–20). One of the aspects of Communion that people often fail to grasp is to do what these men did: realizing we're defiled, that we've taken part in activities which cause death spiritually, that we harbor deadly attitudes internally.

Numbers 9:8
And Moses said unto them, Stand still, and I will hear what the LORD will command concerning you.

"I need to ask the Lord," Moses said. I like that! Too often I'm too ready to give my own opinion. How I want to be more like Moses. How I want to be one whose first inclination is to pray.

Numbers 9:9–12
And the LORD spake unto Moses, saying, Speak unto the children of Israel, saying, if any man of you or of your posterity shall be unclean by reason of a dead body, or be in a journey afar off, yet he shall keep the passover unto the LORD. The fourteenth day of the second month at even they shall keep it, and eat it with unleavened bread and bitter herbs. They shall leave none of it unto the morning, nor break any bone of it: according to all the ordinances of the passover they shall keep it.

If someone touched a dead body, or was away on a journey, they were to celebrate Passover thirty days later—on the fourteenth day of the *second* month. In other words, a period of time was to pass between the defilement and the celebration.

So, too, Communion is not only a time of celebration, but of communication as we ask the Father to show us that of which we might not even be aware that is rotten, that is deadly within us. Communion is not simply a matter of eating a little cracker and gulping some grace juice, but of saying, "Search my heart, Lord. Show me where my attitudes are wrong. Show me where I've been on a journey, going down a dead-end road." Only in confession is there true liberty. Therefore, don't rush through Communion. Instead, spend the time it takes to hear from your Father.

Numbers 9:13, 14
But the man that is clean, and is not in a journey, and forbeareth to keep the passover, even the same soul shall be cut off from among his people: because he brought not the offering of the LORD in his appointed season, that man shall bear his sin. And if a stranger shall sojourn among you, and will keep the passover unto the LORD; according

to the ordinance of the passover, and according to the manner thereof, so shall he do: ye shall have one ordinance, both for the stranger, and for him that was born in the land.

If someone was not on a journey or not defiled by a dead body and didn't celebrate Passover, he was to be cut off from the rest of the congregation and was to bear his sin.

Those who don't come to Communion will inevitably begin to be isolated from God's people because as we all eat of the same loaf, we experience intimacy and unity uniquely. Truly, it is His broken body that brings His living body into oneness. Thus, those who don't participate eventually find themselves increasingly isolated. And they not only carry their sin with them, but find sin in those around them. That's why Paul said that, because some in the Corinthian congregation hadn't given worth to Communion, some were sick and weak and had even died unnecessarily (1 Corinthians 11:30).

Numbers 9:15–23
And on the day that the tabernacle was reared up the cloud covered the tabernacle, namely, the tent of the testimony: and at even there was upon the tabernacle as it were the appearance of fire, until the morning. So it was alway: the cloud covered it by day, and the appearance of fire by night. And when the cloud was taken up from the tabernacle, then after that the children of Israel journeyed: and in the place where the cloud abode, there the children of Israel pitched their tents. At the commandment of the LORD the children of Israel journeyed, and at the commandment of the LORD they pitched: as long as the cloud abode upon the tabernacle they rested in their tents. And when the cloud tarried long upon the tabernacle many days, then the children of Israel kept the charge of the LORD, and journeyed not. And so it was, when the cloud was a few days upon the tabernacle; according to the commandment of the LORD they abode in their tents, and according to the commandment of the LORD they journeyed. And so it was, when the cloud abode from even unto the morning, and that the cloud was taken up in the morning, then they journeyed: whether it was by day or by night that the cloud was taken up, they journeyed. Or whether it were two days, or a month, or a year, that the cloud tarried upon the tabernacle, remaining thereon, the children of Israel abode in their tents, and journeyed not: but when it was taken up, they journeyed. At the commandment of the LORD they rested in the tents, and at the commandment of the LORD they journeyed: they kept the charge of the LORD, at the commandment of the LORD by the hand of Moses.

Isaiah 63 tells us the cloud by day and the pillar of fire by night was the Holy Spirit. Thus, it was the Spirit of God that told the children of Israel where to stop and settle in, when to pack up and move out. Yet although we think it would be wonderful to have a visible, tangible cloud leading us, the children of Israel murmured and complained. And this shows me there's a better way to be led than by the external, the visible, the tangible.

"I'm going to do something new," God told Jeremiah. "I'm going to write My will on the tables of the hearts of My people" (Jeremiah 31:33).

I'm so thankful for the New Covenant—for God directing us by placing impressions on our hearts. And I have found the most satisfying, adventurous, fulfilling life there can possible be is to be led by the Spirit as He writes His will upon my heart.

10

Numbers 10:1, 2 (a)
And the LORD spake unto Moses, saying, Make thee two trumpets of silver; of a whole piece shalt thou make them:

In the days before megaphones, telephones, cell phones, one of the ways to communicate would be through the sounding of trumpets. Two trumpets were to be made of silver to be sounded for four specific reasons . . .

Numbers 10:2 (b)–4
. . . that thou mayest use them for the calling of the assembly, and for the journeying of the camps. And when they shall blow with them, all the assembly shall assemble themselves to thee at the door of the tabernacle of the congregation. And if they blow but with one trumpet, then the princes, which are heads of the thousands of Israel, shall gather themselves unto thee.

The first reason the trumpets sounded was for the *purpose of convocation*—when the people were to assemble together at the door of the tabernacle.

Numbers 10:5–8
When ye blow an alarm, then the camps that lie on the east parts shall go forward. When ye blow an alarm the second time, then the camps that lie on the south side shall take

their journey: they shall blow an alarm for their journeys. But when the congregation is to be gathered together, ye shall blow, but ye shall not sound an alarm. And the sons of Aaron, the priests, shall blow with the trumpets; and they shall be to you for an ordinance for ever throughout your generations.

The second reason the trumpets sounded was for the *purpose of mobilization*—to tell the people it was time to pull up stakes, pack up their tents, and move ahead.

Numbers 10:9
And if ye go to war in your land against the enemy that oppresseth you, then ye shall blow an alarm with the trumpets; and ye shall be remembered before the LORD your God, and ye shall be saved from your enemies.

The third reason the trumpets sounded was for the *purpose of confrontation*—to do battle against the enemies which the children of Israel would encounter in the Promised Land.

Numbers 10:10
Also in the day of your gladness, and in your solemn days, and in the beginnings of your months, ye shall blow with the trumpets over your burnt offerings, and over the sacrifices of your peace offerings; that they may be to you for a memorial before your God: I am the LORD your God.

The fourth and final reason the trumpets were to sound was for the *purpose of celebration*—to signal the feasts and festivals as well as the solemn days.

Everything in the Old Testament is an illustration of New Testament truth—and the trumpets made of silver, the metal of redemption, are no exception, for they give us understanding about that which Paul called a mystery . . .

> Behold, I shew you a mystery; we shall not all sleep, but we shall all be changed, in a moment, in the twinkling of an eye, at the last trump: for the trumpet shall sound, and the dead shall be raised incorruptible, and we shall be changed. 1 Corinthians 15:51, 52

The idea of being changed is that of being metamorphosed—like caterpillars changed miraculously into butterflies. Paul says the same thing is true concerning people. We're not all going to die. But we're all going to be metamorphosed. When? At the last trumpet.

Here in Numbers 10, we see two trumpets. Although the Bible is filled with trumpets, there are only two trumpets of God: the first trump and the last trump. The first trump was sounded in Exodus 19 when God gathered His people at the base of Mt. Sinai and gave them the Ten Commandments. It was during that convocation that Israel became a nation.

But there is a second trumpet, called the last trump. And it has not yet been heard. When it is, even as Numbers 10 illustrates, it will signal a grand convocation as the dead in Christ shall rise—and as we who are alive will be caught up—or raptured—to meet the Lord in the air.

This leads us to mobilization—the second reason the trumpets were sounded here in Numbers 10. When the last trumpet sounds, we'll leave the snares and entanglements of this world behind as we pull up stakes, pack up our tents, and move on to heaven. Oh, glorious day that will be!

This leads us to the third reason the trumpets were sounded, for war also is part of the equation. After we are reunited and taken on our journey to our new home in heaven, Revelation 6—19 describes the war that will break out on earth during the horrendous seven-year period of the Tribulation.

But this leads to celebration—the last reason the trumpet was to sound. At the end of seven years, when Jesus comes back to the earth and we come back with Him, the earth enters into a new day, a day of unparalleled peace and prosperity.

As I read Numbers 10, I realize that these folks in the wilderness were instructed to keep their ears tuned towards the sound of the trumpet. And I need to do the same in the wilderness I'm in. So do you. And we need to remind others to do the same, to keep focused on eternity, to keep their ears tuned for the final trumpet which will sound on a day I believe is not far away.

Numbers 10:11–13
And it came to pass on the twentieth day of the second month, in the second year, that the cloud was taken up from off the tabernacle of the testimony. And the children of Israel took their journeys out of the wilderness of Sinai; and the cloud rested in the wilderness of Paran. And they first took their journey according to the commandment of the LORD by the hand of Moses.

After being redeemed from bondage and slavery, after being instructed in worship and the sacrificial system, after being organized in the order in which they were to march and camp, the children of Israel took their first steps towards the Promised Land.

That's always the way of the Lord. He redeems us from sin and sets us free from the Egyptian mentality of the world. He instructs us about worshiping Him and wants us to be a people who are ordered, linked together on our journey towards heaven.

Numbers 10:14–28
In the first place went the standard of the camp of the children of Judah according to their armies: and over his host was Nahshon the son of Amminadab. And over the host of the tribe of the children of Issachar was Nethaneel the son of Zuar. And over the host of the tribe of the children of Zebulun was Eliab the son of Helon. And the tabernacle was taken down; and the sons of Gershon and the sons of Merari set forward, bearing the tabernacle. And the standard of the camp of Reuben set forward according to their armies: and over his host was Elizur the son of Shedeur. And over the host of the tribe of the children of Simeon was Shelumiel the son of Zurishaddai. And over the host of the tribe of the children of Gad was Eliasaph the son of Deuel. And the Kohathites set forward, bearing the sanctuary: and the other did set up the tabernacle against they came. And the standard of the camp of the children of Ephraim set forward according to their armies: and over his host was Elishama the son of Ammihud. And over the host of the tribe of the children of Manasseh was Gamaliel the son of Pedahzur. And over the host of the tribe of the children of Benjamin was Abidan the son of Gideoni. And the standard of the camp of the children of Dan set forward, which was the rereward of all the camps throughout their hosts: and over his host was Ahiezer the son of Ammishaddai. And over the host of the tribe of the children of Asher was Pagiel the son of Ocran. And over the host of the tribe of the children of Naphtali was Ahira the son of Enan. Thus were the journeyings of the children of Israel according to their armies, when they set forward.

Judah leads the procession. It's interesting to me that, as Scripture unfolds, we see it will be Judah at the front of the parade, at the head of the nation. The tribe of Judah would always be leading the way as the Lord led them. Why? Here are a couple of suggestions:

Jesus, our Leader, would come from the tribe of Judah. Therefore, Judah would always be in a place of priority. Secondly, the name *Judah* literally means "praise." Praise is always to lead the way, for it is through praise that we can enter into Jesus' courts (Psalm 100:4). Practically, to start the parade of your own day personally with praise; to begin any project, any undertaking with an attitude of worship makes all the difference.

Numbers 10:29–32
And Moses said unto Hobab, the son of Raguel the Midianite, Moses' father in law, We are journeying unto the place of which the LORD said, I will give it you: come thou with us, and we will do thee good: for the LORD hath spoken good concerning Israel. And he said unto him, I will not go; but I will depart to mine own land, and to my kindred. And he said, Leave us not, I pray thee; forasmuch as thou knowest how we are to encamp in the wilderness, and thou mayest be to us instead of eyes. And it shall be, if thou go with us, yea, it shall be, that what goodness the LORD shall do unto us, the same will we do unto thee.

Before leaving for the Land of Promise, Moses invited his father-in-law to accompany them on their journey.

***For topical study of Numbers 10:29–32 entitled "You Gotta Come," turn to page* 475.**

Numbers 10:33–35
And they departed from the mount of the LORD three days' journey: and the ark of the covenant of the LORD went before them in the three days' journey, to search out a resting place for them. And the cloud of the LORD was upon them by day, when they went out of the camp. And it came to pass, when the ark set forward, that Moses said, Rise up, LORD, and let thine enemies be scattered; and let them that hate thee flee before thee.

As the cloud moved out, "Rise up, O Lord," Moses says. "Let the enemies be scattered." What a great way to start the day, praying, "Lord, go before us and clear the way. Let the enemies before me be scattered today, as well as the enemies of my fleshly tendencies within me."

Numbers 10:36
And when it rested, he said, Return, O LORD, unto the many thousands of Israel.

When the cloud stopped, so did the company of Israel. And as they did, Moses asked that the Lord return. And is not that the cry of our own hearts? Even so, come, Lord Jesus (Revelation 22:20).

YOU GOTTA COME

A Topical Study of NUMBERS 10:29–32

A number of newspapers carried the story concerning the discoveries indicating that perhaps ninety percent of the universe is black matter. In fact, when one paper referred to it as "outer darkness," I couldn't help but remember that Jesus used that very phrase to describe the place wherein those not a part of the kingdom would be cast (Matthew 22:13).

Although people think the darkness, pain, and isolation of hell is unfair, Jesus said specifically that hell was not created for man, but for the devil and his demons (Matthew 25:41). However, if a person doesn't want God—who is Light—the only other alternative is darkness. If a person doesn't want God—who is Love—the only other alternative is hate. If a person doesn't want God—who is health—the only other alternative is pain and suffering. Hell is the absence of the attributes of God. And if a person says, "I don't want God in my life," the only alternative is to be where God is not—a place of weeping and wailing and gnashing of teeth, a place of outer darkness and eternal fire (Jude 7).

I believe it was because, to a certain degree, Moses had an intrinsic understanding of this that he said to Hobab, "Come with us. You gotta be part of this company because if you're not, you're headed for destruction."

And although Hobab at first refused, Moses didn't give up. "We're going into the desert," he said. "You understand the terrain. You know the region. You can be eyes for us, a guide to us. Hobab, we need you."

To those who say they're not interested in church and don't care much about heaven, we need to follow the example of Moses and say, "We need you. I've seen the way you can hit a softball and our church team is in desperate need of a first baseman. You can help us. You can enrich us." Or, "I've seen the way you work with people, and we could use your abilities." Or, "I've seen your artwork. Could you paint a mural in our Sunday school wing?"

Such is the course Moses took and Hobab responded, for in the Book of Judges (4:11), his family appears again. Thus, Hobab did indeed choose to travel to the Promised Land. When? When he was told, "You're valuable. You can enrich us. We need you."

Are we really to tell unbelievers they are needed?

Jesus did.

He needed the woman at the well to give Him water to drink (John 4:7). He needed the owner of the colt He would ride into Jerusalem to release it to Him (Mark 11:3).

How long has it been since you took someone by the hand, looked him in the eye, and said, "You need to be saved. We're going to heaven. If you don't come with us, the alternative is awful. And on the way, we'll do you good. It will be good for you to travel with us. I know you feel more comfortable in the world, but we need you in the kingdom. Would you pray with me right now?"

Maybe you've invited your unsaved brother-in-law or your nephew to church five Christmases in a row, only to have them decline every time—but do you fully comprehend that they are going to hell unless they understand that God has prepared a land for them, that God places great value upon them, that they can be helpful to the believing community, and that we'll be good to them? We can't let go. We can't give up. We can't stop. The stakes are too high.

C. S. Lewis was right when he said, "If heaven and hell are true, nothing else matters. If heaven and hell aren't true, then nothing matters at all."

I have found that the most effective way to bring people to Jesus is not by discussing doctrine endlessly, debating evolution passionately, or even inviting them to church repeatedly but to share with them the way of salvation clearly and to pray with them immediately. I begin by opening my Bible and showing them Romans 3:23 . . .

For all have sinned, and come short of the glory of God.

"You, me, and everyone have fallen short of the glory, the standard, the requirement of God," I say. Then I turn a few pages to Romans 5:6 . . .

For when we were yet without strength, in due time Christ died for the ungodly.

"When we were pulled down, wiped out, done in by sin, Christ died for us," I say. "It was when we were hopelessly lost that Christ died for you and me." Then I turn the page and show them Romans 6:23 . . .

For the wages of sin is death; but the gift of God is eternal life through Jesus Christ our Lord.

"The wages of sin is certain death," I say. "You'll be dead in your heart internally. Your marriage will fall short of what it was supposed to be. Your family will be dead relationally. And most importantly, sin brings death eternally. But the gift of God is eternal life—which begins now and lasts through eternity." From there, I take them to Romans 8:1 . . .

There is therefore now no condemnation to them which are in Christ Jesus, who walk not after the flesh, but after the Spirit.

"Once we change direction and follow Jesus," I explain, "we experience a resurrection of relationships and emotions as the sentence of death is removed from our lives." Finally, we turn to Romans 10:8 (b)–10 . . .

> *. . . The word is nigh thee, even in thy mouth, and in thy heart: that is, the word of faith, which we preach; that if thou shalt confess with thy mouth the Lord Jesus, and shalt believe in thine heart that God hath raised him from the dead, thou shalt be saved. For with the heart man believeth unto righteousness; and with the mouth confession is made unto salvation.*

"If you confess that Jesus is Lord, you'll be saved," I tell them. "And you'll never regret it."

Known as the "Romans Road," I have found this to be a most effective way to share the gospel.

"What if they don't believe the Bible is God's Word?" you ask. "Don't you have to convince them?"

Not necessarily. When asked how to defend the Bible, C.H. Spurgeon, the "Prince of Preachers," answered, "How does one defend the Bible? The same way he defends a lion. He just opens the door and it will defend itself!"

The greatest blessing on earth is to lead someone into eternal life. The Bible says that when one soul is saved, all of heaven breaks out in cosmic celebration (Luke 15:10). And the same thing will happen in your heart. The issues, problems, concerns facing you will suddenly matter no longer when you've seen someone take their first step towards heaven.

Don't let this week go by without walking with someone down the Romans Road. Because it's the most important thing you'll ever do, how I encourage you to share your faith with the Hobabs around you, to invite them to journey with you, even to tell them they will be helpful to you on your way to heaven.

And if they accept the invitation, they will, like Hobab of old, be amazed by the glorious treasures and experiences awaiting them in the land of milk and honey, in the land of God's promise both presently and eternally.

11

Numbers 11:1 (a)

And when the people complained, it displeased the LORD: and the LORD heard it . . .

The Lord has given instruction to them, appeared unto them, been patient with them. And now at last, the trumpets are sounding. Moses says, "Rise up, O Lord, and go before us," the children of Israel are on their way—and the first thing they do is complain about something evidently so insignificant that Scripture doesn't even bother to record the reason. Oh, it must have seemed important to the Israelites at the time, but from God's perspective, it was not even worth wasting the ink to write it on parchment.

Numbers 11:1 (b)–3

. . . and his anger was kindled; and the fire of the LORD burnt among them, and consumed them that were in the uttermost parts of the camp. And the people cried unto Moses; and when Moses prayed unto the LORD, the fire was quenched. And he called the name of

the place Taberah: because the fire of the LORD burnt among them.

After hearing their complaints, it's as if the Lord gave His people something to complain about through the fire which broke out in their midst. The lesson is a good one for me because through it I understand that complaining causes confusion. If I'm complaining about something in one part of my life, a fire is sure to flare up in another part.

In his letter to the Galatians, Paul tells us that if we bite and devour one another, we ourselves will be consumed (5:15). And here at the outset of the Israelites' journey, God reminds us that we'll get burned if we're a people given to complaining.

Numbers 11:4
And the mixt multitude that was among them fell a lusting: and the children of Israel also wept again, and said, Who shall give us flesh to eat?

The problem of complaining was followed by that of lusting. The children of Israel had been given manna miraculously which sustained them wonderfully—and yet they wanted flesh. Oh, how easily this can happen to me. God has given me all things that pertain to life and godliness (2 Peter 1:3)—and yet my flesh still demands its own way.

Numbers 11:5, 6
We remember the fish, which we did eat in Egypt freely; the cucumbers, and the melons, and the leeks, and the onions, and the garlick: but now our soul is dried away: there is nothing at all, beside this manna, before our eyes.

Memory can indeed be a mirage, for the Israelites never had these things in Egypt. They were slaves baking bricks under the blistering sun while their sons drowned in the Nile. But somehow in their journeying, their memories got all mixed up. And the same thing can happen to us, for while Satan will exaggerate the kicks we used to have, he'll never remind us of the kickbacks, or the reality of the situation.

Numbers 11:7–9
And the manna was as coriander seed, and the colour thereof as the colour of bdellium. And the people went about, and gathered it, and ground it in mills, or beat it in a mortar, and baked it in pans, and made cakes of it: and the taste of it was as the taste of fresh oil. And when the dew fell upon the camp in the night, the manna fell upon it.

Regardless of the fact that the manna was miraculous, healthy, and right, the children of Israel tired of that which God sent their way day after day.

Numbers 11:10
Then Moses heard the people weep throughout their families, every man in the door of his tent: and the anger of the LORD was kindled greatly; Moses also was displeased.

Can you imagine the sound of the weeping of three million people—with the men leading the way?

Numbers 11:11
And Moses said unto the LORD, Wherefore hast thou afflicted thy servant? and wherefore have I not found favour in thy sight, that thou layest the burden of all this people upon me?

The people were complaining and Moses was complaining about their complaining.

Numbers 11:12–15 (a)
Have I conceived all this people? Have I begotten them, that thou shouldest say unto me, Carry them in thy bosom, as a nursing father beareth the sucking child, unto the land which thou swarest unto their fathers? Whence should I have flesh to give unto all this people? For they weep unto me, saying, Give us flesh, that we may eat. I am not able to bear all this people alone, because it is too heavy for me. And if thou deal thus with me, kill me, I pray thee, out of hand, if I have found favour in thy sight . . .

"Just kill me, God," Moses cried. "I've had it. I can't do this any more. This job is too hard."

Numbers 11:15 (b)
. . . and let me not see my wretchedness.

So meek a man was Moses, that in confessing his own wretchedness, He saw himself as no better than the people about whom he complained.

Numbers 11:16
And the LORD said unto Moses, Gather unto me seventy men of the elders of Israel, whom thou knowest to be the elders of the people, and officers over them; and bring them unto the tabernacle of the congregation, that they may stand there with thee.

God's solution to the burden of a people so prone to complain and criticism was to enlist them to help shoulder the burden.

Numbers 11:17
And I will come down and talk with thee there: and I will take of the spirit which is upon thee, and will put it upon them; and they shall bear the burden of the people with thee, that thou bear it not thyself alone.

Here we see the formation of a plurality of elders—a group of men to stand together and bear the burden shoulder to shoulder, with the same spirit upon each of them. In this, we see the foundation for the way the Lord wants His people organized even today. There are to be elders who stand together to bear the burden as they move in unanimity—a model seen clearly in Acts 15 . . .

As debate raged over whether new Gentile believers should become circumcised according to Jewish tradition, the early church didn't take a vote, form a committee, or hold a seminar. They talked and they prayed. And they talked and they prayed until finally James, one of the elders, stood up and gave a word that "seemed good to all and to the Holy Ghost," (Acts 15:28). Thus, there was unanimity, oneness, total agreement.

Numbers 11:18–20
And say thou unto the people, Sanctify yourselves against to morrow, and ye shall eat flesh: for ye have wept in the ears of the LORD, saying, Who shall give us flesh to eat? for it was well with us in Egypt: therefore the LORD will give you flesh, and ye shall eat. Ye shall not eat one day, nor two days, nor five days, neither ten days, nor twenty days; but even a whole month, until it come out at your nostrils, and it be loathsome unto you: because that ye have despised the LORD which is among you, and have wept before him, saying, Why came we forth out of Egypt?

When Moses heard that the Lord would give them meat for a month, he did some calculating . . .

Numbers 11:21, 22
And Moses said, The people, among whom I am, are six hundred thousand footmen; and thou hast said, I will give them flesh, that they may eat a whole month. Shall the flocks and the herds be slain for them, to suffice them? or shall all the fish of the sea be gathered together for them, to suffice them?

"How are You going to feed three million people, Lord?" Moses asked. "Do You want us to kill all the herds and flocks we planned to bring in to the Promised Land—or do You want us to fish all of the fish out of the Red Sea? You have two choices here, Lord: fish or meat. Which will it be?"

Numbers 11:23
And the LORD said unto Moses, Is the LORD's hand waxed short? Thou shalt see now whether my word shall come to pass unto thee or not.

God didn't tell Moses what He was going to do. He doesn't usually do that to us, either. As He did to Moses, He simply says, "Wait and see."

Numbers 11:24–26 (a)
And Moses went out, and told the people the words of the LORD, and gathered the seventy men of the elders of the people, and set them round about the tabernacle. And the LORD came down in a cloud, and spake unto him, and took of the spirit that was upon him, and gave it unto the seventy elders: and it came to pass, that, when the spirit rested upon them, they prophesied, and did not cease. But there remained two of the men in the camp . . .

Sixty-eight of the seventy elders were at the tabernacle, which was pitched outside of the camp. But two were in the camp. They weren't at the meeting. They weren't with the others.

Numbers 11:26 (b)–28
. . . the name of the one was Eldad, and the name of the other Medad: and the spirit rested upon them; and they were of them that were written, but went not out unto the tabernacle: and they prophesied in the camp. And there ran a young man, and told Moses, and said, Eldad and Medad do prophesy in the camp. And Joshua the son of Nun, the servant of Moses, one of his young men, answered and said, My lord Moses, forbid them.

"Because Eldad and Medad are not in our midst," protested one of the seventy, "forbid them from prophesying at all." The protestor's name? Joshua.

Numbers 11:29, 30
And Moses said unto him, Enviest thou for my sake? Would God that all the LORD's people were prophets, and that the LORD would put his spirit upon them! And Moses gat him into the camp, he and the elders of Israel.

"Even though Eldad and Medad are not in our midst, God is still working through them," Moses answered. And his answer reminds me of the answer Jesus gave to a similar protest when He said, "He that is not against us is for us" (Mark 9:40). Thus, Jesus, like Moses, showed that we ought to be as magnanimous as we possibly can be even if someone is not in our camp theologically, or at our church geographically. The fact is, if someone is prophesying, casting out demons, or being used by the Lord in another way, even if they don't do it exactly "our way," that's okay.

Paul picked up the same theme when he said, "I would that all speak in tongues," (1 Corinthians 14:5). Therefore, we need to be careful that we don't quench the Spirit by limiting people. Paul, Moses, and Jesus Himself were all in agreement concerning the necessity of being inclusive and big-hearted.

Numbers 11:31 (a)
And there went forth a wind from the Lord, and brought quails from the sea . . .

Although Moses had limited His choice to "Surf or Turf,"—to fish or livestock—God caused a wind to blow that not only blew in millions of quail, but also must have blown Moses' mind!

Numbers 11:31 (b)
. . . and let them fall by the camp, as it were a day's journey on this side, and as it were a day's journey on the other side, round about the camp, and as it were two cubits high upon the face of the earth.

So abundant was God's provision, that if you were to walk in the same direction for an entire day, you would still be knee-deep in quail.

Numbers 11:32
And the people stood up all that day, and all that night, and all the next day, and they gathered the quails: he that gathered least gathered ten homers: and they spread them all abroad for themselves round about the camp.

He that gathered least gathered ten homers. That's how I know these quail flew right in the spring zone. The weakest hitter on the team had ten homers! Ten homers would have been about fifty bushels of quail—or the equivalent of two hundred family-size buckets of Kentucky Fried Chicken.

Numbers 11:33–35
And while the flesh was yet between their teeth, ere it was chewed, the wrath of the Lord was kindled against the people, and the Lord smote the people with a very great plague. And he called the name of that place Kibroth-hattaavah: because there they buried the people that lusted. And the people journeyed from Kibroth-hattaavah unto Hazeroth; and abode at Hazeroth.

Many speculate that it was actually the overindulgence of the people that brought about the plague. And they could be right . . .

> They soon forgat his works; they waited not for his counsel: But lusted exceedingly in the wilderness, and tempted God in the desert. And he gave them their request; but sent leanness into their soul. Psalm 106:13–15

The Lord sent the children of Israel that which they desired—but it killed them. That's important for me to understand. I think I know what I want. But only God sees what is truly best for me. And He promises to withhold nothing from us that would be good for us (Psalm 84:11). Therefore, we can be the most peaceful people on the planet because, while everyone else is trying to figure out how to get ahead and how to make it happen, we get to say, "Father, You know my situation. You know what's best for me. I trust You."

I'm so glad we don't have to figure out what's best and make our demands accordingly—but rather we can simply say, "Lord, Your will be done today"—fully confident that He will do what's best for you and me.

12

The passage before us deals with Miriam, Aaron, and the subtle sin of envy. Envy gets neither the publicity that murder does, nor the press that adultery can. Yet, although it's unnoticed by many, envy can be just as damaging, just as dangerous, and just as deadly as murder or adultery.

Envy is the whimpering whisper within me which says, "Why him and not me? It's not fair what he has, where he's at, what he enjoys." Envy is different than jealousy, for while jealousy fears that I'll lose what I have, envy wants what someone else has—be it a personality trait or skill, a gift or position.

Envy not only begins at the earliest of ages—most frequently with sibling rivalry—but at the beginning of time itself when envy led Cain to kill Abel.

Numbers 12:1 (a)
And Miriam and Aaron spake against Moses . . .

The fact that Miriam is listed first, as well as that the Hebrew word translated "spake" is in the feminine form, indicates Miriam was the ringleader of the two. Miriam was quite a lady, for she was charismatic, had a powerful personality, and, according to Exodus 15, was a prophetess. As high priest, Aaron had an undeniably important role to play in the congregation. Thus, Miriam and Aaron were important players in the life of the young nation of Israel.

Numbers 12:1 (b)
. . . because of the Ethiopian woman whom he had married: for he had married an Ethiopian woman.

Evidently, after Moses' wife, Zipporah died, he married an Ethiopian woman. Yet as valid as Miriam's and Aaron's concern was that he didn't marry a Jewish woman, it was actually only a smokescreen to cover the real reason for their words against him—which, as seen in verse 2, was envy . . .

Numbers 12:2
And they said, Hath the LORD indeed spoken only by Moses? Hath he not spoken also by us? And the LORD heard it.

"Why is Moses in charge?" Miriam asked Aaron. "He's our little brother. Why him and not us? It's not fair!"

Numbers 12:3
(Now the man Moses was very meek, above all the men which were upon the face of the earth.)

This verse shows me this book must have been inspired by God, for Moses wouldn't have included it if it was up to his own human imagination. I bet he was a bit red-faced when he penned these words. In Deuteronomy 34, we'll read about Moses' death, and he wrote those words as well. How can a man write about his own death—unless it is actually God speaking to him?

Numbers 12:4–8
And the LORD spake suddenly unto Moses, and unto Aaron, and unto Miriam, Come out ye three unto the tabernacle of the congregation. And they three came out. And the LORD came down in the pillar of the cloud, and stood in the door of the tabernacle, and called Aaron and Miriam: and they both came forth. And he said, Hear now my words: If there be a prophet among you, I the LORD will make myself known unto him in a vision, and will speak unto him in a dream. My servant Moses is not so, who is faithful in all mine house. With him will I speak mouth to mouth, even apparently, and not in dark speeches; and the similitude of the LORD shall he behold: wherefore then were ye not afraid to speak against my servant Moses?

"Unlike to a prophet or a prophetess, I speak to Moses directly," said God.

Numbers 12:9, 10
And the anger of the LORD was kindled against them; and he departed. And the cloud departed from off the tabernacle; and, behold, Miriam became leprous, white as snow: and Aaron looked upon Miriam, and, behold, she was leprous.

Although our tendency is to think that the dreaded disease of leprosy is too severe a punishment for simply questioning Moses' choice of a bride, it is actually a picture in which we see how God views envy . . .

First, envy grieves God. When I say, "Why him and not me?" I am actually saying, "You goofed, Lord." And so offensive is this to Him that His response to Miriam was not only to smite her with leprosy, but to depart.

Numbers 12:11–13
And Aaron said unto Moses, Alas, my lord, I beseech thee, lay not the sin upon us, wherein we have done foolishly, and wherein we have sinned. Let her not be as one dead, of whom the flesh is half consumed when he cometh out of his mother's womb. And Moses cried unto the LORD, saying, Heal her now, O God, I beseech thee.

Secondly, envy not only grieves God, but it will eat at me. Miriam was smitten with leprosy—the disease that eats away at one's skin and causes a great stench to emanate from him. Envy does that too. When envy takes root in the soil of my soul, the fruit is stinky. James nails it when he says, "For where envy is, there is confusion and every evil work" (3:16).

Numbers 12:14, 15 (a)
And the LORD said unto Moses, If her father had but spit in her face, should she not be ashamed seven days? Let her be shut out from the camp seven days, and after that let her be received in again. And Miriam was shut out from the camp seven days . . .

Thirdly, envy pulls me away. Miriam was isolated in her leprous condition for a full week.

Envy does that. It causes me to close the door, to pull the shades, to isolate myself from those of whom I am envious.

Numbers 12:15 (b), 16
. . . and the people journeyed not till Miriam was brought in again. And afterward the people removed from Hazeroth, and pitched in the wilderness of Paran.

Finally, envy holds others back. The entire congregation was stuck for seven days, waiting for Miriam to be healed of her leprous, envious condition.

The Book of Romans says we are to rejoice with those who rejoice and weep with those who weep (12:15). Moses modeled this as he rejoiced for Eldad and Medad and wept for Miriam. We, on the other hand, know we're guilty of envy if there is anyone we know to whom, if they came to us and said, "I got promoted," or, "I made the team," we would outwardly say, "Great!" but inwardly say, "Why him and not me?"

Do I rejoice with those who rejoice? Moses did. Envy weeps over those who rejoice and rejoices over those who weep. Moses did just the opposite.

Numbers 12 is not only a practical chapter, but a prophetic chapter as well, as it points to, and is a picture of, Jesus and His older brothers, the Jews. You see, in Deuteronomy 18:18, the prophecy was given that a Prophet would be raised up, greater than Moses, but similar to Moses. Deuteronomy 18:18 is recognized by all as a Messianic prophecy. Thus, Moses is a type of Jesus.

"Moses was the meekest man in all the earth," Moses wrote.

"I am meek and lowly," Jesus declared in Matthew 11:29.

Just as Miriam and Aaron were older siblings to Moses, Jesus had a group of older brothers—the scribes and Pharisees of the religious establishment—who were filled with envy (Matthew 27:18).

Both Moses and Jesus took Gentile brides, for we Gentiles are the Bride of Christ (2 Corinthians 11:2).

When Miriam was struck with leprosy, Moses interceded for the very one who was envying him, accusing him, trying to take him down a peg or two. When Jesus was on the Cross, He asked forgiveness for the very men who were crucifying Him (Luke 23:34).

Miriam being a picture of the Jews, it is only logical that, due to the plague of leprosy, she would have been isolated for seven days—for Israel will be shut away not for seven days, but for seven years during the time of the Tribulation when horrendous plagues will fall upon her. Yet, just as Miriam did indeed rejoin the company of Israel on their way to the Promised Land, so after seven years of Tribulation, Israel will be shaken to the core, and, saved and restored, she, too, will journey to her eternal destiny (Romans 11:26).

The more I study the Word, the more amazed I am at how it lets us see the ultimate plan of the Father—that all things were created for, center around, and point to His Son.

The clearer I understand this prophetically, the more I realize practically that my life will make sense and my days will have meaning to the degree that I center them around Jesus.

13

Numbers 13:1–3
And the LORD spake unto Moses, saying, Send thou men, that they may search the land of Canaan, which I give unto the children of Israel: of every tribe of their fathers shall ye send a man, every one a ruler among them. And Moses by the commandment of the LORD sent them from the wilderness of Paran: all those men were heads of the children of Israel.

The heads of the twelve tribes were to go in and check out the Promised Land.

Numbers 13:4–15
And these were their names: of the tribe of Reuben, Shammua the son of Zaccur. Of the tribe of Simeon, Shaphat the son of Hori. Of the tribe of Judah, Caleb the son of Jephunneh. Of the tribe of Issachar, Igal the son of Joseph. Of the tribe of Ephraim, Oshea the son of Nun. Of the tribe of Benjamin, Palti the son of Raphu. Of the tribe of Zebulun, Gaddiel the son of Sodi. Of the tribe of Joseph, namely, of the tribe of Manasseh, Gaddi the son of Susi. Of the tribe of Dan, Ammiel the son of Gemalli. Of the tribe of Asher, Sethur the son of Michael. Of the tribe of Naphtali, Nahbi the son of Vophsi. Of the tribe of Gad, Geuel the son of Machi.

These men are the twelve spies who will cross the border into the Promised Land.

Numbers 13:16
These are the names of the men which Moses sent to spy out the land. And Moses called Oshea the son of Nun Jehoshua.

Oshea means "to save." *Jehoshua* means "Jehovah saves." *Joshua*, the contracted form, means "The Lord who saves."

Numbers 13:17–20
And Moses sent them to spy out the land of Canaan, and said unto them, Get you up this way southward, and go up into the mountain: and see the land, what it is; and the people that dwelleth therein, whether they be strong or weak, few or many; and what the land is that they dwell in, whether it be good or bad; and what cities they be that they dwell in, whether in tents, or in strong holds; and what the land is, whether it be fat or lean, whether there be wood therein, or not. And be ye of good courage, and bring of the fruit of the land. Now the time was the time of the first ripe grapes.

Watch out, Moses. Don't send in the spies. Just step out in faith and follow the command of the Lord who promised to give you the land of destiny.

I believe Moses is making a mistake at this moment when he sent in the spies.

"Wait," you say. "Wasn't it the Lord who told Moses to send men in to search out the land?"

Turn to the Book of Deuteronomy to see what really happened that day . . .

> And ye came near unto me every one of you, and said, We will send men before us, and they shall search us out the land, and bring us word again by what way we must go up, and into what cities we shall come. And the saying pleased me well: and I took twelve men of you, one of a tribe: and they turned and went up into the mountain, and came unto the valley of Eshcol, and searched it out.
>
> Deuteronomy 1:22–24

The people said, "Send spies to scope out the land to which we're headed."

"Sounds good to me," Moses said of the plan which originated in the hearts of the people.

So finally, God said, "If that's what you want to do, then that's the plan."

The same thing can happen to you and me. If we set our own agenda, if we demand our own way, God very likely will say, "Okay. If that's your plan, go ahead."

That's why it's the wise man or woman who increasingly prays, "Not my will but *Your* will be done. Here's how I see the situation, Lord, but I lay it before You. Please adjust it, modify it, correct it."

Numbers 13:21, 22 (a)
So they went up, and searched the land from the wilderness of Zin unto Rehob, as men come to Hamath. And they ascended by the south, and came unto Hebron; where Ahiman, Sheshai, and Talmai, the children of Anak, were . . .

The children of Anak, or Anakim, were giants, as we shall see, the size of Goliath. Most likely, they were at least 9′6″ and perhaps as tall as 11′2″.

Numbers 13:22 (b)
. . . (Now Hebron was built seven years before Zoan in Egypt.)

Although this phrase is in parentheses, it is wonderfully significant, for it obliterates the theories of the skeptics who question the veracity of the Scripture. You see, Zoan being the secret resort of the Pharaohs, the only people who knew about it were Pharaoh, his family, and his innermost circle of advisers. For many centuries, people read this and said, "Because there is no such place as Zoan, we cannot believe everything in Scripture"—until Zoan was uncovered by the archaeological spade.

Whoever wrote the Book of Numbers had to have inside information, had to be in the inner circle to know about Zoan. Moses grew up as the son of Pharaoh. No other Hebrew writer would have known this.

Numbers 13:23
And they came unto the brook of Eshcol, and cut down from thence a branch with one cluster of grapes, and they bare it between two upon a staff; and they brought of the pomegranates, and of the figs.

The grapes, pomegranates, and figs in the Promised Land were so big that two men were required to carry a single bunch of grapes back to the congregation.

Numbers 13:24, 25
The place was called the brook Eshcol, because of the cluster of grapes which the children of Israel cut down from thence. And they returned from searching of the land after forty days.

Forty is the number of judgment.

Numbers 13:26–29
And they went and came to Moses, and to Aaron, and to all the congregation of the children of Israel, unto the wilderness of Paran, to Kadesh; and brought back word unto them, and unto all the congregation, and shewed them the fruit of the land. And they told him, and said, We came unto the land whither thou sentest us, and surely it floweth with milk and honey; and this is the

fruit of it. Nevertheless the people be strong that dwell in the land, and the cities are walled, and very great: and moreover we saw the children of Anak there. The Amalekites dwell in the land of the south: and the Hittites, and the Jebusites, and the Amorites, dwell in the mountains: and the Canaanites dwell by the sea, and by the coast of Jordan.

The spies saw big grapes, but they also saw big men, and walled cities, and many nations with great military ability.

Numbers 13:30–33
And Caleb stilled the people before Moses, and said, Let us go up at once, and possess it; for we are well able to overcome it. But the men that went up with him said, We be not able to go up against the people; for they are stronger than we. And they brought up an evil report of the land which they had searched unto the children of Israel, saying, The land, through which we have gone to search it, is a land that eateth up the inhabitants thereof; and all the people that we saw in it are men of a great stature. And there we saw the giants, the sons of Anak, which come of the giants: and we were in our own sight as grasshoppers, and so we were in their sight.

Ten spies had an evil report. Two believed God. People can't name one of the ten spies—but all of us know the names of Joshua and Caleb. Here's a key to being forgotten in history, by your family, in the work of the kingdom: Murmur, be cynical, be a doubter, be skeptical, be a critic. Sit back and say, "This isn't right and that will never happen." On the other hand, the men, women, and congregations who leave an imprint on history are those who say, "We believe God will do great things."

- The ten spies saw the foes.
  Joshua and Caleb saw the fruit.
- The ten spies saw the giants.
  Joshua and Caleb saw God.
- The ten spies saw the walls and their faith crumbled.
  Joshua and Caleb had faith and knew the walls would crumble.

It's all a matter of perspective. We will have faith in that which we fear. The ten spies had faith in the giants because they feared them. But Joshua and Caleb feared God, and, therefore, had faith in Him.

I saw a nature movie years ago in which, seeing a mountain lion headed his way, a little bear cub stood on its back legs, raised its little paws, and let forth a high-pitched growl. The mountain lion immediately stopped in his tracks, turned around, and ran away, leaving the little bear cub thinking, This is great! Look what I did! *And then the camera panned back to show that standing behind the little bear was his Mama—a huge grizzly.*

We have a great big God standing with us who makes any giant seem like a grasshopper in comparison. The spies lifted up their eyes to the giants. Joshua and Caleb lifted them higher and saw the Father.

14

Numbers 14:1–3
And all the congregation lifted up their voice, and cried; and the people wept that night. And all the children of Israel murmured against Moses and against Aaron: and the whole congregation said unto them, Would God that we had died in the land of Egypt! or would God we had died in this wilderness! And wherefore hath the LORD brought us unto this land, to fall by the sword, that our wives and our children should be a prey? Were it not better for us to return into Egypt?

"We're going to die in the wilderness. We're going to get wiped out. These giants, these problems, these fortified cities, these various cultures are all too much for us to take on," cried the children of Israel. But the faithlessness of their plea was surpassed by the foolishness of their plan . . .

Numbers 14:4
And they said one to another, Let us make a captain, and let us return into Egypt.

"Let's overthrow Moses and find someone to lead us back into captivity."

Numbers 14:5
Then Moses and Aaron fell on their faces before all the assembly of the congregation of the children of Israel.

After hearing the murmuring, the criticism, the doubts, fears, and frustration of the people, Moses and Aaron did what you and I need to do: They fell on their faces. That was one of the secrets of Moses' greatness. Three million people wanted to overthrow him. And what did He do? He prayed.

Numbers 14:6–8
And Joshua the son of Nun, and Caleb the son of Jephunneh, which were of them that

searched the land, rent their clothes: And they spake unto all the company of the children of Israel, saying, The land, which we passed through to search it, is an exceeding good land. If the LORD delight in us, then he will bring us into this land, and give it us; a land which floweth with milk and honey.

Don't you love Joshua and Caleb? "I don't care what the lawyers say, the statistics say, the doctors say," they said. "God has said that we're to go into the land."

Numbers 14:9
Only rebel not ye against the LORD, neither fear ye the people of the land; for they are bread for us: their defence is departed from them, and the LORD is with us: fear them not.

What builds a body—a Fellowship, a marriage, a family? The bread of affliction. Joshua and Caleb knew this. "These giants are good for us," they said. "This is a great opportunity for us to grow."

Every once in a while you meet people like Joshua and Caleb. "This is great!" they say in tough times. "A wonderful opportunity!" What a radical perspective. What a wonderful way to live.

Numbers 14:10
But all the congregation bade stone them with stones. And the glory of the LORD appeared in the tabernacle of the congregation before all the children of Israel.

"You gotta face facts," the congregation protested. "We're outgunned, outmanned, outnumbered." And they wanted to stone Joshua and Caleb.

Numbers 14:11, 12
And the LORD said unto Moses, How long will this people provoke me? and how long will it be ere they believe me, for all the signs which I have shewed among them? I will smite them with the pestilence, and disinherit them, and will make of thee a greater nation and mightier than they.

"That's it," God said to Moses. "I'm going to destroy these people. Justice demands it. They murmur against Me continually. They have no faith in Me. I'll make a great nation of you instead."

Numbers 14:13–16
And Moses said unto the LORD, Then the Egyptians shall hear it, (for thou broughtest up this people in thy might from among them). And they will tell it to the inhabitants of this land: for they have heard that thou LORD art among this people, that thou LORD art seen face to face, and that thy cloud standeth over them, and that thou goest before them, by day time in a pillar of a cloud, and in a pillar of fire by night. Now if thou shalt kill all this people as one man, then the nations which have heard the fame of thee will speak, saying, Because the LORD was not able to bring this people into the land which he sware unto them, therefore he hath slain them in the wilderness.

"If You don't bring Your people into the Land of Promise," Moses said to God, "the Egyptians and other nations will accuse You of being unable to do what You promised, incapable of seeing them through."

Numbers 14:17–19
And now, I beseech thee, let the power of my Lord be great, according as thou hast spoken, saying, The LORD is longsuffering, and of great mercy, forgiving iniquity and transgression, and by no means clearing the guilty, visiting the iniquity of the fathers upon the children unto the third and fourth generation. Pardon, I beseech thee, the iniquity of this people according unto the greatness of thy mercy, and as thou hast forgiven this people, from Egypt even until now.

"You visit every generation," Moses continued, "giving them a chance to repent and change their ways. That's where Your greatness is."

Numbers 14:20
And the LORD said, I have pardoned according to thy word:

Although on first reading, it appears that God was upset until Moses said, "Calm down. Think it through, Lord,"—in reality, Moses was simply reflecting God's heart all along. You see, justice demanded that the people be punished for their rebelliousness and their lack of faith. Intercession, however, could bring about mercy.

That's why later on we'll see God saying, "I sought for an intercessor, a man to stand in the gap" (Ezekiel 22:30). God is looking for people who will intercede. Justice demands punishment. But intercession ushers in mercy. This makes me wonder how much more could be done in seeing people blessed who don't deserve to be if I would be a man like Moses, a man of intercession.

Who put this heart of intercession in Moses? God. God's justice and holiness demanded judgment. But God's compassion and grace put a heart of intercession into Moses to release mercy. God did the whole thing. And He continues to do so today. For example, when you're watching the news and a story comes on which tugs at your heart, it's the Spirit of God saying, "I want you to be an intercessor through which I can minister mercy."

Numbers 14:21–24 (a)
But as truly as I live, all the earth shall be filled with the glory of the LORD. Because all those men which have seen my glory, and my miracles, which I did in Egypt and in the wilderness, and have tempted me now these ten times, and have not hearkened to my voice; Surely they shall not see the land which I sware unto their fathers, neither shall any of them that provoked me see it: But my servant Caleb, because he had another spirit with him . . .

"God has not given us the spirit of fear, but of power, of love, and of a sound mind," Paul declared, (2 Timothy 1:7). The ten spies had the spirit of fear. Caleb, on the other hand, had the unbeatable combination of power, love, and a sound mind.

Numbers 14:24 (b), 25
. . . and hath followed me fully, him will I bring into the land whereinto he went; and his seed shall possess it. (Now the Amalekites and the Canaanites dwelt in the valley.) To morrow turn you, and get you into the wilderness by the way of the Red sea.

Caleb and Joshua will go in to the Promised Land. But not one other person of their generation would be allowed entrance.

Numbers 14:26–28
And the LORD spake unto Moses and unto Aaron, saying, How long shall I bear with this evil congregation, which murmur against me? I have heard the murmurings of the children of Israel, which they murmur against me. Say unto them, As truly as I live, saith the LORD, as ye have spoken in mine ears, so will I do to you:

"Would to God that we die in the wilderness," the children of Israel had repeatedly said (Numbers 14:2).

And, because life and death are in the power of the tongue (Proverbs 18:21), God said, "Okay. As you have spoken, so shall it be."

Faith and words go hand in hand, for out of the abundance of the heart, the mouth speaks (Matthew 12:34). That is why to be saved, we must believe in our heart as well as confess with our mouth (Romans 10:9, 10).

The longer I live, the more I realize that what I say has huge impact on the unseen world around me. I'm beginning to understand more and more that if I speak critically and cynically even only to my wife, the impact is sure to boomerang back on me. Conversely, if I speak words of faith, I open the door for the Lord to work miraculously.

Numbers 14:29–31
Your carcases shall fall in this wilderness; and all that were numbered of you, according to your whole number, from twenty years old and upward, which have murmured against me, doubtless ye shall not come into the land, concerning which I sware to make you dwell therein, save Caleb the son of Jephunneh, and Joshua the son of Nun. But your little ones, which ye said should be a prey, them will I bring in, and they shall know the land which ye have despised.

"If we go into the land, our wives and children will be destroyed," the Israelites had said (v. 3). Here we see that the ones they thought would be wiped out are the very ones God would bring in.

Numbers 14:32–34
But as for you, your carcases, they shall fall in this wilderness. And your children shall wander in the wilderness forty years, and bear your whoredoms, until your carcases be wasted in the wilderness. After the number of the days in which ye searched the land, even forty days, each day for a year, shall ye bear your iniquities, even forty years, and ye shall know my breach of promise.

The spies were in the land forty days. Therefore, for every day of fear, there was a year of wandering. This is what the Bible refers to as the law of sowing and reaping. In this regard, we have discovered that, although, when a person confesses his sin, he is pardoned immediately, the repercussions are nonetheless felt very definitely.

Some people say, "I have a hard time with a God who sentenced an entire generation to death simply because they demonstrated a lack of faith one day." But that's because they don't understand that God was justified not because they made one mistake on one day, but, according to Amos 5:25 and Acts 7, over a forty-year period of time, God's people didn't offer sacrifices to Him, nor keep the Passover commemoration. They took the tabernacle with them, but all the while they were intrigued by and involved with pagan gods.

Thus, God declared, "This generation must die in the wilderness and a new one will be raised up that will believe in Me, worship Me, have a heart for Me."

Numbers 14:35–38
I the LORD have said, I will surely do it unto all this evil congregation, that are gathered together against me: in this wilderness they shall be consumed, and there they shall die. And the men, which Moses sent to search the land, who returned, and made all the congregation to murmur against him, by bringing up a slander upon the land, even those men that did bring up the evil report upon the land, died by the plague before the LORD. But Joshua the son of Nun, and Caleb the son of Jephunneh, which were of the men that went to search the land, lived still.

Caleb and Joshua lived because holiness brings life whereas the wages of sin is death (Romans 6:23).

Numbers 14:39, 40
And Moses told these sayings unto all the children of Israel: and the people mourned greatly. And they rose up early in the morning, and gat them up into the top of the mountain, saying, Lo, we be here, and will go up unto the place which the LORD hath promised: for we have sinned.

"Here we go," the people said. "We realize we sinned. But now we're going to step out in faith and take the land."

Numbers 14:41–45
And Moses said, Wherefore now do ye transgress the commandment of the LORD? but it shall not prosper. Go not up, for the LORD is not among you; that ye be not smitten before your enemies. For the Amalekites and the Canaanites are there before you, and ye shall fall by the sword: because ye are turned away from the LORD, therefore the LORD will not be with you. But they presumed to go up unto the hill top: nevertheless the ark of the covenant of the LORD, and Moses, departed not out of the camp. Then the Amalekites came down, and the Canaanites which dwelt in that hill, and smote them, and discomfited them, even unto Hormah.

When God said, "Go," they wouldn't. And now they're saying, "We've learned our lesson. We're going to do it now." But God had already spoken. He had already told them they would wander forty years in the wilderness until the entire generation died.

There can be a presumption that looks like faith but in reality is folly. What's the difference between faith and presumption? Simply this: God's Word. Are you launching out because you're trying to prove your spiritual prowess, or because of some fantastic fantasy—or do you have God's Word on the matter? Faith comes by hearing and hearing by the Word of God (Romans 10:17). Therefore, it is the promise of God found in the Word of God upon which we are to stand.

15

In chapters 15 through 25, we see the sad saga of God's people wandering in the wilderness instead of marching into the Land of Promise. It's a sad section of Scripture in one way, but a tremendous warning to you and me today—for we must be people who choose to believe that God will do what He promised to do.

Numbers 15:1, 2 (a)
And the LORD spake unto Moses, saying, Speak unto the children of Israel, and say unto them, When ye be come into the land of your habitations . . .

Even after God said in chapter 14 that the whole generation was to die, even though He knew they wouldn't be obedient to Him, He reiterates His intention to bring His people into the Land when He doesn't say, "*If* you come into the land . . ." but "*when* you come into the land . . . ." And to the nineteen-year-olds, sixteen-year-olds, and eight-year-olds hearing this, it would be just as God declared—for although His people could delay His blessings, they could not destroy His purpose.

I can delay God's blessings in my life for forty minutes or forty hours, forty days, forty weeks, or even forty years. But I cannot delay His purpose . . .

> Having made known unto us the mystery of his will, according to his good pleasure which he hath purposed in himself: That in the dispensation of the fulness of times he might gather together in one all things in Christ, both which are in heaven, and which are on earth; even in him . . . Ephesians 1:9, 10

God's ultimate plan is that in the fullness of time, everything and everyone will be brought into unity in Christ, intimacy with Christ, and conformed to Christ. That is where life is going. Therefore, because God created everything to be brought together in Christ, focused on Christ, united by Christ, the degree to which I do that tomorrow will be the degree to which I will move in the same direction as all of creation. Conversely, the degree to which I do anything other than that is the degree to which I'll go against the flow of that which God has predetermined for all of creation.

It's so wonderful to relax in your inner tube in the center of the river. As you cruise along in the sun, it's refreshing and wonderful with some thrills along the way. If, on the other hand, you're trying to go upstream against the flow, it's miserable. You get tired and go nowhere.

Go with the flow of what God determined all of history to do. Be one with Christ; focus on Christ; live for Christ.

Numbers 15:2 (b)–13

. . . which I give unto you, And will make an offering by fire unto the LORD, a burnt offering, or a sacrifice in performing a vow, or in a freewill offering, or in your solemn feasts, to make a sweet savour unto the LORD, of the herd, or of the flock: Then shall he that offereth his offering unto the LORD bring a meat offering of a tenth deal of flour mingled with the fourth part of an hin of oil. And the fourth part of an hin of wine for a drink offering shalt thou prepare with the burnt offering or sacrifice, for one lamb. Or for a ram, thou shalt prepare for a meat offering two tenth deals of flour mingled with the third part of an hin of oil. And for a drink offering thou shalt offer the third part of an hin of wine, for a sweet savour unto the LORD. And when thou preparest a bullock for a burnt offering, or for a sacrifice in performing a vow, or peace offerings unto the LORD: Then shall he bring with a bullock a meat offering of three tenth deals of flour mingled with half an hin of oil. And thou shalt bring for a drink offering half an hin of wine, for an offering made by fire, of a sweet savour unto the LORD. Thus shall it be done for one bullock, or for one ram, or for a lamb, or a kid. According to the number that ye shall prepare, so shall ye do to every one according to their number. All that are born of the country shall do these things after this manner, in offering an offering made by fire, of a sweet savour unto the LORD.

Not only did God reestablish His intention, but He reiterated His instruction, adding specific details not previously given in Leviticus 2 when He first gave the instructions about this particular offering. This amazes me. I would think at this point, God would say, "Why should I give you further instruction about these offerings when you're only going to disobey Me anyway?" God, however, gives yet more details to His people, added instruction, further information, expanded understanding. He still treats them with dignity and respect.

And He does the same thing with you and me. Even when we are disobedient, out to lunch, off the wall, God still has a way of treating us with dignity. He'll still give information to me, understanding for me. Through conversations I have, books I read, radio broadcasts I hear, I still get input from Him. That's our God.

Numbers 15:14–16

And if a stranger sojourn with you, or whosoever be among you in your generations, and will offer an offering made by fire, of a sweet savour unto the LORD; as ye do, so he shall do. One ordinance shall be both for you of the congregation, and also for the stranger that sojourneth with you, an ordinance for ever in your generations: as ye are, so shall the stranger be before the LORD. One law and one manner shall be for you, and for the stranger that sojourneth with you.

Egyptians, Moabites, Edomites, or any other strangers were welcome to accompany the Israelites to the Promised Land. But there was to be one ordinance, one law for everyone, regardless of culture or nationality. And that one law was to be God's. Everyone was welcome, but everyone was to travel under God's authority.

Numbers 15:17–19

And the LORD spake unto Moses, saying, Speak unto the children of Israel, and say unto them, When ye come into the land whither I bring you, then it shall be, that, when ye eat of the bread of the land, ye shall offer up an heave offering unto the LORD.

Heave offerings were tossed into the air as a way of saying, "God, this is for You."

Numbers 15:20, 21

Ye shall offer up a cake of the first of your dough for an heave offering: as ye do the heave offering of the threshingfloor, so shall ye heave it. Of the first of your dough ye

shall give unto the LORD an heave offering in your generations.

When they reached the Land of Promise, the children of Israel were to offer to their Lord the first of their dough.

"Give us this day our daily bread," we pray—as we ought. "Lord, You know I need bread. Bills are piling up."

"I'll make you some bread," the Lord answers. "Just give Me the dough."

Why does your money disappear through the holes in your pockets? "Because you've ignored My house," the Lord answers (Haggai 1:6). "You can pray all you want, but if you do what I tell you, then you can watch and see how I bless you" (Malachi 3:10).

Numbers 15:22–28
And if ye have erred, and not observed all these commandments, which the LORD hath spoken unto Moses, even all that the LORD hath commanded you by the hand of Moses, from the day that the LORD commanded Moses, and henceforward among your generations; then it shall be, if ought be committed by ignorance without the knowledge of the congregation, that all the congregation shall offer one young bullock for a burnt offering, for a sweet savour unto the LORD, with his meat offering, and his drink offering, according to the manner, and one kid of the goats for a sin offering. And the priest shall make an atonement for all the congregation of the children of Israel, and it shall be forgiven them; for it is ignorance: and they shall bring their offering, a sacrifice made by fire unto the LORD, and their sin offering before the LORD, for their ignorance: And it shall be forgiven all the congregation of the children of Israel, and the stranger that sojourneth among them; seeing all the people were in ignorance. And if any soul sin through ignorance, then he shall bring a she goat of the first year for a sin offering. And the priest shall make an atonement for the soul that sinneth ignorantly, when he sinneth by ignorance before the LORD, to make an atonement for him; and it shall be forgiven him.

Through the offering of a bull as a burnt offering and a goat as a sin offering, provision was made for mistakes, for failing to keep the commandments God had so carefully, so painstakingly given His people. And the same holds true for us. The sins we commit ignorantly or in stupidity are paid for, washed away completely by the sacrifice of the Burnt Offering who took the heat on the altar of Calvary, by the Sin Offering who shed His blood for you and me.

Numbers 15:29
Ye shall have one law for him that sinneth through ignorance, both for him that is born among the children of Israel, and for the stranger that sojourneth among them.

Regardless of one's background, psychological make-up, or culture, there are no excuses for sin. Although this flies in the face of today's conventional wisdom, sin always requires an offering.

Numbers 15:30
But the soul that doeth ought presumptuously, whether he be born in the land, or a stranger, the same reproacheth the LORD; and that soul shall be cut off from among his people.

Be they Moabite or Israelite, whoever presumptuously, intentionally sinned was to be cut off, excommunicated, isolated. Why? Read on . . .

Numbers 15:31
Because he hath despised the word of the LORD, and hath broken his commandment, that soul shall utterly be cut off; his iniquity shall be upon him.

The Hebrew word translated "presumptuously" implies that done with a high hand. What does it mean to sin with a high hand? Turn to Exodus 14 . . .

The Israelites had just been set free from bondage in Egypt. And when they left, verse 8 tells us they left with a high hand, as if to say, "So long, Pharaoh. We're outta here!"

The sin which is unforgivable, unpardonable is not committed by the person struggling with an issue, but by the one who with a "high hand" shakes his fist at God, saying, "I want nothing to do with You. I don't care what You say. Goodbye." And if a person shakes his fist at God day after week after month after year, God won't force him to stay in His kingdom. If a person wants to sin with a high hand, God eventually lets him go (Matthew 12:31).

Numbers 15:32–36
And while the children of Israel were in the wilderness, they found a man that gathered sticks upon the sabbath day. And they that found him gathering sticks brought him unto Moses and Aaron, and unto all the congregation. And they put him in ward, be-

cause it was not declared what should be done to him. And the LORD said unto Moses, The man shall be surely put to death: all the congregation shall stone him with stones without the camp. And all the congregation brought him without the camp, and stoned him with stones, and he died; as the LORD commanded Moses.

We come to the story of a man who was eventually stoned for thinking he could add to what God said He would do.

For topical study of Numbers 15:32–36, see "Stick with Grace" below.

Numbers 15:37–41
And the LORD spake unto Moses, saying, Speak unto the children of Israel, and bid them that they make them fringes in the borders of their garments throughout their generations, and that they put upon the fringe of the borders a ribband of blue: And it shall be unto you for a fringe, that ye may look upon it, and remember all the commandments of the LORD, and do them; and that ye seek not after your own heart and your own eyes, after which ye use to go a whoring: That ye may remember, and do all my commandments, and be holy unto your God. I am the LORD your God, which brought you out of the land of Egypt, to be your God: I am the LORD your God.

Any Israelite over the age of twenty would not enter the Promised Land because, although there is forgiveness of sin, there are also repercussions; although God forgives and forgets, the scars remain. Such is the message of Numbers 15, the first of ten chapters which will chronicle God's dealings with a group of people who had not only failed miserably, but who would continue to do so over the next fifty years.

And yet at the end of this chapter, God says this: "Here's what will make the wilderness wandering which you've brought upon yourselves bearable: Around your garments make a border of blue." Blue in Scripture is the color of heaven. Therefore, God was essentially saying, "Never forget that you're on your way to heaven."

"Let not your heart be troubled," Jesus would echo centuries later, "Believe in God, believe also in Me. In My Father's house are many mansions" (John 14:1, 2). My heart can be troubled. So can yours. But because Jesus will never ask us to do that which He doesn't empower us to do, I don't have to let my heart be troubled. What's the key? heaven—to think about heaven, to be focused on heaven, to be constantly aware that heaven is close at hand. The children of Israel were to have borders of blue on their hems so that when they looked down at their feet as they trudged through the wilderness, they would see a dusty border of blue, reminding them of their higher calling, their grand destination.

The same is true today. When I get dressed each morning until the time I undress each night, I am to see the border of blue. That is, I'm to remember that I'm headed for heaven—where all those things I wish I could redo, where all the opportunities I missed and mistakes I made, will be set right.

If you remove the border of blue from your garments, if you remove heaven from the equation, you'll be depressed in the wilderness, for the key to being happy and joyful on earth is to live for heaven.

STICK WITH GRACE

A Topical Study of NUMBERS 15:32–36

"Sticks and stones may break my bones, but names will never hurt me." While it's true that names can't do physical damage, it's equally true that sticks can get one stoned—as seen in the passage before us . . .

When the elders of the congregation asked the Lord what should be done with a man who gathered sticks on the Sabbath, the Lord said, "Kill him."

"What?" we say. "Isn't that a bit harsh? What's going on?"

I believe the passage before us shows us that God is deadly serious about the sanctity of the Sabbath for some very important reasons . . .

Physical Consideration

As our Creator and Designer, God knows the way we will function most successfully and effectively, most efficiently and fruitfully. That is why He said we are to remember the Sabbath Day and keep it holy (Exodus 20:8)—that one day in seven is set aside for relaxation, refreshment, and renewal. Because we are indeed fearfully and wonderfully made (Psalm 139:14), our Manufacturer, our Father, our Lord gave us some instructions about the way life works. Therefore, it should be no surprise that doctors have recently discovered that, at rest, our heart beats faster in the evening than it does in the morning for six consecutive days. But on the seventh day, it beats faster in the morning than it does in the evening—suggesting that our bodies are energized for six days and run on a different cycle on the seventh. In his excellent book, *Fearfully And Wonderfully Made,* Dr. Paul Brand elucidates the physiological ways the human body operates on a cycle which requires one day in seven to be refreshed and renewed.

It makes sense to follow the Manufacturer's instructions. The owner of a new car who says, "Those guys at the dealership don't know what they're talking about. I know better. I'll just let my car run and wait until 300,000 miles to change the oil," will have problems. Friction will build up in the engine; the viscosity of the oil will break down—and eventually there will be a blow-up. The same thing will happen to those who say, "I don't need to change pace every seven days. Other people might, but not me. I'm a can-do kind of guy."

I believe stress, nervous conditions, depression, and ulcers can be the result of violating the simple, practical instruction of our Manufacturer to kick back, slow down, and refocus one day in seven.

Prophetic Illustration

The Sabbath Day was not to be violated even by an activity as simple as picking up sticks because, as with all Old Testament regulations, ordinances, and holy days, it is a prophetic picture, a portrait, an illustration of One who was to come (Colossians 2:16, 17). Jesus Christ is our Sabbath (Matthew 11:28). Because the work He accomplished on the Cross is complete, Jesus is our rest.

> *There remaineth therefore a rest to the people of God. For he that is entered into his rest, he also hath ceased from his own works, as God did from his. Let us labour therefore to enter into that rest, lest any man fall after the same example of unbelief.* Hebrews 4:9–11

Everything in me wants to work to earn God's favor, to merit God's blessings, to curry something from Him through passion in prayer, discipline in Bible study, faithfulness in giving. But the author of the Book of Hebrews says, "Don't do that." Rather, we are to labor simply to rest.

> "What must we do to do the works of God?" they asked Jesus, no doubt expecting Him to give them a list concerning the keeping of holy days, the giving of offerings.
>
> "This is the singular work of God," He said instead, "that you believe on Him whom the Father hath sent" (John 6:29).

We look for lists of dos and don'ts. Jesus, however, simply draws our attention to Himself.

Practical Application

> *Six days shall work be done, but on the seventh day there shall be to you an holy day, a sabbath of rest to the Lord: whosoever doeth work therein shall be put to death. Ye shall kindle no fire throughout your habitations upon the sabbath day.* Exodus 35:2, 3

For gathering sticks to kindle a fire, the man in our text was put to death. Working on the Sabbath killed him physically just as it will kill us spiritually. You see, I can say, "I realize Jesus died for my sins, that He paid the price, that He is my Rest. But you know what? I can stoke things up a bit. I can get things hotter by my own efforts. So I'm going to gather sticks. I'm going to pray four minutes every day. I'm going to read my Bible at least once a month." And if I do that, I can think I'm pretty hot. But, like any fire, the fire I've kindled demands more. So I find myself saying, "I better read a chapter a week and pray an hour a day," which then becomes, "a chapter and two hours of prayer every day," and pretty soon, "fifteen chapters and six hours of prayer a day"—until finally, I say, "I can't do this anymore. I can't follow through with these obligations and commitments. And now I'm so burned out, I'm going to forget the whole thing."

That's what legalism does. That's what this man in our text was doing. He should have been resting, enjoying the Sabbath, but instead he gathered wood to stoke the fire. And he died in the process because legalism always kills (2 Corinthians 3:6). That's why the Christian life is all about grace. It's not about the sticks I gather or the fire I ignite. It's all about what Jesus did not with sticks but on two beams of wood which formed the Cross of Calvary.

"It is finished," He said.

And so it is.

The person who finally gets it and says, "I'm going to learn to receive grace graciously. I'm going to rest. Instead of trying to impress God, I'm going to enjoy Him," is the one who is truly blessed. Our enemy would have us believe that our Father is a stern God who overreacts in rage to a man innocently picking up sticks—when, in fact, He is a Father who wants us to rest in Him because He is a God of immeasurable grace.

16

Numbers 16:1 (a)
Now Korah, the son of Izhar . . .

Izhar was the brother of Amram. This means Korah and Moses were cousins.

Numbers 16:1 (b), 2
. . . the son of Kohath, the son of Levi, and Dathan and Abiram, the sons of Eliab, and On, the son of Peleth, sons of Reuben, took men: And they rose up before Moses, with certain of the children of Israel, two hundred and fifty princes of the assembly, famous in the congregation, men of renown:

Accompanied by 250 of the most prominent men of the congregation, Korah, Dathan, and Abiram sought an audience with Moses.

Numbers 16:3 (a)
And they gathered themselves together against Moses and against Aaron, and said unto them, Ye take too much upon you, seeing all the congregation are holy, every one of them, and the LORD is among them . . .

The flavor of this passage in Hebrew is as follows: "You have ruled too much, too long. You've had your turn, your time. We're all holy. We all have something to offer. Who do you think you are?"

Numbers 16:3 (b)
. . . wherefore then lift ye up yourselves above the congregation of the LORD?

Accusing Moses of lifting himself above the congregation is groundless particularly in light of his reluctance to accept the role of leader in the first place (Exodus 3:11). As was the case in chapter 12, the real, though unspoken, issue was envy—this time, however directed *toward* Aaron instead of raised *by* him.

Numbers 16:4
And when Moses heard it, he fell upon his face:

Man of humility that he was, instead of getting in Korah's face, Moses fell on his own.

Numbers 16:5 (a)
And he spake unto Korah . . .

Moses spoke unto Korah *after* he fell on his face before the Lord. This is the way a leader, a parent, a boss ought to move—falling on his face before the Lord before confronting people.

Numbers 16:5 (b)–7
. . . and unto all his company, saying, Even to morrow the LORD will shew who are his, and who is holy; and will cause him to come near unto him: even him whom he hath chosen will he cause to come near unto him. This do; Take you censers, Korah, and all his company; And put fire therein, and put incense in them before the LORD to morrow: and it shall be that the man whom the LORD doth choose, he shall be holy: ye take too much upon you, ye sons of Levi.

After falling on his face before the Lord, Moses spoke with utmost humility and yet with the clarity of honesty when he said, "Tomorrow we'll bring our censers before the Lord and see who He chooses."

Numbers 16:8–10
And Moses said unto Korah, Hear, I pray you, ye sons of Levi: Seemeth it but a small thing unto you, that the God of Israel hath separated you from the congregation of Israel, to bring you near to himself to do the service of the tabernacle of the LORD, and to stand before the congregation to minister unto them? And he hath brought thee near to him, and all thy brethren the sons of Levi with thee: and seek ye the priesthood also?

"Why can't you just enjoy and celebrate where God has placed you?" Moses asked Korah. "Why must there be something else, something more? Why can't you be content with the kindness and grace God has shown to you? You men have a role to play—to stand before the congregation and minister to them. Why do you want to take on more?"

Numbers 16:11 (a)
For which cause both thou and all thy company are gathered together against the LORD . . .

"In not accepting where He's placed you, you're actually coming against the Lord," Moses continued.

Numbers 16:11 (b)
. . . and what is Aaron, that ye murmur against him?

Here, Moses magnanimously defends Aaron not very many days after Aaron himself had challenged his authority.

Numbers 16:12, 13
And Moses sent to call Dathan and Abiram, the sons of Eliab: which said, We will not come up: Is it a small thing that thou hast brought us up out of a land that floweth with milk and honey, to kill us in the wilderness, except thou make thyself altogether a prince over us?

Rebellion never has its root in principle. Rebellion has its root in pride. And because of this, the rebellious person doesn't see things right. His perspective is entirely wrong—as seen in Dathan's and Abiram's reference to the land in which they had been beaten for four hundred years as a land of milk and honey.

Numbers 16:14, 15 (a)
Moreover thou hast not brought us into a land that floweth with milk and honey, or given us inheritance of fields and vineyards: wilt thou put out the eyes of these men? we will not come up. And Moses was very wroth . . .

When God said He would make of Moses a new nation, Moses stood in the gap and interceded for the very people whose accusations were so far-fetched and off-base that they would drive even the meekest man on the face of the earth to become "very wroth."

Numbers 16:15 (b)–17
. . . and said unto the LORD, Respect not thou their offering: I have not taken one ass from them, neither have I hurt one of them. And Moses said unto Korah, Be thou and all thy company before the LORD, thou, and they, and Aaron, to morrow: And take every man his censer, and put incense in them, and bring ye before the LORD every man his censer, two hundred and fifty censers; thou also, and Aaron, each of you his censer.

In addition to being the meekest man on the face of the earth, Moses surely must have been one of the wisest—for rather than dealing in anger with this rebellion, he left it in the hands of the Lord.

Numbers 16:18–22
And they took every man his censer, and put fire in them, and laid incense thereon, and stood in the door of the tabernacle of the congregation with Moses and Aaron. And Korah gathered all the congregation against them unto the door of the tabernacle of the congregation: and the glory of the LORD appeared unto all the congregation. And the LORD spake unto Moses and unto Aaron, saying, Separate yourselves from among this congregation, that I may consume them in a moment. And they fell upon their faces, and said, O God, the God of the spirits of all flesh, shall one man sin, and wilt thou be wroth with all the congregation?

That Korah, Dathan, Abiram, and two hundred and fifty leaders came to the tabernacle with censers in hand indicates that they thought they had a case, that they thought they would be vindicated, that they thought God would justify their rebellion.

As I look back over my life, I am amazed by the times I thought I was right only to find out how wrong I was. "We all see through a glass darkly," Paul said (1 Corinthians 13:12)—no doubt understanding this better than anyone. "I know this is the right thing to do," he no doubt said as he dragged Christians from their homes believing they were ruining Judaism and polluting the people of God. What a shock it must have been when, on his way to Damascus one day to imprison more believers, he was knocked to the ground and in that moment realized he of the giant intellect and the spiritual passion had been absolutely, completely, one hundred percent wrong (Acts 9).

Korah, Dathan, and Abiram thought they were right, but what they failed to factor in to the equation was God's sovereignty. God's on the throne. God's in control. Therefore, it's not up to us to pull people down or prop people up. Sometimes I mistakenly think, "I need to straighten this guy out or pull that group down because if it's gonna be, it's up to me."

God, however, says, "Promotion does not come from the east, the west, or the south. *I* am the Lord who raises up one and puts down the other" (Psalm 75:6, 7).

It's a great day when a person finally realizes that because God is on the throne and is in control, he can simply say, "Lord, You're the One who will raise up one and put down another—be it the boss of my company or the leaders of our country. Therefore, I'm going to be submitted to You as I submit to those in authority over me."

We can't learn to be humble without being humiliated, to be forgiving without being wronged, to be sweet without bitter experiences. Therefore God uses people and situations in our lives to allow us to experience these things personally rather than just to propound them intellectually.

Numbers 16:23–26
And the LORD spake unto Moses, saying, Speak unto the congregation, saying, Get you up from about the tabernacle of Korah, Dathan, and Abiram. And Moses rose up and went unto Dathan and Abiram; and the elders of Israel followed him. And he spake unto the congregation, saying, Depart, I pray you, from the tents of these wicked men, and touch nothing of theirs, lest ye be consumed in all their sins.

A warning was issued for people to keep distance from those with the spirit of rebellion—an equally important message today.

Numbers 16:27–29
So they gat up from the tabernacle of Korah, Dathan, and Abiram, on every side: and Dathan and Abiram came out, and stood in the door of their tents, and their wives, and their sons, and their little children. And Moses said, Hereby ye shall know that the LORD hath sent me to do all these works; for I have not done them of mine own mind. If these men die the common death of all men, or if they be visited after the visitation of all men; then the LORD hath not sent me.

"If Korah, Dathan, and Abiram live to a ripe old age and die of natural causes, God has not sent me," Moses declared.

Numbers 16:30
But if the LORD make a new thing, and the earth open her mouth, and swallow them up, with all that appertain unto them, and they go down quick into the pit; then ye shall understand that these men have provoked the LORD.

"But if the earth swallows them," Moses continued, "you'll know they were wrong."

When I try to make a case against those in positions of authority over me, like Korah, Dathan, and Abiram, I always end up in the pit of despair and despondency.

Numbers 16:31–34
And it came to pass, as he had made an end of speaking all these words, that the ground clave asunder that was under them: And the earth opened her mouth, and swallowed them up, and their houses, and all the men that appertained unto Korah, and all their goods. They, and all that appertained to them, went down alive into the pit, and the earth closed upon them: and they perished from among the congregation. And all Israel that were round about them fled at the cry of them: for they said, Lest the earth swallow us up also.

The earth opened up—and the rebellious men, along with their possessions were all wiped out. But it would get even worse . . .

Numbers 16:35
And there came out a fire from the LORD, and consumed the two hundred and fifty men that offered incense.

God "fired" these men who were once men of renown, who once had a prominent role to play. But it would get worse still . . .

Numbers 16:36–38
And the LORD spake unto Moses, saying, Speak unto Eleazar the son of Aaron the priest, that he take up the censers out of the burning, and scatter thou the fire yonder; for they are hallowed. The censers of these sinners against their own souls, let them make them broad plates for a covering of the altar: for they offered them before the LORD, therefore they are hallowed: and they shall be a sign unto the children of Israel.

Moses was to make a brass covering for the altar from the censers of the rebellious company as a reminder to future generations of the cost of rebellion.

Numbers 16:39, 40
And Eleazar the priest took the brasen censers, wherewith they that were burnt had offered; and they were made broad plates for a covering of the altar: To be a memorial unto the children of Israel, that no stranger, which is not of the seed of Aaron, come near to offer incense before the LORD; that he be not as Korah, and as his company: as the LORD said to him by the hand of Moses.

According to Exodus 25:38, the censers used by the priests were to be made of gold. Why, then, were the censers seen here made of brass? Evidently because they didn't have any gold. Why? Most likely because the gold which should have been used for the censers had instead been used to make the golden calf (Exodus 32:4).

Numbers 16:41
But on the morrow all the congregation of the children of Israel murmured against Moses and against Aaron, saying, Ye have killed the people of the LORD.

Isn't this amazing? After seeing the earth open up and fire come down, the people have the audacity to murmur.

Numbers 16:42–45 (a)
And it came to pass, when the congregation was gathered against Moses and against Aaron, that they looked toward the tabernacle of the congregation: and, behold, the cloud covered it, and the glory of the LORD appeared. And Moses and Aaron came before the tabernacle of the congregation. And the LORD spake unto Moses, saying, Get you up from among this congregation, that I may consume them as in a moment . . .

"That's it," the Lord said to Moses. "I've had it with these people."

Numbers 16:45 (b)
. . . And they fell upon their faces.

Yet again we see Moses and Aaron on their faces before the Lord. We're sure to recognize Moses in heaven—he'll be the one with the flat nose!

Numbers 16:46, 47 (a)
And Moses said unto Aaron, Take a censer, and put fire therein from off the altar, and put on incense, and go quickly unto the congregation, and make an atonement for them: for there is wrath gone out from the LORD; the plague is begun. And Aaron took as Moses commanded, and ran into the midst of the congregation . . .

Could it be that Aaron ran because he knew what it was like to get mixed up, to become rebellious, to be full of envy? Could it be that Aaron has the heart of an intercessor because of his own weaknesses, his own history?

Numbers 16:47 (b), 48
. . . and, behold, the plague was begun among the people: and he put on incense, and made an atonement for the people. And he stood between the dead and the living; and the plague was stayed.

Aaron, the high priest, is a picture of our High Priest, Jesus Christ, who stands between the dead and the living, who intercedes for you and me, who stops the plague of sin which would consume us and ultimately bring us into the hell fire of damnation. We are rebellious. We are those who murmur. We are those who have constantly strayed away—and yet day after day, Jesus ever lives to make intercession for us, to be an Advocate on behalf of us (Hebrews 7:25).

Numbers 16:49
Now they that died in the plague were fourteen thousand and seven hundred, beside them that died about the matter of Korah.

Who were these 14,700? They were the ones who were hanging around. They're the ones who paid the price in this plague. And their fate causes me to say, "I don't want to even be in the neighborhood, to be an observer of rebellion. Rebelliousness causes people to get burned up, to lose what they once had or what they could have been. It causes people to fade into oblivion. And I want nothing to do with that."

Numbers 16:50
And Aaron returned unto Moses unto the door of the tabernacle of the congregation: and the plague was stayed.

Like Korah and company, we think we know who should be in power. In reality, however, we know oh, so little—as verified by the following newspaper article . . .

Suppose tomorrow is election day. It's time to elect a new world leader—and your vote counts. Here are the choices: Candidate A consults with astrologers. He's had two mistresses, chain smokes and drinks eight to ten martinis a day. Candidate B was kicked out of office twice, sleeps until noon, used opium in college, and drinks a quart of brandy every evening. Candidate C is a decorated war hero, a vegetarian, is monogamous, doesn't smoke, and drinks only an occasional beer. Candidate A was FDR, Candidate B was Winston Churchill. Candidate C was Adolf Hitler.

If you're not happy with your boss, your spouse, or your parents, you'll not be happy with anyone because God in His sovereignty allowed the very situation in which you find yourself presently.

May we learn from the example of Korah.

May we walk humbly.

17

Following the rebellion of Korah, Dathan and Abiram, here in chapter 17, we see God give a tool to His people by which they might be protected from future deception . . .

Numbers 17:1–5
And the LORD spake unto Moses, saying, Speak unto the children of Israel, and take of every one of them a rod according to the house of their fathers, of all their princes

according to the house of their fathers twelve rods: write thou every man's name upon his rod. And thou shalt write Aaron's name upon the rod of Levi: for one rod shall be for the head of the house of their fathers. And thou shalt lay them up in the tabernacle of the congregation before the testimony, where I will meet with you. And it shall come to pass, that the man's rod, whom I shall choose, shall blossom: and I will make to cease from me the murmurings of the children of Israel, whereby they murmur against you.

That God would use the rod as a validation for true ministry is only fitting, for in Isaiah 11:1, 2, we see a rod come forth from the stem of Jesse, from the lineage of David, upon whom the Spirit of the Lord would rest, and in whom would be the spirit of wisdom and understanding, the spirit of counsel and might, the spirit of knowledge and of the fear of the Lord. The rod, of course, speaks of Jesus.

Numbers 17:6–8 (a)
And Moses spake unto the children of Israel, and every one of their princes gave him a rod apiece, for each prince one, according to their fathers' houses, even twelve rods: and the rod of Aaron was among their rods. And Moses laid up the rods before the LORD in the tabernacle of witness. And it came to pass, that on the morrow Moses went into the tabernacle of witness; and, behold, the rod of Aaron for the house of Levi was budded, and brought forth buds, and bloomed blossoms . . .

How were the children of Israel to know which leader spoke with true authority? By the blossoming of the rod.

How do we know Jesus is the One to whom we should be linked, after whom we should follow? By His blossoming, by His life . . .

"Give us a sign," they said to Jesus.

"One sign I'll give you," He answered. "The sign of Jonah. As Jonah was in the belly of the whale, so shall the Son of Man be in the grave" (Matthew 12:40).

The one sign that proves Jesus is the One who has all authority is His resurrection from the grave, His "blossoming" back to life.

Numbers 17:8 (b)–10
. . . and yielded almonds. And Moses brought out all the rods from before the LORD unto all the children of Israel: and they looked, and took every man his rod. And the LORD said unto Moses, Bring Aaron's rod again before the testimony, to be kept for a token against the rebels; and thou shalt quite take away their murmurings from me, that they die not.

Not only did Aaron's rod blossom, but it yielded fruit. No one before Jesus, no one since Him has borne the fruit of the Spirit—of love characterized by joy, peace, and longsuffering, by gentleness, goodness, and faith, by meekness and temperance like He did.

Secondarily, we can recognize those to whom we are to be linked, those to whom we are to listen, those to whom we are to submit by the presence of the fruit of the Spirit in their lives.

Mom and Dad, if you're wishing you had more impact on your teenage daughter or junior-high grandson, the key is not to beat them with the rod, but to let them see your passion for God, to let them see the fruit of the Spirit in your life. Kids and adults alike can sense if a person is walking with the Lord and full of the Spirit because such a life manifests itself in love.

When you have decisions to make about people who claim to have authority, remember Numbers 17 and look for the budding, the blossoming, the fruit.

Numbers 17:11–13
And Moses did so: as the LORD commanded him, so did he. And the children of Israel spake unto Moses, saying, Behold, we die, we perish, we all perish. Whosoever cometh any thing near unto the tabernacle of the LORD shall die: shall we be consumed with dying?

The children of Israel had reason to say this. After all, in chapter 16, they saw the earth swallow Korah, Dathan, and Abiram as well as their families, followed by a fire which consumed two hundred and fifty of their leaders, and a plague which killed an additional 14,700—all in the vicinity of the tabernacle (vv. 19 and 42). No wonder they felt the tabernacle was a dangerous place to be.

We sometimes think church is a dangerous place to be. We can feel like we're "swallowed up" in the pit of depression as we're made aware of our rebellious natures. We can find ourselves on the "hot seat" as we hear the Word speak to specific struggles in our lives. Or we can feel "plagued" as the sin is addressed which seems to dominate us. As a result, all too often, we hear ourselves say, "Life is tough enough. Every time I come to church, it seems I'm cut up or cut down. I don't need this."

This wouldn't surprise us if we understood that

opening the Scriptures is very dangerous. Why? Because Hebrews 4:12 says the Word of God is living and powerful, sharper than any two-edged sword. No wonder, then, that we feel cut up. The Word divides the soul and the spirit—my intellect and emotions from my true self that will live forever. It divides my joints and marrow—an act that, if done physically, would immobilize and kill me. It divides the thoughts and intents of my heart, as it gets to the true heart of any given matter.

No wonder when I hear or read the Word I can feel pierced and poked, sliced and diced. That's what the Word does, not only to those who hear it, but those who speak it . . .

> *Mistakenly thinking Jeremiah was yelling at them, was coming down on them, lacked understanding of them, the people captured him and threw him into a pit. "That's it," Jeremiah said. "I quit. I'm tired of the pit. Enough is enough. I will speak no more in the name of the Lord"—until the Word was like fire in his bones and he couldn't keep quiet (Jeremiah 20:9).*

We've all felt that way. When you share the Word, you can be convicted by the very things you share. Because the Word is a *two*-edged sword, it cuts both ways. Yes, it comforts, inspires, delights. But because it's a two-edged sword, it also pierces and penetrates, prods and provokes.

"Shall we be consumed in dying?" the children of Israel asked.

The answer is "Yes."

Jesus said, "If any man come after Me, let him deny himself, take up his cross, die daily, and follow Me" (Luke 9:23).

"I die daily," said Paul (1 Corinthians 15:31).

In other words, there is no real Spirit-filled living without there being a radical flesh-dying. The flesh must die before the Spirit can live. And because my flesh seems to reawaken every day, like Paul, I must die daily.

How?

The only way I know to deal with the flesh is with the sword of the Spirit. That's why I need to allow the Word to kill my flesh day after day. And as it does, like the resurrected Jesus, I find I am able to walk through walls and locked doors (John 20:26).

"My son won't talk to me," a father sighs.

"My daughter has shut me out," a mother cries.

"My wife has locked the door," says a weary husband.

"He's built a wall," says the devastated wife.

I suggest that when I allow my flesh to be sliced and diced by the piercing and poking of the Word every day, although it's painful in some ways, humbling and difficult in others, the end result is that I have entry into places I would never have had otherwise. High walls, locked doors, pulled shades begin to open as my critical, cynical, harsh nature softens, giving me access into places which were previously closed.

I'm convinced it's our own flesh that keeps us out of places we long to enter. There's no resurrection and life without crucifixion and death. There's no Easter Sunday without Good Friday. There's no way to enter in without first being broken down. It's a process that must happen daily, continually. And the way it happens is through the Word of God very simply, very powerfully, very definitely.

Thomas was a doubter; others were cynical; many were skeptics. But when they saw Jesus—His flesh broken, beaten, buried, and resurrected—they realized something incredible had transpired.

Die daily, gang. It's the way you'll be free. Let the Word do its work in your life and you will see doors open for you and people impacted by you.

"Shall we all utterly die?"

I hope so!

18 **Numbers 18:1**
And the LORD said unto Aaron, Thou and thy sons and thy father's house with thee shall bear the iniquity of the sanctuary: and thou and thy sons with thee shall bear the iniquity of your priesthood.

The word "and" connects this passage to the previous chapter. God's words in one of only two times He would speak directly to Aaron must have stunned him, for after having his authority validated by God through the miraculous blossoming and budding of his rod, God essentially says to Aaron, "I am now holding you responsible for the iniquity which happens in the ministry which I've entrusted to your care."

The Lord would say to you, "If there is any person in your life who, like Korah, is in the pits, you have no reason to feel smug, for you are responsible to a certain degree. You must bear responsibility. Is there something else you could have done? Could you have prayed more effectively? Could you have shown more compassion?"

Am I my brother's keeper? If, like Aaron, I am involved in ministry to any degree, the answer is "Yes."

Numbers 18:2 (a)
And thy brethren also of the tribe of Levi, the tribe of thy father, bring thou with thee, that they may be joined unto thee and minister unto thee . . .

After a word of caution, comes a word of encouragement. The tribe of Levi were the ones who were to practically serve, assist, and support Aaron and his sons. Thus, God gave Aaron an entire tribe to assist him in the work he was called to do.

Numbers 18:2 (b)
. . . but thou and thy sons with thee shall minister before the tabernacle of witness.

Although the tribe of Levi would assist him, only Aaron and his sons were to perform the sacred duties.

Numbers 18:3
And they shall keep thy charge, and the charge of all the tabernacle: only they shall not come nigh the vessels of the sanctuary and the altar, that neither they, nor ye also, die.

Aaron was to make sure the Levites understood and remained in their calling—for if they went beyond it, they would die. It is important for us not to arrogantly attempt to go beyond the gifts and calling the Lord has given us—to do everything we're called to do, yet not step ahead of the Lord. Many people die in ministry. That is, they just burn out or give up because they step into areas they aren't called to step into, take on responsibilities they aren't called to fulfill. And ministry becomes a burden rather than a blessing.

Numbers 18:4
And they shall be joined unto thee, and keep the charge of the tabernacle of the congregation, for all the service of the tabernacle: and a stranger shall not come nigh unto you.

Sometimes in the name of quality or excellence we use people who aren't necessarily even walking with the Lord. "Be careful," God would say to us. "None outside the family is to assist you in the ministry to which I've called you."

Numbers 18:5
And ye shall keep the charge of the sanctuary, and the charge of the altar: that there be no wrath any more upon the children of Israel.

In King James English, the word "ye" is plural. Thus, it wasn't only Aaron, but all of the priests collectively who would ensure that there would be no more plagues, no more fires, no more earthquakes, no more wrath of God poured out upon them.

Likewise, although our great High Priest, Jesus Christ, has finished the work, as a royal priesthood (1 Peter 2:9), we get to partner in the process to see people spared from the wrath of hell, to see people saved. And whether this happens here in the sanctuary, in a corporate prayer meeting, or in private times of devotion, ours is a huge responsibility.

Numbers 18:6
And I, behold, I have taken your brethren the Levites from among the children of Israel: to you they are given as a gift for the LORD, to do the service of the tabernacle of the congregation.

If you have people working for you or under you, the godly perspective is to see them as gifts.

Numbers 18:7 (a)
Therefore thou and thy sons with thee shall keep your priest's office for every thing of the altar, and within the vail; and ye shall serve: I have given your priest's office unto you as a service of gift . . .

It is not only the people who serve under us who are gifts—but the very job or ministry itself is a gift. Once we think we deserve to be used in ministry because of our spirituality or our intensity, we are in big trouble.

Numbers 18:7 (b)
. . . and the stranger that cometh nigh shall be put to death.

Far from limiting people, God here is loving them by saving them from that which would wipe them out. Because God knows where each of us will function best, it's a wise man who trusts God to place him where he will be most productive, where he will be most at peace.

Numbers 18:8, 9
And the LORD spake unto Aaron, Behold, I also have given thee the charge of mine heave offerings of all the hallowed things of the children of Israel; unto thee have I given them by reason of the anointing, and to thy sons, by an ordinance for ever. This shall be thine of the most holy things, reserved from the fire: every oblation of theirs, every meat offering of theirs, and every sin

offering of theirs, and every trespass offering of theirs, which they shall render unto me, shall be most holy for thee and for thy sons.

Concerning the offerings given to the Lord, He said to those who were serving Him, "This has been offered to Me, but now I'm giving it to you." That is, when a heave offering was made, God didn't receive it physically, but rather gave it to the priests. And when a sin offering or trespass offering was made, although a portion of it went up in smoke to the Lord, the majority of meat remained and was given to the priests.

Numbers 18:10
In the most holy place shalt thou eat it; every male shall eat it: it shall be holy unto thee.

In offering meat to the Lord on behalf of the people, the priests themselves would be fed. That's always the way it is. If you feel like you're not being fed, teach Sunday school; start a Bible study at work; disciple someone; have family devotions. The priests would be fed to the degree they fed others. And the principle is still true.

Numbers 18:11
And this is thine; the heave offering of their gift, with all the wave offerings of the children of Israel: I have given them unto thee, and to thy sons and to thy daughters with thee, by a statute for ever: every one that is clean in thy house shall eat of it.

Not only would the priests be fed, but their families would be fed as well.

Numbers 18:12
All the best of the oil, and all the best of the wine, and of the wheat, the firstfruits of them which they shall offer unto the LORD, them have I given thee.

Those who served God would be blessed with His best. And haven't each of us found this to be so? When we're serving Him, He meets our needs and satisfies our souls in the most wonderful ways.

Numbers 18:13
And whatsoever is first ripe in the land, which they shall bring unto the LORD, shall be thine; every one that is clean in thine house shall eat of it.

So often, people give the Lord leftovers. If they have money left over, they'll tithe. If they have a surplus, they'll give it to the Lord's work or to His people. But over and over again, the Lord lovingly challenges us in the Word, saying, "Give Me your best and watch and see how I will give back to you and your family in amazing ways."

Numbers 18:14–19 (a)
Every thing devoted in Israel shall be thine. Every thing that openeth the matrix in all flesh, which they bring unto the LORD, whether it be of men or beasts, shall be thine: nevertheless the firstborn of man shalt thou surely redeem, and the firstling of unclean beasts shalt thou redeem. And those that are to be redeemed from a month old shalt thou redeem, according to thine estimation, for the money of five shekels, after the shekel of the sanctuary, which is twenty gerahs. But the firstling of a cow, or the firstling of a sheep, or the firstling of a goat, thou shalt not redeem; they are holy: thou shalt sprinkle their blood upon the altar, and shalt burn their fat for an offering made by fire, for a sweet savour unto the Lord. And the flesh of them shall be thine, as the wave breast and as the right shoulder are thine. All the heave offerings of the holy things, which the children of Israel offer unto the LORD, have I given thee, and thy sons and thy daughters with thee, by a statute for ever:

"Seek ye first the kingdom of God and His righteousness, and all these things shall be added unto you," Jesus said (Matthew 6:33). If you're making excuses now as to why you can't do what you've been called to do, there will be a whole new set of obstacles five years from now. Therefore, it's foolish for a person to think that down the road, it will be easier to serve the Lord. We are to seek the Lord *now*, believe the Lord *now*, trust Him *now*—and watch Him bless us as He has promised (Malachi 3:10).

Numbers 18:19 (b)
. . . it is a covenant of salt for ever before the LORD unto thee and to thy seed with thee.

Because salt doesn't break down under heat, it shouldn't be surprising that the word "salary" comes from the same root word—for the employee who earns a salary is guaranteed a certain wage no matter how much heat the company takes in any given month. So, too, through the covenant of salt, God declares, "Aaron, do what I've called you to do and I will take care of your sons and daughters. Regardless of what comes up or what goes down, I will see you through."

Numbers 18:20
And the LORD spake unto Aaron, Thou shalt have no inheritance in their land, neither shalt thou have any part among them: I am thy part and thine inheritance among the children of Israel.

The Levites would have no less than God Himself for their inheritance.

Numbers 18:21–24
And, behold, I have given the children of Levi all the tenth in Israel for an inheritance, for their service which they serve, even the service of the tabernacle of the congregation. Neither must the children of Israel henceforth come nigh the tabernacle of the congregation, lest they bear sin, and die. But the Levites shall do the service of the tabernacle of the congregation, and they shall bear their iniquity: it shall be a statute for ever throughout your generations, that among the children of Israel they have no inheritance. But the tithes of the children of Israel, which they offer as an heave offering unto the LORD, I have given to the Levites to inherit: therefore I have said unto them, Among the children of Israel they shall have no inheritance.

The priests would eventually receive the tithe that was given to the Lord.

Numbers 18:25, 26
And the LORD spake unto Moses, saying, Thus speak unto the Levites, and say unto them, When ye take of the children of Israel the tithes which I have given you from them for your inheritance, then ye shall offer up an heave offering of it for the LORD, even a tenth part of the tithe.

Pastors, leaders, Christian workers, take note: The Levites were to tithe of that which came to them. In other words, God's mind and God's heart is that none are exempt from the tithe.

Numbers 18:27, 28
And this your heave offering shall be reckoned unto you, as though it were the corn of the threshingfloor, and as the fulness of the winepress. Thus ye also shall offer an heave offering unto the LORD of all your tithes, which ye receive of the children of Israel; and ye shall give thereof the LORD's heave offering to Aaron the priest.

Without exception, every Christian worker needs to understand God's heart and not exempt themselves from giving to our great High Priest, Jesus Christ.

Numbers 18:29
Out of all your gifts ye shall offer every heave offering of the LORD, of all the best thereof, even the hallowed part thereof out of it.

Again, this verse directed to the servants of the Lord, they're to take the best of what they get and give it back to the Lord, to the high priest.

Numbers 18:30–32
Therefore thou shalt say unto them, When ye have heaved the best thereof from it, then it shall be counted unto the Levites as the increase of the threshingfloor, and as the increase of the winepress. And ye shall eat it in every place, ye and your households: for it is your reward for your service in the tabernacle of the congregation. And ye shall bear no sin by reason of it, when ye have heaved from it the best of it: neither shall ye pollute the holy things of the children of Israel, lest ye die.

Our hearts lifted to God in prayer and praise constitute a present-day heave offering.

19

In chapter 19, we come to the very interesting section of Scripture which deals with the sacrifice of the red heifer—a sacrifice unique in that it was introduced decades after all of the other sacrifices; unique in that it has an entire chapter devoted to it; and unique in that it was to be offered outside the camp rather than in the tabernacle . . .

Numbers 19:1, 2
And the LORD spake unto Moses and unto Aaron, saying, This is the ordinance of the law which the LORD hath commanded, saying, Speak unto the children of Israel, that they bring thee a red heifer without spot, wherein is no blemish, and upon which never came yoke:

Who is the only One without spot or blemish, the only One who was never yoked by the plans or demands of men (John 10:18)? Jesus Christ.

Numbers 19:3 (a)
And ye shall give her unto Eleazar the priest, that he may bring her forth without the camp . . .

Where was Jesus crucified? Outside the camp, outside Jerusalem.

Numbers 19:3 (b), 4
. . . and one shall slay her before his face: And Eleazar the priest shall take of her blood with his finger, and sprinkle of her blood directly before the tabernacle of the congregation seven times:

Unlike any other sacrifice, the priest would not slaughter the red heifer but would stand by as someone else did. Why? Because although Caiaphas, the high priest, ordered that Jesus be put to death, it was actually the Romans who carried out the sentence.

Numbers 19:5
And one shall burn the heifer in his sight; her skin, and her flesh, and her blood, with her dung, shall he burn:

The heifer was to be burned even as Jesus would be burned by the fire of God's wrath poured out upon Him.

Numbers 19:6
And the priest shall take cedar wood, and hyssop, and scarlet, and cast it into the midst of the burning of the heifer.

The priest was to cast cedar wood, hyssop, and scarlet into the fire with the red heifer—just as Jesus was nailed to a Cross very likely made of cedar, was offered vinegar to deaden the pain on a pole of hyssop, and shed scarlet blood for you and me.

Numbers 19:7–9
Then the priest shall wash his clothes, and he shall bathe his flesh in water, and afterward he shall come into the camp, and the priest shall be unclean until the even. And he that burneth her shall wash his clothes in water, and bathe his flesh in water, and shall be unclean until the even. And a man that is clean shall gather up the ashes of the heifer, and lay them up without the camp in a clean place, and it shall be kept for the congregation of the children of Israel for a water of separation: it is a purification for sin.

After the entire heifer was consumed by fire outside the camp, the ashes were scooped up and put aside for the purpose of separation and purification.

Numbers 19:10–13
And he that gathereth the ashes of the heifer shall wash his clothes, and be unclean until the even: and it shall be unto the children of Israel, and unto the stranger that sojourneth among them, for a statute for ever. He that toucheth the dead body of any man shall be unclean seven days. He shall purify himself with it on the third day, and on the seventh day he shall be clean: but if he purify not himself the third day, then the seventh day he shall not be clean. Whosoever toucheth the dead body of any man that is dead, and purifieth not himself, defileth the tabernacle of the LORD; and that soul shall be cut off from Israel: because the water of separation was not sprinkled upon him, he shall be unclean; his uncleanness is yet upon him.

The one who came into contact with a dead body was to wash on the third and seventh days with water into which the ashes from the red heifer had been sprinkled. If the red heifer pictures Jesus, why was it a red heifer rather than a red bull? I suggest it was for the same reason that Jesus was betrayed for thirty pieces of silver—the price a woman paid for dedication rather than for fifty pieces, the price for a man (Leviticus 27), and for the same reason Aceldama, the name of the field purchased with the thirty pieces of silver is in the feminine form (Acts 1:19). That is, Jesus is not only the Son of Man, the perfect Man, but He also has qualities of the woman that make Him so complete.

You see, Adam was at one time complete as well, but when God took a rib from his side and from it fashioned a woman, he not only lost a rib, but the tenderness, the ability to communicate, the sensitivity, the intuition which went to the woman. That's why when man and woman come together, there is oneness, unity, dependency, and completion. Enter the second Adam, the Last Adam, Jesus Christ (1 Corinthians 15:45). He's not only the bull of the burnt offering—the epitome of strength, but He is also the red heifer—the essence of sensitivity. When a wife realizes her husband will always be missing something, and when a husband realizes his wife has qualities he will always lack, they no longer put pressure on each other to be what they're not, but instead log in time with the One who is altogether lovely, the One who is perfectly complete, and find their deepest needs met.

Numbers 19:14
This is the law, when a man dieth in a tent: all that come into the tent, and all that is in the tent, shall be unclean seven days.

Even if a man hadn't physically come into contact with a dead body, if he even went into the tent of one who had died, he was considered unclean. Even though we might not be directly involved with the dark and deadly stuff of this world, even being around it renders us needful of the forgiveness and cleansing only our red heifer, Jesus Christ, can give.

Numbers 19:15–22
And every open vessel, which hath no covering bound upon it, is unclean. And whosoever toucheth one that is slain with a sword in the open fields, or a dead body, or a bone of a man, or a grave, shall be unclean seven days. And for an unclean person they shall take of the ashes of the burnt heifer of purification for sin, and running water shall be put thereto in a vessel: And a clean person shall take hyssop, and dip it in the water, and sprinkle it upon the tent, and upon all the vessels, and upon the persons that were there, and upon him that touched a bone, or one slain, or one dead, or a grave: And the clean person shall sprinkle upon the unclean on the third day, and on the seventh day: and on the seventh day he shall purify himself, and wash his clothes, and bathe himself in water, and shall be clean at even. But the man that shall be unclean, and shall not purify himself, that soul shall be cut off from among the congregation, because he hath defiled the sanctuary of the LORD: the water of separation hath not been sprinkled upon him; he is unclean. And it shall be a perpetual statute unto them, that he that sprinkleth the water of separation shall wash his clothes; and he that toucheth the water of separation shall be unclean until even. And whatsoever the unclean person toucheth shall be unclean; and the soul that toucheth it shall be unclean until even.

The careful attention given to those who came in contact with death addressed two issues. First, the issue of health. This side of the discovery of bacteria and infection, it seems only common sense to stay away from disease and death. But in Numbers, only God knew these things. Thus, His instructions were vital for His people. In addition to the issue of health, however, was the issue of holiness. By distancing His people from death, God was also distancing them from the Egyptian practices and superstitions of keeping the mummified remains of ancestors in one's home.

Health and holiness belong to any today who choose to keep a distance from the death sin brings, from the disease and decay the superstitions of the world inflict upon those who dabble with them.

20

In Numbers 20, we come to the end of an era. That is, we come to the end of the wilderness wanderings. For thirty-eight-plus years, the people of Israel have been wandering in the wilderness, a story told in chapters 14 through 19. It should not be surprising that thirty-eight years are chronicled in only six chapters, for when we wander around in the wilderness because we didn't step up and go in to the place God called us, not a whole lot happens. Consequently, not a whole lot is recorded for posterity in God's economy. On the other hand, do that which He's told you to do and it will be noteworthy eternally.

Numbers 20:1–5
Then came the children of Israel, even the whole congregation, into the desert of Zin in the first month: and the people abode in Kadesh; and Miriam died there, and was buried there. And there was no water for the congregation: and they gathered themselves together against Moses and against Aaron. And the people chode with Moses, and spake, saying, Would God that we had died when our brethren died before the LORD! And why have ye brought up the congregation of the LORD into this wilderness, that we and our cattle should die there? And wherefore have ye made us to come up out of Egypt, to bring us in unto this evil place? it is no place of seed, or of figs, or of vines, or of pomegranates; neither is there any water to drink.

Listen to what the children of Israel said when they were here at Kadesh thirty-eight years earlier . . .

> And all the children of Israel murmured against Moses and against Aaron: and the whole congregation said unto them, Would God that we had died in the land of Egypt! or would God we had died in this wilderness! And wherefore hath the Lord brought us unto this land, to fall by the sword, that our wives and our children should be a prey? Were it not better for us to return into Egypt? Numbers 14:2, 3

This sobers me because I realize it is possible for a man or congregation to murmur or complain in the same way we murmured or complained a generation earlier. When we're younger, we think we'll outgrow certain tendencies. "When I'm seventy, I'm going to be a patriarch," we tell ourselves. "My family will highly esteem me. People will want to listen to me. Sure, I'm busy now at age thirty-five or forty. But when I'm seventy, I'll have made a mark spiritually."

Time itself does not make one mature. The only way we will be wise at age seventy is to make wise decisions at age forty. You're making that choice by studying the Word right now, for God has determined that people grow in wisdom by taking heed to His Word chapter by chapter, verse by verse. How I pray that if the Lord tarries, I will not be as foolish at age seventy as I am at age forty-seven. "Lord," I pray, "deepen me." How does that happen? By spending time in, and obeying the Word.

Numbers 20:6

And Moses and Aaron went from the presence of the assembly unto the door of the tabernacle of the congregation, and they fell upon their faces: and the glory of the LORD appeared unto them.

Just as the people murmured the same way they had murmured thirty-eight years earlier, Moses and Aaron fell on their faces before God as they had done all along. They have stayed true to the course that is right in God's sight. When the pressure mounted, when the people complained, these men did what we get to do. They fell on their faces before the Lord and in so doing experienced His presence.

Numbers 20:7–13

And the LORD spake unto Moses, saying, Take the rod, and gather thou the assembly together, thou, and Aaron thy brother, and speak ye unto the rock before their eyes; and it shall give forth his water, and thou shalt bring forth to them water out of the rock: so thou shalt give the congregation and their beasts drink. And Moses took the rod from before the LORD, as he commanded him. And Moses and Aaron gathered the congregation together before the rock, and he said unto them, Hear now, ye rebels; must we fetch you water out of this rock? And Moses lifted up his hand, and with his rod he smote the rock twice: and the water came out abundantly, and the congregation drank, and their beasts also. And the LORD spake unto Moses and Aaron, because ye believed me not, to sanctify me in the eyes of the children of Israel, therefore ye shall not bring this congregation into the land which I have given them. This is the water of Meribah; because the children of Israel strove with the LORD, and he was sanctified in them.

Without question, Moses was one of the greatest men in history. He had an awesome responsibility. He led three million people out of slavery on a journey towards the land of their destiny. He also had a glorious opportunity, for he heard from the Lord directly (Numbers 12:8). Moses was a uniquely blessed and godly man—but he was still a man. And here we see the humanity of Moses in what would be his greatest sin.

If you were to ask Moses' contemporaries what his great sin was, some would point to his murdering the Egyptian in Exodus 2. Others might point to his failure to tend his own children in Exodus 4. Others might point to his marriage to the Ethiopian woman in Numbers 12. But none of those things disqualified Moses in the way this sin does.

The people were thirsty. They were murmuring. They wanted water to drink. In response, God told Moses to take the rod that had blossomed and budded three chapters earlier and speak to the rock. Moses took the rod but then looked at the people and called them rebels. In the Greek Septuagint, the word translated "rebels" is *moros*—from which we get the word "moron." "You morons, must we fetch you water?" Moses cried as he smote the rock twice.

And although God provided water, He said, "Because of this, Moses, you will not be allowed to go into the Promised Land."

Moses had been leading this congregation for decades. He had put up with the murmuring, the complaining, the sins of three million people. How, then, can it be that God would disqualify him when he's so close to the finish line? What was the sin Moses committed that disqualified him, that marred his record? The sin was obviously related to anger. We know this not only from the context, but from the Psalms . . .

> They angered him also at the waters of strife, so that it went ill with Moses for their sakes: Because they provoked his spirit, so that he spake unadvisedly with his lips. Psalm 106:32, 33

As I read the Bible, I understand that the point of a man's greatest strength is more often than not the point of his greatest failure. Known for his meekness—which the Greeks defined as strength under control—Moses failed when he lost control and lost his temper. Peter was a man known for his courage—as one who walked on water in the midst of a storm, as one who chopped off Malchus' ear. But where did he fail? He failed when he became a coward before a servant girl (Matthew 26:69). Job was a man who was abundantly patient—and yet he was rebuked by the Lord for a lack of patience (Job 40). David was a man after God's heart, a lover of God—and yet he fell because he lusted after a woman (2 Samuel

11). Unlike the others around him, Noah was a righteous man—yet he failed when he got drunk in his tent (Genesis 9:21).

The same is true of us. Where we think we are strongest will be the point of our greatest vulnerability. If you think your marriage is so strong that you will never be in danger, be careful. If you think you have so much integrity that you would never cheat on your taxes, wait a minute. If you think you're so honest you would never tell a lie, beware. Where I'm weak, I'm aware of my vulnerability. I know I've got to pray about it. I know I've got to keep my guard up. But where I think I'm together, I fail to pray and I don't watch as carefully as I ought to. I rely on my own strength, not realizing that my own strength is very limited.

Secondly, Moses' sin included taking credit for what God alone could do. "Must *we* fetch you water?" he said—implying that he was the one meeting the needs of the people. "When you do good works," Jesus said, "let your light so shine before men that they may see your good works and glorify *your Father*" (Matthew 5:16).

Thirdly and most importantly, Moses misrepresented the nature and character of the Father. In blowing his top, Moses signaled to the people that God must be angry with them. But He wasn't. Psalm 103 says our Father has compassion on us, remembering our frames, knowing that we are dust. Our God is a God of incredible mercy, a Father of intense compassion. And because Moses misrepresented Him, he would not be able to lead the congregation into the Land of Promise.

> Moreover, brethren, I would not that ye should be ignorant, how that all our fathers were under the cloud, and all passed through the sea; And were all baptized unto Moses in the cloud and in the sea; And did all eat the same spiritual meat; And did all drink the same spiritual drink: for they drank of that spiritual Rock that followed them: and that Rock was Christ.
> 1 Corinthians 10:1–4

When the children of Israel began their journey, God told Moses to smite the rock. And out of the rock came water (Exodus 17:6). The Rock is Christ. Christ was smitten once, never to be smitten again. Yes, our sin demanded the Rock be smitten. But He died once for all—for all sin, for all time, for all men. The price has been paid and now Moses was to speak to the rock. The rock was only to be smitten once because Christ's sacrifice was sufficient. But Moses ruined the picture by striking the rock again.

It's not our job to beat people up or straighten them out. Yes, we are to share the truth with them in love, but anger or bitterness will disqualify us from true leadership, for the wrath of man never works the righteousness of God (James 1:20). Moses no doubt thought, "This is it. It's been almost forty years and these people never stop complaining. Certainly, God, You must have had it up to here with Your people." God's mercy, however, is inexhaustible. It extends all the way to the heavens (Psalm 36:5).

"Your mercies are new every morning," the prophet proclaimed (Lamentations 3:22, 23). Like Moses, we think God surely must be exhausted, upset, angry with us and the rest of the sinners surrounding us. But He's not. His mercy is new every morning, and where sin abounds grace abounds *more* (Romans 5:20).

For the above reasons, Moses could not enter the Promised Land. But God is so merciful and gracious that 1,500 years later, who stands on the Mount of Transfiguration in the Promised Land? Moses himself (Matthew 17:3). God snuck him in! Oh, the grace and goodness of our God.

Numbers 20:14 (a)
And Moses sent messengers from Kadesh unto the king of Edom,

Marching towards the Promised Land, the children of Israel come to a point where they must pass through the land of the Edomites.

Numbers 20:14 (b)–17
. . . Thus saith thy brother Israel, Thou knowest all the travail that hath befallen us: How our fathers went down into Egypt, and we have dwelt in Egypt a long time; and the Egyptians vexed us, and our fathers: And when we cried unto the LORD, he heard our voice, and sent an angel, and hath brought us forth out of Egypt: and, behold, we are in Kadesh, a city in the uttermost of thy border: Let us pass, I pray thee, through thy country: we will not pass through the fields, or through the vineyards, neither will we drink of the water of the wells: we will go by the king's high way, we will not turn to the right hand nor to the left, until we have passed thy borders.

"We're related to you," Moses said to the king of Edom "—cousins, in a sense. Can we pass through your land?"

Numbers 20:18
And Edom said unto him, Thou shalt not pass by me, lest I come out against thee with the sword.

Moses' request was denied.

Numbers 20:19
And the children of Israel said unto him, We will go by the high way: and if I and my cattle drink of thy water, then I will pay for it: I will only, without doing any thing else, go through on my feet.

"We'll just take the highway," the Israelites said. "We'll stick to the outskirts. And we'll pay for any water we consume."

Numbers 20:20, 21
And he said, Thou shalt not go through. And Edom came out against him with much people, and with a strong hand. Thus Edom refused to give Israel passage through his border: wherefore Israel turned away from him.

The Edomites were the descendants of Esau. If you want to know how evil they were, read the Book of Obadiah. God was justified in saying, "Jacob have I loved and Esau have I hated" (Romans 9:13), because as you read their history, you realize the Edomites were a hateful, cruel people.

Numbers 20:22
And the children of Israel, even the whole congregation, journeyed from Kadesh, and came unto mount Hor.

How were the children of Israel led? By day, it was a cloud. By night, it was a pillar of fire that guided them. Here, however, it seems as though Moses takes his cue not from the direction of God but from the threat of the Edomites. The same thing can happen to us. People can say, "No. You can't do that"—even though you know in your heart that God has told you to do it. And, as it was for Moses, the question at that time is singular: Am I going to obey God—or fear man?

Numbers 20:23, 24 (a)
And the LORD spake unto Moses and Aaron in mount Hor, by the coast of the land of Edom, saying, Aaron shall be gathered unto his people . . .

Aaron was going to die; he was going to be gathered unto his people. So, unless we're raptured first, we will be gathered to our people. The question is, who are our people? Jesus said, "By this shall all men know that you are my disciples: By your love one to another" (John 13:35). John said we would know if we were truly born again by our love for the brethren (1 John 3:14). Therefore if a person says he can't stand Christians, that he has no use for the church, he must take another look at his salvation because he won't be gathered into the company of believers when he dies.

Numbers 20:24 (b)–29
. . . for he shall not enter into the land which I have given unto the children of Israel, because ye rebelled against my word at the water of Meribah. Take Aaron and Eleazar his son, and bring them up unto mount Hor: And strip Aaron of his garments, and put them upon Eleazar his son: and Aaron shall be gathered unto his people, and shall die there. And Moses did as the LORD commanded: and they went up into mount Hor in the sight of all the congregation. And Moses stripped Aaron of his garments, and put them upon Eleazar his son; and Aaron died there in the top of the mount: and Moses and Eleazar came down from the mount. And when all the congregation saw that Aaron was dead, they mourned for Aaron thirty days, even all the house of Israel.

The Lord takes Aaron home, and His work goes on through Eleazar.

I'm so glad our High Priest never changes (Hebrews 13:8). Jesus is our Rock. He doesn't change from generation to generation. Therefore, I know the same Lord who has been so good to me will be good to my children and their children. Unlike Aaron, our great High Priest *ever liveth* to make intercession for us (Hebrews 7:25).

21

Numbers 21:1, 2
And when king Arad the Canaanite, which dwelt in the south, heard tell that Israel came by the way of the spies; then he fought against Israel, and took some of them prisoners. And Israel vowed a vow unto the LORD, and said, If thou wilt indeed deliver this people into my hand, then I will utterly destroy their cities.

With the Promised Land in sight, the children of Israel are attacked. And when some of their number are taken captive, they make a vow to the Lord, saying, "If You will give us victory over those who captured our people, we'll destroy the pagan cities."

Numbers 21:3
And the LORD hearkened to the voice of Israel, and delivered up the Canaanites; and they utterly destroyed them and their cities: and he called the name of the place Hormah.

Hormah means "Complete destruction." The Lord did indeed give victory to the Israelites. I suggest to you that whenever we say, "That which is pagan in my life—be it blatant sin or subtle attitudes—is going to be destroyed because I want to see my daughter, my neighbor, or my coworker set free from the captivity of sin," the Lord hearkens unto us as well.

Numbers 21:4
And they journeyed from mount Hor by the way of the Red sea, to compass the land of Edom: and the soul of the people was much discouraged because of the way.

I suggest that it was when the people circled around Edom rather than facing the king of Edom and saying, "This is the direction God is guiding us; this is the way He's leading us; this is what we're going to do," that they became discouraged. I'm discovering in my own walk that when I make concessions to the king of Edom rather than following the Lord's leading, when I say, "I don't want to hassle this," or, "I don't want to confront that situation," discouragement is the end result.

Numbers 21:5
And the people spake against God, and against Moses, Wherefore have ye brought us up out of Egypt to die in the wilderness? for there is no bread, neither is there any water; and our soul loatheth this light bread.

Deuteronomy 8:4 tells us that in all the years of the wilderness wandering, the feet of the Israelites didn't swell—which is one indication of a well-balanced diet. Thus, they were tired of the very food that was perfect for them.

Numbers 21:6 (a)
And the LORD sent fiery serpents among the people, and they bit the people . . .

Some say the snakes were called fiery snakes because of their brilliant colors. Much more likely, however, they were called fiery because of the burning sensation caused by their deadly poison.

Numbers 21:6 (b)
. . . and much people of Israel died.

Why would it be here—only weeks away from their entering the Promised Land—that God would have poisonous serpents bite His people? Because if they're not taught in the wilderness, they will be distraught in the Land of Promise. God is willing to go to great extremes to get us to understand that if we're not happy today, we'll not be happy tomorrow regardless of what comes our way or where we might be. Happiness is an inside job.

God allows His children to feel a lot of pain and even to die in order that they might see and understand that He is with them, that He is enough for them, that He will take care of them. If they don't learn to quit their complaining here, they'll not experience it even in the Land of Promise.

How about you? Has it been a week of complaining? Have you heard yourself say, "This is hard right now, but as soon as I get the job or as soon as I retire, as soon as she marries me or as soon as my wife leaves me, as soon as we have kids or as soon as the kids move out, I'll be happy."

If you're not happy today, you'll not be happy tomorrow unless you get to the root issue. We get so deceived about this. We think we're going to be happy "just as soon as"—but "just as soon as" never comes.

Numbers 21:7, 8 (a)
Therefore the people came to Moses, and said, We have sinned, for we have spoken against the LORD, and against thee; pray unto the LORD, that he take away the serpents from us. And Moses prayed for the people. And the LORD said unto Moses, Make thee a fiery serpent, and set it upon a pole . . .

When the people repented and asked Moses to pray that the Lord would remove the fiery snakes, God told him to make a snake and fasten it to a pole. The Hebrew word translated "pole" is *nec* and refers to what a flag would fly from—or the cross-shaped mast to which a sail on a ship would be attached.

Numbers 21:8 (b), 9
. . . and it shall come to pass, that every one that is bitten, when he looketh upon it, shall live. And Moses made a serpent of brass, and put it upon a pole, and it came to pass, that if a serpent had bitten any man, when he beheld the serpent of brass, he lived.

What does this mean? Jesus explained it perfectly . . .

"Master, I know no man can do the works You do except God be with Him," Nicodemus said to Him.

"Truly, I say unto you, unless a man is born again, he cannot see the kingdom of God," Jesus answered as if to say, "Let's not talk about miracles, Nicodemus. I want to get to the root: You must be born again."

"Born again?" Nicodemus asked. "Can a man enter into his mother's womb a second time?"

"That which is born of flesh is flesh, but that which is born of spirit is spirit," Jesus said. And then He reached back to this story in Numbers 21 when He said, "And as Moses lifted up the serpent in the wilderness, so must the Son of Man be lifted up, that whosoever believeth in Him should not perish but have eternal life" (John 3).

Jesus likens Himself to the serpent—the very creature that caused Eve to question God's goodness in the Garden of Eden and thereby plunged all mankind into sin, because He who knew no sin was made sin that we might be made the righteousness of God (2 Corinthians 5:21).

Here in Numbers 21, there were no doubt those who said, "You're telling me all I have to do to be healed is look at a pole and see a brass snake? What good will that do? I need some anti-venom." Or, "If I can get the right prescription, I can get over this infection." And, because of their stubbornness, they would die unnecessarily.

There are people today who will not look to the One who hung on the pole of the Cross. "All I need is some Prozac," they say, "or a beer," or "a hot fudge sundae. All I need is something to fill up the hole in my soul."

God said the only thing we must do is to realize we've been bitten and look to the Serpent on the Cross. The one who does so will be made whole. It's just that simple.

> Look unto me, and be ye saved, all the ends of the earth: for I am God, and there is none else.
> Isaiah 45:22

We don't have to climb the pole and hang there with Him. We don't have to do something for Him. We just have to look to Him. "Even as ye have received Christ, so walk in Him," Paul would write (Colossians 2:6). We looked to Him when we were saved. And that's what we get to do each and every day.

Numbers 21:10–14

And the children of Israel set forward, and pitched in Oboth. And they journeyed from Oboth, and pitched at Ijeabarim, in the wilderness which is before Moab, toward the sunrising. From thence they removed, and pitched in the valley of Zared. From thence they removed, and pitched on the other side of Arnon, which is in the wilderness that cometh out of the coasts of the Amorites: for Arnon is the border of Moab, between Moab and the Amorites. Wherefore it is said in the book of the wars of the LORD, What he did in the Red sea, and in the brooks of Arnon,

Because God evidently did not think it necessary that we have the book of the wars of the Lord, it was not preserved in the same way as were the other books of our Bible.

Numbers 21:15–18

And at the stream of the brooks that goeth down to the dwelling of Ar, and lieth upon the border of Moab. And from thence they went to Beer: that is the well whereof the LORD spake unto Moses, Gather the people together, and I will give them water. Then Israel sang this song, Spring up, O well; sing ye unto it: The princes digged the well, the nobles of the people digged it, by the direction of the lawgiver, with their staves. And from the wilderness they went to Mattanah:

The children of Israel sang and water gushed forth. That's always the way it is. When we come to dry times and difficult days in our pilgrimage, we can either choose to murmur or to make music.

> Sing, O barren, thou that didst not bear; break forth into singing, and cry aloud, thou that didst not travail with child: for more are the children of the desolate than the children of the married wife, saith the LORD. Isaiah 54:1

"Are you barren?" the Lord asks you and me. "I don't want you to grumble about your situation. I want you to sing out." An overriding principle seen throughout the Word is that when people are in barren conditions, dry times, or locked in jail cells, power and blessing are released when they choose not to murmur but to praise the Lord. The children of Israel did this. Water gushed forth. And they moved on.

Numbers 21:19–26

And from Mattanah to Nahaliel: and from Nahaliel to Bamoth: And from Bamoth in the valley, that is in the country of Moab, to the top of Pisgah, which looketh toward Jeshimon. And Israel sent messengers unto Sihon king of the Amorites, saying, Let me pass through thy land: we will not turn into the fields, or into the vineyards; we will not drink of the waters of the well: but we will go along by the king's high way, until we be past thy borders. And Sihon would not suffer Israel to pass through his border: but Sihon gathered all his people together, and went out against Israel into the wilderness: and he came to Jahaz, and fought against

Israel. And Israel smote him with the edge of the sword, and possessed his land from Arnon unto Jabbok, even unto the children of Ammon: for the border of the children of Ammon was strong. And Israel took all these cities: and Israel dwelt in all the cities of the Amorites, in Heshbon, and in all the villages thereof. For Heshbon was the city of Sihon the king of the Amorites, who had fought against the former king of Moab, and taken all his land out of his hand, even unto Arnon.

Rather than giving in to the king of the Amorites as they had done to the king of Edom, Moses said, "No more backing away. No more compromise. No more trying to appease people. We're going to stay true to the Word of God." And in so doing, they possessed the land.

Numbers 21:27–30
Wherefore they that speak in proverbs say, Come into Heshbon, let the city of Sihon be built and prepared: For there is a fire gone out of Heshbon, a flame from the city of Sihon: it hath consumed Ar of Moab, and the lords of the high places of Arnon. Woe to thee, Moab! thou art undone, O people of Chemosh: he hath given his sons that escaped, and his daughters, into captivity unto Sihon king of the Amorites. We have shot at them; Heshbon is perished even unto Dibon, and we have laid them waste even unto Nophah, which reacheth unto Medeba.

Sung previously by the Amorites when they beat the Moabites in battle, this was the Amorite victory song, their number one hit. And when the Israelites beat the Amorites, they used it to taunt the Amorites themselves. In other words, they gave the world's song a whole new meaning. I believe this is what we are to do as well. We're to take the stuff the world has used and turn it around for God's glory.

Numbers 21:31–34 (a)
Thus Israel dwelt in the land of the Amorites. And Moses sent to spy out Jaazer, and they took the villages thereof, and drove out the Amorites that were there. And they turned and went up by the way of Bashan: and Og the king of Bashan went out against them, he, and all his people, to the battle at Edrei. And the LORD said unto Moses, Fear him not . . .

Even though Og was a man of gigantic stature who ruled over sixty separate communities, God said, "Fear him not."

Numbers 21:34 (b), 35
. . . for I have delivered him into thy hand, and all his people, and his land; and thou shalt do to him as thou didst unto Sihon king of the Amorites, which dwelt at Heshbon. So they smote him, and his sons, and all his people, until there was none left him alive: and they possessed his land.

Why were the Israelites victorious? Because the sword was used (v. 24), the song was sung (v. 27), and the Spirit was heard (v. 34). That is, backing down no more, they obeyed God's Word, hijacked the world's song for God's glory, listened to the Spirit saying, "Fear not"—and continued on . . .

22

We meet a man in this chapter who I can't figure out. His name is Balaam, and he's talked about in the Books of Numbers, Deuteronomy, Joshua, Nehemiah, Micah, Peter, Jude, and Revelation. In fact, he's talked about much more than is Mary, the mother of Jesus—and yet he remains a mystery . . .

Numbers 22:1–4
And the children of Israel set forward, and pitched in the plains of Moab on this side Jordan by Jericho. And Balak the son of Zippor saw all that Israel had done to the Amorites. And Moab was sore afraid of the people, because they were many: and Moab was distressed because of the children of Israel. And Moab said unto the elders of Midian, Now shall this company lick up all that are round about us, as the ox licketh up the grass of the field. And Balak the son of Zippor was king of the Moabites at that time.

Having heard reports of what the Israelites did to the Amorites, Balak, king of Moab, was filled with fear as he saw the children of Israel camped in his backyard.

Numbers 22:5 (a)
He sent messengers therefore unto Balaam the son of Beor . . .

Also having heard that the people whom a prophet named Balaam blessed were blessed, and those he cursed were cursed, Balak sent messengers to talk with him.

Numbers 22:5 (b), 6
. . . to Pethor, which is by the river of the land of the children of his people, to call him, say-

ing, Behold, there is a people come out from Egypt: behold, they cover the face of the earth, and they abide over against me: Come now therefore, I pray thee, curse me this people; for they are too mighty for me: peradventure I shall prevail, that we may smite them, and that I may drive them out of the land: for I wot that he whom thou blessest is blessed, and he whom thou cursest is cursed.

Balaam was a prophet of the Lord. He heard from the Lord—and yet he didn't live with the people of the Lord.

Numbers 22:7 (a)
And the elders of Moab and the elders of Midian departed with the rewards of divination in their hand . . .

To better his odds against Israel, Balak forms an alliance with the Midianites.

Numbers 22:7 (b)
. . . and they came unto Balaam, and spake unto him the words of Balak.

"Come and curse the Israelites," the elders of Moab and Midian say to Balaam.

Numbers 22:8
And he said unto them, Lodge here this night, and I will bring you word again, as the LORD shall speak unto me: and the princes of Moab abode with Balaam.

"Stay here tonight," Balaam said, "and I'll ask the Lord if I can go with you."

Numbers 22:9–12
And God came unto Balaam, and said, What men are these with thee? And Balaam said unto God, Balak the son of Zippor, king of Moab, hath sent unto me, saying, Behold, there is a people come out of Egypt, which covereth the face of the earth: come now, curse me them; peradventure I shall be able to overcome them, and drive them out. And God said unto Balaam, Thou shalt not go with them; thou shalt not curse the people: for they are blessed.

God's word to Balaam was singular. It was simple and definitive. It was "No."

Numbers 22:13–17
And Balaam rose up in the morning, and said unto the princes of Balak, Get you into your land: for the LORD refuseth to give me leave to go with you. And the princes of Moab rose up, and they went unto Balak, and said, Balaam refuseth to come with us. And Balak sent yet again princes, more, and more honourable than they. And they came to Balaam, and said to him, Thus saith Balak the son of Zippor, Let nothing, I pray thee, hinder thee from coming unto me: For I will promote thee unto very great honour, and I will do whatsoever thou sayest unto me: come therefore, I pray thee, curse me this people.

Refusing to take "No" for an answer, Balak sent a group of emissaries to Balaam more impressive than the first, who told Balaam he would be promoted if he cursed the Israelites.

Numbers 22:18, 19
And Balaam answered and said unto the servants of Balak, if Balak would give me his house full of silver and gold, I cannot go beyond the word of the LORD my God, to do less or more. Now therefore, I pray you, tarry ye also here this night, that I may know what the LORD will say unto me more.

"Even if Balak gave me a house full of silver and gold, I can't go with you," said Balaam. "But stay here tonight and I'll see what the Lord says." Balaam already knew the heart of the Lord, for His word had already been given. But this prophet saw a profit and wanted to see if God would change His mind.

"Honey," said the preacher, "we just got an invitation to go to a bigger church in a bigger city with a bigger salary. So I'm going to go upstairs to pray about it."

"Do you want me to pray with you?" asked his wife.

"No," the preacher answered. "You stay down here and start packing."

Such a man was Balaam.

Numbers 22:20–22 (a)
And God came unto Balaam at night, and said unto him, If the men come to call thee, rise up, and go with them; but yet the word which I shall say unto thee, that shalt thou do. And Balaam rose up in the morning, and saddled his ass, and went with the princes of Moab. And God's anger was kindled because he went . . .

Why was God's anger kindled? Hadn't He told Balaam to go? When, like Balaam, we beg and insist on our own way, God might say, "Okay." But it's not necessarily His plan or His will.

If you're a parent, you will sometimes let your kids go the way they insist on going—even though you know there will be needless pain and heartache down the road. Sometimes God will do the same with His children. That's why the "Name It and Claim It" movement is so frightening to me. I don't want to name and claim anything God knows isn't best for me. I want to pray like Jesus: "Father, not My will but Thine be done."

Numbers 22:22 (b)
. . . and the angel of the LORD stood in the way for an adversary against him.

The "angel of the Lord" refers to a *Christophany*—an appearance of Jesus before He came as the Babe of Bethlehem.

Numbers 22:22 (c), 23 (a)
. . . Now he was riding upon his ass, and his two servants were with him. And the ass saw the angel of the LORD standing in the way, and his sword drawn in his hand: and the ass turned aside out of the way, and went into the field . . .

Sometimes donkeys see what prophets miss. Maybe you look at your husband or wife, your mom or dad, your coach or boss as a donkey. But sometimes that "donkey" sees things you never would.

Numbers 22:23 (b)–25
. . . and Balaam smote the ass, to turn her into the way. But the angel of the LORD stood in a path of the vineyards, a wall being on this side, and a wall on that side. And when the ass saw the angel of the LORD, she thrust herself unto the wall, and crushed Balaam's foot against the wall: and he smote her again.

More concerned about his foot than about his soul, Balaam hits the donkey a second time.

Numbers 22:26–30
And the angel of the LORD went further, and stood in a narrow place, where was no way to turn either to the right hand or to the left. And when the ass saw the angel of the LORD, she fell down under Balaam: and Balaam's anger was kindled, and he smote the ass with a staff. And the LORD opened the mouth of the ass, and she said unto Balaam, What have I done unto thee, that thou hast smitten me these three times? And Balaam said unto the ass, Because thou hast mocked me: I would there were a sword in mine hand, for now would I kill thee. And the ass said unto Balaam, Am not I thine ass, upon which thou hast ridden ever since I was thine unto this day? Was I ever wont to do so unto thee? And he said, Nay.

To me, more surprising than the donkey speaking to Balaam is Balaam answering the donkey as if it were a normal occurrence.

Numbers 22:31–35
Then the LORD opened the eyes of Balaam, and he saw the angel of the LORD standing in the way, and his sword drawn in his hand: and he bowed down his head, and fell flat on his face. And the angel of the LORD said unto him, Wherefore hast thou smitten thine ass these three times? Behold, I went out to withstand thee, because thy way is perverse before me: And the ass saw me, and turned from me these three times: unless she had turned from me, surely now also I had slain thee, and saved her alive. And Balaam said unto the angel of the LORD, I have sinned; for I knew not that thou stoodest in the way against me: now therefore, if it displease thee, I will get me back again. And the angel of the LORD said unto Balaam, Go with the men: but only the word that I shall speak unto thee, that thou shalt speak. So Balaam went with the princes of Balak.

At last, Balaam sees what his donkey saw all along. He sees the Lord.

Numbers 22:36–41
And when Balak heard that Balaam was come, he went out to meet him unto a city of Moab, which is in the border of Arnon, which is in the utmost coast. And Balak said unto Balaam, Did I not earnestly send unto thee to call thee? wherefore camest thou not unto me? Am I not able indeed to promote thee to honour? And Balaam said unto Balak, Lo, I am come unto thee: have I now any power at all to say any thing? The word that God putteth in my mouth, that shall I speak. And Balaam went with Balak, and they came unto Kirjath-huzoth. And Balak offered oxen and sheep, and sent to Balaam, and to the princes that were with him. And it came to pass on the morrow, that Balak took Balaam, and brought him up into the high places of Baal, that thence he might see the utmost part of the people.

Giving Balaam a bird's eye view of the children of Israel would prove to be a big mistake for Balak . . .

23 Numbers 23:1–5
And Balaam said unto Balak, Build me here seven altars, and prepare me here seven oxen and seven rams. And Balak did as Balaam had spoken; and Balak and Balaam offered on every altar a bullock and a ram. And Balaam said unto Balak, Stand by thy burnt offering, and I will go: peradventure the LORD will come to meet me: and whatsoever he sheweth me I will tell thee. And he went to an high place. And God met Balaam: and he said unto him, I have prepared seven altars, and I have offered upon every altar a bullock and a ram. And the LORD put a word in Balaam's mouth, and said, Return unto Balak, and thus thou shalt speak.

As outlined in Numbers 2, the children of Israel camped in the configuration of a cross.

Numbers 23:6–10
And he returned unto him, and, lo, he stood by his burnt sacrifice, he, and all the princes of Moab. And he took up his parable, and said, Balak the king of Moab hath brought me from Aram, out of the mountains of the east, saying, Come, curse me Jacob, and come, defy Israel. How shall I curse, whom God hath not cursed? or how shall I defy, whom the LORD hath not defied? For from the top of the rocks I see him, and from the hills I behold him: lo, the people shall dwell alone, and shall not be reckoned among the nations. Who can count the dust of Jacob, and the number of the fourth part of Israel? Let me die the death of the righteous, and let my last end be like his!

Instead of a curse upon the children of Israel, a blessing comes out of Balaam's mouth.

Numbers 23:11–15
And Balak said unto Balaam, What hast thou done unto me? I took thee to curse mine enemies, and, behold, thou hast blessed them altogether. And he answered and said, Must I not take heed to speak that which the LORD hath put in my mouth? And Balak said unto him, Come, I pray thee, with me unto another place, from whence thou mayest see them: thou shalt see but the utmost part of them, and shalt not see them all: and curse me them from thence. And he brought him into the field of Zophim, to the top of Pisgah, and built seven altars, and offered a bullock and a ram on every altar. And he said unto Balak, Stand here by thy burnt offering, while I meet the LORD yonder.

Infuriated, Balak takes Balaam to another vantage point. And yet it is still the shape of a cross Balaam sees as he looks down upon the children of Israel.

Numbers 23:16–24
And the LORD met Balaam, and put a word in his mouth, and said, Go again unto Balak, and say thus. And when he came to him, behold, he stood by his burnt offering, and the princes of Moab with him. And Balak said unto him, What hath the LORD spoken? And he took up his parable, and said, Rise up, Balak, and hear; hearken unto me, thou son of Zippor: God is not a man, that he should lie; neither the son of man, that he should repent: hath he said, and shall he not do it? Or hath he spoken, and shall he not make it good? Behold, I have received commandment to bless: and he hath blessed; and I cannot reverse it. He hath not beheld iniquity in Jacob, neither hath he seen perverseness in Israel: the LORD his God is with him, and the shout of a king is among them. God brought them out of Egypt; he hath as it were the strength of an unicorn. Surely there is no enchantment against Jacob, neither is there any divination against Israel: according to this time it shall be said of Jacob and of Israel, What hath God wrought! Behold, the people shall rise up as a great lion, and lift up himself as a young lion: he shall not lie down until he eat of the prey, and drink the blood of the slain.

Once again, Balaam could do nothing other than bless Israel.

Numbers 23:25–30
And Balak said unto Balaam, Neither curse them at all, nor bless them at all. But Balaam answered and said unto Balak, Told not I thee, saying, All that the LORD speaketh, that I must do? And Balak said unto Balaam, Come, I pray thee, I will bring thee unto another place; peradventure it will please God that thou mayest curse me them from thence. And Balak brought Balaam unto the top of Peor, that looketh toward Jeshimon. And Balaam said unto Balak, Build me here seven altars, and prepare me here seven bullocks and seven rams. And Balak did as Balaam had said, and offered a bullock and a ram on every altar.

With the count two to zero, Balak takes Balaam up yet another mountain . . .

24

Numbers 24:1–9

And when Balaam saw that it pleased the LORD to bless Israel, he went not, as at other times, to seek for enchantments, but he set his face toward the wilderness. And Balaam lifted up his eyes, and he saw Israel abiding in his tents according to their tribes; and the spirit of God came upon him. And he took up his parable, and said, Balaam the son of Beor hath said, and the man whose eyes are open hath said: He hath said, which heard the words of God, which saw the vision of the Almighty, falling into a trance, but having his eyes open: How goodly are thy tents, O Jacob, and thy tabernacles, O Israel! As the valleys are they spread forth, as gardens by the river's side, as the trees of lign aloes which the LORD hath planted, and as cedar trees beside the waters. He shall pour the water out of his buckets, and his seed shall be in many waters, and his king shall be higher than Agag, and his kingdom shall be exalted. God brought him forth out of Egypt; he hath as it were the strength of an unicorn: he shall eat up the nations his enemies, and shall break their bones, and pierce them through with his arrows. He couched, he lay down as a lion, and as a great lion: who shall stir him up? Blessed is he that blesseth thee, and cursed is he that curseth thee.

Balaam opens his mouth a third time to curse the children of Israel, and, again, all that comes out is a blessing—a blessing uniquely and specifically fulfilled 1,500 years later in the Person of Jesus Christ.

Numbers 24:10, 11 (a)

And Balak's anger was kindled against Balaam, and he smote his hands together: and Balak said unto Balaam, I called thee to curse mine enemies, and, behold, thou hast altogether blessed them these three times. Therefore now flee thou to thy place:

The third time he blessed the children of Israel, in Balak's scorebook, Balaam struck out.

Numbers 24:11 (b)–17 (a)

. . . I thought to promote thee unto great honour; but, lo, the LORD hath kept thee back from honour. And Balaam said unto Balak, Spake I not also to thy messengers which thou sentest unto me, saying, If Balak would give me his house full of silver and gold, I cannot go beyond the commandment of the LORD, to do either good or bad of mine own mind; but what the LORD saith, that will I speak? And now, behold, I go unto my people: come therefore, and I will advertise thee what this people shall do to thy people in the latter days. And he took up his parable, and said, Balaam the son of Beor hath said, and the man whose eyes are open hath said: He hath said, which heard the words of God, and knew the knowledge of the most High, which saw the vision of the Almighty, falling into a trance, but having his eyes open: I shall see him, but not now: I shall behold him, but not nigh: there shall come a Star out of Jacob, and a Sceptre shall rise out of Israel . . .

This reference to the Star of Jacob was no doubt the verse that caused the wise men to recognize the star in the East and to follow it to the stable in Bethlehem wherein they indeed found the King of kings.

Numbers 24:17 (b), 18

. . . and shall smite the corners of Moab, and destroy all the children of Sheth. And Edom shall be a possession, Seir also shall be a possession for his enemies; and Israel shall do valiantly.

Balaam goes on to talk about how Israel will overcome both Edom and Moab (Psalm 108:9).

Numbers 24:19, 20

Out of Jacob shall come he that shall have dominion, and shall destroy him that remaineth of the city. And when he looked on Amalek, he took up his parable, and said, Amalek was the first of the nations; but his latter end shall be that he perish for ever.

Amalek, the oldest and most powerful nation in Balaam's time, was exterminated in the days of Hezekiah (1 Chronicles 4:41–43).

Numbers 24:21, 22

And he looked on the Kenites, and took up his parable, and said, Strong is thy dwellingplace, and thou puttest thy nest in a rock. Nevertheless the Kenite shall be wasted, until Asshur shall carry thee away captive.

Although they thought they were invincible in the cliffs of En-gedi, the Kenites would be carried away captive by the Assyrians (1 Chronicles 2:55).

Numbers 24:23, 24

And he took up his parable, and said, Alas, who shall live when God doeth this! And ships shall come from the coast of Chittim,

and shall afflict Asshur, and shall afflict Eber, and he also shall perish for ever.

The Assyrians would be overthrown by both the Greeks and the Romans.

Numbers 24:25
And Balaam rose up, and went and returned to his place: and Balak also went his way.

Three times Balaam is used in Scripture as an example of what not to be. In 2 Peter 2:15, he's mentioned as one who loved the wages of unrighteousness. That is, he was a man given to coveting. In Jude 11, we read of the error of Balaam—his misunderstanding, because he failed to factor the Cross into the equation, that God wanted to curse His people for their rebelliousness. The third time he is mentioned is with regard to the doctrine of Balaam, which is compromise. In Revelation 2, Jesus brings up his name in connection with the stumbling block he placed in Israel's path. Numbers 31 tells us that, knowing he couldn't curse God's people, Balaam told Balak he could get them to bring a curse on themselves by having his women seduce the Jewish men, incorporating idol worship in their seduction.

Did Balak take Balaam up on his advice? Read on . . .

25

Numbers 25:1
And Israel abode in Shittim, and the people began to commit whoredom with the daughters of Moab.

Evidently, Balaam's advice to Balak to have his women seduce the Israelite men was indeed followed.

Numbers 25:2, 3 (a)
And they called the people unto the sacrifices of their gods: and the people did eat, and bowed down to their gods. And Israel joined himself unto Baal-peor . . .

Baal worship—which included sexual perversion—was practiced at Mt. Peor.

Numbers 25:3 (b)
. . . and the anger of the LORD was kindled against Israel.

The Hebrew word translated "anger" literally refers to the reddening of the nose. And it implies not only that the Lord was angry to the point that His face was red, but also that His face was red because of crying, because of a broken heart. Thus, while the Lord's face was flushed, so to speak, with anger, it's equally true that His heart was broken as He saw what His children were doing.

Numbers 25:4
And the LORD said unto Moses, Take all the heads of the people, and hang them up before the LORD against the sun, that the fierce anger of the LORD may be turned away from Israel.

"Take the leaders—those who should know better, those who should have stopped this from happening, but didn't do so, those who went along with it, who didn't stand against it—and hang them in the sun as a spectacle, as a lesson for everyone."

Numbers 25:5
And Moses said unto the judges of Israel, Slay ye every one his men that were joined unto Baal-peor.

Moses ordered the judges of Israel to slay every man caught up in immorality, every man seduced by the Moabite and Midianite women.

Numbers 25:6
And, behold, one of the children of Israel came and brought unto his brethren a Midianitish woman in the sight of Moses, and in the sight of all the congregation of the children of Israel, who were weeping before the door of the tabernacle of the congregation.

The anger of the Lord is kindled, His heart broken. The leaders are hung. The sinners are slain. Blood is flowing. People are weeping—and in the midst of it all, one man has the audacity to bring a Midianite woman to the very door of the tabernacle.

Numbers 25:7, 8
And when Phinehas, the son of Eleazar, the son of Aaron the priest, saw it, he rose up from among the congregation, and took a javelin in his hand; And he went after the man of Israel into the tent, and thrust both of them through, the man of Israel, and the woman through her belly. So the plague was stayed from the children of Israel.

Phineas, the grandson of Aaron, thrusts a javelin through both the Israelite man and the Midianite woman.

Numbers 25:9–13
And those that died in the plague were twenty and four thousand. And the Lord spake unto Moses, saying, Phinehas, the son of Eleazar, the son of Aaron the priest, hath turned my wrath away from the children of Israel, while he was zealous for my sake among them, that I consumed not the children of Israel in my jealousy. Wherefore say, Behold, I give unto him my covenant of peace: And he shall have it, and his seed after him, even the covenant of an everlasting priesthood; because he was zealous for his God, and made an atonement for the children of Israel.

Phineas and his children would be blessed because he dealt with the sin which was sweeping through the congregation—a promise so sure, it would be repeated in Psalm 106:30, 31.

Numbers 25:14, 15
Now the name of the Israelite that was slain, even that was slain with the Midianitish woman, was Zimri, the son of Salu, a prince of a chief house among the Simeonites. And the name of the Midianitish woman that was slain was Cozbi, the daughter of Zur; he was head over a people, and of a chief house in Midian.

Zimri, whose name means "Remember him," who came from an upstanding family, walked into sin with *Cozbi*, whose name means "Deception."

Numbers 25:16–18
And the Lord spake unto Moses, saying, Vex the Midianites, and smite them: For they vex you with their wiles, wherewith they have beguiled you in the matter of Peor, and in the matter of Cozbi, the daughter of a prince of Midian, their sister, which was slain in the day of the plague for Peor's sake.

Although this account is graphic and gory, it's necessary for in Numbers 22—24, encamped in the cross, the children of Israel couldn't be cursed. Because of Jesus' finished work on the Cross of Calvary, we can't be cursed because there is therefore now no condemnation to those who are in Christ Jesus (Romans 8:1).

And yet we see the very people who were blessed in chapters 22 through 24 cursed in chapter 25 because of the sin they brought upon themselves.

When I first moved to Oregon, we lived out in the country. And every summer, the ditches which surrounded our property would be filled with water to flood-irrigate the fields. But before the ditches could be filled with water, our landlady would hire a crew of guys to clean them—knowing that the blackberry bushes, old pieces of timber, and rusted car parts which accumulated in them every winter would restrict the flow of water. It wasn't the water master who said, "I'm going to inspect your ditches and see how clean they are for that will determine how much water I'll send." No, the water master opened the spigot fully. But if the ditches were full of debris, the debris itself would restrict the flow of water to the fields.

God is not saying, "Your righteousness will determine how much I bless you." No, God opens the spigot and says, "You're in the Cross. Here comes the blessing." The problem is, if there are blackberry bushes, old tires, and timber in my pipeline, the flow through me and to me is restricted. It's not God. It's my own carnality that clogs the pipe.

What do I have to do to get God to bless my family, my marriage? God has already released blessings for generations to come. The only question is, do I get the point? Will I, like Phinehas, grab the spear? Will I clean my ditch?

Of Jesus it was said, "And the whole multitude sought to touch Him, for there went virtue out of Him" (Luke 6:19). Virtue speaks of both purity and power. Because Jesus was pure, because He had an "open ditch," power flowed from Him in such a way that people who even touched the hem of His robe were helped, healed, set free (Matthew 14:36).

If those around you aren't interested in spiritual things, maybe it's because virtue is not flowing from you. And maybe virtue isn't flowing from you because your ditch is clogged by the timber of compromise, the blackberry vine of carnality. Whatever Midianite God is drawing your attention to right now, pierce it through. Kill it. Whether it be an attitude or an activity, a habit or a tendency, deal it a death blow and let God's blessings flow. He's already opened the spigot. The blessings have already been sent. The only question is, Will you clear the ditch and let the blessings of God flood you and bless your family?

26

Numbers 26:1–4
And it came to pass after the plague, that the Lord spake unto Moses and unto Eleazar the son of Aaron the priest, saying, Take the sum of all the congregation of the children of Israel, from twenty years old and upward, throughout their father's

house, all that are able to go to war in Israel. And Moses and Eleazar the priest spake with them in the plains of Moab by Jordan near Jericho, saying, Take the sum of the people, from twenty years old and upward; as the LORD commanded Moses and the children of Israel, which went forth out of the land of Egypt.

In Numbers 1, verses 1 through 3, the Lord commanded Moses to number all the males in the congregation twenty years and older. Here, twenty-five chapters and nearly forty years later, he's told to number them again for the two-fold purpose of warfare and welfare. On the brink of entering the Promised Land, it was necessary that the Israelites know the size of their army for the inevitable battles facing them. It was also vital to know the size of each tribe in order that the Land be divided equitably among them.

In the result of the census that comprises the next forty-six verses, I draw your attention to the following insertion. . . .

Numbers 26:9, 10
And the sons of Eliab; Nemuel, and Dathan, and Abiram. This is that Dathan and Abiram, which were famous in the congregation, who strove against Moses and against Aaron in the company of Korah, when they strove against the LORD: And the earth opened her mouth, and swallowed them up together with Korah, when that company died, what time the fire devoured two hundred and fifty men: and they became a sign.

The names of Korah, Dathan, and Abiram appear as if to underscore and to remind the people of the tragic results of rebellion.

Numbers 26:11
Notwithstanding the children of Korah died not.

Korah's kids didn't die in the plague. They were not destined to be dysfunctional because their dad was a rebel. They were not burned up or wiped out. Instead, they went on to become worship leaders in the congregation, appearing no less than eleven times in the Psalms.

Numbers 26:51
These were the numbered of the children of Israel, six hundred thousand and a thousand seven hundred and thirty.

Forty years earlier, Jewish males twenty years and older had numbered 605,550. Here, their number is 601,730—a difference of 1,820. Manasseh gained 20,500. Simeon, however lost 37,000. Why did Simeon lose so many men? According to Jewish scholars, it was because the man who took the Midianite woman to the door of the tabernacle was from the tribe of Simeon (Numbers 25), his sin cost his entire tribe.

Numbers 26:52–54
And the LORD spake unto Moses, saying, Unto these the land shall be divided for an inheritance according to the number of names. To many thou shalt give the more inheritance, and to few thou shalt give the less inheritance: to every one shall his inheritance be given according to those that were numbered of him.

The bigger tribes would get the bigger piece of property. Jesus talked about this when He said, "To those who have, more shall be given. To those who have not, what they have shall be taken from them" (Luke 19:26). In other words, we will be given more if we do well with that which God has entrusted to us. And we will lose what He gives us if we fail to tend it properly.

Numbers 26:55, 56
Notwithstanding the land shall be divided by lot: according to the names of the tribes of their fathers they shall inherit. According to the lot shall the possession thereof be divided between many and few.

Although the size of the tribe would determine the size of the property given them, the location of the property would be determined by lot, by "drawing straws."

I find the combination of verses 53 to 54, and 55 to 56 fascinating because in the former we see Jesus' parable of the pounds (Luke 19) in which servants were rewarded according to what they did with an equal number of pounds given to each of them, while in the latter, we see Jesus' parable of the talents (Matthew 25), in which the servants were rewarded according to what they did with differing amounts given sovereignly to them. Thus, man's free will and God's sovereignty both enter into the equation.

Numbers 26:57 (a)
And these are they that were numbered of the Levites . . .

The Levites were not mentioned previously because they were in a different category completely. They did not have a portion of the land given to them because they were to serve in the tabernacle.

Numbers 26:60, 61
And unto Aaron was born Nadab, and Abihu, Eleazar, and Ithamar. And Nadab and Abihu died, when they offered strange fire before the LORD.

After Dathan and Abiram, as well as Korah, were mentioned earlier, now we see Nadab and Abihu. In fact, their story is seen four times in the Books of Exodus, Leviticus, and Numbers—not because God forgot He already told it, but because He wants us to learn well the lesson that the only fire which will keep us burning brightly for Him is the fire which comes from the altar, the finished work of the Cross of Calvary.

Numbers 26:63, 64
These are they that were numbered by Moses and Eleazar the priest, who numbered the children of Israel in the plains of Moab by Jordan near Jericho. But among these there was not a man of them whom Moses and Aaron the priest numbered, when they numbered the children of Israel in the wilderness of Sinai.

Six hundred one thousand, seven hundred and twenty eight of the original 601,730 had died in the wilderness, leaving only two to enter the Promised Land . . .

Numbers 26:65
For the LORD had said of them, They shall surely die in the wilderness. And there was not left a man of them, save Caleb the son of Jephunneh, and Joshua the son of Nun.

In addition to Nadab and Abihu, and Dathan and Abiram, we see a third pair here in Numbers 26: Joshua and Caleb. Whereas the first two men presumed upon God and the second two rebelled against God, the third two simply believed God—and in so doing were able to enter the Promised Land.

27

Numbers 27:1, 2 (a)
Then came the daughters of Zelophehad, the son of Hepher, the son of Gilead, the son of Machir, the son of Manasseh, of the families of Manasseh the son of Joseph: and these are the names of his daughters; Mahlah, Noah, and Hoglah, and Milcah, and Tirzah. And they stood before Moses, and before Eleazar the priest, and before the princes and all the congregation, by the door of the tabernacle of the congregation . . .

Where did the daughters of Zelophehad go with their problem? To the place where sacrifices were being offered, where incense was ascending, where spiritual life was happening—to the door of the tabernacle. When we face challenges, have questions, need prayer, if we come to the place where the Lord is honored and where His people are gathered, we'll receive counsel vastly different than that which we would receive in a clinical setting apart from Him. Through the body of Christ, we'll receive living, vibrant counsel from our living, vibrant Lord.

Numbers 27:2 (b)–4
. . . saying, Our father died in the wilderness, and he was not in the company of them that gathered themselves together against the LORD in the company of Korah; but died in his own sin, and had no sons. Why should the name of our father be done away from among his family, because he hath no son? Give unto us therefore a possession among the brethren of our father.

Because their father had died without a son, Zelophehad's five daughters asked for the possession which would have been given to the male in their family had there been one.

Numbers 27:5
And Moses brought their cause before the LORD.

After forty years, you'd think Moses would have all the answers. He doesn't. Moses says Instead, "That's a tough one. I need to pray." I like this a whole lot because it shows me that it's not what we know that counts. It's who we know. And Moses knew the Lord.

Numbers 27:6, 7 (a)
And the LORD spake unto Moses, saying, The daughters of Zelophehad speak right . . .

In saying that the daughters of Zelophehad were right, is the Lord implying that He neglected to address the question of a lack of a male inheritor, that He simply forgot to put it in the Law? Obviously not. I believe the Lord purposely leaves some things unsaid in the Word in order that we might go to Him for further instruction.

When I was younger, I basically had as my trinity God the Father, God the Son, and God the Holy Bible. I didn't understand that the real key to vibrant Christianity, to a radical faith, lies in the New Covenant—where the Lord says, "I will write My will upon the table of your heart" (Jeremiah 31).

Why was it that the whole known world was

impacted, turned upside down by a group of believers who didn't have a single page of the New Testament? It was because, although they didn't have the Gospel of Luke or the epistle to the Romans, they knew how to listen to the promptings of the Holy Spirit. And, as a result, miracles happened and blessings flowed.

We will be the most radical group of the believers in the world to the degree that, we say, "Lord, lead me today. Write Your will upon my heart; confirm it by Your Word. And what You tell me, I will do."

Numbers 27:7 (b)–11
. . . thou shalt surely give them a possession of an inheritance among their father's brethren; and thou shalt cause the inheritance of their father to pass unto them. And thou shalt speak unto the children of Israel, saying, If a man die, and have no son, then ye shall cause his inheritance to pass unto his daughter. And if he have no daughter, then ye shall give his inheritance unto his brethren. And if he have no brethren, then ye shall give his inheritance unto his father's brethren. And if his father have no brethren, then ye shall give his inheritance unto his kinsman that is next to him of his family, and he shall possess it: and it shall be unto the children of Israel a statute of judgment, as the LORD commanded Moses.

If a man didn't have a son, the inheritance was to go to his daughters. Such was the Word of the Lord to Moses. This would have been shocking in the ears of any person at that time in history, unbelievable in an age in which women had no more rights than cattle. As Galatians 3:28 says, in Christ there is neither male nor female. He's an "Equal Opportunity" Savior. He deals with us all equally. Without question, Jesus Christ is women's greatest Friend, for wherever the gospel has gone, women's rights have flourished, while in every culture which has rejected Christianity, women are still treated as second-class citizens.

Numbers 27:12
And the LORD said unto Moses, Get thee up into this mount Abarim, and see the land which I have given unto the children of Israel.

Mount Abarim is actually a mountain range fifty miles in length, the highest point being Mount Nebo, also called Mount Pisgah.

Numbers 27:13, 14
And when thou hast seen it, thou also shalt be gathered unto thy people, as Aaron thy brother was gathered. For ye rebelled against my commandment in the desert of Zin, in the strife of the congregation, to sanctify me at the water before their eyes: that is the water of Meribah in Kadesh in the wilderness of Zin.

"Your time is about up," God says to His friend, Moses. "It is time for you to be gathered to your people, to be taken to heaven. But first I want you to climb Mt. Nebo, where I will show you the Promised Land."

In this, we see both the grace and the discipline of God. God's grace allowed Moses to view the entire Promised Land. But because he had sinned in misrepresenting God to the people as he struck the rock at Meribah (Numbers 20:11), he would not be able to enter the Land.

The older I get, the more I realize that, although God is indeed gracious and full of mercy, a Father who is inexpressibly patient and kind, there are definite, absolute repercussions of sin. This is why the Bible says the fear of the Lord is the beginning of wisdom (Proverbs 9:10). We ought to walk in the fear of God—not afraid of Him, but afraid of the repercussions of our sin.

Numbers 27:15–17
And Moses spake unto the LORD, saying, Let the LORD, the God of the spirits of all flesh, set a man over the congregation, Which may go out before them, and which may go in before them, and which may lead them out, and which may bring them in; that the congregation of the LORD be not as sheep which have no shepherd.

Rather than arguing about the Lord's decision, Moses is concerned about his congregation. He doesn't want the people to be as a sheep without a shepherd—a phrase used by both Matthew and Mark to describe how Jesus felt when He saw the multitudes and was moved with compassion (Matthew 9:36; Mark 6:34).

Numbers 27:18–23
And the LORD said unto Moses, Take thee Joshua the son of Nun, a man in whom is the spirit, and lay thine hand upon him; And set him before Eleazar the priest, and before all the congregation; and give him a charge in their sight. And thou shalt put some of thine honour upon him, that all the congregation of the children of Israel may be obedient. And he shall stand before Eleazar the priest, who shall ask counsel for him after the judgment of Urim before the LORD: at his word shall they go out, and at his word they shall come in, both he, and all the chil-

dren of Israel with him, even all the congregation. And Moses did as the LORD commanded him: and he took Joshua, and set him before Eleazar the priest, and before all the congregation: And he laid his hands upon him, and gave him a charge, as the LORD commanded by the hand of Moses.

Called a minister, or servant, of Moses (Joshua 1:1), Joshua played second fiddle to Moses. For forty years, he simply served as number two, faithful in whatever he was to do. "Moreover, it is required of stewards that they be found faithful," Paul declared (1 Corinthians 4:2). Many want to be men of faith. But rarer and perhaps more important is to be a faithful man. Joshua was just that. And in due season, after forty years of faithfulness, God tapped him on the shoulder.

God does that with us, too. It might take forty years, but if we faithfully plug away at what God has called us to do—big or small, noticed or unnoticed—He will tap us on the shoulder one day and say, "You've served faithfully. Now is the time for greater ministry."

28

Chapters 28 and 29 are basically a reiteration of what we saw in the Book of Leviticus, dealing with the sacrifices, holy days, and festivals. Why are these laws repeated here? Because this is a new generation. And every generation must be instructed and reminded.

Numbers 28:1, 2
And the LORD spake unto Moses, saying, Command the children of Israel, and say unto them, My offering, and my bread for my sacrifices made by fire, for a sweet savour unto me, shall ye observe to offer unto me in their due season.

It's interesting that the Lord calls the savor of the sacrifices sweet because if you have ever smelled a burning bull or cow—the hide, the hair, the entire animal, as would be the case in the burnt offering—the odor is anything but sweet. Yet whenever the flesh is placed upon the altar, it's always sweet to the Father. The flesh speaks of our inclination towards self. Thus, there is nothing sweeter to God than when I lay my flesh on the altar and let it burn. It's sweet to Him for two reasons . . .

First, because it sets me free. God knows that sin is only pleasurable for a season (Hebrews 11:25). Consequently, whenever He smells the burning of the flesh it's sweet to Him because He knows the one making such an offering is set free. "To be carnally, or fleshly, minded is death," Paul writes. "But to be spiritually minded is life and peace" (see Romans 8:6). Do you want to really live, to have abundant peace? Then put your flesh on the altar and be set free.

Putting my flesh on the altar not only sets me free, but it lets me see. It lets me see God. Moses was one who desperately desired to see God. "If Your Presence doesn't go with me," he said, "I don't want to go on this journey" (see Exodus 33:15). In other words, "I don't want Your hand. I want Your face. I don't want something from You, Lord. I just want You."

Whether or not you are aware of it, what we all crave is the face of God. We often think, however, that we want His hand, as is evidenced by our prayers. "Give me this, Lord. Touch that. Anoint the other. Open this door. Make it happen. My business is in trouble. My kids need Your touch. I'm not feeling very well," we pray. We seek what God gives rather than who He is. And the problem is, once we get whatever is in His hand, it's not enough. It doesn't do what we thought it would do—be it in ministry, family, or any other arena. There's something even more important than anointing. It's called the presence of God.

Second Chronicles 7 says that when the presence of God filled the temple, the priests couldn't even stand in ministry because of it. "Lord," we say, "we want Your presence, Your chabod in our congregation and in our families."

"Are you sure?" asks God, "because no one can see My face and live. You've got to die" (see Exodus 33:20).

Therefore, to the degree we die to ourselves is the degree to which we will experience God's glory and presence, the degree to which we will see His face.

Numbers 28:3–8
And thou shalt say unto them, This is the offering made by fire which ye shall offer unto the LORD; two lambs of the first year without spot day by day, for a continual burnt offering. The one lamb shalt thou offer in the morning, and the other lamb shalt thou offer at even; and a tenth part of an ephah of flour for a meat offering, mingled with the fourth part of an hin of beaten oil. It is a continual burnt offering, which was ordained in mount Sinai for a sweet savour, a sacrifice made by fire unto the LORD. And the drink offering thereof shall be the fourth part of an hin for the one lamb: in the holy place shalt thou cause the strong wine to be poured unto the LORD for a drink offering. And the other lamb shalt thou offer at even: as the meat offering of the morning, and as the drink offering thereof, thou

shalt offer it, a sacrifice made by fire, of a sweet savour unto the LORD.

Every day, a lamb was to be offered both morning and evening. Note the word "continual"—a word that appears seventeen times in the Book of Numbers, a word speaks of consistency.

Numbers 28:9, 10
And on the sabbath day two lambs of the first year without spot, and two tenth deals of flour for a meat offering, mingled with oil, and the drink offering thereof: This is the burnt offering of every sabbath, beside the continual burnt offering, and his drink offering.

On the Sabbath, the sacrifice doubled to two lambs.

Numbers 28:11–15
And in the beginnings of your months ye shall offer a burnt offering unto the LORD; two young bullocks, and one ram, seven lambs of the first year without spot; and three tenth deals of flour for a meat offering, mingled with oil, for one bullock; and two tenth deals of flour for a meat offering, mingled with oil, for one ram; and a several tenth deal of flour mingled with oil for a meat offering unto one lamb; for a burnt offering of a sweet savour, a sacrifice made by fire unto the LORD. And their drink offerings shall be half an hin of wine unto a bullock, and the third part of an hin unto a ram, and a fourth part of an hin unto a lamb: this is the burnt offering of every month throughout the months of the year. And one kid of the goats for a sin offering unto the LORD shall be offered, beside the continual burnt offering, and his drink offering.

At the beginning of each month, the sacrifice increased to two bullocks, one ram, and seven lambs.

Numbers 28:16
And in the fourteenth day of the first month is the passover of the LORD.

Passover was to be commemorated annually with the sacrifice of a lamb for each household.

Numbers 28:17–25
And in the fifteenth day of this month is the feast: seven days shall unleavened bread be eaten. In the first day shall be an holy convocation; ye shall do no manner of servile work therein: But ye shall offer a sacrifice made by fire for a burnt offering unto the LORD; two young bullocks, and one ram, and seven lambs of the first year: they shall be unto you without blemish: And their meat offering shall be of flour mingled with oil: three tenth deals shall ye offer for a bullock, and two tenth deals for a ram; a several tenth deal shalt thou offer for every lamb, throughout the seven lambs: And one goat for a sin offering, to make an atonement for you. Ye shall offer these beside the burnt offering in the morning, which is for a continual burnt offering. After this manner ye shall offer daily, throughout the seven days, the meat of the sacrifice made by fire, of a sweet savour unto the LORD: it shall be offered beside the continual burnt offering, and his drink offering. And on the seventh day ye shall have an holy convocation; ye shall do no servile work.

As seen in Leviticus 23, the Feast of Unleavened Bread speaks of the burial of Christ.

Numbers 28:26–31
Also in the day of the firstfruits, when ye bring a new meat offering unto the LORD, after your weeks be out, ye shall have an holy convocation; ye shall do no servile work: But ye shall offer the burnt offering for a sweet savour unto the LORD; two young bullocks, one ram, seven lambs of the first year; And their meat offering of flour mingled with oil, three tenth deals unto one bullock, two tenth deals unto one ram, A several tenth deal unto one lamb, throughout the seven lambs; And one kid of the goats, to make an atonement for you. Ye shall offer them beside the continual burnt offering, and his meat offering, (they shall be unto you without blemish) and their drink offerings.

Again, as seen in Leviticus 23, I believe the Feast of Firstfruits speaks of Jesus' Resurrection from the dead (1 Corinthians 15:20).

29

Numbers 29:1–6
And in the seventh month, on the first day of the month, ye shall have an holy convocation; ye shall do no servile work: it is a day of blowing the trumpets unto you. And ye shall offer a burnt offering for a sweet savour unto the LORD; one young bullock, one ram, and seven lambs of the first year without blemish: And their meat offering shall be of flour mingled with oil, three tenth deals for a bullock, and two tenth deals for a ram, And one tenth deal

for one lamb, throughout the seven lambs: And one kid of the goats for a sin offering, to make an atonement for you: Beside the burnt offering of the month, and his meat offering, and the daily burnt offering, and his meat offering, and their drink offerings, according unto their manner, for a sweet savour, a sacrifice made by fire unto the LORD.

Following the Feast of Firstfruits, I believe the Feast of Trumpets speaks of the rapture of the church (1 Corinthians 15:52).

Numbers 29:7–11
And ye shall have on the tenth day of this seventh month an holy convocation; and ye shall afflict your souls: ye shall not do any work therein: But ye shall offer a burnt offering unto the LORD for a sweet savour; one young bullock, one ram, and seven lambs of the first year; they shall be unto you without blemish: And their meat offering shall be of flour mingled with oil, three tenth deals to a bullock, and two tenth deals to one ram, a several tenth deal for one lamb, throughout the seven lambs: One kid of the goats for a sin offering; beside the sin offering of atonement, and the continual burnt offering, and the meat offering of it, and their drink offerings.

I believe this feast—the Day of Atonement—speaks of the Tribulation.

Numbers 29:12
And on the fifteenth day of the seventh month ye shall have an holy convocation; ye shall do no servile work, and ye shall keep a feast unto the LORD seven days . . .

I believe this Feast of Tabernacles speaks of the Millennium—the joyous 1,000-year period when Jesus will rule the earth with righteousness.

Numbers 29:13
And ye shall offer a burnt offering, a sacrifice made by fire, of a sweet savour unto the LORD; thirteen young bullocks, two rams, and fourteen lambs of the first year; they shall be without blemish:

From the sacrifice of a single lamb in the morning and in the evening of Numbers 28:4, as seen in verses 13 through 39, the sacrifice has now multiplied to a total of over a ton of flour, 1,000 gallons of wine and oil, 13,000 oxen, and 60,000 sheep given annually.

"That's an awful lot of giving," you say, "a huge sacrifice."

Wait a minute. Father's Day is coming up. Suppose my nine-year-old son, Benjamin, says to me, "Daddy, can I have ten dollars to get you a Father's Day gift?"

"Sure," I say, and give him a crisp ten-dollar bill.

Father's Day morning, sure enough, I get a homemade card from Benny and inside the card is the crisp ten-dollar bill.

"Thanks Ben!" I would say excitedly—even though it was I who gave him the money to give to me.

That the Israelites gave thousands of livestock, a ton of flour, and thousands of gallons of wine and oil meant that God had blessed them with these things in the first place. As I did to Benny, God gave them everything they would give back to Him.

God gave us all that we have, all that we are. If we lay down our lives for God, it's only because He gave them to us in the first place.

Numbers 29:40
And Moses told the children of Israel according to all that the LORD commanded Moses.

As God is getting His people organized, developing them for their destiny, the sacrificial system is recorded. That is, a lamb was to be sacrificed every morning, every evening, every day. Weekly, an additional lamb was to be sacrificed. Monthly, a greater sacrifice was to be made at the beginning of each month. Annually, there were feasts with accompanying sacrifices that God's people were to celebrate.

In this, I understand that there is a rhythm to spiritual life. Many people have a hard time with this because they view spiritual life as being random. But as we look at God's calendar, it's impossible to deny the rhythm therein. Therefore, wise is the man, woman, or family who understands God's heart is for us to begin and end our days focused on the Lamb—unlocking the blessings for the day in the morning, closing up the blessings securely in the evening.

In addition, one day a week should be set aside to make twice the expenditure—to be focused on God singularly, offering to Him the day in praise, worship, and fellowship.

In addition, at the beginning of the month, we have opportunity to get away and say, "What's on Your heart for me for the coming month, Lord?" as we carve out time for refreshment and review, for vision and correction.

In addition, the children of Israel observed seven feasts that drew their hearts and minds back to God's goodness to them, His faithful provision for them. When the people of Israel followed this pattern, they did well. They deviated from it, they stumbled. God is not wasting pages in His Word to go over arcane, meaningless sacrifices. No, He's teaching us, reminding us that this is the way our lives will count.

Is there a pattern, a rhythm to your spiritual life? Or are you one who is haphazard and inconsistent? As much as we may not like to hear it, God designed us to be disciplined. Therefore, if you want to be prosperous and productive in claiming the promises of the Spirit-filled life, listen to what God told His people on the eve of their setting forth into the Promised Land and follow the pattern, the rhythm of spiritual life as seen here in the book which tells us how to make our lives count, the Book of Numbers.

30 To prepare the children of Israel for the battles that faced them in the Promised Land, in the chapter before us, God deals with the subject of accountability and integrity. After all, if you're headed into battle, it's imperative that the guy next to you means what he says when he says, "Go one hundred yards ahead and I'll cover you." You've got to be sure that he's not going to change his mind, that he'll come through.

Numbers 30:1, 2
And Moses spake unto the heads of the tribes concerning the children of Israel, saying, This is the thing which the LORD hath commanded. If a man vow a vow unto the LORD, or swear an oath to bind his soul with a bond; he shall not break his word, he shall do according to all that proceedeth out of his mouth.

God is serious about vows, promises, and commitments. And that makes me happy because God doesn't hold us to a higher standard than that to which He holds Himself. Therefore, the fact that God tells us we are to keep our word means He keeps His. This book is packed with promises—at the very least, three hundred in number. God makes promise after promise to you and me. And what He says, He will do. He told us, for example, that if we believe on Him, we'll not perish but have everlasting life (John 3:16). That's a promise He makes and a promise He'll keep.

Numbers 30:3 (a)
If a woman also vow a vow unto the LORD . . .

After talking about the importance of keeping one's vows, the Lord goes on to give some exceptions—all dealing with women . . .

Numbers 30:3 (b)–5
. . . and bind herself by a bond, being in her father's house in her youth; and her father hear her vow, and her bond wherewith she hath bound her soul, and her father shall hold his peace at her: then all her vows shall stand, and every bond wherewith she hath bound her soul shall stand. But if her father disallow her in the day that he heareth; not any of her vows, or of her bonds wherewith she hath bound her soul, shall stand: and the LORD shall forgive her, because her father disallowed her.

If the father of a woman living at home vows a vow (i.e., a book or record club commitment), her vow will be of none effect if he steps in and says, "She means well, but she's unable to fulfill her obligation."

Numbers 30:6–8
And if she had at all an husband, when she vowed, or uttered ought out of her lips, wherewith she bound her soul; and her husband heard it, and held his peace at her in the day that he heard it: then her vows shall stand, and her bonds wherewith she bound her soul shall stand. But if her husband disallowed her on the day that he heard it; then he shall make her vow which she vowed, and that which she uttered with her lips, wherewith she bound her soul, of none effect: and the LORD shall forgive her.

Secondly, a husband could disavow his wife's vow if he knew she couldn't keep it.

Numbers 30:9
But every vow of a widow, and of her that is divorced, wherewith they have bound their souls, shall stand against her.

The vow of a woman disconnected from her husband either by divorce or widowhood was to stand.

Numbers 30:10, 11
And if she vowed in her husband's house, or bound her soul by a bond with an oath; And her husband heard it, and held his peace at her, and disallowed her not: then all her vows shall stand, and every bond wherewith she bound her soul shall stand.

If the husband of a woman making a vow was silent, her vow would stand.

Numbers 30:12–14
But if her husband hath utterly made them void on the day he heard them; then whatsoever proceeded out of her lips concerning her vows, or concerning the bond of her soul, shall not stand: her husband hath made them void; and the LORD shall forgive her. Every vow, and every binding oath to afflict the soul, her husband may establish it, or her husband may make it void. But if her husband altogether hold his peace at her from day to day; then he establisheth all her vows, or all her bonds, which are upon her: he confirmeth them, because he held his peace at her in the day that he heard them.

In other words, if a husband heard his wife make a vow and didn't step in immediately, the vow she made was to stand.

Numbers 30:15, 16
But if he shall any ways make them void after that he hath heard them; then he shall bear her iniquity. These are the statutes, which the LORD commanded Moses, between a man and his wife, between the father and his daughter, being yet in her youth in her father's house.

If, four days after his wife made a vow, her husband said, "I'm not comfortable with that contract you signed, with that commitment you made," it would be too late to back out, leaving him responsible for fulfilling the obligation.

In this chapter, we see God holding men to their word, but making exceptions for women. Is this chauvinistic discrimination? No. It's a wonderful illustration. You see, on one hand, God wants me to be a man of integrity. On the other hand, as the Bride of Christ, we are all women. And we have a Husband who ever lives to make intercession for us, who steps up, steps in, who's at the right hand of the Father as an Advocate for us (1 John 2:1).

Tempted in all points like us (Hebrews 4:15), He understands our pressures, our frailties, our infirmities, our desire to keep promises, but our inability to do so. So He steps in, intercedes, intervenes on our behalf. It's a wonderful picture and illustration.

This is exactly what happened in Luke 22 . . .

Only hours before He was to be crucified, Jesus told Peter he would deny Him.

"Not me," Peter argued. "Lord, even if everyone else denies You, I won't. I'll die alongside of You if it comes to that. You can count on me."

Hearing Peter's heart but also knowing he couldn't do what he promised, Jesus said, "Satan has desired to sift you like wheat. But I have prayed for you that your faith fail not. And when you make it through, strengthen the brothers."

From there, Peter would eventually find himself at Jerusalem, preaching at the service in which 3,000 were saved (Acts 2:41). Because Jesus prayed for the man who made a vow he couldn't keep, thousands were saved.

You have a Friend in Jesus Christ. You have a Bridegroom who knows all about your fickleness. You have One who steps up and steps in on your behalf, Who ever lives to make intercession for you (Hebrews 7:25). No matter what vows you made at any given time, Jesus will see you through. He promised to, and He keeps every promise perfectly. If, however, if you are a divorcee or a widow—if you turn your back on Him, walk away from Him, are no longer covered by Him, you're on your own.

Numbers 30 has much to say about integrity, but also about our security as the Bride of Christ.

31

Numbers 31:1, 2
And the LORD spake unto Moses, saying, Avenge the children of Israel of the Midianites: afterward shalt thou be gathered unto thy people.

Moses had already been told he was about to die (Numbers 27:12, 13). Here, however, the Lord gives him another assignment—to do battle with the Midianites, the people who, following the counsel of Balaam, caused the Israelites to fall.

Hope deferred makes the heart sick (Proverbs 13:12). Therefore, God is a good Father who doesn't want us to be under the illusion that somehow, someday everything will be hunky dory. It doesn't work that way. There are battles until the day we go to heaven. "Moses," God said, "you're going to heaven, but before you do, there's a battle to fight."

So, too, we battle against our flesh, against the world system, against our enemy every day until the day we die. This is a key to spiritual maturity, for once we understand this, we'll not be disappointed or depressed by hope deferred.

Numbers 31:3–8
And Moses spake unto the people, saying, Arm some of yourselves unto the war, and let them go against the Midianites, and avenge the LORD of Midian. Of every tribe a thousand, throughout all the tribes of Israel, shall ye send to the war. So there were delivered out of the thousands of Israel, a thousand of every tribe, twelve thousand armed for war. And Moses sent them to the

war, a thousand of every tribe, them and Phinehas the son of Eleazar the priest, to the war, with the holy instruments, and the trumpets to blow in his hand. And they warred against the Midianites, as the LORD commanded Moses; and they slew all the males. And they slew the kings of Midian, beside the rest of them that were slain; namely, Evi, and Rekem, and Zur, and Hur, and Reba, five kings of Midian: Balaam also the son of Beor they slew with the sword.

Balaam—he who said, "Let me die the death of the righteous" (Numbers 23:10)—died in the midst of the unrighteous, killed by the very people he had caused to stumble.

Numbers 31:9–12
And the children of Israel took all the women of Midian captives, and their little ones, and took the spoil of all their cattle, and all their flocks, and all their goods. And they burnt all their cities wherein they dwelt, and all their goodly castles, with fire. And they took all the spoil, and all the prey, both of men and of beasts. And they brought the captives, and the prey, and the spoil, unto Moses, and Eleazar the priest, and unto the congregation of the children of Israel, unto the camp at the plains of Moab, which are by Jordan near Jericho.

The troops return to Moses, bringing the women of Midian with them.

Numbers 31:13–16
And Moses, and Eleazar the priest, and all the princes of the congregation, went forth to meet them without the camp. And Moses was wroth with the officers of the host, with the captains over thousands, and captains over hundreds, which came from the battle. And Moses said unto them, Have ye saved all the women alive? Behold, these caused the children of Israel, through the counsel of Balaam, to commit trespass against the LORD in the matter of Peor, and there was a plague among the congregation of the LORD.

"What are you guys doing bringing the women as captives?" Moses said, "They're the very ones who brought the plague upon us. What are you thinking?"

They were probably thinking what we think. "Yes, we got seduced by these women, and yes, it took a toll on our nation, but that's not a problem any more. Don't worry, Moses. We've learned our lesson." Oh, but let he who thinks he stands take heed lest he fall (1 Corinthians 10:12).

Numbers 31:17
Now therefore kill every male among the little ones, and kill every woman that hath known man by lying with him.

This is very harsh, we think. But, while He kept His own people at bay in Egypt, God had given the people of Canaan four hundred years to repent, to turn from their sin, to come to Him. Instead, they only became more perverted. So finally God said, "Put them out of their misery. Annihilate them."

Numbers 31:18
But all the women children, that have not known a man by lying with him, keep alive for yourselves.

The young men would grow up to war against them, the women had already brought death to them, but the young girls had done neither, so they would live.

Numbers 31:19, 20
And do ye abide without the camp seven days: whosoever hath killed any person, and whosoever hath touched any slain, purify both yourselves and your captives on the third day, and on the seventh day. And purify all your raiment, and all that is made of skins, and all work of goats' hair, and all things made of wood.

Following the principle of Numbers 19, those who dealt with the death of the Midianites were to be purified with the ashes of the red heifer.

Numbers 31:21–24
And Eleazar the priest said unto the men of war which went to the battle, This is the ordinance of the law which the LORD commanded Moses; Only the gold, and the silver, the brass, the iron, the tin, and the lead, Every thing that may abide the fire, ye shall make it go through the fire, and it shall be clean: nevertheless it shall be purified with the water of separation: and all that abideth not the fire ye shall make go through the water. And ye shall wash your clothes on the seventh day, and ye shall be clean, and afterward ye shall come into the camp.

The spoils the Israelites had taken from the Midiantes—the gold, silver, brass, and iron—were to be purified by fire and water. In the war we wage daily, everything we have, everything we are must be purified by the trials of fire and by the truth of the water of the Word.

I will not know what is gold, silver, and precious stones versus what is wood, hay, and stubble in my life until I go through trials—for they alone reveal to me where I'm really at.

> *"Abraham, take your son, your only son who you love, and offer him as a sacrifice to Me," God said. Abraham obeyed, took Isaac to Mt. Moriah, put him on the altar, ready to plunge the knife in his hand into the chest of his son.*
>
> *"Lay not thine hand upon the lad," God then said, "neither do thou anything unto him; for now I know that thou fearest God, seeing thou hast not withheld thy son, thine only son from me" (Genesis 22:12).*
>
> *The result of this incredible trial was that Abraham knew that God knew that he loved God more than he loved his son.*

How are we purified? By the water of the Word (Psalm 119:9). And we'll see the results by how we react in the trials we face.

Numbers 31:25–27
And the LORD spake unto Moses, saying, Take the sum of the prey that was taken, both of man and of beast, thou, and Eleazar the priest, and the chief fathers of the congregation: And divide the prey into two parts; between them that took the war upon them, who went out to battle, and between all the congregation:

The entire nation of Israel benefited from the 12,000 who engaged themselves on the front lines of battle. All the spoils were split in two—half went to the 12,000, half to the remaining three million.

That's always the way it is in spiritual life. Yes, we're blessed because others have paid the price, paved the way by waging war in prayer and getting laboring in ministry—but when we choose to be one of the 12,000, we discover we're a whole lot richer in the things of God than had we remained on the sidelines.

Numbers 31:28–30
And levy a tribute unto the LORD of the men of war which went out to battle: one soul of five hundred, both of the persons, and of the beeves, and of the asses, and of the sheep: Take it of their half, and give it unto Eleazar the priest, for an heave offering of the LORD. And of the children of Israel's half, thou shalt take one portion of fifty, of the persons, of the beeves, of the asses, and of the flocks, of all manner of beasts, and give them unto the Levites, which keep the charge of the tabernacle of the LORD.

As if to underscore the principle of the previous passage, the men who did battle were to give 1/500th of their reward to the work of the ministry while those who didn't were to give 1/50th.

Numbers 31:31–34
And Moses and Eleazar the priest did as the LORD commanded Moses. And the booty, being the rest of the prey which the men of war had caught, was six hundred thousand and seventy thousand and five thousand sheep, And threescore and twelve thousand beeves, And threescore and one thousand asses,

Of the 61,000 donkeys taken from Midian, one of them must have been able to talk (Numbers 22:28).

Numbers 31:35–41
And thirty and two thousand persons in all, of woman that had not known man by lying with him. And the half, which was the portion of them that went out to war, was in number three hundred thousand and seven and thirty thousand and five hundred sheep: And the LORD's tribute of the sheep was six hundred and threescore and fifteen. The beeves were thirty and six thousand; of which the LORD's tribute was threescore and twelve. And the asses were thirty thousand and five hundred; of which the LORD's tribute was threescore and one. And the persons were sixteen thousand; of which the LORD's tribute was thirty and two persons. And Moses gave the tribute, which was the LORD's heave offering, unto Eleazar the priest, as the LORD commanded Moses.

This is the portion that went to the army, including the portion they gave to the Lord.

Numbers 31:42–47
And of the children of Israel's half, which Moses divided from the men that warred, (Now the half that pertained unto the congregation was three hundred thousand and thirty thousand and seven thousand and five hundred sheep, And thirty and six thousand beeves, And thirty thousand asses and five hundred, And sixteen thousand persons;) Even of the children of Israel's half, Moses took one portion of fifty, both of man and of beast, and gave them unto the Levites, which kept the charge of the tabernacle of the LORD; as the LORD commanded Moses.

This was the portion given to the congregation, including the portion they gave to the Lord.

Numbers 31:48–50
And the officers which were over thousands of the host, the captains of thousands, and captains of hundreds, came near unto Moses: And they said unto Moses, Thy servants have taken the sum of the men of war which are under our charge, and there lacketh not one man of us. We have therefore brought an oblation for the LORD, what every man hath gotten, of jewels of gold, chains, and bracelets, rings, earrings, and tablets, to make an atonement for our souls before the LORD.

Something amazing happened in the war with the Midianites, for 12,000 Israelites went out to battle and 12,000 came back. They didn't lose a single man. So blown away by the goodness of God were these experienced men of war that they brought an offering to the Lord of that which they had plundered. The Lord didn't ask for this, but these leaders had an eye to see the grace and goodness of God at work. And they said, "God has been so good to us. How can we not go above and beyond the call of duty?"

Numbers 31:51–54
And Moses and Eleazar the priest took the gold of them, even all wrought jewels. And all the gold of the offering that they offered up to the LORD, of the captains of thousands, and of the captains of hundreds, was sixteen thousand seven hundred and fifty shekels. (For the men of war had taken spoil, every man for himself.) And Moses and Eleazar the priest took the gold of the captains of thousands and of hundreds, and brought it into the tabernacle of the congregation, for a memorial for the children of Israel before the LORD.

The men of war brought four hundred and twenty pounds of gold to the tabernacle as a memorial to the Lord. We talk a lot about making memories with our kids and our families. But these men made a memory for God. "You've been so good to us," they said. "Let this be a memory for You."

I read this and I say, "Make me that kind of man, Lord—a man who makes memories for I'm so calloused and cold. Circumcise my heart. Let me see what You've done for me and my family."

I miss my daughter, Jessie. Oh, I'm so glad she's in heaven. And I'm glad for the memories we have. But I miss her a lot. If you have a daughter you're able to tuck in tonight, who's still with you, you need to be thankful. I don't care how bad your day, the hard times you might be going through, if you can tuck your daughter in, it's time for you to make a memory for the Lord, a memorial unto Him. It's time for you to bring Him the jewels and gold of thankgiving and praise for His abundant goodness to us all.

32

Jesus and His disciples had just gone through a storm so terrifying to the disciples that these experienced fishermen thought they were going to die. On the other side of the Sea of Galilee they found themselves in another difficult place—at a cemetery surrounded by pigs. It was not only unclean due to the pigs, but it was unsafe because in it was a man demon-possessed by a legion of hellions. "What do you want?" screamed the demons. Jesus wanted what He always wants—He wanted the man back.

"Don't send us away from here," the demons said. "Just send us into the swine," a pig being as good as a man, a man as good as a pig in their view. The demons entered into the swine and the pigs ran into the Sea of Galilee. Hearing this report, people in the city came out to see what had been done to their cash crop. They saw the man sitting, clothed, and in his right mind. And it was at this point that the people in Gadera were afraid.

"Leave Gadera," they said to Jesus. But the man spread the news in Decapolis concerning the great things Jesus had done for him (Mark 5).

Why, there on the edge of the Sea of Galilee, was there a thriving pig industry? After all, pigs were forbidden by the Law of God. And why does this man go to Decapolis—a Greek city? Of the ten Greek cities comprising Decapolis, why were nine were on the Eastern side, the Gadarene side of the Jordan? Why did the people of Gadera tell Jesus to go back to the west side of the Jordan from whence He came?

For the answers to these questions, turn to our text, Numbers 32 . . .

Numbers 32:1–5
Now the children of Reuben and the children of Gad had a very great multitude of cattle: and when they saw the land of Jazer, and the land of Gilead, that, behold, the place was a place for cattle; The children of Gad and the children of Reuben came and spake unto Moses, and to Eleazar the priest, and unto the princes of the congregation, saying, Ataroth, and Dibon, and Jazer, and Nimrah, and Heshbon, and Elealeh, and Shebam, and Nebo, and Beon, Even the country which the LORD smote before the congregation of Israel, is a land for cattle, and thy servants have cattle: Wherefore,

said they, if we have found grace in thy sight, let this land be given unto thy servants for a possession, and bring us not over Jordan.

Here were the children of Israel—poised to at last cross the Jordan River into the Land of Promise. But wait. Reuben and Gad say, "Moses, we don't want to cross over the Jordan. We like it here on the east side. We've got cattle and there's lots of grass here. This is a great place for business, for economic prosperity, for us. We don't want to press in further or go deeper. We want to stay here on the edge, on the east side." Who wanted to stay on the east side? The tribe of Reuben and the tribe of Gad—from which came the word Gad-era.

Numbers 32:6, 7
And Moses said unto the children of Gad and to the children of Reuben, Shall your brethren go to war, and shall ye sit here? And wherefore discourage ye the heart of the children of Israel from going over into the land which the LORD hath given them?

"It's not just about you," Moses said. "If you stay here, you'll discourage the others."

How sad it is when people say, "I don't see him or her pressing in to the things of God, so I guess it's okay for me to kick back. After all, they've been around longer than I have. And if they don't want to go further, why should I?"

Numbers 32:8, 9
Thus did your fathers, when I sent them from Kadesh-barnea to see the land. For when they went up unto the valley of Eshcol, and saw the land, they discouraged the heart of the children of Israel, that they should not go into the land which the LORD had given them.

Moses knew all too well the effects of discouragement—for when the ten spies discouraged the hearts of the people by saying, "It's scary in there. There are giants to fight, a price to pay," an entire generation was lost.

Numbers 32:10–15
And the LORD's anger was kindled the same time, and he sware, saying, Surely none of the men that came up out of Egypt, from twenty years old and upward, shall see the land which I sware unto Abraham, unto Isaac, and unto Jacob; because they have not wholly followed me: Save Caleb the son of Jephunneh the Kenezite, and Joshua the son of Nun: for they have wholly followed the LORD. And the LORD's anger was kindled against Israel, and he made them wander in the wilderness forty years, until all the generation, that had done evil in the sight of the LORD, was consumed. And, behold, ye are risen up in your fathers' stead, an increase of sinful men, to augment yet the fierce anger of the LORD toward Israel. For if ye turn away from after him, he will yet again leave them in the wilderness; and ye shall destroy all this people.

Moses likened Gad and Reuben to the generation before them, men who were afraid to enter the Land the Lord had promised them.

Numbers 32:16–19
And they came near unto him, and said, We will build sheepfolds here for our cattle, and cities for our little ones: But we ourselves will go ready armed before the children of Israel, until we have brought them unto their place: and our little ones shall dwell in the fenced cities because of the inhabitants of the land. We will not return unto our houses, until the children of Israel have inherited every man his inheritance. For we will not inherit with them on yonder side Jordan, or forward; because our inheritance is fallen to us on this side Jordan eastward.

"We'll leave our wives and kids here on this side," said the men of Reuben and Gad. "But we'll cross over and fight the battles. And once the battles are won in the Promised Land, we'll come back and live here on the east side of the Jordan, on the east side of the Sea of Galilee, in Gadera."

This is a lot like those today who say, "If there's something to do, I'll step in and do my best to help those who want to press in and move on. But don't expect me to actually *live* in the territory that requires faith or commitment. After all, my home is in Gadera."

Numbers 32:20–24
And Moses said unto them, If ye will do this thing, if ye will go armed before the LORD to war, and will go all of you armed over Jordan before the LORD, until he hath driven out his enemies from before him, and the land be subdued before the LORD: then afterward ye shall return, and be guiltless before the LORD, and before Israel; and this land shall be your possession before the LORD. But if ye will not do so, behold, ye have sinned against the LORD: and be sure your sin will find you out. Build you cities for your little ones, and folds for your sheep; and do that which hath proceeded out of your mouth.

Because God will never take us one step further in spiritual life than we want to go, Moses agreed to Reuben's and Gad's proposal—but warned them that if they didn't live up to their agreement, their sin would find them out.

This is a pivotal, foundational principle. Notice Moses didn't say it was God who would track them down, do them in, find them out. No, should Reuben and Gad fail to keep their end of the bargain, it was their sin which would find them out. And the same is true with us.

Due to the finished work of the Cross, God not only forgives our sin, but buries it in the sea of His forgetfulness (Hebrews 10:17). Yet I must understand that, as Galatians 6 declares, whatever I sow, I'll reap. It isn't God who says, "Aha! I'm going to expose that sin to embarrass you." That's not the nature of our Father. No, it is the sin itself that will come to fruition. I am firmly persuaded and deeply convinced that there is no exception to this. Every time I sin, that sin will sooner or later track me down, find me out, and humiliate me. But it's not God doing so. Rather, it's the work of the enemy to not only seduce us into sin, but to expose and humiliate us through it.

Numbers 32:25–33

And the children of Gad and the children of Reuben spake unto Moses, saying, Thy servants will do as my lord commandeth. Our little ones, our wives, our flocks, and all our cattle, shall be there in the cities of Gilead: But thy servants will pass over, every man armed for war, before the LORD to battle, as my lord saith. So concerning them Moses commanded Eleazar the priest, and Joshua the son of Nun, and the chief fathers of the tribes of the children of Israel: And Moses said unto them, If the children of Gad and the children of Reuben will pass with you over Jordan, every man armed to battle, before the LORD, and the land shall be subdued before you; then ye shall give them the land of Gilead for a possession: But if they will not pass over with you armed, they shall have possessions among you in the land of Canaan. And the children of Gad and the children of Reuben answered, saying, As the LORD hath said unto thy servants, so will we do. We will pass over armed before the LORD into the land of Canaan, that the possession of our inheritance on this side Jordan may be ours. And Moses gave unto them, even to the children of Gad, and to the children of Reuben, and unto half the tribe of Manasseh the son of Joseph, the kingdom of Sihon king of the Amorites, and the kingdom of Og king of Bashan, the land, with the cities thereof in the coasts, even the cities of the country round about.

Joined by half of the tribe of Manasseh, the tribes of Reuben and Gad did indeed remain on the east side of the Jordan. Oh, they went into the Promised Land occasionally, but they didn't live there. And, as we'll see in Joshua 22, when they built an altar on their side of the Jordan, the other tribes said, "What are you doing building an altar? There is only to be one altar—at the tabernacle."

"Wait a minute," said the men of Gad. "We're not building an altar to offer sacrifices, but so that in the coming days you won't disavow us. It's not a working altar, but simply a monument so that future generations will know we're linked with you." Yet, although they made peace that day, the problems had begun—leading to suspicion and division in the nation between those who wanted to stay and those who wanted to go on.

Although they established cities, as evidenced by the remainder of the chapter, it would eventually be these who didn't go in, who didn't go on who were picked off first by the Syrians and the Assyrians. And it would be they who would become corrupted—for when Jesus came on the scene, the prized property of Reuben and Gad, the land of the Gadarenes, was filled with pigs, demons, and pagan Greek culture.

Why?

Because we either move further and deeper into the presence of the Lord—or we move in the other direction and become more and more interested in the things of the world. Right now, you are either deeper than you were five years ago, or you are more shallow. But you are not the same. Either my knowledge of the Lord is deeper, my walk stronger, my faith larger—or it is less. It's a great misconception to think we can put our spiritual lives on cruise control, to think that because we know the plan of salvation and basic biblical principles that we can coast from here on out. We can't.

Reuben and Gad made a monumental mistake choosing a place of comfort rather than one of commitment, by opting for affluence rather than obedience. "This land is good for our cattle and for our families," they said. And yet by the time Jesus walked their land, there was not a cow in sight. If you want your cattle to do well, take them into the Promised Land, otherwise they'll turn into pigs. And if you want your kids to do well, take them with you, otherwise they'll be the ones who prefer that Jesus depart from their coasts.

Nevertheless I have somewhat against thee, because thou hast left thy first love. Remember therefore from whence thou art fallen, and repent, and do the first works; or else I will come unto thee quickly, and will remove thy candlestick out of his place, except thou repent.

Revelation 2:4, 5

Is your praise more fervent, your prayer more intense, your commitment to the kingdom greater, your time in the Word longer, your knowledge of God larger, your love for the Lord deeper than it was two years ago? Press in. Go on. Don't stop.

Numbers 32:34 (a)
And the children of Gad built Dibon . . .

Verse 34 to the end of the chapter lists the cities either built or conquered by the children of Israel.

33

Numbers 33:1–49

These are the journeys of the children of Israel, which went forth out of the land of Egypt with their armies under the hand of Moses and Aaron. And Moses wrote their goings out according to their journeys by the commandment of the LORD: and these are their journeys according to their goings out. And they departed from Rameses in the first month, on the fifteenth day of the first month; on the morrow after the passover the children of Israel went out with an high hand in the sight of all the Egyptians. For the Egyptians buried all their firstborn, which the LORD had smitten among them: upon their gods also the LORD executed judgments. And the children of Israel removed from Rameses, and pitched in Succoth. And they departed from Succoth, and pitched in Etham, which is in the edge of the wilderness. And they removed from Etham, and turned again unto Pi-hahiroth, which is before Baal-zephon: and they pitched before Migdol. And they departed from before Pi-hahiroth, and passed through the midst of the sea into the wilderness, and went three days' journey in the wilderness of Etham, and pitched in Marah. And they removed from Marah, and came unto Elim: and in Elim were twelve fountains of water, and threescore and ten palm trees; and they pitched there. And they removed from Elim, and encamped by the Red sea. And they removed from the Red sea, and encamped in the wilderness of Sin. And they took their journey out of the wilderness of Sin, and encamped in Dophkah. And they departed from Dophkah, and encamped in Alush. And they removed from Alush, and encamped at Rephidim, where was no water for the people to drink. And they departed from Rephidim, and pitched in the wilderness of Sinai. And they removed from the desert of Sinai, and pitched at Kibroth-hattaavah. And they departed from Kibroth-hattaavah, and encamped at Hazeroth. And they departed from Hazeroth, and pitched in Rithmah. And they departed from Rithmah, and pitched at Rimmon-parez. And they departed from Rimmon-parez, and pitched in Libnah. And they removed from Libnah, and pitched at Rissah. And they journeyed from Rissah, and pitched in Kehelathah. And they went from Kehelathah, and pitched in mount Shapher. And they removed from mount Shapher, and encamped in Haradah. And they removed from Haradah, and pitched in Makheloth. And they removed from Makheloth, and encamped at Tahath. And they departed from Tahath, and pitched at Tarah. And they removed from Tarah, and pitched in Mithcah. And they went from Mithcah, and pitched in Hashmonah. And they departed from Hashmonah, and encamped at Moseroth. And they departed from Moseroth, and pitched in Bene-jaakan. And they removed from Bene-jaakan, and encamped at Hor-hagidgad. And they went from Hor-hagidgad, and pitched in Jotbathah. And they removed from Jotbathah, and encamped at Ebronah. And they departed from Ebronah, and encamped at Ezion-gaber. And they removed from Ezion-gaber, and pitched in the wilderness of Zin, which is Kadesh. And they removed from Kadesh, and pitched in mount Hor, in the edge of the land of Edom. And Aaron the priest went up into mount Hor at the commandment of the LORD, and died there, in the fortieth year after the children of Israel were come out of the land of Egypt, in the first day of the fifth month. And Aaron was an hundred and twenty and three years old when he died in mount Hor. And king Arad the Canaanite, which dwelt in the south in the land of Canaan, heard of the coming of the children of Israel. And they departed from mount Hor, and pitched in Zalmonah. And they departed from Zalmonah, and pitched in Punon. And they departed from Punon, and pitched in Oboth. And they departed from Oboth, and pitched in Ije-abarim, in the border of Moab. And they departed from Iim, and pitched in Dibon-gad. And they removed from Dibon-gad, and encamped in Almon-diblathaim. And they removed from Almon-diblathaim, and pitched in the mountains of Abarim, before Nebo. And they departed from the mountains of

Abarim, and pitched in the plains of Moab by Jordan near Jericho. And they pitched by Jordan, from Beth-jesimoth even unto Abel-shittim in the plains of Moab.

I know what you're thinking—that that is the most boring passage of Scripture you've ever read. Why, you might ask, did God command Moses to record every place the children of Israel pitched their tents?

I suggest it was because this is God's scrapbook, His slide show, His video, His journal. You see, He was traveling with His children for forty years, and these places are memorable to Him. They might seem boring to you or insignificant to us, but this should not be surprising. After all, we've all had the experience of being at a friend's house only to see him proudly bring out the video, the slide projector, or the scrapbook of his summer vacation. And although he's really into it, we find ourselves somewhat bored by it. It's important to him—but not necessarily important to us.

On the other hand, when we're showing our own slides of our family vacation it's fascinating. Our kids find themselves in every picture and we relive our trip together. That's essentially what's happening here. At the end of this forty-year camping trip, God says, "I want our journey recorded in perfect order. Make a record of all the places we went together."

"Okay," you say. "This record might have brought back some memories to those who were on that journey—but what's the point of it for us today?"

I believe there are a couple of important principles this passage teaches us, for the God of the children of Israel is our Father as well. He's made us a holy nation, adopted us into His family, and He's taking us on our own journey, a journey toward the Promised Land of heaven . . .

Our Father Remembers Where We've Been

Every stop along the way, every place we've pitched our tent, every time we've pulled up stakes to move on, He remembers. I wish that could be said of me. My kids will say, "Dad, remember when we did that?" But I don't. I forget the places we stopped and some of the things we've done. Not so our Father. He remembers it all. In Hebrews 6:10, we read that God is not unrighteous to forget your work and your labor of love. God never forgets anything we've done. Whenever we've done what He's led us to do, He records it, remembers it, and eventually rewards it (Matthew 10:42). He never forgets—not a single work.

God has led you from stop to stop, from place to place that you have long since forgotten about—like the time your coworker was bogged down with a bunch to do and you chose to stay an extra twenty minutes to help him, the time you helped in the nursery when it wasn't even your turn, the time you stood by the one in your seventh-grade class who everyone else was picking on. "I remember when you chose to do what I led you to do, when you pitched your tent where I told you to pitch," God says. "It's in My scrapbook. It might be boring to others, forgotten by you—but it's important to Me."

Which of us as parents doesn't have a box or a trunk filled with pictures and paintings, birthday cards and drawings from our kids? I have a painting matted and framed on my wall made by Peter-John when he was two years old—some green and blue brush strokes slapped on a piece of paper. You would look at it and say, "What's that?" But what would be unimportant and insignificant to you is treasured by me. That's the idea here.

Each one of these names stands for a place where God said to His people, "I want you to pitch your tent here." And they did. Thus, their obedience was treasured by Him.

Our Father Forgets about Our Sin

In verses 3 and 4, we see the children of Israel leaving Egypt. In verses 5 through 8, they go to and through the Red Sea. In verses 9 through 15, they go from Marah to Mt. Sinai, where they received the Law and instructions for building the tabernacle and the sacrificial system. In verses 16 through 36, they go from Mt. Sinai to Kadesh-barnea. And in verses 37 through 49, they go from Kadesh-barnea to the Jordan River, into the Land of Promise.

In this account, there is something huge missing, a glaring omission—namely, the thirty-eight years the children of Israel wandered in the wilderness due to their unbelief. In other words, the Father records exactingly and carefully every single spot where they pitched their tents in obedience to His leading. But when they were in sin, there's no mention, no record, no memory as far as He is concerned.

How I like that! He remembers where we've been, but He forgets about our sin. He edits it out of the video, throws away the slide, erases it from His journal. That's the kind of God we serve.

Why doesn't He remember our sin? Because He sent His Son to die on the Cross in our place and shed His blood in order that it could be cleansed. What a price the Father paid to eradicate that memory, to clean up my story.

Our Father Will Take Us In

Listen to what God declares a few pages later in the Book of Deuteronomy . . .

> The LORD your God which goeth before you, he shall fight for you, according to all that he did for you in Egypt before your eyes; And in the wilderness, where thou hast seen how that the LORD thy God bare thee, as a man doth bear his son, in all the way that ye went, until ye came into this place. Deuteronomy 1:30, 31

"I went before you," God says. "Each of your stops was scouted out by Me. I was leading the way." That's the nature of our Father. And that's what He does for you and me. God became a Man and walked through life ahead of us. He knows where we're camping. He knows how we're struggling. And yet He's going to take us in.

Where?

To the Promised Land of the Spirit-filled life.

But it doesn't stop there. He not only will see us through this life, but He's preparing a place for us in heaven, our ultimate destiny (John 14:2).

Numbers 33:50, 51
And the LORD spake unto Moses in the plains of Moab by Jordan near Jericho, saying, Speak unto the children of Israel, and say unto them, When ye are passed over Jordan into the land of Canaan;

God didn't say, "*If* you pass over," He said, "*when* you pass over. . . ." He promised to bring them in—and He would. He who began a good work in us will continue to perform it until the day of Jesus Christ (Philippians 1:6).

Numbers 33:52, 53
Then ye shall drive out all the inhabitants of the land from before you, and destroy all their pictures, and destroy all their molten images, and quite pluck down all their high places: And ye shall dispossess the inhabitants of the land, and dwell therein: for I have given you the land to possess it.

"When I cause you to cross over the Jordan—and I will do that for you—" God said to His people, "you're to rid the land of the reminders of the false gods which have dominated it for the last four hundred years."

Numbers 33:54–56
And ye shall divide the land by lot for an inheritance among your families: and to the more ye shall give the more inheritance, and to the fewer ye shall give the less inheritance: every man's inheritance shall be in the place where his lot falleth; according to the tribes of your fathers ye shall inherit. But if ye will not drive out the inhabitants of the land from before you; then it shall come to pass, that those which ye let remain of them shall be pricks in your eyes, and thorns in your sides, and shall vex you in the land wherein ye dwell. Moreover it shall come to pass, that I shall do unto you, as I thought to do unto them.

Just as the children of Israel were to drive out the Canaanites, my flesh and my spirit cannot coexist. There can be no peace treaty between them. The only peace there can be is the peace of God through the One who travels every step with us on our journey to heaven (Romans 5:1).

34

Numbers 34:1, 2
And the LORD spake unto Moses, saying, Command the children of Israel, and say unto them, When ye come into the land of Canaan; (this is the land that shall fall unto you for an inheritance, even the land of Canaan with the coasts thereof).

Verses 2 through 15 describe the borders of the land given to the Jews.

Numbers 34:16–18
And the LORD spake unto Moses, saying, These are the names of the men which shall divide the land unto you: Eleazar the priest, and Joshua the son of Nun. And ye shall take one prince of every tribe, to divide the land by inheritance.

Verses 19 through 28 list the names of the representative of each tribe for the purpose of dividing the Land.

Numbers 34:29
These are they whom the LORD commanded to divide the inheritance unto the children of Israel in the land of Canaan.

The Israelites never came close to taking all of the territory God had given them. God had so much for them. He had given so much to them. He had such grand plans for them. Yet they never took advantage of them. And as I read this, I can't help but wonder, *Lord, how much more do You have in mind for me, for my family, for the congregation?* As I do, I realize I can get very comfortable on this side of Jordan and miss out on what God wants to do through me and in me. I also realize that if I don't deal decisively with the carnal tendencies of my heart, like the children of

Israel, I'll possess only a fraction of what the Lord had for me.

35 In these final two chapters of the Book of Numbers, we come to the end of a journey that entails thirty-nine years in totality—years in which the children of Israel wandered through the wilderness. We have heard their murmuring, seen their rebellion, observed their sinning. It's been an amazing story . . .

> Moreover, brethren, I would not that ye should be ignorant, how that all our fathers were under the cloud, and all passed through the sea; And were all baptized unto Moses in the cloud and in the sea; And did all eat the same spiritual meat; And did all drink the same spiritual drink: for they drank of that spiritual Rock that followed them: and that Rock was Christ. But with many of them God was not well pleased: for they were overthrown in the wilderness. Now these things were our examples, to the intent we should not lust after evil things, as they also lusted. Neither be ye idolaters, as were some of them; as it is written, the people sat down to eat and drink, and rose up to play. Neither let us commit fornication, as some of them committed, and fell in one day three and twenty thousand. Neither let us tempt Christ, as some of them also tempted, and were destroyed of serpents. Neither murmur ye, as some of them also murmured, and were destroyed of the destroyer.
>
> 1 Corinthians 10:1–10

Over and over, Paul reaches back to the Book of Numbers and brings to remembrance the stories we've been studying, summing up the whole discussion by saying, "All these things happened unto them for examples." As has been rightly said, experience is the best teacher—if you can afford to pay the tuition. Therefore, wise is the man or woman who learns from the experience of others.

Numbers 35:1 (a)
And the LORD spake unto Moses in the plains of Moab by Jordan near Jericho . . .

Still on the east side of the Jordan River, directly across from the city of Jericho, three million people are gathered, ready to cross over into the Promised Land, wandering around in the wilderness no longer, but ready to enter into the land of milk and honey, the land of prosperity. And that's what the Lord wants for you and me spiritually.

Numbers 35:1 (b)–5
. . . saying, Command the children of Israel, that they give unto the Levites of the inheritance of their possession cities to dwell in; and ye shall give also unto the Levites suburbs for the cities round about them. And the cities shall they have to dwell in; and the suburbs of them shall be for their cattle, and for their goods, and for all their beasts. And the suburbs of the cities, which ye shall give unto the Levites, shall reach from the wall of the city and outward a thousand cubits round about. And ye shall measure from without the city on the east side two thousand cubits, and on the south side two thousand cubits, and on the west side two thousand cubits, and on the north side two thousand cubits and the city shall be in the midst: this shall be to them the suburbs of the cities.

Serving as ministers in the tabernacle, the tribe of Levi was not given any portion of the Promised Land. Instead, the Levites were to be scattered throughout the entire country. The rest of the tribes were told to give certain cities to the Levites as places in which they could dwell. As we shall see, these cities would number forty-eight.

If the Levites were only in one tribal region, people who weren't close to them wouldn't get the proper ministry. So they were scattered throughout the entire country. And that's what the Lord does with us. The Lord has snuck His servants into the most amazing places. He sneaks Christian teachers into high schools to be subversive, secret agents, Levites, reflections of Jesus Christ. He sneaks Christian salesmen, secretaries, and accountants into the workplace to be examples of what it means to be a believer. He sneaks Christian doctors into hospital rooms as ministers of the gospel.

This is such a key. Each of us who is serious about Jesus is in ministry. We are a royal priesthood (1 Peter 2:9). And He's stationed you in that work place, that neighborhood, that family to be a servant of His. It's a great day indeed when a believer looks at his work as his ministry and says, "I'm surrounded by people professional pastors would never have an opportunity to reach. I'm here on campus, at the store, in the neighborhood not just to work for a paycheck or to raise my family, but to be a minister. So I'm going to keep my eyes open and my antennae up in order to determine the part I am to play in this place for God's glory."

Numbers 35:6–8
And among the cities which ye shall give unto the Levites there shall be six cities for

refuge, which ye shall appoint for the manslayer, that he may flee thither: and to them ye shall add forty and two cities. So all the cities which ye shall give to the Levites shall be forty and eight cities: them shall ye give with their suburbs. And the cities which ye shall give shall be of the possession of the children of Israel: from them that have many ye shall give many; but from them that have few ye shall give few: every one shall give of his cities unto the Levites according to his inheritance which he inheriteth.

Of the forty-eight Levitical cities, six were designated to be cities of refuge—places to which those who unintentionally killed someone could flee.

Numbers 35:9–12
And the LORD spake unto Moses, saying, Speak unto the children of Israel, and say unto them, When ye be come over Jordan into the land of Canaan; Then ye shall appoint you cities to be cities of refuge for you; that the slayer may flee thither, which killeth any person at unawares. And they shall be unto you cities for refuge from the avenger; that the manslayer die not, until he stand before the congregation in judgment.

In Bible days, there was no such thing as a police force. There was no constable, no sheriff, no deputy, and no patrolman. It was up to the family to keep law and order. Therefore, the way it worked was as follows: If my brother Jimmy was crossing the street and you accidentally hit and killed him, as his brother, it would be up to me to avenge his death, to track you down and kill you. No matter how long it might take, culture required that I kill you.

The idea of the avenger was neither created nor condoned by God. God here is simply controlling the reality of the day—similar to when He gave rules and regulations concerning practices such as divorce and slavery. Why didn't He simply do away with these practices altogether? Because He's treating His people as a family.

When Ben and Mary were little, I didn't have the same requirements, the same expectations for them that I do now that they're twelve and thirteen. And they'll have still greater obligations when they're seventeen and eighteen. As our kids grow older, we expect more out of them. But we don't burden them immediately. We let them grow. That's what our Father does with His family. Here in the very early stages of their nationhood, because these customs were already deeply imbedded in their culture, God placed boundaries around customs like that of the avenger, dealing with them more fully as they grew (Luke 6:29).

To this end, He singled out six cities in which people who accidentally killed someone would be safe until a trial could be held.

Numbers 35:13, 14
And of these cities which ye shall give six cities shall ye have for refuge. Ye shall give three cities on this side Jordan, and three cities shall ye give in the land of Canaan, which shall be cities of refuge.

Although nine and one-half tribes were on the west side of the Jordan and only two and one-half tribes on the east side, three of the cities of refuge were on each side of the Jordan evidently because the two and one-half eastern tribes would commit as much sin as the nine and one-half western tribes. Because they didn't push on, the eastern tribes would experience more sin, more sorrow, more sadness. And the same is true of us.

Numbers 35:15
These six cities shall be a refuge, both for the children of Israel, and for the stranger, and for the sojourner among them: that every one that killeth any person unawares may flee thither.

When you look at these six cities, you realize that no one would have to cross a river or climb a mountain range to reach one of them. Jesus said that if we've been angry with anyone, bitter towards anyone, upset with anyone, cynical about anyone, we're guilty of murder (Matthew 5:21, 22). But Jesus is our Refuge (Hebrews 6:18). And, like the cities of refuge, He's easily available . . .

> Say not in thine heart, Who shall ascend into heaven? (that is, to bring Christ down from above:) Or, Who shall descend into the deep? (that is, to bring up Christ again from the dead.) But what saith it? The word is nigh thee, even in thy mouth, and in thy heart:
>
> Romans 10:6 (b)–8 (a)

Some people say that to find enlightenment, we must either ascend into heaven with the third eye of mystical wisdom, or explore the deep, deep understandings of the Christ consciousness. Paul, however, says, we neither have to climb up nor dig deep, but rather, the Word of salvation is as near as our own heart and mouth. Thus, Jesus is a Refuge easily accessible to all.

Numbers 35:16–21
And if he smite him with an instrument of iron, so that he die, he is a murderer: the murderer shall surely be put to death. And if he smite him with throwing a stone, wherewith he may die, and he die, he is a murderer: the murderer shall surely be put to death. Or if he smite him with an hand weapon of wood, wherewith he may die, and he die, he is a murderer: the murderer shall surely be put to death. The revenger of blood himself shall slay the murderer: when he meeteth him, he shall slay him. But if he thrust him of hatred, or hurl at him by laying of wait, that he die; Or in enmity smite him with his hand, that he die: he that smote him shall surely be put to death; for he is a murderer: the revenger of blood shall slay the murderer, when he meeteth him.

If a man beat someone with iron, a rock, a wooden club, or if he was angry with another man—even if he made it to a city of refuge, he was to be brought out the city, for his crime was neither accidental nor unintentional.

Numbers 35:22–25
But if he thrust him suddenly without enmity, or have cast upon him any thing without laying of wait, Or with any stone, wherewith a man may die, seeing him not, and cast it upon him, that he die, and was not his enemy, neither sought his harm: Then the congregation shall judge between the slayer and the revenger of blood according to these judgments: And the congregation shall deliver the slayer out of the hand of the revenger of blood, and the congregation shall restore him to the city of his refuge, whither he was fled: and he shall abide in it unto the death of the high priest, which was anointed with the holy oil.

He who committed murder unintentionally was to stay in the city of refuge until the high priest died—be that a year, a decade or longer.

Numbers 35:26–29
But if the slayer shall at any time come without the border of the city of his refuge, whither he was fled; And the revenger of blood find him without the borders of the city of his refuge, and the revenger of blood kill the slayer; he shall not be guilty of blood: Because he should have remained in the city of his refuge until the death of the high priest: but after the death of the high priest the slayer shall return into the land of his possession. So these things shall be for a statute of judgment unto you throughout your generations in all your dwellings.

If the unintentional murderer left the city of refuge before the high priest died, he was open game. The avenger of blood would not be found guilty of his death.

The person who was guilty—as we all are—was kept safe in the city by the life of the high priest. But he was declared not guilty by the death of the high priest. The picture should be obvious. We are kept safe by the life of our great High Priest, Jesus Christ. He is the One who intercedes for us, the One who gives instruction to us, the One who lives through us. But while we are kept safe by His life, we are saved by His death, for our sins have been washed away by His blood.

For New Testament confirmation of this Old Testament illustration, turn to Acts 27 . . .

The storm is raging. The boat is bobbing up and down. The soldiers are panicked and the sailors are frightened. "We're going down!" they cry.

But as they fight for their lives on the furious sea, Paul says, "Be of good cheer. There shall be no loss of life."

As the storm continued, however, the sailors let down a lifeboat to escape the impending crash. "Except the sailors abide in the ship," Paul said, "you can't be saved." So the ropes were cut, the lifeboats fell empty into the sea, and all on board the ship were saved.

As long as we're on board the Good Ship Salvation, we'll be saved. As long as we're in Jesus, our Refuge, we're OK. But if we choose to wander off, to bail out, to back away and live a life of drunkenness and fornication, of adultery and bitterness, the Bible says we'll not inherit the kingdom of God (1 Corinthians 6:9, 10; Galatians 5:19–21; Ephesians 5:5).

Am I teaching contrary to the doctrine of eternal security? No. I believe in eternal security. I know I'm eternally secure because I have no intention of going anywhere other than staying on board the ship of faith. I know I need the Lord. I know I can't make it without Him. He is my city of refuge, my ship of salvation. And I have no intention of leaving.

"You'll be saved," Paul says, "if you stay on board."

What board?

The board of the Cross of Jesus—following Him, loving Him, living for Him.

"Make your calling and election sure," Peter writes (2 Peter 1:10). How? It's so simple, as easily accessible as a city of refuge. You don't have to climb a mountain or swim an ocean. You simply confess with your mouth that Jesus is Lord and believe in your heart that He died for your sin and rose from the dead (Romans 10:9).

When I lead people in the sinners' prayer, I pray right along with them. Is it because I doubt my own salvation? No, I know I'm saved—but what does it hurt? Why not make sure? Why not take every opportunity to say, "Lord I love You and I understand my great need for You. And rather than be doctrinally arrogant, I want to make sure You're in my heart and that You hear from me again. Lord, I confess You as Lord and am so thankful that You died for me, that You live in heaven, interceding for me."

I say this time and time again—not because I'm insecure and worried about losing my salvation, but simply because in the city of Refuge I have reason for great celebration.

Numbers 35:30–34
Whoso killeth any person, the murderer shall be put to death by the mouth of witnesses: but one witness shall not testify against any person to cause him to die. Moreover ye shall take no satisfaction for the life of a murderer, which is guilty of death: but he shall be surely put to death. And ye shall take no satisfaction for him that is fled to the city of his refuge, that he should come again to dwell in the land, until the death of the priest. So ye shall not pollute the land wherein ye are: for blood it defileth the land: and the land cannot be cleansed of the blood that is shed therein, but by the blood of him that shed it. Defile not therefore the land which ye shall inhabit, wherein I dwell: for I the LORD dwell among the children of Israel.

If a man was found guilty of intentional, purposeful, premeditated murder, he was to be executed. This system which incorporated both cities of refuge and capital punishment was one in which the requirements of both humanity and justice were met.

36

Numbers 36:1
And the chief fathers of the families of the children of Gilead, the son of Machir, the son of Manasseh, of the families of the sons of Joseph, came near, and spake before Moses, and before the princes, the chief fathers of the children of Israel:

Here we see the leaders from the tribe of Manasseh approaching Moses and the other elders of the congregation with a problem . . .

Numbers 36:2
And they said, The LORD commanded my lord to give the land for an inheritance by lot to the children of Israel: and my lord was commanded by the LORD to give the inheritance of Zelophehad our brother unto his daughters.

In chapter 27, the daughters of Zelophehad had come to Moses saying, "Our father died in the wilderness. It's not fair that his name and property should be lost simply because he had no sons." After seeking counsel from the Lord, Moses concurred with Zelophehad's daughters that if there were no sons in a family, the inheritance was to go to the daughters in order to perpetuate the father's name.

Numbers 36:3, 4
And if they be married to any of the sons of the other tribes of the children of Israel, then shall their inheritance be taken from the inheritance of our fathers, and shall be put to the inheritance of the tribe whereunto they are received: so shall it be taken from the lot of our inheritance. And when the jubile of the children of Israel shall be, then shall their inheritance be put unto the inheritance of the tribe whereunto they are received: so shall their inheritance be taken away from the inheritance of the tribe of our fathers.

"Wait a minute," said the leader of Manasseh. "If these daughters marry men from other tribes, the property will belong to their husbands and we'll lose territory that is rightly ours."

Numbers 36:5–9
And Moses commanded the children of Israel according to the word of the LORD, saying, The tribe of the sons of Joseph hath said well. This is the thing which the LORD doth command concerning the daughters of Zelophehad, saying, Let them marry to whom they think best; only to the family of the tribe of their father shall they marry. So shall not the inheritance of the children of Israel remove from tribe to tribe: for every one of the children of Israel shall keep himself to the inheritance of the tribe of his fathers. And every daughter, that possesseth an inheritance in any tribe of the children of Israel, shall be wife unto one of the family of the tribe of her father, that the children of Israel may enjoy every man the

inheritance of his fathers. Neither shall the inheritance remove from one tribe to another tribe; but every one of the tribes of the children of Israel shall keep himself to his own inheritance.

"You've raised a valid point," Moses said to the leaders of Manasseh. "And here is what the Lord says: If a woman receives the inheritance of her father, she can marry whoever she wants as long as she marries within her tribe."

This is an important principle, for as we come to the final chapter of the Book of Numbers, the final word is simply this: Marry within your tribe or you'll lose ground.

Can two walk together, except they be agreed?
Amos 3:3

Be ye not unequally yoked together with unbelievers: for what fellowship hath righteousness with unrighteousness? And what communion hath light with darkness? 2 Corinthians 6:14

As parents, make sure your kids know that it's non-negotiable, not open for discussion, not even a consideration that they marry outside of the tribe of those who believe in God.

Even more, the daughters of Zelophehad weren't only to have no dealings with pagan men—but they were to marry within their own tribe.

The night before my daughter was taken to heaven, my final word to her was this word from Numbers 36. "You must not marry a person who is spiritually weaker than you," I told her. "You must marry someone with whom you can yoke, who has the same heart for God that you do, who can lead you in the things of the kingdom. Marry within the tribe of your fathers. Marry someone who can lead you in the ways of the Lord."

Numbers 36:10–12
Even as the LORD commanded Moses, so did the daughters of Zelophehad: For Mahlal, Tirzah, and Hoglah, and Milcah, and Noah, the daughters of Zelophehad, were married unto their father's brothers' sons: And they were married into the families of the sons of Manasseh the son of Joseph, and their inheritance remained in the tribe of the family of their father.

I love the fact that the daughters of Zelophehad not only heard the Word of the Lord, but that they obeyed it—for the blessing lies not in simply hearing or agreeing with the Word, but in obeying it (James 1:22–25).

Numbers 36:13
These are the commandments and the judgments, which the LORD commanded by the hand of Moses unto the children of Israel in the plains of Moab by Jordan near Jericho.

And so ends the Book of Numbers, the book that instructs us how to make our lives count, the book that deals with the importance of order and organization, discipline and direction, responsibility and accountability in the lives of those who, rather than wandering aimlessly, seek to claim the Promised Land of God as their own.

DEUTERONOMY

Background to Deuteronomy

We come to the fifth and final book of Moses—the final book of the Pentateuch, the final book of the Torah—and the final address to the people he had led for forty years. It's a lengthy address, but oh, so impacting, for in it Moses reviews and reminds the people of their history—how their fathers failed miserably but how God saw them through mercifully. Then he reiterates and repeats the Law of God—the Word given to the children of Israel in the first year of their journey. That's where this Book gets its name, for *deutero* is the Greek word meaning "second," and *nomos* the Greek word for "law." Thus, in the book before us we see the Law reviewed and repeated.

Your initial reaction might be, "I spent a long time already going through the Law and studying the peoples' history in the wilderness in Exodus, Leviticus, and Numbers. Why would I need to go through it *again?*" Yet it was the Book of Deuteronomy that God commanded the people read audibly, publicly every sabbatical year at the Feast of Tabernacles—the joyous festival wherein the people of Israel celebrated how God faithfully brought them through the wilderness and to the Promised Land.

It's so important to be in the Word—not just to learn practical principles, but, far more importantly, to gain an understanding of, an appreciation for the nature and character of God—for when you learn about the ways and the heart of God, you can't help but lift your hands, bow your knee, and sing His praise.

Without Bible study, worship loses its luster. Without worship, Bible study becomes academic. We need both sides of this equation. We need to be students of the Word and worshipers of the Lord. If I'm only a student and not a worshiper, I will become an intellectual Christian who lacks passion. I might have my theology down and my doctrine right, but my heart will be cold. If, on the other hand, I am involved in worship without grounding myself in the Word, my worship will be shallow, fuzzy, and will eventually fade away completely. Jesus said the Father seeks those who will worship Him in both spirit and truth (John 4:23), for that's the winning combination.

"Do we have to go through the history and the Law again?" we ask.

"Yes," God answers, "because it will inspire you to worship with both passion and intelligence."

Evidently, the New Testament writers understood the importance of the Book of Deuteronomy, for they quote it over one hundred times. But it's importance is seen even more clearly in the fact that Jesus quotes it more than He does Genesis, Psalms, or Isaiah. In fact, He quotes it more than He does any other Old Testament book. That He used it to silence Satan three times in the wilderness speaks not only of His familiarity with it, but of the power within it (Matthew 4:4–10).

If you're like me, you might have a tendency to say, "Oh, no. Not the Law again." But because God commanded it to be read audibly, because the New Testament writers quoted it repeatedly, and because Jesus valued it greatly, wise is the believer who allows the Book of Deuteronomy to be woven into the fabric of his soul.

DEUTERONOMY

1

Deuteronomy 1:1
These be the words which Moses spake unto all Israel on this side Jordan in the wilderness, in the plain over against the Red sea, between Paran, and Tophel, and Laban, and Hazeroth, and Dizahab.

As Moses begins his "farewell address," the children of Israel are camped on the east side of the Jordan River, poised to enter the Promised Land.

Deuteronomy 1:2
(There are eleven days' journey from Horeb by the way of mount Seir unto Kadesh-barnea.)

This parenthetical statement must have been particularly painful for Moses to write. After all, how long would it take a man to walk from Mt. Sinai to Kadesh-barnea, the border of the Promised Land? Eleven days. How long did it take the children of Israel? Forty years.

The number forty being the number of a biblical generation, an entire generation was lost simply for lack of faith. When God brought them to Kadesh-barnea, they were supposed to go from there and take the territory, move in to the Promised Land. But they lacked faith and were fearful of the giants about which they'd heard.

I wonder how many tears will roll down our cheeks in heaven.

"Tears in Heaven?" you say. "I thought there would be no tears in heaven."

Ah, but because Revelation 7:17 says Jesus will wipe away every tear, there must be tears to wipe away—possibly shed as we see how much He would have done for us and through us, in us and with us if only we had believed and claimed the territory of the Spirit-filled life rather than wandering around for a lifetime.

Quoting from this very story, Paul says, "Learn the lesson" (1 Corinthians 10:11). When God puts something on your heart, do it immediately lest you wander around needlessly and waste your days in a desert experience.

Deuteronomy 1:3–6
And it came to pass in the fortieth year, in the eleventh month, on the first day of the month, that Moses spake unto the children of Israel, according unto all that the LORD had given him in commandment unto them; after he had slain Sihon the king of the Amorites, which dwelt in Heshbon, and Og the king of Bashan, which dwelt at Astaroth in Edrei: On this side Jordan, in the land of Moab, began Moses to declare this law, saying, The LORD our God spake unto us in Horeb, saying, Ye have dwelt long enough in this mount:

After forty years, the children of Israel are back at Point A, the place they began, Mount Horeb, or Mt. Sinai, the place where the Ten Commandments were given, the place they began . . .

Deuteronomy 1:7, 8
Turn you, and take your journey, and go to the mount of the Amorites, and unto all the places nigh thereunto, in the plain, in the hills, and in the vale, and in the south, and

by the sea side, to the land of the Canaanites, and unto Lebanon, unto the great river, the river Euphrates. Behold, I have set the land before you: go in and possess the land which the LORD sware unto your fathers, Abraham, Isaac, and Jacob, to give unto them and to their seed after them.

Even at the height of her power, Israel only possessed a fraction of the land promised to them. That's a lot like us. So many promises are given to us, yet we only possess a fraction of them.

Deuteronomy 1:9–18
And I spake unto you at that time, saying, I am not able to bear you myself alone: The LORD your God hath multiplied you, and, behold, ye are this day as the stars of heaven for multitude. (The LORD God of your fathers make you a thousand times so many more as ye are, and bless you, as he hath promised you!) How can I myself alone bear your cumbrance, and your burden, and your strife? Take you wise men, and understanding, and known among your tribes, and I will make them rulers over you. And ye answered me, and said, The thing which thou hast spoken is good for us to do. So I took the chief of your tribes, wise men, and known, and made them heads over you, captains over thousands, and captains over hundreds, and captains over fifties, and captains over tens, and officers among your tribes. And I charged your judges at that time, saying, Hear the causes between your brethren, and judge righteously between every man and his brother, and the stranger that is with him. Ye shall not respect persons in judgment; but ye shall hear the small as well as the great; ye shall not be afraid of the face of man; for the judgment is God's: and the cause that is too hard for you, bring it unto me, and I will hear it. And I commanded you at that time all the things which ye should do.

Here we see the beginning of eldership, where God's people weren't ruled by one man dictatorially but through a plurality of leaders who cared for the flock lest the flock be frustrated by not getting the help they need and lest one man get burned out, trying to do what cannot be done. And the principle still works today if the men chosen are those already doing the work, as was the case here. You'll always find a true shepherd among the sheep. Where was David when Samuel came to Bethlehem looking for the next king? He was out with his father's sheep. Where was Moses when he was called? He, too, was with the sheep.

"Take wise and understanding men who are already known among your tribes," Moses instructed the Israelites. It's a principle that applies to every aspect of ministry and service.

Deuteronomy 1:19–21
And when we departed from Horeb, we went through all that great and terrible wilderness, which ye saw by the way of the mountain of the Amorites, as the LORD our God commanded us; and we came to Kadeshbarnea. And I said unto you, Ye are come unto the mountain of the Amorites, which the LORD our God doth give unto us. Behold, the LORD thy God hath set the land before thee: go up and possess it, as the LORD God of thy fathers hath said unto thee; fear not, neither be discouraged.

After establishing the leadership structure, Moses told the children of Israel not to be afraid to step out, not to be discouraged. I have found when I get discouraged or depressed it's always due to a lack of courage in my life. Whether it be witnessing to the friend at work, beginning family devotions, worshiping with passion—or any other new opportunity the Lord has provided, we must not be discouraged by the size or scope of the task, for "faithful is He who called you who also will do it" (1 Thessalonians 5:24).

Deuteronomy 1:22–24
And ye came near unto me every one of you, and said, We will send men before us, and they shall search us out the land, and bring us word again by what way we must go up, and into what cities we shall come. And the saying pleased me well: and I took twelve men of you, one of a tribe: And they turned and went up into the mountain, and came unto the valley of Eshcol, and searched it out.

"Let's check out the land first," said the people. So Moses sent in twelve spies—one man from each tribe. The problem is, there's no record, no hint that he prayed about doing so.

Deuteronomy 1:25, 26
And they took of the fruit of the land in their hands, and brought it down unto us, and brought us word again, and said, It is a good land which the LORD our God doth give us. Notwithstanding ye would not go up, but rebelled against the commandment of the LORD your God:

God said, "Go take the land." The people said, "Let's send spies to check it out." Big mistake. It's always a mistake when I spy out the land because it shifts me from the place of obedience to the place of evaluation. And evaluation leads more often than not to trepidation. The Bible says we're to walk by faith, not by sight. When we spy out the land, we want sight and insight. But the point where I'm evaluating what I'm seeing is the point faith becomes nonexistent.

Deuteronomy 1:27, 28
And ye murmured in your tents, and said, Because the LORD hated us, he hath brought us forth out of the land of Egypt, to deliver us into the hand of the Amorites, to destroy us. Whither shall we go up? our brethren have discouraged our heart, saying, The people is greater and taller than we; the cities are great and walled up to heaven; and moreover we have seen the sons of the Anakims there.

"And ye murmured in your tents." I'm convinced that the enemy enters most frequently through a conversation between a husband and a wife. Although we mistakenly think we can "let our hair down" with our husband or wife, in reality, if there's any place we should be people of faith, it should be in our tents. Otherwise, doubts creep in, cynicism rises up, and discouragement takes up residence.

Deuteronomy 1:29–31
Then I said unto you, Dread not, neither be afraid of them. The LORD your God which goeth before you, he shall fight for you, according to all that he did for you in Egypt before your eyes; And in the wilderness, where thou hast seen how that the LORD thy God bare thee, as a man doth bear his son, in all the way that ye went, until ye came into this place.

"God brought you out of Egypt, didn't He?" Moses said. "Certainly He won't let you down now that you're moving out, wanting to go deeper, desiring to be used more impactingly for Him."

Deuteronomy 1:32, 33 (a)
Yet in this thing ye did not believe the LORD your God, Who went in the way before you, to search you out a place to pitch your tents in . . .

The reason there was no need to send spies into the Land was because God had already spied it out.

Deuteronomy 1:33 (b)
. . . in fire by night, to shew you by what way ye should go, and in a cloud by day.

God led by both a cloud that shielded the children of Israel from the heat of the sun and by a pillar of fire that illuminated their darkness. And He does the same today. When our path leads through darkness, the temptation is to bemoan the fiery trials that come our way not realizing that God uses the fire itself to lead us. He leads by fire in the darkness, by the comforting cloud in the light. He leads both ways.

Deuteronomy 1:34, 35
And the LORD heard the voice of your words, and was wroth, and sware, saying, Surely there shall not one of these men of this evil generation see that good land, which I sware to give unto your fathers,

When we speak words of faith, God hears, and, as a result, we're saved (Romans 10:9). When we speak words of unbelief, He hears as well, and, as a result, we spend time unnecessarily lost in the wilderness of doubt and despair.

Deuteronomy 1:36
Save Caleb the son of Jephunneh; he shall see it, and to him will I give the land that he hath trodden upon, and to his children, because he hath wholly followed the LORD.

Caleb was one of the twelve spies who, along with Joshua said, "Don't back down."

Deuteronomy 1:37, 38
Also the LORD was angry with me for your sakes, saying, Thou also shalt not go in thither. But Joshua the son of Nun, which standeth before thee, he shall go in thither: encourage him: for he shall cause Israel to inherit it.

Moses was not allowed to go in—and yet he was to encourage the one who would. How do you feel when someone younger than you gets the promotion, when someone newer than you gets the tap on the shoulder, when someone less qualified, less experienced than you seems to be raised up? Something wonderful happens in the lives of those who say, "I want to encourage people who are elevated above me, who are promoted ahead of me, who get recognition instead of me." Moses had such a heart. He couldn't go into the Promised Land, but we'll see him encourage Joshua nonetheless.

Deuteronomy 1:39
Moreover your little ones, which ye said should be a prey, and your children, which in that day had no knowledge between good and evil, they shall go in thither, and unto them will I give it, and they shall possess it.

The very children the Israelites had been worried about would be the ones to possess the Land (Numbers 14:3).

Deuteronomy 1:40–46
But as for you, turn you, and take your journey into the wilderness by the way of the Red sea. Then ye answered and said unto me, we have sinned against the LORD, we will go up and fight, according to all that the LORD our God commanded us. And when ye had girded on every man his weapons of war, ye were ready to go up into the hill. And the LORD said unto me, Say unto them, Go not up, neither fight; for I am not among you; lest ye be smitten before your enemies. So I spake unto you; and ye would not hear, but rebelled against the commandment of the LORD, and went presumptuously up into the hill. And the Amorites, which dwelt in that mountain, came out against you, and chased you, as bees do, and destroyed you in Seir, even unto Hormah. And ye returned and wept before the LORD; but the LORD would not hearken to your voice, nor give ear unto you. So ye abode in Kadesh many days, according unto the days that ye abode there.

The children of Israel didn't do what God had told them to do when He told them to take the Land. Then they did what God had told them not to do when they attacked the Amorites. Why? Because they followed their own counsel rather than God's.

What has God told you to do? What has He put on your heart? I can make a strong case against doing what God told me to do. I can murmur and blame others. But each time I do, I end up wandering and missing the promised land of whatever area the Lord wanted me to possess. Life is either a fantastic adventure or it is an endless detour. And the only difference between the two is faith.

2

Deuteronomy 2:1, 3
Then we turned, and took our journey into the wilderness by the way of the Red sea, as the LORD spake unto me: and we compassed mount Seir many days. And the LORD spake unto me, saying, Ye have compassed this mountain long enough: turn you northward.

"Ye have compassed this mountain long enough." And indeed they had. After spending one year at Mt. Sinai and thirty-eight years in the wilderness, it was time for the children of Israel to go north, time to get back to where they were supposed to be thirty-eight years earlier, time to go back to Kadesh-barnea and into the Promised Land.

Deuteronomy 2:4, 5
And command thou the people, saying, Ye are to pass through the coast of your brethren the children of Esau, which dwell in Seir; and they shall be afraid of you: take ye good heed unto yourselves therefore: Meddle not with them; for I will not give you of their land, no, not so much as a foot breadth; because I have given mount Seir unto Esau for a possession.

On their way toward the Promised Land, when the children of Israel passed through the region of Mt. Seir, they were not to engage in battle because God had given that particular piece of property to the Edomites, the descendants of Esau.

Deuteronomy 2:6
Ye shall buy meat of them for money, that ye may eat; and ye shall also buy water of them for money, that ye may drink.

That the Israelites were to buy meat and water signals a shift in God's provision for them. In their wilderness wandering, God had fed them manna from the sky and water from the rock. Now that they're ready to enter the Promised Land, however, although manna would fall seemingly sporadically (Joshua 5:12), after they celebrated their first Passover in the Promised Land, the manna would stop completely.

The point is simple. God expects us to grow up, to move on. Concerning that which was once given to us, God will say, "You need to participate in the process not because I'm being mean to you or holding back from you but because I want to see maturity in you." As we do with our own kids, God expected His children to participate in their own care.

Deuteronomy 2:7
For the LORD thy God hath blessed thee in all the works of thy hand: he knoweth thy walking through this great wilderness: these forty years the LORD thy God hath been with thee; thou hast lacked nothing.

Each of us who has logged time in with the Lord must, in retrospect, join Moses in saying, "God has seen me through faithfully." For me personally, yes, there were times of doubt and fear and tears, but as I look back over forty years, I have no other honest choice but to say, "God has been nothing but faithful to me."

Deuteronomy 2:8, 9
And when we passed by from our brethren the children of Esau, which dwelt in Seir, through the way of the plain from Elath, and from Ezion-gaber, we turned and passed by the way of the wilderness of Moab. And the LORD said unto me, Distress not the Moabites, neither contend with them in battle: for I will not give thee of their land for a possession; because I have given Ar unto the children of Lot for a possession.

The Edomites were descendants of Esau; the Moabites along with the Ammonites, descendants of Lot and his incestuous relationship with his daughters following the destruction of Sodom.

Deuteronomy 2:10–12
The Emims dwelt therein in times past, a people great, and many, and tall, as the Anakims; Which also were accounted giants, as the Anakims; but the Moabites call them Emims. The Horims also dwelt in Seir beforetime; but the children of Esau succeeded them, when they had destroyed them from before them, and dwelt in their stead; as Israel did unto the land of his possession, which the LORD gave unto them.

Like the Anakims, the Emims and Horims were giant people, fearful, and terrible. Yet here Moses says that the Horims were beaten back by the descendants of Esau. In other words, because the Edomites wiped out the very giants of which God's people were afraid (Numbers 13:31–33), the Edomites possessed the land that should have been the Israelites'.

Sometimes we as believers can be real wimpy. "I'm going through this trial, this persecution, this difficulty," we whine—failing to realize that the unbeliever has just as many trials, just as many problems, just as many difficulties (Matthew 5:45). If you think being a Christian is hard, try being an unbeliever. They have the same problems as you and me, but they don't have the opportunity to approach the throne of grace boldly, to pour out their heart to the Father, to open the Word for inspiration and instruction. The world has the same kinds of problems we do, but without access to the Problem-Solver.

Deuteronomy 2:13–15
Now rise up, said I, and get you over the brook Zered. And we went over the brook Zered. And the space in which we came from Kadesh-barnea, until we were come over the brook Zered, was thirty and eight years; until all the generation of the men of war were wasted out from among the host, as the LORD sware unto them. For indeed the hand of the LORD was against them, to destroy them from among the host, until they were consumed.

Because God held only those who were twenty years old and older responsible for their unbelief (Numbers 14:29), I believe the age of accountability—the age at which a person's eternal destiny is decided—is higher than we tend to think. God's grace is great and His mercy amazing, for even if the eighteen- and nineteen-year-olds were murmuring, God gave them the opportunity to go into the Promised Land.

Deuteronomy 2:16–21 (a)
So it came to pass, when all the men of war were consumed and dead from among the people, That the LORD spake unto me, saying, Thou art to pass over through Ar, the coast of Moab, this day: And when thou comest nigh over against the children of Ammon, distress them not, nor meddle with them: for I will not give thee of the land of the children of Ammon any possession; because I have given it unto the children of Lot for a possession. (That also was accounted a land of giants: giants dwelt therein in old time; and the Ammonites call them Zamzummims; A people great, and many, and tall, as the Anakims . . .

"No temptation has taken you but that which is common to all men," Paul writes (1 Corinthians 10:13). Therefore, I firmly believe everyone has it equally hard. You see, while I've gone through some hard experiences, I've also had great blessings in my life. On the other hand, others might not go through hard times, but neither do they have the blessings. It all equals out. May we not be a people who pout about the Horims and Zamzummims in our lives. Rather, may we be those who say, "On this journey, every step of the way, God has been with us. And how *good* He has been to us."

Deuteronomy 2:21 (b), 22
. . . but the LORD destroyed them before them; and they succeeded them, and dwelt in their stead: As he did to the children of Esau, which dwelt in Seir, when he destroyed

the Horims from before them; and they succeeded them, and dwelt in their stead even unto this day:

In verse 12, we read that the descendants of Esau destroyed the Horims, but here in verse 22, we see that, in reality, it was God who destroyed them. Those who say, "I'm a self-made man. I don't need Jesus or the Bible. I fight my own battles. I take on my own giants," fail to understand that it is God who gave them the ability to succeed in business, to hit a baseball, to think technologically. *Every* good and perfect gift comes from God, James tells us (1:17). Therefore, foolish is the man who takes credit for his success.

Deuteronomy 2:23, 24
And the Avims which dwelt in Hazerim, even unto Azzah, the Caphtorims, which came forth out of Caphtor, destroyed them, and dwelt in their stead.) Rise ye up, take your journey, and pass over the river Arnon: behold, I have given into thine hand Sihon the Amorite, king of Heshbon, and his land: begin to possess it, and contend with him in battle.

Although the Israelites were forbidden from fighting the Edomites, Moabites, and Ammonites because of their relation to them, they were free to do battle against the Amorites.

Deuteronomy 2:25
This day will I begin to put the dread of thee and the fear of thee upon the nations that are under the whole heaven, who shall hear report of thee, and shall tremble, and be in anguish because of thee.

In waging war against the Amorites, God would bless Israel with such decisive victory that all of the surrounding nations would be in awe of them.

Deuteronomy 2:26–29
And I sent messengers out of the wilderness of Kedemoth unto Sihon king of Heshbon with words of peace, saying, Let me pass through thy land: I will go along by the high way, I will neither turn unto the right hand nor to the left. Thou shalt sell me meat for money, that I may eat; and give me water for money, that I may drink: only I will pass through on my feet; (As the children of Esau which dwell in Seir, and the Moabites which dwell in Ar, did unto me) until I shall pass over Jordan into the land which the LORD our God giveth us.

Even though they were permitted to do battle with the Amorites, the Israelites first asked permission of Sihon to pass through his land.

Deuteronomy 2:30, 31
But Sihon king of Heshbon would not let us pass by him: for the LORD thy God hardened his spirit, and made his heart obstinate, that he might deliver him into thy hand, as appeareth this day. And the LORD said unto me, Behold, I have begun to give Sihon and his land before thee: begin to possess, that thou mayest inherit his land.

Sihon's refusal to give safe passage to Israel set the stage for a battle he was unknowingly destined to lose. Maybe today you have a broken heart because of someone else's obstinate heart. Most of us know what it's like to be rejected by someone we care about. Yet happy is the man or woman who remembers God's sovereignty. We can be happy if we don't lose sight of the fact that God is in control. When someone has a hard heart toward me, I must remember that God is the One who causes all things to work out for His perfect, divine plan. A truly radical way to live is to realize that everything that happens is part of God's plan to allow me to possess more of my possession, to be a bigger person, to gain new territory, to experience great victory.

Deuteronomy 2:32–37
Then Sihon came out against us, he and all his people, to fight at Jahaz. And the LORD our God delivered him before us; and we smote him, and his sons, and all his people. And we took all his cities at that time, and utterly destroyed the men, and the women, and the little ones, of every city, we left none to remain: Only the cattle we took for a prey unto ourselves, and the spoil of the cities which we took. From Aroer, which is by the brink of the river of Arnon, and from the city that is by the river, even unto Gilead, there was not one city too strong for us: the LORD our God delivered all unto us: Only unto the land of the children of Ammon thou camest not, nor unto any place of the river Jabbok, nor unto the cities in the mountains, nor unto whatsoever the LORD our God forbad us.

Because of Sihon's obstinate heart, war did indeed break out. But the result was great victory for the children of Israel, just as God had promised. And through it, they gained their first foothold in the Land—the region east of the Jordan where Reuben, Gad, and the half tribe of Manasseh would eventually settle.

3 Deuteronomy 3:1
Then we turned, and went up the way to Bashan: and Og the king of Bashan came out against us, he and all his people, to battle at Edrei.

Having heard what happened to Sihon, king of the Amorites, Og, king of Bashan, set out to do battle with Israel.

Deuteronomy 3:2–11
And the LORD said unto me, Fear him not: for I will deliver him, and all his people, and his land, into thy hand; and thou shalt do unto him as thou didst unto Sihon king of the Amorites, which dwelt at Heshbon. So the LORD our God delivered into our hands Og also, the king of Bashan, and all his people: and we smote him until none was left to him remaining. And we took all his cities at that time, there was not a city which we took not from them, threescore cities, all the region of Argob, the kingdom of Og in Bashan. All these cities were fenced with high walls, gates, and bars; beside unwalled towns a great many. And we utterly destroyed them, as we did unto Sihon king of Heshbon, utterly destroying the men, women, and children, of every city. But all the cattle, and the spoil of the cities, we took for a prey to ourselves. And we took at that time out of the hand of the two kings of the Amorites the land that was on this side Jordan, from the river of Arnon unto mount Hermon; (Which Hermon the Sidonians call Sirion; and the Amorites call it Shenir;) All the cities of the plain, and all Gilead, and all Bashan, unto Salchah and Edrei, cities of the kingdom of Og in Bashan. For only Og king of Bashan remained of the remnant of giants; behold, his bedstead was a bedstead of iron; is it not in Rabbath of the children of Ammon? nine cubits was the length thereof, and four cubits the breadth of it, after the cubit of a man.

Israel's victory over Og was no small one—for not only did he rule over sixty cities, but he himself was so big that his "bedstead," or, more likely, his casket measured thirteen by six feet.

Deuteronomy 3:12–17
And this land, which we possessed at that time, from Aroer, which is by the river Arnon, and half mount Gilead, and the cities thereof, gave I unto the Reubenites and to the Gadites. And the rest of Gilead, and all Bashan, being the kingdom of Og, gave I unto the half tribe of Manasseh; all the region of Argob, with all Bashan, which was called the land of giants. Jair the son of Manasseh took all the country of Argob unto the coasts of Geshuri and Maachathi; and called them after his own name, Bashan-havoth-jair, unto this day. And I gave Gilead unto Machir. And unto the Reubenites and unto the Gadites I gave from Gilead even unto the river Arnon half the valley, and the border even unto the river Jabbok, which is the border of the children of Ammon; The plain also, and Jordan, and the coast thereof, from Chinnereth even unto the sea of the plain, even the salt sea, under Ashdoth-pisgah eastward.

The victory over both Og and Sihon left the territory east of the Jordan available to the Israelites. And, as seen in Numbers 32, the tribes of Gad and Reuben and half of the tribe of Manasseh asked Moses that it be given to them.

Deuteronomy 3:18–20
And I commanded you at that time, saying, The LORD your God hath given you this land to possess it: ye shall pass over armed before your brethren the children of Israel, all that are meet for the war. But your wives, and your little ones, and your cattle, (for I know that ye have much cattle,) shall abide in your cities which I have given you; until the LORD have given rest unto your brethren, as well as unto you, and until they also possess the land which the LORD your God hath given them beyond Jordan: and then shall ye return every man unto his possession, which I have given you.

Although Reuben, Gad, and half of the tribe of Manasseh didn't have to go with the rest of the children of Israel, they nonetheless had to assist their brethren in battle. If you have a heart for missions or a desire to serve in ministry but feel unable to do so at this time, God would have you support those who do step up, who do claim territory, who do take their place on the front lines in the battle for men's souls. Pray for those in ministry; give financially to missionaries; do your part to help others be victorious. Don't miss the opportunity to fight alongside your brothers.

Deuteronomy 3:21, 22
And I commanded Joshua at that time, saying, Thine eyes have seen all that the LORD your God hath done unto these two kings: so shall the LORD do unto all the kingdoms whither thou passest. Ye shall not fear them: for the LORD your God he shall fight for you.

The children of Israel had seen miraculous victory over Sihon and Og—but that would be only a sneak preview of coming attractions, just a hint of how God would prove to be faithful to them in the Land of Promise.

Deuteronomy 3:23–26
And I besought the LORD at that time, saying, O Lord GOD, thou hast begun to shew thy servant thy greatness, and thy mighty hand: for what God is there in heaven or in earth, that can do according to thy works, and according to thy might? I pray thee, let me go over, and see the good land that is beyond Jordan, that goodly mountain, and Lebanon. But the LORD was wroth with me for your sakes, and would not hear me: and the LORD said unto me, Let it suffice thee; speak no more unto me of this matter.

Because Moses had misrepresented the Lord when he smote the rock at Meribah (Numbers 20), he was not allowed to go into the Land of Promise, until 1,500 years later when we see him talking with Jesus on the Mount of Transfiguration. I love our Lord! It's amazing to me how He has ways of making things happen that we could never imagine. And I believe Moses will be in the Promised Land again—one of the two witnesses of the Tribulation Period in Jerusalem (Revelation 11:3).

Deuteronomy 3:27
Get thee up into the top of Pisgah, and lift up thine eyes westward, and northward, and southward, and eastward, and behold it with thine eyes: for thou shalt not go over this Jordan.

Even though Moses couldn't go into the Land, the Lord gave him a supernatural sneak preview of it in its entirety.

For topical study of Deuteronomy 3:23–28, see "The Mountain of Vision" below.

Deuteronomy 3:28, 29
But charge Joshua, and encourage him, and strengthen him: for he shall go over before this people, and he shall cause them to inherit the land which thou shalt see. So we abode in the valley over against Bethpeor.

The name *Joshua* in the Old Testament is *Jesus* in the New Testament. Moses couldn't go in to the Promised Land. Joshua would be the one to lead the people in. And Jesus does just that. Jesus is the One who leads us into the Promised Land, the place of salvation, the Spirit-filled life. Even as the Law prepares the way for us to see our need to receive Jesus (Galatians 3:24), Moses was to encourage Joshua to do that which Joshua alone could do then, which Jesus alone can do now.

THE MOUNTAIN OF VISION

A Topical Study of DEUTERONOMY 3:23–28

After leading the congregation through the wilderness for forty years, Moses desperately desired to see the Land of Promise. But he couldn't go in because of the sin he committed at Meribah when he implied that God was upset with His people (Numbers 20:10). Consequently, because he misrepresented the nature and character, the goodness and grace of the Father, Moses was unable to accompany the congregation into the Promised Land.

Maybe today in your journey through life, you're a bit discouraged, confused by what you cannot do. You're not sure where to go from here. It seems like plans you once had have been altered, that doors have been shut. Maybe things haven't worked out for you in the way you thought they should or the way you hoped they would. Moses can relate to you. And he has good news: The solution to your confusion, the prescription for your pain is found at the top of Mt. Pisgah . . .

The Mountain of Vision

Although Moses could not accompany the children of Israel in to the Promised Land, the Lord told Moses to climb Mt. Pisgah, or Mt. Nebo—where he would be given a supernatural view of the entire land.

Where there is no vision, the people perish (Proverbs 29:18). The Hebrew word translated "perish" is *pahrah,* which simply means "naked." Without vision, people feel naked, unsure, exposed, undone. Without vision, people want to hole up and hide away. Without vision, people perish. Yesterday, I went to the mountaintop and was reminded that it's in getting away to a quiet place at a quiet time with a quiet heart that we hear what God would say to us, that we receive fresh vision.

From this point on, Pisgah in Scripture is known as the mount of vision. And it was at this point that Moses knew what he was to do. He was to encourage Joshua, for as a representative of the Law, Moses could not be the one to lead the children of Israel into the Promised Land, but as a picture of Jesus, Joshua could and would.

How about you? Is it clear to you what you're to do? Is it clear what those who follow after you are to be? If not, could I encourage you to get to a quiet place, away from distractions and interruptions, and say, "Lord, I need vision. I'm perishing. I'm confused. I'm in the dark."

Get away, brothers and sisters, and seek the Lord. Find your Nebo, your Pisgah, and go there regularly.

The Mountain of Seduction

Jesus was also taken to a high mountain. "Look at all the kingdoms of the world," Satan said to Him. "They're all Yours if you just bow down to me." What a vision. "You can rule over all these people. You can bring peace to the earth, prosperity to the nations. You can solve the problems in the world. Just bow down to me and Your kingdom can come."

But Jesus said, "No." Why? Because it wasn't a vision from God, but a seduction of Satan (Matthew 4:8–10).

You see, although Jesus could have ruled and reigned over the earth, people would still have ended up in hell. He had to die for the sins of humanity, not just rule over people governmentally. Sure, it would have been a good thing for Jesus to rule and reign temporally—but terrible in light of eternity. So what if people have peace and prosperity on earth if they spend eternity in hell? What does it profit a man if he gain the whole world but lose his soul (Mark 8:36)? It seemed to be a good, noble vision Satan suggested seductively. But it ended up with people being doomed and damned eternally.

So as we're on the mountain, how do we know if the vision is from God or a temptation from Satan? The third mountain is the key . . .

Mount Moriah

The ridge that runs right through Jerusalem and out of the north side of the Old City peaks and crests at Mt. Moriah—a place we know more commonly as Golgotha, or Calvary. Rather than buy into the seduction of Satan, Jesus went to Mt. Moriah and laid down His life to save people like you and me.

If I told you about some of the thoughts and dreams I've had, they would sound noble and exciting. But I know in my soul they were to make my own life more interesting, more fulfilled, more exciting, more comfortable—not about laying down my life for the redemptive purposes of God, not about giving up my life in order that others might do better. You will know if any given vision truly is of God or if it's a subtle seduction of Satan by asking yourself if it is about making your life more comfortable—or if it's about dying to yourself, laying down your life, doing whatever it takes to help people do better. Redemption is the nature of a true vision of God.

Is the vision you're considering all about you? Or is it about getting butchered, slaughtered, kicked around, beat up, crucified in order that others might live? Because Jesus chose the latter, He would find Himself on yet another mountain . . .

The Mount of Olives

Forty days after shedding His blood for you and me on Mt. Calvary, Jesus stood on the Mount of Olives before ascending to heaven triumphantly. And since whatever goes up must come down, guess who is coming back to the Mount of Olives. The Bible says that when He does, He will walk through the Kidron Valley, through the Eastern Gate, and into Jerusalem as the Prince of Peace to rule over all the kingdoms of the world for 1,000 years (Zechariah 14:4). In other words, by opting to go to Mt. Moriah, by doing what was best for the greatest number, Jesus is not only rewarded in heaven and exalted eternally, but He gets the very thing Satan was offering previously. It's a win/win situation. It all works out perfectly.

When we choose to take up the cross and say, "It's not about what's easiest for me. It's about what's best for the most people I can possibly touch and reach and help—be it Applegate or Africa, be it on the East Coast or Alaska—it's about whatever You would have me do, Lord, even if it kills me," we'll get whatever Satan may have tried to seduce us with because Jesus said that if we seek first the kingdom, everything we need would be thrown in (Matthew 6:33).

On Tuesday, I spent some time with a bunch of pastors going through the Book of Ezra and dealing with some pastoral issues. When I was done, I had a couple meetings and then did a radio show. On my way home, I felt really fatigued and weary of soul. Yet the Lord, I believe, gave me a very simple vision, a simple stirring, a simple directive to go and see our brother Jeff, who, at thirty-five years of age, was dying of brain cancer. But after getting lost twice trying to find his house and having been up since before four in the morning, knowing that my kids weren't home that night and that Tammy had a nice dinner planned, I thought, *I'm tired. I'll go home and pick it up tomorrow.* Yet even as I made my way home, I knew that it wasn't right. I knew it wasn't the way of the Cross for me at that moment at that time. So I made a U-turn and, by God's grace, I found the house.

Jeff's three sons were there with a few pastors, worshiping the Lord, praying, and sharing. And I talked to him and read Scriptures because I believe that even though the mind may not be working, the spirit still perceives and receives prayer, praise, and the Word. So we were sharing together, talking to him about heaven, even though he was unable to comprehend mentally. Then, after an hour or so, something happened I'll never forget. As I sat by his bed, suddenly Jeff looked at me. His eyes were crystal clear, his focus laser-sharp. He grabbed my hand and held it for forty-five seconds as our eyes met. And I found myself weeping as he gripped my hand with the strongest grip I've felt in a long time. Then he let go and returned to his previous state.

He went to heaven the next day.

"I'm going to go and do this," I had said. "It's the way of the Cross." What I didn't know was Mt. Calvary turned into the Mount of Olives. I was caught up in heavenly places. That's the way it always is. I was the one who was blessed. Jeff ministered to me in that forty-five-second window of opportunity. I can't explain it, but I went home with tears in my eyes because I was so deeply touched. And to think I almost missed it because I almost opted for what was more comfortable for me. I almost missed the supernatural blessing God had flowing through Jeff into my heart at that moment.

Discouraged today? You need a fresh vision. How do you get that? Go to the mountain. How will you know the vision is from God? It will not be what's easiest for you, what's most comfortable for you. Mount Moriah will mean death to yourself. But Mount Moriah will turn into the Mount of Olives very quickly.

Are you doing that which is most helpful to the most people, or are you making your choices based on what's easiest for you?

I need to go to the mountain constantly and say, "Father, give me Your vision even though it leads to my death because it will ultimately mean resurrection and ecstasy not only for others, but for me."

---

4 "Tell Pharaoh to let My people go," the Lord said to Moses.

"I can't," said Moses. "I'm slow of speech. You're asking me to do something I'm not cut out to do" (see Exodus 4:10).

Yet here in Deuteronomy, we see Moses going on and on and on, chapter after chapter—the antithesis of a man "slow of speech." When did Moses become such an orator, such a speaker? The rabbis have an interesting perspective on this. They say when Moses was initially called to speak to Pharaoh, the issue was political. And when it came to politics, Moses was indeed slow of speech when it came to speaking diplomatic jargon. But here in Deuteronomy, he's not talking politics. He's talking morality and theology—and, because of that, he can go on and on and on—a preacher after my own heart!

Deuteronomy 4:1, 2
Now therefore hearken, O Israel, unto the statutes and unto the judgments, which I teach you, for to do them, that ye may live, and go in and possess the land which the LORD God of your fathers giveth you. Ye shall not add unto the word which I command you, neither shall ye diminish ought from it, that ye may keep the commandments of the LORD your God which I command you.

Contrary to the warm, fuzzy family commercials inviting you to call an 800 number to learn about "another gospel of the Lord Jesus Christ," there *is* no other gospel. The Mormon church claims they have another gospel which came from an angel Moroni. But if Joseph Smith had read his Bible, he would know that Paul said that "if we or an angel preach any other gospel, let him be accursed" (Galatians 1:8, 9).

Jesus reiterated this when He told the Pharisees and scribes that they had made the Word of God powerless because they had taught for doctrines the commandments of men (Mark 7:7). In other words, they had added layers of complicated meanings to the simplicity of the Scriptures.

Therefore, I say, "Lord, show me where we have added traditions to Your Word. Are there things we are teaching or doing simply out of habit rather than out of a biblical base for such actions?" It's a question we need to ask ourselves personally as well as corporately.

Deuteronomy 4:3
Your eyes have seen what the LORD did because of Baal-peor: for all the men that followed Baal-peor, the LORD thy God hath destroyed them from among you.

Unable to curse God's people, Balaam told the king of the Midianites that the Israelites could bring a curse upon themselves through immorality. And Balaam proved to be tragically right when 24,000 men were killed as a result of immorality with Midianite women (Numbers 25:9). As he reminds the Israelites of this event in their recent history, Moses says, "Remember what happened when you didn't listen, when you thought the Word of God didn't apply to you."

Deuteronomy 4:4
But ye that did cleave unto the LORD your God are alive every one of you this day.

Those who didn't listen were dead. Those who did were alive. How true that still is. When I don't listen to the Lord, I experience deadness, dearth, and drought in my soul. On the other hand, there is a liveliness and vitality about those who do indeed listen to the Lord.

Deuteronomy 4:5–8
Behold, I have taught you statutes and judgments, even as the LORD my God commanded me, that ye should do so in the land whither ye go to possess it. Keep therefore and do them; for this is your wisdom and your understanding in the sight of the nations, which shall hear all these statutes, and say, Surely this great nation is a wise and understanding people. For what nation is there so great, who hath God so nigh unto them, as the LORD our God is in all things that we call upon him for? And what nation is there so great, that hath statutes and judgments so righteous as all this law, which I set before you this day?

Not only were the Israelites to obey God's Word that they might live—but that they might be a light in order that other nations might see the way life was meant to be lived (Isaiah 49:6).

I'm so glad we have God's Word. It's so right. We're so blessed.

> Wherein in time past ye walked according to the course of this world, according to the prince of the power of the air, the spirit that now worketh in the children of disobedience: Among whom also we all had our conversation in times past in the lusts of our flesh, fulfilling the desires of the flesh and of the mind; and were by nature the children of wrath, even as others. But God, who is rich in mercy, for his great love wherewith he loved us, Even when we were dead in sins, hath quickened us together with Christ . . . Ephesians 2:2–5 (a)

In times past, we didn't have a clue Someone was going to come to save souls and save the world from its dark, depraved, sinful state. We didn't have a clue. We didn't have the promises. We didn't have hope. It's good for us to reflect on this from time to time. Paul says, "Remember where you once were and rejoice in where you are now."

We have God. We have Christ. We have the promises of the Word. We have the hope of heaven. I'm so thankful, so grateful, so glad I'm saved. We're so blessed—every one of us.

Deuteronomy 4:9 (a)
Only take heed to thyself, and keep thy soul diligently, lest thou forget the things which thine eyes have seen, and lest they depart from thy heart all the days of thy life . . .

You've been blessed, but be careful because you can become so familiar with the Word that you no longer take heed to it. You've been given such a wonderful treasure in the Scriptures, but watch out lest it no longer be a priority for you, a passion within you to know the heart of God, the Word of the Lord.

Deuteronomy 4:9 (b), 10
. . . but teach them thy sons, and thy sons' sons; Specially the day that thou stoodest before the LORD thy God in Horeb, when the LORD said unto me, Gather me the people together, and I will make them hear my words, that they may learn to fear me all the days that they shall live upon the earth, and that they may teach their children.

Take heed to yourself because it's not just about you, but about your kids and grandchildren as well. Here is your job: to be familiar with the Word, to be constantly learning more about the Word so that you can teach your children and grandchildren.

"Your mother and brothers are calling for You," the disciples said to Jesus.

"My mother and brothers are those who hear and do the Word," Jesus said (see Matthew 12:48–50).

Jesus' disciples were His family, but your family is your disciples. This is such an important understanding. "What's my ministry?" people often ask. And my question to them is, "Do you have kids or grandchildren? Pray for them, share the things you're learning about the Lord with them day by day. And in so doing, you will be in ministry."

If you raise godly kids or are involved in seeing godly grandchildren raised up, yours is a fruitful, successful, rewarding, fulfilling, thrilling, eternity-impacting ministry indeed. There can be no greater blessing. That's why my personal favorite ministry time is the time I get to spend with my family in family devotions.

Deuteronomy 4:11–13
And ye came near and stood under the mountain; and the mountain burned with fire unto the midst of heaven, with darkness, clouds, and thick darkness. And the LORD spake unto you out of the midst of the fire: ye heard the voice of the words, but saw no similitude; only ye heard a voice. And he declared unto you his covenant, which he commanded you to perform, even ten commandments; and he wrote them upon two tables of stone.

When the Law was given, Mt. Sinai was on fire. The earth quaked. Thunder rolled. God's voice was heard. And He wrote the commandments not on an Etch-a-Sketch but in stone because they're not suggestions. They're nonnegotiable, irrevocable, everlasting commands.

Deuteronomy 4:14–20
And the LORD commanded me at that time to teach you statutes and judgments, that ye might do them in the land whither ye go over to possess it. Take ye therefore good heed unto yourselves; for ye saw no manner of similitude on the day that the LORD spake unto you in Horeb out of the midst of the fire: Lest ye corrupt yourselves, and make you a graven image, the similitude of any figure, the likeness of male or female, The likeness of any beast that is on the earth, the likeness of any winged fowl that flieth in the air, The likeness of any thing that creepeth on the ground, the likeness of any fish that is in the waters beneath the earth: And lest thou lift up thine eyes unto heaven, and when thou seest the sun, and the moon, and the stars, even all the host of heaven, shouldest be driven to worship them, and serve them, which the LORD thy God hath divided unto all nations under the whole heaven. But the LORD hath taken you, and brought you forth out of the iron furnace, even out of Egypt, to be unto him a people of inheritance, as ye are this day.

When the Law was given, the children of Israel heard the Word, but saw nothing physical or tangible of God's Person. Therefore, they were not to make any images to represent Him. And because of this, of all cultures of antiquity, the Jewish people are the only culture without artistic treasures or monuments. Instead, they directed their energies elsewhere, which partially explains the fact that, although they constitute less than one-half of one percent of the world's population, the Jewish people as an ethnic group have won almost twenty-five percent of all Nobel prizes.

Deuteronomy 4:21–24
Furthermore the LORD was angry with me for your sakes, and sware that I should not go over Jordan, and that I should not go in

unto that good land, which the LORD thy God giveth thee for an inheritance: But I must die in this land, I must not go over Jordan: but ye shall go over, and possess that good land. Take heed unto yourselves, lest ye forget the covenant of the LORD your God, which he made with you, and make you a graven image, or the likeness of any thing, which the LORD thy God hath forbidden thee. For the LORD thy God is a consuming fire, even a jealous God.

For we who know Him, the fact that our God is a consuming fire should be anything but frightening, for anything fire touches soon becomes fire, too. Aren't you kind of sick of yourself? I'm so tired of me. Consequently, I find myself praying, "Consume me, Lord. Set me free from my fleshly inclinations. Make me burn bright and pure, holy and hot for You."

Deuteronomy 4:25–28

When thou shalt beget children, and children's children, and ye shall have remained long in the land, and shall corrupt yourselves, and make a graven image, or the likeness of any thing, and shall do evil in the sight of the LORD thy God, to provoke him to anger: I call heaven and earth to witness against you this day, that ye shall soon utterly perish from off the land whereunto ye go over Jordan to possess it; ye shall not prolong your days upon it, but shall utterly be destroyed. And the LORD shall scatter you among the nations, and ye shall be left few in number among the heathen, whither the LORD shall lead you. And there ye shall serve gods, the work of men's hands, wood and stone, which neither see, nor hear, nor eat, nor smell.

The Jewish people would turn away from the true and living God and become immersed in idolatry and materialism. Consequently, in 586 B.C., God allowed the Babylonians to besiege and destroy Jerusalem, to burn the temple, and to carry His people to Babylon, where they were held captive for seventy years. After seventy years, the Spirit began to stir in the hearts of a remnant of Jews who would rebuild the city of Jerusalem and, eventually, the temple. But as time passed, so radically did the nation again turn its back on God that of His Son they would cry, "Away with Him! Crucify Him! We have no king but Caesar" (John 19:15). Consequently, within forty years, in the year A.D. 70, the Romans besieged the city, destroyed the temple and killed one million Jews. When Hadrian became emperor of Rome, the persecution of the Jews intensified further. And, of course, in World War II, the Jewish population was nearly obliterated by Hitler.

"... and ye shall be left few in number ..."

Indeed.

Deuteronomy 4:29, 30 (a)

But if from thence thou shalt seek the LORD thy God, thou shalt find him, if thou seek him with all thy heart and with all thy soul. When thou art in tribulation ...

"When thou art in tribulation. ..." The Jews will indeed be present in the Tribulation—the seven-year period described in Revelation 6 through 19. But because God is faithful to His promise to Israel, 144,000 Jewish evangelists will be sent throughout the world preaching the gospel of Jesus Christ; Elijah and Moses will come back and preach on the streets of Jerusalem; and angels will proclaim the message of salvation. As a result, Romans 11 tells us that all Israel will be saved.

Deuteronomy 4:30 (b), 31

... and all these things are come upon thee, even in the latter days, if thou turn to the LORD thy God, and shalt be obedient unto his voice; (For the LORD thy God is a merciful God;) he will not forsake thee, neither destroy thee, nor forget the covenant of thy fathers which he sware unto them.

Perhaps you are enduring your own personal tribulation even now. Maybe you feel scattered, unsure of what is going on. This promise is not only for the Jew. It's for you.

> When the LORD shall build up Zion, he shall appear in his glory. He will regard the prayer of the destitute, and not despise their prayer. This shall be written for the generation to come: and the people which shall be created shall praise the LORD. For he hath looked down from the height of his sanctuary; from heaven did the LORD behold the earth; to hear the groaning of the prisoner; to loose those that are appointed to death; to declare the name of the LORD in Zion, and his praise in Jerusalem;
>
> Psalm 102:16–21

We have seen Zion built up in our generation. The Lord is coming. We're going to heaven. And things will be at last what you thought and hoped and dreamed they would be.

Deuteronomy 4:32–34

For ask now of the days that are past, which were before thee, since the day that God created man upon the earth, and ask from the

one side of heaven unto the other, whether there hath been any such thing as this great thing is, or hath been heard like it? Did ever people hear the voice of God speaking out of the midst of the fire, as thou hast heard, and live? Or hath God assayed to go and take him a nation from the midst of another nation, by temptations, by signs, and by wonders, and by war, and by a mighty hand, and by a stretched out arm, and by great terrors, according to all that the LORD your God did for you in Egypt before your eyes?

As proof of God's faithfulness, Moses asks, "Have you ever heard of God rescuing a people from the grip of another nation as He did when He rescued you from bondage in Egypt?"

Deuteronomy 4:35–40
Unto thee it was shewed, that thou mightest know that the LORD he is God; there is none else beside him. Out of heaven he made thee to hear his voice, that he might instruct thee: and upon earth he shewed thee his great fire; and thou heardest his words out of the midst of the fire. And because he loved thy fathers, therefore he chose their seed after them, and brought thee out in his sight with his mighty power out of Egypt; To drive out nations from before thee greater and mightier than thou art, to bring thee in, to give thee their land for an inheritance, as it is this day. Know therefore this day, and consider it in thine heart, that the LORD he is God in heaven above, and upon the earth beneath: there is none else. Thou shalt keep therefore his statutes, and his commandments, which I command thee this day, that it may go well with thee, and with thy children after thee, and that thou mayest prolong thy days upon the earth, which the LORD thy God giveth thee, for ever.

"Which I command thee this day"—the phrase implies that God must be rediscovered each day. Every day, we get to rediscover the nature and beauty of our Father. Every day, there ought to be a rediscovery of the grace and glory and grandeur of our God.

"Take heed to My Word," God says. "Rediscover Me each day. Listen to what I have to say once more. Go over the Scriptures; pray them in; think them through; act them out and it will go well for you and for your family."

A story is told in the Mishnah, the collection of Jewish teaching and writings, of a certain Persian king named Arteban who sent to Judah, the prince in Jerusalem, the largest diamond known in existence at that time. Upon receiving this gift, Judah sent back to Arteban a copy of the Book of Deuteronomy with the accompanying note: What you sent me requires guards to protect it. What I have sent you will guard and protect you.

I'm so thankful for God's Word. I really am—because I know, as you do, that it works. When we take heed and do what we're told to, it is well with us and with our families, too.

Deuteronomy 4:41–43
Then Moses severed three cities on this side Jordan toward the sunrising; That the slayer might flee thither, which should kill his neighbour unawares, and hated him not in times past; and that fleeing unto one of these cities he might live: Namely, Bezer in the wilderness, in the plain country, of the Reubenites; and Ramoth in Gilead, of the Gadites; and Golan in Bashan, of the Manassites.

Here we see the three cities of refuge located east of the Jordan wherein a person who committed second-degree murder could flee, as first seen in Numbers 35.

Deuteronomy 4:44–49
And this is the law which Moses set before the children of Israel: These are the testimonies, and the statutes, and the judgments, which Moses spake unto the children of Israel, after they came forth out of Egypt, On this side Jordan, in the valley over against Beth-peor, in the land of Sihon king of the Amorites, who dwelt at Heshbon, whom Moses and the children of Israel smote, after they were come forth out of Egypt: And they possessed his land, and the land of Og king of Bashan, two kings of the Amorites, which were on this side Jordan toward the sunrising; From Aroer, which is by the bank of the river Arnon, even unto mount Sion, which is Hermon, And all the plain on this side Jordan eastward, even unto the sea of the plain, under the springs of Pisgah.

The once-invincible kingdoms of Og and Sihon are toppled—replaced by three million Jews, listening to Moses, ready to cross the Jordan into the Promised Land.

5

Deuteronomy 5:1
And Moses called all Israel, and said unto them, Hear, O Israel, the statutes and judgments which I speak in your ears this

day, that ye may learn them, and keep, and do them.

Moses' command to the children of Israel is a vital one for us: to learn the Word of God, as we're doing now; to keep it not only on the pages of a notebook or a journal but in our hearts; and, finally, to do it.

Deuteronomy 5:2, 3
The LORD our God made a covenant with us in Horeb. The LORD made not this covenant with our fathers, but with us, even us, who are all of us here alive this day.

"The Lord made a contract not with our ancestors but with us. How blessed we are," Moses would say, "that God made a covenant with us by which we might experience success."

Deuteronomy 5:4, 5
The LORD talked with you face to face in the mount out of the midst of the fire, (I stood between the LORD and you at that time, to shew you the word of the LORD: for ye were afraid by reason of the fire, and went not up into the mount;) saying,

And now Moses will remind the people what the Lord said on the mountain when He gave them the commandments.

Deuteronomy 5:6
I am the LORD thy God, which brought thee out of the land of Egypt, from the house of bondage.

The commandments were based upon the love God demonstrated when He freed them from bondage in Egypt. We, too, were in bondage to our own sin, headed for eternal damnation. And God purchased us with the blood of His Son, rescued us from our sinful condition. Because of that, we ought to give earnest heed to what He says to you and me, knowing it springs from a heart of love toward us.

Deuteronomy 5:7, 8
Thou shalt have none other gods before me. Thou shalt not make thee any graven image, or any likeness of any thing that is in heaven above, or that is in the earth beneath, or that is in the waters beneath the earth:

Any image a person tries to conjure up in their mind about the Lord is going to be, at best, very inadequate for God is bigger than anything we can imagine. Therefore, God says, "Don't try to represent Me with some image because it's going to fail terribly in capturing My essence and My greatness." Even crucifixes fail unspeakably short not only in depicting the suffering Jesus went through when, according to Isaiah 52 and 53 He was marred more than any other human being has ever been, but in failing to represent the fact that, although He was mangled in a way we can't depict or understand, three days later He left the Cross behind and rose again.

Deuteronomy 5:9, 10
Thou shalt not bow down thyself unto them, nor serve them: for I the LORD thy God am a jealous God, visiting the iniquity of the fathers upon the children unto the third and fourth generation of them that hate me, And shewing mercy unto thousands of them that love me and keep my commandments.

What God is declaring here is that if a dad sins and his son sins, God will keep on visiting them, that He'll neither change His mind about their sin nor give up on showing the way of deliverance to them.

Deuteronomy 5:11
Thou shalt not take the name of the LORD thy God in vain: for the LORD will not hold him guiltless that taketh his name in vain.

The word "vain" means "empty." Therefore, the reference here is to much more than simply cursing. We can also take God's name in vain, make it empty, by saying, "The Lord told me to tell you . . ." or, "The Lord wants you to know . . ." without any basis to do so. On the other hand, we also take the name of the Lord in vain if we ignore it—as seen in the present attempts by our legal system to remove it whenever possible.

Deuteronomy 5:12–14
Keep the sabbath day to sanctify it, as the LORD thy God hath commanded thee. Six days thou shalt labour, and do all thy work: But the seventh day is the sabbath of the LORD thy God: in it thou shalt not do any work, thou, nor thy son, nor thy daughter, nor thy manservant, nor thy maidservant, nor thine ox, nor thine ass, nor any of thy cattle, nor thy stranger that is within thy gates; that thy manservant and thy maidservant may rest as well as thou.

Keep in mind that the concept of a Sabbath was a new concept. No other culture in history up to this point had the concept that people could take a day off. Here God makes it not only a possibility but a requirement. And yet this is the only one of the Ten Commandments not repeated in the New Testament. Why? Because, although the Sabbath is an important covenantal point to and for the Jew (Exodus 31:12–17; Nehemiah 9:13–15; Ezekiel 20:12, 20), the church does not seem to be held under the same legal mandate. Why? Because we don't have a Sabbath day. We have a Sabbath life in Christ Jesus. Because of the work He did on the Cross, we can rest every day in Him. Therefore, as New Testament believers, keeping the Sabbath is a wise thing for us to do, but not a legalistic requirement.

Deuteronomy 5:15
And remember that thou wast a servant in the land of Egypt, and that the Lord thy God brought thee out thence through a mighty hand and by a stretched out arm: therefore the Lord thy God commanded thee to keep the sabbath day.

"I want you to have a different lifestyle than you had in Egypt with your nose to the grindstone perpetually," God said. It's amazing that this was a commandment reiterated repeatedly in the Old Testament. Here God wanted to bless His people with rest. And yet they would continually break this wonderful commandment.

Deuteronomy 5:16
Honour thy father and thy mother, as the Lord thy God hath commanded thee; that thy days may be prolonged, and that it may go well with thee, in the land which the Lord thy God giveth thee.

Honor thy father and thy mother that thy days may be elongated, or enriched—that you might stay a long time in the Land. Conversely, failure to honor the family structure leads to shortened days in the land, a destruction of the culture. Any serious student of history knows that within one generation after the family structure breaks down, the culture is destroyed. God said we are to honor mother and father. And unless we do, we'll not be long in the land.

Deuteronomy 5:17
Thou shalt not kill.

There are those who say that, on the basis of this command, Christians shouldn't go to war. Yet the God who gave this commandment to the Jews would tell them to go to war against all kinds of people. Jesus explains this seeming contradiction when He said, "Thou shalt not murder"—making a distinction between murdering and killing. God allowed His own Son to be killed that we might be saved. There are men who have shed their blood that we might be set free as a nation. Thus, risking one's life in order that others might be free can actually be very Jesus-like.

Deuteronomy 5:18–20
Neither shalt thou commit adultery. Neither shalt thou steal. Neither shalt thou bear false witness against thy neighbour.

Bearing false witness is not only about telling whoppers. It can also refer to giving the right information with a wrong implication.

"Destroy this temple and in three days, I will build it up," Jesus said. Yet the Bible calls those who quoted Him false witnesses (Matthew 26:60, 61), for although they quoted Him accurately, they missed the point of what He was saying entirely.

We can be guilty of this as well. "That's what she said," we say. Yes, but what did she say before that and after that? What was the context? Christians are vulnerable to telling what they heard—but not the whole story. That's what false witnessing is. Be oh, so careful that you don't quote people out of context. It really hurts them.

Anytime you're talking about someone, imagine him or her being there. Would you say the same things in the same way—with the same tone of voice and the same look in your eye? This will serve you well because somehow, as Christians, we have learned to be adept liars. "That's what she said." But that's not all she said. "That's what he did." But that's not all he did. Help us, Lord, to be people who are rich in integrity and lovers of people.

Deuteronomy 5:21, 22 (a)
Neither shalt thou desire thy neighbour's wife, neither shalt thou covet thy neighbour's house, his field, or his manservant, or his maidservant, his ox, or his ass, or any thing that is thy neighbour's. These words the Lord spake unto all your assembly in the mount out of the midst of the fire, of the cloud, and of the thick darkness, with a great voice: and he added no more . . .

". . . and He added no more." I like that. God gave us ten succinct, simple, and profound commandments that give us the key to living life successfully. And He added no more.

Deuteronomy 5:22 (b)–28
. . . And he wrote them in two tables of stone, and delivered them unto me. And it came to pass, when ye heard the voice out of the midst of the darkness, (for the mountain did burn with fire,) that ye came near unto me, even all the heads of your tribes, and your

elders; and ye said, Behold, the LORD our God hath shewed us his glory and his greatness, and we have heard his voice out of the midst of the fire: we have seen this day that God doth talk with man, and he liveth. Now therefore why should we die? For this great fire will consume us: if we hear the voice of the LORD our God any more, then we shall die. For who is there of all flesh, that hath heard the voice of the living God speaking out of the midst of the fire, as we have, and lived? Go thou near, and hear all that the LORD our God shall say: and speak thou unto us all that the LORD our God shall speak unto thee; and we will hear it, and do it. And the LORD heard the voice of your words, when ye spake unto me; and the LORD said unto me, I have heard the voice of the words of this people, which they have spoken unto thee: they have well said all that they have spoken.

If I were God and heard the people say, "Moses, you go talk to Him and tell us what He says, and everything He says we'll do," I'd sarcastically say, "Yeah, right. Sure they're going to do everything I say." But our Father is so wonderful that even though He knows the frailty and fickleness of His family, He still approves of what they said. This is precious to me because I wouldn't have shown anywhere near this kind of grace.

Deuteronomy 5:29–33
O that there were such an heart in them, that they would fear me, and keep all my commandments always, that it might be well with them, and with their children for ever! Go say to them, Get you into your tents again. But as for thee, stand thou here by me, and I will speak unto thee all the commandments, and the statutes, and the judgments, which thou shalt teach them, that they may do them in the land which I give them to possess it. Ye shall observe to do therefore as the LORD your God hath commanded you: ye shall not turn aside to the right hand or to the left. Ye shall walk in all the ways which the LORD your God hath commanded you, that ye may live, and that it may be well with you, and that ye may prolong your days in the land which ye shall possess.

If the children of Israel had only done all that the Lord commanded, it would have been well with them and their children forever.

6

Deuteronomy 6:1–3
Now these are the commandments, the statutes, and the judgments, which the LORD your God commanded to teach you, that ye might do them in the land whither ye go to possess it: That thou mightest fear the LORD thy God, to keep all his statutes and his commandments, which I command thee, thou, and thy son, and thy son's son, all the days of thy life; and that thy days may be prolonged. Hear therefore, O Israel, and observe to do it; that it may be well with thee, and that ye may increase mightily, as the LORD God of thy fathers hath promised thee, in the land that floweth with milk and honey.

Milk is a staple. Honey is a luxury. Milk gives you strength. Honey is sweet. God says, "I want to bring you into the land of milk and honey—the place of strength and sweetness. How does that happen? Listen to Me and it will go well with you."

Deuteronomy 6:4 (a)
Hear, O Israel:

So begins the great *Shema*, which means "Listen"—recited throughout the world by every observant Jew every morning and every evening . . .

Deuteronomy 6:4 (b)
. . . The LORD our God is one LORD:

The Hebrew word translated "one" is *echod*, which refers to a compound unity. *Echod* is used in Genesis 2:24 with regard to Adam and Eve as well as in Exodus 26 to describe the curtains and coverings in the tabernacle. The Hebrew word translated "God" is *Elohim*, also a compound unity. *El* is singular. *Elo* is used for two. *Elohim* refers to three or more. "Hear, O Israel, the Lord your God, *Elohim*, is one compound unity." Listen carefully to the Shema, and you'll hear the Trinity.

Deuteronomy 6:5, 6
And thou shalt love the LORD thy God with all thine heart, and with all thy soul, and with all thy might. And these words, which I command thee this day, shall be in thine heart:

Can love be commanded? If you think of love only as a noun, the answer is no. But love in the Bible is not a noun. It's a verb—something you do rather than something you feel. Divorce is rampant today because we have lost our understanding of what love is.

"Why do you have so many songs about rain?" an anthropologist asked the Hopi Indians he was studying.

"We live in the desert," they answered. "We sing about rain because it is so rare."

I wonder if that's why so many of our songs are about love. Love is a fantasy in the way it's being hyped today.

Jesus taught us wherever our treasure is, there will our heart be also (Matthew 6:21). In other words, choose to love and then the feeling will follow. So God here commands love. He doesn't say, "I hope you feel love for Me." He says, "I'm commanding you to show love to Me."

Deuteronomy 6:7
And thou shalt teach them diligently unto thy children, and shalt talk of them when thou sittest in thine house, and when thou walkest by the way, and when thou liest down, and when thou risest up.

When you get up in the morning, when you go to bed at night, when you're walking, when you're relaxing, talk to your kids about loving God. My brother, Dave, modeled this wonderfully. Every time he would go anywhere—to the post office, to 7–11, to the hardware store—he would take one of his boys, knowing he could spend time with him.

If you haven't been teaching your kids, consider the Chinese proverb which says, "The best time to plant a tree is twenty years ago. The second best time is today." We should have done things twenty years ago. All of us know that. But the second best time to do it is now. And if your kids have grown up and moved out of the house—there's always grandchildren, nieces, nephews, or neighbor kids with whom you can share the Lord.

Deuteronomy 6:8
And thou shalt bind them for a sign upon thine hand, and they shall be as frontlets between thine eyes.

The Jews literally had boxes, or phylacteries, which were worn on their head or on their wrists containing the Shema.

Deuteronomy 6:9
And thou shalt write them upon the posts of thy house, and on thy gates.

Like the phylacteries worn on one's person, a *mezuzah* is a box containing the Shema, attached near the front door of one's house. God's intent was not for His people to have mezuzahs and phylacteries, but that His Word be written in the fabric of their homes and minds.

Deuteronomy 6:10 (a)
And it shall be, when the LORD thy God shall have brought thee into the land which he sware unto thy fathers, to Abraham, to Isaac, and to Jacob . . .

Moses didn't say, "If the Lord brings you into the Land," or, "Should the Lord bring you in," or, "Perhaps the Lord will bring you in." He said, "*When* the Lord brings you in." In other words, "You're going to make it. God will see you through. God will bring you in. Of that there is no doubt."

The same thing is true for you and me, for He who has begun a good work in us will be faithful to complete it (Philippians 1:6). The message of Moses to that congregation is the message the Master gives to us today as well. He's going to bring us in. He's going to see us through. It's as good as done.

Deuteronomy 6:10 (b)–19
. . . to give thee great and goodly cities, which thou buildedst not, And houses full of all good things, which thou filledst not, and wells digged, which thou diggedst not, vineyards and olive trees, which thou plantedst not; when thou shalt have eaten and be full; Then beware lest thou forget the LORD, which brought thee forth out of the land of Egypt, from the house of bondage. Thou shalt fear the LORD thy God, and serve him, and shalt swear by his name. Ye shall not go after other gods, of the gods of the people which are round about you; (For the LORD thy God is a jealous God among you) lest the anger of the LORD thy God be kindled against thee, and destroy thee from off the face of the earth. Ye shall not tempt the LORD your God, as ye tempted him in Massah. Ye shall diligently keep the commandments of the LORD your God, and his testimonies, and his statutes, which he hath commanded thee. And thou shalt do that which is right and good in the sight of the LORD: that it may be well with thee, and that thou mayest go in and possess the good land which the LORD sware unto thy fathers, To cast out all thine enemies from before thee, as the LORD hath spoken.

"When you take possession of houses you didn't build, vineyards and olive trees you didn't plant, and wells you didn't dig, beware," Moses warned, "lest you forget the Lord who brought you out of bondage."

There is a peril in prosperity. When things are going well, when things come our way which bless and amaze us, there is an insidious danger, for it is in those days that we can forget the Lord and think that it's our energy, our effort, our creativity, ingenuity, or hard work which got us where we are.

In Deuteronomy 8, God will remind the people that it was He who gave them everything they had. And it is He who does the same for us, for truly, the foundational essence of our Father is that He is a Giver . . .

> I am the LORD thy God, which brought thee out of the land of Egypt: open thy mouth wide, and I will fill it. Psalm 81:10

> Ask, and it shall be given you; seek, and ye shall find; knock, and it shall be opened unto you: Matthew 7:7

> For God so loved the world, that he gave his only begotten Son . . . John 3:16 (a)

> He that spared not his own Son, but delivered him up for us all, how shall he not with him also freely give us all things? Romans 8:32

> Now unto him that is able to do exceeding abundantly above all that we ask or think, according to the power that worketh in us, Ephesians 3:20

> Every good gift and every perfect gift is from above, and cometh down from the Father of lights, with whom is no variableness, neither shadow of turning. James 1:17

"You're in for a treat," Moses said. "God is going to give you cities and houses you didn't build; olive trees, vineyards, and wells you neither had to plant nor dig." And yet he would also have to warn the people that whenever there is prosperity, God is forgotten.

Can prosperity be navigated successfully? I believe so. Turn to Matthew's Gospel to see how.

> When the even was come, there came a rich man of Arimathaea, named Joseph, who also himself was Jesus' disciple: Matthew 27:57

Joseph of Arimathaea was a mover and shaker, a rich man, a powerful person. He was also a secret disciple of Jesus. But when Jesus was crucified, Joseph no longer cared about what others thought of him and came out of the spiritual closet.

> He went to Pilate, and begged the body of Jesus. Then Pilate commanded the body to be delivered. Matthew 27:58

Joseph went to Pontius Pilate—the most powerful political person in the region, the one who had ordered the execution of Jesus—and begged the body of Jesus. Mark says he craved the body of Jesus (15:43). When Pilate commanded the body be given him, Joseph took the body, wrapped it in a clean linen cloth, and laid it in his own new tomb. Only very wealthy men in those days were able to have their own tombs prepared ahead of time. And Joseph was one of them.

There's nothing inherently wrong with being wealthy or prosperous, as long as you don't forget the Lord. "This is My body broken for you," Jesus said. "Do this in remembrance of Me." When a person truly understands how good the Lord has been to him, he craves to remember the Lord's body at Communion. Secondly, he desires to minister to the body of believers. Joseph used what he had for the body of Christ. And what a great thing it is to see a person's wealth or possessions used for the body of Christ. That's the way it's supposed to be. That's what God wants to do in us and through us. He wants to give us good things and bless us for the purpose of taking care of His body.

I believe Joseph of Arimathaea provides a pattern for successfully navigating prosperity. May we be those who, like him, crave the body of Jesus both mystically and practically.

Deuteronomy 6:20–23

And when thy son asketh thee in time to come, saying, What mean the testimonies, and the statutes, and the judgments, which the LORD our God hath commanded you? Then thou shalt say unto thy son, We were Pharaoh's bondmen in Egypt; and the LORD brought us out of Egypt with a mighty hand: And the LORD shewed signs and wonders, great and sore, upon Egypt, upon Pharaoh, and upon all his household, before our eyes: And he brought us out from thence, that he might bring us in, to give us the land which he sware unto our fathers.

"Son, let me tell you something" we can say. "The reason I go to Bible study week after week and listen to this pastor as he goes on and on and on is because I was in bondage and the Lord miraculously, wonderfully, lovingly set me free." Do your kids know your story? They need to. They need to know why you do what you do, where you once were, what God saved you from and how good He's been to you. That makes great dinnertime conversation. Instead of complaining about your job situation or murmuring about other people, talk about what God has done for you today or in your past.

Moses didn't say, "*If* thy son asketh thee . . ." He said, "*When* he asketh thee . . ." because every kid is curious about his parents. Your kids will ask about your story in one way or another. When they do, seize the opportunity and let them hear your heart. Let them know why you're so committed to Christ, why you're so radical for Jesus.

Deuteronomy 6:24
And the LORD commanded us to do all these statutes, to fear the LORD our God, for our good always, that he might preserve us alive, as it is at this day.

Do you fear the Lord? I believe there is a huge lack in the body of Christ in our day because people don't fear God. "It's a fearful thing," the writer of Hebrews said, "to fall into the hands of the living God" (10:31). God's hands are loving and tender to be sure—but He will also chasten and discipline His wayward children. And the repercussions and scars of sin go on and on and on.

Deuteronomy 6:25
And it shall be our righteousness, if we observe to do all these commandments before the LORD our God, as he hath commanded us.

In twenty-five years of ministry, I have yet to talk to one person who said, "I'm glad I sinned. Oh, it was a little rough for awhile, but it paid big dividends in the long run."

Moses here is saying, "This is for your *good.*"

Maybe these commandments, statutes, and judgments seem confining and restricting, but these words are given that it might be well with us now and eternally.

7 **Deuteronomy 7:1, 2**
When the LORD thy God shall bring thee into the land whither thou goest to possess it, and hath cast out many nations before thee, the Hittites, and the Girgashites, and the Amorites, and the Canaanites, and the Perizzites, and the Hivites, and the Jebusites, seven nations greater and mightier than thou; And when the LORD thy God shall deliver them before thee; thou shalt smite them, and utterly destroy them; thou shalt make no covenant with them, nor shew mercy unto them:

"When you go into the Land," Moses instructs the people, "God will deliver seven formidable foes into your hand. And you shall smite them."

The same is true for us . . .

There hath no temptation taken you but such as is common to man: but God is faithful, who will not suffer you to be tempted above that ye are able; but will with the temptation also make a way to escape, that ye may be able to bear it. 1 Corinthians 10:13

No temptation will ever come our way without the Lord providing a way for victory at that time. But we need to participate. In other words, the Lord will deliver us, but we have a role to play as well. At the moment of temptation, when the battle is raging, when the enemy is looming, the Lord will give me victory if I choose to participate. There will always be a way of escape, a way of victory.

Knowing this, that our old man is crucified with him, that the body of sin might be destroyed, that henceforth we should not serve sin.
Romans 6:6

Because the word translated "crucified" literally means "rendered inactive," we can say, "I'm not going to get beaten up by the enemy of temptation or of depression or of seduction because not only has the Lord promised that there is a way of escape, but that the sin of anger or hostility or lust can't dominate me any more. When Christ Jesus died on the Cross, anything contrary to Christ was crucified, paralyzed. Therefore, all the old nature can do is yell at me, scream at me, and try to intimidate me. But it cannot touch me unless I choose to listen."

Some people say, "I just can't seem to get over this. I can't deal with that. Where's the Lord?" The answer is that the Lord has done His part. Now He's waiting for you to do yours and smite the enemy.

Deuteronomy 7:3, 4
Neither shalt thou make marriages with them; thy daughter thou shalt not give unto his son, nor his daughter shalt thou take unto thy son. For they will turn away thy son from following me, that they may serve other gods: so will the anger of the LORD be kindled against you, and destroy thee suddenly.

"Mixed marriages will be disastrous because they'll pull your sons and daughters away from the Lord," Moses says. And, again, the same is still true, for compromised relationships slow us down, hold us back, pull us away from where we ought to be.

Deuteronomy 7:5
But thus shall ye deal with them; ye shall destroy their altars, and break down their

images, and cut down their groves, and burn their graven images with fire.

Can't you hear the heart of Pastor Moses here as he pleads with his people? They know this. They've heard it before. But here is a shepherd, a man of God, saying, "Please listen again. Understand that these things are important: Smite both the enemy and their idols."

Deuteronomy 7:6
For thou art an holy people unto the LORD thy God: the LORD thy God hath chosen thee to be a special people unto himself, above all people that are upon the face of the earth.

The children of Israel were not to be eroded, lessened, diminished by the worship of false gods but were to be a uniquely whole and holy people.

Deuteronomy 7:7, 8 (a)
The LORD did not set his love upon you, nor choose you, because ye were more in number than any people; for ye were the fewest of all people: But because the LORD loved you . . .

I love this Scripture. Moses says I want you to know the Lord didn't select you to be His, to be holy, to be different, because you were mightier than others. No, He chose you simply because He loved you. God loves you and me not because we are mighty or together or have something awesome to offer. Quite the opposite, He loves us just because He loves us. Period. His love is not based upon how good I'm doing or how much you're doing, how poorly I'm faring or how much you're erring. God's love for us is honestly, truly, absolutely unconditional. And once we grasp this, we can go through our day expecting the Lord to bless us, to shower grace upon us—not because of who we are or what we've done but simply and solely because of who He is.

Deuteronomy 7:8 (b)
. . . and because he would keep the oath which he had sworn unto your fathers, hath the LORD brought you out with a mighty hand, and redeemed you out of the house of bondmen, from the hand of Pharaoh king of Egypt.

"God made a promise to your fathers," Moses reminded the children of Israel. "And He's will keep His Word."

Deuteronomy 7:9, 10
Know therefore that the LORD thy God, he is God, the faithful God, which keepeth covenant and mercy with them that love him and keep his commandments to a thousand generations; And repayeth them that hate him to their face, to destroy them: he will not be slack to him that hateth him, he will repay him to his face.

Those who arrogantly shake their fist at God, turn their back on God, or make fun of God, will feel the wrath of God.

Deuteronomy 7:11–13
Thou shalt therefore keep the commandments, and the statutes, and the judgments, which I command thee this day, to do them. Wherefore it shall come to pass, if ye hearken to these judgments, and keep, and do them, that the LORD thy God shall keep unto thee the covenant and the mercy which he sware unto thy fathers: And he will love thee, and bless thee, and multiply thee: he will also bless the fruit of thy womb, and the fruit of thy land, thy corn, and thy wine, and thine oil, the increase of thy kine, and the flocks of thy sheep, in the land which he sware unto thy fathers to give thee.

In verse 7, Moses told the people the Lord loved them unconditionally. Here, he tells them the Lord would love and bless them if they obeyed His Words. Is this contradictory? No.

I love my kids whether they're good or bad. I love them simply because they're my kids. But if they say, "We're not going to be here for breakfast, lunch, or dinner, for Christmas, Thanksgiving, or Easter"—although I'll still love them, they'll not enjoy the blessings which would have come their way if they remained close to me.

That's what Jude meant when he said, "Keep yourselves in the love of God" (v. 21). He didn't mean to try to earn or work for or merit God's love. He meant we are to just "keep ourselves under the spout where God's blessings come out."

Here in Deuteronomy, God says, "You'll experience all kinds of blessings if you hearken to the judgments, if you take heed to the Word, if you let Me love you."

Deuteronomy 7:14, 15
Thou shalt be blessed above all people: there shall not be male or female barren among you, or among your cattle. And the LORD will take away from thee all sickness, and will put none of the evil diseases of Egypt, which thou knowest, upon thee; but will lay them upon all them that hate thee.

Having lived in Egypt 400 years, the children of Israel were all too familiar with the diseases of Egypt. Egypt being a type of the world, we, too, see the sickness of the world in which we live.

Keep in mind that everything in the Old Testament is a physical picture of a New Testament spiritual truth . . .

- The children of Israel were delivered from the bondage of Egypt and brought to the Promised Land.
  We've been delivered from the world system and ushered into the Spirit-filled life.
- Their citizenship was in a land.
  Ours is in heaven.
- They fought with swords and spears.
  The weapons of our warfare are spiritual.
- They were to smite their enemies.
  We are to reckon dead the enemy of our soul.

If you don't understand this, the Old Testament will be troubling and impractical to you. There are those who say if we walk with the Lord, we'll have no diseases, that we'll never be sick. Yet Paul had a thorn in his flesh (2 Corinthians 12:7). He left Trophimus sick (2 Timothy 4:20). He told Timothy to take wine for his stomach problems (1 Timothy 5:23). The diseases the Old Testament talks about which were physical for them are spiritual for us. The Lord wants to make us a peculiar, special people, different from the Egyptians that surround us. And He says that will happen if we do what He tells us to do.

Deuteronomy 7:16–18 (a)
And thou shalt consume all the people which the LORD thy God shall deliver thee; thine eye shall have no pity upon them: neither shalt thou serve their gods; for that will be a snare unto thee. If thou shalt say in thine heart, These nations are more than I; how can I dispossess them? Thou shalt not be afraid of them . . .

Moses says, "When you come to the place where you're tempted to say in your heart, deep within you, that there's no solution, no victory, no way out, you must remember not to succumb to fear."

Deuteronomy 7:18 (b), 19
. . . but shalt well remember what the LORD thy God did unto Pharaoh, and unto all Egypt; The great temptations which thine eyes saw, and the signs, and the wonders, and the mighty hand, and the stretched out arm, whereby the LORD thy God brought thee out: so shall the LORD thy God do unto all the people of whom thou art afraid.

Fear is more a loss of memory than it is a lack of faith. That is why Moses says, "When you begin to feel afraid, remember what the Lord did for you in setting you free from the bondage of Egypt."

"Do this in remembrance of Me," Jesus said (Luke 22:19). As I go the Lord's Table and am reminded that He gave everything to save my soul, I know He'll see me through whatever it is that's frightening me presently. The Bible says there is one thing that casts out fear. It isn't faith. It's perfect love (1 John 4:18). When I realize how much the Lord has already loved me, I won't be afraid of anything or anyone. What he'll say, what she'll think, how they will respond will no longer be the issue.

Are you fearful? Are you saying, "I'd like to do this, but what will my boss, husband, friends, kids, wife think?" Don't let fear dominate you. Choose to do what's right. How? Remember what Jesus has already done on your behalf and trust Him to see you through.

Deuteronomy 7:20
Moreover the LORD thy God will send the hornet among them, until they that are left, and hide themselves from thee, be destroyed.

In Isaiah 7, the Assyrians are called bees. Thus, it could be that the Lord is saying, "I will use other nations to come down to Canaan to deal with your enemies." But my personal opinion is that the reference here is to literal hornets. The Lord has amazing ways at His disposal to drive out His enemies so that His people can be all they can "bee."

Deuteronomy 7:21 (a)
Thou shalt not be affrighted at them . . .

What do you fear? At any given moment I am living in fear and so are you—either the fear of the Lord, which is the beginning of wisdom and success (Psalm 111:10), or the fear of man, which is a snare (Proverbs 29:25).

> *"What are your goals for the coming school year?" I asked my two youngest kids.*
> *About to start seventh grade, Ben looked at me and said, "I have two goals, Dad. The first is to remember where my locker is, the second is to be able to open it."*

Ben was kidding—sort of. But remember seventh grade? Lockers and combinations and PE? Remember all those fears? Well, guess what. You made it! You're here. You got through those junior high years. The exhortation of Moses to the congregation at Jordan was, "Remember how much God has done for you already. He's not going to let you down now."

God loves you, gang. He proved it to us on the Cross. So do what He's called you to do and don't fear. Don't listen to the whisper of the enemy. Instead, say, "Lord, You've loved me so passionately, I'm going to do what You direct me to, let the chips fall where they may."

"Good," He'll say. "I'll surprise you with an army of hornets going before you—the ultimate sting operation."

Jesus put it this way: "Fear not, little flock. It is the Father's good pleasure to give you the kingdom" (Luke 12:32). Fear not and watch and see how God will bless you.

Deuteronomy 7:21 (b)
. . . for the Lord thy God is among you, a mighty God and terrible.

Preaching from this text, at the Westminster Chapel in London, G. Campbell Morgan ended his sermon by saying, "Is this not a most wonderful promise for you and me?"

Following his sermon, however, he was greeted at the door by two sisters who said to him, "Pastor Morgan, that is not a promise. It's reality."

And G. Campbell Morgan said, "How true."

A promise tends to imply that which is to be. But the reality is that God is with us presently.

Deuteronomy 7:22, 23
And the Lord thy God will put out those nations before thee by little and little: thou mayest not consume them at once, lest the beasts of the field increase upon thee. But the Lord thy God shall deliver them unto thee, and shall destroy them with a mighty destruction, until they be destroyed.

Had God driven the enemy out of the land quickly, wild beasts would eat the crops which would otherwise have nourished God's people. So He drove the enemies out a little at a time until the children of Israel were ready to take on more territory.

God is working in you and on me. "But it's going so slowly," you say. "I thought I would be a lot further along by now." I know. I thought I would be, too.

But God would say to you and me, "Be patient and trust Me. I'm not going to drive out your enemies immediately, but little by little, I'll give you more territory, more possibilities, more responsibilities."

Deuteronomy 7:24
And he shall deliver their kings into thine hand, and thou shalt destroy their name from under heaven: there shall no man be able to stand before thee, until thou have destroyed them.

In other words, God says, "No one will be able to stop you from doing what I've called you to do."

Deuteronomy 7:25, 26
The graven images of their gods shall ye burn with fire: thou shalt not desire the silver or gold that is on them, nor take it unto thee, lest thou be snared therein: for it is an abomination to the Lord thy God. Neither shalt thou bring an abomination into thine house, lest thou be a cursed thing like it: but thou shalt utterly detest it, and thou shalt utterly abhor it; for it is a cursed thing.

At the last junior high camp, after I shared with the kids around the campfire about what Christians went through in days of old—stories of martyrdom and persecution and the blessings of taking a stand for the Lord, an eighth grader reached in his sweatshirt, pulled out some CDs and chucked them into the fire. It was a very powerful moment when this young man did precisely what the Word says ought to be done.

"Fear not. The Lord is in your midst. He will drive out your enemies little by little. But you have a part to play as well." The exhortation of Moses here in Deuteronomy 7 is one I need to hear constantly.

---

8 Deuteronomy 8:1, 2
All the commandments which I command thee this day shall ye observe to do, that ye may live, and multiply, and go in and possess the land which the Lord sware unto your fathers. And thou shalt remember all the way which the Lord thy God led thee these forty years in the wilderness, to humble thee, and to prove thee, to know what was in thine heart, whether thou wouldest keep his commandments, or no.

"Do what you know is right in God's sight," Moses instructed the children of Israel. "Remember how the Lord took you through the wilderness for forty years to humble you, to prove you, to test you, that you might know where you're truly at, what's really taking place within your hearts."

It's easy to say, "I'm going to keep the commandments of the Lord. I'm going to do what He tells me." The proof, however, is in the wilderness. It's when the days are dry and difficult and when the heat is rising that we get to see if we are truly those who obey what the Lord tells us to do.

Maybe you are in a wilderness season, in the desert of difficulty. If so, this is such an important time for you to realize it's an opportunity to see what's going on deep within your heart. Just as we don't know what's in a sponge until it's squeezed, I can't know what's taking place deep within me until I'm squeezed. Oh, I can quote the verses, sing the songs, say the phrases—but the fact is, I won't know what's truly going on until and unless I'm squeezed by days of difficulty and times of trouble.

Deuteronomy 8:3
And he humbled thee, and suffered thee to hunger, and fed thee with manna, which thou knewest not, neither did thy fathers know; that he might make thee know that man doth not live by bread only, but by every word that proceedeth out of the mouth of the LORD doth man live.

The Israelites welcomed God's provision of manna because they were in a place of hunger. That's always the way it is. We get hungry in the wilderness, in the day of difficulty. And it is then that we long for God's provision for us. Jesus put it this way: "Blessed are you when you hunger and thirst for righteousness, for then you'll be filled" (Matthew 5:6). Too often, we don't crave the Bread of the Word or the Bread of Life because we're not hungry. There's a progression seen here: My reaction in the wilderness makes me hungry for righteousness. So I go to church once again, have devotions once more, exchange *Newsweek* for the Word, turn off talk radio and listen to teaching tapes. But this doesn't happen until I'm hungry. And I don't know I'm hungry until I'm in the wilderness. It's all part of the program.

Jesus quoted this verse in His own wilderness experience. He was tested for forty days as Satan came and said, "If you're the Son of God, turn those stones into bread. Take care of yourself. Find a way to satisfy your own needs."

"No," Jesus said, and quoted this verse. In fact, all three times He dealt with Satan in Matthew 4, Jesus quoted from Deuteronomy. That is why I suggest Deuteronomy was where He was having devotions at that time. As a result, He was empowered to withstand the temptation and to obey His Father—the same opportunity each of us has who eats freely of the Bread of Life, who partakes consistently of the manna of the Word.

Deuteronomy 8:4
Thy raiment waxed not old upon thee, neither did thy foot swell, these forty years.

One commentator suggests that, because deficiency in diet causes feet to swell, this text proves that the manna that came from heaven every morning was perfectly suited for the Israelites' needs in the wilderness.

Deuteronomy 8:5, 6
Thou shalt also consider in thine heart, that, as a man chasteneth his son, so the LORD thy God chasteneth thee. Therefore thou shalt keep the commandments of the LORD thy God, to walk in his ways, and to fear him.

Are we aware of the fact that God will chasten us because He cares passionately about our well being and will discipline us when we're out of line? I fear that we don't fear the Lord these days. Somehow, we think we can hide our carnality. But our Father loves us so much He won't let us go on a path that will be destructive to us. He'll discipline and chasten us when we're out of line.

Deuteronomy 8:7–9
For the LORD thy God bringeth thee into a good land, a land of brooks of water, of fountains and depths that spring out of valleys and hills; a land of wheat, and barley, and vines, and fig trees, and pomegranates; a land of oil olive, and honey; a land wherein thou shalt eat bread without scarceness, thou shalt not lack any thing in it; a land whose stones are iron, and out of whose hills thou mayest dig brass.

All of this testing and proving and chastening was for a purpose: to bring the children of Israel into a land of honey and olive oil, of pomegranates and blessing. And such is the Lord's desire for you: to bring you into the wonderful land of the Spirit-filled life that He has planned and prepared for you personally.

Deuteronomy 8:10
When thou hast eaten and art full, then thou shalt bless the LORD thy God for the good land which he hath given thee.

When you've eaten until you're full, make sure you give thanks to the One who has taken such good care of you.

Deuteronomy 8:11–18
Beware that thou forget not the LORD thy God, in not keeping his commandments, and

his judgments, and his statutes, which I command thee this day: Lest when thou hast eaten and art full, and hast built goodly houses, and dwelt therein; And when thy herds and thy flocks multiply, and thy silver and thy gold is multiplied, and all that thou hast is multiplied; Then thine heart be lifted up, and thou forget the LORD thy God, which brought thee forth out of the land of Egypt, from the house of bondage; Who led thee through that great and terrible wilderness, wherein were fiery serpents, and scorpions, and drought, where there was no water; who brought thee forth water out of the rock of flint; Who fed thee in the wilderness with manna, which thy fathers knew not, that he might humble thee, and that he might prove thee, to do thee good at thy latter end; And thou say in thine heart, My power and the might of mine hand hath gotten me this wealth. But thou shalt remember the LORD thy God: for it is he that giveth thee power to get wealth, that he may establish his covenant which he sware unto thy fathers, as it is this day.

"The time to engage in worship, to be a man or woman of prayer, to be a student of the Scriptures, to remember how good God has been is when you're in the Promised Land," Moses reminds the people.

And yet the irony is, it is when people prosper that they often drift away. They don't have time for the Lord. Their passion diminishes. Their devotion decreases. They begin to say, "It is my hard work which has allowed me to have that ski boat or this vacation home. And I've got to maintain it, so I don't have time to serve the Lord."

Deuteronomy 8:19, 20
And it shall be, if thou do at all forget the LORD thy God, and walk after other gods, and serve them, and worship them, I testify against you this day that ye shall surely perish. As the nations which the LORD destroyeth before your face, so shall ye perish; because ye would not be obedient unto the voice of the LORD your God.

Was there ever a time when you were serving the Lord more diligently and more consistently than you are today? If your answer is yes, I plead with you to take this passage to heart, for if you do not, you'll perish. Oh, maybe not physically—but your marriage will diminish; your family will diminish; your joy will diminish. Your life will get smaller and smaller. On the other hand, when you say, "God's been good to me. Therefore, I'm going to learn His ways, give Him praise, and serve Him with all of my heart and soul, mind and strength"—you'll find yourself truly blessed in every way.

9

Deuteronomy 9:1–3
Hear, O Israel: Thou art to pass over Jordan this day, to go in to possess nations greater and mightier than thyself, cities great and fenced up to heaven, A people great and tall, the children of the Anakims, whom thou knowest, and of whom thou hast heard say, Who can stand before the children of Anak! Understand therefore this day, that the LORD thy God is he which goeth over before thee; as a consuming fire he shall destroy them, and he shall bring them down before thy face: so shalt thou drive them out, and destroy them quickly, as the LORD hath said unto thee.

"Don't fear," Moses tells the people. "Don't panic. God is going to blaze a trail before you. As a consuming fire, He's going to take care of those seemingly insurmountable problems, the Anakims."

Deuteronomy 9:4–7
Speak not thou in thine heart, after that the LORD thy God hath cast them out from before thee, saying, For my righteousness the LORD hath brought me in to possess this land: but for the wickedness of these nations the LORD doth drive them out from before thee. Not for thy righteousness, or for the uprightness of thine heart, dost thou go to possess their land: but for the wickedness of these nations the LORD thy God doth drive them out from before thee, and that he may perform the word which the LORD sware unto thy fathers, Abraham, Isaac, and Jacob. Understand therefore, that the LORD thy God giveth thee not this good land to possess it for thy righteousness; for thou art a stiffnecked people. Remember, and forget not, how thou provokedst the LORD thy God to wrath in the wilderness: from the day that thou didst depart out of the land of Egypt, until ye came unto this place, ye have been rebellious against the LORD.

"Don't think that the blessings you enjoy are because of your power or your ability," Moses continues. "And don't think when the enemy is driven out it's because of your righteousness. It's not about your righteousness, but about God's divine purpose."

This comforts me because I realize what happens in this ministry, in my family, in my life personally is not dependent upon my righteousness but upon God's purpose. Therefore, because He wants to do certain things in this community, in this fellowship, in my family, I can expect Him to go before me as a flaming fire. And that way, He gets all the glory.

Deuteronomy 9:8–14
Also in Horeb ye provoked the LORD to wrath, so that the LORD was angry with you to have destroyed you. When I was gone up into the mount to receive the tables of stone, even the tables of the covenant which the LORD made with you, then I abode in the mount forty days and forty nights, I neither did eat bread nor drink water: And the LORD delivered unto me two tables of stone written with the finger of God; and on them was written according to all the words, which the LORD spake with you in the mount out of the midst of the fire in the day of the assembly. And it came to pass at the end of forty days and forty nights, that the LORD gave me the two tables of stone, even the tables of the covenant. And the LORD said unto me, Arise, get thee down quickly from hence; for thy people which thou hast brought forth out of Egypt have corrupted themselves; they are quickly turned aside out of the way which I commanded them; they have made them a molten image. Furthermore the LORD spake unto me, saying, I have seen this people, and, behold, it is a stiffnecked people: Let me alone, that I may destroy them, and blot out their name from under heaven: and I will make of thee a nation mightier and greater than they.

While Moses was on the mountain alone with God for forty days, the people were sinning down below. "I'm going to destroy these people and make of you a new nation," God said to him. Would Moses accept the offer? Wait a minute. This sounds strangely familiar to another test after a forty-day fast . . .

"Bow down to me," Satan said to Jesus, "and the entire world will be yours" (see Matthew 4:8, 9). The similarities are neither coincidental nor accidental. Rather, they show us that what God uses to test us, Satan uses to tempt us. God tests us to work good in us, to show Himself strong through us. Satan, on the other hand, tempts us in order to destroy us.

Whenever you're tempted, realize that God uses what Satan means as a temptation for a test. Conversely, whenever you're going through a test from God, Satan will jump on it and make it a temptation.

James makes it clear that God does not tempt any man to do evil (1:13). Like a car manufacturer who puts his car through rigorous tests in order to showcase its capabilities, when God tests you, He's not saying, "I hope you don't fall apart." No, He says, "I know what I've built into you. And I will not allow you to be tested above what you're able" (1 Corinthians 10:13). The test He sends our way is not Him saying, "I wonder what's going to happen." It's Him saying, "Look what I've done."

This makes murmuring or complaining or whining a sin. "Pipe down," God would say to us. "It's only a test. I know what I've built into you. I know the work I've done deep within you." God knew Moses would pass this test. He wasn't tempting him to sin. Rather, He was testing him, knowing he would come through with flying colors.

If you're tempted by Satan, God intends it as a test to see you through. If you're tested by the Father, Satan will jump on it to tempt you. That's why the Greek word for "test" and "temptation" is the same word. Moses would pass the test. Jesus would beat back the temptation. So when that temptation comes strolling up to you tomorrow, know it's a test from God and He won't test you above that which you are able.

Deuteronomy 9:15–21
So I turned and came down from the mount, and the mount burned with fire: and the two tables of the covenant were in my two hands. And I looked, and, behold, ye had sinned against the LORD your God, and had made you a molten calf: ye had turned aside quickly out of the way which the LORD had commanded you. And I took the two tables, and cast them out of my two hands, and brake them before your eyes. And I fell down before the LORD, as at the first, forty days and forty nights: I did neither eat bread, nor drink water, because of all your sins which ye sinned, in doing wickedly in the sight of the LORD, to provoke him to anger. For I was afraid of the anger and hot displeasure, wherewith the LORD was wroth against you to destroy you. But the LORD hearkened unto me at that time also. And the LORD was very angry with Aaron to have destroyed him: and I prayed for Aaron also the same time. And I took your sin, the calf which ye had made, and burnt it with fire, and stamped it, and ground it very small, even until it was as small as dust: and I cast the dust thereof into the brook that descended out of the mount.

As he recounts his time on Mount Sinai, Moses say, "The first forty days, I was worshiping. The second forty, I was warring. The first time, my heart was touched and I came down with God's Word. The second time, I fought for you in intercession lest you be destroyed because of your sin and rebellion." Anyone who wants to minister must be both a worshiper and a warrior, battling in prayer on behalf of people.

Yet lest we think were it not for Moses' intercession, the people would have been destroyed, that Moses had to "calm God down," who put a heart of intercession in Moses in the first place? Justice demanded judgment, but, looking for a reason to show mercy, God put it in the heart of Moses to be an intercessor. God did it all.

Deuteronomy 9:22 (a)
And at Taberah . . .

The account of what happened at Taberah is found in Numbers 11. The people complained; the Lord heard them; and a fire was kindled which consumed them. What were they complaining about? Evidently it was something so insignificant that Scripture doesn't even record it.

Deuteronomy 9:22 (b)
. . . and at Massah . . .

At Massah the people complained about a lack of water (Exodus 17).

Deuteronomy 9:22 (c)
. . . and at Kibroth-hattaavah, ye provoked the LORD to wrath.

"We want meat to eat," the people had said. "We're tired of this manna." So God sent them so much quail to eat that it came out of their nostrils. And many of the people were killed by their own lust (Numbers 11:33).

Deuteronomy 9:23
Likewise when the LORD sent you from Kadesh-barnea, saying, Go up and possess the land which I have given you; then ye rebelled against the commandment of the LORD your God, and ye believed him not, nor hearkened to his voice.

When they came to the boundary of the Promised Land, the Lord said, "Take it." The people, however, refused. Why? There were giants in the land.

"Why should we go in there? Our children might die," the fathers might have said.

"I know it's a land that flows with milk and honey," the wives might have said, "but the wilderness isn't such a bad place. We're together as a family. We home-school our kids. God is in our midst. The tabernacle is close by. The Shekinah glory is seen. Manna comes down every day. This is a fine place to be."

"But it's not the Promised Land," God would say. "There aren't grapes the size of basketballs. There's no milk and honey. There's no destiny."

"Yes," the people would say, "but there's also no risk."

"Trust and Obey," we sing. But what we often declare is, "I like it here. Why should I take my kids out of school and make that move? Why should I jeopardize the convenience? I really kind of like the wilderness." Yet, all the while, there's territory to take, work to do, blessings ahead.

I have observed that when people don't step out and step up and move in to the Promised Land—whatever that may be for them—they end up slowly dying in the wilderness. Oh, it's imperceptible at first, but after wandering around for years, they realize they're going in circles. At a certain point, a man says, "Stop this carousel. There's a call upon my life. I know what the Lord wants me to do."

I'm afraid we can be vulnerable to saying, "I'm blessed here. I like this." But in our hearts, we know that God has said, "Step up. Step out. And go where you're needed. There are jobs to do, battles to fight, people to touch."

I don't know what that means for you personally, but I'll tell you this: We cannot stay the same in our spiritual walk day after month after year. I am either getting more radical for Jesus, taking steps of faith, launching out in service, plunging ahead—or I'm falling back and wandering in circles. Sure, my family might be safe. But something is missing in my soul.

Go in. Possess the land God has told you to take. Yes, you'll take some blows. Certainly there will be challenges and difficulties. But it's only in the Promised Land where the fruit will blow your mind, where the blessings will cause your soul to expand, where life will no longer be routine. "There's got to be something more to life," you say. There is—the Land God called you to, the Land God told me to press into. Especially in the time of prosperity, it's easy to say, "I just bought my house," or, "I just got that promotion. The wilderness is fine."

Who will dare to say to the Father, "I want to do what You want me to do, to go where You have told me to go, to give what You have commanded me to give. I don't want to settle for just playing it safe. I don't want to die in the wilderness of missed opportunity."?

The saddest thing of all is to see people who were once big in stature spiritually, who cut a wide swath for the kingdom of God, who accomplished great things for eternity, but are now shrinking in obscurity. There are people who used to be giants of faith but aren't anymore because when God spoke to their hearts and told them to start a Bible study, to share with their neighbor, to go to the mission field, they opted out in the name of convenience or comfort.

"Remember what you saw in the generation that died off in the wilderness," Moses said. "They didn't go in. And they ended up complaining and murmuring, wandering and dying. Learn the lesson," Moses said to the children of Israel—and to us. Do what God has called you to do. Go where God has told you to go. Don't say, "Later." Don't say, "As soon as . . . ." Don't say, "But I like it here." Instead, say, "Lord, what You tell me to do, I'm going to do by Your grace."

Let's be those who don't shrink before the eyes of each other. Let's be those who grow and are stretched, who get bigger in the Lord, who grow stronger for the Lord and step out on behalf of the Lord as we leave the wilderness behind and claim the Land of Promise.

Deuteronomy 9:24
Ye have been rebellious against the LORD from the day that I knew you.

"Don't you see where you've been as a people?" Moses says lovingly but honestly to the congregation, for in rebelling against the Lord, they lost the Promised Land.

Are you happy tonight? When I'm not happy, I know it's because I've not done what the Lord told me to do. I have not gone where He commanded me to go.

Deuteronomy 9:25–29
Thus I fell down before the LORD forty days and forty nights, as I fell down at the first; because the LORD had said he would destroy you. I prayed therefore unto the LORD, and said, O Lord GOD, destroy not thy people and thine inheritance, which thou hast redeemed through thy greatness, which thou hast brought forth out of Egypt with a mighty hand. Remember thy servants, Abraham, Isaac, and Jacob; look not unto the stubbornness of this people, nor to their wickedness, nor to their sin: Lest the land whence thou broughtest us out say, Because the LORD was not able to bring them into the land which he promised them, and because he hated them, he hath brought them out to slay them in the wilderness. Yet they are thy people and thine inheritance, which thou broughtest out by thy mighty power and by thy stretched out arm.

"For forty days I fought on behalf of you, I prayed for you," Moses reminds the people. I'm so glad God raised up an even Greater than Moses for me—my Lord and Savior, Jesus Christ who ever lives to intercede for me (Hebrews 7:25).

THE PERIL OF PRIDE

A Topical Study of DEUTERONOMY 8—9

In chapter 8, Moses began giving a warning to the congregation of Israel concerning the peril of pride, the danger of arrogance . . .

The Possessions We Have

Beware that thou forget not the LORD thy God, in not keeping his commandments, and his judgments, and his statutes, which I command thee this day: Lest when thou hast eaten and art full, and hast built goodly houses, and dwelt therein; And when thy herds and thy flocks multiply, and thy silver and thy gold is multiplied, and all that thou hast is multiplied; Then thine heart be lifted up, and thou forget the LORD thy God, which brought thee forth out of the land of Egypt, from the house of bondage; Deuteronomy 8:11–14

When the bull market is roaring and the economy is soaring, the tendency is to forget the Lord rather than to thank Him. "I've been a clever entrepreneur, a careful businessman, I've handled my money well—and look what I've accomplished. My business is going great; my bank account is growing; my car is new; my house is grand." Oh, we're too wise, too sophisticated to say this with our lips, but in our hearts, we say, "I've done alright."

"Beware," Moses would say. The possessions we have—the gold, the silver, the portfolio, house, and car are all due to God's grace exclusively. What you have, what I enjoy, what we possess is a gift from God to you and me not because of who we are but in spite of us!

"But I've worked hard" you may say.

Wait a minute. Who gave you the energy to work hard? Who gave you the ability to be wise? Sometimes we forget. Sometimes we say in our heart, "I'm pretty sharp." But it's nothing more than arrogance. Pride creeps in during times of prosperity. And pride is the only disease known to man that makes everyone sick except the one who has it. Everything we have and all that we enjoy is solely because of God's grace—His unmerited, undeserved, unearned favor.

While most of us would agree with that, the next point is more subtle—even jarring and somewhat shocking . . .

The Position We're In

> *Speak not thou in thine heart, after that the LORD thy God hath cast them out from before thee, saying, For my righteousness the LORD hath brought me in to possess this land: but for the wickedness of these nations the LORD doth drive them out from before thee.* Deuteronomy 9:4

Why did God bring you and me into the Promised Land of His kingdom? Because He saw we would want to be righteous? No. Like the children of Israel, we were stiff-necked and rebellious from the beginning (Deuteronomy 9:7). He did so because of the wickedness of our enemy.

We have an enemy who, from before time began, has questioned the goodness and kindness, mercy and grace of God. "Can't you eat of that tree, Eve?" Satan hissed. "God knows that in the day you eat of it, you'll become godly. In other words, God is not as good as He purports to be. He's holding something back from you, Eve. He knows that if you eat of that tree that it would be wonderful for you. And He doesn't want you to have good things" (see Genesis 3:1–5).

Satan not only challenged the goodness of the Father in the garden, but in heaven. "Of course Job serves You," he said to God. "You've blessed him. But if those blessings weren't there, he would turn his back on You" (see Job 1:9–11).

Psalm 73:1 says God is good.

Satan says, "No He's not."

So God says, "I will prove My goodness and grace by bringing stiffnecked people like those at Applegate into My kingdom, by showering rebellious people like Jon Courson with blessing."

Blessed be the God and Father of our Lord Jesus Christ, who hath blessed us with all spiritual blessings in heavenly places in Christ: According as he hath chosen us in him before the foundation of the world, that we should be holy and without blame before him in love: Having predestinated us unto the adoption of children by Jesus Christ to himself, according to the good pleasure of his will, To the praise of the glory of his grace, wherein he hath made us accepted in the beloved. Ephesians 1:3–6

Paul says we were elected and redeemed not because God saw we were a good, sincere people who wanted to be spiritual, but in order that angels and demons alike would marvel, saying, "Look how *gracious* God is to bless a guy like Jon!"

Whether you're prospering materially or moving into the Promised Land of the kingdom and enjoying blessings spiritually, don't think it's because of your righteousness. The greatest danger to the children of Israel would not be the persecution or the battles in the Promised Land. The greatest danger would occur when things were going well because it would be then that they would forget the Lord.

How do you know when you've forgotten the Lord? It's quite simple: You no longer have time for Him. After all, there are ski boats to use, vacations to take, money to spend. In times of persecution people don't forget God. They gather together. They pray with passion. Their roots sink deep into the soil of the Scriptures. But in times of prosperity, people have toys to play with, places to go, hobbies to pursue. And, although they don't admit it, they forget about God.

Statistics confirm that people forget the Lord in time of prosperity not only by withdrawing from the body, but by failing to give sacrificially. Ironically, people give much more generously in times of difficulty than in times of prosperity. In times of prosperity, they say, "I can't tithe because I bought the second house, the newer car, and I'm overextended"—failing to remember that it was God who gave them the ability to do what they do, to bless them with every single thing they have.

If we truly believe that God has blessed us, we'll say, "This is not my wealth. It's God's. Therefore, in giving my tithe I recognize that what came my way this week is not because of my cleverness or ability but because of Him."

The Posture We Take

Let us therefore come boldly unto the throne of grace, that we may obtain mercy, and find grace to help in time of need. Hebrews 4:16

I can come boldly before the throne of grace because God loves to help sinners like me. And as I do, I bow my knee in humility, humbled by how good God has been to me. And even though I'm stiff-necked and rebellious, I raise my hands in appreciation and raise my head in expectation not because of my worthiness, but solely because of His grace.

"When you have eaten and are full, bless the Lord and beware of pride," Moses cautioned the people. And he would say the same to us.

God wants us to be those who come before His throne of grace and expect to be blessed—not because of who we are, but because of who He is.

10

Deuteronomy 10:1, 2
At that time the LORD said unto me, Hew thee two tables of stone like unto the first, and come up unto me into the mount, and make thee an ark of wood. And I will write on the tables the words that were in the first tables which thou brakest, and thou shalt put them in the ark.

"Carve two more stone tablets and come back to the mountain," the Lord had said to Moses after Moses had broken the original tablets when he saw the children of Israel worshiping the golden calf (Exodus 32). "Bring the ark, and I will write the commandments again."

Notice that God didn't change His mind and say, "I gave you ten commandments before, but the people didn't seem to be too good at keeping them, so let's just try five this time." No, God doesn't do that. God's Word is immutable. It doesn't change. Whether people succeed at keeping it or whether they fail in it, God's Word remains written in stone.

Deuteronomy 10:3–5
And I made an ark of shittim wood, and hewed two tables of stone like unto the first, and went up into the mount, having the two tables in mine hand. And he wrote on the tables, according to the first writing, the ten commandments, which the LORD spake unto you in the mount out of the midst of the fire in the day of the assembly: and the LORD gave them unto me. And I turned myself and came down from the mount, and put the tables in the ark which I had made; and there they be, as the LORD commanded me.

As Moses continues to remind the people of their history, he says, "This time I didn't carry the commandments in my hand as I had done previously, for God instructed me to put them in the ark."

The lid on top of the ark was called the mercy seat. And it was at the mercy seat that God would meet with His people (Exodus 25:22). In this, I find a wonderful balance. You see, because the Law of the Lord is perfect, I must bow my knee and say to Him constantly, "What You say is true, Lord. And by Your grace, I will do what You tell me to do." And I also realize that because the Law is perfect, it points out my failings and shortcomings. But God doesn't meet us in the ark, where the Law is kept. He meets us at the mercy seat—where the blood is sprinkled. And I'm so glad about that.

Deuteronomy 10:6–9
And the children of Israel took their journey from Beeroth of the children of Jaakan to Mosera: there Aaron died, and there he was buried; and Eleazar his son ministered in the priest's office in his stead. From thence they journeyed unto Gudgodah; and from Gudgodah to Jotbath, a land of rivers of waters. At that time the LORD separated the tribe of Levi, to bear the ark of the covenant of the LORD, to stand before the LORD to minister unto him, and to bless in his name, unto this day. Wherefore Levi hath no part nor inheritance with his brethren; the LORD is his inheritance, according as the LORD thy God promised him.

The tribe of Levi was to be those to minister to the Lord. Why? The story is told in Exodus 32—when Moses came down the mountain the first time, seeing the children of Israel worshiping the golden calf, he said, "Who is on the Lord's side? Who will deal with this situation?" Only one tribe stepped up: the tribe of Levi. From that point on, Levi would be the tribe of ministry because they took the sword in the fear of the Lord. The other tribes said, "We don't want to get involved." And that can all too often be our tendency as well. Yet if we're not willing to wield the sword of Scripture in love and say, "This cannot go on. This needs to be thought through and cut away," we cannot be servants of the Lord.

Paul said, "If we seek to please men, we cannot be the servants of God" (Galatians 1:10). We need to be those who are merciful and loving enough to say to the people we care about those who are involved in sin, "I care about you and am committed to you. Therefore, I'm not going to hold back the truth from you." This is not anger and hostility, judgment and condemnation. It's love and compassion, kindness and mercy. Only Levi was willing to unsheathe the sword and deal with the cancer that would corrupt the whole congregation. Thus, only Levi would qualify for ministry.

Deuteronomy 10:10
And I stayed in the mount, according to the first time, forty days and forty nights; and the LORD hearkened unto me at that time also, and the LORD would not destroy thee.

God had offered Moses a very interesting opportunity when He said He would destroy the people and make of Moses a new nation. Moses said, "No, Lord, don't do that. The Egyptians will say that You slaughtered Your own people, that You were unable to keep the promises You made to Abraham, Isaac, and Jacob that their seed would inherit the land. You can't go back on Your Word."

And I'm sure Moses' answer brought a smile to the heart of God, showing as it did, that he cared more about God's reputation than his own opportunity to be the head of a mighty nation.

Deuteronomy 10:11–13
And the LORD said unto me, Arise, take thy journey before the people, that they may go in and possess the land, which I sware unto their fathers to give unto them. And now, Israel, what doth the LORD thy God require of thee, but to fear the LORD thy God, to walk in all his ways, and to love him, and to serve the LORD thy God with all thy heart and with all thy soul, To keep the commandments of the LORD, and his statutes, which I command thee this day for thy good?

"God spared you," Moses said to the congregation. "And now what does He require of you? Simply that you love Him with all your heart and do what His Word tells you for your own *good*."

Deuteronomy 10:14, 15
Behold, the heaven and the heaven of heavens is the LORD's thy God, the earth also, with all that therein is. Only the LORD had a delight in thy fathers to love them, and he chose their seed after them, even you above all people, as it is this day.

"Everything is God's, but He chose *you* to be His children."

Deuteronomy 10:16
Circumcise therefore the foreskin of your heart, and be no more stiffnecked.

As He did with Israel, God chose us. He has shown great mercy to us. Therefore, let's be tenderhearted towards our Father, thankful to Him for all He's done.

Deuteronomy 10:17–19
For the LORD your God is God of gods, and Lord of lords, a great God, a mighty, and a terrible, which regardeth not persons, nor taketh reward: He doth execute the judgment of the fatherless and widow, and loveth the stranger, in giving him food and raiment. Love ye therefore the stranger: for ye were strangers in the land of Egypt.

"Love God and love the stranger, too, because you were once strangers yourselves," Moses said. Sometimes we forget that, like Israel, we were strangers, sinners in bondage to the world of which Egypt is a picture.

Jesus both loved and was loved by strangers—by lepers, prostitutes, and tax collectors. He confronted the self-righteous yet loved the sinner. All too often, we have this reversed. Jesus was embraced by the masses, but the religious establishment was uncomfortable around Him. All too often, the religious establishment is comfortable with me, while the sinner is uncomfortable. And this ought not be.

Deuteronomy 10:20–22
Thou shalt fear the LORD thy God; him shalt thou serve, and to him shalt thou cleave, and swear by his name. He is thy praise, and he is thy God, that hath done for thee these great and terrible things, which thine eyes have seen. Thy fathers went down into Egypt with threescore and ten persons; and now the LORD thy God hath made thee as the stars of heaven for multitude.

"Look how you've grown," Moses said. "Look what God has done. Seventy people became three million."

And so I say to you. Look how you've grown. Look what God has done. You're bigger people, deeper in your understanding of the Lord, more passionate in your love for the Lord. God has multiplied you. He's done great and glorious things in you—all because of His mercy, His goodness, His grace.

11

Deuteronomy 11:1 (a)
Therefore . . .

"Because God has blessed you, multiplied you, prospered you, taken care of you . . ." Moses continues in his farewell address to Israel . . .

Deuteronomy 11:1 (b)–9
. . . thou shalt love the LORD thy God, and keep his charge, and his statutes, and his judgments, and his commandments, alway. And know ye this day: for I speak not with your children which have not known, and which have not seen the chastisement of the LORD your God, his greatness, his mighty hand, and his stretched out arm, And his miracles, and his acts, which he did in the midst of Egypt unto Pharaoh the king of Egypt, and unto all his land; And what he did unto the army of Egypt, unto their horses, and to their chariots; how he made the water of the Red sea to overflow them as they pursued after you, and how the LORD hath destroyed them unto this day; And what he did unto you in the wilderness, until ye came into this place; And what he did unto Dathan and Abiram, the sons of Eliab, the son of Reuben: how the earth opened her mouth, and swallowed them up, and their households, and their tents, and all the substance that was in their possession, in the midst of all Israel: But your eyes have seen all the great acts of the LORD which he did. Therefore shall ye keep all the commandments which I command you this day, that ye may be strong, and go in and possess the land, whither ye go to possess it; And that ye may prolong your days in the land, which the LORD sware unto your fathers to give unto them and to their seed, a land that floweth with milk and honey.

"I'm not talking to your children, I'm talking to you who have seen the mighty hand of God, the outstretched arm of the Lord," Moses says. "You were the ones who saw what He did when He parted the Red Sea and drowned the armies of Pharaoh miraculously. You are the ones who saw how He took care of the rebellions in the wilderness, how He conquered your enemies, how He was there every step of the way day by day. You know, you saw what the Lord has done. I'm talking to you who have been blessed, you who know the truth, you who have seen the work of the Lord."

I find it interesting that Moses would address this to the adults, to those who had seen so much, who know a lot because, as adults, we have a tendency to say, "I hope my kids heard that sermon," or, "I hope my kids got that lesson," or, "I'm going to send the tape to my son-in-law or my granddaughter." There's nothing wrong with that, but our kids want *us* to be godly, to live lives that are exemplary, to have integrity, to be holy, to be godly. It's not about learning something to pass on to our kids, but about applying it to our own lives.

Deuteronomy 11:10–12
For the land, whither thou goest in to possess it, is not as the land of Egypt, from whence ye came out, where thou sowedst thy seed, and wateredst it with thy foot, as a garden of herbs: But the land, whither ye go to possess it, is a land of hills and valleys, and drinketh water of the rain of heaven: A land which the LORD thy God careth for: the eyes of the LORD thy God are always upon it, from the beginning of the year even unto the end of the year.

"Be strong," Moses said. "Keep the commandments that you may take the land God has laid before you. And, unlike Egypt, the land is a great land." Although the Egyptians were a sophisticated and mighty civilization, the land itself gets less than one inch of rain per year. The only way Egypt could prosper was by taking water out of the Nile and irrigating sections around the river that would provide the agricultural base for their civilization. How did they do this? Verse 10 tells us. They would use foot pumps. Day after day, perpetually, exhaustingly, continually they would have to pump water out of the Nile into the fields in order that their crops might grow. It was hard work.

Moses said, "The land you're going to is not like that. The Lord keeps His eye upon this land and sends rain. You don't have to sweat to see the water flow."

Deuteronomy 11:13–15
And it shall come to pass, if ye shall hearken diligently unto my commandments which I command you this day, to love the LORD your God, and to serve him with all your heart and with all your soul, That I will give you the rain of your land in his due season, the first rain and the latter rain, that thou mayest gather in thy corn, and thy wine, and thine oil. And I will send grass in thy fields for thy cattle, that thou mayest eat and be full.

The mention of "latter rain" also appears in Jeremiah 5, Hosea 6, Joel 2, and James 5—where it speaks of the outpouring of the Holy Spirit. "There's coming a time," the Lord says, "when I will pour out My Spirit upon all flesh. Your sons and daughters shall prophesy. Your young men shall see visions, your old men shall dream dreams." (Joel 2:28)

We are already seeing the beginning of a wonderful last day's outpouring, where people are being filled and empowered by the Holy Spirit. But it's only the beginning. The Lord wants to save souls and bring in a huge harvest in these last days. And He's going to empower us to an even greater degree.

How will this happen? It's not going to come through the Egyptian methodology—where we pump it up. I've been to meetings where there is an attempt to get people worked up, pumped up through fervor and emotion. But sometimes such meetings remind me of the prophets of Baal on Mt. Carmel who jumped up and down and slashed their bodies with knives to try and get the attention of their gods. After a full day of futility, Elijah said, "My turn," and prayed a simple ten-second prayer so powerful it brought fire down from heaven (1 Kings 18:36–38). Therefore, I'm always cautious about situations where the Egyptian mentality is used to try and get the fire to come down, the latter rain to fall, the Spirit to move.

The latter rain is not something we pump up emotionally, but that which the Lord pours out upon those who simply love Him and give themselves in service to Him. "You shall receive power when the Holy Ghost comes upon you to be My witnesses in Jerusalem, Judaea, Samaria, and the uttermost parts of the earth," Jesus said (Acts 1:8).

Power is given for the purpose of service. Therefore, it is to any of us who say, "Lord, I love You. That's why I'm here. And I want to serve You. Use me," that the Lord will pour out His Spirit in order that we might be His witnesses.

Deuteronomy 11:16, 17
Take heed to yourselves, that your heart be not deceived, and ye turn aside, and serve other gods, and worship them; And then the LORD's wrath be kindled against you, and he shut up the heaven, that there be no rain, and that the land yield not her fruit; and lest ye perish quickly from off the good land which the LORD giveth you.

Although the Lord pours out His Spirit to those who give themselves to serve Him, the outpouring will cease if we turn aside and serve the gods of our hobbies, our desires, our flesh. Once I start serving these gods, the heavens are shut up and my soul gets dry.

Elijah—he who called down fire from heaven—stormed into wicked King Ahab's court and said, "Be it known unto you, it shall not rain these years but according to my word." And indeed it didn't rain for over three years (1 Kings 17:1). James tells us that although Elijah was a man just like you and me, he knew how to pray (James 5:17). Therefore, he evidently knew this text, for Jesus said if His words abide in us our prayers will be answered (John 15:7).

That is why we come out on a night like this. That's why we attend Bible studies year after year after year. That's why I read the Word. I want to know what this book has to say that I might pray effectively. Elijah models this. The Word of the Lord was evidently in his heart, enabling him to pray effectively. The more Bible study you take in, the more Scripture you know, the more effectively you can pray. And the effectual, fervent prayer of a righteous man avails, or accomplishes, *much* (James 5:16).

Deuteronomy 11:18
Therefore shall ye lay up these my words in your heart and in your soul, and bind them for a sign upon your hand, that they may be as frontlets between your eyes.

Although the Jews took this literally by wearing phylacteries, or boxes, on their wrists or foreheads containing the Shema (Deuteronomy 6:4), that's not what Moses meant. The idea is to keep the Word close at hand and between your eyes, in your mind.

Deuteronomy 11:19
And ye shall teach them your children, speaking of them when thou sittest in thine house, and when thou walkest by the way, when thou liest down, and when thou risest up.

When Peter-John was in fourth or fifth grade, we were on our way to a Giants game. As we left the Rogue Valley on our way to Candlestick Park, the sky became cloudy and looked rather threatening. "Let's pray it doesn't rain," Peter said.

Aha! I thought. *This is an opportunity to teach.* So I said, "Peter, what you have to remember is that we're in a drought and there's a whole bunch of farmers, prayer warriors, who have been praying for rain."

"Okay, Dad," he said, "Their prayer warriors are praying for rain. You and me are going to pray that it won't rain. Let the strongest army win!"

We might think our kids aren't aware of what we're telling them. But your son, daughter, or grandchild is taking in a lot more than you know. So use every opportunity to expand their knowledge of the Word, of God's kingdom, of the ways of the Lord.

Deuteronomy 11:20
And thou shalt write them upon the door posts of thine house, and upon thy gates:

The Word of God should be woven into the very fabric of your home. People should sense that your house is a sanctified spot.

Deuteronomy 11:21–23 (a)
That your days may be multiplied, and the days of your children, in the land which the LORD sware unto your fathers to give them, as the days of heaven upon the earth. For if ye shall diligently keep all these commandments which I command you, to do them, to love the LORD your God, to walk in all his ways, and to cleave unto him; Then will the LORD drive out all these nations from before you . . .

"But there are so many problems in our house," you might say.

The Lord says, "If you love Me and do what I tell you to, I will drive out the forces causing those problems."

When you love the Lord and keep His Word at the front door, close at hand, and between your eyes; when you teach your kids what God will do, He promises to drive out the enemy that would otherwise drive you crazy.

Deuteronomy 11:23 (b), 24
. . . and ye shall possess greater nations and mightier than yourselves. Every place whereon the soles of your feet shall tread shall be yours: from the wilderness and Lebanon, from the river, the river Euphrates, even unto the uttermost sea shall your coast be.

Although the children of Israel would take control of only approximately one tenth of what God intended for them, this description is of a huge amount of territory—all the way to present-day Iraq and Iran.

God is able to do "exceedingly abundantly above all we can ask or even think," Paul tells us (Ephesians 3:20). So take a step of faith. Believe the Lord. Obey His commands. Claim the territory He's already declared would be yours—for your kids, your family, your service for Him. God wants to do so much for us. Let's go for it.

Deuteronomy 11:25–32
There shall no man be able to stand before you: for the LORD your God shall lay the fear of you and the dread of you upon all the land that ye shall tread upon, as he hath said unto you. Behold, I set before you this day a blessing and a curse; A blessing, if ye obey the commandments of the LORD your God, which I command you this day: And a curse, if ye will not obey the commandments of the LORD your God, but turn aside out of the way which I command you this day, to go after other gods, which ye have not known. And it shall come to pass, when the LORD thy God hath brought thee in unto the land whither thou goest to possess it, that thou shalt put the blessing upon mount Gerizim, and the curse upon mount Ebal. Are they not on the other side Jordan, by the way where the sun goeth down, in the land of the Canaanites, which dwell in the champaign over against Gilgal, beside the plains of Moreh? For ye shall pass over Jordan to go in to possess the land which the LORD your God giveth you, and ye shall possess it, and dwell therein. And ye shall observe to do all the statutes and judgments which I set before you this day.

In Joshua 8, we'll see half of the tribes of the children of Israel on Mount Gerizim, the other half on Mount Ebal with Joshua and the priests and Levites in the valley between. Joshua will say a certain commandment to which was attached a blessing, and all the tribes on Mt. Gerizim will say, "Amen!" Then he will give a command with a curse—something which they're not to do—and those on Mt. Ebal will also say, "Amen!" In so doing, the nation of Israel will acknowledge that if they obey God, they shall put the blessing on Gerizim. It was on Mt. Ebal that sacrifice was to be made. I love this because where there are curses, an altar is made to make provision. I'm so glad about that because I've been on both sides of the valley. I've experienced the blessings of Gerizim. But I've also wandered over to Ebal. Thus, I am so grateful for the altar, the provision for my sin and stupidity.

Joshua is, of course, a picture of Jesus. Where is Jesus right now? Between two mountains. He's already been on the mountain of cursing, where He who knew no sin was made sin for us as He hung on the Cross of Calvary (2 Corinthians 5:21). But He's coming back to another mountain—the Mount of Olives, which will split in two when He returns as the Prince of Peace (Zechariah 14:4).

"I've heard you talk about being blessed if we obey the commandments," you might say. "I've done my best, tried my hardest. But I'm not being blessed like I thought I would be. You talk about taking territory, but it hasn't happened for me."

Wait. You're in the valley. Wait until Jesus gets back. Oh, we're blessed right now without question, but the Mount of Olives tells me the best is yet to come. When you read these blessings and promises, realize that, although they apply to you, to your marriage, to your family, to your ministry—the best is yet to come. And I'm so looking forward to that. Obey the Lord. Keep His commandments. Bind His Word before your eyes. Keep it close at hand. Teach your children.

And God will bless you, yes in this life—but especially, most importantly, most fully in the age of the kingdom, throughout eternity, in heaven.

12

Deuteronomy 12:1–3

These are the statutes and judgments, which ye shall observe to do in the land, which the LORD God of thy fathers giveth thee to possess it, all the days that ye live upon the earth. Ye shall utterly destroy all the places, wherein the nations which ye shall possess served their gods, upon the high mountains, and upon the hills, and under every green tree: And ye shall overthrow their altars, and break their pillars, and burn their groves with fire; and ye shall hew down the graven images of their gods, and destroy the names of them out of that place.

As we watched the painful situation in Jerusalem, we could see the wisdom of this command from God to His people. The command was simply this: "When you go into the Land I give to you, make sure you utterly destroy the places where the Canaanites worshiped their false gods."

This might sound harsh. It's certainly not politically correct, but it's right and it's practical, for you see, God knew that if they didn't destroy those groves and tear down those altars, that there would be a tendency for problems down the road to crop up, where the people of Israel's curiosity about those false gods would grow, where the Canaanites and pagans in the area would still have a foothold. Consequently, God ordered the absolute eradication of those holy spots. And I can't help but think of the events of the past twelve days. For in Jerusalem, we see a pagan spot—the shrine known as the Dome of the Rock—built in A.D. 690 by the followers of Mohammed, is proving to be a problem even now, centuries later.

Allah is not a name for the True and Living God, but the name of the moon god Mohammed chose to be his god. Allah is not the same God as the God of Abraham, Isaac, and Jacob. Furthermore, the Dome of the Rock was erected under false pretenses as a result of a battle within the Islamic Empire.

The Israelis had an opportunity to destroy it completely in 1967. When they captured the city of Jerusalem in the six-Day War of 1967, the Israeli Defense Forces made its way immediately to the Temple Mount and were ready to blow up the Dome of the Rock monument. You might have seen the famous footage of what took place in Germany during World War II when our troops went into Berlin and blew up the huge Nazi insignia that stood above the coliseum. That's what soldiers do. That's the way war works. The victor has the right to eradicate the emblems of the enemy. In 1967, the Israelis had the opportunity to do this, but General Moshe Dayan stopped the commanders from giving that particular order and instead turned over the day-to-day control of the Temple Mount to the Islamic authorities. Thus, although Israel is still sovereign over the Temple Mount, the daily operation has been overseen by the Islamic police and has proven to be a huge mistake. Compromise always is.

No doubt the Israelis were thinking at the time that if they did indeed touch the mosque, it would have been tantamount to a declaration of war against all of Islam. But I believe the real reason they stopped is because there was a higher Force at work—the hand of God—knowing that there are certain events that must take place to fulfill prophecy, to cause Jerusalem to become the troubled spot it is presently.

But God's initial plan, His intention for His people—whether Jews in ancient times, Israelis today, or believers like you and me—is that we deal a death blow to the enemy. We don't compromise. We totally eradicate the strongholds of Satan. Ephesians 4 tells us we are to give no place to the devil. And whether it's in my life personally or the Temple Mount geographically, unnecessary pain, problems, and difficulty are always the result of compromise. When Jesus said the kingdom of God is taken by violence, or by force (Matthew 11:12), He wasn't talking about physically taking a sword or shouldering an M16 but about the fact that if we want to experience the kingdom to the greatest degree, we've got to deal violently with the enemy.

If there is something in your home where shady things take place via cable TV or the Internet, get rid of it. Don't make any compromises with it. Deal violently in the area of the Spirit and say, "That's got to go. I can't afford to have that grove, that altar, that high place in my home or in my heart."

Deuteronomy 12:4–12

Ye shall not do so unto the LORD your God. But unto the place which the LORD your God shall choose out of all your tribes to put his name there, even unto his habitation shall ye seek, and thither thou shalt come: And thither ye shall bring your burnt offerings, and your sacrifices, and your tithes, and heave offerings of your hand, and your vows, and your freewill offerings, and the firstlings of

your herds and of your flocks: And there ye shall eat before the LORD your God, and ye shall rejoice in all that ye put your hand unto, ye and your households, wherein the LORD thy God hath blessed thee. Ye shall not do after all the things that we do here this day, every man whatsoever is right in his own eyes. For ye are not as yet come to the rest and to the inheritance, which the LORD your God giveth you. But when ye go over Jordan, and dwell in the land which the LORD your God giveth you to inherit, and when he giveth you rest from all your enemies round about, so that ye dwell in safety; Then there shall be a place which the LORD your God shall choose to cause his name to dwell there; thither shall ye bring all that I command you; your burnt offerings, and your sacrifices, your tithes, and the heave offering of your hand, and all your choice vows which ye vow unto the LORD: And ye shall rejoice before the LORD your God, ye, and your sons, and your daughters, and your menservants, and your maidservants, and the Levite that is within your gates; forasmuch as he hath no part nor inheritance with you. Take heed to thyself that thou offer not thy burnt offerings in every place that thou seest: But in the place which the LORD shall choose in one of thy tribes, there thou shalt offer thy burnt offerings, and there thou shalt do all that I command thee.

"Tear down their altars. Cut down their groves. Destroy their high places," God declares. "Instead, go to the place I tell you of and there you shall worship Me. There you shall bring your tithes and offerings to Me. There you shall make your vows to Me. There you shall seek Me."

Where was "there"?

Jerusalem.

"Why do we have to tithe? Who says we have to go to church on Sunday? I'm going to do what I want to do," some people say. But theirs is a wilderness mentality. They might be sincere, but God says once we have crossed into the Promised Land—which speaks of the Spirit-filled life, the deeper life, the productive life, the fruitful life—it's not up to us what to do.

"Our fathers say we are to worship on Mt. Gerizim, yet you Jews say we are to worship in Jerusalem," the woman at the well said to Jesus.

"In reality," Jesus answered, "the Father is seeking those who will worship Him in spirit and in truth" (John 4:23).

Why do we get together and worship the Lord with uplifted hands, on our knees, at His Table? Because we're worshiping the Lord in spirit. Why do we go through the Bible month after month, year after year, decade after decade? Because we're worshiping Him in truth.

Deuteronomy 12:15 (a)
Notwithstanding thou mayest kill and eat flesh in all thy gates, whatsoever thy soul lusteth after . . .

The only place to offer the sacrifice is in the place God chooses—which would ultimately be Jerusalem. If the children of Israel wanted to have a BBQ for themselves or their friends, they could kill the bull anywhere, but if it was for a spiritual purpose, they had to go to the place God chose. They had to go to Jerusalem.

Deuteronomy 12:15 (b), 16
. . . according to the blessing of the LORD thy God which he hath given thee: the unclean and the clean may eat thereof, as of the roebuck, and as of the hart. Only ye shall not eat the blood; ye shall pour it upon the earth as water.

"You can kill the animal where you wish, you can have him when you want, but make sure you remember the sanctity of the blood," Moses said, "for the life of the flesh is in the blood" (Leviticus 17:11). The blood was to be drained from the animal because it is symbolic of life—pointing ultimately to the blood that would be poured out from the veins of our Lord Jesus Christ, even as the blood of the sacrifice was to be poured out upon the ground.

Deuteronomy 12:17–19
Thou mayest not eat within thy gates the tithe of thy corn, or of thy wine, or of thy oil, or the firstlings of thy herds or of thy flock, nor any of thy vows which thou vowest, nor thy freewill offerings, or heave offering of thine hand: But thou must eat them before the LORD thy God in the place which the LORD thy God shall choose, thou, and thy son, and thy daughter, and thy manservant, and thy maidservant, and the Levite that is within thy gates: and thou shalt rejoice before the LORD thy God in all that thou puttest thine hands unto. Take heed to thyself that thou forsake not the Levite as long as thou livest upon the earth.

There are those who say "I'll figure out what to do with my tithe. I'll have my own little account and I'll put it where I think it ought to go." No. God says the tithe is to be brought to the place *He* chooses.

Deuteronomy 12:20–22
When the LORD thy God shall enlarge thy border, as he hath promised thee, and thou shalt say, I will eat flesh, because thy soul longeth to eat flesh; thou mayest eat flesh, whatsoever thy soul lusteth after. If the place which the LORD thy God hath chosen to put his name there be too far from thee, then thou shalt kill of thy herd and of thy flock, which the LORD hath given thee, as I have commanded thee, and thou shalt eat in thy gates whatsoever thy soul lusteth after. Even as the roebuck and the hart is eaten, so thou shalt eat them: the unclean and the clean shall eat of them alike.

Verses 20–24 repeat that a man was allowed to eat meat in his home or town. But if it was a sacrifice, he was to go to Jerusalem.

Deuteronomy 12:23–28
Only be sure that thou eat not the blood: for the blood is the life; and thou mayest not eat the life with the flesh. Thou shalt not eat it; thou shalt pour it upon the earth as water. Thou shalt not eat it; that it may go well with thee, and with thy children after thee, when thou shalt do that which is right in the sight of the LORD. Only thy holy things which thou hast, and thy vows, thou shalt take, and go unto the place which the LORD shall choose: And thou shalt offer thy burnt offerings, the flesh and the blood, upon the altar of the LORD thy God: and the blood of thy sacrifices shall be poured out upon the altar of the LORD thy God, and thou shalt eat the flesh. Observe and hear all these words which I command thee, that it may go well with thee, and with thy children after thee for ever, when thou doest that which is good and right in the sight of the LORD thy God.

When Cain killed Abel, God said, "The blood of your brother cries out" (Genesis 4:10). Today, with the sophistication of DNA testing, in murder cases, for example we hear blood literally crying out. Ultimately, of course, this doesn't speak of the blood that cries out, "Guilty," but of the blood that cries out "Forgiven!"—the blood of Jesus Christ. How grateful I am that I can come to Communion, that I can take of the cup, drink of the blood, and know that my sins are washed away.

Deuteronomy 12:29, 30
When the LORD thy God shall cut off the nations from before thee, whither thou goest to possess them, and thou succeedest them, and dwellest in their land; Take heed to thyself that thou be not snared by following them, after that they be destroyed from before thee; and that thou inquire not after their gods, saying, How did these nations serve their gods? Even so will I do likewise.

Moses tells the Israelites that if they became entangled in the worship of the gods of the people God destroyed, they themselves would be destroyed.

Deuteronomy 12:31, 32
Thou shalt not do so unto the LORD thy God: for every abomination to the LORD, which he hateth, have they done unto their gods; for even their sons and their daughters they have burnt in the fire to their gods. What thing soever I command you, observe to do it: thou shalt not add thereto, nor diminish from it.

It is a dangerous thing for people to study and inquire after false gods. I know people who are now caught up in a cult because they became interested in it initially so they could argue against it.

> But sanctify the Lord God in your hearts: and be ready always to give an answer to every man that asketh you a reason of the hope that is in you with meekness and fear:
>
> 1 Peter 3:15

There are those who use this verse to say we should be able to defend our faith to those who are involved in cults. The context of 1 Peter 3:15, however, deals not with false doctrine but with suffering. In other words, we should be able to tell people who see us go through trials, heartbreaks, and difficulty the reason for our hope. But Paul tells us clearly that if someone knocks on the door who's a heretic, we're to send them on their way without even saying, "God bless you" (2 John 10). The best way to study cults is to stay in the Word because then you will recognize that which doesn't ring true.

13

Deuteronomy 13:1–9 (a)
If there arise among you a prophet, or a dreamer of dreams, and giveth thee a sign or a wonder, And the sign or the wonder come to pass, whereof he spake unto thee, saying, Let us go after other gods, which thou hast not known, and let us serve them; Thou shalt not hearken unto the

words of that prophet, or that dreamer of dreams: for the LORD your God proveth you, to know whether ye love the LORD your God with all your heart and with all your soul. Ye shall walk after the LORD your God, and fear him, and keep his commandments, and obey his voice, and ye shall serve him, and cleave unto him. And that prophet, or that dreamer of dreams, shall be put to death; because he hath spoken to turn you away from the LORD your God, which brought you out of the land of Egypt, and redeemed you out of the house of bondage, to thrust thee out of the way which the LORD thy God commanded thee to walk in. So shalt thou put the evil away from the midst of thee. If thy brother, the son of thy mother, or thy son, or thy daughter, or the wife of thy bosom, or thy friend, which is as thine own soul, entice thee secretly, saying, Let us go and serve other gods, which thou hast not known, thou, nor thy fathers; Namely, of the gods of the people which are round about you, nigh unto thee, or far off from thee, from the one end of the earth even unto the other end of the earth; Thou shalt not consent unto him, nor hearken unto him; neither shall thine eye pity him, neither shalt thou spare, neither shalt thou conceal him: But thou shalt surely kill him . . .

So we're to kill the Mormon missionary? Of course not! But we're to put to death the relationship where we're giving time and listening to what he says. Even if he's a friend or a brother, we're not to give ear to those who would entice us by saying, "There's a god you don't know about, something you're not aware of, something more. The Bible is fine. But there's more." Put that relationship to death because there are demonic powers in false religious systems.

Wise is the person who says, "I'm going to keep my eyes on Jesus Christ all the days of my life. Nothing less, nothing more, nothing else."

Deuteronomy 13:9 (b)–11
. . . thine hand shall be first upon him to put him to death, and afterwards the hand of all the people. And thou shalt stone him with stones, that he die; because he hath sought to thrust thee away from the LORD thy God, which brought thee out of the land of Egypt, from the house of bondage. And all Israel shall hear, and fear, and shall do no more any such wickedness as this is among you.

The Israelites were to physically stone the person who tried to pull them away from God—for that is the way they would put an end not only to that person, but also to the problem. And in this, God declares that capital punishment is indeed a deterrent to crime.

Notice that the first stone was to be thrown by the accuser—which would, in itself, be a deterrent to false accusation or accusation made lightly. Notice, too, that the entire community was to take part in the stoning, for one person's sin will indeed affect an entire community.

In Joshua 7, Achan hid that which he stole from Jericho, and the whole nation was defeated at Ai. I wish we could understand more fully that when someone sins in our fellowship, it directly affects us all. We're one body, one community, one church, one family. Therefore, the whole community must be involved in the purging process. That is why Paul would write to Timothy, "Openly rebuke those who openly sin in order that *all* may hear" (see 1 Timothy 5:20).

Deuteronomy 13:12–18
If thou shalt hear say in one of thy cities, which the LORD thy God hath given thee to dwell there, saying, Certain men, the children of Belial, are gone out from among you, and have withdrawn the inhabitants of their city, saying, Let us go and serve other gods, which ye have not known; Then shalt thou inquire, and make search, and ask diligently; and, behold, if it be truth, and the thing certain, that such abomination is wrought among you; Thou shalt surely smite the inhabitants of that city with the edge of the sword, destroying it utterly, and all that is therein, and the cattle thereof, with the edge of the sword. And thou shalt gather all the spoil of it into the midst of the street thereof, and shalt burn with fire the city, and all the spoil thereof every whit, for the LORD thy God: and it shall be an heap for ever; it shall not be built again. And there shall cleave nought of the cursed thing to thine hand: that the LORD may turn from the fierceness of his anger, and shew thee mercy, and have compassion upon thee, and multiply thee, as he hath sworn unto thy fathers; When thou shalt hearken to the voice of the LORD thy God, to keep all his commandments which I command thee this day, to do that which is right in the eyes of the LORD thy God.

"Even if this might seem to hurt your nation economically or militarily," Moses said, "the city that causes you to rebel against God is to be destroyed and never rebuilt."

CHARACTERISTICS OF CULTS

A Topical Study of DEUTERONOMY 12—13

A few weeks ago, I talked with a man who has become quite confused and very troubled because he began to inquire about a false god. When he went to the open house of the Mormon Temple recently dedicated in the Rogue Valley, he was intrigued by what he saw and began to buy into certain things he heard, impressed by the closeness of the Mormon community. And now he doesn't know what to think—all because he did what our text tells us we ought to be on guard against.

As a shepherd, Moses knew there would be a temptation for the flock of God to be intrigued by the gods of the Canaanites. So he warned the people about inquiring after them. In the New Testament, another shepherd of God's flock gave the same warning in his own farewell address to the elders at Ephesus. "You know that after my departing, ravenous wolves will rise up from your midst" Paul said in Acts 20:29, 30.

As an under-shepherd, it is my joy, privilege, and responsibility to feed the flock of God. We need to be fed. And we do that as we graze in the Word. But if I feed the flock and never warn the flock, I might simply be fattening the flock for the kill. There must be feeding, but there must also be warning. That is why I want to draw your attention to five characteristics common to all cults as seen in our text . . .

Cults Distance the Father

Thou shalt not do so unto the LORD thy God: for every abomination to the LORD, which he hateth, have they done unto their gods; for even their sons and their daughters they have burnt in the fire to their gods. What thing soever I command you, observe to do it: thou shalt not add thereto, nor diminish from it.

Deuteronomy 12:31, 32

"It's not that simple," the cultist says to the believer. "You can't come boldly before the throne of grace. You've got to prove your sincerity."

In Moses' day, the Canaanites proved they were sincere seekers of their gods by literally burning their sons and daughters. Five-foot high iron idols dedicated to Moloch were constructed with a hole in them in which a fire would burn, causing the idol to become incandescent. Sincere worshipers would place their firstborn child on the red-hot arms of these idols in the valley of Tophet, also known as the valley of Gehenna, which is another name for Hell.

I talked to a young lady after first service who said, "I just came out of Mormonism, a belief full of barriers. You have to wear holy underwear; you can't drink Coke. It's not enough to believe—you've got to prove it." People might be able to do this for a little while, but they can't do it forever, and ultimately they get burned out. She tried to be a "good Mormon," to earn the blessings that would come her way if she did this and didn't do the other, but eventually she rebelled against the Lord completely. Legalism does that. That's where Mormonism is wrong. That's why Jehovah's Witnesses are wrong. They say it's not enough simply to believe in Jesus Christ. And that is what separates biblical Christianity from all other cults, every other religion.

Every cult and false religion is based upon man working his way up the ladder of sincerity, good works, obedience to a system. Christianity alone is not based upon man working up to God, but God reaching down to man. "For by grace are ye saved," Paul declares. And what is grace? It is unmerited, undeserved, unearned favor. It is a gift of God, *not* of works (Ephesians 2:8, 9 italics added).

What must a man do to be saved? Simply believe in the Lord Jesus Christ. Period. (Acts 16:30, 31). "It is *finished*," Jesus said (John 19:30). My standing with God is not about what I do to prove my sincerity, but about what He's already done to prove His love and mercy. And all that's left is for me to respond to His free gift of salvation.

Cults Diminish the Son

If there arise among you a prophet, or a dreamer of dreams, and giveth thee a sign or a wonder, And the sign or the wonder come to pass, whereof he spake unto thee, saying, Let us go after other gods, which thou hast not known, and let us serve them; Thou shalt not hearken unto the words of that prophet, or that dreamer of dreams: for the LORD your God proveth you, to know whether ye love the LORD your God with all your heart and with all your soul.

Deuteronomy 13:1–3

In 1820, a fifteen-year-old boy named Joseph Smith claimed he had a vision and a dream. He also claimed he was a prophet from God. The so-called angel, Moroni, came to Joseph Smith to give him "another gospel," the "full truth." Four years later, he would supposedly find golden tablets with hieroglyphics inscribed on them that would reveal the truth completely. Joseph went to the spot pointed out by Moroni. He saw the golden tablets, which were indecipherable until he put on magic glasses called the Urim and the Thummim. With them, he could make sense of the golden tablets that, incidentally, were written in King James English. And this is what this so-called prophet had to say about Jesus Christ. Jesus is not the Creator of all things, but a created being, the brother of Lucifer. Jehovah's Witnesses say He is the archangel, Michael.

All cults diminish the Person of Jesus. They make Him less than He is. Who is

He? He is God. And if you don't believe that, according to Romans 10:9, 10, you can't be saved.

You're splitting hairs, you might be thinking. *So the Mormons believe Jesus was a created being, so the Jehovah's Witnesses believe he's an angel, don't they both believe that He died, that His blood was shed?*

It's far more than splitting hairs. The cults have staked out a horrible position in saying that God didn't die for us, but that He created a Being to take the hit, to pay the price, to shed His blood.

> If a house suddenly erupted in flames and I knew there were people inside, if, instead of going in myself, I grabbed Benjamin and tossed him in to rescue the people, what kind of person would I be?

The Bible says that God was in Christ reconciling the world (2 Corinthians 5:19). He didn't create a Being other than Himself to pay the price, to go into the fire, to take the heat of the Cross. His name, Isaiah tells us, shall be both Everlasting Father *and* Prince of Peace (9:6). God didn't create Someone to do the work of salvation. God Himself became a Man. God was in the Son. That's why a man can't be saved if he doesn't believe that Jesus Christ is Lord, that Jesus Christ is God.

> Let's say I do storm into the burning house. And I pull a ten-year-old boy to safety. But it costs me greatly. My eyesight is lost. My skin is scorched. And the boy I rescued comes to see me in the hospital. As he enters my room, the nurse says, "Here's the man who saved you."
>
> "No, he didn't," the boy says. "He didn't really save me. It was just an image of him, an emanation of him."
>
> Hearing this, I would say, "You little rat. How dare you deny what I did for you. I stormed into a burning house, took the heat, paid the price, and became permanently scarred to save you—yet you won't even acknowledge me?"

There are those in the cults today who have the audacity to say God merely created Someone to die on the Cross in His place. "I have a problem with that," God would say. "*I* paid the price. And if you don't believe that, you can't be saved."

Cults Demand Allegiance

> *Ye shall walk after the* LORD *your God, and fear him, and keep his commandments, and obey his voice, and ye shall serve him, and cleave unto him.*
>
> Deuteronomy 13:4

"We do not seek to have dominion over you," Paul declared. "Rather, we are helpers of your joy, for by faith you stand" (2 Corinthians 1:24).

Cults, on the other hand, say, "We'll tell you how to believe and how to act. If you don't give us your total allegiance, then you'll not make it to heaven."

Cults Defy the Spirit

> *And that prophet, or that dreamer of dreams, shall be put to death; because he hath spoken to turn you away from the LORD your God, which brought you out of the land of Egypt, and redeemed you out of the house of bondage, to thrust thee out of the way which the LORD thy God commanded thee to walk in. So shalt thou put the evil away from the midst of thee.* Deuteronomy 13:5

You've seen the Mormon commercials on TV. They invite you to call for the Book of Mormon they call another gospel. Yet the Spirit of God inspired Paul to write specifically that any person or angel who preached another gospel was to be damned (Galatians 1:6–8).

"Put to death those who would want to lure you away from God," Moses says. And Paul would add, "Even if it's an angel named Moroni."

Cults Divide the Body

> *If thy brother, the son of thy mother, or thy son, or thy daughter, or the wife of thy bosom, or thy friend, which is as thine own soul, entice thee secretly, saying, Let us go and serve other gods, which thou hast not known, thou, nor thy fathers; Namely, of the gods of the people which are round about you, nigh unto thee, or far off from thee, from the one end of the earth even unto the other end of the earth; Thou shalt not consent unto him, nor hearken unto him; neither shall thine eye pity him, neither shalt thou spare, neither shalt thou conceal him: But thou shalt surely kill him . . .* Deuteronomy 13:6–9 (a)

The body of Christ is huge. But the cults say, "Everyone but our group is wrong." Joseph Smith was told by Moroni that every Christian group was in absolute heresy. Whenever any group suggests that they alone know the truth about Jesus Christ and that every other Christian is wrong, it's the sign of a cult dividing the body, coming between brothers and sisters, ripping apart the church.

Because no Scripture is of private interpretation (2 Peter 1:20), when someone comes your way saying, "This is the truth and everyone else is wrong," I would encourage you to stick with the vast majority of believers throughout history who, although they have different flavors, different strengths, different emphases, stand shoulder to shoulder behind the simplicity of the gospel and the finished work of the Cross.

I need to hear this warning and share it with you. I am not going to be one who inquires after other gods. I'm not going to be interested in them or seduced by them because Jesus Christ has delivered me from Egypt, from the house of bondage. He's changed my life; He saved my soul. And it's so freeing, so exhilarating, so wonderful to know that I don't have to jump through hoops or work my way into the presence of God, but that I can simply receive what He's done for me and worship Him passionately.

And not only can I come boldly before the throne of grace, but I can go to a person on his deathbed with only moments to live and say, "You can be born again. You can live forever. Just open your heart to Jesus," rather than, "Sorry, you don't have time to put on your holy underwear or distribute *Watchtower* magazine. Therefore, you won't make it to Heaven." I'm so thankful that I'm not part of a group that makes it impossible to share the Good News of the gospel so simple a three-year-old can understand it. I was three when I opened my heart to Jesus. I know how simple it is. It's profoundly simple and simply profound.

Dear brothers and sisters, rejoice in the profound simplicity of the gospel of Jesus Christ and make no other inquiry. Stay focused on the Author and Perfector of faith, Jesus Christ. And I guarantee you will find that He is all you'll ever need to give you a life of freedom, of love, of peace. Don't become ensnared by the gods around you. Don't inquire of them or be intrigued by them lest you be burnt by the worship of a false god.

"I alone am the door," Jesus said. "All others are thieves and robbers" (John 10:7–9). Sorry, Joseph and Brigham, I have no doubt that Jesus is exactly who He claimed to be: God in the flesh, who died for our sins and rose again that we might be set free.

14

Deuteronomy 14:1, 2
Ye are the children of the LORD your God: ye shall not cut yourselves, nor make any baldness between your eyes for the dead. For thou art an holy people unto the LORD thy God, and the LORD hath chosen thee to be a peculiar people unto himself, above all the nations that are upon the earth.

When someone died in the Canaanite culture, the mourners would mark their bodies and shave the middle of their heads. "You are not to do that," God said to His people, as if to say, "Rather than mutilate yourselves, you're to celebrate the fact that those who die in your midst are with Me."

The teenage delivery boy dropped the first order of flowers off and proceeded to the second delivery spot, the grand opening of a new store. The owner took the flowers, opened the card, and read, "Our deepest sympathy on this most sad day."

"Oh, no!" said the delivery boy. "I gave you the wrong bouquet!"

"That's okay," the owner said. "The flowers will do fine."

"It's not that," the delivery boy said. "The problem is, I sent your flowers to a funeral with a card that read: Congratulations on your new location."

For a believer, such a card would be entirely appropriate. Sure, we passionately and deeply miss those who die, but we don't cut our flesh or tear ourselves apart emotionally because we know he or she is in the best place possible.

Deuteronomy 14:3
Thou shalt not eat any abominable thing.

In this section, Moses reiterates the dietary laws for the people of Israel—which meats were considered to be clean, which unclean. These kosher laws served the people of Israel well not only in Moses' generation, but for centuries to come . . .

In the Middle Ages, when plagues and disease devastated the continent of Europe, the Jewish people were singularly protected from many of them. Mistakenly thinking their protection came from magic or witchcraft, the Jews were persecuted. As time has passed, however, we now know that the reason the Jewish people in Europe were protected was because of their adherence to the sanitary and dietary regulations found here in the Book of Deuteronomy.

The wisdom of God's Word becomes all the more clear in light of the contemporary writings of other cultures. For example, an Egyptian scroll written at approximately the same time Moses wrote Deuteronomy propagated the following: To prevent gray hair, take blood from a black cat, mix it with the fat of a rattlesnake and eat it twice daily. Or to reverse baldness, take fat from a cat, a horse, a crocodile, a hippo, a snake, and an ibex and mix it together and eat it. If you have a severe case of baldness, add to it a tooth of a donkey that has been cooked in honey.

When we read these things, we chuckle because of its absurdity. But when we study the Scriptures, written at the same time as this papyrus, we see them proving to be medically correct and profound and healthy. They are not dated, not absurd—and should the Lord tarry, I have a sneaking suspicion that as we learn more, we'll discover even more how God's dietary regulations are the best possible plan for the human condition.

When Jesus came on the scene, He said, "The issue is not what you eat physically, but what goes on in your heart" (see Mark 7:15). With this in mind, we can understand that these laws are not only to be followed by the Jewish people of Moses' day, but that they're applicable for you and me spiritually—that we might be careful what we take in, what we put in our soul.

Deuteronomy 14:4–21

These are the beasts which ye shall eat: the ox, the sheep, and the goat, The hart, and the roebuck, and the fallow deer, and the wild goat, and the pygarg, and the wild ox, and the chamois. And every beast that parteth the hoof, and cleaveth the cleft into two claws, and cheweth the cud among the beasts, that ye shall eat. Nevertheless these ye shall not eat of them that chew the cud, or of them that divide the cloven hoof; as the camel, and the hare, and the coney: for they chew the cud, but divide not the hoof; therefore they are unclean unto you. And the swine, because it divideth the hoof, yet cheweth not the cud, it is unclean unto you: ye shall not eat of their flesh, nor touch their dead carcase. These ye shall eat of all that are in the waters: all that have fins and scales shall ye eat: And whatsoever hath not fins and scales ye may not eat; it is unclean unto you. Of all clean birds ye shall eat. But these are they of which ye shall not eat: the eagle, and ossifrage, and the ospray, And the glede, and the kite, and the vulture after his kind, And every raven after his kind, And the owl, and the night hawk, and the cuckow, and the hawk after his kind, The little owl, and the great owl, and the swan, And the pelican, and the gier eagle, and the cormorant, And the stork, and the heron after her kind, and the lapwing, and the bat. And every creeping thing that flieth is unclean unto you: they shall not be eaten. But of all clean fowls ye may eat. Ye shall not eat of any thing that dieth of itself: thou shalt give it unto the stranger that is in thy gates, that he may eat it; or thou mayest sell it unto an alien: for thou art an holy people unto the LORD thy God. Thou shalt not seethe a kid in his mother's milk.

Two characteristics would determine whether an animal was clean, kosher, or unclean: how he walked and what he ate. In other words, is there a division in the way the animal walks? And does it chew the cud, or does it simply spew out stuff half-digested?

When I'm reading a book, watching a TV show, or reading a magazine, I must ask, "Is it clean or unclean?" And I can determine this by looking at those who wrote the book or directed the show. How do they walk? Is there a division? Do they know right from wrong, bad from good, dark from light? Do they understand that there is a division in life—a high way and a low way? Has he or she really chewed on the issues and produced something refined—or is it just a bunch of half-thoughts being spewed out?

"Be careful," Jesus said. "It's more important what you put into your soul than what you put into your body."

Deuteronomy 14:22, 23

Thou shalt truly tithe all the increase of thy seed, that the field bringeth forth year by year. And thou shalt eat before the LORD thy God, in the place which he shall choose to place his name there, the tithe of thy corn, of thy wine, and of thine oil, and the firstlings of thy herds and of thy flocks; that thou mayest learn to fear the LORD thy God always.

How does a man learn to fear the Lord—to be in awe of Him, to be amazed by Him, to have respect for Him? One of the ways is by tithing because when a person tithes, they begin to see miracles take place.

"Test Me," God says, "and see if I will not open

up the windows of heaven and pour out a blessing so big your barns can't contain it" (see Malachi 3:10). It's the only place in all of Scripture where God says, "Test Me."

More than once, people have said to me, "When you talked on tithing, I resented it—until I began to tithe. And then I began to see just how awesome God is, what He does, and the blessings He sends to us when we tithe."

Deuteronomy 14:24, 25
And if the way be too long for thee, so that thou art not able to carry it; or if the place be too far from thee, which the LORD thy God shall choose to set his name there, when the LORD thy God hath blessed thee: Then shalt thou turn it into money, and bind up the money in thine hand, and shalt go unto the place which the LORD thy God shall choose:

If the temple was too far for the people to take their tithe—their corn or ox—they could convert it to money and bring the money to the temple, the place God chose to place His name—in Jerusalem.

Deuteronomy 14:26
And thou shalt bestow that money for whatsoever thy soul lusteth after, for oxen, or for sheep, or for wine, or for strong drink, or for whatsoever thy soul desireth: and thou shalt eat there before the LORD thy God, and thou shalt rejoice, thou, and thine household,

When the children of Israel brought their tithe, it was to be with rejoicing. "The Lord loves a cheerful giver," Paul would write to the Corinthians (2 Corinthians 9:7). The Greek word translated "cheerful" is *hilaros*—from which we get the word "hilarious." God loves a person who gives hilariously, cheerfully, gladly. Therefore, I think it's a mistake to feel obligated to give. It's a privilege to be able to say, "Lord, I'm honoring You in the way You've asked me." If it's not a privilege for you, don't do it. You'll find, however, that things don't work for you in your budgeting and your own financial situation. Over and over I've watched people miss out on blessings all because of a failure to understand that they couldn't possibly out give God.

Deuteronomy 14:27
And the Levite that is within thy gates; thou shalt not forsake him; for he hath no part nor inheritance with thee.

Separated for service, unlike the other tribes, the Levites had no land. Thus, they were to be cared for by the other tribes.

Deuteronomy 14:28, 29
At the end of three years thou shalt bring forth all the tithe of thine increase the same year, and shalt lay it up within thy gates: And the Levite, (because he hath no part nor inheritance with thee,) and the stranger, and the fatherless, and the widow, which are within thy gates, shall come, and shall eat and be satisfied; that the LORD thy God may bless thee in all the work of thine hand which thou doest.

Every third year a second tithe was taken to take care of people who were poor—the fatherless, the widow, the stranger. And that money was to be used for their well being and welfare. If you add together the tithes of Deuteronomy 14, Deuteronomy 16, and Numbers 18, they come to an average of twenty-three percent annually. While it may be that even in our Godless society we are contributing a portion of this through taxes, this we do know for certain: God's ways are right. His heart is *for* us. Therefore, when He asks us to give to Him, it's not only for His glory, but for our good.

15

Deuteronomy 15:1, 2
At the end of every seven years thou shalt make a release. And this is the manner of the release: Every creditor that lendeth ought unto his neighbour shall release it; he shall not exact it of his neighbour, or of his brother; because it is called the LORD's release.

Every seventh year was to be a sabbatical year. The land was to rest. No crops were to be planted or harvested. The people were to rest. No work was to be done. And the debts were to be released every seventh year. Were they cancelled in totality or just for that year? I believe the latter because in the year of Jubilee that occurred every fifty years, debts were cancelled completely.

Deuteronomy 15:3
Of a foreigner thou mayest exact it again: but that which is thine with thy brother thine hand shall release;

An outsider living in the land still had to make his payment.

Deuteronomy 15:4 (a)
Save when there shall be no poor among you . . .

If Israel tithed for the poor every third year as seen in chapter 14, if they released debts every seven years and cancelled them completely every fifty, if they followed God's economic plan for them, poverty would be entirely eradicated from their nation.

Deuteronomy 15:4 (b)
. . . for the LORD shall greatly bless thee in the land which the LORD thy God giveth thee for an inheritance to possess it:

Canceling debts for a year, canceling debts entirely, and giving money to the poor doesn't make sense financially. But God said, "If you trust Me and be obedient to Me, you'll be blessed. Poverty will be nonexistent in your culture. How? By being generous, by being merciful, by giving with a rejoicing heart." But guess what. It didn't work out that way for Israel, for as far as we know, never once in their history did they celebrate the year of Jubilee. It didn't make sense to them. After all, there were bills to pay, budgets to keep. Consequently, the nation never did experience a release from poverty because it just didn't make sense to them—just like God's principles don't make sense to us. And we are the poorer for it.

Deuteronomy 15:5, 6
Only if thou carefully hearken unto the voice of the LORD thy God, to observe to do all these commandments which I command thee this day. For the LORD thy God blesseth thee, as he promised thee: and thou shalt lend unto many nations, but thou shalt not borrow; and thou shalt reign over many nations, but they shall not reign over thee.

"If you do what the Lord commands, you'll be the financiers—the lenders rather than the borrowers," Moses told the people of Israel. The Jewish people did indeed become the great financiers of world economy when, during the Middle Ages, a papal edict forbade Christians from lending money. Thus, the Jews became the bankers of Europe. And if you poke around very closely in Wall Street, you'll see the great brokerage firms are almost invariably founded by or led by people of Jewish origin.

Deuteronomy 15:7–10
If there be among you a poor man of one of thy brethren within any of thy gates in thy land which the LORD thy God giveth thee, thou shalt not harden thine heart, nor shut thine hand from thy poor brother: But thou shalt open thine hand wide unto him, and shalt surely lend him sufficient for his need, in that which he wanteth. Beware that there be not a thought in thy wicked heart, saying, The seventh year, the year of release, is at hand; and thine eye be evil against thy poor brother, and thou givest him nought; and he cry unto the LORD against thee, and it be sin unto thee. Thou shalt surely give him, and thine heart shall not be grieved when thou givest unto him: because that for this thing the LORD thy God shall bless thee in all thy works, and in all that thou puttest thine hand unto.

Here is a great piece of business advice, a very important principle that doesn't make sense to us rationally. God says, "Be careful when the sixth year is coming that you don't refuse to lend money because it won't be paid back in the seventh year. Rather, share and open your hand wide to the people who need help from you at any time no matter what year it might be. If you do this, if you don't close your heart and close your hand, I will bless you in whatever you do."

If you're a businessman, be as generous as you can. Find people to whom you can give your treasure, your energy, your talent, your abilities. "I'm having a tough time making ends meet as it is," we protest.

But God says, "If you will have a generous heart and an open hand, watch and see how I will bless you."

Deuteronomy 15:11–18
For the poor shall never cease out of the land: therefore I command thee, saying, Thou shalt open thine hand wide unto thy brother, to thy poor, and to thy needy, in thy land. And if thy brother, an Hebrew man, or an Hebrew woman, be sold unto thee, and serve thee six years; then in the seventh year thou shalt let him go free from thee. And when thou sendest him out free from thee, thou shalt not let him go away empty: Thou shalt furnish him liberally out of thy flock, and out of thy floor, and out of thy winepress: of that wherewith the LORD thy God hath blessed thee thou shalt give unto him. And thou shalt remember that thou wast a bondman in the land of Egypt, and the LORD thy God redeemed thee: therefore I command thee this thing to day. And it shall be, if he say unto thee, I will not go away from thee; because he loveth thee and thine house, because he is well with thee; Then thou shalt take an aul, and thrust it through his ear unto the door, and he shall be thy servant for ever. And also unto thy maidservant thou shalt do likewise. It shall not seem hard unto thee, when thou sendest him away free from thee; for he hath been worth a double hired servant to thee, in serving thee six years: and the LORD thy God shall bless thee in all that thou doest.

The reference here is to the slave serving as an indentured servant to pay his bills. On the seventh year he was to be released and set free. But if he so chose, he could remain in his master's service for the rest of his days, signified by the hole that would be pierced in his ear.

For topical study of Deuteronomy 15:12–17, see "Bondservants: Give It Your 'Awl'" below.

Deuteronomy 15:19–23
All the firstling males that come of thy herd and of thy flock thou shalt sanctify unto the LORD thy God: thou shalt do no work with the firstling of thy bullock, nor shear the firstling of thy sheep. Thou shalt eat it before the LORD thy God year by year in the place which the LORD shall choose, thou and thy household. And if there be any blemish therein, as if it be lame, or blind, or have any ill blemish, thou shalt not sacrifice it unto the LORD thy God. Thou shalt eat it within thy gates: the unclean and the clean person shall eat it alike, as the roebuck, and as the hart. Only thou shalt not eat the blood thereof; thou shalt pour it upon the ground as water.

Only sacrifices without blemish were to be offered to God. Yet we who are blind, lame, and full of blemishes are accepted as sacrifices (Romans 12:1, 2) because we are covered by the blood of the perfect, spotless Lamb of God.

BONDSERVANTS: GIVE IT YOUR "AWL"

A Topical Study of DEUTERONOMY 15:12–17

This past week, I had one of those weeks that we all have from time to time, where I found myself feeling physically fatigued and weary. You know the feeling. We've all been there.

Last weekend, I was in the San Bernardino Mountains speaking at a men's conference. Coming back late Saturday night, I enjoyed teaching the Word here Sunday. The leadership meeting following Sunday night's service was interesting and challenging. Then I headed over to the coast to speak at Lake Bradley, and from there, went south again to speak at a single's retreat. When I was done teaching Friday night, I plopped in a pew completely exhausted. But when a bunch of guys approached me with questions about raising kids as single dads, we ended up talking past midnight. When I finally got back to my room, I sat down on the bed no longer feeling exhausted but now elated and energized.

I share that story with you because it's the basis of our text. You see, Moses is reiterating, repeating the Law to the people of Israel. And in so doing, he reminds them of the Law of the bondslave. Simply put, this text says if a Jew found himself in debt from which he was unable to extricate himself, he could sell himself into slavery—a form of bankruptcy, but one which made people think twice before filing!

Such an indentured servant could only serve for six years before being set free in the seventh. There was an exception, however. If a slave wanted to remain in his owner's service, his owner was to pierce his ear with an awl. And the ring that would hang from it would signify he was a slave by choice. Paul the apostle refers to himself as such a bondslave, using the Greek word *doulos* (Romans 1:1).

But in Psalm 40, we read of the ultimate Bondslave . . .

> *Sacrifice and offering thou didst not desire; mine ears hast thou opened: burnt offering and sin offering hast thou not required. Then said I, Lo, I come: in the volume of the book it is written of me, I delight to do thy will, O my God: yea, thy law is within my heart.* Psalm 40:6–8

The ear of Jesus Christ was opened, pierced not with an awl but by the wood of the Cross of Calvary. Jesus is the perfect Bondslave who came not to be served but to serve (Mark 10:45), Who came not to do His own will, but His Father's (Matthew 26:39). For the joy set before Him, He endured the Cross, despising the shame (Hebrews 12:2). He knew there would be suffering and bleeding, but He also knew that on the other side, there would be joy which would far outweigh and supercede even the pain.

And such can be the same for you and me . . .

Doulos, the Greek word for servant, refers to an under rower. Think of a ship sailing across the Mediterranean Sea. While the passengers on the deck are enjoying the view, below them were men expending great energy, toiling at the oars. That's what it means to be a servant. You slave away hour after hour, day after day in order to get the people above you to their destination. The true servant says, "I want to get you to where you're supposed to be—out of the slough of despondency, out of the place where you're discouraged, confused, or damned eternally. I want to do whatever I can to get you to your destination."

"That sounds awful," you say, "rowing day after day under the deck just to get someone else to his or her destination."

But here's what you must remember: If the people on deck are headed to Maui, guess where you will end up. It's true. If I'm helping someone else to have a better day, I arrive at the same port. If I'm helping someone overcome discouragement, I myself end up overcoming my own discouragement. If I'm helping someone else with their marriage, my own marriage grows stronger, richer, deeper. If I'm helping someone else who is confused about the nature of the Father, as I row for them, my own understanding of the Father becomes so much clearer.

This should not be as surprising as it is to us. After all, Jesus said, "Give and it shall be given unto you; good measure, pressed down, and shaken together, and running over, shall men give into your bosom, For with the same measure that ye mete withal it shall be measured to you again" (Luke 6:38).

Next time you have a week where you feel physically, emotionally, spiritually, or mentally fatigued, here's the key: Serve others. Talk to others. Pray with others. And maybe people will notice your labor of love on their behalf.

But it may be that your work will take place under the deck where, out of sight, unnoticed by others, as a bondslave, you row faithfully to get them to their destination.

Choose today to say, "Lord, I want to be a bondslave. Open my ear. Pierce my flesh." Give Him your "awl"—and set sail for islands of joy and fulfillment never before imagined.

---

16 Chapter 16 reviews the three major feasts of Israel . . .

Deuteronomy 16:1–8
Observe the month of Abib, and keep the passover unto the LORD thy God: for in the month of Abib the LORD thy God brought thee forth out of Egypt by night. Thou shalt therefore sacrifice the passover unto the LORD thy God, of the flock and the herd, in the place which the LORD shall choose to place his name there. Thou shalt eat no leavened bread with it; seven days shalt thou eat unleavened bread therewith, even the bread of affliction; for thou camest forth out of the land of Egypt in haste: that thou mayest remember the day when thou camest forth out of the land of Egypt all the days of thy life. And there shall be no leavened bread seen with thee in all thy coast seven days; neither shall there anything of the flesh, which thou sacrificedst the first day at even, remain all night until the morning. Thou mayest not sacrifice the passover within any of thy gates, which the LORD thy God giveth thee: But at the place which the LORD thy God shall choose to place his name in, there thou shalt sacrifice the passover at even, at the going down of the sun, at the season that thou camest forth out of Egypt. And thou shalt roast and eat it in the place which the LORD thy God shall choose: and thou shalt turn in the morning, and go unto thy tents. Six days thou shalt eat unleavened bread: and on the seventh day shall be a solemn assembly to the LORD thy God: thou shalt do no work therein.

Passover took place in the spring and commemorated the way the children of Israel were released from Egypt.

Deuteronomy 16:9–12
Seven weeks shalt thou number unto thee: begin to number the seven weeks from such time as thou beginnest to put the sickle to the corn. And thou shalt keep the feast of weeks unto the LORD thy God with a tribute of a freewill offering of thine hand, which thou shalt give unto the LORD thy God, according as the LORD thy God hath blessed thee: And thou shalt rejoice before the LORD thy God, thou, and thy son, and thy daughter, and thy manservant, and thy maidservant, and the Levite that is within thy gates, and the stranger, and the fatherless, and the widow, that are among you, in the place which the LORD thy God hath chosen to place his name there. And thou shalt remember that thou wast a bondman in Egypt: and thou shalt observe and do these statutes.

Pentecost, or the Feast of Weeks took place fifty days after Passover in anticipation of God's provision as His people waved the first harvest of the summer season before Him.

Deuteronomy 16:13–15
Thou shalt observe the feast of tabernacles seven days, after that thou hast gathered in thy corn and thy wine: And thou shalt rejoice in thy feast, thou, and thy son, and thy daughter, and thy manservant, and thy maidservant, and the Levite, the stranger, and the fatherless, and the widow, that are within thy gates. Seven days shalt thou keep a solemn feast unto the LORD thy God in the place which the LORD shall choose: because the LORD thy God shall bless thee in all thine increase, and in all the works of thine hands, therefore thou shalt surely rejoice.

The Feast of Tabernacles took place in the fall as the Jews dwelt in lean-to's in celebration of the way God brought the children of Israel through the wilderness.

Deuteronomy 16:16, 17
Three times in a year shall all thy males appear before the LORD thy God in the place which he shall choose; in the feast of unleavened bread, and in the feast of weeks, and in the feast of tabernacles: and they shall not appear before the LORD empty: Every man shall give as he is able, according to the blessing of the LORD thy God which he hath given thee.

Although the women and children were invited to attend these three feasts, the men were required to do so. And they were not to come empty-handed. The same is true today. When we come before the Lord, when we meet together, we're to come ready to give. We're to come, saying, "Who can I pray for? Who can I encourage? Who can I help?" The brother or sister who understands this is the one who leaves times of fellowship and corporate worship with a heart full, excited for the Lord.

Deuteronomy 16:18
Judges and officers shalt thou make thee in all thy gates, which the LORD thy God giveth thee, throughout thy tribes: and they shall judge the people with just judgment.

The gates referred to here were actually more like a room through which the people entered and exited the city and in which disputes were settled—more like a city hall.

Deuteronomy 16:19–21
Thou shalt not wrest judgment; thou shalt not respect persons, neither take a gift: for a gift doth blind the eyes of the wise, and pervert the words of the righteous. That which is altogether just shalt thou follow, that thou mayest live, and inherit the land which the LORD thy God giveth thee. Thou shalt not plant thee a grove of any trees near unto the altar of the LORD thy God, which thou shalt make thee.

This is a reference to the groves and high places of pagan worship. "Do not make any provision for the flesh," we are told in Romans 13:14. Don't allow any groves in your home. Don't allow yourselves to be in a position where you can veer off into "shady" areas—be they books, magazines, movies, music, Internet sites, or anything else which obstructs your view of the true and living God.

Deuteronomy 16:22
Neither shalt thou set thee up any image; which the LORD thy God hateth.

If you want a clear image of Jesus, read the description found in Revelation 1:11–16. Anything less limits our understanding of the King of kings.

17

Deuteronomy 17:1
Thou shalt not sacrifice unto the LORD thy God any bullock, or sheep, wherein is blemish, or any evilfavouredness: for that is an abomination unto the LORD thy God.

While the Lord freely accepts the sacrifice of our lives—blemished as we are—we are not to bring Him our castoffs. It's amazing what people bring to the Helps Ministry: one shoe, a single glove. There's a tendency for us to say, "I don't need that anymore, I'll just give it to the Lord." Such ought not be.

Deuteronomy 17:2–7 (a)
If there be found among you, within any of thy gates which the LORD thy God giveth thee, man or woman, that hath wrought wickedness in the sight of the LORD thy God, in transgressing his covenant, And hath gone and served other gods, and worshipped them, either the sun, or moon, or any of the host of heaven, which I have not commanded; And it be told thee, and thou hast heard of it, and inquired diligently, and, behold, it be true, and the thing certain, that such abomination is wrought in Israel: Then shalt thou bring forth that man or that woman, which have committed that wicked thing, unto thy gates, even that man or that woman, and shalt stone them with stones, till they die. At the mouth of two witnesses, or three witnesses, shall he that is worthy of death be put to death; but at the mouth of one witness he shall not be put to death. The hands of the witnesses shall be first upon him to put him to death, and afterward the hands of all the people . . .

If, after careful investigation, a person was found guilty of worshiping false gods, his accusers were to be his executioners and were to be joined by the entire community base, as seen in the sad story of Achan (Joshua 7), one man's sin affects everyone to whom he is linked.

Deuteronomy 17:7 (b)
. . . So thou shalt put the evil away from among you.

In God's economy, capital punishment is a definite deterrent to sin.

Deuteronomy 17:8, 9
If there arise a matter too hard for thee in judgment, between blood and blood, between plea and plea, and between stroke and stroke, being matters of controversy within thy gates: then shalt thou arise, and get thee up into the place which the LORD thy God shall choose; And thou shalt come unto the priests the Levites, and unto the judge that

shall be in those days, and inquire; and they shall shew thee the sentence of judgment:

The person at odds with someone was to go to the temple for resolution. The same is true today. I firmly believe that the best place for arbitration between believers is at the church. "Don't you know you will one day judge angels?" Paul asks the Corinthians. "Why, then, can't you handle your own disputes and squabbles presently?" (1 Corinthians 6:1–4).

Deuteronomy 17:10, 11
And thou shalt do according to the sentence, which they of that place which the LORD shall choose shall shew thee; and thou shalt observe to do according to all that they inform thee: According to the sentence of the law which they shall teach thee, and according to the judgment which they shall tell thee, thou shalt do: thou shalt not decline from the sentence which they shall shew thee, to the right hand, nor to the left.

He who went to the temple to resolve a dispute was to abide by the decision made.

Deuteronomy 17:12, 13
And the man that will do presumptuously, and will not hearken unto the priest that standeth to minister there before the LORD thy God, or unto the judge, even that man shall die: and thou shalt put away the evil from Israel. And all the people shall hear, and fear, and do no more presumptuously.

He who came to the temple for arbitration but refused to abide by the decision made therein was to be put to death.

People who come to the church for counsel must come submitted to what the Lord instructs and what the Word declares rather than going to other people, lawyers, or clinics until they find someone who agrees with them or feels sorry for them. Knowing our tendency to travel around until we hear what we want to hear, God says, "If you don't do what you're told, you'll die." And that's exactly what happens. When I don't do what God tells me to do, joy dies. Relationships die. Ministry dies.

Deuteronomy 17:14, 15
When thou art come unto the land which the LORD thy God giveth thee, and shalt possess it, and shalt dwell therein, and shalt say, I will set a king over me, like as all the nations that are about me; Thou shalt in any wise set him king over thee, whom the LORD thy God shall choose: one from among thy brethren shalt thou set king over thee: thou mayest not set a stranger over thee, which is not thy brother.

God knew His people would want a king once they were in the Land. But that was not His original intent for them. His heart was that Israel be a theocracy. But as a Father, He knew the nature of His kids. And He knew that when they went into the Land, they would eventually desire to be like the nations round about them. The other nations had kings, so His people would want a king, too.

And that's precisely what happened. In 1 Samuel 8, we read that the people came to Samuel the prophet and said, "Make us a king that we might be like the other nations." Their request broke Samuel's heart, for he knew that their request was a step down, a step back from what God intended for them. But God instructed him to grant their request.

How did other nations select their kings? They would appoint the tallest, best-looking, most charismatic man they could find. Therefore, in instructing Samuel to anoint Saul king, it's as if God was saying, "If My people want to be like other nations, I'll give them a king like those of other nations."

Way back in Genesis 49:10, God had declared that the scepter—the symbol of kingly authority—would not depart from Judah. Saul, however, was from the tribe of Benjamin. Thus, we know that God allowed Saul to be king because He wanted His people to feel the full force of their foolishness. But after Saul was killed in battle, God's mercy kicked in, His grace broke through, and He did indeed give Israel a king from Judah, a man after His own heart (Acts 13:22).

God instructed Samuel to anoint David. And from David's line would come the Lion of the Tribe of Judah, the King of kings, Jesus Christ.

Deuteronomy 17:16, 17
But he shall not multiply horses to himself, nor cause the people to return to Egypt, to the end that he should multiply horses: forasmuch as the LORD hath said unto you, Ye shall henceforth return no more that way. Neither shall he multiply wives to himself, that his heart turn not away: neither shall he greatly multiply to himself silver and gold.

God instituted three prohibitions to those who would rule His people. Kings were not to be power-hungry, signified by the number of horses they amassed. Neither were they to be woman-crazy, signified by multiple wives. Nor were they to be money-mad.

What drives politics in our country today? Power, women, and money. And while none of us is likely to rule a country, this passage is nonetheless vital for anyone who wants to exert authority in family, ministry, or vocation. What's to keep the king from falling prey to the lure of power, women, and wealth? David said, "Thy Word have I hid in my heart that I might not sin against Thee" (Psalm 119:11)—which is exactly what Moses said . . .

Deuteronomy 17:18
And it shall be, when he sitteth upon the throne of his kingdom, that he shall write him a copy of this law in a book out of that which is before the priests the Levites:

The first act the king was to perform upon taking the throne was not to go to an inaugural ball, throw a party for his donors, or watch a parade in his honor. God declared the first thing a king was to do was to make a copy of the Law. Why? Because in writing down every line, every word, the Law would be embedded in the king's mind.

I have found that if I have pencil and paper in hand when I have devotions or go to a Bible study, I never come away empty-handed. And even if I never refer to those notes again, taking notes forces me to be engaged in the process of listening.

Deuteronomy 17:19 (a)
And it shall be with him . . .

Not only are we to write the Word down, but we're to pack it around. I have several pocket Bibles I carry, not because I'm trying to be a holy Joe or some kind of Pharisee, but because I've found I can redeem a bunch of time—be it waiting for a stoplight, waiting for an appointment, or standing in line at the grocery store. You will be amazed at how much Scripture you can absorb in a single year simply by keeping the Word close at hand.

Deuteronomy 17:19 (b)
. . . and he shall read therein all the days of his life . . .

In other words, the king was to read the Word every day. Sometimes I hear people say, "I don't have devotions because I've already read the Bible through three times." But that's not the point. God says if you want to be effective, you need to read it over and over and over again.

Deuteronomy 17:19 (c)
. . . that he may learn to fear the Lord his God, to keep all the words of this law and these statutes, to do them:

In addition to writing it down and packing it around, the king was not only to read the Word consistently, but to take it seriously. When I read the Bible, I fear the Lord. Why? Not because I'm condemned, but because I'm convicted. I realize the Word is right and I'm not, that it is good and I'm not, that it is true and I'm not. In other words, when I read the Word, I realize that I need Jesus every single day.

Deuteronomy 17:20 (a)
That his heart be not lifted up above his brethren . . .

When do I find fault with others? When do I come down on others? When is my heart lifted up above others? When I'm not in the Word. When I'm in the Word, however, I realize how far I have yet to go. In reading the Word, the king would be reminded of his own need for mercy and forgiveness and would thereby be merciful and forgiving towards those he ruled.

Deuteronomy 17:20 (b)
. . . and that he turn not aside from the commandment, to the right hand, or to the left: to the end that he may prolong his days in his kingdom, he, and his children, in the midst of Israel.

If, like Israel's kings were instructed to do, I read the Word consistently and take it seriously, not only will I walk in the ways of the Lord, but also my children will follow. What a simple premise. What a glorious promise.

18

Deuteronomy 18:1
The priests the Levites, and all the tribe of Levi, shall have no part nor inheritance with Israel: they shall eat the offerings of the Lord made by fire, and his inheritance.

With the exception of the Levites, every tribe had been assigned a portion of the Promised Land. As ministers to the Lord, the Levites were to be scattered throughout Israel.

Deuteronomy 18:2–5
Therefore shall they have no inheritance among their brethren: the Lord is their inheritance, as he hath said unto them. And this shall be the priest's due from the people, from them that offer a sacrifice, whether it be ox or sheep; and they shall give unto the priest the shoulder, and the two cheeks, and the maw. The firstfruit also of thy corn, of thy wine, and of thine oil, and the first of

the fleece of thy sheep, shalt thou give him. For the LORD thy God hath chosen him out of all thy tribes, to stand to minister in the name of the LORD, him and his sons for ever.

In other words, those who ministered to the people of God were to be cared for by the people of God.

Deuteronomy 18:6–8 (a)
And if a Levite come from any of thy gates out of all Israel, where he sojourned, and come with all the desire of his mind unto the place which the LORD shall choose; Then he shall minister in the name of the LORD his God, as all his brethren the Levites do, which stand there before the LORD. They shall have like portions to eat . . .

The Levites would serve for two weeks at a time in the temple. But if a Levite wanted to serve longer, he could, in which case he was to be supported through the tithes, offerings, and sacrifices, as were the other Levites.

Deuteronomy 18:8 (b)
. . . beside that which cometh of the sale of his patrimony.

Although the Levites had no land deeded to them, they were permitted to buy houses, goods, and cattle.

Deuteronomy 18:9, 10 (a)
When thou art come into the land which the LORD thy God giveth thee, thou shalt not learn to do after the abominations of those nations. There shall not be found among you any one that maketh his son or his daughter to pass through the fire . . .

This refers to the worship of Molech in which parents placed their babies on the incandescent arms of his statue in hopes that in so doing they would prosper as a family. We do the same thing in our culture. We burn our unborn children with saline solution because we think we can't afford them. Prosperity rules either way. And it's an abomination to God.

Deuteronomy 18:10 (b), 11
. . . or that useth divination, or an observer of times, or an enchanter, or a witch, Or a charmer, or a consulter with familiar spirits, or a wizard, or a necromancer.

Anything having to do with divination—be it psychic hot lines or astrology, ouija boards or tarot cards—is to be scrupulously avoided.

Deuteronomy 18:12
For all that do these things are an abomination unto the LORD: and because of these abominations the LORD thy God doth drive them out from before thee.

The Canaanites were driven out of the land because of their involvement in the very activities God forbade His people from doing.

Deuteronomy 18:13, 14
Thou shalt be perfect with the LORD thy God. For these nations, which thou shalt possess, hearkened unto observers of times, and unto diviners: but as for thee, the LORD thy God hath not suffered thee so to do.

If we can't read our horoscopes or get our palms read, what are we to do?

Deuteronomy 18:15–19
The LORD thy God will raise up unto thee a Prophet from the midst of thee, of thy brethren, like unto me; unto him ye shall hearken; According to all that thou desiredst of the LORD thy God in Horeb in the day of the assembly, saying, Let me not hear again the voice of the LORD my God, neither let me see this great fire any more, that I die not. And the LORD said unto me, They have well spoken that which they have spoken. I will raise them up a Prophet from among their brethren, like unto thee, and will put my words in his mouth; and he shall speak unto them all that I shall command him. And it shall come to pass, that whosoever will not hearken unto my words which he shall speak in my name, I will require it of him.

As word reached Herod that there was One in Israel who was casting out demons and healing people, he thought it was John the Baptist—whom he himself had beheaded—risen from the dead. Others, however, told him it was Elijah or possibly the Prophet, referring to the Prophet spoken of here in Deuteronomy 18 (Mark 6:14, 15).

> God, who at sundry times and in divers manners spake in time past unto the fathers by the prophets, Hath in these last days spoken unto us by his Son, whom he hath appointed heir of all things, by whom also he made the worlds;
> Hebrews 1:1, 2

God doesn't want to give us knowledge about the future. He wants to give us strength for today. And for that, we're not to look to the stars, but to the Son.

Deuteronomy 18:20
But the prophet, which shall presume to speak a word in my name, which I have not commanded him to speak, or that shall speak in the name of other gods, even that prophet shall die.

The prophet who spoke in the name of a false god was to be put to death.

Deuteronomy 18:21, 22
And if thou say in thine heart, How shall we know the word which the LORD hath not spoken? When a prophet speaketh in the name of the LORD, if the thing follow not, nor come to pass, that is the thing which the LORD hath not spoken, but the prophet hath spoken it presumptuously: thou shalt not be afraid of him.

The people were not to be afraid of—or literally, not to respect—he who gave a prophecy that failed to come to pass.

It's knowing the Word, it's meditating on the Word, it's living in the Word that keeps us from pursuing the dead-end paths of those who promise things that don't come to pass, of those who predict things that never happen. Stay in the Word, precious people.

19 **Deuteronomy 19:1–7**
When the LORD thy God hath cut off the nations, whose land the LORD thy God giveth thee, and thou succeedest them, and dwellest in their cities, and in their houses; Thou shalt separate three cities for thee in the midst of thy land, which the Lord thy God giveth thee to possess it. Thou shalt prepare thee a way, and divide the coasts of thy land, which the LORD thy God giveth thee to inherit, into three parts, that every slayer may flee thither. And this is the case of the slayer, which shall flee thither, that he may live: Whoso killeth his neighbour ignorantly, whom he hated not in time past; As when a man goeth into the wood with his neighbour to hew wood, and his hand fetcheth a stroke with the axe to cut down the tree, and the head slippeth from the helve, and lighteth upon his neighbour, that he die; he shall flee unto one of those cities, and live: Lest the avenger of the blood pursue the slayer, while his heart is hot, and overtake him, because the way is long, and slay him; whereas he was not worthy of death, inasmuch as he hated him not in time past. Wherefore I command thee, saying, Thou shalt separate three cities for thee.

Upon entering the Promised Land, the children of Israel were to establish three cities as cities of refuge for the person who committed second-degree murder. As outlined in Numbers 35, a man who unintentionally killed another would be safe from revenge as long as he remained in a city of refuge.

"He who is angry with his brother is guilty of murder," Jesus said (see Matthew 5:22). And who among us has not been angry with our brother? We're all guilty. We're all murderers. We all need Jesus as our Refuge (Hebrews 6:18).

Deuteronomy 19:8–10
And if the LORD thy God enlarge thy coast, as he hath sworn unto thy fathers, and give thee all the land which he promised to give unto thy fathers; If thou shalt keep all these commandments to do them, which I command thee this day, to love the LORD thy God, and to walk ever in his ways; then shalt thou add three cities more for thee, beside these three: That innocent blood be not shed in thy land, which the LORD thy God giveth thee for an inheritance, and so blood be upon thee.

If the children of Israel obeyed the Lord and claimed more land, they were to add three additional cities of refuge.

Deuteronomy 19:11–13
But if any man hate his neighbour, and lie in wait for him, and rise up against him, and smite him mortally that he die, and fleeth into one of these cities: Then the elders of his city shall send and fetch him thence, and deliver him into the hand of the avenger of blood, that he may die. Thine eye shall not pity him, but thou shalt put away the guilt of innocent blood from Israel, that it may go well with thee.

He who committed first-degree murder, he who intentionally killed another had no place in the city of refuge. The Bible is full of warnings to those who try to use the grace of God as a cloak to cover their own sin. Those who are truly born of God do not commit sin (1 John 3:9). Does this mean believers lead sinless lives? No. The Greek word translated "commit" refers to one who habitually, continually practices sin the way others practice golf or the piano. We all struggle with sin, but there is a difference between a person who struggles with or even succumbs to sin, and one who practices sin in order to get better at sinning.

Deuteronomy 19:14
Thou shalt not remove thy neighbour's landmark, which they of old time have set in thine inheritance, which thou shalt inherit in the land that the LORD thy God giveth thee to possess it.

Turning his attention from the cities of refuge to cities in general, Moses told the children of Israel they were not to remove the old boundaries. And the same is true today. In the Promised Land of the Spirit-filled life, we're not to remove the old boundaries because they're there for a reason. For example, those who say homosexuality ought to be allowed and celebrated in the Christian community are wrong because such teaching has never been acknowledged or embraced at any time in church history. Although there is pressure to change the boundaries, God's Word says the boundaries are to remain.

Deuteronomy 19:15–18 (a)
One witness shall not rise up against a man for any iniquity, or for any sin, in any sin that he sinneth: at the mouth of two witnesses, or at the mouth of three witnesses, shall the matter be established. If a false witness rise up against any man to testify against him that which is wrong; Then both the men, between whom the controversy is, shall stand before the LORD, before the priests and the judges, which shall be in those days; And the judges shall make diligent inquisition . . .

Accusation must be followed by confirmation. That is, a second witness must be found before judgment could be made. If, however, there was no second witness, accuser and accused were to come before the priest, where diligent inquisition would be made.

Deuteronomy 19:18 (b)–20
. . . and, behold, if the witness be a false witness, and hath testified falsely against his brother; Then shall ye do unto him, as he had thought to have done unto his brother: so shalt thou put the evil away from among you. And those which remain shall hear, and fear, and shall henceforth commit no more any such evil among you.

If the witness proved to be a false witness, his punishment would be that which would have otherwise been given to the accused. That is why Haman, falsely accusing the Jews, was hung on the very gallows he had built for them (Esther 7:9).

Deuteronomy 19:21
And thine eye shall not pity; but life shall go for life, eye for eye, tooth for tooth, hand for hand, foot for foot.

While at the outset, this may sound harsh, it is, in fact, merciful considering our propensity for "one-upmanship." You see, if you blacken my eye, my fleshly tendency is to want to blacken both of yours. God, however, calls for an equitable, measured response: only one eye for an eye, only one tooth for a tooth. Jesus, however, would reinstitute the idea of "one-upmanship" by telling us to offer two cheeks when struck on one, to give two coats when asked for one (Matthew 5:38–42).

20

Deuteronomy 20:1
When thou goest out to battle against thine enemies, and seest horses, and chariots, and a people more than thou, be not afraid of them: for the LORD thy God is with thee, which brought thee up out of the land of Egypt.

To the children of Israel, Moses didn't say, "*If* you see the enemy more numerous than you . . ." He said, "*When* you see the enemy . . ." In other words, battles were inevitable. Every one of us will have encounters when we feel outgunned and outmaneuvered, when we feel under-prepared and overwhelmed. At such times, we are not to be afraid. Why? Because they provide invaluable opportunities for us to see how God will come through for us.

Deuteronomy 20:2–4
And it shall be, when ye are come nigh unto the battle, that the priest shall approach and speak unto the people, And shall say unto them, Hear, O Israel, ye approach this day unto battle against your enemies: let not your hearts faint, fear not, and do not tremble, neither be ye terrified because of them; For the LORD your God is he that goeth with you, to fight for you against your enemies, to save you.

There is no way to know how great God is until you are in a situation you can't handle, until you don't know what to do, until it is seemingly impossible to solve the problem. The only way we'll know how great God is, how loving our Lord is, is to be over our heads, completely at a loss. I've been there. So have you. Maybe you're there tonight. The priest is to say, "Don't freak out. The Lord is with you. He brought you out of Egypt, out of the world, out of hell. He's not going to let you go now."

Deuteronomy 20:5–7
And the officers shall speak unto the people, saying, What man is there that hath built a new house, and hath not dedicated it? Let him go and return to his house, lest he die in the battle, and another man dedicate it. And what man is he that hath planted a vineyard, and hath not yet eaten of it? Let him also go and return unto his house, lest he die in the battle, and another man eat of it. And what man is there that hath betrothed a wife, and hath not taken her? Let him go and return unto his house, lest he die in the battle, and another man take her.

Three groups of men were exempt from battle: those who hadn't finished building their houses, those who hadn't yet eaten of their vineyards, and those who were engaged, but not yet married. In this, we see God's desire that people delight in His blessings before they devote themselves to battle.

For ye know the grace of our Lord Jesus Christ, that, though he was rich, yet for your sakes he became poor, that ye through his poverty might be rich. 2 Corinthians 8:9

Jesus left the blessings of heaven in order to bless us. And, while there is definitely a time for battle, there is also a time to delight in the blessings that are ours through the grace of the One Who became poor that we might be rich.

Deuteronomy 20:8
And the officers shall speak further unto the people, and they shall say, What man is there that is fearful and fainthearted? Let him go and return unto his house, lest his brethren's heart faint as well as his heart.

A fourth group deferred from battle was comprised of those who were afraid. When people lack faith, they often begin to speak negatively to justify their own fears. Cynicism and criticism are often a cowardly covering for fear. And they're contagious. That's why those who were afraid were to go home.

Deuteronomy 20:9
And it shall be, when the officers have made an end of speaking unto the people, that they shall make captains of the armies to lead the people.

If you want to be used by the Lord, go back over the preceding four verses and ask yourself if your household is stable, if the work of your hands is thriving, if your marriage is healthy, if your heart is full of faith. If a man doesn't have a home for his family, he ought to tend that first. If a man doesn't have a job and wants to be supported by others, he should get a job and succeed at that. If a man has a lousy marriage, he shouldn't be taking on further ministry. If a man is full of fear, he shouldn't try to hide behind ministry or missions. This passage is an important checklist for anyone who wants to be used by the Lord, to be engaged in His work.

Deuteronomy 20:10–15
When thou comest nigh unto a city to fight against it, then proclaim peace unto it. And it shall be, if it make thee answer of peace, and open unto thee, then it shall be, that all the people that is found therein shall be tributaries unto thee, and they shall serve thee. And if it will make no peace with thee, but will make war against thee, then thou shalt besiege it: And when the LORD thy God hath delivered it into thine hands, thou shalt smite every male thereof with the edge of the sword: But the women, and the little ones, and the cattle, and all that is in the city, even all the spoil thereof, shalt thou take unto thyself; and thou shalt eat the spoil of thine enemies, which the LORD thy God hath given thee. Thus shalt thou do unto all the cities which are very far off from thee, which are not of the cities of these nations.

The pagan cities the children of Israel would encounter upon entry into the Promised Land were to be destroyed. This passage, however, speaks of cities outside the boundaries of the Promised Land. Before engaging in battle with such cities, the Israelites were to first offer to be at peace with them if they would surrender. At this time in history, the offer of peace and surrender were completely foreign concepts.

Deuteronomy 20:16–18
But of the cities of these people, which the LORD thy God doth give thee for an inheritance, thou shalt save alive nothing that breatheth: But thou shalt utterly destroy them; namely, the Hittites, and the Amorites, the Canaanites, and the Perizzites, the Hivites, and the Jebusites; as the LORD thy God hath commanded thee: That they teach you not to do after all their abominations, which they have done unto their gods; so should ye sin against the LORD your God.

No offer of peace was to be made to the cities within the Promised Land and lest this sounds cruel, remember that in Genesis 15, God told Abraham that his descendants would go to Egypt a full four hundred years while God gave the Canaanites opportunity to repent of their sin and turn to Him. When they refused to do so, He used the Israelites to put them out of their misery lest they inflect others with their wickedness and perversion.

Deuteronomy 20:19, 20
When thou shalt besiege a city a long time, in making war against it to take it, thou shalt not destroy the trees thereof by forcing an axe against them: for thou mayest eat of them, and thou shalt not cut them down (for the tree of the field is man's life) to employ them in the siege: Only the trees which thou knowest that they be not trees for meat, thou shalt destroy and cut them down; and thou shalt build bulwarks against the city that maketh war with thee, until it be subdued.

When the Israelites went to battle, their axes were not to fly indiscriminately. That is, they were not to cut down any fruit-bearing tree. This is a good word for us because in our battle against principalities and powers, against the devil, our Adversary, if we're not careful, we can cut down trees that bear fruit, other believers, denominations, or churches who might have an entirely different flavor than ours, but from which we can be nourished. Wise is the believer who says, "Lord, help me to see what I can glean from that group, what I can learn from those people."

So much of what I've learned has been from trees that, in my own fleshly tendency, I would have chopped down. Wouldn't it be something if all the energy we expend analyzing ministry and criticizing Christians was harnessed against the real enemy? Yes, there's a war to wage, a battle to fight. And some trees are apostate indeed. But others have fruit that we can glean, through which we can grow, from which we can gain strength for the battle against the enemy of our souls.

21

Before they charge on to the field for the opening game, a good coach will review with his team the game plan they worked on all summer long. So, too, "Coach Moses," knowing that his team is about to charge into the Promised Land, reminds the children of Israel of certain truths, underscores certain principles in order that they might be successful in the Land of Promise . . .

Deuteronomy 21:1–9
If one be found slain in the land which the LORD thy God giveth thee to possess it, lying in the field, and it be not known who hath slain him: Then thy elders and thy judges shall come forth, and they shall measure unto the cities which are round about him that is slain: And it shall be, that the city which is next unto the slain man, even the elders of that city shall take an heifer, which hath not been wrought with, and which hath not drawn in the yoke; And the elders of that city shall bring down the heifer unto a rough valley, which is neither eared nor sown, and shall strike off the heifer's neck there in the valley: And the priests the sons of Levi shall come near; for them the LORD thy God hath chosen to minister unto him, and to bless in the name of the LORD; and by their word shall every controversy and every stroke be tried: And all the elders of that city, that are next unto the slain man, shall wash their hands over the heifer that is beheaded in the valley: And they shall answer and say, Our hands have not shed this blood, neither have our eyes seen it. Be merciful, O LORD, unto thy people Israel, whom thou hast redeemed, and lay not innocent blood unto thy people of Israel's charge. And the blood shall be forgiven them. So shalt thou put away the guilt of innocent blood from among you, when thou shalt do that which is right in the sight of the LORD.

Concerning the unsolved murders that would take place even in the Promised Land, rather than shrugging their shoulders and ignoring them, the children of Israel were to investigate and make atonement for them.

The elders closest to the scene of the crime were to offer sacrifices and intercession in order that the people of the region could be protected.

During a staff meeting at Lake Bradley one afternoon, hail began to fall. The roof overhead took the pounding and absorbed the beating, thereby allowing us to remain dry and protected. Every organization, every community needs people of maturity who will act as a covering to absorb the inevitable poundings in order that those beneath them can grow and function in safety.

There comes a point in the life of a mature person when he or she says, "Even though this isn't my problem personally, it's time I take some responsibility." This is what was to be modeled by the elders of Israel—and by any who want to be used by the Lord to a greater capacity.

Deuteronomy 21:10, 11
When thou goest forth to war against thine enemies, and the LORD thy God hath delivered them into thine hands, and thou hast taken them captive, And seest among the captives a beautiful woman, and hast a desire unto her, that thou wouldest have her to thy wife;

Keep in mind, in every culture at this time in history, and even until relatively recently, when there was a war, invading soldiers would wreak havoc upon the populace—especially upon the women. The Lord, however, instituted something shockingly new when He said, "If you see a woman who interests you, you are to treat her honorably in the following manner. . . ."

Deuteronomy 21:12
Then thou shalt bring her home to thine house; and she shall shave her head, and pare her nails;

If an Israelite soldier wanted to marry a woman of a conquered city, he was to take her to his house, where she would shave her head and "pare" or, as perhaps your margin might more correctly render this word, let her nails grow, which, in Old Testament times, would have been considered an oddity.

Deuteronomy 21:13 (a)
And she shall put the raiment of her captivity from off her, and shall remain in thine house, and bewail her father and her mother a full month . . .

The bride-to-be was to put on mourning clothes, most likely sackcloth, and mourn for her mother and father, who were either killed in battle or left behind.

Deuteronomy 21:13 (b), 14
. . . and after that thou shalt go in unto her, and be her husband, and she shall be thy wife. And it shall be, if thou have no delight in her, then thou shalt let her go whither she will; but thou shalt not sell her at all for money, thou shalt not make merchandise of her, because thou hast humbled her.

If the Israelite still wanted to marry her after hearing her mourn for a month, he was free to do so. If, however, he later changed his mind, he was to let her go and she would be free. Again, while this scenario sounds odd to us, the month-long waiting period, the commitment to marry, and the freedom granted should the marriage not work elevated women in a day when the women in surrounding nations had no more rights than did livestock.

Deuteronomy 21:15–17
If a man have two wives, one beloved, and another hated, and they have born him children, both the beloved and the hated; and if the firstborn son be hers that was hated: Then it shall be, when he maketh his sons to inherit that which he hath, that he may not make the son of the beloved firstborn before the son of the hated, which is indeed the firstborn: But he shall acknowledge the son of the hated for the firstborn, by giving him a double portion of all that he hath: for he is the beginning of his strength; the right of the firstborn is his.

As the Word unfolds, God will move His family from this practice of polygamy. But at this time, He's putting restrictions around it before He will eventually wean them from it. The reality of multiple wives is that one is loved, the others hated. And the same is true today. Part of the reason God hates divorce (Malachi 2:16) is that there is no final decree in divorce. There are always repercussions and difficulties and problems, most often having to do with children. If you've gone through the heartache of divorce, this is not a word of condemnation, but rather one of evaluation: Don't forget your firstborn. Don't forget your children from your previous marriage. Divorce happens. But we are not to complicate an already complicated situation by ignoring the firstborn.

Deuteronomy 21:18–20
If a man have a stubborn and rebellious son, which will not obey the voice of his father, or the voice of his mother, and that, when they have chastened him, will not hearken unto them: Then shall his father and his mother lay hold on him, and bring him out unto the elders of his city, and unto the gate of his place; and they shall say unto the elders of his city, This our son is stubborn and rebellious, he will not obey our voice; he is a glutton, and a drunkard.

According to this passage, it was not an option but an obligation for the parents of a son determined to live a life of rebelliousness to bring him to the elders of the city.

Deuteronomy 21:21
And all the men of his city shall stone him with stones, that he die: so shalt thou put

evil away from among you; and all Israel shall hear, and fear.

All the men of the city were to stone the rebellious son. Why? I suggest three reasons . . .

- *Motivation.* Communities being small in Bible times, the men of the city would know the son in question. They would know his family. Therefore, so difficult would it be to stone him, they would go home resolved to do whatever it took to make sure their own sons didn't follow the same path of rebellion.
- *Evaluation.* Participating in the stoning would cause the men in the community to ask themselves if there was something they could have done to turn him from his rebellious ways. If one of our kids in the Fellowship is out of line, all of us have to take a certain degree of responsibility; all of us must ask ourselves, *Could I have prayed more? Is there something I could have said?*
- *Proclamation.* The stoning proclaimed to the community that rebellion was neither a "stage" nor an inevitable part of growing up. It was simply not to be tolerated.

If you've either been or raised a rebellious child, I call your attention to another rebellious son—the prodigal son of Luke 15. When this rebellious son returned, his father ran out to meet him not with rocks in his hand, but with a robe for his son. Why? Did God change His mind somewhere between Deuteronomy and Luke about the severity of rebellion?

No. The punishment for rebellion is always death (Romans 6:23). But because a third Son—not the rebellious son, not the prodigal son, but the perfect Son—became sin and took my place on the Cross, rebellious son that I am, I am forgiven completely.

Deuteronomy 21:22, 23
And if a man have committed a sin worthy of death, and he be to be put to death, and thou hang him on a tree: His body shall not remain all night upon the tree, but thou shalt in any wise bury him that day; (for he that is hanged is accursed of God;) that thy land be not defiled, which the LORD thy God giveth thee for an inheritance.

Deuteronomy 21:23 is quoted in Galatians 3:13 and was fulfilled by the One who took our curse and our sin, by the One who died in our place. I deserve to be put to death and stoned for my stubbornness and rebellion. But my Father sent His only begotten Son, the One who never rebelled (John 8:29), in order that I might be robed in His righteousness (Isaiah 61:10).

22

Deuteronomy 22:1–4
Thou shalt not see the brother's ox or his sheep go astray, and hide thyself from them: thou shalt in any case bring them again unto thy brother. And if thy brother be not nigh unto thee, or if thou know him not, then thou shalt bring it unto thine own house, and it shall be with thee until thy brother seek after it, and thou shalt restore it to him again. In like manner shalt thou do with his ass; and so shalt thou do with his raiment; and with all lost thing of thy brother's, which he hath lost, and thou hast found, shalt thou do likewise: thou mayest not hide thyself. Thou shalt not see thy brother's ass or his ox fall down by the way, and hide thyself from them: thou shalt surely help him to lift them up again.

This passage addresses sins of omission rather than sins of commission—failing to do what's right rather than overtly doing wrong, missed deeds rather than misdeeds. Seeing their brother's runaway sheep or fallen cow, the children of Israel were not to ignore the problem, but to make it right. And we are to do the same (James 4:17).

Deuteronomy 22:5
The woman shall not wear that which pertaineth unto a man, neither shall a man put on a woman's garment: for all that do so are abomination unto the LORD thy God.

Knowing that confusion about identity can lead to all manner of perversion, the Lord clearly prohibits anything which would blur the lines between men and women.

Deuteronomy 22:6, 7
If a bird's nest chance to be before thee in the way in any tree, or on the ground, whether they be young ones, or eggs, and the dam sitting upon the young, or upon the eggs, thou shalt not take the dam with the young: But thou shalt in any wise let the dam go, and take the young to thee; that it may be well with thee, and that thou mayest prolong thy days.

If I saw a bird's nest on the ground, I would think, *Lucky day! Fried bird and scrambled eggs!* But God says, "No. You can take the eggs if you choose, but let the mother bird go." And in this I begin to understand that many of the present-day bureaucratic regulations that admittedly irritate me have their origins in God's Word, in God's heart. Like many of you, I have very real political stands, but I must measure them against what the Father declares in His Word and follow His wisdom rather than my opinion on any given matter.

Deuteronomy 22:8
When thou buildest a new house, then thou shalt make a battlement for thy roof, that thou bring not blood upon thine house, if any man fall from thence.

Rooftops being used as patios, railings would be necessary to keep people from falling off. As in the previous passage, we see God instituting ordinances that, to me, seem bureaucratic and unnecessary. After all, if someone was on my roof, my fleshly tendency would be to think that his safety was his own responsibility. "That might be your tendency, but it's not My heart," God would say. "I want you to be concerned about the welfare of others. I want you to be like Me."

Deuteronomy 22:9–12
Thou shalt not sow thy vineyard with divers seeds: lest the fruit of thy seed which thou hast sown, and the fruit of thy vineyard be defiled. Thou shalt not plow with an ox and an ass together. Thou shalt not wear a garment of divers sorts, as of woollen and linen together. Thou shalt make thee fringes upon the four quarters of thy vesture, wherewith thou coverest thyself.

Planting a variety of seeds, plowing with an ox and an ass, wearing wool and linen all speak of mixture. "Either be hot or cold," Jesus said, "but not lukewarm" (see Revelation 3:15). Why? Because lukewarm is a mixture of hot and cold. I like hot tea and iced tea, but I don't like room-temperature tea. And the same is true with the Lord. If we're hot, He can use us. If we're cold, He can break us. But if we're neither hot nor cold, not only will He "spew us out of His mouth," but we'll be miserable as well because we'll have too much of the Lord in us to enjoy the world and too much of the world in us to seek the Lord. That's why He wants us to be hot or cold, linen or wool, yea or nay (Matthew 5:37), all or nothing.

Deuteronomy 22:13–19
If any man take a wife, and go in unto her, and hate her, And give occasions of speech against her, and bring up an evil name upon her, and say, I took this woman, and when I came to her, I found her not a maid: Then shall the father of the damsel, and her mother, take and bring forth the tokens of the damsel's virginity unto the elders of the city in the gate: And the damsel's father shall say unto the elders, I gave my daughter unto this man to wife, and he hateth her; And, lo, he hath given occasions of speech against her, saying, I found not thy daughter a maid; and yet these are the tokens of my daughter's virginity. And they shall spread the cloth before the elders of the city. And the elders of that city shall take that man and chastise him; And they shall amerce him in an hundred shekels of silver, and give them unto the father of the damsel, because he hath brought up an evil name upon a virgin of Israel: and she shall be his wife; he may not put her away all his days.

He who wrongly accused a woman concerning her virginity was to be fined one hundred shekels—a considerable sum of money.

Deuteronomy 22:20, 21
But if this thing be true, and the tokens of virginity be not found for the damsel: Then they shall bring out the damsel to the door of her father's house, and the men of her city shall stone her with stones that she die: because she hath wrought folly in Israel, to play the whore in her father's house: so shalt thou put evil away from among you.

Although we think stoning for promiscuity is an awfully harsh sentence, when we see the entire continent being devastated by AIDS, suddenly purity doesn't seem like such a bad idea. When we look and see what happens to a culture that ignores this standard or calls it archaic, we see a culture contaminated and dying.

Deuteronomy 22:22
If a man be found lying with a woman married to an husband, then they shall both of them die, both the man that lay with the woman, and the woman: so shalt thou put away evil from Israel.

In an adulterous situation, both the man and woman were to be put to death. "Unfair!" we cry, thinking death to be the worst thing that could happen to someone. But such is not the way God views death. To those headed for heaven, it is, in fact, the best thing that could happen. With the moral purity, the physical safety, and the emotional stability of His people at stake, God constructed a very strong fence around the marriage relationship.

Deuteronomy 22:23, 24
If a damsel that is a virgin be betrothed unto an husband, and a man find her in the city, and lie with her; Then ye shall bring them both out unto the gate of that city, and ye shall stone them with stones that they die; the damsel, because she cried not, being in the city; and the man, because he hath humbled his neighbour's wife: so thou shalt put away evil from among you.

Why was the woman to be stoned if the man took advantage of her? Because if the act took place in the city, her failure to cry out meant she didn't do all she could to stop it. As parents, we need to insist that our daughters be in places where they can "cry out," where they're not putting themselves in situations which will lead to unnecessary problems.

Deuteronomy 22:25–27
But if a man find a betrothed damsel in the field, and the man force her, and lie with her: then the man only that lay with her shall die: But unto the damsel thou shalt do nothing; there is in the damsel no sin worthy of death: for as when a man riseth against his neighbour, and slayeth him, even so is this matter: For he found her in the field, and the betrothed damsel cried, and there was none to save her.

As seen in the Book of Ruth, women worked in the fields harvesting wheat or barley. If such a woman was taken advantage of physically, unlike the woman in the city, she was to be exonerated because even her cry would not have saved her.

Deuteronomy 22:28, 29
If a man find a damsel that is a virgin, which is not betrothed, and lay hold on her, and lie with her, and they be found; Then the man that lay with her shall give unto the damsel's father fifty shekels of silver, and she shall be his wife; because he hath humbled her, he may not put her away all his days.

In God's sight, marriage is not defined by a man in a tuxedo and a woman in a beautiful gown saying, "I do," but rather by two people becoming one flesh. An understanding of this would curb the promiscuous mindset presently pervading our culture.

Deuteronomy 22:30
A man shall not take his father's wife, nor discover his father's skirt.

The reference here is most likely to the case of a stepmother, and was a law acted upon by Solomon in 1 Kings 2:13–25.

23

Deuteronomy 23:1
He that is wounded in the stones, or hath his privy member cut off, shall not enter into the congregation of the LORD.

This passage is here to say, among other things, that in the congregation, God expects His people to reproduce. I like that. A healthy congregation witnesses, shares, and talks to others about Jesus.

Deuteronomy 23:2
A bastard shall not enter into the congregation of the LORD; even to his tenth generation shall he not enter into the congregation of the LORD.

God doesn't have stepsons, foster kids, or illegitimate children. It is only to as many as receive Him personally that He gives the power, the authority to become His sons (John 1:12). The fact that your great-grandfather was a minister doesn't make you part of the kingdom of God. Each man must believe and receive for himself.

Deuteronomy 23:3–6
An Ammonite or Moabite shall not enter into the congregation of the LORD; even to their tenth generation shall they not enter into the congregation of the LORD for ever: Because they met you not with bread and with water in the way, when ye came forth out of Egypt; and because they hired against thee Balaam the son of Beor of Pethor of Mesopotamia, to curse thee. Nevertheless the LORD thy God would not hearken unto Balaam; but the LORD thy God turned the curse into a blessing unto thee, because the LORD thy God loved thee. Thou shalt not seek their peace nor their prosperity all thy days for ever.

Due to Balaam's sin which eventually resulted in the deaths of 24,000 Israelites (Numbers 25:9), and also to their mean-spiritedness in refusing to share food and water with the people of God during their wilderness wandering, the Ammonite and Moabite were not allowed into the congregation.

Deuteronomy 23:7, 8
Thou shalt not abhor an Edomite; for he is thy brother: thou shalt not abhor an Egyptian; because thou wast a stranger in his

land. The children that are begotten of them shall enter into the congregation of the LORD in their third generation.

As opposed to their dealing with the Moabites and Ammonites, the children of Israel were not to exclude the Edomites because, as sons of Esau, they were related to Israel. Neither were they to exclude the Egyptians due to their early care of Israel on Joseph's behalf and because of the kindness shown to Israel by individual Egyptians (Exodus 1:17, 12:36).

Deuteronomy 23:9–14
When the host goeth forth against thine enemies, then keep thee from every wicked thing. If there be among you any man, that is not clean by reason of uncleanness that chanceth him by night, then shall he go abroad out of the camp, he shall not come within the camp: But it shall be, when evening cometh on, he shall wash himself with water: and when the sun is down, he shall come into the camp again. Thou shalt have a place also without the camp, whither thou shalt go forth abroad: And thou shalt have a paddle upon thy weapon; and it shall be, when thou wilt ease thyself abroad, thou shalt dig therewith, and shalt turn back and cover that which cometh from thee: For the LORD thy God walketh in the midst of thy camp, to deliver thee, and to give up thine enemies before thee; therefore shall thy camp be holy: that he see no unclean thing in thee, and turn away from thee.

At this time in history, such a command was revolutionary. Keep in mind, the camp was large. Yet the Israelites were to leave the camp to "go to the restroom."

"This is legalistic," they could have protested. Yet, rather than explaining the connection between bacteria and disease, God simply told them they were to do this because He was in the camp and He was holy.

God doesn't always give us understanding or reasons. Sometimes He wants us to obey Him even if it doesn't make sense at the time. And if we do, in due season, we'll see the wisdom of His Word as science catches up to what He knew all along.

Deuteronomy 23:15, 16
Thou shalt not deliver unto his master the servant which is escaped from his master unto thee: He shall dwell with thee, even among you, in that place which he shall choose in one of thy gates, where it liketh him best: thou shalt not oppress him.

Apart from indentured service for financial reasons, Israelites were not allowed to enslave fellow Israelites. Therefore, this passage speaks of slaves of other nations being given refuge in Israel.

Deuteronomy 23:17, 18
There shall be no whore of the daughters of Israel, nor a sodomite of the sons of Israel. Thou shalt not bring the hire of a whore, or the price of a dog, into the house of the LORD thy God for any vow: for even both these are abomination unto the LORD thy God.

As we will see in the context of this passage, pagan religions of the Canaanite culture included temple prostitution—a practice obviously forbidden by God.

Deuteronomy 23:19, 20
Thou shalt not lend upon usury to thy brother; usury of money, usury of victuals, usury of any thing that is lent upon usury: Unto a stranger thou mayest lend upon usury; but unto thy brother thou shalt not lend upon usury: that the LORD thy God may bless thee in all that thou settest thine hand to in the land whither thou goest to possess it.

When the children of Israel loaned money, they were not to charge each other interest.

Deuteronomy 23:21, 22
When thou shalt vow a vow unto the LORD thy God, thou shalt not slack to pay it: for the LORD thy God will surely require it of thee; and it would be sin in thee. But if thou shalt forbear to vow, it shall be no sin in thee.

The children of Israel weren't required to make a vow to the Lord, but those who did were required to keep the vow they made.

Deuteronomy 23:23
That which is gone out of thy lips thou shalt keep and perform; even a freewill offering, according as thou hast vowed unto the LORD thy God, which thou hast promised with thy mouth.

In verse 19, the Israelites were told not to charge their brothers interest, to be generous. Yet here, it appears God is saying, "If you make a financial vow to Me, be sure to pay Me." Was God asking the Israelites to be more generous than He Himself was? Of course not. It's not that God wants His children to pay up—but rather that He wants them to grow up. It's not a matter of money, but of integrity.

Deuteronomy 23:24, 25
When thou comest into thy neighbour's vineyard, then thou mayest eat grapes thy fill at thine own pleasure; but thou shalt not put any in thy vessel. When thou comest into the standing corn of thy neighbour, then thou mayest pluck the ears with thine hand; but thou shalt not move a sickle unto thy neighbour's standing corn.

In the days before mini-marts, travelers were allowed to eat of the crops along the way. It was a law generated by the kindness of the Father and put into practice by the disciples of the Son (Matthew 12:1).

24

Deuteronomy 24:1, 2
When a man hath taken a wife, and married her, and it come to pass that she find no favour in his eyes, because he hath found some uncleanness in her: then let him write her a bill of divorcement, and give it in her hand, and send her out of his house. And when she is departed out of his house, she may go and be another man's wife.

For centuries, this was a controversial passage in the life and history of Israel. In fact, when Jesus came on the scene there was a red-hot debate taking place in the culture concerning the definition of "uncleanness." One opinion was voiced by a famous scholar named Hillel. Liberal in his perspective, Hillel said a woman was to be considered unclean—and, therefore, a candidate for divorce—if she caused uncleanness in her home. For example, if she over-salted her husband's eggs, thereby causing him to be angry, the resulting "unclean" atmosphere of the home would be her fault. Hillel went on to say that if a man saw a woman who was "cleaner" than his wife, his wife would become "unclean" by comparison. The other opinion was voiced by a scholar named Shammai, who insisted that uncleanness applied exclusively to immorality.

When asked His opinion on the matter, Jesus answered, "What God has joined together, let no man put asunder."

"Why, then, did Moses give permission to divorce?" the Pharisees asked Him.

"Because of the hardness of your hearts," Jesus explained (Matthew 19:3–9). As evidenced by Jesus' answer, the answer to the question of divorce doesn't lie in loopholes.

"I want a divorce because I'm being abused," says a wife.

"How are you being abused?" I ask.

"Verbally," she answers.

"I want a divorce because my wife is hindering my spiritual growth," a husband says.

"No," Jesus says. "Go back to the Garden of Eden and see that God's plan is that one woman and one man stay together until death separates them." Does this mean the divorced person has committed the unpardonable sin? Not at all. It means they've committed a sin—just like we all have. But divorce being something God hates (Malachi 2:16), it must be an absolute last resort, not a first option. And there must be the admission that it is only the hardness of one's own heart that makes it even a possibility.

Deuteronomy 24:3, 4
And if the latter husband hate her, and write her a bill of divorcement, and giveth it in her hand, and sendeth her out of his house; or if the latter husband die, which took her to be his wife; her former husband, which sent her away, may not take her again to be his wife, after that she is defiled; for that is abomination before the LORD: and thou shalt not cause the land to sin, which the LORD thy God giveth thee for an inheritance.

Divorce is so painful and brutal, so heartbreaking and gut-wrenching with scars so deep and hurts so real that God essentially declares that the marriage severed by divorce ought to be buried. Upon occasion, there are miracles where God brings about resurrection. But such is not the norm and it takes nothing short of a miracle.

Deuteronomy 24:5
When a man hath taken a new wife, he shall not go out to war, neither shall he be charged with any business: but he shall be free at home one year, and shall cheer up his wife which he hath taken.

Upon getting married, a man was to spend the first year at home with his wife in order to cheer her up—the implication being she would need cheering up after marrying him!

"Wherever a man's treasure is, there will his heart be also," Jesus said (see Luke 12:34). Therefore, if a man took one year off to make his wife his treasure, he would inevitably lose interest in everything else that would otherwise vie for his attention. He would find himself wanting to be with her more than wanting anything else.

Deuteronomy 24:6
No man shall take the nether or the upper millstone to pledge: for he taketh a man's life to pledge.

Millstones could not be used as collateral because they were necessary for cooking. In other words, lenders were not to be hard-hearted, not to take from the poor anything necessary for their survival.

Deuteronomy 24:7
If a man be found stealing any of his brethren of the children of Israel, and maketh merchandise of him, or selleth him; then that thief shall die; and thou shalt put evil away from among you.

Kidnapping was to be a capital offense.

Deuteronomy 24:8, 9
Take heed in the plague of leprosy, that thou observe diligently, and do according to all that the priests the Levites shall teach you: as I commanded them, so ye shall observe to do. Remember what the LORD thy God did unto Miriam by the way, after that ye were come forth out of Egypt.

In Numbers 12, we read how Moses' sister, Miriam, was struck with leprosy for finding fault with Moses. After Moses interceded on her behalf, she was healed—but not before she was quarantined for seven days. Leprosy was, in Miriam's case, a picture of the sin of jealousy. So, too, we are to intercede for those in our midst who are jealous. And, just as Miriam was quarantined, we are to keep a watchful eye lest their jealousy, contagious disease that it is, infect others in the congregation.

Deuteronomy 24:10, 11
When thou dost lend thy brother any thing, thou shalt not go into his house to fetch his pledge. Thou shalt stand abroad, and the man to whom thou dost lend shall bring out the pledge abroad unto thee.

Here is a second admonition for the lender to be respectful of the borrower.

Deuteronomy 24:12, 13
And if the man be poor, thou shalt not sleep with his pledge: In any case thou shalt deliver him the pledge again when the sun goeth down, that he may sleep in his own raiment, and bless thee: and it shall be righteousness unto thee before the LORD thy God.

If one's blanket or cloak was used as collateral, the lender was not to be cold-hearted, but was to return it at night lest the borrower be cold.

Deuteronomy 24:14, 15
Thou shalt not oppress an hired servant that is poor and needy, whether he be of thy brethren, or of thy strangers that are in thy land within thy gates: At his day thou shalt give him his hire, neither shall the sun go down upon it; for he is poor, and setteth his heart upon it: lest he cry against thee unto the LORD, and it be sin unto thee.

Continuing with the theme of respect for those who were prone to be disrespected, employers were to pay those who worked for them daily rather than to string them along with promises.

Deuteronomy 24:16
The fathers shall not be put to death for the children, neither shall the children be put to death for the fathers: every man shall be put to death for his own sin.

If convicted of a capital offense, I can't say, "Take Peter-John instead." If I have committed a crime, my sons aren't to pay the price in my place. This is why the cults are so damnable, implying as they do, that, rather than dying for the sin of the world, God created Jesus to do it. In stripping Jesus of His deity, they make God the Father a violator of His own Law.

Deuteronomy 24:17–22
Thou shalt not pervert the judgment of the stranger, nor of the fatherless; nor take a widow's raiment to pledge: But thou shalt remember that thou wast a bondman in Egypt, and the LORD thy God redeemed thee thence: therefore I command thee to do this thing. When thou cuttest down thine harvest in thy field, and hast forgot a sheaf in the field, thou shalt not go again to fetch it: it shall be for the stranger, for the fatherless, and for the widow: that the LORD thy God may bless thee in all the work of thine hands. When thou beatest thine olive tree, thou shalt not go over the boughs again: it shall be for the stranger, for the fatherless, and for the widow. When thou gatherest the grapes of thy vineyard, thou shalt not glean it afterward: it shall be for the stranger, for the fatherless, and for the widow. And thou shalt remember that thou wast a bondman in the land of Egypt: therefore I command thee to do this thing.

When harvesting their crops, God's people were to leave a remnant for the poor. In this chapter particularly, God's heart and passion for the poor is impossible to miss. Therefore, He commanded His people to think differently, to be as kind as they could be, to see how much they could give away.

And the same is true for us. We're to be as generous as we can be towards as many as we can be. And then we'll see how God, a debtor to no man, blesses in return.

25 Deuteronomy 25:1–3

If there be a controversy between men, and they come unto judgment, that the judges may judge them; then they shall justify the righteous, and condemn the wicked. And it shall be, if the wicked man be worthy to be beaten, that the judge shall cause him to lie down, and to be beaten before his face, according to his fault, by a certain number. Forty stripes he may give him, and not exceed: lest, if he should exceed, and beat him above these with many stripes, then thy brother should seem vile unto thee.

Although we might initially recoil at the thought of public beatings, we must also admit that our penal system doesn't work—which is why we must continue to build prisons and why it costs more to keep a man in prison for a year than it does to send him to Yale for the same period. God's Law makes no mention of prisons. If a man was found guilty of committing a capital crime, he was to be stoned by the community. If his was a minor infraction, he was to be beaten before the community.

Deuteronomy 25:4

Thou shalt not muzzle the ox when he treadeth out the corn.

An ox grinding corn was to be able to eat that which he treaded. In 1 Corinthians 9:9, Paul used this verse to justify providing for those in ministry.

Deuteronomy 25:5, 6

If brethren dwell together, and one of them die, and have no child, the wife of the dead shall not marry without unto a stranger: her husband's brother shall go in unto her, and take her to him to wife, and perform the duty of an husband's brother unto her. And it shall be, that the firstborn which she beareth shall succeed in the name of his brother which is dead, that his name be not put out of Israel.

If a man died, his brother was to marry his widow. Their firstborn would bear the dead husband's name in order that his lineage would continue.

"Am I my brother's keeper?" Cain asked impudently.

Here, God answers, "Yes."

Deuteronomy 25:7–10

And if the man like not to take his brother's wife, then let his brother's wife go up to the gate unto the elders, and say, My husband's brother refuseth to raise up unto his brother a name in Israel, he will not perform the duty of my husband's brother. Then the elders of his city shall call him, and speak unto him: and if he stand to it, and say, I like not to take her; Then shall his brother's wife come unto him in the presence of the elders, and loose his shoe from off his foot, and spit in his face, and shall answer and say, So shall it be done unto that man that will not build up his brother's house. And his name shall be called in Israel, The house of him that hath his shoe loosed.

If a man refused to marry his deceased brother's wife, his brother's widow was to take off his shoe and spit in his face. As do verses 1 through 3 of this chapter, this passage points prophetically to Jesus—for it was by His stripes that we are healed (Isaiah 53:5), and it was He whose shoe was removed, whose face was spit upon as He hung on the Cross of Calvary in our place.

Deuteronomy 25:11, 12

When men strive together one with another, and the wife of the one draweth near for to deliver her husband out of the hand of him that smiteth him, and putteth forth her hand, and taketh him by the secrets: Then thou shalt cut off her hand, thine eye shall not pity her.

The scenario here is of two men fighting and a wife unfairly intervening. The same thing happens still. Two guys will be at odds because of a bad business deal. And, although they eventually work it out, their wives remain hostile towards each other because each has heard only her husband's side of the story. Wise, therefore, is the wife who doesn't get involved in her husband's battles, lest she only muddy the waters and get hurt in the process.

Deuteronomy 25:13–16

Thou shalt not have in thy bag divers weights, a great and a small. Thou shalt not have in thine house divers measures, a great

and a small. But thou shalt have a perfect and just weight, a perfect and just measure shalt thou have: that thy days may be lengthened in the land which the LORD thy God giveth thee. For all that do such things, and all that do unrighteously, are an abomination unto the LORD thy God.

Once again, God tells His people that they are to be people of integrity and honesty.

Deuteronomy 25:17–19
Remember what Amalek did unto thee by the way, when ye were come forth out of Egypt; How he met thee by the way, and smote the hindmost of thee, even all that were feeble behind thee, when thou wast faint and weary; and he feared not God. Therefore it shall be, when the LORD thy God hath given thee rest from all thine enemies round about, in the land which the LORD thy God giveth thee for an inheritance to possess it, that thou shalt blot out the remembrance of Amalek from under heaven; thou shalt not forget it.

God's people were not to lag behind, but to be front and center in their walk with Him, in their commitment to Him, because it is those at the back who get attacked . . .

THE ATTACK IS AT THE BACK

A Topical Study of
DEUTERONOMY 25:17–19

C. S. Lewis said that the primary task of teaching is not so much to reveal as it is to remind. And evidently Moses would agree, for, as we have seen, the entire Book of Deuteronomy is a reminder to the children of Israel of what God had done for them, of what He had taught them, of what He expects of them.

The passage before us is no exception, beginning as it does with the word "Remember" and ending with the words, "You shall not forget."

What were the children of Israel not to forget? They were not to forget how, during their wilderness wandering, the Amalekites attacked them not man-to-man, not face-to-face, but from the back. The Israelites were to remember how the Amalekites would wait in hiding until they passed by, how they would attack those who were weary and feeble.

We, too, have an enemy who attacks us constantly. "Be sober," Peter said. "Be vigilant because your adversary goes about as a roaring lion, seeking whom he may devour" (see 1 Peter 5:8). It is said that in the jungle, the lion wakes up each day knowing that he simply must outrun the slowest prey. And the same is true spiritually, for, like the lion, Satan attacks the weariest or feeblest among us; and like Amalek, he finds them at the back of the pack.

This is a word I need to remember, a word of which we need to be reminded constantly because we can say, "I've been walking with the Lord for a number of years. I've been involved in a lot of battles. I need to kick back a bit, to cruise awhile"—not realizing that those who think they deserve a break are the very ones most vulnerable to an attack . . .

He was a great man, a godly man. Year after year he had led his troops into battle. He was their commander, their king. But at the age of fifty, he said, "I've fought long enough. I'm going to kick back awhile." So he sent another to lead the troops while he stayed behind. On the roof of his palace one night, enjoying the view of the golden city of Jerusalem, his eye came across a woman taking a bath. Intrigued with her, he had an affair with her and tried to cover it up by murdering her husband. He should have been fully engaged. He should have been front and center in battle. Instead, he thought he deserved a break. And as a result, life was never the same for David, for his family, for his kingdom.

The same thing can happen to you and me. "Hey," we say, "I've been walking with the Lord for forty years. Who says I have to have devotions and go to Bible study? Why not let someone else teach Sunday school? Why not let someone else work in the nursery? Why not let someone else go to prayer meeting? I'm tired."

We are currently seeing a rash of middle-aged men in our own community falling into immorality. The number of people who have been sucked into sin at this point in life is astonishing to me. And the common thread among them seems to be their misconception that they were justified in pulling away from fellowship, in drifting away from worship because they thought they had paid their dues, because they thought that spending time with the Lord or with His people no longer needed to be a priority.

Precious people, be oh, so careful that you don't grow weary somewhere in middle life, saying, "I've fought the fight. Now it's time to cruise." Amalek attacks the back of the pack. He'll be waiting for you.

At only thirty years of age, he wasn't weary. But he was feeble. He hadn't always been that way. "Smite the shepherd and the sheep will scatter," the Lord had said.

"Not me," he had boldly answered. "My name is Peter. I'm solid as a rock. You can count on me" (see Matthew 26:31–35).

But when, hours later, Jesus was led away to the trial that would ultimately lead to His crucifixion, Peter did what he said he would never do: He ran. And then, feeling feeble, he followed Jesus afar off. He still followed Jesus, but no longer at His side. Now there was a distance between them (Matthew 26:58).

> The enemies of Jesus lit fires that night to take the chill away. And Peter was chilled indeed—not only outwardly, but his soul was chilled. He knew he was not where he was supposed to be, where he said he would be, where he used to be. Instead, he stood by the fires of the enemy.
>
> "We know you," one of those who stood by said to him. "You're one of His followers."
>
> "No, I'm not," Peter answered.
>
> "Weren't you with Jesus?" asked a young girl.
>
> "No," Peter insisted.
>
> "I'm sure you're a Galilean," said another.

> And at this point Peter swore, the original text indicating that he took an oath as if to say, "My soul be damned if I know that Man" (Matthew 26:74).

Be careful when you feel feeble that you don't say, "I'm not what I should be or not what I used to be so I'm going to follow Jesus afar off." When you follow Jesus from afar, there's a chill in your soul that will drive you to the fires of the enemy in search of warmth. You'll visit web sites you know you ought not to look at. You'll turn to movies or to alcohol, to drugs or to fantasies, hoping they'll warm your soul. You'll fall prey to the attack of the enemy when you allow former sins or tendencies to needlessly drive you to the back of the pack.

What are you supposed to do when you're weary or feeble?

Don't go to the back. Go to the front. Become more engaged than ever, more involved than you ever were before in your spiritual work and devotional life, more committed to service and ministry, to worship and Bible study.

> *But they that wait upon the LORD shall renew their strength; they shall mount up with wings as eagles; they shall run, and not be weary; and they shall walk, and not faint.*
>
> Isaiah 40:31

Why should we remain front and center in the things of the Lord even when we're tired, even if we're feeble? Because in so doing, our strength is not diminished. It's renewed, replenished, restored.

I am amazed by the number of times over my forty-plus years of walking with the Lord that He has met me just because I simply chose to press in and step up rather than following my fleshly inclination to go to the back of the pack. And I guarantee He'll do the same for you.

We're involved in a battle to be sure. But the last verse of our text reminds us that this won't always be so, for there's coming a day when even the memory of Amalek will be blotted out when Satan is cast into the lake of fire (Revelation 20:10).

Isaiah tells us that we're going to "narrowly look" on Satan (14:16, 17). That is, with furrowed brow, we'll scratch our heads and say, "Is *this* the one who kept people captive, who shook kingdoms, who brought destruction? We were tricked by *him?*"

And then we'll see how greatly the lion seeking whom he may devour pales in comparison to the Lion of the Tribe of Judah.

Until then, remain fully engaged in your devotional life, in your personal walk, in your service for the King. In so doing, not only will you please Him greatly, not only will your strength be renewed daily, but the arrows of Amalek will never reach you way up there at the front.

26 Deuteronomy 26:1–3

And it shall be, when thou art come in unto the land which the LORD thy God giveth thee for an inheritance, and possessest it, and dwellest therein; That thou shalt take of the first of all the fruit of the earth, which thou shalt bring of thy land that the LORD thy God giveth thee, and shalt put it in a basket, and shalt go unto the place which the LORD thy God shall choose to place his name there. And thou shalt go unto the priest that shall be in those days, and say unto him, I profess this day unto the LORD thy God, that I am come unto the country which the LORD sware unto our fathers for to give us.

When the children of Israel entered the Promised Land, they were to place the firstfruits of the land in a basket and bring them to the tabernacle—ultimately the temple—where they were to audibly testify of the Lord's goodness in bringing them to the land He had promised to give their fathers.

Deuteronomy 26:4–9

And the priest shall take the basket out of thine hand, and set it down before the altar of the LORD thy God. And thou shalt speak and say before the LORD thy God, A Syrian ready to perish was my father, and he went down into Egypt, and sojourned there with a few, and became there a nation, great, mighty, and populous: And the Egyptians evil entreated us, and afflicted us, and laid upon us hard bondage: And when we cried unto the LORD God of our fathers, the LORD heard our voice, and looked on our affliction, and our labour, and our oppression: And the LORD brought us forth out of Egypt with a mighty hand, and with an outstretched arm, and with great terribleness, and with signs, and with wonders: And he hath brought us into this place, and hath given us this land, even a land that floweth with milk and honey.

Not only were the children of Israel to confess and profess that the Lord had brought them in to the Promised Land, but also that He had brought them out of Egypt.

The Lord wants to do the same thing for us. All of us who are born again have been brought out of Egypt—set free from the sin that once held us captive. But it doesn't end there. He also wants to take us from that point into the Land of Promise—the Spirit-filled, abundant life. In other words, just as He did with the children of Israel, God brought us out in order to bring us in.

Deuteronomy 26:10, 11

And now, behold, I have brought the firstfruits of the land, which thou, O LORD, hast given me. And thou shalt set it before the LORD thy God, and worship before the LORD thy God: And thou shalt rejoice in every good thing which the LORD thy God hath given unto thee, and unto thine house, thou, and the Levite, and the stranger that is among you.

For you and me, the firstfruits are the tithe. We're to say, "Lord, You've blessed us. You've done so much for us. You've been so patient with us. You've been so good to us. And now we bring You the firstfruit of what You gave us." Notice that this is to be done with rejoicing. Tithing is not a time of tears, but a time for cheers (2 Corinthians 9:7).

Deuteronomy 26:12, 13

When thou hast made an end of tithing all the tithes of thine increase the third year, which is the year of tithing, and hast given it unto the Levite, the stranger, the fatherless, and the widow, that they may eat within thy gates, and be filled; Then thou shalt say before the LORD thy God, I have brought away the hallowed things out of mine house, and also have given them unto the Levite, and unto the stranger, to the fatherless, and to the widow, according to all thy commandments which thou hast commanded me: I have not transgressed thy commandments, neither have I forgotten them:

The year of tithing seen in verse 12 was addressed previously in chapter 14. Every third year an extra tithe was given for the purpose of helping those in need—the widow, the fatherless, the stranger.

Deuteronomy 26:14, 15

I have not eaten thereof in my mourning, neither have I taken away ought thereof for any unclean use, nor given ought thereof for the dead: but I have hearkened to the voice of the LORD my God, and have done according to all that thou hast commanded me. Look down from thy holy habitation, from heaven, and bless thy people Israel, and the land which thou hast given us, as thou swarest unto our fathers, a land that floweth with milk and honey.

The children of Israel were to say, "Lord, we've done what You told us to do. We've brought You the firstfruits. We've given You the tithe. We've honored You in this way. Now, Lord, we ask that You bless our land."

Deuteronomy 26:16–18 (a)
This day the LORD thy God hath commanded thee to do these statutes and judgments: thou shalt therefore keep and do them with all thine heart, and with all thy soul. Thou hast avouched the LORD this day to be thy God, and to walk in his ways, and to keep his statutes, and his commandments, and his judgments, and to hearken unto his voice: And the LORD hath avouched thee this day to be his peculiar people . . .

Peculiar doesn't mean bizarre. It means blessed. Peter would use this same term to describe the church (1 Peter 2:9). Of Jesus, Scripture says He did not cry in the streets (Matthew 12:19). And when the soldiers came to arrest Jesus in the Garden of Gethsemane, so ordinary looking was He that Judas had to identify Him with a kiss (Luke 22:47). Jesus was not One to make a public spectacle. Therefore, neither should His church. That which makes us identifiable is not to be bizarre behavior but love (John 13:35). And in these days, it's peculiar indeed for people to love each other, to enjoy being together, to be kind and merciful towards each other.

Deuteronomy 26:18 (b), 19
. . . as he hath promised thee, and that thou shouldest keep all his commandments; And to make thee high above all nations which he hath made, in praise, and in name, and in honour; and that thou mayest be an holy people unto the LORD thy God, as he hath spoken.

Those who keep the Lord's commands will be holy. The word "holy" essentially means "whole"—not eroded by sin, not fragmented, not missing something. That is the way God wants to bless His people.

27

Deuteronomy 27:1, 2
And Moses with the elders of Israel commanded the people, saying, Keep all the commandments which I command you this day. And it shall be on the day when ye shall pass over Jordan unto the land which the LORD thy God giveth thee, that thou shalt set thee up great stones, and plaister them with plaister:

When the children of Israel crossed the Jordan River into the Promised Land, they were to construct a monument of stones which they were to cover with plaster, and upon which they would write the Law.

Deuteronomy 27:3–5
And thou shalt write upon them all the words of this law, when thou art passed over, that thou mayest go in unto the land which the LORD thy God giveth thee, a land that floweth with milk and honey; as the LORD God of thy fathers hath promised thee. Therefore it shall be when ye be gone over Jordan, that ye shall set up these stones, which I command you this day, in mount Ebal, and thou shalt plaister them with plaister. And there shalt thou build an altar unto the LORD thy God, an altar of stones: thou shalt not lift up any iron tool upon them.

At Mount Ebal, the children of Israel were to build a simple altar of stones. Throughout His Law, God declares that when an altar was made, it was to be made only of stone or earth. It was to be common and uncarved because otherwise the tendency would be for people to focus on the altar rather than on the sacrifice.

Deuteronomy 27:6, 7
Thou shalt build the altar of the LORD thy God of whole stones: and thou shalt offer burnt offerings thereon unto the LORD thy God: And thou shalt offer peace offerings, and shalt eat there, and rejoice before the LORD thy God.

As outlined in Leviticus 1, the burnt offering spoke of sober dedication. As seen in Leviticus 3, the peace offering spoke of joyful celebration, as the one bringing it celebrated his peace with God through a "barbeque" with the Lord. Both offerings were necessary, and both dedication and celebration are still vital to the life of faith.

Deuteronomy 27:8
And thou shalt write upon the stones all the words of this law very plainly.

When do we get to the place of soberly dedicating our lives to the Lord and joyfully celebrating what He's done for us? When we read the Word and see therein the rightness of God's ways, the Sacrifice He made.

Deuteronomy 27:9–13
And Moses and the priests the Levites spake unto all Israel, saying, Take heed, and hearken, O Israel; this day thou art become the people of the LORD thy God. Thou shalt therefore obey the voice of the LORD thy God, and do his commandments and his statutes, which I command thee this day. And Moses charged the people the same day, saying, These shall stand upon mount Geri-

zim to bless the people, when ye are come over Jordan; Simeon, and Levi, and Judah, and Issachar, and Joseph, and Benjamin: And these shall stand upon mount Ebal to curse; Reuben, Gad, and Asher, and Zebulun, Dan, and Naphtali.

Mount Gerizim and Mount Ebal are each about 2,000 feet high. Between them is a valley that served as a natural "amphitheater." With six tribes on each mountain and the priests and leaders in between, the stage was set for an illustrated sermon the children of Israel would not soon forget . . .

Deuteronomy 27:14–26
And the Levites shall speak, and say unto all the men of Israel with a loud voice, Cursed be the man that maketh any graven or molten image, an abomination unto the LORD, the work of the hands of the craftsman, and putteth it in a secret place. And all the people shall answer and say, Amen. Cursed be he that setteth light by his father or his mother. And all the people shall say, Amen. Cursed be he that removeth his neighbour's landmark. And all the people shall say, Amen. Cursed be he that maketh the blind to wander out of the way. And all the people shall say, Amen. Cursed be he that perverteth the judgment of the stranger, fatherless, and widow. And all the people shall say, Amen. Cursed be he that lieth with his father's wife; because he uncovereth his father's skirt. And all the people shall say, Amen. Cursed be he that lieth with any manner of beast. And all the people shall say, Amen. Cursed be he that lieth with his sister, the daughter of his father, or the daughter of his mother. And all the people shall say, Amen. Cursed be he that lieth with his mother in law. And all the people shall say, Amen. Cursed be he that smiteth his neighbour secretly. And all the people shall say, Amen. Cursed be he that taketh reward to slay an innocent person. And all the people shall say, Amen. Cursed be he that confirmeth not all the words of this law to do them. And all the people shall say, Amen.

As the Law was read, the tribes on Mount Ebal would say, "Amen" to the curses, while those on Mount Gerizim would affirm the blessings. And lest you think you would rather be on Mount Gerizim affirming the blessings, don't forget that the altar—the place where blood is shed, where forgiveness is made—was on Mount Ebal.

You might be aware of failings and shortcomings in your life—of times you've dropped the ball and cursed yourself or others because of stupidity and sin. But where sin abounds, grace abounds more (Romans 5:20). Therefore, the greater awareness I have of my sin, the more thankful I am for the grace of God. It is not surprising that the one who is forgiven much loves much (Luke 7:47), making Mount Ebal—the place where blood is shed—the place where there is, ultimately, peace and joy.

28

Deuteronomy 28:1, 2
And it shall come to pass, if thou shalt hearken diligently unto the voice of the LORD thy God, to observe and to do all his commandments which I command thee this day, that the LORD thy God will set thee on high above all nations of the earth: And all these blessings shall come on thee, and overtake thee, if thou shalt hearken unto the voice of the LORD thy God.

As he continues to prepare the people of Israel to enter the Promised Land, Moses tells them that if they do what the Lord tells them to do, they won't have to search for His blessings. On the contrary, His blessings will find them and will overwhelm them in most wonderful ways.

Deuteronomy 28:3
Blessed shalt thou be in the city, and blessed shalt thou be in the field.

The first blessing given here is that of location. Those who obey God's commandments will be blessed, or happy, wherever they are.

Deuteronomy 28:4 (a)
Blessed shall be the fruit of thy body . . .

Not only the location, but future generations of those who follow the way of the Lord will be blessed.

Deuteronomy 28:4 (b)
. . . and the fruit of thy ground, and the fruit of thy cattle, the increase of thy kine, and the flocks of thy sheep.

To those who follow Him, God extends His blessing to their vocation.

Deuteronomy 28:5
Blessed shall be thy basket and thy store.

The provisions of those who follow the Lord will be blessed.

Deuteronomy 28:6
Blessed shalt thou be when thou comest in, and blessed shalt thou be when thou goest out.

The daily routine of those who put God first will not be mundane but magnificent.

Deuteronomy 28:7
The LORD shall cause thine enemies that rise up against thee to be smitten before thy face: they shall come out against thee one way, and flee before thee seven ways.

Victory in battle belongs to those who follow God.

Deuteronomy 28:8
The LORD shall command the blessing upon thee in thy storehouses, and in all that thou settest thine hand unto; and he shall bless thee in the land which the LORD thy God giveth thee.

The Lord promises a secure future to those who follow Him.

Deuteronomy 28:9
The LORD shall establish thee an holy people unto himself, as he hath sworn unto thee, if thou shalt keep the commandments of the LORD thy God, and walk in his ways.

Saving the best for last, the Lord promises spiritual intimacy and stability to those who follow Him.

For topical study of Deuteronomy 28:1–9 entitled "Be Blessed!" turn to page **614.**

Deuteronomy 28:10
And all people of the earth shall see that thou art called by the name of the LORD; and they shall be afraid of thee.

God's divine design was that Israel would be an example to the pagan nations surrounding her of what a people looked like who followed the true and living God.

Deuteronomy 28:11–14
And the LORD shall make thee plenteous in goods, in the fruit of thy body, and in the fruit of thy cattle, and in the fruit of thy ground, in the land which the LORD sware unto thy fathers to give thee. The LORD shall open unto thee his good treasure, the heaven to give the rain unto thy land in his season, and to bless all the work of thine hand: and thou shalt lend unto many nations, and thou shalt not borrow. And the LORD shall make thee the head, and not the tail; and thou shalt be above only, and thou shalt not be beneath; if that thou hearken unto the commandments of the LORD thy God, which I command thee this day, to observe and to do them: And thou shalt not go aside from any of the words which I command thee this day, to the right hand, or to the left, to go after other gods to serve them.

If the Israelites walked in God's ways, they would be the head, not the tail; they would be above, not beneath. In other words, they would set the standard other nations would strive to follow.

Deuteronomy 28:15 (a)
But . . .

Blessing, security, prosperity were Israel's for the taking if she followed the Law God so carefully and painstakingly spelled out to her. If, however, she chose not to walk in His ways, an entirely different scenario would unfold . . .

Deuteronomy 28:15 (b), 16
. . . it shall come to pass, if thou wilt not hearken unto the voice of the LORD thy God, to observe to do all his commandments and his statutes which I command thee this day; that all these curses shall come upon thee, and overtake thee: Cursed shalt thou be in the city, and cursed shalt thou be in the field.

If Israel chose not to follow the Lord, wherever God's people went—city or country—it wouldn't be quite right.

Deuteronomy 28:17, 18 (a)
Cursed shall be thy basket and thy store. Cursed shall be the fruit of thy body . . .

If Israel chose not to walk in God's ways, the children would feel the unmistakable effects of the curse.

Deuteronomy 28:18 (b)–20
. . . and the fruit of thy land, the increase of thy kine, and the flocks of thy sheep. Cursed shalt thou be when thou comest in, and cursed shalt thou be when thou goest out. The LORD shall send upon thee cursing, vexation, and rebuke, in all that thou settest thine hand unto for to do, until thou be destroyed, and until thou perish quickly; because of the wickedness of thy doings, whereby thou hast forsaken me.

God won't allow you to continue on in a path of rebellion or sin any more than He would allow the children of Israel to do the same because He knows doing so will affect your eternal state. And He's more concerned about your eternal state than He is about your present comfort. Yes, there is pleasure in sin for a season (Hebrews 11:25), but sin will come crashing down on you eventually, leaving heartache and pain in its wake.

Deuteronomy 28:21, 22
The LORD shall make the pestilence cleave unto thee, until he have consumed thee from off the land, whither thou goest to possess it. The LORD shall smite thee with a consumption, and with a fever, and with an inflammation, and with an extreme burning, and with the sword, and with blasting, and with mildew; and they shall pursue thee until thou perish.

Although we've all tried at one time or another, no one beats the rap. If you choose to go your own way, the curse will catch up with you. Guaranteed.

Deuteronomy 28:23–29
And thy heaven that is over thy head shall be brass, and the earth that is under thee shall be iron. The LORD shall make the rain of thy land powder and dust: from heaven shall it come down upon thee, until thou be destroyed. The LORD shall cause thee to be smitten before thine enemies: thou shalt go out one way against them, and flee seven ways before them: and shalt be removed into all the kingdoms of the earth. And thy carcase shall be meat unto all fowls of the air, and unto the beasts of the earth, and no man shall fray them away. The LORD will smite thee with the botch of Egypt, and with the emerods, and with the scab, and with the itch, whereof thou canst not be healed. The LORD shall smite thee with madness, and blindness, and astonishment of heart: And thou shalt grope at noonday, as the blind gropeth in darkness, and thou shalt not prosper in thy ways: and thou shalt be only oppressed and spoiled evermore, and no man shall save thee.

If the children of Israel forsook the Lord, their land would turn to dust, their physical health would disappear, their emotional stability would crumble. A grimmer picture could not be imagined—and yet it gets worse . . .

Deuteronomy 28:30
Thou shalt betroth a wife, and another man shall lie with her: thou shalt build an house, and thou shalt not dwell therein: thou shalt plant a vineyard, and shalt not gather the grapes thereof.

In chapter 20, those men who were engaged but not yet married, those who had built a house but hadn't yet moved in, those who had planted a vineyard but hadn't yet harvested the fruit were all excused from battle. Here in chapter 28, however, rather than being protected, those same groups were singled out for their failure to walk in the way of the Lord. Their marriages would fall apart; their houses would be abandoned; their vineyards would fail. This is powerful stuff. This is God declaring to people the way it will be for those who turn their back on Him.

Deuteronomy 28:31, 32
Thine ox shall be slain before thine eyes, and thou shalt not eat thereof: thine ass shall be violently taken away from before thy face, and shall not be restored to thee: thy sheep shall be given unto thine enemies, and thou shalt have none to rescue them. Thy sons and thy daughters shall be given unto another people, and thine eyes shall look, and fail with longing for them all the day long: and there shall be no might in thine hand.

If Israel turned her back on God, her sons and daughters would be carried away into captivity. And indeed they were. The nation underwent unspeakable devastation at the hands of the Assyrians, the Babylonians, and finally under the iron foot of the Romans.

Deuteronomy 28:33–37
The fruit of thy land, and all thy labours, shall a nation which thou knowest not eat up; and thou shalt be only oppressed and crushed alway: So that thou shalt be mad for the sight of thine eyes which thou shalt see. The LORD shall smite thee in the knees, and in the legs, with a sore botch that cannot be healed, from the sole of thy foot unto the top of thy head. The LORD shall bring thee, and thy king which thou shalt set over thee, unto a nation which neither thou nor thy fathers have known; and there shalt thou serve other gods, wood and stone. And thou shalt become an astonishment, a proverb, and a byword, among all nations whither the LORD shall lead thee.

God told the Israelite congregation that they would be a high and holy nation, the head and not the tail, the most blessed of all people if they walked with Him. But if they chose to go their own way, their name would be a byword, or something contemptible, on the lips of the nations.

Deuteronomy 28:38–41
Thou shalt carry much seed out into the field, and shalt gather but little in; for the locust shall consume it. Thou shalt plant vineyards, and dress them, but shalt neither drink of the wine, nor gather the grapes; for the worms shall eat them. Thou shalt have olive trees throughout all thy coasts, but thou shalt not anoint thyself with the oil; for thine olive shall cast his fruit. Thou shalt beget sons and daughters, but thou shalt not enjoy them; for they shall go into captivity.

Even today, there are parents who don't enjoy their kids because their kids are held captive by the enemy.

Deuteronomy 28:42–47
All thy trees and fruit of thy land shall the locust consume. The stranger that is within thee shall get up above thee very high; and thou shalt come down very low. He shall lend to thee, and thou shalt not lend to him: he shall be the head, and thou shalt be the tail. Moreover all these curses shall come upon thee, and shall pursue thee, and overtake thee, till thou be destroyed; because thou hearkenedst not unto the voice of the LORD thy God, to keep his commandments and his statutes which he commanded thee: And they shall be upon thee for a sign and for a wonder, and upon thy seed for ever. Because thou servedst not the LORD thy God with joyfulness, and with gladness of heart, for the abundance of all things;

The Bible says we are to rejoice evermore (1 Thessalonians 5:16). The Bible says we are to give thanks in everything (1 Thessalonians 5:18). The Bible says happy is the people whose God is the Lord (Psalm 144:15). Therefore, I believe we are to be those who put aside the tendency to be heavy, those who forego the tendency to want to be pitied, those who abandon the thought that it's hard to serve the Lord. Instead, we're to be those who lift up those around us; to be those who serve the Lord from a heart overflowing with joy and gladness.

Deuteronomy 28:48
Therefore shalt thou serve thine enemies which the LORD shall send against thee, in hunger, and in thirst, and in nakedness, and in want of all things: and he shall put a yoke of iron upon thy neck, until he have destroyed thee.

Serve the Lord with gladness (Psalm 100:2)—or serve the enemy with sadness. That is the choice we make each day.

Deuteronomy 28:49–52
The LORD shall bring a nation against thee from far, from the end of the earth, as swift as the eagle flieth; a nation whose tongue thou shalt not understand; a nation of fierce countenance, which shall not regard the person of the old, nor shew favour to the young: and he shall eat the fruit of thy cattle, and the fruit of thy land, until thou be destroyed: which also shall not leave thee either corn, wine, or oil, or the increase of thy kine, or flocks of thy sheep, until he have destroyed thee. And he shall besiege thee in all thy gates, until thy high and fenced walls come down, wherein thou trustedst, throughout all thy land: and he shall besiege thee in all thy gates throughout all thy land, which the LORD thy God hath given thee.

First the Assyrians, then the Babylonians, but ultimately this speaks of the Romans, the eagle being the imperial emblem of the Roman Empire.

Deuteronomy 28:53–55 (a)
And thou shalt eat the fruit of thine own body, the flesh of thy sons and of thy daughters, which the LORD thy God hath given thee, in the siege, and in the straitness, wherewith thine enemies shall distress thee: So that the man that is tender among you, and very delicate, his eye shall be evil toward his brother, and toward the wife of his bosom, and toward the remnant of his children which he shall leave: So that he will not give to any of them of the flesh of his children whom he shall eat: because he hath nothing left him in the siege . . .

In the year A.D. 70, when the Romans came into Jerusalem, burned the temple, and destroyed the city, 600,000 Jews were slaughtered in the first wave. Starvation ensued and cannibalism followed. That was only the beginning, for in A.D. 135, Emperor Hadrian came back to Jerusalem with his troops in answer to a Jewish revolt. And unbelievable atrocities ensued unlike anything in history.

Deuteronomy 28:55 (b)–64
. . . and in the straitness, wherewith thine enemies shall distress thee in all thy gates. The tender and delicate woman among you, which would not adventure to set the sole

of her foot upon the ground for delicateness and tenderness, her eye shall be evil toward the husband of her bosom, and toward her son, and toward her daughter, And toward her young one that cometh out from between her feet, and toward her children which she shall bear: for she shall eat them for want of all things secretly in the siege and straitness, wherewith thine enemy shall distress thee in thy gates. If thou wilt not observe to do all the words of this law that are written in this book, that thou mayest fear this glorious and fearful name, THE LORD THY GOD; Then the LORD will make thy plagues wonderful, and the plagues of thy seed, even great plagues, and of long continuance, and sore sicknesses, and of long continuance. Moreover he will bring upon thee all the diseases of Egypt, which thou wast afraid of; and they shall cleave unto thee. Also every sickness, and every plague, which is not written in the book of this law, them will the LORD bring upon thee, until thou be destroyed. And ye shall be left few in number, whereas ye were as the stars of heaven for multitude; because thou wouldest not obey the voice of the LORD thy God. And it shall come to pass, that as the LORD rejoiced over you to do you good, and to multiply you; so the LORD will rejoice over you to destroy you, and to bring you to nought; and ye shall be plucked from off the land whither thou goest to possess it. And the LORD shall scatter thee among all people, from the one end of the earth even unto the other; and there thou shalt serve other gods, which neither thou nor thy fathers have known, even wood and stone.

As the Jews were scattered throughout the world, they would get caught up in the gods of the age: the gods of materialism, intellectualism, and social position.

Deuteronomy 28:65, 66
And among these nations shalt thou find no ease, neither shall the sole of thy foot have rest: but the LORD shall give thee there a trembling heart, and failing of eyes, and sorrow of mind: And thy life shall hang in doubt before thee; and thou shalt fear day and night, and shalt have none assurance of thy life:

If they forsook God, wherever the Israelites went their security would be doubtful. And, of course, this is exactly what happened, as evidenced most notably, though far from exclusively, in the Holocaust. Read the history of the Jewish people and you will find that—for reasons that don't make sense at all other than for the fulfillment of prophecy and the intent of Satan to destroy God's people—wherever they went, they would ultimately be persecuted, put down, kicked out.

Deuteronomy 28:67, 68
In the morning thou shalt say, Would God it were even! and at even thou shalt say, Would God it were morning! for the fear of thine heart wherewith thou shalt fear, and for the sight of thine eyes which thou shalt see. And the LORD shall bring thee into Egypt again with ships, by the way whereof I spake unto thee, thou shalt see it no more again: and there ye shall be sold unto your enemies for bondmen and bondwomen, and no man shall buy you.

Following the Roman destruction of Jerusalem, the Jews were deported to Egypt, where they were sold as slaves. Although Moses' words to them would go on to include hope and promise, perhaps it's good that this particular chapter ends here—for through it, we see the lengths to which the Lord went in order to warn His people about the effects of apostasy.

May we be those who earnestly take heed to these warnings, and may God's Word be written clearly on the plaster of our hearts.

BE BLESSED!

A Topical Study of DEUTERONOMY 28:1–9

When I see the blessings in Deuteronomy 28, I can't help but say, "That's exactly what I want. I want to see my family blessed. I want my location to be satisfying to me. I want to see my cupboards full. I want to experience stability and spiritual intimacy. I want to see the work of my hands blessed, to have a daily routine that's fulfilling, to know my future is secure."

But this is hardly surprising, for who of us doesn't want these blessings?

So when I hear Moses saying, "If you hearken diligently to the Lord, if you obey all of His commandments, these blessings will be yours," I say, "Wonderful!"—until I try, but inevitably and consistently fail.

You see, the key to success and blessing lies in obeying *all* of the commandments. It can't be ninety percent or even ninety-nine percent. To get the victory that brings the blessings, one must do it *all* (James 2:10) because the Ten Commandments are interwoven in such a way that to break one is ultimately to break all ten . . .

> You're out at sea, two miles from shore, when you notice that, although nine of the floorboards in your boat are shipshape, one is rotting away in the salt water. Therefore, even though only one in ten is faulty, even though nine are in perfect order, you're sunk.

Moses said if you want these blessings, you've got to obey *all* the commandments. And therein lies the problem. I want to. I try. But I can't.

There is One, however, who came to earth and walked among people like me, who did indeed keep *all* the commandments. In fact, so perfectly did He keep them that even His enemies could find no fault in Him (Luke 23:4). And because Jesus kept all the commandments, because He fulfilled every expectation and requirement of the Law, He gets all of the blessings. In other words, every Old Testament blessing, every glorious promise made to those who would walk in God's ways, who would obey God's Word, who would seek God's heart is His because He did all of those things (2 Corinthians 1:19, 20).

And here's the amazing news: When you became a Christian, not only did Christ come in you, but you were placed in Him (2 Corinthians 5:17). Therefore, all the promises are yours as well.

How?

Think of it this way . . .

My phone rings. I pick up the receiver and hear a voice saying, "Hello, Jon. This is Coach Erickson from Oregon State University. We've got a big game today. Our Quarterback is a good athlete and a great guy. But he's small. So I want some back-up insurance and you're the man."

"I haven't played football for . . . five years," I say.

"That's okay," he says. "Come and join us."

So I go to Corvallis and put on the uniform as the rest of the team says, "Who's *he?*"

At the end of four quarters, Oregon State wins. And when the game is over, the photographers come. The reporters are there. The parties begin. And guess what. Even though I never got off the bench, I'm part of it all. Why? Because of who I am? No. Because of what I did? No. I'm part of the celebration simply because I'm wearing the uniform, simply because I'm on the team.

You are in Christ, "uniformed" in His righteousness (Isaiah 61:10). You don't deserve to be. Neither do I. But the Coach called us to come and we accepted His invitation. It just so happens that the team we're on is championed by Jesus Christ, who wins the game single-handedly, who executes the plays perfectly. And because we're on His team, His victory is undeservedly and unbelievably ours as well.

This means we who are in Christ, we who are on His team, we who wear His uniform can expect to be blessed in our going out and our coming in. We can expect to be blessed in our profession. We can expect our kids will be fruitful and successful. We can expect to be blessed in everything we do—not because of what we do, not because of who we are, but because God has chosen to use foolish and weak things to confound the wise and the strong (1 Corinthians 1:27).

That all sounds good, you might be thinking. *But why don't I see those blessings in my life?*

Maybe God has blessed you more than you realize. Maybe you haven't taken the time to think through the way He's blessed you in the city and in the country, blessed the fruit of your body, blessed you in the storehouse, blessed you in your basket, blessed you with victory over the enemy that threatened to crush and destroy you. Maybe He's blessed you more than you think. And maybe part of the issue is to stop and review what He's done for you and rejoice in that. But secondly, and perhaps more importantly, maybe you don't see God's blessings in your life because you're working too hard to even notice them . . .

After wasting his father's money in the far country, the prodigal son returned—not to punishment, but to a party. "Unfair!" said his older brother to their father. "I've been with you every day, working faithfully. But you never threw a party on my behalf."

"Son," the father answered. "All that I have is yours" (see Luke 15:31). In other words, "Any time you wanted, you could have had anything and everything you desired. But you were too busy being self-righteous, working in the field trying to impress me, trying to earn something from me to come out of the field and into the party."

Many of us also have said, "I'm going to pray more. I'm going to work harder. I'm going to worship with greater intensity. I'm going to give more money. I'm going to teach Sunday school or work in the nursery so that I will be blessed"—only to find that it never works.

Then why be obedient at all? Why pray or study or worship or give or serve at all? Why not, like the prodigal son, waste our time and our Father's resources in the "far country" of sin?

For the answer, go back to Oregon State . . .

If Coach Erickson said, "Courson, I want you to come back next season and play for us again," I would undergo rigorous and radical preparation. I would study the playbook. I would throw passes. I would go to the Y. Why? Not so that I might make the team, but because I'm already on the team. You see, it's great to be on a winning team, even if you're on the bench. But it's a whole lot better to be on a winning team and also on the field.

We're blessed, gang, no matter what we do or don't do simply because we're on the team. But now God wants to use us. Isn't it amazing that God would want to use *us?*

> *I am crucified with Christ: nevertheless I live; yet not I, but Christ liveth in me: and the life which I now live in the flesh I live by the faith of the Son of God, who loved me, and gave himself for me.* Galatians 2:20

Because Christ lives in us, we can go out on the field and expect to complete passes, to make blocks, to throw tackles in a way we never dreamed possible. And the more we allow Him to work in and through us, the more He taps us on the shoulder, saying, "I've already blessed you. Now I want to use you. Go out there and play for My glory."

---

29 In chapter 28, we saw how the Lord warned His people that if they turned their backs on Him and walked away from Him that they would experience some very dire repercussions. In chapters 29 and 30, however, God declares what will happen to the Jewish nation when they turn away from their rebelliousness and back towards Him. In so doing, He makes a covenant, an agreement with His people. The covenant He makes, seen here in chapters 29 and 30, is known as the Palestinian Covenant because it relates to the land we know as Israel, but which, before 1948, was known only as Palestine.

Deuteronomy 29:1
These are the words of the covenant, which the LORD commanded Moses to make with the children of Israel in the land of Moab, beside the covenant which he made with them in Horeb.

Mt. Horeb is another name for Mount Sinai. The covenant God made there was the Mosaic Covenant.

Deuteronomy 29:2, 3
And Moses called unto all Israel, and said unto them, Ye have seen all that the LORD did before your eyes in the land of Egypt unto Pharaoh, and unto all his servants, and unto all his land; The great temptations which thine eyes have seen, the signs, and those great miracles:

Newer translations properly render the word "temptations" as "plagues"—referring to the plagues which descended upon Pharaoh and the people of Egypt before Pharaoh finally let God's people go.

Deuteronomy 29:4
Yet the LORD hath not given you an heart to perceive, and eyes to see, and ears to hear, unto this day.

"God has shown you miracles, signs and wonders," Moses said to the children of Israel. "But what you saw with your eyes made no impact on your hearts."

Deuteronomy 29:5, 6
And I have led you forty years in the wilderness: your clothes are not waxen old upon you, and thy shoe is not waxen old upon thy foot. Ye have not eaten bread, neither have ye drunk wine or strong drink: that ye might know that I am the LORD your God.

As the children of Israel were so prone to do, how easy it is for us to murmur and complain. Instead of being thankful that our shoes last for forty years, we complain that they're out of style. God's been so good to us. But oh, how easily we lose sight of it.

Deuteronomy 29:7
And when ye came unto this place, Sihon the king of Heshbon, and Og the king of Bashan, came out against us unto battle, and we smote them:

Think back to the times in your own life when it felt as though the problems, like Sihon and Og, were too big and too heavy to bear, that you were sure to be crushed and wiped out under their weight. Yet here you are tonight. God saw you through.

Deuteronomy 29:8, 9
And we took their land, and gave it for an inheritance unto the Reubenites, and to the Gadites, and to the half tribe of Manasseh. Keep therefore the words of this covenant, and do them, that ye may prosper in all that ye do.

God's heart is that His people prosper. Thus, His commandments are given to that end.

Deuteronomy 29:10–15
Ye stand this day all of you before the LORD your God; your captains of your tribes, your elders, and your officers, with all the men of Israel, Your little ones, your wives, and thy stranger that is in thy camp, from the hewer of thy wood unto the drawer of thy water: That thou shouldest enter into covenant with the LORD thy God, and into his oath, which the LORD thy God maketh with thee this day: That he may establish thee to day for a people unto himself, and that he may be unto thee a God, as he hath said unto thee, and as he hath sworn unto thy fathers, to Abraham, to Isaac, and to Jacob. Neither with you only do I make this covenant and this oath; But with him that standeth here with us this day before the LORD our God, and also with him that is not here with us this day:

This covenant was not only for those in attendance the day it was made, but for future generations.

Deuteronomy 29:16–18
(For ye know how we have dwelt in the land of Egypt; and how we came through the nations which ye passed by; And ye have seen their abominations, and their idols, wood and stone, silver and gold, which were among them:) Lest there should be among you man, or woman, or family, or tribe, whose heart turneth away this day from the LORD our God, to go and serve the gods of these nations; lest there should be among you a root that beareth gall and wormwood;

"You'll be bitter. You'll be unhappy. You won't be prosperous if you follow the gods of other nations. Materialism, seeking your own ease, serving yourselves will leave a bad taste in your mouth," Moses warned the people.

Deuteronomy 29:19, 20
And it come to pass, when he heareth the words of this curse, that he bless himself in his heart, saying, I shall have peace, though I walk in the imagination of mine heart, to add drunkenness to thirst: The LORD will not spare him, but then the anger of the LORD and his jealousy shall smoke against that man, and all the curses that are written in this book shall lie upon him, and the LORD shall blot out his name from under heaven.

In this introduction to the Palestinian Covenant, God is speaking through Moses, saying to His people, "I took care of you in the wilderness. Now do what I'm telling you to do that you might prosper in the Promised Land." Yet even as He gave this warning, God knew there would be those who mistakenly thought they could walk in the imagination of their own hearts, that the commands didn't apply to them, that they could do whatever they wanted.

Deuteronomy 29:21–23
And the LORD shall separate him unto evil out of all the tribes of Israel, according to all the curses of the covenant that are written in this book of the law: So that the generation to come of your children that shall rise up after you, and the stranger that shall come from a far land, shall say, when they see the plagues of that land, and the sicknesses which the LORD hath laid upon it; And that the whole land thereof is brimstone, and salt, and burning, that it is not sown, nor beareth, nor any grass groweth therein, like the overthrow of Sodom, and Gomorrah, Admah, and Zeboim, which the LORD overthrew in his anger, and in his wrath:

The Jews did indeed turn their back on the Lord not only individually, but as a nation. And so the land of honey would become, as it was even one hundred years ago, a land of brimstone and salt, a land where even grass wouldn't grow.

Deuteronomy 29:24–29
Even all nations shall say, Wherefore hath the LORD done thus unto this land? what meaneth the heat of this great anger? Then men shall say, Because they have forsaken the covenant of the LORD God of their fathers, which he made with them when he brought them forth out of the land of Egypt: For they went and served other gods, and worshiped them, gods whom they knew not, and whom he had not given unto them: And the anger of the LORD was kindled against this land, to bring upon it all the curses that are written in this book: And the LORD rooted them out of their land in anger, and in wrath, and in great indignation, and cast them into another land, as it is this day. The secret things belong unto the LORD our God: but those things which are revealed belong unto us and to our children for ever, that we may do all the words of this law.

The Land itself became a testimony of the state of the hearts of God's people. When a people walks with God, there is a blessing on him or them, a fruitfulness in them, a beauty of holiness about them. On the other hand, there is a barrenness, an emptiness, a dryness in the lives of those who walk in the imagination of their own hearts. God will use our lives one way or the other—either as an illustration of the effects of rebellion or to show what happens when people walk in obedience to the commandments God writes both on their hearts and in His Word, to the word He whispers in their ears (Isaiah 30:21).

30 Here in chapter 30, we come to the heart of the Palestinian Covenant, made with the people of Israel prior to their entry into the Promised Land . . .

Deuteronomy 30:1–5
And it shall come to pass, when all these things are come upon thee, the blessing and the curse, which I have set before thee, and thou shalt call them to mind among all the nations, whither the LORD thy God hath driven thee, And shalt return unto the LORD thy God, and shalt obey his voice according to all that I command thee this day, thou and thy children, with all thine heart, and with all thy soul; That then the LORD thy God will turn thy captivity, and have compassion upon thee, and will return and gather thee from all the nations, whither the LORD thy God hath scattered thee. If any of thine be driven out unto the outmost parts of heaven, from thence will the LORD thy God gather thee, and from thence will he fetch thee: And the LORD thy God will bring thee into the land which thy fathers possessed, and thou shalt possess it; and he will do thee good, and multiply thee above thy fathers.

"When your land has been destroyed, when bitterness has filled your heart, when things have fallen apart and the situation looks grim, if you turn to Me, I will bring you back to this land again," God tells His people.

Deuteronomy 30:6
And the LORD thy God will circumcise thine heart, and the heart of thy seed, to love the LORD thy God with all thine heart, and with all thy soul, that thou mayest live.

Not only will the children of Israel be returned to their land, but their hearts will one day be tender toward God.

Deuteronomy 30:7
And the LORD thy God will put all these curses upon thine enemies, and on them that hate thee, which persecuted thee.

In their land once again, with hearts tender toward God, the children of Israel will themselves be blessed even as their enemies experience God's curse.

Deuteronomy 30:8–10
And thou shalt return and obey the voice of the LORD, and do all his commandments which I command thee this day. And the LORD thy God will make thee plenteous in every work of thine hand, in the fruit of thy body, and in the fruit of thy cattle, and in the fruit of thy land, for good: for the LORD will again rejoice over thee for good, as he rejoiced over thy fathers: If thou shalt hearken unto the voice of the LORD thy God, to keep his commandments and his statutes which are written in this book of the law, and if thou turn unto the LORD thy God with all thine heart, and with all thy soul.

All of this has yet to happen. Many of the Jews of the world are back in the land of Israel—but certainly not the majority. There is coming a time, however, when the Lord shall gather His elect from every corner of the world and bring them back. When? Matthew 24:32 tells us it will happen when Jesus comes back.

Deuteronomy 30:11–20
For this commandment which I command thee this day, it is not hidden from thee, nei-

ther is it far off. It is not in heaven, that thou shouldest say, Who shall go up for us to heaven, and bring it unto us, that we may hear it, and do it? Neither is it beyond the sea, that thou shouldest say, Who shall go over the sea for us, and bring it unto us, that we may hear it, and do it? But the word is very nigh unto thee, in thy mouth, and in thy heart, that thou mayest do it. See, I have set before thee this day life and good, and death and evil; In that I command thee this day to love the LORD thy God, to walk in his ways, and to keep his commandments and his statutes and his judgments, that thou mayest live and multiply: and the LORD thy God shall bless thee in the land whither thou goest to possess it. But if thine heart turn away, so that thou wilt not hear, but shalt be drawn away, and worship other gods, and serve them; I denounce unto you this day, that ye shall surely perish, and that ye shall not prolong your days upon the land, whither thou passest over Jordan to go to possess it. I call heaven and earth to record this day against you, that I have set before you life and death, blessing and cursing: therefore choose life, that both thou and thy seed may live: That thou mayest love the LORD thy God, and that thou mayest obey his voice, and that thou mayest cleave unto him: for he is thy life, and the length of thy days: that thou mayest dwell in the land which the LORD sware unto thy fathers, to Abraham, to Isaac, and to Jacob, to give them.

The Palestinian Covenant reminds me that God has a plan for the Jew, that He's not through with the Jew. And this is important because it means He's not through with you or me. God will be faithful to every covenant He makes, to every promise He proclaims.

God made promises to you that everything is working together for good (Romans 8:28), that there's no condemnation to them who are in Christ Jesus (Romans 8:1), that nothing shall separate you from the love of God (Romans 8:38, 39). Can you count on these promises? "Look at the Jew," Paul would answer in Romans 9 through 11, "for just as God will be faithful to the Jew, He'll be faithful to you."

The Palestinian Covenant is in play. God's going to do exactly what He said He would do—for the Jew, for me, and for you.

THE PROXIMITY OF HIS PRECEPTS AND PRESENCE

A Topical Study of DEUTERONOMY 30:11–20

As we come to chapter 30, nearing the end of Moses' farewell sermon to the children of Israel, I can almost hear Moses pause, sigh, and look the congregation in the eye as he begins to share with them from his soul.

He's been going on and on, repeating the commandments of the Lord. And now he says God's commandment is not secret, mystical, abstract, or hard to reach. It's not in the heavens, but is very near to them. How near? As close as it can be. It's embedded in their hearts and on the tip of their tongues.

After twenty-nine chapters of preaching, Moses pauses and essentially says, "You know what to do. And you know that it's true." People do know. They might not want to admit it, but deep within, they know that the best way to live is to love God and keep His commandments. After all, who does even the unsaved person want to move in to the vacant house next to them—a person who loves God and honors the Ten Commandments, or one who hates God and believes that murder and adultery, stealing, lying, and killing are acceptable?

Or think of it this way . . .

You run out of gas in the middle of a big city just before midnight. You leave your car by the side of a poorly lit street and begin walking to the nearest gas station. After a block or two, sensing you're not alone, you look over your shoulder and see four big guys following you. Would it make a difference if you know they were coming out of an evening Bible study and prayer meeting rather than out of a bar?

In our hearts, we know the right way to live is to love God and obey the commands He's given us. "So choose life," Moses says. "Don't violate what you know is true, what you know you ought to do, what you know is best for you."

Jesus said all of the commandments are summed up in a single word: love. "Love the Lord your God with all your heart, soul, mind, and strength," He said. "And love your neighbor as yourself" (Matthew 22:37–40). We're to love God passionately and to love our neighbor compassionately. It's just that simple.

"I know what to do," you might be saying, "I know God's ways are true, that they're best for me and you. But here's the problem: I don't come through. There are times when I don't do what I know is the right thing to do. And there are times when I do things I ought not to do. I understand what is right and good and true. But I fail to do so in so many ways, on so many days."

Wait. There's hope because this very passage pops up again in the New Testament. Paul reaches back to Deuteronomy 30 and look what he says concerning these very things . . .

> *But the righteousness which is of faith speaketh on this wise, Say not in thine heart, Who shall ascend into heaven? (that is, to bring Christ down from above:) Or, Who shall descend into the deep? (that is, to bring up Christ again from the dead.)*
> Romans 10:6, 7

Inspired by the Spirit, Paul says, "There's another way. Not the word of the Law, but the word of faith . . ."

> *But what saith it? The word is nigh thee, even in thy mouth, and in thy heart: that is, the word of faith, which we preach; That if thou shalt confess with thy mouth the Lord Jesus, and shalt believe in thine heart that God hath raised him from the dead, thou shalt be saved. For with the heart man believeth unto righteousness; and with the mouth confession is made unto salvation.*
> Romans 10:8–10

There's no need to try to attain a spiritual high or dig into the depths of your soul. There's no need to come forward, go to the prayer room, meet with a pastor, or even be baptized, for salvation is in none of those places. Where is it? It's on the tip of your tongue, if you'll simply confess that you want Jesus to be your Lord.

> *For whosoever shall call upon the name of the Lord shall be saved.*
> Romans 10:13

Salvation lies in saying, "Jesus, I believe in my heart that You died for me and rose again."

Then why come forward or be baptized? Why go to the prayer room or meet with a pastor?

Because these are wonderful expressions of faith, and invaluable opportunities for growth. But they're not prerequisites to salvation.

I recently talked to a lady who became a Christian last year during one of our services. She was eighty-four years old and her life has been absolutely, radically changed. I'm so glad I didn't have to say to her, "If you want spiritual reality, you need to sit in the lotus position and concentrate on the candle flickering before you. And perhaps if you give yourself to this and work hard at that, maybe you'll come into divine illumination."

No! What a joy it is to be able to say to someone who's eighty-four, "It's so simple. You already know it's true. Jesus died and rose again and wants to live in you by His Spirit. All you have to do is believe in your heart and say with your mouth that Jesus is your Lord." It's shockingly and scandalously simple.

And the same thing is true for you. Whosoever shall call on the name of the Lord shall be saved—not just from past sin, but from present problems. If you believe in your heart that Jesus is risen from the dead and call upon His name, you'll be saved even in your present struggle.

Here's the problem. We'll go across town to get medication to help us out of depression; we'll scour the country to find a retreat center to help us with our addiction; we'll search the phone book to find a psychiatrist to help us cope with problems in our childhood—all while ignoring the power of salvation which lies on the very tip of our tongue.

Unlimited power is ours for the asking. Inexhaustible grace is ours for the believing. The question is, Will we?

It's such a glorious promise found here in Deuteronomy 30 that Paul repeated it centuries later. May we be those who take it to heart. And may we remind others to do the same.

---

31 "Thy Word is a lamp unto my feet and a light unto my path," the Psalmist wrote (Psalm 119:105). Knowing this to be true, Moses wanted the people to whom he had faithfully ministered for forty years to enter the new season, the new phase of their history, the new Land having enlightenment from the Word . . .

Deuteronomy 31:1–5

And Moses went and spake these words unto all Israel. And he said unto them, I am an hundred and twenty years old this day; I can no more go out and come in: also the LORD hath said unto me, Thou shalt not go over this Jordan. The LORD thy God, he will go over before thee, and he will destroy these nations from before thee, and thou shalt possess them: and Joshua, he shall go over before thee, as the LORD hath said. And the LORD shall do unto them as he did to Sihon and to Og, kings of the Amorites, and unto the land of them, whom he destroyed. And the LORD shall give them up before your face, that ye may do unto them according unto all the commandments which I have commanded you.

"Even though I will not be accompanying you into the Promised Land, in the same way you have seen the Lord come through for you previously, He will come through for you when you cross over the Jordan and face a whole new set of enemies," Moses declared. In other words, "God has shown you His faithfulness in the past, that you might have peace about the future."

Deuteronomy 31:6
Be strong and of a good courage, fear not, nor be afraid of them: for the Lord thy God, he it is that doth go with thee; he will not fail thee, nor forsake thee.

Fear is to the devil what faith is to the Lord. That is, Satan responds to, takes advantage of, and delights in fear the same way our Lord responds to, works through, and delights in faith. When I don't know how the bills will get paid or if the relationship will be restored, the devil will try to get me to become full of anxiety and fear. God, however, "has not given us the spirit of fear, but of power, love, and a sound mind." (2 Timothy 1:7).

The disciples were on the Sea of Galilee, toiling at the oars. The wind was howling; the waves were rolling; and the disciples, many of whom were seasoned fishermen were afraid of the ferocity of the storm. Suddenly they saw Someone walking on the waves, headed in their direction. "It's a ghost!" they shouted, perhaps alluding to the legend that said when a boat was about to go down, a ghost would come to deliver the message that the lives of the men on board were over.

But then they heard the words, "Be of good cheer. It is I. Be not afraid" (Matthew 14:27).

Faith is like a muscle. It doesn't grow unless it's exercised. And we need to exercise faith in a most practical way. We need to choose in the midst of the storm, when it seems as though our boat is sunk, to be of good cheer. I have discovered over and over that when I make the decision to be strong, to be of good cheer, to not give in to tears and fears, that the Lord is truly near.

Romans 10:17 says faith comes by hearing and hearing by the Word of God. We take faith in as we hear the promises of God's Word, the preaching of the Scripture. Faith is worked in by the hearing of the Word—but it's worked out by the speaking of the Word. That's why Romans 10 also says we must confess with our mouth (vv. 9, 10). Faith comes in through the ear, but is worked out through the mouth.

A lot of times we take in a Scripture, but then have a tendency to complain or murmur—and wonder why faith isn't impacting our situation. Jesus said, "*Say* to the mountain be removed . . ." (Matthew 21:21, italics added). This is such a key, but is forgotten so easily. Faith that works is not only a matter of having devotions in the morning or going to Bible study in the evening, but it's a matter of speaking out that which we have taken in.

If I hear the Word in a Bible study and go my way saying, "I don't know what's going to happen. I don't know how things are going to work," my faith is short-circuited by my words of fear and frustration. Proverbs 18:21 tells us that the power of life and death is in the tongue. How often we kill our faith either by the words we say or fail to say.

> . . . for he hath said, I will never leave thee, nor forsake thee. So that we may boldly say, The Lord is my helper, and I will not fear what man shall do unto me. Hebrews 13:5 (b), 6

"He hath said . . . that we may boldly say . . ." Next time you are fearful about the future, boldly speak out what He has already said—and watch your faith grow.

Deuteronomy 31:7
And Moses called unto Joshua, and said unto him in the sight of all Israel, Be strong and of a good courage: for thou must go with this people unto the land which the Lord hath sworn unto their fathers to give them; and thou shalt cause them to inherit it.

Moses couldn't take the people into the Promised Land not only because He misrepresented the Lord at Meribah (Numbers 20:10, 11), but because He was the Law-giver—and the Law never leads to the fruitful, Spirit-filled life of which the Promised Land is a picture. On the other hand, "Joshua" is the Old Testament name for "Jesus." Therefore, Joshua was the one who would lead the children of Israel into the Promised Land, just as Jesus is the way into the Spirit-filled life for us.

Deuteronomy 31:8
And the Lord, he it is that doth go before thee; he will be with thee, he will not fail thee, neither forsake thee: fear not, neither be dismayed.

With a promise like this, how can we fear?

Deuteronomy 31:9
And Moses wrote this law, and delivered it unto the priests the sons of Levi, which bare the ark of the covenant of the Lord, and unto all the elders of Israel.

There always seems to be a debate among scholars concerning the authorship of Deuteronomy. If they would just read it, however, they would find the answer right here!

Deuteronomy 31:10 (a)
And Moses commanded them, saying, At the end of every seven years, in the solemnity of the year of release . . .

As outlined in Exodus 23, Leviticus 25, and Deuteronomy 15, the year of release was the Sabbatical year, when debts were forgiven, when slaves were released, when both land and people were to rest.

Deuteronomy 31:10 (b)
. . . in the feast of tabernacles,

The Feast of Tabernacles was the week-long celebration in the fall that was the happiest time of the year for the people of Israel as they camped out in pup tents to commemorate God's faithfulness in bringing them through the wilderness.

Deuteronomy 31:11, 12
When all Israel is come to appear before the LORD thy God in the place which he shall choose, thou shalt read this law before all Israel in their hearing. Gather the people together, men, and women, and children, and thy stranger that is within thy gates, that they may hear, and that they may learn, and fear the LORD your God, and observe to do all the words of this law:

In the time of release, refreshment, and rejoicing, the people of God were to read the Word. Why? Because there's a link between reading the Word and experiencing release and refreshment. In the reading of the Word, there will be refreshment in my soul, release in my spirit, rejoicing in my heart.

Deuteronomy 31:13–18
And that their children, which have not known any thing, may hear, and learn to fear the LORD your God, as long as ye live in the land whither ye go over Jordan to possess it. And the LORD said unto Moses, Behold, thy days approach that thou must die: call Joshua, and present yourselves in the tabernacle of the congregation, that I may give him a charge. And Moses and Joshua went, and presented themselves in the tabernacle of the congregation. And the LORD appeared in the tabernacle in a pillar of a cloud: and the pillar of the cloud stood over the door of the tabernacle. And the LORD said unto Moses, Behold, thou shalt sleep with thy fathers; and this people will rise up, and go a whoring after the gods of the strangers of the land, whither they go to be among them, and will forsake me, and break my covenant which I have made with them. Then my anger shall be kindled against them in that day, and I will forsake them, and I will hide my face from them, and they shall be devoured, and many evils and troubles shall befall them; so that they will say in that day, Are not these evils come upon us, because our God is not among us? And I will surely hide my face in that day for all the evils which they shall have wrought, in that they are turned unto other gods.

Here, God tells Moses that all of the people he'd been leading would turn away from Him to serve false gods. What a heartbreak—not only for Moses, but for God. Because there's nothing hidden from the Lord (Hebrews 4:13), all the while He had been patient with His people, all the while He had led them, provided for them, protected them, He knew they would eventually walk away from Him.

Deuteronomy 31:19–21
Now therefore write ye this song for you, and teach it the children of Israel: put it in their mouths, that this song may be a witness for me against the children of Israel. For when I shall have brought them into the land which I sware unto their fathers, that floweth with milk and honey; and they shall have eaten and filled themselves, and waxen fat; then will they turn unto other gods, and serve them, and provoke me, and break my covenant. And it shall come to pass, when many evils and troubles are befallen them, that this song shall testify against them as a witness; for it shall not be forgotten out of the mouths of their seed: for I know their imagination which they go about, even now, before I have brought them into the land which I sware.

God told Moses about the future rebellion of His people because He wanted Moses to write a song for them. It's as if God said, "Moses, you've preached thirty chapters. But the people won't remember your sermon. What they will remember is a song."

Deuteronomy 31:22
Moses therefore wrote this song the same day, and taught it the children of Israel.

Moses wrote the song and taught it to the people that very day. Oh for men like Moses, men who don't say, "That's a great idea. I'll get to it when I have a moment of inspiration. I'll get to it when I can clear my schedule," but who say, "I'll do it right now."

Deuteronomy 31:23–26
And he gave Joshua the son of Nun a charge, and said, Be strong and of a good courage: for thou shalt bring the children of Israel into the land which I sware unto them: and I will be with thee. And it came to pass, when Moses had made an end of writing the words of this law in a book, until they were finished, That Moses commanded the Levites, which bare the ark of the covenant of the LORD, saying, Take this book of the law, and put it in the side of the ark of the covenant of the LORD your God, that it may be there for a witness against thee.

In 2 Kings 22, we read that when King Josiah remodeled the temple, the only copy of the Law to be found in all Israel was discovered therein—placed there because of this Scripture.

Deuteronomy 31:27–29 (a)
For I know thy rebellion, and thy stiff neck: behold, while I am yet alive with you this day, ye have been rebellious against the LORD; and how much more after my death? Gather unto me all the elders of your tribes, and your officers, that I may speak these words in their ears, and call heaven and earth to record against them. For I know that after my death ye will utterly corrupt yourselves, and turn aside from the way which I have commanded you; and evil will befall you in the latter days;

I believe this is a reference to the time of Jacob's trouble, the great Tribulation of Revelation 6—19. Because they would turn their back on the Lord, Israel will be cast into the Tribulation in order that, in the process, she will at last realize that Jesus is Messiah, her Savior.

Deuteronomy 31:29 (b), 30
. . . because ye will do evil in the sight of the LORD, to provoke him to anger through the work of your hands. And Moses spake in the ears of all the congregation of Israel the words of this song, until they were ended.

In chapter 32, we'll see Moses' song—one that is sure to put a melody in your own heart.

32

The congregation Moses had been leading would, after his departure, rebel against the Lord and turn their back on the Lord. In light of this, the Lord said to Moses, "There's one more thing I want you to do before I take you to heaven. I want you to write a song and teach it to the people so that when they go through times of tribulation and days of difficulty, they will turn back to Me."

And here is the song Moses wrote . . .

Deuteronomy 32:1–3
Give ear, O ye heavens, and I will speak; and hear, O earth, the words of my mouth. My doctrine shall drop as the rain, my speech shall distil as the dew, as the small rain upon the tender herb, and as the showers upon the grass: Because I will publish the name of the LORD: ascribe ye greatness unto our God.

Throughout Scripture, the Word is likened to water. And here Moses declares the Word will come down not like a fire hydrant, blasting people, but like a gentle spring rain, blessing those who heard it.

Deuteronomy 32:4
He is the Rock, his work is perfect: for all his ways are judgment: a God of truth and without iniquity, just and right is he.

Everything God does is good.

Deuteronomy 32:5, 6
They have corrupted themselves, their spot is not the spot of his children: they are a perverse and crooked generation. Do ye thus requite the LORD, O foolish people and unwise? Is not he thy father that hath bought thee? Hath he not made thee, and established thee?

Remember, this song was composed to remind the children of Israel who God is and why they would be going through tribulation.

Deuteronomy 32:7, 8
Remember the days of old, consider the years of many generations: ask thy father, and he will shew thee; thy elders, and they will tell thee. When the most High divided to the nations their inheritance, when he separated the sons of Adam, he set the bounds of the people according to the number of the children of Israel.

"Ask the elders if you don't know your history," Moses said, "about how God divided humanity." Seventy nations are listed in Genesis 10 following the Flood. Later, in Genesis 46, we see seventy who went to Egypt. Thus, seventy represents all of humanity. And God is sovereign over all.

Deuteronomy 32:9
For the LORD's portion is his people; Jacob is the lot of his inheritance.

Of all humanity, God claimed Israel for Himself in a unique way. But He also claimed us, for Paul tells us we are His inheritance as well (Ephesians 1). How can we understand this? Paul said God proved His love for us in that while we were yet sinners, Christ died for us (Romans 5:8). The value of an object is known by how much a person is willing to pay for it. What was God willing to pay for you? His very life. Thus, it is the Cross of Calvary that shows me how much He loves me.

Deuteronomy 32:10 (a)
He found him in a desert land, and in the waste howling wilderness . . .

God's people were found in a desert land. It was when we felt deserted—unloved, uncared for, unimportant, dry, thirsty—that the Lord found us. He found us in the "waste howling wilderness"—where we were wasting our lives, talent, time, and energy in stupidity.

Deuteronomy 32:10 (b)
. . . he led him about . . .

The Hebrew word translated "led" means "encompassed." In other words, God says, "When My people were in the desert, wasting away, howling in emptiness, I encompassed them. I threw My arms around them. I enveloped them in Myself."

Deuteronomy 32:10 (c)
. . . he instructed him . . .

God not only found and enveloped us, rescued and saved us, but He instructs us by His Word, a Word that converts our soul, rejoices our heart, enlightens our eyes, and makes us wise (Psalm 19:7, 8).

Deuteronomy 32:10 (d)
. . . he kept him as the apple of his eye.

The "apple of the eye" refers to the pupil. Those who study such things tell us the fastest reflex in our bodies is that of the eyelid covering the eyeball. If there is an object coming towards your eye, instinctively, intuitively, immediately your eye closes in 1/1000th of a second. So in calling us the apple of His eye, God is saying, "When danger is headed your way, I am there to close you in, to take care of you. I treasure and protect you as you would treasure and protect your own eye."

Deuteronomy 32:11, 12
As an eagle stirreth up her nest, fluttereth over her young, spreadeth abroad her wings, taketh them, beareth them on her wings: So the LORD alone did lead him, and there was no strange god with him.

In using a mother eagle as an analogy for the Father-love of God, Moses drew on a subject with which the children of Israel, trudging through the wilderness, would have been very familiar . . .

For topical study of Deuteronomy 32:7–12 entitled "Singing and Soaring," turn to page 629.

Deuteronomy 32:13
He made him ride on the high places of the earth, that he might eat the increase of the fields; and he made him to suck honey out of the rock, and oil out of the flinty rock;

In Israel, bees make their honeycombs and olive trees take root in crevasses or fissures in the rocks. Therefore, what would seem to be an unproductive place actually produces sweetness and sustenance.

"I'm on the rocks," we cry. "This is it. I'm through."

And yet God would say, "There's honey and oil in those rocks, for in them you will discover sweetness you never knew about, empowering and anointing you never would have experienced."

If you're between a rock and a hard place, realize that it is there that you will find honey and oil you never knew existed.

Deuteronomy 32:14 (a)
Butter of kine, and milk of sheep, with fat of lambs, and rams of the breed of Bashan, and goats, with the fat of kidneys of wheat . . .

All of this describes richness and fullness.

Deuteronomy 32:14 (b)
. . . and thou didst drink the pure blood of the grape.

I like this because it brings to mind, of course, the imagery of redemption, of Communion.

Deuteronomy 32:15 (a)
But Jeshurun waxed fat, and kicked: thou art waxen fat, thou art grown thick, thou art covered with fatness . . .

Jeshurun literally means "upright ones," and is another name for Israel.

Deuteronomy 32:15 (b)
. . . then he forsook God which made him, and lightly esteemed the Rock of his salvation.

This is such a sad story, yet one we've all experienced. When we're fat and happy, when everything is hunky dory, we forget about God.

Deuteronomy 32:16, 17
They provoked him to jealousy with strange gods, with abominations provoked they him to anger. They sacrificed unto devils, not to God; to gods whom they knew not, to new gods that came newly up, whom your fathers feared not.

In 1 Corinthians 10:20, Paul says that idols were not simply stone carvings or brass objects, but that demons were actually linked to them. And the same is still true.

Deuteronomy 32:18, 19
Of the Rock that begat thee thou art unmindful, and hast forgotten God that formed thee. And when the LORD saw it, he abhorred them, because of the provoking of his sons, and of his daughters.

God gave His people honey and oil, livestock and vineyards—and yet in their prosperity they forget Him and became interested in other gods, passions, and ideologies.

Deuteronomy 32:20, 21
And he said, I will hide my face from them, I will see what their end shall be: for they are a very froward generation, children in whom is no faith. They have moved me to jealousy with that which is not God; they have provoked me to anger with their vanities: and I will move them to jealousy with those which are not a people; I will provoke them to anger with a foolish nation.

Paul alludes to this verse in Romans 10:19, when he says that the Lord will provoke His people to jealousy by bringing the gospel to the Gentiles and allowing them to be the Bride of Christ. "I will provoke My people to anger with a foolish nation," God says. Guess who the foolish nation is. It's us.

Deuteronomy 32:22–24
For a fire is kindled in mine anger, and shall burn unto the lowest hell, and shall consume the earth with her increase, and set on fire the foundations of the mountains. I will heap mischiefs upon them; I will spend mine arrows upon them. They shall be burnt with hunger, and devoured with burning heat, and with bitter destruction: I will also send the teeth of beasts upon them, with the poison of serpents of the dust.

I believe this is a very accurate description of the horror of the Holocaust—a result of Israel turning away from the Lord and walking in rebellion against the Lord.

Deuteronomy 32:25–27
The sword without, and terror within, shall destroy both the young man and the virgin, the suckling also with the man of gray hairs. I said, I would scatter them into corners, I would make the remembrance of them to cease from among men: Were it not that I feared the wrath of the enemy, lest their adversaries should behave themselves strangely, and lest they should say, Our hand is high, and the LORD hath not done all this.

While conquering nations would erroneously think it was their own strength that defeated Israel, Israel's defeat would have nothing to do with the strength of other nations and everything to do with the chastening hand of God.

Deuteronomy 32:28, 29
For they are a nation void of counsel, neither is there any understanding in them. O that they were wise, that they understood this, that they would consider their latter end!

"I wish the people were wise," Moses says. "Instead, they're intrigued by their idols, seduced by paganism. I wish they would consider the end of that path." That's what the Bible does for us. That's why it is so important. It lets us see where the road of sin leads.

Deuteronomy 32:30
How should one chase a thousand, and two put ten thousand to flight, except their Rock had sold them, and the LORD had shut them up?

The Jewish people are heroic fighters. Look at David and Joshua, at Moshe Dayan and David Ben Gurion, at Old Testament stories and present-day heroes. How, then, could it be that they would go through periods in their history where a single enemy soldier could chase 1,000 of them? There's only one explanation: the Lord's hand against them.

Deuteronomy 32:31 (a)
For their rock is not as our Rock . . .

The rock of the Third Reich, the rock of any nation is incomparable to the Rock of Israel.

Deuteronomy 32:31 (b)–35
. . . even our enemies themselves being judges. For their vine is of the vine of Sodom, and of the fields of Gomorrah: their grapes are grapes of gall, their clusters are bitter: Their wine is the poison of dragons, and the cruel venom of asps. Is not this laid up in store with me, and sealed up among my treasures? To me belongeth vengeance, and recompence; their foot shall slide in due time: for the day of their calamity is at hand, and the things that shall come upon them make haste.

This was the text of the most famous sermon preached in American history. A man named Jonathan Edwards ushered in the Great Awakening with his message entitled, "Sinners in the Hands of an Angry God." Drawing from this text, Edwards said men are walking over a fiery pit on an icy plank, dangling by a thread over the fires of hell. An unassuming man with a high voice and poor eyesight, it was hardly Edwards' demeanor that caused revival. Rather, it was the power of the Word and the anointing of the Spirit that caused people to pour down the aisles of his church.

People came to this country and worshiped God. But they had forgotten about Him, falsely secure in their theology and caught up in material prosperity even in the earliest days of our country's history. So God used Edwards and others to do what we so often fail to do today—to call a nation to repentance.

Deuteronomy 32:36–40
For the LORD shall judge his people, and repent himself for his servants, when he seeth that their power is gone, and there is none shut up, or left. And he shall say, Where are their gods, their rock in whom they trusted, Which did eat the fat of their sacrifices, and drank the wine of their drink offerings? let them rise up and help you, and be your protection. See now that I, even I, am he, and there is no god with me: I kill, and I make alive; I wound, and I heal: neither is there any that can deliver out of my hand. For I lift up my hand to heaven, and say, I live for ever.

We like to think of God as One who heals. And He does. But, as seen in verse 39, He also wounds. When I read about God and study His Word, I realize that He is much bigger than my ability to package Him neatly. He is, after all, God.

"I'm thirsty," Lucy said to Aslan.

"Drink of the water, Lucy," Aslan replied.

She looked at the big lion with the bushy mane, powerful claws, and sharp teeth. "If I drink of that water, will you promise not to eat me?" she asked.

"No," Aslan answered. "I devour humans and destroy nations. I do what I choose. And there is none that can stop me. I make no promise to you."

Lucy looked at him, "If you won't promise not to eat me," she said, "I'm not going to drink of the water."

"Then you'll thirst to death, Lucy," Aslan answered.

In his classic series, *The Chronicles of Narnia*, C. S. Lewis drove home a very real point. That is, God doesn't make deals with me or you. He's God. And He can wound, heal, kill, and resurrect whenever He wants. Our God is indeed an awesome God, a fearful and terrible God. He loves us. He proved it in sending His Son to die for us. But never forget this song. The people who forget this do so to their own destruction.

Deuteronomy 32:41–43
If I whet my glittering sword, and mine hand take hold on judgment; I will render vengeance to mine enemies, and will reward them that hate me. I will make mine arrows drunk with blood, and my sword shall devour flesh; and that with the blood of the slain and of the captives, from the beginning of revenges upon the enemy. Rejoice, O ye nations, with his people: for he will avenge the blood of his servants, and will render vengeance to his adversaries, and will be merciful unto his land, and to his people.

I'm glad the song ends this way—with vengeance for God's enemies and mercy for His people.

Deuteronomy 32:44–47
And Moses came and spake all the words of this song in the ears of the people, he, and

Hoshea the son of Nun. And Moses made an end of speaking all these words to all Israel: And he said unto them, Set your hearts unto all the words which I testify among you this day, which ye shall command your children to observe to do, all the words of this law. For it is not a vain thing for you; because it is your life: and through this thing ye shall prolong your days in the land, whither ye go over Jordan to possess it.

Mom and Dad, lots of things we do with our kids are vain or empty. But teaching them the Word, talking to them about the Lord, sharing with them where we're at in our own walk with Him does not fall into that category. I have yet to regret any time I've spent teaching my kids the ways and the Word of God. I've yet to look back once and wish that we'd gone bowling instead.

Deuteronomy 32:48, 49
And the LORD spake unto Moses that selfsame day, saying, Get thee up into this mountain Abarim, unto mount Nebo, which is in the land of Moab, that is over against Jericho; and behold the land of Canaan, which I give unto the children of Israel for a possession:

"Go up into the mountain," the Lord said to Moses, "and you can see the Promised Land. You'll not be able to cross over the Jordan with the people, but I'll give you a sneak preview of coming attractions."

Deuteronomy 32:50, 51
And die in the mount whither thou goest up, and be gathered unto thy people; as Aaron thy brother died in mount Hor, and was gathered unto his people: Because ye trespassed against me among the children of Israel at the waters of Meribah-kadesh, in the wilderness of Zin; because ye sanctified me not in the midst of the children of Israel.

"Speak to the rock," the Lord had told Moses when the people cried for water. Instead, Moses struck the rock (Numbers 20:11). There had been a time previously when he was to strike the rock (Exodus 17:6)—but this time he was simply to speak to it. The first time speaks of the first coming of the Rock of Ages, when Jesus was smitten on the Cross. The second time, however, speaks of the Second Coming, when He will come not as the smitten Servant but as the conquering King.

It's a dangerous thing to misrepresent the nature of God to people. God help us to properly represent our Lord rather than to imply that He's upset or angry.

Deuteronomy 32:52
Yet thou shalt see the land before thee; but thou shalt not go thither unto the land which I give the children of Israel.

While Moses didn't get to enter the Promised Land with the children of Israel, he did, in fact, make it there—for in Matthew 17, as Jesus was transfigured on Mount Hermon, Moses was right there with Him. God snuck him in!

SINGING AND SOARING
A Topical Study of
DEUTERONOMY 32:7–12

Eagles can be found on every continent of the world except Antarctica. Eagles fly higher than any other bird and uniquely, among all of the animals of the animal kingdom, can look directly into the sun because of the "built-in sunglasses" which protect their eyes.

The eagle is not only the symbol of America, but was, in Czarist days, the symbol of Russia and was, in Bible times, the symbol of the Roman Empire.

The African eagle, with which the children of Israel would have been familiar, makes its home in the Middle East and has a wingspan of up to ten feet.

Once a year, the female eagle lays an egg in a nest high over a bluff or ravine, inaccessible to predators. For the six weeks following its hatching, the eaglet has it made in the shade. He can see lots of things from his vantage point. He's fed hourly by his mother. And he grows fat and plump.

By week five, he has grown quite large. And then something begins to happen. Unbeknownst to him, his mother designed the nest in such a way that sticks point inward. So as he gets fatter, the sticks begin to poke him. And no doubt Ernie Eaglet wonders why his parents didn't make a more comfortable nest—never realizing that its design was all part of the plan to get him to do something he never would have done otherwise: to get him to fly.

The same thing can happen to you and me. We're comfy. We're cozy. We're chubby. But all of a sudden, something begins to happen that agitates us, that pokes at us. "My boss shouldn't treat me this way," we squawk. "My friend shouldn't ignore me that way," we screech.

Wait a minute. It's all part of a divine design, a grand plan. Therefore, wise is the man or woman who doesn't blame the sticks, but realizes they're part of the plan of the Father.

At about this time, Mom returns to the nest one day and, with her ten-foot wings, stirs it and bumps it. And Ernie is thrown out, causing him to fall hundreds of feet towards the ravine below. Feathers fly. Ernie squawks. The ground gets closer, the rocks bigger—when Mama swoops underneath Ernie and carries him on her back to the nest once again.

Whew! Ernie thinks. *That was close! I hope Mom learned a lesson about being clumsy.* But three days later, Mama stirs the nest once again, sending Ernie screeching and tumbling once more. And once again, she swoops underneath him at seemingly the last minute, returning him to the nest at last.

The same process is repeated over and over again. But somewhere after the sixth or seventh time, Ernie catches air. No longer sore at his mother, he soars with her. And he can't believe it. He didn't have any idea that he could fly—until he was dumped out of the nest.

"What are You doing, God?" we cry. "If I'm Your inheritance, if You keep me as the apple of Your eye, then why am I headed for the rocks?" But right before we crash—maybe only a moment or so before we crash—He swoops in, bears us on His back, and returns us to the nest. Then, days later, He stirs the nest and begins the process all over again.

You see, God loves you and me too much to allow us to settle in the comfort of mediocrity. So He makes our nest uncomfortable as He gets us ready to do something new. He's not going to let us settle for a perch on a cliff when He knows we could soar in the heavenlies.

Maybe you feel like you're freefalling right now. Maybe you've been squawking a bit. Know this: You'll not hit bottom. You might get real close, but the Lord is going to bear you on His wings and take you back up to the nest again to catch your breath for a day or two. And then you'll get knocked around once more. It's all for a reason: To teach you how to fly, how to soar.

"If it's true that the Lord is going to turn over my nest of mediocrity, what should I do?" you ask. "Is there anything I can do to speed up the process? Is there any way I can learn to fly more quickly?"

Yes.

> *But they that wait upon the* L*ORD shall renew their strength; they shall mount up with wings as eagles; they shall run, and not be weary; and they shall walk, and not faint.* Isaiah 40:31

To learn to fly, wait on the Lord.

- "But I'm about to hit the rocks," you say.
  Wait.
- "But you don't understand my situation," you cry.
  Wait.
- "You don't realize the seriousness and the sadness, the pain and the problems," you squawk.
  Wait.

Waiting on the Lord does not mean passively doing nothing. Waiting on the Lord means doing what a waiter in an upscale restaurant does. "How can I help you?" he asks. "Is everything alright? Can I get you some more coffee? Can I bring you dessert?"

That's what it means to wait on the Lord. To wait on the Lord is to say, "Enough about me and my problems. I'm here to serve You, Lord, to honor You with thanksgiving, to give You a feast of praise."

Wait on the Lord. Reestablish your morning devotional time. Praise Him throughout the day. He is teaching you how to fly, taking you to a new dimension. I guarantee that if you wait on Him, you'll soar a whole lot quicker than if you just keep squawking.

"There was no strange god with him," Moses declared. That is not surprising, for when you're soaring in the heavenlies, the "strange gods," the things of this world grow strangely dim. When you're soaring high, the things of the world become unimportant and unappealing. When people go through tough times, they often lose weight. Why? Because in tough times, the flesh just isn't important. And the same principle is true spiritually. In hard times, when we seem to be headed for disaster, God frees us from the strange gods that so easily capture our attention. And in their place, like the eagle, we find ourselves looking at the Son.

That's what the Lord will do for you and me when He teaches us to soar higher and to fly in new dimensions. You watch. You wait. You'll see.

33 **Deuteronomy 33:1**
And this is the blessing, wherewith Moses the man of God blessed the children of Israel before his death.

Chapter 32 ended with a reiteration of God's refusal to allow Moses to enter the Promised Land with the children of Israel. Chapter 33 begins with Moses blessing the people. And this, among other things, is what qualifies Moses to be called "a man of God," a phrase seen here in Scripture for the first time. When God denied Moses' requests to accompany the people into the Promised Land, Moses could have said, "If, after forty years, this is the thanks I get; if, after I've given my life for these people and lead them through the wilderness to the best of my ability, I'm disqualified because of one mistake, I'm outta here." But he didn't. Rather than running away and licking his wounds, Moses blessed the people.

Greatness is found in what a man does within the boundaries placed around him. Many people say, "If I can't do this, if I can't be that, I won't do anything." Not Moses. He shows us the way to greatness, to being a man of God, is not by pulling back, but by being a blessing.

Deuteronomy 33:2
And he said, The Lord came from Sinai, and rose up from Seir unto them; he shined forth from mount Paran, and he came with ten thousands of saints: from his right hand went a fiery law for them.

Moses begins his blessing by reminding the people how the Lord came from Mt. Sinai with 10,000 saints, or literally, angels, to give them the Law.

Deuteronomy 33:3 (a)
Yea, he loved the people . . .

The Lord gave the Law to His people for one reason: Because He loved them. As parents, we should be able to understand this. "Put your seatbelts on," we say to our kids.

"Oh, but we just want to move around and do what we want," they say.

"I don't care. Put them on," we say. Why? Because we love them.

Deuteronomy 33:3 (b)–5
. . . all his saints are in thy hand: and they sat down at thy feet; every one shall receive of thy words. Moses commanded us a law, even the inheritance of the congregation of Jacob. And he was king in Jeshurun, when the heads of the people and the tribes of Israel were gathered together.

After reflecting on God's love in entrusting to them His Law, Moses begins to bless the Twelve Tribes.

Deuteronomy 33:6, 7
Let Reuben live, and not die; and let not his men be few. And this is the blessing of Judah: and he said, Hear, Lord, the voice of Judah, and bring him unto his people: let his hands be sufficient for him; and be thou an help to him from his enemies.

"Lord," Moses said, "Cause Reuben to prosper. May his tribe increase. Help him when he encounters the enemy." As the people of Israel marched through the wilderness and, again, as they will march into the Land of Promise, which tribe lead the way? Judah. *Judah* means "Praise." We enter into His gates with thanksgiving and into His courts with praise (Psalm 100:4). Praise is always the key.

All of these requests for Judah were indeed answered in the Lion of the tribe of Judah, in the Person of Jesus Christ (Matthew 1:2).

Deuteronomy 33:8 (a)
And of Levi he said, Let thy Thummim and thy Urim be with thy holy one . . .

"I don't know what to do. I don't know which way to go," we are prone to say. Even in these New Testament times, the Urim and the Thummim give us real understanding about finding God's will and getting His direction, for in whose care were the Urim and the Thummim? They were in the charge of the high priest (Numbers 27:21).

"I am the Way," said Jesus, our great High Priest. He didn't say, "I'll tell you the way," or, "I'll point you to the way." He said, "I *am* the Way" (John 14:6).

One of my tasks as a pastor and teacher is to remind people of this constantly. People come seeking an answer, asking for direction. But what they need to do is simply cling to Jesus every hour, every minute. And then, because He *is* the way, they'll end up in the right place.

At six months old, my granddaughter, Bailey, doesn't say, "Mommy, how do I get to the mall?" She just stays close to Amanda, and, believe me, she'll get there! Like Bailey, we can say to the Lord, "I'm not going to be anxious about what I should do tomorrow. I'm just going to abide in You, cling to You today, close to Your heart, right by Your side. And I know I'll end up exactly where I'm supposed to be."

Deuteronomy 33:8 (b)–11
. . . whom thou didst prove at Massah, and with whom thou didst strive at the waters of Meribah; Who said unto his father and to his mother, I have not seen him; neither did he acknowledge his brethren, nor knew his own children: for they have observed thy word, and kept thy covenant. They shall teach Jacob thy judgments, and Israel thy law: they shall put incense before thee, and whole burnt sacrifice upon thine altar. Bless, LORD, his substance, and accept the work of his hands: smite through the loins of them that rise against him, and of them that hate him, that they rise not again.

Those who tried to keep the Levites from their priestly duties were to be smitten.

Deuteronomy 33:12
And of Benjamin he said, The beloved of the LORD shall dwell in safety by him; and the LORD shall cover him all the day long, and he shall dwell between his shoulders.

The location of the tribe of Benjamin in the southern part of the nation was shaped like two shoulders—between which was the city of Jerusalem. This, then, is the first hint that, as dwelling place of the Lord, Jerusalem would be His Holy City.

Deuteronomy 33:13–17
And of Joseph he said, Blessed of the LORD be his land, for the precious things of heaven, for the dew, and for the deep that coucheth beneath, And for the precious fruits brought forth by the sun, and for the precious things put forth by the moon, And for the chief things of the ancient mountains, and for the precious things of the lasting hills, And for the precious things of the earth and fulness thereof, and for the good will of him that dwelt in the bush: let the blessing come upon the head of Joseph, and upon the top of the head of him that was separated from his brethren. His glory is like the firstling of his bullock, and his horns are like the horns of unicorns: with them he shall push the people together to the ends of the earth: and they are the ten thousands of Ephraim, and they are the thousands of Manasseh.

"May Joseph have glorious blessings from the land and from the fruit ripened by the sun."

Deuteronomy 33:18, 19
And of Zebulun he said, Rejoice, Zebulun, in thy going out; and, Issachar, in thy tents. They shall call the people unto the mountain; there they shall offer sacrifices of righteousness: for they shall suck of the abundance of the seas, and of treasures hid in the sand.

The land of the tribe of Zebulun extends to the coast at Haifa. Interestingly, it is said that after reading of tar in the Old Testament, J. D. Rockefeller chose to construct a massive pipeline from Iraq to Haifa, 1,000 miles away. When his Standard Oil Company struck oil, tankers would pump the oil, "the treasures hid in the sand," right to the seacoast of Zebulun—just as Moses prophesied.

Deuteronomy 33:20
And of Gad he said, Blessed be he that enlargeth Gad: he dwelleth as a lion, and teareth the arm with the crown of the head.

In 1 Chronicles 12:8, the men of Gad are likened unto lions because of their ferocity in battle.

Deuteronomy 33:21
And he provided the first part for himself, because there, in a portion of the lawgiver, was he seated; and he came with the heads of the people, he executed the justice of the LORD, and his judgments with Israel.

Gad got the best piece of property because he was willing to deal with problems. He executed justice. There's a real lesson in that for us. You see, under the inspiration of God's Spirit, Moses said that because lion-like Gad was willing to do what was necessary, he would get the best of the land. And the same is true for us. If, for example, as parents we choose to parent our kids rather than to be liked by them, in so doing, we will procure for our families a strong, stable, spiritual place for them to dwell.

Deuteronomy 33:22
And of Dan he said, Dan is a lion's whelp: he shall leap from Bashan.

Whereas Zebulun was a lion, Dan was a cub. Dan found the portion of land he was given too difficult, so he headed north, and inadvertently ended up in the worst place he could have chosen, in the place where all the invading armies came through and where paganism took root.

Deuteronomy 33:23
And of Naphtali he said, O Naphtali, satisfied with favour, and full with the blessing

of the LORD: possess thou the west and the south.

The Hebrew term "satisfied with favor" means "content." Naphtali was a tribe that was content—which is also the kind of tribe we are to be.

Deuteronomy 33:24, 25
And of Asher he said, Let Asher be blessed with children; let him be acceptable to his brethren, and let him dip his foot in oil. Thy shoes shall be iron and brass; and as thy days, so shall thy strength be.

The land given to Asher was shaped like a leg, with the "toe" located near Zebulun at Mt. Carmel. Although the reference to oil could very well be that of olive oil, due to the phrase "let him dip his foot in oil," this area is being explored as a potential oil field.

Deuteronomy 33:26, 27 (a)
There is none like unto the God of Jeshurun, who rideth upon the heaven in thy help, and in his excellency on the sky. The eternal God is thy refuge, and underneath are the everlasting arms . . .

Having finished the pronunciation of blessing upon the congregation of Israel, this great man of God reminds them again who their God is. If the sun, moon, and stars are the work of God's fingers (Psalm 8:3), what must be the power of His everlasting arms?

I can recall as a three-year-old in Portland when my dad would drive in to our driveway after work at the bank, I would scramble to the top of the wood box on the side of our house. After parking the car, he would walk to the wood box and, with outstretched arms, say, "Okay, Jon. Jump." And, although I was scared, I'd jump. He always caught me. Every time.

Moses is hoping the children of Israel will come to understand the same thing—that their Father has strong arms and that He will never let them fall.

Deuteronomy 33:27 (b)–29
. . . and he shall thrust out the enemy from before thee; and shall say, Destroy them. Israel then shall dwell in safety alone: the fountain of Jacob shall be upon a land of corn and wine; also his heavens shall drop down dew. Happy art thou, O Israel: who is like unto thee, O people saved by the LORD, the shield of thy help, and who is the sword of thy excellency! and thine enemies shall be found liars unto thee; and thou shalt tread upon their high places.

"You will be victorious," Moses said to the people, "because of the strength of your God."

34

Deuteronomy 34:1–5
And Moses went up from the plains of Moab unto the mountain of Nebo, to the top of Pisgah, that is over against Jericho. And the LORD shewed him all the land of Gilead, unto Dan, And all Naphtali, and the land of Ephraim, and Manasseh, and all the land of Judah, unto the utmost sea, And the south, and the plain of the valley of Jericho, the city of palm trees, unto Zoar. And the LORD said unto him, This is the land which I sware unto Abraham, unto Isaac, and unto Jacob, saying, I will give it unto thy seed: I have caused thee to see it with thine eyes, but thou shalt not go over thither. So Moses the servant of the LORD died there in the land of Moab, according to the word of the LORD.

Although Moses couldn't go into the Land, God gave Moses a supernatural sneak preview—to be added to centuries later when he would view it from atop the Mount of Transfiguration (Matthew 17).

Deuteronomy 34:6
And he buried him in a valley in the land of Moab, over against Beth-peor: but no man knoweth of his sepulchre unto this day.

Jude 9 tells us that when Moses was buried, the devil fought for his body. Why would the devil want the body of Moses? I believe it's because Moses will be one of the two witnesses of Revelation 11, calling down fire, preaching the truth, telling people about antichrist, sharing the gospel.

Deuteronomy 34:7–9
And Moses was an hundred and twenty years old when he died: his eye was not dim, nor his natural force abated. And the children of Israel wept for Moses in the plains of Moab thirty days: so the days of weeping and mourning for Moses were ended. And Joshua the son of Nun was full of the spirit of wisdom; for Moses had laid his hands upon him: and the children of Israel hearkened unto him, and did as the LORD commanded Moses.

That we know the events regarding the death of Moses means Moses was writing his own obituary. Some believe Joshua wrote this section. But I believe it was, in fact, Moses.

Deuteronomy 34:10–12
And there arose not a prophet since in Israel like unto Moses, whom the LORD knew face to face, In all the signs and the wonders, which the LORD sent him to do in the land of Egypt to Pharaoh, and to all his servants, and to all his land, And in all that mighty hand, and in all the great terror which Moses shewed in the sight of all Israel.

Stuck in prison, John sent messengers to ask Jesus if He was indeed the Messiah. If not, he would look for another. Jesus' answer to the messengers was for them to tell John how He had healed the blind, made the lame to walk, cleansed the leper, raised the dead. Then Jesus added, "And blessed is he who is not offended in Me." When John received this message, I wonder if he beat himself for his lack of faith. He had been so bold up to that point, I wonder if he felt his ministry was, after all, a failure.

Certainly Moses would be able to understand. Faithful for forty years, his obedience had faltered at a moment of frustration. Yet Moses knew the end of his story. John didn't. You see, right after his messengers left, Jesus called John the greatest man ever born (Matthew 11:11). But, unlike Moses, John never heard this.

So if you feel like a failure, like you've let the Lord down once too often, like He will never again be able to use you, remember that He sees you as perfect, robed in the righteousness of His Son (Isaiah 61:10). That makes we who are "least in the kingdom" greater even than John the Baptist (Matthew 11:11). Messengers may not tell you this, your prison walls may not confirm it, failure at Meribah may say otherwise—but you, dear saint are God's prize and His inheritance. And, as seen in the lives of Moses and John the Baptist, those God uses to the greatest degree are often the very ones who question their own effectiveness.

Press on, precious brother; be strong, dear sister. The Promised Land of the Spirit-filled life is yours for the taking. And the Promised Land of heaven is just around the bend.

JOSHUA

Background to Joshua

"I have come that you might have life and that you might have it more abundantly," Jesus declared (John 10:10). We who have been born again have life. We have eternal life—but do we have abundant life? It's wonderful and important to be saved. But there's more to the life of faith than simply being saved, for as He did His people, God not only takes us out of Egypt, which is a picture of the world. He desires to bring us into the Land of Promise.

Perhaps you've heard sermons on, or sung hymns about the Promised Land in reference to heaven. But as we make our way through the Book of Joshua, we will see that, although there is abundant fruit in the Promised Land, there are also battles to fight and wars to wage. Therefore, the Promised Land cannot speak of heaven, for in heaven, we will "learn war no more" (Isaiah 2:4).

> *Moreover, brethren, I would not that ye should be ignorant, how that all our fathers were under the cloud, and all passed through the sea; And were all baptized unto Moses in the cloud and in the sea; And did all eat the same spiritual meat; And did all drink the same spiritual drink: for they drank of that spiritual Rock that followed them: and that Rock was Christ. Now all these things happened unto them for ensamples: and they are written for our admonition, upon whom the ends of the world are come.* 1 Corinthians 10:1–4, 11

"Don't be ignorant of the fact that these Old Testament pictures were painted for our benefit," says Paul. "The Rock speaks of Christ. The manna speaks of spiritual nourishment. The parting of the Red Sea speaks of baptism." Here in the Book of Joshua, God's chosen people have been set free from the brutal bondage of Egypt just as we have been set free from our own sin and carnality. They have been baptized in the Red Sea just as we have been baptized in water. They have wandered for forty years in the dusty, dreary wilderness just as we have wondered and wandered through dry days in our own spiritual experience.

But now we see the people about to undergo a second baptism not in the Red Sea, but in the Jordan River. The parting of the Red Sea speaks of the water baptism of salvation. But the parting of the Jordan speaks of the baptism of the Holy Spirit that Jesus promised in Luke 24.

The baptism in the Holy Spirit can happen simultaneously with water baptism. It can happen simultaneously with salvation. But for most of us, although it can happen that way, it didn't happen that way. Most of us were born again and saved and thankful for that. But we found ourselves wandering in circles and confusion in the wilderness. At least that's what happened to me.

I was born again at a very young age and had devoted my life to the Lord. But in my late teens and early twenties, I began to realize that I was not experiencing the abundant life I was reading about in the Word. I knew something was missing. Then one day, when I was twenty-one, I was teaching the story of Jonah to about three hundred high-school kids. And in a watershed moment, during our last session together, the Lord seemed to hold up a mirror to me to let me see the condition of my own soul. And as He did, I realized I didn't care at all about the kids I was teaching. This realization was so devastating to me that after the conference was over, I got in my 1964 Ford Econoline van and drove all night up and down the coast. I loved the Lord. I was studying for the ministry. I had already been a youth pastor and a camp speaker. But I knew in my soul that there was a lack of power and a lack of love.

In the morning, I found myself driving into the parking lot of Calvary Chapel, the church I attended. "I've been involved in ministry," I said to a young pastor there. "But there's a sadness in my soul, a dryness in my spirit. Something's not right."

"You need the baptism of the Holy Spirit," he said. "Let me pray for you." So he laid hands on me and prayed in the Spirit. And as he did, I didn't go into some kind of a trance—but something happened in the deepest part of my soul and spirit. I began to pray just a few simple phrases in tongues and felt my spirit touched and warmed. I then went into the sanctuary, where I knelt and prayed for a few hours before I got into my van and drove back to my apartment a changed man.

Everything changed for me that day. From the way I understood grace and the way I looked at Romans to the way I worshiped and witnessed, everything was affected. I had told the Lord I felt called to the ministry, but couldn't go on with the dryness that was in my soul. "Either meet me or I'll take it as though You're guiding me in some other direction," I had said. And He met me because I was desperate. "Blessed are those who hunger and thirst after righteousness," Jesus said, "for they shall be filled" (Matthew 5:6).

There comes a moment when a man realizes that, although he's born again, he's tired of the wilderness. In the Book of Joshua, the people of Israel are at that very place. That's why I believe this study will be very enlightening and very exciting. The Book of Joshua deals with what it means to step into the Jordan after already being baptized in the Red Sea. The Book of Joshua deals with what it means to move into the Promised Land of the Spirit-filled life.

JOSHUA

1 **Joshua 1:1 (a)**
Now after the death of Moses the servant of the LORD it came to pass, that the LORD spake unto Joshua the son of Nun . . .

Moses was dead. A representative, a picture, a type of the Law, Moses brought the people to the edge of the Promised Land, but it would be Joshua, whose name is the Old Testament name for *Jesus,* who would actually bring them in to the Promised Land.

In Numbers 13:8, we read that Joshua's name was originally Hoshea. *Hoshea* means "salvation." Joshua was indeed saved when the blood was applied to the house of Nun during the Passover. As firstborn, he would have died otherwise. So his name, "Salvation," was an appropriate one. But Moses changed his name from *Hoshea* to *Joshua,* from "Salvation" to "Jehovah is Salvation," signifying that Jehovah alone brings salvation.

Joshua 1:1 (b)
. . . Moses' minister . . .

The word *minister* means "servant." We see Joshua serving Moses in Exodus 17 when Moses ordered him to lead the Israelites in battle against the Amalekites. We see Joshua serving Moses in Exodus 24 as he accompanied Moses part way up Mount Sinai. We see Joshua serving Moses in Numbers 13 as one of the twelve Moses sent to spy out the Land. As seen in the life of Joshua, to minister means to serve. Somehow, the passage of time has made the ministry an exalted position when in fact it is simply one of service, exemplified no more clearly than in the life of Jesus, the One who came to be the servant of all (John 13).

Joshua 1:1 (c)–3
. . . saying, Moses my servant is dead; now therefore arise, go over this Jordan, thou, and all this people, unto the land which I do give to them, even to the children of Israel. Every place that the sole of your foot shall tread upon, that have I given unto you, as I said unto Moses.

God didn't say, "I *will* give you the land upon which you walk." He said, "I *have* given it to you." The same is true today. Concerning the things of God, whenever you choose to step out and engage your "sole," that land is already yours. It's a matter of possessing your possession. It's a matter of appropriation. Where do you want to put your soul? Where do you want to plant your foot and say, "I believe You for this, Lord. I'm stepping out in this. I'm going after this"?

I read about a man who was arrested in a futile attempt to rob a convenience store. The amazing part of the story is that the gun he used was actually a Civil War-era pistol worth $23,000. He had robbed the store for $125 when all the time, right there in his hand, he held a $23,000 treasure.

Isn't that like us? We strive for peanuts when the Lord has grapes for us the size of bowling balls. The Lord says, "I've already given you the land. It's already a done deal. It's just a matter of how much of it you want. I won't take you any farther than you choose. But I'll take you as far as you want to go." How far did the Israelites go? The Promised Land covers 30,000 square miles. At the height of their power, in Solomon's reign, the Israelites claimed 3,000 square miles. They took one-tenth of what God had already given them. And I can't help but wonder if we have even done that.

Concerning the Spirit-filled life and the appropriation of the power of the Holy Ghost, many people say, "If the Lord wants to empower me and baptize me, I'm open." But in Genesis 8, we see Noah on the ark, with the dove—a symbol of the Holy Spirit—circling overhead. Noah stretched out his hand and brought the dove in unto him. I believe the Spirit of God is looking for a person, a people, a congregation to land upon. But this will not happen through passivity. Rather, like Noah, He responds to those who see the opportunity and extend their hand to pull Him in unto them.

Here in Joshua 1:3, the Lord says, "The land is already yours. It's up to you how far you want to go, how deep you want to be."

Joshua 1:4, 5 (a)
From the wilderness and this Lebanon even unto the great river, the river Euphrates, all the land of the Hittites, and unto the great sea toward the going down of the sun, shall be your coast. There shall not any man be able to stand before thee all the days of thy life . . .

God goes on to tell Joshua that no one would be able to stop him, that there would be no limitation as he led the congregation.

Joshua 1:5 (b)–7 (a)
. . . as I was with Moses, so I will be with thee: I will not fail thee, nor forsake thee. Be strong and of a good courage: for unto this people shalt thou divide for an inheritance the land, which I sware unto their

fathers to give them. Only be thou strong and very courageous . . .

Joshua could only be strong and very courageous "not by might, nor by power, but by God's spirit" (Zechariah 4:6). Jesus, our Greater than Joshua, was Himself baptized in the Spirit when, following His baptism in the Jordan, the Holy Spirit descended upon Him in the form of a dove (Matthew 3:16). The powerful works He did were done in obedience to the Father's direction and through the power of the Spirit upon Him. This means that what Jesus did is a model for you and me.

I didn't know this for many years. "Of course Jesus fed thousands, healed lepers, and walked on water," I thought. "He's Jesus." But my entire understanding of the ministry of my Master changed when I understood that, according to Philippians 2, Jesus laid aside His power when He became a Man and instead relied on the same Spirit available to me.

Joshua 1:7 (b), 8 (a)
. . . that thou mayest observe to do according to all the law, which Moses my servant commanded thee: turn not from it to the right hand or to the left, that thou mayest prosper whithersoever thou goest. This book of the law shall not depart out of thy mouth . . .

God didn't tell Joshua that His Word was not to depart out of his hand or out of his back pocket, but that it was not to depart out of his *mouth.*

Joshua 1:8 (b)
. . . but thou shalt meditate therein day and night . . .

The word *meditate* simply means "to mutter." Thus, biblical meditation consists of speaking the Scriptures over and over. It is not a matter of thinking about the Scriptures because merely thinking about them allows our minds to wander. Meditation means to speak verbally, quoting Scriptures audibly, talking to others about them constantly.

Joshua 1:8 (c)
. . . that thou mayest observe to do according to all that is written therein: for then thou shalt make thy way prosperous, and then thou shalt have good success.

Prosperity, success, and the abundant life are hallmarks of the Spirit-filled life. And the Spirit is inextricably linked to the Word . . .

> Let the word of Christ dwell in you richly in all wisdom; teaching and admonishing one another in psalms and hymns and spiritual songs, singing with grace in your hearts to the Lord. And whatsoever ye do in word or deed, do all in the name of the Lord Jesus, giving thanks to God and the Father by him. Wives, submit yourselves unto your own husbands, as it is fit in the Lord. Husbands, love your wives, and be not bitter against them. Children, obey your parents in all things: for this is well pleasing unto the Lord. Fathers, provoke not your children to anger, lest they be discouraged. Servants, obey in all things your masters according to the flesh; not with eyeservice, as menpleasers; but in singleness of heart, fearing God. Colossians 3:16–22

The result of letting the Word of Christ dwell in us will be that we'll speak to ourselves and to each other with psalms and hymns. We'll be submitted to each other. We'll be the kind of husband, wife, or child we ought to be and the kind of worker that honors God.

> And be not drunk with wine, wherein is excess; but be filled with the Spirit; Speaking to yourselves in psalms and hymns and spiritual songs, singing and making melody in your heart to the Lord; Giving thanks always for all things unto God and the Father in the name of our Lord Jesus Christ; Submitting yourselves one to another in the fear of God. Wives, submit yourselves unto your own husbands, as unto the Lord . . . Husbands, love your wives, even as Christ also loved the church, and gave himself for it . . . Children, obey your parents in the Lord: for this is right . . . And, ye fathers, provoke not your children to wrath: but bring them up in the nurture and admonition of the Lord. Servants, be obedient to them that are your masters according to the flesh, with fear and trembling, in singleness of your heart, as unto Christ; Not with eyeservice, as menpleasers; but as the servants of Christ, doing the will of God from the heart. Ephesians 5:18–22, 25; 6:1, 4–6

The result of being filled with the Spirit is that we'll speak to ourselves with psalms and hymns. We'll be submitted to each other. We'll be the kind of husband, wife, or child we ought to be and the kind of worker that honors God. In other words, being filled with the Spirit and being filled with the Word are linked together.

Spirit-filled people or congregations are those who meditate in the Word, devote themselves to the study of the Word, and gain more understanding about the Word. And as that happens, they are continually filled with the Spirit in fresh ways. I used to think a believer was either a Spirit-filled person or a student of the Word. Not so. Jesus said the Father seeks those who will worship Him in Spirit *and* in truth (John 4:23, 24).

At the very beginning of his ministry, Joshua is told to meditate in the Word day and night because that is the key to appropriating the power of the Spirit he would need to accomplish that which God had called him to do.

For topical study of Joshua 1:8, see "Meditation: The Key to Prosperity," turn to page 640.

Joshua 1:9–11
Have not I commanded thee? Be strong and of a good courage; be not afraid, neither be thou dismayed: for the LORD thy God is with thee whithersoever thou goest. Then Joshua commanded the officers of the people, saying, Pass through the host, and command the people, saying, Prepare you victuals; for within three days ye shall pass over this Jordan, to go in to possess the land, which the LORD your God giveth you to possess it.

"Three days from now, we're crossing over the Jordan," Joshua told the people.

For me, it wasn't three days before I crossed the Jordan, but three years. For three years, I wrestled with the question of whether baptism in the Holy Spirit was theologically correct. But I'm glad I went through those three years because I know the arguments of those who don't believe in the baptism of the Spirit, of those who don't believe the gifts of the Spirit are for today. If you're going through a time of questioning presently, don't despair. The Lord will use it to prepare you just as He did the children of Israel.

Joshua 1:12–15
And to the Reubenites, and to the Gadites, and to half the tribe of Manasseh, spake Joshua, saying, Remember the word which Moses the servant of the LORD commanded you, saying, The LORD your God hath given you rest, and hath given you this land. Your wives, your little ones, and your cattle, shall remain in the land which Moses gave you on this side Jordan; but ye shall pass before your brethren armed, all the mighty men of valour, and help them; Until the LORD have given your brethren rest, as he hath given you, and they also have possessed the land which the LORD your God giveth them: then ye shall return unto the land of your possession, and enjoy it, which Moses the LORD's servant gave you on this side Jordan toward the sunrising.

As seen in Numbers 32, the tribes of Reuben, Gad, and half of the tribe of Manasseh said, "We don't want to go into the Promised Land. We like it here on the east side of the Jordan. It's a great place for our families and cattle, a great place to retire."

"If you want to stay where it's seemingly comfortable, that's okay," Moses said. "But when the rest go into the Promised Land, your soldiers must help fight the battle."

Tragically, the place that seemed safe proved to be unsafe, for in Luke 8, we see that it was the Gadarenes, those of the tribe of Gad, whose land was filled with pigs and demons and who asked Jesus to leave.

Joshua 1:16–18
And they answered Joshua, saying, All that thou commandest us we will do, and whithersoever thou sendest us, we will go. According as we hearkened unto Moses in all things, so will we hearken unto thee: only the LORD thy God be with thee, as he was with Moses. Whosoever he be that doth rebel against thy commandment, and will not hearken unto thy words in all that thou commandest him, he shall be put to death: only be strong and of a good courage.

"We're with you, Joshua," the people of Israel said. "We'll go where you send us. We'll do what you tell us. But we have one requirement of you. That is, you must be strong and courageous."

Our Greater than Joshua, Jesus Christ, is strong and courageous. Indeed. Let's go with Him into the Promised Land of the Spirit-filled life. The choice is yours and mine to step out and move in to the promise of the Father to an even greater degree.

MEDITATION: THE KEY TO PROSPERITY

A Topical Study of JOSHUA 1:8

Poised to enter the Promised Land, the people of Israel were about to turn a new page in their history. And a new man had been raised up to lead them.

In Joshua 1, we see God say to this man, "This book of the Law shall not depart out of thy mouth. But thou shalt meditate therein day and night that thou mayest observe, or literally, in order that you'll be able to observe, to do all that is commanded therein."

God promises to Joshua—and to all those who choose to follow in his footsteps—prosperity and success if he meditated in His Word. Most people have the mistaken idea that meditation is silent contemplation. The problem with silent meditation, however, is that our minds wander very easily. We start thinking about a verse or a spiritual principle, but before we know it, we're thinking about what we're going to have for lunch. Audibly speaking the Word, however, keeps our minds on track.

For example, Joshua 1:7 says, "Be strong and very courageous." Therefore, if I want to have good success, if I want to prosper, I am to go throughout my day, muttering, "Lord, You want me to be strong. You want me to have courage. Thank You for the strength and courage You give." That's what biblical meditation is. Biblical meditation is simply taking a phrase, a verse, or a small portion of Scripture and muttering it over and over.

People might look at you and say, "What's the mutter with you, anyway?" That's okay! Let them think what they may. When I'm driving in my car, walking down the road, or lying on my bed, I'm to be speaking Scripture. God's Word is not to depart out of my mouth.

Most Christians look at their Bibles like a fax machine through which God sends faxes to them one after another. The Bible is not a fax machine, gang. It's a cell phone. It allows us to converse with our Father. I'm to speak Scripture back to God and to my own heart. If you don't talk to your Bible, your Bible won't talk to you. A lot of believers don't know this. They read their Bibles—and there's a place for reading. They study their Bibles—and that's also commanded. But there's more than reading and studying. It's called meditation—where you're talking to the Lord, where day and night a chunk of the Word is in your mind and on your lips, flowing from you and taking root deep within you.

In addition to being like a cell phone, the Word is like a telescope. The telescope is not to look at. It's to look through. Look through a telescope and a whole new world opens up. This is the way a lot of people look at their Bibles. They read them for doctrine and history. Yet while that's all well and good, the Word was given to us in order that we might look through it to see our Father in heaven.

The second Hebrew word for meditation literally means "to chew the cud." This means you come to a Bible study on Sunday or Wednesday night and you don't just go your way, but you take that which the Lord put on your heart and whispered in your ear and chew on it as you drive in the car, walk down the road, lay in your bed. You take what you hear and extract every bit of nutrition available. Meditation is different from reading the Bible. Reading produces information. Meditation produces transformation.

Why does God want us to meditate? In Proverbs 23, we read, "As a man thinks in his heart, so is he." In other words, what you mutter to yourself, what you think on, is what you become. Therefore, God says, "I want you to mutter My Word. I want you to think about Scripture because you'll become like Me.'"

"That sounds good," you might be thinking. "But I'm too busy to meditate."

Are you busier than Joshua? He had to lead three million people into a land they would have to fight their way through. If there was ever a man who didn't have time to meditate night and day, it was Joshua. Yet God said to the busiest man on the planet at that time, "Take time to meditate on Scripture day and night. If you do, you will be prosperous and you will have good success."

Maybe you think you can't meditate because you're busy looking for a husband or wife. But what was Isaac doing when God brought him his bride? He was meditating in the field in the evening (Genesis 24:63).

Maybe you think you can't meditate because you're busy raising a family. Certainly Mary could have said she was too busy. But she was one who pondered and meditated upon what she heard from the Lord (Luke 2:19).

Maybe you're a pastor, busy taking care of the stuff of the church. Yet Paul said to Timothy, a pastor, "I know you have many responsibilities. But don't neglect the importance of meditation" (1 Timothy 4:15).

David, the one the Bible calls a man after God's own heart, prospered and had good success to an incredible degree. Therefore, it shouldn't be surprising that he talks about meditation more than anyone else in Scripture . . .

- "Blessed is the man that walks not in the counsel of the ungodly," David wrote (Psalm 1). This means you can forget about all the books, tapes, and seminars given by people who don't know God.
- "The happy man's delight is in the law of the Lord. And in His law he meditates day and night." In other words, the Word is integrated into his soul.
- "He shall be like a tree planted by the river of water that brings forth fruit in its season. And its leaf shall not wither." When others dry up because of the drought that inevitably comes, when others shrivel and fade away as the years go by, the one who meditates is more engaged than ever in the things of God.
- "And whatsoever he does shall prosper." The one who chews on the Word and speaks it out will prosper in whatever he does.

In the seasons when I have meditated on the Word, my leaf doesn't wither. Fruit inevitably abounds. I'm successful and prosper. In the seasons when I mistakenly thought I was too busy to meditate, I have found myself withering, being blown about, fruitless. In other words, I have found what David said to be absolutely true.

"Let not My Word depart from your mouth," God said to Joshua. And He says the same thing to us. Meditate on the Word. And as you do, you will prosper and have good success. Keep in the Word more than ever before. Stay in the Word. Learn from the Word. Be involved in Bible study. But don't stop there. As you take it in, speak it out. Chew on it. Meditate on the Word as you drive in traffic and as you walk down the road, as you mow the lawn and as you make dinner. Mutter it over and over so that your mind stays focused. And prosperity and success will be the result. Guaranteed!

2

Joshua 2:1 (a)
And Joshua the son of Nun sent out of Shittim two men to spy secretly . . .

Joshua, a picture of Jesus, is about to take the Israelites across the Jordan River into the Land of Promise. But before he does, he does something that reminds me of what Jesus did. That is, he sends two men to go before him into the Land. In Luke 10, we read that Jesus sent seventy men out in groups of two to go before Him, to be His witnesses. The two men Joshua sends think they're going to spy. But in reality, they'll be witnesses. The same is true of you and me as well. We think we're schoolteachers, insurance salesmen, or stockbrokers. But we're not. We're undercover agents for the kingdom. God has planted us in those positions to be His witnesses. The two men Joshua sent out were the first of the Israelites to experience the Promised Land. And it is as we witness that we will experience it as well.

Joshua 2:1 (b)
. . . saying, Go view the land, even Jericho . . .

Surrounded by at least one massive wall—and very possibly two according to recent archaeological findings—Jericho was a seemingly impenetrable city.

Joshua 2:1 (c)
. . . And they went, and came into an harlot's house, named Rahab, and lodged there.

Although the Hebrew word translated "harlot" can also refer to a female innkeeper, each time Rahab's name appears in the New Testament, it is in conjunction with a word in Greek that can only be translated "harlot." Why did these men go into a harlot's house? Most likely it was because, as enemies in the gated city of Jericho, Rahab's house was the only place they could hide in anonymity.

Joshua 2:2
And it was told the king of Jericho, saying, Behold, there came men in hither to night of the children of Israel to search out the country.

While Rahab's house was the safest place for the men of Israel to be, it wasn't safe enough. Word leaked out anyway.

Joshua 2:3–6
And the king of Jericho sent unto Rahab, saying, Bring forth the men that are come to thee, which are entered into thine house: for they be come to search out all the country. And the woman took the two men, and hid them, and said thus, There came men unto me, but I wist not whence they were: And it came to pass about the time of shutting of the gate, when it was dark, that the men went out: whither the men went I wot not: pursue after them quickly; for ye shall overtake them. But she had brought them up to the roof of the house, and hid them with the stalks of flax, which she had laid in order upon the roof.

Flax was commonly laid on the flat roofs to dry. So Rahab hid the two men under the flax.

Joshua 2:7–11
And the men pursued after them the way to Jordan unto the fords: and as soon as they which pursued after them were gone out, they shut the gate. And before they were laid down, she came up unto them upon the roof; And she said unto the men, I know that the LORD hath given you the land, and that your terror is fallen upon us, and that all the inhabitants of the land faint because of you. For we have heard how the LORD dried up the water of the Red sea for you, when ye came out of Egypt; and what ye did unto the two kings of the Amorites, that were on the other side Jordan, Sihon and

Og, whom ye utterly destroyed. And as soon as we had heard these things, our hearts did melt, neither did there remain any more courage in any man, because of you: for the LORD your God, he is God in heaven above, and in earth beneath.

As a harlot, Rahab was in a degenerate position. But then she had a dramatic conversion. She had faith in God, as evidenced by her belief that God had given the land to the Israelites (v. 9). She knew the facts about God, as evidenced by her knowledge of what He had done for His people (v. 10). And she feared God, as evidenced by the condition of her heart (v. 11).

Rahab's dramatic conversion was proved by a definite confession. In letting down the scarlet cord, she was essentially confessing to God that she was wholly and completely dependent upon His blood for her salvation. Secondly, Rahab confessed not only to God but before men when she said to the spies, "for the Lord your God, he is God in heaven above and in earth beneath" (v. 11). Romans 10:9 tells us that in order to be saved, a man must believe in his heart and confess with his mouth. And Rahab did just that.

In addition to Rahab's degenerate position, dramatic conversion, and definite confession, notice her dynamic commendation. In Hebrews 11, a small number of people are singled out as heroes in God's "hall of faith." Isaiah didn't make it. Jeremiah didn't make it. Daniel didn't make it. Elisha didn't make it. But one who did make it into the hall of faith was Rahab the prostitute. Rahab's name appears again in James 2 as an example of what it means to have faith that is real. But the most important place Rahab's name appears is in Matthew 1, as she takes her place with only three other women in the genealogy of Jesus Christ.

Rahab is honored by James as an example of faith. She's inducted into the hall of faith of Hebrews. She's in the lineage of Jesus. But there's a problem—for not only is she a harlot, but she's a liar. The Bible says we are to honor the king. She lied to his face. The Bible says we are not to bear false witness. She certainly did. How, then, could Rahab be so exalted?

In 2 Corinthians 5, we read that every believer will stand before the judgment seat of Christ—not to be judged for our sin because our sin was washed away by the blood Jesus shed on the Cross of Calvary—but to be rewarded for what we've done. In 1 Corinthians 3, we read that all of our works will be tried by fire wherein the wood, hay, and stubble—that which was done with mixed motives and carnality—will burn away, leaving only gold, silver, and precious stones. Revelation 1 describes Jesus as One whose eyes are like a burning fire. Therefore, I believe it is as He looks on us that all the stuff that's polluted and defiled by mixed motives and carnality will evaporate and disappear.

What will be left? Based on the story of Rahab, I suggest what's left will be a lot more than you think. You see, in Jeremiah 15, the Lord said, "Jeremiah, you will be My spokesman if you can extract the valuable from the vile." We tend to notice only the vile. Not so the Lord. He does the opposite. He pokes around in the pile of our rubble and stubble and finds the jewels. We would call Rahab a harlot and a liar. Not God. Simply because she believed in Him, He calls her a hero.

We have a tendency to listen to Satan who perches on our shoulder, saying, "You're not going to be rewarded for that. Your motive wasn't pure. Your thoughts weren't right. Your attitude was amiss."

But God would say, "I specialize in extracting the precious from the vile. Oh, I know there's all kinds of weakness even in your best deeds and ministry. But I will find the gold, silver, and precious stones others don't see even in your simply giving a cup of cold water in My name" (Matthew 10:42).

Joshua 2:12, 13
Now therefore, I pray you, swear unto me by the LORD, since I have shewed you kindness, that ye will also shew kindness unto my father's house, and give me a true token: And that ye will save alive my father, and my mother, and my brethren, and my sisters, and all that they have, and deliver our lives from death.

"Save us," said Rahab. "We don't want to be destroyed. We believe in your God. We know He's given you our land."

Joshua 2:14–16
And the men answered her, Our life for yours, if ye utter not this our business. And it shall be, when the LORD hath given us the land, that we will deal kindly and truly with thee. Then she let them down by a cord through the window: for her house was upon the town wall, and she dwelt upon the wall. And she said unto them, Get you to the mountain, lest the pursuers meet you; and hide yourselves there three days, until the pursuers be returned: and afterward may ye go your way.

The mountains to which Rahab refers were to the west. The Jordan River was to the east. So as Rahab sent the king's men east, she sent the two spies west to hide for three days before they would eventually travel east to return to the camp of Israel.

Joshua 2:17
And the men said unto her, We will be blameless of this thine oath which thou hast made us swear.

The spies told Rahab she would indeed be spared.

Joshua 2:18, 19
Behold, when we come into the land, thou shalt bind this line of scarlet thread in the window which thou didst let us down by: and thou shalt bring thy father, and thy mother, and thy brethren, and all thy father's household, home unto thee. And it shall be, that whosoever shall go out of the doors of thy house into the street, his blood shall be upon his head, and we will be guiltless: and whosoever shall be with thee in the house, his blood shall be on our head, if any hand be upon him.

Rahab was to keep her family in the house and hang a scarlet cord from her window. In this way, her family would be saved in the day Israel conquered Jericho.

Joshua 2:20, 21 (a)
And if thou utter this our business, then we will be quit of thine oath which thou hast made us to swear. And she said, According unto your words, so be it. And she sent them away, and they departed: and she bound the scarlet line . . .

In Rahab's day, ropes were made not of hemp like our ropes but of flax. Flax also was the material from which linen was made. This means that the Israelites on the roof, the priests wearing their priestly garments, and Rahab the harlot were all covered with the same material. They were all covered with flax. The same is still true today. The blood of Jesus Christ covers believing saints and sinners alike. We are saved, covered, and hidden by the righteousness of Christ so freely given to us (Colossians 3:3).

Joshua 2:21 (b)
. . . in the window.

Rahab would be saved by letting down a scarlet cord. In these days, prostitutes would paint their windowsills bright red. Therefore, by hanging a scarlet cord over her red windowsill, Rahab would be forming a cross. The same image that saved the people of Israel in the Passover when they applied blood to the top, sides, and bottom of their doors, would save the pagans in Jericho. Whether to a Jew or a Gentile, the message is the same. It is the Cross that saves from destruction.

Joshua 2:22–24
And they went, and came unto the mountain, and abode there three days, until the pursuers were returned: and the pursuers sought them throughout all the way, but found them not. So the two men returned, and descended from the mountain, and passed over, and came to Joshua the son of Nun, and told him all things that befell them: And they said unto Joshua, Truly the LORD hath delivered into our hands all the land; for even all the inhabitants of the country do faint because of us.

Even as the seventy apostles returned to Jesus amazed, saying, "Lord, even the demons are subject to us in Your name" (Luke 10:17), so Joshua's witnessing spies returned amazed by what they had seen. That's always the way it is. Whenever we set out to witness to someone else, we are witnessed to by God's power and provision. Conversely, in failing to witness, we miss out on so much.

There are people on my street I have never talked to directly about Jesus Christ because I've listened to Satan's lie that says they don't want to hear, that they're not ready, or that they're too busy. The story of Rahab says just the opposite. "Where have you been?" she asked the spies. "We've heard about what your god has done."

Isaiah 14:16 says that when we see Satan, we're going to look at him narrowly—or squint at him—saying, "Is this the one that terrorized the world? *This* is the one who intimidated us? *This* is the one we believed when he told us our friends, family, and neighbors didn't want to hear about Jesus?"

The power of the Holy Spirit is like electricity. It won't enter something from which it can't exit. We want the power of the Holy Spirit. The question is, will there be a place for it to go? When we witness, the power of the Spirit surges through us. There is unbelievable joy in sharing the gospel. A lot of believers go from meeting to meeting looking for some "Holy Ghost high" because they're not witnessing. They go to this convention and that seminar—and the high lasts for a week or two. But after that, they're back in the wilderness because the Holy Ghost was given for the sole purpose of empowering us to share with the Rahabs around us the Good News of the gospel.

When we say, "Lord, I'm tired of wandering in the wilderness," He baptizes us in the Jordan and empowers us to be His witnesses. When we say, "I want to share the plan of salvation with my secretary. Empower me," or, "I want to talk to my buddy about You, Lord. Make me bold," we'll be empowered in ways we never could have imagined.

How long has it been since you've shared the gospel, the plan of salvation, the scarlet cord with someone who's not a believer? By faith, receive the power to be a witness. Awaiting you is a land of milk and honey, fruit and abundance. And you get there by going in as a witness. It's time to cross over the Jordan into the Promised Land of the Spirit-filled life. Come join us on our journey.

3 There was excitement in the air and anticipation in their hearts. At long last, they were about to enter the land of their destiny, the Land of Promise. The congregation of three million could smell the fruit and see the greenery. But first they had to go through a second baptism as they crossed the Jordan.

Joshua 3:1 (a)
And Joshua rose early in the morning . . .

Here, Joshua arises early in the day just as our Greater than Joshua did (Mark 1:35). Isaiah prophesied that Messiah would rise morning by morning that He might hear from the Father concerning what He was to do, what He was to say, where He was to go (Isaiah 50:4).

Joshua 3:1 (b), 2
. . . and they removed from Shittim, and came to Jordan, he and all the children of Israel, and lodged there before they passed over. And it came to pass after three days, that the officers went through the host.

Following three days of preparation, it was time for the people of Israel to move off the banks of the Jordan and into the Land of Promise. Time spent in preparation for the baptism of the Holy Spirit—of which the crossing of the Jordan speaks—is time well spent.

Of the believers worshiping the Lord and speaking in tongues, some said, "Those guys must be drunk."

"They're not drunk," Peter answered. "This is that which was spoken by the prophet Joel" (Acts 2:15). Peter then quoted Joel who said, "In the last days, I will pour out My spirit upon all flesh. And your sons and daughters shall prophesy. Your young men shall see visions, your old men shall dream dreams" (Joel 2:28–32).

It's not a waste of time to wait for three days, three months, or even three years on the bank of the Jordan if, like Peter, you can say, "I'm not simply caught up in an emotion or seeking an experience, but I understand the biblical foundation and base for the direction into which I'm moving."

Joshua 3:3
And they commanded the people, saying, When ye see the ark of the covenant of the LORD your God, and the priests the Levites bearing it, then ye shall remove from your place, and go after it.

"When you see the presence of God move, go after it," the officers of the congregation said. I like that! Our God is on the move. And we must be those who go after Him.

Joshua 3:4
Yet there shall be a space between you and it, about two thousand cubits by measure: come not near unto it, that ye may know the way by which ye must go: for ye have not passed this way heretofore.

When they saw the ark move, the Israelites were to follow it. Yet they were to follow at a distance of approximately half a mile. In this, it's as if God was saying, "Follow Me, but don't push Me."

People say, "I'm going to have the same experience that he or she or they had." God, however, wants to take us where we've never been before. Therefore, it's the wise man or woman who says, "Lord, I want Your anointing. And I'm going to give You space to work it out any way you choose."

Joshua 3:5
And Joshua said unto the people, Sanctify yourselves for to morrow the LORD will do wonders among you.

The word "sanctify" is *quodosh* in Hebrew. It means "to set apart" or "to prepare." If you filled a glass full of rocks and then attempted to pour a pitcher of water into it, the amount of water that could be poured in would be limited by the rocks in the glass. If you really wanted more water in the glass, the key wouldn't be to keep pouring more water because it would just spill out. The key would be to remove the rocks.

The same thing is true spiritually. A lot of people are trying to be filled with the Spirit when in reality they need to be emptied of sin. They need to say, "Search my heart, Lord. Show me the things that are restricting the flow of Your Spirit. Show me the rocks."

Joshua 3:6, 7
And Joshua spake unto the priests, saying, Take up the ark of the covenant, and pass over before the people. And they took up the ark of the covenant, and went before the people. And the LORD said unto Joshua, This day will I begin to magnify thee in the sight of all Israel, that they may know that, as I was with Moses, so I will be with thee.

Joshua was magnified in the sight of Israel the day he crossed the Jordan. So it was when our Greater than Joshua, Jesus Christ, was baptized in the Jordan that God said, "This is My beloved Son in whom I am well pleased" (Matthew 3:17). Empowered with the Spirit, Jesus' public ministry began at that point.

Joshua 3:8
And thou shalt command the priests that bear the ark of the covenant, saying, When ye are come to the brink of the water of Jordan, ye shall stand still in Jordan.

Historically, the Jordan River was usually one hundred feet wide except during the fall when it would be one mile wide. The story before us taking place in the fall, it was a formidable river the Israelites were commanded to cross.

Joshua 3:9, 10
And Joshua said unto the children of Israel, Come hither, and hear the words of the LORD your God. And Joshua said, Hereby ye shall know that the living God is among you, and that he will without fail drive out from before you the Canaanites, and the Hittites, and the Hivites, and the Perizzites, and the Girgashites, and the Amorites, and the Jebusites.

The Canaanites, Hittities, Hivites, Perizzites, Girgashites, Amorites, and Jebusites would be overcome by God's might through the Israelites.

Josh 3:11–14 (a)
Behold, the ark of the covenant of the Lord of all the earth passeth over before you into Jordan. Now therefore take you twelve men out of the tribes of Israel, out of every tribe a man. And it shall come to pass, as soon as the soles of the feet of the priests that bear the ark of the LORD, the Lord of all the earth, shall rest in the waters of Jordan, that the waters of Jordan shall be cut off from the waters that come down from above; and they shall stand upon an heap . . .

When the priests and representatives from each tribe put their feet into the river, the water would divide. Forty years previously, when the children of Israel crossed the Red Sea, the water parted before they stepped in (Exodus 14). But not this time. When it comes to the issues of the Spirit, we're to step in by faith.

"But what if hands are laid upon me and I seek the Lord's power aggressively, yet nothing happens? I'll feel like a big drip," we say. So we stay on the bank where it's safe and dry—real dry, dusty dry, wilderness dry.

Why doesn't God part the water first? I'm convinced it's because the language of eternity is faith. This life is only eighty years long at best. So God uses every opportunity to teach us to see and hear with the eyes and ears of faith. "Step out. Step in. Step up in faith," He says. "And watch and see what I'll do."

Joshua 3:14 (b), 15
. . . And it came to pass, when the people removed from their tents, to pass over Jordan, and the priests bearing the ark of the covenant before the people; And as they that bare the ark were come unto Jordan, and the feet of the priests that bare the ark were dipped in the brim of the water (for Jordan overfloweth all his banks all the time of harvest).

The Israelites weren't commanded to step into a trickling stream but into a raging river. But how could it have been otherwise? In reference to the Holy Ghost, Jesus said, "If any man thirst, let him come unto Me and drink. And out of his innermost being shall gush forth torrents of living water" (see John 7:37, 38). Thus, it's appropriate that, as a symbol of the power and presence of the Holy Spirit, the Jordan would have been a roaring river.

Joshua 3:16
That the waters which came down from above stood and rose up upon an heap very far from the city Adam, that is beside Zaretan: and those that came down toward the sea of the plain, even the salt sea, failed, and were cut off: and the people passed over right against Jericho.

For the Jordan to part at the point the priests stepped in, God actually built a supernatural dam nineteen miles upriver. This means that because Joshua and the people of Israel couldn't see that far, God was working out of sight. And He still works that way today. That's why He says, "Trust Me. Don't walk by sight. Walk by faith. I'm doing things nineteen miles upriver that you can't see."

Joshua 3:17
And the priests that bare the ark of the covenant of the LORD stood firm on dry ground in the midst of Jordan, and all the Israelites passed over on dry ground, until all the people were passed clean over Jordan.

The priests stepped in and said, "We're not leaving until all have passed over." And they stood firm while three million people passed through the Jordan. They stood until the work was done.

Evangelist D. L. Moody locked himself in a hotel room in New York City for three and a half days, saying, "I'm not coming out of this room until I know the power of the Spirit has come upon me." On the fourth day, God overwhelmed and overpowered Him to such a degree that he knew without a doubt that he was empowered to do the work God had called him to do.

As I read the Book of Joshua, I say, "Lord, I don't want to miss out on anything You have ordained for me."

Has there been a moment, a time when you stepped in and stood firm until you knew the Holy Spirit had come upon you? If you're not sure, don't miss chapter 4.

4 The apostle Paul proclaimed that the three greatest and most important components of life are faith, hope, and love. In the Book of Joshua, we see the people had hearts of hope in chapter 2 when the spies came back and said, "Truly the Lord has delivered the Land into our hands." In chapter 3, they took steps of faith as they put the soles of their feet into the Jordan River, believing God would meet them in the process. And here in chapter 4, we see the third component—a picture of love . . .

Joshua 4:1
And it came to pass, when all the people were clean passed over Jordan, that the LORD spake unto Joshua, saying,

The Israelites had passed over the Jordan River. The illustration is that they had been "baptized" in the Spirit. How do we know if we're truly Spirit-filled? Is speaking in tongues the sign? Although speaking in tongues is a wonderful tool in the toolbox of the believer, I don't believe speaking in tongues is proof one has been filled with the Spirit. Rather, I believe the proof is seen in the chapter before us . . .

Joshua 4:2–7
Take you twelve men out of the people, out of every tribe a man, And command ye them, saying, Take you hence out of the midst of Jordan, out of the place where the priests' feet stood firm, twelve stones, and ye shall carry them over with you, and leave them in the lodging place, where ye shall lodge this night. Then Joshua called the twelve men, whom he had prepared of the children of Israel, out of every tribe a man: And Joshua said unto them, Pass over before the ark of the LORD your God into the midst of Jordan, and take ye up every man of you a stone upon his shoulder, according unto the number of the tribes of the children of Israel: That this may be a sign among you, that when your children ask their fathers in time to come, saying, What mean ye by these stones? Then ye shall answer them, That the waters of Jordan were cut off before the ark of the covenant of the LORD; when it passed over Jordan, the waters of Jordan were cut off: and these stones shall be for a memorial unto the children of Israel for ever.

Twelve men were to place twelve stones from the bed of the Jordan River on the west bank of the Jordan. Of them, they were to make a monument, a memorial. In our country, sites like the Vietnam Memorial and Lincoln Memorial help us to remember and to reflect just as the twelve stones would enable the Israelite fathers to tell their children how God miraculously stopped the Jordan for His people.

I like the fact that it was the fathers who would talk to their children about God. When children were brought to Jesus for blessing, the pronoun Mark uses makes it clear that it was the fathers who brought them (10:14). Obviously, when a father is unable or unwilling to talk to his kids about spiritual things, the mother is to take that role. But how much better it is for both Mom and Dad to teach their kids the ways of God.

Joshua 4:8–10
And the children of Israel did so as Joshua commanded, and took up twelve stones out of the midst of Jordan, as the LORD spake unto Joshua, according to the number of the tribes of the children of Israel, and carried them over with them unto the place where they lodged, and laid them down there. And Joshua set up twelve stones in the midst of Jordan, in the place where the feet of the priests which bare the ark of the covenant stood: and they are there unto this day. For the priests which bare the ark stood in the midst of Jordan, until everything was fin-

ished that the LORD commanded Joshua to speak unto the people, according to all that Moses commanded Joshua: and the people hasted and passed over.

In addition to the twelve stones placed on the "Spirit-filled" side of the Jordan, Joshua was instructed to place twelve stones in the midst of the Jordan itself. This means that when the water came rushing in after everyone had passed over, Joshua's monument would not be seen by any man—only by God. There were two monuments. One was visible. One was out of sight. And that's the way it is with any work of the Spirit. The outward manifestations are only as valid as the inward, hidden work in one's heart.

Joshua 4:11–13
And it came to pass, when all the people were clean passed over, that the ark of the LORD passed over, and the priests, in the presence of the people. And the children of Reuben, and the children of Gad, and half the tribe of Manasseh, passed over armed before the children of Israel, as Moses spake unto them: About forty thousand prepared for war passed over before the LORD unto battle, to the plains of Jericho.

The two and one-half tribes that chose to settle on the east side of the Jordan weren't forced to go with the rest of the children of Israel into the Promised Land. God won't force you or me to cross over and reside in the Spirit-filled life. He'll take us as far as we want to go—but not one step further.

Joshua 4:14
On that day the LORD magnified Joshua in the sight of all Israel; and they feared him, as they feared Moses, all the days of his life.

According to John 1:28, Jesus was baptized in the Jordan at Bethabara. *Bethabara* means "house of passage." Therefore, Jesus was baptized in the same place Joshua was as he passed over into the Promised Land. To the Pharisees and Sadducees who cynically watched him baptize, John said, "And think not to say within yourselves, We have Abraham to our father: for I say unto you, that god is able of these stones to raise up children unto Abraham" (Matthew 3:9). And no doubt he would have been pointing to the stones that would still be there in his day, the twelve stones placed as a memorial in Joshua's day.

Joshua 4:15–18
And the LORD spake unto Joshua, saying, Command the priests that bear the ark of the testimony, that they come up out of Jordan. Joshua therefore commanded the priests, saying, Come ye up out of Jordan. And it came to pass, when the priests that bare the ark of the covenant of the LORD were come up out of the midst of Jordan, and the soles of the priests' feet were lifted up unto the dry land, that the waters of Jordan returned unto their place, and flowed over all his banks, as they did before.

Again, in the overflowing of its banks, the Jordan River is a fitting picture of the power of the Spirit (John 7:38, 39).

Joshua 4:19–24
And the people came up out of Jordan on the tenth day of the first month, and encamped in Gilgal, in the east border of Jericho. And those twelve stones, which they took out of Jordan, did Joshua pitch in Gilgal. And he spake unto the children of Israel, saying, When your children shall ask their fathers in time to come, saying, What mean these stones? Then ye shall let your children know, saying, Israel came over this Jordan on dry land. For the LORD your God dried up the waters of Jordan from before you, until ye were passed over, as the LORD your God did to the Red sea, which he dried up from before us, until we were gone over: That all the people of the earth might know the hand of the LORD, that it is mighty: that ye might fear the LORD your God for ever.

Twelve stones stacked together in one monument, twelve stones representing the Twelve Tribes, fit together in unity would be the sign that the Israelites had crossed over the Jordan, that they had been "baptized" a second time. Peter says that, as believers, we are living stones fit together in unity (1 Peter 2:5). When you come to church not out of obligation but because you want to be linked together with fellow blockheads and stones, your love for them is a sure sign of your being touched deeply by the Spirit. "All men shall know you are My disciples," said Jesus. "By your speaking in tongues? No. By your gift of healing? No. They'll know you are My disciples by your love" (see John 13:35).

In 1 Corinthians 12 and 14, Paul discusses spiritual gifts and their manifestations. But packed between them is chapter 13, a chapter that deals exclusively with love because love is the defining characteristic of one who has had an encounter with the Spirit.

"Father, let them be one," Jesus prayed in John 17, "that the world might know that I am in You and that You are in Me." In other words, love within the body of Christ is proof positive to a world that is skeptical that Jesus is risen and real, alive and well.

5 **Joshua 5:1 (a)**
And it came to pass, when all the kings of the Amorites, which were on the side of Jordan westward, and all the kings of the Canaanites, which were by the sea, heard that the LORD had dried up the waters of Jordan from before the children of Israel, until we were passed over, that their heart melted . . .

As seen in Joshua 2:9–11, the inhabitants of the Land west of the Jordan had heard what God had done for His people forty years earlier when He parted the Red Sea. But here in chapter 5, we see they also heard what He had done presently when He parted the Jordan.

Some people rejoice over that which the Lord did forty years ago. That's okay. But the Lord wants to do even greater things today.

Joshua 5:1 (b)
. . . neither was there spirit in them any more, because of the children of Israel.

The enemy was demoralized, intimidated, and afraid. This would have been the perfect time to attack. But God chose otherwise . . .

Joshua 5:2
At that time the LORD said unto Joshua, Make thee sharp knives, and circumcise again the children of Israel the second time.

General Joshua must have said, "What? Make sharp knives? Surely, Lord, You mean we are to make sharp swords to take into battle. If we circumcise all of our men, we'll be left vulnerable in enemy territory."

Joshua 5:3–5
And Joshua made him sharp knives, and circumcised the children of Israel at the hill of the foreskins. And this is the cause why Joshua did circumcise: All the people that came out of Egypt, that were males, even all the men of war, died in the wilderness by the way, after they came out of Egypt. Now all the people that came out were circumcised: but all the people that were born in the wilderness by the way as they came forth out of Egypt, them they had not circumcised.

Despite any misgivings, Joshua obeyed the Lord—which is precisely why he would be used so mightily.

Joshua 5:6–9
For the children of Israel walked forty years in the wilderness, till all the people that were men of war, which came out of Egypt, were consumed, because they obeyed not the voice of the LORD: unto whom the LORD sware that he would not shew them the land, which the LORD sware unto their fathers that he would give us, a land that floweth with milk and honey. And their children, whom he raised up in their stead, them Joshua circumcised: for they were uncircumcised, because they had not circumcised them by the way. And it came to pass, when they had done circumcising all the people, that they abode in their places in the camp, till they were whole. And the LORD said unto Joshua, This day have I rolled away the reproach of Egypt from off you. Wherefore the name of the place is called Gilgal unto this day.

Gilgal, or literally, "the place of rolling," was the place where the reproach of Egypt was rolled away, or literally cut away as the Israelites reinstituted the practice of circumcision that had been abandoned in their wilderness wanderings. The Israelites had been "baptized" in the Jordan River. And Gilgal is a picture, an illustration of what happens next in the Spirit-filled life. You see, after we put our foot in the Jordan River and say, "Lord, fill me, flood me, and use me," how do we get things "rolling"? I believe the key is circumcision. I personally believe that, among other things circumcision illustrates, it correlates to speaking in tongues. Here's why . . .

In Genesis 17, God said to Abraham, "I want to give you a token of the covenant I've made with you."

"Wonderful," Abraham must have thought. *"I get to have a badge that I can pin on my robe. Or maybe a crown I can wear on my head so people will know that I'm in a covenant relationship with the Almighty God."*

But then God told him the token would be circumcision.

"What?!" Abraham must have thought. *"That's the token? That's the sign? That's the seal? Circumcision? I'd rather have a badge."*

In circumcision, the flesh is dealt with literally. Circumcision sensitizes and purifies a man in a way he otherwise wouldn't be. Circumcision is a mark known only privately, but of which a man is reminded daily. Circumcision being ridiculed and mocked by the surrounding nations, in ordering His people to be circumcised, God said to them, "I want you to be marked. It will be ridiculed by those who don't understand. But it will make you more sensitive. It will bring you a degree of purity. It will remind you of our covenant constantly."

Reproduction and sensitivity, a private mark, a sign and seal are all aspects of speaking in tongues. How do we get things rolling? My flesh hates speaking in tongues because it doesn't seem to me to be intellectually acceptable. But that's the point. In 1 Corinthians 14:13, Paul said, "My mind is unfruitful, but my spirit is edified when I pray in tongues." Speaking in tongues marks me. I'm in a new relationship with the Lord. The people around me might make fun of it, but it provides in me a new sensitivity to the work and reality of the Holy Ghost."

In 1 Corinthians 14, we see the "Gilgal" of Spirit-filled living . . .

> Follow after charity, and desire spiritual gifts, but rather that ye may prophesy. For he that speaketh in an unknown tongue speaketh not unto men, but unto God: for no man understandeth him; howbeit in the spirit he speaketh mysteries. 1 Corinthians 14:1, 2

Oftentimes, my mind either doesn't know how to pray or is limited in expressions of thanksgiving, love, and appreciation. But when my spirit prays, I'm set free from the limitations of my own mental abilities.

> He that speaketh in an unknown tongue edifieth himself . . . 1 Corinthians 14:4 (a)

Speaking in tongues is the least of the gifts because it doesn't edify others. But it's an important gift because it edifies the one speaking. When I pray in the spirit, I'm built up because I'm free from my own mental limitations of trying to come up with logical phrases and expressions.

> For if I pray in an unknown tongue, my spirit prayeth, but my understanding is unfruitful. 1 Corinthians 14:14

When I pray in the Spirit, my flesh doesn't get it. My mind doesn't comprehend it. But my spirit—the real me—is released as the flesh is rolled away.

> What is it then? I will pray with the spirit, and I will pray with the understanding also: 1 Corinthians 14:15

Notice Paul says, "I will pray." Praying in the Spirit is not done in some kind of a mysterious trance. Rather, it's something one chooses to do. And when I do, Satan is right there to challenge me. But that should not be surprising, for it's what he does with every spiritual experience from the moment we're born again.

In the Book of Romans, we are given further light on this illustration . . .

> For he is not a Jew, which is one outwardly; neither is that circumcision, which is outward in the flesh: But he is a Jew, which is one inwardly; and circumcision is that of the heart, in the spirit, and not in the letter; whose praise is not of men, but of God. Romans 2:28, 29

> And he received the sign of circumcision, a seal of the righteousness of the faith which he had yet being uncircumcised: Romans 4:11

In Acts 2, we read that when the Holy Spirit moved on the Day of Pentecost, the disciples in the Upper Room spoke with other tongues. In Acts 8, the next time the Holy Spirit came upon a group of people, we don't know if they spoke in tongues, but something happened that was noticed because a magician named Simon offered to buy the "trick." In Acts 9, when Ananias laid hands on Paul and prayed, Paul was empowered. Did Paul speak in tongues? Scripture doesn't say whether he did right then. But later on, he would say, "I speak in tongues more than you all" (1 Corinthians 14:18). In Acts 10, as Peter was preaching, the Holy Spirit fell upon the listeners and they began to speak in tongues. In Acts 19, Paul laid his hands on those in Ephesus and they spoke in tongues.

There seems to be a pattern that indicates that speaking in tongues is the norm in relation to the empowering of the Spirit.

> For we are the circumcision, which worship God in the spirit, and rejoice in Christ Jesus, and have no confidence in the flesh. Philippians 3:3

Who is the true circumcision? Those who worship God in the Spirit. I take this to, at least partially, allude to worshiping God in the Spirit rather than solely with one's understanding.

> I thank my God, I speak with tongues more than ye all: Yet in the church I had rather speak five words with my understanding, 1 Corinthians 14:18, 19

Paul is encouraging the private devotional usage of tongues and discouraging the public outbursts. I pray often in tongues. It's an important part of my prayer life because I need to be built up, because I get discouraged, because I don't know how to pray, because I'm limited in my expression. As I pray in the Spirit, I am free to pray from my innermost being. Joshua was instructed to make sharp knives to cut away the flesh. Sharper than any two-edged sword, the Word of God is the sharpest knife I know (Hebrews 4:12). Therefore, I encourage you to unsheathe the sharp knife of the Word and, with an open mind and heart, study the Word and see if the Lord confirms these things in your heart.

Joshua 5:10, 11
And the children of Israel encamped in Gilgal, and kept the passover on the fourteenth day of the month at even in the plains of Jericho. And they did eat of the old corn of the land on the morrow after the passover, unleavened cakes, and parched corn in the selfsame day.

The first time the Israelites celebrated Passover was forty years earlier. Here, after the flesh had been dealt with through circumcision, they celebrate it again. I have noticed that the person who is moving in the Spirit finds himself drawn to the New Testament Passover—the Lord's Table of Communion. I have also noticed that when I'm in the wilderness, I just don't seem to find the time or expend the energy to come to Communion. But when I'm walking in the Spirit, I find myself at the Table once again.

When is the last time you sought the Lord, saying, "I need to eat and drink of You"? If you make your way to the Lord's Table, even though you, like the children of Israel, might be surrounded by enemies, trials, and problems, you'll find yourself participating in the Spirit-filled life once again.

Joshua 5:12
And the manna ceased on the morrow after they had eaten of the old corn of the land; neither had the children of Israel manna any more; but they did eat of the fruit of the land of Canaan that year.

It is interesting to me that it was in the Promised Land, a picture of the Spirit-filled life, that the miracle of manna ceased. If there was ever going to be manna from heaven, I would think it would be when we're Spirit-filled, when we're moving in the arena of the miraculous, when we have the anointing of the Holy Ghost. But this passage tells me differently, for when the Israelites were in the wilderness—which speaks of carnality and dryness—miracles abounded. But now that they're in the Promised Land, the manna stops.

In the Azusa Street Revival of the early 1900s, during which there was a fresh outpouring of the Holy Spirit, the leader of the movement prophesied that three things would cause the movement of the Spirit to be quenched: more attention given to the Holy Spirit than to Jesus Christ, more attention given to praise than to prayer, and more attention given to the gifts of the Spirit than the fruit of the Spirit.

When they were released from Egypt and as they wandered in the wilderness, the children of Israel saw more signs and wonders than any other group of people in history. Yet it was unbelief that kept them from entering the Promised Land (Hebrews 3:19) because faith doesn't come through seeing miracles. It comes from hearing the Word. Therefore, the new generation would eat the formidable fruit produced in the land of God's promise rather than the manna of the miraculous.

Joshua 5:13 (a)
And it came to pass, when Joshua was by Jericho, that he lifted up his eyes . . .

Throughout the Word, when men find themselves at a crossroads, we see them lifting up their eyes (Genesis 13:10, 18:2, 24:63; Numbers 24:2; 1 Chronicles 21:16; Daniel 10:5). In this case, Jericho is looming over Joshua. It's a formidable problem, a massive, walled city. Yet he didn't look down, hide out, or hole up. He lifted his eyes.

Joshua 5:13 (b)
. . . and looked, and, behold, there stood a man over against him with his sword drawn in his hand . . .

As we will see, this Man is none other than a preincarnate appearance of Jesus Christ. Because Joshua was on the verge of battle, the Lord appeared to him as a man of war. On the plains of Mamre, the Lord appeared to Abraham as a traveler because Abraham was a pilgrim (Genesis 18). So we need to watch for the Lord to appear to us through the circumstances and people around us.

Joshua 5:13 (c), 14 (a)
. . . and Joshua went unto him, and said unto him, Art thou for us, or for our adversaries? And he said, Nay; but as captain of the host of the LORD am I now come . . .

"Are you for us or against us?" Joshua asked. But the Lord simply answered, "No," for the issue wasn't whose side the Lord was on. It was whose side Joshua was on.

Joshua 5:14 (b)
. . . And Joshua fell on his face to the earth, and did worship . . .

We know from this verse that the man of war was not an angel because angels do not accept worship (Revelation 19:10; 22:8)

Joshua 5:14 (c), 15
. . . and said unto him, What saith my lord unto his servant? And the captain of the LORD's host said unto Joshua, Loose thy shoe from off thy foot; for the place whereon thou standest is holy. And Joshua did so.

When the Lord appeared to Moses, He said, "Take off your shoes. The ground you're standing on is holy" (see Exodus 3:5). Therefore, in telling Joshua to loose his shoe, the Lord was essentially saying, "As I was with Moses, so I am with you. Even though there's a giant difficulty called Jericho looming over you, I'm with you as your Captain."

6 **Joshua 6:1–4 (a)**
Now Jericho was straitly shut up because of the children of Israel: none went out, and none came in. And the LORD said unto Joshua, See, I have given into thine hand Jericho, and the king thereof, and the mighty men of valour. And ye shall compass the city, all ye men of war, and go round about the city once. Thus shalt thou do six days. And seven priests . . .

As the Captain of the Lord's host, Jesus Himself, outlined the strategy of how the Israelites were to conquer the city of Jericho, Joshua must have grown more confused with each step. Here we see the priests were to take part in the operation. Yet according to the law, the priests were exempt from all military duty in order to devote themselves to serving in the tabernacle and, later on, in the temple.

Joshua 6:4 (b)
. . . shall bear before the ark. . . .

The ark of the covenant was never to be taken into battle. In fact, the one time the Israelites tried it, not only were they defeated, but the ark was captured (1 Samuel 4—5).

Joshua 6:4 (c)
. . . seven trumpets of rams' horns . . .

Numbers 10 states specifically that it wasn't rams' horns that were to be used in battle but two silver trumpets.

Joshua 6:4 (d)
. . . and the seventh day ye shall compass the city seven times, and the priests shall blow with the trumpets.

According to the Law, there was to be no traveling on the Sabbath. But the Israelites were here commanded to travel around the city of Jericho seven times more, seven times farther than they had on any of the previous six days.

Joshua 6:5
And it shall come to pass, that when they make a long blast with the ram's horn, and when ye hear the sound of the trumpet, all the people shall shout with a great shout; and the wall of the city shall fall down flat, and the people shall ascend up every man straight before him.

The actual confrontation with Jericho was to take place on the seventh day, the day of rest, the Sabbath. So devoted to keeping the Sabbath were the Jews that throughout history, many atrocities were committed against Jewish soldiers on the Sabbath because their enemies knew they wouldn't fight back.

At Moses' side when the Law was given, Joshua was now being told to violate it. Why? I believe the answer lies in the Book of Zechariah . . .

> Then shall the LORD go forth, and fight against those nations, as when he fought in the day of battle. Zechariah 14:3

In this prophecy concerning Jesus' Second Coming and the battle of Armageddon, Zechariah says Jesus will fight like He did before. The question is, when did Jesus fight before? Read the Gospels and you'll never see Jesus fighting. You never see Him with a drawn sword. You'll never see Him leading the charge. He's the Prince of peace. So when did He fight? Here in Joshua 5. You see, as Captain of the host of the Lord, Jesus was the One who led the Israelites around the walls of Jericho once each day for six days. Jesus was the One who compassed the city with them seven times on the Sabbath. Jesus was the One who told Joshua to shout and the walls would come down. Joshua was along for the ride. Jesus was the One who led the way.

And because Jesus was in the midst of His people physically, the rules and regulations of the Law were no longer necessary.

> Let no man therefore judge you in meat, or in drink, or in respect of an holyday, or of the

new moon, or of the Sabbath days: Which are a shadow of things to come; but the body is of Christ. Colossians 2:16, 17

The priests, the ark, and the rams' horns that were all part of the procession around the walls of Jericho all point to Jesus. Even the Sabbath on which the Israelites marched points to Jesus, for He is our Sabbath rest (Hebrews 4).

It's Valentines Day. You walk in your house and see your wife hugging and kissing your picture. "Surprise!" you say as you hold out candy and roses, expecting her to run towards you. But if she remains more infatuated with your picture than with you, you would say, "Why are you so wrapped up with the picture, when the one it portrays is right here?"

When Jesus was on the scene, of Joshua's day He would say, "I am the fulfillment of the Sabbath and of the silver trumpets. I am the fulfillment of the priesthood and of the ark of the covenant. They're just pictures. Focus on Me."

I wonder how many of us are focused on rules, regulations and religion even in the Promised Land of the Spirit-filled life. I wonder how many of us subconsciously say, "It's Sunday. That's a holy day. I'm off to church. It's morning. I'm disciplined. It's time for devotions."

To us, Jesus would say, "Rules, regulations, and rituals are only necessary if I'm not present. But if I'm present, those things are replaced by relationship with Me."

Gang, we know more than the early church knew about typology and illustrations. The question is, Do we know who they knew? They knew Jesus. And they responded to His leading moment by moment. We, too, will be free from religion and predictability, from legalism and traditions, from habits, ruts, and routines to the degree that we realize that the Captain of the host of the Lord, the Captain of our salvation, Jesus Himself is in our midst.

***For topical study of Joshua 5:13—6:5 entitled "The Wall Will Fall!" turn to page* 656.**

Joshua 6:6–15

And Joshua the son of Nun called the priests, and said unto them, Take up the ark of the covenant, and let seven priests bear seven trumpets of rams' horns before the ark of the LORD. And he said unto the people, Pass on, and compass the city, and let him that is armed pass on before the ark of the LORD. And it came to pass, when Joshua had spoken unto the people, that the seven priests bearing the seven trumpets of rams' horns passed on before the LORD, and blew with the trumpets: and the ark of the covenant of the LORD followed them. And the armed men went before the priests that blew with the trumpets, and the rereward came after the ark, the priests going on, and blowing with the trumpets. And Joshua had commanded the people, saying, Ye shall not shout, nor make any noise with your voice, neither shall any word proceed out of your mouth, until the day I bid you shout; then shall ye shout. So the ark of the LORD compassed the city, going about it once: and they came into the camp, and lodged in the camp. And Joshua rose early in the morning, and the priests took up the ark of the LORD. And seven priests bearing seven trumpets of rams' horns before the ark of the LORD went on continually, and blew with the trumpets: and the armed men went before them; but the rereward came after the ark of the LORD, the priests going on, and blowing with the trumpets. And the second day they compassed the city once, and returned into the camp: so they did six days. And it came to pass on the seventh day, that they rose early about the dawning of the day, and compassed the city after the same manner seven times: only on that day they compassed the city seven times. And it came to pass at the seventh time, when the priests blew with the trumpets, Joshua said unto the people, Shout; for the LORD hath given you the city.

As His people marched around the walls of Jericho, God prepared them in several ways. First, He gave them a realization of the impossibility of their situation. The first time the Israelites circled the city, the walls must have looked huge. And they must have looked bigger and more foreboding with each successive trip. Thus, in their repeated journeys around the Jericho, the Lord was showing His people that victory would not come through their might nor through their power, but only by His Spirit (Zechariah 4:6).

Right now there might be a huge wall between you and a family member, neighbor or fellow believer. God will have you go around it again and again until you finally say, "I can't manipulate the situation. I can't solve the problem. I can't do a thing about this, Lord. Only You can solve this." And when at last you come to this realization, I promise you that in due season, He will do something earth-shattering. Oh, it might take six months or even six years—but there will come a time when you'll say, "It was the Lord who brought that wall down. It wasn't my cleverness or my ingenuity because as I went in circles day after week after month, it just got thicker and higher."

Secondly, as His people circled the walls of Jericho, God taught them the importance of patience. Hebrews 6:12 says that it is through faith and patience that His promises are obtained. Do you have faith? Great. God wants you to have patience, too. You see, His agenda is bigger than just knocking down walls. His purpose is to develop patience in us in order that we might be perfect, lacking nothing (James 1:4).

Thirdly, as His people circled the walls of Jericho, God taught them discipline. His job was to work, theirs to be absolutely silent. If I can't control my tongue, I won't conquer the enemy. My tongue will get me in big trouble. So will yours (James 3:5, 6). Therefore, it is the wise man or woman who silently—without complaint or opinion—gives God time and room to work.

God's strategy for conquering Jericho served not only to prepare the children of Israel but to provide a witness to the people of Jericho. I believe that the people walking in quietness and tranquility, the ark of the covenant, the trumpets playing were all to be a witness to the inhabitants of Jericho. According to Rahab, their hearts were already melted. Thus, I believe God was giving them one last opportunity to come to Him. While His people were in Egypt, God gave the inhabitants of Canaan four hundred years to repent. Then He gave them forty more years while His people wandered in the wilderness. Here, He gives them six more days as they watched His children walk in devotion and order.

What will impress around you? Seeing you walk patiently and quietly, neither panicking nor complaining, but simply walking under the authority of your Captain. Seeing the way your homes, marriages, and lives are ordered in this march towards heaven is a witness to the people of our own Jerichos.

Joshua 6:17–25

And the city shall be accursed, even it, and all that are therein, to the LORD: only Rahab the harlot shall live, she and all that are with her in the house, because she hid the messengers that we sent. And ye, in any wise keep yourselves from the accursed thing, lest ye make yourselves accursed, when ye take of the accursed thing, and make the camp of Israel a curse, and trouble it. But all the silver, and gold, and vessels of brass and iron, are consecrated unto the LORD: they shall come into the treasury of the LORD. So the people shouted when the priests blew with the trumpets: and it came to pass, when the people heard the sound of the trumpet, and the people shouted with a great shout, that the wall fell down flat, so that the people went up into the city, every man straight before him, and they took the city. And they utterly destroyed all that was in the city, both man and woman, young and old, and ox, and sheep, and ass, with the edge of the sword. But Joshua had said unto the two men that had spied out the country, Go into the harlot's house, and bring out thence the woman, and all that she hath, as ye sware unto her. And the young men that were spies went in, and brought Rahab, and her father, and her mother, and her brethren, and all that she had; and they brought out all her kindred, and left them without the camp of Israel. And they burnt the city with fire, and all that was therein: only the silver, and the gold, and the vessels of brass and of iron, they put into the treasury of the house of the LORD. And Joshua saved Rahab the harlot alive, and her father's household, and all that she had; and she dwelleth in Israel even unto this day; because she hid the messengers, which Joshua sent to spy out Jericho.

Because it was the wall of Jericho that fell, the wall would have been the most dangerous place to live—unless you knew God. Rahab's house was part of the wall of Jericho (Joshua 2:15). Yet because she knew God, the most dangerous place in the city was, for her, the safest place to be. When the wall fell, the scarlet cord hanging from Rahab's window was hardly necessary to identify Rahab's house, for evidently hers was the only part of the wall left standing. But the scarlet cord was an outward sign of an inward belief. It wasn't necessary for salvation, but was an indication of what was taking place in Rahab's heart. The same is true of baptism. We don't need to be baptized to be saved. But it is an outward sign to others of our faith in the One who died and rose for us, in the One who rescued us from the walls of sin surrounding us.

Joshua 6:26, 27

And Joshua adjured them at that time, saying, Cursed be the man before the LORD, that riseth up and buildeth this city Jericho: he shall lay the foundation thereof in his firstborn, and in his youngest son shall he set up the gates of it. So the LORD was with Joshua; and his fame was noised throughout all the country.

He who tried to rebuild the walls of Jericho would pay a steep price. His oldest and youngest son would die. In 1 Kings 16, we read of a man named Hiel who did this. He rebuilt Jericho—but his oldest and youngest son died in the process.

If God knocks down a wall between you and another and you say, "Maybe I shouldn't be so forgiving. Maybe I'm being taken advantage of," there will be no shortage of people to hand you all the bricks and mortar you need to rebuild the wall. But you'll pay a terrible price. Don't undo what God has done. Don't harden your heart. Don't let your soul become like concrete. Instead, with the wall flat on the ground, enter into fresh fellowship with the One from whom, by God's grace and mercy, you are no longer estranged.

THE WALL WILL FALL!

A Topical Study of JOSHUA 5:13—6:5

At long last the children of Israel had entered the Land of Promise, the Land that flowed with milk and honey, the Land that speaks to you and me of the Spirit-filled abundant life. To enter into the heart of the Land, however, they would have to conquer Jericho. And with Jericho's walls seemingly absolutely impregnable, the situation looked humanly impossible.

Maybe you can relate to Joshua and the people of Israel. You've been set free from Egypt and baptized in the Spirit. But looking before you is a wall, a fortress, a barrier between you and someone else that is keeping you from going all the way into the heart of the Land of Promise. As a father, it might be between you and your junior high son. As a mother, it might be between you and your teenage daughter. As a husband or wife, it might be between you and your spouse. As a believer, it might be between you and a brother or sister in the Lord.

In the life of Joshua, I believe we see three elements that deal directly with the walls of separation that can keep us from the heart of the Promised Land . . .

Submission to the Lord

As Joshua scoped out the city of Jericho, a Man with a sword in His hand appeared to him. "Are You for us or for our enemies?" Joshua asked. "Which side are You on?"

But as Captain of the host of the Lord, the issue wasn't whose side He was on. It was whose side Joshua was on.

If we're to see walls flattened, the first thing we have to realize is that it's not "us against them." When there are walls or barriers in a marriage, a family, or a church, the issue will inevitably become one of us against them, the good guys vs. the bad guys.

"Whose side are You on, Lord?" we ask, sure that He will answer that He is on ours.

But when He simply answers, "No," wise is the man or woman who does what Joshua did, who bows the knee and changes the question to, "What saith my Lord to His servant?"

Before he understood who he was talking to, perhaps it was rather gruffly that General Joshua asked, "Whose side are you on?" But once he realized who it was, he no longer gave orders. He simply reported for duty. And that's the way prayer ought always to be. We're re-learning that God always gives His best to those who leave the choice to Him.

I used to think that prayer in faith meant I was to give the plan to the Lord, stand on it in faith, and expect it to come about. I've since learned, however, that because we all see through a glass only darkly at best (1 Corinthians 13:12), I would be a fool to order the Lord around. The Bible says to have faith in God. He sees things we don't see. So we ask in faith. We share our thoughts with the Lord in humility and transparence. But we leave the choice and results with the One who sees the end from the beginning, who sees all things clearly.

Waiting for the Lord

For six days, the congregation of Israel marched around the walls of the city of Jericho. God has you and me go round and round in circles until finally we get dizzy and realize the wall is too high, the breach too great, the estrangement too severe. Although we do everything we know how to do, the wall only gets higher. Before there can be a moment of the miraculous, there must be a lengthy season of helplessness.

Perhaps in wanting to see a relationship restored or a wall removed, you've tried everything. But finally you get to a place where you say, "I can't go around this circle again. I've tried everything but nothing's working. Lord, it will have to be You who brings this wall down." Some may say it's ludicrous to just wait. But the truth is, there's nothing we can do until God moves in and does what only He can.

Believing in the Lord

When their circling was complete, the Israelites were not to point, not to doubt, but to shout. While I'm waiting for God to flatten the walls in my life, I'm not to wring my hands in anxiety. I'm to clap them in expectancy (Psalm 47:1).

Notice that the Israelites were commanded to shout before the walls fell. Not when they fell, not after they fell, the children of Israel shorted *before* they fell. Thus, theirs was an expression of anticipation, a proclamation of faith.

Let's join their ranks. Let's be those who have free access to the heart of all that God has for us as we believe in Him, wait for Him and submit to Him—for that's where the walls begin to fall.

7

Joshua 7:1 (a)
But . . .

As a picture of the Spirit-filled life, it should not surprise us to find the word "but" in our text—for just as the children of Israel are about to experience defeat following their glorious victory at Jericho, we can experience defeat even in the Spirit-filled life. How? By grieving or quenching the Spirit.

You see, just as there are three relationships a person can have with the Spirit, there are three negative responses a person can make towards the Spirit. Every person who has ever lived has had the experience of the Holy Spirit being *with* him as He comes to every man and whispers the truth in his ear about his need for God. If a person continues to resist the Spirit, however, He will eventually go His way, leaving that individual stuck in his lost condition. This is called the blasphemy of the Holy Spirit (Matthew 12:31).

But when a man says yes to the Spirit and asks Jesus to be his Savior, he moves into the second relationship with the Spirit. That is, the Spirit comes *in* him (John 20:22). However, even though a believer has the Spirit within him, he can grieve the Spirit by allowing sin, malice and evil speaking to creep into his life (Ephesians 4:30, 31).

The third relationship with the Spirit is the "coming upon" of the Spirit to empower a person for service (Acts 1:8). Yet in this relationship the Spirit can be quenched. That is, a person can say, "I'm uncomfortable with prophecy, speaking in tongues, or gifts of healing. Give me a good solid Bible study and a hymn or two, and that will be fine for me." And while the Spirit will still be in him, the empowering will be greatly diminished (1 Thessalonians 5:19).

Here in Joshua 7, we will see both the grieving of the Spirit and the quenching of the Spirit. And because the same can be true of us, this chapter has much to say to us . . .

Joshua 7:1 (b)
. . . the children of Israel committed a trespass in the accursed thing . . .

In chapter 6, we saw how God miraculously gave the city of Jericho to the people of Israel. But, although they would be able to keep the spoil of the subsequent cities they would conquer, they were to take nothing from Jericho because the first of everything belongs to the Lord.

Joshua 7:1 (c)
. . . for Achan, the son of Carmi, the son of Zabdi, the son of Zerah, of the tribe of Judah, took of the accursed thing: and the anger of the LORD was kindled against the children of Israel.

The entire nation felt the consequences of one man's sin because, in the Spirit, we are one body (1 Corinthians 12:20). If I shoplift, my whole body goes to jail—not just my hand. When one person in our fellowship family strays, it affects the whole body of believers. Thus, because Achan sinned, God was grieved with the entire congregation.

Joshua 7:2
And Joshua sent men from Jericho to Ai, which is beside Beth-aven, on the east side of Bethel, and spake unto them, saying, Go up and view the country. And the men went up and viewed Ai.

Its name literally meaning "heap," *Ai* was a little town that appeared to be no problem for the people of Israel in their conquest of the Promised Land.

Joshua 7:3, 4 (a)
And they returned to Joshua, and said unto him, Let not all the people go up; but let about two or three thousand men go up and smite Ai; and make not all the people to labour thither; for they are but few. So there went up thither of the people about three thousand men . . .

Although it was Achan's sin that grieved the Spirit, it was Joshua's failure to seek the Lord before going into battle that quenched the Spirit.

> And the LORD said unto Moses, Take thee Joshua the son of Nun, a man in whom is the spirit, and lay thine hand upon him; And set him before Eleazar the priest, and before all the congregation; and give him a charge in their sight. And thou shalt put some of thine honour upon him, that all the congregation of the children of Israel may be obedient. And he shall stand before Eleazar the priest, who shall ask counsel for him after the judgment of Urim before the LORD: at his word shall they go out, and at his word they shall come in, both he, and all the children of Israel with him, even all the congregation. Numbers 27:18–21

Instruction for crossing the Jordan had been given to Joshua by divine revelation (Joshua 3). Instruction for dealing with the flesh once they were in the Promised Land had been given to Joshua by divine revelation (Joshua 5). Instruction for taking Jericho had been given to Joshua by divine revelation (Joshua 6). In other words, all along the way, Joshua had been seeking the Lord. But when he thought he could handle Ai by himself, the Spirit was quenched.

Paul put it this way when he asked the Galatians, "Are you so foolish? Having begun in the Spirit, are you now made perfect by the flesh?" (Galatians 3:3) And the same can be true of us.

Although we were once open to the mystery and intimacy of God's Word specifically and personally given to us, a "Joshua chapter 7" mentality can kick in which causes us to say, "I can handle this little problem with my own energy, insight and ability. After all, it's just Ai." And as a result, the Spirit is quenched.

Joshua 7:4 (b)–6
. . . and they fled before the men of Ai. And the men of Ai smote of them about thirty and six men: for they chased them from before the gate even unto Shebarim, and smote them in the going down: wherefore the hearts of the people melted, and became as water. And Joshua rent his clothes, and fell to the earth upon his face before the ark of the LORD until the eventide, he and the elders of Israel, and put dust upon their heads.

The combination of Joshua's sin which quenched the Spirit and Achan's sin which grieved the Spirit led to the defeat of a nation that was previously invincible. And the same will be the result in our lives.

Joshua 7:7–9
And Joshua said, Alas, O Lord GOD, wherefore hast thou at all brought this people over Jordan, to deliver us into the hand of the Amorites, to destroy us? would to God we had been content, and dwelt on the other side Jordan! O Lord, what shall I say, when Israel turneth their backs before their enemies! For the Canaanites and all the inhabitants of the land shall hear of it, and shall environ us round, and cut off our name from the earth: and what wilt thou do unto thy great name?

Just as Joshua questioned God, our Greater than Joshua, Jesus Himself, questioned His Father when He who knew no sin became sin for us (2 Corinthians 5:21). "My God, My God, why hast Thou forsaken Me?" Jesus cried as the Father turned His back on the Son in the only time in eternity that there was estrangement between them (Matthew 27:46). The only time Jesus ever addressed His Father as "my God" was when there was distance and separation because of our sin.

Joshua 7:10
And the LORD said unto Joshua, Get thee up; wherefore liest thou thus upon thy face?

"Don't lay with your face down," the Lord said to Joshua. "Instead, face up to some issues."

Joshua 7:11, 12
Israel hath sinned, and they have also transgressed my covenant which I commanded them: for they have even taken of the accursed thing, and have also stolen, and dissembled also, and they have put it even among their own stuff. Therefore the children of Israel could not stand before their enemies, but turned their backs before their enemies, because they were accursed: neither will I be with you any more, except ye destroy the accursed from among you.

Sin results in a loss of God's power and the sense of His presence. It strangles and stifles the abundant life. It paralyzes and immobilizes ministry and service. It pulls us down, tears us up, wipes us out.

Joshua 7:13
Up, sanctify the people, and say, Sanctify yourselves against to morrow: for thus saith the LORD God of Israel, There is an accursed thing in the midst of thee, O Israel: thou canst not stand before thine enemies, until ye take away the accursed thing from among you.

"Why aren't things working out? Why aren't things opening up? Why aren't things coming to pass?," we cry. And the Lord would say, "It is because I love you too much to let you continue on in your sin which will destroy you. Therefore, I'm holding back My provision and presence, My power and blessing not because I'm mad at you, but because I grieve for you."

Joshua 7:14, 15
In the morning therefore ye shall be brought according to your tribes: and it shall be, that the tribe which the LORD taketh shall come according to the families thereof; and the family which the LORD shall take shall come by households; and the household which the LORD shall take shall come man by man. And it shall be, that he that is taken with the accursed thing shall be burnt with fire, he and all that he hath: because he hath transgressed the covenant of the LORD, and because he hath wrought folly in Israel.

Sometimes I get confused when I hear conflicting stories about a single situation. And sometimes, even after a great length of time passes, I just can't get to the bottom of it. But God does. Whether it's here in Joshua 7 or in Acts 5 concerning Ananias and Sapphira, God works.

There can be a tendency for us to think that, like Achan, we have our sin covered. God, however says otherwise. "Be sure your sin will find you out," He declares (Numbers 32:23). Therefore, we would be a wise group of people to make right those situations we think we have hidden. For if we choose to do that, we will diminish what the repercussions would otherwise have been when God brings about full disclosure. Conversely, if you've been lied about or accused wrongly, know that God is on the throne and in control. And in due season, by divine revelation, He will bring to light the truth of the situation.

Joshua 7:16–19
So Joshua rose up early in the morning, and brought Israel by their tribes; and the tribe of Judah was taken: And he brought the family of Judah; and he took the family of the Zarhites: and he brought the family of the Zarhites man by man; and Zabdi was taken: And he brought his household man by man; and Achan, the son of Carmi, the son of Zabdi, the son of Zerah, of the tribe of Judah, was taken. And Joshua said unto Achan, My son, give, I pray thee, glory to the LORD God of Israel, and make confession unto him; and tell me now what thou hast done; hide it not from me.

Joshua, a picture of Jesus, didn't call Achan an idiot. He called him his son. And such is the picture of the grieving of the Spirit.

Joshua 7:20, 21 (a)
And Achan answered Joshua, and said, Indeed I have sinned against the LORD God of Israel, and thus and thus have I done: When I saw among the spoils. . . .

In referring to the garment and the silver as spoils, Achan is subtly justifying his sin. After all, spoils were the rightful property of conquering armies. The problem is, Achan didn't take spoils. He took that which was devoted to God. And whenever we refer to adultery as an affair, drunkenness as alcoholism, or murmuring as melancholy, we do the same thing.

Joshua 7:21 (b)
. . . a goodly Babylonish garment, and two hundred shekels of silver, and a wedge of gold of fifty shekels weight, then I coveted them, and took them; and, behold, they are hid in the earth in the midst of my tent, and the silver under it.

Achan's sin began when he saw. Then he coveted. Then he took. Then he hid. The longer I observe spiritual life, the more I'm convinced that the eye is the portal of the devil (Psalm 101:3) and the ear is the portal of the Spirit (Romans 10:17). Our culture is increasingly enamored with and drawn to the things of the eyes. As a result, we can't sit very long for the teaching of the Word. We don't want to just hear a message. We want a dramatic presentation. But because faith is the evidence of things not seen (Hebrews 11:1), we need to be people who learn to listen.

Joshua 7:22–25
So Joshua sent messengers, and they ran unto the tent; and, behold, it was hid in his tent, and the silver under it. And they took them out of the midst of the tent, and brought them unto Joshua, and unto all the children of Israel, and laid them out before the LORD. And Joshua, and all Israel with him, took Achan the son of Zerah, and the silver, and the garment, and the wedge of gold, and his sons, and his daughters, and his oxen, and his asses, and his sheep, and his tent, and all that he had: and they brought them unto the valley of Achor. And Joshua said, Why hast thou troubled us? The LORD shall trouble thee this day. And all Israel stoned him with stones, and burned them with fire, after they had stoned them with stones.

Whenever we sin and cover it up, other people are made to ache as well.

Joshua 7:26
And they raised over him a great heap of stones unto this day. So the LORD turned from the fierceness of his anger. Wherefore the name of that place was called, the valley of Achor, unto this day.

Although *Achor* means "Trouble," Hosea tells us the valley of Achor shall be a door of hope (2:15). The trouble that Achan brought upon himself, his family, and his nation would only truly be dealt with by what Jesus, the Door of John 10:7, would do in being burned with the fire of God's wrath on the Cross and "stoned" as the great stone was placed in front of His tomb. Isaiah 65 tells us the flock shall lie down in the valley of Achor. That's what God can do.

If we come clean and say, "Lord, I've erred. But You took the blame and the heat and the pain on my behalf," although we'll still feel the repercussions of our sin, will be at peace in hope.

In referring to the Tribulation as the time of Jacob's trouble, Jeremiah uses the word *achor* (Jeremiah 30:7). It's a fitting word indeed for in the Tribulation, Israel will be stoned with one hundred-pound hailstones and burned in the fire of persecution. But even this will be a door of hope because in the midst of their difficulty, the people of Israel will be singled out and shown the truth. All of Israel will be saved (Romans 11:26). And what a grand and glorious day that will be.

8 **Joshua 8:1**
And the LORD said unto Joshua, Fear not, neither be thou dismayed: take all the people of war with thee, and arise, go up to Ai: see, I have given into thy hand the king of Ai, and his people, and his city, and his land:

Whereas chapter 7 began with a big "but," chapter 8 begins with a grand "and." We can grieve the Spirit by sin. We can quench the Spirit when we fail to wait on the Lord to receive direction. But the Lord doesn't give up. There's always an "and." Once Achan's sin was exposed, the Lord said, "Don't be dismayed. I'm giving you the victory."

The successful person in life is the one who gets up one more time than he or she is knocked down. Too many Christians, when they are dealt a blow, lay in the dust day after day and don't get up. "Forgetting the things which lie behind, I press toward the mark of the prize of the high calling of God in Christ Jesus" Paul declared (Philippians 3:13, 14). How could Paul accomplish what he did? By forgetting that which was behind and looking ahead instead.

Joshua 8:2 (a)
And thou shalt do to Ai and her king as thou didst unto Jericho and her king: only the spoil thereof, and the cattle thereof, shall ye take for a prey unto yourselves . . .

In Jericho, the first city conquered, the Israelites weren't to take anything. But here they were to spoil the city of Ai. Therefore, if Achan had been just a little more patient, the spoils of Ai would have been his. If we'll just wait, God will bless us exceeding abundantly above all we can ask or think (Ephesians 3:20).

Josh 8: 2 (b), 3 (a)
. . . lay thee an ambush for the city behind it. So Joshua arose, and all the people of war, to go up against Ai: and Joshua chose out thirty thousand mighty men of valour . . .

Two or three thousand men went out to fight Ai the first time. This time, 30,000 are going. And they are only the ambush team.

Joshua 8:3 (b)–6
. . . and sent them away by night. And he commanded them, saying, Behold, ye shall lie in wait against the city, even behind the city: go not very far from the city, but be ye all ready: And I, and all the people that are with me, will approach unto the city: and it shall come to pass, when they come out against us, as at the first, that we will flee before them, (For they will come out after us) till we have drawn them from the city; for they will say, They flee before us, as at the first: therefore we will flee before them.

Not realizing the Israelites had moved from chapter 7 to chapter 8, the men of Ai would chase them with confidence.

Joshua 8:7, 8 (a)
Then ye shall rise up from the ambush, and seize upon the city: for the LORD your God will deliver it into your hand. And it shall be, when ye have taken the city, that ye shall set the city on fire . . .

May this be true of us. May our cities be taken and set on fire for Jesus Christ.

Joshua 8:8 (b)
. . . according to the commandment of the LORD shall ye do. See, I have commanded you.

With 30,000 valiant men lying in wait, the rest of the army would attack with a frontal assault. Then they would turn around and seemingly run for their lives. The men of Ai would pour out and the ambush team would rush in, take the city, and burn it to the ground. This being a cowardly way to fight, it's as if God said, "You were so proud and sure of yourselves last time around. This time, you'll win through a coward's strategy so that you won't be so arrogant and sure of yourselves."

Jericho was taken by day. Ai was to be taken at night. At Jericho, the Israelites were united. At Ai, they were divided into two companies. The battle of Jericho was a marvelous miracle. Ai was a military maneuver. At Jericho, the Israelites simply had to watch. At Ai, they were to work. With regard to the Spirit-filled life, we cannot box in what God desires to do in our lives concerning the battles that come to us. The Spirit-filled life means I walk in the Spirit hour by hour, day by day, saying, "Lord what do You want to do today?" rather than expecting Him to repeat that which He did yesterday.

Joshua 8:9–12
Joshua therefore sent them forth: and they went to lie in ambush, and abode between Bethel and Ai, on the west side of Ai: but Joshua lodged that night among the people. And Joshua rose up early in the morning, and numbered the people, and went up, he and the elders of Israel, before the people to Ai. And all the people, even the people of war that were with him, went up, and drew nigh, and came before the city, and pitched on the north side of Ai: now there was a valley between them and Ai. And he took about five thousand men, and set them to lie in ambush between Bethel and Ai, on the west side of the city.

The job of the 5,000 men positioned between Ai and Bethel five miles away was to cut off the escape route from Ai.

Joshua 8:13–17
And when they had set the people, even all the host that was on the north of the city, and their liers in wait on the west of the city, Joshua went that night into the midst of the valley. And it came to pass, when the king of Ai saw it, that they hasted and rose up early, and the men of the city went out against Israel to battle, he and all his people, at a time appointed, before the plain; but he wist not that there were liers in ambush against him behind the city. And Joshua and all Israel made as if they were beaten before them, and fled by the way of the wilderness. And all the people that were in Ai were called together to pursue after them: and they pursued after Joshua, and were drawn away from the city. And there was not a man left in Ai or Bethel, that went not out after Israel: and they left the city open, and pursued after Israel.

Running outside the city, the men of Ai thought they had won because Joshua and the men of Israel seemed to be beaten. Satan also thought he was victorious when Jesus was beaten and nailed to the Cross outside the city. I believe every demon from hell was at the foot of the Cross hissing, "He's beaten! We won!"

Joshua 8:18–20 (a)
And the LORD said unto Joshua, Stretch out the spear that is in thy hand toward Ai; for I will give it into thine hand. And Joshua stretched out the spear that he had in his hand toward the city. And the ambush arose quickly out of their place, and they ran as soon as he had stretched out his hand: and they entered into the city, and took it, and hasted and set the city on fire. And when the men of Ai looked behind them, they saw, and, behold, the smoke of the city ascended up to heaven, and they had no power . . .

Although a spear was thrust seemingly victoriously into Jesus' side, what a shock it must have been to Satan and the hordes of hell when, three days later, they realized their plan had backfired.

Joshua 8:20 (b), 21
. . . to flee this way or that way: and the people that fled to the wilderness turned back upon the pursuers. And when Joshua and all Israel saw that the ambush had taken the city, and that the smoke of the city ascended, then they turned again, and slew the men of Ai.

When the men of Ai turned around to see 30,000 Israelites behind them, they knew they were in big trouble. Satan knows that, too. That's why he causes all the problems he can for you and me.

When you're standing by the edge of a pool, eating a hamburger, and you see a group of guys walking ominously towards you, you know you're going for a swim. But you also know you're going to take as many as you can with you. To that end, you grab arms and legs and shirts and whatever else you can.

That's what Satan is doing. He knows he's doomed. He knows he's headed for the lake of fire. And, determined to take as many as he can with him, he seeks to neutralize God's saints.

Joshua 8:22–26
And the other issued out of the city against them; so they were in the midst of Israel, some on this side, and some on that side: and they smote them, so that they let none of them remain or escape. And the king of Ai they took alive, and brought him to Joshua. And it came to pass, when Israel had made an end of slaying all the inhabitants of Ai in the field, in the wilderness wherein they chased them, and when they were all fallen on the edge of the sword, until they were consumed, that all the Israelites returned unto Ai, and smote it with the edge of the sword. And so it was, that all that fell that day, both of men and women, were twelve thousand, even all the men of Ai. For Joshua drew not his hand back, wherewith he stretched out the spear,

until he had utterly destroyed all the inhabitants of Ai.

Here, Joshua follows the example Moses set at Rephidim when he held up his staff until Joshua, a young man at that time, was victorious against the Amalekites (Exodus 17).

***For topical study of Joshua 8:18–26 entitled "The Point Is Passion," turn to page* 664.**

Joshua 8:27, 28
Only the cattle and the spoil of that city Israel took for a prey unto themselves, according unto the word of the LORD which he commanded Joshua. And Joshua burnt Ai, and made it an heap for ever, even a desolation unto this day.

Satan will be cast into the lake of fire with his henchmen where they will burn forever.

Joshua 8:29
And the king of Ai he hanged on a tree until eventide: and as soon as the sun was down, Joshua commanded that they should take his carcase down from the tree, and cast it at the entering of the gate of the city, and raise thereon a great heap of stones, that remaineth unto this day.

Deuteronomy 21:22, 23 says everyone that hangs on a tree is cursed. In Galatians 3:13, Paul says this speaks of Jesus, who hung on a tree as He who knew no sin was made sin (2 Corinthians 5:21). Thus, we see in this snapshot that it is not only Joshua who pictures Jesus, but the king of Ai does as well because only Jesus loved us so much that He would become cursed for us and placed in a tomb even as the king of Ai was placed under a heap of stones.

Joshua 8:30 (a)
Then . . .

The Israelites lost the battle at Ai the first time. But now the city is theirs because our God is the God of the second chance.

Joshua 8:30 (b)
. . . Joshua built an altar unto the LORD God of Israel in mount Ebal,

Located in the present-day west bank of Israel, Mt. Ebal is the mountain on which the cursings of Deuteronomy 27 were repeated by half of the nation of Israel while the other half repeated the blessings five hundred yards away on Mt. Gerazim. Why was it Mt. Ebal upon which Joshua built an altar? Because the only way our lives can be "altared" is through the Cross of Calvary upon which Jesus sacrificed His life to pay for the curse of our sin.

Joshua 8:31
As Moses the servant of the LORD commanded the children of Israel, as it is written in the book of the law of Moses, an altar of whole stones, over which no man hath lift up any iron: and they offered thereon burnt offerings unto the LORD, and sacrificed peace offerings.

This altar was to be very simple because the focus was not to be on man's artistic ability, skill, or craftsmanship but upon the sacrifice on the altar.

Joshua 8:32
And he wrote there upon the stones a copy of the law of Moses, which he wrote in the presence of the children of Israel.

Along with the altar on the mount of cursing, there was to be a big monument upon which the Law of Moses was written. The Book of Joshua portraying the Spirit-filled life, the picture here says that the key to living in the Spirit successfully is to heed the Law of God seriously.

Joshua 8:33, 34
And all Israel, and their elders, and officers, and their judges, stood on this side the ark and on that side before the priests the Levites, which bare the ark of the covenant of the LORD, as well the stranger, as he that was born among them; half of them over against mount Gerizim, and half of them over against mount Ebal; as Moses the servant of the LORD had commanded before, that they should bless the people of Israel. And afterward he read all the words of the law, the blessings and cursings, according to all that is written in the book of the law.

The key to having a continued successful run against the enemy is to hear and heed the Word. How shall a young man cleanse his way? By taking heed to the Word (Psalm 119:9).

Joshua 8:35
There was not a word of all that Moses commanded, which Joshua read not before all the congregation of Israel, with the women, and the little ones, and the strangers that were conversant among them.

At the beginning of their conquest of the Promised Land, all of Israel and those in their company stopped to hear the Word. Have your kids heard the Word? The tremendous task before us is to read and discuss the Word of God with our kids over and over, day after day. "We don't have time," you might say. "There are battles to fight, wars to win, Little League games to play, staff meetings to attend." Joshua could have easily said the same thing. But he realized that if we're not talking to our kids about the Word of God, then we're missing the mark completely.

And the stakes are getting higher because we're living in the last days. Dark will get darker and the dangers will become greater. Mom and Dad, if you care about your son or daughter, you will take this responsibility seriously. It is a big mistake to assume our kids know the Word. That's why Joshua said, "I know you're anxious to conquer the land. I know you can't wait to drive out the enemy so you can settle in, grow your crops, and enjoy your family. But we're stopping here and now to go over the Word again."

The Word will be plastered on the wall of your soul and imprinted in your mind if you will take the time to review it time after time after time.

THE POINT IS PASSION

A Topical Study of JOSHUA 8:18–26

"The effectual, fervent prayer of a righteous man availeth much," James declared (5:16). God is not interested in mindless chatter, religious repetition, or lazy liturgy. What our Father is after is people who pray passionately, thoughtfully, and expectantly.

I think of Abraham. When God told him that Sodom was about to be destroyed, Abraham engaged in a passionate conversation with God. "Will not the judge of all the earth do righteously? Surely You'll not destroy the city if there are fifty righteous people in the city," he said.

And God said, "If there are fifty righteous people, I won't."

Abraham came back and said, "If there are forty-five righteous people in the city, surely You'll not destroy it, will You?"

"No," said God.

"What about forty?" countered Abraham. "Thirty, twenty, ten?"

"Even if there are ten righteous men, I won't destroy the city," God replied.

Oh, the audacity, the boldness of Abraham to bargain with God. There was dialogue and desperation, intensity and sincerity. Abraham's relationship with God wasn't based on religion, morning devotions, or a church session. It was based on passion. And as a result, God called him His friend (James 2:23).

I think of Abraham's grandson, Jacob. In his own hour of need, Jacob grabbed God and said, "I'm not going to let You go until You bless me." And there they were, rolling in the dirt by the brook Jabok, wrestling all night long. When morning broke, Jacob was broken as well. But the Lord said, "You've prevailed. And My blessing is upon you" (Genesis 32).

I think of Elijah. When a drought gripped the land and drained life from crop, cattle, and man, Elijah put his head between his knees and prayed not once, twice, or three times but seven times. In assuming the birthing position of the day, Elijah prayed and prayed until he birthed what God desired to do (1 Kings 18).

I think of Elisha. "The Syrians are threatening you and your kingdom," he said to Joash. "Take these arrows out of the quiver and smite them on the ground. They are symbolic of the Lord's deliverance and your victory over Syria." Joash took the arrows and tapped them three times. After all, how could smiting arrows bring about victory? But Elisha said, "Joash, because you only tapped the arrow three times and didn't smite it, your victory over the Syrians will only be partial rather than the total victory God intended for you" (2 Kings 13).

We can think of story after story concerning people of passion who pray with passion—friends of God like Abraham or prophets who birth answers like Elijah. And Joshua is in their company. "I've given Ai into your hands. Now take the spear and hold it up in the air," the Lord said to Joshua. And Joshua held the spear in the air and kept it there until he utterly destroyed all the inhabitants of Ai. He prevailed in prayer and held up the spear not only at the beginning of the battle but all the way through to the end.

Where did he get this idea? I suggest it was forty years earlier at Rephidim. The Amalekites were fighting the Israelites. And Moses said to Joshua, "You lead the troops in the valley. I'll go to the mountain and pray." Moses held high the rod of God. And as he held it up, Joshua and the troops were victorious. But when his hands grew weary and the rod began to fall, the Amalekites gained the upper hand. Moses lifted his hands once again, and Israel took the lead. The battle seesawed back and forth until Aaron and Hur held up Moses' hands until the victory was completely secure for the Israelites.

"Write this scene in a book," God said to Moses. "And rehearse it in the ears of Joshua so that he will know that the reason for his victory in the valley was not due to his strategy or ability but rather because there was intercession and prayer on the mountain."

A lot of us have lost our passion for God. Devotions have become drowsy. Prayer, if we bother, is routine and repetitious chatter. But here's the good news: God cares so passionately about you and me that He will not allow us to remain in a state of passionless religiosity.

C. S. Lewis nailed it when he said that God whispers to us in our pleasure, but shouts to us in our pain. Pain and passion walk hand in hand. If you're married, you understand this. Things get routine, mundane, boring. But when she says something she ought not to, or when he does something he ought not to, there's pain. Feelings are released. Frustrations are vented. Tears flow. But it all leads to passion as the couple is engaged once again.

"I want you either hot or cold," says the Lord (see Revelation 3:16). Yes, you have morning devotions and evening prayer. But there's no smiting of the arrow, no holding up of the spear throughout the whole day, no putting your head between your knees until there's death, drought, or the specter of a Syrian attack. God will not let you reside in a passionless state with Him indefinitely. He will send you pain.

The reason Joshua held up his spear is because he was tired of seeing his friends dead and defeated. *I can't afford this any more,* he must have thought. *The stakes are high, so I will stand here. I will prevail.* And he did.

G. Campbell Morgan said that faith answers questions and is, therefore, out of business when no question is asked. If there are no questions, there is no need for faith. And when do questions arise? When I'm going through difficulty and pain. As Christians, we can have a unique outlook on pain and setbacks if we see them as the fuel of passion.

Why does God desire passion? Because He knows that from passion comes intimacy. And intimacy brings transformation as we are changed from Jacob to Israel, from one who is self-sufficient to one governed by God.

If there has been an absence of passion in your life, expect pain. And when it comes, realize it's not punishment, but a loving Father saying, "I miss you. And you're missing out on being one with Me."

"I'm not going to let go," Joshua said. "I've seen pain. I've seen the death of my comrades in battle. I won't put the spear down. I won't pull it back until the victory is won." That's passion. That's the effectual, fervent prayer that births God's work in our lives.

9 **Joshua 9:1–3**

And it came to pass, when all the kings which were on this side Jordan, in the hills, and in the valleys, and in all the coasts of the great sea over against Lebanon, the Hittite, and the Amorite, the Canaanite, the Perizzite, the Hivite, and the Jebusite, heard thereof; That they gathered themselves together, to fight with Joshua and with Israel, with one accord. And when the inhabitants of Gibeon heard what Joshua had done unto Jericho and to Ai,

In their conquest of the Promised Land, the Israelites took no prisoners because God declared to Joshua that all of the inhabitants of the land of the Canaanites were to be killed—every woman, man, boy, and girl.

"What kind of God would order the extermination of an entire group of people?" many say. "That sounds terribly cruel and brutal." But actually, it's quite merciful. You see, God had given the Canaanites four hundred years to repent from their terrible debauchery and depravity. Theirs was a very evil civilization. Yet God was patient with them and gave them four centuries to repent and get right. But they wouldn't. Therefore, God was as justified in doing what He did as I would be in killing a rabid dog in my house—for in killing him, not only would I spare him further pain, but would save my own kids in the process. As a father, I have no other choice than to protect my children. So, too, in killing people who were already dying in their own sin, God was putting them out of their misery and protecting His own children in the process.

Joshua 9:4 (a)

They did work wilily . . .

The base of the word "wilily" appears in Ephesians 6:11, where Paul instructs the Ephesians to put on the whole armor of God that they would be able to stand against the wiles of the devil. In the war he wages against us, Satan is wily indeed, employing trickery and deception at every turn.

Joshua 9:4 (b)–13
. . . and went and made as if they had been ambassadors, and took old sacks upon their asses, and wine bottles, old, and rent, and bound up; And old shoes and clouted upon their feet, and old garments upon them; and all the bread of their provision was dry and mouldy. And they went to Joshua unto the camp at Gilgal, and said unto him, and to the men of Israel, We be come from a far country: now therefore make ye a league with us. And the men of Israel said unto the Hivites, Peradventure ye dwell among us; and how shall we make a league with you? And they said unto Joshua, We are thy servants. And Joshua said unto them, Who are ye? and from whence come ye? And they said unto him, From a very far country thy servants are come because of the name of the LORD thy God: for we have heard the fame of him, and all that he did in Egypt, And all that he did to the two kings of the Amorites, that were beyond Jordan, to Sihon king of Heshbon, and to Og king of Bashan, which was at Ashtaroth. Wherefore our elders and all the inhabitants of our country spake to us, saying, Take victuals with you for the journey, and go to meet them, and say unto them, We are your servants: therefore now make ye a league with us. This our bread we took hot for our provision out of our houses on the day we came forth to go unto you; but now, behold, it is dry, and it is mouldy: And these bottles of wine, which we filled, were new; and, behold, they be rent: and these our garments and our shoes are become old by reason of the very long journey.

"We are from a far country," said the men of Gibeon. "Our wineskins are torn and our bread is moldy even though they were fresh when we began our journey. We're no threat to you. So let's make a treaty."

Joshua 9:14, 15
And the men took of their victuals, and asked not counsel at the mouth of the LORD. And Joshua made peace with them, and made a league with them, to let them live: and the princes of the congregation sware unto them.

Rather than taking this matter to the Lord, Joshua was taken in by the deception of the Gibeonites.

Joshua 9:16–20
And it came to pass at the end of three days after they had made a league with them, that they heard that they were their neighbours, and that they dwelt among them. And the children of Israel journeyed, and came unto their cities on the third day. Now their cities were Gibeon, and Chephirah, and Beeroth, and Kirjath-jearim. And the children of Israel smote them not, because the princes of the congregation had sworn unto them by the LORD God of Israel. And all the congregation murmured against the princes. But all the princes said unto all the congregation, We have sworn unto them by the LORD God of Israel: now therefore we may not touch them. This we will do to them; we will even let them live, lest wrath be upon us, because of the oath which we sware unto them.

Three days after signing the treaty, the men of Israel discovered that the men of Gibeon lived only a stone's throw away. Why was Israel deceived? For the same reason we are.

"Don't be so uptight about this sin or that compromise. Don't worry about who we are," the hellish ambassadors whisper in our ears. "We'll give you space. We're no threat to you. We want to be friends. Don't worry about being grouchy. Don't worry about losing your temper. Don't worry about seeing that movie. Just be at peace." And whenever I fail to partake of the wine of the blood of Christ and the bread of His broken body, I am deceived by the empty wineskin and the moldy bread of the world.

When I don't go to the Lord's Table—when the wineskin is empty and the bread moldy—I lose sight of the reality of what sin does. But when I come and eat of the fresh bread of the broken body and the shed blood of my Savior, I realize once again that sin slaughters and destroys, that there's no such thing as a small one, a friendly one, an allowable one.

Concerning the sin we think is no big deal, Jesus says, "Eat of My body and drink of My blood. This is what that sin did to Me."

"Wait a minute," you say. "When Jesus died on the Cross, He died for the sins of the whole world—not just for my sin of grumpiness."

That is true. But we need to understand that in the Old Testament, when a man or woman sinned, they had to place their hand on lamb, ox, bull, or goat and confess each sin singularly. Their confession wasn't generic because each sin had to be paid for individually. Therefore, as the fulfillment of the Old Testament sacrificial system, when Jesus died on the Cross, He was paying for each individual sin.

"How could that be?" you ask. "How could He die for the sins of all humanity in just six hours one spring day in A.D. 32"?

Revelation 13:8 tells us that Jesus Christ is the Lamb slain before the foundation of the world.

Go back in your mind before the creation of the world. Then go back further before time began. Then go back further still until there's nothing in your mind. And in the middle of that nothingness, if you look carefully, you'll see the Lamb hanging on the Cross.

When we see the Lord, Revelation 5 says there will be an outpouring of praise, an explosion of adoration not because some worship leader on the stage is saying, "Let's all praise the Lord," but because we're going to understand only then what Jesus did for us. Seeing the Lamb slain will cause everyone to fall down with tears running down our faces, casing everything we have and are at His feet, saying, "Thou art worthy."

Paul wrote to the Corinthians that many of them were sick, weak, and even dying unnecessarily because they had not given worth the Lord's body and blood (1 Corinthians 11:29, 30). He also wrote that in coming to Communion, they showed the Lord's death until He comes (1 Corinthians 11:26). In other words, the way we will understand what sin does and what Christ did for us is not to go to another Bible study or praise gathering. The way to preach the reality of the Lord's death is at Communion.

And yet Christians today will flock to sermons, Christian concerts, or even praise gatherings. But Communion is, at best, optional. Perhaps it is because the Catholic community centers the Mass around Communion, that Protestants err in going too far in the other direction. How many Bible studies, sermons, or praise gatherings have you attended in the past year compared to how many times you've come to the Lord's Table? It's an important question for each person. Communion is the most powerful sermon, the most important teaching that could ever be given.

When I come to the Lord's Table, I see through the deception and treachery of the enemy. Unlike the wine of the world, the wine of the Lord's blood has a sobering effect.

Joshua 9:21–23

And the princes said unto them, Let them live; but let them be hewers of wood and drawers of water unto all the congregation; as the princes had promised them. And Joshua called for them, and he spake unto them, saying, Wherefore have ye beguiled us, saying, We are very far from you; when ye dwell among us? Now therefore ye are cursed, and there shall none of you be freed from being bondmen, and hewers of wood and drawers of water for the house of my God.

If you've been deceived like the Israelites were, if you haven't taken seriously the wine and the bread, do what Joshua did. Make your mistakes work for you. "You've tricked us," he said to the Gibeonites. "We can't kill you because we make an oath. But we're putting you to work. You will chop down trees and carry water. With wood on your shoulders and water in buckets at your side, you're to haul them to the temple for refreshment and redemption."

Joshua 9:24–27

And they answered Joshua, and said, Because it was certainly told thy servants, how that the LORD thy God commanded his servant Moses to give you all the land, and to destroy all the inhabitants of the land from before you, therefore we were sore afraid of our lives because of you, and have done this thing. And now, behold, we are in thine hand: as it seemeth good and right unto thee to do unto us, do. And so did he unto them, and delivered them out of the hand of the children of Israel, that they slew them not. And Joshua made them that day hewers of wood and drawers of water for the congregation, and for the altar of the LORD, even unto this day, in the place which he should choose.

Centuries later, in the Books of Ezra and Nehemiah, we see the Gibeonites, called Nethinims, still serving in the temple. The word *nethinim* means "sent ones" or "given ones." They were given to the task. God so loved the world that He gave His only Son who bore the wood of the Cross on His shoulders and from Whose side water was poured out (John 19:34). He who knew no sin was made sin for us. He is the ultimate sent One, the ultimate given One. And even though I stray from His Table and forget what sin did to Him, He yet invites me to come and dine and to eat of Him, my daily Bread.

10

Joshua 10:1–4

Now it came to pass, when Adoni-zedek king of Jerusalem had heard how Joshua had taken Ai, and had utterly destroyed it; as he had done to Jericho and her king, so he had done to Ai and her king; and how the inhabitants of Gibeon had made peace with Israel, and were among them; That they feared greatly, because Gibeon was a great city, as one of the royal cities, and because it was greater than Ai, and all the men thereof were mighty. Wherefore Adoni-zedek king of Jerusalem sent unto Hoham king of Hebron, and unto Piram king of Jarmuth, and unto Japhia king of Lachish, and unto Debir king of Eglon, saying, Come up unto me, and help me, that

we may smite Gibeon: for it hath made peace with Joshua and with the children of Israel.

When Adoni-zedek, king of then-Canaanite Jerusalem, heard that the Gibeonites were in league with the people who had already conquered Jericho and Ai, he and a confederation of four other kinds decided to launch a war against the Gibeonites in order to discourage other nations from following their example and joining forces with Israel.

Joshua 10:5, 6
Therefore the five kings of the Amorites, the king of Jerusalem, the king of Hebron, the king of Jarmuth, the king of Lachish, the king of Eglon, gathered themselves together, and went up, they and all their hosts, and encamped before Gibeon, and made war against it. And the men of Gibeon sent unto Joshua to the camp to Gilgal, saying, Slack not thy hand from thy servants; come up to us quickly, and save us, and help us: for all the kings of the Amorites that dwell in the mountains are gathered together against us.

If I were Joshua, I would have simply refused to answer the Gibeonites' cry for help. After all, there had been no agreement that Israel would provide protection for Gibeon. And besides that, located twenty-five miles away from Gilgal and four thousand feet higher, it would have been an arduous and dangerous undertaking for the Israelites. But Joshua wasn't like me. He was, in fact, a picture of Jesus.

Joshua 10:7, 8
So Joshua ascended from Gilgal, he, and all the people of war with him, and all the mighty men of valour. And the LORD said unto Joshua, Fear them not: for I have delivered them into thine hand; there shall not a man of them stand before thee.

As a picture of Jesus, Joshua set out to rescue the very people who had lied to him and were now far from him. Jesus comes to our rescue when we are undeserving and unworthy because, even though we are faithless, He is faithful still (2 Timothy 2:13).

Joshua 10:9
Joshua therefore came unto them suddenly, and went up from Gilgal all night.

Traveling all night, Joshua moved his troops double-time twenty-five miles and 4,000 feet in elevation.

Joshua 10:10
And the LORD discomfited them before Israel, and slew them with a great slaughter at Gibeon, and chased them along the way that goeth up to Beth-horon, and smote them to Azekah, and unto Makkedah.

Why did God allow five powerful kings to attack the Gibeonites? Because in this single battle, Israel would be able to wipe out all five of them. Yes, it was a big mistake for Joshua to have relied on his own wisdom. Yes, it was a big mistake for Joshua to have signed a treaty with the Gibeonites. But the God he served was able to turn his blunder into a blessing. And He does the same for us.

Joshua 10:11
And it came to pass, as they fled from before Israel, and were in the going down to Beth-horon, that the LORD cast down great stones from heaven upon them unto Azekah, and they died: they were more which died with hailstones than they whom the children of Israel slew with the sword.

Why were these men stoned? Because that was the Old Testament punishment for blasphemy (Leviticus 24:14, 15). In the New Testament, the one unpardonable sin is the blasphemy of the Holy Spirit (Matthew 12). The one unpardonable, unforgivable sin is saying No to the Holy Spirit as He speaks to us of our need to be saved.

Joshua 10:12, 13 (a)
Then spake Joshua to the LORD in the day when the LORD delivered up the Amorites before the children of Israel, and he said in the sight of Israel, Sun, stand thou still upon Gibeon; and thou, Moon, in the valley of Ajalon. And the sun stood still, and the moon stayed, until the people had avenged themselves upon their enemies. Is not this written in the book of Jasher?

Jasher was a book known to the people of the time, but is unavailable to us. The divine Editor knows what to preserve and what to delete.

Joshua 10:13 (b)
. . . So the sun stood still in the midst of heaven, and hasted not to go down about a whole day.

"We know that the sun doesn't really move. We know it is the earth that revolves around the sun. So this is wrong," scoffs the cynic. People sometimes get all upset about this verse, failing to realize that sunrises and sunsets are figures of speech we use to this day.

Joshua 10:14
And there was no day like that before it or after it, that the LORD hearkened unto the voice of a man: for the LORD fought for Israel.

In this vignette, we see Joshua doing four things that not only elongated his day but that also ensured his victory. First, we see Joshua believing God's Word. In verse 8, God told Joshua that He would give him victory. And Joshua acted on that promise. We can do the same concerning the three thousand-plus promises given to us in the Word.

Secondly, Joshua did his best. He traveled quickly all night to reach the Gibeonites. Because faith without works is dead (James 2:20), the Lord expects me to partner with Him in getting the job done. A lot of people believe a Scripture, but never stay up all night and march out to see it come to pass.

Thirdly, in verse 12, Joshua called on God. "Without Me," Jesus said, "you can do nothing" (John 15:5). And James echoes that we have not because we ask not (James 4:2).

Finally, Joshua spoke in faith. It was in the midst of all the congregation that he said, "Sun, stand still. And moon, stay."

This is where the rubber meets the road for me. You see, it's one thing to believe the Word, to do my best, and to pray. It's another to go on record before my family or the congregation and say, "The victory is won." That is why the Bible says it's not enough to believe in your heart to be saved. It's not enough to raise your hand. It's not enough to come forward. Salvation comes to the one who believes in his heart and confesses with his mouth (Romans 10:9, 10). We have to go on record in the sight of heaven and in the ears of hell not only concerning our salvation, but concerning anything over which we want victory.

Why don't we go on record? Because we're afraid of failure. And fear is the opposite of faith. Without faith it is impossible to please God (Hebrews 11:6). Therefore, there comes a moment, a day when we must go on record and exercise our faith verbally. That's when we're saved. That's when things happen.

***For topical study of Joshua 10:12–14 entitled "Speak to the Son," turn to page* 672.**

Joshua 10:15, 16
And Joshua returned, and all Israel with him, unto the camp to Gilgal. But these five kings fled, and hid themselves in a cave at Makkedah.

Monarchs of cultures that worshiped the moon and the sun, it is no wonder that the five defeated kings went into hiding when the sun and moon stood still at Joshua's command.

Joshua 10:17–20
And it was told Joshua, saying, The five kings are found hid in a cave at Makkedah. And Joshua said, Roll great stones upon the mouth of the cave, and set men by it for to keep them: And stay ye not, but pursue after your enemies, and smite the hindmost of them; suffer them not to enter into their cities: for the LORD your God hath delivered them into your hand. And it came to pass, when Joshua and the children of Israel had made an end of slaying them with a very great slaughter, till they were consumed, that the rest which remained of them entered into fenced cities.

With the kings held prisoner, Joshua sent his troops on a mop-up operation to complete the victory.

Joshua 10:21–25
And all the people returned to the camp to Joshua at Makkedah in peace: none moved his tongue against any of the children of Israel. Then said Joshua, Open the mouth of the cave, and bring out those five kings unto me out of the cave. And they did so, and brought forth those five kings unto him out of the cave, the king of Jerusalem, the king of Hebron, the king of Jarmuth, the king of Lachish, and the king of Eglon. And it came to pass, when they brought out those kings unto Joshua, that Joshua called for all the men of Israel, and said unto the captains of the men of war which went with him, Come near, put your feet upon the necks of these kings. And they came near, and put their feet upon the necks of them. And Joshua said unto them, Fear not, nor be dismayed, be strong and of good courage: for thus shall the LORD do to all your enemies against whom ye fight.

In chapter 1, God said to Joshua, "Fear not, but be strong and of good courage." And now, as time goes on, Joshua, who has lived this out, is now telling those with him not to be afraid. Because Joshua had seen God do exactly what He promised, he could teach with authority that which he had experienced personally. The best things to teach your kids are the things you've found to be true in your own life. The best thing to share in Sunday school or in a Bible study are the things you yourself have experienced. What have you lived out? What have you been through? What's real to you personally? That's where the power is because that's where the Word becomes incarnational, tangible, touchable.

Joshua 10:26, 27
And afterward Joshua smote them, and slew them, and hanged them on five trees: and they were hanging upon the trees until the evening. And it came to pass at the time of the going down of the sun, that Joshua commanded, and they took them down off the trees, and cast them into the cave wherein they had been hid, and laid great stones in the cave's mouth, which remain until this very day.

Five kings were hung on five trees, put in a cave, and covered by stones. Our King, the King of kings was also hung on a tree and put in a cave covered by a stone. But guess what. He didn't stay there. When the stone was rolled away, it was evident that He had risen.

Joshua 10:28–30
And that day Joshua took Makkedah, and smote it with the edge of the sword, and the king thereof he utterly destroyed, them, and all the souls that were therein; he let none remain: and he did to the king of Makkedah as he did unto the king of Jericho. Then Joshua passed from Makkedah, and all Israel with him, unto Libnah, and fought against Libnah: And the LORD delivered it also, and the king thereof, into the hand of Israel; and he smote it with the edge of the sword, and all the souls that were therein; he let none remain in it; but did unto the king thereof as he did unto the king of Jericho.

Joshua is doing exactly what he was commanded to do. He's not leaving any of the enemy in the land.

Joshua 10:31–40
And Joshua passed from Libnah, and all Israel with him, unto Lachish, and encamped against it, and fought against it: And the LORD delivered Lachish into the hand of Israel, which took it on the second day, and smote it with the edge of the sword, and all the souls that were therein, according to all that he had done to Libnah. Then Horam king of Gezer came up to help Lachish; and Joshua smote him and his people, until he had left him none remaining. And from Lachish Joshua passed unto Eglon, and all Israel with him; and they encamped against it, and fought against it: And they took it on that day, and smote it with the edge of the sword, and all the souls that were therein he utterly destroyed that day, according to all that he had done to Lachish. And Joshua went up from Eglon, and all Israel with him, unto Hebron; and they fought against it: And they took it, and smote it with the edge of the sword, and the king thereof, and all the cities thereof, and all the souls that were therein; he left none remaining, according to all that he had done to Eglon; but destroyed it utterly, and all the souls that were therein. And Joshua returned, and all Israel with him, to Debir; and fought against it: And he took it, and the king thereof, and all the cities thereof; and they smote them with the edge of the sword, and utterly destroyed all the souls that were therein; he left none remaining: as he had done to Hebron, so he did to Debir, and to the king thereof; as he had done also to Libnah, and to her king. So Joshua smote all the country of the hills, and of the south, and of the vale, and of the springs, and all their kings: he left none remaining, but utterly destroyed all that breathed, as the LORD God of Israel commanded.

With the conquest of Jericho, Ai, and the five kings confederated against Gibeon, the country had been split in two in this northern campaign. After dividing the land, Joshua went south, smiting the cities there with the edge of the sword. Joshua smote his enemies with a single-edged sword. We, however, have the double-edged sword of the Word with which to wage war against the sin that so easily besets us (Hebrews 4:12).

Joshua 10:41 (a)
And Joshua smote them from Kadesh-barnea . . .

It was at Kadesh-barnea that the children of Israel had lost heart and lacked faith forty years earlier. Now they're at Kadesh-barnea again—this time experiencing victory.

Joshua 10:41 (b)–43
. . . even unto Gaza, and all the country of Goshen, even unto Gibeon. And all these kings and their land did Joshua take at one time, because the LORD God of Israel fought for Israel. And Joshua returned, and all Israel with him, unto the camp to Gilgal.

The same year Galileo invented the telescope, he discovered there were four moons orbiting the planet Jupiter—a surprising discovery considering the fact that prior to this, there was no knowledge of any moon other than our own. In the 1780s, a mathematician/astronomer named William Herschel discovered two more moons around Saturn and two moons around Uranus. In 1846, Asaph Hall discovered Mars had two moons that rose in the west and set in the east. The reason they were not discovered for 250 years after

Galileo invented the telescope is because, with only three percent of the ability to reflect light, they were the darkest objects in the solar system.

In 1726, one hundred and fifty years before Asaph Hall discovered the two moons of Mars, there was an Irish satirist named Jonathan Swift. In his political satire, *Gulliver's Travels,* Swift gave the precise dimensions of the two moons of Mars, including the fact that they traveled from west to east and were dark. How could it be that Swift would be able to nail with such precision the two moons of Mars one hundred and fifty years before they were discovered? There has been much speculation that Swift would base his stories upon ancient legends of history.

As evidenced by England's Stonehenge and Egypt's pyramids, the ancients of every culture were very knowledgeable about the planets. And every culture contains a story of either a long night or a long day. In 1950, Emmanuel Belakowski authored a best-selling book entitled *Worlds in Collision* in which he contends that, due to the universal understanding of a long day on one half of the world and a long night on the other, a planet must have suddenly moved out of its normal orb. He suggests that when Venus was introduced into the solar system after breaking off from a larger planet, the result was cataclysmic repercussions—including the slowing down of the rotation of our earth.

Since 1950, there have been numerous studies suggesting that Mars fits Belakowski's theory better than does Venus. What appears to have happened is that, due to some cosmic disturbance, Mars made a pass by earth. This would explain not only how Jonathan Swift could have known about the two moons of Mars, but also how there could be a five-day increase in the calendar year—from the 360-day calendar of the Aztecs, Mayas, Incas, and Egyptians to our present 365-day calendar year.

Joshua's longest day could very possibly have been brought about by Mars sweeping close to earth. Yet there is still the unmistakable element of the miraculous in this story—for God would have had to set this plan in motion one hundred and eighty years in advance in order for the longest day to be the very one on which Joshua prayed. In Jeremiah 32, we hear the Lord say, "I am the Lord. Is there anything too hard for Me?" The Psalmist declares, "The day is Thine and the night is Thine also" (Psalm 74:16). Day and night are God's. He is the Creator, Sustainer, and Maintainer. He can do whatever He wants with any given day—seen nowhere more clearly than in Joshua 10.

Although it does so begrudgingly and reluctantly, science has to admit that there is nothing in the Bible that ultimately won't prove to be absolutely true. You can bank on it. What I learned in my high school science class has changed many times since I was there. But what I learned in my kindergarten Sunday school class has not changed a bit. And I'm so thankful.

SPEAK TO THE SON

A Topical Study of JOSHUA 10:12–14

Do you ever come to the end of a day feeling frustrated, tense, or anxious because the day slipped away before you could accomplish even half of the things you intended to do? Does it ever seem to you like there's just not enough "day" in your day? There are so many obligations and responsibilities, opportunities and activities that the day seems to dissipate. And sometimes that can fill us with a great degree of frustration.

If you feel that way, the story before us is custom-made for you. In this story, as Joshua fought the enemy in the Promised Land, the sun began to set and the moon began to appear. Running out of time to do what he was supposed to do, Joshua did something radical. Before all of the congregation of Israel, he looked up at the sun and said, "Sun, stand still." And he looked at the moon and said, "Stay." And the sun and moon both stopped.

With the day elongated, Joshua was able to do what the Lord commanded him to do. He finished the work—which reminds me of Another who was able to come through at the end of the day successfully and finish the work perfectly. "Father, I have glorified You and finished the work You gave Me to do," Jesus said (John 17:4). What did Jesus do that enabled Him to say at the end of the day, "I have finished the work"? I believe the answer can be found in Mark's Gospel . . .

Mark tells us that all those who were diseased and demon-possessed were brought to Jesus after He had spent the day teaching the Word and blessing the people in Capernaum (1:32). After preaching all day and ministering to the people personally through the night, verse 33 leaps out at me because it says Jesus rose a great while before daybreak the next morning to pray. If there was ever a time when Jesus would have been justified in kicking back and sleeping in, it would have been here. But He didn't. He rose early for prayer because it was His habit to do so. How do I know? In Isaiah 50, a messianic passage, we read the following:

> *The Lord God hath given me the tongue of the learned, that I should know how to speak a word in season to him that is weary: he wakeneth mine ear to hear as the learned.* Isaiah 50:4

In other words, morning by morning the Father educated, inspired, and directed the Son concerning what to say and how to say it to those who were weary. Jesus always knew not only what to say, but how to say what needed to be said because a great while before the day broke, He sought His Father. And in Mark 1, we see how this worked out practically in His life . . .

> *And Simon and they that were with him followed after him. And when they had found him, they said unto him, All men seek for thee.* Mark 1:36, 37

Jesus' disciples were elated to learn that their Master was in great demand. But watch what Jesus said . . .

> *And he said unto them, Let us go into the next towns, that I may preach there also: for therefore came I forth.* Mark 1:38

The Greek word translated "towns" is seen only here in all of the New Testament. It doesn't speak of a typical town but rather of an unwalled village. In other words, the towns to which Jesus wanted to go were not even big enough to have a wall. Why? "For this reason came I forth," He said—not, I suggest, from heaven, but from His time of prayer. It was as if He said, "I already have instruction for the day. I already know what I'm to do."

This was why Jesus was able to move with such serenity and such tranquility. This is why, at the end of the day, He was able to say, "I've finished the work You've given Me to do." He didn't live according to the obligations, expectations, or even the needs of others. Rather, a great while before the sun rose, this Son had risen and was in the posture and place of prayer. I believe this is the reason that, although He was accused of being a glutton and a winebibber, of being demonized, illegitimate, and crazy, He was never accused of being busy. He moved in such order, such peace, and such tranquility that such an accusation was never hurled at Him.

In our world, to be busy is to be important. But such is not the case in God's economy. To Him, busyness is more of a curse than an asset. That is why Jesus says, "My burden is easy and My load is light. Come unto Me all that are weary and heavy laden, and I will give you rest. Learn of Me and you will find rest in your soul" (Matthew 11:28–30).

If, like Joshua, you and I speak to the Son, things will stand still because He'll whisper in our ear, "Now that you've spent a bit of time with Me, talked things over, made confession of sin, read some Scripture, here's a couple things I want you to do today. . . ."

When I get up before the beginning of the day to find a quiet place with a quiet heart for a quiet time, I find the Lord instructs me about what I should do with my discretionary time. We waste so much time trying to figure out what we should do next. And when we don't get to it, we feel condemned about it. In reality, the decision ought to have been made early in the day. I'm not saying there's no room for flexibility, but for the most part, I have discovered that the real key is to say early in the day, "Lord, what do You want me to do? By Your grace and with Your help, that's what I'll do."

And as I do those things, as I come to the end of the day, I realize the sun has indeed stood still. Therefore, like Jesus, I'm able to say, "Father, I've finished the work You gave me to do." The tensions disappear; the burdens dissipate; and I find myself living a life of serenity and tranquility to a much greater degree.

What God gives us to do is doable. Do what our Greater than Joshua did day by day. Before the day begins, find a quiet place and have a quiet time with a quiet heart. Let God direct your day. You will have fewer decisions to make and you'll be victorious in a whole new way.

---

11 Utilizing the foundational military strategy still used today of "divide and conquer," chapter 10 dealt with Joshua's southern campaign. Here in chapter 11, we see the northern campaign.

Joshua's strategy was essentially based upon three elements: stealth, speed, and knowledge of the terrain. But the real secret of Joshua's success was that he "wholly followed after the Lord his God" (Joshua 14:8). Joshua was one who had a passion for God and followed hard after God.

Sometimes in the Spirit-filled life, people say, "Strategy and organization are not necessary. We're just going to go with the flow." But when I read Joshua, I see in his Spirit-filled model a great emphasis on strategy. Yet although organization is a very good servant, it's a very bad master. It must not be what determines what we do. We know if organization is our master by how we start our day. Do we begin it on our knees in prayer—or with our Daytimer?

If I begin my day on my knees saying, "Lord, by Your Spirit, inspire my thoughts, write upon the table of my heart what You would have me to do," then organization is in its proper place.

Joshua 11:1, 2 (a)
And it came to pass, when Jabin king of Hazor had heard those things, that he sent to Jobab king of Madon, and to the king of Shimron, and to the king of Achshaph, And to the kings that were on the north of the mountains, and of the plains south of Chinneroth . . .

Meaning "harp" *Chinneroth* appears in Scripture again and again. It's another name for the harp-shaped Sea of Galilee, the Sea of Tiberius.

Joshua 11:2 (b)–4
. . . and in the valley, and in the borders of Dor on the west, And to the Canaanite on the east and on the west, and to the Amorite, and the Hittite, and the Perizzite, and the Jebusite in the mountains, and to the Hivite under Hermon in the land of Mizpeh. And they went out, they and all their hosts with them, much people, even as the sand that is upon the sea shore in multitude, with horses and chariots very many.

Led by Jabin, king of Hazor, a massive coalition was formed among the kings of the northern region. The historian Josephus tells us this coalition numbered 300,000 infantrymen, 10,000 cavalrymen, and 20,000 chariots. Chariots being like tanks in those days, this was a formidable army indeed.

Joshua 11:5
And when all these kings were met together, they came and pitched together at the waters of Merom, to fight against Israel.

The waters of Merom being in the valley of Megiddo, we see how this event pictures the prophecies of Revelation. This massive army gathers in the valley of Megiddo to come against Joshua just as they will one day come together to fight our Greater than Joshua, Jesus Christ.

Joshua 11:6, 7
And the LORD said unto Joshua, Be not afraid because of them: for to morrow about this time will I deliver them up all slain before Israel: thou shalt hough their horses, and burn their chariots with fire. So Joshua came, and all the people of war with him, against them by the waters of Merom suddenly; and they fell upon them.

According to Deuteronomy 17, kings were not to multiply horses for themselves. Why? Second Kings 23:11 links horses to the worship of the sun. As you read the history of the Jewish people, you see they did very well without horses . . .

- At the Red Sea, the children lived while the Egyptians on horseback drowned (Exodus 14).
- Deborah and Barak were victorious while Sisera's chariots got stuck in the mud (Judges 4).
- David was given victory over Hadadezer and his thousand horses (2 Samuel 8).

We are not to trust in horses (Psalm 20:7). In this day of incredible technology, we must never think it is technology that will win the world or make an impact evangelistically.

Joshua 11:8–18
And the LORD delivered them into the hand of Israel, who smote them, and chased them unto great Zidon, and unto Misrephothmaim, and unto the valley of Mizpeh eastward; and they smote them, until they left them none remaining. And Joshua did unto them as the LORD bade him: he houghed their horses, and burnt their chariots with fire. And Joshua at that time turned back, and took Hazor, and smote the king thereof with the sword: for Hazor beforetime was the head of all those kingdoms. And they smote all the souls that were therein with the edge of the sword, utterly destroying them: there was not any left to breathe: and he burnt Hazor with fire. And all the cities of those kings, and all the kings of them, did Joshua take, and smote them with the edge of the sword, and he utterly destroyed them, as Moses the servant of the LORD commanded. But as for the cities that stood still in their strength, Israel burned none of them, save Hazor only; that did Joshua burn. And all the spoil of these cities, and the cattle, the children of Israel took for a prey unto themselves; but every man they smote with the edge of the sword, until they had destroyed them, neither left they any to breathe. As the LORD commanded Moses his servant, so did Moses command Joshua, and so did Joshua; he left nothing undone of all that the LORD commanded Moses. So Joshua took all that land, the hills, and all the south country, and all the land of Goshen, and the valley, and the plain, and the mountain of Israel, and the valley of the same; Even from the mount Halak, that goeth up to Seir, even unto Baal-gad in the valley of Lebanon under mount Hermon: and all their kings he took, and smote them, and slew them. Joshua made war a long time with all those kings.

In this description of the northern campaign, we see the war continue. Given Caleb's age, we know it would be a seven-year operation. That is, Joshua would spend seven years clearing out the enemy and taking control of the territory. This rings a bell prophetically, for this is exactly what our Greater than Joshua will do during the seven years of the Tribulation.

Joshua 11:19
There was not a city that made peace with the children of Israel, save the Hivites the inhabitants of Gibeon: all other they took in battle.

The Gibeonites had a peace treaty with Israel. But every other nation came against her. They thought they could challenge Joshua even as the armies of the world will think they can challenge Jesus in the last days.

Joshua 11:20
For it was of the LORD to harden their hearts, that they should come against Israel in battle, that he might destroy them utterly, and that they might have no favour, but that he might destroy them, as the LORD commanded Moses.

After giving them four hundred years to repent, God was at last determined to destroy the Canaanites. And so defiled, perverted, and polluted were they that God was actually merciful in putting them out of their misery.

Joshua 11:21, 22
And at that time came Joshua, and cut off the Anakims from the mountains, from Hebron, from Debir, from Anab, and from all the mountains of Judah, and from all the mountains of Israel: Joshua destroyed them utterly with their cities. There was none of the Anakims left in the land of the children of Israel: only in Gaza, in Gath, and in Ashdod, there remained.

In 1 Samuel we'll read of Goliath, who stood at least 9′9″ tall and possibly even 12′6″. Goliath fought for Gath. But Gath, Gaza, and Ashdod were Philistine cities and the Philistines were not a people of large stature. Those of large stature were the Anakim, first seen in Genesis 6:4. Thus, Goliath must have been a hired soldier.

So too, strange things take place in Spirit-filled living. When you say, "Lord, baptize me in the Spirit. Use me," all hell breaks loose against you as you enter into an intensity of spiritual warfare perhaps previously unknown to you. Suddenly, you're aware of an entirely different dimension. You're cognizant of the fact that you wrestle not against flesh and blood but against principalities and powers in high places (Ephesians 6:12). You no longer blame people but instead see the forces manipulating and dominating them.

Yet although we fight against seeming giants, there's great news . . .

Joshua 11:23 (a)
So Joshua took the whole land, according to all that the LORD said unto Moses; and Joshua gave it for an inheritance unto Israel according to their divisions by their tribes . . .

Because He who is in us is greater than he who comes against us (1 John 4:4), we, like Joshua, can take the whole land as we wield the sword of the Word, don the helmet of salvation, and employ the shield of faith (Ephesians 6:14–17).

Joshua 11:23 (b)
. . . And the land rested from war.

Jesus won the victory for you and me when He cried, "It is finished" (John 19:30). The work is done. The war is won. And we have rest because of what our Greater than Joshua did for us.

12

Joshua 12:1
Now these are the kings of the land, which the children of Israel smote, and possessed their land on the other side Jordan toward the rising of the sun, from the river Arnon unto mount Hermon, and all the plain on the east:

Chapter 12 is review of the battles the Israelites won on the east side of the Jordan, before they crossed the Jordan River into the Promised Land.

Joshua 12:2, 3
Sihon king of the Amorites, who dwelt in Heshbon and ruled from Aroer, which is upon the bank of the river Arnon, and from the middle of the river, and from half Gilead, even unto the river Jabbok, which is the border of the children of Ammon; And from the plain to the sea of Chinneroth on the east, and unto the sea of the plain, even the salt sea on the east, the way to Beth-jeshimoth; and from the south, under Ashdoth-pisgah:

The Israelites conquered Sihon under the leadership of Moses.

Joshua 12:4–6
And the coast of Og king of Bashan, which was of the remnant of the giants, that dwelt at Ashtaroth and at Edrei, And reigned in mount Hermon, and in Salcah, and in all Bashan, unto the border of the Geshurites and the Maachathites, and half Gilead, the border of Sihon king of Heshbon. Them did Moses the servant of the LORD and the children of Israel smite: and Moses the servant of

the Lord gave it for a possession unto the Reubenites, and the Gadites, and the half tribe of Manasseh.

Og was a powerful king, a giant of a man. Along with Sihon, however, he was destroyed by the Israelites under the leadership of Moses.

Joshua 12:7, 8
And these are the kings of the country which Joshua and the children of Israel smote on this side Jordan on the west from Baal-gad in the valley of Lebanon even unto the mount Halak, that goeth up to Seir; which Joshua gave unto the tribes of Israel for a possession according to their divisions; In the mountains, and in the valleys, and in the plains, and in the springs, and in the wilderness, and in the south country; the Hittites, the Amorites, and the Canaanites, the Perizzites, the Hivites, and the Jebusites:

Verses 7 through 24 comprise the list of kings over which Joshua and Israel were victorious on the west side of the Jordan.

Joshua 12:9–24
The king of Jericho, one; the king of Ai, which is beside Bethel, one; The king of Jerusalem, one; the king of Hebron, one; The king of Jarmuth, one; the king of Lachish, one; The king of Eglon, one; the king of Gezer, one; The king of Debir, one; the king of Geder, one; The king of Hormah, one; the king of Arad, one; The king of Libnah, one; the king of Adullam, one; The king of Makkedah, one; the king of Bethel, one; The king of Tappuah, one; the king of Hepher, one; The king of Aphek, one; the king of Lasharon, one; The king of Madon, one; the king of Hazor, one; The king of Shimron-meron, one; the king of Achshaph, one; The king of Taanach, one; the king of Megiddo, one; The king of Kedesh, one; the king of Jokneam of Carmel, one; The king of Dor in the coast of Dor, one; the king of the nations of Gilgal, one; The king of Tirzah, one: all the kings thirty and one.

In their day, these kings would have been well known throughout the region. They were the famous people, the ones on the cover of *People* magazine. Yet, although the kings are listed, their names aren't given because today, we don't even know who they were.

In the paper today, I read that to hire Jennifer Lopez to sing at an event costs $750,000 per hour. Elton John, *NSYNC, and the Backstreet Boys charge one million dollars an hour. Former President George Bush, Al Gore, or Jay Leno charge $100,000 per lecture. But 1,000 years from now, people will say, "Jennifer who? Backstreet what?" Like the kings of verses 9–24, the people in the world's *Who's Who* today will be in *Who Cares* tomorrow.

Heaven. That's what counts. The names written in the Lamb's Book of Life are recorded *eternally.*

13

Joshua 13:1–6
Now Joshua was old and stricken in years; and the Lord said unto him, Thou art old and stricken in years, and there remaineth yet very much land to be possessed. This is the land that yet remaineth: all the borders of the Philistines, and all Geshuri, From Sihor, which is before Egypt, even unto the borders of Ekron northward, which is counted to the Canaanite: five lords of the Philistines; the Gazathites, and the Ashdothites, the Eshkalonites, the Gittites, and the Ekronites; also the Avites: From the south, all the land of the Canaanites, and Mearah that is beside the Sidonians, unto Aphek, to the borders of the Amorites: And the land of the Giblites, and all Lebanon, toward the sunrising, from Baal-gad under mount Hermon unto the entering into Hamath. All the inhabitants of the hill country from Lebanon unto Misrephoth-maim, and all the Sidonians, them will I drive out from before the children of Israel: only divide thou it by lot unto the Israelites for an inheritance, as I have commanded thee.

In Joshua 11:23, we read that Joshua took the whole land and that the land rested from war. Here, we read that very much land remained to be possessed. Is this a contradiction? No, for although the victory was secure, there were still "mop-up operations" to complete in pockets of resistance where the enemy was holed up.

In our soul, there are pockets of resistance as well. However, in the Spirit-filled life we don't fight for victory because Jesus already was victorious on our behalf when He died on the Cross. The roaring lion has had his teeth kicked in. We don't fight *for* victory, but *from* victory. Positionally, we're the righteousness of God in Christ Jesus (2 Corinthians 5:21), but practically, there are still enemies lurking around my soul that need to be rooted out.

***For topical study of Joshua 11:23; 13:1 entitled "Take Your Position," turn to page* 678.**

Joshua 13:7–13
Now therefore divide this land for an inheritance unto the nine tribes, and the half tribe of Manasseh, With whom the Reubenites and the Gadites have received their inheritance,

which Moses gave them, beyond Jordan eastward, even as Moses the servant of the LORD gave them; From Aroer, that is upon the bank of the river Arnon, and the city that is in the midst of the river, and all the plain of Medeba unto Dibon; And all the cities of Sihon king of the Amorites, which reigned in Heshbon, unto the border of the children of Ammon; And Gilead, and the border of the Geshurites and Maachathites, and all mount Hermon, and all Bashan unto Salcah; All the kingdom of Og in Bashan, which reigned in Ashtaroth and in Edrei, who remained of the remnant of the giants: for these did Moses smite, and cast them out. Nevertheless the children of Israel expelled not the Geshurites, nor the Maachathites: but the Geshurites and the Maachathites dwell among the Israelites until this day.

Gad, Reuben, and half of the tribe of Manasseh were the ones who chose to remain on the east side of the Jordan rather than crossing with the rest of the tribes into the Promised Land. Their decision wasn't based upon God's best for their families but seemingly upon what was best for their cattle and bank accounts. History shows, however, that Reuben, Gad, and the half-tribe of Manasseh were the first ones to be carried away when the enemies of Israel attacked the nation.

The same thing happens to you and me. If you say, "I'm just going to hang out in the back," watch out. That is sure to be the most dangerous, most depressing place ultimately. God will not make me go in and go on in my walk with Him. The choice is up to me. He will take me as deep as I want to go—but He won't take me one step further than I want to go.

Joshua 13:14
Only unto the tribe of Levi he gave none inheritance; the sacrifices of the LORD God of Israel made by fire are their inheritance, as he said unto them.

Jacob, whose name was changed to Israel, had twelve sons, which comprised the Twelve Tribes of Israel. The tribe of Joseph, however, was represented by Joseph's sons, Manasseh and Ephraim, which, technically, meant there were thirteen tribes. Yet the fact that the Levites, the priestly tribe, was given no territory in order that they could minister throughout the nation, meant that the tribes inheriting land remained twelve in number.

Joshua 13:15–23
And Moses gave unto the tribe of the children of Reuben inheritance according to their families. And their coast was from Aroer, that is on the bank of the river Arnon, and the city that is in the midst of the river, and all the plain by Medeba; Heshbon, and all her cities that are in the plain; Dibon, and Bamoth-baal, and Beth-baal-meon, And Jahazah, and Kedemoth, and Mephaath, And Kirjathaim, and Sibmah, and Zareth-shahar in the mount of the valley, And Beth-peor, and Ashdoth-pisgah, and Beth-jeshimoth, And all the cities of the plain, and all the kingdom of Sihon king of the Amorites, which reigned in Heshbon, whom Moses smote with the princes of Midian, Evi, and Rekem, and Zur, and Hur, and Reba, which were dukes of Sihon, dwelling in the country. Balaam also the son of Beor, the soothsayer, did the children of Israel slay with the sword among them that were slain by them. And the border of the children of Reuben was Jordan, and the border thereof. This was the inheritance of the children of Reuben after their families, the cities and the villages thereof.

Verses 24–33 describe the region given to Gad, Reuben, and the half tribe of Manasseh—for although they chose not to step into the Jordan River and press on to deeper waters in kingdom life, they were still part of the family, still part of the congregation of God.

TAKE YOUR POSITION

A Topical Study of JOSHUA 11:23; 13:1

So Joshua took the whole land, according to all that the LORD said unto Moses; and Joshua gave it for an inheritance unto Israel according to their divisions by their tribes. And the land rested from war. Joshua 11:23

Now Joshua was old and stricken in years; and the LORD said unto him, Thou art old and stricken in years, and there remaineth yet very much land to be possessed.
Joshua 13:1

Although skeptics cry, "Contradiction!" concerning these two passages, there is no contraction whatsoever. You see, the first passage refers to the fact that, after seven years of battle, under God's providence and Joshua's leadership, the Israelites were successful in their conquest of the Promised Land. And yet there were pockets where the Canaanites were holed up and hiding out. So in chapter 13, the Lord told Joshua that there were many places where the property had not yet been possessed, that there was a mop-up operation to do.

We see the same thing in our history. In WWII, we convincingly defeated the Japanese Imperial Army. They lost the war. But there were pockets of Imperial soldiers on islands and atolls throughout the South Seas that remained on for many years after the war was over. That's the idea here. The war was over, but the Israelites had yet to "mop up" and take control.

What does this have to do with us?

Lots.

The Old Testament is a grand picture book. It illustrates truths for you and me in the stories it tells, in the portraits it paints. For every New Testament truth or principle, there's an Old Testament picture. I need that. In this Book of Joshua, there are many glorious pictures painted. One such picture is that of the difference between positional and practical truth.

Positional Truth

Joshua won the war. The inheritance was given out. The land had rest. This pictures exactly what our Joshua, Jesus, did when He won the victory on the Cross. "Te telestai," He cried. "It is finished." His wasn't the whimpering cry of a quitter. No, it was the victorious shout of a warrior. "It is finished. The price is paid. The work is done." We have rest because of what Jesus did for you and me on the Cross of Calvary. Because He fought the war and won, we get the inheritance of eternal life—just like the Israelites got the inheritance.

Before Jesus died on the Cross, only the high priest could enter the Holy Place of the Lord's presence—and then only one day each year on Yom Kippur, the Day of Atonement. After Jesus died, however, the veil separating the Holy Place from the rest of the temple was rent from top to bottom, as if God said, "Open House! Everyone, anyone, any time can come into My presence." Because Jesus won the victory, we get the inheritance and we rest in that fact.

Because of what Jesus did, we are righteous. The war is over. Second Corinthians 5:21 tells us we are the righteousness of God in Christ Jesus. That is, when the Father looks at us, He doesn't see our frailties and foibles, flaws and foolishness.

No, He sees us surrounded by, cloaked with, hidden in Christ. There is therefore now no condemnation to those who are in Christ Jesus (Romans 8:1). That's our position.

Think of it this way . . .

Midway into spring training, Dusty Baker, manager of the San Francisco Giants, calls and says, "Jon, we're a little weak on our shortstop position. Can you come and give us a hand?"

"Sure, Dusty. I'll be right there," I say.

As I begin to train with the Giants, however, it suddenly becomes clear that I can't play baseball. *This guy can't play baseball,* thinks Dusty. *He can't handle a grounder, can't make the pivot at second, can't throw accurately to first. He can't hit a curve ball, fastball, slowball, or even a softball.*

But because I signed a no-cut contract, I remain on the team. The Giants go on to win the divisional championships, the playoffs, and the World Series. I don't take the field or get up to bat a single time because I'm awful. But I'm on the team. And when the ticker tape parade takes place, when all the fans are waving, I'm in the parade because I'm on the team. I'm in the team picture. I have the World Series ring on my finger, and the World Series bonus in my wallet. I'm still lousy—but, because I'm on the team, I get the benefits.

That's positional truth. That's the standing I have. It's not based on what I do, but on what God's done. It's not based on who I am, but on where He's placed me—in His Son. And the same thing is true for each of us. Great is the day when a man or woman finally sees that, positionally, they're in Christ, righteous, forgiven, free. They can come boldly before His throne and expect to find mercy and help whenever they need it. I wake up every day expecting to be blessed—not because of who I am, but because of what Jesus has done.

Practical Truth

Now suppose Dusty Baker says, "Jon, you've got the ring and the bonus. You were in the picture and parade. But I've got plans for you. Next season, I don't want you to be on the bench every inning of every game. I want to get you in occasionally. I want you to be a real contributing part of the team. So this winter, I'm going to work with you. Every single day, I'm going to knock you grounders. I'm going to put a plastic ball on a plastic tee and you're going to hit it with a big plastic bat. I'm going to work with you day after day, week after week, and we're going to get you to where you're not only positionally on the team, but practically you're on the field, in the game. I'm going to train and teach you and help you to be successful not just in theory but practically."

That's what chapter 13 is talking about. The war is over. The land is at rest. The inheritance has been given. However, there are still Canaanites to be rooted out, to be dealt with practically. The Canaanites of carnality in our lives need to be rooted out and taken away so that we can be productive.

Maybe at this point you're thinking you would rather sit on the bench with your World Series ring and World Series bonus. Why should we want to be out there in the war mopping up? If the victory is won, why should we want to mop up?

Three reasons . . .

For Your Own Sake

The Israelites allowed the Canaanites to remain. Consequently, as the years went on, the Canaanites increased in number and began to launch guerilla warfare against the people of Israel. The Israelites watched their kids being attacked and the land destroyed because they didn't deal with the Canaanites when they had opportunity. The same thing is true of you and me.

I can say, "Positionally I'm the righteousness of God in Christ. Positionally, I can come before His throne of grace. Positionally, I'm on the winning team eternally." That's all true. But if I say, "So I'm not going to worry about what I say when my temper flares. I'm not going to worry about the lust in my heart, or the drink I must have to calm my nerves. I'm not going to worry about what's on TV because I'm forgiven. I'm going to just let those things slide," I will be attacked without question. Positionally, we are righteous. But practically, any Canaanites we allow in our lives will gain ground and bring great harm to us and to those around us.

I have yet to talk to a man who says, "I'm glad I kept swearing year after year," or, "I'm so thankful I had one adulterous affair after another. It made my life successful and made my family happy." No one has said to me in all my years of ministry, "I'm really glad I've been a gossip." What people say is, "The thing I regret is the alcohol I was in bondage to, the pornography I was caught up in, the adulterous relationships I pursued. I once had opportunity to see them rooted out. Instead, I let the Canaanites have control of pockets in my soul. Now they're causing misery and destroying my family."

The Canaanites of carnality will make you miserable. Drive them out. Don't let them take root because they'll grow and bring about incalculable pain and misery. For your own sake, drive them out.

For Heaven's Sake

I recently attended a memorial service for Peter-John's great-grandmother who was one hundred and two years old. Alice Elder impacted people. She loved the Lord and raised her three sons in the ways of God. As I listened to people talk about how she had influenced them, I wondered what people would say about us. What will be your lasting legacy? If you were to die today, what would the people you live and work with say about you? What would they truly think and feel about you?

Here is a key to living life successfully: Live it backwards. Live as though you're going to die by Saturday. How would you treat your husband, wife, or kids? How would you treat people at work if you knew you were going to die before this week is over? Jesus lived His entire life backwards. He came to earth, knowing He had come to die. The Cross was ever before Him. Everything pointed to that moment. Even as a babe in Bethlehem, He was born in a cave, which pictures a tomb, and was wrapped in swaddling cloths, which picture grave clothes. Jesus lived an abundant life because He knew He had come to die.

When I see Jesus face to face, will I hear Him say, "Well done, good and faithful servant! You accepted My positional gift of salvation and you worked it out practically in your daily life. You rooted out the Canaanite. You didn't tolerate that, you got rid of the other. Well done!"? That's what I want to hear.

For Christ's Sake

Joshua was "old and stricken in years." Praise the Lord, our Joshua, our Jesus, never gets old. Jesus is the same today, yesterday, and forever. What do the people around your house, at your job, or in your family think about Christ? Is He old and stricken, or is He virile, vital, and real?

Most of the people you work with or live near will never read their Bible seriously. Most of them won't come to Bible study. Therefore, you are the Bible to them. They will get their impression about who Jesus is by looking at you day after day. What will they see? Is Christ old and stricken, powerless and impotent?

"I heard stories in Sunday school where Jesus fed 5,000 miraculously, calmed the stormy sea incredibly, turned water into wine amazingly. So where is this same Jesus today? I don't see that kind of power," people say. And they get this impression of Jesus by what they see in our lives day to day.

A skeptic stood up in a church service and said, "I don't believe in the Jesus you talk about because the Jesus in the Bible was powerful and did miracles."

A man in the back raised his hand and said, "Sir, Jesus is still doing miracles today, only in an even greater way. You talked about Jesus turning water into wine. In my life, He turned beer into furniture. I used to be an alcoholic. My family was falling apart, my money was spent on alcohol. Then I met Jesus and He changed my life. I don't drink any more. The money I used to spend on beer, I spend on my family."

Based upon what you do practically, the cynic will either view Christ as old and stricken or powerful and virile. He will draw his conclusions about Christ based not on positional truth but on the truth he sees you live out before him.

I want people to see that Jesus still changes lives, sees people through, and brings abundance and blessing.

How do I root out the enemy? Here's the great news. Positionally, I enjoy the riches and inheritance because of Christ's *death*. Practically, I have victory over that which would make me miserable, ruin my testimony, and rob me eternally through Christ's resurrected *life*. You see, Jesus not only died to wash our sins away positionally, but He rose again on the third day to live within us practically. So when the Canaanites rise up, when the temptation threatens, the good news is that Christ is right there with you. The good news is that God will not allow you to be tempted above what you are able, but will provide a way of escape, a way of victory—every single time (1 Corinthians 10:13).

The Lord not only tells us what to do, but He sets up residence inside of us. Positionally, we're cleansed by His death. Practically, we're set free by His life.

14

Joshua 14:1
And these are the countries which the children of Israel inherited in the land of Canaan, which Eleazar the priest, and Joshua the son of Nun, and the heads of the fathers of the tribes of the children of Israel, distributed for inheritance to them.

With Reuben, Gad, and the half tribe of Manasseh remaining on the east side of the Jordan, the rest of the nine and one-half tribes claimed their territory on the west side, in the Promised Land. Each tribe was given a certain region, described in chapters 13 through 21. These descriptions might seem tedious to us, but they were important and wonderful to the Israelites. Why? Because the descriptions were of their own inheritance.

God has a wonderful plan for you. It might be boring to others, but for you, it's of utmost importance to know what territory God has given to you, where your place is in the body of Christ, what God wants you to do. If your heart desires to know His will, be sure He will give the parameters to you. As time goes on, what you're to do will become clear to you.

"I am careful that I do not stretch myself beyond measure," Paul declared (2 Corinthians 10:14–16). In other words, "I realize what God has called me to do and I want to take it all. But I'm not going to stretch myself beyond what He's called me to do and to be."

God has exacting boundaries for you. And it's our privilege and responsibility to explore, to pursue, to pray, to seek the Lord, study, to wait on Him and say, "Lord, what territory have You mapped out as mine? Help me to stick to it and be faithful in it that I might take all the territory you have for me."

Joshua 14:2
By lot was their inheritance, as the LORD commanded by the hand of Moses, for the nine tribes, and for the half tribe.

The word "lot" in Hebrew is actually *gowral*, which means "pebble." "To cast lots" in Greek is *lanchano*, which literally means "to launch." In other words, "lot" here speaks of the rolling of some sort of dice—a practice seen throughout the Old Testament. In Deuteronomy 34, Moses declared that the land was to be divided by lot. It was by lot that the sailors determined it was Jonah who caused the storm that threatened their lives (Jonah 1:7). In Proverbs 16:33, we read, "The lot is cast into the lap; but the whole disposing thereof is of the Lord." In other words, "You can cast lots, but in reality, the whole thing is determined by the Lord."

"If people cast dice in Deuteronomy and Joshua, shouldn't we do this as well?" some might ask. Casting lots was indeed prescribed and utilized in Old Testament times, but in the New Testament, we see a better way.

After Judas hung himself, there was a vacancy in the apostolic company. The remaining eleven disciples placed stipulations upon who could fulfill the office, saying, "It must be a man who's been with us and who has seen Jesus." Two men met the criterion, so they cast lots and Matthias was chosen. But Acts 1 comes before Acts 2, and Acts 2 was when the disciples were empowered by the Holy Ghost. As the Book of Acts unfolds, we meet a man who was uniquely raised up by the Spirit, a man named Paul. We never hear of Matthias again, but Paul's impact was huge. Therefore, I believe had the disciples waited until after the Spirit was poured out upon them, they would have chosen Paul to fill Judas' vacancy.

In Old Testament times, it was allowable to cast lots. But in New Testament days, we have an entirely different way to discern direction. We don't cast lots or roll dice to find God's will, get rich, or get ahead. Rather, we wait on the Spirit. I think rolling dice, choosing straws, or playing the lottery grieves the Lord and short-circuits what He wants to do with us, through us, and for us. An infinitely better way is to be guided by the Spirit day by day.

Joshua 14:3–6
For Moses had given the inheritance of two tribes and an half tribe on the other side Jordan: but unto the Levites he gave none inheritance among them. For the children of Joseph were two tribes, Manasseh and Ephraim: therefore they gave no part unto the Levites in the land, save cities to dwell in, with their suburbs for their cattle and for their substance. As the LORD commanded Moses, so the children of Israel did, and they divided the land. Then the children of Judah came unto Joshua in Gilgal: and Caleb the son of Jephunneh the Kenezite said unto him, Thou knowest the thing that the LORD said unto Moses the man of God concerning me and thee in Kadesh-barnea.

Joshua and Caleb were two of the twelve spies who went into the Promised Land at Kadesh-barnea. They were the two who believed in God, who had faith that He would give the people of Israel the land. The congregation, however, chose to believe the ten who didn't believe God. Here, Caleb reminds Joshua of their story.

Joshua 14:7–12
Forty years old was I when Moses the servant of the LORD sent me from Kadesh-barnea to espy out the land; and I brought him word again as it was in mine heart. Nevertheless my brethren that went up with me made the heart of the people melt: but I wholly followed the LORD my God. And Moses sware on that day, saying, Surely the land whereon thy feet have trodden shall be thine inheritance, and thy children's for ever, because thou hast wholly followed the LORD my God. And now, behold, the LORD hath kept me alive, as he said, these forty and five years, even since the LORD spake this word unto Moses, while the children of Israel wandered in the wilderness: and now, lo, I am this day fourscore and five years old. As yet I am as strong this day as I was in the day that Moses sent me: as my strength was then, even so is my strength now, for war, both to go out, and to come in. Now therefore give me this mountain, whereof the LORD spake in that day; for thou heardest in that day how the Anakims were there, and that the cities were great and fenced: if so be the LORD will be with me, then I shall be able to drive them out, as the LORD said.

Caleb didn't claim a beachfront condo on the Mediterranean, a cabin on the Sea of Galilee, or a loft apartment in Jerusalem for his inheritance. Rather, he said, "Give me the area where the giants are." Oh, may the Lord make us like Caleb—people who don't back away from challenges or problems, but who instead understand that they're actually good for us.

Joshua 14:13–15
And Joshua blessed him, and gave unto Caleb the son of Jephunneh Hebron for an inheritance. Hebron therefore became the inheritance of Caleb the son of Jephunneh the Kenezite unto this day, because that he wholly followed the LORD God of Israel. And the name of Hebron before was Kirjath-arba; which Arba was a great man among the Anakims. And the land had rest from war.

Arba means "large and loud." *Kirjath* means "city." *Hebron* means "fellowship." The city of the big and loud became the city of fellowship. That's always the way it is. Big loud problems cause us to call out to the Lord, to depend on the Lord, and to fellowship with the Lord in ways we never would have otherwise.

"I thought the Spirit-filled life was supposed to be the abundant life. So why do I have these big headaches and problems?," we cry. It is because they bring us to Hebron. Without them, we would become complacent and lazy.

It was an eighty-five-year-old Caleb who said, "I'm as strong as I've ever been, so give me the place where the giants are." Don't let old age creep in spiritually. Stay vibrant and youthful by taking on new challenges, by not shrinking away from problems. It's the giants who will keep you in Hebron, the difficulties that will keep you in fellowship.

WONDER BREAD!

A Topical Study of JOSHUA 14:6–15

"A man ripens until the age of thirty. After thirty, he rots," said philosopher Henry David Thoreau. Yet here in our text is a man who, at the age of eighty-five, said, "I am as vibrant and as vigorous as I've ever been." His name is Caleb, and his story is an amazing one.

At this point in the Book of Joshua, Joshua is dividing the Promised Land among the tribes of Israel. As he does, his friend, Caleb came to him, telling him what he wanted for his inheritance. Now, one would think that, at eighty-five, Caleb would say, "What I want is a condo on the beach on the Mediterranean seashore." Or perhaps, "Give me a cabin on the shore of the Sea of Galilee." But that's not what Caleb said.

He said, "What I want is the high country, the mountainous territory where the Anakims—the giants—are."

Joshua and Caleb knew about giants. Years earlier, they were two of the twelve spies sent in to check out the Promised Land. In Caleb's story, we see a very practical and important lesson that will help us to remain vigorous spiritually even as we age physically. You see, God does not want us to fade away, to retire, or to pull back. Rather, the Bible says He wants to take you and me from glory to *greater* glory (2 Corinthians 3:18). He wants us to become stronger and deeper, richer and better, year after year until the day He takes us to heaven. That's God's intention.

I question that, you might be thinking. *My grandmother loves the Lord—but she's been in a hospital, a rest home, or even a coma for many years. How do you explain that?*

Even though a person has Alzheimers or does not think clearly, it doesn't mean there's not a lot going on in his spirit. As he lays in bed day after day, year after year, people might say, "Why is God keeping him here?" Yet God is putting His finishing touches on him and using him in ways we can't understand. "When I pray in the Spirit, my mind is unfruitful," Paul said (1 Corinthians 14:14). In other words, a person can pray in the Spirit even though his mind isn't tracking.

Caleb is an example for you, a model for me of how to stay spiritually vibrant. In Numbers 13, we see his story . . .

Forty-five years before the account in Joshua 14, God had lead His people to a place called Kadesh-barnea. Poised to go into the Promised Land, the people of Israel sent one man from each of the twelve tribes to check it out. The tribe of Ephraim was represented by Joshua, the tribe of Judah by Caleb. Ten of the spies returned, saying, "We can't go up against the people because they're stronger than us. Compared to them, we're just grasshoppers."

Joshua and Caleb, however, ripped their clothes in grief and said, "The land is an exceedingly good land. If the Lord delight in us, He will bring us into this land and give it to us. Do not fear the people of the land. For they are bread for us."

When others said, "We're going to get crunched and stomped on," Caleb said. "No, God's with us. And those giants are bread for us. We're going to eat them up" (Numbers 14:9). When he was eighty-five years old, this same Caleb said, "I want the Anakims. I want food. I don't want to kick back. I don't want an easier load. I don't want to retire. What I want, what's keeping me strong and vigorous is giants. I thrive on them."

Why would Caleb say this? Because he understood that what God's people need is not comfort but challenges because it is the giant difficulty, the giant heartbreak, the giant heartache that brings them to Hebron. Hebron, the place Abraham first built an altar, means "Fellowship." That's what giant problems do—they bring me to the place where I cry out to the Lord, call on the Lord, and look to the Lord. They bring me to fellowship. When things are comfy and cozy, I can find myself pulling away from fellowship. I can find myself spiritually putting my feet up, kicking back, retiring.

And that makes me old, grumpy, cranky, diminished. Why? Because it's in the place where I'm battling heartbreak and heartache, where I'm doing battle in the spiritual realm that I am forced to be on my knees, forced to say, "Lord, I can't make it without You."

And the Lord says, "That's why I've allowed these Anakims to come to you. They're bread for you. They actually make you stronger because they bring you into Hebron."

"Give us this day our daily bread," Jesus taught us to pray. When I think of bread, I think of sourdough with butter and strawberry jelly. While the Lord does indeed give us bread to sustain us physically, He also gives us the bread of giant problems to make us strong and energetic spiritually.

I want to be like Caleb. I want to say I'm strong like I was at my peak.

The Lord says, "OK, then I'm going to send bread your way—Anakims that will force you to come to Hebron."

That's what Jesus did. Such an abundance of bread did He provide for the multitude that there were twelve baskets left over. If this meant each disciple was given his own basket, I can picture them enjoying their "leftovers" on the grassy hillside, overlooking the Sea of Galilee. That very evening, they were on the Sea of Galilee facing giant problems. "We're dying!" they cried, as they fought the storm hour after hour. Yet it was then—in the midst of a giant storm—that Jesus, the Bread of Life, came to them, walking on the water (Matthew 14:27).

When we're eating bread on the grassy hillside, we don't understand who Jesus is. But when the seas are angry and the wind is howling, when there are giants around us and everything seems to be going down, it's then we hear His voice and see His face. It is then we understand that He is our Bread.

As believers, we're the luckiest people in the world because we are the only ones who can count it all joy when various trials come our way (James 1:2). We're the only ones who know that all things are working together for good (Romans 8:28). We're the only ones who can say, "There's a giant of a problem in my life—and I know it's bread for me."

How do I know that every storm the Lord sends my way will ultimately be good for me? Because the Bread of Life was broken on the Cross of Calvary to pay for my sins. Our Lord, our Joshua, our Jesus says to us, "I care about you deeply. I love you passionately. And anything that comes your way is Wonder Bread. It will build your body, keep you young, and bring you into fellowship with Me."

15

Joshua 15:1 (a)
This then was the lot of the tribe of the children of Judah . . .

In chapter 15, we see a description of the land given to Judah. Again, while this may be tedious to us, it was as important to the people of Judah as discovering our own unique place and function in the body of Christ is to us.

Joshua 15:13–19
And unto Caleb the son of Jephunneh he gave a part among the children of Judah, according to the commandment of the LORD to Joshua, even the city of Arba the father of Anak, which city is Hebron. And Caleb drove thence the three sons of Anak, Sheshai, and Ahiman, and Talmai, the children of Anak. And he went up thence to the inhabitants of Debir: and the name of Debir before was Kirjath-sepher. And Caleb said, He that smiteth Kirjath-sepher, and taketh it, to him will I give Achsah my daughter to wife. And Othniel the son of Kenaz, the brother of Caleb, took it: and he gave him Achsah his daughter to wife. And it came to pass, as she came unto him, that she moved him to ask of her father a field: and she lighted off her ass; and Caleb said unto her, What wouldest thou? Who answered, Give me a blessing; for thou hast given me a south land; give me also springs of water. And he gave her the upper springs, and the nether springs.

As a member of the tribe of Judah, we again see Caleb. And in this vignette concerning him, I believe a most interesting parallel can be drawn. That is, I believe Caleb is a picture of the Holy Spirit . . .

First, I believe Caleb pictures the Holy Spirit because, of the twelve spies, he alone traveled into the Promised Land with Joshua, who is himself a picture of our Lord Jesus. Likewise, the ministry of the Spirit is to point people not to Himself, but to Jesus (1 Corinthians 12:3).

Secondly, Caleb was victorious over giants—just as the Spirit gives us victory over our adversary (Ephesians 6:17).

Third, here we see Caleb giving a bride away. What is the ministry of the Holy Spirit? To form a church, a Bride for Jesus.

Fourth, Caleb provided both the upper and lower springs. Springs are a picture of the work of the Spirit. "If any man thirst," Jesus said, "let him come to Me and out of his innermost being shall gush forth torrents of living water. This spake He of the Holy Spirit (John 7:38).

"I don't want only the lower springs," Achsah said. And guess what. Because she asked, she got just what she asked for. You see, there are two baptisms that deal with the Holy Spirit. The first, seen in 1 Corinthians 12, took place when you became a believer, when you were baptized by the Spirit into the body of Christ. But there's a second baptism—when you are baptized not by the Spirit into the body, but by Jesus into the Spirit. Every Christian is baptized by the Spirit into the body of Christ. But there's a difference between that and being baptized by Jesus into the Spirit. Achsah wanted both.

I believe most of us would say, "I do, too."

Finally, *Caleb's* name literally means "dog." And I can't help but think of the "Hound of heaven,"—the Holy Spirit—who tracks people down to let them know they're loved by God.

Joshua 15:20
This is the inheritance of the tribe of the children of Judah according to their families.

The remainder of chapter 15 continues to describe the boundaries of the tribe of Judah.

16

Joshua 16:1–5 (a)
And the lot of the children of Joseph fell from Jordan by Jericho, unto the water of Jericho on the east, to the wilderness that goeth up from Jericho throughout mount Bethel, And goeth out from Bethel to Luz, and passeth along unto the borders of Archi to Ataroth, And goeth down westward to the coast of Japhleti, unto the coast of Beth-horon the nether, and to Gezer: and the goings out thereof are at the sea. So the children of Joseph, Manasseh and Ephraim, took their inheritance. And the border of the children of Ephraim according to their families was thus:

Chapters 16 and 17 describe the inheritance given to Joseph's two sons, Ephraim and Manasseh. Although Manasseh was the older brother, Ephraim is mentioned first. And therein lies a story . . .

Hearing that his father was sick, Joseph brought his two sons to be blessed by their grandfather, carefully positioning them so that Manasseh was on Jacob's right side and Ephraim on his left. After pronouncing blessing upon Joseph, Jacob prepared to bless Joseph's sons by placing his right hand—the hand of priority—on Ephraim and his left on Manasseh. "Wait a minute, Dad," Joseph said. "You're confused. Manasseh is the firstborn. Therefore, your right hand should be on *his* head."

"I know what I'm doing," Jacob insisted. "Manasseh will be a great people—but Ephraim shall indeed be greater" (Genesis 48:19).

This is often the way of God . . .

It was Abel and not Cain who was blessed, even though Cain was the firstborn. Jacob and Esau were twins, but Esau was older. Jacob, however, was the blessed one. Ishmael was Abraham's firstborn. Isaac, however, was the child of promise. Aaron was the elder son of Amram and Jochebed, yet it was their second-born son, Moses, who was called to deliver God's people. David was the youngest of Jesse's sons, yet it was he, a man after God's own heart, who was anointed king.

This pattern is seen throughout Scripture.

Why?

I suggest it shows you and me that God forgets about our firstborn and blesses our second born. Kids? No, our lives. That is, our first life is forgotten about. Our new life is what God focuses on and blesses.

"You must be born again," Jesus told Nicodemus (John 3).

"Therefore if any man be in Christ, he is a new creature: old things are passed away; behold, all things are become new," Paul told the Corinthians (2 Corinthians 5:17).

"Knowing this, that our old man is crucified with him, that the body of sin might be destroyed, that henceforth we should not serve sin," he told the Romans (Romans 6:6).

Ours is the God of the second-born and the second chance.

And for that, I'm oh, so grateful.

17

Joshua 17:1, 2

There was also a lot for the tribe of Manasseh; for he was the firstborn of Joseph; to wit, for Machir the firstborn of Manasseh, the father of Gilead: because he was a man of war, therefore he had Gilead and Bashan. There was also a lot for the rest of the children of Manasseh by their families; for the children of Abiezer, and for the children of Helek, and for the children of Asriel, and for the children of Shechem, and for the children of Hepher, and for the children of Shemida: these were the male children of Manasseh the son of Joseph by their families.

Chapter 16 detailed the inheritance given to Joseph's second son, Ephraim. Here in chapter 17, we see the inheritance given to Manasseh, his firstborn son.

The Book of Joshua illustrates what it means to move into and live out the Spirit-filled life. The people of Israel were set free from bondage in Egypt the night the blood was placed on the doorposts of their homes. We were also set free from bondage to the world by the blood of the Lamb on the doorposts of our hearts.

After they were set free, the people of Israel made their way to the Red Sea, where they were baptized when the waters parted (1 Corinthians 10:2) just as the baptism of believers signifies death and resurrection to a whole new way of living.

When their faith faltered shortly thereafter, the Israelites found themselves wandering in the wilderness for an entire generation—approximately forty years.

That can happen to you and me as well. We're born again, baptized in water, but then we get distracted. Oh, we're still Christians, but we're wandering in the wilderness, swatting flies, and eating dust. Things are dry, not like they used to be, not like they're supposed to be. We wander and we wonder sometimes year after year until, like the Israelites, we come to a second baptism—the Jordan River, which speaks of the baptism in the Spirit.

A new generation came to those waters, and as they obeyed the command of the Lord to put the soles of their feet into the water, they entered into the Promised Land. When you and I engage our souls and say, "Lord, I want to step out. I want to press in. I want to take hold of all You have for me," a new dimension of spiritual life begins. The baptism in the Spirit transforms those who were wandering and weak into those who are dynamic and fruitful.

We're coming to the point where we're saying, "Lord, I love You, but I'm tired of the dryness of my soul. I'm tired of wandering around aimlessly. I want You to take control. I want to see Your

Spirit come upon me and flow through me. I'm going to do whatever You tell me to do. I'm going to step out. I'm going to take a risk and begin to press in to what You say is available for me this very day."

As we receive by faith the empowering of the Spirit, we enter into the Promised Land—a land filled with milk, honey, and grapes the size of bowling balls. That's where the people of Israel are at this point in the Book of Joshua. Oh, there are battles to fight and wars to wage—but it's a place of fruitfulness and abundance.

We continue on with the land being divided because the Spirit-filled life is not only about moving in and enjoying the fruit, but about responsibilities as well. There is work for us to do because the Holy Spirit is given for the purpose of impacting the world around us.

Joshua 17:3–6
But Zelophehad, the son of Hepher, the son of Gilead, the son of Machir, the son of Manasseh, had no sons, but daughters: and these are the names of his daughters, Mahlah, and Noah, Hoglah, Milcah, and Tirzah. And they came near before Eleazar the priest, and before Joshua the son of Nun, and before the princes, saying, The LORD commanded Moses to give us an inheritance among our brethren. Therefore according to the commandment of the LORD he gave them an inheritance among the brethren of their father. And there fell ten portions to Manasseh, beside the land of Gilead and Bashan, which were on the other side Jordan; Because the daughters of Manasseh had an inheritance among his sons: and the rest of Manasseh's sons had the land of Gilead.

Because the inheritance was passed to the firstborn son in every family, when Zelophehad died, his daughters came to Moses in Numbers 27 and said, "Just because our father had no sons, does that mean we don't get any inheritance? Are we left out of the equation?" When he sought the Lord, the Lord told Moses that the daughters were to indeed receive the inheritance. However, in Numbers 36, further information was given when the stipulation was made that they had to marry within their tribe lest their inheritance be transferred to another tribe, causing the boundaries to change.

The implications of this seemingly obscure incident were so far-reaching that they affected Jesus' role as King of the Jews. You see, the genealogy of Matthew 1 traces Jesus' lineage from Abraham to Isaac to Jacob to Jesse to David to Solomon to Reheboam. But there's a problem in verse 11, were we read that Josiah begat Jeconiah, or Coniah, as he was also known. Jeconiah was such a wicked king that Jeremiah declared none of his seed would sit on the throne of David (Jeremiah 22:28–30).

This means that, although Joseph was a legal heir to the throne of David, due to the curse of Coniah, he was not a spiritual heir. In Luke's genealogy, however, we see not Joseph's lineage, but Mary's. While Joseph's genealogy goes from David through Solomon ultimately to Coniah, Mary's genealogy goes from David to another of David's sons named Nathan, avoiding Coniah altogether. If this little obscure ruling about the daughters of Zelophehad had not kicked in, the inheritance could never have been claimed through His mother. Yet, because His mother had no brothers, the inheritance passed to Mary—giving Jesus not only the legal right to the throne, but the spiritual right as well.

What an amazing and awesome God we serve. His ways are absolutely letter-perfect.

Joshua 17:11–13
And Manasseh had in Issachar and in Asher Beth-shean and her towns, and Ibleam and her towns, and the inhabitants of Dor and her towns, and the inhabitants of Endor and her towns, and the inhabitants of Taanach and her towns, and the inhabitants of Megiddo and her towns, even three countries. Yet the children of Manasseh could not drive out the inhabitants of those cities; but the Canaanites would dwell in that land. Yet it came to pass, when the children of Israel were waxen strong, that they put the Canaanites to tribute; but did not utterly drive them out.

Although they taxed them, the tribe of Manasseh was unable to drive out the Canaanites hiding out in their land.

Joshua 17:14
And the children of Joseph spake unto Joshua, saying, Why hast thou given me but one lot and one portion to inherit, seeing I am a great people, forasmuch as the LORD hath blessed me hitherto?

"Why were we given only one portion?" asked the children of Manasseh. "We have lots of people in our tribe." Puffed up with pride, the children of Manasseh wanted more land, yet they failed to destroy the Canaanites from the land they already had.

People sometimes say, "I should have more responsibility. I should have greater authority. I should have a bigger role to play in ministry, in my family, or on the job. I'm a great guy. I'm a great person. I've got great talent, great ability."

I like Joshua's answer . . .

Joshua 17:15
And Joshua answered them, If thou be a great people, then get thee up to the wood country, and cut down for thyself there in the land of the Perizzites and of the giants, if mount Ephraim be too narrow for thee.

"Don't tell me what you think you deserve," Joshua said. "Go to the wooded area. Go to the mountains. Cut down the timber. Drive out the giants."

"I think I should have a larger role in the ministry. In my job, I should have more responsibility. I think I should be more appreciated by my family because I'm a great guy," some say.

"Don't expect people to see how great you are," Joshua would say. "Go to the mountain. Go where the wood is."

Upon which mountain was there wood? On a mountain called Calvary stood a wooden cross. Come to Communion. There's no higher place than that. There's no greater ministry than bowing at the Lord's Table and pouring out praise to the Lord, giving honor to the Lord, spending time with the Lord. Many people want roles other than that, but there's no more important ministry.

Joshua's exhortation is a powerful one. One Sunday, as he was away from his congregation, a well-known preacher visited a church in a different city. At the end of the service, he asked the pastor how long it took him to prepare his sermon.

"Four hours," the young preacher answered.

And the older preacher said, "That's funny. It took me twenty hours to prepare the same one."

When the younger preacher realized to whom he was talking, he was embarrassed because he realized he did not do what the older preacher had done. He hadn't gone to the mountain, chopped down the timber, or wrestled with the Lord in order to hear His heart and receive His Word. Instead, he found an easier way.

"If you want to be great," the older preacher wisely said, "you'll have to learn how to chop your own timber."

This doesn't apply only to preachers or teachers—but to every area of spirituality. We've got to go to the mountain. There's no shortcut. There's no other way.

Joshua 17:16
And the children of Joseph said, The hill is not enough for us: and all the Canaanites that dwell in the land of the valley have chariots of iron, both they who are of Bethshean and her towns, and they who are of the valley of Jezreel.

"The hill is not enough," the children of Manasseh insisted. "Yet the valleys have chariots of iron"—the Abrams tanks of the day.

Joshua 17:17, 18
And Joshua spake unto the house of Joseph, even to Ephraim and to Manasseh, saying, Thou art a great people, and hast great power: thou shalt not have one lot only: But the mountain shall be thine; for it is a wood, and thou shalt cut it down: and the outgoings of it shall be thine: for thou shalt drive out the Canaanites, though they have iron chariots, and though they be strong.

This is leadership at its best. This is "Jesus stuff." "If you're so great," Joshua had said, "go up to the mountain. Drive out the giants. Carve out territory."

"But we're afraid," the children of Manasseh, in essence, answered.

First, Joshua acted with the necessary toughness of a father telling his children to grow up. Here, however, he answers with the tenderness of a mother saying, "You really are great. And you will indeed chop down those trees and drive out those giants. You will indeed overcome the chariots that strike terror in your hearts presently."

This is a paradigm of powerful leadership—and, more importantly, of the ultimate Leader, Jesus Christ. He exhorts us, yes. But He also shows great and glorious tenderness to us.

18

Joshua 18:1
And the whole congregation of the children of Israel assembled together at Shiloh, and set up the tabernacle of the congregation there. And the land was subdued before them.

The entire congregation set up the tabernacle at Shiloh, a central location, where it would remain for hundreds of years until King David would move it to Jerusalem.

Joshua 18:2–7
And there remained among the children of Israel seven tribes, which had not yet received their inheritance. And Joshua said unto the children of Israel, How long are ye slack to go to possess the land, which the LORD God of your fathers hath given you? Give out from among you three men for each tribe: and I will send them, and they

shall rise, and go through the land, and describe it according to the inheritance of them; and they shall come again to me. And they shall divide it into seven parts: Judah shall abide in their coast on the south, and the house of Joseph shall abide in their coasts on the north. Ye shall therefore describe the land into seven parts, and bring the description hither to me, that I may cast lots for you here before the LORD our God. But the Levites have no part among you; for the priesthood of the LORD is their inheritance: and Gad, and Reuben, and half the tribe of Manasseh, have received their inheritance beyond Jordan on the east, which Moses the servant of the LORD gave them.

It was evidently up to the leaders of the tribes to approach Joshua and say, "We're here to receive our lot, our inheritance." Yet at this point, seven of the twelve tribes had not yet done so. Why? I suggest it was that, without a specific region appropriated to them, they would have no battles to fight. They could be on the coast for a while and then go into the valley of Jezreel or on to Jerusalem. Whenever difficulties arose, they could simply pack up and move. And there are Christians who are just like them.

There are people who have left the wilderness of carnality and who have received the baptism of the Holy Spirit. They've entered the Promised Land of the Spirit-filled life, and are experiencing something of abundance—yet they don't want to be locked in to a specific territory, a specific congregation. "I want to attend this meeting over here and that church over there," they say—until the pastor makes them angry and they head in a different direction. "When the building project is complete, I'll be back," they say. Although people with this mindset might think they're being led by the Spirit, in reality, they're simply neither accountable to nor responsible for anyone. They're involved as is comfortable for them, but if they're asked to do something that stretches them, they'll leave.

The majority of the tribes failed to claim their inheritance. And, sadly, Joshua's question still needs to be asked in our generation: "When are you going to quit floating around, sink some roots, put your hand to the plow, and claim territory for the kingdom?"

Joshua 18:8–10
And the men arose, and went away: and Joshua charged them that went to describe the land, saying, Go and walk through the land, and describe it, and come again to me, that I may here cast lots for you before the LORD in Shiloh. And the men went and passed through the land, and described it by cities into seven parts in a book, and came again to Joshua to the host at Shiloh. And Joshua cast lots for them in Shiloh before the LORD: and there Joshua divided the land unto the children of Israel according to their divisions.

The word "describe" seen here in verse 9 and previously in verse 4, literally means "to survey." Three men from each of the seven tribes who hadn't claimed their inheritance were sent to survey the land. Here's the question: Where did they learn how to survey? Did they learn while wandering in the wilderness? I don't think so. Did they learn while fighting in the Promised Land? Not likely. I suggest they learned the art of surveying while in Egypt. Those who were twenty years of age when they left Egypt, would have been involved in all kinds of construction projects requiring surveying skills.

Sometimes, young people say, "I want to be a missionary. I want to start a church. Why do I need to know math, history, or science?" They ask because they don't yet realize that because the Lord doesn't waste a thing, the skills and understandings gained and gleaned in school will be extremely beneficial and important in days to come. Therefore, I think we ought to remind our kids that learning is important because God will use it for His purposes in ways we don't yet see.

Joshua 18:11
And the lot of the tribe of the children of Benjamin came up according to their families: and the coast of their lot came forth between the children of Judah and the children of Joseph.

In the history of Israel, Judah and Ephraim were often rivals. Located in between them, Benjamin played the role of peacemaker. Benjamin was the smallest of the tribes territorially—but what a wonderful inheritance he was given, for in his borders were Shiloh, Jericho, Hebron, Gibeon—and Jerusalem.

The remainder of the chapter describes the inheritance given to Benjamin. And just as the borders were carefully given, never forget that God has an exacting plan, custom-designed for you and me. Therefore, part of Spirit-filled living is to say, "Lord, what do You want me to do? What's *Your* plan for me this day?"

19

Joshua 19:1
And the second lot came forth to Simeon, even for the tribe of the children

of Simeon according to their families: and their inheritance was within the inheritance of the children of Judah.

The land given to Simeon was surrounded by the land given to the tribe of Judah. Judah being a powerful tribe, Simeon essentially disappears. As you read the history of Israel, it is evident that Simeon is essentially swallowed up. Oh, there would still be Simeonites in Israel, but their territory would become fuzzy and indefinable, as prophesied in Genesis 49 . . .

As Jacob pronounced a final blessing on his sons, he declared that, because they were instruments of cruelty, Simeon and Levi would have no inheritance in the land. This was in reference to the account in Genesis 30, when Dinah, the sister of the twelve brothers who became the twelve tribes, was raped by Shechem. Jacob didn't seem to do anything about this initially, so two of his sons—Simeon and Levi—took matters into their own hands. After he raped Dinah, Shechem wanted to marry her, so Simeon and Levi said, "We'll let you marry our sister if all your men become like us—if they all are circumcised."

So the men of Shechem were indeed circumcised. While they were recovering, Simeon and Levi unsheathed their swords and killed all of the Shechemites. When Jacob realized what his sons had done, he said, "You've caused me to stink in this land." On his deathbed, his appraisal of Simeon and Levi was evident.

Joshua 19:10
And the third lot came up for the children of Zebulun according to their families: and the border of their inheritance was unto Sarid:

Zebulun was given an area north between the Sea of Galilee and the Mediterranean. This was also a fulfillment of prophecy because in Genesis 49, Jacob had said to Zebulun, "You will be a haven for ships." Indeed he became just that with his land stretching to the Mediterranean on one side and the fresh-water Sea of Galilee on the other.

Joshua 19:17
And the fourth lot came out to Issachar, for the children of Issachar according to their families.

Issachar's was the region south of the Sea of Galilee, where there is a magnificent valley called the Valley of Jezreel, more commonly known as Megiddo.

Joshua 19:24
And the fifth lot came out for the tribe of the children of Asher according to their families.

Although Asher does not go down in history as a very prominent or important tribe, there is one specific mention of Asher that stands out. It relates to the story of Jesus. When Mary and Joseph brought Jesus to the temple to be dedicated, a woman in the temple recognized Him immediately as Messiah. Luke identifies her as Anna. I find it interesting that it wasn't the strength of its army or the mighty deeds of its people that caused the tribe of Asher to be uniquely known. Rather, it was the spiritual sensitivity of an eighty-four-year-old widow who brought notoriety to the tribe of Asher.

Joshua 19:32
The sixth lot came out to the children of Naphtali, even for the children of Naphtali according to their families.

The inheritance of Zebulun and Naphtali is called "the Galilee of the Gentiles" in Matthew 4. Throughout Israel's history, Zebulun and Naphtali were always being beat up because the enemies of Israel—the Babylonians, Assyrians, Greeks, Persians, and Romans came from the north. Consequently, Zebulun and Naphtali resided in "the Galilee of the Gentiles" because Gentiles resided there ultimately.

Isaiah prophesied that the land of Zebulun and Naphtali would see a great light (Isaiah 9:1, 2). Indeed, those who were depressed, in bondage, and under attack were those who saw a great light because where did Jesus base His ministry? Where did He spend virtually all of His time except when He traveled to Jerusalem? Galilee. You might be in the dark today—depressed and beat up. If so, you're just the person the Lord wants especially to visit. If you're in a place of being wiped out, understand that it was the people who sat in great darkness who saw a great, great Light (Matthew 4:13–16).

Joshua 19:35
And the fenced cities are Ziddim, Zer, and Hammath, Rakkath, and Chinnereth,

Chinnereth means "harp" and refers to the Sea of Galilee because the Sea of Galilee is harp-shaped.

Joshua 19:40
And the seventh lot came out for the tribe of the children of Dan according to their families.

Although the children of Dan were to settle near Joppa—the place of Simon the tanner's house, a part of present-day Tel Aviv on the coast of Southern Israel, they went north instead . . .

Joshua 19:47
And the coast of the children of Dan went out too little for them: therefore the children of Dan went up to fight against Leshem, and took it, and smote it with the edge of the sword, and possessed it, and dwelt therein, and called Leshem, Dan, after the name of Dan their father.

Why did Dan go north? Because the southern region was too hard for them to control. They left the region to which they were assigned and went north because it was easier—or so they thought. In reality, they fell into idolatry, made a golden calf eventually, and were attacked constantly. Thus, by trying to avoid struggle, they found themselves in an infinitely worse situation They were under attack to a greater degree and had a tough time throughout history because they didn't stay in the place the Lord knew would be best for them. And oh, how often we have found the same to be true in our lives.

Joshua 19:49, 50
When they had made an end of dividing the land for inheritance by their coasts, the children of Israel gave an inheritance to Joshua the son of Nun among them: According to the word of the LORD they gave him the city which he asked, even Timnath-serah in mount Ephraim: and he built the city, and dwelt therein.

It was only after everyone else had an assigned section that Joshua claimed his territory. Timnath-serah was hill country. It was similar to Caleb's territory—a tough assignment.

Philippians 2 tells us we're to have the same mind as Jesus, Who came in humility and gave up His rights to die on the Cross in order to provide redemption for lost sinners like you and me.

Timnath-serah literally means "abundant portion" because abundance is always found when we lay down our rights. It's the hard stuff that brings abundance. It's when you have to roll up your sleeves and put your hand to the plow, it's when you get involved and engaged that you find abundant life. The abundant life is found in walking in the Spirit, seeking first the kingdom, taking on the territory you've been assigned, and not giving up. Joshua claimed Timnath-serah as his own. Yet Jesus took on an infinitely tougher assignment when He took on my salvation.

20

Joshua 20:1, 2
The Lord also spake unto Joshua, saying, Speak to the children of Israel, saying, Appoint out for you cities of refuge, whereof I spake unto you by the hand of Moses:

Chapter 20 lists the cities of refuge, first seen in Numbers 35.

Joshua 20:3–6
That the slayer that killeth any person unawares and unwittingly may flee thither: and they shall be your refuge from the avenger of blood. And when he that doth flee unto one of those cities shall stand at the entering of the gate of the city, and shall declare his cause in the ears of the elders of that city, they shall take him into the city unto them, and give him a place, that he may dwell among them. And if the avenger of blood pursue after him, then they shall not deliver the slayer up into his hand; because he smote his neighbour unwittingly, and hated him not beforetime. And he shall dwell in that city, until he stand before the congregation for judgment, and until the death of the high priest that shall be in those days: then shall the slayer return, and come unto his own city, and unto his own house, unto the city from whence he fled.

Simply put, because there was neither a police force nor a penal system in Israel, it was up to the families to make sure that law and order prevailed. Therefore, the relatives of a man who was killed would track down the murderer and avenge the death of their slain relative. Such a system was not unique to Israel, for the practice of revenge and retaliation is seen in virtually every society of antiquity. But the Lord provided a refuge for His people. That is, a man who killed another by accident could run to one of six cities—three on each side of the Jordan River—and there be protected from retaliation. The elders of the city would then call for witnesses and if his offense was found to be accidental, or second-degree murder, he could remain in the city of refuge and be safe there until the death of the high priest—at which time he would be free to leave the city without fear of retribution.

This speaks beautifully of our salvation—for not only do we have refuge in Christ, but we're also free because our High Priest died for us on the Cross of Calvary.

Joshua 20:7–9
And they appointed Kedesh in Galilee in mount Naphtali, and Shechem in mount Ephraim, and Kirjath-arba, which is Hebron, in the mountain of Judah. And on the other side Jordan by Jericho eastward, they

assigned Bezer in the wilderness upon the plain out of the tribe of Reuben, and Ramoth in Gilead out of the tribe of Gad, and Golan in Bashan out of the tribe of Manasseh. These were the cities appinted for all the children of Israel, and for the stranger that sojourneth among them, that whosoever killeth any person at unawares might flee thither, and not die by the hand of the avenger of blood, until he stood before the congregation.

With three cities on each side of the Jordan, no one would have to cross water or a mountain range to reach one. The cities of refuge were strategically located, available, and accessible—just like Jesus is available and accessible to each person who says, "I'm guilty. I need protection. I need refuge. I need salvation."

---

21 Joshua 21:1–3

Then came near the heads of the fathers of the Levites unto Eleazar the priest, and unto Joshua the son of Nun, and unto the heads of the fathers of the tribes of the children of Israel; And they spake unto them at Shiloh in the land of Canaan, saying, The LORD commanded by the hand of Moses to give us cities to dwell in, with the suburbs thereof for our cattle. And the children of Israel gave unto the Levites out of their inheritance, at the commandment of the LORD, these cities and their suburbs.

Although the Levites were not given territory, as were the other tribes, they were given cities within the territories of the other tribes. The Levites were those who worked in the tabernacle, those who cared for the spiritual life of the people of Israel. The priests all came from the tribe of Levi, but not all Levites were priests. To be a priest, one had to be a descendant of Aaron. The Levites were spread out over forty-eight cities. This meant that every Israelite was near to a Levitical community, near to men who knew the Scriptures and were dedicated to serving the Lord.

As we have seen, Levi, along with Simeon, was to have no inheritance due to his dealing with Shechem (Genesis 32, 49). Yet the curse on Levi was reversed and transformed into a major blessing when the Lord said, "Levi, I will be your inheritance. You'll be scattered everywhere in order to serve Me, and your cities will be protected by the rest of the nation." Simeon and Levi were both cursed, but God reversed the curse upon Levi. Why? I believe the answer lies in Exodus 32:28.

The day Moses came down from Mount Sinai with the Ten Commandments in hand, the people were dancing around a golden calf. "Who is on the Lord's side?" Moses said. "Who will deal with this sin?" Only one tribe volunteered—the tribe of Levi. The Levites unsheathed their swords and went throughout the congregation dealing with their friends and relatives. It was painful, but they had to do it because the tribe of Levi knew, perhaps better than anyone, that sin cannot go unchecked.

God can take our sin and turn it around for good. He can reverse the curse even today. Wherever you've been, whatever you've done, if you repent and say, "Lord, from here on out, I'm going Your way," He'll turn the mistakes you've made around for good. Oh, the scars will still be there. But God will open new doors and do wonderful things in your life. You'll be more blessed than you could have ever imagined if—and only if—you repent. Simeon didn't. Evidently the men of Simeon didn't want to offend their friends or family, so they stood on the sidelines. As a result, centuries later, the land Simeon was given was eventually swallowed up.

Say, "I know I shouldn't be doing that anymore, but I don't want to be different. My teammates, my roommates, everyone is going there and doing that and I don't want to stand out. I don't want to be too radical, so I'll just go to church when I can, fit in there as much as I can, and then when I'm with the guys, I'll fit in with them," and you'll end up like Simeon. You'll disappear into nothingness. Oh, you'll still go to heaven, but your life and impact will be tragically diminished. You'll look in the mirror at age fifty, sixty, or seventy, and say, "I'm basically nothing because I wanted to fit in."

On the other hand, say, "I was wrong. I messed up badly. Lord, I repent"—and God will use even your mistakes. You'll minister to Him, make an impact for Him, and be blessed by Him. I know you've dropped the ball. I know you've messed up. We all have because *all* we like sheep have gone astray (Isaiah 53:6). But the curse can be reversed. God can give you a dynamic life and a dynamic ministry if you, like Levi, unsheathe the sword and say, "Enough is enough. I'm going on record. I'm standing for the Lord from here on out." It's all a matter of repentance, of changing directions. Simeon didn't and he's in the middle of Judah, swallowed up by a greater tribe. Levi did, and they're involved in ministry throughout forty-eight cities, serving in the temple. Two men committed the same sin. One chose to repent, the other didn't, and the difference in their lives is unmistakable.

Joshua 21:43–45
And the LORD gave unto Israel all the land which he sware to give unto their fathers; and they possessed it, and dwelt therein. And the LORD gave them rest round about, according to all that he sware unto their fathers: and there stood not a man of all their enemies before them; the LORD delivered all their enemies into their hand. There failed not ought of any good thing which the LORD had spoken unto the house of Israel; all came to pass.

Following the list of the forty-eight cities given to the Levites, chapter 21 closes with one of my favorite verses in all of Scripture: "There failed not ought of any good thing which the Lord had spoken unto the house of Israel; *all* came to pass." And because *Israel* means "governed by God," if your house or your life is governed by God, this applies to you, too.

IT *ALL* CAME TO PASS

A Topical Study of JOSHUA 21:43–45

An eerie discovery was made when the contents of a leather suitcase salvaged from the *Titanic* were dry enough to make an ironic letter legible. The suitcase belonged to a seventeen-year-old young man named Edgar Samuel Andrew. Andrew, a citizen of Argentina, boarded the *Titanic* in Southampton, England, not far from where he was attending school. He had initially purchased a ticket to board the steamship, *Oceanic,* but, due to a coal strike, he was forced to change his ticket and boarded the *Titanic* instead. In the letter addressed to his girlfriend, Josie, he wrote: "You figure, Josie. I had to leave on the seventeenth this month aboard the *Oceanic,* but due to the coal strike that steamer cannot depart. So I have to go one week earlier aboard the *Titanic*. It really seems unbelievable that I have to leave a few days before your arrival here. There's no help for it. I've got to go. You figure, Josie. I'm boarding the greatest steamship in the world, but I don't really feel proud of it at all. Right now, I wish the *Titanic* were laying at the bottom of the ocean."

Likewise, this past week, I've "salvaged" some Scriptures I have known very well and have taught on before. Yet as I looked at them again, I was most touched by the passage before us. It was a discovery that impacted me, a rediscovery that encouraged me. You see, the last time I taught on this passage, I was twenty-three years old. And, as a twenty-three-year-old, concerning Joshua 21:45, I said, "I know this is true. God said it. Let's believe it, and see what He'll do." Twenty-five years later, I know this is true not only because it's in Scripture—which would be reason enough—but because, over the past twenty-five years, God has kept every promise He has ever made to me. Without exception, He has done everything He said He would do.

"I have come that you might have life and life more abundantly," Jesus said (John 10:10). And I have that. I have an abundant, full life. If I were to die today, I would die a very happy man. Even if in theory there was no heaven—which there is—if I could go back and live my life again, I would give my heart to the Lord, offer my life in service for the Lord, and daily walk with the Lord because I have had an absolutely abundant life—just like He promised.

"Peace I leave with you, my peace I give unto you: not as the world giveth, give I unto you. Let not your heart be troubled, neither let it be afraid," Jesus said (John 14:27). I have peace. Even yesterday, which would have been my daughter Jessie's twenty-third birthday, as I spent time at her grave, I realized that the Lord has done precisely what He said He would do. I have peace in my heart. I'm happy for my daughter. I'm delighted that she is in the arms of her Love, and that she's having a better time than she could ever have with us here on earth.

"But my God shall supply all your need according to his riches in glory by Christ Jesus," Paul declared (Philippians 4:19). Guess what. God has done exactly that. Oh, there were times in those early years and even sometimes presently when I wonder how everything will work practically—but it always does. "I have been young and now I am old, but I have never seen the righteous forsaken, nor his seed begging for bread," David wrote (Psalm 37:25). God will do exactly as He said. He will supply your needs. He will fulfill your desires.

Flipping through my journals yesterday, I was amazed to see entries I made when I was twenty-three, twenty-four, and twenty-five years old concerning questions I had, dilemmas I was in, problems I was wrestling through. As I turned the now-yellowing pages of those journals, I had no other choice but to say, "Lord, You came through in every instance, in every way, point by point. The stuff I thought would never work out has worked out marvelously. The battles I thought would never end have given way to peace presently. You've done everything You said You would do. It has *all* come to pass."

As an older brother, I'm telling you that you will discover the same thing. As the years unfold, and as you begin to look back and read through old prayer logs or journals, you, too, will say, "The Lord has come through in every way He promised."

Is this true for everyone? It can be. God wants it to be. That's His intention for you and me. There is one issue, however, that will stand in His way. In the Book of Hebrews, we see what will keep us from experiencing all of the blessings God wants to bestow upon us . . .

So we see that they could not enter in because of unbelief. Hebrews 3:19

The parents and grandparents of those who reaped the blessings of the Promised Land also had an opportunity to do so. They were at the border. They could see it. They could smell it. They could even taste it in the grapes brought to them by the twelve spies. They were oh, so close. But they couldn't go in. Why? It wasn't because they had danced around the golden calf in sin and rebellion. It wasn't their complaining and murmuring that kept them from entering the land of their destiny. It wasn't their carnality that popped up time and time again that kept them out of the Promised Land. It wasn't any of the issues we would think would be a barrier to experiencing the abundance and blessings of God. It was a very simple, singular issue. The previous generation wasted away in the wilderness due entirely and exclusively to unbelief. They just didn't believe God would do what He promised.

Their kids, however, learned the lesson. Their kids said, "We're going to believe what God says, and if He says we can go in and be blessed and have victory and enjoy prosperity, then we are going to step up and step in and believe that the Lord will take us through.

> *Let us therefore fear, lest, a promise being left us of entering into his rest, any of you should seem to come short of it. For unto us was the gospel preached, as well as unto them: but the word preached did not profit them, not being mixed with faith in them that heard it.* Hebrews 4:1, 2

The previous generation heard the Word. The promises were proclaimed to them. The invitation was extended to them. But they didn't mix them with faith. That is why the writer of Hebrews says to you and me, "Be careful. The Good News has come to you, but it will profit you nothing if you don't mix it with faith." Unbelief is the only thing that will keep us from experiencing the promises God has so freely given to us.

> *And we desire that every one of you do shew the same diligence to the full assurance of hope unto the end: That ye be not slothful, but followers of them who through faith and patience inherit the promises.* Hebrews 6:11, 12

God gives a promise and then keeps it—but there is often a period of time between when the promise is given and the fulfillment of it is seen. God says, "Hear the Word. Mix it with faith. Don't be slothful. Don't be cynical. Don't give up. Instead, keep to the course to which God has called you. Believe the promises He's given to you in the Word. And, with faith and patience, you'll inherit them." I wonder how many people give up a month, a day, or an hour too soon and just miss God's blessing.

> *For when God made promise to Abraham, because he could swear by no greater, he sware by himself, Saying, Surely blessing I will bless thee, and multiplying I will multiply thee. And so, after he had patiently endured, he obtained the promise.* Hebrews 6:13–15

Abraham goes down in history and is celebrated throughout eternity as a man of faith. He heard the Word. He mixed it with faith. He patiently endured, and it came to pass.

Perhaps you're thinking, *Believing might have been simple for Abraham, but me? I don't have faith that God will bless my marriage, my kids, or my job. I can't believe because my faith is so weak.* Are you sure? I suggest that your faith is huge, colossal, titanic in size. After all, you're in the hall of faith, in the company of Moses, Abraham, Sarah, Gideon, and Samson.

> *Through faith we understand that the worlds were framed by the word of God, so that things which are seen were not made of things which do appear.*
>
> Hebrews 11:3

Your belief that God created all things is itself an indication of the colossal size and strength of your faith. Believing God created the world out of nothing is the hardest thing to believe. Everything else is a piece of cake by comparison. The second biggest issue deals with the Resurrection of Jesus Christ . . .

"I won't believe Jesus is alive unless I can put my fingers in the holes in His side and touch His wounds with my hands," Thomas said.

After allowing Thomas to touch His wounds, Jesus said, "You have seen and believed. But blessed are those who have not seen and yet believe," Jesus said (John 20:29).

That's us.

Do you believe Jesus rose from the dead? If so, I suggest with a sparkle in His eye and a grin on His face, Jesus would say, "Awesome! You have not seen Me physically, but you believe in Me. You are a blessed person."

Therefore, when the enemy whispers in your ear, "You're not going to see that happen. You're never going to see that work out because your faith is too weak," you need to say, "I believe creation was accomplished by my Father. I also believe Jesus rose from the dead. I couldn't believe either one of those things had not the Father given me huge, colossal-sized faith. He has given me faith for the big issues, and everything else—health, finances, relationships—are miniscule by comparison."

Mix the Word with faith, gang. Patiently endure, and in the coming days and years, you'll have no choice but to say, "There failed not ought of any good thing which the Lord had spoken unto me. It *all* came to pass."

22

Joshua 22:1(a)
Then . . .

After wandering in the wilderness for forty years, the Israelites were camped by the Jordan River, poised to enter the Promised Land, the land of their destiny. The tribes of Reuben, Gad, and half the tribe of Manasseh, however, chose to remain on the east side of the Jordan because the lush land seemed like an ideal place to raise cattle. Moses gave them permission to do so—with the stipulation that they were to join the other nine and one-half tribes in warfare. Reuben, Gad, and Manasseh agreed and fought for seven years on the west side of the Jordan until the Promised Land was conquered.

Joshua 22:1(b)–9
. . . Joshua called the Reubenites, and the Gadites, and the half tribe of Manasseh, And

said unto them, Ye have kept all that Moses the servant of the LORD commanded you, and have obeyed my voice in all that I commanded you: Ye have not left your brethren these many days unto this day, but have kept the charge of the commandment of the LORD your God. And now the LORD your God hath given rest unto your brethren, as he promised them: therefore now return ye, and get you unto your tents, and unto the land of your possession, which Moses the servant of the LORD gave you on the other side Jordan. But take diligent heed to do the commandment and the law, which Moses the servant of the LORD charged you, to love the LORD your God, and to walk in all his ways, and to keep his commandments, and to cleave unto him, and to serve him with all your heart and with all your soul. So Joshua blessed them, and sent them away: and they went unto their tents. Now to the one half of the tribe of Manasseh Moses had given possession in Bashan: but unto the other half thereof gave Joshua among their brethren on this side Jordan westward. And when Joshua sent them away also unto their tents, then he blessed them, And he spake unto them, saying, Return with much riches unto your tents, and with very much cattle, with silver, and with gold, and with brass, and with iron, and with very much raiment: divide the spoil of your enemies with your brethren. And the children of Reuben and the children of Gad and the half tribe of Manasseh returned, and departed from the children of Israel out of Shiloh, which is in the land of Canaan, to go unto the country of Gilead, to the land of their possession, whereof they were possessed, according to the word of the LORD by the hand of Moses.

Joshua said to the tribes of Reuben, Gad, and half of Manasseh, "Return to your wives, children, and cattle." And we see them going back over the Jordan to the east side of the river.

Joshua 22:10
And when they came unto the borders of Jordan, that are in the land of Canaan, the children of Reuben and the children of Gad and the half tribe of Manasseh built there an altar by Jordan, a great altar to see to.

As we will see in verses 27 and 28, the Israelites on the east side of the Jordan built an altar not for sacrifice or worship, but, rather, as a symbol of their solidarity with their brothers on the west side of the Jordan. So incensed by this were their brothers on the west side, however, that civil war nearly ensued.

The nine and one-half tribes were in the Promised Land, but the enemy sought to divide them from their brothers on the other side of the Jordan. Satan's strategy is still the same: divide and conquer. His goal is always to get believers to separate, to distance, to analyze. In this passage, we see four ways the nine and one-half tribes fell prey to the destructive division that almost led to civil war . . .

Joshua 22:11, 12
And the children of Israel heard say, Behold, the children of Reuben and the children of Gad and the half tribe of Manasseh have built an altar over against the land of Canaan, in the borders of Jordan, at the passage of the children of Israel. And when the children of Israel heard of it, the whole congregation of the children of Israel gathered themselves together at Shiloh, to go up to war against them.

The first step towards division was taken when the nine and one-half tribes acted on hearsay. They didn't see the altar the two and one-half tribes had built—they only heard about it. That's always how Satan begins to bring people into division and opposition. So often, divisions in families or churches are based simply on what is heard. Rumors take on a life of their own and fires are fanned when people act on hearsay.

Joshua 22:13, 14
And the children of Israel sent unto the children of Reuben, and to the children of Gad, and to the half tribe of Manasseh, into the land of Gilead, Phinehas the son of Eleazar the priest, And with him ten princes, of each chief house a prince throughout all the tribes of Israel; and each one was an head of the house of their fathers among the thousands of Israel.

The second mistake of the nine and one-half tribes was that they got worked up before they checked the situation out. That is, they sharpened their swords and grabbed their shields before they established the facts. "He that answers a matter before he hears it, it is a folly and a shame unto him" (Proverbs 18:13). Making a decision without learning the whole story leads to folly and shame ultimately.

Joshua 22:15–18
And they came unto the children of Reuben, and to the children of Gad, and to the half tribe of Manasseh, unto the land of Gilead, and they spake with them, saying, Thus saith the whole congregation of the LORD,

What trespass is this that ye have committed against the God of Israel, to turn away this day from following the LORD, in that ye have builded you an altar, that ye might rebel this day against the LORD? Is the iniquity of Peor too little for us, from which we are not cleansed until this day, although there was a plague in the congregation of the LORD, But that ye must turn away this day from following the LORD? and it will be, seeing ye rebel to day against the LORD, that to morrow he will be wroth with the whole congregation of Israel.

The third misstep the nine and one-half tribes made was using the Lord's name loosely. That can happen to Spirit-filled believers as well. We hear something. Our righteous indignation flares up. And then we use the name of the Lord quite liberally when we say, "The Lord showed me this," or, "The Lord wants you to know that." But we must be careful. Are we sure it's the Lord? It might simply be our own opinion or perspective.

Joshua 22:19, 20
Notwithstanding, if the land of your possession be unclean, then pass ye over unto the land of the possession of the LORD, wherein the LORD's tabernacle dwelleth, and take possession among us: but rebel not against the LORD, nor rebel against us, in building you an altar beside the altar of the LORD our God. Did not Achan the son of Zerah commit a trespass in the accursed thing, and wrath fell on all the congregation of Israel? and that man perished not alone in his iniquity.

The fourth mistake the nine and one-half tribes made was when they bore false witness in accusing their brothers of rebelling against God. We usually think of bearing false witness as telling a whopper of a lie. While it can be that, it's not limited to that. Bearing false witness means giving the right information, but with the wrong implication.

When Jesus was being tried, false witnesses pointed to Him and said, "He said to destroy the temple and in three days, He would raise it up" (Matthew 26:60, 61). While Jesus did, in fact, utter those words, He wasn't referring to the temple in Jerusalem, but to His own body (John 2:19–21).

Although the two and one-half tribes did indeed build an altar, it was not a sign of rebellion. That said, however, Reuben, Gad, and the half tribe of Manasseh were also responsible for the division that nearly led to civil war. Why? They were on the wrong side of the Jordan River. God wanted His people on the west side of the Jordan. But the two and one-half tribes said, "No. We have business interests and family obligations, so we'll just stay here on the east side."

In reality, the east side of the Jordan was a place of carnality. You see, the word, *carnal*, simply means "fleshly." As seen in 1 Corinthians 3, it refers to those who are interested in the seen rather than in the unseen, in the material rather than in the spiritual, in the temporal rather than in the eternal. How do you know when you're carnal? How do you know that, although you're part of God's family and part of the kingdom, you're on the wrong side of the Jordan? In the response of Reuben, Gad, and Manasseh, we see three indications of the state of the heart of one who is carnal . . .

Joshua 22:21–24
Then the children of Reuben and the children of Gad and the half tribe of Manasseh answered, and said unto the heads of the thousands of Israel, The LORD God of gods, the LORD God of gods, he knoweth, and Israel he shall know; if it be in rebellion, or if in transgression against the LORD, (save us not this day,) That we have built us an altar to turn from following the LORD, or if to offer thereon burnt offering or meat offering, or if to offer peace offerings thereon, let the LORD himself require it; And if we have not rather done it for fear of this thing, saying, In time to come your children might speak unto our children, saying, What have ye to do with the LORD God of Israel?

When they were accused and challenged by the nine and one-half tribes for building an altar, the two and one-half tribes said, "The Lord knows." This is what carnal people often say.

"Don't judge me," says the carnal believer. "God knows my heart." Yes, God does know our hearts. The problem is, we don't. "The heart is deceitful above all things, and desperately wicked: who can know it?" Jeremiah asks. (Jeremiah 17:9). We can't know our own heart—but the Word of God can because it is a "discerner of the thoughts and intents of the heart" (Hebrews 4:12). Therefore, it doesn't matter what your heart tells you. It matters what God's Word declares.

Joshua 22:25 (a)
For the LORD hath made Jordan a border between us and you, ye children of Reuben and children of Gad; ye have no part in the LORD . . .

Secondly, carnal people blame the Lord either directly or indirectly for any given problem. Reuben, Gad, and Manasseh blamed the Lord for the division. Carnal people blame the Lord—and sometimes others—for their own sins and shortcomings. "It was because of the woman *You* gave me that I sinned," Adam said to God as an excuse for his own rebellion (Genesis 3:12).

Joshua 22:25 (b)
. . . so shall your children make our children cease from fearing the LORD.

Thirdly, carnal people blame their family problems on churches or other believers. Blaming the church is always an indication of carnality. "If your kids were better behaved, our kids wouldn't be rebellious," say the carnal parents. It is the mature believer who understands that it's not up to the church, Boy Scouts, or the school system to raise his kids. It's up to him. When his kids struggle, it's the mature believer who says, "Lord, *I* have dropped the ball. Show me what I need to do."

Joshua 22:26–28
Therefore we said, Let us now prepare to build us an altar, not for burnt offering, nor for sacrifice: But that it may be a witness between us, and you, and our generations after us, that we might do the service of the LORD before him with our burnt offerings, and with our sacrifices, and with our peace offerings; that your children may not say to our children in time to come, Ye have no part in the LORD. Therefore said we, that it shall be, when they should so say to us or to our generations in time to come, that we may say again, Behold the pattern of the altar of the LORD, which our fathers made, not for burnt offerings, nor for sacrifices; but it is a witness between us and you.

Finally, carnal believers say, "I'm going to worship how I want to worship, where I want to worship, in the way I want to worship." God never told the two and one-half tribes to build an altar. He wanted His people to gather around the single altar of the tabernacle. But the two and one-half tribes did it their way.

The same is still true today. Carnal Christians say, "I can worship just as well out on the golf course as I can in church." The Word, however, clearly says, "Do not forsake the assembling of yourselves together" (Hebrews 10:25) and "Behold, how good, and how pleasant it is for brethren to dwell together in unity" (Psalm 133:1).

The nine and one-half tribes were in error because, in righteous indignation, they wanted to correct their brothers before they understood the problem. However, the two and one-half tribes were also in error because, by remaining on the east side of the Jordan, they placed themselves in a position to be misunderstood.

The lesson for us is clear. You who are spiritual, you who love the Lord and are walking with Him, be careful that in your Spirit-filled desire for rightness, you don't judge and criticize those on the other side of the river. The enemy would love to see you at odds with your brothers and sisters, waging war against them, critical of them, losing patience with them. In Galatians 6:1, we read, "Brethren, if any of you be overtaken in a fault, you who are spiritual"—which means Spirit-filled people—"restore such a one in the spirit of meekness." The word, "restore," is a medical term referring to the way a doctor would carefully reset a broken bone. He who is spiritual must deal with people gently and meekly in order that the bones of others might mend, in order that their walk might be restored. If you're spiritual, be careful.

If you're carnal, be cautioned. If you say, "I like being on the fringe. I don't want to get too radical," be cautioned because Gad, Reuben, and Manasseh were the first people to be led hundreds of miles across the desert when the Assyrians attacked the nation of Israel and led them into captivity. If you're a carnal believer, understand that, although you'll go to heaven ultimately, you'll experience unnecessary heartbreak and agony before then because the wages of sin is still and always death (Romans 6:23).

Joshua 22:32–34
And Phinehas the son of Eleazar the priest, and the princes, returned from the children of Reuben, and from the children of Gad, out of the land of Gilead, unto the land of Canaan, to the children of Israel, and brought them word again. And the thing pleased the children of Israel; and the children of Israel blessed God, and did not intend to go up against them in battle, to destroy the land wherein the children of Reuben and Gad dwelt. And the children of Reuben and the children of Gad called the altar Ed: for it shall be a witness between us that the LORD is God.

Ed means "witness." This altar was meant to be a witness to the unity of the twelve tribes. Jesus said that our *ed*—the witness of our unity as the body of Christ—is love. The world will know we're believers not by our bumper stickers or the size of the Bible we carry. "They'll know you are My disciples," Jesus said, "by your love" (John 13:35).

"Father, let them be one that the world might know that I am in You and You are in Me," Jesus prayed (John 17:21).

Gang, we get to love people and love each other. Love is the key. Love is our witness. Where is unity found? At the altar of the Cross of Calvary. It is neither our eschatology nor our pneumatology—neither how we view the end times nor how we view the manifestations of the Holy Spirit—that make us one. We are one because we all believe in the same Lord. We eat of His body. We drink of His blood. Unity is found at the foot of the Cross, at the altar called Calvary. Whether regarding division among family members, churches, or brothers and sisters in the congregation, unity is found only at the altar where the Lamb was slain for you and me.

The enemy wants to cause believers to wage war with each other. Be warned. Be wise. And just love people in Jesus' name.

23

Joshua 23:1
And it came to pass a long time after that the LORD had given rest unto Israel from all their enemies round about, that Joshua waxed old and stricken in age.

Many years had passed since Joshua and the children of Israel crossed over the Jordan River and entered into the land of destiny. It took them seven years to defeat the enemies inhabiting the land of Canaan. Then thirteen years passed before the land was divided among the tribes. After tackling the remnants of their enemies hiding in the hills and valleys, the land had been given rest. So when we read that Joshua was old and stricken in age, this is no exaggeration. At one hundred and ten years of age, however, he was still going strong, still encouraging, exhorting, instructing, and inspiring.

Roman philosopher, Cato, wrote commentaries on the Greek language. Yet he didn't learn Greek until he was eighty-one. Tennyson wrote *Crossing the Bar* at eighty-three years of age. John Wesley, the circuit-riding preacher who traveled 250,000 miles on horseback going from town to town preaching the gospel wrote four hundred books, preached 40,000 messages, traveled 250,000 miles and became a self-taught scholar in ten different languages. When he got to be eighty-one, he wrote in his journal that he was angry because he could only read for five hours at one sitting before his eyes began to bother him. At the age of eighty-six, he wrote that he was upset because he had to cut back to two sermons a day. At eighty-eight, he complained that he had a tendency to occasionally sleep in until 5:30 A.M. John Wesley had a passion in his heart because he had a calling on his life to share the Good News, to tell people about Jesus, to see people make it to heaven, to watch people do better in their walk with the Lord. It burned in his soul like fire, and he kept going and going in an amazing way.

Joshua was that kind of man. Moses didn't even begin his public ministry until he was eighty. And yet today we have a tendency to say, "I'm thirty-six. I'm just about through." Or, "I'm forty-one. There's not much left for me to do." Be careful. I believe God wants you to finish the race with a burst of energy. I believe God wants to use us until the day He calls us home. I believe there are things for you to do today no matter how old you are or how late a start you had. The Scriptures indicate over and over that God has a grand plan even for men and women who are in the winter season of their lives.

Joshua 23:2
And Joshua called for all Israel, and for their elders, and for their heads, and for their judges, and for their officers, and said unto them, I am old and stricken in age.

The first use of the word, "and," being in italics, it doesn't appear in the original text. Therefore, the idea here is that Joshua gathered the leaders of the nation to give them a final word of exhortation. In chapter 24, he'll call for the congregation in its entirety.

Joshua 23:3
And ye have seen all that the LORD your God hath done unto all these nations because of you; for the LORD your God is he that hath fought for you.

When people get old, they can have a tendency to want applause or approval, credit or recognition. Joshua is bigger than that. He says, "It wasn't my military strategy, my great ability, or my ingenuity that gave you victory. It was the Lord exclusively." In this, Joshua is, again, a wonderful picture of Jesus—for every time Jesus did a miracle, without exception, Scripture records that people glorified God. Jesus was able to minister in such a way that no matter how spectacular His acts, the attention, honor, and glory always went to His Father.

Joshua 23:4, 5
Behold, I have divided unto you by lot these nations that remain, to be an inheritance for your tribes, from Jordan, with all the nations that I have cut off, even unto the

great sea westward. And the LORD your God, he shall expel them from before you, and drive them from out of your sight; and ye shall possess their land, as the LORD your God hath promised unto you.

I like this. Joshua says, "Consider what the Lord has done, and know there's more He's going to do. He'll expel your enemies, and you'll possess their land." The Lord will expel—but we're to possess. That's the key. God will do His part, but we've got to do our part.

An example of this principle can be seen in the practice of speaking in tongues. In Acts 2:4, we read that those in the Upper Room spoke "with other tongues, as the Spirit gave them utterance." The Spirit prompted. They spoke. You can sit hour after hour, day after day, saying, "I'm open. If God wants me to speak in tongues, He'll move my tongue." But that won't work any more than if you said, "I'm open to praying in English. If God wants me to pray in English, He'll move my tongue." No, when I begin to pray in English, then the Lord begins to meet me and inspire me to continue. The same is true of the prayer language.

In all areas of spiritual life, God will do—but we must cooperate, too. That's what Joshua meant when he said, "God will expel—but you must possess." God will do His part, but we've got to do ours. There is so much God wants to do for me and with me, through me, and in me. But I've got to do my part. I can't just sit passively.

Joshua 23:6
Be ye therefore very courageous to keep and to do all that is written in the book of the law of Moses, that ye turn not aside therefrom to the right hand or to the left . . .

The first responsibility Joshua gave to the leaders of the nation was to be obedient to the Word. Keep in the Word, gang. Satan will tell you you're too old, too tired. He'll tell you that you don't have to meet with us for Bible study because the music is too loud, the seats too hard, or the pastor talks too long! Don't listen to him. Make study of the Word the priority of your life.

Joshua 23:7
That ye come not among these nations, these that remain among you; neither make mention of the name of their gods, nor cause to swear by them, neither serve them, nor bow yourselves unto them:

Joshua told the elders that, in addition to being obedient to the Word, they were to be separate from the world. They were not to be experts on the gods of the nations surrounding them. According to Romans 16:19, we are to be simple, or naive, concerning evil.

Joshua 23:8–11
But cleave unto the LORD your God, as ye have done unto this day. For the LORD hath driven out from before you great nations and strong: but as for you, no man hath been able to stand before you unto this day. One man of you shall chase a thousand: for the LORD your God, he it is that fighteth for you, as he hath promised you. Take good heed therefore unto yourselves, that ye love the LORD your God.

The leaders of Israel were to be obedient to the Word, separate from the world, and affectionate towards the Lord. How can we love God? By spending time with Him. It's real simple. If you spend time with the Lord tomorrow morning, you will become intrigued by Him and experience intimacy with Him. It's all about time. After all, if you spend five minutes every third day with your wife, what kind of marriage will you have? If you spend ten minutes every fifth day with your girlfriend or boyfriend, what kind of relationship will you have? Friendships are formed over time. I'm not talking about a legalistic, pharisaical schedule. I'm talking about saying, "I have a half hour open here, or twenty minutes there. I don't need to watch that show or read that magazine. Maybe I'll just go for a walk with my Bible and talk to the Lover of my soul." Do this and you'll be amazed by the things He'll whisper in your ear, the things He'll speak to your heart, the way the Word will come alive.

I absolutely know this to be so. The way to love God is to spend time with Him because the more time you spend with Him, the more you can't help but love the One who is altogether lovely (Song of Solomon 5:16).

Joshua 23:12
Else if ye do in any wise go back, and cleave unto the remnant of these nations, even these that remain among you, and shall make marriages with them, and go in unto them, and they to you:

How could it be that people who had seen the blessings of God and who had been given a grand and glorious land would be in danger of going back, of pulling away from God? We're involved in a very real war, attacked constantly by a very real adversary—a roaring lion who prowls about, seeking whom he may devour (1 Peter 5:8). It can happen at any time. You might be twenty-eight, forty-eight, sixty-eight, or eighty-eight—but you're not home free until you get to heaven.

No matter how long you've walked with the Lord, how deep your love is for Him, or how broad your knowledge is of Him, there's a war going on. It's a real war, and we're all vulnerable. So Joshua warns these leaders, these men of maturity, of very real danger. They had seen God bless them. They knew how good He had been to them. But if they chose to go back, they would experience tragic consequences . . .

Joshua 23:13 (a)
Know for a certainty that the LORD your God will no more drive out any of these nations from before you . . .

If the Israelites joined themselves with heathen gods, the True and Living God would no longer fight for them, and their defeat would be certain.

Joshua 23:13 (b)
. . . but they shall be snares and traps unto you, and scourges in your sides, and thorns in your eyes, until ye perish from off this good land which the LORD your God hath given you.

Not only would the Israelites be defeated if they failed to cleave to the Lord, but they would be discomforted. Their enemies would be scourges in their sides and thorns in their eyes. In this, I can't help but think of the One who, although He knew no sin, became sin for us (2 Corinthians 5:21). Thorns were in His eyes when a crown of thorns was placed upon His forehead. A scourge ripped open His back; a spear cut through His side. That's what sin does—not His sin, but mine.

If you're toying with the idea of backsliding, know this: what happened to Jesus will happen to you. Sooner or later, it will kill you because the wages of sin is still, and always, death (Romans 6:23).

Joshua 23:14–16
And, behold, this day I am going the way of all the earth: and ye know in all your hearts and in all your souls, that not one thing hath failed of all the good things which the LORD your God spake concerning you; all are come to pass unto you, and not one thing hath failed thereof. Therefore it shall come to pass, that as all good things are come upon you, which the LORD your God promised you; so shall the LORD bring upon you all evil things, until he have destroyed you from off this good land which the LORD your God hath given you. When ye have transgressed the covenant of the LORD your God, which he commanded you, and have gone and served other gods, and bowed yourselves to them; then shall the anger of the LORD be kindled against you, and ye shall perish quickly from off the good land which he hath given unto you.

In addition to defeat and discomfort, God's people are sure to experience disgrace whenever they turn from Him. In 722 B.C., after Israel turned away from the Lord and worshiped other gods, the Assyrians invaded their land and marched them across the desert with fishhooks in their mouths to Assyria, where they were held captive. But that was only the beginning of their disgrace. In 586 B.C., the Babylonians came into Jerusalem, burned the temple, destroyed the city, and carried the Jews into captivity. In 165 B.C., a madman named Antiochus Epiphanes humiliated the Jews when he slaughtered a pig in the temple. In A.D. 70, the Romans destroyed the second temple and burned the city of Jerusalem. In A.D. 130, Roman Emperor Hadrian decreed that if any two Jews were seen talking together in Jerusalem, they would be executed. During the Spanish Inquisition, tens of thousands of Jews were tortured and killed. In our own twentieth century, the Jews faced the horror of Auschwitz and Treblinka.

Joshua said, "If you choose to go back and serve other gods, this is what you can count on: defeat, discomfort, and disgrace." The same applies to us—which is why obedience to the Lord (v. 6), separation from the world (v. 7), and affection for the Lord (v. 11) are all of utmost importance.

24

Joshua 24:1
And Joshua gathered all the tribes of Israel to Shechem, and called for the elders of Israel, and for their heads, and for their judges, and for their officers; and they presented themselves before God.

After addressing the leaders of Israel in chapter 23, here in chapter 24, he addresses the entire nation.

Joshua 24:2
And Joshua said unto all the people, Thus saith the LORD God of Israel, Your fathers dwelt on the other side of the flood in old time, even Terah, the father of Abraham, and the father of Nachor: and they served other gods.

"The Flood" speaks of the Euphrates River. God called Abraham from the land of Ur, where false gods were worshiped to a new land, to become a new nation—comprised of the people to whom Joshua spoke.

Joshua 24:3–12
And I took your father Abraham from the other side of the flood, and led him throughout all the land of Canaan, and multiplied his seed, and gave him Isaac. And I gave unto Isaac Jacob and Esau: and I gave unto Esau mount Seir, to possess it; but Jacob and his children went down into Egypt. I sent Moses also and Aaron, and I plagued Egypt, according to that which I did among them: and afterward I brought you out. And I brought your fathers out of Egypt: and ye came unto the sea; and the Egyptians pursued after your fathers with chariots and horsemen unto the Red sea. And when they cried unto the LORD, he put darkness between you and the Egyptians, and brought the sea upon them, and covered them; and your eyes have seen what I have done in Egypt: and ye dwelt in the wilderness a long season. I brought you into the land of the Amorites, which dwelt on the other side Jordan; and they fought with you: and I gave them into your hand, that ye might possess their land; and I destroyed them from before you. Then Balak the son of Zippor, king of Moab, arose and warred against Israel, and sent and called Balaam the son of Beor to curse you: But I would not hearken unto Balaam; therefore he blessed you still: so I delivered you out of his hand. And ye went over Jordan, and came unto Jericho: and the men of Jericho fought against you, the Amorites, and the Perizzites, and the Canaanites, and the Hittites, and the Girgashites, the Hivites, and the Jebusites; and I delivered them into your hand. And I sent the hornet before you, which drave them out from before you, even the two kings of the Amorites; but not with thy sword, nor with thy bow.

Through His servant, Joshua, God reminds the nation of Israel of His care for them throughout their history. Notice God's active involvement in the lives of His people: "I took. I gave. I sent. I brought. I destroyed. I delivered," He says.

Joshua 24:13
And I have given you a land for which ye did not labour, and cities which ye built not, and ye dwell in them; of the vineyards and oliveyards which ye planted not do ye eat.

Speaking at a retreat in the Hamptons, I was walking along a small boardwalk, looking up at homes bigger than anything I've ever seen. "Lord," I said, "You are so awesome. You have given these people so much—and most of them don't even know You. Truly, every good and perfect gift comes from Your hand. You just bless everyone."

The generosity of our God is amazing, as seen in His undeserved goodness to the Israelites—and to us.

Joshua 24:14, 15
Now therefore fear the LORD, and serve him in sincerity and in truth: and put away the gods which your fathers served on the other side of the flood, and in Egypt; and serve ye the LORD. And if it seem evil unto you to serve the LORD, choose you this day whom ye will serve; whether the gods which your fathers served that were on the other side of the flood, or the gods of the Amorites, in whose land ye dwell: but as for me and my house, we will serve the LORD.

At one hundred and ten years of age, Joshua was still saying, "As for me and my house, we will serve the Lord."

***For topical study of Joshua 24:14, 15 entitled "As for Me and My House," turn to page* 707.**

Joshua 24:16–19
And the people answered and said, God forbid that we should forsake the LORD, to serve other gods; For the LORD our God, he it is that brought us up and our fathers out of the land of Egypt, from the house of bondage, and which did those great signs in our sight, and preserved us in all the way wherein we went, and among all the people through whom we passed: And the LORD drave out from before us all the people, even the Amorites which dwelt in the land: therefore will we also serve the LORD; for he is our God. And Joshua said unto the people, Ye cannot serve the LORD: for he is an holy God; he is a jealous God; he will not forgive your transgressions nor your sins.

"As for me and my house, we will serve the Lord," Joshua declared with certainty.

"We want to serve the Lord, too," the people said.

"You can't," Joshua said.

Why? Because he knew it was "idle" talk. As we shall see, Joshua knew the people had idols in their tents and in their homes. He knew they were talking the talk but not prepared to walk the walk. He knew they would say, "Hip, hip, hooray for the Lord" in the midst of the congregation. But in reality, their idols would be at home waiting for them.

The Israelites had already begun to worship idols—the multi-breasted Ashteroth that spoke of sensuality, Baal that spoke of the intellect, Mammon that spoke of money. They had already begun to collect these idols—symbols of hedonism, intellectualism, materialism. Joshua knew this.

Concerning idols, the Lord said to Ezekiel,

> Son of man, these men have set up their idols in their heart, and put the stumblingblock of their iniquity before their face: should I be inquired of at all by them? Therefore speak unto them, and say unto them, Thus saith the Lord GOD; Every man of the house of Israel that setteth up his idols in his heart, and putteth the stumblingblock of his iniquity before his face, and cometh to the prophet; I the LORD will answer him that cometh according to the multitude of his idols. Ezekiel 14:3, 4

I've often been baffled by people who say, "God has given me peace about having an affair," or, "I've prayed about leaving my husband," or, "I have peace about having this cable channel in my house." How could it be that a person could look us in the eye and say, "God has told me . . ." something that is exactly contrary to the Word? Ezekiel says if there's an idol in your heart and you seek the Lord, you'll hear the voice of your idol and think it's the voice of God.

Stay away from idols, gang. I'm not talking about statues. I'm talking about passions, compromises, flirting with stuff you know is not right. They will lie to you and tell you you're in God's will. But you'll be deceived, disgraced, and carried away captive into a foreign country—into a place or a situation in which you don't want to be—just like the Israelites would be.

Joshua 24:20
If ye forsake the LORD, and serve strange gods, then he will turn and do you hurt, and consume you, after that he hath done you good.

"God has blessed you," Joshua said to Israel. "But if you turn to other gods, you'll be badly hurt."

Joshua 24:21–23
And the people said unto Joshua, Nay; but we will serve the LORD. And Joshua said unto the people, Ye are witnesses against yourselves that ye have chosen you the LORD, to serve him. And they said, We are witnesses. Now therefore put away, said he, the strange gods which are among you, and incline your heart unto the LORD God of Israel.

"If you're serious about following God, put away your idols," Joshua said.

Joshua 24:24, 25
And the people said unto Joshua, The LORD our God will we serve, and his voice will we obey. So Joshua made a covenant with the people that day, and set them a statute and an ordinance in Shechem.

"Okay," Joshua said. "You've been heard. You've promised to put away the strange gods—not just talk the talk in the congregation, but walk the walk in your own situations."

Joshua 24:26, 27
And Joshua wrote these words in the book of the law of God, and took a great stone, and set it up there under an oak, that was by the sanctuary of the LORD. And Joshua said unto all the people, Behold, this stone shall be a witness unto us; for it hath heard all the words of the LORD which he spake unto us: it shall be therefore a witness unto you, lest ye deny your God.

How could a stone be a witness? "If the disciples pipe down, even the rocks will cry out and be a witness of Me," Jesus said (Luke 19:40). The ultimate witness was the stone that was rolled away from the tomb when Jesus conquered death and rose on Easter morning.

Joshua 24:28, 29
So Joshua let the people depart, every man unto his inheritance. And it came to pass after these things, that Joshua the son of Nun, the servant of the LORD, died, being an hundred and ten years old.

Joshua kept going strong until the day he went home. How did he do it? Isaiah declared that they that wait upon the Lord shall renew their strength. They shall mount up with wings as eagles. They shall run and not be weary. They shall walk and not faint (Isaiah 40:31). The older and more tired you are is the time to wait on the Lord, to learn about Him, to spend time with Him. And as you do, you'll mount up with wings as eagles. You'll run and not be weary. You'll walk and not faint. When fatigue sets in to the soul of a man, it's indicative of a failure to wait on the Lord—because the promise of God's Word is that if we wait on Him, He'll renew our strength.

Joshua 24:30–33
And they buried him in the border of his inheritance in Timnathserah, which is in mount Ephraim, on the north side of the hill of Gaash. And Israel served the LORD all the days of Joshua, and all the days of the elders that overlived Joshua, and which had known all the works of the LORD, that

he had done for Israel. And the bones of Joseph, which the children of Israel brought up out of Egypt, buried they in Shechem, in a parcel of ground which Jacob bought of the sons of Hamor the father of Shechem for an hundred pieces of silver: and it became the inheritance of the children of Joseph. And Eleazar the son of Aaron died; and they buried him in a hill that pertained to Phinehas his son, which was given him in mount Ephraim.

The last chapter of the Book of Joshua—the book that pictures the Spirit-filled life—includes a strong exhortation for a reason. You see, whenever God gives us a warning, it's because we need to be warned. God never gives warnings just because. He always warns for a reason. Therefore, it would do us well to heed them. Just like the people of Israel heard the word of Joshua and responded, so too, may we hear the word of our Joshua, our Jesus, and respond—to put away any and every idol in our homes or hearts and say, "No more. That's it. I've been warned."

May the Lord give us wisdom.

***For topical study of Joshua 1—24 entitled "A Prophetic Overview of Joshua," turn to page* 711.**

AS FOR ME AND MY HOUSE

A Topical Study of JOSHUA 24:14, 15

Great historical figures are often remembered for their powerful quotations . . .

- "Give me liberty or give me death," Patrick Henry thundered in the days of the American Revolution.
- "We have nothing to fear but fear itself," said Franklin Delano Roosevelt in the dark days of the Great Depression.
- "Ask not what your country can do for you. Ask what you can do for your country," said John F. Kennedy in his first inaugural address.
- "One small step for man, one giant leap for mankind," were the words of Neil Armstrong, the first man to put his foot on the surface of the moon.
- "As for me and my house, we will serve the Lord," Joshua declared on the plains of Shechem.

An Important Realization

"As for me *and my house, we will serve the Lord."*

If I say, "As for me and my house, we will serve the Lord," I must realize it begins with me. I lead the way. Where I am will set the stage for where my kids will end up. What am I doing? Who am I privately? If I watch questionable stuff on TV late at night and sneak off to the movies, I cannot expect my kids not to do the same.

"Oh, but my kids don't know," you might protest.

Jesus declares that what you do in secret the Father sees and will reward openly (Matthew 6). Therefore, if you want your sons and daughters to be Bible lovers, love the Bible yourself. Develop a deep devotional life personally and privately. If you want your kids to be pure, then live in purity in your secret life because what you do in secret will inevitably impact what your children and grandchildren end up doing in their own lives.

I think of David. When he was just a teenager, he killed Goliath. The years went by and we see him on his deathbed, surrounded by the group known as David's "mighty men." Scripture records that they were giant-killers as well (2 Samuel 23). They never saw David kill Goliath. Yet fearlessly waging war against evil was part of David's character, and it was transferred to the men who spent time with him. On the other hand, in the list of men who surrounded Saul, we find not one giant-killer because Saul, who was afraid to do battle with Goliath, never killed a giant himself.

Dad, your kids or grandchildren will take on aspects not of what they see you do, but of who you *are*. When Achan sinned, his whole family paid the price because what he did in secret in due time affected his entire family (Joshua 7).

A man shared his testimony, saying he was a born-again Christian who enjoyed alcohol. One Thanksgiving, the snow was falling, and, after the family feast was over, he wanted something to drink. Finding his liquor cabinet empty, he put on his hat, coat, and boots, and went outside to walk three blocks away to the liquor store. Halfway to his destination, he sensed that someone was following him. Turning around, he saw his four-year-old son with his hat, coat, and galoshes on, taking giant steps, putting his feet in the newly fallen snow where his father had left his own footprints.

Hey, buddy, what are you doing?" the father asked.

"Daddy, I'm just walking in your footsteps," his son proudly answered.

"He's walking in my footsteps," thought the man, "and I'm going to the liquor store. Is that what I want for my boy?"

Immediately, he turned around, went home with his son, and never drank again.

"I can have beer and wine," you might be thinking.

Sure, you can. But do you want your kids to go there?

No?

Then don't lead them there.

What are my kids and grandchildren seeing? For better or worse, they're following in my footsteps.

A Grand Celebration

"As for me and my house, *we will serve the Lord."*

The Book of Joshua illustrates not only the Spirit-filled life, but also our Joshua, our Leader, Jesus. "Who are My sisters and brothers?" He asked. "They who do the will of God," He answered (Matthew 12:48–50). That's us. We're His family. We're His house. Jesus served His Father perfectly. That gives me great hope because I realize that even when I drop the ball, mess up, and miss the mark, I'm in the house of One who never fails. Even if I'm faithless, He will be faithful still (2 Timothy 2:13).

"Lord, even though everyone else forsakes You, I won't," Peter boasted. "I'll die beside you." By the time the rooster crowed, however, Peter had denied Jesus three times (John 18). After Jesus rose from the dead, He found Peter and said, "Do you love Me?" Three times, Peter had denied Him. Now Jesus gave him the opportunity to say three times, "I love You."

"Feed My lambs," Jesus said, as if to say, "You're not disqualified. It's a new day. Your sin is forgiven" (John 21:15).

You might have been more concerned about your kids liking you than about parenting them properly. But it's not too late. It's a new day. Starting here and now, God will see you through if you let Him. And if your kids are grown, you can still be involved with grandchildren or kids in the congregation. They're lambs for you to feed.

A Strong Declaration

"As for me and my house, we *will serve the Lord."*

We need men today who will not turn to their wives and say, "What do you think, honey? Should we serve the Lord?" We need men like Joshua who will declare directly, powerfully and boldly that they will indeed serve the Lord. Joshua, however, was not evidently always a strong leader. After Moses died, God told Joshua three times in chapter 1 to be strong and very courageous. Even the people said, "We'll follow you, Joshua. Only be strong and very courageous" (1:18). Evidently, Joshua needed this exhortation from the Lord and this encouragement from the congregation.

We live in a day when men "wimp-out" all too frequently. We want to be tender, sensitive, and politically correct. The Bible example, however, is that we ought to be men who say with strength and certainty, "We're not going to back away. This is the way it's got to be. This is the way it will be. As for me and my house, we will serve the Lord." We need strong men once again.

I'm not talking about arrogance or brutality. I'm talking about men who will say with firmness and love, "Son, I don't care if everyone else has those posters on their walls, you're not going to. I don't care if everyone else is listening to those songs, they won't be played in this house. I don't care if everyone else watches every movie, you're not going to. Why? Because as for me and my house, we will serve the Lord. As long as you're under my roof, I'm responsible for you, and I care about you. I want the best to come your way, and I know those things will pollute and destroy you. Although you might be angry with me, I care more about you than what you think of me."

Much of today's parenting is rooted in sinful selfishness. Parents want their kids to like them—but that is not what parenting is about. Oh, it's wonderful if and when our kids like us, but that's not the goal. The goal is to raise your kids in the way that will be beneficial to them in the days to come and on into eternity. Children are like cassette tapes. They're always running and always recording. The question is, what do you want to be on the tape of your child's soul and mind?

The congregation of Israel said to Joshua, "We'll follow you, only be strong and of good courage." Dad, your wife, kids, and grandchildren are saying the same thing. Whether it's articulated or not, your family wants you to be strong and courageous. They want you to hold the line spiritually.

If you're a single mom or married to a man who won't take leadership, you need to step up and step in yourself. You need to do what Deborah did in Old Testament days. When Barak, the general of Israel's fighting forces, wouldn't take the lead, Deborah said, "If you won't lead, then I will." And she did just that. As a result, she goes down in history as an example of what a woman ought to do if a man won't do the things he's called to do. If there is no man to lead, the woman needs to step up and step in because the kids are too important. It is essential that they are trained properly by a loving parent who will say, "As for me and my house, we will serve the Lord."

A Wonderful Expectation

"As for me and my house, we will *serve the Lord."*

"We *will* serve the Lord," said Joshua. "I expect this to be reality. My kids will serve the Lord right beside me."

The Bible says that without faith it is impossible to please God (Hebrews 11:6). Therefore, dad, husband, or grandpa, you need to say, "I have faith that God will do what He's promised." What has God promised? He has promised that He who has begun a good work will be faithful to perform it (Philippians 1:6); that He is able to keep that which is committed to Him (2 Timothy 1:12); that if you train up a child in the way he should go, even when he is old, he will not depart from it (Proverbs 22:6).

"Believe in the Lord Jesus Christ, and thou shalt be saved—and thy house," Paul told the Philippian jailer (Acts 16:31). In other words, "If you believe, not only will you be saved, but in due time, your family will be saved, too." That's God's heart.

For one hundred and twenty years, Noah pounded away on the ark, preparing it not only for the animals, but for his wife, three sons, and their wives, too. What amazes me is that he prepared these rooms twenty years before his sons were even born. *That's* faith!

You can do the same thing, Dad and Grandpa. In faith say, "I believe my family will indeed serve the Lord. I believe my kids won't be wiped out and washed away, but that they'll be on the ark of salvation." Have faith. Believe. It's important because without faith, it's impossible to please Him.

"As for me and my house, we will serve the Lord."

Declare this for your own family.

Expect it to be so.

Realize it begins with you.

And then break out in celebration as you remember heaven, where we will serve the Lord perfectly and eternally.

A PROPHETIC OVERVIEW OF JOSHUA

A Topical Study of JOSHUA 1—24

Let there be no question about it. Jesus Christ is coming back! The Bible speaks of the return of Jesus Christ clearly and constantly. In fact, almost one-third of the Bible deals with prophetic themes or issues. This is not surprising, for looking and longing for the coming of our Lord is such a key in navigating the Christian life successfully. The apostle John said, "Whoever has this hope purifies himself, even as He Himself is pure" (1 John 3:3). Looking for the coming of the Lord has a purifying effect on our lives because it keeps us focused on heaven.

Not only does looking for Jesus' coming purify our lives, but it produces peace in our hearts. "Don't let your heart be troubled," Jesus said. "You believe in God, believe also in Me. In My Father's house are many mansions. I go to prepare a place for you" (John 14:1, 2). So often, people lack peace because they've lost the air of expectancy.

The Bible talks about prophecy in principles, precepts—and also in pictures. One of the pictures I have found to be absolutely intriguing is the picture portrayed in the Book of Joshua. Following are a few of the parallels, portraits, "sneak previews" of the end times presented in the Book of Joshua . . .

Joshua and Jesus

The Book of Joshua is a wonderful illustration of what it means to live the Spirit-filled life. But there's another dimension of the Book of Joshua. That is, it relates to the coming of the kingdom.

It all begins with Joshua himself. Joshua pictures and portrays Jesus. The names, "Joshua," and "Jesus" are the same name. *Yeshua* is the Hebrew rendering; "Joshua, the Greek rendering; and "Jesus" the English pronunciation of the Greek.

Driving Out the Usurpers

We see Joshua driving out the usurpers in the land of Canaan. You see, different countries had taken up residence in the land God had given to Abraham, Isaac, and Jacob while their descendants were in Egypt for four hundred years. As Joshua returns to the Land, he was to drive out these usurpers.

This parallels the situation we're in today, for this world has been usurped by Satan. War, famine, disease, and rape are all due to his hand. Satan has been given temporary control of this planet. That's why Jesus called him the prince of this world (John 12:31), and why Paul called him the god of this world (2 Corinthians 4:4). Yet although Satan was handed the title deed to this planet when they sinned in the Garden of Eden, when Jesus died on the Cross, He paid for the sins of all humanity—including Adam's rebellion. Consequently, the sin has been paid for. And there's coming a day—not too far away—when Jesus will come back to the earth to take control.

The Canaanites, hellions, demons, and Satan are presently having their way on this planet. But there's coming a day when the Lord will take control. The Book of Joshua pictures this fact, as we see Joshua driving out the usurpers, sending them packing, wiping them out.

It took Joshua seven years to drive out the usurpers. We know this by comparing Deuteronomy 2:14 with Joshua 14:7–10. In Joshua 14, Caleb declares he was forty years of age when he went in to spy out the Promised Land, and that he was eighty-five years old when it was time to claim his inheritance. If he was eighty-five in Joshua 14 when the Land was conquered, and forty when he spied out the Land, forty-five years had passed. Deuteronomy 2:14 says the Israelites wandered in the wilderness for thirty-eight years. That makes a seven-year difference, which is interesting because a seven-year theme appears in prophecy, as well. The Tribulation period described in Revelation 6—19 is a seven-year period in which God pours out His wrath on a Christ-rejecting world. The Tribulation deals with the usurping of Satan and the rising of antichrist, culminating in a final confrontation in the battle of Armageddon.

It took seven years for Joshua to conquer the Promised Land—just as it will take seven years after we are raptured to set the stage for the Second Coming of Christ when He will be Ruler and reign in Jerusalem.

The Seven Nations

In Joshua 3:10, we read of seven nations that would be driven out. But there's a problem because in Genesis 15, when God told first told Abraham about the Promised Land, He named ten nations—the seven nations of Joshua 3:10, plus three more. This means something as it relates to what antichrist will do. In Daniel 7, we are told that antichrist—the usurper, the coming world figure who will bring the world under his thumb during the Tribulation—will rule over an empire of ten nations, three of which are uprooted—just as portrayed in Genesis 15 and Joshua 3.

Adoni-zedek and Antichrist

Antichrist is a world leader who will be extremely charismatic and powerful—an amalgamation of every quality the world admires. There is an antichrist picture in the Book of Joshua painted with uncanny accuracy. In Joshua 10, we see a man named Adoni-zedek. He is the king of Jerusalem, whose name means "The lord of righteousness." He's the "lord of righteousness" and he rules from Jerusalem, which is the city of peace. Antichrist will also appear to be righteous and a man of peace.

There was another figure who was king of Salem, but was not a false entity. Appearing in the Genesis account in the days of Abraham, his name was not Adoni-zedek, but Melchi-zedek, and his name meant "king of righteousness." The Book of Hebrews tells us Melchi-zedek was either an incredible picture of Jesus Christ, or, as I believe personally, an incarnate appearance of Christ. Abraham tithed to Melchi-zedek and worshiped him. Melchi-zedek, in turn, gave to Abraham bread and wine, the symbols of Communion.

Adoni-zedek apppears to be like Melchi-zedek, but he's a false Christ. Defeated in battle, he hid in a cave (Joshua 10). In Revelation 6, we read that the kings of the earth shall hide themselves in the mountains during the time of the Tribulation, where they will ask the rocks to fall upon them. What happened in Joshua 10? Stones did indeed fall from the sky—either hailstones or a meteor shower. Joshua then told the sun to stand still. According to Zechariah 14:8, during the coming of our Lord, the evening shall be light. In other words, the sun will stand still once again.

The Gibeonites and the Tribulation Believers

In Joshua 10, we read that Adoni-zedek organized a coalition of nations to wage war against Gibeon. Why? Because the Gibeonites had made peace with Joshua. You remember the story . . .

Having heard about Joshua's victories, the men of Gibeon wanted to be on the winning side so they tricked Joshua by sending emissaries from their number with ragged clothes, dry wineskins, and crusty bread, saying they came from a far country. When Joshua discovered they were not from a far country at all, he would not destroy them because he honored his treaty with them (Joshua 9).

In the Tribulation period, when the wrath of the Lamb is poured out, many people will be like the Gibeonites. Seeing the destruction round about them, they'll choose to be on the winning side and will become believers. Antichrist will wage war against them, just like Adoni-zedek waged war against the Gibeonites.

What happened to the Gibeonites? They become known as the Nethinims, those whose job was to carry water and hew wood for the temple. The people who get saved in the Tribulation will be in heaven, but, unlike us, they won't be the Bride of Christ. They'll serve in the temple—not a bad place to be! The Tribulation believers will have a different position in heaven than we will have because they waited until they saw angels flying across the sky and prophets speaking in Jerusalem before they believed.

"Thomas," Jesus said, "you've seen and believed. But blessed is the one who hasn't seen and yet has believed" (John 20:29).

The Two Spies and the Two Witnesses

In Joshua 2, at the very beginning of the unfolding of the seven-year battles, two spies were sent in as witnesses because there was a woman named Rahab who needed to hear. "You and your family can be saved," they told her. "Hang a scarlet cord out your window"—picturing the bloodline of the blood of the Lamb that runs from cover to cover through the Scriptures.

As seen in Revelation 11, two witnesses will appear—probably Elijah and Moses—to share the truth of the gospel on the streets of Jerusalem. Like the two witnesses in Joshua, they will bring hope and understanding.

When the king of Jericho heard about these two men, Rahab eventually sent them away to hide in the mountains for three days. In Revelation 11, the two witnesses will be killed and lie in the streets of Jerusalem for three days. After three days, just as the two spies were seen again, the two witnesses will appear again, for all the world to see. For many years, people wondered how it could possibly be that the whole world would be able to see them. Then came CNN.

Ruling and Reigning

When the Land had been conquered, Joshua charged the people to rule the territory they had been given, taking care to deal with any remaining opposition. At the end of the Tribulation, Jesus will come back—and we will come with Him (Jude 14). Just as the Promised Land was divided among the Twelve Tribes of Israel in Joshua's day, each of us will have a role to play in the millennial kingdom, ruling over a certain area, having specific responsibilities (Ezekiel 45—48).

Making a Choice and Taking a Stand

After the Promised Land was divided, Joshua told the people to choose whom they would serve (Joshua 24:15). At the end of the Millennium, a choice must be made. You see, as believers, we will rule and reign with Christ during the Millennium in our glorified bodies. But those who become believers during the Tribulation will be ushered into the Millennium and will have families. As a result, those born during the Millennium will know nothing but peace, prosperity, and righteousness. Therefore, Satan—who will have been in the pit for 1,000 years—will be let loose for a little while to give them an opportunity to choose whom they will follow. Tragically, many will choose to follow Satan, and there will be one last massive conflict, after which Satan and his followers will be cast into outer darkness (Matthew 25).

Jesus may come tonight. If not, then tomorrow we'll lift up our heads and say, "It could be today." That's the way the Lord wants you to live. Of that, I have no doubt. I know the Lord wants me to live every day, saying, "No matter what pressures might come upon me or what problems might plague me, the fact is, I'm going to heaven."

For those who don't believe, life on earth is the best it will ever be. On the other hand, for believers, life on earth is the worst it will ever be. Don't lose sight of heaven. If you're not heavenly minded, you'll get bogged down, depressed, and discouraged. But if you're heavenly minded, your heart is not troubled (John 14:1, 2). Sure, there are challenges and difficulties—but there is also an overarching optimism, peace, happiness, and freedom that transpires when men and women seek first the kingdom (Matthew 6:33).

May the Lord bless you as you do just that. Talk about heaven. Look for the coming of the Lord. You're one day closer than you were yesterday, that's for sure! Lift up your head. Things are going to be glorious. The best is yet to come.

JUDGES

Background to Judges

Entitled *Shopethaim* in Hebrew, the Book of Judges speaks of judges not in a judicial sense, but rather in a heroic sense. That is, Old Testament judges didn't wear black robes, sit on a high bench, or hold gavels. They were deliverers—which is what *shopethaim* means. The twelve men and one woman whose stories are told in this book were the instruments through which God judged those who had wandered away from Him, and through which He delivered those who were held captive, yet sought Him.

These thirteen judges lived between the time of Joshua and Samuel—during a span of four hundred years. The author of the Book of Judges is believed to be Samuel. Tradition seems to indicate that he indeed was the writer, although of this we cannot be dogmatic.

Throughout this book, we will see a cycle that is repeated seven times, a cycle very similar to the one in which we so often find ourselves:

- First, we see the people of Israel serving God.
- Next, we see them succumbing to sin.
- Then they are enslaved by sin.
- Fourthly, they are sorry about their sin.
- And finally, they are saved from their sin.

If there's one message to be found in the Book of Judges, it's that sin doesn't pay. Sin will wipe you out and trip you up.

The story is told of a man who walked into a butcher shop and decided to steal a hot dog. Hot dog in hand, he started to run out of the store—completely unaware that his frank was only one on a string forty feet long. As he stumbled over the doorjamb, the butcher called the police, and the man was eventually arrested—ensnared by a string of hot dogs.

That's just the way it is with sin. "It's insignificant," we say at the outset. "I'm just doing something small." But when we grab on, there's a whole string of sins following that will entangle us, trouble us, and trip us up.

The good news, however, in the Book of Judges is that, although the people of Israel stumbled into sin and became enslaved by sin, they were also delivered from sin when they called upon the Lord. And, praise God, that is true of us as well.

JUDGES

1

Judges 1:1 (a)
Now after the death of Joshua . . .

In contrast to the Book of Joshua, which talks about entering into the Promised Land by faith, the Book of Judges deals with enjoying the Land by faithfulness. The application for us is that we have entered into the land of our heavenly inheritance apart from anything we've done or haven't done. We've received salvation as a free gift of God (Ephesians 2:8). Yet, if we are going to be a people who *enjoy* our salvation, we must be a people who walk in faithfulness to the Lord. While we enter the kingdom simply by faith, we enjoy our presence in the kingdom by our obedience and faithfulness to the Lord and to His Word.

If you're miserable today, if you feel as though life is a great big disappointment, it could very well be due to an area in your life where you are being disobedient, where you are not being faithful to the things God has shown you and to which He has called you. Take heart, dear saint—you're at the right place, for the Book of Judges is built on the premise that faithfulness and obedience are not only necessary for victory in the land, but for enjoyment of the kingdom.

Judges 1:1 (b)
. . . it came to pass, that the children of Israel asked the LORD, saying, Who shall go up for us against the Canaanites first, to fight against them?

Although the Israelites were in the Promised Land, there were pockets of Canaanites there as well. Consequently, there was still much guerilla activity throughout the land of Israel.

The same is true of us. Our salvation is secure. Jesus won the war when He hung on the Cross and cried victoriously, "It is finished." But there's still work for us to do, still pockets of resistance in our flesh.

Judges 1:2
And the LORD said, Judah shall go up: behold, I have delivered the land into his hand.

"Where do we begin? What should we do first?" asked the children of Israel concerning the mop-up operation before them.

"Start with Judah," the Lord said.

Judah means "praise." Praise always has priority in warfare. On the Day of Pentecost, before Peter stood up to deliver the message in which three thousand would be saved, we first see the Holy Spirit inspiring the people of God to worship Him, magnify Him, and glorify Him as they spoke praise in other tongues (Acts 2:11). Something unique happens when we praise the Lord. Praise prepares the way, clears the air, sets the stage. Praise is powerful.

I need to be reminded of this a lot. Praise paves the way to victory. When you're discouraged and don't know what to do, call for Judah. Lift up your hands, bow your knee, express your heart energetically and watch and see how the enemy is beaten back.

Judges 1:3
And Judah said unto Simeon his brother, Come up with me into my lot, that we may fight against the Canaanites; and I likewise will go with thee into thy lot. So Simeon went with him.

Simeon and Judah were blood brothers. In addition to this, the tribe of Simeon was small and was surrounded by the much larger tribe of Judah. So it made sense both relationally and geographically that the tribe of Judah would say to the tribe of Simeon, "If you help us, we'll help you." But was it right?

Some commentators believe this shows cooperation. And that may be. But I suggest to you it's not so much an illustration of cooperation as it is an indication of cowardice. Judah's response to the command and promise of God in verse 1 was, "I don't feel adequate. I don't feel able. I need help."

The old adage is true: You and God are a majority. You don't need anyone else to do what God has called you to do. He may tell you to include others—but don't pull back or pull away because you feel inadequate and alone. If God calls you, He will also empower you (1 Thessalonians 5:24).

Judges 1:4–6
And Judah went up; and the LORD delivered the Canaanites and the Perizzites into their hand: and they slew of them in Bezek ten thousand men. And they found Adoni-bezek in Bezek: and they fought against him, and

they slew the Canaanites and the Perizzites. But Adoni-bezek fled; and they pursued after him, and caught him, and cut off his thumbs and his great toes.

It was fairly common practice to cut off the thumbs and big toes of one's captives because without a thumb, it's impossible to hold a sword, and without a big toe, it's impossible to run.

Judges 1:7
And Adoni-bezek said, Threescore and ten kings, having their thumbs and their great toes cut off, gathered their meat under my table: as I have done, so God hath requited me. And they brought him to Jerusalem, and there he died.

In Leviticus 8, we read that when a priest was ordained for service, blood was placed upon his thumbs and his big toes, illustration that sacrifice had to be made for what he did with his hands and where he walked with his feet. Evidence exists for the suggestion by some that placing blood on thumbs and toes was not unique to Israel, but was practiced throughout the land of Canaan by people in pagan religions as well. The king of a city would often be its priest. This being the case, the cutting off of thumbs and toes disabled them not only from escape and warfare, but from serving their false gods.

"I cut off the thumbs and toes of seventy kings," Adoni-bezek said. "I made them eat the crumbs that fell on the floor under my table. I not only incapacitated them, but I humiliated them. Therefore, as I have done, so God hath required me. I did this to others, and now it's coming back to me."

In Galatians 6:7, we read, "Be not deceived. God is not mocked. Whatever a man sows, that shall he also reap." It's a law of God. And Adoni-bezek innately understood it. God would have us to understand that this is an absolutely irrevocable principle of life.

"Give, and it shall be given unto you; good measure, pressed down, and shaken together, and running over, shall men give into your bosom," Jesus said. "For with the same measure that ye mete withal it shall be measured to you again" (Luke 6:38). You may have heard this verse used to encourage people to give financially. But Jesus wasn't talking about financial giving. The context of the verse deals with mercy and forgiveness. The context says, "Give mercy and forgiveness, kindness and love—and they will come back to you. Men will show mercy and kindness to you. But if you are critical, judgmental, grumpy, and cynical, others will analyze you in the same way" (Luke 6:27–37).

This is elementary, but a pagan Adoni-bezek understood it in a way we have yet to. Sooner or later, I will reap what I have sown. Knowing this makes me a whole lot more understanding when people are critical of me or angry with me because I know I deserve their criticism and anger. I've sowed some seeds of anger and criticism somewhere along the way—maybe yesterday, maybe last year—and now I'm reaping the harvest. It's a great day when a man or woman realizes that they deserve the things they're going through or the attack upon them. "Lord, I deserve this," the mature believer says. "I ruined that relationship, so no wonder my relationship is not what it should be. I ripped them off, so no wonder I'm getting ripped off today. Truly, I deserve whatever comes my way."

And if you've sown a whole lot of seed that haven't come up yet, I have great news for you. Second Corinthians 5 says that if any man be in Christ, he is a new creation. Old things are passed away. All things are become new. Why? Because the thumbs and toes, the hands and feet of our Lord were pierced with a nail. Our sin has been paid for by One who didn't simply give His thumbs and toes, but His hands and His feet, His back and His side, His very life. He died on the Cross that we might be forgiven, that we might be free. "Come and eat," He says—"not crumbs under My table, but bread and wine at My table. Come and dine. I know you've sinned, but My body is broken and My blood is shed, making available a grand meal constantly."

We all have sinned. What we have done in killing others with comments and murdering others in our hearts will come back on us. But the gift of God is eternal life through Jesus Christ our Lord (Romans 6:23). Therefore, we can have a fresh start when we go to His Table and say, "Lord, I deserve nothing but judgment. What's come down on me is not even a tenth of what ought to come down on me. I've lopped off thumbs and toes. I've ripped out hearts. I'm a sinner. But, I eat of You and drink again, thanking You that I'm forgiven, thanking You that You paid the price for me now, tomorrow, and into eternity. I will take the repercussions that come my way. But I thank You that, I can come to You with my cares and receive from You new and wonderful mercies each and every day."

Gang, today is the day of salvation, of new life, of a fresh start. You can be "toe-tally" forgiven. You can have "toe-tal" peace. You can have abundant life if you open your hearts to Jesus.

Judges 1:8
Now the children of Judah had fought against Jerusalem, and had taken it, and

smitten it with the edge of the sword, and set the city on fire.

How is a city "set on fire"? By the edge of the sword. You get the Word out. You talk about the things of the Word. You give teachings from the Word. You talk about the truths found in the Word, and they begin to ignite in the hearts of people—just like they ignite in you.

Judges 1:9–11
And afterward the children of Judah went down to fight against the Canaanites, that dwelt in the mountain, and in the south, and in the valley. And Judah went against the Canaanites that dwelt in Hebron: (now the name of Hebron before was Kirjath-arba:) and they slew Sheshai, and Ahiman, and Talmai. And from thence he went against the inhabitants of Debir: and the name of Debir before was Kirjath-sepher:

Debir means "sanctuary." *Kirjath-sepher* means "city of books"—which means it most likely was a scholastic center.

Judges 1:12
And Caleb said, He that smiteth Kirjath-sepher, and taketh it, to him will I give Achsah my daughter to wife.

Caleb evidently wanted to turn the city of learning into a sanctuary.

Judges 1:13
And Othniel the son of Kenaz, Caleb's younger brother, took it: and he gave him Achsah his daughter to wife.

This story reminds me of a similar situation in the life of David, when, desiring to conquer Jerusalem, he said to his men, "The first one of you guys who finds a way to break into the city shall be general of my army" (see 1 Chronicles 11:6).

Here, Caleb says, "The first one who takes the city of Debir gets to marry my daughter"—who must have been quite a prize. As it so happened, Caleb's nephew was the first one to make it inside the city, and thus he was rewarded.

The principle in both the story of David and Caleb is that God blesses and honors the individual who is an initiator. Too often, people hold back and wait, thinking, "I really can't start a home Bible study," or, "I can't disciple some junior high kids. Nobody has asked me." That's not the point. Perhaps no one will ask you to do anything, but the Holy Spirit will lay upon your heart certain things *He* desires you to do, and God will bless you as you initiate, instigate, and move out in those specific areas and visions.

This week, ask the Lord what Debir He has for you to conquer. If God is calling you to assemble an intercession group, don't call the church office and ask permission—just do it! If He is calling you to China, God bless you! I encourage and exhort you in the name of Jesus to respond to the varied, creative, needful avenues of ministry He will open before you via the promptings of the Holy Ghost.

Judges 1:14, 15
And it came to pass, when she came to him, that she moved him to ask of her father a field: and she lighted from off her ass; and Caleb said unto her, What wilt thou? And she said unto him, Give me a blessing: for thou hast given me a south land; give me also springs of water. And Caleb gave her the upper springs and the nether springs.

Throughout Scripture, in addition to being a picture of the Word, water is a type, or picture, of the Holy Spirit. Thus, in Achsah's request for a second blessing—for the springs of water in addition to the land given her—we see a picture of what we are to do as well. If you haven't yet asked the Father for the second blessing, for the Holy Spirit, do what Achsah did. Jesus said, "If ye, being evil, know how to give good gifts unto your children, how much more shall your heavenly Father give the Holy Spirit to them that ask Him?" (Luke 11:13). The "upper springs and the nether springs"—water in abundance, the power of the Spirit—are available to you. All you need to do is ask.

Judges 1:16–18
And the children of the Kenite, Moses' father in law, went up out of the city of palm trees with the children of Judah into the wilderness of Judah, which lieth in the south of Arad; and they went and dwelt among the people. And Judah went with Simeon his brother, and they slew the Canaanites that inhabited Zephath, and utterly destroyed it. And the name of the city was called Hormah. Also Judah took Gaza with the coast thereof, and Askelon with the coast thereof, and Ekron with the coast thereof.

Jericho is the city of palm trees. Gaza is in the southwest part of Israel, on the Mediterranean shore. Ashkelon and Ekron were Philistine cities, even as today they are controlled by the Palestinians.

Judges 1:19
And the LORD was with Judah; and he drave out the inhabitants of the mountain; but could not drive out the inhabitants of the valley, because they had chariots of iron.

Why couldn't Judah drive out the inhabitants of the valley? Because their eyes were fixed on the iron chariots rather than on Almighty God. If your eyes are fixed on the Lord, I care not how formidable your foe might be, it can be overcome. But if your eyes are on the obstacle—if you're focused on the problem, if you're in bondage to your past—you will not drive it out. You've got to lift your eyes higher, and fix them on the Father. Yes, the enemies of Judah had chariots of iron, but if Judah had lifted their eyes higher and focused upon the One who has twenty thousand chariots at His command (Psalm 68:17), they would have been victorious.

Judah was successful in the mountains. But he was discouraged and defeated in the valley. We sometimes tend to live in our past. We think that, because we've had problems with iron chariots previously, we need always be fearful whenever we see them on the horizon. Not true. We need to be a people who put the past behind us—past defeats, past discouragements, past wounds, past failures, past sins. "This one thing I do," said our brother, Paul, "forgetting those things which are behind, and reaching forth unto those things which are before, I press toward the mark for the prize of the high calling of God in Christ Jesus" (Philippians 3:13, 14). We need to put the past away, and lift our eyes higher—to the high calling of God.

Judges 1:20
And they gave Hebron unto Caleb, as Moses said: and he expelled thence the three sons of Anak.

Eighty-five years old at this point, not only had Caleb been given the mountains country wherein the giants lived, but he was successful in driving them out.

Judges 1:21
And the children of Benjamin did not drive out the Jebusites that inhabited Jerusalem; but the Jebusites dwell with the children of Benjamin in Jerusalem unto this day.

The Jebusites would remain in Jerusalem until David took control of the city and drove them out completely.

Judges 1:22–25
And the house of Joseph, they also went up against Bethel: and the LORD was with them. And the house of Joseph sent to descry Bethel. (Now the name of the city before was Luz.) And the spies saw a man come forth out of the city, and they said unto him, Shew us, we pray thee, the entrance into the city, and we will shew thee mercy. And when he shewed them the entrance into the city, they smote the city with the edge of the sword; but they let go the man and all his family.

Surrounded by walls, the city of Bethel, formerly called Luz, was a city with no visible entrance. Thus, the men of Israel were confused about how to enter—until they happened to see a man walking outside. Knowing he had somehow exited the city, they said, "Show us the way into the city, and we'll spare you." Evidently understanding that the Lord was with the people of Israel, the man showed them the entry into the city, perhaps an underground passage, and his life was spared.

Judges 1:26
And the man went into the land of the Hittites, and built a city, and called the name thereof Luz: which is the name thereof unto this day.

This man was spared and saved—but what did he do? Did he join the people of God? No. After experiencing deliverance, he went into an area of present-day northern Syria, and built another city called Luz—just like the city that had been destroyed.

The same thing happens today. When people go through hard times, they receive the blessing, mercy, and forgiveness of God. But then they soon find themselves going back to the old areas, rebuilding the old cities, and doing the old things once again. If the Lord has touched your life, if He has called you into His kingdom, if He has brought you into His family, when things start getting easier, don't give in to the temptation of saying, "I don't have to be as intense anymore. I can sort of kick back. I can go back up to northern Syria where I came from and kind of rebuild old ways."

Don't do it! That's what this man did. What happened to him? The Bible doesn't say. His name isn't mentioned; his deeds are not recorded from this point on. Thus, it seems his life didn't count for much in the economy of God.

How about your life? How about mine? Oh, we've been saved. God has shown us mercy. But when all is said and done, will the Lord be able to say to us, "Well done, good and faithful servant?"

Judges 1:27, 28
Neither did Manasseh drive out the inhabitants of Beth-shean and her towns, nor Ta-

anach and her towns, nor the inhabitants of Dor and her towns, nor the inhabitants of Ibleam and her towns, nor the inhabitants of Megiddo and her towns: but the Canaanites would dwell in that land. And it came to pass, when Israel was strong, that they put the Canaanites to tribute, and did not utterly drive them out.

In verse 19, we saw the men of Judah were too mired in the valley of despair to do the work they could have done, that they should have done. They put their eyes on the problems, on the iron chariots and could not drive them out. Here, however, in verse 28, we see Manasseh has a different problem. It's not that Manasseh *could* not drive out their enemies. It's that they *would* not drive them out because they saw an opportunity to make money by taxing them.

This is always a fatal mistake, a grave error, and one we often make. "I don't really have to drive that sin out of my life," we say smugly. "I can control it. I can harness it." But, as we will see, the Canaanites Manasseh failed to drive out would soon plague them and eventually control them.

Judges 1:29–36
Neither did Ephraim drive out the Canaanites that dwelt in Gezer; but the Canaanites dwelt in Gezer among them. Neither did Zebulun drive out the inhabitants of Kitron, nor the inhabitants of Nahalol; but the Canaanites dwelt among them, and became tributaries. Neither did Asher drive out the inhabitants of Accho, nor the inhabitants of Zidon, nor of Ahlab, nor of Achzib, nor of Helbah, nor of Aphik, nor of Rehob: But the Asherites dwelt among the Canaanites, the inhabitants of the land: for they did not drive them out. Neither did Naphtali drive out the inhabitants of Beth-shemesh, nor the inhabitants of Bethanath; but he dwelt among the Canaanites, the inhabitants of the land: nevertheless the inhabitants of Beth-shemesh and of Beth-anath became tributaries unto them. And the Amorites forced the children of Dan into the mountain: for they would not suffer them to come down to the valley: But the Amorites would dwell in mount Heres in Aijalon, and in Shaalbim: yet the hand of the house of Joseph prevailed, so that they became tributaries. And the coast of the Amorites was from the going up to Akrabbim, from the rock, and upward.

What's keeping us from inheriting the blessings of God? Is it that we *cannot* drive our enemies out because, like Judah, our eyes are fixed on past problems? Is it that, like Manasseh, we *will not* drive them out because we think we can control them ourselves? Or is it due to any one of a number of the other unnamed reasons Ephraim and Zebulun, Asher and Naphtali failed to drive the Canaanites from the land God had given them? While the reasons for our failure may vary, the root cause is the same. The failure to obey what God commands is always the result of failure to believe what He has promised. Grab hold of the promises of God, gang, and through them drive out the enemies that keep you from enjoying His presence.

2

Judges 2:1 (a)
And an angel of the LORD . . .

Angel means "messenger." The messenger of the Lord is Jesus Christ, the Word made flesh. Jesus would appear from time to time in Old Testament days before He came as Jesus of Nazareth.

Judges 2:1 (b), 2
. . . came up from Gilgal to Bochim, and said, I made you to go up out of Egypt, and have brought you unto the land which I sware unto your fathers; and I said, I will never break my covenant with you. And ye shall make no league with the inhabitants of this land; ye shall throw down their altars: but ye have not obeyed my voice: why have ye done this?

"Drive out your enemies," the Lord commanded. "Just as I brought you out of Egypt, I will give you victory in this land." But the people of Bochim botched it by allowing their enemies to remain in their midst.

Judges 2:3–5 (a)
Wherefore I also said, I will not drive them out from before you; but they shall be as thorns in your sides, and their gods shall be a snare unto you. And it came to pass, when the angel of the LORD spake these words unto all the children of Israel, that the people lifted up their voice, and wept. And they called the name of that place Bochim . . .

Bochim means "weeping"—which is fitting because sin always causes sorrow. You see, gang, Satan *never* has a good day. He never says, "I feel pretty nice today. I think I'll let up a bit and kind of bless people as they sin." No. He is a murderer and a destroyer. He is out to rip you off and wipe you out. Refusal to do battle with the sin in our lives always leads to Bochim—to the place of sorrow and weeping.

Judges 2:5 (b)
. . . and they sacrificed there unto the LORD.

They sacrificed to the Lord, but, as we shall see, theirs wasn't godly sorrow that resulted in repentance for their sin. It was emotional sorrow regarding the consequences of their sin. Godly sorrow works repentance (2 Corinthians 7:10). And repentance results in a change of direction. The Bible says Esau wept—or, in Hebrew, "cried profusely"—when he realized he had lost his blessing (Genesis 27:38). But there is no mention of Esau repenting. The same is true of the people of Bochim, as we shall see.

Judges 2:6–10
And when Joshua had let the people go, the children of Israel went every man unto his inheritance to possess the land. And the people served the LORD all the days of Joshua, and all the days of the elders that outlived Joshua, who had seen all the great works of the LORD, that he did for Israel. And Joshua the son of Nun, the servant of the LORD, died, being an hundred and ten years old. And they buried him in the border of his inheritance in Timnath-heres, in the mount of Ephraim, on the north side of the hill Gaash. And also all that generation were gathered unto their fathers: and there arose another generation after them, which knew not the LORD, nor yet the works which he had done for Israel.

Following the death of Joshua, under whose leadership the Israelites served the Lord, here we see them poised to take the second step in the cycle of sin repeated throughout the Book of Judges.

Judges 2:11
And the children of Israel did evil in the sight of the LORD, and served Baalim:

Step two: Here we see Israel succumbing to sin by serving Baal. Baal was the rain god, the god of the intellect. Because the people of the region were dependent on rain, and because weather was a mystery to them, Baal was their explanation for everything they couldn't understand. Later on, it would be the prophets of Baal Elijah would challenge to send forth rain upon a drought-stricken land (1 Kings 18).

Judges 2:12, 13
And they forsook the LORD God of their fathers, which brought them out of the land of Egypt, and followed other gods, of the gods of the people that were round about them, and bowed themselves unto them, and provoked the LORD to anger. And they forsook the LORD, and served Baal and Ashtaroth.

Ashtaroth, also known as the Babylonian god, Ishtar, and in Rome as "Easter," was the goddess of fertility, whose signs were, interestingly, the rabbit and the egg. Baal and Ashtaroth—the god of the intellect and the goddess of the senses—are two gods our own society still serves. Truly, behind every *Penthouse* and *Playboy* magazine looms the goddess Ashtaroth. And on every college campus where men flaunt their intellect and think themselves too wise to bow the knee to the God who reigns in heaven, there lurks Baal.

Judges 2:14
And the anger of the LORD was hot against Israel, and he delivered them into the hands of spoilers that spoiled them, and he sold them into the hands of their enemies round about, so that they could not any longer stand before their enemies.

Step 3: After succumbing to sin, the people of Israel are enslaved by sin.

Judges 2:15
Whithersoever they went out, the hand of the LORD was against them for evil, as the LORD had said, and as the LORD had sworn unto them: and they were greatly distressed.

Step 4: Feeling the hand of the Lord heavy against them, Israel is made to feel sorry for sin.

Judges 2:16
Nevertheless the LORD raised up judges, which delivered them out of the hand of those that spoiled them.

Step 5: Compassionate toward His people, the Lord saves them from their sin. But notice verse 17 . . .

Judges 2:17, 18
And yet they would not hearken unto their judges, but they went a whoring after other gods, and bowed themselves unto them: they turned quickly out of the way which their fathers walked in, obeying the commandments of the LORD; but they did not so. And when the LORD raised them up judges, then the LORD was with the judge, and delivered them out of the hand of their enemies all the days of the judge: for it repented the LORD because of their groanings by reason of them that oppressed them and vexed them.

Here we see Steps 1 through 5, as the people of Israel go from serving God to being saved by Him after becoming ensnared by their own sin. Yes, God cares. Yes, He's merciful. Yes, He hears the groaning of people and responds compassionately. Yet—the repercussions of sin are unavoidable (Galatians 6:7).

Judges 2:19
And it came to pass, when the judge was dead, that they returned, and corrupted themselves more than their fathers, in following other gods to serve them, and to bow down unto them; they ceased not from their own doings, nor from their stubborn way.

Here the Israelites are, back at Step 2 all over again.

Judges 2:20–23
And the anger of the LORD was hot against Israel; and he said, Because that this people hath transgressed my covenant which I commanded their fathers, and have not hearkened unto my voice; I also will not henceforth drive out any from before them of the nations which Joshua left when he died: That through them I may prove Israel, whether they will keep the way of the LORD to walk therein, as their fathers did keep it, or not. Therefore the LORD left those nations, without driving them out hastily; neither delivered he them into the hand of Joshua.

Because the Israelites continually disobeyed Him, the Lord said, "I'm going to allow their enemies to remain." Thus, the Canaanites, Hittites, Perizzites, Jebusites, Gergashites, Ammonites, and the Amorites served as instruments whereby the Lord could test His people.

First Corinthians talks about the testing we face. You see, many of the problems we go through are the results of our own stupidity. Many of the difficulties we encounter are the direct result of our own disobedience. Yet the Lord will use those very difficulties and problems in order to test us, to prove us, to show us where we stand.

You will be tested, gang, and it is during the time of testing—when fire sweeps through your life, your marriage, your family—that you will discover whether you have been building with wood, hay, and stubble, or with gold, silver, and precious stones. If everything burns in the time of testing, then you need to deal with it, saying, "Father, I have been building with the wrong material. Correct me."

Whenever fire sweeps through your life, don't try and put the fire out. You'll only get burned. Instead, let the fire go. Let it burn. And then when it's over, come back and poke around. See in the midst of the ashes if there's any gold, silver, or precious stones—and rebuild with them.

I believe it is crucial for us not to be those who try and put out fires in our church, in our marriages, at our jobs. Don't be one who puts out fires. It won't work. Oh, you might delay the fire a bit. Or you might diffuse it somewhat—but only for a while. Instead, let the fire burn because you will never know what you're building with in life, in ministry, in your occupation until the day of trial comes and the fire is unleashed.

That's why, as Christians, we must never be defensive. We must never answer accusations or protect ourselves in any area. We must welcome the fires that sweep through our lives, our families, our ministries, our jobs in order that in the light of the flames, we might see clearly the true nature of our building materials.

Let the fire rage. Let the Canaanites—those who might be attacking you, misunderstanding you, or accusing you—stand, for through them, you'll be able to see exactly where you're at, how you're developing, how you're maturing.

That's what Jesus did.

If there was ever justification for someone to get tough and take a stand, it would have been Him. If there was ever a time for someone to say, "This isn't right, and it must not happen," it was when His enemies accused and cursed Him. But He didn't. He submitted. He went to the Cross.

How can you stop a Man who doesn't fight back? How can you stop a church who will embrace difficult times? How can you stop a family or a marriage that actually welcomes fires? How can you stop people like that?

You can't.

---

3 Spiritual collapse in the life of the believer is rarely the result of a blowout, but almost always the result of a slow leak. Compromises are made. Devotional life is ignored. And slowly but surely, spiritual strength we once enjoyed is dissipated until finally we find ourselves unable to go on.

As we continue in the Book of Judges, we see the spiritual collapse of the people of God. The reason is not so much that they were blown away *by* their enemies, but rather that they compromised *with* their enemies. It was a slow leak that dissipated their spiritual stamina and destroyed their potential potency.

That's always the way it is. As a Christian, you

will not be vulnerable to the big blowout as much as to the slow, subtle leak.

Judges 3:1–4
Now these are the nations which the LORD left, to prove Israel by them, even as many of Israel as had not known all the wars of Canaan; Only that the generations of the children of Israel might know, to teach them war, at the least such as before knew nothing thereof; Namely, five lords of the Philistines, and all the Canaanites, and the Sidonians, and the Hivites that dwelt in mount Lebanon, from mount Baal-hermon unto the entering in of Hamath. And they were to prove Israel by them, to know whether they would hearken unto the commandments of the LORD, which he commanded their fathers by the hand of Moses.

As seen in chapter 2, the Israelites were supposed to destroy their enemies. When they failed to do so, however, the Lord used their enemies to reveal their heart.

Judges 3:5
And the children of Israel dwelt among the Canaanites, Hittites, and Amorites, and Perizzites, and Hivites, and Jebusites.

First, the children of Israel dwelt with their enemies. This is the beginning of the slow leak that led to their collapse.

Judges 3:6 (a)
And they took their daughters to be their wives, and gave their daughters to their sons . . .

Secondly, the children of Israel had relations with their enemies.

Judges 3:6 (b)
. . . and served their gods.

Finally, the children of Israel worshiped with their enemies.

In this, we see a pattern repeated in our own lives if we're not oh, so careful. We dwell with the world. We start relating to the world. We end up worshiping with the world. Let me remind you once again that none of us falls into sin. We walk into it one step at a time. All along the way, the Lord is saying, "Wait. Stop."

"Oh, Lord, this is okay," we say. "I just won't do *that.*" But when we end up doing *that,* we say, "Well, Lord, that's okay, but I sure won't do the next"—until we end up doing the next.

Sin is not fallen into—it's walked into one step at a time—which is why we are to make no provision for the flesh (Romans 13:14). When we fail to do this, the slow leak of compromise is bound to take its toll.

Judges 3:7
And the children of Israel did evil in the sight of the LORD, and forgat the LORD their God, and served Baalim and the groves.

The groves were dedicated to pagan deities—places trees were planted for the purpose of idolatry and immorality.

Judges 3:8 (a)
Therefore the anger of the LORD was hot against Israel . . .

The anger of the Lord was a holy indignation, a righteous anger because He knew His people were headed for disaster.

Judges 3:8 (b)
. . . and he sold them into the hand of Chushan-rishathaim king of Mesopotamia: and the children of Israel served Chushan-rishathaim eight years.

Chushan-rishathaim means "double darkness." And that's what the king Mesopotamia was—a very evil, wicked ruler. The Lord used Chushan-rishathaim as an instrument of chastening, that through him the Israelites might come to their senses and realize they couldn't give their sons and daughters. We're given over to double darkness when we don't destroy those things we know must go. Depression sets in. Confusion fills our thinking. We're in the dark about what we're supposed to do, where we should go, who we are. It's a double darkness. It's the reality of sin.

Judges 3:9 (a)
And when the children of Israel cried unto the LORD . . .

No doubt the Israelites prayed all the while they were in bondage to Chushan-rishathaim. But it evidently took eight years for them to cry to the Lord, to reach a place of desperation and intensity in their prayer.

"Dear God," we pray, "It's really been (ho hum) a long day, so I don't have much energy to talk to You tonight (yawn), but I really need help with my car payment (zzzz)."

If the Lord responded to us in the same degree of intensity and passion that we talk to Him, He would say, "(Yawn) Really? It has been a long day (stretch). And maybe I can get to it, but I can't promise . . ." Then He would nod off.

This was not the way Elijah prayed. When he prayed for rain, Scripture says he put his head between his knees and prayed seven times (1 Kings 18:42, 43). I suggest this was because this was the position of birthing in that culture. There was something being birthed by Elijah that day as he labored in prayer—once, again, a third time, four, five, six, seven times. And in answering his prayer, it is as if the Lord said, "I like that. In a world plagued by mediocrity, apathy, and laziness, it's good to see a man who knows it's dry in his soul or in his land and prays passionately and fervently for rain."

Judges 3:9 (b)
. . . the LORD raised up a deliverer to the children of Israel . . .

I love this verse—one that is repeated over and over again throughout Judges. Do you find yourself in bondage today? Do you find yourself in bondage presently? Do you find yourself ensnared today? Let me tell you what the answer is: Cry out to the Lord. I'm convinced that we as Christians do too much talking *about* the Lord, and not enough talking *to* Him. We are very ready, very eager to receive counsel, but very reluctant to cry out. The reason counseling offices are filled in Christendom today is because people do not bow their knee and call out to the Lord in fervency. Throughout Scripture, God is consistently seen responding to His people when they cry out. Truly, the effectual fervent prayer of a righteous man availeth *much* (James 5:16).

Judges 3:9 (c), 10 (a)
. . . who delivered them, even Othniel the son of Kenaz, Caleb's younger brother. And the Spirit of the LORD came upon him, and he judged Israel . . .

The first of the named judges was a man named Othniel. What was his secret? The Spirit of the Lord came upon him. There is no substitute for the Spirit of God. Jesus said, "You shall receive power when the Holy Ghost comes upon you and you shall be My witnesses: (Acts 1:8). We must be those who seek the fullness, the power, the anointing of the Spirit if we are to be used effectively for the kingdom, for while the Spirit indwells every believer at the moment of conversion, His "coming upon" ministry uniquely empowers every believer for service. Every believer has the Holy Spirit. The question is, Does the Holy Spirit have every believer?

How does the Spirit come upon us? When, like the Israelites, we cry out and say, "Father I need the power of the Spirit. I'm tired of being in bondage. I'm tired of the drought within. I want to be filled with You and used by You for Your glory. Jesus said, "If you, being evil, know how to give good gifts to your children, how much more will the Heavenly Father give the Holy Ghost to them that ask" (Luke 11:13).

Judges 3:10 (b), 11
. . . and went out to war: and the LORD delivered Chushan-rishathaim king of Mesopotamia into his hand; and his hand prevailed against Chushan-rishathaim. And the land had rest forty years. And Othniel the son of Kenaz died.

Othniel had the singular job of seeing his generation set free from oppression. After the Spirit of God came upon him, he accomplished this task—and the land rested for forty years. I want to see the Spirit of God come upon us so that those in our generation might be set free, might experience rest.

Judges 3:12
And the children of Israel did evil again in the sight of the LORD: and the LORD strengthened Eglon the king of Moab against Israel, because they had done evil in the sight of the LORD.

Eglon was aptly named in that he looked like an egg. The only man in the Bible called "a very fat man" (Judges 3:17), Eglon was a great big, tubby oppressor. His story provides a perfect illustration of how to deal with the heavyweight, heavy-duty oppressors that threaten us.

Judges 3:13 (a)
And he gathered unto him the children of Ammon and Amalek . . .

After leaving Sodom, Lot's daughters were worried that they would never have children. So they seduced their father and gave birth to two sons—Moab and Ammon. This explains why Eglon, a Moabite, would join forces with the Ammonites and a third group—the Amalekites, the descendants of Esau. All three of these nations had their roots in carnality, sin, and iniquity.

Judges 3:13 (b)
. . . and went and smote Israel, and possessed the city of palm trees.

The city of palm trees is Jericho. Jericho was where fruits and vegetables grew prolifically. The region's "Food 4 Less," Eglon, a very fat man, looked at Jericho and knew that was the city for him!

Judges 3:14, 15 (a)
So the children of Israel served Eglon the king of Moab eighteen years. But when the children of Israel cried unto the LORD the LORD raised them up a deliverer . . .

During the eighteen years they served Eglon, I'm sure the children of Israel prayed and talked to each other about somehow getting free from Eglon. But they weren't in a place of desperation. It was only when they cried to the Lord—when there was energy expended, when lethargy was shaken off—that the Lord hearkened to them.

Judges 3:15 (b)
. . . Ehud, the son of Gera, a Benjamite, a man lefthanded . . .

Benjamin means "son of my right hand." The right hand speaks of authority, prowess, and ability. In this culture, the left hand spoke of shortcoming, and was considered a curse. Therefore, as Ehud grew up, he probably wondered, "Lord, why am I, a Benjamite, *left*-handed?" It could be simply that Ehud was born left-handed. Or, as the text could indicate, his right hand may have been handicapped in some way.

Judges 3:15 (c)
. . . and by him the children of Israel sent a present unto Eglon the king of Moab.

I suggest the present the Israelites sent to King Eglon was a gift of food in hopes it would appease him. We also are prone to appease and feed the Eglons, the temptations in our lives. But it never works because temptation is just like fire: the more you feed it, the more it demands. It's always a bad idea to try and appease that which is oppressing you. It will only make the enemy bigger, fatter, and heavier.

Judges 3:16 (a)
But Ehud made him a dagger which had two edges, of a cubit length . . .

While others sent food to appease Eglon, Ehud went to his workshop and made an eighteen inch, two-edged sword.

Judges 3:16 (b)
. . . and he did gird it under his raiment . . .

Notice Ehud put his sword under his clothes. Of the two-edged sword of the Word (Hebrews 4:12), the psalmist writes, "Thy Word have I hid in my heart that I might not sin against Thee" (Psalm 119:11).

Judges 3:16 (c)
. . . upon his right thigh.

Because daggers were drawn across one's body, being left-handed, Ehud strapped his dagger to his right thigh.

Judges 3:17, 18
And he brought the present unto Eglon king of Moab: and Eglon was a very fat man. And when he had made an end to offer the present, he sent away the people that bare the present.

Any time you try to appease the enemy, you'll always be sent away. The Lord won't be able to use you. It's not condemnation, but simply the reality of the situation. Compromise is never the answer.

Judges 3:19
But he himself turned again from the quarries that were by Gilgal, and said, I have a secret errand unto thee, O king: who said, Keep silence. And all that stood by him went out from him.

Having already been presented with a gift from the Israelites, Eglon must have been eager to hear Ehud's message. Ehud, however, returned to Eglon not with a gift, but with a sword.

Judges 3:20 (a)
And Ehud came unto him; and he was sitting in a summer parlour which he had for himself alone . . .

Eglon was in the *aleah*—the rooftop sitting room that provided a cool retreat from the heat of the day on palaces and well-to-do homes.

Judges 3:20 (b), 21
. . . And Ehud said, I have a message from God unto thee. And he arose out of his seat. And Ehud put forth his left hand, and took the dagger from his right thigh, and thrust it into his belly.

Like our modern-day monarchs and presidents, Eglon would have been surrounded by "Secret Service" agents. But historians tell us these bodyguards would become careless and only frisk men on their left side—the side where weapons were carried. That's how Ehud made it in with his sword. *That's* why he was left-handed.

God never makes mistakes. You may wonder why you are the way you are. There's a reason. Psalm 139 declares that when you were in your mother's womb, God was fitting you together and ordaining your days. Everything about you is the way God desires it to be—from your personality to your physical appearance. It's all by Divine design. Ask Ehud. I'm sure as he drew his sword, he said, "Thank You, Lord, for making me left-handed. It's not a curse after all."

Judges 3:22 (a)
And the haft also went in after the blade; and the fat closed upon the blade, so that he could not draw the dagger out of his belly . . .

According to historical records, the handle of Ehud's knife would have been twelve to fifteen inches; the blade itself, eighteen inches. I can see Ehud's eyes getting big as saucers as the knife kept going in a full thirty inches!

When Jesus was attacked in the wilderness by Satan, the heavyweight from hell, He quoted Scripture three times—once for each temptation (Matthew 4). Jesus unsheathed the sword of the Word hidden in His heart and beat back the enemy.

Judges 3:22 (b)
. . . and the dirt came out.

Some translators have translated the word, "dirt," as "intestines" or "entrails." Others have left it as literal dirt. I don't know if this means Eglon was chewing on dirt clods, or if he just didn't wash his food. But I do know that the illustration is appropriate. "How shall a young man cleanse his way?" asked the psalmist. "By taking heed thereto according to Thy Word" (Psalm 119:9). When the Word goes in, the dirt comes out.

That's why what you're doing right now is so important. You see, it's not so much going through the Bible that makes a difference as it is the Bible going through us. When the Word goes in, something miraculous and mystical happens. Every time you are in the Word—studying, meditating, reading—a cleansing process takes place.

"Well, then, why aren't all Christians spotless?" you ask. Or, "Why isn't the person sitting next to me perfect? After all, he's been coming to Bible study for eight years."

Listen—instead of looking at other believers and wondering why they're not better, we should realize how much worse we'd all be if not for the Lord. I hate to even think what I would be if not for the Word of God going through me. To be sure, it's a long, hard process. But step by step, day by day, month by month, year by year, decade by decade, we're being changed as the Word goes in and the dirt comes out. If you want to be Spirit-filled and experience abundant life, be one who is committed to the Word—studying the Word, meditating in the Word, memorizing chunks of the Word.

For topical study of Judges 3:12–22 entitled "The Word Goes In and the Dirt Comes Out," turn to page 728.

Judges 3:23, 24
Then Ehud went forth through the porch, and shut the doors of the parlour upon him, and locked them. When he was gone out, his servants came; and when they saw that, behold, the doors of the parlour were locked, they said, Surely he covereth his feet in his summer chamber.

"He covereth his feet" was a polite way of saying, "He's in the bathroom."

Judges 3:25–28
And they tarried till they were ashamed: and, behold, he opened not the doors of the parlour; therefore they took a key, and opened them: and, behold, their lord was fallen down dead on the earth. And Ehud escaped while they tarried, and passed beyond the quarries, and escaped unto Seirath. And it came to pass, when he was come, that he blew a trumpet in the mountain of Ephraim, and the children of Israel went down with him from the mount, and he before them. And he said unto them, Follow after me: for the LORD hath delivered your enemies the Moabites into your hand. And they went down after him, and took the fords of Jordan toward Moab, and suffered not a man to pass over.

"Follow me," said this one who wielded his sword so effectively. If you want to be a leader in your family, be one who has a handle on the sword of the Word and who knows how to use it effectively. It makes a huge difference, Mom and Dad, when you speak from authority other than your own, when you can say, "This is what God says concerning this issue . . ."

If you aspire to any kind of leadership, be like Ehud. "Follow me," he said because he was a man who knew the power of the Sword and used it effectively.

Judges 3:29, 30
And they slew of Moab at that time about ten thousand men, all lusty, and all men of valour; and there escaped not a man. So Moab was subdued that day under the hand of Israel. And the land had rest fourscore years.

Through Ehud's effective use of the sword, the oppressor was destroyed and the land had rest. The same thing can be true in our lives. "Sanctify them through thy truth; thy word is truth," Jesus prayed (John 17:17). "And ye shall know the truth, and the truth shall make you free," He declared (John 8:32). If you are facing heavy problems, dark days, tough times, get in the Word. Spend more time than ever with the sword of the Scriptures in your hand, talking to the Lord about what you're reading, crying out with passion, hearing His voice through meditation. No matter how heavy, how Ehud-like the problem, you *will* be set free. Jesus promised this, and I've found this to be true in my own life over and over again.

Judges 3:31
And after him was Shamgar the son of Anath, which slew of the Philistines six hundred men with an ox goad: and he also delivered Israel.

The third judge, Shamgar, used an ordinary instrument to do an extraordinary work for God. It's true. God will use whatever's in your hand for His glory if you allow Him—even something as unlikely as an ox goad. What's in your hand? Don't just make a living—make a life by using what God has put in your hand for His glory.

In the three judges of chapter 3, I see the power of the Spirit in Othniel, the power of the sword in Ehud, and the power of service in Shamgar. These three elements—the Spirit of God upon you, the Word of the Lord within you, and service for the Lord through you—will lead you into much fruitfulness as you do battle in the land to which God has brought you.

***For topical study of Judges 3:31 entitled "The Ox Goad Incident," turn to page* 730.**

THE WORD GOES IN AND THE DIRT COMES OUT

A Topical Study of JUDGES 3:12–22

Sin is not bad because it's forbidden. Sin is forbidden because it's bad. Most people think God capriciously declares what is good and bad. That's not the way it is. God sees what will be a blessing and what will be a curse. And because certain things will defile, destroy, and damage because certain things bring headaches and heartaches, sadness and sorrow, pain and problems, He says, "Stay away from those things." It's not that God is mad at me when I sin, but rather He's grieved for me, knowing I'm headed down a path that will bring me unnecessary pain and sorrow.

When Peter-John was a baby, we lived in a cabin on the edge of a pasture. When he learned to walk, I thought PJ would immediately go outside and pet Bessie and Daisy, the cows. But that's not what he did. He made his way out the door and headed straight for the nearest "pasture patty."

"No!" I said. "No, no, no."

Looking at me rather defiantly, he made his way to the next "meadow muffin" he saw and put both hands in it.

"No, Peter-John," I said, as I spanked, then washed, his hands.

With tears filling his eyes, he looked up at me. If he could have talked, I know he would have said, "You great big bully. You don't understand the ecstasy and the pleasure of a pasture patty. Why are you so mean?"

As Peter-John has grown up, he agrees that pasture patties are disgusting.

And the same thing happens spiritually. "Why can't I go here, do this, or have that?" we wonder, sure that God is robbing us of some wonderful pleasure.

But our loving Father says, "It's a pasture patty, a meadow muffin. And as a spiritual toddler, you might think it's fun and pleasurable—but in reality, it will cause you pain and problems. That's why I can't allow you to plunge in, grab hold, or get involved with that thing."

Most of us have pasture patties and meadow muffins in our lives—sins that fascinate us, oppress us, dominate us, and dictate to us; issues, habits, or tendencies we might conceal quite well from those around us, but which secretly, and repeatedly control us.

Are you tired of the dirt within your soul—the bad attitude, anger, or addiction; the bitterness, bigotry, or hostility that seems to hold you captive? If you want to be free from the Eglon you know is leading you down a path of heartache and heartbreak, realize God has already given you the weapon you need—the sword of the Spirit, which is the Word of God (Ephesians 6:17).

Are you saturating your soul in the Word of God? If I'm not in the Word, Eglon is sure to rear up and take control. But as I give priority to the Scriptures—as Ehud discovered—the sword goes in and the dirt comes out.

Read Consistently

Read your Bible every day. Get involved in Bible study. Learn the Word. Hide it in your heart.

"But my mind is like a sieve," you say. "I can't even remember what I read yesterday."

That's OK. The Word is like water. So even if your mind is like a sieve—if you read the Word, at least it will be clean!

Read your Bible consistently. Find a Bible study that will take you through the Word, chapter by chapter, verse by verse so that you can get the full counsel of God (Acts 20:27).

"But it's so dry," you say.

I know. It can be dry for me, too.

After marching their troops and livestock seven days in the wilderness without water, the kings of Judah and Israel went to Elisha for help. "Thus saith the Lord," Elijah said. "Make this valley full of ditches." For thus saith the Lord, "You shall not see wind, nor shall you see rain; yet that valley shall be filled with water, so that your cattle and your animals may drink."

The kings obeyed. And the next day, the ditches were filled with water (2 Kings 3).

Sometimes Bible study may feel dry. You can't remember what you've read—and even if you could, it doesn't make sense to you. That's OK. You're digging ditches that the Lord will fill the next day, week, month, or year. The best advice I can give anyone is to learn the Scriptures. A young man cleanses his way—an old man, too—by taking heed to the Word, by hiding it in his heart, by making it part of the fabric of his being so that he thinks biblically.

Read Expectantly

When you read the Word, read it with a spirit of expectation. Come to the Word prepared to hear from God. For me, that means having pencil and paper in hand.

Wrestling through some issues, Habakkuk said, "I will go to the tower and wait upon the Lord to see what He shall say to me."

"Write the vision," the Lord answered, "and make it plain" (see Habakkuk 2:1, 2). I doubt Habakkuk had to ask to borrow a pencil.

For me, a pencil and paper in hand shows I expect God is going to say something worth noting. If you want to have victory, become a student of the Word. Read it with the spirit of expectation, saying, "Lord, I need to hear from You today, and I know I will."

Read Conversationally

Read the Word consistently. Come with expectancy. Read conversationally. That is, allow the Lord to talk with you as you read a verse. Then talk to Him about that verse through prayer. Read a verse or two more, think them through, and talk to God once again. It's a dialogue. It's not Bible study *then* prayer. It's Bible study *with* prayer. It's a conversation.

Read Obediently

If I'm not going to do what the Lord tells me to do through His Word on any given morning, I can't expect to receive more instruction from Him that evening. You see, God doesn't pile our spiritual "in-boxes" higher and higher with "To Do" lists. He simply gives us one thing to do at a time. Therefore, as you open the Word, purpose in your heart to do what He tells you to do that day.

The only way to be free from the Eglons that bring oppression and depression to you is to allow the Word of God to do its work within you. The key to Ehud's victory was a hidden, two-edged sword, rightly used.

And the key to our victory is the same.

THE OX GOAD INCIDENT

A Topical Study of JUDGES 3:31

Bigfoot, King Kong, Superman, the Incredible Hulk—there is something within people, something within every generation, searching for heroes—for people who are larger than life, people who accomplish extraordinary feats. The Book of Judges chronicles the lives of seven individuals—six men and one woman—who were used by God to mete out judgment to the enemies of Israel. What impresses me about these judges, these heroes, is the fact that they were, by and large, extraordinarily ordinary. They didn't have a lot going for them; they didn't have an abundance of abilities. Yet every one of them had the most important ability necessary to be used by God. They had availability.

As we look at these judges, I pray we will gain insight as to how we, too, might be used by the Lord to accomplish great things for Him. The particular judge in the passage before us is an unlikely, unknown, unsung hero named Shamgar . . .

Shamgar was an unlikely hero indeed. His name gives us insight into his personality, for in the Hebrew culture, names carried great significance and were given according to one's personality or prophecy concerning him. Shamgar's father was named *Anath*, or "Afflicted." Shamgar's own name means "The Desolate Dragged Away One"—not a very likely name for a hero.

Shamgar is also an unknown hero, for there is no mention of him anywhere in Scripture except for this single verse. Consequently, we don't know about his past, nor do we know what happened to him after this incident took place.

Unlikely, unknown, and unsung—that's Shamgar. After all, how many of you proclaim the heroics of Shamgar? How many name him as one of their favorite Bible heroes? And yet Shamgar was utilized in God's work and recorded in God's Word as one whom the Lord used mightily.

What did Shamgar do? This man—unknown, unlikely, and unsung—accomplished an incredible feat. He took on six hundred Philistines and whipped them singlehandedly—six hundred Philistines who so oppressed the people of Israel that men were afraid to travel on the highways, six hundred Philistines who virtually brought village life to a standstill. The Philistines were brutal oppressors, yet Shamgar killed six hundred of them with only an ox goad.

Why did he use an ox goad? I believe it was because Shamgar was one who worked with oxen—a rancher, a herdsman. You see, the ox goad—a stick used to prod cattle—was a common instrument, easily accessible to anyone who worked with livestock.

I point this out to remind you that the Lord delights in using whatever is in your hand in order to bring about His purposes through your life. God has gifted you with talents, given you abilities, placed within you certain desires and interests—and those are the very components He desires to utilize for the work of His kingdom through you. Truly, He will use whatever is in your hand.

When God called Moses to go before Pharaoh, Moses balked, fearing no one would listen to him.

"What is that in your hand?" asked the Lord.

"A rod," answered Moses.

"Throw it down," said God.

As Moses threw the rod to the ground, it miraculously became a snake. And when he picked it up, it became a rod once again.

God used a common, ordinary, everyday shepherd's rod to accomplish His plan through Moses (Exodus 4).

David grew up slinging stones against trees, fence posts, and any other target he could find as he watched his father's flocks. So what did the Lord utilize in David's life to slay a giant? A simple sling and a few stones (1 Samuel 17:49).

I think of Peter and Andrew. What was in their hands when the Lord called them for service? They were casting fishing nets into the sea. Thus, Jesus said, "Follow Me, and I will make you fishers of men" (Matthew 4:19).

Among five thousand hungry people on the hillside was a little boy. What did he have in his hand? Five loaves and two fish—which the Lord used to feed the entire crowd (John 6:9).

I am reminded of the apostle Paul. What was in his hand when he was converted? A pen, for he was a scholar whose command of the Greek language exceeded every other scholar in history. So what did God use most powerfully in Paul's life? A pen, as Paul authored one epistle after another.

Gang, the Lord can use whatever skills, interests, or abilities you have. He will use whatever is in your hand for His glory. He will give you insights and open doors. Great things will take place through you. The kingdom of darkness, the kingdom of selfishness, the kingdom of greed will be beaten back as you take whatever ox goad is in your life and say, "Lord, use it for *Your* glory."

"But I have nothing in my hand," you say. "I can't do anything."

Oh, yes you can. Can you babysit? Can you sew clothes or chop wood? Can you fix cars? There are a number of people in this body, in this community, who would welcome your skills. Make them available. God will use them powerfully if you simply say, "Lord, show me."

Why am I stressing serve so strongly?

For two reasons . . .

One is because I am totally, absolutely convinced it is in serving the Lord that we find ourselves fulfilled. If you just take in and never give out, you'll find yourself feeling grumpy and discouraged, depressed and defeated. Before long, you will notice you have no appetite to take in any more, and your walk will grow stale and stagnant. Jesus said, "Whatever measure with which you give out will be the measure with which it will be given back to you" (Matthew 7:2). Thus, for fulfillment in this life, it is essential that I be used in the things of God. We are not saved to set, soak, and sour. We're saved to serve.

Secondly, service has eternal ramifications. In Matthew 24, we see some enlightening insights on the eternal nature of service. We find ourselves at the center of the Olivet Discourse—the teaching Jesus gave dealing with end times and events. In verse 32, Jesus says, "When you see the budding of the fig tree, know My coming is nigh." Scripturally, the fig tree speaks of the nation of Israel. The budding or blossoming of the nation of Israel came to pass May 14, 1948, when Israel was declared a nation. We have seen the fig tree blossom. We have seen this very prophecy fulfilled. Therefore, the return of Jesus Christ is nigh—even at the very door.

We are living in the final hours of the last days. In light of this, consider two illustrations Jesus gave . . .

The Scenario of the Season

> *Who then is a faithful and wise servant, whom his lord hath made ruler over his household, to give them meat in due season? Blessed is that servant, whom his lord when he cometh shall find so doing. Verily I say unto you, That he shall make him ruler over all his goods. But and if that evil servant shall say in his heart, My lord delayeth his coming; And shall begin to smite his fellowservants, and to eat and drink with the drunken; The lord of that servant shall come in a day when he looketh not for him, and in an hour that he is not aware of, And shall cut him asunder, and appoint him his portion with the hypocrites: there shall be weeping and gnashing of teeth.* Matthew 24:45–51

I believe this heavy-duty passage has wonderful application to us as believers. The Greek word translated "evil" in verse 48 is *kakos.* Kakos doesn't mean evil in the sense of being wicked, unregenerate, or lost. It refers to one who was once good but has gone bad. Specifically, it was used to describe an apple that had become rotten, or a musical instrument that had fallen out of tune. Thus, the Lord is speaking of one who once served, but has gone bad, has gotten out of tune. It's not that he has walked away from his master—he just stopped serving.

What does Jesus say concerning such a one? When the master returns and finds him living for his own pleasures and beating his fellow servants, he will cut him in two and appoint him his portion with the hypocrites. What is a hypocrite? A hypocrite is simply one who is two-faced.

After careful study of this passage, I am convinced that Jesus is speaking to believers. You see, when our Master comes back, suddenly our lives will be divided. That which we have done for ourselves, that which we have done hypocritically, will suddenly be cut asunder—causing weeping, wailing, and gnashing of teeth. We will weep not because God will punish us, but because, at His appearance, we will see our lives cut in two: That which has been done for ourselves in our own energy, for our own glory vs. what we did out of a heart of love for God. And we will cry out, "Father, why did I waste my time and energy, money and ability on things which have no lasting value? All those hours I spent on that project, all the money I spent on that hobby are gone." And we will fall before God, saying, "I was a fool. I wasted my life, my skills, my talents."

"Be careful," Jesus says. "When the master comes, there will be a dividing asunder whereby you will be made aware of the mission and ministry you could have enjoyed in eternity had you not wasted your earthly life on trivial pursuits."

The Sobering of the Saints

> *Then shall the kingdom of heaven be likened unto ten virgins, which took their lamps, and went forth to meet the bridegroom. And five of them were wise, and five were foolish. They that were foolish took their lamps, and took no oil with them: But the wise took oil in their vessels with their lamps. While the bridegroom tarried, they all slumbered and slept. And at midnight there was a cry made, Behold, the bridegroom cometh; go ye out to meet him. Then all those virgins arose, and trimmed their lamps. And the foolish said unto the wise, Give us of your oil; for our lamps are gone out. But the wise answered, saying, Not so; lest there be not enough for us and you: but go ye rather to them that sell, and buy for yourselves. And while they went to buy, the bridegroom came; and they that were ready went in with him to the marriage: and the door was shut. Afterward came also the other virgins, saying, Lord, Lord, open to us. But he answered and said, Verily I say unto you, I know you not. Watch therefore, for ye know neither the day nor the hour wherein the Son of man cometh.* Matthew 25:1–13

In this second illustration, Jesus likens the community of believers to a wedding party. Again, due to the fact that all ten virgins were part of the wedding party, I believe this passage refers to believers.

According to the custom of the day, the bridegroom would come unexpectedly to the house of his bride, at which time the wedding procession would begin. In this case, the five foolish virgins said to the five others, "Oh, no! The bridegroom is here, but we don't have any oil for our lamps. Give us some of yours so we can join the procession."

"No," said the wise virgins. "There's not enough. You can't rely upon our oil. Go buy your own."

Maybe you're relying on the oil of your husband, your wife, or your parents. Maybe you're thinking you will be rewarded or blessed on the basis of those around you. Not so. It doesn't work that way. You cannot gain anything eternally from the experience of others.

The story continues, and I find it very intriguing. The five who were watching and ready were allowed into the wedding feast. When the other five realized what had taken place, they knocked on the door, saying, "Lord, let us in."

"I don't know you," the Lord replied.

This Greek phrase doesn't mean, "I don't know who you are," but rather, "I don't know you personally." Could this mean that, although the entire body of Christ will be present in heaven, not everyone will be ushered in to that time of intimacy, into that time of special relationship with Jesus at the marriage feast? It seems to solve some problems in my own understanding of Revelation 7, where you'll find there are those who are seated with Christ, but there are also those who are serving—standing on the outside, removed from the inner circle.

I believe the possibility exists that those who are burning brightly, serving the Lord fervently, living their lives daily for Him will be ushered into the marriage feast when Jesus Christ comes back. But those who are playing the foolish virgin—they're born-again, but not living for the Lord, working for the Lord, or looking for the Lord—although they will be in heaven, they will hold a different position due to their distant relationship with Him here on earth.

I am increasingly convinced that this life is significant because it reflects our capacity to enjoy eternity. If I'm living for puny, petty pursuits here on earth, my ability to enjoy eternity will be equally small.

> Four-year-old Christy carries around her purple Care Bear. She talks to it, kisses it, hugs it. Her Care Bear makes her happy. Now, I could hug the same Care Bear, but it wouldn't do a whole lot for me because my capacity for satisfaction and enjoyment is past the Care Bear stage.

The same is true in heaven. There will be those who will be happy to hold little Care Bears. But there will also be those who will be involved in the cosmic purposes of God. That's what I want. I want to be all I can be for Him in eternity. Gang, what we're doing today affects what we will be doing for the next billion years.

That's why Jesus says, "Be ready. Don't be out of tune. Don't be an evil servant, lest when I return and your life is divided, you will see the majority of it dissipate into nothingness." That's why Jesus says, "Don't be a foolish virgin. Be ready, lest you find yourself excluded from real intimacy with Me."

Saint, whatever ox goad is in your hand, whatever little lunch you're clutching, whatever sling you are swinging, whatever pen you're holding—dedicate it to God, and I promise you will not be disappointed.

You will never say, "Oh, I really wish I hadn't given that skill to God's service. I wish I had made more money for myself. I wish I had spent more time on myself. No, the only weeping, the only regret in eternity will be that we didn't give *more*, didn't do *more*, didn't serve *more*.

Shamgar was not a man of great abilities—just a prodder of oxen, a guy who poked cattle. But his life is recorded in Scripture because he gave his ability to God and accomplished great things for God.

Life is short, gang, and eternity long. I plead with you, even as I plead with myself, don't fall out of tune. Don't run out of oil. Take whatever is in your hand and say, "Lord, it's Yours. Show me how this can be used for Your glory."

Amen.

4 In chapter 4, we come to the fourth judge—a woman . . .

Judges 4:1
And the children of Israel again did evil in the sight of the LORD, when Ehud was dead.

From before the turn of the century into the days of the Great Depression, a colorful evangelist named Billy Sunday preached with an intensity unrivaled to this day. A professional baseball player before his conversion, Sunday caroused continually, partied frequently, and experienced the effects of sin most definitely. No doubt that is why he said, "I am against sin. I will kick it as long as I've got a foot. I'll fight it as long as I've got a fist. I'll butt it as long as I've got a head. I'll bite it as long as I've got a tooth. And when I'm old and fistless and footless and toothless, I'll gum it till I go home to glory and it goes to perdition."

The wages of sin is death, as the children of Israel would discover. And even in our day of inflation, sin's wages remain the same.

Judges 4:2 (a)
And the LORD sold them into the hand of Jabin king of Canaan, that reigned in Hazor . . .

Evidently the king of a confederation of Canaanite nations, Jabin ruled from Hazor, fifteen miles north of the Sea of Galilee.

Judges 4:2 (b), 3
. . . the captain of whose host was Sisera, which dwelt in Harosheth of the Gentiles. And the children of Israel cried unto the LORD: for he had nine hundred chariots of iron; and twenty years he mightily oppressed the children of Israel.

With nine hundred chariots of iron, Sisera had a seemingly invincible military machine at his disposal.

Judges 4:4, 5
And Deborah, a prophetess, the wife of Lapidoth, she judged Israel at that time. And she dwelt under the palm tree of Deborah between Ramah and Bethel in mount Ephraim: and the children of Israel came up to her for judgment.

I find it fitting that Deborah's name means "bee" . . .

The wax with which beehives are constructed is the most heat-resistant wax known to man and can withstand temperatures up to 140 degrees. However, at 141 degrees, the wax begins to melt. So when the hive nears the 141 degree mark, the bees begin to cluster around their hive and fan it by fluttering their wings 190 times per second, or 11,400 times per minute. No wonder bees are called industrious! They are also very discerning, with antennae containing between 2,000 and 3,000 plates through which they identify the proper flower from which to draw their nectar. Finally, bees are known for the sweetness of the honey they produce.

In Deborah, I see these same three characteristics: She was very industrious, very discerning, and very sweet. But she also packed a wallop of a sting, as we will see.

Judges 4:6–8
And she sent and called Barak the son of Abinoam out of Kedesh-naphtali, and said unto him, Hath not the LORD God of Israel commanded, saying, Go and draw toward mount Tabor, and take with thee ten thousand men of the children of Naphtali and of the children of Zebulun? And I will draw unto thee to the river Kishon Sisera, the captain of Jabin's army, with his chariots and his multitude; and I will deliver him into thine hand. And Barak said unto her, If thou wilt go with me, then I will go: but if thou wilt not go with me, then I will not go.

Although God found someone He could use mightily in Deborah, it is an indictment against the men of Israel that God's people lacked male leadership at this time.

Judges 4:9 (a)
And she said, I will surely go with thee: notwithstanding the journey that thou takest shall not be for thine honour; for the LORD shall sell Sisera into the hand of a woman . . .

Deborah's prophecy did indeed come to pass. Barak would not be given credit for Sisera's demise. Instead, as we will see, the honor would go to a woman named Jael.

Judges 4:9 (b), 10
. . . And Deborah arose, and went with Barak to Kedesh. And Barak called Zebulun and Naphtali to Kedesh; and he went up with ten thousand men at his feet: and Deborah went up with him.

Barak called Zebulun and Naphtali—the two tribes in the region—to join him.

Judges 4:11
Now Heber the Kenite, which was of the children of Hobab the father in law of Moses, had severed himself from the Kenites, and pitched his tent unto the plain of Zaanaim, which is by Kedesh.

Heber means "crossed over"—just as *Hebrew* means "crossing over." The Kenites lived in Israel, but were not Israelites. They were descendants of Moses' father-in-law, Hobab (Numbers 10:29). Although they had settled in Israel, the Kenites were in alliance with Jabin. But Heber left this group and began to dwell with the people of Israel. He "crossed over" and joined the Israelites.

Judges 4:12
And they shewed Sisera that Barak the son of Abinoam was gone up to mount Tabor.

Why did Heber alert Sisera? Evidently, it was because he was setting Sisera up for defeat.

Judges 4:13
And Sisera gathered together all his chariots, even nine hundred chariots of iron, and all the people that were with him, from Harosheth of the Gentiles unto the river of Kishon.

This second mention of Sisera's nine hundred chariots speaks of their importance. At this point in history, without iron weapons of any kind, Israel had not even entered the Iron Age. Thus, the odds were heavily stacked against Barak and his men.

Judges 4:14
And Deborah said unto Barak, Up; for this is the day in which the LORD hath delivered Sisera into thine hand: is not the LORD gone out before thee? So Barak went down from mount Tabor, and ten thousand men after him.

Mount Tabor is a hill in the middle of the valley of Jezreel, also known as the valley of Megiddo, or Armageddon.

Judges 4:15
And the LORD discomfited Sisera, and all his chariots, and all his host, with the edge of the sword before Barak; so that Sisera lighted down off his chariot, and fled away on his feet.

I like this! The one who trusted in his arms is now relying on his feet.

Judges 4:16, 17
But Barak pursued after the chariots, and after the host, unto Harosheth of the Gentiles: and all the host of Sisera fell upon the edge of the sword; and there was not a man left. Howbeit Sisera fled away on his feet to the tent of Jael the wife of Heber the Kenite: for there was peace between Jabin the king of Hazor and the house of Heber the Kenite.

Jabin and Sisera controlled the Kenites. Therefore, thinking Heber and Jael were still under their dominion, Sisera headed to their house for protection.

A court jester served in the court of Henry VIII, a man known for his fits of rage. After a certain performance that displeased him, the king said to the jester, "Sir, you will die for that particular act." Thinking himself a bit rash, however, the king said, "Die you must. The decree has been given. But I will allow you to die in the manner you choose."

The clever jester replied, "Very well, sire. I choose to die by old age."

That's just the way it is with our old sin nature, our old man (Colossians 3:9). He doesn't die easily. He's always showing up on the scene.

Judges 4:18
And Jael went out to meet Sisera, and said unto him, Turn in, my lord, turn in to me; fear not. And when he had turned in unto her into the tent, she covered him with a mantle.

No longer afraid of Sisera, Jael sets out to engage in aggressive battle against him as she invites him in to her tent and covers him with a blanket.

Judges 4:19 (a)
And he said unto her, Give me, I pray thee, a little water to drink; for I am thirsty . . .

This, too, is just like our old man, our old sin nature. He orders us around, beginning in small ways. "Give me a little water to drink," he says. "Give me a little space. Give me a little room. Give me a little satisfaction."

Sin is tricky. Little sins don't stay little. Little compromises don't remain little compromises. Give in a little, and you'll find yourself in big trouble.

Judges 4:19 (b)
. . . And she opened a bottle of milk, and gave him drink, and covered him.

After running for his life, it is no wonder Sisera's body cried for water. But what did Jael give him? Unrefrigerated, room-temperature milk, which, due to the climate, most likely resembled a cottage cheese/yogurt mixture, and which would have been the last thing Sisera wanted.

We are to overcome our sin nature, our old man who seeks to order us around, by giving him the milk of the Word (1 Peter 2:2). Saints—especially you older Christians—be careful you read 1 Peter 2:2 correctly. It doesn't say newborn babes desire the sincere milk of the Word. It says that *as* newborn babes, we are *all* to crave the milk of the Word. Never think you're beyond milk. We need to be continually refreshed by, renewed in, and reminded of the milk truths of the Word of God, for it's when we no longer receive and enjoy the milk that we begin to lose our appetite for the meat of the Word as well.

Judges 4:20
Again he said unto her, Stand in the door of the tent, and it shall be, when any man doth come and inquire of thee, and say, Is there any man here? that thou shalt say, No.

At first, Sisera cruised in and said, "Can I have a little drink of water?" Now, he's saying, "Go stand at the door and lie for me. Don't acknowledge that I'm here. Don't let anyone know you're struggling with this." That's what the old man of our sin nature always does. Open the door a crack, and he'll come in and attempt to totally control and dominate every part of your life.

Judges 4:21
Then Jael Heber's wife took a nail of the tent, and took an hammer in her hand, and went softly unto him, and smote the nail into his temples, and fastened it into the ground: for he was fast asleep and weary. So he died.

After giving Sisera milk instead of water, after ignoring his command to stand in the door and lie for him, Jael pinned him to the ground with a tent stake. In the Bedouin society of which Jael was a part, it was the women who pitched the tents and set up camp. Thus, as a shepherd boy named David would do after her, she used what was in her hand to slay the giant that held the people of God in the grip of fear.

Judges 4:22
And, behold, as Barak pursued Sisera, Jael came out to meet him, and said unto him, Come, and I will shew thee the man whom thou seekest. And when he came into her tent, behold, Sisera lay dead, and the nail was in his temples.

In chapter 3, we saw Ehud thrusting the sword of the Word into Eglon (Hebrews 4:12). Here in chapter 4, we see Jael pounding the hammer of the Word into Sisera (Jeremiah 23:29).

Judges 4:23, 24
So God subdued on that day Jabin the king of Canaan before the children of Israel. And the hand of the children of Israel prospered, and prevailed against Jabin the king of Canaan, until they had destroyed Jabin king of Canaan.

If Sisera represents the old man of our sin nature, Jabin represents Satan. Satan, the one whose goal it is to oppress and suppress you and me, works through our old sin nature just as surely as Jabin kept Israel in bondage through Sisera. Consequently, once we apply the hammer of the Word and the nail of the Cross to our old sin nature in any given area of our life, like Jabin, Satan capitulates in that area as well.

NAILING THE OLD MAN

A Topical Study of JUDGES 4:17–21

The guy was tough. My eighth grade Pop Warner football coach, Dennis Bennett, was always yelling, always rapping our helmets, always kicking us. That's why we quaked whenever he was around. After the season was over, I remember being in a store and seeing Coach Bennett walk by. My initial reaction was to hide. But then I thought, "Wait a minute. The season's over. I'm not on his team anymore. He can yell at me if he wants to, he can threaten me if he likes, but the point is, he no longer is my coach. I've been delivered, set free, released!"

Now, if Coach Bennett wanted to, he could have come over and ordered me to do fifty push-ups and thirty laps around the store—but I wouldn't have had to do them. If I did give in to his demands, it would have been because I didn't know a very simple fact: Coach Bennett's authority over me had been rendered inactive because I was no longer on his team.

In Romans 6 we find one of the most powerful passages to be found in all of Scripture. If you begin to understand it and apply it, it will be extremely helpful to you in overcoming the sin that can so easily entangle you and set you free from the Coach Bennetts who threaten and intimidate you.

All of us wrestle with sin. *All* of us fight sin. The story is told that playwright Noel Coward, quite a practical joker, one day sent a letter to twenty of his friends that simply read: "All is discovered. Flee while you can ." Two days later, he called all twenty, only to discover that, without exception, all had left town.

All have sinned, declared Paul, and come short of the glory of God (Romans 3:23). Sin is something with which each of us wrestles. I pray the Holy Spirit might bring to your mind even now some particular sin to which you are vulnerable, with which you wrestle, over which you want victory.

In Romans 5, Paul tells us the penalty of sin has been removed. Jesus Christ died for all of our sin—past, present, and future. On the Cross, He cried, "It is finished"—and, dear friend, it is. There is no sin that is not forgiven except one. That is the blasphemy of the Holy Ghost, which is one's failure to accept Jesus as Lord and Savior (Matthew 12:31).

The penalty of sin is gone. But in Romans 6, Paul goes further and says that we are not only free from the penalty of sin, but from the power of sin as well (Romans 6:2, 3). When we were baptized, we were buried in the waters of baptism, signifying our identification with Jesus and our death to sin. At Calvary, Jesus died *for* sin. In baptism, we die *to* sin. The old is buried, freeing us to walk in newness of life (Romans 6:4).

"Well that *sounds* nice," you say, "but it doesn't always work that way. I know theologically I was buried with Christ, and I know I'm to be walking in newness of life—but in this particular area of my life, it doesn't seem to work. I'm struggling. I'm succumbing. What hope is there for me?"

As Paul continues in Romans 6, he gives three steps to experiencing victory over the sin that grips us . . .

Know

Knowing this, that our old man is crucified with him, that the body of sin might be destroyed, that henceforth we should not serve sin. For he that is dead is freed from sin. Romans 6:6, 7

Step 1 is to know. What we are told to know is the mystery, the miracle, the marvel that our old man, our old nature, the sin within us that seeks to dictate to us and have power over us was crucified with Christ Jesus on the Cross of Calvary. Before you were a Christian, the old man of your sin nature controlled you. But once you became a Christian, you tapped in and have access to an entirely different power. When Christ died on the Cross, His blood was shed to wash away your sin. But His body was broken to break the power of sin. That is why there are two elements in Communion: The broken body and the shed blood.

The word translated "destroyed" in Romans 6:6 is *catargao* in Greek, and it means "rendered inactive," or "paralyzed." It does not mean that my old man is done away with. He's still there. But he has been rendered inactive. "*Know* this," said Paul, "something miraculous took place at Calvary. Your sin nature, although still present, was completely paralyzed."

Reckon

Likewise reckon ye also yourselves to be dead indeed unto sin, but alive unto God through Jesus Christ our Lord. Romans 6:11

Step 2 is to reckon. The word translated "reckon" is an accounting term, meaning "add it up; figure it out." The old man is crucified. Reckon it to be so. Add it up. Figure it out. Respond accordingly.

If your boss deposited $10,000 in your bank account because of your faithful service on the job, you would have a choice to make: Whether to make purchases and pay bills—or whether to say, "Nah, he told me that, but I don't believe it." Now, even if you didn't believe it, the fact would remain that he made the deposit and you would be the poorer because you didn't reckon it to be so.

The "knowing" of verse 6 refers to the mind. The "reckoning" of verse 11 refers to the soul, the part of you that puts your knowledge into practice.

Yield

Neither yield ye your members as instruments of unrighteousness unto sin: but yield yourselves unto God, as those that are alive from the dead, and your members as instruments of righteousness unto God. Romans 6:13

Step 3 is to yield. In Genesis 1:26, man was given dominion over the earth. Instead, man became dominated by sin, for whoever commits sin is the servant of sin

(John 8:34). But for the believer, the dominion was broken when Jesus died on the Cross not only to free us from the penalty of sin, but from its power.

Know this factually. Reckon it spiritually. Respond to it physically. How? Just like Jael did—by nailing the old man.

Jeremiah 23:29 likens the Word of God to a hammer. Therefore, the hammer we are to use is the Word of God. And the nail we are to use is the same one that pierced the hands and feet of Christ on the Cross of Calvary.

When Jesus died—when nails pierced His hands and feet—my old man was there being paralyzed, rendered inactive, broken, done away with as well. Thus, in the moment of temptation, I have a choice to make. I can either succumb to sin; I can give in a little and then find myself dominated completely and destroyed ultimately. Or, like Jael, I can take the hammer of the Word, the nail of the Cross, and say, "I do not have to succumb. Right now, I yield my body as an instrument of righteousness instead of sin."

If you do the latter, you can be absolutely free. You will never again have to sin. You will never again have to succumb. You can choose to give in if you want. When the Coach Bennett of your life barks, "Give me fifty," you can hit the floor and do fifty push-ups. But you don't have to. You can look the old man in the eye and say, "On the basis of the Word of God and the work of Christ on Calvary, I am free. You no longer have dominion over me. I will not succumb." And you can walk away free.

There are those who say, "Your sin is particularly powerful and problematic. You're going to need lots of counseling and lots of work to walk your way out of your sinful condition."

Yet the Bible teaches nothing of this. Romans 6 is shocking because in it Paul declares, "If you can believe this to be true, you don't have to give in to that sin ever again." Whatever sin hounds you has been rendered inactive—gossip, murder, homosexuality, a lousy attitude, drunkenness, lying—have all been paralyzed by Jesus' death on the Cross.

> With the fudge cascading down the sides, the whipped cream piled high, and the cherry perched proudly on top, the hot fudge sundae calls out to me. I can listen to the voice inside that says, "Jon, you have to give in. The only way you'll not succumb is to ease off slowly over many months. You'll have to attend hot fudge sundae group meetings and listen to special speakers. This sin is too big for you."
>
> Or—I can say, "The Bible says that sin was paralyzed. I do not have to give in." And right then and there, I experience victory. The next time a hot fudge sundae screams out to me, I do the same thing again. And I am free once more.

All we have to do is believe, receive, and respond to the finished work of the Cross. In the moment of temptation, gang, take the hammer of the Word and the nail of the Cross of Calvary and nail the old man.

In Jesus' name.

5 **Judges 5:1–3**
Then sang Deborah and Barak the son of Abinoam on that day, saying, Praise ye the LORD for the avenging of Israel, when the people willingly offered themselves. Hear, O ye kings; give ear, O ye princes; I, even I, will sing unto the LORD; I will sing praise to the LORD God of Israel.

Although Barak and Deborah were perhaps not as gifted in the area of singing as they were in the arena of battle, they said, "I even I will sing." If you have a lousy voice, claim this verse as you worship! Even *I* will sing to the Lord.

Judges 5:4, 5
LORD, when thou wentest out of Seir, when thou marchedst out of the field of Edom, the earth trembled, and the heavens dropped, the clouds also dropped water. The mountains melted from before the LORD, even that Sinai from before the LORD God of Israel.

Here we see what happened in the battle with Sisera. History verifies that the Lord sent a rainstorm and all of Sisera's nine hundred chariots got stuck in the mud. In other words, the highest technology of the day was rendered useless by rain.

The largest expenditure in our country's Department of Defense is spent trying to disable our enemy's technology. With every nation of the world depending increasingly upon technology, if any nation is successful in messing up the computerized systems of its enemy, enemy forces are rendered useless. Therefore, my personal suspicion is that when the armies converge for the battle of Armageddon, technology will at some point be rendered absolutely useless, ushering in the scenario in the Battle of Armageddon in which men will resort to hand-to-hand combat in the most primitive ways.

"We have iron chariots," boasted Sisera. Yes, but what happened when it rained?

Judges 5:6, 7 (a)
In the days of Shamgar the son of Anath, in the days of Jael, the highways were unoccupied, and the travellers walked through byways. The inhabitants of the villages ceased, they ceased in Israel, until that I Deborah arose . . .

The highways were unoccupied because people lived in fear of their enemies.

Judges 5:7 (b)
. . . that I arose a mother in Israel.

Notice it does not say Deborah is the mother of Israel. It says she is *a* mother in Israel. Here was a woman who was a poet, a prophetess, a judge, a genuine hero in the history of God's people—and yet what does she take pride in? The fact that she's a mother. There is no higher calling than motherhood because mothers have the unique opportunity to shape lives and affect the future.

Judges 5:8 (a)
They chose new gods . . .

Israel chose apostasy; she chose to worship other gods. Reading the Old Testament, you might wonder how Israel could be so foolish as to worship other gods. But in our society, we're even more foolish. We worship ourselves. To me, polytheism is not nearly as foolish as atheism. And yet atheism is accepted, respected, even protected in our society.

Judges 5:8 (b)
. . . then was war in the gates: was there a shield or spear seen among forty thousand in Israel?

Because the people of Israel found themselves new gods, they also found themselves wiped out—with war in their gates and with no defense.

Judges 5:9, 10
My heart is toward the governors of Israel, that offered themselves willingly among the people. Bless ye the LORD. Speak, ye that ride on white asses, ye that sit in judgment, and walk by the way.

Those who gave godly counsel to others rode on white donkeys. Jesus, of course, rode into Jerusalem on a donkey (Matthew 21). And it wouldn't surprise me if it was a white one.

Judges 5:11
They that are delivered from the noise of archers in the places of drawing water, there shall they rehearse the righteous acts of the LORD, even the righteous acts toward the inhabitants of his villages in Israel: then shall the people of the LORD go down to the gates.

Those who got involved and engaged in the battle with Sisera, those who stood up and gave wise counsel, were singled out.

Judges 5:12
Awake, awake, Deborah: awake, awake, utter a song: arise, Barak, and lead thy captivity captive, thou son of Abinoam.

Certain men did rise up and were willing to be used. Barak is even graciously included in this company.

Judges 5:13
Then he made him that remaineth have dominion over the nobles among the people: the LORD made me have dominion over the mighty.

The Canaanites were brought under the dominion of Israel. The tables were turned. The good guys were in control.

Judges 5:14, 15 (a)
Out of Ephraim was there a root of them against Amalek; after thee, Benjamin, among thy people; out of Machir came down governors, and out of Zebulun they that handle the pen of the writer. And the princes of Issachar were with Deborah; even Issachar, and also Barak: he was sent on foot into the valley . . .

Benjamin, Ephraim, Manasseh, Zebulun, and Issachar were commended as those who entered the battle against Sisera and Jabin. But Deborah and Barak's song continues . . .

Judges 5:15 (b), 16
. . . For the divisions of Reuben there were great thoughts of heart. Why abodest thou among the sheepfolds, to hear the bleatings of the flocks? For the divisions of Reuben there were great searchings of heart.

Reuben didn't get involved. He stayed in the sheepfold, stayed where it was safe. Why? Because he gave it a lot of thought.

The "paralysis of analysis" is a dangerous, yet common problem today. "Should I witness to him, or not?," we ask. "Should I go there, or not? Should I be kind to that person, or not?" And we find ourselves becoming introspective to the place where, like Reuben, we do nothing. Reuben debated so long that he missed the entire battle.

Could that happen to you or me? Absolutely. God says, "I want you to do this, to experience that, to have victory here, to gain spoil there." But we sit back and analyze—and thereby miss what He has for us. Be like Ephraim, Benjamin, Manasseh, Zebulun, and Issachar. Get involved. Get engaged. Be part of what the Lord is doing as He wages war against sin and does battle for the souls of men.

Judges 5:17 (a)
Gilead abode beyond Jordan . . .

Gilead opted not to fight, saying, "It's not our turf, not our area. We're beyond the Jordan." The same is still true. A need arises, and it is the Gilead within us that says, "That's not my area of expertise. I don't feel comfortable doing that." And in so doing, we miss the battle.

Judges 5:17 (b)
. . . and why did Dan remain in ships?

Rather than entering the battle, Dan went sailing and missed it altogether.

Judges 5:17 (c)
. . . Asher continued on the sea shore, and abode in his breaches.

Asher remained at the beach. And, along with Gilead and Dan, missed the opportunity to join the battle and share the victory.

Judges 5:18
Zebulun and Naphtali were a people that jeoparded their lives unto the death in the high places of the field.

Unlike Gilead, Dan, and Asher, Zebulun and Naphtali risked their lives. They took steps of faith. They engaged in battle and took on the enemy.

We see the nation of Israel divided into two groups: Those who responded to the call to arms and those who remained with their flocks, in their ships, or on the shore. And we see the same division today. Some are rushing into battle, saying, "God use me," while others are content to stay with their flocks, take a cruise, or hang out at the beach.

Judges 5:19–22
The kings came and fought, then fought the kings of Canaan in Taanach by the waters of Megiddo; they took no gain of money. They fought from heaven; the stars in their courses fought against Sisera. The river of Kishon swept them away, that ancient river, the river Kishon. O my soul, thou hast trodden down strength. Then were the horsehoofs broken by the means of the pransings, the pransings of their mighty ones.

Of all those who entered the battle, it was the Lord of hosts who secured the victory.

Judges 5:23
Curse ye Meroz, said the angel of the LORD, curse ye bitterly the inhabitants thereof; because they came not to the help of the LORD, to the help of the LORD against the mighty.

Although we don't know its exact location, Meroz was a city of Israel in the region of the battle.

But its inhabitants were cursed for their failure to get involved in the battle.

The same is still true. Cursed will be the man or woman who does not get involved in the battle, who does not get involved in service. Where will he or she be cursed? In heaven.

You see, when we stand before the judgment seat of Christ, those who didn't get involved—who sat back day after week after month after year after decade, missing opportunities in their own communities to be part of God's plan for the area—will weep. "Why did I waste my life?" they will cry. "What was I thinking? Why did I have time for this and that—but not to get involved in what God called me to do, in what He gave me the ability to do?"

There will be cursing in eternity—not from God, but from people who will curse themselves.

It was the unrighteous servant who said, "The Lord delays His coming. I've got lots of time. No worry, no hurry." But when the master comes unexpectedly, he's cut asunder (Matthew 24:51).

We might die tonight. And once we're dead, it will be too late to say, "I'm going to use the abilities You gave me, Lord—the money you entrusted to me, the doors you opened before me." And in that day, we, too, could be cut asunder as we realize the capacity of our spiritual life is forever diminished, that we'll be spiritual midgets for eternity, that we'll not rule over ten cities, five cities, or even one city (Luke 19).

God has things in store for us that are mind-blowing, gang, but this is the only opportunity we have to be able to be at the top or middle level—ruling ten or five cities. There will be many in heaven who make it, "yet so as by fire" (1 Corinthians 3:15). They will be there, but they'll have no rewards because they buried the personality, intellectual ability, musical skill or finances God entrusted to them. As a result, they'll curse themselves.

The way to be sad today is to not serve the Lord—to focus on your problems, your situation, your hurts, your needs, your life. Everything is discouraging when we live for ourselves. Instead of worrying about what shape you're in emotionally, financially, or physically, forget about yourself and start serving others. Jesus said, "The measure you give out will be the measure returned to you" (Matthew 7:2). Start serving others and I guarantee you'll find yourself free from the curse of self-absorption today, and free from cursing yourself in the days to come.

Judges 5:24–27
Blessed above women shall Jael the wife of Heber the Kenite be, blessed shall she be above women in the tent. He asked water, and she gave him milk; she brought forth butter in a lordly dish. She put her hand to the nail, and her right hand to the workmen's hammer; and with the hammer she smote Sisera, she smote off his head, when she had pierced and stricken through his temples. At her feet he bowed, he fell, he lay down: at her feet he bowed, he fell: where he bowed, there he fell down dead.

No one was more fully engaged in the battle than Jael. She was one tough lady!

Judges 5:28–30
The mother of Sisera looked out at a window, and cried through the lattice, Why is his chariot so long in coming? why tarry the wheels of his chariots? Her wise ladies answered her, yea, she returned answer to herself, Have they not sped? have they not divided the prey; to every man a damsel or two; to Sisera a prey of divers colours, a prey of divers colours of needlework, of divers colours of needlework on both sides, meet for the necks of them that take the spoil?

A mother herself, Deborah writes of Sisera's mother, speculating why her son is late in returning home.

Judges 5:31
So let all thine enemies perish, O LORD: but let them that love him be as the sun when he goeth forth in his might. And the land had rest forty years.

Over and over throughout Judges, we read that the land had rest for forty years. Forty years is a generation. It seems as though every generation has its own deliverance, its own revival, its own encounter with the Lord. How I thank the Lord that we are seeing the outpouring of His Spirit in *this* generation. What a joy it is to be part of a people who love the Lord, love the Word, and love each other.

6

Judges 6:1 (a)
And the children of Israel did evil in the sight of the LORD . . .

It was the year 1256 B.C. Approximately two hundred years had passed since Joshua had led the children of Israel on their famous march around the walled city of Jericho. Under the guidance of God, the people of Israel had stormed not only through the walls of Jericho, but through the entire region of Canaan, conquering the Amorites and the Ammonites, the Hittites and the Jebusites.

But because they failed to obey the Lord fully, because they failed to totally drive out the pagan people of Palestine, because they allowed pockets of Canaanites to remain in the land—like a disease in seeming remission, two hundred years later the Canaanites regained strength and began to dominate and regulate the lives of the people of Israel.

Judges 6:1 (b)
. . . and the LORD delivered them into the hand of Midian seven years.

After Sarah died, Abraham married a woman named Keturah, with whom he had six sons—one of whom was a boy named Midian. To keep Isaac, the son of promise, from being hassled by the sons of Keturah, Abraham sent Keturah's sons away, and, over the years, the Midianites became enemies of Israel. Throughout Scripture, we see the sons of Midian constantly attacking the people of Israel.

Judges 6:2 (a)
And the hand of Midian prevailed against Israel . . .

An arrogant, brutal, nomadic people, the Midianites were the first people in history to domesticate the camel. This gave them a huge military advantage. If you've ever stood next to a camel, you know their size can be terrifying—yet they are very maneuverable in battle.

Judges 6:2 (b)
. . . and because of the Midianites the children of Israel made them the dens which are in the mountains, and caves, and strong holds.

We talk about men becoming mice—but the Israelites had actually descended lower than mice. They became moles, hiding in underground caves, holing up in dens, terrified of the Midianites, humiliated by their enemies.

Judges 6:3
And so it was, when Israel had sown, that the Midianites came up, and the Amalekites, and the children of the east, even they came up against them;

The Amalekites were the descendants of Esau. It is fairly well established that the Bedouin people of today are of this same line.

Judges 6:4, 5 (a)
And they encamped against them, and destroyed the increase of the earth, till thou come unto Gaza, and left no sustenance for Israel, neither sheep, nor ox, nor ass. For they came up with their cattle and their tents, and they came as grasshoppers for multitude . . .

The Midianites and Amalekites would wait until the Israelites had harvested their crops. Then they would sweep into the area and take all of the grain. This equivalent today would be if someone robbed you every payday. It would be frustrating, to say the least!

Judges 6:5 (b), 6 (a)
. . . for both they and their camels were without number: and they entered into the land to destroy it. And Israel was greatly impoverished because of the Midianites . . .

The speed of the camels allowed the Midianites to conduct guerilla warfare because they could ride into an area and attack quickly.

Judges 6:6 (b)
. . . and the children of Israel cried unto the LORD.

After seven long years of being ripped off by the Midianites, of being dominated by the Midianites, of being intimidated by the Midianites, Israel finally cried to the Lord.

What is it in our nature that is so stubborn? Why is it that we so desperately desire to work things out in our own strength? Why does it take us sometimes years to find ourselves in a position of brokenness before God?

If you're as old as I am, you remember the series of commercials Bayer aspirin ran in which a daughter would say to her well-meaning mother, "Mother, I'd rather do it myself." And that long-running series of commercials struck a chord within the heart of everyone because there's something within each of us that says, "I want to do it myself. I can work it out." Meanwhile, the Lord watches and waits for us to cry out to Him.

Judges 6:7–10
And it came to pass, when the children of Israel cried unto the LORD because of the Midianites, That the LORD sent a prophet unto the children of Israel, which said unto them, Thus saith the LORD God of Israel, I brought you up from Egypt, and brought you forth out of the house of bondage; And I delivered you out of the hand of the Egyptians, and out of the hand of all that op-

pressed you, and drave them out from before you, and gave you their land; And I said unto you, I am the LORD your God; fear not the gods of the Amorites, in whose land ye dwell: but ye have not obeyed my voice.

Psalm 34:6 declares that when we cry out to the Lord, He hearkens to our cry, answers our prayers. When we get to the place of total desperation and brokenness, He always responds. The question is, when was the last time you really cried out to the Lord? How long has it been since there have been tears streaming down your cheeks before Him?

If you wonder why you are dominated, why you are struggling, could it be because you have failed to cry out to God with intensity and sincerity? For seven years, the children of Israel lived in caves. But when at last they cried to the Lord, He answered by first sending a prophet, and then coming Himself . . .

Judges 6:11
And there came an angel of the LORD, and sat under an oak which was in Ophrah, that pertained unto Joash the Abi-ezrite: and his son Gideon threshed wheat by the winepress, to hide it from the Midianites.

The threshing of wheat was usually done at a higher elevation in order to allow the wind to blow the chaff away. Gideon, however, realized that every time he threshed wheat, the Midianites would sweep in and rip him off. So he threshed wheat not on a mountaintop but in a winepress, a lower spot, a hidden area.

Judges 6:12 (a)
And the angel of the LORD appeared unto him, and said unto him . . .

The "angel of the Lord" in the Old Testament is a Christophany—an appearance of Jesus Christ before He came as Jesus of Nazareth.

Judges 6:12 (b)
. . . the LORD is with thee, thou mighty man of valour.

I love this! Here's Gideon, hiding from the Midianites, knees knocking, shaking with fright—yet the Lord calls him a mighty man of valor. Why? Because He sees His own not in their present problems, but as finished products. How do I know? Turn to Romans 8 . . .

And I said unto you, I am the LORD your God; fear not the gods of the Amorites, in whose land ye dwell: but ye have not obeyed my voice.

And we know that all things work together for good to them that love God, to them who are the called according to his purpose. For whom he did foreknow, he also did predestinate to be conformed to the image of his Son, that he might be the firstborn among many brethren. Moreover whom he did predestinate, them he also called: and whom he called, them he also justified: and whom he justified, them he also glorified. Romans 8:28–30

Please hang on to this. God is saying that you who are part of the elect were predestined by Him, called by Him, made just by Him, and glorified by Him. It doesn't say you *will be* glorified. It says you *are* glorified. That is why in Ephesians 5:27, Paul talks about the church as being a glorious church without spot or wrinkle. When we look at each other, we see lots of wrinkles and a whole bunch of spots. But God transcends the time/space dimension and views us in our eternal state. Yes, He's aware of our present struggles, but He also sees us as glorified.

This is fabulous, folks, because I am one of the few who, throughout the history of humanity, have been selected, elected, chosen by God to be part of His eternal family. So are you.

Judges 6:13
And Gideon said unto him, Oh my Lord, if the LORD be with us, why then is all this befallen us? and where be all his miracles which our fathers told us of, saying, Did not the LORD bring us up from Egypt? but now the LORD hath forsaken us, and delivered us into the hands of the Midianites.

With Gideon, we cry, "If God has chosen me, if God is with me, I have two questions: Why is everything crashing all around me? And where are all the miracles I read about in the Bible and hear about in the lives of others?"

Watch Jesus' response . . .

Judges 6:14
And the LORD looked upon him, and said, Go in this thy might, and thou shalt save Israel from the hand of the Midianites: have not I sent thee?

Jesus doesn't answer Gideon's question. Instead, He gives Gideon a commission. This is so important for us to understand, as well. "Why is this happening?" we cry. "How will this ever work out?" we ask.

"I'm not going to answer that," the Lord answers. "I have things for you to do today—people to share with, people to witness to, people to pray for, people to love."

If you are prone to asking about the whys and hows, to hiding away in the winepress day after day until you get answers, God would tell you the same thing He told Gideon: "Here's what you're to do . . ." as He uses you to set people free.

Judges 6:15, 16
And he said unto him, Oh my Lord, wherewith shall I save Israel? behold, my family is poor in Manasseh, and I am the least in my father's house. And the LORD said unto him, Surely I will be with thee, and thou shalt smite the Midianites as one man.

"Who am I?" Gideon asked in verse 15.

"That's not the issue," the Lord says in verse 16. "The question is: Who am *I*, for *I* will be with you. And that is all you need."

The key to service, to ministry, to being used by the Lord and being an instrument of the Lord is to say, "It's not who I am. It's who You are, Lord. And if You choose to use the foolish things of the world to confound the wise, if You choose the weak things to show Your strength, then I qualify. And if You choose to use me, You'll get all the glory because it's obvious I can do nothing on my own."

What has God called you to do? What's on your agenda this week? Is there something you know you should be engaged in, but don't feel capable to do? Through this story, God would say to you, "It's not about you. It's about Me. I'm with you."

Judges 6:17
And he said unto him, If now I have found grace in thy sight, then shew me a sign that thou talkest with me.

"If You want to use me as an instrument to free your people from the Midianites, give me a sign," Gideon said.

I think it's a good thing when people say, "Lord, if I'm hearing You correctly, if this really is of You, give me confirmation." I think too many people have an impression, a thought, an idea—and sometimes they'll launch out in a way that ultimately proves to be foolhardy because, unlike Gideon, they didn't seek confirmation. I don't think a person should ever sell his house, quit his job, and leave the country, thinking he's heard the Lord, without first getting confirmation. God responds to honest doubt.

Judges 6:18, 19
Depart not hence, I pray thee, until I come unto thee, and bring forth my present, and set it before thee. And he said, I will tarry until thou come again. And Gideon went in, and made ready a kid, and unleavened cakes of an ephah of flour: the flesh he put in a basket, and he put the broth in a pot, and brought it out unto him under the oak, and presented it.

In these days of famine—when bread was worth more than silver, and meat was more valuable than gold—Gideon prepares both as an offering, as an act of worship to the Lord.

"That's a waste," some might say.

No, that's worship. People who worship the Lord are often accused of being wasteful. Do you recall the story of Mary? When she took ointment out of an alabaster box and poured it upon Jesus, one of the disciples said, "That is wasteful. The money could have been used much more wisely in caring for the poor" (John 12:5).

Who was the disciple?

Judas Iscariot.

Those who don't understand worship will always call it wasteful.

Judges 6:20, 21
And the angel of God said unto him, Take the flesh and the unleavened cakes, and lay them upon this rock, and pour out the broth. And he did so. Then the angel of the LORD put forth the end of the staff that was in his hand, and touched the flesh and the unleavened cakes; and there rose up fire out of the rock, and consumed the flesh and the unleavened cakes. Then the angel of the LORD departed out of his sight.

Where was confirmation found in Gideon's story? At the Table of the Lord—the unleavened bread, the flesh. Where will we find confirmation? I can't tell you how frequently I have found confirmation at the Table of the Lord, the Table of Communion. It's where I'm re-ignited. Remembering the fire Jesus absorbed when He hung on the Cross for me, I pray, "Lord, ignite my soul that I might leave this Table on fire for You, doing what You want me to do."

When you're going through struggles, wondering what the Lord would have you do, oftentimes, you'll find your answer at His Table. You'll find your answer as you reflect on what Jesus did for you.

Judges 6:22
And when Gideon perceived that he was an angel of the LORD, Gideon said, Alas, O Lord GOD! for because I have seen an angel of the LORD face to face.

In verse 13, Gideon was afraid because he didn't see the hand of the Lord. Here in verse 22, he's terrified because he does. After all, hadn't

God clearly said, "There shall no man see Me and live"? (Exodus 33:20)

Gideon did indeed look at God face to face—not upon God the Father, but upon God the Son, the One who would eventually come to dwell with man (John 1:14). And in looking upon Him, the sweat of fear is replaced by the sweetness of fellowship.

Judges 6:23, 24
And the LORD said unto him, Peace be unto thee; fear not: thou shalt not die.
Then Gideon built an altar there unto the LORD, and called it Jehovah-shalom: unto this day it is yet in Ophrah of the Abi-ezrites.

After seeing the Lord, Gideon was an altered man. Therefore, it is only logical that he would build an altar. *Jehovah-shalom* means "The Lord is peace." About to face the fight of his life, Gideon didn't feel particularly courageous. Rather, he felt unqualified, uncertain, unsure, knowing he had been called to do something out of the realm of human possibility. Yet, in meeting with the Lord at the table, he had peace.

When the disciples were afraid because Jesus told them He would be betrayed, He said, "Don't let your heart be troubled. In My Father's house are many mansions. I go to prepare a place for you" (see John 14:1, 2). What's the key to not being troubled? I believe, as this story portrays, it's to go to the Lord's Table and realize there will be peace beyond this present day, beyond this present problem. I can let my heart be troubled, or I can let my heart not be troubled. It's up to me. And I make that choice every day. By focusing on eternity—on Jehovah-shalom—Gideon left with peace in his heart and a new perspective on his mind . . . at least for now.

Judges 6:25, 26
And it came to pass the same night, that the LORD said unto him, Take thy father's young bullock, even the second bullock of seven years old, and throw down the altar of Baal that thy father hath, and cut down the grove that is by it: And build an altar unto the LORD thy God upon the top of this rock, in the ordered place, and take the second bullock, and offer a burnt sacrifice with the wood of the grove which thou shalt cut down.

After revelation comes consecration. After the Lord revealed Himself to Gideon, He said, "There's a problem in your family, Gideon. Your dad had an altar to Baal that must be torn down. Before you deal with the men of Midian, I want you to deal with your own family."

This reminds me of Moses. On his way to lead the people of Israel from captivity in Egypt to the Land of Promise, the Lord actually pinned him to the ground because he hadn't circumcised his own son. You see, there was no point in Moses leading a nation if he wouldn't lead his own family (Exodus 4).

Family is top priority. Ministry begins at home. The highest pleasure and priority you'll have in ministry is to your own family.

Judges 6:27 (a)
Then Gideon took ten men of his servants, and did as the LORD had said unto him . . .

Gideon is now becoming what God said he would be: A mighty man of valor. He's willing to stand up to his father and to society, willing to become an iconoclast as he tears down his father's altar.

Judges 6:27 (b)
. . . and so it was, because he feared his father's household, and the men of the city, that he could not do it by day, that he did it by night.

Afraid to face his father, Gideon still has a way to go—but he's progressing!

Judges 6:28–31
And when the men of the city arose early in the morning, behold, the altar of Baal was cast down, and the grove was cut down that was by it, and the second bullock was offered upon the altar that was built. And they said one to another, Who hath done this thing? And when they inquired and asked, they said, Gideon the son of Joash hath done this thing. Then the men of the city said unto Joash, Bring out thy son, that he may die: because he hath cast down the altar of Baal, and because he hath cut down the grove that was by it. And Joash said unto all that stood against him, Will ye plead for Baal? will ye save him? he that will plead for him, let him be put to death whilst it is yet morning: if he be a god, let him plead for himself, because one hath cast down his altar.

When Joash saw the boldness of his son, something stirred within his heart. Once a worshiper of God, he had been sucked into worshiping Baal. But the action of his son inspired him once again as he realized the stupidity of serving a god who couldn't defend himself.

Judges 6:32–34 (a)
Therefore on that day he called him Jerubbaal, saying, Let Baal plead against him,

because he hath thrown down his altar. Then all the Midianites and the Amalekites and the children of the east were gathered together, and went over, and pitched in the valley of Jezreel. But the Spirit of the LORD came upon Gideon . . .

Throughout the entire Old Testament and into the pages of the New Testament, we read of the Spirit of God coming upon people to empower them for service. That's what the baptism of the Spirit is all about. That's what the fullness of the Holy Ghost really is. It is the power of the Spirit to enable people for service. God not only called Gideon to serve, but empowered Him to do so.

Judges 6:34 (b), 35
. . . and he blew a trumpet; and Abi-ezer was gathered after him. And he sent messengers throughout all Manasseh; who also was gathered after him: and he sent messengers unto Asher, and unto Zebulun, and unto Naphtali; and they came up to meet them.

The bugle blast was heard throughout the land, and the effect was electrifying. Suddenly, men from throughout Israel rallied around this common farm boy. Why?

- It was not because of Gideon, but because of God.
- It was not a program of Gideon's doing, but the power of the Spirit moving.
- It was not indoctrination, but inspiration.

Apart from a moving of the Spirit of God, there's no way men would have rallied around Gideon. He had no reputation upon which to stand, no credentials with which to impress. But God was moving, and when Gideon blew the trumpet, issuing a sound that hadn't been heard in seven years, people immediately joined him, ready to do battle.

Judges 6:36, 37
And Gideon said unto God, If thou wilt save Israel by mine hand, as thou hast said, Behold, I will put a fleece of wool in the floor; and if the dew be on the fleece only, and it be dry upon all the earth beside, then shall I know that thou wilt save Israel by mine hand, as thou hast said.

Gideon is doubting once again. He's seen amazing things happen. He's had an encounter with the angel of the Lord. He's seen his dad's altar pulled down and his dad coming around. He's seen a lot, but he still has doubts and questions. I can relate to Gideon, can't you?

Judges 6:38–40
And it was so: for he rose up early on the morrow, and thrust the fleece together, and wringed the dew out of the fleece, a bowl full of water. And Gideon said unto God, Let not thine anger be hot against me, and I will speak but this once: let me prove, I pray thee, but this once with the fleece; let it now be dry only upon the fleece, and upon all the ground let there be dew. And God did so that night: for it was dry upon the fleece only, and there was dew on all the ground.

Gideon had worshiped God intensely, and stood up to his entire society unashamedly. Now, as he is about to lead his countrymen in a battle in which the odds are heavily against them, he pauses to make sure he is hearing God right. All too often, believers look only at Gideon setting a fleece and ignore the worship and the tearing down of the altars that preceded it. Isolated in such a way, this passage loses all perspective and this practice becomes nothing more than an option for any who are too lazy to really seek God.

Having said that, however, we come to an interesting illustration that raises some practical questions about finding God's will. Is it right to put a "fleece" before God?

Some people believe that to test is not to trust—that if you put a test before the Lord, it proves you don't have trust in the Lord. I, however, do not believe this to be so . . .

In Genesis 24, Abraham sent his servant, Eliezer to find a bride for his son, Isaac. To complete this assignment, Eliezer told the Lord that if a woman came to the well and offered to draw water for him and for his camels, he would know she was the chosen one.

In 1 Samuel 14, in order to determine whether it was God's will that he and his armor-bearer take on the entire Philistine army, Jonathan said, "We'll shout. If the Philistines threaten to come to us, we'll know God's not with us and we'll split. But if they challenge us to come to them, we'll know God is with us." So Jonathan and his armor-bearer made their way to the periphery of the Philistine camp, let out a yell, and were immediately ordered into the camp to do battle.

"Alright!" said Jonathan. "God is with us. Let's go get 'em!"

And the entire Philistine army was defeated.

In Isaiah 7, God Himself instructed Ahaz to ask for a sign from Him.

Thus, there are many accounts throughout Scripture wherein we see the reality and rightness of "setting a fleece" before the Lord. However, I want to qualify this with a couple of very important principles . . .

1. A fleece before the Lord is valid only if the Word of God has not already spoken. As ludicrous as it would be for us to say, "Lord, when I hand the teller this note, if she puts money in the bag I give her, I'll know You want me to rob the bank. But if she pushes the buzzer, I'll know You don't" it was for Satan to say to Jesus, "If You're the Son of God, then turn these stones into bread" (Matthew 4).
2. When you "lay a fleece" before the Lord, make sure you are not limiting Him. "Lord, if You want me to purchase this car," we say, "then allow five thousand dollars to come in the mail by noon on Monday"—when, in fact, He might have a package due to arrive on our doorstep at eight o'clock on Tuesday.
3. God will only honor the practice of laying out a fleece if I am serious and not merely curious. "Jump off the cliff, and see if Your angels will really catch You," Satan taunted Jesus (Matthew 4). Sadly, in my own life, I have set all kinds of fleeces out of curiosity. Not so Gideon. He was dead serious about what he was doing.

Finally, in addition to the practical aspect of setting a fleece before God, there is a spiritual understanding as well. You see, throughout the Old Testament, dew was likened to the power of the Spirit of God coming upon His people (e.g., Hosea 14:5). Thus, I see Gideon praying,

"Before I lead any attempt at conquering the Midianites, I must be filled with Your Spirit, Lord. I lay out my life as a fleece before You. Saturate me. Drench me. Flood me with Your Spirit, or I cannot go."

And indeed the fleece was saturated. But then it's as if Gideon took it a step further when he prayed,

"Lord, I want a second understanding of this situation. Even should my own life become dry, I want the ground round about me, the lives next to me, the work connected to me to go on in the anointing and power of Your Spirit. Even if I should dry out, dry up, or fail, Lord, I want Your name to be glorified and Your work to be done."

And I believe God honored Gideon's request by saying, "Yes, Gideon, even if you fail, My work shall go on."

7 God loves to work in the realm of the impossible. Therefore, He puts you and me in impossible situations in order that we can see that *He* is the One who comes through and works things out. Surely this is the reason for the story before us . . .

Judges 7:1, 2
Then Jerubbaal, who is Gideon, and all the people that were with him, rose up early, and pitched beside the well of Harod: so that the host of the Midianites were on the north side of them, by the hill of Moreh, in the valley. And the LORD said unto Gideon, The people that are with thee are too many for me to give the Midianites into their hands, lest Israel vaunt themselves against me, saying, Mine own hand hath saved me.

Thirty-two thousand men responded to Gideon's trumpet call to arms. Facing a Midianite army of 135,000, the odds were 4:1 against the Israelites. Yet what does God say?

"The odds are too heavily stacked in your favor, Gideon."

Gideon must have thought, *You're kidding. We're outnumbered 4 to 1!* But God knows the tendency within the heart of man to take the credit for what He alone does.

Judges 7:3
Now therefore go to, proclaim in the ears of the people, saying, Whosoever is fearful and afraid, let him return and depart early from mount Gilead. And there returned of the people twenty and two thousand; and there remained ten thousand.

When God told Gideon to send home the men who were fearful, twenty-two thousand men said, "We're out of here!" This made the odds 14:1 in favor of the Midianites.

Judges 7:4–7
And the LORD said unto Gideon, The people are yet too many; bring them down unto the water, and I will try them for thee there: and it shall be, that of whom I say unto thee, This shall go with thee, the same shall go with thee; and of whomsoever I say unto thee, This shall not go with thee, the same shall not go. So he brought down the people unto the water: and the LORD said unto Gideon, Every one that lappeth of the water with his tongue, as a dog lappeth, him shalt thou set by himself; likewise every one that boweth down upon his knees to drink. And the number of them that lapped, putting their hand to their mouth, were three hundred men: but all the

rest of the people bowed down upon their knees to drink water. And the LORD said unto Gideon, By the three hundred men that lapped will I save you, and deliver the Midianites into thine hand: and let all the other people go every man unto his place.

Why were these three hundred chosen? Possibly for the following reasons . . .

First, they were free from fear. Twenty-two thousand were sent home because fear and faith are mutually exclusive. Only ten thousand men were free from fear. Why did they have no fear? I suggest it was because they had an understanding of eternity. As Christians, we know the reality of eternity. Therefore, we must not fear the difficulties or dangers of this life. Those with eternity's values in view are those who serve the Lord with abandon.

Secondly, the three hundred were chosen because they were men of humility. You see, in Israeli culture, the dog was despicable. To be called a dog, to look like a dog, to be associated with a dog was to be avoided. Yet here, the men who were chosen scooped up water with their hands and lapped it like dogs.

Thirdly, the three hundred were men of priority. That is, they didn't spend unnecessary time doing necessary things. Yes, they needed to drink, but they never lost sight of the possibility of attack from the Midianites. There are things in this life to which we must tend. There are chores and responsibilities to which each of us is obligated. But the man or woman used by God will not devote unnecessary time to doing necessary things. They will streamline their life as much as possible because they realize the battle is raging, the time is short, the calling is great.

Eternity, humility, priority—these were all characteristics held by the three hundred chosen men. Yet an equally possible scenario was that these three hundred guys were not necessarily depicting noble qualities at all. It could be that these were broken-down, fat guys who simply couldn't get into the water. It could be that their knees were bad and their backs were out. It could be that in choosing the men who couldn't put their faces in the water, God was saying, "I want to use the old fat guys—guys the world would laugh at, ignore, or discard."

The three hundred may have lacked the ability to lay down and drink from the stream, but the one thing they had was availability—and that's the one ability that matters most.

Judges 7:8
So the people took victuals in their hand, and their trumpets: and he sent all the rest of Israel every man unto his tent, and retained those three hundred men: and the host of Midian was beneath him in the valley.

The odds went from 4:1 to 14:1 to 450:1 as only three hundred men were allowed to move with Gideon into battle against the Midianites. We read of those same odds in 1 Kings 18, where Elijah alone was victorious against four hundred and fifty prophets of Baal.

Maybe today you feel as though the odds are stacked terribly against you, that your circumstances look impossible. Rejoice! Be glad! God has set you up to bring you through and to show Himself strong. That's His intention, that's His purpose for you—to put you in an impossible situation so He can show you and those around you just how strong, how wonderful, how glorious He is.

Judges 7:9–12
And it came to pass the same night, that the LORD said unto him, Arise, get thee down unto the host; for I have delivered it into thine hand. But if thou fear to go down, go thou with Phurah thy servant down to the host: And thou shalt hear what they say; and afterward shall thine hands be strengthened to go down unto the host. Then went he down with Phurah his servant unto the outside of the armed men that were in the host. And the Midianites and the Amalekites and all the children of the east lay along in the valley like grasshoppers for multitude; and their camels were without number, as the sand by the sea side for multitude.

Fear had once again fastened itself to the heart of Gideon. Knowing this, God doesn't condemn Gideon. Instead, He commissions him . . .

Judges 7:13, 14
And when Gideon was come, behold, there was a man that told a dream unto his fellow, and said, Behold, I dreamed a dream, and, lo, a cake of barley bread tumbled into the host of Midian, and came unto a tent, and smote it that it fell, and overturned it, that the tent lay along. And his fellow answered and said, This is nothing else save the sword of Gideon the son of Joash, a man of Israel: for into his hand hath God delivered Midian, and all the host.

As Gideon and his servant spied on the Midianites, they overheard a conversation through which, much to his surprise, Gideon was made aware of the fact that the Midianites were afraid of him.

Amazing! This man, who, just a few days previous, was hiding in a winepress, frightened, worried, intimidated, now had a reputation throughout the whole host of Midian as being a fearless warrior. Why? No doubt the Midianites heard how he had pulled down the altar of Baal, effect challenging Baal face to face. Even though only a few people saw Gideon do this, even though only a few people were initially aware of it, word spread that he was a man of power.

The same is true today. Many times we are afraid of the demons of the enemy—but in reality, the enemy knows we who name the name of Jesus Christ can utilize His name, stand in His authority, and be unstoppable. If you have been moving out for Jesus Christ—even if it's not widely known by those around you—your name is known in hell. If you're being attacked, persecuted, hassled, bombarded—rejoice. It means they're talking about you a lot down there. If you're never persecuted, never attacked, never hassled—*that's* when you need to worry.

"Yea all those who live godly in Christ Jesus shall suffer persecution," Paul told Timothy (2 Timothy 3:12). He didn't say all Christians shall suffer persecution, because not all Christians will. But all who live godly—who make a mark, who impact this world—*will* suffer persecution.

Judges 7:15 (a)

And it was so, when Gideon heard the telling of the dream, and the interpretation thereof, that he worshipped . . .

Notice that Gideon was likened not to a huge boulder rumbling down the mountain and destroying the camp of Midian. No, he was likened to a barley loaf. In that culture, barley was the food of slaves and animals. It was the lowest type of grain used in that society. Yet what does Gideon do? Does he say, "Barley loaf? That's what You think of me? Thanks a lot, Lord"? No, he worships.

Judges 7:15 (b)–18

. . . and returned into the host of Israel, and said, Arise; for the LORD hath delivered into your hand the host of Midian. And he divided the three hundred men into three companies, and he put a trumpet in every man's hand, with empty pitchers, and lamps within the pitchers. And he said unto them, Look on me, and do likewise: and, behold, when I come to the outside of the camp, it shall be that, as I do, so shall ye do. When I blow with a trumpet, I and all that are with me, then blow ye the trumpets also on every side of all the camp, and say, The sword of the LORD, and of Gideon.

"Look on me and do likewise," said Gideon.

"Follow me as I follow Christ," echoed Paul (2 Thessalonians 3:9).

Gideon was a man of action. He was a doer, not simply a talker. He sought the Lord, selected three hundred troops out of 32,000, risked his life by sneaking into the Midianite camp, surveyed the situation, overheard a conversation, came back, developed a strategy, supplied his troops, and then did battle. No committees, no dialogues, no discussions. He was a doer. He made things happen. And that's the kind of men God is looking for today—men who see the need and fill it, men who go for it. Gideon was a man who understood that leadership was not about lecturing, but simply about leading; not saying, "You go," but saying, "*Let's* go."

Judges 7:19–23

So Gideon, and the hundred men that were with him, came unto the outside of the camp in the beginning of the middle watch; and they had but newly set the watch: and they blew the trumpets, and brake the pitchers that were in their hands. And the three companies blew the trumpets, and brake the pitchers, and held the lamps in their left hands, and the trumpets in their right hands to blow withal: and they cried, The sword of the LORD, and of Gideon. And they stood every man in his place round about the camp: and all the host ran, and cried, and fled. And the three hundred blew the trumpets, and the LORD set every man's sword against his fellow, even throughout all the host: and the host fled to Beth-shittah in Zererath, and to the border of Abel-meholah, unto Tabbath. And the men of Israel gathered themselves together out of Naphtali, and out of Asher, and out of all Manasseh, and pursued after the Midianites.

This was a brilliant strategy because, although the Midianites were brutal, powerful, arrogant warriors, due to the fact that they were steeped in superstition and occultist practices, nighttime terrorized them. A second factor to keep in mind in understanding this strategy is that the Midianites were very suspicious of each other due to the skirmishes fought between tribes within their ranks.

So here they are. It's the middle of the night. They're all tucked in. Suddenly, there's a loud crash and a shout from the hills surrounding the valley. They stumble out of their tents to find three hundred torches surrounding them. Because it was normal military practice in that day for a company of 1,000 soldiers to march behind a single torch, the Midianites assumed they were encompassed not by three hundred men, but by 300,000. When they heard the crashing of the broken pitchers, saw the torches light up the night sky, and heard the cry of the trumpets, they thought they were doomed. And in the chaos and confusion, in their suspicion and superstition, they began to butcher each other.

What application does this have for us today? Earthen vessels that we are (2 Corinthians 4:7), whenever we are broken, the light shines forth from our lives, causing Satan to be as confused and defeated as the host of Midian . . .

For topical study of Judges 7:19–21, see "The Blessedness of Brokenness" below.

Judges 7:24, 25 (a)
And Gideon sent messengers throughout all mount Ephraim, saying, Come down against the Midianites, and take before them the waters unto Beth-barah and Jordan. Then all the men of Ephraim gathered themselves together, and took the waters unto Beth-barah and Jordan. And they took two princes of the Midianites, Oreb and Zeeb . . .

Oreb means "Raven"; *Zeeb* means "Wolf." These two were formidable leaders.

Judges 7:25 (b)
. . . and they slew Oreb upon the rock Oreb, and Zeeb they slew at the winepress of Zeeb, and pursued Midian, and brought the heads of Oreb and Zeeb to Gideon on the other side Jordan.

Here come the men of Ephraim, carrying the bloody heads of Oreb and Zeeb. But, as we will see in Chapter 8, rather than rejoicing in the victory, they complained about the strategy.

THE BLESSEDNESS OF BROKENNESS

A Topical Study of JUDGES 7:19–21

The odds were absolutely brutal, yet the strategy was incredibly brilliant, as Gideon gathered three hundred select soldiers and marched into battle against 135,000 Midianite men of war. Statistically, Gideon was outnumbered 450 to 1. Yet, miraculously, incredibly, the Lord gave victory to Gideon and his band of three hundred.

Here's what happened: While the Midianites snoozed in their tents in the valley below him, Gideon gave each of his men a trumpet and an earthenware pitcher with a smoldering torch inside. Then he ordered his men to quietly surround the Midianite camp. On signal, Gideon had his men shout, "The sword of the Lord and of Gideon," as they smashed the pitchers, causing air to rush into the broken vessels and the smoldering embers to burst into flame.

Hearing the crashing and clanging sound of broken glass, and the shouts coming from the hills around them, the Midianites came stumbling out of their tents to see torches encircling them. Since it was customary for companies of 1,000 soldiers to be led by a single torch, the Midianites assumed that behind every one of the three hundred torches, marched a division of men. Thus, in their panic, they grabbed their swords, and, still in a sleepy stupor, began to fight one another.

An incredible story—a brilliant, God-given, inspired strategy, as three hundred Israeli soldiers overcame unbelievable odds, destroying 135,000 Midianites. I would like to focus on one particular segment of this story. I would like to use stop-action instant replay and freeze one frame. I would like us to look at a seemingly minor detail which actually is hugely significant.

We live in a world oppressed by Midianites, dominated by Midianites, controlled by Midianites. I'm not speaking of an external race of people, but of an internal struggle within people. The dominion of Satan, the control of self, the oppression of sin is within the heart of every human being, for, like David, we are all born into sin (Psalm 51:5). We have all been tainted by sin; we have all succumbed to sin. But praise be to God, we can be liberated. We can be rescued. We can be free. God has called us into His glorious gospel—the good news that Jesus Christ died for our sins, paid the price for all of our iniquity, rose from the dead, and wants to set up residence within our hearts, to free us, to liberate us, to lead us into life that is both abundant and eternal. That's the gospel.

And we who have come into this saving knowledge of Jesus are to trumpet this gospel to all who are still dominated, controlled, oppressed by the Midianites of sin, Satan, and self. We have the answer. The Light of the world, Jesus Christ, dwells within us. His light is inside of us—but it is also to be radiating from us. And there's the rub.

You see, most of us understand that Jesus is the Light because most of us have walked in His light—and yet all too often His light remains inside, all bottled up. The Lord wants to release the light of Jesus which He has placed in you. He wants His light to shine out from you in order that others can be saved and freed and satisfied. How does this happen? Only by breaking—for just as the light of the torch was hidden within the earthen vessel until the pitcher was broken, so, too, if our lives are going to be a blessing, there must first be a breaking.

Turn to 2 Corinthians 4, where Paul capitalizes on this particular illustration . . .

> *For God, who commanded the light to shine out of darkness, hath shined in our hearts, to give the light of the knowledge of the glory of God in the face of Jesus Christ. But we have this treasure in earthen vessels, that the excellency of the power may be of God, and not of us.* 2 Corinthians 4:6, 7

The light is *in* the earthen vessel. But the light cannot shine forth *from* the vessel until there is a breaking *of* the vessel.

> *We are troubled on every side, yet not distressed; we are perplexed, but not in despair; Persecuted, but not forsaken; cast down, but not destroyed; Always*

> *bearing about in the body the dying of the Lord Jesus, that the life also of Jesus might be made manifest in our body. For we which live are always delivered unto death for Jesus' sake, that the life also of Jesus might be made manifest in our mortal flesh. So then death worketh in us, but life in you.*
>
> 2 Corinthians 4:8–12

This is the breaking of the vessel. What's happening in us, says Paul, is difficult on us, but necessary for you.

Gang, you cannot be a blessing until you first go through breaking. Why? Because we live in a broken world.

We live in a broken world indeed. The baby in his playpen cries over a broken toy. The little boy is upset because of his broken bike. The junior higher is in agony over a broken arm. The high school Sophomore is in pain because of a broken heart. The young wife is crying because of broken marriage vows. The businessman is in despair because of broken hopes. The middle-aged man is hurting because of broken health. Wherever you look, wherever you observe people you see hurts. People are broken. People are in tough situations. And we who have the Light and Life of Jesus Christ can only touch them to the degree that we are able to relate to them.

> I shared breakfast with a fellow yesterday who has gone through tough times. His wife left him, and took his two boys with her. As we were sharing, he related how certain people came to him with certain ideas and understandings, and very kindly, yet very emphatically he said, "You know, they just don't understand. They mean well, but they don't understand. They haven't suffered. They haven't felt it. They can't relate to it."

During the times of breaking in my own life, I have observed that basically all of the people who have approached me fall into one of two categories: those who help, and those who hinder. In thinking about people who have helped me, I have noticed a common denominator which can be summed up in one word: brokenness. The people who were a hindrance to me with their advice, exhortations, and prophetic utterances had not really been broken themselves. But without exception, at some point in their lives, in some area of their lives, each of those who have helped me have themselves experienced breaking. Indeed, there's something about a broken heart, a broken spirit, a broken man which blesses unbelievably.

Brokenness. There is no other way to be effective in touching others' lives. Job knew this. He went through more breaking than any of us could possibly imagine. He lost it all, and yet it was Job's suffering which silenced Satan.

You see, Satan cruised by God and said, "Sure Job serves You. Sure he worships You. Look how You've blessed him. Look what You've given him. No wonder he walks with You. Big deal. But if those things were taken away, he would curse You. He would walk away from You" (Job 1:9–11).

But when everything was taken away from Job, listen to how he responded:

Behold I go forward, but he is not there; and backward, but I cannot perceive him. Job 23:8

Ever feel like that? Wherever you go, you can't feel or sense the Lord.

On the left hand, where he doth work, but I cannot behold him: he hideth himself on the right hand, that I cannot see him: But he knoweth the way that I take: when he hath tried me, I shall come forth as gold. Job 23:9, 10

"I don't know the way He's taking, I don't know what He's doing," says Job, "but *He* knows the way I take. *He* knows where I'm at. *He* knows what He's doing."

And with that, Satan's accusations went up in smoke.

Not only does suffering silence Satan, but suffering is necessary for service.

> A five-dollar iron bar can be pounded into a couple of ten-dollar horseshoes. Or, that same iron bar can be pounded further into $350 worth of needles. Or, that same iron bar can be pounded even further to produce $250,000 worth of fine watch springs. It all depends on how much pounding is done.

Maybe you feel as though you have been pounded on, worked on, broken this week. Rejoice and be exceedingly glad, for it means God is making you into something fine, something useful, something valuable for His glory.

"I don't know about this teaching," you say. "I think I would rather control my own destiny than submit to the breaking of God. Thanks, but no thanks. I'll go it alone." Those of you who, so saying, want to captain your own ship, turn with me to Acts 27 . . .

En route to Rome, where he was to stand trial before Caesar, Paul advised his shipmates they were headed for treacherous waters. Ignoring his warning, the captain sailed on—right into a storm so fierce the ship was tossed to and fro on the waves, eventually running aground, where it was broken into pieces. All on board were saved, however, by clinging to the broken remains of the very boat of which they were previously so proud and confident. It was the broken pieces which saved them.

Storms will come into your life, gang. There is not a man or woman who is exempt from this. And when they do, each of us will have a choice to make: Either to flail about in our own efforts, or to grab on to the splinters and say, "I don't have much to offer, Lord—just a bunch of shattered pieces of my life. But take control and bring me to dry land."

If you choose the latter, guess what. The Lord will take the breakings, the hurts, the heartaches of your life, and He will bring you not only safely to shore, but He will use the remnants of your ship to bring others as well. You will touch, pray, and relate to people in an entirely different way—for you will have been broken.

Christian, if you're going through a time of breaking right now, know this: The process keeps going. It just keeps on. You might be a horseshoe, and He's making you into a needle—or you might be a needle which He's shaping into a watchspring. Wherever you are, He's working on you, breaking you in order that the light of Jesus Christ may shine from you. The world is impressed and blessed, moved and touched when they see people who not only rejoice and praise the Lord in times of prosperity, but who worship God and hang tough when the times are difficult, for it is then that the light of the gospel shines forth. It is then that the trumpet of Jesus Christ is heard throughout the land. It is then that the Midianites which oppress and depress people are defeated.

Hang in there, gang. Don't give up. Don't question, wonder, or fret about what God is doing. "I don't know His ways," said Job. "But He knows mine—and that's all that matters."

8

Judges 8:1
And the men of Ephraim said unto him, Why hast thou served us thus, that thou calledst us not, when thou wentest to fight with the Midianites? And they did chide with him sharply.

Carrying the bloody, blackened heads of Oreb and Zeeb, the men of Ephraim came down on Gideon. "Why didn't you involve us in the initial battle plans? How come you called us in at the tail end?" Instead of saying, "Wow! God is good!" they said, "How come we only got the mop up operation?"

Throughout the Old Testament, Ephraim was the most negative of the Twelve Tribes—always complaining about something.

A few months ago, a large department store was being picketed not only by picketers protesting store policy but by picketers protesting the anti-department store signs which had been printed in a non-union shop. Incredible: Picketers picketing picketers.

Yet that's just like Christians. We ignore the decisive victory of the Cross, the great mercy with which we are all forgiven, and instead like Ephraim, find the smallest things about which to disagree.

The trumpet had sounded throughout the land. Anyone who could come was invited to join the battle. Thirty-two thousand men showed up. The men of Ephraim, however, stayed home. But now they're upset because a great victory had been won. Spoils were divided. And rather than rejoicing in the victory, they criticized the strategy.

Judges 8:2, 3
And he said unto them, What have I done now in comparison of you? Is not the gleaning of the grapes of Ephraim better than the vintage of Abi-ezer? God hath delivered into your hands the princes of Midian, Oreb and Zeeb: and what was I able to do in comparison of you? Then their anger was abated toward him, when he had said that.

I like this! If there were a Nobel Peace Prize in 1256 B.C., Gideon would have won it hands down. He demonstrated diplomacy, tact, and love when he said, "You guys won a far greater victory than we did. What we've done is inconsequential compared to the work you've done in capturing Oreb and Zeeb."

Ronald Reagan wisely said, "There's no limit to what a man can accomplish if he doesn't care who gets the credit." There's no limit to what the body of Christ can accomplish if we don't care who gets the credit—just that Jesus gets the glory.

Judges 8:4
And Gideon came to Jordan, and passed over, he, and the three hundred men that were with him, faint, yet pursuing them.

One hundred twenty thousand Midianites had been killed, but fifteen thousand were still left, and Gideon and his three hundred available—though possibly not very agile—men were in pursuit of them.

Judges 8:5–7
And he said unto the men of Succoth, Give, I pray you, loaves of bread unto the people that follow me; for they be faint, and I am pursuing after Zebah and Zalmunna, kings of Midian. And the princes of Succoth said, Are the hands of Zebah and Zalmunna now in thine hand, that we should give bread unto thine army? And Gideon said, Therefore when the LORD hath delivered Zebah and Zalmunna into mine hand, then I will tear your flesh with the thorns of the wilderness and with briers.

Arriving in Succoth, Gideon said, "My men are hungry. Give us some bread so we can continue on."

"Not so fast," said the men of Succoth. "Is the victory totally secure? If not, we don't want to get involved."

Judges 8:8, 9
And he went up thence to Penuel, and spake unto them likewise: and the men of Penuel answered him as the men of Succoth had answered him. And he spake also unto the men of Penuel, saying, When I come again in peace, I will break down this tower.

Lest you think Gideon sounds like anything but a man of humility, you need to understand that, although Israel had obtained victory in this battle, Gideon intuitively understood that the real key is not obtaining victory but maintaining it. Whether in a church, in a family, or on the jobsite, obtaining victory in battle is exciting. The real trick, however, is maintaining it in the days that follow. Gideon understood this.

Judges 8:10–16
Now Zebah and Zalmunna were in Karkor, and their hosts with them, about fifteen thousand men, all that were left of all the hosts of the children of the east: for there fell an hundred and twenty thousand men that drew sword. And Gideon went up by the way of them that dwelt in tents on the east of Nobah and Jogbehah, and smote the host: for the host was secure. And when Zebah and Zalmunna fled, he pursued after them, and took the two kings of Midian, Zebah and Zalmunna, and discomfited all the host. And Gideon the son of Joash returned from battle before the sun was up, And caught a young man of the men of Succoth, and inquired of him: and he described unto him the princes of Succoth, and the elders thereof, even threescore and seventeen men. And he came unto the men of Succoth, and said, Behold Zebah and Zalmunna, with whom ye did upbraid me, saying, Are the hands of Zebah and Zalmunna now in thine hand, that we should give bread unto thy men that are weary? And he took the elders of the city, and thorns of the wilderness and briers, and with them he taught the men of Succoth.

The ancient practice of "teaching" men with briers and thorns was such that the "pupil" would lay face down on the ground while his body was beaten with thorns and briers. Following this, he would be drug through the dirt until he was near death. It was a relatively common method of teaching a lesson in a most severe manner.

The seventy-seven men of Succoth who didn't want to help Gideon because they didn't want to risk their standing with Zebah and his men ended up losing on all sides. That's always the way it is. When you try and straddle both worlds, you'll fall and miss out on both—which is why Jesus said to be hot or cold but not lukewarm (Revelation 3:16).

Judges 8:17
And he beat down the tower of Penuel, and slew the men of the city.

"That's pretty harsh," you might say, "beating and whipping the elders of Succoth, and killing the men of Penuel. Why was Gideon so brutal?"

I believe there's an important principle embedded here. That is, to attain success is not as difficult as it is to maintain success. The Israelites were successful—they had just beaten the Midianites against incredible odds. On the heels of their success, no doubt, the temptation would have been to think, *What's the big deal? We beat the Midianites! We're scoring big victories. So what if the men of Succoth kind of blew it?* But Gideon knew he had to discipline these men in order to maintain success under his administration.

Parents, take note of this. There may be times when everything's running fairly smoothly at home. Sure, your kids are way out of line, but you think, *I don't want to discipline them. Things are going pretty well, and I don't want to upset the cart.* But listen: Success can only be maintained through loving discipline and correction when necessary. Gideon knew this, and so instead of just sitting back and enjoying the plaudits and applause of his people, he said, "I must discipline for the sake of the whole country." Yes it was brutal, but it was necessary.

Judges 8:18, 19 (a)
Then said he unto Zebah and Zalmunna, What manner of men were they whom ye slew at Tabor? And they answered, As thou art, so were they; each one resembled the children of a king. And he said, They were my brethren, even the sons of my mother . . .

"The men we killed looked just like you." In other words, these guys were the reason Gideon was hiding in the winepress. It was these two princes, with their murdering marauders, who had swept through the area and killed his family.

Judges 8:19 (b)–21
. . . as the LORD liveth, if ye had saved them alive, I would not slay you. And he said unto Jether his firstborn, Up, and slay them. But the youth drew not his sword: for he feared, because he was yet a youth. Then Zebah and Zalmunna said, Rise thou, and fall upon us: for as the man is, so is his strength. And Gideon arose, and slew Zebah and Zalmunna, and took away the ornaments that were on their camels' necks.

Gideon thought he was giving a blessing to his eldest son by saying, "Avenge the death of your uncles." But Gideon's son was afraid. So it was left up to Gideon to slay the men of whom he himself was once afraid.

Judges 8:22, 23
Then the men of Israel said unto Gideon, Rule thou over us, both thou, and thy son, and thy son's son also: for thou hast delivered us from the hand of Midian. And Gideon said unto them, I will not rule over you, neither shall my son rule over you: the LORD shall rule over you.

Amen! I love it! The people came to Gideon and said, "You're a hero. Rule over us."

"No way," said Gideon. "I will not rule over you; my son will not rule over you. The Lord is the One who will rule over you."

Please let that sink in, precious people. You see, the Lord is the One who is to rule over you—not men, not elders, not pastors, not apostles, not people. People who are in ministry are to serve and to assist not to rule (2 Corinthians 1:24). Why do I say this? Because there's a tendency in the heart of each of us to want to look to a man to give us direction. Why? Because it's easier to go to someone and say, "Tell me what I should do," rather than to seek the Lord and say, "Father, what is Your desire and intention for me in this matter?"

How important it is that we learn to seek the Lord and to seek His face.

Judges 8:24–27 (a)
And Gideon said unto them, I would desire a request of you, that ye would give me every man the earrings of his prey. (For they had golden earrings, because they were Ishmaelites.) And they answered, We will willingly give them. And they spread a garment, and did cast therein every man the earrings of his prey. And the weight of the golden earrings that he requested was a thousand and seven hundred shekels of gold; beside ornaments, and collars, and purple raiment that was on the kings of Midian, and beside the chains that were about their camels' necks. And Gideon made an ephod thereof . . .

An ephod was the vest-like garment worn by the high priest. Upon the ephod were the Urim and the Thumim, which were used to determine the will of God. Gideon made a golden ephod, possibly with the intention of keeping people focused on the priestly ministry and not upon him as a person.

Judges 8:27 (b)
. . . and put it in his city, even in Ophrah: and all Israel went thither a whoring after it: which thing became a snare unto Gideon, and to his house.

Gideon made an ephod, and guess what happened. The people began to worship it. I suggest to you a real danger here: Gideon wisely and correctly said, "I will not rule over you"—but perhaps he thought, *Neither do I want to be forgotten by you. So I'll make an ephod from the gold we plundered which will point to God, but which will also remind you of the victory we experienced together.* Thus, in becoming a monument to his own ministry, the ephod became a snare.

As you study church history, you will see an interesting pattern unfold. That is, revival often starts with a man who is gifted by God, whose ministry grows and blossoms into a movement. So far, so good. God is moving. God is blessing. But then the movement begins to construct a monument and the monument becomes a mausoleum. Man, ministry, movement, monument, mausoleum. It happens over and over and over again. The great church buildings, the great cathedrals in Europe and in the major cities of America at one time where thriving, bustling, pulsating, energetic centers of revival. But monuments built to glorify men are destined to become mausoleums.

Here's what happens: God blesses, and as He blesses facilities begin to be constructed—and that's good and right. But the tragedy occurs when the machine which was originally set up to serve and bless the people becomes so ingrained and established that the people exist to serve the machine. And it happens in church after church. May that not be so with us.

Judges 8:28–31
Thus was Midian subdued before the children of Israel, so that they lifted up their heads no more. And the country was in quietness forty years in the days of Gideon. And Jerubbaal the son of Joash went and dwelt in his own house. And Gideon had threescore and ten sons of his body begotten: for he had many wives. And his concubine that was in Shechem, she also bare him a son, whose name he called Abimelech.

In the time of battle and difficulty, Gideon did well and excelled. The real danger, however, lay in the time of peace and prosperity, for it was then that Gideon pulled away. Oh, he didn't become a king—but he began to live like one, as seen, for example, in the number of women he married. In chapter 9, we will see the tragic result of Gideon's multiple marriages. Throughout the Old Testament, when you see men who had more than one wife, their lives are invariably marked with tragedy and heartache.

In today's society, we are seeing another move towards multiple marriages as people discard wives and husbands and move into marriage after marriage. And the resulting heartache and tragedy are the same as they were in Gideon's day.

Judges 8:32
And Gideon the son of Joash died in a good old age, and was buried in the sepulchre of Joash his father, in Ophrah of the Abiezrites.

Gideon—this one who needed sign after sign when God had made it so clear from the very beginning that He was calling him; this one who vacillated, whose heart was filled with doubts, whose mind was flooded with confusion—is one of only a handful of men who made it into God's "Hall of Faith," found in Hebrews 11. Moses isn't there. David isn't there. Elisha, Elijah, and Ezekiel aren't there. Why is *Gideon* there?

I suggest it's because when you read the story of Gideon or the accounts of Barak and Samson, also seen in Hebrews 11, all you can say is, "Lord, for these guys to be in Your hall of faith is truly an indication of Your grace, Your kindness, Your generosity, Your incredible mercy." As I read the life of Gideon, the conclusion I come to is not that Gideon is a great guy—but that God used an ordinary guy in an extraordinary way.

It's pure grace that Gideon was used like he was. It's pure grace that he is listed in the hall of faith. And it's even greater grace that God chooses to call and to use people like us.

Judges 8:33–35
And it came to pass, as soon as Gideon was dead, that the children of Israel turned again, and went a whoring after Baalim, and made Baal-berith their god. And the children of Israel remembered not the Lord their God, who had delivered them out of the hands of all their enemies on every side: Neither shewed they kindness to the house of Jerubbaal, namely, Gideon, according to all the goodness which he had shewed unto Israel.

Yet again, Israel takes the first step on the downward cycle of sin. Oh, the forgetfulness and fickleness of God's people.

Our God takes us from glory to greater glory. Therefore, we must be those who allow the Lord to keep us current. There ought to be so much going on in our hearts and lives presently that we're caught up in rejoicing for what He's doing *today*. Oh, that God would keep us fresh and vibrant for His glory.

9

It has been wisely said that no man's life is completely worthless, for anyone can serve as a horrible example. In chapter 9, we have a man who fits that description. His name is Abimelech . . .

Judges 9:1 (a)
And Abimelech the son of Jerubbaal . . .

Jerubbaal being another name for Gideon, Abimelech was Gideon's son, the fruit of his relations with one of his concubines (8:30).

Abimelech literally means "My father is king." This is interesting because, when the people in Israel wanted to make Gideon king, he said, "I will not be king over you—neither I nor my sons nor my son's sons. Your king is to be God exclusively." Perhaps Gideon, so adamant about not being a king, was having second thoughts. Or perhaps the concubine who bore Abimelech named him in order to gain recognition. Whatever the case, Abimelech was one who desired to be king, a man of ambition.

Judges 9:1 (b)
. . . went to Shechem unto his mother's brethren, and communed with them, and with all the family of the house of his mother's father . . .

In Gideon's day, when a man took a concubine, he did not bring her into his own house. She remained in her father's house, and was visited on occasion by the man who had taken her as his concubine. That is why we see Abimelech's mother still residing in her father's house.

Judges 9:1 (c), 2
. . . saying, Speak, I pray you, in the ears of all the men of Shechem, Whether is better for you, either that all the sons of Jerubbaal, which are threescore and ten persons, reign over you, or that one reign over you? remember also that I am your bone and your flesh.

Abimelech goes to his mother's family, saying, "Allow me instead of all seventy of my brothers to rule and reign over this territory." Because Gideon had made it clear that neither Abimelech nor any of his sons were to rule the people (8:23), Abimelech is operating on a completely erroneous presupposition as he seeks to wrest power for himself.

Judges 9:3, 4
And his mother's brethren spake of him in the ears of all the men of Shechem all these words: and their hearts inclined to follow Abimelech; for they said, He is our brother. And they gave him threescore and ten pieces of silver out of the house of Baal-berith, wherewith Abimelech hired vain and light persons, which followed him.

Abimelech's uncles went to the temple of Baal and gave him seventy pieces of silver, with which he hired some hit men.

Judges 9:5 (a)
And he went unto his father's house at Ophrah, and slew his brethren the sons of Jerubbaal, being threescore and ten persons, upon one stone . . .

Abimelech had the ruffians he hired place the heads of his brothers on a single stone and lop them off.

Judges 9:5 (b), 6
. . . notwithstanding yet Jotham the youngest son of Jerubbaal was left; for he hid himself. And all the men of Shechem gathered together, and all the house of Millo, and went, and made Abimelech king, by the plain of the pillar that was in Shechem.

Abimelech wasn't king of Israel, but simply a local ruler, ruling over the Shechemites.

Judges 9:7 (a)
And when they told it to Jotham, he went and stood in the top of mount Gerizim . . .

About eight hundred feet in elevation, Mount Gerizim was the mountain on which the people of Israel spoke blessing when they entered the Promised Land (Deuteronomy 27:12). Mount Gerizim overlooks the city of Shechem. Jotham made his way up to the top of that mountain.

Judges 9:7 (b)
. . . and lifted up his voice, and cried, and said unto them, Hearken unto me, ye men of Shechem, that God may hearken unto you.

Standing atop Mount Gerizim, Jotham—Gideon's one remaining son—had a huge pulpit from which to preach. Now, he's going to share a parable—the first in the Bible—with the people below. It's a parable that gives us great insight concerning God's heart toward leadership.

Judges 9:8–14
The trees went forth on a time to anoint a king over them; and they said unto the olive tree, Reign thou over us. But the olive tree said unto them, Should I leave my fatness, wherewith by me they honour God and man, and go to be promoted over the trees? And the trees said to the fig tree, Come thou, and reign over us. But the fig tree said unto them, Should I forsake my sweetness, and my good fruit, and go to be promoted over the trees? Then said the trees unto the vine, Come thou, and reign over us. And the vine said unto them, Should I leave my wine, which cheereth God and man, and go to be promoted over the trees? Then said all the trees unto the bramble, Come thou, and reign over us.

The bramble is a thorn bush, the most worthless plant in the Middle East. It produces no fruit and is too low to the ground to produce any shade. Its wood cannot be used for any kind of construction because it splits too easily. All it can do is burn.

Judges 9:15 (a)
And the bramble said unto the trees, If in truth ye anoint me king over you, then come and put your trust in my shadow . . .

Remember, a bramble is too low to the ground to produce any usable shade.

Judges 9:15 (b)
. . . and if not, let fire come out of the bramble, and devour the cedars of Lebanon.

The olive tree, fig tree, and vine were all of great value. Not so the bramble. Thus, in this parable, the trees that deserved leadership the most desired it the least because they knew ruling the other trees meant they would have to cease fruit-bearing. Only the bramble—the worthless tree—grasped at leadership.

There are still brambles who love to rule other people—not to minister to people—but simply to rule. Be wary of them.

As Jesus walked through the crowd, a woman who had been hemorrhaging for twelve years reached out and touched Him.

"Who touched me?" Jesus asked. "I perceive virtue has gone forth from Me" (Luke 8:46).

Jesus Himself was aware of the draining that takes place in ministry. Therefore, before you seek leadership, understand it will be draining. It will be demanding. I'm often suspicious of those who want to thrust themselves into any kind of position of leadership before they've counted the cost.

Judges 9:16–21
Now therefore, if ye have done truly and sincerely, in that ye have made Abimelech king, and if ye have dealt well with Jerubbaal and his house, and have done unto him according to the deserving of his hands; (For my father fought for you, and adventured his life far, and delivered you out of the hand of Midian: And ye are risen up against my father's house this day, and have slain his sons, threescore and ten persons, upon one stone, and have made Abimelech, the son of his maidservant, king over the men of Shechem, because he is your brother;) If ye then have dealt truly and sincerely with Jerubbaal and with his house this day, then rejoice ye in Abimelech, and let him also rejoice in you: But if not, let fire come out from Abimelech, and devour the men of Shechem, and the house of Millo; and let fire come out from the men of Shechem, and from the house of Millo, and devour Abimelech. And Jotham ran away, and fled, and went to Beer, and dwelt there, for fear of Abimelech his brother.

After likening Abimelech to a worthless bramble who deserved nothing more than to be burned, Jotham wisely ran for his life.

Parables always speak a simple truth, and Jotham's is no exception. "Fruitful trees wouldn't do this," he said. "Only a bramble. And that's who Abimelech is."

Judges 9:22, 23 (a)
When Abimelech had reigned three years over Israel, Then God sent an evil spirit between Abimelech and the men of Shechem . . .

Notice that it was God who sent a spirit of ill will between Abimelech and the men of Shechem. We see the same thing in 1 Samuel 11:6, when God sent a spirit of jealousy upon Saul, and again in Isaiah 19:14, when God sent a spirit of perverseness upon the people.

Mark it well: Demons, evil spirits, even Satan himself cannot function outside of God's permissive will (Job 1). But why would God want tools like demons or Satan? In order to provide mankind an alternative. You see, man must have an alternative in order for him to *choose* a relationship with God. "I will give mankind a choice," says God. "He can either choose Satan and his hellish henchmen, or he can walk with Me. The choice is that simple."

Demons and Satan himself are actually tools of the Lord and cannot move apart from His permission. Therefore, when there is a spirit of ill will, a spirit of jealousy, a spirit of perverseness moving in people, my attitude towards them must not be one of condemnation. Rather, my attitude must be one of compassion. Instead of looking at people as vicious, I must look at them as victims.

Nothing can happen to us without the Lord allowing it. Take comfort in that. God actually uses the enemy to accomplish His purpose. "I'm being attacked," we cry.

Yet the Lord would say, "I've allowed it for important reasons. Trust Me, seek Me, and you'll see why I've allowed this to be."

Judges 9:23 (b)—25
. . . and the men of Shechem dealt treacherously with Abimelech: That the cruelty done to the threescore and ten sons of Jerubbaal might come, and their blood be laid upon Abimelech their brother, which slew them; and upon the men of Shechem, which aided him in the killing of his brethren. And the men of Shechem set liers in wait for him in the top of the mountains and they robbed all that came along that way by them: and it was told Abimelech.

After three years, bad blood developed between the men who were ruled by the bramble, and Abimelech himself. No longer enamored with Abimelech, the men of Shechem decided to raid caravans passing through their area in order to deal a financial blow to Abimelech's kingdom.

Judges 9:26–29
And Gaal the son of Ebed came with his brethren, and went over to Shechem: and the men of Shechem put their confidence in him. And they went out into the fields, and gathered their vineyards, and trode the grapes, and made merry, and went into the house of their god, and did eat and drink, and cursed Abimelech. And Gaal the son of Ebed said, Who is Abimelech, and who is Shechem, that we should serve him? is not he the son of Jerubbaal? and Zebul his officer? serve the men of Hamor the father of Shechem: for why should we serve him? And would to God this people were under my hand! then would I remove Abimelech. And he said to Abimelech, Increase thine army, and come out.

Abimelech wasn't even present, yet Gaal cursed and challenged him. Why? I believe it was because Gaal had been drinking. Let me suggest to you if there's no other reason (and there are many) to stay away from alcohol, this should be valid in and of itself: People say things they wish they had never said when they are under the influence of alcohol.

Judges 9:30–36 (a)
And when Zebul the ruler of the city heard the words of Gaal the son of Ebed, his anger was kindled. And he sent messengers unto Abimelech privily, saying, Behold, Gaal the son of Ebed and his brethren be come to Shechem; and, behold, they fortify the city against thee. Now therefore up by night, thou and the people that is with thee, and lie in wait in the field: And it shall be, that in the morning, as soon as the sun is up, thou shalt rise early, and set upon the city: and, behold, when he and the people that is with him come out against thee, then mayest thou do to them as thou shalt find occasion. And Abimelech rose up, and all the people that were with him, by night, and they laid wait against Shechem in four companies. And Gaal the son of Ebed went out, and stood in the entering of the gate of the city: and Abimelech rose up, and the people that were with him, from lying in wait. And when Gaal saw the people, he said to Zebul, Behold, there come people down from the top of the mountains . . .

Gaal didn't realize Zebul was a double agent.

Judges 9:36 (b)
. . . And Zebul said unto him, Thou seest the shadow of the mountains as if they were men.

"You're just seeing things," Zebul assured Gaal.

Judges 9:37, 38
And Gaal spake again and said, See there come people down by the middle of the land, and another company come along by the plain of Meonenim. Then said Zebul unto him, Where is now thy mouth, wherewith thou saidst, Who is Abimelech, that we should serve him? is not this the people that thou hast despised? go out, I pray now, and fight with them.

Able to deceive Gaal no longer, Zebul changes tactics and says to Gaal, "Put your money where your mouth is. You wanted to fight Abimelech. Here's your chance."

Judges 9:39–45
And Gaal went out before the men of Shechem, and fought with Abimelech. And Abimelech chased him, and he fled before him, and many were overthrown and wounded, even unto the entering of the gate. And Abimelech dwelt at Arumah: and Zebul thrust out Gaal and his brethren, that they should not dwell in Shechem. And it came to pass on the morrow, that the people went out into the field; and they told Abimelech. And he took the people, and divided them into three companies, and laid wait in the field, and looked, and, behold, the people were come forth out of the city; and he rose up against them, and smote them. And Abimelech, and the company that was with him, rushed forward, and stood in the entering of the gate of the city: and the two other companies ran upon all the people that were in the fields, and slew them. And Abimelech fought against the city all that day; and he took the city, and slew the people that was therein, and beat down the city, and sowed it with salt.

What had Jotham said in his parable? He said, "If you guys aren't right in this, Abimelech will burn you." And now Abimelech is doing just that as he unleashes his fury towards Gaal on the men of Shechem. Abimelech not only destroyed all of the people in his own hometown, but he also put salt in the land so nothing would ever grow there again.

Judges 9:46, 47
And when all the men of the tower of Shechem heard that, they entered into an hold

of the house of the god Berith. And it was told Abimelech, that all the men of the tower of Shechem were gathered together.

All of the men who were supposed to be guarding the city ran into the temple of their god, Berith.

Judges 9:48, 49
And Abimelech gat him up to mount Zalmon, he and all the people that were with him; and Abimelech took an axe in his hand, and cut down a bough from the trees, and took it, and laid it on his shoulder, and said unto the people that were with him, What ye have seen me do, make haste, and do as I have done. And all the people likewise cut down every man his bough, and followed Abimelech, and put them to the hold, and set the hold on fire upon them; so that all the men of the tower of Shechem died also, about a thousand men and women.

"Abimelech will burn you," Jotham had warned. And that is exactly what's happening here.

Judges 9:50
Then went Abimelech to Thebez, and encamped against Thebez, and took it.

A city ten miles away, Thebez was evidently in alliance with Shechem.

Judges 9:51–53
But there was a strong tower within the city, and thither fled all the men and women, and all they of the city, and shut it to them, and gat them up to the top of the tower. And Abimelech came unto the tower, and fought against it, and went hard unto the door of the tower to burn it with fire. And a certain woman cast a piece of a millstone upon Abimelech's head, and all to brake his skull.

Reminiscent of Jael before her, a woman in the tower of Thebez took the upper part of a millstone—eighteen or twenty inches in diameter, and two or three inches thick—and threw it right on Abimelech's head. Talk about a splitting headache!

Judges 9:54
Then he called hastily unto the young man his armourbearer, and said unto him, Draw thy sword, and slay me, that men say not of me, A woman slew him. And his young man thrust him through, and he died.

The unnamed woman of Thebez joins Deborah and Jael as women God used to overcome seemingly invincible warriors.

Judges 9:55–57
And when the men of Israel saw that Abimelech was dead, they departed every man unto his place. Thus God rendered the wickedness of Abimelech, which he did unto his father, in slaying his seventy brethren: And all the evil of the men of Shechem did God render upon their heads: and upon them came the curse of Jotham the son of Jerubbaal.

Please note two things about this story . . .

First, the peril of ambition. Abimelech's problem was ambition. The Word says God resists the proud, but gives grace to the humble (see James 4:6)—which is why we are to humble ourselves under His mighty hand in order that *He* will exalt us in due time (see 1 Peter 5:6).

We live in a very caustic society that says, "Watch out for Number One."

Jesus says, however, "Blessed are the meek, for they shall inherit the earth" (Matthew 5:5).

Secondly, notice the principle of sowing and reaping. Whatever a man sows, that shall he also reap (Galatians 6:7). Abimelech sowed a seed when he put the heads of his seventy brothers upon the chopping block. He shouldn't have been surprised, then, when a stone fell upon his own head. He wanted to be crowned, and was indeed crowned—with a millstone.

The peril of ambition, the principle of sowing and reaping. May God deliver us from walking in the steps of Abimelech.

10

Judges 10:1, 2
And after Abimelech there arose to defend Israel Tola the son of Puah, the son of Dodo, a man of Issachar; and he dwelt in Shamir in mount Ephraim. And he judged Israel twenty and three years, and died, and was buried in Shamir.

I frequently find myself gleaning lessons from the more obscure characters in the Bible. This shouldn't be surprising because Jesus said the last shall be first (Matthew 19:30), and that the Father, who sees in secret will reward openly (Matthew 6:4). Therefore, because it won't necessarily be the guys up front or in the limelight who will be rewarded, I suspect it might be that we will see Tola rewarded greatly in eternity.

Who is Tola? In this Book of Judges, it is uniquely said of him that he was one who arose to defend Israel. The Hebrew word translated "to defend" can mean "to save" or "to deliver." The King James translators chose to translate the word "to defend" because, as far as we know, Tola didn't deliver Israel from an invading army, nor did he save them from a foreign power.

For topical study of Judges 10:1, 2 entitled "Defender of God's People," turn to page 767.

Judges 10:3–5
And after him arose Jair, a Gileadite, and judged Israel twenty and two years. And he had thirty sons that rode on thirty ass colts, and they had thirty cities, which are called Havoth-jair unto this day, which are in the land of Gilead. And Jair died, and was buried in Camon.

The donkey was the police car of the day. Therefore, the fact that Jair's sons each had one meant they held positions of authority. Jair was the main judge, but his thirty boys were his "deputy judges" as they followed in their father's footsteps.

Dad, you might say, "I wish I could be a missionary to Asia." However, the most important, the most satisfying ministry you'll ever have is with your own children. There is no more thrilling or fulfilling ministry than that of raising your kids, teaching them everything you know, leading them in the Word and ways of God, pouring out your heart with them in prayer. Whether as a parent, grandparent, aunt, or uncle, you'll always have opportunity to share the Lord with your family. And that's the best legacy there is.

Judges 10:6
And the children of Israel did evil again in the sight of the LORD, and served Baalim, and Ashtaroth, and the gods of Syria, and the gods of Zidon, and the gods of Moab, and the gods of the children of Ammon, and the gods of the Philistines, and forsook the LORD, and served not him.

Under Tola and Jair, Israel had experienced forty-five years of peace and prosperity. You'd think the result would be that the people of Israel would seek God, glory in God, and draw close to God. But that's not what happened. Instead, we read that, after those two judges were off the scene, after forty-five years of peace and prosperity, the people did evil in the sight of the Lord. This, however, came as no surprise to God . . .

When thou hast eaten and art full, then thou shalt bless the LORD thy God for the good land which he hath given thee. Beware that thou forget not the LORD thy God, in not keeping his commandments, and his judgments, and his statutes, which I command thee this day: Lest when thou hast eaten and art full, and hast built goodly houses, and dwelt therein; And when thy herds and thy flocks multiply, and thy silver and thy gold is multiplied, and all that thou hast is multiplied; Then thine heart be lifted up, and thou forget the LORD thy God, which brought thee forth out of the land of Egypt, from the house of bondage.

Deuteronomy 8:10–14

Israel had experienced prosperity and peace for forty-five years—but instead of drawing close to the Lord and being built up in Him, they got caught up in the gods, toys, trinkets, and baubles of the world.

The same thing can happen to me. When things go smoothly, if I'm not careful, I can find I'm not praying with the same passion, that I'm not as disciplined in my devotion as I was when times were harder. Many people can quote sticker prices and consumer guide information, but they don't have a basic understanding of the Book of Judges. Why? Because things are going pretty well for them. God has blessed them. As a result, they're interested in the things of the world—in Baal, the god of the intellect; in Ashtaroth, the god of sensuality; in Mammon, the god of money—the same gods that intrigued and seduced the children of Israel.

Judges 10:7
And the anger of the LORD was hot against Israel, and he sold them into the hands of the Philistines, and into the hands of the children of Ammon.

Because the children of Israel were interested in the world, they became controlled by the world. Because they were intrigued by the gods of the Ammonites, they found themselves in bondage to the Ammonites.

Judges 10:8, 9
And that year they vexed and oppressed the children of Israel: eighteen years, all the children of Israel that were on the other side Jordan in the land of the Amorites, which is in Gilead. Moreover the children of Ammon passed over Jordan to fight also against Judah, and against Benjamin, and against the house of Ephraim; so that Israel was sore distressed.

Whenever you see the word "oppressed" in the Old Testament, you can put the word "depressed" in its place because external oppression speaks of internal depression.

"Why am I so depressed?" people ask. "I've got a nice car. I've got a nice home. Why should I be depressed?" Maybe it's because they have given themselves to those things.

Judges 10:10 (a)
And the children of Israel cried unto the Lord . . .

After eighteen years, the children of Israel cried to the Lord. How long does it take before you and I cry to the Lord? How much time passes before we say, "Lord, I am oppressed, distressed, and depressed. I became intrigued with and seduced by my job, my hobby, or that person." How long before we say, "I've been living for my career and it's been unfulfilling," or, "I've been living for my children and I'm miserable. I've strayed away from a real, vital, intimate relationship with You, and now I'm distressed."

Don't wait eighteen years to cry to the Lord, gang. Because of His finished work on the Cross, we can come before His throne of grace *whenever* we have need (Hebrews 4:16).

Judges 10:10 (b)
. . . saying, We have sinned against thee, both because we have forsaken our God, and also served Baalim.

What is a god? The master passion of one's life. What is the master passion of your life? Where do you spend your time and energy on any given day? What is the driving force within you? That's your god.

Judges 10:11–13
And the Lord said unto the children of Israel, Did not I deliver you from the Egyptians, and from the Amorites, from the children of Ammon, and from the Philistines? The Zidonians also, and the Amalekites, and the Maonites, did oppress you; and ye cried to me, and I delivered you out of their hand. Yet ye have forsaken me, and served other gods: Wherefore I will deliver you no more.

The worst thing that can happen to us is not for the Father to raise His voice or lift His hand to discipline us, but for Him to turn His back and say, "I've blessed you with so much. I've seen you through time and time again. But if you persist in going there or pursuing that, I'll let you."

Judges 10:14
Go and cry unto the gods which ye have chosen; let them deliver you in the time of your tribulation.

Please know this, folks: The day of distress will come into your life. I guarantee it. I say this not as a prophet of doom, but as a pastor who knows and cares. The day of distress *will* come into your life. It does unto every man, for rain falls on the just and the unjust alike (Matthew 5:45). In that day, cry out to the god you have chosen. If you are living for materialism, cry out to your things and see how much satisfaction and help you get. If you're living for pleasure, cry out to pleasure, and see what help it offers. But if you choose the true and living God, if you walk with the Lord, He will be real to you. He will deliver you. He will strengthen you, comfort you, and help you in the day of your distress.

We don't know what tomorrow holds. Someday you will have to call out to the god you've chosen—and I hope it's the true and living God, for there's no help anywhere else.

Judges 10:15, 16 (a)
And the children of Israel said unto the Lord, We have sinned: do thou unto us whatsoever seemeth good unto thee; deliver us only, we pray thee, this day. And they put away the strange gods from among them, and served the Lord . . .

This is really important. Forty-five years of peace and prosperity under two judges. One defended them, the other sent out his sons to keep the peace and allow prosperity to take root in the land. But they ignored the Lord. And now, seduced by other gods, God said, "Let your gods deliver you." What did they do? The Word says they first of all confessed. Secondly, they submitted. They didn't explain their sin or justify it. They simply said, We have sinned. That is where it begins. We have sinned. Period. Not we have sinned because, or we have sinned, however. Just we've sinned. We've missed the mark. Confession.

Submission. So now, Lord, do whatever You want to do to me. I realize I've been out of line, missed the mark, dropped the ball. If you want me to run laps or do push-ups, if You want to send me to my room for a day or a year or two, do unto me what You see is good. Have Your way. I want to be changed and chastened. I want to be disciplined and developed.

Thirdly, destruction. They put away the foreign gods. Put away sounds like they put them in their drawer. A lot of folks do that. I know I shouldn't have alcohol in my house, so I'll put it in the basement. No. The word "put away" in Hebrew means they utterly destroyed it. When something's got to go, you don't say, I'm going to lock it up and put it in the closet because that thing will call out to you at some point. We will not allow these gods to be in our homes or in our land, the Israelites said.

Confession, submission, destruction—anything less is not true biblical repentance (2 Corinthians 7:10).

Judges 10:16 (b)
. . . and his soul was grieved for the misery of Israel.

God saw that they were sincere. They confessed, they submitted, they destroyed. God hurt for them, and would once again deliver His children from oppression.

Judges 10:17 (a)
Then the children of Ammon were gathered together, and encamped in Gilead.

Gilead is in the northern part, on the east side of the Jordan River, out of the country proper. You might remember that Gad, Reuben, and Manasseh said they wanted to stay on the east side of the Jordan.

Judges 10:17 (b)
. . . And the children of Israel assembled themselves together, and encamped in Mizpeh.

Mizpeh is a city in the region of Gilead.

Judges 10:18
And the people and princes of Gilead said one to another, What man is he that will begin to fight against the children of Ammon? he shall be head over all the inhabitants of Gilead.

The children of Israel had confessed. They had submitted. They had destroyed their gods. But there was not a capable leader found among them initially because a country will only get the leaders it deserves. Following confession, submission, and destruction, Israel was ready for action. But, because, they had been living in idolatry, when they tried to rally the troops, they couldn't find a man to lead them—until chapter 11 . . .

DEFENDER OF GOD'S PEOPLE

A Topical Study of JUDGES 10:1, 2

When Jesus "expounded in all the Scriptures the things concerning Himself" to the two disciples on the road to Emmaus (Luke 24:27), the Book of Judges must have been part of the discourse, for the judges therein do indeed portray definite aspects of the One who was "ordained by God to be the Judge of the living and dead" (Acts 10:42) . . .

- Othniel fought to win Caleb's daughter as a bride.
  Jesus fought the ultimate battle on the Cross of Calvary to win you and me as His bride.
- Shamgar used that which was in his hand—an ox goad—to do battle against the Philistines.
  After using His hands to heal, bless, and feed multitudes, Jesus allowed His hand to be nailed to a Cross, and the "ox goad" of a spear to pierce His side in order to pay for our sins.

- Ehud drove a sword into the oppressor Eglon.
  Jesus used the sword of the Word to beat back Satan (Matthew 4).
- Deborah, a mother in Israel, sought deliverance for the people of Israel.
  Jesus wept for Jerusalem, desiring to gather His people under His wings as a mother hen gathers her chicks (Matthew 23:37).
- Samson pushed apart the pillars of the temple of Dagon with his outstretched arms and brought the temple down.
  Jesus stretched out His arms on the Cross and brought down the house of hell.
- Gideon was a man of humility who allowed light to shine from broken jars.
  Jesus, One who was meek and lowly (Matthew 11:29), allowed the light of God's love to shine forth when He was broken on the Cross.

Truly, one can see aspects of the personality of the true Judge, Jesus Christ, in the judges, and Tola is no exception . . .

Celebrate

Tola's dad's name, *Puah*, means "splendid." His grandfather's name, *Dodo*, means "beloved one." *Tola's* name, however, meant neither "splendid" nor "beloved," but "worm." This being the case, Tola was probably as obscure in his own time as he is today. He was a man of Issachar who dwelt in Ephraim. That is, he wasn't dwelling among his own people.

Jesus is depicted here. Not only did He leave His home in heaven to dwell among people who wouldn't receive Him (John 1:11), but in Psalm 22:6, He says, prophetically, "I am a worm and not a man."

The Hebrew word, *tola*—the plural of which is *tolaith*—is translated two ways in the Bible: as either "scarlet" or "worm." Why would the same word be used for both "scarlet" and "worm"? Because in Bible days, when people needed scarlet cloth, they would grind worms into a pasty, blood-red substance that would be used as a dye.

Why would Jesus say, "I am a worm?" Because, to reproduce, the tola would climb the trunk of a tree and fasten on a limb. Then the worm would lay the larva and cover the eggs with its body. Although the eggs would hatch, the worm wouldn't budge. So the larva would begin to feed on the body of the one who had given them life. As the tola gave its life for its young, its blood would leave a scarlet mark on the tree. After the dead worm fell, the bloody spot left on the limb of the tree would dry after three days, becoming a white, flaky substance that would fall to the ground like snow.

"Though your sins be as scarlet—*tola*—they shall be white as snow," Isaiah declares (1:18). Fastened to the tree of the Cross of Calvary, Jesus wouldn't budge until the work was finished. What work? The work that would allow you and me to be "hatched," to be born again. "Eat of My Body," He says. "Drink of My blood. I give My life for you" (Mark 14:22–24).

By His blood, Jesus not only saved us, but, like Tola in the text before us, He is the Judge who defends us. You see, Revelation 12:10 tells us that Satan accuses us day and night, going before the throne of the Father, saying, "Look at him. Look at her. They've blown it here. They've messed up there." But the Bible says the accuser was overcome by the blood of the Lamb and the word of testimony.

"If any man sin, we have an Advocate, a Defender with the Father—that is, Jesus Christ the righteous," John declares (see 1 John 2:1). This means that when we sin, although Satan will be at the throne of God pointing out our failures and shortcomings, we have a Defender—the Tola, the scarlet Worm, Jesus—who says, "Father, she has eaten of My body. He has tasted of My blood. They are clean."

Hearing the accusations of the prosecuting attorney, and listening to the defense of His Son, the Father hits the gavel in the courtroom of heaven and says, "Case dismissed for lack of evidence."

And celebration breaks forth.

Imitate

Unlike Samson, you might not be able to take down the temple of Dagon. Unlike Gideon, you might not be able to attack a massive army of 135,000 men. You may not be like any of the judges or heroes of the Old Testament. But you *can* be like Tola. Every single believer can go down in history as a "tola," as a defender of God's people simply by saying, "I refuse to be part of the accusatory nature and tactics of Satan. I will not listen to or talk about anything that is negative concerning any of God's people. I will not listen to 'prayer requests' that are mixed with gossip. I will not get involved in discussions about any of the sins or problems of believers. I will deal with the person directly, but I will not deal with gossip."

The Bible says that where there is no wood, the fire goes out (Proverbs 26:20). In other words, if we refuse to give ear to gossip, the mean-spirited fire of gossip and backbiting dies. When someone approaches me with information they feel is important for me to know regarding someone else in the Fellowship, I say, "Before you begin speaking, know that I will quote you on everything you say." And nine times out of ten, people change their minds about talking to me about someone else. I am not saying we are to ignore problems. I am, however, saying that we are to defend God's people rather than listen to gossip.

May we be those who take every opportunity to defend God's people even as we celebrate the fact that we are defended by our Tola, our Hero, Jesus Christ. May we be those who celebrate and imitate in His name.

11 **Judges 11:1**
Now Jephthah the Gileadite was a mighty man of valour, and he was the son of an harlot: and Gilead begat Jephthah.

Talk about an unlikely hero! Jephthah was the result of his father's relations with a harlot. In Jephthah's time and culture, being born illegitimately carried a terrible social stigma. Wherever he went, he would be the butt of jokes, teased, and taunted. Yet in Hebrews 11, Jephthah's name is recorded for all eternity as one of the giants of faith, one of the heroes of God's people.

Dear brother, precious sister—regardless of your past, no matter your reputation, if God used Jephthah, He can use you—for God loves to use the most unlikely, unqualified people.

"Look to the rock from which you were hewn and to the hole of the pit from which you were dug," declares the Lord (see Isaiah 51:1). In other words, "Consider where you've come from. And upon the basis of what I have already done in your life, look forward to how I will bless you and make your life fruitful in the future."

Every one of us was brought out of the pit, gang. There are no exceptions. Just look at the pit out of which we were brought . . .

- Look at Abraham. Even after he was called by God, even after he was ordained to be the father of faith, he still wavered, foundered, and fell. Fearing Pharaoh, he lied not once, but twice about his wife in order to save his own skin.
- Look at Moses. After he was called into ministry, he murdered a man, buried him in the sand, and ran for his life to the desert.
- Look at Jonah. He was called by God to usher in the world's greatest revival. But when the Ninevites began to acknowledge God and repent, Jonah was totally discouraged, wishing the Ninevites would have been blasted instead of blessed.
- Look at Peter. After spending three years with Jesus, watching His miracles, hearing His teaching, sharing meals with Him, conversing constantly with Him, he stood by the fire of the enemy and denied ever knowing Him.
- Look at Paul. He was a man so cruel and callous, so barbaric and brutal that when he finally did get saved, the early church initially refused to believe it.
- Look at John Mark. After receiving a call to the mission field, he got homesick and high-tailed it back home.

No matter where you look in the Word, you will find individuals who were in the pit, brought out of the pit by the One who had no fault whatsoever—Jesus Christ Himself.

Knowing this allows me to move on. I can say, "Lord, in spite of my failures, I'm still moving on in You according to Your grace, mercy, and love." Secondly, it allows me to reach out. When other people fail and fall, instead of coming down on them, talking about them, or finding fault with them, I'm free to reach out in love to them.

Folks, that tough guy who seems so hopeless and so out of it to you might be the next Jephthah in a future move of God. That fellow you think is bizarre, raunchy, or rude just might be the man God is tapping on the shoulder to lead the next revival.

Judges 11:2
And Gilead's wife bare him sons; and his wife's sons grew up, and they thrust out Jephthah, and said unto him, Thou shalt not inherit in our father's house; for thou art the son of a strange woman.

Growing up unwanted and unloved, Jephthah compensated by becoming the toughest kid on the block. How do I know? Read what happened after he left home . . .

Judges 11:3 (a)
Then Jephthah fled from his brethren, and dwelt in the land of Tob . . .

Jephthah headed for Tob—an area known for its marauders and murderers, its raiders and robbers.

Judges 11:3 (b)
. . . and there were gathered vain men to Jephthah, and went out with him.

I can see Jephthah and his men now: The Tob Mob, dressed in black leather jackets, riding loud, unmuffled donkeys from party to party.

Judges 11:4–7
And it came to pass in process of time, that the children of Ammon made war against Israel. And it was so, that when the children of Ammon made war against Israel, the elders of Gilead went to fetch Jephthah out of the land of Tob: And they said unto Jephthah, Come, and be our captain, that we may fight with the children of Ammon. And Jephthah said unto the elders of Gilead, Did not ye hate me, and expel me out of my father's house? and why are ye come unto me now when ye are in distress?

Threatened by the Ammonites, the Israelites turned to the toughest man they knew—Jephthah. "Fight for us," they begged. Now, asking Jephthah to fight would be like asking Mario Andretti for a ride to the grocery store, like asking Michael Jordan if he could help out the church basketball team. Jephthah fight? This was something he could do!

Judges 11:8–11
And the elders of Gilead said unto Jephthah, Therefore we turn again to thee now, that thou mayest go with us, and fight against the children of Ammon, and be our head over all the inhabitants of Gilead. And Jephthah said unto the elders of Gilead, If ye bring me home again to fight against the children of Ammon, and the LORD deliver them before me, shall I be your head? And the elders of Gilead said unto Jephthah, The LORD be witness between us, if we do not so according to thy words. Then Jephthah went with the elders of Gilead, and the people made him head and captain over them: and Jephthah uttered all his words before the LORD in Mizpeh.

This tough guy from Tob was made head of the entire Israelite army. And the story goes on . . .

Judges 11:12, 13
And Jephthah sent messengers unto the king of the children of Ammon, saying, What hast thou to do with me, that thou art come against me to fight in my land? And the king of the children of Ammon answered unto the messengers of Jephthah, Because Israel took away my land, when they came up out of Egypt, from Arnon even unto Jabbok, and unto Jordan: now therefore restore those lands again peaceably.

Before engaging in battle, Jephthah sought to bring about peace through diplomatic channels.

Judges 11:14–19
And Jephthah sent messengers again unto the king of the children of Ammon: And said unto him, Thus saith Jephthah, Israel took not away the land of Moab, nor the land of the children of Ammon: But when Israel came up from Egypt, and walked through the wilderness unto the Red sea, and came to Kadesh; Then Israel sent messengers unto the king of Edom, saying, Let me, I pray thee, pass through thy land: but the king of Edom would not hearken thereto. And in like manner they sent unto the king of Moab: but he would not consent: and Israel abode in Kadesh. Then they went along through the wilderness, and compassed the land of Edom, and the land of Moab, and came by the east side of the land of Moab, and pitched on the other side of Arnon, but came not within the border of Moab: for Arnon was the border of Moab. And Israel sent messengers unto Sihon king of the Amorites, the king of Heshbon; and Israel said unto him, Let us pass, we pray thee, through thy land into my place.

Jephthah recounts Israel's history in the land by reminding the king of Arnon that three hundred years earlier, as the Israelites came out of Egypt on their way to the Promised Land, they asked Sihon, who was king of the area, if they could pass through to go into Canaan.

Judges 11:20
But Sihon trusted not Israel to pass through his coast: but Sihon gathered all his people together, and pitched in Jahaz, and fought against Israel.

Not only did Sihon refuse passage, but he rallied his army and launched an offensive attack against Israel.

Judges 11:21, 22
And the LORD God of Israel delivered Sihon and all his people into the hand of Israel, and they smote them: so Israel possessed all the land of the Amorites, the inhabitants of that country. And they possessed all the coasts of the Amorites, from Arnon even unto Jabbok, and from the wilderness even unto Jordan.

God was with Israel, and when Sihon's men went down in defeat, the land became Israel's—a fact that has great bearing upon the Middle East situation to this day.

Judges 11:23, 24
So now the LORD God of Israel hath dispossessed the Amorites from before his people Israel, and shouldest thou possess it? Wilt not thou possess that which Chemosh thy god giveth thee to possess? So whomsoever the LORD our God shall drive out from before us, them will we possess.

Jephthah continues his argument by saying, "You take whatever Chemosh brings to you. Let us take what our God, Jehovah, has given us."

Judges 11:25–27
And now art thou any thing better than Balak the son of Zippor, king of Moab? did he ever strive against Israel, or did he ever fight

against them, While Israel dwelt in Heshbon and her towns, and in Aroer and her towns, and in all the cities that be along by the coasts of Arnon, three hundred years? why therefore did ye not recover them within that time? Wherefore I have not sinned against thee, but thou doest me wrong to war against me: the LORD the Judge be judge this day between the children of Israel and the children of Ammon.

Jephthah's third diplomatic argument is as follows: "We've been here three hundred years. Why are you choosing to raise this question *now?* No other country has."

Judges 11:28, 29
Howbeit the king of the children of Ammon hearkened not unto the words of Jephthah which he sent him. Then the Spirit of the LORD came upon Jephthah, and he passed over Gilead, and Manasseh, and passed over Mizpeh of Gilead, and from Mizpeh of Gilead he passed over unto the children of Ammon.

Jephthah was an illegitimate son, a hoodlum, a marauder—yet God said to him, "You're My man, Jephthah. You're the one for the job."

Judges 11:30, 31
And Jephthah vowed a vow unto the LORD, and said, If thou shalt without fail deliver the children of Ammon into mine hands, Then it shall be, that whatsoever cometh forth of the doors of my house to meet me, when I return in peace from the children of Ammon, shall surely be the LORD's, and I will offer it up for a burnt offering.

"If You give me victory over the Ammonites," Jephthah prayed, "I'll give You whatever is in the front yard of my house upon my return," no doubt thinking it would be a bull, a sheep, or a goat.

Judges 11:32, 33
So Jephthah passed over unto the children of Ammon to fight against them; and the LORD delivered them into his hands. And he smote them from Aroer, even till thou come to Minnith, even twenty cities, and unto the plain of the vineyards, with a very great slaughter. Thus the children of Ammon were subdued before the children of Israel.

The Lord heard Jephthah's prayer and honored his vow.

Judges 11:34, 35
And Jephthah came to Mizpeh unto his house, and, behold, his daughter came out to meet him with timbrels and with dances: and she was his only child; beside her he had neither son nor daughter. And it came to pass, when he saw her, that he rent his clothes, and said, Alas, my daughter! thou hast brought me very low, and thou art one of them that trouble me: for I have opened my mouth unto the LORD, and I cannot go back.

It would seem as though Jephthah did not expect his daughter to be home when he returned. Maybe she was away at college. Maybe she had moved out of the house. I don't know the specifics. But I'm certain that Jephthah was completely shocked when upon his arrival, the first one through his door was his daughter, his only child.

Judges 11:36
And she said unto him, My father, if thou hast opened thy mouth unto the LORD, do to me according to that which hath proceeded out of thy mouth; forasmuch as the LORD hath taken vengeance for thee of thine enemies, even of the children of Ammon.

In this verse, I hear Jephthah's daughter saying, "Dad, you're a man of integrity. Don't back down now." Parents, our kids want us to be godly. Our kids want us to be people of integrity. Our kids want us to excel in the things of God.

I'm sure at this point, all kinds of feelings and thoughts flooded Jephthah's mind . . .

"Nobody really heard me say that vow, so maybe I don't really need to keep it," or, *"Lord, You know I was under a lot of stress . . ."* or, *"Carrying out that vow will contradict my love for my daughter, so I can't keep it."*

How easy it would have been for Jephthah to rationalize this vow away. But watch what happens . . .

Judges 11:37–40
And she said unto her father, Let this thing be done for me: let me alone two months, that I may go up and down upon the mountains, and bewail my virginity, I and my fellows. And he said, Go. And he sent her away for two months: and she went with her companions, and bewailed her virginity upon the mountains. And it came to pass at the end of two months, that she returned unto her father, who did with her according to his vow which he had vowed: and she knew no man. And it was a custom in Israel, That the daughters of Israel went yearly to lament

the daughter of Jephthah the Gileadite four days in a year.

Did Jephthah really kill his daughter? Many scholars throughout history have said he indeed offered her to the Lord as a burnt offering. Others, however, have asked how that could be when God abhors such offerings. No, they insist, Jephthah didn't kill her—he simply set her aside to live a cloistered nun-like existence in the mountains, worshiping and serving God all the days of her life.

The second argument has real credence, for many translators have used the word "or" in place of "and" in verse 31, thus rendering the verse: "Then it shall be, that whatsoever cometh forth of the doors of my house to meet me, when I return in peace from the children of Ammon, shall surely be the Lord's dedicated to Him, *or* I will sacrifice it as a burnt offering." Even the King James Version gives the word "or" as an option.

Another translator's choice appears in verse 40, where, in the newer translations, the word "lament" is rendered "commemorate" or "communicate"—implying that for four days each year, Jephthah's daughter had interaction with other women.

So which is it? Did Jephthah's daughter die—or did she live out her days in seclusion?

I don't know. As I've studied both arguments, I find each very convincing. But this I do know: Whether Jephthah killed his daughter, or whether he sent her away, either way it was a tremendous sacrifice.

Was Jephthah right in either killing her or sending her away? For many years, I believed Jephthah's story was recorded simply as an illustration of what we *shouldn't* do, that he is an illustration of the kind of people we *shouldn't* be—making rash vows and then keeping them no matter the cost to others. But then I read Hebrews 11:32, where Jephthah is listed as one of the heroes of faith.

What does this mean?

Turn to Psalm 15 . . .

LORD, who shall abide in thy tabernacle? who shall dwell in thy holy hill? He that walketh uprightly, and worketh righteousness, and speaketh the truth in his heart. He that backbiteth not with his tongue, nor doeth evil to his neighbour, nor taketh up a reproach against his neighbour. In whose eyes a vile person is contemned; but he honoureth them that fear the LORD. He that sweareth to his own hurt, and changeth not. He that putteth not out his money to usury, nor taketh reward against the innocent. He that doeth these things shall never be moved. Psalm 15

God says we can be immovable, solid in our relationship with Him, when we swear to our own hurt and do not change. Gang, I believe the reason we are spiritually impotent both personally and corporately is because we do not keep our commitments. We make vows to the Lord and then when they start to hurt a little, we drop them . . .

- "It's January first, Lord. *This* is the year I'm going to read through the Bible. *This* is the year I'm going to seriously study Your Word. And I'm going to begin just as soon as the Rose Bowl is over. . . ."
- "I know I said I'd be at Bible study every Wednesday, but I didn't know *Law and Order* would be on. . . ."
- "Lord, I know I promised at the start of my marriage that not a day would go by that we wouldn't pray together—but that was before I knew he'd be such a doof . . ."

As a young lawyer, Attorney Black was invited to deliver the welcome address to the Governor of Georgia on a Monday night. With great care, he prepared his address—until a telegram arrived saying that the Governor's visit would be moved to Wednesday night. Mr. Black immediately wrote the committee that a previous engagement would prevent his being present on Wednesday night, saying, "No service to man or state could ever make me swerve from my commitment." Besides the pastor of his church, few people knew that the previous engagement to which Mr. Black referred was the regular Wednesday night prayer meeting which the young lawyer had committed to the Lord.

Why did Judge Black become a well-known judge in Georgia?

I believe it was because God responds to sacrificial commitments . . .

- I think of Hannah as she prayed, "Lord, I have no children. But if You bless me with a child, he shall be Yours." You know the story. After this sacrificial commitment, Hannah gave birth to Samuel—one of the greatest prophets of antiquity (1 Samuel 1).
- I think of Shammah. When the Philistines attacked and his companions fled in fear, Shammah said, "I'm not leaving." We read that the Spirit of God came upon him and he singlehandedly whipped the entire Philistine army (2 Samuel 23).
- I think of the widow who placed her last two mites in the temple treasury, little knowing that across the way, Jesus was sitting, watch-

ing, observing her sacrificial commitment (Mark 12).

- I think of Mary as she broke open her alabaster box and poured the ointment it contained over Jesus. So important was her commitment to Him, He said, "Wherever the gospel is preached, this deed will be talked about" (Matthew 26).

Sacrificial commitment moves the heart of God. And God not only responds to it, but He requires it. "I'll follow You anywhere," said the young man. "But first let me go home and have a goodbye party."

"After putting his hand to the plow, no man who turns back is worthy of the kingdom of God," Jesus answered (see Luke 9:62).

Why does the Lord require commitment? Is He some kind of ogre who takes pleasure in burdening His children?

Quite the opposite. There are three reasons why commitment is necessary. Mark them well . . .

First, *commitment cures complacency.* Think about it. When were you most in love with Jesus Christ? It might have been ten months ago or ten years ago, but I suggest it was when you were keeping your commitment to Him. You were up in the morning, seeking His face. Bible study was a priority. Carrying out the tasks He gave you was of highest importance. You were committed.

I have found that when I grow lazy in my commitment, my love begins to grow cold. I can't explain it, but I have certainly experienced it. If I don't keep my commitments to the Lord, I begin to lose my love for Him. That is why in Revelation 2, Jesus said to the church at Ephesus, "I have something against you. You have left your first love." He didn't say, "You have lost it." He said "You *left* it. Remember from whence thou art fallen. Repent and do thy first works again."

Church, please hear this. Remember how it was when you were doing well, and do those works again. What works? Were you reading the Word in the morning? Get up tomorrow morning and read it again. Were you going to worship on Sunday night? Go again. Were you taking time with your husband or wife to pray together every day? Do it again. The formula is so practical and so powerful: Go back and do the things you were doing when you were radically following and deeply in love with Jesus Christ. Do them again, and you'll find your love rekindled. Commitment cures complacency.

"That sounds legalistic," you say. And well it can . . .

When I stand on the bathroom scale and realize I've put on a few pounds, my tendency is to put on jogging shorts and shoes and run nine miles. Then I come back and say, "I will never do that again. And I don't run for about two months. Then I think, I gotta get in shape. *So out come my shoes and shorts once again.*

We do the same thing spiritually. "Okay," we say. "Commitment. I hear it. I see it. I'm going for it. Starting at three A.M. I'm going to spend four hours a day in prayer." We set the alarm for three o'clock and we're out of bed. But after a few days, we realize we'll never be able to keep it up.

Listen, folks—when you make your commitments, count the cost and make them practical and doable. Don't go for nine miles—start with nine yards and work your way up. Wouldn't it be wonderful if every one of us said, "Lord, I'm committing myself right now to spending five minutes in prayer every morning, where I will talk to You, worship You, and meet with You." Five minutes may sound like nothing—but if the truth were known, it's probably a lot more than most of us have been doing. Start with five minutes and ten verses every day. If you don't know where to start, start with the Gospel of John, and I promise you, you'll tap into a reality in your relationship with Jesus Christ that will whet your appetite for more as you begin to feel your first love rekindled and revived.

Secondly, *commitment rewards eternally.* Whatever you commit to Jesus Christ will be kept for you and given back to you in eternity (2 Timothy 1:12). When we get to heaven, no one will say, "Wow, I wish I would have slept in more on earth. I really wish I wouldn't have given so much to the church. I wish I would have spent more on toys for myself." No, every one of us will fall before the Lord, saying, "Thank You, Lord, for allowing us the opportunity to commit to You"—for even the smallest commitment of energy, money, time, talents, abilities, or gifts will impact our capacity to enjoy eternity.

Thirdly, *commitment is a response to Calvary.* "I beseech you, brethren, present your bodies to God, which is your reasonable service," said Paul (see Romans 12:1). Why is it reasonable to commit ourselves to developing a walk with Jesus? Because of what He's done for us. Great is the mystery of godliness that God was manifest in the flesh (1 Timothy 3:16)—that God became a Man and hung on the Cross of Calvary. Jesus' suffering is far deeper than we'll ever understand this side of heaven, for the fact remains that when He set aside His godly attributes and became a Man, He locked Himself into humanity forever. Why did He take such a huge step down? Because He loves me, and knew I desperately need a Savior. That is why Communion is so important, for as I consider the Cross, I cannot help but say, "Lord, I need to be committed to You."

Keep your commitments, precious people, and you will find yourself walking in the footsteps of that hero of faith, Jephthah. Oh, it will cost you. Yes, there will be some pain, some hurt, some sacrifice. But you'll find them far outweighed by the life and love of Jesus Christ burning in your heart, the anointing of the Spirit upon your life, and the blessing of God upon your service.

Jephthah pictures Jesus . . .

> *Jesus was born seemingly illegitimately, shunned by brothers who didn't believe in Him, and surrounded by some rough, tough Galilean fishermen. "Save us," Israel said to Jephthah. And one day, Jesus will do just that. The Spirit of the Lord came upon Jephthah as he crossed the Jordan. The Spirit of the Lord came upon Jesus when He was baptized in the Jordan. Jephthah sacrificed to the Lord. Jesus became a sacrifice to the Lord. Jesus kept His commitment—*
>
> *And yet even when we are faithless, our Greater than Jephthah is faithful still, for He cannot deny Himself (2 Timothy 2:13). That means, even if we choose not to keep our commitments, He remains faithful.*
>
> If Jesus remains faithful, I can be apathetic, *you might be thinking. Yes, you can—but you'll miss out on blessings that otherwise would have been yours both in this life and eternally. On the other hand, if you follow through on the commitments you made in the desperate times and rough days when you were on your knees with tears streaming down your cheeks, watch and see how momentum builds and your faith grows stronger than ever before.*
>
> *And even if you can't remember what you promised to do, ask the Lord, and He'll remind you. Say, "What have I committed to You in past days or years? What vows did I make? What promises did I give?"*

Watch and hear Him say, "You promised this. You committed to that. You have your word about this. You heard My heart on that." And do it. Remember from whence you're fallen. Repent, and do your first works again. Keep your commitments and watch and see how God will bless. He'll pick you up, take you on, and see you through if you give Him the opportunity today.

12 When you feel dog-tired at the end of a day, make sure it's not because you've been biting and barking, for nothing will wear you out or tear you down faster than being one who bites, devours, and complains. Paul warns us in Galatians 5 that if we bite and devour one another, we are to beware lest we be consumed by one another. Truly, biting and devouring, murmuring and complaining will cause one to feel dog-tired.

Here in chapter 12, we come across a group of people who were chronic complainers: the men of Ephraim. In chapter 8, when Gideon led the Israelites into battle against the Midianites, the men of Ephraim said, "How come we weren't part of the first wave of the attack? Why did we only get to take part in the mop-up operation?" Instead of rejoicing in the victory, they complained about the strategy. And here in chapter 12, on the heels of Jephthah's victory, we see the men of Ephraim complaining once again . . .

Judges 12:1
And the men of Ephraim gathered themselves together, and went northward, and said unto Jephthah, Wherefore passedst thou over to fight against the children of Ammon, and didst not call us to go with thee? we will burn thine house upon thee with fire.

In other words, the men of Ephraim not only wanted to fire Jephthah as judge—they wanted to burn him out completely.

Judges 12:2–4 (a)
And Jephthah said unto them, I and my people were at great strife with the children of Ammon; and when I called you, ye delivered me not out of their hands. And when I saw that ye delivered me not, I put my life in my hands, and passed over against the children of Ammon, and the LORD delivered them into my hand: wherefore then are ye come up unto me this day, to fight against me? Then Jephthah gathered together all the men of Gilead, and fought with Ephraim . . .

The tact and diplomacy that Gideon used so masterfully in chapter 8 to talk these men out of their jealousy didn't get very far in this situation. So here the tactic is changed as Jephthah, the tough fighter from Tob, said, "If that's the way you want to play, let's fight."

Judges 12:4 (b)
. . . and the men of Gilead smote Ephraim, because they said, Ye Gileadites are fugitives of Ephraim among the Ephraimites, and among the Manassites.

When the Israelites first entered the Promised Land, Gad, Reuben, and half the tribe of Manasseh chose to remain on the east side of the Jordan (Numbers 32). Because of this, they were often discriminated against by the other nine and a half tribes. So, when the men of Ephraim implied that the Gileadites were wimps, Gilead took Ephraim on in battle and whipped them.

Judges 12:5 (a)
And the Gileadites took the passages of Jordan before the Ephraimites . . .

Heading home in defeat, the Ephraimites were met by the Gileadites, who had reached the Jordan before them.

Judges 12:5 (b), 6 (a)
. . . and it was so, that when those Ephraimites which were escaped said, Let me go over; that the men of Gilead said unto him, Art thou an Ephraimite? If he said, Nay; Then said they unto him, Say now Shibboleth: and he said Sibboleth: for he could not frame to pronounce it right . . .

As is the case in our own country, different dialects began to develop throughout Israel, Using this to their advantage, the Gileadites required everyone waiting to cross the Jordan to say, *shibboleth,* which means "crossing" or "flowing stream." You see, the closest the Ephraimites could come to "shibboleth" was *sibboleth*—and their pronunciation was a dead giveaway. One word would cost them their lives. One word would make the difference between living and dying. Their destiny hinged on a single word.

Judges 12:6 (b), 7
. . . Then they took him, and slew him at the passages of Jordan: and there fell at that time of the Ephraimites forty and two thousand. And Jephthah judged Israel six years. Then died Jephthah the Gileadite, and was buried in one of the cities of Gilead.

Forty-two thousand men were killed because their speech betrayed them.

"I don't know Him. I have never had contact with Him," declared Peter.

"Ah, but your speech betrays you," said a little girl. "You are from Galilee" (see Mark 14:70).

Jesus said our words will either justify or betray us (Matthew 12:37). Truly, our speech condemns us over and over again. But there is a word, a single word that will allow us to cross Jordan into the Promise of heaven. And that word is *kuriat,* or "Lord."

Romans 10 says that, to be saved, we must believe in our heart and confess with our mouth that Jesus is Lord. Those who think Jesus is anything less than God—that He is a moral teacher or a good man—are not pronouncing His name correctly. To confess Him as Lord means to submit to His authority rather than to simply live life according to how one thinks it should be lived.

Because Satan has blinded men's eyes (2 Corinthians 4:4), no man can say Jesus is Lord except by the Holy Ghost (1 Corinthians 12:3). Therefore, if you have made the proclamation that Jesus is Lord, it was through the miraculous, marvelous work of the Holy Spirit, who gave you the ability to see the truth.

"No man can come to me except the Father draws Him," Jesus declared (see John 6:44). You weren't "talked into" becoming a Christian because the Bible says there is none that seeks after God (Romans 3:11).

Do you realize how blessed you are? Satan blinded you—but God saved you. How wonderful it is that we are able to say "Jesus is Lord" on this side of the Jordan, on this side of eternity.

Judges 12:8–10
And after him Ibzan of Bethlehem judged Israel. And he had thirty sons, and thirty daughters, whom he sent abroad, and took in thirty daughters from abroad for his sons. And he judged Israel seven years. Then died Ibzan, and was buried at Bethlehem.

This verse doesn't say the Spirit of God came upon Ibzan, or that he did anything particularly noteworthy. Evidently, he had his hands full with his thirty sons, especially considering the Jews taught that every father owed his sons three things: to teach him the Law, to teach him a trade, and to find him a wife.

Bible commentator J. Vernon McGee called Ibzan a picture of mediocrity because Ibzan seemed to place all of his emphasis on his family. Contrary to the present flow of teaching today in the body of Christ, it's an observation worth considering—for although Ibzan had the position, he didn't move in power because his priority was his family.

Mom and Dad, we must spend time with our children—nurturing them, disciplining them, helping them. But they must not be the priority of our lives. Seek ye first the kingdom of God, Jesus said. I think a lot of times if we would spend more time seeking God and less time seeking how to be a better parent or husband or wife, we would find ourselves being better parents, better husbands, better wives (Matthew 6:33).

Judges 12:11–15
And after him Elon, a Zebulonite, judged Israel; and he judged Israel ten years. And Elon the Zebulonite died, and was buried in Aijalon in the country of Zebulun. And after him Abdon the son of Hillel, a Pirathonite, judged Israel. And he had forty sons and thirty nephews, that rode on threescore and ten ass colts: and he judged Israel eight years. And Abdon the son of Hillel the Pirathonite died, and was buried in Pirathon in the land of Ephraim, in the mount of the Amalekites.

Elon means "plain"—and that is what Elon was. Like Ibzan, Elon and Abdon held the position of judge, but didn't take advantage of it. They had opportunity, but evidently did nothing with it.

13

In chapter 13, we come to one of the all-time interesting and instructive stories: the story of Samson . . .

Judges 13:1
And the children of Israel did evil again in the sight of the LORD; and the LORD delivered them into the hand of the Philistines forty years.

The Philistines were a strong, sea-faring people who originally came from the island of Crete. Settling in the southern coastal region of Israel, they built five cities and dominated the area for several hundred years. Proficient in smelting iron, they had weapons the Israelites and Canaanites had never even seen.

Judges 13:2–5
And there was a certain man of Zorah, of the family of the Danites, whose name was Manoah; and his wife was barren, and bare not. And the angel of the LORD appeared unto the woman, and said unto her, Behold now, thou art barren, and bearest not: but thou shalt conceive, and bear a son. Now therefore beware, I pray thee, and drink not wine nor strong drink, and eat not any unclean thing: For, lo, thou shalt conceive, and bear a son; and no rasor shall come on his head: for the child shall be a Nazarite unto God from the womb: and he shall begin to deliver Israel out of the hand of the Philistines.

The Hebrew word, *Nazar,* means "separated one." *Nazarites* were men who took a vow to separate themselves from the world in order to be fully consecrated to God for a given period of time—usually six months to a year. Samson, however, was unique in that he was to be a Nazarite all the days of his life.

From Numbers 6, we know that a Nazarite was one who was consecrated to serve God in three specific ways: He was to touch no wine—not even grapes. He was to let his hair grow. And he was to stay away from anything that had died.

Why were these three things the mark of a Nazarite?

Wine is a symbol of earthly joy. "Be not drunk with wine, but rather be filled with the Spirit," Paul declares (Ephesians 5:18). The long hair of a Nazarite was to serve as an identifiable outward sign of his consecration—just as we are to be identified by the outward signs of love (John 13:35). To keep himself pure, the Nazarite was to keep away from decay and death. We are also to be very careful we don't become involved with the dead things of this world, unequally yoked with unbelievers lest we find ourselves becoming defiled, dried up, dead.

Judges 13:6–8
Then the woman came and told her husband, saying, A man of God came unto me, and his countenance was like the countenance of an angel of God, very terrible: but I asked him not whence he was, neither told he me his name: But he said unto me, Behold, thou shalt conceive, and bear a son; and now drink no wine nor strong drink, neither eat any unclean thing: for the child shall be a Nazarite to God from the womb to the day of his death. Then Manoah intreated the LORD, and said, O my Lord, let the man of God which thou didst send come again unto us, and teach us what we shall do unto the child that shall be born.

I like this! When his wife told him she had seen the angel of the Lord, Manoah didn't say, "You flipped out, lady." No, realizing his wife had some sort of very special dynamic spiritual revelation and understanding, he wisely said, "Lord, please confirm it."

Listen carefully, guys: The nature of women is such that they will often be more spiritually perceptive than you are. So when they share with you a revelation or an understanding, don't reject it. Be like Manoah, and ask the Lord to confirm it.

Judges 13:9
And God hearkened to the voice of Manoah; and the angel of God came again unto the woman as she sat in the field: but Manoah her husband was not with her.

God heard the prayer of Manoah, but then sent an angel to his wife. Why? Perhaps it was because she was sitting in the field. More than likely, as provider for his family, Manoah was plowing the field. His wife, on the other hand, was sitting in the field, in a place of receptivity.

Your wife can be a tremendous help to you, brother, because she may have even more time to sit in the presence of the Lord than you do. Don't chafe against or feel threatened by this—take advantage of it! The angel came again to the woman, but it was in response to the prayer of her husband.

Judges 13:10, 11 (a)
And the woman made haste, and ran, and shewed her husband, and said unto him, Behold, the man hath appeared unto me, that came unto me the other day. And Manoah arose, and went after his wife . . .

Guys, there is a time to follow your wife—and here is a perfect example. Manoah's wife was the one through whom the Lord dealt with this matter—and Manoah was wise, secure, and strong enough to follow her.

Judges 13:11 (b), 12
. . . and came to the man, and said unto him, Art thou the man that spakest unto the woman? And he said, I am. And Manoah said, Now let thy words come to pass. How shall we order the child, and how shall we do unto him?

Manoah was right on when he asked, "How are we supposed to raise this child?"

The Bible says, "Train up a child in the way he should go" (Proverbs 22:6).

Judges 13:13, 14
And the angel of the LORD said unto Manoah, Of all that I said unto the woman let her beware. She may not eat of any thing that cometh of the vine, neither let her drink wine or strong drink, nor eat any unclean thing: all that I commanded her let her observe.

Although Manoah had asked God how He wanted Samson to be raised, the angel immediately speaks of the behavior of Samson's mother, for unbeknownst to Manoah, the issue wasn't the child. The issue was the parent.

The same is still true. We might be tempted to think, *My kids can't do that, but I can. My kids can't go there, but I can. My kids can't watch that, but I can because I have the maturity to handle it.* Wait a minute. It's not what you say, but rather who you are that will affect your kids. It's not a matter of laying down rules for them to follow, but rather of providing an example they can follow. It's who you are personally—even when they're not around or when you think they can't see you—that will most greatly impact who they will become ultimately. That is why the best thing you can do for your kids is to maintain your own walk with the Lord.

Judges 13:15–18
And Manoah said unto the angel of the LORD, I pray thee, let us detain thee, until we shall have made ready a kid for thee. And the angel of the LORD said unto Manoah, Though thou detain me, I will not eat of thy bread: and if thou wilt offer a burnt offering, thou must offer it unto the LORD. For Manoah knew not that he was an angel of the LORD. And Manoah said unto the angel of the LORD, What is thy name, that when thy sayings come to pass we may do thee honour? And the angel of the LORD said unto him, Why askest thou thus after my name, seeing it is secret?

The word translated "secret" is literally "wonderful." Whose name is Wonderful? Isaiah 9:6 says His name shall be called Wonderful, Counselor, Almighty God, the Everlasting Father, the Prince of Peace. It's Jesus.

Judges 13:19–22
So Manoah took a kid with a meat offering, and offered it upon a rock unto the LORD: and the angel did wondrously; and Manoah and his wife looked on. For it came to pass, when the flame went up toward heaven from off the altar, that the angel of the LORD ascended in the flame of the altar. And Manoah and his wife looked on it, and fell on their faces to the ground. But the angel of the LORD did no more appear to Manoah and to his wife. Then Manoah knew that he was an angel of the LORD. And Manoah said unto his wife, We shall surely die, because we have seen God.

"Show us the Father," said Philip, "and it will suffice us."

"Have I been with you so long, Philip? Don't you know that he that hath seen Me hath seen the Father?," answered Jesus (John 14:9).

Exodus 33:20 says no man can see God and live. Manoah and his wife saw God—but because it was the second Person of the Godhead, Jesus Christ, they did not die.

Judges 13:23, 24
But his wife said unto him, If the LORD were pleased to kill us, he would not have received a burnt offering and a meat offering at our hands, neither would he have shewed us all these things, nor would as at this time have told us such things as these. And the woman bare a son, and called his name Samson: and the child grew, and the LORD blessed him.

Samson literally means, "Shining as the sun." No doubt it was the prayer of his parents that their miracle son would be a light to his people in the dark days of the judges.

Judges 13:25
And the Spirit of the LORD began to move him at times in the camp of Dan between Zorah and Eshtaol.

"The Spirit of the Lord began to move upon him." The secret of Samson's strength was not in his arms, although with his arms he would take the jawbone of an ass and kill 1,000 Philistines. The secret of his strength was not in his back, although upon his back he would carry a city gate thirty-eight miles. The secret of his strength was not in his hair, although his hair would be thick enough to weave upon a loom. No, the secret of Samson's strength was the Spirit of God alone.

When you think about Samson, erase the mental image of a huge Charles Atlas strolling down the streets of Gaza. You see, as we read his story, we'll see Samson move throughout the Philistine cities rather unknown. If he was a huge individual with bulging muscles and unbelievable size, he would have been spotted and recognized by all. That is why I suggest that Samson was probably very average, very ordinary—corroborated by the fact that the Philistines told Delilah to figure out the secret of his strength. Surely, they thought, he had some magical charm on his body, or some sort of idol in his pocket.

When the Spirit of God didn't move in his life, you could probably have kicked sand in Samson's face. But when the Spirit of God moved upon him—watch out!

14

Judges 14:1 (a)
And Samson went down to Timnath, and saw a woman . . .

Here lies the summation of Samson's life: He went down. He saw a woman. As has been rightly said, "Samson was a he-man with a she-weakness."

Judges 14:1 (b), 2 (a)
. . . in Timnath of the daughters of the Philistines. And he came up, and told his father and his mother, and said, I have seen a woman . . .

These, Samson's first recorded words, are telling indeed.

Judges 14:2 (b), 3
. . . in Timnath of the daughters of the Philistines: now therefore get her for me to wife. Then his father and his mother said unto him, Is there never a woman among the daughters of thy brethren, or among all my people, that thou goest to take a wife of the uncircumcised Philistines? And Samson said unto his father, Get her for me; for she pleaseth me well.

Samson is already showing chinks in his armor. Not only is he seeking to link himself to the world, but he's not respecting his parents.

Judges 14:4
But his father and his mother knew not that it was of the LORD, that he sought an occasion against the Philistines: for at that time the Philistines had dominion over Israel.

What Satan means for evil, God uses for good (Genesis 50:20). Even though Samson is rebellious, God will still use the situation to accomplish His purposes.

Judges 14:5 (a)
Then went Samson down, and his father and his mother, to Timnath, and came to the vineyards of Timnath:

A Nazarite was to stay away from grapes. Watch out, Samson.

Judges 14:5 (b)
. . . and, behold, a young lion roared against him.

First Peter 5:8 says Satan is a roaring lion, seeking whom he may devour. Here, in a place where he shouldn't have been, Samson comes face to face with just such a lion.

Judges 14:6 (a)
And the Spirit of the LORD came mightily upon him, and he rent him as he would have rent a kid, and he had nothing in his hand . . .

Truly, this is the only way to deal with the Adversary. Satan is a roaring lion who cannot be dealt with in our own strength.

Satan tempted Jesus three times in the wilderness with heavy-duty temptations (Matthew 4). But Jesus was victorious because the Spirit of God had already descended upon Him (Matthew 3:16). Apart from the Spirit, you and I will get eaten up, munched on, and wiped out. Satan is sneaky, subtle, and strong. Don't underestimate him. But the Spirit of God upon your life will give you victory as you seek His anointing daily, as you call upon Him in the morning hours. And when Satan comes later on in the day, even if, like Samson, you're by a vineyard where you shouldn't be, God's Spirit will give you power to do battle against him.

Judges 14:6 (b)–9
. . . but he told not his father or his mother what he had done. And he went down, and talked with the woman; and she pleased Samson well. And after a time he returned to take her, and he turned aside to see the carcase of the lion: and, behold, there was a swarm of bees and honey in the carcase of the lion. And he took thereof in his hands, and went on eating, and came to his father and mother, and he gave them, and they did eat: but he told not them that he had taken the honey out of the carcase of the lion.

Why didn't Samson tell his parents? Because the lion was dead, and he was a Nazarite. He knows he's in error here—but it seemed so sweet; it seemed so right.

Judges 14:10
So his father went down unto the woman: and Samson made there a feast; for so used the young men to do.

First, Samson walked through the vineyard (v. 5). Then he reached into the carcass (v. 9). Here, he's throwing a party—a drunken brawl, really—as was the Philistine custom.

Judges 14:11
And it came to pass, when they saw him, that they brought thirty companions to be with him.

This being a "bachelor party," since Samson didn't bring his own groomsmen, the Philistines supplied thirty men to serve in that capacity.

Judges 14:12–14
And Samson said unto them, I will now put forth a riddle unto you: if ye can certainly declare it me within the seven days of the feast, and find it out, then I will give you thirty sheets and thirty change of garments: But if ye cannot declare it me, then shall ye give me thirty sheets and thirty change of garments. And they said unto him, Put forth thy riddle, that we may hear it. And he said unto them, Out of the eater came forth meat, and out of the strong came forth sweetness. And they could not in three days expound the riddle.

The custom remains today wherein the groom gives the groomsmen in his wedding party small gifts as tokens of his appreciation. With so many guys to buy for, Samson devised a way where he wouldn't be out the money for thirty gifts.

Judges 14:15 (a)
And it came to pass on the seventh day, that they said unto Samson's wife . . .

When these guys realized they weren't going to get any wedding prizes, they appealed to Samson's bride . . .

Judges 14:15 (b), 16 (a)
. . . Entice thy husband, that he may declare unto us the riddle, lest we burn thee and thy father's house with fire: have ye called us to take that we have? is it not so? And Samson's wife wept before him . . .

"If you don't find the answer to that riddle," the Philistines threatened, "we're going to burn you and your father's house." So Samson's wife cried to her husband . . .

Judges 14:16 (b)–18 (a)
. . . and said, Thou dost but hate me, and lovest me not: thou hast put forth a riddle unto the children of my people, and hast not told it me. And he said unto her, Behold, I have not told it my father nor my mother, and shall I tell it thee? And she wept before him the seven days, while their feast lasted: and it came to pass on the seventh day, that he told her, because she lay sore upon him: and she told the riddle to the children of her people. And the men of the city said unto him on the seventh day before the sun went down, What is sweeter than honey? and what is stronger than a lion?

This, of course, was the answer to the riddle.

Judges 14:18 (b), 19 (a)
. . . And he said unto them, If ye had not plowed with my heifer, ye had not found out my riddle. And the Spirit of the LORD came upon him, and he went down to Ashkelon, and slew thirty men of them, and took their

spoil, and gave change of garments unto them which expounded the riddle . . .

Samson's groomsmen got the clothes they were promised—but Ashkelon being a Philistine city, the garments were stained with the blood of their Philistine brothers.

Judges 14:19 (b), 20
. . . And his anger was kindled, and he went up to his father's house. But Samson's wife was given to his companion, whom he had used as his friend.

With Samson in a furious rage, his wife was given to his best man.

15

Judges 15:1–3
But it came to pass within a while after, in the time of wheat harvest, that Samson visited his wife with a kid; and he said, I will go in to my wife into the chamber. But her father would not suffer him to go in. And her father said, I verily thought that thou hadst utterly hated her; therefore I gave her to thy companion: is not her younger sister fairer than she? take her, I pray thee, instead of her. And Samson said concerning them, Now shall I be more blameless than the Philistines, though I do them a displeasure.

Now Samson is really burned up. Watch what he does in the heat of anger.

Judges 15:4 (a)
And Samson went and caught three hundred foxes . . .

The Hebrew word translated "foxes," can either mean foxes or jackals. Since jackals travel in packs, this reference is probably to jackals.

Judges 15:4 (b), 5
. . . and took firebrands, and turned tail to tail, and put a firebrand in the midst between two tails. And when he had set the brands on fire, he let them go into the standing corn of the Philistines, and burnt up both the shocks, and also the standing corn, with the vineyards and olives.

Interestingly enough, Samson's wife was initially fearful of getting burned (14:15). Yet when she betrayed her husband, she set into motion events that would cause the entire area to erupt in flames.

Judges 15:6
Then the Philistines said, Who hath done this? And they answered, Samson, the son in law of the Timnite, because he had taken his wife, and given her to his companion. And the Philistines came up, and burnt her and her father with fire.

It's never right to do wrong to do right. Samson's wife may have thought she was protecting her father by betraying her husband—but her plan "backfired" completely.

Judges 15:7, 8 (a)
And Samson said unto them, Though ye have done this, yet will I be avenged of you, and after that I will cease. And he smote them hip and thigh with a great slaughter . . .

The idiom, "hip and thigh" means "top to bottom." In other words, Samson walloped the Philistines.

Judges 15:8 (b)
. . . and he went down and dwelt in the top of the rock Etam.

After walloping the Philistines, Samson heads for the hills to wait and see what would happen next.

Judges 15:9–11
Then the Philistines went up, and pitched in Judah, and spread themselves in Lehi. And the men of Judah said, Why are ye come up against us? And they answered, To bind Samson are we come up, to do to him as he hath done to us. Then three thousand men of Judah went to the top of the rock Etam, and said to Samson, Knowest thou not that the Philistines are rulers over us? what is this that thou hast done unto us? And he said unto them, As they did unto me, so have I done unto them.

This is Samson's Golden Rule. As they did to me, I'm doing to them.

"They burned me, so I burned them," Samson said.

Jesus, however, said, "As you want others to do to you, do to them" (Luke 6:31).

Judges 15:12, 13
And they said unto him, We are come down to bind thee, that we may deliver thee into the hand of the Philistines. And Samson said unto them, Swear unto me, that ye will not fall upon me yourselves. And they spake unto him, saying, No; but we will bind thee fast, and deliver thee into their hand: but

surely we will not kill thee. And they bound him with two new cords, and brought him up from the rock.

In this account, the only time we see the Israelites mustering an army was to capture one of their own. That's the way it can be with us sometimes. All too often, we seek to capture our own men when we fight other believers who don't look at doctrine precisely the same way we do.

Judges 15:14, 15
And when he came unto Lehi, the Philistines shouted against him: and the Spirit of the LORD came mightily upon him, and the cords that were upon his arms became as flax that was burnt with fire, and his bands loosed from off his hands. And he found a new jawbone of an ass, and put forth his hand, and took it, and slew a thousand men therewith.

Here's Samson—tied up by the men of Judah, turned over to the Philistines—when suddenly, the Spirit of God comes upon him. He pops the ropes and starts swinging the jawbone of a donkey. When he's done, one thousand Philistines lay dead.

This cracks me up. I mean, the Philistines had the most advanced weapon system of their day. But in Judges 3, Shamgar killed six hundred of them with an ox goad. And here, twelve chapters later, one thousand more are beaten with the jawbone of a donkey. Later on, Goliath—the greatest Philistine of them all—will be beaten with a stone and a sling. Isn't that just like the Lord to use the foolish things of the world to confound the wise, the weak to show up the strong? Look at us—ox goads, jawbones, stones and all. We're perfect examples of the foolish things of the world confounding the wise (1 Corinthians 1:27).

In your own personal battles, God can use whatever is in your hand. "That's nothing," the world will scoff. But with the Spirit of God—it becomes something mighty.

Judges 15:16, 17
And Samson said, With the jawbone of an ass, heaps upon heaps, with the jaw of an ass have I slain a thousand men. And it came to pass, when he had made an end of speaking, that he cast away the jawbone out of his hand, and called that place Ramath-lehi.

Ramath-lehi means "The place of the lifting up of the jawbone," or, "Jawbone Heights." Samson names this area after his great exploit.

Judges 15:18
And he was sore athirst, and called on the LORD, and said, Thou hast given this great deliverance into the hand of thy servant: and now shall I die for thirst, and fall into the hand of the uncircumcised?

Wait a minute. Hadn't Samson just said, "With the jaw of an ass *I* have slain a thousand men"? (v. 16) But as his throat gets drier, realizing how helpless he really is, he calls out to the Lord. God has ways of tempering our triumphs with trial because otherwise triumphs become points of pride.

Judges 15:19 (a)
But God clave an hollow place that was in the jaw, and there came water thereout; and when he had drunk, his spirit came again, and he revived:

This is truly the goodness and matchless grace of God.

Judges 15:19 (b)
. . . wherefore he called the name thereof En-hakkore, which is in Lehi unto this day.

Enhakkore means "The well of him who cried." Before, Samson christened the area "Jawbone Heights." But now it's "The well of him who cried." Let's be careful, folks. If the Lord uses us, let's always remember it's *Him.* Without Him, we couldn't last a moment.

Judges 15:20
And he judged Israel in the days of the Philistines twenty years.

It was a time of peace, a time of prosperity. For twenty years, Samson did real well. When you think of Samson, please don't only remember his sins. He was a man who was mightily used by God, who had a real love for God, and who is singled out in the New Testament as one of the giants of faith (Hebrews 11:32).

16

For twenty years, Samson did well—and then he went to Gaza . . .

Judges 16:1–3
Then went Samson to Gaza, and saw there an harlot, and went in unto her. And it was told the Gazites, saying, Samson is come hither. And they compassed him in, and laid wait for him all night in the gate of the city, and were quiet all the night, saying, In the morning, when it is day, we shall kill him.

And Samson lay till midnight, and arose at midnight, and took the doors of the gate of the city, and the two posts, and went away with them, bar and all, and put them upon his shoulders, and carried them up to the top of an hill that is before Hebron.

Seeing Samson in the lodging of a harlot, the Gazites said, "We got him! We'll wait by the gate, and when he leaves in the morning, we'll kill him." But in the middle of the night, Samson strode past the Gazites, uprooted the gates, and carried them to a hill outside Hebron. The hill could either be one four and one-half miles or thirty-eight miles from Gaza. Carrying the massive city gates on his shoulders, Samson's feat was amazing.

Judges 16:4 (a)
And it came to pass afterward, that he loved a woman in the valley of Sorek . . .

Sorek means "Valley of the choice vine." Sorek was a border town with the reputation of a border town. Again, Samson was to stay away from grapes, but he keeps toying with the things that he is supposed to avoid. He keeps lingering on the border, straddling the fence.

Judges 16:4 (b)
. . . whose name was Delilah.

Oh, Samson, her name should have tipped you off, for the Hebrew word *delal* means "to weaken or impoverish."

Judges 16:5
And the lords of the Philistines came up unto her, and said unto her, Entice him, and see wherein his great strength lieth, and by what means we may prevail against him, that we may bind him to afflict him: and we will give thee every one of us eleven hundred pieces of silver.

The source of Samson's strength wasn't bulging biceps, massive muscles, terrific triceps, or powerful thighs. These would have been obvious to his enemies and they wouldn't have had to bribe Delilah to discover the source of his strength. No, the source of Samson's strength was singular: it was the Holy Spirit.

Judges 16:6–10
And Delilah said to Samson, Tell me, I pray thee, wherein thy great strength lieth, and wherewith thou mightest be bound to afflict thee. And Samson said unto her, If they bind me with seven green withs [bowstrings] that were never dried, then shall I be weak, and be as another man. Then the lords of the Philistines brought up to her seven green withs which had not been dried, and she bound him with them. Now there were men lying in wait, abiding with her in the chamber. And she said unto him, The Philistines be upon thee, Samson. And he brake the withs, as a thread of tow is broken when it toucheth the fire. So his strength was not known. And Delilah said unto Samson, Behold, thou hast mocked me, and told me lies: now tell me, I pray thee, wherewith thou mightest be bound.

Isn't this an amazing story?

Judges 16:11–13
And he said unto her, If they bind me fast with new ropes that never were occupied, then shall I be weak, and be as another man. Delilah therefore took new ropes, and bound him therewith, and said unto him, The Philistines be upon thee, Samson. And there were liers in wait abiding in the chamber. And he brake them from off his arms like a thread. And Delilah said unto Samson, Hitherto thou hast mocked me, and told me lies: tell me wherewith thou mightest be bound. And he said unto her, If thou weavest the seven locks of my head with the web.

Watch out, Samson. Now you're speaking of your hair, a sign of your vow as a Nazarite, a symbol of your consecration.

Judges 16:14
And she fastened it with the pin, and said unto him, The Philistines be upon thee, Samson. And he awaked out of his sleep, and went away with the pin of the beam, and with the web.

Samson must have thought he was doing pretty well in not letting Delilah get to him. That can happen to us, too. We say, "I haven't really been honest with those who ask me the reason I am the way I am. I've kind of hinted at it, but I haven't come out and said, 'The reason I'm not going to the party you're inviting me to is because I'm a believer. Jesus Christ has changed my life. I want to keep my life focused on Him. I want to be filled with Him. I want to be used by Him. I'm a Christian.'" The problem is, if you're not being honest, like Samson, you'll be invited again and again. Don't play games. Say, "This is who I am. This is why I am the way I am," and you'll save yourself lots of heartache and heartbreak.

Judges 16:15, 16
And she said unto him, How canst thou say, I love thee, when thine heart is not with me? thou hast mocked me these three times, and hast not told me wherein thy great strength lieth. And it came to pass, when she pressed him daily with her words, and urged him, so that his soul was vexed unto death;

So constantly did Delilah pester him, Samson wanted to die—which, ironically, was the end result of her pestering.

Judges 16:17
That he told her all his heart, and said unto her. There hath not come a rasor upon mine head; for I have been a Nazarite unto God from my mother's womb: if I be shaven, then my strength will go from me, and I shall become weak, and be like any other man.

Rather than keeping his vow of consecration, Samson gives in to Delilah, doubtless knowing he was in for a haircut.

Judges 16:18
And when Delilah saw that he had told her all his heart, she sent and called for the lords of the Philistines, saying, Come up this once, for he hath shewed me all his heart. Then the lords of the Philistines came up unto her, and brought money in their hand.

This time, the Philistines brought money because they must have heard in Delilah's voice that she had finally discovered the source of Samson's strength. Indeed she had.

If you want to be strong in the things of God, the source of strength is the Holy Spirit, and the secret of that strength lies in consecration, in choosing to say, "I'm not going to weaken or impoverish my spirit in Gaza, in Sorek, or with Delilah."

Judges 16:19 (a)
And she made him sleep upon her knees . . .

Every time Samson is tied up, he's sleeping. Therefore, I can't help but wonder if Samson wasn't unusually vulnerable to this kind of stupidity because he was tired. Even for those who love God and serve Him, there is a danger in becoming fatigued, weary, tired. Be warned and be wise because that's when Delilah's voice suddenly sounds reasonable.

"Come unto Me, and you'll find rest for your souls," Jesus says. This story could have ended so differently. This giant of faith could have come out, could have kept on going—but he was lulled to sleep on Delilah's knees, rather than praying on his.

Judges 16:19 (b), 20 (a)
. . . and she called for a man, and she caused him to shave off the seven locks of his head; and she began to afflict him, and his strength went from him. And she said, The Philistines be upon thee, Samson. And he awoke out of his sleep, and said, I will go out as at other times before, and shake myself . . .

The source of Samson's strength was the Holy Spirit. The secret of his strength was his consecration. Some people are consecrated—disciplined and dedicated. But they are not recipients of the power of the Spirit. Although they understand the secret of strength, they don't have the source of power. Others have received the power of the Spirit—they move in the arena of the miraculous—but there's no consecration, dedication, or discipline. The winning combination is the source *and* the secret, inward filling *and* outward, noticeable consecration.

Judges 16:20 (b)
. . . And he wist not that the Lord was departed from him.

This verse is the most tragic in the entire book. *How could Samson be so stupid?* we wonder. I suggest he knew Delilah was no good, that he knew Delilah was setting him up. I mean, he had already seen that three times previously. He wasn't dumb. But I believe what was happening in his mind was the same thing that happens in ours. You see, God had told him that, as a Nazarite, he must not touch grapes, must not touch carcasses, must not cut his hair. He touched grapes—and nothing happened. He touched a carcass—and nothing happened. So, he must have thought that if he cut his hair nothing would happen.

We may also think *Maybe the Bible isn't really as strict as it sounds. Maybe it doesn't really matter if I compromise a little here and a little there. Maybe I can get away with it. Maybe it's OK.* But it's not, and we won't, for it doesn't work that way.

What a shock it must have been to Samson when he suddenly found himself weak, helpless, and wiped out.

Judges 16:21 (a)
But the Philistines took him, and put out his eyes . . .

This verse perfectly portrays the progression of sin. First, sin blinds. Long before his eyes were put out, Samson was blinded because he thought there would be no repercussions of his sin. Dear saint, if you are persisting in sin right now, I'll tell you what will happen: A blinding will take place, and you'll think your sin doesn't really matter. But notice what happened to Samson, for there is a second step . . .

Judges 16:21 (b)
. . . and brought him down to Gaza, and bound him with fetters of brass . . .

Secondly, sin binds. Just as Samson's arms were bound with fetters, sin in our lives holds us captive. We no longer move in the same way we once moved. We no longer experience the same joy we once experienced, the same power we once knew. But there's a third step . . .

Judges 16:21 (c)
. . . and he did grind in the prison house.

Sin grinds. Around and around and around Samson went, grinding at a wheel like an ox grinding grain. His life literally was spent going round and round in circles. "Why is my life such a grind?" we ask. "Why do I feel like I'm going in circles?" It's the result of sin.

Judges 16:22 (a)
Howbeit . . .

How I love this word! This giant of a man who had giant problems with sin would yet experience the goodness and grace of God upon his life.

Judges 16:22 (b)
. . . the hair of his head began to grow again after he was shaven.

Our God is the God of the second chance—and the third chance, and the thirty-third chance. Samson was about to be given a second chance, but mark it well: It took time. Yet, although Samson had to go through a season of pain, slowly but surely, his hair began to grow.

Samson's hair grew—but his eyesight never returned. Certain things are lost forever because of sin. The longer you live, the more you see the grace of God. He restores the years the locust has eaten (Joel 2:25). He gives beauty for ashes, the oil of joy for mourning, and the garment of praise for the spirit of heaviness (Isaiah 61:3). But it is also true that there are permanent repercussions when we sin. Be not deceived. God is not mocked. As seen in Samson's life, whatever a man sows, that shall he also reap (Galatians 6:7).

Judges 16:23 (a)
Then the lords of the Philistines gathered them together for to offer a great sacrifice unto Dagon their god . . .

The Philistines borrowed Dagon, the fish god, from the Assyrians. That's why when Jonah was sent to the Assyrians, God delivered him to them in a fish.

Judges 16:23 (b), 24
. . . and to rejoice: for they said, Our god hath delivered Samson our enemy into our hand. And when the people saw him, they praised their god: for they said, Our god hath delivered into our hands our enemy, and the destroyer of our country, which slew many of us.

One of the greatest tragedies of sin is that it gives the enemies of God a reason to rejoice.

Judges 16:25–28
And it came to pass, when their hearts were merry, that they said, Call for Samson, that he may make us sport. And they called for Samson out of the prison house; and he made them sport: and they set him between the pillars. And Samson said unto the lad that held him by the hand, Suffer me that I may feel the pillars whereupon the house standeth, that I may lean upon them. Now the house was full of men and women; and all the lords of the Philistines were there; and there were upon the roof about three thousand men and women, that beheld while Samson made sport. And Samson called unto the LORD, and said, O Lord GOD, remember me, I pray thee, and strengthen me, I pray thee, only this once, O God, that I may be at once avenged of the Philistines for my two eyes.

In these three relatively short verses, we see a reversal of the events of the previous three chapters. You see, although as a Nazarite, Samson exhibited a certain degree of dedication, he previously had no devotion. Yes, he was dedicated to his work. Yes, he took on the Philistines—but, as far as we know, he never offered sacrifice to the Lord. He never expressed worship to the Lord. He was a man dedicated to service, but he had no devotional life. Here, however, we see Samson offering his life to God rather than making demands from God.

Secondly, although Samson had authority, he

previously thought he had no accountability. He thought he had no accountability to his countrymen, to his parents, or to God—as seen in his breaking of all three of his Nazarite vows. Yet here we see him led to the temple by a mere lad because he couldn't get there alone. Accountability is linked to humility, and humility to humiliation. I wish it didn't work that way—but it does.

Finally, although Samson had great power, he previously had no purity. Jesus said, "If your right eye offend you pluck it out" (Matthew 5:29). Here, with both of his eyes plucked out, Samson was able to see past the realm of the physical world that had dominated his life.

Judges 16:29, 30 (a)
And Samson took hold of the two middle pillars upon which the house stood, and on which it was borne up, of the one with his right hand, and of the other with his left. And Samson said, Let me die with the Philistines . . .

Samson had experienced great success and great failure. And at this point, he's saying, "Lord, just one more exploit, then get me out. I want to die. I want to go home." I point this out because it's my personal belief that, had Samson prayed differently and desired differently, he could have gone on to be used of God yet again. I know some of you feel that, because you have failed in the past, you can never be used in the future. Not so. The Lord could have used Samson again, but instead answered Samson's prayer and called him home.

Judges 16:30 (b)
. . . And he bowed himself with all his might; and the house fell upon the lords, and upon all the people that were therein. So the dead which he slew at his death were more than they which he slew in his life.

Samson's greatest moment was not twenty years of beating back the Philistines in his life, but at the moment of his death.

For topical study of Judges 16:27–30, see "Dying to Greatness" below.

Judges 16:31
Then his brethren and all the house of his father came down, and took him, and brought him up, and buried him between Zorah and Eshtaol in the burying place of Manoah his father. And he judged Israel twenty years.

Although Samson flirted with sin throughout his life, God used him powerfully and remained faithful even in his death.

DYING TO GREATNESS

A Topical Study of JUDGES 16:27–30

Samson was a man with unparalleled potential. He was born into a godly home. He was dedicated and consecrated to God from the day of his birth. He was called to significant ministry even before he was born. He could have and should have done so much. But in the end, his life has been summarized by some as a life of mediocrity.

Yet, although Samson missed fantastic opportunity, we read in Hebrews 11 that he is one of the few men who were inducted into God's "Hall of Faith." This means that, although in our estimation, Samson might be described up as mediocre, God saw something in Samson that placed him in a very select group that made him a giant in God's economy.

I suggest to you that Samson plays a monumental role in God's economy because he portrays the Person of Jesus Christ in a most wonderful way.

"How can this be?" you ask. "Samson ignored the counsel of his godly parents. He was ensnared with Philistine women. He was proud and arrogant. How can it be that he is a picture of Jesus?"

In Matthew 12:40, Jesus reached back to the story of a mediocre man named Jonah and said, "As Jonah was in the belly of the whale for three days and nights, so will the Son of Man be in the center of the earth, buried. And even as Jonah was spewed out, so will I rise again." In other words, Jesus was able to reach back to Jonah and say, "This guy pictures My Resurrection." And I suggest He could do the same with Samson.

I suggest He could say, "Samson pictures Me—not My Resurrection, but My death. As he stood with his hands outstretched, pushing against the pillars, saying, 'Let me die that the enemies of Israel might perish,' so, too, with arms outstretched, I died that the hordes of hell might be beaten back."

To me, this is very liberating . . .

Liberating

I know that I am a man of mediocrity. I have blessing, potential, and opportunity that God graciously entrusted to me. You do, too. But we have messed up. We haven't followed through. We haven't been good stewards. Like Samson, every one of us has dropped the ball. Like Samson, every one of us has missed the mark. Like Samson, every one of us has messed up. As a result, we hear the voices of the Philistines as they make fun, boo, and make sport, saying, "You're supposed to be a Christian? You're supposed to be a godly woman? You're supposed to be a leader, a servant? How can that be? Look how you've dropped the ball."

Then Jesus comes on the scene. When He cried triumphantly on the Cross, "It is finished," He brought the house down and silenced our enemies. When He toppled Satan's house of cards, He paid the price for all of our sins and all of our mediocrity.

"There is therefore now no condemnation to them who are in Christ Jesus" (Romans 8:1). "Their sin and iniquity I will remember no more" (Hebrews 8:12). You're forgiven. I'm forgiven. We're free.

Illuminating

I might not be able to kill Philistines or to judge Israel. I may not be able to be a conqueror or a mighty man. But I can do what Samson did. You see, Samson's moment of greatness came not in the life he lived, but in the death he chose. The enemy was dealt a devastating blow on the day he said, "Let me die."

You might not be able to kill Goliaths. You might not be able to take on Philistines. You might not be able to call down fire like the heroes of old. But this you can do: You can die. Jesus said, "If any man come after Me, let him deny himself, take up his cross, and follow Me" (Matthew 16:24). You will do more damage to the kingdom of hell; you will have a greater impact for God; you will be rewarded by the Lord to the extent that you die.

Any of us can choose to die. Any of us can say, "Lord, what they're saying about me isn't right. What's happening to me isn't fair. But I'm choosing to let go of my rights, of my reputation, of what I think. I'm choosing to die."

You see, there can be no reconciliation apart from death (Hebrews 9:22). If a man and wife are at odds, there can be no reconciliation until one of them chooses to die. If a child and parent are at odds, there can be no reconciliation until one of them chooses to die. If two neighbors or brothers are at odds, there is only one way to reconciliation: death. Someone must say, "I'm not going to defend myself. I'm not going to stand up for my rights. I'm not going to do what I think ought to be done. I'm going to follow Jesus, who, when He was wronged said, 'Father, forgive them.' I'm going to follow the One who didn't deserve to be crucified, but who chose to die for me that I might be reconciled to the Father."

What about this, husband? You can't understand why your wife isn't as submissive as Scripture commands her to be. Die.

What about this, wife? You can't believe your husband wants to go there, do this, or lead you in that way. Die.

What about this, teenager? You think your dad's an idiot or that your mom is unfair. You might not be able to lead a Bible study on your campus, but the greatest thing you can do is to give up your own point of view and die.

When the Roman soldiers came to break the legs of Jesus, they found that He was already dead. Why did He die so quickly? I suggest it is because He knew that the sooner He died, the sooner would come His resurrection. If He had hung on the Cross, insisting on His rights, His way, His turn to defend Himself, He would have struggled hour after hour, day after day. But the sooner He died, the sooner He let go, the sooner there was Resurrection and glory. The same is true for us.

Let go. Give up. Die. And watch what will happen. The sooner you die, the sooner there will be resurrection. Right now you can let go of the axe you've been grinding, of the battle you've been fighting, of the grudge you've been holding. Right now you can say, "Let me die that the demons might be brought down, that Satan might be beaten back, that God's kingdom might be brought about in my heart and in my home."

When a man takes up the cross, it means he's choosing something that might be painful for him, but that will be redemptive to others round about him. Therefore, I challenge you as I challenge myself to move from mediocrity to greatness not by what we do in life, but in how we let go and choose to die. If we do, the temple of Dagon will collapse, and we'll go down in God's economy as men and women of greatness.

17 The final five chapters of the Book of Judges are fairly well summed up in verse 6 of chapter 17, where we read: "In those days, there was no king in Israel, but every man did that which was right in his own eyes." Such was the case in the house of Micah—a man who wanted riches, religion, and respectability. But, playing by his own rules and doing what was right in his own eyes, we'll see how he ends up losing all three . . .

Judges 17:1, 2 (a)
And there was a man of mount Ephraim, whose name was Micah. And he said unto his mother, The eleven hundred shekels of silver that were taken from thee, about which thou cursedst, and spakest of also in mine ears, behold, the silver is with me; I took it . . .

In the days of the judges, the average annual wage would be ten shekels of silver. This being the case, no wonder Micah's mother was upset when she discovered 1,100 shekels of silver were missing. This would have been her life's savings, her retirement fund. No wonder she pronounced a curse on the one who stole her money. Knowing his mother had placed a curse on the person who had taken her money, Micah owned up to his actions and confessed to the theft.

Judges 17:2 (b)
. . . And his mother said, Blessed be thou of the Lord, my son.

A blessing came from the same mouth that had uttered a curse. This ought not to have been (James 3:10). Our speech should always be seasoned with grace (Colossians 4:6). Our words should always be gracious, redemptive, restorative, healing, and helpful.

Judges 17:3, 4
And when he had restored the eleven hundred shekels of silver to his mother, his mother said, I had wholly dedicated the silver unto the Lord from my hand for my son, to make a graven image and a molten image: now therefore I will restore it unto thee. Yet he restored the money unto his mother; and his mother took two hundred shekels of silver, and gave them to the founder, who made thereof a graven image and a molten image: and they were in the house of Micah.

"Because this money is dedicated to the Lord," said Micah's mother, "I'm going to use it to make you two images." So she paid a silversmith two hundred shekels to make a couple of idols for her boy. Some commentators believe the graven image was a replica of the ark of the covenant.

What could possibly have been Micah's mother's rationale? I suggest she sincerely believed she would be helping her son to worship the Lord by giving him some statues to assist him in focusing on the Lord's presence. The Second Commandment is: "Thou shalt make no graven image" (Exodus 20:4)—but Micah's mother was doing right in her own eyes.

Judges 17:5 (a)
And the man Micah had an house of gods, and made an ephod, and teraphim . . .

An ephod was worn by the high priest. Teraphim were small statues or figurines that served as family gods.

Judges 17: 5 (b), 6
. . . and consecrated one of his sons, who became his priest. In those days there was no king in Israel, but every man did that which was right in his own eyes.

By making his son a priest, Micah completes his collection. Now he has his own private gods, his own private priest, his own private interpretation of what should be done in worship.

"Know this," Peter warns. "No prophecy of Scripture is of any private interpretation, for prophecy never came by the will of man, but holy men of God spoke as they were moved by the Holy Spirit" (2 Peter 1:21).

Judges 17:7–10
And there was a young man out of Bethlehem Judah of the family of Judah, who was a Levite, and he sojourned there. And the man departed out of the city from Bethlehem Judah to sojourn where he could find a place: and he came to mount Ephraim to the house of Micah, as he journeyed. And Micah said unto him, Whence comest thou? And he said unto him, I am a Levite of Bethlehem Judah, and I go to sojourn where I may find a place. And Micah said unto him, Dwell with me, and be unto me a father and a priest, and I will give thee ten shekels of silver by the year, and a suit of apparel, and thy victuals. So the Levite went in.

Although Micah had already appointed his son as priest, his private religion was evidently not working like he had hoped. So when a genuine Levite came by, Micah offered him a new suit, ten shekels of silver, and free room and board to be his private priest. The Levite, also doing what was right in his own eyes, and perhaps thinking he could steer Micah away from idolatry, thought, *Why not?*

Judges 17:11–13
And the Levite was content to dwell with the man; and the young man was unto him as one of his sons. And Micah consecrated the Levite; and the young man became his priest, and was in the house of Micah. Then said Micah, Now know I that the LORD will do me good, seeing I have a Levite to my priest.

Does every Levite qualify to be a priest? No. Only the sons of Aaron. Levites who were not direct descendants of Aaron were simply to assist in the tabernacle and the temple. So, once again, we see Micah's theology amiss, his understanding skewed. Nonetheless, he feels like he's headed for tremendous blessing.

- "I did it my way," crooned Frank Sinatra.
- "Have it your way," says Burger King.
- "It's your thing, do what you want to do; born free, as free as the wind blows; I gotta be me," everyone sang in the 60s.

That's what was happening in the days of the judges. "Don't put restrictions on me," the people of Israel said. "I'll determine what's best for me." And in our generation, the same thing is happening. Existential philosophy planted in the 50s bore fruit in the 60s, causing people to say today, "The only absolute is that there are no absolutes."

What has been the fruit of this?

Oppression and depression.

We think we see what's best for our lives. But the Bible says we only see through a glass darkly at best (1 Corinthians 13:12). If you do what's right in your own sight you might experience a little bit of pleasure now, but a lifetime of pain will follow. On the other hand, if you do what's right in God's sight, you might experience a little pain now, but you'll experience pleasure for eternity (Psalm 16:11).

18

Judges 18:1
In those days there was no king in Israel: and in those days the tribe of the Danites sought them an inheritance to dwell in; for unto that day all their inheritance had not fallen unto them among the tribes of Israel.

The portion of land given to the tribe of Dan was in the south, near that given to the tribes of Benjamin and Judah. But we read in chapter 1 how the Danites were unable to defeat the Canaanites dwelling in their territory. With Philistines to the west of them, Amonites to the east of them, and Judah to the south of them, the tribe of Dan is about to make a mass migration to the very northernmost part of Israel in search of an easier place to live.

Maybe, like the Danites, you're looking for an easier place to live. Maybe you're tired of your situation, your surroundings, your circumstances. But let me tell you, the Danites are about to embark on a huge mistake because when they go north, they will meet all sorts of problems that will plague them throughout their history. In the north, they will become a weakened, idolatrous tribe. They should have stuck it out where God had sent them. They should have fought the fight and become the people God intended them to be. But they wanted out. And they're jumping out of the proverbial frying pan into the fire as they migrate north.

Judges 18:2–4
And the children of Dan sent of their family five men from their coasts, men of valour, from Zorah, and from Eshtaol, to spy out the land, and to search it; and they said unto them, Go, search the land: who when they came to mount Ephraim, to the house of Micah, they lodged there. When they were by the house of Micah, they knew the voice of the young man the Levite: and they turned in thither, and said unto him, Who brought thee hither? and what makest thou in this place? and what hast thou here? And he said unto them, Thus and thus dealeth Micah with me, and hath hired me, and I am his priest.

Jesus warned about hirelings—ministers or servants whose only interest is in wages and earnings (John 10:12, 13). Micah's priest is the quintessential hireling.

Judges 18:5, 6
And they said unto him, Ask counsel, we pray thee, of God, that we may know whether our way which we go shall be prosperous. And the priest said unto them, Go in peace: before the LORD is your way wherein ye go.

Micah's "priest" couldn't have been more mistaken. How could the tribe of Dan go in peace when they were running away from the very place God told them to be?

Judges 18:7–10
Then the five men departed, and came to Laish, and saw the people that were therein, how they dwelt careless, after the manner of the Zidonians, quiet and secure; and there

was no magistrate in the land, that might put them to shame in any thing; and they were far from the Zidonians, and had no business with any man. And they came unto their brethren to Zorah and Eshtaol: and their brethren said unto them, What say ye? And they said, Arise, that we may go up against them: for we have seen the land, and, behold, it is very good: and are ye still? be not slothful to go, and to enter to possess the land. When ye go, ye shall come unto a people secure, and to a large land: for God hath given it into your hands; a place where there is no want of any thing that is in the earth.

Sidonians were Phoenicians living in the region of present-day Lebanon. A quiet people, they looked like easy pickings. Besides, the land was fruitful and productive. So, doing right in their own eyes, the Danites prepared for war.

Judges 18:11–13
And there went from thence of the family of the Danites, out of Zorah and out of Eshtaol, six hundred men appointed with weapons of war. And they went up, and pitched in Kirjath-jearim, in Judah: wherefore they called that place Mahaneh-dan unto this day: behold, it is behind Kirjath-jearim. And they passed thence unto mount Ephraim, and came unto the house of Micah.

Micah's house was a busy place—everyone seemed to drop by!

Judges 18:14
Then answered the five men that went to spy out the country of Laish, and said unto their brethren, Do ye know that there is in these houses an ephod, and teraphim, and a graven image, and a molten image? now therefore consider what ye have to do.

In other words, "You know what to do."

Judges 18:15, 16
And they turned thitherward, and came to the house of the young man the Levite, even unto the house of Micah, and saluted him. And the six hundred men appointed with their weapons of war, which were of the children of Dan, stood by the entering of the gate.

Imagine you're Micah. You open your door to find the five men who had been in your house earlier—and behind them are six hundred men armed to the teeth.

Judges 18:17–19
And the five men that went to spy out the land went up, and came in thither, and took the graven image, and the ephod, and the teraphim, and the molten image: and the priest stood in the entering of the gate with the six hundred men that were appointed with weapons of war. And these went into Micah's house, and fetched the carved image, the ephod, and the teraphim, and the molten image. Then said the priest unto them, What do ye? And they said unto him, Hold thy peace, lay thine hand upon thy mouth, and go with us, and be to us a father and a priest: is it better for thee to be a priest unto the house of one man, or that thou be a priest unto a tribe and a family in Israel?

"Come with us," said the Danites to the Levite, after raiding Micah's shrine. "Now you're priest for only one man. We'll let you be priest of our entire tribe."

Judges 18:20 (a)
And the priest's heart was glad . . .

"Far out! A promotion! God is honoring me," the priest thought mistakenly.

Judges 18:20 (b)–22
. . . and he took the ephod, and the teraphim, and the graven image, and went in the midst of the people. So they turned and departed, and put the little ones and the cattle and the carriage before them. And when they were a good way from the house of Micah, the men that were in the houses near to Micah's house were gathered together, and overtook the children of Dan.

Micah and his neighbors caught up with the tribe of Dan.

Judges 18:23, 24 (a)
And they cried unto the children of Dan. And they turned their faces, and said unto Micah, What aileth thee, that thou comest with such a company? And he said, Ye have taken away my gods which I made . . .

How impressive could gods be that not only had to be made, but that could be stolen?

Judges 18:24 (b)–27
. . . and the priest, and ye are gone away: and what have I more? And what is this that ye say unto me, What aileth thee? And the children of Dan said unto him, Let not thy voice be heard among us, lest angry fellows

run upon thee, and thou lose thy life, with the lives of thy household. And the children of Dan went their way: and when Micah saw that they were too strong for him, he turned and went back unto his house. And they took the things which Micah had made, and the priest which he had, and came unto Laish . . .

Micah wanted riches, religion, respectability—but he lost all three. He lost his silver idols that were worth a lot of money; he lost his gods; he lost his respectability when he had to back down in front of his neighbors. He lost it all.

Why?

Because he was doing what was right in his own eyes—and it was so very wrong. We have to be careful not to move upon what we think is right in any given situation. How we must be a people who seek the Lord in all things great and small. We must not trust our own wisdom or our own understanding. We must seek wisdom, guidance, and direction from God about *every* matter.

Judges 18:27 (b), 28
. . . unto a people that were at quiet and secure: and they smote them with the edge of the sword, and burnt the city with fire. And there was no deliverer, because it was far from Zidon, and they had no business with any man; and it was in the valley that lieth by Beth-rehob. And they built a city, and dwelt therein.

The Sidonians should not have been smitten because they were not Canaanites. On the contrary, Deuteronomy 13:12–15 declares that if any Jewish city was involved in idolatry, that city was to be burned. Therefore, the guys from Dan were the ones who should have been burned. Instead, they burned the Sidonians.

The same is still true. I've often noticed that when we burn someone in our heart, it's often indicative of our own sin.

Judges 18:29–31
And they called the name of the city Dan, after the name of Dan their father, who was born unto Israel: howbeit the name of the city was Laish at the first. And the children of Dan set up the graven image: and Jonathan, the son of Gershom, the son of Manasseh, he and his sons were priests to the tribe of Dan until the day of the captivity of the land. And they set them up Micah's graven image, which he made, all the time that the house of God was in Shiloh.

The "designer faith" Micah developed had several things going for it . . .

First, it had practical convenience. With a "priest" in his own house, Micah didn't have to go far to get to church. He didn't have to fight traffic. He didn't get stuck in the parking lot. And there are people today who don't come to church for those very reasons.

Secondly, Micah's religion had family involvement. With his son as a priest and money coming in from his mom, it was a real family endeavor.

Thirdly, it could boast cultural tolerance. Everyone in his day had teraphim—family idols—and Micah was no exception.

Fourth, it had a positive message. "Go in peace. God is with you," Micah's "priest" said—even though the people were headed in the wrong direction.

We see the same tendencies today. Yet practical convenience, family involvement, cultural tolerance, and a positive message notwithstanding, Micah's religion was tragically impotent. Whether it's national events or personal crises, the fact is, only the true and living God can see us through. That's the problem with boutique religions, designer faith, and stay-at-home spirituality. In the day of trouble—and trouble will come—it doesn't work. That's what Micah discovered.

Not only was Micah's religion tragically impotent, but it was also truly unnecessary. Micah was a man looking for riches, religion, respectability—spending all of his energy and all of his time developing his own religious system. Yet right over the hill from where he lived was the house of God, the ark of the covenant, the place where he could have received true guidance, fulfillment, and help. Shiloh, the house of God, was right over the hill.

Precious people—right over the hill from where you are, lies that which you truly seek. Tonight, you can be on your knees before the Lord—talking to Him, worshiping Him, receiving from Him, being blessed by Him. The choice is yours: You can continue to play religious games, doing what you think is right, going through religious motions—or you can be in the presence of the true and living God intimately, personally, in reality.

How long has it been since you've really been in the presence of God? I'm not asking how long it has been since you've been to a Bible study, or to church. I'm asking how long it's been since you've really been in the presence of God. God's tabernacle was at Shiloh—where the true ark sat, where real priests served, where the Shekinah glory of God abode. All that Micah longed for was right there all the time. Granted, it was eighty miles away. Granted, it would take effort to get there. But if he had only gone to Shiloh, he would have been blessed.

What does *Shiloh* mean? "The sent one." Who is the ultimate sent One? Jesus. Where is Jesus? He said He would be wherever two or three are gathered in His name. Don't fall for designer religiosity, gang. Instead, say, "All of my days, I'm going to be where Jesus is. I'm going to be at Shiloh, where people gather in His name."

Our privileged responsibility is to tell people, "You need to be in the presence of Jesus. There is a special awareness of His 'there-ness' when people gather together at Shiloh, when people meet together in His name. Don't fall into the error of Micah because someday you'll need to be strong. And when that day comes, it will be too late to gain strength. You need to be in the place where you're seeking His face and experiencing His grace *now.* You need to be at Shiloh."

19 Judges 19, 20, and 21 dramatically depict the depravity and darkness of the people of Israel at this point in their history. These are grim and gruesome chapters, but they are important, for I believe there are lessons for us both personally and nationally . . .

Judges 19:1 (a)
And it came to pass in those days, when there was no king in Israel . . .

"There was no king in Israel." We've heard this phrase before, but here it appears again as a summary statement of the people of Israel. They had no king; they were not submitted to authority; and every man did right in his own sight.

We hear this yet today. "Every person must determine what is right for him personally," our culture declares. "What's right for me may not be right for you. There are no absolutes." This thinking is absolutely wrong. There *are* absolutes. The entire universe is governed by absolute laws—one of which is gravity. If you defy it and try to bend the rules, you'll find yourself bruised, battered, and bloody. And that's precisely what happened to the people of Israel.

Judges 19:1 (b)
. . . that there was a certain Levite sojourning on the side of mount Ephraim, who took to him a concubine out of Bethlehem Judah.

Although the practice of taking a concubine was allowable in the Old Testament Law, it wasn't ordained or approved by the Lord. Yet, because the people were already practicing this, there is regulation in the Old Testament. However, as you move through the redemptive history of God's people, you see that He makes it clear it was not His divine design. Of all people, a Levite ought not to have been involved in this practice.

Judges 19:2
And his concubine played the whore against him, and went away from him unto her father's house to Bethlehem Judah, and was there four whole months.

When his concubine was unfaithful to him, the Levite tasted the bitter fruit of the choice he made.

Judges 19:3
And her husband arose, and went after her, to speak friendly unto her, and to bring her again, having his servant with him, and a couple of asses: and she brought him into her father's house: and when the father of the damsel saw him, he rejoiced to meet him.

It is no wonder that the concubine's father rejoiced to meet the Levite. After all, the Levite was a seemingly religious man who was evidently willing to try to tame his wild, flirtatious daughter.

Judges 19:4–8
And his father in law, the damsel's father, retained him; and he abode with him three days: so they did eat and drink, and lodged there. And it came to pass on the fourth day, when they arose early in the morning, that he rose up to depart: and the damsel's father said unto his son in law, Comfort thine heart with a morsel of bread, and afterward go your way. And they sat down, and did eat and drink both of them together: for the damsel's father had said unto the man, Be content, I pray thee, and tarry all night, and let thine heart be merry. And when the man rose up to depart, his father in law urged him: therefore he lodged there again. And he arose early in the morning on the fifth day to depart: and the damsel's father said, Comfort thine heart, I pray thee. And they tarried until afternoon, and they did eat both of them.

So persuasive was the concubine's father that one night's lodging for the Levite turned into five.

Judges 19:9
And when the man rose up to depart, he, and his concubine, and his servant, his father in law, the damsel's father, said unto him, Behold, now the day draweth toward evening, I pray you tarry all night: behold, the day groweth to an end, lodge here, that thine

heart may be merry; and to morrow get you early on your way, that thou mayest go home.

It seems this father-in-law is doing what was right in his own eyes because when the Levite came for his wife, he was detained by her father. Why? I suggest it's because the father thought he could be part of the redeeming, healing process. But such is not the case. Dear dad, precious mom—the best thing you can do for your married children is to make them seek the Lord and spend time with their mates. Don't try to be a mediator. Don't try to be part of the solution. Don't try to keep them dependent on you.

And kids—if you're married, don't go running home to mom and dad every time you have a fight or a difficulty because, even though you will eventually make up with your mate, your parents will have a hard time forgetting the problem. Resentment will be inevitable, which is probably why the third leading cause of divorce is in-law problems.

Judges 19:10 (a)
But the man would not tarry that night, but he rose up and departed . . .

On the evening of the fifth day, the Levite could be persuaded to stay no longer.

Judges 19:10 (b)–12
. . . and came over against Jebus, which is Jerusalem; and there were with him two asses saddled, his concubine also was with him. And when they were by Jebus, the day was far spent; and the servant said unto his master, Come, I pray thee, and let us turn in into this city of the Jebusites, and lodge in it. And his master said unto him, We will not turn aside hither into the city of a stranger, that is not of the children of Israel; we will pass over to Gibeah.

Gibeah was about four miles from Jerusalem. Although the Levite thought he would be safer with his own people, we'll see that this will prove to be disastrous. Some believers think they must isolate and insulate themselves from the world—even to the point of patronizing only dentists, mechanics, or carpet cleaners that display the sign of the fish on their business cards. This was evidently the mindset of the Levite. When my car is broken, however, I'm not primarily concerned if the guy's a Christian. I just want him to fix my car.

Judges 19:13–15
And he said unto his servant, Come, and let us draw near to one of these places to lodge all night, in Gibeah, or in Ramah. And they passed on and went their way; and the sun went down upon them when they were by Gibeah, which belongeth to Benjamin. And they turned aside thither, to go in and to lodge in Gibeah: and when he went in, he sat him down in a street of the city: for there was no man that took them into his house to lodging.

Night having fallen, the Levite sits in the town square, where, according to custom, someone would offer him lodging. It was supposed to be the city's responsibility to take in those who were passing through in need of a place to stay. But none offered him lodging.

Judges 19:16–20
And, behold, there came an old man from his work out of the field at even, which was also of mount Ephraim; and he sojourned in Gibeah: but the men of the place were Benjamites. And when he had lifted up his eyes, he saw a wayfaring man in the street of the city: and the old man said, Whither goest thou? and whence comest thou? And he said unto him, We are passing from Bethlehem Judah toward the side of mount Ephraim; from thence am I: and I went to Bethlehem Judah, but I am now going to the house of the LORD; and there is no man that receiveth me to house. Yet there is both straw and provender for our asses; and there is bread and wine also for me, and for thy handmaid, and for the young man which is with thy servants: there is no want of any thing. And the old man said, Peace be with thee; howsoever let all thy wants lie upon me; only lodge not in the street.

Finally, a man of Ephraim—from the same region as the Levite—offered lodging in his home.

Judges 19:21–22
So he brought him into his house, and gave provender unto the asses: and they washed their feet, and did eat and drink. Now as they were making their hearts merry, behold, the men of the city, certain sons of Belial, beset the house round about, and beat at the door, and spake to the master of the house, the old man, saying, Bring forth the man that came into thine house, that we may know him.

This, of course, brings to mind the story of Lot in Genesis 19. Keep in mind, these are Israelites.

The Bible says homosexuality was not to be allowed in any city of God's people. But they were doing what was right in their own sight—just like we do today. The problem is, God is our Creator, Designer. And, as Creator, He is all-wise. He says, "I made you. I know how you work individually and as a society. If you take the path of homosexuality, it will lead to disaster." But the Benjamites thought otherwise.

Judges 19:23
And the man, the master of the house, went out unto them, Nay, my brethren, nay, I pray you, do not so wickedly; seeing that this man is come into mine house, do not this folly.

To this day in the Middle East, there is an understanding that if someone comes into your home, even if he is your worst enemy, you are obligated to give him lodging and protection for three days. That's not what the Bible said. It's what the culture decreed.

Judges 19:24
Behold, here is my daughter a maiden, and his concubine; them I will bring out now, and humble ye them, and do with them what seemeth good unto you: but unto this man do not so vile a thing.

Here, the old man, the master of the house, is doing right in his own eyes. You see, in that culture, when a man entered a home, it was imperative that the host go to every means possible to insulate his guest from any difficulty. So, culturally, the old man is doing right by saying, "Take my daughter and the concubine—just don't bother my guest." But Scripturally, morally, even logically, what he's doing is an abomination.

How could this be? We wonder. And yet it's the result of a culture doing what's right in their sight. Women, be thankful for Jesus Christ because He is the true Liberator of women. Wherever the gospel has gone, women have been elevated, for in Christ, there is neither male nor female. In Christ, we are co-heirs (Galatians 3:28).

Judges 19:25
But the men would not hearken to him: so the man took his concubine, and brought her forth unto them; and they knew her, and abused her all the night until the morning: and when the day began to spring, they let her go.

This was a cowardly act indeed with horrific repercussions.

Judges 19:26–28 (a)
Then came the woman in the dawning of the day, and fell down at the door of the man's house where her lord was, till it was light. And her lord rose up in the morning, and opened the doors of the house, and went out to go his way: and, behold, the woman his concubine was fallen down at the door of the house, and her hands were upon the threshold. And he said unto her, Up, and let us be going. But none answered . . .

The concubine was dead.

Judges 19:28 (b)–30
. . . Then the man took her up upon an ass, and the man rose up, and gat him unto his place. And when he was come into his house, he took a knife, and laid hold on his concubine, and divided her, together with her bones, into twelve pieces, and sent her into all the coasts of Israel. And it was so, that all that saw it said, There was no such deed done nor seen from the day that the children of Israel came up out of the land of Egypt unto this day: consider of it, take advice, and speak your minds.

The Levite chops his concubine into twelve pieces, and sends a piece of her body to each one of the Twelve Tribes. It was a telegram they would never forget. When the people of Israel received this very graphic message, they had a right to be outraged. But, as the story goes on, it is clear they did not seek the Lord in response.

Thus, we've seen a man who as doing right in his own eyes in protecting his guest, even though it cost the life of a woman. We've seen a Levite who did right in his own eyes by seeking retaliation. And we're about to see an entire nation doing right in their own eyes in response to this tragedy—each scene darker than the one before as the glory of God is shunned.

20

Judges 20:1, 2
Then all the children of Israel went out, and the congregation was gathered together as one man, from Dan even to Beer-sheba, with the land of Gilead, unto the LORD in Mizpeh. And the chief of all the people, even of all the tribes of Israel, presented themselves in the assembly of the people of God, four hundred thousand footmen that drew sword.

After receiving a piece of the corpse of the concubine, the Twelve Tribes of Israel mustered an army of 400,000.

Judges 20:3–6
(Now the children of Benjamin heard that the children of Israel were gone up to Mizpeh.) Then said the children of Israel, Tell us, how was this wickedness? And the Levite, the husband of the woman that was slain, answered and said, I came into Gibeah that belongeth to Benjamin, I and my concubine, to lodge. And the men of Gibeah rose against me, and beset the house round about upon me by night, and thought to have slain me: and my concubine have they forced, that she is dead. And I took my concubine, and cut her in pieces, and sent her throughout all the country of the inheritance of Israel: for they have committed lewdness and folly in Israel.

The Levite recounts the tragedy.

Judges 20:7
Behold, ye are all children of Israel; give here your advice and counsel.

Notice he's not saying, "Let's seek God; let's pray; let's wait on the Lord"—but rather, "What are *we* going to do with these evil Benjamites?"

Judges 20:8, 9
And all the people arose as one man, saying, We will not any of us go to his tent, neither will we any of us turn into his house. But now this shall be the thing which we will do to Gibeah; we will go up by lot against it;

Israel decided to launch a civil war and wipe out the Benjamite city of Gibeah.

Judges 20:10
And we will take ten men of an hundred throughout all the tribes of Israel, and an hundred of a thousand, and a thousand out of ten thousand, to fetch victual for the people, that they may do, when they come to Gibeah of Benjamin, according to all the folly that they have wrought in Israel.

Ten percent of the men of Israel were to be drafted to go to war against the brutal butchers of Benjamin.

Judges 20:11
So all the men of Israel were gathered against the city, knit together as one man.

The children of Israel were incensed and united because of a treacherous terrorist act. The nation had been sinning, with every man doing right in his own eyes. But tragedy aroused the nation and forced it to look at its own spiritual condition. Tragedy brought about mobilization and unification.

Does this ring a bell as to our own situation? September eleventh shook us. We mobilized our men. We became united. But watch where the story goes . . .

Judges 20:12
And the tribes of Israel sent men through all the tribe of Benjamin, saying, What wickedness is this that is done among you?

Israel dispatched diplomats.

Judges 20:13
Now therefore deliver us the men, the children of Belial, which are in Gibeah, that we may put them to death, and put away evil from Israel. But the children of Benjamin would not hearken to the voice of their brethren the children of Israel:

An outraged nation said, "Turn over those butchers to us." But the men of Benjamin refused.

Judges 20:14, 15
But the children of Benjamin gathered themselves together out of the cities unto Gibeah, to go out to battle against the children of Israel. And the children of Benjamin were numbered at that time out of the cities twenty and six thousand men that drew sword, beside the inhabitants of Gibeah, which were numbered seven hundred chosen men.

This small group of 26,700 consisted of amazing fighters.

Judges 20:16, 17
Among all this people there were seven hundred chosen men lefthanded; every one could sling stones at an hair breadth, and not miss. And the men of Israel, beside Benjamin, were numbered four hundred thousand men that drew sword: all these were men of war.

The battle lines were drawn: 400,000 Israelites *vs.* 26,700 Benjamites. The fact that seven hundred Benjamites were left-handed puts one in mind of perhaps one of the bravest left-handed Benjamites of all time: Ehud (Judges 3). The fact that they could sling stones to within an hair breadth of their target calls to mind a crack-shot shepherd boy named David.

Judges 20:18 (a)
And the children of Israel arose, and went up to the house of God, and asked counsel of God . . .

At last, the Israelites asked counsel of God—but wait . . .

Judges 20:18 (b)
. . . said, Which of us shall go up first to the battle against the children of Benjamin?

The Israelites didn't pray, "Should we attack?" but "Which of us should attack first?" That's the way we often pray.

We don't open our hearts to the Lord and say, "Lord, what do You want?" No, we say, "Here's Your choice, Lord: A or B." We give Him one or two options when there's an entire set of alternatives about which we know nothing. It's a dangerous way to pray, folks. When we pray, we must seek the Lord's heart in quietness and humility, saying, "Lord what do *You* want?"

Judges 20:18 (c)
. . . And the LORD said, Judah shall go up first.

As He did with Hezekiah (2 Kings 20), the Lord answered Israel's prayer according to His permissive will rather than His perfect will. "If that's what You want to do," He said, "send Judah first."

Judges 20:19–23
And the children of Israel rose up in the morning, and encamped against Gibeah. And the men of Israel went out to battle against Benjamin; and the men of Israel put themselves in array to fight against them at Gibeah. And the children of Benjamin came forth out of Gibeah, and destroyed down to the ground of the Israelites that day twenty and two thousand men. And the people the men of Israel encouraged themselves, and set their battle again in array in the place where they put themselves in array the first day. (And the children of Israel went up and wept before the LORD until even, and asked counsel of the LORD, saying, Shall I go up again to battle against the children of Benjamin my brother? And the LORD said, Go up against him.)

It was an amazing military upset when the tribe of Benjamin, the rock-throwers, mowed down 22,000 Israelites. *How could this be?* Israel wondered. *Didn't we pray?* So Israel prayed again.

Judges 20:24, 25
And the children of Israel came near against the children of Benjamin the second day. And Benjamin went forth against them out of Gibeah the second day, and destroyed down to the ground of the children of Israel again eighteen thousand men; all these drew the sword.

In their second defeat, 18,000 Israelites were slain. How could this be? Here, the good guys have their prayer meeting and seek God's blessing. Their numbers are far greater. It should have been a cakewalk. But they were mowed down—22,000 on the first day, 18,000 the next.

Judges 20:26–31
Then all the children of Israel, and all the people, went up, and came unto the house of God, and wept, and sat there before the LORD, and fasted that day until even, and offered burnt offerings and peace offerings before the LORD. And the children of Israel inquired of the LORD, (for the ark of the covenant of God was there in those days, And Phinehas, the son of Eleazar, the son of Aaron, stood before it in those days,) saying, Shall I yet again go out to battle against the children of Benjamin my brother, or shall I cease? And the LORD said, Go up; for to morrow I will deliver them into thine hand. And Israel set liers in wait round about Gibeah. And the children of Israel went up against the children of Benjamin on the third day, and put themselves in array against Gibeah, as at other times. And the children of Benjamin went out against the people, and were drawn away from the city; and they began to smite of the people, and kill, as at other times, in the highways, of which one goeth up to the house of God, and the other to Gibeah in the field, about thirty men of Israel.

This was the strategy Israel had used successfully in the battle against Ai. Why, then, did Israel lose men this time? I suggest it was because they committed themselves to a course of confrontation rather than to attempt reconciliation. You see, the Lord could have chastened the people of Benjamin apart from the Israelites marching against them. He could have sent hailstones down on the men of Benjamin. He could have opened the earth under their feet to swallow them. But, because the men of Israel were eager to be the instrument of chastisement against their brother, they suffered as well.

I believe there's an important principle here. "That person needs to be corrected," we declare, "and *I'm* going to do it." If that is your attitude, the Lord will allow you to go, but I firmly believe you will find yourself in Israel's shoes—bloodied and unnecessarily beaten down.

It's interesting to me that the last miracle Jesus did, the very final miracle of His earthly ministry, took place when He healed an ear one of His own disciples had chopped off (Luke 22:51). We Christians still do this today. We take the Sword of the Spirit and use it as a weapon to brutalize and beat people. And it's wrong, the Sword of the Spirit is not meant to chop people down—it's meant to do battle against the enemy, the forces of darkness.

The pressure's off, gang! We don't have to go to every Christian in error and straighten them out, beating them over the head with the Word of God as we point out their flaws and failures. There's a better way: praying, "Lord, here's the situation. You know what to do. I don't."

The men of Israel chose confrontation rather than intercession. Yes, the Lord will use them, but it will cost them dearly.

Judges 20:32–48
And the children of Benjamin said, They are smitten down before us, as at the first. But the children of Israel said, Let us flee, and draw them from the city unto the highways. And all the men of Israel rose up out of their place, and put themselves in array at Baal-tamar: and the liers in wait of Israel came forth out of their places, even out of the meadows of Gibeah. And there came against Gibeah ten thousand chosen men out of all Israel, and the battle was sore: but they knew not that evil was near them. And the LORD smote Benjamin before Israel: and the children of Israel destroyed of the Benjamites that day twenty and five thousand and an hundred men: all these drew the sword. So the children of Benjamin saw that they were smitten: for the men of Israel gave place to the Benjamites, because they trusted unto the liers in wait which they had set beside Gibeah. And the liers in wait hasted, and rushed upon Gibeah; and the liers in wait drew themselves along, and smote all the city with the edge of the sword. Now there was an appointed sign between the men of Israel and the liers in wait, that they should make a great flame with smoke rise up out of the city. And when the men of Israel retired in the battle, Benjamin began to smite and kill of the men of Israel about thirty persons: for they said, Surely they are smitten down before us, as in the first battle. But when the flame began to arise up out of the city with a pillar of smoke, the Benjamites looked behind them, and, behold, the flame of the city ascended up to heaven. And when the men of Israel turned again, the men of Benjamin were amazed: for they saw that evil was come upon them. Therefore they turned their backs before the men of Israel unto the way of the wilderness; but the battle overtook them; and them which came out of the cities they destroyed in the midst of them. Thus they inclosed the Benjamites round about, and chased them, and trode them down with ease over against Gibeah toward the sunrising. And there fell of Benjamin eighteen thousand men; all these were men of valour. And they turned and fled toward the wilderness unto the rock of Rimmon: and they gleaned of them in the highways five thousand men; and pursued hard after them unto Gidom, and slew two thousand men of them. So that all which fell that day of Benjamin were twenty and five thousand men that drew the sword; all these were men of valour. But six hundred men turned and fled to the wilderness unto the rock Rimmon, and abode in the rock Rimmon four months. And the men of Israel turned again upon the children of Benjamin, and smote them with the edge of the sword, as well the men of every city, as the beast, and all that came to hand: also they set on fire all the cities that they came to.

All that remained of the tribe of Benjamin were six hundred men. The rock of Rimmon was a fortress in the rocks. So these six hundred survivors hung out there for four months.

What's going on here? Why did God allow 22,000 of the "good guys" to die on Day 1, and 18,000 to die on Day 2? It should have been an easy battle. But when you read the story carefully, you see something happen. "Which of us do You want to go first?" Israel prayed in the beginning. The second day, they prayed, "Are You sure You want us to go at all?" But after that, something happened that was different from the two previous occasions of prayer and inquiry. The third time, they wept, fasted, offered burnt offerings, and offered peace offerings. In other words, they repented. They didn't unfurl their flags. They didn't print bumper stickers that proclaimed "United We Stand." They didn't sing, "God Bless Israel." They repented. They said, "Lord, we have sinned." And after they fasted, cried, and sacrificed, after they recognized the sin in their own country, they had victory.

Yes, it was God's intention that the enemy would be dealt with. But first there needed to be a realization of sin in their own tribes. They had to acknowledge the need for the blood of sacrifice before the need for the blood of revenge.

My prayer is that the Lord would work in us personally, corporately, and nationally a spirit of true repentance and brokenness before Him. This will be brought about and evidenced not by the offering of burnt offerings, but by partaking of the Lamb of God, who Himself became the only Sacrifice potent enough to deal with our sin.

21

Judges 21:1
Now the men of Israel had sworn in Mizpeh, saying, There shall not any of us give his daughter unto Benjamin to wife.

Before they attacked Benjamin, in a moment of passion and emotional upheaval, the 400,000 Israelites vowed none of their daughters would marry a Benjamite. The Bible warns about taking vows or making oaths because the implication of taking a vow is often, "I can pull this off. I can see this through." Therefore, for the most part, making a vow is a foolish thing to do.

Judges 21:2, 3
And the people came to the house of God, and abode there till even before God, and lifted up their voices, and wept sore; And said, O LORD God of Israel, why is this come to pass in Israel, that there should be to day one tribe lacking in Israel?

If it weren't so tragic, this would be almost humorous. After all, Benjamin had outrageously rebelled by standing up for sexual perverts, causing the rest of Israel to overwhelmingly react. Thus, although there was rebellion and reaction on the part of the people, they held God responsible as they cried, "Lord, one of our tribes is about to become extinct. Why did You let this happen?"

Isn't that just like us? We violate the precepts of God; we ignore the statutes of God; we don't listen to the leading of God; we either rebel or overreact—and then we say, "Thanks a lot, Lord. My life is a mess."

Gang, the Lord is so perfect and merciful, loving and pure. He is genuinely *good.* Therefore, if things are going wrong, I have no right in shaking my fist at Him. It's not His fault. He did everything He possibly could to make my life prosperous and wonderful, fulfilled and right. He gave me the Word, gave me His Spirit, and saved my soul.

Judges 21:4
And it came to pass on the morrow, that the people rose early, and built there an altar, and offered burnt offerings and peace offerings.

The people seem to be worshiping, but they're not waiting on the Lord, for they're about to push every panic button in sight, trying to figure out what they can do to rescue the tribe of Benjamin on their own.

Judges 21:5–7
And the children of Israel said, Who is there among all the tribes of Israel that came not up with the congregation unto the LORD? For they had made a great oath concerning him that came not up to the LORD to Mizpeh, saying, He shall surely be put to death. And the children of Israel repented them for Benjamin their brother, and said, There is one tribe cut off from Israel this day. How shall we do for wives for them that remain, seeing we have sworn by the LORD that we will not give them of our daughters to wives?

After having their time of worship, their obligatory "morning devotions" so to speak, the Israelites immediately set about to come up with their own plan to rescue Benjamin, expecting God to bless it.

Judges 21:8–11
And they said, What one is there of the tribes of Israel that came not up to Mizpeh to the LORD? And, behold, there came none to the camp from Jabesh-gilead to the assembly. For the people were numbered, and, behold, there were none of the inhabitants of Jabesh-gilead there. And the congregation sent thither twelve thousand men of the valiantest, and commanded them, saying, Go and smite the inhabitants of Jabesh-gilead with the edge of the sword, with the women and the children. And this is the thing that ye shall do, Ye shall utterly destroy every male, and every woman that hath lain by man.

"What are we going to do?" asked the Israelites. "Our poor brethren don't have wives. Hey, what about that oath we made? We said whoever didn't join our crusade against the Benjamites would be put to death. Well, the men of Jabesh-gilead didn't join us, so let's kill them, and give their virgins to the Benjamites."

Now, it's entirely possible that the men of Jabesh-gilead never even received the message concerning the attack on Gibeah. But that didn't matter to the Israelites. There was no attempt to seek the truth, to help, or to heal. They just wanted to patch up the Benjamite problem—and it seemed right in their own eyes to use Jabesh-gilead to do it.

Judges 21:12
And they found among the inhabitants of Jabesh-gilead four hundred young virgins, that had known no man by lying with any male: and they brought them unto the camp to Shiloh, which is in the land of Canaan.

The Israelites found four hundred virgins—but they were still two hundred short. Do they seek God at this point? No. Do they wait on the Lord? No. They keep going with their own plan and program.

Judges 21:13–18
And the whole congregation sent some to speak to the children of Benjamin that were in the rock Rimmon, and to call peaceably unto them. And Benjamin came again at that time; and they gave them wives which they had saved alive of the women of Jabesh-gilead: and yet so they sufficed them not. And the people repented them for Benjamin, because that the LORD had made a breach in the tribes of Israel. Then the elders of the congregation said, How shall we do for wives for them that remain, seeing the women are destroyed out of Benjamin? And they said, There must be an inheritance for them that be escaped of Benjamin, that a tribe be not destroyed out of Israel. Howbeit we may not give them wives of our daughters: for the children of Israel have sworn, saying, Cursed be he that giveth a wife to Benjamin.

On to Plan Two . . .

Judges 21:19–22
Then they said, Behold, there is a feast of the LORD in Shiloh yearly in a place which is on the north side of Bethel, on the east side of the highway that goeth up from Bethel to Shechem, and on the south of Lebonah. Therefore they commanded the children of Benjamin, saying, Go and lie in wait in the vineyards; And see, and, behold, if the daughters of Shiloh come out to dance in dances, then come ye out of the vineyards, and catch you every man his wife of the daughters of Shiloh, and go to the land of Benjamin. And it shall be, when their fathers or their brethren come unto us to complain, that we will say unto them, Be favourable unto them for our sakes: because we reserved not to each man his wife in the war: for ye did not give unto them at this time, that ye should be guilty.

The two hundred Benjamites without wives were instructed to kidnap the daughters of Shiloh. This way, the Israelites would not be technically breaking their oath because they weren't really giving their daughters to the Benjamites. They were simply allowing them to be "kidnapped."

Judges 21:23–25
And the children of Benjamin did so, and took them wives, according to their number, of them that danced, whom they caught: and they went and returned unto their inheritance, and repaired the cities, and dwelt in them. And the children of Israel departed thence at that time, every man to his tribe and to his family, and they went out from thence every man to his inheritance. In those days there was no king in Israel: every man did that which was right in his own eyes.

The land is confused and chaotic, bloodied and beaten.

Why?

Because there was no king, and everyone did what was right in his own eyes.

Just as my life becomes chaotic and confused, your life will become bruised and battered unless you acknowledge Jesus as King, and say, "Lord, it doesn't matter what is right in my eyes. It only matters what is right according to Your Word."

And so ends the Book of Judges—with God's people greatly in need of a righteous King, a true Judge, the only Hero who will not only deliver them from their oppressors, but who will save them from the cycle of sin which does "so easily beset them."

And Who will that be?

Good News: He is pictured on the very next page as our Kinsman Redeemer in the person of Boaz—for even in the dark days of the judges, Jesus, the Light of the world, remains close at hand.

May He be your King, your Hero, your Redeemer this day and forever.

RUTH

Background to Ruth

The story is told that, when Benjamin Franklin was Ambassador to France, he spoke to a group of intellectuals who continually scoffed at his belief in the Bible. Unconvinced that these men were familiar with the book they mocked, Franklin said, "By the way, gentlemen, I have come across a most intriguing love story that I would like to read for you tonight. I think you'll find it interesting." He then proceeded to read a handwritten copy of the Book of Ruth.

After he finished the four short chapters, his audience was ecstatic. "That is the greatest love story we have ever heard," they exclaimed. "You must publish it at once."

Franklin answered, "It has already been published. It's in the Bible."

And the scoffers were silenced.

The Book of Ruth is divided into four chapters, each taking place in a different setting—a four-act drama, if you will:

- Chapter One takes place in the country of Moab.
- Chapter Two—in the fields of Boaz in Bethlehem.
- Chapter Three—on the threshingfloor of Boaz.
- Chapter Four—at the city gate of Bethlehem.

The main character, of course, is *Ruth*. Her name means "Friendship," and she is the great-grandmother of King David. She is a picture or a representative of us—the Bride of Christ.

The hero of this drama is Boaz, who is a picture or type of our Hero, our Kinsman Redeemer, our *Goel*—Jesus Christ.

The three themes of the Book of Ruth are: Redemption, revival, and restoration.

This powerful little love story shows us clearly how the Lord can breathe life into a situation that appears lifeless. Our Lord is a Restorer; He is a Rebuilder; He is a Reviver—and the Book of Ruth ministers the message of hope to any who feel wiped-out, hurting, or hopeless.

RUTH

1 Ruth 1:1, 2 (a)
Now it came to pass in the days when the judges ruled, that there was a famine in the land. And a certain man of Bethlehem Judah went to sojourn in the country of Moab, he, and his wife, and his two sons. And the name of the man was Elimelech, and the name of his wife Naomi, and the name of his two sons Mahlon and Chilion, Ephrathites of Bethlehem Judah.

In chapter 1, we are introduced to a happy Hebrew family residing in the country of Judah, in the city of Bethlehem.

How do I know they were happy?

Check out their names. *Elimelech* means, "God is my King;" *Naomi* means "Pleasant;" and, according to *Our Nearest Kinsman* by Roy Hession, *Mahlon* means "Song;" while *Chilion* means "Satisfaction."

This family was one where God was King; where there was pleasantness, song, and satisfaction.Why? Because they resided in the city of Bethlehem.

Bethlehem means, "House of Bread," and it is the city where Jesus, the Bread of Life would be born centuries later. No wonder there was satisfaction and pleasantness in Elimelech's family. No wonder there were songs and happiness. God was their King and they were living in the House of Bread.

Gang, we will always be a happy, blessed, successful people if we dwell in the House of Bread, which is the Word of God. When we eat of heavenly manna, we will experience earthly happiness.

How do I know this?

Psalm 1 declares that the man who meditates in the Word, and who delights in the Law of the Lord will be like a tree whose leaf does not wither, a tree which prospers in whatever it does. Picture, if you would, a strong oak tree. What is an oak tree? An oak tree is simply a little nut that refused to give ground. I like that! Because that's what we are. We're all little nuts, and all a little nutty. But if we refuse to give ground and plant our roots in the Word of God—if we study it, meditate on it, devour it, and make it top priority in our lives—we will find ourselves growing in strength and stability. We will find ourselves experiencing God's blessing.

Notice also that Elimelech's family not only resided in the city of Bethlehem, but in the tribe of Judah. Throughout the Book of Ruth, Bethlehem is always hyphenated with Judah. *Judah* means, "Praise."

I find the connection more than coincidental, for there is an intimate, intricate correlation between the House of Bread—which is the Word of God—and Praise—which ascends toward God. David, the sweet psalmist of Israel, declared this in Psalm 119: "I will praise thee O Lord, when I have learned thy statutes." A person who is learning about the ways of God and the character of God through the Word of God cannot help but overflow in praise to God.

As I was meditating on Genesis 1:2, the phrase, "The Spirit of God moved upon the face of the waters," jumped off the page and spoke to my heart. The Spirit of God *moved*. Peter said the same thing when he wrote: "Holy men spake as they were *moved* by the Holy Ghost" (2 Peter 1:21).

Suddenly I realized our God is on the move. And everything in creation, everything which He has touched is also perpetually and continually moving. The chair on which you're sitting right now is vibrating and moving millions of times per second. Why? Because the atoms which make up the chair are in constant motion. In fact, any individual atom is continually, perpetually in motion, for the electron which spins around the nucleus of the atom is moving at a tremendous rate of speed in an unpredictable path.

This amazes me!

Because the electron is spinning around in an unpredictable path at an unbelievable speed, in 1936, a scientist named Dr. Heisenberg said, "Since all matter is in motion, nothing is predictable." His statement came to be known as the Principle of Uncertainty. And unbeknownst to Dr. Heisenberg, his Principle of Uncertainty threw the door wide open to the practicality of miracles.

Is it scientifically possible that a man can walk on water? Yes. The Principle of Uncertainty allows for that possibility. The chances are very remote, but the possibility exists.

Is it possible for a man to feed 5,000 people with a single loaf of bread? Yes. The Principle of Uncertainty allows for that possibility. The chances are very remote, but the possibility exists.

I thank the Lord for Dr. Heisenberg. As far as I know, he didn't know the Lord, but he certainly opened a can of worms for the scientist who denies the miraculous. Miracles are possible because everything is in motion.

The writer to the Hebrews tells us that Jesus Christ is the same yesterday, today, and forever (Hebrews 13:8). And so in a world where everything appears uncertain and unpredictable—guess what. We have a solid Rock in Jesus Christ.

Our God is on the move. And yet He remains a sure foundation (Isaiah 28:16).

If you're having a difficult time praising and worshiping, if you feel far removed from Judah, the Place of Praise—it could be because you're not dwelling in Bethlehem, the House of Bread, the Word of God. Once you're dwelling in the Word, you can't help but become a worshiper.

Ruth 1:2 (b)
. . . And they came into the country of Moab, and continued there.

Elimelech and his family left Bethlehem-judah when famine came to the land. "I don't get it." you say. "How could a famine inflict the House of Bread, the Place of Praise?"

In 2 Chronicles 7, God told His people that if they turned from Him and began to serve other gods, He would send famine to their land. Evidently that is what happened here. Oh, it might have been subtle, even imperceptible at first, but there was nonetheless a turning away from the Lord. The result? Dry times.

Amos wrote about a famine not of food, but of hearing the Word of the Lord (Amos 8:11). Maybe you can relate to that. Perhaps you no longer feel like you're hearing from God or in communion with God. There was a time when every time you opened the Word, God seemed to speak to you. There was a time when coming to Bible study was the most exciting thing for you. But not now. There is famine in your land. The days are dry, dreary, and difficult.

Precious people, I don't care who you are or how close to God you might be. You can bet your bottom dollar that there will come into your walk seasons of dryness and times of difficulty. The question is not whether times of famine will come. The question is: "Where will you go when they do?"

Second Chronicles 7 teaches that the cure for famine is to remain where you are and call upon God. But Elimelech and his family went to Moab instead.

This is a fundamental mistake we often make. In the Book of Isaiah, the Lord declared that He would go with us *through* the fire (Isaiah 43:2). But so often we want to *avoid* the fire. We want to change our circumstances. We want to run from the difficulties.

So, when famine came, Elimelech, upon the prodding of his wife Naomi, decided that instead of praying it through and remaining in the land until God graciously blessed again, they would make a move, a short sojourn in Moab, where they heard there was plenty of food and an abundance of water. It seemed to be the chance of a lifetime. In reality, however, it was a death march toward the grave.

Moab had its beginning in a cave. Maybe you recall the story found in Genesis 19 . . .

Lot and his family had left Sodom just as God's judgment fell. Lot's wife, of course, was turned into a pillar of salt as she looked back on Sodom with the intent of going back. So it was, that following the destruction of Sodom, Lot and his two daughters took refuge in a cave overlooking the city. While living in this cave, Lot's two daughters got their father drunk and seduced him.

The children born from that incestuous relationship were Moab and Benammi, progenitors of the Moabites and the Ammonites—two peoples who would continually haunt the children of Israel. Thus, Moab had its beginning in a cave and, according to Zephaniah, its ending in a grave (Zephaniah 2:8–11).

In Psalm 108, God refers to Moab as His washpot. A more correct literal translation would be, "Moab is My toilet bowl." So, in taking a trip to Moab, Elimelech and Naomi were saying, "It's getting tough here in the House of Bread, the Place of Praise. Let's go swim in the toilet for awhile."

Isn't that just like you and me? "Where's the Lord? My devotions are dry. Times are tough. Wonder what I can find on cable TV to swim around in for a while," we say as we head to Moab. "Don't worry, Lord, I'm not moving out permanently. I'm just taking a little break from the intensity of the House of Bread and the Place of Praise. I'll be back."

Don't be fooled, folks. Moab is like a black hole—easy to get sucked in, but extremely difficult to get back out. Ask Naomi. She'll spend ten years there.

Ruth 1:3
And Elimelech Naomi's husband died; and she was left, and her two sons.

In Moab, Elimelech died. "God is King" always dies in Moab. If I'm swimming in the toilet bowl of the world, I can no longer say, "God is my King." Once I leave Bethlehem-judah—the House of Bread and the Place of Praise—the rule and reign of God in my life will dissipate and die.

Ruth 1:4 (a)
And they took them wives of the women of Moab . . .

Following Elimelech's death, and against Old Testament Law, Mahlon and Chilion married Moabite women.

Dad and Mom, listen carefully. When we journey into Moab—when we kick back, pull away, and pursue worldly things—do you know who pays the price? Our kids. Kids end up marrying Moabitish women when parents choose Moab over Bethlehem.

Ruth 1:4 (b)
. . . the name of the one was Orpah, and the name of the other Ruth: and they dwelled there about ten years.

Orpah's name means "Youthful" or "Immature." We will see her exhibit those qualities as the story progresses.

Ruth's name means "Friendship." The Midrach—the Hebrew commentary respected by all biblical historians—declares that Ruth was none other than the daughter of Eglon.

Think back to the Book of Judges—Eglon was the king of Moab who oppressed the Israelites for eighteen years. The only man in the Bible referred to as a "very fat man" (Judges 3:17), Eglon met his death when the Lord raised up Ehud to kill him with a double-edged dagger.

Ruth 1:5
And Mahlon and Chilion died also both of them; and the woman was left of her two sons and her husband.

When God is no longer my King, it is only a matter of time before the song on my lips ceases to exist. Whereas at one time, there was a beautiful flow of praise and adoration to the Lord—there is now cynicism and sourness, murmuring and complaining because Mahlon is dead.

Chilion was the next to die. Have you ever thought, *What's wrong with me? Why has the satisfaction which was once so sweet to me departed?* Could it be that you left the House of Bread and the Place of Praise?

You see, Naomi's experience is a perfect picture of exactly what takes place when we leave the House of Bread and the Place of Praise: First, God is no longer our King; then the song departs from our heart; finally, satisfaction leaves our soul. It's an order that is absolute and irrefutable. And we have all experienced it to some degree.

Ruth 1:6 (a)
Then she arose with her daughters in law, that she might return from the country of Moab . . .

"God is my King" is dead. "Song" is dead. "Satisfaction" is dead. And now Naomi finally realizes that allowing her family to go to Moab was an unmitigated disaster. At last she longed for Bethlehem.

Ruth 1:6 (b)
. . . for she had heard in the country of Moab how that the Lord had visited his people in giving them bread.

While Naomi was in Moab, in misery and in rebellion, she heard reports of how God was blessing Bethlehem. It's always that way, folks. Those who waited it out in Bethlehem were indeed blessed. Those who wait upon the Lord *will* renew their strength (Isaiah 40:31). Meat *will* come in due season to those who faint not (Psalm 145:15).

Second Chronicles 6 declares that if God's people turn away from Him, He will stop the rain and curse the land. But the next chapter goes on to say that if His people humble themselves and pray, He will hear from heaven and heal their land.

Therefore, while many were playing, there must have been someone praying. As a result, a prophet must have come on the scene, calling the people to forsake their heathen idols and turn once again to the True and Living God. When they did, God revived and rebuilt the land which had become so fruitless and dry. And Naomi heard the report of God's blessing.

This intrigues me because it was Naomi's loss that led her to listen. Please keep this in mind: This story is not to show God punishing Naomi for wandering off into Moab. Her loss was not punitive—it was corrective. Its purpose was to get her back on track—back to Bethlehem, the House of Bread; back to Judah, the Place of Praise.

In your life and in mine, when there is loss, it is not for punishment. Why? Because the punishment for our sin could never be severe enough. I know you; you're like me. We all deserve to be totally consumed. Whatever God could send our way could never be punishment enough for our sin. The punishment which should have come upon us was poured out upon Jesus Christ, who died in our place. Therefore, His work in our lives is not punitive. It's corrective.

If you have been in a place of loss—materially or internally, vocationally or relationally—know this: You are experiencing loss not because God is mad *at* you, angry *with* you, or disappointed *in* you—but because He wants to speak *to* you. And He knows that sometimes the only time we will listen is when we are at a place of loss where we can do nothing else.

Ruth 1:7
Wherefore she went forth out of the place where she was, and her two daughters in law with her; and they went on the way to return unto the land of Judah.

Naomi, the Prodigal Daughter, goes back home. And I am reminded of Luke 15 . . .

When the prodigal son—after leaving his father's house, going to a far country, and spending his father's fortune on wine, women, and song—finally came to his senses, he realized he was sitting in a pigpen eating pig slop.

The difference between a prodigal and a pig is that although the prodigal might spend some time in the pigpen, he doesn't make it his home. If the pigpen is your home today, you need to seriously evaluate your relationship to your Father. But if you find yourself in the pigpen today, wanting desperately to get out—take hope. Take the first step back home towards your Father, and, like the prodigal son, you will see Him running to meet you.

The only time in the Bible when God is seen to be in a hurry is in the person of the prodigal son's father, who hitched up his robes and ran down the road with abandon to meet his son. What a beautiful picture of restoration and redemption, renewal and revival. That's our Father.

Ruth 1:8, 9
And Naomi said unto her two daughters in law, Go, return each to her mother's house: the LORD deal kindly with you, as ye have dealt with the dead, and with me. The LORD grant you that ye may find rest, each of you in the house of her husband. Then she kissed them; and they lifted up their voice, and wept.

As Naomi, Ruth, and Orpah are on their way to Bethlehem, Naomi turns to her daughters-in-law and says, "Why are you traveling with me? I'm going back *with* nothing and I'm going back *to* nothing. I lost everything in Moab, but you have been good to me. May the Lord bless you. Now go back to your people."

Ruth 1:10–13 (a)
And they said unto her, Surely we will return with thee unto thy people. And Naomi said, Turn again, my daughters: why will ye go with me? are there yet any more sons in my womb, that they may be your husbands? Turn again, my daughters, go your way; for I am too old to have an husband. If I should say, I have hope, if I should have an husband also to night, and should also bear sons; Would ye tarry for them till they were grown? would ye stay for them from having husbands? nay, my daughters . . .

Naomi is referring to the practice outlined in Deuteronomy 25, whereby if a woman lost her husband, it was the responsibility of his younger unmarried brother to marry his sister-in-law. Their children would then bear the name of the deceased brother.

In reference to this, Naomi is saying, "Even if I married right now and bore sons, it would be ridiculous for you to wait until they were old enough to assume the responsibility of marrying you."

Ruth 1:13 (b)
. . . for it grieveth me much for your sakes that the hand of the LORD is gone out against me.

Not true, Naomi. Yes, you've felt the brutal, bitter repercussions of being in Moab. But God is not against you. He has a good plan for you, a divine design. He's at work. He takes even our backsliding blunders and is able to transform them into beautiful blossoms. It's an amazing thing. It's called redemption.

Ruth 1:14
And they lifted up their voice, and wept again: and Orpah kissed her mother in law; but Ruth clave unto her.

In this verse we see Naomi grieving, Orpah leaving, and Ruth cleaving.

Orpah, whose name means "Youthful" or "Immature," shows the reaction of an immature believer—much emotion, but no devotion; conviction, but no commitment. Jesus talked about this in the parable of the sower (Mark 4) . . .

> *Some hear the Word and spring up quickly, but when the hot sun comes out, they dry up and wither away because they have no roots.*
>
> *Some believers get totally excited when they hear a sermon, or a testimony, or a concert—but their roots are not grounded in the Word of God. There is no devotional life, simply an emotional hype. And when the hard times come—when there's a price to pay to follow Jesus—like Orpah, they turn away.*

Ruth, on the other hand, cleaves to Naomi.

The same remains true today, for, there are those who kiss with emotion—but others who cleave with devotion. The Bible indicates that God isn't impressed with how high we jump, but how straight we walk. Ruth stayed with Naomi. She walked the walk.

Ruth 1:15 (a)
And she said, Behold, thy sister in law is gone back unto her people, and unto her gods . . .

This doesn't mean Oprah is a bad person. It does mean she is no longer in the narrative of this drama. Her name never appears again.

There are times when you have to let people go. Far too often, people cling to some past experience or relationship. Let them go. They're not part of your story any more.

Ruth 1:15 (b)–17
. . . return thou after thy sister in law. And Ruth said, Intreat me not to leave thee, or to return from following after thee: for whither thou goest, I will go; and where thou lodgest, I will lodge: thy people shall be my people, and thy God my God: Where thou diest, will I die, and there will I be buried: the LORD do so to me, and more also, if ought but death part thee and me.

"Even if God's hand is against you, Naomi," Ruth said, "the worst God gives is better than the best the world offers." What a sentiment expressed by Ruth! This intrigues me because it means that Ruth saw in a broken embittered Naomi a spiritual reality that superseded anything she had seen in Moab.

I say this to encourage you who perhaps have been in Moab recently. You may be like Naomi—coming back *to* nothing, and coming back *with* nothing. But, like Ruth, there will be those who will see your brokenness and repentance and follow you right into the kingdom.

Why?

Because "good people" usually do not draw sinners. Naomi realized she herself needed to get back to the Lord—and that is the person with whom the sinner feels most inclined to travel.

If you have been in a place where you know you haven't been what you should be, or doing what you should do—you still have the opportunity, like Naomi, to bring someone back with you.

Ruth 1:18, 19 (a)
When she saw that she was stedfastly minded to go with her, then she left speaking unto her. So they two went until they came to Bethlehem . . .

Here we see the backslider returning home and the outsider coming home. Naomi and Ruth—Jew and Moabite—traveled together to the House of Bread.

Ruth 1:19 (b)
. . . And it came to pass, when they were come to Bethlehem, that all the city was moved about them, and they said, Is this Naomi?

"Is this Pleasant?" asked Naomi's neighbors incredulously. "Look at the lines in her face and the sadness in her eyes." Naomi came back—but without "God is my King," without "Satisfaction," without "Song." The effects of sin were bitter upon her.

Ruth 1:20
And she said unto them, Call me not Naomi, call me Mara: for the Almighty hath dealt very bitterly with me.

The woman who was once called "Pleasant" says, "That's not my name anymore. Call me *Mara*. Call me "Bitter," for the Lord has dealt severely with me. To get my attention, heavy things have happened to me." Naomi was not complaining. She was confessing—acknowledging the chastening hand of God upon her life (Hebrews 12:6).

Ruth 1:21 (a)
I went out full, and the LORD hath brought me home again empty:

Would you please underline this verse in your Bible and underscore it in your mind? This is the reason backsliding is so ridiculous. When you leave Bethlehem-judah—the House of Bread, the Place of Praise—and wander off to sojourn in Moab, you will always leave full, but come back empty. Sin always brings sorrow and sadness. Be not deceived, God is not mocked—whatsoever a man sows that shall he also reap (Galatians 6:7).

Naomi went through ten years of proverbial hell on earth and would carry scars for the rest of her life because she left the land of the true and living God.

Gang, the mathematics of sin are always the same, for sin adds to your sorrows, subtracts from your energy, multiplies your troubles, and divides your loyalty.

Naomi went out full, but returned empty. But praise be to our Lord—the remaining three chapters of the Book of Ruth will chronicle Naomi's refilling and recharging as the Lord renews and revives her. Naomi's story is truly one of the interesting subplots of this magnificent little book.

Ruth 1:21 (b)
. . . why then call ye me Naomi, seeing the LORD hath testified against me, and the Almighty hath afflicted me?

Naomi has it wrong. God is not against her. He's for her—even in the ramifications and repercussions of her own choices.

Ruth 1:22 (a)
So Naomi returned, and Ruth the Moabitess, her daughter in law, with her, which returned out of the country of Moab . . .

Often, when you and I backslide, the tragedy is that we take others with us.

"I'm going fishing," Peter said. "I'm not good enough. I'm not worthy enough to follow Jesus Christ any longer" (see John 21:3).

What did the other disciples say?

"We'll go with you," they said, as they boarded the boat of backsliding together.

But here is Naomi coming back, returning to the place of blessing and look—she is bringing Ruth with her—Ruth who will be so instrumental in the very genealogy of Jesus Christ; Ruth, who is herself an illustration of the body of Christ. Ruth is brought into the Land of Promise by a broken Naomi.

When was Ruth brought into the place of blessing? It wasn't when she was impressed with Naomi's pleasantness and perfectness. It was when she saw Naomi's brokenness and bitterness.

Precious people, I am convinced that very often our friends, family, colleagues, and neighbors are not getting saved and not responding to the gospel because they look at us and see the life we are presenting to them as being totally together and they say, "God is the God of the together person, the perfect person—which is fine for you because you're together and you're perfect. But I'm not. Therefore He could not be my God."

Why is it we try so hard to present ourselves as perfect? We know we're not. Who are we kidding? We all know we have problems and weaknesses, temptations and difficulties. And yet we carefully cultivate an impeccable image to present to the world. I suggest to you that people are touched and moved not when you and I preach from the pulpit of perfection, but rather when we share from the place of brokenness and humility—not pointing to our togetherness, but to God's graciousness.

Marrying into Naomi's happy Hebrew family did not convert Ruth. You see, it was not until Naomi—Miss Pleasant—became humble and confessed freely that the Lord had dealt bitterly with her that Ruth said, "Your God shall be my God because I can relate to a God like that."

When the sinner can see that you and I are real—that we have weaknesses and vulnerabilities which the Lord is slowly but surely working out—they will be drawn to follow Him with us. I'm firmly persuaded of this.

Paul said it this way: "But we have this treasure [Jesus Christ] in earthen vessels, that the excellency of the power may be of God, and not of us" (2 Corinthians 4:7). Why is it, folks, that we attempt to cover up the "earthenness" of our vessels by painting them, glazing them, shining them, polishing them—and then wonder why nobody's getting saved? When the attention is on the earthen vessel and not on the Treasure within, we are doomed to failure in our efforts to draw people to Christ.

The Treasure is to be exalted. The Treasure is to be lifted up. And there is only one Treasure—the Person of Jesus Christ. It's not "churchianity;" it's not intellectual study; it's not pious spirituality. The Treasure is *Jesus.* We applaud *Jesus.* We praise *Him.* We point to *Him* and to Him alone—not to our doctrines, or theologies, or lifestyles, for *He* is the One who has rescued us, who has redeemed us, who has been so good to us.

When we can say with transparency to those around us, I am earthen. I am flawed. I have difficulties and struggles and weaknesses and scars and hurts—but there is One who is redemptive. There is One who is perfect. There is One who is all-loving, always available. And I'm going back to Bethlehem to be with Him," those around us will want to come with us.

It is time for reality, saints. It is time to applaud the Person of Jesus Christ, not our own religious lifestyles. Oh, that we might be like John the Baptist who said, "He must increase and I must decrease" (John 3:30).

Even if you have sojourned in Moab for a long season, even though you left full and are now coming back empty, know this: First of all, God can and will refill and revive you. Secondly, if you will extol His grace and His goodness, He will actually use you to bring a whole lot of Ruths back with you.

Am I suggesting that we should sin in order to be relatable? In the words of the apostle Paul, "God forbid!" (Romans 6:2) If you do, you're a fool. I know Scripturally and experientially that, although God will still love you and receive you and bless you, you will carry scars and hurts and pains which are totally unnecessary.

I am not suggesting we sin in order to be relatable. I am saying we need to be very careful that we are not trying to lift up a lifestyle and present ourselves only in the best possible light. We need to be real. We need to share with people our setbacks and the hard knocks we've had to go through to learn lessons. Above all, we need to share the grace and glory of God through it all.

And if we do—many a Moabitess, many a worldling, many a lost soul will say, "I want your God to be my God."

Ruth 1:22 (b)

. . . and they came to Bethlehem in the beginning of barley harvest.

Naomi and Ruth came to Bethlehem at the beginning of barley harvest—which is the time of Passover.

When do the backslider and the baby Christian, so to speak, come into Bethlehem, the House of Bread—and Judah, the Place of Praise? During Passover—through the death and Resurrection of Jesus Christ. That's always where it starts—when we recognize and realize that Jesus Christ is the One who died for our sin.

Fifty days later—during Pentecost—we will see Boaz marry Ruth. The experience of Pentecost is the culmination of our salvation—when we allow Jesus Christ to fill us and overflow us with His Holy Spirit.

2 Ruth 2:1
And Naomi had a kinsman of her husband's, a mighty man of wealth, of the family of Elimelech; and his name was Boaz.

Boaz, whose name means "Standing in Strength," was an impressive fellow indeed. Look at his pedigree—he came from the tribe of Judah. Look at his posterity—from him came David, Israel's greatest king prior to the reign of the King of kings, Jesus Christ.

David's son, Solomon, so impressed with his great-great grandfather Boaz, named one of the two main pillars of the temple after him (1 Kings 7:21). After all, "Standing in Strength" would be a good name for a pillar.

Truly Boaz was a man who stood in strength. He lived during the days of the Judges, when the Bible says that every man did right in his own eyes (Judges 21:25). The country was corrupt and bankrupt as a result. Yet Boaz stood strong in the days of famine and stayed true in the days of darkness.

Boaz was of good pedigree, good posterity, and above all—was a picture of our Kinsman Redeemer, Jesus Christ.

The word translated "kinsman" is *goel* in Hebrew. *Goel* means "Redeemer" and has its roots in the twenty-fifth chapters of Numbers and Leviticus wherein God outlined a plan to prevent capitalism from getting out of hand. Every fifty years, in the Year of Jubilee, all properties purchased by corporations or wealthy individuals due to bankruptcy were to revert back to the original owner. In the Year of Jubilee, all debts were canceled. It was the Father's safeguard against the greed which causes such disparity between rich and poor.

As gracious as the Year of Jubilee was, however, fifty years is a long time to be without your land—especially if you're a farmer. So the Lord made another provision: The closest kinsman had the right at any time to buy back property which had been lost through bankruptcy, poor business practices, or mismanagement. That is why the word, *goel* is translated both "kinsman" and "redeemer."

This is an important concept because Jesus Christ is our *Goel*. We're bankrupt. We're out of it. Like Ruth and Naomi, we have nothing. But there is One who is wealthy. There is One who stands in strength. He is our Kinsman Redeemer, Jesus Christ.

Boaz is about to redeem Ruth and bring her under his covering—even as Jesus Christ has redeemed us, the church, and brought us under His covering.

Ruth 2:2
And Ruth the Moabitess said unto Naomi, Let me now go to the field, and glean ears of corn after him in whose sight I shall find grace. And she said unto her, Go, my daughter.

In Deuteronomy 24:18–20, the Father provided another compassionate law which stated that a poor person could go into the fields during the time of harvest and gather whatever was left behind by the reapers—a "work-fare" system. Familiar with Old Testament Law perhaps through conversations with Naomi, Ruth said "Let me go glean for us. It's better than starving."

Ruth 2:3
And she went, and came, and gleaned in the field after the reapers: and her hap was to light on a part of the field belonging unto Boaz, who was of the kindred of Elimelech.

Her "hap" was to end up in the field of Boaz. I like that! Although Ruth certainly didn't know that this wealthy, strong landowner was a kinsman of Elimelech, the Lord had directed her steps. Nothing just happens. God is at work. There's a grand plan coming into play.

Ruth is a picture of you and me, as we shall see. We're the Bride of Christ. But we were lost, impoverished, hungry—and it just so "happened" that we found ourselves in His field. One day, someone invited us to church, to Bible study. It is all part of God's grand plan to send people your way, allowing you to come into contact with our Boaz—Jesus Christ.

Ruth 2:4
And behold, Boaz came from Bethlehem, and said unto the reapers, The LORD be with you. And they answered him, The LORD bless thee.

I love this! Boaz walked among his reapers, saying, "The Lord be *with* you," even as our

Greater than Boaz is called *Emmanuel*, or "God *with* us."

God has always chosen to walk among men . . .

- In the Garden of Eden, He walked with man in the cool of the day (Genesis 3:8). But then man fell, was expelled from the Garden, and the world became corrupted.
- God walked among man in the nation of Israel. His glory was in the midst of the camp (Deuteronomy 23:14). But Israel rebelled and rejected the True and Living God.
- Then God came and walked among man in the Person of Jesus Christ. John 1 says He tabernacled, or dwelt, among us. But the world rejected Jesus and nailed Him to a cross.
- Today, God walks among man in the church of Jesus Christ. But the church is experiencing rejection, persecution, and difficulty because wherever God has walked among man, He has been rejected by the world.

The day is coming, however, when Jesus Christ will come back and suddenly Eden will bloom again. The world will be what it was supposed to be all along. The whole earth will burst forth into blooming and blossoming. Israel will be the head of all nations, as she was intended to be in the first place. Jesus Christ will reign forever as King of kings. Today, men resent the Lord walking among them—but soon that will all change. There will be no more arguments, no more strife, no more tension, because Emmanuel will be with us—and we shall be with Him. What a fabulous hope that is.

Ruth 2:5
Then said Boaz unto his servant that was set over the reapers, Whose damsel is this?

I want you to take note of this unnamed servant. Who is he? He is the same unnamed servant—not physically, but spiritually—who was sent to find a bride for Isaac in Genesis 24. He is the Holy Ghost—the One who seeks a bride for Jesus Christ; the One who moves in secrecy, never speaking of Himself, always pointing to Jesus—the One who drew you and me into a relationship with Jesus.

***For topical study of Ruth 2:1–5 entitled "Nothing Just Happens," turn to page* 816.**

Ruth 2:6, 7
And the servant that was set over the reapers answered and said, It is the Moabitish damsel that came back with Naomi out of the country of Moab: And she said, I pray you, let me glean and gather after the reapers among the sheaves: so she came, and hath continued even from the morning until now, that she tarried a little in the house.

The unnamed servant was set over the reapers, even as the Holy Spirit is set over us (Ephesians 1:13).

Ruth 2:8
Then said Boaz unto Ruth, Hearest thou not, my daughter? Go not to glean in another field, neither go from hence, but abide here fast by my maidens:

"Go not to glean in another field." This is what our Greater than Boaz would say to you today. Do not look for some deeper theological truth, some exciting esoteric experience, some new slant on doctrine.

Stay in the field of redemption. Simply say, "I will spend all of my days marvelling that I've been redeemed by the blood of the Lamb."

Ruth 2:9 (a)
Let thine eyes be on the field that they do reap, and go thou after them: have I not charged the young men that they shall not touch thee?

"The young man shall not touch thee." Boaz realized that the reapers serving in his field would be vulnerable and susceptible to involvement with Ruth. In this glorious task to which we are called—serving in the field of our Greater than Boaz—we must be so careful that as we touch the things of God together, we do not touch the men or the maidens the Lord has lined up alongside of us.

Why is there such a problem in the church today with the issue of morality?

I am convinced it's because there is an enjoyment and a realization of the love of God. It's a beautiful thing to enjoy the Lord together, to worship together, to laugh together; but Satan seeks to exploit this by turning agape love into emotional or even physical love. Boaz here acknowledges the danger and the reality. He says, "I have warned the young men not to touch you."

In 1 Corinthians 7:1, Paul writes that it is good for a man not to touch a woman. There is wisdom in that. I think it's wonderful and appropriate and Scriptural to be a people who are affectionate—but you and I know when holy affection becomes carnal inclination. When that happens, back off. People might think you're cold and you're weird. Let them think what they want. You be one who listens to the words of Boaz and "touch not the maiden."

Ruth 2:9 (b)
. . . and when thou art athirst, go unto the vessels, and drink of that which the young men have drawn.

Ruth didn't even have to draw her own water. It was provided for her, the same way our Greater than Boaz invites us to drink *freely* from the wells of salvation (Isaiah 12:3).

Ruth 2:10
Then she fell on her face, and bowed herself to the ground, and said unto him, Why have I found grace in thine eyes, that thou shouldest take knowledge of me, seeing I am a stranger?

Not only a stranger, Ruth was a Moabitess. God had cursed the Moabites and proclaimed they could not come near the tabernacle for ten generations (Deuteronomy 23:3). This meant if your great-great-great-great-great-great-great-great grandmother had Moabite blood in her, you could not come into the Sanctuary, even though you were an Israelite. Indeed the Moabites were a cursed people—and Ruth knew it. That is why she was blown away by Boaz. The "big man in Bethlehem" was so good to her. "Why have *I*— a Moabitess—found grace?" she asked.

That's exactly how I feel. How could it be that *I* have found grace in God's sight?

Ruth 2:11, 12
And Boaz answered and said unto her, It hath fully been shewed me, all that thou hast done unto thy mother in law since the death of thine husband: and how thou hast left thy father and thy mother, and the land of thy nativity, and art come unto a people which thou knewest not heretofore. The LORD recompense thy work, and a full reward be given thee of the LORD God of Israel, under whose wings thou art come to trust.

Boaz said, "I know you, Ruth. I've heard about you."

The same is true of us. We fall before our Greater than Boaz and say, "Why have *I* found grace in Your sight?"

And He answers, "I know you."

Romans 8 declares that, "whom He did foreknow He predestined; whom He predestined, He called; whom He called, He justified; whom He justified, He glorified." It all begins with the foreknowledge of God. He says,"I know you guys. I see your hearts. And I'm choosing you. I'm electing you. I've chosen to be gracious unto you."

I can't help but think of Nathanel—

When Philip came to him in John 1, saying he had found the Messiah, Nathanael cynically said, "Can any good thing come out of Nazareth?"

"Come and see," Philip said.

When Jesus later saw Nathanael coming, He said, "Behold an Israelite in whom there is no guile—one who is not easily tricked."

I like that! Jesus could have condemned Nathanael for his cynicism. Instead, he commended him for his caution.

"How do you know me?" asked Nathanael.

"Before Philip came to you, I saw you sitting under the fig tree," Jesus answered (John 1:48).

The Lord sees us. The Lord knows us. And the Lord has chosen to show grace unto us. I don't understand it. I don't deserve it. But I am so grateful for it.

Good news, gang. The Lord does not condemn you. He commends you. He doesn't focus on your sin. He hears your sigh. He hears your heart saying,"I want more of You, Lord. Even though I am a Moabite, even though I have problems, I want to be right in your sight." And He responds with grace.

Ruth 2:13, 14
Then she said, Let me find favour in thy sight, my lord; for that thou hast comforted me, and for that thou hast spoken friendly unto thine handmaid, though I be not like unto one of thine handmaidens. And Boaz said unto her, At mealtime come thou hither, and eat of the bread, and dip thy morsel in the vinegar. And she sat beside the reapers: and he reached her parched corn, and she did eat, and was sufficed, and left.

Here is an interesting and beautiful analogy for you students of the Word. Boaz invites Ruth, his bride-to-be, to come and eat bread and vinegar, or wine. Bread and wine—a picture of Communion.

Ruth 2:15, 16
And when she was risen up to glean, Boaz commanded his young men, saying, Let her glean even among the sheaves, and reproach her not: And let fall also some of the handfuls of purpose for her, and leave them, that she may glean them, and rebuke her not.

In other words, "Let her glean in the best places and don't bother her. In fact, spill some of the good grain you're harvesting right in her path."

The workers could have protested that this wasn't fair. But grace is never fair. Grace is unmerited, undeserved, unearned favor. Grace is God dropping buckets and truckloads of good things upon us.

Ruth 2:17–19 (a)
So she gleaned in the field until even, and beat out that she had gleaned: and it was about an epah of barley. And she took it up, and went into the city: and her mother in law saw what she had gleaned: and she brought forth, and gave to her that she had reserved after she was sufficed. And her mother in law said unto her, Where hast thou gleaned to day?

In the previous generation, this was a question frequently asked among Christians: "Where has thou gleaned today?" I propose we revive it. I think it's a good greeting for those who love the Word of God.

Where have you gleaned today? We're so busy with the menus of Moab, we often find it difficult to answer this question.

Can you talk more readily about the latest movie you've seen than about the latest spiritual understanding you've received?

Is it easier to talk about the TV show you watched last night than about the truths of the Word you missed this morning?

Where are you eating? Where are you gleaning?

It might be a little unnerving, but I believe it would be healthy and right for us to greet each other saying, "Where have you gleaned today?"

Ruth 2:19 (b), 20
. . . and where wroughtest thou? blessed be he that did take knowledge of thee. And she shewed her mother in law with whom she had wrought, and said, The man's name with whom I wrought to day is Boaz. And Naomi said unto her daughter in law, Blessed be he of the Lord, who hath not left off his kindness to the living and to the dead. And Naomi said unto her, The man is near of kin unto us, one of our next kinsmen.

The word *goel* is used sixty-four times in the Old Testament, translated either as "redeemer" or "kinsman." Here, Naomi said, "Boaz! He's related to Elimelech. He can be our goel, our redeemer. He can rescue us from our poverty."

Ruth 2:21
And Ruth the Moabitess said, He said unto me also, Thou shalt keep fast by my young men, until they have ended all my harvest.

Wait a minute, Ruth. You're showing your Moab-ness. What did Boaz say in verse 8? He said, "Abide here fast by my *maidens.*" Why? Harvest time was a time of tremendous celebration for youth. It was a time of partying in the best sense of the word. Being a young woman, Ruth probably would have just as soon been by the young men, and so perhaps she took liberty in reporting the words of Boaz to Naomi.

But Naomi smelled a skunk . . .

Ruth 2:22
And Naomi said unto Ruth her daughter in law, It is good, my daughter, that thou go out with his maidens, that they meet thee not in any other field.

Notice that Naomi underscored Boaz's instructions when she told Ruth to "Go out with his *maidens.*"

Ruth 2:23
So she kept fast by the maidens of Boaz to glean unto the end of barley harvest and of wheat harvest; and dwelt with her mother in law.

Ruth listened to the counsel of her elders. Boaz, an older man said, "Stay with the maidens." Naomi, her mother-in-law, said the same thing. And Ruth was wise enough to listen.

As I read the Scriptures more and more, I see a linkage of elders and youth, of young and old. Young people have zeal, but it is often without knowledge. Older people have wisdom, but often lack vision. The two are needed together. Thus, we see Moses with Joshua, Elijah with Elisha, Eli with Samuel.

There's a need for young and old—for vision and wisdom; for energy and experience—to work together.

We need each other!

3

Ruth 3:1, 2 (a)
Then Naomi her mother in law said unto her, My daughter, shall I not seek rest for thee, that it may be well with thee? And now is not Boaz of our kindred, with whose maidens thou wast?

When Naomi realized Ruth had found grace in the eyes of Boaz, a near kinsman, the plot thickened!

Ruth 3:2 (b)
. . . Behold, he winnoweth barley to night in the threshingfloor.

Taking advantage of the night breezes, the men would harvest in the daytime and winnow the harvest at night. That is, they would throw the grain into the air and the chaff—the waste—would be blown away, leaving the barley to fall to the ground to be gathered. When their work was done, they would sleep on the threshingfloor to protect the harvest.

Ruth 3:3 (a)
Wash thyself therefore . . .

A new day was dawning. Naomi told Ruth she was to prepare for something good. If Boaz is a picture of Jesus, Ruth is a picture of His bride, the church—you and me. Paul says we are washed by the water of the Word (Ephesians 5). Therefore, there is nothing more important than keeping in the Word day after week after month after year.

Ruth 3:3 (b)
. . . and anoint thee . . .

Anointing is always a picture of the work of the Spirit. Jesus said we are to ask the Father for the gift of the Holy Ghost (Luke 11:13). We ought to do this continually. A new day is coming your way. If you want to really grab hold of it, to extract everything from it, wash yourself in the Word and anoint yourself in the Spirit.

Ruth 3:3 (c)
. . . and put thy raiment upon thee . . .

Thirdly, Ruth was to change her raiment. As we are commanded to do, she was to put away the garment of heaviness and don instead the garment of praise (Isaiah 61). The psalmist said that praise from the upright is comely (Psalm 33:1). I can make a choice on any given day to be blessed in a big way if I wash myself in the water of the Word, anoint myself in the Spirit, and praise the Lord.

Ruth 3:3 (d)–5
. . . and get thee down to the floor: but make not thyself known unto the man, until he shall have done eating and drinking. And it shall be, when he lieth down, that thou shalt mark the place where he shall lie, and thou shalt go in, and uncover his feet, and lay thee down; and he will tell thee what thou shalt do. And she said unto her, All that thou sayest unto me I will do.

Ruth was to go to the place where Boaz lay. I cannot help but think of the angel's words to the women at the tomb: "Come, see the place where the Lord lay" (Matthew 28:6).

Ruth 3:6
And she went down unto the floor, and did according to all that her mother in law bade her.

Why was Boaz at the threshingfloor?

It was at the threshingfloor that the reapers would take the grain and throw it into the air, allowing the nighttime breeze to sift out the wheat from the chaff.

Listen, gang—in the field, Ruth gleaned for herself. At the threshingfloor, Ruth gave of herself. What a difference this is. Are you one who is still in the field, simply taking all you can get? Or have you moved on to greater maturity at the threshingfloor?

Throughout Scripture, the threshingfloor speaks of separation and sacrifice.

- In 2 Samuel, we read how David purchased the threshingfloor of Ornan. After plague had swept the country for three days and thousands had died, David approached Ornan and said, "I want to buy this spot to build a place of sacrifice to Jehovah."
- Ornan offered to give it to David, but David replied, "I will not give to the Lord of that which costs me nothing" (2 Samuel 24:24) and he paid full price.
- It was at the threshingfloor, where Gideon hid from the Midianites, that God commissioned him for service (Judges 6).
- Jesus used the analogy of the threshingfloor when He told Peter that Satan sought to sift him like wheat on the eve of His betrayal (Luke 22:31).

The threshingfloor speaks of sacrifice. Have you come to the place where you are not simply in the field gleaning *for* yourself, but at the threshingfloor giving *of* yourself? See the place where He lay. Go to the tomb and see what Christ has done for you.

"I beseech you therefore brethren," wrote Paul, "by the mercies of God to present your bodies a living sacrifice, holy and acceptable unto Him, which is your reasonable service" (Romans 12:1). When we see the place where He lay, it becomes very reasonable to go to the threshingfloor and offer ourselves to Him—just as Ruth did.

Perhaps you're in a "threshingfloor" season, where you feel up in the air, separated, and blown away. Whenever you come to a time like this, you have the opportunity to be great. It's an opportunity that comes your way only very infrequently—to do something for the Lord, to give yourself to Him, to say, "Lord, do what You want to do; be glorified in this; and have Your way this day."

Ruth 3:7
And when Boaz had eaten and drunk, and his heart was merry, he went to lie down at the end of the heap of corn: and she came softly, and uncovered his feet, and laid her down.

Ruth laid at the *feet* of Boaz. Look at the feet of our Greater than Boaz. John's Gospel declares it was when John the Baptist saw Jesus *walking* that he said, "Behold the Lamb of God" (John 1:36).

Look at the feet of Jesus. He is the Lord of the calm as He walks along the seashore. He is the Lord of the storm as He walks upon the water. Look at His feet—feet that were pierced, feet that not only walked in the temple, but walked up Mount Calvary.

Sculptor Thors Walden chiseled a glorious statue of Jesus Christ. Due to the position of His body, however, it is impossible to see His face. A sign next to the statue says this: If you desire to see His face, you must first sit at His feet. And as you sit at the feet of that sculpture and look up, it is then and only then that you see His face.

Eve sought to be at Adam's head, and she fell. Ruth sought to be at Boaz's feet, and she's about to be redeemed.

Ruth 3:8
And it came to pass at midnight, that the man was afraid, and turned himself: and, behold, a woman lay at his feet.

There is nothing immodest or immoral about this. By her actions, Ruth was declaring to Boaz that she desired him to be a spiritual covering for her.

Ruth 3:9
And he said, Who art thou? And she answered, I am Ruth thine handmaid: spread therefore thy skirt over thine handmaid; for thou art a near kinsman.

"You are a near kinsman," said Ruth—"my redeemer, my goel, my only hope. Please cover me."

Here's the question, gang: Would Boaz do it? Would this wealthy, strong individual stretch his robe to cover a Moabitish woman, a new kid on the block, one who had no credibility, no credentials, nothing to offer him? What would he do? Would he be a *goel?* Would his garment stretch that far?

That's the question many of us wrestle with right now. "I'm bankrupt," we say, "I'm Moabitish in my nature. Would the Lord spread His covering over *me?*"

Understand this, dear friend: Redeemer is a word that indicates a *continual* work of redemption. When the Lord says, "I'm a Redeemer," it means He's continually redeeming—not only in relation to your salvation ten years ago. He remains continually and constantly willing to cloak you, to redeem you, to claim you no matter where you've been, no matter how far Moab has drawn you.

Ruth 3:10
And he said, Blessed be thou of the Lord, my daughter: for thou hast shewed more kindness in the latter end than at the beginning, inasmuch as thou followedst not young men, whether poor or rich.

"You have showed more kindness in the latter end than at the beginning." This is what our Greater than Boaz says to you.

"When you came into My field, that was a blessing. When you showed up at church, when you had morning devotions, when you came into the field to glean the wheat of My Word—you blessed Me. I know you could have gone water skiing. I know you could have stayed home. I know you could have slept in—but you came into My field and you blessed Me.

And now you're blessing Me even more by wanting Me to cover you, to redeem you, to rescue you. It's not an obligation *to* Me—it's an elation *for* Me. You could have sought some young man, some new fad, some exciting trip—but you sought Me, the Ancient of Days. You put aside other alluring pursuits and you sought Me to cover you. You've blessed Me."

Boaz had strength and wealth, pedigree and prosperity. He had everything—except one upon which to pour out his love.

Jesus Christ is the Creator of all things. He, too, has it all. But what He desires is a Bride. And guess what we are! Anyone who will fall before His nail-pierced feet and say, "Cover me"—He will in no wise cast out (John 6:37).

Ruth 3:11
And now, my daughter, fear not; I will do to thee all that thou requirest: for all the city

of my people doth know that thou art a virtuous woman.

Ruth knew she was a Gentile, and a stranger. Boaz, however, saw her as a virtuous woman. One translator renders his statement, "Thou art a bride worth winning."

This is honestly the Lord's heart toward us. We think He's stuck with us, when in actuality He's in love with us because He sees us as a bride worth winning.

Ruth 3:12, 13
And now it is true that I am thy near kinsman: howbeit there is a kinsman nearer than I. Tarry this night, and it shall be in the morning, that if he will perform unto thee the part of a kinsman, well; let him do the kinsman's part: but if he will not do the part of a kinsman to thee, then will I do the part of a kinsman to thee, as the LORD liveth: lie down until the morning.

It is true that Jesus is my Kinsman, my near Kinsman—that He, God Himself, became flesh, became like me, and was tempted in all points like I am. Hebrews 2 teaches the incredible concept of the Incarnation—how Jesus is a High Priest who relates to you and me because He became just like us.

But there's a problem. There's a *nearer* kinsman—one who came before the Incarnation of Jesus, one who has prior claim to us.

Who is this?

Watch and see . . .

Ruth 3:14 (a)
And she lay at his feet until the morning: and she rose up before one could know another . . .

Ruth was at Boaz's feet, then rose up before the break of day. The best place for us to be is at the feet of the Lord before we rise up to start our day.

Ruth 3:14 (b), 15
. . . And he said, Let it not be known that a woman came into the floor. Also he said, Bring the vail that thou hast upon thee, and hold it. And when she held it, he measured six measures of barley, and laid it on her: and she went into the city.

Why did Boaz give Ruth *six* measures of barley?

I suggest it was because God worked six days in creation. He didn't rest until the seventh day—when His work was complete. Boaz is sending a message through Ruth to Naomi, saying: "I'm going to work and not rest until my work is complete—until she's my wife."

It was a tricky message which passed right over the head of Ruth, a young convert. But Naomi understood, as evidenced by her response in verse 18.

Ruth 3:16
And when she came to her mother in law, she said, Who art thou, my daughter? And she told her all that the man had done to her.

"Who art thou?" doesn't mean, "Who are you?"—but, "Who are you becoming?" In other words, "How did it go?"

Ruth 3:17, 18
And she said, These six measures of barley gave he me; for he said to me, Go not empty unto thy mother in law. Then said she, Sit still, my daughter, until thou know how the matter will fall: for the man will not be in rest, until he have finished the thing this day.

"The man will not rest."

Naomi understood Boaz's message.

"Sit still, Ruth. Rest, and watch, and see what he'll do."

4

Ruth 4:1 (a)
Then went Boaz up to the gate, and sat him down there . . .

The next day, Boaz went to the city gate, where business transactions took place. No doubt amazed that Ruth would see him as her kinsman redeemer, he was eager to complete the process of redemption.

Ruth 4:1 (b)
. . . and, behold, the kinsman of whom Boaz spake came by; unto whom he said, Ho, such a one! turn aside, sit down here. And he turned aside, and sat down.

This was the nearer kinsman of whom Boaz spoke in chapter 3. Who was he? Read on!

Ruth 4:2–4
And he took ten men of the elders of the city, and said, Sit ye down here. And they sat down. And he said unto the kinsman, Naomi, that is come again out of the country of Moab, selleth a parcel of land, which was our brother Elimelech's: And I thought to advertise thee, saying, Buy it before the inhabitants, and before the elders of my peo-

ple. If thou wilt redeem it, redeem it: but if thou wilt not redeem it, then tell me, that I may know: for there is none to redeem it beside thee; and I am after thee. And he said, I will redeem it.

The *ten* elders of the city are an illustration of who our nearer kinsman is. It's the Law. The Law came first. Before Jesus came to earth to redeem us, the Law was already in place. With its do's and don'ts it was an unmerciful nearer kinsman which laid claim to you and me.

Ruth 4:5
Then said Boaz, What day thou buyest the field of the hand of Naomi, thou must buy it also of Ruth the Moabitess, the wife of the dead, to raise up the name of the dead upon his inheritance.

According to Deuteronomy 25, the *goel*—the nearer kinsman—not only had the right to redeem the property, but an obligation to take care of the family. If the nearer kinsman refused to meet his responsibility to the family—in this case, if he refused to marry Ruth—the Law said he was to be spat upon. Then his shoe was to be removed from his foot, signifying that he was walking away from his responsibility—that he was a "heel," that he had no "sole."

Ruth 4:6
And the kinsman said, I cannot redeem it for myself, lest I mar mine own inheritance: redeem thou my right to thyself; for I cannot redeem it.

"I already have a family," said the nearer kinsman. "I cannot take on the responsibility of another one. I cannot redeem."

Although we initially think the Law can save us through our good works, we realize in the end that it cannot redeem. In 1 Corinthians 15, Paul writes that the strength of sin is in the Law. The more you read the Law, study the Law, and know the Law—the more you realize that the Law is not your redeemer. It's your condemner. The Law points out your weaknesses, your failings, and your flaws.

It is only when you stop trying to earn your salvation and merit brownie points with God in your Christian walk that you are free. Once you realize your rules and regulations—joining the right clubs, working on the right committees, and being nice to your dog and cat—will not redeem you, you look to your Greater than Boaz. You look to Jesus Christ. You see, it's not what we're doing that counts—it's what *He* has done that matters.

Ruth 4:7, 8
Now this was the manner in former time in Israel concerning redeeming and concerning changing, for to confirm all things; a man plucked off his shoe, and gave it to his neighbour: and this was a testimony in Israel. Therefore the kinsman said unto Boaz, Buy it for thee. So he drew off his shoe.

Biblically, the shoe always refers to possession.

In Joshua 1:3, the Lord said to Joshua, "Wherever you put the soles of your foot, *that shall be your inheritance."*

When the Israelites came to the Jordan River, it was when the priests put the soles of their feet *into the water that it parted (Joshua 3:13).*

Now, think with me: The true Kinsman Redeemer, Jesus Christ, who came to redeem the nation Israel, had His heel bared as He was nailed to a Cross, and received spittle in His face when the nation rejected Him. Thus, although they didn't know it consciously, Scripturally what Israel said was, "You will not be our *goel.* We spit in Your face. We take off Your shoe. We will not have You rule over us."

Today, if you have not acknowledged Jesus as your Redeemer, you, too, have taken off His shoe. You have spat in the face of the One who died for you and wants to live inside you. Your rejection of Him is the greatest insult that could ever take place. It's called the blasphemy of the Holy Spirit, and it is the one sin which is eternally unforgivable (Matthew 12:31).

Ruth 4:9, 10
And Boaz said unto the elders, and unto all the people, Ye are witnesses this day, that I have bought all that was Elimelech's, and all that was Chilion's and Mahlon's, of the hand of Naomi. Moreover Ruth the Moabitess, the wife of Mahlon, have I purchased to be my wife, to raise up the name of the dead upon his inheritance, that the name of the dead be not cut off from among his brethren, and from the gate of his place: ye are witnesses this day.

Boaz stepped up and said, "Since the nearer kinsman cannot redeem, I will!" And that is exactly what our Greater than Boaz says concerning us.

- Jesus alone has the *right to redemption.* Rules and regulations do not, will not, and cannot.
- Jesus alone has the *resource for redemption.* He purchased us with the richness of the blood that flowed through His veins and onto the ground at Calvary.

- Jesus alone has a *reason for redemption.* It is His grace, his undeserved, unmerited, unearned favor which brings us into His family.

Finally, Jesus alone gives us *rest in redemption.* Like Boaz, He says, "Glean not in another man's field. Stay in the field of My redemption and you will find the ultimate satisfaction."

Ruth 4:11 (a)
And all the people that were in the gate, and the elders, said, We are witnesses . . .

Acts 10:39–43 says that the Law and the prophets are a witness *of* Him. And we are witnesses *for* Him as the Holy Spirit enables us.

Ruth 4:11 (b), 12
. . . The LORD make the woman that is come into thine house like Rachel and like Leah, which two did build the house of Israel: and do thou worthily in Ephratah, and be famous in Bethlehem: And let thy house be like the house of Pharez, whom Tamar bare unto Judah, of the seed which the LORD shall give thee of this young woman.

Ephratah is an old name for Bethlehem. No longer is Ruth a stranger. Never again is she called a Moabitess because now she has been absorbed in the covering of Boaz, her kinsman redeemer.

Ruth 4:13–16
So Boaz took Ruth, and she was his wife: and when he went in unto her, the LORD gave her conception, and she bare a son. And the women said unto Naomi, Blessed be the LORD, which hath not left thee this day without a kinsman, that his name may be famous in Israel. And he shall be unto thee a restorer of thy life, and a nourisher of thine old age: for thy daughter in law, which loveth thee, which is better to thee than seven sons, hath born him. And Naomi took the child, and laid it in her bosom, and became nurse unto it.

You left full, Naomi. You came back empty. And now God is blessing you once again. The women told Naomi that Ruth was better than seven sons, seven being the number of perfection. Their words were prophetic indeed for out of Ruth's line would come forth not only King David, but the Perfect One—Jesus Christ.

Naomi, this prodigal daughter of the Old Testament, came back to Bethlehem, where God rebuilt, rebirthed, restored, and renewed her.

And that's what He'll do with us—if we'll just come back to Him.

Ruth 4:17–22
And the women her neighbours gave it a name, saying, There is a son born to Naomi; and they called his name Obed: he is the father of Jesse, the father of David. Now these are the generations of Pharez: Pharez begat Hezron, And Hezron begat Ram, and Ram begat Amminadab, And Amminadab begat Nahshon, and Nahshon begat Salmon, And Salmon begat Boaz, and Boaz begat Obed, And Obed begat Jesse, and Jesse begat David.

According to Deuteronomy 23:2, 3, no descendant of an illegitimate child could enter the tabernacle until ten generations had passed. Judah's son, Pharaz, was illegitimite—the result of Judah's union with Tamar (Genesis 38). That is why we see ten generations between Pharez and David—ten generations between the illegitimate son and the rightful king.

Ruth, Naomi, and Boaz now fade from the scene. David will take center stage as he points to the Son of David, our Greater than Boaz—Jesus Christ.

***For topical study of Ruth 1—4 entitled "A Prophetic Overview of Ruth," turn to page* 818.**

NOTHING JUST HAPPENS

A Topical Study of RUTH 2:1–5

Three tenacious women tied together by the common thread of suffering and sorrow, pain and death. A gracious man named Boaz—a man of incredible wealth and sterling character. This book does more to explain God's grand plan for the nation Israel and the church and how they come together in the end times.

Something is taking place in chapter 2 that appeared to be circumstantial, accidental, coincidental. That is, we read that Ruth's hap was to light on a part of the field that belonged to Boaz. It "just so happened" that she made her way to the part of the field that Boaz was gleaning in that day. "It just so happened," I suggest that was written with a twinkle in the eye and a smile on the face because nothing just happens. It was all part of a grand plan, all part of a Divine Design.

"I went out full . . ." That strikes me. I went out full? When she left ten years earlier, she thought she was empty then. We don't have enough food. We don't have enough money. We've got to do something. So they went to Moab. But now, looking back, ten years later, she says I was full. Oh, I might not have had money or bread physically. But I had my husband and I had my two sons. I had family. Even though I thought I was poor, I realize I was rich. Listen—the thing you are anxious about today, worried about—the financial pressure, the rejection by that person you cared for, the job situation, the retirement plan—whatever it might be that has caused you to feel anxious and worried, and as though you don't have much is nothing in comparison to what you have with you tonight—that wife or husband sitting next to you, those kids with you, being able to share with brothers and sisters in the congregation, your health. Whatever you're anxious or worried about—making the team, paying the mortgage—is nothing in comparison to what you have. You are full right now even though you might not think so. You never know what you have until you lose it. And when you lose it, like Naomi, you say, "What was I thinking? I was full in the time of famine because I had my husband, my family. Now I realize I went out full and tried to make stuff happen financially, physically, and I come back empty. I realize what I had, even though I didn't realize it when I had it."

Count your blessings, folks. Realize that whatever anxieties or worry you might have pales in comparison to the blessings you've already been given, which you're surrounded with even today. Naomi realized this ten years too late.

Even though Naomi was late in realizing this, she made her way back to Bethlehem, back to where she belonged. Satan will whisper in your ear, "It's too late for you. It's been ten years. Your time to be involved in serving the Lord or your time to draw close to the Lord or your time to receive blessing has passed. You've been in Moab too long." Naomi didn't buy into this lie. She said. "This is it. Time to quit. Gonna split. Moab don't fit. I'm going back to where I belong." And as we'll see, it wasn't too late at all. It's never too late.

Your people shall be my people: Ruth and Naomi, the Moabitess and the Jew didn't have a lot in common. But they did share a common thread—the common thread of suffering. The Bible talks about the fellowship of suffering. Both women had lost their husbands, both had gone through pain and heartache. It's true. The people you're closest to are not the ones you laugh with but the ones you cry with because of the fellowship of suffering. Nothing just happens. All of these things are being put into play to cause God's story to unfold perfectly.

Nothing just happens. God is in control of every step you take, every move you make. His plan is being unfolded. No matter where you are, what you've done, God is in control. He's sovereign. He's a Father who cares about you. What if you're in rebellion? Naomi and Elimelech were in rebellion, but God used their story as an illustration of His Son, Israel, and the church. Even Jonah. God said, Go to Nineveh. No way, he said. But God has His way. Jonah was in the belly of a great fish for three days before he was barfed up on the beach. And Jesus would say "Even as Jonah was in the belly of the whale three days and three nights, even so the Son of Man will be in the center of the earth for three days and three nights. Jonah is a picture of Me—that I might receive glory. Just as Jonah disappeared and reappeared, so, too, will I."

You might be going through a whale of a problem, you might have all kinds of storms swirling about, you might be going in the opposite direction of where God wants you—but God can use even that. Think of your greatest joy—when she said, "yes!" When the doctor said, "It's a boy." When the boss said, "Here's your bonus."—those things didn't just happen. God brought them about. Every good and perfect gift comes from above. God has given you every thing that you enjoy. Think of your worst times—your greatest miseries, your heartache, your heartbreak didn't just happen either. Psalm 139 declares, "If I'm in hell, You're there, too. You're always with me." Nothing just happens. If it's a wonderful experience or a difficult time, a season of sadness or even rebellion, God is on the throne. God is in control.

Therefore, whatever comes my way—good or bad—I can be happy because I know ultimately all things work together for good—not some things, not lots of things, not the majority of things but ALL things work together for good. God is doing something. A story is being written. Bethelehem is unfolding.

A PROPHETIC OVERVIEW OF RUTH

A Topical Study of
RUTH 1—4

In the historic Hebrew Bible, this book is placed with the prophets because, as we shall see, it really is a book that deals with prophecy. In Hebrew tradition historically and presently, the Book of Ruth is read during the Feast or the Celebration of Pentecost. Pentecost was that annual celebration that took place fifty days after the Passover. It was celebrating the harvesting of the wheat which was so crucial to the Israelite economy. So the wheat would be harvested and there would be a celebration as it would be offered up in thanksgiving to the Lord. It was not only celebrating, but comemorating an event that took place historically.

That is, it commemorated the giving of the Law. The rabbis and scholars came to the conclusion that the giving of the Law—when God spoke audibly on Mt. Sinai and gave Moses the two tables of stone—was during this time. It celebrated the wheat harvest, and commemorated the giving of the Law. Both of these are aspects of the feast of Pentecost.

Why would Ruth be read during Pentecost?

First, the wheat harvest is mentioned (2:23). The barley harvest was during Passover, the wheat harvest during Pentecost. Passover was in the springtime, Pentecost was fifty days later, in early summer.

But an even more important reason is due to what took place in the church on the Day of Pentecost, as seen in Acts 2. Fifty days after Jesus had died and risen from the dead. The disciples were in the Upper Room, numbering one hundred and twenty, praying, wondering what would happen next. They had been told to go to that place and wait for the promise of the Father. Jesus said, "You shall receive power when the Holy Ghost comes upon you." And there on the very day of Pentecost, as the disciples were in the Upper Room—waiting on the Lord, talking to the Lord, there was sent from the Lord an anointing and empowering of the Holy Spirit. A rushing mighty wind blew through the room and there were tongues of fire on each of the disciples' heads and they began to speak with other tongues and on that day, Pentecost, was the birthday of the church. The Holy Spirit was given to them. And the church was born.

It's interesting because Pentecost is the birthday of the church on one hand, but also the birthday of Judaism because it was on that same day 2,000 years earlier when the Law was given. So Judaism and Christianity have the same birthday—the day of Pentecost. This explains why they would take two loaves of wheat bread in OT times and wave them before the Lord, celebrating the harvest, it's true. But there's something unusual about those loaves of bread that was exclusive to that particular day. Those loaves were made with leaven. Leaven is a picture of sin. So when you ask the Jews today what do those two loaves stand for, they will say—We're celebrating the giving of the Law, and the Law was given on two tablets. So the waving of the two loaves speak of the Law being given, which sustains and nourishes our soul like bread sustains and nourishes the body. The problem with that is, leaven is in those loaves—the only time leaven is allowed in any offering to the Lord. Is the Law leavened? Does the Law have sin? No, the Law is perfect. Therefore, it's not primarily speaking of the Law, but something pictured here in the Book of Ruth. That is, the church.

Why two loaves? Jew and Gentile—sinners, both—coming together into a new entity called the church. No longer am I a Gentile. Now I'm in a new entity—the church. You see, in OT times, the world was divided into two groups: Jews and Gentiles. But something happened on the Day of Pentecost. Those two groups became one—a new entity called the church. Does the church have sin? If you've been around church very much, you know it's true. We're righteous positionally, but we're all dealing with leaven practically. And that's what's going on. Jew and Gentile walk together—just like those two loaves would be held together by the priest who would wave them before the Lord, two coming together.

But on the birthday of Judaism something happened. On the day the Law was given, when Moses comes down, what happened? The people were already sinning, dancing around the golden calf—which led to punishment and 3,000 were killed that day. On the birthday of the church, 3,000 were not killed, but saved because, as Paul would say, the Law kills, but the Spirit gives life.

So we see Jew and Gentile coming together into a third entity, called the church—comprised of former Jews and former Gentiles. We are now Christians. And that's what this book talks about. We have a Jew and a Gentile being brought together in this prophetic portrait. They come together and something marvelous happens.

Boaz is a portrait of Jesus Christ. The lord of the harvest, the owner of the field, a wealthy man, a gracious man, a good man, a generous man. His name literally means Standing in Strength.

Ruth is a picture of the church because she was a Moabite. In Deuteronomy 23, a Moabite was cursed for ten generations. In other words, the Law would shut you out. You moved in from Moab, and the Law would say, "Sorry. Even though you've come to Israel, even though you've left Moab, in your lifetime, you're never going to make it into the house of God." Ten generations is a long time. The Law shut the Moabite out. And the Law shut us out, too. There's no way we can go in to the house of the Lord, stand in the presence of God if it's by the Law. But what the Law shuts out, grace finds a way. And that's what blew Ruth's mind and warmed her heart. She said, "How could it be that I a Moabite (2:10) would find grace in thine eyes?" She can't believe Boaz would be so kind to her. But what the Law shuts out, grace finds a way.

Ruth was washed, anointed, and clothed with new raiment just like we have been washed in the blood of the Lamb, anointed by the Holy Spirit, and robed in His righteousness. She's washed. She's anointed. She's robed. She's amazed.

Notice that she finds herself at the feet of her goel, her groom at the threshingfloor. The threshingfloor in OT Scriptures is a picture of the time prophetically when the world will go through a threshing. It's called the Tribulation. It will be brutal. It will be a time of separation—the sheep from the goats (Matthew 25), the wheat from the chaff, when a Christ-rejecting sinful world will be dealt with. Now people have closed ears and hard hearts. But in that day, there will be a great awakening and there will be the greatest revival in world history during the seven-year Tribulation (Revelation 6—19). When the world is being tossed up and the winds of difficulty are blowing about, the harvest has already been brought in. We are the harvest. We are Ruth. And where is Ruth? She's at his feet. Where will we be when the world is being threshed? We will be at Jesus' feet—just like Ruth. In the place of intimacy, safety, security.

Boaz spotted her before she spotted him. Boaz was interested in her. Boaz cared about her. Boaz wanted to be a blessing to her. But—it was up to her. Boaz didn't force himself. He waited to see if she would respond to the goodness he was showing her, but he left it up to her to make the first move. He didn't force her into a relationship.

Thirdly, we see the servant. When Boaz is in his field. The unnamed servant is the one who identifies the bride-to-be. It's the unnamed servant who's involved in the linking of the bride, Ruth, with the bridegroom, Boaz. The unnamed servant, of course, is an illustration of the Holy Spirit. Why is he unnamed? Because in John 16, Jesus said concerning the Spirit, that when He comes, he will not speak of Himself, but will speak all things concerning Me.

Boaz wanted to be a goel for Ruth, but there was a nearer relative that had first dibs. The nearer kinsman was offered Naomi's property. Great! Said the kinsman. But if you choose to exercise the option, you need to take Ruth as well. With her you need to have a child that will not count as yours. Oh, no, this will mess up my inheritance for my own kids. The nearer kinsman represents the Law. The Law is indeed interested in property and principles and procedures, but not in people. The nearer kinsman is a picture of the Law. While the nearer kinsman wasn't interested in Ruth, Ruth is exactly who Boaz was interested in. He had enough property. He wanted people. Not so the Law. The Law can't deal with you and me. It's perfect. We're not. We mar its inheritance. Which came first, the Law or the coming of Jesus Christ? The Law came first.

Naomi is a picture of Israel. First, it was necessary for her to be in exile until the bride, Ruth, was ready to be brought into union with the bridegroom. Israel was in exile from A.D. 70, when the temple was destroyed until a miracle took place in May, 1948, when Israel became a nation. That's why when Israel became a nation, the stage was set for the return of Christ. In Matthew 24, Jesus said the generation that sees the fig tree blossom—always a picture of Israel in Scripture—will not pass away. In Romans 11, Paul says Let their eyes be darkened, through their fall, salvation is come unto the Gentile. The Jewish people were cut off, or sent away, but God has a plan. They're going to be brought back in. Israel is in exile, out of her homeland until the bride is ready—just like Naomi. She was from Israel—out in Moab until Ruth was ready to be brought in to meet the Bridegroom during the threshing season. God is at work with the Gentiles. He was primarily working through the Jew, but the Jews rejected His Son. Consequently, they would be exiled while the Bride—you and me, the Gentiles—were brought in. But once Naomi goes back home, the marriage feast of Boaz and Ruth is at hand.

While she was exiled, Naomi changed her name from Pleasant to Bitter. When Israel was in her land, was enjoying the blessings of the Lord, it was pleasant. In fact, Israel is called just that—the pleasant land. But when she was kicked out, driven away, there was bitterness. The Jewish people were hunted, haunted, and hounded everywhere they went. Persecution and execution followed them.

While Naomi was gone, the land was being destroyed. While the Jewish people were gone from A.D. 70 until 1948, the land was destroyed.

Boaz and Naomi never meet until the marriage feast. When will Israel meet Jesus? When the church is raptured. It is at that time that the veil will be lifted. Her eyes will be opened. There are a remnant now who are part of the kingdom. But the majority don't get it because Paul says there is a veil over their eyes. But when the marriage happens, guess who's going to meet Boaz—Naomi. Naomi learns of Boaz' whereabouts through Ruth. She knows there is a man named Boaz, but she doesn't know if he's dead or alive until Ruth comes home and says, Guess who I met. Israel does not know if Messiah is dead or alive. The only way she'll hear about her Messiah is through the church.

Israel learns of the whereabouts of Boaz through the church, but equally true is that Ruth learns the ways of Boaz through Naomi. That's why this book is such a key. It's a Jew and a Gentile walking together. Together something happens. Ruth and Boaz have a baby named *Obed,* which means "Worshiped one." And guess what happens to this worshiped one. The baby is then given to Naomi. We, the Bride of Christ, have been impregnated by the Spirit and the Lord is birthed in and through us. Then, as we are caught up and taken away, the baby is handed to Naomi. When you share with Jewish people, when you're on your honeymoon, the baby will be nursed and nurtured by Naomi. Ruth does not take the place of Naomi. Naomi is not displaced by Ruth. Rather, Ruth creates a family for Naomi. Gentile and Jew, dependent on each other, gleaning from each other, gaining because of each other. And the two travel together in this glorious story. God doesn't give up on His people. Ever.

1 SAMUEL

Background to 1 & 2 Samuel

Approximately 1,100 years before Christ, the books before us were written. Their title notwithstanding, the identity of their human author is uncertain, for Samuel dies six chapters before the end of 1 Samuel. While the identity of this author remains a mystery, it is clear that the true Author not only of 2 Samuel, but also of the entire Bible, is the Holy Spirit. The Spirit Himself inspired these books, and you'll be inspired as well by the lessons within—lessons gleaned from the lives of Samuel and David, Jonathan and Saul.

Samuel was a transitional figure in that he was the last of the judges. However, although the Philistines were plaguing the land and the people of Israel, Samuel didn't deliver the people of God physically, as the other judges were wont to do. Instead, he delivered them spiritually. He didn't lead armies, but he was a spiritual deliverer. He was a godly man who ministered to the people in the difficult days of transition between the time of the judges and the rule of kings.

1 SAMUEL

1 1 Samuel 1:1, 2 (a)

Now there was a certain man of Ramathaim-zophim, of mount Ephraim, and his name was Elkanah, the son of Jeroham, the son of Elihu, the son of Tohu, the son of Zuph, an Ephrathite: And he had two wives . . .

When reading verses like this, some people mistakenly think that the Bible condones polygamy. Polygamy is not condoned by the Bible, but simply reported as what was taking place. When a newspaper reports a crime, it is not condoning it, but simply reporting the story. It is true that the Law of God contains regulations concerning a man having more than one wife. This, however, is not an indication of God's approval. Rather, God is simply regulating an always-difficult situation. As you go through the Word, you see the practice of polygamy increasingly prohibited. Without exception, wherever you see polygamy in Scripture, it always results in problems.

1 Samuel 1:2 (b)

. . . the name of the one was Hannah, and the name of the other Peninnah: and Peninnah had children, but Hannah had no children.

Hannah means "Favored." *Peninnah* means "Ruby." Yet, although she's stone cold and rock hard, as we shall see, Peninnah is no gem.

1 Samuel 1:3 (a)

And this man went up out of his city yearly to worship and to sacrifice unto the LORD of hosts in Shiloh . . .

Shiloh was the worship center of Israel—where the tabernacle was pitched and where sacrifices were offered. I like the fact that both the words "worship" and "sacrifice" are used because worship and sacrifice truly walk hand in hand. "Let us continually offer the sacrifice of praise to God," the writer to Hebrews declares (13:15). Worship is often just that—a sacrifice of one's time, finances, or energy.

1 Samuel 1:3 (b)–5 (a)
. . . And the two sons of Eli, Hophni and Phinehas, the priests of the LORD, were there. And when the time was that Elkanah offered, he gave to Peninnah his wife, and to all her sons and her daughters, portions: But unto Hannah he gave a worthy portion; for he loved Hannah . . .

The person offering a peace offering was not only to offer it to the Lord but would eat of it himself (Leviticus 7:11–36). The fact that Elkanah gave Hannah a "worthy" or double portion spoke of his heart for her.

1 Samuel 1:5 (b)
. . . but the LORD had shut up her womb.

God commanded Adam and Eve to be fruitful and multiply (Genesis 1:22). Therefore, the rabbis considered barrenness to be a curse from God—an indication of sin or something wrong spiritually in one's life. As a result, Hannah's barren condition would have weighed on her greatly.

1 Samuel 1:6
And her adversary also provoked her sore, for to make her fret, because the LORD had shut up her womb.

Peninnah had sons and daughters, Hannah had none. Here, we see Peninnah badgering Hannah over this fact.

1 Samuel 1:7
And as he did so year by year, when she went up to the house of the LORD, so she provoked her; therefore she wept, and did not eat.

Like Hannah, we have an Adversary who often seems to provoke us on our way to the house of the Lord. Don't be surprised that Satan will do whatever he can to keep you from coming to church. Hannah was about to be greatly blessed. And so will be the believer who makes coming to the house of the Lord a priority. The fact that Satan continually tries to keep us from fellowship with other believers means something grand and glorious must be waiting there for us.

1 Samuel 1:8
Then said Elkanah her husband to her, Hannah, why weepest thou? and why eatest thou not? and why is thy heart grieved? am not I better to thee than ten sons?

Elkanah must surely have known the reason for Hannah's tears. That must be why she didn't answer him.

1 Samuel 1:9, 10
So Hannah rose up after they had eaten in Shiloh, and after they had drunk. Now Eli the priest sat upon a seat by a post of the temple of the LORD. And she was in bitterness of soul, and prayed unto the LORD, and wept sore.

Although Elkanah knows what the problem is, he can't solve it. Only God could. The same is true for us. So often, we look to our spouse to solve the problem of the depression in our heart, the discouragement in our mind, the barrenness in our soul. And while they may lend a listening ear or give helpful advice, God alone can solve the problem—most often in ways we could never imagine.

1 Samuel 1:11
And she vowed a vow, and said, O LORD of hosts, if thou wilt indeed look on the affliction of thine handmaid, and remember me, and not forget thine handmaid, but wilt give unto thine handmaid a man child, then I will give him unto the LORD all the days of his life, and there shall no rasor come upon his head.

"Lord, if You give me a son," Hannah prays, "he'll be Yours." No doubt Hannah had prayed countless times about her situation. But now her prayer would be answered. This doesn't mean God didn't hear her before, for every time she prayed she was heard (Psalm 34:17, 69:33; Proverbs 15:29; Jeremiah 33:3; John 9:31).

God can say, "Yes" to our requests. He can say, "No." Or He can say, "Wait." If He says, "No," that's just as much an answer as if He said, "Yes." If He says, "Wait," that's okay because that is exactly what was happening to Hannah. Here, she prayed "Lord give me a son, and I'll give him to You." And that's what God was waiting for. Previously, she wanted a son to give to her husband. God, however, wanted a prophet to give to a nation. God had something much bigger and bolder, greater and grander in mind than Hannah did.

If you've prayed about your barren condition, if you're weeping bitterly, that is okay. It might be that God is simply waiting to get you into harmony with His heart, which means He wants to do something larger than your prayer. This is really encouraging to me because I've discovered that my "unanswered' prayers grow larger for those people or situations I'm forced to bring before the Lord over a long period of time. And I'm reminded once again that prayer is not about getting God to do *my* will, but about getting me in line with what *He* wants to do in and through me.

1 Samuel 1:12–16
And it came to pass, as she continued praying before the LORD, that Eli marked her mouth. Now Hannah, she spake in her heart; only her lips moved, but her voice was not heard: therefore Eli thought she had been drunken. And Eli said unto her, How long wilt thou be drunken? put away thy wine from thee. And Hannah answered and said, No, my lord, I am a woman of a sorrowful spirit: I have drunk neither wine nor strong drink, but have poured out my soul before the LORD. Count not thine handmaid for a daughter of Belial: for out of the abundance of my complaint and grief have I spoken hitherto.

As he watched her pray, Eli thought Hannah must have been drinking. The same thing happened centuries later when, on the Day of Pentecost, the disciples were thought to be drunk because they spoke in other tongues after the Spirit came upon them (Acts 2). Notice that Hannah was immediately able to explain what she was doing. So was Peter on the Day of Pentecost. If you're in a place where the Spirit is at work, be wary of people who say, "We can't explain what's going on. We're just all caught up in this ecstatic experience." As seen in both Hannah's and Peter's situations, where the Spirit of the Lord is, all things are done decently and in order (1 Corinthians 14:40).

1 Samuel 1:17, 18
Then Eli answered and said, Go in peace: and the God of Israel grant thee thy petition that thou hast asked of him. And she said, Let thine handmaid find grace in thy sight. So the woman went her way, and did eat, and her countenance was no more sad.

When Hannah was told her prayer was answered, although she had no tangible evidence of this, she chose to believe. Are you discouraged or depressed? The cure lies not in seeing your situation change, but in hearing the Word and choosing to believe it. What has God whispered in your ear? Hang on to it. Believe it. Don't despair. Live a life of rejoicing, for in so doing, you will prevent Satan from aborting that which God wants to conceive in you and birth through you.

1 Samuel 1:19, 20
And they rose up in the morning early, and worshipped before the LORD, and returned, and came to their house to Ramah: and Elkanah knew Hannah his wife; and the LORD remembered her. Wherefore it came to pass, when the time was come about after Hannah had conceived, that she bare a son, and called his name Samuel, saying, Because I have asked him of the LORD.

Samuel means "Asked of God." In naming her baby, Hannah remembered that his delivery was in response to her prayer made nine months earlier. I'm convinced the biggest problem in our prayer lives is forgetting what we prayed for. When the answer to our prayer comes nine days, months, or years after we asked, we say, "Wonderful!" but forget it is in answer to what we were praying for previously.

Forgetting what I prayed for previously causes me to think God is not responding to my prayers presently. For example, in a moment of honesty before the Lord, I pray, "Lord, there are things in me that need to be changed. Make me a man who is broken before You and totally dependent on You. Lord, change me." And He begins that process. But then, three weeks later, I pray, "Lord, I need a raise desperately." But the raise doesn't come. Why? Because God is still answering my prayer that I be dependent on Him. Since we don't remember what we pray for, we often end up offering contradictory prayers.

When I look back over my journals, inevitably I hear myself saying, "No wonder I'm going through this now. I prayed for it way back then." Forgetting what we pray for is a problem most of us have that keeps us from being men and women of prayer. Such was not the case with Hannah.

1 Samuel 1:21–24
And the man Elkanah, and all his house, went up to offer unto the LORD the yearly sacrifice, and his vow. But Hannah went not up; for she said unto her husband, I will not go up until the child be weaned, and then I will bring him, that he may appear before the LORD, and there abide for ever. And Elkanah her husband said unto her, Do what seemeth thee good; tarry until thou have weaned him; only the LORD establish his word. So the woman abode, and gave her son suck until she weaned him. And when she had weaned him, she took him up with her, with three bullocks, and one ephah of flour, and a bottle of wine, and brought him unto the house of the LORD in Shiloh: and the child was young.

Samuel is believed to be about three years old here. I like what Hannah packed when she took him to the tabernacle, for meat speaks of the strong meat of the Word (Hebrews 5:12–14), and flour and wine speak of the bread and wine of Communion.

1 Samuel 1:25–27
And they slew a bullock, and brought the child to Eli. And she said, Oh my lord, as thy soul liveth, my lord, I am the woman that stood by thee here, praying unto the LORD. For this child I prayed; and the LORD hath given me my petition which I asked of him:

"Remember me, Eli?" Hannah said. "I'm the lady who was praying for a child. And here he is!" A number of times over the years, I've prayed for couples that want to have a child. And nothing could be better than being given the opportunity to dedicate the child the Lord gives them.

1 Samuel 1:28 (a)
Therefore also I have lent him to the LORD; as long as he liveth he shall be lent to the LORD . . .

The Hebrew word translated "lent" literally means "returned." Hannah vowed she would give her child to the Lord—and here she honors her vow.

1 Samuel 1:28 (b)
. . . And he worshipped the LORD there.

In the presentation of little Samuel to the Lord, we see the model for baby dedication. Although it's not commanded specifically in the Word, we see Jesus Himself brought to the temple to be dedicated (Luke 2). Does a parent have to do this? No. But God will take any territory we give Him. And if you present your child, the house you're building, or the relationship you're in to the Lord, He'll surely use it for His glory.

2 In chapter 1, we heard the prayer of a barren woman. Here in chapter 2, we hear the praise of a blessed woman . . .

1 Samuel 2:1 (a)
And Hannah prayed . . .

Hannah's prayer is interesting because it's remarkably similar to the Magnificat in Luke 1—the prayer Mary offered after learning she would bear a Son. This means Mary was familiar with the prayer of Hannah, that she was a student of the Word. Although only a teenage girl, Mary would have heard the Word in the synagogue and evidently she absorbed and embraced it, treasured and memorized it.

The language of Hannah's prayer is heavenly—but don't miss the earthy accent in the not-so-subtle references to her rival, Peninnah. Sometimes our prayers are so lofty that they hide our true emotions. To such prayers, I believe the Lord would say, "Tell Me what you're really feeling. I can handle it. After all, I already know all about it" (Hebrews 4:13).

1 Samuel 2:1 (b)
. . . and said, My heart rejoiceth in the LORD, mine horn is exalted in the LORD: my mouth is enlarged over mine enemies . . .

"Mine horn is exalted," or "I'm lifted up," Hannah prayed. "My mouth is enlarged, for now I have something to say. I don't have to bite my tongue any longer."

1 Samuel 2:1 (c)–4
. . . because I rejoice in thy salvation. There is none holy as the LORD: for there is none beside thee: neither is there any rock like our God. Talk no more so exceeding proudly; let not arrogancy come out of your mouth: for the LORD is a God of knowledge, and by him actions are weighed. The bows of the mighty men are broken, and they that stumbled are girded with strength.

"Let not arrogancy come out of your mouth." Here, we hear an earthy accent because to whom is Hannah referring? Peninnah.

1 Samuel 2:5
They that were full have hired out themselves for bread; and they that were hungry ceased: so that the barren hath born seven; and she that hath many children is waxed feeble.

Hannah had borne one child at this point. As we'll see, she'll have five more.

1 Samuel 2:6, 7
The LORD killeth, and maketh alive: he bringeth down to the grave, and bringeth up. The LORD maketh poor, and maketh rich: he bringeth low, and lifteth up.

The Lord makes things right; He brings things about in an equitable way.

1 Samuel 2:8
He raiseth up the poor out of the dust, and lifteth up the beggar from the dunghill, to set them among princes, and to make them inherit the throne of glory: for the pillars of the earth are the LORD's, and he hath set the world upon them.

The Lord is in control. He's the One who holds everything together, the One who works everything out.

1 Samuel 2:9 (a)
He will keep the feet of his saints . . .

The Lord will walk with His saints. He'll see them through. He'll keep their steps from slipping.

1 Samuel 2:9 (b), 10
. . . and the wicked shall be silent in darkness; for by strength shall no man prevail. The adversaries of the LORD shall be broken to pieces; out of heaven shall he thunder upon them: the LORD shall judge the ends of the earth; and he shall give strength unto his king, and exalt the horn of his anointed.

Thus ends the prayer of Hannah—full of lofty praise and exaltation, but revealing the humanness of her soul as well. Hannah's prayer encourages me. The fact that God includes it in His Word gives me great freedom to be honest and open before Him.

1 Samuel 2:11
And Elkanah went to Ramah to his house. And the child did minister unto the LORD before Eli the priest.

Just as she promised, Hannah brought Samuel to the temple and left him there to be trained for ministry. And as a young boy, he's left there to be trained up in the ministry and to minister to the Lord personally from a young age.

1 Samuel 2:12
Now the sons of Eli were sons of Belial; they knew not the LORD.

In other words, Eli's sons were worthless and wicked.

1 Samuel 2:13, 14
And the priests' custom with the people was, that, when any man offered sacrifice, the priest's servant came, while the flesh was in seething, with a fleshhook of three teeth in his hand; And he struck it into the pan, or kettle, or caldron, or pot; all that the fleshhook brought up the priest took for himself. So they did in Shiloh unto all the Israelites that came thither.

According to Old Testament Law, with the exception of burnt offerings, priests would be allowed portions of the sacrifices after they were offered to the Lord. Hophni and Phinehas, however, didn't wait for the Lord. They took their portion *before* it was offered to the Lord.

1 Samuel 2:15, 16
Also before they burnt the fat, the priest's servant came, and said to the man that sacrificed, Give flesh to roast for the priest; for he will not have sodden flesh of thee, but raw. And if any man said unto him, Let them not fail to burn the fat presently, and then take as much as thy soul desireth; then he would answer him, Nay; but thou shalt give it me now: and if not, I will take it by force.

In Leviticus 3 through 9, God declared that the fat of the sacrifice was to be completely burned on the altar, signifying the offering of it to Him. In Old Testament times, the fat was considered to be the best part of the meat. Therefore, God could have been accused of keeping the best part for Himself. We now know that the fat is actually the worst part of the meat. Therefore, God was protecting His people from that which would have harmed them.

That's always the way it is with God. We say, "Why can't I have that? Why can't I go there? Why can't I do that? God must be keeping something good from me."

But the Lord would say, "I'm not going to explain what I'm doing because I want you to trust Me. But as time goes on, you'll see that the things, people, or places I withheld from you would have been harmful to you."

1 Samuel 2:17
Wherefore the sin of the young men was very great before the LORD: for men abhorred the offering of the LORD.

What a sad situation. Some ministers have a wealth of thought; others have only thoughts of wealth. Eli's sons were of the latter type.

1 Samuel 2:18
But Samuel ministered before the LORD, being a child, girded with a linen ephod.

Even though he was young, Samuel didn't let Eli and his sons discourage, distract, or deter him from what he knew he should do. Samuel would become the greatest of all judges because he ministered to the Lord even though others were messing up. The way to greatness is simply to say, "Regardless of what others do, I'm going to do what I know is pleasing to You, Lord."

1 Samuel 2:19
Moreover his mother made him a little coat, and brought it to him from year to year, when she came up with her husband to offer the yearly sacrifice.

Once a year, Hannah would bring Samuel a new garment because he would grow over a year's time and need new clothes.

1 Samuel 2:20, 21
And Eli blessed Elkanah and his wife, and said, The LORD give thee seed of this woman for the loan which is lent to the LORD. And they went unto their own home. And the LORD visited Hannah, so that she conceived, and bare three sons and two daughters. And the child Samuel grew before the LORD.

Hannah gave one child to the Lord and received five in return. It's a great illustration of the glorious fact that you can't out give God. Many believers never really understand God's math. They don't understand His ways or His economy. They go through a lifetime never understanding that they can't out give God. Give God what is His, and you'll get back much more than you could ever imagine. Ask Hannah.

1 Samuel 2:22
Now Eli was very old, and heard all that his sons did unto all Israel; and how they lay with the women that assembled at the door of the tabernacle of the congregation.

"Laying with women" obviously speaks of immorality, fornication, and adultery. There are two schools of thought on this. It may be that Hophni and Phinehas forced themselves upon the women who came to worship the Lord. Or it could mean that they put together a troop—as the original language suggests—of temple prostitutes, as did the pagans of the region. They're introducing to the people of Israel temple prostitution. Either way, it's a deplorable situation that came to Eli's attention.

1 Samuel 2:23–25 (a)
And he said unto them, Why do ye such things? for I hear of your evil dealings by all this people. Nay, my sons; for it is no good report that I hear: ye make the LORD's people to transgress. If one man sin against another, the judge shall judge him: but if a man sin against the LORD, who shall intreat for him?

"If you sin against a man, you go to court. But if you sin against God, you have no defense," Eli said.

1 Samuel 2:25 (b)
. . . Notwithstanding they hearkened not unto the voice of their father, because the LORD would slay them.

The Lord already intended that it was time for Eli's sons to be taken out of the ministry permanently. Hophni and Phinehas were destined to die. They had crossed the line. They had gone too far.

1 Samuel 2:26
And the child Samuel grew on, and was in favour both with the LORD, and also with men.

Hophni and Phinehas were bad guys who would die prematurely. Samuel, on the other hand, kept growing in God. And what happened? He not only found favor in the eyes of the Lord, but also in the eyes of men. Our kids sometimes have the mistaken idea that if they stand for the Lord and walk with Him, they'll be put down or left out. Not true. Yes, there will be a certain degree of persecution in the Christian walk, but notice what happened to Samuel. He found favor in the eyes of God and of men, too.

Blessed is the man who doesn't walk with the ungodly and sit in the seat of the scornful, but whose delight is in the Law of the Lord. Whatever he does will prosper (Psalm 1). As parents, we need to remind our kids that the real key to having a prosperous, exciting life, the key to finding favor in the eyes of both God and men is to do what Samuel did. He walked with the Lord, and God blessed him indeed.

1 Samuel 2:27
And there came a man of God unto Eli, and said unto him, Thus saith the LORD, Did I plainly appear unto the house of thy father, when they were in Egypt in Pharaoh's house?

The reference, of course, is to Aaron, the first high priest.

1 Samuel 2:28–30
And did I choose him out of all the tribes of Israel to be my priest, to offer upon mine altar, to burn incense, to wear an ephod before me? and did I give unto the house of thy father all the offerings made by fire of the children of Israel? Wherefore kick ye at my sacrifice and at mine offering, which I have com-

manded in my habitation; and honourest thy sons above me, to make yourselves fat with the chiefest of all the offerings of Israel my people? Wherefore the LORD God of Israel saith, I said indeed that thy house, and the house of thy father, should walk before me for ever: but now the LORD saith, Be it far from me; for them that honour me I will honour, and they that despise me shall be lightly esteemed.

Here, through a prophet, God says to Eli, "You and your family have a heritage reaching all the way back to Aaron in the days of the Exodus. You were given the privilege to walk with Me and stand before Me day after day. But you despised it by allowing your sons to sin. You honored your sons above Me. You cared more about them liking you than about what I thought of the situation."

Mom and Dad, take note. If your primary goal as a parent is to have your kids like you, you will not like what your kids become. Your primary goal should be to want your kids to know what's right in God's sight. If that means discipline, so be it. If they hate you in the process, so be it. But you must honor God more than you honor your kids. Eli wanted to be cool in the eyes of his boys. And it would lead to their downfall.

1 Samuel 2:31–34
Behold, the days come, that I will cut off thine arm, and the arm of thy father's house, that there shall not be an old man in thine house. And thou shalt see an enemy in my habitation, in all the wealth which God shall give Israel: and there shall not be an old man in thine house for ever. And the man of thine, whom I shall not cut off from mine altar, shall be to consume thine eyes, and to grieve thine heart: and all the increase of thine house shall die in the flower of their age. And this shall be a sign unto thee, that shall come upon thy two sons, on Hophni and Phinehas; in one day they shall die both of them.

In other words, not only would Eli's family disintegrate, but the enemy would eventually enter the house of God.

1 Samuel 2:35, 36
And I will raise me up a faithful priest, that shall do according to that which is in mine heart and in my mind: and I will build him a sure house; and he shall walk before mine anointed for ever. And it shall come to pass, that every one that is left in thine house shall come and crouch to him for a piece of silver and a morsel of bread, and shall say, Put me, I pray thee, into one of the priests' offices, that I may eat a piece of bread.

Who is the faithful priest? It could be Samuel. Although Samuel was not a priest but a prophet because he was not of the tribe of Levi, we will see him minister like a priest in the offering of sacrifices.

Others suggest the faithful priest refers to Zadok because this verse is alluded to in 1 Kings 2:27 and 35 when Zadok takes over the priesthood from a man named Abiezar. Abiezar was the last descendant of Eli. When Abiezar is moved off the scene, the whole family disappears from Israel's history. The problem with this suggestion is that Zadok didn't "walk before mine anointed forever." Therefore, some suggest the reference is to the sons of Zadok, who continue all the way through the Millennium (Ezekiel 40:46).

Obviously, this prophecy is most completely fulfilled in the One who would come and be the perfect High Priest forever. People will let you down—but there is One who will walk in perfection for all eternity. That One is our great High Priest, Jesus Christ.

3

1 Samuel 3:1
And the child Samuel ministered unto the LORD before Eli. And the word of the LORD was precious in those days; there was no open vision.

The word of the Lord was precious—or rare. Speaking to believers in Revelation 3:20, Jesus says, "Behold, I stand at the door and knock. If any man hear My voice and open the door, I will come in and sup with him and he with Me." In other words, the question isn't whether Jesus is speaking. The question is: Are we listening?

There's no question God speaks. Psalm 29 tells us His voice is so powerful that it moves mountains and clears forests. The question is, are God's people tuning in? Are they able to perceive and receive the word He speaks constantly? There are numerous voices speaking via radio and television waves traveling through any given location. The fact that we don't hear them is not because those voices aren't present, but because we're not tuned in to them. Our antenna isn't up, our TV sets aren't on. The same thing is true spiritually (John 10:27). Our Shepherd speaks constantly. The question is, are we tuned in to His frequency? Am I picking up and receiving what He's saying?

I see four questions answered in the passage before us . . .

To Whom Does God Speak?

1 Samuel 3:2

And it came to pass at that time, when Eli was laid down in his place, and his eyes began to wax dim, that he could not see;

In the temple, there was an experienced, professional priest named Eli. He may have had all his seminary degrees, but he didn't hear God's voice. God bypassed him and spoke to a child instead. Jesus said, "Unless you become as a little child, you cannot enter the kingdom" (Luke 18:17).

Children have an amazing receptivity and expectancy. As people get older and more knowledgeable, they begin to look down on hearing the voice of the Lord. "God doesn't speak to us in that way today," they say. Eli represents the old order and what can happen when one loses his sense of wonder and expectancy.

Have you become an old professional? Are you saying in your soul, "I've heard all this. I know all that"? If so, you'll not hear the voice of the Lord. It's when you retain a childlike excitement about the things of God that He will speak to you.

When Did God Speak?

1 Samuel 3:3, 4 (a)

And ere the lamp of God went out in the temple of the LORD, where the ark of God was, and Samuel was laid down to sleep; That the LORD called Samuel . . .

Samuel was ministering to the Lord when God spoke to him. Ministering *to* the Lord is different from ministering *for* Him. Ministering *for* the Lord is teaching a lesson, giving a sermon, helping someone in His name. Ministering *to* the Lord, on the other hand, is drawing near to Him personally and privately. Ministry *to* the Lord takes place not on stage, but in the pew. Ministry *to* the Lord is not about what others see us do, but what the Lord alone enjoys as we spend time with Him. Ministering *to* the Lord is the highest calling in life, and every single one of us can do it.

I love it when my wife makes a meal for me or irons my shirt. But those things can't begin to compare to the love I feel when she's ministering *to* me—being by my side, sharing with me, loving me. The same is true of the Lord. When you minister *to* Him, it's a far higher calling than ministering *for* Him (Ezekiel 44).

1 Samuel 3:4 (b)–7

. . . and he answered, Here am I. And he ran unto Eli, and said, Here am I; for thou calledst me. And he said, I called not; lie down again. And he went and lay down. And the LORD called yet again, Samuel. And Samuel arose and went to Eli, and said, Here am I; for thou didst call me. And he answered, I called not, my son; lie down again. Now Samuel did not yet know the LORD, neither was the word of the LORD yet revealed unto him.

Notice at this point, Samuel didn't know the Lord personally. He hadn't yet heard from the Lord audibly. But he knew about the Lord. Samuel knew that, as God, He deserved worship and affection. Samuel didn't yet know the Lord, but here he is, year after year, ministering to the Lord.

Ministering *to* the Lord before ministering *for* Him is also seen in the Book of Acts . . .

As they ministered to the Lord, and fasted, the Holy Ghost said, Separate me Barnabas and Saul for the work whereunto I have called them. Acts 13:2

This verse should be noted by anyone who wants to be a servant of Jesus Christ, for it was as Paul and Barnabas ministered *to* the Lord that He separated them for ministry. Find ways you can minister to the Lord, where no one else sees what you're doing, but where you are pleasing the Lord simply because He's worthy.

Where Did the Lord Speak?

1 Samuel 3:8–10

And the LORD called Samuel again the third time. And he arose and went to Eli, and said, Here am I; for thou didst call me. And Eli perceived that the LORD had called the child. Therefore Eli said unto Samuel, Go, lie down: and it shall be, if he call thee, that thou shalt say, Speak, LORD; for thy servant heareth. So Samuel went and lay down in his place. And the LORD came, and stood, and called as at other times, Samuel, Samuel. Then Samuel answered, Speak; for thy servant heareth.

Samuel was in the temple. Growing up, I heard the voice of the Lord most clearly at church, youth group meetings, and Sunday school classes. And as the years go by, I still hear His voice most clearly and most frequently in the temple—at church.

If you want the Lord to speak to you and give guidance to you, be in the temple. As the days go by, you'll discover that it's the place He'll speak to you most frequently. I can't tell you the number of times I've stood at the door after a service and heard people tell me things in my message that morning that ministered to them—things I never even said! Why did they hear them? Because, as

He did to Samuel, it was God speaking to them in the temple.

Why Did God Speak to Samuel?

1 Samuel 3:11–14

And the LORD said to Samuel, Behold, I will do a thing in Israel, at which both the ears of every one that heareth it shall tingle. In that day I will perform against Eli all things which I have spoken concerning his house: when I begin, I will also make an end. For I have told him that I will judge his house for ever for the iniquity which he knoweth; because his sons made themselves vile, and he restrained them not. And therefore I have sworn unto the house of Eli, that the iniquity of Eli's house shall not be purged with sacrifice nor offering for ever.

God didn't speak to Eli. He spoke to Samuel. Why? I suggest it was because Samuel got out of bed. God talks to us in the middle of the night as well. But we think it's the pizza or our husband's snoring or the caffeine from the double latte we ordered earlier that keeps us up. I am convinced, however, the Lord speaks to our souls at night because it's the only time our hearts are quiet enough to hear Him. The question is, "Will I respond?"

When I do, I hear Him say, "There's something I want to talk over with you. I have direction to give you. I have a word of correction for you." If you want your dreams to come true, gang, you've got to get out of bed! Four times in one night, Samuel got out of bed to check out what was going on. On the fourth time, he discovered it was the Lord all along. God interrupts your sleep or your life, your plans and your schedule, because He wants you to hear from Him.

1 Samuel 3:15–21

And Samuel lay until the morning, and opened the doors of the house of the LORD. And Samuel feared to shew Eli the vision. Then Eli called Samuel, and said, Samuel, my son. And he answered, Here am I. And he said, What is the thing that the LORD hath said unto thee? I pray thee hide it not from me: God do so to thee, and more also, if thou hide any thing from me of all the things that he said unto thee. And Samuel told him every whit, and hid nothing from him. And he said, It is the LORD: let him do what seemeth him good. And Samuel grew, and the LORD was with him, and did let none of his words fall to the ground. And all Israel from Dan even to Beer-sheba knew that Samuel was established to be a prophet of the LORD. And the LORD appeared again in Shiloh: for the LORD revealed himself to Samuel in Shiloh by the word of the LORD.

God not only spoke to Samuel because of his responsiveness, but because of his tenderness. Samuel didn't want to say to Eli, "Eli, you're in trouble. You haven't disciplined your sons. Now judgment is coming to you and your family. And it's too late for any sacrifices to make up for what you've done."

Living in the temple, Samuel no doubt observed Eli's sons and was aware of their immorality and problems. Therefore, he could have said, "Aha! At last these guys are getting what they deserve." But that wasn't the heart of Samuel. Nor was it the heart of Daniel.

Before Daniel gave Nebuchadnezzar the interpretation of his dream, he said, "I wish this dream applied to your worst enemy rather than to you, for you're going to go insane like an animal for seven years and eat grass like a cow in the fields." Daniel could have said, "Great! It's about time God brings Nebuchadnezzar down a notch or two." But that wasn't the heart of Daniel, nor is it the heart of anyone who is in tune with God.

Whatever God speaks to you must be enveloped in tenderness and love. Even if the message is a difficult one, it's always to be delivered in humility and kindness.

4

1 Samuel 4:1 (a)

And the word of Samuel came to all Israel . . .

Samuel is now a prophet, doing what he was called to do—giving the word of the Lord to the people of God.

1 Samuel 4:1 (b)

. . . Now Israel went out against the Philistines to battle, and pitched beside Ebenezer: and the Philistines pitched in Aphek.

The armies of the Israelites and the armies of the Philistines are facing off.

1 Samuel 4:2, 3

And the Philistines put themselves in array against Israel: and when they joined battle, Israel was smitten before the Philistines: and they slew of the army in the field about four thousand men. And when the people were come into the camp, the elders of Israel said, Wherefore hath the LORD smitten us to day before the Philistines? Let us fetch the ark of the covenant of the LORD out of Shiloh

unto us, that, when it cometh among us, it may save us out of the hand of our enemies.

With four thousand casualties, Israel had taken a beating. They called for the ark of the covenant, certain it would deliver them. But God doesn't work that way because He wants His people to look to Him. He wants us to give all glory and honor to Him—not to our "box" of religious practices or customs. All too often, Christian books and seminars present four steps to deliverance, six steps to victory, twelve principles of success. Many of us have walked with the Lord long enough to have jumped through countless hoops, or checked off numerous "boxes"—the latest fad, the hottest trend in spiritual life—only to find they don't work. God wants us to be Spirit-led day by day. He wants to show us what *He* has for us to do, rather than what some program will do for us.

The Israelites were in error, sure that God-in-a-box would give them victory.

1 Samuel 4:4 (a)
So the people sent to Shiloh, that they might bring from thence the ark of the covenant of the LORD of hosts, which dwelleth between the cherubims . . .

The ark of the covenant was the most important object in the Israelites' possession. Yet here, it's importance was tragically misapplied.

1 Samuel 4:4 (b)
. . . and the two sons of Eli, Hophni and Phinehas, were there with the ark of the covenant of God.

It's not surprising that Hophni and Phinehas accompanied the ark. They were carnal indeed, and carnality always relies on programs or formulas.

1 Samuel 4:5
And when the ark of the covenant of the LORD came into the camp, all Israel shouted with a great shout, so that the earth rang again.

The old adage is true: God does not care about how high we jump, but about how straight we walk. I've been in meetings where there was lots of sky-high jumping, but not straight walking in the lives of those who attend because they haven't been taught the Word of God. They've been given clever sayings and admonitions, but nothing of substance to help them walk straight the next day. God's Word is the key.

Here, the Israelites weren't interested in hearing the Word of the Lord. They were simply whooping and hollering because the ark was there.

1 Samuel 4:6, 7
And when the Philistines heard the noise of the shout, they said, What meaneth the noise of this great shout in the camp of the Hebrews? And they understood that the ark of the LORD was come into the camp. And the Philistines were afraid, for they said, God is come into the camp. And they said, Woe unto us! for there hath not been such a thing heretofore.

"God is in their camp!" the Philistines said. Yes, the symbol of His presence was there, but the context was all wrong because His people were more taken up with the symbol than with Him.

1 Samuel 4:8–10
Woe unto us! who shall deliver us out of the hand of these mighty Gods? these are the Gods that smote the Egyptians with all the plagues in the wilderness. Be strong, and quit yourselves like men, O ye Philistines, that ye be not servants unto the Hebrews, as they have been to you: quit yourselves like men, and fight. And the Philistines fought, and Israel was smitten, and they fled every man into his tent: and there was a very great slaughter; for there fell of Israel thirty thousand footmen.

Thirty thousand men died. This was a horrible defeat; a brutal, bloody battle in which the Philistines butchered the people of Israel.

The same thing can happen to me. I bring the "ark" into my camp. My boxes are all checked off on my spiritual To Do list. Therefore, it's sure to be a great day. But I've discovered that sometimes when my boxes are all checked off, the day goes horribly. "Lord," I cry, "I checked my boxes. I read my Bible, prayed, and went to church. I even tithed eleven percent last week! Why don't I have victory?"

And the Lord would say to me, "It's not about bringing a box into your camp or checking a box off on a list. Only a relationship with Me will bring victory as I guide you step by step, day by day."

Reading two chapters a day or attending church two times a week won't guarantee victory any more than bringing the box into the camp brought victory to the Israelites. God doesn't work that way. If, however, reading two chapters a day or attending church two times a week is done for the purpose of meeting *Him*, of learning more about *Him*, of spending time with *Him*—He has promised to meet us there (James 4:8).

1 Samuel 4:11–13 (a)
And the ark of God was taken; and the two sons of Eli, Hophni and Phinehas, were slain. And there ran a man of Benjamin out of the army, and came to Shiloh the same day with his clothes rent, and with earth upon his head. And when he came, lo, Eli sat upon a seat by the wayside watching: for his heart trembled for the ark of God . . .

Eli's heart didn't tremble for his sons; he knew they were deserving of death. Eli was worried about the ark. For he knew taking the ark into battle was a travesty.

1 Samuel 4:13 (b)–18 (a)
. . . And when the man came into the city, and told it, all the city cried out. And when Eli heard the noise of the crying, he said, What meaneth the noise of this tumult? And the man came in hastily, and told Eli. Now Eli was ninety and eight years old; and his eyes were dim, that he could not see. And the man said unto Eli, I am he that came out of the army, and I fled to day out of the army. And he said, What is there done, my son? And the messenger answered and said, Israel is fled before the Philistines, and there hath been also a great slaughter among the people, and thy two sons also, Hophni and Phinehas, are dead, and the ark of God is taken. And it came to pass, when he made mention of the ark of God, that he fell from off the seat backward by the side of the gate, and his neck brake, and he died: for he was an old man, and heavy . . .

Hearing the ark had been taken, Eli died just as the prophet said he would—on the same day as his sons.

1 Samuel 4:18 (b)–22
. . . And he had judged Israel forty years. And his daughter in law, Phinehas' wife, was with child, near to be delivered: and when she heard the tidings that the ark of God was taken, and that her father in law and her husband were dead, she bowed herself and travailed; for her pains came upon her. And about the time of her death the women that stood by her said unto her, Fear not; for thou hast born a son. But she answered not, neither did she regard it. And she named the child I-chabod, saying, The glory is departed from Israel: because the ark of God was taken, and because of her father in law and her husband. And she said, The glory is departed from Israel: for the ark of God is taken.

It is in the Book of Exodus that we first see the Hebrew word, *chabod*, meaning "weight" or "splendor" used in reference to God's presence. It was the *chabod* that was present on Mt Sinai (Exodus 24:16), the *chabod* that appeared to Moses (Exodus 33:22), the *chabod* that filled the tabernacle (Exodus 40:34). Now, with the ark gone and the people of God defeated, *I-chabod's* name, meaning, "Where is the glory?" was fitting, for it seemed the glory of God had departed. Yet even though God's people are faithless toward Him, He remains faithful to them (2 Timothy 2:13), for not too far down the road, His glory, His splendor, His presence will fill the temple (1 Kings 8). God never gave up on Israel—and He'll never give up on you. Aren't you glad?

5

1 Samuel 5:1
And the Philistines took the ark of God, and brought it from Eben-ezer unto Ashdod.

Ashdod was one of the five Philistine cities on the Mediterranean seacoast of Southern Israel.

1 Samuel 5:2
When the Philistines took the ark of God, they brought it into the house of Dagon, and set it by Dagon.

Half fish and half man, Dagon was the god of the Philistines. Also worshiped by the Assyrians, he was considered by the people in the region of Canaan to be the father of Baal.

1 Samuel 5:3
And when they of Ashdod arose early on the morrow, behold, Dagon was fallen upon his face to the earth before the ark of the LORD. And they took Dagon, and set him in his place again.

I once talked to a man who desperately wanted to be free from a certain addiction. Although he had tried numerous programs and counseling sessions, nothing worked. This story of Dagon proved to be a key for him. Dagon could not stand in the presence of the Lord. Therefore, I told this man that if he tried to get victory over the "Dagon" of his addiction in his own power, he would only become obsessed with it all the more. "Forget about Dagon," I said. "Instead, bring in the ark. Bring in the presence of the Lord. Spend time in His Word, in prayer, in fellowship with

Him—and Dagon will fall." And that's exactly what happened.

The key to overcoming darkness is not to curse, cajole, or karate chop the darkness. The key is simply to turn on the light. Bring the ark into any situation and watch Dagon go down because darkness and light are mutually exclusive. Light always eventually wins (1 John 1:5).

1 Samuel 5:4
And when they arose early on the morrow morning, behold, Dagon was fallen upon his face to the ground before the ark of the LORD; and the head of Dagon and both the palms of his hands were cut off upon the threshold; only the stump of Dagon was left to him.

When the statue of Dagon fell, its head and hands fell off and rolled to the door of the temple. Now, if you walked into the temple of your god and discovered his head cut off and his hands missing, wouldn't you think something was "fishy"?

1 Samuel 5:5
Therefore neither the priests of Dagon, nor any that come into Dagon's house, tread on the threshold of Dagon in Ashdod unto this day.

One would think that having to step over Dagon's head as they walked in the door of the temple would prove to the people that Dagon was no god at all. Instead, however, the people honored the threshold as holy ground. The only explanation for this is the fact that pagan religions—including the worship of Dagon—required many bizarre practices and immoral procedures. The Philistines knew Dagon wasn't a real god. But they justified his false religious system because it gave them license to indulge their flesh.

1 Samuel 5:6
But the hand of the LORD was heavy upon them of Ashdod, and he destroyed them, and smote them with emerods, even Ashdod and the coasts thereof.

The Philistines were smitten with hemorrhoids. If they wouldn't stand before God, they wouldn't be able to sit before Dagon, either.

1 Samuel 5:7
And when the men of Ashdod saw that it was so, they said, The ark of the God of Israel shall not abide with us: for his hand is sore upon us, and upon Dagon our god.

Instead of saying, "Lord, we're going to seek You, call upon You, turn to You, and believe in You, the Philistines said, "We'll go with the fishy one, the headless god, Dagon." Amazing.

1 Samuel 5:8
They sent therefore and gathered all the lords of the Philistines unto them, and said, What shall we do with the ark of the God of Israel? And they answered, Let the ark of the God of Israel be carried about unto Gath. And they carried the ark of the God of Israel about thither.

Gath was a Philistine city twelve miles southeast of Ashdod. "Let's send the ark to Gath, our sister city," said the city fathers of Ashdod. Misery must surely love company.

1 Samuel 5:9
And it was so, that, after they had carried it about, the hand of the LORD was against the city with a very great destruction: and he smote the men of the city, both small and great, and they had emerods in their secret parts.

The people of Gath were also smitten with hemorrhoids.

1 Samuel 5:10
Therefore they sent the ark of God to Ekron. And it came to pass, as the ark of God came to Ekron, that the Ekronites cried out, saying, They have brought about the ark of the God of Israel to us, to slay us and our people.

The people of Gath sent the ark to Ekron, the next Philistine city on the map.

1 Samuel 5:11, 12
So they sent and gathered together all the lords of the Philistines, and said, Send away the ark of the God of Israel, and let it go again to his own place, that it slay us not, and our people: for there was a deadly destruction throughout all the city; the hand of God was very heavy there. And the men that died not were smitten with the emerods: and the cry of the city went up to heaven.

Evidently, it was some type of plague that killed many in Ekron. Instead of turning to the Lord when His hand was upon them, however, the people of Ekron said, "We have to get rid of this ark."

6

1 Samuel 6:1, 2
And the ark of the LORD was in the country of the Philistines seven months. And

the Philistines called for the priests and the diviners, saying, What shall we do to the ark of the LORD? tell us wherewith we shall send it to his place.

Having had their fill of the plagues associated with the ark, the Philistines were ready to send it back to Israel.

1 Samuel 6:3–5
And they said, If ye send away the ark of the God of Israel, send it not empty; but in any wise return him a trespass offering: then ye shall be healed, and it shall be known to you why his hand is not removed from you. Then said they, What shall be the trespass offering which we shall return to him? They answered, Five golden emerods, and five golden mice, according to the number of the lords of the Philistines: for one plague was on you all, and on your lords. Wherefore ye shall make images of your emerods, and images of your mice that mar the land; and ye shall give glory unto the God of Israel: peradventure he will lighten his hand from off you, and from off your gods, and from off your land.

The Philistine priests and wise men decided that the ark could not be returned empty. So they made replicas of five mice and hemorrhoids out of gold to accompany it. Five represented the five Philistine cities. Mice evidently represented those who died in the plague, and hemorrhoids evidently represented those who, although they felt the hand of God, survived.

1 Samuel 6:6
Wherefore then do ye harden your hearts, as the Egyptians and Pharoah hardened their hearts? when he had wrought wonderfully among them, did they not let the people go, and they departed?

"Learn a lesson from the Egyptians," the Philistine priests said. "When Pharaoh hardened his heart, the result was deadly. Let the ark go."

1 Samuel 6:7–9
Now therefore make a new cart, and take two milch kine, on which there hath come no yoke, and tie the kine to the cart, and bring their calves home from them: And take the ark of the LORD, and lay it upon the cart; and put the jewels of gold, which ye return him for a trespass offering, in a coffer by the side thereof; and send it away, that it may go. And see, if it goeth up by the way of his own coast to Beth-shemesh, then he hath done us this great evil: but if not, then we shall know that is not his hand that smote us; it was a chance that happened to us.

"Fasten the cart to these two mother cows and send them on their way," the Philistine priests said. "If the cows go towards Beth-shemesh, we'll know that it is God who has smitten us. If the cows don't go, it means it just so happened that these plagues came our way." The Philistines were correct in thinking only God could cause cows to willingly leave their young.

1 Samuel 6:10–12
And the men did so; and took two milch kine, and tied them to the cart, and shut up their calves at home: And they laid the ark of the LORD upon the cart, and the coffer with the mice of gold and the images of their emerods. And the kine took the straight way to the way of Beth-shemesh, and went along the highway, lowing as they went, and turned not aside to the right hand or to the left; and the lords of the Philistines went after them unto the border of Beth-shemesh.

Leaving their calves behind and going against all natural instincts, it was obvious the cows were supernaturally led by the Lord.

1 Samuel 6:13–15
And they of Beth-shemesh were reaping their wheat harvest in the valley: and they lifted up their eyes, and saw the ark, and rejoiced to see it. And the cart came into the field of Joshua, a Beth-shemite, and stood there, where there was a great stone: and they clave the wood of the cart, and offered the kine a burnt offering unto the LORD. And the Levites took down the ark of the LORD, and the coffer that was with it, wherein the jewels of gold were, and put them on the great stone: and the men of Beth-shemesh offered burnt offerings and sacrificed sacrifices the same day unto the LORD.

The ark had been missing for seven months. So it was with hearts of thanksgiving and rejoicing that the Israelites offered sacrifices to the Lord upon its return.

1 Samuel 6:16–20
And when the five lords of the Philistines had seen it, they returned to Ekron the same day. And these are the golden emerods which the Philistines returned for a trespass offering unto the LORD; for Ashdod one, for Gaza one, for Askelon one, for Gath one, for Ekron one; And the golden mice, according to the number of all the cities of the Philistines

belonging to the five lords, both of fenced cities, and of country villages, even unto the great stone of Abel, whereon they set down the ark of the LORD: which stone remaineth unto this day in the field of Joshua, the Beth-shemite. And he smote the men of Beth-shemesh, because they had looked into the ark of the LORD, even he smote of the people fifty thousand and threescore and ten men: and the people lamented, because the LORD had smitten many of the people with a great slaughter. And the men of Beth-shemesh said, Who is able to stand before this holy LORD God? and to whom shall he go up from us?

On this day of celebration, rejoicing, and thanksgiving, 50,070 Israelites died. Many scholars say the number 50,070 is not accurate—that a scribe mistakenly wrote 50,070 instead of 70, or that it refers to 70 men who died out of a city of 50,000. While these suggestions are indeed possible, I believe 50,070 died because verse 19 tells us it was a great slaughter. In this story of the ark, we saw 4,000 slain in 1 Samuel 4:2, and 30,000 slain in 1 Samuel 4:10. In comparison to those figures, the deaths of seventy men would hardly constitute a "great slaughter." It seems to me that it was a horrific price that was paid for removing the mercy seat . . .

1 Samuel 6:21
And they sent messengers to the inhabitants of Kirjath-jearim, saying, The Philistines have brought again the ark of the LORD; come ye down, and fetch it up to you.

Kirjath-jearim was ten miles north east of Beth-shemesh. In the wake of devastation associated with it, the men of Beth-shemesh sent word to the men of Kirjath-jearim, saying, "Come and get this ark."

PUT A LID ON IT

A Topical Study of 1 SAMUEL 6:13–20

They were out in the field harvesting when they saw an oxcart coming, pulled by two cows. As the cart drew nearer, the men of Beth-shemesh saw that on the back of the cart was their stolen, most precious ark. The ark of the covenant was a box approximately three feet long, two feet wide, and two feet high inside of which were the Ten Commandments, the Law. On top of it was a lid called the mercy seat. It was at the mercy seat that God declared He would meet with His people (Exodus 25:22).

One day each year—Yom Kippur—the high priest would enter the Holy of Holies, wherein stood the ark, and sprinkle blood seven times on the mercy seat. Then he would make his way out of the Holy of Holies to the congregation waiting outside and announce that they were forgiven. The people would then know that their sins were covered, and great celebration would follow.

No wonder, then, that the men of Bethshemesh rejoiced to see the ark making its way across Joshua's field. What happened next, however, is shocking—for the Lord smote the men of Beth-shemesh simply because they looked into the ark.

Two questions come to mind. The first is: Why did the men of Beth-shemesh look into the ark? I suggest it was because they wanted to see if the Philistines had stolen the Ten Commandments from within. The second question is: Why was this so wrong in God's sight?

In the Book of Numbers, God specifically declared that no man was to look into the holy things that were covered (4:20). In the case of the ark, this meant that the Law was not to be looked upon without the covering of mercy. I know about this. Maybe you do, too. "I need to look into this situation," I'll say. "There seems to be a violation. I need to get to the bottom of this matter." So I'll lay aside mercy and look into the Law to try to get to the bottom of the issue. But every time I do, something in me dies. Whenever mercy is removed—even for a moment—whenever mercy is set aside, something in me will always die.

One day, the prophet Nathan, came to David and said, "A rich man in the kingdom wanted to fix a dinner for his friend. So, instead of taking one of his own numerous sheep, he took his neighbor's only lamb—a family pet—and served it to his friend.

"What?!" David said. "That man must surely die!"

Nathan looked at him and said, "David, that man is you. You have everything you could want. But you took another man's little lamb when you stole Bathsheba from Uriah the Hittite" (2 Samuel 12:1–9).

"Restore unto me the joy of Thy salvation," David later prayed (Psalm 51). Why? Because when he removed the mercy seat to deal with the matter of the hypothetical rich man who took another man's lamb, joy died within his own soul.

When Jesus taught His disciples to pray, the only part of His prayer He made additional comment on dealt with mercy. "If you forgive men their trespasses," He said, "your heavenly Father will forgive you. But if you forgive not men their trespasses, neither will your Father forgive your trespasses" (Matthew 6:14). Notice that Jesus said, "If you forgive men their trespasses, your heavenly Father will forgive *you*, but if you don't forgive men their trespasses, your heavenly Father won't forgive your *trespasses*." In other words, if you choose not to forgive someone, you'll still be forgiven, but your trespass won't. It will remain in your heart, pulling you down, holding you back, killing your joy. The joy of your salvation will depart whenever the mercy seat is removed.

> *Be ye therefore merciful, as your Father also is merciful. Judge not, and ye shall not be judged: condemn not, and ye shall not be condemned: forgive, and ye shall be forgiven: Give, and it shall be given unto you; good measure, pressed down, and shaken together, and running over, shall men give into your bosom. For with the same measure that ye mete withal it shall be measured to you again.*
>
> Luke 6:36–38

Luke 6:38 is probably most often heard in reference to money. But that's not the context. It's about showing mercy. Jesus said to the degree that you forgive others is the degree that you will receive forgiveness from others in your own hour of need.

Every one of us without exception will come to a day when we need mercy, when tears will run down our face and our soul will ache, when we'll know we missed the mark and dropped the ball. And in that day, we'll receive mercy to the exact degree that we've given it. Remove the mercy seat, and the joy of your salvation will die. But if you choose to keep a lid on it—to cover the Law with mercy—kindness, forgiveness, and grace will be shown to you when you need it most.

I understand what you're saying theoretically, you might be thinking. *But he hurt me* or *she crushed me. How do you expect me to keep a lid on this and forgive him, to go my way and forgive her?*

Jesus would say, "I provided justice the day I hung on the Cross. The sin that hurts you so badly, that bruises you so deeply killed Me. My body was broken for that specific sin. Therefore, you don't need to look into it. Put a lid on it. And look instead to the hill where stands the Cross. The price for the sin of the one who is hurting you was paid for with My very life so that the mercy seat could be sprinkled with My own blood."

The mother of a nine-year-old boy received a phone call in the middle of the afternoon. It was her son's teacher. "Mrs. Walden, something unusual happened today. Your son did something that surprised me so much I thought you should know about it immediately."

The mother began to worry.

The teacher continued, "Nothing like this has happened in all my years of teaching. This morning I was teaching a lesson on creative writing. And as I always do, I told the story of the ant and the grasshopper. The ant works hard all summer and stores plenty of food. But the grasshopper plays all summer and does no work at all. Then winter comes. The grasshopper begins to starve because he has no food. So he says, 'Please Mr. Ant. You have so much food. Let me eat, too.'" Then I said, "Boys and girls, it's your job to write the ending to the story."

"Your son raised his hand. 'Teacher, may I draw a picture?'"

"'Yes, but first you must write the ending to the story,' I said."

She continued, "As in all past years, most of the students wrote: 'The ant shares his food in the winter, and both the ant and the grasshopper lived.' A few children wrote, 'No, Mr. Grasshopper, you should have worked in the summer. Now I have just enough food for myself. Sorry.' So the ant lives and the grasshopper dies."

"But your son ended the story in a different way from any child I've ever taught. He wrote: 'So the ant gave all of his food to the grasshopper. The grasshopper lived through the winter. The ant died.' And the picture? At the bottom of the page, he had drawn a cross."

Who's bugging you? A boss? A spouse? A child? Someone who turned his back and walked away? Someone who said she loved you and you never heard from her again? Maybe you've forgiven just about everyone—but who is it you're still angry with?

"I took care of the matter," Jesus says. "I paid the price. Justice has been done.

Now you get to be free from the weight on your soul that comes when there's a lack of mercy. You get to be free simply to love people."

Every sin was individually paid for. Every sin was individually dealt with. Every sin was absorbed by our Lord. He felt the heat. He took the hit. He plunged into the damnation that sin would bring. How can we then say, "I'm still going to poke around. I'm not going to forgive her because someone needs to bring this to justice." If that's what you're feeling, bitterness, depression, sadness, and a judgmental heart will be the result. And it will kill you. Put a lid on the matter. Cover it with mercy. And you'll be free.

7

1 Samuel 7:1, 2

And the men of Kirjath-jearim came, and fetched up the ark of the LORD, and brought it into the house of Abinadab in the hill, and sanctified Eleazar his son to keep the ark of the LORD. And it came to pass, while the ark abode in Kirjath-jearim, that the time was long; for it was twenty years: and all the house of Israel lamented after the LORD.

After hearing what happened to the Philistines and the men of Beth-shemesh, the Israelites were understandably cautious. It is true that God is loving, gracious, and merciful. But He's also an awesome God who must be respected and deeply reverenced. The Israelites, it seems, were at a place where they understood this.

1 Samuel 7:3

And Samuel spake unto all the house of Israel, saying, If ye do return unto the LORD with all your hearts, then put away the strange gods and Ashtaroth from among you, and prepare your hearts unto the LORD, and serve him only: and he will deliver you out of the hand of the Philistines.

If there's ever a Scripture appropriate for us today, surely it's this one. If we want to be free from the terror of our enemies, we are to serve the Lord only.

"How could God be so narrow?" some ask. "How could it be that God would provide only one way to Heaven, only one way to know Him?"

The answer is, "Because He is good."

You see, if there were five ways to heaven, five ways to know Him, Satan would provide five hundred counterfeits. So God keeps it real simple. "There's only one way, "He says. "The one Way is My Son."

1 Samuel 7:4, 5

Then the children of Israel did put away Baalim and Ashtaroth, and served the LORD only. And Samuel said, Gather all Israel to Mizpeh, and I will pray for you unto the LORD.

Notice that before the convocation, before the prayer of blessing, there was a turning away from false gods. The sin of Israel was not that they turned their back on the Lord. It was that they added other gods to the land. "We're not rejecting the Lord," the Israelites could have said. "We're simply being open-minded."

1 Samuel 7:6 (a)

And they gathered together to Mizpeh, and drew water, and poured it out before the LORD . . .

Because water was a precious commodity in the Middle East, this act signified the pouring out of their hearts before the Lord.

1 Samuel 7:6 (b)

. . . and fasted on that day, and said there, We have sinned against the LORD. And Samuel judged the children of Israel in Mizpeh.

Samuel judged—or gave wisdom—to Israel.

1 Samuel 7:7–9

And when the Philistines heard that the children of Israel were gathered together to Mizpeh, the lords of the Philistines went up against Israel. And when the children of Israel heard it, they were afraid of the Philistines. And the children of Israel said to Samuel, Cease not to cry unto the LORD our God for us, that he will save us out of the hand of the Philistines. And Samuel took a sucking lamb, and offered it for a burnt offering wholly unto the LORD: and Samuel cried unto the LORD for Israel; and the LORD heard him.

A lamb was offered. A prayer was made. And God heard.

The same is true for our country in this day. The Lamb has been offered. Prayers need to be made. And God will hear (2 Chronicles 7:14).

1 Samuel 7:10
And as Samuel was offering up the burnt offering, the Philistines drew near to battle against Israel: but the LORD thundered with a great thunder on that day upon the Philistines, and discomfited them; and they were smitten before Israel.

The people of this region believed that Baal, the son of Dagon, was the thunder god. Here, the true and living God thunders on this people who honored Baal.

1 Samuel 7:11, 12
And the men of Israel went out of Mizpeh, and pursued the Philistines, and smote them, until they came under Beth-car. Then Samuel took a stone, and set it between Mizpeh and Shen, and called the name of it Eben-ezer, saying, Hitherto hath the LORD helped us.

Ebenezer means "stone of help." In setting up this stone, Samuel was saying, "Up to this point, the Lord has helped us."

Why is this important to do? Because sometimes we think, *Oh, no. Things will never work out. My marriage is on the rocks. My finances are down the drain. Everything looks grim."* What we need in times like this is an "Ebenezer stone" that reminds us that God has never failed us, that what we fear doesn't come to pass. Yes, there are definite challenges that come our way—but in those challenges, God always shows Himself strong. He's always there for us.

I have found journaling to be a wonderful "Ebenezer stone." Reading through my journals, I am reminded again and again that God has never let me down in the past, which gives me confidence that He won't let me down in the future. Whether through journaling or songwriting, letters or pictures, I encourage you to put your own "Ebenzer stone" in place, where you can be reminded of God's faithfulness in the past, draw strength for the present, and hope for the future.

1 Samuel 7:13–16
So the Philistines were subdued, and they came no more into the coast of Israel: and the hand of the LORD was against the Philistines all the days of Samuel. And the cities which the Philistines had taken from Israel were restored to Israel, from Ekron even unto Gath; and the coasts thereof did Israel deliver out of the hands of the Philistines. And there was peace between Israel and the Amorites. And Samuel judged Israel all the days of his life. And he went from year to year in circuit to Bethel, and Gilgal, and Mizpeh, and judged Israel in all those places.

These cities were in a fourteen-mile radius. Samuel, a "circuit-riding" judge, visited each one, counseling the inhabitants in the ways and wisdom of God.

1 Samuel 7:17
And his return was to Ramah; for there was his house; and there he judged Israel; and there he built an altar unto the LORD.

Samuel built an altar where he lived. This principle remains of utmost importance. If you want to minister, it all begins at home (Deuteronomy 6:7).

8

In chapter 8, we see that Samuel was on this circuit, preaching from town to town, place to place. The circuit evidently took a toll on his family . . .

1 Samuel 8:1–3
And it came to pass, when Samuel was old, that he made his sons judges over Israel. Now the name of his firstborn was Joel; and the name of his second, Abiah: they were judges in Beer-sheba. And his sons walked not in his ways, but turned aside after lucre, and took bribes, and perverted judgment.

Samuel's sons succumbed to the seduction of money, taking bribes from God's people. How could it be that Samuel, who saw the sons of Eli succumb to lust, allowed his own sons to give themselves to money? What happened? Chapter 7 ended with Samuel traveling from town to town. It could be that this took a toll on his own family. Although we read that he built an altar at his house, it would seem that he was gone a lot. Yes, he was serving the Lord, caring for God's people, but his top priority—his family—was not being instructed and tended.

This can happen so easily in the ministry, in serving the Lord. It takes time to parent properly—not only the structured devotional times which are imperative, or the planned activities which are wonderful, but also the unstructured, unplanned, occasions to share with our kids. Looking back, I see that two of the most important conversations I've had with my kids were spontaneous occasions, times when I was just there. If you're involved in any type of ministry, the example of Samuel tells us we must be those who constantly pray for our kids.

What a heartbreak it must have been for Samuel, as it must have been for Eli before him, to realize his own sons were not walking in the ways of the Lord. Samuel had a heart for God, a passion to serve God. He was a good man, a great man, a godly man—but he was evidently gone too much to be cognizant of what was really going on in the souls of his kids as they grew up. The apostle John was right when he said he had no greater joy than to hear that his children walked in truth (3 John 4). This requires constant evaluation, saying, "Lord, am I really on Your circuit—or am I just going around in circles?"

Samuel failed to learn the lesson of Eli. May God help us as parents to be those who don't go in circles, mistakenly thinking we're serving Him, when in reality, we're ignoring our primary ministry—spending not only quality, but a quantity of time with our kids.

1 Samuel 8:4, 5
Then all the elders of Israel gathered themselves together, and came to Samuel unto Ramah, And said unto him, Behold, thou art old, and thy sons walk not in thy ways: now make us a king to judge us like all the nations.

Israel had prophets, priests, and judges—but God was their King. Now they wanted a man for a king.

1 Samuel 8:6
But the thing displeased Samuel, when they said, Give us a king to judge us. And Samuel prayed unto the Lord.

Instead of lashing out at the people, Samuel looked up to the Lord—a wise thing to do because the wrath of man never works the righteousness of God (James 1:20). Instead of coming down on the people, Samuel simply prayed.

When you feel frustration churn in your stomach, it's always a good thing to slip away to a quiet spot and talk it over with the Lord. When you return, you'll have an entirely different perspective, countenance, and attitude—and the outcome will be entirely different. When I don't do this—when I blow my top, let off steam, or give someone a piece of my mind—I never fail to regret it.

1 Samuel 8:7, 8
And the Lord said unto Samuel, Hearken unto the voice of the people in all that they say unto thee: for they have not rejected thee, but they have rejected me, that I should not reign over them. According to all the works which they have done since the day that I brought them up out of Egypt even unto this day, wherewith they have forsaken me, and served other gods, so do they also unto thee.

Evidently, Samuel felt personally rejected. But as he prays, he hears God say, "It's not about you, Samuel. It's all about Me."

1 Samuel 8:9
Now therefore hearken unto their voice: howbeit yet protest solemnly unto them, and shew them the manner of the king that shall reign over them.

Samuel was to let the people know the repercussions of their request.

1 Samuel 8:10–12
And Samuel told all the words of the Lord unto the people that asked of him a king. And he said, This will be the manner of the king that shall reign over you: He will take your sons, and appoint them for himself, for his chariots, and to be his horsemen; and some shall run before his chariots. And he will appoint him captains over thousands, and captains over fifties; and will set them to ear his ground, and to reap his harvest, and to make his instruments of war, and instruments of his chariots.

"Are you sure you want a king?" Samuel asked the people. "He will draft your sons into his army and into his service."

1 Samuel 8:13
And he will take your daughters to be confectionaries, and to be cooks, and to be bakers.

"Are you sure you want a king?" Samuel asked the people. "He'll draft your daughters into his kitchens."

1 Samuel 8:14
And he will take your fields, and your vineyards, and your oliveyards, even the best of them, and give them to his servants.

"Are you sure you want a king?" Samuel asked the people. "He'll take the fruit of your own labor. You're going to be paying a big price for this monarchy you want to establish."

Government is expensive indeed. In our country, one of every fourteen people works for the government. To pay them, the wages we earn from January first to May sixteenth go to pay our taxes. Israel wanted to be like the nations around them—but it would cost them greatly.

1 Samuel 8:15–17
And he will take the tenth of your seed, and of your vineyards, and give to his officers, and to his servants. And he will take your menservants, and your maidservants, and your goodliest young men, and your asses, and put them to his work. He will take the tenth of your sheep: and ye shall be his servants.

The Babylonians, Assyrians, Persians, and other ancient empires demanded that ten percent of all that was produced was to be turned over to the king. Now, if those pagan kings received ten percent, how much more should the King of kings, our God, receive the tithe from us.

1 Samuel 8:18
And ye shall cry out in that day because of your king which ye shall have chosen you; and the LORD will not hear you in that day.

"You will have cast your vote," Samuel warns. "You will have made your decision. There will be no higher courts to appeal to. When you have a king, you will need to live with the decision you've made. You'll cry out. You'll protest. You'll be upset—but the choice will have been yours."

1 Samuel 8:19, 20
Nevertheless the people refused to obey the voice of Samuel; and they said, Nay; but we will have a king over us; That we also may be like all the nations; and that our king may judge us, and go out before us, and fight our battles.

At this point, the people still had an opportunity to admit they had made a mistake in asking for a king. But that's not what they did.

1 Samuel 8:21
And Samuel heard all the words of the people, and he rehearsed them in the ears of the LORD.

I so admire Samuel because he goes back to the Lord once more. He talks to God about the issue. God knows all things. He wasn't in need of information from Samuel. But Samuel was in need of spending time with Him.

1 Samuel 8:22
And the LORD said to Samuel, Hearken unto their voice, and make them a king. And Samuel said unto the men of Israel, Go ye every man unto his city.

Although it was not His plan for them, God gave His people what they wanted.

O Israel, thou hast destroyed thyself; but in me is thine help. I will be thy king: where is any other that may save thee in all thy cities? and thy judges of whom thou saidst, Give me a king and princes? I gave thee a king in mine anger, and took him away in my wrath.
Hosea 13:9–11

God can give us what we ask for. This is one of the real dangers of the "Name it and claim it" school of thought. God is the King. He knows what's best for me. He knows what will make me happy. I think I do—but I'm almost always wrong. I believe this is where the radical faith movement is in grave error. The assumption there is, "God, I know this thing, that person, or that career is perfect for me, so I claim it in faith." In so doing, people become their own king, using God to bring about their own demands.

I have discovered that it is infinitely wiser to say, "Lord, here's the way I see it. Here are my thoughts about this. But, Lord, You see what I don't. You know what I can't. So I gladly, happily defer to Your perfect plan for me."

The old adage remains true: God always gives His best to those who leave the choice with Him. Always.

9 Up until this time, Israel had been a theocracy. God was the leader of the nation. Wanting to be like the countries surrounding them, however, Israel called for a king. And here in chapter 9, they will get what they thought they wanted . . .

1 Samuel 9:1
Now there was a man of Benjamin, whose name was Kish, the son of Abiel, the son of Zeror, the son of Bechorath, the son of Aphiah, a Benjamite, a mighty man of power.

"A mighty man of power" means Kish was wealthy.

1 Samuel 9:2 (a)
And he had a son, whose name was Saul . . .

Saul was appropriately named, for *Saul* means "Requested," and the people had requested a king to lead them.

1 Samuel 9:2 (b)
. . . a choice young man, and a goodly: and there was not among the children of Israel a goodlier person than he: from his shoulders and upward he was higher than any of the people.

Saul was not only "goodly," or handsome, but he was tall. Certainly height would be an asset, for the Philistines were the primary enemies of Israel at this time. The Philistines were known to have a few big guys in their midst—like Goliath and his brothers. So Saul, the tallest guy in the land of Israel, would seem to be a perfect choice to lead them. The problem is, man looks only on the outward appearance, while God looks on the heart (1 Samuel 16:7).

1 Samuel 9:3 (a)
And the asses of Kish Saul's father were lost . . .

The pick-up trucks of the day, donkeys, or asses, were valuable—to a certain degree, a measure of one's wealth.

1 Samuel 9:3 (b)–5
. . . And Kish said to Saul his son, Take now one of the servants with thee, and arise, go seek the asses. And he passed through mount Ephraim, and passed through the land of Shalisha, but they found them not: then they passed through the land of Shalim, and there they were not: and he passed through the land of the Benjamites, but they found them not. And when they were come to the land of Zuph, Saul said to his servant that was with him, Come, and let us return; lest my father leave caring for the asses, and take thought for us.

"Even though we haven't found the donkeys, I don't want my father worrying about us, so let's return home," said Saul.

1 Samuel 9:6
And he said unto him, Behold now, there is in this city a man of God, and he is an honourable man; all that he saith cometh surely to pass: now let us go thither; peradventure he can shew us our way that we should go.

"Wait a minute," Saul's servant said. "We're at a place where there is a prophet. Let's ask him if he knows anything about the missing donkeys."

1 Samuel 9:7–9
Then said Saul to his servant, But, behold, if we go, what shall we bring the man? for the bread is spent in our vessels, and there is not a present to bring to the man of God: what have we? And the servant answered Saul again, and said, Behold, I have here at hand the fourth part of a shekel of silver: that will I give to the man of God, to tell us our way. (Beforetime in Israel, when a man went to inquire of God, thus he spake, Come, and let us go to the seer: for he that is now called a Prophet was beforetime called a Seer.)

In these days, prophets were known as seers because they could see things others couldn't.

1 Samuel 9:10–16
Then said Saul to his servant, Well said; come, let us go. So they went unto the city where the man of God was. And as they went up the hill to the city, they found young maidens going out to draw water, and said unto them, Is the seer here? And they answered them, and said, He is; behold, he is before you: make haste now, for he came to day to the city; for there is a sacrifice of the people to day in the high place: As soon as ye be come into the city, ye shall straightway find him, before he go up to the high place to eat: for the people will not eat until he come, because he doth bless the sacrifice; and afterwards they eat that be bidden. Now therefore get you up; for about this time ye shall find him. And they went up into the city: and when they were come into the city, behold, Samuel came out against them, for to go up to the high place. Now the LORD had told Samuel in his ear a day before Saul came, saying, To morrow about this time I will send thee a man out of the land of Benjamin, and thou shalt anoint him to be captain over my people Israel, that he may save my people out of the hand of the Philistines: for I have looked upon my people, because their cry is come unto me.

The day previously, Samuel heard the Lord say, "Tomorrow a man is going to come—the one I have chosen to be the captain, the king of the nation." I find it interesting that the Lord whispered in Samuel's ear the day before this event took place—to let him know what was ahead. In 1 Samuel 8:21, we read that Samuel heard all the words of the people and he rehearsed them in the ears of the Lord. Those who whisper in the ears of the Lord will hear the Word whispered in their ear as well. I'm convinced that many times I don't hear what the Lord wants to say in my ear because I haven't first spoken in His ear. Samuel was a man who understood what it meant to pray without ceasing. As a result, the Lord whispered in his ear, telling him the man who would be king was on his way.

1 Samuel 9:17–19
And when Samuel saw Saul, the LORD said unto him, Behold the man whom I spake to thee of! this same shall reign over my people. Then Saul drew near to Samuel in the gate, and said, Tell me, I pray thee, where the seer's house is. And Samuel answered Saul, and said, I am the seer: go up before me unto the high place; for ye shall eat with me to day, and to morrow I will let thee go, and will tell thee all that is in thine heart.

"I'm the man you're looking for," Samuel said to Saul and his servant. "Today, let's eat together. Tomorrow, I'll tell you all you want to know."

1 Samuel 9:20
And as for thine asses that were lost three days ago, set not thy mind on them; for they are found. And on whom is all the desire of Israel? Is it not on thee, and on all thy father's house?

"Don't worry about the donkeys," said Samuel. "You have a far greater purpose for being here."

1 Samuel 9:21
And Saul answered and said, Am not I a Benjamite, of the smallest of the tribes of Israel? and my family the least of all the families of the tribe of Benjamin? wherefore then speakest thou so to me?

"I'm from the smallest tribe," Saul protested. "And my family is the smallest family in the tribe."

1 Samuel 9:22, 23
And Samuel took Saul and his servant, and brought them into the parlour, and made them sit in the chiefest place among them that were bidden, which were about thirty persons. And Samuel said unto the cook, Bring the portion which I gave thee, of which I said unto thee, Set it by thee.

"Bring that special chunk of meat I ordered set aside," Samuel said to the cook.

1 Samuel 9:24
And the cook took up the shoulder, and that which was upon it, and set it before Saul. And Samuel said, Behold that which is left! set it before thee, and eat: for unto this time hath it been kept for thee since I said, I have invited the people. So Saul did eat with Samuel that day.

The shoulder was considered to be one of the prime pieces of meat. There is a second piece of meat that was considered to be a special delicacy. That was the breast. Saul was given the shoulder, but not the breast because Saul was a man known to be head and shoulders above others. He was a man who showed real strength—but he didn't have a heart for God. Because of this, it's appropriate he was given the shoulder.

1 Samuel 9:25
And when they were come down from the high place into the city, Samuel communed with Saul upon the top of the house.

Keep in mind that houses in that region were flat-roofed, providing a place where people could sit in the evening and enjoy the cool breezes.

1 Samuel 9:26, 27
And they arose early: and it came to pass about the spring of the day, that Samuel called Saul to the top of the house, saying, Up, that I may send thee away. And Saul arose, and they went out both of them, he and Samuel, abroad. And as they were going down to the end of the city, Samuel said to Saul, Bid the servant pass on before us, (and he passed on,) but stand thou still a while, that I may shew thee the word of God.

"Send your servant away," Samuel said to Saul, "but you stand still because there's something I must tell you. There's something more the Lord wants to do through me for you. Stand still. I know you're anxious to get back. I know you're worried about your dad and the donkeys. But stand still. Slow down. Listen up because there's a word from the Lord for you."

10

1 Samuel 10:1
Then Samuel took a vial of oil, and poured it upon his head, and kissed him, and said, Is it not because the LORD hath anointed thee to be captain over his inheritance?

Here we see the anointing of Saul as king of Israel. The idea of anointing a king was not unique to Israel. The nations surrounding Israel also anointed their kings and leaders. But they used animal fat to anoint because they believed that by pouring on the fat of a bull or an ox and rubbing it into a man's head, somehow the individual would be infused with the strength and power of the bull or ox. When God gave anointing to His people, it wasn't from the fat of an animal, but from oil of the olive tree mixed with spices. God's anointing wasn't to make men like animals, but to show that they were to be rooted and grounded in the things of God in order to bring fruit to the glory of God.

1 Samuel 10:2
When thou art departed from me to day, then thou shalt find two men by Rachel's sepulchre in the border of Benjamin at Zelzah; and they will say unto thee, The asses which thou wentest to seek are found: and, lo, thy father hath left the care of the asses, and sorroweth for you, saying, What shall I do for my son?

I like what Samuel says because there are times when we, too, lose our donkeys—when we feel very real burdens, tensions, and anxieties. And as He did to Saul, God says, "I want to help you with that."

As a seer, Samuel is a type of the Holy Spirit, who searches out the deep things of God (1 Corinthians 2:10). "You've come to the right place," Samuel said. "But before I give you information about your lost donkeys, I want you to sit at the table with me."

Saul could have said, "My dad is worried. I have a job to do. Thanks, but no thanks. I can't take time to sit at the table." But Saul didn't do that. To his credit, he heard what the seer said, and sat down. I suggest that a practical picture is painted in this vignette. That is, like Saul, we're worried about stuff that is ultimately not all that important. God will take care of it—but there's a bigger calling, a grander picture. There's a big plan for us. There's a divine design for our lives. Therefore, when you feel overwhelmed by problems and tensions, burdens and frustrations, slow down. Come to the Table. Come to Communion. Come and dine. Wait on the Lord. It's not about your problem. It's not about the donkeys. It's about your being anointed as royalty to be used by God eternally.

If Saul had said, "Sorry, I don't have time. I've got to get home," I suggest he would never have been king. I wonder who of us has missed out because we were worried about our donkeys, failing to realize the Lord was simply using them to call us away to commune with Him. When you're uptight or upset, come to the Lord's Table and dine with Him. Go to the top of the house—get above the situation—and say, "Lord, what do You want to say to me?" As it was to Saul, His answer will most likely be different than you thought, and bigger than what you could imagine.

1 Samuel 10:3–6
Then shalt thou go on forward from thence, and thou shalt come to the plain of Tabor, and there shall meet thee three men going up to God to Bethel, one carrying three kids, and another carrying three loaves of bread, and another carrying a bottle of wine: And they will salute thee, and give thee two loaves of bread; which thou shalt receive of their hands. After that thou shalt come to the hill of God, where is the garrison of the Philistines: and it shall come to pass, when thou art come thither to the city, that thou shalt meet a company of prophets coming down from the high place with a psaltery, and a tabret, and a pipe, and a harp, before them; and they shall prophesy: And the Spirit of the LORD will come upon thee, and thou shalt prophesy with them, and shalt be turned into another man.

"You'll see that what I'm telling you is true," Samuel said to Saul, "because you're going to meet a group of men who will tell you your father is concerned about you. Then you'll see another group who will offer you bread and wine. Another group will be prophets, who will play music and speak the things of the Lord. Then the Spirit of the Lord will come upon you, too, and you'll prophesy right along with them.

In this passage, I see three experiences a man or woman must have in order to be effective in ministry: the care of the Father, communion with the Son, and a heart changed by the Spirit.

The message of the first group of men Saul would meet was that his father missed him. So, too, before anyone can impact others for the Lord, he or she must know the Father's love in his or her own heart. Secondly, just as Saul met a group carrying bread and wine—the elements of Communion—there must be fellowship with the Son. Finally, Saul became a changed man and prophesied with the prophets, just as anyone who truly wants to communicate God's Word today must be changed by, and filled with the Spirit.

If you don't have a firm understanding that the Father cares for you, that He is on your side, that He cares about everything you're going through and dealing with, you'll never be a minister of grace. You'll be one who talks about principles and procedures, but you'll never have the tender, gracious, compassionate kind of ministry that God desires. It's when a person realizes the nature of the Father, has communion with the Son, and is changed by the Spirit that he becomes a true minister.

1 Samuel 10:7–12
And let it be, when these signs are come unto thee, that thou do as occasion serve thee; for God is with thee. And thou shalt go down before me to Gilgal; and, behold, I will come down unto thee, to offer burnt offerings, and to sacrifice sacrifices of peace offerings:

seven days shalt thou tarry, till I come to thee, and shew thee what thou shalt do. And it was so, that when he had turned his back to go from Samuel, God gave him another heart: and all those signs came to pass that day. And when they came thither to the hill, behold, a company of prophets met him; and the Spirit of God came upon him, and he prophesied among them. And it came to pass, when all that knew him beforetime saw that, behold, he prophesied among the prophets, then the people said one to another, What is this that is come unto the son of Kish? Is Saul also among the prophets? And one of the same place answered and said, But who is their father? Therefore it became a proverb, Is Saul also among the prophets?

Concerning something incredible or outrageous, we say, "That will happen when pigs fly."

"Is Saul among the prophets?" became a similar statement of unlikelihood.

1 Samuel 10:13–16
And when he had made an end of prophesying, he came to the high place. And Saul's uncle said unto him and to his servant, Whither went ye? And he said, To seek the asses: and when we saw that they were no where, we came to Samuel. And Saul's uncle said, Tell me, I pray thee, what Samuel said unto you. And Saul said unto his uncle, He told us plainly that the asses were found. But of the matter of the kingdom, whereof Samuel spake, he told him not.

Saul didn't tell his uncle that he would one day be king. Instead, as Mary would later do, he simply heard the Word of the Lord and pondered it in his heart (Luke 2:19, 51).

I believe this is a great word for us as well. There should be more pondered in our heart than we ever speak about. Some people speak about everything they hear. On the other hand, deep people seem to know a lot more than they talk about. Deep people have experiences they don't share, intimate secrets between them and the Lord. Saul begins this way. Something very special happened to him, but he kept it to himself.

1 Samuel 10:17–19
And Samuel called the people together unto the Lord to Mizpeh; And said unto the children of Israel, Thus saith the Lord God of Israel, I brought up Israel out of Egypt, and delivered you out of the hand of the Egyptians, and out of the hand of all kingdoms, and of them that oppressed you: And ye have this day rejected your God, who himself saved you out of all your adversities and your tribulations; and ye have said unto him, Nay, but set a king over us. Now therefore present yourselves before the Lord by your tribes, and by your thousands.

"You wanted a king. You're going to get a king," Samuel told the people.

1 Samuel 10:20–22
And when Samuel had caused all the tribes of Israel to come near, the tribe of Benjamin was taken. When he had caused the tribe of Benjamin to come near by their families, the family of Matri was taken, and Saul the son of Kish was taken: and when they sought him, he could not be found. Therefore they inquired of the Lord further, if the man should yet come thither. And the Lord answered, Behold, he hath hid himself among the stuff.

Saul began so well. Rather than heralding himself, he humbly hid.

1 Samuel 10:23–26
And they ran and fetched him thence: and when he stood among the people, he was higher than any of the people from his shoulders and upward. And Samuel said to all the people, See ye him whom the Lord hath chosen, that there is none like him among all the people? And all the people shouted, and said, God save the king. Then Samuel told the people the manner of the kingdom, and wrote it in a book, and laid it up before the Lord. And Samuel sent all the people away, every man to his house. And Saul also went home to Gibeah; and there went with him a band of men, whose hearts God had touched.

Saul had been anointed king, and had been revealed to the people as the one God had chosen, yet he makes his way home again to farm.

1 Samuel 10:27 (a)
But the children of Belial said, How shall this man save us? And they despised him, and brought him no presents . . .

Belial means "foolishness." Of Saul, the foolish men said, "He's just a farm boy. How can he save us?" In bringing him no presents, they rejected him.

For topical study of 1 Samuel 10:27 entitled "Wise Men Bring Gifts," turn to page 847.

1 Samuel 10:27 (b)
. . . But he held his peace.

Again, we see Saul acting with great wisdom. Moses—the man who would lead the nation of Israel not as a king but as a fellow pilgrim—told the people that, because the Lord would fight for them, they could hold their peace (Exodus 14:14). Here, Saul walks in the wisdom of Moses. Rather than giving the sons of Belial a piece of his mind, he wisely held his peace.

WISE MEN BRING GIFTS

A Topical Study of 1 SAMUEL 10:27

After He had died and risen again, Jesus opened the Scriptures to two travelers on the road to Emmaus. Beginning with Moses and going through all the prophets, Luke tells us He explained all things concerning Himself (24:27). The key to good Bible study is to understand that all Scripture points to Jesus—and 1 Samuel is no exception, for in the anointing of Saul as king, we see a Polaroid picture develop before our eyes of our King, Jesus Christ . . .

Even as Saul was anointed king, Jesus is the *Christos,* or "Anointed One." He is the King of kings, for that is the name written on His thigh and across His vest in Revelation 19.

After Saul was anointed king, the Holy Spirit came upon him and he began to prophesy. When Jesus was baptized in the Jordan River, not only did the Holy Spirit come upon Him, but the Father spoke from heaven, saying, "This is My beloved Son, in whom I am well pleased" (Matthew 3:17).

Saul was announced by a prophet—just as Jesus would be announced by the greatest of prophets, John the Baptist who said, "Prepare the way. The King is coming" (see Matthew 3:3).

Even as a group of men whose hearts God had touched traveled with Saul, the disciples traveled with Jesus. Saul traveled to *Gibeah,* which means "Hill." Jesus would also travel to a hill called Calvary where He would be crucified.

After Saul made his way to Gibeah, some rejoiced, but the foolish men said, "How shall this man save us?" When the King of kings was sent to this planet, the angels sang with joy in the Bethlehem skies; the shepherds were filled with awe; the wise men made their way from the east, bringing gifts. But the religious leaders of the day brought no gifts (Matthew 2).

The same story is being told in our world today. There are those who are children of Belial—fools who say, "How can Jesus save us?"

On the other hand, there are wise men who come from a long way to bring gifts to Him. And we are invited to join their company. What gifts can we bring?

The wise men from the east brought gold, frankincense, and myrrh—three gifts which correspond to the three offices of Christ. Gold is the metal of monarchy. Jesus is the King of kings. Frankincense, burned in the tabernacle and temple speaks of the priestly ministry. Jesus is our great High Priest. Myrrh, used in the burial process, speaks of the martyrdom of a prophet. Jesus is the incomparable Prophet.

We, too, can bring gold to Jesus. We can bring the gold of our tithes and offerings. We can bring the gold of our faith (1 Peter 1:7). We can bring the gold of the words we speak one to another (Proverbs 25:11, 12).

We, too, can bring frankincense to Jesus. The word *frankincense* means "whitened," most likely due to the fact that when it was burned, the smoke would ascend in white puffs. Frankincense comes from a small tree that requires very little soil to grow, but rather roots itself in rocks. That's like us. We're small indeed—but we can root ourselves in the Rock of our salvation, Jesus Christ (1 Corinthians 10:4). Revelation 5 tells us that the frankincense burned by the priests speaks of prayer. As we bring our gift of prayer and our sacrifice of praise to the Lord, not only are they a sweet-smelling savor to Him, but we are "whitened"—purified—in the process.

We, too, can bring myrrh to Jesus. He didn't ask us to build a monument or erect an impressive tower in His honor. He simply asks us to remember what He has done by coming to His Table (Luke 22:19). As we partake of His body and blood at the Communion Table, we remember His work on the Cross on our behalf. And our doing so is myrrh to Him.

The sons of Belial—the foolish men—brought no gifts to Saul. And it is the foolish man today who brings no gifts to Jesus. But wise is the man, wise the woman, who brings gifts to the King of kings, our great High Priest, our martyred Prophet.

God chooses the foolish things of the world to confound the wise (1 Corinthians 1:27). By His grace and mercy, He has reached out to fools like us, and all that remains for us to do is respond.

11

1 Samuel 11:1 (a)

Then Nahash the Ammonite came up, and encamped against Jabesh-gilead . . .

Nahash means "serpent." Jabesh-gilead was an Israelite town on the east side of the Jordan River in the territory given to Manasseh.

1 Samuel 11:1 (b)

. . . and all the men of Jabesh said unto Nahash, Make a covenant with us, and we will serve thee.

Fearing for their lives, the men of Jabesh-gilead offered to sign a peace treaty with Nahash. "We'll serve you if you don't destroy us," they said.

1 Samuel 11:2

And Nahash the Ammonite answered them, On this condition will I make a covenant with you, that I may thrust out all your right eyes, and lay it for a reproach upon all Israel.

"I won't destroy you if you poke out the right eyes of all your men," Nahash said. This, of course, would not only disable the troops, but also would distress and dishearten all of the people of Jabesh-gilead.

1 Samuel 11:3
And the elders of Jabesh said unto him, Give us seven days' respite, that we may send messengers unto all the coasts of Israel: and then, if there be no man to save us, we will come out to thee.

Why would Nahash agree to give Jabesh-gilead a week to find reinforcements? I suggest it was because they knew the story of Judges 21. You see, when civil war broke out in Israel between Benjamin and the other eleven tribes, the only men who didn't fight were the men of Jabesh-gilead. Perhaps knowing this, Nahash was sure no one would come to their aid.

In this, we see a lesson for us. That is, just as Nahash, "the serpent," based his plan of attack on past performance, the devil continually whispers in our ears today that past failures prevent future rescues; that past failures mean there won't be future blessings. But just as Nahash would prove to be wrong, in God's economy, there's always a second chance.

1 Samuel 11:4–6
Then came the messengers to Gibeah of Saul, and told the tidings in the ears of the people: and all the people lifted up their voices, and wept. And, behold, Saul came after the herd out of the field; and Saul said, What aileth the people that they weep? And they told him the tidings of the men of Jabesh. And the Spirit of God came upon Saul when he heard those tidings, and his anger was kindled greatly.

While the results of the Spirit of God coming upon a person can indeed be peace and harmony, anger and righteous indignation can also be the result. Here, Saul was upset because his brothers were in trouble. Even though they had chosen to remain on the other side of the Jordan River, when the Spirit of God came upon him, he felt compassion for them and was grieved on their behalf.

1 Samuel 11:7 (a)
And he took a yoke of oxen, and hewed them in pieces, and sent them throughout all the coasts of Israel by the hands of messengers, saying, Whosoever cometh not forth after Saul and after Samuel, so shall it be done unto his oxen . . .

In butchering an ox—the "tractor" of this agrarian society—the message Saul sent was: You're going to go bankrupt if you don't join me in helping our brothers who are in jeopardy.

1 Samuel 11:7 (b)–9
. . . And the fear of the LORD fell on the people, and they came out with one consent. And when he numbered them in Bezek, the children of Israel were three hundred thousand, and the men of Judah thirty thousand. And they said unto the messengers that came, Thus shall ye say unto the men of Jabesh-gilead, To morrow, by that time the sun be hot, ye shall have help. And the messengers came and shewed it to the men of Jabesh; and they were glad.

A message was sent to the men of Jabesh-gilead that help was on the way.

1 Samuel 11:10, 11
Therefore the men of Jabesh said, To morrow we will come out unto you, and ye shall do with us all that seemeth good unto you. And it was so on the morrow, that Saul put the people in three companies; and they came into the midst of the host in the morning watch, and slew the Ammonites until the heat of the day: and it came to pass, that they which remained were scattered, so that two of them were not left together.

Saul marched all night long, gathering 300,000 men along the way. Saul was not a soldier. He was a farmer. But when the Holy Spirit comes upon a man, he is given a sense of exactly what to do. Don't ever underestimate the power of the Holy Spirit to give you abilities or insights you never had before.

1 Samuel 11:12, 13
And the people said unto Samuel, Who is he that said, Shall Saul reign over us? bring the men, that we may put them to death. And Saul said, There shall not a man be put to death this day: for to day the LORD hath wrought salvation in Israel.

Saul wisely attributed the Israelite victory to God alone.

1 Samuel 11:14, 15
Then said Samuel to the people, Come, and let us go to Gilgal, and renew the kingdom there. And all the people went to Gilgal; and there they made Saul king before the LORD in Gilgal; and there they sacrificed sacrifices of peace offerings before the LORD; and there Saul and all the men of Israel rejoiced greatly.

What was it that finally unified Israel? Love. When the Israelites saw Saul take the reins and march the troops to rescue men about to be blinded by the serpent, the nation said, "He's our man." It wasn't when Saul prophesied or even when he was presented by Samuel that the nation supported him. It was not until they saw that Saul was a man who cared about all of his countrymen that they rallied behind him.

If I speak with the tongues of men and angels, if I know all things, if I prophesy, if I give my body to be burned, if I have faith to move mountains but have not love, I am nothing (1 Corinthians 13). The point at which people sense that you'd march all night to be there for them is the point they say, "We want you to have input and impact in our lives." Love is the key. It's not prophecy, tongues, or knowledge. If you pray for one thing, ask the Lord to make you a man or woman of love.

12

All prayer is basically divided into two categories: "Thy will be done" and "my will be done." I am learning that when I pray the latter, when I insist on my way, I never fail to eventually regret it. The people of Israel insisted upon having a king like the nations surrounding them. God heard their heart and let them have their way. Israel wanted a king, and God gave Israel Saul.

At first, it seemed to be exciting. Head and shoulders above everyone else, Saul was a man they could be proud of, a man they could look up to. But, as we shall see in the chapters before us, he was terribly flawed and would be a heartbreak to the nation . . .

1 Samuel 12:1, 2
And Samuel said unto all Israel, Behold, I have hearkened unto your voice in all that ye said unto me, and have made a king over you. And now, behold, the king walketh before you: and I am old and grayheaded; and, behold, my sons are with you: and I have walked before you from my childhood unto this day.

There seems to be an assumption that, even if only for a brief period, all kids inevitably stray from their faith. Parents seem to almost expect that their kids will rebel before ultimately coming around again. I suggest, however, that we would do better by praying, believing, trusting, and assuming that, like Samuel, our kids will walk with the Lord all of their days.

1 Samuel 12:3–12
Behold, here I am: witness against me before the Lord, and before his anointed: whose ox have I taken? or whose ass have I taken? or whom have I defrauded? whom have I oppressed? or of whose hand have I received any bribe to blind mine eyes therewith? and I will restore it you. And they said, Thou hast not defrauded us, nor oppressed us, neither hast thou taken ought of any man's hand. And he said unto them, The Lord is witness against you, and his anointed is witness this day, that ye have not found ought in my hand. And they answered, He is witness. And Samuel said unto the people, It is the Lord that advanced Moses and Aaron, and that brought your fathers up out of the land of Egypt. Now therefore stand still, that I may reason with you before the Lord of all the righteous acts of the Lord, which he did to you and to your fathers. When Jacob was come into Egypt, and your fathers cried unto the Lord, then the Lord sent Moses and Aaron, which brought forth your fathers out of Egypt, and made them dwell in this place. And when they forgat the Lord their God, he sold them into the hand of Sisera, captain of the host of Hazor, and into the hand of the Philistines, and into the hand of the king of Moab, and they fought against them. And they cried unto the Lord, and said, We have sinned, because we have forsaken the Lord, and have served Baalim and Ashtaroth: but now deliver us out of the hand of our enemies, and we will serve thee. And the Lord sent Jerubbaal, and Bedan, and Jephthah, and Samuel, and delivered you out of the hand of your enemies on every side, and ye dwelled safe And when ye saw that Nahash the king of the children of Ammon came against you, ye said unto me, Nay; but a king shall reign over us: when the Lord your God was your king.

"I have done nothing bad, and God has done nothing but good," Samuel says. "Why, then, did you turn your back on Him and demand a king?"

1 Samuel 12:13
Now therefore behold the king whom ye have chosen, and whom ye have desired! and, behold, the Lord hath set a king over you.

"You wanted a king. You got a king," Samuel said.

At this point, if I were God, I would say, "So long. Good luck." But watch what God declares through Samuel . . .

1 Samuel 12:14
If ye will fear the Lord, and serve him, and obey his voice, and not rebel against the commandment of the Lord, then shall both ye

and also the king that reigneth over you continue following the LORD your God:

"Even though you've messed up and basically rejected God's reign over you, if you'll serve Him, He promises to reign over both you and your king," Samuel declares.

1 Samuel 12:15
But if ye will not obey the voice of the LORD, but rebel against the commandment of the LORD, then shall the hand of the LORD be against you, as it was against your fathers.

God is unbelievably gracious. He says, "If you choose to obey Me, I'll reign over you. But if you rebel, My hand will be against you."

The Bible says whom the Lord loves, He chastens (Hebrews 12:6). Therefore, God's chastening hand is a sign of His love. In one way or another, all of us have rebelled. But the great news is that, on the basis of this text, God says, "Even though you've rebelled against Me or ignored Me, if you'll obey what I say and fear again today, I'll be with you. If you don't, I'll chasten you because I am still your Father, and I still love you."

Many people who know they married the wrong person, made a wrong move, or took a wrong turn feel that there's no hope from that point on. God, however, says otherwise. "You wanted him. You got him. You wanted that job. It's yours. But I'm still here, and I always will be. If you choose to turn to Me today, and if you choose to once again obey, I'll reign over you."

That's grace, gang. God doesn't give up on Israel—and He won't give up on you.

1 Samuel 12:16–18
Now therefore stand and see this great thing, which the LORD will do before your eyes. Is it not wheat harvest to day? I will call unto the LORD, and he shall send thunder and rain; that ye may perceive and see that your wickedness is great, which ye have done in the sight of the LORD, in asking you a king. So Samuel called unto the LORD; and the LORD sent thunder and rain that day: and all the people greatly feared the LORD and Samuel.

Harvest took place during the dry season. Therefore, the thunderstorm that arose as a result of Samuel's prayer validated his words to the people.

1 Samuel 12:19
And all the people said unto Samuel, Pray for thy servants unto the LORD thy God, that we die not: for we have added unto all our sins this evil, to ask us a king.

It is no surprise that the people asked Samuel to pray. His name literally means "Asked for," because he was the result of answered prayer (1 Samuel 2). Not only was he the result of answered prayer, but Samuel grew up in the temple—the house of prayer. Throughout his life, Samuel was a man of prayer. Prayer was the secret to his effectiveness in ministry.

1 Samuel 12:20–22
And Samuel said unto the people, Fear not: ye have done all this wickedness: yet turn not aside from following the LORD, but serve the LORD with all your heart; And turn ye not aside: for then should ye go after vain things, which cannot profit nor deliver; for they are vain. For the LORD will not forsake his people for his great name's sake: because it hath pleased the LORD to make you his people.

"Because His name is on you, the Lord will not forsake you," Samuel declared. As Christians, the name of Christ is on us. This means the Lord won't give up on, or turn away from us. No matter where we've been or how stupid we've been, the Lord won't give up on us because we carry His name. It pleased God to make us His people. Why would it please the Lord to have a person like me carry His name? Beats me! That God would entrust *us* with the name of His precious Son is indeed a mystery to me.

1 Samuel 12:23–25
Moreover as for me, God forbid that I should sin against the LORD in ceasing to pray for you: but I will teach you the good and the right way: Only fear the LORD, and serve him in truth with all your heart: for consider how great things he hath done for you. But if ye shall still do wickedly, ye shall be consumed, both ye and your king.

When the people asked him to pray for them, Samuel said, "God forbid that I should sin against the Lord in ceasing to pray for you." Prayerlessness is the epitome of selfishness because my failure to intercede for others means I am withholding that which would so greatly bless them. That is why Samuel was shocked at the suggestion that he wouldn't pray.

Prayer is the proof of love, and love is the product of prayer. If I love someone, I will pray for him. And if I pray for him, I will love him. That's why Jesus told us to pray for our enemies. If you pray for someone—even someone you don't like—

something happens within you. You find your heart knit to those for whom you pray.

Intercession is the common denominator of all godly men and women. Whether it's in the Bible or in biographies, you'll notice that, without exception, the people who have really left a mark for the Lord and have made a difference in this world are men and women given to intercession . . .

- Abraham was a friend of God, but he interceded for Sodom—a sick and sinful city.
- Elijah was a man who moved in the arena of the miraculous, but he prayed passionately for the people of Israel.
- Esther was the bride of the king, yet she risked her own life to intercede for the people.

"My heart's prayer and desire for Israel is that they should be saved," Paul said. "In fact, I would be accursed for the sake of my kinsman" (see Romans 9:3). Where did Paul get this kind of love? I suggest it was through passionate and consistent prayer for the people who were out to do him in. Because he prayed passionately for Israel, he loved Israel even above his own life.

The best gauge I know to measure my humility or lack thereof is to monitor my prayer life. A person who doesn't pray is proud because he is, in essence, saying, "I can provide for my kids. I can excel in my career. I can fix this difficulty. I can get through this day." A person who is given to prayer, however, is humble because he knows that without the Lord he can't do anything.

Prayer is not only the gauge of humility, but is the priority of true ministry. Note that Samuel said he would pray before he said he would teach (v. 23). If you're one who aspires to be used in Christian service, understand that it is not teaching, counseling, discipling, or even witnessing that is the priority of true ministry. It's prayer. The apostles who were setting the pace, leading the way in ministry, said, "It is not reasonable that we should leave the ministry of prayer and the Word to tend to the practical needs in the church in Jerusalem" (Acts 6). What came first? Prayer.

Most Christian leaders know this theoretically, but they don't understand it practically. May we be the exception. Greatness awaits the man or woman who will make prayer a priority. Therefore, let us be people given to prayer.

13

1 Samuel 13:1–4

Saul reigned one year; and when he had reigned two years over Israel, Saul chose him three thousand men of Israel; whereof two thousand were with Saul in Michmash and in mount Bethel, and a thousand were with Jonathan in Gibeah of Benjamin: and the rest of the people he sent every man to his tent. And Jonathan smote the garrison of the Philistines that was in Geba, and the Philistines heard of it. And Saul blew the trumpet throughout all the land, saying, Let the Hebrews hear. And all Israel heard say that Saul had smitten a garrison of the Philistines, and that Israel also was had in abomination with the Philistines. And the people were called together after Saul to Gilgal.

It was Jonathan who slew the Philistines but Saul who blew the trumpet, trying to make it appear as though the victory was his own. Gifts had been given to Saul. Grace had been poured out upon him. But now we see the cracks in his character that will lead to his tragic downfall.

The limb that bears the most fruit always hangs the lowest. If we're truly fruitful, there won't be a lifting up, but a bending down. This was not the case with Saul.

1 Samuel 13:5–9

And the Philistines gathered themselves together to fight with Israel, thirty thousand chariots, and six thousand horsemen, and people as the sand which is on the sea shore in multitude: and they came up, and pitched in Michmash, eastward from Beth-aven. When the men of Israel saw that they were in a strait, (for the people were distressed,) then the people did hide themselves in caves, and in thickets, and in rocks, and in high places, and in pits. And some of the Hebrews went over Jordan to the land of Gad and Gilead. As for Saul, he was yet in Gilgal, and all the people followed him trembling. And he tarried seven days, according to the set time that Samuel had appointed: but Samuel came not to Gilgal; and the people were scattered from him. And Saul said, Bring hither a burnt offering to me, and peace offerings. And he offered the burnt offering.

Samuel had told Saul to wait seven days before engaging in battle against the Philistines. When seven days had come and almost gone and Samuel hadn't shown up, Saul said, "My troops are leaving. I've got to do something." So he assumed the role of priest and offered a sacrifice himself rather than waiting for Samuel so that he could engage in battle.

1 Samuel 13:10–14

And it came to pass, that as soon as he had made an end of offering the burnt offering,

behold, Samuel came; and Saul went out to meet him, that he might salute him. And Samuel said, What hast thou done? And Saul said, Because I saw that the people were scattered from me, and that thou camest not within the days appointed, and that the Philistines gathered themselves together at Michmash; Therefore said I, The Philistines will come down now upon me to Gilgal, and I have not made supplication unto the LORD: I forced myself therefore, and offered a burnt offering. And Samuel said to Saul, Thou hast done foolishly: thou hast not kept the commandment of the LORD thy God, which he commanded thee: for now would the LORD have established thy kingdom upon Israel for ever. But now thy kingdom shall not continue: the LORD hath sought him a man after his own heart, and the LORD hath commanded him to be captain over his people, because thou hast not kept that which the LORD commanded thee.

No sooner had Saul finished offering the sacrifice than Samuel showed up. This is so often the way of God. So often the Lord waits until the last moment to step in. Why? It's not to tease us, but to test us. He takes us right down to the wire not to taunt but to train us in order that we might have endurance (see James 1:3). You see, the race we run as believers isn't a sprint. It's a marathon. And God knows how desperately we need endurance. The only way to get endurance is to go through testing that will force us to wait on Him in order that we might not panic, not run off the track, not throw in the towel. C.H. Spurgeon said the snails made it safely to the ark because they had endurance. You might be a snail. I might be a slug. We might move very, very slowly—but we will make it to the ark if we simply endure.

"Time is running out!" we cry. "We've got to do something!"

Do we? I can give you all kinds of advice and recommendations, but it's only when God steps in that there will be a real solution. The sage was right when he said that the brave man is not braver than any other, but simply braver for ten minutes longer. Who is the brave man? Who is the mature brother, the wise sister, the deep Christian among us? It's not one who is necessarily super-spiritual. It's simply one who has learned to wait and not panic.

Has God promised to show up? Has God promised you that He is going to work all things for good? Has God promised you that He will take the cares you cast on Him? Has God promised you that He will give a peace deep within? Has God promised that the desires deep within your heart will come to pass? If He has, wait for Him. Don't panic, dear people. Be brave. Saul thought he waited seven days—but seven days hadn't completely passed. He didn't wait the full course.

"Lord make me a man of God," we pray. "Produce in me depth of character and wisdom."

"Okay," God says. "I'm going to take you through some experiences in which you will have the choice either to panic and try to solve the problem by sacrificing this or looking to them—or to trust Me."

1 Samuel 13:15
And Samuel arose, and gat him up from Gilgal unto Gibeah of Benjamin. And Saul numbered the people that were present with him, about six hundred men.

Samuel walked away heartbroken. Saul, on the other hand, continued with his activities.

1 Samuel 13:16–18
And Saul, and Jonathan his son, and the people that were present with them, abode in Gibeah of Benjamin: but the Philistines encamped in Michmash. And the spoilers came out of the camp of the Philistines in three companies: one company turned unto the way that leadeth to Ophrah, unto the land of Shual: And another company turned the way to Beth-horon: and another company turned to the way of the border that looketh to the valley of Zeboim toward the wilderness.

The Philistines dominated the countryside. They were in control of the territory.

1 Samuel 13:19–21
Now there was no smith found throughout all the land of Israel: for the Philistines said, Lest the Hebrews make them swords or spears: But all the Israelites went down to the Philistines, to sharpen every man his share, and his coulter, and his axe, and his mattock. Yet they had a file for the mattocks, and for the coulters, and for the forks, and for the axes, and to sharpen the goads.

When the Philistines controlled the country, they would not allow the men of Israel to have swords. So to sharpen their plows and other implements of farming, the Israelites had to go to the Philistines.

It is always the way of the enemy to take away your sword. "You can still farm. You can still do your work. I'll give you tools," Satan says. "I'll help you financially or educationally. I'll give you the instruments you need to succeed. But I don't want you to have the sword." Self-help and advice books fill the shelves of many who won't open the sword of the Word because Satan has tricked them into thinking they don't need it. I suggest, however, that the sixty-six-book library you hold in your hand contains enough material to keep you busy studying for the rest of your life.

I truly thought that by this point in my life I would have a much better handle on this book than I do. I know the Word not nearly like I ought to, not nearly like I want to. I don't have Zephaniah down like I ought to. I don't have passages in Romans memorized like I wanted to. I'm still sketchy on the flow of certain sections of Revelation. Time is running out. My memory is fading and I need to give myself to the Sword. I am more and more convinced that everything I need to know is in this book—about parenting and grandparenting, about finances and family, about faith and the future. It's all right here. Satan will try to give us other tools—but it is the Sword we need.

1 Samuel 13:22, 23
So it came to pass in the day of battle, that there was neither sword nor spear found in the hand of any of the people that were with Saul and Jonathan: but with Saul and with Jonathan his son was there found. And the garrison of the Philistines went out to the passage of Michmash.

The swords were stripped away, but God was still at work, as we'll see in chapter 14 . . .

14

1 Samuel 14:1
Now it came to pass upon a day, that Jonathan the son of Saul said unto the young man that bare his armour, Come, and let us go over to the Philistines' garrison, that is on the other side. But he told not his father.

We saw in chapter 13 that there was a garrison of Philistines near Michmash ready to do battle with the people of Israel.

1 Samuel 14:2
And Saul tarried in the uttermost part of Gibeah under a pomegranate tree which is in Migron: and the people that were with him were about six hundred men;

Many of the soldiers were garrisoned with Jonathan. Saul, however, was at home with six hundred of his personal bodyguards.

1 Samuel 14:3–5
And Ahiah, the son of Ahitub, I-chabod's brother, the son of Phinehas, the son of Eli, the LORD's priest in Shiloh, wearing an ephod. And the people knew not that Jonathan was gone. And between the passages, by which Jonathan sought to go over unto the Philistines' garrison, there was a sharp rock on the one side and a sharp rock on the other side: and the name of the one was Bozez, and the name of the other Seneh. The forefront of the one was situate northward over against Michmash, and the other southward over against Gibeah.

Bozez or "glistening" and *Seneh* or "thorny" were two rocks that stood between Jonathan and the enemy. That's the way it is for us as well. There are all kinds of glistening rewards and riches if we'll engage in battle. But there is also no shortage of thorny challenges and difficulties.

1 Samuel 14:6
And Jonathan said to the young man that bare his armour, Come, and let us go over unto the garrison of these uncircumcised: it may be that the LORD will work for us: for there is no restraint to the LORD to save by many or by few.

Deuteronomy 32:30 tells us that one with the Lord will put to flight 1,000 and two with the Lord will put to flight 10,000. I like the Lord's mathematics because if one would put to flight 1,000, you would think that two would put to flight 2,000. But God's economy is exponential and explosive, allowing two to have victory over ten times as many as one would.

Daniel 11:32 says that those who know their God shall do great exploits. In other words, the more I know about the Lord, the more faith I'll have to do great things for Him. William Carey, famous missionary of generations past said, "Attempt great things for God and expect great things from God." Every believer ought to be involved in something so big that, unless God is in it, it's doomed to fail. Go in over your head. Do something that is so much bigger than you are, that unless God is in it, it can't work. Jonathan models this mindset.

1 Samuel 14:7
And his armour-bearer said unto him, Do all that is in thine heart: turn thee; behold, I am with thee according to thy heart.

It's easy to be negative. It's easy to say, "What are you thinking? We don't have a chance!" Instead, Jonathan's armor-bearer said to him, "If it's on your heart, I'm with you."

1 Samuel 14:8–10
Then said Jonathan, Behold, we will pass over unto these men, and we will discover ourselves unto them. If they say thus unto us, Tarry until we come to you; then we will stand still in our place, and will not go up unto them. But if they say thus, Come up unto us; then we will go up: for the LORD hath delivered them into our hand: and this shall be a sign unto us.

Although Jonathan and his armor-bearer said, "Let's step out and see what the Lord might want to do," they weren't being presumptuous because they said, "If the Lord doesn't want us to go, we're not going to plunge ahead." In this, I see a wonderful balance.

A lot of people wait for something to happen—but they wait at a great distance. They say, "Lord if You want to do something with me, you have my number." I think a better way is to do what Jonathan did. He stood on the edge. He was at the door. He wasn't going to force it, but he was in place to storm through it.

Perhaps you're in a place vocationally, relationally, or in ministry where the Lord is telling you to step up, move out, and get ready.

"But what if it doesn't work out?" you ask.

The Lord has promised to close doors no man can open and to open doors no man can shut (Revelation 3:7), but you can't see the door from a long distance. You've got to be there. That's what Jonathan did.

1 Samuel 14:11
And both of them discovered themselves unto the garrison of the Philistines: and the Philistines said, Behold, the Hebrews come forth out of the holes where they had hid themselves.

Afraid of the Philistines, the Israelites had taken to hiding in caves.

1 Samuel 14:12
And the men of the garrison answered Jonathan and his armour-bearer, and said, Come up to us, and we will shew you a thing. And Jonathan said unto his armour-bearer, Come up after me: for the LORD hath delivered them into the hand of Israel.

In Matthew 16, Jesus told us that He would build His church and the gates of hell would not prevail against it. For many years, I thought that verse meant Satan would not conquer us. But that's obviously not what Jesus was saying because gates don't attack. No, Jesus was saying, "You will storm through the gates of hell. You'll go on the offense and take territory previously held by the enemy." If Jonathan were put in a defensive position, his plan was to split. But the enemy egged him on to an offensive position, and in taking the offense, he and his armor-bearer were able to conquer that which was previously held by the enemy. We are to do the same thing. We get to go on the offense and see Jesus free people previously held by the enemy.

1 Samuel 14:13–15
And Jonathan climbed up upon his hands and upon his feet, and his armour-bearer after him: and they fell before Jonathan; and his armour-bearer slew after him. And that first slaughter, which Jonathan and his armour-bearer made, was about twenty men, within as it were an half acre of land, which a yoke of oxen might plow. And there was trembling in the host, in the field, and among all the people: the garrison, and the spoilers, they also trembled, and the earth quaked: so it was a very great trembling.

The Philistines were blown away. They couldn't believe that only two men were wiping out their army. And as if that weren't bad enough, the earth began to quake.

1 Samuel 14:16
And the watchmen of Saul in Gibeah of Benjamin looked; and, behold, the multitude melted away, and they went on beating down one another.

Evidently, they were disoriented and confused, the Philistines began to attack each other.

1 Samuel 14:17–19
Then said Saul unto the people that were with him, Number now, and see who is gone from us. And when they had numbered, behold, Jonathan and his armour-bearer were not there. And Saul said unto Ahiah, Bring hither the ark of God. For the ark of God was at that time with the children of Israel. And it came to pass, while Saul talked unto the priest, that the noise that was in the host of the Philistines went on and increased: and Saul said unto the priest, Withdraw thine hand.

Hearing the noise from the Philistine camp grow louder, and still not understanding the need to slow down and wait on the Lord, Saul called for the ark and told the priest there wasn't time to seek the Lord.

1 Samuel 14:20–22
And Saul and all the people that were with him assembled themselves, and they came to the battle: and, behold, every man's sword was against his fellow, and there was a very great discomfiture. Moreover the Hebrews that were with the Philistines before that time, which went up with them into the camp from the country round about, even they also turned to be with the Israelites that were with Saul and Jonathan. Likewise all the men of Israel which had hid themselves in mount Ephraim, when they heard that the Philistines fled, even they also followed hard after them in the battle.

As this amazing victory unfolded, the Israelites who previously sided with the enemy suddenly found courage to change alliances. Others, hiding away because they were intimidated left their caves and began to move in glorious unity. It took only two young men who were willing to say, "Let's go see what the Lord might want to do" to cause fearful men to surface and join the battle.

I wonder who is young of heart tonight. I wonder who is tired of the mundane and predictable, tired of that which is easy to do in your own energy. Maybe the Lord is saying to you, "There's something I want to do that will be ground-shaking, something that will cause other people to get fired up and to get right." I wonder who God is speaking to even now.

1 Samuel 14:23, 24
So the LORD saved Israel that day: and the battle passed over unto Beth-aven. And the men of Israel were distressed that day: for Saul had adjured the people, saying, Cursed be the man that eateth any food until evening, that I may be avenged on mine enemies. So none of the people tasted any food.

As the Philistines fought each other and fled in their confusion, Saul suddenly got involved and said, "No one is to eat anything all day long. I want you to be focused like a laser on chasing down the enemy."

1 Samuel 14:25, 26
And all they of the land came to a wood; and there was honey upon the ground. And when the people were come into the wood, behold, the honey dropped; but no man put his hand to his mouth: for the people feared the oath.

The Israelites had been working, fighting, running. They were hungry—and honey was there for the taking.

We are told that the Law of the Lord is sweeter than honey (Psalm 19:10). But it is the Saul mentality that says, "You don't have time for honey. You don't have time for devotions. You don't have time to go to Bible study. There's work to do. The business needs attention. The lawn needs mowing. You don't have time to stop, to eat, to grow."

The Lord, however, would say, "You need to slow down and take time to eat the honey of the Word if you're going to overcome and overtake the enemy."

1 Samuel 14:27
But Jonathan heard not when his father charged the people with the oath: wherefore he put forth the end of the rod that was in his hand, and dipped it in an honeycomb, and put his hand to his mouth; and his eyes were enlightened.

Jonathan's eyes were enlightened, meaning he was energized. The commandment of the Lord is pure, enlightening the eyes (Psalm 19:8).

1 Samuel 14:28, 29
Then answered one of the people, and said, Thy father straitly charged the people with an oath, saying, Cursed be the man that eateth any food this day. And the people were faint. Then said Jonathan, My father hath troubled the land: see, I pray you, how mine eyes have been enlightened, because I tasted a little of this honey.

Jonathan realized the command of his father was foolish because he was more effective after he had tasted the honey.

1 Samuel 14:30, 31
How much more, if haply the people had eaten freely to day of the spoil of their enemies which they found? for had there not been now a much greater slaughter among the Philistines? And they smote the Philistines that day from Michmash to Aijalon: and the people were very faint.

Aijalon is fourteen miles northwest of Jerusalem.

1 Samuel 14:32
And the people flew upon the spoil, and took sheep, and oxen, and calves, and slew them on the ground: and the people did eat them with the blood.

So hungry were the people from the battle that they ate the food before them—the food of the enemy. It was unclean. It wasn't kosher. It wasn't prepared properly.

The same thing happens to me. If I don't partake of the meat of the Word, I'll end up eating the unclean meat of the world. If I've worked hard, focused like a laser, done battle—but haven't taken time to dip into the honey of the Word, when the day is over, I'll dive into a scoop of ice cream—or two—or a gallon. Then I'll turn on TV and watch a political debate where political analysts scream at each other for two hours. By that time, I'll think I need a bowl of cereal. And before I know it, it's two in the morning and I'm still hungry. But when I open the Bible, the most amazing thing happens. My eyes are enlightened. My soul is satiated. Suddenly I'm talking with the Lord and hearing from Him. And it's wonderful—for it's what I wanted all along.

Eat the honey before you get so discouraged and weary that you dive into carnal stuff. The best thing you can do to remain healthy and happy is to eat of the honey regularly. It will keep you from eating the unclean meat of the world. Pack a pocket New Testament instead of a calorie counter in your purse or pocket. Always keep at least a section of Scripture close at hand.

1 Samuel 14:33–35
Then they told Saul, saying, Behold, the people sin against the LORD, in that they eat with the blood. And he said, Ye have transgressed: roll a great stone unto me this day. And Saul said, Disperse yourselves among the people, and say unto them, Bring me hither every man his ox, and every man his sheep, and slay them here, and eat; and sin not against the LORD in eating with the blood. And all the people brought every man his ox with him that night, and slew them there. And Saul built an altar unto the LORD: the same was the first altar that he built unto the LORD.

It was Saul who kept the honey from the people—but now not only is he blaming the people for his sin, but he's once again assuming the role of priest and trying to correct the situation in a way he wasn't called to do. This is all so symptomatic of what happens when we try to fix things in the strength of our flesh.

1 Samuel 14:36
And Saul said, Let us go down after the Philistines by night, and spoil them until the morning light, and let us not leave a man of them. And they said, Do whatsoever seemeth good unto thee. Then said the priest, Let us draw near hither unto God.

As Saul barks order, the priest says, "Could we pray first?"

1 Samuel 14:37
And Saul asked counsel of God, Shall I go down after the Philistines? wilt thou deliver them into the hand of Israel? But he answered him not that day.

In Psalm 66, David declared, "If I regard iniquity in my heart, the Lord will not hear me." When our prayers aren't answered, it is God's way of saying, "Something is not right. Something is out of order. There's an issue that needs to be adjusted." God didn't answer Saul a word because Saul was caught up in himself.

1 Samuel 14:38
And Saul said, Draw ye near hither, all the chief of the people: and know and see wherein this sin hath been this day.

Saul knew something was wrong, but he failed to understand that he was the problem.

1 Samuel 14:39
For, as the LORD liveth, which saveth Israel, though it be in Jonathan my son, he shall surely die. But there was not a man among all the people that answered him.

Saul came to the irrational conclusion that the reason God didn't answer his prayer was because someone ate some honey. That he singled out Jonathan suggests to me that he realized that, as a man of faith and a courageous warrior, his son was a threat to him.

1 Samuel 14:40, 41
Then said he unto all Israel, Be ye on one side, and I and Jonathan my son will be on the other side. And the people said unto Saul, Do what seemeth good unto thee. Therefore Saul said unto the LORD God of Israel, Give a perfect lot. And Saul and Jonathan were taken: but the people escaped.

Saul and Jonathan stood on one side; the people stood on the other. They drew straws to discover who had sinned—and Saul and Jonathan drew the short one.

1 Samuel 14:42, 43
And Saul said, Cast lots between me and Jonathan my son. And Jonathan was taken. Then Saul said to Jonathan, Tell me what

thou hast done. And Jonathan told him, and said, I did but taste a little honey with the end of the rod that was in mine hand, and, lo, I must die.

Rather than defending himself or blaming his father, Jonathan said, "I must die." Jonathan's conclusion is correct for anyone involved in conflict with another, for the only way peace can be attained is through someone dying to his point of view, his opinion, his rights.

1 Samuel 14:44
And Saul answered, God do so and more also: for thou shalt surely die, Jonathan.

Saul was a failure as a father, as a leader, as a king.

1 Samuel 14:45
And the people said unto Saul, Shall Jonathan die, who hath wrought this great salvation in Israel? God forbid: as the LORD liveth, there shall not one hair of his head fall to the ground; for he hath wrought with God this day. So the people rescued Jonathan, that he died not.

The people stepped in and stood up for Jonathan.

1 Samuel 14:46, 47
Then Saul went up from following the Philistines: and the Philistines went to their own place. So Saul took the kingdom over Israel, and fought against all his enemies on every side, against Moab, and against the children of Ammon, and against Edom, and against the kings of Zobah, and against the Philistines: and whithersoever he turned himself, he vexed them.

Saul turned his attention to fighting the enemies of Israel.

1 Samuel 14:48, 49
And he gathered an host, and smote the Amalekites, and delivered Israel out of the hands of them that spoiled them. Now the sons of Saul were Jonathan, and Ishui, and Melchishua: and the names of his two daughters were these; the name of the firstborn Merab, and the name of the younger Michal:

Jonathan means "Gift from God." *Ishui* means "Just like me." Saul is regressing. At the birth of his firstborn son, he acknowledged God. Here, he simply boasts in himself.

1 Samuel 14:50
And the name of Saul's wife was Ahinoam, the daughter of Ahimaaz: and the name of the captain of his host was Abner, the son of Ner, Saul's uncle.

Ner means "light" or "lamp." *Ab* means "son." Thus, *Abner* means "son of light."

1 Samuel 14:51, 52
And Kish was the father of Saul; and Ner the father of Abner was the son of Abiel. And there was sore war against the Philistines all the days of Saul: and when Saul saw any strong man, or any valiant man, he took him unto him.

The young, strong men were drafted into Saul's army—just as Samuel had prophesied.

15

In the chapter before us, the cracks we have seen in Saul's character become crevices into which he will fall. Here, we see the sad story of the downward spiral of a man who began well, who had the anointing of the Spirit, who had the call of God, but whose flaws will ultimately destroy him.

1 Samuel 15:1
Samuel also said unto Saul, The LORD sent me to anoint thee to be king over his people, over Israel: now therefore hearken thou unto the voice of the words of the LORD.

Although Saul had already dropped the ball, the Lord sends Samuel to give him yet another opportunity to do something right.

That's what the Lord always does to His children. He sends messenger after messenger, gives us opportunity after opportunity to walk wisely, to live successfully. But there does come an end to those opportunities to do right. Ultimately, as we shall see, Saul just doesn't get it, and his poor decisions destroy him. Therefore, as we look at the story before us and see Saul's plight, God would say to us what He said to Saul: "Hearken"—take heed, give ear, listen up—"to My Word."

1 Samuel 15:2, 3
Thus saith the LORD of hosts, I remember that which Amalek did to Israel, how he laid wait for him in the way, when he came up from Egypt. Now go and smite Amalek, and utterly destroy all that they have, and spare them not; but slay both man and woman, infant and suckling, ox and sheep, camel and ass.

In the Bible, Amalek is a picture of the flesh. In Deuteronomy 25, we are told that the Amalekites would attack the back of the pack as the people of Israel marched through the wilderness on their way to the Promised Land. In other words, the Amalekites would pick off those who were sick, feeble, or elderly.

That's exactly how the flesh works. It exploits the areas of our lives where we are weak, feeble, or holding back. Concerning the Amalekites who harassed the people of Israel, God said, "It's time to deal a death blow to these people."

To some who read this story that may sound mean or cruel. "How could God call for the destruction of an entire civilization?" they ask. But the Amalekites were so corrupt and so polluted that they were actually destroying themselves in their perversity and sin. Throughout the Old Testament, we see God ordering the annihilation of certain civilizations because they were so corrupt and polluted that it was actually an act of mercy for Him to take them out of their misery.

1 Samuel 15:4–6
And Saul gathered the people together, and numbered them in Telaim, two hundred thousand footmen, and ten thousand men of Judah. And Saul came to a city of Amalek, and laid wait in the valley. And Saul said unto the Kenites, Go, depart, get you down from among the Amalekites, lest I destroy you with them: for ye shewed kindness to all the children of Israel, when they came up out of Egypt. So the Kenites departed from among the Amalekites.

Although the Kenites were neighbors of the Amalekites, they had shown kindness to Israel—perhaps because Jethro, Moses' father-in-law, was a Kenite. "We don't want you to get caught in the middle of this war with the Amalekites," Saul warned them. They wisely heeded Saul's warning and left.

1 Samuel 15:7–9
And Saul smote the Amalekites from Havilah until thou comest to Shur, that is over against Egypt. And he took Agag the king of the Amalekites alive, and utterly destroyed all the people with the edge of the sword. But Saul and the people spared Agag, and the best of the sheep, and of the oxen, and of the fatlings, and the lambs, and all that was good, and would not utterly destroy them: but every thing that was vile and refuse, that they destroyed utterly.

Agag's name literally means "I will overcome." What a great name for the king of the flesh: "I will overcome. I will succeed. I will not be wiped out or done in or removed easily." Agag, the king of the flesh, was spared by Saul, which will prove to be a costly error. You see, because Saul didn't utterly destroy the Amalekites, years later, when he is wounded on Mt. Gilboa in a battle against the Philistines, it will be an Amalekite who will ultimately run a sword through him (2 Samuel 1:6–8).

What a great illustration. If I don't kill the flesh, the flesh will kill me. Ask Saul. He thought he could control Agag, but found that Agag's descendants eventually destroyed him. If you think that, because you've destroyed certain aspects of your flesh and have Agag in chains, you don't have to worry—watch out. Agag will prove to be one that gives birth to another fleshly tendency that will do you in. Ask Saul. It happened to him.

A couple hundred years after this, we come to the story of Esther. The Book of Esther deals with a villain named Haman who was determined to destroy the Jews. Haman was an Agagite (Esther 3:1). Thus, two hundred-plus years after Saul, the nation feels the ramifications of his failure to deal with the flesh.

Sometimes we fall into the folly of Saul, thinking we have our flesh under control. But we fail to realize that our failure to deal with it completely will have ramifications on our kids and grandchildren, our friends, neighbors, and the church family—perhaps even years later.

1 Samuel 15:10, 11
Then came the word of the Lord unto Samuel, saying, It repenteth me that I have set up Saul to be king: for he is turned back from following me, and hath not performed my commandments. And it grieved Samuel; and he cried unto the Lord all night.

How I like Samuel's heart. He wasn't ticked off. He didn't stomp around the room or put his fist through the wall. He was simply heartbroken. He hurt for Saul.

1 Samuel 15:12–15
And when Samuel rose early to meet Saul in the morning, it was told Samuel, saying, Saul came to Carmel, and, behold, he set him up a place, and is gone about, and passed on, and gone down to Gilgal. And Samuel came to Saul: and Saul said unto him, Blessed be thou of the Lord: I have performed the commandment of the Lord. And Samuel said, What meaneth then this bleating of the sheep in mine ears, and the lowing of the oxen which I hear? Saul said, They have brought them from the Amalekites: for the people spared the best of the

sheep and of the oxen, to sacrifice unto the LORD thy God; and the rest we have utterly destroyed.

"Praise the Lord. Hallelujah. Glory to God! I've had victory!" Saul said. But his spiritual jargon could barely be heard above the bleating of the very sheep he was supposed to have destroyed (v. 3).

1 Samuel 15:16, 17
Then Samuel said unto Saul, Stay, and I will tell thee what the LORD hath said to me this night. And he said unto him, Say on. And Samuel said, When thou wast little in thine own sight, wast thou not made the head of the tribes of Israel, and the LORD anointed thee king over Israel?

"Humble yourselves under the mighty hand of God that He may exalt you in due time," James declares (4:10). It's when Saul was small in his own sight that God tapped him to be king. Humility brings about productivity. But humility was no longer part of Saul's character.

1 Samuel 15:18–21
And the LORD sent thee on a journey, and said, Go and utterly destroy the sinners the Amalekites, and fight against them until they be consumed. Wherefore then didst thou not obey the voice of the LORD, but didst fly upon the spoil, and didst evil in the sight of the LORD? And Saul said unto Samuel, Yea, I have obeyed the voice of the LORD, and have gone the way which the LORD sent me, and have brought Agag the king of Amalek, and have utterly destroyed the Amalekites. But the people took of the spoil, sheep and oxen, the chief of the things which should have been utterly destroyed, to sacrifice unto the LORD thy God in Gilgal.

"Don't blame me," Saul insisted. "It's the peoples' fault, not mine."

People still say this. "My parents, my grandparents, or my kindergarten teacher are the reason I have these fleshly problems and evil tendencies," they insist.

1 Samuel 15:22
And Samuel said, Hath the LORD as great delight in burnt offerings and sacrifices, as in obeying the voice of the LORD? Behold, to obey is better than sacrifice, and to hearken than the fat of rams.

Many people give to a charity or ministry in order to assuage a guilty conscience or to appear more selfless than they are. Obeying is infinitely more important than giving because obedience isn't self-serving.

1 Samuel 15:23
For rebellion is as the sin of witchcraft, and stubbornness is as iniquity and idolatry. Because thou hast rejected the word of the LORD, he hath also rejected thee from being king.

The margin of your Bible most likely renders the word "witchcraft" as "divination." Rebellion is as witchcraft because when I rebel, I'm basically saying, "Lord, I will divine, I will determine what's best for me." According to this text, rebellion against the Lord is equal to involvement with the occult. Because of this, Saul lost the kingdom.

1 Samuel 15:24
And Saul said unto Samuel, I have sinned: for I have transgressed the commandment of the LORD, and thy words: because I feared the people, and obeyed their voice.

Even in his confession, Saul made excuses. He should have simply said, "I've sinned. I'm wrong. Period." Instead, he added "because." If I begin to justify why I have a sinful tendency, I'm in trouble. I need to simply say, "I sinned. Period."

1 Samuel 15:25–28
Now therefore, I pray thee, pardon my sin, and turn again with me, that I may worship the LORD. And Samuel said unto Saul, I will not return with thee: for thou hast rejected the word of the LORD, and the LORD hath rejected thee from being king over Israel. And as Samuel turned about to go away, he laid hold upon the skirt of his mantle, and it rent. And Samuel said unto him, The LORD hath rent the kingdom of Israel from thee this day, and hath given it to a neighbour of thine, that is better than thou.

The kingdom would be taken from Saul and given to a neighbor. That neighbor would, of course, be David.

1 Samuel 15:29
And also the Strength of Israel will not lie nor repent: for he is not a man, that he should repent.

God doesn't repent. That is, He doesn't change His mind. God never says, "Oops. I'm going the wrong way. I'd better change direction." Because God never makes a mistake, He has no need to repent.

1 Samuel 15:30, 31
Then he said, I have sinned: yet honour me now, I pray thee, before the elders of my people, and before Israel, and turn again with me, that I may worship the LORD thy God. So Samuel turned again after Saul; and Saul worshipped the LORD.

"Come with me to worship thy God," Saul said to Samuel—referring to God as Samuel's God, but evidently no longer his own.

1 Samuel 15:32, 33
Then said Samuel, Bring ye hither to me Agag the king of the Amalekites. And Agag came unto him delicately. And Agag said, Surely the bitterness of death is past. And Samuel said, As thy sword hath made women childless, so shall thy mother be childless among women. And Samuel hewed Agag in pieces before the LORD in Gilgal.

Can't we all get along? Agag asked—just as the flesh always tries to strike a bargain with us. But Samuel dealt a deathblow to this representative of the flesh. And so must we.

1 Samuel 15:34, 35
Then Samuel went to Ramah; and Saul went up to his house to Gibeah of Saul. And Samuel came no more to see Saul until the day of his death: nevertheless Samuel mourned for Saul: and the LORD repented that he had made Saul king over Israel.

In verse 29, we read that the Lord is not a man that he should repent. The word "repent" can mean "to change direction"—or it can mean, as it does forty-one times in the Old Testament—"to regret." God is simply regretting that the people demanded a king. In Deuteronomy 17:15, provision is made for a king. But the people got ahead of God because the king He intended for them was David.

Perhaps that's a word for some of us. "Delight yourself in the Lord, and He will give you the desires of your heart," Psalm 37:4 tells us. We cling to and claim this verse, as well we should—but not apart from its context, for three verses later, David tells us to wait patiently for God. God has a plan for our lives—and no small part of it requires patience. If we get ahead of God, we end up with Ishmael instead of Isaac, with Saul instead of David. It's a recurring lesson throughout Scripture (Psalm 27:14; Proverbs 20:22; Isaiah 40:31; Jeremiah 14:22; Lamentations 3:26; Hosea 12:6; Micah 7:7; Habakkuk 2:3; Zephaniah 3:8; Acts 1:4; Romans 8:25; 1 Thessalonians 1:10). Wait, wait, wait on the Lord.

16

1 Samuel 16:1
And the LORD said unto Samuel, How long wilt thou mourn for Saul, seeing I have rejected him from reigning over Israel? fill thine horn with oil, and go, I will send thee to Jesse the Bethlehemite: for I have provided me a king among his sons.

"Quit your mourning and moaning, Samuel, there's work to do," God said.

"But I have reason to mourn. My heart is broken," Samuel could have said.

"I regret it, too, but I've moved on," God might have answered.

We need to move on, gang. Yes, there are incidents in our lives that are hurtful, even regrettable—sad things, hard times, raw deals; pain, problems, and disappointments. But we must move on. Why? Because we serve a God who is on the move (Genesis 1:2). If I remain in the past problem or the past disappointment, I will miss the present move of God.

1 Samuel 16:2 (a)
And Samuel said, How can I go? if Saul hear it, he will kill me . . .

So bad had Saul become that Samuel, a man of God, now feared for his life.

1 Samuel 16:2 (b)–4
. . . And the LORD said, Take an heifer with thee, and say, I am come to sacrifice to the LORD. And call Jesse to the sacrifice, and I will shew thee what thou shalt do: and thou shalt anoint unto me him whom I name unto thee. And Samuel did that which the LORD spake, and came to Bethlehem. And the elders of the town trembled at his coming, and said, Comest thou peaceably?

I've known a few men who have truly been called into prophetic ministry. They speak God's heart and share God's Word in a way that is so impacting that when they knock on my door, like the elders of Bethlehem, I tremble a bit!

1 Samuel 16:5–7
And he said, Peaceably: I am come to sacrifice unto the LORD: sanctify yourselves, and come with me to the sacrifice. And he sanctified Jesse and his sons, and called them to the sacrifice. And it came to pass, when they were come, that he looked on Eliab, and said, Surely the LORD's anointed is before him. But the LORD said unto Samuel, Look not on his countenance, or on the height of

his stature; because I have refused him: for the LORD seeth not as man seeth; for man looketh on the outward appearance, but the LORD looketh on the heart.

In this life, we most often judge people by how they look, behave, dress, talk, or carry themselves. But God sees through all of that. He looks straight at the heart.

1 Samuel 16:8–11 (a)
Then Jesse called Abinadab, and made him pass before Samuel. And he said, Neither hath the LORD chosen this. Then Jesse made Shammah to pass by. And he said, Neither hath the LORD chosen this. Again, Jesse made seven of his sons to pass before Samuel. And Samuel said unto Jesse, The LORD hath not chosen these. And Samuel said unto Jesse, Are here all thy children? And he said, There remaineth yet the youngest, and, behold, he keepeth the sheep . . .

With the sheep—what a great place to find a shepherd for the nation.

1 Samuel 16:11 (b), 12
. . . And Samuel said unto Jesse, Send and fetch him: for we will not sit down till he come hither. And he sent, and brought him in. Now he was ruddy, and withal of a beautiful countenance, and goodly to look to. And the LORD said, Arise, anoint him: for this is he.

David is anointed as king—but Saul is still on the throne. Jesus is the Christ, or, literally, "Anointed One." Jesus will rule and reign on this planet someday. In the meantime, a usurper is on the throne. Jesus calls the devil the prince of this world (John 14:30). Paul calls him the god of this world (2 Corinthians 4:4).

"If Jesus is King of kings, why is this world so crazy? Why are there so many problems?" people ask. The answer is that, according to God's perfect plan, Jesus is anointed, but not yet enthroned.

1 Samuel 16:13 (a)
Then Samuel took the horn of oil, and anointed him . . .

When Saul was anointed, it was with a vial of oil (1 Samuel 10:1). David, on the other hand, was anointed with a big flask. Why? Because oil in the Word is a symbol of the Holy Spirit and David is a picture of the true Anointed One, the Christos, Jesus, who would be anointed with the oil of gladness more than any of His brethren (Hebrews 1:9).

1 Samuel 16:13 (b)
. . . in the midst of his brethren: and the Spirit of the LORD came upon David from that day forward . . .

Notice that Samuel anoints David in the midst of his brethren. David will eventually be anointed three times. The first time is here. The second time is in 2 Samuel 2:4, when he is anointed over the tribe of Judah. The third time is in 2 Samuel 5, when he is anointed as king over all Israel.

Sometimes a man will think he's anointed for ministry. His mom might agree. A few others might even recognize his anointing—and he'll wonder why everyone else doesn't see it. Most likely it's because it's not time. There is an unfolding of God's plan for a man or woman in service or ministry. You cannot rush it. Anointing is recognized by others in stages. It doesn't happen quickly. As it did with David, it comes when you fight battles on behalf of others, when you gain victory for others by caring for them, standing by them, helping them. David was an incredible man—a man after God's own heart, unlike anyone the world had ever seen—yet it took many years before his anointing was recognized. Saul was impatient. David, on the other hand, patiently waited. So must we.

1 Samuel 16:13 (c), 14
. . . So Samuel rose up, and went to Ramah. But the Spirit of the LORD departed from Saul, and an evil spirit from the LORD troubled him.

How could an evil spirit be sent from the Lord? Evil spirits and Satan himself can do nothing without the Lord's permission. As such, demons actually serve the purpose of God. How? By providing people a choice. If there were no Satan, people would have no choice. Thus, we would never know if our love for God was genuine. In this area, God is pro-choice. He says, "If you don't want to love Me, walk with Me, or believe in Me, you have another option. You can be deceived by the devil."

If I tell my son, Ben, I want him to stay home this afternoon—and then I lock him in his room, bolt his door, and board up his windows, it would be meaningless for me to come home later and tell him how proud I was of him for staying home. Unless there was an open door for Ben to make a decision, my praise of him would be pointless. That is why God leaves the door open and uses Satan as a tool to give people a choice.

1 Samuel 16:15–18
And Saul's servants said unto him, Behold now, an evil spirit from God troubleth thee.

Let our lord now command thy servants, which are before thee, to seek out a man, who is a cunning player on an harp: and it shall come to pass, when the evil spirit from God is upon thee, that he shall play with his hand, and thou shalt be well. And Saul said unto his servants, Provide me now a man that can play well, and bring him to me. Then answered one of the servants, and said, Behold, I have seen a son of Jesse the Bethlehemite, that is cunning in playing, and a mighty valiant man, and a man of war, and prudent in matters, and a comely person, and the LORD is with him.

What a resume! David had confidence, courage, and charisma. He was a conqueror, yet was careful. On top of it all, the Lord was with him.

1 Samuel 16:19–21
Wherefore Saul sent messengers unto Jesse, and said, Send me David thy son, which is with the sheep. And Jesse took an ass laden with bread, and a bottle of wine, and a kid, and sent them by David his son unto Saul. And David came to Saul, and stood before him: and he loved him greatly; and he became his armour-bearer.

David never was bitter, never felt anger, never allowed hatred to rule his heart. He was always an admirer of Saul, even though Saul was out to kill him. Amazing.

1 Samuel 16:22, 23
And Saul sent to Jesse, saying, Let David, I pray thee, stand before me; for he hath found favour in my sight. And it came to pass, when the evil spirit from God was upon Saul, that David took an harp, and played with his hand: so Saul was refreshed, and was well, and the evil spirit departed from him.

When music was played by this godly man, the demons fled. That is not surprising, for there is power in praise. Worship works wonders. When I'm depressed or blue, when I feel attacked by the enemy, when I feel the demons harassing me, I have found that one of the best things I can do is worship the Lord.

17

The chapter before us tells one of the best-known and best-loved stories in all of Scripture: the story of David and Goliath. While it is a story filled with lessons of God's faithfulness even in the most seemingly impossible situations, I would like us to look at this account as yet another picture of our Champion, Jesus Christ, and His victory over Satan, a giant of an enemy.

1 Samuel 17:1–3
Now the Philistines gathered together their armies to battle, and were gathered together at Shochoh, which belongeth to Judah, and pitched between Shochoh and Azekah, in Ephes-dammim. And Saul and the men of Israel were gathered together, and pitched by the valley of Elah, and set the battle in array against the Philistines. And the Philistines stood on a mountain on the one side, and Israel stood on a mountain on the other side: and there was a valley between them.

The Philistines were encamped in Judah, the place of praise, where they ought not be.

1 Samuel 17:4
And there went out a champion out of the camp of the Philistines, named Goliath, of Gath, whose height was six cubits and a span.

Goliath means "strip"—which is exactly what our Adversary does as he strips us of our joy, happiness, purpose, and peace.

1 Samuel 17:5
And he had an helmet of brass upon his head, and he was armed with a coat of mail; and the weight of the coat was five thousand shekels of brass.

Five thousand shekels of brass would be approximately two hundred pounds.

1 Samuel 17:6, 7
And he had greaves of brass upon his legs, and a target of brass between his shoulders. And the staff of his spear was like a weaver's beam; and his spear's head weighed six hundred shekels of iron: and one bearing a shield went before him.

Six hundred shekels would be approximately twenty-five pounds—an amazing weight for a spear, considering a shot-put weighs only sixteen pounds.

1 Samuel 17:8
And he stood and cried unto the armies of Israel, and said unto them, Why are ye come out to set your battle in array? am not I a Philistine, and ye servants to Saul? choose you a man for you, and let him come down to me.

"Send a man down to me," Goliath roared. I like that phrase because there would indeed be a Man—the Son of Man—who would come down from heaven to do battle with the enemy that seeks to devour us.

1 Samuel 17:9–11
If he be able to fight with me, and to kill me, then will we be your servants: but if I prevail against him, and kill him, then shall ye be our servants, and serve us. And the Philistine said, I defy the armies of Israel this day; give me a man, that we may fight together. When Saul and all Israel heard those words of the Philistine, they were dismayed, and greatly afraid.

It's no wonder Saul was dismayed. After all, being the tallest man in Israel made him the logical choice to face Goliath.

1 Samuel 17:12–14
Now David was the son of that Ephrathite of Bethlehem Judah, whose name was Jesse; and he had eight sons: and the man went among men for an old man in the days of Saul. And the three eldest sons of Jesse went and followed Saul to the battle: and the names of his three sons that went to the battle were Eliab the firstborn, and next unto him Abinadab, and the third Shammah. And David was the youngest: and the three eldest followed Saul.

David was the eighth son. Eight is the biblical number of sanctification and new beginnings. The other brothers were thought to be more qualified, but God said to Samuel, "This is the one. This is the man. I've set him apart. I've sanctified him."

1 Samuel 17:15
But David went and returned from Saul to feed his father's sheep at Bethlehem.

David had been in Saul's presence earlier when he played the harp for Saul. Here, having left Saul's court, he's back home in Bethlehem, taking care of his father's sheep—a picture of the One who would one day not only take care of His Father's sheep, but lay down His life for them (John 10:11).

1 Samuel 17:16
And the Philistine drew near morning and evening, and presented himself forty days.

Forty, in the Bible, is the number of testing and trial . . .

- Rain pelted Noah's ark for forty days.
- The children of Israel wandered forty years.
- Jesus was tested in the wilderness for forty days.

1 Samuel 17:17–19
And Jesse said unto David his son, Take now for thy brethren an ephah of this parched corn, and these ten loaves, and run to the camp to thy brethren; And carry these ten cheeses unto the captain of their thousand, and look how thy brethren fare, and take their pledge. Now Saul, and they, and all the men of Israel, were in the valley of Elah, fighting with the Philistines.

David and Jesus were both sent by their fathers—David to bring his brothers bread, Jesus to be Bread for His brothers (John 6:48; Hebrews 2:11).

1 Samuel 17:20–25
And David rose up early in the morning, and left the sheep with a keeper, and took, and went, as Jesse had commanded him; and he came to the trench, as the host was going forth to the fight, and shouted for the battle. For Israel and the Philistines had put the battle in array, army against army. And David left his carriage in the hand of the keeper of the carriage, and ran into the army, and came and saluted his brethren. And as he talked with them, behold, there came up the champion, the Philistine of Gath, Goliath by name, out of the armies of the Philistines, and spake according to the same words: and David heard them. And all the men of Israel, when they saw the man, fled from him, and were sore afraid. And the men of Israel said, Have ye seen this man that is come up? surely to defy Israel is he come up: and it shall be, that the man who killeth him, the king will enrich him with great riches, and will give him his daughter, and make his father's house free in Israel.

The reward promised to the one who slew Goliath was great riches, a bride, and freedom for his family. What did the Son of David, Jesus Christ, gain by defeating Satan? We are His inheritance (Ephesians 1), His treasure (Matthew 13:44), His pearl of great price (Matthew 13:46). We are also His bride (Revelation 21:9). And we are the ones who have been set free (John 8:36).

1 Samuel 17:26–29
And David spake to the men that stood by him, saying, What shall be done to the man that killeth this Philistine, and taketh away the reproach from Israel? for who is this

uncircumcised Philistine, that he should defy the armies of the living God? And the people answered him after this manner, saying, So shall it be done to the man that killeth him. And Eliab his eldest brother heard when he spake unto the men; and Eliab's anger was kindled against David, and he said, Why camest thou down hither? and with whom hast thou left those few sheep in the wilderness? I know thy pride, and the naughtiness of thine heart; for thou art come down that thou mightest see the battle. And David said, What have I now done? Is there not a cause?

Sanctified by the Spirit, sent by the Father, seeking a treasure, like David, Jesus was scorned by His brothers without cause (Luke 23:21, 22).

1 Samuel 17:30–33
And he turned from him toward another, and spake after the same manner: and the people answered him again after the former manner. And when the words were heard which David spake, they rehearsed them before Saul: and he sent for him. And David said to Saul, Let no man's heart fail because of him; thy servant will go and fight with this Philistine. And Saul said to David, Thou art not able to go against this Philistine to fight with him: for thou art but a youth, and he a man of war from his youth.

"I'll take Goliath on," David said.

"You don't have a chance," Saul said. "You're just a kid and he's a giant who's been a warrior from his youth."

1 Samuel 17:34–37
And David said unto Saul, Thy servant kept his father's sheep, and there came a lion, and a bear, and took a lamb out of the flock: And I went out after him, and smote him, and delivered it out of his mouth: and when he arose against me, I caught him by his beard, and smote him, and slew him. Thy servant slew both the lion and the bear: and this uncircumcised Philistine shall be as one of them, seeing he hath defied the armies of the living God. David said moreover, The LORD that delivered me out of the paw of the lion, and out of the paw of the bear, he will deliver me out of the hand of this Philistine. And Saul said unto David, Go, and the LORD be with thee.

David and Jesus were both strengthened by experience. David was strengthened as he battled the lion in the field. When He overcame the temptation of Satan, the roaring lion, in the wilderness, Jesus was strengthened for the battle not in the valley of Elah, but on the mountain of Calvary.

1 Samuel 17:38, 39
And Saul armed David with his armour, and he put an helmet of brass upon his head; also he armed him with a coat of mail. And David girded his sword upon his armour, and he assayed to go; for he had not proved it. And David said unto Saul, I cannot go with these; for I have not proved them. And David put them off him.

Perhaps feeling guilty about sending a boy into battle, Saul gave David his armor. But David laid aside this armor, just as Jesus laid aside His godly powers and abilities to become a Man like us (Philippians 2).

1 Samuel 17:40
And he took his staff in his hand, and chose him five smooth stones out of the brook, and put them in a shepherd's bag which he had, even in a scrip; and his sling was in his hand: and he drew near to the Philistine.

Why did David grab five stones? It could be because Goliath had four brothers. But it could also be because five in the Bible is the number of grace and David knew that the victory would come not because of who he was or what he had done, but solely because of God's grace.

1 Samuel 17:41–46
And the Philistine came on and drew near unto David; and the man that bare the shield went before him. And when the Philistine looked about, and saw David, he disdained him: for he was but a youth, and ruddy, and of a fair countenance. And the Philistine said unto David, Am I a dog, that thou comest to me with staves? And the Philistine cursed David by his gods. And the Philistine said to David, Come to me, and I will give thy flesh unto the fowls of the air, and to the beasts of the field. Then said David to the Philistine, Thou comest to me with a sword, and with a spear, and with a shield: but I come to thee in the name of the LORD of hosts, the God of the armies of Israel, whom thou hast defied. This day will the LORD deliver thee into mine hand; and I will smite thee, and take thine head from thee; and I will give the carcases of the host of the Philistines this day unto the fowls of the air, and to the wild beasts of the earth; that all the earth may know that there is a God in Israel.

Both David and Jesus were strong in faith.

"This day will the Lord deliver you into my hands," David said in the ears of Goliath as well as in the hearing of his countrymen.

"Destroy this temple and in three days I will raise it up," Jesus declared in the ears of the Jews as well as His disciples (John 2:19–22).

Faith abides in the heart and is released through the mouth (Romans 10:10). It's one thing to believe in your heart silently. It's something else to make a statement publicly.

1 Samuel 17:47–49
And all this assembly shall know that the LORD saveth not with sword and spear: for the battle is the LORD's, and he will give you into our hands. And it came to pass, when the Philistine arose, and came and drew nigh to meet David, that David hasted, and ran toward the army to meet the Philistine. And David put his hand in his bag, and took thence a stone, and slang it, and smote the Philistine in his forehead, that the stone sunk into his forehead; and he fell upon his face to the earth.

Recent discoveries indicate that Philistine armor was made in such a way that the helmets had visors. But David was so little that when Goliath lifted his visor to see him, David used the "window of opportunity" to sink a stone in his forehead.

1 Samuel 17:50–53
So David prevailed over the Philistine with a sling and with a stone, and smote the Philistine, and slew him; but there was no sword in the hand of David. Therefore David ran, and stood upon the Philistine, and took his sword, and drew it out of the sheath thereof, and slew him, and cut off his head therewith. And when the Philistines saw their champion was dead, they fled. And the men of Israel and of Judah arose, and shouted, and pursued the Philistines, until thou come to the valley, and to the gates of Ekron. And the wounded of the Philistines fell down by the way to Shaaraim, even unto Gath, and unto Ekron. And the children of Israel returned from chasing after the Philistines, and they spoiled their tents.

Both David and Jesus snatched the enemy's weapons and used them against them. David lopped off Goliath's head with Goliath's own sword—just as Jesus set the captives free by way of the Cross (Ephesians 4:8).

1 Samuel 17:54
And David took the head of the Philistine, and brought it to Jerusalem; but he put his armour in his tent.

Both David and Jesus singularly secured the victory. According to Goliath's own rules, one man would win the victory for the entire army (1 Samuel 17:9). And according to the Word, Jesus won the battle for all mankind (John 12:32). All the Israelites had to do was pick up the spoils—and the same is true with us. We can expect our lives to be blessed, our kids to do well, our prayers to be answered—all because of what Jesus did on our behalf.

1 Samuel 17:55–58
And when Saul saw David go forth against the Philistine, he said unto Abner, the captain of the host, Abner, whose son is this youth? And Abner said, As thy soul liveth, O king, I cannot tell. And the king said, Inquire thou whose son the stripling is. And as David returned from the slaughter of the Philistine, Abner took him, and brought him before Saul with the head of the Philistine in his hand. And Saul said to him, Whose son art thou, thou young man? And David answered, I am the son of thy servant Jesse the Bethlehemite.

David having grown up since the time he played the harp for Saul, Saul no longer recognizes him. So David introduces himself as the son of Jesse, a resident of Bethlehem, little knowing he was a precursor of the Son who would leave His Father to be born in Bethlehem in order to save us from the Goliath of an enemy out to destroy us.

18

When David reported to Saul, Saul said, "Who are you?" When he finished telling Saul who he was, the soul of Jonathan was knit with the soul of David . . .

1 Samuel 18:1–4
And it came to pass, when he had made an end of speaking unto Saul, that the soul of Jonathan was knit with the soul of David, and Jonathan loved him as his own soul. And Saul took him that day, and would let him go no more home to his father's house. Then Jonathan and David made a covenant, because he loved him as his own soul. And Jonathan stripped himself of the robe that was upon him, and gave it to David, and his garments, even to his sword, and to his bow, and to his girdle.

Jonathan—the crown prince, the next in line to the throne—looks at this unlikely hero, stripped himself of the robe he was wearing and the weapons he was carrying, and gave them to David.

Jonathan was a hero in his own right. He could have looked at David as competition. But he didn't. Instead, he gave up his power and prestige to ally himself with this one-time shepherd boy from Bethlehem.

You might have a program, a plan, a passion. But the Lord would say to you today, "Let go. Give Me your robe and your weapons. Knit your soul with Mine, and what you'll find is freedom and fulfillment like you've never known."

Saul was determined to remain on the throne and in control. Jonathan does just the opposite. Saul goes down in infamy; Jonathan is exalted eternally. When you talk to people at work, on the campus, or in the neighborhood, the issue is always the same: Are you willing to get off the throne of your life? Are you willing to give control to the God who loves you so much that He became the Good Shepherd who gave His life for you?

This is a daily issue for those of us who know the Lord, as well. Who will be on the throne today? Will I give up my abilities and appearance to follow the One who gave up the throne of heaven to die for me?

1 Samuel 18:5
And David went out whithersoever Saul sent him, and behaved himself wisely: and Saul set him over the men of war, and he was accepted in the sight of all the people, and also in the sight of Saul's servants.

This man after God's own heart behaved himself wisely. Even though he had outshone Saul in the valley of Elah, even though he had been anointed with the horn of oil, he went wherever Saul sent him. He realized God had a perfect plan unfolding and he trusted the sovereign ability of God to work things out at the right time.

1 Samuel 18:6–9
And it came to pass as they came, when David was returned from the slaughter of the Philistine, that the women came out of all cities of Israel, singing and dancing, to meet king Saul, with tabrets, with joy, and with instruments of musick. And the women answered one another as they played, and said, Saul hath slain his thousands, and David his ten thousands. And Saul was very wroth, and the saying displeased him; and he said, They have ascribed unto David ten thousands, and to me they have ascribed but thousands: and what can he have more but the kingdom? And Saul eyed David from that day and forward.

Saul loved the first verse of this number one song on the charts. But the second verse enraged him.

1 Samuel 18:10, 11
And it came to pass on the morrow, that the evil spirit from God came upon Saul, and he prophesied in the midst of the house: and David played with his hand, as at other times: and there was a javelin in Saul's hand. And Saul cast the javelin; for he said, I will smite David even to the wall with it. And David avoided out of his presence twice.

In David's hand was a harp—an instrument of worship. In Saul's hand was a javelin—an instrument of war. In Saul's hand was an instrument of hurting. In David's hand was an instrument of healing. What is in your hand—worship or war, healing or hurting? Saul and David are both leaders. Both have been anointed. But one is on his way down, while the other is on his way up. You can always tell if you're on the way up or on the way down by what instrument is in your hand. A person who is losing the anointing, who is diminishing in calling, will be throwing spears, cutting people down with harsh words. Have you thrown a spear today? Have you made your "point"? When Saul threw the spear at David, this one who slew a giant didn't throw it back.

1 Samuel 18:12, 13
And Saul was afraid of David, because the LORD was with him, and was departed from Saul. Therefore Saul removed him from him, and made him his captain over a thousand; and he went out and came in before the people.

Saul sent David to war, perhaps hoping he'd die in battle.

1 Samuel 18:14–16
And David behaved himself wisely in all his ways; and the LORD was with him. Wherefore when Saul saw that he behaved himself very wisely, he was afraid of him. But all Israel and Judah loved David, because he went out and came in before them.

One with the people, David led them in battle, and they loved him.

1 Samuel 18:17
And Saul said to David, Behold my elder daughter Merab, her will I give thee to wife: only be thou valiant for me, and fight the LORD's battles. For Saul said, Let not mine hand be upon him, but let the hand of the Philistines be upon him.

In Chapter 17, the reward promised to the victor over Goliath was Saul's daughter. Here, the list of requirements for her hand in marriage grows as Saul continues to try to remove David from the scene.

1 Samuel 18:18–21
And David said unto Saul, Who am I? and what is my life, or my father's family in Israel, that I should be son in law to the king? But it came to pass at the time when Merab Saul's daughter should have been given to David, that she was given unto Adriel the Meholathite to wife. And Michal Saul's daughter loved David: and they told Saul, and the thing pleased him. And Saul said, I will give him her, that she may be a snare to him, and that the hand of the Philistines may be against him. Wherefore Saul said to David, Thou shalt this day be my son in law in the one of the twain.

Hoping his daughter, Michal, would trip David up, Saul gave him her hand.

1 Samuel 18:22–25
And Saul commanded his servants, saying, Commune with David secretly, and say, Behold, the king hath delight in thee, and all his servants love thee: now therefore be the king's son in law. And Saul's servants spake those words in the ears of David. And David said, Seemeth it to you a light thing to be a king's son in law, seeing that I am a poor man, and lightly esteemed? And the servants of Saul told him, saying, On this manner spake David. And Saul said, Thus shall ye say to David, The king desireth not any dowry, but an hundred foreskins of the Philistines, to be avenged of the king's enemies. But Saul thought to make David fall by the hand of the Philistines.

The Philistines constantly made fun of the Israelites because they were circumcised.

1 Samuel 18:26, 27
And when his servants told David these words, it pleased David well to be the king's son in law: and the days were not expired. Wherefore David arose and went, he and his men, and slew of the Philistines two hundred men; and David brought their foreskins, and they gave them in full tale to the king, that he might be the king's son in law. And Saul gave him Michal his daughter to wife.

Saul thought David would die in this attempt. But David came through, slaying twice as many of the enemy as Saul requested.

1 Samuel 18:28–30
And Saul saw and knew that the LORD was with David, and that Michal Saul's daughter loved him. And Saul was yet the more afraid of David; and Saul became David's enemy continually. Then the princes of the Philistines went forth: and it came to pass, after they went forth, that David behaved himself more wisely than all the servants of Saul; so that his name was much set by.

The more David was exalted, the more jealous Saul became. Jonathan, however, had an even greater right to be jealous of David because they were of the same generation. But Jonathan is free from jealousy because he decided to help David accomplish his goal rather than to stand against him. Thus, in helping David, Jonathan is free from jealousy, goes down in history as a great man, and is rewarded eternally.

I guarantee there has been or will be a situation in your life similar to this. You'll have a choice to feel threatened and to throw spears—or to rejoice and help others excel. If you try to keep someone else down, you will spiral downward yourself. But if you help someone else go higher, you will inevitably be on an upward path as well. On a daily basis, let go of the spear, and pick up the harp.

19

1 Samuel 19:1
And Saul spake to Jonathan his son, and to all his servants, that they should kill David.

Jealous of, and threatened by David, Saul is determined to kill him. We, too, have an enemy who, targets us as believers because he does not want us to influence others to leave his kingdom of death, darkness, and damnation for God's kingdom of love, light, and salvation. As real and as powerful as our Adversary is, however, this chapter shows that God will protect us in the same four ways He protected David . . .

1 Samuel 19:2–7
But Jonathan Saul's son delighted much in David: and Jonathan told David, saying, Saul my father seeketh to kill thee: now therefore, I pray thee, take heed to thyself until the morning, and abide in a secret place, and hide thyself: And I will go out and stand beside my father in the field where thou art, and I will commune with my father of thee; and what I see, that I will tell thee. And Jonathan spake good of David unto Saul his father, and said unto him, Let not the king sin against his servant, against

David; because he hath not sinned against thee, and because his works have been to thee-ward very good: For he did put his life in his hand, and slew the Philistine, and the LORD wrought a great salvation for all Israel: thou sawest it, and didst rejoice: wherefore then wilt thou sin against innocent blood, to slay David without a cause? And Saul hearkened unto the voice of Jonathan: and Saul sware, As the LORD liveth, he shall not be slain. And Jonathan called David, and Jonathan shewed him all those things. And Jonathan brought David to Saul, and he was in his presence, as in times past.

The first way God protected David was through a prince who pled his case. An advocate for David, Jonathan talked to his father about David's situation. This all points to a far greater prince than Jonathan—the Prince of peace, our Savior, Jesus Christ—who pleads our case to the King of kings (1 John 2:1). Jonathan pled for David on the basis of David's works—that he slew Goliath. Jesus, on the other hand, pleads our case not on the basis of our works, but on the basis of His work for us.

1 Samuel 19:8–10
And there was war again: and David went out, and fought with the Philistines, and slew them with a great slaughter; and they fled from him. And the evil spirit from the LORD was upon Saul, as he sat in his house with his javelin in his hand: and David played with his hand. And Saul sought to smite David even to the wall with the javelin; but he slipped away out of Saul's presence, and he smote the javelin into the wall: and David fled, and escaped that night.

When David returned victorious from battle, the spirit of jealousy rose up again within the heart of Saul, causing him to go back on his word that he wouldn't kill David. When Saul threw a spear at him a third time, David realized it was time for him to leave.

1 Samuel 19:11–17
Saul also sent messengers unto David's house, to watch him, and to slay him in the morning: and Michal David's wife told him, saying, If thou save not thy life to night, to morrow thou shalt be slain. So Michal let David down through a window: and he went, and fled, and escaped. And Michal took an image, and laid it in the bed, and put a pillow of goats' hair for his bolster, and covered it with a cloth. And when Saul sent messengers to take David, she said, He is sick. And Saul sent the messengers again to see David, saying, Bring him up to me in the bed, that I may slay him. And when the messengers were come in, behold, there was an image in the bed, with a pillow of goats' hair for his bolster. And Saul said unto Michal, Why hast thou deceived me so, and sent away mine enemy, that he is escaped? And Michal answered Saul, He said unto me, Let me go; why should I kill thee?

God protected David through a bride who saved his life. "There are men who will ambush you," Michal told her husband. "Go out the back window and I'll cover for you."

It was David's bride who saved his life. The people in the body of Christ are the Bride of Christ—and they are the ones who will save your life. You might think people in the church are liars. That's okay, so was Michal. You might think the people in the church are idolators. That's okay, so was Michal. On a practical level, we are a blemished Bride indeed. But in God's eyes, because we have been washed in the blood of the Lamb and robed in the righteousness of our Lord, we are a glorious church without spot or wrinkle, a holy priesthood, a spotless Bride (Revelation 19:8; Ephesians 5:27; 1 Peter 2:5).

I have discovered that when I go through valleys, difficulties, and tragedies, it's the body of Christ I'm most thankful for. When the enemy is out to destroy you, it's the blemished Bride of Christ who will rescue you.

1 Samuel 19:18
So David fled, and escaped, and came to Samuel to Ramah, and told him all that Saul had done to him. And he and Samuel went and dwelt in Naioth.

Realizing Saul was determined to destroy him, David made his way to the prophet, Samuel. Samuel not only talked to David, but walked with him to the next town. How this must have strengthened David's heart.

I have a Prince who pleads my case. I am part of a Bride who saves my life. And I, too, know prophets who not only tell me what to do, but walk with me every step of the way. In this book, Isaiah, Jeremiah, and Ezekiel walk with me. When I walk down the street, you wouldn't believe the company that travels with me. This book saves my life when the enemy is in hot pursuit.

1 Samuel 19:19, 20
And it was told Saul, saying, Behold, David is at Naioth in Ramah. And Saul sent messengers to take David: and when they saw the company of the prophets prophesying,

and Samuel standing as appointed over them, the Spirit of God was upon the messengers of Saul, and they also prophesied.

Saul's men came to apprehend David, but the Spirit of God came upon them and they began to prophesy.

1 Samuel 19:21
And when it was told Saul, he sent other messengers, and they prophesied likewise. And Saul sent messengers again the third time, and they prophesied also.

In John 7, we read that the Pharisees and scribes sent soldiers to arrest Jesus. When the soldiers returned empty-handed, the leaders asked why. "Something happened," the soldiers answered. "No man spoke like this Man."

1 Samuel 19:22, 23
Then went he also to Ramah, and came to a great well that is in Sechu: and he asked and said, Where are Samuel and David? And one said, Behold, they be at Naioth in Ramah. And he went thither to Naioth in Ramah: and the Spirit of God was upon him also, and he went on, and prophesied, until he came to Naioth in Ramah.

"Is Saul also among the prophets?" This question was asked earlier when Saul was a humble man (1 Samuel 10:11). In that case, it was a confirmation that he was the one being raised up by the Lord. At this point, however, nine chapters later, he's in an entirely different situation. It's not confirmation—but conviction.

1 Samuel 19:24
And he stripped off his clothes also, and prophesied before Samuel in like manner, and lay down naked all that day and all that night. Wherefore they say, Is Saul also among the prophets?

The Spirit of God comforts and confirms. But, as seen here, He will also convict and strip when necessary. The same Saul who at one time prophesied in the power of the Spirit in chapter 10 is prophesying again—but no longer a confirmation of his ministry, it's an indication that he is in deep trouble.

20

1 Samuel 20:1
And David fled from Naioth in Ramah, and came and said before Jonathan, What have I done? what is mine iniquity? and what is my sin before thy father, that he seeketh my life?

"What have I done?" we hear David ask. Like David, oftentimes we think trouble comes our way because of something we've done. Perhaps God is indeed disciplining, chastening, correcting us. But hard times are not always about punishment. Sometimes they're about preparation. As we see the story unfold, we see God knocking some rough edges off David as He prepares him for the calling on his life.

The same thing is true for you and me. Tribulation brings about patience and patience brings about perfection (Romans 5:3; James 1:4).

1 Samuel 20:2
And he said unto him, God forbid; thou shalt not die: behold, my father will do nothing either great or small, but that he will shew it me: and why should my father hide this thing from me? it is not so.

In insisting that David wouldn't die and that Saul wasn't out to get him, Jonathan is both right and wrong. He was wrong because Saul was indeed out to get David. But he was right because David wouldn't die by Saul's hand. God's plan would not be thwarted. And the same is true for you. God has a plan and nothing can cause that plan to come undone. As long as you're walking with Him, nothing will derail you.

1 Samuel 20:3
And David sware moreover, and said, Thy father certainly knoweth that I have found grace in thine eyes; and he saith, Let not Jonathan know this, lest he be grieved: but truly as the LORD liveth, and as thy soul liveth, there is but a step between me and death.

"There is but a step between me and death." What a great truth. Because we are truly but one step away from eternity, I believe one of the wisest ways to live life is to live every day as if it was our last opportunity to get things right, to straighten things out.

1 Samuel 20:4
Then said Jonathan unto David, Whatsoever thy soul desireth, I will even do it for thee.

"In light of the fact that you feel you're only one step away from death, what do you want me to do?" Jonathan asks.

1 Samuel 20:5–7
And David said unto Jonathan, Behold, to morrow is the new moon, and I should not

fail to sit with the king at meat: but let me go, that I may hide myself in the field unto the third day at even. If thy father at all miss me, then say, David earnestly asked leave of me that he might run to Bethlehem his city: for there is a yearly sacrifice there for all the family. If he say thus, It is well; thy servant shall have peace: but if he be very wroth, then be sure that evil is determined by him.

As a member of Saul's court, David would be expected to be at the feast of the new moon. David's plan was not to attend—and then to gauge Saul's feelings for him by Saul's response to his absence. If Saul became upset, David would know Saul was scheming to do him in.

1 Samuel 20:8, 9
Therefore thou shalt deal kindly with thy servant; for thou hast brought thy servant into a covenant of the LORD with thee: notwithstanding, if there be in me iniquity, slay me thyself; for why shouldest thou bring me to thy father? And Jonathan said, Far be it from thee: for if I knew certainly that evil were determined by my father to come upon thee, then would not I tell it thee?

If Jonathan felt that David was worthy of death, David told him he was to kill him on the spot. Stress sires suspicions; pressure produces paranoia. When you're under stress—as David was—you can begin to get suspicious. Always take lightly the emotions you feel when you're under pressure because even David sounds paranoid here.

1 Samuel 20:10–13
Then said David to Jonathan, Who shall tell me? or what if thy father answer thee roughly? And Jonathan said unto David, Come, and let us go out into the field. And they went out both of them into the field. And Jonathan said unto David, O LORD God of Israel, when I have sounded my father about to morrow any time, or the third day, and, behold, if there be good toward David, and I then send not unto thee, and shew it thee; The LORD do so and much more to Jonathan: but if it please my father to do thee evil, then I will shew it thee, and send thee away, that thou mayest go in peace: and the LORD be with thee, as he hath been with my father.

Jonathan promised he would show David of his father's intent to do David harm.

1 Samuel 20:14, 15
And thou shalt not only while yet I live shew me the kindness of the LORD, that I die not: But also thou shalt not cut off thy kindness from my house for ever: no, not when the LORD hath cut off the enemies of David every one from the face of the earth.

A famous conductor identified the greatest quality of a concert violinist not as the ability to play first violin, but the willingness to play second. Such was the heart of Jonathan.

1 Samuel 20:16, 17
So Jonathan made a covenant with the house of David, saying, Let the LORD even require it at the hand of David's enemies. And Jonathan caused David to swear again, because he loved him: for he loved him as he loved his own soul.

To make a covenant, or, literally to "cut covenant" meant the two parties would divide an animal, stand in the middle of the carcass, and state their commitment to each other. In doing this, they were saying, "I'm deadly serious about this. If I don't follow through on my end of the bargain, let me be as the dead animal that surrounds us."

1 Samuel 20:18, 19
Then Jonathan said to David, To morrow is the new moon: and thou shalt be missed, because thy seat will be empty. And when thou hast stayed three days, then thou shalt go down quickly, and come to the place where thou didst hide thyself when the business was in hand, and shalt remain by the stone Ezel.

Ezel means "the rock that shows the way." Therefore, David was to stay by the rock that shows the way. Like David, you might be at a crossroads, worried you won't figure out where you're supposed to go. I have great news for you: God will direct you. All you have to do is stay close to "the Rock that shows the way." That is, all you have to do is stay in touch with Jesus day by day by day. Even if your devotional life isn't what it should be, even if there are struggles with which you wrestle continually, even if you feel like you missed the boat previously, God is faithful. God blesses us in spite of ourselves if we simply plop ourselves by the Rock that shows the way.

As a father of five, I don't direct my kids on the basis of how they're doing. That is, I don't say to one, "Since you're being good, I'm going to give you lots of direction," and to another, "I can't direct you because you're struggling with this or dealing with that." No, I direct my kids wherever they're at. I want to give them as much direction, help, and assistance as they'll allow me to give them. The same is true of our heavenly Father. He sees our needs and is aware of our frailty. Yet even when we are faithless, He is faithful still (2 Timothy 2:13).

1 Samuel 20:20–23
And I will shoot three arrows on the side thereof, as though I shot at a mark. And, behold, I will send a lad, saying, Go, find out the arrows. If I expressly say unto the lad, Behold, the arrows are on this side of thee, take them; then come thou: for there is peace to thee, and no hurt; as the LORD liveth. But if I say thus unto the young man, Behold, the arrows are beyond thee; go thy way: for the LORD hath sent thee away. And as touching the matter which thou and I have spoken of, behold, the LORD be between thee and me for ever.

Jonathan instructed David to hide in a certain field. After three days, Jonathan and his servant would come to this field under the pretense of target practice. As his servant set out to retrieve the arrows, Jonathan would either say, "Keep going; the arrows are further," or, "You're too far; come on in." If he said the former, David would know he had to flee. If he said the latter, David would know it was safe to return.

1 Samuel 20:24–26
So David hid himself in the field: and when the new moon was come, the king sat him down to eat meat. And the king sat upon his seat, as at other times, even upon a seat by the wall: and Jonathan arose, and Abner sat by Saul's side, and David's place was empty. Nevertheless Saul spake not any thing that day: for he thought, Something hath befallen him, he is not clean; surely he is not clean.

When Saul noticed David's absence, he assumed either something had happened to David or he was ceremonially unclean.

1 Samuel 20:27–31
And it came to pass on the morrow, which was the second day of the month, that David's place was empty: and Saul said unto Jonathan his son, Wherefore cometh not the son of Jesse to meat, neither yesterday, nor to day? And Jonathan answered Saul, David earnestly asked leave of me to go to Bethlehem: And he said, Let me go, I pray thee; for our family hath a sacrifice in the city; and my brother, he hath commanded me to be there: and now, if I have found favour in thine eyes, let me get away, I pray thee, and see my brethren. Therefore he cometh not unto the king's table. Then Saul's anger was kindled against Jonathan, and he said unto him, Thou son of the perverse rebellious woman, do not I know that thou hast chosen the son of Jesse to thine own confusion, and unto the confusion of thy mother's nakedness? For as long as the son of Jesse liveth upon the ground, thou shalt not be established, nor thy kingdom. Wherefore now send and fetch him unto me, for he shall surely die.

When David was absent the second day of the feast, Saul asked Jonathan the reason. When Jonathan said David had asked him for permission to go to Jerusalem, Saul said, "I know what you're up to. You're siding with David. But don't you understand that as long as David is on the scene, you'll never be king?"

1 Samuel 20:32, 33
And Jonathan answered Saul his father, and said unto him, Wherefore shall he be slain? what hath he done? And Saul cast a javelin at him to smite him: whereby Jonathan knew that it was determined of his father to slay David.

Jesus told us to love our enemies because if I don't love my enemies, like Saul, I'll find myself out to get even with my own family. You see, we think we can confine hatred toward this person or control it toward that group—not realizing that hatred or judgment of someone will ultimately spill over into the lives of everyone around us.

For a topical study of 1 Samuel 20:32, 33 entitled "Saul's Sin-Drome," turn to page 873.

1 Samuel 20:34–37
So Jonathan arose from the table in fierce anger, and did eat no meat the second day of the month: for he was grieved for David, because his father had done him shame. And it came to pass in the morning, that Jonathan went out into the field at the time appointed with David, and a little lad with him. And he said unto his lad, Run, find out now the arrows which I shoot. And as the lad ran, he shot an arrow beyond him. And when the lad was come to the place of the arrow which Jonathan had shot, Jonathan cried after the lad, and said, Is not the arrow beyond thee?

This was the sign that David was to flee.

1 Samuel 20:38–42
And Jonathan cried after the lad, Make speed, haste, stay not. And Jonathan's lad gathered

up the arrows, and came to his master. But the lad knew not any thing: only Jonathan and David knew the matter. And Jonathan gave his artillery unto his lad, and said unto him, Go, carry them to the city. And as soon as the lad was gone, David arose out of a place toward the south, and fell on his face to the ground, and bowed himself three times: and they kissed one another, and wept one with another, until David exceeded. And Jonathan said to David, Go in peace, forasmuch as we have sworn both of us in the name of the LORD, saying, The LORD be between me and thee, and between my seed and thy seed for ever. And he arose and departed: and Jonathan went into the city.

What a hero Jonathan is. I pray everyone of us at some point might have a Jonathan linked to us. Even more, may we be a Jonathan—perhaps having the ability to play first chair, but providing harmony in second chair.

SAUL'S SIN-DROME

A Topical Study of 1 SAMUEL 20:32, 33

In the text before us, we see King Saul throwing a javelin at his own son. And Saul's "sin-drome" can affect us as well. But God is faithful to let us know when we are being afflicted by it. We get warning signs—like I did a couple of days ago . . .

I like my 1974 VW, but it's old. And when things get old, they fall apart. So, driving down the road a couple of days ago, the glove box door fell open. Because my glove box is full of everything but gloves, I slammed it shut. About twenty seconds later, I hit another bump and it flipped open again. I shut it once more. About a minute later, it fell open again. I then pulled over and saw that the latch that secures the door had been worn away. I slammed the door shut and continued on my way. It flopped open again. I shut it again. It flopped open again. I shut it again. I knew the latch was broken. I knew it couldn't stay shut. But that didn't stop me from slamming it shut every ten seconds, saying, "Stay shut!"

When I reached my destination, I found myself in a conversation with a close friend. Feeling irritated, I fired away at him in a quiet voice, thinking I was "on target" about this, that I needed to make "a point" about that. When I was done, I knew something was really wrong. I got back in my car, talked it over with the Lord, and realized that He had shown me on the way to the meeting that something was wrong not with my glove box but with my soul.

We think we feel hostility or anger because we've been wronged. In reality, however, the irritation, the frustration, the bump in our path doesn't produce the hostility, anger, or frustration within us, but simply reveals the anger, hostility, or frustration already within us.

I see a sponge in my kitchen sink. I can see it's wet—but I don't know what's in it. It could be apple juice. It could be milk. It could be water. The only way I'll know what's in it is to squeeze it. Then, what's already in it will flow out. My squeeze won't put the liquid there—it will simply reveal what was already there. So, when you're squeezed, when I'm bumped, when we feel under the gun or under pressure, the way we respond will reveal what's already in our soul.

You see, Saul was already in a state of insanity before he realized his son was befriending his enemy. After all, he had already thrown a spear two times previously (18:10, 19:10). Thus, it wasn't that Jonathan provoked his father to anger. Anger was already within him.

Was David the problem? No, because when we read about Saul chucking spears at David, 1 Samuel 19:9 tells us an evil spirit was upon Saul. Yet it wasn't even the evil spirit's fault because the evil spirit came upon Saul only because Saul was already a man of rebellion and disobedience. In other words, because Saul was disobedient, he became vulnerable to an evil spirit plaguing him that caused him to throw spears not only at David but also at his own son.

The same can be true of us. If we don't understand this, we will lash out at him or her, at our boss or neighbor, at our sister or brother—never understanding the real issue is within our own heart. What are we to do if we realize we're throwing spears? How can we know if we're right or wrong? The answer is very simple: At any given moment, we will either be Spirit-led, or we'll "spear it dead." If I'm Spirit-led, there will be compassion. If I'm "spearing it dead," there will be confusion—for it was because Saul was terribly confused himself that he accused Jonathan of confusion (v. 30).

I see another King who was put down and attacked brutally. Pinned to a Cross, what did He pray? He said, "Father, forgive them. They don't know what they do" (Luke 23:34). That's compassion. When He was offered a sponge filled with vinegar and myrrh to deaden the pain, He refused it. Sometimes when we're hurt, we might think we're justified in numbing the pain through gossip or through making our "points." But Jesus wouldn't take the vinegar. He wouldn't take that which was bitter. Consequently, when a spear was thrust into His side, what came out? Not vinegar, but blood and water; not bitterness, but redemption and refreshment (John 19:34). What comes out of me? Is it redemptive and refreshing—or is it bitter?

Confusion is transformed into compassion through Communion and confession because Jesus said the one who is forgiven much loves much (Luke 7:47). It is at the Lord's Table that I see the irony of trying to take a speck out of your eye when there is a beam in my own. It is at the Lord's Table that I lose my appetite to make my point or hit my target.

When I throw spears, it's indicative of the fact that I don't realize my own miserable, sinful condition. That's why we are to confess our sins specifically. Bitterness becomes redemption and refreshment when I say, "*I'm* the sinner, Lord. *I* broke Your body. *I* break Your heart." Then I take the cup and say, "Lord, thank You for the fresh start that is mine because my sin is washed by Your blood."

And as I do, I no longer desire to make my point, throw a spear—or even slam a glove box door, for I understand the problem isn't with you or with my VW. The problem is with me, and the solution is the Cross.

21

1 Samuel 21:1 (a)
Then came David to Nob . . .

Envious of and threatened by David, Saul is out to kill him. So, running for his life, David comes to Nob, a city of priests, in the southern part of Israel, approximately three miles north of Jerusalem.

1 Samuel 21:1 (b)
. . . to Ahimelech the priest: and Ahimelech was afraid at the meeting of David, and said unto him, Why art thou alone, and no man with thee?

David was Saul's son-in-law, a member of his court. Therefore, Ahimelech wondered why an official retinue of men wasn't traveling with David.

1 Samuel 21:2
And David said unto Ahimelech the priest, The king hath commanded me a business, and hath said unto me, Let no man know any thing of the business whereabout I send thee, and what I have commanded thee: and I have appointed my servants to such and such a place.

David lied that he was traveling undercover in the service of Saul.

1 Samuel 21:3, 4
Now therefore what is under thine hand? give me five loaves of bread in mine hand, or what there is present. And the priest answered David, and said, There is no common bread under mine hand, but there is hallowed bread; if the young men have kept themselves at least from women.

The only bread on hand was the holy bread, or shewbread, which was to be consumed only by the priests.

1 Samuel 21:5, 6
And David answered the priest, and said unto him, Of a truth women have been kept from us about these three days, since I came out, and the vessels of the young men are holy, and the bread is in a manner common, yea, though it were sanctified this day in the vessel. So the priest gave him hallowed bread: for there was no bread there but the shewbread, that was taken from before the LORD, to put hot bread in the day when it was taken away.

Jesus, our Greater than David, reaches back to this story in Luke 6:3, 4 and commends Ahimelech for what he does here. Why? Because Jesus uses it as an illustration in His teaching that there is something more important than the Law—that is love. Human need always has a higher priority than religious traditions or regulations. More important than anything else is that we love people.

1 Samuel 21:7
Now a certain man of the servants of Saul was there that day, detained before the LORD; and his name was Doeg, an Edomite, the chiefest of the herdmen that belonged to Saul.

Doeg literally means "Fearful," which means he struck fear in the hearts of those around him. Why? He was Saul's one-man "CIA."

1 Samuel 21:8
And David said unto Ahimelech, And is there not here under thine hand spear or sword? for I have neither brought my sword nor my weapons with me, because the king's business required haste.

After asking for bread, David asks Ahimelech for weapons, lying that he couldn't bring his own due to the urgency of his mission.

1 Samuel 21:9
And the priest said, The sword of Goliath the Philistine, whom thou slewest in the valley of Elah, behold, it is here wrapped in a cloth behind the ephod: if thou wilt take that, take it: for there is no other save that here. And David said, There is none like that; give it me.

David is on a downward spiral. He's a lover of God, but now he's trusting in his lies and in Goliath's sword. Before, when he was in the Spirit, he refused to take Saul's weapons, choosing instead to rely on the God who had given him victory over the bear and the lion (1 Samuel 17:36). But now he seeks material weapons. The weapons of our warfare are not carnal, but spiritual (2 Corinthians 10:4). But when we're in a carnal place, we start depending on carnal weapons.

1 Samuel 21:10
And David arose, and fled that day for fear of Saul, and went to Achish the king of Gath.

Gath is a Philistine city, Achish a Philistine king. David walks into Gath carrying the sword of Gath's most famous citizen—not the smartest thing to do. Why did David go to Gath? Perhaps he thought that, because Saul was so intent on hunting him down, there was no sanctuary for him anywhere in Israel.

1 Samuel 21:11, 12
And the servants of Achish said unto him, Is not this David the king of the land? did they not sing one to another of him in dances, saying, Saul hath slain his thousands, and David his ten thousands? And David laid up these words in his heart, and was sore afraid of Achish the king of Gath.

David realized Gath wasn't a safe place for him to be. That's always the way it is. When we wander into the world to find safety, security, or satisfaction, we're spotted a mile away. If you're tempted to return to the world, you'll be a colossal failure because you have too much of the Lord in you to fit into the world like you once did.

1 Samuel 21:13–15
And he changed his behaviour before them, and feigned himself mad in their hands, and scrabbled on the doors of the gate, and let his spittle fall down upon his beard. Then said Achish unto his servants, Lo, ye see the man is mad: wherefore then have ye brought him unto me? Have I need of mad men, that ye have brought this fellow to play the mad man in my presence? shall this fellow come into my house?

Clawing at the gates and drooling, David pretended to be insane. Yet, even though he's spiraling downward, even though he appears to be out of control, the psalms he pens at this period reveal that, although outwardly he was a mess, he still had a heart for God.

DAVID IN GATH

A Topical Study of 1 SAMUEL 21:10–15

I will bless the LORD at all times: his praise shall continually be in my mouth. My soul shall make her boast in the LORD: the humble shall hear thereof, and be glad. O magnify the LORD with me, and let us exalt his name together. I sought the LORD, and he heard me, and delivered me from all my fears. They looked unto him, and were lightened: and their faces were not ashamed. This poor man cried, and the LORD heard him, and saved him out of all his troubles. The angel of the LORD encampeth round about them that fear him, and delivereth them. O taste and see that the LORD is good: blessed is the man that trusteth in him. O fear the LORD, ye his saints: for there is no want to them that fear him. The young lions do lack, and suffer hunger: but they that seek the LORD shall not want any good thing. Psalm 34:1–10

As we read this Psalm of David, this tribute to the faithfulness of God, it would be easy to assume he composed it at the tabernacle—the place where sacrifices were offered, where incense filled the air, where praise ascended to heaven. No wonder he would write, "I will bless the Lord at all times."

Or perhaps it would be easy to assume David composed it on the hills overlooking Bethlehem. It's easy to imagine that, as his flock was grazing, David's mind would begin working—meditating on the goodness and greatness of God. No wonder he would write, "The young lions do lack, and suffer hunger: but they that seek the Lord shall not want any good thing."

Or perhaps it would be easy to assume David composed it while he was in the grand and glorious city of Jerusalem. No wonder he would write, "The angel of the Lord encampeth round about them that fear him, and delivereth them."

As plausible as any of these scenarios might be, however, they're not possible, for the heading of Psalm 34 tells us exactly where David was when he wrote it: *A Psalm of David, when he changed his behaviour before A-bim'-e-lech; who drove him away, and he departed.*

What if you lived in David's day? What if you watched this story unfold? What would you think? I'm afraid I know all too well what I would say. "Remember David—the one who showed such courage in killing Goliath, the one Samuel anointed? I hate to tell you this, but he has become insane. He's gone over to the side of the enemy. It's so sad. He had such potential."

That's what I would have said. But God would say otherwise. "That's not the way it really is. You might write David off, but you don't see him the way I do. Oh, it's true he's in Gath. It's true he's acting crazy. It's true he lied. All of that is true. But what you don't see is his heart."

God's acceptance and forgiveness is indeed conditional. But it's conditioned only upon what a person desires in his or her heart. If a person says, "I want nothing to do with God; I care nothing about God; I'm not interested in God," he will not be forgiven or accepted by God because God sees the heart. Our forgiveness toward others, on the other hand, must be unconditional because we don't see anyone's heart. From outward appearances, David is lost, hopeless. But God saw his heart.

What heart did God see? In addition to Psalm 34, penned when he was let out of the city gate, David wrote Psalm 56 when he was still in the city, clawing at the gates . . .

> *Thou tellest my wanderings: put thou my tears into thy bottle: are they not in thy book? When I cry unto thee, then shall mine enemies turn back: this I know; for God is for me. In God will I praise his word: in the* LORD *will I praise his word. In God have I put my trust: I will not be afraid what man can do unto me. Thy vows are upon me, O God: I will render praises unto thee. For thou hast delivered my soul from death: wilt not thou deliver my feet from falling, that I may walk before God in the light of the living?*
>
> Psalm 56:8–13

We would have written David off. God, however, knew what he would write.

I wonder how many people I have written off because they're in Gath, because they have withdrawn from fellowship, because they're acting crazy.

Put on therefore, as the elect of God, holy and beloved, bowels of mercies, kindness, humbleness of mind, meekness, longsuffering . . . Colossians 3:12

David's story tells me I must not write anyone off, count anyone out, turn anyone away. Paul's words tell me the deepest part of me is to be nothing but merciful, meek, and kind, knowing that only God sees the longing of the soul and the heart of the matter.

22

1 Samuel 22:1 (a)
David therefore departed thence, and escaped to the cave Adullam . . .

A cave is not an easy place to be. It's dark and discouraging. But Psalms 57 and 142, written while David was in the cave at Adullam, show a deep work going on in his soul . . .

> Be thou exalted, O God, above the heavens; let thy glory be above all the earth. They have prepared a net for my steps; my soul is bowed down: they have digged a pit before me, into the midst whereof they are fallen themselves. Selah. My heart is fixed, O God, my heart is fixed: I will sing and give praise. Awake up, my glory; awake, psaltery and harp: I myself will awake early. I will praise thee, O Lord, among the people: I will sing unto thee among the nations. For thy mercy is great unto the heavens, and thy truth unto the clouds. Be thou exalted, O God, above the heavens: let thy glory be above all the earth. Psalm 57:5–11

> When my spirit was overwhelmed within me, then thou knewest my path. In the way wherein I walked have they privily laid a snare for me. I looked on my right hand, and beheld, but there was no man that would know me: refuge failed me; no man cared for my soul. I cried unto thee, O LORD: I said, Thou art my refuge and my portion in the land of the living. Attend unto my cry; for I am brought very low: deliver me from my persecutors; for they are stronger than I. Bring my soul out of prison, that I may praise thy name: the righteous shall compass me about; for thou shalt deal bountifully with me. Psalm 142:3–7

We want to be comfortable—but God knows that our souls do not grow in times of comfort (Romans 5:3–5). Therefore, He puts us in places where His work can be done, where His Word takes root. If you're in a cave today, you're in good company because God does deep work in hard places.

1 Samuel 22:1 (b), 2
. . . and when his brethren and all his father's house heard it, they went down thither to him. And every one that was in distress, and every one that was in debt, and every one that was discontented, gathered themselves unto him; and he became a captain over them: and there were with him about four hundred men.

The group of four hundred men who were in debt, distressed, and discontented will eventually become David's mighty men, an elite fighting unit. David was flawed indeed, yet more is written of him than any other man in Scripture because he was a man after God's heart—a man who pursued God. And as these four hundred men spent time with him, they became like him.

Like David's men, we, too, are in debt, distressed, and often discontented. But as we hang around the Son of David, Jesus Christ, an amazing thing happens: we become like Him (2 Corinthians 3:18). The key to greatness is to hang around Jesus constantly. Choose to make Jesus your identity and your passion and slowly but surely you'll be conformed into the image of the One captivating your heart.

1 Samuel 22:3, 4
And David went thence to Mizpeh of Moab: and he said unto the king of Moab, Let my father and my mother, I pray thee, come forth, and be with you, till I know what God will do for me. And he brought them before the king of Moab: and they dwelt with him all the while that David was in the hold.

Although David is in a better place than he was in chapter 21, why would he choose to hide his family in Moab? I suggest it was because he was related to the Moabites. Ruth was the grandmother of David's dad (Matthew 1:5, 6).

1 Samuel 22:5
And the prophet Gad said unto David, Abide not in the hold; depart, and get thee into

the land of Judah. Then David departed, and came into the forest of Hareth.

"Leave this stronghold. Leave this fortress in the wilderness and get back to Judah, back to the place of praise," God said to David. Still today, this is a word for any who have put walls up, for any who have pulled away, for any who have battles to fight. Let the songs of deliverance flow from your lips. Let the songs of praise fill your car, your house, and your heart—and, like David, you'll hear from the Lord once again.

1 Samuel 22:6
When Saul heard that David was discovered, and the men that were with him, (now Saul abode in Gibeah under a tree in Ramah, having his spear in his hand, and all his servants were standing about him;)

With spear in hand, as always, Saul was in Ramah, approximately five miles from Jerusalem.

1 Samuel 22:7, 8
Then Saul said unto his servants that stood about him, Hear now, ye Benjamites; will the son of Jesse give every one of you fields and vineyards, and make you all captains of thousands, and captains of hundreds; That all of you have conspired against me, and there is none that sheweth me that my son hath made a league with the son of Jesse, and there is none of you that is sorry for me, or sheweth unto me that my son hath stirred up my servant against me, to lie in wait, as at this day?

"Doesn't anyone feel bad for me?" Saul asked his servants. "You knew my son was in a league with David, yet you didn't tell me." Why does Saul refer to his servants as Benjamites? I suggest his implication is that, because Saul was from the tribe of Benjamin and David was from Judah, they would do better having one of their own tribesman on the throne.

When David does indeed come to power, where does he make his capital? Jerusalem—which straddles the two tribes of Benjamin and Judah. David was a shrewd politician as well as a deeply spiritual leader.

1 Samuel 22:9, 10
Then answered Doeg the Edomite, which was set over the servants of Saul, and said, I saw the son of Jesse coming to Nob, to Ahimelech the son of Ahitub. And he inquired of the LORD for him, and gave him victuals, and gave him the sword of Goliath the Philistine.

Falsely implying that David inquired of the Lord so he could do battle against Saul, Doeg takes advantage of Saul's growing paranoia.

1 Samuel 22:11–15
Then the king sent to call Ahimelech the priest, the son of Ahitub, and all his father's house, the priests that were in Nob: and they came all of them to the king. And Saul said, Hear now, thou son of Ahitub. And he answered, Here I am, my lord. And Saul said unto him, Why have ye conspired against me, thou and the son of Jesse, in that thou hast given him bread, and a sword, and hast inquired of God for him, that he should rise against me, to lie in wait, as at this day? Then Ahimelech answered the king, and said, And who is so faithful among all thy servants as David, which is the king's son in law, and goeth at thy bidding, and is honourable in thine house? Did I then begin to inquire of God for him? be it far from me: let not the king impute any thing unto his servant, nor to all the house of my father: for thy servant knew nothing of all this, less or more.

Ahimelech pleads his case, saying he knew nothing of what was going on. He thought David was simply on an errand for Saul.

1 Samuel 22:16, 17
And the king said, Thou shalt surely die, Ahimelech, thou, and all thy father's house. And the king said unto the footmen that stood about him, Turn, and slay the priests of the LORD; because their hand also is with David, and because they knew when he fled, and did not shew it to me. But the servants of the king would not put forth their hand to fall upon the priests of the LORD.

Consumed with paranoia and jealousy, Saul ordered his servants to kill the priests because they had assisted David. To their eternal credit, Saul's servants wisely and courageously refused his order.

1 Samuel 22:18
And the king said to Doeg, Turn thou, and fall upon the priests. And Doeg the Edomite turned, and he fell upon the priests, and slew on that day fourscore and five persons that did wear a linen ephod.

Doeg stepped in to commit this horrendous act of cruelty as the blood of eighty-five priests was shed. As wrong as Doeg is in doing this, he is fulfilling what God told Samuel would happen as a result of Eli's failure to correct his sons (1 Samuel 3:11–14).

1 Samuel 22:19
And Nob, the city of the priests, smote he with the edge of the sword, both men and women, children and sucklings, and oxen, and asses, and sheep, with the edge of the sword.

Doeg's murderous rampage was a direct result of David's lie. David thought he was simply protecting himself—but when you twist the truth, the repercussions are most often much more severe than you can imagine.

1 Samuel 22:20, 21
And one of the sons of Ahimelech the son of Ahitub, named Abiathar, escaped, and fled after David. And Abiathar shewed David that Saul had slain the Lord's priests.

One of Ahimelech's sons escapes and follows David. Now, I would think the last guy he would want to see would be David. After all, it was David's lie that set in motion the events that would kill his family. But God's hand is seen because Abiathar will go on to become priest in David's kingdom (2 Samuel 8:17). And in this, it's as if God is putting together something that humanly would have been impossible.

Maybe the same is true in your situation. Maybe a relationship has been cut off to such a degree that it makes no sense to even think it could be put back together. But what you haven't factored into the equation is God. God can do things men can't.

1 Samuel 22:22, 23
And David said unto Abiathar, I knew it that day, when Doeg the Edomite was there, that he would surely tell Saul: I have occasioned the death of all the persons of thy father's house. Abide thou with me, fear not: for he that seeketh my life seeketh thy life: but with me thou shalt be in safeguard.

"It's my fault," David said. "I brought about the tragedy that killed your family. But I will stand by you. You'll be safe with me. Stick around, Abiathar." And we'll see Abiathar do just that.

23

1 Samuel 23:1
Then they told David, saying, Behold, the Philistines fight against Keilah, and they rob the threshingfloors.

An Israelite city in the lowlands of Judah, Keilah was northwest of the city of Hebron. Perpetual enemies of the people of Israel, the Philistines were robbing the food supply of the people of Keilah.

1 Samuel 23:2
Therefore David inquired of the LORD, saying, Shall I go and smite these Philistines? And the LORD said unto David, Go, and smite the Philistines, and save Keilah.

I like David. He does what we get to do. He asked the Lord if he should go to battle on behalf of his countrymen. And the Lord said, "Go."

1 Samuel 23:3
And David's men said unto him, Behold, we be afraid here in Judah: how much more then if we come to Keilah against the armies of the Philistines?

Numbering six hundred at this time, David's men said. "We're being chased by Saul and his army. We've got big problems of our own. We can't take on the burden or responsibility of fighting for the men of Keilah because we're under attack ourselves."

1 Samuel 23:4
Then David inquired of the LORD yet again. And the LORD answered him and said, Arise, go down to Keilah; for I will deliver the Philistines into thine hand.

David didn't berate his men for their lack of faith or compassion. He simply inquired of the Lord once again, and the Lord reaffirmed that He wanted David to fight for the men of Keilah.

1 Samuel 23:5
So David and his men went to Keilah, and fought with the Philistines, and brought away their cattle, and smote them with a great slaughter. So David saved the inhabitants of Keilah.

David did what the Lord commanded him to do and God gave him victory.

1 Samuel 23:6
And it came to pass, when Abiathar the son of Ahimelech fled to David to Keilah, that he came down with an ephod in his hand.

An ephod was the vest worn by the high priest. Attached to it were twelve stones representing the Twelve Tribes of Israel. This comprised the Urim and the Thummim, used by the high priest to determine God's will.

1 Samuel 23:7
And it was told Saul that David was come to Keilah. And Saul said, God hath delivered him into mine hand; for he is shut in, by entering into a town that hath gates and bars.

Because David was trapped in the city, Saul mistakenly assumed God was handing David over to him.

1 Samuel 23:8
And Saul called all the people together to war, to go down to Keilah, to besiege David and his men.

As Saul gathered his troops to go to Keilah, ostensibly the men would think they were headed to war against the Philistines. But that wasn't Saul's plan.

1 Samuel 23:9
And David knew that Saul secretly practised mischief against him; and he said to Abiathar the priest, Bring hither the ephod.

David called for the ephod in order to determine God's will.

1 Samuel 23:10–12
Then said David, O LORD God of Israel, thy servant hath certainly heard that Saul seeketh to come to Keilah, to destroy the city for my sake. Will the men of Keilah deliver me up into his hand? will Saul come down, as thy servant hath heard? O LORD God of Israel, I beseech thee, tell thy servant. And the LORD said, He will come down. Then said David, Will the men of Keilah deliver me and my men into the hand of Saul? And the LORD said, They will deliver thee up.

When David got word that Saul knew his location, he once again prayed, "Lord, are the men of Keilah going to betray me and turn me over to Saul?"

The Lord said, "Yes, that's precisely what will happen. The very ones you helped, that you set free, that you risked your lives for are going to turn you over to your enemy."

Here, David had risked his own life and the lives of his men to liberate the people of Keilah. Yet the men of Keilah were the very ones who were going to hand him over to Saul. I wish I could tell you that the men of Keilah were an anomaly, that no one will betray you, that the people you help will be appreciative all your days. But that would be untrue. The reality is, it's often the people you care most about who will let you down the greatest.

Why, then, help people at all?

I suggest three reasons . . .

The first is *present satisfaction.* When people don't appreciate what you've done, or when you've been betrayed, don't have a cow. Don't say, "This is an "udder" disgrace. Don't "milk it" for all it's worth. Don't have a cow. Instead, have a steak. You see, as we read the story of David's men, we see they were often hungry. On the run, supplies were often scant. But on this day, because they fought for the men of Keilah, they walked away with steaks (v. 5). Even though the men of Keilah threatened to do them in, David's men had steaks.

Jesus told us whatever measure we give out will be given back to us (Luke 6:38). Haven't you found this to be true? When I share with someone else, my own faith grows. When I pray for someone else, my own prayers become passionate and real again.

Jesus modeled this principle in John 4 . . .

Tired and hungry, He sat at the edge of a well while His disciples went into the city to get food for themselves and for Him. While they were gone, a woman came to the well. Jesus began to talk to her. She listened to Him and was so excited that she left her water pots to go to the city to tell everyone about Him. Meanwhile, the disciples returned with food, but Jesus didn't eat it.

"Aren't You hungry?" they asked.

I can see a big smile on His face as He answered, "I have food you know not of. My food is to do the will of Him who sent Me. I was hungry. But then I had the opportunity to share with someone else—and I'm hungry no more."

The second reason to help people who might betray us is *eternal remuneration* . . .

> Blessed are ye, when men shall revile you, and persecute you, and shall say all manner of evil against you falsely, for my sake. Rejoice, and be exceeding glad: for great is your reward in heaven: for so persecuted they the prophets which were before you. Matthew 5:11, 12

In other words, if you're put down or betrayed for doing right, Jesus would say, "You're going to have a great reward some day. You're in good company. People did the same thing to the prophets."

The third reason to help people is our own *personal situations.* I suggest the reason there is no mention in our text of David being angry at, disappointed in, or upset with the men of Keilah is because in the verses preceding this story, David had dropped the ball himself when he lied to Ahimelech. It is easy for us to forget about all the people we have betrayed, all the people we've let down. Therefore, because we ourselves are in need of mercy, the only logical choice we have is to extend mercy to others.

1 Samuel 23:13, 14 (a)
Then David and his men, which were about six hundred, arose and departed out of Kei-

lah, and went whithersoever they could go. And it was told Saul that David was escaped from Keilah; and he forbare to go forth. And David abode in the wilderness in strong holds, and remained in a mountain in the wilderness of Ziph. And Saul sought him every day . . .

Ziph literally means "refining place." What a great place for David to go—to a place where God will refine him. In the refining process, a smelter would heat ore to the point that it became liquid, with all of the impurities burned away. The smelter would know the process was complete when he could look in the pot of liquid ore and see his own face. The Lord says, "I'm going to allow the heat to be turned up a bit, to burn out the impurities so that people might see something of Me in your life."

C. H. Spurgeon said that affliction is the tuner of the harp and the sanctifier of the son. I like that. How did David have such intimacy with the Lord, such passion for the Lord, such understanding of the Lord that He could write the psalms he wrote? His passion, wisdom, and understanding came from places like Ziph and Keilah—where people were chasing him down, where he was betrayed by people he had helped, where he would feel forsaken and alone—where God could deal with Him.

How long does the process of affliction or refining go on? Longer than you might think. It takes a while for the impurities to be burnt off, for the reflection of His face to be seen from my life or yours.

1 Samuel 23:14 (b)
. . . but God delivered him not into his hand.

"But God . . ." How I love this phrase that appears throughout Scripture. Saul is after David. But God was there for him. And the same thing is true for you. Satan seeks to devour you as a roaring lion, but God is with you. And greater is He that is in you than the one who comes against you (1 John 4:4).

1 Samuel 23:15, 16
And David saw that Saul was come out to seek his life: and David was in the wilderness of Ziph in a wood. And Jonathan Saul's son arose, and went to David into the wood, and strengthened his hand in God.

Jonathan doesn't wring his hands in anxiety, but strengthens David's hand in God. Lots of people will worry with you. But those aren't the people you need. You need people who will strengthen your hand in God, who will say to you, "Trust in the Lord. Put away your sorrow. Put away your fear because God is here. The Lord will see you through." We look for sympathy—at least I do. But the Lord knows that's not what I need ultimately. But what I need is for someone to come my way and strengthen my hand in God. That's what we all need. Jonathan was that kind of man.

1 Samuel 23:17–20
And he said unto him, Fear not: for the hand of Saul my father shall not find thee; and thou shalt be king over Israel, and I shall be next unto thee; and that also Saul my father knoweth. And they two made a covenant before the LORD: and David abode in the wood, and Jonathan went to his house. Then came up the Ziphites to Saul to Gibeah, saying, Doth not David hide himself with us in strong holds in the wood, in the hill of Hachilah, which is on the south of Jeshimon? Now therefore, O king, come down according to all the desire of thy soul to come down; and our part shall be to deliver him into the king's hand.

Not only was David nearly betrayed by the men of Keilah, but here he is in jeopardy of being betrayed by the men of Ziph.

1 Samuel 23:21
And Saul said, Blessed be ye of the LORD; for ye have compassion on me.

Saul knows how to speak the language of piety and spirituality—but it's not based in reality. Rather than walking with the Lord, Saul simply knows how to talk about Him.

1 Samuel 23:22
Go, I pray you, prepare yet, and know and see his place where his haunt is, and who hath seen him there: for it is told me that he dealeth very subtilly.

"Go track David down," Saul said. "And don't take your eye off him because he's very sneaky."

1 Samuel 23:23–26
See therefore, and take knowledge of all the lurking places where he hideth himself, and come ye again to me with the certainty, and I will go with you: and it shall come to pass, if he be in the land, that I will search him out throughout all the thousands of Judah. And they arose, and went to Ziph before Saul: but David and his men were in the wilderness of Maon, in the plain on the south of Jeshimon. Saul also and his men went to seek him. And they told David: wherefore he

came down into a rock, and abode in the wilderness of Maon. And when Saul heard that, he pursued after David in the wilderness of Maon. And Saul went on this side of the mountain, and David and his men on that side of the mountain: and David made haste to get away for fear of Saul; for Saul and his men compassed David and his men round about to take them.

Backed up against a mountain range and surrounded on both sides, the situation doesn't look good for David.

1 Samuel 23:27
But there came a messenger unto Saul, saying, Haste thee, and come; for the Philistines have invaded the land.

"Saul! Get back home! The Philistines are mounting an attack against us!" cried a messenger. God has a way of moving in and protecting us even—or especially—when there seems to be no way out.

1 Samuel 23:28
Wherefore Saul returned from pursuing after David, and went against the Philistines: therefore they called that place Sela-hammahlekoth.

Sela-hammahlekoth means "rock of protection." David had no place to go. He was hemmed in, surrounded by the enemy. But there was a rock of protection between him and Saul. Likewise, our Rock, the Rock of Ages, Jesus Christ, has never let me down, never dropped the ball. So many times I've thought, "I just can't figure this out. I don't know how this is going to work," but the Lord has always come through for me. And He'll always come through for you. Even when we are faithless, He is faithful still because He cannot deny Himself (2 Timothy 2:13).

Without striking a blow, shooting an arrow, or hurling a spear, David was delivered. Sometimes when we try to take things into our hands, we only make matters worse. God would say, "Let the Rock be your protection. Watch and see what I'll do as you trust in Me."

1 Samuel 23:29
And David went up from thence, and dwelt in strong holds at En-gedi.

En-gedi means "the mount of the kid" because, as it is even today, it was a place where mountain goats hung out. This isn't surprising, for En-gedi remains a beautiful spot in the desert area surrounding the Dead Sea, an oasis in an otherwise barren region.

24

After dealing with the Philistines, Saul makes his way south near the Dead Sea to resume his hunt for David . . .

1 Samuel 24:1–3
And it came to pass, when Saul was returned from following the Philistines, that it was told him, saying, Behold, David is in the wilderness of En-gedi. Then Saul took three thousand chosen men out of all Israel, and went to seek David and his men upon the rocks of the wild goats. And he came to the sheepcotes by the way, where was a cave; and Saul went in to cover his feet: and David and his men remained in the sides of the cave.

With temperatures soaring to one hundred and twenty degrees in this region, Saul chose to take a nap in a cave to escape the heat. But it just so happened that the cave he chose was the same cave in which David and his men were hiding.

1 Samuel 24:4 (a)
And the men of David said unto him, Behold the day of which the LORD said unto thee, Behold, I will deliver thine enemy into thine hand, that thou mayest do to him as it shall seem good unto thee . . .

David's advisors thought this was a God-given opportunity for him to lop off Saul's head. David, however, knew otherwise.

Those who trust in the Lord will not make haste, Isaiah 28:16 tells us. One of the hardest lessons for me is to wait, to slow down. David's men thought this opportunity to kill Saul was God's blessing when, in reality, it was God's testing. God will often test us with what seems to be a blessing that's ours for the taking. But unless we wait on and for God, that which we thought would be a delight will always prove to be a disaster.

1 Samuel 24:4 (b)
. . . Then David arose, and cut off the skirt of Saul's robe privily.

David snipped the hem of Saul's robe. In those days, the border of a garment was highly significant. Called the *zitsiot,* you can still see them today on clothing in Israel. In Numbers 15, God commanded Moses to tell the people of Israel to make blue borders on their garments (15:37–39). Why blue? Because blue is the color of heaven, when the people of Israel looked at the hems of their garments, they would be reminded that they were a heavenly people, that they were not to be enamored with the world.

According to the Numbers 15 passage, the blue hems were to remind the people not only that they were destined for heaven, but of the commandments their God in heaven had given them. So the people tied the fringes of their hems in six hundred and thirteen knots—one for each commandment the Rabbis declared were in the Scriptures.

The dye to make the blue borders came from a certain kind of sea snail. Extracting the dye was a costly and lengthy process. Perhaps this is why Jesus would indict the scribes and Pharisees for having large borders as a sign of their wealth (Matthew 23:5).

In Bible days, one could determine another's wealth and family history by the size of the border and the tying of knots on the hem of his garment. Thus, when Ruth said to Boaz, "Cover me," she was essentially saying, "I want to come under the covering of your family pedigree" (Ruth 3:9).

In Revelation 19, we read that when Jesus returns, the title "King of kings and Lord of lords" will be written on His thigh. These words are not tattooed on His thigh—but would be evident by the border of His garment, which would be pulled up to his thigh as he sits astride the horse that will carry Him.

In cutting the fringe of Saul's garment, David was saying in essence that Saul's pedigree, position, power, and authority were to be given to him. And that is precisely why David's heart smote him. He was grabbing Saul's position, questioning Saul's authority—and he knew he ought not to have done this.

1 Samuel 24:5, 6
And it came to pass afterward, that David's heart smote him, because he had cut off Saul's skirt. And he said unto his men, The LORD forbid that I should do this thing unto my master, the LORD's anointed, to stretch forth mine hand against him, seeing he is the anointed of the LORD.

The Lord's anointed? Wasn't David the Lord's anointed? David would say, "Yes, I am anointed to be king, but Saul is the instrument God is using to work in my life to bring me to the place I need to be. And by my nicking him, I am in error."

What's being said here is incredible. You see, it wasn't just kings who were anointed with oil. Nor was it only prophets and priests who were anointed with oil. The altar and instruments used in the tabernacle were anointed with oil as well. In other words, David recognized that anointing did not have to imply deserving. That is why he could say, "I shouldn't have done this. I shouldn't have touched the Lord's anointed, for Saul is the anointed instrument of God to stretch me, to change me, to make me the man I'm supposed to be."

1 Samuel 24:7–15
So David stayed his servants with these words, and suffered them not to rise against Saul. But Saul rose up out of the cave, and went on his way. David also arose afterward, and went out of the cave, and cried after Saul, saying, My lord the king. And when Saul looked behind him, David stooped with his face to the earth, and bowed himself. And David said to Saul, Wherefore hearest thou men's words, saying, Behold, David seeketh thy hurt? Behold, this day thine eyes have seen how that the LORD had delivered thee to day into mine hand in the cave: and some bade me kill thee: but mine eye spared thee; and I said, I will not put forth mine hand against my lord; for he is the LORD's anointed. Moreover, my father, see, yea, see the skirt of thy robe in my hand: for in that I cut off the skirt of thy robe and killed thee not, know thou and see that there is neither evil nor transgression in mine hand, and I have not sinned against thee; yet thou huntest my soul to take it. The LORD judge between me and thee, and the LORD avenge me of thee: but mine hand shall not be upon thee. As saith the proverb of the ancients, Wickedness proceedeth from the wicked: but mine hand shall not be upon thee. After whom is the king of Israel come out? after whom dost thou pursue? after a dead dog, after a flea. The LORD therefore be judge, and judge between me and thee, and see, and plead my cause, and deliver me out of thine hand.

David's insights into the Lord, his dependence upon the Lord, his passion for the Lord are revealed in the psalms he wrote during the time he was fleeing from Saul because the man who had nothing but anger towards him was God's instrument to make him into the man he desired to be.

The same is true with us. "Lord, change me," I pray. "I'm tired of the smallness of my soul, the hardness of my heart. Make me different than I am."

"Okay," the Lord says. "I'll send you an anointed instrument to help accomplish this change."

"Good!" I say, thinking it will be an anointed teacher, a Christian book, a close friend.

But He sends a Saul or two throwing spears at me.

Who has the Lord allowed to be in your life who throws spears at you, who brings grief to you? That person is the anointed instrument of God to work in you the love, kindness, and tenderness you long for. There's no other way for the Lord to change you but to send a Saul or two your way. The question is, what will you do? Will you cut the fringe?

I doubt that the blind man in John 9 would have washed in the pool of Siloam—or literally "sent one"—had there not been mud in his eyes. Why does God allow people we think are mud to get in our face? The reason is to cause us to go to the true Sent One and wash again. When everything is going well, I have a tendency to cruise on automatic pilot. But when there's mud thrown at me, I make my way to the Lord in desperation. I pour out my heart to the Lord and get into the water of the Word once again.

David said to Saul, "the Lord will judge between you and me. The Lord will work things out. The Lord will deal with you eventually. But I'm not to touch you because you are God's anointed instrument in my life."

What about that person who breaks your heart? Are you going to take them down a peg or two—or, like David, will you wisely choose not to touch the Lord's anointed?

1 Samuel 24:16–22

And it came to pass, when David had made an end of speaking these words unto Saul, that Saul said, Is this thy voice, my son David? And Saul lifted up his voice, and wept. And he said to David, Thou art more righteous than I: for thou hast rewarded me good, whereas I have rewarded thee evil. And thou hast shewed this day how that thou hast dealt well with me: forasmuch as when the LORD had delivered me into thine hand, thou killedst me not. For if a man find his enemy, will he let him go well away? wherefore the LORD reward thee good for that thou hast done unto me this day. And now, behold, I know well that thou shalt surely be king, and that the kingdom of Israel shall be established in thine hand. Swear now therefore unto me by the LORD, that thou wilt not cut off my seed after me, and that thou wilt not destroy my name out of my father's house. And David sware unto Saul. And Saul went home; but David and his men gat them up unto the hold.

Saul may have been sincere. He may have had great intentions. The problem, however, is the flesh. Lots of people make promises of reformation. They attend twelve-step programs, make appointments at counseling clinics, or write inspiring words on note cards to tape to their mirror. But the reality is that, although the spirit might be willing, the flesh is weak (Mark 14:38). Therefore, the issue isn't reformation. The issue is regeneration. We've got to be born again.

"Without Me, you can do nothing," Jesus said (John 15:5). No matter how good the program is, no matter how sincere the people might be, no matter how hard one tries, the flesh ultimately wells up again. Saul may have been sincere—but he lacked the ability to keep his word. He was no longer walking with the Lord and, therefore, no longer drawing strength from the Lord. Thus, even if Saul had been sincere, he was unable to control his flesh.

25

1 Samuel 25:1, 2

And Samuel died; and all the Israelites were gathered together, and lamented him, and buried him in his house at Ramah. And David arose, and went down to the wilderness of Paran. And there was a man in Maon, whose possessions were in Carmel; and the man was very great, and he had three thousand sheep, and a thousand goats: and he was shearing his sheep in Carmel.

Maon is a city of Judah, eight miles south of Hebron. There are two Carmels in Israel—one north by Haifa, and this smaller Carmel, located near Maon in the southern part of Judah.

1 Samuel 25:3

Now the name of the man was Nabal; and the name of his wife Abigail: and she was a woman of good understanding, and of a beautiful countenance: but the man was churlish and evil in his doings; and he was of the house of Caleb.

With 3,000 sheep and 1,000 goats, *Nabal* was a wealthy man. His name, however, literally means "Fool." *Abigail* means "Joy of the Father" What a combination. Abigail is a real jewel, in God's economy. Nabal came from good stock in Caleb, but he's a fool, as we shall see . . .

1 Samuel 25:4–9

And David heard in the wilderness that Nabal did shear his sheep. And David sent out ten young men, and David said unto the young men, Get you up to Carmel, and go to Nabal, and greet him in my name: And thus shall ye say to him that liveth in prosperity, Peace be both to thee, and peace be to thine house, and peace be unto all that thou hast. And now I have heard that thou hast shearers: now thy shepherds which were with us, we hurt them not, neither was there ought missing unto them, all the while

they were in Carmel. Ask thy young men, and they will shew thee. Wherefore let the young men find favour in thine eyes: for we come in a good day: give, I pray thee, whatsoever cometh to thine hand unto thy servants, and to thy son David. And when David's young men came, they spake to Nabal according to all those words in the name of David, and ceased.

David sent ten of his men with the following message to where Nabal was shearing his sheep: "This is a great day for you. You've been blessed. You have all this profit coming in. And not one of your sheep has been taken because we protected your property from sheep rustlers. Therefore, help us out. We're short on supplies."

This was customary in those days. If you were protected, you would pay accordingly. Therefore, this wasn't a matter of extortion but of protection.

1 Samuel 25:10, 11
And Nabal answered David's servants, and said, Who is David? and who is the son of Jesse? there be many servants now a days that break away every man from his master. Shall I then take my bread, and my water, and my flesh that I have killed for my shearers, and give it unto men, whom I know not whence they be?

"Who do you think you are?" Nabal thundered. "Your leader, David, is nothing more than a fugitive from Saul."

1 Samuel 25:12
So David's young men turned their way, and went again, and came and told him all those sayings.

David's men informed him that Nabal was not about to help them.

1 Samuel 25:13
And David said unto his men, Gird ye on every man his sword. And they girded on every man his sword; and David also girded on his sword: and there went up after David about four hundred men; and two hundred abode by the stuff.

David had just shown incredible wisdom and restraint in not lopping off Saul's head. But the truth of spiritual life is that when you have a victory over a great temptation, you are vulnerable to a smaller one. As the Song of Solomon declares, it is the little foxes that destroy (2:15). I think of Peter. Such courage did he show in the Garden of Gethsemane that he drew his sword and was ready to take on the entire company of soldiers that came to arrest Jesus. Yet a few hours later, when a little servant girl accused him of being a follower of Jesus, he crumbled in fear.

That's the way it is. It's not the big battles that will get you. It's not the big temptations or the big challenges. It's the little problems, the little foxes.

1 Samuel 25:14–17
But one of the young men told Abigail, Nabal's wife, saying, Behold, David sent messengers out of the wilderness to salute our master; and he railed on them. But the men were very good unto us, and we were not hurt, neither missed we any thing, as long as we were conversant with them, when we were in the fields: They were a wall unto us both by night and day, all the while we were with them keeping the sheep. Now therefore know and consider what thou wilt do; for evil is determined against our master, and against all his household: for he is such a son of Belial, that a man cannot speak to him.

It was common practice that, if you had a group of men in your region who were a wall around you, providing protection for you, you were obligated to help the men with their needs.

1 Samuel 25:18
Then Abigail made haste, and took two hundred loaves, and two bottles of wine, and five sheep ready dressed, and five measures of parched corn, and an hundred clusters of raisins, and two hundred cakes of figs, and laid them on asses.

Abigail goes out to intercede on behalf of her foolish husband. I would think this would be an opportunity for her to say, "This is my chance to be set free. If my husband gets his head lopped off, so be it." But that's not what she does. When she hears this report, she determines to intercede on Nabal's behalf.

1 Samuel 25:19
And she said unto her servants, Go on before me; behold, I come after you. But she told not her husband Nabal.

Abigail goes behind Nabal's back not to be sneaky or treacherous, but to protect him from his own stupidity.

1 Samuel 25:20–24
And it was so, as she rode on the ass, that she came down by the covert of the hill, and,

behold, David and his men came down against her; and she met them. Now David had said, Surely in vain have I kept all that this fellow hath in the wilderness, so that nothing was missed of all that pertained unto him: and he hath requited me evil for good. So and more also do God unto the enemies of David, if I leave of all that pertain to him by the morning light any that pisseth against the wall. And when Abigail saw David, she hasted, and lighted off the ass, and fell before David on her face, and bowed herself to the ground, And fell at his feet, and said, Upon me, my lord, upon me let this iniquity be: and let thine handmaid, I pray thee, speak in thine audience, and hear the words of thine handmaid.

"It's my fault," Abigail said. "Let this sin that has understandably angered you be accounted to me."

1 Samuel 25:25–27
Let not my lord, I pray thee, regard this man of Belial, even Nabal: for as his name is, so is he; Nabal is his name, and folly is with him: but I thine handmaid saw not the young men of my lord, whom thou didst send. Now therefore, my lord, as the LORD liveth, and as thy soul liveth, seeing the LORD hath withholden thee from coming to shed blood, and from avenging thyself with thine own hand, now let thine enemies, and they that seek evil to my lord, be as Nabal. And now this blessing which thine handmaid hath brought unto my lord, let it even be given unto the young men that follow my lord.

"I have come to prevent you from shedding blood," Abigail declared. "This food is for you and your young men to enjoy."

1 Samuel 25:28
I pray thee, forgive the trespass of thine handmaid: for the LORD will certainly make my lord a sure house; because my lord fighteth the battles of the LORD, and evil hath not been found in thee all thy days.

"You have great days ahead, David," Abigail said. "Your destiny is certain."

1 Samuel 25:29
Yet a man is risen to pursue thee, and to seek thy soul: but the soul of my lord shall be bound in the bundle of life with the LORD thy God; and the souls of thine enemies, them shall he sling out, as out of the middle of a sling.

Abigail's reference to a sling indicates that, as well as knowing David's destiny, she was aware of David's history.

1 Samuel 25:30, 31
And it shall come to pass, when the LORD shall have done to my lord according to all the good that he hath spoken concerning thee, and shall have appointed thee ruler over Israel; That this shall be no grief unto thee, nor offence of heart unto my lord, either that thou hast shed blood causeless, or that my lord hath avenged himself: but when the LORD shall have dealt well with my lord, then remember thine handmaid.

"Don't do anything today that you will regret when you come into a position of power," Abigail told David.

1 Samuel 25:32–35
And David said to Abigail, Blessed be the LORD God of Israel, which sent thee this day to meet me: And blessed be thy advice, and blessed be thou, which hast kept me this day from coming to shed blood, and from avenging myself with mine own hand. For in very deed, as the LORD God of Israel liveth, which hath kept me back from hurting thee, except thou hadst hasted and come to meet me, surely there had not been left unto Nabal by the morning light any that pisseth against the wall. So David received of her hand that which she had brought him, and said unto her, Go up in peace to thine house; see, I have hearkened to thy voice, and have accepted thy person.

Like Deborah before her and Esther after her, Abigail altered the course of history simply by being obedient to the Lord.

1 Samuel 25:36
And Abigail came to Nabal; and, behold, he held a feast in his house, like the feast of a king; and Nabal's heart was merry within him, for he was very drunken: wherefore she told him nothing, less or more, until the morning light.

Here, Nabal was about to be wiped out, yet he's having a party. His very life was in peril, yet he doesn't even realize it.

1 Samuel 25:37
But it came to pass in the morning, when the wine was gone out of Nabal, and his wife had told him these things, that his heart died within him, and he became as a stone.

After Nabal sobered up a bit, hearing how close he had come to losing his head, he had a stroke.

1 Samuel 25:38, 39 (a)
And it came to pass about ten days after, that the LORD smote Nabal, that he died. And when David heard that Nabal was dead, he said, Blessed be the LORD, that hath pleaded the cause of my reproach from the hand of Nabal, and hath kept his servant from evil: for the LORD hath returned the wickedness of Nabal upon his own head . . .

Nabal got what he deserved—but not because David took matters into his own hands. What a lesson for us. I want to fix things. I want to take stuff into my own hands. I want to make things happen. David did, too. But he was refrained by Abigail and was wise enough to listen.

1 Samuel 25:39 (b)
. . . And David sent and communed with Abigail, to take her to him to wife.

No doubt David was impressed not only with Abigail's beautiful countenance, but also by her humility and spiritual sensitivity.

1 Samuel 25:40–42
And when the servants of David were come to Abigail to Carmel, they spake unto her, saying, David sent us unto thee to take thee to him to wife. And she arose, and bowed herself on her face to the earth, and said, Behold, let thine handmaid be a servant to wash the feet of the servants of my lord. And Abigail hasted, and arose, and rode upon an ass, with five damsels of hers that went after her; and she went after the messengers of David, and became his wife.

Let this be a word of encouragement to any of you who are married to "Nabals." You might say, "I can't believe I'm stuck with him or her. How can I get out of this?" Abigail provides a real key in helping anyone in such a relationship. That is, regardless of whether or not your spouse is the person he or she is supposed to be, if you are the person you're supposed to be, God will work in amazing ways. Abigail did what was right even though her husband was a fool. She stood up for him, took responsibility for him, and tried to do everything she could to protect him. Had she not done so, she would never have been the bride of the king.

One day, a Greater than David will whisk you away to His kingdom—where you'll be free from the Nabal to whom you're married. You'll be His Bride. And may He say to you in that day, "Well done. You did what you were supposed to do." Life is so short in comparison to eternity. You'll never regret doing what is right.

Abigail is a picture of you and me . . .

- Like Abigail, we have good understanding and are of a beautiful countenance. God has given us good understanding from His Word, and we're robed in the beauty of His holiness.
- Abigail was yoked to Nabal. We, too, are yoked to fools—the fools of our sin and self and Satan. She was stuck with an idiot. So are we. We're stuck with ourselves.
- Abigail was barren. She had no children with Nabal. We, too, were barren. Without the Lord there was no fruit in our lives of eternal importance.
- Abigail heard the word of impending doom (v. 17). So did we. Jesus, our Greater than David, talked more about hell than about heaven.
- Abigail humbled herself before David (v. 24). That's what happened to you and me, as well. We heard the word of doom and realized our need for a Savior.
- Abigail sought forgiveness (v. 28). Some people think they don't need to be forgiven, that they have no need of salvation. Like Abigail, however, we know otherwise.
- Abigail was persuaded of David's goodness (v. 28). So, too, we say, "Lord, Thou art worthy."
- Abigail's request was granted (v. 35). The real issue of salvation is not that we accept the Lord, but that the Lord accepts us. And because He does, we are no longer at war with Him, but have peace with God through Jesus Christ.

1 Samuel 25:43, 44
David also took Ahinoam of Jezreel; and they were also both of them his wives. But Saul had given Michal his daughter, David's wife, to Phalti the son of Laish, which was of Gallim.

David's first wife, Michal, having been given to another man, David now has two wives: Abigail and Ahinoam. Although not ordained or condoned by God (Deuteronomy 17:17), this was a common practice in this day. But it was a practice that, throughout Scripture, never failed to end in disaster. And Ahinoam being the mother of Amnon, who would later rape his sister and destroy David's family, this marriage would prove to be no exception.

26

1 Samuel 26:1, 2
And the Ziphites came unto Saul to Gibeah, saying, Doth not David hide himself in the hill of Hachilah, which is before Jeshimon? Then Saul arose, and went down to the wilderness of Ziph, having three thousand chosen men of Israel with him, to seek David in the wilderness of Ziph.

David had already been in Ziph. The men of Ziph had betrayed him once before (chapter 23). So why would he go back to Ziph? Our text gives us no answer as to what David was thinking. But we do have revelation about the state of his heart at this time . . .

> To the chief Musician on Neg'-i-noth, Mas'-chil, A Psalm of David, when the Ziph'ims came and said to Saul, Doth not David hide himself with us?
>
> Save me, O God, by thy name, and judge me by thy strength. Hear my prayer, O God; give ear to the words of my mouth. For strangers are risen up against me, and oppressors seek after my soul: they have not set God before them. Selah. Behold, God is mine helper: the Lord is with them that uphold my soul. He shall reward evil unto mine enemies: cut them off in thy truth. I will freely sacrifice unto thee: I will praise thy name, O LORD; for it is good. For he hath delivered me out of all trouble: and mine eye hath seen his desire upon mine enemies. Psalm 54

Men are curious about thoughts. God, however, is more interested in our hearts. Here, David was writing poetry to the Lord, inspired by the Lord, and praising the Lord passionately even while he was doing something that didn't make sense logically.

1 Samuel 26:3, 4
And Saul pitched in the hill of Hachilah, which is before Jeshimon, by the way. But David abode in the wilderness, and he saw that Saul came after him into the wilderness. David therefore sent out spies, and understood that Saul was come in very deed.

The last time David encountered Saul, he heard Saul say, "David, I've done wrong in chasing you. You're a greater man, a better man than I am" (24:16–22). Our text indicates that, although David knew Saul's army was coming, he didn't believe Saul himself was leading the charge. Evidently, David believed Saul meant what he said at En-gedi—until his spies confirmed the worst.

Although Saul chucked spears at him, caused problems for him, and showed hatred toward him, David still wanted to believe the best about Saul. Yet David was wise enough to find out the facts so as not to jeopardize the lives of his men. I like this balance in David, a wise leader indeed.

1 Samuel 26:5
And David arose, and came to the place where Saul had pitched: and David beheld the place where Saul lay, and Abner the son of Ner, the captain of his host: and Saul lay in the trench, and the people pitched round about him.

Saul was in the center of the camp, with 3,000 of his special forces protecting him.

1 Samuel 26:6 (a)
Then answered David and said to Ahimelech the Hittite, and to Abishai the son of Zeruiah, brother to Joab, saying, Who will go down with me to Saul to the camp?

A dictator says, "Go." A leader says, "*Let's* go." David is a true leader. Jesus, our Greater than David, neither asks us to go where He hasn't gone before (Hebrews 4:15), nor where He won't go with us (Matthew 28:20).

1 Samuel 26:6 (b)–8
. . . And Abishai said, I will go down with thee. So David and Abishai came to the people by night: and, behold, Saul lay sleeping within the trench, and his spear stuck in the ground at his bolster: but Abner and the people lay round about him. Then said Abishai to David, God hath delivered thine enemy into thine hand this day: now therefore let me smite him, I pray thee, with the spear even to the earth at once, and I will not smite him the second time.

A second time, it would seem God had given David an opportunity to get rid of his enemy. But it wasn't an opportunity. It was a test for David to prove whether he would take things into his own hands or wait upon the Lord.

1 Samuel 26:9–11
And David said to Abishai, Destroy him not: for who can stretch forth his hand against the LORD's anointed, and be guiltless? David said furthermore, As the LORD liveth, the LORD shall smite him; or his day shall come to die; or he shall descend into battle, and perish. The LORD forbid that I should stretch forth mine hand against the LORD's anointed: but, I pray thee, take thou now the spear that is at his bolster, and the cruse of water, and let us go.

Sometimes danger comes to us not only from unspiritual enemies like Saul, but from overzealous friends like Abishai. David knew Saul was still the anointed instrument in God's hand to work in his own life. Therefore, he wisely refused Abishai's offer to kill Saul.

1 Samuel 26:12–14
So David took the spear and the cruse of water from Saul's bolster; and they gat them away, and no man saw it, nor knew it, neither awaked: for they were all asleep; because a deep sleep from the LORD was fallen upon them. Then David went over to the other side, and stood on the top of an hill afar off; a great space being between them: And David cried to the people, and to Abner the son of Ner, saying, Answerest thou not, Abner? Then Abner answered and said, Who art thou that criest to the king?

As day was breaking, David and Abishai made their way to a hill across from Saul's camp and called out to Abner, "Rise and shine!"

1 Samuel 26:15, 16
And David said to Abner, Art not thou a valiant man? and who is like to thee in Israel? wherefore then hast thou not kept thy lord the king? for there came one of the people in to destroy the king thy lord. This thing is not good that thou hast done. As the LORD liveth, ye are worthy to die, because ye have not kept your master, the LORD's anointed. And now see where the king's spear is, and the cruse of water that was at his bolster.

Here, we see David modeling the truth that the righteous are as bold as a lion (Proverbs 28:1). Not only did he sneak into Saul's camp, but he challenges Abner's authority. This reminds me of Paul before Agrippa at the amphitheater at Caesarea, of Martin Luther before the Diet of Worms, of John Knox before Queen Mary.

I will not tremble in the presence of man if I have trembled in the presence of God. When I find myself afraid of people, it's always indicative that I haven't been in the presence of the Lord because when I spend time with Him, I have boldness, peace, and confidence.

1 Samuel 26:17–19 (a)
And Saul knew David's voice, and said, Is this thy voice, my son David? And David said, It is my voice, my lord, O king. And he said, Wherefore doth my lord thus pursue after his servant? for what have I done? or what evil is in mine hand? Now therefore, I pray thee, let my lord the king hear the words of his servant. If the LORD have stirred thee up against me, let him accept an offering . . .

"If the Lord has stirred your heart to punish me because I've been wrong, if you are the instrument of chastening because I'm out of line, I need to bring an offering of sacrifice to the Lord," David said. "My heart is to be right with the Lord."

1 Samuel 26:19 (b)
. . . but if they be the children of men, cursed be they before the LORD . . .

"On the other hand," David continued, "if men have been lying to you about me or stoking the fires within you to feel animosity toward me, let those men be cursed." . . .

1 Samuel 26:19 (c)
. . . for they have driven me out this day from abiding in the inheritance of the LORD, saying, Go, serve other gods.

Notice that David's primary complaint against his enemies was not that they had forced him into exile, but that they had prevented him access to worshiping with His people.

1 Samuel 26:20, 21
Now therefore, let not my blood fall to the earth before the face of the LORD: for the king of Israel is come out to seek a flea, as when one doth hunt a partridge in the mountains. Then said Saul, I have sinned: return, my son David: for I will no more do thee harm, because my soul was precious in thine eyes this day: behold, I have played the fool, and have erred exceedingly.

Although Saul doesn't know it, he's about to die. Therefore, this is his epitaph.

I wonder what it must feel like to be seventy, eighty, or ninety—headed toward your eternal destiny—and say, "I've been a fool. I've pursued things I shouldn't have pursued." I believe one of the primary messages of the Bible is to teach us to live as though this is our last day. That's the beauty of watching for the Lord's coming every day.

1 Samuel 26:22–25
And David answered and said, Behold the king's spear! and let one of the young men come over and fetch it. The LORD render to every man his righteousness and his faithfulness: for the LORD delivered thee into my hand to day, but I would not stretch forth

mine hand against the LORD's anointed. And, behold, as thy life was much set by this day in mine eyes, so let my life be much set by in the eyes of the LORD, and let him deliver me out of all tribulation. Then Saul said to David, Blessed be thou, my son David: thou shalt both do great things, and also shalt still prevail. So David went on his way, and Saul returned to his place.

Saul goes back to his palace and never sees David again. He slinks off the pages of Scripture with the summary conclusion: I have played the fool. I have erred greatly.

The first time David had a chance to deal with Saul, he touched the hem of his garment, and later was convicted. Now, David's heart does not smite him because he doesn't touch Saul at all.

I guarantee before the week is over, you'll have an opportunity to lop off a head, to snip a garment, or to make a comment. But perhaps the Lord would say to you, "There's a better way." I pray that the power of the Word being heard and received will change us from glory to glory—from a Saul to a David.

27 Jealous of David, threatened by David, Saul was determined to kill David. But God had spared David time and time again—not only from the attacks of Saul, but also from David's fleshly temptation to attack Saul. Yet although his enemy had verified the fact that David would emerge victorious (26:25), depression descended upon the soul of David . . .

1 Samuel 27:1 (a)
And David said in his heart, I shall now perish one day by the hand of Saul . . .

David was a lover of God who talked to the Lord constantly and wrote psalms about the Lord very expressively. In this situation, however, we see him not talking to the Lord, but talking to his heart. The Hebrew phrase translated "in his heart" literally means David talked to himself. And in so doing, he got mixed up. He came to wrong conclusions. He fell into depression. He ends up living in enemy territory for almost a year and a half because he talked to himself rather than talking to the Lord.

I can do the same thing oh, so easily. I talk to myself and convince myself of all kinds of things that are completely untrue. As I drive home from church, I overhear myself saying,

"Now, Jon, what do you think about that?"

"I think what he said was unfair."

"I do, too!"

"I think she could have been a little kinder. What do you think, Jon?"

"I completely agree. I don't know what's gotten into her."

"I've been wondering the same thing! It seems like they used to be so nice and so pleasant, but something's wrong with them now."

"I concur! You need to do something about them. You need to yell at them."

"You're right, Jon. Excellent advice!"

I think a lot of us talk to ourselves from time to time. Driving to church, walking the dog, mowing the lawn, we convince ourselves that we're right, as we make our way to Gath, as we defect, as we rebel.

You will persuade yourself. You'll build up a case that's airtight. You will be your own best ally. You'll feel more justified with each passing moment as you talk to yourself. But here's the danger with talking to yourself, with talking to your heart: According to Jeremiah 17:9, the heart is deceitful and desperately wicked. This means that when you're having a good "heart to heart" talk with yourself, you're getting counsel that is desperately wicked. When I talk to myself, I am being deceived and I am becoming wicked. And the end result is that you'll take a detour—be it sixteen seconds, sixteen months, or sixteen years—into Gath.

What are we to do? Philippians 4 says, "Be anxious for nothing. But in everything with prayer and supplication with thanksgiving, let your requests be made known"—not to yourself, not to your pastor, not to your spouse—"unto God. And the peace of God will keep your hearts and minds in Christ Jesus."

Imagine two stopwatches in your hands. One starts every time you talk to yourself or to others about a situation. The other starts every time you talk to your Father about the matter, communicating in articulate, intelligent, understandable prayer. After three days, what would these clocks look like? How much time would have been spent talking to yourself? How much time would have been spent talking to your Father?

There are some people with whom spending time is a joy. Why? Because their hearts and minds are at peace. Why? Because they're people of prayer. They have no fish to fry, no axes to grind, no battles to fight, no points to prove because they have learned to say, "Father, I don't know what to do about this. I'm tired of mulling it over in my mind or talking to people round about me. I'm just going to talk to You."

The only way to have this peace is to pray. If you talk to yourself more than you talk to your

Father, you'll make big mistakes. But if you choose to talk to the Father, there will be a genuine peace about you that is winsome and attractive, pleasant and contagious. Bend your knee, open your heart, and wait on Him. The end result will be a peace that will keep your heart and mind in Christ, and will keep you out of Gath.

1 Samuel 27:1 (b), 2
. . . There is nothing better for me than that I should speedily escape into the land of the Philistines; and Saul shall despair of me, to seek me any more in any coast of Israel: so shall I escape out of his hand. And David arose, and he passed over with the six hundred men that were with him unto Achish, the son of Maoch, king of Gath.

When he was first running from Saul, David went to Gath to find refuge. Why does he now return to Gath? Perhaps it is because when he was there previously, the people of Gath thought he was a madman (1 Samuel 21:13, 14). Returning with a band of six hundred soldiers would prove to them otherwise.

1 Samuel 27:3–5
And David dwelt with Achish at Gath, he and his men, every man with his household, even David with his two wives, Ahinoam the Jezreelitess, and Abigail the Carmelitess, Nabal's wife. And it was told Saul that David was fled to Gath: and he sought no more again for him. And David said unto Achish, If I have now found grace in thine eyes, let them give me a place in some town in the country, that I may dwell there: for why should thy servant dwell in the royal city with thee?

I don't want to crowd you," David said to Achish. "I have six hundred men with me—along with their families. So we'll just live in one of your other cities."

1 Samuel 27:6
Then Achish gave him Ziklag that day: wherefore Ziklag pertaineth unto the kings of Judah unto this day.

No doubt hearing reports that Saul and David were at war, Achish would welcome an enemy of Saul. Ziklag was originally given to Judah (Joshua 15:31). The problem was, the people of Judah never possessed it, so the Philistines gained control of it. Here, David makes Ziklag his base of operation—and the city would remain in the hands of the Jews until the time this book was written.

1 Samuel 27:7
And the time that David dwelt in the country of the Philistines was a full year and four months.

David must have thought, *Saul isn't chasing me. The enemy isn't hounding me. I've got it made here in Philistine country.*

This can happen to you and me as well. We can say, "I'm tired of struggling with the people of God, so I'll just hang out with the world in Philistine country." And for awhile, it will seem good because the enemy will no longer chase you. If you stop going to church, if you pull away from fellowship, if you isolate yourself from Christians, Satan won't bug you. But what will eventually happen to David is highly instructive because, although his situation will be easier initially, it will be disastrous ultimately.

I find it interesting that Psalms 8, 81, and 84 are to be played on an instrument called a *gittih*, an instrument evidently invented in Gath. You see, when David was in Gath for sixteen months, he must have heard instruments that were new to him and ultimately employed them in the praise of God. Thus, even though David was where he ought not to have been, God eventually brought glory to Himself through it.

1 Samuel 27:8
And David and his men went up, and invaded the Geshurites, and the Gezrites, and the Amalekites: for those nations were of old the inhabitants of the land, as thou goest to Shur, even unto the land of Egypt.

The Geshurites, Gezrites, and Amalekites were groups living in the southern regions of Judah and northern regions of Philistine country. David and his men launched guerrilla raids on these Canaanite tribes—tribes that were never rooted out by the Jews as they were supposed to have been when they first took possession of the land.

1 Samuel 27:9
And David smote the land, and left neither man nor woman alive, and took away the sheep, and the oxen, and the asses, and the camels, and the apparel, and returned, and came to Achish.

This shows me that energetic activity is not a sign of true spirituality. David is attacking the enemy because, no doubt, he has a guilty conscience about living in Philistine country. We can do the same thing. We can pull away from fellowship with other believers, but make up for it by becoming active in a myriad of service organizations. Thus, oftentimes when a person is the most active, it's not because he's the most spiritual. It might be because he's trying to overcome his own awareness of carnality.

Secondly, this shows me that success is not necessarily an indication of true spirituality. Here, David was highly successful. After all, he won every battle. Nonetheless, he wasn't doing what was right in God's sight.

1 Samuel 27:10
And Achish said, Whither have ye made a road to day? And David said, Against the south of Judah, and against the south of the Jerahmeelites, and against the south of the Kenites.

By saying he was in the area of Judah, David falsely implied that he was waging war against his fellow Israelites.

1 Samuel 27:11, 12
And David saved neither man nor woman alive, to bring tidings to Gath, saying, Lest they should tell on us, saying, So did David, and so will be his manner all the while he dwelleth in the country of the Philistines. And Achish believed David, saying, He hath made his people Israel utterly to abhor him; therefore he shall be my servant for ever.

Thinking David was killing his own countrymen, Achisch was delighted. Surely David would be loyal to him, he thought. But Achish didn't know of David's propensity to lie. At Saul's table, we see David telling Jonathan to lie for him (1 Samuel 20:6). David lied to Ahimelech that he was on a secret mission for Saul (1 Samuel 21:2). He will lie to Uriah to cover his sin with Bathsheba (2 Samuel 11).

How could a man after God's own heart lie?

Because God uses imperfect people—aren't you glad?

Others might say, "How could God use him, or her, or them?" But God sees the heart. This doesn't justify David's lying—for it not only will get him in all kinds of trouble, but others died as a result. Therefore, this is not a justification for lying, but rather an indication that God sees man's heart.

God doesn't give up on David—and David will eventually come to the point where he will cry, "Remove me from the way of lying lips" (Psalm 120:2).

28

1 Samuel 28:1, 2
And it came to pass in those days, that the Philistines gathered their armies together for warfare, to fight with Israel. And Achish said unto David, Know thou assuredly, that thou shalt go out with me to battle, thou and thy men. And David said to Achish, Surely thou shalt know what thy servant can do. And Achish said to David, Therefore will I make thee keeper of mine head for ever.

"I've been watching you, David," Achish said. "You've been fighting your own people. I trust you. Now we're going to go to war against the Israelites, and I want you and your men to join us."

Uh-oh. Were you counting on this, David, when you backslid? Were you counting on this when you cut yourself off from your people, when you went into Philistine country? Sure, the pressure was off when you were in Philistine country. But now there's a bigger problem. Now you're going to have to come against the people of God. There's a price to pay for your sixteen-month vacation.

There's always a price to pay. Every temptation the devil sends our way is gift-wrapped as a present. Yes, David was given Ziklag. But sixteen months later, the bill comes due.

1 Samuel 28:3–5
Now Samuel was dead, and all Israel had lamented him, and buried him in Ramah, even in his own city. And Saul had put away those that had familiar spirits, and the wizards, out of the land. And the Philistines gathered themselves together, and came and pitched in Shunem: and Saul gathered all Israel together, and they pitched in Gilboa. And when Saul saw the host of the Philistines, he was afraid, and his heart greatly trembled.

That the war between the Philistines and Saul was to take place in the northern city of Gilboa meant that the Philistines had penetrated deeply into Israel and that Saul was boxed in. No wonder his heart greatly trembled.

How did this happen? How did Saul lose control of the land of Israel? There's a very simple reason: He was spending his time fighting the wrong enemy. He was chasing David. So now when there is a genuine war to fight, he is completely, totally unprepared.

The same thing can happen to us. If we get all tangled up in the little problems that arise among Christians, when it comes time to do battle against our true enemy, we'll be powerless.

1 Samuel 28:6
And when Saul inquired of the LORD, the LORD answered him not, neither by dreams nor by Urim, nor by prophets.

God wasn't speaking to Saul through dreams, through the priests, or through prophecy. Even Samuel was now dead. Here, Saul is in for the battle of his life—and God's not talking to him.

1 Samuel 28:7, 8

Then said Saul unto his servants, Seek me a woman that hath a familiar spirit, that I may go to her, and inquire of her. And his servants said to him, Behold, there is a woman that hath a familiar spirit at Endor. And Saul disguised himself, and put on other raiment, and he went, and two men with him, and they came to the woman by night: and he said, I pray thee, divine unto me by the familiar spirit, and bring me him up, whom I shall name unto thee.

Although Saul had ordered the deportation of wizards and fortune tellers, his heart was still inclined toward their practice. So, under the cover of night, he seeks help from a "psychic."

I think of another man who sought counsel at night: Nicodemus. Unlike Saul, however, Nicodemus would not remain in the dark, for he sought counsel from the Light of the world (John 3).

1 Samuel 28:9–12

And the woman said unto him, Behold, thou knowest what Saul hath done, how he hath cut off those that have familiar spirits, and the wizards, out of the land: wherefore then layest thou a snare for my life, to cause me to die?

And Saul sware to her by the Lord, saying, As the Lord liveth, there shall no punishment happen to thee for this thing. Then said the woman, Whom shall I bring up unto thee? And he said, Bring me up Samuel. And when the woman saw Samuel, she cried with a loud voice: and the woman spake to Saul, saying, Why hast thou deceived me? for thou art Saul.

How low are you going to go, Saul? God is not speaking to you—and instead of repenting before Him, confessing your need of Him, and turning away from your sin, you're going to a psychic. This is not innocent because the Bible specifically tells us we are to have nothing to do with activities involving necromancy. Are these things bad simply because God forbids them? No. Like all sin, God forbids them because they're bad. They open doors to demonic deception.

Although in this case, Saul would hear the truth from Samuel rather than the lie of a demon, how better off he would have been had he humbled himself and sought the Lord.

1 Samuel 28:13–19

And the king said unto her, Be not afraid: for what sawest thou? And the woman said unto Saul, I saw gods ascending out of the earth. And he said unto her, What form is he of? And she said, An old man cometh up; and he is covered with a mantle. And Saul perceived that it was Samuel, and he stooped with his face to the ground, and bowed himself. And Samuel said to Saul, Why hast thou disquieted me, to bring me up? And Saul answered, I am sore distressed; for the Philistines make war against me, and God is departed from me, and answereth me no more, neither by prophets, nor by dreams: therefore I have called thee, that thou mayest make known unto me what I shall do. Then said Samuel, Wherefore then dost thou ask of me, seeing the Lord is departed from thee, and is become thine enemy? And the Lord hath done to him, as he spake by me: for the Lord hath rent the kingdom out of thine hand, and given it to thy neighbour, even to David: Because thou obeyedst not the voice of the Lord, nor executedst his fierce wrath upon Amalek, therefore hath the Lord done this thing unto thee this day. Moreover the Lord will also deliver Israel with thee into the hand of the Philistines: and to morrow shalt thou and thy sons be with me: the Lord also shall deliver the host of Israel into the hand of the Philistines.

"What should I do?" Saul said to Samuel in desperation. Samuel never tells Saul what he should do. Instead he says, "Here's what's going to happen: Because you disobeyed when the Lord asked you to destroy the Amalekites, the kingdom has been taken from you and given to David. Furthermore, you and your sons will die tomorrow.

1 Samuel 28:20–22

Then Saul fell straightway all along on the earth, and was sore afraid, because of the words of Samuel: and there was no strength in him; for he had eaten no bread all the day, nor all the night. And the woman came unto Saul, and saw that he was sore troubled, and said unto him, Behold, thine handmaid hath obeyed thy voice, and I have put my life in my hand, and have hearkened unto thy words which thou spakest unto me. Now therefore, I pray thee, hearken thou also unto the voice of thine handmaid, and let me set a morsel of bread before thee; and eat, that thou mayest have strength, when thou goest on thy way.

This woman's apparent kindness to Saul may have been due to the fact that if he had died in her house, she would have been in big trouble since witches were outlawed (v. 3).

1 Samuel 28:23–25
But he refused, and said, I will not eat. But his servants, together with the woman, compelled him; and he hearkened unto their voice. So he arose from the earth, and sat upon the bed. And the woman had a fat calf in the house; and she hasted, and killed it, and took flour, and kneaded it, and did bake unleavened bread thereof: And she brought it before Saul, and before his servants; and they did eat. Then they rose up, and went away that night.

Saul slips away into the night. The next time we read of him, he'll be in the battle that will take his life.

29

1 Samuel 29:1, 2
Now the Philistines gathered together all their armies to Aphek: and the Israelites pitched by a fountain which is in Jezreel. And the lords of the Philistines passed on by hundreds, and by thousands: but David and his men passed on in the rereward with Achish.

In Achish's army, David is actually poised to begin fighting for the Philistines against his own people.

1 Samuel 29:3–5
Then said the princes of the Philistines, What do these Hebrews here? And Achish said unto the princes of the Philistines, Is not this David, the servant of Saul the king of Israel, which hath been with me these days, or these years, and I have found no fault in him since he fell unto me unto this day? And the princes of the Philistines were wroth with him; and the princes of the Philistines said unto him, Make this fellow return, that he may go again to his place which thou hast appointed him, and let him not go down with us to battle, lest in the battle he be an adversary to us: for wherewith should he reconcile himself unto his master? should it not be with the heads of these men? Is not this David, of whom they sang one to another in dances, saying, Saul slew his thousands, and David his ten thousands?

The song that aroused Saul's anger toward David initially (1 Samuel 18:7, 8), is the same song that would rescue him presently. God is the great Orchestrator, the Master Composer of the symphony of our lives. At times, we might think, we're hearing a song that's off-key, flat, out of tune. *This is awful,* we think. *Why is this happening to me? Why are people saying those things about me? I don't understand.* But in reality, the song that seems to be sour often proves down the road to be the very song God uses to rescue us from the disaster that would have been ours.

1 Samuel 29:6–11
Then Achish called David, and said unto him, Surely, as the LORD liveth, thou hast been upright, and thy going out and thy coming in with me in the host is good in my sight: for I have not found evil in thee since the day of thy coming unto me unto this day: nevertheless the lords favour thee not. Wherefore now return, and go in peace, that thou displease not the lords of the Philistines. And David said unto Achish, But what have I done? and what hast thou found in thy servant so long as I have been with thee unto this day, that I may not go fight against the enemies of my lord the king? And Achish answered and said to David, I know that thou art good in my sight, as an angel of God: notwithstanding the princes of the Philistines have said, He shall not go up with us to the battle. Wherefore now rise up early in the morning with thy master's servants that are come with thee: and as soon as ye be up early in the morning, and have light, depart. So David and his men rose up early to depart in the morning, to return into the land of the Philistines. And the Philistines went up to Jezreel.

The Lord kept David from doing something he would have regretted all the days of his life, something that would have changed not only his personal history, but that of the entire nation. God stepped in. Even though David had failed, even though he's in enemy territory, God steps in and rescues him. I get myself in all sorts of predicaments, in all kinds of jams. But even when I make a mess of things, God doesn't walk away or turn from me. He steps up. He moves in. He saves me because He is faithful even when I am faithless (2 Timothy 2:13).

I trust God not because I have my act together or because I know lots of Bible verses. I trust Him for one reason: He's proven Himself to be trustworthy. The greatest thing we can give God is trust, where say,

"It's not about how worthy or worthless I am.
It's not about how bad or how good I might

be. It's all about You, Lord. No matter whether I'm faithful or faithless, good or bad, glad or sad, You do exactly what You promise to do. You never leave or forsake me. You cause all things to work together for good in my life. You draw near to me when I draw near to You. You answer me when I call. Surely, You have proven Yourself to be nothing but trustworthy."

We often say, "Lord, I love You." But I wonder if it isn't more meaningful to say, "Lord, I trust You." I think it thrills the heart of the Father to be trusted.

May the Lord cause you to be one who trusts in Him. Whether or not you're where you should be, ought to be, or want to be—there is one thing I promise you: He is trustworthy. He's faithful. I'm so grateful. Aren't you?

30 Having been delivered from the near-disaster of fighting his own countrymen, David and his men return to Ziklag. But when they arrive, their hearts break . . .

1 Samuel 30:1, 2
And it came to pass, when David and his men were come to Ziklag on the third day, that the Amalekites had invaded the south, and Ziklag, and smitten Ziklag, and burned it with fire; And had taken the women captives, that were therein: they slew not any, either great or small, but carried them away, and went on their way.

Ziklag means "winding road." Life is like that. You think you have things all straightened out, all your ducks in the proverbial row, with nothing but smooth sailing ahead—until you come to a curve you weren't counting on, a pothole you didn't see. That's the way it will always be this side of heaven. But one day, when we're called away, the streets will be straight (Isaiah 40:4) and paved with gold (Revelation 21:21)—no more winding roads, no more potholes.

David finds a curve he wasn't counting on. He and his boys make it back to Ziklag to reunite with their families only to discover that the Amalekites had invaded the town, burned down their homes, and carried their families away. It was a brutal, devastating, heartbreaking situation.

Amalekite means "dweller in the valley." Each time the Amalekites are seen in Scripture, they're an illustration of the flesh, warring against the people of God. That is why God said to Moses, "You shall war against Amalek from generation to generation" (Exodus 17:16).

Whether it's due to the fleshly tendencies within us or to external enemies that seek to pull us down, you can count on a fight from Amalek. Right when you think you have things all figured out, another generation of Amalekites will rise up and war against you. Knowing this, aren't you thankful that He who is within you is greater than any Amalekite who comes against you? (1 John 4:4).

1 Samuel 30:3–5
So David and his men came to the city, and, behold, it was burned with fire; and their wives, and their sons, and their daughters, were taken captives. Then David and the people that were with him lifted up their voice and wept, until they had no more power to weep. And David's two wives were taken captives, Ahinoam the Jezreelitess, and Abigail the wife of Nabal the Carmelite.

Their city had been burned. Their families had been taken away. David understood why his men were grieving. His house had been burned, too. His family had been carried off as well. Thus, the captain of this rag-tag group of renegades was feeling exactly what his men were feeling.

The Captain of our salvation (Hebrews 2:10) relates to whatever trials and difficulties we face because He was tested in the very same areas (Hebrews 4:15). He knows what you're going through. He knows why you feel the way you do because He, too, has felt the heat of the attack of the enemy.

1 Samuel 30:6 (a)
And David was greatly distressed; for the people spake of stoning him, because the soul of all the people was grieved, every man for his sons and for his daughters . . .

Not only did David lose his house and his family, but his own men turned against him, ready to stone him. No doubt, they felt that David had dropped the ball and let them down. Already grieving over his own loss, yet seeing rocks in the hands of his men, he had reason to be distressed.

Maybe you were fired. Maybe your household is under attack. Maybe your spouse has drifted away. Maybe your kids have been carried away by the enemy. This is a story for you because there are four things I want you to see that allowed David to eventually recover all that he had lost . . .

1 Samuel 30:6 (b)
. . . but David encouraged himself in the LORD his God.

David encouraged himself in the Lord. This is where it starts. This is what we must do to get back all that's been ripped off by the enemy. David couldn't depend on his men. They were angry with him. There was no one to pat him on the back and say, "It'll be okay." There was no one to wipe away his tears. But that's the way it usually is. Don't wait for a pastor to come, a friend to show up, a neighbor to drop by when you're depressed. If you do, you might have a long wait. David knew what he had to do. Everything looked grim. But he chose to encourage himself in the Lord.

How?

We see the answer in Psalm 42 . . .

> Why art thou cast down, O my soul? and why art thou disquieted in me? hope thou in God: for I shall yet praise him for the help of his countenance. Psalm 42:5

I can be depressed, discouraged, despairing continually—or I can say, "Why are you this way, soul? Hope in God. Give praise to Him. Offer thanks to Him."

When I receive news that my city has been burned down, the first thing I must do is encourage myself in the Lord by thanking Him for the ways He has been so faithful time and time again. I reflect and remember—and begin to talk to the Lord audibly giving Him thanks for what He has done.

Little Tommy didn't understand this. When his mommy said, "You're going to have a baby brother or a baby sister," he was so thrilled that he told his kindergarten teacher. He told her again the next day. In fact, every day without fail he told her that he was going to have a baby brother or a baby sister.

One day, his mother said, "Tommy, come here." As she placed his hand on her stomach, she said, "Feel that? That's your baby brother or sister kicking!"

Tommy smiled faintly and walked away.

The next day when he went to school he didn't tell his teacher he was going to have a baby brother or a baby sister. He didn't bring it up the second, third, or fifth day, either. Finally, after a couple of weeks, his teacher said, "Tommy, you haven't talked about the baby that's coming."

Tommy burst into tears. "The baby's not coming," he cried. "My mommy ate it!"

Like Tommy, we don't understand things very well. *Oh, this is awful,* we think—failing to realize that God is up to something wonderful.

1 Samuel 30:7, 8

And David said to Abiathar the priest, Ahimelech's son, I pray thee, bring me hither the ephod. And Abiathar brought thither the ephod to David. And David inquired at the LORD, saying, Shall I pursue after this troop? shall I overtake them? And he answered him, Pursue: for thou shalt surely overtake them, and without fail recover all.

After encouraging himself in the Lord, *David inquired of the Lord.* "What do You want me to do, Lord?" The Lord answered him directly and quickly. And God will do the same with you.

It doesn't take as much as you think. Satan will say, "So you want to hear from the Lord? That's going to require three hours of constant prayer, three days of fasting, three weeks of getting away. You only have thirty minutes? God's not going to hear you. Ten minutes? Forget about it. Three minutes? You've got to be kidding. God's not going to give you direction in a three-minute prayer."

I challenge that. Ask Peter. He was on the Sea of Galilee. He had been walking on the water, but now he's sinking quickly. He didn't pray for three days, three months, three hours, or even three minutes. He prayed three words: "Lord, save me." And the Lord grabbed him by the hand and pulled him out of the water (Matthew 14:30, 31).

Satan will say, "It takes a lot more. That's not enough."

But Jesus said, "Do not think you're going to be heard because of your much speaking, your long praying. That's a heathen concept. When you pray, be simple" (see Matthew 6:7, 8).

1 Samuel 30:9, 10 (a)

So David went, he and the six hundred men that were with him, and came to the brook Besor, where those that were left behind stayed. But David pursued, he and four hundred men . . .

Thirdly, *David was engaged with the Lord.* Following praise and prayer, we see pursuit. Many times, people sit back and say, "Lord, if You want good things to come my way, bring them to me."

The Lord, however, says, "Take a step of faith. I'll be with you. I'll fight for you. But I want you to be engaged with Me. I don't want you passive because I want to prepare you for eternity."

To Elijah—another man who was depressed and holed up in a cave—God said, "Why are you in this cave of depression? You know better than this. I want you to go to Syria. I want you to anoint a new king. I want you to go to Israel and raise up a leader. I want you to find a young man named Elisha and mentor him. I have work for you to do" (1 Kings 19).

The Lord says the same thing to us. "Why are you in this cave? You know better than that. Do what you know, and you'll know what to do."

Having been encouraged, having inquired, now being engaged, the story goes on . . .

1 Samuel 30:10 (b)–15 (a)
. . . for two hundred abode behind, which were so faint that they could not go over the brook Besor. And they found an Egyptian in the field, and brought him to David, and gave him bread, and he did eat; and they made him drink water; And they gave him a piece of a cake of figs, and two clusters of raisins: and when he had eaten, his spirit came again to him: for he had eaten no bread, nor drunk any water, three days and three nights. And David said unto him, To whom belongest thou? and whence art thou? And he said, I am a young man of Egypt, servant to an Amalekite; and my master left me, because three days agone I fell sick. We made an invasion upon the south of the Cherethites, and upon the coast which belongeth to Judah, and upon the south of Caleb; and we burned Ziklag with fire. And David said to him, Canst thou bring me down to this company?

Finding a servant of an Amalekite left in the wilderness to die, David said, "Do you know where the Amalekites are? Can you take me to them?"

1 Samuel 30:15 (b)
. . . And he said, Swear unto me by God, that thou wilt neither kill me, nor deliver me into the hands of my master, and I will bring thee down to this company.

David gave his word that the Amalekite would be spared.

1 Samuel 30:16, 17
And when he had brought him down, behold, they were spread abroad upon all the earth, eating and drinking, and dancing, because of all the great spoil that they had taken out of the land of the Philistines, and out of the land of Judah. And David smote them from the twilight even unto the evening of the next day: and there escaped not a man of them, save four hundred young men, which rode upon camels, and fled.

Four hundred seems like a large number of escapees—unless there were thousands of Amalekites killed. Because David encouraged himself in the Lord, inquired of the Lord, and became engaged for the Lord, he was used mightily by the Lord.

1 Samuel 30:18, 19
And David recovered all that the Amalekites had carried away: and David rescued his two wives. And there was nothing lacking to them, neither small nor great, neither sons nor daughters, neither spoil, nor any thing that they had taken to them: David recovered all.

David recovered all that the Amalekites carried away—not some, not a lot, not a good percentage—but *all*. This is the Lord's will for you and His heart for me. He wants us to recover all that has been ripped off by sin, our flesh, and the enemy.

1 Samuel 30:20–22
And David took all the flocks and the herds, which they drave before those other cattle, and said, This is David's spoil. And David came to the two hundred men, which were so faint that they could not follow David, whom they had made also to abide at the brook Besor: and they went forth to meet David, and to meet the people that were with him: and when David came near to the people, he saluted them. Then answered all the wicked men and men of Belial, of those that went with David, and said, Because they went not with us, we will not give them ought of the spoil that we have recovered, save to every man his wife and his children, that they may lead them away, and depart.

Some of the four hundred men who accompanied David into battle insisted that the two hundred men who stayed behind to guard the supplies were not entitled to any of the spoil.

1 Samuel 30:23–25
Then said David, Ye shall not do so, my brethren, with that which the LORD hath given us, who hath preserved us, and delivered the company that came against us into our hand. For who will hearken unto you in this matter? but as his part is that goeth down to the battle, so shall his part be that tarrieth by the stuff: they shall part alike. And it was so from that day forward, that he made it a statute and an ordinance for Israel unto this day.

David encouraged himself in the Lord. David inquired of the Lord. David engaged himself for the Lord. Here, *David is inspired by the Lord* when he insisted that the men who guarded the supplies were as important as those on the front line.

You might not be a warrior. You might not be front and center. But if you're keeping the supply lines going by praying faithfully, giving financially, serving humbly, our Captain will insist that you get equal share of the reward. That's God's economy.

1 Samuel 30:26–31
And when David came to Ziklag, he sent of the spoil unto the elders of Judah, even to his friends, saying, Behold a present for you of the spoil of the enemies of the LORD; To them which were in Bethel, and to them which were in south Ramoth, and to them which were in Jattir, And to them which were in Aroer, and to them which were in Siphmoth, and to them which were in Eshtemoa, And to them which were in Rachal, and to them which were in the cities of the Jerahmeelites, and to them which were in the cities of the Kenites, And to them which were in Hormah, and to them which were in Chor-ashan, and to them which were in Athach, And to them which were in Hebron, and to all the places where David himself and his men were wont to haunt.

The story ends gloriously. David and his men got back more than they had lost—enough to share with the entire nation—"good measure, pressed down, and running over" (Luke 6:38). And that's God's heart for us, as well.

31 We come to the end of the sad, sorry saga of Saul. The first king of Israel had tragically hardened his heart against the Lord, turned his back on the Lord, and now will be judged by the Lord . . .

1 Samuel 31:1–7
Now the Philistines fought against Israel: and the men of Israel fled from before the Philistines, and fell down slain in mount Gilboa. And the Philistines followed hard upon Saul and upon his sons; and the Philistines slew Jonathan, and Abinadab, and Malchishua, Saul's sons. And the battle went sore against Saul, and the archers hit him; and he was sore wounded of the archers. Then said Saul unto his armour-bearer, Draw thy sword, and thrust me through therewith; lest these uncircumcised come and thrust me through, and abuse me. But his armour-bearer would not; for he was sore afraid. Therefore Saul took a sword, and fell upon it. And when his armour-bearer saw that Saul was dead, he fell likewise upon his sword, and died with him. So Saul died, and his three sons, and his armour-bearer, and all his men, that same day together. And when the men of Israel that were on the other side of the valley, and they that were on the other side Jordan, saw that the men of Israel fled, and that Saul and his sons were dead, they forsook the cities, and fled; and the Philistines came and dwelt in them.

Battling the Philistines, Saul saw his soldiers—including his own sons—fall round about him before he himself felt the piercing pain of a Philistine arrow.

So Saul died for his transgression which he committed against the LORD, even against the word of the LORD, which he kept not, and also for asking counsel of one that had a familiar spirit, to inquire of it; And inquired not of the LORD: therefore he slew him, and turned the kingdom unto David the son of Jesse.
1 Chronicles 10:13, 14

As his life drained from him, he told his armor-bearer to kill him. When the armor-bearer refused, Saul did that which was unethical, immoral, and sinful. Once again, taking matters into his own hands, he killed himself in an attempt to keep himself from being abused by the Philistines.

1 Samuel 31:8–10
And it came to pass on the morrow, when the Philistines came to strip the slain, that they found Saul and his three sons fallen in mount Gilboa. And they cut off his head, and stripped off his armour, and sent into the land of the Philistines round about, to publish it in the house of their idols, and among the people. And they put his armour in the house of Ashtaroth: and they fastened his body to the wall of Beth-shan.

Saul's suicide did not accomplish that which he intended, for his head was lopped off and passed around from city to city, and his naked corpse was nailed to the wall of a Philistine city as a spectacle for all to see.

1 Samuel 31:11–13
And when the inhabitants of Jabesh-gilead heard of that which the Philistines had done to Saul; All the valiant men arose, and went all night, and took the body of Saul and the bodies of his sons from the wall of Beth-shan, and came to Jabesh, and burnt them there. And they took their bones, and buried

them under a tree at Jabesh, and fasted seven days.

When the men of Jabesh-gilead received word that Saul's corpse was pinned to the wall of a Philistine city, their hearts were stirred with compassion. Marching all night, the men of Jabesh-gilead risked their lives to recover the bodies of Saul and his sons. The bodies were so mutilated that they eventually had to burn them. But they buried their bones under a tree in their own city.

What moved these men? Why would they risk their lives outnumbered and out manned to recover the headless corpse of a judged king?

I suggest it's because of something that happened forty years previously, when Saul was presented to Israel as her king. Certain people applauded. "Long live the king," they said. But others said, "We're not going to have this farmer from the tribe of Benjamin rule over us." And Saul realized that the opinion about him was divided. So he went back to his farm and plowed away—until word reached him that the men of Jabesh-gilead were in trouble.

When Nahash the Ammonite threatened to wage war against the men of Jabesh-gilead, Saul was moved with compassion and rallied the men of Israel. With the 330,000 men who answered his call, Saul marched all night to rescue the inhabitants of Jabesh-gilead. And the men of Jabesh-gilead never forgot it. And forty years later, when he was naked and humiliated, the men to whom Saul and shown mercy returned the favor.

In Luke 6:38, when Jesus said, "Whatever is measured out will be measured back to you," he was talking about mercy. If we are those who learn mercy (Matthew 9:13), if we are those who love mercy (Micah 6:8), mercy will be shown to us. It might not happen for forty years—but when we need it most, it will be there (Matthew 5:7).

There was another King whose body was pinned—not to a wall, but to a Cross. The agony was unbelievable; the humiliation, unspeakable. He was spiritually decapitated as well, for He was the Head—but where was His body. Except for John, all of His disciples had fled. He was burned in the fire of God's righteous indignation poured out upon Him. Yet, even as we see in our text, His bones were not broken.

And so we come to His Table day after day to say, "I remember what You did for me. We were about to be done in by the enemy, but You came from heaven to rescue us. Others might not remember. Others might not care. But we of Jabesh-gilead remember what You did when You marched all night and came to this world to save us."

2 SAMUEL

1 At the end of First Samuel, we saw Saul and his army fighting a losing battle against the Philistines on Mount Gilboa. Saul's soldiers were falling. Even his sons died near him. Finally, an arrow from a Philistine soldier pierced his own body. As his life was draining from him, he ordered his armor-bearer to kill him lest the Philistines torture him. When the armor-bearer refused, Saul fell on his own sword and died on Mount Gilboa.

Here, In 2 Samuel 1, we are given some additional information regarding this account . . .

2 Samuel 1:1, 2
Now it came to pass after the death of Saul, when David was returned from the slaughter of the Amalekites, and David had abode two days in Ziklag; It came even to pass on the third day, that, behold, a man came out of the camp from Saul with his clothes rent, and earth upon his head: and so it was, when he came to David, that he fell to the earth, and did obeisance.

Running from Saul, David and his band of renegades were holed up in Philistine country when a survivor of the battle on Mount Gilboa appeared before him.

2 Samuel 1:3, 4 (a)
And David said unto him, From whence comest thou? And he said unto him, Out of the camp of Israel am I escaped. And David said unto him, How went the matter? I pray thee, tell me . . .

Eager to hear of the outcome of the battle, David asks this man for information.

2 Samuel 1:4 (b)–7
. . . And he answered, That the people are fled from the battle, and many of the people also are fallen and dead; and Saul and Jonathan his son are dead also. And David said unto the young man that told him, How knowest thou that Saul and Jonathan his son be dead? And the young man that told him said, As I happened by chance upon mount Gilboa, behold, Saul leaned upon his spear; and, lo, the chariots and horsemen followed hard after him. And when he looked behind him, he saw me, and called unto me. And I answered, Here am I.

It would seem as though Saul had attempted suicide, but was unsuccessful.

2 Samuel 1:8–10 (a)
And he said unto me, Who art thou? And I answered him, I am an Amalekite. And he said unto me again, Stand, I pray thee, upon me, and slay me: for anguish is come upon me, because my life is yet whole in me. So I stood upon him, and slew him, because I was sure that he could not live after that he was fallen:

Twenty-five years earlier, God said to Saul, "I want you to kill every Amalekite." Why? The Amalekites were a constant problem for the people of Israel. As the Israelites made their way to the Promised Land, the Amalekites would attack the back of the pack—where the older folks, mothers with babies, and the sick and feeble would walk. Therefore, because they showed no mercy, God declared to Moses that he would war against the Amalekites from generation to generation (Exodus 17).

In 1 Samuel, God reiterated his charge against the Amalekites when he told Saul to destroy them—every man, woman, child, and all that they owned. Saul dutifully led the Israelite army in war against the Amalekites. When the battle was over, he said to Samuel, "Blessed be the Lord. We have obeyed what the Lord told us to do. We have been victorious over the Amalekites."

"If that's true," said Samuel, "what's the bleating I hear in my ear?"

"Oh," said Saul, "we saved a few of the sheep to sacrifice to the Lord."

"Who's that?" Samuel asked.

"Him? Oh, that's Agag, king of the Amalekites," Saul answered. "I brought him back here as a trophy."

Samuel then said to Saul, "Because you have not obeyed the Lord, the kingdom has been taken from you. You have lost your authority, opportunity, and ministry. You were supposed to kill every Amalekite, but because you compromised, because you did things your way, you're in trouble."

At the end of Saul's life, who finally does him in? Ironically, it was an Amalekite.

2 Samuel 1:10 (b)
. . . and I took the crown that was upon his head, and the bracelet that was on his arm, and have brought them hither unto my lord.

With Saul's crown and bracelet in hand, I'm sure this Amalekite was as pleased as punch. After all, knowing Saul had been chasing David, he would assume David would be delighted to hear that Saul was no longer on the scene. No doubt the Amalekite expected to be rewarded by David for killing his enemy.

2 Samuel 1:11–14
Then David took hold on his clothes, and rent them; and likewise all the men that were with him: And they mourned, and wept, and fasted until even, for Saul, and for Jonathan his son, and for the people of the Lord, and for the house of Israel; because they were fallen by the sword. And David said unto the young man that told him, Whence art thou? And he answered, I am the son of a stranger, an Amalekite. And David said unto him, How wast thou not afraid to stretch forth thine hand to destroy the Lord's anointed?

"Who do you think you are?" David said to the Amalekite. "How dare you stretch forth your hand and take the life of one anointed by the Lord." Even though Saul had hardened his heart against God, David recognized that Saul was king because the Lord allowed him to be. That is why, when he himself had opportunity to kill Saul on two separate occasions, he didn't do so. We're not to take matters into our own hands. David understood this.

2 Samuel 1:15, 16
And David called one of the young men, and said, Go near, and fall upon him. And he smote him that he died. And David said unto him, Thy blood be upon thy head; for thy mouth hath testified against thee, saying, I have slain the Lord's anointed.

The Amalekite thought he deserved a reward. Instead, he is killed. Throughout Scripture Amalek is an illustration of the flesh. We are to mortify—or kill—the flesh because if we don't annihilate and eradicate it, it will kill us (Romans 8:13). This Amalekite would have never existed had Saul obeyed God in the first place.

"Who are you?" asked Saul.

"I am an Amalekite—one of the guys you should have killed."

Saul lost the monarchy because he didn't understand that Amalek had to be dealt with. There are no excuses for sin, only a cure. And the cure is repentance. We aren't to explore, explain, or excuse sin. We're simply to acknowledge, confess, repent, and go our way free (John 8:11).

2 Samuel 1:17, 18
And David lamented with this lamentation over Saul and over Jonathan his son: (Also he bade them teach the children of Judah the use of the bow: behold, it is written in the book of Jasher.)

During this period of lamentation and mourning, David says, "We need to teach the young people to be archers." Why would he say this at that time? First Samuel 13 tells us that the Philistines had taken away all weapons and instruments of iron from the Israelites to ensure their own military advantage as they ruled the region. It would seem that it was Jonathan and Saul who introduced the bow and arrow to the people of Israel. The arrows would be tipped with stone, thus eliminating the need for iron.

The lesson for us is simple and practical. That is, if there's been a loss in your life, a hurt in your heart, an ache in your soul—here's the key: Get back in the battle. Wage war against the enemy. Serve the Lord with new intensity. Give Him more than you have ever given previously. If you don't you will remain in a state of depression and heaviness.

David showed great insight here. His call to arms would provide both a fitting commemoration of Saul and Jonathan, and needed restoration to the nation.

The chapter ends with the song David penned to honor his friend, Jonathan . . .

2 Samuel 1:19–21
The beauty of Israel is slain upon thy high places: how are the mighty fallen! Tell it not in Gath, publish it not in the streets of Askelon; lest the daughters of the Philis-

tines rejoice, lest the daughters of the uncircumcised triumph. Ye mountains of Gilboa, let there be no dew, neither let there be rain, upon you, nor fields of offerings: for there the shield of the mighty is vilely cast away, the shield of Saul, as though he had not been anointed with oil.

To this day, Mount Gilboa is completely barren because here, David cursed it as the place where Saul and Jonathan fell.

2 Samuel 1:22–27
From the blood of the slain, from the fat of the mighty, the bow of Jonathan turned not back, and the sword of Saul returned not empty. Saul and Jonathan were lovely and pleasant in their lives, and in their death they were not divided: they were swifter than eagles, they were stronger than lions. Ye daughters of Israel, weep over Saul, who clothed you in scarlet, with other delights, who put on ornaments of gold upon your apparel. How are the mighty fallen in the midst of the battle! O Jonathan, thou was slain in thine high places. I am distressed for thee, my brother Jonathan: very pleasant hast thou been unto me: thy love to me was wonderful, passing the love of women. How are the mighty fallen, and the weapons of war perished!

This is the sincere expression of a broken heart—not only for Jonathan, his close friend and brother—but also for Saul, the man who relentlessly chased him.

Maybe there's someone after you—throwing verbal spears in your direction, chasing you mercilessly. Would you write a song like this for him? In verse 19, David writes of Saul's and Jonathan's glory. In verse 21, he speaks of their strength and dignity. Verse 23 refers to their military prowess. In verse 24 is a tribute to Saul's economic leadership. In this, we see David's wonderful ability to approve the things that were excellent in Saul. This is what Paul said we are all to do (Philippians 1:10).

In fact, Paul goes on to say that we are to esteem others as better than ourselves (Philippians 2:3). Why? Because it's true. Every person you meet is better than you at something. He might pray with more intensity. He might be more artistic. He might have a greater understanding of certain spiritual principles. He might be able to fix a car.

All men are created in the image of God. The rabbis teach that the reason for the billions of people that inhabit the earth is that it takes billions of people to portray God properly. Every one of us has a little piece to contribute. Our job, therefore, is to look for the piece that speaks of God in the life of another.

"But I don't see anything good in him," you might say.

To you, I say, "Explore deeper. Watch and see what the Lord will do."

2

2 Samuel 2:1 (a)
And it came to pass after this . . .

"It came to pass after this"—after what? After Saul died. As David first comes into power, notice what he does . . .

2 Samuel 2:1 (b)
. . . that David inquired of the LORD, saying, Shall I go up into any of the cities of Judah? And the LORD said unto him, Go up. And David said, Whither shall I go up? And he said, Unto Hebron.

Here we see a real secret of David's success—why it was that he was used so effectively, why his life had so great an impact that we study him to this day. David was a man who inquired of the Lord.

"Is this the right time to go into the cities of Judah?" David asked.

"Yes," the Lord answered.

"Where should I go?" David asked.

"Go to Hebron," the Lord answered.

When David asked if it was time for him to go into the cities of Judah, God could have said, "Yes. Go to Hebron first." But He didn't do that. He gave David the specific information David asked for and waited until David asked for more.

The Lord does the same with us. He isn't reluctant to give guidance, but there's something more important than guidance. It's called intimacy. If you've prayed repeatedly for direction concerning a given situation but still aren't sure what the Lord would have you do, perhaps it's because He loves you so much that He wants to keep hearing from you. He wants you to come into His presence time and again. He wants you to feel the embrace of His grace.

Corrie Ten Boom asked this pointed question: "Is prayer your steering wheel, or is it your spare tire?" Many of us pull prayer out of the trunk when we're feeling flat or when there's a blowout. However, prayer ought to be the steering wheel guiding us through the day, keeping us out of the ruts and ditches of life. Some days I act like I can get through my day without prayer. How dumb of me. Prayer is the highest, most important calling of any believer. It will keep you out of the ditches of depression, the ruts of predictability, the snares of seduction. At the outset of his reign, David models the absolute necessity of prayer.

2 Samuel 2:2, 3
So David went up thither, and his two wives also, Ahinoam the Jezreelitess, and Abigail Nabal's wife the Carmelite. And his men that were with him did David bring up, every man with his household: and they dwelt in the cities of Hebron.

David asked the Lord what to do—and then did exactly what the Lord told him, bringing his rag-tag band of renegades along with him.

2 Samuel 2:4
And the men of Judah came, and there they anointed David king over the house of Judah. And they told David, saying, That the men of Jabesh-gilead were they that buried Saul.

I strongly suspect that the intention of the men of Judah was, "Now that you're in power, David, you should nail the men of Jabesh-gilead for showing compassion to your enemy."

2 Samuel 2:5–7
And David sent messengers unto the men of Jabesh-gilead, and said unto them, Blessed be ye of the LORD, that ye have shewed this kindness unto your lord, even unto Saul, and have buried him. And now the LORD shew kindness and truth unto you: and I also will requite you this kindness, because ye have done this thing. Therefore now let your hands be strengthened, and be ye valiant: for your master Saul is dead, and also the house of Judah have anointed me king over them.

"I'm proud of you," David said to the men of Jabesh-gilead. "Yes, I'm king. But I'm not out to get you."

2 Samuel 2:8–11
But Abner the son of Ner, captain of Saul's host, took Ish-bosheth the son of Saul, and brought him over to Mahanaim; And made him king over Gilead, and over the Ashurites, and over Jezreel, and over Ephraim, and over Benjamin, and over all Israel. Ish-bosheth Saul's son was forty years old when he began to reign over Israel, and reigned two years. But the house of Judah followed David. And the time that David was king in Hebron over the house of Judah was seven years and six months.

Wanting to retain power for Saul's family and for himself personally, Saul's cousin, Abner, grabs Saul's one remaining son and makes him king over all the tribes of Israel except Judah.

2 Samuel 2:12, 13
And Abner the son of Ner, and the servants of Ish-bosheth the son of Saul, went out from Mahanaim to Gibeon. And Joab the son of Zeruiah, and the servants of David, went out, and met together by the pool of Gibeon: and they sat down, the one on the one side of the pool, and the other on the other side of the pool.

David's nephew, Joab, called for a meeting with Abner, Saul's cousin.

2 Samuel 2:14, 15
And Abner said to Joab, Let the young men now arise, and play before us. And Joab said, Let them arise. Then there arose and went over by number twelve of Benjamin, which pertained to Ish-bosheth the son of Saul, and twelve of the servants of David.

"Why should we involve our entire armies?" Abner said. "I'll pick twelve of my best men, you do the same, and we'll let them battle it out. The winner will take all."

2 Samuel 2:16
And they caught every one his fellow by the head, and thrust his sword in his fellow's side; so they fell down together: wherefore that place was called Helkath-hazzurim, which is in Gibeon.

Abner's and Joab's experiment ended in a tie—with all twenty-four men dead.

2 Samuel 2:17 (a)
And there was a very sore battle that day; and Abner was beaten, and the men of Israel, before the servants of David . . .

When at last the armies got involved, Abner and his men were beaten by the men of Judah.

2 Samuel 2:17 (b)–19
. . . And there were three sons of Zeruiah there, Joab, and Abishai, and Asahel: and Asahel was as light of foot as a wild roe. And Asahel pursued after Abner; and in going he turned not to right hand nor to the left from following Abner.

As the battle drew to a close, Joab's brothers pursued Abner.

2 Samuel 2:20, 21
Then Abner looked behind him, and said, Art thou Asahel? And he answered, I am. And Abner said to him, Turn thee aside to thy right hand or to thy left, and lay thee hold on one of the young men, and take thee his armour.

"You're just a young man," Abner warned Asahel. "I'm an experienced warrior. You don't know what you're getting into. Go find someone else to chase."

2 Samuel 2:22, 23
And Abner said again to Asahel, Turn thee aside from following me: wherefore should I smite thee to the ground? how then should I hold up my face to Joab thy brother? Howbeit he refused to turn aside: wherefore Abner with the hinder end of the spear smote him under the fifth rib, that the spear came out behind him; and he fell down there, and died in the same place: and it came to pass, that as many as came to the place where Asahel fell down and died stood still.

After twice warning Asahel, Abner poked him with the blunt end of his spear in an apparent attempt to stop him without killing him.

2 Samuel 2:24, 25
Joab also and Abishai pursued after Abner: and the sun went down when they were come to the hill of Ammah, that lieth before Giah by the way of the wilderness of Gibeon. And the children of Benjamin gathered themselves together after Abner, and became one troop, and stood on the top of an hill.

Asahel's brothers, Joab and Abishai, take off after Abner. The Benjamites—Saul's tribe—show up on the scene with fresh reinforcements.

2 Samuel 2:26
Then Abner called to Joab, and said, Shall the sword devour for ever? knowest thou not that it will be bitterness in the latter end? how long shall it be then

"This will go on and on," Abner called to Joab. "It will be a feud that will never be resolved. Let's stop now before it becomes a bitter burden to both of us and to our nation."

2 Samuel 2:27, 28
And Joab said, As God liveth, unless thou hadst spoken, surely then in the morning the people had gone up every one from following his brother. So Joab blew a trumpet, and all the people stood still, and pursued after Israel no more, neither fought they any more.

Joab heeded Abner's words. The men of Judah stopped chasing the men of Israel.

2 Samuel 2:29–31
And Abner and his men walked all that night through the plain, and passed over Jordan, and went through all Bithron, and they came to Mahanaim. And Joab returned from following Abner: and when he had gathered all the people together, there lacked of David's servants nineteen men and Asahel. But the servants of David had smitten of Benjamin, and of Abner's men, so that three hundred and threescore men died.

A census of Joab's troops showed that nineteen of his men had died. However, three hundred and sixty men of Benjamin had died. Therefore, Abner's call for a cease-fire was a wise move on his part.

2 Samuel 2:32
And they took up Asahel, and buried him in the sepulchre of his father, which was in Bethlehem. And Joab and his men went all night, and they came to Hebron at break of day.

After beating Abner's army, Joab and his men return to Hebron.

3

2 Samuel 3:1
Now there was long war between the house of Saul and the house of David: but David waxed stronger and stronger, and the house of Saul waxed weaker and weaker.

At this time, David is ruling over Judah. At war against Abner and the household of Saul, there are battles raging, but Saul's forces are growing weaker and weaker. David, on the other hand, grows stronger.

Spiritually, Saul is a symbol of sin and self; David, a symbol of our Savior. There's a war going on in my soul that will last for a lifetime. But the house of Saul, the house of self, the house of sin grows weaker and weaker, while the kingdom of God grows stronger. Sure, there are setbacks along the way. There are defeats we have on certain days. But as I look back and chart the course, I can see that He who has begun a good work in me is indeed being faithful to complete it (Philippians 1:6). And because the One who resides in you is greater than the one who comes against you (1 John 4:4), even though you might have discouraging days, you can be sure that David becomes stronger as Saul grows weaker.

2 Samuel 3:2, 3
And unto David were sons born in Hebron: and his firstborn was Amnon, of Ahinoam the Jezreelitess; And his second, Chileab, of Abigail the wife of Nabal the Carmelite; and the third, Absalom the son of Maacah the daughter of Talmai king of Geshur;

David marries a pagan woman, the daughter of a Canaanite king. The product of that relationship will be a man named Absalom, who will cause David's heart to be broken and division in his kingdom.

"Be not unequally yoked," Paul warns (2 Corinthians 6:14). If you choose to be yoked with an unbeliever, it will break your heart down the road—guaranteed.

2 Samuel 3:4, 5
And the fourth, Adonijah the son of Haggith; and the fifth, Shephatiah the son of Abital; And the sixth, Ithream, by Eglah David's wife. These were born to David in Hebron.

David already had three wives, but as he adds more and more, the story gets worse and worse. According to Deuteronomy 17:17, kings were not to multiply horses, store gold, or multiply wives. Knowing the Word, David knows this.

David is very flawed. He has a propensity to lie. He's tempted by women. He has an ego that we'll see in the next part of the chapter. And yet overarching, he had a passion for God. We can have a tendency to say, "Sure, I sin. But I don't sin nearly to the degree David did." But that's the wrong perspective entirely. Don't measure your sins against David's. Instead, measure your virtues against his. David killed a giant. David danced before the Lord with passion. David wrote psalms. David was a lover of God. David was given to prayer. David praised God continually.

Am I a giant killer? Am I laying down everything for my Lord? Am I a poet and a prophet, a singer, dancer, and warrior for God? Are you? How strong is my passion for God? Can I truly say, "Only one thing have I desired of the Lord, and that will I seek after—to behold the beauty of the Lord and to inquire in His temple"?

Where did David get this passion for God? It was developed in the pastures as he watched his sheep and in the caves as he fled from Saul. It was developed through prayer, through spending time with God.

Maybe the Lord is whispering in your ear, "I see in you the same potential."

"How can this be?" you ask.

"Because I put David in that place," He answers. "I gave David that kind of grace. All He did was respond to My tugging and whispering."

The path to passion is not mysterious or even mystical. It's very simple and practical. When the Lord says, "Get up and pray," you say, "okay." When He tells you to take on that giant and share your faith, say, "Yes." When He inspires you to write a love letter to Him, grab your pen. It is not up to us to generate the fire of passion. Our job is simply to stir the coals (2 Timothy 1:6) through faithfulness and obedience.

2 Samuel 3:6
And it came to pass, while there was war between the house of Saul and the house of David, that Abner made himself strong for the house of Saul.

David has already been acknowledged as king by Samuel the prophet. But the people are waiting to see whether David can step up and take control. Consequently, there will be a seven and one-half-year battle to see who will ultimately gain control of the throne. During this time, Abner sees that Saul's son, *Ish-bosheth*, is a man who is not particularly gifted, strong, or capable. In fact, his name means, "man of shame." Abner realizes that if Saul's dynasty is to continue, it will be up to him. So he begins to consolidate an even greater degree of power.

2 Samuel 3:7
And Saul had a concubine, whose name was Rizpah, the daughter of Aiah: and Ish-bosheth said to Abner, Wherefore hast thou gone in unto my father's concubine?

At this time, when a man took another man's concubine he was, in essence, saying, "I'm stepping in to his shoes." That's why, a few chapters from now, when Absalom rebels against his dad, he is advised to take his dad's concubines as a sign to the nation that he is in control.

2 Samuel 3:8
Then was Abner very wroth for the words of Ish-bosheth, and said, Am I a dog's head, which against Judah do shew kindness this day unto the house of Saul thy father, to his brethren, and to his friends, and have not delivered thee into the hand of David, that thou chargest me to day with a fault concerning this woman?

"I have stood by you, Ish-bosheth," Abner said, defending his action. "the only reason you're still in power is because of me. How dare you treat me like a dog in this way."

2 Samuel 3:9–11
So do God to Abner, and more also, except, as the LORD hath sworn to David, even so I do to him; To translate the kingdom from the house of Saul, and to set up the throne of David over Israel and over Judah, from Dan even to Beer-sheba. And he could not answer Abner a word again, because he feared him.

Abner was so upset at Ish-bosheth for challenging him concerning the concubine that he said, "I'm going to see to it that God's promise to David comes to pass. I'm going to see to it that the kingdom is translated from Saul to David."

Paul uses the same word in Colossians 1 when he says, "We give thanks unto the Father, which hath made us meet to be partakers of the inheritance of the saints in light: Who hath delivered us from the power of darkness, and hath translated us into the kingdom of his dear Son" (see Colossians 1:12, 13). We have been translated. Once in the kingdom of darkness, we are now in the kingdom of light. Like Abner, once we were fighting against the Son of David, but now we follow after Him.

2 Samuel 3:12
And Abner sent messengers to David on his behalf, saying, Whose is the land? saying also, Make thy league with me, and, behold, my hand shall be with thee, to bring about all Israel unto thee.

"I'm here to negotiate with you, David," Abner said.

2 Samuel 3:13
And he said, Well; I will make a league with thee: but one thing I require of thee, that is, Thou shalt not see my face, except thou first bring Michal Saul's daughter, when thou comest to see my face.

Saul promised his daughter, Michal, to the man who could kill one hundred Philistines (1 Samuel 18:25). When David killed two hundred, Michal became his wife. But when David fled for his life, Saul gave Michal to another man. Here, David says, "I'll negotiate with you, Abner if you bring my wife back."

What's David doing? One thing he doesn't need is another wife. He already has six, and will add more as the story continues. It's an ego thing, no doubt. But perhaps it was also political. That is, if he could get Saul's daughter back, it would broaden his base of power.

2 Samuel 3:14–18
And David sent messengers to Ish-bosheth Saul's son, saying, Deliver me my wife Michal, which I espoused to me for an hundred foreskins of the Philistines. And Ish-bosheth sent, and took her from her husband, even from Phaltiel the son of Laish. And her husband went with her along weeping behind her to Bahurim. Then said Abner unto him, Go, return. And he returned. And Abner had communication with the elders of Israel, saying, Ye sought for David in times past to be king over you: Now then do it: for the LORD hath spoken of David, saying, By the hand of my servant David I will save my people Israel out of the hand of the Philistines, and out of the hand of all their enemies.

After switching his allegiance to David, Abner tells everyone to switch. "You delighted in David and wanted to follow him," he said. "Now do it."

Gang, that's the message I bring to you today: In the past, you've heard the gospel preached; you've understood something of the loveliness of Jesus Christ; you've desired to walk with Him; you've desired to devote your life to Him in service. Now is the time to do it. Not tomorrow, not next week, but *now* is the time to go for it (2 Corinthians 6:2).

2 Samuel 3:19, 20
And Abner also spake in the ears of Benjamin: and Abner went also to speak in the ears of David in Hebron all that seemed good to Israel, and that seemed good to the whole house of Benjamin. So Abner came to David to Hebron, and twenty men with him. And David made Abner and the men that were with him a feast.

Abner comes to Hebron to deliver Israel into David's hand.

2 Samuel 3:21
And Abner said unto David, I will arise and go, and will gather all Israel unto my lord the king, that they may make a league with thee, and that thou mayest reign over all that thine heart desireth. And David sent Abner away; and he went in peace.

Abner left to gather the people in order to anoint David as king of the entire nation.

2 Samuel 3:22–24
And, Behold, the servants of David and Joab came from pursuing a troop, and brought in a great spoil with them: but Abner was not with David in Hebron; for he had sent him

away, and he was gone in peace. When Joab and all the host that was with him were come, they told Joab, saying, Abner the son of Ner came to the king, and he hath sent him away, and he is gone in peace. Then Joab came to the king, and said, What hast thou done? behold, Abner came unto thee; why is it that thou hast sent him away, and he is quite gone?

When Joab learned that David had made a treaty with Abner, he was upset. After all, Joab had no use for Abner because Abner had killed his brother.

2 Samuel 3:25
Thou knowest Abner the son of Ner, that he came to deceive thee, and to know thy going out and thy coming in, and to know all that thou doest.

"Abner is spying out the situation so he can ultimately defeat you," Joab said.

2 Samuel 3:26
And when Joab was come out from David, he sent messengers after Abner, which brought him again from the well of Sirah: but David knew it not.

Unbeknownst to David, Joab sent messengers telling Abner to come back.

2 Samuel 3:27
And when Abner was returned to Hebron, Joab took him aside in the gate to speak with him quietly, and smote him there under the fifth rib, that he died, for the blood of Asahel his brother.

Tragically, Joab avenged the blood of his brother when he killed Abner under his fifth rib—just as Abner had done to Asahel (2:23).

2 Samuel 3:28, 29
And afterward when David heard it, he said, I and my kingdom are guiltless before the Lord for ever from the blood of Abner the son of Ner: Let it rest on the head of Joab, and on all his father's house; and let there not fail from the house of Joab one that hath an issue, or that is a leper, or that leaneth on a staff, or that falleth on the sword, or that lacketh bread.

"May Joab's family and all his descendants be cursed perpetually with leprosy, starvation, disease, and war," David said. "May what Joab has done come crashing down upon his head and upon his family as well."

I point this out because, as we'll see in the next chapter, Joab becomes David's chief of staff and will hold this post throughout David's entire forty-year reign. Like Joab, we are flawed. Yet, just as David used Joab, the Son of David will use us if we make ourselves available to Him.

2 Samuel 3:30, 31
So Joab and Abishai his brother slew Abner, because he had slain their brother Asahel at Gibeon in the battle. And David said to Joab, and to all the people that were with him, Rend your clothes, and gird you with sackcloth, and mourn before Abner. And king David himself followed the bier.

David walked behind Abner's coffin in the funeral procession.

2 Samuel 3:32–34
And they buried Abner in Hebron: and the king lifted up his voice, and wept at the grave of Abner; and all the people wept. And the king lamented over Abner, and said, Died Abner as a fool dieth? Thy hands were not bound, nor thy feet put into fetters: as a man falleth before wicked men, so fellest thou. And all the people wept again over him.

"What happened to Abner is not right," David said at Abner's funeral service. "He didn't deserve to die like he did. He wasn't imprisoned because of some wrong he had committed. He died foolishly because he was seduced, tricked, and lured out of the city."

You see, in Old Testament times, if a man killed someone unintentionally—as Abner had done—he could find protection from his victim's avengers by running to one of six cities of refuge located throughout Israel. If, however, he stepped outside of the gate of the city, he would no longer be protected. Hebron was a city of refuge. That is why Joab had to meet with Abner at the gate (v. 27) in order to kill him.

Jesus Christ is our refuge. Don't be lured away from Him, gang, or else you'll lose the safety, security, satisfaction, and protection He offers to you. Abner was a great warrior, a true leader, loyal to a fault, a wise man—but he died as a fool because he stepped away from the city of refuge. Don't let this happen to you. Stay within the city of refuge, under the shadow of the wings of Jesus (Luke 13:34).

2 Samuel 3:35, 36
And when all the people came to cause David to eat meat while it was yet day, David sware, saying, So do God to me, and more also, if I taste bread, or ought else, till the

sun be down. And all the people took notice of it, and it pleased them: as whatsoever the king did pleased all the people.

"This is good," the people said. "David isn't rejoicing that the man who fought against him is now dead. David is a man of compassion and forgiveness, grace and mercy. This is the kind of man we can follow."

2 Samuel 3:37–39
For all the people and all Israel understood that day that it was not of the king to slay Abner the son of Ner. And the king said unto his servants, Know ye not that there is a prince and a great man fallen this day in Israel? And I am this day weak, though anointed king; and these men the sons of Zeruiah be too hard for me: the LORD shall reward the doer of evil according to his wickedness.

Abner means "enlightening." Abner was a man who spent most of his life fighting against David. But there came a time when he turned around and joined with David. As such, he is a wonderful illustration, an important picture of people who spend much of their lives fighting against the Son of David, Jesus Christ. But finally, they become enlightened and follow Him.

In preaching a simple message, telling his people to follow David, little did Abner know that 18,000 fighting men would transfer their allegiance from the household of Ish-bosheth to become part of the kingdom of David. The same can be true of you. The one simple message you preach as you change allegiance can make all the difference in the world. Therefore, I call upon lukewarm Christians to consider if the Lord is allowing unhappiness and uneasiness to take place in your life because your allegiance is not solid, your commitment not sincere. Who are you fighting for? What side are you really on? Turn to Him today. He will abundantly pardon.

4

2 Samuel 4:1–4
And when Saul's son heard that Abner was dead in Hebron, his hands were feeble, and all the Israelites were troubled. And Saul's son had two men that were captains of bands: the name of the one was Baanah, and the name of the other Rechab, the sons of Rimmon a Beerothite, of the children of Benjamin: (for Beeroth also was reckoned to Benjamin: And the Beerothites fled to Gittaim, and were sojourners there until this day.) And Jonathan, Saul's son, had a son that was lame of his feet. He was five years old when the tidings came of Saul and Jonathan out of Jezreel, and his nurse took him up, and fled: and it came to pass, as she made haste to flee, that he fell, and became lame. And his name was Mephibosheth.

The death of Saul would mean there would be a new king. The custom of the day was that, when a new king ascended to power, everyone in the previous king's family would be killed. Therefore, hearing that Saul and Jonathan had died, Jonathan's son's nurse grabbed him and ran to protect him from what she knew would otherwise come his way.

2 Samuel 4:5, 6
And the sons of Rimmon the Beerothite, Rechab and Baanah, went, and came about the heat of the day to the house of Ish-bosheth, who lay on a bed at noon. And they came thither into the midst of the house, as though they would have fetched wheat; and they smote him under the fifth rib: and Rechab and Baanah his brother escaped.

Pretending to be delivering wheat, Ishbosheth's captains killed him in his sleep.

2 Samuel 4:7, 8
For when they came into the house, he lay on his bed in his bedchamber, and they smote him, and slew him, and beheaded him, and took his head, and gat them away through the plain all night. And they brought the head of Ish-bosheth unto David to Hebron, and said to the king, Behold the head of Ish-bosheth the son of Saul thine enemy, which sought thy life; and the LORD hath avenged my lord the king this day of Saul, and of his seed.

Ish-bosheth's captains brought his head to David, no doubt thinking he would reward them for killing the one man who stood between him and the throne.

2 Samuel 4:9, 10
And David answered Rechab and Baanah his brother, the sons of Rimmon the Beerothite, and said unto them, As the LORD liveth, who hath redeemed my soul out of all adversity, When one told me, saying, Behold, Saul is dead, thinking to have brought good tidings, I took hold of him, and slew him in Ziklag, who thought that I would have given him a reward for his tidings:

In response, David told the two captains about another who thought he would be rewarded for the death of David's enemy (2 Samuel 1).

2 Samuel 4:11, 12
How much more, when wicked men have slain a righteous person in his own house upon his bed? shall I not therefore now require his blood of your hand, and take you away from the earth? And David commanded his young men, and they slew them, and cut off their hands and their feet, and hanged them up over the pool in Hebron. But they took the head of Ish-bosheth, and buried it in the sepulchre of Abner in Hebron.

The repugnance of the punishment of this crime was matched only by David's abhorrence of the murder of an innocent man upon his bed.

5

2 Samuel 5:1–3
Then came all the tribes of Israel to David unto Hebron, and spake, saying, Behold, we are thy bone and thy flesh. Also in time past, when Saul was king over us, thou wast he that leddest out and broughtest in Israel: and the LORD said to thee, Thou shalt feed my people Israel, and thou shalt be a captain over Israel. So all the elders of Israel came to the king to Hebron; and king David made a league with them in Hebron before the LORD: and they anointed David king over Israel.

Anointing speaks of the empowering, the authority, the ability to do that which God has called one to do. The first time David was anointed was in 1 Samuel 16 when he was anointed before his family. This is always where the first anointing comes. If it doesn't work at home, it doesn't work at all. If you're interested in some ministry, but it isn't manifested at home in the eyes of your family, forget about it. David's brothers looked at their younger sibling and saw Samuel pour out the oil from the horn upon his head. They couldn't figure it out—but they knew it was real.

That's not the way it works, they may have thought. *It's supposed to be the oldest, the strongest, or the most handsome one who is anointed—not David, the shepherd boy.* His brothers questioned him, even chastised him (1 Samuel 17:28)—until they saw him kill Goliath.

Your calling begins at the point your brothers, your family, your husband, wife, or kids say, "There is an anointing on you. I can't figure out why. It seems like I should be the one. But I have to admit that giants are falling; things are getting done; you are truly communing with the Lord." As his brothers castigated, questioned, and doubted him, David learned to say, "I know that even if my brothers don't fully understand, even if it doesn't seem I'm the most likely candidate, I know God has called me. So I'm going to trust the Lord will do what He's called me to do. I'll watch my father's sheep. I'll take my brothers' taunts. I'll do the menial jobs and let them go off to war. If I stay home and don't go to the battlefield—or the mission field—that's okay. I'm going to live my life in hope and humility."

David was anointed again in 2 Samuel 2:4 before his tribe, the men of Judah. Why? For seven and one-half years, he didn't take things into his own hands. He didn't kill Saul when he had an opportunity. He didn't kill Ish-bosheth. He didn't even want to see Abner killed. Instead, he had faith in God and plugged away day after month after year. I'm sure his advisors were saying, "Take control of the situation, David." But David wouldn't do it. He simply faithfully served his tribe and had faith that God would do what was right in due season.

Likewise, not only your family, but also your peers will sense that the Lord is doing something in and through you as you are faithful in whatever task God puts before you. "Despise not the day of small beginnings," Zechariah declares (4:10). You might not be at the full orb of what you desire to be or to do. But if you are faithful to do what is before you—regardless of how big or small it might be—your "tribe" will confirm that God's hand is upon you.

The third time David is anointed is here in chapter 5, when he is anointed before the entire nation. Before his family, David exhibited humility and hope. Before his tribe, he was faithful. Before the nation, David proved his love. How? We read in verse 1 "*Then* came all the tribes of Israel to David . . ." When did the tribes come? After Saul had died, after Abner had died, after his enemies were removed from the scene, and after David had mourned for them all. David was anointed when the people saw him as a man of grace, of mercy, of love.

The three great attributes identified in 1 Corinthians 13 are faith, hope, and love. David embodies all three. He shows hope and humility as he serves his family, faith and faithfulness as he leads his tribe, and love as he rules the nation. What qualities do you desire as a person, as a parent, as a preacher? As seen in the three-fold anointing of David, they will take longer to develop than you think. But they will come to full fruition when, like David, you show you truly care about people because the greatest of qualities is indeed love (1 Corinthians 13:13).

2 Samuel 5:4, 5
David was thirty years old when he began to reign, and he reigned forty years. In He-

bron he reigned over Judah seven years and six months: and in Jerusalem he reigned thirty and three years over all Israel and Judah.

Throughout Scripture, the age of thirty seems to be significant. Joseph began his reign as prime minister of Egypt when he was thirty. The priests began their ministry in Israel when they reached the age of thirty. And, of course, our Lord Jesus began His public ministry when He was thirty.

2 Samuel 5:6 (a)
And the king and his men went to Jerusalem unto the Jebusites, the inhabitants of the land . . .

David knew the city of Jerusalem was strategic. It was geographically strategic because it was surrounded on three sides by a valley, making it a hard place to attack. It was also politically strategic because it straddled the boundary line between Judah and Benjamin, making it impossible for any one tribe to claim it. It was also historically significant, dating back to the days of the patriarchs.

2 Samuel 5:6 (b)
. . . which spake unto David, saying, Except thou take away the blind and the lame, thou shalt not come in hither: thinking, David cannot come in hither.

This was not only a taunt, but also a tactic, for the Jebusites would place their blind and lame on top of the city walls as an alarm system. You see, if an enemy attempted to enter the city, the finely tuned ears of the blind would hear them. The lame, unable to run to safety, would simply holler for help, thereby alerting the city.

2 Samuel 5:7 (a)
Nevertheless David took the strong hold of Zion . . .

This is the first time Zion is mentioned in the Bible. Zion is another name for Jerusalem, and it eventually refers to the Temple Mount area. I find it appropriate that the word *Zion* can be translated either "parched place" or "sunny spot." It all depends on one's perspective. Either way, it was a "hot spot"—just as it is to this day.

2 Samuel 5:7 (b)
. . . the same is the city of David.

There are two places referred to as the city of David. One is Jerusalem. The other is the place he was born—the city of Bethlehem.

2 Samuel 5:8
And David said on that day, Whosoever getteth up to the gutter, and smiteth the Jebusites, and the lame and the blind, that are hated of David's soul, he shall be chief and captain. Wherefore they said, The blind and the lame shall not come into the house.

David wanted the city of Jerusalem for both spiritual and strategic reasons. So he said to his men, "The first guy who can find a way into the walled city of Zion will be my general." The fact that Jerusalem was surrounded by valleys on three sides and a mountain on the fourth made David's challenge seem impossible. Yet, with no water source on the inside, David knew that, because the Jebusites couldn't survive without water, there had to be a camouflaged shaft descending seventy-five feet to the Kidron River below.

First Chronicles 11 tells us the name of the man who found the shaft was Joab. As we have seen, Joab was not the most upstanding man. But one thing he did do: He found a way to get into the city. Joab's example is vital for us. You see, we serve a Greater than David—the Son of David—Jesus Christ. Like David, Jesus desires to take cities. But He also desires to take countries, families, and individuals. He wants to beat back the spiritual Jebusites who keep people in bondage. So what does He do? He comes to people like you and me and says, "I want to talk to him; I want to see her saved; I want to touch them. And the first person who will shimmy up the shaft will be My man." Like Joab, we might not be the greatest, the most worthy, or the most spiritual. But if we are simply willing to shimmy up the shaft, He'll use us mightily.

There are desires the Lord places on your heart, thoughts He puts in your mind, things you know the Lord would want to do—to talk to your neighbor, to teach a Bible study, to reach your coworkers. But as sure as you feel that tug on the strings of your soul, you hear the taunting of the enemy, saying, "You're blind. You're lame. There's no way you can make an impact." If that's the way you see yourself, you are in a perfect position to be blessed, for it was especially the blind and lame whom Jesus healed (Matthew 21).

William Carey, the great missionary who opened the continent of India for the gospel, said, "Attempt great things for God and expect great things from God." In other words—"Shimmy up the shaft."

The Jebusites will say you don't have a prayer. Jesus, however, says, "I've healed your blind eyes and lame feet. Now look to Me and step out because there are people, families, and cities I want to claim through you."

2 Samuel 5:9
So David dwelt in the fort, and called it the city of David. And David built round about from Millo and inward.

Millo refers to the northern, vulnerable side of Jerusalem. David built terraces on the northern side, thus making any who attacked from the north easy targets and virtual sitting ducks.

2 Samuel 5:10
And David went on, and grew great, and the LORD God of hosts was with him.

David went on and grew great, or, literally in the Hebrew text, "David went going and growing." I like that. "Lord, let that be me. Help me to keep going and help me to keep growing." The Lord will take you as far as you want to go—but not one step further.

David was a man after God's heart. He wanted more of Him, wanted to be closer to Him, wanted to gain more knowledge about Him. What about you? Was there ever a time in your walk when you were closer to the Lord than you are now, when you felt His presence to a greater degree, when you were drawn to Him in greater intimacy? If so, I have great news for you. Right here, right now, you can say, "Lord, I'm here. I've been bogged down. But here I am. Take me deeper. Take me further. I want to keep going and I want to keep growing." And I guarantee He'll hear your prayer.

2 Samuel 5:11
And Hiram king of Tyre sent messengers to David, and cedar trees, and carpenters, and masons: and they built David an house.

Hiram was in Tyre—or present-day Lebanon, thirty-five miles north of Haifa. Although Hiram was not a Jew, he was wise enough to recognize that David's God was blessing Israel mightily and that it would be wise for him to assist David and to ally himself with Israel. To this end, he sent supplies and workers to construct a palace for David.

2 Samuel 5:12
And David perceived that the LORD had established him king over Israel, and that he had exalted his kingdom for his people Israel's sake.

David understood that God was blessing his kingdom for His people's sake. In other words David said, "God has blessed me to be a blessing." What a key understanding this is. I'm convinced God is looking for people to bless who want to be blessed for one purpose: that they might be a blessing to others.

"Lord, make me a servant," we say. But the true test of servanthood is very simple: How do we respond when people treat us like servants—when they order us around, never say thanks, and don't even notice what we do? If we get offended and upset, we're not yet servants. May we be those who, like David, understand that blessing is bestowed upon us in order that we might be a blessing to others.

2 Samuel 5:13–16
And David took him more concubines and wives out of Jerusalem, after he was come from Hebron: and there were yet sons and daughters born to David. And these be the names of those that were born unto him in Jerusalem; Shammua, and Shobab, and Nathan, and Solomon, Ibhar also, and Elishua, and Nepheg, and Japhia, And Elishama, and Eliada, and Eliphalet.

David is a godly man, but he has real flaws. Not only does he struggle with lying, but with a tendency to be attracted to many women. Here, he does what is forbidden in Deuteronomy 17 by gathering numerous wives and concubines. Although God will continue to use David, the consequences of these concubines and multiple wives will be difficulty and heartbreak, as we will see.

David has problems to be sure—but he also has a passion for God like no other. Oh, that we would long for that as well.

2 Samuel 5:17 (a)
But when the Philistines heard that they had anointed David king over Israel, all the Philistines came up to seek David . . .

The five Philistine cities joined forces and attacked David. When? Right after he had gained a great victory in conquering Jerusalem. This is often what happens. It was after Abraham built an altar to the Lord that there was strife among his and Lot's herdsmen. It was after Joseph had a dream and God gave him revelation that his brothers turned against him. It was after Elijah called down fire from heaven and there was a great victory on Mount Carmel that Jezebel threatened to take his life.

Note and remember that, following victory, there will usually come an attack from the enemy. Count that there will come an attack from the enemy. Whenever you take Jerusalem, capture new territory, step out in ministry, the enemy will hear about it and show up.

2 Samuel 5:17 (b)
. . . and David heard of it, and went down to the hold.

I like this. David didn't go *up* to fight. He didn't go *out* to battle. He went *down* to the hold. This speaks to me of humility. He didn't stand up to the Philistines that day. Instead, he went down before God to pray.

2 Samuel 5:18, 19 (a)
The Philistines also came and spread themselves in the valley of Rephaim. And David inquired of the LORD, saying, Shall I go up to the Philistines? wilt thou deliver them into mine hand?

Rephaim means "Valley of the Giants." Although David was a giant-killer, he didn't say, "I've already killed the biggest giant of them all. This will be no problem." No, he said, "Lord what do You want me to do?"

2 Samuel 5:19 (b)
. . . And the LORD said unto David, Go up: for I will doubtless deliver the Philistines into thine hand.

You might be a giant-killer. You might think, *I can handle this problem. I know how to deal with those things—I've done it before.* But David didn't think that way. This man who has a heart for God stops and prays. "Is this what *You* want, Lord?"

2 Samuel 5:20
And David came to Baal-perazim, and David smote them there, and said, The LORD hath broken forth upon mine enemies before me, as the breach of waters. Therefore he called the name of that place Baal-perazim.

Baal-perazim means "breach of waters," or "breakthrough."

"The Lord has given me this breakthrough," David declared. "It wasn't my strategy. It wasn't my ability. It wasn't my energy. I prayed to the Lord, and *He* secured the victory."

2 Samuel 5:21
And there they left their images, and David and his men burned them.

In Deuteronomy 7, God declared that the images of the enemies were to be burned. In Deuteronomy 17, God declared that kings were not to gather to themselves multiple wives. Although David had a hard time with Deuteronomy 17, he nails Deuteronomy 7. We must do the same. Any images that are of the enemy—be they books, magazines, music, or videos—must be destroyed—not controlled, not saved, not sold—but destroyed.

2 Samuel 5:22, 23 (a)
And the Philistines came up yet again, and spread themselves in the valley of Rephaim. And when David inquired of the LORD . . .

David had already beaten the same people in the same place. But David was a man who sought a fresh word from the Lord for each and every situation. He didn't assume anything. How I want to be more like him.

2 Samuel 5:23 (b)
. . . he said, Thou shalt not go up; but fetch a compass behind them, and come upon them over against the mulberry trees.

Earlier, David went right into the valley and confronted the enemy head to head. Here, he's in the same valley, facing the same enemy, but the Lord gave him a different strategy. And in this, it's as if God says to us, "Forget about yesterday's strategy. It was good for then, but not for today. Stay in constant touch with Me."

2 Samuel 5:24, 25
And let it be, when thou hearest the sound of a going in the tops of the mulberry trees, that then thou shalt bestir thyself: for then shall the LORD go out before thee, to smite the host of the Philistines. And David did so, as the LORD had commanded him; and smote the Philistines from Geba until thou come to Gazer.

The leaves of the mulberry trees in Israel are so light that even the slightest breeze will cause them to move. In fact, even an army would provide sufficient breeze to cause the mulberry leaves to move. If this massive Philistine army suddenly began to mobilize and move toward Jerusalem, that would indeed generate a large enough breeze to move the leaves—which would be a signal to David as to which direction they were marching.

In John 3:8, Jesus likened the Spirit to the wind. In Acts 2, the Spirit came with the sound of a mighty rushing wind. In other words, the work of the Spirit is supernaturally natural. "That's just soldiers on the move," the world says. But the believer who chooses to have eyes to see will see God's hand behind everything.

Driving home today, I saw beautiful poppies blossoming beside the road. "Lord, this is so wonderful," I said. "Thank You for these bouquets."

And it was as if the Lord said, "These are for everyone and anyone who has eyes to see that I love them."

"What do you mean?" the cynic scoffs. "Those poppies are simply the result of seeds that fell or were blown there."

If that's how you choose to look at them, you can. But I chose to look at them as bouquets from God because *every* good and perfect gift is from above (James 1:17). If you cultivate this kind of mindset, you will see the work of the Spirit constantly. To live in the Spirit means you see everything as from God's hand—no matter what means He uses to bring it about.

6 David has just become king of the entire nation of Israel. And in the chapter before us, we see one of his first acts as king. David desired that his people experience what he experienced. He had experienced the glory of God, and he wanted everyone in the nation to experience God's glory.

When Adam and Eve walked with God in the cool of the day in the Garden of Eden, they were surrounded by the *chabod*, the glory of God. When they sinned, when they ate of the forbidden fruit, the chabod departed and suddenly they sought to cover their nakedness, their emptiness with fig leaves. Ever since that time, people have been on a quest to cover themselves—to experience the weight, the substance of God's glory.

In Old Testament times, the glory of God, the *chabod*, was directly linked to the ark of the covenant because it was at the mercy seat that He chose to meet with His people (Leviticus 16:2). Therefore, David wanted the ark of the covenant to be brought to Jerusalem so that the people in the nation could experience the glory, the *chabod*, the presence of God. The problem was, the ark wasn't in Jerusalem. It was thirteen miles away at a place called Kirjath-jearim (1 Samuel 6:21).

2 Samuel 6:1, 2
Again, David gathered together all the chosen men of Israel, thirty thousand. And David arose, and went with all the people that were with him from Baale of Judah, to bring up from thence the ark of God, whose name is called by the name of the LORD of hosts that dwelleth between the cherubims.

Baale is another name for Kirjath-jearim because years previously, Baal was worshiped there. A huge parade accompanied the return of the ark from Kirjath-jearim. That's often what people still try today. "How can we see the glory of God in this church or in our family?" they ask. "We'll have a big parade and gather a stadium full of people."

2 Samuel 6:3 (a)
And they set the ark of God upon a new cart . . .

What is a cart? It's nothing more than boards and big wheels. I like the analogy because all too often when we want to see God's glory in the church we think the answer begins with a board meeting and some big wheels.

2 Samuel 6:3 (b), 4
. . . and brought it out of the house of Abinadab that was in Gibeah: and Uzzah and Ahio, the sons of Abinadab, drave the new cart. And they brought it out of the house of Abinadab which was at Gibeah, accompanying the ark of God: and Ahio went before the ark.

The man steering the car was *Uzzah*, whose name means "Strength." The man in front, leading the way, was *Ahio*, whose name means "Friendly." Catch the scene: Mr. Friendly was out in front slapping backs, passing out bulletins, giving high fives. Mr. Strong was driving the cart. And a parade of people followed behind.

2 Samuel 6:5
And David and all the house of Israel played before the LORD on all manner of instruments made of fir wood, even on harps, and on psalteries, and on timbrels, and on cornets, and on cymbals.

The word "cornets" is better translated "castanets." All of these instruments were played with the hand. It was a "hands-on" experience because the people mistakenly thought they could "handle" the situation themselves.

2 Samuel 6:6
And when they came to Nachon's threshingfloor, Uzzah put forth his hand to the ark of God, and took hold of it; for the oxen shook it.

The cart is rolling along. Mr. Friendly is out in front. Mr. Strong is at the wheel. The people are playing their guitars—when suddenly they hit a bump and the ark begins to teeter. "No problem," Mr. Strong must have thought as he reached back to stabilize the ark, to give God a hand.

I've been here. Perhaps you have, too. We have our parades, our programs, our big ideas, our grand plans. And even if we hit a bump, we think we can solve the problem by our own efforts. I find it more than coincidental that the problem occurred at a threshingfloor. You see, when a farmer harvested his wheat, he would bring it to the threshingfloor, throw it up in the air, and let the wind blow away the chaff, leaving the grain itself to fall to the ground. The threshingfloor was the place where the grain was separated from the chaff, where the substantial was separated from the trivial.

2 Samuel 6:7
And the anger of the LORD was kindled against Uzzah; and God smote him there for his error; and there he died by the ark of God.

Suddenly, the parade stopped. Everyone was at a standstill.

2 Samuel 6:8 (a)
And David was displeased, because the LORD had made a breach upon Uzzah . . .

David thought he was doing something for God—but now realizes it wasn't accepted by God.

2 Samuel 6:8 (b)
. . . and he called the name of the place Perez-uzzah to this day.

Perez-uzzah literally means "the falling of Uzzah."

2 Samuel 6:9
And David was afraid of the LORD that day, and said, How shall the ark of the LORD come to me?

"How shall the ark of the Lord come to me?" This is the key question for every parent, church, and ministry. How will God's glory fill my house, my family, my church?

2 Samuel 6:10, 11 (a)
So David would not remove the ark of the LORD unto him into the city of David: but David carried it aside into the house of Obed-edom the Gittite. And the ark of the LORD continued in the house of Obed-edom the Gittite three months . . .

For three months, the ark was kept in the house of a man named Obed-edom.

2 Samuel 6:11 (b), 12 (a)
. . . and the LORD blessed Obed-edom, and all his household. And it was told king David, saying, The LORD hath blessed the house of Obed-edom, and all that pertaineth unto him, because of the ark of God . . .

When David received reports that Obed-edom had been blessed, he realized the ark needed to be in Jerusalem.

2 Samuel 6:12 (b)
. . . So David went and brought up the ark of God from the house of Obed-edom into the city of David with gladness.

In verse 8, David was displeased. In verse 9, he was afraid. Here in verse 12, he's glad. Why? Because evidently during the three months the ark was in the house of Obed-edom, David searched the Scriptures and found how the ark was to be carried (Exodus 25:14).

2 Samuel 6:13 (a)
And it was so, that when they that bare the ark of the LORD . . .

This time, there are no boards or big wheels. This time, there are no parades or tambourines. This time, the ark was carried in simplicity and humility on the shoulders of four priests.

2 Samuel 6:13 (b)
. . . had gone six paces, he sacrificed oxen and fatlings.

To sacrifice an animal required great energy and effort—yet David expended this energy and effort every six steps. The world places great value on efficiency. Moving the ark on a cart would have been vastly more efficient than carrying it and stopping every six steps. God, however, values effectiveness. Efficiency is doing things right. Effectiveness is doing the right thing. What's the right thing? Stopping every six steps.

You see, throughout Scripture, six is the number of man and the flesh. Therefore, offering sacrifice every six steps says, "Because I'm a man who deals with my flesh, I've got to stop every six steps, build an altar, and lay my dreams, my objectives, and my life down." Stopping every six steps says, "Lord, it's not about what I want to do. It's about what You want me to do. Therefore, I'm going to offer You the sacrifice of praise. I'm going to confess my fleshly tendencies every six steps throughout the day."

It's in stopping throughout the day to be "altared" that the *chabod,* the presence of God will enter your city, your ministry, your family, your soul.

2 Samuel 6:14
And David danced before the LORD with all his might; and David was girded with a linen ephod.

As the new king, David could have been adorned in regal robes. David, however, cared more about how he worshiped than about what he wore. So he danced before the Lord in his undergarments.

2 Samuel 6:15
So David and all the house of Israel brought up the ark of the LORD with shouting, and with the sound of the trumpet.

On the ark's ill-fated first journey, it was accompanied by music played with the hands: castanets, harps, lyres. Here, it's accompanied by wind instruments—the mouth and trumpets—because breath is symbolic of the Spirit, and it is not by might nor by power but by the Spirit that anything of significance is ever accomplished (Zechariah 4:6).

2 Samuel 6:16
And as the ark of the LORD came into the city of David, Michal Saul's daughter looked through a window, and saw king David leaping and dancing before the LORD; and she despised him in her heart.

Because the Lord inhabits the praise of His people (Psalm 22:3), the ark of the Lord was accompanied by those who praised. Because Michal was one who despised praise, we will see barrenness enter her life.

2 Samuel 6:17, 18
And they brought in the ark of the LORD, and set it in his place, in the midst of the tabernacle that David had pitched for it: and David offered burnt offerings and peace offerings before the LORD. And as soon as David had made an end of offering burnt offerings and peace offerings, he blessed the people in the name of the LORD of hosts.

Notice that David offered sacrifice to the Lord before he blessed the people. Dear brother, precious sister, follow David's example and bless the Lord first. Offer the sacrifice of praise. Be a worshiper—and then you can go out and bless those around you. It is only after you spend time blessing the Lord that you can be a true blessing to others.

2 Samuel 6:19
And he dealt among all the people, even among the whole multitude of Israel, as well to the women as men, to every one a cake of bread, and a good piece of flesh, and a flagon of wine. So all the people departed every one to his house.

"To every one a cake of bread, and a good piece of flesh, and a flagon of wine." Bread and wine are the symbols of Communion. Hebrews 5 tells us that meat is a symbol of the substance of the Word. When we're "altared" every six steps, when we're worshiping the Lord with simplicity and sincerity, when we're waiting on Him, there is Communion and substance for everyone.

2 Samuel 6:20
Then David returned to bless his household. And Michal the daughter of Saul came out to meet David, and said, How glorious was the king of Israel to day, who uncovered himself to day in the eyes of the handmaids of his servants, as one of the vain fellows shamelessly uncovereth himself!

Michal greeted David by berating him.

2 Samuel 6:21, 22
And David said unto Michal, It was before the LORD, which chose me before thy father, and before all his house, to appoint me ruler over the people of the LORD, over Israel: therefore will I play before the LORD. And I will yet be more vile than thus, and will be base in mine own sight: and of the maidservants which thou hast spoken of, of them shall I be had in honour.

David responded by telling Michal that God chose him over her father, Saul. Therefore, it was to God he owed his allegiance and his praise, regardless of how he appeared in her eyes or the eyes of anyone else.

2 Samuel 6:23
Therefore Michal the daughter of Saul had no child unto the day of her death.

Because Michal despised passionate worship and simple expressions of praise, she would have no children. She would bear no fruit. So, too, the person, family, or church that doesn't praise will be fruitless. God doesn't desire big parades or flashy drama. Rather, He desires simplicity, sincerity, and passion. I pray the Lord would help us be people who would be expanded not only in our forms of worship, but in our desire to worship.

Perhaps you're at the threshingfloor today. Maybe you've hit a bump at work. Maybe things are a bit shaky in your marriage. Maybe you've thought you can straighten things out in your own strength. I can't tell you how many parades I've organized in my day—only to see them end in disaster. Initially, I would say, "Why didn't You bless that, Lord? You missed a great opportunity."

Time and time again, God would say, "I want you to draw close to Me and to experience My glory. But you've got to get back to simplicity. You've got to get back to humility."

It's not about the parade, gang. It's about the Person. We must humble ourselves before God. We must confess our sins before Him and offer worship to Him. And as we do, we'll experience the *chabod*—His presence—in our lives from glory to greater glory day by day.

7 **2 Samuel 7:1**
And it came to pass, when the king sat in his house, and the LORD had given him rest round about from all his enemies;

Here, we see David in a rare season of rest. With no one attacking her, Israel was experiencing peace and tranquility.

2 Samuel 7:2 (a)
That the king said unto Nathan the prophet . . .

David is an interesting man because, during this season of rest, notice what he's doing. He's mulling over godly matters in the presence of a godly man. The way a man spends his leisure time says a great deal about him. In Psalm 119:63, David declared that his friends were those who feared God. That is not surprising, for in Proverbs 13:20 we read that he who walks with the wise shall also be wise. So, here's David spending time with God's prophet, Nathan, thinking about what he could do for the God who had been so gracious to him.

2 Samuel 7:2 (b)
. . . See now, I dwell in an house of cedar . . .

In conquering his enemies round about him and receiving gifts and tribute, David would eventually possess the equivalent of over one billion dollars. No wonder that, according to the historian, Josephus, his palace was magnificent in size and splendor.

2 Samuel 7:2 (c)
. . . but the ark of God dwelleth within curtains.

David could have been like Nebuchadnezzar. He could have taken credit for what he had accomplished. That's usually what happens. Statistically, the wealthier a person becomes, the smaller percentage of his income will he give to the work of the Lord. David, however, was different. Here, he's saying, "I want to do more for the Lord than I've done before."

2 Samuel 7:3
And Nathan said to the king, Go, do all that is in thine heart; for the LORD is with thee.

David's desire to build God a house was biblical, for in Deuteronomy 12, God declared that there would come a time when He Himself would choose a spot in the Land of Promise wherein people could seek Him continually.

Like David, we can have visions, ideas, and dreams that are biblical, spiritual, and noble—but that are not right. And, like Nathan, we can say to others, "That's a great idea! Go for it!" without seeking the Lord.

How important it is that we be those who say, "Lord, I've got lots of ideas, plans, and dreams. I've got all kinds of ways to accomplish big things for Your glory—but only if they're part of *Your* plan. That is why we are told in 1 John 4:1 to "try the spirits." Prophets are fallible. So are pastors. This doesn't mean Nathan is a false prophet. It simply means there needs to be evaluation and confirmation regarding any prophecy.

2 Samuel 7:4–8
And it came to pass that night, that the word of the LORD came unto Nathan, saying, Go and tell my servant David, Thus saith the LORD, Shalt thou build me an house for me to dwell in? Whereas I have not dwelt in any house since the time that I brought up the children of Israel out of Egypt, even to this day, but have walked in a tent and in a tabernacle. In all the places wherein I have walked with all the children of Israel spake I a word with any of the tribes of Israel, whom I commanded to feed my people Israel, saying, Why build ye not me an house of cedar? Now therefore so shalt thou say unto my servant David, Thus saith the LORD of hosts, I took thee from the sheepcote, from following the sheep, to be ruler over my people, over Israel:

"You're a shepherd, David," God said through Nathan. "That's why I called you. That's what I saw in you. That's what I like about you. You're not a builder of buildings, you're a herder of sheep. You cared for them, you went after them, you had a heart for them. That's who you are. That's where I found you. That's why I called you."

2 Samuel 7:9
And I was with thee whithersoever thou wentest, and have cut off all thine enemies

out of thy sight, and have made thee a great name, like unto the name of the great men that are in the earth.

"I fought the enemies that came against you, and I brought honor and glory to you," God reminds David.

2 Samuel 7:10
Moreover I will appoint a place for my people Israel, and will plant them, that they may dwell in a place of their own, and move no more; neither shall the children of wickedness afflict them any more, as beforetime,

"I have a plan to establish a center of worship—but not now, and not by you," God continued.

2 Samuel 7:11
And as since the time that I commanded judges to be over my people Israel, and have caused thee to rest from all thine enemies. Also the LORD telleth thee that he will make thee an house.

When God says no, He always tempers our disappointments with wonderful blessings—greater than any we could have anticipated or expected. "Tell David he can't build Me a house," God said to Nathan. "Instead, tell him I'm going to build him a house."

2 Samuel 7:12
And when thy days be fulfilled, and thou shalt sleep with thy fathers, I will set up thy seed after thee, which shall proceed out of thy bowels, and I will establish his kingdom.

"From your seed will come the true King."

2 Samuel 7:13
He shall build an house for my name, and I will stablish the throne of his kingdom for ever.

Who is this? It's the Seed of David, the Son of David, Jesus Christ. "David," God said through Nathan, "there will come one long after you're dead who will build a house for My name, and I will establish His kingdom forever."

2 Samuel 7:14 (a)
I will be his father, and he shall be my son . . .

The author of Hebrews applies this verse to Jesus (1:5).

2 Samuel 7:14 (b)
. . . If he commit iniquity, I will chasten him with the rod of men, and with the stripes of the children of men:

Newer translations correctly render this verse, "When he carries the iniquity, he shall be beaten." And indeed, Jesus was beaten when He bore our sin.

2 Samuel 7:15–17
But my mercy shall not depart away from him, as I took it from Saul, whom I put away before thee. And thine house and thy kingdom shall be established for ever before thee: thy throne shall be established for ever. According to all these words, and according to all this vision, so did Nathan speak unto David.

"You can't do what you want to do, David. But God's going to build a house that you won't believe. From your seed will come One whose kingdom will be established forever." Somehow, David understood this. Somehow, by the Spirit, David got it. He knew somehow that Nathan was talking to him about something that was bigger than anything he dreamed of or could have imagined.

2 Samuel 7:18
Then went king David in, and sat before the LORD, and he said, Who am I, O Lord GOD? and what is my house, that thou hast brought me hitherto?

"Why would You allow me to be a part of this grand plan?" David said, as he sat in the presence of the Lord.

2 Samuel 7:19, 20
And this was yet a small thing in thy sight, O Lord GOD; but thou hast spoken also of thy servant's house for a great while to come. And is this the manner of man, O Lord GOD? And what can David say more unto thee? for thou, Lord GOD, knowest thy servant.

A poet and a songwriter, David was a very verbal man. But here he was tongue-tied, silenced by God's grace and kindness.

2 Samuel 7:21, 22
For thy word's sake, and according to thine own heart, hast thou done all these great things, to make thy servant know them. Wherefore thou art great, O LORD God: for there is none like thee, neither is there any God beside thee, according to all that we have heard with our ears.

Able to keep quiet no longer, praise begins to flow from David's heart . . .

2 Samuel 7:23–29

And what one nation in the earth is like thy people, even like Israel, whom God went to redeem for a people to himself, and to make him a name, and to do for you great things and terrible, for thy land, before thy people, which thou redeemedst to thee from Egypt, from the nations and their gods? For thou hast confirmed to thyself thy people Israel to be a people unto thee for ever: and thou, LORD, art become their God. And now, O LORD God, the word that thou hast spoken concerning thy servant, and concerning his house, establish it for ever, and do as thou hast said. And let thy name be magnified for ever, saying, The LORD of hosts is the God over Israel: and let the house of thy servant David be established before thee. For thou, O LORD of hosts, God of Israel, hast revealed to thy servant, saying, I will build thee an house: therefore hath thy servant found in his heart to pray this prayer unto thee. And now, O Lord GOD, thou art that God, and thy words be true, and thou hast promised this goodness unto thy servant: Therefore now let it please thee to bless the house of thy servant, that it may continue for ever before thee: for thou, O Lord GOD, hast spoken it: and with thy blessing let the house of thy servant be blessed for ever.

Here, we see David receiving grace graciously. First, he gives praise *for* the promise—then he prays *in* the promise. That's a winning combination. When you read the Scriptures, give praise for what you're reading, then pray it in.

My prayer is that you would marvel that God has built you a house, that He lives in your heart, and that He'll build your house to the glory of His Son.

8

2 Samuel 8:1 (a)

And after this it came to pass, that David smote the Philistines, and subdued them . . .

In chapter 7, David was given rest *by* the Lord and then communed *with* the Lord. Here, in chapter 8, he's on the attack *for* the Lord as he takes territory—which is exactly what the church is called to do (Matthew 16:18).

2 Samuel 8:1 (b)

. . . and David took Metheg-ammah out of the hand of the Philistines.

Metheg-ammah, or "the bridle of Ammah"—the chief city of the Philistines—most likely refers to the city of Gath.

2 Samuel 8:2

And he smote Moab, and measured them with a line, casting them down to the ground; even with two lines measured he to put to death, and with one full line to keep alive. And so the Moabites became David's servants, and brought gifts.

In dealing with the enemy, David had to decide who would be a threat to his kingdom. In this case, the big guys would. The smaller men were allowed to be servants. The bigger men were put to death.

David made a decision. And Jesus told you and me to do the same thing. "Don't cast your pearls before swine," He said (Matthew 7:6). This means we are to determine where people are spiritually. Some people have no interest in the gospel, but only want to argue. We need discernment regarding where we should most wisely spend our time. How do we get discernment? Pray. "Lord, show me what I should do with my day, with my time. Give me wisdom. Help me, like David, to measure correctly, to assess the situation as You would."

2 Samuel 8:3, 4 (a)

David smote also Hadadezer, the son of Rehob, king of Zobah, as he went to recover his border at the river Euphrates. David took from him a thousand chariots, and seven hundred horsemen, and twenty thousand footmen . . .

These are big battles. David is fully engaged, completely committed.

2 Samuel 8:4 (b)

. . . and David houghed all the chariot horses, but reserved of them for an hundred chariots.

David disabled all the horses of the enemy. I find this interesting because in Deuteronomy 17, God declared that when a man became a king, he was not to multiply to himself horses or wives. David chose to follow the first injunction.

That's like us. We specialize in certain things. Tithing? Got it down. Witnessing? You bet. Gossiping? Ouch. All of us are specialists in certain areas, and we tend to talk about those areas. The real issue, however, is not what we talk about, but what we're silent about. Oftentimes, our silence indicates where the correction needs to be.

2 Samuel 8:5, 6 (a)
And when the Syrians of Damascus came to succour Hadadezer king of Zobah, David slew of the Syrians two and twenty thousand men. Then David put garrisons in Syria of Damascus: and the Syrians became servants to David, and brought gifts . . .

David is taking territory and making these areas tributaries of his kingdom.

2 Samuel 8:6 (b)
. . . And the LORD preserved David whithersoever he went.

God knew about David's weaknesses and vulnerabilities. God knew David thoroughly. Yet He preserved him still. Even though we struggle, God is faithful. I'm so glad about that.

2 Samuel 8:7–10
And David took the shields of gold that were on the servants of Hadadezer, and brought them to Jerusalem. And from Betah, and from Berothai, cities of Hadadezer, king David took exceeding much brass. When Toi king of Hamath heard that David had smitten all the host of Hadadezer, Then Toi sent Joram his son unto king David, to salute him, and to bless him, because he had fought against Hadadezer, and smitten him: for Hadadezer had wars with Toi. And Joram brought with him vessels of silver, and vessels of gold, and vessels of brass:

Toi was an enemy of Hadadezer, so he thanked David for getting rid of his enemy.

2 Samuel 8:11, 12
Which also king David did dedicate unto the LORD, with the silver and gold that he had dedicated of all nations which he subdued; Of Syria, and of Moab, and of the children of Ammon, and of the Philistines, and of Amalek, and of the spoil of Hadadezer, son of Rehob, king of Zobah.

Here, David brought the spoil to Jerusalem and dedicated it to the Lord in order that it might eventually be used in the building of the temple. You see, even though David could not build the temple himself, he didn't pout. He didn't quit. He didn't get angry. He simply set to work, gathering all the necessary supplies for Solomon.

I point this out because sometimes people say, "If I can't be on the worship team, I'm not going to sing at all. If I can't be recognized or utilized in the way I think I ought to be, I won't do anything." David was used mightily because, even with all of his faults and failures, he served the Lord every way he could.

You might never be an evangelist, write a book, go to the mission field, or preach a sermon—but you can do what David did. You can work behind the scenes, providing the supplies through intercession and prayer. The temple is known commonly as Solomon's temple, but in reality, it was the heart of David behind it. And he will be credited eternally.

2 Samuel 8:13–15
And David gat him a name when he returned from smiting of the Syrians in the valley of salt, being eighteen thousand men. And he put garrisons in Edom; throughout all Edom put he garrisons, and all they of Edom became David's servants. And the LORD preserved David whithersoever he went. And David reigned over all Israel; and David executed judgment and justice unto all his people.

David gave good counsel and was equitable to all his people.

2 Samuel 8:16
And Joab the son of Zeruiah was over the host; and Jehoshaphat the son of Ahilud was recorder;

Joab was in charge of the army. Jehoshaphat kept the journals, remembering and recording the goodness of God. I encourage you to follow Jehoshaphat's lead. I suppose one of the things that causes me to praise the Lord as much as anything else is reading through my own journals and seeing the things that once bothered me—but that God worked out perfectly.

2 Samuel 8:17, 18
And Zadok the son of Ahitub, and Ahimelech the son of Abiathar, were the priests; and Seraiah was the scribe; And Benaiah the son of Jehoiada was over both the Cherethites and the Pelethites; and David's sons were chief rulers.

This was the organization of David's kingdom. At this point, he has taken on the enemy and ordered the goods for the temple. Now his thoughts turn toward the house of Saul . . .

9

2 Samuel 9:1
And David said, Is there yet any that is left of the house of Saul, that I may shew him kindness for Jonathan's sake?

At this point in the story, David has been on the throne for approximately fifteen years. I don't know what jarred David's memory—but, in reflecting on the past, his thoughts turned toward his dear friend, Jonathan. "Are there any survivors from Saul's family to whom I can show kindness?" he asked.

2 Samuel 9:2–6 (a)
And there was of the house of Saul a servant whose name was Ziba. And when they had called him unto David, the king said unto him, Art thou Ziba? And he said, Thy servant is he. And the king said, Is there not yet any of the house of Saul, that I may shew the kindness of God unto him? And Ziba said unto the king, Jonathan hath yet a son, which is lame on his feet. And the king said unto him, Where is he? And Ziba said unto the king, Behold, he is in the house of Machir, the son of Ammiel, in Lo-debar. Then king David sent, and fetched him out of the house of Machir, the son of Ammiel, from Lo-debar. Now when Mephibosheth, the son of Jonathan, the son of Saul, was come unto David, he fell on his face, and did reverence . . .

In Old Testament times, if a king from a different family than the previous one came to power, he would kill all of the relatives of the previous king in order to eliminate any rival. *Lo-debar* means "pasture less place." Consisting of only rocks and sand, Lo-debar would have been a terrible place to live. Why did Mephibosheth live in such a desolate place? Because he no doubt feared the new king.

Mephibosheth means "shameful breath." This more than likely means that he had asthma, or some other breathing ailment. On top of that, he was lame. Second Samuel 4 tells us that when Saul and Jonathan died on Mount Gilboa, Mephibosheth was five years old. His nanny scooped him up to rush him to safety, but in her haste, she tripped. Mephibosheth fell to the ground, evidently injuring his spinal cord.

Here was Mephibosheth—hiding in a dry place, unable to breathe easily, and unable to walk at all. Perhaps that describes you or someone you know. Maybe you feel suffocated spiritually, in a dry place, unable to make any progress because you, too, were dropped . . .

- "He told me he was going to marry me, and I gave myself to him completely. Then he dropped me. My heart is broken and now I'm crippled."
- "My mom left my dad. She was a Christian, but she left and never came back. So here I am, hiding out in a desolate place."
- "I thought I was the best baseball player on the team. But my coach cut me. That might not seem important to some, but to me, it's had a crippling effect."
- "I was a good worker. I deserved better, but my boss dropped me to cut back on the budget."

There are countless stories of people who are crippled. I'm convinced that if we knew the secret stories of even our worst enemies, we would have nothing but compassion for them, nothing but love toward them.

There is One who does know their stories. And He knows yours, as well. He's the King, the Son of David, calling out to those who are in pastureless places, to those with crippled feet. If you feel lame or crippled a bit, listen, and you'll hear the King calling—sending a messenger to you. Just as David sent messengers to the pastureless place, the King calls still.

2 Samuel 9:6 (b)
. . . And David said, Mephibosheth. And he answered, Behold thy servant!

David spoke one word that changes the entire scene. He said Mephibosheth's name. And something in the way David spoke his name ministered to Mephibosheth's heart. I cannot help but think of Jesus at the Garden tomb. Mary was there weeping over the fact that His body was no longer in the tomb. In her turmoil she was conversing with a man she thought to be the gardener. But when He said, "Mary," suddenly, in the very way He spoke her name, she identified Him as her Master.

John 10 declares that Jesus knows the names of His sheep. He knows your name, and He calls you individually. Do you hear His voice calling you today?

2 Samuel 9:7 (a)
And David said unto him, Fear not . . .

"It's okay," David said to Mephibosheth. "Don't be afraid. It's not what you think."

A lot of times it's not what we think. We think, "I'm so lame. I've been far from His pasture. And if the King is calling for me today, it's probably because He wants to lop off my head, or at least shake me up." But the next verse shows us that things are not always what we think . . .

2 Samuel 9:7 (b)
. . . for I will surely shew thee kindness for Jonathan thy father's sake, and will restore thee all the land of Saul thy father . . .

Because Mephibosheth was linked to Jonathan, David would show him kindness in two ways. First, he would restore his land. You see, although Mephibosheth lived in a barren, desolate place, he was heir to the best land in all of the nation. Here, David promises to restore that inheritance to Mephibosheth. And He promises to do the same for us . . .

> And I will restore to you the years that the locust hath eaten, the cankerworm, and the caterpiller, and the palmerworm, my great army which I sent among you. Joel 2:25

What an amazing God we serve. He not only seeks and saves those who are lost, but makes up for their lost time as well.

2 Samuel 9:7 (c)
. . . and thou shalt eat bread at my table continually.

In addition to restoring Mephibosheth's land, David promised to reserve his place—at the king's table. Historian Josephus tells us that a meal on King Solomon's table consisted of 22,000 oxen, 20,000 sheep and fowl beyond description. In other words, there was plenty for everyone at the king's table.

The same is still true, for it is at the Table of our King that mercy abounds. The Lord would say to you today, "I've prepared a Table before you. Take. Eat. This is My body, broken for you. If any man hear My voice and open his heart, I will come in and sup with him. Come to the Table."

If your soul has been dry, it is to you especially that the Lord says, "Come and dine. And let Me restore all you've lost."

2 Samuel 9:8
And he bowed himself, and said, What is thy servant, that thou shouldest look upon such a dead dog as I am?

"Why would you show such kindness to me?" Mephibosheth asked. And his question is mine. "Lord, why would You be so good to *me?* I ran from You and did my own thing. Yet You offer to make up that which I lost and to dine with me continually? *Amazing.*"

2 Samuel 9:9–11
Then the king called to Ziba, Saul's servant, and said unto him, I have given unto thy master's son all that pertained to Saul and to all his house. Thou therefore, and thy sons, and thy servants, shall till the land for him, and thou shalt bring in the fruits, that thy master's son may have food to eat: but Mephibosheth thy master's son shall eat bread alway at my table. Now Ziba had fifteen sons and twenty servants. Then said Ziba unto the king, According to all that my lord the king hath commanded his servant, so shall thy servant do. As for Mephibosheth, said the king, he shall eat at my table, as one of the king's sons.

David's servants were to provide food for Mephibosheth's entire family, but Mephibosheth himself was to eat with David as if he were a son of David.

> But as many as received him, to them gave he power to become the sons of God, even to them that believe on his name. John 1:12

We crippled people, we lame-brains, we who have spent so much time in a pastureless place, running from His face have been invited to dine as His sons at the King's table. The only question is, will we?

2 Samuel 9:12, 13 (a)
And Mephibosheth had a young son, whose name was Micha. And all that dwelt in the house of Ziba were servants unto Mephibosheth. So Mephibosheth dwelt in Jerusalem: for he did eat continually at the king's table . . .

Hearing the generous, gracious offer of the king, Mephibosheth didn't say, "Thanks, king. I'll see if I can drop in occasionally to have a bite with you now and then." No, he said, "King, I can't believe you would do this for a man like me. I will eat at your table continually."

2 Samuel 9:13 (b)
. . . and was lame on both his feet.

When he came to David's table, did Mephibosheth walk straight? No. He was still lame in both his feet. He was still affected by the sin of the fall. So why is it that, when Jesus says "Come and dine," we say, "I can't. I'm too lame"? The Lord calls us just as we are to come and dine with Him. He calls you in the state you're in to receive the grace and abundance He has for you. The Table is set. And the Table is the only place where lame, twisted, crippled feet can't be seen.

Are you burdened because you're always looking at your flaws and your shortcomings—or are you blessed as you partake of the abundance of grace and mercy at the King's Table? I understand that many of us have been dropped brutally. But you must understand that you don't have to remain in your lame condition day after year after decade. Jesus was broken that you might be healed. And his blood was shed to wash away the sin and the memory of that which haunts you. Come and dine, and you'll find yourself back in the land where you perhaps once were or where you long to be. Mephibosheth accepted the king's invitation. May we do the same.

10

2 Samuel 10:1, 2
And it came to pass after this, that the king of the children of Ammon died, and Hanun his son reigned in his stead. Then said David, I will shew kindness unto Hanun the son of Nahash, as his father shewed kindness unto me. And David sent to comfort him by the hand of his servants for his father. And David's servants came into the land of the children of Ammon.

When Nahash, king of Ammon—present-day Jordan—died, David sent servants to express condolence and comfort to Hanun, his son.

2 Samuel 10:3
And the princes of the children of Ammon said unto Hanun their lord, Thinkest thou that David doth honour thy father, that he hath sent comforters unto thee? hath not David rather sent his servants unto thee, to search the city, and to spy it out, and to overthrow it?

"This is a trick," Hanun's advisors said. "You can't trust David. These men are only here to spy out our land so that they can wage war against us."

2 Samuel 10:4
Wherefore Hanun took David's servants, and shaved off the one half of their beards, and cut off their garments in the middle, even to their buttocks, and sent them away.

According to Torah and Jewish tradition, the beard was a symbol of masculinity. Thus, this was an act of incredible humiliation.

As messengers of the King of kings, we're to share the best and prepare for the worst. That is, we're to say to people, "I've got great news for you: God loves you. Your sins—past, present, and future—are all forgiven."

Yet, even though we're sharing the best, people like Hanun will cut us and expose us. "All those who live godly in Christ Jesus shall suffer persecution," Paul told Timothy (2 Timothy 3:12).

Blessed are ye, when men shall revile you, and persecute you, and shall say all manner of evil against you falsely, for my sake. Rejoice, and be exceeding glad: for great is your reward in heaven: for so persecuted they the prophets which were before you. Matthew 5:11, 12

Share the best. Prepare for the worst. And watch and see how the Lord will bless as the enemy is driven back.

2 Samuel 10:5 (a)
When they told it unto David, he sent to meet them, because the men were greatly ashamed: and the king said, Tarry at Jericho . . .

The messengers were told to stay in Jericho rather than to avenge themselves. David defended his servants. And the Son of David will defend you.

2 Samuel 10:5 (b)
. . . until your beards be grown, and then return.

Jesus had His beard plucked out. And it wasn't just the back side of His robe that was cut off, but His entire robe was stripped as He hung on the Cross. But when He arose on Easter Sunday, He did so with a new robe and a full-grown beard.

Maybe today you feel ashamed or embarrassed. Take hope, for as a messenger of the Son of David, your beard will grow back and you will be given a new robe. Sometimes, it just takes time.

2 Samuel 10:6
And when the children of Ammon saw that they stank before David, the children of Ammon sent and hired the Syrians of Beth-rehob, and the Syrians of Zoba, twenty thousand footmen, and of king Maacah a thousand men, and of Ish-tob twelve thousand men.

Thirty-three thousand men were mustered as an army to fight against David when the Ammonites saw how much their treatment of his men offended him.

2 Samuel 10:7
And when David heard of it, he sent Joab, and all the host of the mighty men.

Joab would lead the troops of Israel against Ammon and their hired guns, the Syrians.

2 Samuel 10:8–12
And the children of Ammon came out, and put the battle in array at the entering in of the gate: and the Syrians of Zoba, and of Re-

hob, and Ish-tob, and Maacah, were by themselves in the field. When Joab saw that the front of the battle was against him before and behind, he chose of all the choice men of Israel, and put them in array against the Syrians: And the rest of the people he delivered into the hand of Abishai his brother, that he might put them in array against the children of Ammon. And he said, If the Syrians be too strong for me, then thou shalt help me: but if the children of Ammon be too strong for thee, then I will come and help thee. Be of good courage, and let us play the men for our people, and for the cities of our God: and the LORD do that which seemeth him good.

David divided his troops into two companies. Joab led one contingency, Abishai the other. "We have our work cut out for us," Joab said to Abishai. "If I can't get victory over these Syrians before me, come and help me. If you get in trouble fighting the men of Ammon, I'll help you. We'll trust in the Lord and see what He will do."

Joab's plan was a good one—and remains so today. The battle is great. Others might have a different flavor in their fellowship or denomination. But the fact is, we need *every* brother.

2 Samuel 10:13–17
And Joab drew nigh, and the people that were with him, unto the battle against the Syrians: and they fled before him. And when the children of Ammon saw that the Syrians were fled, then fled they also before Abishai, and entered into the city. And when the Syrians saw that they were smitten before Israel, they gathered themselves together. And Hadarezer sent, and brought out the Syrians that were beyond the river: and they came to Helam; and Shobach the captain of the host of Hadarezer went before them. And when it was told David, he gathered all Israel together, and passed over Jordan, and came to Helam. And the Syrians set themselves in array against David, and fought with him.

The second phase of the war is underway. With their reinforcements, their fresh troops, the Syrians are now battling against David directly.

2 Samuel 10:18, 19
And the Syrians fled before Israel; and David slew the men of seven hundred chariots of the Syrians, and forty thousand horsemen, and smote Shobach the captain of their host, who died there. And when all the kings that were servants to Hadarezer saw that they were smitten before Israel, they made peace with Israel, and served them. So the Syrians feared to help the children of Ammon any more.

When was peace made with Israel? When the enemy was smitten. There has never been a successful peace treaty without a victory over the enemy—without a winner and a loser. David's dealing with the Ammonites began in kindness. But when his kindness was rejected, he became engaged in the battle and brought about a destruction of the enemy so complete that, rather than fighting him, they served him.

Our King, the Son of David, has commissioned you and me as servants to be communicators of kindness, messengers of mercy. It's so important to see that Mephibosheth received David's kindness. Hanun didn't. Mephibosheth was poor, broken, lame, weak. Hanun was rich, proud, self-centered, and arrogant. As a servant of the King, I understand that those who are poor in spirit and meek, that those who mourn their own sin will receive the kind word I bring about the kindness of the King. But there will also be those who, like Hanun, who will not receive the word we bring. Therefore, if you want to be fruitful in ministry, hang out with the people who are lame, the Mephibosheths. Spend your time with people who are weak, broken, and needy. Don't make your priority the millionaire athlete, the movie star, the political leader. It's not that they can't be saved—but that's not where the abundant harvest will be. David sent his servants to both Mephibosheth and Hanun. We're to exclude no one, but we're to realize that the most fruit will be found not with the beautiful people, but with those who are crippled, with those who can't breathe right, with Mephibosheth.

11

After speaking at a men's conference in Georgia years ago, Peter-John and I stopped at a place called Stone Mountain, home of the world's biggest boulder. We took a tram to the top and it was really quite impressive. It is huge and smooth and rounded—but it drops off almost imperceptibly. Our guide said that years earlier—before it was fenced off—a couple of guys were walking down the boulder, when they found themselves slowly sliding down with nothing to grab. It wasn't as if they were falling off a cliff. They were just slowly sliding down—all the way to their deaths.

The same is true of sin. "I know what I'm doing. I'm in control. I can get back up again," we tell ourselves. But when the weight, the gravity of carnality kicks in, we find ourselves sliding to destruction. And that's what happened to David . . .

2 Samuel 11:1
And it came to pass, after the year was expired, at the time when kings go forth to battle, that David sent Joab, and his servants with him, and all Israel; and they destroyed the children of Ammon, and besieged Rabbah. But David tarried still at Jerusalem.

Instead of baseball, basketball, or football season, Old Testament cultures had war season. Wars were generally fought in the springtime—when the mud wouldn't cause chariots to get stuck. In this particular season of war, David remained in Jerusalem.

This is Step 1 in David's downfall. He was supposed to be leading his troops, engaged in battle, confronting the enemy. But at fifty years of age, he evidently decided to take a break and let the younger men go without him.

2 Samuel 11:2 (a)
And it came to pass in an eveningtide, that David arose from off his bed, and walked upon the roof of the king's house . . .

On this warm spring evening, David went out to his flat rooftop to take advantage of the cooling evening breezes.

2 Samuel 11:2 (b)–4
. . . and from the roof he saw a woman washing herself; and the woman was very beautiful to look upon. And David sent and inquired after the woman. And one said, Is not this Bath-sheba, the daughter of Eliam, the wife of Uriah the Hittite? And David sent messengers, and took her; and she came in unto him, and he lay with her; for she was purified from her uncleanness: and she returned unto her house.

There are those who believe that, knowing her house was in view of the king's rooftop, Bathsheba was an active participant in this drama. The Bible, however, doesn't say this. And even though Proverbs 11 says a woman without discretion is like a jewel in the snout of a pig, the Bible lays the responsibility for this sin exclusively at the feet of David. In other words, Bathsheba's possible lack of discretion provides no justification for David's actions.

2 Samuel 11:5–8
And the woman conceived, and sent and told David, and said, I am with child. And David sent to Joab, saying, Send me Uriah the Hittite. And Joab sent Uriah to David. And when Uriah was come unto him, David demanded of him how Joab did, and how the people did, and how the war prospered. And David said to Uriah, Go down to thy house, and wash thy feet. And Uriah departed out of the king's house, and there followed him a mess of meat from the king.

David's intention was to have Uriah spend the night with his wife and her pregnancy would be the assumed result.

2 Samuel 11:9, 10
But Uriah slept at the door of the king's house with all the servants of his lord, and went not down to his house. And when they had told David, saying, Uriah went not down unto his house, David said unto Uriah, Camest thou not from thy journey? why then didst thou not go down unto thine house?

"Why didn't you take advantage of this opportunity, Uriah?" David asks.

2 Samuel 11:11
And Uriah said unto David, The ark, and Israel, and Judah, abide in tents; and my lord Joab, and the servants of my lord, are encamped in the open fields; shall I then go into mine house, to eat and to drink, and to lie with my wife? as thou livest, and as thy soul liveth, I will not do this thing.

"I'm not going to have a night of luxury when my fellow soldiers are in a place of danger," said this man of integrity.

2 Samuel 11:12, 13
And David said to Uriah, Tarry here to day also, and to morrow I will let thee depart. So Uriah abode in Jerusalem that day, and the morrow. And when David had called him, he did eat and drink before him; and he made him drunk: and at even he went out to lie on his bed with the servants of his lord, but went not down to his house.

David sought to get Uriah drunk because he knew, as the devil does, that alcohol lowers the resistance of moral fortitude. I could tell you story after story of godly men and women who began toying with alcohol and found their spiritual lives eroding. You are a wise person if you realize the danger of alcohol and say, "I have a hard enough time thinking right when I'm sober. I don't need to make it harder on myself."

Bathsheba, Solomon's mother would say, "It is not for kings to drink wine or princes to drink strong drink. Let drink be given to those who are perishing and those that be of a depressed spirit"

(Proverbs 31:4–7). Therefore, if you want to be a king or a prince, if you've discovered there's power in prayer and liberty in praise, you won't need the crutch of alcohol to get through a day or a situation.

2 Samuel 11:14
And it came to pass in the morning, that David wrote a letter to Joab, and sent it by the hand of Uriah.

Realizing Uriah still didn't take the bait, David came up with Plan B . . .

2 Samuel 11:15
And he wrote in the letter, saying, Set ye Uriah in the forefront of the hottest battle, and retire ye from him, that he may be smitten, and die.

Here we see David not only committing adultery, but murder. Remember, David was a man after God's own heart, a man who was singularly held up in the Old Testament as one of the greatest men of faith who ever lived. What's going on? It all started seemingly so simple. He neglected his duty to go to battle. Then his eyes wandered. His curiosity was aroused. He committed adultery, and now murder. David is stumbling badly. But that's the way sin is. Sin has a sneaky way of compounding itself. Before you know it, you're more deeply involved in it than you ever thought you would be. That is why it is absolutely essential to not give in at that first point of temptation. You cannot control the course of your destiny once you allow yourself to begin to flirt with sin. It will capture you. It will ensnare you. And ultimately it will destroy you. David once killed giants. Now this giant is killing him.

2 Samuel 11:16, 17
And it came to pass, when Joab observed the city, that he assigned Uriah unto a place where he knew that valiant men were. And the men of the city went out, and fought with Joab: and there fell some of the people of the servants of David; and Uriah the Hittite died also.

The plan went exactly as David desired. Uriah was positioned in the most dangerous place of the battle, and died as a result.

2 Samuel 11:18–21
Then Joab sent and told David all the things concerning the war; And charged the messenger, saying, When thou hast made an end of telling the matters of the war unto the king, And if so be that the king's wrath arise, and he say unto thee, Wherefore approached ye so nigh unto the city when ye did fight? knew ye not that they would shoot from the wall? Who smote Abimelech the son of Jerubbesheth? did not a woman cast a piece of a millstone upon him from the wall, that he died in Thebez? why went ye nigh the wall? then say thou, Thy servant Uriah the Hittite is dead also.

A messenger was dispatched to relay the result of the battle to David. If David asked him why his army fought so close to the wall of the city, the messenger was instructed to tell him that Uriah was dead—thereby justifying this otherwise foolish strategy.

2 Samuel 11:22–25
So the messenger went, and came and shewed David all that Joab had sent him for. And the messenger said unto David, Surely the men prevailed against us, and came out unto us into the field, and we were upon them even unto the entering of the gate. And the shooters shot from off the wall upon thy servants; and some of the king's servants be dead, and thy servant Uriah the Hittite is dead also. Then David said unto the messenger, Thus shalt thou say unto Joab, Let not this thing displease thee, for the sword devoureth one as well as another: make thy battle more strong against the city, and overthrow it: and encourage thou him.

"Don't worry, Joab. You win some and you lose some." David said, understanding that the reason Joab lost the battle was because Uriah had to die.

2 Samuel 11:26, 27
And when the wife of Uriah heard that Uriah her husband was dead, she mourned for her husband. And when the mourning was past, David sent and fetched her to his house, and she became his wife, and bare him a son. But the thing that David had done displeased the LORD.

David no doubt thought he got away with his sin by cleverly covering his tracks. But God knew otherwise.

"Be sure your sins will find you out," we are warned (Numbers 32:23). No matter how well I think I've covered my tracks, the reality is that the sin will track me down. That's Satan's strategy. He sucks you into sin, and then he makes sure that the sin surfaces to expose you, to humiliate and condemn you. After nine or ten months of thinking he got away with this sin, David will have to face up to its repercussions.

I pray that the Lord might remind us again that the most dangerous place to be in spiritual life is kicking back, pulling away, saying, "I taught Sunday school for years. I paid my dues. It's time for me to let someone else fight the battles and do the work." When that mentality creeps in, you're being set up to be taken down. The safest place to be is on the front lines, fully engaged in serving the Lord, in battling against the enemy. May God help us to truly learn the lessons we read about in His Word.

Through all of this, David goes down in history as one of the greatest of the greats because he had a heart for God. Yes, he failed miserably, but there was something about his heart that God loved. The Son of David said that the one who is forgiven much loves much (Luke 7:47). It is when we realize how sinful we are that we realize how merciful God is. And such realization causes us to love Him all the more.

God sees the heart. May He see in you a heart that is amazed by His mercy, grateful for His grace, a heart that loves Him passionately and loves to seek His face. If the choice is between a congregation that errs constantly but loves God passionately and a congregation of self-righteous Pharisees, I'll take the former. And, according to Jesus, so would God.

12

2 Samuel 12:1 (a)
And the LORD sent Nathan unto David . . .

God didn't send an enemy of David to talk to him about his sin. He sent a friend. This is most often the way of the Lord. When He has a word of correction to bring us, inevitably it will be by someone who has a heart for us. Conversely, unless your heart is filled with compassion for the person you are about to correct, it is probably not your responsibility to correct him.

As Jesus arrived at the Upper Room, He found His disciples arguing with each other concerning who was the greatest among them. He also noticed that their feet were dirty. Instead of chastising them for arguing, He girded Himself with a towel and washed their feet. Therefore, I have no right to point out the dirt on other peoples' feet unless I'm willing to wash them myself—time and again. Nathan, evidently, was such a man.

2 Samuel 12:1 (b)–4
. . . And he came unto him, and said unto him, There were two men in one city; the one rich, and the other poor. The rich man had exceeding many flocks and herds: But the poor man had nothing, save one little ewe lamb, which he had bought and nourished up: and it grew up together with him, and with his children; it did eat of his own meat, and drank of his own cup, and lay in his bosom, and was unto him as a daughter. And there came a traveller unto the rich man, and he spared to take of his own flock and of his own herd, to dress for the wayfaring man that was come unto him; but took the poor man's lamb, and dressed it for the man that was come to him.

Nathan told David of a rich man who killed his neighbor's one and only lamb in order to feed his friend.

2 Samuel 12:5, 6
And David's anger was greatly kindled against the man; and he said to Nathan, As the LORD liveth, the man that hath done this thing shall surely die: And he shall restore the lamb fourfold, because he did this thing, and because he had no pity.

Upset that a rich man would steal from a poor man, David was right in saying the rich man should give four lambs to the poor man, for that was the restitution decreed in the Law (Exodus 22:1). The problem was that David didn't stop there. He went on to issue the death sentence upon the rich man. This was neither God's Word nor His heart. In David's awareness of his own sin, he was judging another harshly.

That's always the way it is. We will be harshest with the people who commit the same sin with which we struggle. My sins look terrible on someone else. The Master of mercy, the Model of grace was Jesus Christ. He stood up for the woman taken in adultery; He was tender with the woman living in sin. Why? Because He Himself was free of sin.

2 Samuel 12:7
And Nathan said to David, Thou art the man.

Suddenly David understood. Whenever there's a finger pointing at another, three are pointing back. This sobers me. We're all guilty. The Old Testament as well as the Sermon on the Mount drive us to the place where we say, "I'm a sinner. I need grace."

2 Samuel 12:7, 8
Thus saith the LORD God of Israel, I anointed thee king over Israel, and I delivered thee out of the hand of Saul; And I gave thee thy master's house, and thy master's wives into thy bosom, and gave thee the house of Israel

and of Judah; and if that had been too little, I would moreover have given unto thee such and such things.

"David, I've given you everything. But if that wasn't enough, I would give you more still," the Lord said. With all of his flaws and shortcomings, God's heart was for David because David's heart was after God.

2 Samuel 12:9, 10 (a)
Wherefore hast thou despised the commandment of the Lord, to do evil in his sight? thou hast killed Uriah the Hittite with the sword, and hast taken his wife to be thy wife, and hast slain him with the sword of the children of Ammon. Now therefore the sword shall never depart from thine house . . .

"David, because you have brought adultery, lies, deception, and murder into your home, your family will be plagued with problems."

2 Samuel 12:10 (b), 11
. . . because thou hast despised me, and hast taken the wife of Uriah the Hittite to be thy wife. Thus saith the Lord, Behold, I will raise up evil against thee out of thine own house, and I will take thy wives before thine eyes, and give them unto thy neighbour, and he shall lie with thy wives in the sight of this sun.

"You're going to be humiliated, David. Your wives will be taken."

2 Samuel 12:12
For thou didst it secretly: but I will do this thing before all Israel, and before the sun.

"What you did in the darkness will be made known in the light."

2 Samuel 12:13 (a)
And David said unto Nathan, I have sinned against the Lord . . .

David didn't defend himself or try to blame Bathsheba. He simply and succinctly said, "I've sinned against the Lord. Period." No amplification, no raw emotion, just a simple declaration and honest confession.

"After murdering a man, stealing his wife, deceiving the country? All he can say is one sentence? That's not enough," we might protest. But that's a dangerous stance to take because we do not see a man's heart. A person can be crying on national TV and go out and do the same thing again and again. Someone else might not have a tear in his eye, but he can be sincere to the point where he never sins in that particular way again. David made a single statement. And that was enough.

In Psalm 51, we are given additional information concerning what was going on in David's heart . . .

To the chief Musician, A Psalm of David, when Nathan the prophet came unto him, after he had gone in to Bath-she'-ba . . . Psalm 51:1 (a)

Psalm 51 deals with this exact moment in time, as recorded by David in his "journal" . . .

. . . Have mercy upon me, O God, according to thy lovingkindness: according unto the multitude of thy tender mercies blot out my transgressions. Wash me thoroughly from mine iniquity, and cleanse me from my sin. For I acknowledge my transgressions: and my sin is ever before me. Psalm 51:1 (b)–3

David thought about his sin constantly.

Against thee, thee only, have I sinned, and done this evil in thy sight . . . Psalm 51:4 (a)

"Wait a minute, David," we might say. "What about Bathsheba? What about Uriah? What about the men who died in battle? Surely you sinned against them." But what David is acknowledging, under the inspiration of the Spirit, is that whatever happens to anyone—as sad as it might seem, as tragic as it may be—is nothing compared to what they deserve. You see, there is none righteous, no not one (Romans 3:10). This is a shock to our culture, but it's true. What David is saying here is true because the Lord is the only One who ought not to be treated that way.

. . . that thou mightest be justified when thou speakest, and be clear when thou judgest. Behold, I was shapen in iniquity; and in sin did my mother conceive me. Psalm 51:4 (b), 5

People aren't sinners because they sin. People sin because they're sinners—from the very moment of conception.

Behold, thou desirest truth in the inward parts: and in the hidden part thou shalt make me to know wisdom. Purge me with hyssop, and I shall be clean: wash me, and I shall be whiter than snow. Make me to hear joy and gladness; that the bones which thou hast broken may rejoice. Psalm 51:6–8

As a former shepherd, David refers to a certain practice of Middle Eastern shepherds. That is, if a lamb continually wandered away, jeopardizing its own life by going into areas containing poisonous plants or wolves and foxes, the shepherd had no other recourse but to break its legs. Then he would reset the bones, splint them, and carry the lamb on his shoulders until the bone was healed. When the splint was taken off, the lamb would never leave the shepherd's side, so closely had it bonded with the shepherd.

God declares that He will do whatever it takes to draw His children to be close to Him, that they might understand how much His heart is for them, that they might not wander away and get beaten up or poisoned unnecessarily.

> Hide thy face from my sins, and blot out all mine iniquities. Create in me a clean heart, O God; and renew a right spirit within me. Cast me not away from thy presence; and take not thy holy spirit from me. Restore unto me the joy of thy salvation; and uphold me with thy free spirit. Then will I teach transgressors thy ways; and sinners shall be converted unto thee. Psalm 51:9–13

"Lord, I'll share what I found in You with others You send my way," David prays.

> Deliver me from bloodguiltiness, O God, thou God of my salvation: and my tongue shall sing aloud of thy righteousness. O Lord, open thou my lips; and my mouth shall shew forth thy praise. For thou desirest not sacrifice; else would I give it: thou delightest not in burnt offering. The sacrifices of God are a broken spirit: a broken and a contrite heart, O God, thou wilt not despise. Psalm 51:14–17

That which was happening in David's soul was real. We don't see a person's heart. Only God sees the heart. David said one simple sentence in verse 13. Psalm 51, however, speaks volumes.

2 Samuel 12:13 (b)
. . . And Nathan said unto David, The LORD also hath put away thy sin; thou shalt not die.

"David, your sin is forgiven," the Lord declared through Nathan. "Because you murdered a man you should die, but God is showing great mercy to you."

2 Samuel 12:14 (a)
Howbeit . . .

There's always a "howbeit." Please note two things here. David was fully forgiven. But there would still be repercussions. The Bible says, "Don't be deceived. God is not mocked. Whatever a man sows, that shall he reap" (Galatians 6:7). Over the years, I've noticed that there is often a year cycle that takes place from the planting to the harvesting of sin. David will go through heartbreak and heartache that will last much longer than a year. But this first year is especially difficult for him.

2 Samuel 12:14 (b)
. . . because by this deed thou hast given great occasion to the enemies of the LORD to blaspheme . . .

Who points out, discusses, and focuses on sin? The enemy. Therefore, if I'm talking about someone else's sin, it means I'm acting as an enemy.

2 Samuel 12:14 (c)
. . . the child also that is born unto thee shall surely die.

When we're being seduced by sin, we think, *I know there will be a price to pay, but I've calculated the cost. I've added the columns, and I can handle it.* The problem is, the cost is never what you think. It's never what you calculated. It's never what you thought. The cost is always infinitely higher than what we thought when we took the first step into sin. That's why God hates sin so much.

2 Samuel 12:15–23 (a)
And Nathan departed unto his house. And the LORD struck the child that Uriah's wife bare unto David, and it was very sick. David therefore besought God for the child; and David fasted, and went in, and lay all night upon the earth. And the elders of his house arose, and went to him, to raise him up from the earth: but he would not, neither did he eat bread with them. And it came to pass on the seventh day, that the child died. And the servants of David feared to tell him that the child was dead: for they said, Behold, while the child was yet alive, we spake unto him, and he would not hearken unto our voice: how will he then vex himself, if we tell him that the child is dead? But when David saw that his servants whispered, David perceived that the child was dead: therefore David said unto his servants, Is the child dead? And they said, He is dead. Then David arose from the earth, and washed, and anointed himself, and changed his apparel, and came into the house of the LORD, and worshipped: then he came to his own house; and when he required, they set bread before him, and

he did eat. Then said his servants unto him, What thing is this that thou hast done? thou didst fast and weep for the child, while it was alive; but when the child was dead, thou didst rise and eat bread. And he said, While the child was yet alive, I fasted and wept: for I said, Who can tell whether GOD will be gracious to me, that the child may live? But now he is dead, wherefore should I fast? can I bring him back again?

There is divine healing. There is also divine sickness. No matter how fervently David fasted and prayed, it was not God's will that his child recover.

2 Samuel 12:23 (b)
. . . I shall go to him, but he shall not return to me.

I believe this tells us something concerning the death of children. That is, when a child dies before the age of accountability or understanding, he goes to be in the presence of the Lord.

2 Samuel 12:24, 25
And David comforted Bath-sheba his wife, and went in unto her, and lay with her: and she bare a son, and he called his name Solomon: and the LORD loved him. And he sent by the hand of Nathan the prophet; and he called his name Jedidiah, because of the LORD.

Solomon had two names. *Solomon* means "peaceful," which specifically speaks of the fact that David is at peace with God and with himself. *Jedediah,* on the other hand, means "Beloved of God." This encourages me because the Lord could have said, "I'm not going to honor your relationship with Bathsheba. You've blown it and nothing good is going to come out of that." But our God is the God of the second chance. Our God is the God who exchanges beauty for ashes, the oil of joy for mourning (Isaiah 61:3). Our God turns that which is hurtful into something beautiful. David repented. He's been chastened. He's been forgiven. And now God would bless his relationship, for from this union would come Solomon.

Take hope, dear friend. There is hope. Confess your sin. Turn to the Lord. He can turn a dark night into a bright morning if you'll simply come to Him.

2 Samuel 12:26
And Joab fought against Rabbah of the children of Ammon, and took the royal city.

When David sinned with Bath-sheba, Joab was fighting against the Ammonites. Verses 26–31 pick up the story and recount what happened immediately after David committed adultery with Bathsheba and sentenced Uriah to death.

2 Samuel 12:27, 28
And Joab sent messengers to David, and said, I have fought against Rabbah, and have taken the city of waters. Now therefore gather the rest of the people together, and encamp against the city, and take it: lest I take the city, and it be called after my name.

"David," said Joab, "we've won the battle. Leave Jerusalem and come down here. We're ready to take the city and we want you to come in and lead the way.

2 Samuel 12:29
And David gathered all the people together, and went to Rabbah, and fought against it, and took it.

At this point, David was living in sin. He had not confessed his sin. He had not been broken by sin. He thought he had covered his sin. Here, he claimed outward victory, but in his soul, there was disharmony.

2 Samuel 12:30
And he took their king's crown from off his head, the weight whereof was a talent of gold with the precious stones: and it was set on David's head.

Earlier, whenever David reaped gold and silver, he presented it to the Lord. This time, however, he takes the crown for his own head.

2 Samuel 12:30, 31 (a)
And he brought forth the spoil of the city in great abundance. And he brought forth the people that were therein, and put them under saws, and under harrows of iron, and under axes of iron, and made them pass through the brickkiln . . .

David is sentencing the Ammonites to incredibly cruel deaths. Due to the disharmony in his own heart and spirit, this was not the same David.

2 Samuel 12:31 (b)
. . . and thus did he unto all the cities of the children of Ammon. So David and all the people returned unto Jerusalem.

Nine or ten months later, Nathan the prophet would confront him.

13

2 Samuel 13:1 (a)
And it came to pass after this . . .

It has been rightly said that experience is the best teacher—if you can afford the tuition. It's expensive to learn the hard way! Therefore, I would rather learn from accounts like the one before us than to pay the high price of learning on my own.

2 Samuel 13:1 (b)
. . . that Absalom the son of David had a fair sister, whose name was Tamar; and Amnon the son of David loved her.

Amnon was David's oldest son—a half brother to Absalom and Tamar. In our day, for Amnon to love his half-sister would be scandalous. This was not the case in Bible times, for there was no direct prohibition against a man marrying his half-sister.

2 Samuel 13:2
And Amnon was so vexed, that he fell sick for his sister Tamar; for she was a virgin; and Amnon thought it hard for him to do any thing to her.

Amnon was lovesick, or, more accurately, "lustsick." But he couldn't act on this because in these days, all of a king's sons would live on one side of the palace, and all of his daughters on the opposite side.

2 Samuel 13:3, 4 (a)
But Amnon had a friend, whose name was Jonadab, the son of Shimeah David's brother: and Jonadab was a very subtil man. And he said unto him, Why art thou, being the king's son, lean from day to day? wilt thou not tell me?

Jonadab was a subtle, tricky guy. "What's wrong?" he asked his cousin.

2 Samuel 13:4 (b)
. . . And Amnon said unto him, I love Tamar, my brother Absalom's sister.

As we will see, Amnon wasn't in love. He was in lust. There's a big difference. Love is patient. Love is kind. Love does not seek its own. Lust, on the other hand, is impatient. Lust wants its own way immediately.

2 Samuel 13:5
And Jonadab said unto him, Lay thee down on thy bed, and make thyself sick: and when thy father cometh to see thee, say unto him, I pray thee, let my sister Tamar come, and give me meat, and dress the meat in my sight, that I may see it, and eat it at her hand.

"Pretend you're sick," Jonadab said. "Then ask your dad to send Tamar to bring you some chicken soup."

2 Samuel 13:6–9
So Amnon lay down, and made himself sick: and when the king was come to see him, Amnon said unto the king, I pray thee, let Tamar my sister come, and make me a couple of cakes in my sight, that I may eat at her hand. Then David sent home to Tamar, saying, Go now to thy brother Amnon's house, and dress him meat. So Tamar went to her brother Amnon's house; and he was laid down. And she took flour, and kneaded it, and made cakes in his sight, and did bake the cakes. And she took a pan, and poured them out before him; but he refused to eat. And Amnon said, Have out all men from me. And they went out every man from him.

Amnon ordered all of the palace guards to leave.

2 Samuel 13:10–13 (a)
And Amnon said unto Tamar, Bring the meat into the chamber, that I may eat of thine hand. And Tamar took the cakes which she had made, and brought them into the chamber to Amnon her brother. And when she had brought them unto him to eat, he took hold of her, and said unto her, Come lie with me, my sister. And she answered him, Nay, my brother, do not force me; for no such thing ought to be done in Israel: do not thou this folly. And I, whither shall I cause my shame to go?

"Don't do this," Tamar pleaded.

2 Samuel 13:13 (b), 14
. . . and as for thee, thou shalt be as one of the fools in Israel. Now therefore, I pray thee, speak unto the king; for he will not withhold me from thee. Howbeit he would not hearken unto her voice: but, being stronger than she, forced her, and lay with her.

What a sad story. Tamar tries to appeal to Amnon's logic, but he doesn't listen. He ignores the warnings given to him. That's what lust does. It doesn't listen to the warnings. It blocks out what's being said by a concerned parent, friend, or pastor.

2 Samuel 13:15
Then Amnon hated her exceedingly; so that the hatred wherewith he hated her was greater than the love wherewith he had loved her. And Amnon said unto her, Arise, be gone.

Rapists often kill their victims because when they've done what they do, they hate themselves. And not knowing what to do with that hate, they transfer their hatred, frustration, and guilt to their victims.

Once Amnon has Tamar, he hates her. It's a story we hear over and over and over again.

2 Samuel 13:16, 17
And she said unto him, There is no cause: this evil in sending me away is greater than the other that thou didst unto me. But he would not hearken unto her. Then he called his servant that ministered unto him, and said, Put now this woman out from me, and bolt the door after her.

Young lady, are you listening to this story? Dear sister, this is reality. Once Amnon gets what he wants, he kicks Tamar out and locks the door behind her, leaving her to go her way, crying.

2 Samuel 13:18, 19
And she had a garment of divers colours upon her: for with such robes were the king's daughters that were virgins apparelled. Then his servant brought her out, and bolted the door after her. And Tamar put ashes on her head, and rent her garment of divers colours that was on her, and laid her hand on her head, and went on crying.

How could he do this to me? Tamar wondered. *He claimed he had this deep love for me.* Oh, precious people, may the Holy Spirit give you understanding that this is what happens when lust is the main ingredient, when lust dominates a relationship. It always ends up in sorrow—ultimately in death . . .

2 Samuel 13:20
And Absalom her brother said unto her, Hath Amnon thy brother been with thee? but hold now thy peace, my sister: he is thy brother; regard not this thing. So Tamar remained desolate in her brother Absalom's house.

"I'll take care of this," Absalom told his sister. Although his statement sounds noble, Absalom will use this situation to destroy Amnon—one of the heirs to the throne.

2 Samuel 13:21
But when king David heard of all these things, he was very wroth.

David is angry. His eldest son raped his daughter, and he's understandably upset. Yet, although David is very upset, he does nothing. How could this be? The answer, I believe, is very simple. He succumbed to what we can succumb to as well. You see, a few years earlier, David himself gave in to his own lust with Bathsheba and actually murdered her husband to cover his tracks. Therefore, he felt as though he didn't have any right to address Amnon's sin.

Mom, Dad, listen carefully. This is Satan's favorite tactic to get you to allow your kids to see movies they ought not see, to listen to music they ought not hear. "Who are you to tell your kids what to do? Think of all the sins you commit every day," he hisses. But he's wrong because truth is truth regardless of who speaks it. If you're doing well, you will have great authority. But even if you didn't do well or aren't doing as well presently as you could or should, you are to still share the truth and say, "This is the way it works. This is what you must do."

David was crippled by the condemnation of Satan. And there are men and women who will not tell their sons and daughters what to do and what to avoid because they've given in to the "David syndrome." We need men and women who have courage to speak the truth. Mom and Dad, be wise. Young person, understand that God records this story for a reason—to tell you and me that lust kills.

2 Samuel 13:22, 23
And Absalom spake unto his brother Amnon neither good nor bad: for Absalom hated Amnon, because he had forced his sister Tamar. And it came to pass after two full years, that Absalom had sheepshearers in Baalhazor, which is beside Ephraim: and Absalom invited all the king's sons.

Two years later, Absalom throws a traditional "sheep-shearing party."

2 Samuel 13:24, 25
And Absalom came to the king, and said, Behold now, thy servant hath sheepshearers; let the king, I beseech thee, and his servants go with thy servant. And the king said to Absalom, Nay, my son, let us not all now go, lest we be chargeable unto thee. And he pressed him: howbeit he would not go, but blessed him.

David declined Absalom's invitation to the party but allowed his sons to go.

2 Samuel 13:26–29 (a)
Then said Absalom, If not, I pray thee, let my brother Amnon go with us. And the king said unto him, Why should he go with thee? But Absalom pressed him, that he let Amnon and all the king's sons go with him. Now Absalom had commanded his servants, saying, Mark ye now when Amnon's heart is merry with wine, and when I say unto you, Smite Amnon; then kill him, fear not: have not I commanded you? be courageous and be valiant . . .

We need to realize that sin has serious consequences. The older I get, the longer I live, the more I've gone through, the greater I hate sin because I see what it does. Sin brings about destruction and death, hurts and heartache. Learn the lesson carefully. May God help us to listen to His Word and follow His way lest we, too, find ourselves reaping the results of sin—for it's an ugly crop.

2 Samuel 13:29 (b)
. . . And the servants of Absalom did unto Amnon as Absalom had commanded. Then all the king's sons arose, and every man gat him up upon his mule, and fled.

This is the story of lust. It ends in death. Now you have a dead man, a broken-hearted dad, a depressed sister—and it's all because of lust.

Girls, if you allow lust to be a part of a relationship, death will follow. Your reputation will be slaughtered. Your joy will wither. One of two marriages ends in divorce. A huge percentage is due to sexual dissatisfaction, which is based on premarital activities and pornography. Lust brings forth sin; and sin brings forth death—the death of marriage, the death of joy, the death of what could have been.

What can we do to overcome the power of lust? Listen to what Peter says:

> Dearly beloved, I beseech you as strangers and pilgrims, abstain from fleshly lusts, which war against the soul. 1 Peter 2:11

The battleground is the same for everyone: It's the soul. The soul consists of the mind and emotions. The soul relates to people. The body is material and relates to the physical world. The spirit is the deepest part of a person and relates to God. It is the spirit that will live eternally.

In Genesis 2, we read that God formed a body out of dust, but man was not alive until God breathed a spirit into him and he became a soul. It was the common stuff of earth combined with the highest stuff of heaven that resulted in the soul. In the Garden of Eden, it was the spirit that controlled man. The soul was in subjection to the spirit, the body in subjection to the soul—until man rebelled against God. At that point, the spirit died. The soul is always in the middle. The question is, will your soul be controlled by your spirit, or by the stuff of the world? The battle is always for the soul.

The body controls the soul until a man is born again. At that point, the spirit is in control once again. Then, a battle begins that will be fought in every believer until he dies: Will the spirit dominate the soul, or will the body call the shots. Back and forth the battle goes. The Bible says if your body is controlling your mind and emotions, your soul, you're in trouble because the flesh always leads to death.

> Flee also youthful lusts . . . 2 Timothy 2:22 (a)

This is not mystical. It's so simple. "Youthful lusts" refers to the fact that the same lust that bugged you when you were young will plague you all of your days. The appetites of the flesh are always there. However old you are, this word applies to you. David, after all, was fifty years old when he sinned with Bathsheba.

> . . . but follow righteousness, faith, charity, peace, with them that call on the Lord out of a pure heart. 2 Timothy 2:22 (b)

Flee youthful lusts, and follow righteousness with them that call on the Lord out of a pure heart. In other words, run from the sin and to the saints. Spend time with fellow believers. The way to overcome lust is to flee and follow.

I have noticed in my own walk that God never wastes His warnings, be they through Scripture, through a sermon, or through a conversation. Whenever there is a word shared, it is intended for me personally. And this word is no exception. Make a decision today to abstain from those things that war against your soul. If you give in to lust, you'll have a little pleasure followed by a lifetime of pain. If you flee lust, you'll have a little pain followed by a lifetime of pleasure. It's your choice. Make the right one.

2 Samuel 13:30, 31
And it came to pass, while they were in the way, that tidings came to David, saying, Absalom hath slain all the king's sons, and there is not one of them left. Then the king arose, and tare his garments, and lay on the

earth; and all his servants stood by with their clothes rent.

How many of David's sons died? One.

2 Samuel 13:32, 33
And Jonadab, the son of Shimeah David's brother, answered and said, Let not my lord suppose that they have slain all the young men the king's sons; for Amnon only is dead: for by the appointment of Absalom this hath been determined from the day that he forced his sister Tamar. Now therefore let not my lord the king take the thing to his heart, to think that all the king's sons are dead: for Amnon only is dead.

Jonadab set the record straight.

2 Samuel 13:34–37
But Absalom fled. And the young man that kept the watch lifted up his eyes, and looked, and, behold, there came much people by the way of the hill side behind him. And Jonadab said unto the king, Behold, the king's sons come: as thy servant said, so it is. And it came to pass, as soon as he had made an end of speaking, that, behold, the king's sons came, and lifted up their voice and wept: and the king also and all his servants wept very sore. But Absalom fled, and went to Talmai, the son of Ammihud, king of Geshur. And David mourned for his son every day.

Running for his life, Absalom fled to Geshur most likely because his mother was from Geshur.

2 Samuel 13:38, 39
So Absalom fled, and went to Geshur, and was there three years. And the soul of king David longed to go forth unto Absalom: for he was comforted concerning Amnon, seeing he was dead.

After three years, David longed to see Absalom . . .

14

2 Samuel 14:1–3
Now Joab the son of Zeruiah perceived that the king's heart was toward Absalom. And Joab sent to Tekoah, and fetched thence a wise woman, and said unto her, I pray thee, feign thyself to be a mourner, and put on now mourning apparel, and anoint not thyself with oil, but be as a woman that had a long time mourned for the dead: And come to the king, and speak on this manner unto him. So Joab put the words in her mouth.

Two chapters earlier, David was convicted when Nathan told the story of a man with a lamb. Here, he will be trapped by a tale once again.

2 Samuel 14:4–7
And when the woman of Tekoah spake to the king, she fell on her face to the ground, and did obeisance, and said, Help, O king. the king said unto her, What aileth thee? And she answered, I am indeed a widow woman, and mine husband is dead. And thy handmaid had two sons, and they two strove together in the field, and there was none to part them, but the one smote the other, and slew him. And, behold, the whole family is risen against thine handmaid, and they said, Deliver him that smote his brother, that we may kill him, for the life of his brother whom he slew; and we will destroy the heir also: and so they shall quench my coal which is left, and shall not leave to my husband neither name nor remainder upon the earth.

In this story inspired by Joab, the woman of Tekoah said, "My husband is dead. My two sons got in a fight in which one was killed. Now the rest of the family wants to kill my only remaining son."

2 Samuel 14:8
And the king said unto the woman, Go to thine house, and I will give charge concerning thee.

"I'll take care of it," David said.

2 Samuel 14:9
And the woman of Tekoah said unto the king, My lord, O king, the iniquity be on me, and on my father's house: and the king and his throne be guiltless.

"I know you're bending the rules on this matter," the woman said. "But I'll take responsibility."

2 Samuel 14:10
And the king said, Whosoever saith ought unto thee, bring him to me, and he shall not touch thee any more.

"If anyone bothers you, bring him to me and he won't bother you again," David promised.

2 Samuel 14:11–18
Then said she, I pray thee, let the king remember the LORD thy God, that thou wouldest not suffer the revengers of blood to destroy any more, lest they destroy my son. And he said, As the LORD liveth, there shall not one hair of thy son fall to the earth. Then the

woman said, Let thine handmaid, I pray thee, speak one word unto my lord the king. And he said, Say on. And the woman said, Wherefore then hast thou thought such a thing against the people of God? for the king doth speak this thing as one which is faulty, in that the king doth not fetch home again his banished. For we must needs die, and are as water spilt on the ground, which cannot be gathered up again; neither doth God respect any person: yet doth he devise means, that his banished be not expelled from him. Now therefore that I am come to speak of this thing unto my lord the king, it is because the people have made me afraid: and thy handmaid said, I will now speak unto the king; it may be that the king will perform the request of his handmaid. For the king will hear, to deliver his handmaid out of the hand of the man that would destroy me and my son together out of the inheritance of God. Then thine handmaid said, The word of my lord the king shall now be comfortable: for as an angel of God, so is my lord the king to discern good and bad: therefore the LORD thy God will be with thee. Then the king answered and said unto the woman, Hide not from me, I pray thee, the thing that I shall ask thee. And the woman said, Let my lord the king now speak.

"You're a hypocrite," said the woman to David, "for you have allowed mercy to be extended to my son, but have withheld it from your own son."

This is faulty logic because the cases were entirely dissimilar. In her story, the death was not intentional. Nonetheless, David is trapped because he gave advice according to his own reasoning instead of according to the Word of God.

2 Samuel 14:19, 20
And the king said, Is not the hand of Joab with thee in all this? And the woman answered and said, As thy soul liveth, my lord the king, none can turn to the right hand or to the left from ought that my lord the king hath spoken: for thy servant Joab, he bade me, and he put all these words in the mouth of thine handmaid: To fetch about this form of speech hath thy servant Joab done this thing: and my lord is wise, according to the wisdom of an angel of God, to know all things that are in the earth.

David realized he had been set up.

2 Samuel 14:21, 22
And the king said unto Joab, Behold now, I have done this thing: go therefore, bring the young man Absalom again. And Joab fell to the ground on his face, and bowed himself, and thanked the king: and Joab said, To day thy servant knoweth that I have found grace in thy sight, my lord, O king, in that the king hath fulfilled the request of his servant.

Why is Joab so committed to restoring Absalom to David? I suggest it is because he wanted to make his future secure. After all, following the murder of Abner, David said to Joab, "Cursed be you and your house. Leprosy be upon thee forevermore" (2 Samuel 3:29). Therefore, perhaps Joab was trying to butter up Absalom, the heir apparent, by bringing him out of exile.

2 Samuel 14:23, 24
So Joab arose and went to Geshur, and brought Absalom to Jerusalem. And the king said, Let him turn to his own house, and let him not see my face. So Absalom returned to his own house, and saw not the king's face.

"Absalom can come home, but I don't want to see him," David said.

2 Samuel 14:25, 26
But in all Israel there was none to be so much praised as Absalom for his beauty: from the sole of his foot even to the crown of his head there was no blemish in him. And when he polled his head, (for it was at every year's end that he polled it: because the hair was heavy on him, therefore he polled it:) he weighed the hair of his head at two hundred shekels after the king's weight.

Absalom was extolled for his physical appearance. His hair weighed four pounds.

2 Samuel 14:27, 28
And unto Absalom there were born three sons, and one daughter, whose name was Tamar: she was a woman of a fair countenance. So Absalom dwelt two full years in Jerusalem, and saw not the king's face.

For three years, Absalom was exiled in Geshur. For two years in Jerusalem, he still didn't see his father's face.

2 Samuel 14:29–31
Therefore Absalom sent for Joab, to have sent him to the king; but he would not come to him: and when he sent again the second time, he would not come. Therefore he said unto his servants, See, Joab's field is near mine, and he hath barley there; go and set it on fire. And Absalom's servants set the field on fire. Then Joab arose, and came to

Absalom unto his house, and said unto him, Wherefore have thy servants set my field on fire?

When even Joab refused to see him, Absalom ordered his field to be set on fire in order to get his attention.

2 Samuel 14:32
And Absalom answered Joab, Behold, I sent unto thee, saying, Come hither, that I may send thee to the king, to say, Wherefore am I come from Geshur? it had been good for me to have been there still: now therefore let me see the king's face; and if there be any iniquity in me, let him kill me.

"I can't reach my dad," Absalom said to Joab. "If he wants to kill me, let him do it. If not, let me see him."

2 Samuel 14:33
So Joab came to the king, and told him: and when he had called for Absalom, he came to the king, and bowed himself on his face to the ground before the king: and the king kissed Absalom.

Reconciliation is made—but it's too late. For five years, bitterness had been growing in the heart of Absalom. David was a man who sinned greatly, yet he was forgiven completely. Now he cannot completely forgive his son. He loves him, but he can't forgive him. He puts conditions upon his forgiveness.

God forgives you unconditionally. As far as the east is from the west, that's how far away your sins and iniquities are (Psalm 103:12). Once you have confessed, your sin is forgiven and forgotten. Yes, due to an irrevocable, absolute law of nature—the law of sowing and reaping—the results of your sin will crop up indeed. But your Father has forgotten them completely (Hebrews 10:17).

This is fabulous to me. When I go to the Lord and say, "Father, I've blown it again," He says, "Again? I don't recall what you're talking about." God forgave David that way. The problem is, he doesn't forgive his own son with that same unconditional gracious forgiveness. This created in Absalom a spirit of bitterness that festered within him for five years.

Dad, do you have a son that feels alienated from you. Embrace him and say, "I forgive you even as I have been forgiven time and time again." You might need to discipline and chasten him, even as our heavenly Father disciplines us. But you must forgive him unconditionally. If you don't, you will find rebellion brewing within his heart.

15

2 Samuel 15:1, 2 (a)
And it came to pass after this, that Absalom prepared him chariots and horses, and fifty men to run before him. And Absalom rose up early, and stood beside the way of the gate . . .

Here, we see the beginning of Absalom's insurrection.

2 Samuel 15:2 (b), 3
. . . and it was so, that when any man that had a controversy came to the king for judgment, then Absalom called unto him, and said, Of what city art thou? And he said, Thy servant is of one of the tribes of Israel. And Absalom said unto him, See, thy matters are good and right; but there is no man deputed of the king to hear thee.

The gate of the city was where legal transactions took place and where counsel was given. Absalom began his revolution by sitting at the gate and saying to the people, "I sympathize with you. I wish I could help you. The king is obviously too busy. Now, if *I* were king, I would take care of your concern."

2 Samuel 15:4–6
Absalom said moreover, Oh that I were made judge in the land, that every man which hath any suit or cause might come unto me, and I would do him justice! And it was so, that when any man came nigh to him to do him obeisance, he put forth his hand, and took him, and kissed him. And on this manner did Absalom to all Israel that came to the king for judgment: so Absalom stole the hearts of the men of Israel.

As Absalom undermined his dad's authority, he stole the hearts of the men of Israel.

2 Samuel 15:7 (a)
And it came to pass after forty years . . .

This could only refer to the time that had passed since David's anointing.

2 Samuel 15:7 (b)–10
. . . that Absalom said unto the king, I pray thee, let me go and pay my vow, which I have vowed unto the LORD, in Hebron. For thy servant vowed a vow while I abode at Geshur in Syria, saying, If the LORD shall bring me again indeed to Jerusalem, then I will serve the LORD. And the king said unto him, Go in peace. So he arose, and went to Hebron.

But Absalom sent spies throughout all the tribes of Israel, saying, As soon as ye hear the sound of the trumpet, then ye shall say, Absalom reigneth in Hebron.

Why did Absalom set up his kingdom in Hebron? Hebron was his hometown. But more importantly, Hebron was the capital city of Israel before David moved it to Jerusalem. When David moved the capital to Jerusalem, the men of Hebron were obviously upset. Absalom capitalized on their dissatisfaction with David.

2 Samuel 15:11, 12
And with Absalom went two hundred men out of Jerusalem, that were called; and they went in their simplicity, and they knew not any thing. And Absalom sent for Ahithophel the Gilonite, David's counseller, from his city, even from Giloh, while he offered sacrifices. And the conspiracy was strong; for the people increased continually with Absalom.

David greatly valued Ahithophel's wise counsel. Why, then, did Absalom think Ahithophel would transfer allegiance and defect to his cause? I suggest the reason may have been that Ahithophel was Bathsheba's grandfather. No doubt Ahithophel was aware of the fact that David had done injustice to his family in killing Bathsheba's husband. If that was in fact the case, Absalom could have exploited this weakness for his own purposes.

I point this out to show you the danger of allowing bitterness to take root within your soul. It will lead to your destruction. Ahithophel obviously never dealt with this matter of David. So he defected from David and we'll see him siding with Absalom and ultimately dying, so upset was he by the situation.

May the Lord keep us from any type of unforgiveness or bitterness. Like Absalom, we'll find ourselves hung up, if we don't deal with it directly.

2 Samuel 15:13
And there came a messenger to David, saying, The hearts of the men of Israel are after Absalom.

"You are bone of our bone and flesh of our flesh," the men of Israel said to David in chapter 5, begging him to be their king. Here, they reject David's leadership and side with this one who had stolen their hearts.

"I urge you brethren," Paul would write to the church at Rome, "to avoid those who cause divisions and offenses" (see Romans 16:17). Absalom is the quintessential example of one who should have been avoided.

2 Samuel 15:14–16
And David said unto all his servants that were with him at Jerusalem, Arise, and let us flee; for we shall not else escape from Absalom: make speed to depart, lest he overtake us suddenly, and bring evil upon us, and smite the city with the edge of the sword. And the king's servants said unto the king, Behold, thy servants are ready to do whatsoever my lord the king shall appoint. And the king went forth, and all his household after him. And the king left ten women, which were concubines, to keep the house.

With the forces of Absalom gathered outside the city, David desires to spare Jerusalem from destruction. So He gathers his household and splits—leaving ten of his concubines behind to keep his house while he was gone.

2 Samuel 15:17, 18
And the king went forth, and all the people after him, and tarried in a place that was far off. And all his servants passed on beside him; and all the Cherethites, and all the Pelethites, and all the Gittites, six hundred men which came after him from Gath, passed on before the king.

The six hundred men with David were part of the group we read about in 1 Samuel 22. When David was fleeing from Saul in the wilderness, men who were discontent, in debt, and distressed gathered around David. David used these ragtag renegades as the base of his army. And this group is a perfect picture of us. We are in debt, distressed, and discontent, yet we find ourselves gathering around a Greater than David, the Son of David, Jesus Christ. These men were transformed into a crack unit of excellent troops. Because they were around David, they became like him. And because they endured real difficulties and tribulations with David, they formed into a tight group of loyal, capable soldiers.

We, too, gathering around our Greater than David, Jesus Christ, endure trials. But those very trials produce in us abilities and capabilities for service.

> Wherein ye greatly rejoice, though now for a season, if need be, ye are in heaviness through manifold temptations: That the trial of your faith, being much more precious than of gold that perisheth, though it be tried with fire, might be found unto praise and honour and glory at the appearing of Jesus Christ.
>
> 1 Peter 1:6, 7

In Bible times, gold was purified by melting it to a liquid state. The smelter knew the purification process was complete when he looked into the liquid gold and saw his face. But until he could see his face, he kept the heat on. What's the Lord doing in our lives? He's keeping the heat on until we become a reflection of Him, until we are formed in the image of His likeness.

You might wonder why you've had some fiery, heavy trials. Know this: You're precious. You're gold. And the Lord says, "I'm going to purify you so that My reflection might be seen in you, so that when people see you, they'll see Me."

2 Samuel 15:19–21
Then said the king to Ittai the Gittite, Wherefore goest thou also with us? return to thy place, and abide with the king: for thou art a stranger, and also an exile. Whereas thou camest but yesterday, should I this day make thee go up and down with us? seeing I go whither I may, return thou, and take back thy brethren: mercy and truth be with thee. And Ittai answered the king, and said, As the LORD liveth, and as my lord the king liveth, surely in what place my lord the king shall be, whether in death or life, even there also will thy servant be.

Ittai the Gittite—what a guy! He stood by David even though doing so might have meant death. Are you an Ittai? Do you say, "Lord, wherever You lead and whatever it means, I'm with You"?

2 Samuel 15:22, 23
And David said to Ittai, Go and pass over. And Ittai the Gittite passed over, and all his men, and all the little ones that were with him. And all the country wept with a loud voice, and all the people passed over: the king also himself passed over the brook Kidron, and all the people passed over, toward the way of the wilderness.

Outside the Eastern Gate of Jerusalem, there is a small valley. In Bible days, the Brook Kidron flowed through this valley. The word *Kidron* means "dark." The reason it's called "Dark" is because the Brook Kidron was where much of the waste and sewage of Jerusalem was poured. The temple wastes also poured into the Kidron—which meant that, at the time of Passover when upwards of 1,000 lambs were sacrificed, the brook would take on a red color.

In John 18 we see the Son of David, Jesus Christ, also leaving Jerusalem, also having the masses against Him, also experiencing rebellion and betrayal by one He cared about—Judas Iscariot. He left and crossed the same brook David crosses here. However, when Jesus crossed the Brook Kidron on the night of the Last Supper, it was at the time of the Passover. Thus, He crossed over a blood-red river, emblematic and symbolic of what He was to endure on the Cross.

2 Samuel 15:24–26
And lo Zadok also, and all the Levites were with him, bearing the ark of the covenant of God: and they set down the ark of God; and Abiathar went up, until all the people had done passing out of the city. And the king said unto Zadok, Carry back the ark of God into the city: if I shall find favour in the eyes of the LORD, he will bring me again, and shew me both it, and his habitation: But if he thus say, I have no delight in thee; behold, here am I, let him do to me as seemeth good unto him.

"Take the ark back to Jerusalem," David said to Zadok. "If God wants me to survive, He'll bring me back to the city in due time, and I'll see the ark again. But if He wants to destroy me in the wilderness, so be it."

This heart is sadly lacking in Christians today. It seems we are always trying to tell God what to do and trying to manipulate Him through the exercise of our faith. Oh, for a heart that says, "Not my will, but *Thine* be done."

2 Samuel 15:27–30
The king said also unto Zadok the priest, Art not thou a seer? return into the city in peace, and your two sons with you, Ahimaaz thy son, and Jonathan the son of Abiathar. See, I will tarry in the plain of the wilderness, until there come word from you to certify me. Zadok therefore and Abiathar carried the ark of God again to Jerusalem: and they tarried there. And David went up by the ascent of mount Olivet, and wept as he went up, and had his head covered, and he went barefoot: and all the people that was with him covered every man his head, and they went up, weeping as they went up.

Even as Jesus crossed over the Kidron and went up the Mount of Olives to the Garden of Gethsemane, we see David preceding Him to the Mount of Olives, weeping as he went.

2 Samuel 15:31
And one told David, saying, Ahithophel is among the conspirators with Absalom.

Ahithophel, David's trusted counselor, had betrayed him very possibly due to the fact that he was Bathsheba's grandfather. The root of bitterness deep within his heart surfaced as he sided with Absalom in rebellion.

2 Samuel 15:32
And it came to pass, that when David was come to the top of the mount, where he worshipped God,

David was weeping, but his weeping did not deter his worship. Perhaps you, too, are weeping or brokenhearted. Isaiah 61:3 says God gives us beauty for ashes, the oil of joy for mourning, the garment of praise for the spirit of heaviness. Therefore, in times of weeping, worship. Fight against the tendency to hole up, to pull back, to feel sorry for yourself. It is especially when you feel depressed, discouraged, unloved, or upset that you need to extol the Lord.

2 Samuel 15:32–37
behold, Hushai the Archite came to meet him with his coat rent, and earth upon his head: Unto whom David said, If thou passest on with me, then thou shalt be a burden unto me: But if thou return to the city, and say unto Absalom, I will be thy servant, O king; as I have been thy father's servant hitherto, so will I now also be thy servant: then mayest thou for me defeat the counsel of Ahithophel. And hast thou not there with thee Zadok and Abiathar the priests? therefore it shall be, that what thing soever thou shalt hear out of the king's house, thou shalt tell it to Zadok and Abiathar the priests. Behold, they have there with them their two sons, Ahimaaz Zadok's son, and Jonathan Abiathar's son; and by them ye shall send unto me every thing that ye can hear. So Hushai David's friend came into the city, and Absalom came into Jerusalem.

David sent Hushai to Jerusalem as a "double agent," both to send word of Absalom's plans and to counter the wise advice Absalom was sure to receive from Ahithophel.

16

2 Samuel 16:1–3
And when David was a little past the top of the hill, behold, Ziba the servant of Mephibosheth met him, with a couple of asses saddled, and upon them two hundred loaves of bread, and an hundred bunches of raisins, and an hundred of summer fruits, and a bottle of wine. And the king said unto Ziba, What meanest thou by these? And Ziba said, The asses be for the king's household to ride on; and the bread and summer fruit for the young men to eat; and the wine, that such as be faint in the wilderness may drink. And the king said, And where is thy master's son? And Ziba said unto the king, Behold, he abideth at Jerusalem: for he said, To day shall the house of Israel restore me the kingdom of my father.

As seen in chapter 9, Saul's sole surviving relative was Mephibosheth, Jonathan's son. Ziba, who had been Jonathan's servant, was Mephibosheth's servant. Here, Ziba appears to David and lies that Mephibosheth was rebelling against him.

2 Samuel 16:4
Then said the king to Ziba, Behold, thine are all that pertained unto Mephibosheth. And Ziba said, I humbly beseech thee that I may find grace in thy sight, my lord, O king.

David was fooled. His rash decision to give Ziba Saul and Jonathan's vast inheritance reminds me of Joshua's decision to sign a peace treaty with the Gibeonites (Joshua 9). Whether regarding a business deal or a marriage proposal, be careful you don't make decisions in the time of trial and heat. During those times, your thinking isn't as clear as it would be otherwise. Instead, slow down and seek the Lord.

2 Samuel 16:5, 6
And when king David came to Bahurim, behold, thence came out a man of the family of the house of Saul, whose name was Shimei, the son of Gera: he came forth, and cursed still as he came. And he cast stones at David, and at all the servants of king David: and all the people and all the mighty men were on his right hand and on his left.

This self-proclaimed prophet has the audacity to hurl stones and curses at one of the greatest men of God who ever lived. "Let he who is without sin cast the first stone," Jesus said (John 8:7). Thus, Jesus alone had the right to throw stones. But He never did. Instead, He carried a Cross.

2 Samuel 16:7, 8
And thus said Shimei when he cursed, Come out, come out, thou bloody man, and thou man of Belial: The LORD hath returned upon thee all the blood of the house of Saul, in whose stead thou hast reigned; and the LORD hath delivered the kingdom into the hand of Absalom thy son: and, behold, thou art taken in thy mischief, because thou art a bloody man.

"You're paying the price for overthrowing Saul," Shimei said. This is interesting because Shimei's assessment of the situation is totally wrong. David did not overthrow Saul. In fact, time and time again, when he had the opportunity to annihilate Saul, David spared his life.

2 Samuel 16:9
Then said Abishai the son of Zeruiah unto the king, Why should this dead dog curse my lord the king? let me go over, I pray thee, and take off his head.

"Let me chop this pipsqueak down to size," said Abishai. Did he have the right to say this? In a sense, yes, for in Exodus 22:28, the Law specifically says, "Curse not the ruler of thy people." Ecclesiastes 10:20 goes on to say that we are not to curse rulers in word or even in thought. Abishai had a right to make this statement. But watch David's response . . .

2 Samuel 16:10 (a)
And the king said, What have I to do with you, ye sons of Zeruiah?

"What am I going to do with you, Abishai?" Abishai was with David in the wilderness of Ziph, hiding from Saul who sought David's life. One day, David and Abishai came upon Saul sleeping in a cave. "Let me pin him to the ground. The Lord has delivered him into our hands," Abishai said.

"No," David answered. "The Lord forbid that I should stretch forth my hand against the Lord's anointed" (1 Samuel 26:11).

As Peter would do centuries later in the Garden of Gethsemane, Abishai seemed determined to defend his king with a sword. But David knew better.

2 Samuel 16:10 (b)
. . . so let him curse, because the Lord hath said unto him, Curse David. Who shall then say, Wherefore hast thou done so?

How I appreciate David's attitude here. Notice how he handled this criticism . . .

First, he looked up. At this point in his life, David understood that God was in all things. Earlier, he didn't have such understanding. Earlier, he was pugnacious, a fighter. Earlier, it was only the kindness of Abigail that kept him from destroying Nabal (1 Samuel 25). But now David understood that this attack upon him could not come forth without the Lord allowing it. Oh, that we might have this same understanding.

Dear saint, the Lord has allowed that person to criticize you not to destroy you, but to develop you. Norman Vincent Peale said, "I am concerned that Christians are more willing to be destroyed by praise than to be saved by criticism." It's true. We are more willing to march off to battle with the applause of men ringing in our ears than to hear a valid criticism—one the Lord has allowed to surface.

Several years ago, the manager of New York's Grand Union Hotel was addressing a group of hotel managers. Asked to give a seminar on how to be successful, he said, "You don't need to know anything about running a hotel to run a hotel. Just open the doors and your customers will tell you exactly how it should be run." Wise counsel indeed!

2 Samuel 16:11
And David said to Abishai, and to all his servants, Behold, my son, which came forth of my bowels, seeketh my life: how much more now may this Benjamite do it? let him alone, and let him curse; for the Lord hath bidden him.

Secondly, David looked about. "If you think Shimei's words are harsh, they're nothing in comparison to what Absalom is trying to do," David said. "I've erred greatly. My own family is in utter disorder."

When someone puts you down, do what David did. Look around. See the mistakes you've made, the blunders on your record. However brutal the put-down is, it's not even a fraction of what you deserve.

"In my flesh dwells no good thing," Paul declared (Romans 7:18). It's a pivotal day when you finally realize that there's nothing good in your flesh, for at that point, you no longer seek to defend, extol, or protect yourself, and you're free.

2 Samuel 16:12
It may be that the Lord will look on mine affliction, and that the Lord will requite me good for his cursing this day.

Thirdly, David looked ahead. "God's hearing these words of Shimei," he said. "And maybe He will be kind and merciful to me because of Shimei's cursing."

When my kids are put down, even though they might deserve it, my heart is grieved. We love our kids. We know what they are, but we love them anyway! Now, if we, being evil, care about our kids, how much more does our heavenly Father care about His (see Matthew 7:11). "Blessed are you when men revile you and persecute you and say all manner of evil against you falsely for My sake," Jesus said (Matthew 5:11). Look ahead. God knows what you're going through. And He promises blessing.

2 Samuel 16:13
And as David and his men went by the way, Shimei went along on the hill's side over against him, and cursed as he went, and threw stones at him, and cast dust.

Shimei first hurled rocks and then he cast dust. In this culture, this was equivalent to saying, "I wish you were buried." This is almost always what happens. Start throwing stones at someone and you will eventually wish he were dead. That's why we're not to give place to unforgiveness, bitterness, or a critical spirit. Those things will destroy us.

What happened to Shimei? On his deathbed, David's final word to Solomon was to kill Shimei (1 Kings 2:8). I believe this was because David realized that, although he had the maturity and experience to handle Shimei, his young son, Solomon, would be tripped up by him.

2 Samuel 16:14
And the king, and all the people that were with him, came weary, and refreshed themselves there.

David looked up, looked about, and looked ahead. We have a privilege he didn't yet have. That is, we can look afresh at Jesus Christ (1 Peter 2:21). Jesus was reviled, insulted, mocked, and killed. Yet He never defended Himself, never put down those who were putting Him down.

Greek philosopher Publius said, "I have often regretted my speech, but never my silence."

Solomon said, "In the multitude of words, there wanteth not sin" (Proverbs 10:19).

James said, "Let every man be swift to hear and slow to speak" (James 1:19).

Jesus died without defending Himself, without standing up for His rights, His reputation, or His ministry. And we are to follow in His steps. The secret of life is death. When you finally die, the pressure is off. When you truly realize you are crucified with Christ, you won't exalt yourself, protect yourself, or be concerned about yourself. The secret of the Christian life is to die to self, to get your eyes off yourself and to quit wondering why you're discouraged, why you're depressed, why you're not happy.

The way to abundant life is not to seek to be blessed, but to seek to be a blessing to others; not to seek to be understood, but to seek to understand others; not to seek to receive, but to seek to reach out to others. We look for anything and everything but death. But there is no other way. David recognized this.

2 Samuel 16:15–21
And Absalom, and all the people the men of Israel, came to Jerusalem, and Ahithophel with him. And it came to pass, when Hushai the Archite, David's friend, was come unto Absalom, that Hushai said unto Absalom, God save the king, God save the king. And Absalom said to Hushai, Is this thy kindness to thy friend? why wentest thou not with thy friend? And Hushai said unto Absalom, Nay; but whom the LORD, and this people, and all the men of Israel, choose, his will I be, and with him will I abide. And again, whom should I serve? should I not serve in the presence of his son? as I have served in thy father's presence, so will I be in thy presence. Then said Absalom to Ahithophel, Give counsel among you what we shall do. And Ahithophel said unto Absalom, Go in unto thy father's concubines, which he hath left to keep the house; and all Israel shall hear that thou art abhorred of thy father: then shall the hands of all that are with thee be strong.

Ahithophel said, "Absalom, now that you're in the city, have physical relations with David's concubines. In so doing, you will show all of the people that you despise your father. Knowing you are completely committed to a course of rebellion and that reconciliation with your father is out of the question, they won't be afraid to follow you wholeheartedly."

2 Samuel 16:22, 23
So they spread Absalom a tent upon the top of the house; and Absalom went in unto his father's concubines in the sight of all Israel. And the counsel of Ahithophel, which he counselled in those days, was as if a man had inquired at the oracle of God: so was all the counsel of Ahithophel both with David and with Absalom.

Here we see the fulfillment of 2 Samuel 12:11, 12 when Nathan the prophet said, "Because you have taken the wife of your neighbor, your wives shall be taken in the sight of your countrymen."

Was Ahithophel's counsel righteous and holy? No. But it was clever, cunning, and pragmatic.

17

2 Samuel 17:1–3
Moreover Ahithophel said unto Absalom, Let me now choose out twelve thousand men, and I will arise and pursue

after David this night: And I will come upon him while he is weary and weak handed, and will make him afraid: and all the people that are with him shall flee; and I will smite the king only: And I will bring back all the people unto thee: the man whom thou seekest is as if all returned: so all the people shall be in peace.

"Now is the time to strike," Ahithophel said. "David's on the run. He's tired. He's weary. We can crush him with a small force of 12,000 men."

2 Samuel 17:4
And the saying pleased Absalom well, and all the elders of Israel.

Strategically, this again was excellent counsel.

2 Samuel 17:5–13
Then said Absalom, Call now Hushai the Archite also, and let us hear likewise what he saith. And when Hushai was come to Absalom, Absalom spake unto him, saying, Ahithophel hath spoken after this manner: shall we do after his saying? if not; speak thou. And Hushai said unto Absalom, The counsel that Ahithophel hath given is not good at this time. For, said Hushai, thou knowest thy father and his men, that they be mighty men, and they be chafed in their minds, as a bear robbed of her whelps in the field: and thy father is a man of war, and will not lodge with the people. Behold, he is hid now in some pit, or in some other place: and it will come to pass, when some of them be overthrown at the first, that whosoever heareth it will say, There is a slaughter among the people that follow Absalom. And he also that is valiant, whose heart is as the heart of a lion, shall utterly melt: for all Israel knoweth that thy father is a mighty man, and they which be with him are valiant men. Therefore I counsel that all Israel be generally gathered unto thee, from Dan even to Beer-sheba, as the sand that is by the sea for multitude; and that thou go to battle in thine own person. So shall we come upon him in some place where he shall be found, and we will light upon him as the dew falleth on the ground: and of him and of all the men that are with him there shall not be left so much as one. Moreover, if he be gotten into a city, then shall all Israel bring ropes to that city, and we will draw it into the river, until there be not one small stone found there.

Double Agent Hushai said, "David is as angry as a mother bear robbed of her cubs. Therefore, let's wait. Let's gather troops from Dan to Beersheba, from north to south, and pursue him when his passion has cooled."

2 Samuel 17:14
And Absalom and all the men of Israel said, The counsel of Hushai the Archite is better than the counsel of Ahithophel. For the LORD had appointed to defeat the good counsel of Ahithophel, to the intent that the LORD might bring evil upon Absalom.

In 2 Samuel 15:31, David prayed that Ahithophel would give foolish counsel. Ahithophel's counsel, however, was brilliant.

God does not need our advice, gang. He doesn't need us to figure out the situation. I can't tell you how thankful I am that Jesus Christ ever lives to make intercession for the saints (Hebrews 7:25). This means that right now, at the right hand of the Father, my Lord Jesus is saying, "Father, what Jon means is . . ." The older I get in the Lord, the more I understand the foolishness of presumption—of dictating to the Lord what He must do or how He must work—and the wisdom of saying, "Father, You know what's right in this situation. Here's what I think, but only You know what's right. Therefore, *Thy* kingdom come, Lord. *Thy* will be done."

2 Samuel 17:15, 16
Then said Hushai unto Zadok and to Abiathar the priests, Thus and thus did Ahithophel counsel Absalom and the elders of Israel; and thus and thus have I counselled. Now therefore send quickly, and tell David, saying, Lodge not this night in the plains of the wilderness, but speedily pass over; lest the king be swallowed up, and all the people that are with him.

Hushai sent a message to David, saying, "I've bought you some time, David. Now split."

2 Samuel 17:17–22
Now Jonathan and Ahimaaz stayed by En-rogel; for they might not be seen to come into the city: and a wench went and told them; and they went and told king David. Nevertheless a lad saw them, and told Absalom: but they went both of them away quickly, and came to a man's house in Bahurim, which had a well in his court; whither they went down. And the woman took and spread a covering over the well's mouth, and spread ground corn thereon; and the thing was not known. And when Absalom's servants came to the woman to the house, they said, Where is Ahimaaz and Jonathan? And the woman said unto them, They be gone over the brook

of water. And when they had sought and could not find them, they returned to Jerusalem. And it came to pass, after they were departed, that they came up out of the well, and went and told king David, and said unto David, Arise, and pass quickly over the water: for thus hath Ahithophel counselled against you. Then David arose, and all the people that were with him, and they passed over Jordan: by the morning light there lacked not one of them that was not gone over Jordan.

I am reminded of Rahab, another brave woman who hid two spies, and saved her own life in the process (Joshua 2).

2 Samuel 17:23
And when Ahithophel saw that his counsel was not followed, he saddled his ass, and arose, and gat him home to his house, to his city, and put his household in order, and hanged himself, and died, and was buried in the sepulchre of his father.

When Ahithophel realized Absalom was not going to take his counsel, he knew David would eventually return to power, and that he would be hung as a traitor.

Why was Ahithophel so intent on bringing David down? In 2 Samuel 23:34, we read that Ahithophel had a son named Eliam. In 2 Samuel 11:3, we read that Eliam had a daughter named Bathsheba. This means Ahithophel was the grandfather of Bathsheba—the same Bathsheba whose husband David ordered to be killed in battle (2 Samuel 11:15). Now, it's eleven years later and evidently feelings of bitterness had been festering in Ahithophel's soul.

If I allow bitterness to be under the surface of the soil of my soul, it will eventually bear murderous fruit. It might take a month, a year, or eleven years to surface, but surface it will.

> Let all bitterness, and wrath, and anger, and clamour, and evil speaking, be put away from you, with all malice: And be ye kind one to another, tenderhearted, forgiving one another, even as God for Christ's sake hath forgiven you. Ephesians 4:31, 32

Was Ahithophel's anger justified? Yes. But although he had a reason to be angry, he couldn't afford the price, for his anger cost him his life.

"How many times shall my brother sin against me and I forgive him," asked Peter. "Seven times?" I'm sure Peter felt smug about this, for, based on Amos 1:3, the rabbis taught one was required to forgive someone only three times. Jesus, however, told Peter he was to forgive not seven times, but 490 times—more times than a person was able to keep track of (Matthew 18).

It has been said that bitterness is like swallowing a bottle of poison, and waiting for the other person to die. David doesn't die in this story. Ahithophel does.

Like Ahithophel, Jesus came to us with wise counsel. But, as collective humanity, we rejected His counsel. Ahithophel saddled an ass. So did Jesus. Ahithophel rode into the city. So did Jesus. Ahithophel put his household in order. Jesus went to the Upper Room and gave instructions to His disciples. Ahithophel hanged himself. Jesus went willingly to the Cross, where He, too, hung for you and me. Ahithophel was buried in a sepulchre. Jesus was placed in a sepulchre. But, unlike Ahithophel, Jesus rose again.

I might have reason to be upset or bitter. But I can either be hung up by my bitterness, or I can see that Jesus took the reason for my bitterness upon Himself. We need not be bitter with anyone because Jesus understands our hurt, and it killed Him. Happy indeed is the man whose sins are forgiven (Romans 4:7), not only the sins he's committed, but also the sins committed toward him. The gospel frees us not only from our own sin, but also from the sin round about us. And I'm so glad.

2 Samuel 17:24–26
Then David came to Mahanaim. And Absalom passed over Jordan, he and all the men of Israel with him. And Absalom made Amasa captain of the host instead of Joab: which Amasa was a man's son, whose name was Ithra an Israelite, that went in to Abigail the daughter of Nahash, sister to Zeruiah Joab's mother. So Israel and Absalom pitched in the land of Gilead.

David and Absalom both readied for battle. But God sent three special men uniquely to David . . .

2 Samuel 17:27–29
And it came to pass, when David was come to Mahanaim, that Shobi the son of Nahash of Rabbah of the children of Ammon, and Machir the son of Ammiel of Lo-debar, and Barzillai the Gileadite of Rogelim, Brought beds, and basons, and earthen vessels, and wheat, and barley, and flour, and parched corn, and beans, and lentiles, and parched pulse, And honey, and butter, and sheep, and cheese of kine, for David, and for the people that were with him, to eat: for they said, The people is hungry, and weary, and thirsty, in the wilderness.

Shobi was the son of Nahash. His brother was Hanun, who shaved the beards and cut the garments of David's servants (2 Samuel 10). David, in turn, waged war against him. Therefore, Shobi could have easily said, "Me help David? No way. He killed my family." But he didn't.

Machir was the man who hid and cared for Mephibosheth for many years. Therefore, he could have said, "Me help David? I've been taking care of a crippled guy for years. It's someone else's turn to help." But he didn't.

Barzillai, as we'll see two chapters from now, was eighty years old at this time. He could have said, "Me haul beds and earthen vessels, grain and honey, sheep and cheese? I'm too old." But he didn't.

These are the same three excuses I hear and can give all too easily. "I'm hurt because Brother so and so ignored me." Or, "I helped last time. It's someone else's turn." Or, "I've done my time. I've paid my dues. I deserve a rest."

Shobi, Machir, and Barzillai realized now wasn't the time to back out but to press on. Time is short, precious people. "Feed My sheep," Jesus said (John 21). Therefore, if you love Jesus Christ, be like Shobi, Machir, and Barzillai. Go where people are hungry and weary. Go to the wilderness and give.

18

2 Samuel 18:1, 2 (a)
And David numbered the people that were with him, and set captains of thousands and captains of hundreds over them. And David sent forth a third part of the people under the hand of Joab, and a third part under the hand of Abishai the son of Zeruiah, Joab's brother, and a third part under the hand of Ittai the Gittite . . .

Because Ittai was willing to simply walk *with* David, he was given the honor of working *for* David.

2 Samuel 18:2 (b)
. . . And the king said unto the people, I will surely go forth with you myself also.

"I will surely go forth with you myself," David said.

"Lo, I am with you always," says our Greater than David (Matthew 28:20).

2 Samuel 18:3, 4
But the people answered, Thou shalt not go forth: for if we flee away, they will not care for us; neither if half of us die, will they care for us: but now thou art worth ten thousand of us: therefore now it is better that thou succour us out of the city. And the king said unto them, What seemeth you best I will do. And the king stood by the gate side, and all the people came out by hundreds and by thousands.

"What seemeth you best I will do." David—a man who had been given more authority than anyone in the known world—was also a man of true submission.

2 Samuel 18:5–8
And the king commanded Joab and Abishai and Ittai, saying, Deal gently for my sake with the young man, even with Absalom. And all the people heard when the king gave all the captains charge concerning Absalom. So the people went out into the field against Israel: and the battle was in the wood of Ephraim; Where the people of Israel were slain before the servants of David, and there was there a great slaughter that day of twenty thousand men. For the battle was there scattered over the face of all the country: and the wood devoured more people that day than the sword devoured.

The battle between Absalom's and David's forces took place in a heavily wooded area. In the hubbub and fury of battle, more men were wounded by the trees and brush than by the sword.

2 Samuel 18:9
And Absalom met the servants of David. And Absalom rode upon a mule, and the mule went under the thick boughs of a great oak, and his head caught hold of the oak, and he was taken up between the heaven and the earth; and the mule that was under him went away.

Astride a mule, Absalom's hair got caught in the bough of a tree. Absalom's hair was his source of pride. Thus, it was his point of pride that brought him down.

2 Samuel 18:10–13
And a certain man saw it, and told Joab, and said, Behold, I saw Absalom hanged in an oak. And Joab said unto the man that told him, And, behold, thou sawest him, and why didst thou not smite him there to the ground? and I would have given thee ten shekels of silver, and a girdle. And the man said unto Joab, Though I should receive a thousand shekels of silver in mine hand, yet would I not put forth mine hand against the king's son: for in our hearing the king charged thee and

Abishai and Ittai, saying, Beware that none touch the young man Absalom. Otherwise I should have wrought falsehood against mine own life: for there is no matter hid from the king, and thou thyself wouldest have set thyself against me.

"Why didn't you kill Absalom when you saw him stuck in the tree?" Joab asked one of the men.

"Had I killed him, you would have come down on me," the man wisely answered, "for the wish of the king was that Absalom live."

2 Samuel 18:14
Then said Joab, I may not tarry thus with thee. And he took three darts in his hand, and thrust them through the heart of Absalom, while he was yet alive in the midst of the oak.

Joab shot three arrows in Absalom's heart. Thus, the man who once stole hearts was now stilled in his heart (2 Samuel 15:6).

2 Samuel 18:15–17
And ten young men that bare Joab's armour compassed about and smote Absalom, and slew him. And Joab blew the trumpet, and the people returned from pursuing after Israel: for Joab held back the people. And they took Absalom, and cast him into a great pit in the wood, and laid a very great heap of stones upon him: and all Israel fled every one to his tent.

Absalom ends up in a pit. And whenever you or I attempt to rebel or manipulate, whenever we seek our own kingdom rather than the kingdom of God, the result will always be the same. We'll always end up in a pit. Always. David was a man who learned this lesson. "I will not touch the Lord's anointed," he said, "be it Saul or Shimei." Oh, that we would learn the lesson of letting *God* work.

2 Samuel 18:18
Now Absalom in his lifetime had taken and reared up for himself a pillar, which is in the king's dale: for he said, I have no son to keep my name in remembrance: and he called the pillar after his own name: and it is called unto this day, Absalom's place.

During his life, Absalom erected to himself a huge monument of stones. In his death, a pile of stones was heaped over his body. We read in Deuteronomy 21:18–21 that rebellious sons were to be stoned to death. After Absalom was thrown into a pit, stones were thrown upon him, a fulfillment of the regulation given in Deuteronomy.

2 Samuel 18:19, 20
Then said Ahimaaz the son of Zadok, Let me now run, and bear the king tidings, how that the LORD hath avenged him of his enemies. And Joab said unto him, Thou shalt not bear tidings this day, but thou shalt bear tidings another day: but this day thou shalt bear no tidings, because the king's son is dead.

Zadok was the priest. His son, Ahimaaz, was eager to tell David the news that Absalom was dead. David's general, Joab, however, didn't want Ahimaaz to carry the message to David. Why? When David got the message concerning Saul's death, the messenger was killed (2 Samuel 1:13–15). The same thing happened when Ishbosheth was murdered (2 Samuel 4:12). Therefore, knowing the stakes were high, Joab denied the request of Ahimaaz.

2 Samuel 18:21–23 (a)
Then said Joab to Cushi, Go tell the king what thou hast seen. And Cushi bowed himself unto Joab, and ran. Then said Ahimaaz the son of Zadok yet again to Joab, But howsoever, let me, I pray thee, also run after Cushi. And Joab said, Wherefore wilt thou run, my son, seeing that thou hast no tidings ready? But howsoever, said he, let me run. And he said unto him, Run . . .

Instead of Ahimaaz, Joab appointed a man named Cushi to carry news to David of his son's death. Ahimaaz, however, wouldn't let up. So Joab finally gave him permission.

2 Samuel 18:23 (b)–26
. . . Then Ahimaaz ran by the way of the plain, and overran Cushi. And David sat between the two gates: and the watchman went up to the roof over the gate unto the wall, and lifted up his eyes, and looked, and behold a man running alone. And the watchman cried, and told the king. And the king said, If he be alone, there is tidings in his mouth. And he came apace, and drew near. And the watchman saw another man running: and the watchman called unto the porter, and said, Behold another man running alone. And the king said, He also bringeth tidings.

Had there been a host of men running, David would have known his troops had been defeated and were running for their lives. Two men, however, signaled not defeat but news.

2 Samuel 18:27–32

And the watchman said, Me thinketh the running of the foremost is like the running of Ahimaaz the son of Zadok. And the king said, He is a good man, and cometh with good tidings. And Ahimaaz called, and said unto the king, All is well. And he fell down to the earth upon his face before the king, and said, Blessed be the LORD thy God, which hath delivered up the men that lifted up their hand against my lord the king. And the king said, Is the young man Absalom safe? And Ahimaaz answered, When Joab sent the king's servant, and me thy servant, I saw a great tumult, but I knew not what it was. And the king said unto him, Turn aside, and stand here. And he turned aside, and stood still. And, behold, Cushi came; and Cushi said, Tidings, my lord the king: for the LORD hath avenged thee this day of all them that rose up against thee. And the king said unto Cushi, Is the young man Absalom safe? And Cushi answered, The enemies of my lord the king, and all that rise against thee to do thee hurt, be as that young man is.

Two runners set out. Ahimaaz arrived first and David said, "Tell me, is Absalom alright?"

"I saw some commotion—but I don't really know," said Ahimaaz.

"Stand aside," David said. And he waited until Cushi showed up with the full story.

Are you an Ahimaaz, or are you a Cushi? Are you one who is zealous and eager, but lacking the full message? The Bible warns against zeal without knowledge (Romans 10:2), about people who are zealous to serve the Lord but who lack maturity in Him. That is why it's important that we study to show ourselves approved unto God, workmen that needeth not to be ashamed, rightly dividing the Word of truth (2 Timothy 2:15), so that when we get to the scene, we have something to say.

What is the message the Lord has given you? If you are doubtful, I encourage you to ask Him for clarity of vision so that you would know precisely what He's calling you to do. "Write the vision," the Lord told Habakkuk, "and make it so plain that even those running by can understand it" (Habakkuk 2:2). Habakkuk was given a very clear vision, but it came only after he sought the Lord with fervency and expectancy (Habakkuk 2:2). There is no way to receive vision or understanding apart from seeking the Lord.

2 Samuel 18:33

And the king was much moved, and went up to the chamber over the gate, and wept: and as he went, thus he said, O my son Absalom, my son, my son Absalom! would God I had died for thee, O Absalom, my son, my son!

David was greatly grieved, deeply distressed. Why? When David's child borne by Bathsheba died after seven days, David didn't weep. He simply said, "He cannot be with me, but I will one day be with him (see 2 Samuel 12:23). I believe David had a different understanding here. That is, he knew Absalom was a rebellious, unregenerate son. I believe he sensed Absalom was lost for eternity. And it broke his heart.

19

2 Samuel 19:1–7

And it was told Joab, Behold, the king weepeth and mourneth for Absalom. And the victory that day was turned into mourning unto all the people: for the people heard say that day how the king was grieved for his son. And the people gat them by stealth that day into the city, as people being ashamed steal away when they flee in battle. But the king covered his face, and the king cried with a loud voice, O my son Absalom, O Absalom, my son, my son! And Joab came into the house to the king, and said, Thou hast shamed this day the faces of all thy servants, which this day have saved thy life, and the lives of thy sons and of thy daughters, and the lives of thy wives, and the lives of thy concubines; In that thou lovest thine enemies, and hatest thy friends. For thou hast declared this day, that thou regardest neither princes nor servants: for this day I perceive, that if Absalom had lived, and all we had died this day, then it had pleased thee well. Now therefore arise, go forth, and speak comfortably unto thy servants: for I swear by the LORD, if thou go not forth, there will not tarry one with thee this night: and that will be worse unto thee than all the evil that befell thee from thy youth until now.

"Snap out of it," Joab said to David. "Don't you understand that your people placed their lives on the line for you, yet all they see is that you're moaning and groaning. If you don't wipe the tears from your eyes and wash your face, they will desert you by nightfall.

Our outlook affects others. Therefore, if you are a servant of Jesus Christ, if you are committed to the King, you must not allow yourself the pampered privilege of being discouraged.

When Aaron's sons were killed, the Lord said to him, "Others may mourn, but you cannot for you are anointed (Leviticus 10:6). You have a job to do." And Aaron continued on in ministry.

If the anointing is on your life, you don't have the "right" to pout and whimper. Discouragement, depression, and defeat are instruments the enemy will seek to use to affect your family, friends, and community. It is the mature saint who says, "It's time for me to grow up and to cast my care not upon those around me, but upon the Lord solely" (1 Peter 5:7).

"I have *learned* in whatever state I am to be content," Paul said (Philippians 4:11, italics added). Contentment is the result of a decision you make with your mind rather than a feeling you have in your heart. God intervened on David's behalf. The rebels were defeated. The kingdom was spared. Yet all David could see was that his son was dead.

2 Samuel 19:8
Then the king arose, and sat in the gate. And they told unto all the people, saying, Behold, the king doth sit in the gate. And all the people came before the king: for Israel had fled every man to his tent.

Eventually, David changed his mind and his outlook. We must do the same. Every one of us is blessed beyond words. Every day we awake, we choose either to see burdens or blessings, gaffes or gifts, Absalom or the kingdom. And the choice we make affects everyone around us.

2 Samuel 19:9–13
And all the people were at strife throughout all the tribes of Israel, saying, The king saved us out of the hand of our enemies, and he delivered us out of the hand of the Philistines; and now he is fled out of the land for Absalom. And Absalom, whom we anointed over us, is dead in battle. Now therefore why speak ye not a word of bringing the king back? And king David sent to Zadok and to Abiathar the priests, saying, Speak unto the elders of Judah, saying, Why are ye the last to bring the king back to his house? seeing the speech of all Israel is come to the king, even to his house. Ye are my brethren, ye are my bones and my flesh: wherefore then are ye the last to bring back the king? And say ye to Amasa, Art thou not of my bone, and of my flesh? God do so to me, and more also, if thou be not captain of the host before me continually in the room of Joab.

"The rebellion is over! Bring back the king!" said the people of Israel. And David extends grace by naming Amasa as his general, for Amasa, David's nephew, had been Absalom's general.

2 Samuel 19:14–20
And he bowed the heart of all the men of Judah, even as the heart of one man; so that they sent this word unto the king, Return thou, and all thy servants. So the king returned, and came to Jordan. And Judah came to Gilgal, to go to meet the king, to conduct the king over Jordan. And Shimei the son of Gera, a Benjamite, which was of Bahurim, hasted and came down with the men of Judah to meet king David. And there were a thousand men of Benjamin with him, and Ziba the servant of the house of Saul, and his fifteen sons and his twenty servants with him; and they went over Jordan before the king. And there went over a ferry boat to carry over the king's household, and to do what he thought good. And Shimei the son of Gera fell down before the king, as he was come over Jordan; And said unto the king, Let not my lord impute iniquity unto me, neither do thou remember that which thy servant did perversely the day that my lord the king went out of Jerusalem, that the king should take it to his heart. For thy servant doth know that I have sinned: therefore, behold, I am come the first this day of all the house of Joseph to go down to meet my lord the king.

As David returned to Jerusalem, Shimei was one of the first to greet him, saying, "I'm sorry I threw rocks at you and cursed you and mocked you. No hard feelings, I hope."

2 Samuel 19:21–23 (a)
But Abishai the son of Zeruiah answered and said, Shall not Shimei be put to death for this, because he cursed the LORD's anointed? And David said, What have I to do with you, ye sons of Zeruiah, that ye should this day be adversaries unto me? shall there any man be put to death this day in Israel?

Once again, Abishai asked permission to kill Shimei. And once again, David denied his request (2 Samuel 16:10).

2 Samuel 19:23 (b)
. . . for do not I know that I am this day king over Israel? Therefore the king said unto Shimei, Thou shalt not die. And the king sware unto him.

"I know who I am," David said. "I know what God has called me to do. I don't need to defend my position." Over the years, I have noticed that the most secure individuals, like David, are those least likely to cut down others.

2 Samuel 19:24
And Mephibosheth the son of Saul came down to meet the king, and had neither dressed his feet, nor trimmed his beard, nor washed his clothes, from the day the king departed until the day he came again in peace.

All the while David was gone, Mephibosheth was sad. I think I know how he felt, for I, too, am looking forward to the King coming back—when all arguments will be settled, all relationships will be right. I miss Jesus and long for His return.

2 Samuel 19:25–28
And it came to pass, when he was come to Jerusalem to meet the king, that the king said unto him, Wherefore wentest not thou with me, Mephibosheth? And he answered, My lord, O king, my servant deceived me: for thy servant said, I will saddle me an ass, that I may ride thereon, and go to the king; because thy servant is lame. And he hath slandered thy servant unto my lord the king; but my lord the king is as an angel of God: do therefore what is good in thine eyes. For all of my father's house were but dead men before my lord the king: yet didst thou set thy servant among them that did eat at thine own table. What right therefore have I yet to cry any more unto the king?

When David asked why Mephibosheth didn't join him in exile, Mephibosheth said, "I wanted to go with you. I saddled a donkey so that I could go with you. Ziba lied when he told you I wanted to rebel against you. Nothing could be further from the truth, for I owe my very life to you."

2 Samuel 19:29
And the king said unto him, Why speakest thou any more of thy matters? I have said, Thou and Ziba divide the land.

In telling Mephibosheth to share his inheritance with Ziba, was David saying, "Yes, Ziba slandered you. But split the land anyway and let bygones be bygones"? No. David is showing wisdom in the same way his son, Solomon, would show wisdom. When two women came before Solomon with one living baby, both claiming the baby as their own, Solomon said, "Divide the baby. You may each have half." It was the real mother who said, "No! Let her have it. I give up my rights so that my baby might live" (1 Kings 3).

2 Samuel 19:30
And Mephibosheth said unto the king, Yea, let him take all, forasmuch as my lord the king is come again in peace unto his own house.

When Mephibosheth said to David, "I don't care about the land. I'm just glad you're back," David knew it was Mephibosheth who had been telling the truth all along. It was the fact that Mephibosheth desired the giver more than the gifts that showed his true allegiance.

What about us? Do we say to our King, "I don't care about gifts. I just want You"?

2 Samuel 19:31, 32
And Barzillai the Gileadite came down from Rogelim, and went over Jordan with the king, to conduct him over Jordan. Now Barzillai was a very aged man, even fourscore years old: and he had provided the king of sustenance while he lay at Mahanaim; for he was a very great man.

Barzillai, who had brought goods to David when he was fleeing, now comes to meet David upon his return to Jerusalem.

2 Samuel 19:33
And the king said unto Barzillai, Come thou over with me, and I will feed thee with me in Jerusalem.

"Come with me and you can dine in my palace," a grateful David said to Barzillai.

2 Samuel 19:34–39
And Barzillai said unto the king, How long have I to live, that I should go up with the king unto Jerusalem? I am this day fourscore years old: and can I discern between good and evil? can thy servant taste what I eat or what I drink? can I hear any more the voice of singing men and singing women? wherefore then should thy servant be yet a burden unto my lord the king? Thy servant will go a little way over Jordan with the king: and why should the king recompense it me with such a reward? Let thy servant, I pray thee, turn back again, that I may die in mine own city, and be buried by the grave of my father and of my mother. But behold thy servant Chimham; let him go over with my lord the king; and do to him what shall seem good unto thee. And the king answered, Chimham shall go over with me, and I will do to him that which shall seem good unto thee: and whatsoever thou shalt require of me, that will I do for thee. And all the people went over Jordan. And when the king was come over, the king kissed Barzillai, and blessed him; and he returned unto his own place.

2 Samuel 19:40–43
Then the king went on to Gilgal, and Chimham went on with him: and all the people of Judah conducted the king, and also half the people of Israel. And, behold, all the men of Israel came to the king, and said unto the king, Why have our brethren the men of Judah stolen thee away, and have brought the king, and his household, and all David's men with him, over Jordan? And all the men of Judah answered the men of Israel, Because the king is near of kin to us: wherefore then be ye angry for this matter? have we eaten at all of the king's cost? or hath he given us any gift? And the men of Israel answered the men of Judah, and said, We have ten parts in the king, and we have also more right in David than ye: why then did ye despise us, that our advice should not be first had in bringing back our king? And the words of the men of Judah were fiercer than the words of the men of Israel.

"Why do you get to escort David across the Jordan?" the ten northern tribes asked the tribe of Judah.

"Because he's our relative," Judah answered.

"Well, we were the first to want him back," countered the ten northern tribes.

This cracks me up because only a few weeks earlier, they were fighting *against* David and here, they're fighting *over* him.

When you're serving Jesus and ministering to people, know this: The same people who one week cried, "Hosanna!" the next week cried, "Crucify Him!" Unfortunately, we all have these tendencies because the heart is deceitful and desperately wicked (Jeremiah 17:9). That is why Paul said it was the love of Christ that constrained, or motivated him (2 Corinthians 5:14). If you're in ministry for the love of people, you won't last because people change their minds. If you're in ministry for the love of the lost, what will happen is, like Jeremiah, you preach and teach and witness for thirty years to your friends and neighbors, and not one person gets saved? The only true motivation for ministry must be your love for Jesus, regardless of peoples' response and reaction.

20

It has been rightly said that there is no furlough from the fight of faith. There are no breaks in the battle in which we are engaged. It is good for us to realize that there is no real resting place until we are taken home to be with Jesus. In our story, David has put down a rebellion led by his son and has put up with a squabble between the ten northern tribes and the southern tribe of Judah. Now he is about to be put through yet another rebellion. Therefore, we should not be surprised when we find ourselves going through multiple difficulties. Not very much time passes before you, like David, will be rudely reminded that this world is not your home . . .

2 Samuel 20:1, 2
And there happened to be there a man of Belial, whose name was Sheba, the son of Bichri, a Benjamite: and he blew a trumpet, and said, We have no part in David, neither have we inheritance in the son of Jesse: every man to his tents, O Israel. So every man of Israel went up from after David, and followed Sheba the son of Bichri: but the men of Judah clave unto their king, from Jordan even to Jerusalem.

When the ten northern tribes of Israel were offended because Judah alone escorted David back into power, Sheba sought to exploit the situation. "David doesn't care about us," he said, "so let's rebel against him."

2 Samuel 20:3
And David came to his house at Jerusalem; and the king took the ten women his concubines, whom he had left to keep the house, and put them in ward, and fed them, but went not in unto them. So they were shut up unto the day of their death, living in widowhood.

From this point on, David will gather to himself no more wives or concubines. The heartache in his home and the turmoil in his kingdom seem to cause him to settle down. At over fifty years of age, it's about time.

2 Samuel 20:4–6
Then said the king to Amasa, Assemble me the men of Judah within three days, and be thou here present. So Amasa went to assemble the men of Judah: but he tarried longer than the set time which he had appointed him. And David said to Abishai, Now shall Sheba the son of Bichri do us more harm than did Absalom: take thou thy lord's servants, and pursue after him, lest he get him fenced cities, and escape us.

Amasa had been Absalom's general. After Absalom died, David graciously offered Amasa the position of general of his army. Here, Amasa raises suspicions by seemingly going "AWOL." So David sends Abishai to put down Sheba's uprising.

2 Samuel 20:7–10
And there went out after him Joab's men, and the Cherethites, and the Pelethites, and all the mighty men: and they went out of Jerusalem, to pursue after Sheba the son of Bichri. When they were at the great stone which is in Gibeon, Amasa went before them. And Joab's garment that he had put on was girded unto him, and upon it a girdle with a sword fastened upon his loins in the sheath thereof; and as he went forth it fell out. And Joab said to Amasa, Art thou in health, my brother? And Joab took Amasa by the beard with the right hand to kiss him. But Amasa took no heed to the sword that was in Joab's hand: so he smote him therewith in the fifth rib, and shed out his bowels to the ground, and struck him not again; and he died. So Joab and Abishai his brother pursued after Sheba the son of Bichri.

Joab goes to seemingly join forces with Amasa. Remember, it was Joab's position as general that Amasa took. And it was Joab's intent to assassinate his replacement.

Like Joab's sword, the Word of God is quick and powerful, sharper than any two-edged sword (Hebrews 4:12). But let us remember the sword is not to be used in battle against other brothers. Rather, it is to be used in battle against the enemy. I think we should be increasingly cautious against allowing our sword just to happen to fall out and our spiritual prowess to be seen in proving a point, in cutting down, or bringing hurt to a brother. I am tired of Christians using the Bible against one another.

2 Samuel 20:11
And one of Joab's men stood by him, and said, He that favoureth Joab, and he that is for David, let him go after Joab.

"If you're for David, follow Joab." This still happens today. "Whoever is for Jesus Christ and the MX Missile, stand up!" Or, "Whoever is for Jesus Christ and the Republican Party, stand up!" People have a tendency to link Jesus with political or social issues. I think we need to be extremely wary of this kind of linkage.

2 Samuel 20:12–15
And Amasa wallowed in blood in the midst of the highway. And when the man saw that all the people stood still, he removed Amasa out of the highway into the field, and cast a cloth upon him, when he saw that every one that came by him stood still. When he was removed out of the highway, all the people went on after Joab, to pursue after Sheba the son of Bichri. And he went through all the tribes of Israel unto Abel, and to Beth-maachah, and all the Berites: and they were gathered together, and went also after him. And they came and besieged him in Abel of Beth-maachah, and they cast up a bank against the city, and it stood in the trench: and all the people that were with Joab battered the wall, to throw it down.

Sheba takes his rebellion to a city called Abel. The men of Joab surround the city and begin to batter down the walls.

2 Samuel 20:16
Then cried a wise woman out of the city, Hear, hear; say, I pray you, unto Joab, Come near hither, that I may speak with thee.

The city was about to be destroyed when a wise woman appeared. Praise the Lord for wise women!

2 Samuel 20:17–19
And when he was come near unto her, the woman said, Art thou Joab? And he answered, I am he. Then she said unto him, Hear the words of thine handmaid. And he answered, I do hear. Then she spake, saying, They were wont to speak in old time, saying, They shall surely ask counsel at Abel: and so they ended the matter. I am one of them that are peaceable and faithful in Israel: thou seekest to destroy a city and a mother in Israel: why wilt thou swallow up the inheritance of the LORD?

"Our city is a peaceful city, " said the woman. "We're known for our abilities to negotiate rather than fight."

2 Samuel 20:20–22
And Joab answered and said, Far be it, far be it from me, that I should swallow up or destroy. The matter is not so: but a man of mount Ephraim, Sheba the son of Bichri by name, hath lifted up his hand against the king, even against David: deliver him only, and I will depart from the city. And the woman said unto Joab, Behold, his head shall be thrown to thee over the wall. Then the woman went unto all the people in her wisdom. And they cut off the head of Sheba the son of Bichri, and cast it out to Joab. And he blew a trumpet, and they retired from the city, every man to his tent. And Joab returned to Jerusalem unto the king.

Sheba wanted to get ahead, but he ended up losing his head. In our attempts to get ahead, we can end up totally missing the boat. Seek to serve, not to be served. Seek to understand, not to be understood. Seek to give, not to receive.

2 Samuel 20:23–26
Now Joab was over all the host of Israel: and Benaiah the son of Jehoiada was over the Cherethites and over the Pelethites: And Adoram was over the tribute: and Jehoshaphat the son of Ahilud was recorder: And Sheva was scribe: and Zadok and Abiathar were the priests: And Ira also the Jairite was a chief ruler about David.

The chapter ends with a record of the organization of David's government.

21

2 Samuel 21:1 (a)
Then there was a famine in the days of David . . .

Scientists tell us famine is usually the result of changes in climate, from planetary disturbances to sunspot storms. But the simplest believer has a huge advantage over the scientific scholar, for he knows that nothing can happen apart from the Lord allowing it to happen. Climatic changes are all secondary. Primary is the fact that God is in control.

2 Samuel 21:1 (b)
. . . three years, year after year; and David inquired of the LORD. And the LORD answered . . .

It's interesting to me that David waited for three years before inquiring of the Lord. I wonder how many difficulties we go through, how many dry spells we endure all because we do not diligently inquire of the Lord. The Lord was waiting for David to ask, and when he asked, the Lord answered.

2 Samuel 21:1 (c)
. . . It is for Saul, and for his bloody house, because he slew the Gibeonites.

When the Israelites first entered the Promised Land, they wiped out all of the Canaanites, according to the plan of God. One group, however, the Gibeonites tricked Joshua into signing a peace treaty with them. The result was that the Gibeonites became servants to the Israelites. When Saul became king, he attempted to break the treaty, and God took note. Forty years later, the effects of that sin were felt in Israel. Time does not lessen the effects of sin. Our God is incredibly patient. After all, He gave the Canaanites four hundred years to repent. But don't mistake the patience of God for impotence or apathy. He doesn't judge quickly, but He does judge thoroughly.

2 Samuel 21:2–9
And the king called the Gibeonites, and said unto them; (now the Gibeonites were not of the children of Israel, but of the remnant of the Amorites; and the children of Israel had sworn unto them: and Saul sought to slay them in his zeal to the children of Israel and Judah.) Wherefore David said unto the Gibeonites, What shall I do for you? and wherewith shall I make the atonement, that ye may bless the inheritance of the LORD? And the Gibeonites said unto him, We will have no silver nor gold of Saul, nor of his house; neither for us shalt thou kill any man in Israel. And he said, What ye shall say, that will I do for you. And they answered the king, The man that consumed us, and that devised against us that we should be destroyed from remaining in any of the coasts of Israel, Let seven men of his sons be delivered unto us, and we will hang them up unto the LORD in Gibeah of Saul, whom the LORD did choose. And the king said, I will give them. But the king spared Mephibosheth, the son of Jonathan the son of Saul, because of the LORD's oath that was between them, between David and Jonathan the son of Saul. But the king took the two sons of Rizpah the daughter of Aiah, whom she bare unto Saul, Armoni and Mephibosheth; and the five sons of Michal the daughter of Saul, whom she brought up for Adriel the son of Barzillai the Meholathite: And he delivered them into the hands of the Gibeonites, and they hanged them in the hill before the LORD: and they fell all seven together, and were put to death in the days of harvest, in the first days, in the beginning of barley harvest.

To right the wrong Saul had perpetrated upon the Gibeonites, seven of Saul's grandsons were given to the Gibeonites, who hung them on a tree. Seven represents the number of completion. In this, we see the household of Saul being judged because of Saul's sin. Sin will catch up with us sooner or later. It will come to completion. It's unavoidable.

2 Samuel 21:10–14
And Rizpah the daughter of Aiah took sackcloth, and spread it for her upon the rock, from the beginning of harvest until water dropped upon them out of heaven, and suffered neither the birds of the air to rest on

them by day, nor the beasts of the field by night. And it was told David what Rizpah the daughter of Aiah, the concubine of Saul, had done. And David went and took the bones of Saul and the bones of Jonathan his son from the men of Jabesh-gilead, which had stolen them from the street of Beth-shan, where the Philistines had hanged them, when the Philistines had slain Saul in Gilboa: And he brought up from thence the bones of Saul and the bones of Jonathan his son; and they gathered the bones of them that were hanged. And the bones of Saul and Jonathan his son buried they in the country of Benjamin in Zelah, in the sepulchre of Kish his father: and they performed all that the king commanded. And after that God was intreated for the land.

The bodies of Saul's grandsons were left hanging on the tree. One of the mothers stood by for six months, watching the decay take place, fighting off the birds, chasing away the animals of prey. When David heard about this, he ordered the bodies cut down and the bones taken, along with Saul's and Jonathan's, to be buried.

If we or anyone we know is in a time of difficulty, we must seek the Lord because there is very likely sin involved, sin that brings dryness, drought, and famine . . .

> There is no soundness in my flesh because of thine anger; neither is there any rest in my bones because of my sin. For mine iniquities are gone over mine head: as an heavy burden they are too heavy for me. My wounds stink and are corrupt because of my foolishness. I am troubled; I am bowed down greatly; I go mourning all the day long. For my loins are filled with a loathsome disease: and there is no soundness in my flesh. I am feeble and sore broken: I have roared by reason of the disquietness of my heart. Lord, all my desire is before thee; and my groaning is not hid from thee. My heart panteth, my strength faileth me: as for the light of mine eyes, it also is gone from me. My lovers and my friends stand aloof from my sore; and my kinsmen stand afar off. Forsake me not, O LORD: O my God, be not far from me. Make haste to help me, O Lord my salvation. Psalm 38:3–11, 21, 22

When was this Psalm penned? At a time when David himself was living in unconfessed sin. It took a year for David to say, "Father, I have sinned against You." Before he confessed, his heart was heavy, his sparkle was gone, his bones were weary. Life was a drag. When he confessed, his spirit was restored.

It's so simple. Why do we go month after month or even day after day wondering why we're so dry without saying, like David did, "Lord, search my heart"? It is when we do this that we will see the joy of our salvation restored, the rains of revival falling upon our soul.

2 Samuel 21:15, 16
Moreover the Philistines had yet war again with Israel; and David went down, and his servants with him, and fought against the Philistines: and David waxed faint. And Ishbi-benob, which was of the sons of the giant, the weight of whose spear weighed three hundred shekels of brass in weight, he being girded with a new sword, thought to have slain David.

Here's David, fighting against a guy who carried a spear weighing thirty pounds. A college shot-put weighs sixteen pounds. Therefore, I can't fathom throwing a thirty-pound spear. This guy was powerful!

2 Samuel 21:17–22
But Abishai the son of Zeruiah succoured him, and smote the Philistine, and killed him. Then the men of David sware unto him, saying, Thou shalt go no more out with us to battle, that thou quench not the light of Israel. And it came to pass after this, that there was again a battle with the Philistines at Gob: then Sibbechai the Hushathite slew Saph, which was of the sons of the giant. And there was again a battle in Gob with the Philistines, where Elhanan the son of Jaare-oregim, a Bethlehemite, slew the brother of Goliath the Gittite, the staff of whose spear was like a weaver's beam. And there was yet a battle in Gath, where was a man of great stature, that had on every hand six fingers, and on every foot six toes, four and twenty in number; and he also was born to the giant. And when he defied Israel, Jonathan the son of Shimea the brother of David slew him. These four were born to the giant in Gath, and fell by the hand of David, and by the hand of his servants.

Even at the end of his life, David was still fighting giants. Make no mistake, dear brother and sister—the Christian walk does not necessarily get easier. There are giants all the way to the end.

22

2 Samuel 22:1
And David spake unto the LORD the words of this song in the day that the LORD had delivered him out of the hand of all his enemies, and out of the hand of Saul:

In Psalm 18, recorded here in chapter 22, we feel the spiritual pulse of a man who is called a man after God's heart . . .

Paul reaches back to this Psalm himself in Romans and applies it to Jesus Christ.

2 Samuel 22:2–4
And he said, The LORD is my rock, and my fortress, and my deliverer; The God of my rock; in him will I trust: he is my shield, and the horn of my salvation, my high tower, and my refuge, my saviour; thou savest me from violence. I will call on the LORD, who is worthy to be praised: so shall I be saved from mine enemies.

At the end of his life, David thinks back about how God has given him victory over his enemies

2 Samuel 22:5–20
When the waves of death compassed me, the floods of ungodly men made me afraid; The sorrows of hell compassed me about; the snares of death prevented me; In my distress I called upon the LORD, and cried to my God: and he did hear my voice out of his temple, and my cry did enter into his ears. Then the earth shook and trembled; the foundations of heaven moved and shook, because he was wroth. There went up a smoke out of his nostrils, and fire out of his mouth devoured: coals were kindled by it. He bowed the heavens also, and came down; and darkness was under his feet. And he rode upon a cherub, and did fly: and he was seen upon the wings of the wind. And he made darkness pavilions round about him, dark waters, and thick clouds of the skies. Through the brightness before him were coals of fire kindled. The LORD thundered from heaven, and the most High uttered his voice. And he sent out arrows, and scattered them; lightning, and discomfited them. And the channels of the sea appeared, the foundations of the world were discovered, at the rebuking of the LORD, at the blast of the breath of his nostrils. He sent from above, he took me; he drew me out of many waters; He delivered me from my strong enemy, and from them that hated me: for they were too strong for me. They prevented me in the day of my calamity: but the LORD was my stay. He brought me forth also into a large place: he delivered me, because he delighted in me.

Why is this Psalm repeated in two places? I suggest one is for the purpose of history, the other for the purpose of prophecy. The 2 Samuel rendering recounts the history of king David. The Psalm 18 rendering speaks of the life and work of our Greater than David, Jesus Christ.

2 Samuel 22:21, 22
The LORD rewarded me according to my righteousness: according to the cleanness of my hands hath he recompensed me. For I have kept the ways of the LORD, and have not wickedly departed from my God.

In this Psalm, David says, "The Lord has rewarded me because I have not violated his way." What? As I read the life of David, I see lies, adultery, and murder. What, then, is going on? In Psalm 38 and Psalm 51, we hear David acknowledge what a wretch he is, how he has failed the Lord. Before the Lord, he admits his sin. But here, in the presence of his enemies, he says he is righteous.

This is the way it must be. You see, the closer I get to God, the more I am aware of how far I am from Him, of attitudes that are amiss, of activities that are wrong. In the presence of my enemy, however, the accuser of the brethren who accuses me day and night, I say, "Back off. The Word of God says I am the righteousness of God in Christ Jesus" (2 Corinthians 5:21; Revelation 12:10).

You'll never be used by the Lord; you'll never develop a deep relationship with Him until you learn that you are righteous in Christ Jesus. When He died on the Cross and said, "It is finished," it was finished indeed. The price for every sin you have ever committed or will commit has been paid.

Satan's favorite weapon is condemnation. Therefore, he will tell you that you can't be used, that you can't go on, but you can overcome him by the Word.

2 Samuel 22:23–51
For all his judgments were before me: and as for his statutes, I did not depart from them. I was also upright before him, and have kept myself from mine iniquity. Therefore the LORD hath recompensed me according to my righteousness; according to my cleanness in his eye sight. With the merciful thou wilt shew thyself merciful, and with the upright man thou wilt shew thyself upright thyself pure; and with the froward thou wilt shew thyself unsavoury. And the afflicted people thou wilt save: but thine eyes are upon the haughty, that thou mayest bring them down. With the pure thou wilt shew For thou art my lamp, O LORD: and the LORD will lighten my darkness. For by thee I have run through a troop: by my God have I leaped over a wall. As for God, his way is perfect; the word of the LORD is tried: he is a buckler to all them that trust

in him. For who is God, save the LORD? and who is a rock, save our God? God is my strength and power: and he maketh my way perfect. He maketh my feet like hinds' feet: and setteth me upon my high places. He teacheth my hands to war; so that a bow of steel is broken by mine arms. Thou hast also given me the shield of thy salvation: and thy gentleness hath made me great. Thou hast enlarged my steps under me; so that my feet did not slip. I have pursued mine enemies, and destroyed them; and turned not again until I had consumed them. And I have consumed them, and wounded them, that they could not arise: yea, they are fallen under my feet. For thou hast girded me with strength to battle: them that rose up against me hast thou subdued under me. Thou hast also given me the necks of mine enemies, that I might destroy them that hate me. They looked, but there was none to save; even unto the LORD, but he answered them not. Then did I beat them as small as the dust of the earth, I did stamp them as the mire of the street, and did spread them abroad. Thou also hast delivered me from the strivings of my people, thou hast kept me to be head of the heathen: a people which I knew not shall serve me. Strangers shall submit themselves unto me: as soon as they hear, they shall be obedient unto me. Strangers shall fade away, and they shall be afraid out of their close places. The LORD liveth; and blessed be my rock; and exalted be the God of the rock of my And that bringeth me forth from mine enemies: thou also hast lifted me up on high above them that rose up against me: thou hast delivered me from the violent man. Therefore I will give thanks unto thee, O LORD, among the heathen, and I will sing praises unto thy name. He is the tower of salvation for his king: and sheweth mercy to his anointed, unto David, and to his seed for evermore.

These are the last words of David. His last words glorified God and edified people. May our words do the same.

23

2 Samuel 23:1–8

Now these be the last words of David. David the son of Jesse said, and the man who was raised up on high, the anointed of the God of Jacob, and the sweet psalmist of Israel, said, The Spirit of the LORD spake by me, and his word was in my tongue. The God of Israel said, the Rock of Israel spake to me, He that ruleth over men must be just, ruling in the fear of God. And he shall be as the light of the morning, when the sun riseth, even a morning without clouds; as the tender grass springing out of the earth by clear shining after rain. Although my house be not so with God; yet he hath made with me an everlasting covenant, ordered in all things, and sure: for this is all my salvation, and all my desire, although he make it not to grow. But the sons of Belial shall be all of them as thorns thrust away, because they cannot be taken with hands: But the man that shall touch them must be fenced with iron and the staff of a spear; and they shall be utterly burned with fire in the same place. These be the names of the mighty men whom David had: The Tachmonite that sat in the seat, chief among the captains; the same was Adino the Eznite: he lift up his spear against eight hundred, whom he slew at one time.

Three of David's mighty men are singled out. The first is Adino. He lifted up his spear eight hundred times and killed eight hundred. That's a lot of lifting!

If you desire to be mighty for God, the first prerequisite is that you be a person of prayer—lifting up your hands eight hundred times if necessary until the enemy is defeated. On the mountain, Moses lifted up his hands in prayer as Joshua fought the enemy in the valley below (Exodus 17).

To be a mighty man of god, you must be a man of prayer. This is a problem for many believers. "Why should I have to keep praying?" they say. "Why doesn't the Lord hear my prayer the first time and answer immediately?" I suggest the reason is because it is only as I pray repeatedly about a situation that I find my request wasn't the issue at all, that spending time with the Lord was the need of my soul.

2 Samuel 23:9, 10

And after him was Eleazar the son of Dodo the Ahohite, one of the three mighty men with David, when they defied the Philistines that were there gathered together to battle, and the men of Israel were gone away: He arose, and smote the Philistines until his hand was weary, and his hand clave unto the sword: and the LORD wrought a great victory that day; and the people returned after him only to spoil.

The second prerequisite for those who wish to be mighty men and women of God is to be one whose hand cleaves to the sword. Eleazar held on so tightly that his hand molded around the sword.

Are you wearing your Bibles out? I hope so. You must be in the Word consistently and continuously. You cannot grow unless you're taking in consistent Bible teaching and Bible study. Faith comes by hearing and hearing by the Word of God (Romans 10:17). Your faith grows stronger as you take in the nutrients and spiritual calories of the meat of the Word.

2 Samuel 23:11, 12
And after him was Shammah the son of Agee the Hararite. And the Philistines were gathered together into a troop, where was a piece of ground full of lentiles: and the people fled from the Philistines. But he stood in the midst of the ground, and defended it, and slew the Philistines: and the Lord wrought a great victory.

The third prerequisite to be used by God, as seen in Shammah's life, is faithfulness in service. Shammah's job was to guard the beans. When the Philistines attacked, everyone else ran for their lives. Not Shammah. He said, "I have a job to do. Even if I die, I'm going to guard the beans." And because he was faithful in service, he became a mighty man of God.

What has the Lord given you to do? Maybe your job is to change diapers in the nursery, to serve in the rest home, or to teach third grade Sunday school. Stand your ground even when everyone else splits. Be like Shammah—until the King releases you, stick with your job.

Paul says it is required of stewards that they be found faithful (1 Corinthians 4:2). Jesus said the one who is faithful in small things shall be made ruler over great things (Matthew 25:21). God is testing us today. Have we stood our ground? Have we kept our commitment?

2 Samuel 23:13–15
And three of the thirty chief went down, and came to David in the harvest time unto the cave of Adullam: and the troop of the Philistines pitched in the valley of Rephaim. And David was then in an hold, and the garrison of the Philistines was then in Bethlehem. And David longed, and said, Oh that one would give me drink of the water of the well of Bethlehem, which is by the gate!

During a particular battle, holed up in a hot, stuffy, cave overlooking his hometown, David saw a well, which, no doubt, he drank from frequently as a boy. He could taste the water in his mind. "It would be so nice if I had a drink of water from that well," he said. But there was a problem. His hometown of Bethlehem was surrounded by the enemy.

David wasn't giving an order. But his mighty men heard what their king was thinking. Do you hear what your King is thinking? It's one thing to obey the commands of Christ. It's something else to hear His heartbeat.

2 Samuel 23:16 (a)
And the three mighty men brake through the host of the Philistines, and drew water out of the well of Bethlehem . . .

It was hard to obtain the water from Bethlehem because Bethlehem was surrounded by Philistines.

"The words that I speak to you are spirit and life," Jesus said (John 6:63). The Word of God is where you will draw from the well of the water of the Spirit. I guarantee that when you were most refreshed and doing the very best in the Lord was when you were spending time in the Word. But, like Bethlehem, the Word is surrounded by the enemy. I know the water of the Spirit is in it. But the Philistine of fatigue keeps me away. The Philistines of the phone, of chores, and of lethargy encamp around the Word.

How did the three mighty men break through to get water? The Bible doesn't say because breaking through the Philistines that plague you is something that cannot be programmed or preached. It is up to each one of us to seek the Lord and say, "Father, how do I break through? Show me my schedule, my priorities, my obligations that stand between us." I guarantee that if you ask the Lord to show you how to rearrange your schedule in order to break through the Philistines, He will.

2 Samuel 23:16 (b), 17
. . . that was by the gate, and took it, and brought it to David: nevertheless he would not drink thereof, but poured it out unto the Lord. And he said, Be it far from me, O Lord, that I should do this: is not this the blood of the men that went in jeopardy of their lives? therefore he would not drink it. These things did these three mighty men.

The fourth and final prerequisite is seen in the life of David—that is, worship. David poured out that which was most precious to him. What a creative act of worship. My prayer is that I would sincerely and creatively learn to worship like David.

2 Samuel 23:18, 19
And Abishai, the brother of Joab, the son of Zeruiah, was chief among three. And he lifted up his spear against three hundred, and slew them, and had the name among three. Was he not most honourable of three?

therefore he was their captain: howbeit he attained not unto the first three.

Abishai, the brother of Joab, is noted in this list of mighty men. Is Joab? No. In his day, Joab was more prominent, but in God's economy, Abishai, his younger brother, is noted instead. Things are not always what they seem. That is why I'm convinced that in eternity, there will be glorious surprises.

2 Samuel 23:20 (a)
And Benaiah the son of Jehoiada, the son of a valiant man, of Kabzeel, who had done many acts, he slew two lionlike men of Moab . . .

First, Benaiah killed two lion-like men of Moab. This gave him confidence to do subsequent battle with a real lion. Do you know why you've faced lion-like men today, people who are roaring at you, seeking to devour you? They're preparing you to do battle against the real lion—Satan, who seeks to devour your witness, your faith, and your joy.

2 Samuel 23:20 (b)
. . . he went down also and slew a lion in the midst of a pit in time of snow:

Benaiah went down into a pit on a snowy day and slew a lion. If you feel like your walk is cold, your surroundings are snow, and you're trapped in a pit, don't throw a "pit-y" party. Get down on your knees and do battle in prayer. That's what Benaiah did.

2 Samuel 23:21, 22
And he slew an Egyptian, a goodly man: and the Egyptian had a spear in his hand; but he went down to him with a staff, and plucked the spear out of the Egyptian's hand, and slew him with his own spear. These things did Benaiah the son of Jehoiada, and had the name among three mighty men.

After Benaiah slew lions—symbols of Satan—he slew a man from Egypt, symbolic of the world. How did Benaiah overcome the Egyptian? With the Egyptian's own staff. The staff in Scripture is symbolic of a pilgrim. How do we overcome the world? By being a pilgrim.

The world will have no pull over you if you keep your heart set on things above (Colossians 3:2). When I have blown it, it is invariably because I lost sight of the reality of eternity and was locked in to the immediate situation around me. As long as you have a staff in your hand, the world will lose its pull and power over you. Be a pilgrim—one who is just passing through, one who is headed *home*.

2 Samuel 23:23–39
He was more honourable than the thirty, but he attained not to the first three. And David set him over his guard. Asahel the brother of Joab Shammah the Harodite, Elika the Harodite, Helez the Paltite, Ira the son of Ikkesh the Tekoite, Abiezer the Anethothite, Mebunnai the Hushathite, Zalmon the Ahohite, Maharai the Netophathite, Heleb the son of Baanah, a Netophathite, Ittai the son of Ribai out of Gibeah of the children of Benjamin, Benaiah the Pirathonite, Hiddai of the brooks of Gaash, Abi-albon the Arbathite, Azmaveth the Barhumite, Eliahba the Shaalbonite, of the sons of Jashen, Jonathan, Shammah the Hararite, Ahiam the son of Sharar the Hararite, Eliphelet the son of Ahasbai, the son of the Maachathite, Eliam the son of Ahithophel the Gilonite, Hezrai the Carmelite, Paarai the Arbite, Igal the son of Nathan of Zobah, Bani the Gadite, Zelek the Ammonite, Naharai the Beerothite, armourbearer to Joab the son of Zeruiah, Ira an Ithrite, Gareb an Ithrite, Uriah the Hittite: thirty and seven in all.

Our King, our Greater than David, Jesus Christ, also has a list of mighty men, men "of whom the world was not worthy"—who, like Uriah, gave their lives in the service of their King (Hebrews 11).

24

2 Samuel 24:1
And again the anger of the LORD was kindled against Israel, and he moved David against them to say, Go, number Israel and Judah.

If you have a newer translation, it's possible that "he" in this verse is capitalized. That is unfortunate. In the original languages, there are no capital letters. Here, translators added one where it doesn't belong, for in 1 Chronicles 21—the parallel passage to this one—we are told that it wasn't God but Satan who inspired David to number the people.

2 Samuel 24:2, 3
For the king said to Joab the captain of the host, which was with him, Go now through all the tribes of Israel, from Dan even to Beer-sheba, and number ye the people, that I may know the number of the people. Joab said unto the king, Now the LORD thy God add unto the people, how many soever they

be, an hundredfold, and that the eyes of my lord the king may see it: but why doth my lord the king delight in this thing?

"What are you doing?" asked Joab. "May the Lord increase His people, but why are you numbering them?" Here, David is bowing to the dreaded scourge of statistics, counting the people rather than counting on God for strength.

2 Samuel 24:4–9
Notwithstanding the king's word prevailed against Joab, and against the captains of the host. And Joab and the captains of the host went out from the presence of the king, to number the people of Israel. And they passed over Jordan, and pitched in Aroer, on the right side of the city that lieth in the midst of the river of Gad, and toward Jazer: Then they came to Gilead, and to the land of Tahtim-hodshi; and they came to Dan-jaan, and about to Zidon, And came to the strong hold of Tyre, and to all the cities of the Hibites, and of the Canaanites: and they went out to the south of Judah, even to Beer-sheba. So when they had gone through all the land, they came to Jerusalem at the end of nine months and twenty days. And Joab gave up the sum of the number of the people unto the king: and there were in Israel eight hundred thousand valiant men that drew the sword; and the men of Judah were five hundred thousand men.

The census showed there were 1.3 million fighting men at David's disposal.

2 Samuel 24:10
And David's heart smote him after that he had numbered the people. And David said unto the LORD, I have sinned greatly in that I have done: and now, I beseech thee, O LORD, take away the iniquity of thy servant; for I have done very foolishly.

In Genesis 22:17, God had promised that His people would be as innumerable as the stars of the heaven, as the sand upon the seashore. Realizing he should have taken God at His Word, David confessed his sin of submitting to the prompting of Satan to get statistics that would swell his pride and make him independent of God.

2 Samuel 24:11, 12
For when David was up in the morning, the word of the LORD came unto the prophet Gad, David's seer, saying, Go and say unto David, Thus saith the LORD, I offer thee three things; choose thee one of them, that I may do it unto thee.

The Father will scourge, chasten, punish His children. Why? Because He loves us. When Adam ate of the forbidden fruit, even though he was forgiven by the Lord, he was not allowed to enter back into the Garden of Innocence. When Moses sinned against the Lord in smiting the rock, thereby depicting the Father as being angry when He wasn't, the Lord prevented him from entering the Promised Land. God forgives His people. He gives peace to His people, but He doesn't pamper them.

> My son, despise not thou the chastening of the Lord, nor faint when thou art rebuked of him: For whom the Lord loveth he chasteneth, and scourgeth every son whom he receiveth. If ye endure chastening, God dealeth with you as with sons; for what son is he whom the father chasteneth not? But if ye be without chastisement, whereof all are partakers, then are ye bastards, and not sons. Hebrews 12:5–8

2 Samuel 24:13
So Gad came to David, and told him, and said unto him, Shall seven years of famine come unto thee in thy land? or wilt thou flee three months before thine enemies, while they pursue thee? or that there be three days' pestilence in thy land? now advise, and see what answer I shall return to him that sent me.

For his punishment, David was to choose between seven years of famine, seven months of being chased by his enemies, or three days of plague upon the land.

2 Samuel 24:14
And David said unto Gad, I am in a great strait: let us fall now into the hand of the LORD; for his mercies are great: and let me not fall into the hand of man.

The only choice David ruled out was being pursued by his enemies—choosing to place himself in the merciful hands of God rather than in the harsh and cruel hands of man.

2 Samuel 24:15–17
So the LORD sent a pestilence upon Israel from the morning even to the time appointed: and there died of the people from Dan even to Beer-sheba seventy thousand men. And when the angel stretched out his hand upon Jerusalem to destroy it, the LORD repented him of the evil, and said to the angel that destroyed the people, It is enough: stay now thine hand. And the angel of the LORD was by the threshingplace of Araunah the Jebusite. And David spake unto the LORD when

he saw the angel that smote the people, and said, Lo, I have sinned, and I have done wickedly: but these sheep, what have they done? let thine hand, I pray thee, be against me, and against my father's house.

For the second time in this chapter, David is given another statistic. Hearing that 70,000 people died from the plague, he fell before the Lord and said, "Lord, I have sinned. But what have these people done? I have erred. Why are they bearing the brunt of my punishment?"

Dad, when you take your eyes off the Lord, your family will feel the shock waves and bear the brunt of your sin. Student, when you sin, the kids who are watching you will be hurt. Take heed. When one sins, many are affected.

2 Samuel 24:18–25
And Gad came that day to David, and said unto him, Go up, rear an altar unto the Lord in the threshingfloor of Araunah the Jebusite. And David, according to the saying of Gad, went up as the Lord commanded. And Araunah looked, and saw the king and his servants coming on toward him: and Araunah went out, and bowed himself before the king on his face upon the ground. And Araunah said, Wherefore is my lord the king come to his servant? And David said, To buy the threshingfloor of thee, to build an altar unto the Lord, that the plague may be stayed from the people. And Araunah said unto David, Let my lord the king take and offer up what seemeth good unto him: behold, here be oxen for burnt sacrifice, and threshing instruments and other instruments of the oxen for wood. All these things did Araunah, as a king, give unto the king. And Araunah said unto the king, The Lord thy God accept thee. And the king said unto Araunah, Nay; but I will surely buy it of thee at a price: neither will I offer burnt offerings unto the Lord my God of that which doth cost me nothing. So David bought the threshingfloor and the oxen for fifty shekels of silver. And David built there an altar unto the Lord, and offered burnt offerings and peace offerings. So the Lord was intreated for the land, and the plague was stayed from Israel.

In this passage, I think we are given understanding and insight into what made David so great. Why was he alone called a man after God's own heart (1 Samuel 13:14)? It certainly wasn't because he was sinless, for he had a series of failures that I daresay match or exceed any of ours. In fact, if he were on trial before the Christian community, I suggest the Christian community would have had a tendency to write him off long ago. Saul, on the other hand, would be applauded and approved. Saul, too, made mistakes. But not as seemingly blatant as David's. Therefore, I suggest that, in the eyes of human understanding, Saul would be exalted, and David would be dismissed as one who wasted his potential.

But that wasn't God's verdict. Why? Because God looks at the heart, and David had a heart for God.

"Take the property," Araunah said. "Make your sacrifice so the plague might be stopped. It's free. It's yours."

"I will not give the Lord that which costs me nothing," David said.

Hear the heart of David. "I won't skimp," he said. "I won't cheat God. Yes, I failed Him in the past. But my heart is devoted to Him."

If you want to know the heart of David, read the Psalms. Saul never wrote a single psalm because Saul didn't have a heart for the Lord. Saul was outwardly impressive, but he used the things of God to exalt himself. David, on the other hand, used himself to exalt the things of God. When David penned the Psalms, he didn't know they would be preserved and studied for centuries. He was simply writing love letters. He just loved God.

What would you have done had Araunah come to you and said, "Take the property. Here's the wood for the sacrifice. Here's the oxen. Just take it"?

Would you have said, "Great! I can save a few shekels"? Or do you have a heart like David's, a heart that says, "I will give everything I have, everything I am to the One who gave His all for me"?

Many of us are skimpy and small. We give the Lord the leftovers of our time, of our energy. You might not be committing any moral sin. But God sees the heart (1 Samuel 16:7). He's looking for men and women who say, "I'm devoted to worshiping the Lord. I'm devoted to extolling and praising Him. I'm devoted to paying the full price."

Although severely chastened again, even at the end of his life, David is still to be exalted by the Lord and acknowledged throughout history as one of the very greatest of all men who ever lived. Why? Because he had a heart after God.

Do you?

1 KINGS

1 The Books of 1 and 2 Samuel, 1 and 2 Kings, and 1 and 2 Chronicles are a running commentary on the history of the nation of Israel. Most Bible scholars believe Jeremiah was the one inspired by the Holy Spirit to pen the book before us.

First Kings opens at the end of David's life—with one last difficulty for him to face . . .

1 Kings 1:1
Now king David was old and stricken in years; and they covered him with clothes, but he gat no heat.

At seventy years of age, David is exhausted. He had lived a very full, demanding life.

1 Kings 1:2–4
Wherefore his servants said unto him, Let there be sought for my lord the king a young virgin: and let her stand before the king, and let her cherish him, and let her lie in thy bosom, that my lord the king may get heat. So they sought for a fair damsel throughout all the coasts of Israel, and found Abishag a Shunammite, and brought her to the king. And the damsel was very fair, and cherished the king, and ministered to him: but the king knew her not.

To keep David warm, a virgin was brought in to lie with him. Although this was a common custom of the day, my personal belief is that David knew this was not right in the sight of the Lord, for in the next verse, we see the chastening hand of the Lord upon his life . . .

1 Kings 1:5, 6
Then Adonijah the son of Haggith exalted himself, saying, I will be king: and he prepared him chariots and horsemen, and fifty men to run before him. And his father had not displeased him at any time in saying, Why hast thou done so? and he also was a very goodly man; and his mother bare him after Absalom.

Knowing his father was dying, David's son, Adonijah, makes a move to usurp the throne.

1 Kings 1:7
And he conferred with Joab the son of Zeruiah, and with Abiathar the priest: and they following Adonijah helped him.

Why did Joab and Abiathar side with Adonijah in this rebellion? I suggest it's because Joab and Abiathar were both hurt by David . . .

Following Absalom's rebellion, David appointed Amasa general in Joab's place (2 Samuel 19:13). When Joab killed Amasa, he returned to a position of power, but he knew he was not David's first choice.

Likewise, Abiathar, the priest, was aware of the fact that David had exalted and approved of Zadok above him—as perhaps hinted at by the fact that whenever Abiathar and Zadok's names appear together, Zadok's is always first.

Because Joab and Abiathar had their feelings hurt, they chose to rebel. That is why we must be oh, so careful that we do not allow the "root of bitterness" (Hebrews 12:15) to spring up in the soil of our souls.

"Be ye kind one to another," Paul declared, "tenderhearted, forgiving one another even as God for Christ's sake has forgiven you" (Ephesians 4:32). No matter who has wronged you, no matter how they have wronged you, forgive them. If you don't forgive them totally and unconditionally, you will sooner or later find yourself in the shoes of Joab or Abiathar, waging war in a needless and costly battle.

1 Kings 1:8–10
But Zadok the priest, and Benaiah the son of Jehoiada, and Nathan the prophet, and Shimei, and Rei, and the mighty men which belonged to David, were not with Adonijah. Adonijah slew sheep and oxen and fat cattle by the stone of Zoheleth, which is by En-rogel, and called all his brethren the king's sons, and all the men of Judah the king's ser-

vants: But Nathan the prophet, and Benaiah, and the mighty men, and Solomon his brother, he called not.

In his attempt to usurp the throne, Adonijah threw a party for everyone but those loyal to David.

1 Kings 1:11–14
Wherefore Nathan spake unto Bath-sheba the mother of Solomon, saying, Hast thou not heard that Adonijah the son of Haggith doth reign, and David our lord knoweth it not? Now therefore come, let me, I pray thee, give thee counsel, that thou mayest save thine own life, and the life of thy son Solomon. Go and get thee in unto king David, and say unto him, Didst not thou, my lord, O king, swear unto thine handmaid, saying, Assuredly Solomon thy son shall reign after me, and he shall sit upon my throne? why then doth Adonijah reign? Behold, while thou yet talkest there with the king, I also will come in after thee, and confirm thy words.

Nathan told Solomon's mother, Bath-sheba, that Adonijah had taken Solomon's place as king.

1 Kings 1:15
And Bath-sheba went in unto the king into the chamber: and the king was very old; and Abishag the Shunammite ministered unto the king.

Here comes Bath-sheba, David's favorite wife, Solomon's mother.

1 Kings 1:16–21
And Bath-sheba bowed, and did obeisance unto the king. And the king said, What wouldest thou? And she said unto him, My lord, thou swarest by the LORD thy God unto thine handmaid, saying, Assuredly Solomon thy son shall reign after me, and he shall sit upon my throne. And now, behold, Adonijah reigneth; and now, my lord the king, thou knowest it not: And he hath slain oxen and fat cattle and sheep in abundance, and hath called all the sons of the king, and Abiathar the priest, and Joab the captain of the host: but Solomon thy servant hath he not called. And thou, my lord, O king, the eyes of all Israel are upon thee, that thou shouldest tell them who shall sit on the throne of my lord the king after him. Otherwise it shall come to pass, when my lord the king shall sleep with his fathers, that I and my son Solomon shall be counted offenders.

Bath-sheba told David that, although he had promised Solomon would reign after him, Adonijah had claimed the throne instead.

1 Kings 1:22–27
And, lo, while she yet talked with the king, Nathan the prophet also came in. And they told the king, saying, Behold Nathan the prophet. And when he was come in before the king, he bowed himself before the king with his face to the ground. And Nathan said, My lord, O king, hast thou said, Adonijah shall reign after me, and he shall sit upon my throne? For he is gone down this day, and hath slain oxen and fat cattle and sheep in abundance, and hath called all the king's sons, and the captains of the host, and Abiathar the priest; and, behold, they eat and drink before him, and say, God save king Adonijah. But me, even me thy servant, and Zadok the priest, and Benaiah the son of Jehoiada, and thy servant Solomon, hath he not called. Is this thing done by my lord the king, and thou hast not shewed it unto thy servant, who should sit on the throne of my lord the king after him?

No sooner had Bath-sheba given her report to David than, as they had planned, Nathan the prophet came in and confirmed her words. Deuteronomy 19:15 says that it is in the mouth of two witnesses that every word shall be established. That is why Nathan came in to corroborate Bath-sheba's account.

Jesus reiterated this concept in Matthew 18 where He stressed the importance of two people dealing with problems within the Christian community. In 2 Corinthians 13:1 and 1 Timothy 5:19, Paul declares that no accusation is to be received apart from the confirmation of two witnesses.

This Old Testament principle, given in Deuteronomy, seen in the story before us, and woven into the fabric of Scripture all the way to the end of the New Testament is an important one for us to embrace. Often, people come to me with accusations against another brother or sister. I immediately stop that person and say, "May I quote you on that?" I immediately ask. "I need confirmation and I will quote you as a source of this report." And 99 times out of 100, the accusation is dropped.

Whenever you hear accusations, gossip, or innuendo, I would encourage you to try this approach.

1 Kings 1:28–32
Then king David answered and said, Call me Bath-sheba. And she came into the king's presence, and stood before the king. And the king sware, and said, As the LORD liveth, that hath redeemed my soul out of all distress, Even as I sware unto thee by the LORD God of Israel, saying, Assuredly Solomon

thy son shall reign after me, and he shall sit upon my throne in my stead; even so will I certainly do this day. Then Bath-sheba bowed with her face to the earth, and did reverence to the king, and said, Let my lord king David live for ever. And king David said, Call me Zadok the priest, and Nathan the prophet, and Benaiah the son of Jehoiada. And they came before the king.

The very men who weren't called by Adonijah in verses 8–10 are now called by David in verse 35. They missed Adonijah's party, but they will be used, and therefore honored, by the king.

1 Kings 1:33–35
The king also said unto them, Take with you the servants of your lord, and cause Solomon my son to ride upon mine own mule, and bring him down to Gihon: And let Zadok the priest and Nathan the prophet anoint him there king over Israel: and blow ye with the trumpet, and say, God save king Solomon. Then ye shall come up after him, that he may come and sit upon my throne; for he shall be king in my stead: and I have appointed him to be ruler over Israel and over Judah.

Solomon was to ride David's mule. Why wouldn't he ride David's horse? The reason is that the mule was the animal of peace, the horse the animal of conquest. That is why, when Jesus presented Himself as Messiah, He rode upon a mule, offering Himself as the Prince of peace. But the people did not receive Him. "Away with Him!" they cried. "We will not have this Man rule over us." So the next time Jesus comes, Revelation 19:11 tells us He will ride on a horse, not as the Prince of peace, but as the conquering King.

1 Kings 1:36–40
And Benaiah the son of Jehoiada answered the king, and said, Amen: the LORD God of my lord the king say so too. As the LORD hath been with my lord the king, even so be he with Solomon, and make his throne greater than the throne of my lord king David. So Zadok the priest, and Nathan the prophet, and Benaiah the son of Jehoiada, and the Cherethites, and the Pelethites, went down, and caused Solomon to ride upon king David's mule, and brought him to Gihon. And Zadok the priest took an horn of oil out of the tabernacle, and anointed Solomon. And they blew the trumpet; and all the people said, God save king Solomon. And all the people came up after him, and the people piped with pipes, and rejoiced with great joy, so that the earth rent with the sound of them.

Solomon was anointed king and the earth reverberated with the joy of the people.

1 Kings 1:41–49
And Adonijah and all the guests that were with him heard it as they had made an end of eating. And when Joab heard the sound of the trumpet, he said, Wherefore is this noise of the city being in an uproar? And while he yet spake, behold, Jonathan the son of Abiathar the priest came: and Adonijah said unto him, Come in; for thou art a valiant man, and bringest good tidings. And Jonathan answered and said to Adonijah, Verily our lord king David hath made Solomon king. And the king hath sent with him Zadok the priest, and Nathan the prophet, and Benaiah the son of Jehoiada, and the Cherethites, and the Pelethites, and they have caused him to ride upon the king's mule: And Zadok the priest and Nathan the prophet have anointed him king in Gihon: and they are come up from thence rejoicing, so that the city rang again. This is the noise that ye have heard. And also Solomon sitteth on the throne of the kingdom. And moreover the king's servants came to bless our lord king David, saying, God make the name of Solomon better than thy name, and make his throne greater than thy throne. And the king bowed himself upon the bed. And also thus said the king, Blessed be the LORD God of Israel, which hath given one to sit on my throne this day, mine eyes even seeing it. And all the guests that were with Adonijah were afraid, and rose up, and went every man his way.

Upon hearing that Solomon had been anointed king, everyone who had once dined with Adonijah deserted him. That's always the way it is. When people bond around a rebellion, their connection doesn't last very long. Therefore, may the Lord always allow us to be bonded not around a cause, organization, or doctrinal persuasion, but simply around the person of Jesus.

1 Kings 1:50
And Adonijah feared because of Solomon, and arose, and went, and caught hold on the horns of the altar.

The altar in the tabernacle had horns on its corner that were used to tie down the sacrifices that were placed upon the altar. When a man was afraid or in trouble, he would run into the tabernacle, grab hold of the horns of the altar, and plead for mercy.

1 Kings 1:51–53
And it was told Solomon, saying, Behold, Adonijah feareth king Solomon: for, lo, he hath caught hold on the horns of the altar, saying, Let king Solomon swear unto me to day that he will not slay his servant with the sword. And Solomon said, If he will shew himself a worthy man, there shall not an hair of him fall to the earth: but if wickedness shall be found in him, he shall die. So king Solomon sent, and they brought him down from the altar. And he came and bowed himself to king Solomon: and Solomon said unto him, Go to thine house.

When Adonijah appeared before him, Solomon didn't rant; Solomon didn't rave. With the authority of the kingdom behind him, he simply said, "Go to your room." I like that!

2

1 Kings 2:1, 2
Now the days of David drew nigh that he should die; and he charged Solomon his son, saying, I go the way of all the earth: be thou strong therefore, and shew thyself a man;

David was a man who spent time in the wilderness doing battle, killing giants, leaping over walls, risking his life. Solomon, on the other hand, grew up in a palace, never knowing what it meant to be chased by enemies or to be face to face with giants. Therefore, I don't think Solomon was David's favorite son. David mourned Absalom's death perhaps because he sensed in Absalom a manliness that matched his own. So, as he's dying, he exhorts his sixteen-year-old son to get tough and be a man.

1 Kings 2:3, 4
And keep the charge of the LORD thy God, to walk in his ways, to keep his statutes, and his commandments, and his judgments, and his testimonies, as it is written in the law of Moses, that thou mayest prosper in all that thou doest, and whithersoever thou turnest thyself: That the LORD may continue his word which he spake concerning me, saying, If thy children take heed to their way, to walk before me in truth with all their heart and with all their soul, there shall not fail thee (said he) a man on the throne of Israel.

"Walk in God's ways, Solomon," David continued. "Keep His statutes, His commandments, His judgments, His testimonies. Study the Word, follow the Word, and you'll do well."

1 Kings 2:5 (a)
Moreover . . .

After giving general instructions to be strong in the Lord and in His Word, David goes on to give Solomon specific instructions . . .

1 Kings 2:5 (b), 6
. . . thou knowest also what Joab the son of Zeruiah did to me, and what he did to the two captains of the hosts of Israel, unto Abner the son of Ner, and unto Amasa the son of Jether, whom he slew, and shed the blood of war in peace, and put the blood of war upon his girdle that was about his loins, and in his shoes that were on his feet. Do therefore according to thy wisdom, and let not his hoar head go down to the grave in peace.

"Joab wronged me. He killed Absalom. He killed Amasa. He killed Abner. See that he pays for this," David said to Solomon.

1 Kings 2:7 (a)
But shew kindness unto the sons of Barzillai the Gileadite . . .

Barzillai was the man who brought supplies to David as he fled from Jerusalem during Absalom's attempted coup (2 Samuel 17:27–29).

1 Kings 2:7 (b)–10
. . . and let them be of those that eat at thy table: for so they came to me when I fled because of Absalom thy brother. And, behold, thou hast with thee Shimei the son of Gera, a Benjamite of Bahurim, which cursed me with a grievous curse in the day when I went to Mahanaim: but he came down to meet me at Jordan, and I sware to him by the LORD, saying, I will not put thee to death with the sword. Now therefore hold him not guiltless: for thou art a wise man, and knowest what thou oughtest to do unto him; but his hoar head bring thou down to the grave with blood. So David slept with his fathers, and was buried in the city of David.

Shimei was the man who flung curses, rocks, and dust at David (2 Samuel 16:6, 7). "All of this is happening to you because you're a wretch." And during that time of real difficulty and personal tragedy, at that time when he was already heavy and heartbroken, Shimei was the last straw. "Let me lop that guy's head off," one of his men said. "No, David said, God's allowed it. Let him curse."

Then, when Absalom's rebellion was put down

and David was returning to Jerusalem, Shimei met him at the River Jordan saying, "No hard feelings I hope." And David forgave him.

But here, at the end of his life, David's last words were, "You need to take care of Joab and Shimei." Is David being cruel here? I don't think so. I think David looked at his sixteen-year-old son, remembered the cunning and craftiness of Joab and Shimei, and said to himself, *I can handle these guys, but my son doesn't stand a chance.*

1 Kings 2:11
And the days that David reigned over Israel were forty years: seven years reigned he in Hebron, and thirty and three years reigned he in Jerusalem.

Second Samuel 5:4 tells us David was thirty years old when he began his reign. Thirty is a significant number in Scripture. At thirty, the Levites assumed their ministry. At thirty, Joseph became prime minister of Egypt. At thirty, Ezekiel began making his powerful prophetic proclamations. At thirty, John the Baptist began to go throughout the countryside preaching preparation for the kingdom. At thirty, Jesus began His public ministry. Thus, there seems to be something significant about the age of thirty. In God's economy, it would seem as though the years up to thirty are years of training and preparation.

David reigned over Israel for forty years and died at the age of seventy. Interestingly, Psalm 90, penned by Moses, says that the years of a man are seventy years. In other words, seventy years is a normal lifespan.

If you're under thirty, use the time to prepare wisely as you seek the Lord for what He has ahead for you. If you're over thirty, serve Him with maturity and wisdom. If you're under thirty, glean from your elders. If you're over thirty, set the pace for those looking to you. It has been said that the difference between a politician and a statesman is that a politician has his eyes on the next election, while a statesman has his eyes on the next generation. May God make us spiritual statesmen who have a heart for generations to follow.

1 Kings 2:12, 13
Then sat Solomon upon the throne of David his father; and his kingdom was established greatly. And Adonijah the son of Haggith came to Bath-sheba the mother of Solomon. And she said, Comest thou peaceably? And he said, Peaceably.

After his attempted coup, it's no wonder Bath-sheba questioned Adonijah.

1 Kings 2:14–17
He said moreover, I have somewhat to say unto thee. And she said, Say on. And he said, Thou knowest that the kingdom was mine, and that all Israel set their faces on me, that I should reign: howbeit the kingdom is turned about, and is become my brother's: for it was his from the LORD. And now I ask one petition of thee, deny me not. And she said unto him, Say on. And he said, Speak, I pray thee, unto Solomon the king, (for he will not say thee nay,) that he give me Abishag the Shunammite to wife.

Adonijah's words were as smooth as butter, but his heart was as cold as steel. "I've lost the kingdom," he said. "But let me at least have the lady." Why did Adonijah want Abishag? It wasn't because he loved her but because it was customary that if a man took a former leader's concubine or wife, he was assuming the leader's position. That is why, when Absalom went into Jerusalem, the first thing he did was have relations with the ten concubines of David, signifying to the entire nation that he was on the throne (2 Samuel 16:22).

1 Kings 2:18, 19
And Bath-sheba said, Well; I will speak for thee unto the king. Bath-sheba therefore went unto king Solomon, to speak unto him for Adonijah. And the king rose up to meet her, and bowed himself unto her, and sat down on his throne, and caused a seat to be set for the king's mother; and she sat on his right hand.

I like this. Solomon the king sees his mother walk in, gets up, and bows down, paying respect and reverence to her. It's a virtue that is very becoming to any child of God, when they show honor to their parents. Here's Solomon, the king, bowing down before his mother.

1 Kings 2:20–25
Then she said, I desire one small petition of thee; I pray thee, say me not nay. And the king said unto her, Ask on, my mother: for I will not say thee nay. And she said, Let Abishag the Shunammite be given to Adonijah thy brother to wife. And king Solomon answered and said unto his mother, And why dost thou ask Abishag the Shunammite for Adonijah? ask for him the kingdom also; for he is mine elder brother; even for him, and for Abiathar the priest, and for Joab the son of Zeruiah. Then king Solomon sware by the LORD, saying, God do so to me, and more also, if Adonijah have not spoken this word against his own life. Now therefore, as the LORD liveth, which hath established me, and

set me on the throne of David my father, and who hath made me an house, as he promised, Adonijah shall be put to death this day. And king Solomon sent by the hand of Benaiah the son of Jehoiada; and he fell upon him that he died.

Why did Bath-sheba ask Solomon to give Abishag to Adonijah? I believe it was because she knew precisely what Solomon's reaction would be. I believe she knew all along that Adonijah was a threat and seized the opportunity to put an end to it.

1 Kings 2:26
And unto Abiathar the priest said the king, Get thee to Anathoth, unto thine own fields; for thou art worthy of death: but I will not at this time put thee to death, because thou barest the ark of the Lord GOD before David my father, and because thou hast been afflicted in all wherein my father was afflicted.

Like Joab, Abiathar deserved death for his part in Adonijah's attempted coup. (v. 7). He was spared, however, because of his service as priest and because of his history with David.

1 Kings 2:27
So Solomon thrust out Abiathar from being priest unto the LORD; that he might fulfil the word of the LORD, which he spake concerning the house of Eli in Shiloh.

In 1 Samuel 2, a word was given to Eli that his family would be cut off from the priesthood forever. Here, we see the fulfillment of this prophecy as Abiathar, who was of the house of Eli, is removed from the priesthood.

1 Kings 2:28–35
Then tidings came to Joab: for Joab had turned after Adonijah, though he turned not after Absalom. And Joab fled unto the tabernacle of the LORD, and caught hold on the horns of the altar. And it was told king Solomon that Joab was fled unto the tabernacle of the LORD; and, behold, he is by the altar. Then Solomon sent Benaiah the son of Jehoiada, saying, Go, fall upon him. And Benaiah came to the tabernacle of the LORD, and said unto him, Thus saith the king, Come forth. And he said, Nay; but I will die here. And Benaiah brought the king word again, saying, Thus said Joab, and thus he answered me. And the king said unto him, Do as he hath said, and fall upon him, and bury him; that thou mayest take away the innocent blood, which Joab shed, from me, and from the house of my father. And the LORD shall return his blood upon his own head, who fell upon two men more righteous and better than he, and slew them with the sword, my father David not knowing thereof, to wit, Abner the son of Ner, captain of the host of Israel, and Amasa the son of Jether, captain of the host of Judah. Their blood shall therefore return upon the head of Joab, and upon the head of his seed for ever: but upon David, and upon his seed, and upon his house, and upon his throne, shall there be peace for ever from the LORD. So Benaiah the son of Jehoiada went up, and fell upon him, and slew him: and he was buried in his own house in the wilderness. And the king put Benaiah the son of Jehoiada in his room over the host: and Zadok the priest did the king put in the room of Abiathar.

Joab was a man who was never ashamed of his sin and never afraid of punishment all the while he served David. He did whatever he wanted, feeling as though he would experience no repercussions. I suggest the reason for this is that Joab was the only one beside David, Bath-sheba, and Nathan the prophet, who knew that David ordered the execution of Uriah the Hittite (2 Samuel 11:15). Because he knew this secret, he did as he pleased. Once David died, however, the secret no longer mattered. So Joab tried to seek sanctuary in the temple, but was killed at Solomon's command nonetheless.

First Peter 2:16 says we are not to use our liberty as a cloak for sin. Therefore, just because you might be one who clings to the altar of the Cross of Calvary, just because you might recognize the atoning work of Jesus Christ, do not be deceived in thinking you can do whatever you want and not suffer repercussions. Joab was deceived. Here, he finds himself at the very altar, saying, "Surely, they're not going to take me away." But he was wrong.

The Word of God has very strong things to say concerning those who name the name of Jesus but continually, habitually persist in sin—refusing to respond to the chastening of the Lord, refusing to submit to the correction of the Lord—using their "liberty in Jesus" as a covering for sin. The Word of God warns that such people will not inherit the kingdom (1 Corinthians 6:9–11). Joab being dragged away from the altar should sober us to the point where we say, "Lord, have I been clinging to the altar, thinking I'm home free when in reality I've been disobeying Your commands, not learning lessons, not allowing You to speak to me and deal with me?"

Be not deceived, there will be those who will

truly be surprised when the Lord says, "Depart from Me. I never knew you" (Matthew 7:21–23).

"But I was holding on to the altar," they'll say.

Perhaps, but did you obey the command of the King or did you think you knew a secret, that no matter what you did, it wouldn't matter.

My prayer is that none of us who minister to others in any capacity will allow people to be lulled into eternal destruction, but would cause every person with whom we deal to carefully consider if they are truly in the kingdom of God. I would rather see us as His people come before His altar with fear and trepidation, weeping and saying, "Lord, I pray that Your mercy will suffice, that Your grace will cover, that my heart will be right with You." I would rather see us come to the altar too often and commit ourselves too frequently than be lulled by some theology into thinking we were saved, only to find out we weren't.

1 Kings 2:36–46
And the king sent and called for Shimei, and said unto him, Build thee an house in Jerusalem, and dwell there, and go not forth thence any whither. For it shall be, that on the day thou goest out, and passest over the brook Kidron, thou shalt know for certain that thou shalt surely die: thy blood shall be upon thine own head. And Shimei said unto the king, The saying is good: as my lord the king hath said, so will thy servant do. And Shimei dwelt in Jerusalem many days. And it came to pass at the end of three years, that two of the servants of Shimei ran away unto Achish son of Maachah king of Gath. And they told Shimei, saying, Behold, thy servants be in Gath. And Shimei arose, and saddled his ass, and went to Gath to Achish to seek his servants: and Shimei went, and brought his servants from Gath. And it was told Solomon that Shimei had gone from Jerusalem to Gath, and was come again. And the king sent and called for Shimei, and said unto him, Did I not make thee to swear by the LORD, and protested unto thee, saying, Know for a certain, on the day thou goest out, and walkest abroad any wither, that thou shalt surely die? and thou saidst unto me, The word that I have heard is good. Why then hast thou not kept the oath of the LORD, and the commandment that I have charged thee with? The king said moreover to Shimei, Thou knowest all the wickedness which thine heart is privy to, that thou didst to David my father: therefore the LORD shall return thy wickedness upon thine own head; And king Solomon shall be blessed, and the throne of David shall be established before the LORD for ever. So the king commanded Benaiah the son of Jehoiada; which went out, and fell upon him, that he died. And the kingdom was established in the hand of Solomon.

Like Joab, Shimei was not to die in peace (vv. 5–9). Graciously put under "house arrest" by Solomon, Shimei was free to move about the entire city of Jerusalem. But, assuming Solomon either wouldn't notice or wouldn't care, Shimei crossed the boundary of Jerusalem in pursuit of two escaped servants. Thus, it was not only his cursing of David but his disregard for Solomon's grace that brought about Shimei's death.

The same is true of us. Born in sin, we were at enmity with God. But we were offered pardon through His amazing grace. No wonder the writer to the Hebrews asks, "How shall we escape if we neglect so great salvation?" (2:3). Our Savior, our Hero crossed the brook Kidron in our place on His way to the Cross. Therefore, let us not be like Shimei. Let us remain in Jerusalem; let us not stray from His grace.

3 Kings 3:1
And Solomon made affinity with Pharaoh king of Egypt, and took Pharaoh's daughter, and brought her into the city of David, until he had made an end of building his own house, and the house of the LORD, and the wall of Jerusalem round about.

In the Middle Eastern culture of Solomon's day, marriage was often used to cement treaties and to seal alliances between nations. Here, we see Solomon doing this. According to the letter of the law, his action was not wrong for the only women the Israelites were forbidden to marry were Canaanite women. However, Solomon violated the spirit of the law, for in gathering wives from other countries and cultures, he would soon find his own heart entangled in their religious system.

1 Kings 3:2, 3
Only the people sacrificed in high places, because there was no house built unto the name of the LORD, until those days. And Solomon loved the LORD, walking in the statutes of David his father: only he sacrificed and burnt incense in high places.

Throughout the land of Israel were high places, or groves, planted by the Canaanites for the purpose of worshiping their deities. The Jews would use these same groves to offer sacrifice and incense to Jehovah.

These are the statutes and judgments, which ye shall observe to do in the land, which the

LORD God of thy fathers giveth thee to possess it, all the days that ye live upon the earth. Ye shall utterly destroy all the places, wherein the nations which ye shall possess served their gods, upon the high mountains, and upon the hills, and under every green tree: And ye shall overthrow their altars, and break their pillars, and burn their groves with fire; and ye shall hew down the graven images of their gods, and destroy the names of them out of that place. Ye shall not do so unto the LORD your God. But unto the place which the LORD your God shall choose out of all your tribes to put his name there, even unto his habitation shall ye seek, and thither thou shalt come.

Deuteronomy 12:1–5

The law specifies that God's people were to worship Him only in the place He assigned. Because the ark of the covenant was in Jerusalem at this time, Solomon would have been so much wiser and the people so much safer had they offered their sacrifices and incense in Jerusalem, or in Gibeon where the tabernacle was pitched at this time.

What does this have to do with us? Some people say, "I can worship the Lord anywhere I want. I don't need to be in church on Sunday. I can go to a lake and worship the Lord. After all, didn't Jesus preach by the lake? In fact, didn't Jesus preach from a boat? Wouldn't it, then, be understandable to go boating on Sunday?"

"Forsake not the assembling of yourselves together," the writer of the Book of Hebrews clearly tells us (10:25). Those who don't assemble together become vulnerable to all sorts of needless pain and problems. In His infinite wisdom, the Lord set up His church as a body because we find our true calling as we remain linked to each other.

1 Kings 3:4, 5 (a)
And the king went to Gibeon to sacrifice there; for that was the great high place: a thousand burnt offerings did Solomon offer upon that altar. In Gibeon the LORD appeared to Solomon in a dream by night . . .

The Lord appeared to Solomon in Gibeon because that was where the tabernacle was. It was at the place that Solomon abandoned his own ideas about worship and submitted to the Word of the Lord that the Lord appeared to him.

Secondly, notice *when* the Lord spoke to Solomon. It was after he had been busy working for the Lord all day that he was blessed to hear from the Lord at night. When we offer the sacrifice of praise or the sacrifice of service, whenever we find ourselves in the place of giving *to* the Lord, we are in a position to hear from Him.

Finally, notice *how* the message from the Lord came to Solomon. It came in a dream. Throughout both the Old and New Testaments, the Lord speaks through dreams. This doesn't mean every dream you have is significant. But it's not a bad idea before your head hits the pillow to say, "Lord, if You want to minister a truth or understanding to me tonight, I would love that." God doesn't just tuck you in and tune you out. Rather, I believe it's often His desire to minister to us in the night hours because, for most of us, it's the only time we're quiet enough to hear Him!

1 Kings 3:5 (b)
. . . and God said, Ask what I shall give thee.

This is amazing. What if the Lord came to you tonight and said, "Whatever you want, I'll do." How would you answer?

1 Kings 3:6 (a)
And Solomon said . . .

Although the Lord appeared to Solomon in a dream, Solomon answered verbally. In this, I'm reminded of the account in Acts 12, where the angel of the Lord came to Peter in prison, saying, "Follow me." Luke writes that Peter "went out, and followed him; and wist not that it was true which was done by the angel; but thought he saw a vision." In other words, had Peter dismissed the Lord's words as having only ethereal, philosophical meaning, he would have eventually woken up on the hard floor of his prison cell. But, because He took the Lord at His word and obeyed Him physically, He walked out of prison a free man. Solomon could have taken the Lord's appearance as nothing more than an encouraging thought, but he didn't. He opened his mouth and spoke audible words that would result in incredible blessing.

Perhaps the Lord has been speaking to your heart about a certain matter, but you have written it off as little more than a good idea. I encourage you to put feet to your faith, to do whatever it is He is asking of you, and see if your physical action doesn't result in a physical response from Him.

1 Kings 3:6 (b)–10
. . . Thou hast shewed unto thy servant David my father great mercy, according as he walked before thee in truth, and in righteousness, and in uprightness of heart with thee; and thou hast kept for him this great kindness, that thou hast given him a son to sit on his

throne, as it is this day. And now, O LORD my God, thou hast made thy servant king instead of David my father: and I am but a little child: I know not how to go out or come in. And thy servant is in the midst of thy people which thou hast chosen, a great people, that cannot be numbered nor counted for multitude. Give therefore thy servant an understanding heart to judge thy people, that I may discern between good and bad: for who is able to judge this thy so great a people? And the speech pleased the Lord, that Solomon had asked this thing.

"Ask of Me anything," the Lord said. And Solomon asked for wisdom that he might be able to wisely lead the people God had placed under his leadership. The beginning of wisdom is truly to recognize the need for wisdom. You'll know you are becoming wiser when you say to the Lord, "I don't know as much as I used to think I knew."

> If any of you lack wisdom, let him ask of God, that giveth to all men liberally, and upbraideth not; and it shall be given him. James 1:5

The word "upbraideth" means that the Lord won't come down on, or get angry with those who ask for wisdom. On the contrary, as seen in the next verse, God is pleased with such a request.

1 Kings 3:11–13
And God said unto him, Because thou hast asked this thing, and hast not asked for thyself long life; neither hast asked riches for thyself, nor hast asked the life of thine enemies; but hast asked for thyself understanding to discern judgment; Behold, I have done according to thy words: lo, I have given thee a wise and an understanding heart; so that there was none like thee before thee, neither after thee shall any arise like unto thee. And I have also given thee that which thou hast not asked, both riches, and honour: so that there shall not be any among the kings like unto thee all thy days.

Jesus taught us that if we seek first His kingdom and His righteousness, everything else we need will be added to us (Matthew 6:33). Solomon is proof of this. Consider the prayers you prayed today or this week. How many were for the good of the kingdom? How many of your prayers were, "Lord, allow Your kingdom to be expanded. Allow Your name to be exalted," versus "Lord, I need this . . . please help me with that"? Solomon didn't ask for himself. He asked for the kingdom. And the Lord was pleased.

1 Kings 3:14, 15
And if thou wilt walk in my ways, to keep my statutes and my commandments, as thy father David did walk, then I will lengthen thy days. And Solomon awoke; and, behold, it was a dream. And he came to Jerusalem, and stood before the ark of the covenant of the LORD, and offered up burnt offerings, and offered peace offerings, and made a feast to all his servants.

Solomon woke from his dream and immediately sacrificed to the Lord in Jerusalem. Again, Solomon is responding physically to a promise he would soon see fulfilled physically. At this point, however, his response is based solely on faith. The combination reminds me of how we were saved . . .

> That if thou shalt confess with thy mouth the Lord Jesus, and shalt believe in thine heart that God hath raised him from the dead, thou shalt be saved. For with the heart man believeth unto righteousness; and with the mouth confession is made unto salvation. Romans 10:9, 10

It is through the unseen belief of the heart coupled with the spoken word of the mouth that salvation is brought to the sinner. True inward faith is invariably linked to an outward manifestation.

1 Kings 3:16–23
Then came there two women, that were harlots, unto the king, and stood before him. And the one woman said, O my lord, I and this woman dwell in one house; and I was delivered of a child with her in the house. And it came to pass the third day after that I was delivered, that this woman was delivered also: and we were together; there was no stranger with us in the house, save we two in the house. And this woman's child died in the night; because she overlaid it. And she arose at midnight, and took my son from beside me, while thine handmaid slept, and laid it in her bosom, and laid her dead child in my bosom. And when I rose in the morning to give my child suck, behold, it was dead: but when I had considered it in the morning, behold, it was not my son, which I did bear. And the other woman said, Nay; but the living is my son, and the dead is thy son. And this said, No; but the dead is thy son, and the living is my son. Thus they spake before the king. Then said the king, The one saith, This is my son that liveth, and thy son is the dead: and the other saith, Nay; but thy son is the dead, and my son is the living.

Two women who were harlots were living together and gave birth within three days of each other. When one child died in the night, the babies were switched, and suddenly, as one woman looked at the dead baby next to her, she realized it wasn't her baby at all. They came to Solomon to settle their dispute. There were no eyewitnesses to the crime and, because these women were harlots, the baby's fathers would not surface. But in Solomon's amazing answer to them, we see the fruit of the answer to his own prayer, for in it we see unfathomable wisdom . . .

1 Kings 3:24
And the king said, Bring me a sword. And they brought a sword before the king.

The Word of God is quick and powerful, sharper than any two-edged sword (Hebrews 4:12). Dear friend, if you're involved in counseling, sharing with friends or neighbors, or giving advice to people in need, the first words out of your mouth should be those of Solomon: "Bring me a sword. Let's look in the Word." If you want to be effective in ministering to people, let these words be on your lips and may the Word be in your hand.

1 Kings 3:25–28
And the king said, Divide the living child in two, and give half to the one, and half to the other. Then spake the woman whose the living child was unto the king, for her bowels yearned upon her son, and she said, O my lord, give her the living child, and in no wise slay it. But the other said, Let it be neither mine nor thine, but divide it. Then the king answered and said, Give her the living child, and in no wise slay it: she is the mother thereof. And all Israel heard of the judgment which the king had judged; and they feared the king: for they saw that the wisdom of God was in him, to do judgment.

Solomon's answer was absolutely brilliant for it unequivocally determined the rightful mother. You see, a true mother will never tolerate division. A true mother would sooner never see her baby again than to have it divided in any way. Thus, the true mother was immediately and undisputedly identified.

Be it in a marriage, a family, or a church body, division leads either quickly or eventually to one thing: death. May we be as committed to unity as this mother was.

4

1 Kings 4:1–6
So king Solomon was king over all Israel. And these were the princes which he had; Azariah the son of Zadok the priest, Elihoreph and Ahiah, the sons of Shisha, scribes; Jehoshaphat the son of Ahilud, the recorder. And Benaiah the son of Jehoiada was over the host: and Zadok and Abiathar were the priests: And Azariah the son of Nathan was over the officers: and Zabud the son of Nathan was principal officer, and the king's friend: And Ahishar was over the household: and Adoniram the son of Abda was over the tribute.

In verses 1 through 19, we see a picture of church leadership. First, we see one king. In the body of Christ, there is only one King—Jesus Christ. He is the chief Cornerstone, the Alpha and Omega, the Head of the church. Underneath the king, we see a small group of men who are princes, overseers who carried out the work of the king. In this, we see a picture of New Testament elders. The Church of Jesus Christ is not a dictatorship, where only one earthly man rules. Neither is it a democracy, where everyone has a say. It's an oligarchy. There is plurality and collegiality as a group of men seek the face of God together and carry out the commands of their King.

1 Kings 4:7–19
And Solomon had twelve officers over all Israel, which provided victuals for the king and his household: each man his month in a year made provision. And these are their names: The son of Hur, in mount Ephraim: The son of Dekar, in Makaz, and in Shaalbim, and Beth-shemesh, and Elon-beth-hanan: The son of Hesed, in Aruboth; to him pertained Sochoh, and all the land of Hepher: The son of Abinadab, in all the region of Dor; which had Taphath the daughter of Solomon to wife: Baana the son of Ahilud; to him pertained Taanach and Megiddo, and all Beth-shean, which is by Zartanah beneath Jezreel, from Beth-shean to Abel-meholah, even unto the place that is beyond Jokneam: The son of Geber, in Ramoth-gilead; to him pertained the towns of Jair the son of Manasseh, which are in Gilead; to him also pertained the region of Argob, which is in Bashan, threescore great cities with walls and brasen bars: Ahinadab the son of Iddo had Mahanaim: Ahimaaz was in Naphtali; he also took Basmath the daughter of Solomon to wife: Baanah the son of Hushai was in Asher and in Aloth: Jehoshaphat the son of Paruah, in Issachar: Shimei the son of Elah, in Benjamin: Geber the son of Uri was in the country of Gilead, in the country of Sihon king of the Amorites, and of Og king of Bashan; and he was the only officer which was in the land.

Twelve men supplied food for the table. This ministry foreshadows the ministry in Acts 6, whereby the widows were fed, and points to the New Testament office of deacon.

1 Kings 4:20–24
Judah and Israel were many, as the sand which is by the sea in multitude, eating and drinking, and making merry. And Solomon reigned over all kingdoms from the river unto the land of the Philistines, and unto the border of Egypt: they brought presents, and served Solomon all the days of his life. And Solomon's provision for one day was thirty measures of fine flour, and threescore measures of meal, Ten fat oxen, and twenty oxen out of the pastures, and an hundred sheep, beside harts, and roebucks, and fallowdeer, and fatted fowl. For he had dominion over all the region on this side the river, from Tiphsah even to Azzah, over all the kings on this side the river: and he had peace on all sides round about him.

Here, we see peace and incredible prosperity in Solomon's kingdom. Yet the peace and prosperity that Solomon and his people experienced was based upon the war and bloodshed of David, the man who preceded him.

As we gather at His Table, as we feast from His Word, as we come into His presence, we enjoy peace and prosperity because the Son of David, Jesus Christ, went to war on our behalf and shed His blood in our place.

1 Kings 4:25–28
And Judah and Israel dwelt safely, every man under his vine and under his fig tree, from Dan even to Beer-sheba, all the days of Solomon. And Solomon had forty thousand stalls of horses for his chariots, and twelve thousand horsemen. And those officers provided victual for king Solomon, and for all that came unto king Solomon's table, every man in his month: they lacked nothing. Barley also and straw for the horses and dromedaries brought they unto the place where the officers were, every man according to his charge.

This is a prophetic peek into the Millennium. Micah prophesied that, when Jesus Christ comes back, every man shall dwell under his vine and under his fig tree (4:4). In other words, when Jesus comes back, things are going to be right. There will be peace and prosperity, not only internally, but also materially and physically as well.

1 Kings 4:29
And God gave Solomon wisdom and understanding exceeding much, and largeness of heart, even as the sand that is on the sea shore.

In 1 Corinthians 8:1, we are reminded that knowledge puffs up. Oftentimes, the more we know, the colder we can become. The more we know, the more cynical we find ourselves. Not so with Solomon. He grew exceedingly great in understanding, but he also had a correlating largeness of heart.

When we gather together to study the Word, I think we should pray, "Lord, allow me to not become cold or puffed up with knowledge. Give me the largeness of heart you gave Solomon"—for even if you know all things, if you don't have love, you have nothing at all.

1 Kings 4:30–34
And Solomon's wisdom excelled the wisdom of all the children of the east country, and all the wisdom of Egypt. For he was wiser than all men; than Ethan the Ezrahite, and Heman, and Chalcol, and Darda, the sons of Mahol: and his fame was in all nations round about. And he spake three thousand proverbs: and his songs were a thousand and five. And he spake of trees, from the cedar tree that is in Lebanon even unto the hyssop that springeth out of the wall: he spake also of beasts, and of fowl, and of creeping things, and of fishes. And there came of all people to hear the wisdom of Solomon, from all kings of the earth, which had heard of his wisdom.

This guy was incredible. Try making up one proverb worth writing down and passing on. Solomon wrote 3,000. In addition, he wrote 1,005 songs. He was also a dendrologist, a botanist, a zoologist, an ornithologist, an entomologist, and an ichthyologist. Solomon asked for wisdom and God answered "above all he could ask or think" (Ephesians 3:20).

"Call unto Me," the Lord declares, "and I will show you great and mighty things which thou knowest not" (Jeremiah 33:3). His invitation still stands. May we, like Solomon, be wise enough to simply ask.

5

1 Kings 5:1–5
And Hiram king of Tyre sent his servants unto Solomon; for he had heard that they had anointed him king in the room of his father: for Hiram was ever a lover of David. And Solomon sent to Hiram, saying, Thou knowest how that David my father could not build an house unto the name of the LORD his God for the wars which were about him on every side, until the LORD put them under the soles of his feet. But now the LORD my God hath given me rest on every

side, so that there is neither adversary nor evil occurrent. And, behold, I purpose to build an house unto the name of the LORD my God, as the LORD spake unto David my father, saying, Thy son, whom I will set upon thy throne in thy room, he shall build an house unto my name.

Anything you do of significance in life begins when you get to the place of purposing in your heart. Daniel purposed in his heart that he would not defile himself (Daniel 1:8). Solomon purposed to build a house unto the Lord. What have *you* purposed?

1 Kings 5:6
Now therefore command thou that they hew me cedar trees out of Lebanon; and my servants shall be with thy servants: and unto thee will I give hire for thy servants according to all that thou shalt appoint: for thou knowest that there is not among us any that can skill to hew timber like unto the Sidonians.

Solomon realized the Sidonians were better woodcutters than were his own men. So he took advantage of their expertise and abilities. Before him, Moses invited his father-in-law, an unbeliever, to join the Israelites on their journey to the Promised Land, knowing Hobab's knowledge of the wilderness would be invaluable (Numbers 10:31). Some believers choose to do business only with other believers. Moses, however, gives us an example of something more practical on both sides of eternity. That is, not only were the Israelites blessed by the presence of a wise guide in Hobab, but in Judges 4:11, we see Hobab's relatives living in the Promised Land. This means Hobab not only accompanied Moses, but very likely became a believer.

While I certainly encourage the body supporting one another, there is a place to seek practical help and expertise from nonbelievers, and in so doing, to introduce them to the Lord.

1 Kings 5:7–12
And it came to pass, when Hiram heard the words of Solomon, that he rejoiced greatly, and said, Blessed be the LORD this day, which hath given unto David a wise son over this great people. And Hiram sent to Solomon, saying, I have considered the things which thou sentest to me for: and I will do all thy desire concerning timber of cedar, and concerning timber of fir. My servants shall bring them down from Lebanon unto the sea: and I will convey them by sea in floats unto the place that thou shalt appoint me, and will cause them to be discharged there, and thou shalt receive them: and thou shalt accomplish my desire, in giving food for my household. So Hiram gave Solomon cedar trees and fir trees according to all his desire. And Solomon gave Hiram twenty thousand measures of wheat for food to his household, and twenty measures of pure oil: thus gave Solomon to Hiram year by year. And the LORD gave Solomon wisdom, as he promised him: and there was peace between Hiram and Solomon; and they two made a league together.

Jews and Gentiles worked together on the temple. Why? Because in Ephesians 2, we read that, although we as Gentiles were once strangers and far off from the covenants and people of God, God destroyed the middle wall of partition, bringing Jews and Gentiles together.

1 Kings 5:13, 14
And king Solomon raised a levy out of all Israel; and the levy was thirty thousand men. And he sent them to Lebanon ten thousand a month by courses: a month they were in Lebanon, and two months at home: and Adoniram was over the levy.

Here we see the levy—or work crew—that built the temple. Solomon's wisdom was again seen in requiring that his crew spent only one month in three away from home.

1 Kings 5:15 (a)
And Solomon had threescore and ten thousand that bare burdens . . .

Seventy thousand bore burdens. They were intercessors, so to speak, bearing burdens on their backs and shoulders. Oh that the Lord would raise up more intercessors, more people who say, "Lord, I give You permission to wake me at five in the morning, or to cause me in the middle of my lunch break to be pulled away to intercede on behalf of my brothers and sisters."

Prayer is the most important ministry anyone can undertake, and yet it is one of the most neglected. Only heaven can reward those who make the commitment to be a burden-bearer in prayer.

1 Kings 5:15 (b)
. . . and fourscore thousand hewers in the mountains;

Eighty thousand men were stone cutters. Jeremiah likens the Word of God to a hammer (23:29). In this, we see a picture of 80,000 men chipping away, cutting away with the hammer of the Word of God—discipling and teaching. May God continue to raise up those who are willing to hew stone, to teach Sunday school, to lead Bible studies, or to disciple coworkers.

1 Kings 5:16
Beside the chief of Solomon's officers which were over the work, three thousand and three hundred, which ruled over the people that wrought in the work.

The 33,000 who oversaw this vast project speak to me of church leadership, seen nowhere more perfectly than in the One who washed the feet and gave His life for those He led (John 13:5).

1 Kings 5:17 (a)
And the king commanded, and they brought great stones . . .

The king commanded and the workers commenced. There was no hesitation, no reservation, no argument. Gang, that's the way it's always to be. When our King speaks, we're to obey.

I think of Mary. "They're out of wine," she said to her Son at the marriage feast in Cana. Then she went to the servants and said, "Whatsoever He saith unto you do it" (John 2:5). The same word applies to us today. Whatever He says, let's do. Whatever the King commands, let's begin.

1 Kings 5:17 (b), 18
. . . costly stones, and hewed stones, to lay the foundation of the house. And Solomon's builders and Hiram's builders did hew them, and the stonesquarers: so they prepared timber and stones to build the house.

I understand that the stones would need to be large and would need to be hewn. But who of us in building a house would make a foundation from precious, costly stones? We have a tendency to think, *Out of sight, out of mind. If it doesn't show, it doesn't matter.* Perhaps Solomon, however, understood that all things are open and exposed before the Lord (Hebrews 4:13), that nothing is hidden from His sight. Maybe that is why he chose costly stones, for although man wouldn't notice them, he knew they would please the Lord.

6

1 Kings 6:1
And it came to pass in the four hundred and eightieth year after the children of Israel were come out of the land of Egypt, in the fourth year of Solomon's reign over Israel, in the month Zif, which is the second month, that he began to build the house of the LORD.

In 1 Kings 5:5, we saw Solomon purpose to build the temple. Here, we see him actually beginning the work. It has been rightly said that the pathway of Bible studies and conferences is strewn with the intentions of those who purposed but never began. We must both purpose and begin if we are going to complete the work God has called us to do.

When asked how he began his conquest of the world, Alexander the Great is reported to have answered, "By not delaying."

What has the Lord shown you today? *Now* is the time to begin.

1 Kings 6:2, 3
And the house which king Solomon built for the LORD, the length thereof was threescore cubits, and the breadth thereof twenty cubits, and the height thereof thirty cubits. And the porch before the temple of the house, twenty cubits was the length thereof, according to the breadth of the house; and ten cubits was the breadth thereof before the house.

At ninety feet by thirty feet by forty-five feet, the temple was twice as big as the tabernacle. Although the temple provides a picture of the church, it doesn't hold the same significance as the tabernacle. As seen in the Book of Hebrews, especially as it portrays Jesus, the tabernacle rather than the temple is the model.

Why?

The tabernacle was simple; the temple was complex. For example, while there was one candlestick in the tabernacle, there will be ten candlesticks in the temple (1 Chronicles 28). Man prizes the ornate. God, however, values simplicity. The beautiful truths the tabernacle portrayed were somewhat masked by the complication and ornamentation of the temple.

1 Kings 6:4
And for the house he made windows of narrow lights.

The tabernacle had no windows because the Shekinah glory of the Lord provided the light for the Holy of Holies. Here, however, windows were built in the temple evidently because the plans provided for failure—in case the glory of God would not be present.

1 Kings 6:5
And against the wall of the house he built chambers round about, against the walls of the house round about, both of the temple and of the oracle: and he made chambers round about:

The tabernacle was mobile, built for a journeying nation. The temple, on the other hand, was stable, built for a people who had arrived at their destination.

1 Kings 6:6, 7
The nethermost chamber was five cubits broad, and the middle was six cubits broad, and the third was seven cubits broad: for without in the wall of the house he made narrowed rests round about, that the beams should not be fastened in the walls of the house. And the house, when it was in building, was built of stone made ready before it was brought thither: so that there was neither hammer nor axe nor any tool of iron heard in the house, while it was in building.

All of the cutting and carving, all of the chipping and grinding was done in the quarry so that when the massive stones arrived at the temple site, they fit together perfectly. What an amazing sight it must have been to watch the temple going up silently.

We are living stones, gang (1 Peter 2:5). That makes this world the rock quarry. It's the place where we are chipped and cut, polished and ground so that when we get to heaven, the clamor will cease, the work will be complete.

***For a topical study of 1 Kings 6:7 entitled "Foundation Work," turn to page* 973.**

1 Kings 6:8–10
The door for the middle chamber was in the right side of the house: and they went up with winding stairs into the middle chamber, and out of the middle into the third. So he built the house, and finished it; and covered the house with beams and boards of cedar. And then he built chambers against all the house, five cubits high: and they rested on the house with timber of cedar.

As we will see, the temple took seven years to complete.

1 Kings 6:11–13
And the word of the LORD came to Solomon, saying, Concerning this house which thou art in building, if thou wilt walk in my statutes, and execute my judgments, and keep all my commandments to walk in them; then will I perform my word with thee, which I spake unto David thy father: And I will dwell among the children of Israel, and will not forsake my people Israel.

Even while construction is going on, the Lord calls Solomon back to a very important reality. In the midst of this building project, He says, "Walk in My statutes. Execute My judgments. Keep My commandments, and I will perform My word." In other words, the Lord was saying, "I'm not so concerned about building a building as I am about building you."

Dear friend, don't ever mistake activity and ministry for what is happening spiritually internally. You could be buzzing around doing all kinds of things for the Lord, but that doesn't necessarily mean you're doing well. How are you and the Lord doing? That's the issue. That's always the issue.

1 Kings 6:14–19
So Solomon built the house, and finished it. And he built the walls of the house within with boards of cedar, both the floor of the house, and the walls of the cieling: and he covered them on the inside with wood, and covered the floor of the house with planks of fir. And he built twenty cubits on the sides of the house, both the floor and the walls with boards of cedar: he even built them for it within, even for the oracle, even for the most holy place. And the house, that is, the temple before it, was forty cubits long. And the cedar of the house within was carved with knops and open flowers: all was cedar; there was no stone seen. And the oracle he prepared in the house within, to set there the ark of the covenant of the LORD.

The ark of the covenant was the only part of the tabernacle we see in the temple. This is as it should be, for the ark represented the presence of God, and God in Christ Jesus is the same—yesterday, today, and forever (Hebrews 13:8).

1 Kings 6:20–22
And the oracle in the forepart was twenty cubits in length, and twenty cubits in breadth, and twenty cubits in the height thereof: and he overlaid it with pure gold; and so covered the altar which was of cedar. So Solomon overlaid the house within with pure gold: and he made a partition by the chains of gold before the oracle; and he overlaid it with gold. And the whole house he overlaid with gold, until he had finished all the house: also the whole altar that was by the oracle he overlaid with gold.

The Holy of Holies is here called the oracle, because that is where God would speak to the high priest.

1 Kings 6:23–28
And within the oracle he made two cherubims of olive tree, each ten cubits high. And five cubits was the one wing of the cherub, and five cubits the other wing of the cherub: from the uttermost part of the one wing unto the uttermost part of the other were ten cubits. And the other cherub was ten cubits: both the cherubims were of one measure and one size. The height of the one cherub was ten cubits, and so was it of the other cherub. And he set the cherubims within the inner house: and they stretched forth the wings of the cherubims, so that the wing of the one touched the one wall, and the wing of the other cherub touched the other wall; and their wings touched one another in the midst of the house. And he overlaid the cherubims with gold.

Although the cherubim were much larger than those in the tabernacle, unlike their predecessors, they were not solid gold, but rather gold-plated.

1 Kings 6:29–38
And he carved all the walls of the house round about with carved figures of cherubims and palm trees and open flowers, within and without. And the floor of the house he overlaid with gold, within and without. And for the entering of the oracle he made doors of olive tree: the lintel and side posts were a fifth part of the wall. The two doors also were of olive tree; and he carved upon them carvings of cherubims and palm trees and open flowers, and overlaid them with gold, and spread gold upon the cherubims, and upon the palm trees. So also made he for the door of the temple posts of olive tree, a fourth part of the wall. And the two doors were of fir tree: the two leaves of the one door were folding, and the two leaves of the other door were folding. And he carved thereon cherubims and palm trees and open flowers: and covered them with gold fitted upon the carved work. And he built the inner court with three rows of hewed stone, and a row of cedar beams. In the fourth year was the foundation of the house of the LORD laid, in the month Zif: And in the eleventh year, in the month Bul, which is the eighth month, was the house finished throughout all the parts thereof, and according to all the fashion of it. So was he seven years in building it.

Again, the reason we're not looking at the temple in depth is because, although the temple is referred to as a picture of the church (Ephesians 2:21), the tabernacle portrays Jesus.

The tabernacle was simple. The temple was complex. Secondly, the windows of the temple signified a provision for failure because the people wouldn't have to rely solely on the light of the Shekinah glory of God. Thirdly, because the cherubim were not solid gold, as they had been in the tabernacle, the genuineness of the temple was second to that of the tabernacle. They were just covered with gold. There was not the genuineness through and through of the articles that there was in the tabernacle. Finally, as we'll see in chapter 7, Hiram, a son of a man of Tyre, was brought in to complete the work—unlike Aholiab and Bezaliel, the two Jewish men who were filled by the Spirit to produce wonderful work for the tabernacle (Exodus 38:22, 23). In all of this we see that the temple was incomparable to the tabernacle.

FOUNDATION WORK

A Topical Study of
1 KINGS 6:7

In 1 Kings 6, we see the wisest man who ever lived undertaking one of the greatest projects ever attempted as Solomon begins to build a temple unto the Lord. He begins by quarrying large, costly stones to be used in the temple's foundation—always a good place to begin.

The temple constructed by Solomon was not simply a place for the Old Testament saints to worship the Lord, but also a picture of us, as New Testament saints, being built by the Lord . . .

Now therefore ye are no more strangers and foreigners, but fellowcitizens with the saints, and of the household of God; And are built upon the foundation of the apostles and prophets, Jesus Christ himself being the chief corner stone; In whom all the building fitly framed together groweth unto an holy temple in the Lord: Ephesians 2:19–21

We are the temple of God, being built for the glory and pleasure of God. Like the temple of old, we are being built on a hewn foundation, a costly foundation. Paul gives us three elements that comprise the foundation upon which we are built. This is where it all begins. This is foundational understanding. If you miss this, your entire Christian walk will be vulnerable to instability and insecurity. If you grab hold of it, however, you'll stand firm.

Sound Schooling

And ye are built upon the foundation of the apostles and prophets . . .

When thousands came to the temple to radically worship the Lord or fervently pray to Him, Solomon never worried that the building would collapse, for he knew the foundation was strong. He knew the foundation was secure. He was confident that even intense worship and prayer would not cause the temple to wobble or waver.

As the temple of the true and living God, we can feel confident in intense and fervent worship, praise, and prayer as long as we stand upon a solid and strong yet costly foundation. And that strong foundation is solid doctrine. It is costly to become familiar with the Word of God. It will cost you time, energy, and perspiration in order for you to receive inspiration from the Word. But it is worth it, for a fellowship that is built solidly on exegetical, strong teaching and instruction can move into worship fervently and into praise with intensity without worrying it will become unstable.

There was a lovely shade tree growing on a hillside. One day, as the clouds overhead grew dark and the wind began to blow, the shade tree was rocked back and forth, creaking and groaning under the intense pressure of the wind. When the storm passed, the shade tree wisely said to itself, "I've got to become stronger. I must ready myself in the event that another storm should arise." So the shade tree began to branch out, extending itself, producing more leaves. It looked even more beautiful. But no sooner had it begun to branch out than the winds blew once again—this time harder than before. And the tree began to creak and groan as the winds blew against it. Suddenly, it felt itself being pushed over, headed for a terrible crash—when it lodged against a neighboring oak tree. When the storm passed, the shade tree said to the oak tree, "How did you survive the storm? How were you strong enough to not only survive yourself, but to support me when I was falling?"

The oak tree looked at the shade tree and said, "While you were branching out, I was digging in. While you were spreading your leaves above the surface for everyone to see, I was digging in below the surface where real strength is found."

Are you a shade tree or an oak tree? Are you sinking your roots deeper and deeper into the Word of God, understanding and tackling the doctrine written in its pages, or do you say, "That's dry. That's costly. That's too much work. I want to bud, and branch out." Dear saint, before you branch out, dig deep. Then, when your root system is strong in the Word of God, you will be able to be effective for the work of God. Dig deep. Study the Word daily. Come into an understanding of the great doctrines of justification, sanctification, and redemption. Come into the understandings of election and sovereignty, of propitiation and inspiration. And as you grow in the knowledge of God, you will be safe.

A Suffering Savior

. . . Jesus Christ Himself being the chief cornerstone

Paul tells us that the temple of the Lord is built not only on the foundation of the apostles and prophets, but on the foundation of the chief Cornerstone, Jesus Christ. This means that, as we study the Word, we do so not simply to gain an intellectual apprehension of appreciation, but rather a mystical touch with the Lord. The written Word leads me into contact with the Living Word, Jesus Christ.

Before this world was ever spoken into existence, our Lord was suffering for us (Revelation 13:8). God proved His love for us in that while we were yet sinners, Christ died for us (Romans 5:8). When did Jesus die for you? Not when you were coming to church, but when you were completely indifferent toward Him. If the Lord loved you when you were a sinner, be assured that He loves you today, now that you desire to walk with Him.

"Jesus loves me, this I know," we sang as children. And this basic premise must remain foundational. Others can challenge or accuse me, but I stand on the Person of Jesus Christ. He is my strong foundation.

Squirming Saints

In whom all the building fitly framed together groweth unto an holy temple . . .

What kind of a foundation grows? What kind of stones expand? Only one kind: living stones (1 Peter 2:5). We're living stones, gang, built together in this foundation. We are living, squirming stones. This explains why sometimes we have difficulties with each other.

The huge, costly stones for the temple were chipped, carved, and fit together in the quarry so that when they were brought to the temple site, they fit perfectly. This world is the quarry—the place where we, as living stones, are being chiseled and pounded. Why? So that when we get to heaven, we'll fit perfectly.

That means I'm going to be challenged by certain people I'd rather not be challenged by. God says, "They are the living stones next to you, so you better hang in there because they're My instruments to work on you, to shape you, to prepare you for what you're going to be throughout eternity. I'm building a temple for My habitation, and I've got to pound on you for awhile. It's foundational."

Don't fight it, saint. Flow with it. Say, "Okay, Lord. If this is the boss You want me to work under, so be it. If this is the situation You want me to be stretched by, I submit to it." Thank the Lord for one another. Receive from each other, knowing God is building you for His glory.

May the Lord make you solid below the surface. May your foundation be firm where the eyes of people do not notice. May it be strong and rooted in the knowledge of Him, so that as the years go by, you might be steadfast in your knowledge of God and in your love for the Lord.

> *I charge thee therefore before God, and the Lord Jesus Christ, who shall judge the quick and the dead at his appearing and his kingdom; Preach the word; be instant in season, out of season;* 2 Timothy 4:1, 2

That means, take the opportunity or make the opportunity. Sometimes, it's right before you, go for it. Other times, it's difficult, make it happen.

7

1 Kings 7:1
But Solomon was building his own house thirteen years, and he finished all his house.

First Kings 6:38 tells us that Solomon spent seven years building the temple, Here, we read he spent thirteen years building his own house. As we read through the chapter, we can gain some understanding of the immensity and expense of the house he constructed for himself. But I ask you to note something. Although Scripture does record the expense of the project, it took him thirteen years to complete it. In contrast, Solomon completed construction of the temple in only seven years. The temple was a much more difficult project. Yet his own house took him nearly twice as long to build. Why? I suggest it was because Solomon here is at the height of his personal piety, walking with the Lord more closely than he ever would. Thus, when it came to the temple, he had a sense of urgency to complete the project, leaving the construction of his own house much farther towards the bottom of his list of priorities.

Later in Israel's history, the prophet Haggai will indict the people of Judah for being so concerned about building their own homes that they had neglected building the temple of the Lord (1:6–8, 2:15–18). At this point, Solomon's priorities were correct. How about us? Are we like Solomon? As we look at ourselves and allow the Holy Spirit to shine the searchlight of His Word within our hearts, can we say, "Yes, Lord, I'm truly seeking Your kingdom first"? Or are we building our own houses, tending our own needs? If you are doing the latter, you'll find yourself frustrated—for, as the Lord said through Haggai, your pockets will have holes and your stomach will be empty (1:6). Seek first the kingdom, gang, and everything else you need will be added to you (Matthew 6:33).

1 Kings 7:2 (a)
He built also the house of the forest of Lebanon . . .

The Hebrew text here is unclear. This house could either be an extension of the palace, called the house of the forest of Lebanon because of the way it was paneled, or it could be that Solomon constructed a summer cottage in Lebanon.

1 Kings 7:2 (b)–8
. . . the length thereof was an hundred cubits, and the breadth thereof fifty cubits, and the height thereof thirty cubits, upon four rows of cedar pillars, with cedar beams

upon the pillars. And it was covered with cedar above upon the beams, that lay on forty five pillars, fifteen in a row. And there were windows in three rows, and light was against light in three ranks. And all the doors and posts were square, with the windows: and light was against light in three ranks. And he made a porch of pillars; the length thereof was fifty cubits, and the breadth thereof thirty cubits: and the porch was before them: and the other pillars and the thick beam were before them. Then he made a porch for the throne where he might judge, even the porch of judgment: and it was covered with cedar from one side of the floor to the other. And his house where he dwelt had another court within the porch, which was of the like work. Solomon made also an house for Pharaoh's daughter, whom he had taken to wife, like unto this porch.

After constructing his own house, Solomon made a house for his wife and several government buildings relating to his position as king.

1 Kings 7:9, 10
All these were of costly stones, according to the measures of hewed stones, sawed with saws, within and without, even from the foundation unto the coping, and so on the outside toward the great court. And the foundation was of costly stones, even great stones, stones of ten cubits, and stones of eight cubits.

Again, I remind you that it is what is unseen that provides the foundation for that which takes place in our lives, our ministries, our families. The times no one else sees you are up in the morning seeking the Lord or praying in the evening hours that build your foundation. Costly? Yes. Necessary? Absolutely.

1 Kings 7:11–13
And above were costly stones, after the measures of hewed stones, and cedars. And the great court round about was with three rows of hewed stones, and a row of cedar beams, both for the inner court of the house of the Lord, and for the porch of the house. And king Solomon sent and fetched Hiram out of Tyre.

This is not Hiram, king of Tyre, but another Hiram.

1 Kings 7:14, 15
He was a widow's son of the tribe of Naphtali, and his father was a man of Tyre, a worker in brass: and he was filled with wisdom, and understanding, and cunning to work all works in brass. And he came to king Solomon, and wrought all his work. For he cast two pillars of brass, of eighteen cubits high apiece: and a line of twelve cubits did compass either of them about.

Hiram was a skilled craftsman who was greatly involved in the construction of the buildings Solomon erected. Here, he made two huge pillars of brass, twenty-seven feet high.

1 Kings 7:16–22
And he made two chapiters of molten brass, to set upon the tops of the pillars: the height of the one chapiter was five cubits, and the height of the other chapiter was five cubits: And nets of checker work, and wreaths of chain work, for the chapiters which were upon the top of the pillars; seven for the one chapiter, and seven for the other chapiter. And he made the pillars, and two rows round about upon the one network, to cover the chapiters that were upon the top, with pomegranates: and so did he for the other chapiter. And the chapiters that were upon the top of the pillars were of lily work in the porch, four cubits. And the chapiters upon the two pillars had pomegranates also above, over against the belly which was by the network: and the pomegranates were two hundred in rows round about upon the other chapiter. And he set up the pillars in the porch of the temple: and he set up the right pillar, and called the name thereof Jachin: and he set up the left pillar, and he called the name thereof Boaz. And upon the top of the pillars was lily work: so was the work of the pillars finished.

Jachin means "He shall establish." *Boaz* means "In it is strength." Jachin speaks of stability. Boaz speaks of strength. I like that. As you came into the temple, you would see these two huge brass pillars named Stability and Strength. And yet on the top was lily work, beautiful, ornate carvings that were not seen except by someone looking down on them from above. This intrigues me because this beauty wasn't seen by the average person, not by those who would go in and out of the temple. But as God, from His heavenly perspective, looked down on these pillars—strength and stability—there was something beautiful for Him to behold.

As the temple of God, we, too, have some pillars in our midst, some men of strength, some women of stability, who are behind the scenes prayer warriors, burden-bearers, Sunday school teachers, and sacrificial givers. Some people receive honor right now. Others are pillars who may not be noticed by men, but whose lives are full of "lily work," beautiful to the Father, who will one day be rewarded by Him.

1 Kings 7:23
And he made a molten sea, ten cubits from the one brim to the other: it was round all about, and his height was five cubits: and a line of thirty cubits did compass it round about.

This bronze tank, seven and one-half feet high, fifteen feet across, forty-five feet in circumference was used by the priests to wash their hands and feet before they ministered before the Lord.

1 Kings 7:24–26
And under the brim of it round about there were knops compassing it, ten in a cubit, compassing the sea round about: the knops were cast in two rows, when it was cast. It stood upon twelve oxen, three looking toward the north, and three looking toward the west, and three looking toward the south, and three looking toward the east: and the sea was set above upon them, and all their hinder parts were inward. And it was an hand breadth thick, and the brim thereof was wrought like the brim of a cup, with flowers of lilies: it contained two thousand baths.

Twelve brass oxen supported the huge "wash basin" that held 2,000 baths, or 14,000 gallons of water. Who changed the water in this huge bronze tank? You might recall how the Gibeonites had tricked Joshua into thinking they were from a far country and signing a peace treaty with them (Joshua 9). When Joshua discovered they were his neighbors, rather than killing them, he conscripted them to serve in the tabernacle. They became known as Nethinim and it would have been their jobs to tend to the water in this huge brass laver.

1 Kings 7:27–39
And he made ten bases of brass; four cubits was the length of one base, and four cubits the breadth thereof, and three cubits the height of it. And the work of the bases was on this manner: they had borders, and the borders were between the ledges: And on the borders that were between the ledges were lions, oxen, and cherubims: and upon the ledges there was a base above: and beneath the lions and oxen were certain additions made of thin work. And every base had four brasen wheels, and plates of brass: and the four corners thereof had undersetters: under the laver were undersetters molten, at the side of every addition. And the mouth of it within the chapiter and above was a cubit: but the mouth thereof was round after the work of the base, a cubit and an half: and also upon the mouth of it were gravings with their borders, four-square, not round. And under the borders were four wheels; and the axletrees of the wheels were joined to the base: and the height of a wheel was a cubit and a half a cubit. And the work of the wheels was like the work of a chariot wheel: their axletrees, and their naves, and their felloes, and their spokes, were all molten. And there were four undersetters to the four corners of one base: and the undersetters were of the very base itself. And in the top of the base was there a round compass of half a cubit high: and on the top of the base the ledges thereof and the borders thereof were of the same. For on the plates of the ledges thereof, and on the borders thereof, he graved cherubims, lions, and palm trees, according to the proportion of every one, and additions round about. After this manner he made the ten bases: all of them had one casting, one measure, and one size. Then made he ten lavers of brass: one laver contained forty baths: and every laver was four cubits: and upon every one of the ten bases one laver. And he put five bases on the right side of the house, and five on the left side of the house: and he set the sea on the right side of the house eastward over against the south.

Not only was a huge bronze tank that contained 14,000 gallons of water, but there were ten portable tanks, six square feet, that held about two hundred and fifty gallons of water. They had wheels on them, so that wherever there was a need for a priest to wash, they could be wheeled to him.

The brass laver in the tabernacle that preceded the lavers in the temple was made of the mirrors the Israelite women carried out of Egypt (Exodus 38:8). The image is perfect because we are cleansed by the water of the Word (John 15:3), which is also likened to a mirror (James 1:23).

I suggest that the laver containing 14,000 gallons speaks of the full counsel of God (Acts 20:27), the Word in its entirety, while the smaller "portable lavers" speak of the smaller portions of the Word we carry in our hearts upon which we are to meditate throughout the day (Psalm 1:2, 119:105).

1 Kings 7:40–47
And Hiram made the lavers, and the shovels, and the basons. So Hiram made an end of doing all the work that he made king Solomon for the house of the LORD: The two

pillars, and the two bowls of the chapiters that were on the top of the two pillars; and the two networks, to cover the two bowls of the chapiters which were upon the top of the pillars; And four hundred pomegranates for the two networks, even two rows of pomegranates for one network, to cover the two bowls of the chapiters that were upon the pillars; And the ten bases, and ten lavers on the bases; And one sea, and twelve oxen under the sea; And the pots, and the shovels, and the basons: and all these vessels, which Hiram made to king Solomon for the house of the LORD, were of bright brass. In the plain of Jordan did the king cast them, in the clay ground between Succoth and Zarthan. And Solomon left all the vessels unweighed, because they were exceeding many: neither was the weight of the brass found out.

So many vessels and utensils did Hiram make that Solomon said, "Don't even weigh them."

There was one candlestick in the tabernacle. Here in the temple, however, things became more complicated and complex.

1 Kings 7:48–51
And Solomon made all the vessels that pertained unto the house of the LORD: the altar of gold, and the table of gold, whereupon the shewbread was, And the candlesticks of pure gold, five on the right side, and five on the left, before the oracle, with the flowers, and the lamps, and the tongs of gold, And the bowls, and the snuffers, and the basons, and the spoons, and the censers of pure gold; and the hinges of gold, both for the doors of the inner house, the most holy place, and for the doors of the house, to wit, of the temple. So was ended all the work that king Solomon made for the house of the LORD. And Solomon brought in the things which David his father had dedicated; even the silver, and the gold, and the vessels, did he put among the treasures of the house of the LORD.

In 1 Chronicles 29:2, we read that David not only gathered gold, silver, and brass for the temple, but also iron. Yet in the record of the construction of the temple and its utensils, there is no mention of iron whatsoever. There are times in our lives when we will go to a great effort to do something as unto the Lord. But for one reason or another, it will not be used. That's okay. Our job is simply to do the best we can and present it to the Lord. The way He wants to use it is completely, totally up to Him. Our part is to rejoice in His wisdom, His timing, His plan, and in so doing, we will be wonderfully free.

8

1 Kings 8:1–8
Then Solomon assembled the elders of Israel, and all the heads of the tribes, the chief of the fathers of the children of Israel, unto king Solomon in Jerusalem, that they might bring up the ark of the covenant of the LORD out of the city of David, which is Zion. And all the men of Israel assembled themselves unto king Solomon at the feast in the month Ethanim, which is the seventh month. And all the elders of Israel came, and the priests took up the ark. And they brought up the ark of the LORD, and the tabernacle of the congregation, and all the holy vessels that were in the tabernacle, even those did the priests and the Levites bring up. And king Solomon, and all the congregation of Israel, that were assembled unto him, were with him before the ark, sacrificing sheep and oxen, that could not be told nor numbered for multitude. And the priests brought in the ark of the covenant of the LORD unto his place, into the oracle of the house, to the most holy place, even under the wings of the cherubims. For the cherubims spread forth their two wings over the place of the ark, and the cherubims covered the ark and the staves thereof above. And they drew out the staves, that the ends of the staves were seen out in the holy place before the oracle, and they were not seen without: and there they are unto this day.

When the temple was complete, the ark was brought in. Years previously, David had brought the ark to the city of Jerusalem, a convenient place. Here, Solomon takes the baton and brings the ark into a magnificent place.

1 Kings 8:9
There was nothing in the ark save the two tables of stone, which Moses put there at Horeb, when the LORD made a covenant with the children of Israel, when they came out of the land of Egypt.

Hebrews 9:4 tells us that the ark contained the Ten Commandments, a pot of manna, and Aaron's rod. Here, however, we see only the Ten Commandments within the ark. I believe the Holy Spirit included this information to help us to come to a very important understanding. That is, signs and wonders—budding rods and manna—as wonderful as they are, are not lasting. What lasts, what endures, what is absolutely essential is the Word of God.

According to Jesus, the greatest prophet who ever lived was neither Elijah, who called down fire from heaven, nor Moses, who parted the Red Sea. The greatest prophet who ever lived was a man who did no miracles whatsoever. And yet all the things he spoke of Jesus were true. The greatest prophet who ever lived said, "I must decrease, but He must increase." The greatest prophet who ever lived was a man who simply pointed people to Jesus (Matthew 11:11). Like John the Baptist, you might not be one to perform signs, wonders, and miracles. But, like him, you can tell people about Jesus.

1 Kings 8:10–13
And it came to pass, when the priests were come out of the holy place, that the cloud filled the house of the LORD, So that the priests could not stand to minister because of the cloud: for the glory of the LORD had filled the house of the LORD. Then spake Solomon, The LORD said that he would dwell in thick darkness. I have surely built thee an house to dwell in, a settled place for thee to abide in for ever.

Have you ever experienced times in fellowship when, the presence of the Lord is so perceivable that you can hardly stand up? That's what's happening here.

1 Kings 8:14–21
And the king turned his face about, and blessed all the congregation of Israel: (and all the congregation of Israel stood;) And he said, Blessed be the LORD God of Israel, which spake with his mouth unto David my father, and hath with his hand fulfilled it, saying, Since the day that I brought forth my people Israel out of Egypt, I chose no city out of all the tribes of Israel to build an house, that my name might be therein; but I chose David to be over my people Israel. And it was in the heart of David my father to build an house for the name of the LORD God of Israel. And the LORD said unto David my father, Whereas it was in thine heart to build an house unto my name, thou didst well that it was in thine heart. Nevertheless thou shalt not build the house; but thy son that shall come forth out of thy loins, he shall build the house unto my name. And the LORD hath performed his word that he spake, and I am risen up in the room of David my father, and sit on the throne of Israel, as the LORD promised, and have built an house for the name of the LORD God of Israel. And I have set there a place for the ark, wherein is the covenant of the LORD, which he made with our fathers, when he brought them out of the land of Egypt.

When David was forbidden to build the temple, did he pout? Did he pull back? Did he give up? No. This man after God's heart said, "If I can't build the Lord's house, I'll make preparations for it." Although David didn't have the opportunity to participate in the actual construction of the temple, I believe that in eternity, Solomon's temple will be referred to as David's temple because it was in his heart to build it.

1 Kings 8:22–25
And Solomon stood before the altar of the LORD in the presence of all the congregation of Israel, and spread forth his hands toward heaven: And he said, LORD God of Israel, there is no God like thee, in heaven above, or on earth beneath, who keepest covenant and mercy with thy servants that walk before thee with all their heart: Who hast kept with thy servant David my father that thou promisedst him: thou spakest also with thy mouth, and hast fulfilled it with thine hand, as it is this day. Therefore now, LORD God of Israel, keep with thy servant David my father that thou promisedst him, saying, There shall not fail thee a man in my sight to sit on the throne of Israel; so that thy children take heed to their way, that they walk before me as thou hast walked before me.

When God told David he couldn't build Him a house, He tempered his message by saying, "But I'm going to build you a house. There will always be someone from your lineage upon the throne of Israel." Of course, this promise finds its culmination and fulfillment in the Son of David, Jesus Christ, who lives and reigns forever.

1 Kings 8:26–29
And now, O God of Israel, let thy word, I pray thee, be verified, which thou spakest unto thy servant David my father. But will God indeed dwell on the earth? behold, the heaven and heaven of heavens cannot contain thee; how much less this house that I have builded? Yet have thou respect unto the prayer of thy servant, and to his supplication, O LORD my God, to hearken unto the cry and to the prayer, which thy servant prayeth before thee to day: That thine eyes may be open toward this house night and day, even toward the place of which thou hast said, My name shall be there: that thou mayest hearken unto the prayer which thy servant shall make toward this place.

Solomon was right on when he said, "I realize this house I have built cannot possibly contain You, God." How big is God? The Milky Way galaxy we see overhead is 100,000 light-years long and 10,000 light-years wide. This means that, cruising at the speed of light, it would take you 100,000 years to travel from one end of it to the other. And yet Isaiah tells us God holds the heavens in the palm of His hand (40:12).

No wonder David asked, "What is man that Thou art mindful of him?" (Psalm 8:4). We're so puny. And yet this God who is so huge has chosen to relate to us in the Person of Jesus Christ. I understand the heart of the Father, the grace, long-suffering, mercy, and tenderness of God because Jesus is the express image, the exact reflection of Him (Hebrews 1:3).

1 Kings 8:30
And hearken thou to the supplication of thy servant, and of thy people Israel, when they shall pray toward this place: and hear thou in heaven thy dwelling place: and when thou hearest, forgive.

Here, Solomon's prayer shifts from asking God to bless the temple to asking God to forgive the people. In it, he lists seven situations in which only God's intervention would avert either individual or national disaster . . .

1 Kings 8:31, 32
If any man trespass against his neighbour, and an oath be laid upon him to cause him to swear, and the oath come before thine altar in this house: Then hear thou in heaven, and do, and judge thy servants, condemning the wicked, to bring his way upon his head; and justifying the righteous, to give him according to his righteousness.

Doubt. If a man was accused of a crime but there was no evidence against him, only God could rightly judge.

1 Kings 8:33, 34
When thy people Israel be smitten down before the enemy, because they have sinned against thee, and shall turn again to thee, and confess thy name, and pray, and make supplication unto thee in this house: Then hear thou in heaven, and forgive the sin of thy people Israel, and bring them again unto the land which thou gavest unto their fathers.

Defeat. If the nation was defeated in battle, only God could bring them home.

1 Kings 8:35, 36
When heaven is shut up, and there is no rain, because they have sinned against thee; if they pray toward this place, and confess thy name, and turn from their sin, when thou afflictest them: Then hear thou in heaven, and forgive the sin of thy servants, and of thy people Israel, that thou teach them the good way wherein they should walk, and give rain upon thy land, which thou hast given to thy people for an inheritance.

Drought. Only God could send rain to replenish land that had dried up as a result of the rebellion of His people.

1 Kings 8:37–40
If there be in the land famine, if there be pestilence, blasting, mildew, locust, or if there be caterpiller; if their enemy besiege them in the land of their cities; whatsoever plague, whatsoever sickness there be; What prayer and supplication soever be made by any man, or by all thy people Israel, which shall know every man the plague of his own heart, and spread forth his hands toward this house: Then hear thou in heaven thy dwelling place, and forgive, and do, and give to every man according to his ways, whose heart thou knowest; (for thou, even thou only, knowest the hearts of all the children of men;) That they may fear thee all the days that they live in the land which thou gavest unto our fathers.

Destruction. "When the people sin and experience pestilence, when they sin and experience drought, when they sin and are smitten by their enemies, when they call upon You, forgive them," Solomon prayed, "for You know the hearts of men." Only God knows the hearts of men. Only God sees the heart that turns to Him. This means when I forgive people, I must forgive them absolutely unconditionally because I don't know their heart. I have found this to be wonderfully freeing because it means I don't have to judge, analyze, or figure things out. Rather, I'm simply to love and forgive, confident that God will deal with the "heart" of the matter.

1 Kings 8:41–43
Moreover concerning a stranger, that is not of thy people Israel, but cometh out of a far country for thy name's sake; (For they shall hear of thy great name, and of thy strong hand, and of thy stretched out arm;) when he shall come and pray toward this house; Hear thou in heaven thy dwelling place, and do according to all that the stranger calleth to thee for: that all people of the earth may know

thy name, to fear thee, as do thy people Israel; and that they may know that this house, which I have builded, is called by thy name.

Denunciation. "When people of other nations come to the temple and turn their back on their heathen gods after hearing about the great things You're doing, hear their prayers as well," Solomon prayed.

We see Jesus righteously angry in John 2 for there, in the temple, in the court of the Gentiles—which was as far into the temple a Gentile could go—merchants had set up tables to exchange money and to sell animals to sacrifice at exorbitant prices. As evidenced by Solomon's prayer, the court of the Gentiles was to be a place Gentiles could be drawn to the true and living God. No wonder, then, that Jesus was incensed that what was to be a place of outreach and evangelism was nothing more than a business.

We also are called to be salt and light. When we start turning inward, when we start losing our vision for reaching the lost and bringing the lost into a saving knowledge of Jesus Christ, it's over. The church that turns inward will soon grow frustrated. A person who looks inward will soon grow discontent. We must commit ourselves before the Lord to reaching out to the world continually, that when people see us they will sense a loving community whose desire is to lead them into a fuller knowledge of God through Jesus Christ.

Are you concerned about the lost? Solomon was. "Lord, when a stranger joins us, may You hear his prayer, and meet him in his place of need," he prayed.

1 Kings 8:44, 45
If thy people go out to battle against their enemy, whithersoever thou shalt send them, and shall pray unto the LORD toward the city which thou hast chosen, and toward the house that I have built for thy name: Then hear thou in heaven their prayer and their supplication, and maintain their cause.

Deployment. If the nation went to battle in obedience to God's instruction, only He could truly fight for them.

1 Kings 8:46–53
If they sin against thee, (for there is no man that sinneth not,) and thou be angry with them, and deliver them to the enemy, so that they carry them away captives unto the land of the enemy, far or near; Yet if they shall bethink themselves in the land whither they were carried captives, and repent, and make supplication unto thee in the land of them that carried them captives, saying, We have sinned, and have done perversely, we have committed wickedness; And so return unto thee with all their heart, and with all their soul, in the land of their enemies, which led them away captive, and pray unto thee toward their land, which thou gavest unto their fathers, the city which thou hast chosen, and the house which I have built for thy name: Then hear thou their prayer and their supplication in heaven thy dwelling place, and maintain their cause, And forgive thy people that have sinned against thee and all their transgressions wherein they have transgressed against thee, and give them compassion before them who carried them captive, that they may have compassion on them: For they be thy people, and thine inheritance, which thou broughtest forth out of Egypt, from the midst of the furnace of iron: That thine eyes may be open unto the supplication of thy servant, and unto the supplication of thy people Israel, to hearken unto them in all that they call for unto thee. For thou didst separate them from among all the people of the earth, to be thine inheritance, as thou spakest by the hand of Moses thy servant, when thou broughtest our fathers out of Egypt, O Lord GOD.

Defection. If the nation turned from truth to false worship that leads to captivity, only God could turn their hearts back to Him.

1 Kings 8:54
And it was so, that when Solomon had made an end of praying all this prayer and supplication unto the LORD, he arose from before the altar of the LORD, from kneeling on his knees with his hands spread up to heaven.

This is the first time in Scripture we see someone kneeling in prayer. While it is certainly the posture of the heart rather than the posture of the body that matters, I believe it is also true that the posture of the body often reflects the posture of the heart. Haven't you found that when you're really pressed, you naturally find yourself on your knees or face before the Lord? Solomon was so intense in the Spirit, so concerned about the petitions he was raising to the Lord that, although the normal posture of prayer at this time was to stand, he found himself inevitably on his knees with his hand's lifted up, a telling insight regarding the posture of his heart.

Second Chronicles 7 tells us that, after he prayed this prayer, fire was sent from heaven to consume the sacrifices on the altar. This means Solomon literally prayed down fire from heaven. I believe one of the reasons for this was that there was an intensity, a burning within his own heart as he prayed. Oh, that God would give us the ability to pray down fire, that He would give us understanding so that we might be potent and powerful in our prayer lives as well.

1 Kings 8:55, 56
And he stood, and blessed all the congregation of Israel with a loud voice, saying, Blessed be the LORD, that hath given rest unto his people Israel, according to all that he promised: there hath not failed one word of all his good promise, which he promised by the hand of Moses his servant.

After spending time with the Lord, Solomon now stands before the people and begins to bless them, reminding them that God had kept His promises completely.

The same is still true. Can you remember what you were anxious about a year ago? How about three years ago? Yet during those times, you no doubt thought, "God's promise that all things work together for good, His guarantee of blessing and provision are not going to work for me, I just know it." My fears for last year never came to pass. So why should I lose sleep over any situation before me when the Lord keeps His promises without exception?

1 Kings 8:57–61
The LORD our God be with us, as he was with our fathers: let him not leave us, nor forsake us: That he may incline our hearts unto him, to walk in all his ways, and to keep his commandments, and his statutes, and his judgments, which he commanded our fathers. And let these my words, wherewith I have made supplication before the LORD, be nigh unto the LORD our God day and night, that he maintain the cause of his servant, and the cause of his people Israel at all times, as the matter shall require: That all the people of the earth may know that the LORD is God, and that there is none else. Let your heart therefore be perfect with the LORD our God, to walk in his statutes, and to keep his commandments, as at this day.

Solomon pronounces blessing, and yet he was a king, not a priest. The Hebrew word translated "bless" literally means to confer prosperity or happiness upon another. As a royal priesthood (1 Peter 2:9), we have the same opportunity as Solomon to speak God's goodness into peoples' lives.

***For topical study of 1 Kings 8:57–61 entitled "The Building Blocks of Blessing," turn to page* 984.**

1 Kings 8:62, 63
And the king, and all Israel with him, offered sacrifice before the LORD. And Solomon offered a sacrifice of peace offerings, which he offered unto the LORD, two and twenty thousand oxen, and an hundred and twenty thousand sheep. So the king and all the children of Israel dedicated the house of the LORD.

Twenty-two thousand oxen and 120,000 sheep were sacrificed. Not only was this expensive, but it required an incredible amount of effort and energy. But it was a delight to the Lord. As a New Testament priesthood, we are to offer the sacrifice of praise, the fruit of our lips giving thanks to His name (Hebrews 13:15). What if the praises you offered to the Lord were recorded in Scripture. Would it be an impressive figure like this or would it be embarrassingly small?

I have recently reenrolled in the school of praise, working through the Book of Psalms, and learning the language of thanksgiving as I personalize the Psalms in my morning devotions. If you're finding it hard to verbalize praise, I would encourage you to enroll in this school as well. Work through the Psalms and make them yours. Put them in the first person. It's a wonderful tool and it will help you in becoming more expressive in offering praise and thanksgiving to our Lord.

1 Kings 8:64–66
The same day did the king hallow the middle of the court that was before the house of the LORD: for there he offered burnt offerings, and meat offerings, and the fat of the peace offerings: because the brasen altar that was before the LORD was too little to receive the burnt offerings, and meat offerings, and the fat of the peace offerings. And at that time Solomon held a feast, and all Israel with him, a great congregation, from the entering in of Hamath unto the river of Egypt, before the LORD our God, seven days and seven days, even fourteen days. On the eighth day he sent the people away: and they blessed the king, and went unto their tents joyful and glad of heart for all the goodness that the LORD had done for David his servant, and for Israel his people.

After spending time dedicating the temple to the Lord and offering sacrifices unto Him, the people went away joyful and glad. This is not surprising, for whenever we truly have an experience *with* the Lord, we experience the joy *of* the Lord.

THE BUILDING BLOCKS OF BLESSING

A topical Study of 1 KINGS 8:57–61

Upset about the service he received, a man called the small business and said, "I want to talk to someone with a little authority around there."

The clerk on the other end of the line said, "You can talk to me. I've got about as little authority as anyone."

That's the way we often view ourselves. "Who am I to bless others?" we say. "I'm not a priest or a preacher."

That may be, but in Matthew 5, Jesus specifically told us to bless those who curse us and in Luke 10, we are told to pronounce blessing upon homes we enter. Therefore, because all of us are called to bless others, please note with me five characteristics of true biblical blessing as seen in the blessing of Solomon . . .

Preparation

And it was so, that when Solomon had made an end of praying all this prayer and supplication unto the LORD, he arose from before the altar of the LORD, from kneeling on his knees with his hands spread up to heaven. 1 Kings 8:54

Solomon did not stand up on the spur of the moment and speak whatever came to his mind. No, Solomon prayed to the Lord before he stood and blessed. It is prayer that produces power. It is prayer that prepares the heart to speak forth blessing to others. Solomon had spent significant time praying on his knees, with his hands stretched toward heaven.

Blessing begins at the point where I am in the posture of prayer. It starts in the place of prayer. Beginning your day in prayer on your knees before the Lord with hands lifted to Him puts you in a position where blessing can flow through you throughout the day.

Expectation

And he stood, and blessed all the congregation of Israel . . . 1 Kings 8:55 (a)

Solomon stood up, expecting something to happen. When you speak blessing into someone's life, stand up. That is, mix your blessing with faith and *expect* the Lord to respond.

Articulation

> *. . . with a loud voice, saying, Blessed be the* LORD, *that hath given rest unto his people Israel, according to all that he promised: there hath not failed one word of all his good promise, which he promised by the hand of Moses his servant. The* LORD *our God be with us, as he was with our fathers: let him not leave us, nor forsake us: That he may incline our hearts unto him, to walk in all his ways, and to keep his commandments, and his statutes, and his judgments, which he commanded our fathers. And let these my words, wherewith I have made supplication before the* LORD, *be nigh unto the* LORD *our God day and night, that he maintain the cause of his servant, and the cause of his people Israel at all times, as the matter shall require . . .* 1 Kings 8:55–59

Solomon didn't just think about blessing the people or even silently pray about blessing the people. He vocalized it. And it's no wonder that he did, for there is amazing power in the spoken word . . .

> As Joshua chased his enemies, the sun began to set and he knew he could not pursue them after dark. So in faith, Joshua said, "Sun, stand thou still," as the entire camp of Israel listened (Joshua 10).

Would you have been bold enough to make a statement like that? Joshua did, and the Word declares that the Lord hearkened to his voice and the sun did indeed stand still.

Paul said it is not only when we believe in our heart, but it is when we also confess Jesus with our mouth that we are saved (Romans 10:10). There is power in the spoken word. Start blessing people articulately and expectantly and they *will* be blessed. Good things will happen in their lives.

Motivation

> *That all the people of the earth may know that the* LORD *is God, and that there is none else.* 1 Kings 8:60

Solomon sought God's blessing not in order that people would know he was a spiritual heavyweight, but in order that all the earth would know the true and living God. Did that come to pass? Check out what happens two chapters later . . .

> *And when the queen of Sheba heard of the fame of Solomon concerning the name of the* LORD, *she came to prove him with hard questions.* 1 Kings 10:1

Sheba, a Queen from Africa, heard what was happening in Solomon's realm and came, not to glorify Solomon, but to seek the Lord.

If you want to be one who speaks blessing into the lives of others, your motivation must be to see people drawn to the Lord, not that they will be excited about you. If indeed your motivation is to want people to prosper in the Lord, you can expect the Lord to bless them through you.

Exhortation

> *Let your heart therefore be perfect with the* Lord *our God, to walk in his statutes, and to keep his commandments, as at this day.* 1 Kings 8:61

As part of his blessing, Solomon exhorts the people. This is not simply an injunction to them, but it's an infusion. It's not a condemnation, but rather a proclamation of what *will* happen. That is, it's an exhortation based and built on faith. After Solomon rallied the people to believe that they would indeed do well in the Lord, they left that place blessed.

I firmly believe that our country and our world can be affected if we begin to move in the authority and possibility of being a blessing to hurting, diseased people all around us. The man that pumps your gas needs to be blessed. Instead of complaining about the price of oil, instead of listening to the radio, look him in the eye and say, "May the Lord bless you today. As you fill cars, may your heart be filled with God's love."

When you go through the grocery line, instead of making small talk about the headlines of the tabloids, say, "May the Lord bless you, encourage you, and build you in the areas you need to be built up today."

As believers, we are far too often far too concerned about far too many things. Let's change our mindset so that instead of burdening others, we cast our concerns upon the Lord and bless others with a word of faith, a word of encouragement. I challenge us all to stop burdening and start blessing. Why are we so prone to complaining instead of praising? Instead of griping about the price of eggs, why don't we say, "It's so good to see the price of groceries going up. Just think, those farmers that are hit hard will now get a little more help. Maybe the truck drivers will make a little more money to put groceries on their own tables. Praise the Lord!"

Do that, and I guarantee you'll be salt and light. I guarantee you'll be a blessing.

Before He ascended into heaven, Jesus lifted His hands and blessed the people (Luke 24). I encourage us in His name to follow His example as well as the example of Solomon and to speak blessing into the lives of those around us for God's glory.

> *The* Lord *bless thee, and keep thee: The* Lord *make his face shine upon thee, and be gracious unto thee: The* Lord *lift up his countenance upon thee, and give thee peace.* Numbers 6:24–26

Amen!

9 **1 Kings 9:1, 2**
And it came to pass, when Solomon had finished the building of the house of the Lord, and the king's house, and all Solomon's desire which he was pleased to do, That the Lord appeared to Solomon the second time, as he had appeared unto him at Gibeon.

Twenty years earlier, the Lord appeared to Solomon the first time. Here, the Lord appears to him again. This reminds me that there can be great spans of time between the Lord's dealings with us. Therefore, I think it's dangerous to think we need to have a revelation from God or a miraculous experience every day or every week. Abraham went through years where he didn't hear from the Lord, and yet he is called the friend of God (James 2:23). Reading the Book of Acts, it's easy to assume that the early church witnessed miracles daily if not hourly, until you remember that the Book of Acts covers a time span of thirty-eight *years*.

God is interested in developing us for eternity. To this end, He teaches us to walk by faith and not by sight. He wants us to develop discipline, to praise Him when we might not feel His presence, to study His Word even though we might not experience fresh revelation. God wants to develop and deepen you for what He has in store for you.

1 Kings 9:3–5
And the Lord said unto him, I have heard thy prayer and thy supplication, that thou hast made before me: I have hallowed this house, which thou hast built, to put my name there for ever; and mine eyes and mine heart shall be there perpetually. And if thou wilt walk before me, as David thy father walked, in integrity of heart, and in uprightness, to do according to all that I have commanded thee, and wilt keep my statutes and my judgments: Then I will establish the throne of thy kingdom upon Israel for ever, as I promised to David thy father, saying, There shall not fail thee a man upon the throne of Israel.

The Lord promised to establish Solomon's kingdom if he walked before Him with as much integrity as David had. The Hebrew word for integrity speaks of singleness. He fell time after time. David had flaws and failures. But one thing he had was integrity of heart. That is, he never left the Lord to follow false gods. He sinned. He strayed. He erred to be sure. But his heart was always for the Lord, and it is the heart that matters (1 Samuel 16:7). That is why the Lord uses David as a standard by which all other kings in Israel and Judah would be measured.

Regardless of your failing, folly, and faults, God looks at your heart. Therefore, be encouraged in the fact that, if your heart is toward Him and you're not leaving Him to serve other gods, He takes note.

In talking about Jesus, Isaiah was inspired by the Father to write:

> Behold my servant, whom I uphold; mine elect, in whom my soul delighteth; I have put my spirit upon him: he shall bring forth judgment to the Gentiles. He shall not cry, nor lift up, nor cause his voice to be heard in the street. A bruised reed shall he not break, and the smoking flax shall he not quench: he shall bring forth judgment unto truth. Isaiah 42:1–3

In my garden, if plants aren't looking good, out they go. If a campfire isn't providing heat, out it goes. Not so with the Lord. He's tender, compassionate, and exceedingly gracious. Therefore, I am increasingly convinced that, as Christians, we often expect more from each other than the Lord does. As Christians, we often expect more from ourselves than the Lord does. We picture the Lord as an angry God who is out to quench the smoking flax and break the bruised reed. But that's not the way He is.

As I was thinking about a brother in the Lord, I prayed, "Lord, intensify his devotional life. Make him more fervent in his witness. Shake him out of his apathy. Wake him out of his lethargy." And the Lord impressed my heart at that moment, quietly saying, "Be quiet. I'm happy with him. I've chosen him from eternity past. I saved his soul. I've embedded in his life a moral fabric that would have never been there apart from Me. I have a plan for him in eternity. He's doing just fine." And more and more, I'm beginning to see a different perspective. All too often, we punish ourselves and others, but that's not the heart of God. Allow the Lord to minister to you *His* thoughts concerning you. The Lord truly loves you. And if you simply walk in uprightness of heart, like David, you'll be established.

1 Kings 9:6–9
But if ye shall at all turn from following me, ye or your children, and will not keep my commandments and my statutes which I have set before you, but go and serve other gods, and worship them: Then will I cut off Israel out of the land which I have given them; and this house, which I have hallowed

for my name, will I cast out of my sight; and Israel shall be a proverb and a byword among all people: And at this house, which is high, every one that passeth by it shall be astonished, and shall hiss; and they shall say, Why hath the LORD done thus unto this land, and to this house? And they shall answer, Because they forsook the LORD their God, who brought forth their fathers out of the land of Egypt, and have taken hold upon other gods, and have worshipped them, and served them: therefore hath the LORD brought upon them all this evil.

As they prepared to enter the Promised Land, Moses told the Israelites that "if thou shalt hearken diligently unto the voice of the LORD thy God, to observe and to do all his commandments which I command thee this day, that the LORD thy God will set thee on high above all nations of the earth" (Deuteronomy 28:1). The newly completed temple was indeed set on high, both due to its location and size. Here, however, God promises not only to desert His temple, but His own people should they forsake Him and follow other gods.

1 Kings 9:10–14
And it came to pass at the end of twenty years, when Solomon had built the two houses, the house of the LORD, and the king's house, (Now Hiram the king of Tyre had furnished Solomon with cedar trees and fir trees, and with gold, according to all his desire,) that then king Solomon gave Hiram twenty cities in the land of Galilee. And Hiram came out from Tyre to see the cities which Solomon had given him; and they pleased him not. And he said, What cities are these which thou hast given me, my brother? And he called them the land of Cabul unto this day. And Hiram sent to the king sixscore talents of gold.

Verse 14 should read, "Hiram *had sent* to the king threescore talents of gold." During the construction of the temple, Solomon needed some additional funds. So he sent word to his friend Hiram, king of Tyre, and Hiram graciously loaned Solomon one hundred and twenty talents of gold. When it was time to pay back the loan, Solomon gave him twenty cities in the Galilee area. But when Hiram checked them out, he thought they were dumps and called them *Cabul*, or "Dirty."

Why is this incident recorded in Scripture? I suggest two reasons . . .

First, I believe it is tempering. There are those who would say that borrowing money is never right. There are those who say it is never biblical or appropriate to borrow money. But here, Solomon borrowed a significant amount of money to complete the task to which God had called him. Therefore, I believe to be absolutely dogmatic about not borrowing is an unnecessary bondage placed on believers. Is it a good principle? Absolutely. Is it a good warning? You bet.

Yet, in addition to tempering, I believe this incident serves as a warning because this loan caused friction between Solomon and Hiram. If you have to make an error, make it on the side of being too conservative and too safe in order to avoid the problems that borrowing and going into debt can bring about.

1 Kings 9:15–19
And this is the reason of the levy which king Solomon raised; for to build the house of the LORD, and his own house, and Millo, and the wall of Jerusalem, and Hazor, and Megiddo, and Gezer. For Pharaoh king of Egypt had gone up, and taken Gezer, and burnt it with fire, and slain the Canaanites that dwelt in the city, and given it for a present unto his daughter, Solomon's wife. And Solomon built Gezer, and Beth-horon the nether, and Baalath, and Tadmor in the wilderness, in the land, And all the cities of store that Solomon had, and cities for his chariots, and cities for his horsemen, and that which Solomon desired to build in Jerusalem, and in Lebanon, and in all the land of his dominion.

In addition to building the temple, the levy Solomon raised in chapter 5—both of men and of money—was required to finance the vast building projects he undertook. Many kings levied money for war. This wasn't the case with Solomon. He concentrated his efforts on construction and fortification, beginning with the temple, then his own house, a house for his wife, and various cities throughout Israel that were either border towns, such as Hazor, or cities on trade routes such as Megiddo.

1 Kings 9:20–23
And all the people that were left of the Amorites, Hittites, Perizzites, Hivites, and Jebusites, which were not of the children of Israel, Their children that were left after them in the land, whom the children of Israel also were not able utterly to destroy, upon those did Solomon levy a tribute of bondservice unto this day. But of the children of Israel did Solomon make no bondmen: but they were men of war, and his servants, and his princes, and his captains, and rulers of his chariots, and his horsemen. These were the chief of the officers that were over Solomon's work, five hundred and

fifty, which bare rule over the people that wrought in the work.

The people that Israel had conquered provided the workforce of Solomon's construction. The Israelites themselves held more noble positions.

1 Kings 9:24, 25
But Pharaoh's daughter came up out of the city of David unto her house which Solomon had built for her: then did he build Millo. And three times in a year did Solomon offer burnt offerings and peace offerings upon the altar which he built unto the LORD, and he burnt incense upon the altar that was before the LORD. So he finished the house.

The three times a year Solomon offered offerings would have been at Passover, the Feast of Pentecost, and the Feast of Tabernacles.

1 Kings 9:26
And king Solomon made a navy of ships in Ezion-geber, which is beside Eloth, on the shore of the Red sea, in the land of Edom.

Although the Jews fished on the Sea of Galilee, when it came to the open ocean, they shied away from any kind of seafaring activity. Here, and only here in the Bible, do we see a Navy being assembled.

1 Kings 9:27, 28
And Hiram sent in the navy his servants, shipmen that had knowledge of the sea, with the servants of Solomon. And they came to Ophir, and fetched from thence gold, four hundred and twenty talents, and brought it to king Solomon.

It took approximately three years for Solomon to get four hundred and twenty talents of gold through his naval venture into India. However, according to figures recorded in Scripture, David gathered over 100,000 talents of gold in a three-year period. In other words, conquest under David far exceeded commerce under Solomon.

I suggest that the riches in the Lord are not uncovered or discovered in the boardroom, but on the battlefield. In Old Testament days, faith had to be exercised by God's people in battles against real live Philistines and Canaanites. We don't fight Philistines and Canaanites. We fight finances and cash flow. But the battle is just as real. And just as the Philistines and Canaanites were overcome by faith, so finances and cash flow must be dealt with by faith. While I'm not suggesting we have a careless or reckless attitude, I do know that as we step out in faith, God will mature us in the battle.

10

As we come to chapter 10, we find Solomon at the height of both his piety and his prosperity. . . .

1 Kings 10:1
And when the queen of Sheba heard of the fame of Solomon concerning the name of the LORD, she came to prove him with hard questions.

Scholars are divided between two possible locations for Sheba. One is Yemen, the other is Ethiopia. Even if we take the more conservative approach and assume it was Yemen, the 1,500-mile trip from Yemen to Jerusalem would have required a seventy-five-day ride on the back of a camel across the desert. That she came to "prove him with hard question," doesn't mean the queen of Sheba was a skeptic, but that she was a seeker. She went to great lengths to find the truth, and she will not be disappointed.

1 Kings 10:2–9
And she came to Jerusalem with a very great train, with camels that bare spices, and very much gold, and precious stones: and when she was come to Solomon, she communed with him of all that was in her heart. And Solomon told her all her questions: there was not any thing hid from the king, which he told her not. And when the queen of Sheba had seen all Solomon's wisdom, and the house that he had built, And the meat of his table, and the sitting of his servants, and the attendance of his ministers, and their apparel, and his cupbearers, and his ascent by which he went up unto the house of the LORD; there was no more spirit in her. And she said to the king, It was a true report that I heard in mine own land of thy acts and of thy wisdom. Howbeit I believed not the words, until I came, and mine eyes had seen it: and, behold, the half was not told me: thy wisdom and prosperity exceedeth the fame which I heard. Happy are thy men, happy are these thy servants, which stand continually before thee, and that hear thy wisdom. Blessed be the LORD thy God, which delighted in thee, to set thee on the throne of Israel: because the LORD loved Israel for ever, therefore made he thee king, to do judgment and justice.

The queen of Sheba was amazed by everything she saw: Solomon's palace, his furniture, the food at his table, his servants but, because it is mentioned first, above all else, she was amazed by Solomon's wisdom. Wise herself, she praised the God who had given Solomon the wisdom, and thereby the ability, to accomplish all he had.

1 Kings 10:10–13
And she gave the king an hundred and twenty talents of gold, and of spices very great store, and precious stones: there came no more such abundance of spices as these which the queen of Sheba gave to king Solomon. And the navy also of Hiram, that brought gold from Ophir, brought in from Ophir great plenty of almug trees, and precious stones. And the king made of the almug trees pillars for the house of the LORD, and for the king's house, harps also and psalteries for singers: there came no such almug trees, nor were seen unto this day. And king Solomon gave unto the queen of Sheba all her desire, whatsoever she asked, beside that which Solomon gave her of his royal bounty. So she turned and went to her own country, she and her servants.

The queen of Sheba came, saw, and was saved. How do I know? Because Jesus said she will rise up in judgment against those who don't believe (Matthew 12:42). Because the queen of Sheba was a seeker of truth and sought out Solomon, ultimately she found the Greater than Solomon, Jesus Christ.

- Solomon had the wisdom of God.
  Jesus is *the wisdom of God.*
- Solomon was a great king.
  Jesus is the King of kings.
- Solomon had great wealth.
  Jesus has unsearchable riches.
- Solomon spoke practically in proverbs.
  Jesus spoke significantly in the Sermon on the Mount.
- Solomon answered the queen of Sheba's questions.
  Jesus is the answer to all *questions.*
- Solomon revealed his riches to the queen of Sheba.
  Jesus reveals His riches to any who seek His face.
- Solomon loaded the queen of Sheba with a bounty.
  Jesus does exceedingly abundantly above all we can ask or think.

How thankful I am for Jesus Christ, for the wisdom and perfection He embodies, for the riches and blessings He bestows.

1 Kings 10:14, 15
Now the weight of gold that came to Solomon in one year was six hundred threescore and six talents of gold. Beside that he had of the merchantmen, and of the traffick of the spice merchants, and of all the kings of Arabia, and of the governors of the country.

In today's economy, six hundred and sixty-six talents of gold would be equivalent to one billion dollars, a rather hefty sum. How hefty? If a billionaire gave a million dollars to his wife and said, "Go out and spend $1,000 every day and don't come back until you've spent the entire million, his wife wouldn't come back for three years. But if he gave his wife a billion dollars and told her to spend $1,000 a day until it was gone, his wife wouldn't come back for 3,000 *years.* In other words, a billion dollars is a lot of money!

1 Kings 10:16
And king Solomon made two hundred targets of beaten gold: six hundred shekels of gold went to one target.

A target was a shield that covered a soldier's entire body. Solomon was so rich that the shields for his army were solid gold.

1 Kings 10:17
And he made three hundred shields of beaten gold; three pound of gold went to one shield: and the king put them in the house of the forest of Lebanon.

The house of the forest of Lebanon was perhaps Solomon's vacation home.

1 Kings 10:18–20
Moreover the king made a great throne of ivory, and overlaid it with the best gold. The throne had six steps, and the top of the throne was round behind: and there were stays on either side on the place of the seat, and two lions stood beside the stays. And twelve lions stood there on the one side and on the other upon the six steps: there was not the like made in any kingdom.

A throne of ivory would have been impressive enough, but so much gold was at Solomon's disposal that he gold-plated the ivory.

1 Kings 10:21
And all king Solomon's drinking vessels were of gold, and all the vessels of the house of the forest of Lebanon were of pure gold; none were of silver: it was nothing accounted of in the days of Solomon.

Due to the abundance of gold in Solomon's empire, silver was virtually worthless.

1 Kings 10:22, 23
For the king had at sea a navy of Tharshish with the navy of Hiram: once in three years came the navy of Tharshish, bringing gold, and silver, ivory, and apes, and peacocks. So king Solomon exceeded all the kings of the earth for riches and for wisdom.

Solomon was known both for riches and for wisdom. In reality, his riches were the result of his wisdom. "Ask of Me anything," the Lord had said. Solomon asked for wisdom in order that he might rule the people correctly. So pleased was the Lord with his request that, in addition to wisdom beyond comprehension, Solomon received riches beyond measure.

1 Kings 10:24–29
And all the earth sought to Solomon, to hear his wisdom, which God had put in his heart. And they brought every man his present, vessels of silver, and vessels of gold, and garments, and armour, and spices, horses, and mules, a rate year by year. And Solomon gathered together chariots and horsemen: and he had a thousand and four hundred chariots, and twelve thousand horsemen, whom he bestowed in the cities for chariots, and with the king at Jerusalem. And the king made silver to be in Jerusalem as stones, and cedars made he to be as the sycomore trees that are in the vale, for abundance. And Solomon had horses brought out of Egypt, and linen yarn: the king's merchants received the linen yarn at a price. And a chariot came up and went out of Egypt for six hundred shekels of silver, and an horse for an hundred and fifty: and so for all the kings of the Hittites, and for the kings of Syria, did they bring them out by their means.

In Deuteronomy 17:16, the Lord specifically said that the king of Israel was not to multiply to himself horses, gold, or wives. Is this because the Lord is miserly? No, it's because He knows the tendency of our heart—that we'll trust in horses and rely on gold rather than seek Him every step of the way. Solomon multiplied to himself both horses and gold, as well as something else, which we'll see in chapter 11 . . .

11

1 Kings 11:1–3
But king Solomon loved many strange women, together with the daughter of Pharaoh, women of the Moabites, Ammonites, Edomites, Zidonians, and Hittites; Of the nations concerning which the LORD said unto the children of Israel, Ye shall not go in to them, neither shall they come in unto you: for surely they will turn away your heart after their gods: Solomon clave unto these in love. And he had seven hundred wives, princesses, and three hundred concubines: and his wives turned away his heart.

Solomon gathered seven hundred wives and three hundred concubines. Why? One reason is that it was politically prudent for him to do so. You see, in the Middle East culture of the day, alliances were ratified by the king of one country taking the daughter of the king of the other country into his harem. Intermarriage was a way of cementing alliances, and Solomon made many such alliances.

A second reason is obvious. A vast number of wives and concubines would have been sensually satisfying. Both the Book of Proverbs and the Song of Solomon show us that Solomon knew a great deal about women. In Ecclesiastes, we read that Solomon took wives, hoping to find fulfillment in them. Perhaps in search of the perfect woman he thought, *It'll be the next one*—until finally when he came to the thousandth one, he said, "It's all vanity."

There is a misconception in today's society on the part of both men and women that says, "If I just had someone else, I'd be happier. If I was with someone else, I know I'd be more fulfilled." It's a subtle lie of Satan that he whispers in our ears and it was whispered in the ears of Solomon, as well. He thought that happiness was right around the corner—the next relationship, the next concubine, the next marriage—surely then he would be fulfilled. But he wasn't.

Keep Solomon in mind next time you're tempted to think you'd be happier with someone else. Solomon had the opportunity to experiment greatly in that area. It didn't work for him, and it won't for you.

1 Kings 11:4–10
For it came to pass, when Solomon was old, that his wives turned away his heart after other gods: and his heart was not perfect with the LORD his God, as was the heart of David his father. For Solomon went after Ashtoreth the goddess of the Zidonians, and after Milcom the abomination of the Ammonites. And Solomon did evil in the sight of the LORD, and went not fully after the LORD, as did David his father. Then did Solomon build an high place for Chemosh, the abomination of Moab, in the hill that is before Jerusalem, and for Molech, the abomination of the chil-

dren of Ammon. And likewise did he for all his strange wives, which burnt incense and sacrificed unto their gods. And the LORD was angry with Solomon, because his heart was turned from the LORD God of Israel, which had appeared unto him twice, And had commanded him concerning this thing, that he should not go after other gods: but he kept not that which the LORD commanded.

The issue is always the heart. Solomon's heart left the Lord and pursued other gods. The Lord makes mention of the fact that He appeared to Solomon twice. The Lord never appeared unto David. Yet Solomon heard from Him twice. This tells us that miraculous manifestations do not produce spiritual maturation. It's not miracles that produce maturity, it's the Word. David heard the Word of the Lord, responded to the Word of the Lord, and kept the Word of the Lord. David loved God deeply. If you're a lover of God, you're on good ground. If you love the Lord and appreciate Him and are thankful for what He's done in your life and who He is to you, you're on good ground. But if your heart is not toward the Lord, you're on dangerous ground indeed.

Saul had no heart for the Lord. David had a whole heart for the Lord. Solomon had half a heart for the Lord. He began well but ended poorly, for his heart was turned.

1 Kings 11:11–13
Wherefore the LORD said unto Solomon, Forasmuch as this is done of thee, and thou hast not kept my covenant and my statutes, which I have commanded thee, I will surely rend the kingdom from thee, and will give it to thy servant. Notwithstanding in thy days I will not do it for David thy father's sake: but I will rend it out of the hand of thy son. Howbeit I will not rend away all the kingdom; but will give one tribe to thy son for David my servant's sake, and for Jerusalem's sake which I have chosen.

The remaining tribe would, of course, be Judah, from whom Messiah would one day come.

1 Kings 11:14–22
And the LORD stirred up an adversary unto Solomon, Hadad the Edomite: he was of the king's seed in Edom. For it came to pass, when David was in Edom, and Joab the captain of the host was gone up to bury the slain, after he had smitten every male in Edom; (For six months did Joab remain there with all Israel, until he had cut off every male in Edom:) That Hadad fled, he and certain Edomites of his father's servants with him, to go into Egypt; Hadad being yet a little child. And they arose out of Midian, and came to Paran: and they took men with them out of Paran, and they came to Egypt, unto Pharaoh king of Egypt; which gave him an house, and appointed him victuals, and gave him land. And Hadad found great favour in the sight of Pharaoh, so that he gave him to wife the sister of his own wife, the sister of Tahpenes the queen. And the sister of Tahpenes bare him Genubath his son, whom Tahpenes weaned in Pharaoh's house: and Genubath was in Pharaoh's household among the sons of Pharaoh. And when Hadad heard in Egypt that David slept with his fathers, and that Joab the captain of the host was dead, Hadad said to Pharaoh, Let me depart, that I may go to mine own country. Then Pharaoh said unto him, But what hast thou lacked with me, that, behold, thou seekest to go to thine own country? And he answered, Nothing: howbeit let me go in any wise.

When David conquered the Edomites, Hadad, as a little boy, was taken to Egypt in order that his life be spared. As he grew up, he found favor in the eyes of Pharaoh. But one day, he felt a stirring in his heart to leave the comfort of Pharaoh's palace and return to Israel. God caused this stirring because He was raising Hadad to be an adversary against Israel.

1 Kings 11:23–25
And God stirred him up another adversary, Rezon the son of Eliadah, which fled from his lord Hadadezer king of Zobah: And he gathered men unto him, and became captain over a band, when David slew them of Zobah: and they went to Damascus, and dwelt therein, and reigned in Damascus. And he was an adversary to Israel all the days of Solomon, beside the mischief that Hadad did: and he abhorred Israel, and reigned over Syria.

Why did the Lord bring Hadad back into the land? Because He loved Solomon too much to allow him to continue in iniquity and apathy. Hadad and Rezon were used by the Lord to get Solomon off his high horse and back down on his knees.

1 Kings 11:26–28
And Jeroboam the son of Nebat, an Ephrathite of Zereda, Solomon's servant, whose mother's name was Zeruah, a widow woman, even he lifted up his hand against the king. And this was the cause that he lifted up his hand against the king: Solomon built Millo, and repaired the breaches of the city of David his father. And the man Jeroboam was a mighty man of valour: and Solomon seeing

the young man that he was industrious, he made him ruler over all the charge of the house of Joseph.

Here, we are introduced to a man who would become a third thorn in Solomon's flesh: Jeroboam. Not only was Jeroboam industrious, but he was also extremely gifted. Yet, although he had ability, he had no history with God. Although he had talent, he wasn't yet tempered. Although he was an incredibly blessed man, he wasn't a broken man.

1 Kings 11:29–39
And it came to pass at that time when Jeroboam went out of Jerusalem, that the prophet Ahijah the Shilonite found him in the way; and he had clad himself with a new garment; and they two were alone in the field: And Ahijah caught the new garment that was on him, and rent it in twelve pieces: And he said to Jeroboam, Take thee ten pieces: for thus saith the LORD, the God of Israel, Behold, I will rend the kingdom out of the hand of Solomon, and will give ten tribes to thee: (But he shall have one tribe for my servant David's sake, and for Jerusalem's sake, the city which I have chosen out of all the tribes of Israel:) Because that they have forsaken me, and have worshipped Ashtoreth the goddess of the Zidonians, Chemosh the god of the Moabites, and Milcom the god of the children of Ammon, and have not walked in my ways, to do that which is right in mine eyes, and to keep my statutes and my judgments, as did David his father. Howbeit I will not take the whole kingdom out of his hand: but I will make him prince all the days of his life for David my servant's sake, whom I chose, because he kept my commandments and my statutes: But I will take the kingdom out of his son's hand, and will give it unto thee, even ten tribes. And unto his son will I give one tribe, that David my servant may have a light alway before me in Jerusalem, the city which I have chosen me to put my name there. And I will take thee, and thou shalt reign according to all that thy soul desireth, and shalt be king over Israel. And it shall be, if thou wilt hearken unto all that I command thee, and wilt walk in my ways, and do that is right in my sight, to keep my statutes and my commandments, as David my servant did; that I will be with thee, and build thee a sure house, as I built for David, and will give Israel unto thee. And I will for this afflict the seed of David, but not for ever.

Ahijah the prophet came to Jeroboam and said, "Although Solomon's house will keep one tribe, you will be king over ten."

1 Kings 11:40
Solomon sought therefore to kill Jeroboam. And Jeroboam arose, and fled into Egypt, unto Shishak king of Egypt, and was in Egypt until the death of Solomon.

Solomon sought to deter God's judgment by killing Jeroboam. But God's will prevailed and Jeroboam was kept safe.

1 Kings 11:41–43
And the rest of the acts of Solomon, and all that he did, and his wisdom, are they not written in the book of the acts of Solomon? And the time that Solomon reigned in Jerusalem over all Israel was forty years. And Solomon slept with his fathers, and was buried in the city of David his father: and Rehoboam his son reigned in his stead.

Solomon reigned as many years as David, his father, had reigned. However, while David left a unified kingdom, the kingdom Solomon left was soon to be divided. I suggest both are the inevitable result of the state of their hearts. David's heart was singularly God's. Solomon's was divided between the God of his father and the manifold gods of the world.

12

1 Kings 12:1–4
And Rehoboam went to Shechem: for all Israel were come to Shechem to make him king. And it came to pass, when Jeroboam the son of Nebat, who was yet in Egypt, heard of it, (for he was fled from the presence of king Solomon, and Jeroboam dwelt in Egypt;) That they sent and called him. And Jeroboam and all the congregation of Israel came, and spake unto Rehoboam, saying, Thy father made our yoke grievous: now therefore make thou the grievous service of thy father, and his heavy yoke which he put upon us, lighter, and we will serve thee.

To complete his massive building projects (1 Kings 9), Solomon had taxed the peoples' wealth and strength. Here, at the outset of a new administration, the people asked that their burden be made lighter.

1 Kings 12:5
And he said unto them, Depart yet for three days, then come again to me. And the people departed.

"Give me three days to consider your request," Rehoboam said.

1 Kings 12:6, 7
And king Rehoboam consulted with the old men, that stood before Solomon his father while he yet lived, and said, How do ye advise that I may answer this people? And they spake unto him, saying, If thou wilt be a servant unto this people this day, and wilt serve them, and answer them, and speak good words to them, then they will be thy servants for ever.

Before making his decision, Rehoboam first consulted with his father's advisors. "If you will serve, encourage, and bless the people, you won't have a problem," they said. They were right because, truly, the key to authority is humility. The greatest Leader the world will ever know said, "Come unto Me all you who are weary and heavy laden, and I will give you rest. Take My yoke upon you and learn of Me, for My burden is easy. My yoke is light" (see Matthew 11:29, 30).

The night before He was crucified, with the disciples arguing over who was the greatest, Jesus simply began to wash their dusty feet (John 13:5). How I love Jesus. There is no One like Him. Who else would tend and care for us even as we bicker and fight over who is the greatest? How we need to be more like Him.

1 Kings 12:8–11
But he forsook the counsel of the old men, which they had given him, and consulted with the young men that were grown up with him, and which stood before him: And he said unto them, What counsel give ye that we may answer this people, who have spoken to me, saying, Make the yoke which thy father did put upon us lighter? And the young men that were grown up with him spake unto him, saying, Thus shalt thou speak unto this people that spake unto thee, saying, Thy father made our yoke heavy, but make thou it lighter unto us; thus shalt thou say unto them, My little finger shall be thicker than my father's loins. And now whereas my father did lade you with a heavy yoke, I will add to your yoke: my father hath chastised you with whips, but I will chastise you with scorpions.

Rejecting the wise counsel of his father's advisors, Rehoboam sought the counsel of his own peers, who told him to lead not in humility but with force.

1 Kings 12:12–15
So Jeroboam and all the people came to Rehoboam the third day, as the king had appointed, saying, Come to me again the third day. And the king answered the people roughly, and forsook the old men's counsel that they gave him; And spake to them after the counsel of the young men, saying, My father made your yoke heavy, and I will add to your yoke: my father also chastised you with whips, but I will chastise you with scorpions. Wherefore the king hearkened not unto the people; for the cause was from the LORD, that he might perform his saying, which the LORD spake by Ahijah the Shilonite unto Jeroboam the son of Nebat.

Although the decision to rule with an iron fist was entirely Rehoboam's, it coincided perfectly with God's preordained judgment (1 Kings 11:31).

1 Kings 12:16–20
So when all Israel saw that the king hearkened not unto them, the people answered the king, saying, What portion have we in David? neither have we inheritance in the son of Jesse: to your tents, O Israel: now see to thine own house, David. So Israel departed unto their tents. But as for the children of Israel which dwelt in the cities of Judah, Rehoboam reigned over them. Then king Rehoboam sent Adoram, who was over the tribute; and all Israel stoned him with stones, that he died. Therefore king Rehoboam made speed to get him up to his chariot, to flee to Jerusalem. So Israel rebelled against the house of David unto this day. And it came to pass, when all Israel heard that Jeroboam was come again, that they sent and called him unto the congregation, and made him king over all Israel: there was none that followed the house of David, but the tribe of Judah only.

The year was 920 B.C. The ten northern tribes said, "We are not going to serve Rehoboam. We will follow Jeroboam instead."

Judah, the southern tribe, along with the tiny tribe of Benjamin, said, "We'll stick with Rehoboam."

In the year 722 B.C., the ten northern tribes were carried away into captivity by the Assyrians and were eventually lost. The southern tribe of Judah, along with Benjamin, lasted a bit longer.

They lasted until the year 586 when they were carried away by the Babylonians. Out of nineteen kings, they had eight good ones, eleven bad ones. The ten northern tribes, on the other hand, had not a single good king, not a single king who sought the Lord. The Jews that were carried away into Babylon later on were brought back by Ezra, Nehemiah, Zechariah, and Zerubbabel. They rebuilt Jerusalem and the temple and remained there until A.D. 70 when the Roman Empire came crashing down, destroying the Jews, and dispersing them throughout the entire known world.

But the story's not over yet, gang, for in Ezekiel 37, we find a promise that the Jews will come back once again. "Take two sticks," the Lord said to Ezekiel—"one representing Israel, the other representing Judah—and hold them together, for they shall no longer be two but one." We have already seen this happen when the nation of Israel was rebirthed in 1948.

1 Kings 12:21–24
And when Rehoboam was come to Jerusalem, he assembled all the house of Judah, with the tribe of Benjamin, an hundred and fourscore thousand chosen men, which were warriors, to fight against the house of Israel, to bring the kingdom again to Rehoboam the son of Solomon. But the word of God came unto Shemaiah the man of God, saying, Speak unto Rehoboam, the son of Solomon, king of Judah, and unto all the house of Judah and Benjamin, and to the remnant of the people, saying, Thus saith the LORD, Ye shall not go up, nor fight against your brethren the children of Israel: return every man to his house; for this thing is from me. They hearkened therefore to the word of the LORD, and returned to depart, according to the word of the LORD.

Rehoboam chose not to do battle against his brothers in an effort to hold the country together. Instead, he realized that what was happening was from the Lord.

1 Kings 12:25–27
Then Jeroboam built Shechem in mount Ephraim, and dwelt therein; and went out from thence, and built Penuel. And Jeroboam said in his heart, Now shall the kingdom return to the house of David: If this people go up to do sacrifice in the house of the LORD at Jerusalem, then shall the heart of this people turn again unto their lord, even unto Rehoboam king of Judah, and they shall kill me, and go again to Rehoboam king of Judah.

Jeroboam is making a bad blunder here. "Oh, no," he said. "If my people go down to Jerusalem to sacrifice there, their heart will turn towards Judah and Rehoboam." Notice Jeroboam didn't talk to the Lord. He talked to himself. Whenever I talk to myself, I get mixed up. And the same thing will happen to Jeroboam . . .

1 Kings 12:28
Whereupon the king took counsel, and made two calves of gold, and said unto them, It is too much for you to go up to Jerusalem: behold thy gods, O Israel, which brought thee up out of the land of Egypt.

To keep people from going to Jerusalem to sacrifice, Jeroboam made two golden calves and said, "These gods brought you out of Egypt." That should ring a bell, for when Moses was on Mt. Sinai receiving the Ten Commandments, Aaron made a golden calf and the people said, "This is your god that brought you out of Egypt (see Exodus 32:4). The implication in both cases was not that the golden calves replaced God but that they simply represented Him. "It's hard for you to go to Jerusalem. Therefore, let's make a golden calf and it can represent God right here," Jeroboam said.

But such representation always leads to pollution, to idolatry. Jeroboam here is making a huge mistake.

1 Kings 12:29–33
And he set the one in Bethel, and the other put he in Dan. And this thing became a sin: for the people went to worship before the one, even unto Dan. And he made an house of high places, and made priests of the lowest of the people, which were not of the sons of Levi. And Jeroboam ordained a feast in the eighth month, on the fifteenth day of the month, like unto the feast that is in Judah, and he offered upon the altar. So did he in Bethel, sacrificing unto the calves that he had made: and he placed in Bethel the priests of the high places which he had made. So he offered upon the altar which he had made in Bethel the fifteenth day of the eighth month, even in the month which he had devised of his own heart; and ordained a feast unto the children of Israel: and he offered upon the altar, and burnt incense.

Jeroboam went on to assign holy days and to appoint priests in an attempt to hold on to his kingdom. May Jeroboam's sin be a warning to us, for how many concessions are we ready to make in an attempt to hold our own little kingdom or agenda together? What problems are you facing today? Don't be like Jeroboam. Don't talk to yourself. Talk to the Lord. Seek *His* kingdom, not your own.

13 In chapter 13, we come to one of the most interesting stories in the entire Book of First Kings . . .

1 Kings 13:1–3
And, behold, there came a man of God out of Judah by the word of the LORD unto Bethel: and Jeroboam stood by the altar to burn incense. And he cried against the altar in the word of the LORD, and said, O altar, altar, thus saith the LORD; Behold, a child shall be born unto the house of David, Josiah by name; and upon thee shall he offer the priests of the high places that burn incense upon thee, and men's bones shall be burnt upon thee. And he gave a sign the same day, saying, This is the sign which the LORD hath spoken; Behold, the altar shall be rent, and the ashes that are upon it shall be poured out.

As Jeroboam was there sacrificing beside the altar he created, an unnamed man of God prophesied that the Lord would raise up a king named Josiah who would destroy the entire system of false worship. This prophecy was fulfilled over 350 years later when Josiah destroyed the high places and burned the bones of the false prophets (2 Kings 23).

1 Kings 13:4
And it came to pass, when king Jeroboam heard the saying of the man of God, which had cried against the altar in Bethel, that he put forth his hand from the altar, saying, Lay hold on him. And his hand, which he put forth against him, dried up, so that he could not pull it in again to him.

"Take this prophet away," Jeroboam commanded. And right then, his arm shriveled.

1 Kings 13:5, 6
The altar also was rent, and the ashes poured out from the altar, according to the sign which the man of God had given by the word of the LORD. And the king answered and said unto the man of God, Intreat now the face of the LORD thy God, and pray for me, that my hand may be restored me again. And the man of God besought the LORD, and the king's hand was restored him again, and became as it was before.

Rather than holding a grudge, this man of God sought restoration and revitalization for Jeroboam. I like that. It's called love.

1 Kings 13:7–9
And the king said unto the man of God, Come home with me, and refresh thyself, and I will give thee a reward. And the man of God said unto the king, If thou wilt give me half thine house, I will not go in with thee, neither will I eat bread nor drink water in this place: For so was it charged me by the word of the LORD, saying, Eat no bread, nor drink water, nor turn again by the same way that thou camest.

No doubt grateful for the restoration of his arm, Jeroboam invited the prophet to his home. But the prophet refused, due to the command of the Lord. Why did the Lord forbid the prophet any type of reward? I suggest it was to protect him from the compromise that seems to inevitably accompany reward or adulation. In this, I am reminded of Abraham when he said to the king of Sodom, "I will not take from a thread even to a shoelatchet, and that I will not take any thing that is thine, lest thou shouldest say, I have made Abram rich" (Genesis 14:23).

1 Kings 13:10–19
So he went another way, and returned not by the way that he came to Bethel. Now there dwelt an old prophet in Bethel; and his sons came and told him all the works that the man of God had done that day in Bethel: the words which he had spoken unto the king, them they told also to their father. And their father said unto them, What way went he? For his sons had seen what way the man of God went, which came from Judah. And he said unto his sons, Saddle me the ass. So they saddled him the ass: and he rode thereon, And went after the man of God, and found him sitting under an oak: and he said unto him, Art thou the man of God that camest from Judah? And he said, I am. Then he said unto him, Come home with me, and eat bread. And he said, I may not return with thee, nor go in with thee: neither will I eat bread nor drink water with thee in this place: For it was said to me by the word of the LORD, Thou shalt eat no bread nor drink water there, nor turn again to go by the way that thou camest. He said unto him, I am a prophet also as thou art; and an angel spake unto me by the word of the LORD, saying, Bring him back with thee into thine house, that he may eat bread and drink water. But he lied unto him. So he

went back with him, and did eat bread in his house, and drank water.

When an old prophet heard reports of a young prophet doing marvelous things, he found the young prophet and said, "Come to my house and eat bread."

"I can't," the young prophet said. "The word of God to me said I must not."

"But I'm a prophet, too," argued the old man. "An angel came to me and told me you're to come with me and eat and drink."

Why did the old prophet say this? I suggest two possible reasons . . .

It could be that he was hungry for fellowship with someone moving in the anointing of the Spirit and was willing to lie in order to have this kind of fellowship. Or, it could be that he was jealous of the young prophet and wanted him off the scene. Either way, he was wrong. Nonetheless, evidently deferring to the age and experience of the old prophet, the young prophet accepted his invitation.

1 Kings 13:20–22
And it came to pass, as they sat at the table, that the word of the LORD came unto the prophet that brought him back: And he cried unto the man of God that came from Judah, saying, Thus saith the LORD, Forasmuch as thou hast disobeyed the mouth of the LORD, and hast not kept the commandment which the LORD thy God commanded thee, But camest back, and hast eaten bread and drunk water in the place, of the which the LORD did say to thee, Eat no bread, and drink no water; thy carcase shall not come unto the sepulchre of thy fathers.

Midway through the meal, the old prophet said, "Because you disobeyed the word of the Lord, you'll not die a normal death."

1 Kings 13:23–32
And it came to pass, after he had eaten bread, and after he had drunk, that he saddled for him the ass, to wit, for the prophet whom he had brought back. And when he was gone, a lion met him by the way, and slew him: and his carcase was cast in the way, and the ass stood by it, the lion also stood by the carcase. And, behold, men passed by, and saw the carcase cast in the way, and the lion standing by the carcase: and they came and told it in the city where the old prophet dwelt. And when the prophet that brought him back from the way heard thereof, he said, It is the man of God, who was disobedient unto the word of the LORD: therefore the LORD hath delivered him unto the lion, which hath torn him, and slain him, according to the word of the LORD, which he spake unto him. And he spake to his sons, saying, Saddle me the ass. And they saddled him. And he went and found his carcase cast in the way, and the ass and the lion standing by the carcase: the lion had not eaten the carcase, nor torn the ass. And the prophet took up the carcase of the man of God, and laid it upon the ass, and brought it back: and the old prophet came to the city, to mourn and to bury him. And he laid his carcase in his own grave; and they mourned over him, saying, Alas, my brother! And it came to pass, after he had buried him, that he spake to his sons, saying, When I am dead, then bury me in the sepulchre wherein the man of God is buried; lay my bones beside his bones: For the saying which he cried by the word of the LORD against the altar in Bethel, and against all the houses of the high places which are in the cities of Samaria, shall surely come to pass.

What in the world is this story about? In Galatians 1, Paul says, "If we or an angel from heaven preach unto you any other gospel, let that angel be accursed." I don't care who comes to you and says, "An angel spoke to me or a vision has been given to me," if that angel or vision is in contradiction to the Word of God, reject it. If not, you will find yourself being torn up by the lion that Peter identifies as Satan (1 Peter 5:8).

Stick with the Word, gang, and you'll be safe. If you deviate from it, you're lion-bait. Study the Word. Hunger and desire to know the Word of God. Be committed to it. My prayer is that you might know it from cover to cover lest any mixed-up prophet says "The Lord told me to tell you . . ." and you find yourself being ripped up. May God give you a heart for it and the ability to carry out its instructions, not half-heartedly like Solomon, but wholeheartedly and fervently like David.

1 Kings 13:33, 34
After this thing Jeroboam returned not from his evil way, but made again of the lowest of the people priests of the high places: whosoever would, he consecrated him, and he became one of the priests of the high places. And this thing became sin unto the house of Jeroboam, even to cut it off, and to destroy it from off the face of the earth.

Even after God's word was confirmed before his eyes at the beginning of the chapter, Jeroboam continued in false worship—thereby bringing destruction upon the head of his own house, as seen in the next chapter . . .

14

1 Kings 14:1–3
At that time Abijah the son of Jeroboam fell sick. And Jeroboam said to his wife, Arise, I pray thee, and disguise thyself, that thou be not known to be the wife of Jeroboam; and get thee to Shiloh: behold, there is Ahijah the prophet, which told me that I should be king over this people. And take with thee ten loaves, and cracknels, and a cruse of honey, and go to him: he shall tell thee what shall become of the child.

When Jeroboam's son became ill, Jeroboam told his wife to disguise herself and seek out a prophet of God—not for intercession, not for counsel, not for repentance—but simply to find out the future. I find it humorous that Jeroboam told his wife to disguise herself. After all, why trust the word of a prophet who could be that easily fooled?

1 Kings 14:4
And Jeroboam's wife did so, and arose, and went to Shiloh, and came to the house of Ahijah. But Ahijah could not see; for his eyes were set by reason of his age.

Ahijah's eyes were closed, but his ears were open. That is, although he was blind physically, he was tuned-in spiritually.

1 Kings 14:5–10
And the LORD said unto Ahijah, Behold, the wife of Jeroboam cometh to ask a thing of thee for her son; for he is sick: thus and thus shalt thou say unto her: for it shall be, when she cometh in, that she shall feign herself to be another woman. And it was so, when Ahijah heard the sound of her feet as she came in at the door, that he said, Come in, thou wife of Jeroboam; why feignest thou thyself to be another? for I am sent to thee with heavy tidings. Go, tell Jeroboam, Thus saith the LORD God of Israel, Forasmuch as I exalted thee from among the people, and made thee prince over my people Israel, And rent the kingdom away from the house of David, and gave it thee: and yet thou hast not been as my servant David, who kept my commandments, and who followed me with all his heart, to do that only which was right in mine eyes; But hast done evil above all that were before thee: for thou hast gone and made thee other gods, and molten images, to provoke me to anger, and hast cast me behind thy back: Therefore, behold, I will bring evil upon the house of Jeroboam, and will cut off from Jeroboam him that pisseth against the wall, and him that is shut up and left in Israel, and will take away the remnant of the house of Jeroboam, as a man taketh away dung, till it be all gone.

Ahijah's word to Jeroboam's wife—whose disguise proved to be worthless—was that because Jeroboam worshiped false gods, his family would be destroyed.

1 Kings 14:11–13
Him that dieth of Jeroboam in the city shall the dogs eat; and him that dieth in the field shall the fowls of the air eat: for the LORD hath spoken it. Arise thou therefore, get thee to thine own house: and when thy feet enter into the city, the child shall die. And all Israel shall mourn for him, and bury him: for he only of Jeroboam shall come to the grave, because in him there is found some good thing toward the LORD God of Israel in the house of Jeroboam.

Jeroboam's child who was ill would die upon his wife's return. And, as if that wasn't bad enough, everyone else in the family would die a violent death.

1 Kings 14:14–20
Moreover the LORD shall raise him up a king over Israel, who shall cut off the house of Jeroboam that day: but what? even now. For the LORD shall smite Israel, as a reed is shaken in the water, and he shall root up Israel out of this good land, which he gave to their fathers, and shall scatter them beyond the river, because they have made their groves, provoking the LORD to anger. And he shall give Israel up because of the sins of Jeroboam, who did sin, and who made Israel to sin. And Jeroboam's wife arose, and departed, and came to Tirzah: and when she came to the threshold of the door, the child died; And they buried him; and all Israel mourned for him, according to the word of the LORD, which he spake by the hand of his servant Ahijah the prophet. And the rest of the acts of Jeroboam, how he warred, and how he reigned, behold, they are written in the book of the chronicles of the kings of Israel. And the days which Jeroboam reigned were two and twenty years: and he slept with this fathers, and Nadab his son reigned in his stead.

Within two years, Ahijah's prophecy would fully come to pass when a man named Baasha would slay not only Nadab, but also the entire house of Jeroboam (1 Kings 15:28–30). In the meantime, we go back to the south, where Rehoboam was ruling over Judah . . .

1 Kings 14:21
And Rehoboam the son of Solomon reigned in Judah. Rehoboam was forty and one years old when he began to reign, and he reigned seventeen years in Jerusalem, the city which the LORD did choose out of all the tribes of Israel, to put his name there. And his mother's name was Naamah an Ammonitess.

In Jewish genealogies the mother's name is usually never mentioned, but in the Books of Kings and Chronicles, the mother's name often appears. I suggest this is because the Lord is showing us that the mother has a great deal to do with the character of the child.

Moms, your primary ministry is to realize that you are responsible for the discipling and molding of your children. "And Adam was not deceived, but the woman being deceived was in the transgression," Paul wrote to Timothy. "Notwithstanding she shall be saved in childbearing, if they continue in faith and charity and holiness with sobriety" (1 Timothy 2:14, 15). The word "saved" doesn't mean you'll be saved concerning your eternal state. Rather, the Greek word implies being made whole, fulfilled in every area and dimension of your life.

As I understand the Word of God, the ministry of a woman is primarily to minister, mold, develop, and disciple her children. In so doing, she will be saved, fulfilled, content. In the Lord's economy, He has left the ministry of the church primarily to men. But He left the foundation of the church, the home, in the hands of women. There is nothing in my life I value more than my Christian heritage. Sisters, take seriously this glorious responsibility. In so doing, not only will you be fulfilled, but the church will be strong.

1 Kings 14:22–28
And Judah did evil in the sight of the LORD, and they provoked him to jealousy with their sins which they had committed, above all that their fathers had done. For they also built them high places, and images, and groves, on every high hill, and under every green tree. And there were also sodomites in the land: and they did according to all the abominations of the nations which the LORD cast out before the children of Israel. And it came to pass in the fifth year of king Rehoboam, that Shishak king of Egypt came up against Jerusalem: And he took away the treasures of the house of the LORD, and the treasures of the king's house; he even took away all: and he took away all the shields of gold which Solomon had made. And king Rehoboam made in their stead brasen shields, and committed them unto the hands of the chief of the guard, which kept the door of the king's house. And it was so, when the king went into the house of the LORD, that the guard bare them, and brought them back into the guard chamber.

When Shishak, king of Egypt, came to do battle against Jerusalem, he plundered the gold shields that Solomon had made. What did Rehoboam do? He didn't have the resources to make gold shields because the wealth and prosperity of the kingdom was falling rapidly. But he wanted to keep up appearances, so he made brass shields to take their place.

Is that happening in your life? Is the gold gone? Have the riches disappeared, yet you find yourself wanting to maintain the outer front? Rather than do that, the Lord would give back to you the gold and silver you once had spiritually if you'll just say, "Lord, I'm tired of playing games. I'm tired of putting up a front. I want to drink of You right now, Lord. I want to return my heart to You right now. I want to start walking with You once again." If you'll do that right now, the riches and joy of the Lord will be restored to you this very moment.

1 Kings 14:29–31
Now the rest of the acts of Rehoboam, and all that he did, are they not written in the book of the chronicles of the kings of Judah? And there was war between Rehoboam and Jeroboam all their days. And Rehoboam slept with his fathers, and was buried with his fathers in the city of David. And his mother's name was Naamah an Ammonitess. And Abijam his son reigned in his stead.

Although Rehoboam had been forbidden to wage war against the ten tribes, he would defend Judah against border attacks, thus resulting in constant strife, a far cry from the peace experienced during Solomon's reign (1 Kings 5:4).

15

1 Kings 15:1
Now in the eighteenth year of king Jeroboam the son of Nebat reigned Abijam over Judah.

As Jeroboam reigned in the north, Abijam came to the throne in the south and reigned over Judah.

1 Kings 15:2–5
Three years reigned he in Jerusalem. And his mother's name was Maachah, the daughter of Abishalom. And he walked in all the

sins of his father, which he had done before him: and his heart was not perfect with the LORD his God, as the heart of David his father. Nevertheless for David's sake did the LORD his God give him a lamp in Jerusalem, to set up his son after him, and to establish Jerusalem: Because David did that which was right in the eyes of the LORD, and turned not aside from any thing that he commanded him all the days of his life, save only in the matter of Uriah the Hittite.

It's interesting how often David's name appears in the record of Kings and Chronicles. F.B. Meyer said this: "How long after David's sun had set did the light of his life glimmer over his house." Because David shone so brightly, loved God so intensely, worshiped God so fervently, the glow of his life remained upon his family for many generations.

What we enjoy as Christians is because there have been those before us who have prayed on our behalf, who have given of themselves, who have passed a heritage on down the line. Oh, how important it is that we see that our lives have long-term effects years down the road as did David's.

1 Kings 15:6–13
And there was war between Rehoboam and Jeroboam all the days of his life. Now the rest of the acts of Abijam, and all that he did, are they not written in the book of the chronicles of the kings of Judah? And there was war between Abijam and Jeroboam. And Abijam slept with his fathers; and they buried him in the city of David: and Asa his son reigned in his stead. And in the twentieth year of Jeroboam king of Israel reigned Asa over Judah. And forty and one years reigned he in Jerusalem. And his mother's name was Maachah, the daughter of Abishalom. And Asa did that which was right in the eyes of the LORD, as did David his father. And he took away the sodomites out of the land, and removed all the idols that his fathers had made. And also Maachah his mother, even her he removed from being queen, because she had made an idol in a grove; and Asa destroyed her idol, and burnt it by the brook Kidron.

Asa is one of the great kings that we'll see more in depth in Chronicles. He was dedicated to the Lord, broke down the idols that competed against the Lord, and even dealt with his own mother. That might sound brutal, but Jesus said, our love for Him must be so intense that our love for our parents or for any other person seems to be hatred in comparison (Luke 14:26). If it comes down to choosing Mom or choosing the Lord, you've got to choose the Lord. And that's what Asa did.

1 Kings 15:14, 15
But the high places were not removed: nevertheless Asa's heart was perfect with the LORD all his days. And he brought in the things which his father had dedicated, and the things which himself had dedicated, into the house of the LORD, silver, and gold, and vessels.

Although he didn't complete the task, Asa's heart was right, and that's what the Lord looks at (1 Samuel 16:7).

1 Kings 15:16–24
And there was war between Asa and Baasha king of Israel all their days. And Baasha king of Israel went up against Judah, and built Ramah, that he might not suffer any to go out or come in to Asa king of Judah. Then Asa took all the silver and the gold that were left in the treasures of the house of the LORD, and the treasures of the king's house, and delivered them into the hand of his servants: and king Asa sent them to Ben-hadad, the son of Tabrimon, the son of Hezion, king of Syria, that dwelt at Damascus, saying, There is a league between me and thee, and between my father and thy father: behold, I have sent unto thee a present of silver and gold; come and break thy league with Baasha king of Israel, that he may depart from me. So Ben-hadad hearkened unto king Asa, and sent the captains of the hosts which he had against the cities of Israel, and smote Ijon, and Dan, and Abel-beth-maachah, and all Cinneroth, with all the land of Naphtali. And it came to pass, when Baasha heard thereof, that he left off building of Ramah, and dwelt in Tirzah. Then king Asa made a proclamation throughout all Judah; none was exempted: and they took away the stones of Ramah, and the timber thereof, wherewith Baasha had builded; and king Asa built with them Geba of Benjamin, and Mizpah. The rest of all the acts of Asa, and all his might, and all that he did, and the cities which he built, are they not written in the book of the chronicles of the kings of Judah? Nevertheless in the time of his old age he was diseased in his feet. And Asa slept with his fathers, and was buried with his fathers in the city of David his father: and Jehoshaphat his son reigned in his stead.

Asa was a godly man, a great leader, a wonderful king, and yet when he contracted a disease in his feet, 2 Chronicles 16:12 tells us he sought the physicians and not the Lord. Doctors are a gift of God, but I am wrong if I place faith in doctors above placing my hope and faith in the God who heals. The implication in Chronicles is that, had Asa sought the Lord before he sought the physicians, the outcome could have been entirely different. Our faith must never be in human ability or technology, but always in God's sovereignty. Cast *all* your care upon Him—physical, mental, spiritual, financial—and let Him direct from there (1 Peter 5:7).

1 Kings 15:25, 26
And Nadab the son of Jeroboam began to reign over Israel in the second year of Asa king of Judah, and reigned over Israel two years. And he did evil in the sight of the LORD, and walked in the way of his father, and in his sin wherewith he made Israel to sin.

Amazing. One would think the judgment of God that resulted in the death of his brother would have given Nadab pause in so blindly following the false worship instituted by his father, but such was not the case.

1 Kings 15:27–30
And Baasha the son of Ahijah, of the house of Issachar, conspired against him; and Baasha smote him at Gibbethon, which belonged to the Philistines; for Nadab and all Israel laid siege to Gibbethon. Even in the third year of Asa king of Judah did Baasha slay him, and reigned in his stead. And it came to pass, when he reigned, that he smote all the house of Jeroboam; he left not to Jeroboam any that breathed, until he had destroyed him, according unto the saying of the LORD, which he spake by his servant Ahijah the Shilonite: Because of the sins of Jeroboam which he sinned, and which he made Israel sin, by his provocation wherewith he provoked the LORD God of Israel to anger.

In the north, in fulfillment of the prophecy given in chapter 14, the house of Jeroboam is wiped out by assassination and murder.

1 Kings 15:31–34
Now the rest of the acts of Nadab, and all that he did, are they not written in the book of the chronicles of the kings of Israel? And there was war between Asa and Baasha king of Israel all their days. In the third year of Asa king of Judah began Baasha the son of Ahijah to reign over all Israel in Tirzah, twenty and four years. And he did evil in the sight of the LORD, and walked in the way of Jeroboam, and in his sin wherewith he made Israel to sin.

Again, I find it astounding that, even though he was a tool in the hand of the Lord to mete out judgment upon the house of Jeroboam, specifically upon Nadab, Baasha nonetheless followed in the footsteps of the king who was destined for destruction.

16

1 Kings 16:1–4
Then the word of the LORD came to Jehu the son of Hanani against Baasha, saying, Forasmuch as I exalted thee out of the dust, and made thee prince over my people Israel; and thou hast walked in the way of Jeroboam, and hast made my people Israel to sin, to provoke me to anger with their sins;, I will take away the posterity of Baasha, and the posterity of his house; and will make thy house like the house of Jeroboam the son of Nebat. Him that dieth of Baasha in the city shall the dogs eat; and him that dieth of his in the fields shall the fowls of the air eat.

Just as the Lord didn't turn a blind eye to the sins of Jeroboam and Nadab, neither would He allow Baasha to escape judgment for the false worship system that continued under his reign.

1 Kings 16:5–10
Now the rest of the acts of Baasha, and what he did, and his might, are they not written in the book of the chronicles of the kings of Israel? So Baasha slept with his fathers, and was buried in Tirzah: and Elah his son reigned in his stead. And also by the hand of the prophet Jehu the son of Hanani came the word of the LORD against Baasha, and against his house, even for all the evil that he did in the sight of the LORD, in provoking him to anger with the work of his hands, in being like the house of Jeroboam; and because he killed him. In the twenty and sixth year of Asa king of Judah began Elah the son of Baasha to reign over Israel in Tirzah, two years. And his servant Zimri, captain of half his chariots, conspired against him, as he was in Tirzah, drinking himself drunk in the house of Arza steward of his house in Tirzah. And Zimri went in and smote him, and killed him, in the twenty and seventh year of Asa king of Judah, and reigned in his stead.

Elah was killed by Zimri. When? When he was "drinking himself drunk." General Pershing, a man who knew something about war, said, "Drunkenness has killed more men than all of the wars in human history."

President Taft said, "He who drinks is deliberately disqualifying himself for advancement in any field."

By the age of twenty, Alexander the Great was king of the Grecian Empire and conquered the entire known world by the age of thirty-three. At that point, he threw a party, became drunk, fell into a coma, and died three days later. Thus, alcohol conquered the man who conquered the world.

I point this out because I'm tired of dealing with couples whose marriages have been ruined, whose lives have been shipwrecked because of alcohol. It happens more than you know.

1 Kings 16:11–18

And it came to pass, when he began to reign, as soon as he sat on his throne, that he slew all the house of Baasha: he left him not one that pisseth against a wall, neither of his kinsfolks, nor of his friends. Thus did Zimri destroy all the house of Baasha, according to the word of the LORD, which he spake against Baasha by Jehu the prophet, For all the sins of Baasha, and the sins of Elah his son, by which they sinned, and by which they made Israel to sin, in provoking the LORD God of Israel to anger with their vanities. Now the rest of the acts of Elah, and all that he did, are they not written in the book of the chronicles of the kings of Israel? In the twenty and seventh year of Asa king of Judah did Zimri reign seven days in Tirzah. And the people were encamped against Gibbethon, which belonged to the Philistines. And the people that were encamped heard say, Zimri hath conspired, and hath also slain the king: wherefore all Israel made Omri, the captain of the host, king over Israel that day in the camp. And Omri went up from Gibbethon, and all Israel with him, and they besieged Tirzah. And it came to pass, when Zimri saw that the city was taken, that he went into the palace of the king's house, and burnt the king's house over him with fire, and died,

When word got out that Zimri had come into power by killing the king, the people turned to Omri and said, "We don't want Zimri. We want *you* to be our king." When Zimri heard that the people were rebelling against him, he lit his palace on fire and took his own life after reigning only seven days.

1 Kings 16:19–24

For his sins which he sinned in doing evil in the sight of the LORD, in walking in the way of Jeroboam, and in his sin which he did, to make Israel to sin. Now the rest of the acts of Zimri, and his treason that he wrought, are they not written in the book of the chronicles of the kings of Israel? Then were the people of Israel divided into two parts: half of the people followed Tibni the son of Ginath, to make him king; and half followed Omri. But the people that followed Omri prevailed against the people that followed Tibni the son of Ginath: so Tibni died, and Omri reigned. In the thirty and first year of Asa king of Judah began Omri to reign over Israel, twelve years: six years reigned he in Tirzah. And he bought the hill Samaria of Shemer for two talents of silver, and built on the hill, and called the name of the city which he built, after the name of Shemer, owner of the hill, Samaria.

With the palace burned by Zimri's hand, Omri found a new city from which he would reign: Samaria. Thus, Samaria became the capital city of the ten northern tribes.

1 Kings 16:25, 26

But Omri wrought evil in the eyes of the LORD, and did worse than all that were before him. For he walked in all the way of Jeroboam the son of Nebat, and in his sin wherewith he made Israel to sin, to provoke the LORD God of Israel to anger with their vanities.

Omri was a man who, like every other king of Israel, followed the foolish example of Jeroboam, idolatry, immorality, and tragedy. He died, and in his place came the most wicked king of all, one with a particular penchant for perversity, one addicted to evil . . .

1 Kings 16:27–31

Now the rest of the acts of Omri which he did, and his might that he shewed, are they not written in the book of the chronicles of the kings of Israel? So Omri slept with his fathers, and was buried in Samaria: and Ahab his son reigned in his stead. And in the thirty and eighth year of Asa king of Judah began Ahab the son of Omri to reign over Israel: and Ahab the son of Omri reigned over Israel in Samaria twenty and two years. And Ahab the son of Omri did evil in the sight of the LORD above all that were before him. And it came to pass, as if it had been a light thing for him to walk in the sins of Jeroboam the son of Nebat, that

he took to wife Jezebel the daughter of Ethbaal king of the Zidonians, and went and served Baal, and worshipped him.

Ahab, the most wicked of kings, married Jezebel, the most wicked women in known history, and introduced the worship of her god, Baal, to Israel. The god of rain, Baal was the god people worshiped in order to bring rain from heaven that the crops might be productive. Baal worship was intellectually intriguing. It also appealed to the physical senses, as immorality was part of Baal worship.

1 Kings 16:32–34
And he reared up an altar for Baal in the house of Baal, which he had built in Samaria. And Ahab made a grove; and Ahab did more to provoke the LORD God of Israel to anger than all the kings of Israel that were before him. In his days did Hiel the Bethelite build Jericho: he laid the foundation thereof in Abiram his firstborn, and set up the gates thereof in his youngest son Segub, according to the word of the LORD, which he spake by Joshua the son of Nun.

In Joshua 6:26, the Lord cursed the man who would attempt to rebuild Jericho. Here, a man named Hiel does just that, which shows either the ignorance or the contempt the people had at this time for the Word of God. In these dark, disgusting, despicable days, where king to king to king is causing greater pollution and darkness in the land of Israel, a backdrop is being painted, a stage being set, a scene is prepared for someone to burst upon the scene as a bright, shining light. And that someone is Elijah . . .

17

1 Kings 17:1
And Elijah the Tishbite, who was of the inhabitants of Gilead, said unto Ahab, As the LORD God of Israel liveth, before whom I stand, there shall not be dew nor rain these years, but according to my word.

Elijah means "Jehovah is my God." *Tishbite* means "stranger." Gilead is a rocky, rugged region that reaches heat of one hundred and twenty degrees. This man of God from the rugged desert bursts on the scene and goes into the court of Ahab, saying, "The Lord God of Israel lives." Why did he say this? Because the kings of Israel thought God had died. That's why they turned to Baal, Ashteroth, and Mammon.

Proverbs 28:1 tells us that the righteous shall be as bold as a lion. Elijah was a lion-like man. In fact, all of the bold men of Scripture spent time in the desert. Paul spent three years. Moses spent forty years. David spent numerous years in the wilderness running from Saul. Are you in desert experience tonight? Has it been four years or even forty years? Take heart, saint. You're being prepared and molded to be bold for the kingdom.

Here were Ahab and Jezebel, worshiping Baal, the god of rain, when Elijah burst in, saying, "The Lord lives and there won't be any rain."

As far as we know, Elijah wasn't commanded to do this. What gave him the audacity to make such a statement? First, he had a heart for God. He knew God's name was being blasphemed, or, at best, ignored. Secondly, he knew the history of God. Deuteronomy 11 says if the people turned away from God and served idols, God would shut up the heavens. Thirdly, Elijah was heard by God, for James tells us he prayed (5:17). If we have a heart *for* God, know the history *of* God, and are being heard *by* God in prayer, we can move in great faith, and things will happen in our lives.

1 Kings 17:2 (a)
And the word of the LORD came unto him . . .

I like this phrase because so often we talk about seeking or searching for the word of the Lord. In John 10, however, Jesus said, "My sheep hear My voice and they know Me." If you are part of His flock, if you love the Lord, I assure you that the word of the Lord will come to you. Something will be said or a Scripture will be seen that will pierce your heart or provoke your thoughts. And you'll know it's for you.

1 Kings 17:2 (b), 3
. . . saying, Get thee hence, and turn thee eastward, and hide thyself by the brook Cherith, that is before Jordan.

I don't think this was easy for Elijah. Elijah was pumped, ready for the big confrontation, ready to lose his life if necessary, to pay the price right then. He was pumped up for the big game, only to find himself temporarily benched. *Cherith* means "the cutting place." That's interesting because here was a man who was beginning to move in power and prominence and authority, and now he's being hidden away in obscurity as God "cuts him out of the picture."

Why was Elijah put in a place of isolation? I suggest one reason was for preparation. You see, there must be a Cherith before there can be a

Carmel. Before the crown, there must be the Cross. Therefore, if you're in Cherith today, a place where you're not in the limelight, perhaps it's because, like Elijah, you're being prepared for something greater ahead.

1 Kings 17:4
And it shall be, that thou shalt drink of the brook; and I have commanded the ravens to feed thee there.

Leviticus 11:15 declares that ravens were unclean birds and were to be avoided at all costs. In the Middle East, even today, ravens are always associated with doom and death. As if Elijah wasn't already dealing with enough, here, he's bombed with bread from birds that signified doom and death, all part of God's preparation process.

1 Kings 17:5–7
So he went and did according unto the word of the LORD: for he went and dwelt by the brook Cherith, that is before Jordan. And the ravens brought him bread and flesh in the morning, and bread and flesh in the evening; and he drank of the brook. And it came to pass after a while, that the brook dried up, because there had been no rain in the land.

There Elijah sat, day after week after month. And even when the brook began to dry up, he didn't move.

For topical study of 1 Kings 17:1–7 entitled "Drying Brooks," turn to page 1006.

1 Kings 17:8, 9 (a)
And the word of the LORD came unto him, saying, Arise, get thee to Zarephath, which belongeth to Zidon, and dwell there . . .

Zarephath means "refining place." Zarephath wasn't in Israel, but in the hometown of Jezebel, the center of Baal worship.

1 Kings 17:9 (b)
. . . behold, I have commanded a widow woman there to sustain thee.

This would have been incredibly humiliating. First of all, for a Jew to go into Zidon would be humiliating due to the fact that the Jews considered the Gentile nations—the Zidonians, Phoenicians, and all the groups surrounding Israel—to be dogs at best. As if that weren't bad enough, Elijah was to be supported by a woman, and a widow at that.

So here is Elijah, going to the hometown of Jezebel, the center of Baal worship, outside of Israel, in Gentile country, to a woman's home, a widow's home, and there she was going to sustain him. Talk about refining!

1 Kings 17:10
So he arose and went to Zarephath. And when he came to the gate of the city, behold, the widow woman was there gathering of sticks: and he called to her, and said, Fetch me, I pray thee, a little water in a vessel, that I may drink.

This widow was a wonderful woman. I like her because she was industrious. She was down to a handful of meal and a little bit of oil. Yet she wasn't simply waiting for fate to run its course. She was working out in the field, gathering sticks, doing her best. As she gathered, she lifted her eyes and saw a man walking across her property in a dusty robe and sunburned face. "Give me some water," he said. And she did a wonderful thing—she went and got it for him. Water was scarce in that time. And yet she did something I would encourage us to learn from—in the time of her trouble, trial, and difficulty, she gave what she could to someone else.

That's always the secret of life. Haven't you found that to be true? Get your eyes off your own little problems and see someone else crossing the property of this world who is hurting, thirsty, and dry. When you're feeling down yourself, look across the property of your life and you'll see someone with parched lips and sunburned face who is in greater need than you, and reach out to them.

1 Kings 17:11
And as she was going to fetch it, he called to her, and said, Bring me, I pray thee, a morsel of bread in thine hand.

"Wait a minute," this woman could have said. "It's difficult enough for me to share water. But now you're asking me to give you bread on top of that?" Isn't that just like life? You give out to somebody and think you're really doing something nice when, no sooner do you finish, than the person says, "Wait a minute, I want more . . ."

1 Kings 17:12–14
And she said, As the LORD thy God liveth, I have not a cake, but an handful of meal in a barrel, and a little oil in a cruse: and, behold, I am gathering two sticks, that I may go in and dress it for me and my son, that

we may eat it, and die. And Elijah said unto her, Fear not; go and do as thou hast said: but make me thereof a little cake first, and bring it unto me, and after make for thee and for thy son. For thus saith the LORD God of Israel, The barrel of meal shall not waste, neither shall the cruse of oil fail, until the day that the LORD sendeth rain upon the earth.

"Don't worry," Elijah said. "Make me the cake first, and afterwards, there will be a continual supply of meal and oil for you and your son."

I can almost see the widow's wheels turning. *Wait a minute,* she must have thought, *why don't you fill the barrel and the oil jar first—then I'll be happy to give you a cake or two or three.* But the Lord doesn't work that way.

True sacrifice is always out of survival, never out of surplus. We have a tendency to say, "Lord, if You bless me, then I'll give. If You bless us, then we'll move out." That's exactly backwards. You give first, then the blessing is released. Seek ye first the kingdom of God and His righteousness—and *then* all these things shall be added unto you (Matthew 6:33).That's a hard one for us.

"Have the priests put their feet in the water," the Lord said to Joshua, "and the river will part."

Joshua could have said, "Lord, part the water first, then we'll be happy to step in." But he didn't. He obeyed, and the river parted (Joshua 3).

The Father is determined to make us men and women of faith. And He'll put us in situation after situation where faith must be exercised. It takes no faith to give out of surplus. It takes tremendous faith to give out of survival—when you just don't have it—whether it's time, finances, or love.

1 Kings 17:15, 16
And she went and did according to the saying of Elijah: and she, and he, and her house, did eat many days. And the barrel of meal wasted not, neither did the cruse of oil fail, according to the word of the LORD, which he spake by Elijah.

The widow believed. She stepped out in faith, and God blessed. Her needs were met. The Lord will not be a debtor to any man. If you are giving, sharing, sacrificing, He will never be in your debt. He'll more than make it up.

1 Kings 17:17, 18
And it came to pass after these things, that the son of the woman, the mistress of the house, fell sick; and his sickness was so sore, that there was no breath left in him. And she said unto Elijah, What have I to do with thee, O thou man of God? art thou come unto me to call my sin to remembrance, and to slay my son?

Even though the widow experienced a miracle, she was not insulated from further difficulties and problems. Although the meal was always available and the oil was flowing, still sickness came upon her son. And in her frustration, this woman lashed out at Elijah.

1 Kings 17:19
And he said unto her, Give me thy son. And he took him out of her bosom, and carried him up into a loft, where he abode, and laid him upon his own bed.

Elijah didn't retaliate. He didn't fight back. He simply took the widow's son out of sight. Sometimes people who move in the arena of the miraculous take ads out in papers that read: Miracle Meeting Tonight. Don't Miss It. Elijah doesn't do that. He takes this child away from the eyes of people and begins to minister in private.

1 Kings 17:20
And he cried unto the LORD, and said, O LORD my God, hast thou also brought evil upon the widow with whom I sojourn, by slaying her son?

Elijah is not accusing God but inquiring of God. "What is going on here, Lord?" he asks.

1 Kings 17:21, 22
And he stretched himself upon the child three times, and cried unto the LORD, and said, O LORD my God, I pray thee, let this child's soul come into him again. And the LORD heard the voice of Elijah; and the soul of the child came into him again, and he revived.

A dead body was brought back to life. How? In two ways. First there was prayer *for* the dead. Secondly, there was contact *with* the dead as Elijah stretched himself on the dead boy's body, not just once or twice, but three times.

Dear parent, is your child spiritually dead? Dear sister, is your husband spiritually dead, walking in the way of God? Are your parents far from the Lord? Is a friend lost and headed for eternal damnation? If there's a dead corpse in your life, the solution is rather simple: pray for them and establish loving contact with them. Pray and love, and it will surprise you what the Lord will do when we lay down our lives for the lost, when we pray fervently and love practically.

1 Kings 17:23
And Elijah took the child, and brought him down out of the chamber into the house,

and delivered him unto his mother: and Elijah said, See, thy son liveth.

This woman who was once depressed is now delighted. This woman who was once jaded is now joyful. This woman who was once frustrated is now free because her son had been revived. Look around and you'll see a world that's jaded, frustrated, and sad because they're not walking with Jesus Christ. What a privilege is ours to be able to tell them that because the Son lives, they can live, too.

1 Kings 17:24
And the woman said to Elijah, Now by this I know that thou art a man of God, and that the word of the LORD in thy mouth is truth.

It wasn't the miracle of the meal and oil that persuaded the widow of Zarephath that Elijah's God was real. It was resurrection. The same is still true. What is going to convince your world of the reality of your God? Resurrection changed lives.

DRYING BROOKS

A Topical Study of 1 KINGS 17:1–7

They were dark days indeed. Fifty-eight years earlier, king Solomon had passed off the scene. And after he died, the kingdom of Israel was split in two. The south was ruled by a cruel and callous king named Rehoboam. The north was ruled by a gifted but godless king named Jeroboam. After Jeroboam died, there was a series of brutal and bloody revolutions in the northern kingdom. Increasingly sinful and sinister rulers rose to power. And the evil and wickedness reached a crescendo under the reign of King Ahab.

Meanwhile, in the rough and rugged region of Gilead, God was preparing a powerful prophet, a man who would stand in the presence of the Lord, a man who would speak with the power of the Lord, a man who was familiar with the Holy Scriptures, a man who was filled with the Holy Spirit.

Elijah bursts on the scene, confronts wicked king Ahab and proclaims, "It shall not rain according to my word." Our text does not tell us that God told Elijah to do this. Elijah, a man of faith, went into the presence of Ahab and said, It's not going to rain according to my word. What, then, gave him such faith? How could he be so certain?

I suggest three reasons. First, *Elijah had a heart for God.* He wasn't doing this to make history or headlines. In fact, he could have very well lost his head. But he loved God so much that he was willing to risk his neck to go into the presence of Ahab and make this incredible, prophetic prediction. Elijah had a heart for God and God honored that.

Secondly, *Elijah knew the history of God,* for he was a man familiar with the Scriptures. He knew the prophecy of Deuteronomy 11:16, 17 that if the people turned away from God, the heavens would dry up. He must also have known the story of Joshua 10—when the sun stood still at Joshua's command.

Thirdly, *Elijah was heard by God.* James 5 says Elijah was a man of like passions—a man just like us—and yet he prayed and the heavens were shut up. In other words, he was heard by God. James goes on to say that the effectual, fervent prayer of a righteous man avails much. The reason Elijah was so powerful in public was because he was prayerful in private. If you have a heart for God, if you learn the history of God, and if you are being heard by God, you, too, will affect your situation radically. Things will happen all around you. God's power will flow through you if your heart is for Him, if you're familiar with His Word, if you're being heard by Him.

The Lord called Elijah away in order to both protect and provide for him. Ahab would doubtless grow increasingly angry as the drought wore on. So the Lord temporarily placed Elijah out of his reach.

In addition to protection, provision would be made for Elijah as the Lord sent ravens to fly over his head and bomb him with bread. I'm sure Elijah thought, *That idea is for the birds! It'll never work. The birds themselves will be hungry. They'll eat the bread.* Why did the Lord do this? Because if men would have brought bread to Elijah, they would have the tendency to betray him and to blow his cover. If animals had brought the bread to Elijah, they could have been tracked. But birds? Who would ever think of birds! God provided miraculously, but also naturally. For, although the ravens brought bread, Elijah was to draw his own water. In this, I believe we see the perfect balance of the methods and heart of God, on one hand, working miraculously, on the other, working naturally. He still works this way. We do what we can do, and He comes alongside and does what we can't, stretching us, growing us, maturing us, and yet showing us all the while that it is He who is in control.

When the brook began to dry up, Elijah found himself in an interesting situation. As he sat there, day after month after year, he saw the flow slow down. He saw the depth decrease and finally disappear altogether. But Elijah didn't panic.

Are you beside a drying, dying brook? Is there a relationship that is drying up? Are your finances drying up? Is your physical strength drying up? If you're wondering why the brook to which you thought the Lord led you is drying up, I want you to see three possible reasons . . .

Getting Ahead of God

First, the Lord would restrain us from getting ahead of Him. You see, had Elijah panicked and moved prematurely, he would have missed a miracle in the making. It was on the day that a widow in Zarephath was to use her very last bit of meal that Elijah was led by the Lord to show up on the scene and do a miracle. And such an important miracle was it that Jesus Himself later referred to it (Luke 4:26).

Feeling the call of God on his life, Moses went out on his own ahead of God and killed an Egyptian who was beating up an Israelite. When his crime was discovered and the Israelites themselves turned on him, he ran for his life and spent forty years in the desert—all because he got ahead of God.

In order to restrain us from getting ahead of Him, God sometimes restricts us, and that gives me peace. I can say, "Thank You, Lord. Even though the brook is drying up, You're using this to slow me down, to keep me from getting ahead of You."

Getting to Know God

Secondly, the drying brook allows us the opportunity to get to know God. You see, even while the brook was drying up in Cherith, the bread was coming down. And every day, Elijah was no doubt reminded of the incredible power and provision of God. When your brook is drying up, when relationships are going amok, when finances are absent and problems are present, it forces you to look into the Bread of the Word and receive manna from the Father.

It was not in the days of prosperity and ease that you grew closest to the Lord. It was in the days of difficulty and trial that you found yourself searching the Scriptures. In the day of prosperity it's easy for us to set the dial to "cruise." But in the day of adversity, we find ourselves searching the Scriptures and we are renewed in the knowledge of God.

Getting Away from God

In John 4, Jesus said to the woman at the well, "Give Me to drink."

"How is it that You, being a Jew, ask me, a Samaritan to give You drink?" the woman said.

"If you knew the water I had, you would ask Me to give you living water," Jesus said, "for whoever drinks of the water I give shall never thirst again."

Physical, temporal water will never bring satisfaction. If you are thirsty today, I ask you, where are you drawing your water from? If you are feeling drought in your soul, where are you drawing water from? Have you gone back to the old watering hole? If so, it is sure you will thirst again. If you are looking to your job to bring you satisfaction of soul, you are barking up the wrong tree. If you are looking to your husband or wife to satisfy your soul, you are amiss. If you are looking to your ministry to bring you fulfillment, you are in for frustration. Jesus said, "Whoever drinks of that water shall thirst again."

Ministry is for one purpose, to point you to Jesus Christ, where you'll drink of Him. Relationships are for one purpose, to draw you together to Jesus Christ. If you are drinking of any other water, even though it might seem good, it will not satisfy.

"If any man thirst, let him come unto *Me* and drink." That is the invitation of our Lord Jesus. Beside the drying brooks of relationships, of finances, of health, of popularity I am continually reminded that it is only Jesus that can satisfy. With Him, we never thirst again. The brook dries up to remind you that there is no other way, that there is no one else, that there is no other thing that can fulfill you apart from your personal love relationship with Jesus Christ. That is all that will satisfy you. If you love Jesus and walk with Him, you will be filled with His joy. If you are looking to anything else, you will thirst.

My prayer is that when you're beside the drying brook, you might rejoice, knowing God is restraining you from getting ahead of Him, renewing you in your knowledge of Him, or reminding you that no one else can but Him. Don't panic. May God grant you understanding as you sit there and wait until you hear Him say, "Arise."

18

1 Kings 18:1–4

And it came to pass after many days, that the word of the LORD came to Elijah in the third year, saying, Go, shew thyself unto Ahab; and I will send rain upon the earth. And Elijah went to shew himself unto Ahab. And there was a sore famine in Samaria. And Ahab called Obadiah, which was the governor of his house. (Now Obadiah feared the LORD greatly: For it was so, when Jezebel cut off the prophets of the LORD, that Obadiah took an hundred prophets, and hid them by fifty in a cave, and fed them with bread and water.)

Obadiah is an interesting character. His name means "servant of God," and yet he was working for a very wicked king—Ahab. Although some scholars question Obadiah's integrity, I'm not so sure we can judge him so easily. After all, in Philippians 4:22, rather than condemning the believers who were in Caesar's household, Paul greets them. Sometimes God plants believers in ungodly situations to be a light. Even though Obadiah was working under Ahab, even though he was not powerful like Elijah, even though he wasn't a prophet, he certainly was profitable to the prophets, for he hid them from murderous Jezebel.

You might not be powerful like Elijah. But you can be profitable like Obadiah. When asked the secret of his spiritual strength, Spurgeon said, "I have a people who pray for me." You might not be able to preach, but you can pray for those who do. You might not be able to cross the seas as a missionary, but you can pray for them. You might not be able to go door to door, witnessing, but you can pray. I believe that those who are Obadiahs—faithfully working behind the scenes—are not only profitable now, but will be greatly rewarded in heaven.

1 Kings 18:5, 6

And Ahab said unto Obadiah, Go into the land, unto all fountains of water, and unto all brooks: peradventure we may find grass to save the horses and mules alive, that we lose not all the beasts. So they divided the land between them to pass throughout it: Ahab went one way by himself, and Obadiah went another way by himself.

Ahab sought relief from the famine, but he failed to seek the reason for the famine. That's so often true of us. We seek relief from a problem, but we don't get to the root of the problem, asking the Lord what He wants to show us in it.

1 Kings 18:7–12 (a)

And as Obadiah was in the way, behold, Elijah met him: and he knew him, and fell on his face, and said, Art thou that my lord Elijah? And he answered him, I am: go, tell thy lord, Behold, Elijah is here. And he said, What have I sinned, that thou wouldest deliver thy servant into the hand of Ahab, to slay me? As the LORD thy God liveth, there is no nation or kingdom, whither my lord hath not sent to seek thee: and when they said, He is not there; he took an oath of the kingdom and nation, that they found thee not. And now thou sayest, Go, tell thy lord, Behold, Elijah is here. And it shall come to pass, as soon as I am gone from thee, that the Spirit of the LORD shall carry thee whither I know not; and so when I come and tell Ahab, and he cannot find thee, he shall slay me . . .

Knowing how desperately Ahab wanted to find Elijah, Obadiah was afraid that no sooner would he tell Ahab of Elijah's whereabouts than the Lord would hide Elijah once again, leaving Obadiah holding the bag in the face of a furious king.

1 Kings 18:12 (b), 13

. . . but I thy servant fear the LORD from my youth. Was it not told my lord what I did when Jezebel slew the prophets of the LORD, how I hid an hundred men of the LORD's prophets by fifty in a cave, and fed them with bread and water?

Obadiah feared the Lord from his youth, which indicates he had believing parents. In our glorious age of grace, we emphasize the love of the Lord, as well we should. Obadiah, on the other hand, was taught to fear the Lord. Along with the love of the Lord, we need to teach our kids the fear of the Lord, for it is the fear of the Lord that is the beginning of wisdom (Proverbs 9:10). To fear the Lord doesn't mean to be afraid of Him. Rather, it means to realize the power, righteousness, and holiness of God, and the foolishness and fallacy of disobeying Him.

1 Kings 18:14–17
And now thou sayest, Go, tell thy lord, Behold, Elijah is here: and he shall slay me. And Elijah said, As the LORD of hosts liveth, before whom I stand, I will surely shew myself unto him to day. So Obadiah went to meet Ahab, and told him: and Ahab went to meet Elijah. And it came to pass, when Ahab saw Elijah, that Ahab said unto him, Art thou he that troubleth Israel?

When things go bad, God or God's people always seem to get blamed, as evidenced not only by Ahab's question but also by the fact that insurance companies have referred to earthquakes, tornadoes, and hurricanes as "acts of God."

1 Kings 18:18
And he answered, I have not troubled Israel; but thou, and thy father's house, in that ye have forsaken the commandments of the LORD, and thou hast followed Baalim.

"You're the problem, Ahab," Elijah said. And then he set out to prove it . . .

1 Kings 18:19–21
Now therefore send, and gather to me all Israel unto mount Carmel, and the prophets of Baal four hundred and fifty, and the prophets of the groves four hundred, which eat at Jezebel's table. So Ahab sent unto all the children of Israel, and gathered the prophets together unto mount Carmel. And Elijah came unto all the people, and said, How long halt ye between two opinions? if the LORD be God, follow him: but if Baal, then follow him. And the people answered him not a word.

The word "halt" speaks of first standing on one leg, then shifting weight to the other. In other words, the Israelites worshiped the Lord one minute and Baal the next. A double-minded man is unstable in all his ways, James tells us (1:8). "Because you're neither hot nor cold but lukewarm, I'll spew you out of My mouth," Jesus said to the church of Laodicea (see Revelation 3:16). The Lord doesn't want His people "halting" between two opinions, serving Him one day and serving the god of pleasure or prosperity the next.

1 Kings 18:22
Then said Elijah unto the people, I, even I only, remain a prophet of the LORD; but Baal's prophets are four hundred and fifty men.

As we will see in chapter 19, it was not true that Elijah was the only prophet of the Lord.

1 Kings 18:23, 24
Let them therefore give us two bullocks; and let them choose one bullock for themselves, and cut it in pieces, and lay it on wood, and put no fire under: and I will dress the other bullock, and lay it on wood, and put no fire under: And call ye on the name of your gods, and I will call on the name of the LORD: and the God that answereth by fire, let him be God. And all the people answered and said, It is well spoken.

Elijah calls for a bullock because Leviticus 16 says before any minister could enter into the holy place; he first had to offer a bullock for his own sin. Elijah was aware of his own sinfulness. He knew he couldn't call down fire from heaven on his own merit or according to his own righteousness.

Elijah offered a bullock as a sacrifice for his own sin. This is a key to understanding this story because we can think, "Why can't *I* call down fire from heaven? Why don't *I* see miracles happen?" The answer is that we're not worthy of seeing anything happen in the spiritual realm. Why? Because we're sinners. Our appeal to the Lord can never be made on the basis of our spirituality, but only on the basis of His mercy and grace.

1 Kings 18:25, 26
And Elijah said unto the prophets of Baal, Choose you one bullock for yourselves, and dress it first; for ye are many; and call on the name of your gods, but put no fire under. And they took the bullock which was given them, and they dressed it, and called on the name of Baal from morning even until noon, saying, O Baal, hear us. But there was no voice, nor any that answered. And they leaped upon the altar which was made.

These prophets were leaping and screaming and trying to get the attention of their god because they knew he would not otherwise answer. Faith, on the other hand, is quiet. Even in our own day, commotion and emotion all too often indicate a lack of devotion.

1 Kings 18:27–30
And it came to pass at noon, that Elijah mocked them, and said, Cry aloud: for he is a god; either he is talking, or he is pursuing, or he is in a journey, or peradventure he sleepeth, and must be awaked. And they cried aloud, and cut themselves after their manner with knives and lancets, till the blood gushed out upon them. And it came to pass, when midday was past, and they prophesied until the time of the offering of the evening sacrifice, that there was neither voice, nor any to answer, nor any that regarded. And Elijah said unto all the people, Come near unto me. And all the people came near unto him. And he repaired the altar of the LORD that was broken down.

After Baal ignored even the blood of his own prophets, it was Elijah's turn. He began by repairing the altar of the Lord.

1 Kings 18:31, 32 (a)
And Elijah took twelve stones, according to the number of the tribes of the sons of Jacob, unto whom the word of the LORD came, saying, Israel shall be thy name: And with the stones he built an altar in the name of the LORD . . .

Twelve stones—one for each tribe—signified that Jehovah was God of the entire nation of Israel. In Exodus 20, God said very specifically that His altar was to be made of rough stones, stones without carving or engraving. This is because, from the very outset, the simple stone altar was to point to a rock called Golgotha, where the Lamb of God would be sacrificed not only for the sins of the Twelve Tribes of Israel, but for the sins of the whole world.

1 Kings 18:32 (b)–35
. . . and he made a trench about the altar, as great as would contain two measures of seed. And he put the wood in order, and cut the bullock in pieces, and laid him on the wood, and said, Fill four barrels with water, and pour it on the burnt sacrifice, and on the wood. And he said, Do it the second time. And they did it the second time. And he said, Do it the third time. And they did it the third time. And the water ran round about the altar; and he filled the trench also with water.

Four barrels of water filled three times, twelve barrels, one for each tribe. In a time of drought, where did Elijah get twelve barrels of water? Mt. Carmel overlooks the Mediterranean Sea. Thus, the water could have been taken from the sea. If so, it would have been salt water. According to Leviticus 2, no sacrifice was to be made without salt. And here's salt water being poured upon the sacrifice. In Middle Eastern culture, in addition to flavoring, salt was used as a medicine to heal wounds and as a preservative to keep meat from putrefying.

"You are the salt of the earth," Jesus said (Matthew 5:13). As believers, we are to be agents of healing and preserving in addition to creating a thirst within people for the living water Jesus offers. The sacrifice Elijah offered ultimately pointed to salvation through faith in Jesus Christ, the sacrificial Lamb. The salt spoke of the reality of salvation seen through the evidence of a life of faith. "Faith without works is dead," James declares (2:26) because sacrifice without salt is invalid. You may say you believe in Jesus, but if there's no salt in your life—no preserving, no healing, no impact—you have reason to question whether you're really saved.

1 Kings 18:36–38
And it came to pass at the time of the offering of the evening sacrifice, that Elijah the prophet came near, and said, LORD God of Abraham, Isaac, and of Israel, let it be known this day that thou art God in Israel, and that I am thy servant, and that I have done all these things at thy word. Hear me, O LORD, hear me, that this people may know that thou art the LORD God, and that thou hast turned their heart back again. Then the fire of the LORD fell, and consumed the burnt sacrifice, and the wood, and the stones, and the dust, and licked up the water that was in the trench.

When did the fire fall? After Elijah prayed, during the time of the evening sacrifice. The evening and morning sacrifice speak of a consistent devotional life. I call your attention to three characteristics of Elijah's prayer . . .

First, it was abbreviated. Our prayers needn't be lengthy, but they must be constant. Elijah's prayer took less than twelve seconds to pray. Secondly, notice Elijah's attitude. "I am Thy servant," he said. "I'm not here to dictate to You. I'm not here to try and press my point. I am simply Your servant." Finally, notice Elijah's authority. "I have done these things at Thy Word," he said. In John 15, Jesus said that if we abide in Him and His words abide in us, we will ask what we will and it will be done. The one who is effective in prayer and successful in seeking the power of the Lord isn't the one who prays lofty and lengthy prayers. It's the one who has the heart of a servant and who stands on the Word.

1 Kings 18:39
And when all the people saw it, they fell on their faces: and they said, The Lord, he is the God; the Lord, he is the God.

Tragically, although the people acknowledged the Lord as God, they didn't acknowledge Him as *their* God.

1 Kings 18:40
And Elijah said unto them, Take the prophets of Baal; let not one of them escape. And they took them: and Elijah brought them down to the brook Kishon, and slew them there.

The prophets of Baal, finally seen as idolaters, were sentenced to die not by the word of Elijah, but by the Word of God (Deuteronomy 18:20).

1 Kings 18:41
And Elijah said unto Ahab, Get thee up, eat and drink; for there is a sound of abundance of rain.

We often speak of "eyes of faith." Here, Elijah had "ears of faith," hearing the sound of rain before a drop had fallen.

1 Kings 18:42–44
So Ahab went up to eat and to drink. And Elijah went up to the top of Carmel; and he cast himself down upon the earth, and put his face between his knees, And said to his servant, Go up now, look toward the sea. And he went up, and looked, and said, There is nothing. And he said, Go again seven times. And it came to pass at the seventh time, that he said, Behold, there ariseth a little cloud out of the sea, like a man's hand. And he said, Go up, say unto Ahab, Prepare thy chariot, and get thee down, that the rain stop thee not.

According to James 5:17, Elijah's secret was prayer. In public, his prayer was short. But here we see him praying in private, and his prayer takes on an entirely different dimension. He puts his head between his knees and prays. In Middle Eastern cultures, this was the birthing position. Here we see a man of prayer who prayed quickly in public, but in private prayed with intensity and travail.

Do you know what it means to birth something in prayer? Have you experienced what it means to press in and pray through? Do you pray once or twice or three times and give up if nothing happens? That's too often my attitude. Not so with Elijah. He prayed until something was birthed. How I love to be around people who love to pray. It's hard work. Jesus prayed in Gethsemane with such birthing intensity that His face sweat blood. Do we even know what it means to keep asking, keep seeking, keep knocking? Elijah prayed and didn't give up.

Is your marriage a burden tonight? Have you prayed to the place of sweat? Are you experiencing tension over some situation? Have you prayed time and time again? Somehow, dear friend, the Lord teaching us to press in and pray is preparing us for the billions of years that lie beyond. He's not teasing you or making it hard on you. He's developing you and strengthening you. The reason the Lord is stretching us in faith and teaching us in prayer and forcing us to mature is because He's training us for eternity.

Elijah saw a little cloud and said, "Tell Ahab to get moving. A storm's coming!"

"Wait a minute," we say. "A little cloud doesn't mean anything." Oh, but it does to a man of faith.

1 Kings 18:45, 46
And it came to pass in the mean while, that the heaven was black with clouds and wind, and there was a great rain. And Ahab rode, and went to Jezreel. And the hand of the Lord was on Elijah; and he girded up his loins, and ran before Ahab to the entrance of Jezreel.

Here is Elijah, breaking the world's record, arriving at Jezreel ahead of Ahab's chariot. But I think this was a huge mistake. You see, Elijah had gone from Cherith, the place of cutting, to Zarephath, the place of refining, to Carmel, the place of victory and confrontation. Now he's running, but this time, he's not being directed by the Lord. Up to this point, Elijah had obeyed the Lord to the letter. But the Lord didn't tell him to run to Jezreel.

The same thing can happen in our own lives. When we experience an element of power or blessing in our lives, if we're not careful, we can begin to move on the basis of our own desires or vision. Things can still happen, but as Elijah will discover, the side effects can be devastating . . .

19

1 Kings 19:1, 2
And Ahab told Jezebel all that Elijah had done, and withal how he had slain all the prophets with the sword. Then Jezebel sent a messenger unto Elijah, saying, So let the gods do to me, and more also, if I make not thy life as the life of one of them by to morrow about this time.

Having witnessed a whole series of miracles, Ahab still does not give credit to God. Instead, he tells Jezebel all the things *Elijah* had done. Jezebel's response was to vow to destroy Elijah.

1 Kings 19:3, 4
And when he saw that, he arose, and went for his life, and came to Beer-sheba, which belongeth to Judah, and left his servant there. But he himself went a day's journey into the wilderness, and came and sat down under a juniper tree: and he requested for himself that he might die; and said, It is enough; now, O LORD, take away my life; for I am not better than my fathers.

Elijah, the Iron Man of God, was derailed by a woman. This prophet who took on the nation, was afraid by a woman. Consequently, he ran for his life because he was not in the place the Spirit directed.

1 Kings 19:5–8
And as he lay and slept under a juniper tree, behold, then an angel touched him, and said unto him, Arise and eat. And he looked, and, behold, there was a cake baken on the coals, and a cruse of water at his head. And he did eat and drink, and laid him down again. And the angel of the LORD came again the second time, and touched him, and said, Arise and eat; because the journey is too great for thee. And he arose, and did eat and drink, and went in the strength of that meat forty days and forty nights unto Horeb the mount of God.

Mount Horeb—or Mount Sinai—is the place where Moses saw the burning bush. It is the place the Law of the Lord was given. It is the place where the sky thundered and the earth shook. It was the place where things happened.

1 Kings 19:9
And he came thither unto a cave, and lodged there; and, behold, the word of the LORD came to him, and he said unto him, What doest thou here, Elijah?

"Why are you in a cave?" the Lord asks Elijah. "Why are you hiding out, holding back? Why are you in this place of discouragement and depression?"

Such a question is one the Lord would ask of many of us: what are you doing holed-up in the cave of self-pity? F. B. Meyer, renowned Bible scholar, said that self-pity is the most grievous of all sins. Self-pity says to the Lord, "I don't like what You're doing in my life."

Self-pity is nothing more than rebellion, for if I feel sorry for myself, I am actually saying, "God, although Your Word says You are love, I don't buy it. Although Your Word says You are good, I don't believe it. Although Your Word says You are light, I don't see it. Although the Word says You are my Father, I don't relate to it."

1 Kings 19:10–13
And he said, I have been very jealous for the LORD God of hosts: for the children of Israel have forsaken thy covenant, thrown down thine altars, and slain thy prophets with the sword; and I, even I only, am left; and they seek my life, to take it away. And he said, Go forth, and stand upon the mount before the LORD. And, behold, the LORD passed by, and a great and strong wind rent the mountains, and brake in pieces the rocks before the LORD; but the LORD was not in the wind: and after the wind an earthquake; but the LORD was not in the earthquake: And after the earthquake a fire; but the LORD was not in the fire: and after the fire a still small voice. And it was so, when Elijah heard it, that he wrapped his face in his mantle, and went out, and stood in the entering in of the cave. And, behold, there came a voice unto him, and said, What doest thou here, Elijah?

Elijah was on the same mount upon which God had spoken to Moses through a burning bush and where He had given him the Law. Therefore, perhaps Elijah expected the Lord to work in big ways in his situation, as well. Surely the Lord would do something to stop Ahab and Jezebel, he thought. Maybe He would zap Jezebel with lightning and swallow Ahab with an earthquake.

One of the reasons we get depressed is because the Lord doesn't seem to be doing something big. He's not shaking us up with experiences. He's not firing us up with the miraculous. "Lord, where are You?" we cry. "Why aren't You doing anything?"

As He did to Elijah, the Lord says to us, "I'm not in the wind, the earthquake, or the fire. I'm in the still, small voice, just whispering My will and My Word in your heart, leading you one step at a time, one day at a time, causing the circumstances in your life to work on you and direct you and guide you." Elijah had to learn that God was not necessarily going to work in the way, at the time, in the manner he recommended. And so must we.

I am increasingly aware of the Lord working in still, small ways, that He's not panicking, that He's not frustrated, that He's not trying to bomb and blast, but that He just works in spite of me. Listen. God will speak to you, as well. He will direct you through His still, small voice.

1 Kings 19:14
And he said, I have been very jealous for the LORD God of hosts: because the children of Israel have forsaken thy covenant, thrown down thine altars, and slain thy prophets with the sword; and I, even I only, am left; and they seek my life, to take it away.

This is word for word what Elijah said in verse 10. He had his argument down pat.

1 Kings 19:15–18
And the LORD said unto him, Go, return on thy way to the wilderness of Damascus: and when thou comest, anoint Hazael to be king over Syria: And Jehu the son of Nimshi shalt thou anoint to be king over Israel: and Elisha the son of Shaphat of Abel-meholah shalt thou anoint to be prophet in thy room. And it shall come to pass, that him that escapeth the sword of Hazael shall Jehu slay: and him that escapeth from the sword of Jehu shall Elisha slay. Yet I have left me seven thousand in Israel, all the knees which have not bowed unto Baal, and every mouth which hath not kissed him.

"Crawl out of your cave, Elijah," the Lord said. "Get going again. There's work to be done."

For topical study of 1 Kings 19:1–18, see "Dealing with Depression" below.

1 Kings 19:19–21 (a)
So he departed thence, and found Elisha the son of Shaphat, who was plowing with twelve yoke of oxen before him, and he with the twelfth: and Elijah passed by him, and cast his mantle upon him. And he left the oxen, and ran after Elijah, and said, Let me, I pray thee, kiss my father and my mother, and then I will follow thee. And he said unto him, Go back again: for what have I done to thee? And he returned back from him, and took a yoke of oxen, and slew them, and boiled their flesh with the instruments of the oxen, and gave unto the people, and they did eat . . .

Leaving his pity party behind, Elijah was told to disciple a young man named Elisha. Elisha was evidently a rich man based on the number of oxen he had. But he was also humble, as evidenced by the fact that he took the position at the back of the pack. In addition to being rich and humble, Elisha was also determined. When he knew that Elijah wanted to disciple him, he took the very instruments of his livelihood, his oxen, and sacrificed them.

"No man, after putting his hand to the plow, who looks back is fit for the kingdom of God," Jesus said (see Luke 9:62). Accepting Jesus' call to be His disciple is a commitment with no turning back. You burn your bridges, sacrifice the oxen, burn the yokes, and keep going. The road becomes rough and bumpy; there are tests, trials, and challenges to be sure, but the man or woman who makes an impact for the kingdom is the one who says, "My hand is on the plow. I'm not turning back."

1 Kings 19:21 (b)
. . . Then he arose, and went after Elijah, and ministered unto him.

Elisha would spend the next six years serving Elijah. In 2 Kings 3, he was called one who simply poured water on the hands of Elijah. Why was the Lord able to use this man so greatly? Because his heart was so right. Every single person I have known who has been used by the Lord has been more than willing to go through great seasons of "pouring water" on someone else's hands, willing to be a servant. Then, as they were faithful in the small things, the Lord allowed them to minister over more things. How I pray that we might be willing to go through seasons of simply serving, saying, "Lord, it's unto You that I do this task." Elisha was such a man.

DEALING WITH DEPRESSION

A Topical Study of 1 KINGS 19:1–18

Elijah: The name is synonymous with strength. Throughout the ages, he has been called the prophet of power, the Iron Man of God. The days of Elijah were dark, disgusting, despicable days. Carnal king Ahab and his wicked wife Jezebel led the nation of Israel into the folly of idolatry. The people plummeted into pollution beyond belief. The altars of God were replaced by the idols to Baal and Ashteroth, gods of the intellect and sensuality.

In those dark days, Elijah the prophet appeared and stormed into the court of Ahab, saying, "It's not going to rain until I say so." This powerful prophet proclaimed that a judgment was coming upon the nation, that Israel would be afflicted with drought. And for three years, the burning, blistering sun ravaged the crops of Canaan. The people grew hungry. Many, many died.

Elijah was hid away first by a brook at Cherith, and later on he was sent to Zarephath where he lived with a widow. At the end of that three-year period, he sought Ahab and confronted him face to face. There was an authority in his voice, a power in his countenance that caused Ahab to back down. Then Elijah threw out the challenge: Gather the prophets of Baal on Mt. Carmel. Let us both offer sacrifice, one to Baal and one to God. And let the true and living God respond by sending fire from heaven. Four hundred and fifty prophets of Baal built their altar on Mt. Carmel and began to call upon Baal, asking him to prove he was indeed the real god. But Baal didn't answer. So they began to cry louder, to shred their skin, to cut themselves, and to beat themselves with rocks. The hours went by, but still there was no fire.

At the end of the day, Elijah said, "It's my turn." And he prayed a simple prayer to the Lord, a prayer that took only a few seconds to utter. No sooner did he say, "Amen," than fire came down from heaven that not only consumed the bullock, but burned the altar as well. And the people knew then that Jehovah was the true and living God. Elijah then called for the capture of the prophets of Baal. And Elijah slew all four hundred and fifty prophets of Baal.

Then Elijah assumed a posture of prayer and prayed for rain. Seven times he prayed with fervency. First, only a cloud appeared in the sky. But then the rain came down.

Elijah was truly a man of strength, a prophet of power. But in our text, we see this Iron Man of God, this incredibly strong individual, at a place of severe depression. James says Elijah was a man "subject to like passions as we are" (5:17). In other words, he was just like us. That is, he experienced weaknesses even as we do. Here was a man who stopped the skies from raining, called down fire from heaven, prayed and it flooded, and yet suddenly we see him in a cave.

The Lord came to him and said, "What are you doing here, Elijah? Why are you in a cave?" And I believe the Lord would say that same word to some of us. "Why are you in a cave, the slough of despondency, the cave of discouragement?"

Like Elijah, we all deal with depression from time to time. I believe our text gives us an important insight on how we might do so victoriously . . .

Symptoms of Depression

First, what are the symptoms of depression? In our text, we see the first symptom is the exaggeration of problems. You know you are moving in a place of depression when you find yourself exaggerating your problems. Elijah had stormed into the courts of Ahab, telling him it wouldn't rain. Elijah confronted four hundred and fifty prophets of Baal. He had faced problems before. But when one woman said, "I'm going to get you," he panicked. "I want to die," he said. "Lord, just take me home. She's after me." And that is what happens when we find ourselves moving into depression. Problems that previously would have been no sweat loom large over us. In the time of discouragement, things that are rather minor can take on huge dimensions.

Secondly, there was an evaluation of his person. First, he put himself down. "I am not better than my fathers," he said. Yet his fathers were idolaters. He was looking inward, and whenever you look inward, you'll put yourself down. No sooner had he said this, however, than he puffed himself up, boasting that he was the only one who had not bowed the knee to Baal. That's what introspection does. It causes us to either put ourselves down, or to pump ourselves up. If you want to be depressed, just start analyzing yourself. That's why we are to fix our eyes on Jesus.

Thirdly, there was an isolation from people. When we sink into times of discouragement, there is always the tendency to pull back, to pull out, to pull away. "I'm tired of struggling and serving. I'm just going to hole up and feel sorry for myself for awhile." When you hear yourself say this, be assured that discouragement is hovering nearby. God came to Elijah and said, "What are you doing here? You know better than that. You've come farther than this."

Reasons for Depression

First, there is a vulnerability after victory. Whenever your life is being blessed, your ministry is prospering, relationships are growing, or finances are increasing, watch out because you are vulnerable to attack. Noah sailed through problems on the ark, as well as the one hundred years preceding it when people thought he was crazy. It was when he got *out* of the ark that he was vulnerable and drank himself into sin. David took on Goliath and beat him, but it was after that victory that he feigned madness in the city of Gath (1 Samuel 21).

A second factor for Elijah was the factor of fatigue. After he prayed for the Lord to send rain, he outran Ahab's chariot to the city of Jezreel. At this point, he's had huge spiritual confrontation. He's had physical exertion. He's just plain tired. And when you're tired, you're particularly susceptible to depression. There is a close linkage between body, soul, and spirit. If your body is tired, your soul, which is your mind and emotions, will often be affected, as well.

A third factor was disappointed expectations. I'm sure Elijah expected God to immediately deal with Ahab and Jezebel. I'm sure he expected the entire nation to be shook by an earthquake, purged by fire, or blown clean by the wind of the Holy

Ghost. But nothing happened. Ahab still remained in power. Jezebel still sat beside him. And God didn't seem to be doing anything. So Elijah was disappointed. If we expect God to do something and He doesn't, we become vulnerable to depression.

God works at an entirely different pace than we think He should. We are so incredibly pushy and impatient and demanding. And then when the wind doesn't blow and the earth doesn't shake and the fire doesn't appear, we say, "What's going on?" But, as God said to Elijah, He says, "I am not in the earthquake. I am not in the wind. I am not in the fire. I am in the still, small voice."

The Cure for Depression

First, we see the Lord dealing with Elijah by giving him rest. The Lord doesn't rebuke him or find fault with him, but simply says, "Elijah, what are you doing? Here's some food. Go to sleep." Rest is so important. I believe much of the reason we get depressed needlessly is because we have failed to follow the principle of God that tells us we need rest.

In Isaiah 58:13, 14, the Lord says that those who honor His Sabbath will ride on high places. In other words, they won't end up in the valley of depression. God wants us to take a Sabbath. After all, He did. He created for six days and rested on the seventh. He didn't rest because He was tired. He didn't say, "Whew! This creation is really rough. I'm beat." Nor did He rest because He was totally finished with all the possibilities of creation. He could have kept on creating until there would be no room on this planet for us. No, He rested on the seventh day in order to teach us that we, too, must stop, even if we're not tired, even if we're not finished. You might have the capacity to go seven days a week. But it will catch up with you. At some point, you'll burn out and you'll go into a cave.

Interestingly, the Old Testament Sabbath principle was never linked with worship. That only happened in the time period between the Old and New Testaments when synagogue worship was established. I'm not talking about a day of worship. I'm talking about a day of rest. You'll find your marriages strengthened, your attitude changed, your body refreshed.

Secondly, as God spoke to him in the still, small, voice, Elijah realized that God's ways were not his ways. You will move out of depression when you realize that God is on the throne and that nothing happens without His permission. Dear friend, I think it is impossible for a person who believes in the sovereignty of God, in the power of God, in the love of God, to get depressed over circumstances. It's only when I no longer believe God is sovereign or powerful or love that I begin to doubt. That's why God came to Elijah in the still, small voice, in the way he least expected.

Thirdly, God prescribed not only rest and realization, but for Elijah to reach out. After God refreshed Elijah with rest and spoke to him in the still, small voice, He said, "Reach out. You've got work to do. You need to anoint two kings. Then I want you to anoint and disciple Elisha. Get busy. Start serving. There are lives to be touched, work to be done, ministry to move into. Get out of the cave and get going."

I know of no more practical truth than this one. When you're discouraged and despairing, the tendency will be to hide in a cave and feel sorry for yourself. But the cure for that is just the opposite, to find people to disciple, to find folks to pray with, to find situations in which you can be a blessing. Jesus said whatever measure you give out will be given back to you (Matthew 7:2). I have found this to be true over and over again, haven't you? When I talk to others, my own discouragement disappears. When I open the Word to share a truth with someone else, my own questions are answered. When I'm feeling unappreciated or neglected, if I reach out to someone else, my own selfishness dissipates. It's the secret of happiness: Get your eyes off yourself. Quit feeling sorry for yourself and start reaching out for Jesus' sake.

In so doing, you'll feel the presence of the Lord flowing through you, you'll feel a smile on your face, a spring in your step, a fervency of prayer, a joy in your heart. The choice is ours. We can either be a caveman or a man of power and effectiveness, a woman of strength and love. Rest, Realize, and Reach out—it's the cure prescribed by the Great Physician for a man just like us. And it's the same prescription that works for us today.

---

20 As Elijah and Elisha fade from the scene for six years, we read of their archrival Ben-hadad, king of Syria . . .

1 Kings 20:1
And Ben-hadad the king of Syria gathered all his host together: and there were thirty and two kings with him, and horses, and chariots: and he went up and besieged Samaria, and warred against it.

Samaria, of course, was part of Israel.

1 Kings 20:2, 3
And he sent messengers to Ahab king of Israel into the city, and said unto him, Thus saith Ben-hadad, Thy silver and thy gold is mine; thy wives also and thy children, even the goodliest, are mine.

"Ahab, your wife and kids and goods and silver are as good as gone. I'm laying claim to them right now," Ben-hadad boasted.

1 Kings 20:4
And the king of Israel answered and said, My lord, O king, according to thy saying, I am thine, and all that I have.

"Take them," said Ahab.

1 Kings 20:5, 6
And the messengers came again, and said, Thus speaketh Ben-hadad, saying, Although I have sent unto thee, saying, Thou shalt deliver me thy silver, and thy gold, and thy wives, and thy children; Yet I will send my servants unto thee to morrow about this time, and they shall search thine house, and the houses of thy servants; and it shall be, that whatsoever is pleasant in thine eyes, they shall put it in their hand, and take it away.

The messengers of Ben-hadad said, "It's not enough for you just to send us your goods; we're coming down and taking what we think is good."

1 Kings 20:7, 8
Then the king of Israel called all the elders of the land, and said, Mark, I pray you, and see how this man seeketh mischief: for he sent unto me for my wives, and for my children, and for my silver, and for my gold; and I denied him not. And all the elders and all the people said unto him, Hearken not unto him, nor consent.

"Don't give in," said the elders and the people of Israel.

1 Kings 20:9, 10
Wherefore he said unto the messengers of Ben-hadad, Tell my lord the king, All that thou didst send for to thy servant at the first I will do: but this thing I may not do. And the messengers departed, and brought him word again. And Ben-hadad sent unto him, and said, The gods do so unto me, and more also, if the dust of Samaria shall suffice for handfuls for all the people that follow me.

Ben-hadad's response to Ahab was, "If you don't let us come down and take what we want, we're going to come and annihilate you all."

1 Kings 20:11
And the king of Israel answered and said, Tell him, Let not him that girdeth on his harness boast himself as he that putteth it off.

In other words, Ahab said, "Don't count your chickens before they hatch" or, "Just because you get all suited up for the game doesn't mean you're going to win the game."

1 Kings 20:12, 13
And it came to pass, when Ben-hadad heard this message, as he was drinking, he and the kings in the pavilions, that he said unto his servants, Set yourselves in array. And they set themselves in array against the city. And, behold, there came a prophet unto Ahab king of Israel, saying, Thus saith the Lord, Hast thou seen all this great multitude? behold, I will deliver it in to thine hand this day; and thou shalt know that I am the Lord.

"Ahab, do you see all the armies lined up against you? God will deliver them this day into your hand," said a prophet of God.

Ahab was extremely wicked, and yet God is determined to win his heart. That's why I believe Elijah was depressed in the last chapter. Elijah wanted to see Ahab annihilated. But God still had a purpose and a plan for Ahab. So He says, "I'm going to give you victory so that you will truly know that I am the Lord." The heart of our Lord, the grace of our God, is absolutely incredible.

1 Kings 20:14 (a)
And Ahab said, By whom? And he said, Thus saith the Lord, Even by the young men of the princes of the provinces . . .

"I want you to use the young men to lead these troops into battle," said the Lord through His prophet.

1 Kings 20:14 (b)
. . . Then he said, Who shall order the battle? And he answered, Thou.

"Who shall attack first?" Ahab asked.
"You," the Lord answered.

1 Kings 20:15–18
Then he numbered the young men of the princes of the provinces, and they were two hundred and thirty two: and after them he numbered all the people, even all the children of Israel, being seven thousand. And they went out at noon. But Ben-hadad was drinking himself drunk in the pavilions, he and the kings, the thirty and two kings that helped him. And the young men of the princes of the provinces went out first; and Ben-hadad sent out, and they told him, saying, There are men come out of Samaria. And he said, Whether they be come out for peace, take them alive; or whether they be come out for war, take them alive.

In his drunken state, Ben-hadad said, "Just round them up and bring them in." But the men would not come that easily . . .

1 Kings 20:19–22
So these young men of the princes of the provinces came out of the city, and the army which followed them. And they slew every one his man: and the Syrians fled; and Israel pursued them: and Ben-hadad the king of Syria escaped on an horse with the horsemen. And the king of Israel went out, and smote the horses and chariots, and slew the Syrians with a great slaughter. And the prophet came to the king of Israel, and said unto him, Go, strengthen thy self, and mark, and see what thou doest: for at the return of the year the king of Syria will come up against thee.

God gave Ahab victory, but not without warning Ahab that Syria would attack again. If you have experienced victory in the past weeks or months, be warned that in the very area in which you have experienced the Lord's victory, you can expect another attempt of the enemy to destroy you. Be strong in the Lord. Syria will come again.

1 Kings 20:23
And the servants of the king of Syria said unto him, Their gods are gods of the hills; therefore they were stronger than we; but let us fight against them in the plain, and surely we shall be stronger than they.

"The reason we lost," the Syrians said, "is because we fought in the hills and Jehovah is the God of the hills. Move the battle to the valley, and we'll be victorious."

1 Kings 20:24–26
And do this thing, Take the kings away, every man out of his place, and put captains in their rooms: And number thee an army, like the army that thou hast lost, horse for horse, and chariot for chariot: and we will fight against them in the plain, and surely we shall be stronger than they. And he hearkened unto their voice, and did so. And it came to pass at the return of the year, that Ben-hadad numbered the Syrians, and went up to Aphek, to fight against Israel.

With a new battle plan, Ben-hadad again attacked Israel, this time in the valley.

1 Kings 20:27
And the children of Israel were numbered, and were all present, and went against them: and the children of Israel pitched before them like two little flocks of kids; but the Syrians filled the country.

The Israelites were vastly outnumbered. The odds looked grim.

1 Kings 20:28, 29
And there came a man of God, and spake unto the king of Israel, and said, Thus saith the LORD, Because the Syrians have said, The LORD is God of the hills, but he is not God of the valleys, therefore will I deliver all this great multitude into thine hand, and ye shall know that I am the LORD. And they pitched one over against the other seven days. And so it was, that in the seventh day the battle was joined: and the children of Israel slew of the Syrians an hundred thousand footmen in one day.

Even though the battle took place in the valley, the Israelites slew 100,000 Syrians in a single day. Why? Because the Syrians had said that the God of Israel was God only of the mountains. Satan said the same thing when he accused Job of only serving God because God had blessed him (Job 1:9, 10). And he says the same thing today. "Christians are happy as long as their spirits are high. Sure, they can sing and clap and enjoy the Lord as long as they're on the mountaintop. But put them in the valley and, once things don't go well at home or at work or with their finances, they'll be defeated and discouraged just like anyone else." So God lets His people go through valleys to show the world that He is not the God of the mountaintops only, but also of the valley; that even in difficult days, dark times, and deep waters there will be a smile on the faces and a song in the hearts of His people. And that is when the world takes note.

Is your God the God of the valley? Or are you a Christian who only knows God as the God of the mountain, only rejoicing when things go the way you think they should? If God has privileged you to be in the valley, it's to show a watching world that you are not a mercenary, one who serves God only for your own prosperity, but that you are a lover of the Lord regardless of whether you're in the mountain or in the valley.

1 Kings 20:30 (a)
But the rest fled to Aphek, into the city; and there a wall fell upon twenty and seven thousand of the men that were left . . .

As they went to hide out in the city, a wall came down and 27,000 Syrians died.

1 Kings 20:30 (b)–32
. . . And Ben-hadad fled, and came into the city, into an inner chamber. And his servants said unto him, Behold now, we have heard that the kings of the house of Israel are merciful kings: let us, I pray thee, put sackcloth on our loins, and ropes upon our heads, and go out to the king of Israel: peradventure he will save thy life. So they girded sackcloth on their loins, and put ropes on their heads, and came to the king of Israel, and said, Thy servant Ben-hadad saith, I pray thee, let me live. And he said, Is he yet alive? he is my brother.

As Ben-hadad's servants surrendered to Ahab, Ahab asked about Ben-hadad. "He's my brother," Ahab said. Why would Ahab say this? Ben-hadad certainly wasn't his brother racially because he was a Syrian, not an Israelite. He wasn't his brother religiously because he didn't serve or acknowledge Jehovah in any way. But he was his brother in the monarchy. That is, they were both kings. And in this we see the true priority of Ahab's life. More than being an Israelite, more than being a follower of Jehovah, he prided himself and found his identity in his position as king.

1 Kings 20:33, 34
Now the men did diligently observe whether any thing would come from him, and did hastily catch it: and they said, Thy brother Ben-hadad. Then he said, Go ye, bring him. Then Ben-hadad came forth to him; and he caused him to come up into the chariot. And

Ben-hadad said unto him, The cities, which my father took from thy father, I will restore; and thou shalt make streets for thee in Damascus, as my father made in Samaria. Then said Ahab, I will send thee away with this covenant. So he made a covenant with him, and sent him away.

In other words, Ben-hadad said to Ahab, "I'll give you back all the stuff we took."

1 Kings 20:35–40
And a certain man of the sons of the prophets said unto his neighbour in the word of the LORD, Smite me, I pray thee. And the man refused to smite him. Then said he unto him, Because thou hast not obeyed the voice of the LORD, behold, as soon as thou art departed from me, a lion shall slay thee. And as soon as he was departed from him, a lion found him, and slew him. Then he found another man, and said, Smite me, I pray thee. And the man smote him, so that in smiting he wounded him. So the prophet departed, and waited for the king by the way, and disguised himself with ashes upon his face. And as the king passed by, he cried unto the king: and he said, Thy servant went out into the midst of the battle; and, behold, a man turned aside, and brought a man unto me, and said, Keep this man: if by any means he be missing, then shall thy life be for his life, or else thou shalt pay a talent of silver. And as thy servant was busy here and there, he was gone. And the king of Israel said unto him, So shall thy judgment be; thyself hast decided it.

As part of an elaborate object lesson, a prophet of God eventually convinced another man to hit him. He then added ashes to his wound to disguise himself and waited for Ahab to pass by. When Ahab drew near, the prophet approached him, saying, "When I was in battle, I was put in charge of a prisoner and was told that if the prisoner escaped, I would either pay with my life or with a talent of silver (today's equivalent of $3,000). But I got busy, and the prisoner escaped.

"The case is simple," Ahab said. "You must pay."

1 Kings 20:41–43
And he hasted, and took the ashes away from his face; and the king of Israel discerned him that he was of the prophets. And he said unto him, Thus saith the LORD, Because thou hast let go out of thy hand a man whom I appointed to utter destruction, therefore thy life shall go for his life, and thy people for his people. And the king of Israel went to his house heavy and displeased, and came to Samaria.

The prophet answered Ahab by saying, "The word of the Lord is that, because you didn't complete the task I called you to do, because you followed your own logic rather than My direction, you're headed for destruction."

Dear brother, precious sister, if the Lord has been speaking to you about a sin you constantly battle, don't be like Ahab. Don't make excuses for it. Don't compromise with it as Ahab did with Ben-hadad. Destroy it. Otherwise, it will one day destroy you. God has given us the ability to do so because He has made us more than conquerors (Romans 8:37). The only question is, do we have the desire to deal a deathblow to that which continually trips us up and causes others to stumble? Think back, and maybe you'll see that, like the prophet in our text, people in your life have been willing to take a beating in order to warn you about the path you're on. Be wise, dear saint, and heed their warning.

21 If you doubt that the grace of God is available or applicable to you, the text before us is especially for you because in it we see that the grace of God is available to *everyone.* Ahab was the most wicked king in the history of Israel. His idolatry and immorality exceeded that of all before him. And yet the Lord chased hard after him to restore him and minister grace to him. The Lord invested ten years in working with Ahab to bring him to a place of brokenness and repentance.

But at this point, he's not there yet . . .

1 Kings 21:1–3
And it came to pass after these things, that Naboth the Jezreelite had a vineyard, which was in Jezreel, hard by the palace of Ahab king of Samaria. And Ahab spake unto Naboth, saying, Give me thy vineyard, that I may have it for a garden of herbs, because it is near unto my house: and I will give thee for it a better vineyard than it; or, if it seem good to thee, I will give thee the worth of it in money. And Naboth said to Ahab, The LORD forbid it me, that I should give the inheritance of my fathers unto thee.

King Ahab wanted Naboth's garden. But Naboth refused on the grounds that he had inherited it. You see, in Old Testament days, the Lord was determined that His people be treated equally and equitably. To this end, he said that it was only if the family came under dire straits and desperate need that they could sell their land, and even then, it was to be returned in the Year of Jubilee.

1 Kings 21:4
And Ahab came into his house heavy and displeased because of the word which Naboth the Jezreelite had spoken to him: for he had said, I will not give thee the inheritance of my fathers. And he laid him down upon his bed, and turned away his face, and would eat no bread.

Here, Ahab has an entire kingdom and he pouts because he can't have a little garden. In this, we see the fallacy of the materialistic mindset that pervades even our own culture. It doesn't really matter how much you have, if you're materially minded, you always want just a little more.

1 Kings 21:5–7
But Jezebel his wife came to him, and said unto him, Why is thy spirit so sad, that thou eatest no bread? And he said unto her, Because I spake unto Naboth the Jezreelite, and said unto him, Give me thy vineyard for money; or else, if it please thee, I will give thee another vineyard for it: and he answered, I will not give thee my vineyard. And Jezebel his wife said unto him, Dost thou now govern the kingdom of Israel? arise, and eat bread, and let thine heart be merry: I will give thee the vineyard of Naboth the Jezreelite.

After first chiding her husband for being spineless, Jezebel took matters into her own hands . . .

1 Kings 21:8–10
So she wrote letters in Ahab's name, and sealed them with his seal, and sent the letters unto the elders and to the nobles that were in his city, dwelling with Naboth. And she wrote in the letters, saying, Proclaim a fast, and set Naboth on high among the people: And set two men, sons of Belial, before him, to bear witness against him, saying, Thou didst blaspheme God and the king. And then carry him out, and stone him, that he may die.

Jezebel sent letters to the leaders of the city, instructing them to bring in false witnesses to accuse Naboth of blasphemy, and then to stone him.

1 Kings 21:11–16
And the men of his city, even the elders and the nobles who were the inhabitants in his city, did as Jezebel had sent unto them, and as it was written in the letters which she had sent unto them. They proclaimed a fast, and set Naboth on high among the people. And there came in two men, children of Belial, and sat before him: and the men of Belial witnessed against him, even against Naboth, in the presence of the people, saying, Naboth did blaspheme God and the king. Then they carried him forth out of the city, and stoned him with stones, that he died. Then they sent to Jezebel, saying, Naboth is stoned, and is dead. And it came to pass, when Jezebel heard that Naboth was stoned, and was dead, that Jezebel said to Ahab, Arise, take possession of the vineyard of Naboth the Jezreelite, which he refused to give thee for money: for Naboth is not alive, but dead. And it came to pass, when Ahab heard that Naboth was dead, that Ahab rose up to go down to the vineyard of Naboth the Jezreelite, to take possession of it.

Sadly, Jezebel's plan was carried out without a hitch, opening a way for Ahab to seize Naboth's garden.

1 Kings 21:17 (a)
And the word of the LORD came to Elijah the Tishbite . . .

Naboth is dead. The vineyard is now in possession of Ahab. And the word of the Lord comes to Elijah. It had been six years since Elijah had been on the scene. This man of miracles had been through a season of silence. Maybe you're going through a season of silence even presently. Maybe you're wondering why the Lord hasn't spoken to you, or why He isn't using you as He once did or as you hoped. The Lord takes His people through different seasons. It is your responsibility to simply stay filled and be available, filled with the Word and the Holy Spirit, and available to the command of the King. That's all. Should the Lord choose to call upon me once every six years or once every sixty years, that's His prerogative. Elijah was a mighty man of God, a powerful prophet, yet he was off the scene—until now.

1 Kings 21:17 (b)–19
. . . saying, Arise, go down to meet Ahab king of Israel, which is in Samaria: behold, he is in the vineyard of Naboth, whither he is gone down to possess it. And thou shalt speak unto him, saying, Thus saith the LORD, Hast thou killed, and also taken possession? And thou shalt speak unto him, saying, Thus saith the LORD, In the place where dogs licked the blood of Naboth shall dogs lick thy blood, even thine.

"You are in a real mess because of what you did to Naboth," Elijah said to Ahab. Notice that the Lord holds Ahab accountable for Jezebel's actions. Why? First, because he burdened her with his pouting (v. 4). The Word tells us that wives are weaker vessels (1 Peter 3:7), not in the sense of less spiritual, but in the sense of more vulnerable. This means that wives are more likely to carry their husband's concerns even more deeply than their husbands do. Therefore, I believe it is very important for me, as a husband, to protect my wife from unnecessary burdens. I believe I do her a disservice if I unload on her everything I'm going through.

Secondly, Ahab misled her with his whining. Naboth said, "God forbid that I should do this. It's not right that I should do this from God's perspective." But Ahab made it seem like Naboth was just being obstinate. We can all be vulnerable to not quite accurately portraying a given situation. It's natural, but it's not right.

Husbands, let us take note tonight that we need to be careful that our wives don't move in a direction because we have cried to them or because we have failed to give them the whole story.

1 Kings 21:20 (a)
And Ahab said to Elijah, Hast thou found me, O mine enemy?

Wait a minute, Ahab. Elijah's not your enemy at all. Elijah is a great friend of yours because he's speaking the truth to you. Sometimes we see people as enemies who, in reality, are precious friends because they care enough to speak the truth.

1 Kings 21:20 (b)–29
. . . And he answered, I have found thee: because thou hast sold thyself to work evil in the sight of the LORD. Behold, I will bring evil upon thee, and will take away thy posterity, and will cut off from Ahab him that pisseth against the wall, and him that is shut up and left in Israel, And will make thine house like the house of Jeroboam the son of Nebat, and like the house of Baasha the son of Ahijah, for the provocation wherewith thou hast provoked me to anger, and made Israel to sin. And of Jezebel also spake the LORD, saying, The dogs shall eat Jezebel by the wall of Jezreel. Him that dieth of Ahab in the city the dogs shall eat; and him that dieth in the field shall the fowls of the air eat. But there was none like unto Ahab, which did sell himself to work wickedness in the sight of the LORD, whom Jezebel his wife stirred up. And he did very abominably in following idols, according to all things as did the Amorites, whom the LORD cast out before the children of Israel. And it came to pass, when Ahab heard those words, that he rent his clothes, and put sackcloth upon his flesh, and fasted, and lay in sackcloth, and went softly. And the word of the LORD came to Elijah the Tishbite, saying, Seest thou how Ahab humbleth himself before me? because he humbleth himself before me, I will not bring the evil in his days: but in his son's days will I bring the evil upon his house.

There are two things that move God: faith and humility. The Lord responds to humility time and time again throughout Scripture. Here, the most wicked, rotten king in Israel's history humbled himself, and the Lord is excited about it. No one is more wicked than Ahab. Not even you. Therefore, if you humble yourself and repent you, too, can receive the joy of the Lord, the matchless grace of God.

22

1 Kings 22:1–4
And they continued three years without war between Syria and Israel. And it came to pass in the third year, that Jehoshaphat the king of Judah came down to the king of Israel. And the king of Israel said unto his servants, Know ye that Ramoth in Gilead is ours, and we be still, and take it not out of the hand of the king of Syria? And he said unto Jehoshaphat, Wilt thou go with me to battle to Ramoth-gilead? And Jehoshaphat said to the king of Israel, I am as thou art, my people as thy people, my horses as thy horses.

Ahab asked Jehoshaphat, the king of Judah, to join him in battle against Syria in order to reclaim a portion of land belonging to Israel.

1 Kings 22:5
And Jehoshaphat said unto the king of Israel, Inquire, I pray thee, at the word of the LORD to day.

"I'll go with you, but check it out with the Lord first," Jehoshaphat said.

1 Kings 22:6–9
Then the king of Israel gathered the prophets together, about four hundred men, and said unto them, Shall I go against Ramoth-gilead to battle, or shall I forbear? And they said, Go up; for the Lord shall deliver it into the hand of the king. And Jehoshaphat said, Is there not here a prophet of the LORD be-

sides, that we might inquire of him? And the king of Israel said unto Jehoshaphat, There is yet one man, Micaiah the son of Imlah, by whom we may inquire of the LORD: but I hate him; for he doth not prophesy good concerning me, but evil. And Jehoshaphat said, Let not the king say so. Then the king of Israel called an officer, and said, Hasten hither Micaiah the son of Imlah.

Four hundred prophets prophesied victory. Jehoshaphat, however, sensed something was not quite right. So Ahab begrudgingly called for Micaiah, the one prophet who didn't only tell him what he wanted to hear.

1 Kings 22:10–14
And the king of Israel and Jehoshaphat the king of Judah sat each on his throne, having put on their robes, in a void place in the entrance of the gate of Samaria; and all the prophets prophesied before them. And Zedekiah the son of Chenaanah made him horns of iron: and he said, Thus saith the LORD, With these shalt thou push the Syrians, until thou have consumed them. And all the prophets prophesied so, saying, Go up to Ramoth-gilead, and prosper: for the LORD shall deliver it into the king's hand. And the messenger that was gone to call Micaiah spake unto him, saying, Behold now, the words of the prophets declare good unto the king with one mouth: let thy word, I pray thee, be like the word of one of them, and speak that which is good. And Micaiah said, As the LORD liveth, what the LORD saith unto me, that will I speak.

"Everybody's for going to war," the messenger said to Micaiah. "Just this once, join the crowd."

"I can only say what the Lord tells me to say," Micaiah answered.

1 Kings 22:15, 16
So he came to the king. And the king said unto him, Micaiah, shall we go against Ramoth-gilead to battle, or shall we forbear? And he answered him, Go, and prosper: for the LORD shall deliver it into the hand of the king. And the king said unto him, How many times shall I adjure thee that thou tell me nothing but that which is true in the name of the LORD?

Sensing that Micaiah was mocking him, Ahab said, "Tell me the truth."

1 Kings 22:17
And he said, I saw all Israel scattered upon the hills, as sheep that have not a shepherd: and the LORD said, These have no master: let them return every man to his house in peace.

"The sheep are going to be scattered and the leader will be lost," Micaiah finally said.

1 Kings 22:18–23
And the king of Israel said unto Jehoshaphat, Did I not tell thee that he would prophesy no good concerning me, but evil? And he said, Hear thou therefore the word of the LORD: I saw the LORD sitting on his throne, and all the host of heaven standing by him on his right hand and on his left. And the LORD said, Who shall persuade Ahab, that he may go up and fall at Ramoth-gilead? And one said on this manner, and another said on that manner. And there came forth a spirit, and stood before the LORD, and said, I will persuade him. And the LORD said unto him, Wherewith? And he said, I will go forth, and I will be a lying spirit in the mouth of all his prophets. And he said, Thou shalt persuade him, and prevail also: go forth, and do so. Now therefore, behold, the LORD hath put a lying spirit in the mouth of all these thy prophets, and the LORD hath spoken evil concerning thee.

Although Ahab had repented, he began veering back into carnality. So the Lord determined to take him home. "How shall this be done?" the Lord said. There were many suggestions, and then a lying spirit said, "I'll persuade him. I will be a lying spirit in the mouth of all his prophets." How could a lying spirit have this kind of communication in heaven? Satan has access to heaven, but he can do nothing without the Lord's permission (Job 1).

1 Kings 22:24
But Zedekiah the son of Chenaanah went near, and smote Micaiah on the cheek, and said, Which way went the Spirit of the LORD from me to speak unto thee?

"When did the Spirit of God leave me and speak to you?" This alone should witness to the fact that the Spirit of God had already long since left Zedekiah. Why? The fruit of the Spirit is love, joy, and peace (Galatians 5:22). James goes on to say that we'll know that wisdom is from above if it is full of mercy, easy to be entreated, and peaceable (3:17). In 1 Corinthians 13, Paul says prophecy without love is nothing.

1 Kings 22:25–30
And Micaiah said, Behold, thou shalt see in that day, when thou shalt go into an inner

chamber to hide thyself. And the king of Israel said, Take Micaiah, and carry him back unto Amon the governor of the city, and to Joash the king's son; And say, Thus saith the king, Put this fellow in the prison, and feed him with bread of affliction and with water of affliction, until I come in peace. And Micaiah said, If thou return at all in peace, the LORD hath not spoken by me. And he said, Hearken, O people, every one of you. So the king of Israel and Jehoshaphat the king of Judah went up to Ramoth-gilead. And the king of Israel said unto Jehoshaphat, I will disguise myself, and enter into the battle; but put thou on thy robes. And the king of Israel disguised himself, and went into the battle.

Ahab was no dummy. When he heard Micaiah say that the sheep would be scattered and the leader lost, he decided to enter the battle incognito and suggested Jehoshaphat wear his royal robes instead.

1 Kings 22:31
But the king of Syria commanded his thirty and two captains that had rule over his chariots, saying, Fight neither with small nor great, save only with the king of Israel.

The sole mission of the Syrians was to kill the king of Israel.

1 Kings 22:32–34
And it came to pass, when the captains of the chariots saw Jehoshaphat, that they said, Surely it is the king of Israel. And they turned aside to fight against him: and Jehoshaphat cried out. And it came to pass, when the captains of the chariots perceived that it was not the king of Israel, that they turned back from pursuing him. And a certain man drew a bow at a venture, and smote the king of Israel between the joints of the harness: wherefore he said unto the driver of his chariot, Turn thine hand, and carry me out of the host; for I am wounded.

Man can't outsmart God. The Syrians chased Jehoshaphat because he was wearing Ahab's clothes. But they ceased when Jehoshaphat identified himself. Then, an unknown, unnamed man shot an arrow at random and it struck right in the place of vulnerability in Ahab's armor.

1 Kings 22:35, 36
And the battle increased that day: and the king was stayed up in his chariot against the Syrians, and died at even: and the blood ran out of the wound into the midst of the chariot. And there went a proclamation throughout the host about the going down of the sun, saying, Every man to his city, and every man to his own country.

When Israel got word of Ahab's death, they fled. In other words, the shepherd died and the sheep scattered, just as Micaiah had prophesied.

1 Kings 22:37, 38
So the king died, and was brought to Samaria; and they buried the king in Samaria. And one washed the chariot in the pool of Samaria; and the dogs licked up his blood; and they washed his armour; according unto the word of the LORD which he spake.

Thus, Elijah's prophecy was fulfilled (21:19).

1 Kings 22:39, 40
Now the rest of the acts of Ahab, and all that he did, and the ivory house which he made, and all the cities that he built, are they not written in the book of the chronicles of the kings of Israel? So Ahab slept with his fathers; and Ahaziah his son reigned in his stead.

There is no remaining record of the ivory house or the cities Ahab built. What does remain is the account of his life here in 1 Kings that shows him to be a wicked king who God nonetheless pursued.

1 Kings 22:41–45
And Jehoshaphat the son of Asa began to reign over Judah in the fourth year of Ahab king of Israel. Jehoshaphat was thirty and five years old when he began to reign; and he reigned twenty and five years in Jerusalem. And his mother's name was Azubah the daughter of Shilhi. And he walked in all the ways of Asa his father; he turned not aside from it, doing that which was right in the eyes of the LORD: nevertheless the high places were not taken away; for the people offered and burnt incense yet in the high places. And Jehoshaphat made peace with the king of Israel. Now the rest of the acts of Jehoshaphat, and his might that he shewed, and how he warred, are they not written in the book of the chronicles of the kings of Judah?

The antithesis of Ahab, Jehoshaphat is one of the greatest kings in Judah's history, as seen in 2 Chronicles.

1 Kings 22:46–49
And the remnant of the sodomites, which remained in the days of his father Asa, he took out of the land. There was then no king in

Edom: a deputy was king. Jehoshaphat made ships of Tharshish to go to Ophir for gold: but they went not; for the ships were broken at Ezion-geber. Then said Ahaziah the son of Ahab unto Jehoshaphat, Let my servants go with thy servants in the ships. But Jehoshaphat would not.

Second Chronicles 20:35–37 tells us about this incident. Jehoshaphat took part in a venture to send ships for gold. But because it was a joint venture with a wicked king, Jehoshaphat's ships went down on the rocks. Why does the Lord record this? I believe it is as a reminder that if we are unequally yoked with unbelievers—be it in marriage, business, or any other venture—we're headed for the rocks, as well.

1 Kings 22:50–53
And Jehoshaphat slept with his fathers, and was buried with his fathers in the city of David his father: and Jehoram his son reigned in his stead. Ahaziah the son of Ahab began to reign over Israel in Samaria the seventeenth year of Jehoshaphat king of Judah, and reigned two years over Israel. And he did evil in the sight of the LORD, and walked in the way of his father, and in the way of his mother, and in the way of Jeroboam the son of Nebat, who made Israel to sin: For he served Baal, and worshipped him, and provoked to anger the LORD God of Israel, according to all that his father had done.

The book that began with a man after God's own heart sitting on the throne of a united Israel ends with two godless kings on the thrones of a divided nation. "Make us a king to judge us like all the nations," the people had demanded (1 Samuel 8:5). And, in the words of the psalmist, God "gave them their request, but sent leanness into their soul" (106:15).

2 KINGS

1 **2 Kings 1:1, 2 (a)**
Then Moab rebelled against Israel after the death of Ahab. And Ahaziah fell down through a lattice in his upper chamber that was in Samaria, and was sick . . .

Rather than going to battle, Ahaziah thought he would play it safe and stay home. But because he was a sinner, nowhere was safe. We're all only a step away from death no matter where we are, gang. Life is short. Tomorrow is uncertain. Wise is the man or woman who realizes the uncertainty of tomorrow.

2 Kings 1:2 (b), 3
. . . and he sent messengers, and said unto them, Go, inquire of Baal-zebub the god of Ekron whether I shall recover of this disease. But the angel of the LORD said to Elijah the Tishbite, Arise, go up to meet the messengers of the king of Samaria, and say unto them, Is it not because there is not a God in Israel, that ye go to inquire of Baal-zebub the god of Ekron?

"Why are you going to inquire of the Philistine god? Aren't I the true and living God?" the Lord said through Elijah. Before we come down on Ahaziah, we would do well to search our own hearts. For example, when you are hurt, do you first call the doctor or do you call upon the Lord? We are just as guilty as Ahaziah if, when we're hurt or diseased, defeated or wounded, we don't first seek the Lord.

2 Kings 1:4–8
Now therefore thus saith the LORD, Thou shalt not come down from that bed on which thou art gone up, but shalt surely die. And Elijah departed. And when the messengers turned back unto him, he said unto them, Why are ye now turned back? And they said unto him, There came a man up to meet us, and said unto us, Go, turn again unto the king that sent you, and say unto him, Thus saith the LORD, Is it not because there is not a God in Israel, that thou sendest to inquire of Baal-zebub the god of Ekron? therefore thou shalt not come down from that bed on which thou art gone up, but shalt surely die. And he said unto them, What manner of man was he which came up to meet you, and told you these words? And they answered him, He was an hairy man, and girt with a girdle of leather about his loins. And he said, It is Elijah the Tishbite.

A brief description was all Ahaziah needed to recognize Elijah.

2 Kings 1:9
Then the king sent unto him a captain of fifty with his fifty. And he went up to him: and, behold, he sat on the top of an hill. And he spake unto him, Thou man of God, the king hath said, Come down.

Satan, the king of this world, utters the same phrase: "Come down," for he would have us leave the heights of fellowship with God to come down to his level.

2 Kings 1:10
And Elijah answered and said to the captain of fifty, If I be a man of God, then let fire come down from heaven, and consume thee and thy fifty. And there came down fire from heaven, and consumed him and his fifty.

"Lord, they didn't receive You in Samaria. Shall we call down fire and consume them like Elijah did?" thundered James and John, the sons of thunder (Luke 9:54).

"You don't know what spirit you're of," Jesus said. And He rebuked them.

The true proof of a man of God lies in his ability to call down fire from heaven, not to consume other souls, but to consume his own spirit. People asked John Wesley how he drew such great crowds to hear him preach. "I ignite myself in the fire of the Holy Ghost," he is reported to have said, "and people come to watch me burn." I like that! If you are a man or woman of God, you will be able to call down fire, not to blast others, but to ignite your own heart.

"Did not our heart *burn* within us?" asked the travelers to Emmaus after spending time with Jesus (Luke 24:32, italics added). How do you call down fire from heaven? Do what those on the road to Emmaus did: Spend time with Jesus.

2 Kings 1:11
Again also he sent unto him another captain of fifty with his fifty. And he answered and said unto him, O man of God, thus hath the king said, Come down quickly.

This time, Ahaziah commanded Elijah to come down quickly.

2 Kings 1:12–15
And Elijah answered and said unto them, If I be a man of God, let fire come down from heaven, and consume thee and thy fifty. And the fire of God came down from heaven, and consumed him and his fifty. And he sent again a captain of the third fifty with his fifty. And the third captain of fifty went up, and came and fell on his knees before Elijah, and besought him, and said unto him, O man of God, I pray thee, let my life, and the life of these fifty thy servants, be precious in thy sight. Behold, there came fire down from heaven, and burnt up the two captains of the former fifties with their fifties: therefore let my life now be precious in thy sight. And the angel of the LORD said unto Elijah, Go down with him: be not afraid of him. And he arose, and went down with him unto the king.

The third captain approached Elijah differently than the first two. He came with humility. And, as a result, his life was spared.

2 Kings 1:16
And he said unto him, Thus saith the LORD, Forasmuch as thou hast sent messengers to inquire of Baal-zebub the god of Ekron, is it not because there is no God in Israel to inquire of his word? therefore thou shalt not come down off that bed on which thou art gone up, but shalt surely die.

If Ahaziah hoped Elijah would reverse the curse, he was sorely disappointed, for Elijah didn't back down.

2 Kings 1:17, 18
So he died according to the word of the LORD which Elijah had spoken. And Jehoram reigned in his stead in the second year of Jehoram the son of Jehoshaphat king of Judah; because he had no son. Now the rest of the acts of Ahaziah which he did, are they not written in the book of the chronicles of the kings of Israel?

Elijah's prophecy came to pass. God's Word was, as always, true. Ahaziah died, leaving his brother, Jehoram, to succeed him.

2

2 Kings 2:1
And it came to pass, when the LORD would take up Elijah into heaven by a whirlwind, that Elijah went with Elisha from Gilgal.

At the close of Jesus' earthly ministry, He gathered His disciples to Him and said, "It is expedient that I go, for if I go, I will send you another Comforter" (John 16:7). Jesus Himself was quite a Comforter. If you were sailing and a storm suddenly began to beat and batter your boat, it would be a comfort to have Jesus with you because He could simply speak the word and the storm would stop. If you were having a party and ran out of food or drink, Jesus would be a comfort to have with you, for He was able to feed thousands with a few loaves of bread and to turn ordinary water into wine. If you were sick, what a comfort it would be to be in the presence of Jesus, for He could simply speak a word of healing and the sickness would depart. Why, then, would we need *another* Comforter?

The answer is that, while Jesus was on earth, He was physically limited to being in one place at a time. Knowing His church would grow, that His kingdom would expand, He said, "I must depart so I can send you another Comforter, one just like Me, but without the limitations of a physical body." That is why Jesus Christ, by His Holy Spirit is in our midst right now. But He is also in Beijing and Bombay, Alaska and Africa. He is limitless. He is allowed to move in churches and hearts simultaneously all across the globe.

After Jesus died on the Cross and then rose from the dead, validating His claim to be Messiah, He appeared to His disciples again. "Peace," He said. "It is I. Be of good cheer." And then He breathed on them and said, "Receive ye the Holy Spirit" (John 20). The word "spirit" is *pneuma* in Greek and can also be translated "breath" or "wind." The Hebrew word, *ruach*, can also be translated as "breath," "wind," or "spirit." At that point, the disciples had the Holy Spirit, but the Holy Spirit did not have them, for Jesus told those same men to go to Jerusalem and wait until they were empowered with the Spirit from on high. They had the Holy Spirit *in* them, but now they would receive power when the Holy Spirit came *upon* them.

Ten days after Jesus ascended to heaven, the Holy Spirit came upon the group of disciples. These men who were timid and fearful suddenly became bold and powerful. The reason the early church turned the world upside down is because they were plugged in to the power of the Holy Spirit.

Saints throughout all ages have understood that the source and secret of power is the Holy Spirit. In the Old Testament, we read about the Holy Spirit coming upon Moses and upon the seventy elders who ministered alongside him. We read how Othniel was empowered for service, how Samson was supernaturally strengthened, how Gideon stepped out in faith, how David sang songs of praise when the Holy Spirit came upon their lives.

In our text, we see another example of the Holy Spirit coming upon a man. His name was Elisha. For six years as Elisha ministered to Elijah, he observed that the power of the Holy Spirit was the secret to Elijah's ministry. As Elijah was ready to be taken up, he turned to his young protegé and said, "What do you want?"

"I want a double portion of the same Spirit that is upon you," Elisha answered

"You have asked a hard thing. Nevertheless, if you keep your eyes on me, and if you see me depart, it shall be granted to you," Elijah said.

But first, Elijah will take him to four cities. In them, we see the four points of preparation necessary for empowerment to take place.

The first stop was Gilgal, *the place of purification*. When, after forty years of wandering, the children of Israel crossed into the Promised Land, the first place they came to was Gilgal. When they got there, the Lord said, "Stop. Before you fight any battle, you must circumcise the entire generation." Circumcision speaks of radically dealing with the flesh.

The first point of preparation for empowerment is purification. You see, if I am going to be filled with the Holy Spirit, I must first be emptied of the flesh. Too often, too many people are trying to get filled, when in reality they need to be emptied. That is, there is sin in their lives. Their flesh has grown over areas that were once tender and sensitive to the Lord. That is why Gilgal—the place of purification—is still the first step.

2 Kings 2:2 (a)
And Elijah said unto Elisha, Tarry here, I pray thee; for the LORD hath sent me to Bethel. And Elisha said unto him, As the LORD liveth, and as thy soul liveth, I will not leave thee.

At each of the four stops, Elijah says to Elisha, "Stay here. I've got to go on. You hang back." And each time he does, Elisha says, "No way. I'm not leaving. I'm going to follow you wherever you go. I'm going to stick to you like glue."

2 Kings 2:2 (b), 3
So they went down to Bethel. And the sons of the prophets that were at Bethel came forth to Elisha, and said unto him, Knowest thou that the LORD will take away thy master from thy head to day? And he said, Yea, I know it; hold ye your peace.

Bethel is *the place of realization*. In Genesis 28, we read how Jacob tricked his dad into giving him the birthright and blessing. After he got them, he knew his older brother would be angry, so he ran for his life, stopping the first night at a place in the wilderness that seemed God-forsaken. He pulled up a rock for a pillow and went to sleep. That night, God appeared to Jacob. When Jacob awoke, he said, "Surely God is in this place, and I knew it not." Why didn't Jacob know God was there? Because his surroundings were barren and dry. Secondly, he didn't know God was in that place because of his circumstances. He was running from his sin. But when he awoke, he marveled that God was indeed in that place. That is why he called it *Bethel*, or "house of God."

Maybe you look at your circumstances or surroundings and think, "The Lord might want to bless the people around me, but not me. I'm a conniver like Jacob. My surroundings are dry. I'm in a wasted place. I've wasted time, energy, and my whole life." The Lord wants to bless you today. Regardless of where you've been previously or what your circumstances are presently, if you will come to Him, He will bless you abundantly. Jesus said, "If you being evil know how to give good gifts to your children, how much more will the heavenly Father give the Holy Spirit to them that ask" (Matthew 7:11).

2 Kings 2:4
And Elijah said unto him, Elisha, tarry here, I pray thee; for the LORD hath sent me to Jericho. And he said, As the LORD liveth, and as thy soul liveth, I will not leave thee. So they came to Jericho.

The third city was Jericho, *the place of confrontation*. After they were purified at Gilgal, standing before them was the unbelievably difficult task of conquering Jericho. Its walls loomed high. It was thought to be impregnable. The Lord commanded the people to march around the city for six days. On the seventh day, they were to march around it six times and on the seventh time, they were to shout and the walls would come down. It was a fabulous victory, indeed. It was a place of confrontation.

The Holy Spirit is given not to make us feel good, not to make us happy, not to give us a "holy high." The Holy Spirit is given for the purpose of service, to take on Jerichos, to reach out to people who are walled off, and to change lives and situations.

Jesus said, "You shall receive power when the Holy Ghost comes upon you and then you shall be My witnesses" (Acts 1:8). Do you really want to be filled with the Holy Spirit, because that means you're going to be a witness.

2 Kings 2:5
And the sons of the prophets that were at Jericho came to Elisha, and said unto him, Knowest thou that the LORD will take away thy master from thy head to day? And he answered, Yea, I know it; hold ye your peace.

Not only was Elijah testing Elisha by suggesting he hang back, but the guys in the school of prophecy—the seminarians of the day—tried to dissuade him from following a prophet who was destined to die. Yet still, Elisha followed.

2 Kings 2:6
And Elijah said unto him, Tarry, I pray thee, here; for the LORD hath sent me to Jordan. And he said, As the LORD liveth, and as thy soul liveth, I will not leave thee. And they two went on.

Jordan was *the place of expectation.* When the Israelites crossed into the Promised Land, it was as the priests put their feet in the water that the waters parted (Joshua 3:15). They didn't stand on the edge of the bank, saying, "Lord, part the waters and we'll step in." No, they stepped in first, and as they did, a miracle took place.

We will read how Naaman was told by Elisha to dip seven times in the Jordan in order to be cleansed of leprosy. As he did, as he took the step of faith, even though he was at first reluctant, he was healed (2 Kings 5:14).

If you desire to be filled and empowered by the Holy Spirit, you must come to the place of expectation, where you say, "Lord, I'm putting my foot in the water. Lord, I'm dipping seven times if necessary," for without faith, it is impossible to please God (Hebrews 11:6).

2 Kings 2:7
And fifty men of the sons of the prophets went, and stood to view afar off: and they two stood by Jordan.

Elisha passed all four tests. He kept going even though at every juncture Elijah said, "Are you sure you want to keep going?"

Your heart will say the same thing. "Are you sure you want to go deeper and deeper in the things of God?"

In Acts 4, the same group of disciples who were baptized, filled, and empowered with the Holy Spirit on the Day of Pentecost was retouched, refilled and renewed. Likewise, I believe there are many who have had a Holy Spirit experience, but need to be renewed. If you want a double measure, if you want more of the Lord, I would encourage you to follow in Elisha's footsteps: Confess sin. Then confess God is in your situation and expect Him to meet you, to fill you, to empower you.

2 Kings 2:8–10
And Elijah took his mantle, and wrapped it together, and smote the waters, and they were divided hither and thither, so that they two went over on dry ground. And it came to pass, when they were gone over, that Elijah said unto Elisha, Ask what I shall do for thee, before I be taken away from thee. And Elisha said, I pray thee, let a double portion of thy spirit be upon me. And he said, Thou hast asked a hard thing: nevertheless, if thou see me when I am taken from thee, it shall be so unto thee; but if not, it shall not be so.

"Give me a double portion of the Spirit that is upon you," Elisha said. Interestingly, we'll see that Elisha did exactly twice as many miracles as Elijah. In other words, his request was granted. Why? Because he kept his eyes on his master and had been prepared for the Spirit.

2 Kings 2:11
And it came to pass, as they still went on, and talked, that, behold, there appeared a chariot of fire, and horses of fire, and parted them both asunder; and Elijah went up by a whirlwind into heaven.

At the time of his departure, Elijah was walking with and talking with a disciple. I like that. If you are mature in the things of God, do you have an Elisha, someone you're leading closer to the Lord? How I pray that when the Lord comes for me, I might be walking with and talking about the things of the Lord to someone who is growing in Him.

2 Kings 2:12, 13
And Elisha saw it, and he cried, My father, my father, the chariot of Israel, and the horse-

men thereof. And he saw him no more: and he took hold of his own clothes, and rent them in two pieces. He took up also the mantle of Elijah that fell from him, and went back, and stood by the bank of Jordan;

The mantle has fallen upon Elisha. And now the biblical narrative deals with the ministry of Elisha . . . who said, "Give me a double portion." He was granted his request. He was walking with and learning from a powerful prophet. And now he'll carry on.

2 Kings 2:14, 15
And he took the mantle of Elijah that fell from him, and smote the waters, and said, Where is the LORD God of Elijah? and when he also had smitten the waters, they parted hither and thither: and Elisha went over. And when the sons of the prophets which were to view at Jericho saw him, they said, The spirit of Elijah doth rest on Elisha. And they came to meet him, and bowed themselves to the ground before him.

Elisha struck the Jordan with Elijah's mantle, and the water parted. This interests me because the last miracle Elijah did was the same as the first miracle Elisha does.

Elisha watched what his master did, then duplicated it. What was the last miracle our Master did? He healed Malchus' ear after Peter lopped it off with his sword (Luke 22:51). What is the miracle we should be doing? Healing those who have been hurt unnecessarily even by Christians who are wielding the sword upon each other. We must be people who heal, not people who hurt. "Be ye kind one to another," Paul would write, "tenderhearted, forgiving one another, even as God for Christ's sake hath forgiven you" (Ephesians 4:32). May the Lord help us to be healing, forgiving, redemptive people.

2 Kings 2:16–18
And they said unto him, Behold now, there be with thy servants fifty strong men; let them go, we pray thee, and seek thy master: lest peradventure the Spirit of the LORD hath taken him up, and cast him upon some mountain, or into some valley. And he said, Ye shall not send. And when they urged him till he was ashamed, he said, Send. They sent therefore fifty men; and they sought three days, but found him not. And when they came again to him, (for he tarried at Jericho,) he said unto them, Did I not say unto you, Go not?

Fifty men who were devoted to studying the Scriptures said, "We can't believe Elijah really got raptured. Maybe he's stuck on some mountain somewhere. We'd better go find him." The same thing still happens. There are many seminaries who do not believe in a literal interpretation of the Bible. And when the Rapture happens, they'll be searching high and low, wondering where all of those "radical Christians" went!

2 Kings 2:19–22
And the men of the city said unto Elisha, Behold, I pray thee, the situation of this city is pleasant, as my lord seeth: but the water is naught, and the ground barren. And he said, Bring me a new cruse, and put salt therein. And they brought it to him. And he went forth unto the spring of the waters, and cast the salt in there, and said, Thus saith the LORD, I have healed these waters; there shall not be from thence any more death or barren land. So the waters were healed unto this day, according to the saying of Elisha which he spake.

Jesus said that we are the salt of the earth (Matthew 5:13). Paul said, "Let your speech be always with grace, seasoned with salt" (see Colossians 4:6). What are your words like? Are they salt? Do they create in others a thirst for Jesus? Let us commit to be people who, in the power of the Spirit and by the grace of God, speak words seasoned with the salt of grace.

The area around Jericho looked beautiful, but the water was poisoned. Jewish commentators tell us that so poisonous was the water, it was actually causing women to miscarry and the trees to lose their leaves. Outwardly, things looked good, but it was fruitless. Elisha healed the waters by prophesying in the spirit and by pouring in salt.

2 Kings 2:23
And he went up from thence unto Bethel: and as he was going up by the way, there came forth little children out of the city, and mocked him, and said unto him, Go up, thou bald head; go up, thou bald head.

The Hebrew word translated "little children" is *nahar. Nahar* is used to speak of little children, but also of younger men. For example, Isaac, at the age of twenty-eight, and Joseph, at the age of thirty-nine, are both called nahar. In this case, the implication of what these young men were saying was, "Elijah went up, why don't you? We don't want you around."

2 Kings 2:24, 25
And he turned back, and looked on them, and cursed them in the name of the LORD. And

there came forth two she bears out of the wood, and tare forty and two children of them. And he went from thence to mount Carmel, and from thence he returned to Samaria.

In his second epistle, Peter said that there will come scoffers saying, "Why hasn't the Lord come back yet? Where is the promise of His coming?" (3:4). But, like the young men in our text, they will find themselves in an "unbearable" situation, in a time of tremendous tribulation when God pours out His wrath on a Christ-rejecting sinful world during the Tribulation. Those who mock and scoff will find themselves in tough times.

3

2 Kings 3:1–3

Now Jehoram the son of Ahab began to reign over Israel in Samaria the eighteenth year of Jehoshaphat king of Judah, and reigned twelve years. And he wrought evil in the sight of the LORD; but not like his father, and like his mother: for he put away the image of Baal that his father had made. Nevertheless he cleaved unto the sins of Jeroboam the son of Nebat, which made Israel to sin; he departed not therefrom.

Jehoram, the son of Ahab and Jezebel, was a little better than his mom and dad by virtue of the fact that he didn't worship Baal, but he did continue to worship the calves that Jeroboam had made.

2 Kings 3:4, 5

And Mesha king of Moab was a sheepmaster, and rendered unto the king of Israel an hundred thousand lambs, and an hundred thousand rams, with the wool. But it came to pass, when Ahab was dead, that the king of Moab rebelled against the king of Israel.

Mesha was tired of paying tribute. When Ahab died, he felt now was the time to get out from under the heavy taxation that Ahab and Israel had put on him. So he launched a rebellion.

2 Kings 3:6, 7

And king Jehoram went out of Samaria the same time, and numbered all Israel. And he went and sent to Jehoshaphat the king of Judah, saying, The king of Moab hath rebelled against me: wilt thou go with me against Moab to battle? And he said, I will go up: I am as thou art, my people as thy people, and my horses as thy horses.

Jehoshaphat was a great man, but he was a gullible man. This is the exact phrase he said when Ahab, Jehoram's father, asked him to help battle the Syrians. At that time, Jehoshaphat barely escaped with his life (1 Kings 22). It seemed like he would have learned his lesson. But here he makes the same mistake again.

2 Kings 3:8–11

And he said, Which way shall we go up? And he answered, The way through the wilderness of Edom. So the king of Israel went, and the king of Judah, and the king of Edom: and they fetched a compass of seven days' journey: and there was no water for the host, and for the cattle that followed them. And the king of Israel said, Alas! that the LORD hath called these three kings together, to deliver them into the hand of Moab! But Jehoshaphat said, Is there not here a prophet of the LORD, that we may inquire of the LORD by him? And one of the king of Israel's servants answered and said, Here is Elisha the son of Shaphat, which poured water on the hands of Elijah.

Elisha was known as the man who served Elijah. And because he was faithful in little things, he was given greater responsibility (Luke 19:17). Are you willing to serve others? It's an important step in your spiritual development.

2 Kings 3:12, 13

And Jehoshaphat said, The word of the LORD is with him. So the king of Israel and Jehoshaphat and the king of Edom went down to him. And Elisha said unto the king of Israel, What have I to do with thee? get thee to the prophets of thy father, and to the prophets of thy mother. And the king of Israel said unto him, Nay: for the LORD hath called these three kings together, to deliver them into the hand of Moab.

Elisha's first response was, "Go seek your false gods."

But Jehoram said, "We're in trouble. We need to have a word from the Lord."

In days of old, sailors would chart their course by the stars. As we sail through life, it is often only during the dark times that we take the time to look up to heaven and get direction. Why does the Lord cause what St. John of the Cross called "the dark night of the soul" to descend upon our lives? It is because only then are we driven to our knees, only then do we look up and get direction.

2 Kings 3:14

And Elisha said, As the LORD of hosts liveth, before whom I stand, surely, were it not that I regard the presence of Jehoshaphat the

king of Judah, I would not look toward thee, nor see thee.

Jehoshaphat was in the wrong place, but his heart was right. So Elisha said, "Because Jehoshaphat's here, I'll seek the Lord on your behalf." This encourages me because we can find ourselves in the wrong place from time to time. But if our hearts are right, the Lord will not forsake us. He'll still give guidance and direction to us.

2 Kings 3:15
But now bring me a minstrel. And it came to pass, when the minstrel played, that the hand of the LORD came upon him.

As the praise music ascended, Elisha tuned in to the voice of the Lord. Isaiah says, "Break forth into song, you who are barren" (see Isaiah 54:1). If you feel barren, unfruitful, cold, break forth into songs of praise. In Job 38, we read that, when the Lord was creating the heavens and the earth, the angels were singing. The Lord works best to background music. It is in the presence of worship and praise that the Holy Spirit is able to work most creatively and most powerfully.

2 Kings 3:16–20
And he said, Thus saith the LORD, Make this valley full of ditches. For thus saith the LORD, Ye shall not see wind, neither shall ye see rain; yet that valley shall be filled with water, that ye may drink, both ye, and your cattle, and your beasts. And this is but a light thing in the sight of the LORD: he will deliver the Moabites also into your hand. And ye shall smite every fenced city, and every choice city, and shall fell every good tree, and stop all wells of water, and mar every good piece of land with stones. And it came to pass in the morning, when the meat offering was offered, that, behold, there came water by the way of Edom, and the country was filled with water.

In this dry and desert area, the word of the Lord was for the Israelites and Edomites to dig ditches. Only God could give the water, but it was up to them to trench the ground. This is such an important principle. You've got to dig the ditches in the dry times, in the hard times. You've got to daily dig the ditches and the Lord will fill them with water in His time. You might feel like your morning devotions are a rut, as dry as a desert. Dig the ditch anyway. And in the morning, in the Lord's timing, He will fill it with water. It is a principle of God that is irrevocable and absolute. God will fill the ditch, but you must dig it. If the Israelites had only scratched the ground, that's all the water they would have received. The more you dig, the more you'll get. Sometimes it's just plain hard work, but whether it's Bible study, ministry, or prayer, you've got to dig the ditch first. Then the Lord will fill it in due time. May God help us to be those who dig in and prepare for mighty miracles.

2 Kings 3:21–23
And when all the Moabites heard that the kings were come up to fight against them, they gathered all that were able to put on armour, and upward, and stood in the border. And they rose up early in the morning, and the sun shone upon the water, and the Moabites saw the water on the other side as red as blood: And they said, This is blood: the kings are surely slain, and they have smitten one another: now therefore, Moab, to the spoil.

When the Moabites woke up, the sun hit the water in the trenches in such a way as to look to them like it was blood. Therefore, they assumed the Israelite and Edomite kings had all attacked each other. So they went in, thinking they had the victory in hand.

Throughout Scripture, water is a picture of the Word. Some people view the Word as repulsive, a book of blood. But to those of us who have not only viewed it, but also tasted it, it is not repulsive, it is refreshing. If the Moabites had tasted the water, they would have known it was not blood at all. I have never met a man or woman who studied the Word of God who does not love it. The critics of the Word are those who view it from a distance but never taste it.

2 Kings 3:24, 25
And when they came to the camp of Israel, the Israelites rose up and smote the Moabites, so that they fled before them: but they went forward smiting the Moabites, even in their country. And they beat down the cities, and on every good piece of land cast every man his stone, and filled it; and they stopped all the wells of water, and felled all the good trees: only in Kir-haraseth left they the stones thereof; howbeit the slingers went about it, and smote it.

Not only were the Israelites able to defeat the Moabites on the battlefield, but they were also able to defeat them in their own cities.

2 Kings 3:26, 27
And when the king of Moab saw that the battle was too sore for him, he took with him seven hundred men that drew swords, to break

through even unto the king of Edom: but they could not. Then he took his eldest son that should have reigned in his stead, and offered him for a burnt offering upon the wall. And there was great indignation against Israel: and they departed from him, and returned to their own land.

After failing to make a dent in even the Edomite forces, the king of Moab resorted to the unimaginable act of sacrificing his own son, perhaps to obtain the help and favor of Chemosh, his god. No doubt horrified by this act, Israel departed. The battle was over.

What did it take to end the attack of Satan for the conquest of your soul? The death of the Son of the King of the universe. Jesus' death on the Cross, however, was not a frenzied last resort. No, it was planned before the world was even formed (1 Peter 1:20), so much did God love you.

4

2 Kings 4:1–7
Now there cried a certain woman of the wives of the sons of the prophets unto Elisha, saying, Thy servant my husband is dead; and thou knowest that thy servant did fear the LORD: and the creditor is come to take unto him my two sons to be bondmen. And Elisha said unto her, What shall I do for thee? tell me, what hast thou in the house? And she said, Thine handmaid hath not any thing in the house, save a pot of oil. Then he said, Go, borrow thee vessels abroad of all thy neighbours, even empty vessels; borrow not a few. And when thou art come in, thou shalt shut the door upon thee and upon thy sons, and shalt pour out into all those vessels, and thou shalt set aside that which is full. So she went from him, and shut the door upon her and upon her sons, who brought the vessels to her; and she poured out. And it came to pass, when the vessels were full, that she said unto her son, Bring me yet a vessel. And he said unto her, There is not a vessel more. And the oil stayed. Then she came and told the man of God. And he said, Go, sell the oil, and pay thy debt, and live thou and thy children of the rest.

This lady struck oil! She was in debt. Her sons about to be carried away into slavery, she cried to Elisha. Elisha asked what she had. She told him she had but a little bit of oil. "Gather all the vessels you can find, and start pouring," the prophet said. The lady did this, and a miracle took place, for as long as she kept pouring, the oil kept flowing.

Oil, of course, is a symbol of the Holy Spirit. The illustration here is an obvious one. The Lord will continue to flow through you as long as you are giving out to others. Maybe the Holy Spirit isn't flowing in your life. Could it be because there is no empty vessel in your house or in your life? Could it be because you haven't yet said, "I'm determined to minister to this person. I'm going to pour my life out for that person. I'm going to witness radically. I'm going to minister consistently"? Be like this woman. Gather around you empty vessels, empty people in need of the Lord. If you do, the Holy Spirit will fill you and flow from you perpetually. You, too, will strike oil.

2 Kings 4:8 (a)
And it fell on a day, that Elisha passed to Shunem, where was a great woman . . .

The Hebrew word for "great" is *gadol* and is used in the Bible to refer to spiritual greatness, moral greatness, material greatness, and mental greatness. This is the only woman in Scripture who is called a "great woman."

2 Kings 4:8 (b)
. . . and she constrained him to eat bread. And so it was, that as oft as he passed by, he turned in thither to eat bread.

What makes a great woman in the eyes of God? First, she is a woman of hospitality. This woman opened her home to a stranger. Hospitality is spoken of often in Scripture . . .

> He that receiveth a prophet in the name of a prophet shall receive a prophet's reward . . .
> Matthew 10:41 (a)

> Be not forgetful to entertain strangers: for thereby some have entertained angels unawares. Hebrews 13:2

> Be kindly affectioned one to another with brotherly love . . . Distributing to the necessity of saints; given to hospitality.
> Romans 12:10, 13

> . . . When thou makest a dinner or a supper, call not thy friends, nor thy brethren, neither thy kinsmen, nor thy rich neighbours; lest they also bid thee again, and a recompence be made thee. But when thou makest a feast, call the poor, the maimed, the lame, the blind: And thou shalt be blessed; for they cannot recompense thee: for thou shalt be recompensed at the resurrection of the just. Luke 14:12 (b)–14

2 Kings 4:9–11
And she said unto her husband, Behold now, I perceive that this is an holy man of God, which passeth by us continually. Let us

make a little chamber, I pray thee, on the wall; and let us set for him there a bed, and a table, and a stool, and a candlestick: and it shall be, when he cometh to us, that he shall turn in thither. And it fell on a day, that he came thither, and he turned into the chamber, and lay there.

Secondly, a great woman in the eyes of God is a woman of spirituality. Here, the woman perceived that the unknown stranger was a man of God. What did she do with that discernment? Spirituality was translated into practicality when she and her husband built a room for Elisha. She simply provided a quiet place of rest for God's minister.

2 Kings 4:12
And he said to Gehazi his servant, Call this Shunammite. And when he had called her, she stood before him.

Thirdly, a great woman in the eyes of God is a woman of respectability. The dialogue with Elisha passed through Gehazi, the servant. In the name of propriety and wisdom, she refrained from speaking to Elisha directly. Many problems arise due to a lack of propriety. Paul said that even in church matters, if a woman has a question, she is to ask her husband (1 Corinthians 14:35). This isn't chauvinistic. It's for protection, lest people find themselves emotionally involved, unknowingly walking a path that leads to disaster.

2 Kings 4:13–16
And he said unto him, Say now unto her, Behold, thou hast been careful for us with all this care; what is to be done for thee? wouldest thou be spoken for to the king, or to the captain of the host? And she answered, I dwell among mine own people. And he said, What then is to be done for her? And Gehazi answered, Verily she hath no child, and her husband is old. And he said, Call her. And when he had called her, she stood in the door. And he said, About this season, according to the time of life, thou shalt embrace a son. And she said, Nay, my lord, thou man of God, do not lie unto thine handmaid.

Fourthly, a great woman in the eyes of God is a woman of contentment. Only Gehazi spoke of her need.

The story is told of a king who was terribly discontent. He had everything he wanted, but he was still unsatisfied. A sorcerer was called who said, "The solution to your discontentment is simple: Find a man in your realm who is genuinely content. Order the shirt off his back and wear his shirt for two weeks. At the end of two weeks, you'll be totally content." So he sent his soldiers throughout the realm. They searched high and low and finally found a man who was totally content. "Where is his shirt?" the eager king asked.

"He doesn't own one," his soldiers replied.

How true that is. The man or woman who is content is not the one who has the most, but the one who needs the least. "I have *learned* to be content," said Paul (see Philippians 4:11). Contentment is something that comes naturally to no one. It must be learned.

2 Kings 4:17
And the woman conceived, and bare a son at that season that Elisha had said unto her, according to the time of life.

Because she was a great woman, this woman was greatly blessed. She bore a son.

2 Kings 4:18–21
And when the child was grown, it fell on a day, that he went out to his father to the reapers. And he said unto his father, My head, my head. And he said to a lad, Carry him to his mother. And when he had taken him, and brought him to his mother, he sat on her knees till noon, and then died. And she went up, and laid him on the bed of the man of God, and shut the door upon him, and went out.

The woman wasn't preparing a burial. She was preparing for a miracle. Hebrews 11:35 tells us there were women in the Old Testament who, by faith, saw their dead raised again to life. This Shunammite woman is one of two women who saw their sons rise from the dead. The other was the widow in 1 Kings 17. No doubt this woman had heard about that incident. With the same spirit on Elisha that was upon Elijah, she expected a miracle. So she laid her son's body in Elisha's chamber.

2 Kings 4:22, 23
And she called unto her husband, and said, Send me, I pray thee, one of the young men, and one of the asses, that I may run to the man of God, and come again. And he said, Wherefore wilt thou go to him to day? it is neither new moon, nor sabbath. And she said, It shall be well.

"Why are you going to see Elisha?" her husband asked. "It's not the new moon or sabbath."

In other words, "Why are you going to church? It's not Sunday."

2 Kings 4:24, 25 (a)
Then she saddled an ass, and said to her servant, Drive, and go forward; slack not thy riding for me, except I bid thee. So she went and came unto the man of God to mount Carmel . . .

The Shunammite woman found Elisha on Mt. Carmel. That's always where you find men of God, Moses on Mt. Sinai, Elijah on Mt. Carmel, Jesus and the disciples on Mt. Hermon, the Mount of Transfiguration. Are you a mountain man? If you desire to be a man or woman of God, you must learn the secret of the mountain, the place of isolation and elevation.

2 Kings 4:25 (b), 26
. . . And it came to pass, when the man of God saw her afar off, that he said to Gehazi his servant, Behold, yonder is that Shunammite. Run now, I pray thee, to meet her, and say unto her, Is it well with thee? is it well with thy husband? is it well with the child? And she answered, It is well.

Here, this great woman makes a powerful proclamation of faith when she says, "It is well."

2 Kings 4:27, 28
And when she came to the man of God to the hill, she caught him by the feet: but Gehazi came near to thrust her away. And the man of God said, Let her alone; for her soul is vexed within her: and the LORD hath hid it from me, and hath not told me. Then she said, Did I desire a son of my lord? did I not say, Do not deceive me?

Her spirit is strong, but we're seeing her flesh begin to fail. Can you relate to this? At one moment, you make a powerful proclamation of faith. Then, a few moments later, your faith falters. When that happens, understand that you're not alone. In fact, as I read the Scriptures, virtually every man or woman of faith went through times when their faith faltered.

2 Kings 4:29–32
Then he said to Gehazi, Gird up thy loins, and take my staff in thine hand, and go thy way: if thou meet any man, salute him not; and if any salute thee, answer him not again: and lay my staff upon the face of the child. And the mother of the child said, As the LORD liveth, and as thy soul liveth, I will not leave thee. And he arose, and followed her. And Gehazi passed on before them, and laid the staff upon the face of the child; but there was neither voice, nor hearing. Wherefore he went again to meet him, and told him, saying, The child is not awaked. And when Elisha was come into the house, behold, the child was dead, and laid upon his bed.

Elisha sent Gehazi with his staff. Straight and strong, the staff was symbolic of authority and integrity. Elisha felt as though the staff would somehow be instrumental in seeing a miracle happen. But that symbol of authority and integrity was absolutely powerless.

In this picture I see an important principle. That is, sometimes we try and approach people who are dead with a "straight and authoritative" Scripture, with the law or theology. And we wonder why it doesn't move them. Elisha then did something else, and so must we . . .

2 Kings 4:33–35 (a)
He went in therefore, and shut the door upon them twain, and prayed unto the LORD. And he went up, and lay upon the child, and put his mouth upon his mouth, and his eyes upon his eyes, and his hands upon his hands: and he stretched himself upon the child; and the flesh of the child waxed warm. Then he returned, and walked in the house to and fro; and went up, and stretched himself upon him . . .

Authority did nothing. Theology was lifeless. So Elisha made personal contact by laying on the child. It was an act of identification. He identified with him personally. After he laid himself out, throwing himself into the ministry, throwing himself wholeheartedly into this situation, he paced the floor. Why? I believe it was because he was praying intensely. And this is greatly needed in our lives. We must first make personal contact with the dying world around us. And then we must pray for them fervently and faithfully.

2 Kings 4:35 (b)
. . . and the child sneezed seven times, and the child opened his eyes.

When regeneration begins to happen, it doesn't always come with a big splash. Sometimes, it begins with just a little sneeze. We need to listen for those sneezes, even the faint beginning of something happening, and take hope. May they cause us to be even more fervent in prayer and more expectant in faith.

2 Kings 4:36, 37
And he called Gehazi, and said, Call this Shunammite. So he called her. And when she was

come in unto him, he said, Take up thy son. Then she went in, and fell at his feet, and bowed herself to the ground, and took up her son, and went out.

What a marvelous story of resurrection. May the Lord help us to be like Elisha, to make contact personally, to listen for sneezes carefully, to pray expectantly, and to see life in those who were dead spiritually.

2 Kings 4:38 (a)
And Elisha came again to Gilgal: and there was a dearth in the land . . .

A dearth in the land means there was famine.

2 Kings 4:38 (b)
. . . and the sons of the prophets were sitting before him: and he said unto his servant, Set on the great pot, and seethe pottage for the sons of the prophets.

Elisha told his servants to make pottage, vegetable stew, for his students.

2 Kings 4:39–41
And one went out into the field to gather herbs, and found a wild vine, and gathered thereof wild gourds his lap full, and came and shred them into the pot of pottage: for they knew them not. So they poured out for the men to eat. And it came to pass, as they were eating of the pottage, that they cried out, and said, O thou man of God, there is death in the pot. And they could not eat thereof. But he said, Then bring meal. And he cast it into the pot; and he said, Pour out for the people, that they may eat. And there was no harm in the pot.

The pottage was poisoned. The solution was to dilute the poison by pouring in the meal.

Like Elisha's students, we live in a time of drought—not geologically, but spiritually—due to the fact that so few churches teach the Word of God. In addition to the drought, however, there are all kinds of poisonous winds of doctrine being put in the pot, new fads and Christian trends. Our job is not to try and pick out the poison in the pot. Our job is to pour in the meal. Stay in the Scriptures, gang. Study the Word faithfully, consistently, daily. And as you study the Word of God the poison dissipates. Pour in the good stuff, and the bad stuff is naturally flushed out.

2 Kings 4:42
And there came a man from Baal-shalisha, and brought the man of God bread of the firstfruits, twenty loaves of barley, and full ears of corn in the husk thereof. And he said, Give unto the people, that they may eat.

During this time of drought and famine, a man came from the center of Baal worship bringing food to Elisha. A true shepherd, Elisha, in turn, ordered that the food be given to the flock. The Lord loves to do this yet today. He'll bless you through an unexpected person who will come with just the bread you need.

2 Kings 4:43 (a)
And his servitor said, What, should I set this before an hundred men?

"Twenty loaves is not going to be enough to feed one hundred men," said Gehazi. Sound familiar?

2 Kings 4:43 (b), 44
. . . He said again, Give the people, that they may eat: for thus saith the LORD, They shall eat, and shall leave thereof. So he set it before them, and they did eat, and left thereof, according to the word of the LORD.

There was indeed enough, plus leftovers. Of course, this is a preview of a greater Prophet and a mightier miracle that was to take place in John 6, when Jesus would feed 5,000 with only five loaves.

The firstfruits were given and they went far. Do you give the firstfruits of your finances, time, talents, and energy? The firstfruits belong to the Lord. And because this one unknown man gave his firstfruits, one hundred men were fed. Great things will be done whenever the people of God give Him their firstfruits rather than their leftovers.

5

2 Kings 5:1 (a)
Now Naaman, captain of the host of the king of Syria, was a great man with his master, and honourable, because by him the LORD had given deliverance unto Syria: he was also a mighty man in valour, but . . .

Naaman was a man who was well known, a man who was well favored, a man who was mightily used by the Lord, but . . . No matter how good our situation, this side of eternity, there always seems to be a "but."

2 Kings 5:1 (b)
. . . he was a leper.

Leprosy is a picture of sin. It begins small but spreads quickly. Sin is the same way. "This is so small. It's no big deal," we think. But it eats at us, erodes us, and eventually destroys us.

2 Kings 5:2, 3
And the Syrians had gone out by companies, and had brought away captive out of the land of Israel a little maid; and she waited on Naaman's wife. And she said unto her mistress, Would God my lord were with the prophet that is in Samaria! for he would recover him of his leprosy.

This young girl serving in the house of Naaman had been carried from Israel as a captive. She could have been bitter. Instead, she chose to be a blessing. As a result, she was the instrument the Lord would use to tell Naaman that there was hope.

Do you feel like you've been ripped off, like you've been stuck in a bad position or a bad place? You're there for a purpose! Like this servant girl, all you have to do is choose to be used.

2 Kings 5:4–7
And one went in, and told his lord, saying, Thus and thus said the maid that is of the land of Israel. And the king of Syria said, Go to, go, and I will send a letter unto the king of Israel. And he departed, and took with him ten talents of silver, and six thousand pieces of gold, and ten changes of raiment. And he brought the letter to the king of Israel, saying, Now when this letter is come unto thee, behold, I have therewith sent Naaman my servant to thee, that thou mayest recover him of his leprosy. And it came to pass, when the king of Israel had read the letter, that he rent his clothes, and said, Am I God, to kill and to make alive, that this man doth send unto me to recover a man of his leprosy? wherefore consider, I pray you, and see how he seeketh a quarrel against me.

"Oh, no!" said the king of Israel. "The king of Syria has sent a leper for me to cure. How can I do that? I'm not God!"

2 Kings 5:8–11
And it was so, when Elisha the man of God had heard that the king of Israel had rent his clothes, that he sent to the king, saying, Wherefore hast thou rent thy clothes? let him come now to me, and he shall know that there is a prophet in Israel. So Naaman came with his horses and with his chariot, and stood at the door of the house of Elisha. And Elisha sent a messenger unto him, saying, Go and wash in the Jordan seven times, and thy flesh shall come again to thee, and thou shalt be clean. But Naaman was wroth, and went away, and said, Behold, I thought, He will surely come out to me, and stand, and call on the name of the LORD his God, and strike his hand over the place, and recover the leper.

"Behold, I thought," said Naaman, and that's the mistake of every sinner. Instead of praying, instead of repenting, instead of crying out to God, he thinks.

2 Kings 5:12–14 (a)
Are not Abana and Pharpar, rivers of Damascus, better than all the waters of Israel? may I not wash in them, and be clean? So he turned and went away in a rage. And his servants came near, and spake unto him, and said, My father, if the prophet had bid thee do some great thing, wouldest thou not have done it? how much rather then, when he saith to thee, Wash, and be clean? Then went he down, and dipped himself seven times in Jordan, according to the saying of the man of God . . .

Here we see a vivid illustration of the work of salvation . . .

First, leprosy is a picture of sin.

Second, the message of hope was given to a little girl. Paul tells us that the Lord loves to use the weak things of the world to confound the strong (1 Corinthians 1:27). If you feel weak, if you don't consider yourself to be very knowledgeable in the things of God, you are an ideal candidate for God to use because you won't take any glory.

Third, the message was more important than the messenger. Naaman thought Elisha would do something spectacular. Instead, he gave a simple word. Why was Naaman to dip in the Jordan River? The word *Jordan* means "judgment." The number seven speaks of completion. Thus, Naaman was to immerse himself completely in the river of judgment. How are we to be cleansed of our leprosy, of our sin? By immersing ourselves fully in the judgment that Jesus bore for us on the Cross of Calvary.

2 Kings 5:14 (b)
. . . and his flesh came again like unto the flesh of a little child, and he was clean.

"You must become as a little child if you are to be born again," Jesus said (Mark 10:15). And Naaman did just that.

2 Kings 5:15–17
And he returned to the man of God, he and all his company, and came, and stood before

him: and he said, Behold, now I know that there is no God in all earth, but in Israel: now therefore, I pray thee, take a blessing of thy servant. But he said, As the LORD liveth, before whom I stand, I will receive none. And he urged him to take it; but he refused. And Naaman said, Shall there not then, I pray thee, be given to thy servant two mules' burden of earth? for thy servant will henceforth offer neither burnt offering nor sacrifice unto other gods, but unto the LORD.

After Elisha refused his offer of payment, Naaman asked the prophet for permission to take dirt from Israel back to Syria. Why would he want to do this? In the pagan culture of the day, it was thought that deities were localized, that they only had power over specific countries or regions. Thus, by bringing dirt from Israel home with him, Naaman thought he would be bringing home a "base" from which the Israelite God could work.

2 Kings 5:18
In this thing the LORD pardon thy servant, that when my master goeth into the house of Rimmon to worship there, and he leaneth on my hand, and I bow myself in the house of Rimmon: when I bow down myself in the house of Rimmon, the LORD pardon thy servant in this thing.

"As the king's right-hand man, I will have to accompany him into the temple of Rimmon and bow down to this false god," Naaman said. "May the Lord pardon me for this."

2 Kings 5:19
And he said unto him, Go in peace. So he departed from him a little way.

"Go in *peace?*" you say. "Why doesn't Elisha correct Naaman? Why doesn't he tell him he doesn't need dirt from Israel to worship the God of Israel? Why doesn't he forbid him from bowing to the false god, Rimmon?"

I suggest it's because, realizing he was talking to a baby believer, Elisha didn't want to burden him with too many corrections or expectations. Of Jesus, it was said, "A bruised reed He will not break, And smoking flax He will not quench" (Isaiah 42:3). In other words, Jesus responds to even the faintest glimmer of faith.

As we walk with the Lord, He slowly but surely refines us, convicts us, changes us to be sure. But it's over a period of time. The tendency in some Christians is to lay on a brand new believer the convictions and understandings they have acquired over twenty years of walking with the Lord. That's wrong. The Holy Spirit is quite capable of convicting. He doesn't need our help. *Gospel* means "good news." We are to preach the gospel, glad tidings, the message of peace to all people, knowing that the Holy Spirit will tend to the matter of Rimmon in due time.

2 Kings 5:20–23
But Gehazi, the servant of Elisha the man of God, said, Behold, my master hath spared Naaman this Syrian, in not receiving at his hands that which he brought: but, as the LORD liveth, I will run after him, and take somewhat of him. So Gehazi followed after Naaman. And when Naaman saw him running after him, he lighted down from the chariot to meet him, and said, Is all well? And he said, All is well. My master hath sent me, saying, Behold, even now there be come to me from mount Ephraim two young men of the sons of the prophets: give them, I pray thee, a talent of silver, and two changes of garments. And Naaman said, Be content, take two talents. And he urged him, and bound two talents of silver in two bags, with two changes of garments, and laid them upon two of his servants; and they bare them before him.

Taking advantage of the situation, Gehazi caught up with Naaman and said, "Elisha changed his mind. Two prophets' sons came into town and he wants to bless them. So he wants some silver and some clothes after all."

2 Kings 5:24, 25
And when he came to the tower, he took them from their hand, and bestowed them in the house: and he let the men go, and they departed. But he went in, and stood before his master. And Elisha said unto him, Whence comest thou, Gehazi? And he said, Thy servant went no whither.

"Where have you been?" Elisha asked Gehazi.

"Nowhere," Gehazi answered.

2 Kings 5:26, 27
And he said unto him, Went not mine heart with thee, when the man turned again from his chariot to meet thee? Is it a time to receive money, and to receive garments, and oliveyards, and vineyards, and sheep, and oxen, and menservants, and maidservants? The leprosy therefore of Naaman shall cleave unto thee, and unto thy seed for ever. And he went out from his presence a leper as white as snow.

Here, we see the tragic downfall of *Gehazi*. His name means "denier." Many scholars see in him a picture, or type, of Judas Iscariot. Following are four warning signs for any servant of the Lord . . .

From his life, we can see that Gehazi was compassionless. When the woman whose son died grabbed the feet of Elisha, he wanted to push her away (4:27), even as Judas was offended when Mary poured oil on Jesus' feet and wiped them with her hair. "This is a waste," Judas said. "That money could have been used for something better" (John 12:1–6).

Secondly, Gehazi was powerless. He was sent to raise up a woman's son, but he was impotent (4:31). You know you are losing your effectiveness as a servant when you are no longer able to be used in reviving the spiritually dead, when your witness is ineffective, or absent altogether.

Thirdly, Gehazi was faithless. When the man brought the firstfruits, it was he who said, "There's no way this food will feed all these people" (4:42).

Lastly, Gehazi was covetous. He wanted the silver and the garments, just as Judas sold Jesus Christ for a few pieces of silver. Judas was a follower of Jesus. And yet something happened. Compassionless, powerless, faithless, and overcome with covetousness, he ended up denying the Lord. So did Gehazi.

Every one of us is vulnerable. That's why it's imperative that we say, "Lord, search *my* heart. See if there be any wicked way in *me*."

6

2 Kings 6:1, 2

And the sons of the prophets said unto Elisha, Behold now, the place where we dwell with thee is too strait for us. Let us go, we pray thee, unto Jordan, and take thence every man a beam, and let us make us a place there, where we may dwell. And he answered, Go ye.

These men were dedicated to God. They were sons of the prophets, studying the Scriptures, practicing prophecy, and being discipled by Elisha. As the Word went into these men, they began to increase numerically, and it was time for a building project. So they went out to build a bigger place, to expand the ministry, to become more effective.

2 Kings 6:3, 4 (a)

And one said, Be content, I pray thee, and go with thy servants. And he answered, I will go. So he went with them . . .

The request of even one person can constitute a call from God. Let us never succumb to the scourge of statistics, where we analyze what we will do and where we will go according to numbers. In Acts 8, Philip was involved in a huge revival in Samaria. Yet the Spirit called him away to minister to just one man in the desert.

2 Kings 6:4 (b), 5 (a)

. . . And when they came to Jordan, they cut down wood. But as one was felling a beam, the axe head fell into the water . . .

One of the men found himself in a predicament. While he was doing the work of the ministry, the axe head he was using fell in the Jordan River. The axe head in this story is a symbol, a picture of the cutting edge of power, of effectiveness. It speaks of the Holy Spirit.

The only way we'll ever build anything—be it ministry or marriage, families or friendships—is if we build in the power of the Holy Spirit. The Psalmist declares that those who build apart from the Lord labor in vain (127:1). You can follow every principle of marriage, parenting, and ministry, and still fail if you are not doing it in the power of the Holy Ghost, for it is "not by might, nor by power, but by My Spirit saith the Lord" (Zechariah 4:6).

2 Kings 6:5 (b)

. . . and he cried, and said, Alas, master! for it was borrowed.

It was borrowed. Always remember that. The power upon your life is not your own. If you begin to think that the effectiveness of your ministry or the success of your marriage is because of who you are, one day you will wake up like Samson and stand to do battle, only to find, as he did, that the Spirit of the Lord has departed (Judges 16:20).

- "Grieve not the Holy Spirit," the Word declares (Ephesians 4:30).
- "My Spirit shall not strive with man forever," the Father says (Genesis 6:3).
- "Quench not the Spirit," Paul says (1 Thessalonians 5:19).

How did this man lose his axe head? He lost it in the process of service. He was trying to do what was right, but he became careless. You see, an axe head does not fall off suddenly. It becomes loose slowly.

At this point, all the young man had was a wooden axe handle. Wood in Scriptures is symbolic of the flesh (1 Corinthians 3:12). Here's a young man, doing the work of the ministry, and suddenly, the power is gone, leaving him nothing but the wooden handle of the flesh. To his credit, he didn't say, "So what if the axe head is gone?

Who cares if the power has departed? I'll just use this handle." That would have been ridiculous. And yet what do we do? So often, the cutting edge is gone, the power lost, yet we keep on ministering even though the anointing is not there.

This man said, "Alas master." That is always the first step to reclaiming the cutting edge. Open and honest confession that you're not on the cutting edge like you once were is always the place where restoration begins.

2 Kings 6:6 (a)
And the man of God said, Where fell it? And he shewed him the place . . .

Elisha asked one question: "Where did you lose it?" To the church at Ephesus, Jesus said, "I know your good works, your knowledge, your giving. But I have something against you for you have left your first love. Remember from whence you are fallen and repent. And do your first works again" (see Revelation 2:1–5).

Was there a time when you loved the Lord radically, when you worshiped the Lord fervently, when you served the Lord consistently? Was there a time when you couldn't wait to get in the Word, when you found witnessing something that was natural? Was there a time in your life when you were more in love with Jesus and more fervent in serving Him than you are today?

If so, remember how it once was, and then repent. Say, "Lord, I admit to You, I confess before you that I'm not in the place I once was, in the place I long to be. And I repent." Then do your first works again. What were you doing when you loved the Lord? Did you get up early to pray? Do it again. Did you open your house and share the gospel with people? Do it again. Did you come consistently to Bible study and worship meetings? Do it again. It's so simple. Just go back to the place where you lost your cutting edge.

2 Kings 6:6 (b)
. . . And he cut down a stick, and cast it in thither; and the iron did swim.

Elisha took a stick and threw it into the Jordan. And when the flesh was cast into the place of expectation (Joshua 3:13), the cutting edge reappeared. If you think iron can't float, think about the USS *Missouri*. Battleships are iron, and they float quite well.

2 Kings 6:7
Therefore said he, Take it up to thee. And he put out his hand, and took it.

As the axe head floated to the surface, Elisha said, "I've shown it to you. Now it's your responsibility to reach down and grab hold of it." That's always the way it is in the things of God. He causes a truth or understanding to surface, and then He says, "Reach out and grab it." I think of Noah. He released a dove to see if there was dry land, and Genesis 8:9 says that he reached out and brought the dove unto him. The dove is a type of the Holy Spirit and Noah reached out, grabbed hold, and brought it in. May we do the same.

2 Kings 6:8–10
Then the king of Syria warred against Israel, and took counsel with his servants, saying, In such and such a place shall be my camp. And the man of God sent unto the king of Israel, saying, Beware that thou pass not such a place; for thither the Syrians are come down. And the king of Israel sent to the place which the man of God told him and warned him of, and saved himself there, not once nor twice.

Speaking with the word of knowledge (1 Corinthians 12:8), Elisha warned the king of Israel about the ambushes the Syrians tried to set against them.

2 Kings 6:11
Therefore the heart of the king of Syria was sore troubled for this thing; and he called his servants, and said unto them, Will ye not shew me which of us is for the king of Israel?

"How are the Israelites able to avoid our ambushes?" the king of Syria asked. "There must be a spy in our midst."

2 Kings 6:12–14
And one of his servants said, None, my lord, O king: but Elisha, the prophet that is in Israel, telleth the king of Israel the words that thou speakest in thy bedchamber. And he said, Go and spy where he is, that I may send and fetch him. And it was told him, saying, Behold, he is in Dothan. Therefore sent he thither horses, and chariots, and a great host: and they came by night, and compassed the city about.

When it was determined that it was Elisha who was tipping off the Israelites, the king of Syria sent troops to Dathan to capture him.

2 Kings 6:15
And when the servant of the man of God was risen early, and gone forth, behold, an host compassed the city both with horses and chariots. And his servant said unto him, Alas, my master! how shall we do?

Although Elisha's servant was lacking faith, he was at least observant enough to get up early to see that he was surrounded by the enemy. Most people never even see the reality of the enemy. There are all kinds of forces at work against us. We're surrounded by the host of hell because Satan is out to destroy us. Elisha's servant understood this. But he needed further revelation . . .

2 Kings 6:16
And he answered, Fear not: for they that be with us are more than they that be with them.

"Fear not." Elisha first comforted his servant with the Word. And then he prayed . . .

2 Kings 6:17
And Elisha prayed, and said, LORD, I pray thee, open his eyes, that he may see. And the LORD opened the eyes of the young man; and he saw: and, behold, the mountain was full of horses and chariots of fire round about Elisha.

"Lord, open his eyes," Elisha prayed. And when his servant's eyes were fully open, he not only saw the problem, but he saw the solution. That is, he saw that the enemy that surrounded him was itself surrounded by angels and chariots far more powerful than any earthly army.

How I pray that, in every situation we face, we would not only see the problem but that we would see the solution—that the Lord is with us; that His angels are surrounding us; that His promises are applicable to us. He says He will never leave us or forsake us (Hebrews 13:5). He says He will complete the good work He began in us (Philippians 1:6). He says all things work together for good to them that love God (Romans 8:28). He says nothing separates us from His love (Romans 8:35–38). He says all of our needs will be met according to His riches (Philippians 4:19). He says He is the God who heals us (Exodus 15:26). We need to see the reality of the spiritual forces surrounding the enemies that surround us.

Happy is the people whose God is the Lord (Psalm 144:15). The joy of the Lord is your strength (Nehemiah 8:10). Rejoice evermore (1 Thessalonians 5:16). Who is the person who is happy, who rejoices evermore? It's the one whose eyes are open to see the reality of spiritual promises and the presence of God. Who is the sad, depressed, discouraged, defeated one? The one who sees the problem but not the solution. May God give us eyes to see (Ephesians 1:18).

Even though you thought you were doomed, I suggest that you cannot even recall what you were worried about five years ago. Why? Because the promises of God stood. He is faithful. He promised to guide and provide, and He did. Maybe you know someone who thinks he's going down, going under. Do what Elisha did. First, speak a word of exhortation. Tell him to "fear not." Then pray a prayer of intercession. "Lord, open his eyes that he might see the sovereignty of God, the promises of Scripture, the reality of Jesus."

2 Kings 6:18, 19
And when they came down to him, Elisha prayed unto the LORD, and said, Smite this people, I pray thee, with blindness. And he smote them with blindness according to the word of Elisha. And Elisha said unto them, This is not the way, neither is this the city: follow me, and I will bring you to the man whom ye seek. But he led them to Samaria.

In this, Elisha is a picture, or type, of Jesus Christ. Like the Syrians, we were blinded by sin. Then, through some person or circumstance, we heard the voice of our Greater than Elisha, saying, "This is not the way. You're going in the wrong direction," and we followed Him. Where did He lead us? Right into the capital city of God's people, right into His body, His church.

"By this shall all men know that you are My disciples," Jesus said, "by your love one for another" (see John 13:35). Love for the family of God is the proof of our commitment to Jesus.

2 Kings 6:20–23
And it came to pass, when they were come into Samaria, that Elisha said, LORD, open the eyes of these men, that they may see. And the LORD opened their eyes, and they saw; and, behold, they were in the midst of Samaria. And the king of Israel said unto Elisha, when he saw them, My father, shall I smite them? shall I smite them? And he answered, Thou shalt not smite them: wouldest thou smite those whom thou hast taken captive with thy sword and with thy bow? set bread and water before them, that they may eat and drink, and go to their master. And he prepared great provision for them: and when they had eaten and drunk, he sent them away, and they went to their master. So the bands of Syria came no more into the land of Israel.

Instead of killing his enemies, Elisha fed them. Paul tells us to do the same . . .

> Dearly beloved, avenge not yourselves, but rather give place unto wrath: for it is written, Vengeance is mine; I will repay, saith the Lord.

Therefore if thine enemy hunger, feed him; if he thirst, give him drink: for in so doing thou shalt heap coals of fire on his head. Romans 12:19, 20

In Bible days, if a fire went out in her home, a woman would go to her next-door neighbor's with a clay pot on her head and borrow some coals with which she could reignite her fire. Thus, Paul's admonition was given not to burn someone up, but to warm someone up, not to burn him out, but to help him out. That's love. "Be not overcome by evil, but overcome evil with good," Paul went on to say (Romans 12:21). And here, Elisha is doing just that.

2 Kings 6:24, 25
And it came to pass after this, that Ben-hadad king of Syria gathered all his host, and went up, and besieged Samaria. And there was a great famine in Samaria: and, behold, they besieged it, until an ass's head was sold for fourscore pieces of silver, and the fourth part of a cab of dove's dung for five pieces of silver.

Time passed, and Ben-hadad was determined to destroy Samaria once and for all. He surrounded the city and famine followed.

2 Kings 6:26–30
And as the king of Israel was passing by upon the wall, there cried a woman unto him, saying, Help, my lord, O king. And he said, If the LORD do not help thee, whence shall I help thee? out of the barnfloor, or out of the winepress? And the king said unto her, What aileth thee? And she answered, This woman said unto me, Give thy son, that we may eat him to day, and we will eat my son to morrow. So we boiled my son, and did eat him: and I said unto her on the next day, Give thy son, that we may eat him: and she hath hid her son. And it came to pass, when the king heard the words of the woman, that he rent his clothes; and he passed by upon the wall, and the people looked, and, behold, he had sackcloth within upon his flesh.

When the king of Israel heard this story of cannibalism, he tore his clothes, and the people saw that underneath his clothes, he wore sackcloth next to his skin. This was a sign of sorrow. The king was sad about the conditions, but he wasn't repentant. He wasn't seeking the Lord, for the next verse reveals his heart . . .

2 Kings 6:31
Then he said, God do so and more also to me, if the head of Elisha the son of Shaphat shall stand on him this day.

As is so often the case, God and His people were blamed for the tragedy and difficulty in the land.

2 Kings 6:32, 33
But Elisha sat in his house, and the elders sat with him; and the king sent a man from before him: but ere the messenger came to him, he said to the elders, See ye how this son of a murderer hath sent to take away mine head? look, when the messenger cometh, shut the door, and hold him fast at the door: is not the sound of his master's feet behind him? And while he yet talked with them, behold, the messenger came down unto him: and he said, Behold, this evil is of the LORD; what should I wait for the LORD any longer?

Elisha knew by the word of knowledge that his neck was on the line . . .

7

2 Kings 7:1
Then Elisha said, Hear ye the word of the LORD; Thus saith the LORD, To morrow about this time shall a measure of fine flour be sold for a shekel, and two measures of barley for a shekel, in the gate of Samaria.

"Not only will the famine be over tomorrow, but there will be such an abundance of food that it will be cheap to buy," Elisha declared.

2 Kings 7:2 (a)
Then a lord on whose hand the king leaned answered the man of God, and said, Behold, if the LORD would make windows in heaven, might this thing be?

"Even if the Lord opened windows in heaven, a famine can't end in one day," the king's right-hand man scoffed.

2 Kings 7:2 (b)
. . . And he said, Behold, thou shalt see it with thine eyes, but shalt not eat thereof.

"You'll see it happen, but you won't taste it," Elisha prophesied.

2 Kings 7:3
And there were four leprous men at the entering in of the gate: and they said one to another, Why sit we here until we die?

According to Leviticus 13, these leprous men were not allowed to go into the city lest they spread their disease. Normally, they would subsist on leftovers tossed over the wall. But during the famine, there were no leftovers. By abandoning their usual posts, therefore, they knew they had nothing to lose. But they couldn't have imagined how much they had to gain . . .

***For topical study of 2 Kings 7:3 entitled "Why Sit We Here?" turn to page* 1045.**

2 Kings 7:4–6 (a)
If we say, We will enter into the city, then the famine is in the city, and we shall die there: and if we sit still here, we die also. Now therefore come, and let us fall unto the host of the Syrians: if they save us alive, we shall live; and if they kill us, we shall but die. And they rose up in the twilight, to go unto the camp of the Syrians: and when they were come to the uttermost part of the camp of Syria, behold, there was no man there. For the Lord had made the host of the Syrians to hear a noise of chariots, and a noise of horses, even the noise of a great host . . .

I suggest the Syrians heard the same chariots, the same horses, the same army Elisha and his servant had seen. That is, they heard the army of the Lord (2 Kings 6:17).

2 Kings 7:6 (b)–8
. . . and they said one to another, Lo, the king of Israel hath hired against us the kings of the Hittites, and the kings of the Egyptians, to come upon us. Wherefore they arose and fled in the twilight, and left their tents, and their horses, and their asses, even the camp as it was, and fled for their life. And when these lepers came to the uttermost part of the camp, they went into one tent, and did eat and drink, and carried thence silver, and gold, and raiment, and went and hid it; and came again, and entered into another tent, and carried thence also, and went and hid it.

Thinking they were being attacked by both the Hittite and the Egyptian armies, the Syrians had fled across the Jordan, leaving their food, gold, and supplies behind. As a result, the lepers hit the jackpot!

2 Kings 7:9 (a)
Then they said one to another, We do not well: this day is a day of good tidings, and we hold our peace . . .

What about us? We've been given so much. Anytime we want, we can turn on TV or the radio and hear good Bible teaching. We have Christian bookstores and Christian schools. We have countless Christian opportunities and fellowship opportunities. And if we're not careful, we can be just like these lepers, devouring one book, one study, one program after another while all around us are people who are dying. I fear we as Christians are increasingly becoming connoisseurs of fine sermons, critical of Bible studies and theological positions, wondering what new truth we can find, what new insight we can glean, how we can be happier, while our neighbors and coworkers are starving spiritually and headed for hell eternally.

2 Kings 7:9 (b)–12
. . . if we tarry till the morning light, some mischief will come upon us: now therefore come, that we may go and tell the king's household. So they came and called unto the porter of the city: and they told them, saying, We came to the camp of the Syrians, and, behold, there was no man there, neither voice of man, but horses tied, and asses tied, and the tents as they were. And he called the porters; and they told it to the king's house within. And the king arose in the night, and said unto his servants, I will now shew you what the Syrians have done to us. They know that we be hungry; therefore are they gone out of the camp to hide themselves in the field, saying, When they come out of the city, we shall catch them alive, and get into the city.

When advised of the food and wealth available in the Syrian camp, the king thought it was a decoy to lure the Israelites out of the city only to be killed by the Syrian army waiting to ambush them.

2 Kings 7:13
And one of his servants answered and said, Let some take, I pray thee, five of the horses that remain, which are left in the city, (behold, they are as all the multitude of Israel that are left in it: behold, I say, they are even as all the multitude of the Israelites that are consumed:) and let us send and see.

"We have five horses left," said one of the king's servants. "Let's send them out with five riders and see what happens." It has been wisely said that the fear of failure is the father of failure. If you are afraid to try, you are guaranteed to fail.

2 Kings 7:14–17 (a)
They took therefore two chariot horses; and the king sent after the host of the Syrians,

saying, Go and see. And they went after them unto Jordan: and, lo, all the way was full of garments and vessels, which the Syrians had cast away in their haste. And the messengers returned, and told the king. And the people went out, and spoiled the tents of the Syrians. So a measure of fine flour was sold for a shekel, and two measures of barley for a shekel, according to the word of the LORD. And the king appointed the lord on whose hand he leaned to have the charge of the gate . . .

When word came back that the report was true—that the Syrians truly had left their camp—the king posted his right-hand man at the gate in an attempt to control the crowd.

2 Kings 7:17 (b)–20
. . . and the people trode upon him in the gate, and he died, as the man of God had said, who spake when the king came down to him. And it came to pass as the man of God had spoken to the king, saying, Two measures of barley for a shekel, and a measure of fine flour for a shekel, shall be to morrow about this time in the gate of Samaria: And that lord answered the man of God, and said, Now, behold, if the LORD should make windows in heaven, might such a thing be? And he said, Behold, thou shalt see it with thine eyes, but shalt not eat thereof. And so it fell out unto him: for the people trode upon him in the gate, and he died.

Here, we see the tragedy of unbelief. The king's right-hand man could see the food but he was trampled to death before he could taste it. The same thing still happens. Without faith, it is impossible to please God (Hebrews 11:6). You can see what others are experiencing and you can see what others are doing, but you won't enjoy it yourself if you lack faith. You'll be trampled under, feeling like you're stepped on, walked over, missing out. The lepers dined; the counselor of the king died and the difference between them wasn't health, intelligence, riches, or power. It was simply faith.

WHY SIT WE HERE?

A Topical Study of 2 KINGS 7:3

In the days of Elisha, King Ben-hadad of Syria decided to besiege Samaria, the capital city of Israel. His strategy was to surround the city with thousands of his troops. In so doing, he would cut off the supplies that would normally be brought into the city. So effective was his strategy that, as he besieged the city month after month, a great famine ensued so brutal that the Word tells us a donkey's head sold for eighty pieces of silver. I don't know what you can do with a donkey's head other than boil it for soup. Therefore, even donkey-head soup would have been an extravagance.

As the king of Israel cruised through the city of Samaria to assess the situation, a woman cried out, "O, king, help me."

"How can I help you if God doesn't help you?" he said. And his response is all too often ours. If you are facing tough times, be careful. The tendency can be to blame the Lord. But, in reality, the difficulties we experience are often the results of our own foolishness and sin.

In the midst of this devastating famine, a group of lepers decided that it made no sense for them to continue to sit outside the city wall, waiting for the scraps of food that used to be thrown their way. "Let's go to the Syrian camp," they said. "Maybe they'll show mercy to us. We're going to die anyway, so we have nothing to lose."

As they made the journey across the field, what they didn't know was that the Lord had done a miracle. That same evening, He had caused the Syrians to hear sounds of horses, chariots, and soldiers. Hearing the sound of a huge army approaching, the Syrians panicked. So when the lepers cruised into the camp, they were shocked to find it totally deserted. Food was still bubbling in the pots. Bread was left on the table. Amazed by the abundance of silver, gold, and food, the lepers went from tent to tent, gobbling the food and hiding the gold. Finally, one of the lepers said, "What we're doing isn't right. We must go back to the city and share this good news." So they returned to the city and told the gatekeeper that the Syrian camp was deserted and that there was an abundance of food for everyone.

"It's an ambush," the king said. But he sent five horses and riders to check it out. When the lepers' report was verified, the people rushed through the gates, trampling the king's right-hand man, and found enough food to see them through until their crops were restored.

In this story, I see application for three groups of people . . . .

Dining Rather than Doubting

When Elisha told the king that the famine would be over in twenty-four hours, the king's assistant scoffed. "You'll see the food," Elisha then said. "But you won't be able to taste it."

There are those who, like the king's assistant, don't believe what they hear. God says, "I want to forgive your sin. I want to save you. I want to bless you. I want to give you eternal life freely," but they don't believe Him.

A beggar named Lazarus and a rich man both found themselves in eternity with a great gulf separating them. Lazarus was in paradise. The rich man was in the place of torment.

"Lazarus," the rich man said. "Come over here. Dip your finger in the water and cool my tongue. I'm tormented in this flame" (Luke 16). At that point, the rich man clearly saw the reality of paradise. But he never tasted of it.

"O, taste and see that the Lord is good," the psalmist declares (Psalm 34:8).

How?

Simply by believing in your heart and confessing with your mouth that Jesus Christ rose from the dead, for then you're saved (Romans 10:9).

Let us not be trampled under by life. Let us not be those who see what the Word says, but refuse to believe it; who hear the Word, but don't practice it; who know the principles of the Word, but don't apply them. Let us taste and see that the Lord is indeed good. Let us dine rather than doubt.

Stepping Out Rather than Sitting Back

Maybe you're in a place where you feel leprous and famished, relegated to sitting outside the city, barely surviving on crumbs of hope. Our culture says, "Take it easy. Kick back." But I believe the Word of God says, "Take a chance. Step out." Faith is never learned in comfort. We learn faith when we're pressed, when we're hurting, when we're starving. Faith honors God and God honors faith.

These lepers had the faith to step out, to take a chance. If you feel like you're barely surviving spiritually, I would encourage you to follow their lead, to take a chance and step out in faith. Why sit where you are until you die, be it relationally, vocationally, or in ministry? Step out and see what the Lord will do. Exercise the faith God has given you, utilize the gifts He has embedded within you and watch mountains move (Matthew 17:20).

Giving Rather than Gorging

Finally, there are those who, having stepped out in faith, have found abundance. Perhaps you have eaten abundantly, as the lepers did. Maybe you have been enriched spiritually with silver and gold from the Word of God. But it is not good that we should gorge ourselves on more and more of the gospel in a world that is starving and dying. I think it brings grief to the Lord that we go from this seminar to that meeting, trying to find how to be happier, richer, more blessed while there is a world dying of starvation because they don't know the simple plan of salvation. This ought not be.

May the Lord speak to us that we would come to our senses as did the lepers and say, "This is not good. I need to take my eyes off myself, quit worrying about feeding myself, and reach out to those who are dying."

I don't think it's coincidental that the first two letters in "gospel" are "go." May we be a people of faith who share the glad tidings, the truth of the riches God has for all people if they will simply come to Him.

---

8 **2 Kings 8:1**
Then spake Elisha unto the woman, whose son he had restored to life, saying, Arise, and go thou and thine household, and sojourn wheresoever thou canst sojourn: for the LORD hath called for a famine; and it shall also come upon the land seven years.

In the day of Elijah, God sent a terrible famine that lasted three and one-half years. Here, in the day of Elisha, another famine will come, but it will last seven years. That's the way the Lord works. He slowly but surely increases the pressure in our lives until we bow our knee and say, "Lord, *Your* will be done."

When Elisha told the woman whose son he restored to life that famine was coming, he didn't say, "Here's a miracle to see you through." He said, "You'd better do something practical. Go somewhere the famine is not going to hit." Sometimes the Lord does something miraculous. Other times, He works very naturally. Elijah told the widow that if she made bread out of the ingredients she had, the Lord would continue to supply for her all the days of the famine (1 Kings 17). On the other hand, Elisha—who did even more miracles than Elijah—said to this woman, "I'm not promising a miracle. I'm telling you to do something practical: leave."

We can't box the Lord in. He works differently with different individuals in different times. You'll find nothing but frustration if you try to formulize God. God didn't write His Word like a manual. He didn't say, "Here's fifteen steps for healing the sick and ten steps for helping the hurting." I have often wished the Bible were written differently than it was. It seems there should be sections on Marriage, Parenting, and Finances. Why did God write it this way? Because in His Word, we find general principles, but we must seek Him for specifics. Why? Because He wants to hear from us.

Dear saint, the Lord truly loves you and wants to spend time with you. The only difference between a strong believer and a weak one is responsiveness. The times you've been wakened in the night, thinking it was the pie you ate or the problems you face may have been the Lord, tapping you on the shoulder, saying, "I enjoy your company and I'd like to spend some time with you right now." The times you felt a stirring in your heart while you watched TV may have been the Lord calling you to spend a few moments with Him. God doesn't have favorites. He doesn't arbitrarily bless some more than others. No, the people who develop and mature in Him are simply those who have said, "I'll turn off the TV or roll out of bed in response to His call." And I guarantee not a one is disappointed.

2 Kings 8:2
And the woman arose, and did after the saying of the man of God: and she went with her household, and sojourned in the land of the Philistines seven years.

The land of the Philistines was the southern coastal area of Palestine, a beautiful area by the beach.

2 Kings 8:3–6
And it came to pass at the seven years' end, that the woman returned out of the land of the Philistines: and she went forth to cry unto the king for her house and for her land. And the king talked with Gehazi the servant of the man of God, saying, Tell me, I pray thee, all the great things that Elisha hath done. And it came to pass, as he was telling the king how he had restored a dead body to life, that, behold, the woman, whose son he had restored to life, cried to the king for her house and for her land. And Gehazi said, My lord, O king, this is the woman, and this is her son, whom Elisha restored to life. And when the king asked the woman, she told him. So the king appointed unto her a certain officer, saying, Restore all that was hers, and all the fruits of the field since the day that she left the land, even until now.

The famine over, the woman whose son Elisha had healed returned to Israel. At the very same time she made her way to talk to the king about reclaiming her property, Elisha's servant was telling the king about the miracle God had done in the life of her son. Evidently intrigued, the king restored all that was hers.

In this, I am reminded of the account in Acts 23, where we read that Paul's nephew "just so happened" to hear of a plot to kill Paul. Paul's life was spared because God positioned his nephew in the right place at the right time, just as He positioned Gehazi in the right place at the right time to provide for this woman. In a believer's life, nothing is coincidental or accidental. God's hand is in every detail.

2 Kings 8:7–10
And Elisha came to Damascus; and Benhadad the king of Syria was sick; and it was told him, saying, The man of God is come hither. And the king said unto Hazael, Take a present in thine hand, and go, meet the man of God, and inquire of the LORD by him, saying, Shall I recover of this disease? So Hazael went to meet him, and took a present with him, even of every good thing of Damascus, forty camels' burden, and came and stood before him, and said, Thy son Benhadad king of Syria hath sent me to thee, saying, Shall I recover of this disease? And Elisha said unto him, Go, say unto him, Thou mayest certainly recover: howbeit the LORD hath shewed me that he shall surely die.

Elisha told Hazael that the king would, in fact, die but not of the disease he had.

2 Kings 8:11
And he settled his countenance stedfastly, until he was ashamed: and the man of God wept.

Elisha joins the company of Jeremiah, Paul, and Jesus, men who wept not for themselves, but for the sorrow in the world brought about by sin.

2 Kings 8:12, 13
And Hazael said, Why weepeth my lord? And he answered, Because I know the evil that thou wilt do unto the children of Israel: their strong holds wilt thou set on fire, and their young men wilt thou slay with the sword, and wilt dash their children, and rip up their women with child. And Hazael said, But what, is thy servant a dog, that he should do this great thing? And Elisha answered, The LORD hath shewed me that thou shalt be king over Syria.

"The Lord has shown me that you're going to be king, and that you're going to be cruel," Elisha answered.

2 Kings 8:14, 15
So he departed from Elisha, and came to his master; who said to him, What said Elisha

to thee? And he answered, He told me that thou shouldest surely recover. And it came to pass on the morrow, that he took a thick cloth, and dipped it in water, and spread it on his face, so that he died: and Hazael reigned in his stead.

Hazael pretended to be caring for Ben-hadad. In reality, he smothered him and reigned in his place, just as Elisha had prophesied.

2 Kings 8:16–18
And in the fifth year of Joram the son of Ahab king of Israel, Jehoshaphat being then king of Judah, Jehoram the son of Jehoshaphat king of Judah began to reign. Thirty and two years old was he when he began to reign; and he reigned eight years in Jerusalem. And he walked in the way of the kings of Israel, as did the house of Ahab: for the daughter of Ahab was his wife: and he did evil in the sight of the LORD.

"Be not unequally yoked with unbelievers," Paul would write (2 Corinthians 6:14). The reason is seen here. Jehoram married the unbelieving daughter of Ahab and it lead to his downfall.

2 Kings 8:19–24
Yet the LORD would not destroy Judah for David his servant's sake, as he promised him to give him alway a light, and to his children. In his days Edom revolted from under the hand of Judah, and made a king over themselves. So Joram went over to Zair, and all the chariots with him: and he rose by night, and smote the Edomites which compassed him about, and the captains of the chariots: and the people fled into their tents. Yet Edom revolted from under the hand of Judah unto this day. Then Libnah revolted at the same time. And the rest of the acts of Joram, and all that he did, are they not written in the book of the chronicles of the kings of Judah? And Joram slept with his fathers, and was buried with his fathers in the city of David: and Ahaziah his son reigned in his stead.

Joram or Jehoram as he is also called, was a total failure, largely due to the fact that he married an unbeliever who led him in the ways of evil.

2 Kings 8:25–29
In the twelfth year of Joram the son of Ahab king of Israel did Ahaziah the son of Jehoram king of Judah begin to reign. Two and twenty years old was Ahaziah when he began to reign; and he reigned one year in Jerusalem. And his mother's name was Athaliah, the daughter of Omri king of Israel. And he walked in the way of the house of Ahab, and did evil in the sight of the LORD, as did the house of Ahab: for he was the son in law of the house of Ahab. And he went with Joram the son of Ahab to the war against Hazael king of Syria in Ramoth-gilead; and the Syrians wounded Joram. And king Joram went back to be healed in Jezreel of the wounds which the Syrians had given him at Ramah, when he fought against Hazael king of Syria. And Ahaziah the son of Jehoram king of Judah went down to see Joram the son of Ahab in Jezreel, because he was sick.

Ahab had two sons: Ahaziah and Jehoram who reigned not successfully but successively. Jehoshaphat had a son and grandson named Jehoram and Ahaziah who also reigned successively. Joram, king of Israel, and Ahaziah, king of Judah, joined forces to battle Hazael, king of Syria. Wounded in battle, Joram returned to Jezreel to recover. Thus, the stage is set for an intriguing story in chapter 9 . . .

9

2 Kings 9:1–3
And Elisha the prophet called one of the children of the prophets, and said unto him, Gird up thy loins, and take this box of oil in thine hand, and go to Ramoth-gilead: And when thou comest thither, look out there Jehu the son of Jehoshaphat the son of Nimshi, and go in, and make him arise up from among his brethren, and carry him to an inner chamber; Then take the box of oil, and pour it on his head, and say, Thus saith the LORD, I have anointed thee king over Israel. Then open the door, and flee, and tarry not.

Anointing a new king during the reign of an existing one was no easy task. Realizing he was too old for such a treacherous, dangerous mission, Elisha sent one of his protegés to find Jehu and tell him he was to be king of Israel from that point on.

2 Kings 9:4–8 (a)
So the young man, even the young man the prophet, went to Ramoth-gilead. And when he came, behold, the captains of the host were sitting; and he said, I have an errand to thee, O captain. And Jehu said, Unto which of all us? And he said, To thee, O captain. And he arose, and went into the house; and he poured the oil on his head, and said unto him, Thus saith the LORD God of Israel,

I have anointed thee king over the people of the LORD, even over Israel. And thou shalt smite the house of Ahab thy master, that I may avenge the blood of my servants the prophets, and the blood of all the servants of the LORD, at the hand of Jezebel. For the whole house of Ahab shall perish . . .

Joram was the son of Ahab.

2 Kings 9:8 (b)–10
. . . and I will cut off from Ahab him that pisseth against the wall, and him that is shut up and left in Israel: And I will make the house of Ahab like the house of Jeroboam the son of Nebat, and like the house of Baasha the son of Ahijah: And the dogs shall eat Jezebel in the portion of Jezreel, and there shall be none to bury her. And he opened the door, and fled.

"Open the door and flee," Elisha had instructed this young prophet. And, after delivering this message of the destruction of the house of Ahab, including Joram, the reigning king, he wisely heeded Elisha's advice.

2 Kings 9:11 (a)
Then Jehu came forth to the servants of his lord: and one said unto him, Is all well? wherefore came this mad fellow to thee?

The prophets were often thought to be crazy. Paul was thought to be mad (Acts 26:24). Even Jesus was accused of being demon-possessed (Matthew 12:24).

2 Kings 9:11 (b)–13
. . . And he said unto them, Ye know the man, and his communication. And they said, It is false; tell us now. And he said, Thus and thus spake he to me, saying, Thus saith the LORD, I have anointed thee king over Israel. Then they hasted, and took every man his garment, and put it under him on the top of the stairs, and blew with trumpets, saying, Jehu is king.

The captains of the army acknowledged that Jehu was indeed the anointed king.

2 Kings 9:14, 15
So Jehu the son of Jehoshaphat the son of Nimshi conspired against Joram. (Now Joram had kept Ramoth-gilead, he and all Israel, because of Hazael king of Syria. But king Joram was returned to be healed in Jezreel of the wounds which the Syrians had given him, when he fought with Hazael king of Syria.) And Jehu said, If it be your minds, then let none go forth nor escape out of the city to go to tell it in Jezreel.

"Don't let Joram know about this," Jehu said. "Let's keep the element of surprise on our side."

2 Kings 9:16–19
So Jehu rode in a chariot, and went to Jezreel; for Joram lay there. And Ahaziah king of Judah was come down to see Joram. And there stood a watchman on the tower in Jezreel, and he spied the company of Jehu as he came, and said, I see a company. And Joram said, Take an horseman, and send to meet them, and let him say, Is it peace? So there went one on horseback to meet him, and said, Thus saith the king, Is it peace? And Jehu said, What hast thou to do with peace? turn thee behind me. And the watchman told, saying, The messenger came to them, but he cometh not again. Then he sent out a second on horseback, which came to them, and said, Thus saith the king, Is it peace? And Jehu answered, What hast thou to do with peace? turn thee behind me.

Assuming Jehu and his army were returning from battle against the Syrians, Joram sent messengers on horseback to ask if they were victorious in battle. Jehu didn't give an answer, but instead told the messengers to be quiet and fall in.

2 Kings 9:20–22
And the watchman told, saying, He came even unto them, and cometh not again: and the driving is like the driving of Jehu the son of Nimshi; for he driveth furiously. And Joram said, Make ready. And his chariot was made ready. And Joram king of Israel and Ahaziah king of Judah went out, each in his chariot, and they went out against Jehu, and met him in the portion of Naboth the Jezreelite. And it came to pass, when Joram saw Jehu, that he said, Is it peace, Jehu? And he answered, What peace, so long as the whoredoms of thy mother Jezebel and her witchcrafts are so many?

There can be no true peace as long as there is sin that has not been confessed . . .

> I create the fruit of the lips; Peace, peace to him that is far off, and to him that is near, saith the LORD; and I will heal him. But the wicked are like the troubled sea, when it cannot rest, whose waters cast up mire and dirt. There is no peace, saith my God, to the wicked.
>
> Isaiah 57:19–21

A lot of times people wonder why their spirit is churning, why their soul is troubled. One of the reasons could be that there is sin that needs to be confessed. Something is amiss if you find yourself in continual turmoil, for the fruit of the Spirit is love, joy, and peace (Galatians 5:22). The cure for uneasiness and turmoil is so simple, for if we simply confess our sins, God is able to cleanse us from *all* unrighteousness, from all that which robs us of our peace (1 John 1:9).

2 Kings 9:23
And Joram turned his hands, and fled, and said to Ahaziah, There is treachery, O Ahaziah.

Joram suddenly understood that Jehu was launching a rebellion.

2 Kings 9:24–26
And Jehu drew a bow with his full strength, and smote Jehoram between his arms, and the arrow went out at his heart, and he sunk down in his chariot. Then said Jehu to Bidkar his captain, Take up, and cast him in the portion of the field of Naboth the Jezreelite: for remember how that, when I and thou rode together after Ahab his father, the LORD laid this burden upon him; Surely I have seen yesterday the blood of Naboth, and the blood of his sons, saith the LORD; and I will requite thee in this plat, saith the LORD. Now therefore take and cast him into the plat of ground, according to the word of the LORD.

Joram, the son of Ahab, died in the field of Naboth. When Ahab had an entire kingdom, there was a little garden outside his palace that belonged to a man named Naboth. Ahab wanted that little garden. So his wife stirred up false charges against Naboth and had him killed. Then she gave his garden to Ahab. As Ahab was walking in his newly acquired garden, suddenly Elijah said to him, "God has seen this deed. And your blood will He require in this place, and the blood of your wife, as well." Ahab repented when he heard this, and for a season there was a time of reprieve. But he died in battle and the blood in his chariot was rinsed out in this very place. Here, we see his son wiped out in the field of Naboth, as well.

2 Kings 9:27
But when Ahaziah the king of Judah saw this, he fled by the way of the garden house. And Jehu followed after him, and said, Smite him also in the chariot. And they did so at the going up to Gur, which is by Ibleam. And he fled to Megiddo, and died there.

Because he associated with Joram, who was evil, Ahaziah paid the price and lost his life.

2 Kings 9:28–30
And his servants carried him in a chariot to Jerusalem, and buried him in his sepulchre with his fathers in the city of David. And in the eleventh year of Joram the son of Ahab began Ahaziah to reign over Judah. And when Jehu was come to Jezreel, Jezebel heard of it; and she painted her face, and tired her head, and looked out at a window.

Historians tell us Jezebel was one of the world's most beautiful women. She was also one of the most wicked. Here, even in her old age, fourteen years after her husband, Ahab, had died, she tries to seduce Jehu in an attempt to save her life.

2 Kings 9:31
And as Jehu entered in at the gate, she said, Had Zimri peace, who slew his master?

Here, Jezebel switches tactics from flirtation to intimidation. Zimri was a king who came into power because he assassinated the king who had preceded him. His rebellion lasted seven days. After seven days, the people rebelled against him. He went into his house, burned it down and he died in the fire (1 Kings 16:18). Here, Jezebel is saying, "Remember Zimri." The difference is, Zimri was not told by the Lord to do that, whereas Jehu was obeying the command of the Lord.

2 Kings 9:32, 33
And he lifted up his face to the window, and said, Who is on my side? who? And there looked out to him two or three eunuchs. And he said, Throw her down. So they threw her down: and some of her blood was sprinkled on the wall, and on the horses: and he trode her under foot.

Now Jezebel is lying in the same field where the blood of Ahab was washed out, and where her son, Joram, was killed.

2 Kings 9:34–37
And when he was come in, he did eat and drink, and said, Go, see now this cursed woman, and bury her: for she is a king's daughter. And they went to bury her: but they found no more of her than the skull, and the feet, and the palms of her hands. Wherefore they came again, and told him. And he said, This is the word of the LORD, which he spake by his servant Elijah the Tishbite, saying, In the portion of Jezreel shall dogs eat the flesh of Jezebel: And the carcase of Jezebel shall be

as dung upon the face of the field in the portion of Jezreel; so that they shall not say, This is Jezebel.

After Ahab was killed, Jezebel lived fourteen years in luxury and in ease. She thought she had beaten the rap. She must have felt that her position was secured, that the Word of the Lord was not applicable to her.

Maybe you see ungodly people prosper and you wonder what's going on. Their time will come. The Lord is patient, and the wheels of His judgment turn slowly, but they grind thoroughly. Jezebel found this out. She lived a life of sin and rebellion, and she ended up going to the dogs.

10

2 Kings 10:1–3
And Ahab had seventy sons in Samaria. And Jehu wrote letters, and sent to Samaria, unto the rulers of Jezreel, to the elders, and to them that brought up Ahab's children, saying, Now as soon as this letter cometh to you, seeing your master's sons are with you, and there are with you chariots and horses, a fenced city also, and armour; Look even out the best and meetest of your master's sons, and set him on his father's throne, and fight for your master's house.

"Ahab's gone, Jezebel's gone, Joram's gone," said Jehu. "Choose a new king and let's do battle."

2 Kings 10:4, 5
But they were exceedingly afraid, and said, Behold, two kings stood not before him: how then shall we stand? And he that was over the house, and he that was over the city, the elders also, and the bringers up of the children, sent to Jehu, saying, We are thy servants, and will do all that thou shalt bid us; we will not make any king: do thou that which is good in thine eyes.

Knowing they were no match for Jehu, the elders of Judah said, "We will do whatever you want."

2 Kings 10:6, 7
Then he wrote a letter the second time to them, saying, If ye be mine, and if ye will hearken unto my voice, take ye the heads of the men your master's sons, and come to me to Jezreel by to morrow this time. Now the king's sons, being seventy persons, were with the great men of the city, which brought them up. And it came to pass, when the letter came to them, that they took the king's sons, and slew seventy persons, and put their heads in baskets, and sent him them to Jezreel.

Seventy sons of Ahab were brutally murdered because the men around them were not loyal to them.

How I love being part of the body of Christ. What a joy it is to be related to brothers and sisters in Christ who will stand with and for each other. The world knows nothing of this.

2 Kings 10:8
And there came a messenger, and told him, saying, They have brought the heads of the king's sons. And he said, Lay ye them in two heaps at the entering in of the gate until the morning.

In this, Jehu was saying that his coup was deadly serious, that there would be no insurrections, no challenges.

2 Kings 10:9–15
And it came to pass in the morning, that he went out, and stood, and said to all the people, Ye be righteous: behold, I conspired against my master, and slew him: but who slew all these? Know now that there shall fall unto the earth nothing of the word of the LORD, which the LORD spake concerning the house of Ahab: for the LORD hath done that which he spake by his servant Elijah. So Jehu slew all that remained of the house of Ahab in Jezreel, and all his great men, and his kinsfolks, and his priests, until he left him none remaining. And he arose and departed, and came to Samaria. And as he was at the shearing house in the way, Jehu met with the brethren of Ahaziah king of Judah, and said, Who are ye? And they answered, We are the brethren of Ahaziah; and we go down to salute the children of the king and the children of the queen. And he said, Take them alive. And they took them alive, and slew them at the pit of the shearing house, even two and forty men; neither left he any of them. And when he was departed thence, he lighted on Jehonadab the son of Rechab coming to meet him: and he saluted him, and said to him, Is thine heart right, as my heart is with thy heart? And Jehonadab answered, It is. If it be, give me thine hand. And he gave him his hand; and he took him up to him into the chariot.

We'll come across Jehonadab again in the Book of Jeremiah. Jehonadab was a wonderful man of God. A mystic and an ascetic, he was one who sacrificed everything to serve his Lord. Jehu recognized this. Just coming into power, he wanted to be seen with this spiritual giant, hoping it would strengthen his political base as a new king. And then Jehu says something that shows a crack in his character . . .

2 Kings 10:16
And he said, Come with me, and see my zeal for the LORD. So they made him ride in his chariot.

Jehu is showing the early signs of his downfall. Why? He's boasting about his zeal for the Lord and he wants his service for the Lord to be noticed. Those are always two dangers to anyone who serves the Lord.

2 Kings 10:17–28
And when he came to Samaria, he slew all that remained unto Ahab in Samaria, till he had destroyed him, according to the saying of the LORD, which he spake to Elijah. And Jehu gathered all the people together, and said unto them, Ahab served Baal a little; but Jehu shall serve him much. Now therefore call unto me all the prophets of Baal, all his servants, and all his priests; let none be wanting: for I have a great sacrifice to do to Baal; whosoever shall be wanting, he shall not live. But Jehu did it in subtilty, to the intent that he might destroy the worshippers of Baal. And Jehu said, Proclaim a solemn assembly for Baal. And they proclaimed it. And Jehu sent through all Israel: and all the worshippers of Baal came, so that there was not a man left that came not. And they came into the house of Baal; and the house of Baal was full from one end to another. And he said unto him that was over the vestry, Bring forth vestments for all the worshippers of Baal. And he brought them forth vestments. And Jehu went, and Jehonadab the son of Rechab, into the house of Baal, and said unto the worshippers of Baal, Search, and look that there be here with you none of the servants of the LORD, but the worshippers of Baal only. And when they went in to offer sacrifices and burnt offerings, Jehu appointed fourscore men without, and said, If any of the men whom I have brought into your hands escape, he that letteth him go, his life shall be for the life of him. And it came to pass, as soon as he had made an end of offering the burnt offering, that Jehu said to the guard and to the captains, Go in, and slay them; let none come forth. And they smote them with the edge of the sword; and the guard and the captains cast them out, and went to the city of the house of Baal. And they brought forth the images out of the house of Baal, and burned them. And they brake down the image of Baal, and brake down the house of Baal, and made it a draught house unto this day. Thus Jehu destroyed Baal out of Israel.

Jehu does a very noble thing in annihilating Baal worship from Israel. But before we applaud him, the next verse is an indictment against him . . .

2 Kings 10:29
Howbeit from the sins of Jeroboam the son of Nebat, who made Israel to sin, Jehu departed not from after them, to wit, the golden calves that were in Bethel, and that were in Dan.

Jehu wiped out Baal, but he allowed the continuation of calf worship in the nation. It was a political necessity, he thought. After all, if he took away the golden calves, people would have to worship in Jerusalem, and he would lose control over them.

2 Kings 10:30–36
And the LORD said unto Jehu, Because thou hast done well in executing that which is right in mine eyes, and hast done unto the house of Ahab according to all that was in mine heart, thy children of the fourth generation shall sit on the throne of Israel. But Jehu took no heed to walk in the law of the LORD God of Israel with all his heart: for he departed not from the sins of Jeroboam, which made Israel to sin. In those days the LORD began to cut Israel short: and Hazael smote them in all the coasts of Israel; From Jordan eastward, all the land of Gilead, the Gadites, and the Reubenites, and the Manassites, from Aroer, which is by the river Arnon, even Gilead and Bashan. Now the rest of the acts of Jehu, and all that he did, and all his might, are they not written in the book of the chronicles of the kings of Israel? And Jehu slept with his fathers: and they buried him in Samaria. And Jehoahaz his son reigned in his stead. And the time that Jehu reigned over Israel in Samaria was twenty and eight years.

Jehu had a chance to bring about real revival and true reformation, but because he was politically minded and didn't walk in the ways of the law of the Lord, the nation of Israel began at this point to become diminished. This is the beginning of an irrevocable turn of events that will lead to their destruction by the hand of the Assyrians.

11

We now go back down south to Judah. Jehu has been in a position of power in the north for a number of years. In the meantime, incredible things are happening in Judah . . .

2 Kings 11:1
And when Athaliah the mother of Ahaziah saw that her son was dead, she arose and destroyed all the seed royal.

Athaliah was the wife of Jehoshaphat, the daughter of Ahab. When her son, Ahaziah, was killed, she saw an opportunity to grab the power of the throne of Judah. So she had all of her grandchildren killed in order to secure her own position. There was one son who was saved, however . . .

2 Kings 11:2, 3
But Jehosheba, the daughter of king Joram, sister of Ahaziah, took Joash the son of Ahaziah and stole him from among the king's sons which were slain; and they hid him, even him and his nurse, in the bedchamber from Athaliah, so that he was not slain. And he was with her hid in the house of the LORD six years. And Athaliah did reign over the land.

One son survived. His name was Joash. "And he was with her hid in the house of the Lord . . ." How I love that phrase. "One thing have I desired of the Lord," David said, "and that will I seek after: that I may dwell in the house of the Lord all the days of my life" (Psalm 27:4). David found sanctuary in the house of the Lord. And Joash, his descendant, did as well.

2 Kings 11:4
And the seventh year Jehoiada sent and fetched the rulers over hundreds, with the captains and the guard, and brought them to him into the house of the LORD, and made a covenant with them, and took an oath of them in the house of the LORD, and shewed them the king's son.

Jehoiada, a godly priest, called the leaders of Judah together and said, "I've got news for you. But before I tell you what it is, you've got to make a covenant with me." That's always the way of the Lord. Before there is revelation, there must be commitment. Too often, we want to learn about the Lord to satisfy our curiosity. But the Lord looks for commitment first.

2 Kings 11:5–8
And he commanded them, saying, This is the thing that ye shall do; A third part of you that enter in on the sabbath shall even be keepers of the watch of the king's house; And a third part shall be at the gate of Sur; and a third part at the gate behind the guard: so shall ye keep the watch of the house, that it be not broken down. And two parts of all you that go forth on the sabbath, even they shall keep the watch of the house of the LORD about the king. And ye shall compass the king around about, every man with his weapons in his hand: and he that cometh within the ranges, let him be slain: and be ye with the king as he goeth out and as he cometh in.

A plan was made to announce that Joash was the rightful king of Judah. But such an announcement would require a great deal of protection. So the leaders of Judah were armed. Where did they get their weapons? The next verse tells us . . .

2 Kings 11:9, 10
And the captains over the hundreds did according to all things that Jehoiada the priest commanded: and they took every man his men that were to come in on the sabbath, with them that should go out on the sabbath, and came to Jehoiada the priest. And to the captains over hundreds did the priest give king David's spears and shields, that were in the temple of the LORD.

It "just so happened" that the swords and shields David had captured from his enemies hung on one of the walls of the temple. Having been mounted there for years, they were now to be put to very practical use.

You have been given victories by the Lord, and they need to be mounted in the temple of the Lord. The glory needs to go to the Lord for every victory you've experienced, every blessing you've received. We should be abounding in testimonies, saying, "This is what the Lord has done in my life. And, by His grace and mercy, this is what He is doing presently." What is the importance of such testimony? First, it glorifies God. Secondly, it arms the servants of God. They grab the weapons themselves and say, "I'm encouraged. God used you in that insurmountable difficulty. He saw you through and I know He'll do the same for me."

If God answers your prayers and gives you victory, I believe you have a responsibility to share that and to post it in the house of the Lord. No matter how seemingly small they might be, share your victories. They'll be used. They'll be definitely needed by someone at some time.

2 Kings 11:11–21
And the guard stood, every man with his weapons in his hand, round about the king, from the right corner of the temple to the left corner of the temple, along by the altar and the temple. And he brought forth the king's son, and put the crown upon him, and gave him the testimony; and they made him king, and anointed him; and they clapped their hands, and said, God save the king. And when Athaliah heard the noise of the guard and of the people, she came to the people into the temple of the LORD. And when she looked, behold, the king stood by a pil-

lar, as the manner was, and the princes and the trumpeters by the king, and all the people of the land rejoiced, and blew with trumpets: and Athaliah rent her clothes, and cried, Treason, Treason. But Jehoiada the priest commanded the captains of the hundreds, the officers of the host, and said unto them, Have her forth without the ranges: and him that followeth her kill with the sword. For the priest had said, Let her not be slain in the house of the LORD. And they laid hands on her; and she went by the way by the which the horses came into the king's house: and there was she slain. And Jehoiada made a covenant between the LORD and the king and the people that they should be the LORD's people; between the king also and the people. And all the people of the land went into the house of Baal, and brake it down; his altars and his images brake they in pieces thoroughly, and slew Mattan the priest of Baal before the altars. And the priest appointed officers over the house of the LORD. And he took the rulers over hundreds, and the captains, and the guard, and all the people of the land; and they brought down the king from the house of the LORD, and came by the way of the gate of the guard to the king's house. And he sat on the throne of the kings. And all the people of the land rejoiced, and the city was in quiet: and they slew Athaliah with the sword beside the king's house. Seven years old was Jehoash when he began to reign.

In this picture, we see our present situation. There's a usurper, an oppressor named Satan who causes trouble and turmoil on every front. But when our Greater than Joash—Jesus Christ—comes, there will be a clapping of hands as we crown Him as King of kings. The people will rejoice. And there will be peace and quietness in the land.

Jesus is coming back soon and when He does, things will be right. Athaliah—that is, Satan—will be dethroned and cast into a bottomless pit. There shall be peace and love between all brothers. Righteousness shall prevail.

12

2 Kings 12:1, 2

In the seventh year of Jehu Jehoash began to reign; and forty years reigned he in Jerusalem. And his mother's name was Zibiah of Beer-sheba. And Jehoash did that which was right in the sight of the LORD all his days wherein Jehoiada the priest instructed him.

As long as Jehoiada was tutoring and counseling him, Joash did well.

2 Kings 12:3–5

But the high places were not taken away: the people still sacrificed and burnt incense in the high places. And Jehoash said to the priests, All the money of the dedicated things that is brought into the house of the LORD, even the money of every one that passeth the account, the money that every man is set at, and all the money that cometh into any man's heart to bring into the house of the LORD, Let the priests take it to them, every man of his acquaintance: and let them repair the breaches of the house, wheresoever any breach shall be found.

Revival is starting and it begins with the desire to see the temple repaired. Joash was hid in the house of the Lord. Perhaps that is why he had such a heart for the house of the Lord. The temple was in disrepair. So he told the priests to take the money that was given on the occasion of peoples' hearts being stirred and complete the project.

2 Kings 12:6

But it was so, that in the three and twentieth year of king Jehoash the priests had not repaired the breaches of the house.

The priests had been given money to do the job, but they hadn't completed it.

2 Kings 12:7–9

Then king Jehoash called for Jehoiada the priest, and the other priests, and said unto them, Why repair ye not the breaches of the house? now therefore receive no more money of your acquaintance, but deliver it for the breaches of the house. And the priests consented to receive no more money of the people, neither to repair the breaches of the house. But Jehoiada the priest took a chest, and bored a hole in the lid of it, and set it beside the altar, on the right side as one cometh into the house of the LORD: and the priests that kept the door put therein all the money that was brought into the house of the LORD.

A locked box with a hole in it was placed at the right side of the altar for the collection of money to repair the temple.

2 Kings 12:10–16

And it was so, when they saw that there was much money in the chest, that the king's scribe and the high priest came up, and they put up in bags, and told the money that was found in the house of the LORD. And they gave the money, being told, into the hands

of them that did the work, that had the oversight of the house of the LORD: and they laid it out to the carpenters and builders, that wrought upon the house of the LORD, And to masons, and hewers of stone, and to buy timber and hewed stone to repair the breaches of the house of the LORD, and for all that was laid out for the house to repair it. Howbeit there were not made for the house of the LORD bowls of silver, snuffers, basons, trumpets, any vessels of gold, or vessels of silver, of the money that was brought into the house of the LORD: But they gave that to the workmen, and repaired therewith the house of the LORD. Moreover they reckoned not with the men, into whose hand they delivered the money to be bestowed on workmen: for they dealt faithfully. The trespass money and sin money was not brought into the house of the LORD: it was the priests'.

The priests were still provided for by the trespass and sin offerings, but the money raised for the temple was not to be spent on ministry needs. Rather, it was exclusively for temple remodeling. In this, Joash shows real wisdom.

2 Kings 12:17, 18
Then Hazael king of Syria went up, and fought against Gath, and took it: and Hazael set his face to go up to Jerusalem. And Jehoash king of Judah took all the hallowed things that Jehoshaphat, and Jehoram, and Ahaziah, his fathers, kings of Judah, had dedicated, and his own hallowed things, and all the gold that was found in the treasures of the house of the LORD, and in the king's house, and sent it to Hazael king of Syria: and he went away from Jerusalem.

Hearing that Hazael, king of Syria, was about to attack Jerusalem, instead of praying for wisdom, Joash paid him off with money from the temple. In the Book of Chronicles, we see that this was a big mistake.

2 Kings 12:19–21
And the rest of the acts of Joash, and all that he did, are they not written in the book of the chronicles of the kings of Judah? And his servants arose, and made a conspiracy, and slew Joash in the house of Millo, which goeth down to Silla. For Jozachar the son of Shimeath, and Jehozabad the son of Shomer, his servants, smote him, and he died; and they buried him with his fathers in the city of David: and Amaziah his son reigned in his stead.

With a heart for the house of God, Joash began so well. But, as we see in 2 Chronicles, without the godly influence of Jehoiada, Joash would himself fall prey to idolatry.

13

In chapter 13, we head back north to the ten tribes of Israel.

2 Kings 13:1–4
In the three and twentieth year of Joash the son of Ahaziah king of Judah Jehoahaz the son of Jehu began to reign over Israel in Samaria, and reigned seventeen years. And he did that which was evil in the sight of the LORD, and followed the sins of Jeroboam the son of Nebat, which made Israel to sin; he departed not therefrom. And the anger of the LORD was kindled against Israel, and he delivered them into the hand of Hazael king of Syria, and into the hand of Benhadad the son of Hazael, all their days. And Jehoahaz besought the LORD, and the LORD hearkened unto him: for he saw the oppression of Israel, because the king of Syria oppressed them.

Jehoahaz was an evil man. Yet even he knew that the peoples' oppression was the result of their transgression. Here, a wicked king cried out to the Lord, and He heard him.

2 Kings 13:5, 6
(And the LORD gave Israel a saviour, so that they went out from under the hand of the Syrians: and the children of Israel dwelt in their tents, as beforetime. Nevertheless they departed not from the sins of the house of Jeroboam, who made Israel sin, but walked therein: and there remained the grove also in Samaria.)

The Lord raised up a deliverer to free Israel from the hand of the Syrians. And yet these people continued to walk in their sin. Why would people continue in sin when the Lord raised up a savior for them? That's a question we have to ask ourselves. We have to realize that it's only by the grace, mercy, and lovingkindness of God that a Savior was granted to us.

Why did the Lord give these wicked sinners a savior? Here's a better question: Why did He give His Son for *us?*

2 Kings 13:7–9
Neither did he leave of the people to Jehoahaz but fifty horsemen, and ten chariots, and ten thousand footmen; for the king of Syria had destroyed them, and had made them like the dust by threshing. Now the rest of the acts of Jehoahaz, and all that he

did, and his might, are they not written in the book of the chronicles of the kings of Israel? And Jehoahaz slept with his fathers; and they buried him in Samaria: and Joash his son reigned in his stead.

This is a different Joash from chapter 12.

2 Kings 13:10, 11
In the thirty and seventh year of Joash king of Judah began Jehoash the son of Jehoahaz to reign over Israel in Samaria, and reigned sixteen years. And he did that which was evil in the sight of the LORD; he departed not from all the sins of Jeroboam the son of Nebat, who made Israel sin: but he walked therein.

Joash practiced the idolatry which was indigenous to the soil of Israel, and the nation willingly followed.

2 Kings 13:12, 13 (a)
And the rest of the acts of Joash, and all that he did, and his might wherewith he fought against Amaziah king of Judah, are they not written in the book of the chronicles of the kings of Israel? And Joash slept with his fathers . . .

Joash is off the scene, but before his story is over, there are a few parenthetical thoughts recorded . . .

2 Kings 13:13 (b), 14 (a)
. . . and Jeroboam sat upon his throne: and Joash was buried in Samaria with the kings of Israel. Now Elisha was fallen sick of his sickness whereof he died . . .

Elisha is one of the greatest miracle workers in the Bible. He was a man of immense power, of fervent faith. He was able to pray so effectively that the dead were brought back to life. He was able to make iron float. And yet here we see that Elisha was sick himself. Sickness isn't always the result of sin. It can be, but not always. Nor is a lingering illness evidence of a lack of faith. It was Elisha's sickness that ushered him into eternity. Thus, the Lord uses even sickness to accomplish His purposes.

2 Kings 13:14 (b)–19
. . . And Joash the king of Israel came down unto him, and wept over his face, and said, O my father, my father, the chariot of Israel, and the horsemen thereof. And Elisha said unto him, Take bow and arrows. And he took unto him bow and arrows. And he said to the king of Israel, Put thine hand upon the bow. And he put his hand upon it: and Elisha put his hands upon the king's hands. And he said, Open the window eastward. And he opened it. Then Elisha said, Shoot. And he shot. And he said, The arrow of the LORD's deliverance, and the arrow of deliverance from Syria: for thou shalt smite the Syrians in Aphek, till thou have consumed them. And he said, Take the arrows. And he took them. And he said unto the king of Israel, Smite upon the ground. And he smote thrice, and stayed. And the man of God was wroth with him, and said, Thou shouldest have smitten five or six times; then hadst thou smitten Syria till thou hadst consumed it: whereas now thou shalt smite Syria but thrice.

This story is a classic example of the importance of fervency and the danger of lethargy.

***For topical study of 2 Kings 13:14–19 entitled "The Arrows of Deliverance," turn to page* 1058.**

2 Kings 13:20, 21
And Elisha died, and they buried him. And the bands of the Moabites invaded the land at the coming in of the year. And it came to pass, as they were burying a man, that, behold, they spied a band of men; and they cast the man into the sepulchre of Elisha: and when the man was let down, and touched the bones of Elisha, he revived, and stood up on his feet.

In the heat of battle, a dead man was inadvertently thrown into Elisha's tomb. But when his body touched Elisha's bones, he immediately came back to life. Amazing!

Like the dead man in this passage, we must die to self if we are going to truly experience life. "If any man come after Me, let him deny himself, take up his cross and follow Me," Jesus said (Matthew 16:24). He did not say this to burden us but to liberate us because, as we have discovered, the more we think about ourselves and live for ourselves, the more miserable we become. But the more we die to self and take up the cross, the more we spring to life.

If you want to be effective in ministering to other people, even as Elisha was dead, so too in ministry or in service, you've got to die to popularity. "If I please men, I cannot be the servant of God," Paul declared (see Galatians 1:10). If you take a stand for Jesus Christ and do what you believe is right for the Lord, there will be those who will misunderstand. That can be painful. But if you are going to minister, you've got to die in order that life might come forth. Jesus said he who lives for his own life will lose it, but if you give up your life, you'll find it (Matthew 10:39).

I have a hard time with this. I struggle on this point because when I sense that someone is unhappy with me or disappointed in me, my natural tendency is to keep from making waves or causing offense. But James said we offend in all things (3:2). The only solution is to live for the Lord and in such a way that you can say, "Father, I have finished the work which *Thou* hast given me and glorified Thy name (John 17:4). I'm doing what You're telling me to do to the best of my perception and abilities no matter the cost."

If you do that, if you die to self, life will spring forth. People will be touched. Lives will be changed.

Elisha was a man who, even after his death, still influenced and affected peoples' lives. How about you? What if the Lord took you home today? Oh, that we might live our lives in such a way that the memory of our lives, the words we spoke, the truth we shared, the love we showed, the example we set, might cause others to spring to life themselves.

2 Kings 13:22–25

But Hazael king of Syria oppressed Israel all the days of Jehoahaz. And the LORD was gracious unto them, and had compassion on them, and had respect unto them, because of his covenant with Abraham, Isaac, and Jacob, and would not destroy them, neither cast he them from his presence as yet. So Hazael king of Syria died; and Ben-hadad his son reigned in his stead. And Jehoash the son of Jehoahaz took again out of the hand of Ben-hadad the son of Hazael the cities, which he had taken out of the hand of Jehoahaz his father by war. Three times did Joash beat him, and recovered the cities of Israel.

How many times did Joash beat the Syrian forces? Three times. How many times did he beat the arrows? Three times. Yes, there was a victory, but only a partial recovery. The Syrians were not defeated completely.

THE ARROWS OF DELIVERANCE

A Topical Study of 2 KINGS 13:14–19

The kingdom of Syria was oppressing and depressing the nation of Israel. And God desired to bring deliverance to His bruised and battered people by partnering with Joash, the king of Israel. God could have easily brought deliverance apart from Joash, but it was His desire and design to use Joash. Why? Because God was not only interested in delivering Israel, but He was also interested in developing Joash.

The same is still true. We often find ourselves oppressed and depressed, continually bothered and hurt by the kingdom of Satan. Satan is an oppressor. Satan is a destroyer. Paul said we wrestle not against flesh and blood, but against principalities and powers, against spiritual forces in high places (Ephesians 6:12). Sometimes you might feel like a tank has run over you, a bomb has gone off inside of you, or like there are fireworks and explosions all around you. That is because you are involved in battle and the kingdom of Satan is seeking to oppress and depress you just like the kingdom of Syria sought to oppress and depress the kingdom of Israel.

The attack of Satan manifests itself in three primary ways: through sin, through sickness, and through self. God not only desires to bring deliverance *to* you, but also to work deliverance *through* you in such a way that others who are hurting may be delivered as well.

How does deliverance happen? When Joash came to Elisha, Elisha told him to open the window eastward—in the direction of Syria—and to shoot an arrow out the window. Elisha placed his hands upon the hands of Joash so that when Joash drew back the bow, Elisha's hands were on his. In other words, as God's representative, Elisha joined with Joash, who was weak and unable to bring about deliverance himself. And through His Son, God does the same with us . . .

> *The Spirit of the Lord GOD is upon me; because the LORD hath anointed me to preach good tidings unto the meek; he hath sent me to bind up the brokenhearted, to proclaim liberty to the captives, and the opening of the prison to them that are bound; To proclaim the acceptable year of the LORD, and the day of vengeance of our God; to comfort all that mourn; To appoint unto them that mourn in Zion, to give unto them beauty for ashes, the oil of joy for mourning, the garment of praise for the spirit of heaviness; that they might be called trees of righteousness, the planting of the LORD, that he might be glorified.* Isaiah 61:1–3

That's the ministry of our Master. He has come to set the captives free, to liberate the oppressed, to heal the hurting, to bind the brokenhearted, to give the garment of praise, to make beauty for ashes. Jesus has been sent as the "Arrow" of the Lord's deliverance.

"That sounds nice," you might be saying. "But if it's true, why am I so discouraged? Why does sin still have dominion over me? Why aren't I experiencing the oil of joy for mourning? Why don't I have the garment of praise for the spirit of heaviness? Why is my life still ashes and not a thing of beauty?"

The answer to that is very possibly that you need to be delivered. Deliverance is on the heart of the Father. Deliverance is available to you and yet the Lord won't do it apart from your partnering with Him, joining yourself to Him. He will place His hands upon yours but you must grab the arrow, open the window, and say, "I need You."

After the initial arrow was launched, Elisha told Joash to take the rest of the arrows out of the quiver and beat them on the ground. So Joash took the rest of the arrows out of the quiver and beat them once, twice, three times, and then he stopped.

"Why have you stopped after three times?" Elisha asked. "You should have smitten the arrows five or six times. But because you only hit them three times, you'll only have a partial victory over Syria."

What do those arrows speak of? They speak of the arsenal we have been given by the Lord to bring about the deliverance He intends for us to experience daily . . .

The Arrow of Prayer

The most important arrow in your arsenal is prayer. We can do more than pray, but we can't do anything until we first pray. And yet what do we do with this arrow of prayer? All too often, we tap it lazily, lethargically, half-heartedly. Consequently, Elisha would say to us, "You should have taken that arrow of prayer and beaten it six times fervently, energetically, expectantly. But, because your prayers are routine and mindless, your deliverance is only partial."

We are told in James 5 that Elijah was a man like us, and yet he was a man of power because he was a man of prayer. As he prayed for rain to come, he placed his head between his knees and prayed not once, twice, or three times, but seven times in this intensive posture of prayer (1 Kings 18). Why did he put his head between his knees? In that day, this was the position of birthing and he was birthing something through prayer.

That is the kind of prayer we need if we are to prevail against the kingdom of Satan. Oh, how I love to be with men who know how to pray. I desire to be a man of prayer, to press into the presence of God. In Genesis 32, we read that Jacob wrestled all night with the Lord and said, "I will not let You go until You bless me." When you feel oppressed, have you wrestled all night in prayer, saying, "Lord Jesus, I'm not going to let You go until I receive deliverance"? That's the kind of prayer that moves the hand of God.

The Arrow of the Word

A second arrow in our quiver is the Word of God. When Jesus was doing battle against Satan in Matthew 4, every time Satan came at Him, Jesus repelled Him by quoting Scripture. The Word of God is a powerful weapon in your arsenal, an arrow that will bring about deliverance. But how do we handle that arrow?

All too often, we say, "Let's see, I might have time for devotions this morning . . . Where shall I read . . . I don't know . . . Oops, time to go . . ." tap, tap, tap . . .

Elisha would say to us, "Take those arrows and beat them! Memorize the Scriptures. Meditate on the Word. Study to show yourself approved unto God. Verbalize the Scriptures." But we keep this arrow in its quiver and dust it off only occasionally and halfheartedly and then wonder why our deliverance isn't complete. This is the Word of the Lord, gang. Nothing should have higher priority than studying this book. In those who study the Word consistently, there is a continual pattern of growth and victory.

The Arrow of the Word of Faith

Another arrow in our quiver is the word of faith. Jesus said, "*Say* to the mountain be removed and it shall be removed" (see Matthew 17:20). Too often, too much of our talk is about why we're discouraged or why we're upset. Negative attitudes and talk should be done away with. Instead, we should speak words of faith and life.

In Zechariah 4, we read that Zerubbabel was discouraged when the project of rebuilding the temple was stalled. The Lord told him to shout "grace" to the cornerstone of the foundation. Zerubbabel might have thought this was foolish, but he did it anyway, and it released something in the Spirit that brought about the completion of the project.

What project is before you? Is there a mountain in front of you? Speak to it, shout at it, release a word of faith in that situation. Don't talk about why it can't happen. Speak words of faith. Take the arrow of faith and smash it. Say, "I'm not going to settle for this destruction in my marriage or in my family. I shout it out right now." Even if you have to get by yourself in the bathroom or in your car, take the arrow of the word of faith and smite it against the ground. In so doing, you'll experience deliverance.

The Arrow of Praise

As they waged war against their enemies, the armies of Israel were preceded by a choir who sang, "Praise be to the Lord. His mercy endures forever and ever." When the praise ascended from the choir, the enemy was so caught off guard, they began to slay each other. And by the time the army of Israel arrived at the scene, there was nothing more to do than simply collect the spoils of the army that destroyed itself (2 Chronicles 20).

There is power in praise! Think about what you're singing. Don't just tap through a couple of songs. If you put on the garment of praise for the spirit of heaviness, you will find the spirit of heaviness fleeing from you quickly.

The Arrow of Communion

Some people are bored by Communion. And yet in 1 Corinthians 11, Paul said many were sick, weak, or even dying because they didn't value the Table of the Lord. "Take and eat," Jesus said. "This is My body broken for you. Drink. This is My blood shed for you" (see 1 Corinthians 11:24). There is much more power in the Lord's Table than we can even imagine. When you eat of the bread and drink of the cup of Jesus Christ, in a sense, you are being born again—and again. And I need that. When I fail to do that or when I do it haphazardly or sporadically, my deliverance will be only partial.

Come to the Lord's Table expecting a fresh measure of His grace and forgiveness. He'll meet you in that place, and your deliverance will be full.

I'm convinced that far too many people are depressed for no real reason other than a failure to realize that deliverance has been granted in the arrows of the Lord Jesus Christ, a failure to take the arrows He left for us and smash them against the ground of our own unbelief.

The Lord's Table, the power of praise, the spoken word of faith, the written Word of God, passionate prayer, whichever arrow you grab, grab it energetically and beat it expectantly, for without faith, it is impossible to please Him (Hebrews 11:6).

Why didn't Joash smite the arrows more than three times? I suggest three possible reasons . . .

First, perhaps it was because he felt unworthy. Joash was well aware of the fact that he was not considered one of the most righteous kings of Israel. I'm sure he felt, "That's great for Jehoshaphat or Asa or the prophets. But the Lord doesn't really want to deliver me or work through me. Others can pray, but not me. Others can witness, but not me. I'm not quite good enough."

Not true! The ministry, gifts, and work of God are not dependent upon who we are. They are only dependent on Who *He* is—and He is a gracious God who desires to use the foolish things of this world to confound the wise; the weak to show up the strong (1 Corinthians 1:27). God is looking for trophies of His grace and many of us qualify because, like Joash, we know how unworthy we are.

Secondly, perhaps Joash was unconvinced. Maybe he thought, *Here I am, tapping these arrows, claiming deliverance, but the one telling me to do this is sick and dying. If deliverance is real, why is he sick? If the power of God is available, why is he dying?* Here's how to nullify your ministry: look at people. You'll be baffled and beaten. You'll wonder why the Lord is using that person and not the other. Keep your eyes on people, and you'll tap arrows and go away half-defeated. But fix your eyes on Jesus, and your faith will soar (Hebrews 12:2).

Finally, perhaps Joash was unsure whether or not he wanted to see the Syrians really destroyed. Do you really want to be delivered, or is it possible that you enjoy negativity? Is it possible that you enjoy infirmity because it gives you sympathy? Sometimes, it's easier to say, "Woe is me," than it is to take authority. I suggest that there can indeed be a tendency for us to find reasons why we're depressed and oppressed, to justify why we're not moving in faith and fervency. To a man who was lame for thirty-eight years, Jesus said, "Wilt thou be made whole?" Wouldn't you think the answer would be obvious? Yet the man's answer was, "I have no man to put me in the water" (see John 5). He didn't say, "Yes!" Instead, he gave the reason why he couldn't be healed. After thirty-eight years, he had grown accustomed to being lame and perhaps didn't want to deal with the responsibility of what would take place if he was indeed made whole.

As long as I'm mad at the church, I don't have to give to the building project. As long as I'm mad at the elders, I don't have to come to Wednesday night Bible study. As long as I'm mad at the Lord, I don't have to get up early to spend time with Him. We find reasons why we want to be lame. Perhaps Joash didn't want the Syrians totally annihilated. Beaten back a little? Sure. But wiped out? That was another matter altogether.

The Lord desires to shake us out of our lethargy, gang, to give us complete victory. Therefore, let us be those who worship with intensity, who pray with expectancy, who speak the word of faith loudly, who read the Word consistently, who move out energetically—all for *His* great glory.

14 **2 Kings 14:1–3**
In the second year of Joash son of Jehoahaz king of Israel reigned Amaziah the son of Joash king of Judah. He was twenty and five years old when he began to reign, and reigned twenty and nine years in Jerusalem. And his mother's name was Jehoaddan of Jerusalem. And he did that which was right in the sight of the LORD, yet not like David his father: he did according to all things as Joash his father did.

David is the standard by which all other kings are measured. Amaziah did that which was right, but not like David. In other words, he made the right motions, but lacked the right emotion. He did good things, but he didn't have a heart that was truly inclined toward the Lord like David's was.

2 Kings 14:4, 5
Howbeit the high places were not taken away: as yet the people did sacrifice and burnt incense on the high places. And it came to pass, as soon as the kingdom was confirmed in his hand, that he slew his servants which had slain the king his father.

His father was assassinated while he was in office, so Amaziah avenged his father's death.

2 Kings 14:6
But the children of the murderers he slew not: according unto that which is written in the book of the law of Moses, wherein the LORD commanded, saying, The fathers shall not be put to death for the children, nor the children be put to death for the fathers; but every man shall be put to death for his own sin.

The Lord here is approving the fact that, unlike the normal custom, Amaziah killed the servants who killed his father but didn't kill their children. God specifically said that children are not to die for the sins of their fathers (Deuteronomy 24:16). Amaziah honored this.

Both Jeremiah and Ezekiel said, "This proverb shall be said no more: Our fathers ate sour grapes. Therefore our teeth are on edge" (Jeremiah 31:29; Ezekiel 18:2). Twice, the Lord raised up prophets to tell His people to quit blaming their parents. There is validity in the healing of our souls, minds, and emotions. But I believe it is also grievous in the sight of our Lord when people blame their depression and problems on someone else, particularly their parents.

2 Kings 14:7, 8
He slew of Edom in the valley of salt ten thousand, and took Selah by war, and called the name of it Joktheel unto this day. Then Amaziah sent messengers to Jehoash, the son of Jehoahaz son of Jehu, king of Israel, saying, Come, let us look one another in the face.

Second Chronicles 25 tells us Amaziah raised an army that numbered 300,000 men. But that wasn't big enough for him, so, in order to increase it, he hired 100,000 more soldiers from the kingdom of Israel. With this huge army, Amaziah was determined to battle the Edomites.

The Edomites were constantly troubling the Jews and Amaziah decided, with his huge army, he could wipe them out. He was ready to march against Edom when a prophet came and said, "The Lord God is not with Israel, for Israel has gone against Him. Therefore, go into battle, but don't take the soldiers you've hired from Israel." So Amaziah told all of the men from Israel to go back home. He then led his men into battle against the Edomites and was completely victorious.

But while he was gone, the mercenaries from Israel plundered the cities of Judah on their way back to Israel, killing 3,000. When Amaziah came back and heard this, he was understandably upset. So he sent a message to Jehoash, the king of Israel, challenging him to fight.

2 Kings 14:9, 10
And Jehoash the king of Israel sent to Amaziah king of Judah, saying, The thistle that was in Lebanon sent to the cedar that was in Lebanon, saying, Give thy daughter to my son to wife: and there passed by a wild beast that was in Lebanon, and trode down the thistle. Thou hast indeed smitten Edom, and thine heart hath lifted thee up: glory of this, and tarry at home: for why shouldest thou meddle to thy hurt, that thou shouldest fall, even thou, and Judah with thee?

"You had a victory," Jehoash said to Amaziah. "Enjoy it. Don't start looking for battles you're not called to fight." Jehoash's advice is still sound. It is always dangerous for us to take on battles we're not called to fight, mistakenly thinking we're stronger than we are.

2 Kings 14:11 (a)
But Amaziah would not hear . . .

Jehoash was giving a word of warning, trying to keep Amaziah from meddling. But Amaziah would not hear. So often in our Christian experience, we are like Amaziah. We experience victory by the grace and goodness of God. And in those victories, we tend to take on an air of invincibility. "Because the Lord saw me through, nothing can stop me now," we say. As a result, we find ourselves meddling where we shouldn't.

- "Last time I went to a party, I didn't do anything wrong. I didn't join in. I was victorious. So I'll be victorious at this week's party, too."
- "I know I'm strong enough to absorb what is on the movie screen. No problem."
- "Lord," Peter said, "Though all others forsake You, I never will. You can count on me."

Over and over again, men and women of God have been undermined by overconfidence, putting themselves in situations they think won't affect them. And all the while, they hear the Holy Spirit saying, "Don't go. Stay away. You're meddling to your own hurt."

2 Kings 14:11 (b), 12
. . . Therefore Jehoash king of Israel went up; and he and Amaziah king of Judah looked one another in the face at Beth-shemesh, which belongeth to Judah. And Judah was put to the worse before Israel; and they fled every man to their tents.

In this passage, we see four results of overconfidence. The first is that there is disgrace to the nation. Judah lost the battle. Whenever I meddle, I will find myself inevitably bringing disgrace to the people of God. In 2 Samuel 12, when David had sinned, he was approached by Nathan the prophet. Upon David's confession of sin, Nathan said, "The Lord has forgiven you. Nevertheless, you have caused the enemies of Jehovah to blaspheme."

When you and I succumb to sin, when we meddle where we don't belong, we bring disgrace to the people of God. Let us be careful lest we disgrace others.

2 Kings 14:13
And Jehoash king of Israel took Amaziah king of Judah, the son of Jehoash the son of Ahaziah, at Beth-shemesh, and came to Jerusalem, and brake down the wall of Jerusalem from the gate of Ephraim unto the corner gate, four hundred cubits.

The second result of overconfidence is that it decreases defenses. The walls that protected the people were broken down. When you become involved in a little sin, your defenses are torn down and it leads to bigger sins. That is the problem with little sins, they never stay little.

"I would never do *that,*" you say. But then you compromise, and before long, you find yourself asking, "How did I get *here?*" You got there by giving in at the first point, meddling where you didn't belong. There are standards you know the Lord has given you. When you ignore them, what used to bother you no longer affects you because the walls of defense are broken.

2 Kings 14:14 (a)
And he took all the gold and silver, and all the vessels that were found in the house of the LORD, and in the treasures of the king's house . . .

The third result of overconfidence is that it diminishes worship. The temple itself was plundered. Riches were lost. Haven't you found it to be true that once you are meddling, involved in areas you shouldn't be, your desire for worship diminishes proportionately? I have found that one of the best barometers to judge where I'm at spiritually is to look at my desire and capacity for worship. When I have meddled in areas I didn't belong, my desire for worship decreases.

When the people of Israel continued in sin, the glory of God departed from the temple (Ezekiel 10). Worship then became formalized and ritualistic. It became an obligation. It is a tragedy when sin brings about the departing of the glory of God from our lives. When the gold and silver is gone, our worship becomes bankrupt. And it's all because we compromised, all because we were overconfident.

2 Kings 14:14 (b)
. . . and hostages, and returned to Samaria.

The fourth result of overconfidence is that it destroys freedom, for not only was the temple plundered, but hostages were taken.

We who are in Jesus Christ are the freest of all people because in 1 Corinthians 10, Paul declared that all things were lawful. People talk about Christianity being restrictive. But nothing could be farther from the truth. We are not under the law, not under regulations and rules, do's and don'ts. All things are lawful but all things are not expedient. That is, there are things that will ensnare and enslave me if I allow myself to fall into their trap. If I meddle in areas I shouldn't, I'll be carried off, hostage to a certain sin or series of sins that will enslave me. If I repent, God will forgive me, but my liberty will be diminished. That is why our loving heavenly Father has given us the Holy Spirit to continually say to us, "Don't meddle in that. Don't compromise at that point."

Precious brother, dear sister, let us not be overcome by overconfidence. Instead, let us be wise, listening for the Spirit to speak at every juncture.

2 Kings 14:15–22
Now the rest of the acts of Jehoash which he did, and his might, and how he fought with Amaziah king of Judah, are they not written in the book of the chronicles of the kings of Israel? And Jehoash slept with his fathers, and was buried in Samaria with the kings of Israel; and Jeroboam his son reigned in his stead. And Amaziah the son of Joash king of Judah lived after the death of Jehoash son of Jehoahaz king of Israel fifteen years. And the rest of the acts of Amaziah, are they not written in the book of the chronicles of the kings of Judah? Now they made a conspiracy against him in Jerusalem: and he fled to Lachish; but they sent after him to Lachish, and slew him there. And they brought him on horses: and he was buried at Jerusalem with his fathers in the city of David. And all the people of Judah took Azariah, which was sixteen years old, and made him king instead of his father Amaziah. He built Elath, and restored it to Judah, after that the king slept with his fathers.

After Amaziah was defeated in a battle he had no business fighting, his popularity in his nation plummeted. The people of Judah, defeated by their northern neighbors, no longer wanted him. In those days, royalty was risky business. Kings didn't get voted out. They got done in. And Amaziah was no exception. After he was killed, his son, Azariah, reigned in his place.

2 Kings 14:23
In the fifteenth year of Amaziah the son of Joash king of Judah Jeroboam the son of Joash king of Israel began to reign in Samaria, and reigned forty and one years.

We go back up north to Israel. This is not Jeroboam of previous writings but another Jeroboam.

2 Kings 14:24
And he did that which was evil in the sight of the LORD: he departed not from all the sins of Jeroboam the son of Nebat, who made Israel to sin.

During Jeroboam's reign, the Lord raised up four powerful prophets: Jonah, Hosea, Joel, and Micah. But Jeroboam didn't heed their words.

2 Kings 14:25–27
He restored the coast of Israel from the entering of Hamath unto the sea of the plain, according to the word of the LORD God of Israel, which he spake by the hand of his servant Jonah, the son of Amittai, the prophet, which was of Gath-hepher. For the LORD saw the affliction of Israel, that it was very bitter: for there was not any shut up, nor any left, nor any helper for Israel. And the LORD said not that he would blot out the name of Israel from under heaven: but he saved them by the hand of Jeroboam the son of Joash.

In spite of Jeroboam's sin, God remained faithful to Israel and gave them victory.

2 Kings 14:28, 29
Now the rest of the acts of Jeroboam, and all that he did, and his might, how he warred, and how he recovered Damascus, and Hamath, which belonged to Judah, for Israel, are they not written in the book of the chronicles of the kings of Israel? And Jeroboam slept with his fathers, even with the kings of Israel; and Zachariah his son reigned in his stead.

Jeroboam was a wicked king, and yet the Lord used him powerfully. He had a long reign. He was prosperous. And yet he did not love the Lord. Oftentimes, we get confused on this issue. We see someone who is powerful and prosperous, who seems to get all the breaks while we who love the Lord face one trial after another. Why is it that the evil people seem to do so well? Have you ever asked that question? Asaph did . . .

> Truly God is good to Israel, even to such as are of a clean heart. But as for me, my feet were almost gone; my steps had well nigh slipped. For I was envious at the foolish, when I saw the prosperity of the wicked. When I thought to know this, it was too painful for me; Until I went into the sanctuary of God; then understood I their end. Surely thou didst set them in slippery places: thou castedst them down into destruction. Nevertheless I am continually with thee: thou hast holden me by my right hand. Thou shalt guide me with thy counsel, and afterward receive me to glory. Psalm 73:1–3, 16, 18, 23, 24

Asaph was confused and baffled until he came into the house of the Lord. And suddenly his perspective was restored. I can't tell you how many times that has happened to me. Discouraged or confused, I have plopped into a pew and when the Word was opened, it spoke exactly to me and my vision was restored. That's why I love being in the house of the Lord. My perspective is always clarified once again. Let the Jeroboams have their success now. Ours is coming.

15

In the south, a great king arises named Azariah, better known as Uzziah . . .

2 Kings 15:1–3
In the twenty and seventh year of Jeroboam king of Israel began Azariah son of Amaziah king of Judah to reign. Sixteen years old was he when he began to reign, and he reigned two and fifty years in Jerusalem. And his mother's name was Jecholiah of Jerusalem. And he did that which was right in the sight of the LORD, according to all that his father Amaziah had done;

In the Book of Chronicles, we'll see that Uzziah was a truly great king. He was a capable administrator, a valiant warrior, an inventor, and, above all, a lover of God.

2 Kings 15:4–7
Save that the high places were not removed: the people sacrificed and burnt incense still on the high places. And the LORD smote the king, so that he was a leper unto the day of his death, and dwelt in a several house. And Jotham the king's son was over the house, judging the people of the land. And the rest of the acts of Azariah, and all that he did, are they not written in the book of the chronicles of the kings of Judah? So Azariah slept with his fathers; and they buried him with his fathers in the city of David: and Jotham his son reigned in his stead.

What's going on here? If Uzziah loved the Lord, why is he smitten with leprosy? Uzziah who was doing so well made a tragic, fatal error. He went in to the temple and offered sacrifices. The priests warned him, saying, Don't do it. But he felt God would bless him. So he overstepped his parameters. And he found out God is not a respecter of persons. There is only One who is qualified to be both priest and king—Jesus Christ. Thus, Uzziah distorted the picture of Jesus.

In this, I am reminded of Moses. When the children of Israel thirsted in the wilderness, God told him to speak to the rock and water would gush forth. Instead, Moses struck the rock as he had done previously (Exodus 17:6). But because the rock was a picture of Jesus (1 Corinthians 10:4), the picture became distorted because Jesus would be smitten only once through His death on the Cross for our sins. This picture was so important to God that Moses was unable to enter the Promised Land because, like Azariah, he altered the picture.

2 Kings 15:8–12
In the thirty and eighth year of Azariah king of Judah did Zachariah the son of Jeroboam reign over Israel in Samaria six months. And he did that which was evil in the sight of the LORD, as his fathers had done: he departed not from the sins of Jeroboam the son of Nebat, who made Israel to sin. And Shallum the son of Jabesh conspired against him, and smote him before the people, and slew him, and reigned in his stead. And the rest of the acts of Zachariah, behold, they are written in the book of the chronicles of the kings of Israel. This was the word of the LORD which he spake unto Jehu, saying, Thy sons shall sit on the throne of Israel unto the fourth generation. And so it came to pass.

Although there was only one dynasty in the southern kingdom—David's family—there were eight dynasties in the northern kingdom. One of these dynasties was that of Jehu. Because Jehu destroyed Baal worship in Israel, the Lord promised that his family would continue on the throne for four generations. This is the fulfillment of that prophecy.

2 Kings 15:13–16
Shallum the son of Jabesh began to reign in the nine and thirtieth year of Uzziah king of Judah; and he reigned a full month in Samaria. For Menahem the son of Gadi went up from Tirzah, and came to Samaria, and smote Shallum the son of Jabesh in Samaria, and slew him, and reigned in his stead. And the rest of the acts of Shallum, and his conspiracy which he made, behold, they are written in the book of the chronicles of the kings of Israel. Then Menahem smote Tiphsah, and all that were therein, and the coasts thereof from Tirzah: because they opened not to him, therefore he smote it; and all the women therein that were with child he ripped up.

It is believed that Menahem was the general of Zachariah's army. Hearing of Zachariah's death, Menahem killed Zachariah's murderer and proclaimed himself king. When the people of the city of Tiphsah refused to open their gates to him, he stormed in and committed barbarous acts of murder.

2 Kings 15:17–20
In the nine and thirtieth year of Azariah king of Judah began Menahem the son of Gadi to reign over Israel, and reigned ten years in Samaria. And he did that which was evil in the sight of the LORD: he departed not all his days from the sins of Jeroboam the son of Nebat, who made Israel to sin. And Pul the king of Assyria came against the land: and Menahem gave Pul a thousand talents of silver, that his hand might be with

him to confirm the kingdom in his hand. And Menahem exacted the money of Israel, even of all the mighty men of wealth, of each man fifty shekels of silver, to give to the king of Assyria. So the king of Assyria turned back, and stayed not there in the land.

Menahem raised taxes in order to buy off the king of Assyria, who otherwise would have invaded Israel.

2 Kings 15:21–25
And the rest of the acts of Menahem, and all that he did, are they not written in the book of the chronicles of the kings of Israel? And Menahem slept with his fathers; and Pekahiah his son reigned in his stead. In the fiftieth year of Azariah king of Judah Pekahiah the son of Menahem began to reign over Israel in Samaria, and reigned two years. And he did that which was evil in the sight of the LORD: he departed not from the sins of Jeroboam the son of Nebat, who made Israel to sin. But Pekah the son of Remaliah, a captain of his, conspired against him, and smote him in Samaria, in the palace of the king's house, with Argob and Arieh, and with him fifty men of the Gileadites: and he killed him, and reigned in his room.

There is no shortage of chaos and confusion, intrigue and assassination in the history of the kings of Israel.

2 Kings 15:26–29
And the rest of the acts of Pekahiah, and all that he did, behold, they are written in the book of the chronicles of the kings of Israel. In the two and fiftieth year of Azariah king of Judah Pekah the son of Remaliah began to reign over Israel in Samaria, and reigned twenty years. And he did that which was evil in the sight of the LORD: he departed not from the sins of Jeroboam the son of Nebat, who made Israel to sin. In the days of Pekah king of Israel came Tiglath-pileser king of Assyria, and took Ijon, and Abel-beth-maachah, and Jonoah, and Kedesh, and Hazor, and Gilead, and Galilee, all the land of Naphtali, and carried them captive to Assyria.

This is the first of two deportations. Tiglath-pileser, the powerful ruler of Assyria, comes down and begins to carry the people back to Assyria for the purpose of assimilating them into the Assyrian culture, taking away their national identity. Over time, they would no longer be an enemy and no longer pose a threat.

2 Kings 15:30–38
And Hoshea the son of Elah made a conspiracy against Pekah the son of Remaliah, and smote him, and slew him, and reigned in his stead, in the twentieth year of Jotham the son of Uzziah. And the rest of the acts of Pekah, and all that he did, behold, they are written in the book of the chronicles of the kings of Israel. In the second year of Pekah the son of Remaliah king of Israel began Jotham the son of Uzziah king of Judah to reign. Five and twenty years old was he when he began to reign, and he reigned sixteen years in Jerusalem. And his mother's name was Jerusha, the daughter of Zadok. And he did that which was right in the sight of the LORD: he did according to all that his father Uzziah had done. Howbeit the high places were not removed: the people sacrificed and burned incense still in the high places. He built the higher gate of the house of the LORD. Now the rest of the acts of Jotham, and all that he did, are they not written in the book of the chronicles of the kings of Judah? In those days the LORD began to send against Judah Rezin the king of Syria, and Pekah the son of Remaliah. And Jotham slept with his fathers, and was buried with his fathers in the city of David his father: and Ahaz his son reigned in his stead.

From the parallel account in 2 Chronicles 27, we learn that Jotham was able to overthrow the Ammonites and collect from them one hundred talents of silver, 10,000 measures of wheat, and 10,000 measures of barley for three years. Although Hezekiah and Josiah would impact the nation spiritually, Jotham would be the last of the Jewish kings to have a prosperous reign politically.

16

2 Kings 16:1–4
In the seventeenth year of Pekah the son of Remaliah Ahaz the son of Jotham king of Judah began to reign. Twenty years old was Ahaz when he began to reign, and reigned sixteen years in Jerusalem, and did not that which was right in the sight of the LORD his God, like David his father. But he walked in the way of the kings of Israel, yea, and made his son to pass through the fire, according to the abominations of the heathen, whom the LORD cast out from before the children of Israel. And he sacrificed and burnt incense in the high places, and on the hills, and under every green tree.

It was believed that if a person placed his eldest son on the incandescent arms of the statue of the pagan god, Molech, his family would be prosperous. Before we rush to judge Ahaz for doing this, however, we would do well to look at ourselves and our own culture. There are a lot of kids who have been "sacrificed" in order that there might be financial prosperity in the home. They have been ignored in order that a parent's career might prosper. But our kids don't want every thing. They want *us.* They need *us.* We wonder why our kids are burning up with anger and rebellion and frustration. Perhaps it is because we are doing the same thing Ahaz did—sacrificing our kids for the sake of prosperity.

2 Kings 16:5 (a)
Then Rezin king of Syria and Pekah son of Remaliah king of Israel came up to Jerusalem to war . . .

Pekah was the king of Israel. He allied himself with Rezin, king of Syria, to fight the king of Judah.

2 Kings 16:5 (b)–7
. . . and they besieged Ahaz, but could not overcome him. At that time Rezin king of Syria recovered Elath to Syria, and drave the Jews from Elath: and the Syrians came to Elath, and dwelt there unto this day. So Ahaz sent messengers to Tiglath-pileser king of Assyria, saying, I am thy servant and thy son: come up, and save me out of the hand of the king of Syria, and out of the hand of the king of Israel, which rise up against me.

Ahaz asks Tiglath-pileser to come and rescue him from the confederacy of Israel and Syria. He cries out to the king of Assyria instead of crying up to the King of kings in heaven. He's reaching out for human help instead of praying down divine help.

2 Kings 16:8
And Ahaz took the silver and gold that was found in the house of the LORD, and in the treasures of the king's house, and sent it for a present to the king of Assyria.

Ahaz robbed the house of the Lord to pay for help from man. Before we too quickly condemn Ahaz, perhaps the Holy Spirit would convict us and call us to consider our own state. When we feel pressure, when we feel like we're going under, when we're sinking in debt, do we sometimes rob the house of the Lord? "I can't tithe this week because I've got to pay these guys off. Lord, You understand, don't You?" we say.

2 Kings 16:9
And the king of Assyria hearkened unto him: for the king of Assyria went up against Damascus, and took it, and carried the people of it captive to Kir, and slew Rezin.

Ahaz was saved by Tiglath-pileser's assistance. So relieved was he, he went to meet him in the city of Damascus, where Tiglath-pileser was enjoying his success.

2 Kings 16:10–12
And king Ahaz went to Damascus to meet Tiglath-pileser king of Assyria, and saw an altar that was at Damascus: and king Ahaz sent to Urijah the priest the fashion of the altar, and the pattern of it, according to all the workmanship thereof. And Urijah the priest built an altar according to all that king Ahaz had sent from Damascus: so Urijah the priest made it against king Ahaz came from Damascus. And when the king was come from Damascus, the king saw the altar: and the king approached to the altar, and offered thereon.

While in Damascus congratulating Tiglath-pileser, Ahaz saw a heathen altar that caught his attention. So he sent for the priest in Jerusalem to go to Damascus to make notes so that he could reproduce it.

I am increasingly concerned that we in the church are all too often following the example of Ahaz, patterning our ministries upon what the world propagates. In previous generations, Satan attempted to counterfeit the church. But it seems in this present day that the church is seeing the heathen altars of the enemy and copying them. The church should be setting the standard, remaining true to what the Word says rather than what the world does.

2 Kings 16:13, 14
And he burnt his burnt offering and his meat offering, and poured his drink offering, and sprinkled the blood of his peace offerings, upon the altar. And he brought also the brasen altar, which was before the LORD, from the forefront of the house, from between the altar and the house of the LORD, and put it on the north side of the altar.

The brass altar is the one the Lord designed. Here, furniture that was placed by divine design is now being moved by Ahaz's whims.

2 Kings 16:15
And king Ahaz commanded Urijah the priest, saying, Upon the great altar burn the morn-

ing burnt offering, and the evening meat offering, and the king's burnt sacrifice, and his meat offering, with the burnt offering of all the people of the land, and their meat offering, and their drink offerings; and sprinkle upon it all the blood of the burnt offering, and all the blood of the sacrifice: and the brasen altar shall be for me to inquire by.

Ahaz decided the brass altar would be his personal altar.

2 Kings 16:16–20
Thus did Urijah the priest, according to all that king Ahaz commanded. And king Ahaz cut off the borders of the bases, and removed the laver from off them; and took down the sea from off the brasen oxen that were under it, and put it upon a pavement of stones. And the covert for the sabbath that they had built in the house, and the king's entry without, turned he from the house of the LORD for the king of Assyria. Now the rest of the acts of Ahaz which he did, are they not written in the book of the chronicles of the kings of Judah? And Ahaz slept with his fathers, and was buried with his fathers in the city of David: and Hezekiah his son reigned in his stead.

Although he came from an ungodly father, Hezekiah would be a godly king. Hezekiah would do as much to restore the temple as his father did to destroy it. And thus, God's work would continue in spite of the wickedness of man.

17

We come now to a sobering and sad section of Scripture, for in chapter 17, we see the nation of Israel—the ten northern tribes—carried away into captivity . . .

2 Kings 17:1–3
In the twelfth year of Ahaz king of Judah began Hoshea the son of Elah to reign in Samaria over Israel nine years. And he did that which was evil in the sight of the LORD, but not as the kings of Israel that were before him. Against him came up Shalmaneser king of Assyria; and Hoshea became his servant, and gave him presents.

Shalmaneser, king of Assyria, put pressure on Israel. Hoshea, king of Israel, paid him tribute.

2 Kings 17:4
And the king of Assyria found conspiracy in Hoshea: for he had sent messengers to So king of Egypt, and brought no present to the king of Assyria, as he had done year by year: therefore the king of Assyria shut him up, and bound him in prison.

Hoshea is attempting to strike up a rebellious confederacy with the Egyptian king in order to rid himself of the tribute he was paying the Assyrians.

2 Kings 17:5–8
Then the king of Assyria came up throughout all the land, and went up to Samaria, and besieged it three years. In the ninth year of Hoshea the king of Assyria took Samaria, and carried Israel away into Assyria, and placed them in Halah and in Habor by the river of Gozan, and in the cities of the Medes. For so it was, that the children of Israel had sinned against the LORD their God, which had brought them up out of the land of Egypt, from under the hand of Pharoah king of Egypt, and had feared other gods, And walked in the statutes of the heathen, whom the LORD cast out from before the children of Israel, and of the kings of Israel, which they had made.

Carrying people into captivity was a common practice of the day. A conquering country would take the conquered people back into its own region for the purpose of assimilation. Over time, the new arrivals would be absorbed into the host culture and thereby lose their national identity. The people of Israel were divided and placed in various areas in order that separation and isolation would keep them from rebelling. After they carried the people of Israel into Assyria, the Assyrians sent other people they had conquered into the area that was once inhabited by the ten northern tribes.

2 Kings 17:9
And the children of Israel did secretly those things that were not right against the LORD their God, and they built them high places in all their cities, from the tower of the watchmen to the fenced city.

Hebrews 4:13 tells us that all things we do are naked and open before Him with whom we deal. Nothing is done in secret. The Lord sees. Here, Israel's sin caught up with her.

2 Kings 17:10–13
And they set them up images and groves in every high hill, and under every green tree: And there they burnt incense in all the high places, as did the heathen whom the LORD carried away before them; and wrought

wicked things to provoke the LORD to anger: For they served idols, whereof the LORD had said unto them, Ye shall not do this thing. Yet the LORD testified against Israel, and against Judah, by all the prophets, and by all the seers, saying, Turn ye from your evil ways, and keep my commandments and my statutes, according to all the law which I commanded your fathers, and which I sent to you by my servants the prophets.

While they were practicing their secret sins, the Lord was publicly calling them to return to Him. Many prophets were on the scene at this time, preaching, teaching and calling God's people to repentance.

2 Kings 17:14, 15 (a)
Notwithstanding they would not hear, but hardened their necks, like to the neck of their fathers, that did not believe in the LORD their God. And they rejected his statutes, and his covenant that he made with their fathers, and his testimonies which he testified against them; and they followed vanity, and became vain . . .

The word "vanity" in the OT means "empty." The people of Israel followed empty things and became empty themselves. The same is still true. When we feel empty, it is inevitably because we are following after vanity. Do you ever get to the place where you're hungry inside but think that what you really need is a hot fudge sundae? You have one, only to realize you're still empty inside. So you think you need to watch TV. But after watching a two-hour movie, you're still empty. Why? Because those things are empty. Then you take twenty minutes, get on your knees, cry out to the Lord, open the Word—and you're deeply satisfied.

2 Kings 17:15 (b), 16
. . . and went after the heathen that were round about them, concerning whom the LORD had charged them, that they should not do like them. And they left all the commandments of the LORD their God, and made them molten images, even two calves, and made a grove, and worshipped all the host of heaven, and served Baal.

The "host of heaven" refers to astrology, which has its roots in Babylonian religious practices.

2 Kings 17:17, 18
And they caused their sons and their daughters to pass through the fire, and used divination and enchantments, and sold themselves to do evil in the sight of the LORD, to provoke him to anger. Therefore the LORD was very angry with Israel, and removed them out of his sight: there was none left but the tribe of Judah only.

For hundreds of years, the Lord called to His people, but they would not respond. And because they would not respond to His goodness, they began to experience His judgment.

2 Kings 17:19–24
Also Judah kept not the commandments of the LORD their God, but walked in the statutes of Israel which they made. And the LORD rejected all the seed of Israel, and afflicted them, and delivered them into the hand of spoilers, until he had cast them out of his sight. For he rent Israel from the house of David; and they made Jeroboam the son of Nebat king: and Jeroboam drave Israel from following the LORD, and made them sin a great sin. For the children of Israel walked in all the sins of Jeroboam which he did; they departed not from them; Until the LORD removed Israel out of his sight, as he had said by all his servants the prophets. So was Israel carried away out of their own land to Assyria unto this day. And the king of Assyria brought men from Babylon, and from Cuthah, and from Ava, and from Hamath, and from Sepharvaim, and placed them in the cities of Samaria instead of the children of Israel: and they possessed Samaria, and dwelt in the cities thereof.

Not only was there deportation *from* Israel, but occupation in Israel. Assyria is occupying the land of Israel with the goal of annexation.

2 Kings 17:25
And so it was at the beginning of their dwelling there, that they feared not the LORD: therefore the LORD sent lions among them, which slew some of them.

The occupiers of Israel ate from crops they didn't plant and lived in houses they didn't build. They enjoyed benefits and blessings, and yet all without acknowledging the Lord who blessed the land. So He sent lions in their midst.

Peter tells us that our Adversary, Satan, is like a roaring lion, seeking whom he may devour (1 Peter 5:8). Even those who do not fear the Lord in our country enjoy the blessings of health, freedom, Christian heritage, and influence. Yet because they do not acknowledge Him, He allows Satan to bite and devour. Is this to punish them? No, it's to awaken them.

2 Kings 17:26
Wherefore they spake to the king of Assyria, saying, The nations which thou hast removed, and placed in the cities of Samaria, know not the manner of the God of the land: therefore he hath sent lions among them, and, behold, they slay them, because they know not the manner of the God of the land.

"We don't know what to do. Who is the God of this land?" asked Israel's new occupants.

2 Kings 17:27
Then the king of Assyria commanded, saying, Carry thither one of the priests whom ye brought from thence; and let them go and dwell there, and let him teach them the manner of the God of the land.

"Let one of the priests of Israel return to teach the people about the God of the land," the king of Assyria said.

2 Kings 17:28–33
Then one of the priests whom they had carried away from Samaria came and dwelt in Bethel, and taught them how they should fear the LORD. Howbeit every nation made gods of their own, and put them in the houses of the high places which the Samaritans had made, every nation in their cities wherein they dwelt. And the men of Babylon made Succoth-benoth, and the men of Cuth made Nergal, and the men of Hamath made Ashima, And the Avites made Nibhaz and Tartak, and the Sepharvites burnt their children in fire to Adrammelech and Anammelech, the gods of Sepharvaim. So they feared the LORD, and made unto themselves of the lowest of them priests of the high places, which sacrificed for them in the houses of the high places. They feared the LORD, and served their own gods, after the manner of the nations whom they carried away from thence.

They feared the Lord and yet they served their own heathen deities. They were afraid of the consequences, but they had affection for their previous practices. This is what Spurgeon calls a "sham conversion." And the same thing still happens. When a person goes through a hard time—losing a loved one or the pain of divorce, or bankruptcy—he says, "I must seek the Lord. I'm being bitten." And yet, although they fear the Lord in the sense of being afraid of the consequences of sin, there is no change in their lifestyle. Repentance is the beginning of genuine salvation.

2 Kings 17:34
Unto this day they do after the former manners: they fear not the LORD, neither do they after their statutes, or after their ordinances, or after the law and commandment which the LORD commanded the children of Jacob, whom he named Israel;

When the lions backed off, the settlers stopped fearing the Lord altogether. If you fear the Lord only because you've been bitten, once the problem you face goes away, you'll no longer fear Him and you won't be saved in the last day. That is why Peter pleads with us to make our calling and election sure (2 Peter 1:10). Make sure you're saved, not just responding to the growl of a lion or the breath of a beast closing in on you. Make sure your heart is toward the Lord. Seeing a person come forward several times for salvation doesn't bother me a bit. I would rather see people come forward every Sunday, making their election sure than to be part of a sham conversion.

2 Kings 17:35–41
With whom the LORD had made a covenant, and charged them saying, Ye shall not fear other gods, nor bow yourselves to them, nor serve them, nor sacrifice to them: But the LORD, who brought you up out of the land of Egypt with great power and a stretched out arm, him shall ye fear, and him shall ye worship, and to him shall ye do sacrifice. And the statutes, and the ordinances, and the law, and the commandment, which he wrote for you, ye shall observe to do for evermore; and ye shall not fear other gods. And the covenant that I have made with you ye shall not forget; neither shall ye fear other gods. But the LORD your God ye shall fear; and he shall deliver you out of the hand of all your enemies. Howbeit they did not hearken, but they did after their former manner. So these nations feared the LORD, and served their graven images, both their children, and their children's children: as did their fathers, so do they unto this day.

Mixture always leads to disaster. Jesus said, "I would that you were either hot or cold. If you're lukewarm, I will spew you out of My mouth. If you're hot, I'll use you. If you're cold, I'll deal with you. But if you're lukewarm, it's hard for Me to find any use for you at all" (Revelation 3:15, 16).

The Jewish people hated these Samaritans, these new settlers. Some of the Jews had been left behind and they intermarried with people of the Assyrian empire. Thus, they were half-breeds racially. They were also half-breeds religiously because they believed in God, but didn't serve Him wholeheartedly. The Jews despised them. They were the perfect picture of lukewarmness.

There was one Jew, however, who said, "I must go to Samaria." When every other Jew of that day would go miles out of their way to avoid even walking on Samaritan soil, there was One who said, "I must go there" (John 4:4).

In the fourth chapter of John, we see Jesus tenderly but firmly, compassionately yet directly dealing with a Samaritan woman. As a result, there was a revival in Samaria, the home of the half-breed, the home of the lukewarm. And there can be revival in your soul as well.

18 2 Kings 18:1–3
Now it came to pass in the third year of Hoshea son of Elah king of Israel, that Hezekiah the son of Ahaz king of Judah began to reign. Twenty and five years old was he when he began to reign; and he reigned twenty and nine years in Jerusalem. His mother's name also was Abi, the daughter of Zachariah. And he did that which was right in the sight of the LORD, according to all that David his father did.

Along with Asa, Jehoshaphat, and Josiah, Hezekiah is one of the four outstanding kings whose life is recorded in Kings and Chronicles as men who did that which was right in the sight of the Lord.

2 Kings 18:4 (a)
He removed the high places, and brake the images, and cut down the groves . . .

Hezekiah removed the obvious forms of idolatry but he doesn't stop there. He goes on to deal with a more subtle form of idolatry, one to which we as believers can fall prey . . .

2 Kings 18:4 (b)
. . . and brake in pieces the brasen serpent that Moses had made: for unto those days the children of Israel did burn incense to it: and he called it Nehushtan.

Over seven hundred years previously, when the children of Israel were wandering in the wilderness, they were bitten by serpents because of their perpetual murmuring and sin. As they began to fall like flies, they cried to Moses. Moses, in turn, cried to the Lord and was told to make a brass serpent on a brass pole. Brass is the metal of judgment. Therefore, the brass serpent was a picture of Jesus, for He who knew no sin was made sin for you and me and judged on the Cross of Calvary (2 Corinthians 5:21). Anyone who looked upon the brass serpent was healed, just as today, any one of us who look to Jesus Christ will be saved, healed from the snakebite of sin.

Over the years, the brass serpent became an idol. Hezekiah, under the inspiration of the Spirit, called it what it was: *Nehushtan*, or "a thing of brass."

2 Kings 18:5–7
He trusted in the LORD God of Israel; so that after him was none like him among all the kings of Judah, nor any that were before him. For he clave to the LORD, and departed not from following him, but kept his commandments, which the LORD commanded Moses. And the LORD was with him; and he prospered whithersoever he went forth: and he rebelled against the king of Assyria, and served him not.

Why did Hezekiah prosper? Because he clave to the commandments of the Lord. David knew this secret, for in Psalm 1, he said, "Blessed is the man who meditates in the Law of the Lord. Whatsoever he doeth shall prosper."

***For topical study of 2 Kings 18:1–7 entitled "The Subtlety of Idolatry," turn to page* 1074.**

2 Kings 18:8–13
He smote the Philistines, even unto Gaza, and the borders thereof, from the tower of the watchmen to the fenced city. And it came to pass in the fourth year of king Hezekiah, which was the seventh year of Hoshea son of Elah king of Israel, that Shalmaneser king of Assyria came up against Samaria, and besieged it. And at the end of three years they took it: even in the sixth year of Hezekiah, that is the ninth year of Hoshea king of Israel, Samaria was taken. And the king of Assyria did carry away Israel unto Assyria, and put them in Halah and in Habor by the river of Gozan, and in the cities of the Medes: Because they obeyed not the voice of the LORD their God, but transgressed his covenant, and all that Moses the servant of the LORD commanded, and would not hear them, nor do them. Now in the fourteenth year of king Hezekiah did Sennacherib king of Assyria come up against all the fenced cities of Judah, and took them.

Sennacherib, king of Assyria, began his move to conquer Judah.

2 Kings 18:14
And Hezekiah king of Judah sent to the king of Assyria to Lachish, saying, I have offended; return from me: that which thou puttest on me will I bear.

When Sennacherib came down with his mighty Assyrian army, Hezekiah agreed to pay tribute if he would call a halt to his invasion.

2 Kings 18:15, 16
And the king of Assyria appointed unto Hezekiah king of Judah three hundred talents of silver and thirty talents of gold. And Hezekiah gave him all the silver that was found in the house of the LORD, and in the treasures of the king's house. At that time did Hezekiah cut off the gold from the doors of the temple of the LORD, and from the pillars which Hezekiah king of Judah had overlaid, and gave it to the king of Assyria.

Hezekiah is in error here. Rather than calling out to the Lord to supply his need, he removes the golden doors and golden overlay from the temple and uses it to pay Sennacherib. But whenever we seek to appease the enemy, it never works. The more you feed him, the fatter he gets. Sennacherib was no exception. Rather than being satisfied with this initial payment of gold and silver, it just whetted his appetite for more.

2 Kings 18:17
And the king of Assyria sent Tartan and Rabsaris and Rab-shakeh from Lachish to king Hezekiah with a great host against Jerusalem. And they went up and came to Jerusalem. And when they were come up, they came and stood by the conduit of the upper pool, which is in the highway of the fuller's field.

With an army of 200,000 the Assyrians were hoping the Jews would surrender out of intimidation. The fuller's field was sort of the Geneva Conference Center of the day.

2 Kings 18:18–21
And when they had called to the king, there came out to them Eliakim the son of Hilkiah, which was over the household, and Shebna the scribe, and Joah the son of Asaph the recorder. And Rab-shakeh said unto them, Speak ye now to Hezekiah, Thus saith the great king, the king of Assyria, What confidence is this wherein thou trustest? Thou sayest, (but they are but vain words,) I have counsel and strength for the war. Now on whom dost thou trust, that thou rebellest against me? Now, behold, thou trustest upon the staff of this bruised reed, even upon Egypt, on which if a man lean, it will go into his hand, and pierce it: so is Pharoah king of Egypt unto all that trust on him.

"Don't think you can rely on the Egyptians. Pharaoh is nothing more than a broken reed—he can't support you," said Sennacherib's spokesman, Rab-shakeh.

2 Kings 18:22
But if ye say unto me, We trust in the LORD our God: is not that he, whose high places and whose altars Hezekiah hath taken away, and hath said to Judah and Jerusalem, Ye shall worship before this altar in Jerusalem?

Hezekiah honored the Lord in destroying the altars of the heathen deities. But the Assyrians misunderstood what he was doing and thought he was destroying sanctified altars. Therefore, they assumed God would not come to Hezekiah's aid.

2 Kings 18:23
Now therefore, I pray thee, give pledges to my lord the king of Assyria, and I will deliver thee two thousand horses, if thou be able on thy part to set riders upon them.

"If you surrender," Rab-shakeh said, "I'll give you 2,000 horses."

2 Kings 18:24, 25
How then wilt thou turn away the face of one captain of the least of my master's servants, and put thy trust on Egypt for chariots and for horsemen? Am I now come up without the LORD against this place to destroy it? The LORD said to me, Go up against this land, and destroy it.

"Forget the Egyptians," Rab-shakeh said, "because they're weak. Forget the Lord because He's angry. Actually, the Lord told me to destroy this land." But saying "the Lord told me," doesn't make it true.

2 Kings 18:26–31
Then said Eliakim the son of Hilkiah, and Shebna, and Joah, unto Rab-shakeh, Speak, I pray thee, to thy servants in the Syrian language; for we understand it: and talk not with us in the Jews' language in the ears of the people that are on the wall. But Rabshakeh said unto them, Hath my master sent me to thy master, and to thee, to speak these words? hath he not sent me to the men which sit on the wall, that they may eat their own dung, and drink their own piss with you. Then Rab-shakeh stood and cried with a loud voice in the Jews' language, and spake, saying, Hear the word of the great king, the king of Assyria: Thus saith the king, Let not Hezekiah deceive you: for he shall not be able to deliver you out of his hand: Neither let Hezekiah make you trust in the LORD, saying, The LORD will surely deliver us, and this city shall not be delivered

into the hand of the king of Assyria. Hearken not to Hezekiah: for thus saith the king of Assyria, Make an agreement with me by a present, and come out to me, and then eat ye every man of his own vine, and every one of his fig tree, and drink ye every one the waters of his cistern:

Speaking in a loud voice so that the soldiers defending the wall might give up, Rab-shakeh gives a three-fold argument for why they should surrender. First, he promised that if they came to his side, they would have their own vine, their own land, and their own well. In other words, they would be prosperous.

2 Kings 18:32
Until I come and take you away to a land like your own land, a land of corn and wine, a land of bread and vineyards, a land of oil olive and of honey, that ye may live, and not die: and hearken not unto Hezekiah, when he persuadeth you, saying, The LORD will deliver us.

The second promise Rab-shakeh made to whoever would defect to the Assyrian side was that they wouldn't die.

2 Kings 18:33–35
Hath any of the gods of the nations delivered at all his land out of the hand of the king of Assyria? Where are the gods of Hamath, and of Arpad? where are the gods of Sepharvaim, Hena, and Ivah? have they delivered Samaria out of mine hand? Who are they among all the gods of the countries, that have delivered their country out of mine hand, that the LORD should deliver Jerusalem out of mine hand?

Finally, Rab-shakeh sought to plant seeds of doubt in the minds of the Jews by questioning God's ability to withstand the power of the Assyrians.

These three ploys—the promise of prosperity, the denial of death, and the raising of questions—are the same tactics Satan used in the garden of Eden to tempt Eve. This tells me that Satan's playbook is extremely limited. He keeps running the same plays over and over again. "Cheat here and you'll be happy," he says. "You won't die. You have your whole life ahead of you, so live it up," he hisses. "If God is a God of love, why are there starving people in the world?" he taunts.

2 Kings 18:36, 37
But the people held their peace, and answered him not a word: for the king's commandment was, saying, Answer him not. Then came Eliakim the son of Hilkiah, which was over the household, and Shebna the scribe, and Joah the son of Asaph the recorder, to Hezekiah with their clothes rent, and told him the words of Rab-shakeh.

Here is how to deal with the devil. Follow Hezekiah's command: Answer him not. Too often I think we are too ready to do battle with the devil. The sons of Sceva tried to do this against him and got their clothes ripped off in the process (Acts 19). In Jude we read that Michael the archangel did not dare bring a railing accusation against Satan but left the rebuke of Satan to the Lord (v. 9). It's always good to keep the Lord between you and Satan.

THE SUBTLETY OF IDOLATRY

A Topical Study of 2 KINGS 18:1–7

It can be said without hesitation that Hezekiah was one of Judah's greatest rulers. He ascended to the throne when he was twenty-five years old and did that which was right in the sight of the Lord. Under his reign, Judah experienced a very remarkable, radical revival. Hezekiah was an energetic iconoclast. He destroyed images, cut down groves, dismantled the high places, all which were associated with idolatry.

Our Father is radically and vehemently opposed to idolatry. The First Commandment He gave Moses was that there was to be no other god before Him (Exodus 20:3). There is only one true and living God. But there are other gods. In the

Old Testament, these gods had names such as Ashteroth, the goddess of sensuality; Mammon, the god of money; Molech, the god of pleasure; and Baal, the god of the intellect. And although we don't have those same names, our society serves the same gods. Every man will serve some god. There is some master passion of your life that controls you and is a priority for you. If you think you serve no god, in reality, you are worshiping yourself, and that is a terrible god indeed!

In the Second Commandment, God said,

> *Thou shalt not make unto thee any graven image, or any likeness of any thing that is in heaven above, or that is in the earth beneath, or that is in the water under the earth: Thou shalt not bow down thyself to them, nor serve them: for I the* LORD *thy God am a jealous God . . .* Exodus 20:4, 5 (a)

God is not jealous of false gods. No, He is jealous for you. He cares about you and wants the best for you and knows those other gods will mislead and ultimately destroy you. So He says, "You are never to bow down to an image or an idol."

Why is God so vehemently opposed to idolatry?

I'll suggest two reasons . . .

Protection

Idols can be, and often are, more than merely a piece of carved wood or stone. In 1 Corinthians 10, Paul talks about a controversy that was raging in the church of Corinth over whether it was right for Christians to eat meat that had been sacrificed to idols. You see, after the meat was sacrificed, it was taken to shambles—little markets—and sold at a cut rate. Some Christians bought this meat. Others, however, looked down on them for doing so . . .

> *What say I then? that the idol is any thing, or that which is offered in sacrifice to idols is any thing? But I say, that the things which the Gentiles sacrifice, they sacrifice to devils, and not to God: and I would not that ye should have fellowship with devils. Ye cannot drink the cup of the Lord, and the cup of devils: ye cannot be partakers of the Lord's table, and of the table of devils. Do we provoke the Lord to jealousy? are we stronger than he?* 1 Corinthians 10:19–22

Paul is saying that the idol in itself is nothing, but behind the idol is a demonic entity. Thus, it is for our protection that God tells us to stay away from idols.

Not only are idols demonic, but they are also demeaning . . .

> *Their idols are silver and gold, the work of men's hands. They have mouths, but they speak not: eyes have they, but they see not: They have ears, but they hear not: noses have they, but they smell not: They have hands, but they handle not: feet have they, but they walk not: neither speak they through their throat.*

They that make them are like unto them; so is every one that trusteth in them.
O Israel, trust thou in the L*ORD . . .* Psalm 115:4–9 (a)

The psalmist says these idols are deaf, dumb, and lame. And those that make them and worship them become just like them—lamebrains. In other words, we become like whatever we worship. If we worship a loving, holy, great, and gracious God, we begin to take on His characteristics, for as we behold Him, we are changed from glory to greater glory (2 Corinthians 3:18).

Preparation

Secondly, God forbids idolatry for our preparation. They that worship the true and living God must worship Him in spirit and in truth (John 4:23, 24). We live in a world that continually gravitates to the material realm. We want to see, touch, smell, and taste. But our God is Spirit, and He is preparing us for eternity, developing within us the ability to move in the Spirit, free from the constraints of the tangible or touchable.

Hezekiah kept the commandment of the Lord. And revival followed. But then he dealt with even a more subtle manifestation of idolatry. He dealt with the brass serpent . . .

Nehushtan means "a thing of brass." The brass snake was kept first by Moses, then by Joshua for forty years as the nation engaged in warfare. During the reigns of Saul, David, Solomon, and the rest of the kings—for seven hundred years—this pole and serpent were preserved. I'm sure it was saved as something to remember what the Lord had done. But over the years, it became an idol. What was initially used *by* the Lord soon was placed in competition *with* Him. I'm sure the people who burned incense to it thought they were simply using it to draw closer to God. But in reality, it was an idol to them. They were burning incense which was only to be burned before Jehovah. Hezekiah called it what it was, and broke it into pieces.

I believe that, like the children of Israel, we, as the people of God, are in danger of subtle idolatry in exalting, lifting up, and worshiping things, which are in competition with the true and living God . . .

Our past can be an idol. "Oh, yes," we say, "I remember in 1948. That's when things were really happening with the Lord and me." If we glory in the past, live in the past, and talk about the past, our past becomes an idol. In Ezra 3, we read that when the foundation of the temple was laid, the young men shouted for joy. The old men, however, wept, saying, "It's not like it used to be" because the past had become an idol to them.

"Forgetting those things which are behind, I press on toward the high calling of Jesus Christ," Paul declared (Philippians 3:13, 14).The human mind has the tendency to remember only the good things about the past. Therefore, we must, like Paul, continually look ahead.

Procedures or practices can become idols. We have to worship with a guitar. No, they're Nehushtan. We can cling to our doctrines, our practices, our style of ministry—and they can actually become idols. We must be careful.

People can become idols. I'm thankful for men and women of God. But they're men and women nonetheless. There was a man several years before Hezekiah came to the throne that was also a great king. His name was Uzziah. So wise, prosperous, and successful a ruler was he that his name was on the lips of everyone from north to south (2 Chronicles 26:15). During his life, the prophet, Isaiah, was on the scene. Isaiah had a fabulous vision of God. He said, "I saw the Lord high and lifted up, and His train filled the temple." But the interesting thing is that the chapter wherein this vision is recorded begins with these words: In the year that King Uzziah died, I saw the Lord (Isaiah 6:1). When did Isaiah see the Lord? When Uzziah died. As long as Uzziah was on the throne, people trusted in Uzziah. But when he was gone, people set their sights higher.

Dear brothers and sisters, let us be careful that we not fall into the subtlety of idolatry. There is only One worthy of worship: our Lord and Savior, Jesus Christ. For His pleasure, all things are created. Therefore, to Him and Him alone be glory and honor forevermore.

19

2 Kings 19:1

And it came to pass, when king Hezekiah heard it, that he rent his clothes, and covered himself with sackcloth, and went into the house of the LORD.

The house of the Lord is the best place to be. Sometimes, however, it's the hardest place to get to because when the enemy is threatening, sometimes you feel you can't make it to the house of the Lord. Rab-shakeh's railings against God notwithstanding, Hezekiah made it to the house of the Lord.

2 Kings 19:2–5

And he sent Eliakim, which was over the household, and Shebna the scribe, and the elders of the priests, covered with sackcloth, to Isaiah the prophet the son of Amoz. And they said unto him, Thus saith Hezekiah, This day is a day of trouble, and of rebuke, and blasphemy: for the children are come to the birth, and there is not strength to bring forth. It may be the LORD thy God will hear all the words of Rab-shakeh, whom the king of Assyria his master hath sent to reproach the living God; and will reprove the words which the LORD thy God hath heard: wherefore lift up thy prayer for the remnant that are left. So the servants of king Hezekiah came to Isaiah.

With the mighty Assyrian army camped outside his gates and Rab-shakeh's taunts in his ears, Hezekiah sent word to Isaiah the prophet.

2 Kings 19:6, 7

And Isaiah said unto them, Thus shall ye say to your master, Thus saith the LORD, Be not afraid of the words which thou hast heard, with which the servants of the king of Assyria have blasphemed me. Behold, I will send a blast upon him, and he shall hear a rumour, and shall return to his own land; and I will cause him to fall by the sword in his own land.

Isaiah prophesied of a blast, a rumor, and a sword. The blast was no doubt the death of 185,000 Assyrian soldiers in one night (v. 35). The rumor was that Ethiopia had invaded Assyria (v. 9). The sword was the death of Sennacherib by the hands of his own sons (v. 37). In other words, God was not caught off guard by Sennacherib. He was not surprised by Rab-shakeh. He was not worried about the Assyrians.

I am reminded of another godly man who wondered why the Lord seemed to be oblivious to the violence that surrounded him. God's answer to Habakkuk was the same as his answer to Hezekiah:

Behold ye among the heathen, and regard, and wonder marvelously: for I will work a work in your days, which ye will not believe, though it be told you. Habakkuk 1:5

God knew exactly what He would do in Hezekiah's day. He knew exactly what He would do in Habakkuk's day. And He knows exactly what He'll do in whatever faces you today, as well.

2 Kings 19:8–13
So Rab-shakeh returned, and found the king of Assyria warring against Libnah: for he had heard that he was departed from Lachish. And when he heard say of Tirhakah king of Ethiopia, Behold, he is come out to fight against thee: he sent messengers again unto Hezekiah, saying, Thus shall ye speak to Hezekiah king of Judah, saying, Let not thy God in whom thou trustest deceive thee, saying, Jerusalem shall not be delivered into the hand of the king of Assyria. Behold, thou hast heard what the kings of Assyria have done to all lands, by destroying them utterly: and shalt thou be delivered? Have the gods of the nations delivered them which my fathers have destroyed; as Gozan, and Haran, and Rezeph, and the children of Eden which were in Thelasar? Where is the king of Hamath, and the king of Arpad, and the king of the city of Sepharvaim, of Hena, and Ivah?

With his troops spread thin, Sennacherib resumed his attempt to cause Hezekiah to surrender.

2 Kings 19:14–19
And Hezekiah received the letter of the hand of the messengers, and read it: and Hezekiah went up into the house of the LORD, and spread it before the LORD. And Hezekiah prayed before the LORD, and said, O LORD God of Israel, which dwellest between the cherubims, thou art the God, even thou alone, of all the kingdoms of the earth: thou hast made heaven and earth. LORD, bow down thine ear, and hear: open, LORD, thine eyes, and see: and hear the words of Sennacherib, which hath sent him to reproach the living God. Of a truth, LORD, the kings of Assyria have destroyed the nations and their lands, And have cast their gods into the fire: for they were no gods, but the work of men's hands, wood and stone: therefore they have destroyed them. Now therefore, O LORD our God, I beseech thee, save thou us out of his hand, that all the kingdoms of the earth may know that thou art the LORD God, even thou only.

Hezekiah received Sennacherib's letter, read its contents, and responded perfectly: he relied on the Lord.

***For topical study of 2 Kings 19:1–19 entitled "Turn Your Cares into Prayers," turn to page* 1079.**

2 Kings 19:20–22
Then Isaiah the son of Amoz sent to Hezekiah, saying, Thus saith the LORD God of Israel, That which thou hast prayed to me against Sennacherib king of Assyria I have heard. This is the word that the LORD hath spoken concerning him; The virgin the daughter of Zion hath despised thee, and laughed thee to scorn; the daughter of Jerusalem hath shaken her head at thee. Whom hast thou reproached and blasphemed? and against whom hast thou exalted thy voice, and lifted up thine eyes on high? even against the Holy One of Israel.

The Lord is saying, "Sennacherib, you've had it. By attacking My people, you are attacking Me." I'm aware that my kids have shortcomings and I try to correct them. But if someone else seeks to attack my kids, the bear comes out in me. I will fiercely and fervently protect them from attack. Our heavenly Father feels the same way. He knows what we are. He'll deal with us and correct us. The God of Ananias and Sapphira is able indeed to correct His children. We do not need to attack the people of God. When we attack other believers, we are actually attacking God Himself.

2 Kings 19:23–28
By the messengers thou hast reproached the Lord, and hast said, With the multitude of my chariots I am come up to the height of the mountains, to the sides of Lebanon, and will cut down the tall cedar trees thereof, and the choice fir trees thereof: and I will enter into the lodgings of his borders, and into the forest of his Carmel. I have digged and drunk strange waters, and with the sole of my feet have I dried up all the rivers of besieged places. Hast thou not heard long ago how I have done it, and of ancient times that I have formed it? now have I brought it to pass, that thou shouldest be to lay waste fenced cities into ruinous heaps. Therefore their inhabitants were of small power, they were dismayed and confounded; they were as the grass of the field, and as the green herb, as the grass on the housetops, and as corn blasted before it be grown up. But I know thy abode, and thy going out, and thy

coming in, and thy rage against me. Because thy rage against me and thy tumult is come up into mine ears, therefore I will put my hook in thy nose, and my bridle in thy lips, and I will turn thee back by the way by which thou camest.

"You've put your hook in other peoples' noses. Now I'm putting My hook in yours," the Lord said to Sennacherib.

2 Kings 19:29, 30
And this shall be a sign unto thee, Ye shall eat this year such things as grow of themselves, and in the second year that which springeth of the same; and in the third year sow ye, and reap, and plant vineyards, and eat the fruits thereof. And the remnant that is escaped of the house of Judah shall yet again take root downward, and bear fruit upward.

This is always the way it is. There can be no visible fruit without invisible roots. If we are to bear fruit in ministry, in worship, in our families, in our communities, our root system must be developed in the unseen area, in the morning hour of prayer, in the evening hour of Bible study.

2 Kings 19:31, 32
For out of Jerusalem shall go forth a remnant, and they that escape out of mount Zion: the zeal of the LORD of hosts shall do this. Therefore thus saith the LORD concerning the king of Assyria, He shall not come into this city, nor shoot an arrow there, nor come before it with shield, nor cast a bank against it.

Almost 200,000 men were camped outside of Jerusalem, yet the Lord said not a single one of their arrows would land in the city.

2 Kings 19:33, 34
By the way that he came, by the same shall he return, and shall not come into this city, saith the LORD. For I will defend this city, to save it, for mine own sake, and for my servant David's sake.

"I'm going to defend My people not because of how good they are or because of how worthy they are, but for My name's sake and for David's. The Lord will defend us, not for our righteousness but because we carry His name, and because of a promise He made to a Greater than David, the Son of David, Jesus Christ. All you need to do is spread the troubling situation before Him and watch Him fight for you (Exodus 14:14).

2 Kings 19:35–37
And it came to pass that night, that the angel of the LORD went out, and smote in the camp of the Assyrians an hundred fourscore and five thousand: and when they arose early in the morning, behold, they were all dead corpses. So Sennacherib king of Assyria departed, and went and returned, and dwelt at Nineveh. And it came to pass, as he was worshipping in the house of Nisroch his god, that Adrammelech and Sharezer his sons smote him with the sword: and they escaped into the land of Armenia. And Esarhaddon his son reigned in his stead.

Recognizing that something supernatural had taken place, Sennacherib went to the temple and worshiped his god. Historians tell us that his two sons were upset that he was turning his power over to another son. So while he was worshiping, they pushed the idol on top of him, pinned him to the ground, and beheaded him—unknowingly but unmistakably fulfilling Isaiah's prophecy (v. 7).

TURN YOUR CARES INTO PRAYERS

A Topical Study of 2 KINGS 19:1–19

Hezekiah's heart was very heavy. His head was probably pounding. He had just received a very distressing letter from Sennacherib, king of Assyria, commander-in-chief of the most advanced army in the world at that time—a fighting force that had not lost a battle for one hundred and fifty years. Not only were the Assyrians unbeatable in battle, they were also unbelievable in brutality. Hooks were placed in the noses of their captives through which ropes were passed, thus joining them together in a forced death-march to Assyria.

Sennacherib wrote a letter. Maybe a letter has been delivered to you recently that is disturbing. Maybe it didn't come in the mail but some situation has been handed to you that distresses you, discourages you, disheartens you. King Hezekiah certainly had reason to be disturbed. The Assyrians were right outside the city and a letter from their king was in his hand.

We live in a world full of stress, anxiety, and tension. This shouldn't surprise us because in Luke 21:26 we read that one of the signs of the end times would be that men's hearts would fail them for fear. Ours is the first generation in history to actually experience this prophecy as doctors increasingly correlate heart attacks and heart failure with stress. And yet Jesus came on the scene, saying, "Take no thought for what you shall eat, drink, or wear. The birds of the air do not sow or reap, but the Father in heaven takes care of them. Consider the lilies of the field. Even Solomon was not arrayed like one of these" (see Matthew 6:28–30).

"Take no thought for tomorrow," Jesus said, "for today has enough troubles of its own." Jesus told us we are not to be worried or stressed. Now, anyone can say, "Don't worry." Only the Bible tells us how not to . . .

Be careful for nothing . . . Philippians 4:6 (a)

"Be careful for nothing." The King James translators had a different understanding of the word "careful" than we do today. In reference to this verse, they said, "Be full of care about nothing. Don't be anxious." God's intent is that we be carefree.

Paul says, "Be careful for nothing"—but he doesn't leave it there. He gives a plan to help us do just that . . .

. . . but in every thing by prayer and supplication with thanksgiving . . .
Philippians 4:6 (b)

Thanksgiving is so important. A grateful person is a great, full person. Think of the people you know who are great. They're not people who are negative and who complain. They're people who have an attitude of continual thanksgiving. Paul said, "In everything give thanks for this is the will of God in Christ Jesus concerning you" (1 Thessalonians 5:18). I am often asked how to discover God's will. Here it is: Give God thanks in everything. You will be large in stature in the things of God if you are simply grateful.

. . . let your requests be made known unto God. Philippians 4:6 (c)

Be careful for nothing. Give thanks in all things. Pray about everything. Everything means *every* thing. There is nothing too small for God's concern. This is where we often err. We often think of God as being so awesome in size that He could not possible care about my lost key. God is infinite. Infinite means He cannot be measured. He's bigger than time and space. He's also smaller than the smallest electron and molecule. This means the problems I think are small are as big to Him as the problems I think are insurmountable. He is small enough to care about them and big enough to solve them. Nothing is too small to talk to the Lord about. Nothing. Pray about *every* thing.

And the peace of God, which passeth all understanding, shall keep your hearts and minds through Christ Jesus. Philippians 4:7

If we follow this simple plan in obedience to the plan of Jesus Christ—if we are careful for nothing, give thanks in all things, and pray about every thing—we will experience the inexpressible peace of God.

When things are coming down, the world says, "Look out!" The Word, however, says, "When things are coming down, look up! Pray." After I pray, I don't usually have the answer, but I do have peace—peace that comes not from understanding, but that passes understanding.

Paul preached it. Hezekiah practiced it. Hezekiah began his prayer by worshiping (v. 15). That's always a wise thing to do, for worship wipes out worry. My problems can seem so huge to me. But when I begin to worship and experience the glory and majesty of God, my problems shrink proportionately. If you stand at the foot of the Himalayan mountains, at over 29,000 feet they tower over you. But if you go up in a satellite and look down, you won't even notice them. Worship is the way to get above your problems, to get God's perspective.

In his prayer, Hezekiah didn't tell the Lord what to do. He simply spread Sennacherib's letters out before Him. The problem we have in prayer is that we say, "Lord, here's what should be done. Let me give You some advice because I don't know if You see the situation as clearly as I do." Do you find yourself praying that way sometimes? I do. And when I realize it, I am always terribly embarrassed.

Hezekiah laid out Sennacherib's letters and said, "For Your glory, Lord, do something." The Lord has ideas and plans of which we could never dream. He has creative alternatives we can't even imagine.

At the end of the chapter, in verse 35, we read, "And it came to pass." I love that phrase because things *do* pass. The difficulty you face today *will* pass. Don't give up. It only took *one* angel to smite 185,000 Assyrians (v. 35). The battle was won due to a simple prayer by a desperate king. He prayed to the Lord. When you're in a tight spot, pray, gang. And, like Hezekiah, you will experience the peace of God which passes all understanding.

20

2 Kings 20:1 (a)
In those days was Hezekiah sick unto death . . .

When was Hezekiah sick unto death? In the day of victory, the day of the miraculous, the day of answered prayer. Some Bible scholars believe the killing of the 185,000 soldiers was the result of a plague and that Hezekiah contracted the same disease. This is another passage that reminds me that even in times when the Holy Ghost is moving and miracles are happening, godly men are not immune from sickness. We serve a God who heals. But we also serve a God who—as Elisha experienced, as Hezekiah experienced, as Paul makes reference to—sometimes uses sickness for His glory. Here is a case of a man who, although he did right in the sight of God, was sick.

2 Kings 20:1 (b)
. . . And the prophet Isaiah the son of Amoz came to him, and said unto him, Thus saith the LORD, Set thine house in order; for thou shalt die, and not live.

"It's time to go home," the Lord said to Hezekiah through His prophet, Isaiah. "I'm taking you home and sickness is the tool I'm using." What if the Lord came to you and said, "Set your house in order, I'm taking you home." Would you panic? Or are you walking with the Lord in such a way that you would be at peace about it?

2 Kings 20:2, 3
Then he turned his face to the wall, and prayed unto the LORD, saying, I beseech thee, O LORD, remember now how I have walked before thee in truth and with a perfect heart, and have done that which is good in thy sight. And Hezekiah wept sore.

In the original language of a parallel passage, Isaiah tells us Hezekiah turned his face toward the wall and prayed (see 38:2). He didn't want to die, so he cried.

2 Kings 20:4–7
And it came to pass, afore Isaiah was gone out into the middle court, that the word of the LORD came to him, saying, Turn again, and tell Hezekiah the captain of my people, Thus saith the LORD, the God of David thy father, I have heard thy prayer, I have seen thy tears: behold, I will heal thee: on the third day thou shalt go up unto the house of the LORD. And I will add unto thy days fifteen years; and I will deliver thee and this city out of the hand of the king of Assyria; and I will defend this city for mine own sake, and for my servant David's sake. And Isaiah said, Take a lump of figs. And they took and laid it on the boil, and he recovered.

The compound of crushed figs was a common medicine of the day. God's healing comes through prayer, through medicine, through our natural healing processes, or through a combination of all three. It is not prayer that heals, medicine that heals, or our bodies that heal. It's the Lord who heals and He can use any method He chooses.

2 Kings 20:8
And Hezekiah said unto Isaiah, What shall be the sign that the LORD will heal me, and that I shall go up into the house of the LORD the third day?

When Isaiah told Hezekiah that God would heal him and give him fifteen more years to live, Hezekiah asked for confirmation. I commend him for this. In the area of divine healing, we must seek confirmation about what the Lord is doing before we make claims about what He's done.

2 Kings 20:9–11
And Isaiah said, This sign shalt thou have of the LORD, that the LORD will do the thing that he hath spoken: shall the shadow go forth ten degrees, or go back ten degrees? And Hezekiah answered, It is a light thing for the shadow to go down ten degrees: nay, but let the shadow return backward ten degrees. And Isaiah the prophet cried unto the LORD: and he brought the shadow ten degrees backward, by which it had gone down in the dial of Ahaz.

Ten degrees on the sundial was probably forty-five minutes. The miracle was confirmed.

2 Kings 20:12, 13
At that time Berodach-baladan, the son of Baladan, king of Babylon, sent letters and a present unto Hezekiah: for he had heard that Hezekiah had been sick. And Hezekiah hearkened unto them, and shewed them all the house of his precious things, the silver, and the gold, and the spices, and the precious ointment, and all the house of his armour, and all that was found in his treasures: there was nothing in his house, nor in all his dominion, that Hezekiah shewed them not.

So flattered was Hezekiah that bigwigs from Babylon would come to bring him get well wishes that he showed them everything in his empire.

2 Kings 20:14–18
Then came Isaiah the prophet unto king Hezekiah, and said unto him, What said these men? and from whence came they unto thee? And Hezekiah said, They are come from a far country, even from Babylon. And he said, What have they seen in thine house? And Hezekiah answered, All the things that are in mine house have they seen: there is nothing among my treasures that I have not shewed them. And Isaiah said unto Hezekiah, Hear the word of the LORD. Behold, the days come, that all that is in thine house, and that which thy fathers have laid up in store unto this day, shall be carried into Babylon: nothing shall be left, saith the LORD. And of thy sons that shall issue from thee, which thou shalt beget, shall they take away; and they shall be eunuchs in the palace of the king of Babylon.

"Hezekiah, you botched it," Isaiah said. "The Babylonian messengers will go home and tell their king how rich you are. Then you'll be attacked."

We live in a day when transparency is lauded. While I think there's a time to be open, I also think it's foolish to open yourself up to everyone who shows up with a Get Well card. When prophecies were made about Jesus, Luke says Mary pondered them in her heart (10:19). There can be great damage done when a person opens himself up indiscriminately. In the multitude of words, "there wanteth not sin" (Proverbs 2:19). In other words, the more you open your mouth, the more sin comes out. Let every man be quick to hear and slow to speak, James wisely counseled (1:19). I can't count the number of times I have regretted speaking rather than listening. Lord, help us.

2 Kings 20:19
Then said Hezekiah unto Isaiah, Good is the word of the LORD which thou hast spoken. And he said, Is it not good, if peace and truth be in my days?

After seeing Hezekiah's mistake, here we see his maturity, for even though he was told his kingdom would come crashing down and that his sons would be carried away, he willingly submitted to the will of God.

2 Kings 20:20, 21
And the rest of the acts of Hezekiah, and all his might, and how he made a pool, and a conduit, and brought water into the city, are they not written in the book of the chronicles of the kings of Judah? And Hezekiah slept with his fathers: and Manasseh his son reigned in his stead.

When Hezekiah heard the Assyrians were coming, he commanded a tunnel be dug from the spring of Gihon to the pool of Siloam inside the city in order that the Assyrians would be unable to cut off their water source. To accomplish this monumental feat, a 1,777-foot tunnel was dug thirty feet underground through solid rock.

Man can live weeks without food, but only days without water. Water in Scripture refers both to the written word (Ephesians 5:26) and the living Word, Jesus Christ (John 7:37). How deep are we willing to dig? How many obstacles are we willing to tunnel through in order to spend time in the written Word with the living Word in order to keep our souls from dehydrating?

21

2 Kings 21:1
Manasseh was twelve years old when he began to reign, and reigned fifty and five years in Jerusalem. And his mother's name was Hephzi-bah.

Manasseh was the worst of all of the kings, yet he had the longest reign.

2 Kings 21:2, 3
And he did that which was evil in the sight of the LORD, after the abominations of the heathen, whom the LORD cast out before the children of Israel. For he built up again the high places which Hezekiah his father had destroyed; and he reared up altars for Baal, and made a grove, as did Ahab king of Israel; and worshipped all the host of heaven, and served them.

In other words, Manasseh was the "Ahab of Judah."

2 Kings 21:4, 5
And he built altars in the house of the LORD, of which the LORD said, In Jerusalem will I put my name. And he built altars for all the host of heaven in the two courts of the house of the LORD.

Manasseh erected idolatrous altars even in the temple.

2 Kings 21:6
And he made his son pass through the fire, and observed times, and used enchantments, and dealt with familiar spirits and wizards:

he wrought much wickedness in the sight of the LORD, to provoke him to anger.

In addition to using incantations and spells, Manasseh either offered his son as a sacrifice on the red-hot hands of the idol, Molech, or at the very least, consecrated him to Molech.

2 Kings 21:7, 8
And he set a graven image of the grove that he had made in the house, of which the LORD said to David, and to Solomon his son, In this house, and in Jerusalem, which I have chosen out of all tribes of Israel, will I put my name for ever: Neither will I make the feet of Israel move any more out of the land which I gave their fathers; only if they will observe to do according to all that I have commanded them, and according to all the law that my servant Moses commanded them.

Had God's people remained faithful to Him, they would never have been carried out of the land He had given them (2 Samuel 7:10).

2 Kings 21:9
But they hearkened not: and Manasseh seduced them to do more evil than did the nations whom the LORD destroyed before the children of Israel.

Not only were God's people unfaithful to Him, but also they sinned even more than the Canaanites before them had sinned.

2 Kings 21:10–12
And the LORD spake by his servants the prophets, saying, Because Manasseh king of Judah hath done these abominations, and hath done wickedly above all that the Amorites did, which were before him, and hath made Judah also to sin with his idols: Therefore thus saith the LORD God of Israel, Behold, I am bringing such evil upon Jerusalem and Judah, that whosoever heareth of it, both his ears shall tingle.

Through Hosea, Joel, Nahum, Habakkuk, and Isaiah, God spoke so plainly and loudly to His people that their words would echo even after they passed from the scene.

2 Kings 21:13 (a)
And I will stretch over Jerusalem the line of Samaria, and the plummet of the house of Ahab . . .

The line and plummet here refer to the implements used to group together captives doomed to destruction (see 2 Samuel 8:2). Samaria had already been led into captivity. Jerusalem would suffer the same fate.

2 Kings 21:13 (b)
. . . and I will wipe Jerusalem as a man wipeth a dish, wiping it, and turning it upside down.

As polluted as they were, God's people deserved to be wiped out. Instead, God declares He would wipe them up.

2 Kings 21:14–16
And I will forsake the remnant of mine inheritance, and deliver them into the hand of their enemies; and they shall become a prey and a spoil to all their enemies; Because they have done that which was evil in my sight, and have provoked me to anger, since the day their fathers came forth out of Egypt, even unto this day. Moreover Manasseh shed innocent blood very much, till he had filled Jerusalem from one end to another; beside his sin wherewith he made Judah to sin, in doing that which was evil in the sight of the LORD.

"They were sawn in two . . ." (Hebrews 11:37). Bible scholars believe this verse refers to Isaiah, who was sawn in half by Manasseh. Fifteen years earlier, the Lord had said to Hezekiah, "It's time to go home." But Hezekiah cried. So the Lord let him have his way. As a result, not only would the Babylonians have reason to invade Judah and carry God's people into captivity, but also Manasseh, the worst king in Judah's history, would be born.

Be careful, dear saint, what you insist upon, for it could have disastrous results. Unless you are in the center of God's will, the desire of your heart could lead to leanness in your soul (Psalm 106:15).

How much better it would have been had Hezekiah not tried to talk God into his plans, but just said, "Father, Thy will be done." We make so many mistakes by complaining and griping and murmuring about what God is doing in our lives. And sometimes the Father says, "If that's what you want, have your way." Saints, go with the flow of what God is doing. Yes, offer your requests, but always in submission to the perfect will of God.

2 Kings 21:17, 18 (a)
Now the rest of the acts of Manasseh, and all that he did, and his sin that he sinned, are they not written in the book of the chronicles of the kings of Judah? And Manasseh

slept with his fathers, and was buried in the garden of his own house, in the garden of Uzza . . .

In 2 Chronicles 33, we read that after Manasseh was carried captive to Babylon, he repented and sought God. Eventually, he was restored to his kingdom, where he destroyed idolatry and reinstituted worship of the true and living God.

2 Kings 21:18 (b)–22
. . . and Amon his son reigned in his stead. Amon was twenty and two years old when he began to reign, and he reigned two years in Jerusalem. And his mother's name was Meshullemeth, the daughter of Haruz of Jotbah. And he did that which was evil in the sight of the LORD, as his father Manasseh did. And he walked in all the way that his father walked in, and served the idols that his father served, and worshipped them: And he forsook the LORD God of his fathers, and walked not in the way of the LORD.

Rather than following the footsteps of his father's later years, Amon copied the idolatrous practices of Manasseh's earlier years.

2 Kings 21:23
And the servants of Amon conspired against him, and slew the king in his own house.

After only a two-year reign, Amon was killed by his own servants.

2 Kings 21:24–26
And the people of the land slew all them that had conspired against king Amon; and the people of the land made Josiah his son king in his stead. Now the rest of the acts of Amon which he did, are they not written in the book of the chronicles of the kings of Judah? And he was buried in his sepulchre in the garden of Uzza: and Josiah his son reigned in his stead.

In Josiah's ascension to the throne, two of Judah's worst kings were replaced by one of Judah's best kings.

22 At this point, Judah will enter a period of peace and prosperity resulting from revival and reformation during the reign of King Josiah. There were four great reformers, four great kings who ushered in revival in the country of Judah: Asa, Hezekiah, Jehoshaphat, and Josiah. But the reforms under Josiah went further and deeper than the reforms of any of the other reformers. In the life of Josiah, we see the reason for revival, the road to revival and the result of revival.

Revival is what every one of us longs for in some way. If your own heart is dry, you need a personal revival. If your children aren't walking with the Lord in the way you know they should, your family needs revival. If your workplace is an atmosphere of ungodliness and carnality, your colleagues need revival. Our God is the God of continual revival. And He *wants* to revive.

What is the reason for revival? One eight-year-old boy was totally in love with the Lord. And in him, the Lord had a base from which He could work. The reason for revival is found in one individual going all out for the things of God. As you study history and read of revivals, you will find without exception that they begin with one individual excited about the Lord. All it takes is one.

"What difference can I make in my neighborhood or at my workplace?" we ask. "There are so many people, how could I affect that situation?" It only takes one . . .

In the late 1800s, there was a great evangelist named Gypsy Smith. He traveled the world, preaching on every continent. Wherever he preached, revival broke out. One day, a delegation of people came to him and said, "Reverend Smith, we desperately want to see revival in our area. It's so dry and dead. What can we do?"

Gypsy reportedly said, "Go home. Lock yourselves in your bedrooms. Take a piece of chalk. Draw a circle on the floor. Kneel in the circle and pray fervently that God would start a revival in that circle."

Revival doesn't begin by praying for your husband or wife, or praying for your boss. It begins when you get on your face before the Lord and say, "Let it begin with *me*."

2 Kings 22:1, 2
Josiah was eight years old when he began to reign, and he reigned thirty and one years in Jerusalem. And his mother's name was Jedidah, the daughter of Adaiah of Boscath. And he did that which was right in the sight of the LORD, and walked in all the way of David his father, and turned not aside to the right hand or to the left.

A whitewater river guide once told me that the secret of whitewater canoeing is to stay in the "tongue," or the center, of the river because there are currents to the right and left that ultimately lead to a cracked canoe. That's what Josiah did. He didn't go to the right or the left. So often we, as Christians, can go off to the right. We can become very legalistic, thinking we alone are "right." The Pharisees veered off to the right. Or we drift to the left and become so liberal in our theology that we stand for nothing. The Sadducees did this. That is why the Lord calls us, like Josiah, to remain in the center.

2 Kings 22:3–6
And it came to pass in the eighteenth year of king Josiah, that the king sent Shaphan the son of Azaliah, the son of Meshullam, the scribe, to the house of the LORD, saying, Go up to Hilkiah the high priest, that he may sum the silver which is brought into the house of the LORD, which the keepers of the door have gathered of the people: And let them deliver it into the hand of the doers of the work, that have the oversight of the house of the LORD: and let them give it to the doers of the work which is in the house of the LORD, to repair the breaches of the house, Unto carpenters, and builders, and masons, and to buy timber and hewn stone to repair the house.

In the life of Josiah, we see not only the reason for revival, but also seven steps on the road to revival. Step one is that the people repaired the breaches in the temple. According to Paul, we are the temple of God (1 Corinthians 3:16). We are living stones, Peter tells us, being fit together into a holy habitation (1 Peter 2:5). The Lord does not work where there is not love. That is why the first step on the road to revival is to repair the breaches. Jesus said that it was our love for each other that would identify us as His disciples (John 13:35). Love is patient and kind, not easily provoked. Love thinks no evil, believes all things, bears all things, and endures all things. Love never fails (1 Corinthians 13).

When you're truly in love with the Lord, you're no longer interested in strife and faultfinding. "If you come before the altar and there remember that your brother has something against you," Jesus said, "leave your gift, be reconciled with your brother, and then present your gift at the altar" (Matthew 5:23, 24). When you're seeking the Lord at the altar, listen for Him telling you how to repair the breaches.

2 Kings 22:7, 8
Howbeit there was no reckoning made with them of the money that was delivered into their hand, because they dealt faithfully. And Hilkiah the high priest said unto Shaphan the scribe, I have found the book of the law in the house of the LORD. And Hilkiah gave the book to Shaphan, and he read it.

Following the repair of the breaches, the second step on the road to revival is the rediscovery of God's Word. Evidently, Manasseh and Amon had attempted to destroy all of the copies of the Law. But one copy was stuck away in a corner of the temple and was uncovered during the rebuilding project. It intrigues me that the Word of God was lost in the house of God. But, in a sense, that's what often happens today. Churches meet, but there is no emphasis on studying or knowing the Scriptures. As a result, the Word is lost in liturgy, buried in ritual. Manasseh attempted to destroy the Word, but he couldn't, for the Word of God is everlasting (Matthew 5:18).

When revival touches your heart, you inevitably rediscover the Word. The Word can be read aloud from Genesis to Revelation in only seventy hours and forty minutes. The New Testament can be read in eighteen hours and twenty-eight minutes. The Gospel of Luke can be read in two hours and forty-three minutes. In other words, in less than three hours, you can become acquainted or reacquainted with Jesus as you read Luke's Gospel.

This one copy of the Word was uncovered in the day of restoration and revival. That's what always happens in a true revival. There's an appreciation and reemphasis on the Word.

2 Kings 22:9, 10
And Shaphan the scribe came to the king, and brought the king word again, and said, Thy servants have gathered the money that was found in the house, and have delivered it into the hand of them that do the work, that have the oversight of the house of the LORD. And Shaphan the scribe shewed the king, saying, Hilkiah the priest hath delivered me a book. And Shaphan read it before the king.

This single copy of the Law wasn't placed in an airtight container inside a museum. No, it was read. The key is to *read* the Bible, not just have to own one.

2 Kings 22:11
And it came to pass, when the king had heard the words of the book of the law, that he rent his clothes.

Repentance from error is the third step on the road to revival. Realizing how far off course they were from where they should have been, Josiah tore his clothes in a sign of brokenness.

2 Kings 22:12, 13
And the king commanded Hilkiah the priest, and Ahikam the son of Shaphan, and

Achbor the son of Michaiah, and Shaphan the scribe, and Asahiah a servant of the king's, saying, Go ye, inquire of the LORD for me, and for the people, and for all Judah, concerning the words of this book that is found: for great is the wrath of the LORD that is kindled against us, because our fathers have not hearkened unto the words of this book, to do according unto all that which is written concerning us.

A request for instruction is the fourth step on the road to revival. Paul did the same thing. On the road to Damascus, he was knocked to the ground by the Lord. When he realized he was talking to Jesus, Paul said, "Lord, what wilt Thou have me to do?" (Acts 9:6). I don't know what the Lord would have you do when He brings revival to your soul. Maybe He'll have you start a Bible study at your job or in your neighborhood. Maybe He'll have you visit people in the hospital or take care of some kids in the nursery. I do know that as you seek Him, He'll show you something to do practically if, like Josiah, you request instruction.

2 Kings 22:14
So Hilkiah the priest, and Ahikam, and Achbor, and Shaphan, and Asahiah, went unto Huldah the prophetess, the wife of Shallum the son of Tikvah, the son of Harhas, keeper of the wardrobe; (now she dwelt in Jerusalem in the college;) and they communed with her.

At this time, both Jeremiah and Zephaniah were on the scene in Judah. Yet when Josiah heard the Word, he sought out Huldah, a woman who had insight and sensitivity to the Spirit of God.

2 Kings 22:15–20
And she said unto them, Thus saith the LORD God of Israel, Tell the man that sent you to me, Thus saith the LORD, Behold, I will bring evil upon this place, and upon the inhabitants thereof, even all the words of the book which the king of Judah hath read: Because they have forsaken me, and have burned incense unto other gods, that they might provoke me to anger with all the works of their hands; therefore my wrath shall be kindled against this place, and shall not be quenched. But to the king of Judah which sent you to inquire of the LORD, thus shall ye say to him, Thus saith the LORD God of Israel, As touching the words which thou hast heard; Because thine heart was tender, and thou hast humbled thyself before the LORD, when thou heardest what I spake against this place, and against the inhabitants thereof, that they should become a desolation and a curse, and hast rent thy clothes, and wept before me; I also have heard thee, saith the LORD. Behold therefore, I will gather thee unto thy fathers, and thou shalt be gathered into thy grave in peace; and thine eyes shall not see all the evil which I will bring upon this place. And they brought the king word again.

The Lord's answer through Huldah was that hard times would come but, because Josiah's heart was tender and because he humbled himself, Judah would not experience judgment in his lifetime.

If there was a revival taking place and people were getting right with the Lord, why would judgment still come?

The reason is that, because a crop of sin was planted, the harvest would inevitably come. For years, these people had slaughtered their children, forsaken the Lord, and practiced hideous abominations. Consequently, those things that took place would have repercussions. That is why the Bible says, "Be not deceived. God is not mocked. Whatever a man sows, that shall he also reap" (see Galatians 6:7). Sin always brings about repercussions.

Secondly, although Josiah humbled himself and was tenderhearted, the movement of the people toward the Lord was neither very sincere nor very deep (Jeremiah 7:4). In any revival, there are three kinds of believers. Some are rowboats who must be pushed to move in any direction. Others are sailboats who keep changing course depending upon the direction of the wind. But a third group are steamboats, people who make up their minds and go in a given direction regardless of wind or weather. Josiah was a steamboat. He had a heart for the Lord, a love for God, and was determined that nothing would pull him to the right or left.

At this point, if I were Josiah, having heard Huldah's prophecy, I'm afraid I would have said, "If judgment is coming, forget the revival." And yet in chapter 23, he continues bringing about reforms, doing what was right in the sight of the Lord.

Rowboat, sailboat, steamboat—which boat are you?

23

2 Kings 23:1–3
And the king sent, and they gathered unto him all the elders of Judah and of Jerusalem. And the king went up into the house of the LORD, and all the men of Judah and all the inhabitants of Jerusalem with him, and the priests, and the prophets,

and all the people, both small and great: and he read in their ears all the words of the book of the covenant which was found in the house of the LORD. And the king stood by a pillar, and made a covenant before the LORD, to walk after the LORD, and to keep his commandments and his testimonies and his statutes with all their heart and all their soul, to perform the words of this covenant that were written in this book. And all the people stood to the covenant.

After repairing the breaches, rediscovering God's Word, repenting from error, and requesting instruction, the fifth stop on the road to revival is to respond outwardly. Reading the entire Pentateuch would have been quite a lengthy study and yet this was Josiah's outward response to the revival taking place in his own soul.

The same is still true. When revival really happens, you're ready to take your stand, to go to your knees, to come forward to the altar. "Cool" Christianity melts in the fire of revival and you're willing to do whatever it takes to draw near to God.

During the old summer camps, I can recall every Friday night there was a bonfire service in which all of us were given a little pinecone. Those who had been touched by the Lord would walk down to the fire and throw their pinecone in as if to say, "Lord, that's my life. I give it to You. Consume me. Burn through me." Some people dismiss practices like this as nothing more than an emotional release. I, however, disagree. I praise the Lord for the hundreds of pinecones I chucked into summer camp fires because, to me, each one was meaningful. Sure, they were emotional moments but the Lord made us emotional beings. There's a time to express our emotions and to take a stand. Josiah took his by reading the Word.

2 Kings 23:4–7

And the king commanded Hilkiah the high priest, and the priests of the second order, and the keepers of the door, to bring forth out of the temple of the LORD all the vessels that were made for Baal, and for the grove, and for all the host of heaven: and he burned them without Jerusalem in the fields of Kidron, and carried the ashes of them unto Bethel. And he put down the idolatrous priests, whom the kings of Judah had ordained to burn incense in the high places in the cities of Judah, and in the places round about Jerusalem; them also that burned incense unto Baal, to the sun, and to the moon, and to the planets, and to all the host of heaven. And he brought out the grove from the house of the LORD, without Jerusalem, unto the brook Kidron, and burned it at the brook Kidron, and stamped it small to powder, and cast the powder thereof upon the graves of the children of the people. And he brake down the houses of the sodomites, that were by the house of the LORD, where the women wove hangings for the grove.

In the sixth step of revival, we see the removal of sin. Inside the temple, there were actually altars and idols to false gods. Josiah ordered them removed, burned, ground to powder, and stomped on.

Too often, we think this sixth step of revival should actually be the first step—that there must be removal of sin before revival can be experienced. But such is not the case. Throughout Scripture, we see repentance only as a response to the movement of God. In other words, we are so carnal that we cannot remove sin ourselves. God moves first and we simply respond.

Paul tells us it is the goodness of God that leads men to repentance (Romans 2:4). We have it all backwards. Too often, we preach the conviction of sin before we preach the goodness of God. But when you begin to know and experience, to taste and see the goodness of God, your taste for sin turns sour.

In 1904 one of the greatest revivals in history took place in Wales. A coal miner named Evans Robert was touched by the grace of God. Unlearned and ineloquent, he nonetheless began to teach and preach in the streets. People responded to his message to such a degree that within one year, there was not one functioning pub in Wales. They all closed, not because Christians picketed, but because no one was going. Morality cannot be legislated. Revival is what is needed because when people are touched by the Lord, their lives begin to change and sin begins to be removed. You don't fight darkness by fighting darkness. You turn on the light. When the Lord's love and light come into a life, the darkness is dispelled automatically.

2 Kings 23:8–10

And he brought all the priests out of the cities of Judah, and defiled the high places where the priests had burned incense, from Geba to Beer-sheba, and brake down the high places of the gates that were in the entering in of the gate of Joshua the governor of the city, which were on a man's left hand at the gate of the city. Nevertheless the priests of the high places came not up to the altar of the LORD in Jerusalem, but they did eat of the unleavened bread among their brethren. And he defiled Topheth, which is in the valley of the children of Hinnom, that

no man might make his son or his daughter to pass through the fire to Molech.

Directly below Jerusalem is a small valley called the valley of Hinnom, which became synonymous with Gehenna of hell because it was the place the Jews sacrificed their children to Molech. They called this area *Topheth,* which refers to the drums that were played loudly and steadily to drown out the cries.

2 Kings 23:11–14
And he took away the horses that the kings of Judah had given to the sun, at the entering in of the house of the LORD, by the chamber of Nathan-melech the chamberlain, which was in the suburbs, and burned the chariots of the sun with fire. And the altars that were on the top of the upper chamber of Ahaz, which the kings of Judah had made, and the altars which Manasseh had made in the two courts of the house of the LORD, did the king beat down, and brake them down from thence, and cast the dust of them into the brook Kidron. And the high places that were before Jerusalem, which were on the right hand of the mount of corruption, which Solomon the king of Israel had builded for Ashtoreth the abomination of the Zidonians, and for Chemosh the abomination of the Moabites, and for Milcom the abomination of the children of Ammon, did the king defile. And he brake in pieces the images, and cut down the groves, and filled their places with the bones of men.

Josiah transformed the places where idolatrous worship practices had taken place into cemeteries. Why? Because the Jews respected places of burial and, thus, would not turn these places back into centers of idolatry.

2 Kings 23:15
Moreover the altar that was at Bethel, and the high place which Jeroboam the son of Nebat, who made Israel to sin, had made, both that altar and the high place he brake down, and burned the high place, and stamped it small to powder, and burned the grove.

Here we see Josiah ushering in revival not only in Judah, but also in Bethel, which was to the north in Israel. That's always the way it is with true revival—it always spreads beyond its own boundaries. Even though at this point most of Israel had been carried away into Assyria, some of God's people remained in the area and Josiah was concerned about this remnant.

2 Kings 23:16–20
And as Josiah turned himself, he spied the sepulchres that were there in the mount, and sent, and took the bones out of the sepulchres, and burned them upon the altar, and polluted it, according to the word of the LORD which the man of God proclaimed, who proclaimed these words. Then he said, What title is that that I see? And the men of the city told him, It is the sepulchre of the man of God, which came from Judah, and proclaimed these things that thou hast done against the altar of Bethel. And he said, Let him alone; let no man move his bones. So they let his bones alone, with the bones of the prophet that came out of Samaria. And all the houses also of the high places that were in the cities of Samaria, which the kings of Israel had made to provoke the LORD to anger, Josiah took away, and did to them according to all the acts that he had done in Bethel. And he slew all the priests of the high places that were there upon the altars, and burned men's bones upon them, and returned to Jerusalem.

When Jeroboam built an altar in Bethel in order to keep his people from traveling to Jerusalem to offer sacrifices, a man of God prophesied of the day when the altar would be destroyed by a man named Josiah and that the bones of the prophets would be burned upon it. Three hundred years had passed and the prophecy was now being fulfilled to the letter (1 Kings 13:2).

If you're wondering why certain promises the Lord has either spoken to you through His Word, or written on your heart have yet to be fulfilled, don't give up. The Lord's timing is not ours. His is perfect.

2 Kings 23:21–23
And the king commanded all the people, saying, Keep the passover unto the LORD your God, as it is written in the book of this covenant. Surely there was not holden such a passover from the days of the judges that judged Israel, nor in all the days of the kings of Israel, nor of the kings of Judah; But in the eighteenth year of king Josiah, wherein this passover was holden to the LORD in Jerusalem.

The seventh and last step on the road to revival is the restoration of the ordinances. For hundreds of years, Passover had been forgotten. The celebration commemorating deliverance from Egypt and pointing to the Lamb of God—Jesus Christ—was ignored for centuries. But in the midst of revival, it was celebrated and observed again.

During the days of true revival, New Testament believers desire to return to the New Testament equivalent of Passover, the Lord's Table. This should not be surprising, for the result of real revival in the heart of people is a love for Jesus.

2 Kings 23:24, 25
Moreover the workers with familiar spirits, and the wizards, and the images, and the idols, and all the abominations that were spied in the land of Judah and in Jerusalem, did Josiah put away, that he might perform the words of the law which were written in the book that Hilkiah the priest found in the house of the LORD. And like unto him was there no king before him, that turned to the LORD with all his heart, and with all his soul, and with all his might, according to all the law of Moses; neither after him arose there any like him.

Josiah was a singularly spiritual man—a great man in the eyes of God.

2 Kings 23:26–28
Notwithstanding the LORD turned not from the fierceness of his great wrath, wherewith his anger was kindled against Judah, because of all the provocations that Manasseh had provoked him withal. And the LORD said, I will remove Judah also out of my sight, as I have removed Israel, and will cast off this city Jerusalem which I have chosen, and the house of which I said, My name shall be there. Now the rest of the acts of Josiah, and all that he did, are they not written in the book of the chronicles of the kings of Judah?

The life of Josiah is seen in greater depth in the Book of Second Chronicles. But there is one final note concerning his life. He was a great man and godly king and yet, in a sense, he died prematurely, for the next passage tells us something he did that was unwise . . .

2 Kings 23:29, 30
In his days Pharaoh-nechoh king of Egypt went up against the king of Assyria to the river Euphrates: and king Josiah went against him; and he slew him at Megiddo, when he had seen him. And his servants carried him in a chariot dead from Megiddo, and brought him to Jerusalem, and buried him in his own sepulchre. And the people of the land took Jehoahaz the son of Josiah, and anointed him, and made him king in his father's stead.

Pharaoh-nechoh, king of Egypt, marched his troops to war against the Assyrians. Although this was none of his business, Josiah decided to get involved. Second Chronicles explains the situation more fully. "Do not meddle in this matter," Pharaoh-nechoh said to Josiah. But Josiah hearkened not to the word of God coming through Pharaoh-nechoh and it cost him his life (2 Chronicles 35).

Sometimes, like Josiah, we think we must jump into a situation or straighten out a matter, only to find ourselves defeated in the process. When we realize we don't have to jump into every fight, figure out every problem, or solve every situation, we spare ourselves much needless hurt and pain. Be careful. Josiah was a good king, a great man, but he got involved in a battle not meant for him.

2 Kings 23:31–33
Jehoahaz was twenty and three years old when he began to reign; and he reigned three months in Jerusalem. And his mother's name was Hamutal, the daughter of Jeremiah of Libnah. And he did that which was evil in the sight of the LORD, according to all that his fathers had done. And Pharaoh-nechoh put him in bands at Riblah in the land of Hamath, that he might not reign in Jerusalem; and put the land to a tribute of an hundred talents of silver, and a talent of gold.

Pharaoh-nechoh taxed Judah three and three-fourth tons of silver and seventy-five pounds of gold.

2 Kings 23:34
And Pharaoh-nechoh made Eliakim the son of Josiah king in the room of Josiah his father, and turned his name to Jehoiakim, and took Jehoahaz away: and he came to Egypt, and died there.

Pharaoh-nechoh installed Josiah's brother, Jehoahaz, as king of Judah and changed his name to Jehoiakim. It was a custom in that culture that if you ruled over someone else, you would change his name as a reminder of his subordination to you and of your authority over him.

2 Kings 23:35–37
And Jehoiakim gave the silver and the gold to Pharaoh; but he taxed the land to give the money according to the commandment of Pharaoh: he exacted the silver and the gold of the people of the land, of every one

according to his taxation, to give it unto Pharaoh-nechoh. Jehoiakim was twenty and five years old when he began to reign; and he reigned eleven years in Jerusalem. And his mother's name was Zebudah, the daughter of Pedaiah of Rumah. And he did that which was evil in the sight of the LORD, according to all that his fathers had done.

Jehoiakim's chief function was to collect taxes for Pharaoh-necoh. In this, I am reminded of another tax collector who collected money from God's people to give to a foreign ruler. Yet while Matthew and Jehoiakim performed the same duty, they didn't share the same devotion. Jehoiakim turned away from God. Matthew, on the other hand, heard the call of the Son of God and followed Him.

24

During this time, world power was in the process of shifting from Assyria to Babylon. The Assyrians swept away the ten northern tribes into captivity. But now there's a transition taking place. In 612 B.C., the capital city of Assyria fell and the Babylonians emerged on the scene.

2 Kings 24:1 (a)
In his days Nebuchadnezzar king of Babylon came up, and Jehoiakim became his servant three years . . .

As Nebuchadnezzar swept through the Middle East, he stopped off in Judah and in the year 605 B.C., he put Jehoiakim in his control and carried away the cream of the crop of the young men of Judah—a group that included a young man named Daniel.

2 Kings 24:1 (b)–4
. . . then he turned and rebelled against him. And the LORD sent against him bands of the Chaldees, and bands of the Syrians, and bands of the Moabites, and bands of the children of Ammon, and sent them against Judah to destroy it, according to the word of the LORD, which he spake by his servants the prophets. Surely at the commandment of the LORD came this upon Judah, to remove them out of his sight, for the sins of Manasseh, according to all that he did; And also for the innocent blood that he shed: for he filled Jerusalem with innocent blood; which the LORD would not pardon.

Notice how Manasseh's name keeps resurfacing. At this point, fifty years had passed since he died, but the effects of his sin were still being felt. This sobers me because it shows that sin has a rippling effect for a long time. God puts this in His Word to warn and caution us. "Be sure your sins will find you out," God declares (Numbers 32:23). If you're involved in sin, stop now. Confess, repent, and stay away from it because the Lord warns us that the effects of sin have far-reaching repercussions for years to come.

2 Kings 24:5–12
Now the rest of the acts of Jehoiakim, and all that he did, are they not written in the book of the chronicles of the kings of Judah? So Jehoiakim slept with his fathers: and Jehoiachin his son reigned in his stead. And the king of Egypt came not again any more out of his land: for the king of Babylon had taken from the river of Egypt unto the river Euphrates all that pertained to the king of Egypt. Jehoiachin was eighteen years old when he began to reign, and he reigned in Jerusalem three months. And his mother's name was Nehushta, the daughter of Elnathan of Jerusalem. And he did that which was evil in the sight of the LORD, according to all that his father had done. At that time the servants of Nebuchadnezzar king of Babylon came up against Jerusalem, and the city was besieged. And Nebuchadnezzar king of Babylon came against the city, and his servants did besiege it. And Jehoiachin the king of Judah went out to the king of Babylon, he, and his mother, and his servants, and his princes, and his officers: and the king of Babylon took him in the eighth year of his reign.

The year now is 597 B.C. In 605 B.C., Nebuchadnezzar made his first sweep through the area. Here is his second sweep. This time, he takes all of the treasures out of the house of the Lord.

2 Kings 24:13, 14
And he carried out thence all the treasures of the house of the LORD, and the treasures of the king's house, and cut in pieces all the vessels of gold which Solomon king of Israel had made in the temple of the LORD, as the LORD had said. And he carried away all Jerusalem, and all the princes, and all the mighty men of valour, even ten thousand captives, and all the craftsmen and smiths: none remained, save the poorest sort of the people of the land.

The poor people were left behind—an illustration of the fact that wealth is oftentimes more trouble than it's worth.

2 Kings 24:15–20
And he carried away Jehoiachin to Babylon, and the king's mother, and the king's wives, and his officers, and the mighty of the land, those carried he into captivity from Jerusalem to Babylon. And all the men of might, even seven thousand, and craftsmen and smiths a thousand, all that were strong and apt for war, even them the king of Babylon brought captive to Babylon. And the king of Babylon made Mattaniah his father's brother king in his stead, and changed his name to Zedekiah. Zedekiah was twenty and one years old when he began to reign, and he reigned eleven years in Jerusalem. And his mother's name was Hamutal, the daughter of Jeremiah of Libnah. And he did that which was evil in the sight of the LORD, according to all that Jehoiakim had done. For through the anger of the LORD it came to pass in Jerusalem and Judah, until he had cast them out from his presence, that Zedekiah rebelled against the king of Babylon.

Here is Zedekiah, an evil "puppet" ruler in charge of a peasant people. After ruling for eleven years, he rebelled, which brought Nebuchadnezzar down for a third time, this time determined to destroy Judah completely.

25

2 Kings 25:1–3
And it came to pass in the ninth year of his reign, in the tenth month, in the tenth day of the month, that Nebuchadnezzar king of Babylon came, he, and all his host, against Jerusalem, and pitched against it; and they built forts against it round about. And the city was besieged unto the eleventh year of king Zedekiah. And on the ninth day of the fourth month the famine prevailed in the city, and there was no bread for the people of the land.

As Nebuchadnezzar and his forces surround the city of Jerusalem, famine and fear set in.

2 Kings 25:4
And the city was broken up, and all the men of war fled by night by the way of the gate between two walls, which is by the king's garden: (now the Chaldees were against the city round about:) and the king went the way toward the plain.

There seems to be historical proof that Zedekiah escaped through a secret passageway carved by Solomon.

2 Kings 25:5–7
And the army of the Chaldees pursued after the king, and overtook him in the plains of Jericho: and all his army were scattered from him. So they took the king, and brought him up to the king of Babylon to Riblah; and they gave judgment upon him. And they slew the sons of Zedekiah before his eyes, and put out the eyes of Zedekiah, and bound him with fetters of brass, and carried him to Babylon.

This solves a mystery in prophecy. Concerning Zedekiah, Jeremiah said, "Your eyes shall behold the king of Babylon" (see Jeremiah 34:3). At the same time, however, Ezekiel said, "Your eyes shall not see Babylon" (Ezekiel 12:13). Zedekiah was captured as he ran from Jerusalem. He was brought before the king of Babylon in Judah. There, his eyes were poked out and he was carried captive to Babylon. Two prophets were on the scene, both making seemingly opposite statements. Who was right? History shows they both were.

2 Kings 25:8, 9
And in the fifth month, on the seventh day of the month, which is the nineteenth year of king Nebuchadnezzar king of Babylon, came Nebuzar-adan, captain of the guard, a servant of the king of Babylon, unto Jerusalem: And he burnt the house of the LORD, and the king's house, and all the houses of Jerusalem, and every great man's house burnt he with fire.

The temple, palace, and the costliest homes of Jerusalem were burned.

2 Kings 25:10–12
And all the army of the Chaldees, that were Now the rest of the people that were left in the city, and the fugitives that fell away to the king of Babylon, with the remnant of the multitude, did Nebuzar-adan the captain of the guard carry away. But the captain of the guard left of the poor of the land to be vinedressers and husbandmen.

The poor were allowed to remain in Judah in order to keep the land from reverting to wilderness.

2 Kings 25:13–21
And the pillars of brass that were in the house of the LORD, and the bases, and the brasen sea that was in the house of the LORD, did the Chaldees break in pieces, and carried the brass of them to Babylon. And the pots, and the shovels, and the snuffers,

and the spoons, and all the vessels of brass wherewith they ministered, took they away. And the firepans, and the bowls, and such things as were of gold, in gold, and of silver, in silver, the captain of the guard took away. The two pillars, one sea, and the bases which Solomon had made for the house of the Lord; the brass of all these vessels was without weight. The height of the one pillar was eighteen cubits, and the chapiter upon it was brass: and the height of the chapiter three cubits; and the wreathen work, and pomegranates upon the chapiter round about, all of brass: and like unto these had the second pillar with wreathen work. And the captain of the guard took Seraiah the chief priest, and Zephaniah the second priest, and the three keepers of the door: And out of the city he took an officer that was set over the men of war, and five men of them that were in the king's presence, which were found in the city, and the principal scribe of the host, which mustered the people of the land, and threescore men of the people of the land that were found in the city: And Nebuzar-adan captain of the guard took these, and brought them to the king of Babylon to Riblah: And the king of Babylon smote them, and slew them at Riblah in the land of Hamath. So Judah was carried away out of their land.

This was the third and final deportation. Jerusalem is now smoldering. The temple is destroyed; the palace is gone; the neighborhoods are ransacked.

2 Kings 25:22–24
And as for the people that remained in the land of Judah, whom Nebuchadnezzar king of Babylon had left, even over them he made Gedaliah the son of Ahikam, the son of Shaphan, ruler. And when all the captains of the armies, they and their men, heard that the king of Babylon had made Gedaliah governor, there came to Gedaliah to Mizpah, even Ishmael the son of Nethahiah, and Johanan the son of Careah, and Seraiah the son of Tanhumeth the Netophathite, and Jaazaniah the son of a Maachathite, they and their men. And Gedaliah sware to them, and to their men, and said unto them, Fear not to be the servants of the Chaldees: dwell in the land, and serve the king of Babylon; and it shall be well with you.

From Jeremiah 26:24, we know that Gedaliah was Jeremiah's friend. Nebuchadnezzar put him in a position of authority over the remnant in Judah. Gedaliah wisely counseled them to dwell peaceably under Babylonian rule.

2 Kings 25:25
But it came to pass in the seventh month, that Ishmael the son of Nethaniah, the son of Elishama, of the seed royal, came, and ten men with him, and smote Gedaliah, that he died, and the Jews and the Chaldees that were with him at Mizpah.

Gedaliah was warned in Jeremiah 40:13–16 that Ishmael was going to do him in. But, failing to take heed to the warning, Gedaliah lost his life.

2 Kings 25:26, 27
And all the people, both small and great, and the captains of the armies, arose, and came to Egypt: for they were afraid of the Chaldees. And it came to pass in the seven and thirtieth year of the captivity of Jehoiachin king of Judah, in the twelfth month, on the seven and twentieth day of the month, that Evil-merodach king of Babylon in the year that he began to reign did lift up the head of Jehoiachin king of Judah out of prison;

Here, thirty-six years after Jehoiachin was carried into captivity, Evil-merodach, the son of Nebuchadnezzar comes into power. Upon ascending the throne, he freed Jehoiachin.

2 Kings 25:28–30
And he spake kindly to him, and set his throne above the throne of the kings that were with him in Babylon; And changed his prison garments: and he did eat bread continually before him all the days of his life. And his allowance was a continual allowance given him of the king, a daily rate for every day, all the days of his life.

Why did Evil-merodach show kindness to Jehoiachin? History tells us he was in prison himself for a short time. Possibly having been in prison himself, he felt compassion for others in prison. Some Jewish writers say that Evil-merodach was converted to a true understanding of God by Daniel. That is very possible.

Perhaps, like Daniel, you feel like you're in a confusing or foreign situation. That's okay. The Lord might have an Evil-merodach with whom you're to share.

An infinitely Greater than Evil-merodach came to us when we were blinded and imprisoned by sin, for Jesus Himself came to us. We don't deserve it, but because of what He endured, He came to us compassionately and lovingly.

Is your head down? Are you discouraged and

depressed and defeated? The Lord longs to lift up your head and speak kindly to you. No wonder people marveled at the gracious words He spoke (Luke 4:22). Want to hear kind words? Read the Gospel of Matthew and listen to Jesus.

Evil-merodach set Jehoiachin above other kings. Paul tells us we have been seated with Christ in heavenly places (Ephesians 2:6). Evil-merodach changed Jehoiachin's prison garments. We have been robed in Jesus' righteousness (Isaiah 61:10). Evil-merodach provided food for Jehoiachin all the days of his life. Jesus invites us to dine at His Table continually.

The Book of Second Kings ends with the brightness of Evil-merodach set against the darkness of Judah's captivity. If you find yourself "held captive" by one dark circumstance or another, look for the brightness of the inexplicable grace and kindness of Jesus to meet you there, and fellowship with you all the days of your life.

1 CHRONICLES

Background to 1 & 2 Chronicles

Although we can't be dogmatic, it is believed that the author of 1 and 2 Chronicles was Ezra the scribe. First and Second Chronicles are, in a sense, a repetition of the Books of 1 and 2 Kings. There is a difference, however, because 1 and 2 Kings deal both with the kingdom of Judah in the south and the kingdom of Israel in the north, while 1 and 2 Chronicles deal exclusively with the kingdom of Judah.

Although many of the stories in these books also appear in 1 and 2 Kings, we must remember that whenever the Father repeats Himself in His Word, it is not because He is at a loss for new things to say. No, He repeats that we might receive. The gospels are repeated four times because the Father does not want any of us to miss the message of Jesus. These stories concerning David and the kings are important illustrations of practical truth.

1 CHRONICLES

1 The first nine chapters of the Book of 1 Chronicles deal primarily with genealogies. Genealogies were important to the Jews for ministry and they are important to us prophetically. You see, anyone who desired to serve the Lord in the temple had to prove that he was of the tribe of Levi. Priests themselves were further required to be descendants of Aaron. Therefore, genealogies were vital to establish pedigree. In addition, they are also important prophetically, for they are exacting records for the skeptic to see how Jesus of Nazareth was the Messiah promised centuries before He appeared on the scene.

1 Chronicles 1:1 (a)
Adam . . .

Adam is always a good place to begin any genealogy.

1 Chronicles 1:1 (b)–4 (a)
. . . Sheth, Enosh, Kenan, Mahalaleel, Jered, Henoch, Methuselah, Lamech, Noah . . .

The first ten names that appear in the genealogy of Genesis 2 take us back to the very beginning of humanity. The meaning of these first ten names shed light on a most intriguing revelation . . .

- *Adam* means "Man."
- *Seth* means "Appointed."
- *Enosh* means "Subject to death."
- *Kenan* means "Sorrowful."
- *Mahaleel* means "From the presence of God."
- *Jered* means "One comes down."
- *Henoch* means "Dedicated."
- *Methuselah* means "Dying, he shall send."
- *Lamech* means "To the poor brought very low."
- *Noah* means "Comfort, or rest."

Read together, these literal meanings form the gospel: Man, appointed, subject to death, sorrowful. From the presence of God, One comes down, dedicated. Dying, He shall send to the poor brought very low, comfort, or rest.

1 Chronicles 1:4 (b)–7
. . . Shem, Ham, and Japheth. The sons of Japheth; Gomer, and Magog, and Madai, and Javan, and Tubal, and Meshech, and Tiras. And the sons of Gomer; Ashchenaz, and Riphath, and Togarmah. And the sons of Javan; Elishah, and Tarshish, Kittim, and Dodanim.

The sons of Japheth eventually inhabited present-day Europe.

1 Chronicles 1:8–16
The sons of Ham; Cush, and Mizraim, Put, and Canaan. And the sons of Cush; Seba, and Havilah, and Sabta, and Raamah, and Sabtecha. And the sons of Raamah; Sheba, and Dedan. And Cush begat Nimrod: he began to be mighty upon the earth. And Mizraim begat Ludim, and Anamim, and Lehabim, and Naphtuhim, And Pathrusim, and Casluhim, (of whom came the Philistines,) and Caphthorim. And Canaan begat Zidon his firstborn, and Heth, The Jebusite also, and the Amorite, and the Girgashite, And the Hivite, and the Arkite, and the Sinite, And the Arvadite, and the Zemarite, and the Hamathite.

The sons of Ham eventually migrated south, inhabiting Africa.

1 Chronicles 1:17, 18 (a)
The sons of Shem; Elam, and Asshur, and Arphaxad, and Lud, and Aram, and Uz, and Hul, and Gether, and Meshech. And Arphaxad begat Shelah . . .

The sons of Shemor—Semites—remained in the region of the Middle East.

1 Chronicles 1:18 (b)
. . . and Shelah begat Eber.

Eber is the name from which we get the word "Hebrew."

1 Chronicles 1:19
And unto Eber were born two sons: the name of the one was Peleg; because in his days the earth was divided: and his brother's name was Joktan.

There are two possible meanings of this phrase, "the earth was divided." It could refer to the dispersion that took place at the tower of Babel. Or, it could refer to a geological movement of the continents—today called "the continental drift."

1 Chronicles 1:20–27
And Joktan begat Almodad, and Sheleph, and Hazarmaveth, and Jerah, Hadoram also, and Uzal, and Diklah, And Ebal, and Abimael, and Sheba, And Ophir, and Havilah, and Jobab. All these were the sons of Joktan. Shem, Arphaxad, Shelah, Eber, Peleg, Reu, Serug, Nahor, Terah, Abram; the same is Abraham.

The line is traced from Shem to Abraham and, at this point, the genealogical record changes from that of the world population to that of a specific family. Adam is the father of all flesh, but Abraham is the father of all faithful.

1 Chronicles 1:28
The sons of Abraham; Isaac, and Ishmael.

These are the fathers of the Jews and Arabs. Because Abraham decided to help God out, he birthed Ishmael through Hagar instead of waiting for the promised child through Sarah.

If you are feeling impatient concerning a given situation, don't try to work it out in your own fleshly abilities or understanding. It can lead to real difficulty. Ask Isaac and Ishmael.

1 Chronicles 1:29–32
These are their generations: The firstborn of Ishmael, Nebaioth; then Kedar, and Adbeel, and Mibsam, Mishma and Dumah, Massa, Hadad, and Tema, Jetur, Naphish, and Kedemah. These are the sons of Ishmael. Now the sons of Keturah, Abraham's concubine: she bare Zimran, and Jokshan, and Medan, and Midian, and Ishbak, and Shuah. And the sons of Jokshan; Sheba, and Dedan.

After Sarah died, Abraham married a woman named Keturah, who gave birth to Midian. The Midianites were a continual problem to the Israelites, but they, like the Ishmaelites, had a common father in Abraham.

1 Chronicles 1:33, 34
And the sons of Midian; Ephah, and Epher, and Henoch, and Abida, and Eldaah. All these are the sons of Keturah. And Abraham begat Isaac. The sons of Isaac; Esau and Israel.

Israel's name was originally Jacob, or "heel snatcher." But when God changed his character from one who tripped people up to one who was governed by God, his name was correspondingly changed from Jacob to Israel.

1 Chronicles 1:35
The sons of Esau; Eliphaz, Reuel, and Jeush, and Jaalam, and Korah.

The sons of Esau are known as the Edomites (Genesis 25:30).

1 Chronicles 1:36–43 (a)
The sons of Eliphaz; Teman, and Omar, Zephi, and Gatam, Kenaz, and Timna, and Amalek. The sons of Reuel; Nahath, Zerah, Shammah, and Mizzah. And the sons of Seir; Lotan, and Shobal, and Zibeon, and Anah, and Dishon, and Ezer, and Dishan. And the sons of Lothan; Hori, and Homam: and Timna was Lotan's sister. The sons of Shobal; Alian, and Manahath, and Ebal, Shephi, and Onam. And the sons of Zibeon; Aiah, and Anah. The sons of Anah; Dishon. And the sons of Dishon; Amram, and Eshban, and Ithran, and Cheran. The sons of Ezer; Bilhan, and Zavan, and Jakan. The sons of Dishan; Uz, and Aran. Now these are the kings that reigned in the land of Edom before any king reigned over the children of Israel . . .

The Edomites established a royal heirarchy. The descendants of Jacob, on the other hand, were not to have a king over them because God was to be their Sovereign.

1 Chronicles 1:43 (b), 44
. . . Bela the son of Beor: and the name of his city was Dinhabah. And when Bela was dead, Jobab the son of Zerah of Bozrah reigned in his stead.

Some Bible scholars believe Jobab was Job. If this is true, his position as ruler would explain his wealth, as well as his standing in the community.

1 Chronicles 1:45–54
And when Jobab was dead, Husham of the land of the Temanites reigned in his stead. And when Husham was dead, Hadad the son of Bedad, which smote Midian in the field of Moab, reigned in his stead: and the name of his city was Avith. And when Hadad was dead, Samlah of Masrekah reigned in his stead. And when Samlah was dead, Shaul of Rehoboth by the river reigned in his stead. And when Shaul was dead, Baalhanan the son of Achbor reigned in his stead. And when Baalhanan was dead, Hadad reigned in his stead: and the name of his city was Pai; and his wife's name was Mehetabel, the daughter of Matred, the daughter of Mezahab. Hadad died also. And the dukes of Edom were; duke Timnah, duke Aliah, duke Jetheth, Duke Aholibamah, duke Elah, duke Pinon, Duke Kenaz, duke Teman, duke Mibzar, Duke Magdiel, duke Iram. These are the dukes of Edom.

According to archaeological evidence, the kingdom of Edom was founded during the thirteenth century B.C. In the ensuing four centuries, the government changed from being run by tribal chiefs to that of a monarchy. It was one of the kings of Edom who refused to allow the Israelites to pass through his country on the way to the Promised Land (Numbers 20:14–21).

2

1 Chronicles 2:1, 2
These are the sons of Israel; Reuben, Simeon, Levi, and Judah, Issachar, and Zebulun, Dan, Joseph, and Benjamin, Naphtali, Gad, and Asher.

These, of course, are the twelve patriarchs of Israel.

1 Chronicles 2:3
The sons of Judah; Er, and Onan, and Shelah: which three were born unto him of the daughter of Shua the Canaanitess. And Er, the firstborn of Judah, was evil in the sight of the LORD; and he slew him.

Here, the genealogy follows the line of Judah.

1 Chronicles 2:4–7
And Tamar his daughter in law bare him Pharez and Zerah. All the sons of Judah were five. The sons of Pharez; Hezron, and Hamul. And the sons of Zerah; Zimri, and Ethan, and Heman, and Calcol, and Dara: five of them in all. And the sons of Carmi; Achar, the troubler of Israel, who transgressed in the thing accursed.

The lives of both Er and Acher, or Achan, are summed up by the sins that characterized them. No doubt Er and Achan did good things in their lives. But those things are not recorded. Rather, the sin they committed characterized them. Therefore, I wonder if it wouldn't be good for us to say, "If my life had to be summed up in one sentence, what would that one sentence be?" I think it's a good thing to occasionally say, "What is the sum total of my life thus far? If my name were in this record, what would be written?"

1 Chronicles 2:8–11
And the sons of Ethan; Azariah. The sons also of Hezron, that were born unto him; Jerahmeel, and Ram, and Chelubai. And Ram begat Amminadab; and Amminadab begat Nahshon, prince of the children of Judah; And Nahshon begat Salma, and Salma begat Boaz,

The wonderful story of Boaz, a picture of our own Kinsman Redeemer—Jesus Christ—is seen in the Book of Ruth.

1 Chronicles 2:12
And Boaz begat Obed, and Obed begat Jesse,

Jesse would have eight sons, his most famous, of course, being David, the man after God's own heart.

1 Chronicles 2:13–15
And Jesse begat his firstborn Eliab, and Abinadab the second, and Shimma the third, Nethaneel the fourth, Raddai the fifth, Ozem the sixth, David the seventh:

David was Jesse's eighth son (1 Samuel 16:10, 11). Why are only seven listed here? No doubt because one died during childhood.

1 Chronicles 2:16
Whose sisters were Zeruiah, and Abigail. And the sons of Zeruiah; Abishai, and Joab, and Asahel, three.

Abishai, Joab, and Asahel, nephews of David, would become generals in his army.

1 Chronicles 2:17
And Abigail bare Amasa: and the father of Amasa was Jether the Ishmeelite.

Amasa, a cousin of Abishai, Joab, and Asahel, sided with another cousin named Absalom. Absalom was David's rebellious son and Amasa would be his general.

1 Chronicles 2:18–20
And Caleb the son of Hezron begat children of Azubah his wife, and of Jerioth: her sons are these; Jesher, and Shobab, and Ardon. And when Azubah was dead, Caleb took unto him Ephrath, which bare him Hur. And Hur begat Uri, and Uri begat Bezaleel.

The majority of those listed in the remainder of chapter 2 are mentioned nowhere else in Scripture. Bezaleel, however, is an exception as he was uniquely gifted by God to work on the tabernacle (Exodus 31:2).

1 Chronicles 2:21–55
And afterward Hezron went in to the daughter of Machir the father of Gilead, whom he married when he was threescore years old; and she bare him Segub. And Segub begat Jair, who had three and twenty cities in the land of Gilead. And he took Geshur, and Aram, with the towns of Jair, from them, with Kenath, and the towns thereof, even threescore cities. All these belonged to the sons of Machir the father of Gilead. And after that Hezron was dead in Calebephratah, then Abiah Hezron's wife bare him Ashur the father of Tekoa. And the sons of Jerahmeel the firstborn of Hezron were, Ram the firstborn, and Bunah, and Oren, and Ozem, and Ahijah. Jerahmeel had also another wife, whose name was Atarah; she was the mother of Onam. And the sons of Ram the firstborn of Jerahmeel were, Maaz, and Jamin, and Eker. And the sons of Onam were, Shammai, and Jada. And the sons of Shammai; Nadab, and Abishur. And the name of the wife of Abishur was Abihail, and she bare him Ahban, and Molid. And the sons of Nadab; Seled, and Appaim: but Seled died without children. And the sons of Appaim; Ishi. And the sons of Ishi; Sheshan. And the children of Sheshan; Ahlai. And the sons of Jada the brother of Shammai; Jether and Jonathan: and Jether died without children. And the sons of Jonathan; Peleth, and Zaza. These were the sons of Jerahmeel. Now Sheshan had no sons, but daughters. And Sheshan had a servant, an Egyptian, whose name was Jarha. And Sheshan gave his daughter to Jarha his servant to wife; and she bare him Attai. And Attai begat Nathan, and Nathan begat Zabad, And Zabad begat Ephlal, and Ephlal begat Obed, And Obed begat Jehu, and Jehu begat Azariah, And Azariah begat Helez, and Helez begat Eleasah, And Eleasah begat Sisamai, and Sisamai begat Shallum, And Shallum begat Jekamiah, and Jekamiah begat Elishama. Now the sons of Caleb the brother of Jerahmeel were, Mesha his firstborn, which was the father of Ziph; and the sons of Mareshah the father of Hebron. And the sons of Hebron; Korah, and Tappuah, and Rekem, and Shema. And Shema begat Raham, the father of Jorkoam: and Rekem begat Shammai. And the son of Shammai was Maon: and Maon was the father of Bethzur. And Ephah, Caleb's concubine, bare Haran, and Moza, and Gazez: and Haran begat Gazez. And the sons of Jahdai; Regem, and Jotham, and Geshan, and Pelet, and Ephah, and Shaaph. Maachah, Caleb's concubine, bare Sheber, and Tirhanah. She bare also Shaaph the father of Madmannah, Sheva the father of

Machbenah, and the father of Gibea: and the daughter of Caleb was Achsah. These were the sons of Caleb the son of Hur, the firstborn of Ephratah; Shobal the father of Kirjath-jearim, Salma the father of Bethlehem, Hareph the father of Beth-gader. And Shobal the father of Kirjath-jearim had sons; Haroeh, and half of the Manahethites. And the families of Kirjath-jearim; the Ithrites, and the Puhites, and the Shumathites, and the Mishraites; of them came the Zareathites, and the Eshtaulites. The sons of Salma; Bethlehem, and the Netophathites, Ataroth, the house of Joab, and half of the Manahethites, the Zorites. And the families of the scribes which dwelt at Jabez; the Tirathites, the Shimeathites, and Suchathites. These are the Kenites that came of Hemath, the father of the house of Rechab.

So ends the list of the descendants of Judah—David's ancestors and the tribe into which the Son of David would be born.

---

3 In chapter 3, we come to David's personal genealogy.

1 Chronicles 3:1 (a)
Now these were the sons of David, which were born unto him in Hebron . . .

David had nineteen sons, the best of which was Solomon. And even Solomon became entangled in fleshly pursuits in his latter years. It has been suggested that the reason David, who was a man after God's own heart, had nineteen bad sons is because he was so busy tending the kingdom, he didn't take time to train his children, setting in motion the classic example of the "preacher's kid" syndrome. We can indeed get so involved in the work of the kingdom that we neglect the training of our children. This must not be. Therefore, pray for those in the ministry because Satan likes nothing better than to cause havoc in the family in order to discredit one's ministry.

1 Chronicles 3:1 (b)–5
. . . the firstborn Amnon, of Ahinoam the Jezreelitess; the second Daniel, of Abigail the Carmelitess: The third, Absalom the son of Maachah the daughter of Talmai king of Geshur: the fourth, Adonijah the son of Haggith: The fifth, Shephatiah of Abital: the sixth, Ithream by Eglah his wife. These six were born unto him in Hebron; and there he reigned seven years and six months: and in Jerusalem he reigned thirty and three years. And these were born unto him in Jerusalem; Shimea, and Shobab, and Nathan, and Solomon, four, of Bathshua the daughter of Ammiel:

One of David's sons was named Nathan. I call this to your attention because Nathan the prophet was the one who pointed out David's otherwise secret sins of adultery with Bathsheba and the murder of Uriah. The Bible says that "faithful are the wounds of a friend" (Proverbs 27:6). In other words, it is a sign of love when someone speaks the truth (Ephesians 4:15). So much did David value Nathan's honesty that he evidently named one of his sons after him.

1 Chronicles 3:6–16
Ibhar also, and Elishama, and Eliphelet, And Nogah, and Nepheg, and Japhia, And Elishama, and Eliada, and Eliphelet, nine. These were all the sons of David, beside the sons of the concubines, and Tamar their sister. And Solomon's son was Rehoboam, Abia his son, Asa his son, Jehoshaphat his son, Joram his son, Ahaziah his son, Joash his son, Amaziah his son, Azariah his son, Jotham his son, Ahaz his son, Hezekiah his son, Manasseh his son, Amon his son, Josiah his son. And the sons of Josiah were, the firstborn Johanan, the second Jehoiakim, the third Zedekiah, the fourth Shallum. And the sons of Jehoiakim: Jeconiah his son, Zedekiah his son.

The names in verses 1 through 16 represent the succession of David's throne to the point when Judah was carried into captivity.

1 Chronicles 3:17–24
And the sons of Jeconiah; Assir, Salathiel his son, Malchiram also, and Pedaiah, and Shenazar, Jecamiah, Hoshama, and Nedabiah. And the sons of Pedaiah were, Zerubbabel, and Shimei: and the sons of Zerubbabel; Meshullam, and Hananiah, and Shelomith their sister: And Hashubah, and Ohel, and Berechiah, and Hasadiah, Jushabhesed, five. And the sons of Hananiah; Pelatiah, and Jesaiah: the sons of Rephaiah, the sons of Arnan, the sons of Obadiah, the sons of Shechaniah. And the sons of Shechaniah; Shemaiah; and the sons of Shemaiah; Hattush, and Igeal, and Bariah, and Neariah, and Shaphat, six. And the sons of Neariah; Elioenai, and Hezekiah, and Azrikam, three. And the sons of Elioenai were, Hodaiah, and Eliashib, and Pelaiah, and Akkub, and Johanan, and Dalaiah, and Anani, seven.

The names in verses 17 through 24 delineate the royal line following the return of the Jews to the Promised Land.

---

4 1 Chronicles 4:1–9
The sons of Judah; Pharez, Hezron, and Carmi, and Hur, and Shobal. And Reaiah the son of Shobal begat Jahath; and Jahath begat Ahumai and Lahad. These are the families of the Zorathites. And these were of the father of Etam; Jezreel, and Ishma, and Idbash: and the name of their sister was Hazelelponi: And Penuel the father of Gedor and Ezer the father of Hushah. These are the sons of Hur, the firstborn of Ephratah, the father of Bethlehem. And Ashur the father of Tekoa had two wives, Helah and Naarah. And Naarah bare him Ahuzam, and Hepher, and Temeni, and Haahashtari. These were the sons of Naarah. And the sons of Helah were, Zereth, and Jezoar, and Ethnan. And Coz begat Anub, and Zobebah, and the families of Aharhel the son of Harum. And Jabez was more honourable than his brethren: and his mother called his name Jabez, saying, Because I bare him with sorrow.

Jabez was one who experienced such success and prosperity that he had more honor than his brothers. In 1 Chronicles 2:55, we read that a city dedicated to the scribes, the intellectual community of the day, was named after him. Jabez was a man who was singularly blessed and very successful. But it wasn't always that way, for here we see that when he was born, his mother called him "sorrowful." Why? Perhaps it was because he had a birth defect, or perhaps he was an unwanted child coming into an already-crowded home. Jabez experienced prosperity to be sure, but he also had problems to overcome. How did he do this? Read on . . .

1 Chronicles 4:10
And Jabez called on the God of Israel, saying, Oh that thou wouldest bless me indeed, and enlarge my coast, and that thine hand might be with me, and that thou wouldest keep me from evil, that it may not grieve me! And God granted him that which he requested.

The secret of Jabez's success wasn't due to a seminar he attended or to a book he purchased. Jabez's success was due to the fact that he was a man of prayer. James says we have not because we ask not (4:2). It's that simple. The Lord is continually asking His people to ask. "Call unto Me," He says in Jeremiah 33, "and I will show you great and mighty things which you know not."

"Ask, seek, and knock that you might receive and the door might be opened unto you," Jesus said (see Matthew 7:7).

How is your prayer life? Are you experiencing success and prosperity? The pathway to prosperity is prayer. Pray. And pray more. And pray still more.

Prayer is vital. We know that. But here's the problem: Because we know it, we think we're doing it. If the stopwatch was on this past week, how much time would it show that you've actually spent in prayer? God loves you no matter whether you're praying or not. But the blessings He is waiting to pour out upon you, your ministry, your marriage, your family and your friends can only be released through prayer.

***For topical study of 1 Chronicles 4:10 entitled "Prayer: The Pathway to Prosperity," turn to page* 1102.**

1 Chronicles 4:11–14
And Chelub the brother of Shuah begat Mehir, which was the father of Eshton. And Eshton begat Bethrapha, and Paseah, and Tehinnah the father of Irnahash. These are the men of Rechah. And the sons of Kenaz; Othniel, and Seraiah: and the sons of Othniel; Hathath. And Meonothai begat Ophrah: and Seraiah begat Joab, the father of the valley of Charashim; for they were craftsmen.

Here we see a community of craftsmen, a custom seen throughout history wherein those of the same trade or occupation inhabited the same street or neighborhood. According to Nehemiah 11:35, this particular community was located outside of Jerusalem.

1 Chronicles 4:15–18
And the sons of Caleb the son of Jephunneh; Iru, Elah, and Naam: and the sons of Elah, even Kenaz. And the sons of Jehaleleel; Ziph, and Ziphah, Tiria, and Asareel. And the sons of Ezra were, Jether, and Mered, and Epher, and Jalon: and she bare Miriam, and Shammai, and Ishbah the father of Eshtemoa. And his wife Jehudiajah bare Jered the father of Gedor, and Heber the father of Socho, and Jekuthiel the father of Zanoah. And these are the sons of Bithiah the daughter of Pharoah, which Mered took.

The marriage of this Egyptian princess to a descendant of Caleb would have been recognized only if the Egyptian princess had renounced the idolatry of Egypt and embraced the true and living God of Israel. The fact that she appears in the genealogy indicates that this is exactly what she did.

1 Chronicles 4:19–21
And the sons of his wife Hodiah the sister of Naham, the father of Keilah the Garmite, and Eshtemoa the Maachathite. And the sons of Shimon were, Amnon, and Rinnah, Benhanan, and Tilon. And the sons of Ishi were, Zoheth, and Benzoheth. The sons of Shelah the son of Judah were, Er the father of Lecah, and Laadah the father of Mareshah, and the families of the house of them that wrought fine linen, of the house of Ashbea.

It is most likely that the skill to make fine linen was carried out of Egypt along with the gold, silver, and clothing given to the Israelites (Exodus 12:35, 36).

1 Chronicles 4:22, 23
And Jokim, and the men of Chozeba, and Joash, and Saraph, who had the dominion in Moab, and Jashubilehem. And these are ancient things. These were the potters, and those that dwelt among plants and hedges: there they dwelt with the king for his work.

I like this verse! It lists a group of men who were potters and gardeners. These were common jobs done by common workers. And yet here we read that they had a place in the palace. In other words, because they worked for the king, they dwelt with the king.

If you're a potter or a gardener, a mechanic or a banker, a dishwasher or a teacher, and you're doing it as unto the King, you'll dwell with the King at that very place. Your occupation can become a real ministry if you'll do it as unto the King. For example, if you plant plants and say, "Lord, this is for You, a garden for Your glory," if you give back change as a teller and say, "Lord, bless this person with wisdom on how they will use this money," you can make any occupation a ministry, and if you do it, you'll dwell with the King at that very point as you experience His presence in a powerful, practical way.

1 Chronicles 4:24–43
The sons of Simeon were, Nemuel, and Jamin, Jarib, Zerah, and Shaul: Shallum his son, Mibsam his son, Mishma his son. And the sons of Mishma; Hamuel his son, Zachur his son, Shimei his son. And Shimei had sixteen sons and six daughters; but his brethren had not many children, neither did all their family multiply, like to the children of Judah. And they dwelt at Beer-sheba, and Moladah, and Hazarshual, And at Bilhah, and at Ezem, and at Tolad, And at Bethuel, and at Hormah, and at Ziklag, And at Bethmarcaboth, and Hazarsusim, and at Bethbirei, and at Shaaraim. These were their cities unto the reign of David. And their villages were, Etam, and Ain, Rimmon, and Tochen, and Ashan, five cities: And all their villages that were round about the same cities, unto Baal. These were their habitations, and their genealogy. And Meshobab, and Jamlech, and Joshah the son of Amaziah, And Joel, and Jehu the son of Josibiah, the son of Seraiah, the son of Asiel, And Elioenai, and Jaakobah, and Jeshohaiah, and Asaiah, and Adiel, and Jesimiel, and Benaiah, And Ziza the son of Shiphi, the son of Allon, the son of Jedaiah, the son of Shimri, the son of Shemaiah; These mentioned by their names were princes in their families: and the house of their fathers increased greatly. And they went to the entrance of Gedor, even unto the east side of the valley, to seek pasture for their flocks. And they found fat pasture and good, and the land was wide, and quiet, and peaceable; for they of Ham had dwelt there of old. And these written by name came in the days of Hezekiah king of Judah, and smote their tents, and the habitations that were found there, and destroyed them utterly unto this day, and dwelt in their rooms: because there was pasture there for their flocks. And some of them, even of the sons of Simeon, five hundred men, went to mount Seir, having for their captains Pelatiah, and Neariah, and Rephaiah, and Uzziel, the sons of Ishi. And they smote the rest of the Amalekites that were escaped, and dwelt there unto this day.

As the family of Simeon increased numerically, they felt constricted in their territory. So they looked over their boundaries and saw a land that was very blessed, a land that was fertile, a land that could support their flocks and herds. So they wiped out the enemy to expand their territory for the blessing of their people.

Perhaps you feel restricted in some area of your life or ministry. The key is to look beyond your borders, find some area the enemy is still holding, and go after it. Carve out new territory in your ministry, in your life. Carve out new areas of new visions of ministry and opportunity beyond your own borders. That's what the sons of Simeon did.

Increasingly, my prayer is that God would

make us a people of vision, that we would see beyond our own boundaries and borders, that we would see the possibilities that exist all around us, the opportunities that abound on every side of us and claim them for the glory of God and for the furtherance of the gospel.

PRAYER: THE PATHWAY TO PROSPERITY

A Topical Study of 1 CHRONICLES 4:10

In Jabez, we see not only a man whose family looked up to him, but one who had a city named after him. Jabez was a blessed individual indeed. And yet because his name means "sorrowful," his birth was somehow marked with sorrow. Thus, although Jabez would experience prosperity, he also experienced problems.

Prayer

And Jabez called on the God of Israel . . . 1 Chronicles 4:10 (a)

Jabez overcame his adversity by calling upon the God of Israel. In other words, he prayed. Prayer is not a subject that draws a lot of attention or creates a lot of excitement. People think the answer to their problems lies in a practice or a program they've never heard of before. But the life of this one who was named "Sorrowful"—this one who had a family that looked up to him and a city named after him—is recorded in the Word because he prayed simply and effectively.

Jabez called on the God of Israel. Israel was a nation, but also a person. You might know him as Jacob. Jacob was another man born in an interesting manner, for even at the time of his birth, he exhibited a quality that would characterize his entire life. That is, he grabbed on to his twin brother's heel in an apparent attempt to be firstborn. This caused his mother to name him *Jacob,* or, literally, "Heel snatcher." Jacob grabbed his brother's heel and would spend the rest of his life trying to trip people up that he might get ahead.

After he connived his way into receiving both the blessing and birthright that should have been his brother's, he fled to Padanaram, where he lived with his uncle Laban—also a conniver. After twenty years, he out-connived Laban and ended up prospering with so much wealth that Laban said, "Get out of here. If I see you again, you're dead."

So, taking his kids, family, herds, and riches, Jacob headed back home, hoping that Esau would forgive him. As he neared his home territory, he sent messengers to Esau, saying, "I'm coming home. I'm successful. I'm bringing gifts."

The messengers returned, saying, "Esau is coming to greet you with four hundred armed men."

Jacob knew he was in trouble. What could he do? How could he connive his way out of this? Kicked out of Padanaram, with his brother and four hundred men coming to do him in, he was at the end of his rope.

That night, he crossed the river Jabok and attempted to get a good night's sleep, knowing that in the morning, he would have his work cut out for him. As he tried to settle down, suddenly an angel of the Lord—Jesus Christ—appeared to him.

"I will not let You go until You bless me," Jacob said. Hosea tells us he did so with tears and a broken heart (12:4).

Genesis 32 tells us they wrestled all night long. As morning dawned, the angel of the Lord touched Jacob's hip and it became dislocated. Then the Lord looked at this pathetic figure with a dislocated hip and tears streaming down his face, and said, "Jacob, thou hast prevailed with God and with man. Henceforth, you'll no longer be called Jacob, but *Israel*"—which means "governed by God."

No longer did he depend on his mental ability. No longer did he walk proudly. He limped, but in greater strength than he ever had before because he was depending on God, governed by God, and looking to God.

You might be extremely clever. You might be very able, intelligent, or gifted. But no matter how clever or able you are, those qualities have limitations. There will always be someone more clever than you, always some problem bigger than you, always some challenge greater than you. But when, like Jacob, you say, "My heel grabbing won't make it any more. I can't walk. I can't run. I can't connive. I can't figure things out. I need You, Lord. I can't go on without You," you become Israel—governed by God.

Jabez was hurting. And he called to the God of Israel—the God of the conniver who learned the secret of being ruled by God as he wrestled with the Lord in prayer.

Passion

. . . *"Oh, that thou wouldest bless me indeed . . ."* 1 Chronicles 4:10 (b)

The word, "oh," gives us a clue as to the passion of Jabez's prayer. It was said of George Whitefield, the great evangelist, that when he simply said the word, "oh," hundreds of people would repent on the spot because he spoke with such passion. I sense something of this in Jabez's prayer.

Paul says the Spirit prays through us with groanings that cannot be uttered (Romans 8:26). Sometimes the most effective prayer times we have consist of groaning. You're praying for your own situation or for that of someone else and you don't know how to pray, so you let the Spirit groan through you. That's prayer. In this, I sense a passion in Jabez's prayer that moved the hand of God.

Purpose

. . . and enlarge my coast . . . 1 Chronicles 4:10 (c)

"Enlarge my coasts or borders," Jabez prayed. "Make me bigger and larger than I am presently." It is important that, as believers, we are expanding. Are your borders being expanded?

William Carey, the great missionary, said, "Attempt great things for God and expect great things from God." Do something radical. Take a risk in life. Take a risk in your ministry. Take a risk in your understanding of worship and devotion. Enlarge your vision. Attempt something for the Lord so big that, unless God is in it, it's doomed to fail. Such was the heart of Jabez.

Presence

. . . and that thine hand might be with me . . . 1 Chronicles 4:10 (d)

Jabez didn't just want the gifts. He wanted the Giver to be with him. This is something we need to see because so often we can say, "Lord, I need this answer to prayer." And when the answer comes, we run away.

Not Jabez. He said, "*Keep* Your hand upon me. I want You to be with me, directing my steps, guiding my actions." And that's a prayer the Father honors.

Protection

. . . and that thou wouldest keep me from evil, that it may not grieve me!" 1 Chronicles 4:10 (e)

At this point in his life, Jabez understood that sin always brings sadness. Even in the age of inflation, the wages of sin remain the same: death (Romans 6:23). Realizing this, Jabez said, "Keep me from sin lest it grieve me and bring sorrow into my life."

As we read in verse 10, God granted Jabez his request. Jabez was blessed, or enlarged. He experienced both the presence and the protection of God.

If we truly believed that the prayer of Jabez had practical application to our situation, we would be people of prayer. But we don't really believe it. Oh, we believe in God's ability to bless us. But we doubt His willingness to do so. Most of us have an entirely wrong understanding of the nature of our Father. We know He's wealthy, but we think He's stingy.

There are three types of wealthy people. The first is the one who will give money if your presentation for cancer research is good enough. The second type is one who is happy to give regardless of the cause. But the third type doesn't wait for the knock on the door. Instead, he walks around, looking for opportunities to give.

Most of us believe our Father is in the first category, that God is wealthy, but that we have to plead and beg to persuade Him that our cause is worthy of His blessing. Some might even think He's eager to give to us regardless of the worth of our request. But, in reality, our Father is neither of these types. He is the third type, going to and fro throughout the whole world, looking for a man in whom He can show Himself strong (2 Chronicles 16:9). God is looking for Jabezes who have problems, who have difficulty, but who call out to Him.

Jabez's prayer wasn't long. But he did what you and I need to do. He called upon the God of Israel. In brokenness and openness, he poured out his heart and said, "Lord, bless me." And the Lord granted him his request. Precious people, spend time with your Father in the posture of prayer, and you'll be on the pathway to prosperity. I guarantee it because the Word declares it.

5

Chapter 5 deals with the tribes of Reuben and Gad . . .

1 Chronicles 5:1, 2
Now the sons of Reuben the firstborn of Israel, (for he was the firstborn; but, forasmuch as he defiled his father's bed, his birthright was given unto the sons of Joseph the son of Israel: and the genealogy is not to be reckoned after the birthright. For Judah prevailed above his brethren, and of him came the chief ruler; but the birthright was Joseph's)

Although Reuben was Jacob's firstborn, Judah's genealogy was given first for two reasons. First, the "chief ruler"—both David and the Son of David, Jesus Christ—would come from the tribe of Judah. Secondly, Reuben forfeited his rights as firstborn when he took his father's concubine (Genesis 35:22, 49:4).

1 Chronicles 5:3–9
The sons, I say, of Reuben the firstborn of Israel were, Hannoch, and Pallu, Hezron, and Carmi. The sons of Joel; Shemaiah his son, Gog his son, Shimei his son, Micah his son, Reaia his son, Baal his son, Beerah his son, whom Tiglath-pileser king of Assyria carried away captive: he was prince of the Reubenites. And his brethren by their families, when the genealogy of their generations was reckoned, were the chief, Jeiel, and Zechariah, And Bela the son of Azaz, the son of Shema, the son of Joel, who dwelt in Aroer, even unto Nebo and Baal-meon: And eastward he inhabited unto the entering in of the wilderness from the river Euphrates: because their cattle were multiplied in the land of Gilead.

Along with Gad and half the tribe of Manasseh, the tribe of Reuben dwelt east of the Jordan (Numbers 32).

1 Chronicles 5:10
And in the days of Saul they made war with the Hagarites, who fell by their hand: and they dwelt in their tents throughout all the east land of Gilead.

The Hagarites would have been the children of Hagar, or Arabs.

1 Chronicles 5:11–20
And the children of Gad dwelt over against them, in the land of Bashan unto Salchah: Joel the chief, and Shapham the next, and Jaanai, and Shaphat in Bashan. And their brethren of the house of their fathers were, Michael, and Meshullam, and Sheba, and Jorai, and Jachan, and Zia, and Heber, seven. These are the children of Abihail the son of Huri, the son of Jaroah, the son of Gilead, the son of Michael, the son of Jeshishai, the son of Jahdo, the son of Buz; Ahi the son of Abdiel, the son of Guni, chief of the house of their fathers. And they dwelt in Gilead in Bashan, and in her towns, and in all the suburbs of Sharon, upon their borders. All these were reckoned by genealogies in the days of Jotham king of Judah, and in the days of Jeroboam king of Israel. The sons of Reuben, and the Gadites, and half the tribe of Manasseh, of valiant men, men able to bear buckler and sword, and to shoot with bow, and skilful in war, were four and forty thousand seven hundred and threescore, that went out to the war. And they made war with the Hagarites, with Jetur, and Nephish, and Nodab. And they were helped against them, and the Hagarites were delivered into

their hand, and all that were with them: for they cried to God in the battle, and he was intreated of them; because they put their trust in him.

Reuben, Gad, and the half tribe of Manasseh were equipped and prepared to wage war. But in the midst of battle, they realized that, apart from prayer, they would sink. So in the middle of the battle, they cried to the Lord and put their trust in Him.This encourages me because it tells me that it's never too late to pray. God heard the prayers of His people and responded graciously and victoriously.

1 Chronicles 5:21–26
And they took away their cattle; of their camels fifty thousand, and of sheep two hundred and fifty thousand, and of asses two thousand, and of men an hundred thousand. For there fell down many slain, because the war was of God. And they dwelt in their steads until the captivity. And the children of the half tribe of Manasseh dwelt in the land: they increased from Bashan unto Baal-hermon and Senir, and unto mount Hermon. And these were the heads of the house of their fathers, even Epher, and Ishi, and Eliel, and Azriel, and Jeremiah, and Hodaviah, and Jahdiel, mighty men of valour, famous men, and heads of the house of their fathers. And they transgressed against the God of their fathers, and went a whoring after the gods of the people of the land, whom God destroyed before them. And the God of Israel stirred up the spirit of Pul king of Assyria, and the spirit of Tiglath-pileser king of Assyria, and he carried them away, even the Reubenites, and the Gadites, and the half tribe of Manasseh, and brought them unto Halah, and Habor, and Hara, and to the river Gozan, unto this day.

Reuben, Gad, and half of the tribe of Manasseh said, "We like it here on the east bank of the Jordan. We don't want to go all the way in to the Promised Land. We'll just stay here at the boundary." But because they didn't go into the Land of Promise, they were the first ones carried away by the Assyrian enemy.

I have observed that it's at the times when we're on the outer edges, not really going in, that we have a tendency to be carried off. We need to go for it all the way in the Lord. If we're just hanging out, observing but not really involved in the things of God in worship, ministry, and prayer, there's a tendency, a vulnerability for us to be carried away.

Every shepherd knows that the sheep straggling on the outer edges of the flock is the one that will be picked off. It is the sheep who are in the center of the flock, close to the shepherd, who are in the place of safety and protection. May we be those sheep.

6 The genealogy of the Levites—the tribe dedicated to serving the Lord—is given in chapter 6 . . .

1 Chronicles 6:1, 2
The sons of Levi; Gershon, Kohath, and Merari. And the sons of Kohath; Amram, Izhar, and Hebron, and Uzziel.

Three families are mentioned. The Gershonites carried the tent of the tabernacle. The Kohathites bore the furniture of the tabernacle. The Merarites carried the boards of the tabernacle. Each one of these family groups had a specific job and function. Everyone serving the Lord had a specific assignment to carry out, which enabled God's people as a whole to move efficiently in their wilderness wanderings.

I encourage you to ask the Lord to show you what your job is in this pilgrimage we're on together. I believe it is a good goal for every brother and sister to be able to state clearly exactly what their ministry is, to be able to say, "This is what I'm called to do." If you don't know what it is, pray about it and begin to experiment in various types and areas of ministry so you'll find your position and place in the body of Christ.

1 Chronicles 6:3–15
And the children of Amram; Aaron, and Moses, and Miriam. The sons also of Aaron; Nadab, and Abihu, Eleazar, and Ithamar. Eleazar begat Phinehas, Phinehas begat Abishua, And Abishua begat Bukki, and Bukki begat Uzzi, And Uzzi begat Zerahiah, and Zerahiah begat Meraioth, Meraioth begat Amariah, and Amariah begat Ahitub, And Ahitub begat Zadok, and Zadok begat Ahimaaz, And Ahimaaz begat Azariah, and Azariah begat Johanan, And Johanan begat Azariah, (he it is that executed the priest's office in the temple that Solomon built in Jerusalem:) And Azariah begat Amariah, and Amariah begat Ahitub, And Ahitub begat Zadok, and Zadok begat Shallum, And Shallum begat Hilkiah, and Hilkiah begat Azariah, And Azariah begat Seraiah, and Seraiah begat Jehozadak, And Jehozadak went into captivity, when the LORD carried away Judah and Jerusalem by the hand of Nebuchadnezzar.

Eleazar was Aaron's successor as high priest. Here, Eleazar's genealogy is traced to the time of the captivity. Thus, the line is drawn from Eleazar—who came out of bondage in Egypt—to Jehozadak, who went into bondage in Babylon.

1 Chronicles 6:16
The sons of Levi; Gershom, Kohath, and Merari.

Here begins the genealogy of the Levites who were not priests . . .

1 Chronicles 6:17–31
And these be the names of the sons of Gershom; Libni, and Shimei. And the sons of Kohath were, Amram, and Izhar, and Hebron, and Uzziel. The sons of Merari; Mahli, and Mushi. And these are the families of the Levites according to their fathers. Of Gershom; Libni his son, Jahath his son, Zimmah his son, Joah his son, Iddo his son, Zerah his son, Jeaterai his son. The sons of Kohath; Amminadab his son, Korah his son, Assir his son, Elkanah his son, and Ebiasaph his son, and Assir his son, Tahath his son, Uriel his son, Uzziah his son, and Shaul his son. And the sons of Elkanah; Amasai, and Ahimoth. As for Elkanah: the sons of Elkanah; Zophai his son, and Nahath his son, Eliab his son, Jeroham his son, Elkanah his son. And the sons of Samuel; the firstborn Vashni, and Abiah. The sons of Merari; Mahli, Libni his son, Shimei his son, Uzza his son, Shimea his son, Haggiah his son, Asaiah his son. And these are they whom David set over the service of song in the house of the Lord, after that the ark had rest.

It should not surprise us that David, the sweet psalmist of Israel, should ordain certain of the Levites to minister in song.

1 Chronicles 6:32
And they ministered before the dwelling place of the tabernacle of the congregation with singing, until Solomon had built the house of the Lord in Jerusalem: and then they waited on their office according to their order.

David was a real warrior. But more than that, he was a worshiper. David was tough, but he was also tender. Consequently, he raised up an army not of warriors but of singers. They continually offered praise and worship through song in the tabernacle and later in the temple.

1 Chronicles 6:33
And these are they that waited with their children. Of the sons of the Kohathites: Heman a singer, the son of Joel, the son of Shemuel,

If you think it is easy to be involved in a praise ministry, check out Psalm 88, where we see one of the songs Heman wrote . . .

> O Lord God of my salvation, I have cried day and night before thee: Let my prayer come before thee: incline thine ear unto my cry; For my soul is full of troubles: and my life draweth nigh unto the grave. I am counted with them that go down into the pit: I am as a man that hath no strength: Free among the dead, like the slain that lie in the grave, whom thou rememberest no more: and they are cut off from thy hand. Thou hast laid me in the lowest pit, in darkness, in the deeps. Thy wrath lieth hard upon me, and thou hast afflicted me with all thy waves. Selah. Thou hast put away mine acquaintance far from me; thou hast made me an abomination unto them: I am shut up, and I cannot come forth. Mine eye mourneth by reason of affliction: Lord, I have called daily upon thee, I have stretched out my hands unto thee. Wilt thou shew wonders to the dead? shall the dead arise and praise thee? Selah. Shall thy lovingkindness be declared in the grave? or thy faithfulness in destruction? Shall thy wonders be known in the dark? and thy righteousness in the land of forgetfulness? But unto thee have I cried, O Lord; and in the morning shall my prayer prevent thee. Lord, why castest thou off my soul? why hidest thou thy face from me? I am afflicted and ready to die from my youth up: while I suffer thy terrors I am distracted. Thy fierce wrath goeth over me; thy terrors have cut me off. They came round about me daily like water; they compassed me about together. Lover and friend hast thou put far from me, and mine acquaintance into darkness.

Psalms are often born of great difficulty. The most effective songs of praise and worship aren't worked out mechanically or musically, but are pressed into the heart of a person through difficulty. Psalmists anointed by God and inspired by the Spirit were men who spent time dealing in spiritual warfare. They were men who came into deep understandings because of the depths they walked personally. So when you go through trials and struggles, know that a song is being birthed and praise will pour forth in due time. Heman wrote other songs—songs of victory, joy, and praise. But this song was preserved to show us he went through some heavy-duty experiences in order to come out on the other side as a man of praise.

1 Chronicles 6:34–39
The son of Elkanah, the son of Jeroham, the son of Eliel, the son of Toah, The son of Zuph, the son of Elkanah, the son of Mahath, the son of Amasai, The son of Elkanah, the son of Joel, the son of Azariah, the son of Zephaniah, The son of Tahath, the son of Assir, the son of Ebiasaph, the son of Korah, The son of Izhar, the son of Kohath, the son of Levi, the son of Israel. And his brother Asaph, who stood on his right hand, even Asaph the son of Berachiah, the son of Shimea,

As you read the Book of Psalms, you will see many written by Asaph, one of the full-time singers David had appointed to minister day and night in the place of worship.

1 Chronicles 6:40–48
The son of Michael, the son of Baaseiah, the son of Malchiah, The son of Ethni, the son of Zerah, the son of Adaiah, The son of Ethan, the son of Zimmah, the son of Shimei, The son of Jahath, the son of Gershom, the son of Levi. And their brethren the sons of Merari stood on the left hand: Ethan the son of Kishi, the son of Abdi, the son of Malluch, The son of Hashabiah, the son of Amaziah, the son of Hilkiah, The son of Amzi, the son of Bani, the son of Shamer, The son of Mahli, the son of Mushi, the son of Merari, the son of Levi. Their brethren also the Levites were appointed unto all manner of service of the tabernacle of the house of God.

There was no shortage of work for the Levites to do: the provision of water and fuel; the washing of the utensils and sweeping of the temple; the killing, butchering, and boiling of the sacrifices themselves.

As believers, we are both a spiritual house and a holy priesthood, as well (1 Peter 2:5). And there remains no shortage of work to do in the provision of the meat and water of the Word, in exhorting one another to purity and holiness, and in presenting ourselves as living sacrifices (Romans 12:1, 2).

1 Chronicles 6:49–53
But Aaron and his sons offered upon the altar of the burnt offering, and on the altar of incense, and were appointed for all the work of the place most holy, and to make an atonement for Israel, according to all that Moses the servant of God had commanded. And these are the sons of Aaron; Eleazar his son, Phinehas his son, Abishua his son, Bukki his son, Uzzi his son, Zerahiah his son, Meraioth his son, Amariah his son, Ahitub his son, Zadok his son, Ahimaaz his son.

The sons of Aaron were already listed in verses 3 through 16. Here, we see a less extensive list.

1 Chronicles 6:54–81
Now these are their dwelling places throughout their castles in their coasts, of the sons of Aaron, of the families of the Kohathites: for theirs was the lot. And they gave them Hebron in the land of Judah, and the suburbs thereof round about it. But the fields of the city, and the villages thereof, they gave to Caleb the son of Jephunneh. And to the sons of Aaron they gave the cities of Judah, namely, Hebron, the city of refuge, and Libnah with her suburbs, and Jattir, and Eshtemoa, with their suburbs, And Hilen with her suburbs, Debir with her suburbs, And Ashan with her suburbs, and Beth-shemesh with her suburbs: And out of the tribe of Benjamin; Geba with her suburbs, and Alemeth with her suburbs, and Anathoth with her suburbs. All their cities throughout their families were thirteen cities. And unto the sons of Kohath, which were left of the family of that tribe, were cities given out of the half tribe, namely, out of the half tribe of Manasseh, by lot, ten cities. And to the sons of Gershom throughout their families out of the tribe of Issachar, and out of the tribe of Asher, and out of the tribe of Naphtali, and out of the tribe of Manasseh in Bashan, thirteen cities. Unto the sons of Merari were given by lot, throughout their families, out of the tribe of Reuben, and out of the tribe of Gad, and out of the tribe of Zebulun, twelve cities. And the children of Israel gave to the Levites these cities with their suburbs. And they gave by lot out of the tribe of the children of Judah, and out of the tribe of the children of Simeon, and out of the tribe of the children of Benjamin, these cities, which are called by their names. And the residue of the families of the sons of Kohath had cities of their coasts out of the tribe of Ephraim. And they gave unto them, of the cities of refuge, Shechem in mount Ephraim with her suburbs; they gave also Gezer with her suburbs, And Jokmeam with her suburbs, and Beth-horon with her suburbs, And Aijalon with her suburbs, and Gath-rimmon with her suburbs: And out of the half tribe of Manasseh; Aner with her suburbs, and

Bileam with her suburbs, for the family of the remnant of the sons of Kohath. Unto the sons of Gershom were given out of the family of the half tribe of Manasseh, Golan in Bashan with her suburbs, and Ashtaroth with her suburbs: And out of the tribe of Issachar; Kedesh with her suburbs, Daberath with her suburbs, And Ramoth with her suburbs, and Anem with her suburbs: And out of the tribe of Asher; Mashal with her suburbs, and Abdon with her suburbs, And Hukok with her suburbs, and Rehob with her suburbs: And out of the tribe of Naphtali; Kedesh in Galilee with her suburbs, and Hammon with her suburbs, and Kirjathaim with her suburbs. Unto the rest of the children of Merari were given out of the tribe of Zebulun. Rimmon with her suburbs, Tabor with her suburbs: And on the other side Jordan by Jericho, on the east side of Jordan, were given them out of the tribe of Reuben, Bezer in the wilderness with her suburbs, and Jahzah with her suburbs, Kedemoth also with her suburbs, and Mephaath with her suburbs: And out of the tribe of Gad; Ramoth in Gilead with her suburbs, and Mahanaim with her suburbs, And Heshbon with her suburbs, and Jazer with her suburbs.

Verses 55 through 81 list the cities given to the Levites. The cities represent a fulfillment of Jacob's prophecy that the tribe of Levi would be scattered throughout Israel (Genesis 49:7). This dispersion of Levites throughout the land would ensure that instruction concerning God's Word and God's ways would be available to all. Included in the Levites' portion were the cities of refuge established in Joshua 21.

7 1 Chronicles 7:1–5
Now the sons of Issachar were, Tola, and Puah, Jashub, and Shimron, four. And the sons of Tola; Uzzi, and Rephaiah, and Jeriel, and Jahmai, and Jibsam, and Shemuel, heads of their father's house, to wit, of Tola: they were valiant men of might in their generations; whose number was in the days of David two and twenty thousand and six hundred. And the sons of Uzzi; Izrahiah: and the sons of Izrahiah; Michael, and Obadiah, and Joel, Ishiah, five: all of them chief men. And with them, by their generations, after the house of their fathers, were bands of soldiers for war, six and thirty thousand men: for they had many wives and sons. And their brethren among all the families of Issachar were valiant men of might, reckoned in all by their genealogies fourscore and seven thousand.

Here we see the genealogy of the tribe of Issachar. In Genesis 49:14, Jacob prophesied that Issachar would be strong. Issachar spoken of here as "valiant men of might," Jacob's prophecy finds its fulfillment.

1 Chronicles 7:6–12
The sons of Benjamin; Bela, and Becher, and Jediael, three. And the sons of Bela; Ezbon, and Uzzi, and Uzziel, and Jerimoth, and Iri, five; heads of the house of their fathers, mighty men of valour; and were reckoned by their genealogies twenty and two thousand and thirty and four. And the sons of Becher; Zemira, and Joash, and Eliezer, and Elioenai, and Omri, and Jerimoth, and Abiah, and Anathoth, and Alameth. All these are the sons of Becher. And the number of them, after their genealogy by their generations, heads of the house of the fathers, mighty men of valour, was twenty thousand and two hundred. The sons also of Jediael; Bilhan: and the sons of Bilhan; Jeush, and Benjamin, and Ehud, and Chenaanah, and Zethan, and Tharshish, and Ahishahar. All these the sons of Jediael, by the heads of their fathers, mighty men of valour, were seventeen thousand and two hundred soldiers, fit to go out for war and battle. Shuppim also, and Huppim, the children of Ir, and Hushim, the sons of Aher.

Here we find the genealogy of the tribe of Benjamin. Two towering figures in Israel's history—both named Saul—would hail from the tribe of Benjamin. One was the first king of Israel. The other was the first champion of grace (Philippians 3:5).

1 Chronicles 7:13
The sons of Naphtali; Jahziel, and Guni, and Jezer, and Shallum, the sons of Bilhah.

Naphtali's genealogy included Barak, the general who accompanied Deborah into battle (Judges 5).

1 Chronicles 7:14–19
The sons of Manasseh; Ashriel, whom she bare: (but his concubine the Aramitess bare Machir the father of Gilead: And Machir took to wife the sister of Huppim and Shuppim, whose sister's name was Maachah;) and the name of the second was Zelophehad: and Zelophehad had daughters. And Maachah the wife of Machir bare a son, and she called his name Peresh; and the name of his

brother was Sheresh; and his sons were Ulam and Rakem. And the sons of Ulam; Bedan. These were the sons of Gilead, the son of Machir, the son of Manasseh. And his sister Hammoleketh bare Ishod, and Abiezer, and Mahalah. And the sons of Shemida were, Ahian, and Shechem, and Likhi, and Aniam.

Manasseh was a tribe divided, for in Numbers 32:33, we read that half of them remained on the east side of the Jordan.

1 Chronicles 7:20–27
And the sons of Ephraim; Shuthelah, and Bered his son, and Tahath his son, and Eladah his son, and Tahath his son, And Zabad his son, and Shuthelah his son, and Ezer, and Elead, whom the men of Gath that were born in that land slew, because they came down to take away their cattle. And Ephraim their father mourned many days, and his brethren came to comfort him. And when he went in to his wife, she conceived, and bare a son, and he called his name Beriah, because it went evil with his house. (And his daughter was Sherah, who built Beth-horon the nether, and the upper, and Uzzen-sherah.) And Rephah was his son, also Resheph, and Telah his son, and Tahan his son, Laadan his son, Ammihud his son, Elishama his son, Non his son, Jehoshua his son.

Samuel, the last of Israel's judges and the first of her prophets, was of the tribe of Ephraim.

1 Chronicles 7:28, 29
And their possessions and habitations were, Bethel and the towns thereof, and eastward Naaran, and westward Gezer, with the towns thereof; Shechem also and the towns thereof, unto Gaza and the towns thereof: And by the borders of the children of Manasseh, Beth-shean and her towns, Taanach and her towns, Megiddo and her towns, Dor and her towns. In these dwelt the children of Joseph the son of Israel.

In addition to the towns of Ephraim listed here was the town of Shiloh, where the tabernacle was pitched before the temple was constructed (Joshua 18:1).

1 Chronicles 7:30–40
The sons of Asher; Imnah, and Isuah, and Ishuai, and Beriah, and Serah their sister. And the sons of Beriah; Heber, and Malchiel, who is the father of Birzavith. And Heber begat Japhlet, and Shomer, and Hotham, and Shua their sister. And the sons of Japhlet; Pasach, and Bimhal, and Ashvath. These are the children of Japhlet. And the sons of Shamer; Ahi, and Rohgah, Jehubbah, and Aram. And the sons of his brother Helem; Zophah, and Imna, and Shelesh, and Amal. The sons of Zophah; Suah, and Harnepher, and Shual, and Beri, and Imrah, Bezer, and Hod, and Shamma and Shilshah, and Ithran, and Beera. And the sons of Jether; Jephunneh, and Pispah, and Ara. And the sons of Ulla; Arah, and Haniel, and Rezia. All these were the children of Asher, heads of their father's house, choice and mighty men of valour, chief of the princes. And the number throughout the genealogy of them that were apt to the war and to battle was twenty and six thousand men.

Although the tribe of Asher consisted of "mighty men of valour," it is Anna—a woman of the tribe of Asher—who is singularly mentioned in the New Testament solely because of her recognition of the Messiah (Luke 2:36).

Regardless of our "valour" in business, in our families, or even in ministry, the only noteworthy portion of our lives is that which looks for and recognizes Jesus.

8 In chapter 8, we see the genealogy of Benjamin, specifically as it relates to Saul and Jonathan.

1 Chronicles 8:1–5
Now Benjamin begat Bela his firstborn, Ashbel the second, and Aharah the third, Nohah the fourth, and Rapha the fifth. And the sons of Bela were, Addar, and Gera, and Abihud, And Abishua, and Naaman, and Ahoah, And Gera, and Shephuphan, and Huram.

In Judges 19 and 20, the account is given wherein the tribe of Benjamin was reduced to only six hundred men. Here, however, we see the tribe of Benjamin as strong as any of the tribes. Such is the mercy and power of our God.

1 Chronicles 8:6
And these are the sons of Ehud: these are the heads of the fathers of the inhabitants of Geba, and they removed them to Manahath:

Ehud is the brave, left-handed man we see in Judges 3 who, with a dagger hidden in his robe, was able to free Israel from an overweight Moabite despot named Eglon.

1 Chronicles 8:7–28
And Naaman, and Ahiah, and Gera, he removed them, and begat Uzza, and Ahihud.

And Shaharaim begat children in the country of Moab, after he had sent them away; Hushim and Baara were his wives. And he begat of Hodesh his wife, Jobab, and Zibia, and Mesha, and Malcham, And Jeuz, and Shachia, and Mirma. These were his sons, heads of the fathers. And of Hushim he begat Abitub, and Elpaal. The sons of Elpaal; Eber, and Misham, and Shamed, who built Ono, and Lod, with the towns thereof: Beriah also, and Shema, who were heads of the fathers of the inhabitants of Aijalon, who drove away the inhabitants of Gath: And Ahio, Shashak, and Jeremoth, And Zebadiah, and Arad, and Ader, And Michael, and Ispah, and Joha, the sons of Beriah; And Zebadiah, and Meshullam, and Hezeki, and Heber, Ishmerai also, and Jezliah, and Jobab, the sons of Elpaal; And Jakim, and Zichri, and Zabdi, And Elienai, and Zilthai, and Eliel, And Adaiah, and Beraiah, and Shimrath, the sons of Shimhi; And Ishpan, and Heber, and Eliel, And Abdon, and Zichri, and Hanan, And Hananiah, and Elam, and Antothijah, And Iphedeiah, and Penuel, the sons of Shashak; And Shamsherai, and Shehariah, and Athaliah, And Jaresiah, and Eliah, and Zichri, the sons of Jeroham. These were heads of the fathers, by their generations, chief men. These dwelt in Jerusalem.

The notation that these men dwelt in Jerusalem refers to their willingness to return to their desolate city rather than remain in the established city of Babylon following their release from captivity (Nehemiah 11:2).

1 Chronicles 8:29–33
And at Gibeon dwelt the father of Gibeon; whose wife's name was Maachah: And his firstborn son Abdon, and Zur, and Kish, and Baal, and Nadab, And Gedor, and Ahio, and Zacher. And Mikloth begat Shimeah. And these also dwelt with their brethren in Jerusalem, over against them. And Ner begat Kish, and Kish begat Saul, and Saul begat Jonathan, and Malchi-shua, and Abinadab, and Esh-baal.

Here, of course, we see Israel's first king, Saul.

1 Chronicles 8:34–40
And the son of Jonathan was Merib-baal; and Merib-baal begat Micah. And the sons of Micah were, Pithon, and Melech, and Tarea, and Ahaz. And Ahaz begat Jehoadah; and Jehoadah begat Alemeth, and Azmaveth, and Zimri; and Zimri begat Moza, And Moza begat Binea: Rapha was his son, Eleasah his son, Azel his son: And Azel had six sons, whose names are these, Azrikam, Bocheru, and Ishmael, and Sheariah, and Obadiah, and Hanan. All these were the sons of Azel. And the sons of Eshek his brother were, Ulam his firstborn, Jehush the second, and Eliphelet the third. And the sons of Ulam were mighty men of valour, archers, and had many sons, and sons' sons, an hundred and fifty. All these are of the sons of Benjamin.

To be an archer at this point in history required great strength and skill as the bow—which was made of steel—was held steady by the foot while the string was pulled with both hands.

9

Chapter 9 deals with the priests and the Levites . . .

1 Chronicles 9:1, 2
So all Israel were reckoned by genealogies; and, behold, they were written in the book of the kings of Israel and Judah, who were carried away to Babylon for their transgression. Now the first inhabitants that dwelt in their possessions in their cities were, the Israelites, the priests, Levites, and the Nethinims.

Following the captivity, those who first dwelt in the cities given to Israel were those who were involved in the service of the Lord. In this, we see once again the priority of God's work. Those who were committed and devoted to serving God were those who were sent throughout the land in order to assume positions of ministry to the people of the land.

1 Chronicles 9:3–9
And in Jerusalem dwelt of the children of Judah, and of the children of Benjamin, and of the children of Ephraim, and Manasseh; Uthai the son of Ammihud, the son of Omri, the son of Imri, the son of Bani, of the children of Pharez the son of Judah. And of the Shilonites; Asaiah the firstborn, and his sons. And of the sons of Zerah; Jeuel, and their brethren, six hundred and ninety. And of the sons of Benjamin; Sallu the son of Meshullam, the son of Hodaviah, the son of Hasenuah, And Ibneiah the son of Jeroham, and Elah the son of Uzzi, the son of Michri, and Meshullam the son of Shephathiah, the son of Reuel, the son of Ibnijah; And their brethren, according to their generations, nine hundred and fifty and six. All these men were chief of the fathers in the house of their fathers.

Here, we see the fulfillment of Ezekiel's and Hosea's prophecies that the children of Judah and Israel would be gathered together, becoming one nation again (Ezekiel 37:22; Hosea 1:11).

1 Chronicles 9:10–16
And of the priests; Jedaiah, and Jehoiarib, and Jachin, And Azariah the son of Hilkiah, the son of Meshullam, the son of Zadok, the son of Meraioth, the son of Ahitub, the ruler of the house of God; And Adaiah the son of Jeroham, the son of Pashur, the son of Malchijah, and Maasiai the son of Adiel, the son of Jahzerah, the son of Meshullam, the son of Meshillemith, the son of Immer; And their brethren, heads of the house of their fathers, a thousand and seven hundred and threescore; very able men for the work of the service of the house of God. And of the Levites; Shemaiah the son of Hasshub, the son of Azrikam, the son of Hashabiah, of the sons of Merari; And Bakbakkar, Heresh, and Galal, and Mattaniah the son of Micah, the son of Zichri, the son of Asaph; And Obadiah the son of Shemaiah, the son of Galal, the son of Jeduthun, and Berechiah the son of Asa, the son of Elkanah, that dwelt in the villages of the Netophathites.

The priests and Levites were "very able men" indeed (v. 13), possessing not only great faithfulness, but also great courage as they reestablished worship in a hostile environment (Nehemiah 4:17, 18).

1 Chronicles 9:17–27
And the porters were, Shallum, and Akkub, and Talmon, and Ahiman, and their brethren: Shallum was the chief; Who hitherto waited in the king's gate eastward: they were porters in the companies of the children of Levi. And Shallum the son of Kore, the son of Ebiasaph, the son of Korah, and his brethren, of the house of his father, the Korahites, were over the work of the service, keepers of the gates of the tabernacle: and their fathers, being over the host of the LORD, were keepers of the entry. And Phinehas the son of Eleazar was the ruler over them in time past, and the Lord was with him. And Zechariah the son of Meshelemiah was porter of the door of the tabernacle of the congregation. All these which were chosen to be porters in the gates were two hundred and twelve. These were reckoned by their genealogy in their villages, whom David and Samuel the seer did ordain in their set office. So they and their children had the oversight of the gates of the house of the Lord, namely, the house of the tabernacle, by wards. In four quarters were the porters, toward the east, west, north, and south. And their brethren, which were in their villages, were to come after seven days from time to time with them. For these Levites, the four chief porters, were in their set office, and were over the chambers and treasuries of the house of God. And they lodged round about the house of God, because the charge was upon them, and the opening thereof every morning pertained to them.

The only ministry of a certain group of Levites consisted of opening and closing the doors. Their ministry was twofold: they prohibited access to the unclean—the lepers, the disqualified, the uncircumcised—and they granted access to those who had need, perhaps unable to come in on their own strength. In this we see precisely what the ministry of intercession is all about: keeping away the hosts of hell, demonic spirits, and influences of Satan that seek to cause havoc and destruction in the lives of the people of God; and opening the door of blessing for those who are hurting.

If you are an intercessor, I bless you in the name of Jesus. The prayer warriors of the ministry will be those who, in eternity, will receive great reward (Matthew 6:6).

1 Chronicles 9:28–30
And certain of them had the charge of the ministering vessels, that they should bring them in and out by tale. Some of them also were appointed to oversee the vessels, and all the instruments of the sanctuary, and the fine flour, and the wine, and the oil, and the frankincense, and the spices. And some of the sons of the priests made the ointment of the spices.

The priests who washed the utensils used in worship could have said to the priests who prepared the incense, "My job stinks compared to yours." But the job of each was equally vital to tabernacle and temple worship. As New Testament believers, Paul likens the ministry to a body in which every part is needed, even those positions which seem less attractive than others (1 Corinthians 12). God has a certain place for each of us, and He wants us to function in that place, even if it's to be a "dishwasher."

1 Chronicles 9:31–34
And Mattithiah, one of the Levites, who was the firstborn of Shallum the Korahite, had the set office over the things that were made in the pans. And other of their brethren, of the sons of the Kohathites, were over the

shewbread, to prepare it every sabbath. And these are the singers, chief of the fathers of the Levites, who remaining in the chambers were free: for they were employed in that work day and night. These chief fathers of the Levites were chief throughout their generations; these dwelt at Jerusalem.

In Job 38, we read that the morning stars sang together when God created the world. In Luke 2, we read that the angels sang when Jesus was born. Here, we read that the singers in the temple sang day and night. Therefore, it would seem that God works best with "background music." No wonder Paul would exhort us to make "melody in our hearts to the Lord" (Ephesians 5:19).

1 Chronicles 9:35–44
And in Gibeon dwelt the father of Gibeon, Jehiel, whose wife's name was Maachah: And his firstborn son Abdon, then Zur, and Kish, and Baal, and Ner, and Nadab, And Gedor, and Ahio, and Zechariah, and Mikloth. And Mikloth begat Shimeam. And they also dwelt with their brethren at Jerusalem, over against their brethren. And Ner begat Kish; and Kish begat Saul; and Saul begat Jonathan, and Malchi-shua, and Abinadab, and Esh-baal. And the son of Jonathan was Merib-baal: and Merib-baal begat Micah. And the sons of Micah were, Pithon, and Melech, and Tahrea, and Ahaz. And Ahaz begat Jarah; and Jarah begat Alemeth, and Azmaveth, and Zimri; and Zimri begat Moza; And Moza begat Binea; and Rephaiah his son, Eleasah his son, Azel his son. And Azel had six sons, whose names are these, Azrikam, Bocheru, and Ishmael, and Sheariah, and Obadiah, and Hanan: these were the sons of Azel.

In chapter 8, verses 29 through 38, we see this same genealogy. There, it served as the conclusion of the genealogy of Benjamin. Here, it serves as an introduction to Saul . . .

10

1 Chronicles 10:1–10
Now the Philistines fought against Israel; and the men of Israel fled from before the Philistines, and fell down slain in mount Gilboa. And the Philistines followed hard after Saul, and after his sons; and the Philistines slew Jonathan, and Abinadab, and Malchi-shua, the sons of Saul. And the battle went sore against Saul, and the archers hit him, and he was wounded of the archers. Then said Saul to his armour-bearer, Draw thy sword, and thrust me through therewith; lest these uncircumcised come and abuse me. But his armour-bearer would not; for he was sore afraid. So Saul took a sword, and fell upon it. And when his armour-bearer saw that Saul was dead, he fell likewise on the sword, and died. So Saul died, and his three sons, and all his house died together. And when all the men of Israel that were in the valley saw that they fled, and that Saul and his sons were dead, then they forsook their cities, and fled: and the Philistines came and dwelt in them. And it came to pass on the morrow, when the Philistines came to strip the slain, that they found Saul and his sons fallen in mount Gilboa. And when they had stripped him, they took his head, and his armour, and sent into the land of the Philistines round about, to carry tidings unto their idols, and to the people. And they put his armour in the house of their gods, and fastened his head in the temple of Dagon.

After being severely wounded in a battle against the Philistines, Saul killed himself when his armor-bearer refused. When the Philistines found him, they chopped off his head and paraded it through their cities before placing it in the temple of Dagon as a trophy.

1 Chronicles 10:11, 12
And when all Jabeshgilead heard all that the Philistines had done to Saul, They arose, all the valiant men, and took away the body of Saul, and the bodies of his sons, and brought them to Jabesh, and buried their bones under the oak in Jabesh, and fasted seven days.

The men of Jabesh-gilead risked their lives to bring back the body of Saul. Why? Years earlier, when the Amorites threatened to destroy them, the men of Jabesh-gilead sent word to Saul that they were in trouble. Saul and his troops, in turn, marched all night and rescued them.

Know this, gang: if you sow seeds of mercy and love, they will come back to you. Saul was not a particularly honorable man, but in this one case, he did something that was good, merciful, and kind. He rescued Jabesh-gilead and here his kindness is repaid because whatever a man sows, that shall he also reap (Galatians 6:7).

1 Chronicles 10:13, 14
So Saul died for his transgression which he committed against the LORD, even against the word of the LORD, which he kept not, and also for asking counsel of one that had a familiar spirit, to inquire of it; And inquired not of the LORD: therefore he slew him, and turned the kingdom unto David the son of Jesse.

Saul was a man who had incredible potential. He was handsome. He was hand-picked by God to be the first king of Israel. He had Samuel at his side. He had a group of men round about him who were loyal to him. He had a change of heart in his own life when the Holy Spirit came upon him. Saul had so much going for him, but his life ended up a miserable failure because he sought a demonic spirit rather than seeking the Lord.

How I pray we would be people who read the Word daily and seek the Lord continually. Don't be like Saul. Don't needlessly lose your head tomorrow in a battle you can't win on your own. Call upon the name of the Lord. Do what He tells you to do in His Word. And, like the shepherd who would become Israel's second king, you'll prosper.

11

With Saul off the scene, we come to the section in Chronicles that deals with the life of David, a man after God's own heart.

1 Chronicles 11:1–3

Then all Israel gathered themselves to David unto Hebron, saying, Behold, we are thy bone and thy flesh. And moreover in time past, even when Saul was king, thou wast he that leddest out and broughtest in Israel: and the LORD thy God said unto thee, Thou shalt feed my people Israel, and thou shalt be ruler over my people Israel. Therefore came all the elders of Israel to the king to Hebron; and David made a covenant with them in Hebron before the LORD; and they anointed David king over Israel, according to the word of the LORD by Samuel.

I find it interesting that the Lord told David that he would both feed His people and rule over them. There is a close connection between feeding and leading. If you want to be a leader, you need to be a feeder, be it in your home, in your ministry, or on the jobsite.

"If you love Me, feed My sheep," the Lord said to Peter (John 21:15).

Peter, in turn, exhorted the elders in a church to "feed the flock" (1 Peter 5:2).

David was a shepherd, the quintessential example of what God desires in a leader. He was a feeder of sheep, and thus became a ruler over God's people. In whatever your sphere of influence, the Lord wants you to be a leader by being a feeder as you share principles from the Word of God.

1 Chronicles 11:4

And David and all Israel went to Jerusalem, which is Jebus; where the Jebusites were, the inhabitants of the land.

The city of Jerusalem was originally called Jebus and was thus inhabited by the Jebusites, enemies of the people of God. David, however, desired to make Jerusalem his capital.

1 Chronicles 11:5

And the inhabitants of Jebus said to David, Thou shalt not come hither. Nevertheless David took the castle of Zion, which is the city of David.

"You can't come hither," the Jebusites said. And Satan constantly says the same thing to us. "You can't do that," he hisses. "You can't accomplish that. You can't witness. You can't minister. You can't take on that challenge." Our enemy perpetually propagates negativity.

Paul, on the other hand, said, "I *can* do all things through Christ who strengthens me" (Philippians 4:13, italics added).

Fear says you can't. Faith says, "Oh, yeah? Watch me."

It's such a joy to be around men who don't give reasons why things can't get done, but who make a way to make things happen. Without faith it is impossible to please God (Hebrews 11:6). I am convinced that the greatest curse upon the people of God today is that we make all of our decisions based upon logical assumptions. We need to be people of faith. The Bible dwells in and centers on faith. And David was such a man.

1 Chronicles 11:6, 7

And David said, Whosoever smiteth the Jebusites first shall be chief and captain. So Joab the son of Zeruiah went first up, and was chief. And David dwelt in the castle; therefore they called it the city of David.

"We're taking Jerusalem and nothing's stopping us," David declared. Then he turned to his men and said, "The first one inside the city will be my general." A man named Joab found his way in by sliding into the sewer and coming up inside the city (2 Samuel 5:8). He smote the Jebusites, opened the gates, and the other soldiers rushed in.

Who are the men and women God uses? Not the ones who say, "It can't be done" but those who say, "We'll find a way even if it means sliding through the sewers," for that's what the Son of David did for us (2 Corinthians 5:21).

1 Chronicles 11:8, 9

And he built the city round about, even from Millo round about: and Joab repaired the rest of the city. So David waxed greater and greater: for the LORD of hosts was with him.

David became great for one reason: God was with him.

1 Chronicles 11:10
These also are the chief of the mighty men whom David had, who strengthened themselves with him in his kingdom, and with all Israel, to make him king, according to the word of the LORD concerning Israel.

In verse 10 we have a listing or a catalogue of David's mighty men. These were the six hundred ragtag renegades who came to David when he was fighting off the attacks of Saul. In debt, discontent, and distressed, they joined themselves to David (1 Samuel 22:2). They were a motley crew indeed. But an interesting transformation took place, for as they hung around David, they began to take on his characteristics and, over a period of time, became a band of six hundred mighty warriors.

I like this because we're a group of ragtag renegades ourselves. We have troubles and problems to be sure. But our Leader is perfect. And the more we hang around Him, the more we begin to become like Him. It's a long process indeed, but slowly, yet surely, we are changed from glory to even greater glory as we behold Him (2 Corinthians 3:18).

1 Chronicles 11:11
And this is the number of the mighty men whom David had; Jashobeam, and Hachmonite, the chief of the captains: he lifted up his spear against three hundred slain by him at one time.

Jashobeam, also known as Adino in 2 Samuel 23:8, single-handedly took on three hundred enemies. This speaks to us very powerfully about the importance of lifting up our hands in prayer (1 Timothy 2:8). If you want to be a mighty man or woman of God, prerequisite number one is that you persist in prayer.

"But my hands are tired," you protest. "I've been praying about this issue for a long time and I'm getting worn out and beaten down." Do you recall what Moses did? He was on the mountaintop praying for the Israelites while the battle was raging with the Amalekites. When his hands were in the air, the Israelites would advance, but when his hands grew weary and began to fall, the Amalekites gained momentum. Finally, observing what was happening, Aaron stood on one side of him and Hur on the other to prop Moses' hands up until victory was secure (Exodus 17:12).

We're all like Moses. We all need people to hold up our hands. Therefore, we need to pray for, and cultivate relationships that will enable us to hold up one another's hands in times of weakness.

1 Chronicles 11:12
And after him was Eleazar the son of Dodo, the Ahohite, who was one of the three mighties.

Eleazar means "God is my help." In 2 Samuel 10, we read that Eleazar held on so hard for so long that his hand "clave to the sword." The second prerequisite for any who desire to be mighty men or women of God is that their hands must hold tight to the sword of the Word of God.

1 Chronicles 11:13–16
He was with David at Pas-dammim, and there the Philistines were gathered together to battle, where was a parcel of ground full of barley; and the people fled from before the Philistines. And they set themselves in the midst of that parcel, and delivered it, and slew the Philistines; and the LORD saved them by a great deliverance. Now three of the thirty captains went down to the rock to David, into the cave of Adullam; and the host of the Philistines encamped in the valley of Rephaim. And David was then in the hold, and the Philistines' garrison was then at Bethlehem.

Bethlehem was David's hometown. No doubt with his mouth dry and his lips parched, holed up in a cave on a hot fall day with the Philistines down below surrounding his hometown, David must have thought of the days when, as a boy, he would draw cool, sweet water out of the well in Bethlehem.

1 Chronicles 11:17, 18 (a)
And David longed, and said, Oh that one would give me drink of the water of the well of Bethlehem, that is at the gate! And the three brake through the host of the Philistines, and drew water out of the well of Bethlehem, that was by the gate, and took it, and brought it to David . . .

Three mighty men—Shammah, Eleazar, and Adino—risked their lives to bring their king what he desired.

I love this because that's what mighty men and women of God do. They don't simply obey the commands of the King, but they sense His desire. Perhaps you are obeying God's commands. That's good, but are you sensing His desires? Even though it might be costly and difficult, do you break through and give Him what He desires?

1 Chronicles 11:18 (b)
. . . but David would not drink of it, but poured it out to the LORD,

David took that which was most precious to him and offered it to the Lord. Some might say it was a waste, even as one did when another poured out her most precious possession on the head and feet of the Son of David.

"It's a waste," Judas protested. "That money could have been spent on the poor."

But Jesus corrected Judas and said, "Throughout world history, this deed will be remembered" (see John 12; Mark 14).

Whatever you pour out to Jesus is never a waste. Others might say, "Be practical. That's a waste of time, or a waste of energy." But nothing you give to the Lord is ever a waste.

1 Chronicles 11:19–22 (a)
And said, My God forbid it me, that I should do this thing: shall I drink the blood of these men that have put their lives in jeopardy? for with the jeopardy of their lives they brought it. Therefore he would not drink it. These things did these three mightiest. And Abishai the brother of Joab, he was chief of the three: for lifting up his spear against three hundred, he slew them, and had a name among the three. Of the three, he was more honourable than the two; for he was their captain: howbeit he attained not to the first three. Benaiah the son of Jehoiada, the son of a valiant man of Kabzeel, who had done many acts; he slew two lionlike men of Moab . . .

Benaiah means "edified." How was Benaiah edified? First, he took on two lion-like men of Moab. In the Bible, the lion is a symbol for the devil (1 Peter 5:8). Saints, before you ever do battle with the lion himself, like Benaiah, you'll deal with lion-like situations. "If you can't keep up with the footmen, how will you run against the horses?" Jeremiah asked (see Jeremiah 12:5). In other words, if you're not able to handle the race you're in today, how will you handle tomorrow? I need to remember that the difficult, lion-like situations I face today prepare me because the lion himself could show up tomorrow. The struggles, battles, difficulties, temptations, trials, and snares we face today are building us up for the battles the Father knows we will face in the near future.

1 Chronicles 11:22 (b)
. . . also he went down and slew a lion in a pit in a snowy day.

After he took on the two lion-like men, Benaiah faced the lion himself on a snowy day. Isn't it just like the enemy to come when we're coldest, when our heart is cold, when the situation is chilly, when things are brutal? Not only was it a snowy day, but Benaiah was in a pit. That's where the enemy always seeks to pull us.

But Benaiah was ready. The initiator of the battle, he went down into the pit and killed the lion. "Greater is he that is in you than he that is in the world," John tells us (1 John 4:4). This means we can go into a pit even on a snowy day and do battle with the enemy because we've not only been prepared, but because we're indwelt. The Spirit of God lives within us.

1 Chronicles 11:23, 24
And he slew an Egyptian, a man of great stature, five cubits high; and in the Egyptian's hand was a spear like a weaver's beam; and he went down to him with a staff, and plucked the spear out of the Egyptian's hand, and slew him with his own spear. These things did Benaiah the son of Jehoiada, and had the name among the three mighties.

In addition to the lion-like men and the lion itself, Benaiah faced a seven-foot Egyptian. Egypt speaks of the world. Sometimes, the world looms large over us. Maybe we have victory over the devil, but then the whole world system—the pressure of our peers, the pull of society—threatens us. But we can have victory if we do what Benaiah did, if we take the world's own weapons and use them against it . . .

When a woman wanted to know how to have victory over her dependence upon nicotine, we counseled her to use her cigarettes as a weapon against the enemy. That is, every time she felt an urge to smoke, she was to quietly intercede for people she knew were headed for hell. She did that. She interceded fervently for the lost. And guess what happened. Her desire to smoke vanished because the enemy was getting beaten by his own weapon.

You can take the very things Satan uses against you and turn them around (Genesis 50:20). That's what Benaiah did.

1 Chronicles 11:25–47
Behold, he was honourable among the thirty, but attained not to the first three: and David set him over his guard. Also the valiant men of the armies were, Asahel the brother of Joab, Elhanan the son of Dodo of Bethlehem, Shammoth the Harorite, Helez the Pelonite, Ira the son of Ikkesh the Tekoite,

Abi-ezer the Antothite, Sibbecai the Hushathite, Ilai the Ahohite, Maharai the Netophathite, Heled the son of Baanah the Netophathite, Ithai the son of Ribai of Gibeah, that pertained to the children of Benjamin, Benaiah the Pirathonite, Hurai of the brooks of Gaash, Abiel the Arbathite, Azmaveth the Baharumite, Eliahba the Shaalbonite, The sons of Hashem the Gizonite, Jonathan the son of Shage the Hararite, Ahiam the son of Sacar the Hararite, Eliphal the son of Ur, Hepher the Mecherathite, Ahijah the Pelonite, Hezro the Carmelite, Naarai the son of Ezbai, Joel the brother of Nathan, Mibhar the son of Haggeri, Zelek the Ammonite, Naharai the Berothite, the armourbearer of Joab the son of Zeruiah, Ira the Ithrite, Gareb the Ithrite, Uriah the Hittite, Zabad the son of Ahlai, Adina the son of Shiza the Reubenite, a captain of the Reubenites, and thirty with him, Hanan the son of Maachah, and Joshaphat the Mithnite, Uzzia the Ashterathite, Shama and Jehiel the sons of Hothan the Aroerite, Jediael the son of Shimri, and Joha his brother, the Tizite, Eliel the Mahavite, and Jeribai, and Joshaviah, the sons of Elnaam, and Ithmah the Moabite, Eliel, and Obed, and Jasiel the Mesobaite.

"It is easier for heaven and earth to pass than one tittle of the law to fail," Jesus declared (Luke 16:17). This means the names of these valiant men are more securely recorded than those of the most powerful rulers that have ever appeared on the world stage. Your name most likely will not be recorded in history books. But if it is recorded in the Lamb's Book of Life (Revelation 21:27), it is written with the indelible ink of Jesus' blood.

12 In chapter 12, we see the men who joined David in Ziklag, where he hung out while hiding from Saul . . .

1 Chronicles 12:1, 2
Now these are they that came to David to Ziklag, while he yet kept himself close because of Saul the son of Kish: and they were among the mighty men, helpers of the war. They were armed with bows, and could use both the right hand and the left in hurling stones and shooting arrows out of a bow, even of Saul's brethren of Benjamin.

The Benjamites began to defect to David's side and were particularly valuable in war because, being ambidextrous, they could fight with both hands.

1 Chronicles 12:3–8
The chief was Ahiezer, then Joash, the sons of Shemaah the Gibeathite; and Jeziel, and Pelet, the sons of Azmaveth; and Berachah, and Jehu the Antothite, And Ismaiah the Gibeonite, a mighty man among the thirty, and over the thirty; and Jeremiah, and Jahaziel, and Johanan, and Josabad the Gederathite, Eluzai, and Jerimoth, and Bealiah, and Shemariah, and Shephatiah the Haruphite, Elkanah, and Jesiah, and Azareel, and Joezer, and Jashobeam, the Korhites, And Joelah, and Zebadiah, the sons of Jeroham of Gedor. And of the Gadites there separated themselves unto David into the hold to the wilderness men of might, and men of war fit for the battle, that could handle shield and buckler, whose faces were like the faces of lions, and were as swift as the roes upon the mountains;

A buckler was a spear. This means the men of Gad were capable warriors both offensively with the spear and defensively with the shield. In addition to this, they were fierce as lions and swift as deers,

1 Chronicles 12:9–17
Ezer the first, Obadiah the second, Eliab the third, Mishmannah the fourth, Jeremiah the fifth, Attai the sixth, Eliel the seventh, Johanan the eighth, Elzabad the ninth, Jeremiah the tenth, Machbanai the eleventh. These were of the sons of Gad, captains of the host: one of the least was over an hundred, and the greatest over a thousand. These are they that went over Jordan in the first month, when it had overflown all his banks; and they put to flight all them of the valleys, both toward the east, and toward the west. And there came of the children of Benjamin and Judah to the hold unto David. And David went out to meet them, and answered and said unto them, If ye be come peaceably unto me to help me, mine heart shall be knit unto you: but if ye be come to betray me to mine enemies, seeing there is no wrong in mine hands, the God of our fathers look thereon, and rebuke it.

David couldn't have known whether these men joined David out of sincerity or whether they were trying to infiltrate his camp as double agents. So what did he do? He said, "If you're coming to join me, our hearts will be knit together. But if you're coming to betray me, the Lord will see it and rebuke you." David was a man who recognized that God was his Defender and that God saw all things.

How grateful I am that I can rest in the God of

Ananias and Sapphira. Because only God sees the heart of a man, only He is able to judge. I realize how little I know, how incapable I am of seeing another person's heart. So I do what David did. I leave everything with God.

1 Chronicles 12:18

Then the spirit came upon Amasai, who was chief of the captains, and he said, Thine are we, David, and on thy side, thou son of Jesse: peace, peace be unto thee, and peace be to thine helpers; for thy God helpeth thee. Then David received them, and made them captains of the band.

David held no grudge against these who once fought against him. The graciousness of David is exceeded only by the graciousness of the Son of David, Jesus Christ.

1 Chronicles 12:19–22

And there fell some of Manasseh to David, when he came with the Philistines against Saul to battle: but they helped them not: for the lords of the Philistines upon advisement sent him away, saying, He will fall to his master Saul to the jeopardy of our heads. As he went to Ziklag, there fell to him of Manasseh, Adnah, and Jozabad, and Jediael, and Michael, and Jozabad, and Elihu, and Zilthai, captains of the thousands that were of Manasseh. And they helped David against the band of the rovers: for they were all mighty men of valour, and were captains in the host. For at that time day by day there came to David to help him, until it was a great host, like the host of God.

When the armies of Saul began to experience setbacks, as the popularity of Saul began to decline, more and more people joined David. Initially, there were six hundred renegades who came to his side. They stayed with him when he was not popular. They hung by him in his days of difficulty. When things were going badly, they demonstrated a remarkable degree of loyalty. But the tide is turning, and suddenly thousands of men join David.

1 Chronicles 12:23

And these are the numbers of the bands that were ready armed to the war, and came to David to Hebron, to turn the kingdom of Saul to him, according to the word of the LORD.

Between verses 22 and 23, Saul died and his kingdom was transferred to David in Hebron.

1 Chronicles 12:24–37

The children of Judah that bare shield and spear were six thousand and eight hundred, ready armed to the war. Of the children of Simeon, mighty men of valour for the war, seven thousand and one hundred. Of the children of Levi four thousand and six hundred. And Jehoiada was the leader of the Aaronites, and with him were three thousand and seven hundred; And Zadok, a young man mighty of valour, and of his father's house twenty and two captains. And of the children of Benjamin, the kindred of Saul, three thousand: for hitherto the greatest part of them had kept the ward of the house of Saul. And of the children of Ephraim twenty thousand and eight hundred, mighty men of valour, famous throughout the house of their fathers. And of the half tribe of Manasseh eighteen thousand, which were expressed by name, to come and make David king. And of the children of Issachar, which were men that had understanding of the times, to know what Israel ought to do; the heads of them were two hundred; and all their brethren were at their commandment. Of Zebulun, such as went forth to battle, expert in war, with all instruments of war, fifty thousand, which could keep rank: they were not of double heart. And of Naphtali a thousand captains, and with them with shield and spear thirty and seven thousand. And of the Danites expert in war twenty and eight thousand and six hundred. And of Asher, such as went forth to battle, expert in war, forty thousand. And on the other side of Jordan, of the Reubenites, and the Gadites, and of the half tribe of Manasseh, with all manner of instruments of war for the battle, an hundred and twenty thousand.

Up until this point, Israel had been at civil war. For six years, there had been strife between the house of Saul and the renegade army of David. Now, the strife had ceased. At last, there was unity and tranquility. And the soldiers came forth with one heart, to coronate David as their king. Thousands came from each tribe. But Issachar sent only two hundred men. Was this a sign of their reservation about making David king?

I don't think so. I suggest it wasn't a matter of reservation, but of representation. That is, these two hundred men represented the tribe in its entirety. They had a powerful influence in the tribe of Issachar because they had prophetic insight. They were influential because they were insightful. They were useful because they were knowledgeable. They could oversee the tribe because they understood the times—politically, nationally, prophetically.

We live in a world caught up in terrible confusion. People don't know what's coming down or what to do. But we in the body of Christ can be those who, like these men of Issachar, are very influential because we also have understanding of the times and we know what ought to be done.

1 Chronicles 12:38–40
All these men of war, that could keep rank, came with a perfect heart to Hebron, to make David king over all Israel: and all the rest also of Israel were of one heart to make David king. And there they were with David three days, eating and drinking: for their brethren had prepared for them. Moreover they that were nigh them, even unto Issachar and Zebulun and Naphtali, brought bread on asses, and on camels, and on mules, and on oxen, and meat, meal, cakes of figs, and bunches of raisins, and wine, and oil, and oxen, and sheep abundantly: for there was joy in Israel.

There had been feuding and fighting, battles and bitterness between the armies of Saul and David. But on the day of David's coronation, all those difficulties were forgotten. When the Son of David, Jesus Christ, comes back to rule and reign, every wrong will be righted. Every question will be answered. Every hurt will be healed. Every problem will be forgotten. There will be true celebration at the coming and coronation of our King. Don't miss it!

13

1 Chronicles 13:1
And David consulted with the captains of thousands and hundreds, and with every leader.

Here we see a picture of the practice of plurality as David sought advice and wisdom from the leaders surrounding him.

1 Chronicles 13:2, 3
And David said unto all the congregation of Israel, If it seem good unto you, and that it be of the LORD our God, let us send abroad unto our brethren every where, that are left in all the land of Israel, and with them also to the priests and Levites which are in their cities and suburbs, that they may gather themselves unto us: And let us bring again the ark of our God to us: for we inquired not at it in the days of Saul.

The country had gone through some tough times under Saul's administration. Morale was low. David wanted to see the glory enjoyed in the land once more and he knew that true glory is found only in the presence of the Lord. So he sought to bring back the ark of the covenant. The ark was the gold-covered box that represented and symbolized the glory of God, for it was upon the mercy seat that covered the ark that God said He would meet with man (Exodus 25:22). In the days of Samuel, during a battle between Israel and the Philistines, someone had the bad idea to bring the ark into the battle, thinking the ark would give God's people victory. Even though the Philistines thought they were doomed at that point, they continued fighting and eventually not only beat the Israelites, but captured the ark. In this, it was as if God was reminding His people that He would not be boxed, that His presence would not be reduced to a good luck charm.

Gang, if you are looking to a church or an individual to win your battles, it won't work. If you're looking to a book, a program, or a seminar to see you through, you're headed for defeat. Even fellowship, Bible study, and worship are not ends in themselves. Their purpose is to draw us to Jesus, the only One who can give us true victory.

1 Chronicles 13:4–7
And all the congregation said that they would do so: for the thing was right in the eyes of all the people. So David gathered all Israel together, from Shihor of Egypt even unto the entering of Hamath, to bring the ark of God from Kirjath-jearim. And David went up, and all Israel, to Baalah, that is, to Kirjath-jearim, which belonged to Judah, to bring up thence the ark of God the LORD, that dwelleth between the cherubims, whose name is called on it. And they carried the ark of God in a new cart out of the house of Abinadab: and Uzza and Ahio drave the cart.

In his desire to bring back the ark so that the people might experience the glory of God, David does the right thing, but in the wrong way. He put the ark on a cart, which was the Philistine method, but not God's. In the Book of Numbers, the Lord specifically said the ark was not to be carried by anyone but the Levites—by people who were dedicated to praise.

What is a cart? Nothing more than boards and big wheels. So often, churches try to bring in the glory of God by calling a board meeting and seeing what kind of "big wheels" they can bring in. But that's not the way of the Lord. The presence and glory of God are always brought in on the shoulders of people who praise and worship Him.

1 Chronicles 13:8, 9
And David and all Israel played before God with all their might, and with singing, and

with harps, and with psalteries, and with timbrels, and with cymbals, and with trumpets. And when they came unto the threshingfloor of Chidon, Uzza put forth his hand to hold the ark; for the oxen stumbled.

When the oxen pulling the cart stumbled, *Uzza*, whose name means "strong," did what was natural: he put out his hand to try to stabilize the ark. This seemed so right, but proved to be so wrong, for it is impossible for anyone to truly stabilize a situation in his own strength.

1 Chronicles 13:10–12
And the anger of the LORD was kindled against Uzza, and he smote him, because he put his hand to the ark: and there he died before God. And David was displeased, because the LORD had made a breach upon Uzza: wherefore that place is called Perezuzza to this day. And David was afraid of God that day, saying, How shall I bring the ark of God home to me?

David had done his best to bring the ark back to Jerusalem. But his best wasn't good enough. "How can I do this?" he asks. But no answer from God is recorded because He had already spoken in the Scriptures concerning what should be done. He had already clearly, unmistakably, carefully declared how the ark was to be carried.

If you're at a point where you're saying, "Lord, what do You want me to do? How come this isn't working? What's going on?" and the Lord seems strangely silent, it could be because He's already revealed His heart, His plan, His principles, and He's simply waiting for you to discover them in His Word.

1 Chronicles 13:13, 14
So David brought not the ark home to himself to the city of David, but carried it aside into the house of Obed-edom the Gittite. And the ark of God remained with the family of Obed-edom in his house three months. And the LORD blessed the house of Obed-edom, and all that he had.

Would you have taken the ark into your house? I wonder. After all, when it was in the hands of the Philistines, they were plagued. When the men of Beth-shemesh opened the lid to check its contents, thousands were killed. Here, Uzza touches it and falls down dead. Would *you* have taken the ark into your home? Obed-edom was willing to take the risk. And the Lord blessed him for his willingness.

14

1 Chronicles 14:1
Now Hiram king of Tyre sent messengers to David, and timber of cedars, with masons and carpenters, to build him an house.

Hiram was not a believer and yet he provided materials and skilled workmen to build a house for David. In this, I am reminded of the time Jesus asked a Samaritan woman for a drink of water in order to give her the opportunity to give something to Him (John 4). Sometimes I feel that we in the Christian community have so barricaded ourselves in some ways that we have not allowed the Hirams or Samaritan women of the world to interact with us and, in the process, be exposed to the things of God. I think there are times when the Lord would have us involved with people who don't know Him in order to open the way for the gospel.

1 Chronicles 14:2, 3
And David perceived that the LORD had confirmed him king over Israel, for his kingdom was lifted up on high, because of his people Israel. And David took more wives at Jerusalem: and David begat more sons and daughters.

David increased the number of his wives. But that doesn't mean that God approves the practice. And as David's life unfolds, we'll see his home life is a mess. The Lord lets us see this, I believe, to warn us of the problem of multiple marriages.

1 Chronicles 14:4–9
Now these are the names of his children which he had in Jerusalem; Shammua, and Shobab, Nathan, and Solomon, And Ibhar, and Elishua, and Elpalet, And Nogah, and Nepheg, and Japhia, And Elishama, and Beeliada, and Eliphalet. And when the Philistines heard that David was anointed king over all Israel, all the Philistines went up to seek David. And David heard of it, and went out against them. And the Philistines came and spread themselves in the valley of Rephaim.

Whenever a person is anointed for a task, he can expect the enemy to gather forces and attack him. David was no exception. The greater the anointing, the more intense the attack. If the enemy senses you are moving out in any area of ministry or any sphere of service, he will not take it sitting down. Here, it was when David was anointed king that the Philistines attacked.

1 Chronicles 14:10
And David inquired of God, saying, Shall I go up against the Philistines? and wilt thou deliver them into mine hand? And the LORD said unto him, Go up; for I will deliver them into thine hand.

When faced with the Philistines, David didn't take a poll asking what he should do. He simply asked God.

1 Chronicles 14:11–13
So they came up to Baal-perazim; and David smote them there. Then David said, God hath broken in upon mine enemies by mine hand like the breaking forth of waters: therefore they called the name of that place Baal-perazim. And when they had left their gods there, David gave a commandment, and they were burned with fire. And the Philistines yet again spread themselves abroad in the valley.

Philistines don't give up easily. Perhaps you've experienced a victory in your life over an attack of the enemy. But one victory doesn't mean the enemy gives up. He retreats only to regroup.

1 Chronicles 14:14
Therefore David inquired again of God; and God said unto him, Go not up after them; turn away from them, and come upon them over against the mulberry trees.

David had already asked God if he should wage war against the Philistines in verse 10. Here, in verse 14, he asks Him again. My tendency would be to say, "Why inquire of the Lord again? After all, it's the same situation, the same battle, the same enemy, the same place." But David, a man after God's own heart, sought God's heart in the matter. And this time, God told him not to attack. This time His answer was different.

Gang, if we're not careful, we can say, "Well, the Lord did this for me back in 1976. Now that I'm in the same situation, the same formula will work." Not necessarily. The Lord wants us to be in tune with Him and dependent upon Him in every circumstance. I believe this is the secret of David's success. He kept on inquiring at every juncture.

1 Chronicles 14:15
And it shall be, when thou shalt hear a sound of going in the tops of the mulberry trees, that then thou shalt go out to battle: for God is gone forth before thee to smite the host of the Philistines.

If I were instructed to wait until I heard the sound of leaves blowing in the wind before I did something, I think my tendency would be to say, "How will I really know that's You, Lord, and not just normal wind?" This is a question we often ask. Events transpire and we wonder whether they are the result of our prayer or simply the result of natural circumstance. The answer, however, is that the Lord is in just as much control of natural circumstances as He is of supernatural ones. Therefore, we can rest in His sovereignty over every situation.

1 Chronicles 14:16, 17
David therefore did as God commanded him: and they smote the host of the Philistines from Gibeon even to Gazer. And the fame of David went out into all lands; and the LORD brought the fear of him upon all nations.

Although David's fame is spreading and his fortune is increasing, he's still restless inside. Why? The answer is seen in chapter 15 . . .

15

1 Chronicles 15:1
And David made him houses in the city of David, and prepared a place for the ark of God, and pitched for it a tent.

The word, "glory," in Hebrew is *chabod* and means "weighty or heavy." Whether he knows it or not, every person hungers for the glory of God in his life. We seek to satisfy that hunger sometimes by eating, going to a movie, or watching TV. Yet the emptiness remains. Then we come into the presence of the Lord, spend time on our knees or in praise and suddenly we're satisfied.

Dear brother, precious sister, the aching in your heart, the stirring in your soul, is the cry of your spirit for the glory of God. David knew this. He had fame and fortune but they were not enough. He longed for the chabod, and knew it was to be experienced most fully at the mercy seat atop the ark.

1 Chronicles 15:2
Then David said, None ought to carry the ark of God but the Levites: for them hath the LORD chosen to carry the ark of God, and to minister unto him for ever.

David's previous failure in his attempt to move the ark was not meant to frustrate him, but rather to motivate him to search the Scriptures. This verse tells us David did just that. Evidently, he spent three months studying and finally he found the passage that said the Levites were the ones who were to carry the ark.

Have you failed recently in some area? God is not trying to frustrate you, but to motivate you to spend time in His Word as you seek Him more diligently.

1 Chronicles 15:3–14
And David gathered all Israel together to Jerusalem, to bring up the ark of the LORD unto his place, which he had prepared for it. And David assembled the children of Aaron, and the Levites: Of the sons of Kohath; Uriel the chief, and his brethren an hundred and twenty: Of the sons of Merari; Asaiah the chief, and his brethren two hundred and twenty: Of the sons of Gershom; Joel the chief, and his brethren an hundred and thirty: Of the sons of Elizaphan; Shemaiah the chief, and his brethren two hundred: Of the sons of Hebron; Eliel the chief, and his brethren fourscore: Of the sons of Uzziel; Amminadab the chief, and his brethren an hundred and twelve. And David called for Zadok and Abiathar the priests, and for the Levites, for Uriel, Asaiah, and Joel, Shemaiah, and Eliel, and Amminadab, And said unto them, Ye are the chief of the fathers of the Levites: sanctify yourselves, both ye and your brethren, that ye may bring up the ark of the LORD God of Israel unto the place that I have prepared for it. For because ye did it not at the first, the LORD our God made a breach upon us, for that we sought him not after the due order. So the priests and the Levites sanctified themselves to bring up the ark of the LORD God of Israel.

David had prepared a place for the ark. Here, he prepares the people for the ark.

1 Chronicles 15:15–22
And the children of the Levites bare the ark of God upon their shoulders with the staves thereon, as Moses commanded according to the word of the LORD. And David spake to the chief of the Levites to appoint their brethren to be the singers with instruments of musick, psalteries and harps and cymbals, sounding, by lifting up the voice with joy. So the Levites appointed Heman the son of Joel; and of his brethren, Asaph the son of Berechiah; and of the sons of Merari their brethren, Ethan the son of Kushaiah; And with them their brethren of the second degree, Zechariah, Ben, and Jaaziel, and Shemiramoth, and Jehiel, and Unni, Eliab, and Benaiah, and Maaseiah, and Mattithiah, and Elipheleh, and Mikneiah, and Obed-edom, and Jeiel, the porters. So the singers, Heman, Asaph, and Ethan, were appointed to sound with cymbals of brass; And Zechariah, and Aziel, and Shemiramoth, and Jehiel, and Unni, and Eliab, and Maaseiah, and Benaiah, with psalteries on Alamoth; And Mattithiah, and Elipheleh, and Mikneiah, and Obed-edom, and Jeiel, and Azaziah, with harps on the Sheminith to excel. And Chenaniah, chief of the Levites, was for song: he instructed about the song, because he was skilful.

The musicians were divided into three groups under the leadership of Heman, Asaph, and Ethan.

1 Chronicles 15:23–26
And Berechiah and Elkanah were doorkeepers for the ark. And Shebaniah, and Jehoshaphat, and Nethaneel, and Amasai, and Zechariah, and Benaiah, and Eliezer, the priests, did blow with the trumpets before the ark of God: and Obed-edom and Jehiah were doorkeepers for the ark. So David, and the elders of Israel, and the captains over thousands, went to bring up the ark of the covenant of the LORD out of the house of Obed-edom with joy. And it came to pass, when God helped the Levites that bare the ark of the covenant of the LORD, that they offered seven bullocks and seven rams.

Considering the number of people who had died (1 Samuel 5:9, 6:19; 1 Chronicles 13:10), being in proximity to the ark was risky business. Yet here, the ark is carried with joy. Why? Because they knew God would help them. Thus it was, no doubt, with a spirit of relief and hearts of thanksgiving that the Levites offered sacrifice to the Lord.

Samuel tells us this sacrifice was offered every six steps (2 Samuel 6:13). This was not very efficient, to say the least. Efficiency is doing things right. But God is not interested in efficiency. He's interested in effectiveness—which is doing the right thing. Six is the number of the flesh. Consequently, here we see the need to continually say, "Oh, Lord, my flesh is welling up again. I am vulnerable to doing things in my flesh and to hearing my flesh take credit for that which only You can do. I must buld an altar to remind me of You."

Maybe you are experiencing problems in your marriage, your family, your business, or your relationships. Wherever you see problems—the lack of God's glory and substance—the solution is to worship. The glory of God will enter not by might, nor by power, but by His Spirit (Zechariah 4:6), brought in upon the shoulders of people who praise.

1 Chronicles 15:27, 28
And David was clothed with a robe of fine linen, and all the Levites that bare the ark, and the singers, and Chenaniah the master of the song with the singers: David also had upon him an ephod of linen. Thus all Israel brought up the ark of the covenant of the LORD with shouting, and with sound of the cornet, and with trumpets, and with cymbals, making a noise with psalteries and harps.

On the basis of verses 22 and 25, I believe this music was both skillful and joyful.

1 Chronicles 15:29
And it came to pass, as the ark of the covenant of the LORD came to the city of David, that Michal the daughter of Saul looking out at a window saw king David dancing and playing: and she despised him in her heart.

Samuel tells us that because Michal rebuked David for his worship, she would be barren all the days of her life (2 Samuel 6:23). The same is still true. Those who put down worship bring into their own lives a barrenness and an emptiness.

Parenthetically, many commentators suggest it was at this point—when Michal rebuked David—that the seeds were sown in David's heart which eventually culminated in his affair with Bathsheba. Dear brother, precious sister, if you're not joining your husband or wife on the pathway to a closer, deeper walk with the Lord, you're setting yourself up for heartbreak. Don't make Michal's mistake. Serve the Lord together with passion and intensity, and not only will your heart be drawn closer to the Lord, but you will draw closer to each other as well.

16

1 Chronicles 16:1–3
So they brought the ark of God, and set it in the midst of the tent that David had pitched for it: and they offered burnt sacrifices and peace offerings before God. And when David had made an end of offering the burnt offerings and the peace offerings, he blessed the people in the name of the LORD. And he dealt to every one of Israel, both man and woman, to every one a loaf of bread, and a good piece of flesh, and a flagon of wine.

The wine and bread given to the people in celebration of the return of the ark speak to me of the celebration we experience at the Lord's Table where we, too, experience the mercy and glory of God. The piece of meat they were given speaks to me of the joy that is ours as we partake of the meat of God's Word (Jeremiah 15:16).

1 Chronicles 16:4–6
And he appointed certain of the Levites to minister before the ark of the LORD, and to record, and to thank and praise the LORD God of Israel: Asaph the chief, and next to him Zechariah, Jeiel, and Shemiramoth, and Jehiel, and Mattithiah, and Eliab, and Benaiah, and Obed-edom: and Jeiel with psalteries and with harps; but Asaph made a sound with cymbals; Benaiah also and Jahaziel the priests with trumpets continually before the ark of the covenant of God.

It was the job of certain of the Levites simply to record the Lord's blessings. I encourage you to try keeping a record of the blessings of God in your life. At the end of the day, write down the various ways God provided for you. I guarantee you will be surprised at His faithfulness every step of every day.

1 Chronicles 16:7–22
Then on that day David delivered first this psalm to thank the LORD into the hand of Asaph and his brethren. Give thanks unto the LORD, call upon his name, make known his deeds among the people. Sing unto him, sing psalms unto him, talk ye of all his wondrous works. Glory ye in his holy name: let the heart of them rejoice that seek the LORD. Seek the LORD and his strength, seek his face continually. Remember his marvellous works that he hath done, his wonders, and the judgments of his mouth; O ye seed of Israel his servant, ye children of Jacob, his chosen ones. He is the LORD our God; his judgments are in all the earth. Be ye mindful always of his covenant; the word which he commanded to a thousand generations; Even of the covenant which he made with Abraham, and of his oath unto Isaac; And hath confirmed the same to Jacob for a law, and to Israel for an everlasting covenant, Saying, Unto thee will I give the land of Canaan, the lot of your inheritance; When ye were but few, even a few, and strangers in it. And when they went from nation to nation, and from one kingdom to another people; He suffered no man to do them wrong: yea, he reproved kings for their sakes, Saying, Touch not mine anointed, and do my prophets no harm.

This first portion of David's psalm is also seen in Psalm 105.

1 Chronicles 16:23–36 (a)
Sing unto the LORD, all the earth; shew forth from day to day his salvation. Declare his glory among the heathen; his marvellous works among all nations. For great is the LORD, and greatly to be praised: he also is to be feared above all gods. For all the gods of the people are idols: but the LORD made the heavens. Glory and honour are in his presence; strength and gladness are in his place. Give unto the LORD, ye kindreds of the people, give unto the LORD glory and strength. Give unto the LORD the glory due unto his name: bring an offering, and come before him: worship the LORD in the beauty of holiness. Fear before him, all the earth: the world also shall be stable, that it be not moved. Let the heavens be glad, and let the earth rejoice: and let men say among the nations, The LORD reigneth. Let the sea roar, and the fulness thereof: let the fields rejoice, and all that is therein. Then shall the trees of the wood sing out at the presence of the LORD, because he cometh to judge the earth. O give thanks unto the LORD; for he is good; for his mercy endureth for ever. And say ye, Save us, O God of our salvation, and gather us together, and deliver us from the heathen, that we may give thanks to thy holy name, and glory in thy praise. Blessed be the LORD God of Israel for ever and ever . . .

This second half of David's song is found in Psalm 96. Sometimes people ask how to worship. David's Psalm provides a great answer. Work your way right through it. Give thanks. Make known His deeds. Glory in His name. Seek His face. The Psalms in their entirety provide a workbook on worship. If you don't know how to worship, read the Book of Psalms and do what they say. When a Psalm says, "Shout," shout; when it says, "Clap," clap; when it says, "Sing," sing; when it says, "Bow down," bow down, and see if your heart doesn't rejoice as you draw close to the Lord in wonderful ways.

1 Chronicles 16:36 (b)
. . . And all the people said, Amen, and praised the LORD.

All the people said, "Amen," or, literally, "So be it." In this, they were not simply encouraging David, but were themselves establishing what was being spoken. When people pray publicly, we also have an opportunity to say, "Amen." First Corinthians 14 tells us that the early church practiced the saying of "Amen." It's a wonderful opportunity indeed to establish our prayers through speaking faith together.

1 Chronicles 16:37–43
So he left there before the ark of the covenant of the LORD Asaph and his brethren, to minister before the ark continually, as every day's work required: And Obed-edom with their brethren, threescore and eight; Obed-edom also the son of Jeduthun and Hosah to be porters: And Zadok the priest, and his brethren the priests, before the tabernacle of the LORD in the high place that was at Gibeon, To offer burnt offerings unto the LORD upon the altar of the burnt offering continually morning and evening, and to do according to all that is written in the law of the LORD, which he commanded Israel; And with them Heman and Jeduthun, and the rest that were chosen, who were expressed by name, to give thanks to the LORD, because his mercy endureth for ever; And with them Heman and Jeduthun with trumpets and cymbals for those that should make a sound, and with musical instruments of God. And the sons of Jeduthun were porters. And all the people departed every man to his house: and David returned to bless his house.

Notice that it was after being in God's house that the people returned to bless their own houses. Some people think church interferes with family. I believe just the opposite. I believe that church inspires the family. I believe that when families come and hear the Word, the time they spend together is infinitely richer and more profitable than anything else they could do.

17

1 Chronicles 17:1
Now it came to pass, as David sat in his house, that David said to Nathan the prophet, Lo, I dwell in an house of cedars, but the ark of the covenant of the LORD remaineth under curtains.

At last, the ark was safely in Jerusalem. For any other man, that would have been enough. But not for David. This man in relentless pursuit of the heart of his God longed to do more.

1 Chronicles 17:2
Then Nathan said unto David, Do all that is in thine heart; for God is with thee.

Nathan was a godly man, but, like all men, he was fallible. What sounded so right was not the Lord's plan.

1 Chronicles 17:3–15
And it came to pass the same night, that the word of God came to Nathan, saying, Go

and tell David my servant, Thus saith the LORD, Thou shalt not build me an house to dwell in: For I have not dwelt in an house since the day that I brought up Israel unto this day; but have gone from tent to tent, and from one tabernacle to another. Wheresoever I have walked with all Israel, spake I a word to any of the judges of Israel, whom I commanded to feed my people, saying, Why have ye not built me an house of cedars? Now therefore thus shalt thou say unto my servant David, Thus saith the LORD of hosts, I took thee from the sheepcote, even from following the sheep, that thou shouldest be ruler over my people Israel: And I have been with thee whithersoever thou hast walked, and have cut off all thine enemies from before thee, and have made thee a name like the name of the great men that are in the earth. Also I will ordain a place for my people Israel, and will plant them, and they shall dwell in their place, and shall be moved no more; neither shall the children of wickedness waste them any more, as at the beginning, And since the time that I commanded judges to be over my people Israel. Moreover I will subdue all thine enemies. Furthermore I tell thee that the LORD will build thee an house. And it shall come to pass, when thy days be expired that thou must go to be with thy fathers, that I will raise up thy seed after thee, which shall be of thy sons; and I will establish his kingdom. He shall build me an house, and I will stablish his throne for ever. I will be his father, and he shall be my son: and I will not take my mercy away from him, as I took it from him that was before thee: But I will settle him in mine house and in my kingdom for ever: and his throne shall be established for evermore. According to all these words, and according to all this vision, so did Nathan speak unto David.

"Nathan, tell David that although he can't build Me a house, I will build him a house, for from his seed will come One who will reign forever." This is so like the Lord. He tempers our earthly disappointments with eternal blessings.

1 Chronicles 17:16–27

And David the king came and sat before the LORD, and said, Who am I, O LORD God, and what is mine house, that thou hast brought me hitherto? And yet this was a small thing in thine eyes, O God; for thou hast also spoken of thy servant's house for a great while to come, and hast regarded me according to the estate of a man of high degree, O LORD God. What can David speak more to thee for the honour of thy servant? for thou knowest thy servant. O LORD, for thy servant's sake, and according to thine own heart, hast thou done all this greatness, in making known all these great things. O LORD, there is none like thee, neither is there any God beside thee, according to all that we have heard with our ears. And what one nation in the earth is like thy people Israel, whom God went to redeem to be his own people, to make thee a name of greatness and terribleness, by driving out nations from before thy people, whom thou hast redeemed out of Egypt? For thy people Israel didst thou make thine own people for ever; and thou, LORD, becamest their God. Therefore now, LORD, let the thing that thou hast spoken concerning thy servant and concerning his house be established for ever, and do as thou hast said. Let it even be established, that thy name may be magnified for ever, saying, The LORD of hosts is the God of Israel, even a God to Israel: and let the house of David thy servant be established before thee. For thou, O my God, hast told thy servant that thou wilt build him an house: therefore thy servant hath found in his heart to pray before thee. And now, LORD, thou art God, and hast promised this goodness unto thy servant: Now therefore let it please thee to bless the house of thy servant, that it may be before thee for ever: for thou blessest, O LORD, and it shall be blessed for ever.

David understood that the prophecy was messianic that he would be an ancestor of the Messiah. What a glorious promise. But, saint, God has given you an even greater promise, for you are not simply an ancestor of Messiah. Rather, you are linked to Messiah. You are the Bride of Christ. Consequently, no matter what the Lord is doing or not doing in your life, regardless of whether your ministry opens up as you hoped, or your dream is fulfilled as you desired, like David, you should sit before the Lord and marvel, saying, "Lord, the fact that You would let me be a lover of You, related to You, a part of You causes me to praise You forever and ever. I'll worship You enthusiastically, consistently, throughout eternity. I'll love You forevermore."

I believe it wearies our Lord to hear His children continually complain and groan about what they don't have, about what's not going right. We of all people should rejoice evermore because of what the Lord has done. I encourage you to ask Him to show you what He has already done for you. If you do, I guarantee that, like David, you'll be rendered speechless.

WHEN GOD SAYS NO

A Topical Study of 1 CHRONICLES 17

When my daughters, Jessie and Christy, were young, I ended up looking like the heavy in their eyes every week because it seemed like almost every Sunday, on our way to church, someone was giving away kittens.

"Daddy, can we take a kitten home today?" they would ask.

And my answer would always be the same: "No."

The reason I said no every week was because we already had a cat named Gabriel. Gabriel was a mellow cat. But one day he did something that I couldn't tell my daughters about. You see, one day, a little kitten wandered into our yard. The girls named it Snowball. I sent them around the neighborhood to ask if anyone had lost a kitten. But no one had. So we kept Snowball. It wasn't long, however, before there was trouble between Gabriel and the newcomer. Gabriel eyed him suspiciously. Then, about four or five days after his arrival, Snowball had the audacity and the poor judgment to eat Gabriel's food. When Gabriel came by, the kitten arched its back, hissed, and clawed Gabriel's face. That did it. Gabriel's fur stood up and he took off after the kitten. Snowball ran for his life—and I never saw him again.

So, because I had seen another side of Gabriel, I became reluctant to bring any other kitten home. Consequently, when Christy and Jessie asked if they could have a kitten, I always said, *No.* But I didn't explain the whole story because I didn't want them to think badly of Gabriel. Even though I came across as the heavy, as a father, I had a responsibility to do what was best for my household, even if my girls didn't understand.

Our heavenly Father has that same responsibility. Oftentimes, He says *No* to our requests without giving a reason why.

Our Father is ready and desirous to answer our prayers but His answer can be one of three: He can say, *Yes,* and grant our request. Or, He can say, *Wait.* Or He can say, *No.* No matter how spiritual you are, how mature you might be in the things of the Lord, there will come times when He says *No* to you. There was never a more spiritual man in all of the Bible than David, for he alone was called a man after God's own heart. David had a love for the Lord and was in love with the Lord and yet sometimes the Lord said *No,* even to him.

Such is the case in the text before us. At this time, although David was not yet forty years old, he was remarkably successful. He had established his kingdom, subdued his enemies, and prospered materially. Yet as he sat in his palace, his heart and mind wandered outside, to the ark of the covenant. Feeling it wasn't right that he lived in a palace while the ark was in a tent, David declared he wanted to build a temple for God.

"A wonderful idea," the prophet Nathan declared.

But the Lord corrected both Nathan and David.

"Tell David he can't build Me a house." But then He went on to do something so characteristic of Him: He tempered David's disappointment with a new appointment.

Perhaps today you are confused by why the Lord seems to be saying *No* to you.

"Lord," you say, "I've offered myself to go to the mission field. Why have You closed the door?"

"Lord, I wanted to adopt that child, to bring that baby into our home. Why hasn't the door opened?"

"Lord, I started that business, desiring that it would prosper financially so that I could give the profits to Your work. Instead, I'm bankrupt. It failed. Why?"

"Lord, I wanted to marry him and be a help to him. Why hasn't that relationship developed?"

There are so many areas we offer to the Lord. All seem like good ideas, inspired ideas, right ideas, but the Lord shuts the door and simply says *No*. If we're not careful, at that point, we are vulnerable to becoming bitter. How do we keep from blaming God and becoming bitter? The answer is to do what David did when the Lord said *No* to him . . .

Don't Stomp Out. Sit Down.

And David the king came and sat before the LORD *. . .* 1 Chronicles 17:16 (a)

David could have been very hurt. He could have stood up to the Lord. He could have stomped out from the Lord. Instead, he sat before the Lord.

When God says *No*, the first thing we must do is what David did: sit down, slow down, quiet down. Because David sat before the Lord, he was both enlightened and encouraged. In chapter 22:7, we read that David understood the reason he couldn't build the temple was because he was a man of war, whereas Solomon would be a man of peace. Surely, David would never have received this enlightenment had he stomped out angrily.

Secondly, in addition to enlightenment he received encouragement. In 2 Chronicles 6:8, we read that, as Solomon dedicated the temple, the Lord whispered in the ear of David, "For inasmuch as it was in thine heart, thou didst well." Dear folks, when the Lord says *No* to you—and He will—don't stomp out. Sit down. And, in due time, you'll hear words of both enlightenment and encouragement.

Don't Fret. Focus.

. . . for thou hast also spoken of thy servant's house for a great while to come, and hast regarded me according to the estate of a man of high degree, O LORD *God.* 1 Chronicles 17:17 (b)

When the Lord says *No*, don't fret and fuss and fume. Instead, focus on the blessing. We should be continually blown away and blessed by what God has already done. God chose us before the beginning of the world. He sent His Son to save us. He placed His Spirit within our hearts. He is preparing a place for us to live with Him eternally. Let us never, ever forget what God has *already* done for us.

Don't Pout on the Premises. Pray in the Promises.

And now, LORD, thou art God, and hast promised this goodness unto thy servant . . . 1 Chronicles 17:26 (a)

After he blessed the Lord for what He said He would do, David prayed on the basis of His promise. We must do the same. If bills are piling up, say, "On the basis of Your promise to supply all our needs, Lord, I trust in You." If you long to be married, say, "Lord, Your Word says if I delight in You, You will give me the desire of my heart. Therefore, on the basis of that promise, I'm asking that you fulfill my desires or change my heart." If you're worried, say, "Lord, Your Word says You will keep him in perfect peace whose mind is stayed on You. Therefore, according to Your promise, I ask that You inject me with Your peace."

Gang, with over 3,000 promises in the Word, there is no shortage of things to pray in!

Don't Complain about What You Can't Do. Do What You Can.

Now, behold, in my trouble I have prepared for the house of the LORD an hundred thousand talents of gold . . . 1 Chronicles 22:14 (a)

In the coming chapters, we'll see David gathering his army to raid the enemy territory surrounding Israel. The gold, silver, and other riches from those territories were brought to Jerusalem and laid in store for the temple David knew his son would build. He gathered the architects to draw up plans for the temple. He hired workers to go into the quarries to prepare the stones. He raised taxes, gathered materials, and gave of his own wealth. He did everything he possibly could, short of building it himself.

I like that! Maybe you can't go to the mission field. Do what you can do. Pray for those who are ministering overseas. Give ten percent above your tithe to support other missionaries. If you can't adopt a child, help support one either here or abroad. If your business didn't work out, join someone else's business and help him. It is the man after God's own heart who does what he can rather than complain about what he can't.

Our Father knows best. He really does. Jessie and Christy didn't know why I wouldn't let them have a kitten. But I knew why. Our heavenly Father, who knows your situation better than you do yourself, says, "Child, even though you don't see it and I can't explain it, I want you to trust Me."

And I guarantee that, as you look back over the years at the times God said *No*, you'll say, "Glory to You, Father. You're always right. Veto my plans whenever You want."

18 1 Chronicles 18:1–4
Now after this it came to pass, that David smote the Philistines, and subdued them, and took Gath and her towns out of the hand of the Philistines. And he smote Moab; and the Moabites became David's servants, and brought gifts. And David smote Hadarezer king of Zobah unto Hamath, as he went to stablish his dominion by the river Euphrates. And David took from him a thousand chariots, and seven thousand horsemen, and twenty thousand footmen: David also houghed all the chariot horses, but reserved of them an hundred chariots.

In Deuteronomy 17, the word was given to kings that they were not to multiply to themselves horses because the Lord wanted His people to be dependent only upon Him. Therefore, wanting to be obedient to the Lord, when he captured these horses, David destroyed them.

1 Chronicles 18:5, 6
And when the Syrians of Damascus came to help Hadarezer king of Zobah, David slew of the Syrians two and twenty thousand men. Then David put garrisons in Syriadamascus; and the Syrians became David's servants, and brought gifts. Thus the LORD preserved David whithersoever he went.

Wherever David went, the Lord protected him. In this, we must realize that, as the people of God, we are indestructible until the Lord's time comes for us to go home. "It is appointed unto man once to die," we read in Hebrews 9:27. There is a day, an hour predetermined by the Lord in which you will go home. But until that time comes, you're indestructible. That is the reason that, although the crowd reacted so unfavorably to Jesus' first sermon in a synagogue that they wanted to throw Him over a cliff, He was able to walk right through them unharmed (Luke 4).

1 Chronicles 18:7, 8
And David took the shields of gold that were on the servants of Hadarezer, and brought them to Jerusalem. Likewise from Tibhath, and from Chun, cities of Hadarezer, brought David very much brass, wherewith Solomon made the brasen sea, and the pillars, and the vessels of brass.

David desired to build a temple for the Lord. The Lord, however, forbade him, saying his son would build the temple. Instead of complaining about what he couldn't do, David set out to do all he possibly could. Here, he's gathering materials for that very purpose.

A little boy was given a brand new toy sailboat. Thrilled with the gift, he took it out to a little lake nearby. As he held the string, the boat sailed out to the middle of the lake. Then, suddenly, a huge wind arose that snapped the string and capsized the boat. As he watched his brand new boat sink, the boy said, "Wow! What a great day to fly a kite!"

I like that! Instead of complaining about the wind that sank his boat, he got a kite and flew it. That's the heart of David. He didn't bemoan the fact that he couldn't build the temple. Instead he said, "I'm a man of war and I'll utilize that ability to gather material for the temple."

1 Chronicles 18:9–11
Now when Tou king of Hamath heard how David had smitten all the host of Hadarezer king of Zobah; He sent Hadoram his son to king David, to inquire of his welfare, and to congratulate him, because he had fought against Hadarezer, and smitten him; (for Hadarezer had war with Tou;) and with him all manner of vessels of gold and silver and brass. Them also king David dedicated unto the LORD, with the silver and the gold that he brought from all these nations; from Edom, and from Moab, and from the children of Ammon, and from the Philistines, and from Amalek.

Tou was a smart man. When he saw everyone else getting wiped out, he evidently decided, "If you can't beat 'em, join 'em." So he sent a word of congratulations and some gifts to appease David, which David, in turn, dedicated to the work of the Lord.

1 Chronicles 18:12–15
Moreover Abishai the son of Zeruiah slew of the Edomites in the valley of salt eighteen thousand. And he put garrisons in Edom; and all the Edomites became David's servants. Thus the LORD preserved David whithersoever he went. So David reigned over all Israel, and executed judgment and justice among all his people. And Joab the son of Zeruiah was over the host; and Jehoshaphat the son of Ahilud, recorder.

Joab was the general and Jehoshaphat was the recorder, the one who kept notes of all that God was doing.

1 Chronicles 18:16, 17
And Zadok the son of Ahitub, and Abimelech the son of Abiathar, were the priests; and Shavsha was scribe; And Benaiah the son of Jehoiada was over the Cherethites and the Pelethites; and the sons of David were chief about the king.

Zadok and Abimelech were both high priests—Zadok at Gibeon and Abimelech at Jerusalem.

19

1 Chronicles 19:1–5
Now it came to pass after this, that Nahash the king of the children of Ammon died, and his son reigned in his stead. And David said, I will shew kindness unto Hanun the son of Nahash, because his father shewed kindness to me. And David sent messengers to comfort him concerning his father. So the servants of David came into the land of the children of Ammon to Hanun, to comfort him. But the princes of the children of Ammon said to Hanun, Thinkest thou that David doth honour thy father, that he hath sent comforters unto thee? are not his servants come unto thee for to search, and to overthrow, and to spy out the land? Wherefore Hanun took David's servants, and shaved them, and cut off their garments in the midst hard by their buttocks, and sent them away. Then there went certain, and told David how the men were served. And he sent to meet them: for the men were greatly ashamed. And the king said, Tarry at Jericho until your beards be grown, and then return.

David was genuinely trying to express a heart of love and compassion toward Nahash's son, Hanun. But the sin of suspicion was in the heart of Hanun and his men. "These guys aren't really here to give condolences," they said. They're nothing more than spies." So Hanun shaved their beards—a disgrace in that day—and exposed their backsides in order to humiliate them. When David heard about it, he told them to wait in Jericho until their beards grew back.

Jesus told us to share both love and the gospel with those who are in the world. But He also warned us that even as the world persecuted Him, so it would persecute us (John 15:20). Therefore, we must not be surprised when we are humiliated, embarrassed, and put down. Due to the tendency toward suspicion in all of us, people who don't know Jesus will treat you like you're trying to rip them off when all you're trying to do is help them out.

"Blessed are ye when men shall revile you and persecute you and say all manner of evil against you falsely for My sake," Jesus said, "for so persecuted they the prophets before you" (see Matthew 5:11, 12). Therefore, if people are coming against you, you're in good company—the company of the prophets.

"But I'll never recover from that criticism or suspicion," you say.

Yes you will. Your beard will grow back and you'll be strengthened to serve all the more.

1 Chronicles 19:6–10
And when the children of Ammon saw that they had made themselves odious to David, Hanun and the children of Ammon sent a thousand talents of silver to hire them chariots and horsemen out of Mesopotamia, and out of Syria-maachah, and out of Zobah. So they hired thirty and two thousand chariots, and the king of Maachah and his people; who came and pitched before Medeba. And the children of Ammon gathered themselves together from their cities, and came to battle. And when David heard of it, he sent Joab, and all the host of the mighty men. And the children of Ammon came out, and put the battle in array before the gate of the city: and the kings that were come were by themselves in the field. Now when Joab saw that the battle was set against him before and behind, he chose out of all the choice of Israel, and put them in array against the Syrians.

David sent Joab to lead the troops against the soldiers Hanun had hired from Mesopotamia and Syria. Take heart, dear saint. You might be embarrassed or humiliated, put down, made fun of, persecuted, mocked, or wrongly accused. But there is One who will fight for you (Exodus 14:14). David's servants were put down, but David came to their defense, just as the Son of David will come to your defense in due time.

1 Chronicles 19:11, 12
And the rest of the people he delivered unto the hand of Abishai his brother, and they set themselves in array against the children of Ammon. And he said, If the Syrians be too strong for me, then thou shalt help me: but

if the children of Ammon be too strong for thee, then I will help thee.

Not only were Joab and Abishai brothers by birth, but they were also brothers in battle, fighting a common foe. "If you get overpowered, I'll bring my troops and help you," Abishai said to Joab. "If I get overpowered, you bring your troops and help me."

Gang, this is exactly what we need in the church of Jesus Christ. We need to realize we're fighting a common foe—Satan and the hordes of hell. Therefore, we must not fight each other or fault each other. Yes, we're in different places on the battlefield—different positions, different ministries, different callings. But when some other part of the body is in need, let us be the first to rush to their aid, to support them, stand by them, and assist them in any way we can.

1 Chronicles 19:13
Be of good courage, and let us behave ourselves valiantly for our people, and for the cities of our God: and let the LORD do that which is good in his sight.

These men were armed, trained, and ready to do battle, but they realized the results would have to be left to the Lord. They did what they could, but realized only the Lord could bring about ultimate victory.

I feel it's important we adopt a similar attitude—that we do the very best we can do in situations of spiritual warfare and ministry, and leave the rest with the Lord. I fear that we are sometimes reluctant to pray for the sick because we're worried they won't be healed. I fear we're hesitant to pray for those who are worried or depressed for fear that they will remain in their state. The Lord will do what's right in His sight. Our job is simply to prepare for the battle, to place ourselves in positions to do whatever we can do.

If you say to someone, "Dear brother, let me pray for you," and you pray the prayer of faith and seek the Lord—even if that situation does not seemingly or immediately improve or change, you will have done what you can do. Not only is that pleasing in the sight of the Lord, but it will inevitably be appreciated by the person for whom you pray. All too often, we don't pray or move in faith because we fear people will get disillusioned or disappointed if things don't work out the way we think they should.

I suggest that we should say, "We're going to do everything we can. We're going to pray fervently. We're going to work hard. We're going to see what we can do to the best of our ability. But then, Lord, we submit to Your sovereignty and Your wisdom to do what is right."

Pray for each other, dear saints. And don't let fear quench your desire or your aggressiveness in prayer.

1 Chronicles 19:14–18
So Joab and the people that were with him drew nigh before the Syrians unto the battle; and they fled before him. And when the children of Ammon saw that the Syrians were fled, they likewise fled before Abishai his brother, and entered into the city. Then Joab came to Jerusalem. And when the Syrians saw that they were put to the worse before Israel, they sent messengers, and drew forth the Syrians that were beyond the river: and Shophach the captain of the host of Hadarezer went before them. And it was told David; and he gathered all Israel, and passed over Jordan, and came upon them, and set the battle in array against them. So when David had put the battle in array against the Syrians, they fought with him. But the Syrians fled before Israel; and David slew of the Syrians seven thousand men which fought in chariots, and forty thousand footmen, and killed Shophach the captain of the host.

Why were the Israelites victorious? Because they did their best and trusted the Lord.

1 Chronicles 19:19
And when the servants of Hadarezer saw that they were put to the worse before Israel, they made peace with David, and became his servants: neither would the Syrians help the children of Ammon any more.

Not only did Israel win the battle, but the servants of Hadarezer switched sides and became servants of David. I believe this is what it means to be "more than a conqueror" (Romans 8:37)—to not only gain victory against the sin that seeks to dominate us, but, to make it our servant as it serves to show us our need for the Lord every step of the way.

20

1 Chronicles 20:1 (a)
And it came to pass, that after the year was expired, at the time that kings go out to battle, Joab led forth the power of the army, and wasted the country of the children of Ammon, and came and besieged Rabbah . . .

Israel is one of very few countries in the world that has no indigenous sport. In Old Testament times, the Israelites didn't have time for sports. Their national life consisted of two activites: war and worship. Spring was "the time that kings go out to battle" because it wouldn't be too cold and the chariot wheels wouldn't get stuck in the mud.

1 Chronicles 20:1 (b)
. . . But David tarried at Jerusalem . . .

This is when David committed adultery with Bathsheba. David should have been in battle with Joab, but because he wasn't, he was vulnerable to sin. I find it interesting that the text makes no mention of David's sin. We would know nothing of it were it not for the parallel passage in 2 Samuel. In 1 Samuel 25, Samuel died. Therefore, most scholars believe the ending of 1 Samuel and all of 2 Samuel were the work of David. If this is true, it was David who wrote of his own sin in great detail while Ezra, the author of 1 Chronicles, doesn't even mention it. This tells me that any man can deal publicly with his own sin if he feels it would serve as a warning to others. But no one else has a right to talk about someone else's sin. Ezra simply and wisely said, "David tarried in Jerusalem."

1 Chronicles 20:1 (c), 2
. . . And Joab smote Rabbah, and destroyed it. And David took the crown of their king from off his head, and found it to weigh a talent of gold, and there were precious stones in it; and it was set upon David's head: and he brought also exceeding much spoil out of the city.

After the victory was secured, Joab called for David to symbolically enter the city and take the king's crown.

1 Chronicles 20:3
And he brought out the people that were in it, and cut them with saws, and with harrows of iron, and with axes. Even so dealt David with all the cities of the children of Ammon. And David and all the people returned to Jerusalem.

Why did David cut the people with saws and axes? I suggest it was for the same reason that he imposed the death penalty on a man who stole a lamb (2 Samuel 12:5). There is a tendency within people to become harsh, critical, and cruel when they are themselves involved in sin. The most godly people I know are also the most gracious people I know. The most spiritual people I know are also the most merciful people I know. Mercy, grace, and love are characteristics of godliness and holiness. Harshness, judgment, and criticism are often indicative of sin in one's own life.

Once David made confession, as seen in Psalm 51, once repentance took place, as Acts 20:21 says, David's fellowship with the Lord was immediately restored. And the same is true of us. When we fail, when we err, when we miss the mark, once we repent to the Lord, we are immediately forgiven by the Lord. That doesn't mean we won't experience the problems and repercussions of our sin, but it does mean relationship is restored.

"Against Thee, Thee only, have I sinned," David declared (Psalm 51:4). True, Scriptural repentance is always directed toward God. Once we understand this, we are loosed from the burden of judging those who sin against us and free instead just to love them.

1 Chronicles 20:4–8
And it came to pass after this, that there arose war at Gezer with the Philistines; at which time Sibbechai the Hushathite slew Sippai, that was of the children of the giant: and they were subdued. And there was war again with the Philistines; and Elhanan the son of Jair slew Lahmi the brother of Goliath the Gittite, whose spear staff was like a weaver's beam. And yet again there was war at Gath, where was a man of great stature, whose fingers and toes were four and twenty, six on each hand, and six on each foot: and he also was the son of the giant. But when he defied Israel, Jonathan the son of Shimea David's brother slew him. These were born unto the giant in Gath; and they fell by the hand of David, and by the hand of his servants.

Here we see the servants of David slaying the sons of Goliath even as we can have victory over the demonic forces of Satan because of what our Greater than David did for us on the Cross.

OVERCOMING GIANTS
A Topical Study of 1 CHRONICLES 20:5–8

One of the best-known beaches in southern California is called "The Wedge." The Wedge is an area of the Newport coast that is normally fairly tranquil and peaceful. But every once in awhile, huge swells mount up and slam into the beach with incredible force. When this happens, there are invariably two reactions. When the waders see the swells begin to rise, they turn their backs on the waves and begin to run as fast as they can toward the shore—only to be inevitably knocked down by the very waves they were hoping to escape. The bodysurfers, on the other hand, don't run from the waves, but swim toward them, dive under them, and come up safely on the other side. In life, waves of difficulty inevitably arise in our lives. When they do, we have a decision to make: whether to turn and run from them, and, in so doing, get knocked out, or to face them head-on and come up on the other side.

"That sounds nice, theoretically," you say. "But you don't know the waves that are coming up against me. I've got some big challenges, some difficult dilemmas, some brutal situations headed my way." You're right. I don't know the problems that face you, but I do know they couldn't be bigger than the giants in our text . . .

Unbelievable Giants

One was a brother of Goliath, the others were the sons of Goliath—and they were big. Goliath himself was at least nine feet and four inches tall and perhaps as tall as eleven feet. In addition to their size, Scripture records that they had six fingers on each hand and six toes on each foot. Biologically, this speaks of the fact that they were abnormal. Spiritually, six is the number of man, and speaks of their carnality.

These big, bad giants were stomping through the valleys of Israel. Forty years earlier, David had killed their father and brother. But, as our text says, "there was war again with the Philistines." Take note of this because in the area of spiritual warfare, in your pilgrimage through life, you'll face the same battles over and over again. Just because Goliath went down once doesn't mean he doesn't have some brothers or sons waiting in the wings.

In 2 Samuel 21:16, we read that, although David led his servants out to do battle against these sons of Goliath, his life was threatened. So his servants advised him to go back to Jerusalem. David heeded their advice and went back to his capital, where he was kept safe. But his servants did battle against the giants and were successful. Why? The servants of David were successful in killing giants for one simple reason: years earlier, David had killed Goliath. Thus, David was an inspiration for them and an example to them.

Remember, these men were not even born when David did battle against Goliath. They were not on the scene in the valley of Elah. They didn't see his bravery. They didn't observe his courage. But what David did out of their sight before they were even born was passed on to these servants years later. The giants you are killing in secret presently, the victories you are experiencing in prayer, in spiritual warfare, in witnessing, in giving, in serving will have an effect on the lives of your sons and daughters, your friends and neighbors, even if they don't observe these activities.

In the list of David's mighty men, there are a number of them who are mentioned as killing giants. But among the names of Saul's followers, not one is identified as killing a giant. Why? Because Saul was afraid. Saul never stepped out in faith. And because he never killed a giant, neither did his sons nor his servants.

Who is our Captain? The Son of David, Jesus Christ. Who is the one He defeated thoroughly and completely? Satan. The author of fear, the perpetuator of problems was dealt a death blow on the Cross of Calvary. But Satan still has his "sons"—demonic entities he releases to do battle against us, for the Bible says we wrestle not against flesh and blood, but against principalities and powers, spiritual wickedness in high places (Ephesians 6:12). Satan has been defeated. But he has released his henchmen to put fear in your heart, to smash you in the sand as wave after wave of problems come your way.

Unseen Forces

Do you ever wake up in the morning and wonder why you're depressed, why you just want to stay in bed, why you're discouraged when there's no real reason? It is because, even in the night hours, your spirit can battle against oppressive, demonic entities. But because our Captain, our Hero, our Leader, Jesus Christ, beat Satan, we can enjoy the victory He secured for us. Even though these giants loom over us, they have no authority in our lives. Why? Because they don't belong here. Where did the Philistines come from? From the island of Crete. But they were kicked out of their home and ended up in the territory of God's people. Where do demons come from? They were kicked out of heaven and ended up on this planet.

Unworthy No Longer

There are two difficulties that cause us to be afraid of doing battle against demonic entities. First, we feel unworthy. But check out what the Word says about this . . .

> *Blotting out the handwriting of ordinances that was against us, which was contrary to us, and took it out of the way, nailing it to his cross.*
>
> Colossians 2:14

"The handwriting of ordinances" is a shopping list of all the wrong things we've done and all the right things we haven't done. For all of us, that list is rather lengthy. But even the longest list was placed on the Cross of Christ at Calvary. All of the things that cause me to say, "I can't have victory; I can't be powerful spiritually; I can't accomplish that in ministry" were nailed to the Cross of Calvary and the blood of Jesus blotted them out completely. Every sin you have ever done has been blotted out totally by the blood of Christ.

Unable No More

In addition to feeling unworthy to do battle, we also feel unable. But, again, look at what Paul said to the Colossians . . .

And having spoiled principalities and powers, he made a shew of them openly, triumphing over them in it. Colossians 2:15

The Greek word translated "spoiled" literally means "stripped." It was used to describe what took place when the Roman army defeated another army: the general of the defeated army would be stripped, tied to his horse, and paraded through the streets of Rome as the citizens lined up to mock him. Suppose this general suddenly stopped and said, "People of Rome, listen to me. I am a great general and I demand you follow me right now." The people hearing this would not be scared in the least. No one would follow a naked general, no matter how loudly he yelled, no matter how much he threatened.

The same is true of demonic spirits that were once powerful and authoritative over you. Because they were stripped of their authority on the Cross of Calvary, they cannot touch you unless you give in to them.

For Christ also hath once suffered for sins, the just for the unjust, that he might bring us to God, being put to death in the flesh, but quickened by the Spirit: By which also he went and preached unto the spirits in prison; Which sometime were disobedient, when once the longsuffering of God waited in the days of Noah, while the ark was a preparing, wherein few, that is, eight souls were saved by water. 1 Peter 3:18–20

Following His death on the Cross, Jesus went to a place called Hades, where, according to Peter, He preached unto disobedient spirits. Who are these disobedient spirits? Genesis 6 says that at the time of Noah, there were particularly hideous demons in the world who seduced human women. The result of that demonic union was giants—such as those of the six-fingered and six-toed variety. It was to these demons that Jesus preached, placing limitations and boundaries around them, telling them their authority had been broken, their power stripped. That's what Paul is talking about in Colossians 2 when he says, "He spoiled, or stripped, principalities and powers." They're still alive. But, like a defeated general, all they can do is yell at you.

It is true that Satan goes about as a roaring lion seeking whom he may devour. But it is equally true that this roaring lion has had his teeth kicked out by Jesus Christ on the Cross. Now, all the enemy can do is gum you to death by saying, "Watch out. You're going to fail. You're going to be discouraged. Your marriage is going to collapse. Your job is going to go bad." The spirit of fear that Paul talks about in 2 Timothy is just that—a spirit. But God has not given us the spirit of fear but of power and of love and a sound mind (2 Timothy 1:7).

You can either be like the soldiers of Saul that were intimidated by the giants they saw, or you can be like the servants of David who said, "Because of what David did, we can take on the sons of Goliath and be victorious over them."

Too often, we view the enemy like a cat and ourselves like little mice as we hide in corners and scamper behind chairs. The reality is that you are the cat and Satan is the rat. You have been given authority and victory because of what Jesus did on Calvary. Therefore, refuse to accept the lying demands and commands of the spirits who say, "You'll never be spiritual. You'll never be successful. God can't use you, isn't using you, won't use you" because you've sinned once too often. They are Philistines, usurpers that don't belong in your life and you can command that they leave.

Follow the example of the Son of David, Jesus Christ. Take on the sons of Goliath—six fingers and all—and do them in. They must flee, and they will flee as you use Jesus' name.

21 If you took a poll concerning David's greatest sin, the average person would say it was either murder or adultery. But in God's eyes, it was pride. The sins of murder and adultery in chapter 20 were not even worth mentioning. But the sin of pride is recorded here in chapter 21 as a warning for those wise enough to heed it.

1 Chronicles 21:1
And Satan stood up against Israel, and provoked David to number Israel.

To attack Israel, Satan went after David, the leader of the nation.

1 Chronicles 21:2
And David said to Joab and to the rulers of the people, Go, number Israel from Beersheba even to Dan; and bring the number of them to me, that I may know it.

When David took on Goliath, he depended totally on God. Here, he's planning to rely on the strength of his army.

1 Chronicles 21:3
And Joab answered, The Lord make his people an hundred times so many more as they be: but, my lord the king, are they not all my lord's servants? Why then doth my lord require this thing? Why will he be a cause of trespass to Israel?

Joab—hardly a spiritual giant himself—says, "David, don't do it. May God bless you with more people, but don't count them. I know why you're doing this; I sense pride in your heart."

1 Chronicles 21:4 (a)
Nevertheless the king's word prevailed against Joab . . .

The Lord created us to be dependent upon Him, but in numbering the people, David was attempting to assess his own success apart from the Lord. In Isaiah 14, we read the account of Satan's downfall, and there we see that Satan himself fell because of pride. "I will be like God," he said. And this is always the essence of pride. He didn't say, "I will be greater than God," or, "I will obliterate God, but simply, "I will be like God."

Pride says, "I can do it myself. I don't need to seek the Lord. I can handle the bills and take care of my kids myself." How can you know if you've succumbed to the sin of pride? The answer is quite simple: pride always manifests itself in prayerlessness.

1 Chronicles 21:4 (b)–6
. . . Wherefore Joab departed, and went throughout all Israel, and came to Jerusalem. And Joab gave the sum of the number of the people unto David. And all they of Israel were a thousand thousand and an hundred thousand men that drew sword: and Judah was four hundred threescore and ten thousand men that drew sword. But Levi

and Benjamin counted he not among them: for the king's word was abominable to Joab.

Against his better judgment, Joab numbered the people and 1,100,000 were counted.

1 Chronicles 21:7, 8
And God was displeased with this thing; therefore he smote Israel. And David said unto God, I have sinned greatly, because I have done this thing: but now, I beseech thee, do away the iniquity of thy servant; for I have done very foolishly.

To his credit, David never argues with God. Rather, he submits to the conviction of the Lord and says, "Forgive me, Lord. I was wrong."

1 Chronicles 21:9, 10
And the LORD spake unto Gad, David's seer, saying, Go and tell David, saying, Thus saith the LORD, I offer thee three things: choose thee one of them, that I may do it unto thee.

"Whom the Lord loves, He chastens and disciplines every son" (see Hebrews 12:6). Here, David is about to be disciplined.

1 Chronicles 21:11, 12
So God came to David, and said unto him, Thus saith the LORD, Choose thee Either three years' famine; or three months to be destroyed before thy foes, while that the sword of thine enemies overtaketh thee; or else three days the sword of the LORD, even the pestilence, in the land, and the angel of the LORD destroying throughout all the coasts of Israel. Now therefore advise thyself what word I shall bring again to him that sent me.

God gave David three choices of punishment: three years of famine, three months of being wiped out by his enemies, or three days of pestilence.

1 Chronicles 21:13
And David said unto God, I am in a great strait: let me fall now into the hand of the LORD; for very great are his mercies: but let me not fall into the hand of man.

Forty-eight times in Psalm 136, the psalmist says of God, "Thy mercy endureth forever." This is why David wisely chose to place himself in God's hand rather than in the hand of man.

1 Chronicles 21:14–17
So the LORD sent pestilence upon Israel: and there fell of Israel seventy thousand men. And God sent an angel unto Jerusalem to destroy it: and as he was destroying, the LORD beheld, and he repented him of the evil, and said to the angel that destroyed, It is enough, stay now thine hand. And the angel of the LORD stood by the threshingfloor of Ornan the Jebusite. And David lifted up his eyes, and saw the angel of the LORD stand between the earth and the heaven, having a drawn sword in his hand stretched out over Jerusalem. Then David and the elders of Israel, who were clothed in sackcloth, fell upon their faces. And David said unto God, Is it not I that commanded the people to be numbered? even I it is that have sinned and done evil indeed; but as for these sheep, what have they done? let thine hand, I pray thee, O LORD my God, be on me, and on my father's house; but not on thy people, that they should be plagued.

As the angel was destroying the citizens of Jerusalem, David cried out to the Lord and demonstrated the heart of a shepherd, saying, "Let the people go. It's my sin. Don't let them be plagued. *I* am the one who should be punished."

Sin always affects others. That's part of its tragedy. Here, David's sin affected 70,000 people directly. But before we feel too sorry for those who were slain, we must realize that in 2 Samuel 24, a parallel passage, we see that even as David was preparing to number the people, the anger of the Lord was already kindled against Israel (24:1). Satan was the one who tempted David to number Israel, but God was the One who was angry with the nation as a whole. And God allowed David to be tempted and to succumb because He not only wanted to deal with David personally, but also with the nation corporately.

This is so important to see. God is in absolute control. He works all the situations together. This keeps us from saying, "If He hadn't messed up, I wouldn't be in the mess I'm in." God is on the throne. And no one can say, "It's not fair that I am a victim." God is sovereign, in absolute control of every situation. When you begin to see this and live in it, you can truly praise the Lord in *all* things.

1 Chronicles 21:18–23
Then the angel of the LORD commanded Gad to say to David, that David should go up, and set up an altar unto the LORD in the threshingfloor of Ornan the Jebusite. And David went up at the saying of Gad, which he spake in the name of the LORD. And Ornan turned back, and saw the angel; and his four sons with him hid themselves. Now Ornan was threshing wheat. And as David

came to Ornan, Ornan looked and saw David, and went out of the threshingfloor, and bowed himself to David with his face to the ground. Then David said to Ornan, Grant me the place of this threshingfloor, that I may build an altar therein unto the LORD: thou shalt grant it me for the full price: that the plague may be stayed from the people. And Ornan said unto David, Take it to thee, and let my lord the king do that which is good in his eyes: lo, I give thee the oxen also for burnt offerings, and the threshing instruments for wood, and the wheat for the meat offering; I give it all.

"If it will stop the plague, take my threshingfloor, my oxen, my wood, my wheat—take everything," Ornan said to David.

1 Chronicles 21:24, 25
And king David said to Ornan, Nay; but I will verily buy it for the full price: for I will not take that which is thine for the LORD, nor offer burnt offerings without cost. So David gave to Ornan for the place six hundred shekels of gold by weight.

This man after God's own heart said, "I will not give to the Lord that which costs me nothing" (see 2 Samuel 24:24). Sacrifice always costs. God so loved the world that He gave His only begotten Son. God gave everything. David reflects this.

1 Chronicles 21:26
And David built there an altar unto the LORD, and offered burnt offerings and peace offerings, and called upon the LORD; and he answered him from heaven by fire upon the altar of burnt offering.

As David prepared the offering, the Lord poured out fire upon it—even as Jesus was burned on the Cross by the righteous wrath of the Father for our sins.

1 Chronicles 21:27–30
And the LORD commanded the angel; and he put up his sword again into the sheath thereof. At that time when David saw that the LORD had answered him in the threshingfloor of Ornan the Jebusite, then he sacrificed there. For the tabernacle of the LORD, which Moses made in the wilderness, and the altar of the burnt offering, were at that season in the high place at Gibeon. But David could not go before it to inquire of God: for he was afraid because of the sword of the angel of the LORD.

The sword which was stretched over Jerusalem, causing 70,000 to die was placed in the sheath.

After they sinned, Adam and Eve were kept out of the garden with a flaming sword (Genesis 3:24). Here, we see a sword once again, sheathed, but still at hand. In Zechariah 13:7, we read that Jesus absorbed the blow of the sword when a spear was thrust in His side. At that point, the battle was over. The way into Eden was opened once again. Peace with God was made possible at last (Romans 5:1).

22

1 Chronicles 22:1
Then David said, This is the house of the LORD God, and this is the altar of the burnt offering for Israel.

David decided the temple would be built where the full price was paid, where sacrifice was offered, where fire came down, and where the sword was sheathed.

1 Chronicles 22:2–5
And David commanded to gather together the strangers that were in the land of Israel; and he set masons to hew wrought stones to build the house of God. And David prepared iron in abundance for the nails for the doors of the gates, and for the joinings; and brass in abundance without weight; Also cedar trees in abundance: for the Zidonians and they of Tyre brought much cedar wood to David. And David said, Solomon my son is young and tender, and the house that is to be builded for the LORD must be exceeding magnifical, of fame and of glory throughout all countries: I will therefore now make preparation for it. So David prepared abundantly before his death.

The house built to the Lord was not to be cutrate, bargain-basement, missionary-barrel. It was to be "exceeding magnifical." We need not be extravagant, but we should do our very best in anything we undertake in the name of the Lord.

1 Chronicles 22:6–10
Then he called for Solomon his son, and charged him to build an house for the LORD God of Israel. And David said to Solomon, My son, as for me, it was in my mind to build an house unto the name of the LORD my God: But the word of the LORD came to me, saying, Thou hast shed blood abundantly, and hast made great wars: thou shalt not build an house unto my name, because thou hast shed much blood upon the earth

in my sight. Behold, a son shall be born to thee, who shall be a man of rest; and I will give him rest from all his enemies round about: for his name shall be Solomon, and I will give peace and quietness unto Israel in his days. He shall build an house for my name; and he shall be my son, and I will be his father; and I will establish the throne of his kingdom over Israel for ever.

"David, you're a warrior," the Lord said. "My house is to be connected with peace. So I will use your son, whose name means 'Peace,' to build it."

It wasn't until David sat before the Lord (1 Chronicles 17:16) that he understood why he was not allowed to build the temple. Maybe you're wondering why the Lord isn't letting you do what's on your heart in service for Him. As time passes, His plans and purpose will unfold. His reasons will be made known if you, like David, quiet your heart before Him.

1 Chronicles 22:11 (a)
Now, my son, the LORD be with thee; and prosper thou . . .

In David's blessing upon his son, we see some wonderful truths concerning prosperity. First, we see the prayer for prosperity. "The Lord be with you," David said, because prosperity of soul, family, finances, and health always begins in prayer.

1 Chronicles 22:11 (b)
. . . and build the house of the LORD thy God, as he hath said of thee.

Here, we see the purpose of prosperity. The purpose of prosperity is not to kick back or to be comfortable. The purpose of prosperity is to glorify the Lord. I'm increasingly convinced that the Lord is looking for men and women He can bless exceedingly who will allow His blessings to flow through them to others for His glory. The Lord is looking for people to bless abundantly who will pass on His blessing freely.

1 Chronicles 22:12, 13
Only the LORD give thee wisdom and understanding, and give thee charge concerning Israel, that thou mayest keep the law of the LORD thy God. Then shalt thou prosper, if thou takest heed to fulfil the statutes and judgments which the LORD charged Moses with concerning Israel: be strong, and of good courage; dread not, nor be dismayed.

Finally, we see the pathway to prosperity. Why do Jewish people today prosper around the world? It is because, even though they are not believers, they have adhered to the precepts and principles of the Word of God. God's Laws and principles are absolute. Just like gravity, they affect believer and non-believer alike. If you follow the direction, instruction, and wisdom of the Word, you'll prosper.

1 Chronicles 22:14 (a)
Now, behold, in my trouble I have prepared for the house of the LORD an hundred thousand talents of gold . . .

Three thousand seven hundred and fifty tons of gold would equal six billion dollars today.

1 Chronicles 22:14 (b)–16
. . . and a thousand thousand talents of silver; and of brass and iron without weight; for it is in abundance: timber also and stone have I prepared; and thou mayest add thereto. Moreover there are workmen with thee in abundance, hewers and workers of stone and timber, and all manner of cunning men for every manner of work. Of the gold, the silver, and the brass, and the iron, there is no number. Arise therefore, and be doing, and the LORD be with thee.

David had given Solomon everything he would need to build the temple. All Solomon needed to provide was obedience. The same is true of us. We have been given "all things that pertain to life and godliness" (2 Peter 1:3). Our part is simply to obey.

1 Chronicles 22:17–19
David also commanded all the princes of Israel to help Solomon his son, saying, Is not the LORD your God with you? and hath he not given you rest on every side? for he hath given the inhabitants of the land into mine hand; and the land is subdued before the LORD, and before his people. Now set your heart and your soul to seek the LORD your God; arise therefore, and build ye the sanctuary of the LORD God, to bring the ark of the covenant of the LORD, and the holy vessels of God, into the house that is to be built to the name of the LORD.

Notice the order. Seeking always comes before serving. Too often we say, "What can I do? Give me a job, Lord, and I'll get right on it."

But the Lord says, "No, I want *you*—not what you can do. Seek Me first, and as you begin to know Me, as we begin to walk together and cultivate a deeper relationship, I'll give you assignments, tasks, and ministries."

Gang, Satan would love to get us serving so much we're no longer seeking. He would love to keep us real busy. But once we're too busy to seek the Lord, we're just too busy. Slow it down. Wait on Him. And you'll be blessed.

23 As David comes to the end of his life, he begins the great task of organizing both the religious life and civil life of Israel.

1 Chronicles 23:1–3
So when David was old and full of days, he made Solomon his son king over Israel. And he gathered together all the princes of Israel, with the priests and the Levites. Now the Levites were numbered from the age of thirty years and upward: and their number by their polls, man by man, was thirty and eight thousand.

From Numbers 8, we know that the Levites, up to this point, served between the ages of thirty and fifty. Between the ages of twenty-five and thirty, they were trained. Beyond fifty, they would train younger men. In this, we see the possibility of using every year of our lives for the Lord.

1 Chronicles 23:4 (a)
Of which, twenty and four thousand were to set forward the work of the house of the LORD . . .

From the earliest days of the wilderness wanderings, it had been the job of the Levites to care for and transport the tabernacle. With the establishment of a permanent place of worship, David gives new duties to the Levites. Twenty-four thousand of them were to maintain the temple.

1 Chronicles 23:4 (b)
. . . and six thousand were officers and judges:

Six thousand Levites were appointed to be leaders.

1 Chronicles 23:5 (a)
Moreover four thousand were porters . . .

Four thousand Levites were appointed the job of opening and closing the doors of the temple.

1 Chronicles 23:5 (b)
. . . and four thousand praised the LORD with the instruments which I made, said David, to praise therewith.

David appointed 4,000 Levites to be full-time worshipers, to praise the Lord with instruments he himself had designed. Not only was David a warrior, but he was also an inventor of musical instruments, a musician, and a poet.

1 Chronicles 23:6–23
And David divided them into courses among the sons of Levi, namely, Gershon, Kohath, and Merari. Of the Gershonites were, Laadan, and Shimei. The sons of Laadan; the chief was Jehiel, and Zetham, and Joel, three. The sons of Shimei; Shelomith, and Haziel, and Haran, three. These were the chief of the fathers of Laadan. And the sons of Shimei were, Jahath, Zina, and Jeush, and Beriah. These four were the sons of Shimei. And Jahath was the chief, and Zizah the second: but Jeush and Beriah had not many sons; therefore they were in one reckoning, according to their father's house. The sons of Kohath; Amram, Ishar, Hebron, and Uzziel, four. The sons of Amram; Aaron and Moses: and Aaron was separated, that he should sanctify the most holy things, he and his sons for ever, to burn incense before the LORD, to minister unto him, and to bless in his name for ever. Now concerning Moses the man of God, his sons were named of the tribe of Levi. The sons of Moses were, Gershom, and Eliezer. Of the sons of Gershom, Shebuel was the chief. And the sons of Eliezer were, Rehabiah the chief. And Eliezer had none other sons; but the sons of Rehabiah were very many. Of the sons of Izhar; Shelomith the chief. Of the sons of Hebron; Jeriah the first, Amariah the second, Jahaziel the third, and Jekameam the fourth. Of the sons of Uzziel; Michah the first, and Jesiah the second. The sons of Merari; Mahli, and Mushi. The sons of Mahli; Eleazar, and Kish. And Eleazar died, and had no sons, but daughters: and their brethren the sons of Kish took them. The sons of Mushi; Mahli, and Eder, and Jeremoth, three.

The Levites were divided into three groups to bring about effective, efficient, organized service in the house of the Lord.

1 Chronicles 23:24–28
These were the sons of Levi after the house of their fathers; even the chief of the fathers, as they were counted by number of names by their polls, that did the work for the service of the house of the LORD, from the age of twenty years and upward. For David said, The LORD God of Israel hath given rest unto his people, that they may

dwell in Jerusalem for ever: And also unto the Levites; they shall no more carry the tabernacle, nor any vessels of it for the service thereof. For by the last words of David the Levites were numbered from twenty years old and above: Because their office was to wait on the sons of Aaron for the service of the house of the LORD, in the courts, and in the chambers, and in the purifying of all holy things, and the work of the service of the house of God;

As seen in verse 3, the traditional age for a Levite to begin ministry was at the age of thirty. Here, on David's deathbed, he lowers the age to twenty. In so doing, David allowed more Levites to fill the necessary positions in the temple. My personal opinion is that, in these last days, we are seeing a similar dynamic take place as the Lord raises up more young men and women who are giving themselves for His service. Before, it was difficult to be involved in service for the Lord. If you thought about being a missionary, for example, it meant four years of Bible school, three years of seminary and then applying to a mission board. But in these last days, as the need is so great, as the revival is so wonderful, the Lord is raising opportunities for many to serve who previously would not have had such opportunity.

1 Chronicles 23:29, 30
Both for the shewbread, and for the fine flour for meat offering, and for the unleavened cakes, and for that which is baked in the pan, and for that which is fried, and for all manner of measure and size; And to stand every morning to thank and praise the LORD, and likewise at even;

Every morning and evening, these Levites stood and praised the Lord. So often, we think of ministry only as it relates to people. Here, we see an aspect of ministry directed exclusively to the Lord—a wonderful picture, indeed.

1 Chronicles 23:31, 32
And to offer all burnt sacrifices unto the LORD in the sabbaths, in the new moons, and on the set feasts, by number, according to the order commanded unto them, continually before the LORD: And that they should keep the charge of the tabernacle of the congregation, and the charge of the holy place, and the charge of the sons of Aaron their brethren, in the service of the house of the LORD.

In this temple structure, the high priest correlates with our great High Priest, Jesus Christ. Priests are the Old Testament picture of New Testament elders—men who minister to people on behalf of the Lord and who intercede to the Lord on behalf of people. Levites were those who did the practical service in the temple and correlate to the present-day ministry of deacons. I find it interesting that the Levites were to keep charge of the priests. This created an equality in ministry—a beautiful and wise check and balance system in spiritual leadership.

24 Whereas chapter 23 dealt with the Levites, chapter 24 deals with the priests. Again, although genealogies such as the one that follows seem redundant to us, they would prove to be vital for the reestablishment of the priestly ministry after the Babylonian captivity. Maybe you're going through some seemingly redundant, mundane dry times in your own life and you're wondering why the Lord isn't doing something more exciting. Take heart, dear saint. He's writing the story of your life according to what He knows lies ahead. Therefore, the "genealogies" where nothing seems to be happening are actually preparatory for future days.

1 Chronicles 24:1–5
Now these are the divisions of the sons of Aaron. The sons of Aaron; Nadab, and Abihu, Eleazar, and Ithamar. But Nadab and Abihu died before their father, and had no children: therefore Eleazar and Ithamar executed the priest's office. And David distributed them, both Zadok of the sons of Eleazar, and Ahimelech of the sons of Ithamar, according to their offices in their service. And there were more chief men found of the sons of Eleazar than of the sons of Ithamar; and thus were they divided. Among the sons of Eleazar there were sixteen chief men of the house of their fathers, and eight among the sons of Ithamar according to the house of their fathers. Thus were they divided by lot, one sort with another; for the governors of the sanctuary, and governors of the house of God, were of the sons of Eleazar, and of the sons of Ithamar.

The priests were divided by lot so that their order of service would be fair and effective. Solomon noted that the lot "causeth contention to cease" (Proverbs 18:18). It must have been this example the disciples followed in choosing a replacement for Judas (Acts 1:26).

1 Chronicles 24:6–10
And Shemaiah the son of Nethaneel the scribe, one of the Levites, wrote them before the king, and the princes, and Zadok the

priest, and Ahimelech the son of Abiathar, and before the chief of the fathers of the priests and Levites: one principal household being taken for Eleazar, and one taken for Ithamar. Now the first lot came forth to Jehoiarib, the second to Jedaiah, The third to Harim, the fourth to Seorim, The fifth to Malchijah, the sixth to Mijamin, The seventh to Hakkoz, the eighth to Abijah,

The longevity of these courses is seen in the fact that at the time of Christ, Zechariah, the father of John the Baptist, was identified as being of the division of Abijah.

1 Chronicles 24:11–31
The ninth to Jeshua, the tenth to Shecaniah, The eleventh to Eliashib, the twelfth to Jakim, The thirteenth to Huppah, the fourteenth to Jeshebeab, The fifteenth to Bilgah, the sixteenth to Immer, The seventeenth to Hezir, the eighteenth to Aphses, The nineteenth to Pethahiah, the twentieth to Jehezekel, The one and twentieth to Jachin, the two and twentieth to Gamul, The three and twentieth to Delaiah, the four and twentieth to Maaziah. These were the orderings of them in their service to come into the house of the LORD, according to their manner, under Aaron their father, as the LORD God of Israel had commanded him. And the rest of the sons of Levi were these: Of the sons of Amram; Shubael: of the sons of Shubael; Jehdeiah. Concerning Rehabiah: of the sons of Rehabiah, the first was Isshiah. Of the Izharites; Shelomoth: of the sons of Shelomoth; Jahath. And the sons of Hebron; Jeriah the first, Amariah the second, Jahaziel the third, Jekameam the fourth. Of the sons of Uzziel; Michah: of the sons of Michah; Shamir. The brother of Michah was Isshiah: of the sons of Isshiah; Zechariah. The sons of Merari were Mahli and Mushi: the sons of Jaaziah; Beno. The sons of Merari by Jaaziah; Beno, and Shoham, and Zaccur, and Ibri. Of Mahli came Eleazar, who had no sons. Concerning Kish: the son of Kish was Jerahmeel. The sons also of Mushi; Mahli, and Eder, and Jerimoth. These were the sons of the Levites after the house of their fathers. These likewise cast lots over against their brethren the sons of Aaron in the presence of David the king, and Zadok, and Ahimelech, and the chief of the fathers of the priests and Levites, even the principal fathers over against their younger brethren.

The priests were separated into twenty-four courses, or divisions. There were about 6,000 men in each course, and each course served for two weeks. What did the priests do when they were not serving in the temple? They were the leaders, teachers, and counselors of their cities. It was a wonderful, practical, workable system.

25

1 Chronicles 25:1 (a)
Moreover David and the captains of the host separated to the service of the sons of Asaph, and of Heman, and of Jeduthun, who should prophesy with harps . . .

From 1 Corinthians chapters 12—14, we know that prophecy was a spiritual manifestation that functioned in the NT church. Prophecy is for the purpose of edification, exhortation, and comfort. I find it intriguing that Asaph, Heman, and Jeduthun prophesied with the harp. One of the best ways prophecy can be ministered is through music. If you are a musician, I encourage you to pray that the Lord would give you songs that correlate with what He's doing specifically in your own fellowship of believers.

1 Chronicles 25:1 (b)–3
. . . with psalteries, and with cymbals: and the number of the workmen according to their service was: Of the sons of Asaph; Zaccur, and Joseph, and Nethaniah, and Asarelah, the sons of Asaph under the hands of Asaph, which prophesied according to the order of the king. Of Jeduthun: the sons of Jeduthun; Gedaliah, and Zeri, and Jeshaiah, Hashabiah, and Mattithiah, six, under the hands of their father Jeduthun, who prophesied with a harp, to give thanks and to praise the LORD.

There were two purposes for music in the temple. One was to give God's Word to men. The other was to direct praise to God. Those purposes have not changed. The highest calling of a musician is still to meet those two requirements.

1 Chronicles 25:4–6 (a)
Of Heman: the sons of Heman; Bukkiah, Mattaniah, Uzziel, Shebuel, and Jerimoth, Hananiah, Hanani, Eliathah, Giddalti, and Romamti-ezer, Joshbekashah, Mallothi, Hothir, and Mahazioth: All these were the sons of Heman the king's seer in the words of God, to lift up the horn. And God gave to Heman fourteen sons and three daughters. All these were under the hands of their father . . .

Even though Heman devoted himself to the ministry of worship, his sons were under his hand. For what purpose? Read on . . .

1 Chronicles 25:6 (b)
. . . for song in the house of the Lord, with cymbals, psalteries, and harps, for the service of the house of God, according to the king's order to Asaph, Jeduthun, and Heman.

Heman was amazing. He was one who wrote, worshiped, prophesied, and raised a big family that followed in his footsteps, becoming part of the ministry team. Heman provides wonderful proof that time spent ministering to the Lord and time spent raising a family do not have to be mutually exclusive.

1 Chronicles 25:7
So the number of them, with their brethren that were instructed in the songs of the Lord, even all that were cunning, was two hundred fourscore and eight.

Two hundred and eighty eight—"all that were cunning"—were in the "orchestra." "Cunning" means "skilled" or "gifted." There was order to worship and beauty in it.

1 Chronicles 25:8–31
And they cast lots, ward against ward, as well the small as the great, the teacher as the scholar. Now the first lot came forth for Asaph to Joseph: the second to Gedaliah, who with his brethren and sons were twelve: The third to Zaccur, he, his sons, and his brethren, were twelve: The fourth to Izri, he, his sons, and his brethren, were twelve: The fifth to Nethaniah, he, his sons, and his brethren, were twelve: The sixth to Bukkiah, he, his sons, and his brethren, were twelve: The seventh to Jesharelah, he, his sons, and his brethren, were twelve: The eighth to Jeshaiah, he, his sons, and his brethren, were twelve: The ninth to Mattaniah, he, his sons, and his brethren, were twelve: The tenth to Shimei, he, his sons, and his brethren, were twelve: The eleventh to Azareel, he, his sons, and his brethren, were twelve: The twelfth to Hashabiah, he, his sons, and his brethren, were twelve: The thirteenth to Shubael, he, his sons, and his brethren, were twelve: The fourteenth to Mattithiah, he, his sons, and his brethren, were twelve: The fifteenth to Jeremoth, he, his sons, and his brethren, were twelve: The sixteenth to Hananiah, he, his sons, and his brethren, were twelve: The seventeenth to Joshbekashah, he, his sons, and his brethren, were twelve: The eighteenth to Hanani, he, his sons, and his brethren, were twelve: The nineteenth to Mallothi, he, his sons, and his brethren, were twelve: The twentieth to Eliathah, he, his sons, and his brethren, were twelve: The one and twentieth to Hothir, he, his sons, and his brethren, were twelve: The two and twentieth to Giddalti, he, his sons, and his brethren, were twelve: The three and twentieth to Mahazioth, he, his sons, and his brethren, were twelve: The four and twentieth to Romamti-ezer, he, his sons, and his brethren, were twelve.

The musicians were divided into twenty-four companies, with twelve in each company. Lots were cast to determine order of service. As seen in verse 8, this was done equitably.

"Let all things be done decently and in order," Paul would write (1 Corinthians 14:40), as he gave direction for the New Testament temple—the church. "And the eye cannot say to the hand, I have no need of thee; nor again the head to the feet, I have no need of thee," Paul would contend (1 Corinthians 12:21).

The world is greatly concerned about position and preeminence. But that has never been the way of the Lord. In His economy, humility is what matters (1 Peter 5:6)—as seen in the way He structured both His temple and His church.

26

In chapter 26, we see the office of porter—men who were to tend to the doors of the temple. These men numbered 4,000 and were divided into four groups—one for each door . . .

1 Chronicles 26:1–6
Concerning the divisions of the porters: Of the Korhites was Meshelemiah the son of Kore, of the sons of Asaph. And the sons of Meshelemiah were, Zechariah the firstborn, Jediael the second, Zebadiah the third, Jathniel the fourth, Elam the fifth, Jehohanan the sixth, Elioenai the seventh. Moreover the sons of Obed-edom were, Shemaiah the firstborn, Jehozabad the second, Joah the third, and Sacar the fourth, and Nethaneel the fifth, Ammiel the sixth, Issachar the seventh, Peulthai the eighth: for God blessed him. Also unto Shemaiah his son were sons born, that ruled throughout the house of their father: for they were mighty men of valour.

It is not surprising that the porters are referred to as "mighty man of valor," for not only did they open and close the heavy gates of the temple, but they provided a military guard against would-be plunderers.

1 Chronicles 26:7, 8
The sons of Shemaiah; Othni, and Rephael, and Obed, Elzabad, whose brethren were strong men, Elihu, and Semachiah. All these of the sons of Obed-edom: they and their sons and their brethren, able men for strength for the service, were threescore and two of Obed-edom.

Obed-edom had virtually risked his life to house the ark before David brought it to Jerusalem. Here, we see the fruits of his obedience, as all sixty-two in his lineage were employed in the service of God.

1 Chronicles 26:9–15
And Meshelemiah had sons and brethren, strong men, eighteen. Also Hosah, of the children of Merari, had sons; Simri the chief, (for though he was not the firstborn, yet his father made him the chief;) Hilkiah the second, Tebaliah the third, Zechariah the fourth: all the sons and brethren of Hosah were thirteen. Among these were the divisions of the porters, even among the chief men, having wards one against another, to minister in the house of the LORD. And they cast lots, as well the small as the great, according to the house of their fathers, for every gate. And the lot eastward fell to Shelemiah. Then for Zechariah his son, a wise counseller, they cast lots; and his lot came out northward. To Obed-edom southward; and to his sons the house of Asuppim.

Scholars believe the house of Assumpim—or collections—speaks of the storehouse containing the supplies for the daily needs of the priests.

1 Chronicles 26:16
To Shuppim and Hosah the lot came forth westward, with the gate Shallecheth, by the causeway of the going up, ward against ward.

Scholars believe this gate was the one through which rubbish was carried.

1 Chronicles 26:17
Eastward were six Levites, northward four a day, southward four a day, and toward Asuppim two and two.

Because the eastern gate had the most traffic, it also required the most porters.

1 Chronicles 26:18
At Parbar westward, four at the causeway, and two at Parbar.

If Parbar is the same as Parvar as some scholars suggest (2 Kings 23:11), this gate led to the dwelling places in the city.

1 Chronicles 26:19
These are the divisions of the porters among the sons of Kore, and among the sons of Merari.

I praise the Lord for porters—those who opened and closed the doors. Spiritually, this office speaks of a more important calling than even that—those who watch what goes in and out in prayer. We are the temple of the Lord and there are people who are praying for our body. Once every other week I get a letter from someone who specifically states what they are praying for, how they are in a time of prayer and fasting, standing at the door, saying, *No,* we reject that. We're not going to be penetrated by that, we're not going to be influenced by that." If you're a porter in prayer—keeping out the enemy, as well as opening the doors of blessing—heaven will reward you.

1 Chronicles 26:20
And of the Levites, Ahijah was over the treasures of the house of God, and over the treasures of the dedicated things.

Certain Levites had specific callings. Ahijah, for example, kept track of the money used for the operation of the temple.

1 Chronicles 26:21–28
As concerning the sons of Laadan; the sons of the Gershonite Laadan, chief fathers, even of Laadan the Gershonite, were Jehieli. The sons of Jehieli; Zetham, and Joel his brother, which were over the treasures of the house of the LORD. Of the Amramites, and the Izharites, the Hebronites, and the Uzzielites: And Shebuel the son of Gershom, the son of Moses, was ruler of the treasures. And his brethren by Eliezer; Rehabiah his son, and Jeshaiah his son, and Joram his son, and Zichri his son, and Shelomith his son. Which Shelomith and his brethren were over all the treasures of the dedicated things, which David the king, and the chief fathers, the captains over thousands and hundreds, and the captains of the host, had dedicated. Out of the spoils won in battles did they dedicate to maintain the house of the LORD. And all that Samuel the seer, and Saul the

son of Kish, and Abner the son of Ner, and Joab the son of Zeruiah, had dedicated; and whosoever had dedicated any thing, it was under the hand of Shelomith, and of his brethren.

Throughout Israel's history, the leaders of God's people, including Moses, Samuel, David, Saul, Abner, and Joab had dedicated the spoils of battle to the Lord.

1 Chronicles 26:29–32
Of the Izharites, Chenaniah and his sons were for the outward business over Israel, for officers and judges. And of the Hebronites, Hashabiah and his brethren, men of valour, a thousand and seven hundred, were officers among them of Israel on this side Jordan westward in all the business of the LORD, and in the service of the king. Among the Hebronites was Jerijah the chief, even among the Hebronites, according to the generations of his fathers. In the fortieth year of the reign of David they were sought for, and there were found among them mighty men of valour at Jazer of Gilead. And his brethren, men of valour, were two thousand and seven hundred chief fathers, whom king David made rulers over the Reubenites, the Gadites, and the half tribe of Manasseh, for every matter pertaining to God, and affairs of the king.

Although 1,700 Levites served the ten tribes on the west side of the Jordan, 2,700 were needed to serve the two and one-half tribes on the east side because the two and one-half tribes were more susceptible to the pagan culture that surrounded them. That's always the way it is. The closer we are to the center of God's will, the more tightly we are in fellowship with His people, the more we are protected from the enemy that seeks to trip us up in our walk with Him.

27

In chapter 27, we see the administration of civil aspects for the nation.

1 Chronicles 27:1–15
Now the children of Israel after their number, to wit, the chief fathers and captains of thousands and hundreds, and their officers that served the king in any matter of the courses, which came in and went out month by month throughout all the months of the year, of every course were twenty and four thousand. Over the first course for the first month was Jashobeam the son of Zabdiel: and in his course were twenty and four thousand. Of the children of Perez was the chief of all the captains of the host for the first month. And over the course of the second month was Dodai an Ahohite, and of his course was Mikloth also the ruler: in his course likewise were twenty and four thousand. The third captain of the host for the third month was Benaiah the son of Jehoiada, a chief priest: and in his course were twenty and four thousand. This is that Benaiah, who was mighty among the thirty, and above the thirty: and in his course was Ammizabad his son. The fourth captain for the fourth month was Asahel the brother of Joab, and Zebadiah his son after him: and in his course were twenty and four thousand. The fifth captain for the fifth month was Shamhuth the Izrahite: and in his course were twenty and four thousand. The sixth captain for the sixth month was Ira the son of Ikkesh the Tekoite: and in his course were twenty and four thousand. The seventh captain for the seventh month was Helez the Pelonite, of the children of Ephraim: and in his course were twenty and four thousand. The eighth captain for the eighth month was Sibbecai the Hushathite, of the Zarhites: and in his course were twenty and four thousand. The ninth captain for the ninth month was Abiezer the Anetothite, of the Benjamites: and in his course were twenty and four thousand. The tenth captain for the tenth month was Maharai the Netophathite, of the Zarhites: and in his course were twenty and four thousand. The eleventh captain for the eleventh month was Benaiah the Pirathonite, of the children of Ephraim: and in his course were twenty and four thousand. The twelfth captain for the twelfth month was Heldai the Netophathite, of Othniel: and in his course were twenty and four thousand.

The military force of Israel consisted of twelve divisions of 24,000 each. Each man served only one month a year. Thus, David had a standing army of 24,000, which could be enlarged to 288,000 when necessary.

1 Chronicles 27:16–22
Furthermore over the tribes of Israel: the ruler of the Reubenites was Eliezer the son of Zichri: of the Simeonites, Shephatiah the son of Maachah: Of the Levites, Hashabiah the son of Kemuel: of the Aaronites, Zadok: Of Judah, Elihu, one of the brethren of David: of Issachar, Omri the son of Michael: Of Zebulun, Ishmaiah the son of Obadiah: of Naphtali, Jerimoth the son of Azriel: Of the children of Ephraim, Hoshea the son of

Azaziah: of the half tribe of Manasseh, Joel the son of Pedaiah: Of the half tribe of Manasseh in Gilead, Iddo the son of Zechariah: of Benjamin, Jaasiel the son of Abner: Of Dan, Azareel the son of Jeroham. These were the princes of the tribes of Israel.

These are the leaders of the Twelve Tribes at the time of David's reign and order first instituted by Moses (Exodus 18:25).

1 Chronicles 27:23, 24
But David took not the number of them from twenty years old and under: because the LORD had said he would increase Israel like to the stars of the heavens. Joab the son of Zeruiah began to number, but he finished not, because there fell wrath for it against Israel; neither was the number put in the account of the chronicles of king David.

Reference is here made to the calamitous census ordered by David—incomplete, perhaps, due to the plague that fell upon the nation (1 Chronicles 21).

1 Chronicles 27:25–31
And over the king's treasures was Azmaveth the son of Adiel: and over the storehouses in the fields, in the cities, and in the villages, and in the castles, was Jehonathan the son of Uzziah: And over them that did the work of the field for tillage of the ground was Ezri the son of Chelub: And over the vineyards was Shimei the Ramathite: over the increase of the vineyards for the wine cellars was Zabdi the Shiphmite: And over the olive trees and the sycomore trees that were in the low plains was Baal-hanan the Gederite: and over the cellars of oil was Joash: And over the herds that fed in Sharon was Shitrai the Sharonite: and over the herds that were in the valleys was Shaphat the son of Adlai: Over the camels also was Obil the Ishmaelite: and over the asses was Jehdeiah the Meronothite: And over the flocks was Jaziz the Hagerite. All these were the rulers of the substance which was king David's.

These were the officers in charge of David's vast private estate.

> Blessed is the man that walketh not in the counsel of the ungodly, nor standeth in the way of sinners, nor sitteth in the seat of the scornful. But his delight is in the law of the LORD; and in his law doth he meditate day and night. And he shall be like a tree planted by the rivers of water, that bringeth forth his fruit in his season; his leaf also shall not wither; and whatsoever he doeth shall prosper. Psalm 1:1–3

We know that financial wealth is not synonymous with godliness, but I wonder if our tendency isn't to subconsciously equate financial poverty with spirituality. Moses—the friend of God, and David, a man after God's own heart—stand in contrast to this false supposition. Man judges by the outward appearance, but, truly, God sees the heart of the matter (1 Samuel 16:7).

1 Chronicles 27:32–34
Also Jonathan David's uncle was a counseller, a wise man, and a scribe: and Jehiel the son of Hachmoni was with the king's sons: And Ahithophel was the king's counseller: and Hushai the Archite was the king's companion: And after Ahithophel was Jehoiada the son of Benaiah, and Abiathar: and the general of the king's army was Joab.

"For by wise counsel thou shalt make thy war: and in multitude of counsellers there is safety," Solomon would later write (Proverbs 24:6). Men who had proven faithful to him in the past, these were David's advisors.

28

1 Chronicles 28:1, 2 (a)
And David assembled all the princes of Israel, the princes of the tribes, and the captains of the companies that ministered to the king by course, and the captains over the thousands, and captains over the hundreds, and the stewards over all the substance and possession of the king, and of his sons, with the officers, and with the mighty men, and with all the valiant men, unto Jerusalem. Then David the king stood up upon his feet, and said, Hear me, my brethren, and my people . . .

Approaching the end of his life, David called the leadership of Israel to Jerusalem, where he would pass the torch of leadership to a new generation . . .

1 Chronicles 28:2 (b), 3
. . . As for me, I had in mine heart to build an house of rest for the ark of the covenant of the LORD, and for the footstool of our God, and had made ready for the building: But God said unto me, Thou shalt not build an house for my name, because thou hast been a man of war, and hast shed blood.

Without a trace of self-pity or animosity, David explained what he wanted to do and why God didn't allow him to do it.

1 Chronicles 28:4–8
Howbeit the LORD God of Israel chose me before all the house of my father to be king over Israel for ever: for he hath chosen Judah to be the ruler; and of the house of Judah, the house of my father; and among the sons of my father he liked me to make me king over all Israel: And of all my sons, (for the LORD hath given me many sons,) he hath chosen Solomon my son to sit upon the throne of the kingdom of the LORD over Israel. And he said unto me, Solomon thy son, he shall build my house and my courts: for I have chosen him to be my son, and I will be his father. Moreover I will establish his kingdom for ever, if he be constant to do my commandments and my judgments, as at this day. Now therefore in the sight of all Israel the congregation of the LORD, and in the audience of our God, keep and seek for all the commandments of the LORD your God: that ye may possess this good land, and leave it for an inheritance for your children after you for ever.

David went on to explain the amazing promise God gave him—that he would be linked to the One whose kingdom will never end.

1 Chronicles 28:9 (a)
And thou, Solomon my son, know thou the God of thy father . . .

Notice that David didn't say, "Know the God of the universe," or, "Know the God of Israel." He said, "Know my God." Why? Because David found such satisfaction, fulfillment, excitement in the Lord that he wanted Solomon to have that same experience.

Dad, would you be excited if your son followed in your footsteps, or would you say, "Oh, son, do not know the god of your father because my god—the master passion of my life—will lead you to frustration, misery, and heartache.

1 Chronicles 28:9 (b)
. . . and serve him . . .

We must know God before we can serve Him. In Daniel 11:32, we read that the people who know their God shall be strong and do great exploits. When you know the Lord, you can't help but want to serve Him. But if you don't know Him, your service will be burdensome and legalistic. Sunday school teacher, youth group worker, elder, deacon, Bible study leader—the order here is essential. Know first and then serve. You can become so busy serving the Lord that you no longer have time to walk with Him, and then you're in trouble. Know Him first.

1 Chronicles 28:9 (c)
. . . with a perfect heart and with a willing mind: for the LORD searcheth all hearts, and understandeth all the imaginations of the thoughts . . .

There are ways we can serve the Lord that are not with a perfect heart. That is, we can serve Him halfheartedly. The prophet Malachi indicted the people for sacrificing bulls and rams that were leftovers (1:8). We can do the same with the time, energy, talent, or finances we bring to Him. Secondly, we can serve Him with a cold heart. Through Isaiah, the Lord indicted the people of Israel for drawing near to Him with their lips and mouth but not with their heart (29:13). Finally, we can serve the Lord with an evil heart. Jesus indicted the Pharisees for this kind of service because they sought only to draw attention to themselves when giving alms (Matthew 6:1, 2).

1 Chronicles 28:9 (d)
. . . if thou seek him, he will be found of thee; but if thou forsake him, he will cast thee off for ever.

"If thou seek Him, He will be found of thee." That's a promise. And the same Spirit that inspired David to say this to Solomon also put it in the mind of James to write to us: "Draw near to God and He will draw near to you" (see James 4:8).

1 Chronicles 28:10
Take heed now; for the LORD hath chosen thee to build an house for the sanctuary: be strong, and do it.

In John 15, Jesus said, "You have not chosen Me, but I have chosen you and ordained you . . ." Just as surely as the Lord chose Solomon, He chose you to build a house. Solomon built a physical temple. Ours is a spiritual temple.

"What? Know ye not that your bodies are the temple of the living God?" Paul asked the Corinthians (1 Corinthians 6:19). God has chosen to dwell on this earth through your life. Is the temple of your life vibrant or is it in disrepair? You are chosen by God just as surely as Solomon was to build a temple. Therefore, be strong and do it. How? Read on . . .

1 Chronicles 28:11 (a)
Then David gave to Solomon his son the pattern . . .

David gave Solomon the pattern, the playbook, the program. What is that pattern? The pattern of what God wants you to be and to do and how to get there is in the Word. Here, David says, "Here's the pattern, son. Start building." And the Son of David, Jesus Christ, says the same thing to us. As you study the pattern of the Word, you'll find yourself more and more in line with what He wants to do in and through you.

1 Chronicles 28:11 (b)–19
. . . of the porch, and of the houses thereof, and of the treasuries thereof, and of the upper chambers thereof, and of the inner parlours thereof, and of the place of the mercy seat, And the pattern of all that he had by the spirit, of the courts of the house of the LORD, and of all the chambers round about, of the treasuries of the house of God, and of the treasuries of the dedicated things: Also for the courses of the priests and the Levites, and for all the work of the service of the house of the LORD, and for all the vessels of service in the house of the LORD. He gave of gold by weight for things of gold, for all instruments of all manner of service; silver also for all instruments of silver by weight, for all instruments of every kind of service: Even the weight for the candlesticks of gold, and for their lamps of gold, by weight for every candlestick, and for the lamps thereof: and for the candlesticks of silver by weight, both for the candlestick, and also for the lamps thereof, according to the use of every candlestick. And by weight he gave gold for the tables of shewbread, for every table; and likewise silver for the tables of silver: Also pure gold for the fleshhooks, and the bowls, and the cups: and for the golden basons he gave gold by weight for every bason; and likewise silver by weight for every bason of silver: And for the altar of incense refined gold by weight; and gold for the pattern of the chariot of the cherubims, that spread out their wings, and covered the ark of the covenant of the LORD. All this, said David, the LORD made me understand in writing by his hand upon me, even all the works of this pattern.

The pattern, or the plan, for the temple was inspired by the Lord. Even as Moses got a pattern on Mt. Sinai, so David received a pattern for the temple.

1 Chronicles 28:20
And David said to Solomon his son, Be strong and of good courage, and do it: fear not, nor be dismayed: for the LORD God, even my God, will be with thee; he will not fail thee, nor forsake thee, until thou hast finished all the work for the service of the house of the LORD.

Paul was "confident of this very thing, that He who began a good work in you will perform it until the day of Jesus Christ" (see Philippians 1:6). Therefore, as sure as a promise was made to Solomon, so the same promise is given to you. You can come to a point in your life where you realize that the dreams you had, the goals you set aren't going to happen. That can, if you're not careful, send you into an introspective crisis. But if you're a believer, there won't be a crisis because the promise of God is that what He wants to do in you will be completed. Period.

Zacharias was a priest. His wife, Elisabeth, was a priest's daughter. For years, they prayed that they might have a child. Suddenly, as Zacharias was serving in the temple, an angel appeared and told him his prayer had been heard. Now, I'll bet Zacharias had stopped praying when Elisabeth passed the age of childbearing. I'm sure he had forgotten all about the prayer he had prayed. Maybe you can relate to that. At one time, you felt you were praying in harmony with God's heart, but nothing happened. Don't give up. The promise is that the work *will* be completed. It might take an entirely different course than what you thought, but God will complete His work for your life.

1 Chronicles 28:21
And, behold, the courses of the priests and the Levites, even they shall be with thee for all the service of the house of God: and there shall be with thee for all manner of workmanship every willing skilful man, for any manner of service: also the princes and all the people will be wholly at thy commandment.

David not only gave Solomon the plan, but also the servants to assist him. He purchased the ground, gathered all the materials, lined up the workers. He's done everything. And yet the temple is called Solomon's temple. That's just like Jesus. He gives us the plan. He empowers us with His Spirit. He opens opportunity. He gives us energy. He makes it easy for us. And then, He says, "Well done, good and faithful servant" (Matthew 25:21). It's incredible that He would say, "Well done," to us when He's done it all.

29

1 Chronicles 29:1–4

Furthermore David the king said unto all the congregation, Solomon my son, whom alone God hath chosen, is yet young and tender, and the work is great: for the palace is not for man, but for the LORD God. Now I have prepared with all my might for the house of my God the gold for things to be made of gold, and the silver for things of silver, and the brass for things of brass, the iron for things of iron, and wood for things of wood; onyx stones, and stones to be set, glistering stones, and of divers colours, and all manner of precious stones, and marble stones in abundance. Moreover, because I have set my affection to the house of my God, I have of mine own proper good, of gold and silver, which I have given to the house of my God, over and above all that I have prepared for the holy house, Even three thousand talents of gold, of the gold of Ophir, and seven thousand talents of refined silver, to overlay the walls of the houses withal:

At this point, David is not only giving materials gathered through warfare, but he is opening his own treasury. He's drawing on his own resources. He's putting his treasure where his heart is (Matthew 6:21).

1 Chronicles 29:5

The gold for things of gold, and the silver for things of silver, and for all manner of work to be made by the hands of artificers. And who then is willing to consecrate his service this day unto the LORD?

David didn't command the people to give. Rather, he modeled the spirit of giving before them and asked those who were willing to do the same. The only way God wants us to give is with a willing heart (2 Corinthians 9:7). God doesn't need our money. It is we who need to give. By nature, we are selfish, but every time we give, we give away part of our selfish tendencies and become a little more like Him.

1 Chronicles 29:6–8

Then the chief of the fathers and princes of the tribes of Israel, and the captains of thousands and of hundreds, with the rulers of the king's work, offered willingly, And gave for the service of the house of God of gold five thousand talents and ten thousand drams, and of silver ten thousand talents, and of brass eighteen thousand talents, and one hundred thousand talents of iron. And they with whom precious stones were found gave them to the treasure of the house of the LORD, by the hand of Jehiel the Gershonite.

Notice that it was the leaders who responded initially and willingly. If you claim to be a leader and you are not a giver, you're kidding yourself. If finances hang you up, I believe you should take a break from leadership and say, "Lord, if I cannot trust You with money, I'm not at a place of maturity and not ready to serve You in ministry. Help me." And He will.

1 Chronicles 29:9

Then the people rejoiced, for that they offered willingly, because with perfect heart they offered willingly to the LORD: and David the king also rejoiced with great joy.

First David gave. Then the leaders gave. Then the people gave. And the result was great joy. That's always the way it is. Those who are misery live in misery. But those who are generous are those who are glad.

1 Chronicles 29:10–14

Wherefore David blessed the LORD before all the congregation: and David said, Blessed be thou, LORD God of Israel our father, for ever and ever. Thine, O LORD, is the greatness, and the power, and the glory, and the victory, and the majesty: for all that is in the heaven and in the earth is thine; thine is the kingdom, O LORD, and thou art exalted as head above all. Both riches and honour come of thee, and thou reignest over all; and in thine hand is power and might; and in thine hand it is to make great, and to give strength unto all. Now therefore, our God, we thank thee, and praise thy glorious name. But who am I, and what is my people, that we should be able to offer so willingly after this sort? for all things come of thee, and of thine own have we given thee.

"Lord, we are not giving what is ours at all," David prayed. "It all came from You in the first place. Thank You for the privilege of giving back to You that which is Yours."

1 Chronicles 29:15

For we are strangers before thee, and sojourners, as were all our fathers: our days on the earth are as a shadow, and there is none abiding.

Jim Eliot, martyred missionary to the Auca Indians said, "He is no fool who gives what he cannot keep to gain what he cannot lose." It's true.

Anything you give to God you won't regret. Make eternal investments, gang. Be wise. Time is short.

1 Chronicles 29:16–19
O LORD our God, all this store that we have prepared to build thee an house for thine holy name cometh of thine hand, and is all thine own. I know also, my God, that thou triest the heart, and hast pleasure in uprightness. As for me, in the uprightness of mine heart I have willingly offered all these things: and now have I seen with joy thy people, which are present here, to offer willingly unto thee. O LORD God of Abraham, Isaac, and of Israel, our fathers, keep this for ever in the imagination of the thoughts of the heart of thy people, and prepare their heart unto thee: And give unto Solomon my son a perfect heart, to keep thy commandments, thy testimonies, and thy statutes, and to do all these things, and to build the palace, for the which I have made provision.

After worshiping the Lord with a heart of thanksgiving, David intercedes for the people and for his son, that their hearts would be toward Him.

1 Chronicles 29:20
And David said to all the congregation, Now bless the LORD your God. And all the congregation blessed the LORD God of their fathers, and bowed down their heads, and worshipped the LORD, and the king.

The people worshiped the Lord as their God, and acknowledged Solomon as His appointed leader over them.

1 Chronicles 29:21, 22 (a)
And they sacrificed sacrifices unto the LORD, and offered burnt offerings unto the LORD, on the morrow after that day, even a thousand bullocks, a thousand rams, and a thousand lambs, with their drink offerings, and sacrifices in abundance for all Israel: And did eat and drink before the LORD on that day with great gladness . . .

It is no wonder that the people experienced great gladness as they sacrificed "in abundance." Didn't Jesus tell us that it is more blessed to give than to receive (Acts 20:35)? If you're feeling down or discouraged today, find a way to give—even if it's just a word of encouragement to someone else or a prayer of thanksgiving to the Lord—and see if your own spirit isn't buoyed up in blessing.

1 Chronicles 29:22 (b)–25
. . . And they made Solomon the son of David king the second time, and anointed him unto the LORD to be the chief governor, and Zadok to be priest. Then Solomon sat on the throne of the LORD as king instead of David his father, and prospered; and all Israel obeyed him. And all the princes, and the mighty men, and all the sons likewise of king David, submitted themselves unto Solomon the king. And the LORD magnified Solomon exceedingly in the sight of all Israel, and bestowed upon him such royal majesty as had not been on any king before him in Israel.

The first time Solomon was proclaimed king was when his brother, Adonijah, usurped the throne (1 Kings 1:39). Here, he's anointed king peacefully rather than in a state of emergency.

1 Chronicles 29:26–28
Thus David the son of Jesse reigned over all Israel. And the time that he reigned over Israel was forty years; seven years reigned he in Hebron, and thirty and three years reigned he in Jerusalem. And he died in a good old age, full of days, riches, and honour: and Solomon his son reigned in his stead.

Even though David was a warrior, he died full of days. Even though the Lord was his heart's desire, he died full of riches. Even though a large part of his life was spent hiding from Saul, he died full of honor.

1 Chronicles 29:29, 30
Now the acts of David the king, first and last, behold, they are written in the book of Samuel the seer, and in the book of Nathan the prophet, and in the book of Gad the seer, With all his reign and his might, and the times that went over him, and over Israel, and over all the kingdoms of the countries.

And so we come to the end of the life of the shepherd who became a king, the giant-killer who invented musical instruments, the fugitive who wrote psalms, the sinner who would be in the lineage of the Messiah. We come to the end of the life of David, the man after God's own heart.

2 CHRONICLES

1 **2 Chronicles 1:1**
And Solomon the son of David was strengthened in his kingdom, and the LORD his God was with him, and magnified him exceedingly.

In 2 Chronicles, we come to the apex of Jewish history, a time of unparalleled peace and prosperity. The reign of *Solomon,* whose name means "peaceful," is a prophetic picture of the reign of Jesus, for when He comes back as the Prince of peace and establishes His throne on the earth, there will be perfect peace and incredible prosperity. But please remember that the peace and prosperity that was taking place under the reign of Solomon was made possible only through the blood and battles David had fought previously. Thus, it is David's reign that prophetically pictures the First Coming of Christ, for when He came as a Suffering Savior, He was victorious over the enemy as He died on the Cross of Calvary.

2 Chronicles 1:2–5
Then Solomon spake unto all Israel, to the captains of thousands and of hundreds, and to the judges, and to every governor in all Israel, the chief of the fathers. So Solomon, and all the congregation with him, went to the high place that was at Gibeon; for there was the tabernacle of the congregation of God, which Moses the servant of the LORD had made in the wilderness. But the ark of God had David brought up from Kirjath-jearim to the place which David had prepared for it: for he had pitched a tent for it at Jerusalem. Moreover the brasen altar, that Bezaleel the son of Uri, the son of Hur, had made, he put before the tabernacle of the LORD: and Solomon and the congregation sought unto it.

At the beginning of his reign, Solomon gathered the nation to seek the Lord. To do this, he went to Gibeon because, although the ark was now in Jerusalem, the tabernacle was seven miles northwest, in Gibeon. Why didn't David bring the original tabernacle back with the ark to Jerusalem? No one knows. For whatever, reason, David chose to make his own tabernacle for the ark.

Isn't that similar to what happens today? The Lord wants His people to be one (John 17). We should worship as one, love as one, be united as one. But everyone seems to want to make his own tent, to establish his own center of worship. In the chapters before us, Solomon will eventually unify worship. When Jesus comes back, there will be one church comprised of one loving family. Doctrinal differences will be set aside. Personality clashes will exist no more. How I am looking forward to that day.

2 Chronicles 1:6, 7
And Solomon went up thither to the brasen altar before the LORD, which was at the tabernacle of the congregation, and offered a thousand burnt offerings upon it. In that night did God appear unto Solomon, and said unto him, Ask what I shall give thee.

We burn out giving one offering. Solomon gave 1,000. He spent the day worshiping the Lord, praising the Lord, giving to the Lord, blessing the Lord. And following this inspiration came revelation. Haven't you found that it is as you worship the Lord that His Word becomes alive?

2 Chronicles 1:8, 9
And Solomon said unto God, Thou hast shewed great mercy unto David my father, and hast made me to reign in his stead. Now, O LORD God, let thy promise unto David my father be established: for thou hast made me king over a people like the dust of the earth in multitude.

"What do you want?" the Lord asked Solomon. And Solomon began by acknowledging what the Lord had already done for him. That's always a good place to start. Before you ask the Lord for something, stop and reflect what He's already done for you. You were a captive of Satan, ensnared by sin. So the Father ransomed you from the kingdom of Satan with a heavy-duty price—the blood of His own Son.

Not only are you saved, but you're part of His kingdom. "Lord, You've been merciful in allowing me to reign," Solomon prayed. So, too, the Lord has allowed us to reign with Him (Romans 8:17).

2 Chronicles 1:10 (a)
Give me now wisdom . . .

Where did Solomon get the wisdom to ask for wisdom? It was the answer to his father's prayer (1 Chronicles 22:11).

2 Chronicles 1:10 (b)
. . . and knowledge, that I may go out and come in before this people: for who can judge this thy people, that is so great?

"Seek first the kingdom," Jesus said, "and everything you need will be added to you" (see Matthew 6:33). Solomon practiced what Jesus preached. He didn't seek wealth, honor, power, or glory. In asking for knowledge to wisely rule, he sought not for himself, but for his kingdom.

2 Chronicles 1:11, 12
And God said to Solomon, Because this was in thine heart, and thou hast not asked riches, wealth, or honour, nor the life of thine enemies, neither yet hast asked long life; but hast asked wisdom and knowledge for thyself, that thou mayest judge my people, over whom I have made thee king: Wisdom and knowledge is granted unto thee; and I will give thee riches, and wealth, and honour, such as none of the kings have had that have been before thee, neither shall there any after thee have the like.

In 2 Chronicles 16:9, we read that the eyes of the Lord run to and fro throughout the whole earth to show Himself strong in the heart of them whose heart is perfect toward Him. In other words, the Lord looks for men and women He can trust with His blessing. Are you such an individual? Can the Lord trust you with the blessings He desires to pour out upon you? Solomon sought first the kingdom and God was then able to trust him with much blessing. Are you seeking first His kingdom? It's never too late to start.

2 Chronicles 1:13–17
Then Solomon came from his journey to the high place that was at Gibeon to Jerusalem, from before the tabernacle of the congregation, and reigned over Israel. And Solomon gathered chariots and horsemen: and he had a thousand and four hundred chariots, and twelve thousand horsemen, which he placed in the chariot cities, and with the king at Jerusalem. And the king made silver and gold at Jerusalem as plenteous as stones, and cedar trees made he as the sycomore trees that are in the vale for abundance. And Solomon had horses brought out of Egypt, and linen yarn: the king's merchants received the linen yarn at a price. And they fetched up, and brought forth out of Egypt a chariot for six hundred shekels of silver, and an horse for an hundred and fifty: and so brought they out horses for all the kings of the Hittites, and for the kings of Syria, by their means.

As a businessman, Solomon became extremely wealthy. But in the process, he gathered horses for himself. In Deuteronomy 17, the Lord said the king was not to multiply horses, gold and silver, or wives to himself. Why, then, did Solomon accumulate these very things if he was so wise? Solomon asked for wisdom to govern the people. And he did indeed govern wisely. But in his personal life, he let his guard down and in so doing fell prey to the wiles of the world.

2

The nation of Israel reached its greatest power, peace, and prosperity under Solomon's reign. Yet the fact that five-sixths of the record of his life in 2 Chronicles deals with the building of the temple is indicative of what God saw as important.

2 Chronicles 2:1
And Solomon determined to build an house for the name of the LORD, and an house for his kingdom.

The temple has a three-fold application in the Bible. First, it speaks of the body of Christ (John 2:21). Secondly, it speaks of the body of an individual believer (1 Corinthians 3). Thirdly, it speaks of the body of believers corporately (Ephesians 2:21, 22).

2 Chronicles 2:2
And Solomon told out threescore and ten thousand men to bear burdens, and fourscore thousand to hew in the mountain, and three thousand and six hundred to oversee them.

Solomon was determined to build the temple, but he needed others to help him. "I will build My church and the gates of hell shall not prevail against it," our Greater than Solomon declared (Matthew 16:18). And He graciously has chosen us as His tools.

Seventy thousand were to bear burdens. Burden-bearers speak of prayer warriors. How we need people to pray and bear burdens. Eighty thousand were chosen to carve stones. These are "disciplers"—Sunday school teachers, Bible study leaders, and evangelists who smooth the rough edges of living stones (1 Peter 2:5). Thirty-six hundred were overseers and speak of those involved in leadership ministries.

2 Chronicles 2:3–6
And Solomon sent to Huram the king of Tyre, saying, As thou didst deal with David my father, and didst send him cedars to build him an house to dwell therein, even so deal with me. Behold, I build an house to the name of the LORD my God, to dedicate it to him, and to burn before him sweet incense, and for the continual shewbread, and for the burnt offerings morning and evening, on the sabbaths, and on the new moons, and on the solemn feasts of the LORD our God. This is an ordinance for ever to Israel. And the house which I build is great: for great is our God above all gods. But who is able to build him an house, seeing the heaven and heaven of heavens cannot contain him? who am I then, that I should build him an house, save only to burn sacrifice before him?

Through his request to the king of Tyre, Solomon was not only able to explain the worship practices that would take place within the temple, but also the magnitude of the God he served, for unlike the gods of the surrounding nations, Solomon's God could not be contained in any building.

2 Chronicles 2:7
Send me now therefore a man cunning to work in gold, and in silver, and in brass, and in iron, and in purple, and crimson, and blue, and that can skill to grave with the cunning men that are with me in Judah and in Jerusalem, whom David my father did provide.

Phoenicians were known around the world as the best architects and construction workers. I like the fact that Solomon says, "I'm building a great house for a great God. Send me your best."

2 Chronicles 2:8–10
Send me also cedar trees, fir trees, and algum trees, out of Lebanon: for I know that thy servants can skill to cut timber in Lebanon; and, behold, my servants shall be with thy servants, Even to prepare me timber in abundance: for the house which I am about to build shall be wonderful great. And, behold, I will give to thy servants, the hewers that cut timber, twenty thousand measures of beaten wheat, and twenty thousand measures of barley, and twenty thousand baths of wine, and twenty thousand baths of oil.

The servants would be rewarded with wine and oil, which speak to us of the Spirit, and with wheat and barley, which speak to us of the sustenance found in the Word of God.

2 Chronicles 2:11
Then Huram the king of Tyre answered in writing, which he sent to Solomon, Because the LORD hath loved his people, he hath made thee king over them.

Charles Spurgeon saw in this verse a prophetic picture of Jesus Christ. "Because God has loved His people," he said, "He has made Jesus king over them."

"For God sent not His Son into the world to condemn the world," John writes, "but that the world through Him might be saved" (John 3:17). Jesus did not come to condemn people, but to liberate them.

2 Chronicles 2:12–14
Huram said moreover, Blessed be the LORD God of Israel, that made heaven and earth, who hath given to David the king a wise son, endued with prudence and understanding, that might build an house for the LORD, and an house for his kingdom. And now I have sent a cunning man, endued with understanding, of Huram my father's, The son of a woman of the daughters of Dan, and his father was a man of Tyre, skilful to work in gold, and in silver, in brass, in iron, in stone, and in timber, in purple, in blue, and in fine linen, and in crimson; also to grave any manner of graving, and to find out every device which shall be put to him, with thy cunning men, and with the cunning men of my lord David thy father.

One of the ways the king of Tyre answered Solomon's request was by sending him his top craftsman, the son of an Israelite woman and a man of Tyre.

2 Chronicles 2:15–18
Now therefore the wheat, and the barley, the oil, and the wine, which my lord hath spoken of, let him send unto his servants: And

we will cut wood out of Lebanon, as much as thou shalt need: and we will bring it to thee in floats by sea to Joppa; and thou shall carry it up to Jerusalem. And Solomon numbered all the strangers that were in the land of Israel, after the numbering wherewith David his father had numbered them; and they were found an hundred and fifty thousand and three thousand and six hundred. And he set threescore and ten thousand of them to be bearers of burdens, and fourscore thousand to be hewers in the mountain, and three thousand and six hundred overseers to set the people a work.

If the temple speaks of the body of Christ; if the burden-bearers speak of prayer warriors, the stonecutters of disciples, the overseers of leaders—why would they all be strangers? Because Israel rejected the message of the kingdom. The Jews did not respond to the invitation of Jesus. No wonder, then, that, as a picture of the church, the burden-bearers, stonecutters, and overseers were not of Jewish heritage.

3

2 Chronicles 3:1 (a)
Then Solomon began to build the house of the LORD . . .

In verse 1 of chapter 2, Solomon determined to build the house. Here, in verse 1 of chapter 3, he began to build the house. It's one thing to determine. It's an entirely different thing to begin, to make application, not just proclamation.

2 Chronicles 3:1 (b)
. . . at Jerusalem in mount Moriah, where the LORD appeared unto David his father, in the place that David had prepared in the threshingfloor of Ornan the Jebusite.

Solomon built the temple, a house of sacrifice, on Mt. Moriah, the mount of sacrifice. Mt. Moriah is where Abraham offered his son Isaac. Mt. Moriah is where David paid the full price when he bought the threshingfloor from Ornan. Mt. Moriah peaks at a place called Golgotha, or Calvary.

This tells me the place of beginning is always the place of sacrifice, of time, of money, of energy. At some point, there will be sacrifice made if I'm going to begin to do what God is calling me to do.

2 Chronicles 3:2, 3
And he began to build in the second day of the second month, in the fourth year of his reign. Now these are the things wherein Solomon was instructed for the building of the house of God. The length by cubits after the first measure was threescore cubits, and the breadth twenty cubits.

The temple would be ninety feet long, thirty feet wide, forty-five feet high—twice as big as the tabernacle, but still relatively small. And yet the cost would be approximately ten billion dollars.

2 Chronicles 3:4–8
And the porch that was in the front of the house, the length of it was according to the breadth of the house, twenty cubits, and the height was an hundred and twenty: and he overlaid it within with pure gold. And the greater house he cieled with fir tree, which he overlaid with fine gold, and set thereon palm trees and chains. And he garnished the house with precious stones for beauty: and the gold was gold of Parvaim. He overlaid also the house, the beams, the posts, and the walls thereof, and the doors thereof, with gold; and graved cherubims on the walls. And he made the most holy house, the length whereof was according to the breadth of the house, twenty cubits, and the breadth thereof twenty cubits: and he overlaid it with fine gold, amounting to six hundred talents.

Like the tabernacle, the temple was divided into three main areas: the courtyard, the holy place, and the Holy of Holies. While the courtyard was visible to everyone, the holy place was seen only by the priest. The Holy of Holies was seen only by the high priest only once a year on Yom Kippur, the Day of Atonement.

Even as the temple has three parts, you are a triune being. Your body, seen by all, is the outer court. Your soul, consisting of your mind and emotions, is seen by only a few people, and is thus equivalent to the holy place. Finally, your spirit, like the Holy of Holies, is reserved exclusively for our great High Priest, Jesus Christ. If you want to be a whole person, you must give attention to all three areas—body, soul, and spirit—for they are intricately connected. If I am physically run down, the rest of my temple will be adversely affected. If my mind is not being stimulated or developed, I will be hampered spiritually and physically as well. If I am not taking time to talk to the Lord and to seek Him, my body and soul will suffer the consequences. Therefore, it is the wise person who worships the Lord while he's working out at the gym, who praises the Lord for what he's learning in school. Wherever you're at, take care of the whole person as much as possible.

The more important application, however, is that these three parts of the temple serve as good indicators of where you're at in your walk with the Lord. Maybe you're in the outer court, the place where sacrifice was offered. That's a great first step, but there will come a time when you'll long to be in the holy place, the place of service. Serving the Lord is truly a high calling, but, as Mary discovered, the best place to be is in the Holy of Holies, sitting at His feet (Luke 10:42).

2 Chronicles 3:9
And the weight of the nails was fifty shekels of gold. And he overlaid the upper chambers with gold.

These golden nails were costly indeed. But their cost was nothing in comparison to that of the nails that pierced the hands of Jesus. Therefore, nothing we do for the Lord is too extravagant.

2 Chronicles 3:10–14
And in the most holy house he made two cherubims of image work, and overlaid them with gold. And the wings of the cherubims were twenty cubits long: one wing of the one cherub was five cubits, reaching to the wall of the house: and the other wing was likewise five cubits, reaching to the wing of the other cherub. And one wing of the other cherub was five cubits, reaching to the wall of the house: and the other wing was five cubits also, joining to the wing of the other cherub. The wings of these cherubims spread themselves forth twenty cubits: and they stood on their feet, and their faces were inward. he made the vail of blue, and purple, and crimson, and fine linen, and wrought cherubims thereon.

In Revelation 19, we read that John was so impressed by the angels in heaven that he fell down in worship until he was told by the angel to worship God alone (19:10). Here we see the cherubim facing inward, standing to give worship rather than sitting, facing outward, waiting to accept worship.

2 Chronicles 3:15, 16
Also he made before the house two pillars of thirty and five cubits high, and the chapiter that was on the top of each of them was five cubits. And he made chains, as in the oracle, and put them on the heads of the pillars and made an hundred pomegranates, and put them on the chains.

The chains on the pillars speak of linkage or unity. The pomegranates speak of fruitfulness. Truly, where there is unity, there will be fruit. Where there is division, there will be barrenness. As believers, we must embrace *all* who know Jesus as Savior. And together we'll bring forth fruit.

2 Chronicles 3:17
And he reared up the pillars before the temple, one on the right hand, and the other on the left; and called the name of that on the right hand Jachin, and the name of that on the left Boaz.

In front of the temple stood two huge pillars. One was named *Jachin,* or "He shall establish." The other was named *Boaz,* or "In His strength", because not only was the temple built by God, but it would be maintained by Him as well.

4

The first nine chapters of the Book of 2 Chronicles deal with the reign of Solomon. Yet of those nine chapters, six are devoted to the construction and dedication of the temple. Here in chapter 4, we see the furniture of the temple, every piece symbolic of an aspect of Jesus.

2 Chronicles 4:1
Moreover he made an altar of brass, twenty cubits the length thereof, and twenty cubits the breadth thereof, and ten cubits the height thereof.

The first thing one would see upon entering the courtyard of the temple was the altar. The altar is still where everything begins. Jesus is our Sacrifice. This is what differentiates Christianity from every other religion. Other religions tell people how to live, but make no provision for failure. Christianity not only tells us how to live, but provides provision for inevitable failure through the blood of Jesus Christ.

2 Chronicles 4:2–5
Also he made a molten sea of ten cubits from brim to brim, round in compass, and five cubits the height thereof; and a line of thirty cubits did compass it round about. And under it was the similitude of oxen, which did compass it round about: ten in a cubit, compassing the sea round about. Two rows of oxen were cast, when it was cast. It stood upon twelve oxen, three looking toward the north, and three looking toward the west, and three looking toward the south, and three looking toward the east: and the sea was set above upon them, and all their hinder parts were inward. And the thickness of it was an handbreadth, and the brim of it like the work of the brim of a cup,

with flowers of lilies; and it received and held three thousand baths.

This tank measured approximately fifteen feet across, seven and one-half feet high, and forty-five feet in circumference. After sacrifices were made at the altar, the priests would wash themselves in this huge tank that speaks of Christ, our Purifier. "Now ye are clean through the word which I have spoken unto you," He said (John 15:3). As we spend time in the Word and meditate therein, we, like the priests, are cleansed.

2 Chronicles 4:6
He made also ten lavers, and put five on the right hand, and five on the left, to wash in them: such things as they offered for the burnt offering they washed in them; but the sea was for the priests to wash in.

The ten small tanks that the sacrifices were washed in speak of Christ, our Intercessor. We don't know how to pray as we should, so Jesus takes our prayers and "cleans them up" as He intercedes on our behalf, saying, "Father, what Jon really means is . . ."

2 Chronicles 4:7
And he made ten candlesticks of gold according to their form, and set them in the temple, five on the right hand, and five on the left.

The candlesticks, of course, speak of Christ, our Light (John 8:12).

2 Chronicles 4:8 (a)
He made also ten tables, and placed them in the temple, five on the right side, and five on the left . . .

The tables of showbread speak of Jesus, our Bread (John 6:35).

2 Chronicles 4:8 (b), 9
. . . And he made an hundred basons of gold. Furthermore he made the court of the priests, and the great court, and doors for the court, and overlaid the doors of them with brass.

The doors speak of Jesus, our Door to the Father (John 10:9). Why were they made of brass? Because, throughout Scripture, brass is the metal of judgment and the only way we enter into the presence of God is by realizing that Jesus Christ, our Door, was judged for our sin.

2 Chronicles 4:10–16
And he set the sea on the right side of the east end, over against the south. And Huram made the pots, and the shovels, and the basons. And Huram finished the work that he was to make for king Solomon for the house of God; To wit, the two pillars, and the pommels, and the chapiters which were on the top of the two pillars, and the two wreaths to cover the two pommels of the chapiters which were on the top of the pillars; And four hundred pomegranates on the two wreaths; two rows of pomegranates on each wreath, to cover the two pommels of the chapiters which were upon the pillars. He made also bases, and lavers made he upon the bases; One sea, and twelve oxen under it. The pots also, and the shovels, and the fleshhooks, and all their instruments, did Huram his father make to king Solomon for the house of the LORD of bright brass.

"I have finished the work which thou gavest me to do," Jesus prayed (John 17:4).

"I have finished my course," Paul declared (2 Timothy 4:7).

Here, we see the work that Huram finished. What work has God called *you* to do? Oh, that we would be faithful to finish the task, the work, the course that God has both called us to do and equipped us to complete.

2 Chronicles 4:17, 18
In the plain of Jordan did the king cast them, in the clay ground between Succoth and Zeredathah. Thus Solomon made all these vessels in great abundance: for the weight of the brass could not be found out.

Again, brass speaks of judgment. Just as the weight of the brass used in the temple was too great to weigh, the judgment Jesus absorbed on our behalf cannot be measured.

2 Chronicles 4:19–22
And Solomon made all the vessels that were for the house of God, the golden altar also, and the tables whereon the shewbread was set; Moreover the candlesticks with their lamps, that they should burn after the manner before the oracle, of pure gold; And the flowers, and the lamps, and the tongs, made he of gold, and that perfect gold; And the snuffers, and the basons, and the spoons, and the censers, of pure gold: and the entry of the house, the inner doors thereof for the most holy place, and the doors of the house of the temple, were of gold.

Gold speaks of deity. Yes, brass is emblematic of the judgment Jesus bore on our behalf. But the story doesn't end there. For after Jesus endured the Cross, despising the shame, He sat down at the right hand of the throne of God (Hebrews 12:2).

5

2 Chronicles 5:1 (a)
Thus all the work that Solomon made for the house of the LORD was finished . . .

The temple took seven years to complete. This shows me that when God builds—whether it's us personally or His church corporately—it takes time. Maybe you look at yourself and think you're not growing. But the Lord is working on us, chipping away, strengthening us, and developing us. It just takes time. I'm less and less inclined to judge people or ministries because I know it is only as the years go by that results are seen.

2 Chronicles 5:1 (b), 2
. . . and Solomon brought in all the things that David his father had dedicated; and the silver, and the gold, and all the instruments, put he among the treasures of the house of God. Then Solomon assembled the elders of Israel, and all the heads of the tribes, the chief of the fathers of the children of Israel, unto Jerusalem, to bring up the ark of the covenant of the LORD out of the city of David, which is Zion.

The ark was made of shittim, or acacia wood (Exodus 25:10). Shittim wood never rots and is found in dry ground. Its exterior has thorns and its interior contains a gum-like substance that is used as medicine in the Middle East even to this day. It is not coincidental that this was the wood chosen for the ark because the ark pictures Jesus. Wood that never rots speaks of the fact that Jesus is the same yesterday, today, and forever (Hebrews 13:8). As Isaiah declared, Jesus is a root out of dry ground (Isaiah 53:2). Jesus wore a crown of thorns, and it is by His stripes that we are healed (Isaiah 53:5). The wood was covered with gold. Gold is the metal of deity. Wood speaks of humanity. Together, they paint a picture of Jesus as the God-man.

2 Chronicles 5:3–8
Wherefore all the men of Israel assembled themselves unto the king in the feast which was in the seventh month. And all the elders of Israel came; and the Levites took up the ark. And they brought up the ark, and the tabernacle of the congregation, and all the holy vessels that were in the tabernacle, these did the priests and the Levites bring up. Also king Solomon, and all the congregation of Israel that were assembled unto him before the ark, sacrificed sheep and oxen, which could not be told nor numbered for multitude. And the priests brought in the ark of the covenant of the LORD unto his place, to the oracle of the house, into the most holy place, even under the wings of the cherubims: For the cherubims spread forth their wings over the place of the ark, and the cherubims covered the ark and the staves thereof above.

Inside the ark were the Ten Commandments given to Moses. On top of the ark was the mercy seat. It was at the mercy seat that God met with man (Exodus 25). I'm so glad God meets us not on the basis of the law, but at the place of mercy. Otherwise, none of us would have a prayer or a chance.

Why was the Law kept in the ark at all? Because Jesus Christ was the only One who kept the Law. And because Jesus kept the Law, the Lord meets with us in mercy.

2 Chronicles 5:9
And they drew out the staves of the ark, that the ends of the staves were seen from the ark before the oracle; but they were not seen without. And there it is unto this day.

Why did the priests pull the poles out that were used to carry the ark? Because the temple speaks of permanence. The tabernacle spoke of pilgrimage. The tabernacle speaks of Jesus in His First Coming when He literally "tabernacled" among us (John 1:14). But when He comes again, His kingdom will be established. Therefore, poles were no longer needed.

2 Chronicles 5:10
There was nothing in the ark save the two tables which Moses put therein at Horeb, when the LORD made a covenant with the children of Israel, when they came out of Egypt.

Originally, the ark contained Aaron's rod that budded and a pot of manna along with the tablets of the law (Hebrews 9:4). Here, only the Law remained.

2 Chronicles 5:11, 12
And it came to pass, when the priests were come out of the holy place: (for all the priests that were present were sanctified, and did not then wait by course: Also the Levites which were the singers, all of them of Asaph, of Heman, of Jeduthun, with their sons and their brethren, being arrayed in white linen, having cymbals and psalteries

and harps, stood at the east end of the altar, and with them an hundred and twenty priests sounding with trumpets:)

The priests, arrayed in the white linen of righteousness, stood around the altar, the place of sacrifice. Clothed in the righteousness of God in Christ Jesus (Isaiah 61:10; 2 Corinthians 5:21), we are to stand at the altar of sacrifice and die to our own pride.

2 Chronicles 5:13
It came even to pass, as the trumpeters and singers were as one, to make one sound to be heard in praising and thanking the LORD; and when they lifted up their voice with the trumpets and cymbals and instruments of musick, and praised the LORD, saying, For he is good; for his mercy endureth for ever: that then the house was filled with a cloud, even the house of the LORD;

The trumpeters and singers were as one. When we meet together to worship the Lord, our own problems begin to shrink; our own needs are diminished as we are united in praise. I have a tremendous desire to be part of something bigger than myself, don't you? I find that fulfillment in the place of worship, when I am melted together with brothers and sisters in praise.

2 Chronicles 5:14
So that the priests could not stand to minister by reason of the cloud: for the glory of the LORD had filled the house of God.

So blessed was the Lord by the praise and worship of His people that there was room for nothing else but His presence.

THIS TEMPLE: A PLACE OF PRAISE

A Topical Study of 2 CHRONICLES 5:11–14

There was a government that spent ten billion dollars on a building that was only ninety feet long and thirty feet wide. In the specs for this building, every nail was to be made of solid gold. Was this extravagant? Wasteful? Not when you consider that the building was Solomon's temple. Solomon's temple was costly indeed, but it was extremely important and spiritually significant for two reasons. It was a picture *from* God and a place *for* God.

A Picture from God

Knowing that we are children, our heavenly Father painted all sorts of pictures in the Old Testament to illustrate spiritual truths. The temple is one such picture and illustrates three things.

First, it illustrates Jesus Himself. The Pharisees came to Jesus and said, "Show us a sign to validate who you are."

"One sign I'll give you," He answered. "Destroy this temple and in three days, I'll raise it up again" (John 2:19).

The tabernacle was half the size of the temple, with an outward appearance that was extremely ordinary. Inside, however, it was magnificent. According to Hebrews 8 and 9, the tabernacle speaks of Jesus in His First Coming. But the temple, a magnificent structure both inside and out, speaks of Jesus in His Second Coming.

- Initially, Jesus came alone as the babe of Bethlehem.
  When He comes again, He'll come with 10,000 of His saints (Jude 14).
- When Jesus came the first time, He wore a crown of thorns.
  When He comes again, He'll wear the crown of a conquering King (Revelation 6:2).
- When Jesus came the first time, He was mocked and rejected.
  When He comes again, He'll be worshiped as King of kings and Lord of lords (Philippians 2:10).

Secondly, the temple illustrates who we are individually. First Corinthians 3 and 6 both tell us our bodies are the temple of God. Are our bodies valuable? In a sense, no. If all the elements of your body were sold, the price would be somewhere between ten dollars and fifteen dollars. And yet ten billion dollars would not begin to pay the price to build a computer that could function one tenth as well as your brain. Fearfully and wonderfully made, we are valuable indeed (Psalm 139:14).

Thirdly, the temple is a picture of our body corporately. In Ephesians 2, Paul tells us we are a holy habitation, being fit together that God might dwell in our midst in the person of His Spirit.

A Place for God

Solomon was wiser than to think that the temple could contain God. In 2 Chronicles 2, he said, "I realize even the heavens can't contain Him." Thus, he constructed the temple not to place parameters around God, but to bring pleasure to Him. As His people, we exist not so much to get as to give.

The Church of Jesus Christ exists for three reasons. The third most important reason is to evangelize the world. The second most important reason is for the edification of the believers—that we might be taught the Word and grow in the knowledge of God. But our primary reason for existence, both corporately and individually is to give God pleasure (Revelation 4:11). What a difference it would make in coming to church if we said, "I'm not coming to be impressed or to find fault. I come to church to assemble with the temple of God, to praise Him and give Him pleasure."

Our text says the people praised Him because He is good and His mercy endures forever. The same is true. I come to church because God is good. He's been so good to me that the least I can do is worship Him with the saints. We complain so quickly and gripe so readily, but the mercy and lovingkindness of God is heaped upon us daily (Psalm 68:19).

Whether we know it or not, every one of us craves the glory of God in our life. Where do we find it? In the temple of God. As it did in Solomon's temple, those who bring glory *to* the Lord will experience the glory *of* the Lord as His presence fills the temple of their lives.

How do we bring glory to God? Following are three ways . . .

We Can Glorify Him with Our Mouths . . .

And after these things I heard a great voice of much people in heaven, saying, Alleluia; Salvation, and glory, and honour, and power, unto the Lord our God.

Revelation 19:1

Sing, O barren, thou that didst not bear; break forth into singing, and cry aloud, thou that didst not travail with child . . . Isaiah 54:1 (a)

Do you feel barren or sterile? Sing out and you'll find a dynamic released in your spirit that wouldn't have been otherwise.

We Can Glorify God with Our Hands . . .

O clap your hands, all ye people; shout unto God with the voice of triumph.

Psalm 47:1

Thus will I bless thee while I live: I will lift up my hands in thy name.

Psalm 63:4

When we clap our hands, it's an act of celebration *in* God. When we lift our hands, it's an act of surrender *to* Him.

We Can Glorify God with Our Feet . . .

O come, let us worship and bow down: let us kneel before the LORD *our maker.*

Psalm 95:6

Ye that stand in the house of the Lord, in the courts of the house of our God, Praise the LORD*; for the* LORD *is good . . .* Psalm 135:2, 3 (a)

Let them praise his name in the dance . . . Psalm 149:3 (a)

Bowing before the Lord is an expression of humility. Standing in the house of the Lord is an expression of respect. Dancing before the Lord is an expression of joy in the Lord.

When we worship the Lord, we'll experience greater and greater dimensions of His glory. Is that the purpose we should worship Him? No. That's just a side benefit. We worship Him to give Him glory and to praise His name because indeed He is *good*.

6 2 Chronicles 6:1, 2
Then said Solomon, The LORD hath said that he would dwell in the thick darkness. But I have built an house of habitation for thee, and a place for thy dwelling for ever.

It has been said that if an atomic bomb were detonated, anyone within fifty miles who glanced in its direction would be permanently blinded. If the glory and greatness of God were revealed, it would make an atomic detonation look like the lighting of a match. That is why the Lord dwells in thick darkness. He protects us until we have new bodies and can relate to Him without getting blown away (Philippians 3:21).

2 Chronicles 6:3–6
And the king turned his face, and blessed the whole congregation of Israel: and all the congregation of Israel stood. And he said, Blessed be the LORD God of Israel, who hath with his hands fulfilled that which he spake with his mouth to my father David, saying, Since the day that I brought forth my people out of the land of Egypt I chose no city among all the tribes of Israel to build an house in, that my name might be there; neither chose I any man to be a ruler over my people Israel: But I have chosen Jerusalem, that my name might be there; and have chosen David to be over my people Israel.

Jerusalem is an extremely beautiful city. But God didn't choose it because it was beautiful. Rather, it is beautiful because God chose it. You see, Jerusalem is really very ordinary. The prettiest spot is actually in Samaria, where Ahab and Jezebel chose to build their palace. From their palace, they could look to the west and see the Mediterranean Sea. They could look east and see the Jordan Valley and the Jordan River. From the north, they could see Mt. Hermon. Looking south, they overlooked the city of Jerusalem. It was beautiful. But God didn't choose that area. He chose an ordinary place, just as He chooses ordinary people like you and me. He uses the foolish things of this world and then beautifies them, just as, slowly but surely, He's beautifying us (1 Corinthians 1:26–31).

2 Chronicles 6:7–11
Now it was in the heart of David my father to build an house for the name of the LORD God of Israel. But the LORD said to David my father, Forasmuch as it was in thine heart to build an house for my name, thou didst well in that it was in thine heart: Notwithstanding thou shalt not build the house; but thy son which shall come forth out of thy loins, he shall build the house for my name. The LORD therefore hath performed his word that he hath spoken: for I am risen up in the room of David my father, and am set on the throne of Israel, as the LORD promised, and have built the house for the name of the LORD God of Israel. And in it have I put the ark, wherein is the covenant of the LORD, that he made with the children of Israel.

David had at least eight wives and at least twenty sons. But it always impresses me that the Lord chose Solomon to build the temple and rule the country at the very time the kingdom would come to its apex in history. Solomon was the child of David and Bathsheba. After the Lord dealt with David and Bathsheba by taking their firstborn child home, He turned right around and blessed them with Solomon. God could have chosen one of David's other sons, but in choosing Solomon, it's as if the Father is saying, "I want this to be an illustration of the fact that after I chasten, I bless."

Dear saint, regardless of the mistakes or blunders in your past, if you come to the Lord, He can take any situation and begin to turn it around. Our God is the God of the second chance. He really is.

2 Chronicles 6:12, 13
And he stood before the altar of the LORD in the presence of all the congregation of Israel, and spread forth his hands: For Solomon had made a brasen scaffold, of five cubits long, and five cubits broad, and three cubits high, and had set it in the midst of the court: and upon it he stood, and kneeled down upon his knees before all the congregation of Israel, and spread forth his hands toward heaven.

The temple was complete. The ark was in place. The glory had descended. And now, after preaching to the people, Solomon prayed for the temple. Note his posture. He was on his knees. You don't need to be on your knees when you pray. And yet prayer on our knees is an outward sign of submission and humility before the Lord. The side benefits of kneeling in prayer are that it's a lot harder to stumble in pride or to fall asleep when you're on your knees.

2 Chronicles 6:14
And said, O LORD God of Israel, there is no God like thee in the heaven, nor in the earth; which keepest covenant, and shewest mercy

unto thy servants, that walk before thee with all their hearts:

Solomon begins by acknowledging the greatness of God and then the goodness of God. Haven't you found that, when you consider how big and powerful God is, suddenly the problems that seemed so overwhelming to you shrink in size? Solomon wisely begins his prayer by worshiping the Lord. Then he moves into praise . . .

2 Chronicles 6:15
Thou which hast kept with thy servant David my father that which thou hast promised him; and spakest with thy mouth, and hast fulfilled it with thine hand, as it is this day.

Gang, when your prayer life seems to be dry, praise and thank the Lord, and soon you'll find yourself swimming in an ocean of gratitude. After worshiping and praising, Solomon makes his petition . . .

2 Chronicles 6:16–20
Now therefore, O LORD God of Israel, keep with thy servant David my father that which thou hast promised him, saying, There shall not fail thee a man in my sight to sit upon the throne of Israel; yet so that thy children take heed to their way to walk in my law, as thou hast walked before me. Now then, O LORD God of Israel, let thy word be verified, which thou hast spoken unto thy servant David. But will God in very deed dwell with men on the earth? behold, heaven and the heaven of heavens cannot contain thee; how much less this house which I have built! Have respect therefore to the prayer of thy servant, and to his supplication, O LORD my God, to hearken unto the cry and the prayer which thy servant prayeth before thee: That thine eyes may be open upon this house day and night, upon the place whereof thou hast said that thou wouldest put thy name there; to hearken unto the prayer which thy servant prayeth toward this place.

One of the most effective, powerful ways to pray is to pray with your Bible open. When you pray the promises of God, you can be sure that He will answer. "Let thy word be verified," Solomon prayed, holding the Lord to His Word.

2 Chronicles 6:21
Hearken therefore unto the supplications of thy servant, and of thy people Israel, which they shall make toward this place: hear thou from thy dwelling place, even from heaven; and when thou hearest, forgive.

Here, in the midst of his prayer, foreseeing the problems the people will encounter, Solomon wisely intercedes for them before the problems arise. Solomon wasn't the first man in Scripture to do this. In Job 1, we read that every morning, Job offered sacrifice for his kids lest they sinned. It is still the wise parent who prays for his kids *before* they run into problems.

In verses 22 through 39, we see Solomon pray about neighbor problems, national problems, and natural problems . . .

2 Chronicles 6:22, 23
If a man sin against his neighbour, and an oath be laid upon him to make him swear, and the oath come before thine altar in this house; Then hear thou from heaven, and do, and judge thy servants, by requiting the wicked, by recompensing his way upon his own head; and by justifying the righteous, by giving him according to his righteousness.

"If a man sins, and he comes to the temple to swear his innocence, You judge him, Lord," Solomon prayed. I like this because it's letting the Lord be the judge. We don't need to judge each other. That's for the Lord to do because only He sees the full picture (1 Samuel 16:7).

2 Chronicles 6:24, 25
And if thy people Israel be put to the worse before the enemy, because they have sinned against thee; and shall return and confess thy name, and pray and make supplication before thee in this house; Then hear thou from the heavens, and forgive the sin of thy people Israel, and bring them again unto the land which thou gavest to them and to their fathers.

"If the people sin and go through a season of defeat and pray to You, Lord hear their prayers in days of national difficulty," Solomon prayed.

2 Chronicles 6:26–31
When the heaven is shut up, and there is no rain, because they have sinned against thee; yet if they pray toward this place, and confess thy name, and turn from their sin, when thou dost afflict them; Then hear thou from heaven, and forgive the sin of thy servants, and of thy people Israel, when thou hast taught them the good way, wherein they should walk; and send rain upon thy land, which thou hast given unto thy people for an inheritance. If there be dearth in the land, if there be pestilence, if there be blasting, or mildew, locusts, or caterpillers; if their enemies besiege them in the cities

of their land; whatsoever sore or whatsoever sickness there be: Then what prayer or what supplication soever shall be made of any man, or of all thy people Israel, when every one shall know his own sore and his own grief, and shall spread forth his hands in this house: Then hear thou from heaven thy dwelling place, and forgive, and render unto every man according unto all his ways, whose heart thou knowest; (for thou only knowest the hearts of the children of men:) That they may fear thee, to walk in thy ways, so long as they live in the land which thou gavest unto our fathers.

"Lord, once Your people humble themselves, forgive their sin and bless them once again."

1 Chronicles 6:32, 33
Moreover concerning the stranger, which is not of thy people Israel, but is come from a far country for thy great name's sake, and thy mighty hand, and thy stretched out arm; if they come and pray in this house; Then hear thou from the heavens, even from thy dwelling place, and do according to all that the stranger calleth to thee for; that all people of the earth may know thy name, and fear thee, as doth thy people Israel, and may know that this house which I have built is called by thy name.

In this, we see the calling of Israel to be an apostolic nation. That is, Israel was to extend an invitation to the stranger, to the Gentile. Israel was not to be simply a group of people enjoying the blessings of God for themselves. Rather, they were blessed so that others could see the reality of God and to be drawn to Him. Israel's message was to be "Come and see." Jesus' message to His church, on the other hand, was "Go and tell" (Matthew 28:19, 20).

Both the church and Israel were to be missionary-minded. This is true personally as well as corporately, for if you turn inward and consider only how you can be more successful or how you can be happier, your experience with the Lord will sour. We were saved to serve. If we lose that vision, we'll lose our effectiveness, both individually and as a church family.

2 Chronicles 6:34–39
If thy people go out to war against their enemies by the way that thou shalt send them, and they pray unto thee toward this city which thou hast chosen, and the house which I have built for thy name; Then hear thou from the heavens their prayer and their supplication, and maintain their cause. If they sin against thee, (for there is no man which sinneth not) and thou be angry with them, and deliver them over before their enemies, and they carry them away captives unto a land far off or near; Yet if they bethink themselves in the land whither they are carried captive, and turn and pray unto thee in the land of their captivity, saying, We have sinned, we have done amiss, and have dealt wickedly; If they return to thee with all their heart and with all their soul in the land of their captivity, whither they have carried them captives, and pray toward their land, which thou gavest unto their fathers, and toward the city which thou hast chosen, and toward the house which I have built for thy name: Then hear thou from the heavens, even from thy dwelling place, their prayer and their supplications, and maintain their cause, and forgive thy people which have sinned against thee.

Solomon goes on to pray more specifically for the people in times when they would be taken away into captivity. And in captivity, if they would turn to the Lord and remember from whence they had fallen, he asked that God would forgive them. Israel was indeed carried away into captivity in Babylon, where they remained for seventy years. Perhaps it was on the basis of this prayer of Solomon that there was a man in Babylon who, three times a day, opened his window and prayed. That man was Daniel. And God heard his prayers, and restored the people back to their land.

2 Chronicles 6:40–42
Now, my God, let, I beseech thee, thine eyes be open, and let thine ears be attent unto the prayer that is made in this place. Now therefore arise, O LORD God, into thy resting place, thou, and the ark of thy strength: let thy priests, O LORD God, be clothed with salvation, and let thy saints rejoice in goodness. O LORD God, turn not away the face of thine anointed: remember the mercies of David thy servant.

So ends this eloquent yet humble prayer of Solomon, a prayer so effective that it literally brought down fire from heaven . . .

7

2 Chronicles 7:1, 2
Now when Solomon had made an end of praying, the fire came down from heaven, and consumed the burnt offering and the sacrifices; and the glory of the LORD filled the house. And the priests could not enter into the house of the LORD, because the glory of the LORD had filled the LORD's house.

The glory of the Lord filled the house previously when the people praised the Lord (2 Chronicles 5:13, 14). Here, the glory of the Lord fills the house when Solomon prays. This tells me that the glory of God—the substance, fullness, and reality I crave—will fill us both personally and corporately when we praise and when we pray. Two ways you can experience the glory of God flooding into your life is by praising and praying.

2 Chronicles 7:3–5
And when all the children of Israel saw how the fire came down, and the glory of the LORD upon the house, they bowed themselves with their faces to the ground upon the pavement, and worshipped, and praised the LORD, saying, For he is good; for his mercy endureth for ever. Then the king and all the people offered sacrifices before the LORD. And king Solomon offered a sacrifice of twenty and two thousand oxen, and an hundred and twenty thousand sheep: so the king and all the people dedicated the house of God.

Twenty-two thousand oxen and 120,000 sheep is a substantial sacrifice. Yet even twenty-two million oxen and one hundred and twenty million sheep would not compare to the sacrifice of the single Lamb of God. People cringe when we talk about sacrifices numbering this many. Why was there such a slaughter? Because God is painting a picture, showing us the seriousness of sin. The immensity of sacrifices offered point out that the price Jesus paid is immense, incomprehensible.

2 Chronicles 7:6, 7
And the priests waited on their offices: the Levites also with instruments of musick of the LORD, which David the king had made to praise the LORD, because his mercy endureth for ever, when David praised by their ministry; and the priests sounded trumpets before them, and all Israel stood. Moreover Solomon hallowed the middle of the court that was before the house of the LORD: for there he offered burnt offerings, and the fat of the peace offerings, because the brasen altar which Solomon had made was not able to receive the burnt offerings, and the meat offerings, and the fat.

So numerous were the offerings that the altar was not able to contain them. So additional altars were set up in the temple.

2 Chronicles 7:8, 9
Also at the same time Solomon kept the feast seven days, and all Israel with him, a very great congregation, from the entering in of Hamath unto the river of Egypt. And in the eighth day they made a solemn assembly: for they kept the dedication of the altar seven days, and the feast seven days.

The dedication of the temple took place immediately preceding the Feast of Tabernacles (1 Kings 8:1–12).

2 Chronicles 7:10
And on the three and twentieth day of the seventh month he sent the people away into their tents, glad and merry in heart for the goodness that the LORD had shewed unto David, and to Solomon, and to Israel his people.

Because a large number of the offerings were peace offerings, joy abounded. Gladness and merriment of heart are the result of being in God's presence (Psalm 16:11).

2 Chronicles 7:11–14
Thus Solomon finished the house of the LORD, and the king's house: and all that came into Solomon's heart to make in the house of the LORD, and in his own house, he prosperously effected. And the LORD appeared to Solomon by night, and said unto him, I have heard thy prayer, and have chosen this place to myself for an house of sacrifice. If I shut up heaven that there be no rain, or if I command the locusts to devour the land, or if I send pestilence among my people; If my people, which are called by my name, shall humble themselves, and pray, and seek my face, and turn from their wicked ways; then will I hear from heaven, and will forgive their sin, and will heal their land.

This passage is so important because it says God's people have a responsibility for the society in which they live. We can't just curse our society and the sin therein. We must say, "Lord, forgive *us,*" for Jesus said that we are the salt and light of the earth (Matthew 5:13, 14). If our country is going down the tubes, we must take personal responsibility because we're responsible to heal wounds and light the way. If we're going through difficulty and chaos as a nation, we as believers must say, "Lord, have we been failing? Have we been playing and not praying? Forgive us." Anyone can curse the darkness of our society. We must be those who are lights, praying rather than complaining.

2 Chronicles 7:15–22

Now mine eyes shall be open, and mine ears attent unto the prayer that is made in this place. For now have I chosen and sanctified this house, that my name may be there for ever: and mine eyes and mine heart shall be there perpetually. And as for thee, if thou wilt walk before me, as David thy father walked, and do according to all that I have commanded thee, and shalt observe my statues and my judgments; Then will I stablish the throne of thy kingdom, according as I have covenanted with David thy father, saying, There shall not fail thee a man to be ruler in Israel. But if ye turn away, and forsake my statutes and my commandments, which I have set before you, and shall go and serve other gods, and worship them; Then will I pluck them up by the roots out of my land which I have given them; and this house, which I have sanctified for my name, will I cast out of my sight, and will make it to be a proverb and a byword among all nations. And this house, which is high, shall be an astonishment to every one that passeth by it; so that he shall say, Why hath the LORD done thus unto this land, and unto this house? And it shall be answered, Because they forsook the LORD God of their fathers, which brought them forth out of the land of Egypt, and laid hold on other gods, and worshipped them, and served them: therefore hath he brought all this evil upon them.

The Jewish people have indeed become "a proverb and a byword among all nations" for there is anti-Semitism in virtually every part of the civilized world. The Lord said this would happen. "If My people ignore Me, this house which is high shall be cast down and the people scattered," He warned. Four centuries later, that's precisely what happened. The people had ignored the Lord and returned to idolatry. As a result, He ordered them plucked out of the land and the temple destroyed.

I remind you once again that the Lord will let you go, but you're going to come back. He'll let you pursue your own pleasure. The question is, how hard do you want to hit when you return? If you're flirting with sin, you'll come home because the Lord loves you too much to let you be lost. The question is, what will it take to bring you back?

SPLAT!

A Topical Study of 2 CHRONICLES 7:17–22

Just as we as earthly parents know the importance of disciplining our children, so our heavenly Father knows the necessity of disciplining us. In the text before us, God the Father speaks to Solomon, concerning the children of Israel, saying, "If they forsake Me, if they forget about Me, if they ignore Me or turn away from Me, I will pluck them out of this land and destroy this temple. And all nations shall mock them."

I believe the Bible teaches "rubber band theology." That is, God will give you lots of space; the Father will give you lots of room. You can wander far away from Him. You can ignore the need for Bible study and fellowship. You can pray only inconsistently and routinely if at all. He'll let you move into times of carnality and sin, but you're going to come back. The question is, how hard do you want to hit when you do?

Like a rubber band being stretched, the farther you wander, the harder you'll hit. It's your choice. Jesus said no man can pluck us out of His hand (John 10:27–30). Therefore, we *will* come back. The only question is, how painful and brutal do you want it to be?

The people of Israel found this out historically. The temple had just been constructed. It was a magnificent structure—ten billion dollars perhaps was spent on this project. There were 80,000 men carving stones in such a way that when the stones were brought to the temple mount, they fit together so perfectly that historian Josephus tells us a knife blade couldn't fit between the stones. Seventy thousand men gathered materials. Thirty-five hundred men oversaw the project. Over 150,000 men worked for over seven years to complete this glorious structure. Finally, the day came when it was completed. The glory of God descended and filled the temple so fully and completely that there was not any room to minister.

Then Solomon prayed. And God sent fire from heaven to consume the sacrifice on the altar. The people experienced the glory of God falling upon them. They worshiped and went their way rejoicing. After this dedication took place, God visited Solomon and gave him this warning: "Your prayer has been heard. Know this, however. If My people turn from Me, they will experience difficult days."

Now, if God knows we have a tendency to stray, why doesn't He just keep us from straying in the first place? For the answer to this question, turn to Luke 15, where we find a story known virtually in every culture—the story of the prodigal son . . .

A son went to his father and said, "Dad, why should I wait until you die to get my inheritance? By that time, I'll be too old to enjoy it." So the son took his inheritance, went to a far country, and spent it on partying. When famine hit, he found himself in a most peculiar place for a Jew: he found himself in a pigpen. When he finally came to his senses, he said, "This is crazy. The servants in my father's house fare better than this. I'll go home and ask if I can be a servant in his household."

Now what would have happened had the father, hearing his son was having hard times in the far country, sent one of his servants to bring him back? The servant would have traveled to the far country, grabbed the son by the collar, and marched him home, where his father would have said, "Son, I hope you learned your lesson. I want you to go to your room and stay there until you're sorry." If he was like most kids, the son would have gone to his room, but instead of feeling sorry for his sin, he would have felt sorry for himself, thinking he was on the brink of making it big in the bacon and sausage business, until his dad ruined everything.

That's our tendency. If we were rescued, or forced to come home, our tendency would be to say, "I wasn't doing that bad." So the father wisely let the prodigal reach the end of his own rope.

There is something unique about us. We are the only part of God's creation that refuses to get into harmony with His purpose. Look at the trees. Without exception, every single one is fulfilling its purpose. They are all participating in a program designed by God called photosynthesis. That is, they take in pollution and convert it into oxygen. Not one tree folds its branches and pouts. Every single tree is in beautiful harmony with the purpose of God.

Look at the stars above. They are set in position so perfectly and so consistently that captains can navigate in the open sea. Not one star says, "I want to be a superstar. I want to be where I want to be."

Wherever you look in creation, you'll see every part in harmony with its purpose. But there is one exception: the funny, two-legged creatures on planet earth. We go our own way. Why? Because God gave us the choice each day to either walk in harmony with Him or to rebel against Him. Why did God do this? Because He loves us, and true love must have a choice. Love is not love if it is forced. Therefore, God is willing to take a risk and say, "I'll give you your choice: whether to serve Me and flow with My purpose for your life or to be rebellious, to go into the far country, to live in the pigpen.

The Jews opted for the second alternative. They forgot God. Oh, they gave Him lip service and went through the motions of worship, until the Lord allowed the Babylonians to come down and carry them into captivity for seventy years. Finally, in captivity, a group of them, like the prodigal son, came to their senses and began to seek God. And like the father in Luke 15, God restored His people and brought them back to their land again.

Will the Father have to allow you to be carried off into captivity? Will He allow you to be carried off into some unbelievable difficulty because you have ignored Him and refused to participate in the plan and program He has for your life? He'll give you that freedom. But you'll come back. The question is, how hard do you want to hit?

Hear the heart of our Father and learn the lesson of history. Don't allow your temple to be destroyed. Don't allow your life to be carried away captive, your attitude to grow bitter, your heart to grow cold, your life to be needlessly hurt. You don't have to go through it if you'll cleave to the Lord and stay close to Him.

---

8 **2 Chronicles 8:1, 2**

And it came to pass at the end of twenty years, wherein Solomon had built the house of the LORD, and his own house, That the cities which Huram had restored to Solomon, Solomon built them, and caused the children of Israel to dwell there.

In 1 Kings 9:11–13, we read that the king of Tyre had given Solomon gold to build his palace. When Solomon paid him back with twenty cities of Galilee, Hiram declared they were substandard and refused to accept them. So here we see Solomon rebuilding them.

2 Chronicles 8:3

And Solomon went to Hamath-zobah, and prevailed against it.

This is the only war recorded in Scripture in which Solomon was engaged. He was not a fighter, but a man of peace.

2 Chronicles 8:4–8

And he built Tadmor in the wilderness, and all the store cities, which he built in Hamath. Also he built Beth-horon the upper, and Beth-horon the nether, fenced cities, with walls, gates, and bars; And Baalath, and all the store cities that Solomon had, and all the chariot cities, and the cities of the horsemen, and all that Solomon desired to build in Jerusalem, and in Lebanon, and throughout all the land of his dominion. As for all the people that were left of the Hittites, and the Amorites, and the Perizzites, and the Hivites, and the Jebusites, which were not of Israel, But of their children, who were

left after them in the land, whom the children of Israel consumed not, them did Solomon make to pay tribute until this day.

Although the Canaanites were to have been exterminated when the children of Israel entered the Promised Land, many of them remained in the land. Solomon taxed them heavily, but did not harm them physically. Why? Because they were a source of revenue. Here, Solomon begins compromising—and he'll pay a price as his reign continues.

Sometimes, like Solomon, we say, "I can't get rid of that sin. I can't rectify that business matter. Oh, I know it isn't right, but I've got to be practical." All too often, we think we get away with sin because we don't experience immediate repercussions. But we don't. "God is not mocked," Paul would write to the Galatians. "Whatever a man sows, that will he reap." (see Galatians 6:7). Because Solomon did not deal with the Canaanites, they would reintroduce idolatry to the people of Israel, and it would lead to disaster.

2 Chronicles 8:9, 10
But of the children of Israel did Solomon make no servants for his work; but they were men of war, and chief of his captains, and captains of his chariots and horsemen. And these were the chief of king Solomon's officers, even two hundred and fifty, that bare rule over the people.

Only the Canaanites were taxed. The Israelites were in positions of leadership.

2 Chronicles 8:11
And Solomon brought up the daughter of Pharaoh out of the city of David unto the house that he had built for her: for he said, My wife shall not dwell in the house of David king of Israel, because the places are holy, whereunto the ark of the LORD hath come.

Solomon continues his compromise by taking an Egyptian woman and keeping her outside of the city. Why did Solomon have seven hundred wives? Some commentators suggest it was for political reasons—that by marrying the daughter of a king, he would be less vulnerable to attack. That is possible. But were *seven hundred* political alliances necessary?

2 Chronicles 8:12–14
Then Solomon offered burnt offerings unto the LORD on the altar of the LORD, which he had built before the porch, Even after a certain rate every day, offering according to the commandment of Moses, on the sabbaths, and on the new moons, and on the solemn feasts, three times in the year, even in the feast of unleavened bread, and in the feast of weeks, and in the feast of tabernacles. And he appointed, according to the order of David his father, the courses of the priests to their service, and the Levites to their charges, to praise and minister before the priests, as the duty of every day required: the porters also by their courses at every gate: for so had David the man of God commanded.

Every day there was praise, sacrifice, and music ascending to the Lord.

2 Chronicles 8:15–18
And they departed not from the commandment of the king unto the priests and Levites concerning any matter, or concerning the treasures. Now all the work of Solomon was prepared unto the day of the foundation of the house of the LORD, and until it was finished. So the house of the LORD was perfected. Then went Solomon to Ezion-geber, and to Eloth, at the sea side in the land of Edom. And Huram sent him by the hands of his servants ships, and servants that had knowledge of the sea; and they went with the servants of Solomon to Ophir, and took thence four hundred and fifty talents of gold, and brought them to king Solomon.

The Jews at this time were very suspicious of the ocean and reluctant to go into the sea at all. Yet here Solomon establishes a navy in a joint business venture with Hiram, king of Tyre. The Phoenicians were excellent sailors. So Israel joined them and sailed off to India on what was probably a three-year voyage, netting four hundred and fifty talents of gold in the process. Compare this to the 120,000 talents of gold David was able to acquire not through compromise but through conquest. Solomon went the safe route. David took a more bold approach. Their gain shows the difference. Which do you want? I'd rather fight the war in faith.

9 Because the nation of Israel had an apostolic calling, part of the purpose for the dedication of the temple was so that the rest of the world might see the glory and blessing of God and be drawn to Him. In other words, the world was invited to come to Israel to see what God was doing. As history unfolded, however, Israel made a tragic mistake when she lost this vision and turned inward, concerned only about her own

welfare. But at this point in her story, Israel did indeed influence the world, for 1,500 miles away, a queen heard of Solomon's splendor and came to Jerusalem to see it for herself . . .

2 Chronicles 9:1 (a)
And when the queen of Sheba heard of the fame of Solomon, she came . . .

Where was Sheba? There are two possibilities: one was in Arabia, the other in Ethiopia. In the 1980s, there were news stories of Jews leaving Ethiopia, demanding acceptance in Israel as Jewish citizens. How did these Ethiopians become converts to Judaism? Their answer was that they were descendants of the queen of Sheba and of those who converted to Judaism under her reign in approximately 1000 B.C. This is very possible. But even if Sheba was in Arabia, the journey would have been over 1,500 miles from there to Jerusalem—a trip that would have taken this queen seventy-five days on the back of a camel.

2 Chronicles 9:1 (b)
. . . to prove Solomon with hard questions at Jerusalem . . .

Most people think of themselves as seekers of truth. But in reality, are we, or do we simply raise questions intellectually as long as they don't touch us personally? I think of Pontius Pilate who asked Jesus, "What is truth?," but walked away before Jesus answered (John 18:38).

Many people ask, "What is truth?" But, like Pilate, they don't really want to stick around for the answer. Because the queen of Sheba was a genuine seeker of truth, her record is preserved for all eternity in the passage before us, and her character was commended by no less than Jesus Himself (Matthew 12:42).

2 Chronicles 9:1 (c)
. . . with a very great company, and camels that bare spices, and gold in abundance, and precious stones: and when she was come to Solomon, she communed with him of all that was in her heart.

The queen of Sheba didn't simply want her curiosity satisfied, but came with riches to give to Solomon. In other words, she came to commit herself to his belief if indeed she found it to be correct.

2 Chronicles 9:2, 3
And Solomon told her all her questions: and there was nothing hid from Solomon which he told her not. And when the queen of Sheba had seen the wisdom of Solomon, and the house that he had built,

The queen of Sheba saw not only the wisdom of Solomon, but also the house he had built. Gang, our Greater than Solomon is building a far greater house, a holy temple of brothers and sisters throughout the world and throughout history (Ephesians 2:19–22).

2 Chronicles 9:4 (a)
And the meat of his table . . .

The meat at Solomon's table was impressive indeed. From 1 Kings 4:22, 23, we know one day's provision consisted of 190 bushels of fine flour, 390 bushels of meal, 10 fat oxen, 20 oxen from pastures, and 100 sheep. The queen of Sheba saw the magnificence of this food spread every day before Solomon and his staff. But our Greater than Solomon has spread before us a Table infinitely richer (1 Corinthians 11:23–27).

2 Chronicles 9:4 (b)
. . . and the sitting of his servants, and the attendance of his ministers, and their apparel; his cupbearers also, and their apparel . . .

Not only was the queen of Sheba impressed with Solomon's wisdom and riches, but she was also impressed with Solomon's servants and their apparel. The apparel of those who attend our Greater than Solomon is far more magnificent than the apparel of Solomon's court, for Isaiah 61:10 says we are arrayed in robes of righteousness.

You might not feel righteous. Others might not say you're righteous. But, as a believer, the Father looks at you as being robed in righteousness because of the finished work of the Cross. Jesus Christ paid the price for our sin and robed us with His righteousness. Then He opens up opportunities for service, tells us how to serve, energizes us for service, and, finally, rewards us for service. *Amazing* grace!

2 Chronicles 9:4 (c)
. . . and his ascent by which he went up into the house of the LORD; there was no more spirit in her.

The ascent most likely speaks of the stairs to the altar. That Solomon would be able to ascend to the house of the Lord is incredible. But it's not anything compared to the ascent of our Greater than Solomon when He returned to His Father after He rose from the dead.

2 Chronicles 9:5, 6 (a)
And she said to the king, It was a true report which I heard in mine own land of thine acts, and of thy wisdom: Howbeit I believed not their words, until I came, and mine eyes had seen it: and, behold, the one half of the greatness of thy wisdom was not told me . . .

When the queen of Sheba saw these things, she melted. Give your life to Jesus, listen to His wisdom, eat at His Table, spend time in His temple, became a servant at His feet, experience His resurrected life within you, and your heart will melt, too.

2 Chronicles 9:6 (b)
. . . for thou exceedest the fame that I heard.

Solomon was extremely famous. His name was known throughout the world for a number of reasons. First, he was incredibly wealthy. As we see in verse 13, he received twenty-five tons—or one billion dollars' worth—of gold annually. So much gold did Solomon possess that the shields of his soldiers were made of solid gold. No wonder people throughout the world heard of his wealth! They also heard of his intellectual abilities. He was a biologist, a botanist, an ichthyologist, a writer of over 3,000 proverbs and 1,005 songs (1 Kings 4:32).

Hearing accounts of this magnificent king ruling in Jerusalem—so wise and wealthy—the queen of Sheba decided to investigate for herself and check out what she had heard. She came to prove Solomon with hard questions—not as a skeptic to trick him, but as a seeker to learn from him.

2 Chronicles 9:7–12
Happy are thy men, and happy are these thy servants, which stand continually before thee, and hear thy wisdom. Blessed be the Lord thy God, which delighted in thee to set thee on his throne, to be king for the Lord thy God: because thy God loved Israel, to establish them for ever, therefore made he thee king over them, to do judgment and justice. And she gave the king an hundred and twenty talents of gold, and of spices great abundance, and precious stones: neither was there any such spice as the queen of Sheba gave king Solomon. And the servants also of Huram, and the servants of Solomon, which brought gold from Ophir, brought algum trees and precious stones. And the king made of the algum trees terraces to the house of the Lord, and to the king's palace, and harps and psalteries for singers: and there were none such seen before in the land of Judah. And king Solomon gave to the queen of Sheba all her desire, whatsoever she asked, beside that which she had brought unto the king. So she turned, and went away to her own land, she and her servants.

Solomon answered the queen of Sheba with such wisdom that she was not only impressed but converted. How do we know this? Turn to Matthew 12 . . .

> The men of Nineveh shall rise in judgment with this generation, and shall condemn it: because they repented at the preaching of Jonas; and, behold, a greater than Jonas is here. The queen of the south shall rise up in the judgment with this generation, and shall condemn it: for she came from the uttermost part of the earth to hear the wisdom of Solomon; and, behold, a greater than Solomon is here.
> Matthew 12:41, 42

Just as the entire city of Nineveh turned to the Lord, the implication here is that the queen of Sheba did likewise. And it is no wonder that she did, for Jesus is indeed greater than Solomon . . .

- Solomon had wisdom from God.
  Jesus is *the wisdom of God.*
- Solomon was a great king.
  Jesus is the King of kings.
- Solomon spoke practically to his nation.
  Jesus spoke powerfully to all creation.
- Solomon gave the queen all her heart desired.
  Jesus gives exceedingly abundantly above *all we can ask or think.*
- Solomon answered the queen's questions.
  Jesus is *the Answer to every question.*

2 Chronicles 9:13
Now the weight of gold that came to Solomon in one year was six hundred and threescore and six talents of gold;

This would be equivalent to one billion dollars. Think of one billion dollars this way: if Solomon spent one thousand dollars a day, it would take him three thousand years to spend one billion. Solomon was wealthier than anyone who had ever lived. How did he get his wealth? Read on . . .

2 Chronicles 9:14
Beside that which chapmen and merchants brought. And all the kings of Arabia and governors of the country brought gold and silver to Solomon.

Chapmen were traders. At this time in history, 1000 B.C., the camel was domesticated. That changed the complexion of the Middle East completely because a camel can travel quite easily for three to four days between watering spots. This meant trade routes were opened between Egypt and Mesopotamia. The path that led from Egypt and Mesopotamia went right through Israel. So Solomon took advantage of the situation and constructed toll roads.

2 Chronicles 9:15
And king Solomon made two hundred targets of beaten gold: six hundred shekels of beaten gold went to one target.

A target was a large shield that covered one's entire body. The value of these targets was about $400,000 each.

2 Chronicles 9:16–19
And three hundred shields made he of beaten gold: three hundred shekels of gold went to one shield. And the king put them in the house of the forest of Lebanon. Moreover the king made a great throne of ivory, and overlaid it with pure gold. And there were six steps to the throne, with a footstool of gold, which were fastened to the throne, and stays on each side of the sitting place, and two lions standing by the stays: And twelve lions stood there on the one side and on the other upon the six steps. There was not the like made in any kingdom.

Solomon's throne was gold-plated ivory with images of lions on either side. It would have been impressive and magnificent indeed. And yet our Lord has chosen instead to be enthroned on the praises of His people (Psalm 22:3). This means that when you lift up thanksgiving and praise to the Lord, you are actually building Him a throne more precious to Him than even the most magnificent throne on earth.

2 Chronicles 9:20
And all the drinking vessels of king Solomon were of gold, and all the vessels of the house of the forest of Lebanon were of pure gold: none were of silver; it was not any thing accounted of in the days of Solomon.

There was so much gold in Solomon's kingdom that silver was no longer counted.

2 Chronicles 9:21
For the king's ships went to Tarshish with the servants of Huram: every three years once came the ships of Tarshish bringing gold, and silver, ivory, and apes, and peacocks.

Apes and peacocks were imported for entertainment.

2 Chronicles 9:22–28
And king Solomon passed all the kings of the earth in riches and wisdom. And all the kings of the earth sought the presence of Solomon, to hear his wisdom, that God had put in his heart. And they brought every man his present, vessels of silver, and vessels of gold, and raiment, harness, and spices, horses, and mules, a rate year by year. And Solomon had four thousand stalls for horses and chariots, and twelve thousand horsemen; whom he bestowed in the chariot cities, and with the king at Jerusalem. And he reigned over all the kings from the river even unto the land of the Philistines, and to the border of Egypt. And the king made silver in Jerusalem as stones, and cedar trees made he as the sycomore trees that are in the low plains in abundance. And they brought unto Solomon horses out of Egypt, and out of all lands.

Uh-oh. Deuteronomy 17 specifies that a king in Israel was not to multiply unto himself gold, wives, or horses. But here's Solomon, accumulating thousands of horses. Isaiah 30 gives us further understanding for there the Lord indicts His people for relying on horses, on military prowess, instead of resting in Him.

2 Chronicles 9:29–31
Now the rest of the acts of Solomon, first and last, are they not written in the book of Nathan the prophet, and in the prophecy of Ahijah the Shilonite, and in the visions of Iddo the seer against Jeroboam the son of Nebat? And Solomon reigned in Jerusalem over all Israel forty years. And Solomon slept with his fathers, and he was buried in the city of David his father: and Rehoboam his son reigned in his stead.

Solomon was wise, wealthy, and successful, but, nonetheless, miserable. In Ecclesiastes, we see from Solomon's own hand that, during this time of incredible prosperity, his life was full of misery. Solomon threw unbelievable parties, gained impressive education, had power, wealth, and influence that was unrivaled in the world. Yet he declared it all to be empty.

All of us think that happiness lies right around the corner—a little more money, and we'll be happy; a little more education or job security, and we'll be content. So did poor Solomon. He was at the top of every conceivable arena. He had nowhere else to go, nothing else for which to strive or hope, and he was still wanting.

It is the wise person who learns from the wisest man who ever lived and sees the fallacy that can so easily penetrate our hearts in thinking that happiness lies right around the corner with the next job, raise, acquisition, spouse, or degree.

At the end of his days, Solomon turned to the Lord, realizing that He was what he was looking for all along . . . .

> Let us hear the conclusion of the whole matter: Fear God, and keep his commandments: for this is the whole duty of man.
>
> Ecclesiastes 12:13

10

2 Chronicles 10:1, 2
And Rehoboam went to Shechem: for to Shechem were all Israel come to make him king. And it came to pass, when Jeroboam the son of Nebat, who was in Egypt, whither he had fled from the presence of Solomon the king, heard it, that Jeroboam returned out of Egypt.

Jeroboam was a very talented, capable, and gifted young man. But he was also cocky, conceited, and rebellious. Seeing that Jeroboam had great potential but also many problems, Solomon sought to kill him. So Jeroboam split and hung out in Egypt. Hearing Solomon was dead and his son Rehoboam was king, Jeroboam returns to Israel.

2 Chronicles 10:3, 4
And they sent and called him. So Jeroboam and all Israel came and spake to Rehoboam, saying, Thy father made our yoke grievous: now therefore ease thou somewhat the grievous servitude of thy father, and his heavy yoke that he put upon us, and we will serve thee.

All the magnificent building projects and expansion of the kingdom over forty years having placed a heavy tax burden upon the people, Jeroboam and the people of Israel came to Rehoboam and said, "Give us a break. The yoke was heavy upon us for years. Ease up somewhat and we'll serve you."

2 Chronicles 10:5
And he said unto them, Come again unto me after three days. And the people departed.

"Come back in three days," Rehoboam said, "and I will give you an answer."

2 Chronicles 10:6–8
And king Rehoboam took counsel with the old men that had stood before Solomon his father while he yet lived, saying, What counsel give ye me to return answer to this people? And they spake unto him, saying, If thou be kind to this people, and please them, and speak good words to them, they will be thy servants for ever. But he forsook the counsel which the old men gave him, and took counsel with the young men that were brought up with him, that stood before him.

The elderly, wise, mature men counseled Rehoboam to deal kindly with the people. The same principle still holds, for James writes that the wisdom from above is gentle and merciful (3:17). Therefore, it would follow that the longer a person walks with the Lord, the more gentle and merciful he will be. After hearing this advice, however, Rehoboam turned to his contemporaries to see what they would say.

2 Chronicles 10:9–11
And he said unto them, What advice give ye that we may return answer to this people, which have spoken to me, saying, Ease somewhat the yoke that thy father did put upon us? And the young men that were brought up with him spake unto him, saying, Thus shalt thou answer the people that spake unto thee, saying, Thy father made our yoke heavy, but make thou it somewhat lighter for us; thus shalt thou say unto them, My little finger shall be thicker than my father's loins. For whereas my father put a heavy yoke upon you, I will put more to your yoke: my father chastised you with whips, but I will chastise you with scorpions.

The young men advised Rehoboam to tell the people that if they thought Solomon's rule was heavy, they hadn't seen anything yet.

2 Chronicles 10:12–14
So Jeroboam and all the people came to Rehoboam on the third day, as the king bade, saying, Come again to me on the third day. And the king answered them roughly; and king Rehoboam forsook the counsel of the old men, And answered them after the advice of the young men, saying, My father made your yoke heavy, but I will add thereto: my father chastised you with whips, but I will chastise you with scorpions.

Rehoboam didn't listen to the counsel of maturity, but instead took his advice from his contemporaries. Those who are younger, either chronologically or spiritually in the Lord, would do well to listen to those who have greater maturity and experience.

2 Chronicles 10:15
So the king hearkened not unto the people: for the cause was of God, that the LORD might perform his word, which he spake by the hand of Ahijah the Shilonite to Jeroboam the son of Nebat.

In 1 Kings 11, the prophet Ahijah predicted that the kingdom would split. Here, the prophesied division is about to take place.

2 Chronicles 10:16
And when all Israel saw that the king would not hearken unto them, the people answered the king, saying, What portion have we in David? and we have none inheritance in the son of Jesse: every man to your tents, O Israel: and now, David, see to thine own house. So all Israel went to their tents.

"We're pulling out," said the ten northern tribes. "We have no influence on the sons of David. Our voice isn't being heard. You're on your own."

2 Chronicles 10:17–19
But as for the children of Israel that dwelt in the cities of Judah, Rehoboam reigned over them. Then king Rehoboam sent Hadoram that was over the tribute; and the children of Israel stoned him with stones, that he died. But king Rehoboam made speed to get him up to his chariot, to flee to Jerusalem. And Israel rebelled against the house of David unto this day.

In a misguided effort, Rehoboam sent a tax collector to make peace with the northern tribes. But the people stoned him on the spot. From this point on, the ten northern tribes would be known as Israel, while Benjamin and Judah would now be called the nation of Judah.

Although the ten northern tribes called themselves "Israel" and, although the two southern tribes referred to themselves as "Judah," God calls both nations "Israel" because He didn't acknowledge their division. Yes, there will be fighting and continual tension, but through the prophets, God nonetheless called both groups "Israel."

How does the Lord look at denominational divisions, church splits, personality clashes, doctrinal differences? He sees us as one—one body, one kingdom, one church, one people. It would do us so well to get in line with the heart of God on this matter. Jesus did, for in John 17, we see Him praying, "Father, let them be one, even as we are one."

11

2 Chronicles 11:1–4
And when Rehoboam was come to Jerusalem, he gathered of the house of Judah and Benjamin an hundred and fourscore thousand chosen men, which were warriors, to fight against Israel, that he might bring the kingdom again to Rehoboam. But the word of the LORD came to Shemaiah the man of God, saying, Speak unto Rehoboam the son of Solomon, king of Judah, and to all Israel in Judah and Benjamin, saying, Thus saith the LORD, Ye shall not go up, nor fight against your brethren: return every man to his house: for this thing is done of me. And they obeyed the words of the LORD, and returned from going against Jeroboam.

Realizing his empire was divided, Rehoboam sought to reunite it by force. But the Lord sent a prophet, saying, "Don't fight your brethren in striving for unity."

The Lord never desired division, but He allowed it. Why? Under the reign of Solomon that lasted forty years, Israel experienced incredible prosperity. But at the same time, the nation was cracking and crumbling because of moral decay. So the Lord would actually allow the kingdom to split in order to save it.

From this, I understand that although division is not the Lord's best, He sometimes allows it to accomplish His purpose. In Acts 2, we read that the Lord added to the church such as should be saved. In Acts 6, we read that the Lord multiplied the church. But in between Acts 2 and Acts 6 is Acts 5, where we see not addition, not multiplication, but subtraction. Ananias and Sapphira were subtracted because they lied to the Holy Spirit. So, before there could be a further explosion of growth in the church, there first had to be a purging of the church.

In my own life, this same principle holds true. The Lord adds to my life and wants to multiply abundantly. But He sees He must do some subtracting first. So a season of purging follows. If you're wondering why you're being purged, why you seem to be in a season of subtraction or division, it could very well be because the Lord is getting ready to do a great work of multiplication through you.

2 Chronicles 11:5–12
And Rehoboam dwelt in Jerusalem, and built cities for defence in Judah. He built even Bethlehem, and Etam, and Tekoa, And Beth-zur, and Shoco, and Adullam, And Gath, and Mareshah, and Ziph, And Adoraim, and Lachish, and Azekah, And Zorah, and Aijalon, and Hebron, which are in Judah and in Benjamin fenced cities. And he fortified the strong holds, and put captains in them, and store of victual, and of oil and wine. And in every several city he put shields and spears, and made them exceeding strong, having Judah and Benjamin on his side.

With Israel as his enemy, Rehoboam fortified the cities on his borders against the likelihood of attack.

2 Chronicles 11:13–15
And the priests and the Levites that were in all Israel resorted to him out of all their coasts. For the Levites left their suburbs and their possession, and came to Judah and Jerusalem: for Jeroboam and his sons had cast them off from executing the priest's office unto the LORD: And he ordained him priests for the high places, and for the devils, and for the calves which he had made.

Knowing his people would head south to Jerusalem to worship the Lord, Jeroboam was worried their loyalty would be compromised. So he expelled the priests and Levites and developed his own idolatrous system of worship.

2 Chronicles 11:16, 17 (a)
And after them out of all the tribes of Israel such as set their hearts to seek the LORD God of Israel came to Jerusalem, to sacrifice unto the LORD God of their fathers. So they strengthened the kingdom of Judah, and made Rehoboam the son of Solomon strong, three years . . .

Those with a heart for the true God left Israel and cruised down to Judah. As a result, the kingdom of Judah was strengthened. The same principle is still true, for the secret of the strength of any nation is due to the godly people therein.

2 Chronicles 11:17 (b)
. . . for three years they walked in the way of David and Solomon.

Rehoboam followed the godly path of David and Solomon for three years before he began to backslide and fall into all sorts of sin.

2 Chronicles 11:18–20
And Rehoboam took him Mahalath the daughter of Jerimoth the son of David to wife, and Abihail the daughter of Eliab the son of Jesse; Which bare him children; Jeush, and Shamariah, and Zaham. And after her he took Maachah the daughter of Absalom; which bare him Abijah, and Attai, and Ziza, and Shelomith.

"What portion have we in David?" the ten tribes asked before splitting from Benjamin and Judah (2 Chronicles 10:16). Perhaps it was to counter this complaint that Rehoboam married into the line of David in an attempt to validate his right to the throne.

2 Chronicles 11:21, 22
And Rehoboam loved Maachah the daughter of Absalom above all his wives and his concubines: (for he took eighteen wives, and threescore concubines; and begat twenty and eight sons, and threescore daughters.) And Rehoboam made Abijah the son of Maachah the chief, to be ruler among his brethren: for he thought to make him king.

The implication is that Abijah was not Rehoboam's eldest son. Therefore, his appointment as king contradicted not only custom but the law (Deuteronomy 21:15).

2 Chronicles 11:23
And he dealt wisely, and dispersed of all his children throughout all the countries of Judah and Benjamin, unto every fenced city: and he gave them victual in abundance. And he desired many wives.

The wisdom spoken of here refers not to godly wisdom but to Rehoboam's political wisdom of broadening his base by positioning his sons throughout his kingdom.

12

2 Chronicles 12:1
And it came to pass, when Rehoboam had established the kingdom, and had strengthened himself, he forsook the law of the LORD, and all Israel with him.

From 2 Chronicles 11:17, we know that Rehoboam, king of Judah, walked in the way of his grandfather, David and honored the Lord until he became strong. Then he forgot the Lord.

An elephant and a flea walked over a creaky wooden bridge. When they reached the other side, the flea said to the elephant, "Wow! We sure made that bridge shake, didn't we?" Rehoboam had that same mentality. And so can we. We walk with the Lord. God's blessing is poured out, and we begin to think, "We sure did something great, didn't we, Lord?" Are you in that place? Be careful. It's when we're doing well that we're most vulnerable.

When Paul had a vision of heaven, the Lord sent a thorn in the flesh to buffet him. "Lord," he prayed, "take this thorn from me."

"Lord, remove this thorn from me," he prayed a second time.

After he prayed the same prayer a third time, the Lord said, "No, Paul. My grace is sufficient for you, for when you are weak, then you will be strong."

Paul went on to glory in his weakness, saying, "If God has to keep me weak that I might be dependent upon Him, so be it. I do not want to be strong if it means I'll be independent of Him" (see 2 Corinthians 12).

Why has God sent you a thorn in the flesh? Maybe it's a person. Maybe it's a physical problem or a situation that pokes and prods. It is very possible that its purpose is to keep you from making the mistake of Rehoboam, the mistake of relying upon yourself.

2 Chronicles 12:2–4
And it came to pass, that in the fifth year of king Rehoboam Shishak king of Egypt came up against Jerusalem, because they had transgressed against the LORD, With twelve hundred chariots, and threescore thousand horsemen: and the people were without number that came with him out of Egypt; the Lubims, the Sukkiims, and the Ethiopians. And he took the fenced cities which pertained to Judah, and came to Jerusalem.

In the fifth year of his reign, two years after he departed from following the way of the Lord, a massive army came from Egypt to fight against Rehoboam.

2 Chronicles 12:5, 6
Then came Shemaiah the prophet to Rehoboam, and to the princes of Judah, that were gathered together to Jerusalem because of Shishak, and said unto them, Thus saith the LORD, Ye have forsaken me, and therefore have I also left you in the hand of Shishak. Whereupon the princes of Israel and the king humbled themselves; and they said, The LORD is righteous.

Here Rehoboam does something surprising. He listens to the words of Shemaiah the prophet, humbles himself before the Lord, and declares that the Lord is righteous. I can't help but think of Revelation 19, where, at the end of the Tribulation, we see the world undergoing cataclysmic disaster. "Righteous and true are Your judgments, O Lord," cries a great host in heaven.

Even in the day of Tribulation, the host of heaven says the Lord is righteous. This is a sign of true maturity. "The Lord is righteous," declared Rehoboam, even on the brink of war. Whether regarding Rehoboam's tribulation, the Tribulation at the end of world history, or the tribulation you face today in your own situation, it is the mature man who says, "The Lord is righteous."

2 Chronicles 12:7, 8
And when the LORD saw that they humbled themselves, the word of the LORD came to Shemaiah, saying, They have humbled themselves; therefore I will not destroy them, but I will grant them some deliverance; and my wrath shall not be poured out upon Jerusalem by the hand of Shishak. Nevertheless they shall be his servants; that they may know my service, and the service of the kingdoms of the countries.

"I'm not going to destroy My people," the Lord declared. "But they'll have to pay taxes to Shishak in order that they might appreciate Me. Let My people serve him for awhile. Then they'll see how good they had it with Me." Sometimes the Lord lets us get taxed by heavy situations in order to show us how good *He* is by comparison.

2 Chronicles 12:9–11
So Shishak king of Egypt came up against Jerusalem, and took away the treasures of the house of the LORD, and the treasures of the king's house; he took all: he carried away also the shields of gold which Solomon had made. Instead of which king Rehoboam made shields of brass, and committed them to the hands of the chief of the guard, that kept the entrance of the king's house. And when the king entered into the house of the LORD, the guard came and fetched them, and brought them again into the guard chamber.

After Shishak took the shields of gold, Rehoboam did something we have a tendency to do. He made brass ones and set guards over them, even though they were no longer valuable.

"I know my relationship with the Lord isn't what it once was," we say, "but I'll pretend. I'll polish the brass of my flesh. I'll use the vocabulary and play the game so people won't know the gold is gone."

2 Chronicles 12:12
And when he humbled himself, the wrath of the LORD turned from him that he would not destroy him altogether: and also in Judah things went well.

Rehoboam again humbled himself and began to experience once again the grace and blessing of God.

2 Chronicles 12:13–16
So king Rehoboam strengthened himself in Jerusalem, and reigned: for Rehoboam was one and forty years old when he began to reign, and he reigned seventeen years in Jerusalem, the city which the LORD had chosen out of all the tribes of Israel, to put his name there. And his mother's name was Naamah an Ammonitess. And he did evil, because he prepared not his heart to seek the LORD. Now the acts of Rehoboam, first and last, are they not written in the book of Shemaiah the prophet, and of Iddo the seer concerning genealogies? And there were wars between Rehoboam and Jeroboam continually. And Rehoboam slept with his fathers, and was buried in the city of David: and Abijah his son reigned in his stead.

The word translated "prepared" literally means "fixed." Although there were times when he humbled himself, Rehoboam didn't *fix* his heart to seek the Lord. In other words, when tragedy or difficulty arose, he would humble himself. But otherwise his life lacked discipline. I can't stress enough the importance of a disciplined walk. The word "disciple" means "disciplined one."

"My yoke is easy. My burden is light," Jesus declared (Matthew 11:30). He doesn't crack a whip over us or make heavy demands of us. Yet he wants hearts disciplined to seek Him daily.

Is your heart fixed on the Lord, or are you polished brass? Learn the lesson of Rehoboam.

13

In chapter 13, we come to the account of the reign of Rehoboam's son, Abijah . . .

2 Chronicles 13:1, 2 (a)
Now in the eighteenth year of king Jeroboam began Abijah to reign over Judah. He reigned three years in Jerusalem . . .

From 1 Kings 15, we know Abijah was a man who did evil in the sight of the Lord.

2 Chronicles 13:2 (b)
. . . His mother's name also was Michaiah the daughter of Uriel of Gibeah. And there was war between Abijah and Jeroboam.

During Abijah's reign, civil war broke out between Judah and the ten northern tribes.

2 Chronicles 13:3
And Abijah set the battle in array with an army of valiant men of war, even four hundred thousand chosen men: Jeroboam also set the battle in array against him with eight hundred thousand chosen men, being mighty men of valour.

Outnumbered two to one, Abijah tries to talk his way into a truce . . .

2 Chronicles 13:4–12
And Abijah stood up upon mount Zemaraim, which is in mount Ephraim, and said, Hear me, thou Jeroboam, and all Israel; Ought ye not to know that the LORD God of Israel gave the kingdom over Israel to David for ever, even to him and to his sons by a covenant of salt? Yet Jeroboam the son of Nebat, the servant of Solomon the son of David, is risen up, and hath rebelled against his lord. And there are gathered unto him vain men, the children of Belial, and have strengthened themselves against Rehoboam the son of Solomon, when Rehoboam was young and tenderhearted, and could not withstand them. And now ye think to withstand the kingdom of the LORD in the hand of the sons of David; and ye be a great multitude, and there are with you golden calves, which Jeroboam made you for gods. Have ye not cast out the priests of the LORD, the sons of Aaron, and the Levites, and have made you priests after the manner of the nations of other lands? so that whosoever cometh to consecrate himself with a young bullock and seven rams, the same may be a priest of them that are no gods. But as for us, the LORD is our God, and we have not forsaken him; and the priests, which minister unto the LORD, are the sons of Aaron, and the Levites wait upon their business: And they burn unto the LORD every morning and every evening burnt sacrifices and sweet incense: the shewbread also set they in order upon the pure table; and the candlestick of gold with the lamps thereof, to burn every evening: for we keep the charge of the LORD our God; but ye have forsaken him. And, behold, God himself is with us for our captain, and his priests with sounding trumpets to cry alarm against you. O children of

Israel, fight ye not against the LORD God of your fathers; for ye shall not prosper.

To the ten northern tribes of Israel, Abijah said, "You guys don't have a prayer for two reasons. First, the promise of the Lord is that David will have a son on the throne forever. It is a covenant of salt." A covenant was an agreement wherein two parties took a bull, split it in half, laid it open, and met between the two sides of beef. In killing a bull, they were saying, "We are deadly serious about this agreement." If they wanted to make this covenant especially strong, they would pour salt on the bull because salt prevents putrefaction.

"The Lord made a covenant of salt"—an unbreakable treaty, especially sealed—"that a descendant of David would be on the throne forever," Abijah said. "I'm a descendant of David. Jeroboam isn't. Therefore, you don't have a chance."

"Secondly—not only prophetically, but practically—you're doomed," Abijah continued. "You kicked out the priests and the Levites, made yourselves golden calves to worship, and forsook the true and living God. We, on the other hand, still worship Jehovah. The priests stand before His temple and offer incense and sacrifice to Him. Practically, you've rejected the Lord. Therefore, you'll be fighting against Him because God is for us." The fact that Abijah was not walking with the Lord didn't negate the promises of God, for God remains true, even if every man is a liar (Romans 3:4).

2 Chronicles 13:13, 14 (a)
But Jeroboam caused an ambushment to come about behind them: so they were before Judah, and the ambushment was behind them. And when Judah looked back, behold, the battle was before and behind . . .

I have found, both in my own life and in the lives of others, that the enemy usually follows this same tactic. He attacks from before and behind. That is, he condemns us about our past—mistakes we made five years ago, last week, or yesterday—as well as getting us to worry about our future. What if the check doesn't come? What if the job doesn't open? What if I say the wrong thing?

"Forgetting the things that are behind, I press on toward the mark of the high calling of Jesus Christ," Paul declared (see Philippians 3:13, 14).

"Take no thought for tomorrow," Jesus taught (Matthew 6:34).

The secret of a happy, successful Christian experience is to neither live in your past nor worry about tomorrow, but to enjoy where you are right now, keeping your eyes on Jesus day by day, moment by moment.

2 Chronicles 13:14 (b)
. . . and they cried unto the LORD . . .

With the outlook looking bleak, Abijah had no other choice but to look up.

2 Chronicles 13:14 (c), 15
. . . and the priests sounded with the trumpets. Then the men of Judah gave a shout: and as the men of Judah shouted, it came to pass, that God smote Jeroboam and all Israel before Abijah and Judah.

Abijah was not walking with the Lord. Yet, in a moment of desperation, he cried out to Him and his prayer was answered.

2 Chronicles 13:16–22
And the children of Israel fled before Judah: and God delivered them into their hand. And Abijah and his people slew them with a great slaughter: so there fell down slain of Israel five hundred thousand chosen men. Thus the children of Israel were brought under at that time, and the children of Judah prevailed, because they relied upon the LORD God of their fathers. And Abijah pursued after Jeroboam, and took cities from him, Bethel with the towns thereof, and Jeshnah with the towns thereof, and Ephrain with the towns thereof. Neither did Jeroboam recover strength again in the days of Abijah: and the LORD struck him, and he died. But Abijah waxed mighty, and married fourteen wives, and begat twenty and two sons, and sixteen daughters. And the rest of the acts of Abijah, and his ways, and his sayings, are written in the story of the prophet Iddo.

I believe this story is recorded for a very simple but significant reason: to remind us of the readiness and willingness of our Father to respond immediately to a prayer offered in sincerity. The enemy will tell you God won't answer your prayer because you haven't prayed in a week or you haven't tithed in a month. The reality, however, is that you're not as far gone as Abijah was, and God answered him.

Our Father is waiting to respond to any who humbly and sincerely call upon His name. Therefore, take hope, dear saint. The Father loves you and will respond to you if you'll just cry out to Him no matter where you've been or what you've done.

14 We now come to the life of a very important and interesting king. His name is Asa . . .

2 Chronicles 14:1
So Abijah slept with his fathers, and they buried him in the city of David: and Asa his son reigned in his stead. In his days the land was quiet ten years.

Why was there quietness in the land? Read on . . .

2 Chronicles 14:2
And Asa did that which was good and right in the eyes of the Lord his God:

Note that Asa did that which was both good and right in the eyes of the Lord. You can do that which is good, but it will not necessarily be right. You can pray, and that's good, but if you're like the Pharisees who prayed simply to be heard by men or to fulfill some obligation, it's not right if your motives are wrong. Giving is good, but if you give like the Pharisees, simply to receive the applause and approval of men, you're missing the mark entirely. Witnessing is good, but if you're witnessing simply to add another notch to your Bible, that's not right. Asa did that which was both good and right, and the result was quietness in the land.

2 Chronicles 14:3, 4
For he took away the altars of the strange gods, and the high places, and brake down the images, and cut down the groves: And commanded Judah to seek the Lord God of their fathers, and to do the law and the commandment.

Here we see the beginning of a revival—the first of five revivals in Judah's history.

2 Chronicles 14:5–7 (a)
Also he took away out of all the cities of Judah the high places and the images: and the kingdom was quiet before him. And he built fenced cities in Judah: for the land had rest, and he had no war in those years; because the Lord had given him rest. Therefore he said unto Judah, Let us build these cities, and make about them walls, and towers, gates, and bars, while the land is yet before us; because we have sought the Lord our God, we have sought him, and he hath given us rest on every side . . .

During the time of rest, Asa didn't kick back. He used the time of rest to prepare for future battles. And I believe his example is invaluable to us. If your life is going smoothly, praise the Lord and enjoy it, but prepare for the battles that are sure to come your way. If you're kicking back and watching TV in the time of peace, watch out because you don't know what tomorrow holds. And when the trial or difficulty confronts you, it will be too late to build your cities then. It will be too late to arm the soldiers then. When the attack comes, you'll kick yourself and say, "Why didn't I prepare when I had the opportunity? I didn't study and pray and meditate like I knew I should have, and now I'm sadly defeated."

Asa is remembered as a godly man because he was wise enough to use the time of peace for a time of preparation.

2 Chronicles 14:7 (b)
. . . So they built and prospered.

They built and they prospered. There are three ways the Bible tells us we can build, or edify. The first is through the Word of God. "As newborn babes, desire the sincere milk of the Word that you may grow thereby" (1 Peter 2:2). The word translated "grow" literally means "be edified." Peter doesn't address this exhortation to newborn babes or new believers. He doesn't say, "*If* you're a newborn babe, desire the sincere milk of the Word." No, He says, "*As* newborn babes, desire the sincere milk of the Word." In other words, it is as imperative for us as believers to take in the Word as it is for a newborn baby to take in a consistent and continual supply of nourishment.

The second way to build or edify is through our own words. Proverbs 18:21 tells us that life and death are in the power of the tongue. Every word you speak will either build up or tear down. You'll either build up your own or someone else's faith through words of encouragement and blessing, or you'll undermine your own or someone else's faith through cynicism and doubt.

Finally, we edify through love. Paul says in 1 Corinthians 8 that knowledge puffs up but love builds up. If you're striving with people, you're eroding the underpinnings of faith. But if you love people, you're building on a firm foundation.

Three practical ways you can build and prosper in the time of peace: Get in the Word; speak positive words; and love. In so doing, you will not only edify others, but your own faith will be built up and strengthened.

2 Chronicles 14:8
And Asa had an army of men that bare targets and spears, out of Judah three hundred

thousand; and out of Benjamin, that bare shields and drew bows, two hundred and fourscore thousand: all these were mighty men of valour.

Some in Asa's army held spears for hand-to-hand, close-quartered combat. Others used bows for long-range attacks. We not only have to be defensive against the obvious sin we can see, but also against the long-range, subtle sins of overwork, self-sufficiency, the failure to maintain a consistent prayer life.

2 Chronicles 14:9–11 (a)
And there came out against them Zerah the Ethiopian with an host of a thousand thousand, and three hundred chariots; and came unto Mareshah. Then Asa went out against him, and they set the battle in array in the valley of Zephathah at Mareshah. And Asa cried unto the LORD his God . . .

Good move, Asa. Whenever you face odds that look bad, cry to the Lord.

2 Chronicles 14:11 (b)
. . . and said, LORD, it is nothing with thee to help, whether with many, or with them that have no power: help us, O LORD our God . . .

Although this prayer is only one verse long, it speaks volumes. Asa could boldly seek the Lord in adversity because he had diligently sought the Lord in prosperity. He had no need for a long prayer of introduction or explanation. His prayer took only seconds to utter, but it had a background of ten years of seeking and walking with the Lord.

"Don't think you will be heard by your much speaking," Jesus taught (see Matthew 6:7). The heathen made that mistake. They thought the longer they prayed and more ornate their prayers, the more responsive God would be. Not so. Here, Asa simply says, "Lord, we're outnumbered. We're trusting in You. Help us."

Notice that Asa puts no limitation on God. God knows nothing of degrees of difficulty. To God, it makes no difference whether you're praying for healing from a cold or from cancer. Everything is equally easy for Him.

2 Chronicles 14:11 (c)
. . . for we rest on thee . . .

"We *rest* on You," Asa said. So often I pray and then I worry. I pray and then I fret. Asa shows us how it's supposed to be done.

2 Chronicles 14:11 (d)
. . . and in thy name we go against this multitude. O LORD, thou art our God; let not man prevail against thee.

"Let not man prevail against *Thee.*" Asa prayed for the glory of God. Prayer is not to move God. It is to move *with* God. It is not to rub the proverbial lamp and have the genie pop out. It's to submit to God and say, "Father, what is *Your* intention in this situation? I want to line up with what You're doing for Your glory."

2 Chronicles 14:12–15
So the LORD smote the Ethiopians before Asa and before Judah; and the Ethiopians fled. And Asa and the people that were with him pursued them unto Gerar: and the Ethiopians were overthrown, that they could not recover themselves; for they were destroyed before the LORD, and before his host; and they carried away very much spoil. And they smote all the cities round about Gerar; for the fear of the LORD came upon them: and they spoiled all the cities; for there was exceeding much spoil in them. They smote also the tents of cattle, and carried away sheep and camels in abundance, and returned to Jerusalem.

Judah not only won the battle, but they plundered the enemy camp and the surrounding cities as well as bringing home much livestock. Thus, God answered Asa's prayer the same way He answers ours, in a way "exceedingly abundantly above all that we can ask or think" (Ephesians 3:20).

15

2 Chronicles 15:1
And the Spirit of God came upon Azariah the son of Oded:

Throughout Scripture, whenever the Spirit comes upon someone, it's always for the purpose of service.

2 Chronicles 15:2
And he went out to meet Asa, and said unto him, Hear ye me, Asa, and all Judah and Benjamin; The LORD is with you, while ye be with him; and if ye seek him, he will be found of you; but if ye forsake him, he will forsake you.

If you're looking for a good "life verse," this might be one to consider.

2 Chronicles 15:3–6
Now for a long season Israel hath been without the true God, and without a teaching priest, and without law. But when they in their trouble did turn unto the LORD God of Israel, and sought him, he was found of them. And in those times there was no peace to him that went out, nor to him that came in, but great vexations were upon all the inhabitants of the countries. And nation was destroyed of nation, and city of city: for God did vex them with all adversity.

Azariah reminded Asa of the periods in Israel's history when, although His people had forsaken Him, God didn't forsake His people but showed Himself strong on their behalf when they returned to Him.

2 Chronicles 15:7
Be ye strong therefore, and let not your hands be weak: for your work shall be rewarded.

"Be strong and you'll be rewarded," Azariah said to Asa concerning the work he had begun so well.

2 Chronicles 15:8
And when Asa heard these words, and the prophecy of Oded the prophet, he took courage, and put away the abominable idols out of all the land of Judah and Benjamin, and out of the cities which he had taken from mount Ephraim, and renewed the altar of the LORD, that was before the porch of the LORD.

Renewed courage is always the result of true prophecy.

2 Chronicles 15:9–13
And he gathered all Judah and Benjamin, and the strangers with them out of Ephraim and Manasseh, and out of Simeon: for they fell to him out of Israel in abundance, when they saw that the LORD his God was with him. So they gathered themselves together at Jerusalem in the third month, in the fifteenth year of the reign of Asa. And they offered unto the LORD the same time, of the spoil which they had brought, seven hundred oxen and seven thousand sheep. And they entered into a covenant to seek the LORD God of their fathers with all their heart and with all their soul; That whosoever would not seek the LORD God of Israel should be put to death, whether small or great, whether man or woman.

"Seek God or die," became the order of the day. Oh, that we would be deadly serious about seeking God ourselves, or even that we would seek Him with the same determination that we seek breakfast each morning.

2 Chronicles 15:14, 15
And they sware unto the LORD with a loud voice, and with shouting, and with trumpets, and with cornets. And all Judah rejoiced at the oath: for they had sworn with all their heart, and sought him with their whole desire; and he was found of them: and the LORD gave them rest round about.

When you make a commitment to seek the Lord, you will experience two things: rejoicing and rest. Rejoicing is the result of a brother or sister who says, "I'm going for it. I might falter. I might fail. I might fall, but I'll get back up and keep going for it over and over again." Secondly, rest comes from the hand of the One who said, "Take My yoke upon you and learn of Me, and you shall find rest in your soul" (Matthew 11:29).

The most dangerous and tiresome place to be is hanging toward the back. That's when your joy disappears, your faith wavers, and you become vulnerable to sin. The front line is the safest place to be. You'll be rested and refreshed on the front line instead of exhausted and burdened at the back.

2 Chronicles 15:16
And also concerning Maachah the mother of Asa the king, he removed her from being queen, because she had made an idol in a grove: and Asa cut down her idol, and stamped it, and burnt it at the brook Kidron.

Asa honored his commitment to God even though it meant challenging the idolatrous practices of his grandmother.

2 Chronicles 15:17
But the high places were not taken away out of Israel: nevertheless the heart of Asa was perfect all his days.

I take great comfort in the fact that God calls Asa's heart perfect even though there was still work yet to be done.

2 Chronicles 15:18, 19
And he brought into the house of God the things that his father had dedicated, and that he himself had dedicated, silver, and gold, and vessels. And there was no more war unto

the five and thirtieth year of the reign of Asa.

Commitment was made; rejoicing and rest followed; peace prevailed.

16

2 Chronicles 16:1
In the six and thirtieth year of the reign of Asa Baasha king of Israel came up against Judah, and built Ramah, to the intent that he might let none go out or come in to Asa king of Judah.

Baasha, king of Israel, built a blockade. Having already beaten one million Ethiopians, Baasha's little blockade was sure to be no problem for Asa. So he decided to handle it himself. Big mistake.

2 Chronicles 16:2–6
Then Asa brought out silver and gold out of the treasures of the house of the LORD and of the king's house, and sent to Ben-hadad king of Syria, that dwelt at Damascus, saying, There is a league between me and thee, as there was between my father and thy father: behold, I have sent thee silver and gold; go, break thy league with Baasha king of Israel, that he may depart from me. And Ben-hadad hearkened unto king Asa, and sent the captains of his armies against the cities of Israel; and they smote Ijon, and Dan, and Abel-maim, and all the store cities of Naphtali. And it came to pass, when Baasha heard it, that he left off building of Ramah, and let his work cease. Then Asa the king took all Judah; and they carried away the stones of Ramah, and the timber thereof, wherewith Baasha was building; and he built therewith Geba and Mizpah.

Asa's plan was logical and seemingly successful. He paid the Syrians to attack Baasha in order to keep Israel so busy defending herself that she wouldn't be able to attack him.

2 Chronicles 16:7–9
And at that time Hanani the seer came to Asa king of Judah, and said unto him, Because thou hast relied on the king of Syria, and not relied on the LORD thy God, therefore is the host of the king of Syria escaped out of thine hand. Were not the Ethiopians and the Lubims a huge host, with very many chariots and horsemen? yet, because thou didst rely on the LORD, he delivered them into thine hand. For the eyes of the LORD run to and fro throughout the whole earth, to shew himself strong in the behalf of them whose heart is perfect toward him. Herein thou hast done foolishly: therefore from henceforth thou shalt have wars.

The eyes of the Lord are looking for men and women whose heart is perfect. That doesn't mean flawless. It means their hearts beat in harmony with God's, not relying upon themselves, but saying, "Lord, I'm depending on You." At one time, Asa had such a heart. Here, however, he was acting on his own behalf.

2 Chronicles 16:10
Then Asa was wroth with the seer, and put him in a prison house; for he was in a rage with him because of this thing. And Asa oppressed some of the people the same time.

Asa began well but ended poorly because he grew increasingly independent of God.

2 Chronicles 16:11
And, behold, the acts of Asa, first and last, lo, they are written in the book of the kings of Judah and Israel.

Asa's acts, from his first to his last, were written in the book of the kings of Judah and Israel. Your acts, from first to last, are written in the book of the Kings of the universe. Are your present acts matching your first acts? It's a question I must ask myself continually. Your story is being written right now. If you died tonight, how would your story read? Would your last acts be more glorious, or would your first acts be the only key to your spiritual life? "Remember your first works and repent," Jesus said to the church at Ephesus. "And do your first works again" (see Revelation 2:5).

2 Chronicles 16:12–14
And Asa in the thirty and ninth year of his reign was diseased in his feet, until his disease was exceeding great: yet in his disease he sought not to the LORD, but to the physicians. And Asa slept with his fathers, and died in the one and fortieth year of his reign. And they buried him in his own sepulchres, which he had made for himself in the city of David, and laid him in the bed which was filled with sweet odours and divers kinds of spices prepared by the apothecaries' art: and they made a very great burning for him.

Initially, Asa sought the Lord in every situation. Now, however, he said, "Why pray when I can call a doctor?" The result? He died. Had he sought the Lord first, perhaps he would have lived and perhaps his last acts would have been even greater than his first.

17 2 Chronicles 17:1–3

And Jehoshaphat his son reigned in his stead, and strengthened himself against Israel. And he placed forces in all the fenced cities of Judah, and set garrisons in the land of Judah, and in the cities of Ephraim, which Asa his father had taken. And the LORD was with Jehoshaphat, because he walked in the first ways of his father David, and sought not unto Baalim;

David and Asa began so well in their walks with the Lord. Because their hearts were totally tuned in to Him, their actions were right in His sight. But toward the end of their lives, both of these great men had difficult times. So what does Jehoshaphat do? He follows that which was good in their lives.

Gang, it is the wise person who can study history or look at another life and say, "I'll take the meat and leave the bones. I'll glean from them what I can even though there might be some inconsistencies."

2 Chronicles 17:4–6 (a)

But sought to the LORD God of his father, and walked in his commandments, and not after the doings of Israel. Therefore the LORD stablished the kingdom in his hand; and all Judah brought to Jehoshaphat presents; and he had riches and honour in abundance. And his heart was lifted up in the ways of the LORD . . .

The Hebrew word translated "lifted up" literally means "lively and affectionate." I like that! Jehoshaphat felt enthusiastically affectionate toward the Lord. Oh, that our hearts might be the same.

2 Chronicles 17:6 (b)–9

. . . moreover he took away the high places and groves out of Judah. Also in the third year of his reign he sent to his princes, even to Ben-hail, and to Obadiah, and to Zechariah, and to Nethaneel, and to Michaiah, to teach in the cities of Judah. And with them he sent Levites, even Shemaiah, and Nethaniah, and Zebadiah, and Asahel, and Shemiramoth, and Jehonathan, and Adonijah, and Tobijah, and Tob-adonijah, Levites; and with them Elishama and Jehoram, priests. And they taught in Judah, and had the book of the law of the LORD with them, and went about throughout all the cities of Judah, and taught the people.

Jehoshaphat not only strengthened his kingdom militarily, but he also strengthened it morally. He sent out teachers who taught the Law of the Lord throughout the entire country. The nation, in turn, prospered spiritually because the people were being taught the Word of God consistently.

Building our armies and increasing our weapons as a nation will not be enough to secure us in this world. We must be right morally. And the best thing our country can do is take time to seek God's face and heart. Yes, Jehoshaphat armed his forces, but he also sent out Levites and leaders to teach the people the word of the Law of the Lord.

2 Chronicles 17:10, 11

And the fear of the LORD fell upon all the kingdoms of the lands that were round about Judah, so that they made no war against Jehoshaphat. Also some of the Philistines brought Jehoshaphat presents, and tribute silver; and the Arabians brought him flocks, seven thousand and seven hundred rams, and seven thousand and seven hundred he goats.

Proverbs 16:7 says that when a man is right with the Lord, he makes even his enemies to be at peace with him. Here, the Philistines and Arabians—who normally fought against Judah—no longer wanted to fight and instead paid tribute.

2 Chronicles 17:12–19

And Jehoshaphat waxed great exceedingly; and he built in Judah castles, and cities of store. And he had much business in the cities of Judah: and the men of war, mighty men of valour, were in Jerusalem. And these are the numbers of them according to the house of their fathers: Of Judah, the captains of thousands; Adnah the chief, and with him mighty men of valour three hundred thousand. And next to him was Jehohanan the captain, and with him two hundred and fourscore thousand. And next him was Amasiah the son of Zichri, who willingly offered himself unto the LORD; and with him two hundred thousand mighty men of valour. And of Benjamin; Eliada a mighty man of valour, and with him armed men with bow and shield two hundred thousand. And next him was Jehozabad, and with him an hundred and fourscore thousand ready prepared for the war. These waited on the king, beside those whom the king put in the fenced cities throughout all Judah.

It is not surprising that, both militarily and economically, Judah thrived under the reign of Jehoshaphat, the king with a heart that was "lively and affectionate" toward the Lord.

18

2 Chronicles 18:1
Now Jehoshaphat had riches and honour in abundance, and joined affinity with Ahab.

Jehoshaphat walked rightly in the sight of the Lord and strengthened his people by exposing them to the Word. Here, in chapter 18, however, he'll make a big blunder by joining with Ahab, one of the most wicked rulers in the history of Israel. Why did Jehoshaphat, who was prospering and walking with the Lord, want to get involved with a character like Ahab? The Bible doesn't say. Many commentators speculate that Jehoshaphat linked himself with Ahab in hopes that the nations might be unified. While His intentions may have been right, however, his story will tell us that we can't build a relationship, be it personal or financial, if it means we must compromise what we believe about the Lord. That is why, in 2 Corinthians 6:14, Paul admonishes us not to be "unequally yoked" with unbelievers.

2 Chronicles 18:2, 3 (a)
And after certain years he went down to Ahab to Samaria. And Ahab killed sheep and oxen for him in abundance, and for the people that he had with him, and persuaded him to go up with him to Ramoth-gilead. And Ahab king of Israel said unto Jehoshaphat king of Judah, Wilt thou go with me to Ramoth-gilead?

Ahab changed his tactic from attacking Jehoshaphat to attracting him. "I'm throwing a big party," he said. "Come on down and we'll have a great time. Then we'll go together to rescue Ramoth-gilead." Ramoth-gilead was a city in Gad on the east side of the Jordan. It was a city of refuge originally, an important city spiritually and politically. But the Syrians had taken it over. So Ahab appealed to Jehoshaphat for help in liberating its people.

2 Chronicles 18:3 (b)
. . . And he answered him, I am as thou art, and my people as thy people; and we will be with thee in the war.

Watch out, Jehoshaphat. You're not as Ahab is. Ahab is a worldling. You're a man of God. Sometimes in our attempt to be relatable, we, like Jehoshaphat, become so vulnerable to sin that we're no longer useful to the work of the Lord.

2 Chronicles 18:4–6
And Jehoshaphat said unto the king of Israel, Inquire, I pray thee, at the word of the LORD to day. Therefore the king of Israel gathered together of prophets four hundred men, and said unto them, Shall we go to Ramoth-gilead to battle, or shall I forbear? And they said, Go up; for God will deliver it into the king's hand. But Jehoshaphat said, Is there not here a prophet of the LORD besides, that we might inquire of him?

Four hundred prophets were brought in to Jehoshaphat and Ahab. "God is with you," they said. "Go for it." But Jehoshaphat sensed something wasn't quite right.

"Isn't there another prophet?" he asked.

Not everyone who says, "The Lord told me to tell you . . ." is really speaking for the Lord. Any time a word of prophecy is given, it can come from any one of three sources. It can indeed be from the Lord; it can be from a demonic spirit coming across as an angel of light; or it can come from the human spirit, just someone wanting to say something that sounds good (see 2 Samuel 7:3). How do you know when it's the Lord speaking? This is where discernment is needed.

How can we be discerning?

Four ways . . .

First, the Holy Spirit gives discernment. First John 2:27 declares that the Holy Spirit will guide and direct every believer seeking direction. Thus, there will either be a confirmation or an uneasiness in your heart regarding any word of prophecy.

Secondly, the Scriptures give discernment. "If we or an angel from heaven preach any other gospel than that which has been preached, let him be accursed," Paul said to the Galatians (1:8). If someone shares something that violates the written Word, throw it out.

Thirdly, fruit gives discernment. Jesus taught us we can know from whence a person is speaking by the fruit he bears (Matthew 7:15, 16). We are to observe the fruitfulness of those who claim to speak in the name of the Lord. Is there love, joy, and peace in their lives? Is there the fruit of salvation and good works (Galatians 5:22; Romans 1:13; Titus 3:14)?

Finally, the body of Christ gives discernment. That is, there are people who, like Jehoshaphat, are particularly gifted concerning the discernment of spirits (1 Corinthians 12:10). That's why the body of Christ is so important. We truly need each other.

2 Chronicles 18:7–12

And the king of Israel said unto Jehoshaphat, There is yet one man, by whom we may inquire of the LORD: but I hate him; for he never prophesied good unto me, but always evil: the same is Micaiah the son of Imla. And Jehoshaphat said, Let not the king say so. And the king of Israel called for one of his officers, and said, Fetch quickly Micaiah the son of Imla. And the king of Israel and Jehoshaphat king of Judah sat either of them on his throne, clothed in their robes, and they sat in a void place at the entering in of the gate of Samaria; and all the prophets prophesied before them. And Zedekiah the son of Chenaanah had made him horns of iron, and said, Thus saith the LORD, With these thou shalt push Syria until they be consumed. And all the prophets prophesied so, saying, Go up to Ramoth-gilead, and prosper: for the LORD shall deliver it into the hand of the king. And the messenger that went to call Micaiah spake to him, saying, Behold, the words of the prophets declare good to the king with one assent; let thy word therefore, I pray thee, be like one of theirs, and speak thou good.

Four hundred prophets were telling Ahab that his venture to liberate Ramoth-gilead would be successful. When Micaiah—the only possible dissenting voice—was brought before him, the messenger asks him to make it easy on everyone and go along with the majority.

2 Chronicles 18:13–15

And Micaiah said, As the LORD liveth, even what my God saith, that will I speak. And when he was come to the king, the king said unto him, Micaiah, shall we go to Ramoth-gilead to battle, or shall I forbear? And he said, Go ye up, and prosper, and they shall be delivered into your hand. And the king said to him, How many times shall I adjure thee that thou say nothing but the truth to me in the name of the LORD?

When Micaiah did indeed go along with the rest of the four hundred prophets, Jehoshaphat sensed sarcasm in his voice.

2 Chronicles 18:16–22

Then he said, I did see all Israel scattered upon the mountains, as sheep that have no shepherd: and the LORD said, These have no master; let them return therefore every man to his house in peace. And the king of Israel said to Jehoshaphat, Did I not tell thee that he would not prophesy good unto me, but evil? Again he said, Therefore hear the word of the LORD; I saw the LORD sitting upon his throne, and all the host of heaven standing on his right hand and on his left. And the LORD said, Who shall entice Ahab king of Israel, that he may go up and fall at Ramoth-gilead? And one spake saying after this manner, and another saying after that manner. Then there came out a spirit, and stood before the LORD, and said, I will entice him. And the LORD said unto him, Wherewith? And he said, I will go out, and be a lying spirit in the mouth of all his prophets. And the LORD said, Thou shalt entice him, and thou shalt also prevail: go out, and do even so. Now therefore, behold, the LORD hath put a lying spirit in the mouth of these thy prophets, and the LORD hath spoken evil against thee.

This is a very controversial passage, for it says that God gave permission for a spirit to lie. While this causes confusion to some, I believe the issue is really quite simple. In both Job 1 and Revelation 2, we see that the devil and his demons have access to heaven. Oh, there is coming a time in the Tribulation period when Satan and his demons will be cast out of heaven permanently, but until that time, they appear before God. Here, in 2 Chronicles, God is using Satan and his demons as tools in His hand. You see, God wants our love. But love demands a choice. Therefore, after Satan rebelled against Him, God used him to give humanity a choice. If there wasn't a choice, there could be no real love. Nonetheless, Satan and his demons are in submission to the will of God in that they can do nothing without God allowing it. Was it because God knew that Ahab's heart was bent on sinning that He allowed demonic spirits to fill the mouths of his false prophets?

2 Chronicles 18:23

Then Zedekiah the son of Chenaanah came near, and smote Micaiah upon the cheek, and said, Which way went the Spirit of the LORD from me to speak unto thee?

Zedekiah exhibits the antithesis of the Spirit because wisdom from above is pure, peaceable, gentle, easy to be entreated, and full of mercy (James 3). In other words, wisdom from above is characterized not by force but by love.

2 Chronicles 18:24–27

And Micaiah said, Behold, thou shalt see on that day when thou shalt go into an inner chamber to hide thyself. Then the king of Israel said, Take ye Micaiah, and carry him back to Amon the governor of the city, and to Joash the king's son; And say, Thus saith

the king, Put this fellow in the prison, and feed him with bread of affliction and with water of affliction, until I return in peace. And Micaiah said, If thou certainly return in peace, then hath not the LORD spoken by me. And he said, Hearken, all ye people.

Micaiah said that time itself would prove whether or not his prophecy of defeat was correct.

2 Chronicles 18:28
So the king of Israel and Jehoshaphat the king of Judah went up to Ramoth-gilead.

After observing this whole scene, seeing the foolishness of Zedekiah, and knowing in his own heart it wasn't right, why did Jehoshaphat accompany Ahab into battle? He went for the same reason we see God's truth in the Word, but still go our way unaffected.

2 Chronicles 18:29
And the king of Israel said unto Jehoshaphat, I will disguise myself, and will go to the battle; but put thou on thy robes. So the king of Israel disguised himself; and they went to the battle.

In convincing Jehoshaphat to wear his robes, Ahab was apparently setting Jehoshaphat up as a target.

2 Chronicles 18:30, 31 (a)
Now the king of Syria had commanded the captains of the chariots that were with him, saying, Fight ye not with small or great, save only with the king of Israel. And it came to pass, when the captains of the chariots saw Jehoshaphat, that they said, It is the king of Israel . . .

In verse 3, Jehoshaphat said to Ahab, "We're one. I am as thou art." Here, sadly, his statement finds fulfillment. Are you mistaken for Ahab? In your attempt to be relatable to the world, are people thinking you're part of the world?

2 Chronicles 18:31 (b)–34
. . . Therefore they compassed about him to fight: but Jehoshaphat cried out, and the LORD helped him; and God moved them to depart from him. For it came to pass, that, when the captains of the chariots perceived that it was not the king of Israel, they turned back again from pursuing him. And a certain man drew a bow at a venture, and smote the king of Israel between the joints of the harness: therefore he said to his chariot man, Turn thine hand, that thou mayest carry me out of the host; for I am wounded. And the battle increased that day: howbeit the king of Israel stayed himself up in his chariot against the Syrians until the even: and about the time of the sun going down he died.

Here, Jehoshaphat, wearing Ahab's royal robes, would seem to be extremely vulnerable. Yet he was protected. Ahab, on the other hand, was cleverly disguised and wearing armor. Yet as the battle drew to an end, a Syrian soldier had an extra arrow in his quiver, shot it, and it went right between a space in Ahab's armor. This tells me that nothing happens circumstantially. Everything is ordered by our Father. Everything happens according to His counsel and wisdom. The arrow shot "at a venture" was, in fact, a guided missile, guided by the hand of God.

19

2 Chronicles 19:1–4
And Jehoshaphat the king of Judah returned to his house in peace to Jerusalem. And Jehu the son of Hanani the seer went out to meet him, and said to king Jehoshaphat, Shouldest thou help the ungodly, and love them that hate the LORD? Therefore is wrath upon thee from before the LORD. Nevertheless there are good things found in thee, in that thou hast taken away the groves out of the land, and hast prepared thine heart to seek God. And Jehoshaphat dwelt at Jerusalem: and he went out again through the people from Beersheba to mount Ephraim, and brought them back unto the LORD God of their fathers.

Jehoshaphat's alliance with Ahab caused his people to backslide. Therein is the tragedy of a compromised walk. It affects more than we know.

2 Chronicles 19:5–7
And he set judges in the land throughout all the fenced cities of Judah, city by city, And said to the judges, Take heed what ye do: for ye judge not for man, but for the LORD, who is with you in the judgment. Wherefore now let the fear of the LORD be upon you; take heed and do it: for there is no iniquity with the LORD our God, nor respect of persons, nor taking of gifts.

Jehoshaphat set out to call people back to a relationship with God. Oh, that his words were posted in every law school and above every judge's bench in our own country.

2 Chronicles 19:8–11
Moreover in Jerusalem did Jehoshaphat set of the Levites, and of the priests, and of the chief of the fathers of Israel, for the judgment of the LORD, and for controversies, when they returned to Jerusalem. And he charged them, saying, Thus shall ye do in the fear of the LORD, faithfully, and with a perfect heart. And what cause soever shall come to you of your brethren that dwell in their cities, between blood and blood, between law and commandment, statutes and judgments, ye shall even warn them that they trespass not against the LORD, and so wrath come upon you, and upon your brethren: this do, and ye shall not trespass. And, behold, Amariah the chief priest is over you in all matters of the LORD; and Zebadiah the son of Ishmael, the ruler of the house of Judah, for all the king's matters: also the Levites shall be officers before you. Deal courageously, and the LORD shall be with the good.

Jehoshaphat instituted a "supreme court" in Jerusalem made up of Levites, priests, and wise leaders of the community. Their instructions were to judge faithfully and courageously in the fear of the Lord and with a pure heart.

20

2 Chronicles 20:1–3
It came to pass after this also, that the children of Moab, and the children of Ammon, and with them other beside the Ammonites, came against Jehoshaphat to battle. Then there came some that told Jehoshaphat, saying, There cometh a great multitude against thee from beyond the sea on this side Syria; and, behold, they be Hazazon-tamar, which is En-gedi. And Jehoshaphat feared, and set himself to seek the LORD, and proclaimed a fast throughout all Judah.

If you're afraid, if you feel the enemy surrounding you, if you feel problems mounting up against you, do what Jehoshaphat did. He set his heart to seek the Lord and called for a fast. Fasting is simply letting go of the physical arena in order to focus on the spiritual arena.

2 Chronicles 20:4–12
And Judah gathered themselves together, to ask help of the LORD: even out of all the cities of Judah they came to seek the LORD. And Jehoshaphat stood in the congregation of Judah and Jerusalem, in the house of the LORD, before the new court, And said, O LORD God of our fathers, art not thou God in heaven? and rulest not thou over all the kingdoms of the heathen? and in thine hand is there not power and might, so that none is able to withstand thee? Art not thou our God, who didst drive out the inhabitants of this land before thy people Israel, and gavest it to the seed of Abraham thy friend for ever? And they dwelt therein, and have built thee a sanctuary therein for thy name, saying, If, when evil cometh upon us, as the sword, judgment, or pestilence, or famine, we stand before this house, and in thy presence, (for thy name is in this house,) and cry unto thee in our affliction, then thou wilt hear and help. And now, behold, the children of Ammon and Moab and mount Seir, whom thou wouldest not let Israel invade, when they came out of the land of Egypt, but they turned from them, and destroyed them not; Behold, I say, how they reward us, to come to cast us out of thy possession, which thou hast given us to inherit. O our God, wilt thou not judge them? for we have no might against this great company that cometh against us; neither know we what to do: but our eyes are upon thee.

Surrounded by the Moabites and the Ammonites, Jehoshaphat said, "We don't know what to do, Lord. Our eyes are upon You."

Where are your eyes?

If your eyes are on people, you'll be disappointed. If your eyes are on circumstances, like Peter when his eyes were on the waves, you'll go down. But if your eyes are on the Lord, you'll be stable and He'll see you through.

If you're in financial straits, spread your bills out before the Lord and say, "Father, help me. Where have I erred? Give me wisdom." If your marriage is floundering, get on your face with your husband or wife and say, "God, have mercy. We're hurting. We need Your help." If your kids are rebelling, humble yourself before your Father on behalf of your kids. Whatever the battle you face, don't read books or get counsel before you seek the Lord. Keep your eyes on *Him*.

2 Chronicles 20:13–17
And all Judah stood before the LORD, with their little ones, their wives, and their children. Then upon Jahaziel the son of Zechariah, the son of Benaiah, the son of Jeiel, the son of Mattaniah, a Levite of the sons of Asaph, came the Spirit of the LORD in the midst of the congregation; And he said, Hearken ye, all Judah, and ye inhabitants of Jerusalem, and thou king Jehoshaphat, Thus saith the LORD unto you, Be not afraid nor dismayed by reason of this great multitude; for the battle is not yours, but God's.

To morrow go ye down against them: behold, they come up by the cliff of Ziz; and ye shall find them at the end of the brook, before the wilderness of Jeruel. Ye shall not need to fight in this battle: set yourselves, stand ye still, and see the salvation of the LORD with you, O Judah and Jerusalem: fear not, nor be dismayed; to morrow go out against them: for the LORD will be with you.

"It's not your battle," the Lord said through the prophet Jahaziel. "Stand still and I will fight for you." And He says the same thing to us concerning the obstacles that face us. "You can't solve that problem or overcome that obstacle in your own energy," He says. "Just stand still." And yet standing still is the hardest thing for us to do.

2 Chronicles 20:18
And Jehoshaphat bowed his head with his face to the ground: and all Judah and the inhabitants of Jerusalem fell before the LORD, worshipping the LORD.

When the people heard that God would fight for them, they immediately worshiped Him. Would you have done that? Why is it that we believe the promises of men but doubt the promises of God? When we know we're getting a tax refund, so sure are we it's coming that we have it spent before it arrives. Yet when we read that God will supply all our needs, we don't believe that particular promise applies to us. In other words, we have more confidence in the government than we do in God. We need to be like Jehoshaphat, a man whose walk God commended (17:3, 4). We need to claim the promises of the Word and say, "Victory is coming. God *will* come through."

2 Chronicles 20:19, 20
And the Levites, of the children of the Kohathites, and of the children of the Korhites, stood up to praise the LORD God of Israel with a loud voice on high. And they rose early in the morning, and went forth into the wilderness of Tekoa: and as they went forth, Jehoshaphat stood and said, Hear me, O Judah, and ye inhabitants of Jerusalem; Believe in the LORD your God, so shall ye be established; believe his prophets, so shall ye prosper.

"If you believe, you will be established." The converse is also true. If you don't believe, you won't be established, for without faith it is impossible to please God (Hebrews 11:6). Study the lives of the great men of Scripture and of the giants of faith throughout history and you will find they had one thing in common: they saw the invisible. Average people only see the obvious. It is the one who sees beyond that, the one who sees with the eyes of faith, who experiences blessing, prosperity, and anointing on his life. Are you one who sees the invisible and claims the promise of God, or are you one who says, "It's never going to work. It's never going to happen. It's doomed to fail"? Like Jehoshaphat, everyone who has left a lasting mark on the history of the church of Jesus Christ has been a man or woman of faith.

Even with his enemies surrounding him on all sides, Jehoshaphat says, "Believe in the Lord."

2 Chronicles 20:21
And when he had consulted with the people, he appointed singers unto the LORD, and that should praise the beauty of holiness, as they went out before the army, and to say, Praise the LORD; for his mercy endureth for ever.

Surrounded by enemy forces, Jehoshaphat sends the choir out first. If you were a member of this choir, what would have been *your* response? The choir went out armed with nothing but worship. Logically, this is insane. Spiritually, however, it's the way of the Lord for faith is released through praise and worship. And it is faith that opens the door for God to work.

2 Chronicles 20:22, 23
And when they began to sing and to praise, the LORD set ambushments against the children of Ammon, Moab, and mount Seir, which were come against Judah; and they were smitten. For the children of Ammon and Moab stood up against the inhabitants of mount Seir, utterly to slay and destroy them: and when they had made an end of the inhabitants of Seir, every one helped to destroy another.

The enemy was so confused by the choir that they began to fight each other. This is not surprising for the enemy is always confounded when God's people praise Him in the place of difficulty. When it seems as though you should be cursing and crying but instead are praising and worshiping, the enemy flees.

2 Chronicles 20:24–30
And when Judah came toward the watch tower in the wilderness, they looked unto the multitude, and, behold, they were dead bodies fallen to the earth, and none escaped. And when Jehoshaphat and his people came to take away the spoil of them, they found among them in abundance both riches with

the dead bodies, and precious jewels, which they stripped off for themselves, more than they could carry away: and they were three days in gathering of the spoil, it was so much. And on the fourth day they assembled themselves in the valley of Berachah; for there they blessed the LORD: therefore the name of the same place was called, The valley of Berachah, unto this day. Then they returned, every man of Judah and Jerusalem, and Jehoshaphat in the forefront of them, to go again to Jerusalem with joy; for the LORD had made them to rejoice over their enemies. And they came to Jerusalem with psalteries and harps and trumpets unto the house of the LORD. And the fear of God was on all the kingdoms of those countries, when they had heard that the LORD fought against the enemies of Israel. So the realm of Jehoshaphat was quiet: for his God gave him rest round about.

Berachah means "blessing." After spoiling the enemy, the people of God worshiped and praised Him. Because faith comes by hearing the Word (Romans 10:17), even as we have studied this Word, I pray our faith might so well up within us, that we would leave our times of study and meditation as members of Jehoshaphat's choir, praising God.

2 Chronicles 20:31–37
And Jehoshaphat reigned over Judah: he was thirty and five years old when he began to reign, and he reigned twenty and five years in Jerusalem. And his mother's name was Azubah the daughter of Shilhi. And he walked in the way of Asa his father, and departed not from it, doing that which was right in the sight of the LORD. Howbeit the high places were not taken away: for as yet the people had not prepared their hearts unto the God of their fathers. Now the rest of the acts of Jehoshaphat, first and last, behold, they are written in the book of Jehu the son of Hanani, who is mentioned in the book of the kings of Israel. And after this did Jehoshaphat king of Judah join himself with Ahaziah king of Israel, who did very wickedly: And he joined himself with him to make ships to go to Tarshish: and they made the ships in Eziongeber. Then Eliezer the son of Dodavah of Mareshah prophesied against Jehoshaphat, saying, Because thou hast joined thyself with Ahaziah, the LORD hath broken thy works. And the ships were broken, that they were not able to go to Tarshish.

As seen throughout his life, Jehoshaphat was a godly king, one who sought to follow God, and one with whom God walked (17:3, 4). And yet, here at the end of his life, two shortcomings are noted. First was his inability to entirely rid the land of the high places that so enticed God's people to worship false gods. The second misstep noted was his alliance with Ahab's son, Ahaziah to embark on a shipping venture to secure gold (1 Kings 22:46–49). Just as they do in our lives, any alliance that compromises our high calling as servants of God is destined for shipwreck just as surely as Jehoshaphat's ships were.

21

2 Chronicles 21:1
Now Jehoshaphat slept with his fathers, and was buried with his fathers in the city of David. And Jehoram his son reigned in his stead.

Jehoram was a sinful son, a brutal brother, and a rotten ruler.

2 Chronicles 21:2–4
And he had brethren the sons of Jehoshaphat, Azariah, and Jehiel, and Zechariah, and Azariah, and Michael, and Shephatiah: all these were the sons of Jehoshaphat king of Israel. And their father gave them great gifts of silver, and of gold, and of precious things, with fenced cities in Judah: but the kingdom gave he to Jehoram; because he was the firstborn. Now when Jehoram was risen up to the kingdom of his father, he strengthened himself, and slew all his brethren with the sword, and divers also of the princes of Israel.

Just as Jehoram slew his brothers with the sword, all too often, we in the family of God can chop up our brothers with the sword of the Word. Why did Jehoram attack his brothers? It was because he saw them as threats to his position. Whenever we chop at each other, even using the Scriptures, it is often indicative of our own insecurity and jealousy.

2 Chronicles 21:5–7
Jehoram was thirty and two years old when he began to reign, and he reigned eight years in Jerusalem. And he walked in the way of the kings of Israel, like as did the house of Ahab: for he had the daughter of Ahab to wife: and he wrought that which was evil in the eyes of the LORD. Howbeit the LORD would not destroy the house of David, because of the covenant that he had made with

David, and as he promised to give a light to him and to his sons for ever.

Some people say, "Whenever I read the Bible, all I see is God's judgment, wrath, and brutality." I don't. Whenever I read the Bible, I see God's mercy, goodness, and grace, as seen in the passage before us. At this point, God had every right to destroy the nations of Israel and Judah. But He didn't. He had made a promise that He would preserve the descendants of David (2 Samuel 7:16)—and He honored His promise.

2 Chronicles 21:8–11
In his days the Edomites revolted from under the dominion of Judah, and made themselves a king. Then Jehoram went forth with his princes, and all his chariots with him: and he rose up by night, and smote the Edomites which compassed him in, and the captains of the chariots. So the Edomites revolted from under the hand of Judah unto this day. The same time also did Libnah revolt from under his hand; because he had forsaken the LORD God of his fathers. Moreover he made high places in the mountains of Judah, and caused the inhabitants of Jerusalem to commit fornication, and compelled Judah thereto.

With rebellion breaking out around his kingdom and moral decay taking place within, Jehoram actually forced his people to become involved in immorality as they worshiped heathen gods.

2 Chronicles 21:12–15
And there came a writing to him from Elijah the prophet, saying, Thus saith the LORD God of David thy father, Because thou hast not walked in the ways of Jehoshaphat thy father, nor in the ways of Asa king of Judah, But hast walked in the way of the kings of Israel, and hast made Judah and the inhabitants of Jerusalem to go a whoring, like to the whoredoms of the house of Ahab, and also hast slain thy brethren of thy father's house, which were better than thyself: Behold, with a great plague will the LORD smite thy people, and thy children, and thy wives, and all thy goods: And thou shalt have great sickness by disease of thy bowels, until thy bowels fall out by reason of the sickness day by day.

Elijah, the prophet of fire, said to Jehoram, "You've had it." I find this intriguing because at this time, Elijah had already transcended into heaven. So how does this writing find its way to Jehoram? Some say this is a mistake in the Bible, that it's really Elisha the prophet, not Elijah. But I believe it was Elijah. He must have written this letter prophetically and it hung around after he died. You'd think this would cause Jehoram to repent. But did it? No.

2 Chronicles 21:16–19
Moreover the LORD stirred up against Jehoram the spirit of the Philistines, and of the Arabians, that were near the Ethiopians: And they came up into Judah, and brake into it, and carried away all the substance that was found in the king's house, and his sons also, and his wives; so that there was never a son left him, save Jehoahaz, the youngest of his sons. And after all this the LORD smote him in his bowels with an incurable disease. And it came to pass, that in process of time, after the end of two years, his bowels fell out by reason of his sickness: so he died of sore diseases. And his people made no burning for him, like the burning of his fathers.

The normal practice at funerals was to burn incense. But the people didn't consider Jehoram worthy of even this. Burned up by him, they didn't want to burn anything for him.

2 Chronicles 21:20
Thirty and two years old was he when he began to reign, and he reigned in Jerusalem eight years, and departed without being desired. Howbeit they buried him in the city of David, but not in the sepulchres of the kings.

What a tragic statement: Jehoram departed without being desired. What about us? What would happen if you died tonight? Are we impacting and influencing lives in such a way that people would genuinely miss us?

22

2 Chronicles 22:1
And the inhabitants of Jerusalem made Ahaziah his youngest son king in his stead: for the band of men that came with the Arabians to the camp had slain all the eldest. So Ahaziah the son of Jehoram king of Judah reigned.

Having seen the tragic, empty story of his father's life, one would think Ahaziah would walk rightly with the Lord.

2 Chronicles 22:2–9 (a)
Forty and two years old was Ahaziah when he began to reign, and he reigned one year in Jerusalem. His mother's name also was Athaliah the daughter of Omri. He also walked

in the ways of the house of Ahab: for his mother was his counseller to do wickedly. Wherefore he did evil in the sight of the LORD like the house of Ahab: for they were his counsellers after the death of his father to his destruction. He walked also after their counsel, and went with Jehoram the son of Ahab king of Israel to war against Hazael king of Syria at Ramoth-gilead: and the Syrians smote Joram. And he returned to be healed in Jezreel because of the wounds which were given him at Ramah, when he fought with Hazael king of Syria. And Azariah the son of Jehoram king of Judah went down to see Jehoram the son of Ahab at Jezreel, because he was sick. And the destruction of Ahaziah was of God by coming to Joram: for when he was come, he went out with Jehoram against Jehu the son of Nimshi, whom the LORD had anointed to cut off the house of Ahab. And it came to pass, that, when Jehu was executing judgment upon the house of Ahab, and found the princes of Judah, and the sons of the brethren of Ahaziah, that ministered to Ahaziah, he slew them. And he sought Ahaziah: and they caught him, (for he was hid in Samaria,) and brought him to Jehu: and when they had slain him, they buried him . . .

This story shows us a very simple but important point. That is, Ahaziah, was caught in the wrong place at the wrong time with the wrong person, and he died because of it. How often we get needlessly beat up when we're in the wrong place with the wrong people.

2 Chronicles 22:9 (b), 10
. . . Because, said they, he is the son of Jehoshaphat, who sought the LORD with all his heart. So the house of Ahaziah had no power to keep still the kingdom. But when Athaliah the mother of Ahaziah saw that her son was dead, she arose and destroyed all the seed royal of the house of Judah.

Ahaziah's mother killed all of her own grandchildren—potential heirs to the throne—in order to secure her own position.

2 Chronicles 22:11 (a)
But Jehoshabeath, the daughter of the king, took Joash the son of Ahaziah, and stole him from among the king's sons that were slain, and put him and his nurse in a bedchamber.

Seeing what Athaliah was doing, Ahaziah's sister hid one of his children.

2 Chronicles 22:11 (b), 12
So Jehoshabeath, the daughter of king Jehoram, the wife of Jehoiada the priest, (for she was the sister of Ahaziah,) hid him from Athaliah, so that she slew him not. And he was with them hid in the house of God six years: and Athaliah reigned over the land.

Completely unaware of the child being raised in the house of God, Athaliah foolishly assumed her position was secure.

23

2 Chronicles 23:1–5
And in the seventh year Jehoiada strengthened himself, and took the captains of hundreds, Azariah the son of Jeroham, and Ishmael the son of Jehohanan, and Azariah the son of Obed, and Maaseiah the son of Adaiah, and Elishaphat the son of Zichri, into covenant with him. And they went about in Judah, and gathered the Levites out of all the cities of Judah, and the chief of the fathers of Israel, and they came to Jerusalem. And all the congregation made a covenant with the king in the house of God. And he said unto them, Behold, the king's son shall reign, as the LORD hath said of the sons of David. This is the thing that ye shall do; A third part of you entering on the sabbath, of the priests and of the Levites, shall be porters of the doors; And a third part shall be at the king's house; and a third part at the gate of the foundation: and all the people shall be in the courts of the house of the LORD.

When Joash was seven years old, Jehoiada called the leaders of the nation together and assigned the Levites to arm themselves and stand guard. After watching the people suffer for six years under the wicked reign of Athaliah, this godly priest was about to present the rightful king.

2 Chronicles 23:6–9
But let none come into the house of the LORD, save the priests, and they that minister of the Levites; they shall go in, for they are holy: but all the people shall keep the watch of the LORD. And the Levites shall compass the king round about, every man with his weapons in his hand; and whosoever else cometh into the house, he shall be put to death: but be ye with the king when he cometh in, and when he goeth out. So the Levites

and all Judah did according to all things that Jehoiada the priest had commanded, and took every man his men that were to come in on the sabbath, with them that were to go out on the sabbath: for Jehoiada the priest dismissed not the courses. Moreover Jehoiada the priest delivered to the captains of hundreds spears, and bucklers, and shields, that had been king David's, which were in the house of God.

In the house of God were trophies from the victories David had won. Now, years later, those swords, shields, and spears were distributed in order that another generation could be victorious. We are also the temple of the Lord and we must display the trophies of the battles the Lord fights for us. That's why it's so important to share testimonies. They're trophies, shields, spears, and swords, that will encourage others in battle.

2 Chronicles 23:10–15
And he set all the people, every man having his weapon in his hand, from the right side of the temple to the left side of the temple, along by the altar and the temple, by the king round about. Then they brought out the king's son, and put upon him the crown, and gave him the testimony, and made him king. And Jehoiada and his sons anointed him, and said, God save the king. Now when Athaliah heard the noise of the people running and praising the king, she came to the people into the house of the LORD: And she looked, and, behold, the king stood at his pillar at the entering in, and the princes and the trumpets by the king: and all the people of the land rejoiced, and sounded with trumpets, also the singers with instruments of musick, and such as taught to sing praise. Then Athaliah rent her clothes, and said, Treason, Treason. Then Jehoiada the priest brought out the captains of hundreds that were set over the host, and said unto them, Have her forth of the ranges: and whoso followeth her, let him be slain with the sword. For the priest said, Slay her not in the house of the LORD. So they laid hands on her; and when she was come to the entering of the horse gate by the king's house, they slew her there.

Under heavily armed guard, Joash was brought out of hiding and made king. The result was both great joy for the people and the swift and sudden death of the one who had usurped the throne for so long.

2 Chronicles 23:16–18
And Jehoiada made a covenant between him, and between all the people, and between the king, that they should be the LORD's people. Then all the people went to the house of Baal, and brake it down, and brake his altars and his images in pieces, and slew Mattan the priest of Baal before the altars. Also Jehoiada appointed the offices of the house of the LORD by the hand of the priests the Levites, whom David had distributed in the house of the LORD, to offer the burnt offerings of the LORD, as it is written in the law of Moses, with rejoicing and with singing, as it was ordained by David.

It was with rejoicing and singing that the people offered burnt offerings to the Lord because happy indeed are the people whose God is the Lord (Psalm 144:15).

2 Chronicles 23:19–21
And he set the porters at the gates of the house of the LORD, that none which was unclean in any thing should enter in. And he took the captains of hundreds, and the nobles, and the governors of the people, and all the people of the land, and brought down the king from the house of the LORD: and they came through the high gate into the king's house, and set the king upon the throne of the kingdom. And all the people of the land rejoiced: and the city was quiet, after that they had slain Athaliah with the sword.

This story paints a picture of our present situation. Athaliah was a usurper. For six years, she was on the throne. For six years, wickedness was in the land. But in the seventh year, everything changed when Joash, who was previously hidden from the eyes of the people, was presented as king.

There is a usurper on the throne of this world. Satan is the god of this world, the prince of this world (2 Corinthians 4:4; John 14:30). That's why there is rebellion and hurt, sorrow, sickness, and disease. But there's coming a Greater than Joash. And even though the usurper might yell, "Treason!" he'll be cast into the bottomless pit. Then, in the seventh year, there will be quietness on this planet. There will be peace and prosperity, answers and solutions, rightness and wholeness.

Whatever is bothering or burdening you now won't be soon. "Fear not, little flock," Jesus said. "It is the Father's good pleasure to give you the kingdom" (Luke 12:32). Time here is short. The return of Christ is soon. And rejoicing will fill the land.

24

2 Chronicles 24:1–4

Joash was seven years old when he began to reign, and he reigned forty years in Jerusalem. His mother's name also was Zibiah of Beer-sheba. And Joash did that which was right in the sight of the LORD all the days of Jehoiada the priest. And Jehoiada took for him two wives; and he begat sons and daughters. And it came to pass after this, that Joash was minded to repair the house of the LORD.

Joash was protected, nurtured, and strengthened in the temple. No wonder it held such an important place in his heart. Week by week, our lives have been changed by spending time in the temple, in the house of the Lord. Why do we teach Sunday school, disciple high-schoolers, give to a building project, serve in the nursery? How can we not? God has done so much for us.

2 Chronicles 24:5, 6

And he gathered together the priests and the Levites, and said to them, Go out unto the cities of Judah, and gather of all Israel money to repair the house of your God from year to year, and see that ye hasten the matter. Howbeit the Levites hastened it not. And the king called for Jehoiada the chief, and said unto him, Why hast thou not required of the Levites to bring in out of Judah and out of Jerusalem the collection, according to the commandment of Moses the servant of the LORD, and of the congregation of Israel, for the tabernacle of witness?

The Levites weren't getting the job done because they didn't have Joash's heart for the temple.

2 Chronicles 24:7–10

For the sons of Athaliah, that wicked woman, had broken up the house of God; and also all the dedicated things of the house of the LORD did they bestow upon Baalim. And at the king's commandment they made a chest, and set it without at the gate of the house of the LORD. And they made a proclamation through Judah and Jerusalem, to bring in to the LORD the collection that Moses the servant of God laid upon Israel in the wilderness. And all the princes and all the people rejoiced, and brought in, and cast into the chest, until they had made an end.

Jehoiada made a big collection box. Second Kings 12:9 tells us he carved a hole in it so people could drop their money in. And as they did, they rejoiced. If you can't give and rejoice, don't give at all. If giving is a burden to you, don't do it. The Lord doesn't need your money. He owns the cattle on a thousand hills. He owns the gold and silver in every mine (Psalm 50:10). He doesn't need us to give. We need to give to eradicate our tendency to become selfish, miserly, and materialistic.

2 Chronicles 24:11–13

Now it came to pass, that at what time the chest was brought unto the king's office by the hand of the Levites, and when they saw that there was much money, the king's scribe and the high priest's officer came and emptied the chest, and took it, and carried it to his place again. Thus they did day by day, and gathered money in abundance. And the king and Jehoiada gave it to such as did the work of the service of the house of the LORD, and hired masons and carpenters to repair the house of the LORD, and also such as wrought iron and brass to mend the house of the LORD. So the workmen wrought, and the work was perfected by them, and they set the house of God in his state, and strengthened it.

The temple was refurbished and rebuilt because the people had a heart to give.

2 Chronicles 24:14–19

And when they had finished it, they brought the rest of the money before the king and Jehoiada, whereof were made vessels for the house of the LORD, even vessels to minister, and to offer withal, and spoons, and vessels of gold and silver. And they offered burnt offerings in the house of the LORD continually all the days of Jehoiada. But Jehoiada waxed old, and was full of days when he died; an hundred and thirty years old was he when he died. And they buried him in the city of David among the kings, because he had done good in Israel, both toward God, and toward his house. Now after the death of Jehoiada came the princes of Judah, and made obeisance to the king. Then the king hearkened unto them. And they left the house of the LORD God of their fathers, and served groves and idols: and wrath came upon Judah and Jerusalem for this their trespass. Yet he sent prophets to them, to bring them again unto the LORD; and they testified against them: but they would not give ear.

Following Jehoiada's death, Joash began listening to the counsel of the princes and politicians, and they proved to be ungodly advisors.

2 Chronicles 24:20–22 (a)
And the Spirit of God came upon Zechariah the son of Jehoiada the priest, which stood above the people, and said unto them, Thus saith God, Why transgress ye the commandments of the LORD, that ye cannot prosper? because ye have forsaken the LORD, he hath also forsaken you. And they conspired against him, and stoned him with stones at the commandment of the king in the court of the house of the LORD. Thus Joash the king remembered not the kindness which Jehoiada his father had done to him, but slew his son . . .

Speaking in the name of the Lord, Jehoiada's son, Zechariah, called the people back to God. But the people didn't listen. Instead, Joash ordered his execution. How can it be that this one who was once so concerned about the house of the Lord is now serving Baal and destroying the prophets of God? I believe the answer is that, when Jehoiada died, everything changed.

It would seem that Joash did not have a personal relationship with the Lord. His was secondhand. As long as Jehoiada was on the scene, he was fine. But when Jehoiada died, Joash spun off into idolatry, immorality, and murder. That is why it is so important to have a personal, genuine link to the Lord. Don't depend on your husband or wife, brother or sister, parents, or friends. If you don't have a real relationship with the Lord, when your "Jehoiada" dies, moves, or disappoints you, you'll collapse and, like Joash, eventually turn against the things of God.

2 Chronicles 24:22 (b)
. . . And when he died, he said, The LORD look upon it, and require it.

Zechariah's final words were: "The Lord sees." Did the Lord see? Yes. Because in Matthew 23:35, in His indictment of the scribes and Pharisees, Jesus makes reference to this event.

2 Chronicles 24:23–27
And it came to pass at the end of the year, that the host of Syria came up against him: and they came to Judah and Jerusalem, and destroyed all the princes of the people from among the people, and sent all the spoil of them unto the king of Damascus. For the army of the Syrians came with a small company of men, and the LORD delivered a very great host into their hand, because they had forsaken the LORD God of their fathers. So they executed judgment against Joash. And when they were departed from him, (for they left him in great diseases,) his own servants conspired against him for the blood of the sons of Jehoiada the priest, and slew him on his bed, and he died: and they buried him in the city of David, but they buried him not in the sepulchres of the kings. And these are they that conspired against him; Zabad the son of Shimeath an Ammonitess, and Jehozabad the son of Shimrith a Moabitess. Now concerning his sons, and the greatness of the burdens laid upon him, and the repairing of the house of God, behold, they are written in the story of the book of the kings. And Amaziah his son reigned in his stead.

Here, the repercussion of the murder of Zechariah comes to fruition as Joash, the boy-king who began so well, is himself slain.

25

2 Chronicles 25:1, 2
Amaziah was twenty and five years old when he began to reign, and he reigned twenty and nine years in Jerusalem. And his mother's name was Jehoaddan of Jerusalem. And he did that which was right in the sight of the LORD, but not with a perfect heart.

Amaziah did that which was right, but his heart wasn't fully dedicated. His actions were right, but his heart was lukewarm to the things of God.

2 Chronicles 25:3, 4
Now it came to pass, when the kingdom was established to him, that he slew his servants that had killed the king his father. But he slew not their children, but did as it is written in the law in the book of Moses, where the LORD commanded, saying, The fathers shall not die for the children, neither shall the children die for the fathers, but every man shall die for his own sin.

Amaziah ascended to the throne when his father, Joash, was assassinated. And once he came to the throne, he rounded up the servants of Joash who assassinated him and had them slain. It was the custom at this time not only to kill the assassins, but to wipe out their families. Amaziah did not do that. He allowed the children to go free. This is commendable.

I think this is applicable to us. We live in a day where it is vogue for people to blame their parents for their present problems. The Lord here specifically says every man shall die for his own sin (Ezekiel 18:2–4). Therefore, I believe it is unbiblical and also illogical to blame our parents or anyone else for our problems.

2 Chronicles 25:5, 6
Moreover Amaziah gathered Judah together, and made them captains over thousands, and captains over hundreds, according to the houses of their fathers, throughout all Judah and Benjamin: and he numbered them from twenty years old and above, and found them three hundred thousand choice men, able to go forth to war, that could handle spear and shield. He hired also an hundred thousand mighty men of valour out of Israel for an hundred talents of silver.

In addition to drafting 300,000 of his own men, Amaziah hired 100,000 mercenaries from the ten northern tribes to assist the armies of Judah.

2 Chronicles 25:7, 8
But there came a man of God to him, saying, O king, let not the army of Israel go with thee; for the LORD is not with Israel, to wit, with all the children of Ephraim. But if thou wilt go, do it, be strong for the battle: God shall make thee fall before the enemy: for God hath power to help, and to cast down.

A prophet came to Amaziah and said, "God is not with the army of Israel. Let the mercenaries go. If you want to go to battle, take only men from your own country."

2 Chronicles 25:9
And Amaziah said to the man of God, But what shall we do for the hundred talents which I have given to the army of Israel? And the man of God answered, The LORD is able to give thee much more than this.

Having already paid the mercenaries three and one-half tons of silver, Amaziah was concerned about his lost investment.

2 Chronicles 25:10
Then Amaziah separated them, to wit, the army that was come to him out of Ephraim, to go home again: wherefore their anger was greatly kindled against Judah, and they returned home in great anger.

The men from the northern tribes had been paid. Why, then, would they be upset about being sent home? Perhaps it was due to wounded pride at not being needed. Or, more likely, perhaps they thought they were getting shortchanged because they wouldn't be able to keep any of the spoils of battle.

2 Chronicles 25:11–13
And Amaziah strengthened himself, and led forth his people, and went to the valley of salt, and smote of the children of Seir ten thousand. And other ten thousand left alive did the children of Judah carry away captive, and brought them unto the top of the rock, and cast them down from the top of the rock, that they all were broken in pieces. But the soldiers of the army which Amaziah sent back, that they should not go with him to battle, fell upon the cities of Judah, from Samaria even unto Beth-horon, and smote three thousand of them, and took much spoil.

Amaziah and the army of Judah were victorious in battle against the Edomites. Unbeknownst to them, however, while they were gone, the mercenaries that were sent home plundered Judah and Samaria.

2 Chronicles 25:14, 15
Now it came to pass, after that Amaziah was come from the slaughter of the Edomites, that he brought the gods of the children of Seir, and set them up to be his gods, and bowed down himself before them, and burned incense unto them. Wherefore the anger of the LORD was kindled against Amaziah, and he sent unto him a prophet, which said unto him, Why hast thou sought after the gods of the people, which could not deliver their own people out of thine hand?

After wiping out the Edomites, Amaziah decided to make their gods his gods. In other words, he chose to serve the gods that were apparently weaker than him.

2 Chronicles 25:16, 17
And it came to pass, as he talked with him, that the king said unto him, Art thou made of the king's counsel? forbear; why shouldest thou be smitten? Then the prophet forbare, and said, I know that God hath determined to destroy thee, because thou hast done this, and hast not hearkened unto my counsel. Then Amaziah king of Judah took advice, and sent to Joash, the son of Jehoahaz, the son of Jehu, king of Israel, saying, Come, let us see one another in the face.

Amaziah, king of Judah, challenged Joash, king of Israel to battle.

2 Chronicles 25:18
And Joash king of Israel sent to Amaziah king of Judah, saying, The thistle that was in Lebanon sent to the cedar that was in

Lebanon, saying, Give thy daughter to my son to wife: and there passed by a wild beast that was in Lebanon, and trode down the thistle.

In response to Amaziah's call to battle, Joash gives him a parable concerning a bush that began ordering a cedar tree around. "Give me your daughter for my son," the bush demanded, until a beast came by and squashed it. In other words, Joash was saying, "Amaziah, you're out of your league. You have as much chance of victory over me as a bush who's challenging a cedar tree."

2 Chronicles 25:19
Thou sayest, Lo, thou hast smitten the Edomites; and thine heart lifteth thee up to boast: abide now at home; why shouldest thou meddle to thine hurt, that thou shouldest fall, even thou, and Judah with thee?

"Why are you meddling to your hurt?" Joash asks Amaziah. "You had victory over the Edomites. Enjoy it. But don't challenge me."

The same question can be asked of us. Why *do* we meddle to our own hurt? Why do we go into places we shouldn't be in, take on challenges we have no business taking on? We have a victory in our lives and think we're strong. Then we meddle to our own hurt by hanging out with the old gang in the old haunts, all the while thinking we're invincible.

2 Chronicles 25:20, 21
But Amaziah would not hear; for it came of God, that he might deliver them into the hand of their enemies, because they sought after the gods of Edom. So Joash the king of Israel went up; and they saw one another in the face, both he and Amaziah king of Judah, at Beth-shemesh, which belongeth to Judah.

Amaziah didn't listen to Joash and in the ensuing battle, we see four results of meddling where we shouldn't . . .

2 Chronicles 25:22
And Judah was put to the worse before Israel, and they fled every man to his tent.

First, Amaziah's meddling disgraced the nation. You will find yourself disgracing yourself and your Lord if you meddle in places you don't belong. When Peter-John was nine years old, he was already a big baseball fan. He knew all the statistics and collected all of the cards. But it was tough for me as a dad to explain to him the headlines linking his favorite ball players with drugs. That's what sin does. It always brings disgrace.

2 Chronicles 25:23
And Joash the king of Israel took Amaziah king of Judah, the son of Joash, the son of Jehoahaz, at Beth-shemesh, and brought him to Jerusalem, and brake down the wall of Jerusalem from the gate of Ephraim to the corner gate, four hundred cubits.

Secondly, Amaziah's meddling decreased Judah's defenses as the walls were broken down around Jerusalem. The problem with a little sin is that it doesn't stay little. The defenses break down and we think we can meddle a little and not be affected.

2 Chronicles 25:24 (a)
And he took all the gold and the silver, and all the vessels that were found in the house of God with Obed-edom, and the treasures of the king's house . . .

Thirdly, Amaziah's meddling diminished worship. The beautiful treasures in the temple used in worshiping the Lord were now gone. When we meddle and find ourselves succumbing to sin, we no longer worship with the intensity or consistency we once did.

2 Chronicles 25:24 (b)
. . . the hostages also, and returned to Samaria.

Finally, Amaziah's meddling destroyed Judah's freedom. They were taken hostage. In 1 Corinthians 10:23, Paul said, "All things are lawful for me, but I will not be brought under the power of any." Hang on to your freedom, gang. Don't become enslaved to sin. As believers, we are the freest of all men because we alone are free not to sin.

2 Chronicles 25:25–28
And Amaziah the son of Joash king of Judah lived after the death of Joash son of Jehoahaz king of Israel fifteen years. Now the rest of the acts of Amaziah, first and last, behold, are they not written in the book of the kings of Judah and Israel? Now after the time that Amaziah did turn away from following the LORD they made a conspiracy against him in Jerusalem; and he fled to Lachish: but they sent to Lachish after him, and slew him there. And they brought him upon horses, and buried him with his fathers in the city of Judah.

When Amaziah was victorious, the people were with him. But when he lost the battle, when the city was broken down, when the temple was plundered, the people called for his head. Thus, in addition to disgrace and decreased defenses; in addition to diminished worship and destroyed freedom, Amaziah's meddling brought what sin always brings in one form or another: the wages of death (Romans 6:23).

26 2 Chronicles 26:1–5
Then all the people of Judah took Uzziah, who was sixteen years old, and made him king in the room of his father Amaziah. He built Eloth, and restored it to Judah, after that the king slept with his fathers. Sixteen years old was Uzziah when he began to reign, and he reigned fifty and two years in Jerusalem. His mother's name also was Jecoliah of Jerusalem. And he did that which was right in the sight of the LORD, according to all that his father Amaziah did. And he sought God in the days of Zechariah, who had understanding in the visions of God: and as long as he sought the LORD, God made him to prosper.

In the life of Uzziah, we see the singular path to prosperity. That is, as long as he sought the Lord, God made Uzziah to prosper. And the path hasn't changed to this day. Seek the Lord, walk with the Lord, love the Lord, and He'll bless you in ways you never dreamed possible.

2 Chronicles 26:6–8
And he went forth and warred against the Philistines, and brake down the wall of Gath, and the wall of Jabneh, and the wall of Ashdod, and built cities about Ashdod, and among the Philistines. And God helped him against the Philistines, and against the Arabians that dwelt in Gur-baal, and the Mehunims. And the Ammonites gave gifts to Uzziah: and his name spread abroad even to the entering in of Egypt; for he strengthened himself exceedingly.

One manifestation of God's blessing upon Uzziah was his victory over his enemies.

2 Chronicles 26:9, 10
Moreover Uzziah built towers in Jerusalem at the corner gate, and at the valley gate, and at the turning of the wall, and fortified them. Also he built towers in the desert, and digged many wells: for he had much cattle, both in the low country, and in the plains: husbandmen also, and vine dressers in the mountains, and in Carmel: for he loved husbandry.

A second manifestation of God's blessing upon Uzziah was in his keen agricultural ability.

2 Chronicles 26:11–15 (a)
Moreover Uzziah had an host of fighting men, that went out to war by bands, according to the number of their account by the hand of Jeiel the scribe and Maaseiah the ruler, under the hand of Hananiah, one of the king's captains. The whole number of the chief of the fathers of the mighty men of valour were two thousand and six hundred. And under their hand was an army, three hundred thousand and seven thousand and five hundred, that made war with mighty power, to help the king against the enemy. And Uzziah prepared for them throughout all the host shields, and spears, and helmets, and habergeons, and bows, and slings to cast stones. And he made in Jerusalem engines, invented by cunning men, to be on the towers and upon the bulwarks, to shoot arrows and great stones withal . . .

A third manifestation of God's blessing upon Uzziah was in his development of innovative and effective weaponry.

I suggest these same three manifestations are seen in the lives of those who walk with God today, for they will indeed be victorious in difficulty (1 John 4:4), bear much fruit for God's glory (John 15:2), and be skilled with the weaponry of spiritual warfare (Ephesians 6:13–17).

2 Chronicles 26:15 (b)
. . . And his name spread far abroad; for he was marvellously helped, till he was strong.

Uzziah was a great king. He sought the Lord. He loved the Lord. He caused prosperity to come to the people of Judah. He enabled their defenses to be strong and their territory to expand. In fact, the people did so well under his rule and loved him so much that his fame spread throughout the entire region. But that can be a danger. For, in Uzziah's day, a prophet named Isaiah wrote that it wasn't until Uzziah died that he saw the Lord high and lifted up (Isaiah 6:1).

You see, it seems as though the eyes of the people were on Uzziah. Their security was in Uzziah rather than in the Lord. So it wasn't until Uzziah died that Isaiah saw the Lord.

In your life, those people or things that become "Uzziahs" to you will invariably die before you because the Lord wants you to see *Him* on the throne high and lifted up. If you are depending upon your husband or wife to be your source of strength in spirituality, something will happen that will disappoint or discourage you in some way until you realize that it's not your husband or wife, but the Lord alone who will see you through. If the church or certain leaders therein are your

"Uzziah," something will happen through which you'll see it's not them at all. Once again, you'll realize it's the Lord who builds the church, in spite of us, not because of us. The Lord will allow the "Uzziahs" in our lives to die in order that we might see Him, love Him, worship Him, and walk with Him, for He alone is the only One who will never disappoint us, totally satisfy us, and bring stability to us.

2 Chronicles 26:16
But when he was strong, his heart was lifted up to his destruction: for he transgressed against the LORD his God, and went into the temple of the LORD to burn incense upon the altar of incense.

Although he was king, and although he was remarkably blessed, Uzziah was not a priest and, therefore, forbidden by Old Testament law to go into the temple to burn incense.

2 Chronicles 26:17, 18
And Azariah the priest went in after him, and with him fourscore priests of the LORD, that were valiant men: And they withstood Uzziah the king, and said unto him, It appertaineth not unto thee, Uzziah, to burn incense unto the LORD, but to the priests the sons of Aaron, that are consecrated to burn incense: go out of the sanctuary; for thou hast trespassed; neither shall it be for thine honour from the LORD God.

When Uzziah thought he was above the law and decided to burn incense himself in the temple, eighty priests begged him not do so.

2 Chronicles 26:19–23 (a)
Then Uzziah was wroth, and had a censer in his hand to burn incense: and while he was wroth with the priests, the leprosy even rose up in his forehead before the priests in the house of the LORD, from beside the incense altar. And Azariah the chief priest, and all the priests, looked upon him, and, behold, he was leprous in his forehead, and they thrust him out from thence; yea, himself hasted also to go out, because the LORD had smitten him. And Uzziah the king was a leper unto the day of his death, and dwelt in a several house, being a leper; for he was cut off from the house of the LORD: and Jotham his son was over the king's house, judging the people of the land. Now the rest of the acts of Uzziah, first and last, did Isaiah the prophet, the son of Amoz, write. So Uzziah slept with his fathers, and they buried him with his fathers in the field of the burial which belonged to the kings; for they said, He is a leper . . .

When Uzziah refused to respond to the warning of the priests, he was immediately stricken with leprosy. Thus, this great man was disgraced at the end of his life because he evidently thought he had earned the right to ignore the direct command of the Lord.

2 Chronicles 26:23 (b)
. . . and Jotham his son reigned in his stead.

Uzziah was a godly man who was eaten by leprosy because of a quarrel in the church. His story serves as a warning to us all, for in the following chapters, we'll see the results of his sin in the life of his own son and grandson. Like Uzziah, you might be a godly person. But if you find fault with church or minimize its importance, there are little ears and eyes listening and watching, developing attitudes about the church based on what they hear and see in you.

27

2 Chronicles 27:1, 2 (a)
Jotham was twenty and five years old when he began to reign, and he reigned sixteen years in Jerusalem. His mother's name also was Jerushah, the daughter of Zadok. And he did that which was right in the sight of the LORD, according to all that his father Uzziah did: howbeit he entered not into the temple of the LORD . . .

Uzziah's son, Jotham, loved the Lord like his dad had. But he saw his dad irritated by the priesthood. So what did he do? He didn't go into the temple at all. Jotham was a good man. But he wasn't what he could have been or should have been because he didn't find his way to the temple.

As parents, we can make a very critical error by criticizing the church, pastor, music leader, or Sunday school teachers in front of our kids. If we do, we can't be surprised when, at age sixteen, they don't want anything to do with the church. The reason Uzziah got leprosy was not because he was in the temple, but because he was in error. Unfortunately, Jotham didn't make this distinction.

A twelve-year-old boy followed his dad across a rapid stream. The father was choosing his steps most carefully when, midstream, he heard his son call, "Dad, choose good rocks. I'm stepping on the same ones you are." Choose to build your life on the Rock of Jesus Christ, Dad, and you'll see the benefit not only in your life but in the lives of your sons and grandsons.

2 Chronicles 27:2 (b)
. . . And the people did yet corruptly.

Although Jotham may have been able to survive without temple worship, those under his rule couldn't and, as a result, the country plunged into chaos.

2 Chronicles 27:3–6
He built the high gate of the house of the LORD, and on the wall of Ophel he built much. Moreover he built cities in the mountains of Judah, and in the forests he built castles and towers. He fought also with the king of the Ammonites, and prevailed against them. And the children of Ammon gave him the same year an hundred talents of silver, and ten thousand measures of wheat, and ten thousand of barley. So much did the children of Ammon pay unto him, both the second year, and the third. So Jotham became mighty, because he prepared his ways before the LORD his God.

Even though Jotham didn't partake in worship, he did have a heart that sought after the Lord.

2 Chronicles 27:7–9
Now the rest of the acts of Jotham, and all his wars, and his ways, lo, they are written in the book of the kings of Israel and Judah. He was five and twenty years old when he began to reign, and reigned sixteen years in Jerusalem. And Jotham slept with his fathers, and they buried him in the city of David: and Ahaz his son reigned in his stead.

I believe Jotham could have been a great king. I believe he had the heart and the background and the potential to be one of the great leaders in the history of Judah. But he didn't reach his potential because he didn't partake of temple worship. We as believers will not be what the Lord would have us be if we forsake the consistent "assembling of ourselves together . . ." (Hebrews 10:25).

28

2 Chronicles 28:1–3
Ahaz was twenty years old when he began to reign, and he reigned sixteen years in Jerusalem: but he did not that which was right in the sight of the LORD, like David his father: For he walked in the ways of the kings of Israel, and made also molten images for Baalim. Moreover he burnt incense in the valley of the son of Hinnom, and burnt his children in the fire, after the abominations of the heathen whom the LORD had cast out before the children of Israel.

Ahaz actually had the audacity to offer his own children on the incandescent arms of a metal idol. Before we are too quick to throw stones, however, we must look at our own society. Studies today indicate that, due to business, hobbies, and projects, the average father spends *seven and one-half minutes* per day with his children. If our kids are getting "burned out" on life, could it be because we're sacrificing them to the idol of success?

2 Chronicles 28:4–8
He sacrificed also and burnt incense in the high places, and on the hills, and under every green tree. Wherefore the LORD his God delivered him into the hand of the king of Syria; and they smote him, and carried away a great multitude of them captives, and brought them to Damascus. And he was also delivered into the hand of the king of Israel, who smote him with a great slaughter. For Pekah the son of Remaliah slew in Judah an hundred and twenty thousand in one day, which were all valiant men; because they had forsaken the LORD God of their fathers. And Zichri, a mighty man of Ephraim, slew Maaseiah the king's son, and Azrikam the governor of the house, and Elkanah that was next to the king. And the children of Israel carried away captive of their brethren two hundred thousand, women, sons, and daughters, and took also away much spoil from them, and brought the spoil to Samaria.

As seen repeatedly throughout the history of God's people, the inevitable result of idolatry is captivity.

2 Chronicles 28:9–11
But a prophet of the LORD was there, whose name was Oded: and he went out before the host that came to Samaria, and said unto them, Behold, because the LORD God of your fathers was wroth with Judah, he hath delivered them into your hand, and ye have slain them in a rage that reacheth up unto heaven. And now ye purpose to keep under the children of Judah and Jerusalem for bondmen and bondwomen unto you: but are there not with you, even with you, sins against the LORD your God? Now hear me therefore, and deliver the captives again, which ye have taken captive of your brethren: for the fierce wrath of the LORD is upon you.

Oded, a prophet of the Lord, said to Israel, "The Lord used you to discipline the people of Judah, but you've taken it way too far. You've slaughtered them without mercy and you're capturing them for your own purposes. Because the Lord is angry, you must let them go."

2 Chronicles 28:12–15
Then certain of the heads of the children of Ephraim, Azariah the son of Johanan, Berechiah the son of Meshillemoth, and Jehizkiah the son of Shallum, and Amasa the son of Hadlai, stood up against them that came from the war, and said unto them, Ye shall not bring in the captives hither: for whereas we have offended against the LORD already, ye intend to add more to our sins and to our trespass: for our trespass is great, and there is fierce wrath against Israel. So the armed men left the captives and the spoil before the princes and all the congregation. And the men which were expressed by name rose up, and took the captives, and with the spoil clothed all that were naked among them, and arrayed them, and shod them, and gave them to eat and to drink, and anointed them, and carried all the feeble of them upon asses, and brought them to Jericho, the city of palm trees, to their brethren: then they returned to Samaria.

To their credit, when the leaders of Israel heard the word of prophecy, they responded accordingly. They clothed and fed the captives, bound their wounds, and sent them home.

2 Chronicles 28:16–21
At that time did king Ahaz send unto the kings of Assyria to help him. For again the Edomites had come and smitten Judah, and carried away captives. The Philistines also had invaded the cities of the low country, and of the south of Judah, and had taken Beth-shemesh, and Ajalon, and Gederoth, and Shocho with the villages thereof, and Timnah with the villages thereof, Gimzo also and the villages thereof: and they dwelt there. For the LORD brought Judah low because of Ahaz king of Israel; for he made Judah naked, and transgressed sore against the LORD. And Tiglath-pileser king of Assyria came unto him, and distressed him, but strengthened him not. For Ahaz took away a portion out of the house of the LORD, and out of the house of the king, and of the princes, and gave it unto the king of Assyria: but he helped him not.

Under attack by the Edomites and Philistines, Ahaz hired the godless Assyrians to be his ally. Yet although the king of Assyria took payment, he didn't keep his end of the bargain.

2 Chronicles 28:22, 23
And in the time of his distress did he trespass yet more against the LORD: this is that king Ahaz. For he sacrificed unto the gods of Damascus, which smote him: and he said, Because the gods of the kings of Syria help them, therefore will I sacrifice to them, that they may help me. But they were the ruin of him, and of all Israel.

Ahaz is struggling, striving, floundering. This evil, wicked man who has burned his kids, who has seen his country taken away into captivity, who is now facing threats from the north and south, who got swindled by the Assyrians, turns to the gods of the Syrians in hopes they will help him. Why is it that people will turn to just about anything or anyone but the Lord? In desperation, we'll seek the help of friends, even foes, but stubbornly refuse the only One who can truly come through.

2 Chronicles 28:24, 25
And Ahaz gathered together the vessels of the house of God, and cut in pieces the vessels of the house of God, and shut up the doors of the house of the LORD, and he made him altars in every corner of Jerusalem. And in every several city of Judah he made high places to burn incense unto other gods, and provoked to anger the LORD God of his fathers.

Ahaz brings this three-generation saga to its inevitable conclusion, for in Uzziah, Jotham, and Ahaz, we see a father who had a quarrel with the church followed by his son who stopped going to church, followed by his grandson who closed the doors of the church. In other words, church attendance is not beneficial only to you, Dad, but the example you set will have a direct effect on your kids and grandchildren.

2 Chronicles 28:26, 27 (a)
Now the rest of his acts and of all his ways, first and last, behold, they are written in the book of the kings of Judah and Israel. And Ahaz slept with his fathers, and they buried him in the city, even in Jerusalem: but they brought him not into the sepulchres of the kings of Israel . . .

So much hurt and harm did Ahaz bring to Israel that they didn't even bury him with the other kings.

2 Chronicles 28:27 (b)
. . . and Hezekiah his son reigned in his stead.

Besides David, Hezekiah would be the greatest king in the history of God's people. In the following four chapters, we'll see revival break out, and in studying them, hopefully we'll see revival ignited in our own hearts, as well.

29 There is so much for us to learn from the life of Hezekiah that eleven chapters in the Books of 2 Kings, 2 Chronicles, and Isaiah are devoted to its record.

2 Chronicles 29:1, 2
Hezekiah began to reign when he was five and twenty years old, and he reigned nine and twenty years in Jerusalem. And his mother's name was Abijah, the daughter of Zechariah. And he did that which was right in the sight of the LORD, according to all that David his father had done.

Hezekiah is one of the greatest leaders and rulers in the history of Judah. He did right in the sight of the Lord, even as did David. Humanly speaking, David had his problems. But from the Father's perspective, David was a man who loved Him and worshiped Him with intensity, fervency, and consistency. Thus, David is held up as the quintessential example of a godly man because his heart was inclined toward the Lord.

2 Chronicles 29:3
He in the first year of his reign, in the first month, opened the doors of the house of the LORD, and repaired them.

In 2 Chronicles 28:24, we read that Hezekiah's father, Ahaz, shut the doors of the house of the Lord. But now here comes his son, Hezekiah who—in the first month of his reign—opened the doors of the house of the Lord. I like that!

When Hezekiah first ascended to the throne, he didn't build a palace or consolidate his power. No, the first thing he did was open the doors of the temple.

"Those who seek Me early shall find Me," the Lord declares (Proverbs 8:17). Hezekiah models this beautifully.

2 Chronicles 29:4, 5
And he brought in the priests and the Levites, and gathered them together into the east street, And said unto them, Hear me, ye Levites, sanctify now yourselves, and sanctify the house of the LORD God of your fathers, and carry forth the filthiness out of the holy place.

Ahaz had allowed the holy place to be desecrated and defiled. Here, Hezekiah tells the Levites to clean it up.

Because we are the temple of the true and living God, there must be a continual cleansing of the filthiness that pollutes and penetrates our lives. It is interesting to me that virtually all of creation is concerned with cleanliness . . .

Mice and rats actually spend the majority of their waking hours grooming themselves. They carry disease, but are actually surprisingly clean. So are elephants. Elephants who become invaded with parasites cover themselves with dust. Then they rub themselves against trees. The dust suffocates the bugs. The tree acts like a towel to wipe the dead bugs from off their back. Finally, they give themselves showers by filling their trunks with water and squirting themselves. The gecko lizards in the southwest desert of our country are interesting because they don't have any eyelids. Yet they live in a place where there is lots of dirt and sand. So what do they do? The gecko lizard has a long tongue which he actually extends all the way to his eyes and thus is able to clean them.

There seems to be innately built into creation a desire to be clean. And yet when it comes to the heart of man, we allow corruption and pollution to affect us internally. Cleansing needs to be carried out daily. How? If we confess our sin, He is faithful and just to forgive us our sin and to cleanse us from all unrighteousness (1 John 1:9). This verse tells us that even if we feel defiled and desecrated, we can solve that problem right now simply by confessing. When you confess your sin, the blood of Jesus is immediately applied and it removes all the filth from the temple of your life.

2 Chronicles 29:6–9
For our fathers have trespassed, and done that which was evil in the eyes of the LORD our God, and have forsaken him, and have turned away their faces from the habitation of the LORD, and turned their backs. Also they have shut up the doors of the porch, and put out the lamps, and have not burned incense nor offered burnt offerings in the holy place unto the God of Israel. Wherefore the wrath of the LORD was upon Judah and Jerusalem, and he hath delivered them to trouble, to astonishment, and to hissing, as ye see with your eyes. For, lo, our fathers have fallen by the sword, and our sons and our daughters and our wives are in captivity for this.

What a contrast the state of the nation was to its state under the rule of Uzziah, when both militarily and economically the nation prospered abundantly (see 2 Chronicles 26:1–15).

2 Chronicles 29:10, 11
Now it is in mine heart to make a covenant with the LORD God of Israel, that his fierce wrath may turn away from us. My sons, be not now negligent: for the LORD hath chosen you to stand before him, to serve him, and that ye should minister unto him, and burn incense.

Hezekiah knew the root of all of the problems in his ailing nation was singular: they had forsaken God.

2 Chronicles 29:12–17
Then the Levites arose, Mahath the son of Amasai, and Joel the son of Azariah, of the sons of the Kohathites: and of the sons of Merari, Kish the son of Abdi, and Azariah the son of Jehalelel: and of the Gershonites; Joah the son of Zimmah, and Eden the son of Joah: And of the sons of Elizaphan; Shimri, and Jeiel: and of the sons of Asaph; Zechariah, and Mattaniah: And of the sons of Heman; Jehiel, and Shimei: and of the sons of Jeduthun; Shemaiah, and Uzziel. And they gathered their brethren, and sanctified themselves, and came, according to the commandment of the king, by the words of the LORD, to cleanse the house of the LORD. And the priests went into the inner part of the house of the LORD, to cleanse it, and brought out all the uncleanness that they found in the temple of the LORD into the court of the house of the LORD. And the Levites took it, to carry it out abroad into the brook Kidron. Now they began on the first day of the first month to sanctify, and on the eighth day of the month came they to the porch of the LORD: so they sanctified the house of the LORD in eight days; and in the sixteenth day of the first month they made an end.

It took the Levites eight days to sanctify the holy place—to carry out the filth and clean out the cobwebs—and eight more days to clean the outer courtyard.

2 Chronicles 29:18, 19
Then they went in to Hezekiah the king, and said, We have cleansed all the house of the LORD, and the altar of burnt offering, with all the vessels thereof, and the shewbread table, with all the vessels thereof. Moreover all the vessels, which king Ahaz in his reign did cast away in his transgression, have we prepared and sanctified, and, behold, they are before the altar of the LORD.

Things are looking good. The temple is clean. The broken instruments are repaired. It's ready to be used.

2 Chronicles 29:20–23
Then Hezekiah the king rose early, and gathered the rulers of the city, and went up to the house of the LORD. And they brought seven bullocks, and seven rams, and seven lambs, and seven he goats, for a sin offering for the kingdom, and for the sanctuary, and for Judah. And he commanded the priests the sons of Aaron to offer them on the altar of the LORD. So they killed the bullocks, and the priests received the blood, and sprinkled it on the altar: likewise, when they had killed the rams, they sprinkled the blood upon the altar: they killed also the lambs, and they sprinkled the blood upon the altar. And they brought forth the he goats for the sin offering before the king and the congregation; and they laid their hands upon them:

When the people laid their hands upon the offerings about to be sacrificed, they realized they were "transferring" their sin to the animals about to be slaughtered. In other words, they would understand that sin is so serious it can only be dealt with by death.

2 Chronicles 29:24 (a)
And the priests killed them, and they made reconciliation with their blood upon the altar, to make an atonement for all Israel . . .

The Hebrew word translated "atonement" is *kapar*. *Kapar* doesn't mean "to cleanse" or "to eradicate." It simply means "to cover up." As the author of Hebrews makes clear, the blood of bulls and goats would cover up the sin of the people, but it could not take it away. Only the blood of Jesus Christ, the perfect Lamb of God, can take away sin (Hebrews 10).

When I spent an afternoon with a leader of a local synagogue, I asked him what he does with the issue of sin since the temple is no longer in service and sacrifices are no longer being made.

"We believe sin is dealt with in two ways," he said, "through confession to God and reconciliation with man. You confess your sin to God and then make things right with the one against whom you've sinned. If you reconcile with man, God will forgive."

"How do you deal with all of the Scriptures in the Old Testament that declare that without the shedding of blood, there is no forgiveness?" I asked.

"If you take those things literally, that's a problem," he said.

We are so blessed as Christians to have proof positive that our sins are forgiven, not based upon our being right with each other, for who among us can say, "I am right with every individual on the face of this planet. No one has anything against me, neither do I have anything against anyone else"? It's a scary position to be in if you base your salvation upon confession and restitution. On the other hand, it is a beautiful place to be in if you base your salvation upon the work of Jesus Christ on Calvary, who declared, "It is *finished.*" The price is paid fully and completely. Oh, happy day!

2 Chronicles 29:24 (b)–29
. . . for the king commanded that the burnt offering and the sin offering should be made for all Israel. And he set the Levites in the house of the LORD with cymbals, with psalteries, and with harps, according to the commandment of David, and of Gad the king's seer, and Nathan the prophet: for so was the commandment of the LORD by his prophets. And the Levites stood with the instruments of David, and the priests with the trumpets. And Hezekiah commanded to offer the burnt offering upon the altar. And when the burnt offering began, the song of the LORD began also with the trumpets, and with the instruments ordained by David king of Israel. And all the congregation worshipped, and the singers sang, and the trumpeters sounded: and all this continued until the burnt offering was finished. And when they had made an end of offering, the king and all that were present with him bowed themselves, and worshipped.

Sacrifice was made. The trumpeters began to play. The cymbals crashed. The people began to sing. And the king and all the people bowed down and worshiped.

One of the beautiful things about worship is that it breaks down barriers. Whether you're a king or a commoner, a prince or a pauper, it doesn't make any difference. In worship, we find unity. I love to worship because I get tired of hearing myself talk. I get weary of my flaws and faults and shortcomings. In worship, we lose our identity. We transcend ourselves. We become part of something bigger than our own individuality. We become linked together, praising the Lord, kings and commoners alike.

2 Chronicles 29:30
Moreover Hezekiah the king and the princes commanded the Levites to sing praise unto the LORD with the words of David, and of Asaph the seer. And they sang praises with gladness, and they bowed their heads and worshipped.

Praising the Lord is to be an expression of joy and gladness.

2 Chronicles 29:31 (a)
Then Hezekiah answered and said, Now ye have consecrated yourselves unto the LORD, come near and bring sacrifices and thank offerings into the house of the LORD . . .

Offerings are truly about the giving of thanks for God's goodness.

2 Chronicles 29:31 (b)
. . . And the congregation brought in sacrifices and thank offerings; and as many as were of a free heart burnt offerings.

The burnt offering signified a total commitment. It wasn't required, but those who had a willing heart made this special sacrifice.

2 Chronicles 29:32–34
And the number of the burnt offerings, which the congregation brought, was threescore and ten bullocks, an hundred rams, and two hundred lambs: all these were for a burnt offering to the LORD. And the consecrated things were six hundred oxen and three thousand sheep. But the priests were too few, so that they could not flay all the burnt offerings: wherefore their brethren the Levites did help them, till the work was ended, and until the other priests had sanctified themselves: for the Levites were more upright in heart to sanctify themselves than the priests.

People were coming with sacrifices and burnt offerings. Revival was breaking out. And the priests were unable to handle the large numbers, so the Levites helped them. The Levites legally did not have this right. Offerings were to be made only by the sons of Aaron, the priests. The Levites were simply to assist in the work of the temple, but not to directly offer sacrifices. Yet the work was so great that here the Lord allows, even blesses the Levites for rolling up their sleeves and offering sacrifices.

In these last days, when the Holy Ghost is being outpoured and revival is breaking out, there is so much need that the days when you used to need a seminary education are no more. Thus, we can send people who are not "credentialed" to go and do the work of the Lord because the work is great. Don't ever feel that, just because you haven't had a lot of intellectual training, you can't be used in ministry. In fact, in Acts we read that the Pharisees looked at Peter and John in amazement because they knew they were ignorant men. And yet the way they spoke and moved impressed them greatly. We read that the Pharisees took note that they had been with Jesus (Acts 4:13). That makes all the difference! That's where your credential lies—in being with Jesus Christ, and having a heart willing to serve Him.

2 Chronicles 29:35, 36
And also the burnt offerings were in abundance, with the fat of the peace offerings, and the drink offerings for every burnt offering. So the service of the house of the LORD was set in order. And Hezekiah rejoiced, and all the people, that God had prepared the people: for the thing was done suddenly.

A beautiful revival took place, and there was rejoicing as the Spirit of God moved.

---

30 Rather than keeping this revival to himself, Hezekiah longed for it to spread even to his sometime-enemies . . .

2 Chronicles 30:1
And Hezekiah sent to all Israel and Judah, and wrote letters also to Ephraim and Manasseh, that they should come to the house of the LORD at Jerusalem, to keep the passover unto the LORD God of Israel.

At this time, the Assyrians were in the process of carrying the ten northern tribes into captivity. Knowing they were in trouble, Hezekiah said to the remnant, "Come on down. Join our revival."

2 Chronicles 30:2–9
For the king had taken counsel, and his princes, and all the congregation in Jerusalem, to keep the passover in the second month. For they could not keep it at that time, because the priests had not sanctified themselves sufficiently, neither had the people gathered themselves together to Jerusalem. And the thing pleased the king and all the congregation. So they established a decree to make proclamation throughout all Israel, from Beer-sheba even to Dan, that they should come to keep the passover unto the LORD God of Israel at Jerusalem: for they had not done it of a long time in such sort as it was written. So the posts went with the letters from the king and his princes throughout all Israel and Judah, and according to the commandment of the king, saying, Ye children of Israel, turn again unto the LORD God of Abraham, Isaac, and Israel, and he will return to the remnant of you, that are escaped out of the hand of the kings of Assyria. And be not ye like your fathers, and like your brethren, which trespassed against the LORD God of their fathers, who therefore gave them up to desolation, as ye see. Now be ye not stiffnecked, as your fathers were, but yield yourselves unto the LORD, and enter into his sanctuary, which he hath sanctified for ever: and serve the LORD your God, that the fierceness of his wrath may turn away from you. For if ye turn again unto the LORD, your brethren and your children shall find compassion before them that lead them captive, so that they shall come again into this land: for the LORD your God is gracious and merciful, and will not turn away his face from you, if ye return unto him.

Those who don't see grace or mercy in the Old Testament just aren't reading their Bibles, for here God says through Hezekiah to the people who had forsaken Him, "If you come back to Me, I will be gracious to you."

2 Chronicles 30:10
So the posts passed from city to city through the country of Ephraim and Manasseh even unto Zebulun: but they laughed them to scorn, and mocked them.

The people of Israel are going through troubles, trials, and difficulty. An invitation comes to be part of a revival, and what do they do? They mock and scorn. Oh, the tragic blindness of sin!

2 Chronicles 30:11
Nevertheless divers of Asher and Manasseh and of Zebulun humbled themselves, and came to Jerusalem.

While most mocked and scorned, a few responded. The same is true today. We are like the "postmen" Hezekiah sent, inviting people to join the revival taking place today. Some will scoff and mock. But there will be those who will listen to what you say and respond and come.

2 Chronicles 30:12–18 (a)
Also in Judah the hand of God was to give them one heart to do the commandment of the king and of the princes, by the word of the LORD. And there assembled at Jerusalem much people to keep the feast of unleavened bread in the second month, a very great congregation. And they arose and took away the altars that were in Jerusalem, and all the altars for incense took they away, and cast them into the brook Kidron. Then they killed the passover on the fourteenth day of

the second month: and the priests and the Levites were ashamed, and sanctified themselves, and brought in the burnt offerings into the house of the LORD. And they stood in their place after their manner, according to the law of Moses the man of God: the priests sprinkled the blood, which they received of the hand of the Levites. For there were many in the congregation that were not sanctified: therefore the Levites had the charge of the killing of the passovers for every one that was not clean, to sanctify them unto the LORD. For a multitude of the people, even many of Ephraim, and Manasseh, Issachar, and Zebulun, had not cleansed themselves, yet did they eat the passover otherwise than it was written . . .

The ones who responded positively came from Israel to Jerusalem to enjoy the revival and eat of the Passover. But because they hadn't gone through the purification ceremony outlined in the Scriptures, they were ceremonially impure. Were they forbidden or kept away? Watch what Hezekiah does when they come . . .

2 Chronicles 30:18 (b)–20
. . . But Hezekiah prayed for them, saying, The good LORD pardon every one That prepareth his heart to seek God, the LORD God of his fathers, though he be not cleansed according to the purification of the sanctuary. And the LORD hearkened to Hezekiah, and healed the people.

"Oh, Lord, pardon these people," Hezekiah prayed. "Their hearts are inclined to seeking You. Ceremonially, they're unclean. But, Lord, have mercy upon them."

May God keep us from becoming "churchy," where people who outwardly may be "impure" because of leftover remnants of the world in their lives are held at arm's length. The church is not a museum, but a hospital for real people who come with real hurts. We must never fail to embrace anyone who responds to the messengers and wants to be part of what God is doing.

2 Chronicles 30:21–23
And the children of Israel that were present at Jerusalem kept the feast of unleavened bread seven days with great gladness: and the Levites and the priests praised the LORD day by day, singing with loud instruments unto the LORD. And Hezekiah spake comfortably unto all the Levites that taught the good knowledge of the LORD: and they did eat throughout the feast seven days, offering peace offerings, and making confession to the LORD God of their fathers. And the whole assembly took counsel to keep other seven days: and they kept other seven days with gladness.

The seven days of the Passover were so joyful, so rich, that the people extended it another seven days.

2 Chronicles 30:24–27
For Hezekiah king of Judah did give to the congregation a thousand bullocks and seven thousand sheep; and the princes gave to the congregation a thousand bullocks and ten thousand sheep: and a great number of priests sanctified themselves. And all the congregation of Judah, with the priests and the Levites, and all the congregation that came out of Israel, and the strangers that came out of the land of Israel, and that dwelt in Judah, rejoiced. So there was great joy in Jerusalem: for since the time of Solomon the son of David king of Israel there was not the like in Jerusalem. Then the priests the Levites arose and blessed the people: and their voice was heard, and their prayer came up to his holy dwelling place, even unto heaven.

There was freedom, gladness and great joy in the revival because there was worship of the Lord and an acceptance of each other.

31

The revival that took place during the reign of Hezekiah was characterized by three things: the reopening of the temple, the reinstitution of Passover, and the rejoicing of God's people. Joy is always a key characteristic in any real revival, whether it's a personal revival or a corporate revival.

2 Chronicles 31:1
Now when all this was finished, all Israel that were present went out to the cities of Judah, and brake the images in pieces, and cut down the groves, and threw down the high places and the altars out of all Judah and Benjamin, in Ephraim also and Manasseh, until they had utterly destroyed them all. Then all the children of Israel returned, every man to his possession, into their own cities.

After the revival began, the people responded by going into the cities and destroying the idols therein. Saint, this is really important to see: Holiness was the result of revival, not the reason for revival. Many times we hear preachers say, "Tear down the images. Get rid of your sin and revival will come." The biblical pattern, however, is that when the grace and goodness of God is seen, they cause people to break down their idols (Acts 19; Romans 2:4). In other words, revival doesn't bring about grace. Grace brings about revival.

2 Chronicles 31:2–5
And Hezekiah appointed the courses of the priests and the Levites after their courses, every man according to his service, the priests and Levites for burnt offerings and for peace offerings, to minister, and to give thanks, and to praise in the gates of the tents of the LORD. He appointed also the king's portion of his substance for the burnt offerings, to wit, for the morning and evening burnt offerings, and the burnt offerings for the sabbaths, and for the new moons, and for the set feasts, as it is written in the law of the LORD. Moreover he commanded the people that dwelt in Jerusalem to give the portion of the priests and the Levites, that they might be encouraged in the law of the LORD. And as soon as the commandment came abroad, the children of Israel brought in abundance the firstfruits of corn, wine, and oil, and honey, and of all the increase of the fields; and the tithe of all things brought they in abundantly.

When Hezekiah told the people to support the ministry, they did so enthusiastically.

2 Chronicles 31:6, 7
And concerning the children of Israel and Judah, that dwelt in the cities of Judah, they also brought in the tithe of oxen and sheep, and the tithe of holy things which were consecrated unto the LORD their God, and laid them by heaps. In the third month they began to lay the foundation of the heaps, and finished them in the seventh month.

The people gave so much to the Lord's work that it took four months just to gather it.

2 Chronicles 31:8–10
And when Hezekiah and the princes came and saw the heaps, they blessed the LORD, and his people Israel. Then Hezekiah questioned with the priests and the Levites concerning the heaps. And Azariah the chief priest of the house of Zadok answered him, and said, Since the people began to bring the offerings into the house of the LORD, we have had enough to eat, and have left plenty: for the LORD hath blessed his people; and that which is left is this great store.

One of the results of true revival is a generous giving by God's people. When the blessings and goodness of God are recognized, there's a natural inclination to respond back.

In 2 Corinthians 8, Paul entreated the Corinthians to give in accordance to what the Lord was doing.

Moreover, brethren, we do you to wit of the grace of God bestowed on the churches of Macedonia . . . 2 Corinthians 8:1

Paul here is saying, "I want to tell you about what the churches in Macedonia are doing . . ."

How that in a great trial of affliction the abundance of their joy and their deep poverty abounded unto the riches of their liberality. For to their power, I bear record, yea, and beyond their power they were willing of themselves; Praying us with much intreaty that we would receive the gift, and take upon us the fellowship of the ministering to the saints.
2 Corinthians 8:2–4

Paul was traveling through the area, telling the churches he planted that there was a need back home in Jerusalem. Famine had struck and the saints were suffering. The churches in Asia Minor responded beautifully. Even though they were going through affliction themselves, they responded liberally and gave out of their poverty that Paul might take their gift to the suffering saints in Jerusalem.

And this they did, not as we hoped, but first gave their own selves to the Lord, and unto us by the will of God. 2 Corinthians 8:5

Giving begins with giving yourself to the Lord. The Lord wants us and not our money. Therefore, we need to give our money because as we give our money, we give something of our energy and skills, effort and time.

Therefore, as ye abound in every thing, in faith, and utterance, and knowledge, and in all diligence, and in your love to us, see that ye abound in this grace also. I speak not by commandment, but by occasion of the forwardness of others, and to prove the sincerity of your love. 2 Corinthians 8:7, 8

Paul here is saying the proof of your love is your willingness to give liberally.

For ye know the grace of our Lord Jesus Christ, that, though he was rich, yet for your sakes he became poor, that ye through his poverty might be rich. 2 Corinthians 8:9

May the Holy Spirit speak to our hearts because there's so much more God is calling us to do. And the funding and resources are already in place if we will simply be obedient and say, "Lord, the tithe is yours. And we will give to prove our love for You and commitment to Your kingdom according to the principles and precepts of Your Word."

2 Chronicles 31:11, 12 (a)
Then Hezekiah commanded to prepare chambers in the house of the LORD; and they prepared them, And brought in the offerings and the tithes and the dedicated things faithfully . . .

To store the abundance of resources that were released in this revival, special chambers were built. Later, in the Book of Malachi, the Lord makes reference to such a structure when He said, "Bring ye the tithes and offerings into the storehouse and test Me and see if I will not pour out upon you a blessing so great that your barns cannot contain it" (see 3:10).

People often ask me, "Where should I tithe?" You should tithe in the storehouse, the place where you are spiritually nourished week by week. There, under the guidance and direction of spiritual covering, those resources will be released according to the leading of the Lord.

2 Chronicles 31:12–14
. . . over which Cononiah the Levite was ruler, and Shimei his brother was the next. And Jehiel, and Azaziah, and Nahath, and Asahel, and Jerimoth, and Jozabad, and Eliel, and Ismachiah, and Mahath, and Benaiah, were overseers under the hand of Cononiah and Shimei his brother, at the commandment of Hezekiah the king, and Azariah the ruler of the house of God. And Kore the son of Imnah the Levite, the porter toward the east, was over the freewill offerings of God, to distribute the oblations of the LORD, and the most holy things.

These were the men who were responsible to oversee the funding and administration of the gifts.

2 Chronicles 31:15, 16 (a)
And next him were Eden, and Miniamin, and Jeshua, and Shemaiah, Amariah, and Shecaniah, in the cities of the priests, in their set office, to give to their brethren by courses, as well to the great as to the small: Beside their genealogy of males, from three years old and upward . . .

The priests were "on salary" from the age of three. This tells me that the people of God invested in the youth of their nation. As believers, we, too, need to invest of our time, prayers, wisdom, and finances in our kids so that they will have a firm footing in their walk with the Lord.

2 Chronicles 31:16 (b)–19
. . . even unto every one that entereth into the house of the LORD, his daily portion for their service in their charges according to their courses; Both to the genealogy of the priests by the house of their fathers, and the Levites from twenty years old and upward, in their charges by their courses; And to the genealogy of all their little ones, their wives, and their sons, and their daughters, through all the congregation: for in their set office they sanctified themselves in holiness: Also of the sons of Aaron the priests, which were in the fields of the suburbs of their cities, in every several city, the men that were expressed by name, to give portions to all the males among the priests, and to all that were reckoned by genealogies among the Levites.

The Levites—those from the tribe of Levi who assisted the priests, the sons of Aaron—received support from the age of twenty.

2 Chronicles 31:20, 21
And thus did Hezekiah throughout all Judah, and wrought that which was good and right and truth before the LORD his God. And in every work that he began in the service of the house of God, and in the law, and in the commandments, to seek his God, he did it with all his heart, and prospered.

Why did Hezekiah prosper? Because he did his work energetically, enthusiastically, and wholeheartedly. There is a way in which we can serve God begrudgingly. Don't do it. Don't teach Sunday school because you feel pressured. Don't give to missions out of guilt. Hezekiah prospered because he served the Lord with all his heart. The word "enthusiasm" comes from *en theos,* and literally means "full of God." May the Lord help us to be like Hezekiah—enthusiastic in our service, in our worship, in our giving, and in our work.

32 You can be sure a revival from heaven will always bring a reaction from hell. Anytime you're going through a personal revival, watch out because the hordes of hell will be released against you. Anytime a church is experiencing revival, the same thing will happen. We are wrestling against demonic entities, and the greater the work, the greater the attack, both in your life personally and in the church corporately.

As the revival under Hezekiah was underway, in chapter 32, we come to an attack of Satan . . .

2 Chronicles 32:1
After these things, and the establishment thereof, Sennacherib king of Assyria came, and entered into Judah, and encamped against the fenced cities, and thought to win them for himself.

The first ones to develop battering rams and the first to build ramps to scale walls, the Assyrian army was thought to be invincible. They were the ones who placed the heads of their enemies around the cities they besieged. And here they come against Hezekiah and the people that had just experienced such a glorious revival.

2 Chronicles 32:2–4
And when Hezekiah saw that Sennacherib was come, and that he was purposed to fight against Jerusalem, He took counsel with his princes and his mighty men to stop the waters of the fountains which were without the city: and they did help him. So there was gathered much people together, who stopped all the fountains, and the brook that ran through the midst of the land, saying, Why should the kings of Assyria come, and find much water?

The Assyrian strategy was to besiege a city, cutting off the food and water supply to the inhabitants within. Knowing this, Hezekiah decided to beat them at their own game by covering the wells that were without the city wall and building a tunnel from the spring of Gihon 1,777 feet outside the wall to the pool of Siloam within the wall. It was a tremendous engineering feat through solid rock. When the Assyrians arrived, they found that this time they were the ones without water.

2 Chronicles 32:5, 6 (a)
Also he strengthened himself, and built up all the wall that was broken, and raised it up to the towers, and another wall without, and repaired Millo in the city of David, and made darts and shields in abundance. And he set captains of war over the people, and gathered them together to him in the street of the gate of the city . . .

Hezekiah dug the tunnel, fortified the city, made shields, darts, and weapons. He appointed captains and set them in their stations. In other words, he did what he could, but realized the final result was up to the Lord.

Many Christians fail at this point. They either do their best but fail to commit themselves to God, or they sit back and say, "If God wants me to get a job, someone will come and knock on my door." The correct balance is to do what you can do, knowing all the while it's all in the Lord's hands.

2 Chronicles 32:6 (b)–8
. . . and spake comfortably to them, saying, Be strong and courageous, be not afraid nor dismayed for the king of Assyria, nor for all the multitude that is with him: for there be more with us than with him: With him is an arm of flesh; but with us is the LORD our God to help us, and to fight our battles. And the people rested themselves upon the words of Hezekiah king of Judah.

As hundreds of thousands of Assyrian soldiers were marching toward Jerusalem, Hezekiah spoke comfortably to his people, saying, "There are more of us than there are of them." How could he say this? It was because he saw into the arena of the supernatural.

When the Syrians surrounded the city where Elisha was, his servant said, "Master, we're doomed."

"Open his eyes, Lord," Elisha prayed. And when the servant's eyes were opened, he saw that, surrounding the Syrians was a huge host of angels (see 2 Kings 6:17).

Oh, that God would give us eyes to see into the supernatural arena. The Bible tells us there are ministering spirits—angels—given to stand by us (Hebrews 1:14). Yes, the attempts of the enemy to destroy us are real. But Revelation 12 tells us that when Satan rebelled, one-third of the angels went with him and became demons. That means two-thirds are left. In other words, Satan is outnumbered 2:1. Now, being that a single angel is able to cast the devil into the bottomless pit (Revelation 20:1–3), not only are the demons numerically outnumbered, but they are physically outmatched. Saints, the angels with us are vastly greater than the hordes of hell that come against us.

2 Chronicles 32:9–12
After this did Sennacherib king of Assyria send his servants to Jerusalem, (but he himself laid siege against Lachish, and all his power with him,) unto Hezekiah king of Judah, and unto all Judah that were at Jerusalem, saying, Thus saith Sennacherib king of Assyria, Whereon do ye trust, that ye abide in the siege in Jerusalem? Doth not Heze-

kiah persuade you to give over yourselves to die by famine and by thirst, saying, The LORD our God shall deliver us out of the hand of the king of Assyria? Hath not the same Hezekiah taken away his high places and his altars, and commanded Judah and Jerusalem, saying, Ye shall worship before one altar, and burn incense upon it?

"Are you trusting Hezekiah?" Sennacherib's messengers said to the people of Jerusalem. "He's the one who tore down the altars and the high places." Thinking the high places were ordained by God, these messengers didn't know what they were talking about.

2 Chronicles 32:13–19
Know ye not what I and my fathers have done unto all the people of other lands? were the gods of the nations of those lands any ways able to deliver their lands out of mine hand? Who was there among all the gods of those nations that my fathers utterly destroyed, that could deliver his people out of mine hand, that your God should be able to deliver you out of mine hand? Now therefore let not Hezekiah deceive you, nor persuade you on this manner, neither yet believe him: for no god of any nation or kingdom was able to deliver his people out of mine hand, and out of the hand of my fathers: how much less shall your God deliver you out of mine hand? And his servants spake yet more against the LORD God, and against his servant Hezekiah. He wrote also letters to rail on the LORD God of Israel, and to speak against him, saying, As the gods of the nations of other lands have not delivered their people out of mine hand, so shall not the God of Hezekiah deliver his people out of mine hand. Then they cried with a loud voice in the Jews' speech unto the people of Jerusalem that were on the wall, to affright them, and to trouble them; that they might take the city. And they spake against the God of Jerusalem, as against the gods of the people of the earth, which were the work of the hands of man.

Sennacherib's messengers made challenges and accusations in an attempt to get the people of Judah to doubt Hezekiah and to falter in their faith in God. Sennacherib sent letters to rail on Hezekiah. And when that didn't work, his messengers shouted at the people.

2 Chronicles 32:20
And for this cause Hezekiah the king, and the prophet Isaiah the son of Amoz, prayed and cried to heaven.

Amid Sennacherib's attacks and accusations, Hezekiah and Isaiah held a prayer meeting and cried unto heaven. How would God deliver them from thousands of Assyrians? The same way He's going to deliver you from Satan's henchmen that wage war against you. He's got ways that are not ours, thoughts that we could never think, plans that we could never dream up. Faith is the key. Hezekiah had already gone on record, saying, "God is going to bring victory." And as he and Isaiah prayed, the Lord answered . . .

2 Chronicles 32:21 (a)
And the LORD sent an angel, which cut off all the mighty men of valour . . .

In a parallel passage in 2 Kings 19, a single angel was dispatched who killed 185,000 Assyrians in one night. When the rest of the troops awoke the next morning and saw their comrades dead, they split.

2 Chronicles 32:21 (b)
. . . and the leaders and captains in the camp of the king of Assyria. So he returned with shame of face to his own land. And when he was come into the house of his god, they that came forth of his own bowels slew him there with the sword.

Sennacherib crept back to his home city and went into his temple, where he was killed by members of his own family.

2 Chronicles 32:22–24
Thus the LORD saved Hezekiah and the inhabitants of Jerusalem from the hand of Sennacherib the king of Assyria, and from the hand of all other, and guided them on every side. And many brought gifts unto the LORD to Jerusalem, and presents to Hezekiah king of Judah: so that he was magnified in the sight of all nations from thenceforth. In those days Hezekiah was sick to the death, and prayed unto the LORD: and he spake unto him, and he gave him a sign.

This story is recorded in 2 Kings 20 and Isaiah 38 as well. From these passages, we know that, when God sent Isaiah to tell Hezekiah that it was time to go home, Hezekiah begged God to let him live. God granted Hezekiah's request and confirmed it by turning the sundial back ten degrees, or approximately forty-five minutes. But was it His will? I wonder. In the following fifteen years a couple of terrible things took place. First, Hezekiah fathered a son named Manasseh, who would be the worst of Judah's kings and whose reign would lead to Judah's captivity.

Secondly, when Hezekiah miraculously recovered, the Babylonians sent a contingent of ambassadors with some get-well cards and congratulations. When Hezekiah took them on a personal tour of his storehouses, their report to their leader, Nebuchadnezzar, led to the attack by the Babylonians.

Hezekiah would have been far better off flowing with what the Lord was doing rather than demanding his own way. I don't want to demand my way because I don't know as much as God does. God knows what's right. My Father knows best. Yes, we are to bring our requests to Him. But ultimately we must say, "Not my will, but Thine be done, Father."

As they wandered in the wilderness, the children of Israel begged God for meat. When He answered their demand, Numbers 11:33 tells us they died even as they ate the quail. Of this the psalmist writes, "The Lord gave them their request, but sent leanness to their soul" (Psalm 106:15).

Be careful, gang, that you don't demand from God without submitting it to His perfect will. He might give you your request, only to find it wasn't what you were hoping.

2 Chronicles 32:25–29

But Hezekiah rendered not again according to the benefit done unto him; for his heart was lifted up: therefore there was wrath upon him, and upon Judah and Jerusalem. Notwithstanding Hezekiah humbled himself for the pride of his heart, both he and the inhabitants of Jerusalem, so that the wrath of the Lord came not upon them in the days of Hezekiah. And Hezekiah had exceeding much riches and honour: and he made himself treasuries for silver, and for gold, and for precious stones, and for spices, and for shields, and for all manner of pleasant jewels; Storehouses also for the increase of corn, and wine, and oil; and stalls for all manner of beasts, and cotes for flocks. Moreover he provided him cities, and possessions of flocks and herds in abundance: for God had given him substance very much.

Monetarily, God gave much to Hezekiah. If you have been given much, rejoice. It is not unscriptural to be rich, but it is not unspiritual to be poor, either. Jesus Christ, who was rich, became poor that we might become rich in spiritual things (2 Corinthians 8:9).

"Lord, don't allow me to be rich lest I forget You, nor poor lest I steal," Proverbs 30:8, 9 declares. There's something to be said for being right in the middle somewhere.

2 Chronicles 32:30–34

This same Hezekiah also stopped the upper watercourse of Gihon, and brought it straight down to the west side of the city of David. And Hezekiah prospered in all his works. Howbeit in the business of the ambassadors of the princes of Babylon, who sent unto him to inquire of the wonder that was done in the land, God left him, to try him, that he might know all that was in his heart. Now the rest of the acts of Hezekiah, and his goodness, behold, they are written in the vision of Isaiah the prophet, the son of Amoz, and in the book of the kings of Judah and Israel. And Hezekiah slept with his fathers, and they buried him in the chiefest of the sepulchres of the sons of David: and all Judah and the inhabitants of Jerusalem did him honour at his death. And Manasseh his son reigned in his stead.

The true test does not necessarily come in adversity but in prosperity. Be careful. The true test often comes when things are going well. Hezekiah failed to give God the glory for his healing and riches, yet although he faltered a bit at the end of his life, he was nonetheless a great man.

33

2 Chronicles 33:1–3 (a)

Manasseh was twelve years old when he began to reign, and he reigned fifty and five years in Jerusalem: But did that which was evil in the sight of the Lord, like unto the abominations of the heathen, whom the Lord had cast out before the children of Israel. For he built again the high places which Hezekiah his father had broken down . . .

Manasseh has the longest reign of any of the kings of Judah. But, because he was the most wicked of all kings, it wasn't because of his worthiness. It was because of God's grace.

Sometimes we wonder why the Lord allows certain people to go on and on in this life. "Lord, why don't You destroy them?" we wonder. The Bible says that God is not willing that any should perish, but that all should come to repentance (2 Peter 3:9). Our Father is so patient. He extends Himself so far, waiting for even the most wicked man to come to repentance if there's any hope for him at all. In fact, the Lord waits fifty-five years for Manasseh to turn to Him.

2 Chronicles 33:3 (b)
. . . and he reared up altars for Baalim, and made groves . . .

Groves were trees that were planted in which the worship of Ashteroth took place.

2 Chronicles 33:3 (c)
. . . and worshipped all the host of heaven, and served them.

Manasseh engaged in astrology. But it gets worse . . .

2 Chronicles 33:4
Also he built altars in the house of the LORD, whereof the LORD had said, In Jerusalem shall my name be for ever.

Manasseh had the audacity to erect altars in the very house of the Lord to his false gods and pagan deities.

2 Chronicles 33:5
And he built altars for all the host of heaven in the two courts of the house of the LORD.

He worshiped the stars in the courts of the house of the Lord.

2 Chronicles 33:6 (a)
And he caused his children to pass through the fire in the valley of the son of Hinnom: also he observed times, and used enchantments, and used witchcraft, and dealt with a familiar spirit, and with wizards . . .

Statues of Molech were set up in the valley south of Jerusalem with hollow bellies so that fires could be ignited within. As the idol became incandescent, parents would place their firstborn sons on the arms of the statues. Why? The thinking was that if you sacrificed your firstborn son, the children you would have after that would be blessed and your family would prosper.

Aren't we doing the same thing? Aren't we burning our babies, not with fire, but with a saline solution, convincing ourselves that the children that follow will do better, that they will be more financially stable, or that our situation will improve?

Listen, gang, the same things are happening in our day as they were in Manasseh's. Stars are worshiped and babies are burned.

2 Chronicles 33:6 (b)
. . . he wrought much evil in the sight of the LORD, to provoke him to anger.

The Lord was righteously angered by what was happening because He saw the damage these sins would do to His people. As we engage in these same kinds of practices, we are setting the stage for the righteous indignation of the Father.

2 Chronicles 33:7–9
And he set a carved image, the idol which he had made, in the house of God, of which God had said to David and to Solomon his son, In this house, and in Jerusalem, which I have chosen before all the tribes of Israel, will I put my name for ever: Neither will I any more remove the foot of Israel from out of the land which I have appointed for your fathers; so that they will take heed to do all that I have commanded them, according to the whole law and the statutes and the ordinances by the hand of Moses. So Manasseh made Judah and the inhabitants of Jerusalem to err, and to do worse than the heathen, whom the LORD had destroyed before the children of Israel.

The Lord had previously destroyed the pagans who were in the land. Some people question the fairness of this. In Genesis 15, God said to Abraham that there would come a day when his descendants would be carried to Egypt, where they would remain for four hundred years "until the iniquity of the Amorites was full." In other words, God gave the Canaanites four hundred years to repent, to turn to Him. When they didn't, He ordered their extermination perhaps, in part, because their practices were growing so bizarre and dangerous that He lovingly put them out of their misery.

2 Chronicles 33:10
And the LORD spake to Manasseh, and to his people: but they would not hearken.

God sent His prophet, Isaiah, to speak not only to Manasseh, but throughout the land. But no one listened. In fact, tradition says it was Manasseh who ordered the death of Isaiah.

2 Chronicles 33:11–13
Wherefore the LORD brought upon them the captains of the host of the king of Assyria, which took Manasseh among the thorns, and bound him with fetters, and carried him to Babylon. And when he was in affliction, he besought the LORD his God, and humbled himself greatly before the God of his fathers, And prayed unto him: and he was intreated of him, and heard his supplication, and brought him again to Jerusalem into

his kingdom. Then Manasseh knew that the LORD he was God.

In this time of his affliction, the Lord, in His amazing grace, heard Manasseh's prayer. Even though Manasseh had been living rebelliously for fifty-five years, the Lord heard his prayers. The psalmist said in Psalm 119:71, "It is good for me to be afflicted; that I might learn thy statutes." It's when we're afflicted that, perhaps for the first time in a long time, we pick up the Bible. It's when we're afflicted that we finally cry out to the Lord in sincerity and desperation. If He heard Manasseh's prayers, don't you know He'll hear your prayer when you cry to Him?

I love to think about the grace of God because I need it. I love the way God my Father has been so very gracious to me. The problem is, when I hear about other guys like Manasseh, who I think are awful and who have done evil, I don't want to hear about the grace of God extended to them. In other words, I have found that I compare their worst with my best. In reality, what the Lord would have for me is to compare my worst with their best—to find something that is good or right in them. If you're having difficulty wondering how God could be so gracious to others, it might be a time for you to compare your worst with their best.

2 Chronicles 33:14
Now after this he built a wall without the city of David, on the west side of Gihon, in the valley, even to the entering in at the fish gate, and compassed about Ophel, and raised it up a very great height, and put captains of war in all the fenced cities of Judah.

Realizing the Lord is God, when Manasseh went back to his city, he built up the walls to keep out the enemy. When God has extended you grace, the first thing you ought to do is to reestablish the walls of discipline in your own life, to set boundaries in order to keep out the enemy.

2 Chronicles 33:15, 16
And he took away the strange gods, and the idol out of the house of the LORD, and all the altars that he had built in the mount of the house of the LORD, and in Jerusalem, and cast them out of the city. And he repaired the altar of the LORD, and sacrificed thereon peace offerings and thank offerings, and commanded Judah to serve the LORD God of Israel.

When the Lord has shown grace to us, like Manasseh, we ought to be "altared" men and women. That is, we ought to share the Word, pray together in the "family altar" or family devotional time. We ought to be "altared" in personal devotions as well, to spend time with the Lord in the morning hour. Understanding his position as a recipient of incredible grace, Manasseh built up walls, moved out the idols, and rebuilt the altars. And so must we.

2 Chronicles 33:17
Nevertheless the people did sacrifice still in the high places, yet unto the LORD their God only.

This proves that devotion can't be dictated. Manasseh commanded his people to serve the Lord God of Israel, but they didn't comply.

2 Chronicles 33:18–23
Now the rest of the acts of Manasseh, and his prayer unto his God, and the words of the seers that spake to him in the name of the LORD God of Israel, behold, they are written in the book of the kings of Israel. His prayer also, and how God was intreated of him, and all his sin, and his trespass, and the places wherein he built high places, and set up groves and graven images, before he was humbled: behold, they are written among the sayings of the seers. So Manasseh slept with his fathers, and they buried him in his own house: and Amon his son reigned in his stead. Amon was two and twenty years old when he began to reign, and reigned two years in Jerusalem. But he did that which was evil in the sight of the LORD, as did Manasseh his father: for Amon sacrificed unto all the carved images which Manasseh his father had made, and served them; And humbled not himself before the LORD, as Manasseh his father had humbled himself; but Amon trespassed more and more.

Sometimes people say, "Because God is gracious and full of mercy, if I go astray, I can always come back and He'll hear me when I call on Him." That may be true. But what they fail to factor in to the equation is that the repercussions of sin aren't ever what we think they'll be. We count the cost and think we can pay the price. But when the repercussions come—and they will—they hit us in ways we hadn't planned. In Manasseh's case, he did get right in God's sight, but the repercussion of his sin is now seen in his son. That's the problem. It impacts and affects others. Sin stinks, gang. And the repercussions are more brutal than we could ever imagine.

2 Chronicles 33:24, 25
And his servants conspired against him, and slew him in his own house. But the people of the land slew all them that had conspired against king Amon; and the people of the land made Josiah his son king in his stead.

Bloody revolution is one of the unforeseen results of Manasseh's sin as Amon is killed in his own house and the people rise up to kill his murderers.

34

2 Chronicles 34:1–5
Josiah was eight years old when he began to reign, and he reigned in Jerusalem one and thirty years. And he did that which was right in the sight of the LORD, and walked in the ways of David his father, and declined neither to the right hand, nor to the left. For in the eighth year of his reign, while he was yet young, he began to seek after the God of David his father: and in the twelfth year he began to purge Judah and Jerusalem from the high places, and the groves, and the carved images, and the molten images. And they brake down the altars of Baalim in his presence; and the images, that were on high above them, he cut down; and the groves, and the carved images, and the molten images, he brake in pieces, and made dust of them, and strowed it upon the graves of them that had sacrificed unto them. And he burnt the bones of the priests upon their altars, and cleansed Judah and Jerusalem.

This intrigues me because three hundred years earlier, when Jeroboam was king, an unnamed prophet came on the scene and we read that he cried against the altar, saying, "A child shall be born unto the house of David, Josiah by name, and upon thee shall he sacrifice the priests of the high places" (see 1 Kings 13). The promises of God come to pass. Oh, they might take a little longer than we anticipate, but they *will* come to pass.

Perhaps God has whispered a promise in your ear, or placed a promise in your heart and time has passed and you're wondering why it hasn't come to be. The Bible says that it was after Abraham *patiently endured* that he obtained the promise (Hebrews 6:15). Sometimes there's a space between the promise and the performance of the promise. God has His reasons, among which are to cause us to draw closer to and trust in Him. But what He says will ultimately come to pass. Guaranteed.

2 Chronicles 34:6–8
And so did he in the cities of Manasseh, and Ephraim, and Simeon, even unto Naphtali, with their mattocks round about. And when he had broken down the altars and the groves, and had beaten the graven images into powder, and cut down all the idols throughout all the land of Israel, he returned to Jerusalem. Now in the eighteenth year of his reign, when he had purged the land, and the house, he sent Shaphan the son of Azaliah, and Maaseiah the governor of the city, and Joah the son of Joahaz the recorder, to repair the house of the LORD his God.

"Let no man despise thy youth," Paul wrote to Timothy, "but be thou an example of the believer" (1 Timothy 4:12). Josiah was young when he began to reign. But he sought the Lord seriously when he was sixteen. He brought reformation to the nation when he was twenty. At twenty-six, he's rebuilding, and restoring the temple. If you're young, this is your time. The Lord is doing something wonderful. Be a part of it. Even as a young man, Josiah was engaged in the things of God and God would use him greatly.

2 Chronicles 34:9
And when they came to Hilkiah the high priest, they delivered the money that was brought into the house of God, which the Levites that kept the doors had gathered of the hand of Manasseh and Ephraim, and of all the remnant of Israel, and of all Judah and Benjamin; and they returned to Jerusalem.

The Levites gathered money for the work that was being done in Jerusalem.

2 Chronicles 34:10–12 (a)
And they put it in the hand of the workmen that had the oversight of the house of the LORD, and they gave it to the workmen that wrought in the house of the LORD, to repair and amend the house: Even to the artificers and builders gave they it, to buy hewn stone, and timber for couplings, and to floor the houses which the kings of Judah had destroyed. And the men did the work faithfully . . .

The workmen put their hands to the plow, rolled up their sleeves, and engaged in the work of restoring the temple. In Exodus 36:1, we are told that God gave wisdom and understanding to Aholiab and Bezaleel, two men who were working to construct the tabernacle. This means that anointing isn't only for the purpose of teaching or healing, but there is also an anointing to fix and build things. Oh, that God would give us more anointed mechanics and carpenters!

2 Chronicles 34:12 (b), 13
. . . and the overseers of them were Jahath and Obadiah, the Levites, of the sons of Merari; and Zechariah and Meshullam, of the sons of the Kohathites, to set it forward; and other of the Levites, all that could skill of instruments of musick. Also they were over the bearers of burdens, and were overseers of all that wrought the work in any manner of service: and of the Levites there were scribes, and officers, and porters.

While the temple restoration was going on, musicians were playing. Music has a powerful impact and effect upon our spiritual lives . . .

As he waited on the Lord for a word from Him, Elisha called for a minstrel. And as the minstrel began to play, the Holy Spirit spoke to Elisha (2 Kings 3:15). How often have you begun to worship the Lord in song—when suddenly He begins to speak to you? How often have you found yourself encouraged as you've listened to praise music? Saul was haunted and hounded by a demonic spirit. He called for David to come and play his harp. As songs were played and worship ascended, Saul experienced relief (1 Samuel 16:23).

If you're discouraged, depressed, or defeated, if you want your temple restored, play music. It will build you up and cause your spirit to soar. In Job 38, God says that as the foundations of the earth were being laid, the angels were singing songs. In other words, He does His best work with background music. These guys created an atmosphere that was right spiritually. The Lord inhabits the praise of His people (Psalm 22:3). The demons are confused by praise. That is why Jehoshaphat sent a choir before he sent an army to do battle (2 Chronicles 20). Be a person of praise. Sing in your car. Sing in your shower. Sing when you're depressed. As Isaiah said, "Sing, O barren one" (see 54:1). If you'll develop this practice, you'll tap into a spiritual dynamic that will aid and assist you in the days of spiritual warfare.

2 Chronicles 34:14, 15
And when they brought out the money that was brought into the house of the LORD, Hilkiah the priest found a book of the law of the LORD given by Moses. And Hilkiah answered and said to Shaphan the scribe, I have found the book of the law in the house of the LORD. And Hilkiah delivered the book to Shaphan.

As the temple was being remodeled, refurbished, and restored, someone found a copy of the Law. Manasseh and Amon evidently had destroyed all the copies of the Law. But one was found in the temple in the midst of the rubble. Bookbinding wasn't developed until 900 A.D. Before that time, books were made from dried papyrus woven together and rolled into lengths of approximately one hundred feet. Because the process was not an easy one, books were not easily copied.

Throughout history, every lasting revival that has taken place has been linked to a rediscovery of the Word. The same thing will happen in our lives personally. That is, if we get into the Word, revival can't help but break out. A Bible that's falling apart usually belongs to a person who isn't. If you want your life to be revived and refurbished and renewed, read your Bible, but know that Bible study isn't always like the fourth of July. When I read the Word in the morning, I'm not always fired up. Sometimes it's just plain discipline. But it's a discipline that will bring about long-term maturity and real stability.

Think about the Christians you know who have a real history in the Lord and are rich in the things of God. I guarantee their walks are not based upon "Holy Spirit goose bumps," or some new experience or hot tip. No, the men and women I've known who are deep and rich in their history and maturity with God are that way because of their knowledge of the Word. If you will center your life on Bible study, I guarantee you will have a rich, stable, mature Christian experience.

2 Chronicles 34:16–19
And Shaphan carried the book to the king, and brought the king word back again, saying, All that was committed to thy servants, they do it. And they have gathered together the money that was found in the house of the LORD, and have delivered it into the hand of the overseers, and to the hand of the workmen. Then Shaphan the scribe told the king, saying, Hilkiah the priest hath given me a book. And Shaphan read it before the king. And it came to pass, when the king had heard the words of the law, that he rent his clothes.

When Josiah heard the Word, he realized how far the nation had strayed from the heart of God.

2 Chronicles 34:20, 21
And the king commanded Hilkiah, and Ahikam the son of Shaphan, and Abdon the son of Micah, and Shaphan the scribe, and Asaiah a servant of the king's, saying, Go, in-

quire of the LORD for me, and for them that are left in Israel and in Judah, concerning the words of the book that is found: for great is the wrath of the LORD that is poured out upon us, because our fathers have not kept the word of the LORD, to do after all that is written in this book.

Josiah sent a committee to find someone who could explain not only information *from* the Word, but application *of* the Word. "We've missed the mark," he said. "We've gone astray. Go and find someone who can help us understand what we must do to make things right."

And that is still the need. You see, it's not just going through the Word that's important, but it's allowing the Word to go through us. It's not simply marking your Bible, but letting your Bible mark you. The question isn't only theology. The question is, how does the Word affect you personally?

2 Chronicles 34:22
And Hilkiah, and they that the king had appointed, went to Huldah the prophetess, the wife of Shallum the son of Tikvath, the son of Hasrah, keeper of the wardrobe; (now she dwelt in Jerusalem in the college:) and they spake to her to that effect.

Josiah's committee went to a woman to get understanding. This intrigues me because, according to Jeremiah 26:24, one of their number, Ahikam, was a friend of Jeremiah the prophet. With Jeremiah on the scene at this time, I would have thought they would have gone to him for understanding of what they ought to do. But they went to a prophetess and her words proved to be correct. Sometimes, it's important to understand that your wife—the "keeper of the wardrobe"—can be a prophetess and the source of great wisdom and revelation from God.

2 Chronicles 34:23–25
And she answered them, Thus saith the LORD God of Israel, Tell ye the man that sent you to me, Thus saith the LORD, Behold, I will bring evil upon this place, and upon the inhabitants thereof, even all the curses that are written in the book which they have read before the king of Judah: Because they have forsaken me, and have burned incense unto other gods, that they might provoke me to anger with all the works of their hands; therefore my wrath shall be poured out upon this place, and shall not be quenched.

The Word had been rediscovered. Josiah was eager to apply it, and yet word came that judgment would be poured out. Why? I suggest two reasons . . .

First, when we ask forgiveness, we are immediately forgiven. But be not deceived. Whatever a man sows, that shall he also reap (Galatians 6:7). The seeds are sown and the crop comes up. As a country, Israel had sinned. Therefore, although there was repentance going on, repercussions would still take place.

Secondly, the repentance was not as deep as it ought to have been. Yes, Josiah turned to the Lord, but the rest of the nation was not as deeply committed, for when the winds changed, their commitment would blow away as well.

2 Chronicles 34:26–28
And as for the king of Judah, who sent you to inquire of the LORD, so shall ye say unto him, Thus saith the LORD God of Israel concerning the words which thou hast heard; Because thine heart was tender, and thou didst humble thyself before God, when thou heardest his words against this place, and against the inhabitants thereof, and humbledst thyself before me, and didst rend thy clothes, and weep before me; I have even heard thee also, saith the LORD. Behold, I will gather thee to thy fathers, and thou shalt be gathered to thy grave in peace, neither shall thine eyes see all the evil that I will bring upon this place, and upon the inhabitants of the same. So they brought the king word again.

"Because you are sincere, Josiah, you will die in peace," the Lord said through Huldah, the prophetess.

When Josiah heard this, did he say, "Whew! I've got it made! Sorry about you"? Did it cause him to be apathetic? No, it only further motivated him . . .

2 Chronicles 34:29
Then the king sent and gathered together all the elders of Judah and Jerusalem.

Even though his own destiny was secure, Josiah was not a man who kicked back and took the easy way out. He could have said, "Judgment has been pronounced. But it doesn't have anything to do with me, so I'll just cruise." Sad to say, sometimes that's our attitude . . .

"The Arabs in Libya might get nuked before too long. Whatever. I'm a Christian. I'm going to heaven. War is breaking out in Central America? Oh, well. That's the way it goes. At least I'm Okay."

The Lord said we are to occupy until He comes (Luke 19:13). So what should be our attitude? One of intensive prayer for the lost. How many of us pray for our enemies personally and nationally? Josiah said, "I'm going to do what I can." And that must be our attitude, as well.

2 Chronicles 34:30
And the king went up into the house of the LORD, and all the men of Judah, and the inhabitants of Jerusalem, and the priests, and the Levites, and all the people, great and small: and he read in their ears all the words of the book of the covenant that was found in the house of the LORD.

Josiah gathered the people together and read the Scriptures to them.

2 Chronicles 34:31, 32
And the king stood in his place, and made a covenant before the LORD, to walk after the LORD, and to keep his commandments, and his testimonies, and his statutes, with all his heart, and with all his soul, to perform the words of the covenant which are written in this book. And he caused all that were present in Jerusalem and Benjamin to stand to it. And the inhabitants of Jerusalem did according to the covenant of God, the God of their fathers. And Josiah took away all the abominations out of all the countries that pertained to the children of Israel, and made all that were present in Israel to serve, even to serve the LORD their God. And all his days they departed not from following the LORD, the God of their fathers.

In Manasseh, I see the importance of calling out to the Lord in prayer. In Josiah, I see a man who rediscovered the Word and shared it with those around him. Oh, that we would incorporate both of these practices into our own lives daily and determinedly.

35

Joan of Arc left her mark in history by the time she died at age nineteen. Romulus founded the city of Rome when he was twenty. St. Francis began his order at the age of twenty-four. Patrick Henry said, "Give me liberty or give me death," at twenty-six years of age. Napoleon conquered all of Europe by the time he was twenty-six. Martin Luther ignited the Reformation at the age of twenty-nine. Alexander the Great conquered the known world by the time he was thirty. Therefore, whatever your age, *now* is the time to say with Josiah, "I'm going to seek the Lord diligently. I'm going to get rid of the idols in my life. I'm going to rediscover the Word."

Having refurbished the temple and rediscovered the Law, Josiah now reinstitutes the Passover . . .

2 Chronicles 35:1
Moreover Josiah kept a passover unto the LORD in Jerusalem: and they killed the passover on the fourteenth day of the first month.

Passover was the celebration commemorating how the Lord had delivered His people from the bondage of the Egyptians, as well as anticipating the coming of God's Son, the Lamb of God.

2 Chronicles 35:2, 3
And he set the priests in their charges, and encouraged them to the service of the house of the LORD, And said unto the Levites that taught all Israel, which were holy unto the LORD, Put the holy ark in the house which Solomon the son of David king of Israel did build; it shall not be a burden upon your shoulders: serve now the LORD your God, and his people Israel,

The ark was to be placed in the temple, in the Holy of Holies. Evidently, the ark had been on the move during the dark days of king Manasseh. Manasseh was so wicked, he put an image in the temple. Because of that, evidently the priests took the ark out and moved it from place to place. But now, a godly king was reigning who said, "Bring the ark back and place it in the temple once again. It's not to be carried on the shoulders anymore. Now it's to find its resting place where God intended—in the Holy of Holies."

2 Chronicles 35:4
And prepare yourselves by the houses of your fathers, after your courses, according to the writing of David king of Israel, and according to the writing of Solomon his son.

Josiah went on to exhort the priests and Levites who would now serve according to course. Twenty-five courses were established that allowed the priests to share responsibilities. That is, the priests were scattered throughout the land and they would make their way once a year to serve in the temple for a two-week period.

2 Chronicles 35:5–7
And stand in the holy place according to the divisions of the families of the fathers of your brethren the people, and after the division of the families of the Levites. So kill

the passover, and sanctify yourselves, and prepare your brethren, that they may do according to the word of the LORD by the hand of Moses. And Josiah gave to the people, of the flock, lambs and kids, all for the passover offerings, for all that were present, to the number of thirty thousand, and three thousand bullocks: these were of the king's substance.

After exhorting the priests and Levites to do what they were ordained to do, Josiah does something wonderful. He presents 30,000 of his own sheep and 3,000 of his own bullocks for sacrifice. I like that!

2 Chronicles 35:8
And his princes gave willingly unto the people, to the priests, and to the Levites: Hilkiah and Zechariah and Jehiel, rulers of the house of God, gave unto the priests for the passover offerings two thousand and six hundred small cattle, and three hundred oxen.

After he made a substantial sacrifice of his own, the men under Josiah followed his lead and gave generously. That's always the way it is. Matthew tells us that the Father, who sees in secret, will reward openly (6:6). Therefore, if I choose to do what's right in God's sight, those around me will be affected. Even if they don't see what I'm doing, the person I become will impact and affect them in a very real way.

When pastors tell me that their congregations aren't tithing, I say, "Are you?" When they tell me their congregations aren't witnessing, I say, "When was the last time you talked about the Lord to the guy who sells you gas or bags your groceries?" What we do privately and personally—whether for good or bad—affects the people around us very definitely. And that is reason enough to walk in integrity.

2 Chronicles 35:9–11
Conaniah also, and Shemaiah and Nethaneel, his brethren, and Hashabiah and Jeiel and Jozabad, chief of the Levites, gave unto the Levites for passover offerings five thousand small cattle, and five hundred oxen. So the service was prepared, and the priests stood in their place, and the Levites in their courses, according to the king's commandment. And they killed the passover, and the priests sprinkled the blood from their hands, and the Levites flayed them.

The priests sprinkled the blood on the altar as they were commanded to do. The Levites filleted the lambs, as was their responsibility. All was done according to the ordinances of the Lord given through Moses. One thing however, was never to be done to the Passover sacrifices. That is, the lamb's bones were not to be broken (Exodus 12:46). Why? Because breaking a man's legs hastened death by crucifixion. When Jesus was crucified, there was no need to break His legs, for He had already died (John 19:33). Thus, the picture painted in the sacrificial system found its fulfillment in the Lamb of God.

2 Chronicles 35:12, 13
And they removed the burnt offerings, that they might give according to the divisions of the families of the people, to offer unto the LORD, as it is written in the book of Moses. And so did they with the oxen. And they roasted the passover with fire according to the ordinance: but the other holy offerings sod they in pots, and in caldrons, and in pans, and divided them speedily among all the people.

With a great multitude to be served, the Levites moved quickly, taking these offerings and dealing with them promptly.

2 Chronicles 35:14
And afterward they made ready for themselves, and for the priests: because the priests the sons of Aaron were busied in offering of burnt offerings and the fat until night; therefore the Levites prepared for themselves, and for the priests the sons of Aaron.

After all others were served, the priests and Levites served themselves.

2 Chronicles 35:15 (a)
And the singers the sons of Asaph were in their place, according to the commandment of David, and Asaph, and Heman, and Jeduthun the king's seer . . .

Worship was ascending. Songs were being sung. Sacrifices were being made. It must have been a grand and glorious day.

2 Chronicles 35:15 (b)
. . . and the porters waited at every gate; they might not depart from their service; for their brethren the Levites prepared for them.

Because the doorkeepers couldn't leave their posts, the Levites brought the Passover meal to them. We must not neglect the taking in of the Word even as we serve others.

2 Chronicles 35:16–18
So all the service of the LORD was prepared the same day, to keep the passover, and to offer burnt offerings upon the altar of the LORD, according to the commandment of king Josiah. And the children of Israel that were present kept the passover at that time, and the feast of unleavened bread seven days. And there was no passover like to that kept in Israel from the days of Samuel the prophet; neither did all the kings of Israel keep such a passover as Josiah kept, and the priests, and the Levites, and all Judah and Israel that were present, and the inhabitants of Jerusalem.

There hadn't been such a glorious Passover celebration since the days of Samuel.

2 Chronicles 35:19
In the eighteenth year of the reign of Josiah was this passover kept.

In Josiah, we see a man who sought the Lord. As he sought the Lord, he was called to the temple to refurbish that which had previously been desecrated. In the temple, he discovered the Law. After being in the temple and rediscovering the Scriptures, he reinstated Passover.

As we come to the house of the Lord day after week after month after year, we rediscover the Word. That ought to lead us to the Table of the Lord, where we do exactly what God's people did in Josiah's day: remember how the Lord delivered us from the stranglehold of sin and death.

2 Chronicles 35:20
After all this, when Josiah had prepared the temple, Necho king of Egypt came up to fight against Carchemish by Euphrates: and Josiah went out against him.

The year is 609 B.C. Josiah is in power. He has done well. But now things get a little bit complicated because three years earlier, the Assyrians had been driven out of their capital city of Nineveh and were being challenged by a new world power: the Babylonians. Regrouped at Carchemish, the Assyrians were now seeking to counterattack the Babylonians with reinforcements from the Egyptians. At this point, as Pharaoh Necho, king of Egypt, is making his way north to help the Assyrians, Josiah faces him down.

2 Chronicles 35:21 (a)
But he sent ambassadors to him, saying, What have I to do with thee, thou king of Judah? I come not against thee this day, but against the house wherewith I have war . . .

"I have no bone to pick with you," Pharaoh Necho said to Josiah. "I'm simply passing through on my way north."

2 Chronicles 35:21 (b)
. . . for God commanded me to make haste: forbear thee from meddling with God, who is with me, that he destroy thee not.

"God has ordained that I go north, so don't try and stop me," Necho continued.

2 Chronicles 35:22
Nevertheless Josiah would not turn his face from him, but disguised himself, that he might fight with him, and hearkened not unto the words of Necho from the mouth of God, and came to fight in the valley of Megiddo.

When, rather than backing off, Josiah disguised himself and engaged in battle against Necho, perhaps it was because he thought, "Who are *you* to tell me what God is up to? You're an Egyptian. I'm a Jew." Yet the Lord often comes to us with words of warning or instruction, direction, or exhortation through the unexpected person at the unexpected time . . .

- When Jesus gave a sermon in His hometown, the people scoffed, "Who are you? Aren't you the carpenter's son?" They didn't realize He was infinitely much more (Mark 6:3)
- There was a storm at sea. The winds were blowing, the waves rolling. When Jesus came walking on the water to His disciples, they thought He was a ghost because they didn't recognize Him (Matthew 14:26).
- After He rose from the dead, Jesus appeared to Mary. But she thought He was a gardener (John 20:15).
- As He walked on the road to Emmaus, His traveling companions mistook Him for a stranger (Luke 24:18).

Sometimes we say, "He's just a gardener." Or, "She's a stranger." Or, "They're ghosts." But in reality, the Lord can come to you and me at the unexpected time through the unexpected person. Was Necho really the instrument of the Lord? Yes. Should Josiah have listened to what the Lord was saying through him? Yes.

How do you know when what someone is saying is really from the Lord?

James said, "The wisdom from above is first pure then peaceable, then gentle, easy to be entreated, full of mercy and good fruit." (3:17). When a word comes your way, James says if it's causing strife and confusion and envying and tension, it's not from heaven. But if it's pure and peaceable and gentle and good fruit, you can know it's from heaven. Necho said, "Go home and be at peace." That should have been a clue to Josiah. But Josiah didn't listen.

If you're involved in situations where there is tension and envy, confusion and strife, it is not of the Lord. On the other hand, mercy, gentleness, and peace are signs of His presence.

2 Chronicles 35:23, 24
And the archers shot at king Josiah; and the king said to his servants, Have me away; for I am sore wounded. His servants therefore took him out of that chariot, and put him in the second chariot that he had; and they brought him to Jerusalem, and he died, and was buried in one of the sepulchres of his fathers. And all Judah and Jerusalem mourned for Josiah.

Josiah, a good man, has now died seemingly unnecessarily because he got involved in a needless battle. Maybe you've been shot or wounded in your heart. Could it be it's because you've meddled where you ought not to, getting involved in needless debates and analysis, gossip and opinions? I don't know why I think I have to have an opinion on everything, weigh in on every discussion, or get involved in every debate when the invariable result is that, like Josiah, I feel wounded and depleted from the battle. We would do well to avoid battles that are full of strife and confusion, condemnation and judgment, and instead to be people who are gentle, peaceable, and merciful.

2 Chronicles 35:25–27
And Jeremiah lamented for Josiah: and all the singing men and the singing women spake of Josiah in their lamentations to this day, and made them an ordinance in Israel: and, behold, they are written in the lamentations. Now the rest of the acts of Josiah, and his goodness, according to that which was written in the law of the LORD, And his deeds, first and last, behold, they are written in the book of the kings of Israel and Judah.

Josiah was a great leader, but he got entangled in a battle that wasn't his. Oh, that we would learn from him and determine to be peacemakers. How? Here's the secret: look inward and you'll be depressed; look outward and you'll be upset; but look upward and you'll be at peace.

36

2 Chronicles 36:1
Then the people of the land took Jehoahaz the son of Josiah, and made him king in his father's stead in Jerusalem.

Josiah had at least four sons, three of whom would become kings of Judah.

2 Chronicles 36:2–4 (a)
Jehoahaz was twenty and three years old when he began to reign, and he reigned three months in Jerusalem. And the king of Egypt put him down at Jerusalem, and condemned the land in an hundred talents of silver and a talent of gold. And the king of Egypt made Eliakim his brother king over Judah and Jerusalem, and turned his name to Jehoiakim . . .

Pharaoh Necho, who was now in the region, replaces Jehoahaz with his brother, Eliakim, whose name he changed to Jehoiakim in order to show his power and his authority over the region.

2 Chronicles 36:4 (b)–5
. . . And Necho took Jehoahaz his brother, and carried him to Egypt. Jehoiakim was twenty and five years old when he began to reign, and he reigned eleven years in Jerusalem: and he did that which was evil in the sight of the LORD his God.

During Jehoiakim's reign, the Egyptians are driven out of the region, only to be replaced by Nebuchadnezzar and the Babylonians.

2 Chronicles 36:6, 7
Against him came up Nebuchadnezzar king of Babylon, and bound him in fetters, to carry him to Babylon. Nebuchadnezzar also carried of the vessels of the house of the LORD to Babylon, and put them in his temple at Babylon.

Here we come to the first deportation—605 B.C. Nebuchadnezzar with his Babylonian army comes on the scene and carries away not only Jehoiakim but also the cream of the crop of the young men of Judah, including one named Daniel.

2 Chronicles 36:8–10
Now the rest of the acts of Jehoiakim, and his abominations which he did, and that which was found in him, behold, they are written in the book of the kings of Israel and Judah: and Jehoiachin his son reigned in his stead. Jehoiachin was eight years old when he began to reign, and he reigned

three months and ten days in Jerusalem: and he did that which was evil in the sight of the Lord. And when the year was expired, king Nebuchadnezzar sent, and brought him to Babylon, with the goodly vessels of the house of the Lord, and made Zedekiah his brother king over Judah and Jerusalem.

Jehoiakim is replaced by his son, Jehoiachin who, in turn, is replaced by his brother, Zedekiah. In Zedekiah, we come to the final and last monarch of the kingdom of Judah. At this time, 597 B.C., there is a second deportation. Further treasures and money are taken out of the temple and Zedekiah is left with only the poorest people in Judah.

2 Chronicles 36:11, 12
Zedekiah was one and twenty years old when he began to reign, and reigned eleven years in Jerusalem. And he did that which was evil in the sight of the Lord his God, and humbled not himself before Jeremiah the prophet speaking from the mouth of the Lord.

Jeremiah is on the scene preaching and sharing, pleading with the people in Jerusalem to repent from their evil and turn toward the Lord. But the people didn't listen to Jeremiah. In fact, Jeremiah preached for forty years and evidently no one responded to his ministry. Yet he goes down in eternity as one of the greats because God doesn't call us to be successful. He calls us simply to be faithful.

2 Chronicles 36:13
And he also rebelled against king Nebuchadnezzar, who had made him swear by God: but he stiffened his neck, and hardened his heart from turning unto the Lord God of Israel.

Zedekiah had taken an oath of loyalty to Nebuchadnezzar, but he didn't keep it.

2 Chronicles 36:14–16
Moreover all the chief of the priests, and the people, transgressed very much after all the abominations of the heathen; and polluted the house of the Lord which he had hallowed in Jerusalem. And the Lord God of their fathers sent to them by his messengers, rising up betimes, and sending; because he had compassion on his people, and on his dwelling place: But they mocked the messengers of God, and despised his words, and misused his prophets, until the wrath of the Lord arose against his people, till there was no remedy.

What a sobering thing it must be when the Lord says, "There is no more remedy." Here, the people had hardened their hearts against the Lord, turned their back on the Lord, closed their ears to the Lord, and had gone too far from the Lord.

2 Chronicles 36:17
Therefore he brought upon them the king of the Chaldees, who slew their young men with the sword in the house of their sanctuary, and had no compassion upon young man or maiden, old man, or him that stooped for age: he gave them all into his hand.

Nebuchadnezzar came first in 605 B.C. and took Daniel in his friends. He came again in 597 for a second deportation of Jews, both times knocking on the doors, saying, "Be careful. Don't mess with me." The third time Nebuchadnezzar shows up, he's not knocking on doors, but kicking them down due to Zedekiah's rebellion.

2 Chronicles 36:18–21
And all the vessels of the house of God, great and small, and the treasures of the house of the Lord, and the treasures of the king, and of his princes; all these he brought to Babylon. And they burnt the house of God, and brake down the wall of Jerusalem, and burnt all the palaces thereof with fire, and destroyed all the goodly vessels thereof. And them that had escaped from the sword carried he away to Babylon; where they were servants to him and his sons until the reign of the kingdom of Persia: To fulfil the word of the Lord by the mouth of Jeremiah, until the land had enjoyed her sabbaths: for as long as she lay desolate she kept sabbath, to fulfil threescore and ten years.

Jeremiah prophesied that the Jews would be taken into captivity for seventy years until the land enjoyed its Sabbaths. In Leviticus 25, the Lord declared that every seventh year, the land was to rest. For six years, the people could sow and reap, plant and harvest, but on the seventh, they were to let the land rest. During the sixth year, God promised to supply them enough to see them through for two years. Not only did this make sense agriculturally, but it would serve as a reminder to the people that everything they had was from God's hand. The people decided, however, to plant on the seventh year in order to increase their crops and financial status. For four hundred and ninety years, the people didn't keep the Sabbath year as they were commanded. They thought they were outsmarting God. But it never works that way, for here the Lord says, "You owe me seventy years. Therefore, the land will rest for seventy years while you're held captive in Babylon."

"If I work seven days, I'm really going to get ahead," we think. Oh, I know that isn't what I'm supposed to do, but I'm an exception." The reality, however, is that you can't outsmart God. If I steal the tithe or don't keep the day of rest, ultimately, like the people taken in captivity, I will miss out in some way.

2 Chronicles 36:22 (a)
Now in the first year of Cyrus king of Persia, that the word of the LORD spoken by the mouth of Jeremiah might be accomplished, the LORD stirred up the spirit of Cyrus king of Persia . . .

Seventy years have passed. The Babylonians have been replaced by the Medo-Persians. They were dark days indeed but, with Cyrus on the throne, there's a promise of light ahead . . .

2 Chronicles 36:22 (b), 23
. . . that he made a proclamation throughout all his kingdom, and put it also in writing, saying, Thus saith Cyrus king of Persia, All the kingdoms of the earth hath the LORD God of heaven given me; and he hath charged me to build him an house in Jerusalem, which is in Judah. Who is there among you of all his people? The LORD his God be with him, and let him go up.

With Cyrus on the throne, whoever was willing was free to "go up," to return to Jerusalem, to go home. How much greater is the invitation extended to "whosoever will" to come and "take the water of life freely" (Revelation 22:17).

All those who would, let them go up. That's the word for us. No matter where we've been, the Lord would say to us, "Let's go up."

Let's rebuild, gang. Let's return once more and say, "Lord, You know what's best." No matter where we've been or how long we've been held captive, may we be those who answer the call of our Greater than Cyrus to return, to rebuild, and to occupy till He comes.

Amen!

EZRA

Background to Ezra

July 18, 586 B.C. was a day of infamy in Jewish history for it was on that day that Nebuchadnezzar led his Babylonian soldiers into Jerusalem, where they burned the temple, destroyed the city, and carried away thousands of Jews into captivity. Watching this scene from a hillside overlooking the city, the prophet Jeremiah wept profusely. For nearly forty years, he had warned the people of judgment unless they repented and returned to the Lord, yet evidently not a single person responded to his message. He preached; he prayed; he prophesied, only to end up in prison.

Daniel and Ezekiel were also alive at this time, but they had already been carried away by Nebuchadnezzar into Babylon during an earlier deportation. Daniel eventually became prime minister, a political power in the kingdom second only to the king himself. Ezekiel's ministry, on the other hand, wasn't to the politicians, but to the people as God used him repeatedly as an illustrated sermon to portray His heart.

Why were God's people carried away to Babylon? Two reasons . . .

First, it was because they scorned God's love by continually serving false gods. The idols they worshiped were not simply images, but they represented a variety of lifestyles. Ashteroth was the goddess of sensuality; Moloch the god of prosperity; Baal the god of the intellect; and Mammon the god of money. God's people found themselves sucked further and further into these lifestyles until finally the Lord sent them to Babylon, the center of all false religions. And during their seventy-year captivity an amazing thing happened: they got burned out on idols to such a degree that, throughout their entire history, we never again see them falling prey to idolatry.

In reference to an individual who continued to live in a state of immorality, Paul instructed the church of Corinth to turn him over to Satan for the destruction of his flesh in order that his spirit might be saved (1 Corinthians 5:5). The objective was not excommunication but restoration, to see him brought back into right relationship with the Lord. And in Babylon—as well as in Corinth—that's exactly what happened.

Secondly, God's people were carried into captivity because they had skirted God's Law. That is, according to Leviticus 25:4, every seventh year, they were to let the land rest. They were neither to till nor to sow. But, thinking this was a waste of valuable time, for four hundred and ninety years, they ignored this law. Unbeknownst to them, however, God was keeping track. As a result, the land did indeed rest for seventy years—one year for every seven they had failed to honor the Sabbath (2 Chronicles 36:21).

Studying the Scriptures and realizing the seventy years were nearly expired (Jeremiah 25), Daniel confessed the sin of the nation (Daniel 9). Then, perhaps due to his position of political power, he was able to share some interesting insights with Cyrus, king of Persia . . .

> *That saith of Cyrus, He is my shepherd, and shall perform all my pleasure: even saying to Jerusalem, Thou shalt be built; and to the temple, Thy foundation shall be laid. Thus saith the* L*ORD to his anointed, to Cyrus, whose right hand I have holden, to subdue nations before him; and I will loose the loins of kings, to open before him the two leaved gates; and the gates shall not be shut; I will go before thee, and make the crooked places straight: I will break in pieces the gates of brass, and cut in sunder the bars of iron: And I will give thee the treasures of darkness, and hidden riches of secret places, that thou mayest know that I, the* L*ORD, which call thee by thy name, am the God of Israel. For Jacob my servant's sake, and Israel mine elect, I have even called thee by thy name: I have surnamed thee, though thou hast not known me. I am the* L*ORD, and there is none else, there is no God beside me: I girded thee, though thou hast not known me: That they may know from the rising of the sun, and from the west, that there is none beside me. I am the* L*ORD, and there is none else.*
>
> Isaiah 44:28; 45:1–6

This is incredible! One hundred and seventy years before Cyrus was even born, Isaiah prophesied that a man named Cyrus would come on the scene and would say, "Build Jerusalem. Let the captives go." Although he didn't know the Lord, the Lord surely knew Cyrus.

The Books of Ezra and Nehemiah deal with the rebuilding of the city of Jerusalem following her seventy-year captivity. Specifically, Ezra deals with the rebuilding of the temple while Nehemiah deals with the rebuilding of the wall. In chapters 1 through 6 of the Book of Ezra, the main character is Zerubbabel, the grandson of Jehoiachin, one of the last kings of Judah. Zerubbabel was the leader of the first group to leave Babylon and travel nine hundred miles back to Jerusalem to rebuild the temple.

In part two of the Book of Ezra, chapters 7 through 10, the main character is Ezra himself, who led the second group back to Jerusalem sixty years after Zerubbabel.

Part one deals with the restoration of the temple. Part two deals with the reformation of the people. Part one deals with rebuilding and construction. Part two deals with revival and instruction.

In chapter 1, we see the king proclaiming. In chapters 2 and 3, we see the people reclaiming—their genealogy in chapter 2 and their theology in chapter 3. In chapter 4, we see the enemy defaming. And in chapters 5 and 6 we see the Lord sustaining—prophetically in chapter 5 and politically in chapter 6.

It has been rightly said that, for every New Testament principle, there's an Old Testament picture. Paul says we are the temple of God (1 Corinthians 3:17). But before we opened the door of our heart to Jesus, we, like the temple of old, were wiped out and in ruins. We, like God's people of old, were carted off into the captivity of our sin. Thus, we, like them, sang a song of sadness . . .

> *By the rivers of Babylon, there we sat down, yea, we wept, when we remembered Zion. We hanged our harps upon the willows in the midst thereof. For there they that carried us away captive required of us a song; and they that wasted us required of us mirth, saying, Sing us one of the songs of Zion. How shall we sing the LORD's song in a strange land? If I forget thee, O Jerusalem, let my right hand forget her cunning. If I do not remember thee, let my tongue cleave to the roof of my mouth; if I prefer not Jerusalem above my chief joy. Remember, O LORD, the children of Edom in the day of Jerusalem; who said, Rase it, rase it, even to the foundation thereof. O daughter of Babylon, who art to be destroyed; happy shall he be, that rewardeth thee as thou hast served us. Happy shall he be, that taketh and dasheth thy little ones against the stones.*
>
> Psalm 137

In Isaiah 44:28 Cyrus was called by God "my shepherd." In Isaiah 45:1 he's referred to as God's anointed. Thus, he is a picture of Jesus, the chief Shepherd, God's true Anointed One.

> *When the LORD turned again the captivity of Zion, we were like them that dream. Then was our mouth filled with laughter, and our tongue with singing: then said they among the heathen, The LORD hath done great things for them. The LORD hath done great things for us; whereof we are glad. Turn again our captivity, O LORD, as the streams in the south. They that sow in tears shall reap in joy. He that goeth forth and weepeth, bearing precious seed, shall doubtless come again with rejoicing, bringing his sheaves with him.* Psalm 126

When Jesus, our Greater than Cyrus, came to rebuild the ruined temple of our lives, our song changed radically. Thus, Ezra's story is ours . . .

EZRA

1 Ezra 1:1 (a)
Now in the first year of Cyrus king of Persia . . .

Persian king, Cyrus, came into power when he overthrew the city of Babylon. One hundred and fifty years before he was even born, he was identified in Isaiah 44 and 45.

Ezra 1:1 (b)
. . . that the word of the LORD by the mouth of Jeremiah might be fulfilled, the LORD stirred up the spirit of Cyrus king of Persia . . .

How did the Lord "stir up" Cyrus' spirit? I believe it was through the prophet, Daniel, who, at the time Cyrus overthrew Babylon, would have been in his nineties. There he was, on the night the Medes and Persians conquered the city as Belshazzar, the Babylonian leader, threw a wild party, drinking from the vessels taken from the temple in Jerusalem. Suddenly a hand appeared, writing on the wall. Belshazzar was understandably stricken with fear. When his mother told him that there was a man in his kingdom in whom was "the spirit of the holy gods," (Daniel 5:11), Daniel was summoned . . .

> This is the interpretation of the thing: MENE; God hath numbered thy kingdom, and finished it. TEKEL; Thou art weighed in the balances, and art found wanting. PERES; Thy kingdom is divided, and given to the Medes and Persians.
> Daniel 5:26–28

Within hours, the Medes and Persians conquered Babylon and it is believed by many that it wasn't long before Daniel had the opportunity to tell the conquering king that his name was written in the Word of God.

So how did the Lord "stir up" Cyrus' spirit? The same way He so often stirs ours: through His Word.

Ezra 1:1 (c), 2
. . . that he made a proclamation throughout all his kingdom, and put it also in writing, saying, Thus saith Cyrus king of Persia, The LORD God of heaven hath given me all the kingdoms of the earth; and he hath charged me to build him an house at Jerusalem, which is in Judah.

Through the prophet Isaiah, the Lord said to Cyrus, "You don't know Me, but I know you." And He says the same thing to you, for not only did He know us when we were still in our mother's womb (Psalm 139:13), but He chose us even before the foundation of the world (Ephesians 1:4). Before you were ever interested in the things of God, God was interested in you. He named you, ordained you, and chose you before the beginning of time. Amazing!

Ezra 1:3
Who is there among you of all his people? his God be with him, and let him go up to Jerusalem, which is in Judah, and build the house of the LORD God of Israel, (he is the God,) which is in Jerusalem.

"Who among you of the people of God wish to go back to rebuild the temple?" Cyrus asks. It has been estimated that there were close to two million Jews living in Babylon. During the seventy years of their captivity, they had, in many cases, prospered quite extensively. So how many would be willing to return? Out of two million, we'll see only about 49,000 willing to leave their Babylonian lifestyle and trade the relative comforts of Babylon for the work that lay ahead in Jerusalem.

Ezra 1:4
And whosoever remaineth in any place where he sojourneth, let the men of his place help him with silver, and with gold, and with goods, and with beasts, beside the freewill offering for the house of God that is in Jerusalem.

"Even if you don't want to go, you have a responsibility to help those who do," Cyrus said. And this is the word of the Lord to His people to this day.

As David fought against the Amalekites, two-thirds of the men who were with him grew faint. "We can't go on," they said. "We're just too tired."

"OK," David said. "You stay here, guard the camp and keep the supply lines going while the rest of us go into battle." When David and the troops returned after their victory over the Amalekites, the men who had fought said to the guys who had stayed behind, "You're not getting any rewards or spoil."

"Not so," David said. "Those who stayed with the stuff shall be rewarded equally with those who went into battle." And from that point on, this was the practice (1 Samuel 30:25).

I like this because it means that even though we might not be able to go to the foreign mission field or pastor a church personally, if we pray consistently and give generously, we're involved in the supply lines and as much a part of the victory as if we were on the front lines.

Ezra 1:5
Then rose up the chief of the fathers of Judah and Benjamin, and the priests, and the Levites, with all them whose spirit God had raised, to go up to build the house of the LORD which is in Jerusalem.

That's the way the Lord still works. He stirs the spirit. Philippians 2:13 says it is God who works in you both to will and to do His good pleasure. He gives you the will and then the power and the way to carry out that which He's stirred up within you.

Ezra 1:6
And all they that were about them strengthened their hands with vessels of silver, with gold, with goods, and with beasts, and with precious things, beside all that was willingly offered.

The only way to offer is willingly. Don't ever give begrudgingly. The Lord loves a cheerful or literally "hilarious" giver—one who enjoys the privilege, the opportunity to make eternal investments. In Mark 11, we read that Jesus sat on the opposite side of the treasury where people deposited their money and watched not *what* they gave, but *how* they gave. The Lord is concerned how we give. Are we giving willingly, joyfully, and hilariously?

Ezra 1:7
Also Cyrus the king brought forth the vessels of the house of the LORD, which Nebuchadnezzar had brought forth out of Jerusalem, and had put them in the house of his gods;

Cyrus returned the vessels Nebuchadnezzar had plundered from the temple.

Ezra 1:8–11
Even those did Cyrus king of Persia bring forth by the hand of Mithredath the treasurer, and numbered them unto Sheshbazzar, the prince of Judah. And this is the number of them: thirty chargers of gold, a thousand chargers of silver, nine and twenty knives, Thirty basons of gold, silver basons of a second sort four hundred and ten, and other vessels a thousand. All the vessels of gold and of silver were five thousand and four hundred. All these did Sheshbazzar bring up with them of the captivity that were brought up from Babylon unto Jerusalem.

Sheshbazzar, which means "joy in affliction," was most likely the Chaldean name given to Zerubbabel. *Zerubbabel* means "a stranger in Babylon." I find both names to be significant for in James 1:2 and 3, we are told to "count it all joy" when we face trials, knowing that the testing of our faith works patience. Captivity was a trial indeed for Zerubbabel, but he evidently found joy even there. Yet, even though he found joy in his affliction in Babylon, he never felt at home there. And perhaps that's why the Lord could use him. God will always use those men and women who say, "This world just isn't my home."

Set your heart on things above, dear saint, for, like Zerubbabel, we're a heavenly people, just "passing through."

---

2 In chapter 1, we saw Cyrus proclaiming. Here, in chapter 2, we see the people reclaiming. Ezra 2 consists of the names and genealogies of those who went to Jerusalem. It should not surprise us that the people are listed by families, for God's desire is that entire families be saved . . .

> *"Believe on the Lord Jesus Christ," Paul and Silas said to the Philippian jailer, "and thou shalt be saved,* and thy house" *(Acts 16:31, italics added).*
>
> *In Hebrews 11:7, we read that Noah prepared an ark for the saving of his house. In other words, he made space for his sons and their wives, even though he was called to build the ark twenty years before his first son was born.*

Mom and Dad, I believe we have the privileged responsibility of believing on the Lord to provide salvation for our kids and spouses.

> Thus saith the LORD; A voice was heard in Ramah, lamentation, and bitter weeping; Rahel weeping for her children refused to be comforted for her children, because they were not. Thus saith the LORD; Refrain thy voice from weeping, and thine eyes from tears: for thy work shall be rewarded, saith the LORD; and they shall come again from the land of the enemy. And there is hope in thine end, saith the LORD, that thy children shall come again to their own border. Jeremiah 31:15–17

Even now, claim this promise for your kids, no matter how old they are or how far they might have strayed. Never give up praying for them, for it is the desire of God's heart to save them and bring them again "to their own border."

In the first thirty-five verses of chapter 2, we see families listed. In verses 36 through 39, we see the priests listed. In verse 40, we see the Levites. In verse 41, we see the singers. In verse 42, we see the gatekeepers. In verse 43, we see the Nethinims.

Who are the Nethinims? In the early days of Joshua's conquest, the Gibeonites knew they would be destroyed. So they disguised themselves as travelers from a far country and made a peace treaty with Joshua. When he discovered he'd been tricked, Joshua honored the treaty nonetheless, but made the Gibeonites servants from that day on, hewers of wood and drawers of water (Joshua 9:21).

I think of another "hewer of wood," another "drawer of water," for Simon the Cyrene carried the wood of the Cross of Calvary and the Samaritan woman drew water for Jesus to drink (Matthew 27:32; John 4:9). And both of them became followers of Jesus. That's why the Lord asks us to do things. He knows that if we serve Him, our hearts will be linked to Him. He's not after our service. He's after our hearts.

Why are the names of families, priests, Levites, singers, gatekeepers, and Nethinims listed? If I were writing the Bible, I would think a list like this would be a waste of valuable space. I would use these pages for something more practical, like tips on marriage or child-rearing. God, however, is infinitely wiser than I am. Hebrews 6 tells us the Lord will not forget our labor in ministry (Hebrews 6:10). He records that which we do and give in His name. Malachi 3:16 tells us that every time one of His people talks about the things of the kingdom, God makes note in a Book of Remembrance. Revelation 21:27 speaks of the Lamb's Book of Life wherein are listed the names of every believer. God cares for and about His people not as a group but as individuals, and the people of Ezra's day were no exception, for He lists those who were willing to leave the comfort, the "good life" of Babylon in order to make the hard journey back to Jerusalem.

Ezra 2:61–63
And of the children of the priests: the children of Habaiah, the children of Koz, the children of Barzillai; which took a wife of the daughters of Barzillai the Gileadite, and was called after their name: These sought their register among those that were reckoned by genealogy, but they were not found: therefore were they, as polluted, put from the priesthood. And the Tirshatha said unto them, that they should not eat of the most holy things, till there stood up a priest with Urim and with Thummim.

Urim and *thummim* mean "lights" and "perfection." The Urim and Thummim were in the breastplate of the high priest and were somehow used to determine God's will. Until a priest came with the Urim and Thummim, those who couldn't prove their genealogy were not allowed to minister. In a sense, the same is still true today because if you're not absolutely convinced that you are a child of God, your service will be shaky at best. You'll doubt and wonder. You'll be hesitant, confused, and timid.

How can you be sure of your spiritual lineage, that you are indeed a child of God? In Romans 8:16, we read that the Holy Spirit bears witness with our spirit that we are the sons of God. In other words, the Spirit of God tells you you're one of His. If you haven't had this experience, get away and seek the Lord. Say, "Lord, I need to have the confidence that I am Your child."

"Make your calling and election sure," Peter declares (2 Peter 1:10). Are you *sure?* You can be. All you need to do is ask.

Ezra 2:64–67
The whole congregation together was forty and two thousand three hundred and threescore, Beside their servants and their maids, of whom there were seven thousand three hundred thirty and seven: and there were among them two hundred singing men and singing women. Their horses were seven hundred thirty and six; their mules, two hundred forty and five; Their camels, four hundred thirty and five; their asses, six thousand seven hundred and twenty.

The number of the congregation, including the servants and singers, was more than twice as large as the number of people initially carried into captivity. This means that, as was the case in Egypt, God's people increased even in a time of affliction (Exodus 1:12). Isn't that the way it is with us? We grow most not during days of ease, but during days of trial (James 1:2–4).

Ezra 2:68–70
And some of the chief of the fathers, when they came to the house of the LORD which is at Jerusalem, offered freely for the house of God to set it up in his place: They gave after their ability unto the treasure of the work threescore and one thousand drams of gold, and five thousand pound of silver, and one hundred priests' garments. So the

priests, and the Levites, and some of the people, and the singers, and the porters, and the Nethinims, dwelt in their cities, and all Israel in their cities.

The sight of the temple in ruins resulted in hearts willing to give. I like that! At the completion of their journey, rather than grumbling angrily, the people of God gave willingly and abundantly.

3 After reclaiming their genealogy in chapter 2, here in chapter 3, we'll see the children of Israel reclaim their theology . . .

Ezra 3:1
And when the seventh month was come, and the children of Israel were in the cities, the people gathered themselves together as one man to Jerusalem.

Because they're united, the people are in the proper position for power. As seen in Acts 2, it was when the disciples were in one accord that the Holy Spirit was poured out upon them. In light of this, I suggest that the reason revival is so often missing in our country today is that, rather than unity, we see division, fighting, and fault-finding among the people of God.

Ezra 3:2, 3 (a)
Then stood up Jeshua the son of Jozadak, and his brethren the priests, and Zerubbabel the son of Shealtiel, and his brethren, and builded the altar of the God of Israel, to offer burnt offerings thereon, as it is written in the law of Moses the man of God. And they set the altar upon his bases; for fear was upon them because of the people of those countries . . .

There is something about the morning and evening hours that is to be sanctified in our lives. Morning devotions and evening devotions—beginning your day with the Lord and ending your day with Him—are key components to a deep and rich walk with God.

Ezra 3:3 (b)
. . . and they offered burnt offerings thereon unto the LORD, even burnt offerings morning and evening.

Before they began constructing the temple or securing the city, the leaders of Israel built an altar. I like that! "That's not practical," some might have protested. "You should build the building first or make sure you're safe before you get too spiritual." But we know that, as we seek first the kingdom, everything else will be added to us (Matthew 6:33). Begin your day by opening its door with devotions. And in the evening, lock it shut with a time of prayer, praise, and worship, and see how everything else falls into place.

Ezra 3:4
They kept also the feast of tabernacles, as it is written, and offered the daily burnt offerings by number, according to the custom, as the duty of every day required;

The Feast of Tabernacles was the week-long celebration wherein God's people took time to remember His faithfulness to them as they made their way from Egypt to the Promised Land.

Ezra 3:5–7
And afterward offered the continual burnt offering, both of the new moons, and of all the set feasts of the LORD that were consecrated, and of every one that willingly offered a freewill offering unto the LORD. From the first day of the seventh month began they to offer burnt offerings unto the LORD. But the foundation of the temple of the LORD was not yet laid. They gave money also unto the masons, and to the carpenters; and meat, and drink, and oil, unto them of Zidon, and to them of Tyre, to bring cedar trees from Lebanon to the sea of Joppa, according to the grant that they had of Cyrus king of Persia.

The men from Tyre and Sidon floated trees down to Joppa, where they were taken from Joppa to Jerusalem. This was the same procedure used when Solomon built the first temple (2 Chronicles 2:16). In this, we see Jews and Gentiles working together in the building of the temple, which is fitting because the New Testament temple is comprised of Jews and Gentiles brought together into a new entity called the church (Ephesians 2:19–22). I find it interesting that it was at Joppa that Jonah refused to go to preach to the Gentiles in Nineveh (Jonah 1:3), but also where Peter was called to minister to Gentiles (Acts 10).

Ezra 3:8
Now in the second year of their coming unto the house of God at Jerusalem, in the second month, began Zerubbabel the son of Shealtiel, and Jeshua the son of Jozadak, and the remnant of their brethren the priests and the Levites, and all they that were come out of the captivity unto Jerusalem; and appointed the Levites, from twenty years old

and upward, to set forward the work of the house of the LORD.

At twenty years of age, here the Levites were ordained to ministry. Initially, the law declared that Levites had to be thirty years old to be ordained (Numbers 4). But here, the age of ordination is twenty in accordance with David's last act as king (1 Chronicles 23:27). Still today, I believe the optimum age for ministry to begin is between the ages of twenty and thirty.

Ezra 3:9–12
Then stood Jeshua with his sons and his brethren, Kadmiel and his sons, the sons of Judah, together, to set forward the workmen in the house of God: the sons of Henadad, with their sons and their brethren the Levites. And when the builders laid the foundation of the temple of the LORD, they set the priests in their apparel with trumpets, and the Levites the sons of Asaph with cymbals, to praise the LORD, after the ordinance of David king of Israel. And they sang together by course in praising and giving thanks unto the LORD; because he is good, for his mercy endureth for ever toward Israel. And all the people shouted with a great shout, when they praised the LORD, because the foundation of the house of the LORD was laid. But many of the priests and Levites and chief of the fathers, who were ancient men, that had seen the first house, when the foundation of this house was laid before their eyes, wept with a loud voice; and many shouted aloud for joy:

As the foundation of the temple was being laid, two things were happening: The young men were saying, "Alright! We're getting it done! A new temple is being built. Praise God! This is exciting!" while the old men were saying, "This is nothing like it was in the old days. Things were really great back then. Solomon's temple was full of gold and silver, but this one is just stone." Thus, the shouts of joy of the young men mingled with the cries and complaints of the old men.

There is a valuable lesson in this for us today for God continues to do something new and fresh. That is why Jesus likened the Holy Spirit to the wind, for no one can predict or tame it (John 3:8). Yet there is a tendency for us to want that which is comfortable and predictable. "This is nothing like it was back in the revival of 1970," we grumble. "That's when the Holy Spirit was *really* moving."

God sent a prophet to tell these people that the glory of the new temple would actually exceed the glory of the old temple (Haggai 2:9). That's always the way of the Lord. He just takes us from glory to even greater glory as we behold Him (2 Corinthians 3:18). That means the days we are in right now far exceed the former days. And the days ten years from now, if the Lord tarries, will exceed these days. Therefore, be on guard against longing after the old days. Stay young in the Spirit. Shout for joy at what God is doing now, for He is doing marvelous things indeed.

Ezra 3:13
So that the people could not discern the noise of the shout of joy from the noise of the weeping of the people: for the people shouted with a loud shout, and the noise was heard afar off.

Haggai would say that the glory of the second temple would exceed the glory of the first (2:9). Why? Because Jesus would walk in the latter temple, and where Jesus is, the glory is infinitely greater.

How do we keep from thinking the old days are best? Jesus told us new wine can't be put into old wineskins because as the wine ferments, it expands and the old wineskins would burst (Matthew 9:17). For "new wine," Jesus used the word *neos.* For "wineskin," He used the word *kinos. Neos* means "brand new." *Kinos* means "renewed." In other words, when the Lord wants to do a new work, He pours the new wine of His Spirit into renewed wineskins. How were wineskins renewed? By soaking them in water. This is great news because it means that the Lord doesn't discard us if we're old, but renews us by soaking us time and again in the water of the Word (Psalm 119:9; John 15:3; Ephesians 5:26).

Stay in the Word, gang, for that is the way to remain flexible, pliable, and usable in the new work the Lord continually desires to do.

4 The temple foundation has been laid. The work is progressing. Construction is moving along, and you can be sure that whenever God begins to build, Satan will seek to destroy. In chapter 4, we see the enemy defaming . . .

Ezra 4:1, 2 (a)
Now when the adversaries of Judah and Benjamin heard that the children of the captivity builded the temple unto the LORD God of Israel; Then they came to Zerubbabel . . .

Notice it was when the adversaries heard that the temple was being built that they came to Zerubbabel and sought to do him in. It wasn't when they were building their own houses or doing their own thing, but when people were serious, committed, and dedicated to building the house of God, that the enemy showed up.

Ezra 4:2 (b), 3
. . . and to the chief of the fathers, and said unto them, Let us build with you: for we seek your God, as ye do; and we do sacrifice unto him since the days of Esar-haddon king of Assur, which brought us up hither. But Zerubbabel, and Jeshua, and the rest of the chief of the fathers of Israel, said unto them, Ye have nothing to do with us to build an house unto our God; but we ourselves together will build unto the LORD God of Israel, as king Cyrus the king of Persia hath commanded us.

Who were the ones who said, "Let's work together. Let's help one another. Let's build the temple cooperatively?" They were Samaritans. Many years earlier, the ten northern tribes had been carried off into Assyria. Assyrians, in turn, took up residence in the land vacated by the ten tribes. But when mountain lions began to wipe out the Assyrians, they sent a message back to Assyria, saying, "Send back some of the priests to help us worship the god of this land. We're getting eaten alive by lions. God is punishing us." So certain priests were sent back who built altars to Jehovah, but who also worshiped the gods of the Assyrians. Intermarriage followed soon after and a new race called "Samaritans" emerged. It was to these people that Zerubbabel said, "You have no part here whatsoever."

You see, the enemy's tricks are always the same. Initially, he persecutes. As you study church history, you see this in the brutality of the Roman empire. But an interesting thing happened. The more the early church was persecuted, the more it prospered. The greatest peril to Christianity, therefore, is not persecution. It's prosperity. We're lulled to sleep. So Satan changed his strategy to something much more devastating. Instead of fighting the church, he decided to join it. As he attempted here, he seeks to mix religion with culture and compromise. And that has proven to be a very effective tactic to this day.

Ezra 4:4–6
Then the people of the land weakened the hands of the people of Judah, and troubled them in building, And hired counsellors against them, to frustrate their purpose, all the days of Cyrus king of Persia, even until the reign of Darius king of Persia. And in the reign of Ahasuerus, in the beginning of his reign, wrote they unto him an accusation against the inhabitants of Judah and Jerusalem.

The enemy began a letter-writing campaign against the people of God. In verse 11, we see a copy of their letter . . .

Ezra 4:7–16
And in the days of Artaxerxes wrote Bishlam, Mithredath, Tabeel, and the rest of their companions, unto Artaxerxes king of Persia; and the writing of the letter was written in the Syrian tongue, and interpreted in the Syrian tongue. Rehum the chancellor and Shimshai the scribe wrote a letter against Jerusalem to Artaxerxes the king in this sort: Then wrote Rehum the chancellor, and Shimshai the scribe, and the rest of their companions; the Dinaites, the Apharsathchites, the Tarpelites, the Apharsites, the Archevites, the Babylonians, the Susanchites, the Dehavites, and the Elamites, And the rest of the nations whom the great and noble Asnappar brought over, and set in the cities of Samaria, and the rest that are on this side the river, and at such a time. This is the copy of the letter that they sent unto him, even unto Artaxerxes the king; Thy servants the men on this side the river, and at such a time. Be it known unto the king, that the Jews which came up from thee to us are come unto Jerusalem, building the rebellious and the bad city, and have set up the walls thereof, and joined the foundations. Be it known now unto the king, that, if this city be builded, and the walls set up again, then will they not pay toll, tribute, and custom, and so thou shalt endamage the revenue of the kings. Now because we have maintenance from the king's palace, and it was not meet for us to see the king's dishonour, therefore have we sent and certified the king; That search may be made in the book of the records of thy fathers: so shalt thou find in the book of the records, and know that this city is a rebellious city, and hurtful unto kings and provinces, and that they have moved sedition within the same of old time: for which cause was this city destroyed. We certify the king that, if this city be builded again, and the walls thereof set up, by this means thou shalt have no portion on this side the river.

The letter said that the very people who were rebuilding had been rebellious and had caused trouble in the past. And, actually, that was correct, for on three occasions, Jerusalem rebelled against the kings seeking to control her. Take note, saint, that the tactic of the enemy is still to go through the records, find out where you failed, and make sure your failure is advertised (Revelation 12:10).

Ezra 4:17–24
Then sent the king an answer unto Rehum the chancellor, and to Shimshai the scribe, and to the rest of their companions that dwell in Samaria, and unto the rest beyond the river, Peace, and at such a time. The letter which ye sent unto us hath been plainly read before me. And I commanded, and search hath been made, and it is found that this city of old time hath made insurrection against kings, and that rebellion and sedition have been made therein. There have been mighty kings also over Jerusalem, which have ruled over all countries beyond the river; and toll, tribute, and custom, was paid unto them. Give ye now commandment to cause these men to cease, and that this city be not builded, until another commandment shall be given from me. Take heed now that ye fail not to do this: why should damage grow to the hurt of the kings? Now when the copy of king Artaxerxes' letter was read before Rehum, and Shimshai the scribe, and their companions, they went up in haste to Jerusalem unto the Jews, and made them to cease by force and power. Then ceased the work of the house of God which is at Jerusalem. So it ceased unto the second year of the reign of Darius king of Persia.

Here we see the effects of condemnation: the work ceases. Why does the enemy condemn you? Why does he comb through your records and bring to light your past failures and flaws? Because he knows it will cause you to become disheartened and hopes it will cause you to give up. God's work stops when God's people feel the effects of accusation and condemnation. Are you being condemned? Has the enemy been having a field day in your life, reminding you of failures and shortcomings? Realize it is never God who condemns because "there is therefore now no condemnation to them who are in Christ Jesus" (Romans 8:1). Yes, the Holy Spirit convicts. But the condemnation of Satan causes you to cease your work, whereas the conviction of the Spirit will always motivate you to continue it.

5 After seeing the enemy defaming, here in chapter 5, we see the Lord sustaining . . .

Ezra 5:1 (a)
Then the prophets, Haggai the prophet, and Zechariah the son of Iddo . . .

At this point, when the people were discouraged and defeated, Haggai and Zechariah prophesied to them. Haggai was intensely practical. Zechariah was amazingly mystical. "It is not time for you to stop working," Haggai said. "How can you dwell in your ceilinged houses while the house of God is still lying in ruins?" (Haggai 1:4). Haggai tells them to get in gear and get going. Zechariah, on the other hand, shared visions and heavenly insights. Both of these men were used, practical, and mystical together, to stimulate the people to get going.

Ezra 5:1 (b)
. . . prophesied unto the Jews that were in Judah and Jerusalem in the name of the God of Israel, even unto them.

Zechariah had an encouraging word for Zerubbabel. "You began a work and it will come to completion," he said. "There's coming a day when the headstone will be in place and the people will shout 'Grace, Grace,'" (see Zechariah 4:7). This is a word for us, as well, for it's not by might, not by power, not by anything we could ever do, but by the Spirit of God that the work goes on (Zechariah 4:6).

Zechariah had a prophecy for Joshua, the high priest, who was also discouraged . . .

> And he shewed me Joshua the high priest standing before the angel of the LORD, and Satan standing at his right hand to resist him. And the LORD said unto Satan, The LORD rebuke thee, O Satan; even the LORD that hath chosen Jerusalem rebuke thee: is not this a brand plucked out of the fire? Now Joshua was clothed with filthy garments, and stood before the angel. And he answered and spake unto those that stood before him, saying, Take away the filthy garments from him. And unto him he said, Behold, I have caused thine iniquity to pass from thee, and I will clothe thee with change of raiment. Zechariah 3:1–4

The angel of the Lord in the Old Testament speaks of Jesus Christ. In this scene, we see Satan ready to condemn Joshua. "Is this not a brand or stick plucked out of the fire?" Jesus said. In other words, "I have plucked this stick out of the fire of judgment and destruction. He's My man." Joshua was in filthy garments, just as even our best works are as filthy rags compared to the Lord (Isaiah 64:6). But the Lord clothed Joshua in clean garments, and He does the same with us. When you opened your heart to Him, Jesus not only took up residence within you, but you were also placed in Him. This means that, when the Father looks at us, He doesn't see our filthy garments. He sees us robed in the righteousness of Jesus. Amazing!

Ezra 5:2
Then rose up Zerubbabel the son of Shealtiel, and Jeshua the son of Jozadak, and began to build the house of God which is at Jerusalem: and with them were the prophets of God helping them.

In 1 Corinthians 14, we read that the purpose of prophecy is for edification, exhortation, and comfort. In other words, the purpose of prophecy is to build up, get moving, and bring comfort. And Haggai and Zechariah were doing just that.

Ezra 5:3–5
At the same time came to them Tatnai, governor on this side the river, and Shethar-boznai, and their companions, and said thus unto them, Who hath commanded you to build this house, and to make up this wall? Then said we unto them after this manner, What are the names of the men that make this building? But the eye of their God was upon the elders of the Jews, that they could not cause them to cease, till the matter came to Darius: and then they returned answer by letter concerning this matter.

A letter was sent to Darius, king of Persia, tattling on the men who were working on the temple.

Ezra 5:6–8
The copy of the letter that Tatnai, governor on this side the river, and Shethar-boznai, and his companions the Apharsachites, which were on this side the river, sent unto Darius the king: They sent a letter unto him, wherein was written thus; Unto Darius the king, all peace. Be it known unto the king, that we went into the province of Judea, to the house of the great God, which is builded with great stones, and timber is laid in the walls, and this work goeth fast on, and prospereth in their hands.

Due to the attack of the enemy, work on the temple had stopped. But, hearing the words of Haggai and Zechariah, the people were recharged and renewed and the work continued to such a degree that their progress couldn't be denied. It shouldn't be surprising that the people were inspired, comforted, and encouraged by Haggai and Zechariah, for that is always the result of true prophecy (1 Corinthians 14:3).

Ezra 5:9–16
Then asked we those elders, and said unto them thus, Who commanded you to build this house, and to make up these walls? We asked their names also, to certify thee, that we might write the names of the men that were the chief of them. And thus they returned us answer, saying, We are the servants of the God of heaven and earth, and build the house that was builded these many years ago, which a great king of Israel builded and set up. But after that our fathers had provoked the God of heaven unto wrath, he gave them into the hand of Nebuchadnezzar the king of Babylon, the Chaldean, who destroyed this house, and carried the people away into Babylon. But in the first year of Cyrus the king of Babylon the same king Cyrus made a decree to build this house of God. And the vessels also of gold and silver of the house of God, which Nebuchadnezzar took out of the temple that was in Jerusalem, and brought them into the temple of Babylon, those did Cyrus the king take out of the temple of Babylon, and they were delivered unto one, whose name was Sheshbazzar, whom he had made governor; And said unto him, Take these vessels, go, carry them into the temple that is in Jerusalem, and let the house of God be builded in his place. Then came the same Sheshbazzar, and laid the foundation of the house of God which is in Jerusalem: and since that time even until now hath it been in building, and yet it is not finished.

"By whose authority do you build this temple?" the leaders of the region asked.

"We're God's servants, and, in addition to that, we have the command of Cyrus to rebuild this temple," the elders of Israel answered. "Yes, we messed up. Yes, because of our sin, we were carried into captivity. But, rather than give up on us, our God allowed us to come back to the land and build this temple."

Ezra 5:17
Now therefore, if it seem good to the king, let there be search made in the king's treasure house, which is there at Babylon, whether it be so, that a decree was made of Cyrus the king to build this house of God at Jerusalem, and let the king send his pleasure to us concerning this matter.

The leaders of the region—enemies of the people of God—told king Darius to check the records to see if his predecessor, Cyrus, had, in fact, ever issued a command that the temple be rebuilt. No doubt, they were sure no such command had ever been issued. But they would soon be proven wrong . . .

6 Ezra 6:1, 2
Then Darius the king made a decree, and search was made in the house of the rolls, where the treasures were laid up in Babylon. And there was found at Achmetha, in the palace that is in the province of the Medes, a roll, and therein was a record thus written:

There was no record in Babylon of Cyrus' decree that the Jews were to rebuild their temple, but three hundred miles away in a library a scroll was found that contained it. The enemy of your soul accuses and condemns you in an attempt to stall what God is doing in and through your life. But tucked away in a faraway palace is a scroll—the Lamb's Book of Life—and, if you're a believer, in it, much to the shock of the enemy, is your name. If your name is written there, all of the sins you have ever committed are erased by the blood of Christ shed on Calvary's Cross while your name is preserved eternally, written in the indelible ink of that same blood.

Ezra 6:3–7
In the first year of Cyrus the king the same Cyrus the king made a decree concerning the house of God at Jerusalem, Let the house be builded, the place where they offered sacrifices, and let the foundations thereof be strongly laid; the height thereof threescore cubits, and the breadth thereof threescore cubits; With three rows of great stones, and a row of new timber: and let the expenses be given out of the king's house: And also let the golden and silver vessels of the house of God, which Nebuchadnezzar took forth out of the temple which is at Jerusalem, and brought unto Babylon, be restored, and brought again unto the temple which is at Jerusalem, every one to his place, and place them in the house of God. Now therefore, Tatnai, governor beyond the river, Shethar-boznai, and your companions the Apharsachites, which are beyond the river, be ye far from thence: Let the work of this house of God alone; let the governor of the Jews and the elders of the Jews build this house of God in his place.

On the basis of the scroll that was found, king Cyrus decreed that the work continue and that the enemies of God be "far from thence." It was on the basis of the Word that Jesus said, "Get thee hence, Satan, for it is written . . ." (Matthew 4:10).

How will you overcome the attacks and condemnation of Satan to get you to cease what you know you could and should be doing? Say, "It is written that the price has been paid, that I am forgiven." Claim the command of the King as recorded in the Word and continue with the work He has called you to do.

Ezra 6:8–10
Moreover I made a decree what ye shall do to the elders of these Jews for the building of this house of God: that of the king's goods, even of the tribute beyond the river, forthwith expenses be given unto these men, that they be not hindered. And that which they have need of, both young bullocks, and rams, and lambs, for the burnt offerings of the God of heaven, wheat, salt, wine, and oil, according to the appointment of the priests which are at Jerusalem, let it be given them day by day without fail: That they may offer sacrifices of sweet savours unto the God of heaven, and pray for the life of the king, and of his sons.

So monumentally did the plan of the enemies of God's people fail that, not only was the rebuilding project allowed to continue, but it would be financed by the Persians! Thus, because the Word was heard, the adversaries were beaten at their own game.

How can we turn the tables on our enemy, the accuser of the brethren, Satan himself? We turn the tables on him at the Lord's Table, the table of Communion. You see, Jesus told us that we're to agree with our Adversary quickly (Matthew 5:25). Our Adversary is the devil agreeing with him that I am a sinner at the Table of the Lord simply causes me to praise the Lord with greater passion than I would have otherwise. After all, he who is forgiven much loves much (Luke 7:47). Jesus wasn't speaking of the amount of sin, but of the awareness of the sin that dwells within us, the sin that He would pay for on the Cross.

Satan accuses us, to be sure. But, because he isn't omniscient, his accusations don't identify even half of our sin. Yet neither do they take into account the unfathomable grace of God that washes us clean. Don't defend yourself against your accuser, gang. Agree with him, and praise God all the more.

Ezra 6:11–13
Also I have made a decree, that whosoever shall alter this word, let timber be pulled down from his house, and being set up, let him be hanged thereon; and let his house be made a dunghill for this. And the God that hath caused his name to dwell there destroy all kings and people, that shall put to their hand to alter and to destroy this house of God which is at Jerusalem. I Darius have

made a decree; let it be done with speed. Then Tatnai, governor on this side the river, Shethar-boznai, and their companions, according to that which Darius the king had sent, so they did speedily.

In this I am reminded of another man who sought to do in the people of God: Haman. In the Book of Esther, we read that Haman thought he had concocted a sure-fire plan to destroy the entire Jewish population, only to see it backfire as he himself was hung on the gallows he had built for another.

Ezra 6:14, 15
And the elders of the Jews builded, and they prospered through the prophesying of Haggai the prophet and Zechariah the son of Iddo. And they builded, and finished it, according to the commandment of the God of Israel, and according to the commandment of Cyrus, and Darius, and Artaxerxes king of Persia. And this house was finished on the third day of the month Adar, which was in the sixth year of the reign of Darius the king.

The temple was finished on the third day. I love the third day, don't you, for that's the day Jesus rose. According to Hosea 6:2, after two days, God will revive us and in the third day, He will raise us up. On the third day, this temple will be finished when we're taken up to heaven. What a grand day that will be!

Ezra 6:16, 17
And the children of Israel, the priests, and the Levites, and the rest of the children of the captivity, kept the dedication of this house of God with joy, And offered at the dedication of this house of God an hundred bullocks, two hundred rams, four hundred lambs; and for a sin offering for all Israel, twelve he goats, according to the number of the tribes of Israel.

Notice that there were no "lost tribes." All twelve tribes were represented in the dedication of the temple.

Ezra 6:18–22
And they set the priests in their divisions, and the Levites in their courses, for the service of God, which is at Jerusalem; as it is written in the book of Moses. And the children of the captivity kept the passover upon the fourteenth day of the first month. For the priests and the Levites were purified together, all of them were pure, and killed the passover for all the children of the captivity, and for their brethren the priests, and for themselves. And the children of Israel, which were come again out of captivity, and all such as had separated themselves unto them from the filthiness of the heathen of the land, to seek the LORD God of Israel, did eat, And kept the feast of unleavened bread seven days with joy: for the LORD had made them joyful, and turned the heart of the king of Assyria unto them, to strengthen their hands in the work of the house of God, the God of Israel.

The temple is now rebuilt and dedicated. Passover is celebrated. The priests and Levites are placed in their proper positions. There is unbelievable joy. That's always the result of working for the Lord and seeing the task come to completion. Jesus said, "Father, I have glorified Thee and finished the work Thou hast given me to do" (John 17:4).

May we be those who, when we come to the end of our days, can say, "Father, I have finished the work, not what culture dictated I do or others suggested I do, but what *You* gave me to do."

7 Between chapters 6 and 7, there is a gap of almost sixty years. During this time, the story of Esther takes place. The temple had been rebuilt. But there was a season of silence. That is, nothing noteworthy was happening in Jerusalem that was recorded in Scripture. Maybe you can relate to this. Maybe you've been born again and rescued from the captivity of your own carnality, and you'll be thankful eternally, but it doesn't seem like a lot is happening presently. Good news—the passage before us speaks to your situation, for this is where Ezra appears on the scene.

Ezra's name means "Help" or "Helper." Ezra was a priest, but unable to function as a priest because he had been in Babylon. So, instead, he became a skilled scribe. Most scholars believe that Ezra wrote First and Second Chronicles, along with Psalm 119. We are also told that he was in charge of the council of one hundred and twenty who put together the canon of Scripture and the one who inaugurated the synagogue, a place where God's people could gather together and study the Scriptures. All of this parallels the ministry of the Holy Spirit . . .

Jesus told us that it was important that He go, for He would send another "Helper," or "Comforter" (John 16:7). The Spirit is a ready scribe indeed for, as Peter tells us, the prophets wrote as He moved them (2 Peter 1:21). The Spirit is also a teacher, bringing all things to our remembrance (John 14:26).

Whereas chapters 1 through 6 deal with the construction of the temple, chapters 7 through 10 deal with the instruction of the people. In chapters 1 through 6, we saw rebuilding. In chapters 7 through 10, we'll see reviving, a sure indication of the presence of the Spirit in the life of an individual, a church, or a nation.

Ezra 7:1–5
Now after these things, in the reign of Artaxerxes king of Persia, Ezra the son of Seraiah, the son of Azariah, the son of Hilkiah, The son of Shallum, the son of Zadok, the son of Ahitub, The son of Amariah, the son of Azariah, the son of Meraioth, The son of Zerahiah, the son of Uzzi, the son of Bukki, The son of Abishua, the son of Phinehas, the son of Eleazar, the son of Aaron the chief priest:

Here, we see Ezra's lineage traced back to Aaron, the high priest.

Ezra 7:6 (a)
This Ezra went up from Babylon; and he was a ready scribe in the law of Moses, which the Lord God of Israel had given . . .

Ezra was a ready, or skilled, scribe. When did he get ready? When he was in captivity in Babylon. He could have pouted. He could have been angry he was not in a greater position of importance. But instead of pouting, he prepared. Even if you're in a place of captivity, even if you feel like you're boxed in, don't pout. Prepare. Study. Pray. Seek the Lord. In due time, at the right time, the Lord will release you for those tasks He has prepared for you. Ezra spent years preparing. Then the Lord tapped him on the shoulder to lead another group out of captivity and back to the Land of Promise.

Ezra 7:6 (b)
. . . and the king granted him all his request, according to the hand of the Lord his God upon him.

Six times we'll hear Ezra say that the good hand of God was upon him. He was definitely one who was in constant touch with the Lord.

Ezra 7:7–10 (a)
And there went up some of the children of Israel, and of the priests, and the Levites, and the singers, and the porters, and the Nethinims, unto Jerusalem, in the seventh year of Artaxerxes the king. And he came to Jerusalem in the fifth month, which was in the seventh year of the king. For upon the first day of the first month began he to go up from Babylon, and on the first day of the fifth month came he to Jerusalem, according to the good hand of his God upon him. For Ezra had prepared his heart to seek the law of the Lord . . .

Ezra prepared his heart to seek the Law of the Lord. Because it is the Spirit who searches the deep things of God (1 Corinthians 2:10), it is the Spirit who will teach us how to understand His Word. Ezra pictures this.

Ezra 7:10 (b)
. . . and to do it, and to teach in Israel statutes and judgments.

Not only does the Spirit tell us what to do, but He empowers us to do it (Ephesians 3:16). Lots of people want to learn the Word and teach the Word. Fewer long to *follow* the Word. But without this, teaching lacks anointing and authority.

Ezra 7:11–13
Now this is the copy of the letter that the king Artaxerxes gave unto Ezra the priest, the scribe, even a scribe of the words of the commandments of the Lord, and of his statutes to Israel. Artaxerxes, king of kings, unto Ezra the priest, a scribe of the law of the God of heaven, perfect peace, and at such a time. I make a decree, that all they of the people of Israel, and of his priests and Levites, in my realm, which are minded of their own freewill to go up to Jerusalem, go with thee.

Ezra was given the authority to take those who wanted to go with him to minister to the Lord in Jerusalem. It is the Holy Spirit who says, "Whosoever will, let him take the water of life freely" (Revelation 22:17), and it is the Spirit who calls men to ministry (Acts 13:2).

Ezra 7:14–18
Forasmuch as thou art sent of the king, and of his seven counsellors, to inquire concerning Judah and Jerusalem, according to the law of thy God which is in thine hand; And to carry the silver and gold, which the king and his counsellors have freely offered unto the God of Israel, whose habitation is in Jerusalem, And all the silver and gold that thou canst find in all the province of Babylon, with the freewill offering of the people, and of the priests, offering willingly for

the house of their God which is in Jerusalem: That thou mayest buy speedily with this money bullocks, rams, lambs, with their meat offerings and their drink offerings, and offer them upon the altar of the house of your God which is in Jerusalem. And whatsoever shall seem good to thee, and to thy brethren, to do with the rest of the silver and the gold, that do after the will of your God.

Ezra was not only a teacher of the Word, and not only a doer of what he taught, but he was instrumental in worship, for here he is charged by Artaxerxes to take that which was needed to establish worship in the temple. It is the Holy Spirit who enables us to worship (John 4:24; Ephesians 5:18–21; Philippians 3:3).

Ezra 7:19–23
The vessels also that are given thee for the service of the house of thy God, those deliver thou before the God of Jerusalem. And whatsoever more shall be needful for the house of thy God, which thou shalt have occasion to bestow, bestow it out of the king's treasure house. And I, even I Artaxerxes the king, do make a decree to all the treasurers which are beyond the river, that whatsoever Ezra the priest, the scribe of the law of the God of heaven, shall require of you, it be done speedily, Unto an hundred talents of silver, and to an hundred measures of wheat, and to an hundred bäths of wine, and to an hundred bäths of oil, and salt without prescribing how much. Whatsoever is commanded by the God of heaven, let it be diligently done for the house of the God of heaven: for why should there be wrath against the realm of the king and his sons?

Ezra was entrusted with great treasures, among them the equivalent of up to four tons of silver and six hundred gallons of wine. But even these pale in comparison to the gifts and treasures the Holy Spirit bestows . . .

> But the manifestation of the Spirit is given to every man to profit withal. For to one is given by the Spirit the word of wisdom; to another the word of knowledge by the same Spirit; To another faith by the same Spirit; to another the gifts of healing by the same Spirit; To another the working of miracles; to another prophecy; to another discerning of spirits; to another divers kinds of tongues; to another the interpretation of tongues: But all these worketh that one and the selfsame Spirit, dividing to every man severally as he will. 1 Corinthians 12:7–11

Ezra was given both the manpower and the financial resources to accomplish the task before Him. And the church is given no less.

Ezra 7:24
Also we certify you, that touching any of the priests and Levites, singers, porters, Nethinims, or ministers of this house of God, it shall not be lawful to impose toll, tribute, or custom, upon them.

I find it interesting that here we see the first example of a state providing tax exemptions for ministry.

Ezra 7:25
And thou, Ezra, after the wisdom of thy God, that is in thine hand, set magistrates and judges, which may judge all the people that are beyond the river, all such as know the laws of thy God; and teach ye them that know them not.

Ezra was commissioned to establish those who knew the Law and to teach it to those who didn't yet know it. As Paul would write to the Galatians, the law was our schoolmaster to bring us to Christ (3:24). Then, once we are brought to Christ and His Spirit takes up residence within, so lovely is the fruit He produces that there is no law against it (Galatians 5:22, 23).

Ezra 7:26, 27
And whosoever will not do the law of thy God, and the law of the king, let judgment be executed speedily upon him, whether it be unto death, or to banishment, or to confiscation of goods, or to imprisonment. Blessed be the LORD God of our fathers, which hath put such a thing as this in the king's heart, to beautify the house of the LORD which is in Jerusalem:

The Lord not only wants to build His house, but to beautify it. He's not only building us as a people, but He wants to beautify us as a people (Psalm 149:4). It's one thing to put us all together, it's something else to beautify us.

Ezra 7:28
And hath extended mercy unto me before the king, and his counsellors, and before all the king's mighty princes. And I was strengthened as the hand of the LORD my God was upon me, and I gathered together out of Israel chief men to go up with me.

Ezra was strengthened for the work that lay ahead. And, through the Spirit, so are we (Ephesians 3:16).

8 Ezra 8:1
These are now the chief of their fathers, and this is the genealogy of them that went up with me from Babylon in the reign of Artaxerxes the king.

The number of men who responded to Ezra's invitation to go to Jerusalem—listed in verses 2 through 14—was approximately 1,500. Keep in mind that most of the Jews carried into Babylon had, over time, become comfortable there. In the first group, led by Zerubbabel, nearly 50,000 went. In this second group, there are 1,500 who go. Most chose to stay.

The Holy Spirit is a perfect gentlemen. He invites. He encourages. He inspires. He enlightens. But He doesn't force. That is why He is likened not to a vulture or an eagle, but to a dove, a bird of peace and gentleness (Matthew 3:16).

In Ezekiel 47, we see Ezekiel being led to a river, often a picture of the Spirit in Scripture (Joshua 3:13), where he stepped in up to his ankles. Then he was led downstream, where he stepped in up to his knees. Further downstream, he stepped in up to his waist. Still further, he found himself over his head. What does this say to us? The Spirit of the Lord invites us to step in. Some step in up to their ankles. That is, they're standing in Christ, believing in Jesus. Others, however, choose to go deeper. They go to their knees, not only believing in the Lord themselves, but prayer for others. Others go deeper still, sharing their faith and seeing others born again. And others ask the Lord to take total control of their lives, allowing the baptism of the Spirit to wash over them completely. At each stage, Ezekiel had a choice whether or not to step in. So do we. Will I do what the Lord invites me to do? Will I ask for the power of the Holy Spirit to come upon me? Will I believe that His Spirit will fill me? Will I witness for Him?

Gang, the Lord will take you as far and as deep in Him as you want to go, but not one step further. Why are some people seemingly so Spirit-filled? I suggest it is simply because they want to be, that they are those who say, "Lord, take total control of me. Do whatever You want with my life. I want to be lost in You."

Ezra 8:15 (a)
And I gathered them together to the river that runneth to Ahava; and there abode we in tents three days:

After gathering the people, Ezra stopped for three days to assess the situation, a wise thing to do in light of the fact that an arduous, nine hundred-mile journey awaited them.

Three days by the river reminds me of the three days Joshua and the children of Israel spent camping by the Jordan River. They had been set free from bondage in Egypt. They had been in the wilderness for forty years. They were being led by the Lord, but had not yet entered into the abundance the Lord intended for them. After three days, the officers commanded the people to follow the ark—the symbol of the visible, tangible presence of God. But they were to leave a space of about a half mile because they had not "passed this way heretofore" (Joshua 3:4). In other words, God desired time and space to do what He wanted to do.

Many people are trying to be filled with the Spirit when in reality what they need is to be emptied of the flesh. That's why it's so important to follow Ezra's example and wait on the Lord.

Ezra 8:15 (b)–20
. . . and I viewed the people, and the priests, and found there none of the sons of Levi. Then sent I for Eliezer, for Ariel, for Shemaiah, and for Elnathan, and for Jarib, and for Elnathan, and for Nathan, and for Zechariah, and for Meshullam, chief men; also for Joiarib, and for Elnathan, men of understanding. And I sent them with commandment unto Iddo the chief at the place Casiphia, and I told them what they should say unto Iddo, and to his brethren the Nethinims, at the place Casiphia, that they should bring unto us ministers for the house of our God. And by the good hand of our God upon us they brought us a man of understanding, of the sons of Mahli, the son of Levi, the son of Israel; and Sherebiah, with his sons and his brethren, eighteen; And Hashabiah, and with him Jeshaiah of the sons of Merari, his brethren and their sons, twenty; Also of the Nethinims, whom David and the princes had appointed for the service of the Levites, two hundred and twenty Nethinims: all of them were expressed by name.

Finding no Levites in the company, Ezra decided to "draft" nearly three hundred, for without them, temple worship would have been an impossibility.

Ezra 8:21–23
Then I proclaimed a fast there, at the river of Ahava, that we might afflict ourselves before our God, to seek of him a right way for us, and for our little ones, and for all our substance. For I was ashamed to require of the king a band of soldiers and horsemen

to help us against the enemy in the way: because we had spoken unto the king, saying, The hand of our God is upon all them for good that seek him; but his power and his wrath is against all them that forsake him. So we fasted and besought our God for this: and he was intreated of us.

Carrying about five million dollars' worth of gold and silver, Ezra realized they were easy targets. Yet he didn't want to ask the king for protection because he had told him that God's hand was upon them. How many times have we felt backed into a corner, thinking our only two choices were defeat or reliance on the world, when, in fact, God has limitless options for us if we would only call out to Him? Ezra wisely took this third option and called for the people to fast and pray.

Fasting is a wonderful and powerful instrument in the arsenal of the believer who desires to move in the Spirit. Fasting is not intended to earn the Father's approval, for giving up a brownie or two doesn't score brownie points with Him. Whether skipping a favorite food or a meal or two, whether for a day or longer, fasting is simply a means by which we can use the time and effort we would otherwise spend on meeting our physical needs to concentrate on our spiritual needs. Fasting says, "I need to know the way to go. I want to be led by the Spirit." Fasting doesn't impress God—it's for our benefit. When you feel afraid or confused, fast. Deny the physical. Concentrate on the spiritual. Seek the Lord.

Ezra 8:24–30
Then I separated twelve of the chief of the priests, Sherebiah, Hashabiah, and ten of their brethren with them, And weighed unto them the silver, and the gold, and the vessels, even the offering of the house of our God, which the king, and his counsellors, and his lords, and all Israel there present, had offered: I even weighed unto their hand six hundred and fifty talents of silver, and silver vessels an hundred talents, and of gold an hundred talents; Also twenty basons of gold, of a thousand drams; and two vessels of fine copper, precious as gold. And I said unto them, Ye are holy unto the LORD; the vessels are holy also; and the silver and the gold are a freewill offering unto the LORD God of your fathers. Watch ye, and keep them, until ye weigh them before the chief of the priests and the Levites, and chief of the fathers of Israel, at Jerusalem, in the chambers of the house of the LORD. So took the priests and the Levites the weight of the silver, and the gold, and the vessels, to bring them to Jerusalem unto the house of our God

The offerings were weighed at the beginning of the journey and would be weighed again at Jerusalem. This was wise leadership and good stewardship. Jesus said in Luke 16:11 that if a man couldn't be found faithful in dealing with unrighteous mammon, money, how could he be entrusted with true spiritual riches? Money, it seems, is the indicator God uses to help us see where our hearts are (Luke 12:34).

Ezra 8:31
Then we departed from the river of Ahava on the twelfth day of the first month, to go unto Jerusalem: and the hand of our God was upon us, and he delivered us from the hand of the enemy, and of such as lay in wait by the way.

Ezra knew the enemies wanting to rob them of five million dollars of gold and silver were laying in wait. The children of Israel had no army, but they knew God was with them because they had prayed and prepared. Consistent prayer is that which gives us protection from the enemies that lay in wait on every road, the ones we don't see, and the ones we would never think would be out to get us. Is it really that important that we rise early to pray? Is it really that crucial that I maintain a consistent prayer life. Stop praying and you'll find out, when an enemy you never expected or suspected appears in your path.

Ezra 8:32
And we came to Jerusalem, and abode there three days.

God was with them indeed, for they made it to their destination.

Ezra 8:33, 34
Now on the fourth day was the silver and the gold and the vessels weighed in the house of our God by the hand of Meremoth the son of Uriah the priest; and with him was Eleazar the son of Phinehas; and with them was Jozabad the son of Jeshua, and Noadiah the son of Binnui, Levites; By number and by weight of every one: and all the weight was written at that time.

Just as the priests and Levites gave account for the gifts entrusted to them, there will come a day when we will give an answer for what we did with that which was given to us. That is why Paul would tell Timothy to "stir up" the gift within him (2 Timothy 1:6). The same exhortation applies to us. Don't let the gifts the Spirit has given you go idle, saint. Utilize what God has entrusted to you.

Ezra 8:35, 36
Also the children of those that had been carried away, which were come out of the captivity, offered burnt offerings unto the God of Israel, twelve bullocks for all Israel, ninety and six rams, seventy and seven lambs, twelve he goats for a sin offering: all this was a burnt offering unto the LORD. And they delivered the king's commissions unto the king's lieutenants, and to the governors on this side the river: and they furthered the people, and the house of God.

I think sometimes we ought to treat people as if they're Christians even when they're not. In the days before self-service gas stations, I don't know how many times I would stop on my way to teach and say to the attendant, "Pray for me. I'm going to speak to a group of high school kids about the Lord. I'll be back next week to tell you how it goes." That's what Jesus did. He talked to people about the kingdom as if they were already believers (Matthew 13, 22). Share the Word with king's lieutenants and with governors, with anyone and everyone, and watch to see how it "furthers the people and the house of God."

9 In chapter 8, we read of preparation for the pilgrimage. Here in chapter 9, we see supplication by the scribe . . .

Ezra 9:1–3
Now when these things were done, the princes came to me, saying, The people of Israel, and the priests, and the Levites, have not separated themselves from the people of the lands, doing according to their abominations, even of the Canaanites, the Hittites, the Perizzites, the Jebusites, the Ammonites, the Moabites, the Egyptians, and the Amorites. For they have taken of their daughters for themselves, and for their sons: so that the holy seed have mingled themselves with the people of those lands: yea, the hand of the princes and rulers hath been chief in this trespass. And when I heard this thing, I rent my garment and my mantle, and plucked off the hair of my head and of my beard, and sat down astonied.

Arriving in Jerusalem, Ezra discovered that the men of Israel had married the daughters of the Canaanites. Ezra couldn't believe it. He had just completed a long, hard journey no doubt expecting to see people worshiping and growing and serving God. Instead, he heard reports that they had intermarried. Rather than preach at the people, however, he sat down before them and ripped out his beard and hair.

Do you hate sin that much? Does sin bother you so much that it causes you to rip out your hair? Would to God I had a heart like that.

What was Ezra worried about? Why was intermarriage such a big issue? I suggest two reasons . . .

The first deals with prophecy. You see, all of the prophecies concerning the Messiah was that He would come through the Jewish lineage. Knowing this, Satan sought to so dilute the lineage that Messiah could not be born. Have you ever wondered how the Jews have been able to preserve their identity even to this day? It is because, regardless of how Satan might try, God's prophecies are never thwarted.

Secondly, intermarriage was of major concern practically, for through it, God's people would inevitably begin to follow pagan customs. Not a week goes by when I don't have a conversation with someone who says, "I shouldn't have married him or her. I thought I could set an example and that they would eventually come to the Lord. But they have no intention of doing that." Everyone feels their own case is the exception, that marrying an unbeliever will be alright in their situation. But it is as a loving Father who knows what He's talking about that God says, "Be not unequally yoked with an unbeliever" (see 2 Corinthians 6:14). If you marry an unbeliever, if you violate the command of God, you will pay the price. Be not deceived. God is not mocked (Galatians 6:7).

Ezra 9:4–6
Then were assembled unto me every one that trembled at the words of the God of Israel, because of the transgression of those that had been carried away; and I sat astonied until the evening sacrifice. And at the evening sacrifice I arose up from my heaviness; and having rent my garment and my mantle, I fell upon my knees, and spread out my hands unto the LORD my God, And said, O my God, I am ashamed and blush to lift up my face to thee, my God, for our iniquities are increased over our head, and our trespass is grown up unto the heavens.

Notice how Ezra prays. He doesn't say, "I'm ashamed of these wretches, of these backsliders." He says, "I'm ashamed of ourselves." He recognized his part in the corporate people of God and recognized he was responsible with them.

Ezra 9:7–15
Since the days of our fathers have we been in a great trespass unto this day; and for our iniquities have we, our kings, and our

priests, been delivered into the hand of the kings of the lands, to the sword, to captivity, and to a spoil, and to confusion of face, as it is this day. And now for a little space grace hath been shewed from the LORD our God, to leave us a remnant to escape, and to give us a nail in his holy place, that our God may lighten our eyes, and give us a little reviving in our bondage. For we were bondmen; yet our God hath not forsaken us in our bondage, but hath extended mercy unto us in the sight of the kings of Persia, to give us a reviving, to set up the house of our God, and to repair the desolations thereof, and to give us a wall in Judah and in Jerusalem. And now, O our God, what shall we say after this? for we have forsaken thy commandments, Which thou hast commanded by thy servants the prophets, saying, The land, unto which ye go to possess it, is an unclean land with the filthiness of the people of the lands, with their abominations, which have filled it from one end to another with their uncleanness. Now therefore give not your daughters unto their sons, neither take their daughters unto your sons, nor seek their peace or their wealth for ever: that ye may be strong, and eat the good of the land, and leave it for an inheritance to your children for ever. And after all that is come upon us for our evil deeds, and for our great trespass, seeing that thou our God hast punished us less than our iniquities deserve, and hast given us such deliverance as this; Should we again break thy commandments, and join in affinity with the people of these abominations? wouldest not thou be angry with us till thou hadst consumed us, so that there should be no remnant nor escaping? O LORD God of Israel, thou art righteous: for we remain yet escaped, as it is this day: behold, we are before thee in our trespasses: for we cannot stand before thee because of this.

In this powerful prayer offered by a brokenhearted priest, we see neither pride nor empty promises to do better. We see thanksgiving for God's care and adoration of His character. We see confession of sin and acknowledgement of undeserved mercy. And through it all we see the beauty of humility. No wonder it was a prayer recorded for eternity.

10 In chapter 10, we come to the purification of the people . . .

Ezra 10:1–4
Now when Ezra had prayed, and when he had confessed, weeping and casting himself down before the house of God, there assembled unto him out of Israel a very great congregation of men and women and children: for the people wept very sore. And Shechaniah the son of Jehiel, one of the sons of Elam, answered and said unto Ezra, We have trespassed against our God, and have taken strange wives of the people of the land: yet now there is hope in Israel concerning this thing. Now therefore let us make a covenant with our God to put away all the wives, and such as are born of them, according to the counsel of my lord, and of those that tremble at the commandment of our God; and let it be done according to the law. Arise; for this matter belongeth unto thee: we also will be with thee: be of good courage, and do it.

Ezra's prayer was more productive than a sermon, for when the people saw him praying, weeping, and in mourning, they realized the severity of their sin. It wasn't a finger pointing or a temper flaring that brought them to their knees, it was the heart of a man of God breaking.

Ezra 10:5–12
Then arose Ezra, and made the chief priests, the Levites, and all Israel, to swear that they should do according to this word. And they sware. Then Ezra rose up from before the house of God, and went into the chamber of Johanan the son of Eliashib: and when he came thither, he did eat no bread, nor drink water: for he mourned because of the transgression of them that had been carried away. And they made proclamation throughout Judah and Jerusalem unto all the children of the captivity, that they should gather themselves together unto Jerusalem; And that whosoever would not come within three days, according to the counsel of the princes and the elders, all his substance should be forfeited, and himself separated from the congregation of those that had been carried away. Then all the men of Judah and Benjamin gathered themselves together unto Jerusalem within three days. It was the ninth month, on the twentieth day of the month; and all the people sat in the street of the house of God, trembling because of this matter, and for the great rain. And Ezra the priest stood up, and said unto them, Ye have transgressed, and have taken strange wives, to increase the trespass of Israel. Now therefore make confession unto the LORD God of your fathers, and do his pleasure: and separate yourselves from the people of the land, and from the strange

wives. Then all the congregation answered and said with a loud voice, As thou hast said, so must we do.

The remainder of the chapter is a list of the one hundred and thirteen men who said, "We will kiss our wives goodbye, say farewell to our kids, and let them go back to the land from whence they came." This would not be easy for any man. But they were willing to do it when they heard the voice of God speaking through Ezra and the leaders of Jerusalem, telling them that confession and separation was what was required of them.

I believe this list—including seventeen priests and ten Levites—is not one of condemnation, but rather of commendation of the men who were willing to do whatever it took to be right with God. "Godly sorrow worketh repentance," we read in 2 Corinthians 7:10. It's one thing to say, "I'm sorry." It's quite another to say, "I'm sorry and I'm changing direction."

"Behold," Peter said to Jesus, "we have forsaken all and followed Thee. What shall we have therefore?"

"Truly every one that hath forsaken houses, or brethren, or sisters, or father, or mother, or wife, or children, or lands, for my name's sake, shall receive an hundredfold, and shall inherit everlasting life," Jesus answered (see Matthew 19:27–29).

Confession and separation have eternal ramifications. And in every one of our lives without exception, there are decisions that must be made regarding these issues in one way or another because the same temptations come to *all* men (1 Corinthians 10:13). Make the right choice, precious people. Learn the lesson of Ezra. You can't out give God. He won't let you down. He'll restore you one hundred-fold. Trust Him.

NEHEMIAH

Background to Nehemiah

In accordance with God's plan for His people, in the year 605 B.C., Nebuchadnezzar, king of Babylon, cruised down to Judah and carried Jews captive to Babylon. Eighteen years later, in 586 B.C., the Babylonians destroyed Jerusalem, wiped out the temple, obliterated the wall, and carried more Jews away captive. Seventy years later, the prophecies of Jeremiah were fulfilled when the Jews were allowed to return to Jerusalem to rebuild and restore the temple first and then the walls surrounding the city itself. In 535 B.C., Zerubbabel led the first contingency from Babylon to Jerusalem. Accompanying him were two prophets named Haggai and Zechariah who spurred the people on, exhorting them to continue the process of rebuilding the temple.

Fifty-seven years later, a second group, led by a priest and scribe named Ezra, returned.

In the book before us, a third contingency is coming back. The year is 445 B.C. and this third group is led by a man named Nehemiah. He is coming back to rebuild the walls around the city in order that the people can worship freely without being attacked by the enemy.

The book before us is one of my favorite books in the Old Testament. And each time I have studied it, I have seen entirely different emphases therein. For example, it is an excellent book to study with regard to leadership, for Nehemiah is the quintessential example of what a leader should be. It is also an excellent book regarding the subject of revival. But one of the most interesting ways to look at it is as a picture of the way the Holy Spirit rebuilds and restores the walls of the human personality.

You see, just as God is a triune Being, and because we are created in His image, we consist of three components as well: body, soul, and spirit. The body relates to the physical world around us. In a believer, the spirit lives forever and relates to the Lord within us. The soul—the personality—consists of mind and emotions and relates to the people around us. When we were saved, the temple that was in ruin, our spirit, was rebuilt and reborn when the Spirit came and dwelt within us. Yet even though that happened when I was born again, sometimes my soul—my emotions and mind—can still lie in ruins. That is, my mind doesn't think the way it ought. My emotions aren't as stable as they need to be. And as a result, I am vulnerable to attack unless and until the Spirit begins to rebuild the walls of my soul, how I think and how I feel.

I think it's not coincidental that *Nehemiah* means "Comforter from God"—for I suggest he paints a wonderful picture of the true Comforter (John 14:16), the Holy Spirit, who wants to rebuild and restore the walls that have been torn down by sin, the gates that have burned up by rebellion.

Many people say, "I've been born again. Why am I still struggling in this area emotionally or mentally?" I suggest it's because the Holy Spirit needs to do a restorative, rebuilding work in the area of the soul. If you're in that place, you're at the right place today, for the book before us gives us some powerful lessons about what the Lord desires to do in us in order to free us to worship Him . . .

NEHEMIAH

1 Nehemiah 1:1–4
The words of Nehemiah the son of Hachaliah. And it came to pass in the month Chisleu, in the twentieth year, as I was in Shushan the palace, That Hanani, one of my brethren, came, he and certain men of Judah; and I asked them concerning the Jews that had escaped, which were left of the captivity, and concerning Jerusalem. And they said unto me, The remnant that are left of the captivity there in the province are in great affliction and reproach: the wall of Jerusalem also is broken down, and the gates thereof are burned with fire. And it came to pass, when I heard these words, that I sat down and wept, and mourned certain days, and fasted, and prayed before the God of heaven,

When Nehemiah heard about the affliction and reproach of those who had already returned to Jerusalem, he was grieved. The Bible tells us that when we're afflicted, when we're not doing as well as we ought, the Spirit of God is grieved (Ephesians 4:30).

Nehemiah 1:5, 6
And said, I beseech thee, O LORD God of heaven, the great and terrible God, that keepeth covenant and mercy for them that love him and observe his commandments: Let thine ear now be attentive, and thine eyes open, that thou mayest hear the prayer of thy servant, which I pray before thee now, day and night, for the children of Israel thy servants, and confess the sins of the children of Israel, which we have sinned against thee: both I and my father's house have sinned.

Even though he wasn't in Jerusalem yet, Nehemiah identifies with the people there. Likewise, the Holy Spirit knows what I'm going through and what you're dealing with. That is why He prays through us and for us with groanings that can't even be articulated (Romans 8:26).

Nehemiah 1:7, 8
We have dealt very corruptly against thee, and have not kept the commandments, nor the statutes, nor the judgments, which thou commandedst thy servant Moses. Remember, I beseech thee, the word that thou commandedst thy servant Moses, saying, If ye transgress, I will scatter you abroad among the nations:

"Remember the word," Nehemiah prayed. That's part of the ministry of the Holy Spirit. In John 14:26, we read that when the Holy Spirit is given, He reminds us of that which we've learned of the Lord. If you want Him to bring these things to your remembrance, however, you've got to put stuff in your "remember-er" because He's not going to bring to mind that which hasn't gone in! That's why Bible study is so vital. In due season, He'll cause these things to come to your remembrance right when you need them.

Nehemiah 1:9–11
But if ye turn unto me, and keep my commandments, and do them; though there were of you cast out unto the uttermost part of the heaven, yet will I gather them from thence,

and will bring them unto the place that I have chosen to set my name there. Now these are thy servants and thy people, whom thou hast redeemed by thy great power, and by thy strong hand. O Lord, I beseech thee, let now thine ear be attentive to the prayer of thy servant, and to the prayer of thy servants, who desire to fear thy name: and prosper, I pray thee, thy servant this day, and grant him mercy in the sight of this man. For I was the king's cupbearer.

"I was the king's cupbearer." This final sentence of chapter 1 gives us an indication of Nehemiah's great humility. You see, being the king's cupbearer was a tremendous honor. Originally, the cupbearer sat next to the king and would sample the food and drink brought before him to determine if it had been poisoned. But as time progressed, the office of cupbearer became one of close adviser. In Nehemiah's day, the cupbearer was no longer sampling food, but a "chief of staff." Thus, Nehemiah was in a place of prominence and power.

If I were Nehemiah, I would have mentioned my position at the beginning of the book. Nehemiah, however, mentions it at the end of the chapter and only as it relates to the story about to unfold. Concerning the Spirit, Jesus said that when He came, He wouldn't speak of Himself (John 16:13, 14). The work of the Spirit is to exalt the Son. Where is the Son most exalted? At the Table of Communion, for when I hold the cup of the King at the Table of the Lord, it is then that the Spirit so often begins to advise, correct, and comfort me.

As he was in a position of power, word came back from Jerusalem nine hundred miles away that the walls were still destroyed, the gates still burned, and things were still a mess. Yet, rather than criticize, Nehemiah agonized. He not only confessed sin, but also quoted Scripture. Referring to Deuteronomy 28, he prayed, "Lord, You promised that if we sinned, we would be scattered. But You also promised that if we returned again to You, You would gather us from wherever we've been."

I'm convinced that God loves to hear His children quote Scripture in prayer, as if to say, "Lord, I understand what You said. I'm placing my faith on what You have spoken." And Nehemiah does just that.

2 Nehemiah had it made in the palace of Shushan—the winter palace of the king of Babylon—but in the chapter before us, we'll see him lay aside his possessions, position, and pride in order to become involved in the work of God . . .

Nehemiah 2:1, 2
And it came to pass in the month Nisan, in the twentieth year of Artaxerxes the king, that wine was before him: and I took up the wine, and gave it unto the king. Now I had not been beforetime sad in his presence. Wherefore the king said unto me, Why is thy countenance sad, seeing thou art not sick? this is nothing else but sorrow of heart. Then I was very sore afraid,

Although it was a capital offense for a cupbearer or close advisor to the king to be sad in his presence, Nehemiah couldn't hide the fact that he was greatly grieved over the condition of his brothers in Jerusalem.

Nehemiah 2:3–5 (a)
And said unto the king, Let the king live for ever: why should not my countenance be sad, when the city, the place of my fathers' sepulchres, lieth waste, and the gates thereof are consumed with fire? Then the king said unto me, For what dost thou make request? So I prayed to the God of heaven. And I said unto the king . . .

Nehemiah prayed to God and then immediately spoke to the king. Certainly, Nehemiah's prayer couldn't have been very long! When Peter took his eyes off Jesus and began to sink, he didn't say, "Oh, great and holy Creator and Sustainer of all things, I beseech You to have mercy upon me and incline Your ear toward me." No, he said, "Lord, save me!" And a three-word prayer saved him (Matthew 14:30, 31).

"Don't think you will be heard because of your much speaking," Jesus warned, "for that's how the heathen pray" (see Matthew 6:7). Both Nehemiah and Peter modeled just the opposite. It's not the length of our prayers that counts, but the strength that matters. You can pray quickly and yet very effectively if your heart is in tune with God.

Nehemiah 2:5 (b)
. . . If it please the king, and if thy servant have found favour in thy sight, that thou wouldest send me unto Judah, unto the city of my fathers' sepulchres, that I may build it.

"Send me to Jerusalem," was Nehemiah's request. It was in Jerusalem where the disciples were told to wait for the power of the Holy Spirit (Luke 24:49).

Nehemiah 2:6
And the king said unto me, (the queen also sitting by him,) For how long shall thy journey be? and when wilt thou return? So it pleased the king to send me; and I set him a time.

Throughout Scripture, we see reference to a "set times" in which the Lord works (Exodus 9:5; Psalm 102:13). There's a designated time, a "set time" for the Holy Spirit to work in and through the church, at the end of which, we'll hear the Lord say, "Come up," and we'll go up and go home! (Revelation 11:12).

Nehemiah 2:7
Moreover I said unto the king, If it please the king, let letters be given me to the governors beyond the river, that they may convey me over till I come into Judah;

Nehemiah requested letters of authority in order that he might be protected and given safe passage. In the Word of God, we, too, have letters of authority that will see us through whatever snares the enemy has laid for us.

Nehemiah 2:8 (a)
And a letter unto Asaph the keeper of the king's forest, that he may give me timber to make beams for the gates of the palace which appertained to the house, and for the wall of the city, and for the house that I shall enter into . . .

In verse 5, Nehemiah asked to be sent. In verse 7, he asked to be kept safe. Here in verse 8, he asks to be supplied.

"Why doesn't God use me?" some people ask.

"Hitherto have ye asked nothing in My name," Jesus said (John 16:24).

If you are one who wonders why God isn't using you, have you, like Nehemiah, asked to be sent?

"If He does send me, will I be kept safe? Will I be able to handle it emotionally or physically?" you wonder.

"I'll never leave you nor forsake you," Jesus answers (Hebrews 13:5).

"But I don't have the supplies, the training, or the qualifications," you might say.

Nehemiah lacked the supplies to build the wall. But that didn't stop him. He asked the king for them. And so must we ask our King, who has promised to give us abundantly above all we could ask or even think (Ephesians 3:20).

Nehemiah 2:8 (b)
. . . And the king granted me, according to the good hand of my God upon me.

Nehemiah's quick prayer was indeed a powerful prayer, for the king granted all three of his requests. I find it interesting that in Ezra 8, we read that when Ezra prepared to go to Jerusalem, he determined not to ask the king for anything because the hand of God was upon him. Here, years later, Nehemiah comes on the scene and asks the king for supplies, also because the hand of God was upon him. Who was right? Ezra or Nehemiah? They both were because God uses different personalities to accomplish His perfect purposes.

Peter and John were incredibly different from each other, yet in the Book of Acts, we see them traveling together because their ministries complemented each other. This is so freeing because, rather than judging or criticizing another's flavor of ministry, if there's fruit in their lives, I can praise the Lord for what He's doing through them.

Nehemiah 2:9, 10
Then I came to the governors beyond the river, and gave them the king's letters. Now the king had sent captains of the army and horsemen with me. When Sanballat the Horonite, and Tobiah the servant, the Ammonite, heard of it, it grieved them exceedingly that there was come a man to seek the welfare of the children of Israel.

Hearing that someone was coming to rebuild the wall, the enemies of God's people were exceedingly grieved. This shouldn't be surprising, for any time the Spirit moves in, the enemy will rise up. You can go to the bank on that.

Nehemiah 2:11–13 (a)
So I came to Jerusalem, and was there three days. And I arose in the night, I and some few men with me; neither told I any man what my God had put in my heart to do at Jerusalem: neither was there any beast with me, save the beast that I rode upon. And I went out by night by the gate of the valley, even before the dragon well . . .

Upon arriving in Jerusalem, Nehemiah quietly surveyed the city by night. There are times in our lives when things are dark, when it seems like nothing is happening. In reality, those can be the very times the Lord is surveying the situation, checking out what needs to be done, allowing you to go through a certain period of dryness or darkness because He's about to do something explosive and powerful. If you're in that place, take hope. God hasn't forsaken you. He's simply preparing you.

Nehemiah 2:13 (b), 14 (a)
. . . and to the dung port, and viewed the walls of Jerusalem, which were broken down, and the gates thereof were consumed with fire. Then I went on to the gate of the fountain, and to the king's pool:

The dung gate and the king's pool were both devastated equally because the judgment of God respects no person (Acts 10:34; Matthew 5:45).

Nehemiah 2:14 (b)
. . . but there was no place for the beast that was under me to pass.

There was so much rubble surrounding the wall that Nehemiah's donkey didn't even have a place to put his foot. Thus, the dark of the night was compounded by the obstacles on the ground. Again, if this sounds like your situation, know that the work of reconstruction can't be far behind . . .

Nehemiah 2:15–18
Then went I up in the night by the brook, and viewed the wall, and turned back, and entered by the gate of the valley, and so returned. And the rulers knew not whither I went, or what I did; neither had I as yet told it to the Jews, nor to the priests, nor to the nobles, nor to the rulers, nor to the rest that did the work. Then said I unto them, Ye see the distress that we are in, how Jerusalem lieth waste, and the gates thereof are burned with fire: come, and let us build up the wall of Jerusalem, that we be no more a reproach. Then I told them of the hand of my God which was good upon me; as also the king's words that he had spoken unto me. And they said, Let us rise up and build. So they strengthened their hands for this good work.

After three days, Nehemiah said, "It's time to get busy. There's work to do." There come times when you sense the Spirit of God saying, "You've been a reproach long enough. People aren't seeing My reality through you. You're not worshiping the way you once did because walls have been destroyed, gates have been burned, things are torn up that once were strong." Maybe even now the Lord is calling you to rebuild and restore certain areas in your family, your marriage, your family, or your life.

Nehemiah 2:19 (a)
But when Sanballat the Horonite, and Tobiah the servant, the Ammonite, and Geshem the Arabian, heard it, they laughed us to scorn, and despised us . . .

In verse 10, Sanballat and Tobiah were grieved. Here, they're laughing. Laughter and scorn are often the first response of the enemy to the Lord's work in our lives. "*You* lead a Bible study?" he hisses. "What a joke! *You* share your faith? Who's going to listen to *you?*"

Nehemiah 2:19 (b)
. . . and said, What is this thing that ye do? will ye rebel against the king?

Like Sanballat and Tobiah, the enemy whispers in our ears, "Who do you think you are, wanting a greater work of the Holy Spirit in your life? You're just trying to build your own kingdom."

Nehemiah 2:20
Then answered I them, and said unto them, The God of heaven, he will prosper us; therefore we his servants will arise and build: but ye have no portion, nor right, nor memorial, in Jerusalem.

Rather than cower at Sanballat's laughter and scorn, Nehemiah said to him, "You have no business being here. Therefore, I'm not going to listen to you. We *will* complete this work because God is with us."

God is with us, as well, gang. And He who began a good work in us will bring it to completion and fruition. That's a promise (Philippians 1:6).

---

3 In chapter 3, the work begins. Here, we see a list of the people who worked as well as the locations in which they worked. It's somewhat laborious, and yet there are excellent lessons tucked away in this chapter. Thirty-eight men are listed in eight different locations. They usually worked closest to their own homes—the place any work we do for the kingdom must begin—because if it doesn't work at home, it won't work at all.

Nehemiah 3:1 (a)
Then Eliashib the high priest rose up with his brethren the priests, and they builded the sheep gate; they sanctified it . . .

The sheep gate is where our Christian walk begins as we realize that Jesus is the Lamb who takes away the sin of the world. All we like sheep have truly gone astray, but the Lord has laid upon Him the iniquity of us all (Isaiah 53:6). Even after we're saved, the rebuilding process always begins with a renewed focus on the Lamb, a greater love for Jesus.

Nehemiah 3:1 (b)–3
. . . and set up the doors of it; even unto the tower of Meah they sanctified it, unto the tower of Hananeel. And next unto him builded the men of Jericho. And next to them builded Zaccur the son of Imri. But the fish gate did the sons of Hassenaah build, who also laid the beams thereof, and set up the doors thereof, the locks thereof, and the bars thereof.

Once we see the Lamb of God and become linked to him, the next thing we're called to do is to be workers for Him. At the fish gate, we do just that as we fish for men's souls (Matthew 4:19). Yet, as we share the good news of the Gospel, people ask us questions, which leads us to the next gate . . .

Nehemiah 3:4–6
And next unto them repaired Meremoth the son of Urijah, the son of Koz. And next unto them repaired Meshullam the son of Berechiah, the son of Meshezabeel. And next unto them repaired Zadok the son of Baana. And next unto them the Tekoites repaired; but their nobles put not their necks to the work of their Lord. Moreover the old gate repaired Jehoiada the son of Paseah, and Meshullam the son of Besodeiah; they laid the beams thereof, and set up the doors thereof, and the locks thereof, and the bars thereof.

When questions arise, we are drawn back to the old gate—the solid teachings and doctrines of the Word—in order to get the firm foundation of faith every believer must know in order to be effective in service.

Nehemiah 3:7–13 (a)
And next unto them repaired Melatiah the Gibeonite, and Jadon the Meronothite, the men of Gibeon, and of Mizpah, unto the throne of the governor on this side the river. Next unto him repaired Uzziel the son of Harhaiah, of the goldsmiths. Next unto him also repaired Hananiah the son of one of the apothecaries, and they fortified Jerusalem unto the broad wall. And next unto them repaired Rephaiah the son of Hur, the ruler of the half part of Jerusalem. And next unto them repaired Jedaiah the son of Harumaph, even over against his house. And next unto him repaired Hattush the son of Hashabniah. Malchijah the son of Harim, and Hashub the son of Pahath-moab, repaired the other piece, and the tower of the furnaces. And next unto him repaired Shallum the son of Halohesh, the ruler of the half part of Jerusalem, he and his daughters. The valley gate repaired Hanun, and the inhabitants of Zanoah; they built it, and set up the doors thereof, the locks thereof, and the bars thereof . . .

After being saved, after witnessing and being driven back to studying the Word, we come to the valley gate—times of trial and difficulty—for, as any teacher knows, testing always follows teaching.

"Don't be surprised concerning the fiery trials that come your way," Peter would say (1 Peter 4:12).

"Count it all joy when you fall into various trials because the testing of your faith works patience," James would echo. "But let patience have her perfect work that you may be entire and complete, lacking nothing" (see James 1:2–4).

In other words, praise the Lord for the valley gate.

Nehemiah 3:13 (b)
. . . and a thousand cubits on the wall unto the dung gate.

The dung gate was where refuse was carried out of the city. When we're in the valley, we invariably say things we shouldn't, do things we ought not, have attitudes that are amiss. So we need to go through the "dung gate," to admit our failure and confess our sin. Then, once confession is made, we come to another gate . . .

Nehemiah 3:14, 15
But the dung gate repaired Malchiah the son of Rechab, the ruler of part of Bethhaccerem; he built it, and set up the doors thereof, the locks thereof, and the bars thereof. But the gate of the fountain repaired Shallun the son of Col-hozeh, the ruler of part of Mizpah; he built it, and covered it, and set up the doors thereof, the locks thereof, and the bars thereof, and the wall of the pool of Siloah by the king's garden, and unto the stairs that go down from the city of David.

There comes a point when we say, "Lord, I know You. I want to serve You as a fisherman. I'm in Your Word. I've gone through the valley. I've made confession of sin. But I need more power and life." The fountain gate speaks of this place. To a man, the people of God who have made a lasting impact upon the world have been those who have come to the fountain gate. D.L. Moody was such a one. He came to a point in his ministry where he locked himself in a hotel room, determined not to leave until he had the power of the Holy Ghost upon his life. Three days later, he emerged, and the world hasn't been the same since.

Nehemiah 3:16–26
After him repaired Nehemiah the son of Azbuk, the ruler of the half part of Beth-zur, unto the place over against the sepulchres of David, and to the pool that was made, and unto the house of the mighty. After him repaired the Levites, Rehum the son of Bani. Next unto him repaired Hashabiah, the ruler of the half part of Keilah, in his part. After him repaired their brethren, Bavai the son of Henadad, the ruler of the half part of Keilah. And next to him repaired Ezer the son of Jeshua, the ruler of Mizpah, another piece over against the going up to the armoury at the turning of the wall. After him Baruch the son of Zabbai earnestly repaired the other piece, from the turning of the wall unto the door of the house of Eliashib the high priest. After him repaired Meremoth the son of Urijah the son of Koz another piece, from the door of the house of Eliashib even to the end of the house of Eliashib. And after him repaired the priests, the men of the plain. After him repaired Benjamin and Hashub over against their house. After him repaired Azariah the son of Maaseiah the son of Ananiah by his house. After him repaired Binnui the son of Henadad another piece, from the house of Azariah unto the turning of the wall, even unto the corner. Palal the son of Uzai, over against the turning of the wall, and the tower which lieth out from the king's high house, that was by the court of the prison. After him Pedaiah the son of Parosh. Moreover the Nethinims dwelt in Ophel, unto the place over against the water gate toward the east, and the tower that lieth out.

It was at the water gate that Ezra would proclaim the Word (Nehemiah 8:1). Having gone through the valley of experience and with the fullness of the Spirit upon you, you can share the Word with authority and effectiveness. The power of the Spirit and the path of experience will give unparalleled authority in your sharing.

Nehemiah 3:27, 28
After them the Tekoites repaired another piece, over against the great tower that lieth out, even unto the wall of Ophel. From above the horse gate repaired the priests, every one over against his house.

Revelation 19:14 tells us that when Jesus returns, He'll be accompanied by a company on white horses. Thus, the horse gate speaks of the rapture and return of Jesus.

Nehemiah 3:29
After them repaired Zadok the son of Immer over against his house. After him repaired also Shemaiah the son of Shechaniah, the keeper of the east gate.

It is the east gate through which Jesus will enter in His Second Coming. In 1100 A.D., when the Turks heard the east gate was the gate Jesus would enter, they walled it up and sealed it shut. But in so doing, they inadvertently fulfilled the prophecy of Ezekiel 44 that says the east gate shall be sealed until He returns.

Nehemiah 3:30, 31
After him repaired Hananiah the son of Shelemiah, and Hanun the sixth son of Zalaph, another piece. After him repaired Meshullam the son of Berechiah over against his chamber. After him repaired Malchiah the goldsmith's son unto the place of the Nethinims, and of the merchants, over against the gate Miphkad, and to the going up of the corner.

Miphkad literally means "Judgment." When Jesus comes back, He'll bring judgment with Him. As believers, we will be judged at the bema seat of Christ—not for our sins because they were already judged on the Cross of Calvary—but for that which we have done in service for Him (2 Corinthians 5:10). Unbelievers, however, will appear before the great white throne judgment and will be cast into eternal damnation (Revelation 20:11–15).

Nehemiah 3:32
And between the going up of the corner unto the sheep gate repaired the goldsmiths and the merchants.

Here, we see the sheep gate mentioned once again. Why? Because everything both begins and ends with Jesus, the Lamb of God.

4

Nehemiah 4:1 (a)
But it came to pass, that when Sanballat heard that we builded the wall, he was wroth, and took great indignation . . .

Sanballat's name literally means "thorn in secret." In other words, he was a pain—the Old Testament equivalent of Paul's own thorn in the flesh (2 Corinthians 12:7). A "sanballat" was sent Paul's way to keep him from being puffed up in pride, to keep him in a place of humility and brokenness. I wonder what Sanballat the Lord has sent you. Maybe you look at him as a big pain or at her as a real problem. But could it be that the person who seems to be poking you or breaking your heart is actually allowed by the Lord to cause you to do what we'll see Nehemiah do—to pray? If so, Satan's tactics will backfire because they will draw you closer to the Lord than you otherwise would have been.

Nehemiah 4:1 (b)
. . . and mocked the Jews.

There were plenty of Sanballats in Jesus' day as well. When Jairus' daughter was nearly dead, he asked Jesus to heal her. As they made their way to his house, they found mourners weeping and wailing. Jesus looked at Jairus and said, "Don't believe them. This isn't the end of the story. She's just sleeping." When the people heard this, Matthew tells us they laughed Jesus to scorn (9:24).

Maybe at one time a promise was given to you, something you know the Lord has placed on your heart or a promise in the Word that practically jumped off the page. But now it seems dead. All you hear are voices inside that mock and laugh. You must do what Jesus did, for it wasn't until Jesus sent the mockers packing that resurrection took place. If you have a promise from the Lord that seems dead and hopeless, the Lord would say to you, "Move out the mockers. Send the voices of cynicism and the whispers of doubt packing."

In the early days of Elisha's ministry, there was a group of young men who laughed at him, calling him a baldheaded man. What did Elisha do? He cursed them in the name of the Lord, and they were immediately devoured by bears (2 Kings 2). When doubts come our way in the temple of our spirit, saying, "It's not going to come about. It's too late. You're too old, baldheaded man," send the bears of the Word upon them. Tell them that all things are still working together for good (Romans 8:28). Tell them that God will indeed complete that which He began (Philippians 1:6). Move out the mockers by standing on the Word of God. And then watch resurrection life surge into the promise that He gave you.

Nehemiah 4:2, 3
And he spake before his brethren and the army of Samaria, and said, What do these feeble Jews? will they fortify themselves? will they sacrifice? will they make an end in a day? will they revive the stones out of the heaps of the rubbish which are burned? Now Tobiah the Ammonite was by him, and he said, Even that which they build, if a fox go up, he shall even break down their stone wall.

Just as Sanballat addressed an army, our Adversary has an army of demons. This life is a battleground, gang. That's why we shouldn't be surprised if sometimes we wake up feeling as though tanks had rolled over us. There's a war going on and sometimes we feel the fallout from it.

"Will these feeble Jews fortify themselves?" Sanballat asks. "Will they launch a rebellion against the king from their walled city? Will they really sacrifice once the walls are up, or will they simply live lives of luxury?" Sanballat's questions are the same ones Satan asks us. All of these questions deal with the future, and the Lord doesn't always answer questions that relate to our future because He tells us to "take no thought for the morrow" (Matthew 6:34).

In John 13, we read that it was because Jesus knew from whence He came and where He was going that He was able to wash the disciples' feet. He wasn't concerned about the past or the future. Consequently, He could minister in the present moment. That's always the way it is. Faith takes care of the past because our sins are washed away. Hope secures the future because we know we're going to heaven. That allows us to live in the present.

We are to walk by faith. Faith means we don't know what's ahead or around the next bend. All we need to know is that God is with us right now. You might be having lots of questions and dealing with lots of issues about the future. But the Lord would have you know that He wants to give you peace not that comes *from* your understanding, but that *passes* it (Philippians 4:7) so that you can say, "I trust You, Lord."

Nehemiah 4:4, 5
Hear, O our God; for we are despised: and turn their reproach upon their own head, and give them for a prey in the land of captivity: And cover not their iniquity, and let not their sin be blotted out from before thee: for they have provoked thee to anger before the builders.

Notice that Nehemiah doesn't respond to Sanballat's accusations. Instead, he prays that the accusations would backfire.

Nehemiah 4:6
So built we the wall; and all the wall was joined together unto the half thereof: for the people had a mind to work.

Despite the threats of Sanballat and Tobiah, the people had a mind to work. "For as he thinketh in his heart, so is he," we read in Proverbs 23:7. It was the strength of their mind rather than the strength of their arms that allowed the people to keep their commitment. That is why Paul would instruct the Philippians to "let this mind be in you which was also in Christ Jesus" (2:5).

Nehemiah 4:7, 8
But it came to pass, that when Sanballat, and Tobiah, and the Arabians, and the Ammonites, and the Ashdodites, heard that the walls of Jerusalem were made up, and that the breaches began to be stopped, then they were very wroth, And conspired all of them together to come and to fight against Jerusalem, and to hinder it.

In chapter 2, verse 10, we saw Sanballat and Tobiah. Nine verses later, they were joined by Geshem. Here, the Arabians, Ammonites and the Ashdodites join them—groups that would normally be at odds with each other, but here united in their persecution of the Jews.

Nehemiah 4:9
Nevertheless we made our prayer unto our God, and set a watch against them day and night, because of them.

Nehemiah prayed and the work continued. The Holy Spirit prays for us and the work goes on as our walls are rebuilt and we're changed ever so slowly.

Nehemiah 4:10
And Judah said, The strength of the bearers of burdens is decayed, and there is much rubbish; so that we are not able to build the wall.

Not only are there attacks from without, but there is discouragement within as Judah, the strongest of the tribes, loses heart by looking at the obstacles rather than to God.

The greatest asset we have is Judah or, literally, praise—for, even though we face outward attacks, rubbish underfoot, and internal problems, the Lord wants us to give thanks in everything, to rejoice evermore. Praise is potent and powerful and it ought to lead the way.

I believe that in every man and woman's life there comes a couple of opportunities when life just seems to be overwhelming, unbearable, the rubbish is great, the problems are many. Yet those rare situations are invaluable opportunities for greatness because only then can we say, "In the midst of all this rubble, I'm choosing to praise the Lord."

Nehemiah 4:11
And our adversaries said, They shall not know, neither see, till we come in the midst among them, and slay them, and cause the work to cease.

While Judah is complaining, the enemy swoops in. That's what happens when we complain: the enemy takes advantage of it.

Nehemiah 4:12
And it came to pass, that when the Jews which dwelt by them came, they said unto us ten times, From all places whence ye shall return unto us they will be upon you.

Catch the scene. The Ammonites, Ashdodites, Tobiah, Sanballat and the boys were cursing. Judah is thinking, "We can't finish this wall."

The Jews living outside of Jerusalem were saying, "You guys better give up and come back to us. Forget what you're trying to do. It's not going to work."

In other words, Nehemiah and his coworkers were being hit from every side, from every angle. Ever feel like that? If so, you're in good company!

Nehemiah 4:13, 14
Therefore set I in the lower places behind the wall, and on the higher places, I even set the people after their families with their swords, their spears, and their bows. And I looked, and rose up, and said unto the nobles, and to the rulers, and to the rest of the people, Be not ye afraid of them: remember the Lord, which is great and terrible, and fight for your brethren, your sons, and your daughters, your wives, and your houses.

Nehemiah had two instructions for his beleaguered companions: "The Lord is with you and your families have need of you." And his instructions apply to us no less. We must be in the Word and walk with the Lord, precious people, because our families are directly affected. Your walk is not yours alone. It affects your family directly. How you walk with the Lord will either bring about fruitfulness or frustration within the hearts of those with whom you are linked. That is why we must consistently be in the Word.

Nehemiah 4:15–18 (a)
And it came to pass, when our enemies heard that it was known unto us, and God had brought their counsel to nought, that we returned all of us to the wall, every one

unto his work. And it came to pass from that time forth, that the half of my servants wrought in the work, and the other half of them held both the spears, the shields, and the bows, and the habergeons; and the rulers were behind all the house of Judah. They which builded on the wall, and they that bare burdens, with those that laded, every one with one of his hands wrought in the work, and with the other hand held a weapon. For the builders, every one had his sword girded by his side, and so builded . . .

The wall was built by men who held a brick in one hand and a sword in the other. And that is still the way God's work is accomplished today. The brick speaks of the practical aspect of that which He calls us to do. "I have ordained you, that ye should bear much fruit," Jesus declared (John 15:16). Therefore, even a brick becomes a tool of ministry in the hand of the one who uses it as unto the Lord (Colossians 3:17).

The sword, of course, speaks of the Word (Hebrews 4:12). "Study to show thyself approved unto God," Paul would admonish Timothy, "a workman that needeth not to be ashamed, rightly dividing the word of truth" (2 Timothy 2:15). The man with a brick in one hand, the Word of God in the other, and a mind to work is the man God uses.

Nehemiah 4:18 (b)–20
. . . And he that sounded the trumpet was by me. And I said unto the nobles, and to the rulers, and to the rest of the people, The work is great and large, and we are separated upon the wall, one far from another. In what place therefore ye hear the sound of the trumpet, resort ye thither unto us: our God shall fight for us.

Yes, the work is hard. The sacrifices are great. The enemy's attacks can be intensive and never-ending. But our eyes are upon the Lord and our ears are tuned to His trumpet. In our hands are the Word of God and a brick to accomplish what He's called us to do. We're going to make it. We're going to get through the tasks and calling and projects and opportunities the Lord has given us both individually and corporately because He promised He would complete that which He has begun (Philippians 1:6). It's all based upon His promise, not upon our worthiness.

Nehemiah 4:21–23
So we laboured in the work: and half of them held the spears from the rising of the morning till the stars appeared. Likewise at the same time said I unto the people, Let every one with his servant lodge within Jerusalem, that in the night they may be a guard to us, and labour on the day. So neither I, nor my brethren, nor my servants, nor the men of the guard which followed me, none of us put off our clothes, saving that every one put them off for washing.

So committed to the task before them were Nehemiah and company that they worked on the wall by day and guarded it by night. To do this, they remained clothed day and night, with the exception of the times they took their clothes off to wash them. We must remain robed in His righteousness, shielded by the armor provided for us (Revelation 19:8; Ephesians 6:11).

---

5 It has been said there are basically three kinds of people in the world: those who make things happen, those who watch things happen, and those who wonder what happened. Nehemiah fits in the first category, for he was a man who made things happen. Nehemiah came to Jerusalem to rebuild the walls that had been left in ruin by Nebuchadnezzar. Here in chapter 5, the wall is halfway done. And, although the external opposition seems to be waning, it will be replaced by inward depression.

The same obstacles are still in place today, for whenever you do anything for God, you can expect outward opposition, inward depression, or even a combination of the two. As the chapter unfolds, we see that a shortage of food contributed to the peoples' depression. Three reasons are given for this shortage . . .

Nehemiah 5:1, 2
And there was a great cry of the people and of their wives against their brethren the Jews. For there were that said, We, our sons, and our daughters, are many: therefore we take up corn for them, that we may eat, and live.

"We . . . are many." When Nehemiah and his contingent showed up, thousands of people flooded into the area, causing a population explosion that must surely have taxed the food supply.

Nehemiah 5:3
Some also there were that said, We have mortgaged our lands, vineyards, and houses, that we might buy corn, because of the dearth.

The second reason for a shortage of food was due to a drought in the land.

Nehemiah 5:4
There were also that said, We have borrowed money for the king's tribute, and that upon our lands and vineyards.

The third reason for a shortage of food could have been that, because the people were actively involved in building the wall around Jerusalem in order that they might have protection from the enemy and freedom to worship without anxiety, the crops and fields were not tended to the degree they had been previously.

Nehemiah 5:5
Yet now our flesh is as the flesh of our brethren, our children as their children: and, lo, we bring into bondage our sons and our daughters to be servants, and some of our daughters are brought unto bondage already: neither is it in our power to redeem them; for other men have our lands and vineyards.

Population increase, a dry season, and the work of the ministry caused the people to buy corn at such exorbitant prices that they were forced to mortgage their homes and vineyards and sell their children into virtual slavery.

I believe this passage has something to say to us because we, too, can go through times we feel depressed, stressed, and malnourished. Perhaps it's due to a population explosion. The Lord adds to the church. New people show up on the scene and pretty soon we no longer get the attention we once did. "Whatever happened to just forty of us meeting together?" we lament.

Or maybe it's due to the inevitable dry season that comes into the life of every believer from time to time. Every one of us will go through seasons of drought. The Lord will allow you to be tested in times you don't feel a spiritual "high" in order that He might develop within you a walk based on faith rather than feeling, a faith that is solid as a rock rather than as unstable as a roller coaster.

Or maybe our times of stress and hunger are due to the fact that we're so busy ministering—be it teaching Sunday school, counseling high schoolers, or even directing cars in the church parking lot Sunday mornings—that we're no longer finding time to feed our souls from the Word.

Nehemiah 5:6, 7 (a)
And I was very angry when I heard their cry and these words. Then I consulted with myself . . .

Before he said anything, Nehemiah called a counseling session with himself, just as David did when he "encouraged himself in the Lord" (1 Samuel 30:6).

Nehemiah 5:7 (b), 8
. . . and I rebuked the nobles, and the rulers, and said unto them, Ye exact usury, every one of his brother. And I set a great assembly against them. And I said unto them, We after our ability have redeemed our brethren the Jews, which were sold unto the heathen; and will ye even sell your brethren? or shall they be sold unto us? Then held they their peace, and found nothing to answer.

These men were Jews themselves, yet they exploited the situation at the expense of their own people. When you find yourself in times of stress or drought, there will be those who will seek to exploit the situation, to manipulate your emotions. In fact, in Acts 20, Paul gathered together a group of elders at the church of Ephesus and said, "Know that after I depart, there will arise some from your own midst who will speak perverse things, seeking to draw men after themselves."

Nehemiah 5:9 (a)
Also I said, It is not good that ye do: ought ye not to walk in the fear of our God . . .

The wisest man who ever lived declared that the fear of God is the beginning of wisdom (Proverbs 9:10). Truly, the fear of the Lord is the key to living the Christian life successfully, not being afraid of Him, but being afraid of doing anything that would cause Him grief or disappointment because He's been so good to us, so generous, so merciful.

Nehemiah 5:9 (b)
. . . because of the reproach of the heathen our enemies?

Nehemiah called a meeting and ripped on the leaders that were ripping off their brothers. He gave two reasons why they were wrong. First, it compromised their witness as it gave their enemies reason to reproach them.

Nehemiah 5:10, 11
I likewise, and my brethren, and my servants, might exact of them money and corn: I pray you, let us leave off this usury. Restore, I pray you, to them, even this day, their lands, their vineyards, their oliveyards, and their houses, also the hundredth part of the money, and of the corn, the wine, and the oil, that ye exact of them.

Not only did charging their brothers interest compromise their interest, but it contradicted the Word, for in Leviticus 25, they were specifically told not to charge usury, or interest. In light of this, may we be those who are ever cognizant both of our witness and of the Word as we deal with people around us.

Nehemiah 5:12, 13
Then said they, We will restore them, and will require nothing of them; so will we do as thou sayest. Then I called the priests, and took an oath of them, that they should do according to this promise. Also I shook my lap, and said, So God shake out every man from his house, and from his labour, that performeth not this promise, even thus be he shaken out, and emptied. And all the congregation said, Amen, and praised the LORD. And the people did according to this promise.

After being rebuked by Nehemiah, the leaders promised to return the interest they had taken from the people. But Nehemiah didn't simply rest on their promise. He called for a priest and made them take an oath, swearing in the presence of the priest that they would return the money and cancel the mortgages.

"I will never leave you nor forsake you," Jesus said (see Hebrews 13:5). This means that, as followers of Jesus, we are in the presence of our High Priest continually. Therefore, we must be people whose dealings are those of integrity, whose words are those of honesty.

Nehemiah 5:14–19
Moreover from the time that I was appointed to be their governor in the land of Judah, from the twentieth year even unto the two and thirtieth year of Artaxerxes the king, that is, twelve years, I and my brethren have not eaten the bread of the governor. But the former governors that had been before me were chargeable unto the people, and had taken of them bread and wine, beside forty shekels of silver; yea, even their servants bare rule over the people: but so did not I, because of the fear of God. Yea, also I continued in the work of this wall, neither bought we any land: and all my servants were gathered thither unto the work. Moreover there were at my table an hundred and fifty of the Jews and rulers, beside those that came unto us from among the heathen that are about us. Now that which was prepared for me daily was one ox and six choice sheep; also fowls were prepared for me, and once in ten days store of all sorts of wine: yet for all this required not I the bread of the governor, because the bondage was heavy upon this people. Think upon me, my God, for good, according to all that I have done for this people.

"We do not rule over you, but are helpers of your joy," Paul wrote to the church at Corinth (2 Corinthians 1:24). That is all a leader, pastor, or elder is to do. And Nehemiah modeled this beautifully. He didn't take from the people—he shared with them. He didn't demand they open their wallets for him, but instead opened his home and heart to them.

6

Nehemiah 6:1, 2 (a)
Now it came to pass, when Sanballat, and Tobiah, and Geshem the Arabian, and the rest of our enemies, heard that I had builded the wall, and that there was no breach left therein; (though at that time I had not set up the doors upon the gates;) That Sanballat and Geshem sent unto me . . .

Unable to stop the work on the wall through depression internally, Satan resumes his attack externally. The same is still true. Satan never has a good day, gang. Do you know that? He just keeps pounding and hounding those who undertake any work of faith.

Nehemiah 6:2 (b)
. . . saying, Come, let us meet together in some one of the villages in the plain of Ono. But they thought to do me mischief.

No longer are Sanballat and Tobiah mocking and laughing. Here, they change their tactics and try to persuade Nehemiah to meet with them.

Nehemiah 6:3 (a)
And I sent messengers unto them, saying, I am doing a great work . . .

Notice that Nehemiah didn't say he was doing a great job. Rather, he said, "I'm involved in a great work. You guys thought it was hapless or hopeless. But I see it as holy and glorious."

The "Nehemiah" within us—the Holy Spirit—is doing a great work in us both corporately and individually. Yet, because the enemy wants us to doubt this, we need to learn the lesson of Simeon. The promise had been given to him that he would not die until he saw the Messiah. After waiting all his life for this promise to be fulfilled, the Spirit led him to the temple.

"This is it!" he must have thought. "I will see Messiah at last!"

I'm sure he listened for the sound of chariot wheels and soldiers marching. Surely Messiah would be a military leader who would rescue the Jews from Roman oppression.

But all Simeon heard was a baby's cry.

At that moment, he had a choice to make. He could have thought, "This is what I've been waiting for all my life? A baby? What a waste!"

Instead, he did what I'm challenging us to do. He took the Baby and said, "I bless You, Father. I believe what You are going to do is mighty and massive" (see Luke 2).

I wonder if the Spirit hasn't given you a vision in your mind or a desire in your heart that you know is of Him. When it comes, will you choose to embrace it regardless of how small or weak it initially might seem? Will you, like Simeon, choose to say, "I believe this is the beginning of the fulfillment of what You promised, Lord"?

"Too much rubbish!" some will proclaim.

"It will never last," others will protest.

"Even a fox will knock it down," others will predict.

Will you be the one to say, "No, it's a great work the Lord is doing"? It might not be exactly what you were expecting or what you envisioned, but if you choose to embrace it as from God, you, like Nehemiah, will exhibit the one quality necessary for His work: faith (Hebrews 11:6).

Nehemiah 6:3 (b)
. . . so that I cannot come down: why should the work cease, whilst I leave it, and come down to you?

"Why should I come down to meet with you?" Nehemiah said. And the same question is valid today. The enemy wants to eat up your time in futile meetings or in arguing for hours with people who have no intention of changing their minds. Sanballat wasn't interested in restoration but only in distraction in order to stop God's work any way he could.

Nehemiah 6:4
Yet they sent unto me four times after this sort; and I answered them after the same manner.

Sanballat issued the same invitation four times, and four times Nehemiah refused.

Nehemiah 6:5–7
Then sent Sanballat his servant unto me in like manner the fifth time with an open letter in his hand; Wherein was written, It is reported among the heathen, and Gashmu saith it, that thou and the Jews think to rebel: for which cause thou buildest the wall, that thou mayest be their king, according to these words. And thou hast also appointed prophets to preach of thee at Jerusalem, saying, There is a king in Judah: and now shall it be reported to the king according to these words. Come now therefore, and let us take counsel together.

When negotiation failed, Sanballat resorted to incrimination, sending an open letter accusing Nehemiah of aspiring to be king. Every sister or brother moving out in ministry will face this same accusation from the enemy. "Why are you doing what you're doing?" the accuser of the brethren will hiss. "You just want to be acknowledged as being some spiritual leader. You're only doing this to exalt yourself."

Nehemiah 6:8, 9
Then I sent unto him, saying, There are no such things done as thou sayest, but thou feignest them out of thine own heart. For they all made us afraid, saying, Their hands shall be weakened from the work, that it be not done. Now therefore, O God, strengthen my hands.

After brushing aside Sanballat's accusation, Nehemiah prayed, "Strengthen my hands, Lord. Let me get this job done."

Nehemiah 6:10, 11
Afterward I came unto the house of Shemaiah the son of Delaiah the son of Mehetabeel, who was shut up; and he said, Let us meet together in the house of God, within the temple, and let us shut the doors of the temple: for they will come to slay thee; yea, in the night will they come to slay thee. And I said, Should such a man as I flee? and who is there, that, being as I am, would go into the temple to save his life? I will not go in.

A cloistered, seemingly spiritual man told Nehemiah he should protect himself by taking refuge in the temple. Was Nehemiah being unreasonable in refusing to take his advice? No, he was being unstoppable. How do you stop a guy like Nehemiah? First, the enemy tried negotiation. Next, he tried incrimination. Here, he tries isolation.

Still today, the enemy will try to isolate you. But God desires us to impact the world around us through the work to which He calls us.

Nehemiah 6:12, 13
And, lo, I perceived that God had not sent him; but that he pronounced this prophecy against me: for Tobiah and Sanballat had hired him. Therefore was he hired, that I should be afraid, and do so, and sin, and that they might have matter for an evil report, that they might reproach me.

Nehemiah perceived something was amiss concerning the invitation to isolation, and indeed there was, for Shemaiah was a hireling who had sold out to the enemy.

One of the hardest things about having the gift of discernment is being accused of a lack of love or compassion. However, it's not a matter of love or compassion. It's a matter of listening to the Lord and following His direction.

Nehemiah 6:14
My God, think thou upon Tobiah and Sanballat according to these their works, and on the prophetess Noadiah, and the rest of the prophets, that would have put me in fear.

If people are coming against you and causing fear in your heart, if even seemingly spiritual people are pronouncing judgment against you, questioning your motives, writing letters about you, recognize it for what it is: nothing more than the enemy. The enemy will always seek to stop what God is doing. Follow the example of Nehemiah, and just keep going.

Nehemiah 6:15
So the wall was finished in the twenty and fifth day of the month Elul, in fifty and two days.

The wall was finished. How? The dynamic of God and the determination of man teamed together and saw the work completed.

Nehemiah 6:16–19
And it came to pass, that when all our enemies heard thereof, and all the heathen that were about us saw these things, they were much cast down in their own eyes: for they perceived that this work was wrought of our God. Moreover in those days the nobles of Judah sent many letters unto Tobiah, and the letters of Tobiah came unto them. For there were many in Judah sworn unto him, because he was the son in law of Shechaniah the son of Arah; and his son Johanan had taken the daughter of Meshullam the son of Berechiah. Also they reported his good deeds before me, and uttered my words to him. And Tobiah sent letters to put me in fear.

One thing that cannot be denied is the reality of God's fruitfulness in or through a life. The wall was completed against overwhelming odds. Thus, Sanballat and Tobiah go down in history as fools because they foolishly and arrogantly tried to hinder the work of God. Nehemiah, on the other hand, goes down in history as a great man, not because he was perfect but because he persevered in the calling God had given him.

---

7 **Nehemiah 7:1, 2**
Now it came to pass, when the wall was built, and I had set up the doors, and the porters and the singers and the Levites were appointed, That I gave my brother Hanani, and Hananiah the ruler of the palace, charge over Jerusalem: for he was a faithful man, and feared God above many.

Here, Nehemiah begins delegating responsibility. I find it interesting that Hananiah is described as being both faithful and fearful. At any given moment, I'll either be living in the fear of God or in the fear of man. The fear of man is a snare that will trip you up every time (Proverbs 29:25). The fear of God, on the other hand, is the beginning of wisdom (Proverbs 9:10). The fear of God is to be afraid of doing anything that would grieve the Lord. The fear of God says, "I want to live my life in such a way that I truly acknowledge Your presence with me in every situation, in every conversation."

Nehemiah 7:3, 4
And I said unto them, Let not the gates of Jerusalem be opened until the sun be hot; and while they stand by, let them shut the doors, and bar them: and appoint watches of the inhabitants of Jerusalem, every one in his watch, and every one to be over against his house. Now the city was large and great: but the people were few therein, and the houses were not builded.

Even though the wall was completed, Nehemiah was wise enough to realize that the attacks would continue. Do not be deceived, gang. Not until we get to heaven will there truly be peace. If you're doing anything for God, there will always be some battle, some attempt to ensnare you, to put you down, to stop what you're doing. Our tendency is to think, "If I can just get through this . . ." But when you get through that, there will be something else. Nehemiah understood this.

Nehemiah 7:5–7
And my God put into mine heart to gather together the nobles, and the rulers, and the people, that they might be reckoned by genealogy. And I found a register of the genealogy of them which came up at the first, and found written therein, These are the children of the province, that went up out of the captivity, of those that had been carried

away, whom Nebuchadnezzar the king of Babylon had carried away, and came again to Jerusalem and to Judah, every one unto his city; Who came with Zerubbabel, Jeshua, Nehemiah, Azariah, Raamiah, Nahamani, Mordecai, Bilshan, Mispereth, Bigvai, Nehum, Baanah. The number, I say, of the men of the people of Israel was this;

The genealogy in the remainder of the chapter is the same as the one in the Book of Ezra (2:2). We might think this is a waste of ink and paper, but in repeating their names, it's as if God says, "These are the names of My children who left the comforts of Babylon to make their way back to the holy city in order to worship Me. Their names are remembered, recorded, and repeated because I love them." And if you are a believer, if your name is recorded in the Lamb's Book of Life, He says the same thing about you.

8

Nearly twenty-five centuries ago, a band of battered people faced up to the embarrassing evidence of their inability to rebuild their ruined past. And then came a man who, with patient persistence, abundant supply, and deep compassion taught them to pray. He taught them how to resist the attacks of their adversaries. He taught them to be compassionate and kind toward their brothers who were more unfortunate than they. He led them in rebuilding that which was ruined. And in fifty-two days, the project was completed.

Nehemiah is in this story, but he's also in your story personally for he is a picture of the Holy Spirit who teaches us to pray, who empowers us to overcome the attacks of the devil, who enables us to be compassionate and kind, who works with us and in us to rebuild the ruined parts of our lives, the walls of our soul that lie in rubble and ruin. Don't miss Him in this story. Don't miss Him in your story.

Nehemiah 8:1, 2
And all the people gathered themselves together as one man into the street that was before the water gate; and they spake unto Ezra the scribe to bring the book of the law of Moses, which the LORD had commanded to Israel. And Ezra the priest brought the law before the congregation both of men and women, and all that could hear with understanding, upon the first day of the seventh month.

Water is a symbol of the Word of God. Therefore, it's appropriate that the people gathered at the water gate. "How shall a young man cleanse his way?" the psalmist asked. By taking heed to the Word (see Psalm 119:9).

"Now you are clean through the Word which I have spoken," Jesus declared (John 15:3).

Along with the church at Ephesus, we are washed by the water of the Word (5:26).

According to Deuteronomy 31:11, the law was to be read publicly every seventh year at the Feast of Tabernacles. Evidently hungry for the Word, the people asked Ezra to reinstitute this practice. The first day of the seventh month was the first day of their civil new year. What a great way to bring in a new year, listening to the Word of God.

Nehemiah 8:3–5
And he read therein before the street that was before the water gate from the morning until midday, before the men and the women, and those that could understand; and the ears of all the people were attentive unto the book of the law. And Ezra the scribe stood upon a pulpit of wood, which they had made for the purpose; and beside him stood Mattithiah, and Shema, and Anaiah, and Urijah, and Hilkiah, and Maaseiah, on his right hand; and on his left hand, Pedaiah, and Mishael, and Malchiah, and Hashum, and Hashbadana, Zechariah, and Meshullam. And Ezra opened the book in the sight of all the people; (for he was above all the people;) and when he opened it, all the people stood up:

A pulpit, or scaffold, was constructed that could support Ezra and the thirteen priests who stood by him and that could allow him to be more easily seen and heard by the people.

Nehemiah 8:6 (a)
And Ezra blessed the LORD, the great God. And all the people answered, Amen, Amen, with lifting up their hands . . .

Here, we see a perfect example of the office of priest as being one who speaks to God on behalf of the people and to the people on behalf of God. When the people said "amen" it was more than simply a word of encouragement. It was a word of establishment, for Jesus said that when we agree together on earth, things happen in heaven (Matthew 18:19).

Nehemiah 8:6 (b)
. . . and they bowed their heads, and worshipped the LORD with their faces to the ground.

Worship is not only a happy hallelujah. Sometimes it's a holy hush. Worship is not about how loud we can be. Sometimes, there needs to be a reverential silence. Sometimes, the most intensive times of worship consist not of singing the loudest but of bowing the lowest.

Nehemiah 8:7, 8
Also Jeshua, and Bani, and Sherebiah, Jamin, Akkub, Shabbethai, Hodijah, Maaseiah, Kelita, Azariah, Jozabad, Hanan, Pelaiah, and the Levites, caused the people to understand the law: and the people stood in their place. So they read in the book in the law of God distinctly, and gave the sense, and caused them to understand the reading.

Catch the scene: Ezra is standing on the pulpit, reading by the hour while men linked to him gave the people understanding, answering questions and making application. Reading the Word distinctly and explaining the Word in simplicity are still the great needs of the church today.

Nehemiah 8:9
And Nehemiah, which is the Tirshatha, and Ezra the priest the scribe, and the Levites that taught the people, said unto all the people, This day is holy unto the LORD your God; mourn not, nor weep. For all the people wept, when they heard the words of the law.

Tirshatha refers to Nehemiah's office or position. It is not surprising that the people wept when they heard the words of the Law, for it is the Law that shows us our sin. The Law was given to show us how far we are from what we could and should be in order to drive us to the Lord and to His grace (Galatians 3:24).

Nehemiah 8:10
Then he said unto them, Go your way, eat the fat, and drink the sweet, and send portions unto them for whom nothing is prepared: for this day is holy unto our Lord: neither be ye sorry; for the joy of the LORD is your strength.

The justice of the Law brings sorrow. But the joy of the Lord brings strength. Notice that it's not joy *in* the Lord but the joy *of* the Lord that brings strength. That is, it's not our joy in Him, but His joy over us that is our strength.

> The LORD thy God in the midst of thee is mighty; he will save, he will rejoice over thee with joy; he will rest in his love, he will joy over thee with singing. Zephaniah 3:17

Nehemiah 8:11, 12
So the Levites stilled all the people, saying, Hold your peace, for the day is holy; neither be ye grieved. And all the people went their way to eat, and to drink, and to send portions, and to make great mirth, because they had understood the words that were declared unto them.

Having understood the Word, the people went their way rejoicing.

Nehemiah 8:13–17
And on the second day were gathered together the chief of the fathers of all the people, the priests, and the Levites, unto Ezra the scribe, even to understand the words of the law. And they found written in the law which the LORD had commanded by Moses, that the children of Israel should dwell in booths in the feast of the seventh month: And that they should publish and proclaim in all their cities, and in Jerusalem, saying, Go forth unto the mount, and fetch olive branches, and pine branches, and myrtle branches, and palm branches, and branches of thick trees, to make booths, as it is written. So the people went forth, and brought them, and made themselves booths, every one upon the roof of his house, and in their courts, and in the courts of the house of God, and in the street of the water gate, and in the street of the gate of Ephraim. And all the congregation of them that were come again out of the captivity made booths, and sat under the booths: for since the days of Jeshua the son of Nun unto that day had not the children of Israel done so. And there was very great gladness.

On the second day, following the great preaching service wherein the people were taught for six hours and sent their way rejoicing, the leaders and elders met with Ezra personally and learned that, according to Leviticus 23, once a year they were to celebrate the Feast of Booths, or the Feast of Tabernacles. This was an eight-day festival in which people lived in little huts and remembered the way God had provided for His people during their wilderness wanderings.

If you're in any way interested in ministry, searching the Word is part of your responsibility. Be like these Old Testament leaders and elders. Be like the New Testament saints at Berea (Acts 17:10, 11). Search the Scriptures and find out what needs to be uncovered and reestablished both in your life personally and in the life of the church corporately.

Leviticus 23 tells us there were actually seven feasts and these feasts have significance, not only to the people of God historically, but to us prophetically . . .

The first feast was Passover, It was to be celebrated in the spring, the fourteenth day of Nissan, or our April. The Passover was when the lamb was slain, commemorating how God delivered His people from bondage in Egypt, as well as to portray Jesus, the Lamb of God, who would take away the sin of the world (John 1:29). At the very time the Passover lamb was being slain in the temple, the Son of God, God's holy Lamb would be pinned to the tree of Calvary.

The next feast, the Feast of Unleavened Bread, took place the day after Passover. Leaven is a picture of sin. Jesus, the Lamb of God, was in the tomb the day after Passover, and if there was sin in Him, He would not have risen from the dead, for the wages of sin is nothing other than death (Romans 6:23).

The third feast, the Feast of Firstfruits, took place on the first day of the week after Passover. At the Feast of Firstfruits, the people would offer their firstfruits to the Lord. Jesus rose from the dead on that day as the Firstfruit of many to come, for because He lives, we shall live also.

Fifty days after Passover was the Feast of Pentecost. Among other things, Pentecost was a celebration of the Law being given. When the Law was given, 3,000 people died because of their sin (Exodus 32:28). Conversely, fifty days after Jesus died, when the Holy Spirit came upon the one hundred and twenty in the Upper Room, the church was birthed and 3,000 were saved (Acts 2:41).

The fifth feast was the Feast of Trumpets, which took place on the first day of the seventh month, corresponding with our month of October. One day not too far away, we're going to hear the trump of God and be whisked away in the Rapture (1 Corinthians 15:52).

The sixth feast, Yom Kippur or the Day of Atonement, took place nine days after the Feast of Trumpets. Yom Kippur was a time of sorrow and repentance. So, too, after the church is raptured, the Tribulation will break out on earth and, during that time, the Jewish people will understand to a great degree that Jesus is indeed their Messiah.

The last feast is the one we see here: the Feast of Tabernacles. In Zechariah 14, we read that after the Lord comes and establishes His kingdom on the earth, all people will be invited to celebrate this feast and in so doing say, "Thank You, Lord. You saw us through and brought us home."

Nehemiah 8:18

Also day by day, from the first day unto the last day, he read in the book of the law of God. And they kept the feast seven days; and on the eighth day was a solemn assembly, according unto the manner.

Every day during the seven days of the Feast of Tabernacles, the priests would make their way to the pool of Siloam. There, they would draw water from the pool and pour it out on the temple mount, commemorating how God had supplied water for His people in the wilderness. But on the last day, the solemn assembly day, the priests would go to Siloam and return with empty pitchers, signifying the One who was to come. You see Siloam means "Sent one," and the people knew that One would be coming who would give them refreshment, who would set them free. Thus, when, on the eighth day, the priests would pour out their empty pitchers and quote Isaiah's prophecy that God would pour out His Spirit upon them (Isaiah 44:3, 4), the people would pray that Messiah would come. In John 7, we see the answer to their prayer, for it was on the eighth day of the Feast of Tabernacles that, as the people prayed silently, Jesus declared, "If any man thirst, let him come unto Me and out of his innermost being shall gush forth torrents of living water" (John 7:37, 38). The pitchers would never need to be empty again. And neither do we, for truly Jesus—the fulfillment of every feast, the culmination of every festival—supplies our every need.

9 Through perseverance and faith, Nehemiah saw the completion of the task to which he was called. When the wall was completed, there was a great celebration among the people. They celebrated intensely. Their joy and gladness was obvious to all. They were excited about serving the Lord. They were encouraged in the Lord. Yet here in chapter 9, we see celebration replaced by humiliation. We see feasting turn to fasting. Why? Was it God who was calling for the people to fast rather than feast? Was it God calling for the people to confess rather than celebrate? No. He had told them that it was His *joy* that was their strength (8:10). But the people themselves felt a need for brokenness. And in this there is an important insight.

The Lord calls us to joy. He calls us to experience His grace, to bask in His goodness. But as we do, as we draw close to Him, we're suddenly made aware of how far we are from where we should be. It was when Isaiah saw the Lord high and lifted up that he cried out, "Woe is me. I am a man of unclean lips" (Isaiah 6:5).

It was when Peter realized Jesus was the Son of God that he fell to his knees and said, "Depart from me for I am a sinful man" (Luke 5:8).

So it is when you draw close to the Lord that you are made aware how far you are from where you could be.

Nehemiah 9:1–3
Now in the twenty and fourth day of this month the children of Israel were assembled with fasting, and with sackclothes, and earth upon them. And the seed of Israel separated themselves from all strangers and stood and confessed their sins, and the iniquities of their fathers. And they stood up in their place, and read in the book of the law of the LORD their God one fourth part of the day; and another fourth part they confessed, and worshipped the LORD their God.

In the midst of rejoicing and renewal, the people realized their need for repentance. Sometimes we think that if we confess our sins the Lord will show goodness to us. In reality, however, it's the other way around. It's the goodness of God that leads to repentance (Romans 2:4). Here, after the people celebrated God's grace and rejoiced in His love, confession was the natural result.

Nehemiah 9:4–6
Then stood up upon the stairs, of the Levites, Jeshua, and Bani, Kadmiel, Shebaniah, Bunni, Sherebiah, Bani, and Chenani, and cried with a loud voice unto the LORD their God. Then the Levites, Jeshua, and Kadmiel, Bani, Hashabniah, Sherebiah, Hodijah, Shebaniah, and Pethahiah, said, Stand up and bless the LORD your God for ever and ever: and blessed be thy glorious name, which is exalted above all blessing and praise. Thou, even thou, art LORD alone; thou hast made heaven, the heaven of heavens, with all their host, the earth, and all things that are therein, the seas, and all that is therein, and thou preservest them all; and the host of heaven worshippeth thee.

The passage before us is the longest prayer in the Bible. It is primarily a prayer of reflection, for after acknowledging that the Lord alone is God, His people reflect upon what He has done.

Why is this prayer recorded? I believe it is to teach us the necessity of remembering our own personal history. How long has it been since you've carved out a chunk of time to reflect with the Lord about the things He's done in you, with you, and for you? I am convinced we get shot down, depressed, discouraged, and defeated because we're always looking ahead to the next day or week or month, failing to look back and see what the Lord has already done in our lives.

When the Israelis bought American F-16 fighter jets in the 1980s, they made a simple modification that saved them countless lives: they added a rearview mirror. This allowed them to see their enemies coming. I'm convinced that many of us who should be flying high are shot down because we don't have a rear view mirror on our spiritual plane. We don't see what's behind us. We don't reflect with the Lord upon how He's blessed us, answered our prayers, seen us through over the years. If you want to get blessed and guard yourself against being shot down, spend a couple of hours with the Lord. Look back and see what the Lord has done.

Nehemiah 9:7–16
Thou art the LORD the God, who didst choose Abram, and broughtest him forth out of Ur of the Chaldees, and gavest him the name of Abraham; And foundest his heart faithful before thee, and madest a covenant with him to give the land of the Canaanites, the Hittites, the Amorites, and the Perizzites, and the Jebusites, and the Girgashites, to give it, I say, to his seed, and hast performed thy words; for thou art righteous: And didst see the affliction of our fathers in Egypt, and heardest their cry by the Red sea; And shewedst signs and wonders upon Pharaoh, and on all his servants, and on all the people of his land: for thou knewest that they dealt proudly against them. So didst thou get thee a name, as it is this day. And thou didst divide the sea before them, so that they went through the midst of the sea on the dry land; and their persecutors thou threwest into the deeps, as a stone into the mighty waters. Moreover thou leddest them in the day by a cloudy pillar; and in the night by a pillar of fire, to give them light in the way wherein they should go. Thou camest down also upon mount Sinai, and spakest with them from heaven, and gavest them right judgments, and true laws, good statutes and commandments: And madest known unto them thy holy sabbath, and commandedst them precepts, statutes, and laws, by the hand of Moses thy servant: And gavest them bread from heaven for their hunger, and broughtest forth water for them out of the rock for their thirst, and promisedst them that they should go in to possess the land which thou hadst sworn to give them. But they and our fathers dealt proudly, and hardened their necks, and hearkened not to thy commandments,

In spite of all God's blessings, the children of Israel remained stiff-necked toward Him.

Nehemiah 9:17–26
And refused to obey, neither were mindful of thy wonders that thou didst among them; but hardened their necks, and in their rebellion appointed a captain to return to their bondage: but thou art a God ready to pardon, gracious and merciful, slow to anger, and of great kindness, and forsookest them not. Yea, when they had made them a molten calf, and said, This is thy God that brought thee up out of Egypt, and had wrought great provocations; Yet thou in thy manifold mercies forsookest them not in the wilderness: the pillar of the cloud departed not from them by day, to lead them in the way; neither the pillar of fire by night, to shew them light, and the way wherein they should go. Thou gavest also thy good spirit to instruct them, and withheldest not thy manna from their mouth, and gavest them water for their thirst. Yea, forty years didst thou sustain them in the wilderness, so that they lacked nothing; their clothes waxed not old, and their feet swelled not. Moreover thou gavest them kingdoms and nations, and didst divide them into corners: so they possessed the land of Sihon, and the land of the king of Heshbon, and the land of Og king of Bashan. Their children also multipliedst thou as the stars of heaven, and broughtest them into the land, concerning which thou hadst promised to their fathers, that they should go in to possess it. So the children went in and possessed the land, and thou subduedst before them the inhabitants of the land, the Canaanites, and gavest them into their hands, with their kings, and the people of the land, that they might do with them as they would. And they took strong cities, and a fat land, and possessed houses full of all goods, wells digged, vineyards, and oliveyards, and fruit trees in abundance: so they did eat, and were filled, and became fat, and delighted themselves in thy great goodness. Nevertheless they were disobedient, and rebelled against thee, and cast thy law behind their backs, and slew thy prophets which testified against them to turn them to thee, and they wrought great provocations.

In spite of God's goodness, protection, and provision, His people constantly rebelled against Him.

Nehemiah 9:27–31
Therefore thou deliveredst them into the hand of their enemies, who vexed them: and in the time of their trouble, when they cried unto thee, thou heardest them from heaven; and according to thy manifold mercies thou gavest them saviours, who saved them out of the hand of their enemies. But after they had rest, they did evil again before thee: therefore leftest thou them in the hand of their enemies, so that they had the dominion over them: yet when they returned, and cried unto thee, thou heardest them from heaven; and many times didst thou deliver them according to thy mercies; And testifiedst against them, that thou mightest bring them again unto thy law: yet they dealt proudly, and hearkened not unto thy commandments, but sinned against thy judgments, (which if a man do, he shall live in them;) and withdrew the shoulder, and hardened their neck, and would not hear. Yet many years didst thou forbear them, and testifiedst against them by thy spirit in thy prophets: yet would they not give ear: therefore gavest thou them into the hand of the people of the lands. Nevertheless for thy great mercies' sake thou didst not utterly consume them, nor forsake them; for thou art a gracious and merciful God.

God's provision and protection, His greatness and goodness are contrasted with the peoples' stubbornness.

Nehemiah 9:32, 33
Now therefore, our God, the great, the mighty, and the terrible God, who keepest covenant and mercy, let not all the trouble seem little before thee, that hath come upon us, on our kings, on our princes, and on our priests, and on our prophets, and on our fathers, and on all thy people, since the time of the kings of Assyria unto this day. Howbeit thou art just in all that is brought upon us; for thou hast done right, but we have done wickedly:

"Lord," the people prayed, "in all that we've gone through recently, including the seventy years in captivity and the challenges facing us presently, You've done right, but we've done wrong."

Nehemiah 9:34–37
Neither have our kings, our princes, our priests, nor our fathers, kept thy law, nor hearkened unto thy commandments and thy testimonies, wherewith thou didst testify against them. For they have not served thee in their kingdom, and in thy great goodness that thou gavest them, and in the large and fat land which thou gavest before them, neither turned they from their wicked works. Behold, we are servants this day, and for the

land that thou gavest unto our fathers to eat the fruit thereof and the good thereof, behold, we are servants in it: And it yieldeth much increase unto the kings whom thou hast set over us because of our sins: also they have dominion over our bodies, and over our cattle, at their pleasure, and we are in great distress.

The people acknowledged that, although God was good to them, patient with them, and gracious toward them, they continued to wander off and go astray. They understood that the reason they were carried into captivity and overtaxed and oppressed presently is because that's what it took for God to get their attention.

I love the way this prayer acknowledges God's mercy and grace even in difficulty. Whatever the Lord does is right. He proved this completely, absolutely, and irrefutably on the Cross of Calvary. Whatever doubts or questions you may have, dear saint, know this to be true beyond a shadow of a doubt: whatever God is doing or not doing in your life is exactly right—for so passionate is His love for you that He died in your place.

Nehemiah 9:38
And because of all this we make a sure covenant, and write it; and our princes, Levites, and priests, seal unto it.

After reflecting on what God had done, the people couldn't help but write down a new covenant with Him, a new commitment to Him. I encourage you to keep a spiritual journal, to write down the things God has done for you, the things He has shown to you, and the commitments you're making to Him, for it will be of tremendous value in the days ahead.

10

Nehemiah 10:1
Now those that sealed were, Nehemiah, the Tirshatha, the son of Hachaliah, and Zidkijah,

Verses 1–28 record the names of the twenty-two priests, forty-four chiefs, and others who were so touched by the Lord that they signed on the dotted line of a new covenant with Him.

Nehemiah 10:28
And the rest of the people, the priests, the Levites, the porters, the singers, the Nethinims, and all they that had separated themselves from the people of the lands unto the law of God, their wives, their sons, and their daughters, every one having knowledge, and having understanding;

We now see the four results of rededication and revival, the outworking of what takes place when there is an inward, real revival in our hearts . . .

Nehemiah 10:29 (a)
They clave to their brethren, their nobles . . .

The first result of revival is unification of the brethren. "By your love for one another, all men will know that you are My disciples," Jesus said (see John 13:35). Love is the proof of the pudding. A person can claim to be righteous, spiritual, insightful, and prophetic, but if there's not love, that person is simply blowing hot air (1 Corinthians 13:1–3).

Nehemiah 10:29 (b)
. . . and entered into a curse, and into an oath, to walk in God's law, which was given by Moses the servant of God, and to observe and do all the commandments of the LORD our Lord, and his judgments and his statutes;

The second result of true revival is a renewed dedication to the Word. This shouldn't be surprising because when you're in love, you want to know all you can about the object of your affection. And, because this is God's love letter, when you're in love with Him, you'll find yourself wanting to know His heart and His thoughts through His Word.

Nehemiah 10:30
And that we would not give our daughters unto the people of the land, nor take their daughters for our sons:

The third result of true revival is separation from the world. No longer would God's people marry the heathen people of the land. The same must still be true. We all know people who at one time were doing well, until they became involved with or linked to someone in the world and down they went. How, then, are we to witness to the lost? I'm not suggesting isolation *from* the world, but rather insulation *in* the world, where we determine not to be involved in situations that negatively affect us. For example, if you're spending time with people who don't know Jesus and they're doing better because you're with them, great. But if you find yourself slowly but surely compromising, separate yourself. We must go to where the sinners are, but only if we go as thermostats and not thermometers. Thermometers merely measure temperature. Thermostats, on the other hand, actually change the temperature. Am I radically impacting any given place, or is that given place impacting me and making me cold toward God? That's always the question.

Nehemiah 10:31–39
And if the people of the land bring ware or any victuals on the sabbath day to sell, that we would not buy it of them on the sabbath, or on the holy day: and that we would leave the seventh year, and the exaction of every debt. Also we made ordinances for us, to charge ourselves yearly with the third part of a shekel for the service of the house of our God; For the shewbread, and for the continual meat offering, and for the continual burnt offering, of the sabbaths, of the new moons, for the set feasts, and for the holy things, and for the sin offerings to make an atonement for Israel, and for all the work of the house of our God. And we cast the lots among the priests, the Levites, and the people, for the wood offering, to bring it into the house of our God, after the houses of our fathers, at times appointed year by year, to burn upon the altar of the LORD our God, as it is written in the law: And to bring the firstfruits of our ground, and the firstfruits of all fruit of all trees, year by year, unto the house of the LORD: Also the firstborn of our sons, and of our cattle, as it is written in the law, and the firstlings of our herds and of our flocks, to bring to the house of our God, unto the priests that minister in the house of our God: And that we should bring the firstfruits of our dough, and our offerings, and the fruit of all manner of trees, of wine and of oil, unto the priests, to the chambers of the house of our God; and the tithes of our ground unto the Levites, that the same Levites might have the tithes in all the cities of our tillage. And the priest the son of Aaron shall be with the Levites, when the Levites take tithes: and the Levites shall bring up the tithe of the tithes unto the house of our God, to the chambers, into the treasure house. For the children of Israel and the children of Levi shall bring the offering of the corn, of the new wine, and the oil, unto the chambers, where are the vessels of the sanctuary, and the priests that minister, and the porters, and the singers: and we will not forsake the house of our God.

The fourth result of true revival is seen in a renewed determination to worship. Here, in an act of worship, the people determined that the first of their crops, dough, and cattle would go to the work of the Lord. Why does God want the first of our money, the first of our effort, the first of our time? For one simple reason. It's not that He needs anything we can give. What He wants is our hearts and wherever our treasure is, there our heart is (Luke 12:34). If your treasure is in the stock market, you'll watch the stock market reports every day. If your treasure is in an IRA, you'll keep track of how much you've built up in it. If your treasure is in gold and silver, you'll wonder how those commodities are doing on the world market. But if your treasure is in the things of God, you'll be interested in the things of God. That's why the Lord wants us to give Him the first of our money, the first of our energy, the first of our ability. If I don't give, my treasure, and therefore my heart, will go somewhere else.

11

Nehemiah 11:1
And the rulers of the people dwelt at Jerusalem: the rest of the people also cast lots, to bring one of ten to dwell in Jerusalem the holy city, and nine parts to dwell in other cities.

The wall was completed, but the people were not excited to move into Jerusalem. Why? Maybe it was because they preferred their homes in the suburbs. Maybe it was because the city itself would be crowded. Maybe the rubble still in the city would be a constant reminder to them that much of the city needed to be rebuilt, that their job wasn't yet done.

"Lord, send Your Spirit. Revive us and renew us," we pray. But do we realize that the answer might mean we will have to leave a place of comfort? The Lord desires to rebuild, renew, and fill us. Consequently, this might mean we'll go places we never thought we'd go or do things we never thought we'd do as the Spirit overflows from us.

Here, the people drew straws to determine the one in ten who would move into the city. With approximately 50,000 people in the region, 5,000 would be called upon to make their residence in Jerusalem. They picked straws and one in ten had to go into the city to live. Approximately 50,000 people were in the region. 5,000 would need to make their residence in the holy city.

Nehemiah 11:2, 3
And the people blessed all the men, that willingly offered themselves to dwell at Jerusalem. Now these are the chief of the province that dwelt in Jerusalem: but in the cities of Judah dwelt every one in his possession in their cities, to wit, Israel, the priests, and the Levites, and the Nethinims, and the children of Solomon's servants.

While one out of every ten was drafted to move into the city, others went willingly and were blessed. The same can be true of you. If you desire to be a part of what God is doing, you will be blessed beyond what you can even dream because, truly, God is a debtor to no man.

Nehemiah 11:4 (a)
And at Jerusalem dwelt certain of the children of Judah, and of the children of Benjamin. Of the children of Judah . . .

In verses 4 through 9, we see the names of the leaders of the tribes of Judah and Benjamin who dwelt in Jerusalem. In verses 10 through 18, we see the names of the priests and Levites who settled in Jerusalem. Verse 19 speaks of the gatekeepers; verse 20 again of the priests and Levites. Verse 21 refers to the Nethinims, the people originally of the tribe of Gibeon who served in the temple (Joshua 9:23). Verses 22 and 23 refer to the singers; verse 24 to the king's representative in Jerusalem.

I believe we see the groups of people listed in verses 4 through 23 in the church of Jesus Christ today. You see, geographically, Jerusalem was part of the territory originally ceded to the tribes of Judah and Benjamin. Therefore, those who were of these tribes speak to me of those who have a long heritage in the church. The priests speak of those whose primary service is in the church. The Levites, were scattered throughout the country, teaching people the things of God. Therefore, the Levites speak of those who serve God in the world as teachers and bankers, as schoolteachers and mechanics. The gatekeepers served a very practical purpose and speak to me of the office of deacon, faithful men who meet the practical needs of the body of Christ. The Nethinims speak of those who, although they have no heritage of faith, come to a saving knowledge of the Lord. The singers speak of the highest act all of us can do in the body: worshiping our Lord. And, finally, above all, the king's representative speaks of none other than the Son Himself.

Nehemiah 11:25 (a)
And for the villages, with their fields, some of the children of Judah dwelt at Kirjath-arba, and in the villages thereof . . .

Verses 25 through 36 list the villages and areas where those who worked in the city dwelt. The majority of the people lived in these surrounding suburbs. Notice that the names of villages are given, but not names of people because they chose to stay away from the holy city. The invitation had gone forth to come, but the majority didn't respond. It is the man or woman who chooses to *abide* in Christ rather than merely to call on Him whenever they're in trouble who will be fruitful and useful in the work of the kingdom (John 15:3).

12

Nehemiah 12:1 (a)
Now these are the priests and the Levites that went up with Zerubbabel the son of Shealtiel, and Jeshua . . .

The first twenty-six verses of chapter 12 consist of a list of the priests and the Levites who had returned to Jerusalem with Zerubbabel and Joshua approximately ninety years earlier and whose families were still in the region.

Nehemiah 12:27–29
And at the dedication of the wall of Jerusalem they sought the Levites out of all their places, to bring them to Jerusalem, to keep the dedication with gladness, both with thanksgivings, and with singing, with cymbals, psalteries, and with harps. And the sons of the singers gathered themselves together, both out of the plain country round about Jerusalem, and from the villages of Netophathi; Also from the house of Gilgal, and out of the fields of Geba and Azmaveth: for the singers had builded them villages round about Jerusalem.

Our God is a God of gladness, no question about it! The first miracle Jesus ever did was to inject gladness into a depressing situation when He turned water into wine. Here the dedication of the wall was a celebration marked with gladness, thanksgiving, and song.

Nehemiah 12:30
And the priests and the Levites purified themselves, and purified the people, and the gates, and the wall.

As the singers gathered and the musical instruments were tuned, the priests purified themselves, the people, the gates, and the wall according to the requirements of the Law.

> Then I brought up the princes of Judah upon the wall, and appointed two great companies of them that gave thanks, whereof one went on the right hand upon the wall toward the dung gate: And after them went Hoshaiah, and half of the princes of Judah, And Azariah, Ezra, and Meshullam, Judah, and Benjamin, and Shemaiah, and Jeremiah, And certain of the priests' sons with trumpets; namely, Zechariah the son of Jonathan, the son of Shemaiah, the son of Mattaniah, the son of Michaiah, the

son of Zaccur, the son of Asaph: And his brethren, Shemaiah, and Azarael, Milalai, Gilalai, Maai, Nethaneel, and Judah, Hanani, with the musical instruments of David the man of God, and Ezra the scribe before them. And at the fountain gate, which was over against them, they went up by the stairs of the city of David, at the going up of the wall, above the house of David, even unto the water gate eastward. And the other company of them that gave thanks went over against them, and I after them, and the half of the people upon the wall, from beyond the tower of the furnaces even unto the broad wall; Numbers 12:31–38

Nehemiah divided the people into two companies. One company took their places on the wall. Another went in the opposite direction, going north. Both gave thanks, sang songs, and played instruments. "Even if you finish your wall, if a fox walks on top of it, it will collapse," Tobiah had predicted (see Nehemiah 4:3). How wrong he was, for here we see the wall supporting an entire parade.

Nehemiah 12:39–43
And from above the gate of Ephraim, and above the old gate, and above the fish gate, and the tower of Hananeel, and the tower of Meah, even unto the sheep gate: and they stood still in the prison gate. So stood the two companies of them that gave thanks in the house of God, and I, and the half of the rulers with me: And the priests; Eliakim, Maaseiah, Miniamin, Michaiah, Elioenai, Zechariah, and Hananiah, with trumpets; And Maaseiah, and Shemaiah, and Eleazar, and Uzzi, and Jehohanan, and Malchijah, and Elam, and Ezer. And the singers sang loud, with Jezrahiah their overseer. Also that day they offered great sacrifices, and rejoiced: for God had made them rejoice with great joy: the wives also and the children rejoiced: so that the joy of Jerusalem was heard even afar off.

The joy of Jerusalem was heard. The work of Nehemiah, the comforter, had come to completion. No wonder there was such joy that even from a great distance, one could hear the celebration.

Nehemiah 12:44–47
And at that time were some appointed over the chambers for the treasures, for the offerings, for the firstfruits, and for the tithes, to gather into them out of the fields of the cities the portions of the law for the priests and Levites: for Judah rejoiced for the priests and for the Levites that waited. And both the singers and the porters kept the ward of their God, and the ward of the purification, according to the commandment of David, and of Solomon his son. For in the days of David and Asaph of old there were chief of the singers, and songs of praise and thanksgiving unto God. And all Israel in the days of Zerubbabel, and in the days of Nehemiah, gave the portions of the singers and the porters, every day his portion: and they sanctified holy things unto the Levites; and the Levites sanctified them unto the children of Aaron.

I wish the book ended here because there is dedication, joy, showering the priests and Levites with gifts, and great gladness. Yet, if it ended here, it wouldn't be real. Life doesn't end on a celebration. There are challenges before us. You can have the most fantastic experience in the Lord, you can be blessed by the Lord one day and face a huge challenge the next. In this life, there is always something facing you. So in chapter 13, we see Brother Nehemiah face to face with a series of problems . . .

13

Nehemiah 13:1–3
On that day they read in the book of Moses in the audience of the people; and therein was found written, that the Ammonite and the Moabite should not come into the congregation of God for ever; Because they met not the children of Israel with bread and with water, but hired Balaam against them, that he should curse them: howbeit our God turned the curse into a blessing. Now it came to pass, when they had heard the law, that they separated from Israel all the mixed multitude.

Reading the Law, the Jews realized that the Ammonites and Moabites were not to be a part of their congregation, so they sent them on their way.

Nehemiah 13:4
And before this, Eliashib the priest, having the oversight of the chamber of the house of our God, was allied unto Tobiah:

Through marriage, the priest was allied to Tobiah. Tobiah was an Ammonite.

Nehemiah 13:5, 6
And he had prepared for him a great chamber, where aforetime they laid the meat offerings, the frankincense, and the vessels, and the tithes of the corn, the new wine, and

the oil, which was commanded to be given to the Levites, and the singers, and the porters; and the offerings of the priests. But in all this time was not I at Jerusalem: for in the two and thirtieth year of Artaxerxes king of Babylon came I unto the king, and after certain days obtained I leave of the king:

Nehemiah was on a leave of absence. As promised, he had returned to Babylon to talk to the king (2:6). In his absence, Eliashib, the priest, had given Tobiah a room in the temple. And we can find ourselves doing the same thing. That is, we experience renewal, excitement, and revival, and then slowly but surely, we find ourselves compromising, returning to our old ways, making room for sin.

Nehemiah 13:7, 8
And I came to Jerusalem, and understood of the evil that Eliashib did for Tobiah, in preparing him a chamber in the courts of the house of God. And it grieved me sore: therefore I cast forth all the household stuff of Tobiah out of the chamber.

Like Nehemiah, the Holy Spirit comes on the scene of our lives to convict us and save us from disaster.

Nehemiah 13:9
Then I commanded, and they cleansed the chambers: and thither brought I again the vessels of the house of God, with the meat offering and the frankincense.

Notice that Nehemiah didn't pray about this. He simply said, "This is wrong. We're neither going to compromise with Tobiah nor seek to control him." We are not to try to win victory over sin or compromise with sin." As Ephesians 4:22 says, we are simply to cast it off.

Nehemiah 13:10–13
And I perceived that the portions of the Levites had not been given them: for the Levites and the singers, that did the work, were fled every one to his field. Then contended I with the rulers, and said, Why is the house of God forsaken? And I gathered them together, and set them in their place. Then brought all Judah the tithe of the corn and the new wine and the oil unto the treasuries. And I made treasurers over the treasuries, Shelemiah the priest, and Zadok the scribe, and of the Levites, Pedaiah: and next to them was Hanan the son of Zaccur, the son of Mattaniah: for they were counted faithful, and their office was to distribute unto their brethren.

In response to Nehemiah's question, the people loosened their purse strings so that the Levites could return to do the work they were called to do.

Nehemiah 13:14
Remember me, O my God, concerning this, and wipe not out my good deeds that I have done for the house of my God, and for the offices thereof.

After dealing with the compromise and negligence of the people, here Nehemiah prays. "I thought we were to pray first," you might say. We absolutely are. But there are certain situations we need to deal with suddenly and decisively. When my daughter, Christy, was a toddler, if she walked into the street, it wouldn't have been God's will that I should have fallen to my knees, saying, "Father, be with Christy." No, His will was that I grab her! So, too, there come times in our lives when we must deal with sin and evil quickly and radically. I think far too much gets by in our Christian life because we are reluctant or reticent to move with authority.

Nehemiah 13:15, 16
In those days saw I in Judah some treading wine presses on the sabbath, and bringing in sheaves, and lading asses; as also wine, grapes, and figs, and all manner of burdens, which they brought into Jerusalem on the sabbath day: and I testified against them in the day wherein they sold victuals. There dwelt men of Tyre also therein, which brought fish, and all manner of ware, and sold on the sabbath unto the children of Judah, and in Jerusalem.

The people had broken the promise they had made previously (10:31). They had violated the covenant by selling and working on the Sabbath.

Nehemiah 13:17–20
Then I contended with the nobles of Judah, and said unto them, What evil thing is this that ye do, and profane the sabbath day? Did not your fathers thus, and did not our God bring all this evil upon us, and upon this city? yet ye bring more wrath upon Israel by profaning the Sabbath. And it came to pass, that when the gates of Jerusalem began to be dark before the sabbath, I commanded that the gates should be shut, and charged that they should not be opened till after the sabbath: and some of my servants set I at the gates, that there should no burden be brought in on the sabbath day. So the

merchants and sellers of all kind of ware lodged without Jerusalem once or twice.

Nehemiah ordered that the gates of Jerusalem be shut before the Sabbath in order to keep it from being violated by the buying and selling of merchandise.

Nehemiah 13:21
Then I testified against them, and said unto them, Why lodge ye about the wall? if ye do so again, I will lay hands on you. From that time forth came they no more on the sabbath.

When the merchants set up camp right outside the city wall, Nehemiah addressed them as well because it wasn't only what went on in the city, but what was taking place around the city that concerned him. We have an obligation concerning not only that which goes on within our own soul, but outside of the walls. It's not just about me feeling good in my own walk with the Lord, but about helping others outside of myself to do better, to walk more closely to Him.

Nehemiah 13:22 (a)
And I commanded the Levites that they should cleanse themselves, and that they should come and keep the gates, to sanctify the sabbath day . . .

After dealing with the problem directly, Nehemiah delegated the care of it to the Levites.

Nehemiah 13:22 (b)
. . . Remember me, O my God, concerning this also, and spare me according to the greatness of thy mercy.

As he moves from one fire to another, dealing with situations, doing what's needed Nehemiah prays as if to say, "If I'm doing wrong, forgive me, Lord. You know my heart. I'm trying to see Your work carried out."

Nehemiah 13:23, 24
In those days also saw I Jews that had married wives of Ashdod, of Ammon, and of Moab: And their children spake half in the speech of Ashdod, and could not speak in the Jews' language, but according to the language of each people.

When you marry someone who doesn't love the Lord at least as much as you do, your kids will speak a language that will ultimately grieve you. One day, the way they think will break your heart.

Nehemiah 13:25–27
And I contended with them, and cursed them, and smote certain of them, and plucked off their hair, and made them swear by God, saying, Ye shall not give your daughters unto their sons, nor take their daughters unto your sons, or for yourselves. Did not Solomon king of Israel sin by these things? yet among many nations was there no king like him, who was beloved of his God, and God made him king over all Israel: nevertheless even him did outlandish women cause to sin. Shall we then hearken unto you to do all this great evil, to transgress against our God in marrying strange wives?

When Nehemiah saw that the people of God had married the heathens surrounding them, he pulled the hair of some of them to make his point. Interestingly, when Ezra saw this same situation, he didn't pull the hair of the people, but pulled the hair of his own beard (Ezra 9:3). I call this to your attention to remind you that leadership works out differently in different individuals. God puts different personalities in us to work out different kinds of influences through us. This is so freeing. You can be so patient with people, so generous, so giving if you realize we're all made and used differently. Thus, I respect Nehemiah for his authority and Ezra for his humility.

Nehemiah 13:28
And one of the sons of Joiada, the son of Eliashib the high priest, was son in law to Sanballat the Horonite: therefore I chased him from me.

Joiada, the son of the high priest, had married Sanballat's daughter. Considering the grief Sanballat had brought the people of God, it is no wonder Nehemiah responded the way he did.

Nehemiah 13:29–31
Remember them, O my God, because they have defiled the priesthood, and the covenant of the priesthood, and of the Levites. Thus cleansed I them from all strangers, and appointed the wards of the priests and the Levites, every one in his business; And for the wood offering, at times appointed, and for the firstfruits. Remember me, O my God, for good.

After dealing with the sinful situations before him, in Nehemiah's prayer, I hear the words of humility, as if he's saying, "Don't give up on me, Lord." No wonder Nehemiah is remembered throughout eternity as a wonderful example of solid biblical leadership.

ESTHER

Background to Esther

Written in approximately 485 B.C., the Book of Esther falls chronologically between the Books of Ezra and Nehemiah, following the seventy-year period the Jews were held captive in Babylon. When the Jews were first carried into captivity, they asked, "How can we sing the Lord's song in a strange land?" (Psalm 137:4). But as the years progressed, apparently they gave up singing the Lord's song altogether, for when they were given the opportunity to return to their homeland, only 60,000 of two million returned. Why? They had evidently grown comfortable in the Babylonian empire. They had built houses. They had established businesses. They had learned to sing the song of Babylon.

This is most likely the reason there is no mention of God in the Book of Esther. Indeed, there is no mention of heaven, hell, prayer, or faith, either. Does this mean God wasn't on the scene? No. Esther is the story of the providence of God, the faithfulness of our Father even in light of the faithlessness of His people. Even though His people are faithless, He still cares about them passionately and is committed to them unquestionably.

One of the reasons I love this book so much is because there are times when I, too, feel faithless and weak. And yet, even when I am faithless, God is faithful (2 Timothy 2:13). Even when we relegate Him to the backstage of our lives, He is still there, behind the scenes, for He has promised never to leave or forsake us (Hebrews 13:5).

God is the unseen Rudder of the ship of state here in this glorious Book of Esther, not seen, yet still very much in control. We begin in the city of Shushan, the capital of Persia . . .

ESTHER

1 **Esther 1:1 (a)**
Now it came to pass in the days of Ahasuerus . . .

Ahasuerus is not a name but a title, like Caesar, Emperor, or King. This king's name is Xerxes.

Esther 1:1 (b)–3
. . . (this is Ahasuerus which reigned, from India even unto Ethiopia, over an hundred and seven and twenty provinces:) That in those days, when the king Ahasuerus sat on the throne of his kingdom, which was in Shushan the palace, In the third year of his reign, he made a feast unto all his princes

and his servants; the power of Persia and Media, the nobles and princes of the provinces, being before him:

Xerxes is ready to mount the greatest military invasion in world history. He had gathered two million men from his empire to invade Greece. He would prove to be successful in this invasion, but it would take a great toll on his army and virtually destroy his navy. He would eventually be stopped at Thalmus, where a great upset took place. Had Xerxes been completely successful, world history would be radically different.

Esther 1:4
When he shewed the riches of his glorious kingdom and the honour of his excellent majesty many days, even an hundred and fourscore days.

For one hundred and eighty days, Xerxes threw a party to gain support for his upcoming invasion by building a coalition of leaders from all over the empire.

Esther 1:5, 6
And when these days were expired, the king made a feast unto all the people that were present in Shushan the palace, both unto great and small, seven days, in the court of the garden of the king's palace; Where were white, green, and blue, hangings, fastened with cords of fine linen and purple to silver rings and pillars of marble: the beds were of gold and silver, upon a pavement of red, and blue, and white, and black, marble.

The party was eventually opened to include all of the people to come and join. There were hangings of beautiful colors and beds to lodge the guests.

Esther 1:7–11
And they gave them drink in vessels of gold, (the vessels being diverse one from another,) and royal wine in abundance, according to the state of the king. And the drinking was according to the law; none did compel: for so the king had appointed to all the officers of his house, that they should do according to every man's pleasure. Also Vashti the queen made a feast for the women in the royal house which belonged to king Ahasuerus. On the seventh day, when the heart of the king was merry with wine, he commanded Mehuman, Biztha, Harbona, Bigtha, and Abagtha, Zethar, and Carcas, the seven chamberlains that served in the presence of Ahasuerus the king, To bring Vashti the queen before the king with the crown royal, to shew the people and the princes her beauty: for she was fair to look on.

In the middle of Xerxes' party, he ordered his queen, *Vashti*, whose name means "beauty," to appear. This command implied immorality, for at the very least she was to unveil her face, which was taboo. The only logical explanation for Xerxes' command is that he had been drinking. Drink is often a catalyst for carnality. One man wisely said, "When wine enters, wisdom exists." How many stories we could tell of people who found themselves in compromising situations that would never have occurred had alcohol not been present.

Esther 1:12
But the queen Vashti refused to come at the king's commandment by his chamberlains: therefore was the king very wroth, and his anger burned in him.

Vashti's refusal to come was a radical move, for in that day a woman didn't say no to her husband, let alone to the king.

Esther 1:13–18
Then the king said to the wise men, which knew the times, (for so was the king's manner toward all that knew law and judgment: And the next unto him was Carshena, Shethar, Admatha, Tarshish, Meres, Marsena, and Memucan, the seven princes of Persia and Media, which saw the king's face, and which sat the first in the kingdom;) What shall we do unto the queen Vashti according to law, because she hath not performed the commandment of the king Ahasuerus by the chamberlains? And Memucan answered before the king and the princes, Vashti the queen hath not done wrong to the king only, but also to all the princes, and to all the people that are in all the provinces of the king Ahasuerus. For this deed of the queen shall come abroad unto all women, so that they shall despise their husbands in their eyes, when it shall be reported, The king Ahasuerus commanded Vashti the queen to be brought in before him, but she came not. Likewise shall the ladies of Persia and Media say this day unto all the king's princes, which have heard of the deed of the queen. Thus shall there arise too much contempt and wrath.

"We're in trouble now," the princes said to Xerxes. "When word gets out that Vashti disobeyed you, how will we handle our own wives?"

Esther 1:19–22
If it please the king, let there go a royal commandment from him, and let it be writ-

ten among the laws of the Persians and the Medes, that it be not altered, That Vashti come no more before king Ahasuerus; and let the king give her royal estate unto another that is better than she. And when the king's decree which he shall make shall be published throughout all his empire, (for it is great,) all the wives shall give to their husbands honour, both to great and small. And the saying pleased the king and the princes; and the king did according to the word of Memucan: For he sent letters into all the king's provinces, into every province according to the writing thereof, and to every people after their language, that every man should bear rule in his own house, and that it should be published according to the language of every people.

For her insubordination, Vashti would no longer be queen. When this decree was published throughout the empire, the princes were sure that no wife would dare disobey her husband.

Letters went out—the law of the Medes and Persians—which was irrevocable that every wife must totally submit to her husband in every situation. Wives are to submit to their husbands, and yet your submission to your husband is always secondary to your submission to the Word of the Lord.

2

Esther 2:1
After these things, when the wrath of king Ahasuerus was appeased, he remembered Vashti, and what she had done, and what was decreed against her.

There's a three-year gap between chapters 1 and 2, during which time Xerxes launched his invasion. He returned a battered, beaten man without even a wife to console him.

Esther 2:2–4
Then said the king's servants that ministered unto him, Let there be fair young virgins sought for the king: And let the king appoint officers in all the provinces of his kingdom, that they may gather together all the fair young virgins unto Shushan the palace, to the house of the women unto the custody of Hege the king's chamberlain, keeper of the women; and let their things for purification be given them: And let the maiden which pleaseth the king be queen instead of Vashti. And the thing pleased the king; and he did so.

It was decided that there was to be a beauty contest to find a new queen.

Esther 2:5
Now in Shushan the palace there was a certain Jew, whose name was Mordecai, the son of Jair, the son of Shimei, the son of Kish, a Benjamite;

Mordecai means "little man," but this particular little man would prove to be of giant stature in the history of God's people.

Esther 2:6, 7
Who had been carried away from Jerusalem with the captivity which had been carried away with Jeconiah king of Judah, whom Nebuchadnezzar the king of Babylon had carried away. And he brought up Hadassah, that is, Esther, his uncle's daughter: for she had neither father nor mother, and the maid was fair and beautiful; whom Mordecai, when her father and mother were dead, took for his own daughter.

Hadassah means "myrtle tree." Hadassah's name was changed to Esther, which means "star" This beautiful star, Esther, was raised by her older cousin after her parents died. Her beauty was legendary.

Esther 2:8
So it came to pass, when the king's commandment and his decree was heard, and when many maidens were gathered together unto Shushan the palace, to the custody of Hegai, that Esther was brought also unto the king's house, to the custody of Hegai, keeper of the women.

According to Josephus and tradition, Mordecai was determined to hide Esther. But this was impossible because her beauty was so well known.

Esther 2:9
And the maiden pleased him, and she obtained kindness of him; and he speedily gave her her things for purification, with such things as belonged to her, and seven maidens, which were meet to be given her, out of the king's house: and he preferred her and her maids unto the best place of the house of the women.

Why did Heger, the keeper of the women, favor Esther? Because God was working behind the scenes, controlling the situation.

Esther 2:10
Esther had not shewed her people nor her kindred: for Mordecai had charged her that she should not shew it.

Per Mordecai's instruction, Esther didn't reveal that she was Jew.

Esther 2:11
And Mordecai walked every day before the court of the women's house, to know how Esther did, and what should become of her.

Mordecai followed Esther's progress day by day. More importantly, so did the Lord.

Esther 2:12 (a)
Now when every maid's turn was come to go in to king Ahasuerus, after that she had been twelve months, according to the manner of the women, (for so were the days of their purifications accomplished . . .

The women spent twelve months preparing themselves in order to make a good impression on the king. Do we do the same for our King?

Esther 2:12 (b)
. . . to wit, six months with oil of myrrh . . .

Used in the embalming process, myrrh speaks of death. It was one of the gifts brought to Jesus by the wisemen because it spoke prophetically of the fact that He would die in order to fulfill God's grand plan of redemption.

How willing are we to saturate ourselves with the oil of myrrh, to die to ourselves, to lose our own lives in order to find our lives in our King?

Esther 2:12 (c)
. . . and six months with sweet odours, and with other things for the purifying of the women;)

The sweet odors, or spices, speak of a pleasant fragrance. Throughout Scripture, that which the Lord finds to be a sweet savour is always associated with sacrifice (see Genesis 8:21; Exodus 29:25; Leviticus 1:9). How can we present a sweet savour to the Lord? By placing our flesh, our self, our ambitions, our own agenda, on the altar. How many of us can truly say that our passion and our priority is not to be used *by* the Lord, but simply to be a sweet-smelling fragrance *to* Him?

When God gave Moses the dimensions of the tabernacle as the place to worship Him and fellowship with Him, I'm sure Moses thought he wasn't hearing right. One hundred fifty feet by seventy-five feet for three million people? Surely they wouldn't fit. But the Lord knew that a building that size would be sufficient for the number of people who would sacrifice of their time and energy to make Him a priority in their lives. The most important ministry of all is not ministry *for* the Lord, but ministry *to* Him, and it's one we all can do.

Esther 2:13, 14
Then thus came every maiden unto the king; whatsoever she desired was given her to go with her out of the house of the women unto the king's house. In the evening she went, and on the morrow she returned into the second house of the women, to the custody of Shaashgaz, the king's chamberlain, which kept the concubines: she came in unto the king no more, except the king delighted in her, and that she were called by name.

After twelve months of a beauty treatment of oils and perfume, the women would appear before the king one at a time. The one who pleased him would be the new queen.

Esther 2:15, 16
Now when the turn of Esther, the daughter of Abihail the uncle of Mordecai, who had taken her for his daughter, was come to go in unto the king, she required nothing but what Hegai the king's chamberlain, the keeper of the women, appointed. And Esther obtained favour in the sight of all them that looked upon her. So Esther was taken unto king Ahasuerus into his house royal in the tenth month, which is the month Tebeth, in the seventh year of his reign.

Esther won the beauty contest.

Esther 2:17, 18
And the king loved Esther above all the women, and she obtained grace and favour in his sight more than all the virgins; so that he set the royal crown upon her head, and made her queen instead of Vashti. Then the king made a great feast unto all his princes and his servants, even Esther's feast; and he made a release to the provinces, and gave gifts, according to the state of the king.

Esther was chosen as queen because God was working in the shadows, not seen directly, but controlling the situation absolutely.

Esther 2:19–21
And when the virgins were gathered together the second time, then Mordecai sat in the king's gate. Esther had not yet shewed her kindred nor her people; as Mordecai had charged her: for Esther did the commandment of Mordecai, like as when she was brought up with him. In those days,

while Mordecai sat in the king's gate, two of the king's chamberlains, Bigthan and Teresh, of those which kept the door, were wroth, and sought to lay hand on the king Ahasuerus.

In his continued effort to watch over his niece, Mordecai overheard an assassination plot against Ahasuerus. I suggest this is no more a coincidence than Paul's nephew hearing of the attempt of a band of Jews to take Paul's life (Acts 23). God had bigger plans for Paul so He spared his life through his nephew. God had big plans for His people, so, as we will see, He spared their lives through Mordecai.

Esther 2:22, 23
And the thing was known to Mordecai, who told it unto Esther the queen; and Esther certified the king thereof in Mordecai's name. And when inquisition was made of the matter, it was found out; therefore they were both hanged on a tree: and it was written in the book of the chronicles before the king.

Mordecai reported the assassination plot. Yet, although the culprits were hung, Mordecai wasn't rewarded or even acknowledged. Maybe he thought, "What a gyp. Here I do something wonderful, something noble, and I don't get any thanks. God must surely have forgotten me." If he did indeed think this, it was only because he couldn't have foreseen God's impeccably perfect timing.

3 Esther 3:1
After these things did king Ahasuerus promote Haman the son of Hammedatha the Agagite, and advanced him, and set his seat above all the princes that were with him.

Esther is now queen. Mordecai has rescued the king's life. And now another thread is woven into the fabric of this story, for it is in chapter 3 that Haman, the Hitler of the Old Testament, appears. Haman was a descendent of Agag, king of the Amalekites. The Amalekites were always warring against the Israelites and represent the flesh that continually wars against our souls. The Lord told Saul to destroy every single one because the flesh must be destroyed unequivocally. Saul killed most of them, but we read in 1 Samuel 15 that he spared Agag. "What damage can one Amalekite do?" Saul must have reasoned. Enter Haman, the result of a failure to deal decisively with the flesh.

Oh, Lord, You don't mean for me to give up every one of those sins, do You? I can save one Agag, can't I? Lord, isn't that kind of legalistic, kind of stringent? Let's be reasonable."

"They that are Christ's have crucified the flesh with the affections and lusts," Paul said to the Galatians (5:24).

"Reckon yourselves to be dead unto sin," he instructed the Romans (6:11).

We follow Paul's admonitions—sometimes. But there's that one thing, that one activity, that one person we think isn't that big a deal. Our Father, however, wants every aspect of the flesh destroyed not because He's legalistic but because He sees the Hamans that will inevitably come, bringing much harm and sorrow with them.

Esther 3:2–6
And all the king's servants, that were in the king's gate, bowed, and reverenced Haman: for the king had so commanded concerning him. But Mordecai bowed not, nor did him reverence. Then the king's servants, which were in the king's gate, said unto Mordecai, Why transgressest thou the king's commandment? Now it came to pass, when they spake daily unto him, and he hearkened not unto them, that they told Haman, to see whether Mordecai's matters would stand: for he had told them that he was a Jew. And when Haman saw that Mordecai bowed not, nor did him reverence, then was Haman full of wrath. And he thought scorn to lay hands on Mordecai alone; for they had shewed him the people of Mordecai: wherefore Haman sought to destroy all the Jews that were throughout the whole kingdom of Ahasuerus, even the people of Mordecai.

Haman's got everything going for him, but there's one Jew who won't bow to him. Incensed, he becomes obsessed with destroying not only Mordecai, but all of the Jews.

Esther 3:7
In the first month, that is, the month Nisan, in the twelfth year of king Ahasuerus, they cast Pur, that is, the lot, before Haman from day to day, and from month to month, to the twelfth month, that is, the month Adar.

By "drawing straws," the day the Jews would be annihilated was determined, a day in the month equivalent to our March.

Esther 3:8, 9
And Haman said unto king Ahasuerus, There is a certain people scattered abroad and dispersed among the people in all the provinces of thy kingdom; and their laws

are diverse from all people; neither keep they the king's laws: therefore it is not for the king's profit to suffer them. If it please the king, let it be written that they may be destroyed: and I will pay ten thousand talents of silver to the hands of those that have the charge of the business, to bring it into the king's treasuries.

Ten thousand talents of silver is equivalent to thirty million dollars. Where would Haman get this money? No doubt from the spoils of the Jews themselves (3:13), which shows how successful they had become in Babylon.

Esther 3:10, 11
And the king took his ring from his hand, and gave it unto Haman the son of Hammedatha the Agagite, the Jews' enemy. And the king said unto Haman, The silver is given to thee, the people also, to do with them as it seemeth good to thee.

Throughout history, there has been a concerted effort to destroy God's people. Pharaoh tried to annihilate them in Egypt. Haman tried to annihilate them in Persia. Herod tried to annihilate them in the days of Christ. Hitler tried to annihilate them in our own day. Why? After failing to destroy the nation that was to give birth to Christ when He came as a babe to Bethlehem, is Satan now attempting to destroy the place where He will rule in His Second Coming? I believe so. I believe if a skeptic truly studies Jewish history, he'll become a believer, for not only will he see the repeated attempts to destroy God's people, but also His miraculous power to preserve them.

Esther 3:12–14
Then were the king's scribes called on the thirteenth day of the first month, and there was written according to all that Haman had commanded unto the king's lieutenants, and to the governors that were over every province, and to the rulers of every people of every province according to the writing thereof, and to every people after their language; in the name of king Ahasuerus was it written, and sealed with the king's ring. And the letters were sent by posts into all the king's provinces, to destroy, to kill, and to cause to perish, all Jews, both young and old, little children and women, in one day, even upon the thirteenth day of the twelfth month, which is the month Adar, and to take the spoil of them for a prey. The copy of the writing for a commandment to be given in every province was published unto all people, that they should be ready against that day.

March thirteenth was to be the day of annihilation.

Esther 3:15 (a)
The posts went out, being hastened by the king's commandment, and the decree was given in Shushan the palace. And the king and Haman sat down to drink . . .

The order to destroy the Jews having been sent, the king and Haman sat down to drink, which is where the problems began in the first place (1:7–12).

Esther 3:15 (b)
. . . but the city Shushan was perplexed.

It is little wonder that the entire city was perplexed. The Jews who didn't go to Jerusalem when they had the opportunity realized they were destined for destruction. Even the Persians in the city would have been fearful of armed mobs with license to not only kill but to keep the spoils for themselves.

God, however, was neither perplexed nor afraid. He was still on the throne, still in complete control. The Jews in Shushan wouldn't hear His prophets like the Jews in Jerusalem would. They wouldn't celebrate feasts like those in Jerusalem would. They wouldn't experience the glory and joy at the completion of the wall or temple. But even though they would miss out on those glorious events, God would not turn His back on even His weak-faithed children.

"Oh, no! I'm not going to make it," we cry.

God, however, says, "I'm in control. I know your frame, that you are dust (Psalm 103:14). And even when you're faltering and lacking faith, I will never turn My back on you. I will never leave or forsake you. I will be at work providing and protecting in ways that will simply amaze you."

As Esther's story continues, we will see the faithfulness of God breaking through—how good He will be to these Jews in Babylon, and how good He is to you and me, too.

4 Seventeen years before the story before us began, the Jews were given a golden opportunity by king Cyrus when he told them they were free to return to Jerusalem to rebuild the temple, restore the worship, and renew the nation. And yet amazingly only a handful of the Jews took up the offer to step up and move out. Although approximately 60,000 responded to the offer, the rest, millions of Jews, stayed in Babylon.

Why?

Perhaps some stayed because of fear and anxiety about leaving the homes they had lived in for seventy years. Others may have been overcome by lethargy at the thought of rebuilding the city. But for most, it was no doubt a question of prosperity. To leave that behind didn't make sense to the overwhelming majority.

Even so, God didn't forsake them.

> Can a woman forget her sucking child, that she should not have compassion on the son of her womb? yea, they may forget, yet will I not forget thee. Behold, I have graven thee upon the palms of my hands; thy walls are continually before me Isaiah 49:15, 16

"You may think I have forgotten about you," the Lord says, "but that's impossible. Can a nursing mother forget she has a baby? And even if that were possible, I will never forget you because your names are engraved on My own hands."

One of the overarching themes, one of the real reasons for the Book of Esther is to let you know that if you're His child, God will never forget you. Your name is written in the palm of His hand.

Esther 4:1–3

When Mordecai perceived all that was done, Mordecai rent his clothes, and put on sackcloth with ashes, and went out into the midst of the city, and cried with a loud and a bitter cry; And came even before the king's gate: for none might enter into the king's gate clothed with sackcloth. And in every province, whithersoever the king's commandment and his decree came, there was great mourning among the Jews, and fasting, and weeping, and wailing; and many lay in sackcloth and ashes.

Understandably there is mourning and weeping, wailing and fasting concerning the decree to annihilate the Jews. But there's no mention of any praying. This is what happens when we're not where we should be, when we're in a backslidden condition. The price of not praying when I'm able to pray is not being able to pray when I need to pray. It's not that the Lord turns His back on me. It's just that I'm out of shape spiritually.

Esther 4:4

So Esther's maids and her chamberlains came and told it her. Then was the queen exceedingly grieved; and she sent raiment to clothe Mordecai, and to take away his sackcloth from him: but he received it not.

Mordecai was not interested in a cover-up. He needed a cure.

Esther 4:5–11

Then called Esther for Hatach, one of the king's chamberlains, whom he had appointed to attend upon her, and gave him a commandment to Mordecai, to know what it was, and why it was. So Hatach went forth to Mordecai unto the street of the city, which was before the king's gate. And Mordecai told him of all that had happened unto him, and of the sum of the money that Haman had promised to pay to the king's treasuries for the Jews, to destroy them. Also he gave him the copy of the writing of the decree that was given at Shushan to destroy them, to shew it unto Esther, and to declare it unto her, and to charge her that she should go in unto the king, to make supplication unto him, and to make request before him for her people. And Hatach came and told Esther the words of Mordecai. Again Esther spake unto Hatach, and gave him commandment unto Mordecai; All the king's servants, and the people of the king's provinces, do know, that whosoever, whether man or woman, shall come unto the king into the inner court, who is not called, there is one law of his to put him to death, except such to whom the king shall hold out the golden sceptre, that he may live: but I have not been called to come in unto the king these thirty days.

To save her honor, Vashti lost her crown. To save her people, Esther risked losing her head because the law of the land stated that whoever approached the king without an invitation risked being put to death.

How thankful I am that our King welcomes us into His court at any time. "Come unto Me all ye that labor and are heavy-laden," He says (Matthew 11:28). Therefore, we can come boldly unto His throne of grace. When? Anytime we have need (Hebrews 4:16).

Esther 4:12, 13

And they told to Mordecai Esther's words. Then Mordecai commanded to answer Esther, Think not with thyself that thou shalt escape in the king's house, more than all the Jews.

"If the Jews are destroyed, you will be, too," Mordecai said to Esther. And the same is true of us. As the body of Christ, we're linked together. We tend to associate only with those who are doing well. In reality, we ought to care equally about the person who is doing poorly because even the weakest among us affects the rest of us (1 Corinthians 12:22–25).

Esther 4:14 (a)
For if thou altogether holdest thy peace at this time, then shall there enlargement and deliverance arise to the Jews from another place; but thou and thy father's house shall be destroyed . . .

"Even if you choose not to step out, deliverance *will* come," Mordecai said to Esther. "But you'll miss a glorious opportunity. And you'll be destroyed in the process."

If you're not interested in God's work, if you'd rather complain about your difficult situation or cruise in your easy one, God will still get His work done, but you'll perish, not physically, but the vibrancy of your walk, the joy of service, the opportunity and blessing of being used will be absent.

Esther 4:14 (b)
. . . and who knoweth whether thou art come to the kingdom for such a time as this?

"Maybe you've come into this place as queen of Persia for such a time as this," Mordecai said to Esther. And the same is true of you, dear saint. You are where you are because God is in the shadows, steering the ship of your life. God is in control and He's placed you in your location for such a time as this because there are people for you to minister to, lives for you to touch, and work for you to do. Nothing is accidental to the child of God. Even if your situation seems difficult, the Lord has you right where He wants you to be. He has you right where you are "for such a time as this," for the sake of the kingdom.

Esther 4:15, 16
Then Esther bade them return Mordecai this answer, Go, gather together all the Jews that are present in Shushan, and fast ye for me, and neither eat nor drink three days, night or day: I also and my maidens will fast likewise; and so will I go in unto the king, which is not according to the law: and if I perish, I perish.

The story is told that, after receiving some advice from Augustine, a young man asked him why he was telling him to stay away from this and to avoid that. "I have to live, don't I?"

"Do you?" Augustine is said to have replied.

"I die daily," Paul said (1 Corinthians 15:31).

"If I perish, I perish," Esther concluded.

"If any man come after Me, let him deny himself, take up his cross, and follow Me," Jesus declared (Matthew 16:24).

Esther 4:17
So Mordecai went his way, and did according to all that Esther had commanded him.

"If I perish, I perish. If I go down, I go down. If it's such a time for this that I exist, I'm going to go for it." What are we afraid of? That someone won't like us, that someone will make fun of us? So what? They're doing that anyway! May we be those who share Esther's commitment and clarity.

5

Esther 5:1–3
Now it came to pass on the third day, that Esther put on her royal apparel, and stood in the inner court of the king's house, over against the king's house: and the king sat upon his royal throne in the royal house, over against the gate of the house. And it was so, when the king saw Esther the queen standing in the court, that she obtained favour in his sight: and the king held out to Esther the golden sceptre that was in his hand. So Esther drew near, and touched the top of the sceptre. Then said the king unto her, What wilt thou, queen Esther? and what is thy request? it shall be even given thee to the half of the kingdom.

Proverbs 21:1 says the king's heart is in the hand of the Lord. As Esther is granted access to the king, we see again that God is behind the scenes, setting things up, working things out.

Esther 5:4
And Esther answered, If it seem good unto the king, let the king and Haman come this day unto the banquet that I have prepared for him.

Esther risked her life to invite the king to dinner. Our King, on the other hand, laid down His life so that we might dine with Him forever (Revelation 19:9).

Esther 5:5, 6
Then the king said, Cause Haman to make haste, that he may do as Esther hath said. So the king and Haman came to the banquet that Esther had prepared. And the king said unto Esther at the banquet of wine, What is thy petition? and it shall be granted thee: and what is thy request? even to the half of the kingdom it shall be performed.

Notice that Esther was to make her request at the banquet of the wine. I have found that the place I can most freely make my request and pour out my heart is at the Lord's Table as I hold the wine of His blood in my hand for it is there that I am reminded once again of how much He loves me.

Esther 5:7, 8
Then answered Esther, and said, My petition and my request is; If I have found favour in the sight of the king, and if it please the king to grant my petition, and to perform my request, let the king and Haman come to the banquet that I shall prepare for them, and I will do to morrow as the king hath said.

What's happening here? Twice Esther is given the opportunity to say what's on her heart, but it seems as if she hedges both times. More than likely, however, Esther sensed the timing to make her request was not right. There is a moment of the miraculous, a moment when the time is right to move in the authority and power of God. We have the power, for example, to pray for the sick and to see them restored. The power has been given to us, but we have to wait until the authority is also present. In other words, two components need to come together: power and permission.

When Peter and John saw the man that had been lame since birth, no doubt they had walked past him dozens if not hundreds of times previously. But this time, something was different. They had received the power of the Spirit, and also must have sensed it was the time to say, "In the name of Jesus Christ, rise up and walk" (Acts 3).

I think many times we, as believers, mistakenly think we can randomly move in the arena of the miraculous. We have been given the power, yes, but we must wait for the authority, the timing that's right. Esther seemingly understood this.

Esther 5:9 (a)
Then went Haman forth that day joyful and with a glad heart . . .

Haman thought he had hit the jackpot. After all, he had been invited to two private parties hosted by no less than Esther, the queen. No wonder he left happy.

Esther 5:9 (b)
. . . but when Haman saw Mordecai in the king's gate, that he stood not up, nor moved for him, he was full of indignation against Mordecai.

Haman had just been in the presence of the king and queen. He had a lot going for him. But he was immediately incensed because a "little man" named Mordecai didn't acknowledge him.

I believe you can take an accurate measure of someone's character by the size of the things that bug him. What does it take to irritate you? We're the bride of Christ. We're welcomed into the presence of the King. Why, then, are we so quickly and easily bugged when someone doesn't acknowledge us or when we experience a situation that doesn't go our way?

Esther 5:10–13
Nevertheless Haman refrained himself: and when he came home, he sent and called for his friends, and Zeresh his wife. And Haman told them of the glory of his riches, and the multitude of his children, and all the things wherein the king had promoted him, and how he had advanced him above the princes and servants of the king. Haman said moreover, Yea, Esther the queen did let no man come in with the king unto the banquet that she had prepared but myself; and to morrow am I invited unto her also with the king. Yet all this availeth me nothing, so long as I see Mordecai the Jew sitting at the king's gate.

"Even though I am second in command, I can't enjoy my riches or power because Mordecai won't bow down to me," Haman said.

Esther 5:14
Then said Zeresh his wife and all his friends unto him, Let a gallows be made of fifty cubits high, and to morrow speak thou unto the king that Mordecai may be hanged thereon: then go thou in merrily with the king unto the banquet. And the thing pleased Haman; and he caused the gallows to be made.

"Curse God and die," Job's wife advised him (Job 2:9). Job wisely resisted this advice and he was rewarded (Job 42:10).

"Build a gallows tall enough to make a public spectacle of Mordecai," Haman's wife and friends said. And Haman foolishly listened—to his own peril.

6 **Esther 6:1, 2**
On that night could not the king sleep, and he commanded to bring the book of records of the chronicles; and they were read before the king. And it was found written, that Mordecai had told of Bigthana and Teresh, two of the king's chamberlains, the keepers of the door, who sought to lay hand on the king Ahasuerus.

As Xerxes reads that Mordecai actually saved his life, it becomes clear to us why Esther didn't sense permission to make her request before this.

Esther 6:3–5
And the king said, What honour and dignity hath been done to Mordecai for this? Then said the king's servants that ministered unto him, There is nothing done for him. And the king said, Who is in the court? Now Haman was come into the outward court of the king's house, to speak unto the king to hang Mordecai on the gallows that he had prepared for him. And the king's servants said unto him, Behold, Haman standeth in the court. And the king said, Let him come in.

Before Haman could bring his request to hang Mordecai, the king had something else to talk to him about . . .

Esther 6:6–9
So Haman came in. And the king said unto him, What shall be done unto the man whom the king delighteth to honour? Now Haman thought in his heart, To whom would the king delight to do honour more than to myself? And Haman answered the king, For the man whom the king delighteth to honour, Let the royal apparel be brought which the king useth to wear, and the horse that the king rideth upon, and the crown royal which is set upon his head: And let this apparel and horse be delivered to the hand of one of the king's most noble princes, that they may array the man withal whom the king delighteth to honour, and bring him on horseback through the street of the city, and proclaim before him, Thus shall it be done to the man whom the king delighteth to honour.

"This is great!" thought Haman. "At this time tomorrow, I'll be riding the king's horse, wearing the king's crown and robes, while people proclaim how wonderful I am."

Esther 6:10 (a)
Then the king said to Haman, Make haste, and take the apparel and the horse, as thou hast said, and do even so to Mordecai the Jew . . .

Wouldn't you have loved to see the look on Haman's face at this moment?

Esther 6:10 (b)–12
. . . that sitteth at the king's gate: let nothing fail of all that thou has spoken. Then took Haman the apparel and the horse, and arrayed Mordecai, and brought him on horseback through the street of the city, and proclaimed before him, Thus shall it be done unto the man whom the king delighteth to honour. And Mordecai came again to the king's gate. But Haman hasted to his house mourning, and having his head covered.

Haman knows he's in big trouble.

Esther 6:13, 14
And Haman told Zeresh his wife and all his friends every thing that had befallen him. Then said his wise men and Zeresh his wife unto him, If Mordecai be of the seed of the Jews, before whom thou hast begun to fall, thou shalt not prevail against him, but shalt surely fall before him. And while they were yet talking with him, came the king's chamberlains, and hasted to bring Haman unto the banquet that Esther had prepared.

Whereas previously, Haman's wife and friends told him to build a gallows to hang Mordecai, here they realize it was actually Haman who was going down.

7

Esther 7:1–4
So the king and Haman came to banquet with Esther the queen. And the king said again unto Esther on the second day at the banquet of wine, What is thy petition, queen Esther? and it shall be granted thee: and what is thy request? and it shall be performed, even to the half of the kingdom. Then Esther the queen answered and said, If I have found favour in thy sight, O king, and if it please the king, let my life be given me at my petition, and my people at my request: For we are sold, I and my people, to be destroyed, to be slain, and to perish. But if we had been sold for bondmen and bondwomen, I had held my tongue, although the enemy could not countervail the king's damage.

At last, Esther made the king aware of the plight of both herself and her people.

Esther 7:5–8 (a)
Then the king Ahasuerus answered and said unto Esther the queen, Who is he, and where is he, that durst presume in his heart to do so? And Esther said, The adversary and enemy is this wicked Haman. Then Haman was afraid before the king and the queen. And the king arising from the banquet of wine in his wrath went into the palace garden: and Haman stood up to make request for his life to Esther the queen; for he saw that there was evil determined against him by the king. Then the king returned out of the palace garden into the place of the ban-

quet of wine; and Haman was fallen upon the bed whereon Esther was . . .

Evidently, Haman was so afraid, he fell atop Esther, right as the king walked in.

Esther 7:8 (b)
. . . Then said the king, Will he force the queen also before me in the house? As the word went out of the king's mouth, they covered Haman's face.

In those days, a Persian king would never look into the eyes of a man about to die. In other words, Haman received the death sentence on the spot.

Esther 7:9, 10 (a)
And Harbonah, one of the chamberlains, said before the king, Behold also, the gallows fifty cubits high, which Haman had made for Mordecai, who had spoken good for the king, standeth in the house of Haman. Then the king said, Hang him thereon . . .

In Proverbs 26:27, we read: "Whoso diggeth a pit shall fall therein: and he that rolleth a stone, it will return upon him." That's exactly what happened to Haman, for it was he himself who had ordered the construction of the gallows.

"Don't be deceived," Paul writes. "What a man sows, that shall he reap" (see Galatians 6:7).

Esther 7:10 (b)
. . . So they hanged Haman on the gallows that he had prepared for Mordecai. Then was the king's wrath pacified.

Our God has an incredible way of taking what Satan means for evil in our lives and turning it around for good. Joseph's brothers sold him into slavery. Years later, Joseph found himself prime minister, second only to Pharaoh. His brothers came before him, begging for food. And Joseph revealed his identity. When his brothers reacted in fear, Joseph said, "Don't fear. You meant it for evil, but God has turned it for good to save many people alive this day" (see Genesis 50:20).

That's a promise for you, as well. "No weapon that is formed against thee shall prosper; and every tongue that shall rise against thee in judgment thou shalt condemn. This is the heritage of the servants of the LORD, and their righteousness is of me, saith the LORD." (Isaiah 54:17). Any attempt of Haman to come against you and destroy you will not prosper. It might seem like it's going to. The gallows might be built. The noose might be readied. And you might think it's all over for you. But if you're a child of His, God will miraculously and faithfully turn it for good.

Adolph Hitler destroyed six million Jews, and yet what did God do? He turned it for good to create what otherwise never would have happened: World sentiment to allow the establishment of a nation called Israel.

I think of Satan putting Jesus Christ on the gallows of the Cross thinking that he had won. But God turned the tables, for it was Satan who was defeated that day. Only God can do that.

8

Esther 8:1
On that day did the king Ahasuerus give the house of Haman the Jews' enemy unto Esther the queen. And Mordecai came before the king; for Esther had told what he was unto her.

Esther finally revealed to the king that Mordecai was the one who raised her.

Esther 8:2
And the king took off his ring, which he had taken from Haman, and gave it unto Mordecai. And Esther set Mordecai over the house of Haman.

Haman used to be second in the kingdom. His ring of authority was now given to Mordecai.

Esther 8:3
And Esther spake yet again before the king, and fell down at his feet, and besought him with tears to put away the mischief of Haman the Agagite, and his device that he had devised against the Jews.

The death decree against the Jews was still in effect because the law of the Medes and the Persians was irrevocable.

Esther 8:4–6
Then the king held out the golden sceptre toward Esther. So Esther arose, and stood before the king, And said, If it please the king, and if I have found favour in his sight, and the thing seem right before the king, and I be pleasing in his eyes, let it be written to reverse the letters devised by Haman the son of Hammedatha the Agagite, which he wrote to destroy the Jews which are in all the king's provinces: For how can I endure to see the evil that shall come unto my people? or how can I endure to see the destruction of my kindred?

The Persian government was a constitutional monarchy. That is, the king had to obey the laws of the land. One of the laws was the law of the Medes and Persians which said once a law was established, it couldn't be reversed—not even by the king himself. That's why King Darius couldn't keep Daniel out of the lions' den even though he did everything he could to do so (Daniel 6:14).

Esther 8:7, 8
Then the king Ahasuerus said unto Esther the queen and to Mordecai the Jew, Behold, I have given Esther the house of Haman, and him they have hanged upon the gallows, because he laid his hand upon the Jews. Write ye also for the Jews, as it liketh you, in the king's name, and seal it with the king's ring: for the writing which is written in the king's name, and sealed with the king's ring, may no man reverse.

The king said to Mordecai, "You've got my ring. We can't reverse the first decree, but you can make another one." So the ball was in Mordecai's court.

Esther 8:9–13
Then were the king's scribes called at that time in the third month, that is, the month Sivan, on the three and twentieth day thereof; and it was written according to all that Mordecai commanded unto the Jews, and to the lieutenants, and the deputies and rulers of the provinces which are from India unto Ethiopia, an hundred twenty and seven provinces, unto every province according to the writing thereof, and unto every people after their language, and to the Jews according to their writing, and according to their language. And he wrote in the king Ahasuerus' name, and sealed it with the king's ring, and sent letters by posts on horseback, and riders on mules, camels, and young dromedaries: Wherein the king granted the Jews which were in every city to gather themselves together, and to stand for their life, to destroy, to slay, and to cause to perish, all the power of the people and province that would assault them, both little ones and women, and to take the spoil of them for a prey, Upon one day in all the provinces of king Ahasuerus, namely, upon the thirteenth day of the twelfth month, which is the month Adar. The copy of the writing for a commandment to be given in every province was published unto all people, and that the Jews should be ready against that day to avenge themselves on their enemies.

Mordecai's decree stated that, although the death decree still stood, the Jews had a right to band together and defend themselves. We have a decree issued against us that reads: "The soul that sinneth shall surely die" (Ezekiel 18:20). But there has been a second decree issued. That is, once we recognize that we are sinners, we can have eternal life through Jesus Christ. The wages of sin is still death, *but* the gift of God is eternal life through Jesus Christ our Lord (Romans 6:23). Because we're sinners, we have to die, but because we're saved, we are born again. That's the grand news of the gospel.

Esther 8:14–17 (a)
So the posts that rode upon mules and camels went out, being hastened and pressed on by the king's commandment. And the decree was given at Shushan the palace. And Mordecai went out from the presence of the king in royal apparel of blue and white, and with a great crown of gold, and with a garment of fine linen and purple: and the city of Shushan rejoiced and was glad. The Jews had light, and gladness, and joy, and honour. And in every province, and in every city, whithersoever the king's commandment and his decree came, the Jews had joy and gladness, a feast and a good day . . .

Hearing the second decree, joy, gladness, and celebration erupted within the Jewish community, and yet there would still be a battle on the thirteenth of March. The second decree didn't keep them *from* the heat of the battle. But it gave them great hope *in* the battle. And that's the way it is for us. The Lord doesn't promise to keep us from the battle, from the difficulty, from the trial. But He gives us great hope in the battle, the difficulty, the trial because He gives us the promise of His presence (Hebrews 13:5). When the war is raging, the fire burning, and the storm brewing, we've all discovered that the Lord is with us in a most profound and special way.

Esther 8:17 (b)
. . . And many of the people of the land became Jews; for the fear of the Jews fell upon them.

Even in the face of coming battles, there was joy and gladness and many became Jews as a result. Why would the Lord have us go through battles and hard times? One reason is for others to see the reality of Jesus in us and be drawn to Him.

9 Esther 9:1, 2
Now in the twelfth month, that is, the month Adar, on the thirteenth day of the same, when the king's commandment and his decree drew near to be put in execution,

in the day that the enemies of the Jews hoped to have power over them, (though it was turned to the contrary, that the Jews had rule over them that hated them;) The Jews gathered themselves together in their cities throughout all the provinces of the king Ahasuerus, to lay hand on such as sought their hurt: and no man could withstand them; for the fear of them fell upon all people.

No wonder fear gripped the hearts of the would-be attackers as they saw the Jews standing together with hope, standing together in the spirit of expectation. God behind the scenes was very much there. Although they weren't in Jerusalem where they could have been, where they should have been, God shows His mercy, faithfulness, and grace. Even though they weren't in the best place, God would still be faithful to His people.

Esther 9:3–5
And all the rulers of the provinces, and the lieutenants, and the deputies, and officers of the king, helped the Jews; because the fear of Mordecai fell upon them. For Mordecai was great in the king's house, and his fame went out throughout all the provinces: for this man Mordecai waxed greater and greater. Thus the Jews smote all their enemies with the stroke of the sword, and slaughter, and destruction, and did what they would unto those that hated them.

How are our enemies—Satan himself, demonic powers—defeated? With the stroke of the sword of the Spirit, the Word of God. As we read in Judges concerning Eglon, as the sword went in, the dirt came out (3:22). How shall a young man cleanse his way? By taking heed to the Word (Psalm 119:9). As the sword goes in, the dirt goes out and our enemy is defeated.

Esther 9:6
And in Shushan the palace the Jews slew and destroyed five hundred men.

In the capital city alone, five hundred of the enemy went down.

Esther 9:7–10 (a)
And Parshandatha, and Dalphon, and Aspatha, And Poratha, and Adalia, and Aridatha, And Parmashta, and Arisai, and Aridai, and Vajezatha, The ten sons of Haman the son of Hammedatha, the enemy of the Jews, slew they . . .

It's not just Haman who goes down, but his sons die, too. If we choose to indulge our flesh, to plunge into sin, so often we will have calculated what we think will be the cost. The problem is, the cost will never be what we calculated. It will always be greater than what we anticipated. Sin affects others in heartbreaking ways.

Esther 9:10 (b)
. . . but on the spoil laid they not their hand.

According to Esther 8:11, the Jews could have taken spoil. But they didn't. They weren't fighting for material goods. They fought simply to save their lives.

Esther 9:11–13
On that day the number of those that were slain in Shushan the palace was brought before the king. And the king said unto Esther the queen, The Jews have slain and destroyed five hundred men in Shushan the palace, and the ten sons of Haman; what have they done in the rest of the king's provinces? now what is thy petition? and it shall be granted thee: or what is thy request further? and it shall be done. Then said Esther, If it please the king, let it be granted to the Jews which are in Shushan to do to morrow also according unto this day's decree, and let Haman's ten sons be hanged upon the gallows.

Esther asked that the Jews be given an additional day to defend themselves against any who wanted to do them in. She also asked that Haman's ten sons be hanged from the gallows as a visual reminder of what happens to those who attack God's people.

Esther 9:14–17
And the king commanded it so to be done: and the decree was given at Shushan; and they hanged Haman's ten sons. For the Jews that were in Shushan gathered themselves together on the fourteenth day also of the month Adar, and slew three hundred men at Shushan; but on the prey they laid not their hand. But the other Jews that were in the king's provinces gathered themselves together, and stood for their lives, and had rest from their enemies, and slew of their foes seventy and five thousand, but they laid not their hands on the prey, On the thirteenth day of the month Adar; and on the fourteenth day of the same rested they, and made it a day of feasting and gladness.

The day of battle came and they were victorious. Some 75,000 were killed outside of the capital city and three hundred inside. The enemy was soundly defeated.

Esther 9:18–26
But the Jews that were at Shushan assembled together on the thirteenth day thereof; and on the fourteenth thereof; and on the fifteenth day of the same they rested, and made it a day of feasting and gladness. Therefore the Jews of the villages, that dwelt in the unwalled towns, made the fourteenth day of the month Adar a day of gladness and feasting, and a good day, and of sending portions one to another. And Mordecai wrote these things, and sent letters unto all the Jews that were in all the provinces of the king Ahasuerus, both nigh and far, To stablish this among them, that they should keep the fourteenth day of the month Adar, and the fifteenth day of the same, yearly, As the days wherein the Jews rested from their enemies, and the month which was turned unto them from sorrow to joy, and from mourning into a good day: that they should make them days of feasting and joy, and of sending portions one to another, and gifts to the poor. And the Jews undertook to do as they had begun, and as Mordecai had written unto them; Because Haman the son of Hammedatha, the Agagite, the enemy of all the Jews, had devised against the Jews to destroy them, and had cast Pur, that is, the lot, to consume them, and to destroy them; But when Esther came before the king, he commanded by letters that his wicked device, which he devised against the Jews, should return upon his own head, and that he and his sons should be hanged on the gallows. Wherefore they called these days Purim after the name of Pur. Therefore for all the words of this letter, and of that which they had seen concerning this matter, and which had come unto them,

"This day must be celebrated every year," Mordecai declared. And indeed it is, for to this day, the Feast of Purim, named after the lots that were cast by Haman to determine the day the Jews would be destroyed, is celebrated from March thirteenth to fifteenth. On the thirteenth day, the Jews fast, in commemoration of the battle that would take place. On the fourteenth, people in the outlying villages celebrate. On the fifteenth, celebration breaks out in Jerusalem. The kids dress up in costumes, some as Esther, some as Mordecai, and some as Haman. They pass out candy and cookies, give gifts, and read the story of Esther.

Esther 9:27–32
The Jews ordained, and took upon them, and upon their seed, and upon all such as joined themselves unto them, so as it should not fail, that they would keep these two days according to their writing, and according to their appointed time every year; And that these days should be remembered and kept throughout every generation, every family, every province, and every city; and that these days of Purim should not fail from among the Jews, nor the memorial of them perish from their seed. Then Esther the queen, the daughter of Abihail, and Mordecai the Jew, wrote with all authority, to confirm this second letter of Purim. And he sent the letters unto all the Jews, to the hundred twenty and seven provinces of the kingdom of Ahasuerus, with words of peace and truth, To confirm these days of Purim in their times appointed, according as Mordecai the Jew and Esther the queen had enjoined them, and as they had decreed for themselves and for their seed, the matters of the fastings and their cry. And the decree of Esther confirmed these matters of Purim; and it was written in the book.

The Feast of Purim was established, a glorious, wonderful celebration.

10

Esther 10:1, 2
And the king Ahasuerus laid a tribute upon the land, and upon the isles of the sea. And all the acts of his power and of his might, and the declaration of the greatness of Mordecai, whereunto the king advanced him, are they not written in the book of the chronicles of the kings of Media and Persia?

The implication is that the kingdom expanded under Mordecai's leadership as prime minister.

Esther 10:3
For Mordecai the Jew was next unto king Ahasuerus, and great among the Jews, and accepted of the multitude of his brethren, seeking the wealth of his people, and speaking peace to all his seed.

Mordecai, a type of the Spirit, sought prosperity and peace for the people of God. Haman, a type of the flesh, ended up hung up and done in because God was ever on the scene, watching over, blessing, protecting, and providing for His people. The story ends with the people of God experiencing peace and prosperity, with Mordecai in the place of prominence and power and with Haman hanging.

The path to peace and prosperity remains the same today: with the Spirit as prime minister, directing the affairs of the state of your soul, and with the flesh, like Haman, crucified and reckoned dead (Romans 6:11). Romans 8:6 says to be carnally minded is death but to be Spiritually minded is life and peace.

The Jews were destined for annihilation, but ended up with a brand new celebration. Haman was top dog, but ended up a dead duck. Mordecai was on death row, but now is prime time. God, in a most amazing way to an undeserving people turned the tables. Will He do that for me? Will He do that for you? If we humble ourselves and cry out to Him, the story of Esther tells us the answer is a resounding YES!

JOB

Background to Job

Although the Book of Job deals with the problem of pain and the mystery of misery, the answers we so often desire concerning pain or problems will not necessarily be answered directly in this book. This is how it must be for in Isaiah 55:8 and 9, God declares, "My thoughts are not your thoughts, neither are your ways My ways. For as the heavens are higher than the earth, so are My ways higher than your ways, and My thoughts than your thoughts."

Translator J. B. Phillips explained it this way: If God was small enough for me to figure out, He wouldn't be big enough for me to worship."

God is so beyond us that there are certain things we won't be able to understand this side of eternity. That's why in Deuteronomy 29:29, we read that the secret things belong to the Lord. The Book of Job, however, does give us insights and inspiration that stir my heart and enlighten my thoughts in a way that is helpful and practical concerning what we should do in times of trouble and days of despair. I pray you'll find the same true for you.

Job is probably the oldest book in the Bible, predating even the Pentateuch. That would explain why there is no mention of the Lord, Israel, or the temple. More than likely, it was written near the year 2000 B.C. This would make it not only the oldest book in the Bible, but one of the oldest books in human history. I find this intriguing because one of the oldest books in the Bible, one of the oldest books in human history, deals with the question we still ask to this day: Why do bad things happen to good people?

"Why do bad things happen to good people?" she asked. I was in Denver International Airport, ready to catch a plane to return to Portland. But the flight had been overbooked and I was about to be bumped.

"I really have to get back," I said to the ticket agent. "It's Saturday night and I have five services to preach tomorrow morning."

"The only available seat is in first class. Would you mind if we upgraded you to first class?" he asked.

That is why, instead of making my way to the back of the plane as I boarded, I settled into one of the luxurious leather seats just inside the door. With the seat next to me empty, I felt doubly thankful for the extra space until, at the very last moment, a heavy-set woman walked in and sat in the seat next to mine.

"Tell me," she said, "are you married?"

Taking the photo book I always carry with me from my backpack, I proudly showed her pictures of my wife, Tammy, my sons Peter-John and Ben, and my daughters, Jessie, Christy, and Mary. Then I saw tears running down her cheeks.

"I'm sorry if I've offended you," I said.

"It's not that," she said. "You're just so lucky. You have a beautiful family. All I've ever wanted was to have a family. I know I would be a wonderful wife and mother. But I'm getting older and I know the chances of my getting married are slim. But you wouldn't understand."

"Maybe I can," I said. "Years ago, my wife and I were on our way to a day of skiing when our car hit a patch of ice, spun around, and hit a redwood tree. The next thing I recall, I was crawling down the highway one hundred yards or so from the car on my hands and knees. I don't remember anything after that except being in the ambulance with an attendant putting something in my arm.

"How's my wife?" I asked him.

"She's ok," he hesitantly said.

"No, she's not." I said. And then I said, "Yes, she is. She's in heaven."

He looked at me with piercing intensity and decided to tell me the truth.

"You're right," he said. "She's no longer with us."

At that point, I heard what I believe to this day to be an audible voice saying, "I know the thoughts I think toward you, thoughts of peace and not of evil to give you a future and a hope." I would discover later it was a verse in Scripture: Jeremiah 29:11.

"Wait a minute," the woman next to me said. "You said you're a pastor. I don't understand why, if there is a God, He would take your wife and leave you with three little kids. Why do bad things happen to good people?"

Why do bad things happen to good people? The Book of Job gives us part of the answer.

"God is good," I said. "And what He did for me, He'll do for you." I told her that after I got out of the hospital, I took my kids to the beach. I hugged my son, Peter-John, who was five at the time, and said, "Peter, Mommy's not going to be with us because she's in heaven."

"Wow!" he said. "Can she fly? Can she see us, Daddy?"

Jessie, who was almost three just looked at me with her great big eyes and said, "Oh, no. Oh, no. Oh, no."

Christy, only one, was too young to understand anything.

I came back a few days later after that trip and was sitting in the front room of my house. It was ten-thirty or eleven on Saturday night. I would preach the next morning. There were piles of laundry all around me. And I just cried like a baby.

"Lord, why?" I asked.

And the Lord spoke to me a second time in a way I'll never forget. He said, "Jonny, I promised you a peace that passes understanding. Have I given that to you these past couple of days?"

"Yes, Lord," I said. "You've given me a peace that passes understanding."

"Then never seek a peace that comes *from* understanding," He said.

"Over the years, the Lord has continued to give me abundant peace and amazing blessings. Three years later, He brought me a beautiful, fantastic wife and two more kids. I'm blessed indeed," I said to my seatmate. "And God will do the same for you. I don't know how. But you watch, you wait, you'll see. He'll give you peace that passes understanding. I guarantee it."

"I'd like that," she said.

So I said, "Let's pray."

She received Jesus in her heart somewhere over Salt Lake City.

She eventually returned to Boston, where she began a ministry to single women that continues, as far as I know, to this day.

"I know the thoughts I think toward you, thoughts of peace and not of evil, to give you a future and hope," the Lord said.

So how thrilled I was, as I sat there in the sanctuary that Monday morning. You see, the previous night, sitting at the dinner table with my daughters, sixteen-year-old Jessie and fourteen-year-old Christy, I said, "I don't want you girls to simply marry a Christian. I want you to marry a Christian who is stronger than you, who can lead you in the ways of the Lord—not just some guy who sits in the pew, but a man who is stronger in the Lord than you are."

This would be no small task, for, even at sixteen, Jessie had an incredibly strong faith and deep walk with the Lord.

"Where am I going to find that man?" Jessie joked. "If I went to a good church, I might have a chance!"

Overhearing the conversation, Peter-John chuckled.

The next morning found me at morning worship—a time when the sanctuary was open from 6:00–7:00 each morning so that people could spend time with the Lord in communion, praise, and prayer before going to work or school. When one of my assistant pastors invited people to lead out in prayer, Jessie stood up.

"Lord, I want to thank You for the promise that You know the thoughts You think toward us, thoughts of peace and not of evil to give us a future and a hope," she prayed.

Having never shared that verse and what it meant to me either publicly or with my family, I was delighted. "Lord, You've blessed me so much with a daughter who knows Your Word and loves You passionately, with kids who are walking with You and serving You wholeheartedly, and with a wife who is a perfect match for me."

After her prayer, Jessie caught my eye and gave me a wink and a "thumbs-up" as she headed off to school.

Ten minutes later, one of my assistant pastors said, "Jon, there's been a wreck."

I jumped in my car, raced down the hill, and into the house. Peter-John came out and grabbed me. He was eighteen at the time.

"Dad, dad, dad," he cried. "She found the Man. She found the Man."

I knew what he meant, for the night before, I had told Jessie, "Wait until you find the man that can lead you."

We headed to where the wreck had taken place and discovered that Jessie had been taken to heaven via the exact injury that had taken her mother. The autopsies were virtually identical.

The last words any of us heard from Jessie were: "I know the thoughts I think toward you, thoughts of peace and not of evil to give you a future and a hope."

The Book of Job deals with just that, for uniquely in this book, God says, "I know what I'm doing."

Alfred Lord Tennyson called the Book of Job the greatest poem of ancient or modern times. Author Victor Hugo called it the greatest masterpiece of the human mind. Essayist Thomas Carlyle declared that there is nothing written in the Bible or out of it of the literary merit of the Book of Job.

The book itself divides into three basic sections. Section 1 consists of chapters 1 and 2 which deal with the dilemma *of* Job. The second section, chapters 3 through 37, deals with the debate *about* Job. In the final section, chapters 38 through 42, we see deliverance *for* Job. My prayer is that this wouldn't be only an academic, intellectual, or theological study. My prayer is that the Book of Job might equip you and inspire you to say, "Lord, whatever You choose to do, we trust You implicitly and completely."

JOB

1

Job 1:1 (a)
There was a man in the land of Uz . . .

We can't be certain where Uz was. It is believed to have been somewhere in the desert area of modern-day Syria. But that is only speculation.

Job 1:1 (b)
. . . whose name was Job . . .

We don't exactly know who Job was historically. It could be that he is the Joban mentioned in Genesis 10. If that be so, he would be a contemporary of Abraham, the patriarch, and that would place him around the year 2000 B.C. *Job* literally means "hated." Indeed, Job would be one who was hated by Satan, yet loved by God.

Job 1:1 (c)
. . . and that man was perfect . . .

We may not know exactly where Uz was or who Job was, but we do know he was perfect. This doesn't mean he was sinless. It means he was spiritually mature (see 2 Samuel 22:33; 1 Kings 8:61; Psalm 101:2).

Job 1:1 (d)
. . . and upright . . .

Job was a straight arrow, a man of integrity.

Job 1:1 (e)
. . . and one that feared God, and eschewed evil.

Job was truly a good man.

Job 1:2
And there were born unto him seven sons and three daughters.

Job had ten kids. Having five kids, I can truly say I am happier than a guy who has five million dollars because a guy with five million dollars wants six! In reality, the psalmist said that children are like arrows. Blessed is the man who has a quiver full of them (127:5). Compared to Job, I have only half a quiver, but it's a full one, indeed. I am blessed.

Job 1:3
His substance also was seven thousand sheep, and three thousand camels, and five hundred yoke of oxen, and five hundred she asses, and a very great household; so that this man was the greatest of all the men of the east.

Not only was Job's quiver full of kids, but he was wealthy beyond description. He was Bill Gates, Warren Buffett, and Donald Trump all rolled up into one.

Job 1:4 (a)
And his sons went and feasted in their houses, every one his day . . .

"His day" could refer to a birthday. Or it could mean that Job's sons took turns hosting parties.

Job 1:4 (b), 5
. . . and sent and called for their three sisters to eat and to drink with them. And it was so, when the days of their feasting were gone about, that Job sent and sanctified them, and rose up early in the morning, and offered burnt offerings according to the number of them all: for Job said, It may be that my sons have sinned, and cursed God in their hearts. Thus did Job continually.

Evidently, Job cared about his children's spiritual welfare so deeply that he offered individual sacrifices on their behalf lest they doubt, ignore, or dishonor God. Lest we think it's tough to get up early and pray blessing on our kids before they go to school, it would do us well to consider what Job did every day. He had to offer a bull as a burnt offering—kill it, filet it, and sacrifice it—for each one of his sons.

Boston University conducted a study recently in which fathers were told to estimate how much meaningful time they spent with their children on a daily basis. The average father said he spent between forty-five and fifty minutes a day in meaningful time with his kids either individually or collectively. But video cameras and microphones revealed that the actual time the average father spent in meaningful interaction with each of his kids on any given day was *thirty-eight seconds*.

We might think we're good dads. But perhaps we can do better by following the example of Job—sacrificing our morning cup of coffee or newspaper if necessary, getting up a great while before morning if that's what it takes to say, "Lord, bless Benjamin. Anoint Peter-John. Keep Your hand on Mary. Lord, embrace Christy."

Of all the places I've been privileged to teach, the place I'm most excited about teaching and feel the greatest Holy Ghost anointing is in my own home during family devotions, sitting down with my kids at every stage of life and simply opening the Bible, talking to them about the stories, telling them how they apply to our lives. That's something every one of us can do. You might not go to seminary. You might not be in vocational ministry. But you have the privilege of carving out some time sacrificially to pray for and with your kids, to teach and sanctify them through a simple Bible story, prayer, and a song or two. It will be a huge blessing not only to your family, but it will be the greatest blessing in your own life. Try it. You'll see!

Job 1:6
Now there was a day when the sons of God came to present themselves before the LORD, and Satan came also among them.

The "sons of God" is a reference to angels in the Old Testament. As they presented themselves before the Lord, Satan was in their number. Although he had been cast out of heaven for his attempt to make himself equal to God (Isaiah 14), he still must give account to God.

Job 1:7
And the LORD said unto Satan, Whence comest thou? Then Satan answered the LORD, and said, From going to and fro in the earth, and from walking up and down in it.

"Where have you been?" God asked Satan, not that He needed information, but in order to begin a conversation.

"From going to and fro in the earth," Satan answered.

Peter tells us that Satan goes about as a roaring lion seeking whom he may devour (1 Peter 5:8). On the other hand, in 2 Chronicles 16:9, we read that the eyes of the Lord go to and fro throughout the earth to find a man whose heart is toward Him on behalf of whom He might show Himself strong. In other words, Satan goes about seeking whom he might devour while the Lord goes about seeking whom He might empower.

Job 1:8
And the LORD said unto Satan, Hast thou considered my servant Job, that there is none like him in the earth, a perfect and an upright man, one that feareth God, and escheweth evil?

The Hebrew word translated "considered" referred to what a spy would do as he scoped out enemy territory to find weakness and vulnerability. Thus, the Lord says to Satan, "What do you think about Job? Have you checked him out? Have you probed? Are you aware of his heart toward Me?"

Job 1:9, 10 (a)
Then Satan answered the LORD, and said, Doth Job fear God for nought? Hast not thou made an hedge about him, and about his house, and about all that he hath on every side?

The implication is that Satan had already probed and tried to get Job to fall. "You've put a hedge all around him and I can't get to him," Satan answered.

Isn't it good to know that the Lord has Satan totally under control. There was a hedge around Job, and there is one around you and me, too. God is our Shield and Protector and, according to 1 Corinthians 10:13, He won't allow us to be tempted above that which we're able to bear, but will, with the temptation, provide a way of escape. Nothing can come to us or at us without the Lord allowing it for His sovereign purpose.

Job 1:10 (b), 11
. . . thou hast blessed the work of his hands, and his substance is increased in the land. But put forth thine hand now, and touch all that he hath, and he will curse thee to thy face.

Satan insists that Job is a mercenary, that the only reason he walks with God is because God blesses him, that Job's only in it for the money. In so doing, Satan questions man before God just as in the Garden of Eden, He had questioned God before man.

"Hath God said you shall not eat of every tree?" he asked Eve, hinting that God was holding something good back from her (Genesis 3:1).

Attempting to build a case against Job, Satan questioned his motives. And that's what he still does. Revelation 12:10 tells us he accuses us before the Father day and night.

A panda walked into a restaurant, sat down, and ate breakfast. When he was finished, he stood up, shot the waitress, and walked out. The owner of the restaurant ran after him, yelling, "What in the world are you doing?"

"I'm a panda," the panda yelled. "Look it up in the dictionary."

So the owner of the restaurant did just that. He looked up "panda" and read "Panda: noun, mammal. Eats shoots and leaves."

Who is Satan? Look it up in the Word. He's the accuser of the brethren. That's what he does. That's his defining characteristic.

Job 1:12
And the LORD said unto Satan, Behold, all that he hath is in thy power; only upon himself put not forth thine hand. So Satan went forth from the presence of the LORD.

"You can take what Job has," God said to Satan. "But don't touch him."

Satan had challenged God's honor, in effect saying, "You have no inherent right to receive worship because people wouldn't worship You if You didn't bribe them with blessings. They don't love You for who You are and wouldn't love You if You took Your blessings away."

As the angels and demons watched, they said, "Is that true?"

So now the issue would be settled in an incredible cosmic duel.

Job 1:13–15
And there was a day when his sons and his daughters were eating and drinking wine in their eldest brother's house: And there came a messenger unto Job, and said, The oxen were plowing, and the asses feeding beside them: And the Sabeans fell upon them, and took them away; yea, they have slain the servants with the edge of the sword; and I only am escaped alone to tell thee.

A messenger came to Job, saying, "You've lost your livestock."

Job 1:16
While he was yet speaking, there came also another, and said, The fire of God is fallen from heaven, and hath burned up the sheep, and the servants, and consumed them; and I only am escaped alone to tell thee.

Before the first messenger had finished speaking, a second messenger told Job his sheep and servants had been killed by lightning.

Job 1:17–19
While he was yet speaking, there came also another, and said, The Chaldeans made out three bands, and fell upon the camels, and have carried them away, yea, and slain the servants with the edge of the sword; and I only am escaped alone to tell thee. While he was yet speaking, there came also another, and said, Thy sons and thy daughters were eating and drinking wine in their eldest brother's house: And, behold, there came a great wind from the wilderness, and smote the four corners of the house, and it fell upon the young men, and they are dead; and I only am escaped alone to tell thee.

Before the second messenger finished speaking, a third told Job his children had been killed by a tornado. Thus, Job's finances and family, his prosperity and posterity were all gone.

Job 1:20–22
Then Job arose, and rent his mantle, and shaved his head, and fell down upon the ground, and worshipped, And said, Naked came I out of my mother's womb, and naked shall I return thither: the LORD gave, and the LORD hath taken away; blessed be the name of the LORD. In all this Job sinned not, nor charged God foolishly.

A man of remarkable insight and maturity, Job released his emotion not through ranting and raving, cursing and complaining, weeping and wailing, but through worship.

When Paul and Silas were in the dank, dark dungeon, they began to sing praises to the Lord. They began to worship the One they loved and served. And as they did, the prison doors opened wide. The amazing thing is, not a single prisoner escaped. Why? I suggest it was because they were so amazed that Paul and Silas praised God in the dungeon that they wanted to stick around and see how the rest of the story would unfold.

The same can be true of us. When you feel as though it's dark and damp and dank and dungeony, when you feel as though everything you were hoping for, everything you trusted in has been taken away, it's your opportunity to do what Job did, to do what Paul and Silas did. That is, you can say, "I'm going to worship You, Lord, because You're in control and You know what's best."

Job didn't have chapter 1 to read. He didn't know what was going on. He wouldn't know anything about Satan's challenge throughout his whole ordeal, and perhaps not until he got to heaven. But that didn't matter. He chose to worship nonetheless and untold millions of lives have been impacted by his story.

2

Job 2:1–3
Again there was a day when the sons of God came to present themselves before the LORD, and Satan came also among them to present himself before the LORD. And the LORD said unto Satan, From whence comest thou? And Satan answered the LORD, and said, From going to and fro in the earth, and from walking up and down in it. And the LORD said unto Satan, Hast thou considered my servant Job, that there is none like him in the earth, a perfect and an upright man, one that feareth God, and escheweth evil? and still he holdeth fast his integrity, although thou movedst me against him, to destroy him without cause.

"I removed the hedge of protection around Job," God said to Satan." Yet his integrity is still intact."

Job 2:4–6
And Satan answered the LORD, and said, Skin for skin, yea, all that a man hath will he give for his life. But put forth thine hand now, and touch his bone and his flesh, and he will curse thee to thy face. And the LORD said unto Satan, Behold, he is in thine hand; but save his life.

Initially, Satan called Job a mercenary. Here, he says Job's life is the most important thing to him.

"You can touch him physically," said the Lord. "But you can't kill him."

Job 2:7, 8
So went Satan forth from the presence of the LORD, and smote Job with sore boils from the sole of his foot unto his crown. And he took him a potsherd to scrape himself withal; and he sat down among the ashes.

Some have suggested the boils Job experienced was actually smallpox. That may be. Others believe it was psychosomatic dermatitis in reaction to the terrible losses he had suffered. This much we know: Job was hit hard, for chapter 19 will speak of the "boiling of his bowels," or diarrhea, of his skin burning black, his breath being the breath of death.

Job 2:9
Then said his wife unto him, Dost thou still retain thine integrity? curse God, and die.

"Curse God and die," Job's wife said. Maybe she said this out of love, wanting to see Job released from his misery. But whatever the reason, it wasn't right.

Job 2:10 (a)
But he said unto her, Thou speakest as one of the foolish women speaketh. What? shall we receive good at the hand of God, and shall we not receive evil?

"Are we simply going to love God in the good times and not trust Him in the dark days?" Job asked his wife.

This is the lesson of Job: God does not exist for you. You exist for Him. All things were made by Him and *for* Him (see Colossians 1:16). God can use us any way He chooses. Therefore He can put us in situations that might seem uncomfortable or difficult for reasons we may not understand this side of eternity.

After setting them free from bondage in Egypt, God positioned His people with their backs to the Red Sea. In other words, they were boxed in with Pharaoh closing in on them. It seemed they were about to be wiped out, but God said, "I'm doing this for a reason. I'm putting you in a tough situation in order that Pharaoh and the Egyptians might see My glory" (see Exodus 14:4). The sea would part. Blessings would be bestowed. God's people would eventually reach the Land of Promise. But not immediately. Therefore, I have to remember as I go through life that the Lord may put me in situations from time to time that are uncomfortable or difficult, in part that I might ultimately see how He'll come through for me, but also that the Egyptians around me might see His glory and come to know Him personally.

If we don't remember this as we both go through the Book of Job and through each day of our life, we'll be confused. Job is fulfilling a huge purpose that deals with the honor and integrity of God in the eyes of all eternity. But he didn't know it at the time.

Job 2:10 (b)
. . . In all this did not Job sin with his lips.

Job is in physical pain and misery. He's distraught and distressed emotionally. He's bankrupt and wiped out financially. Yet he doesn't sin by charging God foolishly. And in his submission to God's sovereignty, he's silencing Satan.

Maybe you wonder what's going on in your own life. Maybe you feel like you're being beaten up and run over and you don't know why. It might be that in your choosing to submit to the sovereignty of God by worshiping Him passionately and spending time in His Word consistently that you, too, are silencing Satan. I guarantee that when Job got to heaven, when he finally saw what had taken place, he didn't say, "What a waste." No, I'm sure he said, "Thank You, Lord, for allowing me the privilege of silencing Satan by simply trusting in Your sovereignty, by worshiping You even though I didn't have a clue what was going on."

Job 2:11
Now when Job's three friends heard of all this evil that was come upon him, they came every one from his own place; Eliphaz the Temanite, and Bildad the Shuhite, and Zophar the Naamathite: for they had made an appointment together to come to mourn with him and to comfort him.

Here, we are introduced to the three friends of Job whose dialogue, along with a fourth—constitutes the bulk of this book. We will have some hard things to say about them, but before we do, we need to commend them because they did three things that are definitely to their credit. First, they came to Job. They traveled great distances simply to be with him.

Job 2:12 (a)
And when they lifted up their eyes afar off, and knew him not . . .

So great was Job's physical and emotional pain that his friends didn't even recognize him.

Job 2:12 (b)
. . . they lifted up their voice, and wept; and they rent every one his mantle, and sprinkled dust upon their heads toward heaven.

As seen in Genesis 50 and Ezekiel 3, this was the reaction to death in that day.

Job 2:13
So they sat down with him upon the ground seven days and seven nights, and none spake a word unto him: for they saw that his grief was very great.

Secondly, not only did Job's friends come *to* him, but they sat *with* him. For seven days, they sat with him without saying a word.

After my wife was taken to heaven, many people shared wonderful insights and Scripture with me. But I especially appreciated the ones who would just show up and say very little. In fact, in the first ten days or so following her home going, one guy came by my house, knocked on the door, let himself in, grabbed me by the arm and said, "Come on, Jon. We're going to watch the George Foreman fight on closed circuit TV at the Medford Armory." This guy being bigger than me, I went. And it turned out to be the best thing he could have done for me.

Sometimes, the best thing a person can do is just be there without giving any advice. Initially, that's exactly what Job's friends did.

And when they did finally talk, the third thing they did right was talk to Job rather than talk about him. Even though their conclusions were amiss, they talked directly to him rather than talking behind his back.

3 **Job 3:1 (a)**
After this opened Job his mouth . . .

Silent sympathy created the opportunity for grief to express itself. When you sit with someone and are there for him, it's amazing how he will open his mouth when he's ready. If I'm there with someone who's hurting day by day, week by week, ultimately it will provide the opportunity for that person to express his grief.

Job 3:1 (b)
. . . and cursed his day.

Yes, Job cursed the day he was born but he didn't curse God.

Job 3:2, 3
And Job spake, and said, Let the day perish wherein I was born, and the night in which it was said, There is a man child conceived.

Notice that it wasn't a blob of tissue that was conceived. It was a man child.

Job 3:4–6
Let that day be darkness; let not God regard it from above, neither let the light shine upon it. Let darkness and the shadow of death stain it; let a cloud dwell upon it; let the blackness of the day terrify it. As for that night, let darkness seize upon it; let it not be joined unto the days of the year, let it not come into the number of the months.

"Let the night of my conception and the day of my birth be blotted off the calendar," Job said.

Job 3:7–12
Lo, let that night be solitary, let no joyful voice come therein. Let them curse it that curse the day, who are ready to raise up their mourning. Let the stars of the twilight thereof be dark; let it look for light, but have none; neither let it see the dawning of the day: Because it shut not up the doors of my mother's womb, nor hid sorrow from mine eyes. Why died I not from the womb? why did I not give up the ghost when I came out of the belly? Why did the knees prevent me? or why the breasts that I should suck?

"Why wasn't I stillborn?" Job asks.

Job 3:13
For now should I have lain still and been quiet, I should have slept: then had I been at rest,

On the basis of this verse, some groups have developed a doctrine of "soul sleep" that says when a believer dies, he sleeps in the grave.

Paul, however, would write that to be absent from the body is to be present with the Lord (2 Corinthians 5:8). And, on the Cross, Jesus declared to the thief who believed on Him, "*Today* you shall be with Me in paradise" (see Luke 23:43).

Doctrine cannot be based on the Book of Job because Job speaks out of frustration rather than revelation. In fact, God will come on the scene ultimately and say to him, "Who is this who darkeneth counsel with words without knowledge?" In other words, "Job, you're talking about things you know nothing about" (38:2).

Job 3:14–17
With kings and counsellors of the earth, which built desolate places for themselves; Or with princes that had gold, who filled their houses with silver: Or as an hidden untimely birth I had not been; as infants which never saw light. There the wicked cease from troubling; and there the weary be at rest.

The quietness and nothingness of the grave sounded very appealing and inviting to Job.

Job 3:18, 19
There the prisoners rest together; they hear not the voice of the oppressor. The small and great are there; and the servant is free from his master.

This speaks of the democracy of death, for in death, all men are truly equal.

Job 3:20, 21
Wherefore is light given to him that is in misery, and life unto the bitter in soul; Which long for death, but it cometh not; and dig for it more than for hid treasures;

"When a man is as miserable as I am, why can't he just die?" Job asks. I think it is important to note that even though he wanted to die, Job never contemplated suicide.

Job 3:22, 23
Which rejoice exceedingly, and are glad, when they can find the grave? Why is light given to a man whose way is hid, and whom God hath hedged in?

Job feels he's in the dark because God has hedged him in. In reality, however, it was because God had removed His hedge of protection that Job felt vulnerable (Job 1:10).

Job 3:24, 25
For my sighing cometh before I eat, and my roarings are poured out like the waters. For the thing which I greatly feared is come upon me, and that which I was afraid of is come unto me.

There are those who use verse 25 to say that if we speak negatively, that which we fear will come our way. But that is simply not true. God is not saying, "If you say one negative thing, one thing that lacks faith, I'm going to get you." That's not our Father. That's the Godfather!

David says our Father remembers our frames. He knows we're dust. He knows our frailty (Psalm 103:14).

Job 3:26
I was not in safety, neither had I rest, neither was I quiet; yet trouble came.

After Job shared with his friends his desire to die in chapter 3, they will begin to speak in chapter 4 . . .

4

Job 4:1, 2 (a)
Then Eliphaz the Temanite answered and said, If we assay to commune with thee, wilt thou be grieved?

"We've been quiet for seven days.," Eliphaz said to Job. "Would you be grieved if we spoke with you now?"

Job 4:2 (b)
. . . but who can withhold himself from speaking?

Certainly Job's friends couldn't withhold from speaking, for, through the course of this book, Eliphaz and Bildad will each give two speeches and Zophar will give one.

I find the first couple chapters of Job to be intriguing. I find the last chapters to be glorious and grand as God comes on the scene and sets the record straight. But I must confess that I wonder why the debates in the middle go on chapter after chapter.

If I were writing the Book of Job, it would be about six chapters long. Yet I believe it's a full forty-two chapters because its very length is a reflection of real life. That is, when a trial first begins, there are things to learn. When it ends, we're glad it's over. It's the middle part that seems to go on and on and on. We have all found this to be true. When tragedy strikes, people rally around to encourage us. When it ends, they gather again to rejoice with us. But in the middle of the trial, people go their way, leaving us stuck in the proverbial rut, dealing with the issues, the loneliness, the pain, the sorrow. Thus, the length of the debate that follows mirrors that reality . . .

Job 4:3–5
Behold, thou hast instructed many, and thou hast strengthened the weak hands. Thy words have upholden him that was falling, and thou hast strengthened the feeble knees. But now it is come upon thee, and thou faintest; it toucheth thee, and thou art troubled.

"You gave advice to others in their day of difficulty," Eliphaz says to Job, "but now that difficulty has entered in your own door, you're not doing so well."

Job 4:6
Is not this thy fear, thy confidence, thy hope, and the uprightness of thy ways?

"This is the very time you ought to be upright," Eliphaz declares.

Job 4:7
Remember, I pray thee, who ever perished, being innocent? or where were the righteous cut off?

"Did an innocent man ever perish or go through suffering?" Eliphaz asks. Of course, we know the answer is yes, for the most innocent Man who ever lived would be crucified. And before even Eliphaz's day, even innocent Abel suffered at the hands of Cain. But Eliphaz continued on in his faulty assumption that if Job was suffering, it must have been due to something in his life that was terribly amiss.

Job 4:8
Even as I have seen, they that plow iniquity, and sow wickedness, reap the same.

"You must have sown some wild oats, Job, because look what you're reaping."

Job 4:9
By the blast of God they perish, and by the breath of his nostrils are they consumed.

"You've felt the blast of God, haven't you, Job, as the winds blew down the homes your kids were in."

Job 4:10, 11
The roaring of the lion, and the voice of the fierce lion, and the teeth of the young lions, are broken. The old lion perisheth for lack of prey, and the stout lion's whelps are scattered abroad.

"As fierce and fit as young lions might be, they'll be broken ultimately," Eliphaz declares. "You might have ruled the land, Job. But now you're broken. The reason? Sin. And even if a lion grows old, he'll end up in a state of misery because that's the inevitable repercussion of sin."

Job 4:12–17
Now a thing was secretly brought to me, and mine ear received a little thereof. In thoughts from the visions of the night, when deep sleep falleth on men, Fear came upon me, and trembling, which made all my bones to shake. Then a spirit passed before my face; the hair of my flesh stood up: It stood still, but I could not discern the form thereof: an image was before mine eyes, there was silence, and I heard a voice, saying, Shall mortal man be more just than God? shall a man be more pure than his maker?

Eliphaz switches from "Here's what I've observed . . ." to "I had a dream . . ." He changed the basis of his argument from physical observation to spiritual revelation.

This is often what happens today. When you're going through a trial or difficulty, there will be people who will say, "God told me to tell you. . . ." Generally, however, God does not choose to sneak up on people that way. In fact, Paul would issue a warning about those who delve into such pseudomysticism. "Let no man beguile you," he writes (see Colossians 2:18).

Job 4:18, 19
Behold, he put no trust in his servants; and his angels he charged with folly: How much less in them that dwell in houses of clay, whose foundation is in the dust, which are crushed before the moth?

"If God doesn't even trust His angels, how much less will he trust people who are houses of clay?" Eliphaz asks.

Paul would agree that we are indeed earthen vessels, houses of clay. But he would go on to say that we have the treasure of the Lord in these clay pots. And that's the reason the Lord allows us to go through challenging days and difficult trials (2 Corinthians 4:7).

Facing 135,000 Midianite soldiers, Gideon and his three hundred men surrounded their camp holding flames in earthen jars. On a given signal, they broke the jars and shouted, and when the Midianites saw the light burst forth, they were so confused that they fled in fear (Judges 7).

We have the Light of the world, Jesus Christ, in earthen vessels. When does the light come forth? When is the enemy beaten back? When is the beauty of our Lord seen most clearly? When our earthen pots are broken. That's when people say, "I see the beauty of the Lord in your life because you've gone through some tough times yet there's still a smile on your face and a twinkle in your eye."

Job 4:20, 21
They are destroyed from morning to evening: they perish for ever without any regarding it. Doth not their excellency which is in them go away? they die, even without wisdom.

"Don't you understand, Job?" Eliphaz says. "If you're being crushed or broken it's because you deserve to be."

These are harsh words from Job's friend, Eliphaz. And he's not finished yet . . .

5 Job 5:1, 2
Call now, if there be any that will answer thee; and to which of the saints wilt thou turn? For wrath killeth the foolish man, and envy slayeth the silly one.

"Call to the saints if you want to, Job. Call the holy men who have gone before you, and you'll see I'm right," Eliphaz said.

Job 5:3
I have seen the foolish taking root: but suddenly I cursed his habitation.

"The foolish seem to be planted initially, but suddenly, their habitation is cursed," Eliphaz said, implying that there was fruit in Job's life only for a season.

Job 5:4
His children are far from safety, and they are crushed in the gate, neither is there any to deliver them.

His heart already broken, Job continues to listen to Eliphaz's theories about his situation.

People always have opinions. After being shipwrecked, when Paul threw sticks on a fire, a snake jumped out and fastened its fangs on Paul's hand. Observing this, the inhabitants of the island immediately deduced that Paul was an evil man. But when he shook off the snake and suffered no harm, they decided he was a god. In reality, of course, he was neither. He was simply a man, a man God used through that particular incident to draw the hearts of the islanders to Him (Acts 28).

Job 5:5
Whose harvest the hungry eateth up, and taketh it even out of the thorns, and the robber swalloweth up their substance.

"The fact that not only your kids, but your crops have been ripped off is indicative that there's something wrong with you," Eliphaz said to Job.

Job 5:6, 7
Although affliction cometh not forth of the dust, neither doth trouble spring out of the ground; Yet man is born unto trouble, as the sparks fly upward.

"Just as surely as sparks fly up in a campfire, you will experience trouble as long as you remain in this state of rebellion," Eliphaz warned Job.

Job 5:8
I would seek unto God, and unto God would I commit my cause:

"If I were you, Job, I would certainly seek the Lord," Eliphaz says.

Job 5:9–14
Which doeth great things and unsearchable; marvellous things without number: Who giveth rain upon the earth, and sendeth waters upon the fields: To set up on high those that be low; that those which mourn may be exalted to safety. He disappointeth the devices of the crafty, so that their hands cannot perform their enterprise. He taketh the wise in their own craftiness: and the counsel of the froward is carried headlong. They meet with darkness in the daytime, and grope in the noonday as in the night.

"Not only does God send blessings, but He also causes those who are tricky to be caught in their own traps," Eliphaz declared.

Paul will reiterate Eliphaz's statement, writing to the church at Corinth that "the wisdom of this world is foolishness with God. For it is written, He taketh the wise in their own craftiness" (1 Corinthians 3:19).

Job 5:15–18
But he saveth the poor from the sword, from their mouth, and from the hand of the mighty. So the poor hath hope, and iniquity stoppeth her mouth. Behold, happy is the man whom God correcteth: therefore despise not thou the chastening of the Almighty: For he maketh sore, and bindeth up: he woundeth, and his hands make whole.

We see Solomon echo verse 17 in Proverbs (3:12 and 13) as well as the writer to the Hebrews quote it (12:5). This proves that Eliphaz isn't completely out to lunch, that he does have some things to say that are of value.

Job 5:19–24
He shall deliver thee in six troubles: yea, in seven there shall no evil touch thee. In famine he shall redeem thee from death: and in war from the power of the sword. Thou shalt be hid from the scourge of the tongue: neither shalt thou be afraid of destruction when it cometh. At destruction and famine thou shalt laugh: neither shalt thou be afraid of the beasts of the earth. For thou

shalt be in league with the stones of the field: and the beasts of the field shall be at peace with thee. And thou shalt know that thy tabernacle shall be in peace; and thou shalt visit thy habitation, and shalt not sin.

"Job, if you get right with the Lord, you will be protected from famine, sword, cruel words, destruction, beasts, earthquakes, and whirlwinds."

Job 5:25–27
Thou shalt know also that thy seed shall be great, and thine offspring as the grass of the earth. Thou shalt come to thy grave in a full age, like as a shock of corn cometh in his season. Lo this, we have searched it, so it is; hear it, and know thou it for thy good.

"If you get right, Job, you will be protected, insulated, built up, and prosperous. If you don't, although you were prosperous for a season, you will only ultimately experience destruction."

Eliphaz was answering the words on Job's lips, but not the pain in his heart. As we work with people, may we be those who, unlike Eliphaz, hear something of the heart of people rather than simply their words.

I'm sorry to say that I have a tendency to judge others by their actions, but myself by my intentions. "Reverse that," the Lord said to me. "Judge others by their intentions and judge yourself by your actions. Don't get hung up on the words someone says or the things he does. Try instead to understand what's going on in his heart."

"If I have the tongues of men and angels, if I have all knowledge, but have not love, I am nothing," Paul would declare (1 Corinthians 13). Some of the things Eliphaz said were actually correct but, because they weren't enveloped in love, they had no real effect upon Job. If you want to be a good counselor, understand that you need to hear people's hearts. Choose to give people the benefit of the doubt. Let God judge them. You love them.

6 Children never seem to tire of asking, "Why?" I can recall the time my daughter Jessie was four and, after walking outside in the Oregon rain, she looked at me and said, "Daddy, why is water wet?"

"What?" I said.

"Why is water wet?" she repeated.

"I don't have a clue," I answered, feeling like a big drip!

Kids are so curious about everything. As we grow older, we lose a degree of that sense of wonder and curiosity but we still ask "Why?"

"Why didn't that work out?"

"Why didn't they come through?"

"Why am I going through this?"

All too often, we have a bitter taste in our mouth even as we ask, *"Why?"*

Job was in this place, wondering why he was going through the ordeal he was enduring, suffering to an unbelievable degree. Here in chapter 6, he responds to the counsel he received from Eliphaz, who essentially said, "Job, the reason you're in the situation you're in is because of sin. Why are you experiencing so much heartache? The issue is sin."

Job 6:1–3
But Job answered and said, Oh that my grief were throughly weighed, and my calamity laid in the balances together! For now it would be heavier than the sand of the sea: therefore my words are swallowed up.

"You don't understand the heaviness I feel," Job said. "It's heavier than all of the sand on all of the beaches of the world."

Job 6:4
For the arrows of the Almighty are within me, the poison whereof drinketh up my spirit: the terrors of God do set themselves in array against me.

Job felt that surely he must be a target of the Lord.

Job 6:5
Doth the wild ass bray when he hath grass? or loweth the ox over his fodder?

"When the donkey and ox are fed, will they bray or moo? No, they'll be content. That's why I am groaning because, instead of feeding me with words of encouragement, you've accused me of a secret sin."

Job 6:6, 7
Can that which is unsavoury be eaten without salt? or is there any taste in the white of an egg? The things that my soul refused to touch are as my sorrowful meat.

"That which you've put on my plate, Eliphaz, is tasteless and bitter, inedible, indigestible. The speech you gave me, the accusation you made against me is impossible to swallow. You don't understand not only my heaviness, my bitterness, but my hopelessness . . .

Job 6:8–10 (a)
Oh that I might have my request; and that God would grant me the thing that I long

for! Even that it would please God to destroy me; that he would let loose his hand, and cut me off! Then should I yet have comfort; yea, I would harden myself in sorrow . . .

"God withholds the one thing I long for: death," said Job. Aren't you glad the Lord doesn't answer all of our prayers with a "Yes"? "No" is just as much an answer as "Yes" is.

"Wipe me out," Job had prayed. But the Lord knew that wouldn't be best for Job. He had a plan for Job. When your prayers don't seem to be answered, rejoice because a "No" is just as much an answer as "Yes" is. Because God understands we're limited in our knowledge, His Son intercedes for us at His right hand. The Spirit prays through us with groaning we don't understand to bring our prayer into perfect harmony with His plan for us (Romans 8:26).

Effective prayer is not directive. God does not need counsel as to how to get the job done and yet so often I catch myself advising God in prayer, saying, "This is the way we can do it, Lord . . ." Prayer is not to direct the Father. It's to commune with the Father, to pour out our burdens upon Him, to spend time with Him, and then to receive from Him a heart more and more like that of Jesus.

Job 6:10 (b)–12
. . . let him not spare; for I have not concealed the words of the Holy One. What is my strength, that I should hope? and what is mine end, that I should prolong my life? Is my strength the strength of stones? or is my flesh of brass?

"Eliphaz," Job asks, "do you think I'm as strong as a rock? Do you think I can go round after round with you?"

Job 6:13–17
Is not my help in me? and is wisdom driven quite from me? To him that is afflicted pity should be shewed from his friend; but he forsaketh the fear of the Almighty. My brethren have dealt deceitfully as a brook, and as the stream of brooks they pass away; Which are blackish by reason of the ice, and wherein the snow is hid: What time they wax warm, they vanish: when it is hot, they are consumed out of their place.

"You are like streams," Job says to his friends. "In the wintertime, they flow with snow and ice. But when things get hot in the summer, there is no refreshment there. I'm going through fiery trials, difficult days. I'm in the heat of unbelievable difficulty, but you have no words of refreshment for me."

Job 6:18–20
The paths of their way are turned aside; they go to nothing, and perish. The troops of Tema looked, the companies of Sheba waited for them. They were confounded because they had hoped; they came thither, and were ashamed.

Contrast Job's cry with the words of the psalmist . . .

Blessed is the man whose strength is in thee; in whose heart are the ways of them. Who passing through the valley of Baca make it a well; the rain also filleth the pools. They go from strength to strength, every one of them in Zion appeareth before God. Psalm 84:5–7

Baca means "weeping." Therefore, the valley of Baca is a valley of difficulties and sorrows, a place where tears are shed. The thing to remember is that, when you're in that valley, going through tough times, the wells formed from the tears that flow down your cheeks can actually refresh others who will come after you in their journey with the Lord.

Viewed through a microscope, the saline crystal of a tear is in the shape of a cross. "Why am I going through this?" we cry. "Why am I in this valley of Baca, this valley of weeping?" we wonder. I suggest one of the primary reasons is so that we won't be like Job's miserable counselors who had nothing to say but words of innuendo and accusation.

"Blessed be the Father of mercies, the God of all comforts, who comforts us in our troubles," Paul declares, "that we may be able to comfort others with the comfort we have received of Him" (see 2 Corinthians 1:3, 4).

Job 6:21, 22
For now ye are nothing; ye see my casting down, and are afraid. Did I say, Bring unto me? or, Give a reward for me of your substance?

"Did I ask you for a gift because of what I'm going through?" Job asks. "My need was simply for compassion and sympathy."

Job 6:23, 24
Or, Deliver me from the enemy's hand? or, Redeem me from the hand of the mighty? Teach me, and I will hold my tongue: and cause me to understand wherein I have erred.

"If you show me where I've erred, I'll be quiet," Job says.

Job 6:25
How forcible are right words! but what doth your arguing reprove?

"Right words carry weight," Job contends.

Job 6:26, 27
Do ye imagine to reprove words, and the speeches of one that is desperate, which are as wind? Yea, ye overwhelm the fatherless, and ye dig a pit for your friend.

"Do you think I'm just blowing hot air?" Job asks his friends.

Job 6:28
Now therefore be content, look upon me; for it is evident unto you if I lie.

Maybe at this point, Job's friends were hanging their heads. "Look at me," Job says. "Am I lying about my situation?"

Job 6:29, 30
Return, I pray you, let it not be iniquity; yea, return again, my righteousness is in it. Is there iniquity in my tongue? cannot my taste discern perverse things?

"I can discern the difference between good and bad," Job protests. "So tell me if there is some error you can see in me."

7 After talking about his own heaviness and the ineffectiveness of his friends' counsel, Job paints a picture of life in its futility, its agony, and its brevity.

Job 7:1–5
Is there not an appointed time to man upon earth? are not his days also like the days of an hireling? As a servant earnestly desireth the shadow, and as an hireling looketh for the reward of his work: So am I made to possess months of vanity, and wearisome nights are appointed to me. When I lie down, I say, When shall I arise, and the night be gone? and I am full of tossings to and fro unto the dawning of the day. My flesh is clothed with worms and clods of dust; my skin is broken, and become loathsome.

Plagued by insomnia, Job's days were a grind and his nights were restless. Thus, his life seemed futile.

Job 7:6–8
My days are swifter than a weaver's shuttle, and are spent without hope. O remember that my life is wind: mine eye shall no more see good. The eye of him that hath seen me shall see me no more: thine eyes are upon me, and I am not.

"Even at best, life is short," Job says. "I will never again experience pleasure."

Job 7:9–11
As the cloud is consumed and vanisheth away: so he that goeth down to the grave shall come up no more. He shall return no more to his house, neither shall his place know him any more. Therefore I will not refrain my mouth; I will speak in the anguish of my spirit; I will complain in the bitterness of my soul.

"I'm going to speak out of the condition of my life, the agony, the futility, and the brevity."

Job 7:12
Am I a sea, or a whale, that thou settest a watch over me?

"Have you come to be entertained?" Job asks.

Job 7:13–16
When I say, My bed shall comfort me, my couch shall ease my complaint; Then thou scarest me with dreams, and terrifiest me through visions: So that my soul chooseth strangling, and death rather than my life. I loathe it; I would not live alway: let me alone; for my days are vanity.

"I long for peace of mind, but you weight me down with your accusations and you scare me with your dreams and visions," Job says.

To discern whether something is from the Lord or of the devil, James says if it causes you to feel strife and confusion, it's from the enemy. But if it's peaceable, without hypocrisy, easily entreated, it's from the Lord (3:17).

Job 7:17, 18
What is man, that thou shouldest magnify him? and that thou shouldest set thine heart upon him? And that thou shouldest visit him every morning, and try him every moment?

Directing his response to God rather than to Eliphaz, Job is awed by God. His counselors talked *about* God. Job talked *to* God. Big difference. I like to be around people who not only talk about God, but talk *to* Him. "Why are You trying me every moment?" Job asks as he cries out directly to God.

Job 7:19–21
How long wilt thou not depart from me, nor let me alone till I swallow down my spittle? I have sinned; what shall I do unto thee, O thou preserver of men? why hast thou set me as a mark against thee, so that I am a burden to myself? And why dost thou not pardon my transgression, and take away mine iniquity? for now shall I sleep in the dust; and thou shalt seek me in the morning, but I shall not be.

Literally, Job prays, "If I have sinned, what do You want from me?" In his prayer, we see respect, reverence, and awe but also a raw honesty as he asks, "Lord, what is going on here?"

And with that, Bildad steps in . . .

8

Job 8:1, 2
Then answered Bildad the Shuhite, and said, How long wilt thou speak these things? and how long shall the words of thy mouth be like a strong wind?

Bildad basically calls Job a windbag.

Job 8:3
Doth God pervert judgment? or doth the Almighty pervert justice?

"How dare you challenge the justice of God?" Bildad asks.

Job 8:4
If thy children have sinned against him, and he have cast them away for their transgression;

"It's not only your sin that's a problem, Job but your kids sinned as well," Bildad says.

Job 8:5, 6
If thou wouldest seek unto God betimes, and make thy supplication to the Almighty; If thou wert pure and upright; surely now he would awake for thee, and make the habitation of thy righteousness prosperous.

"If you would get right, God would bless you, Job," Bildad says. "But your suffering indicates that you're in a backslidden state."

We still hear Bildad's false conclusion today by those who say, "If you're righteous and pure, you can ask the Lord for a yacht and it will be there the next day. If you're strong in faith, you won't be sick. If you're walking with the Lord, you'll get the promotion, the raise, or the new car."

Job 8:7
Though thy beginning was small, yet thy latter end should greatly increase.

"You would have had a happy ending, Job, if you had walked righteously and refrained from whatever sin you're hiding," Bildad says.

Job 8:8–10
For inquire, I pray thee, of the former age, and prepare thyself to the search of their fathers: (For we are but of yesterday, and know nothing, because our days upon earth are a shadow:) Shall not they teach thee, and tell thee, and utter words out of their heart?

"Don't just take my word for it," Bildad says. "Check out history. Listen to the fathers that have gone on before us, the wisdom of men wiser than us. They, too talk of righteousness, that God is just, that if you're not doing well, it's not God's fault. It's yours."

Job 8:11, 12
Can the rush grow up without mire? can the flag grow without water? Whilst it is yet in his greenness, and not cut down, it withereth before any other herb.

Bildad tells Job to not only listen to the instruction of the fathers, but to look at the illustration of nature. The reed can pop up and the grass can grow, but if the reed doesn't have mud and the grass doesn't have water, they'll fade away in the heat of the sun. If something dries up, it's because it's out of touch with the source of water. In other words, there's something wrong with the root system. His implication, of course, was that there was something wrong with Job's root system.

Job 8:13
So are the paths of all that forget God; and the hypocrite's hope shall perish:

"You prospered for a season, Job. You were the wealthiest man in all the east. You seemed to have it all together, but now the truth comes out. Your roots are revealed and you are found lacking."

Job 8:14, 15
Whose hope shall be cut off, and whose trust shall be a spider's web. He shall lean upon his house, but it shall not stand: he shall hold it fast, but it shall not endure.

"If you lean against a spider web, you're a fool. It can't support a man. So, too, your house was due to collapse because it had no firm foundation," Bildad contends.

Job 8:16–19
He is green before the sun, and his branch shooteth forth in his garden. His roots are wrapped about the heap, and seeth the place of stones. If he destroy him from his place, then it shall deny him, saying, I have not seen thee. Behold, this is the joy of his way, and out of the earth shall others grow.

Bildad's third illustration from nature concerns a plant that finds a fertile place among the stones and it grows. But when it's removed, it's not missed. Bildad maintained that Job was in the process of being uprooted and that others would take his place.

Job 8:20–22
Behold, God will not cast away a perfect man, neither will he help the evil doers: Till he fill thy mouth with laughing, and thy lips with rejoicing. They that hate thee shall be clothed with shame; and the dwelling place of the wicked shall come to nought.

"If you get right, Job, if you confess your sin and stop claiming to be right, God can bless you again," Bildad said. Job will protest Bildad's speech in chapter 9.

"Job, there's sin in your life. That's why these things have come upon you," Eliphaz said.

"And you continue to sin by denying that you are in sin," Bildad added.

"God is holy. He judges rightly. Therefore, there must be some sin your life," Eliphaz said.

"How dare you challenge God's justice?" Bildad asked.

Eliphaz and Bildad no doubt thought they were doing God a favor by standing up for Him. They were right that God is just. But they were dead wrong in assuming God's justice was the only issue at play, for there was something going on of which neither they nor Job was aware. Yes, God is just. But God became Man and dwelt among us to teach us that God desires mercy and not sacrifice (Matthew 9:13).

There were only three times that Jesus commanded us to learn . . .

In Matthew 11:29, He said, "Learn of Me."

In Matthew 24, He said, "Learn the parable of the fig tree."

In Matthew 9, He said, "Learn to be merciful."

In other words, we are to be students of humility, Bible prophecy, and mercy.

When the Philistines sent the ark of the covenant back to Israel after capturing it in battle, the men of Bethshemesh were elated. But when they lifted off the mercy seat to make sure the Law was still inside, thousands were killed instantly (1 Samuel 6:19). Sometimes I do that. I set aside mercy to check out the law. And whenever I do, something dies. God declared He would meet with man not on the basis of the law, but at the mercy seat (Exodus 25:22).

Oh, Bildad, you don't understand. You're standing for justice. But you forgot mercy.

9

Why doesn't God break in at this point? We know He will later on. Why does He allow Job to go through this confusion, to feel this depression? I believe the answer is that He is teaching Job how to walk by faith and not by sight. Seeing what's coming down or what's going on doesn't require faith. Faith only kicks in when I can't see. Why does faith need to be developed? Because faith seems to be the *lingua franca* of heaven, the currency of eternity. And faith can only be developed this side of heaven.

As He did with Job, the Lord takes us through tests to cause us to be made perfect in faith in order that we might be equipped to rule with Him in eternity. But He promises He won't test us above what we are able (1 Corinthians 10:13). This means He will only allow us to be tested in relationship to what He has prepared us for in our walk with Him and in our knowledge of Him.

I think of Abraham. Yes, he was told to offer his only son as a sacrifice, but not until "after these things" (Genesis 22:1). What things? For many years previously, God had prepared Abraham for a test of this magnitude. Abraham had already left his homeland in Ur of the Chaldees. He had left his family and friends. He buried his dad at Heron. He had to send his son, Ishmael, out to the desert. In all these things, God was preparing Abraham every step of the way for this great test.

Our God is a Master Teacher who tests us only after we have been thoroughly prepared. And He guarantees we'll pass the tests He sends before us. Oh, we might have to take them a few times, but we'll pass them eventually!

Our hearts go out to Job understandably. But we must remember that he was thoroughly prepared. When someone we know goes through difficult times, we must understand that, if they're a child of God, the Father has prepared them and will not test them above what they are able. Job is confused, yes. He despairs, yes. But he never curses God. And in this, he'll pass the test with flying colors.

Job 9:1, 2
Then Job answered and said, I know it is so of a truth: but how should man be just with God?

Bildad had raised a legal issue, the justice of God. Now Job will speak in legal terms, as well. "I know God is just," he says. "But how can a man plead his case before Him?"

Job 9:3
If he will contend with him, he cannot answer him one of a thousand.

"Under the cross-examination of God, man cannot begin to answer even one of a thousand of His questions," Job says.

Job 9:4
He is wise in heart, and mighty in strength: who hath hardened himself against him, and hath prospered?

"Who has ever opposed God successfully? How can I present my case against Him?" Job asks.

Job 9:5, 6
Which removeth the mountains, and they know not: which overturneth them in his anger. Which shaketh the earth out of her place, and the pillars thereof tremble.

"How can I plead my case before a God who is invincible?"

Job 9:7–9
Which commandeth the sun, and it riseth not; and sealeth up the stars. Which alone spreadeth out the heavens, and treadeth upon the waves of the sea. Which maketh Arcturus, Orion, and Pleiades, and the chambers of the south.

God moves mountains and sets the stars and constellations in place. He is invincible indeed. Not only that, but He is incomprehensible . . ."

Job 9:10
Which doeth great things past finding out; yea, and wonders without number.

"God does things we could never figure out," Job says, and he's right, for Deuteronomy 29:29 declares that the secret things belong to the Lord.

Job 9:11
Lo, he goeth by me, and I see him not: he passeth on also, but I perceive him not.

"Not only is God invincible and incomprehensible, He's also invisible. How, then, can I be right with a God who is so wise that I can't debate Him, so powerful that I can't go against Him, so transcendent that I can't even perceive Him?"

Of course, the answer is Jesus, for "great is the mystery of godliness, that God was manifest in the flesh" (1 Timothy 3:16). Jesus came that we might be able to observe and touch and hear and watch God personally.

"He that hath seen Me has seen the Father," Jesus declared (John 14:9).

It's Jesus who bridges the gap, who brings oneness between sinful man and a perfect Father.

Job 9:12
Behold, he taketh away, who can hinder him? who will say unto him, What doest thou?

"God is unaccountable," Job continues. "In a courtroom, who would say to God, 'You're out of order?' Who's going to say, 'I object?'"

Job 9:13
If God will not withdraw his anger, the proud helpers do stoop under him.

"God is also unrestrainable," Job declares. "What bailiff will take God away for being out of order? It's impossible to plead my case."

Job 9:14, 15
How much less shall I answer him, and choose out my words to reason with him? Whom, though I were righteous, yet would I not answer, but I would make supplication to my judge.

"Even if I were righteous, I would simply plead for mercy."

Job 9:16
If I had called, and he had answered me; yet would I not believe that he had hearkened unto my voice.

"If I prayed and God answered me, I wouldn't even believe it was an answer to prayer," Job confesses. "He's just too vast, too great, too big, too large, too 'other.' I would think it was just coincidence."

How could Job, a righteous man, say this? In Acts 12, Peter was in prison and the believers were in the house of John Mark praying passionately for his release. That night, after an angel sprung him loose, he made his way to the house where this group had been praying fervently. He knocks on the door. The servant girl answers and runs into the meeting saying, "Peter's outside!"

"It can't be Peter. He's in prison," said the giants of faith and went back to praying for his release.

We do the same thing. We pray with not a whole lot of faith, but the great news is that if we pray even with faith the size of a mustard seed, mountains can be moved (Matthew 17:20).

Job 9:17–19
For he breaketh me with a tempest, and multiplieth my wounds without cause. He will not suffer me to take my breath, but filleth me with bitterness. If I speak of strength, lo, he is strong: and if of judgment, who shall set me a time to plead?

"God has put me through the wringer," Job says. "How could I appear before Him to plead my case?"

Job 9:20, 21
If I justify myself, mine own mouth shall condemn me: if I say, I am perfect, it shall also prove me perverse. Though I were perfect, yet would I not know my soul: I would despise my life.

"If I said I was perfect, my own words would condemn me. And even if it were true, I don't know my own soul," Job laments.

Job 9:22
This is one thing, therefore I said it, He destroyeth the perfect and the wicked.

Yes, God was allowing these things to happen to Job, but God is not the destroyer. He's the One who pours His rain of blessing on the just and the unjust (Matthew 5:45). Who causes destruction? The destroyer, Satan (Exodus 12:23; Psalm 17:4; 1 Corinthians 10:10).

Job 9:23, 24
If the scourge slay suddenly, he will laugh at the trial of the innocent. The earth is given into the hand of the wicked: he covereth the faces of the judges thereof; if not, where, and who is he?

"The judges of this world are corrupt," Job says. "The judicial system is flawed." Job was not alone in thinking this. Habakkuk would be another to share his conclusion (1:4).

Job 9:25–29
Now my days are swifter than a post: they flee away, they see no good. They are passed away as the swift ships: as the eagle that hasteth to the prey. If I say, I will forget my complaint, I will leave off my heaviness, and comfort myself: I am afraid of all my sorrows, I know that thou wilt not hold me innocent. If I be wicked, why then labour I in vain?

"If I'm wicked, why should I bother to try and make sense of this?" Job asks.

Job 9:30, 31
If I wash myself with snow water, and make my hands never so clean; Yet shalt thou plunge me in the ditch, and mine own clothes shall abhor me.

This is despair, gang. Job is saying, "I'm afraid to even encourage myself because of what God might do to me."

Job 9:32
For he is not a man, as I am, that I should answer him, and we should come together in judgment.

"This God is so incredible, so powerful, so unknowable that to me He seems illogical. How can I discuss with Him what I'm going through?" Job asks.

Job 9:33
Neither is there any daysman betwixt us, that might lay his hand upon us both.

A daysman is an arbitrator, a mediator, a middleman, an umpire. Praise the Lord that we have a Daysman, a Mediator standing for us, an Advocate on our behalf in the person of Jesus (1 John 2:1).

Job 9:34, 35
Let him take his rod away from me, and let not his fear terrify me: Then would I speak, and not fear him; but it is not so with me.

It was the Father who sent the Son, but it was also the Father who was in the Son, for of Jesus, Isaiah said that, along with Wonderful Counselor and Prince of Peace, His name would be called Everlasting Father (9:6). It was God in Christ who reconciled the world to Himself (2 Corinthians 5:19). Therefore, when you think of Jesus as a Daysman, don't think of God being angry, with Jesus calming Him down. No, it is God Himself who was in Christ Jesus—the mystery of the Trinity.

10

Job 10:1, 2
My soul is weary of my life; I will leave my complaint upon myself; I will speak in the bitterness of my soul. I will

say unto God, Do not condemn me; shew me wherefore thou contendest with me.

"Show me why You are coming against me," Job says to God.

Job 10:3 (a)
Is it good unto thee that thou shouldest oppress, that thou shouldest despise the work of thine hands . . .

"You made me, Lord," Job continues. "I am the work of *Your* hands. Is it good that You are oppressing me in this way?"

Job 10:3 (b)
. . . and shine upon the counsel of the wicked?

"Is it right that You pick on me yet honor the decisions of the wicked? Is that fair?"

Job 10:4–6
Hast thou eyes of flesh? or seest thou as man seeth? Are thy days as the days of man? are thy years as man's days, That thou inquirest after mine iniquity, and searchest after my sin?

"Are You unjust? Are you limited, like man? Do you see things only as men see them?" Job asks God.

Job 10:7, 8
Thou knowest that I am not wicked; and there is none that can deliver out of thine hand. Thine hands have made me and fashioned me together round about; yet thou dost destroy me.

"Did You make me only to destroy me?" Job wonders.

Job 10:9
Remember, I beseech thee, that thou hast made me as the clay; and wilt thou bring me into dust again?

In Psalm 103, we read that our Father remembers that we are made of dust. Oftentimes, I think we expect more out of ourselves than God expects of us. We mistakenly think we're more than dust. No wonder we're shocked by what we find ourselves thinking or doing. God, however, isn't shocked. He's not even surprised. He knows our frames. He knows what we're made of. But He also knows what we're going to be. He sees us as already glorified in Christ Jesus (Romans 8:21).

If the Anaheim Angels called me last summer and said, "Jon, we heard you're in town and we really need a pitcher because we're headed for the World Series," and if I agreed to come and take a few practice pitches, the ball would have gone right over the catcher's head and into the stands. But if, for some reason, the coach and the owner liked me, I would be given a uniform. I would be on the team. Yes, I would sit on the bench but I would be on the team. Then, when the Angels won the World Series and the bonus checks were cut and the rings were distributed, when the team photo was taken and the parade took place at Disneyland—there I would be. Why? I can't pitch my way out of a paper bag but, simply because I was on the team, because I wore the uniform, I would get the ring, the photo, the check, the parade, the whole thing.

That's the gospel. Our heavenly Father is the Owner. Our Lord and Savior is our Coach. They happen to like us and chose us for reasons that are beyond me! We're on their team. We get the photo, the ring, and heaven simply because we're robed in the righteous uniform of Christ Jesus (Isaiah 61:10; 2 Corinthians 5:21). Oh, happy day!

Job 10:10
Hast thou not poured me out as milk, and curdled me like cheese?

This is a poetic description of conception and gestation in the womb.

Job 10:11–14
Thou hast clothed me with skin and flesh, and hast fenced me with bones and sinews. Thou hast granted me life and favour, and thy visitation hath preserved my spirit. And these things hast thou hid in thine heart: I know that this is with thee. If I sin, then thou markest me, and thou wilt not acquit me from mine iniquity.

"You've done all this for me," Job says to God. "I was conceived miraculously and made wondrously. Yet, if I sin, You mark me like a target."

Job 10:15 (a)
If I be wicked, woe unto me; and if I be righteous, yet will I not lift up my head . . .

"If I'm wicked, You'll nail me," Job says to God. "And if I'm righteous, I can't lift my head because I'll get shot at." Job is terrified. He's confused. He doesn't know how to think or what to do.

Job 10:15 (b), 16
. . . I am full of confusion; therefore see thou mine affliction; For it increaseth. Thou

huntest me as a fierce lion: and again thou shewest thyself marvellous upon me.

"You hunt me down like a lion and You show Your marvelous power by crushing me," Job says to God.

Job 10:17
Thou renewest thy witnesses against me, and increasest thine indignation upon me; changes and war are against me.

"You bring in fresh troops to fight against me constantly," Job continues. This great man is going through unbelievable difficulty. He's a man of God, but a man nonetheless and here we see his humanity as he cries out in confusion by his own admission.

Job 10:18, 19
Wherefore then hast thou brought me forth out of the womb? Oh that I had given up the ghost, and no eye had seen me! I should have been as though I had not been; I should have been carried from the womb to the grave.

"Oh, that the first day of my life had been my last," Job laments.

Job 10:20–22
Are not my days few? cease then, and let me alone, that I may take comfort a little, Before I go whence I shall not return, even to the land of darkness and the shadow of death; A land of darkness, as darkness itself; and of the shadow of death, without any order, and where the light is as darkness.

Job asks God simply for a little break before he goes to the grave, to the place of darkness.

11

Listening to Job's argument causes Zophar, the third friend, to speak up. The fact that Zophar spoke last could likely mean that he was the youngest of Job's three friends but he was also the harshest. That's the way it often is. When we're younger, we tend to be a little more critical. As we get older, dashed hopes and failure have a way of smoothing some of our points.

Job 11:1–3
Then answered Zophar the Naamathite, and said, Should not the multitude of words be answered? and should a man full of talk be justified? Should thy lies make men hold their peace? and when thou mockest, shall no man make thee ashamed?

"How can I remain silent in the face of your lies and mockery?" Zophar asks Job.

In so doing, he makes a mistake that we can make oh, so easily. When someone is expressing confusion or dealing with depression, we can think it is up to us to defend God. In reality, however, God would say, "I care deeply about the person you want to correct. I know that, like you, he's made only of dust. I understand his frailty."

Job 11:4, 5
For thou hast said, My doctrine is pure, and I am clean in thine eyes. But oh that God would speak, and open his lips against thee;

"Oh that God would speak," Zophar said. Oh, but He did speak. In verse 8 of chapter 1, God declared that Job was the most righteous man on the face of the earth.

Job 11:6 (a)
And that he would shew thee the secrets of wisdom, that they are double to that which is!

"There are two sides to God's wisdom," Zophar said. In this, he was correct. From our side, things appear to be tangled and confused but from heaven's perspective, there is a beautiful picture being formed.

And when we get there, we're going to say, "Awesome, Lord! Now I see You were doing something grand and glorious all along."

Job 11:6 (b)
. . . Know therefore that God exacteth of thee less than thine iniquity deserveth.

"You think you have it tough? Let me tell you, Job, you should have it twice as bad as you do," Zophar said. As brutal as Zophar's words were, they were true in a sense for, because the wages of sin is death, all of us deserve to die. The question is, where does that leave Zophar?

Job 11:7–11
Canst thou by searching find out God? canst thou find out the Almighty unto perfection? It is as high as heaven; what canst thou do? deeper than hell; what canst thou know? The measure thereof is longer than the earth, and broader than the sea. If he cut off, and shut up, or gather together, then who can hinder him? For he knoweth vain men: he seeth wickedness also; will he not then consider it?

It is true that man cannot find God. Praise be to the Lord, therefore, that He found man.

After years spent reading about the existence

of God and struggling with the issue, C.S. Lewis writes that he was riding in the sidecar of a motorcycle on his way to a zoo outside London when God touched him and he was born again. He spent years searching, thinking wondering, and then God found him. Think of your own pilgrimage. At a certain point in time, God found you. It's not we who choose the Lord. Rather, the Lord chose us before the foundation of the world (Ephesians 1:4).

Job 11:12
For vain man would be wise, though man be born like a wild ass's colt.

An empty-headed man has as much chance of being wise as a donkey does of giving birth to a man.

Job 11:13–15 (a)
If thou prepare thine heart, and stretch out thine hands toward him; If iniquity be in thine hand, put it far away, and let not wickedness dwell in thy tabernacles. For then shalt thou lift up thy face without spot . . .

"Put away your sin, Job. Then you can lift your face to Him in innocence," Zophar declares.

Job 11:15 (b), 16
. . . yea, thou shalt be stedfast, and shalt not fear: Because thou shalt forget thy misery, and remember it as waters that pass away:

"All of your misery will be like water under the bridge the day you confess your sin and repent of the secret iniquity you're involved in," Zophar continues.

Job 11:17–19
And thine age shall be clearer than the noonday; thou shalt shine forth, thou shalt be as the morning. And thou shalt be secure, because there is hope; yea, thou shalt dig about thee, and thou shalt take thy rest in safety. Also thou shalt lie down, and none shall make thee afraid; yea, many shall make suit unto thee.

Not only will you be renewed and revived if you put away your sin, but your insomnia will be cured, your fear will be gone, and people will again come to you for counsel.

Job 11:20
But the eyes of the wicked shall fail, and they shall not escape, and their hope shall be as the giving up of the ghost.

"If they don't turn away from their obvious sin, the only hope the wicked have is death," Zophar insists.

And all the while, God listens.

12

Seeing his condition, Job's friends concluded that he must have done something terrible. After all, they argued, God is just. Therefore, Job must have been a terrible sinner to warrant the treatment he was receiving.

Job 12:1
And Job answered and said,

Here in chapter 12, Job will respond. With three prosecuting attorneys against him, Job will now speak as his own defense attorney.

Job 12:2
No doubt but ye are the people, and wisdom shall die with you.

"When you die, wisdom will leave the face of the earth," Job says to his friends, his words dripping with sarcasm.

Job 12:3
But I have understanding as well as you; I am not inferior to you: yea, who knoweth not such things as these?

"What you guys are telling me about the sovereignty and justice of God is common knowledge," Job continues.

Job 12:4, 5
I am as one mocked of his neighbour, who calleth upon God, and he answereth him: the just upright man is laughed to scorn. He that is ready to slip with his feet is as a lamp despised in the thought of him that is at ease.

It has been wisely said that when life is good, we don't have many questions but when life is bad, we don't have many answers. To his friends, Job says, "You guys are at ease. But I have some questions for you that perhaps you haven't thought through. I'm going to be like a headlight on high beam, shining right in your eyes, making you uncomfortable."

Job 12:6
The tabernacles of robbers prosper, and they that provoke God are secure; into whose hand God bringeth abundantly.

"Look around," Job says. "Notice that the wicked seem to be prospering. It seems as though God gives to them abundantly." Psalm 73 deals with this same issue . . .

> Truly God is good to Israel, even to such as are of a clean heart. But as for me, my feet were almost gone; my steps had well nigh slipped. For I was envious at the foolish, when I saw the prosperity of the wicked. For there are no bands in their death: but their strength is firm. They are not in trouble as other men; neither are they plagued like other men. Behold, these are the ungodly, who prosper in the world; they increase in riches. When I thought to know this, it was too painful for me; Until I went into the sanctuary of God; then understood I their end. Psalm 73:1–5, 12, 16, 17

Where did the psalmist regain the right perspective? In the sanctuary. How many are the times we have slipped and struggled until we plopped in a pew and, when the Word was opened, it spoke so directly and incisively to us that we regained perspective and remembered that it's all about eternity.

Job 12:7
But ask now the beasts, and they shall teach thee; and the fowls of the air, and they shall tell thee:

If you throw a potato chip on the sand, the seagulls don't say to each other, "You first." No, they fight for that chip as if their lives depended on it.

"It's a jungle out there and the strongest one wins. Where's the justice in that?" Job asks.

Job 12:8
Or speak to the earth, and it shall teach thee: and the fishes of the sea shall declare unto thee.

"Check out the fish," Job continues. "Who is the strongest? The shark." In other words, Job is saying that, contrary to his friends' assertion, it's not always the good guy who wins.

Job 12:9, 10
Who knoweth not in all these that the hand of the LORD hath wrought this? In whose hand is the soul of every living thing, and the breath of all mankind.

"Who has created the world to be this way?" Job asks. "The Lord."

Job 12:11
Doth not the ear try words? and the mouth taste his meat?

"Just as the mouth can determine whether food is bitter or sweet, my ears can determine whether your words be true or false," Job declares.

Job 12:12–17
With the ancient is wisdom; and in length of days understanding. With him is wisdom and strength, he hath counsel and understanding. Behold, he breaketh down, and it cannot be built again: he shutteth up a man, and there can be no opening. Behold, he withholdeth the waters, and they dry up: also he sendeth them out, and they overturn the earth. With him is strength and wisdom: the deceived and the deceiver are his. He leadeth counsellors away spoiled, and maketh the judges fools.

"With the ancient is wisdom." I believe Job is alluding to the Ancient of Days (Daniel 7:22). Unlike these guys who are pipsqueak philosophers, Job says there is wisdom in the One who has endless days.

Job 12:18–20
He looseth the bond of kings, and girdeth their loins with a girdle. He leadeth princes away spoiled, and overthroweth the mighty. He removeth away the speech of the trusty, and taketh away the understanding of the aged.

God reduces kings to slaves if He so chooses.

Job 12:21–25
He poureth contempt upon princes, and weakeneth the strength of the mighty. He discovereth deep things out of darkness, and bringeth out to light the shadow of death. He increaseth the nations, and destroyeth them: he enlargeth the nations, and straiteneth them again. He taketh away the heart of the chief of the people of the earth, and causeth them to wander in a wilderness where there is no way. They grope in the dark without light, and he maketh them to stagger like a drunken man.

Job contends that the leaders and governments of earth come and go, but God is King of kings. Thus, He is in complete and absolute control.

13

Job 13:1, 2
Lo, mine eye hath seen all this, mine ear hath heard and understood it. What ye know, the same do I know also: I am not inferior unto you.

After Zophar waxed eloquent about God's sovereignty, Job came back and said, "I can top that" and pushes the boundaries even further, maintaining that God can try the just if He so chooses.

Job 13:3
Surely I would speak to the Almighty, and I desire to reason with God.

"I'm tired of listening to your arguments," Job says. "I wish I could talk directly to the Almighty and reason with Him."

"Come, let us reason together," God says (see Isaiah 1:18).

It is the invitation and heart of our Father to do just that. And we have that opportunity, for James would say, "If any of you lack wisdom, let him ask of God who gives to all men liberally" (1:5).

"Woe be to the rebellious children, who take counsel but not of Me," God declares, "for in returning to Me you will be saved" (Isaiah 30:1, 15). Concerning whatever trial you might be going through, the key is to spend time with the Lord. No doubt there are people you want to talk with or turn to, but just as Job's counselors didn't have a clue, it's only the Father who can truly help you.

In previous generations, church services were followed by extended time at "the altar," where people would pour out their hearts to the Lord. That is, after taking in a Bible study, they would respond by kneeling before the Father and waiting on Him. All too often today, I wonder to what degree the need for counseling would be diminished if we took time to immediately respond to the issues on our hearts by spending time in prayer. May we be those who take time, who make time to come to the altar so that we truly can be "altared."

Job 13:4, 5
But ye are forgers of lies, ye are all physicians of no value. O that ye would altogether hold your peace! and it should be your wisdom.

Concluding that his counselors were no help at all, Job says to them, "The wisest thing you could do would be to shut your mouths."

Job 13:6, 7
Hear now my reasoning, and hearken to the pleadings of my lips. Will ye speak wickedly for God? and talk deceitfully for him?

"In attempting to defend God, you're actually offending Him," Job tells his friends. "You're speaking on His behalf, but what you're saying isn't the whole truth." Indeed, these three put a great deal of value on God's justice, but they forgot to add mercy and grace to the equation.

Job 13:8–10
Will ye accept his person? will ye contend for God? Is it good that he should search you out? or as one man mocketh another, do ye so mock him? He will surely reprove you, if ye do secretly accept persons.

"Are you arguing for God?" Job asks. "Are you prepared to have Him search you, or do you think you can fool Him, too? If you show partiality, you're guilty of hypocrisy."

Job 13:11
Shall not his excellency make you afraid? and his dread fall upon you?

"You lack the fear of God," Job says. "Don't you realize that you should be afraid of Him?"

Job 13:12
Your remembrances are like unto ashes, your bodies to bodies of clay.

"Your platitudes are like ashes. The body of your argument is like clay, frail and breakable."

Job 13:13
Hold your peace, let me alone, that I may speak, and let come on me what will.

"Don't interrupt me," Job says. "I'm going to say what I want and let the chips fall where they may."

Job 13:14, 15 (a)
Wherefore do I take my flesh in my teeth, and put my life in mine hand? Though he slay me, yet will I trust in him . . .

And with these words, Satan lost his bet. Although Job didn't navigate his difficulty perfectly, he completely shuts Satan down right here. "Even if I don't understand what God is doing, even though it seems to be to be unfair, even if He should slay me in the process, yet I will trust Him," Job proclaims. Yes, Job's faith will falter, but here it's ignited.

It's one thing to have faith for healing. It's a greater thing to have faith for sickness. That is, it takes greater faith to say, "I come to You for healing. But, Lord, should You, as You did to Paul, say, 'My grace is sufficient,' I will still trust You. I have faith in You, not faith that I can get You to do what I want You to do, but faith that You will do what's best."

Even if the affliction doesn't go away, even if the problem continues, even if the solution doesn't come, faith says, "Though You slay me, I will still trust You because You were slain for me. You gave up everything because You love me. Therefore, I embrace whatever You decide to do. You see things I don't. You know things I can't."

Here, with his body broken out in boils, with his worldly possession and his family taken from him, with his friends relentlessly accusing him, faith flares up in Job.

Job 13:15 (b)
. . . but . . .

"Though He slay me, yet will I trust Him, but . . ." Oh, Job, not the "but." You should have stopped with, "Yet will I trust Him. Period." That's the way it so often is. We say something great and then follow it up with a "but." Job's greatest statement of faith is followed by a statement of his greatest weakness . . .

Job 13:15 (c)
. . . I will maintain mine own ways before him.

"I'm going to defend my position," said Job.

Job 13:16
He also shall be my salvation: for an hypocrite shall not come before him.

"I will be vindicated," Job insisted, "because He won't allow a hypocrite to be victorious."

Job 13:17, 18
Hear diligently my speech, and my declaration with your ears. Behold now, I have ordered my cause; I know that I shall be justified.

"Yes, I trust God," said Job. "But I'm going to keep making my case."

Job 13:19
Who is he that will plead with me? for now, if I hold my tongue, I shall give up the ghost.

"It's up to me," Job said. "If I don't make my case, if I don't stand up for myself, I'll die."

Job 13:20, 21
Only do not two things unto me: then will I not hide myself from thee. Withdraw thine hand far from me: and let not thy dread make me afraid.

Job now directs his words to the Lord. "I ask two things of You, Lord," he says. "Take Your hand of punishment off of me. And, secondly, don't make me fear what You might do tomorrow."

Job 13:22, 23
Then call thou, and I will answer: or let me speak, and answer thou me. How many are mine iniquities and sins? make me to know my transgression and my sin.

"How much have I sinned?" Job asks. "Does it merit this much misery?"

Job 13:24
Wherefore hidest thou thy face, and holdest me for thine enemy?

"Are You hiding from me, Lord?" Job asks. "Am I an enemy in Your sight?"

Job 13:25, 26
Wilt thou break a leaf driven to and fro? and wilt thou pursue the dry stubble? For thou writest bitter things against me, and makest me to possess the iniquities of my youth.

Evidently, Job concludes that he is being punished for sins of his youth. Many of us can fall into this same error in the midst of trials and troubles. "It must be something I did years ago that's causing the trouble I'm in presently," we say, "something I forgot to confess."

I used to think that if there was one unconfessed sin in my life, God wouldn't hear my prayers. Therefore, as a little boy, I would spend a great deal of time at my bedside going over everything I could think of that I did that day or the previous day or the previous week or year so that I wouldn't be "out of fellowship." Then, one day I understood 1 John 1:9—that if I am faithful to confess whatever the Lord is convicting me of, whatever He brings to my mind or attention, He cleanses me of *all* unrighteousness. And I was wonderfully free!

Job 13:27, 28
Thou puttest my feet also in the stocks, and lookest narrowly unto all my paths; thou settest a print upon the heels of my feet.

And he, as a rotten thing, consumeth, as a garment that is moth eaten.

"I can't move on with my life," Job laments. "I can't move forward because I'm held prisoner by my punishment, eaten away daily by despair."

14

Job 14:1
Man that is born of a woman is of few days, and full of trouble.

"Man doesn't last long and the time he does have on earth is full of trouble," Job concludes.

Job 14:2–4
He cometh forth like a flower, and is cut down: he fleeth also as a shadow, and continueth not. And dost thou open thine eyes upon such an one, and bringest me into judgment with thee? Who can bring a clean thing out of an unclean? not one.

"How can You demand purity from one who is impure?" Job asks God. He's right, for, as David said, "In sin did my mother conceive me" (Psalm 51:5). We are depraved from the very beginning, gang. We are not sinners because we sin. We sin because we are sinners. That is, we were born in sin. It's in our genes. That's why we need a change of jeans—to be clothed in *His* righteousness (Isaiah 61:10).

Job 14:5, 6
Seeing his days are determined, the number of his months are with thee, thou hast appointed his bounds that he cannot pass; Turn from him, that he may rest, till he shall accomplish, as an hireling, his day.

"Life is short," Job says and again asks God for a break from his trial before he dies.

Job 14:7–10
For there is hope of a tree, if it be cut down, that it will sprout again, and that the tender branch thereof will not cease. Though the root thereof wax old in the earth, and the stock thereof die in the ground; Yet through the scent of water it will bud, and bring forth boughs like a plant. But man dieth, and wasteth away: yea, man giveth up the ghost, and where is he?

"If there's water around, even if a tree is cut down, it can spring back to life again," Job says. "What about me? When a man dies, what happens to him?"

Job 14:11, 12
As the waters fail from the sea, and the flood decayeth and drieth up: So man lieth down, and riseth not: till the heavens be no more, they shall not awake, nor be raised out of their sleep.

"Like water that evaporates or a flood that disappears in the ground below, so a man is not seen again," Job observes.

Job 14:13
O that thou wouldest hide me in the grave, that thou wouldest keep me secret, until thy wrath be past, that thou wouldest appoint me a set time, and remember me!

Even in his frustration, Job touches on some important truths. Here, for example, he expresses what happened before Christ came and died on the Cross of Calvary. That is, when a believer died in Old Testament days, he didn't go directly to heaven because his sin had not yet been paid for. So, according to the teaching of Jesus in Luke 16, he would go to the place of death that was divided into two compartments: the bad side where there was torment and flame, and the good side, Abraham's bosom, or paradise. In Ephesians 4:8 and 9, Paul writes that before Jesus ascended to heaven, He descended to the lower parts of the earth, Abraham's bosom, and led captivity captive. That is, He took those who were in the "holding tank" of paradise and took them to heaven.

"Remember me," Job cried.

"Remember me when You come into Your kingdom," the thief on the cross said to Jesus (Luke 23:42).

Job's prayer would be answered eventually. The thief's prayer would be answered immediately because of the finished work of the Cross.

Job 14:14, 15
If a man die, shall he live again? all the days of my appointed time will I wait, till my change come. Thou shalt call, and I will answer thee: thou wilt have a desire to the work of thine hands.

This is the ultimate question: Can man live again? "All of the days of my life, I will wait for that, Lord," Job says. "When You call, I'll answer." Here, again, Job expresses hope.

If you're not going through a trial presently, you will at some point. And when you do, remember Job. When does his faith flare up? Whenever he talks about living again, whenever he remembers the reality of eternity. Although it's hazy to him, when he focuses on heaven, suddenly there's hope in his heart.

That's why Jesus talked about heaven immediately after telling His disciples one of them would betray Him and that He was about to die (John 13:33—14:3). For hopeless and heavy hearts, the solution is always heaven. That's why the people of Israel were commanded by the Lord to put blue on the borders of their garments (Numbers 15:38). Blue is the color of heaven. Thus, they would be reminded that they were just passing through, that they were a heavenly people with every step they took.

"Let not your heart be troubled," Jesus said. "You believe in God, believe also in Me. In My Father's house are many mansions and I go to prepare a place for you, that where I am, you may be also." When we go through difficulties, trials, and heartaches, we can either let our hearts be troubled or keep them from being troubled. The choice is ours. It's not just a matter of positive thinking, but of thinking about what really matters. And what really matters is eternity. With every step you take, may your thoughts be of heaven.

Job 14:16
For now thou numberest my steps: dost thou not watch over my sin?

"Lord," cries Job, "You're judging every step I take." Again, this is how it works—when we go through trials, we have flare-ups of faith that are more often than not followed by dousings of doubt.

Job 14:17
My transgression is sealed up in a bag, and thou sewest up mine iniquity.

"Lord, You're collecting my sin and putting it in a bag," Job said. And, in a sense, he was right for, according to Micah 7:19, God does gather our sin and put it in a bag. But it's not to hold it over our heads—it's to cast it to the bottom of the sea. In Bible days, the Jews were terrified of the ocean. And here, the prophet declares that that's precisely where their sins would be dumped, in the place no one would go.

"As far as the east is from the west, that's how far your sins are from me," the Lord would declare (Psalm 103:12).

"Your sins and iniquities I will remember no more," the Lord declares (see Hebrews 10:17).

Job, it's true that your sins were collected in a bag but only to be cast into the sea of God's forgetfulness, the deepest place imaginable.

Job 14:18, 19 (a)
And surely the mountain falling cometh to nought, and the rock is removed out of his place. The waters wear the stones: thou washest away the things which grow out of the dust of the earth;

Mountains and rocks erode.

Job 14:19 (b)
. . . and thou destroyest the hope of man.

Job is despairing. "Just as mountains erode and rocks are removed on a given day, so, Lord You destroy the hope of man," he says.

Job 14:20, 21
Thou prevailest for ever against him, and he passeth: thou changest his countenance, and sendest him away. His sons come to honour, and he knoweth it not; and they are brought low, but he perceiveth it not of them. But his flesh upon him shall have pain, and his soul within him shall mourn.

"Thou changest his countenance," or, literally, "You make us wrinkled." Again, Job is right. We grow old, memory fades, and we experience pain physically and emotionally because life is tough and it takes a toll.

And so ends Round One of what will be a Three-Round Title fight.

15

The great debate is underway. The bell is about to ring for Round Two in a Three-Round Heavyweight bout between Job and his three friends who are theologically sparring. Job's three friends are trying to "knock some sense" into him by getting him to admit that he is a terrible sinner. We, however, know he's not. With the advantage of the first chapters of this book that bears his name, we know that what's taking place is not because of Job's sinfulness, but actually because of his righteousness.

Job 15:1, 2
Then answered Eliphaz the Temanite, and said, Should a wise man utter vain knowledge, and fill his belly with the east wind?

"You're supposed to be wise, Job, but you're full of hot air," Eliphaz says.

Job 15:3–6
Should he reason with unprofitable talk? or with speeches wherewith he can do no good? Yea, thou castest off fear, and restrainest

prayer before God. For thy mouth uttereth thine iniquity, and thou choosest the tongue of the crafty. Thine own mouth condemneth thee, and not I: yea, thine own lips testify against thee.

"It's not my fault, Job," says Eliphaz. "It's your own words that will condemn you." Eliphaz was more concerned about *being* right than about *doing* right. He makes his case. He states his points—all without compassion or sympathy. Why? I suggest it was because not only did Eliphaz want to be right intellectually, but he was concerned theologically. That is, if Job was right, if problems, pain, and difficulty were not the direct result of sin in a man's life, he himself could be the next target. Thus, for his own peace of mind, he felt he had to make an airtight case that bad things don't happen to good people.

We, too, have a tendency to want to put God in a box, to make things tidy and predictable. But the last people who tried to put Him in a box discovered He wouldn't stay there. Three days later, He rose again. The Lord doesn't stay in boxes you and I construct. "The Lord can't do this," we say. "He doesn't work that way," we insist. Are we sure?

Job 15:7–9
Art thou the first man that was born? or wast thou made before the hills? Hast thou heard the secret of God? and dost thou restrain wisdom to thyself? What knowest thou, that we know not? what understandest thou, which is not in us?

Eliphaz's speech rings a bell. In Numbers 16, Korah, Dathan, and Abiram came to Moses, saying, "You take too much upon yourself. Who set you up in this position? Are we not all endued with wisdom?"

Job 15:10
With us are both the grayheaded and very aged men, much elder than thy father.

Evidently, Job's friends were significantly older than he.

Job 15:11 (a)
Are the consolations of God small with thee?

"Is God's comfort not enough for you, Job?" Eliphaz asks.

Job 15:11 (b)–13
. . . is there any secret thing with thee? Why doth thine heart carry thee away? and what do thy eyes wink at, That thou turnest thy spirit against God, and lettest such words go out of thy mouth?

"What secret sin have you committed that has turned your heart against God and caused you to say things you shouldn't have said?" Eliphaz asks.

Job 15:14
What is man, that he should be clean? and he which is born of a woman, that he should be righteous?

"You claim to be righteous, Job, but can any man claim that?"

Job 15:15 (a)
Behold, he putteth no trust in his saints . . .

Even though to all that be in Rome, beloved of God, were called to be saints (e.g. Romans 1:7), we know that all have sinned (Romans 3:23). Therefore, Eliphaz is correct in saying that God can't trust us.

Job 15:15 (b)
. . . yea, the heavens are not clean in his sight.

Eliphaz is again right for Satan still has access to heaven. But there's coming a day when there will be a new heaven that hasn't been polluted by sin (Revelation 21:1).

Job 15:16
How much more abominable and filthy is man, which drinketh iniquity like water?

I find this intriguing because, although Eliphaz's points are valid, they don't tell the whole story. Yes, it's true that a man is born in iniquity. Yes, it's true that there is none righteous. But what a different heart we hear from a man who was a lover of God . . .

> What is man, that thou art mindful of him? and the son of man, that thou visitest him? For thou hast made him a little lower than the angels, and hast crowned him with glory and honour. Thou madest him to have dominion over the works of thy hands; thou hast put all things under his feet: All sheep and oxen, yea, and the beasts of the field; The fowl of the air, and the fish of the sea, and whatsoever passeth through the paths of the seas. O LORD our Lord, how excellent is thy name in all the earth!
> Psalm 8:4–9

Eliphaz says, "What is man? He drinks of evil continually. He's a sinner. He's unclean." That's true. But David, a lover of God who understands His grace and mercy adds, "But we're loved by You, God." The tone of the heart of David and Eliphaz are vastly different.

In our understanding of biblical principles, it is important that we do not become those who have knowledge but have not love lest we become as a clanging bell or a tinkling cymbal (1 Corinthians 13). Love is the key. Therefore, I believe the overarching lesson the Lord has for us in Job's miserable counselors is that, although they might have a point, they don't have a heart.

Job 15:17–19
I will shew thee, hear me; and that which I have seen I will declare; Which wise men have told from their fathers, and have not hid it: Unto whom alone the earth was given, and no stranger passed among them.

"The wise men of old know the truth and they passed it on to others," Eliphaz declares.

Job 15:20, 21
The wicked man travaileth with pain all his days, and the number of years is hidden to the oppressor. A dreadful sound is in his ears: in prosperity the destroyer shall come upon him.

"Even though the wicked man might prosper at first, destruction will inevitably come upon him," Eliphaz says. Job being the most prosperous man of the east, the application is obvious. Eliphaz is indicting Job.

Job 15:22–24
He believeth not that he shall return out of darkness, and he is waited for of the sword. He wandereth abroad for bread, saying, Where is it? he knoweth that the day of darkness is ready at his hand. Trouble and anguish shall make him afraid; they shall prevail against him, as a king ready to the battle.

The man Eliphaz describes was once prosperous but is now begging for bread, hearing things in his ears, and afraid of the dark. Filled with trepidation and anxiety, he's becoming neurotic. In this, Eliphaz is giving his impression of Job.

Job 15:25–27
For he stretcheth out his hand against God, and strengtheneth himself against the Almighty. He runneth upon him, even on his neck, upon the thick bosses of his bucklers: Because he covereth his face with his fatness, and maketh collops of fat on his flanks.

Eliphaz insists that the only explanation for a man who was once prosperous but later experiences tribulation is that at some point he defied God.

Job 15:28, 29
And he dwelleth in desolate cities, and in houses which no man inhabiteth, which are ready to become heaps. He shall not be rich, neither shall his substance continue, neither shall he prolong the perfection thereof upon the earth.

Continuing his erroneous assessment of Job, Eliphaz says, "Yes, you were fat. Yes, you were prosperous. But it's because you took advantage of people. Such a man will not prosper indefinitely. He'll have a reversal. The bubble will burst. There will be a day of reckoning."

Job 15:30
He shall not depart out of darkness; the flame shall dry up his branches, and by the breath of his mouth shall he go away.

It was fire that consumed Job's sheep and servants. Therefore, Eliphaz is making a heartless and cruel reference to Job's own experience.

Job 15:31, 32
Let not him that is deceived trust in vanity: for vanity shall be his recompence. It shall be accomplished before his time, and his branch shall not be green.

"Not only will emptiness be the wicked man's only reward, but he'll be cut off in the prime of life," Eliphaz says.

Job 15:33
He shall shake off his unripe grape as the vine, and shall cast off his flower as the olive.

This verse is especially cruel for it's an allusion to children. Job had just lost ten children. Eliphaz is referring to Job's personal experience—fire, loss of wealth, and loss of family.

Job 15:34, 35
For the congregation of hypocrites shall be desolate, and fire shall consume the tabernacles of bribery. They conceive mischief, and bring forth vanity, and their belly prepareth deceit.

Eliphaz continues to make his case theologically, but he's absolutely void of any kind of compassion, grace, or mercy. "Not only does the wicked man deceive others, but he deceives himself," he says, referring, of course, to Job as he audaciously and heartlessly weaves Job's painful experience into his sermon.

16

Job 16:1, 2
Then Job answered and said, I have heard many such things: miserable comforters are ye all.

Eliphaz's speech was nothing new to Job. A repeat of Round One, it was a little more cynical and cruel, but offered no new information or insights.

Job 16:3
Shall vain words have an end? or what emboldeneth thee that thou answerest?

"Won't you ever be quiet?" Job asks his friends. "How dare you speak like this!"

Job 16:4, 5
I also could speak as ye do: if your soul were in my soul's stead, I could heap up words against you, and shake mine head at you. But I would strengthen you with my mouth, and the moving of my lips should asswage your grief.

"If you were in my shoes and I in yours, I could come down on you, find fault with you, and point my finger at you," Job says. "But that's not what I would do. I would seek to strengthen you, to take away your grief."

When I desire direction, I always look to men who have gone through difficulties, been involved in battles, experienced breaking because they relate to me in an entirely different way than a man who hasn't been broken, who hasn't gone through very much. That is why it's important for us to realize that difficulties are actually blessings from the Lord, for they keep us from ending up like Job's friends: self-righteous and arrogant, heartless and cynical.

Job 16:6
Though I speak, my grief is not asswaged: and though I forbear, what am I eased?

"If I defend myself or keep silent, either way, I'm not being relieved of this grief," Job says.

Job 16:7, 8
But now he hath made me weary: thou hast made desolate all my company. And thou hast filled me with wrinkles, which is a witness against me: and my leanness rising up in me beareth witness to my face.

"I feel like a wrinkled bag of bones because of what I've been through. I'm aging prematurely," Job laments.

Job 16:9–17
He teareth me in his wrath, who hateth me: he gnasheth upon me with his teeth; mine enemy sharpeneth his eyes upon me. They have gaped upon me with their mouth; they have smitten me upon the cheek reproachfully; they have gathered themselves together against me. God hath delivered me to the ungodly, and turned me over into the hands of the wicked. I was at ease, but he hath broken me asunder: he hath also taken me by my neck, and shaken me to pieces, and set me up for his mark. His archers compass me round about, he cleaveth my reins asunder, and doth not spare; he poureth out my gall upon the ground. He breaketh me with breach upon breach, he runneth upon me like a giant. I have sewed sackcloth upon my skin, and defiled my horn in the dust. My face is foul with weeping, and my eyelids is the shadow of death; Not for any injustice in mine hands: also my prayer is pure.

After calling his friends miserable comforters, Job describes his own situation as though he's been torn, gnashed at with others' teeth, gaped at by others' eyes, smitten on the cheek, delivered to the hands of the ungodly, hung up like a target, poured out upon the ground, yet all the while innocent. But wait, Job. All of these descriptions are prophetic, pointing to the One who was to come who was literally hung up on the Cross like a target for His Father to pour out the wrath that should have been poured out on you and me.

This means, Job, in this whole ordeal you're going through, you're being like Jesus. I know you're struggling, questioning, and wondering, but you're becoming like Jesus in the process of this difficulty. You're going through what He would go through. He's entrusted you with the fellowship of suffering.

> That I may know him, and the power of his resurrection, and the fellowship of his sufferings, being made conformable unto his death;
> Philippians 3:10

A bonding takes place when you're with people who have suffered like you've suffered, who have cried like you've cried, and who have hurt like you've hurt. Even though Abraham's son would be spared, in obedience to God's command to offer him as a sacrifice, Abraham would.

Job 16:18, 19
O earth, cover not thou my blood, and let my cry have no place. Also now, behold, my witness is in heaven, and my record is on high.

Regardless of what his friends said about him, Job declared that God was his witness. When people come down on you, hang in there. Regardless of what they think, just keep loving the Lord, serving others, and celebrating your salvation.

Job 16:20
My friends scorn me: but mine eye poureth out tears unto God.

"I can't depend on my friends, but I can pour out my tears to God," Job concluded.

As often quoted, Corrie ten Boom said, "You'll never know the Lord is all you need until the Lord is all you have." It's true. As long as there are people around us whom we can turn to or lean on, we'll do that. So sometimes, the Lord takes away those props that we might learn to lean on Him and in so doing discover more than our best friends could ever provide.

Job 16:21, 22
O that one might plead for a man with God, as a man pleadeth for his neighbour! When a few years are come, then I shall go the way whence I shall not return.

This cry of Job is fully answered in the person of Jesus Christ, for if any man sin, we have an advocate with the Father in the person of Jesus Christ (1 John 2:1).

17

Job 17:1–3
My breath is corrupt, my days are extinct, the graves are ready for me. Are there not mockers with me? and doth not mine eye continue in their provocation? Lay down now, put me in a surety with thee; who is he that will strike hands with me?

"I can't go on much longer," Job says. "Oh, that there were someone who would take my side."

Job 17:4, 5
For thou hast hid their heart from understanding: therefore shalt thou not exalt them. He that speaketh flattery to his friends, even the eyes of his children shall fail.

"Flattery" in verse 5 literally refers to the idea of preying upon someone. That is, the result of preying on or picking on others is a lack of vision in their own kids. If, for example, kids are continually exposed to gossip and backbiting on the way home from church, their parents can't be surprised if they grow up with no desire to go to church. Therefore, we ought never to speak words of prey toward any sister or brother lest our kids become blind to spiritual things.

Job 17:6–8
He hath made me also a byword of the people; and aforetime I was as a tabret. Mine eye also is dim by reason of sorrow, and all my members are as a shadow. Upright men shall be astonied at this, and the innocent shall stir up himself against the hypocrite.

"I'm being beaten on like a drum," Job says. "My vision and life lack insight. Therefore, fair-minded men will be surprised by my ordeal."

Job 17:9, 10
The righteous also shall hold on his way, and he that hath clean hands shall be stronger and stronger. But as for you all, do ye return, and come now: for I cannot find one wise man among you.

"The righteous will go forward and onward," Job said. "The hypocrite, on the other hand, should just go back where he came from." This latter statement, referring to his friends, sounds caustic until we realize God would essentially say the same thing (42:7).

Job 17:11–16
My days are past, my purposes are broken off, even the thoughts of my heart. They change the night into day: the light is short because of darkness. If I wait, the grave is mine house: I have made my bed in the darkness. I have said to corruption, Thou art my father: to the worm, Thou are my mother, and my sister. And where is now my hope? as for my hope, who shall see it? They shall go down to the bars of the pit, when our rest together is in the dust.

"My good days are behind me. My hopes are dashed. My dreams are dark," Job laments. "And they will all accompany me to the grave."

Oh, Job will do better but not before he goes through even deeper waters . . .

18 George Bernard Shaw said the average conversation is like a phonograph with half a dozen records. You soon grow tired of them all. Certainly I suppose Job felt that way as he heard the same song being sung over and over by his three friends. "God is just," they said. "He rewards the righteous and punishes the wicked. Therefore if you're going through these things, it must be because you are wicked. Confess, Job. Get right."

In Round Two, we hear from Bildad . . .

Job 18:1, 2 (a)
Then answered Bildad the Shuhite, and said, How long will it be ere ye make an end of words?

"Job, when will you pipe down?" Bildad asks. If Bildad is impatient with Job, the feeling is mutual, as seen in the next chapter (19:2).

Job 18:2 (b)
. . . mark, and afterwards we will speak.

"Say something meaningful and then we'll converse," Bildad says.

Job 18:3
Wherefore are we counted as beasts, and reputed vile in your sight?

"You treat us like dumb, stupid animals. Why do you talk to us this way?" Bildad asks.

Job 18:4
He teareth himself in his anger: shall the earth be forsaken for thee? and shall the rock be removed out of his place?

"Job, will tearing your clothes cause the earth to be rocked? Will everything be shaken simply because you're going through this?" Bildad asks. At this point, Bildad will get very specific, likening the wicked man to a darkened light in verses 5 and 6, a trapped traveler in verses 7 through 10, a fugitive in verses 11 through 15, and a rotting tree in verses 16 through 21. And the implication is that they are all pictures of Job . . .

Job 18:5, 6
Yea, the light of the wicked shall be put out, and the spark of his fire shall not shine. The light shall be dark in his tabernacle, and his candle shall be put out with him.

According to Proverbs 20:27, the spirit of man is the candle of the Lord. Bildad's point is that the Lord can take the life of the wicked any time He chooses.

Job 18:7–10
The steps of his strength shall be straitened, and his own counsel shall cast him down. For he is cast into a net by his own feet, and he walketh upon a snare. The gin shall take him by the heel, and the robber shall prevail against him. The snare is laid for him in the ground, and a trap for him in the way.

The Hebrew word translated "snare" speaks of a pit covered by brush. A "gin" is a noose that, if stepped on, can suspend a person upside down. Thus, Bildad says, "The reason your life has been turned upside down, Job, is due to your own wickedness and sin."

Job 18:11–15
Terrors shall make him afraid on every side, and shall drive him to his feet. His strength shall be hungerbitten, and destruction shall be ready at his side. It shall devour the strength of his skin: even the firstborn of death shall devour his strength. His confidence shall be rooted out of his tabernacle, and it shall bring him to the king of terrors. It shall dwell in his tabernacle, because it is none of his: brimstone shall be scattered upon his habitation.

In Israel today, when a suicide bomber is identified, the house of his family is bulldozed. Bildad says that even though a fugitive experiences momentary freedom, his house will ultimately come crashing down around him.

Job 18:16–21
His roots shall be dried up beneath, and above shall his branch be cut off. His remembrance shall perish from the earth, and he shall have no name in the street. He shall be driven from light into darkness, and chased out of the world. He shall neither have son nor nephew among his people, nor any remaining in his dwellings. They that come after him shall be astonied at his day, as they that went before were affrighted. Surely such are the dwellings of the wicked, and this is the place of him that knoweth not God.

"Not only will your own life dry up from the roots, Job, but your family tree will be cut off as well," Bildad warns Job. Keep in mind, Job had just lost seven sons and three daughters, rendering Bildad's words especially cruel.

19

Job 19:1–3
Then Job answered and said, How long will ye vex my soul, and break me in pieces with words? These ten times have ye reproached me: ye are not ashamed that ye make yourselves strange to me.

"Over and over again you accuse me," Job replies. "Aren't you ashamed that you've hardened your heart against me?"

Job 19:4
And be it indeed that I have erred, mine error remaineth with myself.

"Even if I have erred," Job continues, "you haven't proved a thing."

Job 19:5, 6 (a)
If indeed ye will magnify yourselves against me, and plead against me my reproach: Know now that God hath overthrown me . . .

"If you're going to come down on me, you need to understand that what's happened to me has been by the hand of God," Job explains. "It's not what you think. It's not because of iniquity or rebellion. It's God who's doing this for reasons I don't know and can't understand."

Then Job proceeds to paint a more complete illustration of his situation, providing eight analogies, doubling Bildad's four . . .

Now Job says, let me give you a fuller picture, a more complete illustration of my desperate situation. Bildad brought up four analogies. Job will give eight . . .

Job 19:6 (b)
. . . and hath compassed me with his net.

"I'm like an innocent animal that has been trapped by God," Job says.

Job 19:7
Behold, I cry out of wrong, but I am not heard: I cry aloud, but there is no judgment.

"I am a wrongly accused criminal in court."

Job 19:8
He hath fenced up my way that I cannot pass, and he hath set darkness in my paths.

"I am a traveler fenced in without light. God has fenced me in and I can't see any way out," Job says.

Job 19:9
He hath stripped me of my glory, and taken the crown from my head.

"I'm like a king dethroned and defamed."

Job 19:10 (a)
He hath destroyed me on every side, and I am gone . . .

"I am like a structure destroyed."

Job 19:10 (b)
. . . and mine hope hath he removed like a tree.

"I am a tree that has been uprooted," Job says.

Job 19:11, 12
He hath also kindled his wrath against me, and he counteth me unto him as one of his enemies. His troops come together, and raise up their way against me, and encamp round about my tabernacle.

"I'm like a besieged enemy."

Job 19:13–20
He hath put my brethren far from me, and mine acquaintance are verily estranged from me. My kinsfolk have failed, and my familiar friends have forgotten me. They that dwell in mine house, and my maids, count me for a stranger: I am an alien in their sight. I called my servant, and he gave me no answer; I intreated him with my mouth. My breath is strange to my wife, though I intreated for the children's sake of mine own body. Yea, young children despised me; I arose, and they spake against me. All my inward friends abhorred me: and they whom I loved are turned against me. My bone cleaveth to my skin and to my flesh, and I am escaped with the skin of my teeth.

"Finally, I am a man forsaken and forgotten," Job laments.

Job 19:21 (a)
Have pity upon me, have pity upon me, O ye my friends . . .

Abraham Lincoln wisely said that he has a right to criticize who has a heart to help. Job's friends, however, weren't there to help. Oh, initially, they might have come with that in mind. But now they were more interested in being right than in doing right.

Job 19:21 (b)
. . . for the hand of God hath touched me.

Job is not quite right on this point because it is not the hand of God that has caused these things to happen. We know from chapters 1 and 2 that it was actually the work of Satan. But Job didn't know this. All he knew was there was no big sin in his life that merited his treatment.

"Wait," you say. "It might not have been God's hand directly, but He removed His hand of protection from Job and allowed the Adversary to bring these things into Job's life. God could have protected him, couldn't He?"

Yes. But once again, when we look at the hand of God that could have shielded Job, we see a hole where a nail pierced it as He hung on the Cross for you, for me, and for Job. Every time we get into a hard situation, we tend to mentally put God on trial. But the answer will always be found in "Cross-examination"—for as we look at the Cross, we have no other option but to say, "Lord, I understand that You are madly in love with me. You proved it absolutely when You died in my place so that my sins could be washed away and I could live with You forever. Therefore, although I might have lots of questions and confusion, the reality is that every time I hold Your broken body and blood, I realize that You care passionately about me, that, in fact, You love me to death."

Looking back at what Job says concerning himself in chapter 19, we see a picture of Jesus. That's not surprising, for the answer to all Job's questions, as well as the answer to all our confusion is always Jesus . . .

- In verse 7, Job said, "I cry out to God but am not heard."
  "Why hast thou forsaken me?" Jesus cried from the Cross of Calvary.
- In verse 8, Job said, "My path is covered in darkness."
  Darkness covered the face of the earth as Jesus hung on the Cross.
- In verse 9, Job said, "I am stripped of my glory and my crown has been taken."
  Jesus was stripped as He hung on the Cross and the crown of His majesty was replaced by a crown of thorns.
- In verse 10, Job said, "God has destroyed me."
  Jesus was marred, beaten, and disfigured more than any other man, Isaiah tells us (53:5), in ways we can't understand this side of heaven.
- In verse 10, Job said, "My hope has been removed like a tree."
  Jesus was pinned to a tree.
- In verse 11, Job said, "God has kindled His wrath against me."
  The wrath that should have been poured out on us was poured out on Jesus.
- In verse 12, Job said, "God's armies are come together against me."
  Jesus was crucified not only by Roman soldiers, but by all of humanity.
- In verse 13, Job said, "My family is estranged from me.
  Jesus' own brothers didn't believe in Him and His disciples ran from Him.

As Jesus hung on the Cross, the Roman soldiers came to break His legs in order to put Him to death quickly, the next day being a holy day. But when they came to speed up the death process, they marveled that He was already dead. In other words, Jesus died more quickly than they thought He would. He gave up the ghost sooner than they had anticipated. Perhaps sometimes we go through elongated difficulties and trials because, like Job, we're struggling to prove our point, to justify our position, or to have our way. But could it be that the Lord might say, "Just die. Give it up. Lay it down"?

Truly, there can be no reconciliation apart from death (Hebrews 9:16). Reconciliation between any two people cannot take place without death. Somebody's gotta die. The only question is who and when? Wouldn't it have been a tragedy if Jesus had kept on struggling on the Cross hour after hour, day after day? Aren't we glad that Jesus laid His life down after six hours? Why did He die so quickly? I suggest it was because the sooner He died, the sooner He would rise.

So, too, the sooner we die, resurrection and restoration will follow. I wonder if there is a husband or wife who is going through trials in their marriage because you're right and she's wrong. I wonder if there is a friend who is avoiding another because it's her fault not yours. Here's a better idea: Give it up. Let it go. Lay it down. Die.

To ensure that Jesus was indeed dead, the Roman soldiers jabbed a spear in His side and out poured blood and water, the signs of a broken heart. You'll know you're truly dead to your rights, your point, your self if, when the sticking point is jabbed in your side, the only thing that flows from you is water and blood, redemption and refreshment.

Job 19:22, 23
Why do ye persecute me as God, and are not satisfied with my flesh? Oh that my words were now written! oh that they were printed in a book!

Job, your words will indeed be written in a book. In fact, it will be a best-seller.

Job 19:24
That they were graven with an iron pen and lead in the rock for ever!

Job couldn't have known this, but his words have been engraved on countless tombstones throughout history. At this low ebb with friends forsaking him and God confusing him, Job has yet another grand and glorious breakthrough of faith . . .

Job 19:25, 26
For I know that my redeemer liveth, and that he shall stand at the latter day upon the earth: And though after my skin worms destroy this body, yet in my flesh shall I see God:

The word "redeemer" or *goel*, speaks of one who can set free, purchase back, or recoup what has been lost.

In chapter 9, Job said, "I wish I had a daysman."

In chapter 16, he said, "I wish I had an advocate."

Here in chapter 19, he says, "I know I have a Redeemer."

There is an increasingly clear and powerful revelation that takes place as Job's tribulation continues. That's the way it works in spiritual life. Job is confused, but there are fantastic revelations that come his way in the midst of his personal tribulation, and that's what we will discover, as well. In the time of tribulation, there is inevitably grand and glorious revelation of who our Lord is. From Genesis through Revelation, we see this theme over and over again. Whenever God's people go through tribulation and difficulty, testing and trial, they inevitably receive fresh understanding and revelation concerning the nature, the character, and the reality of our Lord.

We see not only revelation, but redirection. That is, when Job was at the bottom, he started thinking about eternity in a way he perhaps never would have had everything remained comfortable. I'm convinced that prosperity is a far greater problem for us than persecution is because when we're prosperous, we tend not to think about eternity or heaven. We start living for this life. So, in His goodness, the Lord says to us, "In order to get you thinking about heaven—where you're going to spend the next gazillion years—to get your focus off of the football game, your backyard, or your car, I will send challenges, trials, and difficulties your way. When you're at the bottom the only place you can look is up."

Tensions in relationships, setbacks in business, debilitating illnesses all make us long for heaven. That's why the Lord allows them to come into our lives. Without them, we would be too rooted in a world that is passing away. And God loves us too much for that.

Job would have greater understanding of who God is and a greater hope for the future solely because of his losses and difficulties. "In my flesh, I will see God," he declares. "This is not the end of the road for me."

Job 19:27
Whom I shall see for myself, and mine eyes shall behold, and not another; though my reins be consumed within me.

"Not another" literally means "not a stranger." In other words, Job said, "I'm going to see God and I'll know Him." How would Job recognize God. Through the time they spent together in the fellowship of suffering.

Job 19:28, 29
But ye should say, Why persecute we him, seeing the root of the matter is found in me? Be ye afraid of the sword: for wrath bringeth the punishments of the sword, that ye may know there is a judgment.

"You guys should be careful," Job warns his friends, "because judgment day is coming."

How do you summarize success? Bildad, Zophar, and Eliphaz would say it is to live a life of ease and prosperity, free from tribulation and difficulty. Jesus' definition of success, however, is to hear Him say, "Well done, good and faithful servant." Unlike his friends, Job was slowly but surely beginning to understand this.

20

Zophar now enters the fray. This will be the last time we hear from him . . .

Job 20:1–5
Then answered Zophar the Naamathite, and said, Therefore do my thoughts cause me to answer, and for this I make haste. I have heard the check of my reproach, and the spirit of my understanding causeth me to answer. Knowest thou not this of old, since

man was placed upon earth, That the triumphing of the wicked is short, and the joy of the hypocrite but for a moment?

"It is the evil man who dies young," Zophar says. How, then, Zophar do you explain Robert Murray McCheyne, the great Scottish preacher who died at twenty-nine, David Brainerd, missionary to the American Indians, who died at twenty-eight, Jim Eliot, missionary to the Auca Indians who died at twenty-four? Once again, Zophar is wrong.

Job 20:6–9
Though his excellency mount up to the heavens, and his head reach unto the clouds; Yet he shall perish for ever like his own dung: they which have seen him shall say, Where is he? He shall fly away as a dream, and shall not be found: yea, he shall be chased away as a vision of the night. The eye also which saw him shall see him no more; neither shall his place any more behold him.

"The godless will be utterly forgotten," Zophar contends.

Job 20:10
His children shall seek to please the poor, and his hands shall restore their goods.

In other words, the children of the godless man will have to repay his debts.

Job 20:11–14
His bones are full of the sin of his youth, which shall lie down with him in the dust. Though wickedness be sweet in his mouth, though he hide it under his tongue; Though he spare it, and forsake it not; but keep it still within his mouth: Yet his meat in his bowels is turned, it is the gall of asps within him.

"Your bones ache, Job," said Zophar. "Your family has been destroyed. And the sin that once seemed so sweet has worked its way down to your belly and is making you sick."

Job 20:15–19
He hath swallowed down riches, and he shall vomit them up again: God shall cast them out of his belly. He shall suck the poison of asps: the viper's tongue shall slay him. He shall not see the rivers, the floods, the brooks of honey and butter. That which he laboured for shall he restore, and shall not swallow it down: according to his substance shall the restitution be, and he shall not rejoice therein. Because he hath oppressed and hath forsaken the poor; because he hath violently taken away an house which he builded not;

Zophar says, "I think I've got the read on you, Job. You exploited the poor. You kicked them out of their homes. You absorbed their property. That's why you're so wealthy."

Job 20:20
Surely he shall not feel quietness in his belly, he shall not save of that which he desired.

"The wicked man won't be able to keep that which he dreamed of. It's all going to disappear," Zophar says.

Job 20:21, 22
There shall none of his meat be left; therefore shall no man look for his goods. In the fulness of his sufficiency he shall be in straits: every hand of the wicked shall come upon him.

"At the pinnacle of his power, at the height of his career, the godless will be in difficulty," Zophar declares.

Job 20:23–26 (a)
When he is about to fill his belly, God shall cast the fury of his wrath upon him, and shall rain it upon him while he is eating. He shall flee from the iron weapon, and the bow of steel shall strike him through. It is drawn, and cometh out of the body; yea, the glittering sword cometh out of his gall: terrors are upon him. All darkness shall be hid in his secret places . . .

"The treasure of the wicked will never be found. It will be lost in the dark," Zophar contends.

Job 20:26 (b)
. . . a fire not blown shall consume him; it shall go ill with him that is left in his tabernacle.

Keep in mind that Job has lost his wealth. Fire has come down and consumed his herds. Therefore, Zophar's accusations are very pointedly aimed at him.

Job 20:27–29
The heaven shall reveal his iniquity; and the earth shall rise up against him. The increase of his house shall depart, and his goods shall flow away in the day of his wrath. This is

the portion of a wicked man from God, and the heritage appointed unto him by God.

I imagine Job was glad that Zophar was finally finished.

21

Job 21:1–3
But Job answered and said, Hear diligently my speech, and let this be your consolations. Suffer me that I may speak; and after that I have spoken, mock on.

"Console me simply by listening to me," Job tells his friends. "Then, after I've spoken, you can continue mocking me if you choose."

Job 21:4
As for me, is my complaint to man? and if it were so, why should not my spirit be troubled?

"My argument isn't with man, but with God," Job says. "No wonder my spirit is troubled. I don't understand what He's doing."

Job 21:5, 6
Mark me, and be astonished, and lay your hand upon your mouth. Even when I remember I am afraid, and trembling taketh hold on my flesh.

"You're going to be shocked by what I have to say," Job says. "My own thoughts cause me to tremble. I know I'm on thin ice. I know I'm out on a limb in questioning Him. But I must be honest."

Job 21:7
Wherefore do the wicked live, become old, yea, are mighty in power?

"How is it that the wicked live to a ripe, old age?" Job asks.

Job 21:8
Their seed is established in their sight with them, and their offspring before their eyes.

"The children of the wicked grow up and take over after them."

Job 21:9–13
Their houses are safe from fear, neither is the rod of God upon them. Their bull gendereth, and faileth not; their cow calveth, and casteth not her calf. They send forth their little ones like a flock, and their children dance. They take the timbrel and harp, and rejoice at the sound of the organ. They spend their days in wealth, and in a moment go down to the grave.

"God doesn't discipline or punish the wicked. Everything goes well with them. And on top of that, they die painlessly," Job says.

Job 21:14, 15
Therefore they say unto God, Depart from us; for we desire not the knowledge of thy ways. What is the Almighty, that we should serve him? and what profit should we have, if we pray unto him?

"The wicked aren't interested in God because they do just fine without Him," Job concludes.

Job 21:16, 17 (a)
Lo, their good is not in their hand: the counsel of the wicked is far from me. How oft is the candle of the wicked put out!

The exclamation mark here would have been better translated as a question mark.

Job 21:17 (b)
. . . and how oft cometh their destruction upon them!

"The wicked don't seem to be snuffed out," Job says. "On the contrary, they seem to do well."

Job 21:17 (c), 18
. . . God distributeth sorrows in his anger. They are as stubble before the wind, and as chaff that the storm carrieth away.

Continuing his argument, Job says, "How often do you see the wicked snuffed out? In reality, it's just the opposite. When the winds of adversity blow, the wicked are like chaff. They just go with the flow, unaffected by it at all."

Job 21:19
God layeth up his iniquity for his children: he rewardeth him, and he shall know it.

Here, Job alludes to an old adage that says God will deal with the children of the wicked.

Job 21:20, 21
His eyes shall see his destruction, and he shall drink of the wrath of the Almighty. For what pleasure hath he in his house after him, when the number of his months is cut off in the midst?

"What does the wicked man care what happens to his family when he dies? He's dead anyway.

He's lived in prosperity, pleasure, and power. And even if his kids were to be judged down the road, what does he care?" Job asks.

Job 21:22
Shall any teach God knowledge? seeing he judgeth those that are high.

"God is the highest court on the earth. There is no higher court of appeals," Job says.

Job 21:23–26
One dieth in his full strength, being wholly at ease and quiet. His breasts are full of milk, and his bones are moistened with marrow. And another dieth in the bitterness of his soul, and never eateth with pleasure. They shall lie down alike in the dust, and the worms shall cover them.

"Rich and poor both end up in the same place. Everything ends in the grave."

Job 21:27, 28
Behold, I know your thoughts, and the devices which ye wrongfully imagine against me. For ye say, Where is the house of the prince? and where are the dwelling places of the wicked?

"I know what you're thinking," Job says. "You're going to tell me stories of the wicked men who were once rich but were later judged."

Job 21:29
Have ye not asked them that go by the way? and do ye not know their tokens,

"Ask the guy on the street if the wicked get away with their wickedness. If it always pays to be righteous."

Job 21:30
That the wicked is reserved to the day of destruction? they shall be brought forth to the day of wrath.

"The wicked seem to be protected from destruction," Job concludes. "They seem to be unaffected by the events that deal a bitter blow to others."

Job 21:31
Who shall declare his way to his face? and who shall repay him what he hath done?

"No one dares to rebuke those who are powerful and prosperous. They seem to get away with behavior that would be unacceptable for anyone else," Job says.

"If you're prospering, you're righteous. If you're suffering, you're wicked," Job's friends said.

"That's not the way it works!" Job protests. "Evil men prosper greatly."

Job 21:32, 33
Yet shall he be brought to the grave, and shall remain in the tomb. The clods of the valley shall be sweet unto him, and every man shall draw after him, as there are innumerable before him.

"When the wicked man dies, there is a large funeral processional, complete with glowing eulogies."

Job 21:34
How then comfort ye me in vain, seeing in your answers there remaineth falsehood?

"Your arguments are illogical," Job says to his friends. But Job's friends have to insist that only the wicked are punished because if they're wrong, anyone—including them—could fall prey to what had befallen Job.

22 Here in chapter 22, as we hear from Eliphaz for the last time, we come to the Third and final round of this Three-Round, Heavyweight bout . . .

Job 22:1–3
Then Eliphaz the Temanite answered and said, Can a man be profitable unto God, as he that is wise may be profitable unto himself? Is it any pleasure to the Almighty, that thou art righteous? or is it gain to him, that thou makest thy ways perfect?

"Do you think it pleases God that you're claiming to be righteous and perfect?" Eliphaz asks Job.

Job 22:4, 5
Will he reprove thee for fear of thee? will he enter with thee into judgment? Is not thy wickedness great? and thine iniquities infinite?

"Admit it, Job. You're the world's biggest sinner," Eliphaz insists.

Job 22:6–9
For thou hast taken a pledge from thy brother for nought, and stripped the naked

of their clothing. Thou hast not given water to the weary to drink, and thou hast withholden bread from the hungry. But as for the mighty man, he had the earth; and the honourable man dwelt in it. Thou has sent widows away empty, and the arms of the fatherless have been broken.

Eliphaz accuses Job of favoring the rich and powerful and ripping off the poor.

Job 22:10, 11
Therefore snares are round about thee, and sudden fear troubleth thee; Or darkness, that thou canst not see; and abundance of waters cover thee.

"Because of your sin, Job, you're in the dark and flooded with judgment, just like in Noah's day," Eliphaz says.

Job 22:12
Is not God in the height of heaven? and behold the height of the stars, how high they are!

"God is higher than the stars and He sees everything. He knows what you've been doing," Eliphaz declares.

Job 22:13–15
And thou sayest, How doth God know? can he judge through the dark cloud? Thick clouds are a covering to him, that he seeth not; and he walketh in the circuit of heaven. Hast thou marked the old way which wicked men have trodden?

"Nothing is hidden from God. He sees you're walking down the same old tired path that the wicked have walked for years," Eliphaz says.

Job 22:16, 17
Which were cut down out of time, whose foundation was overflown with a flood: Which said unto God, Depart from us: and what can the Almighty do for them?

The wicked man says, "We don't want God around. What can He do for us?"

Job 22:18 (a)
Yet he filled their houses with good things . . .

"Even though the wicked man wants nothing to do with God, God blesses him anyway." In this, Eliphaz is right, for Jesus said the sun shines on both the evil and the good (Matthew 5:45). The problem is, for the worldling, this is the best it's going to be. For us, however, this is the worst it's going to be because we're going to heaven.

Job 22:18 (b)–20
. . . but the counsel of the wicked is far from me. The righteous see it, and are glad: and the innocent laugh them to scorn. Whereas our substance is not cut down, but the remnant of them the fire consumeth.

"The righteous will go on," Eliphaz says. "The wicked, however, are ultimately burned and consumed."

Job 22:21, 22
Acquaint now thyself with him, and be at peace: thereby good shall come unto thee. Receive, I pray thee, the law from his mouth, and lay up his words in thine heart.

"Job, get acquainted with God," Eliphaz says. "Receive His Word. Get right with Him."

Job 22:23
If thou return to the Almighty, thou shalt be built up, thou shalt put away iniquity far from thy tabernacles.

"If you'll humble yourself before God, you'll be built up," Eliphaz says.

Job 22:24, 25
Then shalt thou lay up gold as dust, and the gold of Ophir as the stones of the brooks. Yea, the Almighty shall be thy defence, and thou shalt have plenty of silver.

"Get right with God and you'll prosper like you once did before you fell into such obvious sin," Eliphaz says.

How did Eliphaz know about Job's supposed sin of having a hard heart toward the needy and taking advantage of people cruelly? After all, Eliphaz lived in an entirely different region. I suggest he came on the scene and, confused by Job's situation, he did his own investigation, listening to what others said about Job. Because Job was the most prosperous man on earth, no doubt people were jealous of him. Thus, it would not be surprising if their report was negative. Eliphaz, nonetheless, chose to listen and buy in to their appraisal.

All too often, we do exactly the same thing. We form opinions about people based on whatever negative things we hear. We choose to uncover sin rather than to discover a saint, to find fault rather than to find fruit. Our flesh believes the worst. Love, on the other hand, hopes all things (1 Corinthians 13).

In chapter 29, we'll see the accusations leveled against Job are not true at all.

Job 22:26, 27
For then shalt thou have thy delight in the Almighty, and shalt lift up thy face unto God. Thou shalt make thy prayer unto him, and he shall hear thee, and thou shalt pay thy vows.

Eliphaz extends a great invitation. The problem is, it is the wrong situation, for his words don't apply to Job.

Job 22:28
Thou shalt also decree a thing, and it shall be established unto thee: and the light shall shine upon thy ways.

This assumption of Eliphaz is the same one we hear today under the banner of "prosperity teaching." The problem with it is that such teaching assumes that we know what to ask for, that we know what's best. We don't.

Job 22:29, 30
When men are cast down, then thou shalt say, There is lifting up; and he shall save the humble person. He shall deliver the island of the innocent: and it is delivered by the pureness of thine hands.

Eliphaz ends by saying, "God will use you, Job, if you get right and open your heart."

23

Job 23:1–4
Then Job answered and said, Even to day is my complaint bitter: my stroke is heavier than my groaning. Oh that I knew where I might find him! that I might come even to his seat! I would order my cause before him, and fill my mouth with arguments.

In answer to Eliphaz's invitation, Job says, "I need a confrontation with the Lord in order to present my case to Him."

Job 23:5
I would know the words which he would answer me, and understand what he would say unto me.

"I would not only argue my case, but would listen to what God has to say to me."

In this, I'm reminded of the words of another who verbally wrestled with God. "I will stand upon my watch," Habakkuk declared, "and set me upon the tower, and will watch to see what he will say unto me, and what I shall answer when I am reproved" (2:1).

Job 23:6
Will he plead against me with his great power? No; but he would put strength in me.

"God wouldn't argue against me. He would encourage me," Job says.

Job 23:7–9
There the righteous might dispute with him; so should I be delivered for ever from my judge. Behold, I go forward, but he is not there; and backward, but I cannot perceive him: On the left hand, where he doth work, but I cannot behold him: he hideth himself on the right hand, that I cannot see him:

Job looked to the left, to the right, ahead, and behind. But he needed to look up.

Job 23:10 (a)
But he knoweth the way that I take . . .

Even though Job couldn't see God, he knew God would see him. Jesus said the Father seeks those who will worship Him in spirit and in truth (John 4:23). And I have discovered that it's a lot easier for God to find me than for me to find Him. Morning by morning, week by week, year after year, I have found this to be such a wonderful, simple, practical key: Worship the Lord because the Father zeroes in on those who worship Him. Worship Him in spirit and truth and see how He'll make Himself oh, so real to you in those morning hours before the breaking of the day or in the quiet hours of the night.

Psalm 22 says the Lord inhabits—or, literally, is enthroned upon—the praises of His people. Therefore, when I praise Him, I provide a throne for Him to rule over me and to make Himself known to me.

Job 23:10 (b)
. . . when he hath tried me, I shall come forth as gold.

"I don't have a lot of answers," Job admits. "But this I do know: God knows where I am and when He's tried me, I'll come forth as gold."

I believe it is this verse Peter refers to when he writes, "Our faith, tried by fire, is much more precious than gold that perishes" (see 1 Peter 1:7). In Bible days, gold was purified by increasing the temperature of molten gold to the place where the dross would be burned away and the smelter would know the process was complete when he looked into the pot of molten gold and saw the reflection of his own face.

That's what God wants from Job, from me, and from you. He wants to see His reflection in us. So He allows fiery trials to come our way in order that the impurities might be burned off. Why does He want to see His own reflection? Because He knows He is the essence of life, abundant life, real life.

When Jesus said, "I have come that you might have life and life more abundantly," not a single person contested His claim. Multitudes were drawn to Him because of the abundant life that flowed from Him. "I want you to have the abundance I enjoy, the richness, the beauty, the joy, the peace that is Mine," He says to us. "I want you to be like Me because I am life to the greatest degree."

Job 23:11, 12
My foot hath held his steps, his way have I kept, and not declined. Neither have I gone back from the commandment of his lips; I have esteemed the words of his mouth more than my necessary food.

"I have walked in His ways," Job says. "I've kept His commands. And if I have a choice between breakfast and devotions, I go for devotions; between a lunch break with the guys or quiet time with the Lord, I'll opt for time with the Lord." No wonder Job was a righteous man. He had a passion for the Word of God.

Job 23:13–17
But he is in one mind, and who can turn him? and what his soul desireth, even that he doeth. For he performeth the thing that is appointed for me: and many such things are with him. Therefore am I troubled at his presence: when I consider, I am afraid of him. For God maketh my heart soft, and the Almighty troubleth me: Because I was not cut off before the darkness, neither hath he covered the darkness from my face.

"I've walked in His ways, I've prioritized His Word, but I'm still in the dark," Job says. "Therefore, I need to stand before the judge of all the earth and present my case to Him. My questions are for God. I would present my case in such a way that He would hear what I say and would encourage me. But, because I can't stand before Him, I'm just kept in the dark."

After walking this far with Job, after knowing something of his heart, we want to break into the story and say, "Job, your problem is that you want to be the defense attorney when, in fact, you are actually the star witness. You don't understand your role. The case is between the Father and the accuser, the Father and the Adversary, the Father and Satan. You are simply a witness of God's keeping power, of His mercy and grace."

Jesus said, "You shall receive power when the Holy Ghost comes upon you to be My witnesses" (Acts 1:8). He didn't say to witness, primarily, but simply to *be* witnesses of what God can do as we go through hard times, setbacks, and difficulty.

Dear brother, precious sister, you're a witness. What's happening is big. It's eternal. Peter tells us angels are looking in, studying this amazing thing called salvation (1 Peter 1:12). The demons are looking on. Satan is snarling. God is smiling and saying, "Watch and see the reality of My faithfulness."

We don't have to figure it out, gang. We don't have to make a case, argue, or defend. We just have to *be* witnesses of what God has already done.

24

Job 24:1
Why, seeing times are not hidden from the Almighty, do they that know him not see his days?

"Since God is not constrained by time, why do godly people not have their day?" Job asks. Then he goes on to talk about the injustice he sees in the country in verses 2 through 11, followed by the injustice he sees in the city in verses 12 through 17.

Job 24:2
Some remove the landmarks; they violently take away flocks, and feed thereof.

Job notes that people remove property markers and eat stolen sheep.

Job 24:3
They drive away the ass of the fatherless, they take the widow's ox for a pledge.

"Widows and orphans are being ripped off by evil men," Job says.

Job 24:4, 5
They turn the needy out of the way: the poor of the earth hide themselves together. Behold, as wild asses in the desert, go they forth to their work; rising betimes for a prey: the wilderness yieldeth food for them and for their children.

"The poor have to go into the desert place to find food for themselves and their families."

Job 24:6
They reap every one his corn in the field: and they gather the vintage of the wicked.

"The wicked exploit the poor widows and fatherless children."

Job 24:7, 8
They cause the naked to lodge without clothing, that they have no covering in the cold. They are wet with the showers of the mountains, and embrace the rock for want of a shelter.

"The poor lack homes and even clothes to cover and shelter them," Job says.

Job 24:9
They pluck the fatherless from the breast, and take a pledge of the poor.

"So wicked are these men that they even hold kids as collateral," Job says.

Job 24:10, 11
They cause him to go naked without clothing, and they take away the sheaf from the hungry; Which make oil within their walls, and tread their winepresses, and suffer thirst.

"The poor are the ones laboring to produce wine and oil, yet they're not allowed to partake of them," Job says. "They work hard, but don't share in the reward."

Job 24:12
Men groan from out of the city, and the soul of the wounded crieth out: yet God layeth not folly to them.

Job observes problems in the city, as well, where people get beat up.

Job 24:13
They are of those that rebel against the light; they know not the ways thereof, nor abide in the paths thereof.

"Evil men in the city neither walk in the light nor do what's right," Job says.

Job 24:14
The murderer rising with the light killeth the poor and needy, and in the night is as a thief.

Job is intelligent and observant. "Wherever I look," he says, "be it in the city or the countryside, I see injustice."

Job 24:15–17
The eye also of the adulterer waiteth for the twilight, saying, No eye shall see me: and disguiseth his face. In the dark they dig through houses, which they had marked for themselves in the daytime: they know not the light. For the morning is to them even as the shadow of death: if one know them, they are in the terrors of the shadow of death.

"Thieves scope out the houses they want to break into in the daytime and then return at night."

In the following seven verses, Job's frustration seems to mount as he denounces the evil man . . .

Job 24:18
He is swift as the waters; their portion is cursed in the earth: he beholdeth not the way of the vineyards.

A better rendering of the first phrase of this verse would be, "May he be as swift as waters." In other words, "May the evil man pass from the scene quickly."

Job 24:19, 20
Drought and heat consume the snow waters: so doth the grave those which have sinned. The womb shall forget him; the worm shall feed sweetly on him; he shall be no more remembered; and wickedness shall be broken as a tree.

"May the evil man go down to the grave and be remembered no more."

Job 24:21
He evil entreateth the barren that beareth not: and doeth not good to the widow.

"May the evil man have no sons."

Job 24:22–24
He draweth also the mighty with his power: he riseth up, and no man is sure of life. Though it be given him to be in safety, whereon he resteth; yet his eyes are upon their ways. They are exalted for a little while, but are gone and brought low; they are taken out of the way as all other, and cut off as the tops of the ears of corn.

"Though he be popular, prosperous, and powerful, may the evil man be cut down like wheat at harvest," Job says.

Job 24:25
And if it be not so now, who will make me a liar, and make my speech nothing worth?

"Who wouldn't agree with me that there is wickedness both in the country and in the city?" Job asks.

At this point, I think we see something happening in Job that is commendable. He is not simply focused on himself. Even in the midst of his own unbelievable difficulty and trial, he's looking around, saying, "Others are going through deep waters, as well."

When a storm arose on the Sea of Galilee, the disciples were afraid as the waves were rolling and the wind howling. But Mark tells us that on the sea there were also "other little ships" (4:36). In other words, Mark lets us know other guys were in the same "boat" they were.

Sometimes, in the midst of our own trials, the best thing we can do is simply take our eyes off ourselves, look around, and see what others are dealing with. It is often only in the midst of our own difficulties that we gain a greater sensitivity to the storms others are navigating.

25 Here in chapter 25, we come to the last time Bildad will speak . . .

Job 25:1–3
Then answered Bildad the Shuhite, and said, Dominion and fear are with him, he maketh peace in his high places. Is there any number of his armies? and upon whom doth not his light arise?

In response to Job's frustration regarding what he saw around him, Bildad piously says, "God is in control." Although this sounds good, Bildad's theology is actually insulating him from considering the plight of hurting people all around him.

Job 25:4, 5
How then can man be justified with God? or how can he be clean that is born of a woman? Behold even to the moon, and it shineth not; yea, the stars are not pure in his sight.

"You want to stand before God, Job. You want to plead your case and be justified. But the beauty of the moon and the brilliance of the stars aren't considered pure in God's sight. So how much less will you be?" Bildad asks.

Job 25:6
How much less man, that is a worm? and the son of man, which is a worm?

"If even the moon and the stars aren't pure in His sight, the grandeur and glory of the skies, how can you, a worm, maintain your innocence and be justified?" Bildad asks Job.

In Psalm 22, a psalm that prophetically speaks of the Crucifixion of Jesus we read,

> But I am a worm, and no man; a reproach of men, and despised of the people. Psalm 22:6

How would a worm like Job ever be justified? Through Jesus, the Son of Man, who would become a worm in his stead.

26 **Job 26:1–4**
But Job answered and said, How hast thou helped him that is without power? how savest thou the arm that hath no strength? How hast thou counselled him that hath no wisdom? and how hast thou plentifully declared the thing as it is? To whom hast thou uttered words? and whose spirit came from thee?

"What is your basis for speaking?" Job asks Bildad. It is obvious that Bildad wasn't speaking on behalf of God, for the ministry of the Holy Spirit is to comfort, strengthen, edify, and heal.

Job 26:5, 6
Dead things are formed from under the waters, and the inhabitants thereof. Hell is naked before him, and destruction hath no covering.

"God has dominion," Job says. "God sees everything that has passed on."

Job 26:7 (a)
He stretcheth out the north over the empty place . . .

"The stars overhead are unsearchable," Job declares. How right he is, for the more we learn of stars and galaxies, their number increases, leaving us more to learn.

Job 26:7 (b)
. . . and hangeth the earth upon nothing.

Job says this at a time when the Greeks thought the earth was held up on the shoulders of Atlas, when people in India believed it was held on the back of an elephant, and when people in Africa thought it was supported by a giant tortoise.

Job 26:8
He bindeth up the waters in his thick clouds; and the cloud is not rent under them.

"God has dominion not only over the world below and the world above, but the very atmosphere," Job declares.

Job 26:9–12
He holdeth back the face of his throne, and spreadeth his cloud upon it. He hath compassed the waters with bounds, until the day and night come to an end. The pillars of heaven tremble and are astonished at his reproof. He divideth the sea with his power, and by his understanding he smiteth through the proud.

Job understands it is God who keeps the seas and oceans within in their boundaries.

Job 26:13
By his spirit he hath garnished the heavens; his hand hath formed the crooked serpent.

The crooked serpent referred to here is very likely the name of a constellation.

Job 26:14
Lo, these are parts of his ways: but how little a portion is heard of him? but the thunder of his power who can understand?

"Bildad," says Job, "you're talking about God being awesome. I'm aware of that. But you have to understand that what we see is just a whisper of His power. What are you going to do, then, with the shout and the thunder of His power? Who can figure out this One who is so far beyond our understanding?"

"Show us the Father," Philip said, "and it will suffice us."

"He that hath seen me hath seen the Father," Jesus answered (John 14:8, 9).

We can see what neither Bildad nor Job could understand because Jesus Christ is God in the flesh, dwelling among us, giving understanding to us.

27 In chapter 27, we come to the second chapter of a six-chapter discourse Job gives as his final speech, his closing argument . . .

Job 27:1
Moreover Job continued his parable, and said,

Job continues his parable, or literally, his discourse.

Job 27:2–5
As God liveth, who hath taken away my judgment; and the Almighty, who hath vexed my soul; All the while my breath is in me, and the spirit of God is in my nostrils; My lips shall not speak wickedness, nor my tongue utter deceit. God forbid that I should justify you: till I die I will not remove mine integrity from me.

On five previous occasions, Job maintained his innocence. But here he does something new: he backs it up with an oath.

Job 27:6, 7
My righteousness I hold fast, and will not let it go: my heart shall not reproach me so long as I live. Let mine enemy be as the wicked, and he that riseth up against me as the unrighteous.

Why does Job seem to be more insistent than ever regarding his righteousness? Because his friends were attempting to do what you and I can have a tendency to do. That is, they were trying to bring Job under conviction. "You can't be righteous," they said. "No one is." And as they made their case day after day, Job argued all the more energetically and emphatically.

When the Lord finally shows up on the scene, Job will repent. But it is only when the Lord shows up that Job breaks down. It isn't until the Lord comes on the scene that Job gives up his claim of righteousness. Sometimes we can seek to bring people under conviction. Most of the time, however, it just causes people to build barriers and walls of resentment. How much better it is to leave the convicting work of sin to the Spirit. How much better it is if we love people and pray for them, trusting the Holy Spirit will make known to them the issues that need attention.

Jesus said, "It is expedient that I go away. For if I go not away, the Comforter will not come. But if I depart, I will send Him to you. And when He is come, He will reprove the world of sin, of righteousness, and of judgment." (See John 16:7, 8).

Job 27:8–10
For what is the hope of the hypocrite, though he hath gained, when God taketh away his soul? Will God hear his cry when trouble cometh upon him? Will he delight himself

in the Almighty? will he always call upon God?

"I know the hopelessness of the hypocrite," Job says. "And that's not me."

Job 27:11–13
I will teach you by the hand of God: that which is with the Almighty will I not conceal. Behold, all ye yourselves have seen it; why then are ye thus altogether vain? This is the portion of a wicked man with God, and the heritage of oppressors, which they shall receive of the Almighty.

"I know what the portion of the wicked man is," Job says. And then he goes on to describe it . . .

Job 27:14–18
If his children be multiplied, it is for the sword: and his offspring shall not be satisfied with bread. Those that remain of him shall be buried in death: and his widows shall not weep. Though he heap up silver as the dust, and prepare raiment as the clay; He may prepare it, but the just shall put it on, and the innocent shall divide the silver. He buildeth his house as a moth, and as a booth that the keeper maketh.

"The wicked man won't last. His children will experience neither health nor satisfaction. Even his widow doesn't cry. It's a horrible scene."

Job 27:19–23
The rich man shall lie down, but he shall not be gathered: he openeth his eyes, and he is not. Terrors take hold on him as waters, a tempest stealeth him away in the night. The east wind carrieth him away, and he departeth: and as a storm hurleth him out of his place. For God shall cast upon him, and not spare: he would fain flee out of his hand. Men shall clap their hands at him, and shall hiss him out of his place.

Virtually every phrase in verses 14 through 23 was first used by Bildad, Zophar, or Eliphaz to come down on Job.

The Bible says whatever a man sows, that shall he reap (Galatians 6:7). We see this principle throughout the Word from cover to cover . . .

Pharaoh ordered the drowning of baby boys that were born to the Jews. How did he die? He drowned (Exodus 1:22, 14:28).

When Adonibezek, king of the Canaanites, was captured, his thumbs and toes were cut off because he had done the same thing to his own captives (Judges 1:6, 7).

Haman built a gallows to hang Mordecai, only to die on the very gallows he built (Esther 7:10).

Daniel was thrown into the lions' den, but it was the men who ordered that he be thrown in that were eaten (Daniel 6:24).

As you read the Word and observe life, you can't help but see that we do indeed sow what we reap. Job's friends were harsh with Job. And now their own phrases are being used against them. That is why Jesus said we are to be people who dispense mercy and who bestow great grace . . .

> Be ye therefore merciful, as your Father also is merciful. Judge not, and ye shall not be judged: condemn not, and ye shall not be condemned: forgive, and ye shall be forgiven: Give, and it shall be given unto you; good measure, pressed down, and shaken together, and running over, shall men give into your bosom. For with the same measure that ye mete withal it shall be measured to you again. Luke 6:36–38

28

As Job continues his closing argument here in chapter 28, it's as though he's thinking out loud, wondering where wisdom can be found . . .

Job 28:1–4
Surely there is a vein for the silver, and a place for gold where they fine it. Iron is taken out of the earth, and brass is molten out of the stone. He setteth an end to darkness, and searcheth out all perfection: the stones of darkness, and the shadow of death. The flood breaketh out from the inhabitant; even the waters forgotten of the foot: they are dried up, they are gone away from men.

Here we see a description of an underground mining operation, where water is channeled away.

Job 28:5
As for the earth, out of it cometh bread: and under it is turned up as it were fire.

There might be barley and oats on top of the earth, but underneath are gems and jewels.

Job 28:6, 7
The stones of it are the place of sapphires: and it hath dust of gold. There is a path which no fowl knoweth, and which the vulture's eye hath not seen:

Even an eagle with a bird's eye view can't see the riches below the surface of the earth.

Job 28:8–11
The lion's whelps have not trodden it, nor the fierce lion passed by it. He putteth forth his hand upon the rock; he overturneth the mountains by the roots. He cutteth out rivers among the rocks; and his eye seeth every precious thing. He bindeth the floods from overflowing; and the thing that is hid bringeth he forth to light.

Men can move mountains, overturn the earth, and expose what's below.

Job 28:12–28
But where shall wisdom be found? and where is the place of understanding? Man knoweth not the price thereof; neither is it found in the land of the living. The depth saith, It is not in me: and the sea saith, It is not with me. It cannot be gotten for gold, neither shall silver be weighed for the price thereof. It cannot be valued with the gold of Ophir, with the precious onyx, or the sapphire. The gold and the crystal cannot equal it: and the exchange of it shall not be for jewels of fine gold. No mention shall be made of coral, or of pearls: for the price of wisdom is above rubies. The topaz of Ethiopia shall not equal it, neither shall it be valued with pure gold. Whence then cometh wisdom? and where is the place of understanding? Seeing it is hid from the eyes of all living, and kept close from the fowls of the air. Destruction and death say, We have heard the fame thereof with our ears. God understandeth the way thereof, and he knoweth the place thereof. For he looketh to the ends of the earth, and seeth under the whole heaven; To make the weight for the winds; and he weigheth the waters by measure. When he made a decree for the rain, and a way for the lightning of the thunder: Then did he see it, and declare it; he prepared it, yea, and searched it out. And unto man he said, Behold, the fear of the Lord, that is wisdom; and to depart from evil is understanding.

After referring extensively to mining the earth for gems and jewels, Job ponders how to discover the gems and jewels of wisdom. He concludes that the way to do so is to listen to what the Lord declares and decrees. Solomon said it is the fear of the Lord that is the beginning of wisdom (Proverbs 9:10). Paul would go on to say that all the treasures of wisdom and knowledge are found in Jesus (Colossians 2:3). I rediscovered that this morning. Pondering some things, I grabbed my Bible and a cup of coffee and made my way to a small park. Enjoying the stars overhead as they broke through the clouds, I talked to the Lord about what was on my heart and my mind. And I came away from that quiet place having the wisdom I needed for the morning. It's amazing! The Lord will *truly* meet us.

Everything you need to know about how to get through the rest of this day or tomorrow will be found in God—in talking to Him, in walking with Him, and in being in awe of Him. The fear of the Lord is not an abstract concept. The fear of the Lord simply says, "Lord, You're awesome, gracious, and good. And I need You desperately. So I'm going to begin this day with You because in You are all the treasures of wisdom and knowledge."

If we don't fear the Lord, gang, we'll fear everything else. But if we fear Him, we'll have nothing else to fear.

29

In chapter 3, Job cursed the day he was born. Twenty-six chapters later, his perspective is a bit different. Now he's looking back and recalling God's past blessings . . .

Job 29:1–3
Moreover Job continued his parable, and said, Oh that I were as in months past, as in the days when God preserved me; When his candle shined upon my head, and when by his light I walked through darkness;

Job thinks back to the days when he saw the light, when he wasn't walking blindly in the dark.

Job 29:4
As I was in the days of my youth, when the secret of God was upon my tabernacle;

Even as a young child, Job evidently had an understanding of God.

Job 29:5
When the Almighty was yet with me, when my children were about me;

Job remembered the days he spent with his children. If you have kids or grandchildren, how I encourage you to seize the opportunity to share the Word with them, even if it's only a simple Bible story or song for the younger ones or a favorite verse with the older ones. Truly, those are the most special times you'll share.

Job 29:6
When I washed my steps with butter, and the rock poured me out rivers of oil;

This speaks of the success of Job's occupation.

Job 29:7–9
When I went out to the gate through the city, when I prepared my seat in the street! The young men saw me, and hid themselves: and the aged arose, and stood up. The princes refrained talking, and laid their hand on their mouth.

In earlier days, Job had taken his place among the leaders and wise men of the city in order to give counsel and instruction. Out of respect, young men stepped back when they saw him coming. Older men stood up. Everyone wanted to hear what he had to say.

Job 29:10, 11
The nobles held their peace, and their tongue cleaved to the roof of their mouth. When the ear heard me, then it blessed me; and when the eye saw me, it gave witness to me:

"People listened to me gladly," Job says. "The work I did was blessed. My kids gathered around me. I was respected in town." He isn't bragging. He's simply referring to the reality of his situation in earlier days.

Job 29:12
Because I delivered the poor that cried, and the fatherless, and him that had none to help him. The blessing of him that was ready to perish came upon me: and I caused the widow's heart to sing for joy.

Job's friends had accused him of ripping off the poor in order to increase his own wealth (20:19). Here, Job refutes their charge, saying, "People respected me because I was generous with the less fortunate. I shared my wealth freely and helped those who were hurting."

Job 29:14
I put on righteousness, and it clothed me: my judgment was as a robe and a diadem. I was eyes to the blind, and feet was I to the lame.

"I lived righteously and walked wisely," Job says. "I helped the blind and the lame."

Job 29:16
I was a father to the poor: and the cause which I knew not I searched out.

"I cared for those who were disenfranchised, and if I didn't understand a matter, I tried to get to the bottom of it."

Job 29:17, 18
And I brake the jaws of the wicked, and plucked the spoil out of his teeth. Then I said, I shall die in my nest, and I shall multiply my days as the sand.

"I took a stand against evil and assumed I would die peacefully at the end of my days," Job says.

Job 29:19, 20
My root was spread out by the waters, and the dew lay all night upon my branch. My glory was fresh in me, and my bow was renewed in my hand.

Because children are likened to arrows in Scripture (Psalm 127:4, 5), Job seems to be suggesting that he felt renewed by his kids.

Job 29:21–23
Unto me men gave ear, and waited, and kept silence at my counsel. After my words they spake not again; and my speech dropped upon them. And they waited for me as for the rain; and they opened their mouth wide as for the latter rain.

"Men were satisfied with my counsel," Job says, "and found it to be refreshing." My speech settled in their soul.

Job 29:24
If I laughed on them, they believed it not; and the light of my countenance they cast not down.

"I was able to encourage and uplift others."

Job 29:25
I chose out their way, and sat chief, and dwelt as a king in the army, as one that comforteth the mourners.

"I was both a commander and a comforter."

Remembering past blessings actually improves Job's present situation. This should not be surprising. In Deuteronomy 8, God declares, "Thou shalt remember all the ways the Lord thy God led thee." Fourteen more times in the Book of Deuteronomy alone God commands His people to remember. In days of difficulty, in times of despair, in seasons of despondency, how important it is to simply remember God and the gracious blessings He showers upon us daily (Psalm 68:19).

> Will the Lord cast off for ever? and will he be favourable no more? Is his mercy clean gone for ever? doth his promise fail for evermore?

> Hath God forgotten to be gracious? hath he in anger shut up his tender mercies? Selah. And I said, This is my infirmity: but I will remember the years of the right hand of the most High. I will remember the works of the LORD: surely I will remember thy wonders of old. I will meditate also of all thy work, and talk of thy doings. Thy way, O God, is in the sanctuary: who is so great a God as our God? Psalm 77:7–13

Walking through his own dark days, the psalmist says, "Will I ever be blessed again?" Then he adds the word *selah*, an instruction to wait or stop. After that, he goes on to say, "I'm going to look back and remember what God has done for me—the grace He's shown me, the blessings He has sent my way."

In this day when so many are depressed, it's necessary to remember what God has already done and to realize that, because He saw us through in the past, He's sure to see us through in the future. C.H. Spurgeon said that too often too many of us write our blessings in sand and our infirmities in marble. We focus on our pain and problems but that ought not be. We must be those who remember, recall, and reflect upon all God has done for us.

"How can this be?" the host of the wedding party said. "Most men serve the good wine at first and the cheaper wine at the end when no one would notice the difference. But you have kept the best for last." (See John 2). Why was the best wine saved for last? Because that's always the way of the Lord. He always takes us from glory to greater glory (2 Corinthians 3:18).

Job will lament in the next chapter but here, he's saying, "Wait a minute. God has been good to me."

And so must we.

30

We have seen sparks flying, tempers flaring, and fireworks igniting in this series of debates between Job and his three friends, who have been mercilessly accusing him of some serious, secret sin.

Here in chapter 30, we see Job in the midst of his last discourse, his closing argument, in the case he's been pleading. In chapter 29, he recalled his past blessings. Here in chapter 30, he laments his present sufferings, and in chapter 31, he'll wager his future standing.

Job 30:1
But now they that are younger than I have me in derision, whose fathers I would have disdained to have set with the dogs of my flock.

In the previous chapter, Job talked about how the young men made way out of respect when he walked through the city. But now it's a different situation entirely, for even the poorest of them look down on him.

Job 30:2–8
Yea, whereto might the strength of their hands profit me, in whom old age was perished? For want and famine they were solitary; fleeing into the wilderness in former time desolate and waste. Who cut up mallows by the bushes, and juniper roots for their meat. They were driven forth from among men, (they cried after them as after a thief;) To dwell in the clifts of the valleys, in caves of the earth, and in the rocks. Among the bushes they brayed; under the nettles they were gathered together. They were children of fools, yea, children of base men: they were viler than the earth.

Young men acting like a pack of wild animals were the ones who held Job in derision.

Job 30:9
And now am I their song, yea, I am their byword.

Job is amazed by how far he's fallen.

Job 30:10
They abhor me, they flee far from me, and spare not to spit in my face.

Spitting in a man's face was the ultimate sign of disdain and disrespect.

Job 30:11–13
Because he hath loosed my cord, and afflicted me, they have also let loose the bridle before me. Upon my right hand rise the youth; they push away my feet, and they raise up against me the ways of their destruction. They mar my path, they set forward my calamity, they have no helper.

"Because God has let me go," Job says, "these young men have cast off all restraints. They trip me up and block my path. Not one is kind."

Job 30:14–16
They came upon me as a wide breaking in of waters: in the desolation they rolled themselves upon me. Terrors are turned upon me: they pursue my soul as the wind: and my welfare passeth away as a cloud. And now my soul is poured out upon me; the days of affliction have taken hold upon me.

As men pour out contempt upon him, Job feels like a huge wave is breaking over his head.

Job 30:17
My bones are pierced in me in the night season: and my sinews take no rest.

As if his emotional pain wasn't enough to bear, Job's entire body ached, as well.

Job 30:18, 19
By the great force of my disease is my garment changed: it bindeth me about as the collar of my coat. He hath cast me into the mire, and I am become like dust and ashes.

The word translated "garment" can mean "skin." Even Job's skin had taken a beating.

Job 30:20, 21
I cry unto thee, and thou dost not hear me: I stand up, and thou regardest me not. Thou art become cruel to me: with thy strong hand thou opposest thyself against me.

The picture here reminds me of a child in class, waving his hand energetically, trying to get his teacher's attention.

Job 30:22
Thou liftest me up to the wind; thou causest me to ride upon it, and dissolvest my substance.

"Lord, You throw me into the tornado," Job laments.

Job 30:23, 24
For I know that thou wilt bring me to death, and to the house appointed for all living. Howbeit he will not stretch out his hand to the grave, though they cry in his destruction.

The "house appointed for all living" is the grave. "You're not responding to my cry," Job says to the Lord. "You're not saving me when I'm going down."

Job 30:25, 26
Did not I weep for him that was in trouble? was not my soul grieved for the poor? When I looked for good, then evil came unto me: and when I waited for light, there came darkness.

"I felt compassion for those who were in trouble," Job laments. "But now that I'm in trouble, there is no one to feel the same for me."

Job 30:27–31
My bowels boiled, and rested not: the days of affliction prevented me. I went mourning without the sun: I stood up, and I cried in the congregation. I am a brother to dragons, and a companion to owls. My skin is black upon me, and my bones are burned with heat. My harp also is turned to mourning, and my organ into the voice of them that weep.

In earlier days, Job responded to the cries of the hurting. Therefore, he wonders why the Lord won't respond to him, when he is heartbroken and hurting.

31

In this final chapter of his argument, Job wagers his future standing, saying, "If I have done certain things, then I ought to be punished greatly . . .

Job 31:1–4
I made a covenant with mine eyes; why then should I think upon a maid? For what portion of God is there from above? and what inheritance of the Almighty from on high? Is not destruction to the wicked? and a strange punishment to the workers of iniquity? Doth not he see my ways, and count all my steps?

Job begins by declaring he has not been guilty of lust. "I will put no unclean thing before my eyes," the psalmist declares (see 101:3). Here, we learn that Job said the same thing.

Job 31:5–8
If I have walked with vanity, or if my foot hath hasted to deceit; Let me be weighed in an even balance, that God may know mine integrity. If my step hath turned out of the way, and mine heart walked after mine eyes, and if any blot hath cleaved to mine hands; Then let me sow, and let another eat; yea, let my offspring be rooted out.

Verses 5 through 8 speak primarily of dishonesty. Thus, Job is saying, "I haven't walked in deceit."

Job 31:9–12
If mine heart have been deceived by a woman, or if I have laid wait at my neighbour's door; Then let my wife grind unto another, and let others bow down upon her. For this is an heinous crime; yea, it is an iniquity to be punished by the judges. For it is a fire that

consumeth to destruction, and would root out all mine increase.

Verses 9 through 12 speak of adultery. Proverbs says he that commits adultery is unwise because he destroys his own soul. One's mind, emotions, and will are all radically affected by the sin of adultery because sexual union is not just about two bodies coming together, but about two souls becoming one.

Job 31:13–15
If I did despise the cause of my manservant or of my maidservant, when they contended with me; What then shall I do when God riseth up? and when he visiteth, what shall I answer him? Did not he that made me in the womb make him? and did not one fashion us in the womb?

Verses 13 through 15 speak about the misuse of authority, of feeling superior to others, a charge of which Job claimed innocence. Philippians 2 tells us we are to esteem every man better than ourselves. I have found that a simple way to do this is to realize that every single person I meet throughout my life is better than me at something.

Job 31:16–23
If I have withheld the poor from their desire, or have caused the eyes of the widow to fail; Or have eaten my morsel myself alone, and the fatherless hath not eaten thereof; (For from my youth he was brought up with me, as with a father, and I have guided her from my mother's womb;) If I have seen any perish for want of clothing, or any poor without covering; If his loins have not blessed me, and if he were not warmed with the fleece of my sheep; If I have lifted up my hand against the fatherless, when I saw my help in the gate: Then let mine arm fall from my shoulder blade, and mine arm be broken from the bone. For destruction from God was a terror to me, and by reason of his highness I could not endure.

Here Job is saying, "I'm not guilty of hard-heartedness or callousness toward the poor. When they needed covering or food, I cared for them." So sure was Job of this that he said, "If that's not true, let my arm be ripped from my shoulder." The psalmist would later use this same language, saying, "If I forget thee, O Jerusalem, let my right hand forget its cunning" or, literally, "Let my right hand be useless." (Psalm 137).

Job 31:24–28
If I have made gold my hope, or have said to the fine gold, Thou art my confidence; If I rejoiced because my wealth was great, and because mine hand had gotten much; If I beheld the sun when it shined, or the moon walking in brightness; And my heart hath been secretly enticed, or my mouth hath kissed my hand: This also were an iniquity to be punished by the judge: for I should have denied the God that is above.

Here, Job maintains his innocence regarding greed and idolatry.

Job 31:29, 30
If I rejoiced at the destruction of him that hated me, or lifted up myself when evil found him: Neither have I suffered my mouth to sin by wishing a curse to his soul.

"I haven't been guilty of vindictiveness," Job says. "I didn't rejoice when calamity hit those who hated me."

Job 31:31, 32
If the men of my tabernacle said not, Oh that we had of his flesh! we cannot be satisfied. The stranger did not lodge in the street: but I opened my doors to the traveller.

Job was a man of hospitality. He shared freely. He was kind even to strangers.

Job 31:33, 34
If I covered my transgressions as Adam, by hiding mine iniquity in my bosom: Did I fear a great multitude, or did the contempt of families terrify me, that I kept silence, and went not out of the door?

Job was not guilty of hypocrisy. He didn't cover his sin like Adam or hide in his house, fearing he might be discovered.

Job 31:35
Oh that one would hear me! behold, my desire is, that the Almighty would answer me, and that mine adversary had written a book.

Utterly confused as to why his trial just goes on and on, Job mistakenly sees the Lord as his adversary.

Job 31:36
Surely I would take it upon my shoulder, and bind it as a crown to me.

"If God presented His case against me in a book, I would cling to whatever it was He said,"

Job declared. This, however, would render faith unnecessary, for if I can see or hear the Lord telling me why things are happening, faith is superfluous. And, because faith is the currency of eternity, it's a muscle that must be constantly exercised this side of heaven.

Job 31:37–40
I would declare unto him the number of my steps; as a prince would I go near unto him. If my land cry against me, or that the furrows likewise thereof complain; If I have eaten the fruits thereof without money, or have caused the owners thereof to lose their life: Let thistles grow instead of wheat, and cockle instead of barley. The words of Job are ended.

Job maintains that he is innocent of the exploitation of property, saying, "If I haven't been good to the land or if I have taken advantage of the land of others, let thistles and weeds grow where there was once wheat and barley."

Job won't speak again until he's met by the Lord. But before the Lord shows up, another guy appears. His name is Elihu . . .

32

Job 32:1, 2
So these three men ceased to answer Job, because he was righteous in his own eyes. Then was kindled the wrath of Elihu the son of Barachel the Buzite, of the kindred of Ram: against Job was his wrath kindled, because he justified himself rather than God.

The fact that Elihu's pedigree was given means that he was not known like the other three friends. *Elihu* means "He is God." *Barachel* means "Blessed of God." Buz was a nephew of Abraham, (Genesis 22).

Job 32:3–7
Also against his three friends was his wrath kindled, because they had found no answer, and yet had condemned Job. Now Elihu had waited till Job had spoken, because they were elder than he. When Elihu saw that there was no answer in the mouth of these three men, then his wrath was kindled. And Elihu the son of Barachel the Buzite answered and said, I am young, and ye are very old; wherefore I was afraid, and durst not shew you mine opinion. I said, Days should speak, and multitude of years should teach wisdom. But there is a spirit in man: and the inspiration of the Almighty giveth them understanding.

In Elihu's speech, we see five aspects of his character. First, note that he is indignant. Four times he will talk about his wrath being kindled.

Job 32:9, 10
Great men are not always wise: neither do the aged understand judgment. Therefore I said, Hearken to me; I also will shew mine opinion.

Secondly, Elihu believes he is inspired.

Job 32:11–14
Behold, I waited for your words; I gave ear to your reasons, whilst ye searched out what to say. Yea, I attended unto you, and, behold, there was none of you that convinced Job, or that answered his words: Lest ye should say, We have found out wisdom: God thrusteth him down, not man. Now he hath not directed his words against me: neither will I answer him with your speeches.

Thirdly, Elihu is independent, employing his own arguments rather than recycling the previous arguments of Eliphaz, Bildad, and Zophar.

Job 32:15–20
They were amazed, they answered no more: they left off speaking. When I had waited, (for they spake not, but stood still, and answered no more;) I said, I will answer also my part, I also will shew mine opinion. For I am full of matter, the spirit within me constraineth me. Behold, my belly is as wine which hath no vent; it is ready to burst like new bottles. I will speak, that I may be refreshed: I will open my lips and answer.

Fourthly, Elihu is impelled. "I have let you guys speak," he says. "I have listened carefully. I've been respectful. But there are things I must say that are burning within me. They must be released or they'll burst like wine in new wineskins."

Job 35:21, 22
Let me not, I pray you, accept any man's person, neither let me give flattering titles unto man. For I know not to give flattering titles; in so doing my maker would soon take me away.

Finally, Elihu claims to be impartial, not influenced by position or title.

If Eliphaz, Bildad, and Zophar drew from tradition and education, Elihu piously claims to draw from revelation. The problem is, when God comes on the scene in chapter 39, He'll talk about Eliphaz, Bildad, and Zophar. But He'll make no mention of Elihu.

33

Job 33:1–4
Wherefore, Job, I pray thee, hear my speeches, and hearken to all my words. Behold, now I have opened my mouth, my tongue hath spoken in my mouth. My words shall be of the uprightness of my heart: and my lips shall utter knowledge clearly. The Spirit of God hath made me, and the breath of the Almighty hath given me life.

"I'm anointed, empowered by the Spirit," Elihu says.

Job 33:5, 6 (a)
If thou canst answer me, set thy words in order before me, stand up. Behold, I am according to thy wish in God's stead . . .

"I wish one would come and stand in God's stead before me," Job had repeatedly said.

Elihu said, "I'm your man."

Job 33:6 (b), 7
. . . I also am formed out of the clay. Behold, my terror shall not make thee afraid, neither shall my hand be heavy upon thee.

"Unlike the others, I'm not going to come down heavy on you," Elihu promises Job.

Job 33:8, 9
Surely thou hast spoken in mine hearing, and I have heard the voice of thy words, saying, I am clean without transgression, I am innocent; neither is there iniquity in me.

Elihu quotes Job, but not accurately. Job never claimed to be sinless. He claimed to be blameless but never sinless. Elihu is quoting what Zophar said about Job rather than what Job said about himself (11:4). In other words, he's bearing false witness.

"Thou shalt not bear false witness," God commanded (Exodus 20:16). And we assume that to bear false witness means to tell a whopper of a lie. But it's more than that. The term "false witness" is used in reference to the men who testified against Jesus.

"He said that if the temple were destroyed, He would rebuild it in three days," they said (Matthew 26:60, 61).

Jesus did indeed say, "Destroy this temple and in three days I will raise it up." But He was speaking of the temple of His own body.

Being a false witness is so subtle, but so dangerous, where we pass on information that may be technically correct, but the implication is completely wrong.

Job 33:10–13
Behold, he findeth occasions against me, he counteth me for his enemy, He putteth my feet in the stocks, he marketh all my paths. Behold, in this thou art not just: I will answer thee, that God is greater than man. Why dost thou strive against him? for he giveth not account of any of his matters.

"Why are you striving against the One who is greater than you, Job?" Elihu asks. Paul would ask the same question . . .

> Nay but, O man, who art thou that repliest against God? Shall the thing formed say to him that formed it, Why hast thou made me thus? Hath not the potter power over the clay , of the same lump to make one vessel unto honour, and another unto dishonour? Romans 9:20, 21

Like the potter, the Lord has absolute sovereignty. He can do with our lives whatever He chooses. That sounds somewhat scary until we look more closely at the hands of our Potter and see the holes made by a nail driven through them because of His great love for us.

Job 33:14–18
For God speaketh once, yea twice, yet man perceiveth it not. In a dream, in a vision of the night, when deep sleep falleth upon men, in slumberings upon the bed; Then he openeth the ears of men, and sealeth their instruction, That he may withdraw man from his purpose, and hide pride from man. He keepeth back his soul from the pit, and his life from perishing by the sword.

God can indeed speak subtly through dreams to keep man from his purposes. The wise men, for example, were warned in a dream not to return to Herod (Matthew 2:12).

"Don't you understand, Job, that the Lord can speak even through a dream to keep you from going off in a wrong direction?"

Job 33:19–22
He is chastened also with pain upon his bed, and the multitude of his bones with strong pain: So that his life abhorreth bread, and his soul dainty meat. His flesh is consumed away, that it cannot be seen; and his bones

that were not seen stick out. Yea, his soul draweth near unto the grave, and his life to the destroyers.

God can speak quietly through dreams and visions or He can speak loudly through trials. Here, Elihu says, "Your suffering is not punitive, Job. You're not being punished for sin like the other three suggested. It's preventive. The suffering you're going through is to keep you from a direction that would be dangerous and harmful."

In his masterful work, *The Problem of Pain,* C.S. Lewis writes that the Lord whispers to us in our pleasures, speaks to us in our conscience, but shouts to us in our pain. He says that pain is God's megaphone to rouse a deaf world."

Pain has purpose. Ask Dr. Brand. The conventional wisdom of his day was that leprosy destroyed fingers, toes, and noses. But as he observed lepers in India, he discovered that rats would nibble their fingers, toes, and noses while they slept because leprosy had destroyed their nerve endings, rendering them unable to feel any pain.

Pain keeps us awake and alive. Pain alerts us to rats that can nibble at our soul.

Job 33:23–26
If there be a messenger with him, an interpreter, one among a thousand, to shew unto man his uprightness: Then he is gracious unto him, and saith, Deliver him from going down to the pit: I have found a ransom. His flesh shall be fresher than a child's: he shall return to the days of his youth: He shall pray unto God, and he will be favourable unto him: and he shall see his face with joy: for he will render unto man his righteousness.

Here, Elihu shares an insight that is quite amazing when he says, "Job, there is One who has paid the ransom, One who can cause you to be born again, One who can render or impute righteousness to you" (2 Corinthians 5:17). Elihu didn't know it, but, of course, he was talking about Jesus.

Job 33:27, 28
He looketh upon men, and if any say, I have sinned, and perverted that which was right, and it profited me not; He will deliver his soul from going into the pit, and his life shall see the light.

Here we see the gospel: If any man admits he's a sinner, the Lord will deliver him.

Job 33:29–33
Lo, all these things worketh God oftentimes with man, To bring back his soul from the pit, to be enlightened with the light of the living. Mark well, O Job, hearken unto me: hold thy peace, and I will speak. If thou hast any thing to say, answer me: speak, for I desire to justify thee. If not, hearken unto me: hold thy peace, and I shall teach thee wisdom.

Save for a problem with arrogance and false witness, Elihu has done well. He has supplied an important piece of the puzzle: that pain has a purpose. Oh, if only he would have stopped at this point. Yes, he had inspiration from the Spirit, but along with that came a vulnerability. Peter knew all about this . . .

"Who do men say I am?" Jesus asked him.

"Thou art the Christ, the Son of the living God," Peter answered.

"Blessed art thou, Peter, for flesh has not revealed this to you, but My Father. Upon this rock of your confession, I will build My church and the gates of hell shall not prevail against it."

Peter had foundational revelation. No doubt he was feeling good until Jesus talked about how He must go to Jerusalem to die and rise again.

"No, no, no," Peter said.

And Jesus said, "Get thee behind me, Satan" (Matthew 16).

John tells us we are to try, or test, the spirits because even though there might be a revelation from someone or a wonderful work of the Spirit through someone, it doesn't mean they can't turn right around and go off on a tangent or in the wrong direction (1 John 4:1). And in chapter 34, Elihu will do just that . . .

34

Job 34:1 (a)
Furthermore Elihu answered . . .

Even though Job wasn't asking, Elihu continued answering . . .

Job 34:1 (b)–3
. . . and said, Hear my words, O ye wise men; and give ear unto me, ye that have knowledge. For the ear trieth words, as the mouth tasteth meat.

"Chew on my words," Elihu says. "Determine if they're right or wrong."

Job 34:4–8
Let us choose to us judgment: let us know among ourselves what is good. For Job hath

said, I am righteous: and God hath taken away my judgment. Should I lie against my right? my wound is incurable without transgression. What man is like Job, who drinketh up scorning like water? Which goeth in company with the workers of iniquity, and walketh with wicked men.

"Job, you've been hanging around sinners, and you're sounding like them," Elihu says.

Job 34:9
For he hath said, It profiteth a man nothing that he should delight himself with God.

Elihu, you're bearing false witness again. Job didn't say this. He asked, "Does it profit a man that he should pray to God?" (see 21:15) He didn't say it doesn't profit a man.

This is so easy to do. Someone says something in a moment of pain or difficulty, and we quote them later on, out of context.

Job 34:10–15
Therefore hearken unto me, ye men of understanding: far be it from God, that he should do wickedness; and from the Almighty, that he should commit iniquity. For the work of a man shall he render unto him, and cause every man to find according to his ways. Yea, surely God will not do wickedly, neither will the Almighty pervert judgment. Who hath given him a charge over the earth? or who hath disposed the whole world? If he set his heart upon man, if he gather unto himself his spirit and his breath; All flesh shall perish together, and man shall turn again unto dust.

"If God pulls back, man will literally fall apart," Elihu declares.

Job 34:16–19
If now thou hast understanding, hear this: hearken to the voice of my words. Shall even he that hateth right govern? and wilt thou condemn him that is most just? Is it fit to say to a king, Thou art wicked? and to princes, Ye are ungodly? How much less to him that accepteth not the persons of princes, nor regardeth the rich more than the poor? for they all are the work of his hands.

"Job, you wouldn't come across this brashly toward a king or a prince. How dare you, then, be this brash in accusing God."

Job 34:20–29
In a moment shall they die, and the people shall be troubled at midnight, and pass away: and the mighty shall be taken away without hand. For his eyes are upon the ways of man, and he seeth all his goings. There is no darkness, nor shadow of death, where the workers of iniquity may hide themselves. For he will not lay upon man more than right; that he should enter into judgment with God. He shall break in pieces mighty men without number, and set others in their stead. Therefore he knoweth their works, and he overturneth them in the night, so that they are destroyed. He striketh them as wicked men in the open sight of others; Because they turned back from him, and would not consider any of his ways: So that they cause the cry of the poor to come unto him, and he heareth the cry of the afflicted. When he giveth quietness, who then can make trouble? and when he hideth his face, who then can behold him? whether it be done against a nation, or against a man only:

Job wondered why God had chosen to be silent. Elihu answers, "God is in control. He can do as He chooses. If He doesn't respond to the cry of those who are oppressed, if He chooses to be quiet, what can they do? They can't make Him respond."

Job 34:30
That the hypocrite reign not, lest the people be ensnared.

Elihu suggests that if God is not responding to people who feel oppressed, it could be that He knows another ruler would be even worse.

Job 34:31, 32
Surely it is meet to be said unto God, I have borne chastisement, I will not offend any more: That which I see not teach thou me: if I have done iniquity, I will do no more.

Elihu isn't calling Job a sinner, but he's telling Job to ask God to search his heart and show him if there's something amiss within him.

There is truth in Elihu's counsel. If God has been quiet, it's because He knows things we don't know. Therefore, our prayer ought to be, "Lord, if there's something in me that's not right, teach me, that I might cease from that sin."

Job 34:33 (a)
Should it be according to thy mind?

"Job, should God really do things the way you want Him to?" Elihu asks rhetorically.

Again, this is wise counsel from Elihu. All too

often, I think I know more than God does. He's the Father. I'm but a child. So are you. And the fact is, Father knows best.

Job 34:33 (b)–37
. . . he will recompense it, whether thou refuse, or whether thou choose; and not I: therefore speak what thou knowest. Let men of understanding tell me, and let a wise man hearken unto me. Job hath spoken without knowledge, and his words were without wisdom. My desire is that Job may be tried unto the end because of his answers for wicked men. For he addeth rebellion unto his sin, he clappeth his hands among us, and multiplieth his words against God.

Elihu, what's gotten into you? You're the one who said, "I'm going to be kind and gentle. I'm not going to be overbearing. You don't have to be afraid of what I'm saying." But now you're saying, "My desire is that Job be tried to the uttermost. Throw the book at him, Lord."

35

Job 35:1, 2
Elihu spake moreover, and said, Thinkest thou this to be right, that thou saidst, My righteousness is more than God's?

"Job, do you actually think you're more righteous than God?" Elihu asks.

Job 35:3
For thou saidst, What advantage will it be unto thee? and, What profit shall I have, if I be cleansed from my sin?

Again, these were questions Job raised in his pain. They ought not to be held against him.

Job 35:4–8
I will answer thee, and thy companions with thee. Look unto the heavens, and see; and behold the clouds which are higher than thou. If thou sinnest, what doest thou against him? or if thy transgressions be multiplied, what doest thou unto him? If thou be righteous, what givest thou him? or what receiveth he of thine hand? Thy wickedness may hurt a man as thou art; and thy righteousness may profit the son of man.

"Look up, Job," Elihu says. "Does your sin hurt God? No. You're only hurting yourself."

Elihu's question might sound silly but we can fall into saying, "OK, Lord, You're not doing what I think You should, so I'm not going to church this week. I'm not going to tithe this month. I'm not going to pray this year." But in so doing, we only rob ourselves.

Job 35:9
By reason of the multitude of oppressions they make the oppressed to cry: they cry out by reason of the arm of the mighty.

Elihu makes the case that, while wicked men can't hurt God, they can hurt people.

Job 35:10–13
But none saith, Where is God my maker, who giveth songs in the night; Who teacheth us more than the beasts of the earth, and maketh us wiser than the fowls of heaven? There they cry, but none giveth answer, because of the pride of evil men. Surely God will not hear vanity, neither will the Almighty regard it.

The oppressed cry out but not to God. Instead, they say, "We're in pain! This isn't fair! That's not right!" Elihu says if they were truly crying out to God, they would be singing a song of deliverance. Elihu's implication is that Job hadn't been crying out to God, that he needed to pray harder, that his prayer lacked passion.

I've been in meetings or places where people were trying to work up the Spirit in such a way that I thought I was on Mt. Carmel. Four hundred and fifty prophets of Baal were dancing, screaming, and slashing themselves, trying to get God's attention. When it was Elijah's turn to pray, however, he prayed a simple prayer that took about 2.5 seconds to pray and it was answered immediately (1 Kings 18). Therefore, I believe Elihu's accusation is misdirected.

Job 35:14
Although thou sayest thou shalt not see him, yet judgment is before him; therefore trust thou in him.

"You don't see God, but He sees you," Elihu says. Indeed, "all things are naked and opened unto the eyes of him with whom we have to do" (Hebrews 4:13).

Job 35:15, 16
But now, because it is not so, he hath visited in his anger; yet he knoweth it not in great extremity: Therefore doth Job open his mouth in vain; he multiplieth words without knowledge.

"God is not acting irrationally, Job," Elihu says. "You're the one who's out to lunch."

Eliphaz, Bildad, and Zophar presented their case intellectually and theologically. Elihu, on the other hand, claimed to base his case on revelation. And although none were right about Job's situation, intellect, theology, and revelation need not be at odds. I've been in extremely traditional churches where I've been deeply touched by the Lord. I've also been in more emotional settings where I've been equally blessed. But I've also been in settings where it seemed like it was an effort of the flesh to pump people up in the name of the Spirit. The Lord has a better way . . .

> For the land, whither thou goest in to possess it, is not as the land of Egypt, from whence ye came out, where thou sowedst thy seed, and wateredst it with thy foot, as a garden of herbs: But the land, whither ye go to possess it, is a land of hills and valleys, and drinketh water of the rain of heaven: A land which the LORD thy God careth for: the eyes of the LORD thy God are always upon it, from the beginning of the year even unto the end of the year. And it shall come to pass, if ye shall hearken diligently unto my commandments which I command you this day, to love the LORD your God, and to serve him with all your heart and with all your soul, That I will give you the rain of your land in his due season, the first rain and the latter rain, that thou mayest gather in thy corn, and thy wine, and thine oil. Deuteronomy 11:10–14

In Egypt, water was pumped to the fields from the Nile. Egypt is a type of the world, the flesh, where things have to be "pumped up." God said, "I'm taking you to a different land, where water comes down from heaven. You won't have to set some kind of atmosphere or try to manipulate the situation. Just love Me with all your heart and soul, and I will pour out the rain upon you."

I suggest that in these days the Lord is indeed pouring out His Spirit. It need not be pumped up in our own energy or manipulated through careful strategy. Rather, if we simply love God and let Him pour out His Spirit, He'll work anywhere and everywhere He's loved.

36

Job 36:1–4

Elihu also proceeded, and said, Suffer me a little, and I will shew thee that I have yet to speak on God's behalf. I will fetch my knowledge from afar, and will ascribe righteousness to my Maker. For truly my words shall not be false: he that is perfect in knowledge is with thee.

Eliphaz, Bildad, and Zophar had all talked extensively to Job. But here, Elihu says, "Now the guy who really understands is on the scene. He that is perfect in knowledge is here. It's me."

It took the Lord one chapter to talk about the creation of the universe in Genesis. Here in Job, we have thirty-five chapters of seemingly endless debate. Unfortunately, I think we see this same ratio in our own lives. How little time we spend conversing with the Lord about the majesty, glory, beauty of His character His ways, and His Word. And how many endless hours we spend chattering about our problems, our perspectives, our trials and troubles.

Job 36:5–14

Behold, God is mighty, and despiseth not any: he is mighty in strength and wisdom. He preserveth not the life of the wicked: but giveth right to the poor. He withdraweth not his eyes from the righteous: but with kings are they on the throne; yea, he doth establish them for ever, and they are exalted. And if they be bound in fetters, and be holden in cords of affliction; Then he sheweth them their work, and their transgressions that they have exceeded. He openeth also their ear to discipline, and commandeth that they return from iniquity. If they obey and serve him, they shall spend their days in prosperity, and their years in pleasures. But if they obey not, they shall perish by the sword, and they shall die without knowledge. But the hypocrites in heart heap up wrath: they cry not when he bindeth them. They die in youth, and their life is among the unclean.

"Job," Elihu says, "if you want to be right with God, you will rule and reign in prosperity. But if you don't obey, or if you are hypocritical, you'll feel His wrath."

Job 36:15–26

He delivereth the poor in his affliction, and openeth their ears in oppression. Even so would he have removed thee out of the strait into a broad place, where there is no straitness; and that which should be set on thy table should be full of fatness. But thou hast fulfilled the judgment of the wicked: judgment and justice take hold on thee. Because there is wrath, beware lest he take thee away with his stroke: then a great ransom cannot deliver thee. Will he esteem thy riches? no, not gold, nor all the forces of strength. Desire not the night, when people are cut off in their place. Take heed, regard not iniquity: for this hast thou chosen rather than affliction. Behold, God exalteth by his power: who teacheth like him? Who hath enjoined him his way? or who can say, Thou hast wrought iniquity? Remember that thou magnify his work,

which men behold. Every man may see it; man may behold it afar off. Behold, God is great, and we know him not, neither can the number of his years be searched out.

As Elihu talks about God's greatness and how He transcends our understanding, evidently there's a change in the climate. The clouds begin to roll in; the winds begin to blow, perhaps it's beginning to rain . . .

Job 36:27–33
For he maketh small the drops of water: they pour down rain according to the vapour thereof: Which the clouds do drop and distil upon man abundantly. Also can any understand the spreadings of the clouds, or the noise of his tabernacle? Behold, he spreadeth his light upon it, and covereth the bottom of the sea. For by them judgeth he the people; he giveth meat in abundance. With clouds he covereth the light; and commandeth it not to shine by the cloud that cometh betwixt. The noise thereof sheweth concerning it, the cattle also concerning the vapour.

Drawing from his surroundings, Elihu uses the storm to speak not only of God's awesome power, but of His abundant provision.

I give Elihu credit for using the things round about him in the teaching he's giving. Jesus was, of course, the Master of this method as He talked about lilies of the field, sowing seed, and sparrows. I encourage you to utilize what takes place around you when you're sharing with people. Use whatever is at hand to draw peoples' attention to the glory and goodness of God.

37

Job 37:1–12
At this also my heart trembleth, and is moved out of his place. Hear attentively the noise of his voice, and the sound that goeth out of his mouth. He directeth it under the whole heaven, and his lightning unto the ends of the earth. After it a voice roareth: he thundereth with the voice of his excellency; and he will not stay them when his voice is heard. God thundereth marvellously with his voice; great things doeth he, which we cannot comprehend. For he saith to the snow, Be thou on the earth; likewise to the small rain, and to the great rain of his strength. He sealeth up the hand of every man; that all men may know his work. Then the beasts go into dens, and remain in their places. Out of the south cometh the whirlwind: and cold out of the north. By the breath of God frost is given: and the breadth of the waters is straitened. Also by watering he wearieth the thick cloud: he scattereth his bright cloud: And it is turned round about by his counsels: that they may do whatsoever he commandeth them upon the face of the world in the earth.

Here, Elihu continues to wax eloquent—at least in his opinion—about the awesome power of God as seen in the storm rising round about him. He alludes to the rain, the clouds, the thunder, and the lighting. Again, he uses that which is round about him to draw attention to God—a commendable practice.

Job 37:13–19
He causeth it to come, whether for correction, or for his land, or for mercy. Hearken unto this, O Job: stand still, and consider the wondrous works of God. Dost thou know when God disposed them, and caused the light of his cloud to shine? Dost thou know the balancings of the clouds, the wondrous works of him which is perfect in knowledge? How thy garments are warm, when he quieteth the earth by the south wind? Hast thou with him spread out the sky, which is strong, and as a molten looking glass? Teach us what we shall say unto him; for we cannot order our speech by reason of darkness.

In order to prove the limits of Job's knowledge, Elihu asks a series of questions regarding natural phenomena. Two chapters from now, God will do the same thing. The difference, however, is that He knows the answers. Elihu doesn't.

Job 37:20–24
Shall it be told him that I speak? if a man speak, surely he shall be swallowed up. And now men see not the bright light which is in the clouds: but the wind passeth, and cleanseth them. Fair weather cometh out of the north: with God is terrible majesty. Touching the Almighty, we cannot find him out: he is excellent in power, and in judgment, and in plenty of justice: he will not afflict. Men do therefore fear him: he respecteth not any that are wise of heart.

"God is so great that He is past finding out," Elihu declares. And with that, he ends his speech.

Chapters 1 and 2 dealt with Job's *dilemma*. Chapters 3 through 37 dealt with Job's *debates*. Chapters 38 through 42 will deal with Job's *deliverance*. Eliphaz, Bildad, and Zophar said God was disciplining Job. Job thought God wanted to destroy him. Elihu said God sought to direct him. But all five were incorrect, as we will see . . .

38 The demanding debates are over. Job has been knocking on heaven's door, longing for God to answer. Now at last, God comes. But take careful note: He comes not *to* answer, but as the Answer. The peace He brings doesn't come from understanding. It transcends, passes, surpasses, and supercedes understanding. The same is still true. You will never have an answer for many of the questions stirring within you. But you'll find that God Himself is the Answer, and that He'll give you a peace that passes understanding.

Job 38:1 (a)
Then the LORD answered Job out of the whirlwind . . .

The storm was brewing. The wind was blowing and the Lord came to Job and spoke with Job at the time of the storm. How often we find that to be true. The disciples were toiling at the oars on the Sea of Galilee as the wind blew and the waves rolled. Even though many of them were experienced fishermen, the disciples were deathly afraid that they were about to go down. Just then, the Lord appeared to them in the storm, walking on water. Initially, they thought He was a ghost until He said, "Be of good cheer. It is I. Fear not." (Matthew 14:27).

Jesus came to His disciples in the storm. And we have found over and over that He comes to us in the storm, as well. When things are tough, difficult, and challenging, it seems that He draws near to us in profound and special ways.

Job 38:1 (b), 2
. . . and said, Who is this that darkeneth counsel by words without knowledge?

"Who is this who doesn't have a clue what he's talking about?" How would you like to be greeted by the Lord in that way!

Job 38:3 (a)
Gird up now thy loins like a man . . .

"Stand up," God said, and I have a sneaking suspicion that our Father would come to many of us, His pouting children, and say the same thing.

Job 38:3 (b)
. . . for I will demand of thee, and answer thou me.

"Job, you've been questioning and you've all been dialoguing endlessly. Now I have some questions for you." Indeed He does, for God will ask Job sixty questions before He's through.

Job 38:4
Where wast thou when I laid the foundations of the earth? declare, if thou hast understanding.

We think we know so much about the sciences. We have endless theories and hypotheses. But the Lord shows up and says, "What do you know firsthand?"

Job 38:5, 6
Who hath laid the measures thereof, if thou knowest? or who hath stretched the line upon it? Whereupon are the foundations thereof fastened? or who laid the corner stone thereof;

God begins by asking Job, "Where were you when I was designing the earth? Do you understand the underpinnings, the foundation, the history?" We think we have the understanding of geography and paleontology down pat. But, in reality, we know so little.

Job 38:7
When the morning stars sang together, and all the sons of God shouted for joy?

"Morning stars" and "sons of God" are phrases that refer to angels. This means that as God was creating the world, the angels were singing. Therefore, I suggest that when things seem to be chaotic or confusing, dark or empty in our own lives, we should start singing because the Lord evidently does His best work to background music.

"Sing, O barren one," Isaiah declares (54:1). I am convinced that much of depression and discouragement would be done away with if we would put on the "garment of praise for the spirit of heaviness" (Isaiah 61:3). Shout for joy, gang. Sing songs of praise. And watch God create something wondrous out of the darkness.

Job 38:8, 9
Or who shut up the sea with doors, when it brake forth, as if it had issued out of the womb? When I made the cloud the garment thereof, and thick darkness a swaddlingband for it,

This most likely alludes to the water canopy that surrounded the planet before the Flood. Evidently, there was a water vapor canopy above the earth's atmosphere that provided protection from the harmful rays of the sun, creating a greenhouse effect upon the entire planet. This would explain the frozen vegetation that has been discovered below the icecaps in the Arctic Circle.

Job 38:10, 11
And brake up for it my decreed place, and set bars and doors, And said, Hitherto shalt thou come, but no further: and here shall thy proud waves be stayed?

Five-sevenths of our planet is covered by water. "Were you there when I put boundaries upon the oceans?" God asks Job.

Job 38:12
Hast thou commanded the morning since thy days; and caused the dayspring to know his place;

"Do you cause the sun to rise every morning?"

Job 38:13–17
That it might take hold of the ends of the earth, that the wicked might be shaken out of it? It is turned as clay to the seal; and they stand as a garment. And from the wicked their light is withholden, and the high arm shall be broken. Hast thou entered into the springs of the sea? or hast thou walked in the search of the depth? Have the gates of death been opened unto thee? or hast thou seen the doors of the shadow of death?

In chapter 3, Job said, "Why didn't I die when I was born, for then I should have been at rest and peace."

"Do you really know what's beyond this life?" God asked.

Job 38:18–21
Hast thou perceived the breadth of the earth? declare if thou knowest it all. Where is the way where light dwelleth? and as for darkness, where is the place thereof, That thou shouldest take it to the bound thereof, and that thou shouldest know the paths to the house thereof? Knowest thou it, because thou wast then born? or because the number of thy days is great?

"Where does the darkness go when the light comes?"

Job 38:22 (a)
Hast thou entered into the treasures of the snow?

Billions and billions of snowflakes fall every year and the geometric design, the intricacy, the beauty is amazing because no two are alike.

Job 38:22 (b), 23
. . . Or hast thou seen the treasures of the hail, Which I have reserved against the time of trouble, against the day of battle and war?

God says snow and hail would be used in times of war. Have they been? Historically, it was snow that finally thwarted Napoleon's invasion of Russia. Prophetically, hailstones that weigh more than one hundred pounds will pelt the earth during the Tribulation period.

Job 38:24 (a)
By what way is the light parted . . .

We know light can be separated, but we don't know how because, to this day, we're not sure whether light is a wave or a particle.

Job 38:24 (b)–31
. . . which scattereth the east wind upon the earth? Who hath divided a watercourse for the overflowing of waters, or a way for the lightning of thunder; To cause it to rain on the earth, where no man is; on the wilderness, wherein there is no man; To satisfy the desolate and waste ground; and to cause the bud of the tender herb to spring forth? Hath the rain a father? or who hath begotten the drops of dew? Out of whose womb came the ice? and the hoary frost of heaven, who hath gendered it? The waters are hid as with a stone, and the face of the deep is frozen. Canst thou bind the sweet influences of Pleiades, or loose the bands of Orion?

The Pleiades are thought to be the center of the gravitational force of the Milky Way Galaxy. This seems to be an allusion to that.

Job 38:32
Canst thou bring forth Mazzaroth in his season? or canst thou guide Arcturus with his sons?

Arcturus is called the runaway star. It moves very quickly at 125,000 miles per second. I think of our closest star, the sun. The fact is 1,300,000 earths can fit inside our sun. But our sun is rather small compared to Anteres, for it could hold sixty-four of our suns. Yet that's nothing, because in the constellation of Hercules, there is a star that could hold one hundred million Anteres, which can hold sixty-four suns, which could hold

1,300,000 earths. We're talking big, gang! But there's an even bigger star called Epsilon that could hold one to two million Anteres. And God created and guides the whole thing.

Job 38:33, 34
Knowest thou the ordinances of heaven? canst thou set the dominion thereof in the earth? Canst thou lift up thy voice to the clouds, that abundance of waters may cover thee?

"Can you cause something as simple as rain, Job?"

Job 38:35, 36
Canst thou send lightnings, that they may go, and say unto thee, Here we are? Who hath put wisdom in the inward parts? or who hath given understanding to the heart?

God changes gears here a bit. He speaks of instincts, like that of the arctic terns who travel from pole to pole, from the Arctic to Antarctica. The amazing thing is, when the female lays her eggs during the journey, although she continues on without them, once her babies are ready to fly, they'll meet up with Mom and Dad at their destination. How do they know where to go? They are all part of a magnificent design by a magnificent Creator.

Job 38:37–41
Who can number the clouds in wisdom? or who can stay the bottles of heaven, When the dust groweth into hardness, and the clods cleave fast together? Wilt thou hunt the prey for the lion? or fill the appetite of the young lions, When they couch in their dens, and abide in the covert to lie in wait? Who provideth for the raven his food? when his young ones cry unto God, they wander for lack of meat.

The raven is an unclean animal, yet who takes care of him? God does.

Job was asking questions of God. When God comes, however, He doesn't give Job answers, but instead asks Job questions. Why? Because our Father is not One who so much gives the answers as much as He *is* the answer. I want to know the reasons why—about life, events, situations, trials, and tragedies. But God is One who, more often than not, does not answer my questions. Rather, He *is* the Answer in my situation.

"What shape is yellow?" my granddaughter, Bailey, asked my son.

"Yellow isn't a shape, Bailey, it's a color," Peter-John answered.

"No, no, no, Daddy. What shape is yellow?"

"It's not a shape, Bailey. "It's a color."

As much as Peter-John would have wanted, he couldn't answer Bailey's question, for it was unanswerable. I'm convinced that so often we ask questions that can't be answered this side of eternity because we're little kids who are all mixed up. We ask the wrong questions. We're limited in our ability to analyze the situation. And the Lord would say to us that it's not answers that we want but His presence that we need.

The good news is that He's here right now, gang, only a prayer away.

39

We question the Lord oftentimes. Job certainly did. But it's a two-way street because the Lord can question us, as well . . .

"Adam, where art thou?" He asked (Genesis 3:9).

"Elijah, what are you doing here?" He queried (1 Kings 19:13).

"Friend," Jesus asked Judas, "wherefore art thou come?" (Matthew 26:50).

Here in chapter 39, the Lord continues to ask Job question after question—sixty in all—dealing with creation round about him.

Job 39:1
Knowest thou the time when the wild goats of the rock bring forth? or canst thou mark when the hinds do calve?

"Do you maintain and sustain the creatures of the earth?"

Job 39:2–4
Canst thou number the months that they fulfil? or knowest thou the time when they bring forth? They bow themselves, they bring forth their young ones, they cast out their sorrows. Their young ones are in good liking, they grow up with corn; they go forth, and return not unto them.

Being a farmer himself, Job would have been accustomed to helping the animals give birth. But what about the ones man didn't help, like the wild goats and the deer? "Who sees them through?" God asks.

Job 39:5–8
Who hath sent out the wild ass free? or who hath loosed the bands of the wild ass? Whose house I have made the wilderness, and the barren land his dwellings. He scorneth the multitude of the city, neither re-

gardeth he the crying of the driver. The range of the mountains is his pasture, and he searcheth after every green thing.

The donkey scorns the city and doesn't even respond to the driver who attempts to steer him. "Who made the donkey so stubborn?" God asks Job.

Job 39:9
Will the unicorn be willing to serve thee, or abide by thy crib?

Most likely, this refers to the wild ox. "Can you domesticate him?" God asks Job.

Job 39:10–12
Canst thou bind the unicorn with his band in the furrow? or will he harrow the valleys after thee? Wilt thou trust him, because his strength is great? or wilt thou leave thy labour to him? Wilt thou believe him, that he will bring home thy seed, and gather it into thy barn?

"Do you think a wild ox will harvest your seed and bring it into the barn?"

Job 39:13 (a)
Gavest thou the goodly wings unto the peacocks?

"Did you paint the peacocks' wings, Job?" I sense that we're not talking about a God who is angry with Job. He's just firing questions good-naturedly at Job and even introducing some humor because the animals He chooses are so interesting.

Job 39:13 (b)–17
. . . or wings and feathers unto the ostrich? Which leaveth her eggs in the earth, and warmeth them in dust, And forgetteth that the foot may crush them, or that the wild beast may break them. She is hardened against her young ones, as though they were not hers: her labour is in vain without fear; Because God hath deprived her of wisdom, neither hath he imparted to her understanding.

The ostrich is a funny bird indeed. She lays her eggs and forgets where she laid them. "I made the ostrich that way," God says, "without wisdom that other birds have in caring for their eggs and tending their young."

Job 39:18
What time she lifteth up herself on high, she scorneth the horse and his rider.

The Hebrew text says she flaps her wings joyfully. Ostriches can't fly but they can run with great speed. In fact, at 35 mph, an ostrich can outrun a horse for short distances. Through this line of questioning, I wonder if God is saying to Job, "Even though an ostrich lacks wisdom, it can flap its wings joyfully and run effectively."

Sometimes we may lack wisdom concerning a given situation. But that needn't stop us from lifting our hands in praise or from exerting energy to spend time with the Lord. Like the ostrich, we can be joyful even though we're bird-brained from time to time.

Job 39:19–25
Hast thou given the horse strength? hast thou clothed his neck with thunder? Canst thou make him afraid as a grasshopper? the glory of his nostrils is terrible. He paweth in the valley, and rejoiceth in his strength: he goeth on to meet the armed men. He mocketh at fear, and is not affrighted; neither turneth he back from the sword. The quiver rattleth against him, the glittering spear and the shield. He swalloweth the ground with fierceness and rage: neither believeth he that it is the sound of the trumpet. He saith among the trumpets, Ha, ha; and he smelleth the battle afar off, the thunder of the captains, and the shouting.

"The horse is ready to charge into battle. Who made the horse that way? Why would the war horse be so fearless? Job, can you cause these things to happen?"

Job 39:26–30
Doth the hawk fly by thy wisdom, and stretch her wings toward the south? Doth the eagle mount up at thy command, and make her nest on high? She dwelleth and abideth on the rock, upon the crag of the rock, and the strong place. From thence she seeketh the prey, and her eyes behold afar off. Her young ones also suck up blood: and where the slain are, there is she.

The fact that He would allude to verse 30 (Matthew 24:28), tells me Jesus Himself was a student of Job.

40

Job 40:1, 2
Moreover the LORD answered Job, and said, Shall he that contendeth with the Almighty instruct him? he that reproveth God, let him answer it.

"Are you trying to instruct Me?" God asks.

That sounds crazy. But that's what we often do. So often, as we come to Him in prayer, we say, "Lord, here's what needs to happen. . . ." We pray directive prayers. We give the Lord instructions. True prayer, however, is not about giving God orders. It's about simply reporting for duty. Why? Because God always gives His best to those who leave the choice with Him. He knows what's best for me. Therefore, it's ridiculous for me to give instructions to the Lord when I should be saying, "Lord, You know what's best. You see what's best for me. Not my will but Thine be done."

Job 40:3–5
Then Job answered the LORD, and said, Behold, I am vile; what shall I answer thee? I will lay mine hand upon my mouth. Once have I spoken; but I will not answer: yea, twice; but I will proceed no further.

Job is amazed not by the answers God gives, for God simply asks questions. He's amazed by the majesty he sees. In the presence of God, he's silenced completely. How much less talking there would be if we lived in a continual awareness of the presence of God. Job was so prolific with words earlier, but now his hand is to his mouth.

Job 40:6, 7 (a)
Then answered the LORD unto Job out of the whirlwind, and said, Gird up thy loins now like a man:

"Gird up your loins," or, "Brace yourself," God tells Job. How does one brace himself when the winds are blowing and the trees are bending? How can you brace yourself in the presence of the Lord? The only way I know is to fasten yourself to the Cross and say, "Lord, I'm dying to myself right here."

Job 40:7 (b), 8
. . . I will demand of thee, and declare thou unto me. Wilt thou also disannul my judgment? wilt thou condemn me, that thou mayest be righteous?

"Are you going to find fault with Me to make yourself look better?" God asks Job.

Job 40:9–14
Hast thou an arm like God? or canst thou thunder with a voice like him? Deck thyself now with majesty and excellency; and array thyself with glory and beauty. Cast abroad the rage of thy wrath: and behold every one that is proud, and abase him. Look on every one that is proud, and bring him low; and tread down the wicked in their place. Hide them in the dust together; and bind their faces in secret. Then will I also confess unto thee that thine own right hand can save thee.

"Job, if you can do these things, then I'll be impressed with you. Let's see what you can do . . ."

Job 40:15 (a)
Behold now behemoth . . .

Some say *behemoth* refers to a hippo. Others say it refers to an elephant.

Job 40:15 (b)–17 (a)
. . . which I made with thee; he eateth grass as an ox. Lo now, his strength is in his loins, and his force is in the navel of his belly. He moveth his tail like a cedar . . .

The tails of neither the hippo nor the elephant are like a cedar tree . . .

Job 40:17 (b)–24
. . . the sinews of his stones are wrapped together. His bones are as strong pieces of brass; his bones are like bars of iron. He is the chief of the ways of God: he that made him can make his sword to approach unto him. Surely the mountains bring him forth food, where all the beasts of the field play. He lieth under the shady trees, in the covert of the reed, and fens. The shady trees cover him with their shadow; the willows of the brook compass him about. Behold, he drinketh up a river, and hasteth not: he trusteth that he can draw up Jordan into his mouth. He taketh it with his eyes: his nose pierceth through snares.

Very likely, this is the description of a dinosaur. But it gets even more interesting . . .

41

Job 41:1 (a)
Canst thou draw out leviathan with an hook?

Some suggest *leviathan* is a blue whale. It could be. The blue whale is massive in size—ninety-eight feet long and twenty times the weight of an elephant. Others say it's a giant crocodile. Indeed, there are fossil remains of crocs that were fifty to fifty-five feet long. But I suggest the description that follows is that of a water dinosaur . . .

Job 41:1 (b)–8
. . . or his tongue with a cord which thou lettest down? Canst thou put an hook into his nose? or bore his jaw through with a thorn? Will he make many supplications unto thee? will he speak soft words unto thee? Will he make a covenant with thee? wilt thou take him for a servant for ever? Wilt thou play with him as with a bird? or wilt thou bind him for thy maidens? Shall the companions make a banquet of him? shall they part him among the merchants? Canst thou fill his skin with barbed irons? or his head with fish spears? Lay thine hand upon him, remember the battle, do no more.

"If you try to battle leviathan, you'll never battle him again," God says as if to say, "If this creature intimidates you, remember that I was the One who created him."

Job 41:9–20
Behold, the hope of him is in vain: shall not one be cast down even at the sight of him? None is so fierce that dare stir him up: who then is able to stand before me? Who hath prevented me, that I should repay him? whatsoever is under the whole heaven is mine. I will not conceal his parts, nor his power, nor his comely proportion. Who can discover the face of his garment? or who can come to him with his double bridle? Who can open the doors of his face? his teeth are terrible round about. His scales are his pride, shut up together as with a close seal. One is so near to another, that no air can come between them. They are joined one to another, they stick together, that they cannot be sundered. By his neesings a light doth shine, and his eyes are like the eyelids of the morning. Out of his mouth go burning lamps, and sparks of fire leap out. Out of his nostrils goeth smoke, as out of a seething pot or caldron.

Some suggest this is the description of a dragon.

Job 41:21–34
His breath kindleth coals, and a flame goeth out of his mouth. In his neck remaineth strength, and sorrow is turned into joy before him. The flakes of his flesh are joined together: they are firm in themselves; they cannot be moved. His heart is as firm as a stone; yea, as hard as a piece of the nether millstone. When he raiseth up himself, the mighty are afraid: by reason of breakings they purify themselves. The sword of him that layeth at him cannot hold: the spear, the dart, nor the habergeon. He esteemeth iron as straw, and brass as rotten wood. The arrow cannot make him flee: slingstones are turned with him into stubble. Darts are counted as stubble: he laugheth at the shaking of a spear. Sharp stones are under him: he spreadeth sharp pointed things upon the mire. He maketh the deep to boil like a pot: he maketh the sea like a pot of ointment. He maketh a path to shine after him; one would think the deep to be hoary. Upon earth there is not his like, who is made without fear. He beholdeth all high things: he is a king over all the children of pride.

This doesn't sound like that of a crocodile or a whale to me. I'm not even sure it's a dinosaur or a dragon. It could be an animal that existed in Job's day but that we don't know about now. Or, it could be a picture of Satan himself . . .

- Out of his mouth go burning lamps or fiery darts (v. 19). Certainly, Satan launches fiery darts at us (Ephesians 6:16).
- His heart is as hard as a stone (v. 24). Throughout Scripture, when people turn against God, they are described as those with hard hearts.
- In the Book of Revelation, Satan is referred to as a dragon and will be cast into the lake of fire, where he will make the deep to boil like a pot (v. 31).
- Satan is indeed the king over all the children of pride (v. 34), for pride was his own downfall (Isaiah 14:14).

Satan indeed plays a key role in Job's story. Therefore, it could be that, in a sense, the Lord is parading him before Job, saying, "I have a question for you, Job. Can you deal with the very one who brought you such misery and pain?"

42

Job 42:1–3
Then Job answered the LORD, and said, I know that thou canst do every thing, and that no thought can be withholden from thee. Who is he that hideth counsel without knowledge? therefore have I uttered that I understood not; things too wonderful for me, which I knew not.

What a wonderful confession. "Forgive me," Job says. "I spoke things I didn't know anything about." God help us to be those who don't speak merely to hear our own voices, for, truly, "in the multitude of words, there wanteth not sin" (Proverbs 10:19).

Job 42:4–6
Hear, I beseech thee, and I will speak: I will demand of thee, and declare thou unto me. I have heard of thee by the hearing of the ear: but now mine eye seeth thee. Wherefore I abhor myself, and repent in dust and ashes.

I believe this is the key to the entire Book of Job: "I heard about You, but now that I see You, I abhor myself." Remember, Job was the most righteous man on the face of the earth. And yet the most righteous man on the face of the earth realized he was nothing in the presence of God.

You might feel secure in your theology but if you chatter endlessly, perhaps it's indicative that you've heard about God without seeing Him. Many Christians know a lot about God, but many have not had revelation of Him. Notice that Job doesn't say, "I abhor Eliphaz, Bildad, and Zophar. He says, "I abhor *myself*."

If the most righteous man on the face of the earth needed to come to a place of repentance, how much more do I need to come before the Lord and say, "Lord, forgive me. Have mercy upon me. I need You to save me. I need Your blood to cleanse me."

Earlier, Job had maintained his righteousness and integrity. But now that he has seen the Lord, all he can say is, "I repent in dust and ashes." Does this mean he's getting right with God? I don't think this is the idea here. Rather, I think it proves that he has been right with God all along. Even though he had questions, even though he wrestled through problems, once the Lord comes on the scene and raises questions to him about creation, about spiritual issues and mysteries, Job responds accordingly.

Over many years, I have observed that, at summer camp, the kids who respond at the campfire are not necessarily the ones who are just then getting right with God. More often than not, they're the ones who are already right with Him because their heart is sensitive enough to respond. It's the ones who don't respond who often have a problem.

James calls Job an example to us of what godly patience looks like (5:11). In Ezekiel 14, Job is in the category with Noah and Daniel as exceedingly righteous men. I believe these references give God's viewpoint of Job's character throughout his ordeal, not just at the conclusion of it.

Job 42:7
And it was so, that after the LORD had spoken these words unto Job, the LORD said to Eliphaz the Temanite, My wrath is kindled against thee, and against thy two friends: for ye have not spoken of me the thing that is right, as my servant Job hath.

God here declares that Job is right. Yes, Job abhors himself. Yes, he's broken. Yes, he's aware of his insignificance, but he responds. And I suggest this means he passed the test. Yes, he had struggles. Yes, there were down times. Questions were raised. Complaints were issued. But God sorts it all out and concludes that Job passed the test.

Job 42:8
Therefore take unto you now seven bullocks and seven rams, and go to my servant Job, and offer up for yourselves a burnt offering; and my servant Job shall pray for you: for him will I accept: lest I deal with you after your folly, in that ye have not spoken of me the thing which is right, like my servant Job.

"Blessed are the merciful for they shall receive mercy," Jesus said (Matthew 5:7). It's oh, so easy to become self-righteous and condescending. But God deals with us eventually. Therefore, I'm learning not to speak against people lest God come to me and say, "Now I'm going to deal with *you*."

Eliphaz drew his conclusions from personal observation. Bildad from the fathers' teachings and traditions, Zophar from his own dogmatic diagnosis. All three were wrong, for the guy they were calling a sinner was the very one God called upon to intercede for them.

Job 42:9, 10 (a)
So Eliphaz the Temanite and Bildad the Shuhite and Zophar the Naamathite went, and did according as the LORD commanded them: the LORD also accepted Job. And the LORD turned the captivity of Job, when he prayed for his friends . . .

God still isn't answering the cosmological questions raised. Instead, he's saying, "Love is the key." When was Job set free? When he prayed for his friends—friends that had come down on him, friends that had found fault with him.

Jesus taught us to pray for our enemies, to bless those that curse us, to do good to those who cause harm to us (Matthew 5:44). Want to be free from the bondage of bitterness? Pray for the people who bug you, the people who have disappointed you, the people who seem to be thorns in your side.

When Jesus tells us to pray for our enemies, I don't believe He means we are to pray that they'll be knocked down a peg or two, that they'll be judged, or that they'll learn a lesson. No, I believe He means we're to pray for them in the same way we want to be prayed for. If you want to be blessed, prosper, and do well, I encourage you to follow Job's example, to pray God's richest blessings for those who mistreat or misunderstand you.

Job 42:10 (b), 11
. . . also the LORD gave Job twice as much as he had before. Then came there unto him all his brethren, and all his sisters, and all they that had been of his acquaintance before, and did eat bread with him in his house: and they bemoaned him, and comforted him over all the evil that the LORD had brought upon him: every man also gave him a piece of money, and every one an earring of gold.

Now that Job is blessed twice as much as he had been before, all of his friends and family return to his side.

Job 42:12, 13
So the LORD blessed the latter end of Job more than his beginning: for he had fourteen thousand sheep, and six thousand camels, and a thousand yoke of oxen, and a thousand she asses. He had also seven sons and three daughters.

His animals numbered twice as much as they had before. Why not his kids? Because his original ten kids were tucked away in heaven. Therefore, with an additional ten, he had twice as many as he had before.

Job 42:14–17
And he called the name of the first, Jemima; and the name of the second, Kezia; and the name of the third, Kerenhappuch. And in all the land were no women found so fair as the daughters of Job: and their father gave them inheritance among their brethren. After this lived Job an hundred and forty years, and saw his sons, and his sons' sons, even four generations. So Job died, being old and full of days.

Some people find the end of this story a bit unsatisfying. They're happy that Job came out so well, but wonder why God didn't answer the questions Job raised. I suggest it is because, in the presence of the Lord, Job found every answer he needed.

Looking back over Job's incredible journey, I see six lessons for us . . .

First, trials and difficulties prepare us for eternity. God wants to develop our faith. That means we won't often see with our eyes what He's doing.

Second, Satan is silenced by submission to God's sovereignty. I'm convinced that when we get to heaven, we're going to discover that a great deal of the difficulty we experienced on earth was simply God proving to the enemy that we're not mercenaries, that we're not hirelings, that He hasn't bought us off with blessings and ease.

When we go through difficulties and misunderstandings, hurts, pains, and problems financially, mentally or emotionally; when we persevere and, like Job, do not curse God or rebel against Him—even though we might have questions for Him, if our attitude is one of worship—Satan is silenced. And when we see the Lord, He'll embrace us and say, "Well done, good and faithful servant. You silenced Satan and you didn't even know it. Satan was accusing you day and night saying, 'If that marriage isn't healed, she'll curse You; if that job doesn't open, he'll deny You; if that answer doesn't come, he'll backslide from You.' But you didn't. I allowed Satan to touch you within certain parameters to prove that you are not a mercenary, that you really do love Me."

Third, suffering produces clearer vision of ourselves and of God. In suffering, Job finally saw he was a vile man. So, when we go through trials and don't react properly, when we hear ourselves saying foolish things, we realize that we're less mature than we thought and say, "Lord, I need You. I'm vile. I need Your blood." If you've gone through deep waters, your understanding and vision of God will increase exponentially. You'll see the Lord in a new dimension. What does this do? It makes us no longer fear suffering the way we once did. Jesus becomes so real and precious that we begin to reach the point where we say, "Trials and testing are worth it because they allow me to see myself in my vileness and the Lord in His holiness."

Fourth, suffering produces compassion. It was when Job saw he was vile himself that he embraced his friends. When do we have compassion for others who are hurting and troubled? After we've been through our own difficulties and trials. That is why Paul would write, "Blessed be the Father who comforts us that we may be able to comfort others with the comfort we ourselves have received (see 2 Corinthians 1:3, 4).

Fifth, suffering teaches us humility. It was when Job was humble that he saw the Lord. Humiliation always brings revelation, for it's when we're going through hard times that we get fresh insight into the Lord and receive revelation of the Lord.

Finally, suffering has a happy ending. Even if you are never healed, you will be in heaven. Even if you're poor on this earth, you'll live in a mansion in eternity. Peter talks about the trial of faith and about the angels that desire to look into these things (1 Peter 1:12). This means that what we go through is not just about us. It's about eternity. It was for the joy that awaited Him that Jesus endured the Cross (Hebrews 12:2). Even on earth, at the end of the story, Job was given twice as much as he had before. That's always the way of the Lord, as He takes us from glory to greater glory (2 Corinthians 3:18), from sorrow to unspeakable joy (John 16:20).